Profiles of Ohio

2008

Second Edition

Profiles of Ohio

A Universal Reference Book

Grey House Publishing

PUBLISHER: Leslie Mackenzie
EDITORIAL DIRECTOR: Laura Mars-Proietti
EDITOR: David Garoogian
RESEARCH ASSISTANT: Michael Marturana

PRODUCTION MANAGER: Karen Stevens
MARKETING DIRECTOR: Jessica Moody

Grey House Publishing, Inc.
185 Millerton Road
Millerton, NY 12546
518.789.8700
FAX 518.789.0545
www.greyhouse.com
e-mail: books @greyhouse.com

First edition published 2006
Second edition published 2008
Printed in the U.S.A.

ISBN: 978-1-59237-406-9

Table of Contents

Introduction
Introduction vii

User's Guides
Profiles ix
Education xxv
Ancestry xxix
Hispanic Population xxxvii
Asian Population xliii
Climate il

Profiles
Alphabetical by County/Place 1
Alphabetical Place Index 343
Comparative Statistics 351

Education
State Public School Profile 384
School District Rankings 385
National Assessment of Educational Progress (NAEP) 409
Ohio Achievement Tests (OAT) 417
Ohio Graduation Tests (OGT) 420

Ancestry
Ancestry 429

Hispanic Population
Hispanic Population 475

Asian Population
Asian Population 501

Climate
State Summary 523
Weather Stations Map 525
Weather Stations by County 526
Weather Stations by City 528
Weather Stations by Elevation 529
National Weather Service Stations 530
Cooperative Weather Stations 538
Weather Station Rankings 559
Storm Events 566

Demographic & Reference Maps
Populated Places, Transportation and Physical Features 569
Federal Lands and Indian Reservations 570
Core-Based Statistical Areas and Counties 571
Congressional Districts (110th Congress) 572
Population 573
Percent White 574
Percent Black 575
Percent Asian 576
Percent Hispanic 577
Median Age 578
Median Household Income 579
Median Home Value 580
Homeownership Rate 581
High School Graduates 582
College Graduates 583
2004 Presidential Election 584

Introduction

Welcome to the second edition of *Profiles of Ohio - Facts, Figures & Statistics for 1,197 Populated Places in Ohio.* As with the other titles in our *State Profiles* series, we built this work using content from Grey House Publishing's award-winning *Profiles of America* - a 4-volume compilation of data on more than 42,000 places in the United States. We have updated and included the Ohio chapter from *Profiles of America,* and added entire fresh chapters of demographic information and ranking sections, so that *Profiles of Ohio* is the most comprehensive portrait of the state of Ohio ever published.

This second edition provides data on all populated communities and counties in the state of Ohio for which the US Census provides individual statistics. It includes seven major sections that cover everything from **Education** to **Ethnic Backgrounds** to **Climate**. All sections include **Comparative Statistics** or **Rankings**, and full-color **Maps** at the back of the book provide valuable information in a quickly processed, visual format. Here's an overview of each section:

1. Profiles
This section, organized by county, gives detailed profiles of 1,197 places plus 88 counties, and is based on the 2000 Census. This core Census data has been so extensively updated, however, that nearly 80% of this section has 2007 numbers. In addition, we have added current government statistics and original research, so that these profiles pull together statistical and descriptive information on every Census-recognized place in the state. Major fields of information include:

Geography	Housing	Education	Religion
Ancestry	Transportation	Population	Climate
Economy	Industry	Health	

In addition to place profiles, this section includes an **Alphabetical Place Index** and **Comparative Statistics** that compare Ohio' 100 largest communities by dozens of data points.

2. Education
This section begins with an **Educational State Profile,** summarizing number of schools, students, diplomas granted and educational dollars spent. Following the state profile are **School District Rankings** on 16 topics ranging from *Teacher/Student Ratios* to *High School Drop-Out Rates.* Following these rankings are statewide *National Assessment of Educational Progress (NAEP)* results and data from the *Ohio Achievement Tests (OAT)* and *Ohio Graduation Tests (OGT).*

3. Ancestry
This section provides a detailed look at the ancestral and racial makeup of Ohio. 217 ethnic categories are ranked three ways: 1) by number, based on all places regardless of population; 2) by percent, based on all places regardless of population; 3) by percent, based on places with populations of 10,000 or more. You will discover, for example, that Parma has the greatest number of *Ukranians* in the state (3,692), and that 26.1% of the population of Garfield Heights are of *Polish* ancestry.

4. Hispanic Population
This section defines Ohio's Hispanic population by 23 Hispanic backgrounds from *Argentinian* to *Venezuelan.* It ranks each of 15 categories, from Median Age to Median Home Value, by each Hispanic background. For example, you'll see that Elyria has the highest percentage of *Mexicans* who speak English-only at home (82.4%), and that Cincinnati has the highest percentage of *Puerto Ricans* who are four-year college graduates (39.3%).

5. Asian Population
Similar in format to the section on Hispanic Population, this section defines Ohio's Asian population by 21 Asian backgrounds from *Bangladeshi* to *Vietnamese.* It ranks each of 14 categories, from Median Age to Median Home Value, by each Asian background. You will learn that *Asian Indians* in Solon have a median household income of $134,386 and that 93.2% of *Filipinos* in Toledo are high-school graduates.

6. Climate
This important topic is explored in detail in this section, which includes a *State Summary,* a *map* of the state's weather stations, and profiles of both *National and Cooperative Weather Stations.* In addition, you'll find *Weather Station Rankings,* where you'll see that, over the 30-year recorded period, Chardon reported the highest annual snowfall with 97.0 inches.

This section also includes current *Storm* data, with the most destructive weather events ranked by both fatalities and property damage, from January 1950 through May 2008. Here you will learn that a flash flood caused $100 million in property damage in Findlay in August 2007 and an F5 tornado was responsible for 36 fatalities in Greene County in April 1974.

7. Maps
For a more visual point of view, there are 16 full-color maps of Ohio at the back of the book. They provide information on topics such as Populated Places, Transportation and Physical Features, Core-Based Statistical Areas and Counties, Population Demographics, Household Size, Median Age, Income, Median Home Values, Educational Attainment, and another look at who voted for George Bush in 2004.

Note: The extensive **User's Guide** that follows this Introduction is segmented into six sections and examines, in some detail, each data field in the individual profiles and comparative sections for all chapters. It provides sources for all data points and statistical definitions as necessary.

User's Guide: Profiles

Places Covered

All 88 counties.

942 incorporated municipalities. Municipalities are incorporated as either cities or villages.

112 census designated places (CDP). The U.S. Bureau of the Census defines a CDP as "a statistical entity, defined for each decennial census according to Census Bureau guidelines, comprising a densely settled concentration of population that is not within an incorporated place, but is locally identified by a name. CDPs are delineated cooperatively by state and local officials and the Census Bureau, following Census Bureau guidelines. Beginning with Census 2000 there are no size limits."

143 unincorporated communities. The communities included have both their own zip code and statistics for their ZIP Code Tabulation Area (ZCTA) available from the Census Bureau. They are referred to as "postal areas." A ZCTA is a statistical entity developed by the Census Bureau to approximate the delivery area for a US Postal Service 5-digit or 3-digit ZIP Code in the US and Puerto Rico. A ZCTA is an aggregation of census blocks that have the same predominant ZIP Code associated with the mailing addresses in the Census Bureau's Master Address File. Thus, the Postal Service's delivery areas have been adjusted to encompass whole census blocks so that the Census Bureau can tabulate census data for the ZCTAs. ZCTAs do not include all ZIP Codes used for mail delivery and therefore do not precisely depict the area within which mail deliveries associated with that ZIP Code occur. Additionally, some areas that are known by a unique name, although they are part of a larger incorporated place, are also included as "postal areas."

Important Notes

- *Profiles of Ohio* uses the term "community" to refer to all places except counties. The term "county" is used to refer to counties and county-equivalents. All places are defined as of the 2000 Census.
- In each community profile, only school districts that have schools that are physically located within the community are shown. In addition, statistics for each school district cover the entire district, regardless of the physical location of the schools within the district.
- Special care should be taken when interpreting certain statistics for communities containing large colleges or universities. College students were counted as residents of the area in which they were living while attending college (as they have been since the 1950 census). One effect this may have is skewing the figures for population, income, housing, and educational attainment.
- Some information (e.g. unemployment rates) is available for both counties and individual communities. Other information is available for just counties (e.g. election results), or just individual communities (e.g. local newspapers).
- Some statistical information is available only for larger communities. In addition, the larger places are more apt to have services such as newspapers, airports, school districts, etc.
- For the most complete information on any community, you should also check the entry for the county in which the community is located. In addition, more information and services will be listed under the larger places in the county.
- For a more in-depth discussion of geographic areas, please refer to the Census Bureau's Geographic Areas Reference Manual at http://www.census.gov/geo/www/garm.html.

Data Sources

CENSUS 2000

The parts of the data which are from the 2000 Decennial Census are from the following sources: *U.S. Bureau of the Census, Census of Population and Housing, 2000: Summary Files 1 and 3.* Summary File 3 (SF 3) consists of 813 detailed tables of Census 2000 social, economic and housing characteristics compiled from a sample of approximately 19 million housing units (about 1 in 6 households) that received the Census 2000 long-form questionnaire. Summary File 1 (SF 1) contains 286 tables focusing on age, sex, households, families, and housing units. This file presents 100-percent population and housing figures for the total population, for 63 race categories, and for many other race and Hispanic or Latino categories.

Comparing SF 3 Estimates with Corresponding Values in SF 1

As in earlier censuses, the responses from the sample of households reporting on long forms must be weighted to reflect the entire population. Specifically, each responding household represents, on average, six or seven other households who reported using short forms.

One consequence of the weighting procedures is that each estimate based on the long form responses has an associated confidence interval. These confidence intervals are wider (as a percentage of the estimate) for geographic areas with smaller populations and for characteristics that occur less frequently in the area being examined (such as the proportion of people in poverty in a middle-income neighborhood).

In order to release as much useful information as possible, statisticians must balance a number of factors. In particular, for Census 2000, the Bureau of the Census created weighting areas—geographic areas from which about two hundred or more long forms were completed—which are large enough to produce good quality estimates. If smaller weighting areas had been used, the confidence intervals around the estimates would have been significantly wider, rendering many estimates less useful due to their lower reliability.

The disadvantage of using weighting areas this large is that, for smaller geographic areas within them, the estimates of characteristics that are also reported on the short form will not match the counts reported in SF 1. Examples of these characteristics are the total number of people, the number of people reporting specific racial categories, and the number of housing units. The official values for items reported on the short form come from SF 1 and SF 2.

The differences between the long form estimates in SF 3 and values in SF 1 are particularly noticeable for the smallest places, tracts, and block groups. The long form estimates of total population and total housing units in SF 3 will, however, match the SF 1 counts for larger geographic areas such as counties and states, and will be essentially the same for medium and large cities.

SF 1 gives exact numbers even for very small groups and areas, whereas SF 3 gives estimates for small groups and areas such as tracts and small places that are less exact. The goal of SF 3 is to identify large differences among areas or large changes over time. Estimates for small areas and small population groups often do exhibit large changes from one census to the next, so having the capability to measure them is worthwhile.

2007 Estimates and 2012 Projections

Some 2000 Census data has been updated with data provided by Claritas. Founded in 1971, Claritas is the industry leader in applied demography and the preeminent provider of small-area demographic estimates.

Information for Communities

PHYSICAL CHARACTERISTICS

Place Type: Lists the type of place (city, town, village, borough, special city, CDP, township, plantation, gore, district, grant, location, reservation, or postal area). *Source: U.S. Bureau of the Census, Census of Population and Housing, 2000: Summary File 1 and U.S. Postal Service, City State File.*

Land and Water Area: Land and water area in square miles. *Source: U.S. Bureau of the Census, Census of Population and Housing, 2000: Summary File 1.*

Latitude and Longitude: Latitude and longitude in degrees. *Source: U.S. Bureau of the Census, Census of Population and Housing, 2000: Summary File 1.*

Elevation: Elevation in feet. *Source: U.S. Geological Survey, Geographic Names Information System (GNIS).*

HISTORY

History: Historical information. *Source: Columbia University Press, The Columbia Gazetteer of North America; Original research.*

POPULATION

Population: 1990 and 2000 figures are a 100% count of population. 2007 estimates and 2012 projections were provided by Claritas. *Source: Claritas; U.S. Bureau of the Census, Census of Population and Housing, 2000: Summary File 1.*

Population by Race: 2007 estimates includes the U.S. Bureau of the Census categories of White alone; Black alone; Asian alone; and Hispanic of any race. Alone refers to the fact that these figures are not in combination with any other race. 2007 data for American Indian/Alaska Native and Native Hawaiian/Other Pacific Islander was not available.

The concept of race, as used by the Census Bureau, reflects self-identification by people according to the race or races with which they most closely identify. These categories are socio-political constructs and should not be interpreted as being scientific or anthropological in nature. Furthermore, the race categories include both racial and national-origin groups.

- **White.** A person having origins in any of the original peoples of Europe, the Middle East, or North Africa. It includes people who indicate their race as "White" or report entries such as Irish, German, Italian, Lebanese, Near Easterner, Arab, or Polish.
- **Black or African American.** A person having origins in any of the Black racial groups of Africa. It includes people who indicate their race as "Black, African American, or Negro," or provide written entries such as African American, Afro-American, Kenyan, Nigerian, or Haitian.
- **Asian.** A person having origins in any of the original peoples of the Far East, Southeast Asia, or the Indian subcontinent including, for example, Cambodia, China, India, Japan, Korea, Malaysia, Pakistan, the Philippine Islands, Thailand, and Vietnam. It includes "Asian Indian," "Chinese," "Filipino," "Korean," "Japanese," "Vietnamese," and "Other Asian."
- **Hispanic.** The data on the Hispanic or Latino population, which was asked of all people, were derived from answers to long-form questionnaire Item 5, and short-form questionnaire Item 7. The terms "Spanish," "Hispanic origin," and "Latino" are used interchangeably. Some respondents identify with all three terms, while others may identify with only one of these three specific terms. Hispanics or Latinos who identify with the terms "Spanish," "Hispanic," or "Latino" are those who classify themselves in one of the specific Hispanic or Latino categories listed on the questionnaire — "Mexican," "Puerto Rican," or "Cuban" — as well as those who indicate that they are "other Spanish, Hispanic, or Latino." People who do not identify with one of the specific origins listed on the questionnaire but indicate that they are "other Spanish, Hispanic, or Latino" are those whose origins are from Spain, the Spanish-speaking countries of Central or South America, the Dominican Republic, or people identifying themselves generally as Spanish, Spanish-American, Hispanic, Hispano, Latino, and so on. All write-in responses to the "other Spanish/Hispanic/Latino" category were coded. Origin can be viewed as the heritage, nationality group, lineage, or country of birth of the person or the person's parents or ancestors before their arrival in the United States. People who identify their origin as Spanish, Hispanic, or Latino may be of any race.

Population Density: 2007 population estimate divided by the land area in square miles. *Source: Claritas; U.S. Bureau of the Census, Census of Population and Housing, 2000: Summary File 1.*

Average Household Size: Average household size was calculated by dividing the total population by the total number of households. Figures are 2007 estimates. *Source: Claritas.*

Median Age: Figures are 2007 estimates. *Source: Claritas.*

Male/Female Ratio: Number of males per 100 females. Figures are 2007 estimates. *Source: Claritas.*

Marital Status: Percentage of population never married, now married, widowed, or divorced. *Source: U.S. Bureau of the Census, Census of Population and Housing, 2000: Summary File 3.*

The marital status classification refers to the status at the time of enumeration. Data on marital status are tabulated only for the population 15 years old and over. Each person was asked whether they were "Now married," "Widowed," "Divorced," or "Never married." Couples who live together (for example, people in common-law marriages) were able to report the marital status they considered to be the most appropriate.

- **Never married**. Never married includes all people who have never been married, including people whose only marriage(s) was annulled.
- **Now married.** All people whose current marriage has not ended by widowhood or divorce. This category includes people defined as "separated."
- **Widowed**. This category includes widows and widowers who have not remarried.
- **Divorced.** This category includes people who are legally divorced and who have not remarried.

Foreign Born: Percentage of population who were not U.S. citizens at birth. Foreign-born people are those who indicated they were either a U.S. citizen by naturalization or they were not a citizen of the United States. *Source: U.S. Bureau of the Census, Census of Population and Housing, 2000: Summary File 3.*

Ancestry: Largest ancestry groups reported (up to five). Includes multiple ancestries. *Source: U.S. Bureau of the Census, Census of Population and Housing, 2000: Summary File 3.*

The data represent self-classification by people according to the ancestry group or groups with which they most closely identify. Ancestry refers to a person's ethnic origin or descent, "roots," heritage, or the place of birth of the person, the person's parents, or their ancestors before their arrival in the United States. Some ethnic identities, such as Egyptian or Polish, can be traced to geographic areas outside the United States, while other ethnicities such as Pennsylvania German or Cajun evolved in the United States.

The ancestry question was intended to provide data for groups that were not included in the Hispanic origin and race questions. Therefore, although data on all groups are collected, the ancestry data shown in these tabulations are for non-Hispanic and non-race groups. Hispanic and race groups are included in the "Other groups" category for the ancestry tables in these tabulations.

The ancestry question allowed respondents to report one or more ancestry groups, although only the first two were coded. If a response was in terms of a dual ancestry, for example, "Irish English," the person was assigned two codes, in this case one for Irish and another for English. However, in certain cases, multiple responses such as "French Canadian," "Greek Cypriote," and "Scotch Irish" were assigned a single code reflecting their status as unique groups. If a person reported one of these unique groups in addition to another group, for example, "Scotch Irish English," resulting in three terms, that person received one code for the unique group (Scotch-Irish) and another one for the remaining group (English). If a person reported "English Irish French," only English and Irish were coded. Certain combinations of ancestries where the ancestry group is a part of another, such as "German-Bavarian," were coded as a single ancestry using the more specific group (Bavarian). Also, responses such as "Polish-American" or "Italian-American" were coded and tabulated as a single entry (Polish or Italian).

The Census Bureau accepted "American" as a unique ethnicity if it was given alone, with an ambiguous response, or with state names. If the respondent listed any other ethnic identity such as "Italian-American," generally the "American" portion of the response was not coded. However, distinct groups such as "American Indian," "Mexican American," and "African American" were coded and identified separately because they represented groups who considered themselves different from those who reported as "Indian," "Mexican," or "African," respectively.

The data is based on the total number of ancestries reported and coded. Thus, the sum of the counts in this type of presentation is not the total population but the total of all responses.

ECONOMY

Unemployment Rate: June 2008. Includes all civilians age 16 or over who were unemployed and looking for work. *Source: U.S. Department of Labor, Bureau of Labor Statistics, Local Area Unemployment Statistics (http://www.bls.gov/lau/home.htm).*

Total Civilian Labor Force: June 2008. Includes all civilians age 16 or over who were either employed, or unemployed and looking for work. *Source: U.S. Department of Labor, Bureau of Labor Statistics, Local Area Unemployment Statistics (http://www.bls.gov/lau/home.htm).*

Single-Family Building Permits Issued: Building permits issued for new single-family housing units in 2007. *Source: U.S. Census Bureau, Manufacturing and Construction Division (http://www.census.gov/const/www/permitsindex.html).*

Multi-Family Building Permits Issued: Building permits issued for new multi-family housing units in 2007. *Source: U.S. Census Bureau, Manufacturing and Construction Division (http://www.census.gov/const/www/permitsindex.html).*

Statistics on housing units authorized by building permits include housing units issued in local permit-issuing jurisdictions by a building or zoning permit. Not all areas of the country require a building or zoning permit. The statistics only represent those areas that do require a permit. Current surveys indicate that construction is undertaken for all but a very small percentage of housing units authorized by building permits. A major portion typically get under way during the month of permit issuance and most of the remainder begin within the three following months. Because of this lag, the housing unit authorization statistics do not represent the number of units actually put into construction for the period shown, and should therefore not be directly interpreted as "housing starts."

Statistics are based upon reports submitted by local building permit officials in response to a mail survey. They are obtained using Form C-404 const/www/c404.pdf, "Report of New Privately-Owned Residential Building or Zoning Permits Issued." When a report is not received, missing data are either (1) obtained from the Survey of Use of Permits (SUP) which is used to collect information on housing starts, or (2) imputed based on the assumption that the ratio of current month authorizations to those of a year ago should be the same for reporting and non-reporting places.

Employment by Occupation: Percentage of the employed civilian population 16 years and over in management, professional, service, sales, farming, construction, and production occupations. *Source: U.S. Bureau of the Census, Census of Population and Housing, 2000: Summary File 3.*

- **Management** includes management, business, and financial operations occupations:
  - Management occupations, except farmers and farm managers
  - Farmers and farm managers
  - Business and financial operations occupations:
    - Business operations specialists
    - Financial specialists

- **Professional** includes professional and related occupations:
  - Computer and mathematical occupations
  - Architecture and engineering occupations:
    - Architects, surveyors, cartographers, and engineers
    - Drafters, engineering, and mapping technicians
  - Life, physical, and social science occupations
  - Community and social services occupations
  - Legal occupations
  - Education, training, and library occupations
  - Arts, design, entertainment, sports, and media occupations
  - Healthcare practitioners and technical occupations:
    - Health diagnosing and treating practitioners and technical occupations
    - Health technologists and technicians

- **Service** occupations include:
  - Healthcare support occupations
  - Protective service occupations:
    - Fire fighting, prevention, and law enforcement workers, including supervisors

Other protective service workers, including supervisors
Food preparation and serving related occupations
Building and grounds cleaning and maintenance occupations
Personal care and service occupations

- **Sales** and office occupations include:
  Sales and related occupations
  Office and administrative support occupations

- **Farming,** fishing, and forestry occupations

- **Construction,** extraction, and maintenance occupations include:
  Construction and extraction occupations:
    Supervisors, construction, and extraction workers
    Construction trades workers
    Extraction workers
  Installation, maintenance, and repair occupations

- **Production,** transportation, and material moving occupations include:
  Production occupations
  Transportation and material moving occupations:
    Supervisors, transportation, and material moving workers
    Aircraft and traffic control occupations
    Motor vehicle operators
    Rail, water, and other transportation occupations
    Material moving workers

INCOME

Per Capita Income: Per capita income is the mean income computed for every man, woman, and child in a particular group. It is derived by dividing the total income of a particular group by the total population in that group. Per capita income is rounded to the nearest whole dollar. Figures shown are 2007 estimates. *Source: Claritas.*

Median Household Income: Includes the income of the householder and all other individuals 15 years old and over in the household, whether they are related to the householder or not. The median divides the income distribution into two equal parts: one-half of the cases falling below the median income and one-half above the median. For households, the median income is based on the distribution of the total number of households including those with no income. Median income for households is computed on the basis of a standard distribution and is rounded to the nearest whole dollar. Figures shown are 2007 estimates. *Source: Claritas.*

Average Household Income: Average household income is obtained by dividing total household income by the total number of households. Figures shown are 2007 estimates. *Source: Claritas.*

Percent of Households with Income of $100,000 or more: Figures shown are 2007 estimates. *Source: Claritas.*

Poverty Rate: Percentage of population with income in 1999 below the poverty level. Based on individuals for whom poverty status is determined. Poverty status was determined for all people except institutionalized people, people in military group quarters, people in college dormitories, and unrelated individuals under 15 years old. *Source: U.S. Bureau of the Census, Census of Population and Housing, 2000: Summary File 3.*

The poverty status of families and unrelated individuals in 1999 was determined using 48 thresholds (income cutoffs) arranged in a two-dimensional matrix. The matrix consists of family size (from 1 person to 9 or more people) cross-classified by presence and number of family members under 18 years old (from no children present to 8 or more children present). Unrelated individuals and 2-person families were further differentiated by the age of the reference person (RP) (under 65 years old and 65 years old and over).

To determine a person's poverty status, one compares the person's total family income with the poverty threshold appropriate for that person's family size and composition. If the total income of that person's family is less than the threshold appropriate for that family, then the person is considered poor, together with every member of his or her family. If a person is not living with anyone related by birth, marriage, or adoption, then the person's own income is compared with his or her poverty threshold.

TAXES

Total City Taxes Per Capita: Total city taxes collected divided by the population of the city. *Source: U.S. Bureau of the Census, State and Local Government Finances, 2005-06 (http://www.census.gov/govs/www/estimate.html).*

Taxes include:

- Property Taxes
- Sales and Gross Receipts Taxes
- Federal Customs Duties
- General Sales and Gross Receipts Taxes
- Selective Sales Taxes (alcoholic beverages; amusements; insurance premiums; motor fuels; pari-mutuels; public utilities; tobacco products; other)
- License Taxes (alcoholic beverages; amusements; corporations in general; hunting and fishing; motor vehicles motor vehicle operators; public utilities; occupation and business, NEC; other)
- Income Taxes (individual income; corporation net income; other)
- Death and Gift
- Documentary & Stock Transfer
- Severance
- Taxes, NEC

Total City Property Taxes Per Capita: Total city property taxes collected divided by the population of the city. *Source: U.S. Bureau of the Census, State and Local Government Finances, 2005-06 (http://www.census.gov/govs/www/estimate.html).*

Property Taxes include general property taxes, relating to property as a whole, taxed at a single rate or at classified rates according to the class of property. Property refers to real property (e.g. land and structures) as well as personal property; personal property can be either tangible (e.g. automobiles and boats) or intangible (e.g. bank accounts and stocks and bonds). Special property taxes, levied on selected types of property (e.g. oil and gas properties, house trailers, motor vehicles, and intangibles) and subject to rates not directly related to general property tax rates. Taxes based on income produced by property as a measure of its value on the assessment date.

EDUCATION

Educational Attainment: Figures shown are 2007 estimates and show the percent of population age 25 and over with a:

- **High school diploma (including GED) or higher:** includes people whose highest degree was a high school diploma or its equivalent, people who attended college but did not receive a degree, and people who received a college, university, or professional degree. People who reported completing the 12th grade but not receiving a diploma are not high school graduates.
- **Bachelor's degree or higher**
- **Master's degree or higher:** Master's degrees include the traditional MA and MS degrees and field-specific degrees, such as MSW, MEd, MBA, MLS, and Meng. *Source: Claritas.*

School Districts: Lists the name of each school district, the grade range (PK=pre-kindergarten; KG=kindergarten), the student enrollment, and the district headquarters' phone number. In each community profile, only school districts that have schools that are physically located within the community are shown. In addition, statistics for each school district cover the entire district, regardless of the physical location of the schools within the district. *Source: U.S. Department of Education, National Center for Educational Statistics, Directory of Public Elementary and Secondary Education Agencies, 2005-06.*

Four-year Colleges: Lists the name of each four-year college, the type of institution (private or public; for-profit or non-profit; religious affiliation; historically black), the total student enrollment (Fall 2007 estimate), the general telephone number, and the annual tuition (including fees) for full-time, first-time undergraduate students (in-state and out-of-state). *Source: U.S. Department of Education, National Center for Educational Statistics, IPEDS College Data, 2007-08.*

Two-year Colleges: Lists the name of each two-year college, the type of institution (private or public; for-profit or non-profit; religious affiliation; historically black), the total student enrollment (Fall 2007 estimate), the general telephone number, and the annual tuition (including fees) for full-time, first-time undergraduate students (in-state and out-of-state). *Source: U.S. Department of Education, National Center for Educational Statistics, IPEDS College Data, 2007-08.*

Vocational/Technical Schools: Lists the name of each vocational/technical school, the type of institution (private or public; for-profit or non-profit; religious affiliation; historically black), the total student enrollment (Fall 2007 estimate), the general telephone number, and the annual tuition and fees for full-time students. *Source: U.S. Department of Education, National Center for Educational Statistics, IPEDS College Data, 2007-08.*

HOUSING

Homeownership Rate: Percentage of housing units that are owner-occupied. Figures shown are 2007 estimates. *Source: Claritas.*

Median Home Value: Median value of all owner-occupied housing units as reported by the owner. Figures shown are 2007 estimates. *Source: Claritas.*

Median Rent: Median monthly contract rent on specified renter-occupied and specified vacant-for-rent units. Specified renter-occupied and specified vacant-for-rent units exclude 1-family houses on 10 acres or more. Contract rent is the monthly rent agreed to or contracted for, regardless of any furnishings, utilities, fees, meals, or services that may be included. For vacant units, it is the monthly rent asked for the rental unit at the time of enumeration. *Source: U.S. Bureau of the Census, Census of Population and Housing, 2000: Summary File 3.*

Median Age of Housing: Median age of housing was calculated by subtracting median year structure built from 2000 (e.g. if the median year structure built is 1967, the median age of housing in that area is 33 years—2000 minus 1967). Year structure built refers to when the building was first constructed, not when it was remodeled, added to, or converted. For housing units under construction that met the housing unit definition—that is, all exterior windows, doors, and final usable floors were in place—the category "1999 or 2000" was used for tabulations. For mobile homes, houseboats, RVs, etc, the manufacturer's model year was assumed to be the year built. The data relate to the number of units built during the specified periods that were still in existence at the time of enumeration. *Source: U.S. Bureau of the Census, Census of Population and Housing, 2000: Summary File 3.*

HOSPITALS

Lists the hospital name and the number of licensed beds. *Source: Grey House Publishing, Directory of Hospital Personnel, 2007.*

SAFETY

Violent Crime Rate: Number of violent crimes reported per 10,000 population. Violent crimes include murder, forcible rape, robbery, and aggravated assault. *Source: Federal Bureau of Investigation, Uniform Crime Reports 2007 (http://www.fbi.gov/ucr/ucr.htm).*

Property Crime Rate: Number of property crimes reported per 10,000 population. Property crimes include burglary, larceny-theft, and motor vehicle theft. *Source: Federal Bureau of Investigation, Uniform Crime Reports 2007 (http://www.fbi.gov/ucr/ucr.htm).*

NEWSPAPERS

Lists the name, circulation and news focus of daily and weekly newspapers. Includes newspapers with offices located in the community profiled. *Source: MediaContactsPro 2008*

TRANSPORTATION

Commute to Work: Percentage of workers 16 years old and over that use the following means of transportation to commute to work: car; public transportation; walk; work from home. *Source: U.S. Bureau of the Census, Census of Population and Housing, 2000: Summary File 3.*

The means of transportation data for some areas may show workers using modes of public transportation that are not available in those areas (e.g. subway or elevated riders in a metropolitan area where there actually is no subway or elevated service). This result is largely due to people who worked during the reference week at a location that was different from their usual place of work (such as people away from home on business in an area where subway service was available) and people who used more than one means of transportation each day but whose principal means was unavailable where they lived (e.g. residents of non-metropolitan areas who drove to the fringe of a metropolitan area and took the commuter railroad most of the distance to work).

Travel Time to Work: Travel time to work for workers 16 years old and over. Reported for the following intervals: less than 15 minutes; 15 to 30 minutes; 30 to 45 minutes; 45 to 60 minutes; 60 minutes or more. *Source: U.S. Bureau of the Census, Census of Population and Housing, 2000: Summary File 3.*

Travel time to work refers to the total number of minutes that it usually took the person to get from home to work each day during the reference week. The elapsed time includes time spent waiting for public transportation, picking up passengers in carpools, and time spent in other activities related to getting to work.

Amtrak: Indicates if Amtrak rail or bus service is available. Please note that the cities being served continually change. *Source: National Railroad Passenger Corporation, Amtrak National Timetable, 2008 (www.amtrak.com).*

AIRPORTS

Lists the local airport(s) along with type of service and hub size. *Source: U.S. Department of Transportation, Bureau of Transportation Statistics (http://www.bts.gov).*

ADDITIONAL INFORMATION CONTACTS

The following phone numbers are provided as sources of additional information: Chambers of Commerce; Economic Development Agencies; and Convention & Visitors Bureaus. Efforts have been made to provide the most recent area codes. However, area code changes may have occurred in listed numbers. *Source: Original research.*

Information for Counties

PHYSICAL CHARACTERISTICS

Physical Location: Describes the physical location of the county. *Source: Columbia University Press, The Columbia Gazetteer of North America and original research.*

Land and Water Area: Land and water area in square miles. *Source: U.S. Bureau of the Census, Census of Population and Housing, 2000: Summary File 1.*

Time Zone: Lists the time zone. *Source: Original research.*

Year Organized: Year the county government was organized. *Source: National Association of Counties (www.naco.org).*

County Seat: Lists the county seat. If a county has more than one seat, then both are listed. *Source: National Association of Counties (www.naco.org).*

Metropolitan Area: Indicates the metropolitan area the county is located in. Also lists all the component counties of that metropolitan area. The Office of Management and Budget (OMB) defines metropolitan and micropolitan statistical areas. The most current definitions are as of November 2007. *Source: U.S. Bureau of the Census (http://www.census.gov/population/www/estimates/metrodef.html).*

Climate: Includes all weather stations located within the county. Indicates the station name and elevation as well as the monthly average high and low temperatures, average precipitation, and average snowfall. The period of record is generally 1970-1999, however, certain weather stations contain averages going back as far as 1900. *Source: Grey House Publishing, Weather America: A Thirty-Year Summary of Statistical Weather Data and Rankings, 2001.*

POPULATION

Population: 1990 and 2000 figures are a 100% count of population. 2007 estimates and 2012 projections were provided by Claritas. *Source: Claritas; U.S. Bureau of the Census, Census of Population and Housing, 2000: Summary File 1.*

Population by Race: 2007 estimates includes the U.S. Bureau of the Census categories of White alone; Black alone; Asian alone; and Hispanic of any race. Alone refers to the fact that these figures are not in combination with any other race. 2007 data for American Indian/Alaska Native and Native Hawaiian/Other Pacific Islander was not available.

The concept of race, as used by the Census Bureau, reflects self-identification by people according to the race or races with which they most closely identify. These categories are socio-political constructs and should not be interpreted as being scientific or anthropological in nature. Furthermore, the race categories include both racial and national-origin groups.

- **White.** A person having origins in any of the original peoples of Europe, the Middle East, or North Africa. It includes people who indicate their race as "White" or report entries such as Irish, German, Italian, Lebanese, Near Easterner, Arab, or Polish.
- **Black or African American.** A person having origins in any of the Black racial groups of Africa. It includes people who indicate their race as "Black, African American, or Negro," or provide written entries such as African American, Afro-American, Kenyan, Nigerian, or Haitian.
- **Asian.** A person having origins in any of the original peoples of the Far East, Southeast Asia, or the Indian subcontinent including, for example, Cambodia, China, India, Japan, Korea, Malaysia, Pakistan, the Philippine Islands, Thailand, and Vietnam. It includes "Asian Indian," "Chinese," "Filipino," "Korean," "Japanese," "Vietnamese," and "Other Asian."
- **Hispanic.** The data on the Hispanic or Latino population, which was asked of all people, were derived from answers to long-form questionnaire Item 5, and short-form questionnaire Item 7. The terms "Spanish," "Hispanic origin," and "Latino" are used interchangeably. Some respondents identify with all three terms, while others may identify with only one of these three specific terms. Hispanics or Latinos who identify with the terms "Spanish," "Hispanic," or "Latino" are those who classify themselves in one of the specific Hispanic or Latino categories listed on the questionnaire — "Mexican," "Puerto Rican," or "Cuban" — as well as those who indicate that they are "other Spanish, Hispanic, or Latino." People who do not identify with one of the specific origins listed on the questionnaire but indicate that they are "other Spanish, Hispanic, or Latino" are those whose origins are from Spain, the Spanish-speaking countries of

Central or South America, the Dominican Republic, or people identifying themselves generally as Spanish, Spanish-American, Hispanic, Hispano, Latino, and so on. All write-in responses to the "other Spanish/Hispanic/Latino" category were coded. Origin can be viewed as the heritage, nationality group, lineage, or country of birth of the person or the person's parents or ancestors before their arrival in the United States. People who identify their origin as Spanish, Hispanic, or Latino may be of any race.

Population Density: 2007 population estimate divided by the land area in square miles. *Source: Claritas; U.S. Bureau of the Census, Census of Population and Housing, 2000: Summary File 1.*

Average Household Size: Average household size was calculated by dividing the total population by the total number of households. Figures are 2007 estimates. *Source: Claritas.*

Median Age: Figures are 2007 estimates. *Source: Claritas.*

Male/Female Ratio: Number of males per 100 females. Figures are 2007 estimates. *Source: Claritas.*

RELIGION

Religion: Lists the largest religious groups (up to five) based on the number of adherents divided by the population of the county. Adherents are defined as "all members, including full members, their children and the estimated number of other regular participants who are not considered as communicant, confirmed or full members." The data is based on a study of 149 religious bodies sponsored by the Association of Statisticians of American Religious Bodies. The 149 bodies reported 268,254 congregations and 141,371,963 adherents. *Source: Glenmary Research Center, Religious Congregations & Membership in the United States 2000.*

ECONOMY

Unemployment Rate: June 2008. Includes all civilians age 16 or over who were unemployed and looking for work. *Source: U.S. Department of Labor, Bureau of Labor Statistics, Local Area Unemployment Statistics (http://www.bls.gov/lau/home.htm).*

Total Civilian Labor Force: June 2008. Includes all civilians age 16 or over who were either employed, or unemployed and looking for work. *Source: U.S. Department of Labor, Bureau of Labor Statistics, Local Area Unemployment Statistics (http://www.bls.gov/lau/home.htm).*

Leading Industries: Lists the three largest industries (excluding government) based on the number of employees. *Source: U.S. Bureau of the Census, County Business Patterns 2006 (http://www.census.gov/epcd/cbp/view/cbpview.html).*

Farms: The total number of farms and the total acreage they occupy. *Source: U.S. Department of Agriculture, National Agricultural Statistics Service, 2002 Census of Agriculture (http://www.nass.usda.gov/census).*

Companies that Employ 500 or more persons: The numbers of companies that employ 500 or more persons. Includes private employers only. *Source: U.S. Bureau of the Census, County Business Patterns 2006 (http://www.census.gov/epcd/cbp/view/cbpview.html).*

Companies that Employ 100 - 499 persons: The numbers of companies that employ 100 - 499 persons. Includes private employers only. *Source: U.S. Bureau of the Census, County Business Patterns 2006 (http://www.census.gov/epcd/cbp/view/cbpview.html).*

Companies that Employ 1 - 99 persons: The numbers of companies that employ 1 - 99 persons. Includes private employers only. *Source: U.S. Bureau of the Census, County Business Patterns 2006 (http://www.census.gov/epcd/cbp/view/cbpview.html)*

Black-Owned Businesses: Number of businesses that are majority-owned by a Black or African-American person(s). Majority ownership is defined as having 51 percent or more of the stock or equity in the business. Black or African American is defined as a person having origins in any of the black racial groups of Africa, including those who consider themselves to be "Haitian." *Source: U.S. Bureau of the Census, 2002 Economic Census, Survey of Business Owners: Black-Owned Firms, 2002 (http://www.census.gov/csd/sbo/index.html).*

Asian-Owned Businesses: Number of businesses that are majority-owned by an Asian person(s). Majority ownership is defined as having 51 percent or more of the stock or equity in the business. *Source: U.S. Bureau of the Census, 2002 Economic Census, Survey of Business Owners: Black-Owned Firms, 2002 (http://www.census.gov/csd/sbo/index.html).*

Hispanic-Owned Businesses: Number of businesses that are majority-owned by a person(s) of Hispanic or Latino origin. Majority ownership is defined as having 51 percent or more of the stock or equity in the business. Hispanic or Latino origin is defined as a person of Cuban, Mexican, Puerto Rican, South or Central American, or other Spanish culture or origin, regardless of race. *Source: U.S. Bureau of the Census, 2002 Economic Census, Survey of Business Owners: Hispanic-Owned Firms, 2002 (http://www.census.gov/csd/sbo/index.html).*

Women-Owned Businesses: Number of businesses that are majority-owned by a woman. Majority ownership is defined as having 51 percent or more of the stock or equity in the business. *Source: U.S. Bureau of the Census, 2002 Economic Census, Survey of Business Owners: Women-Owned Firms, 2002 (http://www.census.gov/csd/sbo/index.html).*

The Survey of Business Owners (SBO), formerly known as the Surveys of Minority- and Women-Owned Business Enterprises (SMOBE/SWOBE), provides statistics that describe the composition of U.S. businesses by gender, Hispanic or Latino origin, and race. Additional statistics include owner's age, education level, veteran status, and primary function in the business; family- and home-based businesses; types of customers and workers; and sources of financing for expansion, capital improvements, or start-up. Economic policymakers in federal, state and local governments use the SBO data to understand conditions of business success and failure by comparing census-to-census changes in business performances and by comparing minority-/nonminority- and women-/men-owned businesses.

Retail Sales per Capita: Total dollar amount of estimated retail sales divided by the estimated population of the county in 2008. *Source: Editor & Publisher Market Guide 2008*

Single-Family Building Permits Issued: Building permits issued for new, single-family housing units in 2007. *Source: U.S. Census Bureau, Manufacturing and Construction Division (http://www.census.gov/const/www/permitsindex.html).*

Multi-Family Building Permits Issued: Building permits issued for new, multi-family housing units in 2007. *Source: U.S. Census Bureau, Manufacturing and Construction Division (http://www.census.gov/const/www/permitsindex.html).*

Statistics on housing units authorized by building permits include housing units issued in local permit-issuing jurisdictions by a building or zoning permit. Not all areas of the country require a building or zoning permit. The statistics only represent those areas that do require a permit. Current surveys indicate that construction is undertaken for all but a very small percentage of housing units authorized by building permits. A major portion typically get under way during the month of permit issuance and most of the remainder begin within the three following months. Because of this lag, the housing unit authorization statistics do not represent the number of units actually put into construction for the period shown, and should therefore not be directly interpreted as "housing starts."

Statistics are based upon reports submitted by local building permit officials in response to a mail survey. They are obtained using Form C-404 const/www/c404.pdf, "Report of New Privately-Owned Residential Building or Zoning Permits Issued." When a report is not received, missing data are either (1) obtained from the Survey of Use of Permits (SUP) which is used to collect information on housing starts, or (2) imputed based on the assumption that the ratio of current month authorizations to those of a year ago should be the same for reporting and non-reporting places.

INCOME

Per Capita Income: Per capita income is the mean income computed for every man, woman, and child in a particular group. It is derived by dividing the total income of a particular group by the total population in that group. Per capita income is rounded to the nearest whole dollar. Figures shown are 2007 estimates. *Source: Claritas.*

Median Household Income: Includes the income of the householder and all other individuals 15 years old and over in the household, whether they are related to the householder or not. The median divides the income distribution into two equal parts: one-half of the cases falling below the median income and one-half above the median. For households, the median income is based on the distribution of the total number of households including those with no income. Median income for households is computed on the basis of a standard distribution and is rounded to the nearest whole dollar. Figures shown are 2007 estimates. *Source: Claritas.*

Average Household Income: Average household income is obtained by dividing total household income by the total number of households. Figures shown are 2007 estimates. *Source: Claritas.*

Percent of Households with Income of $100,000 or more: Figures shown are 2007 estimates. *Source: Claritas.*

Poverty Rate: Estimated percentage of population with income in 2005 below the poverty level. *Source: U.S. Bureau of the Census, Small Area Income & Poverty Estimates.*

Bankruptcy Rate: The personal bankruptcy filing rate is the number of bankruptcies per thousand residents in 2007. Personal bankruptcy filings include both Chapter 7 (liquidations) and Chapter 13 (reorganizations) based on the county of residence of the filer. *Source: Federal Deposit Insurance Corporation, Regional Economic Conditions (http://www2.fdic.gov/recon/index.html).*

TAXES

Total County Taxes Per Capita: Total county taxes collected divided by the population of the county. *Source: U.S. Bureau of the Census, State and Local Government Finances, 2005-06 (http://www.census.gov/govs/www/estimate.html).*

Taxes include:

- Property Taxes
- Sales and Gross Receipts Taxes
- Federal Customs Duties
- General Sales and Gross Receipts Taxes
- Selective Sales Taxes (alcoholic beverages; amusements; insurance premiums; motor fuels; pari-mutuels; public utilities; tobacco products; other)
- License Taxes (alcoholic beverages; amusements; corporations in general; hunting and fishing; motor vehicles motor vehicle operators; public utilities; occupation and business, NEC; other)
- Income Taxes (individual income; corporation net income; other)
- Death and Gift
- Documentary & Stock Transfer
- Severance
- Taxes, NEC

Total County Property Taxes Per Capita: Total county property taxes collected divided by the population of the county. *Source: U.S. Bureau of the Census, State and Local Government Finances, 2005-06 (http://www.census.gov/govs/www/estimate.html).*

Property Taxes include general property taxes, relating to property as a whole, taxed at a single rate or at classified rates according to the class of property. Property refers to real property (e.g. land and structures) as well as personal property; personal property can be either tangible (e.g. automobiles and boats) or intangible (e.g. bank accounts and stocks and bonds). Special property taxes, levied on selected types of property (e.g. oil and gas properties, house trailers, motor vehicles, and intangibles) and subject to rates not directly related to general property tax rates. Taxes based on income produced by property as a measure of its value on the assessment date.

EDUCATION

Educational Attainment: Figures shown are 2007 estimates and show the percent of population age 25 and over with a:

- **High school diploma (including GED) or higher:** includes people whose highest degree was a high school diploma or its equivalent, people who attended college but did not receive a degree, and people who received a college, university, or professional degree. People who reported completing the 12th grade but not receiving a diploma are not high school graduates.
- **Bachelor's degree or higher**
- **Master's degree or higher:** Master's degrees include the traditional MA and MS degrees and field-specific degrees, such as MSW, MEd, MBA, MLS, and Meng. *Source: Claritas.*

HOUSING

Homeownership Rate: Percentage of housing units that are owner-occupied. Figures shown are 2007 estimates. *Source: Claritas.*

Median Home Value: Median value of all owner-occupied housing units as reported by the owner. Figures shown are 2007 estimates. *Source: Claritas.*

Median Rent: Median monthly contract rent on specified renter-occupied and specified vacant-for-rent units. Specified renter-occupied and specified vacant-for-rent units exclude 1-family houses on 10 acres or more. Contract rent is the monthly rent agreed to or contracted for, regardless of any furnishings, utilities, fees, meals, or services that may be included. For vacant units, it is the monthly rent asked for the rental unit at the time of enumeration. *Source: U.S. Bureau of the Census, Census of Population and Housing, 2000: Summary File 3.*

Median Age of Housing: Median age of housing was calculated by subtracting median year structure built from 2000 (e.g. if the median year structure built is 1967, the median age of housing in that area is 33 years — 2000 minus 1967). Year structure built refers to when the building was first constructed, not when it was remodeled, added to, or converted. For housing units under construction that met the housing unit definition—that is, all exterior windows, doors, and final usable floors were in place—the category "1999 or 2000" was used for tabulations. For mobile homes, houseboats, RVs, etc, the manufacturer's model year was assumed to be the year built. The data relate to the number of units built during the specified periods that were still in existence at the time of enumeration. *Source: U.S. Bureau of the Census, Census of Population and Housing, 2000: Summary File 3.*

HEALTH AND VITAL STATISTICS

Birth Rate: Estimated number of births per 10,000 population in 2007. *Source: U.S. Census Bureau, Annual Components of Population Change, July 1, 2006 - July 1 , 2007 (http://www.census.gov/popest/births.html).*

Death Rate: Estimated number of deaths per 10,000 population in 2007. *Source: U.S. Census Bureau, Annual Components of Population Change, July 1, 2006 - July 1 , 2007 (http://www.census.gov/popest/births.html).*

Age-adjusted Cancer Mortality Rate: Number of age-adjusted deaths from cancer per 100,000 population in 2005. Cancer is defined as International Classification of Disease (ICD) codes C00 - D48.9 Neoplasms. *Source: Centers for Disease Control, CDC Wonder (http://wonder.cdc.gov).*

Age-adjusted death rates are weighted averages of the age-specific death rates, where the weights represent a fixed population by age. They are used because the rates of almost all causes of death vary by age. Age adjustment is a technique for "removing" the effects of age from crude rates, so as to allow meaningful comparisons across populations with different underlying age structures. For example, comparing the crude rate of heart disease in New York to that of California is misleading, because the relatively older population in New York will lead to a higher crude death rate, even if the age-specific rates of heart disease in New York and California are the same. For such a comparison, age-adjusted rates would be preferable. Age-adjusted rates should be viewed as relative indexes rather than as direct or actual measures of mortality risk.

Death rates based on counts of twenty or less (<=20) are flagged as "Unreliable". Death rates based on fewer than three years of data for counties with populations of less than 100,000 in the 1990 Census counts, are also flagged as "Unreliable" if the number of deaths is five or less (<=5).

Air Quality Index: The percentage of days in 2007 the AQI fell into the Good (0-50), Moderate (51-100), Unhealthy for Sensitive Groups (101-150), and Unhealthy (151+) ranges. Data covers January 2007 through December 2007. Counties with less than 100 days of air quality data were excluded. *Source: AirData: Access to Air Pollution Data , U.S. Environmental Protection Agency, Office of Air and Radiation (http://www.epa.gov/air/data/index.html).*

The AQI is an index for reporting daily air quality. It tells you how clean or polluted your air is, and what associated health concerns you should be aware of. The AQI focuses on health effects that can happen within a few hours or days after breathing polluted air. EPA uses the AQI for five major air pollutants regulated by the Clean Air Act: ground-level ozone, particulate matter, carbon monoxide, sulfur dioxide, and nitrogen dioxide. For each of these pollutants, EPA has established national air quality standards to protect against harmful health effects.

The AQI runs from 0 to 500. The higher the AQI value, the greater the level of air pollution and the greater the health danger. For example, an AQI value of 50 represents good air quality and little potential to affect public health, while an AQI value over 300 represents hazardous air quality. An AQI value of 100 generally corresponds to the national air quality standard for the pollutant, which is the level EPA has set to protect public health. So, AQI values below 100 are generally thought of as satisfactory. When AQI values are above 100, air quality is considered to be unhealthy—at first for certain sensitive groups of people, then for everyone as AQI values get higher. Each category corresponds to a different level of health concern. For example, when the AQI for a pollutant is between 51 and 100, the health concern is "Moderate." Here are the six levels of health concern and what they mean:

- "Good" The AQI value for your community is between 0 and 50. Air quality is considered satisfactory and air pollution poses little or no risk.
- "Moderate" The AQI for your community is between 51 and 100. Air quality is acceptable; however, for some pollutants there may be a moderate health concern for a very small number of individuals. For example, people who are unusually sensitive to ozone may experience respiratory symptoms.
- "Unhealthy for Sensitive Groups" Certain groups of people are particularly sensitive to the harmful effects of certain air pollutants. This means they are likely to be affected at lower levels than the general public. For example, children and adults who are active outdoors and people with respiratory disease are at greater risk from exposure to ozone, while people with heart disease are at greater risk from carbon monoxide. Some people may be sensitive to more than one pollutant. When AQI values are between 101 and 150, members of sensitive groups may experience health effects. The general public is not likely to be affected when the AQI is in this range.
- "Unhealthy" AQI values are between 151 and 200. Everyone may begin to experience health effects. Members of sensitive groups may experience more serious health effects.
- "Very Unhealthy" AQI values between 201 and 300 trigger a health alert, meaning everyone may experience more serious health effects.
- "Hazardous" AQI values over 300 trigger health warnings of emergency conditions. The entire population is more likely to be affected.

Number of Physicians: The number of active, non-federal physicians per 10,000 population in 2005. *Source: Area Resource File (ARF). 2006 Release. U.S. Department of Health and Human Services, Health Resources and Services Administration, Bureau of Health Professions, Rockville, MD, June 2007.*

Number of Hospital Beds: The number of hospital beds per 10,000 population in 2004. *Source: Area Resource File (ARF). 2006 Release. U.S. Department of Health and Human Services, Health Resources and Services Administration, Bureau of Health Professions, Rockville, MD, June 2007.*

Number of Hospital Admissions: The number of hospital admissions per 10,000 population in 2004. *Source: Area Resource File (ARF). 2006 Release. U.S. Department of Health and Human Services, Health Resources and Services Administration, Bureau of Health Professions, Rockville, MD, June 2007.*

ELECTIONS

Elections: 2004 Presidential election results. *Source: Dave Leip's Atlas of U.S. Presidential Elections (http://www.uselectionatlas.org).*

NATIONAL AND STATE PARKS

Lists National and State parks located in the area. *Source: U.S. Geological Survey, Geographic Names Information System.*

ADDITIONAL INFORMATION CONTACTS

The following phone numbers are provided as sources of additional information: Chambers of Commerce; Economic Development Agencies; and Convention & Visitors Bureaus. Efforts have been made to provide the most recent area codes. However, area code changes may have occurred in listed numbers. *Source: Original research.*

User's Guide: Education

School District Rankings

Number of Schools: Total number of schools in the district. *Source: U.S. Department of Education, National Center for Education Statistics, Common Core of Data, Public Elementary/Secondary School Universe Survey: School Year 2005-2006.*

Number of Teachers: Teachers are defined as individuals who provide instruction to pre-kindergarten, kindergarten, grades 1 through 12, or ungraded classes, or individuals who teach in an environment other than a classroom setting, and who maintain daily student attendance records. Numbers reported are full-time equivalents (FTE). *Source: U.S. Department of Education, National Center for Education Statistics, Common Core of Data, Local Education Agency (School District) Universe Survey: School Year 2005-2006.*

Number of Students: A student is an individual for whom instruction is provided in an elementary or secondary education program that is not an adult education program and is under the jurisdiction of a school, school system, or other education institution. *Sources: U.S. Department of Education, National Center for Education Statistics, Common Core of Data, Local Education Agency (School District) Universe Survey: School Year 2005-2006 and Public Elementary/Secondary School Universe Survey: School Year 2005-2006*

Individual Education Program (IEP) Students: A written instructional plan for students with disabilities designated as special education students under IDEA-Part B. The written instructional plan includes a statement of present levels of educational performance of a child; statement of annual goals, including short-term instructional objectives; statement of specific educational services to be provided and the extent to which the child will be able to participate in regular educational programs; the projected date for initiation and anticipated duration of services; the appropriate objectives, criteria and evaluation procedures; and the schedules for determining, on at least an annual basis, whether instructional objectives are being achieved. *Source: U.S. Department of Education, National Center for Education Statistics, Common Core of Data, Local Education Agency (School District) Universe Survey: School Year 2005-2006*

English Language Learner (ELL) Students: Formerly referred to as Limited English Proficient (LEP). Students being served in appropriate programs of language assistance (e.g., English as a Second Language, High Intensity Language Training, bilingual education). Does not include pupils enrolled in a class to learn a language other than English. Also Limited-English-Proficient students are individuals who were not born in the United States or whose native language is a language other than English; or individuals who come from environments where a language other than English is dominant; or individuals who are American Indians and Alaskan Natives and who come from environments where a language other than English has had a significant impact on their level of English language proficiency; and who, by reason thereof, have sufficient difficulty speaking, reading, writing, or understanding the English language, to deny such individuals the opportunity to learn successfully in classrooms where the language of instruction is English or to participate fully in our society. *Source: U.S. Department of Education, National Center for Education Statistics, Common Core of Data, Local Education Agency (School District) Universe Survey: School Year 2005-2006*

Migrant Students: A migrant student as defined under federal regulation 34 CFR 200.40: 1) (a) Is younger than 22 (and has not graduated from high school or does not hold a high school equivalency certificate), but (b), if the child is too young to attend school-sponsored educational programs, is old enough to benefit from an organized instructional program; and 2) A migrant agricultural worker or a migrant fisher or has a parent, spouse, or guardian who is a migrant agricultural worker or a migrant fisher; and 3) Performs, or has a parent, spouse, or guardian who performs qualifying agricultural or fishing employment as a principal means of livelihood; and 4) Has moved within the preceding 36 months to obtain or to accompany or join a parent, spouse, or guardian to obtain, temporary or seasonal employment in agricultural or fishing work; and 5) Has moved from one school district to another; or in a state that is comprised of a single school district, has moved from one administrative area to another within such district; or resides in a school district of more than 15,000 square miles, and migrates a distance of 20 miles or more to a temporary residence to engage in a fishing activity. Provision 5 currently applies only to Alaska. *Note: Data covers the 2004-2005 school year. Source: U.S. Department of Education, National Center for Education Statistics, Common Core of Data, Public Elementary/Secondary School Universe Survey: School Year 2005-2006*

Students Eligible for Free Lunch Program: The free lunch program is defined as a program under the National School Lunch Act that provides cash subsidies for free lunches to students based on family size and income criteria. *Source: U.S. Department of Education, National Center for Education Statistics, Common Core of Data, Public Elementary/Secondary School Universe Survey: School Year 2005-2006*

Students Eligible for Reduced-Price Lunch Program: A student who is eligible to participate in the Reduced-Price Lunch Program under the National School Lunch Act. *Source: U.S. Department of Education, National Center for Education Statistics, Common Core of Data, Public Elementary/Secondary School Universe Survey: School Year 2005-2006*

Student/Teacher Ratio: The number of students divided by the number of teachers (FTE). See Number of Students and Number of Teachers above for for information.

Student/Librarian Ratio: The number of students divided by the number of library and media support staff. Library and media support staff are defined as staff members who render other professional library and media services; also includes library aides and those involved in library/media support. Their duties include selecting, preparing, caring for, and making available to instructional staff, equipment, films, filmstrips, transparencies, tapes, TV programs, and similar materials maintained separately or as part of an instructional materials center. Also included are activities in the audio-visual center, TV studio, related-work-study areas, and services provided by audio-visual personnel. Numbers are based on full-time equivalents. *Source: U.S. Department of Education, National Center for Education Statistics, Common Core of Data, Local Education Agency (School District) Universe Survey: School Year 2005-2006.*

Student/Counselor Ratio: The number of students divided by the number of guidance counselors. Guidance counselors are professional staff assigned specific duties and school time for any of the following activities in an elementary or secondary setting: counseling with students and parents; consulting with other staff members on learning problems; evaluating student abilities; assisting students in making educational and career choices; assisting students in personal and social development; providing referral assistance; and/or working with other staff members in planning and conducting guidance programs for students. The state applies its own standards in apportioning the aggregate of guidance counselors/directors into the elementary and secondary level components. Numbers reported are full-time equivalents. *Source: U.S. Department of Education, National Center for Education Statistics, Common Core of Data, Local Education Agency (School District) Universe Survey: School Year 2005-2006.*

Current Spending per Student: Expenditure for Instruction, Support Services, and Other Elementary/Secondary Programs. Includes salaries, employee benefits, purchased services, and supplies, as well as payments made by states on behalf of school districts. Also includes transfers made by school districts into their own retirement system. Excludes expenditure for Non-Elementary/Secondary Programs, debt service, capital outlay, and transfers to other governments or school districts. This item is formally called "Current Expenditures for Public Elementary/Secondary Education."

Instruction: Includes payments from all funds for salaries, employee benefits, supplies, materials, and contractual services for elementary/secondary instruction. It excludes capital outlay, debt service, and interfund transfers for elementary/secondary instruction. Instruction covers regular, special, and vocational programs offered in both the regular school year and summer school. It excludes instructional support activities as well as adult education and community services. Instruction salaries includes salaries for teachers and teacher aides and assistants.

Support Services: Relates to support services functions (series 2000) defined in Financial Accounting for Local and State School Systems (National Center for Education Statistics 2000). Includes payments from all funds for salaries, employee benefits, supplies, materials, and contractual services. It excludes capital outlay, debt service, and interfund transfers. It includes expenditure for the following functions:

- Business/Central/Other Support Services
- General Administration
- Instructional Staff Support
- Operation and Maintenance
- Pupil Support Services
- Pupil Transportation Services
- School Administration
- Nonspecified Support Services

Values shown are dollars per pupil per year. They were calculated by dividing the total dollar amounts by the fall membership. Fall membership is comprised of the total student enrollment on October 1 (or the closest school day to October 1) for all grade levels (including prekindergarten and kindergarten) and ungraded pupils. Membership includes students both present and absent on the measurement day. *Source: U.S. Department of Education, National Center for Education Statistics, Common Core of Data, School District Finance Survey (F-33), Fiscal Year 2005.*

Number of Diploma Recipients: A student who has received a diploma during the previous school year or subsequent summer school. This category includes regular diploma recipients and other diploma recipients. A High

School Diploma is a formal document certifying the successful completion of a secondary school program prescribed by the state education agency or other appropriate body. *Note: The National Center for Education Statistics has not released more current district level data due to privacy issues. Source: U.S. Department of Education, National Center for Education Statistics, Common Core of Data, Local Education Agency (School District) Universe Survey: School Year 2002-2003. State data covers the 2004-2005 school year and comes from the Common Core of Data, State Nonfiscal Survey of Public Elementary/Secondary Education, 2005-06.*

High School Drop-out Rate: A dropout is a student who was enrolled in school at some time during the previous school year; was not enrolled at the beginning of the current school year; has not graduated from high school or completed a state or district approved educational program; and does not meet any of the following exclusionary conditions: has transferred to another public school district, private school, or state- or district-approved educational program; is temporarily absent due to suspension or school-approved illness; or has died. The values shown cover grades 9 through 12. *Note: The National Center for Education Statistics has not released more current district level data due to privacy issues. Source: U.S. Department of Education, National Center for Education Statistics, Common Core of Data, Local Education Agency Universe Dropout File: School Year 2001-2002*

Note: n/a indicates data not available.

State Educational Profile

Please refer to the District Rankings section in the front of this User's Guide for an explanation of data for all items except for the following:

Average Salary: The average teacher salary in 2004-2005. *Source: American Federation of Teachers, Survey & Analysis of Teacher Salary Trends 2005*

College Entrance Exam Scores:

Scholastic Aptitude Test (SAT). *Note: The College Board strongly discourages the comparison or ranking of states on the basis of SAT scores alone. Source: The College Board, Mean SAT Reasoning Test™ Critical Reading, Math, and Writing Scores by State, with Changes for Selected Years, 2006*

American College Testing Program (ACT). *ACT, 2006 Average ACT Scores by State*

National Assessment of Educational Progress (NAEP)

The National Assessment of Educational Progress (NAEP), also known as "the Nation's Report Card," is the only nationally representative and continuing assessment of what America's students know and can do in various subject areas. As a result of the "No Child Left Behind" legislation, all states are required to participate in NAEP.

For more information, visit the U.S. Department of Education, National Center for Education Statistics at http://nces.ed.gov/nationsreportcard.

Ohio Achievement Tests (OAT)

The Ohio Reading and Mathematics Achievement Tests are annual assessments that measure how well students have learned the reading and math concepts taught in grades 3 - 8. The achievement tests are designed specifically for Ohio students and are based on Ohios academic content standards. They do not test a childs intelligence or aptitude and are not meant to compare childrens abilities.

Ohio Graduation Tests (OGT)

Ohio Graduation Tests (OGT) are a key part of Ohio's education reform to establish an aligned system of standards, assessments and accountability for Ohio schools. The testing requirements were established by the Ohio General Assembly in 2001 based on recommendations by the Governor's Commission for Student Success. Tests in reading, writing, mathematics, science and social studies make up the OGT.

The purposes of the OGT are to:

- Ensure that students who receive a high school diploma demonstrate at least high school levels of achievement;
- Measure the level of reading, writing, mathematics, science and social studies skills expected of students at the end of the 10th grade;
- Meet federal requirement for high school testing.

The Ohio Graduation Tests have replaced the Ohio Ninth-Grade Proficiency Tests, effective with the graduating class of 2007. For more information please visit the Ohio Department of Education at http://www.ode.state.oh.us.

User's Guide: Ancestry

Places Covered

The ranking tables are based on **1,054 places** in Ohio. Places covered fall into one of the following categories:

942 incorporated municipalities. Municipalities are incorporated as either cities or villages.

112 census designated places (CDP). The U.S. Bureau of the Census defines a CDP as "a statistical entity, defined for each decennial census according to Census Bureau guidelines, comprising a densely settled concentration of population that is not within an incorporated place, but is locally identified by a name. CDPs are delineated cooperatively by state and local officials and the Census Bureau, following Census Bureau guidelines. Beginning with Census 2000 there are no size limits."

Source of Data

The ancestries shown in this chapter were compiled from three different sections of the 2000 Census: Race; Hispanic Origin; and Ancestry. While the ancestries are sorted alphabetically for ease-of-use, it's important to note the origin of each piece of data. Data for Race and Hispanic Origin was taken from Summary File 1 (SF1) while Ancestry data was taken from Summary File 3 (SF3). The distinction is important because SF1 contains the 100-percent data, which is the information compiled from the questions asked of all people and about every housing unit. SF3 was compiled from a sample of approximately 19 million housing units (about 1 in 6 households) that received the Census 2000 long-form questionnaire.

Ancestries Based on Race

The data on race were derived from answers to the question on race that was asked of all people. The concept of race, as used by the Census Bureau, reflects self-identification by people according to the race or races with which they most closely identify. These categories are sociopolitical constructs and should not be interpreted as being scientific or anthropological in nature. Furthermore, the race categories include both racial and national-origin groups.

If an individual did not provide a race response, the race or races of the householder or other household members were assigned using specific rules of precedence of household relationship. For example, if race was missing for a natural-born child in the household, then either the race or races of the householder, another natural-born child, or the spouse of the householder were assigned. If race was not reported for anyone in the household, the race or races of a householder in a previously processed household were assigned.

- African-American/Black:
  - Not Hispanic
  - Hispanic
- Alaska Native tribes, specified:
  - Alaska Athabascan
  - Aleut
  - Eskimo
  - Tlingit-Haida
  - All other tribes
- Alaska Native tribes, not specified
- American Indian or Alaska Native tribes, not specified
- American Indian tribes, specified:
  - Apache
  - Blackfeet
  - Cherokee
  - Cheyenne
  - Chickasaw
  - Chippewa
  - Choctaw
  - Colville
  - Comanche
  - Cree
  - Creek
  - Crow
  - Delaware
  - Houma
  - Iroquois
  - Kiowa
  - Latin American Indians
  - Lumbee
  - Menominee
  - Navajo
  - Osage
  - Ottawa
  - Paiute
  - Pima
  - Potawatomi
  - Pueblo
  - Puget Sound Salish
  - Seminole
  - Shoshone
  - Sioux
  - Tohono O'Odham
  - Ute
  - Yakama
  - Yaqui
  - Yuman
  - All other tribes
- American Indian tribes, not specified
- Asian:
  - Bangladeshi
  - Cambodian
  - Chinese, except Taiwanese
  - Filipino
  - Hmong
  - Indian
  - Indonesian
  - Japanese
  - Korean
  - Laotian
  - Malaysian
  - Pakistani
  - Sri Lankan
  - Taiwanese
  - Thai
  - Vietnamese
  - Other Asian, specified
  - Other Asian, not specified
- Hawaii Native/Pacific Islander:
  - Melanesian:
    - Fijian
    - Other Melanesian
  - Micronesian:
    - Guamanian/Chamorro
    - Other Micronesian
  - Polynesian:
    - Native Hawaiian
    - Samoan
    - Tongan
    - Other Polynesian
  - Other Pacific Islander, specified
  - Other Pacific Islander, not specified
- White:
  - Not Hispanic
  - Hispanic

African American or Black: A person having origins in any of the Black racial groups of Africa. It includes people who indicate their race as "Black, African Am., or Negro," or provide written entries such as African American, Afro American, Kenyan, Nigerian, or Haitian.

American Indian or Alaska Native: A person having origins in any of the original peoples of North and South America (including Central America) and who maintain tribal affiliation or community attachment. It includes people who classified themselves as described below.

American Indian - Includes people who indicated their race as "American Indian," entered the name of an Indian tribe, or reported such entries as Canadian Indian, French American Indian, or Spanish-American Indian.

Respondents who identified themselves as American Indian were asked to report their enrolled or principal tribe. Therefore, tribal data in tabulations reflect the written entries reported on the questionnaires. Some of the entries (for example, Iroquois, Sioux, Colorado River, and Flathead) represent nations or reservations. The information on tribe is based on self identification and therefore does not reflect any designation of federally or state-recognized tribe. Information on American Indian tribes is presented in summary files. The information for Census 2000 is derived from the American Indian Tribal Classification List for the 1990 census that was updated based on a December 1997 Federal Register Notice, entitled "Indian Entities Recognized and Eligible to Receive Service From the United States Bureau of Indian Affairs," Department of the Interior, Bureau of Indian Affairs, issued by the Office of Management and Budget.

Alaska Native - Includes written responses of Eskimos, Aleuts, and Alaska Indians, as well as entries such as Arctic Slope, Inupiat, Yupik, Alutiiq, Egegik, and Pribilovian. The Alaska tribes are the Alaskan Athabascan, Tlingit, and Haida. The information for Census 2000 is based on the American Indian Tribal Classification List for the 1990 census, which was expanded to list the individual Alaska Native Villages when provided as a written response for race.

Asian: A person having origins in any of the original peoples of the Far East, Southeast Asia, or the Indian subcontinent including, for example, Cambodia, China, India, Japan, Korea, Malaysia, Pakistan, the Philippine Islands, Thailand, and Vietnam. It includes "Asian Indian," "Chinese," "Filipino," "Korean," "Japanese," "Vietnamese," and "Other Asian."

Asian Indian - Includes people who indicated their race as "Asian Indian" or identified themselves as Bengalese, Bharat, Dravidian, East Indian, or Goanese.

Chinese - Includes people who indicate their race as "Chinese" or who identify themselves as Cantonese, or Chinese American.

Filipino - Includes people who indicate their race as "Filipino" or who report entries such as Philipino, Philipine, or Filipino American.

Japanese - Includes people who indicate their race as "Japanese" or who report entries such as Nipponese or Japanese American.

Korean - Includes people who indicate their race as "Korean" or who provide a response of Korean American.

Vietnamese - Includes people who indicate their race as "Vietnamese" or who provide a response of Vietnamese American.

Cambodian - Includes people who provide a response such as Cambodian or Cambodia.

Hmong - Includes people who provide a response such as Hmong, Laohmong, or Mong.

Laotian - Includes people who provide a response such as Laotian, Laos, or Lao.

Thai - Includes people who provide a response such as Thai, Thailand, or Siamese.

Other Asian - Includes people who provide a response of Bangladeshi; Bhutanese; Burmese; Indochinese; Indonesian; Iwo Jiman; Madagascar; Malaysian; Maldivian; Nepalese; Okinawan; Pakistani; Singaporean; Sri Lankan; or Other Asian, specified and Other Asian, not specified.

Native Hawaiian or Other Pacific Islander: A person having origins in any of the original peoples of Hawaii, Guam, Samoa, or other Pacific Islands. It includes people who indicate their race as "Native Hawaiian," "Guamanian or Chamorro," "Samoan," and "Other Pacific Islander."

Native Hawaiian - Includes people who indicate their race as "Native Hawaiian" or who identify themselves as "Part Hawaiian" or "Hawaiian."

Guamanian or Chamorro - Includes people who indicate their race as such, including written entries of Chamorro or Guam.

Samoan - Includes people who indicate their race as "Samoan" or who identify themselves as American Samoan or Western Samoan.

Other Pacific Islander - Includes people who provide a write-in response of a Pacific Islander group, such as Carolinian, Chuukese (Trukese), Fijian, Kosraean, Melanesian, Micronesian, Northern Mariana Islander, Palauan, Papua New Guinean, Pohnpeian, Polynesian, Solomon Islander, Tahitian, Tokelauan, Tongan, Yapese, or Pacific Islander, not specified.

White: A person having origins in any of the original peoples of Europe, the Middle East, or North Africa. It includes people who indicate their race as "White" or report entries such as Irish, German, Italian, Lebanese, Near Easterner, Arab, or Polish.

Ancestries Based on Hispanic Origin

Hispanic or Latino:
- Central American:
  - Costa Rican
  - Guatemalan
  - Honduran
  - Nicaraguan
  - Panamanian
  - Salvadoran
  - Other Central American
- Cuban
- Dominican Republic
- Mexican
- Puerto Rican
- South American:
  - Argentinean
  - Bolivian
  - Chilean
  - Colombian
  - Ecuadorian
  - Paraguayan
  - Peruvian
  - Uruguayan
  - Venezuelan
  - Other South American
- Other Hispanic/Latino

The data on the Hispanic or Latino population were derived from answers to a question that was asked of all people. The terms "Spanish," "Hispanic origin," and "Latino" are used interchangeably. Some respondents identify with all three terms while others may identify with only one of these three specific terms. Hispanics or Latinos who identify with the terms "Spanish," "Hispanic," or "Latino" are those who classify themselves in one of the specific Spanish, Hispanic, or Latino categories listed on the questionnaire ("Mexican," "Puerto Rican," or "Cuban") as well as those who indicate that they are "other Spanish/Hispanic/Latino." People who do not identify with one of the specific origins listed on the questionnaire but indicate that they are "other Spanish, Hispanic, or Latino" are those whose origins are from Spain, the Spanish-speaking countries of Central or South America, the Dominican Republic, or people identifying themselves generally as Spanish, Spanish-American, Hispanic, Hispano, Latino, and so on. All write-in responses to the "other Spanish/Hispanic/Latino" category were coded.

Origin can be viewed as the heritage, nationality group, lineage, or country of birth of the person or the person's parents or ancestors before their arrival in the United States. People who identify their origin as Spanish, Hispanic, or Latino may be of any race.

In all cases where the origin of households, families, or occupied housing units is classified as Spanish, Hispanic, or Latino, the origin of the householder is used. If an individual could not provide a Hispanic origin response, their origin was assigned using specific rules of precedence of household relationship. For example, if origin was missing for a natural-born daughter in the household, then either the origin of the householder, another natural-born child, or spouse of the householder was assigned. If Hispanic origin was not reported for anyone in the household, the Hispanic origin of a householder in a previously processed household with the same race was assigned.

Other Ancestries

Acadian/Cajun
Afghan
African, Subsaharan:
- African
- Cape Verdean
- Ethiopian
- Ghanian
- Kenyan
- Liberian
- Nigerian
- Senegalese
- Sierra Leonean
- Somalian
- South African
- Sudanese
- Ugandan
- Zairian
- Zimbabwean
- Other Subsaharan African

Albanian
Alsatian
Arab:
- Arab/Arabic
- Egyptian
- Iraqi
- Jordanian
- Lebanese
- Moroccan
- Palestinian
- Syrian
- Other Arab

Armenian
Assyrian/Chaldean/Syriac
Australian
Austrian
Basque
Belgian
Brazilian
British
Bulgarian
Canadian
Carpatho Rusyn
Celtic
Croatian
Cypriot
Czech
Czechoslovakian
Danish
Dutch
Eastern European
English
Estonian
European
Finnish
French, except Basque
French Canadian
German
German Russian
Greek
Guyanese
Hungarian
Icelander
Iranian
Irish
Israeli
Italian
Latvian
Lithuanian
Luxemburger
Macedonian
Maltese
New Zealander
Northern European
Norwegian
Pennsylvania German
Polish
Portuguese
Romanian
Russian
Scandinavian
Scotch-Irish
Scottish
Serbian
Slavic
Slovak
Slovene
Soviet Union
Swedish
Swiss
Turkish
Ukrainian
United States or American
Welsh
West Indian, excluding Hispanic:
- Bahamian
- Barbadian
- Belizean
- Bermudan
- British West Indian
- Dutch West Indian
- Haitian
- Jamaican
- Trinidadian and Tobagonian
- U.S. Virgin Islander
- West Indian
- Other West Indian

Yugoslavian

The data on ancestry were derived from answers to long-form questionnaire Item 10, which was asked of a sample of the population. The data represent self-classification by people according to the ancestry group or groups with which they most closely identify. Ancestry refers to a person's ethnic origin or descent, "roots," heritage, or the place of birth of the person, the person's parents, or their ancestors before their arrival in the United States. Some ethnic identities, such as Egyptian or Polish, can be traced to geographic areas outside the United States, while other ethnicities, such as Pennsylvania German or Cajun, evolved in the United States.

The intent of the ancestry question was not to measure the degree of attachment the respondent had to a particular ethnicity. For example, a response of "Irish" might reflect total involvement in an Irish community or only a memory of ancestors several generations removed from the individual. Also, the question was intended to provide data for groups that were not included in the Hispanic origin and race questions. Official Hispanic origin data come from long-form questionnaire Item 5, and official race data come from long-form questionnaire Item 6. Therefore, although data on all groups are collected, the ancestry data shown in these tabulations are for non-Hispanic and non-race groups.

The ancestry question allowed respondents to report one or more ancestry groups, although only the first two were coded. If a response was in terms of a dual ancestry, for example, "Irish English," the person was assigned two codes, in this case one for Irish and another for English. However, in certain cases, multiple responses such as "French Canadian," "Greek Cypriote," and "Scotch Irish" were assigned a single code reflecting their status as unique groups. If a person reported one of these unique groups in addition to another group, for example, "Scotch Irish English," resulting in three terms, that person received one code for the unique group (Scotch-Irish) and another one for the remaining group (English). If a person reported "English Irish French," only English and Irish were coded. Certain combinations of ancestries where the ancestry group is a part of another, such as "German-Bavarian," were coded as a single ancestry using the more specific group (Bavarian). Also, responses such as "Polish-American" or "Italian-American" were coded and tabulated as a single entry (Polish or Italian).

The Census Bureau accepted "American" as a unique ethnicity if it was given alone, with an ambiguous response, or with state names. If the respondent listed any other ethnic identity such as "Italian-American," generally the "American" portion of the response was not coded. However, distinct groups such as "American Indian," "Mexican American," and "African American" were coded and identified separately because they represented groups who considered themselves different from those who reported as "Indian," "Mexican," or "African," respectively.

Census 2000 tabulations on ancestry are presented using two types of data presentations — one using total people as the base, and the other using total responses as the base. This chapter uses total responses as the base and includes the total number of ancestries reported and coded. If a person reported a multiple ancestry such as "French

Danish," that response was counted twice in the tabulations — once in the French category and again in the Danish category. Thus, the sum of the counts in this type of presentation is not the total population but the total of all responses.

An automated coding system was used for coding ancestry in Census 2000. This greatly reduced the potential for error associated with a clerical review. Specialists with knowledge of the subject matter reviewed, edited, coded, and resolved inconsistent or incomplete responses. The code list used in Census 2000, containing over 1,000 categories, reflects the results of the Census Bureau's experience with the 1990 ancestry question, research, and consultation with many ethnic experts. Many decisions were made to determine the classification of responses. These decisions affected the grouping of the tabulated data. For example, the Italian category includes the responses of Sicilian and Tuscan, as well as a number of other responses.

Although some people consider religious affiliation a component of ethnic identity, the ancestry question was not designed to collect any information concerning religion. Thus, if a religion was given as an answer to the ancestry question, it was listed in the "Other groups" category which is not shown in this chapter.

Ancestry should not be confused with a person's place of birth, although a person's place of birth and ancestry may be the same.

Ranking Section

In the ranking section of this chapter, each ancestry has three tables. The first table shows the top 10 places sorted by number (based on all places, regardless of population), the second table shows the top 10 places sorted by percent (based on all places, regardless of population), the third table shows the top 10 places sorted by percent (based on places with populations of 10,000 or more).

Within each table, column one displays the place name, the state, and the county (if a place spans more than one county, the county that holds the majority of the population is shown). Column two displays the number of people reporting each ancestry, and column three is the percent of the total population reporting each ancestry. For tables representing ancestries based on race or Hispanic origin, the 100-percent population figure from SF1 is used to calculate the value in the "%" column. For all other ancestries the sample population figure from SF3 is used to calculate the value in the "%" column.

Alphabetical Ancestry Cross-Reference Guide

Acadian/Cajun
Afghan
African *See African, sub-Saharan: African*
African American/Black
African American/Black: Hispanic
African American/Black: Not Hispanic
African, sub-Saharan
African, sub-Saharan: African
African, sub-Saharan: Cape Verdean
African, sub-Saharan: Ethiopian
African, sub-Saharan: Ghanian
African, sub-Saharan: Kenyan
African, sub-Saharan: Liberian
African, sub-Saharan: Nigerian
African, sub-Saharan: Other
African, sub-Saharan: Senegalese
African, sub-Saharan: Sierra Leonean
African, sub-Saharan: Somalian
African, sub-Saharan: South African
African, sub-Saharan: Sudanese
African, sub-Saharan: Ugandan
African, sub-Saharan: Zairian
African, sub-Saharan: Zimbabwean
Alaska Athabascan *See Alaska Native: Alaska Athabascan*
Alaska Native tribes, not specified
Alaska Native tribes, specified
Alaska Native: Alaska Athabascan
Alaska Native: Aleut
Alaska Native: All other tribes
Alaska Native: Eskimo
Alaska Native: Tlingit-Haida
Albanian
Aleut *See Alaska Native: Aleut*
Alsatian
American *See United States or American*
American Indian or Alaska Native tribes, not specified
American Indian tribes, not specified
American Indian tribes, specified
American Indian: All other tribes
American Indian: Apache
American Indian: Blackfeet
American Indian: Cherokee
American Indian: Cheyenne
American Indian: Chickasaw
American Indian: Chippewa
American Indian: Choctaw
American Indian: Colville
American Indian: Comanche
American Indian: Cree
American Indian: Creek
American Indian: Crow
American Indian: Delaware
American Indian: Houma
American Indian: Iroquois
American Indian: Kiowa
American Indian: Latin American Indians
American Indian: Lumbee
American Indian: Menominee
American Indian: Navajo
American Indian: Osage
American Indian: Ottawa
American Indian: Paiute
American Indian: Pima
American Indian: Potawatomi
American Indian: Pueblo
American Indian: Puget Sound Salish
American Indian: Seminole
American Indian: Shoshone
American Indian: Sioux
American Indian: Tohono O'Odham
American Indian: Ute
American Indian: Yakama
American Indian: Yaqui
American Indian: Yuman
Apache *See American Indian: Apache*
Arab
Arab/Arabic *See Arab: Arab/Arabic*
Arab: Arab/Arabic
Arab: Egyptian
Arab: Iraqi
Arab: Jordanian
Arab: Lebanese
Arab: Moroccan
Arab: Other
Arab: Palestinian
Arab: Syrian
Argentinean *See Hispanic: Argentinean*
Armenian
Asian
Asian: Bangladeshi
Asian: Cambodian
Asian: Chinese, except Taiwanese
Asian: Filipino
Asian: Hmong
Asian: Indian
Asian: Indonesian
Asian: Japanese
Asian: Korean
Asian: Laotian
Asian: Malaysian
Asian: Other Asian, not specified
Asian: Other Asian, specified
Asian: Pakistani
Asian: Sri Lankan
Asian: Taiwanese
Asian: Thai
Asian: Vietnamese
Assyrian/Chaldean/Syriac
Australian
Austrian
Bahamian *See West Indian: Bahamian, excluding Hispanic*
Bangladeshi *See Asian: Bangladeshi*
Barbadian *See West Indian: Barbadian, excluding Hispanic*
Basque
Belgian
Belizean *See West Indian: Belizean, excluding Hispanic*
Bermudan *See West Indian: Bermudan, excluding Hispanic*
Blackfeet *See American Indian: Blackfeet*
Bolivian *See Hispanic: Bolivian*
Brazilian
British
British West Indian *See West Indian: British West Indian, excluding Hispanic*
Bulgarian
Cambodian *See Asian: Cambodian*
Canadian
Cape Verdean *See African, sub-Saharan: Cape Verdean*
Carpatho Rusyn
Celtic
Central American: *See Hispanic: Central American*
Cherokee *See American Indian: Cherokee*
Cheyenne *See American Indian: Cheyenne*
Chickasaw *See American Indian: Chickasaw*
Chilean *See Hispanic: Chilean*
Chinese, except Taiwanese *See Asian: Chinese, except Taiwanese*
Chippewa *See American Indian: Chippewa*
Choctaw *See American Indian: Choctaw*
Colombian *See Hispanic: Colombian*
Colville *See American Indian: Colville*
Comanche *See American Indian: Comanche*
Costa Rican *See Hispanic: Costa Rican*
Cree *See American Indian: Cree*
Creek *See American Indian: Creek*
Croatian
Crow *See American Indian: Crow*
Cuban *See Hispanic: Cuban*
Cypriot
Czech
Czechoslovakian
Danish
Delaware *See American Indian: Delaware*
Dominican Republic *See Hispanic: Dominican Republic*
Dutch
Dutch West Indian *See West Indian: Dutch West Indian, excluding Hispanic*
Eastern European
Ecuadorian *See Hispanic: Ecuadorian*
Egyptian *See Arab: Egyptian*
English
Eskimo *See Alaska Native: Eskimo*
Estonian
Ethiopian *See African, sub-Saharan: Ethiopian*
European
Fijian *See Hawaii Native/Pacific Islander: Fijian*
Filipino *See Asian: Filipino*
Finnish
French Canadian
French, except Basque
German
German Russian
Ghanian *See African, sub-Saharan: Ghanian*
Greek
Guamanian or Chamorro *See Hawaii Native/Pacific Islander: Guamanian or Chamorro*
Guatemalan *See Hispanic: Guatemalan*
Guyanese
Haitian *See West Indian: Haitian, excluding Hispanic*
Hawaii Native/Pacific Islander
Hawaii Native/Pacific Islander: Fijian
Hawaii Native/Pacific Islander: Guamanian or Chamorro
Hawaii Native/Pacific Islander: Melanesian
Hawaii Native/Pacific Islander: Micronesian
Hawaii Native/Pacific Islander: Native Hawaiian

Hawaii Native/Pacific Islander: Other Melanesian
Hawaii Native/Pacific Islander: Other Micronesian
Hawaii Native/Pacific Islander: Other Pacific Islander, not specified
Hawaii Native/Pacific Islander: Other Pacific Islander, specified
Hawaii Native/Pacific Islander: Other Polynesian
Hawaii Native/Pacific Islander: Polynesian
Hawaii Native/Pacific Islander: Samoan
Hawaii Native/Pacific Islander: Tongan
Hispanic or Latino
Hispanic: Argentinean
Hispanic: Bolivian
Hispanic: Central American
Hispanic: Chilean
Hispanic: Colombian
Hispanic: Costa Rican
Hispanic: Cuban
Hispanic: Dominican Republic
Hispanic: Ecuadorian
Hispanic: Guatemalan
Hispanic: Honduran
Hispanic: Mexican
Hispanic: Nicaraguan
Hispanic: Other
Hispanic: Other Central American
Hispanic: Other South American
Hispanic: Panamanian
Hispanic: Paraguayan
Hispanic: Peruvian
Hispanic: Puerto Rican
Hispanic: Salvadoran
Hispanic: South American
Hispanic: Uruguayan
Hispanic: Venezuelan
Hmong *See Asian: Hmong*
Honduran *See Hispanic: Honduran*
Houma *See American Indian: Houma*
Hungarian
Icelander
Indian, American *See American Indian*
Indian, Asian *See Asian: Indian*
Indonesian *See Asian: Indonesian*
Iranian
Iraqi *See Arab: Iraqi*
Irish
Iroquois *See American Indian: Iroquois*
Israeli
Italian
Jamaican *See West Indian: Jamaican, excluding Hispanic*
Japanese *See Asian: Japanese*
Jordanian *See Arab: Jordanian*
Kenyan *See African, sub-Saharan: Kenyan*
Kiowa *See American Indian: Kiowa*
Korean *See Asian: Korean*
Laotian *See Asian: Laotian*
Latin American Indians *See American Indian: Latin American Indians*
Latino *See Hispanic or Latino*
Latvian
Lebanese *See Arab: Lebanese*
Liberian *See African, sub-Saharan: Liberian*
Lithuanian
Lumbee *See American Indian: Lumbee*
Luxemburger
Macedonian
Malaysian *See Asian: Malaysian*
Maltese
Melanesian: *See Hawaii Native/Pacific Islander: Melanesian*
Menominee *See American Indian: Menominee*
Mexican *See Hispanic: Mexican*
Micronesian: *See Hawaii Native/Pacific Islander: Micronesian*
Moroccan *See Arab: Moroccan*
Native Hawaiian *See Hawaii Native/Pacific Islander: Native Hawaiian*
Navajo *See American Indian: Navajo*
New Zealander
Nicaraguan *See Hispanic: Nicaraguan*
Nigerian *See African, sub-Saharan: Nigerian*
Northern European
Norwegian
Osage *See American Indian: Osage*
Ottawa *See American Indian: Ottawa*
Paiute *See American Indian: Paiute*
Pakistani *See Asian: Pakistani*
Palestinian *See Arab: Palestinian*
Panamanian *See Hispanic: Panamanian*
Paraguayan *See Hispanic: Paraguayan*
Pennsylvania German
Peruvian *See Hispanic: Peruvian*
Pima *See American Indian: Pima*
Polish
Polynesian: *See Hawaii Native/Pacific Islander: Polynesian*
Portuguese
Potawatomi *See American Indian: Potawatomi*
Pueblo *See American Indian: Pueblo*
Puerto Rican *See Hispanic: Puerto Rican*
Puget Sound Salish *See American Indian: Puget Sound Salish*
Romanian
Russian
Salvadoran *See Hispanic: Salvadoran*
Samoan *See Hawaii Native/Pacific Islander: Samoan*
Scandinavian
Scotch-Irish
Scottish
Seminole *See American Indian: Seminole*
Senegalese *See African, sub-Saharan: Senegalese*
Serbian
Shoshone *See American Indian: Shoshone*
Sierra Leonean *See African, sub-Saharan: Sierra Leonean*
Sioux *See American Indian: Sioux*
Slavic
Slovak
Slovene
Somalian *See African, sub-Saharan: Somalian*
South African *See African, sub-Saharan: South African*
South American: *See Hispanic: South American*
Soviet Union
Sri Lankan *See Asian: Sri Lankan*
sub-Saharan African *See African, sub-Saharan*
Sudanese *See African, sub-Saharan: Sudanese*
Swedish
Swiss
Syrian *See Arab: Syrian*
Taiwanese *See Asian: Taiwanese*
Thai *See Asian: Thai*
Tlingit-Haida *See Alaska Native: Tlingit-Haida*
Tohono O'Odham *See American Indian: Tohono O'Odham*
Tongan *See Hawaii Native/Pacific Islander: Tongan*
Trinidadian and Tobagonian *See West Indian: Trinidadian and Tobagonian, excluding Hispanic*
Turkish
U.S. Virgin Islander *See West Indian: U.S. Virgin Islander, excluding Hispanic*
Ugandan *See African, sub-Saharan: Ugandan*
Ukrainian
United States or American
Uruguayan *See Hispanic: Uruguayan*
Ute *See American Indian: Ute*
Venezuelan *See Hispanic: Venezuelan*
Vietnamese *See Asian: Vietnamese*
Welsh
West Indian, excluding Hispanic
West Indian: Bahamian, excluding Hispanic
West Indian: Barbadian, excluding Hispanic
West Indian: Belizean, excluding Hispanic
West Indian: Bermudan, excluding Hispanic
West Indian: British West Indian, excluding Hispanic
West Indian: Dutch West Indian, excluding Hispanic
West Indian: Haitian, excluding Hispanic
West Indian: Jamaican, excluding Hispanic
West Indian: Other, excluding Hispanic
West Indian: Trinidadian and Tobagonian, excluding Hispanic
West Indian: U.S. Virgin Islander, excluding Hispanic
West Indian: West Indian, excluding Hispanic
White
White: Hispanic
White: Not Hispanic
Yakama *See American Indian: Yakama*
Yaqui *See American Indian: Yaqui*
Yugoslavian
Yuman *See American Indian: Yuman*
Zairian *See African, sub-Saharan: Zairian*
Zimbabwean *See African, sub-Saharan: Zimbabwean*

User's Guide: Hispanic Population

Places Covered

Ranking tables cover all counties and all places in Ohio with populations of 10,000 or more.

Source of Data

CENSUS 2000

Data for this chapter was derived from following source: *U.S. Bureau of the Census, Census of Population and Housing, 2000: Summary File 4.* Summary File 4 (SF 4) contains sample data, which is the information compiled from the questions asked of a sample (generally 1-in-6) of all people and housing units. Summary File 4 is repeated or iterated for the total population and 335 additional population groups. This chapter focuses on the following 24 population groups:

- Hispanic or Latino (of any race)
  - Central American
    - Costa Rican
    - Guatemalan
    - Honduran
    - Nicaraguan
    - Panamanian
    - Salvadoran
  - Cuban
  - Dominican (Dominican Republic)
  - Mexican
  - Puerto Rican
  - South American
    - Argentinian
    - Bolivian
    - Chilean
    - Colombian
    - Ecuadorian
    - Paraguayan
    - Peruvian
    - Uruguayan
    - Venezuelan
  - Spaniard
  - Other Hispanic or Latino

Please note that the above list only includes Spanish-speaking population groups. Groups such as Brazilian are not classified as Hispanic by the Bureau of the Census because they primarily speak Portugese.

In order for any of the tables for a specific group to be shown in Summary File 4, the data must meet a minimum population threshold. For Summary File 4, all tables are repeated for each race group, American Indian and Alaska Native tribe, and Hispanic or Latino group if the 100-percent count of people of that specific group in a particular geographic area is 100 or more. There also must be 50 or more unweighted people of that specific group in a particular geographic area. For example, if there are 100 or more 100-percent people tabulated as Chilean in County A, and there are 50 or more unweighted people, then all matrices for Chilean are shown in SF 4 for County A.

To maintain confidentiality, the Census Bureau applies statistical procedures that introduce some uncertainty into data for small geographic areas with small population groups. Therefore, tables may contain both sampling and nonsampling error.

In an iterated file such as SF 4, the universes *households, families,* and *occupied housing units* are classified by the race or ethnic group of the householder. In any population table where there is no note, the universe classification is always based on the race or ethnicity of the person. In all housing tables, the universe classification is based on the race or ethnicity of the householder.

Comparing SF 4 Estimates with Corresponding Values in SF 1 and SF 2

As in earlier censuses, the responses from the sample of households reporting on long forms must be weighted to reflect the entire population. Specifically, each responding household represents, on average, six or seven other households who reported using short forms. One consequence of the weighting procedures is that each estimate based on the long form responses has an associated confidence interval. These confidence intervals are wider (as a percentage of the estimate) for geographic areas with smaller populations and for characteristics that occur less frequently in the area being examined (such as the proportion of people in poverty in a middle-income neighborhood). In order to release as much useful information as possible, statisticians must balance a number of factors. In particular, for Census 2000, the Bureau of the Census created weighting areas—geographic areas from which about two hundred or more long forms were completed—which are large enough to produce good quality estimates. If smaller weighting areas had been used, the confidence intervals around the estimates would have been significantly wider, rendering many estimates less useful due to their lower reliability. The disadvantage of using weighting areas this large is that, for smaller geographic areas within them, the estimates of characteristics that are also reported on the short form will not match the counts reported in SF 1 or SF 2. Examples of these characteristics are the total number of people, the number of people reporting specific racial categories, and the number of housing units. The official values for items reported on the short form come from SF 1 and SF 2. The differences between the long form estimates in SF 4 and values in SF 1 or SF 2 are particularly noticeable for the smallest places, tracts, and block groups. The long form estimates of total population and total housing units in SF 4 will, however, match the SF 1 and SF 2 counts for larger geographic areas such as counties and states, and will be essentially the same for medium and large cities. This phenomenon also occurred for the 1990 Census, although in that case, the weighting areas included relatively small places. As a result, the long form estimates matched the short form counts for those places, but the confidence intervals around the estimates of characteristics collected only on the long form were often significantly wider (as a percentage of the estimate). SF 1 gives exact numbers even for very small groups and areas; whereas, SF 4 gives estimates for small groups and areas such as tracts and small places that are less exact. The goal of SF 4 is to identify large differences among areas or large changes over time. Estimates for small areas and small population groups often do exhibit large changes from one census to the next, so having the capability to measure them is worthwhile.

Topics

POPULATION

Total Population: Sample count of total population.

Hispanic Population: The data on the Hispanic or Latino population, which was asked of all people, were derived from answers to long-form questionnaire Item 5, and short-form questionnaire Item 7. The terms "Spanish," "Hispanic origin," and "Latino" are used interchangeably. Some respondents identify with all three terms, while others may identify with only one of these three specific terms. Hispanics or Latinos who identify with the terms "Spanish," "Hispanic," or "Latino" are those who classify themselves in one of the specific Hispanic or Latino categories listed on the questionnaire — "Mexican," "Puerto Rican," or "Cuban" — as well as those who indicate that they are "other Spanish, Hispanic, or Latino." People who do not identify with one of the specific origins listed on the questionnaire but indicate that they are "other Spanish, Hispanic, or Latino" are those whose origins are from Spain, the Spanish-speaking countries of Central or South America, the Dominican Republic, or people identifying themselves generally as Spanish, Spanish-American, Hispanic, Hispano, Latino, and so on. All write-in responses to the "other Spanish/Hispanic/Latino" category were coded. Origin can be viewed as the heritage, nationality group, lineage, or country of birth of the person or the person's parents or ancestors before their arrival in the United States. People who identify their origin as Spanish, Hispanic, or Latino may be of any race.

Population groups whose primary language is not Spanish are not classified as Hispanic by the Bureau of the Census and are not included in this chapter (eg. Brazilian).

AGE

Median Age: Divides the age distribution into two equal parts: one-half of the cases falling below the median age and one-half above the median. Median age is computed on the basis of a single year of age standard distribution.

The data on age, which was asked of all people, were derived from answers to the long-form questionnaire Item 4 and short-form questionnaire Item 6. The age classification is based on the age of the person in complete years as of April 1, 2000. The age of the person usually was derived from their date of birth information. Their reported age was used only when date of birth information was unavailable.

HOUSEHOLD SIZE

Average Household Size: A measure obtained by dividing the number of people in households by the total number of households (or householders). In cases where household members are tabulated by race or Hispanic origin, household members are classified by the race or Hispanic origin of the householder rather than the race or Hispanic origin of each individual. Average household size is rounded to the nearest hundredth.

LANGUAGE SPOKEN AT HOME

English Only: Number and percentage of population 5 years and over who report speaking English-only at home.

Spanish: Number and percentage of population 5 years and over who report speaking Spanish at home.

Language spoken at home data were derived from answers to long-form questionnaire Items 11a and 11b, which were asked of a sample of the population. Data were edited to include in tabulations only the population 5 years old and over. Questions 11a and 11b referred to languages spoken at home in an effort to measure the current use of languages other than English. People who knew languages other than English but did not use them at home or who only used them elsewhere were excluded. Most people who reported speaking a language other than English at home also speak English. The questions did not permit determination of the primary or dominant language of people who spoke both English and another language.

FOREIGN-BORN

Foreign Born: Number and percentage of population who were not U.S. citizens at birth. Foreign-born people are those who indicated they were either a U.S. citizen by naturalization or they were not a citizen of the United States.

Foreign-Born Naturalized Citizens: Number and percentage of population who were not U.S. citizens at birth but became U.S. citizens by naturalization.

The data on place of birth were derived from answers to long-form questionnaire Item 12 which was asked of a sample of the population. Respondents were asked to report the U.S. state, Puerto Rico, U.S. Island Area, or foreign country where they were born. People not reporting a place of birth were assigned the state or country of birth of another family member or their residence 5 years earlier, or were imputed the response of another person with similar characteristics. People born outside the United States were asked to report their place of birth according to current international boundaries. Since numerous changes in boundaries of foreign countries have occurred in the last century, some people may have reported their place of birth in terms of boundaries that existed at the time of their birth or emigration, or in accordance with their own national preference.

EDUCATIONAL ATTAINMENT

High School Graduates: Number and percentage of the population age 25 and over who have a high school diploma or higher. This category includes people whose highest degree was a high school diploma or its equivalent, people who attended college but did not receive a degree, and people who received a college, university, or professional degree. People who reported completing the 12th grade but not receiving a diploma are not high school graduates.

4-Years College Graduates: Number and percentage of the population age 25 and over who have a 4-year college, university, or professional degree.

Data on educational attainment were derived from answers to long-form questionnaire Item 9, which was asked of a sample of the population. Data on attainment are tabulated for the population 25 years old and over.

The order in which degrees were listed on the questionnaire suggested that doctorate degrees were "higher" than professional school degrees, which were "higher" than master's degrees. The question included instructions for people currently enrolled in school to report the level of the previous grade attended or the highest degree received. Respondents who did not report educational attainment or enrollment level were assigned the attainment of a person of the same age, race, Hispanic or Latino origin, occupation and sex, where possible, who resided in the same or a nearby area. Respondents who filled more than one box were edited to the highest level or degree reported.

The question included a response category that allowed respondents to report completing the 12th grade without receiving a high school diploma. It allowed people who received either a high school diploma or the equivalent (Test of General Educational Development—G.E.D.) and did not attend college, to be reported as "high school graduate(s)." The category "Associate degree" included people whose highest degree is an associate degree, which generally requires 2 years of college level work and is either in an occupational program that prepares them for a specific occupation, or an academic program primarily in the arts and sciences. The course work may or may not be transferable to a bachelor's degree. Master's degrees include the traditional MA and MS degrees and field-specific degrees, such as MSW, MEd, MBA, MLS, and MEng. Some examples of professional degrees include medicine, dentistry, chiropractic, optometry, osteopathic medicine, pharmacy, podiatry, veterinary medicine, law, and theology. Vocational and technical training such as barber school training; business, trade, technical, and vocational schools; or other training for a specific trade, are specifically excluded.

INCOME AND POVERTY

Median Household Income (in dollars): Includes the income of the householder and all other individuals 15 years old and over in the household, whether they are related to the householder or not. The median divides the income distribution into two equal parts: one-half of the cases falling below the median income and one-half above the median. For households, the median income is based on the distribution of the total number of households including those with no income. Median income for households is computed on the basis of a standard distribution and is rounded to the nearest whole dollar.

Per Capita Income (in dollars): Per capita income is the mean income computed for every man, woman, and child in a particular group. It is derived by dividing the total income of a particular group by the total population in that group. Per capita income is rounded to the nearest whole dollar.

The data on income in 1999 were derived from answers to long-form questionnaire Items 31 and 32, which were asked of a sample of the population 15 years old and over. "Total income" is the sum of the amounts reported separately for wage or salary income; net self-employment income; interest, dividends, or net rental or royalty income or income from estates and trusts; social security or railroad retirement income; Supplemental Security Income (SSI); public assistance or welfare payments; retirement, survivor, or disability pensions; and all other income.

Receipts from the following sources are not included as income: capital gains, money received from the sale of property (unless the recipient was engaged in the business of selling such property); the value of income "in kind" from food stamps, public housing subsidies, medical care, employer contributions for individuals, etc.; withdrawal of bank deposits; money borrowed; tax refunds; exchange of money between relatives living in the same household; and gifts and lump-sum inheritances, insurance payments, and other types of lump-sum receipts.

The eight types of income reported in the census are defined as follows:

Wage or salary income. Wage or salary income includes total money earnings received for work performed as an employee during the calendar year 1999. It includes wages, salary, armed forces pay, commissions, tips, piece-rate payments, and cash bonuses earned before deductions were made for taxes, bonds, pensions, union dues, etc.

Self-employment income. Self-employment income includes both farm and nonfarm self-employment income. Nonfarm self-employment income includes net money income (gross receipts minus expenses) from one's own business, professional enterprise, or partnership. Gross receipts include the value of all goods sold and services rendered. Expenses include costs of goods purchased, rent, heat, light, power, depreciation charges, wages and salaries paid, business taxes (not personal income taxes), etc. Farm self-employment income includes net money income (gross receipts minus operating expenses) from the operation of a farm by a person on his or her own account, as an owner, renter, or sharecropper. Gross receipts include the value of all products sold, government farm programs, money received from the rental of farm equipment to others, and incidental receipts from the sale of wood, sand, gravel, etc. Operating expenses include cost of feed, fertilizer, seed, and other farming supplies, cash wages paid to farmhands, depreciation charges, cash rent, interest on farm mortgages, farm building repairs, farm taxes (not state and federal personal income taxes), etc. The value of fuel, food, or other farm products used for family living is not included as part of net income.

Interest, dividends, or net rental income. Interest, dividends, or net rental income includes interest on savings or bonds, dividends from stockholdings or membership in associations, net income from rental of property to others and receipts from boarders or lodgers, net royalties, and periodic payments from an estate or trust fund.

Social Security income. Social security income includes social security pensions and survivors benefits, permanent disability insurance payments made by the Social Security Administration prior to deductions for medical insurance, and railroad retirement insurance checks from the U.S. government. Medicare reimbursements are not included.

Supplemental Security Income (SSI). Supplemental Security Income (SSI) is a nationwide U.S. assistance program administered by the Social Security Administration that guarantees a minimum level of income for needy aged, blind, or disabled individuals. The census questionnaire for Puerto Rico asked about the receipt of SSI; however, SSI is not a federally administered program in Puerto Rico. Therefore, it is probably not being interpreted by most respondents as the same as SSI in the United States. The only way a resident of Puerto Rico could have appropriately reported SSI would have been if they lived in the United States at any time during calendar year 1999 and received SSI.

Public assistance income. Public assistance income includes general assistance and Temporary Assistance to Needy Families (TANF). Separate payments received for hospital or other medical care (vendor payments) are excluded. This does not include Supplemental Security Income (SSI).

Retirement income. Retirement income includes: (1) retirement pensions and survivor benefits from a former employer; labor union; or federal, state, or local government; and the U.S. military; (2) income from workers' compensation; disability income from companies or unions; federal, state, or local government; and the U.S. military; (3) periodic receipts from annuities and insurance; and (4) regular income from IRA and KEOGH plans. This does not include social security income.

All other income. All other income includes unemployment compensation, Veterans' Administration (VA) payments, alimony and child support, contributions received periodically from people not living in the household, military family allotments, and other kinds of periodic income other than earnings.

Poverty Status: Number and percentage of population with income in 1999 below the poverty level. Based on individuals for whom poverty status is determined. Poverty status was determined for all people except institutionalized people, people in military group quarters, people in college dormitories, and unrelated individuals under 15 years old.

The poverty status of families and unrelated individuals in 1999 was determined using 48 thresholds (income cutoffs) arranged in a two dimensional matrix. The matrix consists of family size (from 1 person to 9 or more people) cross-classified by presence and number of family members under 18 years old (from no children present to 8 or more children present). Unrelated individuals and 2-person families were further differentiated by the age of the reference person (RP) (under 65 years old and 65 years old and over).

To determine a person's poverty status, one compares the person's total family income with the poverty threshold appropriate for that person's family size and composition. If the total income of that person's family is less than the threshold appropriate for that family, then the person is considered poor, together with every member of his or her family. If a person is not living with anyone related by birth, marriage, or adoption, then the person's own income is compared with his or her poverty threshold.

HOUSING

Homeownership: Number and percentage of housing units that are owner-occupied.

The data on tenure, which was asked at all occupied housing units, were obtained from answers to long-form questionnaire Item 33, and short-form questionnaire Item 2. All occupied housing units are classified as either owner occupied or renter occupied.

A housing unit is owner occupied if the owner or co-owner lives in the unit even if it is mortgaged or not fully paid for. The owner or co-owner must live in the unit and usually is Person 1 on the questionnaire. The unit is "Owned by you or someone in this household with a mortgage or loan" if it is being purchased with a mortgage or some other debt arrangement, such as a deed of trust, trust deed, contract to purchase, land contract, or purchase agreement. The unit is also considered owned with a mortgage if it is built on leased land and there is a mortgage on the unit. Mobile homes occupied by owners with installment loans balances are also included in this category.

Median Gross Rent (in dollars): Median monthly gross rent on specified renter-occupied and specified vacant-for-rent units. Specified renter-occupied and specified vacant-for-rent units exclude 1-family houses on 10 acres or more.

The data on gross rent were obtained from answers to long-form questionnaire Items 45a-d, which were asked on a sample basis. Gross rent is the contract rent plus the estimated average monthly cost of utilities (electricity, gas, water and sewer) and fuels (oil, coal, kerosene, wood, etc.) if these are paid by the renter (or paid for the renter by someone else). Gross rent is intended to eliminate differentials that result from varying practices with respect to the inclusion of utilities and fuels as part of the rental payment. The estimated costs of utilities and fuels are reported on an annual basis but are converted to monthly figures for the tabulations. Renter units occupied without payment of cash rent are shown separately as "No cash rent" in the tabulations.

Housing units that are renter occupied without payment of cash rent are shown separately as "No cash rent" in census data products. The unit may be owned by friends or relatives who live elsewhere and who allow occupancy without charge. Rent-free houses or apartments may be provided to compensate caretakers, ministers, tenant farmers, sharecroppers, or others.

Contract rent is the monthly rent agreed to or contracted for, regardless of any furnishings, utilities, fees, meals, or services that may be included. For vacant units, it is the monthly rent asked for the rental unit at the time of enumeration.

If the contract rent includes rent for a business unit or for living quarters occupied by another household, only that part of the rent estimated to be for the respondent's unit was included. Excluded was any rent paid for additional units or for business premises.

If a renter pays rent to the owner of a condominium or cooperative, and the condominium fee or cooperative carrying charge also is paid by the renter to the owner, the condominium fee or carrying charge was included as rent.

If a renter receives payments from lodgers or roomers who are listed as members of the household, the rent without deduction for any payments received from the lodgers or roomers was to be reported. The respondent was to report the rent agreed to or contracted for even if paid by someone else such as friends or relatives living elsewhere, a church or welfare agency, or the government through subsidies or vouchers.

The median divides the rent distribution into two equal parts: one-half of the cases falling below the median contract rent and one-half above the median. Median contract rents are computed on the basis of a standard distribution and are rounded to the nearest whole dollar. Units reported as "No cash rent" are excluded.

Median Home Value (in dollars): Reported by the owner of specified owner-occupied or specified vacant-for-sale housing units. Specified owner-occupied and specified vacant-for-sale housing units include only 1-family houses on less than 10 acres without a business or medical office on the property. The data for "specified units" exclude mobile homes, houses with a business or medical office, houses on 10 or more acres, and housing units in multi-unit buildings.

The data on value (also referred to as "price asked" for vacant units) were obtained from answers to long-form questionnaire Item 51, which was asked on a sample basis at owner-occupied housing units and units that were being bought, or vacant for sale at the time of enumeration. Value is the respondent's estimate of how much the property (house and lot, mobile home and lot, or condominium unit) would sell for if it were for sale. If the house or mobile home was owned or being bought, but the land on which it sits was not, the respondent was asked to estimate the combined value of the house or mobile home and the land. For vacant units, value was the price asked for the property. Value was tabulated separately for all owner-occupied and vacant-for-sale housing units, owner-occupied and vacant-for-sale mobile homes, and specified owner-occupied and specified vacant-for-sale housing units.

The median divides the value distribution into two equal parts: one-half of the cases falling below the median value of the property (house and lot, mobile home and lot, or condominium unit) and one-half above the median. Median values are computed on the basis of a standard distribution and are rounded to the nearest hundred dollars.

User's Guide: Asian Population

Places Covered

Ranking tables cover all counties and places in Ohio with Asian and/or Native Hawaiian and other Pacific Islander residents.

Source of Data

CENSUS 2000

Data for this chapter was derived from following source: *U.S. Bureau of the Census, Census of Population and Housing, 2000: Summary File 4.* Summary File 4 (SF 4) contains sample data, which is the information compiled from the questions asked of a sample (generally 1-in-6) of all people and housing units. Summary File 4 is repeated or iterated for the total population and 335 additional population groups. This chapter focuses on the following 23 population groups:

- Asian
    - Asian Indian
    - Bangladeshi
    - Cambodian
    - Chinese (except Taiwanese)
    - Filipino
    - Hmong
    - Indonesian
    - Japanese
    - Korean
    - Laotian
    - Malaysian
    - Pakistani
    - Sri Lankan
    - Taiwanese
    - Thai
    - Vietnamese
- Native Hawaiian and Other Pacific Islander
    - Fijian
    - Guamanian or Chamorro
    - Hawaiian, Native
    - Samoan
    - Tongan

Please note that this chapter only includes people who responded to the question on race by indicating only one race. These people are classified by the Census Bureau as the race *alone* population. For example, respondents reporting a single detailed Asian group, such as Korean or Filipino, would be included in the Asian *alone* population. Respondents reporting more than one detailed Asian group, such as Chinese and Japanese or Asian Indian and Chinese and Vietnamese would also be included in the Asian *alone* population. This is because all of the detailed groups in these example combinations are part of the larger Asian race category. The same criteria apply to the Native Hawaiian and Other Pacific Islander groups.

In order for any of the tables for a specific group to be shown in Summary File 4, the data must meet a minimum population threshold. For Summary File 4, all tables are repeated for each race group, American Indian and Alaska Native tribe, and Hispanic or Latino group if the 100-percent count of people of that specific group in a particular geographic area is 100 or more. There also must be 50 or more unweighted people of that specific group in a particular geographic area. For example, if there are 100 or more 100-percent people tabulated as Korean in County A, and there are 50 or more unweighted people, then all matrices for Korean are shown in SF 4 for County A.

To maintain confidentiality, the Census Bureau applies statistical procedures that introduce some uncertainty into data for small geographic areas with small population groups. Therefore, tables may contain both sampling and nonsampling error.

In an iterated file such as SF 4, the universes *households, families,* and *occupied housing units* are classified by the race or ethnic group of the householder. In any population table where there is no note, the universe classification is always based on the race or ethnicity of the person. In all housing tables, the universe classification is based on the race or ethnicity of the householder.

Comparing SF 4 Estimates with Corresponding Values in SF 1 and SF 2

As in earlier censuses, the responses from the sample of households reporting on long forms must be weighted to reflect the entire population. Specifically, each responding household represents, on average, six or seven other households who reported using short forms. One consequence of the weighting procedures is that each estimate based on the long form responses has an associated confidence interval. These confidence intervals are wider (as a percentage of the estimate) for geographic areas with smaller populations and for characteristics that occur less frequently in the area being examined (such as the proportion of people in poverty in a middle-income neighborhood). In order to release as much useful information as possible, statisticians must balance a number of factors. In particular, for Census 2000, the Bureau of the Census created weighting areas—geographic areas from which about two hundred or more long forms were completed—which are large enough to produce good quality estimates. If smaller weighting areas had been used, the confidence intervals around the estimates would have been significantly wider, rendering many estimates less useful due to their lower reliability. The disadvantage of using weighting areas this large is that, for smaller geographic areas within them, the estimates of characteristics that are also reported on the short form will not match the counts reported in SF 1 or SF 2. Examples of these characteristics are the total number of people, the number of people reporting specific racial categories, and the number of housing units. The official values for items reported on the short form come from SF 1 and SF 2. The differences between the long form estimates in SF 4 and values in SF 1 or SF 2 are particularly noticeable for the smallest places, tracts, and block groups. The long form estimates of total population and total housing units in SF 4 will, however, match the SF 1 and SF 2 counts for larger geographic areas such as counties and states, and will be essentially the same for medium and large cities. This phenomenon also occurred for the 1990 Census, although in that case, the weighting areas included relatively small places. As a result, the long form estimates matched the short form counts for those places, but the confidence intervals around the estimates of characteristics collected only on the long form were often significantly wider (as a percentage of the estimate). SF 1 gives exact numbers even for very small groups and areas; whereas, SF 4 gives estimates for small groups and areas such as tracts and small places that are less exact. The goal of SF 4 is to identify large differences among areas or large changes over time. Estimates for small areas and small population groups often do exhibit large changes from one census to the next, so having the capability to measure them is worthwhile.

Topics

POPULATION

Total Population: Sample count of total population of all races.

Asian Population: A person having origins in any of the original peoples of the Far East, Southeast Asia, or the Indian subcontinent including, for example, Cambodia, China, India, Japan, Korea, Malaysia, Pakistan, the Philippine Islands, Thailand, and Vietnam. It includes Asian Indian, Bangladeshi, Cambodian, Chinese (except Taiwanese), Filipino, Hmong, Indonesian, Japanese, Korean, Laotian, Malaysian, Pakistani, Sri Lankan, Taiwanese, Thai, and Vietnamese.

Native Hawaiian or Other Pacific Islander (NHPI) Population: A person having origins in any of the original peoples of Hawaii, Guam, Samoa, or other Pacific Islands. It includes people who indicate their race as Fijian, Guamanian or Chamorro, Native Hawaiian, Samoan, and Tongan.

The data on race, which was asked of all people, were derived from answers to long-form questionnaire Item 6 and short-form questionnaire Item 8. The concept of race, as used by the Census Bureau, reflects self-identification by people according to the race or races with which they most closely identify. These categories are socio-political constructs and should not be interpreted as being scientific or anthropological in nature. Furthermore, the race categories include both racial and national-origin groups.

If an individual did not provide a race response, the race or races of the householder or other household members were assigned using specific rules of precedence of household relationship. For example, if race was missing for a natural-born child in the household, then either the race or races of the householder, another natural-born child, or the spouse of the householder were assigned. If race was not reported for anyone in the household, the race or races of a householder in a previously processed household were assigned.

AGE

Median Age: Divides the age distribution into two equal parts: one-half of the cases falling below the median age and one-half above the median. Median age is computed on the basis of a single year of age standard distribution.

The data on age, which was asked of all people, were derived from answers to the long-form questionnaire Item 4 and short-form questionnaire Item 6. The age classification is based on the age of the person in complete years as of April 1, 2000. The age of the person usually was derived from their date of birth information. Their reported age was used only when date of birth information was unavailable.

HOUSEHOLD SIZE

Average Household Size: A measure obtained by dividing the number of people in households by the total number of households (or householders). In cases where household members are tabulated by race or Hispanic origin, household members are classified by the race or Hispanic origin of the householder rather than the race or Hispanic origin of each individual. Average household size is rounded to the nearest hundredth.

LANGUAGE SPOKEN AT HOME

English Only: Number and percentage of population 5 years and over who report speaking English-only at home.

Language spoken at home data were derived from answers to long-form questionnaire Items 11a and 11b, which were asked of a sample of the population. Data were edited to include in tabulations only the population 5 years old and over. Questions 11a and 11b referred to languages spoken at home in an effort to measure the current use of languages other than English. People who knew languages other than English but did not use them at home or who only used them elsewhere were excluded. Most people who reported speaking a language other than English at home also speak English. The questions did not permit determination of the primary or dominant language of people who spoke both English and another language.

FOREIGN-BORN

Foreign Born: Number and percentage of population who were not U.S. citizens at birth. Foreign-born people are those who indicated they were either a U.S. citizen by naturalization or they were not a citizen of the United States.

Foreign-Born Naturalized Citizens: Number and percentage of population who were not U.S. citizens at birth but became U.S. citizens by naturalization.

The data on place of birth were derived from answers to long-form questionnaire Item 12 which was asked of a sample of the population. Respondents were asked to report the U.S. state, Puerto Rico, U.S. Island Area, or foreign country where they were born. People not reporting a place of birth were assigned the state or country of birth of another family member or their residence 5 years earlier, or were imputed the response of another person with similar characteristics. People born outside the United States were asked to report their place of birth according to current international boundaries. Since numerous changes in boundaries of foreign countries have occurred in the last century, some people may have reported their place of birth in terms of boundaries that existed at the time of their birth or emigration, or in accordance with their own national preference.

EDUCATIONAL ATTAINMENT

High School Graduates: Number and percentage of the population age 25 and over who have a high school diploma or higher. This category includes people whose highest degree was a high school diploma or its equivalent, people who attended college but did not receive a degree, and people who received a college, university, or professional degree. People who reported completing the 12th grade but not receiving a diploma are not high school graduates.

Four-Year College Graduates: Number and percentage of the population age 25 and over who have a 4-year college, university, or professional degree.

Data on educational attainment were derived from answers to long-form questionnaire Item 9, which was asked of a sample of the population. Data on attainment are tabulated for the population 25 years old and over.

The order in which degrees were listed on the questionnaire suggested that doctorate degrees were “higher” than professional school degrees, which were “higher” than master's degrees. The question included instructions for people currently enrolled in school to report the level of the previous grade attended or the highest degree received.

Respondents who did not report educational attainment or enrollment level were assigned the attainment of a person of the same age, race, Hispanic or Latino origin, occupation and sex, where possible, who resided in the same or a nearby area. Respondents who filled more than one box were edited to the highest level or degree reported.

The question included a response category that allowed respondents to report completing the 12th grade without receiving a high school diploma. It allowed people who received either a high school diploma or the equivalent (Test of General Educational Development—G.E.D.) and did not attend college, to be reported as "high school graduate(s)." The category "Associate degree" included people whose highest degree is an associate degree, which generally requires 2 years of college level work and is either in an occupational program that prepares them for a specific occupation, or an academic program primarily in the arts and sciences. The course work may or may not be transferable to a bachelor's degree. Master's degrees include the traditional MA and MS degrees and field-specific degrees, such as MSW, MEd, MBA, MLS, and MEng. Some examples of professional degrees include medicine, dentistry, chiropractic, optometry, osteopathic medicine, pharmacy, podiatry, veterinary medicine, law, and theology. Vocational and technical training such as barber school training; business, trade, technical, and vocational schools; or other training for a specific trade, are specifically excluded.

INCOME AND POVERTY

Median Household Income (in dollars): Includes the income of the householder and all other individuals 15 years old and over in the household, whether they are related to the householder or not. The median divides the income distribution into two equal parts: one-half of the cases falling below the median income and one-half above the median. For households, the median income is based on the distribution of the total number of households including those with no income. Median income for households is computed on the basis of a standard distribution and is rounded to the nearest whole dollar.

Per Capita Income (in dollars): Per capita income is the mean income computed for every man, woman, and child in a particular group. It is derived by dividing the total income of a particular group by the total population in that group. Per capita income is rounded to the nearest whole dollar.

The data on income in 1999 were derived from answers to long-form questionnaire Items 31 and 32, which were asked of a sample of the population 15 years old and over. "Total income" is the sum of the amounts reported separately for wage or salary income; net self-employment income; interest, dividends, or net rental or royalty income or income from estates and trusts; social security or railroad retirement income; Supplemental Security Income (SSI); public assistance or welfare payments; retirement, survivor, or disability pensions; and all other income.

Receipts from the following sources are not included as income: capital gains, money received from the sale of property (unless the recipient was engaged in the business of selling such property); the value of income "in kind" from food stamps, public housing subsidies, medical care, employer contributions for individuals, etc.; withdrawal of bank deposits; money borrowed; tax refunds; exchange of money between relatives living in the same household; and gifts and lump-sum inheritances, insurance payments, and other types of lump-sum receipts.

The eight types of income reported in the census are defined as follows:

Wage or salary income. Wage or salary income includes total money earnings received for work performed as an employee during the calendar year 1999. It includes wages, salary, armed forces pay, commissions, tips, piece-rate payments, and cash bonuses earned before deductions were made for taxes, bonds, pensions, union dues, etc.

Self-employment income. Self-employment income includes both farm and nonfarm self-employment income. Nonfarm self-employment income includes net money income (gross receipts minus expenses) from one's own business, professional enterprise, or partnership. Gross receipts include the value of all goods sold and services rendered. Expenses include costs of goods purchased, rent, heat, light, power, depreciation charges, wages and salaries paid, business taxes (not personal income taxes), etc. Farm self-employment income includes net money income (gross receipts minus operating expenses) from the operation of a farm by a person on his or her own account, as an owner, renter, or sharecropper. Gross receipts include the value of all products sold, government farm programs, money received from the rental of farm equipment to others, and incidental receipts from the sale of wood, sand, gravel, etc. Operating expenses include cost of feed, fertilizer, seed, and other farming supplies, cash wages paid to farmhands, depreciation charges, cash rent, interest on farm mortgages, farm building repairs, farm taxes (not state and federal personal income taxes), etc. The value of fuel, food, or other farm products used for family living is not included as part of net income.

Interest, dividends, or net rental income. Interest, dividends, or net rental income includes interest on savings or bonds, dividends from stockholdings or membership in associations, net income from rental of property to others and receipts from boarders or lodgers, net royalties, and periodic payments from an estate or trust fund.

Social Security income. Social security income includes social security pensions and survivors benefits, permanent disability insurance payments made by the Social Security Administration prior to deductions for medical insurance, and railroad retirement insurance checks from the U.S. government. Medicare reimbursements are not included.

Supplemental Security Income (SSI). Supplemental Security Income (SSI) is a nationwide U.S. assistance program administered by the Social Security Administration that guarantees a minimum level of income for needy aged, blind, or disabled individuals. The census questionnaire for Puerto Rico asked about the receipt of SSI; however, SSI is not a federally administered program in Puerto Rico. Therefore, it is probably not being interpreted by most respondents as the same as SSI in the United States. The only way a resident of Puerto Rico could have appropriately reported SSI would have been if they lived in the United States at any time during calendar year 1999 and received SSI.

Public assistance income. Public assistance income includes general assistance and Temporary Assistance to Needy Families (TANF). Separate payments received for hospital or other medical care (vendor payments) are excluded. This does not include Supplemental Security Income (SSI).

Retirement income. Retirement income includes: (1) retirement pensions and survivor benefits from a former employer; labor union; or federal, state, or local government; and the U.S. military; (2) income from workers' compensation; disability income from companies or unions; federal, state, or local government; and the U.S. military; (3) periodic receipts from annuities and insurance; and (4) regular income from IRA and KEOGH plans. This does not include social security income.

All other income. All other income includes unemployment compensation, Veterans' Administration (VA) payments, alimony and child support, contributions received periodically from people not living in the household, military family allotments, and other kinds of periodic income other than earnings.

Poverty Status: Number and percentage of population with income in 1999 below the poverty level. Based on individuals for whom poverty status is determined. Poverty status was determined for all people except institutionalized people, people in military group quarters, people in college dormitories, and unrelated individuals under 15 years old.

The poverty status of families and unrelated individuals in 1999 was determined using 48 thresholds (income cutoffs) arranged in a two dimensional matrix. The matrix consists of family size (from 1 person to 9 or more people) cross-classified by presence and number of family members under 18 years old (from no children present to 8 or more children present). Unrelated individuals and 2-person families were further differentiated by the age of the reference person (RP) (under 65 years old and 65 years old and over).

To determine a person's poverty status, one compares the person's total family income with the poverty threshold appropriate for that person's family size and composition. If the total income of that person's family is less than the threshold appropriate for that family, then the person is considered poor, together with every member of his or her family. If a person is not living with anyone related by birth, marriage, or adoption, then the person's own income is compared with his or her poverty threshold.

HOUSING

Homeownership: Number and percentage of housing units that are owner-occupied.

The data on tenure, which was asked at all occupied housing units, were obtained from answers to long-form questionnaire Item 33, and short-form questionnaire Item 2. All occupied housing units are classified as either owner occupied or renter occupied.

A housing unit is owner occupied if the owner or co-owner lives in the unit even if it is mortgaged or not fully paid for. The owner or co-owner must live in the unit and usually is Person 1 on the questionnaire. The unit is "Owned by you or someone in this household with a mortgage or loan" if it is being purchased with a mortgage or some other debt arrangement, such as a deed of trust, trust deed, contract to purchase, land contract, or purchase agreement. The unit is also considered owned with a mortgage if it is built on leased land and there is a mortgage on the unit. Mobile homes occupied by owners with installment loans balances are also included in this category.

Median Gross Rent (in dollars): Median monthly gross rent on specified renter-occupied and specified vacant-for-rent units. Specified renter-occupied and specified vacant-for-rent units exclude 1-family houses on 10 acres or more.

The data on gross rent were obtained from answers to long-form questionnaire Items 45a-d, which were asked on a sample basis. Gross rent is the contract rent plus the estimated average monthly cost of utilities (electricity, gas, water and sewer) and fuels (oil, coal, kerosene, wood, etc.) if these are paid by the renter (or paid for the renter by someone else). Gross rent is intended to eliminate differentials that result from varying practices with respect to the inclusion of utilities and fuels as part of the rental payment. The estimated costs of utilities and fuels are reported on an annual basis but are converted to monthly figures for the tabulations. Renter units occupied without payment of cash rent are shown separately as "No cash rent" in the tabulations.

Housing units that are renter occupied without payment of cash rent are shown separately as "No cash rent" in census data products. The unit may be owned by friends or relatives who live elsewhere and who allow occupancy without charge. Rent-free houses or apartments may be provided to compensate caretakers, ministers, tenant farmers, sharecroppers, or others.

Contract rent is the monthly rent agreed to or contracted for, regardless of any furnishings, utilities, fees, meals, or services that may be included. For vacant units, it is the monthly rent asked for the rental unit at the time of enumeration.

If the contract rent includes rent for a business unit or for living quarters occupied by another household, only that part of the rent estimated to be for the respondent's unit was included. Excluded was any rent paid for additional units or for business premises.

If a renter pays rent to the owner of a condominium or cooperative, and the condominium fee or cooperative carrying charge also is paid by the renter to the owner, the condominium fee or carrying charge was included as rent.

If a renter receives payments from lodgers or roomers who are listed as members of the household, the rent without deduction for any payments received from the lodgers or roomers was to be reported. The respondent was to report the rent agreed to or contracted for even if paid by someone else such as friends or relatives living elsewhere, a church or welfare agency, or the government through subsidies or vouchers.

The median divides the rent distribution into two equal parts: one-half of the cases falling below the median contract rent and one-half above the median. Median contract rents are computed on the basis of a standard distribution and are rounded to the nearest whole dollar. Units reported as "No cash rent" are excluded.

Median Home Value (in dollars): Reported by the owner of specified owner-occupied or specified vacant-for-sale housing units. Specified owner-occupied and specified vacant-for-sale housing units include only 1-family houses on less than 10 acres without a business or medical office on the property. The data for "specified units" exclude mobile homes, houses with a business or medical office, houses on 10 or more acres, and housing units in multi-unit buildings.

The data on value (also referred to as "price asked" for vacant units) were obtained from answers to long-form questionnaire Item 51, which was asked on a sample basis at owner-occupied housing units and units that were being bought, or vacant for sale at the time of enumeration. Value is the respondent's estimate of how much the property (house and lot, mobile home and lot, or condominium unit) would sell for if it were for sale. If the house or mobile home was owned or being bought, but the land on which it sits was not, the respondent was asked to estimate the combined value of the house or mobile home and the land. For vacant units, value was the price asked for the property. Value was tabulated separately for all owner-occupied and vacant-for-sale housing units, owner-occupied and vacant-for-sale mobile homes, and specified owner-occupied and specified vacant-for-sale housing units.

The median divides the value distribution into two equal parts: one-half of the cases falling below the median value of the property (house and lot, mobile home and lot, or condominium unit) and one-half above the median. Median values are computed on the basis of a standard distribution and are rounded to the nearest hundred dollars.

User's Guide: Climate

Inclusion Criteria — How the Data and Stations Were Selected

There were two central goals in the preparation of the climate chapter. The first was to select those data elements which would have the broadest possible use by the greatest range of potential users. For most of the National Weather Service stations there is a substantial quantity and variety of climatological data that is collected, however for the majority of stations the data is more limited. After evaluating the available data set, the editors chose nine temperature measures, five precipitation measures, and heating and cooling degree days — sixteen key data elements that are widely requested and are believed to be of the greatest general interest.

The second goal was to provide data for as many weather stations as possible. Although there are over 10,000 stations in the United States, not every station collects data for both precipitation and temperature, and even among those that do, the data is not always complete for the last thirty years. As the editors used a different methodology than that of NCDC to compute data, a formal data sufficiency criteria was devised and applied to the source tapes in order to select stations for inclusion.

Sources of the Data

The data in the climate chapter is compiled from several sources. The majority comes from the original National Climactic Data Center computer tapes (TD-3220 Summary of Month Co-Operative). This data was used to create the entire table for each Cooperative station and part of each National Weather Service station. The remainder of the data for each NWS station comes from the International Station Meteorological Climate Summary, Version 4.0, September 1996, which is also available from the NCDC.

NCDC has two main classes or types of weather stations; first order stations which are staffed by professional meteorologists and cooperative stations which are staffed by volunteers. In the climate chapter all first order stations operated by the National Weather Service are included, as well as every cooperative station that met our selection criteria.

Potential cautions in using *Weather America*

First, as with any statistical reference work of this type, users need to be aware of the source of the data. The information here comes from NOAA, and it is the most comprehensive and reliable core data available. Although it is the best, it is not perfect. Most weather stations are staffed by volunteers, times of observation sometimes vary, stations occasionally are moved (especially over a thirty year period), equipment is changed or upgraded, and all of these factors affect the uniformity of the data. the climate chapter does not attempt to correct for these factors, and is not intended for either climatologists or atmospheric scientists. Users with concerns about data collection and reporting protocols are both referred to NCDC technical documentation, and also, they are perhaps better served by using the original computer tapes themselves as well.

Second, users need to be aware of the methodology used, which is described later in this User's Guide. Although this methodology has produced fully satisfactory results, it is not directly compatible with other methodologies, hence variances in the results published here and those which appear in other publications will doubtlessly arise.

Third, is the trap of that informal logical fallacy known as "hasty generalization," and its corollaries. This may involve presuming the future will be like the past (specifically, next year will be an average year), or it may involve misunderstanding the limitations of an arithmetic average, but more interestingly, it may involve those mistakes made most innocently by generalizing informally on too broad a basis. As weather is highly localized, the data should be taken in that context. A weather station collects data about climatic conditions at that spot, and that spot may or may not be an effective paradigm for an entire town or area. For example, the weather station in Burlington, Vermont is located at the airport about 3 miles east of the center of town. Most of Burlington is a lot closer to Lake Champlain, and that should mean to a careful user that there could be a significant difference between the temperature readings gathered at the weather station and readings that might be gathered at City Hall downtown. How much would this difference be? How could it be estimated? There are no answers here for these sorts of questions, but it is important for users of this book to raise them for themselves. (It is interesting to note that similar situations abound across the country. For example, compare different readings for the multiple stations in San Francisco, CA or for those around New York City.)

Our source of data has been consistent, so has our methodology. The data has been computed and reported consistently as well. As a result, the the climate chapter should prove valuable to the careful and informed reader.

Weather Station Tables

The weather station tables are grouped by type (National Weather Service and Cooperative) and then arranged alphabetically. The station name is almost always a place name, and is shown here just as it appears in NCDC data. The station name is followed by the county in which the station is located, the elevation of the station (at the time beginning of the thirty year period) and the latitude and longitude.

The National Weather Service Station tables contain 30 data elements which were compiled from two different sources, the International Station Meteorological Climate Summary (ISMCS) and NCDC TD-3220 data tapes. The following 14 elements are from the ISMCS: maximum precipitation, minimum precipitation, maximum 24-hour precipitation, maximum snowfall, maximum 24-hour snowfall, thunderstorm days, foggy days, predominant sky cover, relative humidity (morning and afternoon), dewpoint, wind speed and direction, and maximum wind gust. The remaining 16 elements come from the TD-3220 data tapes. The period of record (POR) for data from the TD-3220 data tapes is 1970-1999. The POR for ISMCS data varies from station to station.

Weather Elements (National Weather Service and Cooperative Stations)

The following elements were compiled by the editor from the NCDC TD-3220 data tapes using a period of record of 1970-1999.

The average temperatures (maximum, minimum, and mean) are the average (see Methodology below) of those temperatures for all available values for a given month. For example, for a given station the average maximum temperature for July is the arithmetic average of all available maximum July temperatures for that station. (Maximum means the highest recorded temperature, minimum means the lowest recorded temperature, and mean means an arithmetic average temperature.)

The extreme maximum temperature is the highest temperature recorded in each month over the period 1970-1999. The extreme minimum temperature is the lowest temperature recorded in each month over the same time period.

The days for maximum temperature and minimum temperature are the average number of days those criteria were met for all available instances. The symbol >= means greater than or equal to, the symbol <= means less than or equal to. For example, for a given station, the number of days the maximum temperature was greater than or equal to 90°F in July, is just an arithmetic average of the number of days in all the available Julys for that station.

Heating and cooling degree days are based on the median temperature for a given day and its variance from 65°F. For example, for a given station if the day's high temperature was 50°F and the day's low temperature was 30°F, the median (midpoint) temperature was 40°F. 40°F is 25 degrees below 65°F, hence on this day there would be 25 heating degree days. The also applies for cooling degree days. For example, for a given station if the day's high temperature was 80°F and the day's low temperature was 70°F, the median (midpoint) temperature was 75°F. 75°F is 10 degrees above 65°F, hence on this day there would be 10 cooling degree days. All heating and/or cooling degree days in a month are summed for the month giving respective totals for each element for that month. These sums for a given month for a given station over the past thirty years are again summed and then arithmetically averaged. It should be noted that the heating and cooling degree days do not cancel each other out. It is possible to have both for a given station in the same month.

Precipitation data is computed the same as heating and cooling degree days. Mean precipitation and mean snowfall are arithmetic averages of cumulative totals for the month. All available values for the thirty year period for a given month for a given station are summed and then divided by the number of values. The same is true for days of greater than or equal to 0.1" and 1.0" of precipitation, and days of greater than or equal to 1.0" of snow depth on the ground. The word trace appears for precipitation and snowfall amounts that are too small to measure.

Finally, remember that all values presented in the tables and the rankings are averages of available data (see Methodology below) for that specific data element for the last thirty years (1970-1999).

Weather Elements (National Weather Service Stations Only)

The following elements were taken directly from the International Station Meteorological Climate Summary. The periods of records vary per station.

Maximum precipitation, minimum precipitation, maximum 24-hour precipitation, maximum snowfall, maximum 24-hour snowfall, thunderstorm days, foggy days, relative humidity (morning and afternoon), dewpoint, prevailing wind speed and direction, and maximum wind gust are all self-explanatory.

The word trace appears for precipitation and snowfall amounts that are too small to measure.

Predominant sky cover contains four possible entries: CLR (clear); SCT (scattered); BRK (broken); and OVR (overcast).

How Cooperative Stations Were Selected

The basic criteria is that a station must have data for temperature, precipitation, heating and cooling degree days of sufficient quantity in order to create a meaningful average. More specifically, the definition of sufficiency here has two parts. First, there must be 22 values for a given data element (with the exception of cooling degree days which required only 14 values in order to be considered sufficient- more about this later), and second, eight of the sixteen elements included in the table must pass this sufficiency test. For example, in regard to average maximum temperature (the first element on every data table), a given station needs to have a value for every month of at least 22 of the last thirty years in order to meet the criteria, and, in addition, every station included must have at least eight of the sixteen elements at least this minimal level of completeness in order to fulfill the criteria. By using this procedure, 3,933 stations met these requirements and are included here.

Methodology

The following discussion applies only to data compiled from the NCDC TD-3220 data tapes.

the climate chapter is based on an arithmetic average of all available data for a specific data element at a given station. For example, the average maximum daily high temperature during July for Pontiac, New York was abstracted from NCDC source tapes for the thirty Julys, starting in July, 1970 and ending in July, 1999. These thirty figures were then summed and divided by thirty to produce an arithmetic average. As might be expected, there were not thirty values for every data element on every table. For a variety of reasons, NCDC data is sometimes incomplete. Thus the following standards were established.

For those data elements where there were 26-30 values, the data was taken to be essentially complete and an average was computed. For data elements where there were 22-25 values, the data was taken as being partly complete but still valid enough to use to compute an average. Such averages are shown in ***bold italic*** type to indicate that there was less than 26 values. For the few data elements where there were not even 22 values, no average was computed and 'na' appears in the space. If any of the twelve months for a given data element reported a value of 'na', no annual average was computed and the annual average was reported as 'na' as well.

This procedure was followed for 15 of the 16 data elements. The one exception is cooling degree days. The collection of this data began in 1980 so the following standards were adopted: for those data elements where there were 17-20 values, the data was taken to be essentially complete and an average was computed. For data elements where there were 14-16 values, the data was taken as being partly complete but still valid enough to use to compute an average. Such averages are shown in ***bold italic*** type to indicate that there was 14-16 values. For the few data elements where there were not even 14 values, no average was computed and 'na' appears in the space. If any of the twelve months for a given data element reported a value of 'na', no annual average was computed and the annual average was reported as 'na' as well.

Thus the basic computational methodology of the climate chapter is to provide an arithmetic average. Because of this, such a pure arithmetic average is somewhat different from the special type of average (called a "normal") which NCDC procedures produces and appears in federal publications.

Perhaps the best outline of the contrasting normalization methodology is found in the following paragraph (which appears as part of an NCDC technical document titled, CLIM81 1961-1990 NORMALS TD-9641 prepared by Lewis France of NCDC in May, 1992):

Normals have been defined as the arithmetic mean of a climatological element computed over a long time period. International agreements eventually led to the decision that the appropriate time period would be three consecutive decades (Guttman, 1989). The data record should be consistent (have no changes in location, instruments, observation practices, etc.; these are identified here as "exposure changes") and have no missing values so a normal will reflect the actual average climatic conditions. If any significant exposure changes have occurred, the data record is said to be "inhomogeneous," and the normal may not reflect a true climatic average. Such data need to be adjusted to remove the nonclimatic inhomogeneities. The resulting (adjusted) record is then said to be "homogeneous." If no exposure changes have occurred at a station, the normal is calculated simply by averaging the appropriate 30 values from the 1961-1990 record.

In the main, there are two "inhomogeneities" that NCDC is correcting for with normalization: adjusting for variances in time of day of observation (at the so-called First Order stations data is based on midnight to midnight observation times and this practice is not necessarily followed at cooperative stations which are staffed by volunteers), and second, estimating data that is either missing or incongruent.

A long discussion of the normalization process is not required here but a short note concerning comparative results of the two methodologies is appropriate.

When the editors first started compiling the climate chapter a concern arose because the normalization process would not be replicated: would our methodology produce strikingly different results than NCDC's? To allay concerns, results of the two processes were compared for the time period normalized results are available (1961-1990). In short, what was found was that the answer to this question is no. Never-the-less, users should be aware that because of both the time period covered (1970-1999) and the methodology used, data in the climate chapter is not compatible with data from other sources.

Adams County

Located in southern Ohio; bounded on the south by the Ohio River and the Kentucky border. Covers a land area of 583.91 square miles, a water area of 1.88 square miles, and is located in the Eastern Time Zone. The county was founded in 1797. County seat is West Union.

Population: 25,371 (1990); 27,330 (2000); 28,750 (2007); 29,626 (2012 projected); Race: 97.9% White, 0.3% Black, 0.1% Asian, 0.7% Hispanic of any race (2007); Density: 49.2 persons per square mile (2007); Average household size: 2.53 (2007); Median age: 36.9 (2007); Males per 100 females: 96.9 (2007).

Religion: Five largest groups: 5.2% Christian Churches and Churches of Christ, 4.9% The United Methodist Church, 2.1% Presbyterian Church (U.S.A.), 2.0% Christian Union, 1.5% Church of the Nazarene (2000).

Economy: Unemployment rate: 8.6% (6/2008); Total civilian labor force: 13,569 (6/2008); Leading industries: 22.4% health care and social assistance; 22.0% retail trade; 17.3% manufacturing (2005); Farms: 1,320 totaling 198,277 acres (2002); Companies that employ 500 or more persons: 0 (2006); Companies that employ 100 to 499 persons: 8 (2006); Companies that employ less than 100 persons: 427 (2006); Black-owned businesses: n/a (2002); Hispanic-owned businesses: n/a (2002); Asian-owned businesses: n/a (2002); Women-owned businesses: 628 (2002); Retail sales per capita: $8,946 (2008). Single-family building permits issued: 0 (2007); Multi-family building permits issued: 18 (2007).

Income: Per capita income: $17,451 (2007); Median household income: $34,310 (2007); Average household income: $43,867 (2007); Percent of households with income of $100,000 or more: 7.0% (2007); Poverty rate: 20.5% (2005); Bankruptcy rate: 3.52% (2007).

Education: Percent of population age 25 and over with: High school diploma (including GED) or higher: 68.7% (2007); Bachelor's degree or higher: 7.2% (2007); Master's degree or higher: 2.8% (2007).

Housing: Homeownership rate: 74.5% (2007); Median home value: $86,754 (2007); Median rent: $273 per month (2000); Median age of housing: 26 years (2000).

Health: Birth rate: 141.3 per 10,000 population (2007); Death rate: 104.8 per 10,000 population (2007); Age-adjusted cancer mortality rate: 226.3 deaths per 100,000 population (2005); Air Quality Index: 100.0% good, 0.0% moderate, 0.0% unhealthy for sensitive individuals, 0.0% unhealthy (percent of days in 2007); Number of physicians: 5.3 per 10,000 population (2005); Hospital beds: 13.2 per 10,000 population (2004); Hospital admissions: 599.2 per 10,000 population (2004).

Elections: 2004 Presidential election results: 63.8% Bush, 35.7% Kerry, 0.0% Nader, 0.3% Badnarik

National and State Parks: Adams Lake State Reserve; Ohio State Park; Serpent Mound State Memorial; Shawnee State Wilderness; Tranquility State Wildlife Area

Additional Information Contacts

Adams County Government. . . . . (937) 544-3286
http://www.adamscountyohio.com

Adams County Travel and Visitors Bureau . . . . (937) 544-5454
http://www.adamscountytravel.org

Adams County Communities

BLUE CREEK (unincorporated postal area, zip code 45616). Covers a land area of 69.973 square miles and a water area of 0.027 square miles. Located at 38.78° N. Lat.; 83.31° W. Long. Elevation is 680 feet.

Population: 1,382 (2000); Race: 96.8% White, 0.0% Black, 0.0% Asian, 0.0% Hispanic of any race (2000); Density: 19.8 persons per square mile (2000); Age: 25.8% under 18, 11.3% over 64 (2000); Marriage status: 19.4% never married, 68.7% now married, 5.3% widowed, 6.7% divorced (2000); Foreign born: 0.5% (2000); Ancestry (includes multiple ancestries): 31.8% United States or American, 9.8% German, 7.8% Other groups, 6.2% Irish, 4.1% English (2000).

Economy: Employment by occupation: 7.4% management, 5.9% professional, 21.0% services, 17.2% sales, 1.1% farming, 14.2% construction, 33.3% production (2000).

Income: Per capita income: $13,915 (2000); Median household income: $21,313 (2000); Poverty rate: 31.6% (2000).

Education: Percent of population age 25 and over with: High school diploma (including GED) or higher: 55.3% (2000); Bachelor's degree or higher: 4.6% (2000).

Housing: Homeownership rate: 75.4% (2000); Median home value: $60,600 (2000); Median rent: $281 per month (2000); Median age of housing: 24 years (2000).

Transportation: Commute to work: 88.5% car, 0.0% public transportation, 1.5% walk, 5.8% work from home (2000); Travel time to work: 15.2% less than 15 minutes, 23.1% 15 to 30 minutes, 34.6% 30 to 45 minutes, 13.3% 45 to 60 minutes, 13.8% 60 minutes or more (2000)

CHERRY FORK (village). Covers a land area of 0.122 square miles and a water area of 0 square miles. Located at 38.88° N. Lat.; 83.61° W. Long. Elevation is 899 feet.

Population: 178 (1990); 127 (2000); 141 (2007); 151 (2012 projected); Race: 100.0% White, 0.0% Black, 0.0% Asian, 0.0% Hispanic of any race (2007); Density: 1,154.8 persons per square mile (2007); Average household size: 2.56 (2007); Median age: 30.2 (2007); Males per 100 females: 107.4 (2007); Marriage status: 19.8% never married, 59.4% now married, 1.0% widowed, 19.8% divorced (2000); Foreign born: 0.0% (2000); Ancestry (includes multiple ancestries): 37.8% United States or American, 16.2% German, 12.8% Other groups, 4.1% English, 2.7% Irish (2000).

Economy: Employment by occupation: 0.0% management, 13.8% professional, 24.1% services, 25.9% sales, 0.0% farming, 13.8% construction, 22.4% production (2000).

Income: Per capita income: $17,624 (2007); Median household income: $30,833 (2007); Average household income: $45,182 (2007); Percent of households with income of $100,000 or more: 9.1% (2007); Poverty rate: 26.7% (2000).

Education: Percent of population age 25 and over with: High school diploma (including GED) or higher: 79.8% (2007); Bachelor's degree or higher: 10.1% (2007); Master's degree or higher: 5.6% (2007).

Housing: Homeownership rate: 65.5% (2007); Median home value: $84,000 (2007); Median rent: $296 per month (2000); Median age of housing: 54 years (2000).

Transportation: Commute to work: 96.4% car, 0.0% public transportation, 0.0% walk, 0.0% work from home (2000); Travel time to work: 25.0% less than 15 minutes, 17.9% 15 to 30 minutes, 12.5% 30 to 45 minutes, 16.1% 45 to 60 minutes, 28.6% 60 minutes or more (2000)

MANCHESTER (village). Covers a land area of 1.078 square miles and a water area of 0.015 square miles. Located at 38.69° N. Lat.; 83.60° W. Long. Elevation is 505 feet.

History: Manchester was founded in 1791 by General Nathaniel Massie. The town was an important steamboat landing in the mid-1800's, and in the later 1800's offered excursions on the river and showboats at the wharf.

Population: 2,333 (1990); 2,043 (2000); 2,002 (2007); 1,981 (2012 projected); Race: 97.5% White, 0.2% Black, 0.3% Asian, 0.4% Hispanic of any race (2007); Density: 1,856.5 persons per square mile (2007); Average household size: 2.25 (2007); Median age: 37.4 (2007); Males per 100 females: 91.0 (2007); Marriage status: 21.0% never married, 53.5% now married, 11.2% widowed, 14.4% divorced (2000); Foreign born: 0.1% (2000); Ancestry (includes multiple ancestries): 31.2% United States or American, 9.6% Other groups, 8.6% German, 8.4% Irish, 5.8% English (2000).

Economy: Single-family building permits issued: 0 (2007); Multi-family building permits issued: 0 (2007); Employment by occupation: 11.1% management, 10.0% professional, 18.1% services, 17.8% sales, 0.3% farming, 15.6% construction, 27.2% production (2000).

Income: Per capita income: $15,937 (2007); Median household income: $25,847 (2007); Average household income: $35,848 (2007); Percent of households with income of $100,000 or more: 4.6% (2007); Poverty rate: 23.3% (2000).

Education: Percent of population age 25 and over with: High school diploma (including GED) or higher: 62.9% (2007); Bachelor's degree or higher: 6.3% (2007); Master's degree or higher: 3.5% (2007).

School District(s)

Manchester Local (PK-12)
2005-06 Enrollment: 920 . . . . (937) 549-4777

Housing: Homeownership rate: 62.6% (2007); Median home value: $61,196 (2007); Median rent: $263 per month (2000); Median age of housing: 39 years (2000).

Newspapers: Signal (Community news; Circulation 5,500)

Transportation: Commute to work: 93.0% car, 0.0% public transportation, 3.7% walk, 2.0% work from home (2000); Travel time to work: 34.1% less than 15 minutes, 32.5% 15 to 30 minutes, 11.9% 30 to 45 minutes, 3.9% 45 to 60 minutes, 17.6% 60 minutes or more (2000)

PEEBLES (village). Covers a land area of 1.213 square miles and a water area of 0 square miles. Located at 38.94° N. Lat.; 83.40° W. Long. Elevation is 827 feet.

Population: 1,793 (1990); 1,739 (2000); 1,692 (2007); 1,687 (2012 projected); Race: 97.7% White, 0.7% Black, 0.5% Asian, 0.3% Hispanic of any race (2007); Density: 1,394.7 persons per square mile (2007); Average household size: 2.39 (2007); Median age: 35.5 (2007); Males per 100 females: 91.6 (2007); Marriage status: 23.2% never married, 51.1% now married, 10.8% widowed, 14.9% divorced (2000); Foreign born: 0.0% (2000); Ancestry (includes multiple ancestries): 20.4% United States or American, 9.6% German, 9.4% Other groups, 5.6% Irish, 4.6% English (2000).

Economy: Employment by occupation: 5.4% management, 12.5% professional, 18.0% services, 20.8% sales, 1.3% farming, 12.4% construction, 29.6% production (2000).

Income: Per capita income: $14,801 (2007); Median household income: $23,796 (2007); Average household income: $35,057 (2007); Percent of households with income of $100,000 or more: 4.1% (2007); Poverty rate: 28.2% (2000).

Education: Percent of population age 25 and over with: High school diploma (including GED) or higher: 63.0% (2007); Bachelor's degree or higher: 5.2% (2007); Master's degree or higher: 2.5% (2007).

School District(s)

Adams County/Ohio Valley Local (PK-12)
2005-06 Enrollment: 4,190 .... (937) 544-5586

Housing: Homeownership rate: 57.6% (2007); Median home value: $68,778 (2007); Median rent: $276 per month (2000); Median age of housing: 38 years (2000).

Transportation: Commute to work: 92.3% car, 0.2% public transportation, 4.6% walk, 1.4% work from home (2000); Travel time to work: 32.6% less than 15 minutes, 28.3% 15 to 30 minutes, 11.9% 30 to 45 minutes, 7.1% 45 to 60 minutes, 20.2% 60 minutes or more (2000)

ROME (village). Aka Stout. Covers a land area of 0.266 square miles and a water area of 0.027 square miles. Located at 38.66° N. Lat.; 83.38° W. Long. Elevation is 518 feet.

History: Also called Stout.

Population: 99 (1990); 117 (2000); 106 (2007); 105 (2012 projected); Race: 94.3% White, 0.0% Black, 0.0% Asian, 0.0% Hispanic of any race (2007); Density: 398.4 persons per square mile (2007); Average household size: 2.47 (2007); Median age: 32.5 (2007); Males per 100 females: 96.3 (2007); Marriage status: 20.2% never married, 59.6% now married, 6.4% widowed, 13.8% divorced (2000); Foreign born: 0.0% (2000); Ancestry (includes multiple ancestries): 35.3% Other groups, 25.2% United States or American, 7.6% German, 6.7% Irish, 2.5% English (2000).

Economy: Employment by occupation: 8.6% management, 14.3% professional, 20.0% services, 25.7% sales, 0.0% farming, 11.4% construction, 20.0% production (2000).

Income: Per capita income: $16,604 (2007); Median household income: $38,750 (2007); Average household income: $40,930 (2007); Percent of households with income of $100,000 or more: 4.7% (2007); Poverty rate: 24.4% (2000).

Education: Percent of population age 25 and over with: High school diploma (including GED) or higher: 69.7% (2007); Bachelor's degree or higher: 3.0% (2007); Master's degree or higher: 0.0% (2007).

Housing: Homeownership rate: 67.4% (2007); Median home value: $61,667 (2007); Median rent: $329 per month (2000); Median age of housing: 47 years (2000).

Transportation: Commute to work: 91.2% car, 0.0% public transportation, 8.8% walk, 0.0% work from home (2000); Travel time to work: 17.6% less than 15 minutes, 41.2% 15 to 30 minutes, 23.5% 30 to 45 minutes, 5.9% 45 to 60 minutes, 11.8% 60 minutes or more (2000)

SEAMAN (village). Covers a land area of 1.021 square miles and a water area of 0 square miles. Located at 38.93° N. Lat.; 83.57° W. Long. Elevation is 906 feet.

Population: 1,009 (1990); 1,039 (2000); 899 (2007); 890 (2012 projected); Race: 99.0% White, 0.0% Black, 0.0% Asian, 0.8% Hispanic of any race (2007); Density: 880.5 persons per square mile (2007); Average household size: 2.46 (2007); Median age: 33.6 (2007); Males per 100 females: 87.3 (2007); Marriage status: 24.3% never married, 52.2% now married, 12.0% widowed, 11.5% divorced (2000); Foreign born: 0.4% (2000); Ancestry (includes multiple ancestries): 17.6% United States or American, 14.8% Irish, 12.2% German, 9.9% English, 6.3% Other groups (2000).

Economy: Single-family building permits issued: 0 (2007); Multi-family building permits issued: 0 (2007); Employment by occupation: 9.7% management, 15.8% professional, 14.5% services, 19.9% sales, 0.3% farming, 14.5% construction, 25.3% production (2000).

Income: Per capita income: $16,888 (2007); Median household income: $30,341 (2007); Average household income: $41,596 (2007); Percent of households with income of $100,000 or more: 5.5% (2007); Poverty rate: 21.7% (2000).

Education: Percent of population age 25 and over with: High school diploma (including GED) or higher: 75.8% (2007); Bachelor's degree or higher: 9.0% (2007); Master's degree or higher: 3.2% (2007).

School District(s)

Adams County/Ohio Valley Local (PK-12)
2005-06 Enrollment: 4,190 .... (937) 544-5586

Housing: Homeownership rate: 62.7% (2007); Median home value: $87,500 (2007); Median rent: $316 per month (2000); Median age of housing: 36 years (2000).

Transportation: Commute to work: 93.3% car, 0.0% public transportation, 3.6% walk, 3.1% work from home (2000); Travel time to work: 26.6% less than 15 minutes, 25.0% 15 to 30 minutes, 16.5% 30 to 45 minutes, 12.8% 45 to 60 minutes, 19.1% 60 minutes or more (2000)

WEST UNION (village). County seat. Covers a land area of 2.568 square miles and a water area of 0 square miles. Located at 38.79° N. Lat.; 83.54° W. Long. Elevation is 951 feet.

History: Laid out 1804.

Population: 3,234 (1990); 2,903 (2000); 3,042 (2007); 3,125 (2012 projected); Race: 98.3% White, 0.5% Black, 0.1% Asian, 0.5% Hispanic of any race (2007); Density: 1,184.5 persons per square mile (2007); Average household size: 2.27 (2007); Median age: 39.3 (2007); Males per 100 females: 79.6 (2007); Marriage status: 20.8% never married, 49.2% now married, 15.6% widowed, 14.4% divorced (2000); Foreign born: 0.3% (2000); Ancestry (includes multiple ancestries): 20.7% United States or American, 20.6% German, 12.6% Irish, 6.2% Other groups, 5.4% English (2000).

Economy: Employment by occupation: 2.5% management, 9.6% professional, 19.8% services, 24.7% sales, 1.4% farming, 10.3% construction, 31.6% production (2000).

Income: Per capita income: $15,738 (2007); Median household income: $24,349 (2007); Average household income: $33,960 (2007); Percent of households with income of $100,000 or more: 5.4% (2007); Poverty rate: 21.8% (2000).

Education: Percent of population age 25 and over with: High school diploma (including GED) or higher: 66.8% (2007); Bachelor's degree or higher: 3.8% (2007); Master's degree or higher: 0.7% (2007).

School District(s)

Adams County/Ohio Valley Local (PK-12)
2005-06 Enrollment: 4,190 .... (937) 544-5586

Housing: Homeownership rate: 55.3% (2007); Median home value: $75,922 (2007); Median rent: $256 per month (2000); Median age of housing: 32 years (2000).

Hospitals: Adams County Hospital (60 beds)

Newspapers: People's Defender (Community news; Circulation 9,100)

Transportation: Commute to work: 90.4% car, 0.8% public transportation, 6.3% walk, 2.4% work from home (2000); Travel time to work: 50.3% less than 15 minutes, 20.4% 15 to 30 minutes, 8.7% 30 to 45 minutes, 8.8% 45 to 60 minutes, 11.7% 60 minutes or more (2000)

Additional Information Contacts

Adams County Travel and Visitors Bureau .... (937) 544-5454
http://www.adamscountytravel.org

WINCHESTER (village). Covers a land area of 2.685 square miles and a water area of 0.017 square miles. Located at 38.94° N. Lat.; 83.65° W. Long. Elevation is 971 feet.

History: In agricultural area.

Population: 995 (1990); 1,025 (2000); 938 (2007); 925 (2012 projected); Race: 99.3% White, 0.0% Black, 0.3% Asian, 0.7% Hispanic of any race (2007); Density: 349.4 persons per square mile (2007); Average household size: 2.43 (2007); Median age: 34.3 (2007); Males per 100 females: 90.7 (2007); Marriage status: 18.6% never married, 60.7% now married, 7.9% widowed, 12.8% divorced (2000); Foreign born: 1.0% (2000); Ancestry (includes multiple ancestries): 17.7% United States or American, 16.4% German, 9.6% Irish, 9.4% Other groups, 7.0% English (2000).

Economy: Employment by occupation: 9.7% management, 10.8% professional, 12.9% services, 21.0% sales, 0.0% farming, 14.7% construction, 30.9% production (2000).
Income: Per capita income: $20,011 (2007); Median household income: $37,500 (2007); Average household income: $48,627 (2007); Percent of households with income of $100,000 or more: 8.5% (2007); Poverty rate: 14.2% (2000).
Education: Percent of population age 25 and over with: High school diploma (including GED) or higher: 76.5% (2007); Bachelor's degree or higher: 6.4% (2007); Master's degree or higher: 2.9% (2007).
Housing: Homeownership rate: 61.4% (2007); Median home value: $94,032 (2007); Median rent: $289 per month (2000); Median age of housing: 42 years (2000).
Transportation: Commute to work: 95.4% car, 0.0% public transportation, 4.2% walk, 0.5% work from home (2000); Travel time to work: 21.6% less than 15 minutes, 26.0% 15 to 30 minutes, 14.2% 30 to 45 minutes, 16.0% 45 to 60 minutes, 22.1% 60 minutes or more (2000)

Allen County

Located in western Ohio; crossed by the Ottawa and Auglaize Rivers. Covers a land area of 404.43 square miles, a water area of 2.46 square miles, and is located in the Eastern Time Zone. The county was founded in 1820. County seat is Lima.

Allen County is part of the Lima, OH Metropolitan Statistical Area. The entire metro area includes: Allen County, OH

Weather Station: Lima WWTP Elevation: 849 feet

	Jan	Feb	Mar	Apr	May	Jun	Jul	Aug	Sep	Oct	Nov	Dec
High	33	38	48	61	72	81	85	82	77	64	50	39
Low	18	21	30	40	51	60	64	62	55	44	34	25
Precip	2.2	1.9	2.7	3.5	3.9	4.0	4.4	3.3	3.1	2.4	3.1	2.7
Snow	na	na	na	0.1	0.0	0.0	0.0	0.0	0.0	tr	tr	na

High and Low temperatures in degrees Fahrenheit; Precipitation and Snow in inches

Population: 109,755 (1990); 108,473 (2000); 105,665 (2007); 103,388 (2012 projected); Race: 84.9% White, 11.5% Black, 0.8% Asian, 1.6% Hispanic of any race (2007); Density: 261.3 persons per square mile (2007); Average household size: 2.57 (2007); Median age: 37.2 (2007); Males per 100 females: 96.8 (2007).
Religion: Five largest groups: 22.7% Catholic Church, 7.7% The United Methodist Church, 3.2% Evangelical Lutheran Church in America, 2.2% United Church of Christ, 2.0% Church of the Nazarene (2000).
Economy: Unemployment rate: 7.3% (6/2008); Total civilian labor force: 52,793 (6/2008); Leading industries: 21.4% health care and social assistance; 17.9% manufacturing; 14.7% retail trade (2005); Farms: 968 totaling 188,150 acres (2002); Companies that employ 500 or more persons: 7 (2006); Companies that employ 100 to 499 persons: 80 (2006); Companies that employ less than 100 persons: 2,646 (2006); Black-owned businesses: 255 (2002); Hispanic-owned businesses: n/a (2002); Asian-owned businesses: 111 (2002); Women-owned businesses: 2,361 (2002); Retail sales per capita: $20,343 (2008). Single-family building permits issued: 169 (2007); Multi-family building permits issued: 9 (2007).
Income: Per capita income: $21,455 (2007); Median household income: $43,147 (2007); Average household income: $54,382 (2007); Percent of households with income of $100,000 or more: 11.2% (2007); Poverty rate: 13.4% (2005); Bankruptcy rate: 3.34% (2007).
Taxes: Total county taxes per capita: $263 (2006); County property taxes per capita: $112 (2006).
Education: Percent of population age 25 and over with: High school diploma (including GED) or higher: 83.1% (2007); Bachelor's degree or higher: 14.0% (2007); Master's degree or higher: 5.2% (2007).
Housing: Homeownership rate: 73.0% (2007); Median home value: $99,477 (2007); Median rent: $362 per month (2000); Median age of housing: 41 years (2000).
Health: Birth rate: 139.1 per 10,000 population (2007); Death rate: 102.0 per 10,000 population (2007); Age-adjusted cancer mortality rate: 197.4 deaths per 100,000 population (2005); Air Quality Index: 84.9% good, 13.2% moderate, 1.9% unhealthy for sensitive individuals, 0.0% unhealthy (percent of days in 2007); Number of physicians: 26.3 per 10,000 population (2005); Hospital beds: 66.6 per 10,000 population (2004); Hospital admissions: 2,255.7 per 10,000 population (2004).
Elections: 2004 Presidential election results: 66.1% Bush, 33.4% Kerry, 0.0% Nader, 0.3% Badnarik
Additional Information Contacts

Allen County Government . . . . (419) 228-3700
http://www.co.allen.oh.us
Bluffton Area Chamber of Commerce . . . . (419) 358-5675
http://www.bluffton-ohio.com/Chamber/tabid/61/Default.aspx
City of Lima . . . . (419) 228-5462
http://www.cityhall.lima.oh.us
Delphos Area Chamber of Commerce. . . . . (419) 695-1771
http://www.delphos-ohio.com
Lima-Allen County Chamber of Commerce . . . . (419) 222-6045
http://www.limachamber.com

Allen County Communities

BEAVERDAM (village). Aka Beaver Dam. Covers a land area of 0.629 square miles and a water area of 0 square miles. Located at 40.83° N. Lat.; 83.97° W. Long. Elevation is 856 feet.
Population: 487 (1990); 356 (2000); 375 (2007); 378 (2012 projected); Race: 99.2% White, 0.0% Black, 0.0% Asian, 0.5% Hispanic of any race (2007); Density: 596.5 persons per square mile (2007); Average household size: 2.48 (2007); Median age: 38.3 (2007); Males per 100 females: 91.3 (2007); Marriage status: 22.4% never married, 57.7% now married, 5.2% widowed, 14.7% divorced (2000); Foreign born: 0.9% (2000); Ancestry (includes multiple ancestries): 42.9% German, 7.7% Irish, 6.9% Swiss, 5.1% French (except Basque), 5.1% United States or American (2000).
Economy: Single-family building permits issued: 1 (2007); Multi-family building permits issued: 0 (2007); Employment by occupation: 8.9% management, 5.7% professional, 21.0% services, 12.7% sales, 0.0% farming, 10.2% construction, 41.4% production (2000).
Income: Per capita income: $21,060 (2007); Median household income: $48,438 (2007); Average household income: $52,301 (2007); Percent of households with income of $100,000 or more: 8.6% (2007); Poverty rate: 8.9% (2000).
Education: Percent of population age 25 and over with: High school diploma (including GED) or higher: 75.8% (2007); Bachelor's degree or higher: 2.7% (2007); Master's degree or higher: 0.0% (2007).
Housing: Homeownership rate: 86.1% (2007); Median home value: $63,333 (2007); Median rent: $275 per month (2000); Median age of housing: 60+ years (2000).
Transportation: Commute to work: 95.1% car, 0.0% public transportation, 2.1% walk, 0.0% work from home (2000); Travel time to work: 33.3% less than 15 minutes, 45.1% 15 to 30 minutes, 14.6% 30 to 45 minutes, 5.6% 45 to 60 minutes, 1.4% 60 minutes or more (2000)

BLUFFTON (village). Covers a land area of 3.329 square miles and a water area of 0.030 square miles. Located at 40.89° N. Lat.; 83.89° W. Long. Elevation is 833 feet.
History: Bluffton was founded in 1833 and named for a Mennonite community in Indiana. Many of the early residents were Mennonites of Swiss descent. Limestone outcroppings in the vicinity created a crushed stone and lime industry here.
Population: 3,480 (1990); 3,896 (2000); 3,842 (2007); 3,851 (2012 projected); Race: 97.8% White, 0.7% Black, 0.5% Asian, 1.4% Hispanic of any race (2007); Density: 1,154.0 persons per square mile (2007); Average household size: 2.71 (2007); Median age: 35.9 (2007); Males per 100 females: 76.6 (2007); Marriage status: 33.8% never married, 48.3% now married, 11.9% widowed, 6.0% divorced (2000); Foreign born: 2.3% (2000); Ancestry (includes multiple ancestries): 37.7% German, 12.1% English, 10.4% Swiss, 8.9% Irish, 8.8% Other groups (2000).
Economy: Single-family building permits issued: 5 (2007); Multi-family building permits issued: 2 (2007); Employment by occupation: 11.7% management, 26.1% professional, 21.8% services, 19.5% sales, 0.0% farming, 5.8% construction, 15.1% production (2000).
Income: Per capita income: $25,077 (2007); Median household income: $53,252 (2007); Average household income: $64,915 (2007); Percent of households with income of $100,000 or more: 17.6% (2007); Poverty rate: 5.7% (2000).
Education: Percent of population age 25 and over with: High school diploma (including GED) or higher: 88.3% (2007); Bachelor's degree or higher: 31.4% (2007); Master's degree or higher: 11.8% (2007).

School District(s)

Bluffton Exempted Village (PK-12)
2005-06 Enrollment: 1,144 . . . . (419) 358-5901

Four-year College(s)

Bluffton University (Private, Not-for-profit, Mennonite Church)
Fall 2007 Enrollment: 1,117. . . . . (419) 358-3000
2007-08 Tuition: In-state $21,780; Out-of-state $21,780

Housing: Homeownership rate: 70.5% (2007); Median home value: $127,431 (2007); Median rent: $327 per month (2000); Median age of housing: 42 years (2000).

Safety: Violent crime rate: 15.0 per 10,000 population; Property crime rate: 235.5 per 10,000 population (2007).

Newspapers: Bluffton News (Community news; Circulation 2,900)

Transportation: Commute to work: 71.5% car, 0.0% public transportation, 23.7% walk, 2.4% work from home (2000); Travel time to work: 60.7% less than 15 minutes, 26.3% 15 to 30 minutes, 10.4% 30 to 45 minutes, 0.8% 45 to 60 minutes, 1.8% 60 minutes or more (2000)

Airports: Bluffton (general aviation)

Additional Information Contacts

Bluffton Area Chamber of Commerce . . . . (419) 358-5675
http://www.bluffton-ohio.com/Chamber/tabid/61/Default.aspx

CAIRO (village). Covers a land area of 0.242 square miles and a water area of 0 square miles. Located at 40.83° N. Lat.; 84.08° W. Long. Elevation is 814 feet.

Population: 473 (1990); 499 (2000); 448 (2007); 447 (2012 projected); Race: 98.7% White, 0.2% Black, 0.2% Asian, 0.9% Hispanic of any race (2007); Density: 1,853.0 persons per square mile (2007); Average household size: 2.72 (2007); Median age: 34.7 (2007); Males per 100 females: 89.8 (2007); Marriage status: 20.9% never married, 58.8% now married, 7.9% widowed, 12.5% divorced (2000); Foreign born: 0.0% (2000); Ancestry (includes multiple ancestries): 41.5% German, 15.4% English, 11.9% Irish, 8.5% Other groups, 7.1% Welsh (2000).

Economy: Single-family building permits issued: 0 (2007); Multi-family building permits issued: 0 (2007); Employment by occupation: 5.6% management, 13.1% professional, 15.4% services, 22.9% sales, 0.0% farming, 15.4% construction, 27.6% production (2000).

Income: Per capita income: $15,904 (2007); Median household income: $37,396 (2007); Average household income: $43,182 (2007); Percent of households with income of $100,000 or more: 3.0% (2007); Poverty rate: 6.9% (2000).

Education: Percent of population age 25 and over with: High school diploma (including GED) or higher: 90.2% (2007); Bachelor's degree or higher: 8.4% (2007); Master's degree or higher: 4.0% (2007).

Housing: Homeownership rate: 87.9% (2007); Median home value: $89,375 (2007); Median rent: $469 per month (2000); Median age of housing: 59 years (2000).

Transportation: Commute to work: 99.0% car, 0.0% public transportation, 1.0% walk, 0.0% work from home (2000); Travel time to work: 18.6% less than 15 minutes, 57.6% 15 to 30 minutes, 9.5% 30 to 45 minutes, 6.7% 45 to 60 minutes, 7.6% 60 minutes or more (2000)

DELPHOS (city). Covers a land area of 2.903 square miles and a water area of 0 square miles. Located at 40.84° N. Lat.; 84.33° W. Long. Elevation is 774 feet.

History: Delphos was platted in 1845 by Ferdinand Bredeick. Its location on the Miami & Erie Canal and the Pennsylvania Railroad brought it early growth. Large-scale honey production was one of the leading industries.

Population: 7,436 (1990); 6,944 (2000); 6,909 (2007); 6,820 (2012 projected); Race: 98.1% White, 0.4% Black, 0.3% Asian, 0.7% Hispanic of any race (2007); Density: 2,379.8 persons per square mile (2007); Average household size: 2.48 (2007); Median age: 36.6 (2007); Males per 100 females: 95.8 (2007); Marriage status: 22.8% never married, 60.2% now married, 8.7% widowed, 8.3% divorced (2000); Foreign born: 0.8% (2000); Ancestry (includes multiple ancestries): 53.4% German, 7.3% United States or American, 7.0% Irish, 5.6% Other groups, 4.8% English (2000).

Economy: Single-family building permits issued: 16 (2007); Multi-family building permits issued: 0 (2007); Employment by occupation: 7.8% management, 14.0% professional, 14.7% services, 22.4% sales, 0.2% farming, 8.8% construction, 32.1% production (2000).

Income: Per capita income: $19,584 (2007); Median household income: $40,302 (2007); Average household income: $48,170 (2007); Percent of households with income of $100,000 or more: 6.6% (2007); Poverty rate: 6.8% (2000).

Education: Percent of population age 25 and over with: High school diploma (including GED) or higher: 84.0% (2007); Bachelor's degree or higher: 8.5% (2007); Master's degree or higher: 2.6% (2007).

School District(s)

Delphos City (PK-12)
2005-06 Enrollment: 1,180 . . . . (419) 692-2509

Housing: Homeownership rate: 77.1% (2007); Median home value: $83,626 (2007); Median rent: $347 per month (2000); Median age of housing: 49 years (2000).

Safety: Violent crime rate: 10.3 per 10,000 population; Property crime rate: 194.3 per 10,000 population (2007).

Newspapers: The Delphos Herald (Community news; Circulation 4,000)

Transportation: Commute to work: 95.6% car, 0.2% public transportation, 2.3% walk, 1.7% work from home (2000); Travel time to work: 42.7% less than 15 minutes, 35.6% 15 to 30 minutes, 16.8% 30 to 45 minutes, 1.8% 45 to 60 minutes, 3.1% 60 minutes or more (2000)

Additional Information Contacts

Delphos Area Chamber of Commerce. . . . . (419) 695-1771
http://www.delphos-ohio.com

ELIDA (village). Covers a land area of 1.035 square miles and a water area of 0 square miles. Located at 40.78° N. Lat.; 84.19° W. Long. Elevation is 801 feet.

Population: 1,569 (1990); 1,917 (2000); 1,976 (2007); 2,032 (2012 projected); Race: 94.3% White, 2.5% Black, 1.1% Asian, 1.7% Hispanic of any race (2007); Density: 1,909.1 persons per square mile (2007); Average household size: 2.70 (2007); Median age: 38.3 (2007); Males per 100 females: 95.1 (2007); Marriage status: 21.0% never married, 64.8% now married, 5.7% widowed, 8.5% divorced (2000); Foreign born: 0.7% (2000); Ancestry (includes multiple ancestries): 41.6% German, 13.7% Irish, 7.7% United States or American, 7.6% Other groups, 7.4% English (2000).

Economy: Single-family building permits issued: 1 (2007); Multi-family building permits issued: 0 (2007); Employment by occupation: 14.3% management, 20.7% professional, 15.8% services, 25.5% sales, 0.0% farming, 7.8% construction, 15.9% production (2000).

Income: Per capita income: $25,777 (2007); Median household income: $59,107 (2007); Average household income: $69,583 (2007); Percent of households with income of $100,000 or more: 22.1% (2007); Poverty rate: 3.1% (2000).

Education: Percent of population age 25 and over with: High school diploma (including GED) or higher: 92.7% (2007); Bachelor's degree or higher: 23.0% (2007); Master's degree or higher: 8.6% (2007).

School District(s)

Elida Local (PK-12)
2005-06 Enrollment: 2,459 . . . . (419) 331-4155

Housing: Homeownership rate: 89.6% (2007); Median home value: $129,412 (2007); Median rent: $368 per month (2000); Median age of housing: 32 years (2000).

Transportation: Commute to work: 93.9% car, 0.3% public transportation, 1.7% walk, 4.1% work from home (2000); Travel time to work: 37.7% less than 15 minutes, 49.3% 15 to 30 minutes, 7.8% 30 to 45 minutes, 2.5% 45 to 60 minutes, 2.6% 60 minutes or more (2000)

FORT SHAWNEE (village). Covers a land area of 7.205 square miles and a water area of 0 square miles. Located at 40.68° N. Lat.; 84.13° W. Long. Elevation is 866 feet.

Population: 4,128 (1990); 3,855 (2000); 3,789 (2007); 3,695 (2012 projected); Race: 93.2% White, 3.3% Black, 1.2% Asian, 1.6% Hispanic of any race (2007); Density: 525.9 persons per square mile (2007); Average household size: 2.46 (2007); Median age: 40.7 (2007); Males per 100 females: 94.8 (2007); Marriage status: 20.0% never married, 64.5% now married, 5.0% widowed, 10.5% divorced (2000); Foreign born: 0.3% (2000); Ancestry (includes multiple ancestries): 39.2% German, 14.2% Irish, 9.8% United States or American, 9.7% English, 9.0% Other groups (2000).

Economy: Single-family building permits issued: 0 (2007); Multi-family building permits issued: 0 (2007); Employment by occupation: 5.6% management, 18.0% professional, 15.5% services, 26.3% sales, 0.0% farming, 11.1% construction, 23.4% production (2000).

Income: Per capita income: $24,831 (2007); Median household income: $55,241 (2007); Average household income: $61,128 (2007); Percent of households with income of $100,000 or more: 12.9% (2007); Poverty rate: 2.7% (2000).

Education: Percent of population age 25 and over with: High school diploma (including GED) or higher: 90.1% (2007); Bachelor's degree or higher: 11.3% (2007); Master's degree or higher: 4.5% (2007).

Housing: Homeownership rate: 90.2% (2007); Median home value: $104,525 (2007); Median rent: $424 per month (2000); Median age of housing: 35 years (2000).
Safety: Violent crime rate: 21.4 per 10,000 population; Property crime rate: 77.5 per 10,000 population (2007).
Transportation: Commute to work: 96.7% car, 0.9% public transportation, 0.7% walk, 1.5% work from home (2000); Travel time to work: 37.3% less than 15 minutes, 50.8% 15 to 30 minutes, 5.9% 30 to 45 minutes, 2.4% 45 to 60 minutes, 3.6% 60 minutes or more (2000)

GOMER (unincorporated postal area, zip code 45809). Covers a land area of 0.582 square miles and a water area of 0 square miles. Located at 40.84° N. Lat.; 84.18° W. Long. Elevation is 780 feet.
Population: 208 (2000); Race: 100.0% White, 0.0% Black, 0.0% Asian, 0.0% Hispanic of any race (2000); Density: 357.4 persons per square mile (2000); Age: 18.6% under 18, 12.6% over 64 (2000); Marriage status: 17.9% never married, 60.1% now married, 4.0% widowed, 17.9% divorced (2000); Foreign born: 0.0% (2000); Ancestry (includes multiple ancestries): 26.6% German, 16.1% United States or American, 14.1% Irish, 7.5% Welsh, 3.5% Dutch (2000).
Economy: Employment by occupation: 11.5% management, 23.0% professional, 0.0% services, 28.7% sales, 0.0% farming, 0.0% construction, 36.9% production (2000).
Income: Per capita income: $28,434 (2000); Median household income: $54,583 (2000); Poverty rate: 0.0% (2000).
Education: Percent of population age 25 and over with: High school diploma (including GED) or higher: 100.0% (2000); Bachelor's degree or higher: 12.2% (2000).
Housing: Homeownership rate: 79.2% (2000); Median home value: $83,300 (2000); Median rent: $464 per month (2000); Median age of housing: 60+ years (2000).
Transportation: Commute to work: 95.1% car, 0.0% public transportation, 0.0% walk, 0.0% work from home (2000); Travel time to work: 31.1% less than 15 minutes, 54.1% 15 to 30 minutes, 4.9% 30 to 45 minutes, 4.9% 45 to 60 minutes, 4.9% 60 minutes or more (2000)

HARROD (village). Aka Harrods. Covers a land area of 0.224 square miles and a water area of 0 square miles. Located at 40.70° N. Lat.; 83.92° W. Long. Elevation is 981 feet.
Population: 541 (1990); 491 (2000); 447 (2007); 441 (2012 projected); Race: 98.7% White, 0.0% Black, 0.0% Asian, 0.9% Hispanic of any race (2007); Density: 1,996.6 persons per square mile (2007); Average household size: 2.76 (2007); Median age: 33.9 (2007); Males per 100 females: 98.7 (2007); Marriage status: 22.5% never married, 65.7% now married, 6.5% widowed, 5.2% divorced (2000); Foreign born: 0.4% (2000); Ancestry (includes multiple ancestries): 24.7% German, 18.1% United States or American, 10.0% Irish, 6.2% English, 3.0% Welsh (2000).
Economy: Single-family building permits issued: 0 (2007); Multi-family building permits issued: 0 (2007); Employment by occupation: 5.0% management, 7.1% professional, 19.7% services, 22.6% sales, 0.8% farming, 17.6% construction, 27.2% production (2000).
Income: Per capita income: $18,893 (2007); Median household income: $45,000 (2007); Average household income: $52,130 (2007); Percent of households with income of $100,000 or more: 8.0% (2007); Poverty rate: 7.0% (2000).
Education: Percent of population age 25 and over with: High school diploma (including GED) or higher: 80.9% (2007); Bachelor's degree or higher: 4.4% (2007); Master's degree or higher: 3.3% (2007).

School District(s)

Allen East Local (PK-12)
2005-06 Enrollment: 1,031 . . . . (419) 648-3333
Housing: Homeownership rate: 81.5% (2007); Median home value: $84,545 (2007); Median rent: $342 per month (2000); Median age of housing: 58 years (2000).
Transportation: Commute to work: 95.0% car, 1.7% public transportation, 2.1% walk, 1.3% work from home (2000); Travel time to work: 18.6% less than 15 minutes, 47.0% 15 to 30 minutes, 23.3% 30 to 45 minutes, 5.1% 45 to 60 minutes, 5.9% 60 minutes or more (2000)

LAFAYETTE (village). Aka La Fayette. Covers a land area of 0.205 square miles and a water area of 0 square miles. Located at 40.75° N. Lat.; 83.94° W. Long. Elevation is 928 feet.
Population: 449 (1990); 304 (2000); 292 (2007); 286 (2012 projected); Race: 99.3% White, 0.7% Black, 0.0% Asian, 0.0% Hispanic of any race (2007); Density: 1,424.7 persons per square mile (2007); Average household size: 2.52 (2007); Median age: 36.3 (2007); Males per 100 females: 86.0 (2007); Marriage status: 25.5% never married, 62.1% now married, 3.8% widowed, 8.5% divorced (2000); Foreign born: 0.0% (2000); Ancestry (includes multiple ancestries): 37.3% German, 20.2% United States or American, 13.9% Irish, 11.1% English, 7.0% French (except Basque) (2000).
Economy: Employment by occupation: 2.9% management, 21.9% professional, 10.9% services, 32.1% sales, 0.0% farming, 11.7% construction, 20.4% production (2000).
Income: Per capita income: $23,065 (2007); Median household income: $48,333 (2007); Average household income: $58,060 (2007); Percent of households with income of $100,000 or more: 13.8% (2007); Poverty rate: 3.5% (2000).
Education: Percent of population age 25 and over with: High school diploma (including GED) or higher: 91.7% (2007); Bachelor's degree or higher: 8.3% (2007); Master's degree or higher: 2.6% (2007).

School District(s)

Allen East Local (PK-12)
2005-06 Enrollment: 1,031 . . . . (419) 648-3333
Housing: Homeownership rate: 87.9% (2007); Median home value: $88,125 (2007); Median rent: $338 per month (2000); Median age of housing: 60+ years (2000).
Transportation: Commute to work: 97.8% car, 1.4% public transportation, 0.7% walk, 0.0% work from home (2000); Travel time to work: 18.1% less than 15 minutes, 53.6% 15 to 30 minutes, 8.7% 30 to 45 minutes, 0.0% 45 to 60 minutes, 19.6% 60 minutes or more (2000)

LIMA (city). County seat. Covers a land area of 12.785 square miles and a water area of 0.097 square miles. Located at 40.74° N. Lat.; 84.11° W. Long. Elevation is 879 feet.
History: Lima was laid out on the Ottawa River in 1831 as the seat of Allen County. The name, the suggestion of minister and congressman Patrick Good, was drawn from a hat. Lima was incorporated in 1842. Oil was found here in 1885, bringing prosperity for a time until local industry turned to manufacturing railroad locomotives. It was in Lima that the Dillinger gang murdered Sheriff Jesse Sarber, starting a nation-wide hunt that ended in Dillinger's death and the end of his gang.
Population: 45,620 (1990); 40,081 (2000); 36,337 (2007); 33,869 (2012 projected); Race: 68.8% White, 25.9% Black, 0.8% Asian, 2.4% Hispanic of any race (2007); Density: 2,842.2 persons per square mile (2007); Average household size: 2.50 (2007); Median age: 33.5 (2007); Males per 100 females: 97.8 (2007); Marriage status: 33.6% never married, 43.0% now married, 8.5% widowed, 14.9% divorced (2000); Foreign born: 1.1% (2000); Ancestry (includes multiple ancestries): 27.6% Other groups, 20.9% German, 11.0% Irish, 9.6% United States or American, 5.2% English (2000).
Economy: Unemployment rate: 9.2% (6/2008); Total civilian labor force: 17,446 (6/2008); Single-family building permits issued: 7 (2007); Multi-family building permits issued: 7 (2007); Employment by occupation: 6.4% management, 12.0% professional, 20.8% services, 22.0% sales, 0.5% farming, 8.5% construction, 29.9% production (2000).
Income: Per capita income: $15,844 (2007); Median household income: $29,993 (2007); Average household income: $38,786 (2007); Percent of households with income of $100,000 or more: 4.7% (2007); Poverty rate: 22.7% (2000).
Taxes: Total city taxes per capita: $485 (2006); City property taxes per capita: $34 (2006).
Education: Percent of population age 25 and over with: High school diploma (including GED) or higher: 76.0% (2007); Bachelor's degree or higher: 9.9% (2007); Master's degree or higher: 3.2% (2007).

School District(s)

Allen
2005-06 Enrollment: n/a . . . . (419) 222-1836
Allen East Local (PK-12)
2005-06 Enrollment: 1,031 . . . . (419) 648-3333
Apollo (07-12)
2005-06 Enrollment: n/a . . . . (419) 998-2908
Auglaize County Educational Academy (02-12)
2005-06 Enrollment: 44 . . . . (419) 738-3422
Auglaize County Special Needs School (01-12)
2005-06 Enrollment: 35 . . . . (419) 738-3422
Bath Local (PK-12)
2005-06 Enrollment: 1,984 . . . . (419) 221-0807
Heir Force Community School (KG-08)
2005-06 Enrollment: 250 . . . . (419) 228-9241

Lima City (PK-12)
2005-06 Enrollment: 5,071 . . . . (419) 996-3400
Lima Digital Academy
2005-06 Enrollment: n/a . . . . (419) 998-2400
Perry Local (PK-12)
2005-06 Enrollment: 884 . . . . (419) 221-2770
Quest Academy Community (KG-06)
2005-06 Enrollment: 109 . . . . (419) 227-7730
Shawnee Local (PK-12)
2005-06 Enrollment: 2,674 . . . . (419) 998-8031
West Central Learning Academy (07-12)
2005-06 Enrollment: 74 . . . . (419) 227-9252

Four-year College(s)

Ohio State University-Lima Campus (Public)
Fall 2007 Enrollment: 1,340. . . . . (419) 995-8600
2007-08 Tuition: In-state $5,664; Out-of-state $18,273
University of Northwestern Ohio (Private, Not-for-profit)
Fall 2007 Enrollment: 3,312. . . . . (419) 227-3141
2007-08 Tuition: In-state $13,500; Out-of-state $13,500

Two-year College(s)

James A Rhodes State College (Public)
Fall 2007 Enrollment: 3,385. . . . . (419) 221-1112
2007-08 Tuition: In-state $3,398; Out-of-state $6,721
Ohio State Beauty Academy (Private, For-profit)
Fall 2007 Enrollment: 138 . . . . (419) 229-7896

Vocational/Technical School(s)

Apollo Career Center (Public)
Fall 2007 Enrollment: 233 . . . . (419) 998-3000
2007-08 Tuition: $7,700

Housing: Homeownership rate: 57.4% (2007); Median home value: $66,014 (2007); Median rent: $344 per month (2000); Median age of housing: 51 years (2000).
Hospitals: Lima Memorial Hospital (308 beds); St. Rita's Medical Center (424 beds)
Safety: Violent crime rate: 92.9 per 10,000 population; Property crime rate: 697.2 per 10,000 population (2007).
Newspapers: Lima News (Local news; Circulation 34,084)
Transportation: Commute to work: 94.0% car, 1.7% public transportation, 1.7% walk, 1.6% work from home (2000); Travel time to work: 50.7% less than 15 minutes, 34.3% 15 to 30 minutes, 8.1% 30 to 45 minutes, 3.3% 45 to 60 minutes, 3.5% 60 minutes or more (2000)
Additional Information Contacts
City of Lima . . . . (419) 228-5462
http://www.cityhall.lima.oh.us
Lima-Allen County Chamber of Commerce . . . . (419) 222-6045
http://www.limachamber.com

SPENCERVILLE (village). Covers a land area of 0.910 square miles and a water area of 0 square miles. Located at 40.70° N. Lat.; 84.35° W. Long. Elevation is 830 feet.
History: Laid out 1844-1845, incorporated 1866.
Population: 2,293 (1990); 2,235 (2000); 2,201 (2007); 2,173 (2012 projected); Race: 97.0% White, 0.6% Black, 0.2% Asian, 0.2% Hispanic of any race (2007); Density: 2,417.5 persons per square mile (2007); Average household size: 2.55 (2007); Median age: 35.6 (2007); Males per 100 females: 88.9 (2007); Marriage status: 18.9% never married, 56.6% now married, 9.7% widowed, 14.9% divorced (2000); Foreign born: 0.6% (2000); Ancestry (includes multiple ancestries): 37.0% German, 10.9% United States or American, 8.0% Irish, 5.9% Other groups, 5.8% English (2000).
Economy: Single-family building permits issued: 3 (2007); Multi-family building permits issued: 0 (2007); Employment by occupation: 3.9% management, 13.5% professional, 12.5% services, 21.6% sales, 0.1% farming, 8.8% construction, 39.6% production (2000).
Income: Per capita income: $19,252 (2007); Median household income: $38,239 (2007); Average household income: $48,320 (2007); Percent of households with income of $100,000 or more: 7.0% (2007); Poverty rate: 13.0% (2000).
Education: Percent of population age 25 and over with: High school diploma (including GED) or higher: 82.4% (2007); Bachelor's degree or higher: 8.7% (2007); Master's degree or higher: 2.0% (2007).

School District(s)

Spencerville Local (PK-12)
2005-06 Enrollment: 1,021 . . . . (419) 647-4111

Housing: Homeownership rate: 77.3% (2007); Median home value: $81,800 (2007); Median rent: $309 per month (2000); Median age of housing: 49 years (2000).
Safety: Violent crime rate: 0.0 per 10,000 population; Property crime rate: 105.5 per 10,000 population (2007).
Newspapers: Journal-News (Local news; Circulation 2,080)
Transportation: Commute to work: 90.7% car, 0.6% public transportation, 6.3% walk, 1.2% work from home (2000); Travel time to work: 35.4% less than 15 minutes, 35.2% 15 to 30 minutes, 20.3% 30 to 45 minutes, 3.9% 45 to 60 minutes, 5.2% 60 minutes or more (2000)

Ashland County

Located in north central Ohio; drained by forks of the Mohican River. Covers a land area of 424.37 square miles, a water area of 2.47 square miles, and is located in the Eastern Time Zone. The county was founded in 1846. County seat is Ashland.

Ashland County is part of the Ashland, OH Micropolitan Statistical Area. The entire metro area includes: Ashland County, OH

Weather Station: Ashland 2 SW Elevation: 1,263 feet

	Jan	Feb	Mar	Apr	May	Jun	Jul	Aug	Sep	Oct	Nov	Dec
High	32	36	47	59	70	79	83	81	74	62	49	38
Low	15	18	26	36	47	56	60	58	51	40	31	22
Precip	2.4	2.1	2.8	3.6	4.1	4.0	4.2	4.1	3.4	2.6	3.2	2.7
Snow	10.0	7.9	5.4	1.5	tr	0.0	0.0	0.0	0.0	tr	2.1	7.1

High and Low temperatures in degrees Fahrenheit; Precipitation and Snow in inches

Population: 47,507 (1990); 52,523 (2000); 54,527 (2007); 55,702 (2012 projected); Race: 97.2% White, 1.0% Black, 0.7% Asian, 0.8% Hispanic of any race (2007); Density: 128.5 persons per square mile (2007); Average household size: 2.67 (2007); Median age: 37.1 (2007); Males per 100 females: 95.8 (2007).
Religion: Five largest groups: 8.8% The United Methodist Church, 8.7% Evangelical Lutheran Church in America, 3.6% Catholic Church, 3.2% Greek Orthodox Archdiocese of America, 1.9% Independent, Non-Charismatic Churches (2000).
Economy: Unemployment rate: 6.8% (6/2008); Total civilian labor force: 27,908 (6/2008); Leading industries: 27.8% manufacturing; 13.1% retail trade; 12.9% health care and social assistance (2005); Farms: 1,089 totaling 161,100 acres (2002); Companies that employ 500 or more persons: 4 (2006); Companies that employ 100 to 499 persons: 25 (2006); Companies that employ less than 100 persons: 1,091 (2006); Black-owned businesses: n/a (2002); Hispanic-owned businesses: n/a (2002); Asian-owned businesses: n/a (2002); Women-owned businesses: 671 (2002); Retail sales per capita: $9,111 (2008). Single-family building permits issued: 129 (2007); Multi-family building permits issued: 36 (2007).
Income: Per capita income: $20,361 (2007); Median household income: $44,575 (2007); Average household income: $53,448 (2007); Percent of households with income of $100,000 or more: 10.4% (2007); Poverty rate: 12.7% (2005); Bankruptcy rate: 3.26% (2007).
Education: Percent of population age 25 and over with: High school diploma (including GED) or higher: 83.3% (2007); Bachelor's degree or higher: 15.9% (2007); Master's degree or higher: 5.3% (2007).
Housing: Homeownership rate: 76.4% (2007); Median home value: $130,688 (2007); Median rent: $370 per month (2000); Median age of housing: 41 years (2000).
Health: Birth rate: 128.6 per 10,000 population (2007); Death rate: 94.0 per 10,000 population (2007); Age-adjusted cancer mortality rate: 163.1 deaths per 100,000 population (2005); Number of physicians: 10.6 per 10,000 population (2005); Hospital beds: 13.0 per 10,000 population (2004); Hospital admissions: 654.2 per 10,000 population (2004).
Elections: 2004 Presidential election results: 64.9% Bush, 34.3% Kerry, 0.0% Nader, 0.3% Badnarik
National and State Parks: Mohican State Forest
Additional Information Contacts
Ashland County Government. . . . . (419) 289-0000
http://www.ashlandcounty.org
Ashland Area Chamber of Commerce. . . . . (419) 281-4584
http://www.ashlandoh.com
City of Ashland. . . . . (419) 289-8622
http://www.ashland-ohio.com
Loudonville Chamber of Commerce . . . . (419) 994-2519
http://www.loudonville-mohican.com/chamber.html

Ashland County Communities

ASHLAND (city). County seat. Covers a land area of 10.358 square miles and a water area of 0.038 square miles. Located at 40.86° N. Lat.; 82.31° W. Long. Elevation is 1,066 feet.
History: Ashland was platted in 1815 by William Montgomery, who called it Uniontown. In 1822 the town was renamed Ashland, for Henry Clay's estate at Lexington, Kentucky. A memorial to Johnny Appleseed, who often came through Ashland, was erected in 1915 through the donations of Ashland County children.
Population: 20,355 (1990); 21,249 (2000); 21,694 (2007); 22,043 (2012 projected); Race: 96.0% White, 1.2% Black, 1.4% Asian, 1.0% Hispanic of any race (2007); Density: 2,094.5 persons per square mile (2007); Average household size: 2.55 (2007); Median age: 35.3 (2007); Males per 100 females: 87.3 (2007); Marriage status: 26.6% never married, 54.8% now married, 8.1% widowed, 10.5% divorced (2000); Foreign born: 1.5% (2000); Ancestry (includes multiple ancestries): 31.5% German, 11.7% Irish, 11.3% United States or American, 10.8% English, 7.0% Other groups (2000).
Economy: Single-family building permits issued: 16 (2007); Multi-family building permits issued: 12 (2007); Employment by occupation: 9.6% management, 17.9% professional, 15.5% services, 24.8% sales, 0.4% farming, 6.8% construction, 24.9% production (2000).
Income: Per capita income: $19,082 (2007); Median household income: $37,675 (2007); Average household income: $47,057 (2007); Percent of households with income of $100,000 or more: 7.8% (2007); Poverty rate: 10.5% (2000).
Education: Percent of population age 25 and over with: High school diploma (including GED) or higher: 83.6% (2007); Bachelor's degree or higher: 19.7% (2007); Master's degree or higher: 6.9% (2007).

School District(s)

Ashland City (PK-12)
2005-06 Enrollment: 3,695 . . . . (419) 289-1117
Ashland County-West Holmes (09-12)
2005-06 Enrollment: n/a . . . . (419) 289-3313
Crestview Local (KG-12)
2005-06 Enrollment: 1,250 . . . . (419) 895-1700
Mapleton Local (PK-12)
2005-06 Enrollment: 1,072 . . . . (419) 945-2188

Four-year College(s)

Ashland University (Private, Not-for-profit, Brethren Church)
Fall 2007 Enrollment: 6,493. . . . . (419) 289-4142
2007-08 Tuition: In-state $23,006; Out-of-state $23,006

Vocational/Technical School(s)

Ashland County-West Holmes Career Center (Public)
Fall 2007 Enrollment: 70 . . . . (419) 289-3313
2007-08 Tuition: $5,040

Housing: Homeownership rate: 64.6% (2007); Median home value: $113,586 (2007); Median rent: $370 per month (2000); Median age of housing: 45 years (2000).
Hospitals: Samaritan Regional Health System (110 beds)
Safety: Violent crime rate: 8.7 per 10,000 population; Property crime rate: 251.2 per 10,000 population (2007).
Newspapers: Ashland Times-Gazette (Local news; Circulation 13,500)
Transportation: Commute to work: 90.3% car, 0.6% public transportation, 5.7% walk, 2.4% work from home (2000); Travel time to work: 64.9% less than 15 minutes, 17.9% 15 to 30 minutes, 10.1% 30 to 45 minutes, 2.7% 45 to 60 minutes, 4.4% 60 minutes or more (2000)
Additional Information Contacts
Ashland Area Chamber of Commerce. . . . . (419) 281-4584
http://www.ashlandoh.com
City of Ashland. . . . . (419) 289-8622
http://www.ashland-ohio.com

BAILEY LAKES (village). Covers a land area of 0.406 square miles and a water area of 0.059 square miles. Located at 40.94° N. Lat.; 82.35° W. Long. Elevation is 1,053 feet.
Population: 367 (1990); 397 (2000); 460 (2007); 500 (2012 projected); Race: 99.3% White, 0.0% Black, 0.0% Asian, 0.2% Hispanic of any race (2007); Density: 1,133.4 persons per square mile (2007); Average household size: 2.53 (2007); Median age: 37.2 (2007); Males per 100 females: 112.0 (2007); Marriage status: 24.7% never married, 63.7% now married, 3.4% widowed, 8.2% divorced (2000); Foreign born: 0.2% (2000); Ancestry (includes multiple ancestries): 34.1% German, 20.7% Irish, 10.6% Other groups, 9.7% English, 3.9% Scotch-Irish (2000).
Economy: Employment by occupation: 5.8% management, 27.2% professional, 7.6% services, 18.8% sales, 0.0% farming, 6.3% construction, 34.4% production (2000).
Income: Per capita income: $19,658 (2007); Median household income: $44,615 (2007); Average household income: $49,684 (2007); Percent of households with income of $100,000 or more: 5.5% (2007); Poverty rate: 11.8% (2000).
Education: Percent of population age 25 and over with: High school diploma (including GED) or higher: 84.1% (2007); Bachelor's degree or higher: 15.9% (2007); Master's degree or higher: 6.0% (2007).
Housing: Homeownership rate: 68.1% (2007); Median home value: $132,353 (2007); Median rent: $370 per month (2000); Median age of housing: 38 years (2000).
Transportation: Commute to work: 99.1% car, 0.0% public transportation, 0.0% walk, 0.9% work from home (2000); Travel time to work: 27.6% less than 15 minutes, 47.5% 15 to 30 minutes, 16.1% 30 to 45 minutes, 4.1% 45 to 60 minutes, 4.6% 60 minutes or more (2000)

HAYESVILLE (village). Covers a land area of 0.742 square miles and a water area of 0 square miles. Located at 40.77° N. Lat.; 82.26° W. Long. Elevation is 1,240 feet.
History: Hayesville was laid out in 1830 by Linus Hayes, a tavern owner, and Reverend John Cox. It was in Hayesville that William McKinley pleaded his first law case.
Population: 457 (1990); 348 (2000); 335 (2007); 328 (2012 projected); Race: 97.6% White, 2.4% Black, 0.0% Asian, 0.0% Hispanic of any race (2007); Density: 451.3 persons per square mile (2007); Average household size: 2.50 (2007); Median age: 46.8 (2007); Males per 100 females: 93.6 (2007); Marriage status: 22.2% never married, 64.9% now married, 2.5% widowed, 10.5% divorced (2000); Foreign born: 0.0% (2000); Ancestry (includes multiple ancestries): 20.2% German, 12.7% English, 11.7% United States or American, 8.5% Irish, 5.9% Italian (2000).
Economy: Single-family building permits issued: 0 (2007); Multi-family building permits issued: 0 (2007); Employment by occupation: 6.4% management, 12.1% professional, 17.2% services, 22.9% sales, 0.0% farming, 14.0% construction, 27.4% production (2000).
Income: Per capita income: $26,384 (2007); Median household income: $51,765 (2007); Average household income: $62,071 (2007); Percent of households with income of $100,000 or more: 9.0% (2007); Poverty rate: 8.0% (2000).
Education: Percent of population age 25 and over with: High school diploma (including GED) or higher: 80.4% (2007); Bachelor's degree or higher: 11.4% (2007); Master's degree or higher: 3.9% (2007).

School District(s)

Hillsdale Local (PK-12)
2005-06 Enrollment: 1,184 . . . . (419) 368-8231

Housing: Homeownership rate: 84.3% (2007); Median home value: $105,093 (2007); Median rent: $468 per month (2000); Median age of housing: 60 years (2000).
Transportation: Commute to work: 93.0% car, 2.5% public transportation, 1.9% walk, 1.3% work from home (2000); Travel time to work: 30.3% less than 15 minutes, 52.9% 15 to 30 minutes, 6.5% 30 to 45 minutes, 6.5% 45 to 60 minutes, 3.9% 60 minutes or more (2000)

JEROMESVILLE (village). Covers a land area of 0.365 square miles and a water area of 0 square miles. Located at 40.80° N. Lat.; 82.19° W. Long. Elevation is 1,007 feet.
History: Jeromesville was named for a French trader, Jean Baptiste Jerome, who lived here. The town grew as a rural trading center.
Population: 582 (1990); 478 (2000); 402 (2007); 408 (2012 projected); Race: 96.0% White, 0.5% Black, 0.0% Asian, 3.5% Hispanic of any race (2007); Density: 1,101.4 persons per square mile (2007); Average household size: 2.30 (2007); Median age: 39.0 (2007); Males per 100 females: 89.6 (2007); Marriage status: 24.6% never married, 53.7% now married, 7.3% widowed, 14.4% divorced (2000); Foreign born: 1.2% (2000); Ancestry (includes multiple ancestries): 31.8% German, 11.0% United States or American, 8.4% Irish, 8.2% English, 7.3% Other groups (2000).
Economy: Employment by occupation: 4.4% management, 19.2% professional, 16.4% services, 21.6% sales, 0.8% farming, 9.6% construction, 28.0% production (2000).
Income: Per capita income: $21,144 (2007); Median household income: $46,500 (2007); Average household income: $48,571 (2007); Percent of households with income of $100,000 or more: 4.6% (2007); Poverty rate: 6.1% (2000).

Education: Percent of population age 25 and over with: High school diploma (including GED) or higher: 94.9% (2007); Bachelor's degree or higher: 14.2% (2007); Master's degree or higher: 4.0% (2007).

School District(s)

Hillsdale Local (PK-12)
2005-06 Enrollment: 1,184 . . . . (419) 368-8231

Housing: Homeownership rate: 72.6% (2007); Median home value: $111,944 (2007); Median rent: $373 per month (2000); Median age of housing: 60+ years (2000).

Transportation: Commute to work: 94.4% car, 0.4% public transportation, 2.4% walk, 2.8% work from home (2000); Travel time to work: 23.7% less than 15 minutes, 56.4% 15 to 30 minutes, 14.5% 30 to 45 minutes, 2.1% 45 to 60 minutes, 3.3% 60 minutes or more (2000)

LOUDONVILLE (village). Covers a land area of 2.486 square miles and a water area of 0.010 square miles. Located at 40.63° N. Lat.; 82.23° W. Long. Elevation is 965 feet.

History: Loudonville was laid out in 1814 and named for a Revolutionary War soldier, James Louden Priest, who helped to survey the town. An early industry was the building of buses and ambulances.

Population: 3,142 (1990); 2,906 (2000); 2,924 (2007); 2,931 (2012 projected); Race: 98.9% White, 0.0% Black, 0.2% Asian, 0.6% Hispanic of any race (2007); Density: 1,176.0 persons per square mile (2007); Average household size: 2.43 (2007); Median age: 40.6 (2007); Males per 100 females: 94.7 (2007); Marriage status: 16.9% never married, 58.7% now married, 11.1% widowed, 13.3% divorced (2000); Foreign born: 0.6% (2000); Ancestry (includes multiple ancestries): 36.5% German, 11.3% United States or American, 10.7% English, 9.2% Irish, 3.9% Dutch (2000).

Economy: Single-family building permits issued: 18 (2007); Multi-family building permits issued: 24 (2007); Employment by occupation: 5.9% management, 10.2% professional, 16.4% services, 27.4% sales, 0.4% farming, 5.7% construction, 34.1% production (2000).

Income: Per capita income: $19,614 (2007); Median household income: $41,646 (2007); Average household income: $45,639 (2007); Percent of households with income of $100,000 or more: 5.9% (2007); Poverty rate: 13.2% (2000).

Education: Percent of population age 25 and over with: High school diploma (including GED) or higher: 83.9% (2007); Bachelor's degree or higher: 12.7% (2007); Master's degree or higher: 4.3% (2007).

School District(s)

Loudonville-Perrysville Exempted Village (PK-12)
2005-06 Enrollment: 1,371 . . . . (419) 994-3912

Housing: Homeownership rate: 68.0% (2007); Median home value: $102,990 (2007); Median rent: $358 per month (2000); Median age of housing: 60+ years (2000).

Safety: Violent crime rate: 6.7 per 10,000 population; Property crime rate: 243.7 per 10,000 population (2007).

Newspapers: Loudonville Times (Community news; Circulation 2,300)

Transportation: Commute to work: 89.6% car, 0.3% public transportation, 4.9% walk, 3.1% work from home (2000); Travel time to work: 55.7% less than 15 minutes, 17.4% 15 to 30 minutes, 19.6% 30 to 45 minutes, 1.8% 45 to 60 minutes, 5.5% 60 minutes or more (2000)

Additional Information Contacts

Loudonville Chamber of Commerce . . . . (419) 994-2519
http://www.loudonville-mohican.com/chamber.html

MIFFLIN (village). Covers a land area of 0.260 square miles and a water area of 0 square miles. Located at 40.77° N. Lat.; 82.36° W. Long. Elevation is 1,070 feet.

Population: 162 (1990); 144 (2000); 151 (2007); 151 (2012 projected); Race: 98.7% White, 0.0% Black, 1.3% Asian, 0.0% Hispanic of any race (2007); Density: 580.2 persons per square mile (2007); Average household size: 2.19 (2007); Median age: 40.9 (2007); Males per 100 females: 96.1 (2007); Marriage status: 47.0% never married, 27.8% now married, 5.2% widowed, 20.0% divorced (2000); Foreign born: 0.0% (2000); Ancestry (includes multiple ancestries): 23.5% German, 12.9% Irish, 9.1% Other groups, 5.3% United States or American, 4.5% Dutch (2000).

Economy: Single-family building permits issued: 0 (2007); Multi-family building permits issued: 0 (2007); Employment by occupation: 11.5% management, 3.8% professional, 19.2% services, 23.1% sales, 0.0% farming, 3.8% construction, 38.5% production (2000).

Income: Per capita income: $19,089 (2007); Median household income: $37,083 (2007); Average household income: $41,775 (2007); Percent of households with income of $100,000 or more: 0.0% (2007); Poverty rate: 12.9% (2000).

Education: Percent of population age 25 and over with: High school diploma (including GED) or higher: 78.0% (2007); Bachelor's degree or higher: 0.0% (2007); Master's degree or higher: 0.0% (2007).

Housing: Homeownership rate: 72.5% (2007); Median home value: $85,556 (2007); Median rent: $331 per month (2000); Median age of housing: 50 years (2000).

Transportation: Commute to work: 80.4% car, 7.8% public transportation, 7.8% walk, 3.9% work from home (2000); Travel time to work: 32.7% less than 15 minutes, 44.9% 15 to 30 minutes, 8.2% 30 to 45 minutes, 0.0% 45 to 60 minutes, 14.3% 60 minutes or more (2000)

NOVA (unincorporated postal area, zip code 44859). Covers a land area of 31.226 square miles and a water area of 0.054 square miles. Located at 41.02° N. Lat.; 82.33° W. Long. Elevation is 1,030 feet.

Population: 1,759 (2000); Race: 99.3% White, 0.0% Black, 0.0% Asian, 0.7% Hispanic of any race (2000); Density: 56.3 persons per square mile (2000); Age: 26.2% under 18, 10.8% over 64 (2000); Marriage status: 20.1% never married, 68.1% now married, 3.7% widowed, 8.1% divorced (2000); Foreign born: 1.2% (2000); Ancestry (includes multiple ancestries): 25.2% German, 18.9% United States or American, 12.8% Irish, 7.5% English, 5.9% Italian (2000).

Economy: Employment by occupation: 5.6% management, 6.7% professional, 12.0% services, 17.1% sales, 1.3% farming, 14.9% construction, 42.3% production (2000).

Income: Per capita income: $18,340 (2000); Median household income: $47,667 (2000); Poverty rate: 5.0% (2000).

Education: Percent of population age 25 and over with: High school diploma (including GED) or higher: 80.3% (2000); Bachelor's degree or higher: 6.4% (2000).

School District(s)

Mapleton Local (PK-12)
2005-06 Enrollment: 1,072 . . . . (419) 945-2188

Housing: Homeownership rate: 93.5% (2000); Median home value: $105,000 (2000); Median rent: $398 per month (2000); Median age of housing: 27 years (2000).

Transportation: Commute to work: 92.0% car, 0.6% public transportation, 3.2% walk, 3.4% work from home (2000); Travel time to work: 18.7% less than 15 minutes, 35.6% 15 to 30 minutes, 15.7% 30 to 45 minutes, 15.8% 45 to 60 minutes, 14.2% 60 minutes or more (2000)

PERRYSVILLE (village). Covers a land area of 0.776 square miles and a water area of 0 square miles. Located at 40.65° N. Lat.; 82.31° W. Long. Elevation is 994 feet.

Population: 874 (1990); 816 (2000); 715 (2007); 715 (2012 projected); Race: 98.3% White, 0.7% Black, 0.0% Asian, 0.6% Hispanic of any race (2007); Density: 921.9 persons per square mile (2007); Average household size: 2.44 (2007); Median age: 33.7 (2007); Males per 100 females: 92.2 (2007); Marriage status: 24.0% never married, 52.1% now married, 7.8% widowed, 16.2% divorced (2000); Foreign born: 0.0% (2000); Ancestry (includes multiple ancestries): 29.4% German, 19.4% United States or American, 8.4% Irish, 6.8% English, 6.2% Other groups (2000).

Economy: Single-family building permits issued: 0 (2007); Multi-family building permits issued: 0 (2007); Employment by occupation: 4.0% management, 6.1% professional, 19.8% services, 19.5% sales, 1.3% farming, 10.2% construction, 39.0% production (2000).

Income: Per capita income: $14,598 (2007); Median household income: $32,823 (2007); Average household income: $35,623 (2007); Percent of households with income of $100,000 or more: 1.0% (2007); Poverty rate: 18.3% (2000).

Education: Percent of population age 25 and over with: High school diploma (including GED) or higher: 80.0% (2007); Bachelor's degree or higher: 9.0% (2007); Master's degree or higher: 2.7% (2007).

School District(s)

Department of Youth Services (06-12)
2005-06 Enrollment: 1,478 . . . . (614) 728-2489

Loudonville-Perrysville Exempted Village (PK-12)
2005-06 Enrollment: 1,371 . . . . (419) 994-3912

Housing: Homeownership rate: 66.2% (2007); Median home value: $76,774 (2007); Median rent: $305 per month (2000); Median age of housing: 60+ years (2000).

Transportation: Commute to work: 89.6% car, 0.0% public transportation, 7.4% walk, 1.6% work from home (2000); Travel time to work: 47.5% less than 15 minutes, 23.3% 15 to 30 minutes, 21.7% 30 to 45 minutes, 2.2% 45 to 60 minutes, 5.3% 60 minutes or more (2000)

POLK (village). Covers a land area of 1.008 square miles and a water area of 0.028 square miles. Located at 40.94° N. Lat.; 82.21° W. Long. Elevation is 1,270 feet.
Population: 355 (1990); 357 (2000); 396 (2007); 411 (2012 projected); Race: 98.5% White, 0.0% Black, 0.0% Asian, 0.0% Hispanic of any race (2007); Density: 392.8 persons per square mile (2007); Average household size: 2.79 (2007); Median age: 36.6 (2007); Males per 100 females: 87.7 (2007); Marriage status: 29.2% never married, 58.7% now married, 7.9% widowed, 4.3% divorced (2000); Foreign born: 0.0% (2000); Ancestry (includes multiple ancestries): 30.0% German, 18.3% United States or American, 14.6% Irish, 9.5% English, 5.8% Other groups (2000).
Economy: Single-family building permits issued: 0 (2007); Multi-family building permits issued: 0 (2007); Employment by occupation: 7.3% management, 6.4% professional, 20.5% services, 21.5% sales, 0.0% farming, 10.0% construction, 34.2% production (2000).
Income: Per capita income: $18,529 (2007); Median household income: $47,500 (2007); Average household income: $51,673 (2007); Percent of households with income of $100,000 or more: 4.2% (2007); Poverty rate: 5.0% (2000).
Education: Percent of population age 25 and over with: High school diploma (including GED) or higher: 77.7% (2007); Bachelor's degree or higher: 6.1% (2007); Master's degree or higher: 0.8% (2007).

School District(s)

Mapleton Local (PK-12)
2005-06 Enrollment: 1,072 . . . . (419) 945-2188
Housing: Homeownership rate: 85.9% (2007); Median home value: $102,419 (2007); Median rent: $400 per month (2000); Median age of housing: 59 years (2000).
Transportation: Commute to work: 92.5% car, 0.0% public transportation, 0.9% walk, 6.5% work from home (2000); Travel time to work: 24.5% less than 15 minutes, 55.5% 15 to 30 minutes, 11.5% 30 to 45 minutes, 5.5% 45 to 60 minutes, 3.0% 60 minutes or more (2000)

SAVANNAH (village). Covers a land area of 0.443 square miles and a water area of 0 square miles. Located at 40.96° N. Lat.; 82.36° W. Long. Elevation is 1,099 feet.
Population: 363 (1990); 372 (2000); 416 (2007); 442 (2012 projected); Race: 99.3% White, 0.2% Black, 0.0% Asian, 0.0% Hispanic of any race (2007); Density: 938.3 persons per square mile (2007); Average household size: 2.74 (2007); Median age: 34.0 (2007); Males per 100 females: 99.0 (2007); Marriage status: 27.9% never married, 54.7% now married, 6.2% widowed, 11.2% divorced (2000); Foreign born: 0.0% (2000); Ancestry (includes multiple ancestries): 27.2% United States or American, 19.7% German, 8.3% Irish, 7.5% Other groups, 4.4% Polish (2000).
Economy: Single-family building permits issued: 1 (2007); Multi-family building permits issued: 0 (2007); Employment by occupation: 3.3% management, 13.3% professional, 13.3% services, 19.4% sales, 1.1% farming, 12.8% construction, 36.7% production (2000).
Income: Per capita income: $17,999 (2007); Median household income: $42,188 (2007); Average household income: $49,260 (2007); Percent of households with income of $100,000 or more: 7.2% (2007); Poverty rate: 9.6% (2000).
Education: Percent of population age 25 and over with: High school diploma (including GED) or higher: 74.4% (2007); Bachelor's degree or higher: 14.5% (2007); Master's degree or higher: 3.4% (2007).
Housing: Homeownership rate: 80.9% (2007); Median home value: $106,048 (2007); Median rent: $343 per month (2000); Median age of housing: 60+ years (2000).
Transportation: Commute to work: 98.3% car, 0.0% public transportation, 1.1% walk, 0.6% work from home (2000); Travel time to work: 29.4% less than 15 minutes, 42.4% 15 to 30 minutes, 12.4% 30 to 45 minutes, 5.6% 45 to 60 minutes, 10.2% 60 minutes or more (2000)

SULLIVAN (unincorporated postal area, zip code 44880). Covers a land area of 31.376 square miles and a water area of 0.074 square miles. Located at 41.03° N. Lat.; 82.21° W. Long. Elevation is 1,126 feet.
Population: 2,359 (2000); Race: 97.2% White, 1.1% Black, 0.5% Asian, 0.0% Hispanic of any race (2000); Density: 75.2 persons per square mile (2000); Age: 32.6% under 18, 10.7% over 64 (2000); Marriage status: 22.0% never married, 63.1% now married, 7.1% widowed, 7.8% divorced (2000); Foreign born: 1.4% (2000); Ancestry (includes multiple ancestries): 24.6% German, 18.1% Irish, 9.6% English, 8.9% United States or American, 7.8% Other groups (2000).
Economy: Employment by occupation: 9.8% management, 9.9% professional, 12.7% services, 17.8% sales, 1.9% farming, 12.4% construction, 35.5% production (2000).
Income: Per capita income: $15,646 (2000); Median household income: $43,929 (2000); Poverty rate: 13.0% (2000).
Education: Percent of population age 25 and over with: High school diploma (including GED) or higher: 78.0% (2000); Bachelor's degree or higher: 6.9% (2000).

School District(s)

Black River Local (PK-12)
2005-06 Enrollment: 1,779 . . . . (419) 736-3300
Housing: Homeownership rate: 86.7% (2000); Median home value: $111,800 (2000); Median rent: $480 per month (2000); Median age of housing: 23 years (2000).
Transportation: Commute to work: 87.8% car, 0.0% public transportation, 5.1% walk, 7.1% work from home (2000); Travel time to work: 23.5% less than 15 minutes, 24.2% 15 to 30 minutes, 16.0% 30 to 45 minutes, 28.7% 45 to 60 minutes, 7.6% 60 minutes or more (2000)

Ashtabula County

Located in northeastern Ohio; bounded on the north by Lake Erie; crossed by the Grand and Ashtabula Rivers. Covers a land area of 702.44 square miles, a water area of 666.03 square miles, and is located in the Eastern Time Zone. The county was founded in 1807. County seat is Jefferson.

Ashtabula County is part of the Ashtabula, OH Micropolitan Statistical Area. The entire metro area includes: Ashtabula County, OH

Weather Station: Dorset Elevation: 977 feet

	Jan	Feb	Mar	Apr	May	Jun	Jul	Aug	Sep	Oct	Nov	Dec
High	31	35	44	57	68	77	81	80	73	61	48	37
Low	15	16	25	34	44	53	57	56	50	39	32	22
Precip	2.6	2.3	3.2	3.6	3.7	4.5	4.2	4.1	4.3	3.8	3.9	3.3
Snow	17.5	12.9	12.1	2.9	tr	0.0	0.0	0.0	0.0	0.6	8.7	18.4

High and Low temperatures in degrees Fahrenheit; Precipitation and Snow in inches

Population: 99,821 (1990); 102,728 (2000); 103,387 (2007); 103,513 (2012 projected); Race: 93.7% White, 3.3% Black, 0.3% Asian, 2.8% Hispanic of any race (2007); Density: 147.2 persons per square mile (2007); Average household size: 2.55 (2007); Median age: 39.4 (2007); Males per 100 females: 96.1 (2007).
Religion: Five largest groups: 18.0% Catholic Church, 5.2% The United Methodist Church, 2.1% Evangelical Lutheran Church in America, 1.8% United Church of Christ, 1.8% Church of the Nazarene (2000).
Economy: Unemployment rate: 7.5% (6/2008); Total civilian labor force: 50,611 (6/2008); Leading industries: 29.2% manufacturing; 19.2% health care and social assistance; 16.4% retail trade (2005); Farms: 1,283 totaling 170,424 acres (2002); Companies that employ 500 or more persons: 1 (2006); Companies that employ 100 to 499 persons: 44 (2006); Companies that employ less than 100 persons: 2,115 (2006); Black-owned businesses: n/a (2002); Hispanic-owned businesses: n/a (2002); Asian-owned businesses: 102 (2002); Women-owned businesses: 1,954 (2002); Retail sales per capita: $10,910 (2008). Single-family building permits issued: 135 (2007); Multi-family building permits issued: 0 (2007).
Income: Per capita income: $19,967 (2007); Median household income: $40,592 (2007); Average household income: $50,223 (2007); Percent of households with income of $100,000 or more: 8.7% (2007); Poverty rate: 15.3% (2005); Bankruptcy rate: 4.71% (2007).
Taxes: Total county taxes per capita: $251 (2006); County property taxes per capita: $162 (2006).
Education: Percent of population age 25 and over with: High school diploma (including GED) or higher: 79.9% (2007); Bachelor's degree or higher: 11.1% (2007); Master's degree or higher: 3.6% (2007).
Housing: Homeownership rate: 74.3% (2007); Median home value: $115,810 (2007); Median rent: $374 per month (2000); Median age of housing: 45 years (2000).
Health: Birth rate: 126.1 per 10,000 population (2007); Death rate: 105.2 per 10,000 population (2007); Age-adjusted cancer mortality rate: 216.3 deaths per 100,000 population (2005); Air Quality Index: 85.5% good, 9.7% moderate, 4.5% unhealthy for sensitive individuals, 0.3% unhealthy (percent of days in 2007); Number of physicians: 7.9 per 10,000 population (2005); Hospital beds: 31.5 per 10,000 population (2004); Hospital admissions: 910.7 per 10,000 population (2004).
Elections: 2004 Presidential election results: 46.3% Bush, 53.0% Kerry, 0.0% Nader, 0.3% Badnarik

National and State Parks: Geneva-On-The-Lake State Park; Orwell State Wildlife Area; Pymatuning State Park

Additional Information Contacts

Ashtabula County Government . . . . (440) 576-3750
http://www.co.ashtabula.oh.us

Andover Area Chamber of Commerce. . . . . (440) 293-5895
http://www.andoverohio.com

Ashtabula Area Chamber of Commerce . . . . (440) 998-6998
http://www.ashtabulachamber.net

Ashtabula County Convention & Visitors Bureau. . . . . (440) 275-3202
http://www.visitashtabulacounty.com

City of Ashtabula . . . . (440) 992-7103
http://ci.ashtabula.oh.us

City of Conneaut . . . . (440) 593-7401
http://www.conneaut.net

Conneaut Area Chamber of Commerce . . . . (440) 593-2402
http://www.conneautchamber.org

Geneva Area Chamber of Commerce . . . . (440) 466-8694
http://www.genevachamber.org

Geneva-on-the-Lake Visitor Information Center . . . . (440) 466-8600
http://www.visitgenevaonthelake.com

Village of Orwell . . . . (440) 437-6459
http://www.orwellvillage.org

Ashtabula County Communities

ANDOVER (village). Covers a land area of 1.366 square miles and a water area of 0 square miles. Located at 41.60° N. Lat.; 80.57° W. Long. Elevation is 1,093 feet.

Population: 1,216 (1990); 1,269 (2000); 1,285 (2007); 1,311 (2012 projected); Race: 95.3% White, 3.3% Black, 0.0% Asian, 1.6% Hispanic of any race (2007); Density: 940.9 persons per square mile (2007); Average household size: 3.01 (2007); Median age: 45.8 (2007); Males per 100 females: 89.2 (2007); Marriage status: 22.5% never married, 47.9% now married, 12.8% widowed, 16.8% divorced (2000); Foreign born: 0.5% (2000); Ancestry (includes multiple ancestries): 20.4% German, 17.2% United States or American, 13.4% English, 12.6% Irish, 9.8% Other groups (2000).

Economy: Employment by occupation: 6.8% management, 10.1% professional, 13.8% services, 23.3% sales, 1.4% farming, 7.2% construction, 37.2% production (2000).

Income: Per capita income: $17,138 (2007); Median household income: $34,773 (2007); Average household income: $45,796 (2007); Percent of households with income of $100,000 or more: 7.5% (2007); Poverty rate: 10.7% (2000).

Education: Percent of population age 25 and over with: High school diploma (including GED) or higher: 74.1% (2007); Bachelor's degree or higher: 9.5% (2007); Master's degree or higher: 3.8% (2007).

School District(s)

Pymatuning Valley Local (PK-12)
2005-06 Enrollment: 1,398 . . . . (440) 293-6488

Housing: Homeownership rate: 59.5% (2007); Median home value: $91,765 (2007); Median rent: $355 per month (2000); Median age of housing: 60+ years (2000).

Newspapers: Pymatuning Area News (Community news; Circulation 2,100)

Transportation: Commute to work: 87.3% car, 0.4% public transportation, 6.6% walk, 3.4% work from home (2000); Travel time to work: 58.6% less than 15 minutes, 11.4% 15 to 30 minutes, 8.8% 30 to 45 minutes, 10.1% 45 to 60 minutes, 11.2% 60 minutes or more (2000)

Additional Information Contacts

Andover Area Chamber of Commerce. . . . . (440) 293-5895
http://www.andoverohio.com

ASHTABULA (city). Covers a land area of 7.551 square miles and a water area of 0.172 square miles. Located at 41.87° N. Lat.; 80.79° W. Long. Elevation is 673 feet.

History: The surveying party of Moses Cleaveland stopped here in 1796, and two members of the group remained as settlers. The town that was incorporated in 1831 was named Ashtabula for the river that emptied into Lake Erie at the site. Ashtabula developed as a shipping center for coal and iron ore, and as a fishing and farm trading center. Strong abolitionist sentiment made it a key station on the Underground Railroad.

Population: 21,626 (1990); 20,962 (2000); 20,185 (2007); 19,587 (2012 projected); Race: 82.6% White, 10.9% Black, 0.4% Asian, 6.9% Hispanic of any race (2007); Density: 2,673.0 persons per square mile (2007); Average household size: 2.44 (2007); Median age: 36.2 (2007); Males per 100 females: 89.9 (2007); Marriage status: 27.4% never married, 49.1% now married, 9.8% widowed, 13.8% divorced (2000); Foreign born: 2.7% (2000); Ancestry (includes multiple ancestries): 18.7% Other groups, 16.9% German, 15.0% Italian, 11.5% Irish, 9.2% English (2000).

Economy: Single-family building permits issued: 1 (2007); Multi-family building permits issued: 0 (2007); Employment by occupation: 6.6% management, 13.1% professional, 19.4% services, 23.7% sales, 0.3% farming, 8.4% construction, 28.5% production (2000).

Income: Per capita income: $16,052 (2007); Median household income: $30,843 (2007); Average household income: $38,769 (2007); Percent of households with income of $100,000 or more: 4.2% (2007); Poverty rate: 21.4% (2000).

Education: Percent of population age 25 and over with: High school diploma (including GED) or higher: 77.7% (2007); Bachelor's degree or higher: 10.4% (2007); Master's degree or higher: 3.1% (2007).

School District(s)

Ashtabula Area City (PK-12)
2005-06 Enrollment: 4,434 . . . . (440) 993-2500

Buckeye Local (PK-12)
2005-06 Enrollment: 2,333 . . . . (440) 998-4411

Two-year College(s)

Kent State University-Ashtabula Campus (Public)
Fall 2007 Enrollment: 1,575. . . . . (440) 964-3322
2007-08 Tuition: In-state $4,770; Out-of-state $12,202

Housing: Homeownership rate: 58.4% (2007); Median home value: $90,217 (2007); Median rent: $369 per month (2000); Median age of housing: 52 years (2000).

Hospitals: Ashtabula County Medical Center (241 beds)

Newspapers: Star-Beacon (Local news; Circulation 23,564)

Transportation: Commute to work: 92.6% car, 2.1% public transportation, 2.9% walk, 1.6% work from home (2000); Travel time to work: 50.1% less than 15 minutes, 27.5% 15 to 30 minutes, 9.8% 30 to 45 minutes, 6.7% 45 to 60 minutes, 5.9% 60 minutes or more (2000)

Additional Information Contacts

Ashtabula Area Chamber of Commerce . . . . (440) 998-6998
http://www.ashtabulachamber.net

City of Ashtabula . . . . (440) 992-7103
http://ci.ashtabula.oh.us

AUSTINBURG (unincorporated postal area, zip code 44010). Covers a land area of 18.451 square miles and a water area of 0.144 square miles. Located at 41.75° N. Lat.; 80.86° W. Long. Elevation is 817 feet.

Population: 1,764 (2000); Race: 98.3% White, 0.0% Black, 0.0% Asian, 1.0% Hispanic of any race (2000); Density: 95.6 persons per square mile (2000); Age: 22.3% under 18, 16.8% over 64 (2000); Marriage status: 20.6% never married, 61.5% now married, 8.5% widowed, 9.4% divorced (2000); Foreign born: 1.3% (2000); Ancestry (includes multiple ancestries): 25.8% English, 21.1% German, 16.0% Irish, 7.5% Welsh, 7.2% Italian (2000).

Economy: Employment by occupation: 11.4% management, 15.6% professional, 14.9% services, 18.9% sales, 1.0% farming, 15.1% construction, 23.1% production (2000).

Income: Per capita income: $24,447 (2000); Median household income: $46,490 (2000); Poverty rate: 3.3% (2000).

Education: Percent of population age 25 and over with: High school diploma (including GED) or higher: 89.6% (2000); Bachelor's degree or higher: 20.0% (2000).

School District(s)

Geneva Area City (PK-12)
2005-06 Enrollment: 2,929 . . . . (440) 466-4831

Housing: Homeownership rate: 87.8% (2000); Median home value: $109,900 (2000); Median rent: $237 per month (2000); Median age of housing: 39 years (2000).

Transportation: Commute to work: 94.0% car, 0.5% public transportation, 0.6% walk, 4.9% work from home (2000); Travel time to work: 25.4% less than 15 minutes, 49.8% 15 to 30 minutes, 14.9% 30 to 45 minutes, 7.3% 45 to 60 minutes, 2.6% 60 minutes or more (2000)

Additional Information Contacts

Ashtabula County Convention & Visitors Bureau. . . . . (440) 275-3202
http://www.visitashtabulacounty.com

CONNEAUT (city). Aka Lakeville. Covers a land area of 26.373 square miles and a water area of 0.057 square miles. Located at 41.94° N. Lat.; 80.56° W. Long. Elevation is 646 feet.

History: Conneaut was settled in 1799 by Thomas Montgomery and Aaron Wright. The village grew around the natural harbor, which attracted shipping of coal and ores.

Population: 13,241 (1990); 12,485 (2000); 12,573 (2007); 12,585 (2012 projected); Race: 96.0% White, 1.1% Black, 0.5% Asian, 1.2% Hispanic of any race (2007); Density: 476.7 persons per square mile (2007); Average household size: 2.41 (2007); Median age: 39.5 (2007); Males per 100 females: 95.2 (2007); Marriage status: 21.6% never married, 56.8% now married, 9.7% widowed, 11.8% divorced (2000); Foreign born: 1.0% (2000); Ancestry (includes multiple ancestries): 23.7% German, 16.4% Irish, 14.6% Italian, 14.2% English, 5.9% Finnish (2000).

Economy: Employment by occupation: 7.1% management, 12.6% professional, 19.0% services, 18.9% sales, 0.1% farming, 10.6% construction, 31.6% production (2000).

Income: Per capita income: $17,292 (2007); Median household income: $35,552 (2007); Average household income: $41,236 (2007); Percent of households with income of $100,000 or more: 4.3% (2007); Poverty rate: 13.0% (2000).

Education: Percent of population age 25 and over with: High school diploma (including GED) or higher: 81.2% (2007); Bachelor's degree or higher: 10.0% (2007); Master's degree or higher: 3.7% (2007).

School District(s)

Conneaut Area City (PK-12)
2005-06 Enrollment: 2,438 . . . . (440) 593-7200

Housing: Homeownership rate: 69.9% (2007); Median home value: $95,799 (2007); Median rent: $363 per month (2000); Median age of housing: 57 years (2000).

Hospitals: Brown Memorial Hospital (86 beds)

Safety: Violent crime rate: 27.8 per 10,000 population; Property crime rate: 346.0 per 10,000 population (2007).

Transportation: Commute to work: 94.5% car, 0.6% public transportation, 2.1% walk, 1.6% work from home (2000); Travel time to work: 49.8% less than 15 minutes, 27.6% 15 to 30 minutes, 12.8% 30 to 45 minutes, 3.2% 45 to 60 minutes, 6.6% 60 minutes or more (2000)

Additional Information Contacts

City of Conneaut . . . . (440) 593-7401
http://www.conneaut.net
Conneaut Area Chamber of Commerce . . . . (440) 593-2402
http://www.conneautchamber.org

DORSET (unincorporated postal area, zip code 44032). Covers a land area of 38.633 square miles and a water area of 0.035 square miles. Located at 41.67° N. Lat.; 80.66° W. Long. Elevation is 981 feet.

Population: 1,494 (2000); Race: 98.9% White, 0.6% Black, 0.0% Asian, 0.0% Hispanic of any race (2000); Density: 38.7 persons per square mile (2000); Age: 28.8% under 18, 10.1% over 64 (2000); Marriage status: 21.1% never married, 62.8% now married, 6.4% widowed, 9.7% divorced (2000); Foreign born: 1.1% (2000); Ancestry (includes multiple ancestries): 23.1% German, 17.6% Other groups, 16.7% Irish, 16.0% United States or American, 8.7% English (2000).

Economy: Employment by occupation: 7.5% management, 9.7% professional, 22.1% services, 14.6% sales, 3.8% farming, 15.6% construction, 26.7% production (2000).

Income: Per capita income: $13,828 (2000); Median household income: $37,281 (2000); Poverty rate: 12.0% (2000).

Education: Percent of population age 25 and over with: High school diploma (including GED) or higher: 72.5% (2000); Bachelor's degree or higher: 6.0% (2000).

Housing: Homeownership rate: 83.0% (2000); Median home value: $79,300 (2000); Median rent: $468 per month (2000); Median age of housing: 55 years (2000).

Transportation: Commute to work: 89.8% car, 1.4% public transportation, 4.0% walk, 2.1% work from home (2000); Travel time to work: 14.5% less than 15 minutes, 35.6% 15 to 30 minutes, 16.5% 30 to 45 minutes, 10.8% 45 to 60 minutes, 22.7% 60 minutes or more (2000)

EDGEWOOD (CDP). Covers a land area of 6.748 square miles and a water area of 0.006 square miles. Located at 41.87° N. Lat.; 80.75° W. Long. Elevation is 682 feet.

Population: 5,189 (1990); 4,762 (2000); 4,545 (2007); 4,427 (2012 projected); Race: 96.8% White, 1.3% Black, 0.6% Asian, 1.4% Hispanic of any race (2007); Density: 673.5 persons per square mile (2007); Average household size: 2.25 (2007); Median age: 43.3 (2007); Males per 100 females: 94.1 (2007); Marriage status: 17.7% never married, 61.8% now married, 7.5% widowed, 13.1% divorced (2000); Foreign born: 2.0% (2000); Ancestry (includes multiple ancestries): 23.4% German, 15.6% English, 15.3% Irish, 12.0% Italian, 7.7% Other groups (2000).

Economy: Employment by occupation: 6.5% management, 17.8% professional, 18.0% services, 24.8% sales, 0.3% farming, 9.8% construction, 22.9% production (2000).

Income: Per capita income: $23,631 (2007); Median household income: $44,731 (2007); Average household income: $53,005 (2007); Percent of households with income of $100,000 or more: 7.4% (2007); Poverty rate: 6.8% (2000).

Education: Percent of population age 25 and over with: High school diploma (including GED) or higher: 82.4% (2007); Bachelor's degree or higher: 10.1% (2007); Master's degree or higher: 4.9% (2007).

Housing: Homeownership rate: 79.7% (2007); Median home value: $98,968 (2007); Median rent: $389 per month (2000); Median age of housing: 44 years (2000).

Transportation: Commute to work: 97.4% car, 0.3% public transportation, 0.9% walk, 0.6% work from home (2000); Travel time to work: 57.1% less than 15 minutes, 25.2% 15 to 30 minutes, 6.6% 30 to 45 minutes, 6.4% 45 to 60 minutes, 4.6% 60 minutes or more (2000)

GENEVA (city). Covers a land area of 3.996 square miles and a water area of 0 square miles. Located at 41.80° N. Lat.; 80.94° W. Long. Elevation is 673 feet.

History: Geneva was founded in 1805. In Geneva's cemetery is a monument to Platt R. Spencer (1800-1864) who founded business schools in many cities and created the Spencerian penmanship system.

Population: 6,740 (1990); 6,595 (2000); 6,459 (2007); 6,318 (2012 projected); Race: 94.6% White, 1.4% Black, 0.2% Asian, 7.2% Hispanic of any race (2007); Density: 1,616.4 persons per square mile (2007); Average household size: 2.60 (2007); Median age: 41.4 (2007); Males per 100 females: 94.5 (2007); Marriage status: 26.5% never married, 53.4% now married, 8.6% widowed, 11.6% divorced (2000); Foreign born: 0.7% (2000); Ancestry (includes multiple ancestries): 25.4% German, 16.0% Irish, 11.8% English, 9.4% Other groups, 9.0% United States or American (2000).

Economy: Employment by occupation: 8.8% management, 17.0% professional, 15.4% services, 21.6% sales, 3.3% farming, 7.1% construction, 26.8% production (2000).

Income: Per capita income: $19,509 (2007); Median household income: $39,248 (2007); Average household income: $48,173 (2007); Percent of households with income of $100,000 or more: 7.4% (2007); Poverty rate: 9.4% (2000).

Education: Percent of population age 25 and over with: High school diploma (including GED) or higher: 77.3% (2007); Bachelor's degree or higher: 10.8% (2007); Master's degree or higher: 4.0% (2007).

School District(s)

Geneva Area City (PK-12)
2005-06 Enrollment: 2,929 . . . . (440) 466-4831

Housing: Homeownership rate: 63.7% (2007); Median home value: $116,743 (2007); Median rent: $360 per month (2000); Median age of housing: 46 years (2000).

Hospitals: UHHS Memorial Hospital of Geneva (46 beds)

Transportation: Commute to work: 91.2% car, 3.4% public transportation, 2.5% walk, 1.1% work from home (2000); Travel time to work: 38.1% less than 15 minutes, 27.7% 15 to 30 minutes, 24.5% 30 to 45 minutes, 5.9% 45 to 60 minutes, 3.8% 60 minutes or more (2000)

Additional Information Contacts

Geneva Area Chamber of Commerce . . . . (440) 466-8694
http://www.genevachamber.org

GENEVA-ON-THE-LAKE (village). Covers a land area of 2.030 square miles and a water area of 0.015 square miles. Located at 41.85° N. Lat.; 80.94° W. Long. Elevation is 600 feet.

Population: 1,626 (1990); 1,545 (2000); 1,669 (2007); 1,741 (2012 projected); Race: 95.0% White, 1.0% Black, 0.4% Asian, 3.2% Hispanic of any race (2007); Density: 822.0 persons per square mile (2007); Average household size: 2.24 (2007); Median age: 36.1 (2007); Males per 100 females: 100.8 (2007); Marriage status: 24.9% never married, 48.8% now married, 7.2% widowed, 19.1% divorced (2000); Foreign born: 0.6% (2000); Ancestry (includes multiple ancestries): 26.2% German, 20.4% Irish, 11.5% English, 10.9% Other groups, 8.6% Italian (2000).

Economy: Employment by occupation: 10.5% management, 9.1% professional, 18.1% services, 20.3% sales, 0.4% farming, 9.1% construction, 32.6% production (2000).
Income: Per capita income: $18,493 (2007); Median household income: $34,526 (2007); Average household income: $41,430 (2007); Percent of households with income of $100,000 or more: 5.6% (2007); Poverty rate: 19.1% (2000).
Education: Percent of population age 25 and over with: High school diploma (including GED) or higher: 72.9% (2007); Bachelor's degree or higher: 11.3% (2007); Master's degree or higher: 5.3% (2007).
Housing: Homeownership rate: 52.8% (2007); Median home value: $88,833 (2007); Median rent: $413 per month (2000); Median age of housing: 41 years (2000).
Safety: Violent crime rate: 6.6 per 10,000 population; Property crime rate: 151.1 per 10,000 population (2007).
Transportation: Commute to work: 91.3% car, 0.9% public transportation, 3.5% walk, 3.4% work from home (2000); Travel time to work: 26.5% less than 15 minutes, 31.9% 15 to 30 minutes, 16.3% 30 to 45 minutes, 11.7% 45 to 60 minutes, 13.6% 60 minutes or more (2000)
Additional Information Contacts
Geneva-on-the-Lake Visitor Information Center . . . . (440) 466-8600
http://www.visitgenevaonthelake.com

JEFFERSON (village). County seat. Covers a land area of 2.280 square miles and a water area of 0 square miles. Located at 41.73° N. Lat.; 80.77° W. Long. Elevation is 958 feet.
History: Jefferson was named by Gideon Granger, Postmaster General in Jefferson's cabinet. The Republican Party's first national platform was written here at the law office of Joshua R. Giddings.
Population: 3,389 (1990); 3,572 (2000); 3,643 (2007); 3,690 (2012 projected); Race: 97.2% White, 1.4% Black, 0.1% Asian, 0.7% Hispanic of any race (2007); Density: 1,597.7 persons per square mile (2007); Average household size: 2.58 (2007); Median age: 38.3 (2007); Males per 100 females: 88.4 (2007); Marriage status: 23.0% never married, 52.6% now married, 11.4% widowed, 12.9% divorced (2000); Foreign born: 1.1% (2000); Ancestry (includes multiple ancestries): 20.4% German, 17.4% Irish, 16.2% English, 11.0% Italian, 8.4% United States or American (2000).
Economy: Employment by occupation: 10.0% management, 18.5% professional, 22.1% services, 24.1% sales, 0.0% farming, 5.9% construction, 19.3% production (2000).
Income: Per capita income: $21,137 (2007); Median household income: $43,005 (2007); Average household income: $49,798 (2007); Percent of households with income of $100,000 or more: 8.6% (2007); Poverty rate: 5.8% (2000).
Education: Percent of population age 25 and over with: High school diploma (including GED) or higher: 86.7% (2007); Bachelor's degree or higher: 19.5% (2007); Master's degree or higher: 5.3% (2007).

School District(s)

Ashtabula County (07-12)
2005-06 Enrollment: n/a . . . . (440) 576-6015
Jefferson Area Local (PK-12)
2005-06 Enrollment: 2,175 . . . . (440) 576-9876

Vocational/Technical School(s)

Ashtabula County Joint Vocational School (Public)
Fall 2007 Enrollment: 137 . . . . (440) 576-6015
2007-08 Tuition: $7,610

Housing: Homeownership rate: 61.7% (2007); Median home value: $123,232 (2007); Median rent: $392 per month (2000); Median age of housing: 36 years (2000).
Safety: Violent crime rate: 11.5 per 10,000 population; Property crime rate: 221.1 per 10,000 population (2007).
Newspapers: Courier (Community news; Circulation 3,000); The Gazette (Local news; Circulation 3,058); Sentinel (Community news; Circulation 7,000); Shores News (Local news; Circulation 1,200); Valley News (Community news; Circulation 1,300); Vistas (Senior Lifestyles) (Local news; Circulation 5,000)
Transportation: Commute to work: 93.4% car, 0.0% public transportation, 5.1% walk, 1.0% work from home (2000); Travel time to work: 43.4% less than 15 minutes, 32.1% 15 to 30 minutes, 9.4% 30 to 45 minutes, 9.4% 45 to 60 minutes, 5.7% 60 minutes or more (2000)

KINGSVILLE (unincorporated postal area, zip code 44048). Covers a land area of 30.436 square miles and a water area of 0.043 square miles. Located at 41.86° N. Lat.; 80.65° W. Long. Elevation is 789 feet.
Population: 2,553 (2000); Race: 97.1% White, 0.3% Black, 0.0% Asian, 0.0% Hispanic of any race (2000); Density: 83.9 persons per square mile (2000); Age: 26.2% under 18, 17.4% over 64 (2000); Marriage status: 20.3% never married, 57.8% now married, 11.8% widowed, 10.0% divorced (2000); Foreign born: 1.0% (2000); Ancestry (includes multiple ancestries): 15.9% German, 12.9% United States or American, 12.6% English, 10.2% Irish, 6.1% Finnish (2000).
Economy: Employment by occupation: 5.5% management, 13.7% professional, 19.7% services, 21.7% sales, 0.0% farming, 13.7% construction, 25.6% production (2000).
Income: Per capita income: $16,884 (2000); Median household income: $38,750 (2000); Poverty rate: 6.5% (2000).
Education: Percent of population age 25 and over with: High school diploma (including GED) or higher: 75.6% (2000); Bachelor's degree or higher: 9.5% (2000).

School District(s)

Buckeye Local (PK-12)
2005-06 Enrollment: 2,333 . . . . (440) 998-4411

Housing: Homeownership rate: 82.8% (2000); Median home value: $95,600 (2000); Median rent: $324 per month (2000); Median age of housing: 34 years (2000).
Transportation: Commute to work: 95.7% car, 0.0% public transportation, 1.6% walk, 0.7% work from home (2000); Travel time to work: 32.7% less than 15 minutes, 41.3% 15 to 30 minutes, 10.6% 30 to 45 minutes, 5.9% 45 to 60 minutes, 9.5% 60 minutes or more (2000)

NORTH KINGSVILLE (village). Covers a land area of 8.903 square miles and a water area of 0.019 square miles. Located at 41.91° N. Lat.; 80.67° W. Long. Elevation is 712 feet.
Population: 2,672 (1990); 2,658 (2000); 2,709 (2007); 2,719 (2012 projected); Race: 97.3% White, 0.4% Black, 0.5% Asian, 1.6% Hispanic of any race (2007); Density: 304.3 persons per square mile (2007); Average household size: 2.49 (2007); Median age: 43.3 (2007); Males per 100 females: 97.3 (2007); Marriage status: 18.9% never married, 66.0% now married, 8.7% widowed, 6.4% divorced (2000); Foreign born: 1.5% (2000); Ancestry (includes multiple ancestries): 20.6% German, 18.5% English, 13.4% Italian, 12.8% Irish, 9.8% United States or American (2000).
Economy: Employment by occupation: 8.9% management, 18.1% professional, 13.0% services, 26.7% sales, 0.0% farming, 9.5% construction, 23.7% production (2000).
Income: Per capita income: $25,907 (2007); Median household income: $49,398 (2007); Average household income: $64,447 (2007); Percent of households with income of $100,000 or more: 14.9% (2007); Poverty rate: 7.0% (2000).
Education: Percent of population age 25 and over with: High school diploma (including GED) or higher: 83.7% (2007); Bachelor's degree or higher: 14.2% (2007); Master's degree or higher: 5.6% (2007).

School District(s)

Buckeye Local (PK-12)
2005-06 Enrollment: 2,333 . . . . (440) 998-4411

Housing: Homeownership rate: 86.9% (2007); Median home value: $140,254 (2007); Median rent: $332 per month (2000); Median age of housing: 33 years (2000).
Transportation: Commute to work: 93.8% car, 0.8% public transportation, 1.6% walk, 3.6% work from home (2000); Travel time to work: 41.1% less than 15 minutes, 40.9% 15 to 30 minutes, 7.4% 30 to 45 minutes, 4.1% 45 to 60 minutes, 6.5% 60 minutes or more (2000)

ORWELL (village). Covers a land area of 1.664 square miles and a water area of 0 square miles. Located at 41.53° N. Lat.; 80.85° W. Long. Elevation is 896 feet.
Population: 1,387 (1990); 1,519 (2000); 1,626 (2007); 1,689 (2012 projected); Race: 95.7% White, 1.1% Black, 0.6% Asian, 1.4% Hispanic of any race (2007); Density: 977.3 persons per square mile (2007); Average household size: 2.45 (2007); Median age: 35.2 (2007); Males per 100 females: 92.0 (2007); Marriage status: 23.7% never married, 55.6% now married, 8.4% widowed, 12.3% divorced (2000); Foreign born: 0.9% (2000); Ancestry (includes multiple ancestries): 26.0% German, 16.5% Irish, 13.3% Other groups, 12.3% English, 8.9% Polish (2000).
Economy: Employment by occupation: 8.1% management, 9.1% professional, 13.8% services, 19.9% sales, 0.6% farming, 9.8% construction, 38.8% production (2000).
Income: Per capita income: $19,188 (2007); Median household income: $37,692 (2007); Average household income: $44,853 (2007); Percent of

households with income of $100,000 or more: 5.7% (2007); Poverty rate: 10.9% (2000).
Education: Percent of population age 25 and over with: High school diploma (including GED) or higher: 78.0% (2007); Bachelor's degree or higher: 8.4% (2007); Master's degree or higher: 2.9% (2007).

School District(s)

Grand Valley Local (PK-12)
2005-06 Enrollment: 1,436 . . . . (440) 437-6260
Housing: Homeownership rate: 62.2% (2007); Median home value: $107,169 (2007); Median rent: $395 per month (2000); Median age of housing: 29 years (2000).
Safety: Violent crime rate: 13.3 per 10,000 population; Property crime rate: 233.2 per 10,000 population (2007).
Transportation: Commute to work: 95.2% car, 0.0% public transportation, 4.1% walk, 0.7% work from home (2000); Travel time to work: 36.6% less than 15 minutes, 21.9% 15 to 30 minutes, 25.1% 30 to 45 minutes, 8.9% 45 to 60 minutes, 7.5% 60 minutes or more (2000)
Additional Information Contacts
Village of Orwell . . . . (440) 437-6459
http://www.orwellvillage.org

PIERPONT (unincorporated postal area, zip code 44082). Covers a land area of 33.432 square miles and a water area of 0.020 square miles. Located at 41.76° N. Lat.; 80.57° W. Long. Elevation is 995 feet.
Population: 1,469 (2000); Race: 100.0% White, 0.0% Black, 0.0% Asian, 2.2% Hispanic of any race (2000); Density: 43.9 persons per square mile (2000); Age: 33.1% under 18, 11.0% over 64 (2000); Marriage status: 18.5% never married, 64.9% now married, 6.9% widowed, 9.6% divorced (2000); Foreign born: 2.5% (2000); Ancestry (includes multiple ancestries): 23.3% German, 11.0% English, 6.5% Hungarian, 6.4% Irish, 6.2% Other groups (2000).
Economy: Employment by occupation: 5.7% management, 5.9% professional, 20.0% services, 12.3% sales, 1.4% farming, 15.8% construction, 38.9% production (2000).
Income: Per capita income: $13,594 (2000); Median household income: $36,071 (2000); Poverty rate: 24.1% (2000).
Education: Percent of population age 25 and over with: High school diploma (including GED) or higher: 76.1% (2000); Bachelor's degree or higher: 1.6% (2000).

School District(s)

Buckeye Local (PK-12)
2005-06 Enrollment: 2,333 . . . . (440) 998-4411
Housing: Homeownership rate: 89.5% (2000); Median home value: $84,200 (2000); Median rent: $338 per month (2000); Median age of housing: 27 years (2000).
Transportation: Commute to work: 94.4% car, 1.1% public transportation, 0.0% walk, 4.5% work from home (2000); Travel time to work: 15.8% less than 15 minutes, 42.1% 15 to 30 minutes, 30.5% 30 to 45 minutes, 4.2% 45 to 60 minutes, 7.4% 60 minutes or more (2000)

ROAMING SHORES (village). Covers a land area of 2.079 square miles and a water area of 0.719 square miles. Located at 41.63° N. Lat.; 80.82° W. Long. Elevation is 869 feet.
Population: 790 (1990); 1,239 (2000); 1,330 (2007); 1,386 (2012 projected); Race: 97.0% White, 2.0% Black, 0.0% Asian, 0.5% Hispanic of any race (2007); Density: 639.8 persons per square mile (2007); Average household size: 2.47 (2007); Median age: 42.2 (2007); Males per 100 females: 109.1 (2007); Marriage status: 16.4% never married, 71.8% now married, 4.4% widowed, 7.5% divorced (2000); Foreign born: 1.0% (2000); Ancestry (includes multiple ancestries): 28.4% German, 20.4% Irish, 15.3% English, 10.8% Italian, 8.6% United States or American (2000).
Economy: Employment by occupation: 14.8% management, 21.8% professional, 7.6% services, 25.4% sales, 0.0% farming, 9.0% construction, 21.5% production (2000).
Income: Per capita income: $34,722 (2007); Median household income: $70,941 (2007); Average household income: $85,836 (2007); Percent of households with income of $100,000 or more: 29.0% (2007); Poverty rate: 1.0% (2000).
Education: Percent of population age 25 and over with: High school diploma (including GED) or higher: 90.5% (2007); Bachelor's degree or higher: 20.7% (2007); Master's degree or higher: 4.6% (2007).
Housing: Homeownership rate: 93.9% (2007); Median home value: $196,934 (2007); Median rent: $569 per month (2000); Median age of housing: 18 years (2000).
Safety: Violent crime rate: 0.0 per 10,000 population; Property crime rate: 115.0 per 10,000 population (2007).
Transportation: Commute to work: 96.7% car, 0.0% public transportation, 0.3% walk, 3.0% work from home (2000); Travel time to work: 9.4% less than 15 minutes, 27.6% 15 to 30 minutes, 28.2% 30 to 45 minutes, 17.6% 45 to 60 minutes, 17.2% 60 minutes or more (2000)

ROCK CREEK (village). Covers a land area of 0.904 square miles and a water area of 0 square miles. Located at 41.66° N. Lat.; 80.85° W. Long. Elevation is 804 feet.
Population: 553 (1990); 584 (2000); 602 (2007); 612 (2012 projected); Race: 97.8% White, 1.0% Black, 0.0% Asian, 0.3% Hispanic of any race (2007); Density: 666.1 persons per square mile (2007); Average household size: 2.89 (2007); Median age: 34.3 (2007); Males per 100 females: 92.3 (2007); Marriage status: 32.2% never married, 52.4% now married, 7.3% widowed, 8.2% divorced (2000); Foreign born: 0.0% (2000); Ancestry (includes multiple ancestries): 40.9% German, 21.6% Irish, 10.7% Other groups, 9.5% English, 8.7% Italian (2000).
Economy: Employment by occupation: 4.4% management, 8.1% professional, 19.7% services, 20.7% sales, 0.0% farming, 16.6% construction, 30.5% production (2000).
Income: Per capita income: $16,541 (2007); Median household income: $42,308 (2007); Average household income: $47,873 (2007); Percent of households with income of $100,000 or more: 7.2% (2007); Poverty rate: 9.6% (2000).
Education: Percent of population age 25 and over with: High school diploma (including GED) or higher: 84.8% (2007); Bachelor's degree or higher: 8.0% (2007); Master's degree or higher: 2.1% (2007).

School District(s)

Jefferson Area Local (PK-12)
2005-06 Enrollment: 2,175 . . . . (440) 576-9876
Housing: Homeownership rate: 78.8% (2007); Median home value: $107,576 (2007); Median rent: $428 per month (2000); Median age of housing: 60+ years (2000).
Hospitals: Glenbeigh Hospital of Rock Creek (80 beds)
Transportation: Commute to work: 88.9% car, 0.7% public transportation, 5.4% walk, 2.9% work from home (2000); Travel time to work: 25.8% less than 15 minutes, 30.3% 15 to 30 minutes, 24.7% 30 to 45 minutes, 5.5% 45 to 60 minutes, 13.7% 60 minutes or more (2000)

ROME (unincorporated postal area, zip code 44085). Covers a land area of 46.385 square miles and a water area of 0.141 square miles. Located at 41.61° N. Lat.; 80.83° W. Long. Elevation is 853 feet.
Population: 2,943 (2000); Race: 97.4% White, 0.2% Black, 0.0% Asian, 1.6% Hispanic of any race (2000); Density: 63.4 persons per square mile (2000); Age: 30.8% under 18, 9.0% over 64 (2000); Marriage status: 19.3% never married, 62.9% now married, 6.0% widowed, 11.8% divorced (2000); Foreign born: 3.2% (2000); Ancestry (includes multiple ancestries): 21.9% German, 18.8% Irish, 11.8% English, 11.7% United States or American, 9.6% Polish (2000).
Economy: Employment by occupation: 9.4% management, 11.9% professional, 12.2% services, 18.3% sales, 1.8% farming, 17.1% construction, 29.4% production (2000).
Income: Per capita income: $18,049 (2000); Median household income: $44,514 (2000); Poverty rate: 9.8% (2000).
Education: Percent of population age 25 and over with: High school diploma (including GED) or higher: 84.4% (2000); Bachelor's degree or higher: 8.5% (2000).

School District(s)

Grand Valley Local (PK-12)
2005-06 Enrollment: 1,436 . . . . (440) 437-6260
Housing: Homeownership rate: 84.8% (2000); Median home value: $98,000 (2000); Median rent: $452 per month (2000); Median age of housing: 31 years (2000).
Transportation: Commute to work: 93.9% car, 0.7% public transportation, 0.7% walk, 4.7% work from home (2000); Travel time to work: 14.3% less than 15 minutes, 30.6% 15 to 30 minutes, 26.4% 30 to 45 minutes, 13.0% 45 to 60 minutes, 15.8% 60 minutes or more (2000)

WILLIAMSFIELD (unincorporated postal area, zip code 44093). Covers a land area of 33.132 square miles and a water area of 0.079 square miles. Located at 41.52° N. Lat.; 80.58° W. Long. Elevation is 1,135 feet.
Population: 1,525 (2000); Race: 90.7% White, 4.0% Black, 0.5% Asian, 0.0% Hispanic of any race (2000); Density: 46.0 persons per square mile

(2000); Age: 29.9% under 18, 12.8% over 64 (2000); Marriage status: 23.9% never married, 63.2% now married, 5.2% widowed, 7.7% divorced (2000); Foreign born: 2.8% (2000); Ancestry (includes multiple ancestries): 21.2% German, 14.7% Irish, 11.4% Other groups, 11.1% English, 8.8% Polish (2000).
Economy: Employment by occupation: 6.7% management, 6.8% professional, 24.2% services, 24.5% sales, 2.2% farming, 9.1% construction, 26.5% production (2000).
Income: Per capita income: $13,780 (2000); Median household income: $30,417 (2000); Poverty rate: 14.2% (2000).
Education: Percent of population age 25 and over with: High school diploma (including GED) or higher: 77.6% (2000); Bachelor's degree or higher: 4.2% (2000).
Housing: Homeownership rate: 87.9% (2000); Median home value: $74,900 (2000); Median rent: $408 per month (2000); Median age of housing: 42 years (2000).
Transportation: Commute to work: 94.4% car, 0.0% public transportation, 4.4% walk, 0.0% work from home (2000); Travel time to work: 37.0% less than 15 minutes, 24.6% 15 to 30 minutes, 24.5% 30 to 45 minutes, 7.7% 45 to 60 minutes, 6.2% 60 minutes or more (2000)

WINDSOR (unincorporated postal area, zip code 44099). Covers a land area of 19.249 square miles and a water area of 0.038 square miles. Located at 41.54° N. Lat.; 80.96° W. Long. Elevation is 834 feet.
Population: 1,647 (2000); Race: 97.4% White, 1.2% Black, 0.0% Asian, 0.8% Hispanic of any race (2000); Density: 85.6 persons per square mile (2000); Age: 29.9% under 18, 12.7% over 64 (2000); Marriage status: 24.3% never married, 63.7% now married, 6.3% widowed, 5.7% divorced (2000); Foreign born: 0.8% (2000); Ancestry (includes multiple ancestries): 17.8% German, 17.0% United States or American, 14.0% Other groups, 12.5% Irish, 8.3% Hungarian (2000).
Economy: Employment by occupation: 5.0% management, 4.4% professional, 11.0% services, 18.0% sales, 1.3% farming, 32.2% construction, 28.1% production (2000).
Income: Per capita income: $19,014 (2000); Median household income: $40,586 (2000); Poverty rate: 11.3% (2000).
Education: Percent of population age 25 and over with: High school diploma (including GED) or higher: 65.7% (2000); Bachelor's degree or higher: 10.1% (2000).

School District(s)

Grand Valley Local (PK-12)
2005-06 Enrollment: 1,436 . . . . (440) 437-6260
Housing: Homeownership rate: 86.8% (2000); Median home value: $91,500 (2000); Median rent: $382 per month (2000); Median age of housing: 42 years (2000).
Transportation: Commute to work: 91.6% car, 0.8% public transportation, 0.0% walk, 4.6% work from home (2000); Travel time to work: 10.7% less than 15 minutes, 37.4% 15 to 30 minutes, 17.7% 30 to 45 minutes, 8.4% 45 to 60 minutes, 25.8% 60 minutes or more (2000)

Athens County

Located in southeastern Ohio; bounded on the southeast by the Ohio River and the West Virginia border. Covers a land area of 506.76 square miles, a water area of 1.78 square miles, and is located in the Eastern Time Zone. The county was founded in 1805. County seat is Athens.

Athens County is part of the Athens, OH Micropolitan Statistical Area. The entire metro area includes: Athens County, OH

Population: 59,549 (1990); 62,223 (2000); 61,737 (2007); 60,954 (2012 projected); Race: 93.2% White, 2.2% Black, 2.3% Asian, 1.2% Hispanic of any race (2007); Density: 121.8 persons per square mile (2007); Average household size: 2.67 (2007); Median age: 27.0 (2007); Males per 100 females: 95.0 (2007).
Religion: Five largest groups: 4.5% The United Methodist Church, 3.1% Catholic Church, 3.1% Christian Churches and Churches of Christ, 2.6% The Wesleyan Church, 1.2% Presbyterian Church (U.S.A.) (2000).
Economy: Unemployment rate: 6.7% (6/2008); Total civilian labor force: 31,398 (6/2008); Leading industries: 22.5% retail trade; 21.8% accommodation & food services; 21.2% health care and social assistance (2005); Farms: 673 totaling 104,816 acres (2002); Companies that employ 500 or more persons: 1 (2006); Companies that employ 100 to 499 persons: 15 (2006); Companies that employ less than 100 persons: 1,145 (2006); Black-owned businesses: n/a (2002); Hispanic-owned businesses: n/a (2002); Asian-owned businesses: n/a (2002); Women-owned businesses: 1,157 (2002); Retail sales per capita: $8,933 (2008). Single-family building permits issued: 72 (2007); Multi-family building permits issued: 32 (2007).
Income: Per capita income: $17,478 (2007); Median household income: $31,727 (2007); Average household income: $45,204 (2007); Percent of households with income of $100,000 or more: 9.2% (2007); Poverty rate: 31.5% (2005); Bankruptcy rate: 1.42% (2007).
Taxes: Total county taxes per capita: $254 (2006); County property taxes per capita: $145 (2006).
Education: Percent of population age 25 and over with: High school diploma (including GED) or higher: 83.0% (2007); Bachelor's degree or higher: 25.8% (2007); Master's degree or higher: 13.1% (2007).
Housing: Homeownership rate: 61.0% (2007); Median home value: $99,688 (2007); Median rent: $380 per month (2000); Median age of housing: 30 years (2000).
Health: Birth rate: 95.6 per 10,000 population (2007); Death rate: 74.0 per 10,000 population (2007); Age-adjusted cancer mortality rate: 180.3 deaths per 100,000 population (2005); Number of physicians: 22.8 per 10,000 population (2005); Hospital beds: 23.5 per 10,000 population (2004); Hospital admissions: 563.8 per 10,000 population (2004).
Elections: 2004 Presidential election results: 36.1% Bush, 63.2% Kerry, 0.0% Nader, 0.3% Badnarik
National and State Parks: Gifford State Forest; Stroud Run State Park; Trimble State Wildlife Area; Waterloo State Forest

Additional Information Contacts

Athens County Government. . . . . (740) 592-3219
http://www.athenscountygovernment.com
Athens Area Chamber of Commerce. . . . . (740) 594-2251
http://www.athenschamber.com
City of Athens. . . . . (740) 592-3338
http://www.ci.athens.oh.us

Athens County Communities

ALBANY (village). Covers a land area of 1.244 square miles and a water area of 0.005 square miles. Located at 39.22° N. Lat.; 82.20° W. Long. Elevation is 758 feet.
History: Albany was laid out in 1831 and named for Albany, New York.
Population: 822 (1990); 808 (2000); 738 (2007); 732 (2012 projected); Race: 97.7% White, 0.7% Black, 0.3% Asian, 1.9% Hispanic of any race (2007); Density: 593.3 persons per square mile (2007); Average household size: 2.23 (2007); Median age: 39.9 (2007); Males per 100 females: 92.7 (2007); Marriage status: 22.6% never married, 54.9% now married, 8.9% widowed, 13.7% divorced (2000); Foreign born: 1.6% (2000); Ancestry (includes multiple ancestries): 15.1% United States or American, 14.7% German, 13.4% Irish, 10.2% English, 6.8% Other groups (2000).
Economy: Single-family building permits issued: 3 (2007); Multi-family building permits issued: 0 (2007); Employment by occupation: 5.3% management, 23.0% professional, 20.0% services, 26.5% sales, 0.0% farming, 16.0% construction, 9.3% production (2000).
Income: Per capita income: $20,492 (2007); Median household income: $36,979 (2007); Average household income: $45,279 (2007); Percent of households with income of $100,000 or more: 6.9% (2007); Poverty rate: 13.2% (2000).
Taxes: Total city taxes per capita: $77 (2006); City property taxes per capita: $77 (2006).
Education: Percent of population age 25 and over with: High school diploma (including GED) or higher: 85.4% (2007); Bachelor's degree or higher: 19.0% (2007); Master's degree or higher: 6.7% (2007).

School District(s)

Alexander Local (PK-12)
2005-06 Enrollment: 1,654 . . . . (740) 698-8831
Housing: Homeownership rate: 72.8% (2007); Median home value: $108,991 (2007); Median rent: $355 per month (2000); Median age of housing: 34 years (2000).
Transportation: Commute to work: 94.3% car, 0.5% public transportation, 1.2% walk, 4.0% work from home (2000); Travel time to work: 19.2% less than 15 minutes, 64.0% 15 to 30 minutes, 7.8% 30 to 45 minutes, 1.3% 45 to 60 minutes, 7.8% 60 minutes or more (2000)

AMESVILLE (village). Covers a land area of 0.222 square miles and a water area of 0 square miles. Located at 39.40° N. Lat.; 81.95° W. Long. Elevation is 633 feet.
Population: 250 (1990); 184 (2000); 168 (2007); 162 (2012 projected); Race: 95.8% White, 0.6% Black, 0.0% Asian, 3.0% Hispanic of any race

(2007); Density: 757.7 persons per square mile (2007); Average household size: 2.55 (2007); Median age: 33.1 (2007); Males per 100 females: 95.3 (2007); Marriage status: 20.4% never married, 62.0% now married, 8.8% widowed, 8.8% divorced (2000); Foreign born: 0.0% (2000); Ancestry (includes multiple ancestries): 15.3% German, 14.2% Irish, 12.6% United States or American, 9.5% Dutch, 6.3% Scotch-Irish (2000).
Economy: Employment by occupation: 12.0% management, 20.7% professional, 18.5% services, 34.8% sales, 0.0% farming, 3.3% construction, 10.9% production (2000).
Income: Per capita income: $23,080 (2007); Median household income: $43,333 (2007); Average household income: $58,750 (2007); Percent of households with income of $100,000 or more: 13.6% (2007); Poverty rate: 8.0% (2000).
Education: Percent of population age 25 and over with: High school diploma (including GED) or higher: 88.2% (2007); Bachelor's degree or higher: 24.5% (2007); Master's degree or higher: 6.9% (2007).

School District(s)

Federal Hocking Local (PK-12)
2005-06 Enrollment: 1,312 . . . . (740) 662-6691
Housing: Homeownership rate: 80.3% (2007); Median home value: $90,833 (2007); Median rent: $275 per month (2000); Median age of housing: 60+ years (2000).
Transportation: Commute to work: 90.2% car, 0.0% public transportation, 3.3% walk, 6.5% work from home (2000); Travel time to work: 12.8% less than 15 minutes, 54.7% 15 to 30 minutes, 16.3% 30 to 45 minutes, 8.1% 45 to 60 minutes, 8.1% 60 minutes or more (2000)

ATHENS (city). County seat. Covers a land area of 8.335 square miles and a water area of 0 square miles. Located at 39.32° N. Lat.; 82.09° W. Long. Elevation is 719 feet.
History: Athens was selected by the territorial legislature as the site of a university, which was chartered in 1804 and became Ohio University. Athens was incorporated as a city in 1912.
Population: 21,362 (1990); 21,342 (2000); 20,316 (2007); 19,535 (2012 projected); Race: 88.6% White, 3.5% Black, 5.2% Asian, 1.5% Hispanic of any race (2007); Density: 2,437.3 persons per square mile (2007); Average household size: 3.26 (2007); Median age: 21.8 (2007); Males per 100 females: 87.4 (2007); Marriage status: 70.0% never married, 24.6% now married, 2.3% widowed, 3.1% divorced (2000); Foreign born: 6.3% (2000); Ancestry (includes multiple ancestries): 28.3% German, 17.1% Irish, 12.6% Other groups, 10.6% English, 8.3% Italian (2000).
Economy: Single-family building permits issued: 69 (2007); Multi-family building permits issued: 0 (2007); Employment by occupation: 8.2% management, 37.4% professional, 22.5% services, 24.8% sales, 0.1% farming, 2.3% construction, 4.7% production (2000).
Income: Per capita income: $12,769 (2007); Median household income: $18,885 (2007); Average household income: $37,188 (2007); Percent of households with income of $100,000 or more: 8.5% (2007); Poverty rate: 51.9% (2000).
Taxes: Total city taxes per capita: $473 (2006); City property taxes per capita: $33 (2006).
Education: Percent of population age 25 and over with: High school diploma (including GED) or higher: 93.2% (2007); Bachelor's degree or higher: 61.5% (2007); Master's degree or higher: 36.0% (2007).

School District(s)

Athens City (PK-12)
2005-06 Enrollment: 2,964 . . . . (740) 797-4516

Four-year College(s)

Ohio University-Main Campus (Public)
Fall 2007 Enrollment: 21,089. . . . . (740) 593-1000
2007-08 Tuition: In-state $8,907; Out-of-state $17,871
Housing: Homeownership rate: 30.0% (2007); Median home value: $148,064 (2007); Median rent: $423 per month (2000); Median age of housing: 37 years (2000).
Hospitals: O'Bleness Memorial Hospital (114 beds)
Safety: Violent crime rate: 19.2 per 10,000 population; Property crime rate: 230.9 per 10,000 population (2007).
Newspapers: The Athens Messenger (Local news; Circulation 14,000); Athens News (Local news; Circulation 17,500)
Transportation: Commute to work: 51.1% car, 1.0% public transportation, 40.6% walk, 4.2% work from home (2000); Travel time to work: 74.2% less than 15 minutes, 20.0% 15 to 30 minutes, 3.3% 30 to 45 minutes, 0.6% 45 to 60 minutes, 1.8% 60 minutes or more (2000)
Airports: Ohio University Snyder Field (general aviation)
Additional Information Contacts
Athens Area Chamber of Commerce. . . . . (740) 594-2251
http://www.athenschamber.com
City of Athens. . . . . (740) 592-3338
http://www.ci.athens.oh.us

BUCHTEL (village). Covers a land area of 0.481 square miles and a water area of 0 square miles. Located at 39.46° N. Lat.; 82.18° W. Long. Elevation is 676 feet.
Population: 650 (1990); 574 (2000); 513 (2007); 506 (2012 projected); Race: 96.5% White, 0.2% Black, 0.2% Asian, 2.1% Hispanic of any race (2007); Density: 1,067.3 persons per square mile (2007); Average household size: 2.41 (2007); Median age: 35.8 (2007); Males per 100 females: 92.9 (2007); Marriage status: 21.0% never married, 55.1% now married, 8.6% widowed, 15.3% divorced (2000); Foreign born: 0.0% (2000); Ancestry (includes multiple ancestries): 23.2% United States or American, 13.4% Irish, 12.7% German, 9.3% Other groups, 6.8% English (2000).
Economy: Employment by occupation: 11.8% management, 13.2% professional, 18.9% services, 22.8% sales, 0.9% farming, 9.2% construction, 23.2% production (2000).
Income: Per capita income: $14,016 (2007); Median household income: $28,068 (2007); Average household income: $33,756 (2007); Percent of households with income of $100,000 or more: 3.3% (2007); Poverty rate: 20.5% (2000).
Education: Percent of population age 25 and over with: High school diploma (including GED) or higher: 76.9% (2007); Bachelor's degree or higher: 6.2% (2007); Master's degree or higher: 1.8% (2007).
Housing: Homeownership rate: 80.8% (2007); Median home value: $68,571 (2007); Median rent: $317 per month (2000); Median age of housing: 26 years (2000).
Transportation: Commute to work: 97.3% car, 0.0% public transportation, 1.8% walk, 0.0% work from home (2000); Travel time to work: 37.8% less than 15 minutes, 28.9% 15 to 30 minutes, 8.9% 30 to 45 minutes, 4.9% 45 to 60 minutes, 19.6% 60 minutes or more (2000)

CHAUNCEY (village). Covers a land area of 0.670 square miles and a water area of 0 square miles. Located at 39.40° N. Lat.; 82.12° W. Long. Elevation is 659 feet.
History: Chauncey was first a salt town, and later a coal town.
Population: 1,173 (1990); 1,067 (2000); 934 (2007); 924 (2012 projected); Race: 90.8% White, 2.1% Black, 5.0% Asian, 1.1% Hispanic of any race (2007); Density: 1,393.6 persons per square mile (2007); Average household size: 2.43 (2007); Median age: 34.4 (2007); Males per 100 females: 91.4 (2007); Marriage status: 24.6% never married, 50.5% now married, 9.9% widowed, 15.0% divorced (2000); Foreign born: 5.2% (2000); Ancestry (includes multiple ancestries): 15.3% United States or American, 11.4% English, 10.9% Other groups, 9.6% German, 7.9% Irish (2000).
Economy: Employment by occupation: 6.6% management, 11.7% professional, 28.1% services, 28.1% sales, 0.0% farming, 8.3% construction, 17.1% production (2000).
Income: Per capita income: $14,149 (2007); Median household income: $27,396 (2007); Average household income: $34,325 (2007); Percent of households with income of $100,000 or more: 1.0% (2007); Poverty rate: 25.6% (2000).
Education: Percent of population age 25 and over with: High school diploma (including GED) or higher: 74.0% (2007); Bachelor's degree or higher: 11.6% (2007); Master's degree or higher: 3.1% (2007).

School District(s)

Athens City (PK-12)
2005-06 Enrollment: 2,964 . . . . (740) 797-4516
Housing: Homeownership rate: 66.2% (2007); Median home value: $59,848 (2007); Median rent: $338 per month (2000); Median age of housing: 43 years (2000).
Transportation: Commute to work: 97.8% car, 1.2% public transportation, 0.5% walk, 0.5% work from home (2000); Travel time to work: 34.2% less than 15 minutes, 51.1% 15 to 30 minutes, 4.2% 30 to 45 minutes, 4.7% 45 to 60 minutes, 5.7% 60 minutes or more (2000)

COOLVILLE (village). Covers a land area of 0.842 square miles and a water area of 0.026 square miles. Located at 39.22° N. Lat.; 81.79° W. Long. Elevation is 699 feet.
Population: 663 (1990); 528 (2000); 474 (2007); 475 (2012 projected); Race: 98.7% White, 0.0% Black, 0.0% Asian, 0.0% Hispanic of any race (2007); Density: 563.0 persons per square mile (2007); Average household

size: 2.42 (2007); Median age: 36.6 (2007); Males per 100 females: 99.2 (2007); Marriage status: 22.7% never married, 53.0% now married, 10.4% widowed, 13.9% divorced (2000); Foreign born: 0.6% (2000); Ancestry (includes multiple ancestries): 19.8% German, 18.9% English, 17.0% Irish, 14.3% United States or American, 8.1% Other groups (2000).
Economy: Employment by occupation: 7.4% management, 9.4% professional, 24.1% services, 23.2% sales, 0.0% farming, 13.8% construction, 22.2% production (2000).
Income: Per capita income: $21,055 (2007); Median household income: $38,333 (2007); Average household income: $50,918 (2007); Percent of households with income of $100,000 or more: 7.7% (2007); Poverty rate: 15.6% (2000).
Education: Percent of population age 25 and over with: High school diploma (including GED) or higher: 70.6% (2007); Bachelor's degree or higher: 7.0% (2007); Master's degree or higher: 1.0% (2007).

School District(s)

Federal Hocking Local (PK-12)
2005-06 Enrollment: 1,312 . . . . (740) 662-6691

Housing: Homeownership rate: 80.6% (2007); Median home value: $77,500 (2007); Median rent: $348 per month (2000); Median age of housing: 45 years (2000).
Transportation: Commute to work: 94.5% car, 0.5% public transportation, 2.5% walk, 0.0% work from home (2000); Travel time to work: 24.4% less than 15 minutes, 24.4% 15 to 30 minutes, 30.8% 30 to 45 minutes, 8.0% 45 to 60 minutes, 12.4% 60 minutes or more (2000)

GLOUSTER (village). Covers a land area of 1.341 square miles and a water area of 0 square miles. Located at 39.50° N. Lat.; 82.08° W. Long. Elevation is 679 feet.
Population: 2,037 (1990); 1,972 (2000); 2,143 (2007); 2,179 (2012 projected); Race: 96.0% White, 0.9% Black, 0.0% Asian, 1.4% Hispanic of any race (2007); Density: 1,598.5 persons per square mile (2007); Average household size: 2.45 (2007); Median age: 30.7 (2007); Males per 100 females: 90.3 (2007); Marriage status: 27.4% never married, 49.9% now married, 10.8% widowed, 11.9% divorced (2000); Foreign born: 0.3% (2000); Ancestry (includes multiple ancestries): 14.3% Irish, 12.5% German, 12.3% United States or American, 10.3% English, 7.7% Other groups (2000).
Economy: Employment by occupation: 7.5% management, 14.3% professional, 23.6% services, 19.8% sales, 0.5% farming, 13.8% construction, 20.4% production (2000).
Income: Per capita income: $14,617 (2007); Median household income: $28,690 (2007); Average household income: $35,800 (2007); Percent of households with income of $100,000 or more: 4.1% (2007); Poverty rate: 28.2% (2000).
Education: Percent of population age 25 and over with: High school diploma (including GED) or higher: 71.3% (2007); Bachelor's degree or higher: 5.4% (2007); Master's degree or higher: 2.0% (2007).

School District(s)

Trimble Local (PK-12)
2005-06 Enrollment: 1,046 . . . . (740) 593-8001

Housing: Homeownership rate: 68.0% (2007); Median home value: $58,897 (2007); Median rent: $298 per month (2000); Median age of housing: 60+ years (2000).
Transportation: Commute to work: 96.2% car, 0.5% public transportation, 1.1% walk, 2.2% work from home (2000); Travel time to work: 18.8% less than 15 minutes, 31.6% 15 to 30 minutes, 25.0% 30 to 45 minutes, 6.7% 45 to 60 minutes, 17.9% 60 minutes or more (2000)

GUYSVILLE (unincorporated postal area, zip code 45735). Covers a land area of 51.112 square miles and a water area of 0.006 square miles. Located at 39.26° N. Lat.; 81.93° W. Long. Elevation is 652 feet.
History: Guysville developed as a coal-mining center.
Population: 1,692 (2000); Race: 97.1% White, 0.9% Black, 0.5% Asian, 2.0% Hispanic of any race (2000); Density: 33.1 persons per square mile (2000); Age: 25.1% under 18, 13.0% over 64 (2000); Marriage status: 20.1% never married, 64.0% now married, 5.6% widowed, 10.3% divorced (2000); Foreign born: 1.2% (2000); Ancestry (includes multiple ancestries): 20.4% United States or American, 18.3% English, 15.1% German, 13.9% Irish, 4.2% Other groups (2000).
Economy: Employment by occupation: 10.6% management, 13.1% professional, 17.4% services, 24.8% sales, 0.0% farming, 14.7% construction, 19.4% production (2000).
Income: Per capita income: $13,460 (2000); Median household income: $28,580 (2000); Poverty rate: 23.1% (2000).
Education: Percent of population age 25 and over with: High school diploma (including GED) or higher: 75.6% (2000); Bachelor's degree or higher: 9.3% (2000).
Housing: Homeownership rate: 85.5% (2000); Median home value: $68,300 (2000); Median rent: $268 per month (2000); Median age of housing: 22 years (2000).
Transportation: Commute to work: 89.8% car, 1.1% public transportation, 0.0% walk, 6.7% work from home (2000); Travel time to work: 6.0% less than 15 minutes, 34.9% 15 to 30 minutes, 29.8% 30 to 45 minutes, 14.4% 45 to 60 minutes, 15.0% 60 minutes or more (2000)

JACKSONVILLE (village). Covers a land area of 0.257 square miles and a water area of 0 square miles. Located at 39.47° N. Lat.; 82.08° W. Long. Elevation is 686 feet.
Population: 544 (1990); 544 (2000); 476 (2007); 476 (2012 projected); Race: 97.3% White, 0.0% Black, 0.0% Asian, 0.4% Hispanic of any race (2007); Density: 1,853.3 persons per square mile (2007); Average household size: 2.39 (2007); Median age: 37.4 (2007); Males per 100 females: 88.9 (2007); Marriage status: 21.5% never married, 57.0% now married, 11.7% widowed, 9.8% divorced (2000); Foreign born: 0.2% (2000); Ancestry (includes multiple ancestries): 14.1% United States or American, 13.2% Irish, 10.5% Other groups, 8.8% German, 5.9% English (2000).
Economy: Employment by occupation: 6.8% management, 9.7% professional, 25.6% services, 22.2% sales, 1.0% farming, 13.5% construction, 21.3% production (2000).
Income: Per capita income: $13,866 (2007); Median household income: $26,500 (2007); Average household income: $33,166 (2007); Percent of households with income of $100,000 or more: 2.5% (2007); Poverty rate: 24.5% (2000).
Education: Percent of population age 25 and over with: High school diploma (including GED) or higher: 76.8% (2007); Bachelor's degree or higher: 0.7% (2007); Master's degree or higher: 0.0% (2007).
Housing: Homeownership rate: 75.4% (2007); Median home value: $53,125 (2007); Median rent: $335 per month (2000); Median age of housing: 60+ years (2000).
Transportation: Commute to work: 95.5% car, 0.0% public transportation, 2.0% walk, 2.5% work from home (2000); Travel time to work: 18.3% less than 15 minutes, 39.6% 15 to 30 minutes, 25.9% 30 to 45 minutes, 6.6% 45 to 60 minutes, 9.6% 60 minutes or more (2000)

MILLFIELD (unincorporated postal area, zip code 45761). Covers a land area of 33.193 square miles and a water area of 0.010 square miles. Located at 39.43° N. Lat.; 82.10° W. Long. Elevation is 656 feet.
History: Millfield, a coal town, was the scene of a mine disaster in 1930 when Mine No. 6 of the Sunday Creek Coal Company was engulfed in flames.
Population: 1,773 (2000); Race: 98.9% White, 0.0% Black, 0.3% Asian, 0.5% Hispanic of any race (2000); Density: 53.4 persons per square mile (2000); Age: 29.0% under 18, 8.0% over 64 (2000); Marriage status: 32.0% never married, 51.1% now married, 7.5% widowed, 9.4% divorced (2000); Foreign born: 0.5% (2000); Ancestry (includes multiple ancestries): 18.6% German, 12.4% United States or American, 11.5% Irish, 8.4% English, 5.3% Other groups (2000).
Economy: Employment by occupation: 9.3% management, 10.1% professional, 32.0% services, 16.1% sales, 2.1% farming, 13.3% construction, 17.2% production (2000).
Income: Per capita income: $12,565 (2000); Median household income: $27,083 (2000); Poverty rate: 19.4% (2000).
Education: Percent of population age 25 and over with: High school diploma (including GED) or higher: 78.5% (2000); Bachelor's degree or higher: 11.5% (2000).
Housing: Homeownership rate: 80.6% (2000); Median home value: $72,500 (2000); Median rent: $325 per month (2000); Median age of housing: 25 years (2000).
Transportation: Commute to work: 96.1% car, 0.0% public transportation, 1.0% walk, 3.0% work from home (2000); Travel time to work: 25.9% less than 15 minutes, 42.4% 15 to 30 minutes, 8.8% 30 to 45 minutes, 8.4% 45 to 60 minutes, 14.5% 60 minutes or more (2000)

NELSONVILLE (city). Covers a land area of 4.972 square miles and a water area of 0 square miles. Located at 39.45° N. Lat.; 82.22° W. Long. Elevation is 679 feet.

History: First called Englishtown, the name was changed in 1824 to Nelsonville, in honor of Daniel Nelson, an enterprising citizen. Nelsonville developed as a coal town.
Population: 4,914 (1990); 5,230 (2000); 5,233 (2007); 5,188 (2012 projected); Race: 95.1% White, 2.1% Black, 0.5% Asian, 1.5% Hispanic of any race (2007); Density: 1,052.5 persons per square mile (2007); Average household size: 2.48 (2007); Median age: 27.8 (2007); Males per 100 females: 111.3 (2007); Marriage status: 38.6% never married, 42.8% now married, 7.4% widowed, 11.1% divorced (2000); Foreign born: 2.2% (2000); Ancestry (includes multiple ancestries): 15.7% German, 14.5% United States or American, 11.2% Irish, 11.0% Other groups, 10.7% English (2000).
Economy: Employment by occupation: 8.8% management, 10.1% professional, 28.5% services, 29.3% sales, 1.2% farming, 11.6% construction, 10.5% production (2000).
Income: Per capita income: $13,370 (2007); Median household income: $23,777 (2007); Average household income: $31,832 (2007); Percent of households with income of $100,000 or more: 4.1% (2007); Poverty rate: 33.9% (2000).
Education: Percent of population age 25 and over with: High school diploma (including GED) or higher: 73.4% (2007); Bachelor's degree or higher: 7.2% (2007); Master's degree or higher: 3.0% (2007).

School District(s)

Nelsonville-York City (PK-12)
2005-06 Enrollment: 1,356 . . . . (740) 753-4441
Tri-County (07-12)
2005-06 Enrollment: n/a . . . . (740) 753-3511

Two-year College(s)

Hocking College (Public)
Fall 2007 Enrollment: 4,341. . . . . (740) 753-3591
2007-08 Tuition: In-state $3,546; Out-of-state $7,092

Vocational/Technical School(s)

Tri-County Adult Career Center (Public)
Fall 2007 Enrollment: 40 . . . . (740) 753-5464
2007-08 Tuition: $4,800

Housing: Homeownership rate: 49.7% (2007); Median home value: $73,106 (2007); Median rent: $301 per month (2000); Median age of housing: 40 years (2000).
Hospitals: Doctors Hospital of Nelsonville (50 beds)
Transportation: Commute to work: 88.3% car, 0.3% public transportation, 7.9% walk, 2.5% work from home (2000); Travel time to work: 39.8% less than 15 minutes, 34.0% 15 to 30 minutes, 11.6% 30 to 45 minutes, 4.4% 45 to 60 minutes, 10.2% 60 minutes or more (2000)

NEW MARSHFIELD (unincorporated postal area, zip code 45766). Covers a land area of 30.325 square miles and a water area of 0.017 square miles. Located at 39.32° N. Lat.; 82.25° W. Long. Elevation is 840 feet.
Population: 1,386 (2000); Race: 97.7% White, 0.0% Black, 1.4% Asian, 0.0% Hispanic of any race (2000); Density: 45.7 persons per square mile (2000); Age: 25.9% under 18, 9.7% over 64 (2000); Marriage status: 22.0% never married, 58.4% now married, 5.3% widowed, 14.3% divorced (2000); Foreign born: 1.0% (2000); Ancestry (includes multiple ancestries): 23.4% German, 19.7% Irish, 13.4% English, 9.2% United States or American, 7.4% Other groups (2000).
Economy: Employment by occupation: 1.4% management, 22.3% professional, 20.0% services, 24.3% sales, 0.0% farming, 16.5% construction, 15.5% production (2000).
Income: Per capita income: $15,285 (2000); Median household income: $40,491 (2000); Poverty rate: 14.1% (2000).
Education: Percent of population age 25 and over with: High school diploma (including GED) or higher: 80.6% (2000); Bachelor's degree or higher: 15.2% (2000).

School District(s)

Alexander Local (PK-12)
2005-06 Enrollment: 1,654 . . . . (740) 698-8831

Housing: Homeownership rate: 78.8% (2000); Median home value: $55,000 (2000); Median rent: $276 per month (2000); Median age of housing: 25 years (2000).
Transportation: Commute to work: 93.8% car, 0.0% public transportation, 2.6% walk, 3.6% work from home (2000); Travel time to work: 14.8% less than 15 minutes, 64.6% 15 to 30 minutes, 8.5% 30 to 45 minutes, 5.5% 45 to 60 minutes, 6.6% 60 minutes or more (2000)

SHADE (unincorporated postal area, zip code 45776). Covers a land area of 19.470 square miles and a water area of 0 square miles. Located at 39.19° N. Lat.; 82.01° W. Long. Elevation is 791 feet.
Population: 798 (2000); Race: 96.6% White, 0.6% Black, 0.0% Asian, 0.0% Hispanic of any race (2000); Density: 41.0 persons per square mile (2000); Age: 26.4% under 18, 13.5% over 64 (2000); Marriage status: 14.0% never married, 59.1% now married, 9.7% widowed, 17.2% divorced (2000); Foreign born: 0.0% (2000); Ancestry (includes multiple ancestries): 20.8% Irish, 17.8% German, 13.5% Other groups, 13.4% English, 12.1% United States or American (2000).
Economy: Employment by occupation: 12.6% management, 16.7% professional, 23.6% services, 18.9% sales, 0.0% farming, 10.1% construction, 18.2% production (2000).
Income: Per capita income: $14,626 (2000); Median household income: $29,688 (2000); Poverty rate: 14.3% (2000).
Education: Percent of population age 25 and over with: High school diploma (including GED) or higher: 74.4% (2000); Bachelor's degree or higher: 12.2% (2000).

School District(s)

Alexander Local (PK-12)
2005-06 Enrollment: 1,654 . . . . (740) 698-8831

Housing: Homeownership rate: 88.8% (2000); Median home value: $76,700 (2000); Median rent: $325 per month (2000); Median age of housing: 28 years (2000).
Transportation: Commute to work: 92.8% car, 2.8% public transportation, 0.0% walk, 4.4% work from home (2000); Travel time to work: 4.6% less than 15 minutes, 53.9% 15 to 30 minutes, 26.0% 30 to 45 minutes, 4.9% 45 to 60 minutes, 10.5% 60 minutes or more (2000)

STEWART (unincorporated postal area, zip code 45778). Covers a land area of 28.571 square miles and a water area of 0 square miles. Located at 39.34° N. Lat.; 81.88° W. Long. Elevation is 667 feet.
Population: 960 (2000); Race: 82.8% White, 7.5% Black, 1.4% Asian, 3.1% Hispanic of any race (2000); Density: 33.6 persons per square mile (2000); Age: 35.1% under 18, 4.7% over 64 (2000); Marriage status: 22.9% never married, 64.8% now married, 3.1% widowed, 9.2% divorced (2000); Foreign born: 1.4% (2000); Ancestry (includes multiple ancestries): 20.7% Other groups, 14.1% German, 11.8% Irish, 8.3% United States or American, 4.7% Scottish (2000).
Economy: Employment by occupation: 8.5% management, 10.7% professional, 17.7% services, 26.4% sales, 1.7% farming, 11.4% construction, 23.6% production (2000).
Income: Per capita income: $15,314 (2000); Median household income: $34,063 (2000); Poverty rate: 20.1% (2000).
Education: Percent of population age 25 and over with: High school diploma (including GED) or higher: 74.6% (2000); Bachelor's degree or higher: 8.5% (2000).

School District(s)

Federal Hocking Local (PK-12)
2005-06 Enrollment: 1,312 . . . . (740) 662-6691

Housing: Homeownership rate: 85.5% (2000); Median home value: $63,000 (2000); Median rent: $420 per month (2000); Median age of housing: 26 years (2000).
Transportation: Commute to work: 92.0% car, 0.0% public transportation, 2.9% walk, 1.6% work from home (2000); Travel time to work: 17.9% less than 15 minutes, 42.1% 15 to 30 minutes, 22.0% 30 to 45 minutes, 8.4% 45 to 60 minutes, 9.5% 60 minutes or more (2000)

THE PLAINS (CDP). Covers a land area of 2.297 square miles and a water area of 0 square miles. Located at 39.37° N. Lat.; 82.13° W. Long. Elevation is 715 feet.
Population: 2,523 (1990); 2,931 (2000); 3,241 (2007); 3,399 (2012 projected); Race: 92.5% White, 3.2% Black, 1.8% Asian, 1.2% Hispanic of any race (2007); Density: 1,410.8 persons per square mile (2007); Average household size: 2.35 (2007); Median age: 35.0 (2007); Males per 100 females: 82.3 (2007); Marriage status: 25.7% never married, 56.9% now married, 6.4% widowed, 11.1% divorced (2000); Foreign born: 1.3% (2000); Ancestry (includes multiple ancestries): 14.5% German, 14.4% Irish, 11.3% United States or American, 10.7% English, 7.6% Other groups (2000).
Economy: Employment by occupation: 14.6% management, 23.4% professional, 17.2% services, 28.8% sales, 0.0% farming, 10.0% construction, 6.0% production (2000).

Income: Per capita income: $18,883 (2007); Median household income: $32,722 (2007); Average household income: $43,070 (2007); Percent of households with income of $100,000 or more: 6.0% (2007); Poverty rate: 17.7% (2000).
Education: Percent of population age 25 and over with: High school diploma (including GED) or higher: 86.7% (2007); Bachelor's degree or higher: 25.9% (2007); Master's degree or higher: 9.4% (2007).

School District(s)

Athens City (PK-12)
2005-06 Enrollment: 2,964 . . . . (740) 797-4516

Housing: Homeownership rate: 55.0% (2007); Median home value: $110,904 (2007); Median rent: $402 per month (2000); Median age of housing: 21 years (2000).
Transportation: Commute to work: 94.4% car, 0.0% public transportation, 1.9% walk, 3.7% work from home (2000); Travel time to work: 70.5% less than 15 minutes, 22.0% 15 to 30 minutes, 1.5% 30 to 45 minutes, 2.1% 45 to 60 minutes, 3.9% 60 minutes or more (2000)

TRIMBLE (village). Covers a land area of 0.653 square miles and a water area of 0 square miles. Located at 39.48° N. Lat.; 82.07° W. Long. Elevation is 663 feet.
Population: 441 (1990); 466 (2000); 460 (2007); 461 (2012 projected); Race: 98.3% White, 0.0% Black, 0.2% Asian, 0.0% Hispanic of any race (2007); Density: 704.0 persons per square mile (2007); Average household size: 2.60 (2007); Median age: 31.3 (2007); Males per 100 females: 98.3 (2007); Marriage status: 24.0% never married, 54.9% now married, 7.2% widowed, 13.9% divorced (2000); Foreign born: 0.0% (2000); Ancestry (includes multiple ancestries): 19.4% United States or American, 11.2% English, 9.7% German, 9.1% Other groups, 5.7% Irish (2000).
Economy: Employment by occupation: 5.2% management, 12.6% professional, 17.8% services, 21.8% sales, 0.0% farming, 19.5% construction, 23.0% production (2000).
Income: Per capita income: $15,630 (2007); Median household income: $36,964 (2007); Average household income: $40,621 (2007); Percent of households with income of $100,000 or more: 4.5% (2007); Poverty rate: 26.1% (2000).
Education: Percent of population age 25 and over with: High school diploma (including GED) or higher: 74.1% (2007); Bachelor's degree or higher: 2.2% (2007); Master's degree or higher: 0.0% (2007).
Housing: Homeownership rate: 75.7% (2007); Median home value: $52,381 (2007); Median rent: $292 per month (2000); Median age of housing: 56 years (2000).
Transportation: Commute to work: 85.5% car, 0.0% public transportation, 6.9% walk, 5.7% work from home (2000); Travel time to work: 28.0% less than 15 minutes, 31.3% 15 to 30 minutes, 16.0% 30 to 45 minutes, 5.3% 45 to 60 minutes, 19.3% 60 minutes or more (2000)

Auglaize County

Located in western Ohio; drained by the Auglaize and St. Marys Rivers; includes part of Grand Lake. Covers a land area of 401.25 square miles, a water area of 0.47 square miles, and is located in the Eastern Time Zone. The county was founded in 1848. County seat is Wapakoneta.

Auglaize County is part of the Wapakoneta, OH Micropolitan Statistical Area. The entire metro area includes: Auglaize County, OH

Population: 44,585 (1990); 46,611 (2000); 47,543 (2007); 48,131 (2012 projected); Race: 97.6% White, 0.4% Black, 0.6% Asian, 0.8% Hispanic of any race (2007); Density: 118.5 persons per square mile (2007); Average household size: 2.62 (2007); Median age: 39.1 (2007); Males per 100 females: 96.5 (2007).
Religion: Five largest groups: 26.3% Catholic Church, 10.0% United Church of Christ, 9.0% The United Methodist Church, 6.2% Evangelical Lutheran Church in America, 2.2% The Christian and Missionary Alliance (2000).
Economy: Unemployment rate: 5.3% (6/2008); Total civilian labor force: 27,107 (6/2008); Leading industries: 42.3% manufacturing; 12.5% retail trade; 10.3% health care and social assistance (2005); Farms: 1,020 totaling 217,916 acres (2002); Companies that employ 500 or more persons: 4 (2006); Companies that employ 100 to 499 persons: 23 (2006); Companies that employ less than 100 persons: 1,007 (2006); Black-owned businesses: n/a (2002); Hispanic-owned businesses: n/a (2002); Asian-owned businesses: n/a (2002); Women-owned businesses: 753 (2002); Retail sales per capita: $10,910 (2008). Single-family building permits issued: 134 (2007); Multi-family building permits issued: 8 (2007).
Income: Per capita income: $23,225 (2007); Median household income: $49,464 (2007); Average household income: $60,287 (2007); Percent of households with income of $100,000 or more: 13.1% (2007); Poverty rate: 7.1% (2005); Bankruptcy rate: 2.99% (2007).
Education: Percent of population age 25 and over with: High school diploma (including GED) or higher: 85.8% (2007); Bachelor's degree or higher: 13.4% (2007); Master's degree or higher: 4.7% (2007).
Housing: Homeownership rate: 78.2% (2007); Median home value: $114,905 (2007); Median rent: $360 per month (2000); Median age of housing: 41 years (2000).
Health: Birth rate: 133.3 per 10,000 population (2007); Death rate: 99.1 per 10,000 population (2007); Age-adjusted cancer mortality rate: 193.4 deaths per 100,000 population (2005); Number of physicians: 12.6 per 10,000 population (2005); Hospital beds: 19.4 per 10,000 population (2004); Hospital admissions: 858.1 per 10,000 population (2004).
Elections: 2004 Presidential election results: 73.9% Bush, 25.6% Kerry, 0.0% Nader, 0.3% Badnarik
National and State Parks: Fort Amanda State Park
Additional Information Contacts
Auglaize County Government . . . . (419) 739-6710
http://www.auglaizecounty.org
Saint Marys Area Chamber of Commerce . . . . (419) 300-4611
http://www.stmarysohio.org
Southwestern Auglaize County Chamber of Commerce . . . (419) 629-0313
http://www.swauglaizechamber.com
Village of Minster . . . . (419) 628-3497
http://www.minsteroh.com
Village of New Bremen . . . . (419) 629-2447
http://www.newbremen.com
Village of New Knoxville . . . . (419) 753-2160
http://www.newknoxville.com
Wapakoneta Area Chamber of Commerce . . . . (419) 738-2911
http://www.wapakoneta.com/p2_commerce/p2_commerce.html

Auglaize County Communities

BUCKLAND (village). Covers a land area of 0.256 square miles and a water area of 0 square miles. Located at 40.62° N. Lat.; 84.26° W. Long. Elevation is 850 feet.
Population: 239 (1990); 255 (2000); 238 (2007); 239 (2012 projected); Race: 97.9% White, 0.0% Black, 0.0% Asian, 0.0% Hispanic of any race (2007); Density: 929.1 persons per square mile (2007); Average household size: 2.40 (2007); Median age: 32.6 (2007); Males per 100 females: 95.1 (2007); Marriage status: 18.6% never married, 65.0% now married, 6.6% widowed, 9.8% divorced (2000); Foreign born: 0.8% (2000); Ancestry (includes multiple ancestries): 46.9% German, 18.5% United States or American, 8.2% Irish, 7.0% English, 5.8% Other groups (2000).
Economy: Employment by occupation: 8.7% management, 9.4% professional, 18.1% services, 24.4% sales, 2.4% farming, 7.9% construction, 29.1% production (2000).
Income: Per capita income: $19,853 (2007); Median household income: $40,278 (2007); Average household income: $47,727 (2007); Percent of households with income of $100,000 or more: 6.1% (2007); Poverty rate: 4.9% (2000).
Education: Percent of population age 25 and over with: High school diploma (including GED) or higher: 89.2% (2007); Bachelor's degree or higher: 2.0% (2007); Master's degree or higher: 0.7% (2007).

School District(s)

Wapakoneta City (PK-12)
2005-06 Enrollment: 3,105 . . . . (419) 739-2900

Housing: Homeownership rate: 84.8% (2007); Median home value: $71,538 (2007); Median rent: $250 per month (2000); Median age of housing: 60+ years (2000).
Transportation: Commute to work: 90.5% car, 0.0% public transportation, 7.1% walk, 2.4% work from home (2000); Travel time to work: 26.8% less than 15 minutes, 51.2% 15 to 30 minutes, 17.9% 30 to 45 minutes, 3.3% 45 to 60 minutes, 0.8% 60 minutes or more (2000)

CRIDERSVILLE (village). Covers a land area of 0.912 square miles and a water area of 0 square miles. Located at 40.65° N. Lat.; 84.14° W. Long. Elevation is 886 feet.
Population: 1,930 (1990); 1,817 (2000); 1,790 (2007); 1,772 (2012 projected); Race: 95.5% White, 0.7% Black, 0.1% Asian, 2.9% Hispanic of any race (2007); Density: 1,963.2 persons per square mile (2007); Average household size: 2.42 (2007); Median age: 37.8 (2007); Males per 100

females: 86.8 (2007); Marriage status: 20.2% never married, 57.8% now married, 9.7% widowed, 12.3% divorced (2000); Foreign born: 0.8% (2000); Ancestry (includes multiple ancestries): 33.7% German, 14.9% United States or American, 14.2% Irish, 10.6% Other groups, 6.4% English (2000).
Economy: Single-family building permits issued: 1 (2007); Multi-family building permits issued: 0 (2007); Employment by occupation: 6.4% management, 13.2% professional, 15.6% services, 24.8% sales, 0.0% farming, 8.7% construction, 31.2% production (2000).
Income: Per capita income: $17,415 (2007); Median household income: $35,670 (2007); Average household income: $41,688 (2007); Percent of households with income of $100,000 or more: 4.5% (2007); Poverty rate: 12.3% (2000).
Education: Percent of population age 25 and over with: High school diploma (including GED) or higher: 79.0% (2007); Bachelor's degree or higher: 6.0% (2007); Master's degree or higher: 1.6% (2007).

School District(s)

Wapakoneta City (PK-12)
2005-06 Enrollment: 3,105 . . . . (419) 739-2900
Housing: Homeownership rate: 73.9% (2007); Median home value: $88,727 (2007); Median rent: $324 per month (2000); Median age of housing: 35 years (2000).
Safety: Violent crime rate: 17.2 per 10,000 population; Property crime rate: 177.9 per 10,000 population (2007).
Transportation: Commute to work: 95.1% car, 0.0% public transportation, 3.0% walk, 1.6% work from home (2000); Travel time to work: 33.0% less than 15 minutes, 47.2% 15 to 30 minutes, 15.5% 30 to 45 minutes, 2.6% 45 to 60 minutes, 1.6% 60 minutes or more (2000)

MINSTER (village). Covers a land area of 1.878 square miles and a water area of 0 square miles. Located at 40.39° N. Lat.; 84.37° W. Long. Elevation is 965 feet.
History: Incorporated 1833.
Population: 2,733 (1990); 2,794 (2000); 2,811 (2007); 2,836 (2012 projected); Race: 99.7% White, 0.0% Black, 0.1% Asian, 0.2% Hispanic of any race (2007); Density: 1,497.1 persons per square mile (2007); Average household size: 2.72 (2007); Median age: 39.0 (2007); Males per 100 females: 94.4 (2007); Marriage status: 22.3% never married, 68.5% now married, 6.4% widowed, 2.8% divorced (2000); Foreign born: 0.7% (2000); Ancestry (includes multiple ancestries): 75.4% German, 7.2% Irish, 6.6% French (except Basque), 6.4% United States or American, 1.8% Other groups (2000).
Economy: Single-family building permits issued: 5 (2007); Multi-family building permits issued: 0 (2007); Employment by occupation: 12.2% management, 24.8% professional, 11.3% services, 20.9% sales, 0.2% farming, 5.2% construction, 25.4% production (2000).
Income: Per capita income: $27,186 (2007); Median household income: $66,159 (2007); Average household income: $73,590 (2007); Percent of households with income of $100,000 or more: 23.0% (2007); Poverty rate: 3.6% (2000).
Education: Percent of population age 25 and over with: High school diploma (including GED) or higher: 87.9% (2007); Bachelor's degree or higher: 22.5% (2007); Master's degree or higher: 8.7% (2007).

School District(s)

Minster Community School (01-06)
2005-06 Enrollment: 134 . . . . (419) 628-3397
Minster Local (PK-12)
2005-06 Enrollment: 760 . . . . (419) 628-3397
Housing: Homeownership rate: 83.7% (2007); Median home value: $146,196 (2007); Median rent: $356 per month (2000); Median age of housing: 39 years (2000).
Newspapers: Community Post (Local news; Circulation 2,500)
Transportation: Commute to work: 92.3% car, 0.0% public transportation, 3.1% walk, 1.9% work from home (2000); Travel time to work: 59.6% less than 15 minutes, 25.2% 15 to 30 minutes, 11.9% 30 to 45 minutes, 1.2% 45 to 60 minutes, 2.2% 60 minutes or more (2000)
Additional Information Contacts
Southwestern Auglaize County Chamber of Commerce . . . (419) 629-0313
http://www.swauglaizechamber.com
Village of Minster . . . . (419) 628-3497
http://www.minsteroh.com

NEW BREMEN (village). Covers a land area of 2.062 square miles and a water area of 0 square miles. Located at 40.43° N. Lat.; 84.38° W. Long. Elevation is 945 feet.
History: Incorporated 1833.
Population: 2,797 (1990); 2,909 (2000); 2,950 (2007); 2,991 (2012 projected); Race: 97.7% White, 0.1% Black, 0.9% Asian, 0.4% Hispanic of any race (2007); Density: 1,430.4 persons per square mile (2007); Average household size: 2.64 (2007); Median age: 36.6 (2007); Males per 100 females: 97.6 (2007); Marriage status: 21.7% never married, 65.5% now married, 6.2% widowed, 6.5% divorced (2000); Foreign born: 0.9% (2000); Ancestry (includes multiple ancestries): 66.0% German, 9.2% Irish, 8.8% United States or American, 4.8% English, 4.6% Other groups (2000).
Economy: Single-family building permits issued: 20 (2007); Multi-family building permits issued: 0 (2007); Employment by occupation: 9.2% management, 18.9% professional, 12.9% services, 20.9% sales, 0.0% farming, 7.3% construction, 30.9% production (2000).
Income: Per capita income: $25,138 (2007); Median household income: $60,514 (2007); Average household income: $66,449 (2007); Percent of households with income of $100,000 or more: 16.0% (2007); Poverty rate: 1.4% (2000).
Education: Percent of population age 25 and over with: High school diploma (including GED) or higher: 93.0% (2007); Bachelor's degree or higher: 17.5% (2007); Master's degree or higher: 5.5% (2007).

School District(s)

New Bremen Local (PK-12)
2005-06 Enrollment: 932 . . . . (419) 629-8606
Housing: Homeownership rate: 78.2% (2007); Median home value: $123,745 (2007); Median rent: $399 per month (2000); Median age of housing: 43 years (2000).
Transportation: Commute to work: 89.0% car, 0.0% public transportation, 3.8% walk, 2.5% work from home (2000); Travel time to work: 65.4% less than 15 minutes, 23.9% 15 to 30 minutes, 6.1% 30 to 45 minutes, 2.5% 45 to 60 minutes, 2.2% 60 minutes or more (2000)
Additional Information Contacts
Southwestern Auglaize County Chamber of Commerce . . . (419) 629-0313
http://www.swauglaizechamber.com
Village of New Bremen . . . . (419) 629-2447
http://www.newbremen.com

NEW KNOXVILLE (village). Covers a land area of 0.785 square miles and a water area of 0 square miles. Located at 40.49° N. Lat.; 84.31° W. Long. Elevation is 902 feet.
Population: 854 (1990); 891 (2000); 789 (2007); 793 (2012 projected); Race: 97.6% White, 0.4% Black, 0.6% Asian, 0.3% Hispanic of any race (2007); Density: 1,005.4 persons per square mile (2007); Average household size: 2.49 (2007); Median age: 36.4 (2007); Males per 100 females: 91.0 (2007); Marriage status: 26.6% never married, 60.4% now married, 5.8% widowed, 7.2% divorced (2000); Foreign born: 0.4% (2000); Ancestry (includes multiple ancestries): 64.0% German, 11.4% Irish, 7.0% English, 5.4% Other groups, 4.2% United States or American (2000).
Economy: Single-family building permits issued: 1 (2007); Multi-family building permits issued: 0 (2007); Employment by occupation: 6.6% management, 17.5% professional, 11.0% services, 26.1% sales, 1.6% farming, 10.4% construction, 26.7% production (2000).
Income: Per capita income: $23,647 (2007); Median household income: $49,688 (2007); Average household income: $58,856 (2007); Percent of households with income of $100,000 or more: 13.6% (2007); Poverty rate: 4.7% (2000).
Education: Percent of population age 25 and over with: High school diploma (including GED) or higher: 93.7% (2007); Bachelor's degree or higher: 13.3% (2007); Master's degree or higher: 5.9% (2007).

School District(s)

New Knoxville Local (PK-12)
2005-06 Enrollment: 487 . . . . (419) 753-2431
Housing: Homeownership rate: 75.1% (2007); Median home value: $103,571 (2007); Median rent: $363 per month (2000); Median age of housing: 50 years (2000).
Transportation: Commute to work: 87.8% car, 0.0% public transportation, 7.4% walk, 3.7% work from home (2000); Travel time to work: 54.6% less than 15 minutes, 34.5% 15 to 30 minutes, 5.8% 30 to 45 minutes, 2.1% 45 to 60 minutes, 3.0% 60 minutes or more (2000)
Additional Information Contacts
Southwestern Auglaize County Chamber of Commerce . . . (419) 629-0313
http://www.swauglaizechamber.com
Village of New Knoxville. . . . . (419) 753-2160
http://www.newknoxville.com

SAINT MARYS (city). Covers a land area of 4.330 square miles and a water area of 0.032 square miles. Located at 40.54° N. Lat.; 84.39° W. Long. Elevation is 866 feet.

History: St. Marys began as a trading post, and was organized as a town after 1818. It was called Girty's Town when it served as headquarters and supply depot for Generals Harmar, Wayne, and Harrison. Later, its location on the Miami & Erie Canal made it a shipping center for farm produce, which arrived in St. Marys by boat and was transferred to wagons for the overland haul to the Ohio River.

Population: 8,601 (1990); 8,342 (2000); 8,396 (2007); 8,410 (2012 projected); Race: 96.5% White, 0.6% Black, 1.5% Asian, 0.5% Hispanic of any race (2007); Density: 1,939.1 persons per square mile (2007); Average household size: 2.53 (2007); Median age: 37.3 (2007); Males per 100 females: 94.7 (2007); Marriage status: 20.6% never married, 58.6% now married, 10.2% widowed, 10.6% divorced (2000); Foreign born: 2.6% (2000); Ancestry (includes multiple ancestries): 45.8% German, 13.7% Irish, 8.4% Other groups, 8.2% United States or American, 5.5% English (2000).

Economy: Single-family building permits issued: 19 (2007); Multi-family building permits issued: 6 (2007); Employment by occupation: 8.3% management, 17.6% professional, 16.6% services, 16.8% sales, 0.4% farming, 6.6% construction, 33.7% production (2000).

Income: Per capita income: $19,646 (2007); Median household income: $42,416 (2007); Average household income: $49,431 (2007); Percent of households with income of $100,000 or more: 6.9% (2007); Poverty rate: 7.3% (2000).

Taxes: Total city taxes per capita: $723 (2006); City property taxes per capita: $191 (2006).

Education: Percent of population age 25 and over with: High school diploma (including GED) or higher: 82.0% (2007); Bachelor's degree or higher: 11.7% (2007); Master's degree or higher: 4.0% (2007).

School District(s)

St Marys City (PK-12)
2005-06 Enrollment: 2,413 . . . . (419) 394-4312

Housing: Homeownership rate: 70.6% (2007); Median home value: $95,052 (2007); Median rent: $364 per month (2000); Median age of housing: 47 years (2000).

Hospitals: Joint Township District Memorial Hospital (130 beds)

Newspapers: Evening Leader (Local news; Circulation 5,000); St. Mary's Leader (Local news; Circulation 7,000)

Transportation: Commute to work: 94.3% car, 1.0% public transportation, 1.9% walk, 1.0% work from home (2000); Travel time to work: 53.8% less than 15 minutes, 26.2% 15 to 30 minutes, 13.2% 30 to 45 minutes, 3.7% 45 to 60 minutes, 3.1% 60 minutes or more (2000)

Additional Information Contacts

Saint Marys Area Chamber of Commerce . . . . (419) 300-4611
http://www.stmarysohio.org

UNIOPOLIS (village). Covers a land area of 0.156 square miles and a water area of 0 square miles. Located at 40.60° N. Lat.; 84.08° W. Long. Elevation is 938 feet.

Population: 261 (1990); 256 (2000); 273 (2007); 279 (2012 projected); Race: 98.5% White, 0.4% Black, 0.0% Asian, 2.2% Hispanic of any race (2007); Density: 1,749.2 persons per square mile (2007); Average household size: 2.84 (2007); Median age: 36.1 (2007); Males per 100 females: 110.0 (2007); Marriage status: 11.2% never married, 69.8% now married, 5.6% widowed, 13.4% divorced (2000); Foreign born: 0.8% (2000); Ancestry (includes multiple ancestries): 47.9% German, 13.6% Irish, 13.6% Dutch, 7.6% Other groups, 5.5% French (except Basque) (2000).

Economy: Employment by occupation: 1.6% management, 11.2% professional, 20.8% services, 18.4% sales, 0.0% farming, 13.6% construction, 34.4% production (2000).

Income: Per capita income: $19,038 (2007); Median household income: $45,000 (2007); Average household income: $54,141 (2007); Percent of households with income of $100,000 or more: 5.2% (2007); Poverty rate: 0.0% (2000).

Education: Percent of population age 25 and over with: High school diploma (including GED) or higher: 70.8% (2007); Bachelor's degree or higher: 5.1% (2007); Master's degree or higher: 4.5% (2007).

Housing: Homeownership rate: 88.5% (2007); Median home value: $75,833 (2007); Median rent: $375 per month (2000); Median age of housing: 60+ years (2000).

Transportation: Commute to work: 96.6% car, 0.0% public transportation, 0.8% walk, 2.5% work from home (2000); Travel time to work: 28.7% less than 15 minutes, 56.5% 15 to 30 minutes, 11.3% 30 to 45 minutes, 3.5% 45 to 60 minutes, 0.0% 60 minutes or more (2000)

WAPAKONETA (city). County seat. Covers a land area of 5.657 square miles and a water area of 0.055 square miles. Located at 40.56° N. Lat.; 84.19° W. Long. Elevation is 896 feet.

History: Wapakoneta was platted in 1833 and settled by people of German heritage. Woodworking industries provided the economic base in the late 1800's. The town's name was first Wapaghkonetta, a combination of two Indian names, Wapaugh and Konetta.

Population: 9,559 (1990); 9,474 (2000); 9,541 (2007); 9,575 (2012 projected); Race: 97.5% White, 0.3% Black, 0.4% Asian, 1.1% Hispanic of any race (2007); Density: 1,686.6 persons per square mile (2007); Average household size: 2.43 (2007); Median age: 37.8 (2007); Males per 100 females: 90.8 (2007); Marriage status: 21.6% never married, 54.7% now married, 11.2% widowed, 12.5% divorced (2000); Foreign born: 0.9% (2000); Ancestry (includes multiple ancestries): 43.1% German, 10.6% United States or American, 10.2% Irish, 9.9% English, 6.9% Other groups (2000).

Economy: Single-family building permits issued: 19 (2007); Multi-family building permits issued: 0 (2007); Employment by occupation: 9.5% management, 12.2% professional, 18.5% services, 23.1% sales, 0.3% farming, 10.7% construction, 25.8% production (2000).

Income: Per capita income: $21,919 (2007); Median household income: $42,490 (2007); Average household income: $52,876 (2007); Percent of households with income of $100,000 or more: 8.9% (2007); Poverty rate: 8.9% (2000).

Education: Percent of population age 25 and over with: High school diploma (including GED) or higher: 83.2% (2007); Bachelor's degree or higher: 12.7% (2007); Master's degree or higher: 4.2% (2007).

School District(s)

Auglaize County Ed. Srv. Ctr.
2005-06 Enrollment: n/a . . . . (419) 738-3422
Wapakoneta City (PK-12)
2005-06 Enrollment: 3,105 . . . . (419) 739-2900

Housing: Homeownership rate: 69.8% (2007); Median home value: $94,855 (2007); Median rent: $349 per month (2000); Median age of housing: 41 years (2000).

Safety: Violent crime rate: 8.3 per 10,000 population; Property crime rate: 254.6 per 10,000 population (2007).

Newspapers: East Merchandiser (Community news; Circulation 6,792); Shelby County Review (Community news; Circulation 9,268); Wapakoneta Daily News (Local news; Circulation 5,300)

Transportation: Commute to work: 94.9% car, 0.1% public transportation, 2.2% walk, 1.8% work from home (2000); Travel time to work: 49.6% less than 15 minutes, 30.9% 15 to 30 minutes, 15.2% 30 to 45 minutes, 2.5% 45 to 60 minutes, 1.8% 60 minutes or more (2000)

Airports: Neil Armstrong (general aviation)

Additional Information Contacts

Wapakoneta Area Chamber of Commerce . . . . (419) 738-2911
http://www.wapakoneta.com/p2_commerce/p2_commerce.html

WAYNESFIELD (village). Covers a land area of 0.706 square miles and a water area of 0 square miles. Located at 40.60° N. Lat.; 83.97° W. Long. Elevation is 1,063 feet.

Population: 851 (1990); 803 (2000); 716 (2007); 721 (2012 projected); Race: 96.8% White, 0.0% Black, 0.0% Asian, 1.8% Hispanic of any race (2007); Density: 1,014.2 persons per square mile (2007); Average household size: 2.56 (2007); Median age: 34.2 (2007); Males per 100 females: 95.6 (2007); Marriage status: 17.9% never married, 62.3% now married, 8.2% widowed, 11.6% divorced (2000); Foreign born: 0.5% (2000); Ancestry (includes multiple ancestries): 32.1% German, 14.4% United States or American, 13.3% Irish, 10.2% English, 5.6% Other groups (2000).

Economy: Employment by occupation: 11.5% management, 6.8% professional, 19.7% services, 27.1% sales, 0.0% farming, 9.1% construction, 25.9% production (2000).

Income: Per capita income: $16,693 (2007); Median household income: $34,038 (2007); Average household income: $42,688 (2007); Percent of households with income of $100,000 or more: 6.1% (2007); Poverty rate: 10.6% (2000).

Education: Percent of population age 25 and over with: High school diploma (including GED) or higher: 84.0% (2007); Bachelor's degree or higher: 4.9% (2007); Master's degree or higher: 1.6% (2007).

School District(s)

Waynesfield-Goshen Local (PK-12)
2005-06 Enrollment: 637 . . . . (419) 568-2391

Housing: Homeownership rate: 80.7% (2007); Median home value: $81,000 (2007); Median rent: $333 per month (2000); Median age of housing: 47 years (2000).

Transportation: Commute to work: 92.0% car, 0.0% public transportation, 3.8% walk, 4.1% work from home (2000); Travel time to work: 23.1% less than 15 minutes, 36.0% 15 to 30 minutes, 28.6% 30 to 45 minutes, 6.8% 45 to 60 minutes, 5.5% 60 minutes or more (2000)

Belmont County

Located in eastern Ohio; bounded on the east by the Ohio River and the West Virginia border. Covers a land area of 537.35 square miles, a water area of 4.04 square miles, and is located in the Eastern Time Zone. The county was founded in 1801. County seat is St. Clairsville.

Belmont County is part of the Wheeling, WV-OH Metropolitan Statistical Area. The entire metro area includes: Belmont County, OH; Marshall County, WV; Ohio County, WV

Weather Station: Barnesville Elevation: 1,240 feet

	Jan	Feb	Mar	Apr	May	Jun	Jul	Aug	Sep	Oct	Nov	Dec
High	35	38	49	60	70	78	82	81	75	63	51	40
Low	17	19	28	37	47	56	61	59	52	40	32	24
Precip	3.0	2.7	3.5	3.9	4.4	4.9	4.7	3.9	3.5	3.0	3.7	3.2
Snow	11.6	7.6	5.1	1.2	tr	0.0	0.0	tr	0.0	tr	1.7	5.7

High and Low temperatures in degrees Fahrenheit; Precipitation and Snow in inches

Population: 71,074 (1990); 70,226 (2000); 68,969 (2007); 67,870 (2012 projected); Race: 94.3% White, 4.3% Black, 0.4% Asian, 0.6% Hispanic of any race (2007); Density: 128.4 persons per square mile (2007); Average household size: 2.44 (2007); Median age: 42.5 (2007); Males per 100 females: 98.4 (2007).

Religion: Five largest groups: 13.1% Catholic Church, 10.1% The United Methodist Church, 4.9% Presbyterian Church (U.S.A.), 3.0% Christian Churches and Churches of Christ, 2.0% Churches of Christ (2000).

Economy: Unemployment rate: 6.2% (6/2008); Total civilian labor force: 33,189 (6/2008); Leading industries: 23.7% retail trade; 20.7% health care and social assistance; 12.4% accommodation & food services (2005); Farms: 753 totaling 141,908 acres (2002); Companies that employ 500 or more persons: 2 (2006); Companies that employ 100 to 499 persons: 32 (2006); Companies that employ less than 100 persons: 1,540 (2006); Black-owned businesses: n/a (2002); Hispanic-owned businesses: n/a (2002); Asian-owned businesses: n/a (2002); Women-owned businesses: 937 (2002); Retail sales per capita: $17,128 (2008). Single-family building permits issued: 18 (2007); Multi-family building permits issued: 44 (2007).

Income: Per capita income: $19,617 (2007); Median household income: $35,570 (2007); Average household income: $46,690 (2007); Percent of households with income of $100,000 or more: 7.5% (2007); Poverty rate: 16.1% (2005); Bankruptcy rate: 4.15% (2007).

Taxes: Total county taxes per capita: $362 (2006); County property taxes per capita: $168 (2006).

Education: Percent of population age 25 and over with: High school diploma (including GED) or higher: 80.9% (2007); Bachelor's degree or higher: 11.2% (2007); Master's degree or higher: 4.1% (2007).

Housing: Homeownership rate: 75.2% (2007); Median home value: $79,251 (2007); Median rent: $280 per month (2000); Median age of housing: 46 years (2000).

Health: Birth rate: 107.4 per 10,000 population (2007); Death rate: 129.3 per 10,000 population (2007); Age-adjusted cancer mortality rate: 236.6 deaths per 100,000 population (2005); Air Quality Index: 100.0% good, 0.0% moderate, 0.0% unhealthy for sensitive individuals, 0.0% unhealthy (percent of days in 2007); Number of physicians: 13.8 per 10,000 population (2005); Hospital beds: 52.6 per 10,000 population (2004); Hospital admissions: 1,434.6 per 10,000 population (2004).

Elections: 2004 Presidential election results: 46.8% Bush, 52.7% Kerry, 0.0% Nader, 0.3% Badnarik

National and State Parks: Belmont Lake State Reserve

Additional Information Contacts

Belmont County Government. . . . . (740) 699-2155
http://www.belmontcountyohio.org
Barnesville Area Chamber of Commerce . . . . (740) 425-4300
http://www.barnesvilleohio.com/chamber.htm
Bellaire City Chamber of Commerce . . . . (740) 676-9723
http://www.bellairechamber.com
City of Saint Clairsville . . . . (740) 695-1410
http://www.stclairsville.com
Martins Ferry Area Chamber of Commerce. . . . . (740) 633-2565
http://www.martinsferrychamber.com
Saint Clairsville Chamber of Commerce . . . . (740) 695-9623
http://www.stcchamber.com

Belmont County Communities

ALLEDONIA (unincorporated postal area, zip code 43902). Covers a land area of 7.818 square miles and a water area of 0 square miles. Located at 39.89° N. Lat.; 80.97° W. Long. Elevation is 830 feet.

Population: 212 (2000); Race: 100.0% White, 0.0% Black, 0.0% Asian, 0.0% Hispanic of any race (2000); Density: 27.1 persons per square mile (2000); Age: 25.3% under 18, 11.8% over 64 (2000); Marriage status: 17.2% never married, 65.5% now married, 3.4% widowed, 13.8% divorced (2000); Foreign born: 0.0% (2000); Ancestry (includes multiple ancestries): 29.8% English, 10.7% Czech, 9.0% United States or American, 5.1% Polish, 5.1% German (2000).

Economy: Employment by occupation: 5.1% management, 15.4% professional, 0.0% services, 10.3% sales, 0.0% farming, 28.2% construction, 41.0% production (2000).

Income: Per capita income: $16,104 (2000); Median household income: $52,692 (2000); Poverty rate: 20.5% (2000).

Education: Percent of population age 25 and over with: High school diploma (including GED) or higher: 100.0% (2000); Bachelor's degree or higher: 12.7% (2000).

Housing: Homeownership rate: 100.0% (2000); Median home value: $74,200 (2000); Median rent: $n/a per month (2000); Median age of housing: 48 years (2000).

Transportation: Commute to work: 94.9% car, 0.0% public transportation, 0.0% walk, 5.1% work from home (2000); Travel time to work: 0.0% less than 15 minutes, 33.8% 15 to 30 minutes, 25.7% 30 to 45 minutes, 17.6% 45 to 60 minutes, 23.0% 60 minutes or more (2000)

BARNESVILLE (village). Covers a land area of 1.923 square miles and a water area of 0.005 square miles. Located at 39.98° N. Lat.; 81.17° W. Long. Elevation is 1,270 feet.

Population: 4,350 (1990); 4,225 (2000); 4,093 (2007); 4,023 (2012 projected); Race: 98.7% White, 0.5% Black, 0.2% Asian, 0.4% Hispanic of any race (2007); Density: 2,128.0 persons per square mile (2007); Average household size: 2.34 (2007); Median age: 40.5 (2007); Males per 100 females: 83.5 (2007); Marriage status: 25.3% never married, 49.0% now married, 16.3% widowed, 9.4% divorced (2000); Foreign born: 0.9% (2000); Ancestry (includes multiple ancestries): 18.4% German, 16.7% Irish, 15.7% English, 10.6% United States or American, 4.3% Other groups (2000).

Economy: Single-family building permits issued: 3 (2007); Multi-family building permits issued: 0 (2007); Employment by occupation: 6.0% management, 14.3% professional, 22.4% services, 22.9% sales, 0.9% farming, 12.5% construction, 21.1% production (2000).

Income: Per capita income: $16,576 (2007); Median household income: $28,837 (2007); Average household income: $37,747 (2007); Percent of households with income of $100,000 or more: 3.6% (2007); Poverty rate: 22.1% (2000).

Education: Percent of population age 25 and over with: High school diploma (including GED) or higher: 77.9% (2007); Bachelor's degree or higher: 6.6% (2007); Master's degree or higher: 3.3% (2007).

School District(s)

Barnesville Exempted Village (PK-12)
2005-06 Enrollment: 1,191 . . . . (740) 425-3615

Housing: Homeownership rate: 70.0% (2007); Median home value: $64,612 (2007); Median rent: $218 per month (2000); Median age of housing: 58 years (2000).

Hospitals: Barnesville Hospital (25 beds)

Newspapers: Enterprise (Community news; Circulation 4,825)

Transportation: Commute to work: 89.1% car, 0.5% public transportation, 4.7% walk, 4.6% work from home (2000); Travel time to work: 43.3% less than 15 minutes, 21.4% 15 to 30 minutes, 23.5% 30 to 45 minutes, 4.9% 45 to 60 minutes, 6.9% 60 minutes or more (2000)

Additional Information Contacts

Barnesville Area Chamber of Commerce . . . . (740) 425-4300
http://www.barnesvilleohio.com/chamber.htm

BELLAIRE (village). Covers a land area of 1.759 square miles and a water area of 0.010 square miles. Located at 40.01° N. Lat.; 80.74° W. Long. Elevation is 666 feet.
History: Bellaire was named for the home of a Maryland settler who purchased part of the townsite in 1802. After 1900, coal mining and the manufacture of glass and enamel ware became the leading industries.
Population: 5,736 (1990); 4,892 (2000); 4,679 (2007); 4,511 (2012 projected); Race: 93.1% White, 4.9% Black, 0.2% Asian, 0.5% Hispanic of any race (2007); Density: 2,660.4 persons per square mile (2007); Average household size: 2.29 (2007); Median age: 40.6 (2007); Males per 100 females: 86.5 (2007); Marriage status: 27.2% never married, 45.9% now married, 14.4% widowed, 12.5% divorced (2000); Foreign born: 0.8% (2000); Ancestry (includes multiple ancestries): 20.1% Irish, 20.1% German, 12.9% Italian, 11.5% United States or American, 9.9% Other groups (2000).
Economy: Single-family building permits issued: 0 (2007); Multi-family building permits issued: 0 (2007); Employment by occupation: 7.8% management, 12.4% professional, 28.1% services, 25.4% sales, 0.0% farming, 7.9% construction, 18.4% production (2000).
Income: Per capita income: $14,086 (2007); Median household income: $20,842 (2007); Average household income: $31,641 (2007); Percent of households with income of $100,000 or more: 3.5% (2007); Poverty rate: 27.1% (2000).
Education: Percent of population age 25 and over with: High school diploma (including GED) or higher: 74.0% (2007); Bachelor's degree or higher: 5.8% (2007); Master's degree or higher: 2.1% (2007).

School District(s)

Bellaire Local (PK-12)
2005-06 Enrollment: 1,504 . . . . (740) 676-1826
Housing: Homeownership rate: 55.9% (2007); Median home value: $51,994 (2007); Median rent: $259 per month (2000); Median age of housing: 58 years (2000).
Hospitals: Belmont Community Hospital (99 beds)
Safety: Violent crime rate: 25.7 per 10,000 population; Property crime rate: 109.1 per 10,000 population (2007).
Transportation: Commute to work: 91.9% car, 1.2% public transportation, 5.7% walk, 0.6% work from home (2000); Travel time to work: 41.7% less than 15 minutes, 43.3% 15 to 30 minutes, 8.6% 30 to 45 minutes, 2.3% 45 to 60 minutes, 4.2% 60 minutes or more (2000)

Additional Information Contacts

Bellaire City Chamber of Commerce . . . . (740) 676-9723
http://www.bellairechamber.com

BELMONT (village). Covers a land area of 0.282 square miles and a water area of 0 square miles. Located at 40.02° N. Lat.; 81.04° W. Long. Elevation is 1,191 feet.
Population: 471 (1990); 532 (2000); 507 (2007); 494 (2012 projected); Race: 95.9% White, 1.4% Black, 0.0% Asian, 1.2% Hispanic of any race (2007); Density: 1,798.0 persons per square mile (2007); Average household size: 2.50 (2007); Median age: 40.8 (2007); Males per 100 females: 102.0 (2007); Marriage status: 26.8% never married, 54.1% now married, 7.9% widowed, 11.2% divorced (2000); Foreign born: 0.0% (2000); Ancestry (includes multiple ancestries): 24.4% German, 15.7% United States or American, 13.2% Irish, 8.1% English, 5.0% Italian (2000).
Economy: Single-family building permits issued: 0 (2007); Multi-family building permits issued: 0 (2007); Employment by occupation: 5.8% management, 9.9% professional, 24.7% services, 25.5% sales, 1.2% farming, 11.5% construction, 21.4% production (2000).
Income: Per capita income: $17,249 (2007); Median household income: $34,821 (2007); Average household income: $43,079 (2007); Percent of households with income of $100,000 or more: 4.4% (2007); Poverty rate: 12.0% (2000).
Education: Percent of population age 25 and over with: High school diploma (including GED) or higher: 91.1% (2007); Bachelor's degree or higher: 4.9% (2007); Master's degree or higher: 0.9% (2007).

School District(s)

Union Local (PK-12)
2005-06 Enrollment: 1,480 . . . . (740) 695-5776
Housing: Homeownership rate: 79.3% (2007); Median home value: $56,346 (2007); Median rent: $239 per month (2000); Median age of housing: 60+ years (2000).
Transportation: Commute to work: 95.5% car, 0.0% public transportation, 1.7% walk, 1.7% work from home (2000); Travel time to work: 23.1% less than 15 minutes, 41.6% 15 to 30 minutes, 23.1% 30 to 45 minutes, 3.8% 45 to 60 minutes, 8.4% 60 minutes or more (2000)

BETHESDA (village). Covers a land area of 0.642 square miles and a water area of 0.012 square miles. Located at 40.01° N. Lat.; 81.07° W. Long. Elevation is 1,220 feet.
Population: 1,161 (1990); 1,413 (2000); 1,371 (2007); 1,326 (2012 projected); Race: 99.0% White, 0.1% Black, 0.0% Asian, 0.6% Hispanic of any race (2007); Density: 2,134.3 persons per square mile (2007); Average household size: 2.33 (2007); Median age: 36.3 (2007); Males per 100 females: 92.0 (2007); Marriage status: 22.0% never married, 55.7% now married, 9.0% widowed, 13.3% divorced (2000); Foreign born: 0.6% (2000); Ancestry (includes multiple ancestries): 24.3% German, 16.6% Irish, 12.6% English, 11.5% United States or American, 4.6% Polish (2000).
Economy: Single-family building permits issued: 2 (2007); Multi-family building permits issued: 0 (2007); Employment by occupation: 6.0% management, 12.6% professional, 23.8% services, 28.9% sales, 0.0% farming, 12.0% construction, 16.6% production (2000).
Income: Per capita income: $16,158 (2007); Median household income: $29,045 (2007); Average household income: $37,610 (2007); Percent of households with income of $100,000 or more: 3.1% (2007); Poverty rate: 18.5% (2000).
Education: Percent of population age 25 and over with: High school diploma (including GED) or higher: 81.6% (2007); Bachelor's degree or higher: 5.7% (2007); Master's degree or higher: 1.5% (2007).
Housing: Homeownership rate: 67.4% (2007); Median home value: $80,375 (2007); Median rent: $249 per month (2000); Median age of housing: 47 years (2000).
Transportation: Commute to work: 94.5% car, 0.6% public transportation, 1.7% walk, 1.4% work from home (2000); Travel time to work: 21.0% less than 15 minutes, 48.7% 15 to 30 minutes, 21.0% 30 to 45 minutes, 5.6% 45 to 60 minutes, 3.7% 60 minutes or more (2000)

BRIDGEPORT (village). Covers a land area of 1.393 square miles and a water area of 0 square miles. Located at 40.07° N. Lat.; 80.74° W. Long. Elevation is 656 feet.
History: Bridgeport was platted by Ebenezer Zane in 1806, when it was called Canton. The present name was given in 1836. An early boatbuilding industry was replaced by glass-making in the late 1800's.
Population: 2,318 (1990); 2,186 (2000); 2,088 (2007); 1,991 (2012 projected); Race: 92.3% White, 6.1% Black, 0.2% Asian, 0.6% Hispanic of any race (2007); Density: 1,498.6 persons per square mile (2007); Average household size: 2.20 (2007); Median age: 42.0 (2007); Males per 100 females: 90.5 (2007); Marriage status: 22.5% never married, 50.1% now married, 9.3% widowed, 18.2% divorced (2000); Foreign born: 0.2% (2000); Ancestry (includes multiple ancestries): 27.9% German, 24.9% Irish, 12.8% English, 11.7% Other groups, 7.5% Italian (2000).
Economy: Single-family building permits issued: 0 (2007); Multi-family building permits issued: 0 (2007); Employment by occupation: 5.4% management, 10.9% professional, 26.0% services, 31.5% sales, 0.0% farming, 11.6% construction, 14.7% production (2000).
Income: Per capita income: $18,455 (2007); Median household income: $31,698 (2007); Average household income: $40,347 (2007); Percent of households with income of $100,000 or more: 4.7% (2007); Poverty rate: 16.2% (2000).
Education: Percent of population age 25 and over with: High school diploma (including GED) or higher: 84.1% (2007); Bachelor's degree or higher: 10.6% (2007); Master's degree or higher: 3.7% (2007).

School District(s)

Bridgeport Exempted Village (PK-12)
2005-06 Enrollment: 745 . . . . (740) 635-1713
Housing: Homeownership rate: 64.5% (2007); Median home value: $50,221 (2007); Median rent: $260 per month (2000); Median age of housing: 59 years (2000).
Transportation: Commute to work: 94.3% car, 2.9% public transportation, 1.3% walk, 1.0% work from home (2000); Travel time to work: 48.8% less than 15 minutes, 36.9% 15 to 30 minutes, 10.2% 30 to 45 minutes, 0.8% 45 to 60 minutes, 3.3% 60 minutes or more (2000)

BROOKSIDE (village). Covers a land area of 0.173 square miles and a water area of 0 square miles. Located at 40.07° N. Lat.; 80.76° W. Long. Elevation is 659 feet.

History: Brookside was settled along Wheeling Creek, where grist mills, sawmills, and woolen mills were established. Later it became a coal mining town.
Population: 665 (1990); 644 (2000); 590 (2007); 571 (2012 projected); Race: 98.1% White, 1.5% Black, 0.0% Asian, 0.0% Hispanic of any race (2007); Density: 3,403.2 persons per square mile (2007); Average household size: 2.22 (2007); Median age: 45.4 (2007); Males per 100 females: 85.5 (2007); Marriage status: 19.7% never married, 59.8% now married, 10.2% widowed, 10.4% divorced (2000); Foreign born: 1.6% (2000); Ancestry (includes multiple ancestries): 31.4% German, 22.2% Irish, 15.2% Polish, 13.8% English, 9.3% Italian (2000).
Economy: Single-family building permits issued: 0 (2007); Multi-family building permits issued: 0 (2007); Employment by occupation: 10.5% management, 15.7% professional, 18.1% services, 33.4% sales, 0.0% farming, 9.9% construction, 12.3% production (2000).
Income: Per capita income: $21,780 (2007); Median household income: $40,526 (2007); Average household income: $48,308 (2007); Percent of households with income of $100,000 or more: 3.4% (2007); Poverty rate: 7.8% (2000).
Education: Percent of population age 25 and over with: High school diploma (including GED) or higher: 91.9% (2007); Bachelor's degree or higher: 13.5% (2007); Master's degree or higher: 3.2% (2007).
Housing: Homeownership rate: 79.7% (2007); Median home value: $80,278 (2007); Median rent: $352 per month (2000); Median age of housing: 56 years (2000).
Transportation: Commute to work: 93.1% car, 1.6% public transportation, 1.6% walk, 3.6% work from home (2000); Travel time to work: 40.3% less than 15 minutes, 46.8% 15 to 30 minutes, 7.5% 30 to 45 minutes, 1.7% 45 to 60 minutes, 3.7% 60 minutes or more (2000)

FLUSHING (village). Covers a land area of 0.604 square miles and a water area of 0 square miles. Located at 40.14° N. Lat.; 81.06° W. Long. Elevation is 1,283 feet.
Population: 1,042 (1990); 900 (2000); 813 (2007); 800 (2012 projected); Race: 99.0% White, 0.5% Black, 0.0% Asian, 0.0% Hispanic of any race (2007); Density: 1,346.9 persons per square mile (2007); Average household size: 2.32 (2007); Median age: 41.3 (2007); Males per 100 females: 97.3 (2007); Marriage status: 25.1% never married, 50.5% now married, 8.2% widowed, 16.1% divorced (2000); Foreign born: 0.6% (2000); Ancestry (includes multiple ancestries): 21.4% Irish, 18.9% German, 11.6% Italian, 10.3% English, 9.4% United States or American (2000).
Economy: Employment by occupation: 4.5% management, 11.0% professional, 19.5% services, 29.4% sales, 0.0% farming, 13.2% construction, 22.4% production (2000).
Income: Per capita income: $18,954 (2007); Median household income: $34,545 (2007); Average household income: $44,029 (2007); Percent of households with income of $100,000 or more: 7.1% (2007); Poverty rate: 17.4% (2000).
Education: Percent of population age 25 and over with: High school diploma (including GED) or higher: 80.4% (2007); Bachelor's degree or higher: 7.6% (2007); Master's degree or higher: 2.3% (2007).
Housing: Homeownership rate: 76.9% (2007); Median home value: $63,875 (2007); Median rent: $269 per month (2000); Median age of housing: 58 years (2000).
Transportation: Commute to work: 95.1% car, 0.0% public transportation, 2.6% walk, 1.8% work from home (2000); Travel time to work: 20.5% less than 15 minutes, 52.5% 15 to 30 minutes, 14.4% 30 to 45 minutes, 8.1% 45 to 60 minutes, 4.5% 60 minutes or more (2000)

HOLLOWAY (village). Covers a land area of 0.870 square miles and a water area of 0 square miles. Located at 40.16° N. Lat.; 81.13° W. Long. Elevation is 915 feet.
Population: 349 (1990); 345 (2000); 372 (2007); 376 (2012 projected); Race: 98.9% White, 0.0% Black, 0.0% Asian, 0.0% Hispanic of any race (2007); Density: 427.6 persons per square mile (2007); Average household size: 2.42 (2007); Median age: 38.6 (2007); Males per 100 females: 110.2 (2007); Marriage status: 22.6% never married, 54.7% now married, 10.8% widowed, 11.8% divorced (2000); Foreign born: 2.9% (2000); Ancestry (includes multiple ancestries): 18.3% Irish, 14.6% German, 12.3% Italian, 10.0% Other groups, 9.5% English (2000).
Economy: Single-family building permits issued: 0 (2007); Multi-family building permits issued: 0 (2007); Employment by occupation: 7.4% management, 3.3% professional, 22.1% services, 19.7% sales, 0.0% farming, 18.0% construction, 29.5% production (2000).
Income: Per capita income: $14,657 (2007); Median household income: $30,952 (2007); Average household income: $35,406 (2007); Percent of households with income of $100,000 or more: 2.6% (2007); Poverty rate: 20.3% (2000).
Education: Percent of population age 25 and over with: High school diploma (including GED) or higher: 76.7% (2007); Bachelor's degree or higher: 3.5% (2007); Master's degree or higher: 0.4% (2007).
Housing: Homeownership rate: 87.7% (2007); Median home value: $36,591 (2007); Median rent: $255 per month (2000); Median age of housing: 60+ years (2000).
Transportation: Commute to work: 95.9% car, 0.0% public transportation, 0.8% walk, 1.6% work from home (2000); Travel time to work: 15.0% less than 15 minutes, 24.2% 15 to 30 minutes, 20.0% 30 to 45 minutes, 15.8% 45 to 60 minutes, 25.0% 60 minutes or more (2000)

JACOBSBURG (unincorporated postal area, zip code 43933). Covers a land area of 54.419 square miles and a water area of 0.110 square miles. Located at 39.93° N. Lat.; 80.89° W. Long. Elevation is 1,300 feet.
Population: 1,744 (2000); Race: 98.2% White, 0.8% Black, 0.0% Asian, 0.3% Hispanic of any race (2000); Density: 32.0 persons per square mile (2000); Age: 24.0% under 18, 17.4% over 64 (2000); Marriage status: 19.1% never married, 68.9% now married, 7.4% widowed, 4.6% divorced (2000); Foreign born: 1.0% (2000); Ancestry (includes multiple ancestries): 24.3% German, 12.8% Irish, 12.3% English, 9.1% United States or American, 7.3% Other groups (2000).
Economy: Employment by occupation: 5.0% management, 9.9% professional, 14.9% services, 25.2% sales, 1.9% farming, 17.6% construction, 25.6% production (2000).
Income: Per capita income: $14,331 (2000); Median household income: $31,205 (2000); Poverty rate: 12.8% (2000).
Education: Percent of population age 25 and over with: High school diploma (including GED) or higher: 82.4% (2000); Bachelor's degree or higher: 6.7% (2000).
Housing: Homeownership rate: 86.4% (2000); Median home value: $60,200 (2000); Median rent: $215 per month (2000); Median age of housing: 41 years (2000).
Transportation: Commute to work: 89.3% car, 2.0% public transportation, 1.4% walk, 7.3% work from home (2000); Travel time to work: 10.8% less than 15 minutes, 43.8% 15 to 30 minutes, 24.4% 30 to 45 minutes, 14.6% 45 to 60 minutes, 6.4% 60 minutes or more (2000)

MARTINS FERRY (city). Covers a land area of 2.160 square miles and a water area of 0 square miles. Located at 40.09° N. Lat.; 80.72° W. Long. Elevation is 709 feet.
History: The settlement that formed here in the 1780's was known as Norristown. In 1795 Absalom Martin laid out a town that he called Jefferson, but he later voided his town plat when he failed to get the county seat. Settlers continued to come, and in 1835 Absalom's son, Ebenezer Martin, replatted the town and named it Martinsville. Because Martin owned the ferry, the town became known as Martins Ferry. Writer William Dean Howells was born here in 1837.
Population: 8,085 (1990); 7,226 (2000); 6,848 (2007); 6,554 (2012 projected); Race: 93.5% White, 4.8% Black, 0.0% Asian, 0.9% Hispanic of any race (2007); Density: 3,170.2 persons per square mile (2007); Average household size: 2.21 (2007); Median age: 43.0 (2007); Males per 100 females: 85.8 (2007); Marriage status: 23.0% never married, 51.0% now married, 13.0% widowed, 13.0% divorced (2000); Foreign born: 0.6% (2000); Ancestry (includes multiple ancestries): 26.7% German, 17.9% Irish, 12.7% Polish, 8.1% English, 8.0% Italian (2000).
Economy: Single-family building permits issued: 3 (2007); Multi-family building permits issued: 0 (2007); Employment by occupation: 9.1% management, 12.2% professional, 20.3% services, 31.0% sales, 0.2% farming, 8.2% construction, 19.1% production (2000).
Income: Per capita income: $18,150 (2007); Median household income: $26,770 (2007); Average household income: $39,970 (2007); Percent of households with income of $100,000 or more: 5.0% (2007); Poverty rate: 18.3% (2000).
Taxes: Total city taxes per capita: $227 (2006); City property taxes per capita: $64 (2006).
Education: Percent of population age 25 and over with: High school diploma (including GED) or higher: 80.2% (2007); Bachelor's degree or higher: 10.7% (2007); Master's degree or higher: 3.0% (2007).

School District(s)

Martins Ferry City (PK-12)
2005-06 Enrollment: 1,565 . . . . (740) 633-1732

Housing: Homeownership rate: 62.1% (2007); Median home value: $65,313 (2007); Median rent: $271 per month (2000); Median age of housing: 58 years (2000).

Newspapers: The Times Leader (Martins Ferry, OH) (Local news; Circulation 20,221)

Transportation: Commute to work: 90.2% car, 1.1% public transportation, 5.2% walk, 2.4% work from home (2000); Travel time to work: 41.3% less than 15 minutes, 41.6% 15 to 30 minutes, 9.7% 30 to 45 minutes, 3.2% 45 to 60 minutes, 4.2% 60 minutes or more (2000)

Additional Information Contacts

Martins Ferry Area Chamber of Commerce. . . . . (740) 633-2565
http://www.martinsferrychamber.com

MORRISTOWN (village). Covers a land area of 0.505 square miles and a water area of 0 square miles. Located at 40.06° N. Lat.; 81.07° W. Long. Elevation is 1,266 feet.

History: Morristown was laid out in 1802 and served as a toll station on the National Road.

Population: 296 (1990); 299 (2000); 273 (2007); 263 (2012 projected); Race: 99.3% White, 0.4% Black, 0.0% Asian, 2.9% Hispanic of any race (2007); Density: 540.4 persons per square mile (2007); Average household size: 2.39 (2007); Median age: 41.6 (2007); Males per 100 females: 92.3 (2007); Marriage status: 27.4% never married, 58.5% now married, 8.9% widowed, 5.2% divorced (2000); Foreign born: 1.0% (2000); Ancestry (includes multiple ancestries): 16.1% Irish, 16.1% German, 11.5% English, 9.2% Polish, 8.5% Other groups (2000).

Economy: Employment by occupation: 10.9% management, 17.0% professional, 16.3% services, 30.6% sales, 0.0% farming, 10.9% construction, 14.3% production (2000).

Income: Per capita income: $20,110 (2007); Median household income: $45,000 (2007); Average household income: $48,158 (2007); Percent of households with income of $100,000 or more: 1.8% (2007); Poverty rate: 7.2% (2000).

Education: Percent of population age 25 and over with: High school diploma (including GED) or higher: 85.9% (2007); Bachelor's degree or higher: 14.6% (2007); Master's degree or higher: 1.6% (2007).

Housing: Homeownership rate: 78.9% (2007); Median home value: $85,385 (2007); Median rent: $375 per month (2000); Median age of housing: 60+ years (2000).

Transportation: Commute to work: 93.2% car, 0.0% public transportation, 0.0% walk, 4.1% work from home (2000); Travel time to work: 44.7% less than 15 minutes, 20.6% 15 to 30 minutes, 14.9% 30 to 45 minutes, 9.2% 45 to 60 minutes, 10.6% 60 minutes or more (2000)

NEFFS (CDP). Covers a land area of 4.010 square miles and a water area of 0 square miles. Located at 40.02° N. Lat.; 80.81° W. Long. Elevation is 735 feet.

Population: 1,320 (1990); 1,138 (2000); 984 (2007); 971 (2012 projected); Race: 99.0% White, 0.4% Black, 0.0% Asian, 0.2% Hispanic of any race (2007); Density: 245.4 persons per square mile (2007); Average household size: 2.48 (2007); Median age: 42.9 (2007); Males per 100 females: 99.2 (2007); Marriage status: 18.4% never married, 65.5% now married, 9.4% widowed, 6.8% divorced (2000); Foreign born: 0.0% (2000); Ancestry (includes multiple ancestries): 31.1% Irish, 26.7% German, 19.2% Polish, 9.9% English, 7.3% United States or American (2000).

Economy: Employment by occupation: 14.8% management, 7.0% professional, 21.4% services, 27.5% sales, 0.0% farming, 7.4% construction, 21.8% production (2000).

Income: Per capita income: $18,089 (2007); Median household income: $31,029 (2007); Average household income: $44,836 (2007); Percent of households with income of $100,000 or more: 7.3% (2007); Poverty rate: 13.8% (2000).

Education: Percent of population age 25 and over with: High school diploma (including GED) or higher: 70.6% (2007); Bachelor's degree or higher: 2.5% (2007); Master's degree or higher: 0.0% (2007).

Housing: Homeownership rate: 85.1% (2007); Median home value: $61,724 (2007); Median rent: $237 per month (2000); Median age of housing: 60+ years (2000).

Transportation: Commute to work: 97.1% car, 0.0% public transportation, 2.9% walk, 0.0% work from home (2000); Travel time to work: 10.7% less than 15 minutes, 77.0% 15 to 30 minutes, 5.7% 30 to 45 minutes, 2.5% 45 to 60 minutes, 4.1% 60 minutes or more (2000)

POWHATAN POINT (village). Aka Powhatan. Covers a land area of 1.557 square miles and a water area of 0.150 square miles. Located at 39.86° N. Lat.; 80.80° W. Long. Elevation is 682 feet.

History: Powhatan Point was established in the 1820's along the Ohio River. A coal boom during the 1920's brought growth to the town.

Population: 1,807 (1990); 1,744 (2000); 1,647 (2007); 1,596 (2012 projected); Race: 98.6% White, 0.3% Black, 0.0% Asian, 0.3% Hispanic of any race (2007); Density: 1,057.5 persons per square mile (2007); Average household size: 2.24 (2007); Median age: 42.1 (2007); Males per 100 females: 92.4 (2007); Marriage status: 18.1% never married, 62.5% now married, 10.3% widowed, 9.0% divorced (2000); Foreign born: 0.8% (2000); Ancestry (includes multiple ancestries): 18.5% German, 15.6% Irish, 11.5% United States or American, 10.9% English, 7.4% Polish (2000).

Economy: Single-family building permits issued: 0 (2007); Multi-family building permits issued: 0 (2007); Employment by occupation: 5.9% management, 15.7% professional, 19.4% services, 24.2% sales, 0.0% farming, 15.2% construction, 19.6% production (2000).

Income: Per capita income: $18,786 (2007); Median household income: $30,461 (2007); Average household income: $42,095 (2007); Percent of households with income of $100,000 or more: 7.9% (2007); Poverty rate: 19.8% (2000).

Education: Percent of population age 25 and over with: High school diploma (including GED) or higher: 75.7% (2007); Bachelor's degree or higher: 7.4% (2007); Master's degree or higher: 2.8% (2007).

School District(s)

Switzerland of Ohio Local (PK-12)
2005-06 Enrollment: 2,692 . . . . (740) 472-5801

Housing: Homeownership rate: 71.7% (2007); Median home value: $65,816 (2007); Median rent: $258 per month (2000); Median age of housing: 48 years (2000).

Transportation: Commute to work: 96.5% car, 0.0% public transportation, 1.4% walk, 0.5% work from home (2000); Travel time to work: 23.2% less than 15 minutes, 37.1% 15 to 30 minutes, 24.8% 30 to 45 minutes, 7.3% 45 to 60 minutes, 7.6% 60 minutes or more (2000)

SAINT CLAIRSVILLE (city). County seat. Covers a land area of 2.148 square miles and a water area of 0 square miles. Located at 40.07° N. Lat.; 80.90° W. Long. Elevation is 1,273 feet.

History: St. Clairsville was named for Arthur St. Clair, first governor of the Northwest Territory. It became the seat of Belmont County in 1804.

Population: 5,456 (1990); 5,057 (2000); 5,018 (2007); 5,010 (2012 projected); Race: 94.7% White, 2.3% Black, 1.9% Asian, 0.6% Hispanic of any race (2007); Density: 2,336.0 persons per square mile (2007); Average household size: 2.19 (2007); Median age: 48.2 (2007); Males per 100 females: 83.6 (2007); Marriage status: 16.2% never married, 63.1% now married, 11.9% widowed, 8.8% divorced (2000); Foreign born: 2.9% (2000); Ancestry (includes multiple ancestries): 28.1% German, 14.0% Irish, 13.8% English, 12.9% Italian, 11.3% Polish (2000).

Economy: Single-family building permits issued: 9 (2007); Multi-family building permits issued: 2 (2007); Employment by occupation: 16.3% management, 27.2% professional, 14.0% services, 27.9% sales, 0.0% farming, 6.4% construction, 8.1% production (2000).

Income: Per capita income: $28,553 (2007); Median household income: $42,720 (2007); Average household income: $61,910 (2007); Percent of households with income of $100,000 or more: 12.8% (2007); Poverty rate: 6.7% (2000).

Education: Percent of population age 25 and over with: High school diploma (including GED) or higher: 88.3% (2007); Bachelor's degree or higher: 28.8% (2007); Master's degree or higher: 12.5% (2007).

School District(s)

Belmont-Harrison (09-12)
2005-06 Enrollment: n/a . . . . (740) 695-9130

St Clairsville-Richland City (PK-12)
2005-06 Enrollment: 1,629 . . . . (740) 695-1624

Four-year College(s)

Ohio University-Eastern Campus (Public)
Fall 2007 Enrollment: 751 . . . . (740) 695-1720
2007-08 Tuition: In-state $4,395; Out-of-state $5,715

Two-year College(s)

Belmont Technical College (Public)
Fall 2007 Enrollment: 1,742. . . . . (740) 695-9500
2007-08 Tuition: In-state $4,295; Out-of-state $7,283

Housing: Homeownership rate: 71.5% (2007); Median home value: $123,787 (2007); Median rent: $392 per month (2000); Median age of housing: 36 years (2000).
Transportation: Commute to work: 94.8% car, 0.0% public transportation, 1.7% walk, 3.2% work from home (2000); Travel time to work: 42.6% less than 15 minutes, 37.2% 15 to 30 minutes, 8.8% 30 to 45 minutes, 4.4% 45 to 60 minutes, 7.0% 60 minutes or more (2000)

Additional Information Contacts

City of Saint Clairsville . . . . (740) 695-1410
http://www.stclairsville.com
Saint Clairsville Chamber of Commerce . . . . (740) 695-9623
http://www.stcchamber.com

SHADYSIDE (village). Covers a land area of 0.956 square miles and a water area of 0.020 square miles. Located at 39.97° N. Lat.; 80.75° W. Long. Elevation is 689 feet.
History: Shadyside was platted in 1901. It developed as a residential town, with casket making as a primary industry.
Population: 3,867 (1990); 3,675 (2000); 3,537 (2007); 3,414 (2012 projected); Race: 99.3% White, 0.1% Black, 0.1% Asian, 0.3% Hispanic of any race (2007); Density: 3,700.2 persons per square mile (2007); Average household size: 2.09 (2007); Median age: 46.3 (2007); Males per 100 females: 88.3 (2007); Marriage status: 15.1% never married, 62.0% now married, 14.5% widowed, 8.4% divorced (2000); Foreign born: 1.8% (2000); Ancestry (includes multiple ancestries): 25.4% German, 19.9% Irish, 11.5% United States or American, 9.5% English, 9.3% Italian (2000).
Economy: Single-family building permits issued: 1 (2007); Multi-family building permits issued: 0 (2007); Employment by occupation: 8.5% management, 19.3% professional, 18.9% services, 25.2% sales, 0.0% farming, 10.8% construction, 17.3% production (2000).
Income: Per capita income: $20,459 (2007); Median household income: $34,560 (2007); Average household income: $42,718 (2007); Percent of households with income of $100,000 or more: 6.4% (2007); Poverty rate: 9.2% (2000).
Education: Percent of population age 25 and over with: High school diploma (including GED) or higher: 84.8% (2007); Bachelor's degree or higher: 13.5% (2007); Master's degree or higher: 4.8% (2007).

School District(s)

Shadyside Local (PK-12)
2005-06 Enrollment: 853 . . . . (740) 676-3121
Housing: Homeownership rate: 71.5% (2007); Median home value: $79,744 (2007); Median rent: $355 per month (2000); Median age of housing: 53 years (2000).
Transportation: Commute to work: 93.8% car, 1.9% public transportation, 1.9% walk, 2.4% work from home (2000); Travel time to work: 41.2% less than 15 minutes, 37.7% 15 to 30 minutes, 10.8% 30 to 45 minutes, 3.2% 45 to 60 minutes, 7.1% 60 minutes or more (2000)

Brown County

Located in southwestern Ohio; bounded on the south by the Ohio River and the Kentucky border. Covers a land area of 491.76 square miles, a water area of 3.46 square miles, and is located in the Eastern Time Zone. The county was founded in 1817. County seat is Georgetown.

Brown County is part of the Cincinnati-Middletown, OH-KY-IN Metropolitan Statistical Area. The entire metro area includes: Dearborn County, IN; Franklin County, IN; Ohio County, IN; Boone County, KY; Bracken County, KY; Campbell County, KY; Gallatin County, KY; Grant County, KY; Kenton County, KY; Pendleton County, KY; Brown County, OH; Butler County, OH; Clermont County, OH; Hamilton County, OH; Warren County, OH

Weather Station: Ripley Exp. Farm — Elevation: 879 feet

	Jan	Feb	Mar	Apr	May	Jun	Jul	Aug	Sep	Oct	Nov	Dec
High	38	43	53	64	73	81	85	84	78	66	54	43
Low	20	23	31	41	51	60	64	62	54	42	34	25
Precip	2.8	2.8	4.1	4.2	5.0	4.5	4.6	4.1	3.3	3.1	3.4	3.6
Snow	7.5	5.6	4.1	0.5	tr	0.0	0.0	0.0	0.0	tr	0.9	2.9

High and Low temperatures in degrees Fahrenheit; Precipitation and Snow in inches

Population: 34,966 (1990); 42,285 (2000); 44,865 (2007); 46,407 (2012 projected); Race: 97.9% White, 1.0% Black, 0.2% Asian, 0.4% Hispanic of any race (2007); Density: 91.2 persons per square mile (2007); Average household size: 2.67 (2007); Median age: 37.4 (2007); Males per 100 females: 97.7 (2007).
Religion: Five largest groups: 6.6% Christian Churches and Churches of Christ, 6.5% Catholic Church, 6.1% Southern Baptist Convention, 3.2% The United Methodist Church, 1.5% Church of the Nazarene (2000).
Economy: Unemployment rate: 7.3% (6/2008); Total civilian labor force: 22,586 (6/2008); Leading industries: 22.2% health care and social assistance; 18.1% retail trade; 12.1% accommodation & food services (2005); Farms: 1,400 totaling 220,729 acres (2002); Companies that employ 500 or more persons: 0 (2006); Companies that employ 100 to 499 persons: 6 (2006); Companies that employ less than 100 persons: 581 (2006); Black-owned businesses: n/a (2002); Hispanic-owned businesses: n/a (2002); Asian-owned businesses: n/a (2002); Women-owned businesses: n/a (2002); Retail sales per capita: $6,642 (2008). Single-family building permits issued: 111 (2007); Multi-family building permits issued: 213 (2007).
Income: Per capita income: $20,470 (2007); Median household income: $44,762 (2007); Average household income: $54,231 (2007); Percent of households with income of $100,000 or more: 9.9% (2007); Poverty rate: 14.1% (2005); Bankruptcy rate: 4.23% (2007).
Taxes: Total county taxes per capita: $137 (2006); County property taxes per capita: $63 (2006).
Education: Percent of population age 25 and over with: High school diploma (including GED) or higher: 74.5% (2007); Bachelor's degree or higher: 8.7% (2007); Master's degree or higher: 3.2% (2007).
Housing: Homeownership rate: 79.7% (2007); Median home value: $110,505 (2007); Median rent: $331 per month (2000); Median age of housing: 24 years (2000).
Health: Birth rate: 133.5 per 10,000 population (2007); Death rate: 95.8 per 10,000 population (2007); Age-adjusted cancer mortality rate: 203.3 deaths per 100,000 population (2005); Number of physicians: 8.0 per 10,000 population (2005); Hospital beds: 13.5 per 10,000 population (2004); Hospital admissions: 421.1 per 10,000 population (2004).
Elections: 2004 Presidential election results: 63.6% Bush, 35.9% Kerry, 0.0% Nader, 0.3% Badnarik

Additional Information Contacts

Brown County Government . . . . (937) 378-3956
http://www.county.brown.oh.us

Brown County Communities

ABERDEEN (village). Covers a land area of 1.414 square miles and a water area of 0.284 square miles. Located at 38.66° N. Lat.; 83.76° W. Long. Elevation is 515 feet.
History: Aberdeen was the Ohio River terminus of Zane's Trace, and a ferry point for people and goods going across the river to Kentucky.
Population: 1,586 (1990); 1,603 (2000); 1,682 (2007); 1,733 (2012 projected); Race: 96.1% White, 2.1% Black, 0.2% Asian, 1.0% Hispanic of any race (2007); Density: 1,189.6 persons per square mile (2007); Average household size: 2.29 (2007); Median age: 38.0 (2007); Males per 100 females: 89.0 (2007); Marriage status: 20.4% never married, 49.9% now married, 10.2% widowed, 19.6% divorced (2000); Foreign born: 1.1% (2000); Ancestry (includes multiple ancestries): 34.0% United States or American, 13.6% German, 10.1% Irish, 7.0% English, 6.0% Other groups (2000).
Economy: Employment by occupation: 7.4% management, 12.3% professional, 16.1% services, 23.6% sales, 0.3% farming, 13.2% construction, 27.1% production (2000).
Income: Per capita income: $17,817 (2007); Median household income: $32,615 (2007); Average household income: $40,591 (2007); Percent of households with income of $100,000 or more: 4.8% (2007); Poverty rate: 21.9% (2000).
Education: Percent of population age 25 and over with: High school diploma (including GED) or higher: 75.6% (2007); Bachelor's degree or higher: 7.4% (2007); Master's degree or higher: 3.7% (2007).

School District(s)

Ripley-Union-Lewis-Huntington Local (PK-12)
2005-06 Enrollment: 1,338 . . . . (937) 392-4396
Housing: Homeownership rate: 60.5% (2007); Median home value: $85,800 (2007); Median rent: $305 per month (2000); Median age of housing: 22 years (2000).
Transportation: Commute to work: 93.6% car, 0.0% public transportation, 2.2% walk, 2.8% work from home (2000); Travel time to work: 44.1% less than 15 minutes, 32.4% 15 to 30 minutes, 6.7% 30 to 45 minutes, 3.1% 45 to 60 minutes, 13.6% 60 minutes or more (2000)

FAYETTEVILLE (village). Covers a land area of 0.501 square miles and a water area of 0 square miles. Located at 39.18° N. Lat.; 83.93° W. Long. Elevation is 948 feet.
History: Fayetteville was settled in 1811 and became a village in 1868. St. Aloysius Academy, a Catholic school for boys, was founded here in 1850.
Population: 433 (1990); 372 (2000); 346 (2007); 352 (2012 projected); Race: 99.1% White, 0.6% Black, 0.0% Asian, 0.0% Hispanic of any race (2007); Density: 690.5 persons per square mile (2007); Average household size: 2.54 (2007); Median age: 33.6 (2007); Males per 100 females: 101.2 (2007); Marriage status: 19.9% never married, 60.1% now married, 9.4% widowed, 10.5% divorced (2000); Foreign born: 0.0% (2000); Ancestry (includes multiple ancestries): 31.6% German, 25.9% Irish, 13.2% French (except Basque), 12.2% United States or American, 7.8% English (2000).
Economy: Single-family building permits issued: 0 (2007); Multi-family building permits issued: 0 (2007); Employment by occupation: 9.4% management, 12.3% professional, 7.6% services, 26.3% sales, 0.0% farming, 17.5% construction, 26.9% production (2000).
Income: Per capita income: $22,341 (2007); Median household income: $42,143 (2007); Average household income: $56,838 (2007); Percent of households with income of $100,000 or more: 12.5% (2007); Poverty rate: 8.5% (2000).
Education: Percent of population age 25 and over with: High school diploma (including GED) or higher: 77.4% (2007); Bachelor's degree or higher: 7.7% (2007); Master's degree or higher: 3.6% (2007).

School District(s)

Fayetteville-Perry Local (PK-12)
2005-06 Enrollment: 1,057 . . . . (513) 875-2423
Housing: Homeownership rate: 74.3% (2007); Median home value: $96,429 (2007); Median rent: $375 per month (2000); Median age of housing: 50 years (2000).
Transportation: Commute to work: 91.7% car, 1.2% public transportation, 4.1% walk, 3.0% work from home (2000); Travel time to work: 25.0% less than 15 minutes, 14.6% 15 to 30 minutes, 23.8% 30 to 45 minutes, 16.5% 45 to 60 minutes, 20.1% 60 minutes or more (2000)

GEORGETOWN (village). County seat. Covers a land area of 3.702 square miles and a water area of 0 square miles. Located at 38.86° N. Lat.; 83.90° W. Long. Elevation is 919 feet.
History: Georgetown was surveyed in 1819 and named for Georgetown, Kentucky. In the second half of the 1800's, the town was a distribution point for tobacco grown in the area.
Population: 3,925 (1990); 3,691 (2000); 3,783 (2007); 3,845 (2012 projected); Race: 96.7% White, 1.9% Black, 0.6% Asian, 0.3% Hispanic of any race (2007); Density: 1,021.9 persons per square mile (2007); Average household size: 2.31 (2007); Median age: 36.7 (2007); Males per 100 females: 86.2 (2007); Marriage status: 23.7% never married, 50.3% now married, 10.9% widowed, 15.2% divorced (2000); Foreign born: 0.0% (2000); Ancestry (includes multiple ancestries): 30.5% German, 15.0% Irish, 14.9% United States or American, 11.9% Other groups, 11.7% English (2000).
Economy: Employment by occupation: 7.7% management, 13.3% professional, 18.6% services, 23.8% sales, 1.1% farming, 12.5% construction, 23.0% production (2000).
Income: Per capita income: $20,961 (2007); Median household income: $34,218 (2007); Average household income: $47,117 (2007); Percent of households with income of $100,000 or more: 8.5% (2007); Poverty rate: 14.5% (2000).
Education: Percent of population age 25 and over with: High school diploma (including GED) or higher: 77.3% (2007); Bachelor's degree or higher: 12.1% (2007); Master's degree or higher: 4.3% (2007).

School District(s)

Georgetown Exempted Village (PK-12)
2005-06 Enrollment: 1,092 . . . . (937) 378-3730
Southern Hills (07-12)
2005-06 Enrollment: n/a . . . . (937) 378-6131
Housing: Homeownership rate: 63.3% (2007); Median home value: $97,391 (2007); Median rent: $323 per month (2000); Median age of housing: 38 years (2000).
Hospitals: Brown County General Hospital (127 beds)
Safety: Violent crime rate: 24.8 per 10,000 population; Property crime rate: 551.9 per 10,000 population (2007).
Newspapers: News Democrat (Community news; Circulation 16,900)
Transportation: Commute to work: 96.4% car, 0.0% public transportation, 1.6% walk, 2.0% work from home (2000); Travel time to work: 42.0% less than 15 minutes, 14.8% 15 to 30 minutes, 16.0% 30 to 45 minutes, 8.6% 45 to 60 minutes, 18.7% 60 minutes or more (2000)

HAMERSVILLE (village). Covers a land area of 0.374 square miles and a water area of 0 square miles. Located at 38.91° N. Lat.; 83.98° W. Long. Elevation is 968 feet.
Population: 586 (1990); 515 (2000); 532 (2007); 543 (2012 projected); Race: 99.6% White, 0.2% Black, 0.0% Asian, 0.0% Hispanic of any race (2007); Density: 1,422.0 persons per square mile (2007); Average household size: 2.83 (2007); Median age: 34.6 (2007); Males per 100 females: 92.8 (2007); Marriage status: 23.0% never married, 62.3% now married, 7.3% widowed, 7.3% divorced (2000); Foreign born: 0.4% (2000); Ancestry (includes multiple ancestries): 20.0% German, 18.5% Irish, 14.7% English, 12.3% United States or American, 9.7% Other groups (2000).
Economy: Employment by occupation: 8.4% management, 4.2% professional, 13.1% services, 19.4% sales, 0.8% farming, 14.3% construction, 39.7% production (2000).
Income: Per capita income: $17,538 (2007); Median household income: $40,333 (2007); Average household income: $49,628 (2007); Percent of households with income of $100,000 or more: 8.5% (2007); Poverty rate: 6.4% (2000).
Education: Percent of population age 25 and over with: High school diploma (including GED) or higher: 65.1% (2007); Bachelor's degree or higher: 5.7% (2007); Master's degree or higher: 2.0% (2007).

School District(s)

Western Brown Local (PK-12)
2005-06 Enrollment: 3,386 . . . . (937) 444-2044
Housing: Homeownership rate: 72.3% (2007); Median home value: $95,556 (2007); Median rent: $408 per month (2000); Median age of housing: 45 years (2000).
Transportation: Commute to work: 91.8% car, 0.9% public transportation, 3.4% walk, 3.0% work from home (2000); Travel time to work: 16.9% less than 15 minutes, 24.0% 15 to 30 minutes, 26.2% 30 to 45 minutes, 15.1% 45 to 60 minutes, 17.8% 60 minutes or more (2000)

HIGGINSPORT (village). Covers a land area of 0.223 square miles and a water area of <.001 square miles. Located at 38.79° N. Lat.; 83.96° W. Long. Elevation is 512 feet.
Population: 298 (1990); 291 (2000); 311 (2007); 322 (2012 projected); Race: 100.0% White, 0.0% Black, 0.0% Asian, 0.0% Hispanic of any race (2007); Density: 1,394.7 persons per square mile (2007); Average household size: 2.51 (2007); Median age: 41.1 (2007); Males per 100 females: 93.2 (2007); Marriage status: 19.4% never married, 64.0% now married, 5.8% widowed, 10.7% divorced (2000); Foreign born: 0.0% (2000); Ancestry (includes multiple ancestries): 30.5% German, 11.8% Irish, 9.5% Italian, 8.3% United States or American, 5.2% French (except Basque) (2000).
Economy: Employment by occupation: 5.6% management, 4.0% professional, 12.8% services, 27.2% sales, 0.0% farming, 12.8% construction, 37.6% production (2000).
Income: Per capita income: $16,479 (2007); Median household income: $37,500 (2007); Average household income: $41,331 (2007); Percent of households with income of $100,000 or more: 6.5% (2007); Poverty rate: 11.5% (2000).
Education: Percent of population age 25 and over with: High school diploma (including GED) or higher: 71.2% (2007); Bachelor's degree or higher: 4.2% (2007); Master's degree or higher: 1.9% (2007).
Housing: Homeownership rate: 75.0% (2007); Median home value: $84,500 (2007); Median rent: $360 per month (2000); Median age of housing: 60+ years (2000).
Transportation: Commute to work: 85.6% car, 0.0% public transportation, 7.2% walk, 0.0% work from home (2000); Travel time to work: 11.2% less than 15 minutes, 30.4% 15 to 30 minutes, 15.2% 30 to 45 minutes, 20.0% 45 to 60 minutes, 23.2% 60 minutes or more (2000)

MOUNT ORAB (village). Aka Mount Oreb. Covers a land area of 3.796 square miles and a water area of 0 square miles. Located at 39.03° N. Lat.; 83.92° W. Long. Elevation is 942 feet.
History: The name of Mount Orab was derived from the biblical Horeb.
Population: 2,055 (1990); 2,307 (2000); 2,691 (2007); 2,921 (2012 projected); Race: 99.0% White, 0.2% Black, 0.1% Asian, 0.1% Hispanic of any race (2007); Density: 708.9 persons per square mile (2007); Average household size: 2.59 (2007); Median age: 32.4 (2007); Males per 100 females: 88.3 (2007); Marriage status: 21.1% never married, 58.0% now married, 6.7% widowed, 14.2% divorced (2000); Foreign born: 0.5%

(2000); Ancestry (includes multiple ancestries): 19.7% German, 17.7% United States or American, 13.6% Irish, 8.1% Other groups, 6.9% English (2000).
Economy: Employment by occupation: 7.9% management, 11.0% professional, 16.6% services, 24.3% sales, 0.3% farming, 12.2% construction, 27.7% production (2000).
Income: Per capita income: $20,357 (2007); Median household income: $42,770 (2007); Average household income: $52,288 (2007); Percent of households with income of $100,000 or more: 9.8% (2007); Poverty rate: 14.6% (2000).
Taxes: Total city taxes per capita: $384 (2006); City property taxes per capita: $117 (2006).
Education: Percent of population age 25 and over with: High school diploma (including GED) or higher: 75.5% (2007); Bachelor's degree or higher: 9.0% (2007); Master's degree or higher: 3.9% (2007).

School District(s)

Western Brown Local (PK-12)
2005-06 Enrollment: 3,386 . . . . (937) 444-2044
Housing: Homeownership rate: 61.8% (2007); Median home value: $107,868 (2007); Median rent: $301 per month (2000); Median age of housing: 26 years (2000).
Safety: Violent crime rate: 6.9 per 10,000 population; Property crime rate: 204.1 per 10,000 population (2007).
Newspapers: Brown County Press (Local news; Circulation 15,750)
Transportation: Commute to work: 93.3% car, 0.6% public transportation, 1.5% walk, 2.9% work from home (2000); Travel time to work: 23.4% less than 15 minutes, 26.6% 15 to 30 minutes, 22.9% 30 to 45 minutes, 13.7% 45 to 60 minutes, 13.4% 60 minutes or more (2000)

RIPLEY (village). Covers a land area of 1.013 square miles and a water area of 0.065 square miles. Located at 38.73° N. Lat.; 83.84° W. Long. Elevation is 502 feet.
History: Ripley was laid out in 1812 by Colonel James Poage of Virginia. It was an early center for steamboat building, and for piano manufacturing. The 1937 flooding of the Ohio River ruined Ripley's wharf area. The Rankin House in Ripley was a station on the Underground Railroad.
Population: 1,867 (1990); 1,745 (2000); 1,816 (2007); 1,857 (2012 projected); Race: 90.4% White, 7.8% Black, 0.4% Asian, 0.5% Hispanic of any race (2007); Density: 1,792.2 persons per square mile (2007); Average household size: 2.33 (2007); Median age: 38.6 (2007); Males per 100 females: 86.6 (2007); Marriage status: 22.1% never married, 53.3% now married, 10.7% widowed, 13.9% divorced (2000); Foreign born: 0.2% (2000); Ancestry (includes multiple ancestries): 25.5% German, 16.7% United States or American, 11.8% Other groups, 11.4% English, 10.3% Irish (2000).
Economy: Employment by occupation: 7.4% management, 8.6% professional, 19.2% services, 27.4% sales, 0.6% farming, 8.3% construction, 28.4% production (2000).
Income: Per capita income: $18,778 (2007); Median household income: $36,193 (2007); Average household income: $43,662 (2007); Percent of households with income of $100,000 or more: 6.3% (2007); Poverty rate: 15.5% (2000).
Education: Percent of population age 25 and over with: High school diploma (including GED) or higher: 69.7% (2007); Bachelor's degree or higher: 6.7% (2007); Master's degree or higher: 3.0% (2007).

School District(s)

Ripley-Union-Lewis-Huntington Local (PK-12)
2005-06 Enrollment: 1,338 . . . . (937) 392-4396
Housing: Homeownership rate: 63.8% (2007); Median home value: $86,500 (2007); Median rent: $253 per month (2000); Median age of housing: 49 years (2000).
Newspapers: Ripley Bee (Community news; Circulation 2,100)
Transportation: Commute to work: 85.7% car, 1.0% public transportation, 8.0% walk, 4.6% work from home (2000); Travel time to work: 36.9% less than 15 minutes, 29.6% 15 to 30 minutes, 5.9% 30 to 45 minutes, 11.7% 45 to 60 minutes, 16.0% 60 minutes or more (2000)

RUSSELLVILLE (village). Covers a land area of 0.778 square miles and a water area of 0 square miles. Located at 38.86° N. Lat.; 83.78° W. Long. Elevation is 961 feet.
Population: 459 (1990); 453 (2000); 445 (2007); 442 (2012 projected); Race: 98.2% White, 1.6% Black, 0.0% Asian, 1.1% Hispanic of any race (2007); Density: 572.0 persons per square mile (2007); Average household size: 2.34 (2007); Median age: 37.7 (2007); Males per 100 females: 81.6 (2007); Marriage status: 18.4% never married, 58.5% now married, 13.0% widowed, 10.0% divorced (2000); Foreign born: 0.0% (2000); Ancestry (includes multiple ancestries): 23.2% German, 14.3% United States or American, 14.1% English, 9.6% Irish, 5.3% Other groups (2000).
Economy: Employment by occupation: 10.7% management, 16.5% professional, 12.1% services, 26.7% sales, 0.0% farming, 12.1% construction, 21.8% production (2000).
Income: Per capita income: $17,873 (2007); Median household income: $34,375 (2007); Average household income: $41,079 (2007); Percent of households with income of $100,000 or more: 3.7% (2007); Poverty rate: 7.0% (2000).
Education: Percent of population age 25 and over with: High school diploma (including GED) or higher: 71.8% (2007); Bachelor's degree or higher: 8.7% (2007); Master's degree or higher: 5.7% (2007).

School District(s)

Eastern Local (PK-12)
2005-06 Enrollment: 1,543 . . . . (937) 378-3981
Housing: Homeownership rate: 78.9% (2007); Median home value: $80,000 (2007); Median rent: $317 per month (2000); Median age of housing: 53 years (2000).
Transportation: Commute to work: 89.6% car, 1.0% public transportation, 5.0% walk, 4.5% work from home (2000); Travel time to work: 28.6% less than 15 minutes, 20.3% 15 to 30 minutes, 12.0% 30 to 45 minutes, 12.5% 45 to 60 minutes, 26.6% 60 minutes or more (2000)

SAINT MARTIN (village). Covers a land area of 1.162 square miles and a water area of 0 square miles. Located at 39.21° N. Lat.; 83.89° W. Long. Elevation is 978 feet.
Population: 141 (1990); 91 (2000); 78 (2007); 79 (2012 projected); Race: 100.0% White, 0.0% Black, 0.0% Asian, 1.3% Hispanic of any race (2007); Density: 67.1 persons per square mile (2007); Average household size: 2.79 (2007); Median age: 45.0 (2007); Males per 100 females: 90.2 (2007); Marriage status: 28.8% never married, 65.2% now married, 6.1% widowed, 0.0% divorced (2000); Foreign born: 2.3% (2000); Ancestry (includes multiple ancestries): 31.8% German, 22.7% United States or American, 10.2% English, 9.1% Irish, 5.7% Dutch (2000).
Economy: Employment by occupation: 11.1% management, 6.7% professional, 4.4% services, 55.6% sales, 0.0% farming, 2.2% construction, 20.0% production (2000).
Income: Per capita income: $28,173 (2007); Median household income: $75,000 (2007); Average household income: $78,482 (2007); Percent of households with income of $100,000 or more: 28.6% (2007); Poverty rate: 0.0% (2000).
Education: Percent of population age 25 and over with: High school diploma (including GED) or higher: 87.5% (2007); Bachelor's degree or higher: 21.4% (2007); Master's degree or higher: 14.3% (2007).

Two-year College(s)

Chatfield College (Private, Not-for-profit, Roman Catholic)
Fall 2007 Enrollment: 218 . . . . (513) 875-3344
2007-08 Tuition: In-state $7,715; Out-of-state $7,715
Housing: Homeownership rate: 96.4% (2007); Median home value: $181,250 (2007); Median rent: $375 per month (2000); Median age of housing: 30 years (2000).
Transportation: Commute to work: 80.0% car, 2.2% public transportation, 0.0% walk, 17.8% work from home (2000); Travel time to work: 13.5% less than 15 minutes, 35.1% 15 to 30 minutes, 18.9% 30 to 45 minutes, 16.2% 45 to 60 minutes, 16.2% 60 minutes or more (2000)

SARDINIA (village). Covers a land area of 0.641 square miles and a water area of 0 square miles. Located at 39.00° N. Lat.; 83.80° W. Long. Elevation is 958 feet.
Population: 906 (1990); 862 (2000); 796 (2007); 791 (2012 projected); Race: 98.9% White, 0.0% Black, 0.0% Asian, 0.9% Hispanic of any race (2007); Density: 1,240.9 persons per square mile (2007); Average household size: 2.58 (2007); Median age: 33.7 (2007); Males per 100 females: 90.0 (2007); Marriage status: 19.0% never married, 61.0% now married, 6.7% widowed, 13.3% divorced (2000); Foreign born: 0.4% (2000); Ancestry (includes multiple ancestries): 24.3% German, 15.6% United States or American, 12.5% English, 11.8% Irish, 7.0% Other groups (2000).
Economy: Employment by occupation: 3.6% management, 10.9% professional, 19.6% services, 21.5% sales, 0.0% farming, 18.4% construction, 26.0% production (2000).
Income: Per capita income: $14,959 (2007); Median household income: $33,173 (2007); Average household income: $37,176 (2007); Percent of

households with income of $100,000 or more: 2.3% (2007); Poverty rate: 20.1% (2000).
Education: Percent of population age 25 and over with: High school diploma (including GED) or higher: 70.0% (2007); Bachelor's degree or higher: 6.0% (2007); Master's degree or higher: 4.3% (2007).

School District(s)

Eastern Local (PK-12)
2005-06 Enrollment: 1,543 . . . . (937) 378-3981
Housing: Homeownership rate: 58.6% (2007); Median home value: $75,323 (2007); Median rent: $319 per month (2000); Median age of housing: 49 years (2000).
Transportation: Commute to work: 96.2% car, 0.0% public transportation, 2.5% walk, 1.3% work from home (2000); Travel time to work: 21.3% less than 15 minutes, 27.0% 15 to 30 minutes, 25.4% 30 to 45 minutes, 12.4% 45 to 60 minutes, 14.0% 60 minutes or more (2000)

Butler County

Located in southwestern Ohio; bounded on the west by Indiana; crossed by the Great Miami River. Covers a land area of 467.27 square miles, a water area of 2.93 square miles, and is located in the Eastern Time Zone. The county was founded in 1803. County seat is Hamilton.

Butler County is part of the Cincinnati-Middletown, OH-KY-IN Metropolitan Statistical Area. The entire metro area includes: Dearborn County, IN; Franklin County, IN; Ohio County, IN; Boone County, KY; Bracken County, KY; Campbell County, KY; Gallatin County, KY; Grant County, KY; Kenton County, KY; Pendleton County, KY; Brown County, OH; Butler County, OH; Clermont County, OH; Hamilton County, OH; Warren County, OH

Population: 291,479 (1990); 332,807 (2000); 355,739 (2007); 370,885 (2012 projected); Race: 88.5% White, 6.8% Black, 2.0% Asian, 2.3% Hispanic of any race (2007); Density: 761.3 persons per square mile (2007); Average household size: 2.66 (2007); Median age: 35.3 (2007); Males per 100 females: 96.1 (2007).
Religion: Five largest groups: 13.0% Catholic Church, 6.3% Southern Baptist Convention, 2.8% The United Methodist Church, 2.5% Church of God (Cleveland, Tennessee), 1.5% Presbyterian Church (U.S.A.) (2000).
Economy: Unemployment rate: 6.2% (6/2008); Total civilian labor force: 194,321 (6/2008); Leading industries: 15.4% manufacturing; 12.7% retail trade; 12.1% health care and social assistance (2005); Farms: 1,060 totaling 138,044 acres (2002); Companies that employ 500 or more persons: 16 (2006); Companies that employ 100 to 499 persons: 207 (2006); Companies that employ less than 100 persons: 6,921 (2006); Black-owned businesses: 434 (2002); Hispanic-owned businesses: 180 (2002); Asian-owned businesses: 455 (2002); Women-owned businesses: 5,515 (2002); Retail sales per capita: $10,401 (2008). Single-family building permits issued: 851 (2007); Multi-family building permits issued: 59 (2007).
Income: Per capita income: $25,737 (2007); Median household income: $54,702 (2007); Average household income: $67,790 (2007); Percent of households with income of $100,000 or more: 19.0% (2007); Poverty rate: 11.8% (2005); Bankruptcy rate: 3.84% (2007).
Taxes: Total county taxes per capita: $237 (2006); County property taxes per capita: $154 (2006).
Education: Percent of population age 25 and over with: High school diploma (including GED) or higher: 83.6% (2007); Bachelor's degree or higher: 23.7% (2007); Master's degree or higher: 8.2% (2007).
Housing: Homeownership rate: 72.2% (2007); Median home value: $147,858 (2007); Median rent: $463 per month (2000); Median age of housing: 28 years (2000).
Health: Birth rate: 144.2 per 10,000 population (2007); Death rate: 79.7 per 10,000 population (2007); Age-adjusted cancer mortality rate: 207.7 deaths per 100,000 population (2005); Air Quality Index: 66.8% good, 24.9% moderate, 7.4% unhealthy for sensitive individuals, 0.8% unhealthy (percent of days in 2007); Number of physicians: 13.1 per 10,000 population (2005); Hospital beds: 20.0 per 10,000 population (2004); Hospital admissions: 989.2 per 10,000 population (2004).
Elections: 2004 Presidential election results: 65.9% Bush, 33.7% Kerry, 0.0% Nader, 0.2% Badnarik

Additional Information Contacts

Butler County Government . . . . (513) 887-3247
http://www.butlercountyohio.org
City of Fairfield . . . . (513) 867-5300
http://www.fairfield-city.org
City of Hamilton . . . . (513) 785-7000
http://www.hamilton-city.org
City of Middletown . . . . (513) 425-7730
http://www.ci.middletown.oh.us
City of Monroe . . . . (513) 539-7374
http://www.monroeohio.org
City of Oxford . . . . (513) 524-5200
http://www.cityofoxford.org
City of Trenton . . . . (513) 988-6304
http://www.ci.trenton.oh.us
Fairfield Chamber of Commerce . . . . (513) 881-5500
http://www.fairfieldchamber.com
Greater Hamilton Chamber of Commerce . . . . (513) 844-1500
http://www.hamilton-ohio.com
Oxford Chamber of Commerce . . . . (513) 523-5200
http://www.oxfordchamber.org
Oxford Visitors & Convention Bureau . . . . (513) 523-8687
http://www.enjoyoxford.org
The Chamber of Commerce . . . . (513) 422-4551
http://www.thechamberofcommerce.org

Butler County Communities

BECKETT RIDGE (CDP). Covers a land area of 4.864 square miles and a water area of 0 square miles. Located at 39.34° N. Lat.; 84.43° W. Long. Elevation is 817 feet.
Population: 4,503 (1990); 8,663 (2000); 9,129 (2007); 9,488 (2012 projected); Race: 82.0% White, 8.0% Black, 8.1% Asian, 2.6% Hispanic of any race (2007); Density: 1,876.7 persons per square mile (2007); Average household size: 2.71 (2007); Median age: 36.2 (2007); Males per 100 females: 98.5 (2007); Marriage status: 19.2% never married, 69.0% now married, 2.3% widowed, 9.5% divorced (2000); Foreign born: 8.6% (2000); Ancestry (includes multiple ancestries): 33.6% German, 18.0% Irish, 14.1% Other groups, 13.0% English, 5.4% Italian (2000).
Economy: Employment by occupation: 26.7% management, 29.9% professional, 5.4% services, 29.9% sales, 0.0% farming, 2.4% construction, 5.6% production (2000).
Income: Per capita income: $37,101 (2007); Median household income: $82,254 (2007); Average household income: $100,384 (2007); Percent of households with income of $100,000 or more: 37.8% (2007); Poverty rate: 1.5% (2000).
Education: Percent of population age 25 and over with: High school diploma (including GED) or higher: 96.3% (2007); Bachelor's degree or higher: 54.3% (2007); Master's degree or higher: 21.1% (2007).
Housing: Homeownership rate: 83.8% (2007); Median home value: $198,558 (2007); Median rent: $884 per month (2000); Median age of housing: 9 years (2000).
Transportation: Commute to work: 96.0% car, 0.8% public transportation, 0.2% walk, 2.9% work from home (2000); Travel time to work: 20.0% less than 15 minutes, 47.4% 15 to 30 minutes, 23.6% 30 to 45 minutes, 7.2% 45 to 60 minutes, 1.8% 60 minutes or more (2000)

FAIRFIELD (city). Covers a land area of 20.990 square miles and a water area of 0.087 square miles. Located at 39.33° N. Lat.; 84.54° W. Long. Elevation is 591 feet.
Population: 40,084 (1990); 42,097 (2000); 42,217 (2007); 42,398 (2012 projected); Race: 85.4% White, 9.2% Black, 2.9% Asian, 2.4% Hispanic of any race (2007); Density: 2,011.3 persons per square mile (2007); Average household size: 2.43 (2007); Median age: 36.7 (2007); Males per 100 females: 95.4 (2007); Marriage status: 25.3% never married, 59.1% now married, 5.0% widowed, 10.6% divorced (2000); Foreign born: 3.6% (2000); Ancestry (includes multiple ancestries): 31.7% German, 14.4% Irish, 12.9% Other groups, 11.2% English, 9.0% United States or American (2000).
Economy: Unemployment rate: 5.3% (6/2008); Total civilian labor force: 25,459 (6/2008); Single-family building permits issued: 21 (2007); Multi-family building permits issued: 0 (2007); Employment by occupation: 15.9% management, 23.5% professional, 10.4% services, 30.6% sales, 0.1% farming, 7.1% construction, 12.4% production (2000).
Income: Per capita income: $27,458 (2007); Median household income: $55,571 (2007); Average household income: $66,476 (2007); Percent of households with income of $100,000 or more: 16.3% (2007); Poverty rate: 4.2% (2000).
Taxes: Total city taxes per capita: $642 (2006); City property taxes per capita: $125 (2006).

Education: Percent of population age 25 and over with: High school diploma (including GED) or higher: 89.2% (2007); Bachelor's degree or higher: 27.7% (2007); Master's degree or higher: 8.3% (2007).

School District(s)

Fairfield City (PK-12)
2005-06 Enrollment: 9,857 . . . . (513) 829-6300

Two-year College(s)

Moler-Pickens Beauty Academy (Private, For-profit)
Fall 2007 Enrollment: 143 . . . . (513) 874-5116
2007-08 Tuition: In-state $8,700; Out-of-state $8,700

Housing: Homeownership rate: 65.9% (2007); Median home value: $145,294 (2007); Median rent: $593 per month (2000); Median age of housing: 23 years (2000).
Hospitals: Mercy Hospital - Fairfield (167 beds)
Safety: Violent crime rate: 52.8 per 10,000 population; Property crime rate: 351.8 per 10,000 population (2007).
Newspapers: Fairfield Echo (Community news; Circulation 20,000)
Transportation: Commute to work: 95.7% car, 1.1% public transportation, 0.5% walk, 2.3% work from home (2000); Travel time to work: 27.1% less than 15 minutes, 43.9% 15 to 30 minutes, 20.5% 30 to 45 minutes, 6.1% 45 to 60 minutes, 2.4% 60 minutes or more (2000)

Additional Information Contacts

City of Fairfield . . . . (513) 867-5300
http://www.fairfield-city.org
Fairfield Chamber of Commerce . . . . (513) 881-5500
http://www.fairfieldchamber.com

HAMILTON (city). County seat. Covers a land area of 21.612 square miles and a water area of 0.465 square miles. Located at 39.39° N. Lat.; 84.56° W. Long. Elevation is 594 feet.
History: Settlement at Hamilton began in 1791 when General St. Clair built Fort Hamilton as a military and trading post. The town was platted in 1794 by Colonel Israel Ludlow, and named Fairfield, but the site was abandoned in 1796. When the plat was recorded in 1802, the town was named Hamilton for the fort, and became the seat of Butler County. In 1854 Rossville, settled in 1804 on the other side of the Great Miami River, became part of Hamilton. It was the Hamilton Hydraulic water-power plant completed in 1852 that changed Hamilton into an industrial center. A resident here at that time was William Dean Howells, who describes the city in "A Boy's Town."
Population: 61,618 (1990); 60,690 (2000); 62,285 (2007); 63,448 (2012 projected); Race: 86.6% White, 8.5% Black, 0.6% Asian, 4.2% Hispanic of any race (2007); Density: 2,882.0 persons per square mile (2007); Average household size: 2.45 (2007); Median age: 35.7 (2007); Males per 100 females: 94.0 (2007); Marriage status: 24.7% never married, 52.5% now married, 8.6% widowed, 14.2% divorced (2000); Foreign born: 2.2% (2000); Ancestry (includes multiple ancestries): 21.6% German, 15.0% United States or American, 14.7% Other groups, 11.8% Irish, 8.6% English (2000).
Economy: Unemployment rate: 6.6% (6/2008); Total civilian labor force: 30,938 (6/2008); Single-family building permits issued: 68 (2007); Multi-family building permits issued: 26 (2007); Employment by occupation: 8.8% management, 13.7% professional, 16.7% services, 28.0% sales, 0.1% farming, 10.8% construction, 21.8% production (2000).
Income: Per capita income: $20,121 (2007); Median household income: $39,626 (2007); Average household income: $48,623 (2007); Percent of households with income of $100,000 or more: 7.6% (2007); Poverty rate: 13.4% (2000).
Taxes: Total city taxes per capita: $519 (2006); City property taxes per capita: $133 (2006).
Education: Percent of population age 25 and over with: High school diploma (including GED) or higher: 73.7% (2007); Bachelor's degree or higher: 12.5% (2007); Master's degree or higher: 3.8% (2007).

School District(s)

Butler Technology & Career Development Schools (07-12)
2005-06 Enrollment: n/a . . . . (513) 868-1911
Edgewood City (PK-12)
2005-06 Enrollment: 3,789 . . . . (513) 863-4692
Fairfield City (PK-12)
2005-06 Enrollment: 9,857 . . . . (513) 829-6300
Hamilton City (PK-12)
2005-06 Enrollment: 9,234 . . . . (513) 887-5000
New Miami Local (PK-12)
2005-06 Enrollment: 889 . . . . (513) 863-0833
Richard Allen Academy III (KG-07)
2005-06 Enrollment: 175 . . . . (513) 868-2900
Ross Local (PK-12)
2005-06 Enrollment: 2,897 . . . . (513) 863-1253

Four-year College(s)

Miami University-Hamilton (Public)
Fall 2007 Enrollment: 2,607 . . . . (513) 785-3000
2007-08 Tuition: In-state $4,350; Out-of-state $17,210
University of Phoenix-Cincinnati Campus (Private, For-profit)
Fall 2007 Enrollment: 361 . . . . (513) 772-9600
2007-08 Tuition: In-state $12,930; Out-of-state $12,930

Vocational/Technical School(s)

Butler Tech-D Russel Lee Career Center (Public)
Fall 2007 Enrollment: 327 . . . . (513) 645-8200
2007-08 Tuition: $8,633

Housing: Homeownership rate: 60.9% (2007); Median home value: $104,201 (2007); Median rent: $402 per month (2000); Median age of housing: 47 years (2000).
Hospitals: Fort Hamilton Hospital (307 beds)
Safety: Violent crime rate: 80.4 per 10,000 population; Property crime rate: 664.8 per 10,000 population (2007).
Newspapers: Journal News (Local news; Circulation 46,890)
Transportation: Commute to work: 94.2% car, 1.0% public transportation, 2.5% walk, 1.5% work from home (2000); Travel time to work: 32.2% less than 15 minutes, 36.9% 15 to 30 minutes, 20.0% 30 to 45 minutes, 6.5% 45 to 60 minutes, 4.4% 60 minutes or more (2000)
Airports: Butler County Regional (general aviation)

Additional Information Contacts

City of Hamilton . . . . (513) 785-7000
http://www.hamilton-city.org
Greater Hamilton Chamber of Commerce . . . . (513) 844-1500
http://www.hamilton-ohio.com

JACKSONBURG (village). Covers a land area of 0.019 square miles and a water area of 0 square miles. Located at 39.53° N. Lat.; 84.50° W. Long. Elevation is 961 feet.
History: Sometimes spelled Jacksonburgh.
Population: 50 (1990); 67 (2000); 81 (2007); 88 (2012 projected); Race: 95.1% White, 0.0% Black, 0.0% Asian, 0.0% Hispanic of any race (2007); Density: 4,154.7 persons per square mile (2007); Average household size: 3.00 (2007); Median age: 36.9 (2007); Males per 100 females: 118.9 (2007); Marriage status: 35.3% never married, 54.9% now married, 3.9% widowed, 5.9% divorced (2000); Foreign born: 0.0% (2000); Ancestry (includes multiple ancestries): 31.4% German, 20.0% United States or American, 17.1% Irish, 11.4% English, 7.1% Polish (2000).
Economy: Single-family building permits issued: 0 (2007); Multi-family building permits issued: 0 (2007); Employment by occupation: 7.1% management, 17.9% professional, 7.1% services, 39.3% sales, 0.0% farming, 10.7% construction, 17.9% production (2000).
Income: Per capita income: $15,432 (2007); Median household income: $41,250 (2007); Average household income: $46,296 (2007); Percent of households with income of $100,000 or more: 0.0% (2007); Poverty rate: 0.0% (2000).
Education: Percent of population age 25 and over with: High school diploma (including GED) or higher: 83.0% (2007); Bachelor's degree or higher: 13.2% (2007); Master's degree or higher: 0.0% (2007).
Housing: Homeownership rate: 85.2% (2007); Median home value: $108,750 (2007); Median rent: $563 per month (2000); Median age of housing: 60+ years (2000).
Transportation: Commute to work: 89.3% car, 0.0% public transportation, 0.0% walk, 10.7% work from home (2000); Travel time to work: 16.0% less than 15 minutes, 48.0% 15 to 30 minutes, 16.0% 30 to 45 minutes, 8.0% 45 to 60 minutes, 12.0% 60 minutes or more (2000)

MIDDLETOWN (city). Covers a land area of 25.657 square miles and a water area of 0.144 square miles. Located at 39.50° N. Lat.; 84.37° W. Long. Elevation is 656 feet.
History: Middletown was platted in 1802 by Stephen Vail and James Sutton, who named it for its position midway between Cincinnati and Dayton. It was in Middletown in 1825 that Governor DeWitt Clinton of New York took the first shovelful of dirt to signify the beginning of the Miami & Erie Canal.
Population: 52,003 (1990); 51,605 (2000); 51,325 (2007); 51,275 (2012 projected); Race: 83.8% White, 13.0% Black, 0.5% Asian, 1.4% Hispanic of any race (2007); Density: 2,000.4 persons per square mile (2007); Average

household size: 2.34 (2007); Median age: 36.9 (2007); Males per 100 females: 92.6 (2007); Marriage status: 23.7% never married, 53.5% now married, 8.3% widowed, 14.6% divorced (2000); Foreign born: 1.0% (2000); Ancestry (includes multiple ancestries): 17.2% Other groups, 16.9% German, 15.4% United States or American, 11.5% Irish, 10.0% English (2000).

Economy: Unemployment rate: 7.6% (6/2008); Total civilian labor force: 26,680 (6/2008); Single-family building permits issued: 33 (2007); Multi-family building permits issued: 0 (2007); Employment by occupation: 8.3% management, 16.0% professional, 16.3% services, 25.5% sales, 0.1% farming, 9.6% construction, 24.2% production (2000).

Income: Per capita income: $22,008 (2007); Median household income: $40,002 (2007); Average household income: $51,206 (2007); Percent of households with income of $100,000 or more: 9.7% (2007); Poverty rate: 12.6% (2000).

Taxes: Total city taxes per capita: $474 (2006); City property taxes per capita: $116 (2006).

Education: Percent of population age 25 and over with: High school diploma (including GED) or higher: 77.4% (2007); Bachelor's degree or higher: 13.4% (2007); Master's degree or higher: 5.0% (2007).

School District(s)

Life Skills Center-Middletown (09-12)
2005-06 Enrollment: 228 . . . . (513) 423-1800
Madison Local (PK-12)
2005-06 Enrollment: 1,564 . . . . (513) 420-4750
Middletown City (PK-12)
2005-06 Enrollment: 6,925 . . . . (513) 423-0781
Middletown Fitness & Prep Academy (KG-08)
2005-06 Enrollment: 313 . . . . (513) 424-6110
Summit Academy Secondary School - Middletown (05-09)
2005-06 Enrollment: 37 . . . . (513) 420-9767
Summit Academy-Middletown (01-08)
2005-06 Enrollment: 58 . . . . (513) 420-9767

Four-year College(s)

Miami University-Middletown (Public)
Fall 2007 Enrollment: 1,969 . . . . (513) 727-3200
2007-08 Tuition: In-state $4,350; Out-of-state $17,210

Two-year College(s)

Carousel Beauty College (Private, For-profit)
Fall 2007 Enrollment: 47 . . . . (937) 223-3572

Housing: Homeownership rate: 59.8% (2007); Median home value: $110,892 (2007); Median rent: $414 per month (2000); Median age of housing: 41 years (2000).

Hospitals: Middletown Regional Hospital (310 beds)

Safety: Violent crime rate: 43.5 per 10,000 population; Property crime rate: 788.4 per 10,000 population (2007).

Newspapers: Middletown Journal (Local news; Circulation 22,000)

Transportation: Commute to work: 94.7% car, 1.1% public transportation, 1.8% walk, 1.7% work from home (2000); Travel time to work: 42.5% less than 15 minutes, 32.4% 15 to 30 minutes, 17.0% 30 to 45 minutes, 4.7% 45 to 60 minutes, 3.3% 60 minutes or more (2000)

Additional Information Contacts

City of Middletown . . . . (513) 425-7730
http://www.ci.middletown.oh.us
The Chamber of Commerce . . . . (513) 422-4551
http://www.thechamberofcommerce.org

MILLVILLE (village). Covers a land area of 0.591 square miles and a water area of 0 square miles. Located at 39.38° N. Lat.; 84.65° W. Long. Elevation is 620 feet.

Population: 837 (1990); 817 (2000); 972 (2007); 1,071 (2012 projected); Race: 97.6% White, 1.0% Black, 0.1% Asian, 0.0% Hispanic of any race (2007); Density: 1,645.2 persons per square mile (2007); Average household size: 2.59 (2007); Median age: 39.4 (2007); Males per 100 females: 85.5 (2007); Marriage status: 22.9% never married, 60.0% now married, 4.2% widowed, 12.9% divorced (2000); Foreign born: 1.2% (2000); Ancestry (includes multiple ancestries): 19.3% German, 17.2% United States or American, 10.0% English, 6.6% Irish, 4.9% Dutch (2000).

Economy: Employment by occupation: 8.7% management, 10.8% professional, 12.5% services, 25.5% sales, 0.0% farming, 20.0% construction, 22.6% production (2000).

Income: Per capita income: $23,032 (2007); Median household income: $51,471 (2007); Average household income: $59,541 (2007); Percent of households with income of $100,000 or more: 12.2% (2007); Poverty rate: 7.0% (2000).

Education: Percent of population age 25 and over with: High school diploma (including GED) or higher: 80.4% (2007); Bachelor's degree or higher: 9.1% (2007); Master's degree or higher: 2.2% (2007).

Housing: Homeownership rate: 83.8% (2007); Median home value: $131,386 (2007); Median rent: $408 per month (2000); Median age of housing: 31 years (2000).

Transportation: Commute to work: 97.6% car, 0.5% public transportation, 1.2% walk, 0.7% work from home (2000); Travel time to work: 17.8% less than 15 minutes, 39.4% 15 to 30 minutes, 33.3% 30 to 45 minutes, 6.4% 45 to 60 minutes, 3.2% 60 minutes or more (2000)

MONROE (city). Covers a land area of 15.509 square miles and a water area of 0.023 square miles. Located at 39.44° N. Lat.; 84.36° W. Long. Elevation is 833 feet.

Population: 6,078 (1990); 7,133 (2000); 10,864 (2007); 13,151 (2012 projected); Race: 96.0% White, 2.0% Black, 0.5% Asian, 1.0% Hispanic of any race (2007); Density: 700.5 persons per square mile (2007); Average household size: 2.54 (2007); Median age: 40.3 (2007); Males per 100 females: 93.8 (2007); Marriage status: 16.5% never married, 67.7% now married, 6.9% widowed, 8.9% divorced (2000); Foreign born: 0.9% (2000); Ancestry (includes multiple ancestries): 26.0% German, 13.9% Irish, 13.8% English, 13.1% United States or American, 7.4% Other groups (2000).

Economy: Single-family building permits issued: 100 (2007); Multi-family building permits issued: 0 (2007); Employment by occupation: 12.4% management, 21.7% professional, 7.5% services, 29.0% sales, 0.0% farming, 12.7% construction, 16.7% production (2000).

Income: Per capita income: $28,985 (2007); Median household income: $64,067 (2007); Average household income: $72,457 (2007); Percent of households with income of $100,000 or more: 18.3% (2007); Poverty rate: 1.9% (2000).

Taxes: Total city taxes per capita: $624 (2006); City property taxes per capita: $210 (2006).

Education: Percent of population age 25 and over with: High school diploma (including GED) or higher: 90.7% (2007); Bachelor's degree or higher: 24.5% (2007); Master's degree or higher: 7.2% (2007).

School District(s)

Butler Technology & Career Development Schools (07-12)
2005-06 Enrollment: n/a . . . . (513) 868-1911
Monroe Local (PK-12)
2005-06 Enrollment: 1,877 . . . . (513) 539-2536

Housing: Homeownership rate: 79.0% (2007); Median home value: $150,894 (2007); Median rent: $470 per month (2000); Median age of housing: 27 years (2000).

Safety: Violent crime rate: 38.4 per 10,000 population; Property crime rate: 479.5 per 10,000 population (2007).

Transportation: Commute to work: 96.5% car, 0.3% public transportation, 0.8% walk, 1.8% work from home (2000); Travel time to work: 25.2% less than 15 minutes, 47.0% 15 to 30 minutes, 17.0% 30 to 45 minutes, 5.3% 45 to 60 minutes, 5.5% 60 minutes or more (2000)

Additional Information Contacts

City of Monroe . . . . (513) 539-7374
http://www.monroeohio.org
The Chamber of Commerce . . . . (513) 422-4551
http://www.thechamberofcommerce.org

NEW MIAMI (village). Covers a land area of 0.887 square miles and a water area of 0.042 square miles. Located at 39.43° N. Lat.; 84.54° W. Long. Elevation is 594 feet.

Population: 2,598 (1990); 2,469 (2000); 2,637 (2007); 2,751 (2012 projected); Race: 93.0% White, 4.9% Black, 0.2% Asian, 1.3% Hispanic of any race (2007); Density: 2,971.4 persons per square mile (2007); Average household size: 2.75 (2007); Median age: 34.6 (2007); Males per 100 females: 99.8 (2007); Marriage status: 22.2% never married, 59.9% now married, 7.2% widowed, 10.7% divorced (2000); Foreign born: 1.2% (2000); Ancestry (includes multiple ancestries): 21.4% United States or American, 13.2% Other groups, 9.0% German, 5.7% Irish, 4.9% English (2000).

Economy: Employment by occupation: 5.4% management, 6.9% professional, 19.0% services, 24.8% sales, 0.0% farming, 16.3% construction, 27.6% production (2000).

Income: Per capita income: $17,499 (2007); Median household income: $39,648 (2007); Average household income: $48,118 (2007); Percent of households with income of $100,000 or more: 8.0% (2007); Poverty rate: 11.0% (2000).

Education: Percent of population age 25 and over with: High school diploma (including GED) or higher: 61.9% (2007); Bachelor's degree or higher: 2.4% (2007); Master's degree or higher: 1.0% (2007).
Housing: Homeownership rate: 71.0% (2007); Median home value: $80,047 (2007); Median rent: $407 per month (2000); Median age of housing: 42 years (2000).
Transportation: Commute to work: 98.5% car, 0.3% public transportation, 0.4% walk, 0.0% work from home (2000); Travel time to work: 27.3% less than 15 minutes, 39.1% 15 to 30 minutes, 19.7% 30 to 45 minutes, 7.2% 45 to 60 minutes, 6.7% 60 minutes or more (2000)

OKEANA (unincorporated postal area, zip code 45053). Covers a land area of 26.293 square miles and a water area of 0 square miles. Located at 39.35° N. Lat.; 84.78° W. Long. Elevation is 645 feet.
Population: 3,047 (2000); Race: 98.2% White, 0.0% Black, 0.0% Asian, 0.0% Hispanic of any race (2000); Density: 115.9 persons per square mile (2000); Age: 30.6% under 18, 5.6% over 64 (2000); Marriage status: 21.3% never married, 70.0% now married, 2.3% widowed, 6.5% divorced (2000); Foreign born: 0.9% (2000); Ancestry (includes multiple ancestries): 43.7% German, 15.1% United States or American, 11.9% Irish, 8.5% English, 6.7% Italian (2000).
Economy: Employment by occupation: 14.9% management, 12.9% professional, 8.3% services, 22.5% sales, 1.8% farming, 19.2% construction, 20.5% production (2000).
Income: Per capita income: $23,329 (2000); Median household income: $60,530 (2000); Poverty rate: 4.4% (2000).
Education: Percent of population age 25 and over with: High school diploma (including GED) or higher: 87.9% (2000); Bachelor's degree or higher: 16.3% (2000).
Housing: Homeownership rate: 94.0% (2000); Median home value: $175,600 (2000); Median rent: $465 per month (2000); Median age of housing: 21 years (2000).
Transportation: Commute to work: 94.9% car, 1.3% public transportation, 0.9% walk, 1.3% work from home (2000); Travel time to work: 15.1% less than 15 minutes, 24.6% 15 to 30 minutes, 37.4% 30 to 45 minutes, 14.8% 45 to 60 minutes, 8.1% 60 minutes or more (2000)

OLDE WEST CHESTER (CDP). Covers a land area of 0.348 square miles and a water area of 0 square miles. Located at 39.33° N. Lat.; 84.40° W. Long. Elevation is 669 feet.
Population: 152 (1990); 232 (2000); 213 (2007); 189 (2012 projected); Race: 86.9% White, 7.5% Black, 0.9% Asian, 2.8% Hispanic of any race (2007); Density: 612.2 persons per square mile (2007); Average household size: 2.66 (2007); Median age: 39.9 (2007); Males per 100 females: 95.4 (2007); Marriage status: 37.3% never married, 50.2% now married, 10.1% widowed, 2.3% divorced (2000); Foreign born: 7.9% (2000); Ancestry (includes multiple ancestries): 36.5% German, 12.0% French (except Basque), 10.2% Swiss, 9.4% English, 8.6% United States or American (2000).
Economy: Employment by occupation: 9.4% management, 37.4% professional, 10.1% services, 21.6% sales, 0.0% farming, 13.7% construction, 7.9% production (2000).
Income: Per capita income: $34,554 (2007); Median household income: $79,348 (2007); Average household income: $92,000 (2007); Percent of households with income of $100,000 or more: 26.3% (2007); Poverty rate: 7.9% (2000).
Education: Percent of population age 25 and over with: High school diploma (including GED) or higher: 83.0% (2007); Bachelor's degree or higher: 41.5% (2007); Master's degree or higher: 8.8% (2007).
Housing: Homeownership rate: 78.8% (2007); Median home value: $182,237 (2007); Median rent: $950 per month (2000); Median age of housing: 35 years (2000).
Transportation: Commute to work: 94.2% car, 0.0% public transportation, 0.0% walk, 5.8% work from home (2000); Travel time to work: 29.0% less than 15 minutes, 31.3% 15 to 30 minutes, 27.5% 30 to 45 minutes, 6.1% 45 to 60 minutes, 6.1% 60 minutes or more (2000)

OXFORD (city). Covers a land area of 5.876 square miles and a water area of 0.003 square miles. Located at 39.50° N. Lat.; 84.74° W. Long. Elevation is 928 feet.
History: Named for Oxford, the university town in Oxfordshire, England. Oxford was planned, even before the land had been surveyed and cleared, as the site of Miami University, authorized by the Ohio Legislature in 1809. The University actually opened in 1824, and the town grew around it. It was joined in 1848 by the Oxford College for Women, which flourished for 80 years before it was absorbed by Miami University. One of the instructors at the University was William Holmes McGuffey, whose name became synonymous with the "Eclectic Readers" that he compiled to help children learn to read.
Population: 21,307 (1990); 21,943 (2000); 22,194 (2007); 22,485 (2012 projected); Race: 89.0% White, 5.6% Black, 2.7% Asian, 2.3% Hispanic of any race (2007); Density: 3,777.1 persons per square mile (2007); Average household size: 3.58 (2007); Median age: 21.6 (2007); Males per 100 females: 90.8 (2007); Marriage status: 70.4% never married, 24.1% now married, 2.4% widowed, 3.2% divorced (2000); Foreign born: 3.7% (2000); Ancestry (includes multiple ancestries): 31.6% German, 15.9% Irish, 11.1% Other groups, 10.8% English, 8.2% Italian (2000).
Economy: Single-family building permits issued: 24 (2007); Multi-family building permits issued: 14 (2007); Employment by occupation: 8.3% management, 31.3% professional, 25.6% services, 24.1% sales, 0.1% farming, 3.7% construction, 7.0% production (2000).
Income: Per capita income: $14,876 (2007); Median household income: $28,855 (2007); Average household income: $48,785 (2007); Percent of households with income of $100,000 or more: 13.7% (2007); Poverty rate: 43.7% (2000).
Education: Percent of population age 25 and over with: High school diploma (including GED) or higher: 90.1% (2007); Bachelor's degree or higher: 54.4% (2007); Master's degree or higher: 29.5% (2007).

School District(s)

Talawanda City (PK-12)
2005-06 Enrollment: 3,014 . . . . (513) 523-4716

Four-year College(s)

Miami University-Oxford (Public)
Fall 2007 Enrollment: 15,968. . . . . (513) 529-1809
2007-08 Tuition: In-state $10,554; Out-of-state $24,381
Housing: Homeownership rate: 34.0% (2007); Median home value: $161,994 (2007); Median rent: $443 per month (2000); Median age of housing: 27 years (2000).
Safety: Violent crime rate: 43.6 per 10,000 population; Property crime rate: 271.2 per 10,000 population (2007).
Newspapers: Oxford Press (Community news; Circulation 4,500)
Transportation: Commute to work: 63.5% car, 2.0% public transportation, 27.7% walk, 3.9% work from home (2000); Travel time to work: 63.9% less than 15 minutes, 17.9% 15 to 30 minutes, 8.4% 30 to 45 minutes, 6.1% 45 to 60 minutes, 3.7% 60 minutes or more (2000)
Airports: Miami University (general aviation)
Additional Information Contacts
City of Oxford . . . . (513) 524-5200
http://www.cityofoxford.org
Oxford Chamber of Commerce . . . . (513) 523-5200
http://www.oxfordchamber.org
Oxford Visitors & Convention Bureau . . . . (513) 523-8687
http://www.enjoyoxford.org

ROSS (CDP). Aka Venice. Covers a land area of 1.695 square miles and a water area of 0.021 square miles. Located at 39.31° N. Lat.; 84.64° W. Long. Elevation is 548 feet.
Population: 2,140 (1990); 1,971 (2000); 2,194 (2007); 2,328 (2012 projected); Race: 97.1% White, 0.3% Black, 0.3% Asian, 1.0% Hispanic of any race (2007); Density: 1,294.3 persons per square mile (2007); Average household size: 2.65 (2007); Median age: 36.6 (2007); Males per 100 females: 94.0 (2007); Marriage status: 17.0% never married, 68.1% now married, 8.0% widowed, 7.0% divorced (2000); Foreign born: 0.9% (2000); Ancestry (includes multiple ancestries): 18.9% German, 18.7% Irish, 18.2% United States or American, 12.2% English, 8.9% Other groups (2000).
Economy: Employment by occupation: 4.7% management, 15.2% professional, 9.1% services, 25.4% sales, 0.0% farming, 19.8% construction, 25.7% production (2000).
Income: Per capita income: $21,445 (2007); Median household income: $47,570 (2007); Average household income: $56,892 (2007); Percent of households with income of $100,000 or more: 12.0% (2007); Poverty rate: 3.6% (2000).
Education: Percent of population age 25 and over with: High school diploma (including GED) or higher: 76.1% (2007); Bachelor's degree or higher: 8.4% (2007); Master's degree or higher: 2.3% (2007).
Housing: Homeownership rate: 73.0% (2007); Median home value: $123,451 (2007); Median rent: $422 per month (2000); Median age of housing: 35 years (2000).
Transportation: Commute to work: 94.4% car, 0.0% public transportation, 2.3% walk, 3.4% work from home (2000); Travel time to work: 18.9% less

than 15 minutes, 28.7% 15 to 30 minutes, 32.3% 30 to 45 minutes, 12.7% 45 to 60 minutes, 7.5% 60 minutes or more (2000)

SEVEN MILE (village). Covers a land area of 0.758 square miles and a water area of 0 square miles. Located at 39.48° N. Lat.; 84.55° W. Long. Elevation is 653 feet.

Population: 868 (1990); 678 (2000); 639 (2007); 642 (2012 projected); Race: 97.7% White, 0.6% Black, 1.1% Asian, 0.9% Hispanic of any race (2007); Density: 843.1 persons per square mile (2007); Average household size: 2.61 (2007); Median age: 40.4 (2007); Males per 100 females: 90.7 (2007); Marriage status: 22.9% never married, 62.0% now married, 6.6% widowed, 8.5% divorced (2000); Foreign born: 1.3% (2000); Ancestry (includes multiple ancestries): 27.8% German, 14.2% United States or American, 14.1% English, 9.2% Irish, 8.2% Other groups (2000).

Economy: Employment by occupation: 4.3% management, 15.2% professional, 17.2% services, 24.7% sales, 0.0% farming, 13.8% construction, 24.7% production (2000).

Income: Per capita income: $21,970 (2007); Median household income: $49,318 (2007); Average household income: $56,980 (2007); Percent of households with income of $100,000 or more: 10.2% (2007); Poverty rate: 4.1% (2000).

Education: Percent of population age 25 and over with: High school diploma (including GED) or higher: 81.0% (2007); Bachelor's degree or higher: 9.2% (2007); Master's degree or higher: 3.7% (2007).

School District(s)

Edgewood City (PK-12)
2005-06 Enrollment: 3,789 . . . . (513) 863-4692

Housing: Homeownership rate: 78.8% (2007); Median home value: $117,500 (2007); Median rent: $444 per month (2000); Median age of housing: 56 years (2000).

Transportation: Commute to work: 97.1% car, 0.0% public transportation, 0.6% walk, 2.3% work from home (2000); Travel time to work: 21.4% less than 15 minutes, 43.6% 15 to 30 minutes, 21.4% 30 to 45 minutes, 8.6% 45 to 60 minutes, 5.0% 60 minutes or more (2000)

SOMERVILLE (village). Covers a land area of 0.290 square miles and a water area of 0 square miles. Located at 39.56° N. Lat.; 84.63° W. Long. Elevation is 771 feet.

Population: 279 (1990); 294 (2000); 361 (2007); 402 (2012 projected); Race: 99.4% White, 0.0% Black, 0.6% Asian, 0.0% Hispanic of any race (2007); Density: 1,245.6 persons per square mile (2007); Average household size: 2.69 (2007); Median age: 36.7 (2007); Males per 100 females: 101.7 (2007); Marriage status: 25.5% never married, 54.3% now married, 7.0% widowed, 13.2% divorced (2000); Foreign born: 0.0% (2000); Ancestry (includes multiple ancestries): 29.5% United States or American, 14.6% German, 7.1% Other groups, 3.1% Scottish, 3.1% Italian (2000).

Economy: Employment by occupation: 4.7% management, 2.3% professional, 16.4% services, 27.3% sales, 0.0% farming, 21.9% construction, 27.3% production (2000).

Income: Per capita income: $15,325 (2007); Median household income: $36,538 (2007); Average household income: $41,287 (2007); Percent of households with income of $100,000 or more: 2.2% (2007); Poverty rate: 10.3% (2000).

Education: Percent of population age 25 and over with: High school diploma (including GED) or higher: 59.2% (2007); Bachelor's degree or higher: 0.0% (2007); Master's degree or higher: 0.0% (2007).

Housing: Homeownership rate: 72.4% (2007); Median home value: $89,500 (2007); Median rent: $458 per month (2000); Median age of housing: 60+ years (2000).

Transportation: Commute to work: 82.6% car, 2.5% public transportation, 7.4% walk, 4.1% work from home (2000); Travel time to work: 11.2% less than 15 minutes, 35.3% 15 to 30 minutes, 12.9% 30 to 45 minutes, 25.0% 45 to 60 minutes, 15.5% 60 minutes or more (2000)

SOUTH MIDDLETOWN (CDP). Covers a land area of 0.107 square miles and a water area of 0 square miles. Located at 39.48° N. Lat.; 84.41° W. Long. Elevation is 636 feet.

Population: 288 (1990); 264 (2000); 254 (2007); 244 (2012 projected); Race: 97.6% White, 0.4% Black, 0.0% Asian, 1.2% Hispanic of any race (2007); Density: 2,378.5 persons per square mile (2007); Average household size: 2.67 (2007); Median age: 31.8 (2007); Males per 100 females: 86.8 (2007); Marriage status: 7.3% never married, 60.6% now married, 5.1% widowed, 27.0% divorced (2000); Foreign born: 0.0% (2000); Ancestry (includes multiple ancestries): 52.3% United States or American, 10.3% German, 5.7% Other groups, 5.2% Swedish, 2.9% Scotch-Irish (2000).

Economy: Employment by occupation: 19.5% management, 13.4% professional, 26.8% services, 15.9% sales, 0.0% farming, 3.7% construction, 20.7% production (2000).

Income: Per capita income: $18,002 (2007); Median household income: $48,929 (2007); Average household income: $48,132 (2007); Percent of households with income of $100,000 or more: 7.4% (2007); Poverty rate: 5.7% (2000).

Education: Percent of population age 25 and over with: High school diploma (including GED) or higher: 69.3% (2007); Bachelor's degree or higher: 13.7% (2007); Master's degree or higher: 7.8% (2007).

Housing: Homeownership rate: 61.1% (2007); Median home value: $88,333 (2007); Median rent: $475 per month (2000); Median age of housing: 52 years (2000).

Transportation: Commute to work: 89.0% car, 0.0% public transportation, 11.0% walk, 0.0% work from home (2000); Travel time to work: 46.3% less than 15 minutes, 53.7% 15 to 30 minutes, 0.0% 30 to 45 minutes, 0.0% 45 to 60 minutes, 0.0% 60 minutes or more (2000)

TRENTON (city). Covers a land area of 3.786 square miles and a water area of 0 square miles. Located at 39.48° N. Lat.; 84.45° W. Long. Elevation is 650 feet.

Population: 6,630 (1990); 8,746 (2000); 10,815 (2007); 12,119 (2012 projected); Race: 97.5% White, 0.7% Black, 0.4% Asian, 1.5% Hispanic of any race (2007); Density: 2,856.9 persons per square mile (2007); Average household size: 2.68 (2007); Median age: 33.0 (2007); Males per 100 females: 97.5 (2007); Marriage status: 18.6% never married, 66.1% now married, 5.1% widowed, 10.3% divorced (2000); Foreign born: 1.6% (2000); Ancestry (includes multiple ancestries): 21.3% German, 15.3% United States or American, 12.8% Irish, 9.2% Other groups, 7.7% English (2000).

Economy: Single-family building permits issued: 30 (2007); Multi-family building permits issued: 0 (2007); Employment by occupation: 10.5% management, 13.8% professional, 12.0% services, 25.7% sales, 0.1% farming, 11.7% construction, 26.1% production (2000).

Income: Per capita income: $23,511 (2007); Median household income: $56,566 (2007); Average household income: $62,839 (2007); Percent of households with income of $100,000 or more: 13.2% (2007); Poverty rate: 3.7% (2000).

Education: Percent of population age 25 and over with: High school diploma (including GED) or higher: 84.9% (2007); Bachelor's degree or higher: 10.0% (2007); Master's degree or higher: 2.8% (2007).

School District(s)

Edgewood City (PK-12)
2005-06 Enrollment: 3,789 . . . . (513) 863-4692

Housing: Homeownership rate: 74.3% (2007); Median home value: $136,775 (2007); Median rent: $457 per month (2000); Median age of housing: 25 years (2000).

Transportation: Commute to work: 97.5% car, 0.6% public transportation, 0.5% walk, 1.0% work from home (2000); Travel time to work: 23.6% less than 15 minutes, 45.3% 15 to 30 minutes, 19.2% 30 to 45 minutes, 7.8% 45 to 60 minutes, 4.1% 60 minutes or more (2000)

Additional Information Contacts

City of Trenton . . . . (513) 988-6304
http://www.ci.trenton.oh.us
The Chamber of Commerce . . . . (513) 422-4551
http://www.thechamberofcommerce.org

WETHERINGTON (CDP). Covers a land area of 0.698 square miles and a water area of 0 square miles. Located at 39.36° N. Lat.; 84.37° W. Long. Elevation is 860 feet.

Population: 737 (1990); 1,010 (2000); 1,191 (2007); 1,300 (2012 projected); Race: 93.8% White, 3.5% Black, 1.3% Asian, 2.6% Hispanic of any race (2007); Density: 1,707.4 persons per square mile (2007); Average household size: 2.73 (2007); Median age: 42.6 (2007); Males per 100 females: 98.5 (2007); Marriage status: 10.4% never married, 88.2% now married, 0.0% widowed, 1.5% divorced (2000); Foreign born: 2.7% (2000); Ancestry (includes multiple ancestries): 37.2% German, 11.1% English, 10.1% Irish, 9.3% Polish, 6.1% French (except Basque) (2000).

Economy: Employment by occupation: 32.1% management, 18.2% professional, 3.2% services, 37.8% sales, 0.0% farming, 0.0% construction, 8.7% production (2000).

Income: Per capita income: $89,343 (2007); Median household income: $190,000 (2007); Average household income: $244,054 (2007); Percent of

households with income of $100,000 or more: 81.4% (2007); Poverty rate: 2.4% (2000).
Education: Percent of population age 25 and over with: High school diploma (including GED) or higher: 98.7% (2007); Bachelor's degree or higher: 55.9% (2007); Master's degree or higher: 24.3% (2007).
Housing: Homeownership rate: 98.4% (2007); Median home value: $395,930 (2007); Median rent: $625 per month (2000); Median age of housing: 4 years (2000).
Transportation: Commute to work: 85.5% car, 3.8% public transportation, 0.0% walk, 8.7% work from home (2000); Travel time to work: 6.0% less than 15 minutes, 48.9% 15 to 30 minutes, 32.1% 30 to 45 minutes, 8.2% 45 to 60 minutes, 4.9% 60 minutes or more (2000)

Carroll County

Located in eastern Ohio; drained by Small Sandy, Conotton, and Yellow Creeks. Covers a land area of 394.67 square miles, a water area of 4.33 square miles, and is located in the Eastern Time Zone. The county was founded in 1832. County seat is Carrollton.

Carroll County is part of the Canton-Massillon, OH Metropolitan Statistical Area. The entire metro area includes: Carroll County, OH; Stark County, OH

Population: 26,521 (1990); 28,836 (2000); 29,420 (2007); 29,626 (2012 projected); Race: 98.3% White, 0.6% Black, 0.1% Asian, 0.7% Hispanic of any race (2007); Density: 74.5 persons per square mile (2007); Average household size: 2.53 (2007); Median age: 40.9 (2007); Males per 100 females: 97.0 (2007).
Religion: Five largest groups: 10.0% The United Methodist Church, 6.6% Catholic Church, 4.9% Evangelical Lutheran Church in America, 2.1% Presbyterian Church (U.S.A.), 2.0% Christian Churches and Churches of Christ (2000).
Economy: Unemployment rate: 6.8% (6/2008); Total civilian labor force: 14,257 (6/2008); Leading industries: 42.9% manufacturing; 13.4% retail trade; 11.8% health care and social assistance (2005); Farms: 749 totaling 123,506 acres (2002); Companies that employ 500 or more persons: 1 (2006); Companies that employ 100 to 499 persons: 8 (2006); Companies that employ less than 100 persons: 459 (2006); Black-owned businesses: n/a (2002); Hispanic-owned businesses: n/a (2002); Asian-owned businesses: n/a (2002); Women-owned businesses: 732 (2002); Retail sales per capita: $7,603 (2008). Single-family building permits issued: 4 (2007); Multi-family building permits issued: 0 (2007).
Income: Per capita income: $18,820 (2007); Median household income: $38,994 (2007); Average household income: $47,281 (2007); Percent of households with income of $100,000 or more: 6.3% (2007); Poverty rate: 12.6% (2005); Bankruptcy rate: 4.80% (2007).
Education: Percent of population age 25 and over with: High school diploma (including GED) or higher: 80.0% (2007); Bachelor's degree or higher: 9.2% (2007); Master's degree or higher: 3.0% (2007).
Housing: Homeownership rate: 80.4% (2007); Median home value: $109,973 (2007); Median rent: $322 per month (2000); Median age of housing: 31 years (2000).
Health: Birth rate: 109.4 per 10,000 population (2007); Death rate: 92.2 per 10,000 population (2007); Age-adjusted cancer mortality rate: 137.8 deaths per 100,000 population (2005); Number of physicians: 5.2 per 10,000 population (2005); Hospital beds: 0.0 per 10,000 population (2004); Hospital admissions: 0.0 per 10,000 population (2004).
Elections: 2004 Presidential election results: 54.5% Bush, 44.6% Kerry, 0.0% Nader, 0.4% Badnarik
National and State Parks: Leesville State Wildlife Area
Additional Information Contacts
Carroll County Government . . . . (330) 627-4869
http://www.carrollcountyohio.net
Carroll County Chamber of Commerce . . . . (330) 627-4811
http://www.carrollohchamber.com

Carroll County Communities

CARROLLTON (village). County seat. Covers a land area of 2.379 square miles and a water area of 0 square miles. Located at 40.57° N. Lat.; 81.08° W. Long. Elevation is 1,119 feet.
History: Laid out 1815.
Population: 3,194 (1990); 3,190 (2000); 3,257 (2007); 3,281 (2012 projected); Race: 98.9% White, 0.3% Black, 0.1% Asian, 0.7% Hispanic of any race (2007); Density: 1,369.1 persons per square mile (2007); Average household size: 2.18 (2007); Median age: 43.6 (2007); Males per 100 females: 82.4 (2007); Marriage status: 19.8% never married, 55.9% now married, 12.4% widowed, 11.9% divorced (2000); Foreign born: 0.4% (2000); Ancestry (includes multiple ancestries): 25.5% German, 17.8% Irish, 10.9% United States or American, 10.3% English, 5.3% Other groups (2000).
Economy: Single-family building permits issued: 4 (2007); Multi-family building permits issued: 0 (2007); Employment by occupation: 9.1% management, 17.0% professional, 15.7% services, 23.7% sales, 0.0% farming, 7.7% construction, 26.8% production (2000).
Income: Per capita income: $16,368 (2007); Median household income: $28,111 (2007); Average household income: $34,956 (2007); Percent of households with income of $100,000 or more: 2.5% (2007); Poverty rate: 17.0% (2000).
Education: Percent of population age 25 and over with: High school diploma (including GED) or higher: 76.4% (2007); Bachelor's degree or higher: 11.5% (2007); Master's degree or higher: 2.9% (2007).

School District(s)

Carrollton Exempted Village (PK-12)
2005-06 Enrollment: 2,837 . . . . (330) 627-2181
Housing: Homeownership rate: 61.9% (2007); Median home value: $109,114 (2007); Median rent: $287 per month (2000); Median age of housing: 49 years (2000).
Newspapers: Free Press-Standard (Local news; Circulation 7,550)
Transportation: Commute to work: 86.9% car, 4.1% public transportation, 4.8% walk, 2.9% work from home (2000); Travel time to work: 47.4% less than 15 minutes, 18.6% 15 to 30 minutes, 11.7% 30 to 45 minutes, 14.5% 45 to 60 minutes, 7.8% 60 minutes or more (2000)
Airports: Carroll County-Tolson (general aviation)
Additional Information Contacts
Carroll County Chamber of Commerce . . . . (330) 627-4811
http://www.carrollohchamber.com

DELLROY (village). Covers a land area of 0.171 square miles and a water area of 0.040 square miles. Located at 40.55° N. Lat.; 81.19° W. Long. Elevation is 958 feet.
Population: 314 (1990); 294 (2000); 324 (2007); 343 (2012 projected); Race: 99.4% White, 0.0% Black, 0.0% Asian, 0.0% Hispanic of any race (2007); Density: 1,889.7 persons per square mile (2007); Average household size: 2.36 (2007); Median age: 39.3 (2007); Males per 100 females: 85.1 (2007); Marriage status: 12.3% never married, 66.4% now married, 11.4% widowed, 10.0% divorced (2000); Foreign born: 0.0% (2000); Ancestry (includes multiple ancestries): 25.1% German, 16.9% Irish, 11.2% English, 7.9% French (except Basque), 7.9% Dutch (2000).
Economy: Employment by occupation: 17.6% management, 15.5% professional, 14.2% services, 17.6% sales, 0.0% farming, 8.8% construction, 26.4% production (2000).
Income: Per capita income: $16,806 (2007); Median household income: $30,536 (2007); Average household income: $39,745 (2007); Percent of households with income of $100,000 or more: 5.8% (2007); Poverty rate: 9.1% (2000).
Education: Percent of population age 25 and over with: High school diploma (including GED) or higher: 80.5% (2007); Bachelor's degree or higher: 11.9% (2007); Master's degree or higher: 4.0% (2007).

School District(s)

Carrollton Exempted Village (PK-12)
2005-06 Enrollment: 2,837 . . . . (330) 627-2181
Housing: Homeownership rate: 77.4% (2007); Median home value: $77,692 (2007); Median rent: $321 per month (2000); Median age of housing: 60+ years (2000).
Transportation: Commute to work: 87.6% car, 0.0% public transportation, 10.9% walk, 1.5% work from home (2000); Travel time to work: 23.0% less than 15 minutes, 34.8% 15 to 30 minutes, 23.7% 30 to 45 minutes, 3.7% 45 to 60 minutes, 14.8% 60 minutes or more (2000)

LEESVILLE (village). Covers a land area of 0.257 square miles and a water area of 0 square miles. Located at 40.45° N. Lat.; 81.21° W. Long. Elevation is 997 feet.
Population: 156 (1990); 184 (2000); 178 (2007); 171 (2012 projected); Race: 100.0% White, 0.0% Black, 0.0% Asian, 1.7% Hispanic of any race (2007); Density: 692.5 persons per square mile (2007); Average household size: 2.54 (2007); Median age: 35.7 (2007); Males per 100 females: 95.6 (2007); Marriage status: 21.2% never married, 62.8% now married, 10.9% widowed, 5.1% divorced (2000); Foreign born: 0.0% (2000); Ancestry

(includes multiple ancestries): 29.0% German, 10.1% Other groups, 8.2% English, 6.8% United States or American, 5.8% Welsh (2000).
Economy: Employment by occupation: 10.5% management, 2.3% professional, 24.4% services, 10.5% sales, 0.0% farming, 7.0% construction, 45.3% production (2000).
Income: Per capita income: $18,581 (2007); Median household income: $42,500 (2007); Average household income: $47,250 (2007); Percent of households with income of $100,000 or more: 4.3% (2007); Poverty rate: 0.5% (2000).
Education: Percent of population age 25 and over with: High school diploma (including GED) or higher: 76.1% (2007); Bachelor's degree or higher: 6.0% (2007); Master's degree or higher: 6.0% (2007).
Housing: Homeownership rate: 92.9% (2007); Median home value: $57,500 (2007); Median rent: $n/a per month (2000); Median age of housing: 60+ years (2000).
Transportation: Commute to work: 97.6% car, 2.4% public transportation, 0.0% walk, 0.0% work from home (2000); Travel time to work: 21.4% less than 15 minutes, 32.1% 15 to 30 minutes, 34.5% 30 to 45 minutes, 8.3% 45 to 60 minutes, 3.6% 60 minutes or more (2000)

MALVERN (village). Covers a land area of 0.682 square miles and a water area of 0 square miles. Located at 40.69° N. Lat.; 81.18° W. Long. Elevation is 994 feet.
Population: 1,215 (1990); 1,218 (2000); 1,111 (2007); 1,109 (2012 projected); Race: 91.0% White, 6.8% Black, 0.5% Asian, 1.2% Hispanic of any race (2007); Density: 1,628.0 persons per square mile (2007); Average household size: 2.24 (2007); Median age: 40.5 (2007); Males per 100 females: 92.2 (2007); Marriage status: 23.2% never married, 53.4% now married, 9.6% widowed, 13.7% divorced (2000); Foreign born: 1.0% (2000); Ancestry (includes multiple ancestries): 27.5% German, 13.5% Other groups, 12.1% Irish, 11.7% Italian, 7.7% English (2000).
Economy: Single-family building permits issued: 0 (2007); Multi-family building permits issued: 0 (2007); Employment by occupation: 5.3% management, 12.5% professional, 22.6% services, 18.1% sales, 0.3% farming, 10.0% construction, 31.1% production (2000).
Income: Per capita income: $16,076 (2007); Median household income: $30,774 (2007); Average household income: $35,936 (2007); Percent of households with income of $100,000 or more: 2.0% (2007); Poverty rate: 12.8% (2000).
Education: Percent of population age 25 and over with: High school diploma (including GED) or higher: 74.3% (2007); Bachelor's degree or higher: 9.3% (2007); Master's degree or higher: 2.3% (2007).

School District(s)

Brown Local (PK-12)
2005-06 Enrollment: 772 . . . . (330) 863-1170
Housing: Homeownership rate: 59.2% (2007); Median home value: $92,000 (2007); Median rent: $305 per month (2000); Median age of housing: 53 years (2000).
Transportation: Commute to work: 87.8% car, 0.0% public transportation, 9.4% walk, 1.4% work from home (2000); Travel time to work: 41.7% less than 15 minutes, 30.2% 15 to 30 minutes, 17.9% 30 to 45 minutes, 7.2% 45 to 60 minutes, 2.9% 60 minutes or more (2000)

MECHANICSTOWN (unincorporated postal area, zip code 44651). Covers a land area of 22.988 square miles and a water area of 0.009 square miles. Located at 40.62° N. Lat.; 80.96° W. Long. Elevation is 1,240 feet.
Population: 833 (2000); Race: 99.3% White, 0.0% Black, 0.0% Asian, 0.0% Hispanic of any race (2000); Density: 36.2 persons per square mile (2000); Age: 31.0% under 18, 13.9% over 64 (2000); Marriage status: 15.4% never married, 69.9% now married, 9.8% widowed, 4.8% divorced (2000); Foreign born: 0.0% (2000); Ancestry (includes multiple ancestries): 25.4% German, 20.0% Irish, 9.7% English, 8.3% United States or American, 6.4% Italian (2000).
Economy: Employment by occupation: 8.4% management, 6.4% professional, 14.8% services, 27.2% sales, 1.7% farming, 5.5% construction, 35.9% production (2000).
Income: Per capita income: $12,568 (2000); Median household income: $24,219 (2000); Poverty rate: 16.2% (2000).
Education: Percent of population age 25 and over with: High school diploma (including GED) or higher: 76.8% (2000); Bachelor's degree or higher: 3.6% (2000).

School District(s)

Carrollton Exempted Village (PK-12)
2005-06 Enrollment: 2,837 . . . . (330) 627-2181

Housing: Homeownership rate: 70.9% (2000); Median home value: $85,800 (2000); Median rent: $453 per month (2000); Median age of housing: 38 years (2000).
Transportation: Commute to work: 94.2% car, 0.0% public transportation, 2.4% walk, 3.3% work from home (2000); Travel time to work: 27.4% less than 15 minutes, 34.9% 15 to 30 minutes, 14.8% 30 to 45 minutes, 9.7% 45 to 60 minutes, 13.2% 60 minutes or more (2000)

SHERRODSVILLE (village). Covers a land area of 0.316 square miles and a water area of 0 square miles. Located at 40.49° N. Lat.; 81.24° W. Long. Elevation is 909 feet.
Population: 283 (1990); 316 (2000); 275 (2007); 273 (2012 projected); Race: 97.5% White, 0.4% Black, 0.7% Asian, 0.7% Hispanic of any race (2007); Density: 870.0 persons per square mile (2007); Average household size: 2.52 (2007); Median age: 39.8 (2007); Males per 100 females: 89.7 (2007); Marriage status: 15.2% never married, 61.2% now married, 7.6% widowed, 16.1% divorced (2000); Foreign born: 0.0% (2000); Ancestry (includes multiple ancestries): 27.6% German, 18.8% Irish, 11.5% United States or American, 8.6% English, 7.9% Other groups (2000).
Economy: Employment by occupation: 7.7% management, 7.7% professional, 19.4% services, 31.0% sales, 0.0% farming, 11.6% construction, 22.6% production (2000).
Income: Per capita income: $12,755 (2007); Median household income: $31,029 (2007); Average household income: $32,179 (2007); Percent of households with income of $100,000 or more: 0.9% (2007); Poverty rate: 19.1% (2000).
Education: Percent of population age 25 and over with: High school diploma (including GED) or higher: 87.0% (2007); Bachelor's degree or higher: 4.9% (2007); Master's degree or higher: 1.6% (2007).

School District(s)

Conotton Valley Union Local (PK-12)
2005-06 Enrollment: 571 . . . . (740) 269-2000
Housing: Homeownership rate: 78.9% (2007); Median home value: $60,000 (2007); Median rent: $293 per month (2000); Median age of housing: 50 years (2000).
Transportation: Commute to work: 90.1% car, 3.3% public transportation, 6.6% walk, 0.0% work from home (2000); Travel time to work: 25.8% less than 15 minutes, 38.4% 15 to 30 minutes, 15.2% 30 to 45 minutes, 14.6% 45 to 60 minutes, 6.0% 60 minutes or more (2000)

Champaign County

Located in west central Ohio; crossed by the Mad River, and Darby, Small Buck, and Little Darby Creeks. Covers a land area of 428.56 square miles, a water area of 1.15 square miles, and is located in the Eastern Time Zone. The county was founded in 1805. County seat is Urbana.

Champaign County is part of the Urbana, OH Micropolitan Statistical Area. The entire metro area includes: Champaign County, OH

Weather Station: Urbana WWTP Elevation: 997 feet

	Jan	Feb	Mar	Apr	May	Jun	Jul	Aug	Sep	Oct	Nov	Dec
High	33	37	48	60	71	80	84	83	76	64	50	39
Low	17	19	28	38	49	58	61	59	51	41	32	23
Precip	2.3	2.1	2.9	3.5	4.4	4.5	5.0	3.6	2.9	2.8	3.1	2.9
Snow	na	na	na	0.5	0.0	0.0	0.0	0.0	0.0	0.1	0.3	na

High and Low temperatures in degrees Fahrenheit; Precipitation and Snow in inches

Population: 36,019 (1990); 38,890 (2000); 39,899 (2007); 40,444 (2012 projected); Race: 95.2% White, 2.5% Black, 0.5% Asian, 0.9% Hispanic of any race (2007); Density: 93.1 persons per square mile (2007); Average household size: 2.56 (2007); Median age: 38.7 (2007); Males per 100 females: 96.9 (2007).
Religion: Five largest groups: 7.3% The United Methodist Church, 3.8% American Baptist Churches in the USA, 3.1% Catholic Church, 2.1% Evangelical Lutheran Church in America, 1.6% Church of the Nazarene (2000).
Economy: Unemployment rate: 7.0% (6/2008); Total civilian labor force: 21,151 (6/2008); Leading industries: 32.7% manufacturing; 18.2% health care and social assistance; 10.5% retail trade (2005); Farms: 937 totaling 207,554 acres (2002); Companies that employ 500 or more persons: 4 (2006); Companies that employ 100 to 499 persons: 13 (2006); Companies that employ less than 100 persons: 656 (2006); Black-owned businesses: n/a (2002); Hispanic-owned businesses: n/a (2002); Asian-owned businesses: n/a (2002); Women-owned businesses: 683 (2002); Retail

sales per capita: $8,247 (2008). Single-family building permits issued: 61 (2007); Multi-family building permits issued: 0 (2007).
Income: Per capita income: $22,276 (2007); Median household income: $48,221 (2007); Average household income: $56,268 (2007); Percent of households with income of $100,000 or more: 11.1% (2007); Poverty rate: 9.1% (2005); Bankruptcy rate: 4.48% (2007).
Education: Percent of population age 25 and over with: High school diploma (including GED) or higher: 82.5% (2007); Bachelor's degree or higher: 10.7% (2007); Master's degree or higher: 3.6% (2007).
Housing: Homeownership rate: 76.3% (2007); Median home value: $123,298 (2007); Median rent: $367 per month (2000); Median age of housing: 36 years (2000).
Health: Birth rate: 134.6 per 10,000 population (2007); Death rate: 96.7 per 10,000 population (2007); Age-adjusted cancer mortality rate: 175.1 deaths per 100,000 population (2005); Number of physicians: 4.1 per 10,000 population (2005); Hospital beds: 6.4 per 10,000 population (2004); Hospital admissions: 236.1 per 10,000 population (2004).
Elections: 2004 Presidential election results: 62.4% Bush, 37.1% Kerry, 0.0% Nader, 0.3% Badnarik
National and State Parks: Cedar Bog State Nature Preserve; Kiser Lake State Park

Additional Information Contacts

Champaign County Government . . . . (937) 484-1611
http://www.co.champaign.oh.us
Champaign County Chamber of Commerce . . . . (937) 653-5764
http://www.champaignohio.com
City of Urbana . . . . (937) 652-4300
http://urbanaohio.com

Champaign County Communities

CABLE (unincorporated postal area, zip code 43009). Covers a land area of 33.823 square miles and a water area of 0.044 square miles. Located at 40.17° N. Lat.; 83.64° W. Long. Elevation is 1,170 feet.
Population: 1,775 (2000); Race: 99.3% White, 0.0% Black, 0.0% Asian, 0.7% Hispanic of any race (2000); Density: 52.5 persons per square mile (2000); Age: 28.5% under 18, 7.6% over 64 (2000); Marriage status: 14.9% never married, 74.2% now married, 3.5% widowed, 7.3% divorced (2000); Foreign born: 0.6% (2000); Ancestry (includes multiple ancestries): 22.2% German, 21.3% English, 16.4% Irish, 15.8% United States or American, 4.6% Other groups (2000).
Economy: Employment by occupation: 12.1% management, 11.0% professional, 8.4% services, 24.9% sales, 0.0% farming, 7.8% construction, 35.7% production (2000).
Income: Per capita income: $20,446 (2000); Median household income: $53,105 (2000); Poverty rate: 4.6% (2000).
Education: Percent of population age 25 and over with: High school diploma (including GED) or higher: 85.7% (2000); Bachelor's degree or higher: 10.2% (2000).
Housing: Homeownership rate: 90.8% (2000); Median home value: $108,300 (2000); Median rent: $350 per month (2000); Median age of housing: 32 years (2000).
Transportation: Commute to work: 94.7% car, 0.3% public transportation, 0.9% walk, 4.2% work from home (2000); Travel time to work: 15.8% less than 15 minutes, 48.3% 15 to 30 minutes, 20.7% 30 to 45 minutes, 7.1% 45 to 60 minutes, 8.1% 60 minutes or more (2000)

CHRISTIANSBURG (village). Covers a land area of 0.216 square miles and a water area of 0 square miles. Located at 40.05° N. Lat.; 84.02° W. Long. Elevation is 1,115 feet.
Population: 594 (1990); 553 (2000); 557 (2007); 546 (2012 projected); Race: 98.2% White, 0.7% Black, 0.2% Asian, 0.5% Hispanic of any race (2007); Density: 2,581.8 persons per square mile (2007); Average household size: 2.50 (2007); Median age: 37.6 (2007); Males per 100 females: 92.1 (2007); Marriage status: 22.3% never married, 59.2% now married, 7.9% widowed, 10.6% divorced (2000); Foreign born: 1.2% (2000); Ancestry (includes multiple ancestries): 22.6% German, 16.5% United States or American, 11.8% Other groups, 10.8% Irish, 5.9% English (2000).
Economy: Single-family building permits issued: 0 (2007); Multi-family building permits issued: 0 (2007); Employment by occupation: 5.3% management, 7.8% professional, 10.2% services, 24.6% sales, 0.0% farming, 9.4% construction, 42.6% production (2000).
Income: Per capita income: $18,914 (2007); Median household income: $39,792 (2007); Average household income: $47,242 (2007); Percent of households with income of $100,000 or more: 4.9% (2007); Poverty rate: 6.7% (2000).
Education: Percent of population age 25 and over with: High school diploma (including GED) or higher: 72.2% (2007); Bachelor's degree or higher: 4.9% (2007); Master's degree or higher: 1.3% (2007).
Housing: Homeownership rate: 80.7% (2007); Median home value: $94,375 (2007); Median rent: $305 per month (2000); Median age of housing: 60+ years (2000).
Transportation: Commute to work: 95.0% car, 0.0% public transportation, 2.5% walk, 1.7% work from home (2000); Travel time to work: 10.9% less than 15 minutes, 50.8% 15 to 30 minutes, 29.4% 30 to 45 minutes, 5.5% 45 to 60 minutes, 3.4% 60 minutes or more (2000)

MECHANICSBURG (village). Covers a land area of 1.026 square miles and a water area of 0.007 square miles. Located at 40.07° N. Lat.; 83.55° W. Long. Elevation is 1,083 feet.
Population: 1,803 (1990); 1,744 (2000); 1,725 (2007); 1,716 (2012 projected); Race: 97.7% White, 0.7% Black, 0.0% Asian, 0.9% Hispanic of any race (2007); Density: 1,680.9 persons per square mile (2007); Average household size: 2.42 (2007); Median age: 36.1 (2007); Males per 100 females: 94.7 (2007); Marriage status: 26.5% never married, 52.2% now married, 8.5% widowed, 12.8% divorced (2000); Foreign born: 0.8% (2000); Ancestry (includes multiple ancestries): 17.4% German, 14.0% United States or American, 10.7% Irish, 10.6% English, 6.8% Other groups (2000).
Economy: Employment by occupation: 7.6% management, 8.7% professional, 16.4% services, 21.1% sales, 0.0% farming, 8.2% construction, 37.9% production (2000).
Income: Per capita income: $20,271 (2007); Median household income: $39,082 (2007); Average household income: $48,974 (2007); Percent of households with income of $100,000 or more: 9.1% (2007); Poverty rate: 14.9% (2000).
Education: Percent of population age 25 and over with: High school diploma (including GED) or higher: 74.0% (2007); Bachelor's degree or higher: 7.3% (2007); Master's degree or higher: 2.5% (2007).

School District(s)

Mechanicsburg Exempted Village (PK-12)
2005-06 Enrollment: 860 . . . . (937) 834-2453
Housing: Homeownership rate: 67.2% (2007); Median home value: $100,845 (2007); Median rent: $316 per month (2000); Median age of housing: 60+ years (2000).
Transportation: Commute to work: 94.3% car, 0.2% public transportation, 2.4% walk, 2.1% work from home (2000); Travel time to work: 18.1% less than 15 minutes, 37.2% 15 to 30 minutes, 28.3% 30 to 45 minutes, 11.4% 45 to 60 minutes, 5.1% 60 minutes or more (2000)

MUTUAL (village). Covers a land area of 0.136 square miles and a water area of 0 square miles. Located at 40.07° N. Lat.; 83.63° W. Long. Elevation is 1,194 feet.
Population: 126 (1990); 132 (2000); 143 (2007); 150 (2012 projected); Race: 100.0% White, 0.0% Black, 0.0% Asian, 2.1% Hispanic of any race (2007); Density: 1,050.4 persons per square mile (2007); Average household size: 2.51 (2007); Median age: 37.7 (2007); Males per 100 females: 66.3 (2007); Marriage status: 16.5% never married, 67.1% now married, 11.4% widowed, 5.1% divorced (2000); Foreign born: 0.0% (2000); Ancestry (includes multiple ancestries): 34.9% German, 17.0% United States or American, 13.2% English, 6.6% Other groups, 5.7% Dutch (2000).
Economy: Employment by occupation: 3.4% management, 16.9% professional, 8.5% services, 11.9% sales, 0.0% farming, 5.1% construction, 54.2% production (2000).
Income: Per capita income: $22,325 (2007); Median household income: $55,000 (2007); Average household income: $56,009 (2007); Percent of households with income of $100,000 or more: 8.8% (2007); Poverty rate: 1.0% (2000).
Education: Percent of population age 25 and over with: High school diploma (including GED) or higher: 90.3% (2007); Bachelor's degree or higher: 12.9% (2007); Master's degree or higher: 2.2% (2007).
Housing: Homeownership rate: 86.0% (2007); Median home value: $106,618 (2007); Median rent: $525 per month (2000); Median age of housing: 60+ years (2000).
Transportation: Commute to work: 98.2% car, 0.0% public transportation, 0.0% walk, 1.8% work from home (2000); Travel time to work: 26.8% less than 15 minutes, 33.9% 15 to 30 minutes, 33.9% 30 to 45 minutes, 1.8% 45 to 60 minutes, 3.6% 60 minutes or more (2000)

NORTH LEWISBURG (village). Covers a land area of 0.894 square miles and a water area of 0 square miles. Located at 40.22° N. Lat.; 83.55° W. Long. Elevation is 1,093 feet.

Population: 1,275 (1990); 1,588 (2000); 1,769 (2007); 1,861 (2012 projected); Race: 96.8% White, 1.0% Black, 0.0% Asian, 0.8% Hispanic of any race (2007); Density: 1,979.2 persons per square mile (2007); Average household size: 2.61 (2007); Median age: 32.2 (2007); Males per 100 females: 103.6 (2007); Marriage status: 20.8% never married, 58.8% now married, 5.5% widowed, 14.9% divorced (2000); Foreign born: 0.8% (2000); Ancestry (includes multiple ancestries): 21.5% German, 14.1% United States or American, 11.1% Irish, 9.8% Other groups, 8.8% English (2000).

Economy: Employment by occupation: 8.7% management, 9.9% professional, 10.5% services, 20.1% sales, 0.6% farming, 11.5% construction, 38.6% production (2000).

Income: Per capita income: $21,256 (2007); Median household income: $50,585 (2007); Average household income: $55,379 (2007); Percent of households with income of $100,000 or more: 9.0% (2007); Poverty rate: 7.3% (2000).

Education: Percent of population age 25 and over with: High school diploma (including GED) or higher: 87.2% (2007); Bachelor's degree or higher: 6.7% (2007); Master's degree or higher: 1.3% (2007).

School District(s)

Triad Local (PK-12)
2005-06 Enrollment: 1,099 . . . . (937) 826-4961

Housing: Homeownership rate: 72.2% (2007); Median home value: $109,804 (2007); Median rent: $378 per month (2000); Median age of housing: 22 years (2000).

Transportation: Commute to work: 95.8% car, 0.0% public transportation, 1.8% walk, 2.0% work from home (2000); Travel time to work: 25.3% less than 15 minutes, 46.8% 15 to 30 minutes, 12.6% 30 to 45 minutes, 8.3% 45 to 60 minutes, 6.9% 60 minutes or more (2000)

SAINT PARIS (village). Covers a land area of 0.868 square miles and a water area of 0 square miles. Located at 40.12° N. Lat.; 83.96° W. Long. Elevation is 1,207 feet.

History: St. Paris was settled in 1813 by David Huffman, when it was called simply Paris.

Population: 1,851 (1990); 1,998 (2000); 2,017 (2007); 2,051 (2012 projected); Race: 98.1% White, 0.2% Black, 0.0% Asian, 0.7% Hispanic of any race (2007); Density: 2,324.4 persons per square mile (2007); Average household size: 2.51 (2007); Median age: 34.1 (2007); Males per 100 females: 89.4 (2007); Marriage status: 22.1% never married, 60.8% now married, 6.6% widowed, 10.5% divorced (2000); Foreign born: 0.4% (2000); Ancestry (includes multiple ancestries): 24.2% German, 12.4% United States or American, 11.2% Irish, 11.1% English, 8.7% Other groups (2000).

Economy: Employment by occupation: 6.6% management, 13.1% professional, 12.3% services, 22.8% sales, 0.4% farming, 10.5% construction, 34.3% production (2000).

Income: Per capita income: $19,758 (2007); Median household income: $44,451 (2007); Average household income: $49,506 (2007); Percent of households with income of $100,000 or more: 5.2% (2007); Poverty rate: 8.8% (2000).

Education: Percent of population age 25 and over with: High school diploma (including GED) or higher: 81.2% (2007); Bachelor's degree or higher: 9.8% (2007); Master's degree or higher: 2.8% (2007).

School District(s)

Graham Digital Academy (KG-12)
2005-06 Enrollment: 45 . . . . (937) 663-4123
Graham Local (PK-12)
2005-06 Enrollment: 2,317 . . . . (937) 663-4123

Housing: Homeownership rate: 71.9% (2007); Median home value: $104,818 (2007); Median rent: $375 per month (2000); Median age of housing: 50 years (2000).

Transportation: Commute to work: 93.3% car, 0.7% public transportation, 4.6% walk, 1.2% work from home (2000); Travel time to work: 34.0% less than 15 minutes, 26.0% 15 to 30 minutes, 24.9% 30 to 45 minutes, 10.7% 45 to 60 minutes, 4.3% 60 minutes or more (2000)

URBANA (city). County seat. Covers a land area of 6.822 square miles and a water area of 0 square miles. Located at 40.11° N. Lat.; 83.75° W. Long. Elevation is 1,050 feet.

History: Urbana was laid out in 1805, and selected in 1812 by General Hull as the site of a training camp. After the war, many of the soldiers who had trained here remained as residents.

Population: 11,436 (1990); 11,613 (2000); 11,573 (2007); 11,531 (2012 projected); Race: 90.3% White, 6.4% Black, 0.5% Asian, 1.4% Hispanic of any race (2007); Density: 1,696.4 persons per square mile (2007); Average household size: 2.36 (2007); Median age: 38.3 (2007); Males per 100 females: 89.1 (2007); Marriage status: 22.7% never married, 54.8% now married, 9.1% widowed, 13.4% divorced (2000); Foreign born: 0.6% (2000); Ancestry (includes multiple ancestries): 19.3% German, 16.3% United States or American, 12.7% Irish, 11.7% Other groups, 8.2% English (2000).

Economy: Employment by occupation: 8.6% management, 14.7% professional, 16.5% services, 19.2% sales, 0.7% farming, 10.0% construction, 30.3% production (2000).

Income: Per capita income: $18,942 (2007); Median household income: $35,904 (2007); Average household income: $43,422 (2007); Percent of households with income of $100,000 or more: 5.6% (2007); Poverty rate: 10.9% (2000).

Education: Percent of population age 25 and over with: High school diploma (including GED) or higher: 79.0% (2007); Bachelor's degree or higher: 11.3% (2007); Master's degree or higher: 4.0% (2007).

School District(s)

Urbana City (PK-12)
2005-06 Enrollment: 2,316 . . . . (937) 653-1402
Urbana Community School (KG-12)
2005-06 Enrollment: 49 . . . . (937) 653-1478

Four-year College(s)

Urbana University (Private, Not-for-profit)
Fall 2007 Enrollment: 1,440. . . . . (937) 484-1301
2007-08 Tuition: In-state $17,704; Out-of-state $17,704

Housing: Homeownership rate: 60.8% (2007); Median home value: $107,250 (2007); Median rent: $361 per month (2000); Median age of housing: 48 years (2000).

Hospitals: Mercy Memorial Hospital (73 beds)

Newspapers: Sunday Extra (Community news; Circulation 14,200); Urbana Citizen (Local news; Circulation 7,300)

Transportation: Commute to work: 93.9% car, 0.0% public transportation, 3.5% walk, 1.2% work from home (2000); Travel time to work: 51.3% less than 15 minutes, 24.9% 15 to 30 minutes, 14.5% 30 to 45 minutes, 4.7% 45 to 60 minutes, 4.7% 60 minutes or more (2000)

Additional Information Contacts

Champaign County Chamber of Commerce . . . . (937) 653-5764
http://www.champaignohio.com
City of Urbana . . . . (937) 652-4300
http://urbanaohio.com

WOODSTOCK (village). Covers a land area of 0.272 square miles and a water area of 0 square miles. Located at 40.17° N. Lat.; 83.52° W. Long. Elevation is 1,043 feet.

Population: 296 (1990); 317 (2000); 284 (2007); 288 (2012 projected); Race: 97.5% White, 0.0% Black, 0.0% Asian, 0.0% Hispanic of any race (2007); Density: 1,045.6 persons per square mile (2007); Average household size: 3.09 (2007); Median age: 30.5 (2007); Males per 100 females: 88.1 (2007); Marriage status: 14.7% never married, 70.6% now married, 4.4% widowed, 10.3% divorced (2000); Foreign born: 0.0% (2000); Ancestry (includes multiple ancestries): 18.4% United States or American, 11.6% German, 11.3% Other groups, 5.2% English, 4.2% Irish (2000).

Economy: Single-family building permits issued: 0 (2007); Multi-family building permits issued: 0 (2007); Employment by occupation: 5.5% management, 8.2% professional, 11.8% services, 16.4% sales, 2.7% farming, 20.9% construction, 34.5% production (2000).

Income: Per capita income: $19,542 (2007); Median household income: $50,000 (2007); Average household income: $60,326 (2007); Percent of households with income of $100,000 or more: 5.4% (2007); Poverty rate: 10.9% (2000).

Education: Percent of population age 25 and over with: High school diploma (including GED) or higher: 70.7% (2007); Bachelor's degree or higher: 7.9% (2007); Master's degree or higher: 1.8% (2007).

Housing: Homeownership rate: 80.4% (2007); Median home value: $103,000 (2007); Median rent: $297 per month (2000); Median age of housing: 60+ years (2000).

Transportation: Commute to work: 93.3% car, 0.0% public transportation, 6.7% walk, 0.0% work from home (2000); Travel time to work: 11.4% less

than 15 minutes, 47.6% 15 to 30 minutes, 29.5% 30 to 45 minutes, 10.5% 45 to 60 minutes, 1.0% 60 minutes or more (2000)

Clark County

Located in west central Ohio; crossed by the Mad and Little Miami Rivers. Covers a land area of 399.86 square miles, a water area of 3.70 square miles, and is located in the Eastern Time Zone. The county was founded in 1817. County seat is Springfield.

Clark County is part of the Springfield, OH Metropolitan Statistical Area. The entire metro area includes: Clark County, OH

Weather Station: Springfield New Water Works Elevation: 928 feet

	Jan	Feb	Mar	Apr	May	Jun	Jul	Aug	Sep	Oct	Nov	Dec
High	34	38	49	60	71	80	84	82	76	64	51	40
Low	17	19	28	38	48	58	62	59	52	40	32	23
Precip	2.3	1.8	2.5	3.4	4.3	4.5	4.2	3.6	2.9	2.6	3.0	2.7
Snow	na	na	na	tr	0.0	0.0	0.0	0.0	0.0	tr	0.1	na

High and Low temperatures in degrees Fahrenheit; Precipitation and Snow in inches

Population: 147,540 (1990); 144,742 (2000); 141,967 (2007); 139,749 (2012 projected); Race: 87.5% White, 9.0% Black, 0.6% Asian, 1.6% Hispanic of any race (2007); Density: 355.0 persons per square mile (2007); Average household size: 2.49 (2007); Median age: 39.2 (2007); Males per 100 females: 93.2 (2007).
Religion: Five largest groups: 8.4% Catholic Church, 5.0% The United Methodist Church, 4.1% Evangelical Lutheran Church in America, 2.1% Southern Baptist Convention, 1.9% Christian Churches and Churches of Christ (2000).
Economy: Unemployment rate: 6.6% (6/2008); Total civilian labor force: 71,656 (6/2008); Leading industries: 17.9% health care and social assistance; 16.2% manufacturing; 15.3% retail trade (2005); Farms: 756 totaling 165,366 acres (2002); Companies that employ 500 or more persons: 8 (2006); Companies that employ 100 to 499 persons: 61 (2006); Companies that employ less than 100 persons: 2,522 (2006); Black-owned businesses: 229 (2002); Hispanic-owned businesses: n/a (2002); Asian-owned businesses: 174 (2002); Women-owned businesses: 2,407 (2002); Retail sales per capita: $11,315 (2008). Single-family building permits issued: 191 (2007); Multi-family building permits issued: 204 (2007).
Income: Per capita income: $22,407 (2007); Median household income: $44,523 (2007); Average household income: $55,243 (2007); Percent of households with income of $100,000 or more: 11.6% (2007); Poverty rate: 15.0% (2005); Bankruptcy rate: 4.20% (2007).
Taxes: Total county taxes per capita: $250 (2006); County property taxes per capita: $136 (2006).
Education: Percent of population age 25 and over with: High school diploma (including GED) or higher: 81.5% (2007); Bachelor's degree or higher: 15.1% (2007); Master's degree or higher: 5.5% (2007).
Housing: Homeownership rate: 72.3% (2007); Median home value: $109,731 (2007); Median rent: $376 per month (2000); Median age of housing: 41 years (2000).
Health: Birth rate: 128.5 per 10,000 population (2007); Death rate: 116.3 per 10,000 population (2007); Age-adjusted cancer mortality rate: 200.4 deaths per 100,000 population (2005); Air Quality Index: 74.5% good, 22.5% moderate, 2.7% unhealthy for sensitive individuals, 0.3% unhealthy (percent of days in 2007); Number of physicians: 15.7 per 10,000 population (2005); Hospital beds: 27.7 per 10,000 population (2004); Hospital admissions: 1,362.9 per 10,000 population (2004).
Elections: 2004 Presidential election results: 50.8% Bush, 48.7% Kerry, 0.0% Nader, 0.3% Badnarik
National and State Parks: Buck Creek State Park; Buck Creek State Park
Additional Information Contacts
Clark County Government . . . . (937) 328-2405
http://www.clarkcountyohio.gov
City of Springfield . . . . (937) 324-7700
http://www.ci.springfield.oh.us
Greater Springfield Chamber of Commerce . . . . (937) 325-7621
http://chamber.greaterspringfield.com

Clark County Communities

CATAWBA (village). Covers a land area of 0.255 square miles and a water area of 0 square miles. Located at 40.00° N. Lat.; 83.62° W. Long. Elevation is 1,237 feet.
Population: 268 (1990); 312 (2000); 333 (2007); 344 (2012 projected); Race: 95.2% White, 0.6% Black, 0.0% Asian, 0.0% Hispanic of any race (2007); Density: 1,303.4 persons per square mile (2007); Average household size: 2.85 (2007); Median age: 32.9 (2007); Males per 100 females: 109.4 (2007); Marriage status: 20.4% never married, 59.9% now married, 0.0% widowed, 19.7% divorced (2000); Foreign born: 0.0% (2000); Ancestry (includes multiple ancestries): 25.4% German, 24.9% Irish, 15.0% Dutch, 8.8% Other groups, 7.8% Welsh (2000).
Economy: Employment by occupation: 13.0% management, 4.3% professional, 19.6% services, 18.5% sales, 0.0% farming, 12.0% construction, 32.6% production (2000).
Income: Per capita income: $19,512 (2007); Median household income: $53,500 (2007); Average household income: $55,534 (2007); Percent of households with income of $100,000 or more: 3.4% (2007); Poverty rate: 0.0% (2000).
Education: Percent of population age 25 and over with: High school diploma (including GED) or higher: 84.4% (2007); Bachelor's degree or higher: 13.6% (2007); Master's degree or higher: 10.6% (2007).
Housing: Homeownership rate: 86.3% (2007); Median home value: $92,083 (2007); Median rent: $275 per month (2000); Median age of housing: 60+ years (2000).
Transportation: Commute to work: 100.0% car, 0.0% public transportation, 0.0% walk, 0.0% work from home (2000); Travel time to work: 5.4% less than 15 minutes, 46.7% 15 to 30 minutes, 32.6% 30 to 45 minutes, 5.4% 45 to 60 minutes, 9.8% 60 minutes or more (2000)

CRYSTAL LAKES (CDP). Covers a land area of 0.456 square miles and a water area of 0.033 square miles. Located at 39.88° N. Lat.; 84.02° W. Long. Elevation is 850 feet.
Population: 1,613 (1990); 1,411 (2000); 1,310 (2007); 1,281 (2012 projected); Race: 95.6% White, 0.5% Black, 0.2% Asian, 3.5% Hispanic of any race (2007); Density: 2,869.8 persons per square mile (2007); Average household size: 2.45 (2007); Median age: 38.9 (2007); Males per 100 females: 99.4 (2007); Marriage status: 29.7% never married, 53.7% now married, 1.4% widowed, 15.2% divorced (2000); Foreign born: 1.8% (2000); Ancestry (includes multiple ancestries): 27.2% German, 23.7% United States or American, 19.2% English, 9.0% Irish, 5.9% Other groups (2000).
Economy: Employment by occupation: 3.5% management, 7.8% professional, 16.4% services, 25.9% sales, 0.0% farming, 11.7% construction, 34.7% production (2000).
Income: Per capita income: $18,128 (2007); Median household income: $43,171 (2007); Average household income: $44,471 (2007); Percent of households with income of $100,000 or more: 3.6% (2007); Poverty rate: 14.6% (2000).
Education: Percent of population age 25 and over with: High school diploma (including GED) or higher: 73.9% (2007); Bachelor's degree or higher: 1.2% (2007); Master's degree or higher: 0.3% (2007).
Housing: Homeownership rate: 83.3% (2007); Median home value: $83,598 (2007); Median rent: $360 per month (2000); Median age of housing: 44 years (2000).
Transportation: Commute to work: 100.0% car, 0.0% public transportation, 0.0% walk, 0.0% work from home (2000); Travel time to work: 20.4% less than 15 minutes, 56.4% 15 to 30 minutes, 15.9% 30 to 45 minutes, 1.2% 45 to 60 minutes, 6.1% 60 minutes or more (2000)

DONNELSVILLE (village). Covers a land area of 0.388 square miles and a water area of 0 square miles. Located at 39.91° N. Lat.; 83.94° W. Long. Elevation is 932 feet.
Population: 349 (1990); 293 (2000); 302 (2007); 306 (2012 projected); Race: 94.4% White, 0.7% Black, 0.0% Asian, 4.0% Hispanic of any race (2007); Density: 779.3 persons per square mile (2007); Average household size: 2.93 (2007); Median age: 34.1 (2007); Males per 100 females: 101.3 (2007); Marriage status: 20.1% never married, 66.7% now married, 5.2% widowed, 8.0% divorced (2000); Foreign born: 0.8% (2000); Ancestry (includes multiple ancestries): 15.2% German, 13.2% United States or American, 8.6% Irish, 8.6% English, 6.6% Polish (2000).
Economy: Employment by occupation: 15.9% management, 18.9% professional, 11.4% services, 20.5% sales, 0.0% farming, 16.7% construction, 16.7% production (2000).

Income: Per capita income: $24,478 (2007); Median household income: $71,500 (2007); Average household income: $71,772 (2007); Percent of households with income of $100,000 or more: 21.4% (2007); Poverty rate: 9.5% (2000).
Education: Percent of population age 25 and over with: High school diploma (including GED) or higher: 88.0% (2007); Bachelor's degree or higher: 17.9% (2007); Master's degree or higher: 3.3% (2007).

School District(s)

Tecumseh Local (PK-12)
2005-06 Enrollment: 3,560 . . . . (937) 845-3576
Housing: Homeownership rate: 80.6% (2007); Median home value: $123,438 (2007); Median rent: $383 per month (2000); Median age of housing: 45 years (2000).
Transportation: Commute to work: 95.5% car, 0.0% public transportation, 0.0% walk, 4.5% work from home (2000); Travel time to work: 15.1% less than 15 minutes, 54.0% 15 to 30 minutes, 26.2% 30 to 45 minutes, 0.0% 45 to 60 minutes, 4.8% 60 minutes or more (2000)

ENON (village). Covers a land area of 1.326 square miles and a water area of 0 square miles. Located at 39.87° N. Lat.; 83.93° W. Long. Elevation is 899 feet.
Population: 2,653 (1990); 2,638 (2000); 2,517 (2007); 2,442 (2012 projected); Race: 96.5% White, 0.6% Black, 0.6% Asian, 1.1% Hispanic of any race (2007); Density: 1,898.4 persons per square mile (2007); Average household size: 2.29 (2007); Median age: 46.7 (2007); Males per 100 females: 97.3 (2007); Marriage status: 17.8% never married, 65.7% now married, 7.3% widowed, 9.2% divorced (2000); Foreign born: 2.7% (2000); Ancestry (includes multiple ancestries): 24.9% German, 14.9% Irish, 14.5% English, 12.0% United States or American, 5.9% Other groups (2000).
Economy: Single-family building permits issued: 0 (2007); Multi-family building permits issued: 0 (2007); Employment by occupation: 14.3% management, 20.9% professional, 10.4% services, 33.0% sales, 0.0% farming, 8.9% construction, 12.5% production (2000).
Income: Per capita income: $31,087 (2007); Median household income: $64,919 (2007); Average household income: $71,197 (2007); Percent of households with income of $100,000 or more: 20.0% (2007); Poverty rate: 2.8% (2000).
Education: Percent of population age 25 and over with: High school diploma (including GED) or higher: 91.0% (2007); Bachelor's degree or higher: 28.0% (2007); Master's degree or higher: 13.3% (2007).

School District(s)

Greenon Local (PK-12)
2005-06 Enrollment: 2,031 . . . . (937) 864-1202
Housing: Homeownership rate: 79.9% (2007); Median home value: $149,085 (2007); Median rent: $396 per month (2000); Median age of housing: 30 years (2000).
Newspapers: Times Community Newspapers (Community news; Circulation 3,000)
Transportation: Commute to work: 95.3% car, 0.3% public transportation, 2.1% walk, 1.0% work from home (2000); Travel time to work: 25.1% less than 15 minutes, 48.2% 15 to 30 minutes, 20.3% 30 to 45 minutes, 2.8% 45 to 60 minutes, 3.6% 60 minutes or more (2000)

GREEN MEADOWS (CDP). Covers a land area of 0.609 square miles and a water area of 0 square miles. Located at 39.86° N. Lat.; 83.94° W. Long. Elevation is 892 feet.
Population: 2,526 (1990); 2,318 (2000); 2,234 (2007); 2,169 (2012 projected); Race: 97.1% White, 1.1% Black, 0.5% Asian, 1.0% Hispanic of any race (2007); Density: 3,669.8 persons per square mile (2007); Average household size: 2.47 (2007); Median age: 37.5 (2007); Males per 100 females: 93.9 (2007); Marriage status: 19.0% never married, 63.8% now married, 6.2% widowed, 11.0% divorced (2000); Foreign born: 0.9% (2000); Ancestry (includes multiple ancestries): 30.7% German, 16.1% English, 11.4% Irish, 10.3% United States or American, 9.9% Other groups (2000).
Economy: Employment by occupation: 11.3% management, 21.2% professional, 14.1% services, 24.8% sales, 0.0% farming, 12.5% construction, 16.1% production (2000).
Income: Per capita income: $20,210 (2007); Median household income: $44,007 (2007); Average household income: $49,890 (2007); Percent of households with income of $100,000 or more: 7.0% (2007); Poverty rate: 4.5% (2000).
Education: Percent of population age 25 and over with: High school diploma (including GED) or higher: 87.1% (2007); Bachelor's degree or higher: 16.1% (2007); Master's degree or higher: 6.3% (2007).
Housing: Homeownership rate: 75.2% (2007); Median home value: $118,579 (2007); Median rent: $494 per month (2000); Median age of housing: 35 years (2000).
Transportation: Commute to work: 98.3% car, 0.0% public transportation, 0.3% walk, 0.6% work from home (2000); Travel time to work: 24.9% less than 15 minutes, 48.6% 15 to 30 minutes, 19.9% 30 to 45 minutes, 3.0% 45 to 60 minutes, 3.6% 60 minutes or more (2000)

HOLIDAY VALLEY (CDP). Covers a land area of 2.074 square miles and a water area of 0 square miles. Located at 39.85° N. Lat.; 83.97° W. Long. Elevation is 860 feet.
Population: 1,243 (1990); 1,712 (2000); 1,736 (2007); 1,739 (2012 projected); Race: 95.7% White, 1.5% Black, 0.6% Asian, 1.5% Hispanic of any race (2007); Density: 837.0 persons per square mile (2007); Average household size: 2.87 (2007); Median age: 45.6 (2007); Males per 100 females: 89.3 (2007); Marriage status: 15.9% never married, 63.8% now married, 8.8% widowed, 11.5% divorced (2000); Foreign born: 2.5% (2000); Ancestry (includes multiple ancestries): 28.7% German, 13.2% English, 12.3% Scotch-Irish, 11.6% Irish, 9.7% Other groups (2000).
Economy: Employment by occupation: 17.8% management, 20.9% professional, 11.5% services, 25.8% sales, 0.0% farming, 13.0% construction, 11.0% production (2000).
Income: Per capita income: $24,956 (2007); Median household income: $62,143 (2007); Average household income: $67,798 (2007); Percent of households with income of $100,000 or more: 19.0% (2007); Poverty rate: 12.2% (2000).
Education: Percent of population age 25 and over with: High school diploma (including GED) or higher: 89.2% (2007); Bachelor's degree or higher: 22.9% (2007); Master's degree or higher: 8.9% (2007).
Housing: Homeownership rate: 95.7% (2007); Median home value: $131,703 (2007); Median rent: $664 per month (2000); Median age of housing: 29 years (2000).
Transportation: Commute to work: 94.0% car, 3.0% public transportation, 0.0% walk, 3.1% work from home (2000); Travel time to work: 20.7% less than 15 minutes, 47.1% 15 to 30 minutes, 10.5% 30 to 45 minutes, 7.3% 45 to 60 minutes, 14.5% 60 minutes or more (2000)

LAWRENCEVILLE (village). Covers a land area of 0.135 square miles and a water area of 0 square miles. Located at 39.98° N. Lat.; 83.87° W. Long. Elevation is 1,112 feet.
Population: 304 (1990); 302 (2000); 343 (2007); 362 (2012 projected); Race: 93.9% White, 0.9% Black, 0.0% Asian, 0.0% Hispanic of any race (2007); Density: 2,547.7 persons per square mile (2007); Average household size: 2.70 (2007); Median age: 38.1 (2007); Males per 100 females: 104.2 (2007); Marriage status: 20.6% never married, 59.7% now married, 3.3% widowed, 16.5% divorced (2000); Foreign born: 0.0% (2000); Ancestry (includes multiple ancestries): 28.6% German, 18.7% United States or American, 11.6% Irish, 11.2% English, 10.2% Other groups (2000).
Economy: Employment by occupation: 6.3% management, 20.3% professional, 12.7% services, 31.6% sales, 1.9% farming, 12.0% construction, 15.2% production (2000).
Income: Per capita income: $21,866 (2007); Median household income: $55,417 (2007); Average household income: $59,055 (2007); Percent of households with income of $100,000 or more: 11.0% (2007); Poverty rate: 3.1% (2000).
Education: Percent of population age 25 and over with: High school diploma (including GED) or higher: 84.9% (2007); Bachelor's degree or higher: 13.3% (2007); Master's degree or higher: 2.7% (2007).
Housing: Homeownership rate: 67.7% (2007); Median home value: $118,478 (2007); Median rent: $498 per month (2000); Median age of housing: 47 years (2000).
Transportation: Commute to work: 95.5% car, 0.0% public transportation, 1.3% walk, 3.2% work from home (2000); Travel time to work: 30.9% less than 15 minutes, 48.3% 15 to 30 minutes, 14.1% 30 to 45 minutes, 1.3% 45 to 60 minutes, 5.4% 60 minutes or more (2000)

MEDWAY (unincorporated postal area, zip code 45341). Covers a land area of 7.094 square miles and a water area of 0.214 square miles. Located at 39.88° N. Lat.; 84.02° W. Long. Elevation is 850 feet.
Population: 4,110 (2000); Race: 94.7% White, 0.8% Black, 0.7% Asian, 0.6% Hispanic of any race (2000); Density: 579.3 persons per square mile (2000); Age: 21.8% under 18, 18.4% over 64 (2000); Marriage status: 24.1% never married, 55.4% now married, 7.1% widowed, 13.3% divorced (2000); Foreign born: 1.3% (2000); Ancestry (includes multiple ancestries):

24.8% German, 21.4% United States or American, 14.5% English, 11.2% Irish, 6.8% Other groups (2000).
Economy: Employment by occupation: 8.4% management, 13.0% professional, 12.6% services, 26.2% sales, 0.4% farming, 11.6% construction, 27.8% production (2000).
Income: Per capita income: $19,156 (2000); Median household income: $38,191 (2000); Poverty rate: 7.5% (2000).
Education: Percent of population age 25 and over with: High school diploma (including GED) or higher: 77.1% (2000); Bachelor's degree or higher: 8.4% (2000).

School District(s)

Tecumseh Local (PK-12)
2005-06 Enrollment: 3,560 . . . . (937) 845-3576
Housing: Homeownership rate: 84.4% (2000); Median home value: $81,600 (2000); Median rent: $368 per month (2000); Median age of housing: 37 years (2000).
Transportation: Commute to work: 95.0% car, 0.8% public transportation, 0.5% walk, 1.3% work from home (2000); Travel time to work: 26.0% less than 15 minutes, 52.2% 15 to 30 minutes, 16.5% 30 to 45 minutes, 2.1% 45 to 60 minutes, 3.1% 60 minutes or more (2000)

NEW CARLISLE (city). Covers a land area of 1.932 square miles and a water area of 0.007 square miles. Located at 39.94° N. Lat.; 84.03° W. Long. Elevation is 899 feet.
History: Founded 1810.
Population: 6,066 (1990); 5,735 (2000); 5,624 (2007); 5,533 (2012 projected); Race: 94.9% White, 0.4% Black, 0.3% Asian, 4.1% Hispanic of any race (2007); Density: 2,910.7 persons per square mile (2007); Average household size: 2.56 (2007); Median age: 36.8 (2007); Males per 100 females: 91.6 (2007); Marriage status: 20.6% never married, 59.6% now married, 6.8% widowed, 13.1% divorced (2000); Foreign born: 1.2% (2000); Ancestry (includes multiple ancestries): 22.7% German, 16.4% United States or American, 11.3% Other groups, 11.0% Irish, 10.1% English (2000).
Economy: Employment by occupation: 7.8% management, 14.2% professional, 19.0% services, 25.7% sales, 0.9% farming, 11.2% construction, 21.3% production (2000).
Income: Per capita income: $18,774 (2007); Median household income: $42,871 (2007); Average household income: $47,283 (2007); Percent of households with income of $100,000 or more: 5.7% (2007); Poverty rate: 11.5% (2000).
Education: Percent of population age 25 and over with: High school diploma (including GED) or higher: 82.1% (2007); Bachelor's degree or higher: 12.7% (2007); Master's degree or higher: 3.3% (2007).

School District(s)

Tecumseh Local (PK-12)
2005-06 Enrollment: 3,560 . . . . (937) 845-3576
Housing: Homeownership rate: 73.1% (2007); Median home value: $102,466 (2007); Median rent: $379 per month (2000); Median age of housing: 38 years (2000).
Newspapers: Enon Messenger (Community news; Circulation 2,175); New Carlisle Sun (Community news; Circulation 3,250)
Transportation: Commute to work: 96.9% car, 0.2% public transportation, 1.0% walk, 1.1% work from home (2000); Travel time to work: 27.6% less than 15 minutes, 37.6% 15 to 30 minutes, 27.4% 30 to 45 minutes, 3.7% 45 to 60 minutes, 3.6% 60 minutes or more (2000)

NORTH HAMPTON (village). Covers a land area of 0.257 square miles and a water area of 0 square miles. Located at 39.99° N. Lat.; 83.94° W. Long. Elevation is 1,093 feet.
Population: 417 (1990); 370 (2000); 395 (2007); 410 (2012 projected); Race: 95.7% White, 0.0% Black, 1.5% Asian, 0.0% Hispanic of any race (2007); Density: 1,538.1 persons per square mile (2007); Average household size: 2.65 (2007); Median age: 36.7 (2007); Males per 100 females: 102.6 (2007); Marriage status: 22.5% never married, 67.6% now married, 8.1% widowed, 1.8% divorced (2000); Foreign born: 0.0% (2000); Ancestry (includes multiple ancestries): 23.5% German, 22.5% United States or American, 15.0% English, 13.9% Irish, 4.8% Welsh (2000).
Economy: Employment by occupation: 12.0% management, 22.0% professional, 4.0% services, 10.0% sales, 0.0% farming, 26.0% construction, 26.0% production (2000).
Income: Per capita income: $21,703 (2007); Median household income: $46,806 (2007); Average household income: $57,534 (2007); Percent of households with income of $100,000 or more: 11.4% (2007); Poverty rate: 0.0% (2000).
Education: Percent of population age 25 and over with: High school diploma (including GED) or higher: 90.0% (2007); Bachelor's degree or higher: 21.9% (2007); Master's degree or higher: 13.8% (2007).
Housing: Homeownership rate: 79.2% (2007); Median home value: $117,803 (2007); Median rent: $315 per month (2000); Median age of housing: 46 years (2000).
Transportation: Commute to work: 94.0% car, 0.0% public transportation, 6.0% walk, 0.0% work from home (2000); Travel time to work: 18.0% less than 15 minutes, 50.0% 15 to 30 minutes, 22.0% 30 to 45 minutes, 6.0% 45 to 60 minutes, 4.0% 60 minutes or more (2000)

NORTHRIDGE (CDP). Covers a land area of 3.053 square miles and a water area of 0 square miles. Located at 39.99° N. Lat.; 83.77° W. Long. Elevation is 1,083 feet.
Population: 5,939 (1990); 6,853 (2000); 6,811 (2007); 6,832 (2012 projected); Race: 97.2% White, 1.5% Black, 0.5% Asian, 0.6% Hispanic of any race (2007); Density: 2,230.9 persons per square mile (2007); Average household size: 2.36 (2007); Median age: 43.8 (2007); Males per 100 females: 93.5 (2007); Marriage status: 16.2% never married, 68.0% now married, 8.4% widowed, 7.4% divorced (2000); Foreign born: 0.4% (2000); Ancestry (includes multiple ancestries): 29.9% German, 14.6% United States or American, 13.6% Irish, 9.5% English, 5.6% Other groups (2000).
Economy: Employment by occupation: 9.6% management, 19.5% professional, 14.0% services, 25.7% sales, 0.2% farming, 8.1% construction, 22.8% production (2000).
Income: Per capita income: $24,589 (2007); Median household income: $54,603 (2007); Average household income: $58,111 (2007); Percent of households with income of $100,000 or more: 9.8% (2007); Poverty rate: 2.4% (2000).
Education: Percent of population age 25 and over with: High school diploma (including GED) or higher: 89.9% (2007); Bachelor's degree or higher: 17.6% (2007); Master's degree or higher: 5.2% (2007).
Housing: Homeownership rate: 85.3% (2007); Median home value: $126,761 (2007); Median rent: $436 per month (2000); Median age of housing: 28 years (2000).
Transportation: Commute to work: 96.5% car, 0.7% public transportation, 0.2% walk, 2.6% work from home (2000); Travel time to work: 27.5% less than 15 minutes, 50.1% 15 to 30 minutes, 11.8% 30 to 45 minutes, 7.2% 45 to 60 minutes, 3.4% 60 minutes or more (2000)

PARK LAYNE (CDP). Covers a land area of 1.488 square miles and a water area of 0 square miles. Located at 39.88° N. Lat.; 84.04° W. Long. Elevation is 843 feet.
Population: 4,795 (1990); 4,519 (2000); 4,486 (2007); 4,460 (2012 projected); Race: 95.9% White, 0.6% Black, 0.2% Asian, 2.0% Hispanic of any race (2007); Density: 3,014.3 persons per square mile (2007); Average household size: 2.77 (2007); Median age: 33.6 (2007); Males per 100 females: 95.3 (2007); Marriage status: 21.2% never married, 60.8% now married, 5.1% widowed, 13.0% divorced (2000); Foreign born: 1.2% (2000); Ancestry (includes multiple ancestries): 27.0% United States or American, 17.5% German, 12.3% Irish, 8.1% Other groups, 6.4% English (2000).
Economy: Employment by occupation: 5.3% management, 11.1% professional, 14.9% services, 24.4% sales, 1.8% farming, 14.3% construction, 28.3% production (2000).
Income: Per capita income: $16,505 (2007); Median household income: $40,313 (2007); Average household income: $45,732 (2007); Percent of households with income of $100,000 or more: 5.0% (2007); Poverty rate: 6.6% (2000).
Education: Percent of population age 25 and over with: High school diploma (including GED) or higher: 75.6% (2007); Bachelor's degree or higher: 3.6% (2007); Master's degree or higher: 0.6% (2007).
Housing: Homeownership rate: 79.1% (2007); Median home value: $95,641 (2007); Median rent: $433 per month (2000); Median age of housing: 35 years (2000).
Transportation: Commute to work: 96.8% car, 0.0% public transportation, 1.4% walk, 1.7% work from home (2000); Travel time to work: 22.1% less than 15 minutes, 51.9% 15 to 30 minutes, 16.6% 30 to 45 minutes, 4.4% 45 to 60 minutes, 4.9% 60 minutes or more (2000)

SOUTH CHARLESTON (village). Covers a land area of 1.297 square miles and a water area of 0 square miles. Located at 39.82° N. Lat.; 83.63° W. Long. Elevation is 1,125 feet.
History: South Charleston developed as a rural distributing center.

Population: 1,681 (1990); 1,850 (2000); 1,961 (2007); 2,028 (2012 projected); Race: 96.4% White, 1.5% Black, 0.8% Asian, 0.3% Hispanic of any race (2007); Density: 1,511.6 persons per square mile (2007); Average household size: 2.52 (2007); Median age: 33.8 (2007); Males per 100 females: 88.6 (2007); Marriage status: 22.3% never married, 56.5% now married, 9.4% widowed, 11.9% divorced (2000); Foreign born: 0.3% (2000); Ancestry (includes multiple ancestries): 22.0% German, 14.4% Irish, 12.5% United States or American, 10.5% English, 8.7% Other groups (2000).
Economy: Employment by occupation: 9.8% management, 14.1% professional, 17.2% services, 23.2% sales, 0.4% farming, 10.4% construction, 25.0% production (2000).
Income: Per capita income: $20,186 (2007); Median household income: $44,278 (2007); Average household income: $50,815 (2007); Percent of households with income of $100,000 or more: 6.7% (2007); Poverty rate: 8.4% (2000).
Education: Percent of population age 25 and over with: High school diploma (including GED) or higher: 81.9% (2007); Bachelor's degree or higher: 9.7% (2007); Master's degree or higher: 4.0% (2007).

School District(s)

Southeastern Local (PK-12)
2005-06 Enrollment: 884 . . . . (937) 462-8388
Housing: Homeownership rate: 64.4% (2007); Median home value: $106,863 (2007); Median rent: $369 per month (2000); Median age of housing: 46 years (2000).
Safety: Violent crime rate: 0.0 per 10,000 population; Property crime rate: 132.7 per 10,000 population (2007).
Transportation: Commute to work: 93.8% car, 0.4% public transportation, 2.1% walk, 3.3% work from home (2000); Travel time to work: 20.3% less than 15 minutes, 41.5% 15 to 30 minutes, 21.1% 30 to 45 minutes, 10.8% 45 to 60 minutes, 6.3% 60 minutes or more (2000)

SOUTH VIENNA (village). Aka Vienna. Covers a land area of 0.405 square miles and a water area of 0 square miles. Located at 39.92° N. Lat.; 83.61° W. Long. Elevation is 1,194 feet.
Population: 550 (1990); 469 (2000); 467 (2007); 465 (2012 projected); Race: 97.2% White, 0.4% Black, 0.0% Asian, 2.8% Hispanic of any race (2007); Density: 1,152.8 persons per square mile (2007); Average household size: 2.73 (2007); Median age: 33.7 (2007); Males per 100 females: 93.0 (2007); Marriage status: 20.1% never married, 57.0% now married, 5.0% widowed, 17.9% divorced (2000); Foreign born: 0.8% (2000); Ancestry (includes multiple ancestries): 27.9% German, 15.2% English, 13.9% United States or American, 7.1% Irish, 6.3% Scottish (2000).
Economy: Employment by occupation: 7.5% management, 9.2% professional, 14.0% services, 28.9% sales, 0.4% farming, 8.3% construction, 31.6% production (2000).
Income: Per capita income: $20,059 (2007); Median household income: $44,423 (2007); Average household income: $54,781 (2007); Percent of households with income of $100,000 or more: 8.8% (2007); Poverty rate: 8.2% (2000).
Education: Percent of population age 25 and over with: High school diploma (including GED) or higher: 81.7% (2007); Bachelor's degree or higher: 7.4% (2007); Master's degree or higher: 2.8% (2007).

School District(s)

Northeastern Local (PK-12)
2005-06 Enrollment: 3,823 . . . . (937) 325-7615
Housing: Homeownership rate: 71.3% (2007); Median home value: $116,875 (2007); Median rent: $460 per month (2000); Median age of housing: 60+ years (2000).
Transportation: Commute to work: 86.4% car, 0.9% public transportation, 7.3% walk, 5.5% work from home (2000); Travel time to work: 23.1% less than 15 minutes, 49.5% 15 to 30 minutes, 17.8% 30 to 45 minutes, 5.8% 45 to 60 minutes, 3.8% 60 minutes or more (2000)

SPRINGFIELD (city). County seat. Covers a land area of 22.473 square miles and a water area of 0.045 square miles. Located at 39.92° N. Lat.; 83.80° W. Long. Elevation is 978 feet.
History: Springfield's first settler was James Demint, who came in 1799. Surveyor John Daugherty platted a town in 1801. The settlement was called Springfield for the spring water coming down the cliffs that bordered the valley of Buck Creek. Simon Kenton from Kentucky set up a gristmill and sawmill on the site that was later the International Harvester plant. The National Road, completed in 1838, put Springfield on the route of the Ohio Stage Company and provided a means for the area's produce to get to a market. In the 1850's the Champion Binder Company was producing farm machinery here, its facility later purchased by the McCormick interests, which were subsequently acquired by International Harvester Company.
Population: 71,064 (1990); 65,358 (2000); 61,594 (2007); 58,974 (2012 projected); Race: 76.9% White, 18.7% Black, 0.9% Asian, 1.6% Hispanic of any race (2007); Density: 2,740.8 persons per square mile (2007); Average household size: 2.43 (2007); Median age: 36.0 (2007); Males per 100 females: 90.4 (2007); Marriage status: 29.0% never married, 47.6% now married, 9.7% widowed, 13.6% divorced (2000); Foreign born: 1.2% (2000); Ancestry (includes multiple ancestries): 21.9% Other groups, 17.9% German, 13.8% United States or American, 10.4% Irish, 6.5% English (2000).
Economy: Unemployment rate: 7.3% (6/2008); Total civilian labor force: 29,333 (6/2008); Single-family building permits issued: 84 (2007); Multi-family building permits issued: 200 (2007); Employment by occupation: 8.5% management, 16.0% professional, 17.9% services, 25.2% sales, 0.3% farming, 8.1% construction, 24.1% production (2000).
Income: Per capita income: $18,884 (2007); Median household income: $35,017 (2007); Average household income: $45,127 (2007); Percent of households with income of $100,000 or more: 7.2% (2007); Poverty rate: 16.9% (2000).
Taxes: Total city taxes per capita: $531 (2006); City property taxes per capita: $48 (2006).
Education: Percent of population age 25 and over with: High school diploma (including GED) or higher: 77.0% (2007); Bachelor's degree or higher: 13.0% (2007); Master's degree or higher: 4.8% (2007).

School District(s)

Clark-Shawnee Local (PK-12)
2005-06 Enrollment: 2,503 . . . . (937) 328-5378
Greenon Local (PK-12)
2005-06 Enrollment: 2,031 . . . . (937) 864-1202
Life Skills Center-Springfield (09-12)
2005-06 Enrollment: 169 . . . . (937) 322-2940
Northeastern Local (PK-12)
2005-06 Enrollment: 3,823 . . . . (937) 325-7615
Northwestern Local (PK-12)
2005-06 Enrollment: 1,947 . . . . (937) 964-1318
Springfield Acad of Excellence (KG-06)
2005-06 Enrollment: 274 . . . . (937) 325-0933
Springfield City (PK-12)
2005-06 Enrollment: 8,668 . . . . (937) 505-2800
Springfield Preparatory and Fitness Academy (KG-06)
2005-06 Enrollment: 153 . . . . (937) 323-6250
Springfield-Clark County (07-12)
2005-06 Enrollment: n/a . . . . (937) 325-7368
Urban Youth Academy Inc. (07-12)
2005-06 Enrollment: 105 . . . . (937) 360-5169

Four-year College(s)

Wittenberg University (Private, Not-for-profit, Lutheran Church in America)
Fall 2007 Enrollment: 2,078. . . . . (937) 327-6231
2007-08 Tuition: In-state $31,400; Out-of-state $31,400

Two-year College(s)

Carousel Beauty College (Private, For-profit)
Fall 2007 Enrollment: 38 . . . . (937) 223-3572
Clark State Community College (Public)
Fall 2007 Enrollment: 3,383. . . . . (937) 325-0691
2007-08 Tuition: In-state $3,699; Out-of-state $6,828
Community Hospital School of Nursing (Private, Not-for-profit)
Fall 2007 Enrollment: 159 . . . . (937) 328-8900
2007-08 Tuition: In-state $6,823; Out-of-state $6,823

Vocational/Technical School(s)

Springfield Clark County Joint Vocational School (Public)
Fall 2007 Enrollment: n/a. . . . . (937) 325-7368
Housing: Homeownership rate: 57.9% (2007); Median home value: $85,681 (2007); Median rent: $364 per month (2000); Median age of housing: 50 years (2000).
Hospitals: Community Hospital (324 beds); Mercy Medical Center (329 beds)
Safety: Violent crime rate: 73.8 per 10,000 population; Property crime rate: 866.1 per 10,000 population (2007).
Newspapers: Springfield News-Sun (Local news; Circulation 32,146); Tri County Shopper News (Community news; Circulation 67,100)
Transportation: Commute to work: 91.7% car, 1.5% public transportation, 4.2% walk, 1.6% work from home (2000); Travel time to work: 45.8% less

than 15 minutes, 33.3% 15 to 30 minutes, 11.3% 30 to 45 minutes, 5.4% 45 to 60 minutes, 4.2% 60 minutes or more (2000)
Airports: Springfield-Beckley Municipal (general aviation)
Additional Information Contacts
City of Springfield . . . . (937) 324-7700
http://www.ci.springfield.oh.us
Greater Springfield Chamber of Commerce . . . . (937) 325-7621
http://chamber.greaterspringfield.com

TREMONT CITY (village). Covers a land area of 0.267 square miles and a water area of 0 square miles. Located at 40.01° N. Lat.; 83.83° W. Long. Elevation is 951 feet.
Population: 477 (1990); 349 (2000); 324 (2007); 316 (2012 projected); Race: 96.6% White, 1.9% Black, 0.0% Asian, 0.6% Hispanic of any race (2007); Density: 1,212.9 persons per square mile (2007); Average household size: 2.55 (2007); Median age: 34.2 (2007); Males per 100 females: 92.9 (2007); Marriage status: 24.5% never married, 60.6% now married, 4.8% widowed, 10.0% divorced (2000); Foreign born: 0.6% (2000); Ancestry (includes multiple ancestries): 32.2% German, 15.1% Other groups, 13.6% English, 12.3% Irish, 7.2% United States or American (2000).
Economy: Single-family building permits issued: 0 (2007); Multi-family building permits issued: 0 (2007); Employment by occupation: 2.2% management, 10.6% professional, 14.0% services, 22.9% sales, 0.0% farming, 12.3% construction, 38.0% production (2000).
Income: Per capita income: $23,789 (2007); Median household income: $57,955 (2007); Average household income: $60,689 (2007); Percent of households with income of $100,000 or more: 7.1% (2007); Poverty rate: 5.8% (2000).
Education: Percent of population age 25 and over with: High school diploma (including GED) or higher: 89.9% (2007); Bachelor's degree or higher: 9.7% (2007); Master's degree or higher: 1.4% (2007).
Housing: Homeownership rate: 66.1% (2007); Median home value: $102,083 (2007); Median rent: $460 per month (2000); Median age of housing: 60 years (2000).
Transportation: Commute to work: 98.2% car, 1.2% public transportation, 0.0% walk, 0.6% work from home (2000); Travel time to work: 22.5% less than 15 minutes, 55.0% 15 to 30 minutes, 14.2% 30 to 45 minutes, 5.9% 45 to 60 minutes, 2.4% 60 minutes or more (2000)

Clermont County

Located in southwestern Ohio; bounded on the southwest by the Ohio River and the Kentucky border, and on the northwest by the Little Miami River. Covers a land area of 451.99 square miles, a water area of 5.68 square miles, and is located in the Eastern Time Zone. The county was founded in 1800. County seat is Batavia.

Clermont County is part of the Cincinnati-Middletown, OH-KY-IN Metropolitan Statistical Area. The entire metro area includes: Dearborn County, IN; Franklin County, IN; Ohio County, IN; Boone County, KY; Bracken County, KY; Campbell County, KY; Gallatin County, KY; Grant County, KY; Kenton County, KY; Pendleton County, KY; Brown County, OH; Butler County, OH; Clermont County, OH; Hamilton County, OH; Warren County, OH

Weather Station: Chilo Meldahl Lock & Dam — Elevation: 498 feet

	Jan	Feb	Mar	Apr	May	Jun	Jul	Aug	Sep	Oct	Nov	Dec
High	38	43	53	65	74	82	86	85	79	68	55	44
Low	20	23	31	40	50	59	64	63	56	44	35	26
Precip	3.0	3.0	4.2	3.8	4.5	4.3	3.8	3.9	3.1	2.9	3.3	3.3
Snow	na	na	1.0	0.0	0.0	0.0	0.0	0.0	0.0	0.0	tr	1.5

High and Low temperatures in degrees Fahrenheit; Precipitation and Snow in inches

Weather Station: Milford — Elevation: 518 feet

	Jan	Feb	Mar	Apr	May	Jun	Jul	Aug	Sep	Oct	Nov	Dec
High	37	41	52	64	75	82	87	85	79	67	54	42
Low	19	21	30	39	49	58	63	61	53	40	32	24
Precip	3.1	2.6	3.8	4.2	5.0	4.5	4.0	4.2	3.2	3.1	3.7	3.4
Snow	5.8	4.9	2.1	0.4	tr	0.0	0.0	tr	0.0	0.1	0.4	2.2

High and Low temperatures in degrees Fahrenheit; Precipitation and Snow in inches

Population: 150,129 (1990); 177,977 (2000); 194,299 (2007); 205,410 (2012 projected); Race: 96.3% White, 1.3% Black, 0.8% Asian, 1.2% Hispanic of any race (2007); Density: 429.9 persons per square mile (2007); Average household size: 2.62 (2007); Median age: 36.5 (2007); Males per 100 females: 97.1 (2007).
Religion: Five largest groups: 14.6% Catholic Church, 4.2% The United Methodist Church, 3.5% Southern Baptist Convention, 3.2% Christian Churches and Churches of Christ, 0.8% Church of the Nazarene (2000).
Economy: Unemployment rate: 5.9% (6/2008); Total civilian labor force: 108,291 (6/2008); Leading industries: 21.2% retail trade; 12.4% manufacturing; 11.9% accommodation & food services (2005); Farms: 973 totaling 116,026 acres (2002); Companies that employ 500 or more persons: 6 (2006); Companies that employ 100 to 499 persons: 89 (2006); Companies that employ less than 100 persons: 3,501 (2006); Black-owned businesses: 105 (2002); Hispanic-owned businesses: n/a (2002); Asian-owned businesses: n/a (2002); Women-owned businesses: 3,932 (2002); Retail sales per capita: $14,442 (2008). Single-family building permits issued: 587 (2007); Multi-family building permits issued: 233 (2007).
Income: Per capita income: $26,955 (2007); Median household income: $56,556 (2007); Average household income: $70,273 (2007); Percent of households with income of $100,000 or more: 19.7% (2007); Poverty rate: 8.4% (2005); Bankruptcy rate: 4.61% (2007).
Taxes: Total county taxes per capita: $259 (2006); County property taxes per capita: $128 (2006).
Education: Percent of population age 25 and over with: High school diploma (including GED) or higher: 82.0% (2007); Bachelor's degree or higher: 20.7% (2007); Master's degree or higher: 6.8% (2007).
Housing: Homeownership rate: 75.5% (2007); Median home value: $145,052 (2007); Median rent: $473 per month (2000); Median age of housing: 23 years (2000).
Health: Birth rate: 149.7 per 10,000 population (2007); Death rate: 74.9 per 10,000 population (2007); Age-adjusted cancer mortality rate: 205.8 deaths per 100,000 population (2005); Air Quality Index: 66.3% good, 26.7% moderate, 7.0% unhealthy for sensitive individuals, 0.0% unhealthy (percent of days in 2007); Number of physicians: 14.9 per 10,000 population (2005); Hospital beds: 8.7 per 10,000 population (2004); Hospital admissions: 338.6 per 10,000 population (2004).
Elections: 2004 Presidential election results: 70.7% Bush, 29.1% Kerry, 0.0% Nader, 0.2% Badnarik
National and State Parks: East Fork State Park; Stonelick Lake State Park
Additional Information Contacts
Clermont County Government . . . . (513) 732-7300
http://www.clermontcountyohio.gov
Clermont County Ohio Convention and Visitors Bureau . . . (513) 732-3600
http://www.visitclermontohio.com
Milford-Miami Twp Chamber of Commerce . . . . (513) 831-2411
http://www.milfordmiamitownship.com
Village of Bethel . . . . (513) 734-2243
http://bethel-oh.gov

Clermont County Communities

AMELIA (village). Covers a land area of 1.371 square miles and a water area of 0 square miles. Located at 39.02° N. Lat.; 84.22° W. Long. Elevation is 876 feet.
Population: 2,226 (1990); 2,752 (2000); 3,399 (2007); 3,818 (2012 projected); Race: 95.9% White, 1.0% Black, 0.3% Asian, 1.4% Hispanic of any race (2007); Density: 2,479.1 persons per square mile (2007); Average household size: 2.50 (2007); Median age: 32.0 (2007); Males per 100 females: 91.1 (2007); Marriage status: 23.3% never married, 59.9% now married, 5.6% widowed, 11.3% divorced (2000); Foreign born: 1.9% (2000); Ancestry (includes multiple ancestries): 30.4% German, 16.7% Irish, 16.1% United States or American, 9.0% Other groups, 8.3% English (2000).
Economy: Employment by occupation: 14.9% management, 14.1% professional, 16.4% services, 25.9% sales, 0.3% farming, 13.1% construction, 15.3% production (2000).
Income: Per capita income: $21,300 (2007); Median household income: $50,324 (2007); Average household income: $53,196 (2007); Percent of households with income of $100,000 or more: 8.1% (2007); Poverty rate: 7.6% (2000).
Education: Percent of population age 25 and over with: High school diploma (including GED) or higher: 82.9% (2007); Bachelor's degree or higher: 13.7% (2007); Master's degree or higher: 2.7% (2007).

School District(s)

West Clermont Local (PK-12)
2005-06 Enrollment: 9,272 . . . . (513) 943-5000

Housing: Homeownership rate: 53.5% (2007); Median home value: $135,232 (2007); Median rent: $448 per month (2000); Median age of housing: 20 years (2000).

Safety: Violent crime rate: 2.8 per 10,000 population; Property crime rate: 207.0 per 10,000 population (2007).

Transportation: Commute to work: 94.1% car, 2.4% public transportation, 1.7% walk, 1.8% work from home (2000); Travel time to work: 16.4% less than 15 minutes, 29.4% 15 to 30 minutes, 28.7% 30 to 45 minutes, 18.5% 45 to 60 minutes, 7.0% 60 minutes or more (2000)

BATAVIA (village). County seat. Covers a land area of 1.463 square miles and a water area of 0.025 square miles. Located at 39.07° N. Lat.; 84.17° W. Long. Elevation is 594 feet.

History: Settled c.1797, laid out 1814, incorporated 1842.

Population: 1,700 (1990); 1,617 (2000); 1,673 (2007); 1,737 (2012 projected); Race: 94.3% White, 3.4% Black, 0.2% Asian, 0.5% Hispanic of any race (2007); Density: 1,143.6 persons per square mile (2007); Average household size: 2.47 (2007); Median age: 37.8 (2007); Males per 100 females: 98.7 (2007); Marriage status: 22.0% never married, 61.1% now married, 5.2% widowed, 11.7% divorced (2000); Foreign born: 0.6% (2000); Ancestry (includes multiple ancestries): 30.1% German, 17.2% United States or American, 14.4% Irish, 11.1% English, 9.7% Other groups (2000).

Economy: Employment by occupation: 12.0% management, 17.5% professional, 13.9% services, 33.1% sales, 0.0% farming, 8.3% construction, 15.2% production (2000).

Income: Per capita income: $23,967 (2007); Median household income: $47,378 (2007); Average household income: $59,228 (2007); Percent of households with income of $100,000 or more: 16.4% (2007); Poverty rate: 6.6% (2000).

Education: Percent of population age 25 and over with: High school diploma (including GED) or higher: 90.7% (2007); Bachelor's degree or higher: 17.9% (2007); Master's degree or higher: 8.1% (2007).

School District(s)

Batavia Local (PK-12)
2005-06 Enrollment: 1,959 . . . . (513) 732-2343
Clermont Northeastern Local (PK-12)
2005-06 Enrollment: 1,922 . . . . (513) 625-5478
West Clermont Local (PK-12)
2005-06 Enrollment: 9,272 . . . . (513) 943-5000

Four-year College(s)

University of Cincinnati-Clermont College (Public)
Fall 2007 Enrollment: 2,942. . . . . (513) 732-5200
2007-08 Tuition: In-state $4,542; Out-of-state $11,394

Housing: Homeownership rate: 64.8% (2007); Median home value: $123,599 (2007); Median rent: $463 per month (2000); Median age of housing: 46 years (2000).

Hospitals: Mercy Hospital Clermont (114 beds)

Safety: Violent crime rate: 5.9 per 10,000 population; Property crime rate: 644.6 per 10,000 population (2007).

Newspapers: Clermont Sun (Local news; Circulation 3,300)

Transportation: Commute to work: 91.3% car, 1.4% public transportation, 5.9% walk, 1.5% work from home (2000); Travel time to work: 32.4% less than 15 minutes, 23.4% 15 to 30 minutes, 27.3% 30 to 45 minutes, 11.5% 45 to 60 minutes, 5.4% 60 minutes or more (2000)

Airports: Clermont County (general aviation)

Additional Information Contacts

Clermont County Ohio Convention and Visitors Bureau . . . (513) 732-3600
http://www.visitclermontohio.com

BETHEL (village). Covers a land area of 1.339 square miles and a water area of 0 square miles. Located at 38.96° N. Lat.; 84.08° W. Long. Elevation is 883 feet.

History: Settled 1797.

Population: 2,500 (1990); 2,637 (2000); 2,589 (2007); 2,604 (2012 projected); Race: 97.8% White, 0.2% Black, 0.2% Asian, 1.2% Hispanic of any race (2007); Density: 1,933.3 persons per square mile (2007); Average household size: 2.57 (2007); Median age: 32.5 (2007); Males per 100 females: 89.4 (2007); Marriage status: 24.0% never married, 53.5% now married, 9.4% widowed, 13.1% divorced (2000); Foreign born: 0.4% (2000); Ancestry (includes multiple ancestries): 19.9% German, 16.5% United States or American, 15.5% Irish, 13.5% English, 12.5% Other groups (2000).

Economy: Employment by occupation: 9.2% management, 10.5% professional, 19.9% services, 27.0% sales, 0.0% farming, 16.9% construction, 16.3% production (2000).

Income: Per capita income: $16,596 (2007); Median household income: $34,269 (2007); Average household income: $41,497 (2007); Percent of households with income of $100,000 or more: 5.6% (2007); Poverty rate: 20.1% (2000).

Education: Percent of population age 25 and over with: High school diploma (including GED) or higher: 71.8% (2007); Bachelor's degree or higher: 11.5% (2007); Master's degree or higher: 3.5% (2007).

School District(s)

Bethel-Tate Local (PK-12)
2005-06 Enrollment: 1,985 . . . . (513) 734-2238
U S Grant (11-12)
2005-06 Enrollment: n/a . . . . (513) 734-6222

Vocational/Technical School(s)

US Grant Joint Vocational School (Public)
Fall 2007 Enrollment: 19 . . . . (513) 734-6222
2007-08 Tuition: In-state $4,310; Out-of-state $4,310

Housing: Homeownership rate: 49.8% (2007); Median home value: $108,070 (2007); Median rent: $415 per month (2000); Median age of housing: 48 years (2000).

Safety: Violent crime rate: 23.0 per 10,000 population; Property crime rate: 801.4 per 10,000 population (2007).

Transportation: Commute to work: 90.2% car, 2.3% public transportation, 5.0% walk, 0.8% work from home (2000); Travel time to work: 25.4% less than 15 minutes, 24.2% 15 to 30 minutes, 19.3% 30 to 45 minutes, 19.6% 45 to 60 minutes, 11.5% 60 minutes or more (2000)

Additional Information Contacts

Village of Bethel. . . . . (513) 734-2243
http://bethel-oh.gov

CHILO (village). Covers a land area of 0.199 square miles and a water area of 0.039 square miles. Located at 38.79° N. Lat.; 84.13° W. Long. Elevation is 499 feet.

History: Chilo was a boat-building center and river port before the 1937 floods destroyed most of the town.

Population: 130 (1990); 97 (2000); 124 (2007); 139 (2012 projected); Race: 97.6% White, 0.0% Black, 0.0% Asian, 0.0% Hispanic of any race (2007); Density: 622.9 persons per square mile (2007); Average household size: 2.34 (2007); Median age: 47.3 (2007); Males per 100 females: 121.4 (2007); Marriage status: 18.3% never married, 62.0% now married, 12.7% widowed, 7.0% divorced (2000); Foreign born: 2.2% (2000); Ancestry (includes multiple ancestries): 40.7% German, 17.6% Other groups, 16.5% Irish, 12.1% English, 11.0% United States or American (2000).

Economy: Employment by occupation: 10.7% management, 14.3% professional, 14.3% services, 32.1% sales, 0.0% farming, 17.9% construction, 10.7% production (2000).

Income: Per capita income: $20,565 (2007); Median household income: $43,438 (2007); Average household income: $48,113 (2007); Percent of households with income of $100,000 or more: 3.8% (2007); Poverty rate: 12.4% (2000).

Education: Percent of population age 25 and over with: High school diploma (including GED) or higher: 70.5% (2007); Bachelor's degree or higher: 17.0% (2007); Master's degree or higher: 13.6% (2007).

Housing: Homeownership rate: 75.5% (2007); Median home value: $75,000 (2007); Median rent: $550 per month (2000); Median age of housing: 59 years (2000).

Transportation: Commute to work: 92.9% car, 0.0% public transportation, 3.6% walk, 3.6% work from home (2000); Travel time to work: 37.0% less than 15 minutes, 0.0% 15 to 30 minutes, 7.4% 30 to 45 minutes, 22.2% 45 to 60 minutes, 33.3% 60 minutes or more (2000)

DAY HEIGHTS (CDP). Covers a land area of 1.203 square miles and a water area of 0 square miles. Located at 39.17° N. Lat.; 84.23° W. Long. Elevation is 863 feet.

Population: 2,812 (1990); 2,823 (2000); 2,914 (2007); 2,986 (2012 projected); Race: 96.4% White, 1.7% Black, 0.3% Asian, 0.6% Hispanic of any race (2007); Density: 2,422.7 persons per square mile (2007); Average household size: 2.73 (2007); Median age: 40.7 (2007); Males per 100 females: 100.4 (2007); Marriage status: 20.1% never married, 66.7% now married, 6.7% widowed, 6.5% divorced (2000); Foreign born: 0.5% (2000);

Ancestry (includes multiple ancestries): 36.7% German, 23.9% Irish, 13.1% United States or American, 12.0% English, 6.2% Other groups (2000).
Economy: Employment by occupation: 16.7% management, 17.2% professional, 14.4% services, 29.4% sales, 0.0% farming, 6.3% construction, 15.9% production (2000).
Income: Per capita income: $30,435 (2007); Median household income: $70,184 (2007); Average household income: $82,963 (2007); Percent of households with income of $100,000 or more: 26.1% (2007); Poverty rate: 2.3% (2000).
Education: Percent of population age 25 and over with: High school diploma (including GED) or higher: 85.1% (2007); Bachelor's degree or higher: 22.5% (2007); Master's degree or higher: 6.7% (2007).
Housing: Homeownership rate: 94.5% (2007); Median home value: $142,537 (2007); Median rent: $622 per month (2000); Median age of housing: 35 years (2000).
Transportation: Commute to work: 94.6% car, 2.6% public transportation, 0.0% walk, 2.3% work from home (2000); Travel time to work: 18.7% less than 15 minutes, 35.8% 15 to 30 minutes, 31.1% 30 to 45 minutes, 11.1% 45 to 60 minutes, 3.3% 60 minutes or more (2000)

FELICITY (village). Covers a land area of 0.267 square miles and a water area of 0 square miles. Located at 38.83° N. Lat.; 84.09° W. Long. Elevation is 919 feet.
Population: 775 (1990); 922 (2000); 844 (2007); 865 (2012 projected); Race: 96.8% White, 1.3% Black, 0.4% Asian, 1.1% Hispanic of any race (2007); Density: 3,158.9 persons per square mile (2007); Average household size: 2.58 (2007); Median age: 32.2 (2007); Males per 100 females: 93.1 (2007); Marriage status: 25.4% never married, 51.9% now married, 9.2% widowed, 13.5% divorced (2000); Foreign born: 1.1% (2000); Ancestry (includes multiple ancestries): 22.2% German, 22.1% United States or American, 14.9% English, 14.7% Irish, 8.3% Other groups (2000).
Economy: Employment by occupation: 6.4% management, 15.7% professional, 20.4% services, 21.8% sales, 1.1% farming, 15.7% construction, 18.9% production (2000).
Income: Per capita income: $12,473 (2007); Median household income: $23,452 (2007); Average household income: $32,194 (2007); Percent of households with income of $100,000 or more: 3.7% (2007); Poverty rate: 34.9% (2000).
Education: Percent of population age 25 and over with: High school diploma (including GED) or higher: 57.0% (2007); Bachelor's degree or higher: 7.2% (2007); Master's degree or higher: 2.7% (2007).

School District(s)

Felicity-Franklin Local (PK-12)
2005-06 Enrollment: 1,215 . . . . (513) 876-2113
Housing: Homeownership rate: 45.0% (2007); Median home value: $77,188 (2007); Median rent: $365 per month (2000); Median age of housing: 50 years (2000).
Transportation: Commute to work: 82.1% car, 0.0% public transportation, 14.6% walk, 3.4% work from home (2000); Travel time to work: 29.3% less than 15 minutes, 9.3% 15 to 30 minutes, 15.4% 30 to 45 minutes, 31.7% 45 to 60 minutes, 14.3% 60 minutes or more (2000)

GOSHEN (unincorporated postal area, zip code 45122). Covers a land area of 45.909 square miles and a water area of 0.221 square miles. Located at 39.22° N. Lat.; 84.11° W. Long. Elevation is 820 feet.
Population: 11,406 (2000); Race: 98.3% White, 0.4% Black, 0.2% Asian, 0.7% Hispanic of any race (2000); Density: 248.4 persons per square mile (2000); Age: 27.6% under 18, 8.6% over 64 (2000); Marriage status: 19.3% never married, 65.2% now married, 5.3% widowed, 10.2% divorced (2000); Foreign born: 0.2% (2000); Ancestry (includes multiple ancestries): 24.6% German, 20.8% United States or American, 12.4% Irish, 8.2% English, 7.3% Other groups (2000).
Economy: Employment by occupation: 6.6% management, 9.2% professional, 15.4% services, 26.2% sales, 0.1% farming, 17.2% construction, 25.3% production (2000).
Income: Per capita income: $18,963 (2000); Median household income: $45,513 (2000); Poverty rate: 7.3% (2000).
Education: Percent of population age 25 and over with: High school diploma (including GED) or higher: 73.7% (2000); Bachelor's degree or higher: 6.6% (2000).

School District(s)

Goshen Local (PK-12)
2005-06 Enrollment: 2,548 . . . . (513) 722-2222

Housing: Homeownership rate: 85.4% (2000); Median home value: $98,700 (2000); Median rent: $502 per month (2000); Median age of housing: 25 years (2000).
Transportation: Commute to work: 95.8% car, 0.5% public transportation, 1.5% walk, 1.3% work from home (2000); Travel time to work: 12.0% less than 15 minutes, 30.3% 15 to 30 minutes, 37.3% 30 to 45 minutes, 15.0% 45 to 60 minutes, 5.4% 60 minutes or more (2000)

MILFORD (city). Covers a land area of 3.758 square miles and a water area of 0.067 square miles. Located at 39.17° N. Lat.; 84.28° W. Long. Elevation is 548 feet.
History: Milford was settled in an area of glacial moraines, on the Little Miami River. A prehistoric civilization left mounds in this region.
Population: 5,773 (1990); 6,284 (2000); 6,321 (2007); 6,368 (2012 projected); Race: 93.3% White, 4.9% Black, 0.5% Asian, 1.2% Hispanic of any race (2007); Density: 1,681.9 persons per square mile (2007); Average household size: 2.06 (2007); Median age: 41.0 (2007); Males per 100 females: 84.0 (2007); Marriage status: 20.5% never married, 52.5% now married, 13.5% widowed, 13.5% divorced (2000); Foreign born: 1.5% (2000); Ancestry (includes multiple ancestries): 31.5% German, 15.7% Irish, 14.9% English, 11.2% United States or American, 8.9% Other groups (2000).
Economy: Single-family building permits issued: 0 (2007); Multi-family building permits issued: 0 (2007); Employment by occupation: 12.4% management, 19.3% professional, 19.4% services, 26.5% sales, 0.0% farming, 9.2% construction, 13.2% production (2000).
Income: Per capita income: $26,428 (2007); Median household income: $36,863 (2007); Average household income: $54,061 (2007); Percent of households with income of $100,000 or more: 12.9% (2007); Poverty rate: 7.8% (2000).
Education: Percent of population age 25 and over with: High school diploma (including GED) or higher: 78.2% (2007); Bachelor's degree or higher: 24.2% (2007); Master's degree or higher: 8.9% (2007).

School District(s)

Great Oaks Inst of Technology (PK-12)
2005-06 Enrollment: n/a . . . . (513) 771-8840
Madeira City (PK-12)
2005-06 Enrollment: 1,552 . . . . (513) 985-6070
Milford Exempted Village (PK-12)
2005-06 Enrollment: 6,673 . . . . (513) 831-1314
Housing: Homeownership rate: 50.2% (2007); Median home value: $133,776 (2007); Median rent: $438 per month (2000); Median age of housing: 34 years (2000).
Safety: Violent crime rate: 22.1 per 10,000 population; Property crime rate: 336.9 per 10,000 population (2007).
Transportation: Commute to work: 90.8% car, 1.2% public transportation, 2.1% walk, 4.7% work from home (2000); Travel time to work: 26.7% less than 15 minutes, 41.8% 15 to 30 minutes, 23.4% 30 to 45 minutes, 5.2% 45 to 60 minutes, 2.9% 60 minutes or more (2000)
Additional Information Contacts
Milford-Miami Twp Chamber of Commerce . . . . (513) 831-2411
http://www.milfordmiamitownship.com

MOSCOW (village). Covers a land area of 0.402 square miles and a water area of 0.009 square miles. Located at 38.85° N. Lat.; 84.22° W. Long. Elevation is 499 feet.
History: Moscow was one of the first stations on the Underground Railroad. During the Reconstruction Period, Moscow was a busy shipping point, and a producer of large quantities of brandy.
Population: 269 (1990); 244 (2000); 277 (2007); 296 (2012 projected); Race: 96.8% White, 0.7% Black, 0.4% Asian, 0.0% Hispanic of any race (2007); Density: 688.4 persons per square mile (2007); Average household size: 2.56 (2007); Median age: 40.7 (2007); Males per 100 females: 102.2 (2007); Marriage status: 21.8% never married, 54.8% now married, 7.4% widowed, 16.0% divorced (2000); Foreign born: 0.8% (2000); Ancestry (includes multiple ancestries): 32.2% German, 16.9% English, 11.9% United States or American, 11.5% Irish, 4.6% Other groups (2000).
Economy: Employment by occupation: 4.6% management, 4.6% professional, 16.7% services, 19.4% sales, 1.9% farming, 24.1% construction, 28.7% production (2000).
Income: Per capita income: $16,218 (2007); Median household income: $37,333 (2007); Average household income: $41,597 (2007); Percent of households with income of $100,000 or more: 4.6% (2007); Poverty rate: 19.9% (2000).

Education: Percent of population age 25 and over with: High school diploma (including GED) or higher: 68.6% (2007); Bachelor's degree or higher: 1.6% (2007); Master's degree or higher: 1.6% (2007).
Housing: Homeownership rate: 76.9% (2007); Median home value: $97,500 (2007); Median rent: $388 per month (2000); Median age of housing: 60+ years (2000).
Transportation: Commute to work: 98.1% car, 0.0% public transportation, 0.0% walk, 1.9% work from home (2000); Travel time to work: 12.3% less than 15 minutes, 19.8% 15 to 30 minutes, 37.7% 30 to 45 minutes, 19.8% 45 to 60 minutes, 10.4% 60 minutes or more (2000)

MOUNT CARMEL (CDP). Covers a land area of 1.683 square miles and a water area of 0 square miles. Located at 39.09° N. Lat.; 84.29° W. Long. Elevation is 886 feet.
Population: 4,462 (1990); 4,308 (2000); 3,989 (2007); 3,779 (2012 projected); Race: 96.2% White, 1.1% Black, 0.3% Asian, 1.5% Hispanic of any race (2007); Density: 2,369.8 persons per square mile (2007); Average household size: 2.44 (2007); Median age: 35.9 (2007); Males per 100 females: 98.9 (2007); Marriage status: 26.3% never married, 55.4% now married, 5.4% widowed, 12.9% divorced (2000); Foreign born: 1.9% (2000); Ancestry (includes multiple ancestries): 38.0% German, 15.3% Irish, 13.2% United States or American, 9.8% English, 7.5% Other groups (2000).
Economy: Employment by occupation: 12.6% management, 10.6% professional, 16.5% services, 29.7% sales, 0.0% farming, 10.9% construction, 19.6% production (2000).
Income: Per capita income: $20,154 (2007); Median household income: $40,366 (2007); Average household income: $49,218 (2007); Percent of households with income of $100,000 or more: 9.9% (2007); Poverty rate: 9.3% (2000).
Education: Percent of population age 25 and over with: High school diploma (including GED) or higher: 79.0% (2007); Bachelor's degree or higher: 10.9% (2007); Master's degree or higher: 1.4% (2007).
Housing: Homeownership rate: 64.7% (2007); Median home value: $116,872 (2007); Median rent: $441 per month (2000); Median age of housing: 33 years (2000).
Transportation: Commute to work: 93.6% car, 2.0% public transportation, 1.4% walk, 2.8% work from home (2000); Travel time to work: 32.0% less than 15 minutes, 31.6% 15 to 30 minutes, 27.5% 30 to 45 minutes, 6.6% 45 to 60 minutes, 2.3% 60 minutes or more (2000)

MOUNT REPOSE (CDP). Covers a land area of 1.950 square miles and a water area of 0 square miles. Located at 39.18° N. Lat.; 84.22° W. Long. Elevation is 863 feet.
Population: 4,062 (1990); 4,102 (2000); 4,552 (2007); 4,795 (2012 projected); Race: 96.0% White, 1.5% Black, 1.0% Asian, 1.1% Hispanic of any race (2007); Density: 2,334.3 persons per square mile (2007); Average household size: 2.67 (2007); Median age: 36.8 (2007); Males per 100 females: 96.3 (2007); Marriage status: 20.9% never married, 65.8% now married, 5.9% widowed, 7.4% divorced (2000); Foreign born: 2.1% (2000); Ancestry (includes multiple ancestries): 30.2% German, 16.9% Irish, 13.4% Other groups, 11.5% English, 8.6% United States or American (2000).
Economy: Employment by occupation: 14.0% management, 18.9% professional, 12.0% services, 29.7% sales, 0.0% farming, 12.7% construction, 12.7% production (2000).
Income: Per capita income: $24,734 (2007); Median household income: $62,189 (2007); Average household income: $66,150 (2007); Percent of households with income of $100,000 or more: 15.6% (2007); Poverty rate: 5.1% (2000).
Education: Percent of population age 25 and over with: High school diploma (including GED) or higher: 87.8% (2007); Bachelor's degree or higher: 21.8% (2007); Master's degree or higher: 5.9% (2007).
Housing: Homeownership rate: 84.8% (2007); Median home value: $144,885 (2007); Median rent: $419 per month (2000); Median age of housing: 25 years (2000).
Transportation: Commute to work: 93.8% car, 1.5% public transportation, 1.0% walk, 3.3% work from home (2000); Travel time to work: 18.9% less than 15 minutes, 41.5% 15 to 30 minutes, 26.5% 30 to 45 minutes, 9.5% 45 to 60 minutes, 3.6% 60 minutes or more (2000)

MULBERRY (CDP). Covers a land area of 1.514 square miles and a water area of 0 square miles. Located at 39.19° N. Lat.; 84.25° W. Long. Elevation is 840 feet.
Population: 2,856 (1990); 3,139 (2000); 3,542 (2007); 3,773 (2012 projected); Race: 96.4% White, 1.6% Black, 0.8% Asian, 0.9% Hispanic of any race (2007); Density: 2,338.8 persons per square mile (2007); Average household size: 2.49 (2007); Median age: 44.8 (2007); Males per 100 females: 80.9 (2007); Marriage status: 17.7% never married, 56.0% now married, 13.1% widowed, 13.2% divorced (2000); Foreign born: 2.9% (2000); Ancestry (includes multiple ancestries): 33.6% German, 14.8% Irish, 13.3% English, 8.6% United States or American, 5.5% Other groups (2000).
Economy: Employment by occupation: 17.4% management, 23.9% professional, 10.7% services, 30.3% sales, 0.0% farming, 9.6% construction, 8.0% production (2000).
Income: Per capita income: $30,796 (2007); Median household income: $58,346 (2007); Average household income: $75,215 (2007); Percent of households with income of $100,000 or more: 22.1% (2007); Poverty rate: 4.2% (2000).
Education: Percent of population age 25 and over with: High school diploma (including GED) or higher: 88.9% (2007); Bachelor's degree or higher: 33.3% (2007); Master's degree or higher: 9.4% (2007).
Housing: Homeownership rate: 80.1% (2007); Median home value: $139,268 (2007); Median rent: $537 per month (2000); Median age of housing: 16 years (2000).
Transportation: Commute to work: 95.6% car, 0.7% public transportation, 0.0% walk, 3.0% work from home (2000); Travel time to work: 25.6% less than 15 minutes, 40.2% 15 to 30 minutes, 25.9% 30 to 45 minutes, 7.1% 45 to 60 minutes, 1.1% 60 minutes or more (2000)

NEVILLE (village). Covers a land area of 0.417 square miles and a water area of 0.043 square miles. Located at 38.81° N. Lat.; 84.21° W. Long. Elevation is 499 feet.
History: Neville was founded in 1808 and named for a Virginia officer in the Revolutionary War who was given land here for his military service. More than half of the houses in Neville were destroyed by the 1937 flooding of the Ohio River.
Population: 226 (1990); 127 (2000); 125 (2007); 124 (2012 projected); Race: 98.4% White, 1.6% Black, 0.0% Asian, 0.0% Hispanic of any race (2007); Density: 299.7 persons per square mile (2007); Average household size: 2.60 (2007); Median age: 38.9 (2007); Males per 100 females: 92.3 (2007); Marriage status: 22.9% never married, 56.3% now married, 7.3% widowed, 13.5% divorced (2000); Foreign born: 3.0% (2000); Ancestry (includes multiple ancestries): 26.1% German, 24.6% Irish, 24.6% English, 11.9% United States or American, 4.5% Other groups (2000).
Economy: Employment by occupation: 11.1% management, 3.7% professional, 24.1% services, 35.2% sales, 3.7% farming, 11.1% construction, 11.1% production (2000).
Income: Per capita income: $19,320 (2007); Median household income: $41,667 (2007); Average household income: $50,313 (2007); Percent of households with income of $100,000 or more: 8.3% (2007); Poverty rate: 19.4% (2000).
Education: Percent of population age 25 and over with: High school diploma (including GED) or higher: 61.7% (2007); Bachelor's degree or higher: 4.9% (2007); Master's degree or higher: 0.0% (2007).
Housing: Homeownership rate: 83.3% (2007); Median home value: $84,000 (2007); Median rent: $400 per month (2000); Median age of housing: 48 years (2000).
Transportation: Commute to work: 98.1% car, 0.0% public transportation, 1.9% walk, 0.0% work from home (2000); Travel time to work: 16.7% less than 15 minutes, 20.4% 15 to 30 minutes, 20.4% 30 to 45 minutes, 27.8% 45 to 60 minutes, 14.8% 60 minutes or more (2000)

NEW RICHMOND (village). Covers a land area of 3.442 square miles and a water area of 0.096 square miles. Located at 38.95° N. Lat.; 84.28° W. Long. Elevation is 469 feet.
History: New Richmond was created when two villages were joined. One of them, Susanna, had been laid out in 1816 by Thomas Ashburn as a model town. The 1937 flooding of the Ohio River devastated New Richmond.
Population: 2,408 (1990); 2,219 (2000); 2,603 (2007); 2,830 (2012 projected); Race: 96.2% White, 2.2% Black, 0.1% Asian, 1.1% Hispanic of any race (2007); Density: 756.2 persons per square mile (2007); Average household size: 2.71 (2007); Median age: 34.2 (2007); Males per 100 females: 100.8 (2007); Marriage status: 25.7% never married, 54.8% now married, 6.1% widowed, 13.4% divorced (2000); Foreign born: 0.7% (2000); Ancestry (includes multiple ancestries): 27.3% German, 21.9% Irish, 12.9% United States or American, 10.9% Other groups, 6.0% English (2000).

Economy: Employment by occupation: 10.1% management, 11.6% professional, 19.1% services, 26.5% sales, 0.0% farming, 14.9% construction, 17.6% production (2000).
Income: Per capita income: $20,766 (2007); Median household income: $46,535 (2007); Average household income: $55,751 (2007); Percent of households with income of $100,000 or more: 13.6% (2007); Poverty rate: 17.7% (2000).
Education: Percent of population age 25 and over with: High school diploma (including GED) or higher: 74.0% (2007); Bachelor's degree or higher: 15.7% (2007); Master's degree or higher: 4.6% (2007).

School District(s)

New Richmond Exempted Village (PK-12)
2005-06 Enrollment: 2,502 . . . . (513) 553-2616
Housing: Homeownership rate: 60.1% (2007); Median home value: $130,743 (2007); Median rent: $415 per month (2000); Median age of housing: 53 years (2000).
Transportation: Commute to work: 88.2% car, 1.4% public transportation, 4.8% walk, 1.5% work from home (2000); Travel time to work: 27.1% less than 15 minutes, 30.4% 15 to 30 minutes, 27.4% 30 to 45 minutes, 8.7% 45 to 60 minutes, 6.5% 60 minutes or more (2000)

NEWTONSVILLE (village). Covers a land area of 0.243 square miles and a water area of 0 square miles. Located at 39.18° N. Lat.; 84.08° W. Long. Elevation is 899 feet.
Population: 427 (1990); 492 (2000); 520 (2007); 541 (2012 projected); Race: 99.6% White, 0.0% Black, 0.4% Asian, 0.8% Hispanic of any race (2007); Density: 2,136.9 persons per square mile (2007); Average household size: 2.71 (2007); Median age: 36.7 (2007); Males per 100 females: 100.0 (2007); Marriage status: 27.2% never married, 55.6% now married, 3.4% widowed, 13.8% divorced (2000); Foreign born: 0.0% (2000); Ancestry (includes multiple ancestries): 32.0% United States or American, 17.3% German, 5.3% Other groups, 5.0% Irish, 4.3% English (2000).
Economy: Employment by occupation: 7.6% management, 5.4% professional, 19.6% services, 28.3% sales, 0.0% farming, 13.6% construction, 25.5% production (2000).
Income: Per capita income: $21,760 (2007); Median household income: $48,864 (2007); Average household income: $58,932 (2007); Percent of households with income of $100,000 or more: 11.5% (2007); Poverty rate: 15.5% (2000).
Education: Percent of population age 25 and over with: High school diploma (including GED) or higher: 64.9% (2007); Bachelor's degree or higher: 4.1% (2007); Master's degree or higher: 1.2% (2007).
Housing: Homeownership rate: 78.1% (2007); Median home value: $108,152 (2007); Median rent: $375 per month (2000); Median age of housing: 42 years (2000).
Transportation: Commute to work: 92.7% car, 3.9% public transportation, 2.2% walk, 1.1% work from home (2000); Travel time to work: 16.4% less than 15 minutes, 24.3% 15 to 30 minutes, 27.1% 30 to 45 minutes, 18.1% 45 to 60 minutes, 14.1% 60 minutes or more (2000)

OWENSVILLE (village). Covers a land area of 0.396 square miles and a water area of 0 square miles. Located at 39.12° N. Lat.; 84.13° W. Long. Elevation is 863 feet.
Population: 872 (1990); 816 (2000); 735 (2007); 758 (2012 projected); Race: 96.7% White, 1.0% Black, 0.1% Asian, 2.4% Hispanic of any race (2007); Density: 1,857.0 persons per square mile (2007); Average household size: 2.17 (2007); Median age: 35.1 (2007); Males per 100 females: 89.9 (2007); Marriage status: 27.5% never married, 39.5% now married, 15.1% widowed, 17.9% divorced (2000); Foreign born: 0.6% (2000); Ancestry (includes multiple ancestries): 25.3% German, 19.4% United States or American, 12.9% Irish, 5.1% English, 3.8% Other groups (2000).
Economy: Employment by occupation: 7.7% management, 14.1% professional, 23.3% services, 26.2% sales, 0.0% farming, 11.5% construction, 17.3% production (2000).
Income: Per capita income: $18,499 (2007); Median household income: $27,800 (2007); Average household income: $39,970 (2007); Percent of households with income of $100,000 or more: 8.0% (2007); Poverty rate: 18.6% (2000).
Education: Percent of population age 25 and over with: High school diploma (including GED) or higher: 70.0% (2007); Bachelor's degree or higher: 7.5% (2007); Master's degree or higher: 3.2% (2007).

School District(s)

Clermont Northeastern Local (PK-12)
2005-06 Enrollment: 1,922 . . . . (513) 625-5478
Housing: Homeownership rate: 42.9% (2007); Median home value: $114,461 (2007); Median rent: $264 per month (2000); Median age of housing: 27 years (2000).
Safety: Violent crime rate: 0.0 per 10,000 population; Property crime rate: 299.0 per 10,000 population (2007).
Transportation: Commute to work: 90.3% car, 0.0% public transportation, 2.9% walk, 5.5% work from home (2000); Travel time to work: 15.4% less than 15 minutes, 41.1% 15 to 30 minutes, 28.4% 30 to 45 minutes, 11.0% 45 to 60 minutes, 4.1% 60 minutes or more (2000)

SUMMERSIDE (CDP). Covers a land area of 2.277 square miles and a water area of 0.003 square miles. Located at 39.11° N. Lat.; 84.29° W. Long. Elevation is 879 feet.
Population: 4,573 (1990); 5,523 (2000); 5,934 (2007); 6,291 (2012 projected); Race: 95.0% White, 1.6% Black, 1.3% Asian, 1.5% Hispanic of any race (2007); Density: 2,605.7 persons per square mile (2007); Average household size: 2.42 (2007); Median age: 35.2 (2007); Males per 100 females: 92.5 (2007); Marriage status: 24.0% never married, 60.2% now married, 5.3% widowed, 10.5% divorced (2000); Foreign born: 1.2% (2000); Ancestry (includes multiple ancestries): 32.3% German, 21.0% Irish, 11.5% United States or American, 11.3% English, 9.0% Other groups (2000).
Economy: Employment by occupation: 15.4% management, 17.8% professional, 11.3% services, 31.6% sales, 0.3% farming, 7.6% construction, 15.9% production (2000).
Income: Per capita income: $22,458 (2007); Median household income: $45,909 (2007); Average household income: $54,351 (2007); Percent of households with income of $100,000 or more: 10.6% (2007); Poverty rate: 6.2% (2000).
Education: Percent of population age 25 and over with: High school diploma (including GED) or higher: 83.3% (2007); Bachelor's degree or higher: 21.9% (2007); Master's degree or higher: 4.5% (2007).
Housing: Homeownership rate: 65.3% (2007); Median home value: $129,599 (2007); Median rent: $499 per month (2000); Median age of housing: 25 years (2000).
Transportation: Commute to work: 93.8% car, 2.9% public transportation, 1.0% walk, 2.1% work from home (2000); Travel time to work: 22.6% less than 15 minutes, 36.2% 15 to 30 minutes, 32.5% 30 to 45 minutes, 6.1% 45 to 60 minutes, 2.6% 60 minutes or more (2000)

WILLIAMSBURG (village). Covers a land area of 1.908 square miles and a water area of 0.023 square miles. Located at 39.05° N. Lat.; 84.05° W. Long. Elevation is 814 feet.
History: Incorporated 1800.
Population: 2,552 (1990); 2,358 (2000); 2,553 (2007); 2,688 (2012 projected); Race: 98.4% White, 0.2% Black, 0.1% Asian, 0.2% Hispanic of any race (2007); Density: 1,337.8 persons per square mile (2007); Average household size: 2.45 (2007); Median age: 35.1 (2007); Males per 100 females: 90.4 (2007); Marriage status: 23.8% never married, 53.1% now married, 7.7% widowed, 15.4% divorced (2000); Foreign born: 0.7% (2000); Ancestry (includes multiple ancestries): 25.9% German, 17.1% United States or American, 14.1% English, 12.2% Irish, 12.0% Other groups (2000).
Economy: Employment by occupation: 9.8% management, 10.3% professional, 14.1% services, 30.1% sales, 0.9% farming, 12.5% construction, 22.3% production (2000).
Income: Per capita income: $22,391 (2007); Median household income: $44,630 (2007); Average household income: $54,409 (2007); Percent of households with income of $100,000 or more: 8.8% (2007); Poverty rate: 11.3% (2000).
Education: Percent of population age 25 and over with: High school diploma (including GED) or higher: 73.5% (2007); Bachelor's degree or higher: 10.4% (2007); Master's degree or higher: 3.0% (2007).

School District(s)

Williamsburg Local (PK-12)
2005-06 Enrollment: 1,029 . . . . (513) 724-3077
Housing: Homeownership rate: 59.9% (2007); Median home value: $109,128 (2007); Median rent: $448 per month (2000); Median age of housing: 42 years (2000).
Safety: Violent crime rate: 12.8 per 10,000 population; Property crime rate: 352.9 per 10,000 population (2007).

Transportation: Commute to work: 95.2% car, 0.5% public transportation, 2.3% walk, 0.6% work from home (2000); Travel time to work: 23.4% less than 15 minutes, 26.9% 15 to 30 minutes, 21.9% 30 to 45 minutes, 19.6% 45 to 60 minutes, 8.1% 60 minutes or more (2000)

WITHAMSVILLE (CDP). Covers a land area of 1.750 square miles and a water area of 0 square miles. Located at 39.05° N. Lat.; 84.27° W. Long. Elevation is 879 feet.

Population: 2,720 (1990); 3,145 (2000); 2,986 (2007); 3,053 (2012 projected); Race: 96.3% White, 1.4% Black, 1.1% Asian, 1.1% Hispanic of any race (2007); Density: 1,706.1 persons per square mile (2007); Average household size: 2.32 (2007); Median age: 37.3 (2007); Males per 100 females: 99.2 (2007); Marriage status: 27.3% never married, 57.9% now married, 5.7% widowed, 9.1% divorced (2000); Foreign born: 0.3% (2000); Ancestry (includes multiple ancestries): 28.9% German, 21.3% Irish, 11.5% English, 9.6% United States or American, 9.4% Other groups (2000).

Economy: Employment by occupation: 8.9% management, 14.0% professional, 14.2% services, 29.7% sales, 0.0% farming, 14.4% construction, 18.8% production (2000).

Income: Per capita income: $25,717 (2007); Median household income: $53,750 (2007); Average household income: $59,666 (2007); Percent of households with income of $100,000 or more: 13.8% (2007); Poverty rate: 7.8% (2000).

Education: Percent of population age 25 and over with: High school diploma (including GED) or higher: 81.9% (2007); Bachelor's degree or higher: 15.7% (2007); Master's degree or higher: 4.2% (2007).

Housing: Homeownership rate: 64.0% (2007); Median home value: $139,320 (2007); Median rent: $429 per month (2000); Median age of housing: 32 years (2000).

Transportation: Commute to work: 95.4% car, 0.9% public transportation, 0.0% walk, 3.3% work from home (2000); Travel time to work: 21.0% less than 15 minutes, 28.8% 15 to 30 minutes, 38.5% 30 to 45 minutes, 8.6% 45 to 60 minutes, 3.1% 60 minutes or more (2000)

Clinton County

Located in southwestern Ohio; drained by forks of the Little Miami River and Caesar Creek. Covers a land area of 410.88 square miles, a water area of 1.41 square miles, and is located in the Eastern Time Zone. The county was founded in 1810. County seat is Wilmington.

Clinton County is part of the Wilmington, OH Micropolitan Statistical Area. The entire metro area includes: Clinton County, OH

Weather Station: Wilmington 3 N — Elevation: 1,026 feet

	Jan	Feb	Mar	Apr	May	Jun	Jul	Aug	Sep	Oct	Nov	Dec
High	35	39	50	62	72	80	84	83	77	65	52	41
Low	18	21	30	39	49	58	62	60	53	41	33	24
Precip	2.6	2.4	3.4	4.1	4.8	4.3	4.4	3.3	2.8	2.9	3.4	2.9
Snow	8.2	6.3	3.9	0.7	tr	0.0	0.0	0.0	0.0	0.2	1.4	3.0

High and Low temperatures in degrees Fahrenheit; Precipitation and Snow in inches

Population: 35,415 (1990); 40,543 (2000); 43,129 (2007); 44,779 (2012 projected); Race: 95.2% White, 2.4% Black, 0.7% Asian, 1.4% Hispanic of any race (2007); Density: 105.0 persons per square mile (2007); Average household size: 2.59 (2007); Median age: 36.3 (2007); Males per 100 females: 97.4 (2007).

Religion: Five largest groups: 7.0% The United Methodist Church, 6.1% Catholic Church, 5.5% Christian Churches and Churches of Christ, 3.2% Southern Baptist Convention, 2.1% Friends (Quakers) (2000).

Economy: Unemployment rate: 5.8% (6/2008); Total civilian labor force: 24,625 (6/2008); Leading industries: 41.5% transportation & warehousing; 17.8% manufacturing; 8.0% retail trade (2005); Farms: 811 totaling 238,805 acres (2002); Companies that employ 500 or more persons: 8 (2006); Companies that employ 100 to 499 persons: 21 (2006); Companies that employ less than 100 persons: 790 (2006); Black-owned businesses: n/a (2002); Hispanic-owned businesses: n/a (2002); Asian-owned businesses: n/a (2002); Women-owned businesses: 583 (2002); Retail sales per capita: $16,165 (2008). Single-family building permits issued: 78 (2007); Multi-family building permits issued: 58 (2007).

Income: Per capita income: $21,310 (2007); Median household income: $45,606 (2007); Average household income: $54,766 (2007); Percent of households with income of $100,000 or more: 10.5% (2007); Poverty rate: 10.9% (2005); Bankruptcy rate: 3.88% (2007).

Taxes: Total county taxes per capita: $260 (2006); County property taxes per capita: $127 (2006).

Education: Percent of population age 25 and over with: High school diploma (including GED) or higher: 83.1% (2007); Bachelor's degree or higher: 14.2% (2007); Master's degree or higher: 4.9% (2007).

Housing: Homeownership rate: 69.3% (2007); Median home value: $129,452 (2007); Median rent: $393 per month (2000); Median age of housing: 34 years (2000).

Health: Birth rate: 148.4 per 10,000 population (2007); Death rate: 87.5 per 10,000 population (2007); Age-adjusted cancer mortality rate: 206.2 deaths per 100,000 population (2005); Air Quality Index: 59.1% good, 31.2% moderate, 9.8% unhealthy for sensitive individuals, 0.0% unhealthy (percent of days in 2007); Number of physicians: 18.5 per 10,000 population (2005); Hospital beds: 19.4 per 10,000 population (2004); Hospital admissions: 1,113.7 per 10,000 population (2004).

Elections: 2004 Presidential election results: 70.3% Bush, 29.4% Kerry, 0.0% Nader, 0.2% Badnarik

National and State Parks: Cowan State Park

Additional Information Contacts

Clinton County Government. . . . . (937) 382-2103
http://co.clinton.oh.us

City of Wilmington . . . . (937) 382-5458
http://ci.wilmington.oh.us

Wilmington-Clinton County Chamber of Commerce . . . . . . (937) 382-2737
http://www.wccchamber.com

Clinton County Communities

BLANCHESTER (village). Covers a land area of 2.962 square miles and a water area of 0.052 square miles. Located at 39.29° N. Lat.; 83.98° W. Long. Elevation is 971 feet.

Population: 4,293 (1990); 4,220 (2000); 4,356 (2007); 4,446 (2012 projected); Race: 98.2% White, 0.1% Black, 0.8% Asian, 1.1% Hispanic of any race (2007); Density: 1,470.8 persons per square mile (2007); Average household size: 2.52 (2007); Median age: 36.1 (2007); Males per 100 females: 88.2 (2007); Marriage status: 20.4% never married, 56.2% now married, 12.3% widowed, 11.2% divorced (2000); Foreign born: 0.1% (2000); Ancestry (includes multiple ancestries): 21.6% United States or American, 18.1% German, 11.3% English, 7.6% Irish, 6.3% Other groups (2000).

Economy: Employment by occupation: 8.7% management, 10.7% professional, 16.9% services, 23.1% sales, 0.0% farming, 12.2% construction, 28.4% production (2000).

Income: Per capita income: $18,438 (2007); Median household income: $38,728 (2007); Average household income: $45,826 (2007); Percent of households with income of $100,000 or more: 5.1% (2007); Poverty rate: 11.0% (2000).

Education: Percent of population age 25 and over with: High school diploma (including GED) or higher: 71.5% (2007); Bachelor's degree or higher: 10.9% (2007); Master's degree or higher: 3.7% (2007).

School District(s)

Blanchester Local (PK-12)
2005-06 Enrollment: 1,847 . . . . (937) 783-3523

Little Miami Local (PK-12)
2005-06 Enrollment: 3,624 . . . . (513) 899-2264

Housing: Homeownership rate: 65.2% (2007); Median home value: $112,285 (2007); Median rent: $362 per month (2000); Median age of housing: 38 years (2000).

Newspapers: Star-Republican (Local news; Circulation 21,500)

Transportation: Commute to work: 91.6% car, 0.0% public transportation, 4.5% walk, 3.9% work from home (2000); Travel time to work: 29.6% less than 15 minutes, 17.3% 15 to 30 minutes, 29.1% 30 to 45 minutes, 13.9% 45 to 60 minutes, 10.1% 60 minutes or more (2000)

CLARKSVILLE (village). Covers a land area of 0.485 square miles and a water area of 0 square miles. Located at 39.40° N. Lat.; 83.98° W. Long. Elevation is 820 feet.

Population: 485 (1990); 497 (2000); 426 (2007); 423 (2012 projected); Race: 94.6% White, 0.7% Black, 0.5% Asian, 2.8% Hispanic of any race (2007); Density: 877.5 persons per square mile (2007); Average household size: 2.55 (2007); Median age: 34.1 (2007); Males per 100 females: 91.9 (2007); Marriage status: 30.1% never married, 48.7% now married, 5.6% widowed, 15.7% divorced (2000); Foreign born: 0.0% (2000); Ancestry (includes multiple ancestries): 18.9% United States or American, 16.5% Irish, 15.0% German, 13.0% Other groups, 9.1% English (2000).

Economy: Employment by occupation: 6.1% management, 7.8% professional, 21.2% services, 17.3% sales, 0.0% farming, 14.3% construction, 33.3% production (2000).
Income: Per capita income: $17,447 (2007); Median household income: $40,625 (2007); Average household income: $44,506 (2007); Percent of households with income of $100,000 or more: 3.6% (2007); Poverty rate: 9.0% (2000).
Education: Percent of population age 25 and over with: High school diploma (including GED) or higher: 81.1% (2007); Bachelor's degree or higher: 3.6% (2007); Master's degree or higher: 1.1% (2007).

School District(s)

Clinton-Massie Local (KG-12)
2005-06 Enrollment: 1,815 . . . . (937) 289-2471
Housing: Homeownership rate: 71.9% (2007); Median home value: $92,857 (2007); Median rent: $346 per month (2000); Median age of housing: 60+ years (2000).
Transportation: Commute to work: 90.3% car, 0.0% public transportation, 0.9% walk, 8.8% work from home (2000); Travel time to work: 10.2% less than 15 minutes, 64.6% 15 to 30 minutes, 9.2% 30 to 45 minutes, 7.8% 45 to 60 minutes, 8.3% 60 minutes or more (2000)

MARTINSVILLE (village). Covers a land area of 0.442 square miles and a water area of 0 square miles. Located at 39.32° N. Lat.; 83.81° W. Long. Elevation is 1,086 feet.
Population: 476 (1990); 440 (2000); 485 (2007); 514 (2012 projected); Race: 96.1% White, 1.2% Black, 0.2% Asian, 0.6% Hispanic of any race (2007); Density: 1,098.3 persons per square mile (2007); Average household size: 2.69 (2007); Median age: 36.0 (2007); Males per 100 females: 99.6 (2007); Marriage status: 20.6% never married, 54.1% now married, 12.4% widowed, 12.9% divorced (2000); Foreign born: 0.5% (2000); Ancestry (includes multiple ancestries): 31.4% United States or American, 11.0% Irish, 9.6% Other groups, 9.4% English, 8.2% German (2000).
Economy: Employment by occupation: 6.9% management, 10.3% professional, 17.2% services, 27.9% sales, 1.0% farming, 10.3% construction, 26.5% production (2000).
Income: Per capita income: $16,923 (2007); Median household income: $40,714 (2007); Average household income: $45,597 (2007); Percent of households with income of $100,000 or more: 3.3% (2007); Poverty rate: 8.5% (2000).
Education: Percent of population age 25 and over with: High school diploma (including GED) or higher: 69.4% (2007); Bachelor's degree or higher: 5.4% (2007); Master's degree or higher: 1.3% (2007).
Housing: Homeownership rate: 78.9% (2007); Median home value: $105,469 (2007); Median rent: $454 per month (2000); Median age of housing: 50 years (2000).
Transportation: Commute to work: 91.7% car, 0.0% public transportation, 2.9% walk, 3.4% work from home (2000); Travel time to work: 11.2% less than 15 minutes, 61.4% 15 to 30 minutes, 8.1% 30 to 45 minutes, 5.1% 45 to 60 minutes, 14.2% 60 minutes or more (2000)

MIDLAND (village). Aka Midland City. Covers a land area of 0.352 square miles and a water area of 0 square miles. Located at 39.30° N. Lat.; 83.90° W. Long. Elevation is 984 feet.
History: Midland developed as a junction town for two branches of the Baltimore & Ohio Railroad.
Population: 341 (1990); 265 (2000); 265 (2007); 264 (2012 projected); Race: 94.3% White, 0.0% Black, 0.0% Asian, 4.9% Hispanic of any race (2007); Density: 753.0 persons per square mile (2007); Average household size: 2.68 (2007); Median age: 33.4 (2007); Males per 100 females: 103.8 (2007); Marriage status: 21.8% never married, 69.5% now married, 3.3% widowed, 5.4% divorced (2000); Foreign born: 0.0% (2000); Ancestry (includes multiple ancestries): 30.8% United States or American, 13.4% German, 10.7% Other groups, 7.4% English, 6.0% Irish (2000).
Economy: Employment by occupation: 1.6% management, 0.0% professional, 12.0% services, 24.8% sales, 0.0% farming, 12.0% construction, 49.6% production (2000).
Income: Per capita income: $16,896 (2007); Median household income: $44,750 (2007); Average household income: $45,227 (2007); Percent of households with income of $100,000 or more: 2.0% (2007); Poverty rate: 16.7% (2000).
Education: Percent of population age 25 and over with: High school diploma (including GED) or higher: 64.8% (2007); Bachelor's degree or higher: 2.3% (2007); Master's degree or higher: 1.1% (2007).

School District(s)

Blanchester Local (PK-12)
2005-06 Enrollment: 1,847 . . . . (937) 783-3523
Housing: Homeownership rate: 74.7% (2007); Median home value: $76,000 (2007); Median rent: $410 per month (2000); Median age of housing: 47 years (2000).
Transportation: Commute to work: 96.6% car, 0.0% public transportation, 0.0% walk, 0.0% work from home (2000); Travel time to work: 11.9% less than 15 minutes, 32.2% 15 to 30 minutes, 23.7% 30 to 45 minutes, 14.4% 45 to 60 minutes, 17.8% 60 minutes or more (2000)

NEW VIENNA (village). Covers a land area of 0.799 square miles and a water area of 0 square miles. Located at 39.32° N. Lat.; 83.69° W. Long. Elevation is 1,122 feet.
Population: 961 (1990); 1,294 (2000); 1,285 (2007); 1,291 (2012 projected); Race: 97.6% White, 0.2% Black, 0.2% Asian, 1.2% Hispanic of any race (2007); Density: 1,607.7 persons per square mile (2007); Average household size: 2.56 (2007); Median age: 32.5 (2007); Males per 100 females: 86.5 (2007); Marriage status: 19.7% never married, 56.0% now married, 6.4% widowed, 17.9% divorced (2000); Foreign born: 0.5% (2000); Ancestry (includes multiple ancestries): 25.0% United States or American, 19.2% German, 10.6% Irish, 10.3% Other groups, 7.3% English (2000).
Economy: Single-family building permits issued: 0 (2007); Multi-family building permits issued: 8 (2007); Employment by occupation: 5.8% management, 5.8% professional, 9.5% services, 28.6% sales, 0.7% farming, 12.8% construction, 36.8% production (2000).
Income: Per capita income: $15,800 (2007); Median household income: $35,100 (2007); Average household income: $40,443 (2007); Percent of households with income of $100,000 or more: 3.6% (2007); Poverty rate: 10.8% (2000).
Education: Percent of population age 25 and over with: High school diploma (including GED) or higher: 81.6% (2007); Bachelor's degree or higher: 4.3% (2007); Master's degree or higher: 1.4% (2007).

School District(s)

East Clinton Local (PK-12)
2005-06 Enrollment: 1,552 . . . . (937) 584-2461
Housing: Homeownership rate: 65.7% (2007); Median home value: $88,333 (2007); Median rent: $343 per month (2000); Median age of housing: 29 years (2000).
Transportation: Commute to work: 95.2% car, 0.3% public transportation, 1.2% walk, 1.9% work from home (2000); Travel time to work: 20.1% less than 15 minutes, 55.8% 15 to 30 minutes, 8.1% 30 to 45 minutes, 6.2% 45 to 60 minutes, 9.7% 60 minutes or more (2000)

PORT WILLIAM (village). Covers a land area of 0.116 square miles and a water area of 0 square miles. Located at 39.55° N. Lat.; 83.78° W. Long. Elevation is 1,020 feet.
Population: 250 (1990); 258 (2000); 257 (2007); 264 (2012 projected); Race: 94.9% White, 0.0% Black, 0.0% Asian, 2.7% Hispanic of any race (2007); Density: 2,214.0 persons per square mile (2007); Average household size: 2.62 (2007); Median age: 33.2 (2007); Males per 100 females: 114.2 (2007); Marriage status: 19.4% never married, 60.0% now married, 8.3% widowed, 12.2% divorced (2000); Foreign born: 1.6% (2000); Ancestry (includes multiple ancestries): 27.6% United States or American, 25.5% Other groups, 17.3% German, 8.2% English, 5.8% Irish (2000).
Economy: Employment by occupation: 6.8% management, 6.8% professional, 14.4% services, 28.8% sales, 0.0% farming, 19.5% construction, 23.7% production (2000).
Income: Per capita income: $15,204 (2007); Median household income: $36,765 (2007); Average household income: $39,872 (2007); Percent of households with income of $100,000 or more: 3.1% (2007); Poverty rate: 16.0% (2000).
Education: Percent of population age 25 and over with: High school diploma (including GED) or higher: 74.1% (2007); Bachelor's degree or higher: 6.6% (2007); Master's degree or higher: 0.0% (2007).
Housing: Homeownership rate: 60.2% (2007); Median home value: $99,545 (2007); Median rent: $365 per month (2000); Median age of housing: 60+ years (2000).
Transportation: Commute to work: 95.7% car, 0.0% public transportation, 4.3% walk, 0.0% work from home (2000); Travel time to work: 20.7% less than 15 minutes, 50.9% 15 to 30 minutes, 11.2% 30 to 45 minutes, 6.0% 45 to 60 minutes, 11.2% 60 minutes or more (2000)

SABINA (village). Covers a land area of 1.293 square miles and a water area of 0 square miles. Located at 39.48° N. Lat.; 83.63° W. Long. Elevation is 1,050 feet.
Population: 2,698 (1990); 2,780 (2000); 2,877 (2007); 2,945 (2012 projected); Race: 96.8% White, 0.6% Black, 0.8% Asian, 2.7% Hispanic of any race (2007); Density: 2,224.6 persons per square mile (2007); Average household size: 2.55 (2007); Median age: 34.6 (2007); Males per 100 females: 96.4 (2007); Marriage status: 23.2% never married, 55.2% now married, 7.4% widowed, 14.2% divorced (2000); Foreign born: 0.3% (2000); Ancestry (includes multiple ancestries): 23.7% United States or American, 18.3% German, 10.9% Irish, 8.5% Other groups, 8.0% English (2000).
Economy: Single-family building permits issued: 1 (2007); Multi-family building permits issued: 0 (2007); Employment by occupation: 5.9% management, 7.4% professional, 12.5% services, 25.4% sales, 1.3% farming, 10.3% construction, 37.2% production (2000).
Income: Per capita income: $19,210 (2007); Median household income: $40,000 (2007); Average household income: $48,595 (2007); Percent of households with income of $100,000 or more: 7.9% (2007); Poverty rate: 12.9% (2000).
Education: Percent of population age 25 and over with: High school diploma (including GED) or higher: 78.6% (2007); Bachelor's degree or higher: 7.1% (2007); Master's degree or higher: 1.6% (2007).

School District(s)

East Clinton Local (PK-12)
2005-06 Enrollment: 1,552 . . . . (937) 584-2461
Housing: Homeownership rate: 67.1% (2007); Median home value: $94,867 (2007); Median rent: $354 per month (2000); Median age of housing: 40 years (2000).
Transportation: Commute to work: 93.2% car, 0.0% public transportation, 3.1% walk, 2.6% work from home (2000); Travel time to work: 30.6% less than 15 minutes, 49.5% 15 to 30 minutes, 8.8% 30 to 45 minutes, 2.9% 45 to 60 minutes, 8.2% 60 minutes or more (2000)

WILMINGTON (city). County seat. Covers a land area of 7.451 square miles and a water area of 0 square miles. Located at 39.44° N. Lat.; 83.82° W. Long. Elevation is 1,017 feet.
History: Seat of Wilmington College. Settled 1810, incorporated 1828.
Population: 11,421 (1990); 11,921 (2000); 12,565 (2007); 12,952 (2012 projected); Race: 89.3% White, 7.4% Black, 1.1% Asian, 1.8% Hispanic of any race (2007); Density: 1,686.4 persons per square mile (2007); Average household size: 2.41 (2007); Median age: 33.6 (2007); Males per 100 females: 92.2 (2007); Marriage status: 29.5% never married, 49.0% now married, 8.6% widowed, 12.8% divorced (2000); Foreign born: 2.3% (2000); Ancestry (includes multiple ancestries): 20.6% German, 14.8% United States or American, 13.4% Other groups, 13.3% Irish, 10.2% English (2000).
Economy: Single-family building permits issued: 7 (2007); Multi-family building permits issued: 50 (2007); Employment by occupation: 10.8% management, 15.3% professional, 16.9% services, 23.4% sales, 0.3% farming, 7.9% construction, 25.3% production (2000).
Income: Per capita income: $18,967 (2007); Median household income: $37,164 (2007); Average household income: $44,868 (2007); Percent of households with income of $100,000 or more: 5.7% (2007); Poverty rate: 11.7% (2000).
Taxes: Total city taxes per capita: $522 (2006); City property taxes per capita: $157 (2006).
Education: Percent of population age 25 and over with: High school diploma (including GED) or higher: 85.0% (2007); Bachelor's degree or higher: 16.5% (2007); Master's degree or higher: 6.8% (2007).

School District(s)

Great Oaks Inst of Technology (PK-12)
2005-06 Enrollment: n/a . . . . (513) 771-8840
Wilmington City (PK-12)
2005-06 Enrollment: 3,287 . . . . (937) 382-1641

Four-year College(s)

Wilmington College (Private, Not-for-profit, Friends)
Fall 2007 Enrollment: 1,605. . . . . (800) 341-9318
2007-08 Tuition: In-state $22,078; Out-of-state $22,078
Housing: Homeownership rate: 51.0% (2007); Median home value: $116,607 (2007); Median rent: $405 per month (2000); Median age of housing: 38 years (2000).
Hospitals: Clinton Memorial Hospital (150 beds)
Safety: Violent crime rate: 21.9 per 10,000 population; Property crime rate: 538.8 per 10,000 population (2007).
Newspapers: Wilmington News Journal (Local news; Circulation 10,258)
Transportation: Commute to work: 88.8% car, 1.0% public transportation, 7.2% walk, 2.8% work from home (2000); Travel time to work: 59.1% less than 15 minutes, 19.0% 15 to 30 minutes, 8.2% 30 to 45 minutes, 8.4% 45 to 60 minutes, 5.2% 60 minutes or more (2000)
Additional Information Contacts
City of Wilmington . . . . (937) 382-5458
http://ci.wilmington.oh.us
Wilmington-Clinton County Chamber of Commerce . . . . . . (937) 382-2737
http://www.wccchamber.com

Columbiana County

Located in eastern Ohio; bounded on the east by Pennsylvania, and on the southeast by the Ohio River; drained by the Little Beaver River. Covers a land area of 532.46 square miles, a water area of 2.73 square miles, and is located in the Eastern Time Zone. The county was founded in 1803. County seat is Lisbon.

Columbiana County is part of the East Liverpool-Salem, OH Micropolitan Statistical Area. The entire metro area includes: Columbiana County, OH

Weather Station: Millport 2 NW Elevation: 1,148 feet

	Jan	Feb	Mar	Apr	May	Jun	Jul	Aug	Sep	Oct	Nov	Dec
High	35	39	50	61	71	80	83	82	75	63	51	40
Low	17	19	27	36	45	54	58	56	50	39	31	23
Precip	2.5	2.3	3.1	3.2	4.1	3.8	4.2	3.1	3.3	2.5	3.3	3.1
Snow	7.8	6.7	6.1	1.3	tr	0.0	0.0	0.0	0.0	tr	2.2	6.1

High and Low temperatures in degrees Fahrenheit; Precipitation and Snow in inches

Population: 108,276 (1990); 112,075 (2000); 110,560 (2007); 109,081 (2012 projected); Race: 96.1% White, 2.4% Black, 0.3% Asian, 1.3% Hispanic of any race (2007); Density: 207.6 persons per square mile (2007); Average household size: 2.56 (2007); Median age: 40.5 (2007); Males per 100 females: 99.8 (2007).
Religion: Five largest groups: 11.8% Catholic Church, 6.4% The United Methodist Church, 4.5% Presbyterian Church (U.S.A.), 3.5% Christian Churches and Churches of Christ, 3.0% Evangelical Lutheran Church in America (2000).
Economy: Unemployment rate: 7.3% (6/2008); Total civilian labor force: 53,887 (6/2008); Leading industries: 22.6% manufacturing; 20.8% health care and social assistance; 17.0% retail trade (2005); Farms: 1,184 totaling 136,080 acres (2002); Companies that employ 500 or more persons: 5 (2006); Companies that employ 100 to 499 persons: 27 (2006); Companies that employ less than 100 persons: 2,280 (2006); Black-owned businesses: n/a (2002); Hispanic-owned businesses: n/a (2002); Asian-owned businesses: n/a (2002); Women-owned businesses: 1,877 (2002); Retail sales per capita: $11,126 (2008). Single-family building permits issued: 59 (2007); Multi-family building permits issued: 4 (2007).
Income: Per capita income: $19,409 (2007); Median household income: $39,198 (2007); Average household income: $48,662 (2007); Percent of households with income of $100,000 or more: 8.0% (2007); Poverty rate: 15.3% (2005); Bankruptcy rate: 5.58% (2007).
Taxes: Total county taxes per capita: $196 (2006); County property taxes per capita: $159 (2006).
Education: Percent of population age 25 and over with: High school diploma (including GED) or higher: 80.6% (2007); Bachelor's degree or higher: 10.8% (2007); Master's degree or higher: 3.4% (2007).
Housing: Homeownership rate: 76.4% (2007); Median home value: $97,232 (2007); Median rent: $327 per month (2000); Median age of housing: 43 years (2000).
Health: Birth rate: 114.1 per 10,000 population (2007); Death rate: 110.6 per 10,000 population (2007); Age-adjusted cancer mortality rate: 207.1 deaths per 100,000 population (2005); Air Quality Index: 99.2% good, 0.8% moderate, 0.0% unhealthy for sensitive individuals, 0.0% unhealthy (percent of days in 2007); Number of physicians: 11.6 per 10,000 population (2005); Hospital beds: 28.7 per 10,000 population (2004); Hospital admissions: 1,191.8 per 10,000 population (2004).
Elections: 2004 Presidential election results: 52.1% Bush, 47.4% Kerry, 0.0% Nader, 0.3% Badnarik
National and State Parks: Beaver Creek State Forest; Guilford Lake State Park
Additional Information Contacts

Columbiana County Government . . . . . (330) 424-9511
http://www.columbianacounty.org
Calcutta Area Chamber of Commerce . . . . . (330) 386-6060
http://www.calcuttaohiochamber.com
City of East Liverpool . . . . . (330) 385-3381
http://www.eastliverpool.com
City of East Palestine . . . . . (330) 426-4367
http://www.eastpalestine-oh.gov
City of Salem . . . . . (330) 332-4241
http://www.cityofsalemohio.org
Columbiana Area Chamber of Commerce . . . . . (330) 482-3822
http://www.columbianachamber.com
East Liverpool Chamber of Commerce . . . . . (330) 385-0845
http://www.elchamber.com
Salem Chamber of Commerce . . . . . (330) 337-3473
http://www.salemohiochamber.com
Wellsville Area Chamber of Commerce . . . . . (330) 532-2120
http://www.wellsvilleohiochamber.com

Columbiana County Communities

CALCUTTA (CDP). Covers a land area of 11.748 square miles and a water area of 0.015 square miles. Located at 40.68° N. Lat.; 80.57° W. Long. Elevation is 1,115 feet.

Population: 3,211 (1990); 3,491 (2000); 3,460 (2007); 3,462 (2012 projected); Race: 98.4% White, 0.1% Black, 0.8% Asian, 0.7% Hispanic of any race (2007); Density: 294.5 persons per square mile (2007); Average household size: 2.41 (2007); Median age: 47.0 (2007); Males per 100 females: 88.2 (2007); Marriage status: 20.2% never married, 59.8% now married, 10.1% widowed, 9.9% divorced (2000); Foreign born: 0.3% (2000); Ancestry (includes multiple ancestries): 22.3% German, 16.9% English, 16.4% Irish, 12.3% United States or American, 8.5% Italian (2000).

Economy: Employment by occupation: 11.4% management, 16.7% professional, 14.7% services, 25.9% sales, 1.1% farming, 11.8% construction, 18.3% production (2000).

Income: Per capita income: $21,495 (2007); Median household income: $39,925 (2007); Average household income: $51,165 (2007); Percent of households with income of $100,000 or more: 9.5% (2007); Poverty rate: 8.3% (2000).

Education: Percent of population age 25 and over with: High school diploma (including GED) or higher: 81.0% (2007); Bachelor's degree or higher: 13.3% (2007); Master's degree or higher: 5.9% (2007).

School District(s)

Buckeye On-Line School For Success (KG-12)
2005-06 Enrollment: 498 . . . . . (330) 385-1987

Housing: Homeownership rate: 78.6% (2007); Median home value: $115,142 (2007); Median rent: $268 per month (2000); Median age of housing: 29 years (2000).

Transportation: Commute to work: 94.8% car, 0.0% public transportation, 2.0% walk, 1.4% work from home (2000); Travel time to work: 41.6% less than 15 minutes, 31.1% 15 to 30 minutes, 18.2% 30 to 45 minutes, 4.9% 45 to 60 minutes, 4.2% 60 minutes or more (2000)

Additional Information Contacts

Calcutta Area Chamber of Commerce . . . . . (330) 386-6060
http://www.calcuttaohiochamber.com

COLUMBIANA (city). Covers a land area of 6.057 square miles and a water area of 0.128 square miles. Located at 40.88° N. Lat.; 80.68° W. Long. Elevation is 1,158 feet.

History: Columbiana was laid out in 1805, when it was called Dixonville for its founder, Joshua Dixon. Harvey S. Firestone (1868-1938), who had the idea of making rubber tires for buggies, was born in Columbiana.

Population: 5,443 (1990); 5,635 (2000); 5,984 (2007); 6,194 (2012 projected); Race: 98.6% White, 0.1% Black, 0.3% Asian, 0.3% Hispanic of any race (2007); Density: 988.0 persons per square mile (2007); Average household size: 2.21 (2007); Median age: 47.6 (2007); Males per 100 females: 88.3 (2007); Marriage status: 16.9% never married, 61.6% now married, 11.1% widowed, 10.3% divorced (2000); Foreign born: 0.8% (2000); Ancestry (includes multiple ancestries): 30.8% German, 15.2% English, 14.4% Irish, 6.9% United States or American, 6.2% Italian (2000).

Economy: Single-family building permits issued: 30 (2007); Multi-family building permits issued: 0 (2007); Employment by occupation: 7.6% management, 18.9% professional, 16.5% services, 29.0% sales, 0.5% farming, 9.9% construction, 17.6% production (2000).

Income: Per capita income: $21,519 (2007); Median household income: $36,522 (2007); Average household income: $45,231 (2007); Percent of households with income of $100,000 or more: 7.6% (2007); Poverty rate: 6.5% (2000).

Education: Percent of population age 25 and over with: High school diploma (including GED) or higher: 86.0% (2007); Bachelor's degree or higher: 15.4% (2007); Master's degree or higher: 5.4% (2007).

School District(s)

Columbiana Exempted Village (PK-12)
2005-06 Enrollment: 1,011 . . . . . (330) 482-5352
Crestview Local (PK-12)
2005-06 Enrollment: 1,153 . . . . . (330) 482-5526

Housing: Homeownership rate: 67.4% (2007); Median home value: $114,956 (2007); Median rent: $377 per month (2000); Median age of housing: 37 years (2000).

Transportation: Commute to work: 95.2% car, 0.3% public transportation, 3.1% walk, 1.1% work from home (2000); Travel time to work: 35.7% less than 15 minutes, 42.3% 15 to 30 minutes, 17.2% 30 to 45 minutes, 3.0% 45 to 60 minutes, 1.8% 60 minutes or more (2000)

Additional Information Contacts

Columbiana Area Chamber of Commerce . . . . . (330) 482-3822
http://www.columbianachamber.com

EAST LIVERPOOL (city). Covers a land area of 4.348 square miles and a water area of 0.181 square miles. Located at 40.62° N. Lat.; 80.56° W. Long. Elevation is 768 feet.

History: East Liverpool was called St. Clair in 1798 by its founder, Thomas Fawcett of Ireland. Early residents called it Fawcett's Town, but in 1860 the name became Liverpool, because many of the residents had come from the English pottery city. James Bennett, a young potter from England, arrived here in 1838, and East Liverpool began the pottery production that shaped its character for many years.

Population: 13,654 (1990); 13,089 (2000); 12,211 (2007); 11,553 (2012 projected); Race: 93.7% White, 4.0% Black, 0.1% Asian, 0.6% Hispanic of any race (2007); Density: 2,808.3 persons per square mile (2007); Average household size: 2.47 (2007); Median age: 37.1 (2007); Males per 100 females: 88.3 (2007); Marriage status: 21.9% never married, 56.1% now married, 8.4% widowed, 13.7% divorced (2000); Foreign born: 0.5% (2000); Ancestry (includes multiple ancestries): 16.8% German, 14.9% Irish, 13.4% United States or American, 12.5% English, 12.3% Other groups (2000).

Economy: Single-family building permits issued: 0 (2007); Multi-family building permits issued: 0 (2007); Employment by occupation: 4.4% management, 11.3% professional, 25.0% services, 22.9% sales, 0.2% farming, 9.2% construction, 27.0% production (2000).

Income: Per capita income: $14,574 (2007); Median household income: $26,404 (2007); Average household income: $35,417 (2007); Percent of households with income of $100,000 or more: 4.5% (2007); Poverty rate: 25.2% (2000).

Education: Percent of population age 25 and over with: High school diploma (including GED) or higher: 73.6% (2007); Bachelor's degree or higher: 7.3% (2007); Master's degree or higher: 2.6% (2007).

School District(s)

Beaver Local (PK-12)
2005-06 Enrollment: 2,387 . . . . . (330) 385-6831
Buckeye On-Line School for Success (KG-12)
2005-06 Enrollment: 498 . . . . . (330) 385-1987
East Liverpool City (PK-12)
2005-06 Enrollment: 2,687 . . . . . (330) 385-7132

Two-year College(s)

Kent State University-East Liverpool Campus (Public)
Fall 2007 Enrollment: 902 . . . . . (330) 382-7400
2007-08 Tuition: In-state $4,770; Out-of-state $12,202
Ohio Valley College of Technology (Private, For-profit)
Fall 2007 Enrollment: 128 . . . . . (330) 385-1070
2007-08 Tuition: In-state $7,990; Out-of-state $7,990

Housing: Homeownership rate: 59.8% (2007); Median home value: $52,402 (2007); Median rent: $284 per month (2000); Median age of housing: 60 years (2000).

Hospitals: East Liverpool City Hospital (199 beds)

Newspapers: East Liverpool Review (Community news; Circulation 10,937)

Transportation: Commute to work: 92.2% car, 1.5% public transportation, 4.5% walk, 1.5% work from home (2000); Travel time to work: 48.4% less

than 15 minutes, 22.8% 15 to 30 minutes, 14.5% 30 to 45 minutes, 9.8% 45 to 60 minutes, 4.5% 60 minutes or more (2000)
Airports: Columbiana County (general aviation)
Additional Information Contacts
City of East Liverpool . . . . (330) 385-3381
http://www.eastliverpool.com
East Liverpool Chamber of Commerce . . . . (330) 385-0845
http://www.elchamber.com

EAST PALESTINE (city). Covers a land area of 2.775 square miles and a water area of 0 square miles. Located at 40.83° N. Lat.; 80.54° W. Long. Elevation is 1,001 feet.
History: East Palestine was established in 1828 by Thomas McCalla and William Grate. It developed as a pottery town, first using deposits of local clay, but later employing finer materials.
Population: 5,168 (1990); 4,917 (2000); 4,757 (2007); 4,607 (2012 projected); Race: 98.5% White, 0.4% Black, 0.2% Asian, 0.5% Hispanic of any race (2007); Density: 1,714.4 persons per square mile (2007); Average household size: 2.43 (2007); Median age: 40.6 (2007); Males per 100 females: 94.9 (2007); Marriage status: 22.8% never married, 57.8% now married, 10.5% widowed, 8.9% divorced (2000); Foreign born: 0.8% (2000); Ancestry (includes multiple ancestries): 26.5% German, 20.0% English, 19.9% Irish, 10.8% Italian, 9.0% United States or American (2000).
Economy: Single-family building permits issued: 9 (2007); Multi-family building permits issued: 0 (2007); Employment by occupation: 6.9% management, 13.3% professional, 14.8% services, 29.2% sales, 0.0% farming, 11.3% construction, 24.6% production (2000).
Income: Per capita income: $19,278 (2007); Median household income: $41,316 (2007); Average household income: $46,749 (2007); Percent of households with income of $100,000 or more: 5.3% (2007); Poverty rate: 10.0% (2000).
Education: Percent of population age 25 and over with: High school diploma (including GED) or higher: 84.4% (2007); Bachelor's degree or higher: 12.0% (2007); Master's degree or higher: 4.2% (2007).
School District(s)
East Palestine City (PK-12)
2005-06 Enrollment: 1,380 . . . . (330) 426-4191
Housing: Homeownership rate: 75.4% (2007); Median home value: $93,941 (2007); Median rent: $363 per month (2000); Median age of housing: 60+ years (2000).
Transportation: Commute to work: 91.6% car, 0.4% public transportation, 4.9% walk, 2.7% work from home (2000); Travel time to work: 38.9% less than 15 minutes, 28.0% 15 to 30 minutes, 22.7% 30 to 45 minutes, 7.2% 45 to 60 minutes, 3.2% 60 minutes or more (2000)
Additional Information Contacts
City of East Palestine . . . . (330) 426-4367
http://www.eastpalestine-oh.gov

EAST ROCHESTER (unincorporated postal area, zip code 44625). Covers a land area of 21.408 square miles and a water area of 0.138 square miles. Located at 40.75° N. Lat.; 81.00° W. Long. Elevation is 1,094 feet.
Population: 1,603 (2000); Race: 100.0% White, 0.0% Black, 0.0% Asian, 0.0% Hispanic of any race (2000); Density: 74.9 persons per square mile (2000); Age: 31.3% under 18, 11.2% over 64 (2000); Marriage status: 21.4% never married, 66.7% now married, 3.8% widowed, 8.1% divorced (2000); Foreign born: 0.0% (2000); Ancestry (includes multiple ancestries): 37.8% German, 19.2% Irish, 15.6% English, 6.9% United States or American, 6.8% Italian (2000).
Economy: Employment by occupation: 13.3% management, 7.8% professional, 19.0% services, 17.5% sales, 1.8% farming, 9.3% construction, 31.4% production (2000).
Income: Per capita income: $13,537 (2000); Median household income: $38,068 (2000); Poverty rate: 10.5% (2000).
Education: Percent of population age 25 and over with: High school diploma (including GED) or higher: 81.3% (2000); Bachelor's degree or higher: 4.8% (2000).
School District(s)
Minerva Local (PK-12)
2005-06 Enrollment: 2,176 . . . . (330) 868-4332
Housing: Homeownership rate: 78.7% (2000); Median home value: $85,400 (2000); Median rent: $362 per month (2000); Median age of housing: 39 years (2000).
Transportation: Commute to work: 87.5% car, 0.0% public transportation, 6.2% walk, 5.1% work from home (2000); Travel time to work: 32.7% less than 15 minutes, 39.8% 15 to 30 minutes, 17.9% 30 to 45 minutes, 6.2% 45 to 60 minutes, 3.4% 60 minutes or more (2000)

GLENMOOR (CDP). Covers a land area of 2.797 square miles and a water area of 0 square miles. Located at 40.66° N. Lat.; 80.61° W. Long. Elevation is 1,122 feet.
Population: 2,307 (1990); 2,192 (2000); 2,095 (2007); 2,044 (2012 projected); Race: 97.7% White, 1.1% Black, 0.2% Asian, 0.8% Hispanic of any race (2007); Density: 749.0 persons per square mile (2007); Average household size: 2.44 (2007); Median age: 43.2 (2007); Males per 100 females: 95.1 (2007); Marriage status: 18.8% never married, 59.1% now married, 12.2% widowed, 9.9% divorced (2000); Foreign born: 0.0% (2000); Ancestry (includes multiple ancestries): 13.2% Other groups, 13.1% English, 12.3% United States or American, 9.8% Irish, 8.5% German (2000).
Economy: Employment by occupation: 5.8% management, 12.8% professional, 16.4% services, 24.6% sales, 0.0% farming, 12.6% construction, 27.8% production (2000).
Income: Per capita income: $17,640 (2007); Median household income: $34,409 (2007); Average household income: $43,021 (2007); Percent of households with income of $100,000 or more: 5.5% (2007); Poverty rate: 6.9% (2000).
Education: Percent of population age 25 and over with: High school diploma (including GED) or higher: 77.1% (2007); Bachelor's degree or higher: 7.4% (2007); Master's degree or higher: 1.9% (2007).
Housing: Homeownership rate: 83.6% (2007); Median home value: $81,774 (2007); Median rent: $311 per month (2000); Median age of housing: 41 years (2000).
Transportation: Commute to work: 88.8% car, 0.0% public transportation, 7.5% walk, 1.7% work from home (2000); Travel time to work: 36.8% less than 15 minutes, 41.3% 15 to 30 minutes, 11.9% 30 to 45 minutes, 3.1% 45 to 60 minutes, 6.9% 60 minutes or more (2000)

HANOVERTON (village). Covers a land area of 0.707 square miles and a water area of 0 square miles. Located at 40.75° N. Lat.; 80.93° W. Long. Elevation is 1,129 feet.
Population: 434 (1990); 387 (2000); 370 (2007); 366 (2012 projected); Race: 98.1% White, 0.5% Black, 0.0% Asian, 0.5% Hispanic of any race (2007); Density: 523.3 persons per square mile (2007); Average household size: 2.39 (2007); Median age: 37.9 (2007); Males per 100 females: 88.8 (2007); Marriage status: 20.7% never married, 68.1% now married, 7.4% widowed, 3.7% divorced (2000); Foreign born: 3.9% (2000); Ancestry (includes multiple ancestries): 31.1% German, 14.3% English, 14.3% Irish, 8.5% United States or American, 5.1% Polish (2000).
Economy: Single-family building permits issued: 0 (2007); Multi-family building permits issued: 0 (2007); Employment by occupation: 2.8% management, 16.9% professional, 7.9% services, 19.2% sales, 0.0% farming, 15.8% construction, 37.3% production (2000).
Income: Per capita income: $19,277 (2007); Median household income: $42,917 (2007); Average household income: $46,016 (2007); Percent of households with income of $100,000 or more: 3.2% (2007); Poverty rate: 3.2% (2000).
Education: Percent of population age 25 and over with: High school diploma (including GED) or higher: 82.6% (2007); Bachelor's degree or higher: 9.9% (2007); Master's degree or higher: 0.4% (2007).
School District(s)
United Local (PK-12)
2005-06 Enrollment: 1,439 . . . . (330) 223-1521
Housing: Homeownership rate: 85.2% (2007); Median home value: $88,824 (2007); Median rent: $272 per month (2000); Median age of housing: 60+ years (2000).
Transportation: Commute to work: 95.3% car, 0.0% public transportation, 2.3% walk, 1.2% work from home (2000); Travel time to work: 34.3% less than 15 minutes, 38.5% 15 to 30 minutes, 20.1% 30 to 45 minutes, 4.7% 45 to 60 minutes, 2.4% 60 minutes or more (2000)

HOMEWORTH (unincorporated postal area, zip code 44634). Covers a land area of 16.212 square miles and a water area of 0.028 square miles. Located at 40.83° N. Lat.; 81.05° W. Long. Elevation is 1,155 feet.
Population: 2,083 (2000); Race: 98.1% White, 0.0% Black, 0.8% Asian, 0.0% Hispanic of any race (2000); Density: 128.5 persons per square mile (2000); Age: 27.7% under 18, 10.6% over 64 (2000); Marriage status: 23.7% never married, 65.0% now married, 5.4% widowed, 5.8% divorced

(2000); Foreign born: 1.4% (2000); Ancestry (includes multiple ancestries): 25.8% German, 10.4% Irish, 7.3% Italian, 7.0% United States or American, 6.9% Other groups (2000).
Economy: Employment by occupation: 16.9% management, 14.0% professional, 9.0% services, 16.6% sales, 6.1% farming, 13.0% construction, 24.6% production (2000).
Income: Per capita income: $18,980 (2000); Median household income: $48,393 (2000); Poverty rate: 2.6% (2000).
Education: Percent of population age 25 and over with: High school diploma (including GED) or higher: 90.2% (2000); Bachelor's degree or higher: 14.5% (2000).
Housing: Homeownership rate: 86.1% (2000); Median home value: $100,500 (2000); Median rent: $417 per month (2000); Median age of housing: 42 years (2000).
Transportation: Commute to work: 94.4% car, 0.5% public transportation, 1.2% walk, 3.4% work from home (2000); Travel time to work: 23.1% less than 15 minutes, 46.0% 15 to 30 minutes, 18.5% 30 to 45 minutes, 8.3% 45 to 60 minutes, 4.1% 60 minutes or more (2000)

KENSINGTON (unincorporated postal area, zip code 44427). Covers a land area of 31.741 square miles and a water area of 0.045 square miles. Located at 40.72° N. Lat.; 80.94° W. Long. Elevation is 1,119 feet.
Population: 1,728 (2000); Race: 99.6% White, 0.0% Black, 0.0% Asian, 0.0% Hispanic of any race (2000); Density: 54.4 persons per square mile (2000); Age: 29.1% under 18, 11.0% over 64 (2000); Marriage status: 17.7% never married, 70.3% now married, 3.9% widowed, 8.1% divorced (2000); Foreign born: 0.9% (2000); Ancestry (includes multiple ancestries): 24.6% German, 11.9% Irish, 11.3% United States or American, 7.8% English, 6.0% Dutch (2000).
Economy: Employment by occupation: 9.2% management, 12.0% professional, 16.7% services, 14.8% sales, 1.5% farming, 10.5% construction, 35.2% production (2000).
Income: Per capita income: $21,147 (2000); Median household income: $39,265 (2000); Poverty rate: 21.3% (2000).
Education: Percent of population age 25 and over with: High school diploma (including GED) or higher: 74.1% (2000); Bachelor's degree or higher: 7.0% (2000).
Housing: Homeownership rate: 87.8% (2000); Median home value: $75,500 (2000); Median rent: $325 per month (2000); Median age of housing: 39 years (2000).
Transportation: Commute to work: 88.2% car, 1.4% public transportation, 2.8% walk, 6.5% work from home (2000); Travel time to work: 22.3% less than 15 minutes, 27.7% 15 to 30 minutes, 24.2% 30 to 45 minutes, 16.7% 45 to 60 minutes, 9.1% 60 minutes or more (2000)

LA CROFT (CDP). Covers a land area of 1.139 square miles and a water area of 0 square miles. Located at 40.64° N. Lat.; 80.59° W. Long. Elevation is 1,171 feet.
Population: 1,427 (1990); 1,307 (2000); 1,257 (2007); 1,237 (2012 projected); Race: 98.6% White, 0.6% Black, 0.1% Asian, 0.3% Hispanic of any race (2007); Density: 1,103.8 persons per square mile (2007); Average household size: 2.50 (2007); Median age: 41.4 (2007); Males per 100 females: 98.9 (2007); Marriage status: 19.8% never married, 57.1% now married, 11.4% widowed, 11.7% divorced (2000); Foreign born: 0.0% (2000); Ancestry (includes multiple ancestries): 26.2% English, 16.8% German, 11.2% Irish, 8.8% Other groups, 7.0% United States or American (2000).
Economy: Employment by occupation: 8.1% management, 8.7% professional, 17.0% services, 21.8% sales, 0.0% farming, 6.7% construction, 37.6% production (2000).
Income: Per capita income: $15,788 (2007); Median household income: $33,370 (2007); Average household income: $39,453 (2007); Percent of households with income of $100,000 or more: 3.8% (2007); Poverty rate: 11.5% (2000).
Education: Percent of population age 25 and over with: High school diploma (including GED) or higher: 73.5% (2007); Bachelor's degree or higher: 3.8% (2007); Master's degree or higher: 0.9% (2007).
Housing: Homeownership rate: 86.5% (2007); Median home value: $66,702 (2007); Median rent: $348 per month (2000); Median age of housing: 46 years (2000).
Transportation: Commute to work: 95.4% car, 1.0% public transportation, 1.2% walk, 1.4% work from home (2000); Travel time to work: 44.0% less than 15 minutes, 38.7% 15 to 30 minutes, 7.3% 30 to 45 minutes, 4.1% 45 to 60 minutes, 5.9% 60 minutes or more (2000)

LEETONIA (village). Covers a land area of 2.112 square miles and a water area of 0.006 square miles. Located at 40.87° N. Lat.; 80.75° W. Long. Elevation is 1,017 feet.
History: Laid out 1866.
Population: 2,070 (1990); 2,043 (2000); 1,930 (2007); 1,833 (2012 projected); Race: 99.0% White, 0.2% Black, 0.1% Asian, 0.8% Hispanic of any race (2007); Density: 914.0 persons per square mile (2007); Average household size: 2.64 (2007); Median age: 36.9 (2007); Males per 100 females: 100.6 (2007); Marriage status: 25.5% never married, 56.3% now married, 6.5% widowed, 11.7% divorced (2000); Foreign born: 1.7% (2000); Ancestry (includes multiple ancestries): 29.3% German, 16.3% Irish, 15.5% Italian, 13.8% English, 7.0% United States or American (2000).
Economy: Single-family building permits issued: 3 (2007); Multi-family building permits issued: 2 (2007); Employment by occupation: 12.5% management, 10.7% professional, 19.2% services, 20.2% sales, 0.0% farming, 10.6% construction, 26.8% production (2000).
Income: Per capita income: $17,558 (2007); Median household income: $41,803 (2007); Average household income: $46,421 (2007); Percent of households with income of $100,000 or more: 4.5% (2007); Poverty rate: 7.0% (2000).
Education: Percent of population age 25 and over with: High school diploma (including GED) or higher: 83.7% (2007); Bachelor's degree or higher: 10.0% (2007); Master's degree or higher: 2.2% (2007).

School District(s)

Leetonia Exempted Village (PK-12)
2005-06 Enrollment: 862 . . . . (330) 427-6594
Housing: Homeownership rate: 82.2% (2007); Median home value: $83,158 (2007); Median rent: $398 per month (2000); Median age of housing: 60+ years (2000).
Transportation: Commute to work: 93.0% car, 1.8% public transportation, 0.8% walk, 4.3% work from home (2000); Travel time to work: 36.2% less than 15 minutes, 36.2% 15 to 30 minutes, 16.4% 30 to 45 minutes, 5.7% 45 to 60 minutes, 5.6% 60 minutes or more (2000)

LISBON (village). County seat. Covers a land area of 1.106 square miles and a water area of 0 square miles. Located at 40.77° N. Lat.; 80.76° W. Long. Elevation is 968 feet.
History: Lisbon was founded in 1802, and grew as a coal and pottery town. This was the birthplace of politicians Marcus A. Hanna (1837-1904) and Clement L. Vallandigham (1820-1871).
Population: 3,037 (1990); 2,788 (2000); 2,709 (2007); 2,672 (2012 projected); Race: 97.9% White, 0.8% Black, 0.2% Asian, 0.6% Hispanic of any race (2007); Density: 2,449.6 persons per square mile (2007); Average household size: 2.41 (2007); Median age: 40.0 (2007); Males per 100 females: 90.1 (2007); Marriage status: 24.9% never married, 53.9% now married, 9.8% widowed, 11.5% divorced (2000); Foreign born: 1.4% (2000); Ancestry (includes multiple ancestries): 26.1% German, 18.7% Irish, 15.0% English, 9.7% Italian, 5.9% Other groups (2000).
Economy: Single-family building permits issued: 0 (2007); Multi-family building permits issued: 0 (2007); Employment by occupation: 5.2% management, 16.1% professional, 16.9% services, 28.4% sales, 0.7% farming, 12.4% construction, 20.3% production (2000).
Income: Per capita income: $16,589 (2007); Median household income: $30,678 (2007); Average household income: $39,004 (2007); Percent of households with income of $100,000 or more: 4.8% (2007); Poverty rate: 14.1% (2000).
Education: Percent of population age 25 and over with: High school diploma (including GED) or higher: 78.1% (2007); Bachelor's degree or higher: 12.6% (2007); Master's degree or higher: 4.4% (2007).

School District(s)

Beaver Local (PK-12)
2005-06 Enrollment: 2,387 . . . . (330) 385-6831
Columbiana County (09-12)
2005-06 Enrollment: n/a . . . . (330) 424-9561
Lisbon Exempted Village (PK-12)
2005-06 Enrollment: 1,122 . . . . (330) 424-7714

Two-year College(s)

Columbiana County Vocational School (Public)
Fall 2007 Enrollment: 533 . . . . (330) 424-9561
2007-08 Tuition: In-state $4,310; Out-of-state $4,310
Housing: Homeownership rate: 64.1% (2007); Median home value: $93,611 (2007); Median rent: $341 per month (2000); Median age of housing: 60+ years (2000).

Newspapers: Central Shopper (Community news; Circulation 20,400); Lisbon Morning Journal (Local news; Circulation 13,000)
Transportation: Commute to work: 89.9% car, 3.1% public transportation, 4.2% walk, 2.9% work from home (2000); Travel time to work: 39.7% less than 15 minutes, 40.5% 15 to 30 minutes, 10.4% 30 to 45 minutes, 5.7% 45 to 60 minutes, 3.7% 60 minutes or more (2000)

NEGLEY (unincorporated postal area, zip code 44441). Covers a land area of 15.834 square miles and a water area of 0.198 square miles. Located at 40.77° N. Lat.; 80.55° W. Long. Elevation is 850 feet.
Population: 1,573 (2000); Race: 99.5% White, 0.0% Black, 0.0% Asian, 0.4% Hispanic of any race (2000); Density: 99.3 persons per square mile (2000); Age: 24.1% under 18, 8.0% over 64 (2000); Marriage status: 18.9% never married, 62.0% now married, 5.9% widowed, 13.1% divorced (2000); Foreign born: 0.0% (2000); Ancestry (includes multiple ancestries): 21.6% German, 19.1% English, 18.4% United States or American, 13.6% Irish, 5.6% Italian (2000).
Economy: Employment by occupation: 3.6% management, 7.6% professional, 13.9% services, 25.6% sales, 0.0% farming, 9.2% construction, 40.1% production (2000).
Income: Per capita income: $18,439 (2000); Median household income: $40,288 (2000); Poverty rate: 12.2% (2000).
Education: Percent of population age 25 and over with: High school diploma (including GED) or higher: 77.5% (2000); Bachelor's degree or higher: 7.9% (2000).
Housing: Homeownership rate: 85.2% (2000); Median home value: $103,900 (2000); Median rent: $318 per month (2000); Median age of housing: 27 years (2000).
Transportation: Commute to work: 97.9% car, 0.9% public transportation, 0.0% walk, 1.2% work from home (2000); Travel time to work: 18.0% less than 15 minutes, 34.3% 15 to 30 minutes, 24.1% 30 to 45 minutes, 18.9% 45 to 60 minutes, 4.8% 60 minutes or more (2000)

NEW WATERFORD (village). Covers a land area of 0.889 square miles and a water area of 0 square miles. Located at 40.84° N. Lat.; 80.61° W. Long. Elevation is 1,047 feet.
Population: 1,278 (1990); 1,391 (2000); 1,299 (2007); 1,286 (2012 projected); Race: 98.6% White, 0.2% Black, 0.0% Asian, 0.0% Hispanic of any race (2007); Density: 1,460.6 persons per square mile (2007); Average household size: 2.39 (2007); Median age: 39.1 (2007); Males per 100 females: 94.5 (2007); Marriage status: 22.5% never married, 57.6% now married, 7.1% widowed, 12.7% divorced (2000); Foreign born: 0.1% (2000); Ancestry (includes multiple ancestries): 33.4% German, 14.1% Irish, 11.5% English, 7.5% Italian, 6.9% United States or American (2000).
Economy: Employment by occupation: 10.0% management, 9.4% professional, 17.3% services, 27.1% sales, 0.6% farming, 8.3% construction, 27.3% production (2000).
Income: Per capita income: $21,751 (2007); Median household income: $40,870 (2007); Average household income: $51,939 (2007); Percent of households with income of $100,000 or more: 7.7% (2007); Poverty rate: 9.5% (2000).
Education: Percent of population age 25 and over with: High school diploma (including GED) or higher: 82.9% (2007); Bachelor's degree or higher: 8.6% (2007); Master's degree or higher: 2.4% (2007).
Housing: Homeownership rate: 75.2% (2007); Median home value: $99,853 (2007); Median rent: $288 per month (2000); Median age of housing: 27 years (2000).
Transportation: Commute to work: 97.1% car, 0.6% public transportation, 0.8% walk, 1.2% work from home (2000); Travel time to work: 29.5% less than 15 minutes, 38.1% 15 to 30 minutes, 20.6% 30 to 45 minutes, 6.6% 45 to 60 minutes, 5.3% 60 minutes or more (2000)

ROGERS (village). Covers a land area of 0.235 square miles and a water area of 0 square miles. Located at 40.79° N. Lat.; 80.62° W. Long. Elevation is 1,027 feet.
Population: 247 (1990); 266 (2000); 282 (2007); 296 (2012 projected); Race: 98.6% White, 0.0% Black, 0.0% Asian, 0.7% Hispanic of any race (2007); Density: 1,200.5 persons per square mile (2007); Average household size: 2.74 (2007); Median age: 36.3 (2007); Males per 100 females: 112.0 (2007); Marriage status: 27.5% never married, 60.1% now married, 5.2% widowed, 7.3% divorced (2000); Foreign born: 1.6% (2000); Ancestry (includes multiple ancestries): 21.1% German, 19.9% Irish, 12.9% English, 8.2% Italian, 5.9% Welsh (2000).
Economy: Employment by occupation: 1.9% management, 2.8% professional, 27.1% services, 17.8% sales, 1.9% farming, 11.2% construction, 37.4% production (2000).
Income: Per capita income: $16,259 (2007); Median household income: $37,188 (2007); Average household income: $44,515 (2007); Percent of households with income of $100,000 or more: 8.7% (2007); Poverty rate: 14.7% (2000).
Education: Percent of population age 25 and over with: High school diploma (including GED) or higher: 77.1% (2007); Bachelor's degree or higher: 2.3% (2007); Master's degree or higher: 0.0% (2007).

School District(s)

Beaver Local (PK-12)
2005-06 Enrollment: 2,387 . . . . (330) 385-6831

Housing: Homeownership rate: 81.6% (2007); Median home value: $63,333 (2007); Median rent: $275 per month (2000); Median age of housing: 60+ years (2000).
Transportation: Commute to work: 97.2% car, 0.0% public transportation, 0.0% walk, 1.9% work from home (2000); Travel time to work: 14.3% less than 15 minutes, 62.9% 15 to 30 minutes, 15.2% 30 to 45 minutes, 5.7% 45 to 60 minutes, 1.9% 60 minutes or more (2000)

SALEM (city). Covers a land area of 5.474 square miles and a water area of 0 square miles. Located at 40.90° N. Lat.; 80.85° W. Long. Elevation is 1,227 feet.
History: The Quakers came to Salem in 1801 from Salem, New Jersey, and were joined by others from Pennsylvania and Virginia. The town was a station on the Underground Railroad.
Population: 12,796 (1990); 12,197 (2000); 11,673 (2007); 11,375 (2012 projected); Race: 98.3% White, 0.4% Black, 0.5% Asian, 0.5% Hispanic of any race (2007); Density: 2,132.5 persons per square mile (2007); Average household size: 2.32 (2007); Median age: 41.3 (2007); Males per 100 females: 86.8 (2007); Marriage status: 22.9% never married, 56.4% now married, 9.9% widowed, 10.8% divorced (2000); Foreign born: 1.2% (2000); Ancestry (includes multiple ancestries): 28.3% German, 16.7% Irish, 12.5% English, 10.6% Italian, 6.6% United States or American (2000).
Economy: Single-family building permits issued: 11 (2007); Multi-family building permits issued: 2 (2007); Employment by occupation: 7.8% management, 15.3% professional, 15.8% services, 24.3% sales, 0.6% farming, 8.9% construction, 27.4% production (2000).
Income: Per capita income: $18,945 (2007); Median household income: $33,485 (2007); Average household income: $43,263 (2007); Percent of households with income of $100,000 or more: 5.8% (2007); Poverty rate: 11.7% (2000).
Education: Percent of population age 25 and over with: High school diploma (including GED) or higher: 82.1% (2007); Bachelor's degree or higher: 14.8% (2007); Master's degree or higher: 4.0% (2007).

School District(s)

Salem City (PK-12)
2005-06 Enrollment: 2,337 . . . . (330) 332-0316
West Branch Local (PK-12)
2005-06 Enrollment: 2,485 . . . . (330) 938-9324

Four-year College(s)

Allegheny Wesleyan College (Private, Not-for-profit, Other Protestant)
Fall 2007 Enrollment: 54 . . . . (330) 337-6403
2007-08 Tuition: In-state $4,686; Out-of-state $4,686
Kent State University-Salem Campus (Public)
Fall 2007 Enrollment: 1,268. . . . . (330) 332-0361
2007-08 Tuition: In-state $4,770; Out-of-state $12,202

Vocational/Technical School(s)

Hannah E Mullins School of Practical Nursing (Public)
Fall 2007 Enrollment: 36 . . . . (330) 332-8940
2007-08 Tuition: $7,300

Housing: Homeownership rate: 65.7% (2007); Median home value: $94,223 (2007); Median rent: $361 per month (2000); Median age of housing: 48 years (2000).
Hospitals: Salem Community Hospital (183 beds)
Safety: Violent crime rate: 1.7 per 10,000 population; Property crime rate: 130.9 per 10,000 population (2007).
Newspapers: Salem News (Local news; Circulation 7,531); Vindicator - Salem Bureau (Local news); Yesteryears - The Salem News
Transportation: Commute to work: 92.5% car, 0.4% public transportation, 4.3% walk, 2.5% work from home (2000); Travel time to work: 55.1% less than 15 minutes, 21.1% 15 to 30 minutes, 13.6% 30 to 45 minutes, 6.3% 45 to 60 minutes, 3.9% 60 minutes or more (2000)

Airports: Salem Airpark (general aviation)
Additional Information Contacts
City of Salem . . . . (330) 332-4241
http://www.cityofsalemohio.org
Salem Chamber of Commerce . . . . (330) 337-3473
http://www.salemohiochamber.com

SALINEVILLE (village). Covers a land area of 2.223 square miles and a water area of 0 square miles. Located at 40.62° N. Lat.; 80.83° W. Long. Elevation is 899 feet.
History: Salineville was named for the salt springs nearby. A salt well was sunk here in 1809, and by 1835 twenty wells were operating along Little Yellow Creek. The arrival of the railroad in 1852 led to the opening of drift coal mines, bringing prosperity to Salineville after the Civil War.
Population: 1,474 (1990); 1,397 (2000); 1,326 (2007); 1,298 (2012 projected); Race: 99.0% White, 0.0% Black, 0.0% Asian, 0.6% Hispanic of any race (2007); Density: 596.6 persons per square mile (2007); Average household size: 2.55 (2007); Median age: 35.0 (2007); Males per 100 females: 99.1 (2007); Marriage status: 23.9% never married, 59.2% now married, 8.6% widowed, 8.3% divorced (2000); Foreign born: 0.1% (2000); Ancestry (includes multiple ancestries): 20.4% German, 14.0% Irish, 12.9% English, 12.4% United States or American, 5.8% Other groups (2000).
Economy: Employment by occupation: 4.1% management, 8.7% professional, 14.0% services, 19.9% sales, 0.4% farming, 6.3% construction, 46.8% production (2000).
Income: Per capita income: $16,319 (2007); Median household income: $32,645 (2007); Average household income: $41,310 (2007); Percent of households with income of $100,000 or more: 6.4% (2007); Poverty rate: 15.7% (2000).
Education: Percent of population age 25 and over with: High school diploma (including GED) or higher: 75.1% (2007); Bachelor's degree or higher: 4.4% (2007); Master's degree or higher: 1.7% (2007).

School District(s)

Southern Local (PK-12)
2005-06 Enrollment: 945 . . . . (330) 679-2343
Housing: Homeownership rate: 72.3% (2007); Median home value: $45,392 (2007); Median rent: $281 per month (2000); Median age of housing: 60+ years (2000).
Transportation: Commute to work: 95.5% car, 0.4% public transportation, 0.4% walk, 3.2% work from home (2000); Travel time to work: 21.6% less than 15 minutes, 21.2% 15 to 30 minutes, 31.3% 30 to 45 minutes, 14.4% 45 to 60 minutes, 11.5% 60 minutes or more (2000)

SUMMITVILLE (village). Covers a land area of 0.930 square miles and a water area of 0.024 square miles. Located at 40.67° N. Lat.; 80.88° W. Long. Elevation is 1,109 feet.
Population: 125 (1990); 108 (2000); 116 (2007); 119 (2012 projected); Race: 97.4% White, 0.0% Black, 0.0% Asian, 1.7% Hispanic of any race (2007); Density: 124.7 persons per square mile (2007); Average household size: 2.37 (2007); Median age: 42.0 (2007); Males per 100 females: 78.5 (2007); Marriage status: 7.2% never married, 68.1% now married, 14.5% widowed, 10.1% divorced (2000); Foreign born: 0.0% (2000); Ancestry (includes multiple ancestries): 14.6% Irish, 13.5% German, 11.2% United States or American, 7.9% Scottish, 7.9% English (2000).
Economy: Employment by occupation: 0.0% management, 0.0% professional, 19.1% services, 10.6% sales, 0.0% farming, 8.5% construction, 61.7% production (2000).
Income: Per capita income: $19,310 (2007); Median household income: $33,750 (2007); Average household income: $45,714 (2007); Percent of households with income of $100,000 or more: 8.2% (2007); Poverty rate: 15.7% (2000).
Education: Percent of population age 25 and over with: High school diploma (including GED) or higher: 80.8% (2007); Bachelor's degree or higher: 6.4% (2007); Master's degree or higher: 6.4% (2007).
Housing: Homeownership rate: 81.6% (2007); Median home value: $100,000 (2007); Median rent: $325 per month (2000); Median age of housing: 47 years (2000).
Transportation: Commute to work: 85.1% car, 8.5% public transportation, 6.4% walk, 0.0% work from home (2000); Travel time to work: 23.4% less than 15 minutes, 38.3% 15 to 30 minutes, 8.5% 30 to 45 minutes, 14.9% 45 to 60 minutes, 14.9% 60 minutes or more (2000)

WASHINGTONVILLE (village). Covers a land area of 0.669 square miles and a water area of 0 square miles. Located at 40.89° N. Lat.; 80.76° W. Long. Elevation is 1,056 feet.
Population: 894 (1990); 789 (2000); 789 (2007); 832 (2012 projected); Race: 98.2% White, 0.1% Black, 0.0% Asian, 0.9% Hispanic of any race (2007); Density: 1,179.6 persons per square mile (2007); Average household size: 2.44 (2007); Median age: 35.4 (2007); Males per 100 females: 93.9 (2007); Marriage status: 24.8% never married, 56.3% now married, 4.8% widowed, 14.1% divorced (2000); Foreign born: 0.3% (2000); Ancestry (includes multiple ancestries): 25.4% German, 16.3% English, 13.0% Italian, 11.5% Irish, 11.3% United States or American (2000).
Economy: Employment by occupation: 3.4% management, 12.3% professional, 14.9% services, 22.0% sales, 0.6% farming, 14.9% construction, 32.0% production (2000).
Income: Per capita income: $15,928 (2007); Median household income: $33,750 (2007); Average household income: $38,909 (2007); Percent of households with income of $100,000 or more: 4.0% (2007); Poverty rate: 19.9% (2000).
Education: Percent of population age 25 and over with: High school diploma (including GED) or higher: 81.6% (2007); Bachelor's degree or higher: 10.2% (2007); Master's degree or higher: 3.2% (2007).
Housing: Homeownership rate: 63.8% (2007); Median home value: $79,259 (2007); Median rent: $287 per month (2000); Median age of housing: 54 years (2000).
Safety: Violent crime rate: 0.0 per 10,000 population; Property crime rate: 262.5 per 10,000 population (2007).
Transportation: Commute to work: 92.2% car, 0.0% public transportation, 3.3% walk, 3.9% work from home (2000); Travel time to work: 29.5% less than 15 minutes, 44.4% 15 to 30 minutes, 19.3% 30 to 45 minutes, 4.7% 45 to 60 minutes, 2.2% 60 minutes or more (2000)

WELLSVILLE (village). Covers a land area of 1.760 square miles and a water area of 0.114 square miles. Located at 40.60° N. Lat.; 80.65° W. Long. Elevation is 699 feet.
History: Wellsville was founded in 1797 by William Wells, and grew as a stagecoach stop, a shipping center during the steamboat era, and the location of brickyards, potteries, and tile plants.
Population: 4,508 (1990); 4,133 (2000); 3,973 (2007); 3,854 (2012 projected); Race: 92.3% White, 5.6% Black, 0.1% Asian, 0.4% Hispanic of any race (2007); Density: 2,257.4 persons per square mile (2007); Average household size: 2.41 (2007); Median age: 37.6 (2007); Males per 100 females: 89.6 (2007); Marriage status: 25.9% never married, 50.3% now married, 9.8% widowed, 14.0% divorced (2000); Foreign born: 1.2% (2000); Ancestry (includes multiple ancestries): 15.6% German, 15.2% Italian, 13.5% Other groups, 12.8% United States or American, 10.6% Irish (2000).
Economy: Single-family building permits issued: 0 (2007); Multi-family building permits issued: 0 (2007); Employment by occupation: 7.0% management, 13.6% professional, 17.1% services, 23.1% sales, 0.0% farming, 7.4% construction, 31.6% production (2000).
Income: Per capita income: $16,888 (2007); Median household income: $30,793 (2007); Average household income: $40,505 (2007); Percent of households with income of $100,000 or more: 5.0% (2007); Poverty rate: 17.1% (2000).
Education: Percent of population age 25 and over with: High school diploma (including GED) or higher: 80.1% (2007); Bachelor's degree or higher: 6.4% (2007); Master's degree or higher: 0.8% (2007).

School District(s)

Wellsville Local (PK-12)
2005-06 Enrollment: 972 . . . . (330) 532-2643
Housing: Homeownership rate: 63.6% (2007); Median home value: $48,269 (2007); Median rent: $283 per month (2000); Median age of housing: 60+ years (2000).
Transportation: Commute to work: 89.2% car, 0.5% public transportation, 5.3% walk, 4.9% work from home (2000); Travel time to work: 31.9% less than 15 minutes, 44.8% 15 to 30 minutes, 11.2% 30 to 45 minutes, 7.2% 45 to 60 minutes, 4.9% 60 minutes or more (2000)
Additional Information Contacts
Wellsville Area Chamber of Commerce . . . . (330) 532-2120
http://www.wellsvilleohiochamber.com

Coshocton County

Located in central Ohio; drained by the Muskingum, Tuscarawas, and Walhonding Rivers. Covers a land area of 564.07 square miles, a water area of 3.51 square miles, and is located in the Eastern Time Zone. The county was founded in 1811. County seat is Coshocton.

Coshocton County is part of the Coshocton, OH Micropolitan Statistical Area. The entire metro area includes: Coshocton County, OH

Weather Station: Coshocton Agr. Res. Station Elevation: 1,138 feet

	Jan	Feb	Mar	Apr	May	Jun	Jul	Aug	Sep	Oct	Nov	Dec
High	33	37	47	59	70	78	82	81	74	62	50	39
Low	18	20	29	40	51	59	63	62	55	43	34	24
Precip	2.3	2.0	2.9	3.3	3.8	4.0	4.0	3.5	3.0	2.4	3.1	2.7
Snow	na	na	na	tr	0.0	0.0	0.0	0.0	0.0	tr	0.2	na

High and Low temperatures in degrees Fahrenheit; Precipitation and Snow in inches

Weather Station: Coshocton WPC Plant Elevation: 757 feet

	Jan	Feb	Mar	Apr	May	Jun	Jul	Aug	Sep	Oct	Nov	Dec
High	36	40	51	63	73	80	84	83	76	65	52	41
Low	18	21	29	38	48	57	61	60	52	40	32	24
Precip	2.5	2.4	3.2	3.8	4.1	4.0	4.5	4.2	3.2	2.7	3.5	3.0
Snow	8.8	5.6	3.0	0.8	tr	0.0	0.0	0.0	0.0	tr	0.9	3.6

High and Low temperatures in degrees Fahrenheit; Precipitation and Snow in inches

Population: 35,427 (1990); 36,655 (2000); 36,915 (2007); 36,877 (2012 projected); Race: 97.2% White, 1.2% Black, 0.4% Asian, 0.8% Hispanic of any race (2007); Density: 65.4 persons per square mile (2007); Average household size: 2.52 (2007); Median age: 39.2 (2007); Males per 100 females: 96.7 (2007).
Religion: Five largest groups: 14.6% The United Methodist Church, 4.4% Catholic Church, 2.9% American Baptist Churches in the USA, 2.5% Church of the Nazarene, 2.5% Presbyterian Church (U.S.A.) (2000).
Economy: Unemployment rate: 8.7% (6/2008); Total civilian labor force: 17,668 (6/2008); Leading industries: 29.7% manufacturing; 17.7% health care and social assistance; 12.9% retail trade (2005); Farms: 1,043 totaling 179,643 acres (2002); Companies that employ 500 or more persons: 1 (2006); Companies that employ 100 to 499 persons: 18 (2006); Companies that employ less than 100 persons: 686 (2006); Black-owned businesses: 121 (2002); Hispanic-owned businesses: n/a (2002); Asian-owned businesses: n/a (2002); Women-owned businesses: 747 (2002); Retail sales per capita: $8,883 (2008). Single-family building permits issued: 6 (2007); Multi-family building permits issued: 0 (2007).
Income: Per capita income: $19,045 (2007); Median household income: $38,900 (2007); Average household income: $47,617 (2007); Percent of households with income of $100,000 or more: 7.5% (2007); Poverty rate: 12.4% (2005); Bankruptcy rate: 3.74% (2007).
Taxes: Total county taxes per capita: $286 (2006); County property taxes per capita: $195 (2006).
Education: Percent of population age 25 and over with: High school diploma (including GED) or higher: 78.7% (2007); Bachelor's degree or higher: 9.9% (2007); Master's degree or higher: 3.5% (2007).
Housing: Homeownership rate: 76.4% (2007); Median home value: $101,765 (2007); Median rent: $303 per month (2000); Median age of housing: 39 years (2000).
Health: Birth rate: 131.3 per 10,000 population (2007); Death rate: 108.7 per 10,000 population (2007); Age-adjusted cancer mortality rate: 225.1 deaths per 100,000 population (2005); Number of physicians: 6.8 per 10,000 population (2005); Hospital beds: 36.3 per 10,000 population (2004); Hospital admissions: 1,200.7 per 10,000 population (2004).
Elections: 2004 Presidential election results: 56.9% Bush, 42.6% Kerry, 0.0% Nader, 0.1% Badnarik

Additional Information Contacts

Coshocton County Government. . . . . (740) 622-1753
http://www.co.coshocton.oh.us
City of Coshocton. . . . . (740) 622-1373
http://www.coshoctoncityhall.com
Coshocton County Chamber of Commerce. . . . . (740) 622-5411
http://www.coshoctoncounty.net/agency/chamber

Coshocton County Communities

CONESVILLE (village). Covers a land area of 0.152 square miles and a water area of 0 square miles. Located at 40.18° N. Lat.; 81.89° W. Long. Elevation is 745 feet.
Population: 420 (1990); 364 (2000); 325 (2007); 325 (2012 projected); Race: 99.7% White, 0.0% Black, 0.0% Asian, 1.5% Hispanic of any race (2007); Density: 2,131.6 persons per square mile (2007); Average household size: 2.46 (2007); Median age: 37.8 (2007); Males per 100 females: 103.1 (2007); Marriage status: 18.5% never married, 60.4% now married, 12.2% widowed, 8.9% divorced (2000); Foreign born: 0.0% (2000); Ancestry (includes multiple ancestries): 16.7% German, 12.8% United States or American, 10.8% Other groups, 9.4% English, 5.3% Irish (2000).
Economy: Employment by occupation: 6.1% management, 9.5% professional, 15.0% services, 22.4% sales, 0.0% farming, 8.8% construction, 38.1% production (2000).
Income: Per capita income: $16,292 (2007); Median household income: $30,833 (2007); Average household income: $40,114 (2007); Percent of households with income of $100,000 or more: 3.8% (2007); Poverty rate: 10.0% (2000).
Education: Percent of population age 25 and over with: High school diploma (including GED) or higher: 82.1% (2007); Bachelor's degree or higher: 1.8% (2007); Master's degree or higher: 0.0% (2007).

School District(s)

River View Local (PK-12)
2005-06 Enrollment: 2,432 . . . . (740) 824-3521
Housing: Homeownership rate: 85.6% (2007); Median home value: $70,714 (2007); Median rent: $363 per month (2000); Median age of housing: 60+ years (2000).
Transportation: Commute to work: 92.5% car, 1.4% public transportation, 6.1% walk, 0.0% work from home (2000); Travel time to work: 31.3% less than 15 minutes, 57.1% 15 to 30 minutes, 6.1% 30 to 45 minutes, 1.4% 45 to 60 minutes, 4.1% 60 minutes or more (2000)

COSHOCTON (city). County seat. Covers a land area of 7.479 square miles and a water area of 0.111 square miles. Located at 40.26° N. Lat.; 81.85° W. Long. Elevation is 771 feet.
History: Coshocton was established on a plateau southeast of the juncture of the Walhonding and Tuscarawas Rivers, and developed as an industrial city. The town's name is of Indian origin. An advertising novelty plant built in 1887 by J.F. Meek was a leading industry. Coshocton suffered repeated floodings from the rivers until Wills Creek Dam and Mohawk Dam were built on the Walhonding in the 1930's.
Population: 12,193 (1990); 11,682 (2000); 11,627 (2007); 11,544 (2012 projected); Race: 95.6% White, 1.9% Black, 1.0% Asian, 0.8% Hispanic of any race (2007); Density: 1,554.7 persons per square mile (2007); Average household size: 2.29 (2007); Median age: 41.9 (2007); Males per 100 females: 88.8 (2007); Marriage status: 19.4% never married, 58.8% now married, 11.1% widowed, 10.7% divorced (2000); Foreign born: 2.3% (2000); Ancestry (includes multiple ancestries): 23.1% German, 14.4% United States or American, 12.3% Irish, 11.3% English, 7.7% Other groups (2000).
Economy: Single-family building permits issued: 2 (2007); Multi-family building permits issued: 0 (2007); Employment by occupation: 8.4% management, 15.4% professional, 13.6% services, 22.9% sales, 0.0% farming, 6.7% construction, 33.0% production (2000).
Income: Per capita income: $20,214 (2007); Median household income: $34,328 (2007); Average household income: $45,583 (2007); Percent of households with income of $100,000 or more: 6.8% (2007); Poverty rate: 8.3% (2000).
Taxes: Total city taxes per capita: $354 (2006); City property taxes per capita: $42 (2006).
Education: Percent of population age 25 and over with: High school diploma (including GED) or higher: 80.5% (2007); Bachelor's degree or higher: 13.2% (2007); Master's degree or higher: 4.4% (2007).

School District(s)

Coshocton City (PK-12)
2005-06 Enrollment: 1,967 . . . . (740) 622-1901
Coshocton County (09-12)
2005-06 Enrollment: n/a . . . . (740) 622-0211
Coshocton Opportunity School
2005-06 Enrollment: n/a . . . .
River View Local (PK-12)
2005-06 Enrollment: 2,432 . . . . (740) 824-3521
Housing: Homeownership rate: 65.1% (2007); Median home value: $100,380 (2007); Median rent: $306 per month (2000); Median age of housing: 52 years (2000).
Hospitals: Coshocton County Memorial Hospital (61 beds)
Newspapers: Coshocton Tribune (Local news; Circulation 7,721)
Transportation: Commute to work: 91.9% car, 1.0% public transportation, 3.7% walk, 2.6% work from home (2000); Travel time to work: 62.9% less than 15 minutes, 21.1% 15 to 30 minutes, 8.2% 30 to 45 minutes, 3.9% 45 to 60 minutes, 3.9% 60 minutes or more (2000)

Additional Information Contacts

City of Coshocton. . . . . (740) 622-1373
http://www.coshoctoncityhall.com

Coshocton County Chamber of Commerce . . . . (740) 622-5411
http://www.coshoctoncounty.net/agency/chamber

FRESNO (unincorporated postal area, zip code 43824). Covers a land area of 77.896 square miles and a water area of 0.020 square miles. Located at 40.35° N. Lat.; 81.75° W. Long. Elevation is 900 feet.
Population: 3,396 (2000); Race: 98.0% White, 0.0% Black, 0.1% Asian, 0.0% Hispanic of any race (2000); Density: 43.6 persons per square mile (2000); Age: 31.0% under 18, 9.1% over 64 (2000); Marriage status: 24.9% never married, 65.3% now married, 3.9% widowed, 5.9% divorced (2000); Foreign born: 0.0% (2000); Ancestry (includes multiple ancestries): 24.7% German, 11.8% United States or American, 8.5% English, 7.1% Irish, 3.4% Other groups (2000).
Economy: Employment by occupation: 11.6% management, 11.8% professional, 8.4% services, 17.2% sales, 3.1% farming, 12.4% construction, 35.5% production (2000).
Income: Per capita income: $14,240 (2000); Median household income: $36,820 (2000); Poverty rate: 12.8% (2000).
Education: Percent of population age 25 and over with: High school diploma (including GED) or higher: 67.5% (2000); Bachelor's degree or higher: 5.9% (2000).

School District(s)

Ridgewood Local (PK-12)
2005-06 Enrollment: 1,452 . . . . (740) 545-6354
Housing: Homeownership rate: 89.9% (2000); Median home value: $79,400 (2000); Median rent: $430 per month (2000); Median age of housing: 24 years (2000).
Transportation: Commute to work: 84.4% car, 2.0% public transportation, 5.0% walk, 7.1% work from home (2000); Travel time to work: 20.9% less than 15 minutes, 41.7% 15 to 30 minutes, 22.5% 30 to 45 minutes, 5.4% 45 to 60 minutes, 9.4% 60 minutes or more (2000)

NELLIE (village). Covers a land area of 0.710 square miles and a water area of 0 square miles. Located at 40.33° N. Lat.; 82.06° W. Long. Elevation is 810 feet.
Population: 130 (1990); 134 (2000); 146 (2007); 151 (2012 projected); Race: 97.3% White, 0.7% Black, 0.0% Asian, 0.0% Hispanic of any race (2007); Density: 205.5 persons per square mile (2007); Average household size: 2.47 (2007); Median age: 36.7 (2007); Males per 100 females: 84.8 (2007); Marriage status: 16.3% never married, 75.0% now married, 3.8% widowed, 4.8% divorced (2000); Foreign born: 0.0% (2000); Ancestry (includes multiple ancestries): 24.4% English, 17.0% German, 12.6% Irish, 11.9% United States or American, 4.4% Swiss (2000).
Economy: Single-family building permits issued: 0 (2007); Multi-family building permits issued: 0 (2007); Employment by occupation: 14.7% management, 11.8% professional, 16.2% services, 16.2% sales, 5.9% farming, 8.8% construction, 26.5% production (2000).
Income: Per capita income: $19,503 (2007); Median household income: $44,167 (2007); Average household income: $48,263 (2007); Percent of households with income of $100,000 or more: 3.4% (2007); Poverty rate: 3.0% (2000).
Education: Percent of population age 25 and over with: High school diploma (including GED) or higher: 90.9% (2007); Bachelor's degree or higher: 21.2% (2007); Master's degree or higher: 3.0% (2007).
Housing: Homeownership rate: 91.5% (2007); Median home value: $92,500 (2007); Median rent: $n/a per month (2000); Median age of housing: 36 years (2000).
Transportation: Commute to work: 87.5% car, 0.0% public transportation, 3.1% walk, 9.4% work from home (2000); Travel time to work: 10.3% less than 15 minutes, 43.1% 15 to 30 minutes, 31.0% 30 to 45 minutes, 8.6% 45 to 60 minutes, 6.9% 60 minutes or more (2000)

PLAINFIELD (village). Covers a land area of 0.419 square miles and a water area of 0 square miles. Located at 40.20° N. Lat.; 81.71° W. Long. Elevation is 797 feet.
Population: 178 (1990); 158 (2000); 154 (2007); 150 (2012 projected); Race: 99.4% White, 0.0% Black, 0.0% Asian, 0.0% Hispanic of any race (2007); Density: 367.8 persons per square mile (2007); Average household size: 2.33 (2007); Median age: 40.0 (2007); Males per 100 females: 108.1 (2007); Marriage status: 21.9% never married, 67.2% now married, 7.0% widowed, 3.9% divorced (2000); Foreign born: 1.3% (2000); Ancestry (includes multiple ancestries): 41.0% German, 9.6% English, 8.3% French (except Basque), 6.4% Hungarian, 5.8% Other groups (2000).
Economy: Single-family building permits issued: 1 (2007); Multi-family building permits issued: 0 (2007); Employment by occupation: 2.6% management, 11.7% professional, 19.5% services, 19.5% sales, 0.0% farming, 24.7% construction, 22.1% production (2000).
Income: Per capita income: $19,237 (2007); Median household income: $41,500 (2007); Average household income: $44,886 (2007); Percent of households with income of $100,000 or more: 6.1% (2007); Poverty rate: 2.6% (2000).
Education: Percent of population age 25 and over with: High school diploma (including GED) or higher: 80.7% (2007); Bachelor's degree or higher: 13.8% (2007); Master's degree or higher: 7.3% (2007).

School District(s)

Ridgewood Local (PK-12)
2005-06 Enrollment: 1,452 . . . . (740) 545-6354
Housing: Homeownership rate: 78.8% (2007); Median home value: $82,000 (2007); Median rent: $338 per month (2000); Median age of housing: 60+ years (2000).
Transportation: Commute to work: 96.1% car, 0.0% public transportation, 3.9% walk, 0.0% work from home (2000); Travel time to work: 9.1% less than 15 minutes, 64.9% 15 to 30 minutes, 9.1% 30 to 45 minutes, 6.5% 45 to 60 minutes, 10.4% 60 minutes or more (2000)

WALHONDING (unincorporated postal area, zip code 43843). Covers a land area of 45.353 square miles and a water area of 0 square miles. Located at 40.34° N. Lat.; 82.17° W. Long. Elevation is 897 feet.
Population: 890 (2000); Race: 99.0% White, 0.0% Black, 0.0% Asian, 0.0% Hispanic of any race (2000); Density: 19.6 persons per square mile (2000); Age: 27.6% under 18, 14.5% over 64 (2000); Marriage status: 12.6% never married, 73.0% now married, 8.6% widowed, 5.9% divorced (2000); Foreign born: 0.4% (2000); Ancestry (includes multiple ancestries): 20.3% German, 11.9% United States or American, 5.2% Italian, 4.9% Irish, 4.5% Other groups (2000).
Economy: Employment by occupation: 6.3% management, 17.0% professional, 7.9% services, 11.5% sales, 0.0% farming, 20.0% construction, 37.3% production (2000).
Income: Per capita income: $12,908 (2000); Median household income: $33,657 (2000); Poverty rate: 18.0% (2000).
Education: Percent of population age 25 and over with: High school diploma (including GED) or higher: 74.5% (2000); Bachelor's degree or higher: 6.6% (2000).
Housing: Homeownership rate: 83.6% (2000); Median home value: $48,900 (2000); Median rent: $n/a per month (2000); Median age of housing: 24 years (2000).
Transportation: Commute to work: 86.9% car, 0.0% public transportation, 5.8% walk, 3.6% work from home (2000); Travel time to work: 20.8% less than 15 minutes, 23.7% 15 to 30 minutes, 19.1% 30 to 45 minutes, 18.2% 45 to 60 minutes, 18.2% 60 minutes or more (2000)

WARSAW (village). Covers a land area of 0.436 square miles and a water area of 0.016 square miles. Located at 40.33° N. Lat.; 82.00° W. Long. Elevation is 801 feet.
Population: 758 (1990); 781 (2000); 655 (2007); 657 (2012 projected); Race: 96.8% White, 1.1% Black, 0.0% Asian, 1.5% Hispanic of any race (2007); Density: 1,501.4 persons per square mile (2007); Average household size: 2.47 (2007); Median age: 36.0 (2007); Males per 100 females: 90.4 (2007); Marriage status: 20.9% never married, 55.8% now married, 8.7% widowed, 14.6% divorced (2000); Foreign born: 0.4% (2000); Ancestry (includes multiple ancestries): 30.9% German, 16.0% United States or American, 14.3% Irish, 13.3% English, 8.5% Other groups (2000).
Economy: Single-family building permits issued: 2 (2007); Multi-family building permits issued: 0 (2007); Employment by occupation: 7.1% management, 9.4% professional, 17.1% services, 20.2% sales, 1.1% farming, 9.4% construction, 35.6% production (2000).
Income: Per capita income: $16,508 (2007); Median household income: $35,357 (2007); Average household income: $40,802 (2007); Percent of households with income of $100,000 or more: 5.3% (2007); Poverty rate: 6.7% (2000).
Education: Percent of population age 25 and over with: High school diploma (including GED) or higher: 84.8% (2007); Bachelor's degree or higher: 11.9% (2007); Master's degree or higher: 6.4% (2007).

School District(s)

River View Local (PK-12)
2005-06 Enrollment: 2,432 . . . . (740) 824-3521
Housing: Homeownership rate: 74.7% (2007); Median home value: $82,222 (2007); Median rent: $303 per month (2000); Median age of housing: 40 years (2000).

Transportation: Commute to work: 94.5% car, 0.0% public transportation, 2.9% walk, 2.6% work from home (2000); Travel time to work: 18.8% less than 15 minutes, 54.9% 15 to 30 minutes, 14.6% 30 to 45 minutes, 5.4% 45 to 60 minutes, 6.3% 60 minutes or more (2000)

WEST LAFAYETTE (village). Covers a land area of 0.660 square miles and a water area of 0 square miles. Located at 40.27° N. Lat.; 81.75° W. Long. Elevation is 804 feet.
History: West Lafayette began when John Coles, an Englishman, opened a store here in 1850. The town prospered with the arrival of the Pennsylvania Railroad. Early industries were an enameling plant, a metal-products company, and a novelty factory.
Population: 2,226 (1990); 2,313 (2000); 2,328 (2007); 2,337 (2012 projected); Race: 98.4% White, 0.3% Black, 0.0% Asian, 0.5% Hispanic of any race (2007); Density: 3,526.1 persons per square mile (2007); Average household size: 2.49 (2007); Median age: 37.0 (2007); Males per 100 females: 92.7 (2007); Marriage status: 20.8% never married, 55.8% now married, 9.1% widowed, 14.3% divorced (2000); Foreign born: 0.5% (2000); Ancestry (includes multiple ancestries): 28.1% German, 11.9% United States or American, 11.2% English, 9.9% Irish, 6.8% Other groups (2000).
Economy: Single-family building permits issued: 1 (2007); Multi-family building permits issued: 0 (2007); Employment by occupation: 6.0% management, 14.0% professional, 12.7% services, 25.3% sales, 0.0% farming, 9.2% construction, 32.7% production (2000).
Income: Per capita income: $17,029 (2007); Median household income: $33,796 (2007); Average household income: $42,139 (2007); Percent of households with income of $100,000 or more: 5.8% (2007); Poverty rate: 8.1% (2000).
Education: Percent of population age 25 and over with: High school diploma (including GED) or higher: 77.4% (2007); Bachelor's degree or higher: 10.9% (2007); Master's degree or higher: 4.1% (2007).

School District(s)

Ridgewood Local (PK-12)
2005-06 Enrollment: 1,452 . . . . (740) 545-6354

Housing: Homeownership rate: 74.7% (2007); Median home value: $79,615 (2007); Median rent: $325 per month (2000); Median age of housing: 35 years (2000).
Transportation: Commute to work: 95.5% car, 0.4% public transportation, 2.0% walk, 1.3% work from home (2000); Travel time to work: 31.0% less than 15 minutes, 49.2% 15 to 30 minutes, 9.1% 30 to 45 minutes, 5.3% 45 to 60 minutes, 5.3% 60 minutes or more (2000)

Crawford County

Located in north central Ohio; drained by the Sandusky and Olentangy Rivers. Covers a land area of 402.11 square miles, a water area of 0.72 square miles, and is located in the Eastern Time Zone. The county was founded in 1820. County seat is Bucyrus.

Crawford County is part of the Bucyrus, OH Micropolitan Statistical Area. The entire metro area includes: Crawford County, OH

Weather Station: Bucyrus Elevation: 954 feet

	Jan	Feb	Mar	Apr	May	Jun	Jul	Aug	Sep	Oct	Nov	Dec
High	31	35	46	59	70	79	83	81	75	62	49	37
Low	16	18	27	37	47	57	61	59	51	40	32	22
Precip	2.2	1.9	2.7	3.5	4.0	4.4	4.5	3.8	3.2	2.4	3.1	2.8
Snow	7.9	5.9	3.6	0.8	tr	0.0	0.0	0.0	0.0	tr	1.0	4.0

High and Low temperatures in degrees Fahrenheit; Precipitation and Snow in inches

Population: 47,870 (1990); 46,966 (2000); 45,531 (2007); 44,447 (2012 projected); Race: 97.8% White, 0.7% Black, 0.4% Asian, 1.1% Hispanic of any race (2007); Density: 113.2 persons per square mile (2007); Average household size: 2.42 (2007); Median age: 40.3 (2007); Males per 100 females: 93.4 (2007).
Religion: Five largest groups: 16.1% Catholic Church, 12.1% Evangelical Lutheran Church in America, 8.3% The United Methodist Church, 3.9% United Church of Christ, 2.9% Church of the Nazarene (2000).
Economy: Unemployment rate: 8.0% (6/2008); Total civilian labor force: 22,456 (6/2008); Leading industries: 37.8% manufacturing; 14.3% health care and social assistance; 10.1% retail trade (2005); Farms: 693 totaling 234,204 acres (2002); Companies that employ 500 or more persons: 1 (2006); Companies that employ 100 to 499 persons: 25 (2006); Companies that employ less than 100 persons: 928 (2006); Black-owned businesses: n/a (2002); Hispanic-owned businesses: n/a (2002); Asian-owned businesses: n/a (2002); Women-owned businesses: 931 (2002); Retail sales per capita: $8,285 (2008). Single-family building permits issued: 40 (2007); Multi-family building permits issued: 64 (2007).
Income: Per capita income: $20,776 (2007); Median household income: $41,455 (2007); Average household income: $49,685 (2007); Percent of households with income of $100,000 or more: 8.2% (2007); Poverty rate: 11.2% (2005); Bankruptcy rate: 4.23% (2007).
Education: Percent of population age 25 and over with: High school diploma (including GED) or higher: 80.3% (2007); Bachelor's degree or higher: 9.9% (2007); Master's degree or higher: 3.2% (2007).
Housing: Homeownership rate: 72.8% (2007); Median home value: $105,299 (2007); Median rent: $317 per month (2000); Median age of housing: 46 years (2000).
Health: Birth rate: 125.9 per 10,000 population (2007); Death rate: 114.9 per 10,000 population (2007); Age-adjusted cancer mortality rate: 250.6 deaths per 100,000 population (2005); Number of physicians: 9.5 per 10,000 population (2005); Hospital beds: 33.2 per 10,000 population (2004); Hospital admissions: 551.1 per 10,000 population (2004).
Elections: 2004 Presidential election results: 63.7% Bush, 35.7% Kerry, 0.0% Nader, 0.3% Badnarik

Additional Information Contacts

Crawford County Government . . . . (419) 562-5876
http://www.crawford-co.org
Bucyrus Area Chamber of Commerce . . . . (419) 562-4811
http://www.bucyrusohio.com
City of Galion . . . . (419) 468-1857
http://www.ci.galion.oh.us
Crestline Area Chamber of Commerce . . . . (419) 683-3818
http://www.crestlineoh.com/Chamber%20of%20Commerce.html
Galion Chamber of Commerce . . . . (419) 468-7737
http://www.galionchamber.org
Village of Crestline . . . . (419) 683-3800
http://www.crestlineoh.com

Crawford County Communities

BUCYRUS (city). County seat. Covers a land area of 7.298 square miles and a water area of 0.015 square miles. Located at 40.80° N. Lat.; 82.97° W. Long. Elevation is 994 feet.
History: The site of Bucyrus was purchased by Samuel Norton and Colonel James Kilbourne in 1819, and settled by a group from Pennsylvania. Kilbourne surveyed the village in 1822 and named it for Cyrus, an ancient Persian leader. He prefixed it with "bu" to suggest "beautiful."
Population: 13,632 (1990); 13,224 (2000); 12,733 (2007); 12,363 (2012 projected); Race: 97.0% White, 1.0% Black, 0.7% Asian, 1.4% Hispanic of any race (2007); Density: 1,744.7 persons per square mile (2007); Average household size: 2.32 (2007); Median age: 39.5 (2007); Males per 100 females: 90.6 (2007); Marriage status: 22.6% never married, 52.9% now married, 10.8% widowed, 13.7% divorced (2000); Foreign born: 0.6% (2000); Ancestry (includes multiple ancestries): 30.6% German, 15.2% United States or American, 9.6% Irish, 9.4% English, 8.2% Other groups (2000).
Economy: Single-family building permits issued: 11 (2007); Multi-family building permits issued: 64 (2007); Employment by occupation: 7.9% management, 11.3% professional, 14.2% services, 23.9% sales, 0.3% farming, 8.6% construction, 33.8% production (2000).
Income: Per capita income: $20,397 (2007); Median household income: $36,971 (2007); Average household income: $46,136 (2007); Percent of households with income of $100,000 or more: 7.5% (2007); Poverty rate: 12.0% (2000).
Education: Percent of population age 25 and over with: High school diploma (including GED) or higher: 75.9% (2007); Bachelor's degree or higher: 9.8% (2007); Master's degree or higher: 3.0% (2007).

School District(s)

Bucyrus City (PK-12)
2005-06 Enrollment: 1,748 . . . . (419) 562-4045
Colonel Crawford Local (PK-12)
2005-06 Enrollment: 1,006 . . . . (419) 562-4666
Wynford Local (PK-12)
2005-06 Enrollment: 1,181 . . . . (419) 562-7828

Housing: Homeownership rate: 64.3% (2007); Median home value: $98,104 (2007); Median rent: $316 per month (2000); Median age of housing: 45 years (2000).
Hospitals: Bucyrus Community Hospital (25 beds)

Newspapers: Buckeye Snowmobiler (Regional news); Bucyrus Telegraph-Forum (Local news; Circulation 7,424)
Transportation: Commute to work: 92.0% car, 0.1% public transportation, 3.4% walk, 2.1% work from home (2000); Travel time to work: 55.4% less than 15 minutes, 25.5% 15 to 30 minutes, 14.0% 30 to 45 minutes, 1.8% 45 to 60 minutes, 3.4% 60 minutes or more (2000)
Additional Information Contacts
Bucyrus Area Chamber of Commerce . . . . (419) 562-4811
http://www.bucyrusohio.com

CHATFIELD (village). Covers a land area of 0.297 square miles and a water area of 0 square miles. Located at 40.95° N. Lat.; 82.94° W. Long. Elevation is 981 feet.
Population: 206 (1990); 218 (2000); 211 (2007); 204 (2012 projected); Race: 100.0% White, 0.0% Black, 0.0% Asian, 4.7% Hispanic of any race (2007); Density: 710.5 persons per square mile (2007); Average household size: 2.45 (2007); Median age: 39.5 (2007); Males per 100 females: 104.9 (2007); Marriage status: 25.2% never married, 62.6% now married, 9.2% widowed, 3.1% divorced (2000); Foreign born: 2.7% (2000); Ancestry (includes multiple ancestries): 42.4% German, 6.7% United States or American, 6.3% English, 4.5% Irish, 4.5% Other groups (2000).
Economy: Single-family building permits issued: 0 (2007); Multi-family building permits issued: 0 (2007); Employment by occupation: 13.9% management, 12.0% professional, 10.2% services, 14.8% sales, 4.6% farming, 13.9% construction, 30.6% production (2000).
Income: Per capita income: $18,092 (2007); Median household income: $40,833 (2007); Average household income: $44,390 (2007); Percent of households with income of $100,000 or more: 0.0% (2007); Poverty rate: 5.4% (2000).
Education: Percent of population age 25 and over with: High school diploma (including GED) or higher: 86.6% (2007); Bachelor's degree or higher: 9.9% (2007); Master's degree or higher: 3.5% (2007).
School District(s)
Buckeye Central Local (PK-12)
2005-06 Enrollment: 782 . . . . (419) 492-2864
Housing: Homeownership rate: 91.9% (2007); Median home value: $85,476 (2007); Median rent: $325 per month (2000); Median age of housing: 60+ years (2000).
Transportation: Commute to work: 90.6% car, 0.9% public transportation, 4.7% walk, 1.9% work from home (2000); Travel time to work: 28.8% less than 15 minutes, 46.2% 15 to 30 minutes, 15.4% 30 to 45 minutes, 1.9% 45 to 60 minutes, 7.7% 60 minutes or more (2000)

CRESTLINE (city). Covers a land area of 2.888 square miles and a water area of 0 square miles. Located at 40.78° N. Lat.; 82.74° W. Long. Elevation is 1,142 feet.
History: Crestline (Crest Line) was established when the Pennsylvania Railroad became the second line in the area. It joined Livingston, founded two years earlier when the first railroad came through. When the two villages grew to the point where their borders touched, they joined as Crestline.
Population: 4,947 (1990); 5,088 (2000); 4,900 (2007); 4,734 (2012 projected); Race: 96.9% White, 1.6% Black, 0.3% Asian, 0.9% Hispanic of any race (2007); Density: 1,696.7 persons per square mile (2007); Average household size: 2.42 (2007); Median age: 37.1 (2007); Males per 100 females: 92.8 (2007); Marriage status: 26.0% never married, 53.8% now married, 8.5% widowed, 11.8% divorced (2000); Foreign born: 0.8% (2000); Ancestry (includes multiple ancestries): 30.8% German, 16.3% United States or American, 11.8% Irish, 10.5% Other groups, 8.9% English (2000).
Economy: Single-family building permits issued: 5 (2007); Multi-family building permits issued: 0 (2007); Employment by occupation: 7.2% management, 13.0% professional, 16.7% services, 22.0% sales, 0.4% farming, 8.5% construction, 32.1% production (2000).
Income: Per capita income: $19,634 (2007); Median household income: $37,768 (2007); Average household income: $46,970 (2007); Percent of households with income of $100,000 or more: 7.7% (2007); Poverty rate: 12.4% (2000).
Education: Percent of population age 25 and over with: High school diploma (including GED) or higher: 80.0% (2007); Bachelor's degree or higher: 8.5% (2007); Master's degree or higher: 2.8% (2007).
School District(s)
Crestline Exempted Village (PK-12)
2005-06 Enrollment: 855 . . . . (419) 683-3647
Housing: Homeownership rate: 70.8% (2007); Median home value: $90,872 (2007); Median rent: $298 per month (2000); Median age of housing: 45 years (2000).
Hospitals: MedCentral Health System/Crestline Hospital (40 beds)
Safety: Violent crime rate: 13.8 per 10,000 population; Property crime rate: 118.2 per 10,000 population (2007).
Newspapers: The Crestline Advocate (Community news; Circulation 2,000)
Transportation: Commute to work: 95.6% car, 0.2% public transportation, 3.0% walk, 0.9% work from home (2000); Travel time to work: 39.6% less than 15 minutes, 39.2% 15 to 30 minutes, 12.2% 30 to 45 minutes, 3.3% 45 to 60 minutes, 5.7% 60 minutes or more (2000)
Airports: Galion Municipal (general aviation)
Additional Information Contacts
Crestline Area Chamber of Commerce . . . . (419) 683-3818
http://www.crestlineoh.com/Chamber%20of%20Commerce.html
Village of Crestline . . . . (419) 683-3800
http://www.crestlineoh.com

GALION (city). Covers a land area of 4.960 square miles and a water area of 0.011 square miles. Located at 40.73° N. Lat.; 82.78° W. Long. Elevation is 1,171 feet.
History: Galion was setttled by German Lutherans from Pennsylvania in 1831. In the 1890's C.H. North organized a company for the manufacture of telephone equipment, inventing improvements that made Galion a pioneering center for this industry.
Population: 11,867 (1990); 11,341 (2000); 10,906 (2007); 10,595 (2012 projected); Race: 98.1% White, 0.3% Black, 0.3% Asian, 1.2% Hispanic of any race (2007); Density: 2,198.8 persons per square mile (2007); Average household size: 2.31 (2007); Median age: 38.4 (2007); Males per 100 females: 86.3 (2007); Marriage status: 21.7% never married, 53.9% now married, 9.7% widowed, 14.7% divorced (2000); Foreign born: 0.6% (2000); Ancestry (includes multiple ancestries): 28.1% German, 16.4% United States or American, 10.9% Other groups, 10.8% Irish, 9.3% English (2000).
Economy: Single-family building permits issued: 3 (2007); Multi-family building permits issued: 0 (2007); Employment by occupation: 7.6% management, 13.1% professional, 15.4% services, 22.0% sales, 0.0% farming, 9.2% construction, 32.7% production (2000).
Income: Per capita income: $18,559 (2007); Median household income: $35,398 (2007); Average household income: $42,488 (2007); Percent of households with income of $100,000 or more: 5.1% (2007); Poverty rate: 14.7% (2000).
Education: Percent of population age 25 and over with: High school diploma (including GED) or higher: 77.6% (2007); Bachelor's degree or higher: 8.8% (2007); Master's degree or higher: 2.9% (2007).
School District(s)
Galion City (PK-12)
2005-06 Enrollment: 2,149 . . . . (419) 468-3432
Northmor Local (PK-12)
2005-06 Enrollment: 1,228 . . . . (419) 946-8861
Housing: Homeownership rate: 63.4% (2007); Median home value: $93,054 (2007); Median rent: $328 per month (2000); Median age of housing: 49 years (2000).
Hospitals: Galion Community Hospital (178 beds)
Safety: Violent crime rate: 17.1 per 10,000 population; Property crime rate: 509.3 per 10,000 population (2007).
Newspapers: Galion Inquirer (Local news; Circulation 6,500)
Transportation: Commute to work: 93.6% car, 0.4% public transportation, 3.6% walk, 1.7% work from home (2000); Travel time to work: 46.7% less than 15 minutes, 32.8% 15 to 30 minutes, 13.2% 30 to 45 minutes, 3.1% 45 to 60 minutes, 4.2% 60 minutes or more (2000)
Additional Information Contacts
City of Galion . . . . (419) 468-1857
http://www.ci.galion.oh.us
Galion Chamber of Commerce . . . . (419) 468-7737
http://www.galionchamber.org

NEW WASHINGTON (village). Covers a land area of 1.269 square miles and a water area of 0 square miles. Located at 40.96° N. Lat.; 82.85° W. Long. Elevation is 991 feet.
Population: 1,057 (1990); 987 (2000); 886 (2007); 874 (2012 projected); Race: 99.2% White, 0.0% Black, 0.6% Asian, 0.0% Hispanic of any race (2007); Density: 698.1 persons per square mile (2007); Average household size: 2.46 (2007); Median age: 38.6 (2007); Males per 100 females: 94.7

(2007); Marriage status: 24.3% never married, 61.6% now married, 6.7% widowed, 7.4% divorced (2000); Foreign born: 0.4% (2000); Ancestry (includes multiple ancestries): 50.0% German, 9.6% United States or American, 6.6% Other groups, 4.5% English, 4.2% Irish (2000).
Economy: Single-family building permits issued: 2 (2007); Multi-family building permits issued: 0 (2007); Employment by occupation: 9.2% management, 13.7% professional, 10.0% services, 21.4% sales, 1.4% farming, 10.4% construction, 33.9% production (2000).
Income: Per capita income: $20,366 (2007); Median household income: $47,188 (2007); Average household income: $50,021 (2007); Percent of households with income of $100,000 or more: 5.0% (2007); Poverty rate: 6.3% (2000).
Education: Percent of population age 25 and over with: High school diploma (including GED) or higher: 87.8% (2007); Bachelor's degree or higher: 14.4% (2007); Master's degree or higher: 5.7% (2007).

School District(s)

Buckeye Central Local (PK-12)
2005-06 Enrollment: 782 . . . . (419) 492-2864
Housing: Homeownership rate: 83.3% (2007); Median home value: $95,556 (2007); Median rent: $254 per month (2000); Median age of housing: 60+ years (2000).
Newspapers: Herald (Local news; Circulation 1,500); New Washington Herald (Community news; Circulation 1,500)
Transportation: Commute to work: 89.2% car, 0.0% public transportation, 6.5% walk, 2.0% work from home (2000); Travel time to work: 42.5% less than 15 minutes, 34.8% 15 to 30 minutes, 12.7% 30 to 45 minutes, 7.1% 45 to 60 minutes, 2.9% 60 minutes or more (2000)

NORTH ROBINSON (village). Aka Robinson. Covers a land area of 0.098 square miles and a water area of 0 square miles. Located at 40.79° N. Lat.; 82.85° W. Long. Elevation is 1,073 feet.
Population: 216 (1990); 211 (2000); 225 (2007); 229 (2012 projected); Race: 99.1% White, 0.0% Black, 0.0% Asian, 0.0% Hispanic of any race (2007); Density: 2,296.2 persons per square mile (2007); Average household size: 2.53 (2007); Median age: 44.8 (2007); Males per 100 females: 87.5 (2007); Marriage status: 15.9% never married, 71.6% now married, 5.1% widowed, 7.4% divorced (2000); Foreign born: 0.0% (2000); Ancestry (includes multiple ancestries): 33.9% United States or American, 23.7% German, 5.4% Irish, 4.0% Other groups, 3.1% English (2000).
Economy: Single-family building permits issued: 1 (2007); Multi-family building permits issued: 0 (2007); Employment by occupation: 6.1% management, 0.0% professional, 17.2% services, 26.3% sales, 0.0% farming, 8.1% construction, 42.4% production (2000).
Income: Per capita income: $16,056 (2007); Median household income: $33,929 (2007); Average household income: $40,590 (2007); Percent of households with income of $100,000 or more: 1.1% (2007); Poverty rate: 8.9% (2000).
Education: Percent of population age 25 and over with: High school diploma (including GED) or higher: 76.4% (2007); Bachelor's degree or higher: 1.9% (2007); Master's degree or higher: 0.0% (2007).

School District(s)

Colonel Crawford Local (PK-12)
2005-06 Enrollment: 1,006 . . . . (419) 562-4666
Housing: Homeownership rate: 85.4% (2007); Median home value: $75,882 (2007); Median rent: $357 per month (2000); Median age of housing: 58 years (2000).
Transportation: Commute to work: 97.9% car, 0.0% public transportation, 2.1% walk, 0.0% work from home (2000); Travel time to work: 31.3% less than 15 minutes, 40.6% 15 to 30 minutes, 5.2% 30 to 45 minutes, 7.3% 45 to 60 minutes, 15.6% 60 minutes or more (2000)

TIRO (village). Covers a land area of 0.412 square miles and a water area of 0 square miles. Located at 40.90° N. Lat.; 82.77° W. Long. Elevation is 1,053 feet.
Population: 246 (1990); 281 (2000); 285 (2007); 276 (2012 projected); Race: 97.9% White, 0.0% Black, 1.4% Asian, 2.8% Hispanic of any race (2007); Density: 692.1 persons per square mile (2007); Average household size: 2.66 (2007); Median age: 33.8 (2007); Males per 100 females: 102.1 (2007); Marriage status: 16.4% never married, 68.3% now married, 2.6% widowed, 12.7% divorced (2000); Foreign born: 0.0% (2000); Ancestry (includes multiple ancestries): 20.6% German, 11.4% Other groups, 9.6% United States or American, 8.9% Irish, 7.8% English (2000).
Economy: Employment by occupation: 5.1% management, 2.6% professional, 11.1% services, 12.0% sales, 0.0% farming, 15.4% construction, 53.8% production (2000).
Income: Per capita income: $17,325 (2007); Median household income: $37,500 (2007); Average household income: $46,145 (2007); Percent of households with income of $100,000 or more: 3.7% (2007); Poverty rate: 13.2% (2000).
Education: Percent of population age 25 and over with: High school diploma (including GED) or higher: 69.5% (2007); Bachelor's degree or higher: 0.0% (2007); Master's degree or higher: 0.0% (2007).

School District(s)

Buckeye Central Local (PK-12)
2005-06 Enrollment: 782 . . . . (419) 492-2864
Housing: Homeownership rate: 75.7% (2007); Median home value: $78,750 (2007); Median rent: $318 per month (2000); Median age of housing: 60+ years (2000).
Transportation: Commute to work: 98.2% car, 0.0% public transportation, 0.0% walk, 1.8% work from home (2000); Travel time to work: 10.7% less than 15 minutes, 62.5% 15 to 30 minutes, 24.1% 30 to 45 minutes, 0.0% 45 to 60 minutes, 2.7% 60 minutes or more (2000)

Cuyahoga County

Located in northern Ohio; bounded on the north by Lake Erie; drained by the Cuyahoga and Rocky Rivers. Covers a land area of 458.49 square miles, a water area of 787.07 square miles, and is located in the Eastern Time Zone. The county was founded in 1808. County seat is Cleveland.

Cuyahoga County is part of the Cleveland-Elyria-Mentor, OH Metropolitan Statistical Area. The entire metro area includes: Cuyahoga County, OH; Geauga County, OH; Lake County, OH; Lorain County, OH; Medina County, OH

Weather Station: Cleveland Hopkins Int'l Airport Elevation: 767 feet

	Jan	Feb	Mar	Apr	May	Jun	Jul	Aug	Sep	Oct	Nov	Dec
High	33	36	46	58	69	78	82	80	74	62	50	39
Low	19	21	29	38	48	58	63	61	54	44	35	25
Precip	2.4	2.3	3.0	3.3	3.4	3.9	3.6	3.6	3.8	2.8	3.4	3.1
Snow	16.4	13.4	10.8	2.5	tr	tr	tr	0.0	tr	0.4	4.9	12.6

High and Low temperatures in degrees Fahrenheit; Precipitation and Snow in inches

Population: 1,412,140 (1990); 1,393,978 (2000); 1,317,771 (2007); 1,259,187 (2012 projected); Race: 64.7% White, 29.0% Black, 2.2% Asian, 3.9% Hispanic of any race (2007); Density: 2,874.2 persons per square mile (2007); Average household size: 2.39 (2007); Median age: 39.7 (2007); Males per 100 females: 90.1 (2007).
Religion: Five largest groups: 34.9% Catholic Church, 5.7% Jewish Estimate, 2.2% The United Methodist Church, 1.7% American Baptist Churches in the USA, 1.7% Lutheran Church—Missouri Synod (2000).
Economy: Unemployment rate: 8.1% (6/2008); Total civilian labor force: 666,966 (6/2008); Leading industries: 17.3% health care and social assistance; 12.1% manufacturing; 9.6% retail trade (2005); Farms: 159 totaling 4,086 acres (2002); Companies that employ 500 or more persons: 115 (2006); Companies that employ 100 to 499 persons: 1,011 (2006); Companies that employ less than 100 persons: 35,453 (2006); Black-owned businesses: 9,809 (2002); Hispanic-owned businesses: 1,109 (2002); Asian-owned businesses: 2,712 (2002); Women-owned businesses: 28,243 (2002); Retail sales per capita: $14,506 (2008). Single-family building permits issued: 922 (2007); Multi-family building permits issued: 124 (2007).
Income: Per capita income: $25,736 (2007); Median household income: $44,042 (2007); Average household income: $60,999 (2007); Percent of households with income of $100,000 or more: 14.9% (2007); Poverty rate: 17.1% (2005); Bankruptcy rate: 5.63% (2007).
Taxes: Total county taxes per capita: $430 (2006); County property taxes per capita: $256 (2006).
Education: Percent of population age 25 and over with: High school diploma (including GED) or higher: 81.7% (2007); Bachelor's degree or higher: 25.3% (2007); Master's degree or higher: 9.6% (2007).
Housing: Homeownership rate: 63.4% (2007); Median home value: $136,171 (2007); Median rent: $463 per month (2000); Median age of housing: 46 years (2000).
Health: Birth rate: 122.1 per 10,000 population (2007); Death rate: 109.4 per 10,000 population (2007); Age-adjusted cancer mortality rate: 210.7 deaths per 100,000 population (2005); Air Quality Index: 68.5% good, 27.9% moderate, 3.3% unhealthy for sensitive individuals, 0.3% unhealthy (percent of days in 2007); Number of physicians: 59.6 per 10,000 population (2005); Hospital beds: 49.0 per 10,000 population (2004); Hospital admissions: 2,046.3 per 10,000 population (2004).

Elections: 2004 Presidential election results: 32.9% Bush, 66.6% Kerry, 0.0% Nader, 0.3% Badnarik
National and State Parks: Chagrin State Scenic River; Cleveland Lakefront State Park; Edgewater State Park
Additional Information Contacts
Cuyahoga County Government . . . . . . (216) 443-7000
http://www.cuyahogacounty.us
Beachwood Chamber of Commerce . . . . . . (216) 831-0003
http://www.beachwood.org
Bedford Heights Chamber of Commerce. . . . . . (440) 232-3369
http://www.bedfordheightschamber.com
Berea Chamber of Commerce . . . . . . (440) 243-8415
http://www.bereaohio.com/Business/index.cfm
Brecksville Chamber of Commerce . . . . . . (440) 526-7350
http://www.brecksvillechamber.com
Broadview Heights Chamber of Commerce. . . . . . (440) 838-4510
http://www.broadviewhts.org
Brook Park Chamber of Commerce. . . . . . (216) 898-9755
http://www.bpcoc.com
Chagrin Valley Chamber of Commerce . . . . . . (440) 247-6607
http://www.cvcc.org
City of Bay Village . . . . . . (440) 899-3415
http://www.cityofbayvillage.com
City of Beachwood . . . . . . (216) 464-1070
http://www.beachwoodohio.com
City of Bedford . . . . . . (440) 232-1600
http://www.bedfordoh.gov
City of Bedford Heights . . . . . . (440) 786-3200
http://www.bedfordheights.gov
City of Berea . . . . . . (440) 826-5800
http://www.bereaohio.com
City of Brecksville. . . . . . (440) 526-4351
http://www.brecksville.oh.us
City of Broadview Heights . . . . . . (440) 526-4357
http://www.broadview-heights.org
City of Brook Park . . . . . . (216) 433-1300
http://www.cityofbrookpark.com
City of Brooklyn . . . . . . (216) 351-2133
http://www.brooklynohio.gov
City of Cleveland . . . . . . (216) 664-2000
http://www.city.cleveland.oh.us
City of Cleveland Heights. . . . . . (216) 291-4444
http://www.clevelandheights.com
City of East Cleveland . . . . . . (216) 681-2208
http://www.eastcleveland.org
City of Euclid . . . . . . (216) 289-2751
http://www.ci.euclid.oh.us
City of Fairview Park . . . . . . (440) 333-2200
http://www.fairviewpark.org
City of Garfield Heights . . . . . . (216) 475-1100
http://www.garfieldhts.org
City of Independence. . . . . . (216) 524-4131
http://www.independenceohio.org
City of Lakewood . . . . . . (216) 529-6600
http://www.ci.lakewood.oh.us
City of Lyndhurst . . . . . . (440) 442-5777
http://www.lyndhurst-oh.com
City of Maple Heights. . . . . . (216) 662-6000
http://mapleheights.cuyahogacounty.us
City of Mayfield Heights . . . . . . (440) 442-2626
http://www.mayfieldheights.org
City of Middleburg Heights. . . . . . (440) 234-8811
http://www.middleburgheights.com
City of North Olmsted. . . . . . (440) 777-8000
http://www.north-olmsted.com
City of North Royalton . . . . . . (440) 237-5686
http://www.northroyalton.org
City of Olmsted Falls . . . . . . (440) 235-5550
http://www.olmstedfalls.org
City of Parma . . . . . . (440) 885-8000
http://www.cityofparma-oh.gov
City of Parma Heights . . . . . . (440) 884-9600
http://www.parmaheightsoh.gov
City of Pepper Pike . . . . . . (216) 831-8500
http://www.pepperpike.org
City of Richmond Heights . . . . . . (216) 383-6300
http://www.richmondheightsohio.org
City of Rocky River . . . . . . (440) 331-0600
http://www.rrcity.com
City of Seven Hills . . . . . . (216) 524-4421
http://www.sevenhillsohio.org
City of Shaker Heights. . . . . . (216) 491-1400
http://www.shakeronline.com
City of Solon. . . . . . (440) 248-1155
http://www.solonohio.org
City of South Euclid . . . . . . (216) 381-0400
http://www.cityofsoutheuclid.com
City of Strongsville . . . . . . (440) 580-3100
http://www.strongsville.org
City of University Heights. . . . . . (216) 932-7800
http://www.universityheights.com
City of Warrensville Heights. . . . . . (216) 587-6500
http://www.cityofwarrensville.com
City of Westlake. . . . . . (440) 871-3300
http://www.cityofwestlake.org
Convention & Visitors Bureau of Greater Cleveland . . . . . . (216) 875-6600
http://www.travelcleveland.com
Euclid Chamber of Commerce. . . . . . (216) 731-9322
http://www.euclidchamberofcommerce.com
Greater Cleveland Partnership . . . . . . (216) 621-3300
http://www.gcpartnership.com
Heights-Hillcrest Regional Chamber of Commerce . . . . . . (216) 397-7322
http://www.hrcc.org
Lakewood Chamber of Commerce . . . . . . (216) 226-2900
http://www.lakewoodchamber.org
Mayfield Area Chamber of Commerce. . . . . . (216) 556-4598
http://www.mayfieldareachamber.org
Middleburg Heights Chamber of Commerce . . . . . . (440) 243-5599
http://middleburgheightschamber.com
North Olmsted Chamber of Commerce . . . . . . (440) 777-3368
http://www.nolmstedchamber.org
North Royalton Chamber of Commerce. . . . . . (440) 237-6180
http://www.nroyaltonchamber.com
Olmsted Chamber of Commerce . . . . . . (440) 235-0032
http://www.olmstedchamber.org
Parma Area Chamber of Commerce . . . . . . (440) 886-1700
http://www.parmaareachamber.org
Rocky River Chamber of Commerce . . . . . . (440) 331-1140
http://www.rockyriverchamber.com
Solon Chamber of Commerce . . . . . . (440) 248-5080
http://www.solonchamber.com
Strongsville Chamber of Commerce . . . . . . (440) 238-3366
http://www.strongsvillechamber.com
Tri-City Chamber of Commerce. . . . . . (216) 454-0199
http://www.tricitychamber.com
Village of Bentleyville. . . . . . (440) 247-5055
http://www.villageofbentleyville.com
Village of Chagrin Falls . . . . . . (440) 247-5050
http://www.chagrin-falls.org
Village of Mayfield . . . . . . (440) 461-2210
http://www.mayfieldvillage.com
Village of Moreland Hills . . . . . . (440) 248-1188
http://www.morelandhills.com
Village of Orange . . . . . . (440) 498-4400
http://www.orangevillage.com
Village of Valley View. . . . . . (216) 524-6511
http://www.valleyview.net
West Shore Chamber of Commerce . . . . . . (440) 835-8787
http://www.westshorechamber.org

Cuyahoga County Communities

BAY VILLAGE (city). Aka Bay. Covers a land area of 4.631 square miles and a water area of 2.454 square miles. Located at 41.48° N. Lat.; 81.92° W. Long. Elevation is 633 feet.
History: Named for its location on a bay of Lake Erie. Incorporated 1903.
Population: 17,000 (1990); 16,087 (2000); 14,991 (2007); 14,144 (2012 projected); Race: 97.7% White, 0.4% Black, 0.7% Asian, 1.1% Hispanic of any race (2007); Density: 3,236.8 persons per square mile (2007); Average household size: 2.50 (2007); Median age: 43.4 (2007); Males per 100

females: 91.8 (2007); Marriage status: 19.0% never married, 66.4% now married, 7.0% widowed, 7.6% divorced (2000); Foreign born: 4.4% (2000); Ancestry (includes multiple ancestries): 31.2% German, 26.8% Irish, 15.5% English, 9.6% Italian, 7.0% Polish (2000).
Economy: Single-family building permits issued: 9 (2007); Multi-family building permits issued: 0 (2007); Employment by occupation: 24.0% management, 28.2% professional, 7.7% services, 28.5% sales, 0.1% farming, 4.5% construction, 7.1% production (2000).
Income: Per capita income: $40,862 (2007); Median household income: $80,989 (2007); Average household income: $101,949 (2007); Percent of households with income of $100,000 or more: 36.3% (2007); Poverty rate: 3.1% (2000).
Education: Percent of population age 25 and over with: High school diploma (including GED) or higher: 96.4% (2007); Bachelor's degree or higher: 54.2% (2007); Master's degree or higher: 18.2% (2007).

School District(s)

Bay Village City (PK-12)
2005-06 Enrollment: 2,515 . . . . (440) 617-7300
Housing: Homeownership rate: 92.2% (2007); Median home value: $207,872 (2007); Median rent: $381 per month (2000); Median age of housing: 44 years (2000).
Transportation: Commute to work: 89.2% car, 3.1% public transportation, 0.7% walk, 6.1% work from home (2000); Travel time to work: 26.8% less than 15 minutes, 36.5% 15 to 30 minutes, 26.1% 30 to 45 minutes, 7.4% 45 to 60 minutes, 3.1% 60 minutes or more (2000)
Additional Information Contacts
City of Bay Village . . . . (440) 899-3415
http://www.cityofbayvillage.com

BEACHWOOD (city). Covers a land area of 5.281 square miles and a water area of 0.012 square miles. Located at 41.48° N. Lat.; 81.50° W. Long. Elevation is 1,188 feet.
Population: 10,677 (1990); 12,186 (2000); 11,394 (2007); 10,869 (2012 projected); Race: 84.4% White, 9.8% Black, 4.2% Asian, 0.9% Hispanic of any race (2007); Density: 2,157.5 persons per square mile (2007); Average household size: 2.38 (2007); Median age: 53.8 (2007); Males per 100 females: 79.4 (2007); Marriage status: 13.7% never married, 63.7% now married, 16.4% widowed, 6.1% divorced (2000); Foreign born: 15.5% (2000); Ancestry (includes multiple ancestries): 19.1% Other groups, 15.5% Russian, 9.9% United States or American, 8.2% Polish, 6.8% Hungarian (2000).
Economy: Single-family building permits issued: 10 (2007); Multi-family building permits issued: 0 (2007); Employment by occupation: 19.9% management, 39.7% professional, 5.3% services, 30.0% sales, 0.1% farming, 2.3% construction, 2.7% production (2000).
Income: Per capita income: $43,903 (2007); Median household income: $70,000 (2007); Average household income: $102,961 (2007); Percent of households with income of $100,000 or more: 33.9% (2007); Poverty rate: 4.3% (2000).
Education: Percent of population age 25 and over with: High school diploma (including GED) or higher: 91.7% (2007); Bachelor's degree or higher: 50.4% (2007); Master's degree or higher: 26.3% (2007).

School District(s)

Beachwood City (PK-12)
2005-06 Enrollment: 1,496 . . . . (216) 464-2600

Four-year College(s)

Laura and Alvin Siegal College of Judaic Studies (Private, Not-for-profit, Jewish)
Fall 2007 Enrollment: 121 . . . . (216) 464-4050
2007-08 Tuition: In-state $15,775; Out-of-state $15,775
Housing: Homeownership rate: 65.5% (2007); Median home value: $293,007 (2007); Median rent: $1,076 per month (2000); Median age of housing: 29 years (2000).
Safety: Violent crime rate: 7.1 per 10,000 population; Property crime rate: 397.7 per 10,000 population (2007).
Newspapers: Bedford Sun Banner (Community news; Circulation 5,052); Chagrin Herald Sun (Community news; Circulation 17,695); Euclid Sun Journal (Community news; Circulation 14,909); Solon Herald Sun (Community news; Circulation 17,675); Sun Messenger (Community news; Circulation 14,018); Sun Newspapers - Beachwood Bureau (Regional news); Sun Press (Local news; Circulation 20,040); Sun Scoop Journal (Community news; Circulation 14,909); West Geauga Sun (Community news; Circulation 17,695)
Transportation: Commute to work: 89.7% car, 1.4% public transportation, 0.7% walk, 7.6% work from home (2000); Travel time to work: 32.2% less than 15 minutes, 37.2% 15 to 30 minutes, 25.7% 30 to 45 minutes, 2.4% 45 to 60 minutes, 2.6% 60 minutes or more (2000)
Additional Information Contacts
Beachwood Chamber of Commerce . . . . (216) 831-0003
http://www.beachwood.org
City of Beachwood . . . . (216) 464-1070
http://www.beachwoodohio.com

BEDFORD (city). Covers a land area of 5.357 square miles and a water area of 0 square miles. Located at 41.39° N. Lat.; 81.53° W. Long. Elevation is 948 feet.
History: Named for Bedford in Bedfordshire, England. The first settlement at Bedford was made in 1786 by a group of Moravian missionaries, and was called Pilgerruh, meaning pilgrim's rest. In 1810 the town site was surveyed by the Connecticut Land Company, and in 1813 permanent settlers arrived. Benjamin Fitch, who began the manufacture of chairs in Bedford, was one of the first settlers.
Population: 14,922 (1990); 14,214 (2000); 13,440 (2007); 12,818 (2012 projected); Race: 69.5% White, 26.1% Black, 1.4% Asian, 1.2% Hispanic of any race (2007); Density: 2,508.8 persons per square mile (2007); Average household size: 2.07 (2007); Median age: 41.8 (2007); Males per 100 females: 90.1 (2007); Marriage status: 27.8% never married, 51.3% now married, 9.6% widowed, 11.4% divorced (2000); Foreign born: 3.3% (2000); Ancestry (includes multiple ancestries): 19.8% Other groups, 19.1% German, 13.3% Irish, 11.7% Polish, 10.8% Italian (2000).
Economy: Single-family building permits issued: 5 (2007); Multi-family building permits issued: 0 (2007); Employment by occupation: 9.4% management, 17.6% professional, 14.2% services, 30.2% sales, 0.0% farming, 9.9% construction, 18.7% production (2000).
Income: Per capita income: $22,349 (2007); Median household income: $39,561 (2007); Average household income: $46,124 (2007); Percent of households with income of $100,000 or more: 5.9% (2007); Poverty rate: 7.6% (2000).
Taxes: Total city taxes per capita: $1,133 (2006); City property taxes per capita: $287 (2006).
Education: Percent of population age 25 and over with: High school diploma (including GED) or higher: 83.3% (2007); Bachelor's degree or higher: 18.2% (2007); Master's degree or higher: 5.5% (2007).

School District(s)

Bedford City (PK-12)
2005-06 Enrollment: 3,812 . . . . (440) 439-1500
Housing: Homeownership rate: 59.7% (2007); Median home value: $113,281 (2007); Median rent: $539 per month (2000); Median age of housing: 43 years (2000).
Hospitals: UH Bedford Medical Center (110 beds)
Newspapers: Bedford Times Register (Community news; Circulation 3,400); Maple Heights Press (Community news; Circulation 1,900); Record-Courier - Bedford Bureau (Regional news; Circulation 22,000)
Transportation: Commute to work: 94.7% car, 1.7% public transportation, 2.0% walk, 1.4% work from home (2000); Travel time to work: 30.4% less than 15 minutes, 43.7% 15 to 30 minutes, 19.7% 30 to 45 minutes, 3.7% 45 to 60 minutes, 2.6% 60 minutes or more (2000)
Additional Information Contacts
City of Bedford . . . . (440) 232-1600
http://www.bedfordoh.gov

BEDFORD HEIGHTS (city). Covers a land area of 4.537 square miles and a water area of 0 square miles. Located at 41.40° N. Lat.; 81.50° W. Long. Elevation is 1,040 feet.
History: Named for Bedford in Bedfordshire, England. Incorporated 1951.
Population: 12,131 (1990); 11,375 (2000); 10,682 (2007); 10,139 (2012 projected); Race: 20.9% White, 73.9% Black, 2.0% Asian, 1.9% Hispanic of any race (2007); Density: 2,354.7 persons per square mile (2007); Average household size: 2.18 (2007); Median age: 41.5 (2007); Males per 100 females: 86.7 (2007); Marriage status: 30.9% never married, 46.8% now married, 6.9% widowed, 15.4% divorced (2000); Foreign born: 2.1% (2000); Ancestry (includes multiple ancestries): 62.5% Other groups, 5.8% Italian, 4.6% German, 4.1% Irish, 2.8% Polish (2000).
Economy: Single-family building permits issued: 2 (2007); Multi-family building permits issued: 0 (2007); Employment by occupation: 12.0% management, 18.1% professional, 15.1% services, 26.9% sales, 0.1% farming, 7.5% construction, 20.3% production (2000).
Income: Per capita income: $24,091 (2007); Median household income: $41,725 (2007); Average household income: $51,947 (2007); Percent of

households with income of $100,000 or more: 9.9% (2007); Poverty rate: 7.6% (2000).
Education: Percent of population age 25 and over with: High school diploma (including GED) or higher: 82.6% (2007); Bachelor's degree or higher: 16.3% (2007); Master's degree or higher: 5.3% (2007).
Housing: Homeownership rate: 52.8% (2007); Median home value: $130,744 (2007); Median rent: $551 per month (2000); Median age of housing: 35 years (2000).
Safety: Violent crime rate: 26.5 per 10,000 population; Property crime rate: 320.8 per 10,000 population (2007).
Transportation: Commute to work: 89.7% car, 6.0% public transportation, 2.3% walk, 1.5% work from home (2000); Travel time to work: 24.4% less than 15 minutes, 38.6% 15 to 30 minutes, 26.5% 30 to 45 minutes, 4.6% 45 to 60 minutes, 6.0% 60 minutes or more (2000)
Additional Information Contacts
Bedford Heights Chamber of Commerce. . . . . (440) 232-3369
http://www.bedfordheightschamber.com
City of Bedford Heights . . . . (440) 786-3200
http://www.bedfordheights.gov

BENTLEYVILLE (village). Covers a land area of 2.607 square miles and a water area of 0.011 square miles. Located at 41.41° N. Lat.; 81.41° W. Long. Elevation is 935 feet.
Population: 674 (1990); 947 (2000); 919 (2007); 894 (2012 projected); Race: 96.8% White, 0.7% Black, 2.0% Asian, 1.1% Hispanic of any race (2007); Density: 352.6 persons per square mile (2007); Average household size: 3.18 (2007); Median age: 42.8 (2007); Males per 100 females: 101.1 (2007); Marriage status: 19.1% never married, 76.4% now married, 1.8% widowed, 2.7% divorced (2000); Foreign born: 7.4% (2000); Ancestry (includes multiple ancestries): 24.8% German, 14.8% English, 14.4% Italian, 11.4% Irish, 6.9% Polish (2000).
Economy: Single-family building permits issued: 0 (2007); Multi-family building permits issued: 0 (2007); Employment by occupation: 36.2% management, 34.4% professional, 5.5% services, 21.6% sales, 0.0% farming, 0.5% construction, 1.8% production (2000).
Income: Per capita income: $82,799 (2007); Median household income: $193,125 (2007); Average household income: $263,296 (2007); Percent of households with income of $100,000 or more: 72.7% (2007); Poverty rate: 1.0% (2000).
Education: Percent of population age 25 and over with: High school diploma (including GED) or higher: 99.1% (2007); Bachelor's degree or higher: 77.4% (2007); Master's degree or higher: 37.4% (2007).
Housing: Homeownership rate: 97.9% (2007); Median home value: $609,211 (2007); Median rent: $1,208 per month (2000); Median age of housing: 13 years (2000).
Transportation: Commute to work: 92.4% car, 0.3% public transportation, 1.0% walk, 5.8% work from home (2000); Travel time to work: 24.5% less than 15 minutes, 30.4% 15 to 30 minutes, 34.5% 30 to 45 minutes, 8.1% 45 to 60 minutes, 2.5% 60 minutes or more (2000)
Additional Information Contacts
Village of Bentleyville. . . . . (440) 247-5055
http://www.villageofbentleyville.com

BEREA (city). Covers a land area of 5.458 square miles and a water area of 0.108 square miles. Located at 41.37° N. Lat.; 81.86° W. Long. Elevation is 764 feet.
History: Named for the city in ancient Syria, mentioned in the Bible. Berea was founded by John Baldwin in 1827, on land owned by Gideon Granger, Postmaster General under President Jefferson. Baldwin discovered the vein of abrasive sandstone that provided the early industry for the community.
Population: 19,045 (1990); 18,970 (2000); 18,129 (2007); 17,472 (2012 projected); Race: 90.6% White, 5.4% Black, 1.0% Asian, 1.7% Hispanic of any race (2007); Density: 3,321.8 persons per square mile (2007); Average household size: 2.61 (2007); Median age: 38.1 (2007); Males per 100 females: 90.6 (2007); Marriage status: 33.1% never married, 48.7% now married, 7.3% widowed, 10.9% divorced (2000); Foreign born: 3.2% (2000); Ancestry (includes multiple ancestries): 27.8% German, 17.8% Irish, 13.5% English, 10.7% Polish, 9.8% Italian (2000).
Economy: Single-family building permits issued: 80 (2007); Multi-family building permits issued: 0 (2007); Employment by occupation: 12.1% management, 21.4% professional, 13.3% services, 33.5% sales, 0.3% farming, 6.7% construction, 12.8% production (2000).
Income: Per capita income: $24,192 (2007); Median household income: $50,169 (2007); Average household income: $61,591 (2007); Percent of households with income of $100,000 or more: 15.4% (2007); Poverty rate: 5.5% (2000).
Taxes: Total city taxes per capita: $906 (2006); City property taxes per capita: $324 (2006).
Education: Percent of population age 25 and over with: High school diploma (including GED) or higher: 89.0% (2007); Bachelor's degree or higher: 29.0% (2007); Master's degree or higher: 9.7% (2007).

School District(s)

Berea City (PK-12)
2005-06 Enrollment: 7,821 . . . . (440) 243-6000

Four-year College(s)

Baldwin-Wallace College (Private, Not-for-profit, United Methodist)
Fall 2007 Enrollment: 4,383. . . . . (440) 826-2900
2007-08 Tuition: In-state $22,404; Out-of-state $22,404
Housing: Homeownership rate: 71.1% (2007); Median home value: $145,441 (2007); Median rent: $508 per month (2000); Median age of housing: 42 years (2000).
Safety: Violent crime rate: 7.8 per 10,000 population; Property crime rate: 175.3 per 10,000 population (2007).
Newspapers: News Sun (Community news; Circulation 16,255); Parma Sun Post (Community news); Sun Newspapers - Berea Bureau (Regional news); Sun Star (Local news; Circulation 12,022)
Transportation: Commute to work: 86.6% car, 2.8% public transportation, 7.1% walk, 2.7% work from home (2000); Travel time to work: 33.0% less than 15 minutes, 36.4% 15 to 30 minutes, 21.3% 30 to 45 minutes, 6.0% 45 to 60 minutes, 3.3% 60 minutes or more (2000)
Additional Information Contacts
Berea Chamber of Commerce. . . . . (440) 243-8415
http://www.bereaohio.com/Business/index.cfm
City of Berea . . . . (440) 826-5800
http://www.bereaohio.com

BRATENAHL (village). Covers a land area of 1.025 square miles and a water area of 0.600 square miles. Located at 41.55° N. Lat.; 81.60° W. Long. Elevation is 614 feet.
Population: 1,399 (1990); 1,337 (2000); 1,300 (2007); 1,268 (2012 projected); Race: 81.5% White, 14.9% Black, 0.7% Asian, 1.3% Hispanic of any race (2007); Density: 1,268.0 persons per square mile (2007); Average household size: 1.82 (2007); Median age: 53.5 (2007); Males per 100 females: 93.2 (2007); Marriage status: 21.2% never married, 56.3% now married, 8.6% widowed, 13.9% divorced (2000); Foreign born: 6.7% (2000); Ancestry (includes multiple ancestries): 21.1% German, 16.9% Irish, 15.6% English, 15.0% Other groups, 6.9% Italian (2000).
Economy: Single-family building permits issued: 1 (2007); Multi-family building permits issued: 0 (2007); Employment by occupation: 32.1% management, 33.4% professional, 6.4% services, 22.4% sales, 0.0% farming, 2.0% construction, 3.8% production (2000).
Income: Per capita income: $71,693 (2007); Median household income: $82,328 (2007); Average household income: $128,124 (2007); Percent of households with income of $100,000 or more: 41.4% (2007); Poverty rate: 4.3% (2000).
Education: Percent of population age 25 and over with: High school diploma (including GED) or higher: 96.0% (2007); Bachelor's degree or higher: 63.7% (2007); Master's degree or higher: 35.7% (2007).
Housing: Homeownership rate: 84.6% (2007); Median home value: $245,000 (2007); Median rent: $550 per month (2000); Median age of housing: 39 years (2000).
Transportation: Commute to work: 88.2% car, 2.4% public transportation, 0.9% walk, 7.2% work from home (2000); Travel time to work: 28.8% less than 15 minutes, 53.2% 15 to 30 minutes, 13.4% 30 to 45 minutes, 1.9% 45 to 60 minutes, 2.7% 60 minutes or more (2000)

BRECKSVILLE (city). Covers a land area of 19.611 square miles and a water area of 0.005 square miles. Located at 41.31° N. Lat.; 81.62° W. Long. Elevation is 889 feet.
History: Brecksville was settled about 1811 and named for John and Robert Breck, early residents.
Population: 11,818 (1990); 13,382 (2000); 13,165 (2007); 12,977 (2012 projected); Race: 94.7% White, 1.8% Black, 2.7% Asian, 1.1% Hispanic of any race (2007); Density: 671.3 persons per square mile (2007); Average household size: 2.58 (2007); Median age: 47.0 (2007); Males per 100 females: 99.6 (2007); Marriage status: 19.1% never married, 68.3% now married, 6.6% widowed, 6.0% divorced (2000); Foreign born: 6.6% (2000); Ancestry (includes multiple ancestries): 22.1% German, 18.3% Polish, 13.4% Irish, 12.6% Italian, 8.9% English (2000).

Economy: Single-family building permits issued: 12 (2007); Multi-family building permits issued: 0 (2007); Employment by occupation: 26.9% management, 28.3% professional, 8.1% services, 26.2% sales, 0.0% farming, 4.3% construction, 6.2% production (2000).
Income: Per capita income: $45,418 (2007); Median household income: $85,775 (2007); Average household income: $115,834 (2007); Percent of households with income of $100,000 or more: 41.2% (2007); Poverty rate: 2.5% (2000).
Taxes: Total city taxes per capita: $1,404 (2006); City property taxes per capita: $336 (2006).
Education: Percent of population age 25 and over with: High school diploma (including GED) or higher: 92.8% (2007); Bachelor's degree or higher: 47.4% (2007); Master's degree or higher: 22.2% (2007).

School District(s)

Brecksville-Broadview Heights City (PK-12)
2005-06 Enrollment: 4,720 . . . . (440) 740-4010
Cuyahoga Valley Career Center (09-12)
2005-06 Enrollment: n/a . . . . (440) 526-5200

Vocational/Technical School(s)

School of Nursing at Cuyahoga Valley Career Center (Public)
Fall 2007 Enrollment: 129 . . . . (440) 746-8200
2007-08 Tuition: $9,000

Housing: Homeownership rate: 88.2% (2007); Median home value: $256,414 (2007); Median rent: $999 per month (2000); Median age of housing: 28 years (2000).
Safety: Violent crime rate: 5.4 per 10,000 population; Property crime rate: 44.4 per 10,000 population (2007).
Transportation: Commute to work: 91.2% car, 1.4% public transportation, 1.0% walk, 5.8% work from home (2000); Travel time to work: 20.5% less than 15 minutes, 39.9% 15 to 30 minutes, 30.0% 30 to 45 minutes, 6.8% 45 to 60 minutes, 2.8% 60 minutes or more (2000)

Additional Information Contacts

Brecksville Chamber of Commerce . . . . (440) 526-7350
http://www.brecksvillechamber.com
City of Brecksville. . . . . (440) 526-4351
http://www.brecksville.oh.us

BROADVIEW HEIGHTS (city). Covers a land area of 13.059 square miles and a water area of 0 square miles. Located at 41.32° N. Lat.; 81.67° W. Long. Elevation is 1,198 feet.
History: Named for the beautiful local views. Incorporated 1926.
Population: 12,219 (1990); 15,967 (2000); 18,000 (2007); 19,182 (2012 projected); Race: 94.0% White, 0.8% Black, 3.7% Asian, 1.0% Hispanic of any race (2007); Density: 1,378.4 persons per square mile (2007); Average household size: 2.45 (2007); Median age: 41.5 (2007); Males per 100 females: 92.6 (2007); Marriage status: 23.0% never married, 60.0% now married, 7.2% widowed, 9.8% divorced (2000); Foreign born: 8.9% (2000); Ancestry (includes multiple ancestries): 23.6% German, 16.8% Italian, 16.1% Polish, 13.4% Irish, 7.4% Slovak (2000).
Economy: Single-family building permits issued: 30 (2007); Multi-family building permits issued: 0 (2007); Employment by occupation: 19.6% management, 25.6% professional, 9.6% services, 28.3% sales, 0.1% farming, 5.7% construction, 11.1% production (2000).
Income: Per capita income: $36,880 (2007); Median household income: $66,754 (2007); Average household income: $90,081 (2007); Percent of households with income of $100,000 or more: 29.3% (2007); Poverty rate: 3.2% (2000).
Education: Percent of population age 25 and over with: High school diploma (including GED) or higher: 90.4% (2007); Bachelor's degree or higher: 36.9% (2007); Master's degree or higher: 13.1% (2007).

School District(s)

Brecksville-Broadview Heights City (PK-12)
2005-06 Enrollment: 4,720 . . . . (440) 740-4010
North Royalton City (PK-12)
2005-06 Enrollment: 4,588 . . . . (440) 237-8800

Two-year College(s)

Vatterott College-Cleveland (Private, For-profit)
Fall 2007 Enrollment: 253 . . . . (440) 526-1660
2007-08 Tuition: In-state $9,626; Out-of-state $9,626

Housing: Homeownership rate: 76.3% (2007); Median home value: $213,950 (2007); Median rent: $637 per month (2000); Median age of housing: 25 years (2000).
Safety: Violent crime rate: 4.5 per 10,000 population; Property crime rate: 40.5 per 10,000 population (2007).
Newspapers: The Summit County Women's Journal (Local news)
Transportation: Commute to work: 92.9% car, 1.9% public transportation, 0.6% walk, 3.5% work from home (2000); Travel time to work: 16.6% less than 15 minutes, 43.9% 15 to 30 minutes, 29.4% 30 to 45 minutes, 7.2% 45 to 60 minutes, 2.9% 60 minutes or more (2000)

Additional Information Contacts

Broadview Heights Chamber of Commerce. . . . . (440) 838-4510
http://www.broadviewhts.org
City of Broadview Heights . . . . (440) 526-4357
http://www.broadview-heights.org

BROOK PARK (city). Covers a land area of 7.537 square miles and a water area of 0 square miles. Located at 41.40° N. Lat.; 81.81° W. Long. Elevation is 797 feet.
History: Named for its location near a branch of the Rocky River. Incorporated 1914.
Population: 22,961 (1990); 21,218 (2000); 19,733 (2007); 18,613 (2012 projected); Race: 93.2% White, 2.4% Black, 1.6% Asian, 2.1% Hispanic of any race (2007); Density: 2,618.0 persons per square mile (2007); Average household size: 2.51 (2007); Median age: 43.1 (2007); Males per 100 females: 94.9 (2007); Marriage status: 23.8% never married, 58.2% now married, 8.4% widowed, 9.5% divorced (2000); Foreign born: 4.3% (2000); Ancestry (includes multiple ancestries): 26.5% German, 18.5% Irish, 14.1% Polish, 13.2% Italian, 7.2% English (2000).
Economy: Unemployment rate: 7.8% (6/2008); Total civilian labor force: 10,690 (6/2008); Single-family building permits issued: 8 (2007); Multi-family building permits issued: 0 (2007); Employment by occupation: 9.7% management, 12.3% professional, 16.0% services, 30.1% sales, 0.1% farming, 11.3% construction, 20.6% production (2000).
Income: Per capita income: $23,618 (2007); Median household income: $51,160 (2007); Average household income: $59,007 (2007); Percent of households with income of $100,000 or more: 11.7% (2007); Poverty rate: 4.6% (2000).
Taxes: Total city taxes per capita: $1,272 (2006); City property taxes per capita: $132 (2006).
Education: Percent of population age 25 and over with: High school diploma (including GED) or higher: 80.7% (2007); Bachelor's degree or higher: 9.8% (2007); Master's degree or higher: 2.5% (2007).

School District(s)

Berea City (PK-12)
2005-06 Enrollment: 7,821 . . . . (440) 243-6000

Housing: Homeownership rate: 83.7% (2007); Median home value: $137,180 (2007); Median rent: $565 per month (2000); Median age of housing: 38 years (2000).
Safety: Violent crime rate: 10.8 per 10,000 population; Property crime rate: 148.2 per 10,000 population (2007).
Transportation: Commute to work: 94.1% car, 2.5% public transportation, 0.9% walk, 1.3% work from home (2000); Travel time to work: 30.8% less than 15 minutes, 43.0% 15 to 30 minutes, 18.6% 30 to 45 minutes, 4.5% 45 to 60 minutes, 3.1% 60 minutes or more (2000)

Additional Information Contacts

Brook Park Chamber of Commerce. . . . . (216) 898-9755
http://www.bpcoc.com
City of Brook Park . . . . (216) 433-1300
http://www.cityofbrookpark.com

BROOKLYN (city). Covers a land area of 4.284 square miles and a water area of 0.018 square miles. Located at 41.43° N. Lat.; 81.74° W. Long. Elevation is 764 feet.
Population: 11,706 (1990); 11,586 (2000); 10,709 (2007); 10,055 (2012 projected); Race: 90.4% White, 2.2% Black, 3.1% Asian, 4.7% Hispanic of any race (2007); Density: 2,499.7 persons per square mile (2007); Average household size: 2.12 (2007); Median age: 44.1 (2007); Males per 100 females: 92.4 (2007); Marriage status: 25.4% never married, 50.7% now married, 11.2% widowed, 12.7% divorced (2000); Foreign born: 9.0% (2000); Ancestry (includes multiple ancestries): 23.6% German, 14.1% Polish, 13.6% Irish, 12.4% Italian, 9.4% Slovak (2000).
Economy: Single-family building permits issued: 0 (2007); Multi-family building permits issued: 0 (2007); Employment by occupation: 10.0% management, 14.9% professional, 14.4% services, 31.3% sales, 0.0% farming, 8.2% construction, 21.2% production (2000).
Income: Per capita income: $24,095 (2007); Median household income: $40,699 (2007); Average household income: $50,942 (2007); Percent of households with income of $100,000 or more: 9.0% (2007); Poverty rate: 6.6% (2000).

Education: Percent of population age 25 and over with: High school diploma (including GED) or higher: 80.0% (2007); Bachelor's degree or higher: 13.3% (2007); Master's degree or higher: 4.1% (2007).

School District(s)

Brooklyn City (PK-12)
2005-06 Enrollment: 1,452 . . . . (216) 485-8100

Vocational/Technical School(s)

Kaplan Career Institute (Private, For-profit)
Fall 2007 Enrollment: 478 . . . . (216) 485-0900
2007-08 Tuition: In-state $13,500; Out-of-state $13,500

Housing: Homeownership rate: 62.2% (2007); Median home value: $130,050 (2007); Median rent: $446 per month (2000); Median age of housing: 42 years (2000).

Safety: Violent crime rate: 41.6 per 10,000 population; Property crime rate: 581.6 per 10,000 population (2007).

Transportation: Commute to work: 93.4% car, 2.5% public transportation, 2.3% walk, 1.2% work from home (2000); Travel time to work: 29.8% less than 15 minutes, 50.6% 15 to 30 minutes, 13.6% 30 to 45 minutes, 3.7% 45 to 60 minutes, 2.4% 60 minutes or more (2000)

Additional Information Contacts

City of Brooklyn . . . . (216) 351-2133
http://www.brooklynohio.gov

BROOKLYN HEIGHTS (village). Covers a land area of 1.773 square miles and a water area of 0 square miles. Located at 41.41° N. Lat.; 81.67° W. Long. Elevation is 768 feet.

Population: 1,450 (1990); 1,558 (2000); 1,495 (2007); 1,443 (2012 projected); Race: 96.3% White, 1.1% Black, 1.1% Asian, 1.6% Hispanic of any race (2007); Density: 843.2 persons per square mile (2007); Average household size: 2.57 (2007); Median age: 44.9 (2007); Males per 100 females: 91.9 (2007); Marriage status: 21.2% never married, 58.9% now married, 8.1% widowed, 11.8% divorced (2000); Foreign born: 2.7% (2000); Ancestry (includes multiple ancestries): 25.6% German, 23.3% Polish, 18.2% Italian, 10.7% Irish, 7.6% Slovak (2000).

Economy: Single-family building permits issued: 3 (2007); Multi-family building permits issued: 0 (2007); Employment by occupation: 19.3% management, 22.0% professional, 12.7% services, 24.7% sales, 1.7% farming, 3.5% construction, 15.9% production (2000).

Income: Per capita income: $28,051 (2007); Median household income: $54,079 (2007); Average household income: $69,135 (2007); Percent of households with income of $100,000 or more: 26.3% (2007); Poverty rate: 2.2% (2000).

Education: Percent of population age 25 and over with: High school diploma (including GED) or higher: 86.3% (2007); Bachelor's degree or higher: 26.7% (2007); Master's degree or higher: 7.4% (2007).

Housing: Homeownership rate: 89.8% (2007); Median home value: $181,081 (2007); Median rent: $525 per month (2000); Median age of housing: 42 years (2000).

Safety: Violent crime rate: 0.0 per 10,000 population; Property crime rate: 298.5 per 10,000 population (2007).

Transportation: Commute to work: 97.4% car, 1.0% public transportation, 0.9% walk, 0.0% work from home (2000); Travel time to work: 42.9% less than 15 minutes, 39.1% 15 to 30 minutes, 14.7% 30 to 45 minutes, 0.0% 45 to 60 minutes, 3.4% 60 minutes or more (2000)

CHAGRIN FALLS (village). Covers a land area of 2.071 square miles and a water area of 0.037 square miles. Located at 41.43° N. Lat.; 81.38° W. Long. Elevation is 1,004 feet.

History: Noah Graves from Massachusetts built a grist mill here in 1833, and the town of Chagrin Falls developed as a residential community. The town was named for the Chagrin River, said to have been named by surveyor Moses Cleaveland to express his embarrassment at mistaking it for the Cuyahoga River.

Population: 4,146 (1990); 4,024 (2000); 3,742 (2007); 3,523 (2012 projected); Race: 98.4% White, 0.1% Black, 0.5% Asian, 1.2% Hispanic of any race (2007); Density: 1,807.1 persons per square mile (2007); Average household size: 2.16 (2007); Median age: 45.6 (2007); Males per 100 females: 85.9 (2007); Marriage status: 22.0% never married, 55.3% now married, 11.0% widowed, 11.8% divorced (2000); Foreign born: 3.8% (2000); Ancestry (includes multiple ancestries): 28.7% German, 22.1% English, 17.6% Irish, 8.5% Italian, 4.5% United States or American (2000).

Economy: Single-family building permits issued: 3 (2007); Multi-family building permits issued: 0 (2007); Employment by occupation: 27.8% management, 29.2% professional, 9.6% services, 27.0% sales, 0.1% farming, 2.4% construction, 3.9% production (2000).

Income: Per capita income: $49,162 (2007); Median household income: $72,315 (2007); Average household income: $105,052 (2007); Percent of households with income of $100,000 or more: 35.5% (2007); Poverty rate: 3.6% (2000).

Education: Percent of population age 25 and over with: High school diploma (including GED) or higher: 95.3% (2007); Bachelor's degree or higher: 61.2% (2007); Master's degree or higher: 23.2% (2007).

School District(s)

Chagrin Falls Exempted Village (PK-12)
2005-06 Enrollment: 1,982 . . . . (440) 247-5500
Kenston Local (PK-12)
2005-06 Enrollment: 3,218 . . . . (440) 543-9677

Housing: Homeownership rate: 73.3% (2007); Median home value: $274,199 (2007); Median rent: $799 per month (2000); Median age of housing: 40 years (2000).

Newspapers: Bainbridge Banter (Local news); Chagrin Valley Times/Solon Times (Community news; Circulation 20,000); Currents (Local news; Circulation 20,000); Geauga Times Courier (Community news)

Transportation: Commute to work: 89.5% car, 1.8% public transportation, 3.2% walk, 5.1% work from home (2000); Travel time to work: 28.4% less than 15 minutes, 30.1% 15 to 30 minutes, 27.8% 30 to 45 minutes, 9.5% 45 to 60 minutes, 4.2% 60 minutes or more (2000)

Additional Information Contacts

Chagrin Valley Chamber of Commerce . . . . (440) 247-6607
http://www.cvcc.org
Village of Chagrin Falls . . . . (440) 247-5050
http://www.chagrin-falls.org

CLEVELAND (city). County seat. Covers a land area of 77.580 square miles and a water area of 4.844 square miles. Located at 41.48° N. Lat.; 81.67° W. Long. Elevation is 653 feet.

History: Moses Cleaveland platted the city of Cleveland on the shores of Lake Erie in 1796 for the Connecticut Land Company, but stayed only a few months in the town that would bear his name. It was Lorenzo Carter who pulled the community together, and launched the first boat from Cleveland harbor in 1804, a prophesy of the many freighters and passenger steamers that would one day enter this harbor. The spelling of the town's name changed from Cleaveland to Cleveland about 1832, when a newspaper editor had to drop one letter from his masthead to make it fit the space, and decided to drop the "a" from Cleaveland. Cleveland expanded when the Ohio & Erie Canal was completed, becoming a commercial center. In 1836 it was incorporated as a city, and over the next half-century developed into an industrial giant. The Cuyahoga Steam Furnace Company began making locomotives, the Cleveland Iron Company and the Standard Oil Company were organized, along with many other industries.

Population: 505,333 (1990); 478,403 (2000); 445,680 (2007); 421,286 (2012 projected); Race: 38.0% White, 53.0% Black, 1.7% Asian, 8.4% Hispanic of any race (2007); Density: 5,744.8 persons per square mile (2007); Average household size: 2.47 (2007); Median age: 35.0 (2007); Males per 100 females: 91.0 (2007); Marriage status: 38.9% never married, 38.2% now married, 9.0% widowed, 13.9% divorced (2000); Foreign born: 4.5% (2000); Ancestry (includes multiple ancestries): 50.9% Other groups, 9.2% German, 8.1% Irish, 4.8% Polish, 4.6% Italian (2000).

Economy: Unemployment rate: 10.1% (6/2008); Total civilian labor force: 190,735 (6/2008); Single-family building permits issued: 184 (2007); Multi-family building permits issued: 64 (2007); Employment by occupation: 8.2% management, 14.3% professional, 20.9% services, 26.7% sales, 0.1% farming, 7.5% construction, 22.3% production (2000).

Income: Per capita income: $16,197 (2007); Median household income: $29,186 (2007); Average household income: $39,282 (2007); Percent of households with income of $100,000 or more: 5.5% (2007); Poverty rate: 26.3% (2000).

Taxes: Total city taxes per capita: $931 (2006); City property taxes per capita: $149 (2006).

Education: Percent of population age 25 and over with: High school diploma (including GED) or higher: 69.1% (2007); Bachelor's degree or higher: 11.7% (2007); Master's degree or higher: 3.9% (2007).

School District(s)

Academy of Cleveland (KG-06)
2005-06 Enrollment: 131 . . . . (216) 271-0237
Apex Academy (KG-06)
2005-06 Enrollment: 501 . . . . (216) 451-1725
Cincinnati Lighthouse Charter Community School
2005-06 Enrollment: n/a . . . .

Citizens Academy (KG-05)
2005-06 Enrollment: 377 .... (216) 791-4195
Cleveland Academy for Scholarship Technology (09-12)
2005-06 Enrollment: 101 .... (216) 443-5400
Cleveland Arts and Social Sciences Academy (KG-05)
2005-06 Enrollment: 167 .... (216) 357-2953
Cleveland Lighthouse Charter Community School East (KG-KG)
2005-06 Enrollment: 16 .... (216) 523-1133
Cleveland Municipal City (PK-12)
2005-06 Enrollment: 58,788 .... (216) 574-8193
Cuyahoga Heights Local (PK-12)
2005-06 Enrollment: 874 .... (216) 429-5700
Detroit-Shoreway Community School
2005-06 Enrollment: n/a ....
Entreprenuership Academy
2005-06 Enrollment: n/a .... (216) 456-2080
Garfield Heights Community School
2005-06 Enrollment: n/a ....
Greater Achievement Community School (KG-09)
2005-06 Enrollment: 163 .... (216) 341-8138
Greater Cleveland Academy for Gifted Students (KG-07)
2005-06 Enrollment: 59 .... (216) 651-5209
Greater Heights Academy (01-08)
2005-06 Enrollment: 542 .... (216) 320-1720
Hope Academy Broadway Campus (KG-08)
2005-06 Enrollment: 474 .... (216) 271-7747
Hope Academy Cathedral Campus (KG-08)
2005-06 Enrollment: 599 .... (216) 721-6909
Hope Academy Chapelside Campus (KG-08)
2005-06 Enrollment: 457 .... (216) 283-6589
Hope Academy Cuyahoga Campus (KG-08)
2005-06 Enrollment: 507 .... (216) 251-5450
Hope Academy East Campus (KG-08)
2005-06 Enrollment: 460 .... (216) 383-1214
Hope Academy High School - Cleveland Campus (09-11)
2005-06 Enrollment: 454 .... (216) 431-4927
Hope Academy Lincoln Park (KG-06)
2005-06 Enrollment: 198 .... (216) 263-7008
Hope Academy Northwest Campus (KG-08)
2005-06 Enrollment: 390 .... (216) 226-6800
Hope Northcoast Academy (KG-08)
2005-06 Enrollment: 295 .... (216) 429-0232
Horizon Science Acad Cleveland (07-12)
2005-06 Enrollment: 433 .... (216) 432-3660
Horizon Science Academy-Cleveland Middle School (05-06)
2005-06 Enrollment: 113 .... (216) 432-9940
Horizon Science Academy-Denison Middle School (05-08)
2005-06 Enrollment: 297 .... (216) 739-9911
Intergenerational School The (KG-06)
2005-06 Enrollment: 92 .... (216) 721-0120
International Preparatory School
2005-06 Enrollment: n/a .... (216) 518-9297
Life Skills Center of Metro Cleveland (09-12)
2005-06 Enrollment: 147 .... (216) 431-4938
Life Skills Ctr of Cleveland (09-12)
2005-06 Enrollment: 356 .... (216) 431-7571
Life Skills Ctr of Lake Erie (09-12)
2005-06 Enrollment: 420 .... (216) 631-1090
Life Skills of Northeast Ohio (09-12)
2005-06 Enrollment: 381 .... (216) 421-7587
Madison Community School (KG-04)
2005-06 Enrollment: 118 .... (216) 651-5212
Mansfield Academy for Gifted Students
2005-06 Enrollment: n/a ....
Marcus Garvey Academy (06-08)
2005-06 Enrollment: 134 .... (216) 451-7995
Mayfield City (PK-12)
2005-06 Enrollment: 3,935 .... (440) 995-6800
Ohio City Community School
2005-06 Enrollment: n/a ....
Old Brooklyn Montessori School (KG-08)
2005-06 Enrollment: 278 .... (216) 661-7888
Puritas Community School (KG-05)
2005-06 Enrollment: 174 .... (216) 688-0680
Rising Star Elementary School
2005-06 Enrollment: n/a .... (216) 765-1185
South Euclid-Lyndhurst City (PK-12)
2005-06 Enrollment: 4,528 .... (216) 691-2000
Stockyard Community School (KG-04)
2005-06 Enrollment: 117 .... (216) 651-5209
Village Community School
2005-06 Enrollment: n/a ....
Virtual Schoolhouse Inc. (KG-12)
2005-06 Enrollment: 566 .... (216) 932-2048
Weems School (KG-08)
2005-06 Enrollment: 118 .... (216) 771-6799
Westpark Community-Cleveland (KG-07)
2005-06 Enrollment: 282 .... (216) 688-0271

Four-year College(s)

Bryant and Stratton College-Cleveland (Private, For-profit)
Fall 2007 Enrollment: 621 .... (216) 771-1700
2007-08 Tuition: In-state $13,080; Out-of-state $13,080
Case Western Reserve University (Private, Not-for-profit)
Fall 2007 Enrollment: 9,844 .... (216) 368-2000
2007-08 Tuition: In-state $33,538; Out-of-state $33,538
Cleveland Institute of Art (Private, Not-for-profit)
Fall 2007 Enrollment: 485 .... (216) 421-7000
2007-08 Tuition: In-state $30,090; Out-of-state $30,090
Cleveland Institute of Music (Private, Not-for-profit)
Fall 2007 Enrollment: 453 .... (216) 791-5000
2007-08 Tuition: In-state $31,457; Out-of-state $31,457
Cleveland State University (Public)
Fall 2007 Enrollment: 15,038 .... (216) 687-2000
2007-08 Tuition: In-state $7,945; Out-of-state $10,689
David N Myers University (Private, Not-for-profit)
Fall 2007 Enrollment: 570 .... (216) 391-6937
2007-08 Tuition: In-state $10,950; Out-of-state $10,950
John Carroll University (Private, Not-for-profit, Roman Catholic)
Fall 2007 Enrollment: 3,766 .... (216) 397-1886
2007-08 Tuition: In-state $26,434; Out-of-state $26,434
Notre Dame College (Private, Not-for-profit, Roman Catholic)
Fall 2007 Enrollment: 1,490 .... (216) 381-1680
2007-08 Tuition: In-state $21,090; Out-of-state $21,090

Two-year College(s)

Academy of Court Reporting-Cleveland (Private, For-profit)
Fall 2007 Enrollment: 325 .... (216) 861-3222
2007-08 Tuition: In-state $9,750; Out-of-state $9,750
Cuyahoga Community College District (Public)
Fall 2007 Enrollment: 24,563 .... (800) 954-8742
2007-08 Tuition: In-state $3,194; Out-of-state $6,541
Huron School of Nursing (Private, Not-for-profit)
Fall 2007 Enrollment: 289 .... (216) 761-7996
2007-08 Tuition: In-state $6,016; Out-of-state $6,016
Ohio Technical College (Private, For-profit)
Fall 2007 Enrollment: 919 .... (216) 881-1700
Remington College-Cleveland Campus (Private, For-profit)
Fall 2007 Enrollment: 659 .... (216) 475-7520

Vocational/Technical School(s)

Beatrice Academy of Beauty (Private, For-profit)
Fall 2007 Enrollment: 36 .... (216) 421-2313
2007-08 Tuition: $3,910
Central School of Practical Nursing (Private, Not-for-profit)
Fall 2007 Enrollment: 79 .... (216) 391-8434
2007-08 Tuition: $8,025
Cleveland Industrial Training Center (Private, For-profit)
Fall 2007 Enrollment: n/a .... (216) 459-9292
Cleveland Institute of Dental-Medical Assistants (Private, For-profit)
Fall 2007 Enrollment: 126 .... (216) 241-2930
2007-08 Tuition: $8,295
Cleveland Municipal School District Adult and Cont (Public)
Fall 2007 Enrollment: 97 .... (216) 634-2157
2007-08 Tuition: $4,310

Housing: Homeownership rate: 48.4% (2007); Median home value: $88,857 (2007); Median rent: $379 per month (2000); Median age of housing: 60 years (2000).

Hospitals: Cleveland Clinic (1113 beds); Cleveland Clinic Children's Hospital for Rehabilitation (52 beds); Cleveland VA Medical Center (688 beds); Columbia St. Vincent Charity Hospital (492 beds); Fairview Hospital (511 beds); Grace Hospital (87 beds); Hillcrest Hospital/Cleveland Clinic Health System (311 beds); Huron Hospital (346 beds); Lakewood Hospital (410 beds); Lutheran Hospital (209 beds); Marymount Hospital (279 beds);

Meridia Euclid Hospital (377 beds); MetroHealth Medical Center (728 beds); Northcoast Behavioral Health Care Systems - Cleveland Campus (399 beds); Parma Community General Hospital (348 beds); University Hospitals of Cleveland (1009 beds)
Safety: Violent crime rate: 146.5 per 10,000 population; Property crime rate: 614.2 per 10,000 population (2007).
Newspapers: Ameriska Domovina (Community news); Brooklyn Sun Journal (Community news; Circulation 7,771); CATALYST for Cleveland Schools (Local news); Call & Post (National news; Circulation 10,000); Cincinnati Call & Post (National news; Circulation 12,000); Cleveland Call & Post (Local news; Circulation 32,000); Cleveland Free Times (Local news; Circulation 90,000); Cleveland Jewish News (Local news; Circulation 15,500); Cleveland Point of View (Regional news; Circulation 530); The Cleveland Womens Journal - West Edition (Local news); Crusader Urban News (Local news); Daily Legal News (Local news; Circulation 1,000); Dirva (Community news; Circulation 2,500); East Side Daily News (Community news; Circulation 20,000); El Sol de Cleveland (Community news); Garfield-Maple Sun (Community news; Circulation 8,549); Neighborhood News-Garfield Heights Tribune (Community news; Circulation 20,000); Old Brooklyn News (Community news; Circulation 25,000); Plain Dealer Reporter (Local news; Circulation 50,000); The Plain Dealer (Local news; Circulation 344,704); RSI Extra (Regional news; Circulation 6,000); Sunday Magazine - The Plain Dealer (Local news); Twinsburg Sun (Local news; Circulation 3,334); United Church News (National news; Circulation 315,000)
Transportation: Commute to work: 81.3% car, 12.0% public transportation, 4.0% walk, 1.6% work from home (2000); Travel time to work: 22.0% less than 15 minutes, 45.0% 15 to 30 minutes, 20.7% 30 to 45 minutes, 5.6% 45 to 60 minutes, 6.7% 60 minutes or more (2000); Amtrak: Service available.
Airports: Burke Lakefront (general aviation); Cleveland-Hopkins International (primary service/medium hub); Cuyahoga County (general aviation)
Additional Information Contacts
City of Cleveland . . . . (216) 664-2000
http://www.city.cleveland.oh.us
Convention & Visitors Bureau of Greater Cleveland . . . . . . (216) 875-6600
http://www.travelcleveland.com
Greater Cleveland Partnership . . . . (216) 621-3300
http://www.gcpartnership.com
Heights-Hillcrest Regional Chamber of Commerce . . . . (216) 397-7322
http://www.hrcc.org

CLEVELAND HEIGHTS (city). Covers a land area of 8.110 square miles and a water area of 0.015 square miles. Located at 41.51° N. Lat.; 81.56° W. Long. Elevation is 935 feet.
History: Named for Moses Cleaveland (1754-1806), surveyor of the Western Reserve. Cleveland Heights was established in 1905, and became a city in 1921. It grew as a collection of neighborhoods serving as residential suburbs for Cleveland.
Population: 54,052 (1990); 49,958 (2000); 46,489 (2007); 43,955 (2012 projected); Race: 48.0% White, 45.4% Black, 2.9% Asian, 1.7% Hispanic of any race (2007); Density: 5,732.4 persons per square mile (2007); Average household size: 2.33 (2007); Median age: 38.1 (2007); Males per 100 females: 87.7 (2007); Marriage status: 36.7% never married, 47.5% now married, 6.1% widowed, 9.7% divorced (2000); Foreign born: 8.3% (2000); Ancestry (includes multiple ancestries): 44.5% Other groups, 12.1% German, 10.3% Irish, 7.5% English, 5.8% Italian (2000).
Economy: Unemployment rate: 6.4% (6/2008); Total civilian labor force: 27,404 (6/2008); Single-family building permits issued: 7 (2007); Multi-family building permits issued: 22 (2007); Employment by occupation: 15.3% management, 38.2% professional, 12.0% services, 22.6% sales, 0.0% farming, 3.3% construction, 8.6% production (2000).
Income: Per capita income: $30,376 (2007); Median household income: $51,388 (2007); Average household income: $70,254 (2007); Percent of households with income of $100,000 or more: 18.9% (2007); Poverty rate: 10.6% (2000).
Taxes: Total city taxes per capita: $709 (2006); City property taxes per capita: $223 (2006).
Education: Percent of population age 25 and over with: High school diploma (including GED) or higher: 91.5% (2007); Bachelor's degree or higher: 49.8% (2007); Master's degree or higher: 25.2% (2007).
School District(s)
Cleveland Heights-University Heights City (PK-12)
2005-06 Enrollment: 6,376 . . . . (216) 371-7171

Housing: Homeownership rate: 62.8% (2007); Median home value: $136,892 (2007); Median rent: $580 per month (2000); Median age of housing: 60+ years (2000).
Safety: Violent crime rate: 6.0 per 10,000 population; Property crime rate: 116.9 per 10,000 population (2007).
Transportation: Commute to work: 85.7% car, 5.8% public transportation, 3.6% walk, 3.8% work from home (2000); Travel time to work: 22.3% less than 15 minutes, 44.3% 15 to 30 minutes, 23.8% 30 to 45 minutes, 4.9% 45 to 60 minutes, 4.7% 60 minutes or more (2000)
Additional Information Contacts
City of Cleveland Heights. . . . . (216) 291-4444
http://www.clevelandheights.com

CUYAHOGA HEIGHTS (village). Covers a land area of 3.208 square miles and a water area of 0 square miles. Located at 41.43° N. Lat.; 81.65° W. Long. Elevation is 715 feet.
Population: 682 (1990); 599 (2000); 547 (2007); 507 (2012 projected); Race: 97.8% White, 0.0% Black, 1.3% Asian, 0.0% Hispanic of any race (2007); Density: 170.5 persons per square mile (2007); Average household size: 2.23 (2007); Median age: 45.7 (2007); Males per 100 females: 91.3 (2007); Marriage status: 25.1% never married, 48.4% now married, 12.2% widowed, 14.3% divorced (2000); Foreign born: 6.3% (2000); Ancestry (includes multiple ancestries): 39.9% Polish, 21.0% Italian, 15.9% German, 12.2% Irish, 6.0% Slovak (2000).
Economy: Single-family building permits issued: 1 (2007); Multi-family building permits issued: 0 (2007); Employment by occupation: 13.6% management, 10.7% professional, 24.3% services, 30.1% sales, 0.0% farming, 7.4% construction, 14.0% production (2000).
Income: Per capita income: $23,707 (2007); Median household income: $45,577 (2007); Average household income: $52,929 (2007); Percent of households with income of $100,000 or more: 9.8% (2007); Poverty rate: 5.7% (2000).
Education: Percent of population age 25 and over with: High school diploma (including GED) or higher: 81.7% (2007); Bachelor's degree or higher: 9.0% (2007); Master's degree or higher: 2.0% (2007).
Housing: Homeownership rate: 74.7% (2007); Median home value: $139,329 (2007); Median rent: $427 per month (2000); Median age of housing: 57 years (2000).
Transportation: Commute to work: 90.0% car, 0.0% public transportation, 7.4% walk, 2.2% work from home (2000); Travel time to work: 56.1% less than 15 minutes, 33.0% 15 to 30 minutes, 8.7% 30 to 45 minutes, 1.5% 45 to 60 minutes, 0.8% 60 minutes or more (2000)

EAST CLEVELAND (city). Covers a land area of 3.106 square miles and a water area of 0 square miles. Located at 41.53° N. Lat.; 81.58° W. Long. Elevation is 689 feet.
History: Named for its location east of Cleveland. The original East Cleveland was annexed by Cleveland in 1872, and the name disappeared from the map until 1892, when the neighboring Collamer became East Cleveland Hamlet. In 1911 the village became a city.
Population: 33,096 (1990); 27,217 (2000); 25,329 (2007); 23,928 (2012 projected); Race: 4.3% White, 93.2% Black, 0.2% Asian, 0.8% Hispanic of any race (2007); Density: 8,154.1 persons per square mile (2007); Average household size: 2.37 (2007); Median age: 35.6 (2007); Males per 100 females: 80.3 (2007); Marriage status: 42.3% never married, 32.0% now married, 10.5% widowed, 15.3% divorced (2000); Foreign born: 2.9% (2000); Ancestry (includes multiple ancestries): 80.1% Other groups, 1.1% African, 1.1% United States or American, 0.7% German, 0.6% Italian (2000).
Economy: Unemployment rate: 10.0% (6/2008); Total civilian labor force: 9,885 (6/2008); Single-family building permits issued: 5 (2007); Multi-family building permits issued: 0 (2007); Employment by occupation: 6.6% management, 13.8% professional, 27.4% services, 27.2% sales, 0.0% farming, 6.0% construction, 19.0% production (2000).
Income: Per capita income: $13,834 (2007); Median household income: $22,344 (2007); Average household income: $32,341 (2007); Percent of households with income of $100,000 or more: 3.7% (2007); Poverty rate: 32.0% (2000).
Education: Percent of population age 25 and over with: High school diploma (including GED) or higher: 69.2% (2007); Bachelor's degree or higher: 8.8% (2007); Master's degree or higher: 3.7% (2007).
School District(s)
East Cleveland City (PK-12)
2005-06 Enrollment: 4,355 . . . . (216) 268-6570

New Vision Academy (KG-08)
2005-06 Enrollment: 81 . . . . (216) 851-4682
Housing: Homeownership rate: 35.1% (2007); Median home value: $81,238 (2007); Median rent: $397 per month (2000); Median age of housing: 56 years (2000).
Transportation: Commute to work: 75.5% car, 17.9% public transportation, 3.9% walk, 1.9% work from home (2000); Travel time to work: 17.8% less than 15 minutes, 37.6% 15 to 30 minutes, 26.8% 30 to 45 minutes, 8.1% 45 to 60 minutes, 9.7% 60 minutes or more (2000)
Additional Information Contacts
City of East Cleveland . . . . (216) 681-2208
http://www.eastcleveland.org

EUCLID (city). Covers a land area of 10.708 square miles and a water area of 0.858 square miles. Located at 41.59° N. Lat.; 81.51° W. Long. Elevation is 617 feet.
History: Euclid was settled in 1798 and named for the Greek mathematician by surveyors in the party of Moses Cleaveland. Euclid developed as a residential community near Cleveland.
Population: 54,875 (1990); 52,717 (2000); 48,676 (2007); 45,739 (2012 projected); Race: 57.5% White, 38.8% Black, 1.0% Asian, 1.3% Hispanic of any race (2007); Density: 4,545.8 persons per square mile (2007); Average household size: 2.13 (2007); Median age: 41.6 (2007); Males per 100 females: 85.0 (2007); Marriage status: 30.3% never married, 45.8% now married, 10.4% widowed, 13.5% divorced (2000); Foreign born: 5.3% (2000); Ancestry (includes multiple ancestries): 29.9% Other groups, 15.2% German, 12.6% Irish, 9.6% Italian, 8.8% Slovene (2000).
Economy: Unemployment rate: 8.2% (6/2008); Total civilian labor force: 25,695 (6/2008); Single-family building permits issued: 12 (2007); Multi-family building permits issued: 0 (2007); Employment by occupation: 11.9% management, 18.7% professional, 15.2% services, 30.8% sales, 0.0% farming, 6.8% construction, 16.5% production (2000).
Income: Per capita income: $21,784 (2007); Median household income: $37,741 (2007); Average household income: $46,056 (2007); Percent of households with income of $100,000 or more: 6.7% (2007); Poverty rate: 9.7% (2000).
Taxes: Total city taxes per capita: $578 (2006); City property taxes per capita: $126 (2006).
Education: Percent of population age 25 and over with: High school diploma (including GED) or higher: 82.0% (2007); Bachelor's degree or higher: 19.7% (2007); Master's degree or higher: 5.9% (2007).

School District(s)

Cleveland Municipal City (PK-12)
2005-06 Enrollment: 58,788 . . . . (216) 574-8193
Euclid City (PK-12)
2005-06 Enrollment: 6,509 . . . . (216) 261-2900
New Day Academy Boarding & Day School (04-09)
2005-06 Enrollment: 44 . . . . (216) 451-0619
Pinnacle Academy (KG-06)
2005-06 Enrollment: 570 . . . . (216) 731-0127

Two-year College(s)

Cleveland Clinic Health System-School of Diagnostic Imaging (Private, Not-for-profit)
Fall 2007 Enrollment: 45 . . . . (216) 692-8665

Vocational/Technical School(s)

Euclid Beauty College (Private, For-profit)
Fall 2007 Enrollment: 126 . . . . (216) 261-2600
2007-08 Tuition: $9,950
Housing: Homeownership rate: 58.5% (2007); Median home value: $111,295 (2007); Median rent: $483 per month (2000); Median age of housing: 45 years (2000).
Hospitals: Euclid Hospital (371 beds)
Safety: Violent crime rate: 41.5 per 10,000 population; Property crime rate: 338.5 per 10,000 population (2007).
Transportation: Commute to work: 90.6% car, 5.7% public transportation, 1.7% walk, 1.5% work from home (2000); Travel time to work: 25.1% less than 15 minutes, 43.3% 15 to 30 minutes, 22.7% 30 to 45 minutes, 4.2% 45 to 60 minutes, 4.8% 60 minutes or more (2000)
Additional Information Contacts
City of Euclid . . . . (216) 289-2751
http://www.ci.euclid.oh.us
Euclid Chamber of Commerce. . . . . (216) 731-9322
http://www.euclidchamberofcommerce.com

FAIRVIEW PARK (city). Aka Fairview. Covers a land area of 4.696 square miles and a water area of 0 square miles. Located at 41.44° N. Lat.; 81.85° W. Long. Elevation is 748 feet.
History: Named to promote the town as a good place to live. Incorporated 1950.
Population: 18,028 (1990); 17,572 (2000); 16,231 (2007); 15,244 (2012 projected); Race: 94.9% White, 0.9% Black, 1.8% Asian, 1.8% Hispanic of any race (2007); Density: 3,456.6 persons per square mile (2007); Average household size: 2.18 (2007); Median age: 43.4 (2007); Males per 100 females: 89.5 (2007); Marriage status: 25.7% never married, 55.7% now married, 8.8% widowed, 9.8% divorced (2000); Foreign born: 5.8% (2000); Ancestry (includes multiple ancestries): 29.7% German, 26.7% Irish, 10.7% English, 8.9% Polish, 8.8% Italian (2000).
Economy: Single-family building permits issued: 3 (2007); Multi-family building permits issued: 0 (2007); Employment by occupation: 16.1% management, 25.2% professional, 10.6% services, 31.7% sales, 0.1% farming, 6.7% construction, 9.6% production (2000).
Income: Per capita income: $30,603 (2007); Median household income: $56,413 (2007); Average household income: $66,657 (2007); Percent of households with income of $100,000 or more: 17.8% (2007); Poverty rate: 4.1% (2000).
Taxes: Total city taxes per capita: $667 (2006); City property taxes per capita: $289 (2006).
Education: Percent of population age 25 and over with: High school diploma (including GED) or higher: 91.6% (2007); Bachelor's degree or higher: 36.7% (2007); Master's degree or higher: 11.9% (2007).

School District(s)

Fairview Park City (PK-12)
2005-06 Enrollment: 1,810 . . . . (440) 331-5500

Two-year College(s)

Fairview Beauty Academy (Private, For-profit)
Fall 2007 Enrollment: 61 . . . . (216) 734-5555
Housing: Homeownership rate: 73.7% (2007); Median home value: $162,887 (2007); Median rent: $527 per month (2000); Median age of housing: 44 years (2000).
Transportation: Commute to work: 90.5% car, 4.5% public transportation, 1.6% walk, 3.0% work from home (2000); Travel time to work: 28.7% less than 15 minutes, 40.2% 15 to 30 minutes, 21.5% 30 to 45 minutes, 6.4% 45 to 60 minutes, 3.3% 60 minutes or more (2000)
Additional Information Contacts
City of Fairview Park . . . . (440) 333-2200
http://www.fairviewpark.org

GARFIELD HEIGHTS (city). Covers a land area of 7.226 square miles and a water area of 0.081 square miles. Located at 41.42° N. Lat.; 81.60° W. Long. Elevation is 955 feet.
History: Founded 1904, incorporated 1932.
Population: 31,739 (1990); 30,734 (2000); 28,535 (2007); 26,898 (2012 projected); Race: 78.4% White, 18.4% Black, 1.2% Asian, 1.4% Hispanic of any race (2007); Density: 3,948.7 persons per square mile (2007); Average household size: 2.41 (2007); Median age: 40.6 (2007); Males per 100 females: 88.5 (2007); Marriage status: 26.6% never married, 52.8% now married, 10.4% widowed, 10.2% divorced (2000); Foreign born: 4.4% (2000); Ancestry (includes multiple ancestries): 26.1% Polish, 17.4% Other groups, 14.9% German, 14.0% Italian, 10.2% Irish (2000).
Economy: Unemployment rate: 8.4% (6/2008); Total civilian labor force: 14,855 (6/2008); Single-family building permits issued: 1 (2007); Multi-family building permits issued: 0 (2007); Employment by occupation: 9.7% management, 14.2% professional, 15.1% services, 34.6% sales, 0.0% farming, 8.0% construction, 18.3% production (2000).
Income: Per capita income: $21,615 (2007); Median household income: $43,950 (2007); Average household income: $51,739 (2007); Percent of households with income of $100,000 or more: 7.9% (2007); Poverty rate: 8.5% (2000).
Taxes: Total city taxes per capita: $660 (2006); City property taxes per capita: $307 (2006).
Education: Percent of population age 25 and over with: High school diploma (including GED) or higher: 80.1% (2007); Bachelor's degree or higher: 11.9% (2007); Master's degree or higher: 3.3% (2007).

School District(s)

Garfield Heights City (PK-12)
2005-06 Enrollment: 4,081 . . . . (216) 475-8100

Housing: Homeownership rate: 79.6% (2007); Median home value: $109,693 (2007); Median rent: $483 per month (2000); Median age of housing: 47 years (2000).
Hospitals: Marymount Hospital (312 beds)
Safety: Violent crime rate: 49.6 per 10,000 population; Property crime rate: 317.8 per 10,000 population (2007).
Newspapers: Connection Magazine (Regional news)
Transportation: Commute to work: 92.5% car, 3.2% public transportation, 2.0% walk, 1.6% work from home (2000); Travel time to work: 25.5% less than 15 minutes, 47.0% 15 to 30 minutes, 20.5% 30 to 45 minutes, 3.2% 45 to 60 minutes, 3.9% 60 minutes or more (2000)
Additional Information Contacts
City of Garfield Heights . . . . (216) 475-1100
http://www.garfieldhts.org

GATES MILLS (village). Covers a land area of 9.093 square miles and a water area of 0.005 square miles. Located at 41.53° N. Lat.; 81.41° W. Long. Elevation is 719 feet.
Population: 2,508 (1990); 2,493 (2000); 2,333 (2007); 2,209 (2012 projected); Race: 92.5% White, 1.4% Black, 4.3% Asian, 1.8% Hispanic of any race (2007); Density: 256.6 persons per square mile (2007); Average household size: 2.65 (2007); Median age: 49.3 (2007); Males per 100 females: 96.7 (2007); Marriage status: 17.3% never married, 71.8% now married, 4.8% widowed, 6.0% divorced (2000); Foreign born: 12.3% (2000); Ancestry (includes multiple ancestries): 14.9% Irish, 14.3% German, 12.8% Italian, 12.5% English, 9.8% Other groups (2000).
Economy: Single-family building permits issued: 1 (2007); Multi-family building permits issued: 0 (2007); Employment by occupation: 32.5% management, 35.2% professional, 5.4% services, 23.1% sales, 0.0% farming, 1.3% construction, 2.4% production (2000).
Income: Per capita income: $79,661 (2007); Median household income: $147,955 (2007); Average household income: $209,022 (2007); Percent of households with income of $100,000 or more: 64.7% (2007); Poverty rate: 1.1% (2000).
Education: Percent of population age 25 and over with: High school diploma (including GED) or higher: 96.1% (2007); Bachelor's degree or higher: 66.8% (2007); Master's degree or higher: 37.2% (2007).

School District(s)

Mayfield City (PK-12)
2005-06 Enrollment: 3,935 . . . . (440) 995-6800
Housing: Homeownership rate: 92.9% (2007); Median home value: $510,842 (2007); Median rent: $703 per month (2000); Median age of housing: 36 years (2000).
Safety: Violent crime rate: 0.0 per 10,000 population; Property crime rate: 69.3 per 10,000 population (2007).
Transportation: Commute to work: 83.5% car, 4.5% public transportation, 1.1% walk, 9.8% work from home (2000); Travel time to work: 17.4% less than 15 minutes, 33.8% 15 to 30 minutes, 33.2% 30 to 45 minutes, 8.5% 45 to 60 minutes, 7.1% 60 minutes or more (2000)
Additional Information Contacts
Mayfield Area Chamber of Commerce. . . . . (216) 556-4598
http://www.mayfieldareachamber.org

GLENWILLOW (village). Aka Falls Junction. Covers a land area of 2.715 square miles and a water area of 0.005 square miles. Located at 41.36° N. Lat.; 81.47° W. Long. Elevation is 942 feet.
Population: 455 (1990); 449 (2000); 640 (2007); 750 (2012 projected); Race: 92.0% White, 6.1% Black, 0.0% Asian, 1.1% Hispanic of any race (2007); Density: 235.7 persons per square mile (2007); Average household size: 2.13 (2007); Median age: 44.0 (2007); Males per 100 females: 105.1 (2007); Marriage status: 25.4% never married, 51.6% now married, 6.1% widowed, 17.0% divorced (2000); Foreign born: 1.1% (2000); Ancestry (includes multiple ancestries): 21.8% German, 13.0% Italian, 11.2% Irish, 10.8% Polish, 9.2% English (2000).
Economy: Single-family building permits issued: 10 (2007); Multi-family building permits issued: 0 (2007); Employment by occupation: 12.0% management, 10.3% professional, 20.2% services, 28.8% sales, 0.0% farming, 13.3% construction, 15.5% production (2000).
Income: Per capita income: $27,477 (2007); Median household income: $47,833 (2007); Average household income: $57,882 (2007); Percent of households with income of $100,000 or more: 14.0% (2007); Poverty rate: 5.0% (2000).
Education: Percent of population age 25 and over with: High school diploma (including GED) or higher: 90.8% (2007); Bachelor's degree or higher: 17.1% (2007); Master's degree or higher: 2.4% (2007).
Housing: Homeownership rate: 75.4% (2007); Median home value: $138,750 (2007); Median rent: $194 per month (2000); Median age of housing: 40 years (2000).
Transportation: Commute to work: 97.4% car, 0.9% public transportation, 0.0% walk, 1.8% work from home (2000); Travel time to work: 33.2% less than 15 minutes, 41.3% 15 to 30 minutes, 19.7% 30 to 45 minutes, 2.2% 45 to 60 minutes, 3.6% 60 minutes or more (2000)

HIGHLAND HEIGHTS (city). Covers a land area of 5.131 square miles and a water area of <.001 square miles. Located at 41.55° N. Lat.; 81.47° W. Long. Elevation is 938 feet.
Population: 6,249 (1990); 8,082 (2000); 8,728 (2007); 9,071 (2012 projected); Race: 90.4% White, 2.1% Black, 6.3% Asian, 0.4% Hispanic of any race (2007); Density: 1,700.9 persons per square mile (2007); Average household size: 2.88 (2007); Median age: 44.7 (2007); Males per 100 females: 95.0 (2007); Marriage status: 20.8% never married, 66.4% now married, 8.5% widowed, 4.3% divorced (2000); Foreign born: 11.1% (2000); Ancestry (includes multiple ancestries): 31.3% Italian, 16.0% German, 10.4% Irish, 9.0% Other groups, 8.6% Polish (2000).
Economy: Single-family building permits issued: 12 (2007); Multi-family building permits issued: 6 (2007); Employment by occupation: 20.8% management, 30.6% professional, 10.1% services, 29.7% sales, 0.2% farming, 4.6% construction, 4.0% production (2000).
Income: Per capita income: $40,051 (2007); Median household income: $88,808 (2007); Average household income: $115,020 (2007); Percent of households with income of $100,000 or more: 43.9% (2007); Poverty rate: 4.0% (2000).
Education: Percent of population age 25 and over with: High school diploma (including GED) or higher: 90.0% (2007); Bachelor's degree or higher: 43.0% (2007); Master's degree or higher: 20.3% (2007).

Two-year College(s)

ATS Institute of Technology
Fall 2007 Enrollment: 438 . . . . (440) 449-1700
2007-08 Tuition: In-state $10,190; Out-of-state $10,190
Housing: Homeownership rate: 97.3% (2007); Median home value: $276,685 (2007); Median rent: $828 per month (2000); Median age of housing: 30 years (2000).
Safety: Violent crime rate: 4.6 per 10,000 population; Property crime rate: 109.3 per 10,000 population (2007).
Transportation: Commute to work: 92.3% car, 1.0% public transportation, 0.9% walk, 5.1% work from home (2000); Travel time to work: 32.9% less than 15 minutes, 45.1% 15 to 30 minutes, 18.9% 30 to 45 minutes, 1.8% 45 to 60 minutes, 1.3% 60 minutes or more (2000)
Additional Information Contacts
Mayfield Area Chamber of Commerce. . . . . (216) 556-4598
http://www.mayfieldareachamber.org

HIGHLAND HILLS (village). Covers a land area of 1.978 square miles and a water area of 0.003 square miles. Located at 41.44° N. Lat.; 81.52° W. Long. Elevation is 1,096 feet.
Population: 1,677 (1990); 1,618 (2000); 1,431 (2007); 1,374 (2012 projected); Race: 27.3% White, 68.2% Black, 0.7% Asian, 1.8% Hispanic of any race (2007); Density: 723.6 persons per square mile (2007); Average household size: 6.91 (2007); Median age: 42.8 (2007); Males per 100 females: 187.9 (2007); Marriage status: 56.4% never married, 25.7% now married, 8.9% widowed, 9.0% divorced (2000); Foreign born: 0.7% (2000); Ancestry (includes multiple ancestries): 45.0% Other groups, 7.4% German, 5.2% English, 5.1% Hungarian, 2.2% Dutch (2000).
Economy: Single-family building permits issued: 0 (2007); Multi-family building permits issued: 0 (2007); Employment by occupation: 11.5% management, 14.2% professional, 19.9% services, 26.1% sales, 0.0% farming, 7.5% construction, 20.8% production (2000).
Income: Per capita income: $14,103 (2007); Median household income: $39,063 (2007); Average household income: $49,360 (2007); Percent of households with income of $100,000 or more: 9.2% (2007); Poverty rate: 22.9% (2000).
Education: Percent of population age 25 and over with: High school diploma (including GED) or higher: 61.4% (2007); Bachelor's degree or higher: 18.6% (2007); Master's degree or higher: 5.7% (2007).

School District(s)

Department of Youth Services (06-12)
2005-06 Enrollment: 1,478 . . . . (614) 728-2489
Housing: Homeownership rate: 53.6% (2007); Median home value: $109,191 (2007); Median rent: $469 per month (2000); Median age of housing: 44 years (2000).

Safety: Violent crime rate: 7.2 per 10,000 population; Property crime rate: 72.2 per 10,000 population (2007).
Transportation: Commute to work: 90.5% car, 7.7% public transportation, 1.8% walk, 0.0% work from home (2000); Travel time to work: 16.3% less than 15 minutes, 43.0% 15 to 30 minutes, 29.4% 30 to 45 minutes, 5.9% 45 to 60 minutes, 5.4% 60 minutes or more (2000)
Additional Information Contacts
Tri-City Chamber of Commerce . . . . (216) 454-0199
http://www.tricitychamber.com

HUNTING VALLEY (village). Covers a land area of 7.980 square miles and a water area of 0.002 square miles. Located at 41.47° N. Lat.; 81.40° W. Long. Elevation is 764 feet.
Population: 799 (1990); 735 (2000); 706 (2007); 682 (2012 projected); Race: 98.9% White, 0.1% Black, 0.8% Asian, 0.4% Hispanic of any race (2007); Density: 88.5 persons per square mile (2007); Average household size: 2.54 (2007); Median age: 53.3 (2007); Males per 100 females: 98.3 (2007); Marriage status: 16.2% never married, 74.3% now married, 6.2% widowed, 3.3% divorced (2000); Foreign born: 5.0% (2000); Ancestry (includes multiple ancestries): 23.3% English, 22.3% German, 15.5% Irish, 7.5% Italian, 6.5% Russian (2000).
Economy: Single-family building permits issued: 1 (2007); Multi-family building permits issued: 0 (2007); Employment by occupation: 36.5% management, 30.0% professional, 8.8% services, 17.9% sales, 1.3% farming, 3.3% construction, 2.3% production (2000).
Income: Per capita income: $118,456 (2007); Median household income: $289,474 (2007); Average household income: $300,827 (2007); Percent of households with income of $100,000 or more: 73.0% (2007); Poverty rate: 2.3% (2000).
Education: Percent of population age 25 and over with: High school diploma (including GED) or higher: 98.5% (2007); Bachelor's degree or higher: 73.7% (2007); Master's degree or higher: 35.0% (2007).
Housing: Homeownership rate: 85.6% (2007); Median home value: $1 million+ (2007); Median rent: $725 per month (2000); Median age of housing: 42 years (2000).
Transportation: Commute to work: 85.7% car, 0.0% public transportation, 4.7% walk, 8.3% work from home (2000); Travel time to work: 29.7% less than 15 minutes, 28.3% 15 to 30 minutes, 32.6% 30 to 45 minutes, 6.5% 45 to 60 minutes, 2.9% 60 minutes or more (2000)

INDEPENDENCE (city). Covers a land area of 9.586 square miles and a water area of 0 square miles. Located at 41.38° N. Lat.; 81.64° W. Long. Elevation is 863 feet.
Population: 6,500 (1990); 7,109 (2000); 6,916 (2007); 6,733 (2012 projected); Race: 96.9% White, 0.7% Black, 1.6% Asian, 0.9% Hispanic of any race (2007); Density: 721.5 persons per square mile (2007); Average household size: 2.60 (2007); Median age: 46.3 (2007); Males per 100 females: 90.4 (2007); Marriage status: 22.3% never married, 63.9% now married, 9.0% widowed, 4.8% divorced (2000); Foreign born: 5.3% (2000); Ancestry (includes multiple ancestries): 32.3% Polish, 20.2% German, 16.7% Italian, 10.7% Irish, 7.3% English (2000).
Economy: Single-family building permits issued: 11 (2007); Multi-family building permits issued: 0 (2007); Employment by occupation: 20.0% management, 25.4% professional, 7.9% services, 29.4% sales, 0.3% farming, 8.1% construction, 8.9% production (2000).
Income: Per capita income: $32,014 (2007); Median household income: $67,720 (2007); Average household income: $82,933 (2007); Percent of households with income of $100,000 or more: 32.2% (2007); Poverty rate: 3.6% (2000).
Education: Percent of population age 25 and over with: High school diploma (including GED) or higher: 89.0% (2007); Bachelor's degree or higher: 29.0% (2007); Master's degree or higher: 10.8% (2007).

School District(s)

Independence Local (PK-12)
2005-06 Enrollment: 1,111 . . . . (216) 642-5850

Four-year College(s)

Ohio College of Podiatric Medicine (Private, Not-for-profit)
Fall 2007 Enrollment: 370 . . . . (216) 231-3300
University of Phoenix-Cleveland Campus (Private, For-profit)
Fall 2007 Enrollment: 664 . . . . (216) 447-8807
2007-08 Tuition: In-state $12,930; Out-of-state $12,930
Housing: Homeownership rate: 94.5% (2007); Median home value: $237,825 (2007); Median rent: $497 per month (2000); Median age of housing: 42 years (2000).
Safety: Violent crime rate: 14.8 per 10,000 population; Property crime rate: 278.1 per 10,000 population (2007).
Transportation: Commute to work: 94.8% car, 2.0% public transportation, 0.0% walk, 3.2% work from home (2000); Travel time to work: 25.8% less than 15 minutes, 48.6% 15 to 30 minutes, 20.9% 30 to 45 minutes, 2.0% 45 to 60 minutes, 2.6% 60 minutes or more (2000)
Additional Information Contacts
City of Independence . . . . (216) 524-4131
http://www.independenceohio.org

LAKEWOOD (city). Covers a land area of 5.549 square miles and a water area of 1.150 square miles. Located at 41.48° N. Lat.; 81.80° W. Long. Elevation is 705 feet.
History: Named for its location on the wooded shores of Lake Erie. Lakewood was known as East Rockport until 1889, when its name was changed to Lakewood, refering to its location on the wooded shore of Lake Erie. Lakewood was incorporated as a city in 1911.
Population: 59,718 (1990); 56,646 (2000); 52,313 (2007); 49,165 (2012 projected); Race: 91.0% White, 2.7% Black, 1.7% Asian, 2.5% Hispanic of any race (2007); Density: 9,427.7 persons per square mile (2007); Average household size: 2.08 (2007); Median age: 37.8 (2007); Males per 100 females: 92.9 (2007); Marriage status: 38.3% never married, 43.1% now married, 6.5% widowed, 12.1% divorced (2000); Foreign born: 8.7% (2000); Ancestry (includes multiple ancestries): 25.2% German, 23.6% Irish, 9.8% English, 8.9% Italian, 7.8% Polish (2000).
Economy: Unemployment rate: 7.0% (6/2008); Total civilian labor force: 32,465 (6/2008); Single-family building permits issued: 9 (2007); Multi-family building permits issued: 0 (2007); Employment by occupation: 15.9% management, 25.1% professional, 13.8% services, 28.0% sales, 0.0% farming, 6.7% construction, 10.4% production (2000).
Income: Per capita income: $27,818 (2007); Median household income: $45,231 (2007); Average household income: $57,436 (2007); Percent of households with income of $100,000 or more: 12.8% (2007); Poverty rate: 8.9% (2000).
Taxes: Total city taxes per capita: $618 (2006); City property taxes per capita: $268 (2006).
Education: Percent of population age 25 and over with: High school diploma (including GED) or higher: 88.7% (2007); Bachelor's degree or higher: 35.6% (2007); Master's degree or higher: 11.9% (2007).

School District(s)

Lakewood City (PK-12)
2005-06 Enrollment: 6,361 . . . . (216) 529-4092
Lakewood City Academy (07-12)
2005-06 Enrollment: 105 . . . . (216) 529-4037

Two-year College(s)

Virginia Marti College of Art and Design (Private, For-profit)
Fall 2007 Enrollment: 262 . . . . (216) 221-8584
2007-08 Tuition: In-state $13,406; Out-of-state $13,406
Housing: Homeownership rate: 45.4% (2007); Median home value: $144,689 (2007); Median rent: $492 per month (2000); Median age of housing: 60+ years (2000).
Hospitals: Lakewood Hospital (400 beds)
Safety: Violent crime rate: 17.4 per 10,000 population; Property crime rate: 256.9 per 10,000 population (2007).
Newspapers: The Cleveland Women's Journal-East Edition (Local news); Lakewood Times (Community news)
Transportation: Commute to work: 85.1% car, 7.8% public transportation, 3.6% walk, 2.6% work from home (2000); Travel time to work: 26.4% less than 15 minutes, 45.9% 15 to 30 minutes, 20.4% 30 to 45 minutes, 4.3% 45 to 60 minutes, 2.9% 60 minutes or more (2000)
Additional Information Contacts
City of Lakewood . . . . (216) 529-6600
http://www.ci.lakewood.oh.us
Lakewood Chamber of Commerce . . . . (216) 226-2900
http://www.lakewoodchamber.org

LINNDALE (village). Covers a land area of 0.088 square miles and a water area of 0 square miles. Located at 41.44° N. Lat.; 81.76° W. Long. Elevation is 758 feet.
Population: 159 (1990); 117 (2000); 117 (2007); 117 (2012 projected); Race: 65.8% White, 17.9% Black, 0.0% Asian, 11.1% Hispanic of any race (2007); Density: 1,332.8 persons per square mile (2007); Average household size: 1.98 (2007); Median age: 37.2 (2007); Males per 100 females: 98.3 (2007); Marriage status: 36.8% never married, 25.3% now married, 12.6% widowed, 25.3% divorced (2000); Foreign born: 0.0%

(2000); Ancestry (includes multiple ancestries): 32.2% Other groups, 19.0% Irish, 11.6% German, 7.4% Slovak, 5.8% English (2000).
Economy: Single-family building permits issued: 0 (2007); Multi-family building permits issued: 0 (2007); Employment by occupation: 14.0% management, 10.5% professional, 12.3% services, 15.8% sales, 5.3% farming, 19.3% construction, 22.8% production (2000).
Income: Per capita income: $16,667 (2007); Median household income: $21,786 (2007); Average household income: $33,051 (2007); Percent of households with income of $100,000 or more: 5.1% (2007); Poverty rate: 15.7% (2000).
Education: Percent of population age 25 and over with: High school diploma (including GED) or higher: 77.2% (2007); Bachelor's degree or higher: 0.0% (2007); Master's degree or higher: 0.0% (2007).
Housing: Homeownership rate: 44.1% (2007); Median home value: $75,000 (2007); Median rent: $350 per month (2000); Median age of housing: 60+ years (2000).
Transportation: Commute to work: 80.7% car, 8.8% public transportation, 10.5% walk, 0.0% work from home (2000); Travel time to work: 19.3% less than 15 minutes, 35.1% 15 to 30 minutes, 22.8% 30 to 45 minutes, 8.8% 45 to 60 minutes, 14.0% 60 minutes or more (2000)

LYNDHURST (city). Covers a land area of 4.390 square miles and a water area of 0 square miles. Located at 41.52° N. Lat.; 81.49° W. Long. Elevation is 1,033 feet.
History: Incorporated 1917.
Population: 15,982 (1990); 15,279 (2000); 14,241 (2007); 13,449 (2012 projected); Race: 95.9% White, 1.8% Black, 1.2% Asian, 0.8% Hispanic of any race (2007); Density: 3,243.6 persons per square mile (2007); Average household size: 2.24 (2007); Median age: 46.6 (2007); Males per 100 females: 86.4 (2007); Marriage status: 19.9% never married, 62.1% now married, 11.2% widowed, 6.8% divorced (2000); Foreign born: 7.1% (2000); Ancestry (includes multiple ancestries): 23.9% Italian, 18.4% German, 15.9% Irish, 9.4% English, 8.0% Polish (2000).
Economy: Single-family building permits issued: 7 (2007); Multi-family building permits issued: 0 (2007); Employment by occupation: 20.6% management, 24.1% professional, 10.6% services, 32.5% sales, 0.0% farming, 4.8% construction, 7.5% production (2000).
Income: Per capita income: $32,015 (2007); Median household income: $58,391 (2007); Average household income: $71,019 (2007); Percent of households with income of $100,000 or more: 20.8% (2007); Poverty rate: 2.5% (2000).
Education: Percent of population age 25 and over with: High school diploma (including GED) or higher: 92.7% (2007); Bachelor's degree or higher: 37.8% (2007); Master's degree or higher: 13.6% (2007).

School District(s)

South Euclid-Lyndhurst City (PK-12)
2005-06 Enrollment: 4,528 . . . . (216) 691-2000

Two-year College(s)

Inner State Beauty School (Private, For-profit)
Fall 2007 Enrollment: 141 . . . . (440) 461-1000

Vocational/Technical School(s)

Cleveland Institute of Dental-Medical Assistants (Private, For-profit)
Fall 2007 Enrollment: 93 . . . . (216) 241-2930
2007-08 Tuition: $8,295

Housing: Homeownership rate: 88.4% (2007); Median home value: $163,202 (2007); Median rent: $748 per month (2000); Median age of housing: 44 years (2000).
Safety: Violent crime rate: 2.8 per 10,000 population; Property crime rate: 0.0 per 10,000 population (2007).
Transportation: Commute to work: 93.5% car, 1.5% public transportation, 0.5% walk, 4.2% work from home (2000); Travel time to work: 30.5% less than 15 minutes, 43.6% 15 to 30 minutes, 18.9% 30 to 45 minutes, 4.9% 45 to 60 minutes, 2.0% 60 minutes or more (2000)
Additional Information Contacts
City of Lyndhurst . . . . (440) 442-5777
http://www.lyndhurst-oh.com

MAPLE HEIGHTS (city). Covers a land area of 5.191 square miles and a water area of 0 square miles. Located at 41.41° N. Lat.; 81.56° W. Long. Elevation is 899 feet.
History: Named for its abundance of maple trees. Incorporated 1932.
Population: 27,089 (1990); 26,156 (2000); 24,312 (2007); 22,890 (2012 projected); Race: 41.7% White, 53.4% Black, 2.2% Asian, 1.4% Hispanic of any race (2007); Density: 4,683.8 persons per square mile (2007); Average household size: 2.45 (2007); Median age: 40.0 (2007); Males per 100 females: 88.6 (2007); Marriage status: 27.4% never married, 52.1% now married, 10.0% widowed, 10.6% divorced (2000); Foreign born: 2.9% (2000); Ancestry (includes multiple ancestries): 42.4% Other groups, 10.0% Italian, 9.9% Polish, 8.6% German, 6.4% Irish (2000).
Economy: Unemployment rate: 9.3% (6/2008); Total civilian labor force: 12,896 (6/2008); Single-family building permits issued: 8 (2007); Multi-family building permits issued: 0 (2007); Employment by occupation: 9.7% management, 15.5% professional, 14.8% services, 30.6% sales, 0.2% farming, 7.2% construction, 21.9% production (2000).
Income: Per capita income: $20,436 (2007); Median household income: $43,544 (2007); Average household income: $49,870 (2007); Percent of households with income of $100,000 or more: 6.8% (2007); Poverty rate: 5.9% (2000).
Taxes: Total city taxes per capita: $548 (2006); City property taxes per capita: $240 (2006).
Education: Percent of population age 25 and over with: High school diploma (including GED) or higher: 82.2% (2007); Bachelor's degree or higher: 12.9% (2007); Master's degree or higher: 3.0% (2007).

School District(s)

Education Alternatives Community School (KG-05)
2005-06 Enrollment: 205 . . . . (216) 332-9360
Maple Heights City (PK-12)
2005-06 Enrollment: 3,949 . . . . (216) 587-6100
Preparing Academic Leaders Academy
2005-06 Enrollment: n/a . . . .

Housing: Homeownership rate: 83.6% (2007); Median home value: $102,954 (2007); Median rent: $462 per month (2000); Median age of housing: 45 years (2000).
Transportation: Commute to work: 92.8% car, 4.1% public transportation, 1.5% walk, 1.0% work from home (2000); Travel time to work: 24.9% less than 15 minutes, 43.6% 15 to 30 minutes, 21.7% 30 to 45 minutes, 5.9% 45 to 60 minutes, 3.9% 60 minutes or more (2000)
Additional Information Contacts
City of Maple Heights. . . . . (216) 662-6000
http://mapleheights.cuyahogacounty.us

MAYFIELD (village). Covers a land area of 3.925 square miles and a water area of 0.004 square miles. Located at 41.54° N. Lat.; 81.44° W. Long. Elevation is 925 feet.
Population: 3,462 (1990); 3,435 (2000); 3,183 (2007); 2,989 (2012 projected); Race: 92.9% White, 2.0% Black, 4.2% Asian, 0.9% Hispanic of any race (2007); Density: 811.0 persons per square mile (2007); Average household size: 2.41 (2007); Median age: 48.0 (2007); Males per 100 females: 92.4 (2007); Marriage status: 21.3% never married, 63.7% now married, 8.7% widowed, 6.4% divorced (2000); Foreign born: 11.7% (2000); Ancestry (includes multiple ancestries): 25.1% Italian, 23.0% German, 17.3% Irish, 9.2% English, 7.6% Polish (2000).
Economy: Single-family building permits issued: 4 (2007); Multi-family building permits issued: 0 (2007); Employment by occupation: 22.2% management, 25.7% professional, 11.8% services, 28.4% sales, 0.0% farming, 6.7% construction, 5.2% production (2000).
Income: Per capita income: $41,623 (2007); Median household income: $73,611 (2007); Average household income: $100,293 (2007); Percent of households with income of $100,000 or more: 35.0% (2007); Poverty rate: 2.6% (2000).
Education: Percent of population age 25 and over with: High school diploma (including GED) or higher: 94.0% (2007); Bachelor's degree or higher: 45.4% (2007); Master's degree or higher: 18.1% (2007).

School District(s)

Mayfield City (PK-12)
2005-06 Enrollment: 3,935 . . . . (440) 995-6800

Housing: Homeownership rate: 81.9% (2007); Median home value: $244,211 (2007); Median rent: $978 per month (2000); Median age of housing: 37 years (2000).
Safety: Violent crime rate: 15.8 per 10,000 population; Property crime rate: 231.1 per 10,000 population (2007).
Transportation: Commute to work: 91.3% car, 1.5% public transportation, 1.2% walk, 5.3% work from home (2000); Travel time to work: 30.8% less than 15 minutes, 35.6% 15 to 30 minutes, 24.2% 30 to 45 minutes, 3.2% 45 to 60 minutes, 6.2% 60 minutes or more (2000)
Additional Information Contacts
Mayfield Area Chamber of Commerce. . . . . (216) 556-4598
http://www.mayfieldareachamber.org
Village of Mayfield . . . . (440) 461-2210
http://www.mayfieldvillage.com

MAYFIELD HEIGHTS (city). Covers a land area of 4.218 square miles and a water area of 0 square miles. Located at 41.51° N. Lat.; 81.45° W. Long. Elevation is 1,089 feet.

History: Named either for Mayfield in Derby, England, or for the month of May. Incorporated 1925.

Population: 19,847 (1990); 19,386 (2000); 18,131 (2007); 17,155 (2012 projected); Race: 89.8% White, 3.7% Black, 5.1% Asian, 1.2% Hispanic of any race (2007); Density: 4,298.5 persons per square mile (2007); Average household size: 1.93 (2007); Median age: 46.1 (2007); Males per 100 females: 83.3 (2007); Marriage status: 24.4% never married, 50.7% now married, 14.0% widowed, 10.9% divorced (2000); Foreign born: 18.1% (2000); Ancestry (includes multiple ancestries): 26.1% Italian, 15.4% German, 12.6% Other groups, 9.0% Irish, 6.8% Russian (2000).

Economy: Single-family building permits issued: 27 (2007); Multi-family building permits issued: 0 (2007); Employment by occupation: 14.5% management, 23.5% professional, 14.0% services, 31.5% sales, 0.1% farming, 7.1% construction, 9.3% production (2000).

Income: Per capita income: $28,194 (2007); Median household income: $41,932 (2007); Average household income: $54,209 (2007); Percent of households with income of $100,000 or more: 10.1% (2007); Poverty rate: 6.3% (2000).

Education: Percent of population age 25 and over with: High school diploma (including GED) or higher: 85.8% (2007); Bachelor's degree or higher: 27.7% (2007); Master's degree or higher: 10.7% (2007).

Housing: Homeownership rate: 50.9% (2007); Median home value: $153,376 (2007); Median rent: $624 per month (2000); Median age of housing: 36 years (2000).

Hospitals: Hillcrest Hospital (424 beds)

Safety: Violent crime rate: 5.0 per 10,000 population; Property crime rate: 175.6 per 10,000 population (2007).

Transportation: Commute to work: 91.5% car, 2.1% public transportation, 2.5% walk, 3.1% work from home (2000); Travel time to work: 32.4% less than 15 minutes, 40.3% 15 to 30 minutes, 20.3% 30 to 45 minutes, 4.3% 45 to 60 minutes, 2.7% 60 minutes or more (2000)

Additional Information Contacts

City of Mayfield Heights . . . . (440) 442-2626
http://www.mayfieldheights.org

Mayfield Area Chamber of Commerce . . . . (216) 556-4598
http://www.mayfieldareachamber.org

MIDDLEBURG HEIGHTS (city). Covers a land area of 8.075 square miles and a water area of 0.016 square miles. Located at 41.36° N. Lat.; 81.80° W. Long. Elevation is 850 feet.

Population: 14,667 (1990); 15,542 (2000); 15,394 (2007); 15,220 (2012 projected); Race: 93.4% White, 1.7% Black, 2.5% Asian, 1.5% Hispanic of any race (2007); Density: 1,906.5 persons per square mile (2007); Average household size: 2.27 (2007); Median age: 46.4 (2007); Males per 100 females: 90.1 (2007); Marriage status: 24.3% never married, 55.9% now married, 9.9% widowed, 9.8% divorced (2000); Foreign born: 9.0% (2000); Ancestry (includes multiple ancestries): 26.6% German, 16.1% Irish, 14.3% Italian, 11.9% Polish, 7.9% Slovak (2000).

Economy: Single-family building permits issued: 16 (2007); Multi-family building permits issued: 0 (2007); Employment by occupation: 14.8% management, 20.2% professional, 14.8% services, 32.4% sales, 0.0% farming, 7.5% construction, 10.3% production (2000).

Income: Per capita income: $28,141 (2007); Median household income: $53,101 (2007); Average household income: $62,796 (2007); Percent of households with income of $100,000 or more: 15.5% (2007); Poverty rate: 3.0% (2000).

Education: Percent of population age 25 and over with: High school diploma (including GED) or higher: 85.5% (2007); Bachelor's degree or higher: 24.1% (2007); Master's degree or higher: 7.2% (2007).

School District(s)

Berea City (PK-12)
2005-06 Enrollment: 7,821 . . . . (440) 243-6000

Polaris (09-12)
2005-06 Enrollment: n/a . . . . (440) 891-7600

Two-year College(s)

Sanford-Brown Institute (Private, For-profit)
Fall 2007 Enrollment: 510 . . . . (440) 202-3232

Vocational/Technical School(s)

Polaris Career Center (Public)
Fall 2007 Enrollment: 122 . . . . (440) 891-7600
2007-08 Tuition: In-state $4,419; Out-of-state $4,419

Housing: Homeownership rate: 73.2% (2007); Median home value: $178,836 (2007); Median rent: $577 per month (2000); Median age of housing: 32 years (2000).

Hospitals: Southwest General Health Center (336 beds)

Transportation: Commute to work: 93.6% car, 1.5% public transportation, 1.4% walk, 2.9% work from home (2000); Travel time to work: 30.6% less than 15 minutes, 40.9% 15 to 30 minutes, 19.4% 30 to 45 minutes, 6.3% 45 to 60 minutes, 2.8% 60 minutes or more (2000)

Additional Information Contacts

City of Middleburg Heights . . . . (440) 234-8811
http://www.middleburgheights.com

Middleburg Heights Chamber of Commerce . . . . (440) 243-5599
http://middleburgheightschamber.com

MORELAND HILLS (village). Covers a land area of 7.249 square miles and a water area of 0.004 square miles. Located at 41.44° N. Lat.; 81.42° W. Long. Elevation is 1,040 feet.

Population: 3,354 (1990); 3,298 (2000); 3,161 (2007); 3,048 (2012 projected); Race: 91.5% White, 4.0% Black, 3.5% Asian, 0.8% Hispanic of any race (2007); Density: 436.1 persons per square mile (2007); Average household size: 2.49 (2007); Median age: 50.0 (2007); Males per 100 females: 94.0 (2007); Marriage status: 18.1% never married, 71.1% now married, 6.2% widowed, 4.6% divorced (2000); Foreign born: 10.2% (2000); Ancestry (includes multiple ancestries): 17.0% German, 14.0% English, 10.0% Russian, 9.4% Other groups, 8.1% Irish (2000).

Economy: Single-family building permits issued: 5 (2007); Multi-family building permits issued: 0 (2007); Employment by occupation: 30.3% management, 29.4% professional, 6.5% services, 28.0% sales, 0.0% farming, 2.9% construction, 2.9% production (2000).

Income: Per capita income: $76,358 (2007); Median household income: $124,381 (2007); Average household income: $189,815 (2007); Percent of households with income of $100,000 or more: 57.7% (2007); Poverty rate: 3.3% (2000).

Education: Percent of population age 25 and over with: High school diploma (including GED) or higher: 97.3% (2007); Bachelor's degree or higher: 66.1% (2007); Master's degree or higher: 31.1% (2007).

Housing: Homeownership rate: 95.0% (2007); Median home value: $425,419 (2007); Median rent: $1,000 per month (2000); Median age of housing: 37 years (2000).

Transportation: Commute to work: 86.9% car, 0.8% public transportation, 2.3% walk, 9.7% work from home (2000); Travel time to work: 25.7% less than 15 minutes, 38.1% 15 to 30 minutes, 30.0% 30 to 45 minutes, 2.8% 45 to 60 minutes, 3.4% 60 minutes or more (2000)

Additional Information Contacts

Village of Moreland Hills . . . . (440) 248-1188
http://www.morelandhills.com

NEWBURGH HEIGHTS (village). Covers a land area of 0.582 square miles and a water area of 0 square miles. Located at 41.45° N. Lat.; 81.66° W. Long. Elevation is 692 feet.

Population: 2,495 (1990); 2,389 (2000); 2,204 (2007); 2,062 (2012 projected); Race: 92.0% White, 4.8% Black, 0.1% Asian, 3.1% Hispanic of any race (2007); Density: 3,786.5 persons per square mile (2007); Average household size: 2.20 (2007); Median age: 40.2 (2007); Males per 100 females: 94.0 (2007); Marriage status: 30.7% never married, 42.3% now married, 10.5% widowed, 16.5% divorced (2000); Foreign born: 2.5% (2000); Ancestry (includes multiple ancestries): 29.6% Polish, 21.6% German, 16.7% Irish, 12.2% Other groups, 11.1% Italian (2000).

Economy: Single-family building permits issued: 0 (2007); Multi-family building permits issued: 0 (2007); Employment by occupation: 10.4% management, 10.0% professional, 16.6% services, 29.5% sales, 0.0% farming, 10.8% construction, 22.7% production (2000).

Income: Per capita income: $22,053 (2007); Median household income: $42,852 (2007); Average household income: $48,556 (2007); Percent of households with income of $100,000 or more: 7.5% (2007); Poverty rate: 12.0% (2000).

Education: Percent of population age 25 and over with: High school diploma (including GED) or higher: 77.1% (2007); Bachelor's degree or higher: 10.6% (2007); Master's degree or higher: 3.4% (2007).

School District(s)

Washington Park Community (KG-08)
2005-06 Enrollment: 233 . . . . (216) 271-6055

Housing: Homeownership rate: 62.9% (2007); Median home value: $88,257 (2007); Median rent: $414 per month (2000); Median age of housing: 60+ years (2000).

Transportation: Commute to work: 94.2% car, 3.0% public transportation, 2.2% walk, 0.3% work from home (2000); Travel time to work: 31.2% less than 15 minutes, 51.7% 15 to 30 minutes, 11.1% 30 to 45 minutes, 2.1% 45 to 60 minutes, 3.9% 60 minutes or more (2000)

NORTH OLMSTED (city). Covers a land area of 11.631 square miles and a water area of 0 square miles. Located at 41.41° N. Lat.; 81.91° W. Long. Elevation is 761 feet.
History: Named for Charles H. Olmsted. First U.S. municipal bus line began operations in North Olmstead in 1931. Incorporated as a city 1951.
Population: 34,240 (1990); 34,113 (2000); 32,152 (2007); 30,671 (2012 projected); Race: 92.4% White, 1.3% Black, 3.4% Asian, 1.9% Hispanic of any race (2007); Density: 2,764.3 persons per square mile (2007); Average household size: 2.44 (2007); Median age: 42.5 (2007); Males per 100 females: 93.0 (2007); Marriage status: 23.9% never married, 59.6% now married, 7.3% widowed, 9.2% divorced (2000); Foreign born: 7.8% (2000); Ancestry (includes multiple ancestries): 29.9% German, 22.8% Irish, 10.7% Italian, 9.9% Polish, 9.6% English (2000).
Economy: Unemployment rate: 6.9% (6/2008); Total civilian labor force: 18,565 (6/2008); Single-family building permits issued: 9 (2007); Multi-family building permits issued: 0 (2007); Employment by occupation: 16.1% management, 21.6% professional, 12.4% services, 30.6% sales, 0.2% farming, 7.3% construction, 11.8% production (2000).
Income: Per capita income: $28,362 (2007); Median household income: $58,903 (2007); Average household income: $68,884 (2007); Percent of households with income of $100,000 or more: 19.5% (2007); Poverty rate: 4.1% (2000).
Education: Percent of population age 25 and over with: High school diploma (including GED) or higher: 90.3% (2007); Bachelor's degree or higher: 27.3% (2007); Master's degree or higher: 9.3% (2007).

School District(s)

North Olmsted City (PK-12)
2005-06 Enrollment: 4,613 . . . . (440) 779-3549

Two-year College(s)

Remington College-Cleveland West Campus (Private, For-profit)
Fall 2007 Enrollment: 474 . . . . (440) 777-2560

Housing: Homeownership rate: 79.1% (2007); Median home value: $168,664 (2007); Median rent: $577 per month (2000); Median age of housing: 34 years (2000).
Safety: Violent crime rate: 12.2 per 10,000 population; Property crime rate: 184.3 per 10,000 population (2007).
Newspapers: Lakewood Sun Post (Community news; Circulation 9,981); Sun Herald (Regional news; Circulation 15,830); Sun Newspapers - North Olmsted Bureau (Regional news); The Sun (Community news; Circulation 3,409); West Side Sun News (Community news; Circulation 16,699)
Transportation: Commute to work: 92.4% car, 2.7% public transportation, 1.5% walk, 2.9% work from home (2000); Travel time to work: 25.5% less than 15 minutes, 41.2% 15 to 30 minutes, 23.3% 30 to 45 minutes, 6.6% 45 to 60 minutes, 3.5% 60 minutes or more (2000)

Additional Information Contacts

City of North Olmsted. . . . . (440) 777-8000
http://www.north-olmsted.com
North Olmsted Chamber of Commerce . . . . (440) 777-3368
http://www.nolmstedchamber.org

NORTH RANDALL (village). Covers a land area of 0.782 square miles and a water area of 0 square miles. Located at 41.43° N. Lat.; 81.53° W. Long. Elevation is 1,043 feet.
Population: 977 (1990); 906 (2000); 853 (2007); 809 (2012 projected); Race: 17.2% White, 74.7% Black, 0.8% Asian, 9.6% Hispanic of any race (2007); Density: 1,091.0 persons per square mile (2007); Average household size: 1.99 (2007); Median age: 42.5 (2007); Males per 100 females: 98.8 (2007); Marriage status: 36.6% never married, 35.9% now married, 7.5% widowed, 20.0% divorced (2000); Foreign born: 8.1% (2000); Ancestry (includes multiple ancestries): 72.6% Other groups, 4.3% Polish, 3.3% Italian, 3.0% African, 1.5% German (2000).
Economy: Single-family building permits issued: 0 (2007); Multi-family building permits issued: 0 (2007); Employment by occupation: 9.3% management, 18.1% professional, 20.4% services, 29.0% sales, 5.4% farming, 2.0% construction, 15.9% production (2000).
Income: Per capita income: $22,586 (2007); Median household income: $31,583 (2007); Average household income: $42,442 (2007); Percent of households with income of $100,000 or more: 7.5% (2007); Poverty rate: 11.4% (2000).
Education: Percent of population age 25 and over with: High school diploma (including GED) or higher: 67.7% (2007); Bachelor's degree or higher: 10.9% (2007); Master's degree or higher: 3.5% (2007).
Housing: Homeownership rate: 28.2% (2007); Median home value: $121,011 (2007); Median rent: $527 per month (2000); Median age of housing: 39 years (2000).
Transportation: Commute to work: 76.0% car, 6.3% public transportation, 10.5% walk, 1.2% work from home (2000); Travel time to work: 34.2% less than 15 minutes, 33.6% 15 to 30 minutes, 23.9% 30 to 45 minutes, 5.7% 45 to 60 minutes, 2.6% 60 minutes or more (2000)

Additional Information Contacts

Tri-City Chamber of Commerce . . . . (216) 454-0199
http://www.tricitychamber.com

NORTH ROYALTON (city). Covers a land area of 21.286 square miles and a water area of 0 square miles. Located at 41.32° N. Lat.; 81.74° W. Long. Elevation is 1,201 feet.
History: Dairy-processing and sawmilling center in the 19th century, North Royalton has since developed a variety of light industries. Settled 1811, incorporated as a village 1927, as a city 1960.
Population: 23,197 (1990); 28,648 (2000); 29,673 (2007); 30,190 (2012 projected); Race: 95.4% White, 0.9% Black, 2.3% Asian, 1.1% Hispanic of any race (2007); Density: 1,394.0 persons per square mile (2007); Average household size: 2.49 (2007); Median age: 41.4 (2007); Males per 100 females: 94.7 (2007); Marriage status: 24.8% never married, 59.8% now married, 6.9% widowed, 8.5% divorced (2000); Foreign born: 6.8% (2000); Ancestry (includes multiple ancestries): 25.4% German, 18.4% Polish, 14.0% Irish, 12.3% Italian, 8.3% English (2000).
Economy: Unemployment rate: 6.4% (6/2008); Total civilian labor force: 17,751 (6/2008); Single-family building permits issued: 91 (2007); Multi-family building permits issued: 30 (2007); Employment by occupation: 17.2% management, 19.9% professional, 11.6% services, 30.1% sales, 0.2% farming, 8.4% construction, 12.7% production (2000).
Income: Per capita income: $32,094 (2007); Median household income: $66,000 (2007); Average household income: $79,487 (2007); Percent of households with income of $100,000 or more: 26.3% (2007); Poverty rate: 2.3% (2000).
Taxes: Total city taxes per capita: $471 (2006); City property taxes per capita: $149 (2006).
Education: Percent of population age 25 and over with: High school diploma (including GED) or higher: 88.0% (2007); Bachelor's degree or higher: 29.4% (2007); Master's degree or higher: 8.5% (2007).

School District(s)

North Royalton City (PK-12)
2005-06 Enrollment: 4,588 . . . . (440) 237-8800

Housing: Homeownership rate: 74.2% (2007); Median home value: $209,476 (2007); Median rent: $587 per month (2000); Median age of housing: 21 years (2000).
Transportation: Commute to work: 92.8% car, 1.7% public transportation, 1.0% walk, 3.9% work from home (2000); Travel time to work: 18.3% less than 15 minutes, 37.6% 15 to 30 minutes, 28.6% 30 to 45 minutes, 10.4% 45 to 60 minutes, 5.1% 60 minutes or more (2000)

Additional Information Contacts

City of North Royalton . . . . (440) 237-5686
http://www.northroyalton.org
North Royalton Chamber of Commerce. . . . . (440) 237-6180
http://www.nroyaltonchamber.com

OAKWOOD (village). Covers a land area of 3.459 square miles and a water area of <.001 square miles. Located at 41.36° N. Lat.; 81.50° W. Long. Elevation is 1,047 feet.
Population: 3,385 (1990); 3,667 (2000); 3,618 (2007); 3,572 (2012 projected); Race: 34.8% White, 61.7% Black, 0.4% Asian, 1.7% Hispanic of any race (2007); Density: 1,045.9 persons per square mile (2007); Average household size: 2.52 (2007); Median age: 45.9 (2007); Males per 100 females: 87.8 (2007); Marriage status: 28.1% never married, 44.8% now married, 12.2% widowed, 14.9% divorced (2000); Foreign born: 1.2% (2000); Ancestry (includes multiple ancestries): 53.4% Other groups, 13.6% German, 5.7% English, 5.5% Polish, 4.9% Irish (2000).
Economy: Single-family building permits issued: 40 (2007); Multi-family building permits issued: 0 (2007); Employment by occupation: 12.7% management, 16.2% professional, 11.9% services, 26.1% sales, 0.0% farming, 10.3% construction, 22.9% production (2000).
Income: Per capita income: $24,523 (2007); Median household income: $44,670 (2007); Average household income: $59,797 (2007); Percent of

households with income of $100,000 or more: 15.6% (2007); Poverty rate: 6.3% (2000).
Education: Percent of population age 25 and over with: High school diploma (including GED) or higher: 76.4% (2007); Bachelor's degree or higher: 17.3% (2007); Master's degree or higher: 6.0% (2007).

School District(s)

Paulding Exempted Village (PK-12)
2005-06 Enrollment: 1,728 . . . . (419) 399-4656
Housing: Homeownership rate: 72.0% (2007); Median home value: $147,374 (2007); Median rent: $420 per month (2000); Median age of housing: 36 years (2000).
Transportation: Commute to work: 94.0% car, 1.8% public transportation, 2.2% walk, 1.2% work from home (2000); Travel time to work: 20.3% less than 15 minutes, 43.7% 15 to 30 minutes, 26.3% 30 to 45 minutes, 5.0% 45 to 60 minutes, 4.8% 60 minutes or more (2000)

OLMSTED FALLS (city). Covers a land area of 4.131 square miles and a water area of 0 square miles. Located at 41.36° N. Lat.; 81.90° W. Long. Elevation is 768 feet.
Population: 6,784 (1990); 7,962 (2000); 8,470 (2007); 8,741 (2012 projected); Race: 95.8% White, 1.9% Black, 0.9% Asian, 1.6% Hispanic of any race (2007); Density: 2,050.1 persons per square mile (2007); Average household size: 2.46 (2007); Median age: 39.9 (2007); Males per 100 females: 92.6 (2007); Marriage status: 22.6% never married, 63.2% now married, 5.0% widowed, 9.2% divorced (2000); Foreign born: 2.4% (2000); Ancestry (includes multiple ancestries): 32.4% German, 21.2% Irish, 12.9% Italian, 11.9% English, 10.1% Polish (2000).
Economy: Single-family building permits issued: 10 (2007); Multi-family building permits issued: 0 (2007); Employment by occupation: 17.4% management, 24.1% professional, 10.6% services, 29.7% sales, 0.5% farming, 8.2% construction, 9.4% production (2000).
Income: Per capita income: $31,131 (2007); Median household income: $65,845 (2007); Average household income: $76,603 (2007); Percent of households with income of $100,000 or more: 22.6% (2007); Poverty rate: 2.1% (2000).
Education: Percent of population age 25 and over with: High school diploma (including GED) or higher: 94.0% (2007); Bachelor's degree or higher: 36.6% (2007); Master's degree or higher: 11.7% (2007).

School District(s)

Olmsted Falls City (PK-12)
2005-06 Enrollment: 3,518 . . . . (440) 427-6000
Housing: Homeownership rate: 83.7% (2007); Median home value: $170,057 (2007); Median rent: $552 per month (2000); Median age of housing: 26 years (2000).
Safety: Violent crime rate: 9.6 per 10,000 population; Property crime rate: 115.8 per 10,000 population (2007).
Transportation: Commute to work: 93.0% car, 3.5% public transportation, 0.3% walk, 2.5% work from home (2000); Travel time to work: 20.4% less than 15 minutes, 37.7% 15 to 30 minutes, 26.8% 30 to 45 minutes, 8.9% 45 to 60 minutes, 6.1% 60 minutes or more (2000)
Additional Information Contacts
City of Olmsted Falls . . . . (440) 235-5550
http://www.olmstedfalls.org
Olmsted Chamber of Commerce . . . . (440) 235-0032
http://www.olmstedchamber.org

ORANGE (village). Covers a land area of 3.801 square miles and a water area of 0 square miles. Located at 41.44° N. Lat.; 81.47° W. Long. Elevation is 1,158 feet.
Population: 2,810 (1990); 3,236 (2000); 3,356 (2007); 3,419 (2012 projected); Race: 78.0% White, 14.9% Black, 4.9% Asian, 0.7% Hispanic of any race (2007); Density: 882.9 persons per square mile (2007); Average household size: 2.69 (2007); Median age: 45.8 (2007); Males per 100 females: 97.1 (2007); Marriage status: 18.8% never married, 68.9% now married, 6.8% widowed, 5.6% divorced (2000); Foreign born: 8.9% (2000); Ancestry (includes multiple ancestries): 19.8% Other groups, 10.6% United States or American, 10.3% German, 9.9% Russian, 6.4% Hungarian (2000).
Economy: Single-family building permits issued: 3 (2007); Multi-family building permits issued: 0 (2007); Employment by occupation: 21.5% management, 37.0% professional, 9.9% services, 23.5% sales, 0.0% farming, 4.8% construction, 3.2% production (2000).
Income: Per capita income: $53,578 (2007); Median household income: $101,736 (2007); Average household income: $143,959 (2007); Percent of households with income of $100,000 or more: 50.8% (2007); Poverty rate: 3.6% (2000).
Education: Percent of population age 25 and over with: High school diploma (including GED) or higher: 95.6% (2007); Bachelor's degree or higher: 58.5% (2007); Master's degree or higher: 27.2% (2007).
Housing: Homeownership rate: 95.5% (2007); Median home value: $322,581 (2007); Median rent: $931 per month (2000); Median age of housing: 32 years (2000).
Safety: Violent crime rate: 18.1 per 10,000 population; Property crime rate: 159.8 per 10,000 population (2007).
Transportation: Commute to work: 91.6% car, 2.2% public transportation, 0.6% walk, 5.5% work from home (2000); Travel time to work: 28.4% less than 15 minutes, 33.4% 15 to 30 minutes, 29.4% 30 to 45 minutes, 6.3% 45 to 60 minutes, 2.5% 60 minutes or more (2000)
Additional Information Contacts
Village of Orange . . . . (440) 498-4400
http://www.orangevillage.com

PARMA (city). Covers a land area of 19.960 square miles and a water area of 0.017 square miles. Located at 41.39° N. Lat.; 81.72° W. Long. Elevation is 866 feet.
History: Named for the Italian city of Parma. Population declined between 1970 and 1990, reflecting the pattern in conjunction with the greater Northern Ohio area. Settled 1816. Incorporated 1924.
Population: 87,876 (1990); 85,655 (2000); 80,088 (2007); 75,855 (2012 projected); Race: 94.6% White, 1.3% Black, 1.9% Asian, 1.8% Hispanic of any race (2007); Density: 4,012.4 persons per square mile (2007); Average household size: 2.38 (2007); Median age: 41.8 (2007); Males per 100 females: 91.6 (2007); Marriage status: 24.7% never married, 57.0% now married, 9.7% widowed, 8.7% divorced (2000); Foreign born: 9.1% (2000); Ancestry (includes multiple ancestries): 24.5% German, 18.1% Polish, 14.6% Irish, 13.5% Italian, 9.3% Slovak (2000).
Economy: Unemployment rate: 7.8% (6/2008); Total civilian labor force: 42,948 (6/2008); Single-family building permits issued: 20 (2007); Multi-family building permits issued: 0 (2007); Employment by occupation: 12.3% management, 17.7% professional, 14.2% services, 31.9% sales, 0.0% farming, 8.6% construction, 15.3% production (2000).
Income: Per capita income: $24,252 (2007); Median household income: $48,791 (2007); Average household income: $57,231 (2007); Percent of households with income of $100,000 or more: 11.5% (2007); Poverty rate: 4.9% (2000).
Taxes: Total city taxes per capita: $540 (2006); City property taxes per capita: $88 (2006).
Education: Percent of population age 25 and over with: High school diploma (including GED) or higher: 83.4% (2007); Bachelor's degree or higher: 17.9% (2007); Master's degree or higher: 5.2% (2007).

School District(s)

Parma City (PK-12)
2005-06 Enrollment: 12,988 . . . . (440) 842-5300
Parma Community (KG-08)
2005-06 Enrollment: 319 . . . . (440) 888-5490
Summit Academy Secondary - Parma (07-12)
2005-06 Enrollment: 45 . . . . (440) 888-5407
Summit Academy-Parma (01-08)
2005-06 Enrollment: 92 . . . . (440) 888-5407

Four-year College(s)

Bryant and Stratton College-Parma (Private, For-profit)
Fall 2007 Enrollment: 696 . . . . (216) 265-3151
2007-08 Tuition: In-state $11,920; Out-of-state $11,920
Housing: Homeownership rate: 77.3% (2007); Median home value: $136,924 (2007); Median rent: $534 per month (2000); Median age of housing: 42 years (2000).
Safety: Violent crime rate: 22.7 per 10,000 population; Property crime rate: 215.1 per 10,000 population (2007).
Newspapers: Horizons (Regional news; Circulation 4,395)
Transportation: Commute to work: 93.3% car, 3.1% public transportation, 1.4% walk, 1.6% work from home (2000); Travel time to work: 22.8% less than 15 minutes, 43.1% 15 to 30 minutes, 23.9% 30 to 45 minutes, 6.5% 45 to 60 minutes, 3.7% 60 minutes or more (2000)
Additional Information Contacts
City of Parma . . . . (440) 885-8000
http://www.cityofparma-oh.gov
Parma Area Chamber of Commerce . . . . (440) 886-1700
http://www.parmaareachamber.org

PARMA HEIGHTS (city). Covers a land area of 4.199 square miles and a water area of 0 square miles. Located at 41.38° N. Lat.; 81.76° W. Long. Elevation is 856 feet.

History: Named for the city in Italy. Settled 1818; set off from Parma and incorporated 1912.

Population: 21,448 (1990); 21,659 (2000); 20,328 (2007); 19,319 (2012 projected); Race: 92.8% White, 1.7% Black, 3.2% Asian, 2.0% Hispanic of any race (2007); Density: 4,841.6 persons per square mile (2007); Average household size: 2.17 (2007); Median age: 44.4 (2007); Males per 100 females: 87.2 (2007); Marriage status: 23.6% never married, 53.1% now married, 12.3% widowed, 10.9% divorced (2000); Foreign born: 10.2% (2000); Ancestry (includes multiple ancestries): 25.0% German, 16.3% Irish, 13.1% Polish, 12.0% Italian, 7.8% Slovak (2000).

Economy: Single-family building permits issued: 0 (2007); Multi-family building permits issued: 0 (2007); Employment by occupation: 12.2% management, 18.3% professional, 12.2% services, 35.0% sales, 0.0% farming, 7.9% construction, 14.3% production (2000).

Income: Per capita income: $23,160 (2007); Median household income: $41,282 (2007); Average household income: $49,902 (2007); Percent of households with income of $100,000 or more: 8.6% (2007); Poverty rate: 7.6% (2000).

Education: Percent of population age 25 and over with: High school diploma (including GED) or higher: 82.7% (2007); Bachelor's degree or higher: 18.7% (2007); Master's degree or higher: 5.8% (2007).

School District(s)

Parma City (PK-12)
2005-06 Enrollment: 12,988 . . . . (440) 842-5300

Two-year College(s)

Quest Career College (Private, For-profit)
Fall 2007 Enrollment: n/a. . . . . (440) 886-5544

Housing: Homeownership rate: 59.1% (2007); Median home value: $137,001 (2007); Median rent: $526 per month (2000); Median age of housing: 40 years (2000).

Safety: Violent crime rate: 8.5 per 10,000 population; Property crime rate: 217.8 per 10,000 population (2007).

Transportation: Commute to work: 93.1% car, 3.5% public transportation, 1.2% walk, 1.8% work from home (2000); Travel time to work: 25.7% less than 15 minutes, 41.2% 15 to 30 minutes, 22.2% 30 to 45 minutes, 7.1% 45 to 60 minutes, 3.8% 60 minutes or more (2000)

Additional Information Contacts

City of Parma Heights . . . . (440) 884-9600
http://www.parmaheightsoh.gov
Parma Area Chamber of Commerce . . . . (440) 886-1700
http://www.parmaareachamber.org

PEPPER PIKE (city). Covers a land area of 7.093 square miles and a water area of 0.007 square miles. Located at 41.47° N. Lat.; 81.46° W. Long. Elevation is 1,060 feet.

Population: 6,185 (1990); 6,040 (2000); 5,722 (2007); 5,475 (2012 projected); Race: 88.9% White, 6.0% Black, 3.9% Asian, 1.3% Hispanic of any race (2007); Density: 806.7 persons per square mile (2007); Average household size: 2.67 (2007); Median age: 50.5 (2007); Males per 100 females: 90.3 (2007); Marriage status: 17.0% never married, 73.6% now married, 5.4% widowed, 3.9% divorced (2000); Foreign born: 12.2% (2000); Ancestry (includes multiple ancestries): 13.3% German, 12.7% Other groups, 9.6% English, 9.3% Irish, 9.1% Russian (2000).

Economy: Single-family building permits issued: 15 (2007); Multi-family building permits issued: 0 (2007); Employment by occupation: 25.4% management, 38.5% professional, 5.9% services, 25.9% sales, 0.3% farming, 0.9% construction, 3.0% production (2000).

Income: Per capita income: $76,235 (2007); Median household income: $144,664 (2007); Average household income: $201,389 (2007); Percent of households with income of $100,000 or more: 63.5% (2007); Poverty rate: 3.7% (2000).

Education: Percent of population age 25 and over with: High school diploma (including GED) or higher: 97.3% (2007); Bachelor's degree or higher: 71.8% (2007); Master's degree or higher: 38.1% (2007).

School District(s)

Orange City (PK-12)
2005-06 Enrollment: 2,275 . . . . (216) 831-8600

Four-year College(s)

Ursuline College (Private, Not-for-profit, Roman Catholic)
Fall 2007 Enrollment: 1,550. . . . . (440) 449-4200
2007-08 Tuition: In-state $22,910; Out-of-state $22,910

Housing: Homeownership rate: 95.7% (2007); Median home value: $420,188 (2007); Median rent: $523 per month (2000); Median age of housing: 34 years (2000).

Safety: Violent crime rate: 5.3 per 10,000 population; Property crime rate: 103.5 per 10,000 population (2007).

Transportation: Commute to work: 91.1% car, 1.6% public transportation, 1.5% walk, 5.5% work from home (2000); Travel time to work: 28.2% less than 15 minutes, 40.7% 15 to 30 minutes, 27.4% 30 to 45 minutes, 1.9% 45 to 60 minutes, 1.8% 60 minutes or more (2000)

Additional Information Contacts

City of Pepper Pike . . . . (216) 831-8500
http://www.pepperpike.org

RICHMOND HEIGHTS (city). Covers a land area of 4.370 square miles and a water area of 0.006 square miles. Located at 41.55° N. Lat.; 81.50° W. Long. Elevation is 869 feet.

Population: 9,611 (1990); 10,944 (2000); 10,389 (2007); 9,946 (2012 projected); Race: 58.1% White, 33.4% Black, 5.4% Asian, 1.9% Hispanic of any race (2007); Density: 2,377.4 persons per square mile (2007); Average household size: 2.22 (2007); Median age: 43.6 (2007); Males per 100 females: 89.5 (2007); Marriage status: 29.4% never married, 51.6% now married, 9.0% widowed, 10.0% divorced (2000); Foreign born: 17.4% (2000); Ancestry (includes multiple ancestries): 30.2% Other groups, 12.5% German, 11.6% Italian, 6.6% Polish, 6.3% Irish (2000).

Economy: Single-family building permits issued: 26 (2007); Multi-family building permits issued: 0 (2007); Employment by occupation: 16.6% management, 25.5% professional, 12.8% services, 26.8% sales, 0.2% farming, 4.6% construction, 13.5% production (2000).

Income: Per capita income: $29,651 (2007); Median household income: $48,534 (2007); Average household income: $65,091 (2007); Percent of households with income of $100,000 or more: 18.3% (2007); Poverty rate: 5.3% (2000).

Education: Percent of population age 25 and over with: High school diploma (including GED) or higher: 89.4% (2007); Bachelor's degree or higher: 36.0% (2007); Master's degree or higher: 12.0% (2007).

School District(s)

Richmond Heights Local (PK-12)
2005-06 Enrollment: 1,137 . . . . (216) 692-8485

Housing: Homeownership rate: 63.3% (2007); Median home value: $171,774 (2007); Median rent: $525 per month (2000); Median age of housing: 34 years (2000).

Hospitals: University Hospitals Richmond Medical Center (250 beds)

Transportation: Commute to work: 92.7% car, 2.6% public transportation, 1.1% walk, 3.0% work from home (2000); Travel time to work: 19.4% less than 15 minutes, 44.8% 15 to 30 minutes, 25.1% 30 to 45 minutes, 6.4% 45 to 60 minutes, 4.3% 60 minutes or more (2000)

Additional Information Contacts

City of Richmond Heights . . . . (216) 383-6300
http://www.richmondheightsohio.org

ROCKY RIVER (city). Covers a land area of 4.755 square miles and a water area of 0.873 square miles. Located at 41.47° N. Lat.; 81.84° W. Long. Elevation is 689 feet.

History: Named for its location at the mouth of the Rocky River, so named because of its rocky river bed. The town of Rocky River was established in 1815 on Lake Erie at the mouth of the Rocky River.

Population: 20,410 (1990); 20,735 (2000); 19,379 (2007); 18,339 (2012 projected); Race: 96.2% White, 0.5% Black, 1.4% Asian, 1.4% Hispanic of any race (2007); Density: 4,075.6 persons per square mile (2007); Average household size: 2.08 (2007); Median age: 46.4 (2007); Males per 100 females: 83.0 (2007); Marriage status: 21.0% never married, 57.3% now married, 11.4% widowed, 10.3% divorced (2000); Foreign born: 7.0% (2000); Ancestry (includes multiple ancestries): 28.1% German, 26.9% Irish, 12.4% English, 9.4% Italian, 6.6% Polish (2000).

Economy: Single-family building permits issued: 2 (2007); Multi-family building permits issued: 0 (2007); Employment by occupation: 21.7% management, 27.3% professional, 9.6% services, 32.2% sales, 0.1% farming, 3.8% construction, 5.4% production (2000).

Income: Per capita income: $39,534 (2007); Median household income: $57,585 (2007); Average household income: $81,903 (2007); Percent of households with income of $100,000 or more: 24.1% (2007); Poverty rate: 2.3% (2000).

Education: Percent of population age 25 and over with: High school diploma (including GED) or higher: 93.3% (2007); Bachelor's degree or higher: 46.6% (2007); Master's degree or higher: 17.9% (2007).

School District(s)

Rocky River City (PK-12)
2005-06 Enrollment: 2,641 . . . . (440) 333-6000

Two-year College(s)

Brown Aveda Institute (Private, For-profit)
Fall 2007 Enrollment: 98 . . . . (440) 255-9494

Housing: Homeownership rate: 71.6% (2007); Median home value: $215,385 (2007); Median rent: $614 per month (2000); Median age of housing: 41 years (2000).

Newspapers: Lorain County Times (Community news; Circulation 3,200); Westlaker Times (Local news; Circulation 3,000)

Transportation: Commute to work: 88.7% car, 3.5% public transportation, 2.8% walk, 4.4% work from home (2000); Travel time to work: 27.7% less than 15 minutes, 44.4% 15 to 30 minutes, 21.2% 30 to 45 minutes, 4.5% 45 to 60 minutes, 2.2% 60 minutes or more (2000)

Additional Information Contacts

City of Rocky River . . . . (440) 331-0600
http://www.rrcity.com
Rocky River Chamber of Commerce . . . . (440) 331-1140
http://www.rockyriverchamber.com

SEVEN HILLS (city). Covers a land area of 5.009 square miles and a water area of 0 square miles. Located at 41.38° N. Lat.; 81.67° W. Long. Elevation is 883 feet.

History: Named for the seven hills of Rome. Incorporated as a city 1961. Part of its city hall is an old schoolhouse, built in 1861.

Population: 12,339 (1990); 12,080 (2000); 11,854 (2007); 11,649 (2012 projected); Race: 96.8% White, 0.2% Black, 2.3% Asian, 1.0% Hispanic of any race (2007); Density: 2,366.5 persons per square mile (2007); Average household size: 2.45 (2007); Median age: 49.6 (2007); Males per 100 females: 93.4 (2007); Marriage status: 19.5% never married, 65.5% now married, 9.5% widowed, 5.5% divorced (2000); Foreign born: 11.5% (2000); Ancestry (includes multiple ancestries): 22.6% Polish, 19.1% German, 16.4% Italian, 9.2% Irish, 8.9% Slovak (2000).

Economy: Single-family building permits issued: 22 (2007); Multi-family building permits issued: 0 (2007); Employment by occupation: 15.7% management, 23.0% professional, 11.2% services, 29.2% sales, 0.1% farming, 8.1% construction, 12.8% production (2000).

Income: Per capita income: $29,997 (2007); Median household income: $62,660 (2007); Average household income: $73,401 (2007); Percent of households with income of $100,000 or more: 22.8% (2007); Poverty rate: 2.6% (2000).

Education: Percent of population age 25 and over with: High school diploma (including GED) or higher: 85.0% (2007); Bachelor's degree or higher: 22.1% (2007); Master's degree or higher: 7.6% (2007).

School District(s)

Parma City (PK-12)
2005-06 Enrollment: 12,988 . . . . (440) 842-5300

Housing: Homeownership rate: 96.5% (2007); Median home value: $194,288 (2007); Median rent: $643 per month (2000); Median age of housing: 34 years (2000).

Transportation: Commute to work: 94.5% car, 2.0% public transportation, 0.1% walk, 2.9% work from home (2000); Travel time to work: 19.8% less than 15 minutes, 48.3% 15 to 30 minutes, 25.1% 30 to 45 minutes, 4.2% 45 to 60 minutes, 2.5% 60 minutes or more (2000)

Additional Information Contacts

City of Seven Hills . . . . (216) 524-4421
http://www.sevenhillsohio.org
Parma Area Chamber of Commerce . . . . (440) 886-1700
http://www.parmaareachamber.org

SHAKER HEIGHTS (city). Covers a land area of 6.276 square miles and a water area of 0.043 square miles. Located at 41.47° N. Lat.; 81.55° W. Long. Elevation is 1,050 feet.

History: Named for a community of Shakers founded in the region in the early 1800s. The Shakers founded a religious community here in the early 1800's. The site was acquired in 1905 by O.P. and M.J. VanSweringen, railroad tycoons, who connected it with downtown Cleveland by a rapid transit line. Shaker Heights grew as a residential area.

Population: 30,831 (1990); 29,405 (2000); 27,239 (2007); 25,617 (2012 projected); Race: 55.6% White, 37.0% Black, 3.9% Asian, 1.1% Hispanic of any race (2007); Density: 4,339.9 persons per square mile (2007); Average household size: 2.37 (2007); Median age: 41.8 (2007); Males per 100 females: 84.4 (2007); Marriage status: 25.5% never married, 56.3% now married, 7.6% widowed, 10.6% divorced (2000); Foreign born: 7.2% (2000); Ancestry (includes multiple ancestries): 36.6% Other groups, 13.2% German, 9.4% Irish, 9.2% English, 5.1% Russian (2000).

Economy: Unemployment rate: 6.1% (6/2008); Total civilian labor force: 14,952 (6/2008); Single-family building permits issued: 2 (2007); Multi-family building permits issued: 0 (2007); Employment by occupation: 21.2% management, 42.1% professional, 7.7% services, 21.7% sales, 0.0% farming, 1.7% construction, 5.5% production (2000).

Income: Per capita income: $45,463 (2007); Median household income: $70,809 (2007); Average household income: $107,193 (2007); Percent of households with income of $100,000 or more: 34.1% (2007); Poverty rate: 6.9% (2000).

Taxes: Total city taxes per capita: $1,225 (2006); City property taxes per capita: $269 (2006).

Education: Percent of population age 25 and over with: High school diploma (including GED) or higher: 94.6% (2007); Bachelor's degree or higher: 61.6% (2007); Master's degree or higher: 35.5% (2007).

School District(s)

Shaker Heights City (PK-12)
2005-06 Enrollment: 5,631 . . . . (216) 295-4000

Housing: Homeownership rate: 65.2% (2007); Median home value: $221,489 (2007); Median rent: $679 per month (2000); Median age of housing: 55 years (2000).

Transportation: Commute to work: 85.6% car, 8.1% public transportation, 1.4% walk, 4.1% work from home (2000); Travel time to work: 22.0% less than 15 minutes, 47.9% 15 to 30 minutes, 22.1% 30 to 45 minutes, 5.1% 45 to 60 minutes, 2.9% 60 minutes or more (2000)

Additional Information Contacts

City of Shaker Heights . . . . (216) 491-1400
http://www.shakeronline.com

SOLON (city). Covers a land area of 20.552 square miles and a water area of 0.043 square miles. Located at 41.39° N. Lat.; 81.44° W. Long. Elevation is 1,040 feet.

History: Named for Solon Bull, one of the town's early settlers. Founded 1820. Incorporated as a city 1960.

Population: 18,548 (1990); 21,802 (2000); 22,421 (2007); 22,679 (2012 projected); Race: 84.2% White, 8.0% Black, 6.3% Asian, 0.9% Hispanic of any race (2007); Density: 1,091.0 persons per square mile (2007); Average household size: 2.87 (2007); Median age: 41.7 (2007); Males per 100 females: 95.7 (2007); Marriage status: 18.9% never married, 68.4% now married, 5.2% widowed, 7.5% divorced (2000); Foreign born: 8.6% (2000); Ancestry (includes multiple ancestries): 16.8% German, 14.5% Italian, 13.8% Other groups, 11.6% Irish, 10.0% Polish (2000).

Economy: Single-family building permits issued: 23 (2007); Multi-family building permits issued: 2 (2007); Employment by occupation: 22.8% management, 30.4% professional, 7.9% services, 28.5% sales, 0.0% farming, 3.9% construction, 6.4% production (2000).

Income: Per capita income: $42,375 (2007); Median household income: $92,856 (2007); Average household income: $121,448 (2007); Percent of households with income of $100,000 or more: 45.7% (2007); Poverty rate: 2.5% (2000).

Education: Percent of population age 25 and over with: High school diploma (including GED) or higher: 94.6% (2007); Bachelor's degree or higher: 50.7% (2007); Master's degree or higher: 22.1% (2007).

School District(s)

Solon City (PK-12)
2005-06 Enrollment: 5,345 . . . . (440) 248-1600

Housing: Homeownership rate: 87.6% (2007); Median home value: $264,832 (2007); Median rent: $753 per month (2000); Median age of housing: 23 years (2000).

Safety: Violent crime rate: 9.0 per 10,000 population; Property crime rate: 118.7 per 10,000 population (2007).

Transportation: Commute to work: 94.7% car, 0.5% public transportation, 0.7% walk, 3.9% work from home (2000); Travel time to work: 28.1% less than 15 minutes, 36.7% 15 to 30 minutes, 25.2% 30 to 45 minutes, 7.2% 45 to 60 minutes, 2.8% 60 minutes or more (2000)

Additional Information Contacts

City of Solon . . . . (440) 248-1155
http://www.solonohio.org
Solon Chamber of Commerce . . . . (440) 248-5080
http://www.solonchamber.com

SOUTH EUCLID (city). Aka Bluestone. Covers a land area of 4.689 square miles and a water area of 0 square miles. Located at 41.52° N. Lat.; 81.52° W. Long. Elevation is 958 feet.

History: Named for Euclid, the mathematician of Alexandria. Site of Notre Dame College, a Roman Catholic school for women. Incorporated as a city 1940.
Population: 23,866 (1990); 23,537 (2000); 21,824 (2007); 20,546 (2012 projected); Race: 68.6% White, 27.6% Black, 1.6% Asian, 1.1% Hispanic of any race (2007); Density: 4,653.9 persons per square mile (2007); Average household size: 2.42 (2007); Median age: 40.5 (2007); Males per 100 females: 86.1 (2007); Marriage status: 26.1% never married, 55.2% now married, 8.0% widowed, 10.8% divorced (2000); Foreign born: 9.4% (2000); Ancestry (includes multiple ancestries): 25.6% Other groups, 15.4% Italian, 13.9% German, 13.7% Irish, 6.1% Russian (2000).
Economy: Unemployment rate: 6.8% (6/2008); Total civilian labor force: 12,521 (6/2008); Single-family building permits issued: 9 (2007); Multi-family building permits issued: 0 (2007); Employment by occupation: 13.1% management, 27.2% professional, 12.7% services, 31.4% sales, 0.0% farming, 5.1% construction, 10.4% production (2000).
Income: Per capita income: $25,943 (2007); Median household income: $54,090 (2007); Average household income: $62,468 (2007); Percent of households with income of $100,000 or more: 14.9% (2007); Poverty rate: 4.5% (2000).
Taxes: Total city taxes per capita: $522 (2006); City property taxes per capita: $232 (2006).
Education: Percent of population age 25 and over with: High school diploma (including GED) or higher: 90.0% (2007); Bachelor's degree or higher: 36.6% (2007); Master's degree or higher: 13.0% (2007).

School District(s)

South Euclid-Lyndhurst City (PK-12)
2005-06 Enrollment: 4,528 . . . . (216) 691-2000
Housing: Homeownership rate: 84.1% (2007); Median home value: $128,727 (2007); Median rent: $614 per month (2000); Median age of housing: 47 years (2000).
Safety: Violent crime rate: 19.5 per 10,000 population; Property crime rate: 269.0 per 10,000 population (2007).
Transportation: Commute to work: 91.6% car, 3.3% public transportation, 1.3% walk, 3.3% work from home (2000); Travel time to work: 24.2% less than 15 minutes, 43.9% 15 to 30 minutes, 22.4% 30 to 45 minutes, 6.0% 45 to 60 minutes, 3.6% 60 minutes or more (2000)

Additional Information Contacts

City of South Euclid . . . . (216) 381-0400
http://www.cityofsoutheuclid.com

STRONGSVILLE (city). Covers a land area of 24.645 square miles and a water area of 0.007 square miles. Located at 41.31° N. Lat.; 81.83° W. Long. Elevation is 932 feet.
History: Named for Caleb Strong (1745-1819), a Massachusetts statesman. The city's population doubled between 1970 and 1990. Settled 1816. Incorporated 1927.
Population: 35,308 (1990); 43,858 (2000); 43,708 (2007); 43,303 (2012 projected); Race: 92.9% White, 1.6% Black, 3.8% Asian, 1.4% Hispanic of any race (2007); Density: 1,773.5 persons per square mile (2007); Average household size: 2.65 (2007); Median age: 41.7 (2007); Males per 100 females: 94.7 (2007); Marriage status: 20.7% never married, 66.9% now married, 5.3% widowed, 7.2% divorced (2000); Foreign born: 6.5% (2000); Ancestry (includes multiple ancestries): 29.1% German, 18.0% Irish, 13.4% Italian, 12.6% Polish, 10.7% English (2000).
Economy: Unemployment rate: 6.3% (6/2008); Total civilian labor force: 25,149 (6/2008); Single-family building permits issued: 77 (2007); Multi-family building permits issued: 0 (2007); Employment by occupation: 19.9% management, 22.4% professional, 10.1% services, 30.8% sales, 0.1% farming, 6.3% construction, 10.4% production (2000).
Income: Per capita income: $35,920 (2007); Median household income: $78,837 (2007); Average household income: $94,972 (2007); Percent of households with income of $100,000 or more: 35.4% (2007); Poverty rate: 2.2% (2000).
Education: Percent of population age 25 and over with: High school diploma (including GED) or higher: 93.1% (2007); Bachelor's degree or higher: 37.5% (2007); Master's degree or higher: 13.1% (2007).

School District(s)

Strongsville City (PK-12)
2005-06 Enrollment: 7,400 . . . . (440) 572-7000

Two-year College(s)

ITT Technical Institute-Strongsville (Private, For-profit)
Fall 2007 Enrollment: 550 . . . . (440) 234-9091
2007-08 Tuition: In-state $15,600; Out-of-state $15,600
Stautzenberger College-Strongsville Campus (Private, For-profit)
Fall 2007 Enrollment: 282 . . . . (440) 846-1999
2007-08 Tuition: In-state $7,290; Out-of-state $7,290
Housing: Homeownership rate: 83.0% (2007); Median home value: $208,068 (2007); Median rent: $573 per month (2000); Median age of housing: 21 years (2000).
Transportation: Commute to work: 93.2% car, 2.2% public transportation, 0.7% walk, 3.4% work from home (2000); Travel time to work: 22.9% less than 15 minutes, 34.0% 15 to 30 minutes, 28.5% 30 to 45 minutes, 10.1% 45 to 60 minutes, 4.5% 60 minutes or more (2000)

Additional Information Contacts

City of Strongsville . . . . (440) 580-3100
http://www.strongsville.org
Strongsville Chamber of Commerce . . . . (440) 238-3366
http://www.strongsvillechamber.com

UNIVERSITY HEIGHTS (city). Covers a land area of 1.834 square miles and a water area of 0 square miles. Located at 41.49° N. Lat.; 81.53° W. Long. Elevation is 1,027 feet.
History: Named for it being home to John Carroll University. University Heights grew as a residential community. It took its name from John Carroll University, a liberal arts college founded here by the Jesuit Order in 1886.
Population: 14,790 (1990); 14,146 (2000); 13,045 (2007); 12,254 (2012 projected); Race: 72.1% White, 23.4% Black, 1.9% Asian, 1.8% Hispanic of any race (2007); Density: 7,113.2 persons per square mile (2007); Average household size: 2.71 (2007); Median age: 33.6 (2007); Males per 100 females: 90.7 (2007); Marriage status: 34.5% never married, 52.4% now married, 6.0% widowed, 7.1% divorced (2000); Foreign born: 6.5% (2000); Ancestry (includes multiple ancestries): 27.2% Other groups, 16.1% German, 15.8% Irish, 10.4% Italian, 8.6% Polish (2000).
Economy: Single-family building permits issued: 0 (2007); Multi-family building permits issued: 0 (2007); Employment by occupation: 20.0% management, 33.7% professional, 10.3% services, 26.0% sales, 0.0% farming, 3.2% construction, 6.7% production (2000).
Income: Per capita income: $31,938 (2007); Median household income: $70,198 (2007); Average household income: $84,631 (2007); Percent of households with income of $100,000 or more: 28.2% (2007); Poverty rate: 5.8% (2000).
Education: Percent of population age 25 and over with: High school diploma (including GED) or higher: 93.9% (2007); Bachelor's degree or higher: 55.1% (2007); Master's degree or higher: 27.1% (2007).

School District(s)

Cleveland Heights-University Heights City (PK-12)
2005-06 Enrollment: 6,376 . . . . (216) 371-7171
Housing: Homeownership rate: 74.9% (2007); Median home value: $167,751 (2007); Median rent: $653 per month (2000); Median age of housing: 50 years (2000).
Safety: Violent crime rate: 15.5 per 10,000 population; Property crime rate: 195.9 per 10,000 population (2007).
Transportation: Commute to work: 79.2% car, 6.2% public transportation, 9.2% walk, 4.8% work from home (2000); Travel time to work: 26.8% less than 15 minutes, 41.3% 15 to 30 minutes, 25.2% 30 to 45 minutes, 5.2% 45 to 60 minutes, 1.4% 60 minutes or more (2000)

Additional Information Contacts

City of University Heights. . . . . (216) 932-7800
http://www.universityheights.com

VALLEY VIEW (village). Covers a land area of 5.631 square miles and a water area of 0.004 square miles. Located at 41.38° N. Lat.; 81.61° W. Long. Elevation is 643 feet.
Population: 2,137 (1990); 2,179 (2000); 2,066 (2007); 1,975 (2012 projected); Race: 98.3% White, 0.2% Black, 0.5% Asian, 0.5% Hispanic of any race (2007); Density: 366.9 persons per square mile (2007); Average household size: 2.71 (2007); Median age: 45.6 (2007); Males per 100 females: 98.5 (2007); Marriage status: 22.1% never married, 65.3% now married, 5.6% widowed, 7.0% divorced (2000); Foreign born: 3.8% (2000); Ancestry (includes multiple ancestries): 24.6% Polish, 19.5% German, 19.1% Italian, 16.6% Irish, 8.1% English (2000).
Economy: Single-family building permits issued: 0 (2007); Multi-family building permits issued: 0 (2007); Employment by occupation: 17.6% management, 20.3% professional, 13.1% services, 28.9% sales, 0.4% farming, 9.9% construction, 9.9% production (2000).
Income: Per capita income: $31,574 (2007); Median household income: $75,336 (2007); Average household income: $85,607 (2007); Percent of

households with income of $100,000 or more: 30.7% (2007); Poverty rate: 3.1% (2000).
Education: Percent of population age 25 and over with: High school diploma (including GED) or higher: 86.9% (2007); Bachelor's degree or higher: 22.4% (2007); Master's degree or higher: 7.9% (2007).

Vocational/Technical School(s)

Ohio Center for Broadcasting (Private, For-profit)
Fall 2007 Enrollment: 216 . . . . (216) 447-9117
2007-08 Tuition: $14,616

Housing: Homeownership rate: 92.3% (2007); Median home value: $225,493 (2007); Median rent: $554 per month (2000); Median age of housing: 31 years (2000).
Transportation: Commute to work: 95.1% car, 0.7% public transportation, 0.6% walk, 3.3% work from home (2000); Travel time to work: 30.5% less than 15 minutes, 45.4% 15 to 30 minutes, 17.7% 30 to 45 minutes, 4.2% 45 to 60 minutes, 2.1% 60 minutes or more (2000)

Additional Information Contacts

Village of Valley View. . . . . (216) 524-6511
http://www.valleyview.net

WALTON HILLS (village). Covers a land area of 6.876 square miles and a water area of 0 square miles. Located at 41.36° N. Lat.; 81.55° W. Long. Elevation is 991 feet.
Population: 2,278 (1990); 2,400 (2000); 2,328 (2007); 2,269 (2012 projected); Race: 95.2% White, 2.7% Black, 0.7% Asian, 1.4% Hispanic of any race (2007); Density: 338.6 persons per square mile (2007); Average household size: 2.58 (2007); Median age: 51.8 (2007); Males per 100 females: 92.1 (2007); Marriage status: 20.7% never married, 63.5% now married, 8.4% widowed, 7.5% divorced (2000); Foreign born: 4.0% (2000); Ancestry (includes multiple ancestries): 22.1% German, 20.0% Italian, 18.3% Polish, 10.0% Irish, 9.2% Slovak (2000).
Economy: Single-family building permits issued: 3 (2007); Multi-family building permits issued: 0 (2007); Employment by occupation: 17.9% management, 14.6% professional, 11.1% services, 31.6% sales, 0.0% farming, 12.1% construction, 12.6% production (2000).
Income: Per capita income: $32,018 (2007); Median household income: $68,819 (2007); Average household income: $80,285 (2007); Percent of households with income of $100,000 or more: 25.7% (2007); Poverty rate: 2.1% (2000).
Education: Percent of population age 25 and over with: High school diploma (including GED) or higher: 87.0% (2007); Bachelor's degree or higher: 19.5% (2007); Master's degree or higher: 5.0% (2007).
Housing: Homeownership rate: 96.9% (2007); Median home value: $222,040 (2007); Median rent: $450 per month (2000); Median age of housing: 35 years (2000).
Safety: Violent crime rate: 0.0 per 10,000 population; Property crime rate: 90.9 per 10,000 population (2007).
Transportation: Commute to work: 96.3% car, 0.2% public transportation, 0.0% walk, 3.5% work from home (2000); Travel time to work: 25.6% less than 15 minutes, 37.6% 15 to 30 minutes, 26.9% 30 to 45 minutes, 5.1% 45 to 60 minutes, 4.8% 60 minutes or more (2000)

WARRENSVILLE HEIGHTS (city). Covers a land area of 4.127 square miles and a water area of 0 square miles. Located at 41.43° N. Lat.; 81.52° W. Long. Elevation is 1,037 feet.
History: Named for the David Warren family. Incorporated 1927.
Population: 16,002 (1990); 15,109 (2000); 13,963 (2007); 13,135 (2012 projected); Race: 5.3% White, 91.5% Black, 1.0% Asian, 0.9% Hispanic of any race (2007); Density: 3,383.6 persons per square mile (2007); Average household size: 2.33 (2007); Median age: 39.3 (2007); Males per 100 females: 74.5 (2007); Marriage status: 34.5% never married, 40.6% now married, 8.9% widowed, 16.0% divorced (2000); Foreign born: 3.3% (2000); Ancestry (includes multiple ancestries): 78.6% Other groups, 2.1% African, 1.3% Irish, 1.0% United States or American, 0.9% Polish (2000).
Economy: Single-family building permits issued: 9 (2007); Multi-family building permits issued: 0 (2007); Employment by occupation: 10.0% management, 20.0% professional, 18.6% services, 30.1% sales, 0.1% farming, 4.0% construction, 17.4% production (2000).
Income: Per capita income: $21,839 (2007); Median household income: $40,484 (2007); Average household income: $49,660 (2007); Percent of households with income of $100,000 or more: 9.0% (2007); Poverty rate: 11.4% (2000).
Education: Percent of population age 25 and over with: High school diploma (including GED) or higher: 83.6% (2007); Bachelor's degree or higher: 16.4% (2007); Master's degree or higher: 5.1% (2007).

School District(s)

Warrensville Heights City (PK-12)
2005-06 Enrollment: 2,855 . . . . (216) 295-7710

Two-year College(s)

ITT Technical Institute-Warrensville Heights (Private, For-profit)
Fall 2007 Enrollment: 247 . . . . (216) 896-6500
2007-08 Tuition: In-state $15,600; Out-of-state $15,600

Housing: Homeownership rate: 46.7% (2007); Median home value: $104,474 (2007); Median rent: $545 per month (2000); Median age of housing: 39 years (2000).
Hospitals: South Pointe Hospital (232 beds)
Safety: Violent crime rate: 41.3 per 10,000 population; Property crime rate: 344.6 per 10,000 population (2007).
Newspapers: City News (Community news; Circulation 55,000)
Transportation: Commute to work: 86.3% car, 9.5% public transportation, 2.0% walk, 1.5% work from home (2000); Travel time to work: 20.9% less than 15 minutes, 39.2% 15 to 30 minutes, 25.4% 30 to 45 minutes, 7.3% 45 to 60 minutes, 7.2% 60 minutes or more (2000)

Additional Information Contacts

City of Warrensville Heights. . . . . (216) 587-6500
http://www.cityofwarrensville.com
Tri-City Chamber of Commerce. . . . . (216) 454-0199
http://www.tricitychamber.com

WESTLAKE (city). Aka Dover. Covers a land area of 15.898 square miles and a water area of 0.004 square miles. Located at 41.45° N. Lat.; 81.92° W. Long. Elevation is 709 feet.
History: Named for its location southwest of Lakewood. Incorporated as a city 1956.
Population: 27,018 (1990); 31,719 (2000); 31,153 (2007); 30,624 (2012 projected); Race: 91.4% White, 1.2% Black, 4.9% Asian, 1.4% Hispanic of any race (2007); Density: 1,959.6 persons per square mile (2007); Average household size: 2.41 (2007); Median age: 44.9 (2007); Males per 100 females: 89.5 (2007); Marriage status: 21.4% never married, 61.0% now married, 9.1% widowed, 8.5% divorced (2000); Foreign born: 8.4% (2000); Ancestry (includes multiple ancestries): 26.2% German, 23.3% Irish, 11.6% Italian, 10.0% English, 8.2% Other groups (2000).
Economy: Unemployment rate: 6.5% (6/2008); Total civilian labor force: 16,828 (6/2008); Single-family building permits issued: 72 (2007); Multi-family building permits issued: 0 (2007); Employment by occupation: 26.5% management, 26.4% professional, 8.8% services, 27.8% sales, 0.0% farming, 4.7% construction, 5.8% production (2000).
Income: Per capita income: $45,017 (2007); Median household income: $73,817 (2007); Average household income: $107,174 (2007); Percent of households with income of $100,000 or more: 33.7% (2007); Poverty rate: 2.5% (2000).
Taxes: Total city taxes per capita: $1,026 (2006); City property taxes per capita: $398 (2006).
Education: Percent of population age 25 and over with: High school diploma (including GED) or higher: 92.1% (2007); Bachelor's degree or higher: 45.4% (2007); Master's degree or higher: 17.9% (2007).

School District(s)

Westlake City (PK-12)
2005-06 Enrollment: 4,067 . . . . (440) 871-7300

Housing: Homeownership rate: 75.5% (2007); Median home value: $226,399 (2007); Median rent: $781 per month (2000); Median age of housing: 20 years (2000).
Hospitals: St. John West Shore Hospital (200 beds)
Newspapers: West Life (Community news; Circulation 15,000)
Transportation: Commute to work: 92.6% car, 2.3% public transportation, 0.6% walk, 3.9% work from home (2000); Travel time to work: 23.4% less than 15 minutes, 38.8% 15 to 30 minutes, 27.4% 30 to 45 minutes, 7.2% 45 to 60 minutes, 3.2% 60 minutes or more (2000)

Additional Information Contacts

City of Westlake. . . . . (440) 871-3300
http://www.cityofwestlake.org
West Shore Chamber of Commerce . . . . (440) 835-8787
http://www.westshorechamber.org

WOODMERE (village). Covers a land area of 0.329 square miles and a water area of 0 square miles. Located at 41.45° N. Lat.; 81.48° W. Long. Elevation is 1,171 feet.
Population: 834 (1990); 828 (2000); 766 (2007); 719 (2012 projected); Race: 35.8% White, 51.4% Black, 9.4% Asian, 1.2% Hispanic of any race (2007); Density: 2,327.2 persons per square mile (2007); Average

household size: 1.97 (2007); Median age: 38.9 (2007); Males per 100 females: 100.5 (2007); Marriage status: 40.6% never married, 38.8% now married, 6.2% widowed, 14.4% divorced (2000); Foreign born: 14.2% (2000); Ancestry (includes multiple ancestries): 63.3% Other groups, 5.5% German, 4.8% Polish, 4.5% Italian, 4.5% Irish (2000).
Economy: Single-family building permits issued: 2 (2007); Multi-family building permits issued: 0 (2007); Employment by occupation: 19.2% management, 22.8% professional, 12.4% services, 27.2% sales, 0.0% farming, 8.2% construction, 10.2% production (2000).
Income: Per capita income: $24,357 (2007); Median household income: $34,706 (2007); Average household income: $48,086 (2007); Percent of households with income of $100,000 or more: 10.3% (2007); Poverty rate: 10.7% (2000).
Education: Percent of population age 25 and over with: High school diploma (including GED) or higher: 87.0% (2007); Bachelor's degree or higher: 30.8% (2007); Master's degree or higher: 11.8% (2007).
Housing: Homeownership rate: 31.4% (2007); Median home value: $195,313 (2007); Median rent: $583 per month (2000); Median age of housing: 37 years (2000).
Transportation: Commute to work: 85.3% car, 5.5% public transportation, 3.8% walk, 5.1% work from home (2000); Travel time to work: 40.6% less than 15 minutes, 32.3% 15 to 30 minutes, 22.1% 30 to 45 minutes, 2.1% 45 to 60 minutes, 2.8% 60 minutes or more (2000)

Darke County

Located in western Ohio; bounded on the west by Indiana; drained by Greenville Creek and the Stillwater and Mississinewa Rivers. Covers a land area of 599.80 square miles, a water area of 0.49 square miles, and is located in the Eastern Time Zone. The county was founded in 1809. County seat is Greenville.

Darke County is part of the Greenville, OH Micropolitan Statistical Area. The entire metro area includes: Darke County, OH

Weather Station: Greenville Water Plant — Elevation: 1,023 feet

	Jan	Feb	Mar	Apr	May	Jun	Jul	Aug	Sep	Oct	Nov	Dec
High	32	37	48	60	72	80	84	82	77	64	50	38
Low	15	18	28	38	48	58	61	58	50	39	31	21
Precip	2.2	2.1	2.9	3.6	4.0	4.0	4.2	3.2	2.5	2.7	3.1	2.7
Snow	8.3	5.6	3.0	0.5	tr	0.0	0.0	0.0	0.0	0.2	0.8	3.3

High and Low temperatures in degrees Fahrenheit; Precipitation and Snow in inches

Population: 53,597 (1990); 53,309 (2000); 52,929 (2007); 52,511 (2012 projected); Race: 97.7% White, 0.5% Black, 0.3% Asian, 1.1% Hispanic of any race (2007); Density: 88.2 persons per square mile (2007); Average household size: 2.55 (2007); Median age: 39.5 (2007); Males per 100 females: 96.7 (2007).
Religion: Five largest groups: 13.0% Catholic Church, 7.8% The United Methodist Church, 5.3% Evangelical Lutheran Church in America, 2.7% Southern Baptist Convention, 2.6% Church of the Brethren (2000).
Economy: Unemployment rate: 6.3% (6/2008); Total civilian labor force: 28,625 (6/2008); Leading industries: 28.6% manufacturing; 15.1% retail trade; 12.6% health care and social assistance (2005); Farms: 1,764 totaling 339,055 acres (2002); Companies that employ 500 or more persons: 3 (2006); Companies that employ 100 to 499 persons: 16 (2006); Companies that employ less than 100 persons: 1,193 (2006); Black-owned businesses: n/a (2002); Hispanic-owned businesses: n/a (2002); Asian-owned businesses: n/a (2002); Women-owned businesses: 1,272 (2002); Retail sales per capita: $10,880 (2008). Single-family building permits issued: 65 (2007); Multi-family building permits issued: 0 (2007).
Income: Per capita income: $21,725 (2007); Median household income: $44,457 (2007); Average household income: $54,655 (2007); Percent of households with income of $100,000 or more: 10.1% (2007); Poverty rate: 8.6% (2005); Bankruptcy rate: 3.14% (2007).
Education: Percent of population age 25 and over with: High school diploma (including GED) or higher: 82.9% (2007); Bachelor's degree or higher: 10.1% (2007); Master's degree or higher: 3.6% (2007).
Housing: Homeownership rate: 76.7% (2007); Median home value: $122,648 (2007); Median rent: $346 per month (2000); Median age of housing: 43 years (2000).
Health: Birth rate: 131.2 per 10,000 population (2007); Death rate: 105.7 per 10,000 population (2007); Age-adjusted cancer mortality rate: 173.3 deaths per 100,000 population (2005); Number of physicians: 8.0 per 10,000 population (2005); Hospital beds: 13.8 per 10,000 population (2004); Hospital admissions: 499.6 per 10,000 population (2004).
Elections: 2004 Presidential election results: 69.6% Bush, 29.8% Kerry, 0.0% Nader, 0.3% Badnarik
National and State Parks: Fort Jefferson State Memorial; Treaty Of Greenville State Park
Additional Information Contacts
Darke County Government . . . . (937) 547-7370
http://www.co.darke.oh.us
City of Greenville . . . . (937) 548-1819
http://www.cityofgreenville.org
Darke County Chamber of Commerce. . . . . (937) 548-2102
http://www.darkecountyohio.com
Darke County Visitors Bureau . . . . (937) 548-5158
http://www.visitdarkecounty.org
Village of Versailles . . . . (937) 526-3294
http://www.versaillesohio.cc

Darke County Communities

ANSONIA (village). Covers a land area of 0.667 square miles and a water area of 0.017 square miles. Located at 40.21° N. Lat.; 84.63° W. Long. Elevation is 997 feet.
Population: 1,279 (1990); 1,145 (2000); 1,048 (2007); 1,036 (2012 projected); Race: 99.0% White, 0.0% Black, 0.0% Asian, 2.0% Hispanic of any race (2007); Density: 1,571.5 persons per square mile (2007); Average household size: 2.47 (2007); Median age: 36.1 (2007); Males per 100 females: 100.0 (2007); Marriage status: 21.8% never married, 55.1% now married, 8.9% widowed, 14.2% divorced (2000); Foreign born: 0.0% (2000); Ancestry (includes multiple ancestries): 35.8% German, 18.5% United States or American, 12.9% Irish, 9.7% Other groups, 6.3% English (2000).
Economy: Employment by occupation: 6.3% management, 5.4% professional, 12.1% services, 21.4% sales, 3.7% farming, 10.2% construction, 40.9% production (2000).
Income: Per capita income: $19,325 (2007); Median household income: $41,118 (2007); Average household income: $47,653 (2007); Percent of households with income of $100,000 or more: 5.2% (2007); Poverty rate: 7.0% (2000).
Education: Percent of population age 25 and over with: High school diploma (including GED) or higher: 78.9% (2007); Bachelor's degree or higher: 2.7% (2007); Master's degree or higher: 0.7% (2007).
School District(s)
Ansonia Local (PK-12)
2005-06 Enrollment: 786 . . . . (937) 337-4000
Housing: Homeownership rate: 74.1% (2007); Median home value: $90,610 (2007); Median rent: $345 per month (2000); Median age of housing: 48 years (2000).
Transportation: Commute to work: 93.2% car, 0.0% public transportation, 1.3% walk, 1.5% work from home (2000); Travel time to work: 30.2% less than 15 minutes, 46.5% 15 to 30 minutes, 14.8% 30 to 45 minutes, 5.0% 45 to 60 minutes, 3.5% 60 minutes or more (2000)

ARCANUM (village). Covers a land area of 1.160 square miles and a water area of 0 square miles. Located at 39.99° N. Lat.; 84.55° W. Long. Elevation is 1,050 feet.
Population: 2,059 (1990); 2,076 (2000); 2,133 (2007); 2,133 (2012 projected); Race: 98.7% White, 0.0% Black, 0.3% Asian, 0.7% Hispanic of any race (2007); Density: 1,839.0 persons per square mile (2007); Average household size: 2.38 (2007); Median age: 37.1 (2007); Males per 100 females: 92.2 (2007); Marriage status: 16.8% never married, 63.9% now married, 8.1% widowed, 11.2% divorced (2000); Foreign born: 1.2% (2000); Ancestry (includes multiple ancestries): 31.3% German, 9.3% United States or American, 9.1% English, 7.6% Irish, 7.1% Other groups (2000).
Economy: Employment by occupation: 10.2% management, 20.9% professional, 11.6% services, 23.8% sales, 1.0% farming, 11.9% construction, 20.5% production (2000).
Income: Per capita income: $23,967 (2007); Median household income: $48,083 (2007); Average household income: $56,929 (2007); Percent of households with income of $100,000 or more: 10.5% (2007); Poverty rate: 3.5% (2000).
Education: Percent of population age 25 and over with: High school diploma (including GED) or higher: 88.6% (2007); Bachelor's degree or higher: 13.9% (2007); Master's degree or higher: 5.2% (2007).

School District(s)

Arcanum Butler Local (PK-12)
2005-06 Enrollment: 1,065 . . . . (937) 692-5174
Franklin Monroe Local (PK-12)
2005-06 Enrollment: 769 . . . . (937) 692-8637

Housing: Homeownership rate: 73.6% (2007); Median home value: $131,100 (2007); Median rent: $363 per month (2000); Median age of housing: 46 years (2000).

Safety: Violent crime rate: 5.0 per 10,000 population; Property crime rate: 169.8 per 10,000 population (2007).

Transportation: Commute to work: 94.0% car, 0.4% public transportation, 2.9% walk, 1.5% work from home (2000); Travel time to work: 17.6% less than 15 minutes, 34.3% 15 to 30 minutes, 28.4% 30 to 45 minutes, 10.7% 45 to 60 minutes, 9.0% 60 minutes or more (2000)

CASTINE (village). Covers a land area of 0.076 square miles and a water area of 0 square miles. Located at 39.93° N. Lat.; 84.62° W. Long. Elevation is 1,076 feet.

Population: 163 (1990); 129 (2000); 121 (2007); 119 (2012 projected); Race: 99.2% White, 0.8% Black, 0.0% Asian, 1.7% Hispanic of any race (2007); Density: 1,594.7 persons per square mile (2007); Average household size: 2.95 (2007); Median age: 37.3 (2007); Males per 100 females: 120.0 (2007); Marriage status: 15.4% never married, 75.8% now married, 0.0% widowed, 8.8% divorced (2000); Foreign born: 0.0% (2000); Ancestry (includes multiple ancestries): 17.8% United States or American, 9.3% German, 3.9% Other groups, 3.1% Irish (2000).

Economy: Employment by occupation: 13.9% management, 8.3% professional, 13.9% services, 18.1% sales, 0.0% farming, 22.2% construction, 23.6% production (2000).

Income: Per capita income: $13,636 (2007); Median household income: $33,750 (2007); Average household income: $40,244 (2007); Percent of households with income of $100,000 or more: 0.0% (2007); Poverty rate: 7.0% (2000).

Education: Percent of population age 25 and over with: High school diploma (including GED) or higher: 76.7% (2007); Bachelor's degree or higher: 5.5% (2007); Master's degree or higher: 5.5% (2007).

Housing: Homeownership rate: 70.7% (2007); Median home value: $106,731 (2007); Median rent: $325 per month (2000); Median age of housing: 48 years (2000).

Transportation: Commute to work: 100.0% car, 0.0% public transportation, 0.0% walk, 0.0% work from home (2000); Travel time to work: 29.4% less than 15 minutes, 25.0% 15 to 30 minutes, 23.5% 30 to 45 minutes, 8.8% 45 to 60 minutes, 13.2% 60 minutes or more (2000)

GETTYSBURG (village). Covers a land area of 0.440 square miles and a water area of <.001 square miles. Located at 40.11° N. Lat.; 84.49° W. Long. Elevation is 991 feet.

Population: 539 (1990); 558 (2000); 540 (2007); 535 (2012 projected); Race: 95.2% White, 0.9% Black, 1.5% Asian, 0.7% Hispanic of any race (2007); Density: 1,226.8 persons per square mile (2007); Average household size: 2.90 (2007); Median age: 31.1 (2007); Males per 100 females: 92.2 (2007); Marriage status: 23.2% never married, 60.5% now married, 4.7% widowed, 11.6% divorced (2000); Foreign born: 2.9% (2000); Ancestry (includes multiple ancestries): 37.3% German, 9.3% Other groups, 8.2% Irish, 8.0% United States or American, 7.3% French (except Basque) (2000).

Economy: Single-family building permits issued: 0 (2007); Multi-family building permits issued: 0 (2007); Employment by occupation: 7.7% management, 8.4% professional, 8.8% services, 21.5% sales, 0.8% farming, 11.1% construction, 41.8% production (2000).

Income: Per capita income: $17,718 (2007); Median household income: $42,353 (2007); Average household income: $51,438 (2007); Percent of households with income of $100,000 or more: 7.5% (2007); Poverty rate: 10.7% (2000).

Education: Percent of population age 25 and over with: High school diploma (including GED) or higher: 83.7% (2007); Bachelor's degree or higher: 9.4% (2007); Master's degree or higher: 4.2% (2007).

School District(s)

Greenville City (PK-12)
2005-06 Enrollment: 3,296 . . . . (937) 548-3185

Housing: Homeownership rate: 78.0% (2007); Median home value: $103,125 (2007); Median rent: $333 per month (2000); Median age of housing: 49 years (2000).

Transportation: Commute to work: 88.6% car, 0.0% public transportation, 9.1% walk, 2.0% work from home (2000); Travel time to work: 28.5% less than 15 minutes, 50.2% 15 to 30 minutes, 13.7% 30 to 45 minutes, 5.6% 45 to 60 minutes, 2.0% 60 minutes or more (2000)

GORDON (village). Covers a land area of 0.164 square miles and a water area of 0 square miles. Located at 39.93° N. Lat.; 84.50° W. Long. Elevation is 1,043 feet.

Population: 206 (1990); 190 (2000); 203 (2007); 205 (2012 projected); Race: 100.0% White, 0.0% Black, 0.0% Asian, 0.0% Hispanic of any race (2007); Density: 1,239.0 persons per square mile (2007); Average household size: 2.51 (2007); Median age: 36.9 (2007); Males per 100 females: 97.1 (2007); Marriage status: 12.9% never married, 75.5% now married, 5.8% widowed, 5.8% divorced (2000); Foreign born: 0.0% (2000); Ancestry (includes multiple ancestries): 33.7% German, 23.2% United States or American, 14.2% Irish, 5.8% Scotch-Irish, 5.8% Other groups (2000).

Economy: Employment by occupation: 4.4% management, 7.8% professional, 14.4% services, 22.2% sales, 0.0% farming, 21.1% construction, 30.0% production (2000).

Income: Per capita income: $19,938 (2007); Median household income: $40,417 (2007); Average household income: $49,969 (2007); Percent of households with income of $100,000 or more: 8.6% (2007); Poverty rate: 0.5% (2000).

Education: Percent of population age 25 and over with: High school diploma (including GED) or higher: 83.6% (2007); Bachelor's degree or higher: 1.5% (2007); Master's degree or higher: 0.0% (2007).

Housing: Homeownership rate: 87.7% (2007); Median home value: $106,944 (2007); Median rent: $325 per month (2000); Median age of housing: 60+ years (2000).

Transportation: Commute to work: 97.8% car, 0.0% public transportation, 0.0% walk, 2.2% work from home (2000); Travel time to work: 12.6% less than 15 minutes, 39.1% 15 to 30 minutes, 34.5% 30 to 45 minutes, 12.6% 45 to 60 minutes, 1.1% 60 minutes or more (2000)

GREENVILLE (city). County seat. Covers a land area of 6.025 square miles and a water area of 0 square miles. Located at 40.10° N. Lat.; 84.62° W. Long. Elevation is 1,043 feet.

History: Fort Greenville, established here and named for General Nathanael Greene, was abandoned in 1795. A town was founded here in 1805 by the Swawnee chieftain, Tecumseh, and his brother, Tenakwatawa, known as The Prophet. After Prophet's Town was moved to Indiana, other settlers came and the town of Greenville was founded.

Population: 13,140 (1990); 13,294 (2000); 12,902 (2007); 12,542 (2012 projected); Race: 96.7% White, 0.7% Black, 0.7% Asian, 1.5% Hispanic of any race (2007); Density: 2,141.3 persons per square mile (2007); Average household size: 2.29 (2007); Median age: 42.4 (2007); Males per 100 females: 85.4 (2007); Marriage status: 20.3% never married, 53.3% now married, 13.3% widowed, 13.1% divorced (2000); Foreign born: 1.0% (2000); Ancestry (includes multiple ancestries): 30.9% German, 14.6% United States or American, 10.8% Irish, 10.0% English, 6.1% Other groups (2000).

Economy: Employment by occupation: 8.9% management, 15.1% professional, 16.1% services, 24.5% sales, 0.0% farming, 10.7% construction, 24.6% production (2000).

Income: Per capita income: $20,584 (2007); Median household income: $34,650 (2007); Average household income: $44,974 (2007); Percent of households with income of $100,000 or more: 6.5% (2007); Poverty rate: 13.4% (2000).

Education: Percent of population age 25 and over with: High school diploma (including GED) or higher: 81.0% (2007); Bachelor's degree or higher: 11.9% (2007); Master's degree or higher: 4.4% (2007).

School District(s)

Greenville City (PK-12)
2005-06 Enrollment: 3,296 . . . . (937) 548-3185

Housing: Homeownership rate: 63.0% (2007); Median home value: $111,488 (2007); Median rent: $352 per month (2000); Median age of housing: 43 years (2000).

Hospitals: Wayne Hospital (92 beds)

Safety: Violent crime rate: 37.0 per 10,000 population; Property crime rate: 399.9 per 10,000 population (2007).

Newspapers: Daily Advocate (Local news; Circulation 8,692); Early Bird (Community news; Circulation 26,625)

Transportation: Commute to work: 93.5% car, 0.3% public transportation, 2.9% walk, 2.3% work from home (2000); Travel time to work: 63.3% less than 15 minutes, 16.5% 15 to 30 minutes, 9.1% 30 to 45 minutes, 7.5% 45 to 60 minutes, 3.6% 60 minutes or more (2000)

Additional Information Contacts

City of Greenville . . . . (937) 548-1819
http://www.cityofgreenville.org

Darke County Chamber of Commerce. . . . . (937) 548-2102
http://www.darkecountyohio.com

Darke County Visitors Bureau . . . . (937) 548-5158
http://www.visitdarkecounty.org

HOLLANSBURG (village). Covers a land area of 0.122 square miles and a water area of 0 square miles. Located at 39.99° N. Lat.; 84.79° W. Long. Elevation is 1,161 feet.

Population: 300 (1990); 214 (2000); 218 (2007); 216 (2012 projected); Race: 97.7% White, 0.0% Black, 0.0% Asian, 0.0% Hispanic of any race (2007); Density: 1,791.8 persons per square mile (2007); Average household size: 2.42 (2007); Median age: 34.7 (2007); Males per 100 females: 115.8 (2007); Marriage status: 29.2% never married, 48.5% now married, 10.5% widowed, 11.7% divorced (2000); Foreign born: 0.0% (2000); Ancestry (includes multiple ancestries): 21.3% German, 20.4% United States or American, 10.4% Irish, 8.7% Other groups, 5.2% French (except Basque) (2000).

Economy: Employment by occupation: 7.1% management, 8.2% professional, 22.4% services, 9.2% sales, 0.0% farming, 16.3% construction, 36.7% production (2000).

Income: Per capita income: $15,378 (2007); Median household income: $36,875 (2007); Average household income: $37,250 (2007); Percent of households with income of $100,000 or more: 2.2% (2007); Poverty rate: 4.3% (2000).

Education: Percent of population age 25 and over with: High school diploma (including GED) or higher: 77.0% (2007); Bachelor's degree or higher: 3.6% (2007); Master's degree or higher: 0.0% (2007).

Housing: Homeownership rate: 80.0% (2007); Median home value: $57,647 (2007); Median rent: $350 per month (2000); Median age of housing: 60+ years (2000).

Transportation: Commute to work: 94.7% car, 0.0% public transportation, 5.3% walk, 0.0% work from home (2000); Travel time to work: 10.6% less than 15 minutes, 54.3% 15 to 30 minutes, 21.3% 30 to 45 minutes, 8.5% 45 to 60 minutes, 5.3% 60 minutes or more (2000)

ITHACA (village). Covers a land area of 0.030 square miles and a water area of 0 square miles. Located at 39.93° N. Lat.; 84.55° W. Long. Elevation is 1,033 feet.

Population: 119 (1990); 102 (2000); 97 (2007); 95 (2012 projected); Race: 100.0% White, 0.0% Black, 0.0% Asian, 0.0% Hispanic of any race (2007); Density: 3,198.2 persons per square mile (2007); Average household size: 2.77 (2007); Median age: 37.8 (2007); Males per 100 females: 110.9 (2007); Marriage status: 24.5% never married, 62.8% now married, 10.6% widowed, 2.1% divorced (2000); Foreign born: 0.0% (2000); Ancestry (includes multiple ancestries): 25.2% English, 16.0% German, 14.3% United States or American, 3.4% Irish, 1.7% Other groups (2000).

Economy: Employment by occupation: 0.0% management, 3.8% professional, 13.2% services, 26.4% sales, 0.0% farming, 7.5% construction, 49.1% production (2000).

Income: Per capita income: $18,170 (2007); Median household income: $46,250 (2007); Average household income: $50,357 (2007); Percent of households with income of $100,000 or more: 5.7% (2007); Poverty rate: 0.0% (2000).

Education: Percent of population age 25 and over with: High school diploma (including GED) or higher: 76.2% (2007); Bachelor's degree or higher: 0.0% (2007); Master's degree or higher: 0.0% (2007).

Housing: Homeownership rate: 71.4% (2007); Median home value: $87,000 (2007); Median rent: $458 per month (2000); Median age of housing: 49 years (2000).

Transportation: Commute to work: 100.0% car, 0.0% public transportation, 0.0% walk, 0.0% work from home (2000); Travel time to work: 14.0% less than 15 minutes, 42.0% 15 to 30 minutes, 40.0% 30 to 45 minutes, 0.0% 45 to 60 minutes, 4.0% 60 minutes or more (2000)

NEW MADISON (village). Covers a land area of 0.372 square miles and a water area of 0 square miles. Located at 39.96° N. Lat.; 84.70° W. Long. Elevation is 1,109 feet.

Population: 928 (1990); 817 (2000); 796 (2007); 781 (2012 projected); Race: 97.4% White, 0.3% Black, 0.5% Asian, 0.0% Hispanic of any race (2007); Density: 2,140.0 persons per square mile (2007); Average household size: 2.32 (2007); Median age: 40.1 (2007); Males per 100 females: 98.0 (2007); Marriage status: 15.8% never married, 62.3% now married, 10.6% widowed, 11.3% divorced (2000); Foreign born: 1.8% (2000); Ancestry (includes multiple ancestries): 28.6% German, 17.8% United States or American, 9.1% Irish, 8.9% English, 6.6% Other groups (2000).

Economy: Single-family building permits issued: 0 (2007); Multi-family building permits issued: 0 (2007); Employment by occupation: 6.3% management, 12.5% professional, 14.9% services, 24.0% sales, 0.0% farming, 6.5% construction, 35.8% production (2000).

Income: Per capita income: $19,296 (2007); Median household income: $37,500 (2007); Average household income: $44,781 (2007); Percent of households with income of $100,000 or more: 5.8% (2007); Poverty rate: 7.7% (2000).

Education: Percent of population age 25 and over with: High school diploma (including GED) or higher: 86.1% (2007); Bachelor's degree or higher: 6.9% (2007); Master's degree or higher: 2.8% (2007).

School District(s)

Tri-Village Local (PK-12)
2005-06 Enrollment: 791 . . . . (937) 996-6261

Housing: Homeownership rate: 78.4% (2007); Median home value: $103,343 (2007); Median rent: $397 per month (2000); Median age of housing: 56 years (2000).

Transportation: Commute to work: 95.9% car, 0.5% public transportation, 2.4% walk, 1.2% work from home (2000); Travel time to work: 21.6% less than 15 minutes, 54.9% 15 to 30 minutes, 11.3% 30 to 45 minutes, 10.5% 45 to 60 minutes, 1.7% 60 minutes or more (2000)

NEW WESTON (village). Covers a land area of 0.256 square miles and a water area of 0 square miles. Located at 40.33° N. Lat.; 84.64° W. Long. Elevation is 1,010 feet.

Population: 148 (1990); 135 (2000); 140 (2007); 143 (2012 projected); Race: 97.1% White, 0.0% Black, 0.0% Asian, 0.0% Hispanic of any race (2007); Density: 547.6 persons per square mile (2007); Average household size: 2.75 (2007); Median age: 35.0 (2007); Males per 100 females: 100.0 (2007); Marriage status: 22.7% never married, 70.1% now married, 2.1% widowed, 5.2% divorced (2000); Foreign born: 1.6% (2000); Ancestry (includes multiple ancestries): 25.6% German, 23.3% United States or American, 6.2% French (except Basque), 4.7% Irish, 4.7% Other groups (2000).

Economy: Employment by occupation: 4.8% management, 3.2% professional, 19.0% services, 11.1% sales, 3.2% farming, 20.6% construction, 38.1% production (2000).

Income: Per capita income: $14,946 (2007); Median household income: $42,500 (2007); Average household income: $41,029 (2007); Percent of households with income of $100,000 or more: 0.0% (2007); Poverty rate: 12.6% (2000).

Education: Percent of population age 25 and over with: High school diploma (including GED) or higher: 53.9% (2007); Bachelor's degree or higher: 7.9% (2007); Master's degree or higher: 3.4% (2007).

Housing: Homeownership rate: 80.4% (2007); Median home value: $71,250 (2007); Median rent: $475 per month (2000); Median age of housing: 60+ years (2000).

Transportation: Commute to work: 91.8% car, 0.0% public transportation, 8.2% walk, 0.0% work from home (2000); Travel time to work: 14.8% less than 15 minutes, 62.3% 15 to 30 minutes, 16.4% 30 to 45 minutes, 6.6% 45 to 60 minutes, 0.0% 60 minutes or more (2000)

NORTH STAR (village). Covers a land area of 0.521 square miles and a water area of 0 square miles. Located at 40.32° N. Lat.; 84.56° W. Long. Elevation is 1,004 feet.

History: North Star was founded in 1844 by John Houston and Heronimus Star. This was the birthplace of Annie Oakley, born in 1860, who became an expert markswoman.

Population: 246 (1990); 209 (2000); 207 (2007); 207 (2012 projected); Race: 99.0% White, 0.0% Black, 1.0% Asian, 0.0% Hispanic of any race (2007); Density: 397.6 persons per square mile (2007); Average household size: 2.65 (2007); Median age: 40.5 (2007); Males per 100 females: 109.1 (2007); Marriage status: 19.7% never married, 66.9% now married, 12.1% widowed, 1.3% divorced (2000); Foreign born: 0.0% (2000); Ancestry (includes multiple ancestries): 61.5% German, 24.9% French (except Basque), 18.5% United States or American, 2.0% Other groups, 2.0% Dutch (2000).

Economy: Employment by occupation: 5.7% management, 10.5% professional, 18.1% services, 31.4% sales, 0.0% farming, 0.0% construction, 34.3% production (2000).

Income: Per capita income: $22,452 (2007); Median household income: $60,833 (2007); Average household income: $59,583 (2007); Percent of households with income of $100,000 or more: 9.0% (2007); Poverty rate: 5.4% (2000).
Education: Percent of population age 25 and over with: High school diploma (including GED) or higher: 90.8% (2007); Bachelor's degree or higher: 3.1% (2007); Master's degree or higher: 1.5% (2007).

School District(s)

Versailles Exempted Village (PK-12)
2005-06 Enrollment: 1,406 . . . . (937) 526-4773
Housing: Homeownership rate: 89.7% (2007); Median home value: $121,053 (2007); Median rent: $306 per month (2000); Median age of housing: 38 years (2000).
Transportation: Commute to work: 85.4% car, 0.0% public transportation, 7.8% walk, 6.8% work from home (2000); Travel time to work: 24.0% less than 15 minutes, 65.6% 15 to 30 minutes, 8.3% 30 to 45 minutes, 0.0% 45 to 60 minutes, 2.1% 60 minutes or more (2000)

OSGOOD (village). Covers a land area of 0.344 square miles and a water area of 0 square miles. Located at 40.34° N. Lat.; 84.49° W. Long. Elevation is 961 feet.
Population: 289 (1990); 255 (2000); 254 (2007); 254 (2012 projected); Race: 100.0% White, 0.0% Black, 0.0% Asian, 0.0% Hispanic of any race (2007); Density: 739.2 persons per square mile (2007); Average household size: 2.42 (2007); Median age: 38.4 (2007); Males per 100 females: 101.6 (2007); Marriage status: 14.7% never married, 68.8% now married, 11.0% widowed, 5.5% divorced (2000); Foreign born: 1.1% (2000); Ancestry (includes multiple ancestries): 73.6% German, 18.2% French (except Basque), 6.7% United States or American, 3.0% Dutch, 1.9% Irish (2000).
Economy: Employment by occupation: 8.6% management, 15.7% professional, 15.0% services, 15.0% sales, 0.0% farming, 6.4% construction, 39.3% production (2000).
Income: Per capita income: $21,161 (2007); Median household income: $48,542 (2007); Average household income: $51,190 (2007); Percent of households with income of $100,000 or more: 6.7% (2007); Poverty rate: 0.4% (2000).
Education: Percent of population age 25 and over with: High school diploma (including GED) or higher: 77.3% (2007); Bachelor's degree or higher: 10.5% (2007); Master's degree or higher: 5.8% (2007).
Housing: Homeownership rate: 88.6% (2007); Median home value: $136,979 (2007); Median rent: $381 per month (2000); Median age of housing: 33 years (2000).
Transportation: Commute to work: 89.0% car, 0.0% public transportation, 5.9% walk, 5.1% work from home (2000); Travel time to work: 46.5% less than 15 minutes, 38.0% 15 to 30 minutes, 7.8% 30 to 45 minutes, 6.2% 45 to 60 minutes, 1.6% 60 minutes or more (2000)

PALESTINE (village). Covers a land area of 0.147 square miles and a water area of 0 square miles. Located at 40.05° N. Lat.; 84.74° W. Long. Elevation is 1,109 feet.
Population: 219 (1990); 170 (2000); 174 (2007); 172 (2012 projected); Race: 92.0% White, 8.0% Black, 0.0% Asian, 0.0% Hispanic of any race (2007); Density: 1,180.0 persons per square mile (2007); Average household size: 2.90 (2007); Median age: 35.9 (2007); Males per 100 females: 91.2 (2007); Marriage status: 0.0% never married, 66.7% now married, 33.3% widowed, 0.0% divorced (2000); Foreign born: 0.0% (2000); Ancestry (includes multiple ancestries): 33.3% German (2000).
Economy: Employment by occupation: 0.0% management, 0.0% professional, 0.0% services, 100.0% sales, 0.0% farming, 0.0% construction, 0.0% production (2000).
Income: Per capita income: $11,006 (2007); Median household income: $32,500 (2007); Average household income: $31,917 (2007); Percent of households with income of $100,000 or more: 0.0% (2007); Poverty rate: 0.0% (2000).
Education: Percent of population age 25 and over with: High school diploma (including GED) or higher: 100.0% (2007); Bachelor's degree or higher: 0.0% (2007); Master's degree or higher: 0.0% (2007).
Housing: Homeownership rate: 88.3% (2007); Median home value: $81,875 (2007); Median rent: $n/a per month (2000); Median age of housing: 60+ years (2000).
Transportation: Commute to work: 100.0% car, 0.0% public transportation, 0.0% walk, 0.0% work from home (2000); Travel time to work: 100.0% less than 15 minutes, 0.0% 15 to 30 minutes, 0.0% 30 to 45 minutes, 0.0% 45 to 60 minutes, 0.0% 60 minutes or more (2000)

PITSBURG (village). Covers a land area of 0.190 square miles and a water area of 0 square miles. Located at 39.98° N. Lat.; 84.48° W. Long. Elevation is 1,024 feet.
History: Also spelled Pittsburg.
Population: 425 (1990); 392 (2000); 359 (2007); 353 (2012 projected); Race: 96.7% White, 0.0% Black, 0.0% Asian, 0.8% Hispanic of any race (2007); Density: 1,892.6 persons per square mile (2007); Average household size: 2.85 (2007); Median age: 31.3 (2007); Males per 100 females: 101.7 (2007); Marriage status: 9.9% never married, 81.5% now married, 6.0% widowed, 2.6% divorced (2000); Foreign born: 2.1% (2000); Ancestry (includes multiple ancestries): 37.0% German, 12.8% Irish, 12.8% English, 12.5% Other groups, 11.6% United States or American (2000).
Economy: Employment by occupation: 23.9% management, 17.4% professional, 11.0% services, 22.6% sales, 0.0% farming, 11.0% construction, 14.2% production (2000).
Income: Per capita income: $20,731 (2007); Median household income: $62,500 (2007); Average household income: $59,067 (2007); Percent of households with income of $100,000 or more: 13.5% (2007); Poverty rate: 4.0% (2000).
Education: Percent of population age 25 and over with: High school diploma (including GED) or higher: 98.6% (2007); Bachelor's degree or higher: 8.7% (2007); Master's degree or higher: 5.8% (2007).
Housing: Homeownership rate: 81.7% (2007); Median home value: $130,114 (2007); Median rent: $391 per month (2000); Median age of housing: 36 years (2000).
Transportation: Commute to work: 100.0% car, 0.0% public transportation, 0.0% walk, 0.0% work from home (2000); Travel time to work: 18.7% less than 15 minutes, 36.1% 15 to 30 minutes, 18.1% 30 to 45 minutes, 19.4% 45 to 60 minutes, 7.7% 60 minutes or more (2000)

ROSSBURG (village). Covers a land area of 0.140 square miles and a water area of 0 square miles. Located at 40.28° N. Lat.; 84.63° W. Long. Elevation is 1,030 feet.
Population: 268 (1990); 224 (2000); 231 (2007); 234 (2012 projected); Race: 99.1% White, 0.0% Black, 0.0% Asian, 0.9% Hispanic of any race (2007); Density: 1,650.2 persons per square mile (2007); Average household size: 2.54 (2007); Median age: 36.8 (2007); Males per 100 females: 90.9 (2007); Marriage status: 32.3% never married, 47.6% now married, 11.1% widowed, 9.0% divorced (2000); Foreign born: 1.4% (2000); Ancestry (includes multiple ancestries): 38.6% German, 11.9% Other groups, 11.4% Irish, 10.5% United States or American, 2.9% English (2000).
Economy: Employment by occupation: 9.3% management, 10.9% professional, 14.0% services, 14.7% sales, 3.9% farming, 13.2% construction, 34.1% production (2000).
Income: Per capita income: $15,790 (2007); Median household income: $35,625 (2007); Average household income: $40,082 (2007); Percent of households with income of $100,000 or more: 3.3% (2007); Poverty rate: 4.3% (2000).
Education: Percent of population age 25 and over with: High school diploma (including GED) or higher: 76.7% (2007); Bachelor's degree or higher: 1.3% (2007); Master's degree or higher: 0.0% (2007).
Housing: Homeownership rate: 81.3% (2007); Median home value: $79,000 (2007); Median rent: $339 per month (2000); Median age of housing: 60+ years (2000).
Transportation: Commute to work: 88.6% car, 0.0% public transportation, 9.8% walk, 1.6% work from home (2000); Travel time to work: 22.3% less than 15 minutes, 63.6% 15 to 30 minutes, 9.1% 30 to 45 minutes, 2.5% 45 to 60 minutes, 2.5% 60 minutes or more (2000)

UNION CITY (village). Covers a land area of 0.921 square miles and a water area of 0 square miles. Located at 40.20° N. Lat.; 84.80° W. Long. Elevation is 1,109 feet.
Population: 2,047 (1990); 1,767 (2000); 1,721 (2007); 1,705 (2012 projected); Race: 94.7% White, 1.5% Black, 0.1% Asian, 5.6% Hispanic of any race (2007); Density: 1,869.0 persons per square mile (2007); Average household size: 2.50 (2007); Median age: 35.8 (2007); Males per 100 females: 88.7 (2007); Marriage status: 21.2% never married, 56.1% now married, 9.2% widowed, 13.5% divorced (2000); Foreign born: 2.5% (2000); Ancestry (includes multiple ancestries): 25.1% German, 15.8% Other groups, 11.2% United States or American, 10.2% Irish, 6.3% English (2000).

Economy: Employment by occupation: 4.5% management, 4.1% professional, 18.6% services, 18.8% sales, 2.2% farming, 7.6% construction, 44.1% production (2000).
Income: Per capita income: $16,382 (2007); Median household income: $31,680 (2007); Average household income: $39,325 (2007); Percent of households with income of $100,000 or more: 2.9% (2007); Poverty rate: 20.8% (2000).
Education: Percent of population age 25 and over with: High school diploma (including GED) or higher: 62.5% (2007); Bachelor's degree or higher: 1.0% (2007); Master's degree or higher: 0.3% (2007).

School District(s)

Mississinawa Valley Local (PK-12)
2005-06 Enrollment: 732 . . . . (937) 968-5656
Housing: Homeownership rate: 57.6% (2007); Median home value: $65,076 (2007); Median rent: $283 per month (2000); Median age of housing: 39 years (2000).
Transportation: Commute to work: 93.4% car, 0.6% public transportation, 3.5% walk, 1.7% work from home (2000); Travel time to work: 43.6% less than 15 minutes, 31.4% 15 to 30 minutes, 14.5% 30 to 45 minutes, 4.3% 45 to 60 minutes, 6.1% 60 minutes or more (2000)

VERSAILLES (village). Covers a land area of 1.746 square miles and a water area of 0 square miles. Located at 40.22° N. Lat.; 84.48° W. Long. Elevation is 984 feet.
History: Settled 1819, incorporated 1855.
Population: 2,446 (1990); 2,589 (2000); 2,532 (2007); 2,512 (2012 projected); Race: 99.3% White, 0.0% Black, 0.1% Asian, 0.1% Hispanic of any race (2007); Density: 1,449.9 persons per square mile (2007); Average household size: 2.38 (2007); Median age: 38.3 (2007); Males per 100 females: 93.1 (2007); Marriage status: 18.8% never married, 61.3% now married, 10.2% widowed, 9.7% divorced (2000); Foreign born: 0.1% (2000); Ancestry (includes multiple ancestries): 33.9% German, 21.4% French (except Basque), 9.8% Irish, 9.6% United States or American, 5.2% English (2000).
Economy: Single-family building permits issued: 2 (2007); Multi-family building permits issued: 0 (2007); Employment by occupation: 12.2% management, 11.3% professional, 14.0% services, 23.3% sales, 1.4% farming, 7.7% construction, 30.0% production (2000).
Income: Per capita income: $20,676 (2007); Median household income: $42,382 (2007); Average household income: $48,721 (2007); Percent of households with income of $100,000 or more: 8.6% (2007); Poverty rate: 5.3% (2000).
Education: Percent of population age 25 and over with: High school diploma (including GED) or higher: 84.1% (2007); Bachelor's degree or higher: 12.5% (2007); Master's degree or higher: 4.2% (2007).

School District(s)

Versailles Exempted Village (PK-12)
2005-06 Enrollment: 1,406 . . . . (937) 526-4773
Housing: Homeownership rate: 71.0% (2007); Median home value: $125,900 (2007); Median rent: $327 per month (2000); Median age of housing: 47 years (2000).
Newspapers: Versailles Policy (Local news; Circulation 2,200)
Transportation: Commute to work: 94.1% car, 0.3% public transportation, 2.4% walk, 2.8% work from home (2000); Travel time to work: 52.2% less than 15 minutes, 23.8% 15 to 30 minutes, 15.0% 30 to 45 minutes, 2.8% 45 to 60 minutes, 6.2% 60 minutes or more (2000)
Airports: Darke County (general aviation)
Additional Information Contacts
Village of Versailles . . . . (937) 526-3294
http://www.versaillesohio.cc

WAYNE LAKES (village). Aka Wayne Lakes Park. Covers a land area of 0.546 square miles and a water area of 0.108 square miles. Located at 40.02° N. Lat.; 84.66° W. Long. Elevation is 1,047 feet.
Population: 671 (1990); 684 (2000); 647 (2007); 639 (2012 projected); Race: 97.8% White, 0.5% Black, 0.2% Asian, 1.5% Hispanic of any race (2007); Density: 1,184.9 persons per square mile (2007); Average household size: 2.36 (2007); Median age: 42.1 (2007); Males per 100 females: 97.3 (2007); Marriage status: 22.3% never married, 61.3% now married, 4.3% widowed, 12.1% divorced (2000); Foreign born: 1.2% (2000); Ancestry (includes multiple ancestries): 42.4% German, 14.3% Irish, 13.5% Other groups, 13.3% United States or American, 10.7% English (2000).
Economy: Single-family building permits issued: 0 (2007); Multi-family building permits issued: 0 (2007); Employment by occupation: 10.7% management, 9.9% professional, 9.0% services, 31.4% sales, 0.6% farming, 12.1% construction, 26.3% production (2000).
Income: Per capita income: $23,891 (2007); Median household income: $53,261 (2007); Average household income: $56,414 (2007); Percent of households with income of $100,000 or more: 6.9% (2007); Poverty rate: 2.5% (2000).
Education: Percent of population age 25 and over with: High school diploma (including GED) or higher: 89.4% (2007); Bachelor's degree or higher: 16.2% (2007); Master's degree or higher: 4.2% (2007).
Housing: Homeownership rate: 88.0% (2007); Median home value: $117,689 (2007); Median rent: $463 per month (2000); Median age of housing: 34 years (2000).
Transportation: Commute to work: 94.2% car, 0.3% public transportation, 0.0% walk, 4.6% work from home (2000); Travel time to work: 27.0% less than 15 minutes, 33.3% 15 to 30 minutes, 17.9% 30 to 45 minutes, 12.4% 45 to 60 minutes, 9.4% 60 minutes or more (2000)

YORKSHIRE (village). Covers a land area of 0.282 square miles and a water area of 0 square miles. Located at 40.32° N. Lat.; 84.49° W. Long. Elevation is 981 feet.
Population: 126 (1990); 110 (2000); 110 (2007); 110 (2012 projected); Race: 97.3% White, 1.8% Black, 0.0% Asian, 0.0% Hispanic of any race (2007); Density: 390.1 persons per square mile (2007); Average household size: 2.89 (2007); Median age: 31.7 (2007); Males per 100 females: 83.3 (2007); Marriage status: 38.0% never married, 40.5% now married, 6.3% widowed, 15.2% divorced (2000); Foreign born: 0.0% (2000); Ancestry (includes multiple ancestries): 69.9% German, 25.8% United States or American, 5.4% Scottish, 3.2% Other groups, 2.2% French (except Basque) (2000).
Economy: Employment by occupation: 8.7% management, 4.3% professional, 15.2% services, 21.7% sales, 4.3% farming, 21.7% construction, 23.9% production (2000).
Income: Per capita income: $16,682 (2007); Median household income: $45,000 (2007); Average household income: $48,289 (2007); Percent of households with income of $100,000 or more: 5.3% (2007); Poverty rate: 3.2% (2000).
Education: Percent of population age 25 and over with: High school diploma (including GED) or higher: 75.8% (2007); Bachelor's degree or higher: 9.1% (2007); Master's degree or higher: 0.0% (2007).
Housing: Homeownership rate: 78.9% (2007); Median home value: $125,000 (2007); Median rent: $300 per month (2000); Median age of housing: 60+ years (2000).
Transportation: Commute to work: 87.0% car, 0.0% public transportation, 4.3% walk, 8.7% work from home (2000); Travel time to work: 23.8% less than 15 minutes, 54.8% 15 to 30 minutes, 7.1% 30 to 45 minutes, 9.5% 45 to 60 minutes, 4.8% 60 minutes or more (2000)

Defiance County

Located in northwestern Ohio; bounded on the west by Indiana; intersected by the Maumee, Auglize, and Tiffin Rivers. Covers a land area of 411.16 square miles, a water area of 3.03 square miles, and is located in the Eastern Time Zone. The county was founded in 1845. County seat is Defiance.

Defiance County is part of the Defiance, OH Micropolitan Statistical Area. The entire metro area includes: Defiance County, OH

Weather Station: Defiance Elevation: 698 feet

	Jan	Feb	Mar	Apr	May	Jun	Jul	Aug	Sep	Oct	Nov	Dec
High	31	35	46	59	71	81	85	82	76	63	49	37
Low	15	17	26	36	47	57	61	59	52	41	31	22
Precip	1.9	1.8	2.7	3.5	3.6	3.7	4.0	3.1	3.2	2.6	3.0	2.6
Snow	6.8	5.3	2.4	0.6	tr	0.0	0.0	0.0	0.0	tr	1.2	4.5

High and Low temperatures in degrees Fahrenheit; Precipitation and Snow in inches

Population: 39,350 (1990); 39,500 (2000); 39,074 (2007); 38,700 (2012 projected); Race: 92.5% White, 1.5% Black, 0.3% Asian, 7.7% Hispanic of any race (2007); Density: 95.0 persons per square mile (2007); Average household size: 2.53 (2007); Median age: 38.8 (2007); Males per 100 females: 98.1 (2007).
Religion: Five largest groups: 22.9% Catholic Church, 9.6% The United Methodist Church, 8.8% Lutheran Church—Missouri Synod, 6.3% Evangelical Lutheran Church in America, 2.9% Christian Churches and Churches of Christ (2000).

Economy: Unemployment rate: 9.0% (6/2008); Total civilian labor force: 21,160 (6/2008); Leading industries: 32.0% manufacturing; 16.9% retail trade; 13.0% health care and social assistance (2005); Farms: 982 totaling 208,994 acres (2002); Companies that employ 500 or more persons: 2 (2006); Companies that employ 100 to 499 persons: 21 (2006); Companies that employ less than 100 persons: 822 (2006); Black-owned businesses: n/a (2002); Hispanic-owned businesses: n/a (2002); Asian-owned businesses: n/a (2002); Women-owned businesses: 573 (2002); Retail sales per capita: $17,975 (2008). Single-family building permits issued: 88 (2007); Multi-family building permits issued: 14 (2007).
Income: Per capita income: $23,191 (2007); Median household income: $50,199 (2007); Average household income: $58,447 (2007); Percent of households with income of $100,000 or more: 11.7% (2007); Poverty rate: 8.4% (2005); Bankruptcy rate: 3.37% (2007).
Education: Percent of population age 25 and over with: High school diploma (including GED) or higher: 84.7% (2007); Bachelor's degree or higher: 14.4% (2007); Master's degree or higher: 4.6% (2007).
Housing: Homeownership rate: 80.1% (2007); Median home value: $108,878 (2007); Median rent: $365 per month (2000); Median age of housing: 37 years (2000).
Health: Birth rate: 138.0 per 10,000 population (2007); Death rate: 90.8 per 10,000 population (2007); Age-adjusted cancer mortality rate: 197.3 deaths per 100,000 population (2005); Number of physicians: 16.1 per 10,000 population (2005); Hospital beds: 22.7 per 10,000 population (2004); Hospital admissions: 1,127.8 per 10,000 population (2004).
Elections: 2004 Presidential election results: 61.6% Bush, 37.7% Kerry, 0.0% Nader, 0.4% Badnarik
National and State Parks: Independence Dam State Park; Oxbow Lake State Wildlife Area
Additional Information Contacts
Defiance County Government . . . . (419) 782-4761
http://www.defiance-county.com
City of Defiance . . . . (419) 784-2101
http://www.cityofdefiance.com
Defiance Area Chamber of Commerce . . . . (419) 782-7946
http://www.defiancechamber.com
Hicksville Chamber of Commerce . . . . (419) 542-6161
http://www.hicksvillechamber.org

Defiance County Communities

DEFIANCE (city). County seat. Covers a land area of 10.538 square miles and a water area of 0.488 square miles. Located at 41.28° N. Lat.; 84.36° W. Long. Elevation is 676 feet.
History: General Anthony Wayne built a fort here in 1794 and called it Fort Defiance. It was replaced in 1812 by General William Henry Harrison, who built Fort Winchester near Wayne's old fort. The town that developed after the War of 1812 was spurred by the Wabash & Erie Canal and the Miami & Erie Canal, which joined near here.
Population: 16,822 (1990); 16,465 (2000); 15,881 (2007); 15,460 (2012 projected); Race: 86.8% White, 3.1% Black, 0.3% Asian, 13.7% Hispanic of any race (2007); Density: 1,507.0 persons per square mile (2007); Average household size: 2.43 (2007); Median age: 37.3 (2007); Males per 100 females: 95.0 (2007); Marriage status: 26.2% never married, 55.1% now married, 7.8% widowed, 10.9% divorced (2000); Foreign born: 2.2% (2000); Ancestry (includes multiple ancestries): 34.9% German, 20.0% Other groups, 10.0% Irish, 9.6% United States or American, 6.4% English (2000).
Economy: Single-family building permits issued: 19 (2007); Multi-family building permits issued: 14 (2007); Employment by occupation: 8.0% management, 13.7% professional, 14.4% services, 22.5% sales, 0.3% farming, 7.2% construction, 33.8% production (2000).
Income: Per capita income: $23,132 (2007); Median household income: $46,412 (2007); Average household income: $55,648 (2007); Percent of households with income of $100,000 or more: 10.9% (2007); Poverty rate: 8.8% (2000).
Education: Percent of population age 25 and over with: High school diploma (including GED) or higher: 83.6% (2007); Bachelor's degree or higher: 17.1% (2007); Master's degree or higher: 5.2% (2007).

School District(s)

Ayersville Local (PK-12)
2005-06 Enrollment: 912 . . . . (419) 395-1111
Defiance City (PK-12)
2005-06 Enrollment: 2,530 . . . . (419) 782-0070
Northeastern Local (PK-12)
2005-06 Enrollment: 1,167 . . . . (419) 497-3461

Four-year College(s)

Defiance College (Private, Not-for-profit, United Church of Christ)
Fall 2007 Enrollment: 973 . . . . (419) 784-4010
2007-08 Tuition: In-state $20,630; Out-of-state $20,630
Housing: Homeownership rate: 70.8% (2007); Median home value: $102,334 (2007); Median rent: $375 per month (2000); Median age of housing: 40 years (2000).
Hospitals: Defiance Regional Medical Center (61 beds)
Safety: Violent crime rate: 21.7 per 10,000 population; Property crime rate: 481.5 per 10,000 population (2007).
Newspapers: Crescent-News (Local news; Circulation 16,497)
Transportation: Commute to work: 94.5% car, 0.3% public transportation, 2.7% walk, 1.3% work from home (2000); Travel time to work: 59.2% less than 15 minutes, 21.7% 15 to 30 minutes, 12.7% 30 to 45 minutes, 2.9% 45 to 60 minutes, 3.5% 60 minutes or more (2000)
Additional Information Contacts
City of Defiance . . . . (419) 784-2101
http://www.cityofdefiance.com
Defiance Area Chamber of Commerce . . . . (419) 782-7946
http://www.defiancechamber.com

HICKSVILLE (village). Covers a land area of 2.516 square miles and a water area of 0 square miles. Located at 41.29° N. Lat.; 84.76° W. Long. Elevation is 761 feet.
History: Hicksville was founded in 1836 by Henry Hicks, Isaac Smith, and John Bryan as a trading post dealing in furs. The town's industry passed from lumber, to mills and tanneries, and to canning and wood products.
Population: 3,772 (1990); 3,649 (2000); 3,511 (2007); 3,414 (2012 projected); Race: 96.7% White, 0.1% Black, 0.1% Asian, 3.8% Hispanic of any race (2007); Density: 1,395.5 persons per square mile (2007); Average household size: 2.40 (2007); Median age: 36.9 (2007); Males per 100 females: 90.8 (2007); Marriage status: 20.5% never married, 56.8% now married, 10.7% widowed, 12.0% divorced (2000); Foreign born: 0.4% (2000); Ancestry (includes multiple ancestries): 29.9% German, 17.0% United States or American, 8.2% Other groups, 7.7% Irish, 6.7% English (2000).
Economy: Single-family building permits issued: 0 (2007); Multi-family building permits issued: 0 (2007); Employment by occupation: 9.1% management, 11.1% professional, 10.9% services, 18.8% sales, 0.0% farming, 11.8% construction, 38.3% production (2000).
Income: Per capita income: $20,619 (2007); Median household income: $44,093 (2007); Average household income: $48,923 (2007); Percent of households with income of $100,000 or more: 5.8% (2007); Poverty rate: 3.2% (2000).
Education: Percent of population age 25 and over with: High school diploma (including GED) or higher: 82.3% (2007); Bachelor's degree or higher: 12.8% (2007); Master's degree or higher: 4.6% (2007).

School District(s)

Hicksville Exempted Village (PK-12)
2005-06 Enrollment: 1,039 . . . . (419) 542-7665
Housing: Homeownership rate: 76.2% (2007); Median home value: $91,719 (2007); Median rent: $329 per month (2000); Median age of housing: 47 years (2000).
Hospitals: Community Memorial Hospital (25 beds)
Newspapers: Hicksville News-Tribune (Community news; Circulation 2,350)
Transportation: Commute to work: 91.8% car, 0.0% public transportation, 5.6% walk, 2.6% work from home (2000); Travel time to work: 41.6% less than 15 minutes, 32.9% 15 to 30 minutes, 20.0% 30 to 45 minutes, 3.6% 45 to 60 minutes, 1.9% 60 minutes or more (2000)
Additional Information Contacts
Hicksville Chamber of Commerce . . . . (419) 542-6161
http://www.hicksvillechamber.org

MARK CENTER (unincorporated postal area, zip code 43536). Aka Mark Centre. Covers a land area of 16.866 square miles and a water area of 0 square miles. Located at 41.29° N. Lat.; 84.63° W. Long. Elevation is 721 feet.
Population: 451 (2000); Race: 100.0% White, 0.0% Black, 0.0% Asian, 0.0% Hispanic of any race (2000); Density: 26.7 persons per square mile (2000); Age: 30.6% under 18, 3.1% over 64 (2000); Marriage status: 40.1% never married, 48.3% now married, 7.6% widowed, 4.0% divorced (2000); Foreign born: 0.0% (2000); Ancestry (includes multiple ancestries): 69.1%

German, 11.9% Irish, 10.1% Hungarian, 10.1% French (except Basque), 4.0% English (2000).
Economy: Employment by occupation: 12.5% management, 7.3% professional, 14.7% services, 11.4% sales, 0.0% farming, 3.7% construction, 50.5% production (2000).
Income: Per capita income: $23,773 (2000); Median household income: $80,796 (2000); Poverty rate: 0.0% (2000).
Education: Percent of population age 25 and over with: High school diploma (including GED) or higher: 100.0% (2000); Bachelor's degree or higher: 8.6% (2000).
Housing: Homeownership rate: 75.6% (2000); Median home value: $82,100 (2000); Median rent: $240 per month (2000); Median age of housing: 60+ years (2000).
Transportation: Commute to work: 97.4% car, 0.0% public transportation, 0.0% walk, 2.6% work from home (2000); Travel time to work: 13.5% less than 15 minutes, 51.1% 15 to 30 minutes, 18.4% 30 to 45 minutes, 16.9% 45 to 60 minutes, 0.0% 60 minutes or more (2000)

NEY (village). Covers a land area of 0.412 square miles and a water area of 0 square miles. Located at 41.38° N. Lat.; 84.52° W. Long. Elevation is 709 feet.
Population: 331 (1990); 364 (2000); 358 (2007); 358 (2012 projected); Race: 97.8% White, 0.6% Black, 0.0% Asian, 0.6% Hispanic of any race (2007); Density: 869.8 persons per square mile (2007); Average household size: 2.59 (2007); Median age: 33.6 (2007); Males per 100 females: 98.9 (2007); Marriage status: 12.0% never married, 73.0% now married, 3.1% widowed, 12.0% divorced (2000); Foreign born: 0.0% (2000); Ancestry (includes multiple ancestries): 31.4% German, 11.9% United States or American, 10.5% Other groups, 8.1% Irish, 7.6% English (2000).
Economy: Single-family building permits issued: 1 (2007); Multi-family building permits issued: 0 (2007); Employment by occupation: 3.3% management, 6.0% professional, 9.3% services, 27.5% sales, 0.0% farming, 8.2% construction, 45.6% production (2000).
Income: Per capita income: $20,775 (2007); Median household income: $44,091 (2007); Average household income: $53,895 (2007); Percent of households with income of $100,000 or more: 8.0% (2007); Poverty rate: 4.3% (2000).
Education: Percent of population age 25 and over with: High school diploma (including GED) or higher: 80.4% (2007); Bachelor's degree or higher: 3.7% (2007); Master's degree or higher: 1.4% (2007).
Housing: Homeownership rate: 79.0% (2007); Median home value: $83,421 (2007); Median rent: $361 per month (2000); Median age of housing: 55 years (2000).
Transportation: Commute to work: 85.2% car, 2.2% public transportation, 10.4% walk, 2.2% work from home (2000); Travel time to work: 37.1% less than 15 minutes, 45.5% 15 to 30 minutes, 11.2% 30 to 45 minutes, 2.8% 45 to 60 minutes, 3.4% 60 minutes or more (2000)

SHERWOOD (village). Covers a land area of 1.445 square miles and a water area of 0.009 square miles. Located at 41.28° N. Lat.; 84.55° W. Long. Elevation is 712 feet.
Population: 828 (1990); 801 (2000); 718 (2007); 720 (2012 projected); Race: 95.7% White, 0.6% Black, 0.0% Asian, 3.6% Hispanic of any race (2007); Density: 497.0 persons per square mile (2007); Average household size: 2.58 (2007); Median age: 37.6 (2007); Males per 100 females: 89.9 (2007); Marriage status: 20.0% never married, 61.8% now married, 5.2% widowed, 12.9% divorced (2000); Foreign born: 0.0% (2000); Ancestry (includes multiple ancestries): 37.2% German, 15.3% Other groups, 11.6% Irish, 11.6% United States or American, 5.4% English (2000).
Economy: Single-family building permits issued: 0 (2007); Multi-family building permits issued: 0 (2007); Employment by occupation: 2.4% management, 11.4% professional, 15.7% services, 15.7% sales, 0.0% farming, 10.9% construction, 43.9% production (2000).
Income: Per capita income: $18,645 (2007); Median household income: $44,286 (2007); Average household income: $48,121 (2007); Percent of households with income of $100,000 or more: 6.8% (2007); Poverty rate: 12.5% (2000).
Education: Percent of population age 25 and over with: High school diploma (including GED) or higher: 81.1% (2007); Bachelor's degree or higher: 8.8% (2007); Master's degree or higher: 4.4% (2007).

School District(s)

Central Local (PK-12)
2005-06 Enrollment: 1,220 . . . . (419) 658-2808

Housing: Homeownership rate: 83.8% (2007); Median home value: $77,250 (2007); Median rent: $366 per month (2000); Median age of housing: 50 years (2000).
Transportation: Commute to work: 93.5% car, 0.5% public transportation, 1.3% walk, 3.0% work from home (2000); Travel time to work: 18.6% less than 15 minutes, 52.8% 15 to 30 minutes, 19.4% 30 to 45 minutes, 6.1% 45 to 60 minutes, 3.1% 60 minutes or more (2000)

Delaware County

Located in central Ohio; crossed by the Olentangy and Scioto Rivers. Covers a land area of 442.41 square miles, a water area of 13.56 square miles, and is located in the Eastern Time Zone. The county was founded in 1808. County seat is Delaware.

Delaware County is part of the Columbus, OH Metropolitan Statistical Area. The entire metro area includes: Delaware County, OH; Fairfield County, OH; Franklin County, OH; Licking County, OH; Madison County, OH; Morrow County, OH; Pickaway County, OH; Union County, OH

Weather Station: Delaware Elevation: 918 feet

	Jan	Feb	Mar	Apr	May	Jun	Jul	Aug	Sep	Oct	Nov	Dec
High	33	37	48	61	71	80	84	82	76	64	50	39
Low	16	19	28	37	48	57	61	59	51	40	31	23
Precip	2.3	1.9	2.5	3.4	4.0	4.2	4.1	3.5	2.8	2.5	3.5	2.7
Snow	8.1	4.3	2.9	0.9	0.0	0.0	0.0	0.0	0.0	tr	0.8	3.7

High and Low temperatures in degrees Fahrenheit; Precipitation and Snow in inches

Population: 66,929 (1990); 109,989 (2000); 161,089 (2007); 195,812 (2012 projected); Race: 89.8% White, 3.7% Black, 3.9% Asian, 1.7% Hispanic of any race (2007); Density: 364.1 persons per square mile (2007); Average household size: 2.74 (2007); Median age: 33.9 (2007); Males per 100 females: 98.1 (2007).
Religion: Five largest groups: 18.2% Catholic Church, 5.0% The United Methodist Church, 3.0% Presbyterian Church (U.S.A.), 1.0% American Baptist Churches in the USA, 1.0% Evangelical Lutheran Church in America (2000).
Economy: Unemployment rate: 4.9% (6/2008); Total civilian labor force: 91,358 (6/2008); Leading industries: 16.9% finance & insurance; 15.3% retail trade; 12.3% accommodation & food services (2005); Farms: 785 totaling 162,554 acres (2002); Companies that employ 500 or more persons: 8 (2006); Companies that employ 100 to 499 persons: 94 (2006); Companies that employ less than 100 persons: 3,465 (2006); Black-owned businesses: n/a (2002); Hispanic-owned businesses: n/a (2002); Asian-owned businesses: 225 (2002); Women-owned businesses: 3,393 (2002); Retail sales per capita: $13,717 (2008). Single-family building permits issued: 979 (2007); Multi-family building permits issued: 55 (2007).
Income: Per capita income: $37,141 (2007); Median household income: $78,232 (2007); Average household income: $101,579 (2007); Percent of households with income of $100,000 or more: 36.0% (2007); Poverty rate: 4.5% (2005); Bankruptcy rate: 2.51% (2007).
Taxes: Total county taxes per capita: $308 (2006); County property taxes per capita: $88 (2006).
Education: Percent of population age 25 and over with: High school diploma (including GED) or higher: 93.0% (2007); Bachelor's degree or higher: 40.9% (2007); Master's degree or higher: 12.6% (2007).
Housing: Homeownership rate: 81.5% (2007); Median home value: $242,083 (2007); Median rent: $537 per month (2000); Median age of housing: 11 years (2000).
Health: Birth rate: 173.8 per 10,000 population (2007); Death rate: 47.4 per 10,000 population (2007); Age-adjusted cancer mortality rate: 177.6 deaths per 100,000 population (2005); Air Quality Index: 71.2% good, 24.7% moderate, 4.2% unhealthy for sensitive individuals, 0.0% unhealthy (percent of days in 2007); Number of physicians: 33.1 per 10,000 population (2005); Hospital beds: 5.3 per 10,000 population (2004); Hospital admissions: 171.6 per 10,000 population (2004).
Elections: 2004 Presidential election results: 66.1% Bush, 33.6% Kerry, 0.0% Nader, 0.2% Badnarik
National and State Parks: Alum Creek State Park
Additional Information Contacts
Delaware County Government. . . . . (740) 833-2100
http://www.co.delaware.oh.us
City of Delaware. . . . . (740) 203-1000
http://www.delawareohio.net
Delaware Area Chamber of Commerce. . . . . (740) 369-6221
http://www.delawareohiochamber.com

Powell Area Chamber of Commerce . . . . (614) 888-1090
http://www.powellchamber.com
Sunbury-Big Walnut Area Chamber of Commerce . . . . (740) 965-2860
http://www.sunburybigwalnutchamber.com
Village of Powell. . . . . (614) 885-5380
http://www.cityofpowell.us
Village of Shawnee Hills . . . . (614) 889-2824
http://www.shawneehillsoh.com

Delaware County Communities

ASHLEY (village). Covers a land area of 0.543 square miles and a water area of 0 square miles. Located at 40.40° N. Lat.; 82.95° W. Long. Elevation is 984 feet.

Population: 1,087 (1990); 1,216 (2000); 1,680 (2007); 1,986 (2012 projected); Race: 95.0% White, 1.7% Black, 0.0% Asian, 1.3% Hispanic of any race (2007); Density: 3,096.7 persons per square mile (2007); Average household size: 2.55 (2007); Median age: 32.6 (2007); Males per 100 females: 94.7 (2007); Marriage status: 17.2% never married, 59.4% now married, 9.5% widowed, 13.9% divorced (2000); Foreign born: 0.0% (2000); Ancestry (includes multiple ancestries): 22.8% German, 11.4% Irish, 10.0% United States or American, 8.2% English, 5.5% Other groups (2000).

Economy: Single-family building permits issued: 0 (2007); Multi-family building permits issued: 0 (2007); Employment by occupation: 7.9% management, 9.9% professional, 16.2% services, 26.3% sales, 0.0% farming, 14.9% construction, 24.9% production (2000).

Income: Per capita income: $19,273 (2007); Median household income: $43,534 (2007); Average household income: $48,621 (2007); Percent of households with income of $100,000 or more: 5.6% (2007); Poverty rate: 12.7% (2000).

Education: Percent of population age 25 and over with: High school diploma (including GED) or higher: 80.2% (2007); Bachelor's degree or higher: 7.9% (2007); Master's degree or higher: 2.4% (2007).

School District(s)

Buckeye Valley Local (PK-12)
2005-06 Enrollment: 2,319 . . . . (740) 369-8735

Housing: Homeownership rate: 74.8% (2007); Median home value: $98,246 (2007); Median rent: $358 per month (2000); Median age of housing: 52 years (2000).

Transportation: Commute to work: 95.3% car, 1.0% public transportation, 1.9% walk, 1.4% work from home (2000); Travel time to work: 11.2% less than 15 minutes, 43.5% 15 to 30 minutes, 26.5% 30 to 45 minutes, 13.7% 45 to 60 minutes, 5.2% 60 minutes or more (2000)

DELAWARE (city). County seat. Covers a land area of 15.000 square miles and a water area of 0.100 square miles. Located at 40.29° N. Lat.; 83.07° W. Long. Elevation is 869 feet.

History: Named for Thomas West, Lord Delaware, first British governor of the colony of Virginia. Delaware was established around a sulphur spring, called Medicine Waters by the Mingo and Delaware tribes who lived here in the early 1800's. Joseph Barber settled on the present town site in 1807 and opened a tavern, and the town was platted in 1808. In 1833 a company, formed to exploit the local mineral springs, built a resort hotel. The resort was unsuccessful, but the hotel became the first building of Ohio Wesleyan University, chartered in 1842.

Population: 21,106 (1990); 25,243 (2000); 33,067 (2007); 38,511 (2012 projected); Race: 89.6% White, 4.6% Black, 2.0% Asian, 2.0% Hispanic of any race (2007); Density: 2,204.5 persons per square mile (2007); Average household size: 2.59 (2007); Median age: 31.6 (2007); Males per 100 females: 93.5 (2007); Marriage status: 25.3% never married, 57.4% now married, 5.8% widowed, 11.5% divorced (2000); Foreign born: 1.6% (2000); Ancestry (includes multiple ancestries): 25.7% German, 11.8% Irish, 11.4% English, 10.1% Other groups, 9.0% United States or American (2000).

Economy: Unemployment rate: 5.6% (6/2008); Total civilian labor force: 17,808 (6/2008); Single-family building permits issued: 204 (2007); Multi-family building permits issued: 0 (2007); Employment by occupation: 15.1% management, 22.3% professional, 13.1% services, 28.0% sales, 0.3% farming, 6.5% construction, 14.7% production (2000).

Income: Per capita income: $23,696 (2007); Median household income: $51,475 (2007); Average household income: $60,250 (2007); Percent of households with income of $100,000 or more: 13.7% (2007); Poverty rate: 7.3% (2000).

Education: Percent of population age 25 and over with: High school diploma (including GED) or higher: 88.3% (2007); Bachelor's degree or higher: 27.0% (2007); Master's degree or higher: 8.1% (2007).

School District(s)

Buckeye Valley Local (PK-12)
2005-06 Enrollment: 2,319 . . . . (740) 369-8735
Delaware Area Career Center (08-12)
2005-06 Enrollment: n/a . . . . (740) 548-0708
Delaware City (PK-12)
2005-06 Enrollment: 4,683 . . . . (740) 833-1100
Department of Youth Services (06-12)
2005-06 Enrollment: 1,478 . . . . (614) 728-2489

Four-year College(s)

Methodist Theological School-Ohio (Private, Not-for-profit, United Methodist)
Fall 2007 Enrollment: 234 . . . . (740) 363-1146
Ohio Wesleyan University (Private, Not-for-profit, United Methodist)
Fall 2007 Enrollment: 1,986. . . . . (740) 368-2000
2007-08 Tuition: In-state $31,930; Out-of-state $31,930

Vocational/Technical School(s)

Delaware Area Career Center (Public)
Fall 2007 Enrollment: 90 . . . . (740) 548-0708
2007-08 Tuition: $2,200

Housing: Homeownership rate: 61.5% (2007); Median home value: $156,833 (2007); Median rent: $474 per month (2000); Median age of housing: 25 years (2000).

Hospitals: Grady Memorial Hospital (135 beds)

Safety: Violent crime rate: 28.6 per 10,000 population; Property crime rate: 295.1 per 10,000 population (2007).

Newspapers: Delaware Gazette (Community news; Circulation 8,500); Sunbury News (Local news; Circulation 8,000)

Transportation: Commute to work: 91.2% car, 0.4% public transportation, 4.1% walk, 3.3% work from home (2000); Travel time to work: 31.5% less than 15 minutes, 27.1% 15 to 30 minutes, 23.2% 30 to 45 minutes, 11.4% 45 to 60 minutes, 6.7% 60 minutes or more (2000)

Airports: Delaware Municipal (general aviation)

Additional Information Contacts

City of Delaware. . . . . (740) 203-1000
http://www.delawareohio.net
Delaware Area Chamber of Commerce. . . . . (740) 369-6221
http://www.delawareohiochamber.com

GALENA (village). Covers a land area of 0.598 square miles and a water area of 0.046 square miles. Located at 40.21° N. Lat.; 82.88° W. Long. Elevation is 922 feet.

Population: 355 (1990); 305 (2000); 503 (2007); 639 (2012 projected); Race: 97.0% White, 0.0% Black, 0.0% Asian, 2.6% Hispanic of any race (2007); Density: 840.7 persons per square mile (2007); Average household size: 2.47 (2007); Median age: 35.9 (2007); Males per 100 females: 95.7 (2007); Marriage status: 20.3% never married, 68.5% now married, 2.5% widowed, 8.7% divorced (2000); Foreign born: 0.0% (2000); Ancestry (includes multiple ancestries): 27.2% German, 17.6% Other groups, 13.6% English, 7.0% Irish, 5.0% French (except Basque) (2000).

Economy: Employment by occupation: 16.7% management, 11.7% professional, 21.6% services, 28.4% sales, 0.0% farming, 14.2% construction, 7.4% production (2000).

Income: Per capita income: $26,456 (2007); Median household income: $58,077 (2007); Average household income: $65,233 (2007); Percent of households with income of $100,000 or more: 17.2% (2007); Poverty rate: 9.6% (2000).

Education: Percent of population age 25 and over with: High school diploma (including GED) or higher: 85.3% (2007); Bachelor's degree or higher: 21.3% (2007); Master's degree or higher: 8.6% (2007).

School District(s)

Big Walnut Local (PK-12)
2005-06 Enrollment: 2,732 . . . . (740) 965-2706
Olentangy Local (PK-12)
2005-06 Enrollment: 10,801 . . . . (740) 657-4050

Housing: Homeownership rate: 83.3% (2007); Median home value: $123,980 (2007); Median rent: $458 per month (2000); Median age of housing: 60+ years (2000).

Transportation: Commute to work: 95.1% car, 0.0% public transportation, 3.1% walk, 1.9% work from home (2000); Travel time to work: 24.5% less than 15 minutes, 25.8% 15 to 30 minutes, 28.9% 30 to 45 minutes, 10.7% 45 to 60 minutes, 10.1% 60 minutes or more (2000)

Additional Information Contacts
Sunbury-Big Walnut Area Chamber of Commerce . . . . (740) 965-2860
http://www.sunburybigwalnutchamber.com

LEWIS CENTER (unincorporated postal area, zip code 43035). Covers a land area of 18.635 square miles and a water area of 0 square miles. Located at 40.18° N. Lat.; 82.98° W. Long. Elevation is 942 feet.
Population: 11,261 (2000); Race: 90.2% White, 3.9% Black, 3.1% Asian, 2.1% Hispanic of any race (2000); Density: 604.3 persons per square mile (2000); Age: 30.0% under 18, 3.9% over 64 (2000); Marriage status: 21.8% never married, 69.1% now married, 1.2% widowed, 8.0% divorced (2000); Foreign born: 3.6% (2000); Ancestry (includes multiple ancestries): 28.8% German, 17.4% Irish, 11.3% Other groups, 9.7% Italian, 9.3% English (2000).
Economy: Employment by occupation: 27.6% management, 25.3% professional, 10.4% services, 27.1% sales, 0.0% farming, 4.7% construction, 4.8% production (2000).
Income: Per capita income: $31,478 (2000); Median household income: $71,870 (2000); Poverty rate: 6.0% (2000).
Education: Percent of population age 25 and over with: High school diploma (including GED) or higher: 96.4% (2000); Bachelor's degree or higher: 50.6% (2000).

School District(s)

Olentangy Local (PK-12)
2005-06 Enrollment: 10,801 . . . . (740) 657-4050
Housing: Homeownership rate: 74.3% (2000); Median home value: $216,400 (2000); Median rent: $577 per month (2000); Median age of housing: 3 years (2000).
Newspapers: Clintonville This Week (Local news); Delaware This Week (Community news); Dublin Villager (Local news); Grandview this Week (Local news); Johnstown Independent (Community news); Powell This Week (Local news); Reynoldsburg This Week (Community news); South Side This Week (Local news); This Week Community Papers (Local news); This Week in Clintonville (Community news); This Week in Delaware/Big Walnut/Sunbury (Community news); This Week in Grandview (Community news); This Week in Hilliard (Community news); This Week in New Albany (Community news); This Week in Northland (Community news); This Week in Pickerington (Community news); This Week in Powell (Community news); This Week in Reynoldsburg (Community news); This Week in Southside (Community news); This Week in Upper Arlington (Community news); This Week in West Side (Community news); This Week in Westerville (Community news); This Week in Worthington (Community news); Upper Arlington This Week (Local news); West Side This Week (Local news); Westerville This Week (Local news); Worthington This Week (Local news)
Transportation: Commute to work: 94.8% car, 0.4% public transportation, 0.4% walk, 4.0% work from home (2000); Travel time to work: 19.4% less than 15 minutes, 50.7% 15 to 30 minutes, 21.2% 30 to 45 minutes, 4.9% 45 to 60 minutes, 3.8% 60 minutes or more (2000)

OSTRANDER (village). Covers a land area of 0.332 square miles and a water area of 0 square miles. Located at 40.26° N. Lat.; 83.21° W. Long. Elevation is 932 feet.
Population: 469 (1990); 405 (2000); 673 (2007); 850 (2012 projected); Race: 96.9% White, 0.3% Black, 0.0% Asian, 0.0% Hispanic of any race (2007); Density: 2,024.8 persons per square mile (2007); Average household size: 2.69 (2007); Median age: 33.7 (2007); Males per 100 females: 94.5 (2007); Marriage status: 15.4% never married, 65.1% now married, 7.7% widowed, 11.8% divorced (2000); Foreign born: 0.0% (2000); Ancestry (includes multiple ancestries): 29.4% German, 14.4% United States or American, 11.6% European, 11.1% Irish, 6.6% English (2000).
Economy: Employment by occupation: 12.6% management, 11.2% professional, 17.9% services, 26.5% sales, 0.0% farming, 13.0% construction, 18.8% production (2000).
Income: Per capita income: $24,153 (2007); Median household income: $53,953 (2007); Average household income: $65,020 (2007); Percent of households with income of $100,000 or more: 14.8% (2007); Poverty rate: 5.8% (2000).
Education: Percent of population age 25 and over with: High school diploma (including GED) or higher: 89.2% (2007); Bachelor's degree or higher: 11.0% (2007); Master's degree or higher: 2.2% (2007).

School District(s)

Buckeye Valley Local (PK-12)
2005-06 Enrollment: 2,319 . . . . (740) 369-8735
Housing: Homeownership rate: 90.4% (2007); Median home value: $137,500 (2007); Median rent: $433 per month (2000); Median age of housing: 60+ years (2000).
Transportation: Commute to work: 97.3% car, 0.0% public transportation, 2.7% walk, 0.0% work from home (2000); Travel time to work: 11.3% less than 15 minutes, 52.5% 15 to 30 minutes, 18.6% 30 to 45 minutes, 11.3% 45 to 60 minutes, 6.3% 60 minutes or more (2000)

POWELL (city). Covers a land area of 3.036 square miles and a water area of 0 square miles. Located at 40.15° N. Lat.; 83.07° W. Long. Elevation is 909 feet.
Population: 2,776 (1990); 6,247 (2000); 10,040 (2007); 12,560 (2012 projected); Race: 88.3% White, 2.5% Black, 7.3% Asian, 1.8% Hispanic of any race (2007); Density: 3,306.5 persons per square mile (2007); Average household size: 3.23 (2007); Median age: 33.9 (2007); Males per 100 females: 99.4 (2007); Marriage status: 11.0% never married, 82.6% now married, 1.3% widowed, 5.0% divorced (2000); Foreign born: 3.3% (2000); Ancestry (includes multiple ancestries): 33.4% German, 19.8% Irish, 13.2% English, 9.1% Italian, 8.1% Other groups (2000).
Economy: Single-family building permits issued: 114 (2007); Multi-family building permits issued: 40 (2007); Employment by occupation: 32.4% management, 31.5% professional, 5.3% services, 25.6% sales, 0.0% farming, 3.5% construction, 1.7% production (2000).
Income: Per capita income: $47,656 (2007); Median household income: $126,245 (2007); Average household income: $154,145 (2007); Percent of households with income of $100,000 or more: 67.2% (2007); Poverty rate: 0.4% (2000).
Education: Percent of population age 25 and over with: High school diploma (including GED) or higher: 98.8% (2007); Bachelor's degree or higher: 68.6% (2007); Master's degree or higher: 25.5% (2007).

School District(s)

Dublin City (PK-12)
2005-06 Enrollment: 12,939 . . . . (614) 764-5913
Olentangy Local (PK-12)
2005-06 Enrollment: 10,801 . . . . (740) 657-4050
Worthington City (PK-12)
2005-06 Enrollment: 9,553 . . . . (614) 883-3000
Housing: Homeownership rate: 98.0% (2007); Median home value: $311,018 (2007); Median rent: $1,333 per month (2000); Median age of housing: 6 years (2000).
Transportation: Commute to work: 95.2% car, 0.3% public transportation, 0.3% walk, 4.2% work from home (2000); Travel time to work: 15.8% less than 15 minutes, 46.2% 15 to 30 minutes, 27.2% 30 to 45 minutes, 6.6% 45 to 60 minutes, 4.2% 60 minutes or more (2000)

Additional Information Contacts
Powell Area Chamber of Commerce . . . . (614) 888-1090
http://www.powellchamber.com
Village of Powell. . . . . (614) 885-5380
http://www.cityofpowell.us

RADNOR (unincorporated postal area, zip code 43066). Aka Meredith. Covers a land area of 38.542 square miles and a water area of 0 square miles. Located at 40.40° N. Lat.; 83.15° W. Long. Elevation is 938 feet.
Population: 1,085 (2000); Race: 100.0% White, 0.0% Black, 0.0% Asian, 0.0% Hispanic of any race (2000); Density: 28.2 persons per square mile (2000); Age: 27.0% under 18, 5.7% over 64 (2000); Marriage status: 22.6% never married, 69.6% now married, 1.9% widowed, 5.8% divorced (2000); Foreign born: 0.0% (2000); Ancestry (includes multiple ancestries): 21.0% German, 15.4% Welsh, 11.7% United States or American, 9.8% Irish, 7.0% English (2000).
Economy: Employment by occupation: 11.7% management, 16.6% professional, 23.5% services, 20.0% sales, 1.7% farming, 7.8% construction, 18.8% production (2000).
Income: Per capita income: $16,057 (2000); Median household income: $41,570 (2000); Poverty rate: 8.5% (2000).
Education: Percent of population age 25 and over with: High school diploma (including GED) or higher: 90.3% (2000); Bachelor's degree or higher: 16.1% (2000).

School District(s)

Buckeye Valley Local (PK-12)
2005-06 Enrollment: 2,319 . . . . (740) 369-8735
Housing: Homeownership rate: 76.5% (2000); Median home value: $106,900 (2000); Median rent: $507 per month (2000); Median age of housing: 60+ years (2000).

Transportation: Commute to work: 87.5% car, 1.4% public transportation, 0.0% walk, 9.9% work from home (2000); Travel time to work: 20.8% less than 15 minutes, 47.0% 15 to 30 minutes, 19.3% 30 to 45 minutes, 9.1% 45 to 60 minutes, 3.8% 60 minutes or more (2000)

SHAWNEE HILLS (village). Covers a land area of 0.388 square miles and a water area of 0 square miles. Located at 40.15° N. Lat.; 83.13° W. Long. Elevation is 892 feet.
Population: 423 (1990); 419 (2000); 489 (2007); 547 (2012 projected); Race: 90.2% White, 3.5% Black, 4.3% Asian, 3.7% Hispanic of any race (2007); Density: 1,261.9 persons per square mile (2007); Average household size: 2.29 (2007); Median age: 40.0 (2007); Males per 100 females: 92.5 (2007); Marriage status: 22.2% never married, 57.1% now married, 5.1% widowed, 15.6% divorced (2000); Foreign born: 2.9% (2000); Ancestry (includes multiple ancestries): 24.0% German, 13.2% Other groups, 12.0% Italian, 10.8% Irish, 10.8% English (2000).
Economy: Employment by occupation: 18.6% management, 20.2% professional, 20.7% services, 20.7% sales, 0.0% farming, 10.3% construction, 9.5% production (2000).
Income: Per capita income: $27,858 (2007); Median household income: $62,344 (2007); Average household income: $63,657 (2007); Percent of households with income of $100,000 or more: 17.3% (2007); Poverty rate: 7.8% (2000).
Education: Percent of population age 25 and over with: High school diploma (including GED) or higher: 88.0% (2007); Bachelor's degree or higher: 29.3% (2007); Master's degree or higher: 8.0% (2007).
Housing: Homeownership rate: 79.9% (2007); Median home value: $172,794 (2007); Median rent: $561 per month (2000); Median age of housing: 40 years (2000).
Transportation: Commute to work: 94.1% car, 0.0% public transportation, 5.0% walk, 0.8% work from home (2000); Travel time to work: 21.1% less than 15 minutes, 38.8% 15 to 30 minutes, 26.6% 30 to 45 minutes, 7.6% 45 to 60 minutes, 5.9% 60 minutes or more (2000)
Additional Information Contacts
Village of Shawnee Hills . . . . (614) 889-2824
http://www.shawneehillsoh.com

SUNBURY (village). Covers a land area of 2.541 square miles and a water area of 0.001 square miles. Located at 40.24° N. Lat.; 82.86° W. Long. Elevation is 971 feet.
Population: 2,258 (1990); 2,630 (2000); 3,978 (2007); 4,881 (2012 projected); Race: 96.6% White, 0.6% Black, 0.5% Asian, 2.4% Hispanic of any race (2007); Density: 1,565.4 persons per square mile (2007); Average household size: 2.53 (2007); Median age: 34.1 (2007); Males per 100 females: 91.1 (2007); Marriage status: 20.3% never married, 58.7% now married, 8.3% widowed, 12.6% divorced (2000); Foreign born: 1.3% (2000); Ancestry (includes multiple ancestries): 25.6% German, 13.6% Irish, 12.4% English, 10.8% United States or American, 7.9% Other groups (2000).
Economy: Single-family building permits issued: 20 (2007); Multi-family building permits issued: 0 (2007); Employment by occupation: 13.0% management, 15.6% professional, 13.3% services, 29.8% sales, 0.5% farming, 13.0% construction, 14.9% production (2000).
Income: Per capita income: $24,028 (2007); Median household income: $53,142 (2007); Average household income: $60,489 (2007); Percent of households with income of $100,000 or more: 14.4% (2007); Poverty rate: 4.7% (2000).
Education: Percent of population age 25 and over with: High school diploma (including GED) or higher: 84.1% (2007); Bachelor's degree or higher: 19.4% (2007); Master's degree or higher: 4.6% (2007).

School District(s)

Big Walnut Local (PK-12)
2005-06 Enrollment: 2,732 . . . . (740) 965-2706
Housing: Homeownership rate: 73.7% (2007); Median home value: $149,524 (2007); Median rent: $488 per month (2000); Median age of housing: 33 years (2000).
Transportation: Commute to work: 93.5% car, 0.5% public transportation, 3.0% walk, 2.4% work from home (2000); Travel time to work: 22.9% less than 15 minutes, 34.7% 15 to 30 minutes, 29.1% 30 to 45 minutes, 10.0% 45 to 60 minutes, 3.5% 60 minutes or more (2000)
Additional Information Contacts
Sunbury-Big Walnut Area Chamber of Commerce . . . . (740) 965-2860
http://www.sunburybigwalnutchamber.com

Erie County

Located in northern Ohio; bounded on the north by Lake Erie; drained by the Huron and Vermilion Rivers; includes Kelleys Island. Covers a land area of 254.88 square miles, a water area of 371.27 square miles, and is located in the Eastern Time Zone. The county was founded in 1838. County seat is Sandusky.

Erie County is part of the Sandusky, OH Metropolitan Statistical Area. The entire metro area includes: Erie County, OH

Weather Station: Sandusky Elevation: 583 feet

	Jan	Feb	Mar	Apr	May	Jun	Jul	Aug	Sep	Oct	Nov	Dec
High	32	35	44	56	68	78	82	80	74	62	49	38
Low	18	20	29	39	51	61	65	63	56	45	35	25
Precip	1.9	1.7	2.5	3.1	3.3	4.1	3.4	3.6	3.1	2.3	2.8	2.5
Snow	8.7	6.0	3.0	0.6	tr	0.0	0.0	0.0	0.0	tr	0.3	4.3

High and Low temperatures in degrees Fahrenheit; Precipitation and Snow in inches

Population: 76,918 (1990); 79,551 (2000); 78,434 (2007); 77,398 (2012 projected); Race: 88.5% White, 8.3% Black, 0.6% Asian, 2.5% Hispanic of any race (2007); Density: 307.7 persons per square mile (2007); Average household size: 2.44 (2007); Median age: 41.9 (2007); Males per 100 females: 94.5 (2007).
Religion: Five largest groups: 27.8% Catholic Church, 7.3% Evangelical Lutheran Church in America, 5.4% United Church of Christ, 3.9% The United Methodist Church, 1.3% Assemblies of God (2000).
Economy: Unemployment rate: 5.9% (6/2008); Total civilian labor force: 45,503 (6/2008); Leading industries: 24.1% manufacturing; 15.3% retail trade; 15.1% accommodation & food services (2005); Farms: 392 totaling 94,681 acres (2002); Companies that employ 500 or more persons: 4 (2006); Companies that employ 100 to 499 persons: 40 (2006); Companies that employ less than 100 persons: 1,922 (2006); Black-owned businesses: n/a (2002); Hispanic-owned businesses: n/a (2002); Asian-owned businesses: n/a (2002); Women-owned businesses: 1,627 (2002); Retail sales per capita: $14,929 (2008). Single-family building permits issued: 103 (2007); Multi-family building permits issued: 24 (2007).
Income: Per capita income: $24,929 (2007); Median household income: $47,895 (2007); Average household income: $60,080 (2007); Percent of households with income of $100,000 or more: 13.6% (2007); Poverty rate: 11.6% (2005); Bankruptcy rate: 4.75% (2007).
Education: Percent of population age 25 and over with: High school diploma (including GED) or higher: 84.0% (2007); Bachelor's degree or higher: 16.8% (2007); Master's degree or higher: 5.7% (2007).
Housing: Homeownership rate: 72.6% (2007); Median home value: $132,226 (2007); Median rent: $409 per month (2000); Median age of housing: 39 years (2000).
Health: Birth rate: 118.3 per 10,000 population (2007); Death rate: 109.3 per 10,000 population (2007); Age-adjusted cancer mortality rate: 194.4 deaths per 100,000 population (2005); Number of physicians: 23.8 per 10,000 population (2005); Hospital beds: 47.6 per 10,000 population (2004); Hospital admissions: 1,732.7 per 10,000 population (2004).
Elections: 2004 Presidential election results: 46.4% Bush, 53.4% Kerry, 0.0% Nader, 0.1% Badnarik
National and State Parks: Glacial Grooves State Memorial; Kelleys Island State Park
Additional Information Contacts
Erie County Government . . . . (419) 627-7682
http://www.erie-county-ohio.net
City of Huron . . . . (419) 433-5000
http://www.cityofhuron.org
City of Sandusky . . . . (419) 627-5844
http://www.ci.sandusky.oh.us
Erie County Chamber of Commerce . . . . (419) 625-6421
http://www.eriecountyohiocofc.com
Huron Chamber of Commerce. . . . . (419) 433-5700
http://www.huron.net
Kelleys Island Chamber of Commerce . . . . (419) 746-2360
http://www.kelleysislandchamber.com

Erie County Communities

BAY VIEW (village). Covers a land area of 0.292 square miles and a water area of 0 square miles. Located at 41.46° N. Lat.; 82.82° W. Long. Elevation is 581 feet.

History: Bay View developed as a resort community with swimming, boating, and camping facilities.
Population: 739 (1990); 692 (2000); 654 (2007); 627 (2012 projected); Race: 97.9% White, 0.0% Black, 0.3% Asian, 2.0% Hispanic of any race (2007); Density: 2,242.3 persons per square mile (2007); Average household size: 2.31 (2007); Median age: 44.2 (2007); Males per 100 females: 97.0 (2007); Marriage status: 17.2% never married, 62.9% now married, 9.3% widowed, 10.6% divorced (2000); Foreign born: 0.7% (2000); Ancestry (includes multiple ancestries): 42.3% German, 16.3% Irish, 12.3% English, 8.2% United States or American, 7.7% Polish (2000).
Economy: Single-family building permits issued: 1 (2007); Multi-family building permits issued: 0 (2007); Employment by occupation: 12.8% management, 11.3% professional, 15.5% services, 21.6% sales, 0.0% farming, 11.9% construction, 26.8% production (2000).
Income: Per capita income: $23,899 (2007); Median household income: $47,500 (2007); Average household income: $55,230 (2007); Percent of households with income of $100,000 or more: 11.0% (2007); Poverty rate: 4.0% (2000).
Education: Percent of population age 25 and over with: High school diploma (including GED) or higher: 77.3% (2007); Bachelor's degree or higher: 13.2% (2007); Master's degree or higher: 2.6% (2007).
Housing: Homeownership rate: 87.6% (2007); Median home value: $111,620 (2007); Median rent: $414 per month (2000); Median age of housing: 46 years (2000).
Transportation: Commute to work: 97.5% car, 0.0% public transportation, 1.9% walk, 0.6% work from home (2000); Travel time to work: 26.2% less than 15 minutes, 55.8% 15 to 30 minutes, 10.4% 30 to 45 minutes, 2.2% 45 to 60 minutes, 5.4% 60 minutes or more (2000)
Additional Information Contacts
Erie County Chamber of Commerce . . . . (419) 625-6421
http://www.eriecountyohiocofc.com

BERLIN HEIGHTS (village). Covers a land area of 1.563 square miles and a water area of 0 square miles. Located at 41.32° N. Lat.; 82.49° W. Long. Elevation is 778 feet.
History: Berlin Heights developed as the center of an apple and peach district, begun in 1812 when John Hoak and John Fleming brought from Canada a number of young fruit trees.
Population: 691 (1990); 685 (2000); 663 (2007); 652 (2012 projected); Race: 98.9% White, 0.0% Black, 0.0% Asian, 1.4% Hispanic of any race (2007); Density: 424.2 persons per square mile (2007); Average household size: 2.60 (2007); Median age: 41.0 (2007); Males per 100 females: 93.9 (2007); Marriage status: 24.2% never married, 62.4% now married, 4.9% widowed, 8.5% divorced (2000); Foreign born: 1.2% (2000); Ancestry (includes multiple ancestries): 38.9% German, 10.5% Irish, 9.8% English, 7.9% United States or American, 4.5% Other groups (2000).
Economy: Single-family building permits issued: 0 (2007); Multi-family building permits issued: 0 (2007); Employment by occupation: 7.6% management, 19.4% professional, 17.5% services, 19.1% sales, 1.9% farming, 11.5% construction, 22.9% production (2000).
Income: Per capita income: $22,504 (2007); Median household income: $54,394 (2007); Average household income: $58,510 (2007); Percent of households with income of $100,000 or more: 11.4% (2007); Poverty rate: 6.9% (2000).
Education: Percent of population age 25 and over with: High school diploma (including GED) or higher: 83.3% (2007); Bachelor's degree or higher: 19.7% (2007); Master's degree or higher: 7.8% (2007).

School District(s)

Berlin-Milan Local (PK-12)
2005-06 Enrollment: 1,823 . . . . (419) 499-4272
Housing: Homeownership rate: 82.0% (2007); Median home value: $124,798 (2007); Median rent: $381 per month (2000); Median age of housing: 60+ years (2000).
Transportation: Commute to work: 91.9% car, 0.6% public transportation, 6.2% walk, 1.3% work from home (2000); Travel time to work: 28.0% less than 15 minutes, 37.2% 15 to 30 minutes, 19.1% 30 to 45 minutes, 10.9% 45 to 60 minutes, 4.9% 60 minutes or more (2000)
Additional Information Contacts
Erie County Chamber of Commerce . . . . (419) 625-6421
http://www.eriecountyohiocofc.com

CASTALIA (village). Covers a land area of 1.044 square miles and a water area of 0.006 square miles. Located at 41.40° N. Lat.; 82.80° W. Long. Elevation is 633 feet.
Population: 915 (1990); 935 (2000); 803 (2007); 789 (2012 projected); Race: 96.3% White, 1.4% Black, 0.0% Asian, 4.0% Hispanic of any race (2007); Density: 769.2 persons per square mile (2007); Average household size: 2.53 (2007); Median age: 38.9 (2007); Males per 100 females: 90.7 (2007); Marriage status: 22.0% never married, 57.7% now married, 9.1% widowed, 11.2% divorced (2000); Foreign born: 1.0% (2000); Ancestry (includes multiple ancestries): 37.9% German, 14.1% English, 12.8% Irish, 9.1% Other groups, 7.9% United States or American (2000).
Economy: Single-family building permits issued: 0 (2007); Multi-family building permits issued: 0 (2007); Employment by occupation: 7.8% management, 15.8% professional, 16.9% services, 21.2% sales, 0.5% farming, 8.7% construction, 29.2% production (2000).
Income: Per capita income: $22,201 (2007); Median household income: $48,750 (2007); Average household income: $56,238 (2007); Percent of households with income of $100,000 or more: 12.6% (2007); Poverty rate: 6.1% (2000).
Education: Percent of population age 25 and over with: High school diploma (including GED) or higher: 81.7% (2007); Bachelor's degree or higher: 8.2% (2007); Master's degree or higher: 2.6% (2007).

School District(s)

Margaretta Local (PK-12)
2005-06 Enrollment: 1,418 . . . . (419) 684-5322
Housing: Homeownership rate: 71.0% (2007); Median home value: $130,707 (2007); Median rent: $418 per month (2000); Median age of housing: 51 years (2000).
Transportation: Commute to work: 96.9% car, 0.2% public transportation, 1.9% walk, 1.0% work from home (2000); Travel time to work: 31.6% less than 15 minutes, 47.8% 15 to 30 minutes, 10.2% 30 to 45 minutes, 1.9% 45 to 60 minutes, 8.5% 60 minutes or more (2000)
Additional Information Contacts
Erie County Chamber of Commerce . . . . (419) 625-6421
http://www.eriecountyohiocofc.com

FAIRVIEW LANES (CDP). Covers a land area of 0.365 square miles and a water area of 0 square miles. Located at 41.42° N. Lat.; 82.65° W. Long. Elevation is 584 feet.
Population: 1,120 (1990); 1,015 (2000); 1,128 (2007); 1,196 (2012 projected); Race: 98.7% White, 0.9% Black, 0.3% Asian, 1.4% Hispanic of any race (2007); Density: 3,088.6 persons per square mile (2007); Average household size: 2.50 (2007); Median age: 42.6 (2007); Males per 100 females: 94.5 (2007); Marriage status: 16.6% never married, 68.7% now married, 6.7% widowed, 8.1% divorced (2000); Foreign born: 0.0% (2000); Ancestry (includes multiple ancestries): 49.4% German, 14.9% English, 12.3% Irish, 8.3% Italian, 4.4% Welsh (2000).
Economy: Employment by occupation: 8.7% management, 21.1% professional, 14.2% services, 31.6% sales, 0.0% farming, 7.1% construction, 17.3% production (2000).
Income: Per capita income: $29,683 (2007); Median household income: $60,484 (2007); Average household income: $74,076 (2007); Percent of households with income of $100,000 or more: 18.1% (2007); Poverty rate: 0.0% (2000).
Education: Percent of population age 25 and over with: High school diploma (including GED) or higher: 89.6% (2007); Bachelor's degree or higher: 24.2% (2007); Master's degree or higher: 8.7% (2007).
Housing: Homeownership rate: 94.5% (2007); Median home value: $131,929 (2007); Median rent: $625 per month (2000); Median age of housing: 38 years (2000).
Transportation: Commute to work: 98.5% car, 1.5% public transportation, 0.0% walk, 0.0% work from home (2000); Travel time to work: 52.4% less than 15 minutes, 34.2% 15 to 30 minutes, 6.5% 30 to 45 minutes, 2.4% 45 to 60 minutes, 4.5% 60 minutes or more (2000)

HURON (city). Covers a land area of 4.886 square miles and a water area of 2.845 square miles. Located at 41.40° N. Lat.; 82.56° W. Long. Elevation is 584 feet.
History: A French trading post was established here about 1749. In 1805, trader B.F. Flemond arrived, and the town of Huron soon grew up around the harbor at the mouth of the Huron River. Shipping and shipbuilding supported the town.
Population: 7,074 (1990); 7,958 (2000); 7,888 (2007); 7,795 (2012 projected); Race: 96.5% White, 0.9% Black, 1.0% Asian, 2.1% Hispanic of any race (2007); Density: 1,614.2 persons per square mile (2007); Average household size: 2.33 (2007); Median age: 41.6 (2007); Males per 100 females: 91.5 (2007); Marriage status: 19.0% never married, 65.5% now married, 6.4% widowed, 9.1% divorced (2000); Foreign born: 1.7% (2000);

Ancestry (includes multiple ancestries): 40.0% German, 16.5% Irish, 13.0% Italian, 10.6% English, 5.9% Other groups (2000).
Economy: Single-family building permits issued: 9 (2007); Multi-family building permits issued: 0 (2007); Employment by occupation: 14.5% management, 23.0% professional, 13.3% services, 24.3% sales, 0.2% farming, 6.1% construction, 18.6% production (2000).
Income: Per capita income: $31,269 (2007); Median household income: $60,448 (2007); Average household income: $72,442 (2007); Percent of households with income of $100,000 or more: 22.5% (2007); Poverty rate: 3.6% (2000).
Education: Percent of population age 25 and over with: High school diploma (including GED) or higher: 91.4% (2007); Bachelor's degree or higher: 28.9% (2007); Master's degree or higher: 11.2% (2007).

School District(s)

Huron City (PK-12)
2005-06 Enrollment: 1,518 . . . . (419) 433-3911

Two-year College(s)

Bowling Green State University-Firelands (Public)
Fall 2007 Enrollment: 2,065. . . . . (419) 433-5560
2007-08 Tuition: In-state $4,228; Out-of-state $11,536

Housing: Homeownership rate: 74.1% (2007); Median home value: $157,839 (2007); Median rent: $434 per month (2000); Median age of housing: 35 years (2000).
Safety: Violent crime rate: 0.0 per 10,000 population; Property crime rate: 206.9 per 10,000 population (2007).
Transportation: Commute to work: 95.7% car, 0.0% public transportation, 1.8% walk, 1.9% work from home (2000); Travel time to work: 39.2% less than 15 minutes, 40.8% 15 to 30 minutes, 12.8% 30 to 45 minutes, 2.6% 45 to 60 minutes, 4.6% 60 minutes or more (2000)

Additional Information Contacts

City of Huron . . . . (419) 433-5000
http://www.cityofhuron.org
Erie County Chamber of Commerce . . . . (419) 625-6421
http://www.eriecountyohiocofc.com
Huron Chamber of Commerce. . . . . (419) 433-5700
http://www.huron.net

KELLEYS ISLAND (village). Covers a land area of 4.559 square miles and a water area of 0.061 square miles. Located at 41.60° N. Lat.; 82.69° W. Long. Elevation is 597 feet.
History: In 1833 Irad and Datus Kelley acquired the island in Lake Erie, and settled here. They first harvested the forests of red cedar. In 1846 they planted an acre of grapes, and the island was soon known for its wine, as well as its peaches and grapes. Later, quarrying of the limestone became an important industry.
Population: 172 (1990); 367 (2000); 382 (2007); 392 (2012 projected); Race: 99.2% White, 0.5% Black, 0.0% Asian, 0.3% Hispanic of any race (2007); Density: 83.8 persons per square mile (2007); Average household size: 1.96 (2007); Median age: 54.0 (2007); Males per 100 females: 100.0 (2007); Marriage status: 9.8% never married, 69.5% now married, 9.5% widowed, 11.1% divorced (2000); Foreign born: 1.7% (2000); Ancestry (includes multiple ancestries): 28.0% German, 15.9% English, 15.3% Irish, 8.6% Polish, 7.2% Other groups (2000).
Economy: Single-family building permits issued: 11 (2007); Multi-family building permits issued: 0 (2007); Employment by occupation: 15.6% management, 7.5% professional, 14.3% services, 32.7% sales, 0.0% farming, 11.6% construction, 18.4% production (2000).
Income: Per capita income: $25,342 (2007); Median household income: $39,219 (2007); Average household income: $49,564 (2007); Percent of households with income of $100,000 or more: 11.8% (2007); Poverty rate: 9.8% (2000).
Education: Percent of population age 25 and over with: High school diploma (including GED) or higher: 94.5% (2007); Bachelor's degree or higher: 20.1% (2007); Master's degree or higher: 3.9% (2007).

School District(s)

Kelleys Island Local (PK-12)
2005-06 Enrollment: 25 . . . . (419) 746-2730

Housing: Homeownership rate: 81.5% (2007); Median home value: $197,115 (2007); Median rent: $506 per month (2000); Median age of housing: 31 years (2000).
Transportation: Commute to work: 77.6% car, 2.7% public transportation, 3.4% walk, 16.3% work from home (2000); Travel time to work: 71.5% less than 15 minutes, 10.6% 15 to 30 minutes, 8.9% 30 to 45 minutes, 0.0% 45 to 60 minutes, 8.9% 60 minutes or more (2000)

Additional Information Contacts

Erie County Chamber of Commerce . . . . (419) 625-6421
http://www.eriecountyohiocofc.com
Kelleys Island Chamber of Commerce . . . . (419) 746-2360
http://www.kelleysislandchamber.com

MILAN (village). Covers a land area of 1.175 square miles and a water area of 0 square miles. Located at 41.29° N. Lat.; 82.60° W. Long. Elevation is 659 feet.
History: Several villages occupied this site on the Huron River before the permanent settlement of Milan was laid out in 1816 by Ebenezer Merry. The town became a shipping port in 1839, when residents completed a canal to the Huron River, three miles away. Wheat was the principal cargo of the ships that left Milan. Milan prospered until the river became unnavigable for lake boats and the canal ceased to be used in the 1880's.
Population: 1,464 (1990); 1,445 (2000); 1,444 (2007); 1,451 (2012 projected); Race: 97.7% White, 0.5% Black, 0.3% Asian, 1.2% Hispanic of any race (2007); Density: 1,229.1 persons per square mile (2007); Average household size: 2.62 (2007); Median age: 43.4 (2007); Males per 100 females: 93.3 (2007); Marriage status: 21.4% never married, 62.0% now married, 7.7% widowed, 8.9% divorced (2000); Foreign born: 0.8% (2000); Ancestry (includes multiple ancestries): 45.7% German, 14.7% English, 13.3% Irish, 5.4% Other groups, 5.3% Polish (2000).
Economy: Single-family building permits issued: 0 (2007); Multi-family building permits issued: 0 (2007); Employment by occupation: 9.0% management, 21.8% professional, 12.4% services, 27.1% sales, 0.0% farming, 9.0% construction, 20.6% production (2000).
Income: Per capita income: $25,627 (2007); Median household income: $55,455 (2007); Average household income: $65,507 (2007); Percent of households with income of $100,000 or more: 15.8% (2007); Poverty rate: 4.6% (2000).
Education: Percent of population age 25 and over with: High school diploma (including GED) or higher: 86.5% (2007); Bachelor's degree or higher: 22.5% (2007); Master's degree or higher: 7.4% (2007).

School District(s)

Berlin-Milan Local (PK-12)
2005-06 Enrollment: 1,823 . . . . (419) 499-4272
Ehove (PK-12)
2005-06 Enrollment: n/a . . . . (419) 499-4663

Vocational/Technical School(s)

Ehove Career Center (Public)
Fall 2007 Enrollment: 291 . . . . (419) 499-4663
2007-08 Tuition: $6,500

Housing: Homeownership rate: 79.3% (2007); Median home value: $148,529 (2007); Median rent: $432 per month (2000); Median age of housing: 46 years (2000).
Transportation: Commute to work: 92.4% car, 0.0% public transportation, 4.1% walk, 1.8% work from home (2000); Travel time to work: 49.2% less than 15 minutes, 29.3% 15 to 30 minutes, 12.5% 30 to 45 minutes, 3.4% 45 to 60 minutes, 5.7% 60 minutes or more (2000)

Additional Information Contacts

Erie County Chamber of Commerce . . . . (419) 625-6421
http://www.eriecountyohiocofc.com

SANDUSKY (city). County seat. Covers a land area of 10.050 square miles and a water area of 11.937 square miles. Located at 41.44° N. Lat.; 82.70° W. Long. Elevation is 597 feet.
History: Sandusky was platted in 1818, replacing a smaller tract laid out in 1816 and called Portland. Its location on the southeastern corner of Sandusky Bay (named Lac Sandouske by French explorers, after the Wyandotte San-doos-tee) made the town a tourist and vacation destination, as well as an industrial community. The town was a port of entry and a shipping center, a stopping place for all vessels that sailed the Great Lakes. Sandusky became the seat of Erie County in 1838, but the 1840's brought epidemics of cholera that killed hundreds of people. In the 1850's Sandusky was an important station on the Underground Railroad.
Population: 29,764 (1990); 27,844 (2000); 26,395 (2007); 25,297 (2012 projected); Race: 73.9% White, 20.8% Black, 0.4% Asian, 3.7% Hispanic of any race (2007); Density: 2,626.4 persons per square mile (2007); Average household size: 2.28 (2007); Median age: 37.8 (2007); Males per 100 females: 89.4 (2007); Marriage status: 29.0% never married, 48.9% now married, 9.1% widowed, 13.0% divorced (2000); Foreign born: 1.7% (2000); Ancestry (includes multiple ancestries): 32.1% German, 24.7% Other groups, 12.4% Irish, 7.8% English, 7.4% Italian (2000).
Economy: Unemployment rate: 6.5% (6/2008); Total civilian labor force: 15,106 (6/2008); Single-family building permits issued: 7 (2007);

Multi-family building permits issued: 0 (2007); Employment by occupation: 7.0% management, 12.0% professional, 21.1% services, 24.9% sales, 0.2% farming, 7.8% construction, 27.1% production (2000).
Income: Per capita income: $20,027 (2007); Median household income: $34,128 (2007); Average household income: $45,236 (2007); Percent of households with income of $100,000 or more: 6.4% (2007); Poverty rate: 15.3% (2000).
Taxes: Total city taxes per capita: $575 (2006); City property taxes per capita: $85 (2006).
Education: Percent of population age 25 and over with: High school diploma (including GED) or higher: 79.6% (2007); Bachelor's degree or higher: 11.2% (2007); Master's degree or higher: 3.3% (2007).

School District(s)

Perkins Local (PK-12)
2005-06 Enrollment: 2,192 . . . . (419) 625-0484
Sandusky City (PK-12)
2005-06 Enrollment: 4,109 . . . . (419) 626-6940

Two-year College(s)

Firelands Regional Medical Center School of Nursing (Private, Not-for-profit)
Fall 2007 Enrollment: 126 . . . . (419) 557-7111
2007-08 Tuition: In-state $14,840; Out-of-state $14,840
Ohio Business College (Private, For-profit)
Fall 2007 Enrollment: 248 . . . . (419) 627-8345
2007-08 Tuition: In-state $7,740; Out-of-state $7,740

Vocational/Technical School(s)

Sandusky Career Center (Public)
Fall 2007 Enrollment: 137 . . . . (419) 625-9294
2007-08 Tuition: $7,150

Housing: Homeownership rate: 56.8% (2007); Median home value: $89,679 (2007); Median rent: $387 per month (2000); Median age of housing: 50 years (2000).
Hospitals: Firelands Regional Medical Center (265 beds)
Safety: Violent crime rate: 86.6 per 10,000 population; Property crime rate: 612.1 per 10,000 population (2007).
Newspapers: Sandusky Register (Regional news; Circulation 23,162)
Transportation: Commute to work: 94.6% car, 0.6% public transportation, 2.3% walk, 1.4% work from home (2000); Travel time to work: 59.1% less than 15 minutes, 28.5% 15 to 30 minutes, 6.7% 30 to 45 minutes, 1.8% 45 to 60 minutes, 4.0% 60 minutes or more (2000); Amtrak: Service available.
Airports: Griffing Sandusky (general aviation)
Additional Information Contacts
City of Sandusky . . . . (419) 627-5844
http://www.ci.sandusky.oh.us
Erie County Chamber of Commerce . . . . (419) 625-6421
http://www.eriecountyohiocofc.com

SANDUSKY SOUTH (CDP). Covers a land area of 4.266 square miles and a water area of 0.020 square miles. Located at 41.41° N. Lat.; 82.68° W. Long.
Population: 6,466 (1990); 6,599 (2000); 6,542 (2007); 6,496 (2012 projected); Race: 88.2% White, 8.9% Black, 0.9% Asian, 1.5% Hispanic of any race (2007); Density: 1,533.6 persons per square mile (2007); Average household size: 2.89 (2007); Median age: 47.8 (2007); Males per 100 females: 116.6 (2007); Marriage status: 20.0% never married, 60.8% now married, 9.3% widowed, 10.0% divorced (2000); Foreign born: 1.9% (2000); Ancestry (includes multiple ancestries): 39.4% German, 12.2% Irish, 11.0% Other groups, 10.4% English, 7.1% Italian (2000).
Economy: Employment by occupation: 8.9% management, 19.2% professional, 19.9% services, 22.7% sales, 0.3% farming, 6.8% construction, 22.2% production (2000).
Income: Per capita income: $24,898 (2007); Median household income: $56,272 (2007); Average household income: $66,762 (2007); Percent of households with income of $100,000 or more: 17.6% (2007); Poverty rate: 4.0% (2000).
Education: Percent of population age 25 and over with: High school diploma (including GED) or higher: 79.3% (2007); Bachelor's degree or higher: 15.3% (2007); Master's degree or higher: 5.4% (2007).
Housing: Homeownership rate: 87.9% (2007); Median home value: $135,648 (2007); Median rent: $390 per month (2000); Median age of housing: 36 years (2000).
Transportation: Commute to work: 96.4% car, 0.5% public transportation, 0.2% walk, 2.2% work from home (2000); Travel time to work: 70.1% less than 15 minutes, 19.7% 15 to 30 minutes, 4.6% 30 to 45 minutes, 2.7% 45 to 60 minutes, 2.9% 60 minutes or more (2000)

Fairfield County

Located in central Ohio; drained by the Hocking River; includes part of Buckeye Lake. Covers a land area of 505.11 square miles, a water area of 3.49 square miles, and is located in the Eastern Time Zone. The county was founded in 1800. County seat is Lancaster.

Fairfield County is part of the Columbus, OH Metropolitan Statistical Area. The entire metro area includes: Delaware County, OH; Fairfield County, OH; Franklin County, OH; Licking County, OH; Madison County, OH; Morrow County, OH; Pickaway County, OH; Union County, OH

Weather Station: Lancaster 2 NW Elevation: 859 feet

	Jan	Feb	Mar	Apr	May	Jun	Jul	Aug	Sep	Oct	Nov	Dec
High	35	39	50	62	72	80	84	83	77	65	52	41
Low	17	19	28	37	48	57	62	60	52	40	32	23
Precip	2.3	2.2	2.6	3.2	4.2	3.8	4.4	3.6	2.8	2.5	3.1	2.9
Snow	na	na	na	0.7	0.0	0.0	0.0	0.0	0.0	tr	0.3	na

High and Low temperatures in degrees Fahrenheit; Precipitation and Snow in inches

Population: 103,472 (1990); 122,759 (2000); 142,557 (2007); 155,616 (2012 projected); Race: 90.5% White, 6.5% Black, 1.0% Asian, 1.3% Hispanic of any race (2007); Density: 282.2 persons per square mile (2007); Average household size: 2.65 (2007); Median age: 36.6 (2007); Males per 100 females: 98.8 (2007).
Religion: Five largest groups: 11.7% Catholic Church, 8.3% The United Methodist Church, 4.2% Evangelical Lutheran Church in America, 2.4% Christian Churches and Churches of Christ, 1.3% Southern Baptist Convention (2000).
Economy: Unemployment rate: 5.7% (6/2008); Total civilian labor force: 77,764 (6/2008); Leading industries: 17.6% retail trade; 14.5% manufacturing; 13.2% accommodation & food services (2005); Farms: 1,173 totaling 196,128 acres (2002); Companies that employ 500 or more persons: 3 (2006); Companies that employ 100 to 499 persons: 43 (2006); Companies that employ less than 100 persons: 2,570 (2006); Black-owned businesses: n/a (2002); Hispanic-owned businesses: n/a (2002); Asian-owned businesses: n/a (2002); Women-owned businesses: 2,935 (2002); Retail sales per capita: $10,051 (2008). Single-family building permits issued: 375 (2007); Multi-family building permits issued: 47 (2007).
Income: Per capita income: $26,062 (2007); Median household income: $55,765 (2007); Average household income: $68,628 (2007); Percent of households with income of $100,000 or more: 19.4% (2007); Poverty rate: 7.7% (2005); Bankruptcy rate: 3.88% (2007).
Taxes: Total county taxes per capita: $200 (2006); County property taxes per capita: $119 (2006).
Education: Percent of population age 25 and over with: High school diploma (including GED) or higher: 88.1% (2007); Bachelor's degree or higher: 21.6% (2007); Master's degree or higher: 6.6% (2007).
Housing: Homeownership rate: 77.4% (2007); Median home value: $162,650 (2007); Median rent: $442 per month (2000); Median age of housing: 28 years (2000).
Health: Birth rate: 133.3 per 10,000 population (2007); Death rate: 74.7 per 10,000 population (2007); Age-adjusted cancer mortality rate: 196.7 deaths per 100,000 population (2005); Number of physicians: 16.3 per 10,000 population (2005); Hospital beds: 16.4 per 10,000 population (2004); Hospital admissions: 961.9 per 10,000 population (2004).
Elections: 2004 Presidential election results: 62.9% Bush, 36.5% Kerry, 0.0% Nader, 0.3% Badnarik
National and State Parks: Rock Mill Dam State Wildlife Area; Shallenberger State Nature Reserve; Sherman House State Memorial; Tarlton State Park
Additional Information Contacts
Fairfield County Government . . . . (740) 687-7190
http://www.co.fairfield.oh.us
City of Lancaster . . . . (740) 687-6600
http://www.ci.lancaster.oh.us
City of Pickerington . . . . (614) 837-3974
http://www.ci.pickerington.oh.us
Lancaster-Fairfield County Chamber of Commerce . . . . . . (740) 653-8251
http://www.lancoc.org
Pickerington Area Chamber of Commerce . . . . (614) 837-1958
http://www.pickeringtonchamber.com
Village of Baltimore . . . . (740) 862-4491
http://www.baltimoreohio.org
Village of Thurston . . . . (740) 862-6003
http://www.thurstonohio.com

Fairfield County Communities

AMANDA (village). Covers a land area of 0.327 square miles and a water area of 0 square miles. Located at 39.65° N. Lat.; 82.74° W. Long. Elevation is 922 feet.
Population: 774 (1990); 707 (2000); 686 (2007); 682 (2012 projected); Race: 97.7% White, 0.0% Black, 0.0% Asian, 1.7% Hispanic of any race (2007); Density: 2,096.5 persons per square mile (2007); Average household size: 2.69 (2007); Median age: 35.1 (2007); Males per 100 females: 91.6 (2007); Marriage status: 16.7% never married, 70.0% now married, 4.7% widowed, 8.6% divorced (2000); Foreign born: 0.8% (2000); Ancestry (includes multiple ancestries): 22.5% German, 17.0% United States or American, 10.6% English, 8.3% Irish, 6.8% Other groups (2000).
Economy: Employment by occupation: 8.2% management, 9.8% professional, 18.6% services, 24.8% sales, 1.0% farming, 14.1% construction, 23.5% production (2000).
Income: Per capita income: $18,830 (2007); Median household income: $45,536 (2007); Average household income: $50,657 (2007); Percent of households with income of $100,000 or more: 6.7% (2007); Poverty rate: 3.6% (2000).
Education: Percent of population age 25 and over with: High school diploma (including GED) or higher: 82.0% (2007); Bachelor's degree or higher: 7.0% (2007); Master's degree or higher: 1.6% (2007).

School District(s)

Amanda Clearcreek Digital Academy (KG-KG)
2005-06 Enrollment: 101 . . . . (740) 969-4112
Amanda-Clearcreek Local (PK-12)
2005-06 Enrollment: 1,603 . . . . (740) 969-7250

Housing: Homeownership rate: 72.9% (2007); Median home value: $110,000 (2007); Median rent: $381 per month (2000); Median age of housing: 56 years (2000).
Transportation: Commute to work: 93.6% car, 0.0% public transportation, 5.7% walk, 0.7% work from home (2000); Travel time to work: 15.8% less than 15 minutes, 34.7% 15 to 30 minutes, 19.9% 30 to 45 minutes, 19.2% 45 to 60 minutes, 10.4% 60 minutes or more (2000)

BALTIMORE (village). Covers a land area of 1.782 square miles and a water area of 0 square miles. Located at 39.84° N. Lat.; 82.60° W. Long. Elevation is 863 feet.
Population: 3,004 (1990); 2,881 (2000); 2,958 (2007); 3,031 (2012 projected); Race: 98.5% White, 0.2% Black, 0.3% Asian, 0.4% Hispanic of any race (2007); Density: 1,660.0 persons per square mile (2007); Average household size: 2.41 (2007); Median age: 35.9 (2007); Males per 100 females: 90.8 (2007); Marriage status: 20.1% never married, 56.1% now married, 11.2% widowed, 12.5% divorced (2000); Foreign born: 0.3% (2000); Ancestry (includes multiple ancestries): 31.9% German, 12.8% United States or American, 12.3% Irish, 8.8% English, 6.6% Other groups (2000).
Economy: Single-family building permits issued: 4 (2007); Multi-family building permits issued: 0 (2007); Employment by occupation: 9.8% management, 9.9% professional, 16.8% services, 30.1% sales, 0.3% farming, 19.1% construction, 13.9% production (2000).
Income: Per capita income: $21,430 (2007); Median household income: $45,086 (2007); Average household income: $51,369 (2007); Percent of households with income of $100,000 or more: 8.9% (2007); Poverty rate: 9.5% (2000).
Education: Percent of population age 25 and over with: High school diploma (including GED) or higher: 81.5% (2007); Bachelor's degree or higher: 8.4% (2007); Master's degree or higher: 2.4% (2007).

School District(s)

Liberty Union-Thurston Local (PK-12)
2005-06 Enrollment: 1,434 . . . . (740) 862-4171

Housing: Homeownership rate: 63.1% (2007); Median home value: $117,004 (2007); Median rent: $363 per month (2000); Median age of housing: 47 years (2000).
Transportation: Commute to work: 95.5% car, 0.0% public transportation, 1.6% walk, 2.2% work from home (2000); Travel time to work: 22.9% less than 15 minutes, 26.2% 15 to 30 minutes, 29.0% 30 to 45 minutes, 15.3% 45 to 60 minutes, 6.5% 60 minutes or more (2000)

Additional Information Contacts

Village of Baltimore . . . . (740) 862-4491
http://www.baltimoreohio.org

BREMEN (village). Covers a land area of 0.835 square miles and a water area of 0 square miles. Located at 39.70° N. Lat.; 82.43° W. Long. Elevation is 768 feet.
Population: 1,389 (1990); 1,265 (2000); 1,352 (2007); 1,416 (2012 projected); Race: 99.2% White, 0.0% Black, 0.0% Asian, 0.5% Hispanic of any race (2007); Density: 1,619.5 persons per square mile (2007); Average household size: 2.54 (2007); Median age: 33.6 (2007); Males per 100 females: 88.6 (2007); Marriage status: 21.8% never married, 59.9% now married, 8.8% widowed, 9.5% divorced (2000); Foreign born: 0.2% (2000); Ancestry (includes multiple ancestries): 30.9% German, 16.6% United States or American, 12.7% Irish, 6.3% English, 3.3% Other groups (2000).
Economy: Single-family building permits issued: 3 (2007); Multi-family building permits issued: 0 (2007); Employment by occupation: 8.6% management, 13.6% professional, 20.9% services, 25.1% sales, 0.0% farming, 10.8% construction, 21.0% production (2000).
Income: Per capita income: $19,695 (2007); Median household income: $43,276 (2007); Average household income: $50,052 (2007); Percent of households with income of $100,000 or more: 7.3% (2007); Poverty rate: 6.7% (2000).
Education: Percent of population age 25 and over with: High school diploma (including GED) or higher: 84.0% (2007); Bachelor's degree or higher: 7.8% (2007); Master's degree or higher: 2.6% (2007).

School District(s)

Fairfield Union Local (PK-12)
2005-06 Enrollment: 2,062 . . . . (740) 536-7384

Housing: Homeownership rate: 74.8% (2007); Median home value: $113,321 (2007); Median rent: $356 per month (2000); Median age of housing: 60+ years (2000).
Transportation: Commute to work: 92.3% car, 0.0% public transportation, 4.6% walk, 2.9% work from home (2000); Travel time to work: 24.8% less than 15 minutes, 38.9% 15 to 30 minutes, 14.4% 30 to 45 minutes, 6.9% 45 to 60 minutes, 15.0% 60 minutes or more (2000)

CARROLL (village). Covers a land area of 0.275 square miles and a water area of 0 square miles. Located at 39.79° N. Lat.; 82.70° W. Long. Elevation is 837 feet.
Population: 533 (1990); 488 (2000); 493 (2007); 495 (2012 projected); Race: 99.4% White, 0.0% Black, 0.4% Asian, 0.2% Hispanic of any race (2007); Density: 1,795.5 persons per square mile (2007); Average household size: 2.53 (2007); Median age: 35.8 (2007); Males per 100 females: 90.3 (2007); Marriage status: 35.7% never married, 47.2% now married, 3.2% widowed, 13.9% divorced (2000); Foreign born: 0.2% (2000); Ancestry (includes multiple ancestries): 32.3% German, 15.3% Irish, 13.7% United States or American, 10.9% English, 8.5% Other groups (2000).
Economy: Single-family building permits issued: 0 (2007); Multi-family building permits issued: 0 (2007); Employment by occupation: 5.4% management, 8.3% professional, 10.9% services, 31.5% sales, 0.0% farming, 17.4% construction, 26.4% production (2000).
Income: Per capita income: $22,170 (2007); Median household income: $48,229 (2007); Average household income: $56,051 (2007); Percent of households with income of $100,000 or more: 9.2% (2007); Poverty rate: 5.7% (2000).
Education: Percent of population age 25 and over with: High school diploma (including GED) or higher: 91.9% (2007); Bachelor's degree or higher: 7.8% (2007); Master's degree or higher: 0.0% (2007).

School District(s)

Bloom-Carroll Local (PK-12)
2005-06 Enrollment: 1,578 . . . . (614) 837-6560
Eastland-Fairfield Career/Tech (09-12)
2005-06 Enrollment: n/a . . . . (614) 836-4530

Housing: Homeownership rate: 65.1% (2007); Median home value: $115,625 (2007); Median rent: $464 per month (2000); Median age of housing: 60+ years (2000).
Transportation: Commute to work: 94.9% car, 0.4% public transportation, 2.2% walk, 2.5% work from home (2000); Travel time to work: 25.4% less than 15 minutes, 32.5% 15 to 30 minutes, 26.1% 30 to 45 minutes, 11.9% 45 to 60 minutes, 4.1% 60 minutes or more (2000)

FAIRFIELD BEACH (CDP). Covers a land area of 0.648 square miles and a water area of 0.318 square miles. Located at 39.91° N. Lat.; 82.47° W. Long. Elevation is 928 feet.
Population: 1,084 (1990); 1,163 (2000); 1,310 (2007); 1,373 (2012 projected); Race: 97.1% White, 0.2% Black, 0.0% Asian, 0.2% Hispanic of

any race (2007); Density: 2,022.7 persons per square mile (2007); Average household size: 2.41 (2007); Median age: 39.2 (2007); Males per 100 females: 104.4 (2007); Marriage status: 17.1% never married, 66.0% now married, 8.3% widowed, 8.6% divorced (2000); Foreign born: 1.8% (2000); Ancestry (includes multiple ancestries): 22.7% United States or American, 20.7% German, 11.9% Irish, 10.2% English, 6.4% Other groups (2000).
Economy: Employment by occupation: 12.1% management, 11.7% professional, 12.1% services, 23.6% sales, 0.0% farming, 12.1% construction, 28.3% production (2000).
Income: Per capita income: $20,605 (2007); Median household income: $39,492 (2007); Average household income: $49,619 (2007); Percent of households with income of $100,000 or more: 6.3% (2007); Poverty rate: 6.3% (2000).
Education: Percent of population age 25 and over with: High school diploma (including GED) or higher: 75.7% (2007); Bachelor's degree or higher: 2.9% (2007); Master's degree or higher: 1.7% (2007).
Housing: Homeownership rate: 87.9% (2007); Median home value: $111,964 (2007); Median rent: $675 per month (2000); Median age of housing: 41 years (2000).
Transportation: Commute to work: 98.4% car, 0.0% public transportation, 0.0% walk, 1.6% work from home (2000); Travel time to work: 9.7% less than 15 minutes, 21.1% 15 to 30 minutes, 27.1% 30 to 45 minutes, 27.8% 45 to 60 minutes, 14.2% 60 minutes or more (2000)

LANCASTER (city). County seat. Covers a land area of 18.066 square miles and a water area of 0.010 square miles. Located at 39.71° N. Lat.; 82.60° W. Long. Elevation is 879 feet.
History: Lancaster was established on one of the three sections of land given to Ebenezer Zane for his work in laying out Zane's Trace. In 1800 the settlement on the banks of the Hocking River was named New Lancaster, because settlers had come from Lancaster, Pennsylvania. The first newspaper was printed in German, which was the language used in the early schools.
Population: 35,664 (1990); 35,335 (2000); 36,375 (2007); 37,307 (2012 projected); Race: 95.9% White, 1.3% Black, 0.6% Asian, 1.3% Hispanic of any race (2007); Density: 2,013.5 persons per square mile (2007); Average household size: 2.31 (2007); Median age: 35.9 (2007); Males per 100 females: 90.2 (2007); Marriage status: 22.2% never married, 55.9% now married, 8.3% widowed, 13.6% divorced (2000); Foreign born: 0.9% (2000); Ancestry (includes multiple ancestries): 27.6% German, 15.2% United States or American, 13.4% Irish, 8.8% English, 8.2% Other groups (2000).
Economy: Unemployment rate: 6.4% (6/2008); Total civilian labor force: 19,272 (6/2008); Single-family building permits issued: 26 (2007); Multi-family building permits issued: 26 (2007); Employment by occupation: 9.1% management, 14.7% professional, 17.1% services, 29.2% sales, 0.1% farming, 11.4% construction, 18.5% production (2000).
Income: Per capita income: $20,764 (2007); Median household income: $37,438 (2007); Average household income: $47,805 (2007); Percent of households with income of $100,000 or more: 7.0% (2007); Poverty rate: 10.6% (2000).
Taxes: Total city taxes per capita: $459 (2006); City property taxes per capita: $63 (2006).
Education: Percent of population age 25 and over with: High school diploma (including GED) or higher: 83.5% (2007); Bachelor's degree or higher: 13.6% (2007); Master's degree or higher: 4.4% (2007).

School District(s)

Fairfield Union Local (PK-12)
2005-06 Enrollment: 2,062 . . . . (740) 536-7384
Lancaster City (PK-12)
2005-06 Enrollment: 6,044 . . . . (740) 687-7300
Lancaster Digital Academy (01-12)
2005-06 Enrollment: 44 . . . . (740) 687-7634
Lancaster Fairfield Alternative School (08-12)
2005-06 Enrollment: 44 . . . . (740) 687-7177

Four-year College(s)

Ohio University-Lancaster Campus (Public)
Fall 2007 Enrollment: 1,728. . . . . (740) 654-6711
2007-08 Tuition: In-state $4,581; Out-of-state $8,904

Two-year College(s)

Southeastern Business College (Private, For-profit)
Fall 2007 Enrollment: 14 . . . . (740) 687-6126
Housing: Homeownership rate: 59.8% (2007); Median home value: $114,542 (2007); Median rent: $414 per month (2000); Median age of housing: 43 years (2000).
Hospitals: Fairfield Medical Center (229 beds)
Safety: Violent crime rate: 24.0 per 10,000 population; Property crime rate: 526.2 per 10,000 population (2007).
Newspapers: Lancaster Eagle-Gazette (Local news; Circulation 15,760)
Transportation: Commute to work: 93.3% car, 0.5% public transportation, 3.2% walk, 2.1% work from home (2000); Travel time to work: 40.3% less than 15 minutes, 23.6% 15 to 30 minutes, 14.7% 30 to 45 minutes, 12.8% 45 to 60 minutes, 8.6% 60 minutes or more (2000)
Airports: Fairfield County (general aviation)
Additional Information Contacts
City of Lancaster . . . . (740) 687-6600
http://www.ci.lancaster.oh.us
Lancaster-Fairfield County Chamber of Commerce . . . . . . (740) 653-8251
http://www.lancoc.org

LITHOPOLIS (village). Covers a land area of 0.401 square miles and a water area of 0 square miles. Located at 39.80° N. Lat.; 82.80° W. Long. Elevation is 945 feet.
History: The name of Lithopolis means "stone city" in the Greek, an appropriate name for a town that grew around sandstone quarries.
Population: 563 (1990); 600 (2000); 706 (2007); 775 (2012 projected); Race: 98.2% White, 0.4% Black, 0.0% Asian, 0.6% Hispanic of any race (2007); Density: 1,759.0 persons per square mile (2007); Average household size: 2.34 (2007); Median age: 39.7 (2007); Males per 100 females: 95.6 (2007); Marriage status: 25.2% never married, 60.3% now married, 3.8% widowed, 10.7% divorced (2000); Foreign born: 0.4% (2000); Ancestry (includes multiple ancestries): 29.7% German, 16.0% Irish, 11.0% Other groups, 10.3% United States or American, 8.1% English (2000).
Economy: Single-family building permits issued: 32 (2007); Multi-family building permits issued: 0 (2007); Employment by occupation: 12.5% management, 7.5% professional, 16.2% services, 28.7% sales, 1.1% farming, 17.7% construction, 16.2% production (2000).
Income: Per capita income: $24,405 (2007); Median household income: $46,957 (2007); Average household income: $57,053 (2007); Percent of households with income of $100,000 or more: 10.9% (2007); Poverty rate: 5.6% (2000).
Education: Percent of population age 25 and over with: High school diploma (including GED) or higher: 87.7% (2007); Bachelor's degree or higher: 15.9% (2007); Master's degree or higher: 4.6% (2007).

School District(s)

Bloom-Carroll Local (PK-12)
2005-06 Enrollment: 1,578 . . . . (614) 837-6560
Housing: Homeownership rate: 64.6% (2007); Median home value: $146,983 (2007); Median rent: $410 per month (2000); Median age of housing: 45 years (2000).
Transportation: Commute to work: 90.5% car, 0.0% public transportation, 3.8% walk, 4.2% work from home (2000); Travel time to work: 15.1% less than 15 minutes, 38.2% 15 to 30 minutes, 35.1% 30 to 45 minutes, 5.2% 45 to 60 minutes, 6.4% 60 minutes or more (2000)

MILLERSPORT (village). Covers a land area of 0.995 square miles and a water area of 0.034 square miles. Located at 39.90° N. Lat.; 82.53° W. Long. Elevation is 899 feet.
Population: 1,048 (1990); 963 (2000); 869 (2007); 879 (2012 projected); Race: 97.7% White, 0.0% Black, 0.0% Asian, 1.2% Hispanic of any race (2007); Density: 873.1 persons per square mile (2007); Average household size: 2.31 (2007); Median age: 36.0 (2007); Males per 100 females: 83.7 (2007); Marriage status: 21.5% never married, 58.7% now married, 4.7% widowed, 15.1% divorced (2000); Foreign born: 0.3% (2000); Ancestry (includes multiple ancestries): 28.4% German, 17.7% English, 16.4% United States or American, 11.7% Irish, 7.5% Other groups (2000).
Economy: Single-family building permits issued: 1 (2007); Multi-family building permits issued: 0 (2007); Employment by occupation: 14.7% management, 10.9% professional, 14.5% services, 26.8% sales, 0.8% farming, 9.2% construction, 23.1% production (2000).
Income: Per capita income: $23,639 (2007); Median household income: $47,941 (2007); Average household income: $54,634 (2007); Percent of households with income of $100,000 or more: 10.9% (2007); Poverty rate: 5.9% (2000).
Education: Percent of population age 25 and over with: High school diploma (including GED) or higher: 87.0% (2007); Bachelor's degree or higher: 13.4% (2007); Master's degree or higher: 4.5% (2007).

School District(s)

Walnut Township Local (PK-12)
2005-06 Enrollment: 737 . . . . (740) 467-2802

Housing: Homeownership rate: 68.9% (2007); Median home value: $123,694 (2007); Median rent: $400 per month (2000); Median age of housing: 40 years (2000).

Transportation: Commute to work: 92.5% car, 0.6% public transportation, 1.9% walk, 3.2% work from home (2000); Travel time to work: 18.5% less than 15 minutes, 28.9% 15 to 30 minutes, 30.9% 30 to 45 minutes, 15.2% 45 to 60 minutes, 6.4% 60 minutes or more (2000)

PICKERINGTON (city). Covers a land area of 7.433 square miles and a water area of 0 square miles. Located at 39.89° N. Lat.; 82.76° W. Long. Elevation is 837 feet.

Population: 6,400 (1990); 9,792 (2000); 15,931 (2007); 19,787 (2012 projected); Race: 86.2% White, 9.5% Black, 2.0% Asian, 2.0% Hispanic of any race (2007); Density: 2,143.3 persons per square mile (2007); Average household size: 2.78 (2007); Median age: 34.0 (2007); Males per 100 females: 96.8 (2007); Marriage status: 20.3% never married, 68.3% now married, 2.7% widowed, 8.7% divorced (2000); Foreign born: 2.3% (2000); Ancestry (includes multiple ancestries): 31.4% German, 17.8% Irish, 10.0% English, 9.6% Other groups, 8.3% Italian (2000).

Economy: Single-family building permits issued: 126 (2007); Multi-family building permits issued: 0 (2007); Employment by occupation: 22.3% management, 19.5% professional, 11.9% services, 31.6% sales, 0.0% farming, 6.4% construction, 8.2% production (2000).

Income: Per capita income: $28,849 (2007); Median household income: $70,328 (2007); Average household income: $80,002 (2007); Percent of households with income of $100,000 or more: 26.2% (2007); Poverty rate: 3.2% (2000).

Education: Percent of population age 25 and over with: High school diploma (including GED) or higher: 95.0% (2007); Bachelor's degree or higher: 31.0% (2007); Master's degree or higher: 6.9% (2007).

School District(s)

Pickerington Local (PK-12)
2005-06 Enrollment: 9,787 . . . . (614) 833-2110

Housing: Homeownership rate: 77.7% (2007); Median home value: $169,876 (2007); Median rent: $595 per month (2000); Median age of housing: 12 years (2000).

Safety: Violent crime rate: 8.4 per 10,000 population; Property crime rate: 202.2 per 10,000 population (2007).

Transportation: Commute to work: 96.1% car, 0.4% public transportation, 0.6% walk, 2.4% work from home (2000); Travel time to work: 16.7% less than 15 minutes, 38.7% 15 to 30 minutes, 28.9% 30 to 45 minutes, 9.6% 45 to 60 minutes, 6.0% 60 minutes or more (2000)

Additional Information Contacts

City of Pickerington . . . . (614) 837-3974
http://www.ci.pickerington.oh.us

Pickerington Area Chamber of Commerce . . . . (614) 837-1958
http://www.pickeringtonchamber.com

PLEASANTVILLE (village). Covers a land area of 0.278 square miles and a water area of 0 square miles. Located at 39.81° N. Lat.; 82.52° W. Long. Elevation is 909 feet.

Population: 945 (1990); 877 (2000); 901 (2007); 935 (2012 projected); Race: 96.4% White, 0.1% Black, 1.0% Asian, 0.9% Hispanic of any race (2007); Density: 3,241.8 persons per square mile (2007); Average household size: 2.76 (2007); Median age: 34.5 (2007); Males per 100 females: 88.9 (2007); Marriage status: 26.1% never married, 52.4% now married, 7.5% widowed, 14.0% divorced (2000); Foreign born: 0.2% (2000); Ancestry (includes multiple ancestries): 29.3% German, 18.5% Irish, 11.4% United States or American, 7.7% Other groups, 6.6% English (2000).

Economy: Single-family building permits issued: 1 (2007); Multi-family building permits issued: 0 (2007); Employment by occupation: 6.8% management, 10.3% professional, 23.6% services, 21.2% sales, 0.5% farming, 13.9% construction, 23.6% production (2000).

Income: Per capita income: $15,030 (2007); Median household income: $37,721 (2007); Average household income: $41,330 (2007); Percent of households with income of $100,000 or more: 3.4% (2007); Poverty rate: 11.3% (2000).

Education: Percent of population age 25 and over with: High school diploma (including GED) or higher: 77.2% (2007); Bachelor's degree or higher: 4.6% (2007); Master's degree or higher: 1.1% (2007).

School District(s)

Fairfield Union Local (PK-12)
2005-06 Enrollment: 2,062 . . . . (740) 536-7384

Housing: Homeownership rate: 69.4% (2007); Median home value: $109,142 (2007); Median rent: $317 per month (2000); Median age of housing: 53 years (2000).

Transportation: Commute to work: 95.5% car, 0.0% public transportation, 2.2% walk, 1.4% work from home (2000); Travel time to work: 19.5% less than 15 minutes, 43.1% 15 to 30 minutes, 16.1% 30 to 45 minutes, 15.0% 45 to 60 minutes, 6.2% 60 minutes or more (2000)

RUSHVILLE (village). Covers a land area of 0.226 square miles and a water area of 0 square miles. Located at 39.76° N. Lat.; 82.43° W. Long. Elevation is 1,050 feet.

History: Rushville was the birthplace of Benjamin Russell Hanby (1833-1867), who wrote the song "Darling Nellie Gray." Though it was published and became popular across the country, Hanby never received royalties for his work.

Population: 229 (1990); 268 (2000); 293 (2007); 312 (2012 projected); Race: 96.6% White, 0.0% Black, 0.0% Asian, 0.0% Hispanic of any race (2007); Density: 1,293.8 persons per square mile (2007); Average household size: 2.87 (2007); Median age: 32.0 (2007); Males per 100 females: 107.8 (2007); Marriage status: 25.1% never married, 56.8% now married, 4.9% widowed, 13.1% divorced (2000); Foreign born: 0.8% (2000); Ancestry (includes multiple ancestries): 26.6% German, 16.7% United States or American, 15.5% Irish, 11.9% Other groups, 7.5% English (2000).

Economy: Employment by occupation: 7.3% management, 4.1% professional, 12.2% services, 44.7% sales, 0.0% farming, 13.8% construction, 17.9% production (2000).

Income: Per capita income: $17,526 (2007); Median household income: $41,667 (2007); Average household income: $50,343 (2007); Percent of households with income of $100,000 or more: 7.8% (2007); Poverty rate: 14.7% (2000).

Education: Percent of population age 25 and over with: High school diploma (including GED) or higher: 92.1% (2007); Bachelor's degree or higher: 9.0% (2007); Master's degree or higher: 0.0% (2007).

School District(s)

Fairfield Union Local (PK-12)
2005-06 Enrollment: 2,062 . . . . (740) 536-7384

Housing: Homeownership rate: 73.5% (2007); Median home value: $116,071 (2007); Median rent: $394 per month (2000); Median age of housing: 60+ years (2000).

Transportation: Commute to work: 97.5% car, 0.0% public transportation, 0.8% walk, 1.7% work from home (2000); Travel time to work: 6.0% less than 15 minutes, 27.6% 15 to 30 minutes, 16.4% 30 to 45 minutes, 35.3% 45 to 60 minutes, 14.7% 60 minutes or more (2000)

STOUTSVILLE (village). Covers a land area of 1.333 square miles and a water area of 0 square miles. Located at 39.60° N. Lat.; 82.82° W. Long. Elevation is 971 feet.

Population: 518 (1990); 581 (2000); 727 (2007); 822 (2012 projected); Race: 98.1% White, 0.8% Black, 0.0% Asian, 1.0% Hispanic of any race (2007); Density: 545.3 persons per square mile (2007); Average household size: 2.62 (2007); Median age: 36.4 (2007); Males per 100 females: 97.0 (2007); Marriage status: 19.8% never married, 62.8% now married, 5.8% widowed, 11.6% divorced (2000); Foreign born: 0.0% (2000); Ancestry (includes multiple ancestries): 32.3% German, 17.5% United States or American, 11.0% Irish, 11.0% English, 7.6% Other groups (2000).

Economy: Employment by occupation: 4.6% management, 15.2% professional, 7.8% services, 30.4% sales, 0.0% farming, 12.4% construction, 29.7% production (2000).

Income: Per capita income: $24,481 (2007); Median household income: $53,534 (2007); Average household income: $64,251 (2007); Percent of households with income of $100,000 or more: 13.0% (2007); Poverty rate: 3.8% (2000).

Education: Percent of population age 25 and over with: High school diploma (including GED) or higher: 83.0% (2007); Bachelor's degree or higher: 10.3% (2007); Master's degree or higher: 3.2% (2007).

Housing: Homeownership rate: 79.4% (2007); Median home value: $120,339 (2007); Median rent: $369 per month (2000); Median age of housing: 55 years (2000).

Transportation: Commute to work: 93.2% car, 0.0% public transportation, 3.6% walk, 3.2% work from home (2000); Travel time to work: 22.7% less

than 15 minutes, 39.8% 15 to 30 minutes, 15.6% 30 to 45 minutes, 13.0% 45 to 60 minutes, 8.9% 60 minutes or more (2000)

SUGAR GROVE (village). Covers a land area of 0.205 square miles and a water area of 0 square miles. Located at 39.62° N. Lat.; 82.54° W. Long. Elevation is 781 feet.
Population: 465 (1990); 448 (2000); 446 (2007); 446 (2012 projected); Race: 99.6% White, 0.0% Black, 0.0% Asian, 1.1% Hispanic of any race (2007); Density: 2,172.4 persons per square mile (2007); Average household size: 2.69 (2007); Median age: 31.8 (2007); Males per 100 females: 89.0 (2007); Marriage status: 22.5% never married, 58.6% now married, 5.7% widowed, 13.2% divorced (2000); Foreign born: 0.0% (2000); Ancestry (includes multiple ancestries): 26.3% German, 9.9% Other groups, 8.0% Irish, 6.3% United States or American, 4.8% Welsh (2000).
Economy: Single-family building permits issued: 0 (2007); Multi-family building permits issued: 0 (2007); Employment by occupation: 5.7% management, 13.0% professional, 15.1% services, 25.5% sales, 0.0% farming, 17.7% construction, 22.9% production (2000).
Income: Per capita income: $19,524 (2007); Median household income: $45,000 (2007); Average household income: $52,455 (2007); Percent of households with income of $100,000 or more: 5.4% (2007); Poverty rate: 6.0% (2000).
Education: Percent of population age 25 and over with: High school diploma (including GED) or higher: 93.0% (2007); Bachelor's degree or higher: 6.6% (2007); Master's degree or higher: 1.5% (2007).

School District(s)

Berne Union Local (PK-12)
2005-06 Enrollment: 981 . . . . (740) 746-8341
Housing: Homeownership rate: 66.3% (2007); Median home value: $108,173 (2007); Median rent: $454 per month (2000); Median age of housing: 60+ years (2000).
Transportation: Commute to work: 89.9% car, 1.1% public transportation, 4.8% walk, 3.2% work from home (2000); Travel time to work: 15.8% less than 15 minutes, 37.2% 15 to 30 minutes, 7.1% 30 to 45 minutes, 13.7% 45 to 60 minutes, 26.2% 60 minutes or more (2000)

THURSTON (village). Covers a land area of 0.259 square miles and a water area of 0 square miles. Located at 39.84° N. Lat.; 82.54° W. Long. Elevation is 883 feet.
Population: 556 (1990); 555 (2000); 612 (2007); 652 (2012 projected); Race: 94.3% White, 0.5% Black, 0.5% Asian, 0.3% Hispanic of any race (2007); Density: 2,365.6 persons per square mile (2007); Average household size: 2.65 (2007); Median age: 33.6 (2007); Males per 100 females: 96.8 (2007); Marriage status: 21.2% never married, 59.0% now married, 6.8% widowed, 13.0% divorced (2000); Foreign born: 2.0% (2000); Ancestry (includes multiple ancestries): 27.9% United States or American, 22.7% German, 15.5% Irish, 10.3% Other groups, 8.8% English (2000).
Economy: Employment by occupation: 6.7% management, 7.1% professional, 14.7% services, 28.0% sales, 0.0% farming, 19.6% construction, 24.0% production (2000).
Income: Per capita income: $15,752 (2007); Median household income: $34,079 (2007); Average household income: $41,732 (2007); Percent of households with income of $100,000 or more: 5.2% (2007); Poverty rate: 9.9% (2000).
Education: Percent of population age 25 and over with: High school diploma (including GED) or higher: 75.7% (2007); Bachelor's degree or higher: 4.7% (2007); Master's degree or higher: 1.6% (2007).
Housing: Homeownership rate: 78.4% (2007); Median home value: $104,095 (2007); Median rent: $381 per month (2000); Median age of housing: 49 years (2000).
Transportation: Commute to work: 95.3% car, 0.9% public transportation, 0.0% walk, 3.7% work from home (2000); Travel time to work: 15.5% less than 15 minutes, 31.9% 15 to 30 minutes, 27.5% 30 to 45 minutes, 18.4% 45 to 60 minutes, 6.8% 60 minutes or more (2000)
Additional Information Contacts
Village of Thurston . . . . (740) 862-6003
http://www.thurstonohio.com

WEST RUSHVILLE (village). Covers a land area of 0.061 square miles and a water area of 0 square miles. Located at 39.76° N. Lat.; 82.44° W. Long. Elevation is 1,010 feet.
Population: 134 (1990); 132 (2000); 156 (2007); 174 (2012 projected); Race: 98.7% White, 0.0% Black, 0.0% Asian, 5.8% Hispanic of any race (2007); Density: 2,569.6 persons per square mile (2007); Average household size: 2.60 (2007); Median age: 35.0 (2007); Males per 100 females: 105.3 (2007); Marriage status: 34.0% never married, 50.5% now married, 10.7% widowed, 4.9% divorced (2000); Foreign born: 1.6% (2000); Ancestry (includes multiple ancestries): 22.5% United States or American, 20.9% German, 13.2% Other groups, 13.2% Irish, 3.1% French Canadian (2000).
Economy: Employment by occupation: 1.4% management, 2.8% professional, 15.5% services, 42.3% sales, 0.0% farming, 18.3% construction, 19.7% production (2000).
Income: Per capita income: $21,410 (2007); Median household income: $42,500 (2007); Average household income: $55,667 (2007); Percent of households with income of $100,000 or more: 13.3% (2007); Poverty rate: 6.2% (2000).
Education: Percent of population age 25 and over with: High school diploma (including GED) or higher: 85.0% (2007); Bachelor's degree or higher: 9.0% (2007); Master's degree or higher: 2.0% (2007).
Housing: Homeownership rate: 76.7% (2007); Median home value: $133,333 (2007); Median rent: $386 per month (2000); Median age of housing: 60+ years (2000).
Transportation: Commute to work: 100.0% car, 0.0% public transportation, 0.0% walk, 0.0% work from home (2000); Travel time to work: 24.2% less than 15 minutes, 33.9% 15 to 30 minutes, 16.1% 30 to 45 minutes, 12.9% 45 to 60 minutes, 12.9% 60 minutes or more (2000)

Fayette County

Located in south central Ohio; drained by Paint, Sugar, and Rattlesnakes Creeks. Covers a land area of 406.58 square miles, a water area of 0.50 square miles, and is located in the Eastern Time Zone. The county was founded in 1810. County seat is Washington Court House.

Fayette County is part of the Washington Court House, OH Micropolitan Statistical Area. The entire metro area includes: Fayette County, OH

Weather Station: Washington Court House Elevation: 958 feet

	Jan	Feb	Mar	Apr	May	Jun	Jul	Aug	Sep	Oct	Nov	Dec
High	36	40	51	63	72	79	83	82	76	66	52	41
Low	20	23	32	41	52	61	65	63	56	44	35	26
Precip	2.4	2.4	3.3	3.6	4.7	3.8	4.0	3.9	2.6	2.7	3.0	2.8
Snow	8.7	6.1	4.1	0.7	tr	0.0	0.0	0.0	0.0	0.2	1.0	3.5

High and Low temperatures in degrees Fahrenheit; Precipitation and Snow in inches

Population: 27,466 (1990); 28,433 (2000); 28,234 (2007); 28,081 (2012 projected); Race: 95.6% White, 2.3% Black, 0.5% Asian, 1.4% Hispanic of any race (2007); Density: 69.4 persons per square mile (2007); Average household size: 2.52 (2007); Median age: 39.0 (2007); Males per 100 females: 96.4 (2007).
Religion: Five largest groups: 8.3% The United Methodist Church, 5.8% Christian Churches and Churches of Christ, 2.4% Presbyterian Church (U.S.A.), 2.3% Catholic Church, 1.9% American Baptist Churches in the USA (2000).
Economy: Unemployment rate: 5.9% (6/2008); Total civilian labor force: 16,925 (6/2008); Leading industries: 24.7% manufacturing; 23.7% retail trade; 12.3% health care and social assistance (2005); Farms: 480 totaling 203,212 acres (2002); Companies that employ 500 or more persons: 2 (2006); Companies that employ 100 to 499 persons: 15 (2006); Companies that employ less than 100 persons: 656 (2006); Black-owned businesses: n/a (2002); Hispanic-owned businesses: n/a (2002); Asian-owned businesses: n/a (2002); Women-owned businesses: 252 (2002); Retail sales per capita: $19,213 (2008). Single-family building permits issued: 61 (2007); Multi-family building permits issued: 20 (2007).
Income: Per capita income: $22,146 (2007); Median household income: $44,582 (2007); Average household income: $54,962 (2007); Percent of households with income of $100,000 or more: 9.9% (2007); Poverty rate: 13.4% (2005); Bankruptcy rate: 4.77% (2007).
Taxes: Total county taxes per capita: $285 (2006); County property taxes per capita: $110 (2006).
Education: Percent of population age 25 and over with: High school diploma (including GED) or higher: 78.8% (2007); Bachelor's degree or higher: 10.8% (2007); Master's degree or higher: 3.0% (2007).
Housing: Homeownership rate: 66.4% (2007); Median home value: $119,341 (2007); Median rent: $365 per month (2000); Median age of housing: 40 years (2000).
Health: Birth rate: 137.4 per 10,000 population (2007); Death rate: 121.5 per 10,000 population (2007); Age-adjusted cancer mortality rate: 271.7

deaths per 100,000 population (2005); Number of physicians: 6.7 per 10,000 population (2005); Hospital beds: 12.8 per 10,000 population (2004); Hospital admissions: 611.3 per 10,000 population (2004).
Elections: 2004 Presidential election results: 62.7% Bush, 36.9% Kerry, 0.0% Nader, 0.2% Badnarik

Additional Information Contacts

Fayette County Government . . . . (740) 335-0720
http://www.fayette-co-oh.com
City of Washington Court House . . . . (740) 636-2340
http://www.ci.washington-court-house.oh.us
Fayette County Chamber of Commerce . . . . (740) 335-0761
http://www.fayettecountychamberoh.com

Fayette County Communities

BLOOMINGBURG (village). Covers a land area of 0.697 square miles and a water area of 0 square miles. Located at 39.60° N. Lat.; 83.39° W. Long. Elevation is 994 feet.
Population: 769 (1990); 874 (2000); 843 (2007); 840 (2012 projected); Race: 93.4% White, 3.7% Black, 0.0% Asian, 4.3% Hispanic of any race (2007); Density: 1,209.1 persons per square mile (2007); Average household size: 2.76 (2007); Median age: 31.6 (2007); Males per 100 females: 100.2 (2007); Marriage status: 26.3% never married, 53.4% now married, 5.9% widowed, 14.3% divorced (2000); Foreign born: 0.3% (2000); Ancestry (includes multiple ancestries): 25.9% United States or American, 15.2% Other groups, 11.2% German, 8.0% English, 7.1% Irish (2000).
Economy: Employment by occupation: 1.3% management, 8.6% professional, 15.0% services, 18.7% sales, 2.7% farming, 14.2% construction, 39.6% production (2000).
Income: Per capita income: $14,759 (2007); Median household income: $37,188 (2007); Average household income: $39,492 (2007); Percent of households with income of $100,000 or more: 2.6% (2007); Poverty rate: 16.0% (2000).
Education: Percent of population age 25 and over with: High school diploma (including GED) or higher: 67.5% (2007); Bachelor's degree or higher: 1.8% (2007); Master's degree or higher: 0.4% (2007).

School District(s)

Miami Trace Local (PK-12)
2005-06 Enrollment: 2,770 . . . . (740) 335-3010
Housing: Homeownership rate: 64.9% (2007); Median home value: $86,364 (2007); Median rent: $381 per month (2000); Median age of housing: 36 years (2000).
Transportation: Commute to work: 92.4% car, 2.7% public transportation, 3.8% walk, 0.5% work from home (2000); Travel time to work: 30.5% less than 15 minutes, 39.0% 15 to 30 minutes, 12.8% 30 to 45 minutes, 10.1% 45 to 60 minutes, 7.6% 60 minutes or more (2000)

JEFFERSONVILLE (village). Covers a land area of 1.703 square miles and a water area of 0.035 square miles. Located at 39.65° N. Lat.; 83.55° W. Long. Elevation is 1,050 feet.
Population: 1,318 (1990); 1,288 (2000); 1,267 (2007); 1,245 (2012 projected); Race: 89.6% White, 7.7% Black, 0.0% Asian, 0.4% Hispanic of any race (2007); Density: 743.9 persons per square mile (2007); Average household size: 2.43 (2007); Median age: 34.3 (2007); Males per 100 females: 93.4 (2007); Marriage status: 26.7% never married, 46.8% now married, 8.7% widowed, 17.9% divorced (2000); Foreign born: 0.2% (2000); Ancestry (includes multiple ancestries): 21.2% United States or American, 11.2% German, 10.9% Other groups, 9.8% Irish, 5.0% English (2000).
Economy: Employment by occupation: 6.9% management, 7.1% professional, 16.6% services, 25.0% sales, 0.5% farming, 10.2% construction, 33.6% production (2000).
Income: Per capita income: $19,327 (2007); Median household income: $40,329 (2007); Average household income: $47,001 (2007); Percent of households with income of $100,000 or more: 7.5% (2007); Poverty rate: 17.1% (2000).
Education: Percent of population age 25 and over with: High school diploma (including GED) or higher: 79.0% (2007); Bachelor's degree or higher: 7.7% (2007); Master's degree or higher: 1.5% (2007).

School District(s)

Miami Trace Local (PK-12)
2005-06 Enrollment: 2,770 . . . . (740) 335-3010
Housing: Homeownership rate: 57.6% (2007); Median home value: $103,788 (2007); Median rent: $360 per month (2000); Median age of housing: 28 years (2000).
Transportation: Commute to work: 95.1% car, 0.0% public transportation, 1.6% walk, 2.8% work from home (2000); Travel time to work: 31.9% less than 15 minutes, 34.6% 15 to 30 minutes, 16.3% 30 to 45 minutes, 10.2% 45 to 60 minutes, 7.1% 60 minutes or more (2000)

MILLEDGEVILLE (village). Covers a land area of 0.101 square miles and a water area of 0 square miles. Located at 39.59° N. Lat.; 83.58° W. Long. Elevation is 1,050 feet.
Population: 120 (1990); 122 (2000); 116 (2007); 115 (2012 projected); Race: 97.4% White, 2.6% Black, 0.0% Asian, 0.0% Hispanic of any race (2007); Density: 1,143.1 persons per square mile (2007); Average household size: 2.58 (2007); Median age: 37.8 (2007); Males per 100 females: 118.9 (2007); Marriage status: 22.8% never married, 64.1% now married, 2.2% widowed, 10.9% divorced (2000); Foreign born: 4.4% (2000); Ancestry (includes multiple ancestries): 21.1% Other groups, 7.9% German, 5.3% Irish, 3.5% Dutch, 3.5% United States or American (2000).
Economy: Employment by occupation: 6.0% management, 3.0% professional, 22.4% services, 17.9% sales, 0.0% farming, 6.0% construction, 44.8% production (2000).
Income: Per capita income: $22,522 (2007); Median household income: $48,125 (2007); Average household income: $58,056 (2007); Percent of households with income of $100,000 or more: 6.7% (2007); Poverty rate: 4.4% (2000).
Education: Percent of population age 25 and over with: High school diploma (including GED) or higher: 68.2% (2007); Bachelor's degree or higher: 8.2% (2007); Master's degree or higher: 2.4% (2007).
Housing: Homeownership rate: 82.2% (2007); Median home value: $92,500 (2007); Median rent: $406 per month (2000); Median age of housing: 60+ years (2000).
Transportation: Commute to work: 92.5% car, 0.0% public transportation, 0.0% walk, 7.5% work from home (2000); Travel time to work: 35.5% less than 15 minutes, 38.7% 15 to 30 minutes, 16.1% 30 to 45 minutes, 6.5% 45 to 60 minutes, 3.2% 60 minutes or more (2000)

OCTA (village). Covers a land area of 0.285 square miles and a water area of 0 square miles. Located at 39.60° N. Lat.; 83.61° W. Long. Elevation is 1,043 feet.
Population: 83 (1990); 83 (2000); 78 (2007); 76 (2012 projected); Race: 89.7% White, 10.3% Black, 0.0% Asian, 5.1% Hispanic of any race (2007); Density: 273.7 persons per square mile (2007); Average household size: 2.29 (2007); Median age: 42.2 (2007); Males per 100 females: 110.8 (2007); Marriage status: 18.9% never married, 64.2% now married, 3.8% widowed, 13.2% divorced (2000); Foreign born: 0.0% (2000); Ancestry (includes multiple ancestries): 24.3% German, 21.6% United States or American, 18.9% Dutch, 10.8% Irish, 8.1% Other groups (2000).
Economy: Employment by occupation: 0.0% management, 0.0% professional, 13.8% services, 34.5% sales, 0.0% farming, 13.8% construction, 37.9% production (2000).
Income: Per capita income: $20,896 (2007); Median household income: $40,000 (2007); Average household income: $46,838 (2007); Percent of households with income of $100,000 or more: 5.9% (2007); Poverty rate: 8.1% (2000).
Education: Percent of population age 25 and over with: High school diploma (including GED) or higher: 57.9% (2007); Bachelor's degree or higher: 0.0% (2007); Master's degree or higher: 0.0% (2007).
Housing: Homeownership rate: 61.8% (2007); Median home value: $77,000 (2007); Median rent: $313 per month (2000); Median age of housing: 52 years (2000).
Transportation: Commute to work: 81.5% car, 0.0% public transportation, 0.0% walk, 0.0% work from home (2000); Travel time to work: 25.9% less than 15 minutes, 29.6% 15 to 30 minutes, 25.9% 30 to 45 minutes, 0.0% 45 to 60 minutes, 18.5% 60 minutes or more (2000)

WASHINGTON COURT HOUSE (city). Aka City of Washington (historical). County seat. Covers a land area of 6.438 square miles and a water area of 0.066 square miles. Located at 39.53° N. Lat.; 83.43° W. Long. Elevation is 974 feet.
History: Also known as Washington Court House, the rest of the name was added because the first court of common pleas was held here in 1810 in the cabin of John Devault. The jury deliberated in a nearby hazel patch. The town grew as the center of a stock-raising area.

Population: 13,044 (1990); 13,524 (2000); 13,382 (2007); 13,318 (2012 projected); Race: 94.6% White, 2.8% Black, 0.8% Asian, 1.6% Hispanic of any race (2007); Density: 2,078.7 persons per square mile (2007); Average household size: 2.42 (2007); Median age: 38.2 (2007); Males per 100 females: 92.7 (2007); Marriage status: 22.3% never married, 54.2% now married, 10.0% widowed, 13.5% divorced (2000); Foreign born: 1.3% (2000); Ancestry (includes multiple ancestries): 19.1% German, 18.0% United States or American, 12.4% Irish, 9.5% English, 8.6% Other groups (2000).
Economy: Single-family building permits issued: 18 (2007); Multi-family building permits issued: 20 (2007); Employment by occupation: 10.2% management, 15.4% professional, 14.2% services, 25.3% sales, 0.7% farming, 7.6% construction, 26.7% production (2000).
Income: Per capita income: $22,094 (2007); Median household income: $39,821 (2007); Average household income: $52,132 (2007); Percent of households with income of $100,000 or more: 9.2% (2007); Poverty rate: 12.5% (2000).
Education: Percent of population age 25 and over with: High school diploma (including GED) or higher: 77.3% (2007); Bachelor's degree or higher: 13.2% (2007); Master's degree or higher: 3.8% (2007).

School District(s)

Miami Trace Local (PK-12)
2005-06 Enrollment: 2,770 . . . . (740) 335-3010
Washington Court House City (PK-12)
2005-06 Enrollment: 2,326 . . . . (740) 335-6620

Housing: Homeownership rate: 56.2% (2007); Median home value: $112,263 (2007); Median rent: $361 per month (2000); Median age of housing: 44 years (2000).
Hospitals: Fayette County Memorial Hospital (70 beds)
Newspapers: Record Herald (Local news; Circulation 6,000); South Central Ohio Shopper's Guide (Community news; Circulation 24,000)
Transportation: Commute to work: 92.8% car, 0.3% public transportation, 3.1% walk, 2.5% work from home (2000); Travel time to work: 48.7% less than 15 minutes, 20.6% 15 to 30 minutes, 13.6% 30 to 45 minutes, 6.4% 45 to 60 minutes, 10.7% 60 minutes or more (2000)
Airports: Fayette County (general aviation)
Additional Information Contacts
City of Washington Court House . . . . (740) 636-2340
http://www.ci.washington-court-house.oh.us
Fayette County Chamber of Commerce . . . . (740) 335-0761
http://www.fayettecountychamberoh.com

Franklin County

Located in central Ohio; crossed by the Scioto and Olentangy Rivers. Covers a land area of 539.87 square miles, a water area of 3.45 square miles, and is located in the Eastern Time Zone. The county was founded in 1803. County seat is Columbus.

Franklin County is part of the Columbus, OH Metropolitan Statistical Area. The entire metro area includes: Delaware County, OH; Fairfield County, OH; Franklin County, OH; Licking County, OH; Madison County, OH; Morrow County, OH; Pickaway County, OH; Union County, OH

Weather Station: Columbus Valley Crossing — Elevation: 734 feet

	Jan	Feb	Mar	Apr	May	Jun	Jul	Aug	Sep	Oct	Nov	Dec
High	36	41	52	64	74	82	85	84	78	66	53	42
Low	20	23	32	40	51	60	64	62	55	43	34	26
Precip	2.5	2.0	3.0	3.7	4.3	4.1	4.4	4.3	2.9	2.5	3.3	2.9
Snow	8.4	5.0	1.9	0.6	tr	0.0	0.0	0.0	0.0	tr	0.6	2.8

High and Low temperatures in degrees Fahrenheit; Precipitation and Snow in inches

Weather Station: Columbus-Port Columbus Int'l — Elevation: 807 feet

	Jan	Feb	Mar	Apr	May	Jun	Jul	Aug	Sep	Oct	Nov	Dec
High	35	39	51	62	73	81	85	83	76	65	52	41
Low	20	23	31	40	51	60	64	63	55	43	35	26
Precip	2.5	2.2	2.9	3.3	3.9	4.2	4.6	3.7	2.9	2.3	3.2	2.9
Snow	10.5	6.1	4.3	1.2	tr	tr	tr	0.0	tr	0.2	1.6	4.5

High and Low temperatures in degrees Fahrenheit; Precipitation and Snow in inches

Weather Station: Westerville — Elevation: 807 feet

	Jan	Feb	Mar	Apr	May	Jun	Jul	Aug	Sep	Oct	Nov	Dec
High	36	41	52	64	74	82	85	84	78	66	52	41
Low	18	21	30	39	49	58	62	61	54	42	34	25
Precip	2.5	2.2	2.8	3.6	4.0	4.6	4.0	3.5	2.9	2.6	3.4	2.9
Snow	7.7	5.1	2.3	0.7	tr	0.0	0.0	0.0	0.0	tr	0.5	3.3

High and Low temperatures in degrees Fahrenheit; Precipitation and Snow in inches

Population: 961,437 (1990); 1,068,978 (2000); 1,095,410 (2007); 1,108,918 (2012 projected); Race: 71.9% White, 19.7% Black, 3.6% Asian, 3.5% Hispanic of any race (2007); Density: 2,029.0 persons per square mile (2007); Average household size: 2.41 (2007); Median age: 34.5 (2007); Males per 100 females: 96.0 (2007).
Religion: Five largest groups: 13.7% Catholic Church, 4.1% The United Methodist Church, 2.8% Evangelical Lutheran Church in America, 2.1% Southern Baptist Convention, 1.5% Presbyterian Church (U.S.A.) (2000).
Economy: Unemployment rate: 5.7% (6/2008); Total civilian labor force: 632,812 (6/2008); Leading industries: 13.6% health care and social assistance; 11.9% retail trade; 9.7% finance & insurance (2005); Farms: 561 totaling 81,593 acres (2002); Companies that employ 500 or more persons: 110 (2006); Companies that employ 100 to 499 persons: 902 (2006); Companies that employ less than 100 persons: 27,605 (2006); Black-owned businesses: 7,888 (2002); Hispanic-owned businesses: 887 (2002); Asian-owned businesses: 2,338 (2002); Women-owned businesses: 25,366 (2002); Retail sales per capita: $19,881 (2008). Single-family building permits issued: 2,094 (2007); Multi-family building permits issued: 1,873 (2007).
Income: Per capita income: $27,396 (2007); Median household income: $49,888 (2007); Average household income: $65,533 (2007); Percent of households with income of $100,000 or more: 17.2% (2007); Poverty rate: 14.7% (2005); Bankruptcy rate: 4.51% (2007).
Taxes: Total county taxes per capita: $419 (2006); County property taxes per capita: $305 (2006).
Education: Percent of population age 25 and over with: High school diploma (including GED) or higher: 86.3% (2007); Bachelor's degree or higher: 32.3% (2007); Master's degree or higher: 10.7% (2007).
Housing: Homeownership rate: 57.5% (2007); Median home value: $142,157 (2007); Median rent: $496 per month (2000); Median age of housing: 30 years (2000).
Health: Birth rate: 151.6 per 10,000 population (2007); Death rate: 75.4 per 10,000 population (2007); Age-adjusted cancer mortality rate: 210.5 deaths per 100,000 population (2005); Air Quality Index: 67.1% good, 26.0% moderate, 6.8% unhealthy for sensitive individuals, 0.0% unhealthy (percent of days in 2007); Number of physicians: 39.4 per 10,000 population (2005); Hospital beds: 36.7 per 10,000 population (2004); Hospital admissions: 1,641.5 per 10,000 population (2004).
Elections: 2004 Presidential election results: 45.1% Bush, 54.4% Kerry, 0.0% Nader, 0.3% Badnarik
Additional Information Contacts
Franklin County Government . . . . (614) 462-3322
http://www.co.franklin.oh.us
Bexley Area Chamber of Commerce . . . . (614) 470-4500
http://www.bexleyareachamber.org
Canal Winchester Area Chamber of Commerce . . . . (614) 837-1556
http://www.canalwinchester.com
Canal Winchester Convention & Visitors Bureau. . . . . (614) 920-0649
http://www.cwcvb.com
City of Bexley . . . . (614) 559-4200
http://www.bexley.org
City of Columbus . . . . (614) 645-8100
http://www.ci.columbus.oh.us
City of Dublin . . . . (614) 410-4400
http://www.dublin.oh.us
City of Gahanna . . . . (614) 342-4000
http://www.gahanna.gov
City of Grandview Heights . . . . (614) 481-6217
http://www.grandviewheights.org
City of Grove City. . . . . (614) 277-3000
http://www.grovecityohio.gov
City of Hilliard. . . . . (614) 876-7361
http://www.cityofhilliard.com
City of Reynoldsburg . . . . (614) 322-6800
http://www.ci.reynoldsburg.oh.us
City of Upper Arlington. . . . . (614) 583-5040
http://www.ua-ohio.net
City of Westerville . . . . (614) 901-6400
http://www.westerville.org
City of Whitehall. . . . . (614) 338-3106
http://www.ci.whitehall.oh.us
City of Worthington . . . . (614) 436-3100
http://www.worthington.org

Columbus Chamber . . . . (614) 221-1321
http://www.columbus.org
Dublin Chamber of Commerce . . . . (614) 889-2001
http://www.dublinchamber.org
Dublin Convention and Visitors Bureau . . . . (614) 792-7666
http://www.dublinvisit.org
Gahanna Area Chamber of Commerce . . . . (614) 471-0451
http://www.gahannaareachamber.com
Greater Columbus Convention & Visitors Bureau . . . . (614) 221-6623
http://www.experiencecolumbus.com
Grove City Area Chamber of Commerce . . . . (614) 875-9762
http://www.gcchamber.org
Hilliard Area Chamber of Commerce . . . . (614) 876-7666
http://www.hilliardchamber.org
Hilliard Convention & Visitors Bureau . . . . (614) 876-6911
http://www.hilliardcvb.org
New Albany Chamber of Commerce . . . . (614) 855-4400
http://www.newalbanychamber.com
Reynoldsburg Area Chamber of Commerce . . . . (614) 866-4753
http://www.reynoldsburgchamber.com
Southeastern Franklin County Chamber of Commerce . . . . (614) 836-1138
http://www.groveport.org
Upper Arlington Area Chamber of Commerce . . . . (614) 481-5710
http://www.uachamber.org
Village of Canal Winchester . . . . (614) 837-7493
http://www.canalwinchesterohio.gov
Village of Groveport . . . . (614) 836-5301
http://www.groveport.org
Village of New Albany . . . . (614) 855-3913
http://www.villageofnewalbany.org
Village of Obetz . . . . (614) 491-1080
http://www.obetz.oh.us
Westerville Area Chamber of Commerce . . . . (614) 882-8917
http://www.westervillechamber.com
Whitehall Area Chamber of Commerce . . . . (614) 237-7792
http://www.whitehallchamber.org
Worthington Chamber of Commerce . . . . (614) 888-3040
http://www.worthingtonchamber.org

Franklin County Communities

AMLIN (unincorporated postal area, zip code 43002). Covers a land area of 9.461 square miles and a water area of 0 square miles. Located at 40.06° N. Lat.; 83.18° W. Long. Elevation is 944 feet.
Population: 1,304 (2000); Race: 100.0% White, 0.0% Black, 0.0% Asian, 0.0% Hispanic of any race (2000); Density: 137.8 persons per square mile (2000); Age: 16.0% under 18, 11.9% over 64 (2000); Marriage status: 18.5% never married, 62.0% now married, 6.0% widowed, 13.4% divorced (2000); Foreign born: 1.3% (2000); Ancestry (includes multiple ancestries): 28.8% German, 28.7% United States or American, 16.4% Irish, 16.0% English, 6.9% French (except Basque) (2000).
Economy: Employment by occupation: 6.5% management, 15.6% professional, 17.8% services, 27.8% sales, 0.0% farming, 13.8% construction, 18.5% production (2000).
Income: Per capita income: $23,344 (2000); Median household income: $40,795 (2000); Poverty rate: 7.7% (2000).
Education: Percent of population age 25 and over with: High school diploma (including GED) or higher: 83.5% (2000); Bachelor's degree or higher: 20.2% (2000).
Housing: Homeownership rate: 89.0% (2000); Median home value: $136,700 (2000); Median rent: $364 per month (2000); Median age of housing: 23 years (2000).
Transportation: Commute to work: 96.2% car, 0.0% public transportation, 0.9% walk, 2.9% work from home (2000); Travel time to work: 35.8% less than 15 minutes, 38.7% 15 to 30 minutes, 13.4% 30 to 45 minutes, 6.0% 45 to 60 minutes, 6.0% 60 minutes or more (2000)

BEXLEY (city). Covers a land area of 2.446 square miles and a water area of 0 square miles. Located at 39.96° N. Lat.; 82.93° W. Long. Elevation is 791 feet.
History: Named for Bexley, England. Bexley developed as a residential suburb of Columbus, and as the location of Capital University, founded in 1830 as a Lutheran divinity school.
Population: 13,111 (1990); 13,203 (2000); 12,131 (2007); 11,420 (2012 projected); Race: 90.8% White, 5.2% Black, 1.1% Asian, 1.3% Hispanic of any race (2007); Density: 4,960.1 persons per square mile (2007); Average household size: 2.81 (2007); Median age: 36.0 (2007); Males per 100 females: 90.1 (2007); Marriage status: 29.5% never married, 56.6% now married, 6.1% widowed, 7.8% divorced (2000); Foreign born: 6.4% (2000); Ancestry (includes multiple ancestries): 27.7% German, 14.8% Irish, 13.1% English, 12.9% Other groups, 7.3% Russian (2000).
Economy: Single-family building permits issued: 2 (2007); Multi-family building permits issued: 0 (2007); Employment by occupation: 20.0% management, 38.8% professional, 9.5% services, 26.2% sales, 0.1% farming, 1.9% construction, 3.5% production (2000).
Income: Per capita income: $42,058 (2007); Median household income: $80,795 (2007); Average household income: $116,560 (2007); Percent of households with income of $100,000 or more: 38.5% (2007); Poverty rate: 4.6% (2000).
Education: Percent of population age 25 and over with: High school diploma (including GED) or higher: 96.9% (2007); Bachelor's degree or higher: 66.4% (2007); Master's degree or higher: 31.5% (2007).

School District(s)

Bexley City (PK-12)
2005-06 Enrollment: 2,161 . . . . (614) 231-7611
Housing: Homeownership rate: 77.0% (2007); Median home value: $236,943 (2007); Median rent: $534 per month (2000); Median age of housing: 57 years (2000).
Safety: Violent crime rate: 22.2 per 10,000 population; Property crime rate: 362.6 per 10,000 population (2007).
Transportation: Commute to work: 86.4% car, 1.6% public transportation, 7.0% walk, 4.4% work from home (2000); Travel time to work: 42.0% less than 15 minutes, 43.1% 15 to 30 minutes, 11.3% 30 to 45 minutes, 1.8% 45 to 60 minutes, 1.8% 60 minutes or more (2000)
Additional Information Contacts
Bexley Area Chamber of Commerce . . . . (614) 470-4500
http://www.bexleyareachamber.org
City of Bexley . . . . (614) 559-4200
http://www.bexley.org

BLACKLICK (unincorporated postal area, zip code 43004). Aka Black Lick. Covers a land area of 13.718 square miles and a water area of 0 square miles. Located at 39.99° N. Lat.; 82.80° W. Long. Elevation is 951 feet.
Population: 8,664 (2000); Race: 82.0% White, 13.4% Black, 1.9% Asian, 1.0% Hispanic of any race (2000); Density: 631.6 persons per square mile (2000); Age: 26.7% under 18, 6.5% over 64 (2000); Marriage status: 25.5% never married, 62.4% now married, 3.6% widowed, 8.4% divorced (2000); Foreign born: 3.7% (2000); Ancestry (includes multiple ancestries): 27.6% German, 20.1% Other groups, 17.5% Irish, 9.0% English, 8.2% United States or American (2000).
Economy: Employment by occupation: 20.3% management, 21.3% professional, 9.3% services, 28.9% sales, 0.0% farming, 8.4% construction, 11.8% production (2000).
Income: Per capita income: $30,748 (2000); Median household income: $55,406 (2000); Poverty rate: 7.0% (2000).
Education: Percent of population age 25 and over with: High school diploma (including GED) or higher: 91.9% (2000); Bachelor's degree or higher: 36.9% (2000).

School District(s)

Gahanna-Jefferson City (PK-12)
2005-06 Enrollment: 6,905 . . . . (614) 471-7065
Housing: Homeownership rate: 73.3% (2000); Median home value: $152,500 (2000); Median rent: $539 per month (2000); Median age of housing: 4 years (2000).
Transportation: Commute to work: 96.4% car, 0.4% public transportation, 0.8% walk, 1.8% work from home (2000); Travel time to work: 22.8% less than 15 minutes, 42.8% 15 to 30 minutes, 23.3% 30 to 45 minutes, 6.4% 45 to 60 minutes, 4.6% 60 minutes or more (2000)

BLACKLICK ESTATES (CDP). Covers a land area of 1.993 square miles and a water area of 0 square miles. Located at 39.90° N. Lat.; 82.86° W. Long. Elevation is 751 feet.
Population: 9,850 (1990); 9,518 (2000); 8,735 (2007); 8,268 (2012 projected); Race: 81.3% White, 13.1% Black, 1.2% Asian, 1.8% Hispanic of any race (2007); Density: 4,382.5 persons per square mile (2007); Average household size: 2.81 (2007); Median age: 35.1 (2007); Males per 100 females: 96.5 (2007); Marriage status: 25.2% never married, 59.0% now married, 4.0% widowed, 11.9% divorced (2000); Foreign born: 2.0% (2000); Ancestry (includes multiple ancestries): 26.4% German, 15.3%

Other groups, 12.8% Irish, 12.1% United States or American, 9.5% English (2000).
Economy: Employment by occupation: 10.8% management, 10.3% professional, 13.4% services, 34.6% sales, 0.0% farming, 11.8% construction, 19.0% production (2000).
Income: Per capita income: $21,031 (2007); Median household income: $52,667 (2007); Average household income: $59,033 (2007); Percent of households with income of $100,000 or more: 10.5% (2007); Poverty rate: 5.5% (2000).
Education: Percent of population age 25 and over with: High school diploma (including GED) or higher: 82.8% (2007); Bachelor's degree or higher: 9.5% (2007); Master's degree or higher: 1.9% (2007).
Housing: Homeownership rate: 78.5% (2007); Median home value: $101,956 (2007); Median rent: $490 per month (2000); Median age of housing: 32 years (2000).
Transportation: Commute to work: 95.5% car, 1.6% public transportation, 0.4% walk, 1.8% work from home (2000); Travel time to work: 19.7% less than 15 minutes, 50.3% 15 to 30 minutes, 24.0% 30 to 45 minutes, 3.3% 45 to 60 minutes, 2.7% 60 minutes or more (2000)

BRICE (village). Covers a land area of 0.077 square miles and a water area of 0 square miles. Located at 39.91° N. Lat.; 82.83° W. Long. Elevation is 784 feet.
Population: 91 (1990); 70 (2000); 96 (2007); 113 (2012 projected); Race: 95.8% White, 0.0% Black, 0.0% Asian, 0.0% Hispanic of any race (2007); Density: 1,247.8 persons per square mile (2007); Average household size: 2.82 (2007); Median age: 32.5 (2007); Males per 100 females: 100.0 (2007); Marriage status: 26.7% never married, 66.7% now married, 0.0% widowed, 6.7% divorced (2000); Foreign born: 0.0% (2000); Ancestry (includes multiple ancestries): 40.0% Other groups, 27.7% Irish, 16.9% German, 13.8% English, 7.7% Scotch-Irish (2000).
Economy: Single-family building permits issued: 0 (2007); Multi-family building permits issued: 0 (2007); Employment by occupation: 10.5% management, 10.5% professional, 5.3% services, 21.1% sales, 0.0% farming, 21.1% construction, 31.6% production (2000).
Income: Per capita income: $19,349 (2007); Median household income: $38,750 (2007); Average household income: $54,632 (2007); Percent of households with income of $100,000 or more: 8.8% (2007); Poverty rate: 0.0% (2000).
Education: Percent of population age 25 and over with: High school diploma (including GED) or higher: 69.0% (2007); Bachelor's degree or higher: 0.0% (2007); Master's degree or higher: 0.0% (2007).
Housing: Homeownership rate: 79.4% (2007); Median home value: $106,944 (2007); Median rent: $388 per month (2000); Median age of housing: 60+ years (2000).
Transportation: Commute to work: 73.7% car, 0.0% public transportation, 5.3% walk, 21.1% work from home (2000); Travel time to work: 0.0% less than 15 minutes, 60.0% 15 to 30 minutes, 0.0% 30 to 45 minutes, 26.7% 45 to 60 minutes, 13.3% 60 minutes or more (2000)

CANAL WINCHESTER (village). Covers a land area of 6.371 square miles and a water area of 0 square miles. Located at 39.84° N. Lat.; 82.81° W. Long. Elevation is 761 feet.
History: The town of Canal Winchester developed as a produce center on the Ohio & Erie Canal.
Population: 2,538 (1990); 4,478 (2000); 5,644 (2007); 6,335 (2012 projected); Race: 94.2% White, 3.0% Black, 0.8% Asian, 0.7% Hispanic of any race (2007); Density: 885.9 persons per square mile (2007); Average household size: 2.70 (2007); Median age: 39.9 (2007); Males per 100 females: 89.2 (2007); Marriage status: 15.3% never married, 67.2% now married, 8.7% widowed, 8.8% divorced (2000); Foreign born: 2.2% (2000); Ancestry (includes multiple ancestries): 32.7% German, 15.8% Irish, 15.1% English, 9.1% Other groups, 5.4% United States or American (2000).
Economy: Single-family building permits issued: 77 (2007); Multi-family building permits issued: 0 (2007); Employment by occupation: 22.8% management, 24.1% professional, 13.0% services, 24.1% sales, 0.0% farming, 6.1% construction, 9.9% production (2000).
Income: Per capita income: $29,313 (2007); Median household income: $68,345 (2007); Average household income: $77,769 (2007); Percent of households with income of $100,000 or more: 29.3% (2007); Poverty rate: 2.2% (2000).
Education: Percent of population age 25 and over with: High school diploma (including GED) or higher: 91.3% (2007); Bachelor's degree or higher: 31.9% (2007); Master's degree or higher: 8.7% (2007).

School District(s)
Canal Winchester Local (PK-12)
2005-06 Enrollment: 3,076 . . . . (614) 837-4533
Housing: Homeownership rate: 84.4% (2007); Median home value: $178,516 (2007); Median rent: $485 per month (2000); Median age of housing: 23 years (2000).
Transportation: Commute to work: 94.3% car, 1.0% public transportation, 0.7% walk, 3.6% work from home (2000); Travel time to work: 23.3% less than 15 minutes, 41.4% 15 to 30 minutes, 26.6% 30 to 45 minutes, 6.2% 45 to 60 minutes, 2.6% 60 minutes or more (2000)
Additional Information Contacts
Canal Winchester Area Chamber of Commerce . . . . (614) 837-1556
http://www.canalwinchester.com
Canal Winchester Convention & Visitors Bureau. . . . . (614) 920-0649
http://www.cwcvb.com
Village of Canal Winchester. . . . . (614) 837-7493
http://www.canalwinchesterohio.gov

COLUMBUS (city). County seat. Covers a land area of 210.268 square miles and a water area of 2.281 square miles. Located at 39.99° N. Lat.; 82.99° W. Long. Elevation is 771 feet.
History: The site of Columbus was selected for the capital of Ohio in 1812, and the town was laid out. Columbus' early problems of cholera and lack of transportation were solved by draining the nearby swamps, and by the the Ohio & Erie Canal connected to Columbus by a feeder canal. The National Road reached Columbus in 1833, with stagecoaches arriving daily from the east. By 1872 transportation was being provided by five rail lines, and in 1873 Ohio State University was founded in Columbus.
Population: 648,656 (1990); 711,470 (2000); 732,084 (2007); 742,773 (2012 projected); Race: 63.6% White, 26.8% Black, 4.0% Asian, 3.8% Hispanic of any race (2007); Density: 3,481.7 persons per square mile (2007); Average household size: 2.33 (2007); Median age: 32.9 (2007); Males per 100 females: 96.3 (2007); Marriage status: 38.3% never married, 44.0% now married, 5.4% widowed, 12.4% divorced (2000); Foreign born: 6.7% (2000); Ancestry (includes multiple ancestries): 30.0% Other groups, 19.4% German, 11.7% Irish, 7.9% English, 7.2% United States or American (2000).
Economy: Unemployment rate: 5.7% (6/2008); Total civilian labor force: 427,028 (6/2008); Single-family building permits issued: 1,008 (2007); Multi-family building permits issued: 1,698 (2007); Employment by occupation: 13.9% management, 21.5% professional, 15.2% services, 30.1% sales, 0.1% farming, 6.5% construction, 12.7% production (2000).
Income: Per capita income: $24,196 (2007); Median household income: $44,253 (2007); Average household income: $55,908 (2007); Percent of households with income of $100,000 or more: 12.1% (2007); Poverty rate: 14.8% (2000).
Taxes: Total city taxes per capita: $764 (2006); City property taxes per capita: $55 (2006).
Education: Percent of population age 25 and over with: High school diploma (including GED) or higher: 84.7% (2007); Bachelor's degree or higher: 30.1% (2007); Master's degree or higher: 9.4% (2007).

School District(s)
A+ Arts Academy (06-08)
2005-06 Enrollment: 171 . . . . (614) 338-0767
Academy of Columbus (KG-05)
2005-06 Enrollment: 184 . . . . (614) 433-7510
Arts & College Preparatory Academy (10-12)
2005-06 Enrollment: 101 . . . . (614) 986-9974
Buckeye Community Hope Foundation
2005-06 Enrollment: n/a . . . .
Chase Academy for Communication Arts (KG-05)
2005-06 Enrollment: 196 . . . . (614) 509-2432
Clay Community Schools of Columbus-Gifted Hands (KG-09)
2005-06 Enrollment: 29 . . . . (614) 297-1288
Columbus Arts & Technology Academy (KG-06)
2005-06 Enrollment: 532 . . . . (614) 577-0900
Columbus City (PK-12)
2005-06 Enrollment: 58,961 . . . . (614) 365-5000
Columbus Entrepreneurial Academy
2005-06 Enrollment: n/a . . . .
Columbus Humanities Arts and Technology Academy (KG-06)
2005-06 Enrollment: 303 . . . . (614) 261-7200
Columbus Preparatory Academy (KG-06)
2005-06 Enrollment: 350 . . . . (614) 275-3600
Columbus Preparatory and Fitness Academy (KG-05)
2005-06 Enrollment: 36 . . . . (614) 301-4856

Cornerstone Academy Community (KG-04)
2005-06 Enrollment: 67 .... (614) 225-8924
Crittenton Community School (06-09)
2005-06 Enrollment: 110 .... (614) 737-7520
Crossroads Preparatory Academy - Columbus (06-09)
2005-06 Enrollment: 80 .... (614) 586-1800
Dublin City (PK-12)
2005-06 Enrollment: 12,939 .... (614) 764-5913
Electronic Classroom of Tomorrow (KG-12)
2005-06 Enrollment: 6,245 .... (614) 492-8884
Fci Academy (06-12)
2005-06 Enrollment: 210 .... (614) 471-4527
Graham School The (09-12)
2005-06 Enrollment: 196 .... (614) 262-1111
Grandview Heights City (PK-12)
2005-06 Enrollment: 1,176 .... (614) 481-3600
Granville T Woods Comm Shule (KG-05)
2005-06 Enrollment: 122 .... (614) 252-3630
Great Western Academy (KG-04)
2005-06 Enrollment: 345 .... (614) 276-1028
Greater Cincinnati Community (05-08)
2005-06 Enrollment: 83 .... (614) 509-2440
Groveport Madison Local (PK-12)
2005-06 Enrollment: 6,172 .... (614) 492-2520
Hamilton Local (PK-12)
2005-06 Enrollment: 2,817 .... (614) 491-8044
Hamilton Local Digital Academy (02-12)
2005-06 Enrollment: 55 .... (614) 554-5598
Hilliard City (PK-12)
2005-06 Enrollment: 14,851 .... (614) 771-4273
Horizon Science Acad Columbus (05-12)
2005-06 Enrollment: 519 .... (614) 457-2231
International Acad of Columbus (KG-08)
2005-06 Enrollment: 234 .... (614) 844-5539
Life Skills Center of Northern Columbus (09-12)
2005-06 Enrollment: 356 .... (614) 891-9041
Life Skills Ctr of SE Columbus (09-12)
2005-06 Enrollment: 269 .... (614) 296-5026
Millennium Community (KG-05)
2005-06 Enrollment: 663 .... (614) 255-5585
Montessori Renaissance Exp (KG-05)
2005-06 Enrollment: 52 .... (614) 262-6510
Northland Preparatory and Fitness Academy (KG-06)
2005-06 Enrollment: 113 .... (937) 854-4100
Oakstone Community School (KG-10)
2005-06 Enrollment: 71 .... (614) 865-9643
Ohio School for the Deaf (PK-12)
2005-06 Enrollment: 109 .... (614) 728-4030
Ohio State School for the Blind (KG-12)
2005-06 Enrollment: 118 .... (614) 752-1152
Pschtecin Public School (09-12)
2005-06 Enrollment: 23 .... (614) 985-3428
Scholarts Career Center for Children
2005-06 Enrollment: n/a .... (614) 224-1610
Scholarts Preparatory School (KG-09)
2005-06 Enrollment: 85 .... (614) 224-1610
South-Western City (PK-12)
2005-06 Enrollment: 21,583 .... (614) 801-3000
Summit Academy Columbus (01-08)
2005-06 Enrollment: 58 .... (614) 880-0714
Summit Academy Middle School - Columbus (06-08)
2005-06 Enrollment: 31 .... (614) 880-0714
Summit Academy Secondary School - Columbus
2005-06 Enrollment: n/a ....
The Harte School - Columbus (06-09)
2005-06 Enrollment: 111 .... (614) 586-1800
Virtual Community School of Ohio (KG-12)
2005-06 Enrollment: 1,245 .... (614) 501-9473
Vision Into Action Academy (09-12)
2005-06 Enrollment: 168 .... (614) 324-1492
W C Cupe Community School (KG-07)
2005-06 Enrollment: 362 .... (614) 294-3020
Westerville City (PK-12)
2005-06 Enrollment: 14,062 .... (614) 797-5700
Whitehall Prepartory and Fitness Academy (KG-06)
2005-06 Enrollment: 168 .... (614) 314-6301
Worthington City (PK-12)
2005-06 Enrollment: 9,553 .... (614) 883-3000
Youthbuild Columbus Community (10-12)
2005-06 Enrollment: 38 .... (614) 291-0805
Zenith Academy (KG-09)
2005-06 Enrollment: 257 .... (614) 419-6753

Four-year College(s)

Capital University (Private, Not-for-profit, Evangelical Lutheran Church)
Fall 2007 Enrollment: 3,713 .... (614) 236-6011
2007-08 Tuition: In-state $26,360; Out-of-state $26,360
Columbus College of Art and Design (Private, Not-for-profit)
Fall 2007 Enrollment: 1,545 .... (614) 224-9101
2007-08 Tuition: In-state $22,412; Out-of-state $22,412
DeVry University-Ohio (Private, For-profit)
Fall 2007 Enrollment: 3,674 .... (614) 253-7291
2007-08 Tuition: In-state $13,220; Out-of-state $13,220
Franklin University (Private, Not-for-profit)
Fall 2007 Enrollment: 7,559 .... (614) 797-4700
2007-08 Tuition: In-state $8,246; Out-of-state $8,246
Mount Carmel College of Nursing (Private, Not-for-profit, Roman Catholic)
Fall 2007 Enrollment: 680 .... (614) 234-5800
2007-08 Tuition: In-state $7,596; Out-of-state $7,596
Ohio Dominican University (Private, Not-for-profit, Roman Catholic)
Fall 2007 Enrollment: 3,082 .... (614) 253-2741
2007-08 Tuition: In-state $21,700; Out-of-state $21,700
Ohio State University-Main Campus (Public)
Fall 2007 Enrollment: 52,568 .... (614) 292-6446
2007-08 Tuition: In-state $8,676; Out-of-state $21,285
Pontifical College Josephinum (Private, Not-for-profit, Roman Catholic)
Fall 2007 Enrollment: 194 .... (614) 885-5585
2007-08 Tuition: In-state $15,677; Out-of-state $15,677
Trinity Lutheran Seminary (Private, Not-for-profit, Evangelical Lutheran Church)
Fall 2007 Enrollment: 176 .... (614) 235-4136
University of Phoenix-Columbus Ohio Campus (Private, For-profit)
Fall 2007 Enrollment: 289 .... (614) 443-0095
2007-08 Tuition: In-state $12,930; Out-of-state $12,930

Two-year College(s)

Academy of Court Reporting-Columbus (Private, For-profit)
Fall 2007 Enrollment: 274 .... (614) 221-7770
2007-08 Tuition: In-state $9,825; Out-of-state $9,825
American Institute of Alternative Medicine
Fall 2007 Enrollment: 171 .... (614) 825-6278
Bradford School (Private, For-profit)
Fall 2007 Enrollment: 307 .... (614) 416-6200
2007-08 Tuition: In-state $12,640; Out-of-state $12,640
Columbus State Community College (Public)
Fall 2007 Enrollment: 23,057 .... (614) 287-5353
2007-08 Tuition: In-state $3,074; Out-of-state $6,530
Nationwide Beauty Academy (Private, For-profit)
Fall 2007 Enrollment: 115 .... (614) 252-5252
Ohio Institute of Health Careers (Private, For-profit)
Fall 2007 Enrollment: 323 .... (614) 891-5030
Ohio State College of Barber Styling (Private, For-profit)
Fall 2007 Enrollment: 103 .... (614) 868-1015
Ohio State School of Cosmetology (Private, For-profit)
Fall 2007 Enrollment: 61 .... (614) 252-5252
Ohio State School of Cosmetology & Experts Barber School (Private, For-profit)
Fall 2007 Enrollment: 86 .... (614) 252-5252
Technology Education College (Private, For-profit)
Fall 2007 Enrollment: 465 .... (614) 456-4600
2007-08 Tuition: In-state $14,035; Out-of-state $14,035
The Spa School (Private, For-profit)
Fall 2007 Enrollment: 120 .... (614) 252-5252

Vocational/Technical School(s)

Adult and Community Education-Hudson (Public)
Fall 2007 Enrollment: 190 .... (614) 365-6000
2007-08 Tuition: $10,135
American School of Technology (Private, For-profit)
Fall 2007 Enrollment: 126 .... (614) 436-4820
2007-08 Tuition: $9,940
Roadmaster Truck Driving Institute (Private, For-profit)
Fall 2007 Enrollment: n/a .... (614) 351-1748

Housing: Homeownership rate: 49.8% (2007); Median home value: $124,172 (2007); Median rent: $490 per month (2000); Median age of housing: 30 years (2000).
Hospitals: Children's Hospital, Education Foundation (353 beds); Doctors Hospital (478 beds); Grant Medical Center (337 beds); Mount Carmel East Hospital (287 beds); Mount Carmel East-West Health & Saint Ann (523 beds); Ohio State University Medical Center (156 beds); Riverside Methodist Hospital (1049 beds); The Ohio State University (404 beds)
Safety: Violent crime rate: 85.2 per 10,000 population; Property crime rate: 699.6 per 10,000 population (2007).
Newspapers: Alliance Review - Columbus Bureau (Local news); Booster (Community news; Circulation 18,200); Buckeye Farm News (Local news; Circulation 60,000); Canal Winchester Times (Local news; Circulation 2,308); The Catholic Times (Regional news; Circulation 25,063); Cincinnati Enquirer - State Capitol Bureau (Regional news); Columbus Call & Post (National news; Circulation 13,753); The Columbus Dispatch (Local news; Circulation 352,510); The Columbus Federal Voice (Local news; Circulation 8,000); Columbus Messenger (Local news); Columbus Post (Community news); The Daily Record - Dix Capital Bureau (Local news); Dayton Daily News - State Capitol Bureau (Local news); Dayton Minority Communicator (Community news; Circulation 90,000); The Dublin News (Regional news; Circulation 18,450); Eastside Messenger (Community news; Circulation 51,432); Gahanna News (Community news; Circulation 13,136); Grove City Southwest Messenger (Community news; Circulation 17,664); Hillard Northwest News (Community news; Circulation 20,964); Journal-News - Columbus Bureau (Local news); Madison Messenger (Community news; Circulation 12,466); New Albany News (Community news; Circulation 3,277); Northland News (Community news); The Other Paper (Community news; Circulation 50,000); Outlook News (Local news; Circulation 17,000); Pickerington This Week (Local news; Circulation 12,500); Pickerington Times Sun (Local news; Circulation 11,235); Reynoldsburg News (Community news; Circulation 14,083); Rocky Fork Enterprise (Community news; Circulation 13,231); Southeast Messenger (Local news; Circulation 33,137); Suburban News Publications (Local news); Times (Local news; Circulation 11,035); Tri-Village News (Community news; Circulation 5,950); Union County This Week (Local news; Circulation 14,000); Westerville News/Public Opinion (Local news; Circulation 21,185); Westland News (Community news; Circulation 11,063); Westside Messenger (Local news; Circulation 45,139); Whitehall News (Community news; Circulation 10,225); Worthington News (Community news; Circulation 18,606)
Transportation: Commute to work: 89.7% car, 3.9% public transportation, 3.2% walk, 2.3% work from home (2000); Travel time to work: 26.1% less than 15 minutes, 49.1% 15 to 30 minutes, 17.7% 30 to 45 minutes, 3.6% 45 to 60 minutes, 3.4% 60 minutes or more (2000)
Airports: Bolton Field (general aviation); Ohio State University (general aviation); Port Columbus International (primary service/medium hub); Rickenbacker International (commercial service)
Additional Information Contacts
City of Columbus . . . . (614) 645-8100
http://www.ci.columbus.oh.us
Columbus Chamber . . . . (614) 221-1321
http://www.columbus.org
Greater Columbus Convention & Visitors Bureau . . . . (614) 221-6623
http://www.experiencecolumbus.com

DUBLIN (city). Covers a land area of 21.123 square miles and a water area of 0.018 square miles. Located at 40.10° N. Lat.; 83.14° W. Long. Elevation is 830 feet.
History: Named for Dublin, Ireland. Dublin was laid out in 1818 by John Sells, whose descendants organized the Sells Brothers' Circus. At one time, Dublin was selected to be the state capital by a commission appointed for that purpose, but "political horse trading" changed the selection.
Population: 17,231 (1990); 31,392 (2000); 35,862 (2007); 38,751 (2012 projected); Race: 86.3% White, 2.5% Black, 9.4% Asian, 1.6% Hispanic of any race (2007); Density: 1,697.8 persons per square mile (2007); Average household size: 2.75 (2007); Median age: 35.8 (2007); Males per 100 females: 98.6 (2007); Marriage status: 18.9% never married, 72.2% now married, 2.9% widowed, 6.0% divorced (2000); Foreign born: 9.1% (2000); Ancestry (includes multiple ancestries): 31.3% German, 17.0% Irish, 12.9% Other groups, 12.3% English, 9.4% Italian (2000).
Economy: Unemployment rate: 4.4% (6/2008); Total civilian labor force: 20,058 (6/2008); Single-family building permits issued: 131 (2007); Multi-family building permits issued: 54 (2007); Employment by occupation: 29.9% management, 29.9% professional, 6.5% services, 28.3% sales, 0.1% farming, 2.0% construction, 3.3% production (2000).
Income: Per capita income: $47,352 (2007); Median household income: $102,571 (2007); Average household income: $130,187 (2007); Percent of households with income of $100,000 or more: 51.4% (2007); Poverty rate: 2.7% (2000).
Taxes: Total city taxes per capita: $1,925 (2006); City property taxes per capita: $198 (2006)
Education: Percent of population age 25 and over with: High school diploma (including GED) or higher: 97.2% (2007); Bachelor's degree or higher: 63.6% (2007); Master's degree or higher: 22.2% (2007).

School District(s)

Columbus City (PK-12)
2005-06 Enrollment: 58,961 . . . . (614) 365-5000
Dublin City (PK-12)
2005-06 Enrollment: 12,939 . . . . (614) 764-5913

Housing: Homeownership rate: 75.4% (2007); Median home value: $290,601 (2007); Median rent: $839 per month (2000); Median age of housing: 9 years (2000).
Safety: Violent crime rate: 6.7 per 10,000 population; Property crime rate: 202.8 per 10,000 population (2007).
Transportation: Commute to work: 93.3% car, 0.4% public transportation, 0.5% walk, 5.4% work from home (2000); Travel time to work: 28.2% less than 15 minutes, 37.4% 15 to 30 minutes, 26.3% 30 to 45 minutes, 4.4% 45 to 60 minutes, 3.7% 60 minutes or more (2000)
Additional Information Contacts
City of Dublin . . . . (614) 410-4400
http://www.dublin.oh.us
Dublin Chamber of Commerce . . . . (614) 889-2001
http://www.dublinchamber.org
Dublin Convention and Visitors Bureau . . . . (614) 792-7666
http://www.dublinvisit.org

GAHANNA (city). Covers a land area of 12.396 square miles and a water area of 0 square miles. Located at 40.02° N. Lat.; 82.86° W. Long. Elevation is 794 feet.
History: Named for an Algonquian Indian translation of "stream". Incorporated 1881.
Population: 24,610 (1990); 32,636 (2000); 32,473 (2007); 32,255 (2012 projected); Race: 83.1% White, 9.9% Black, 4.1% Asian, 1.9% Hispanic of any race (2007); Density: 2,619.7 persons per square mile (2007); Average household size: 2.68 (2007); Median age: 38.3 (2007); Males per 100 females: 95.2 (2007); Marriage status: 21.6% never married, 63.5% now married, 4.8% widowed, 10.2% divorced (2000); Foreign born: 4.9% (2000); Ancestry (includes multiple ancestries): 26.3% German, 16.0% Other groups, 14.4% Irish, 12.9% English, 7.8% United States or American (2000).
Economy: Unemployment rate: 5.0% (6/2008); Total civilian labor force: 19,347 (6/2008); Single-family building permits issued: 32 (2007); Multi-family building permits issued: 10 (2007); Employment by occupation: 20.7% management, 25.7% professional, 10.1% services, 29.7% sales, 0.0% farming, 5.7% construction, 8.1% production (2000).
Income: Per capita income: $35,537 (2007); Median household income: $77,820 (2007); Average household income: $95,138 (2007); Percent of households with income of $100,000 or more: 35.2% (2007); Poverty rate: 3.7% (2000).
Education: Percent of population age 25 and over with: High school diploma (including GED) or higher: 93.7% (2007); Bachelor's degree or higher: 41.3% (2007); Master's degree or higher: 14.1% (2007).

School District(s)

Gahanna-Jefferson City (PK-12)
2005-06 Enrollment: 6,905 . . . . (614) 471-7065

Vocational/Technical School(s)

Everest Institute-Gahanna (Private, For-profit)
Fall 2007 Enrollment: 1,032. . . . . (614) 322-3414
2007-08 Tuition: $12,400

Housing: Homeownership rate: 77.8% (2007); Median home value: $184,388 (2007); Median rent: $582 per month (2000); Median age of housing: 18 years (2000).
Hospitals: Woods at Parkside (44 beds)
Safety: Violent crime rate: 36.2 per 10,000 population; Property crime rate: 277.9 per 10,000 population (2007).
Transportation: Commute to work: 94.4% car, 0.9% public transportation, 0.7% walk, 3.7% work from home (2000); Travel time to work: 26.6% less

than 15 minutes, 51.4% 15 to 30 minutes, 15.9% 30 to 45 minutes, 2.4% 45 to 60 minutes, 3.7% 60 minutes or more (2000)

Additional Information Contacts

City of Gahanna . . . . (614) 342-4000
http://www.gahanna.gov

Gahanna Area Chamber of Commerce . . . . (614) 471-0451
http://www.gahannaareachamber.com

GALLOWAY (unincorporated postal area, zip code 43119). Covers a land area of 33.748 square miles and a water area of 0 square miles. Located at 39.94° N. Lat.; 83.16° W. Long. Elevation is 905 feet.

Population: 21,695 (2000); Race: 90.8% White, 4.1% Black, 1.6% Asian, 1.9% Hispanic of any race (2000); Density: 642.9 persons per square mile (2000); Age: 30.7% under 18, 3.8% over 64 (2000); Marriage status: 24.9% never married, 62.3% now married, 2.3% widowed, 10.6% divorced (2000); Foreign born: 2.6% (2000); Ancestry (includes multiple ancestries): 27.5% German, 16.0% Irish, 13.4% United States or American, 12.4% Other groups, 9.8% English (2000).

Economy: Employment by occupation: 14.2% management, 17.5% professional, 11.4% services, 32.1% sales, 0.0% farming, 7.7% construction, 17.0% production (2000).

Income: Per capita income: $22,164 (2000); Median household income: $54,978 (2000); Poverty rate: 5.5% (2000).

Education: Percent of population age 25 and over with: High school diploma (including GED) or higher: 89.2% (2000); Bachelor's degree or higher: 22.4% (2000).

School District(s)

South-Western City (PK-12)
2005-06 Enrollment: 21,583 . . . . (614) 801-3000

Housing: Homeownership rate: 74.3% (2000); Median home value: $122,200 (2000); Median rent: $544 per month (2000); Median age of housing: 8 years (2000).

Transportation: Commute to work: 96.2% car, 0.3% public transportation, 0.5% walk, 2.8% work from home (2000); Travel time to work: 19.1% less than 15 minutes, 47.9% 15 to 30 minutes, 24.7% 30 to 45 minutes, 5.2% 45 to 60 minutes, 3.0% 60 minutes or more (2000)

GRANDVIEW HEIGHTS (city). Covers a land area of 1.347 square miles and a water area of 0 square miles. Located at 39.98° N. Lat.; 83.04° W. Long. Elevation is 774 feet.

Population: 7,041 (1990); 6,695 (2000); 6,214 (2007); 5,886 (2012 projected); Race: 94.8% White, 1.8% Black, 1.1% Asian, 2.1% Hispanic of any race (2007); Density: 4,614.9 persons per square mile (2007); Average household size: 2.21 (2007); Median age: 38.4 (2007); Males per 100 females: 93.9 (2007); Marriage status: 31.0% never married, 49.3% now married, 7.8% widowed, 11.8% divorced (2000); Foreign born: 3.0% (2000); Ancestry (includes multiple ancestries): 32.4% German, 20.4% Irish, 18.8% English, 9.6% Italian, 6.1% Other groups (2000).

Economy: Single-family building permits issued: 2 (2007); Multi-family building permits issued: 0 (2007); Employment by occupation: 19.1% management, 32.3% professional, 8.0% services, 29.4% sales, 0.0% farming, 3.1% construction, 8.0% production (2000).

Income: Per capita income: $33,482 (2007); Median household income: $59,618 (2007); Average household income: $73,936 (2007); Percent of households with income of $100,000 or more: 21.6% (2007); Poverty rate: 4.5% (2000).

Education: Percent of population age 25 and over with: High school diploma (including GED) or higher: 91.9% (2007); Bachelor's degree or higher: 47.2% (2007); Master's degree or higher: 16.1% (2007).

Housing: Homeownership rate: 60.1% (2007); Median home value: $200,234 (2007); Median rent: $553 per month (2000); Median age of housing: 59 years (2000).

Safety: Violent crime rate: 19.5 per 10,000 population; Property crime rate: 265.3 per 10,000 population (2007).

Transportation: Commute to work: 88.8% car, 4.7% public transportation, 3.3% walk, 1.4% work from home (2000); Travel time to work: 42.0% less than 15 minutes, 43.6% 15 to 30 minutes, 9.6% 30 to 45 minutes, 3.0% 45 to 60 minutes, 1.9% 60 minutes or more (2000)

Additional Information Contacts

City of Grandview Heights . . . . (614) 481-6217
http://www.grandviewheights.org

GROVE CITY (city). Covers a land area of 13.948 square miles and a water area of 0.011 square miles. Located at 39.87° N. Lat.; 83.07° W. Long. Elevation is 850 feet.

History: Named for its many tree groves, by William F. Brock. Grove City developed around an agricultural and truck gardening region. Many of its early residents were of German ancestry.

Population: 21,241 (1990); 27,075 (2000); 29,709 (2007); 31,262 (2012 projected); Race: 94.8% White, 2.2% Black, 0.8% Asian, 1.8% Hispanic of any race (2007); Density: 2,130.0 persons per square mile (2007); Average household size: 2.63 (2007); Median age: 36.4 (2007); Males per 100 females: 96.0 (2007); Marriage status: 20.7% never married, 62.7% now married, 5.9% widowed, 10.7% divorced (2000); Foreign born: 1.2% (2000); Ancestry (includes multiple ancestries): 29.6% German, 16.8% Irish, 12.0% United States or American, 11.3% English, 7.4% Other groups (2000).

Economy: Unemployment rate: 5.4% (6/2008); Total civilian labor force: 18,198 (6/2008); Single-family building permits issued: 256 (2007); Multi-family building permits issued: 20 (2007); Employment by occupation: 15.8% management, 18.2% professional, 13.1% services, 32.6% sales, 0.0% farming, 8.6% construction, 11.6% production (2000).

Income: Per capita income: $28,192 (2007); Median household income: $64,320 (2007); Average household income: $73,664 (2007); Percent of households with income of $100,000 or more: 22.8% (2007); Poverty rate: 4.6% (2000).

Education: Percent of population age 25 and over with: High school diploma (including GED) or higher: 89.3% (2007); Bachelor's degree or higher: 23.3% (2007); Master's degree or higher: 5.7% (2007).

School District(s)

Life Skills Ctr of SW Columbus (09-12)
2005-06 Enrollment: 226 . . . . (614) 801-1366

South-Western City (PK-12)
2005-06 Enrollment: 21,583 . . . . (614) 801-3000

Housing: Homeownership rate: 74.4% (2007); Median home value: $151,526 (2007); Median rent: $517 per month (2000); Median age of housing: 23 years (2000).

Safety: Violent crime rate: 20.3 per 10,000 population; Property crime rate: 367.1 per 10,000 population (2007).

Newspapers: Grove City Record (Local news; Circulation 4,273)

Transportation: Commute to work: 95.1% car, 1.1% public transportation, 0.9% walk, 2.0% work from home (2000); Travel time to work: 26.3% less than 15 minutes, 44.3% 15 to 30 minutes, 22.8% 30 to 45 minutes, 3.9% 45 to 60 minutes, 2.7% 60 minutes or more (2000)

Additional Information Contacts

City of Grove City . . . . (614) 277-3000
http://www.grovecityohio.gov

Grove City Area Chamber of Commerce . . . . (614) 875-9762
http://www.gcchamber.org

GROVEPORT (village). Covers a land area of 8.004 square miles and a water area of 0.008 square miles. Located at 39.85° N. Lat.; 82.89° W. Long. Elevation is 741 feet.

Population: 3,192 (1990); 3,865 (2000); 4,566 (2007); 4,984 (2012 projected); Race: 89.3% White, 5.8% Black, 1.6% Asian, 2.1% Hispanic of any race (2007); Density: 570.4 persons per square mile (2007); Average household size: 2.41 (2007); Median age: 38.3 (2007); Males per 100 females: 94.3 (2007); Marriage status: 20.0% never married, 59.8% now married, 7.6% widowed, 12.6% divorced (2000); Foreign born: 1.4% (2000); Ancestry (includes multiple ancestries): 26.1% German, 16.3% Other groups, 14.1% Irish, 11.5% United States or American, 11.1% English (2000).

Economy: Single-family building permits issued: 31 (2007); Multi-family building permits issued: 0 (2007); Employment by occupation: 11.9% management, 13.3% professional, 13.4% services, 34.0% sales, 0.2% farming, 10.6% construction, 16.6% production (2000).

Income: Per capita income: $24,403 (2007); Median household income: $51,328 (2007); Average household income: $58,274 (2007); Percent of households with income of $100,000 or more: 13.5% (2007); Poverty rate: 5.9% (2000).

Education: Percent of population age 25 and over with: High school diploma (including GED) or higher: 82.8% (2007); Bachelor's degree or higher: 12.1% (2007); Master's degree or higher: 2.8% (2007).

School District(s)

Eastland-Fairfield Career/Tech (09-12)
2005-06 Enrollment: n/a . . . . (614) 836-4530

Groveport Madison Local (PK-12)
2005-06 Enrollment: 6,172 . . . . (614) 492-2520

Vocational/Technical School(s)

Eastland-Fairfield Career and Technical Schools (Public)
Fall 2007 Enrollment: 177 . . . . (614) 836-4541
2007-08 Tuition: $4,369

Housing: Homeownership rate: 67.7% (2007); Median home value: $142,007 (2007); Median rent: $477 per month (2000); Median age of housing: 33 years (2000).

Safety: Violent crime rate: 25.6 per 10,000 population; Property crime rate: 416.7 per 10,000 population (2007).

Transportation: Commute to work: 93.8% car, 0.7% public transportation, 2.9% walk, 1.7% work from home (2000); Travel time to work: 32.5% less than 15 minutes, 40.5% 15 to 30 minutes, 21.6% 30 to 45 minutes, 3.4% 45 to 60 minutes, 2.0% 60 minutes or more (2000)

Additional Information Contacts

Southeastern Franklin County Chamber of Commerce . . . . (614) 836-1138
http://www.groveport.org
Village of Groveport . . . . (614) 836-5301
http://www.groveport.org

HARRISBURG (village). Covers a land area of 0.100 square miles and a water area of 0 square miles. Located at 39.81° N. Lat.; 83.17° W. Long. Elevation is 794 feet.

Population: 340 (1990); 332 (2000); 338 (2007); 339 (2012 projected); Race: 95.9% White, 0.6% Black, 0.3% Asian, 1.2% Hispanic of any race (2007); Density: 3,390.4 persons per square mile (2007); Average household size: 2.43 (2007); Median age: 41.2 (2007); Males per 100 females: 104.8 (2007); Marriage status: 24.2% never married, 61.2% now married, 5.7% widowed, 8.9% divorced (2000); Foreign born: 0.0% (2000); Ancestry (includes multiple ancestries): 33.1% German, 18.6% Irish, 13.4% Other groups, 12.5% United States or American, 10.8% English (2000).

Economy: Employment by occupation: 7.3% management, 11.5% professional, 19.9% services, 32.5% sales, 1.0% farming, 7.9% construction, 19.9% production (2000).

Income: Per capita income: $22,663 (2007); Median household income: $51,750 (2007); Average household income: $55,108 (2007); Percent of households with income of $100,000 or more: 7.2% (2007); Poverty rate: 3.2% (2000).

Education: Percent of population age 25 and over with: High school diploma (including GED) or higher: 84.6% (2007); Bachelor's degree or higher: 10.4% (2007); Master's degree or higher: 0.0% (2007).

School District(s)

South-Western City (PK-12)
2005-06 Enrollment: 21,583 . . . . (614) 801-3000

Housing: Homeownership rate: 77.0% (2007); Median home value: $121,875 (2007); Median rent: $382 per month (2000); Median age of housing: 60+ years (2000).

Transportation: Commute to work: 90.9% car, 1.6% public transportation, 2.7% walk, 2.7% work from home (2000); Travel time to work: 17.7% less than 15 minutes, 51.9% 15 to 30 minutes, 24.3% 30 to 45 minutes, 3.3% 45 to 60 minutes, 2.8% 60 minutes or more (2000)

HILLIARD (city). Aka Hilliards. Covers a land area of 11.141 square miles and a water area of 0 square miles. Located at 40.03° N. Lat.; 83.14° W. Long. Elevation is 935 feet.

Population: 12,516 (1990); 24,230 (2000); 27,143 (2007); 28,913 (2012 projected); Race: 89.8% White, 2.2% Black, 4.8% Asian, 2.8% Hispanic of any race (2007); Density: 2,436.3 persons per square mile (2007); Average household size: 2.84 (2007); Median age: 34.9 (2007); Males per 100 females: 97.4 (2007); Marriage status: 19.8% never married, 68.1% now married, 3.6% widowed, 8.4% divorced (2000); Foreign born: 4.2% (2000); Ancestry (includes multiple ancestries): 30.1% German, 17.2% Irish, 12.7% English, 8.4% Other groups, 8.3% United States or American (2000).

Economy: Unemployment rate: 4.4% (6/2008); Total civilian labor force: 15,713 (6/2008); Single-family building permits issued: 92 (2007); Multi-family building permits issued: 34 (2007); Employment by occupation: 19.4% management, 27.3% professional, 10.9% services, 27.9% sales, 0.0% farming, 6.1% construction, 8.4% production (2000).

Income: Per capita income: $35,419 (2007); Median household income: $86,024 (2007); Average household income: $100,215 (2007); Percent of households with income of $100,000 or more: 39.2% (2007); Poverty rate: 2.2% (2000).

Taxes: Total city taxes per capita: $629 (2006); City property taxes per capita: $44 (2006).

Education: Percent of population age 25 and over with: High school diploma (including GED) or higher: 92.5% (2007); Bachelor's degree or higher: 45.9% (2007); Master's degree or higher: 14.4% (2007).

School District(s)

Hilliard City (PK-12)
2005-06 Enrollment: 14,851 . . . . (614) 771-4273

Two-year College(s)

ITT Technical Institute-Hilliard (Private, For-profit)
Fall 2007 Enrollment: 598 . . . . (614) 771-4888
2007-08 Tuition: In-state $15,600; Out-of-state $15,600

Housing: Homeownership rate: 73.9% (2007); Median home value: $201,545 (2007); Median rent: $653 per month (2000); Median age of housing: 9 years (2000).

Safety: Violent crime rate: 12.1 per 10,000 population; Property crime rate: 305.3 per 10,000 population (2007).

Transportation: Commute to work: 93.8% car, 0.7% public transportation, 0.7% walk, 4.4% work from home (2000); Travel time to work: 28.8% less than 15 minutes, 43.7% 15 to 30 minutes, 19.4% 30 to 45 minutes, 4.4% 45 to 60 minutes, 3.7% 60 minutes or more (2000)

Additional Information Contacts

City of Hilliard . . . . (614) 876-7361
http://www.cityofhilliard.com
Hilliard Area Chamber of Commerce . . . . (614) 876-7666
http://www.hilliardchamber.org
Hilliard Convention & Visitors Bureau . . . . (614) 876-6911
http://www.hilliardcvb.org

HUBER RIDGE (CDP). Covers a land area of 1.087 square miles and a water area of 0 square miles. Located at 40.09° N. Lat.; 82.91° W. Long. Elevation is 830 feet.

Population: 5,242 (1990); 4,883 (2000); 4,301 (2007); 3,919 (2012 projected); Race: 88.9% White, 6.8% Black, 1.2% Asian, 1.4% Hispanic of any race (2007); Density: 3,957.1 persons per square mile (2007); Average household size: 2.76 (2007); Median age: 34.2 (2007); Males per 100 females: 91.2 (2007); Marriage status: 22.2% never married, 62.9% now married, 3.9% widowed, 11.0% divorced (2000); Foreign born: 3.1% (2000); Ancestry (includes multiple ancestries): 30.7% German, 16.6% Irish, 12.3% English, 10.9% United States or American, 10.5% Other groups (2000).

Economy: Employment by occupation: 16.4% management, 18.3% professional, 13.2% services, 34.0% sales, 0.0% farming, 7.1% construction, 11.0% production (2000).

Income: Per capita income: $22,651 (2007); Median household income: $55,538 (2007); Average household income: $62,449 (2007); Percent of households with income of $100,000 or more: 11.5% (2007); Poverty rate: 3.8% (2000).

Education: Percent of population age 25 and over with: High school diploma (including GED) or higher: 91.6% (2007); Bachelor's degree or higher: 25.2% (2007); Master's degree or higher: 5.1% (2007).

Housing: Homeownership rate: 73.7% (2007); Median home value: $126,035 (2007); Median rent: $635 per month (2000); Median age of housing: 32 years (2000).

Transportation: Commute to work: 94.4% car, 0.8% public transportation, 1.4% walk, 3.1% work from home (2000); Travel time to work: 25.2% less than 15 minutes, 48.7% 15 to 30 minutes, 21.6% 30 to 45 minutes, 1.3% 45 to 60 minutes, 3.2% 60 minutes or more (2000)

LAKE DARBY (CDP). Covers a land area of 3.405 square miles and a water area of 0 square miles. Located at 39.96° N. Lat.; 83.23° W. Long. Elevation is 925 feet.

Population: 2,798 (1990); 3,727 (2000); 3,913 (2007); 4,083 (2012 projected); Race: 92.2% White, 2.4% Black, 0.6% Asian, 2.2% Hispanic of any race (2007); Density: 1,149.0 persons per square mile (2007); Average household size: 3.05 (2007); Median age: 32.8 (2007); Males per 100 females: 97.7 (2007); Marriage status: 18.2% never married, 70.6% now married, 1.1% widowed, 10.1% divorced (2000); Foreign born: 2.8% (2000); Ancestry (includes multiple ancestries): 27.4% German, 14.4% Irish, 12.9% United States or American, 10.9% Other groups, 6.7% English (2000).

Economy: Employment by occupation: 11.4% management, 18.7% professional, 13.5% services, 28.5% sales, 0.0% farming, 9.2% construction, 18.7% production (2000).

Income: Per capita income: $27,056 (2007); Median household income: $73,583 (2007); Average household income: $82,280 (2007); Percent of

households with income of $100,000 or more: 22.5% (2007); Poverty rate: 1.9% (2000).
Education: Percent of population age 25 and over with: High school diploma (including GED) or higher: 91.1% (2007); Bachelor's degree or higher: 22.2% (2007); Master's degree or higher: 6.0% (2007).
Housing: Homeownership rate: 95.6% (2007); Median home value: $136,343 (2007); Median rent: $708 per month (2000); Median age of housing: 19 years (2000).
Transportation: Commute to work: 98.2% car, 0.0% public transportation, 0.0% walk, 1.8% work from home (2000); Travel time to work: 12.2% less than 15 minutes, 47.2% 15 to 30 minutes, 30.7% 30 to 45 minutes, 8.3% 45 to 60 minutes, 1.5% 60 minutes or more (2000)

LINCOLN VILLAGE (CDP). Covers a land area of 1.869 square miles and a water area of 0 square miles. Located at 39.95° N. Lat.; 83.13° W. Long. Elevation is 909 feet.
Population: 9,994 (1990); 9,482 (2000); 8,505 (2007); 7,917 (2012 projected); Race: 88.7% White, 4.3% Black, 0.6% Asian, 8.2% Hispanic of any race (2007); Density: 4,551.7 persons per square mile (2007); Average household size: 2.31 (2007); Median age: 38.7 (2007); Males per 100 females: 95.0 (2007); Marriage status: 23.5% never married, 52.4% now married, 8.9% widowed, 15.2% divorced (2000); Foreign born: 6.0% (2000); Ancestry (includes multiple ancestries): 17.9% German, 16.8% United States or American, 15.7% Other groups, 12.8% Irish, 10.3% English (2000).
Economy: Employment by occupation: 7.9% management, 11.1% professional, 13.7% services, 31.6% sales, 0.0% farming, 12.8% construction, 22.8% production (2000).
Income: Per capita income: $19,760 (2007); Median household income: $38,740 (2007); Average household income: $45,415 (2007); Percent of households with income of $100,000 or more: 6.1% (2007); Poverty rate: 12.0% (2000).
Education: Percent of population age 25 and over with: High school diploma (including GED) or higher: 76.4% (2007); Bachelor's degree or higher: 10.4% (2007); Master's degree or higher: 3.0% (2007).
Housing: Homeownership rate: 64.8% (2007); Median home value: $104,386 (2007); Median rent: $421 per month (2000); Median age of housing: 38 years (2000).
Transportation: Commute to work: 91.7% car, 2.4% public transportation, 3.9% walk, 1.6% work from home (2000); Travel time to work: 30.4% less than 15 minutes, 45.8% 15 to 30 minutes, 17.7% 30 to 45 minutes, 2.7% 45 to 60 minutes, 3.4% 60 minutes or more (2000)

LOCKBOURNE (village). Covers a land area of 0.095 square miles and a water area of 0 square miles. Located at 39.80° N. Lat.; 82.97° W. Long. Elevation is 712 feet.
Population: 179 (1990); 280 (2000); 275 (2007); 270 (2012 projected); Race: 99.3% White, 0.0% Black, 0.0% Asian, 0.7% Hispanic of any race (2007); Density: 2,897.8 persons per square mile (2007); Average household size: 2.57 (2007); Median age: 39.2 (2007); Males per 100 females: 108.3 (2007); Marriage status: 19.9% never married, 57.4% now married, 7.4% widowed, 15.3% divorced (2000); Foreign born: 0.0% (2000); Ancestry (includes multiple ancestries): 16.7% German, 12.8% English, 12.5% Irish, 11.0% Other groups, 3.2% Hungarian (2000).
Economy: Employment by occupation: 6.6% management, 3.3% professional, 24.6% services, 18.9% sales, 0.0% farming, 17.2% construction, 29.5% production (2000).
Income: Per capita income: $17,000 (2007); Median household income: $36,944 (2007); Average household income: $43,692 (2007); Percent of households with income of $100,000 or more: 5.6% (2007); Poverty rate: 9.5% (2000).
Education: Percent of population age 25 and over with: High school diploma (including GED) or higher: 68.0% (2007); Bachelor's degree or higher: 8.8% (2007); Master's degree or higher: 2.2% (2007).

School District(s)

Hamilton Local (PK-12)
2005-06 Enrollment: 2,817 . . . . (614) 491-8044
Housing: Homeownership rate: 75.7% (2007); Median home value: $93,125 (2007); Median rent: $430 per month (2000); Median age of housing: 60+ years (2000).
Transportation: Commute to work: 97.5% car, 0.0% public transportation, 0.0% walk, 2.5% work from home (2000); Travel time to work: 29.3% less than 15 minutes, 44.0% 15 to 30 minutes, 19.0% 30 to 45 minutes, 3.4% 45 to 60 minutes, 4.3% 60 minutes or more (2000)

MARBLE CLIFF (village). Covers a land area of 0.248 square miles and a water area of 0 square miles. Located at 39.98° N. Lat.; 83.06° W. Long. Elevation is 797 feet.
History: Limestone quarry gave its name.
Population: 636 (1990); 646 (2000); 577 (2007); 531 (2012 projected); Race: 97.7% White, 0.9% Black, 1.2% Asian, 0.0% Hispanic of any race (2007); Density: 2,331.3 persons per square mile (2007); Average household size: 2.21 (2007); Median age: 53.8 (2007); Males per 100 females: 73.3 (2007); Marriage status: 28.3% never married, 48.4% now married, 12.4% widowed, 11.0% divorced (2000); Foreign born: 2.7% (2000); Ancestry (includes multiple ancestries): 34.3% German, 19.2% English, 14.2% Irish, 9.2% Italian, 3.6% Scotch-Irish (2000).
Economy: Single-family building permits issued: 0 (2007); Multi-family building permits issued: 0 (2007); Employment by occupation: 28.4% management, 40.3% professional, 3.8% services, 25.0% sales, 0.0% farming, 1.3% construction, 1.3% production (2000).
Income: Per capita income: $39,810 (2007); Median household income: $55,526 (2007); Average household income: $83,506 (2007); Percent of households with income of $100,000 or more: 29.1% (2007); Poverty rate: 3.4% (2000).
Education: Percent of population age 25 and over with: High school diploma (including GED) or higher: 87.8% (2007); Bachelor's degree or higher: 58.0% (2007); Master's degree or higher: 21.5% (2007).
Housing: Homeownership rate: 57.5% (2007); Median home value: $383,333 (2007); Median rent: $552 per month (2000); Median age of housing: 43 years (2000).
Transportation: Commute to work: 91.8% car, 0.6% public transportation, 1.9% walk, 5.7% work from home (2000); Travel time to work: 38.9% less than 15 minutes, 52.3% 15 to 30 minutes, 8.7% 30 to 45 minutes, 0.0% 45 to 60 minutes, 0.0% 60 minutes or more (2000)

MINERVA PARK (village). Covers a land area of 0.496 square miles and a water area of 0.007 square miles. Located at 40.07° N. Lat.; 82.94° W. Long. Elevation is 846 feet.
Population: 1,314 (1990); 1,288 (2000); 1,219 (2007); 1,221 (2012 projected); Race: 96.5% White, 0.5% Black, 0.4% Asian, 1.1% Hispanic of any race (2007); Density: 2,457.9 persons per square mile (2007); Average household size: 2.37 (2007); Median age: 47.5 (2007); Males per 100 females: 96.9 (2007); Marriage status: 16.6% never married, 70.7% now married, 6.5% widowed, 6.2% divorced (2000); Foreign born: 2.0% (2000); Ancestry (includes multiple ancestries): 31.1% German, 19.9% English, 18.8% Irish, 8.9% United States or American, 8.3% Italian (2000).
Economy: Employment by occupation: 15.4% management, 29.2% professional, 10.4% services, 30.8% sales, 0.0% farming, 6.3% construction, 7.9% production (2000).
Income: Per capita income: $35,029 (2007); Median household income: $71,831 (2007); Average household income: $83,074 (2007); Percent of households with income of $100,000 or more: 29.6% (2007); Poverty rate: 1.3% (2000).
Education: Percent of population age 25 and over with: High school diploma (including GED) or higher: 94.2% (2007); Bachelor's degree or higher: 37.0% (2007); Master's degree or higher: 13.2% (2007).
Housing: Homeownership rate: 96.1% (2007); Median home value: $166,541 (2007); Median rent: $683 per month (2000); Median age of housing: 43 years (2000).
Transportation: Commute to work: 94.0% car, 0.3% public transportation, 0.6% walk, 5.1% work from home (2000); Travel time to work: 22.2% less than 15 minutes, 47.3% 15 to 30 minutes, 24.0% 30 to 45 minutes, 2.0% 45 to 60 minutes, 4.5% 60 minutes or more (2000)

NEW ALBANY (village). Covers a land area of 8.928 square miles and a water area of 0 square miles. Located at 40.07° N. Lat.; 82.82° W. Long. Elevation is 1,024 feet.
Population: 1,879 (1990); 3,711 (2000); 5,213 (2007); 6,069 (2012 projected); Race: 92.1% White, 1.9% Black, 3.9% Asian, 1.3% Hispanic of any race (2007); Density: 583.9 persons per square mile (2007); Average household size: 2.87 (2007); Median age: 38.5 (2007); Males per 100 females: 98.4 (2007); Marriage status: 18.5% never married, 73.1% now married, 3.0% widowed, 5.4% divorced (2000); Foreign born: 5.8% (2000); Ancestry (includes multiple ancestries): 28.8% German, 15.0% Irish, 14.7% English, 11.4% Other groups, 10.3% Italian (2000).
Economy: Single-family building permits issued: 106 (2007); Multi-family building permits issued: 0 (2007); Employment by occupation: 33.0%

management, 28.4% professional, 5.5% services, 21.6% sales, 0.0% farming, 4.5% construction, 7.1% production (2000).
Income: Per capita income: $69,885 (2007); Median household income: $123,438 (2007); Average household income: $200,501 (2007); Percent of households with income of $100,000 or more: 59.5% (2007); Poverty rate: 1.2% (2000).
Education: Percent of population age 25 and over with: High school diploma (including GED) or higher: 95.5% (2007); Bachelor's degree or higher: 53.5% (2007); Master's degree or higher: 20.8% (2007).

School District(s)

New Albany-Plain Local (PK-12)
2005-06 Enrollment: 3,429 . . . . (614) 855-2040
Housing: Homeownership rate: 80.8% (2007); Median home value: $594,178 (2007); Median rent: $648 per month (2000); Median age of housing: 5 years (2000).
Safety: Violent crime rate: 7.4 per 10,000 population; Property crime rate: 104.8 per 10,000 population (2007).
Transportation: Commute to work: 91.8% car, 0.0% public transportation, 0.5% walk, 6.5% work from home (2000); Travel time to work: 19.2% less than 15 minutes, 45.0% 15 to 30 minutes, 26.6% 30 to 45 minutes, 4.9% 45 to 60 minutes, 4.3% 60 minutes or more (2000)

Additional Information Contacts

New Albany Chamber of Commerce . . . . (614) 855-4400
http://www.newalbanychamber.com
Village of New Albany . . . . (614) 855-3913
http://www.villageofnewalbany.org

NEW ROME (village). Covers a land area of 0.030 square miles and a water area of 0 square miles. Located at 39.95° N. Lat.; 83.14° W. Long. Elevation is 922 feet.
Population: 40 (1990); 60 (2000); 85 (2007); 101 (2012 projected); Race: 97.6% White, 0.0% Black, 2.4% Asian, 9.4% Hispanic of any race (2007); Density: 2,824.0 persons per square mile (2007); Average household size: 2.30 (2007); Median age: 38.9 (2007); Males per 100 females: 84.8 (2007); Marriage status: 29.3% never married, 41.5% now married, 12.2% widowed, 17.1% divorced (2000); Foreign born: 4.6% (2000); Ancestry (includes multiple ancestries): 24.6% German, 20.0% Other groups, 13.8% United States or American, 13.8% Yugoslavian, 13.8% Irish (2000).
Economy: Employment by occupation: 13.0% management, 17.4% professional, 43.5% services, 26.1% sales, 0.0% farming, 0.0% construction, 0.0% production (2000).
Income: Per capita income: $18,382 (2007); Median household income: $24,583 (2007); Average household income: $42,230 (2007); Percent of households with income of $100,000 or more: 8.1% (2007); Poverty rate: 18.5% (2000).
Education: Percent of population age 25 and over with: High school diploma (including GED) or higher: 54.5% (2007); Bachelor's degree or higher: 5.5% (2007); Master's degree or higher: 0.0% (2007).
Housing: Homeownership rate: 32.4% (2007); Median home value: $95,000 (2007); Median rent: $463 per month (2000); Median age of housing: 43 years (2000).
Transportation: Commute to work: 56.5% car, 8.7% public transportation, 8.7% walk, 26.1% work from home (2000); Travel time to work: 64.7% less than 15 minutes, 11.8% 15 to 30 minutes, 11.8% 30 to 45 minutes, 0.0% 45 to 60 minutes, 11.8% 60 minutes or more (2000)

OBETZ (village). Covers a land area of 3.769 square miles and a water area of 0 square miles. Located at 39.87° N. Lat.; 82.94° W. Long. Elevation is 748 feet.
Population: 3,339 (1990); 3,977 (2000); 4,105 (2007); 4,178 (2012 projected); Race: 92.7% White, 2.9% Black, 0.2% Asian, 2.3% Hispanic of any race (2007); Density: 1,089.2 persons per square mile (2007); Average household size: 2.63 (2007); Median age: 34.5 (2007); Males per 100 females: 96.6 (2007); Marriage status: 21.4% never married, 56.9% now married, 4.3% widowed, 17.3% divorced (2000); Foreign born: 2.2% (2000); Ancestry (includes multiple ancestries): 20.7% German, 20.5% Other groups, 12.8% English, 11.8% Irish, 11.1% United States or American (2000).
Economy: Single-family building permits issued: 5 (2007); Multi-family building permits issued: 4 (2007); Employment by occupation: 9.8% management, 9.9% professional, 16.5% services, 35.2% sales, 0.3% farming, 9.7% construction, 18.7% production (2000).
Income: Per capita income: $21,125 (2007); Median household income: $52,712 (2007); Average household income: $55,519 (2007); Percent of households with income of $100,000 or more: 7.8% (2007); Poverty rate: 6.4% (2000).
Education: Percent of population age 25 and over with: High school diploma (including GED) or higher: 76.6% (2007); Bachelor's degree or higher: 8.1% (2007); Master's degree or higher: 2.7% (2007).
Housing: Homeownership rate: 79.7% (2007); Median home value: $115,984 (2007); Median rent: $477 per month (2000); Median age of housing: 23 years (2000).
Transportation: Commute to work: 96.4% car, 0.0% public transportation, 0.7% walk, 2.2% work from home (2000); Travel time to work: 29.3% less than 15 minutes, 49.2% 15 to 30 minutes, 14.8% 30 to 45 minutes, 4.0% 45 to 60 minutes, 2.6% 60 minutes or more (2000)

Additional Information Contacts

Village of Obetz . . . . (614) 491-1080
http://www.obetz.oh.us

REYNOLDSBURG (city). Covers a land area of 10.584 square miles and a water area of 0 square miles. Located at 39.96° N. Lat.; 82.80° W. Long. Elevation is 879 feet.
Population: 26,344 (1990); 32,069 (2000); 33,240 (2007); 33,960 (2012 projected); Race: 79.5% White, 14.8% Black, 1.9% Asian, 2.8% Hispanic of any race (2007); Density: 3,140.7 persons per square mile (2007); Average household size: 2.46 (2007); Median age: 37.2 (2007); Males per 100 females: 92.5 (2007); Marriage status: 23.5% never married, 58.4% now married, 5.4% widowed, 12.8% divorced (2000); Foreign born: 3.6% (2000); Ancestry (includes multiple ancestries): 26.8% German, 17.1% Other groups, 14.5% Irish, 10.7% English, 8.6% United States or American (2000).
Economy: Unemployment rate: 5.5% (6/2008); Total civilian labor force: 19,503 (6/2008); Single-family building permits issued: 14 (2007); Multi-family building permits issued: 0 (2007); Employment by occupation: 15.9% management, 20.1% professional, 13.8% services, 31.7% sales, 0.0% farming, 6.6% construction, 11.8% production (2000).
Income: Per capita income: $27,363 (2007); Median household income: $58,484 (2007); Average household income: $67,200 (2007); Percent of households with income of $100,000 or more: 18.4% (2007); Poverty rate: 5.5% (2000).
Education: Percent of population age 25 and over with: High school diploma (including GED) or higher: 90.5% (2007); Bachelor's degree or higher: 27.4% (2007); Master's degree or higher: 7.8% (2007).

School District(s)

Pickerington Local (PK-12)
2005-06 Enrollment: 9,787 . . . . (614) 833-2110
Reynoldsburg City (PK-12)
2005-06 Enrollment: 6,781 . . . . (614) 501-1020

Two-year College(s)

Ohio State School of Cosmetology (Private, For-profit)
Fall 2007 Enrollment: 66 . . . . (614) 252-5252
Housing: Homeownership rate: 65.9% (2007); Median home value: $149,405 (2007); Median rent: $559 per month (2000); Median age of housing: 22 years (2000).
Safety: Violent crime rate: 30.7 per 10,000 population; Property crime rate: 376.1 per 10,000 population (2007).
Transportation: Commute to work: 94.8% car, 1.3% public transportation, 1.2% walk, 2.2% work from home (2000); Travel time to work: 25.1% less than 15 minutes, 44.4% 15 to 30 minutes, 23.3% 30 to 45 minutes, 4.4% 45 to 60 minutes, 2.9% 60 minutes or more (2000)

Additional Information Contacts

City of Reynoldsburg . . . . (614) 322-6800
http://www.ci.reynoldsburg.oh.us
Reynoldsburg Area Chamber of Commerce . . . . (614) 866-4753
http://www.reynoldsburgchamber.com

RIVERLEA (village). Covers a land area of 0.161 square miles and a water area of 0 square miles. Located at 40.08° N. Lat.; 83.02° W. Long. Elevation is 787 feet.
Population: 503 (1990); 499 (2000); 471 (2007); 467 (2012 projected); Race: 94.7% White, 0.0% Black, 1.3% Asian, 2.1% Hispanic of any race (2007); Density: 2,926.1 persons per square mile (2007); Average household size: 2.14 (2007); Median age: 48.9 (2007); Males per 100 females: 87.6 (2007); Marriage status: 16.4% never married, 65.7% now married, 7.0% widowed, 11.0% divorced (2000); Foreign born: 3.0% (2000); Ancestry (includes multiple ancestries): 29.3% German, 23.6% English, 11.4% Irish, 7.2% Italian, 6.8% Scottish (2000).

Economy: Employment by occupation: 17.6% management, 45.2% professional, 5.5% services, 26.5% sales, 0.0% farming, 1.1% construction, 4.0% production (2000).
Income: Per capita income: $54,029 (2007); Median household income: $109,091 (2007); Average household income: $115,670 (2007); Percent of households with income of $100,000 or more: 55.5% (2007); Poverty rate: 0.8% (2000).
Education: Percent of population age 25 and over with: High school diploma (including GED) or higher: 98.0% (2007); Bachelor's degree or higher: 68.2% (2007); Master's degree or higher: 33.8% (2007).
Housing: Homeownership rate: 90.0% (2007); Median home value: $270,833 (2007); Median rent: $579 per month (2000); Median age of housing: 48 years (2000).
Transportation: Commute to work: 87.1% car, 3.3% public transportation, 0.7% walk, 7.7% work from home (2000); Travel time to work: 22.7% less than 15 minutes, 54.2% 15 to 30 minutes, 16.7% 30 to 45 minutes, 3.6% 45 to 60 minutes, 2.8% 60 minutes or more (2000)

UPPER ARLINGTON (city). Covers a land area of 9.764 square miles and a water area of 0.022 square miles. Located at 40.02° N. Lat.; 83.06° W. Long. Elevation is 810 feet.
History: Named for the Upper Arlington Company, a development organization. Incorporated 1918.
Population: 34,171 (1990); 33,686 (2000); 30,952 (2007); 29,049 (2012 projected); Race: 93.6% White, 0.8% Black, 4.0% Asian, 1.4% Hispanic of any race (2007); Density: 3,170.2 persons per square mile (2007); Average household size: 2.39 (2007); Median age: 44.4 (2007); Males per 100 females: 90.5 (2007); Marriage status: 20.2% never married, 63.8% now married, 7.7% widowed, 8.3% divorced (2000); Foreign born: 6.3% (2000); Ancestry (includes multiple ancestries): 30.6% German, 19.2% English, 15.1% Irish, 7.7% Other groups, 6.8% Italian (2000).
Economy: Unemployment rate: 4.7% (6/2008); Total civilian labor force: 16,980 (6/2008); Single-family building permits issued: 41 (2007); Multi-family building permits issued: 0 (2007); Employment by occupation: 24.2% management, 39.9% professional, 6.2% services, 24.7% sales, 0.0% farming, 2.0% construction, 2.9% production (2000).
Income: Per capita income: $48,208 (2007); Median household income: $85,394 (2007); Average household income: $115,017 (2007); Percent of households with income of $100,000 or more: 40.4% (2007); Poverty rate: 2.4% (2000).
Taxes: Total city taxes per capita: $786 (2006); City property taxes per capita: $249 (2006).
Education: Percent of population age 25 and over with: High school diploma (including GED) or higher: 97.9% (2007); Bachelor's degree or higher: 67.5% (2007); Master's degree or higher: 29.8% (2007).

School District(s)

Upper Arlington City (PK-12)
2005-06 Enrollment: 5,629 . . . . (614) 487-5000
Upper Arlington Community High School
2005-06 Enrollment: n/a . . . .
Upper Arlington International Baccalaureate HS (11-12)
2005-06 Enrollment: 65 . . . . (614) 487-5200
Wickliffe Progressive Community School
2005-06 Enrollment: n/a . . . . (614) 487-5007

Housing: Homeownership rate: 81.1% (2007); Median home value: $265,031 (2007); Median rent: $661 per month (2000); Median age of housing: 42 years (2000).
Safety: Violent crime rate: 2.9 per 10,000 population; Property crime rate: 120.6 per 10,000 population (2007).
Transportation: Commute to work: 90.3% car, 1.5% public transportation, 1.4% walk, 5.8% work from home (2000); Travel time to work: 30.7% less than 15 minutes, 55.4% 15 to 30 minutes, 10.1% 30 to 45 minutes, 1.4% 45 to 60 minutes, 2.4% 60 minutes or more (2000)

Additional Information Contacts

City of Upper Arlington. . . . . (614) 583-5040
http://www.ua-ohio.net
Upper Arlington Area Chamber of Commerce . . . . (614) 481-5710
http://www.uachamber.org

URBANCREST (village). Covers a land area of 0.442 square miles and a water area of 0 square miles. Located at 39.89° N. Lat.; 83.08° W. Long. Elevation is 840 feet.
Population: 875 (1990); 868 (2000); 962 (2007); 1,001 (2012 projected); Race: 32.4% White, 46.6% Black, 15.0% Asian, 2.9% Hispanic of any race (2007); Density: 2,174.5 persons per square mile (2007); Average household size: 2.69 (2007); Median age: 24.0 (2007); Males per 100 females: 77.2 (2007); Marriage status: 41.5% never married, 38.7% now married, 7.4% widowed, 12.4% divorced (2000); Foreign born: 4.1% (2000); Ancestry (includes multiple ancestries): 54.7% Other groups, 16.4% United States or American, 9.5% German, 2.6% Irish, 1.7% French (except Basque) (2000).
Economy: Employment by occupation: 5.6% management, 10.3% professional, 19.8% services, 37.5% sales, 0.0% farming, 3.0% construction, 23.7% production (2000).
Income: Per capita income: $13,111 (2007); Median household income: $25,446 (2007); Average household income: $35,329 (2007); Percent of households with income of $100,000 or more: 5.0% (2007); Poverty rate: 32.7% (2000).
Education: Percent of population age 25 and over with: High school diploma (including GED) or higher: 59.0% (2007); Bachelor's degree or higher: 2.5% (2007); Master's degree or higher: 1.3% (2007).
Housing: Homeownership rate: 44.8% (2007); Median home value: $84,737 (2007); Median rent: $255 per month (2000); Median age of housing: 38 years (2000).
Transportation: Commute to work: 87.4% car, 0.0% public transportation, 7.9% walk, 1.9% work from home (2000); Travel time to work: 49.0% less than 15 minutes, 30.5% 15 to 30 minutes, 10.5% 30 to 45 minutes, 8.6% 45 to 60 minutes, 1.4% 60 minutes or more (2000)

VALLEYVIEW (village). Covers a land area of 0.152 square miles and a water area of 0 square miles. Located at 39.96° N. Lat.; 83.07° W. Long. Elevation is 778 feet.
Population: 604 (1990); 601 (2000); 538 (2007); 530 (2012 projected); Race: 95.0% White, 1.5% Black, 3.0% Asian, 0.4% Hispanic of any race (2007); Density: 3,542.8 persons per square mile (2007); Average household size: 2.28 (2007); Median age: 42.0 (2007); Males per 100 females: 90.8 (2007); Marriage status: 19.3% never married, 55.8% now married, 9.6% widowed, 15.3% divorced (2000); Foreign born: 0.7% (2000); Ancestry (includes multiple ancestries): 24.0% German, 19.5% English, 14.8% United States or American, 14.1% Irish, 5.5% Other groups (2000).
Economy: Employment by occupation: 10.2% management, 9.6% professional, 7.2% services, 35.8% sales, 0.0% farming, 17.1% construction, 20.1% production (2000).
Income: Per capita income: $24,554 (2007); Median household income: $45,000 (2007); Average household income: $55,975 (2007); Percent of households with income of $100,000 or more: 8.9% (2007); Poverty rate: 5.7% (2000).
Education: Percent of population age 25 and over with: High school diploma (including GED) or higher: 73.1% (2007); Bachelor's degree or higher: 11.4% (2007); Master's degree or higher: 3.1% (2007).
Housing: Homeownership rate: 90.7% (2007); Median home value: $104,301 (2007); Median rent: $425 per month (2000); Median age of housing: 53 years (2000).
Newspapers: Nordonia Hills Sun (Community news; Circulation 3,334); Sun Courier (Community news; Circulation 7,372); Sun Newspapers (Local news)
Transportation: Commute to work: 95.2% car, 2.4% public transportation, 0.3% walk, 0.7% work from home (2000); Travel time to work: 27.9% less than 15 minutes, 52.4% 15 to 30 minutes, 12.1% 30 to 45 minutes, 4.1% 45 to 60 minutes, 3.4% 60 minutes or more (2000)

WESTERVILLE (city). Covers a land area of 12.387 square miles and a water area of 0 square miles. Located at 40.12° N. Lat.; 82.92° W. Long. Elevation is 869 feet.
History: Named for the Westervelt family, prominent farmers in the area. Westerville was settled in 1813 by Virginia Cavalier families and Quakers from Pennsylvania, and became the headquarters of the Anti-Saloon League in 1909.
Population: 30,722 (1990); 35,318 (2000); 34,490 (2007); 34,123 (2012 projected); Race: 90.9% White, 4.4% Black, 2.3% Asian, 1.6% Hispanic of any race (2007); Density: 2,784.3 persons per square mile (2007); Average household size: 2.74 (2007); Median age: 38.7 (2007); Males per 100 females: 91.4 (2007); Marriage status: 24.6% never married, 63.2% now married, 4.7% widowed, 7.5% divorced (2000); Foreign born: 3.2% (2000); Ancestry (includes multiple ancestries): 29.6% German, 15.4% Irish, 14.3% English, 9.1% United States or American, 8.6% Other groups (2000).
Economy: Unemployment rate: 4.8% (6/2008); Total civilian labor force: 20,305 (6/2008); Single-family building permits issued: 65 (2007); Multi-family building permits issued: 53 (2007); Employment by occupation:

21.6% management, 26.0% professional, 10.8% services, 29.8% sales, 0.1% farming, 4.7% construction, 7.0% production (2000).
Income: Per capita income: $36,517 (2007); Median household income: $83,225 (2007); Average household income: $99,164 (2007); Percent of households with income of $100,000 or more: 39.8% (2007); Poverty rate: 3.5% (2000).
Taxes: Total city taxes per capita: $902 (2006); City property taxes per capita: $299 (2006).
Education: Percent of population age 25 and over with: High school diploma (including GED) or higher: 94.7% (2007); Bachelor's degree or higher: 45.2% (2007); Master's degree or higher: 13.9% (2007).

School District(s)

Westerville City (PK-12)
2005-06 Enrollment: 14,062 . . . . (614) 797-5700
Worthington City (PK-12)
2005-06 Enrollment: 9,553 . . . . (614) 883-3000

Four-year College(s)

Otterbein College (Private, Not-for-profit, United Methodist)
Fall 2007 Enrollment: 3,107. . . . . (614) 890-3000
2007-08 Tuition: In-state $25,065; Out-of-state $25,065

Two-year College(s)

Bohecker College-Columbus (Private, For-profit)
Fall 2007 Enrollment: 393 . . . . (614) 882-2551
2007-08 Tuition: In-state $11,720; Out-of-state $11,720
Hondros College (Private, For-profit)
Fall 2007 Enrollment: 255 . . . . (888) 466-3767
2007-08 Tuition: In-state $7,512; Out-of-state $7,512
Ohio State School of Cosmetology (Private, For-profit)
Fall 2007 Enrollment: 105 . . . . (614) 252-5252

Housing: Homeownership rate: 79.3% (2007); Median home value: $194,111 (2007); Median rent: $530 per month (2000); Median age of housing: 22 years (2000).
Hospitals: Mount Carmel St. Ann's Hospital (180 beds)
Safety: Violent crime rate: 9.7 per 10,000 population; Property crime rate: 263.0 per 10,000 population (2007).
Transportation: Commute to work: 92.6% car, 1.0% public transportation, 2.1% walk, 3.9% work from home (2000); Travel time to work: 29.6% less than 15 minutes, 42.3% 15 to 30 minutes, 22.1% 30 to 45 minutes, 3.1% 45 to 60 minutes, 2.8% 60 minutes or more (2000)

Additional Information Contacts

City of Westerville . . . . (614) 901-6400
http://www.westerville.org
Westerville Area Chamber of Commerce . . . . (614) 882-8917
http://www.westervillechamber.com

WHITEHALL (city). Covers a land area of 5.215 square miles and a water area of 0 square miles. Located at 39.96° N. Lat.; 82.88° W. Long. Elevation is 794 feet.
History: Named for Whitehall, site of government offices in London, England. Incorporated 1948.
Population: 20,645 (1990); 19,201 (2000); 17,572 (2007); 16,565 (2012 projected); Race: 65.8% White, 25.9% Black, 2.2% Asian, 4.9% Hispanic of any race (2007); Density: 3,369.5 persons per square mile (2007); Average household size: 2.27 (2007); Median age: 36.3 (2007); Males per 100 females: 95.1 (2007); Marriage status: 30.8% never married, 45.3% now married, 7.0% widowed, 16.9% divorced (2000); Foreign born: 5.9% (2000); Ancestry (includes multiple ancestries): 25.0% Other groups, 18.5% German, 12.5% Irish, 12.1% United States or American, 7.4% English (2000).
Economy: Single-family building permits issued: 1 (2007); Multi-family building permits issued: 0 (2007); Employment by occupation: 6.6% management, 10.1% professional, 19.9% services, 37.2% sales, 0.0% farming, 9.9% construction, 16.3% production (2000).
Income: Per capita income: $18,586 (2007); Median household income: $35,663 (2007); Average household income: $42,114 (2007); Percent of households with income of $100,000 or more: 4.1% (2007); Poverty rate: 14.9% (2000).
Education: Percent of population age 25 and over with: High school diploma (including GED) or higher: 78.7% (2007); Bachelor's degree or higher: 11.4% (2007); Master's degree or higher: 3.9% (2007).

School District(s)

Whitehall City (PK-12)
2005-06 Enrollment: 2,918 . . . . (614) 417-5000

Housing: Homeownership rate: 45.2% (2007); Median home value: $93,406 (2007); Median rent: $412 per month (2000); Median age of housing: 41 years (2000).
Safety: Violent crime rate: 108.9 per 10,000 population; Property crime rate: 830.2 per 10,000 population (2007).
Transportation: Commute to work: 91.7% car, 4.9% public transportation, 2.2% walk, 0.7% work from home (2000); Travel time to work: 27.0% less than 15 minutes, 43.6% 15 to 30 minutes, 21.2% 30 to 45 minutes, 3.5% 45 to 60 minutes, 4.7% 60 minutes or more (2000)

Additional Information Contacts

City of Whitehall. . . . . (614) 338-3106
http://www.ci.whitehall.oh.us
Whitehall Area Chamber of Commerce . . . . (614) 237-7792
http://www.whitehallchamber.org

WORTHINGTON (city). Covers a land area of 5.662 square miles and a water area of 0 square miles. Located at 40.09° N. Lat.; 83.02° W. Long. Elevation is 863 feet.
History: Worthington was settled in 1803 by a group led by Colonel James Kilbourne, who named the place after a parish in Connecticut. A series of educational institutions opened and closed in Worthington over the next century.
Population: 15,085 (1990); 14,125 (2000); 13,053 (2007); 12,319 (2012 projected); Race: 93.8% White, 1.5% Black, 2.7% Asian, 1.4% Hispanic of any race (2007); Density: 2,305.2 persons per square mile (2007); Average household size: 2.44 (2007); Median age: 46.0 (2007); Males per 100 females: 89.3 (2007); Marriage status: 18.1% never married, 65.7% now married, 7.5% widowed, 8.8% divorced (2000); Foreign born: 4.7% (2000); Ancestry (includes multiple ancestries): 33.5% German, 19.1% English, 15.7% Irish, 9.7% Other groups, 6.9% United States or American (2000).
Economy: Single-family building permits issued: 5 (2007); Multi-family building permits issued: 0 (2007); Employment by occupation: 21.2% management, 37.6% professional, 8.6% services, 24.2% sales, 0.1% farming, 3.9% construction, 4.6% production (2000).
Income: Per capita income: $39,758 (2007); Median household income: $78,242 (2007); Average household income: $95,848 (2007); Percent of households with income of $100,000 or more: 36.1% (2007); Poverty rate: 2.5% (2000).
Education: Percent of population age 25 and over with: High school diploma (including GED) or higher: 96.1% (2007); Bachelor's degree or higher: 60.1% (2007); Master's degree or higher: 25.8% (2007).

School District(s)

Worthington City (PK-12)
2005-06 Enrollment: 9,553 . . . . (614) 883-3000

Housing: Homeownership rate: 84.6% (2007); Median home value: $202,296 (2007); Median rent: $514 per month (2000); Median age of housing: 37 years (2000).
Safety: Violent crime rate: 15.5 per 10,000 population; Property crime rate: 272.0 per 10,000 population (2007).
Newspapers: This Week in Bexley (Community news; Circulation 9,311); This Week in Eastside (Community news; Circulation 13,365)
Transportation: Commute to work: 91.6% car, 1.7% public transportation, 1.3% walk, 5.1% work from home (2000); Travel time to work: 29.4% less than 15 minutes, 51.2% 15 to 30 minutes, 14.6% 30 to 45 minutes, 2.8% 45 to 60 minutes, 1.9% 60 minutes or more (2000)

Additional Information Contacts

City of Worthington . . . . (614) 436-3100
http://www.worthington.org
Worthington Chamber of Commerce . . . . (614) 888-3040
http://www.worthingtonchamber.org

Fulton County

Located in northwestern Ohio; bounded on the north by Michigan; drained by the Tiffin River. Covers a land area of 406.78 square miles, a water area of 0.54 square miles, and is located in the Eastern Time Zone. The county was founded in 1850. County seat is Wauseon.

Fulton County is part of the Toledo, OH Metropolitan Statistical Area. The entire metro area includes: Fulton County, OH; Lucas County, OH; Ottawa County, OH; Wood County, OH

Weather Station: Wauseon Water Plant Elevation: 748 feet

	Jan	Feb	Mar	Apr	May	Jun	Jul	Aug	Sep	Oct	Nov	Dec
High	31	35	46	60	72	81	84	82	76	63	49	36
Low	15	18	27	37	48	57	61	59	51	41	32	22
Precip	1.9	1.6	2.5	3.4	3.4	3.7	3.4	3.7	3.1	2.6	3.0	2.4
Snow	8.7	7.0	4.4	0.9	tr	0.0	0.0	0.0	0.0	tr	2.2	5.8

High and Low temperatures in degrees Fahrenheit; Precipitation and Snow in inches

Population: 38,498 (1990); 42,084 (2000); 43,245 (2007); 43,943 (2012 projected); Race: 95.1% White, 0.4% Black, 0.5% Asian, 6.4% Hispanic of any race (2007); Density: 106.3 persons per square mile (2007); Average household size: 2.66 (2007); Median age: 38.3 (2007); Males per 100 females: 97.4 (2007).
Religion: Five largest groups: 21.2% Catholic Church, 8.8% The United Methodist Church, 5.8% Evangelical Lutheran Church in America, 5.7% Mennonite Church USA, 3.8% Christian Church (Disciples of Christ) (2000).
Economy: Unemployment rate: 7.6% (6/2008); Total civilian labor force: 23,557 (6/2008); Leading industries: 51.5% manufacturing; 10.7% health care and social assistance; 9.2% retail trade (2005); Farms: 783 totaling 197,410 acres (2002); Companies that employ 500 or more persons: 3 (2006); Companies that employ 100 to 499 persons: 25 (2006); Companies that employ less than 100 persons: 1,058 (2006); Black-owned businesses: n/a (2002); Hispanic-owned businesses: n/a (2002); Asian-owned businesses: n/a (2002); Women-owned businesses: n/a (2002); Retail sales per capita: $10,267 (2008). Single-family building permits issued: 69 (2007); Multi-family building permits issued: 28 (2007).
Income: Per capita income: $22,511 (2007); Median household income: $50,317 (2007); Average household income: $59,658 (2007); Percent of households with income of $100,000 or more: 12.5% (2007); Poverty rate: 7.1% (2005); Bankruptcy rate: 3.12% (2007).
Education: Percent of population age 25 and over with: High school diploma (including GED) or higher: 85.3% (2007); Bachelor's degree or higher: 13.1% (2007); Master's degree or higher: 3.8% (2007).
Housing: Homeownership rate: 80.0% (2007); Median home value: $134,104 (2007); Median rent: $368 per month (2000); Median age of housing: 37 years (2000).
Health: Birth rate: 128.5 per 10,000 population (2007); Death rate: 83.9 per 10,000 population (2007); Age-adjusted cancer mortality rate: 169.4 deaths per 100,000 population (2005); Number of physicians: 9.4 per 10,000 population (2005); Hospital beds: 40.4 per 10,000 population (2004); Hospital admissions: 685.6 per 10,000 population (2004).
Elections: 2004 Presidential election results: 62.1% Bush, 37.5% Kerry, 0.0% Nader, 0.2% Badnarik
National and State Parks: Harrison Lake State Reservation
Additional Information Contacts
Fulton County Government . . . . (419) 337-9255
http://www.fultoncountyoh.com
Archbold Chamber of Commerce . . . . (419) 445-2222
http://www.archbold.com/chamber.asp?page=18
Delta Chamber of Commerce . . . . (419) 822-3089
http://www.deltaohio.com/chamber/index.htm
Swanton Area Chamber of Commerce . . . . (419) 826-1941
http://www.swantonareacoc.com
Village of Archbold . . . . (419) 445-4726
http://www.archbold.com
Village of Swanton . . . . (419) 826-9515
http://www.villageofswantonohio.us
Wauseon Chamber of Commerce . . . . (419) 335-9966
http://www.wauseonchamber.com

Fulton County Communities

ARCHBOLD (village). Covers a land area of 4.251 square miles and a water area of 0.093 square miles. Located at 41.51° N. Lat.; 84.30° W. Long. Elevation is 732 feet.
Population: 3,590 (1990); 4,290 (2000); 4,546 (2007); 4,704 (2012 projected); Race: 89.9% White, 1.1% Black, 0.4% Asian, 14.4% Hispanic of any race (2007); Density: 1,069.5 persons per square mile (2007); Average household size: 2.44 (2007); Median age: 39.8 (2007); Males per 100 females: 93.0 (2007); Marriage status: 18.8% never married, 63.3% now married, 9.8% widowed, 8.1% divorced (2000); Foreign born: 1.1% (2000); Ancestry (includes multiple ancestries): 44.0% German, 14.9% Other groups, 7.1% United States or American, 6.8% English, 6.7% Swiss (2000).
Economy: Single-family building permits issued: 7 (2007); Multi-family building permits issued: 0 (2007); Employment by occupation: 11.6% management, 15.5% professional, 13.5% services, 25.2% sales, 0.3% farming, 6.9% construction, 27.1% production (2000).
Income: Per capita income: $25,046 (2007); Median household income: $48,750 (2007); Average household income: $61,021 (2007); Percent of households with income of $100,000 or more: 13.5% (2007); Poverty rate: 4.4% (2000).
Education: Percent of population age 25 and over with: High school diploma (including GED) or higher: 83.0% (2007); Bachelor's degree or higher: 20.8% (2007); Master's degree or higher: 4.8% (2007).

School District(s)

Archbold-Area Local (PK-12)
2005-06 Enrollment: 1,381 . . . . (419) 445-5579
Four County (09-12)
2005-06 Enrollment: n/a . . . . (419) 267-3331
Gorham Fayette Local (PK-12)
2005-06 Enrollment: 516 . . . . (419) 237-2573

Two-year College(s)

Northwest State Community College (Public)
Fall 2007 Enrollment: 2,944. . . . . (419) 267-5511
2007-08 Tuition: In-state $3,264; Out-of-state $5,880
Housing: Homeownership rate: 72.7% (2007); Median home value: $127,772 (2007); Median rent: $356 per month (2000); Median age of housing: 32 years (2000).
Safety: Violent crime rate: 8.8 per 10,000 population; Property crime rate: 158.9 per 10,000 population (2007).
Transportation: Commute to work: 90.7% car, 0.0% public transportation, 4.5% walk, 2.6% work from home (2000); Travel time to work: 70.6% less than 15 minutes, 19.3% 15 to 30 minutes, 5.2% 30 to 45 minutes, 2.6% 45 to 60 minutes, 2.2% 60 minutes or more (2000)
Additional Information Contacts
Archbold Chamber of Commerce . . . . (419) 445-2222
http://www.archbold.com/chamber.asp?page=18
Village of Archbold . . . . (419) 445-4726
http://www.archbold.com

DELTA (village). Covers a land area of 2.601 square miles and a water area of 0 square miles. Located at 41.57° N. Lat.; 84.00° W. Long. Elevation is 722 feet.
Population: 2,916 (1990); 2,930 (2000); 2,889 (2007); 2,865 (2012 projected); Race: 95.7% White, 0.1% Black, 0.1% Asian, 5.7% Hispanic of any race (2007); Density: 1,110.9 persons per square mile (2007); Average household size: 2.52 (2007); Median age: 37.3 (2007); Males per 100 females: 97.2 (2007); Marriage status: 19.9% never married, 64.1% now married, 5.7% widowed, 10.3% divorced (2000); Foreign born: 1.3% (2000); Ancestry (includes multiple ancestries): 40.6% German, 12.1% Other groups, 12.1% English, 11.4% Irish, 7.1% United States or American (2000).
Economy: Single-family building permits issued: 3 (2007); Multi-family building permits issued: 2 (2007); Employment by occupation: 6.5% management, 14.9% professional, 15.4% services, 21.8% sales, 0.5% farming, 13.9% construction, 27.0% production (2000).
Income: Per capita income: $22,252 (2007); Median household income: $46,912 (2007); Average household income: $56,046 (2007); Percent of households with income of $100,000 or more: 9.9% (2007); Poverty rate: 9.2% (2000).
Education: Percent of population age 25 and over with: High school diploma (including GED) or higher: 84.7% (2007); Bachelor's degree or higher: 13.6% (2007); Master's degree or higher: 4.2% (2007).

School District(s)

Pike-Delta-York Local (PK-12)
2005-06 Enrollment: 1,520 . . . . (419) 822-3391
Housing: Homeownership rate: 75.8% (2007); Median home value: $119,380 (2007); Median rent: $380 per month (2000); Median age of housing: 49 years (2000).
Safety: Violent crime rate: 6.8 per 10,000 population; Property crime rate: 296.3 per 10,000 population (2007).
Newspapers: Delta Atlas (Community news; Circulation 2,000)
Transportation: Commute to work: 95.0% car, 1.2% public transportation, 1.1% walk, 2.0% work from home (2000); Travel time to work: 28.6% less than 15 minutes, 35.0% 15 to 30 minutes, 21.9% 30 to 45 minutes, 9.6% 45 to 60 minutes, 4.9% 60 minutes or more (2000)
Additional Information Contacts

Delta Chamber of Commerce . . . . (419) 822-3089
http://www.deltaohio.com/chamber/index.htm

FAYETTE (village). Covers a land area of 0.912 square miles and a water area of 0 square miles. Located at 41.67° N. Lat.; 84.32° W. Long. Elevation is 791 feet.
History: Fayette developed as a grain and livestock shipping center.
Population: 1,268 (1990); 1,340 (2000); 1,238 (2007); 1,239 (2012 projected); Race: 93.7% White, 0.2% Black, 0.0% Asian, 10.1% Hispanic of any race (2007); Density: 1,357.2 persons per square mile (2007); Average household size: 2.44 (2007); Median age: 33.2 (2007); Males per 100 females: 97.4 (2007); Marriage status: 22.0% never married, 56.6% now married, 8.3% widowed, 13.0% divorced (2000); Foreign born: 2.4% (2000); Ancestry (includes multiple ancestries): 29.6% German, 16.3% United States or American, 11.2% Other groups, 8.7% English, 8.2% Irish (2000).
Economy: Single-family building permits issued: 0 (2007); Multi-family building permits issued: 0 (2007); Employment by occupation: 7.4% management, 7.3% professional, 12.1% services, 15.9% sales, 3.4% farming, 10.8% construction, 43.1% production (2000).
Income: Per capita income: $18,564 (2007); Median household income: $39,244 (2007); Average household income: $45,330 (2007); Percent of households with income of $100,000 or more: 4.3% (2007); Poverty rate: 9.7% (2000).
Education: Percent of population age 25 and over with: High school diploma (including GED) or higher: 80.1% (2007); Bachelor's degree or higher: 8.4% (2007); Master's degree or higher: 2.3% (2007).

School District(s)

Gorham Fayette Local (PK-12)
2005-06 Enrollment: 516 . . . . (419) 237-2573
Housing: Homeownership rate: 60.0% (2007); Median home value: $84,231 (2007); Median rent: $347 per month (2000); Median age of housing: 53 years (2000).
Newspapers: Fayette Review (Community news; Circulation 1,300)
Transportation: Commute to work: 93.2% car, 0.0% public transportation, 4.9% walk, 1.9% work from home (2000); Travel time to work: 32.3% less than 15 minutes, 42.4% 15 to 30 minutes, 15.8% 30 to 45 minutes, 4.3% 45 to 60 minutes, 5.1% 60 minutes or more (2000)

LYONS (village). Covers a land area of 0.708 square miles and a water area of 0 square miles. Located at 41.70° N. Lat.; 84.07° W. Long. Elevation is 768 feet.
Population: 562 (1990); 559 (2000); 560 (2007); 555 (2012 projected); Race: 94.8% White, 0.0% Black, 0.0% Asian, 4.8% Hispanic of any race (2007); Density: 790.9 persons per square mile (2007); Average household size: 2.49 (2007); Median age: 37.2 (2007); Males per 100 females: 98.6 (2007); Marriage status: 21.7% never married, 58.9% now married, 11.9% widowed, 7.4% divorced (2000); Foreign born: 0.4% (2000); Ancestry (includes multiple ancestries): 31.6% German, 13.7% Irish, 11.4% Other groups, 10.7% United States or American, 5.6% French (except Basque) (2000).
Economy: Single-family building permits issued: 11 (2007); Multi-family building permits issued: 0 (2007); Employment by occupation: 6.9% management, 8.7% professional, 15.6% services, 25.4% sales, 0.7% farming, 17.0% construction, 25.7% production (2000).
Income: Per capita income: $19,987 (2007); Median household income: $47,833 (2007); Average household income: $49,744 (2007); Percent of households with income of $100,000 or more: 4.9% (2007); Poverty rate: 5.6% (2000).
Education: Percent of population age 25 and over with: High school diploma (including GED) or higher: 89.5% (2007); Bachelor's degree or higher: 9.4% (2007); Master's degree or higher: 1.1% (2007).

School District(s)

Evergreen Local (PK-12)
2005-06 Enrollment: 1,406 . . . . (419) 644-3521
Housing: Homeownership rate: 76.9% (2007); Median home value: $107,045 (2007); Median rent: $368 per month (2000); Median age of housing: 55 years (2000).
Transportation: Commute to work: 90.5% car, 0.0% public transportation, 5.5% walk, 2.6% work from home (2000); Travel time to work: 26.3% less than 15 minutes, 31.6% 15 to 30 minutes, 21.8% 30 to 45 minutes, 15.8% 45 to 60 minutes, 4.5% 60 minutes or more (2000)

METAMORA (village). Covers a land area of 0.425 square miles and a water area of 0 square miles. Located at 41.71° N. Lat.; 83.91° W. Long. Elevation is 722 feet.
Population: 641 (1990); 563 (2000); 582 (2007); 594 (2012 projected); Race: 96.7% White, 1.4% Black, 0.0% Asian, 3.6% Hispanic of any race (2007); Density: 1,368.1 persons per square mile (2007); Average household size: 2.76 (2007); Median age: 36.3 (2007); Males per 100 females: 102.8 (2007); Marriage status: 20.7% never married, 59.2% now married, 10.1% widowed, 10.1% divorced (2000); Foreign born: 1.2% (2000); Ancestry (includes multiple ancestries): 43.5% German, 10.4% French (except Basque), 10.1% English, 9.0% Other groups, 8.1% Irish (2000).
Economy: Single-family building permits issued: 0 (2007); Multi-family building permits issued: 0 (2007); Employment by occupation: 7.5% management, 13.8% professional, 16.5% services, 23.6% sales, 0.0% farming, 11.4% construction, 27.2% production (2000).
Income: Per capita income: $23,020 (2007); Median household income: $52,292 (2007); Average household income: $63,495 (2007); Percent of households with income of $100,000 or more: 15.6% (2007); Poverty rate: 8.5% (2000).
Education: Percent of population age 25 and over with: High school diploma (including GED) or higher: 87.0% (2007); Bachelor's degree or higher: 14.4% (2007); Master's degree or higher: 6.5% (2007).

School District(s)

Evergreen Local (PK-12)
2005-06 Enrollment: 1,406 . . . . (419) 644-3521
Housing: Homeownership rate: 76.8% (2007); Median home value: $124,419 (2007); Median rent: $380 per month (2000); Median age of housing: 60+ years (2000).
Transportation: Commute to work: 93.0% car, 0.0% public transportation, 4.5% walk, 2.0% work from home (2000); Travel time to work: 24.7% less than 15 minutes, 23.4% 15 to 30 minutes, 34.7% 30 to 45 minutes, 11.7% 45 to 60 minutes, 5.4% 60 minutes or more (2000)

SWANTON (village). Covers a land area of 2.382 square miles and a water area of 0 square miles. Located at 41.58° N. Lat.; 83.89° W. Long. Elevation is 682 feet.
Population: 3,687 (1990); 3,307 (2000); 3,514 (2007); 3,636 (2012 projected); Race: 97.9% White, 0.3% Black, 0.2% Asian, 1.8% Hispanic of any race (2007); Density: 1,474.9 persons per square mile (2007); Average household size: 2.60 (2007); Median age: 40.0 (2007); Males per 100 females: 92.1 (2007); Marriage status: 21.0% never married, 59.4% now married, 8.8% widowed, 10.8% divorced (2000); Foreign born: 1.3% (2000); Ancestry (includes multiple ancestries): 43.2% German, 13.9% Irish, 11.9% English, 8.1% Other groups, 7.8% Polish (2000).
Economy: Single-family building permits issued: 6 (2007); Multi-family building permits issued: 0 (2007); Employment by occupation: 11.9% management, 16.7% professional, 11.6% services, 24.8% sales, 2.2% farming, 10.1% construction, 22.8% production (2000).
Income: Per capita income: $22,433 (2007); Median household income: $47,849 (2007); Average household income: $57,206 (2007); Percent of households with income of $100,000 or more: 13.2% (2007); Poverty rate: 4.6% (2000).
Education: Percent of population age 25 and over with: High school diploma (including GED) or higher: 87.1% (2007); Bachelor's degree or higher: 16.8% (2007); Master's degree or higher: 4.4% (2007).

School District(s)

Swanton Local (PK-12)
2005-06 Enrollment: 1,468 . . . . (419) 826-7085
Housing: Homeownership rate: 75.3% (2007); Median home value: $131,965 (2007); Median rent: $431 per month (2000); Median age of housing: 44 years (2000).
Newspapers: Swanton Enterprise (Community news; Circulation 1,400)
Transportation: Commute to work: 94.9% car, 0.5% public transportation, 2.3% walk, 1.6% work from home (2000); Travel time to work: 34.1% less than 15 minutes, 31.8% 15 to 30 minutes, 22.4% 30 to 45 minutes, 9.2% 45 to 60 minutes, 2.5% 60 minutes or more (2000)

Additional Information Contacts

Swanton Area Chamber of Commerce . . . . (419) 826-1941
http://www.swantonareacoc.com
Village of Swanton . . . . (419) 826-9515
http://www.villageofswantonohio.us

WAUSEON (city). County seat. Covers a land area of 4.933 square miles and a water area of 0 square miles. Located at 41.55° N. Lat.; 84.13° W. Long. Elevation is 771 feet.
History: Settled 1835, incorporated 1852.
Population: 6,478 (1990); 7,091 (2000); 7,337 (2007); 7,491 (2012 projected); Race: 92.2% White, 1.0% Black, 0.9% Asian, 10.3% Hispanic of any race (2007); Density: 1,487.4 persons per square mile (2007); Average household size: 2.56 (2007); Median age: 35.7 (2007); Males per 100 females: 91.5 (2007); Marriage status: 21.9% never married, 59.6% now married, 8.2% widowed, 10.3% divorced (2000); Foreign born: 2.2% (2000); Ancestry (includes multiple ancestries): 43.6% German, 12.6% Other groups, 11.8% Irish, 9.9% English, 5.6% French (except Basque) (2000).
Economy: Single-family building permits issued: 6 (2007); Multi-family building permits issued: 2 (2007); Employment by occupation: 9.7% management, 13.9% professional, 13.3% services, 24.5% sales, 0.0% farming, 8.2% construction, 30.4% production (2000).
Income: Per capita income: $20,419 (2007); Median household income: $44,541 (2007); Average household income: $51,975 (2007); Percent of households with income of $100,000 or more: 7.1% (2007); Poverty rate: 5.2% (2000).
Education: Percent of population age 25 and over with: High school diploma (including GED) or higher: 87.6% (2007); Bachelor's degree or higher: 12.9% (2007); Master's degree or higher: 4.7% (2007).

School District(s)

Pike-Delta-York Local (PK-12)
2005-06 Enrollment: 1,520 . . . . (419) 822-3391
Wauseon Exempted Village (PK-12)
2005-06 Enrollment: 2,112 . . . . (419) 335-6616
Housing: Homeownership rate: 70.2% (2007); Median home value: $119,163 (2007); Median rent: $343 per month (2000); Median age of housing: 36 years (2000).
Hospitals: Fulton County Health Center (119 beds)
Newspapers: The Blade - Fulton County Bureau (Local news); Fulton County Expositor (Local news; Circulation 4,506)
Transportation: Commute to work: 94.5% car, 0.4% public transportation, 3.1% walk, 1.1% work from home (2000); Travel time to work: 50.0% less than 15 minutes, 34.4% 15 to 30 minutes, 8.2% 30 to 45 minutes, 3.7% 45 to 60 minutes, 3.7% 60 minutes or more (2000)
Airports: Fulton County (general aviation)
Additional Information Contacts
Wauseon Chamber of Commerce . . . . (419) 335-9966
http://www.wauseonchamber.com

Gallia County

Located in southern Ohio; bounded on the east by the Ohio River and the West Virginia border; crossed by Raccoon Creek. Covers a land area of 468.78 square miles, a water area of 2.36 square miles, and is located in the Eastern Time Zone. The county was founded in 1803. County seat is Gallipolis.

Gallia County is part of the Point Pleasant, WV-OH Micropolitan Statistical Area. The entire metro area includes: Gallia County, OH; Mason County, WV

Weather Station: Gallipolis Elevation: 567 feet

	Jan	Feb	Mar	Apr	May	Jun	Jul	Aug	Sep	Oct	Nov	Dec
High	42	47	57	68	77	84	87	86	80	69	57	47
Low	22	24	32	40	50	59	64	63	56	43	35	27
Precip	2.9	2.9	3.6	3.3	4.0	3.9	4.3	3.7	3.0	2.8	3.1	3.3
Snow	6.1	4.6	2.2	tr	0.0	0.0	0.0	0.0	0.0	tr	0.3	1.0

High and Low temperatures in degrees Fahrenheit; Precipitation and Snow in inches

Population: 30,954 (1990); 31,069 (2000); 31,438 (2007); 31,582 (2012 projected); Race: 95.3% White, 2.8% Black, 0.4% Asian, 0.9% Hispanic of any race (2007); Density: 67.1 persons per square mile (2007); Average household size: 2.51 (2007); Median age: 38.9 (2007); Males per 100 females: 95.8 (2007).
Religion: Five largest groups: 5.9% The United Methodist Church, 4.3% American Baptist Churches in the USA, 3.0% General Association of Regular Baptist Churches, 2.6% Christian Churches and Churches of Christ, 2.4% Southern Baptist Convention (2000
Economy: Unemployment rate: 6.6% (6/2008); Total civilian labor force: 14,458 (6/2008); Leading industries: 28.8% health care and social assistance; 15.9% retail trade; 8.9% accommodation & food services (2005); Farms: 936 totaling 117,944 acres (2002); Companies that employ 500 or more persons: 3 (2006); Companies that employ 100 to 499 persons: 12 (2006); Companies that employ less than 100 persons: 600 (2006); Black-owned businesses: n/a (2002); Hispanic-owned businesses: n/a (2002); Asian-owned businesses: n/a (2002); Women-owned businesses: 810 (2002); Retail sales per capita: $15,350 (2008). Single-family building permits issued: 0 (2007); Multi-family building permits issued: 0 (2007).
Income: Per capita income: $18,330 (2007); Median household income: $35,165 (2007); Average household income: $45,550 (2007); Percent of households with income of $100,000 or more: 8.3% (2007); Poverty rate: 22.8% (2005); Bankruptcy rate: 1.82% (2007).
Education: Percent of population age 25 and over with: High school diploma (including GED) or higher: 73.7% (2007); Bachelor's degree or higher: 11.7% (2007); Master's degree or higher: 4.7% (2007).
Housing: Homeownership rate: 75.3% (2007); Median home value: $86,020 (2007); Median rent: $300 per month (2000); Median age of housing: 27 years (2000).
Health: Birth rate: 131.6 per 10,000 population (2007); Death rate: 108.3 per 10,000 population (2007); Age-adjusted cancer mortality rate: 208.8 deaths per 100,000 population (2005); Number of physicians: 33.6 per 10,000 population (2005); Hospital beds: 55.9 per 10,000 population (2004); Hospital admissions: 2,479.3 per 10,000 population (2004).
Elections: 2004 Presidential election results: 61.3% Bush, 38.3% Kerry, 0.0% Nader, 0.2% Badnarik
National and State Parks: Tycoon Lake State Wildlife Area
Additional Information Contacts
Gallia County Government. . . . . (740) 446-8510
http://www.gallianet.net/Gallia/index.htm
City of Gallipolis . . . . (740) 446-1789
http://www.gallianet.net/Gallipolis/index.htm
Gallia County Chamber of Commerce . . . . (740) 446-0596
http://www.galliacounty.org

Gallia County Communities

BIDWELL (unincorporated postal area, zip code 45614). Covers a land area of 69.546 square miles and a water area of 0.447 square miles. Located at 38.91° N. Lat.; 82.29° W. Long. Elevation is 690 feet.
Population: 4,427 (2000); Race: 91.5% White, 5.8% Black, 1.2% Asian, 0.9% Hispanic of any race (2000); Density: 63.7 persons per square mile (2000); Age: 24.4% under 18, 13.7% over 64 (2000); Marriage status: 20.7% never married, 59.0% now married, 10.0% widowed, 10.3% divorced (2000); Foreign born: 1.3% (2000); Ancestry (includes multiple ancestries): 19.2% United States or American, 14.2% Other groups, 11.3% German, 9.0% English, 6.7% Irish (2000).
Economy: Employment by occupation: 9.0% management, 18.8% professional, 12.3% services, 19.7% sales, 0.7% farming, 14.7% construction, 24.8% production (2000).
Income: Per capita income: $15,561 (2000); Median household income: $29,306 (2000); Poverty rate: 21.3% (2000).
Education: Percent of population age 25 and over with: High school diploma (including GED) or higher: 72.4% (2000); Bachelor's degree or higher: 11.1% (2000).

School District(s)

Gallia County Local (PK-12)
2005-06 Enrollment: 2,492 . . . . (740) 446-7917
Housing: Homeownership rate: 77.3% (2000); Median home value: $78,200 (2000); Median rent: $269 per month (2000); Median age of housing: 25 years (2000).
Transportation: Commute to work: 93.9% car, 0.0% public transportation, 1.7% walk, 3.6% work from home (2000); Travel time to work: 26.1% less than 15 minutes, 46.8% 15 to 30 minutes, 8.9% 30 to 45 minutes, 5.0% 45 to 60 minutes, 13.1% 60 minutes or more (2000)

CENTERVILLE (village). Aka Thurman. Covers a land area of 0.099 square miles and a water area of 0 square miles. Located at 38.89° N. Lat.; 82.44° W. Long. Elevation is 679 feet.
Population: 128 (1990); 134 (2000); 116 (2007); 117 (2012 projected); Race: 96.6% White, 1.7% Black, 0.0% Asian, 0.0% Hispanic of any race (2007); Density: 1,169.4 persons per square mile (2007); Average household size: 2.70 (2007); Median age: 35.6 (2007); Males per 100 females: 103.5 (2007); Marriage status: 25.5% never married, 68.2% now married, 2.7% widowed, 3.6% divorced (2000); Foreign born: 0.0% (2000);

Ancestry (includes multiple ancestries): 16.8% German, 9.8% Irish, 8.4% Scotch-Irish, 8.4% Other groups, 7.0% United States or American (2000).
Economy: Employment by occupation: 6.6% management, 19.7% professional, 23.0% services, 3.3% sales, 0.0% farming, 18.0% construction, 29.5% production (2000).
Income: Per capita income: $20,345 (2007); Median household income: $46,250 (2007); Average household income: $54,884 (2007); Percent of households with income of $100,000 or more: 14.0% (2007); Poverty rate: 15.4% (2000).
Education: Percent of population age 25 and over with: High school diploma (including GED) or higher: 71.8% (2007); Bachelor's degree or higher: 9.9% (2007); Master's degree or higher: 8.5% (2007).

School District(s)

Centerville City (PK-12)
2005-06 Enrollment: 8,196 . . . . (937) 433-8841
Housing: Homeownership rate: 83.7% (2007); Median home value: $51,667 (2007); Median rent: $288 per month (2000); Median age of housing: 48 years (2000).
Transportation: Commute to work: 93.2% car, 0.0% public transportation, 3.4% walk, 0.0% work from home (2000); Travel time to work: 33.9% less than 15 minutes, 42.4% 15 to 30 minutes, 13.6% 30 to 45 minutes, 5.1% 45 to 60 minutes, 5.1% 60 minutes or more (2000)

CHESHIRE (village). Covers a land area of 0.184 square miles and a water area of 0.009 square miles. Located at 38.94° N. Lat.; 82.11° W. Long. Elevation is 568 feet.
Population: 263 (1990); 221 (2000); 211 (2007); 213 (2012 projected); Race: 98.1% White, 1.9% Black, 0.0% Asian, 0.0% Hispanic of any race (2007); Density: 1,146.8 persons per square mile (2007); Average household size: 2.32 (2007); Median age: 41.7 (2007); Males per 100 females: 99.1 (2007); Marriage status: 20.7% never married, 66.3% now married, 6.0% widowed, 7.1% divorced (2000); Foreign born: 0.0% (2000); Ancestry (includes multiple ancestries): 23.1% German, 12.8% United States or American, 9.8% Other groups, 8.1% Irish, 3.8% Scotch-Irish (2000).
Economy: Single-family building permits issued: 0 (2007); Multi-family building permits issued: 0 (2007); Employment by occupation: 6.3% management, 15.6% professional, 19.8% services, 28.1% sales, 0.0% farming, 13.5% construction, 16.7% production (2000).
Income: Per capita income: $20,841 (2007); Median household income: $37,188 (2007); Average household income: $48,324 (2007); Percent of households with income of $100,000 or more: 8.8% (2007); Poverty rate: 12.4% (2000).
Education: Percent of population age 25 and over with: High school diploma (including GED) or higher: 76.4% (2007); Bachelor's degree or higher: 8.3% (2007); Master's degree or higher: 2.8% (2007).

School District(s)

Gallia County Local (PK-12)
2005-06 Enrollment: 2,492 . . . . (740) 446-7917
Housing: Homeownership rate: 74.7% (2007); Median home value: $80,000 (2007); Median rent: $288 per month (2000); Median age of housing: 55 years (2000).
Transportation: Commute to work: 87.0% car, 0.0% public transportation, 2.2% walk, 9.8% work from home (2000); Travel time to work: 20.5% less than 15 minutes, 51.8% 15 to 30 minutes, 6.0% 30 to 45 minutes, 4.8% 45 to 60 minutes, 16.9% 60 minutes or more (2000)

CROWN CITY (village). Covers a land area of 1.094 square miles and a water area of 0.029 square miles. Located at 38.59° N. Lat.; 82.28° W. Long. Elevation is 571 feet.
Population: 445 (1990); 411 (2000); 393 (2007); 392 (2012 projected); Race: 97.7% White, 0.3% Black, 0.0% Asian, 2.0% Hispanic of any race (2007); Density: 359.3 persons per square mile (2007); Average household size: 2.43 (2007); Median age: 39.8 (2007); Males per 100 females: 81.9 (2007); Marriage status: 21.5% never married, 62.5% now married, 8.1% widowed, 7.8% divorced (2000); Foreign born: 0.5% (2000); Ancestry (includes multiple ancestries): 17.6% Other groups, 16.0% German, 15.8% Irish, 13.2% United States or American, 3.8% Polish (2000).
Economy: Employment by occupation: 3.8% management, 18.9% professional, 9.4% services, 38.4% sales, 0.0% farming, 15.1% construction, 14.5% production (2000).
Income: Per capita income: $18,931 (2007); Median household income: $30,000 (2007); Average household income: $45,926 (2007); Percent of households with income of $100,000 or more: 11.1% (2007); Poverty rate: 20.0% (2000).
Education: Percent of population age 25 and over with: High school diploma (including GED) or higher: 72.7% (2007); Bachelor's degree or higher: 4.7% (2007); Master's degree or higher: 3.6% (2007).

School District(s)

Gallia County Local (PK-12)
2005-06 Enrollment: 2,492 . . . . (740) 446-7917
Housing: Homeownership rate: 79.0% (2007); Median home value: $85,000 (2007); Median rent: $270 per month (2000); Median age of housing: 32 years (2000).
Transportation: Commute to work: 92.4% car, 0.0% public transportation, 3.2% walk, 2.5% work from home (2000); Travel time to work: 15.0% less than 15 minutes, 11.8% 15 to 30 minutes, 46.4% 30 to 45 minutes, 17.0% 45 to 60 minutes, 9.8% 60 minutes or more (2000)

GALLIPOLIS (city). County seat. Covers a land area of 3.615 square miles and a water area of 0.224 square miles. Located at 38.81° N. Lat.; 82.19° W. Long. Elevation is 574 feet.
History: Gallipolis was settled in 1790 by French immigrants who had been induced to leave France and purchase land in Ohio. After their long journey, they found that the deeds they had purchased were worthless, and those who stayed in Gallipolis had to buy their land all over again.
Population: 4,944 (1990); 4,180 (2000); 4,038 (2007); 3,997 (2012 projected); Race: 89.7% White, 7.1% Black, 1.2% Asian, 0.6% Hispanic of any race (2007); Density: 1,116.9 persons per square mile (2007); Average household size: 2.20 (2007); Median age: 45.3 (2007); Males per 100 females: 87.3 (2007); Marriage status: 23.9% never married, 47.7% now married, 13.2% widowed, 15.1% divorced (2000); Foreign born: 2.3% (2000); Ancestry (includes multiple ancestries): 15.9% United States or American, 13.7% Other groups, 13.4% German, 10.6% Irish, 6.4% English (2000).
Economy: Single-family building permits issued: 0 (2007); Multi-family building permits issued: 0 (2007); Employment by occupation: 6.0% management, 27.1% professional, 19.8% services, 25.5% sales, 0.0% farming, 8.1% construction, 13.6% production (2000).
Income: Per capita income: $18,771 (2007); Median household income: $27,850 (2007); Average household income: $40,203 (2007); Percent of households with income of $100,000 or more: 6.4% (2007); Poverty rate: 21.5% (2000).
Education: Percent of population age 25 and over with: High school diploma (including GED) or higher: 70.7% (2007); Bachelor's degree or higher: 18.3% (2007); Master's degree or higher: 7.9% (2007).

School District(s)

Gallia County Local (PK-12)
2005-06 Enrollment: 2,492 . . . . (740) 446-7917
Gallipolis City (PK-12)
2005-06 Enrollment: 2,383 . . . . (740) 446-3211

Two-year College(s)

Gallipolis Career College (Private, For-profit)
Fall 2007 Enrollment: 135 . . . . (740) 446-4367
2007-08 Tuition: In-state $9,170; Out-of-state $9,170
Housing: Homeownership rate: 53.2% (2007); Median home value: $93,551 (2007); Median rent: $318 per month (2000); Median age of housing: 55 years (2000).
Hospitals: Holzer Medical Center (243 beds)
Newspapers: Gallipolis Daily Tribune (Local news; Circulation 6,700); Tri County News (Community news; Circulation 15,500); The Tri-County News and River Currents (Local news; Circulation 15,500)
Transportation: Commute to work: 92.1% car, 1.5% public transportation, 4.7% walk, 0.3% work from home (2000); Travel time to work: 54.8% less than 15 minutes, 22.9% 15 to 30 minutes, 10.0% 30 to 45 minutes, 1.6% 45 to 60 minutes, 10.7% 60 minutes or more (2000)

Additional Information Contacts

City of Gallipolis . . . . (740) 446-1789
http://www.gallianet.net/Gallipolis/index.htm
Gallia County Chamber of Commerce . . . . (740) 446-0596
http://www.galliacounty.org

PATRIOT (unincorporated postal area, zip code 45658). Covers a land area of 91.886 square miles and a water area of 0.006 square miles. Located at 38.76° N. Lat.; 82.41° W. Long. Elevation is 730 feet.
Population: 2,315 (2000); Race: 98.4% White, 0.0% Black, 0.0% Asian, 0.0% Hispanic of any race (2000); Density: 25.2 persons per square mile (2000); Age: 33.3% under 18, 9.1% over 64 (2000); Marriage status: 22.3% never married, 63.6% now married, 5.1% widowed, 8.9% divorced (2000); Foreign born: 0.0% (2000); Ancestry (includes multiple ancestries): 13.5%

German, 13.1% United States or American, 12.8% Irish, 7.9% English, 7.4% Other groups (2000).
Economy: Employment by occupation: 6.2% management, 10.7% professional, 17.1% services, 19.1% sales, 4.5% farming, 11.8% construction, 30.5% production (2000).
Income: Per capita income: $11,944 (2000); Median household income: $30,968 (2000); Poverty rate: 26.0% (2000).
Education: Percent of population age 25 and over with: High school diploma (including GED) or higher: 71.1% (2000); Bachelor's degree or higher: 8.4% (2000).

School District(s)

Gallia County Local (PK-12)
2005-06 Enrollment: 2,492 . . . . (740) 446-7917
Housing: Homeownership rate: 83.8% (2000); Median home value: $82,000 (2000); Median rent: $293 per month (2000); Median age of housing: 23 years (2000).
Transportation: Commute to work: 91.9% car, 0.0% public transportation, 3.5% walk, 4.6% work from home (2000); Travel time to work: 9.0% less than 15 minutes, 34.6% 15 to 30 minutes, 32.5% 30 to 45 minutes, 11.0% 45 to 60 minutes, 12.9% 60 minutes or more (2000)

RIO GRANDE (village). Covers a land area of 1.198 square miles and a water area of 0.008 square miles. Located at 38.88° N. Lat.; 82.38° W. Long. Elevation is 650 feet.
History: Rio Grande was settled by Nehemiah Atwood, who served under General William Henry Harrison in the War of 1812 and, in 1818, opened a tavern at this site. Atwood provided the endowment for Rio Grande College, established in 1876 under the supervision of the Baptist church.
Population: 1,076 (1990); 915 (2000); 850 (2007); 832 (2012 projected); Race: 91.2% White, 4.4% Black, 1.9% Asian, 0.8% Hispanic of any race (2007); Density: 709.8 persons per square mile (2007); Average household size: 3.70 (2007); Median age: 21.5 (2007); Males per 100 females: 101.4 (2007); Marriage status: 62.1% never married, 29.3% now married, 0.3% widowed, 8.3% divorced (2000); Foreign born: 2.1% (2000); Ancestry (includes multiple ancestries): 14.8% German, 13.6% Other groups, 9.1% Irish, 5.5% English, 5.4% United States or American (2000).
Economy: Employment by occupation: 9.5% management, 14.3% professional, 20.3% services, 45.1% sales, 0.0% farming, 7.4% construction, 3.3% production (2000).
Income: Per capita income: $12,634 (2007); Median household income: $21,333 (2007); Average household income: $40,120 (2007); Percent of households with income of $100,000 or more: 8.7% (2007); Poverty rate: 35.9% (2000).
Education: Percent of population age 25 and over with: High school diploma (including GED) or higher: 87.2% (2007); Bachelor's degree or higher: 23.5% (2007); Master's degree or higher: 11.7% (2007).

School District(s)

Gallia-Jackson-Vinton (04-12)
2005-06 Enrollment: n/a . . . . (740) 245-5334
Gallipolis City (PK-12)
2005-06 Enrollment: 2,383 . . . . (740) 446-3211

Four-year College(s)

University of Rio Grande (Private, Not-for-profit)
Fall 2007 Enrollment: 2,243. . . . . (740) 245-7206
2007-08 Tuition: In-state $16,400; Out-of-state $16,400

Vocational/Technical School(s)

Gallia Jackson Vinton Joint Vocational School District (Public)
Fall 2007 Enrollment: 157 . . . . (740) 245-5334
2007-08 Tuition: $5,100
Housing: Homeownership rate: 37.4% (2007); Median home value: $106,944 (2007); Median rent: $270 per month (2000); Median age of housing: 30 years (2000).
Transportation: Commute to work: 53.8% car, 0.0% public transportation, 44.0% walk, 1.9% work from home (2000); Travel time to work: 62.4% less than 15 minutes, 18.9% 15 to 30 minutes, 7.0% 30 to 45 minutes, 4.3% 45 to 60 minutes, 7.3% 60 minutes or more (2000)

THURMAN (unincorporated postal area, zip code 45685). Aka Centerville. Covers a land area of 26.138 square miles and a water area of 0 square miles. Located at 38.87° N. Lat.; 82.40° W. Long. Elevation is 691 feet.
Population: 918 (2000); Race: 98.7% White, 0.6% Black, 0.0% Asian, 0.1% Hispanic of any race (2000); Density: 35.1 persons per square mile (2000); Age: 25.9% under 18, 11.3% over 64 (2000); Marriage status: 21.5% never married, 66.8% now married, 5.7% widowed, 6.0% divorced (2000); Foreign born: 0.2% (2000); Ancestry (includes multiple ancestries): 20.2% German, 13.5% Welsh, 10.5% Other groups, 9.9% United States or American, 9.9% Irish (2000).
Economy: Employment by occupation: 10.2% management, 16.9% professional, 9.9% services, 20.3% sales, 0.0% farming, 7.9% construction, 34.7% production (2000).
Income: Per capita income: $15,330 (2000); Median household income: $30,938 (2000); Poverty rate: 20.6% (2000).
Education: Percent of population age 25 and over with: High school diploma (including GED) or higher: 81.7% (2000); Bachelor's degree or higher: 11.4% (2000).
Housing: Homeownership rate: 80.5% (2000); Median home value: $80,800 (2000); Median rent: $325 per month (2000); Median age of housing: 27 years (2000).
Transportation: Commute to work: 98.8% car, 0.0% public transportation, 0.6% walk, 0.0% work from home (2000); Travel time to work: 21.3% less than 15 minutes, 46.8% 15 to 30 minutes, 22.5% 30 to 45 minutes, 1.5% 45 to 60 minutes, 7.9% 60 minutes or more (2000)

VINTON (village). Covers a land area of 1.115 square miles and a water area of 0 square miles. Located at 38.97° N. Lat.; 82.34° W. Long. Elevation is 614 feet.
Population: 293 (1990); 324 (2000); 326 (2007); 325 (2012 projected); Race: 97.5% White, 0.6% Black, 0.6% Asian, 0.3% Hispanic of any race (2007); Density: 292.3 persons per square mile (2007); Average household size: 2.55 (2007); Median age: 39.4 (2007); Males per 100 females: 101.2 (2007); Marriage status: 14.2% never married, 65.3% now married, 9.9% widowed, 10.6% divorced (2000); Foreign born: 0.0% (2000); Ancestry (includes multiple ancestries): 22.9% United States or American, 13.2% German, 8.2% Irish, 7.3% English, 7.3% French (except Basque) (2000).
Economy: Employment by occupation: 4.2% management, 12.6% professional, 10.1% services, 25.2% sales, 0.0% farming, 26.1% construction, 21.8% production (2000).
Income: Per capita income: $15,391 (2007); Median household income: $31,667 (2007); Average household income: $39,199 (2007); Percent of households with income of $100,000 or more: 7.8% (2007); Poverty rate: 16.4% (2000).
Education: Percent of population age 25 and over with: High school diploma (including GED) or higher: 63.6% (2007); Bachelor's degree or higher: 7.1% (2007); Master's degree or higher: 3.1% (2007).

School District(s)

Gallia County Local (PK-12)
2005-06 Enrollment: 2,492 . . . . (740) 446-7917
Housing: Homeownership rate: 79.7% (2007); Median home value: $73,636 (2007); Median rent: $271 per month (2000); Median age of housing: 45 years (2000).
Transportation: Commute to work: 86.2% car, 0.0% public transportation, 3.4% walk, 6.0% work from home (2000); Travel time to work: 32.1% less than 15 minutes, 47.7% 15 to 30 minutes, 6.4% 30 to 45 minutes, 3.7% 45 to 60 minutes, 10.1% 60 minutes or more (2000)

Geauga County

Located in northeastern Ohio; drained by the Cuyahoga, Chagrin, and Grand Rivers; includes several lakes. Covers a land area of 403.66 square miles, a water area of 4.63 square miles, and is located in the Eastern Time Zone. The county was founded in 1805. County seat is Chardon.

Geauga County is part of the Cleveland-Elyria-Mentor, OH Metropolitan Statistical Area. The entire metro area includes: Cuyahoga County, OH; Geauga County, OH; Lake County, OH; Lorain County, OH; Medina County, OH

Weather Station: Chardon Elevation: 1,128 feet

	Jan	Feb	Mar	Apr	May	Jun	Jul	Aug	Sep	Oct	Nov	Dec
High	31	34	44	56	68	76	80	79	72	60	48	37
Low	14	15	24	34	44	53	58	56	49	39	32	22
Precip	3.2	2.7	3.4	3.8	4.1	4.4	4.0	4.6	4.5	3.9	4.3	4.1
Snow	26.2	18.9	14.4	2.9	tr	0.0	0.0	0.0	0.0	0.9	10.1	23.6

High and Low temperatures in degrees Fahrenheit; Precipitation and Snow in inches

Population: 81,100 (1990); 90,895 (2000); 96,334 (2007); 99,720 (2012 projected); Race: 96.9% White, 1.5% Black, 0.6% Asian, 0.8% Hispanic of any race (2007); Density: 238.7 persons per square mile (2007); Average household size: 2.81 (2007); Median age: 41.0 (2007); Males per 100 females: 97.3 (2007).

Religion: Five largest groups: 28.1% Catholic Church, 4.4% Old Order Amish Church, 2.8% United Church of Christ, 2.6% The United Methodist Church, 1.7% Episcopal Church (2000).
Economy: Unemployment rate: 6.3% (6/2008); Total civilian labor force: 51,966 (6/2008); Leading industries: 34.9% manufacturing; 11.9% health care and social assistance; 11.9% retail trade (2005); Farms: 975 totaling 66,474 acres (2002); Companies that employ 500 or more persons: 3 (2006); Companies that employ 100 to 499 persons: 40 (2006); Companies that employ less than 100 persons: 2,702 (2006); Black-owned businesses: n/a (2002); Hispanic-owned businesses: n/a (2002); Asian-owned businesses: n/a (2002); Women-owned businesses: 1,982 (2002); Retail sales per capita: $10,560 (2008). Single-family building permits issued: 226 (2007); Multi-family building permits issued: 0 (2007).
Income: Per capita income: $33,246 (2007); Median household income: $70,259 (2007); Average household income: $92,853 (2007); Percent of households with income of $100,000 or more: 30.8% (2007); Poverty rate: 5.4% (2005); Bankruptcy rate: 2.22% (2007).
Taxes: Total county taxes per capita: $382 (2006); County property taxes per capita: $266 (2006).
Education: Percent of population age 25 and over with: High school diploma (including GED) or higher: 85.9% (2007); Bachelor's degree or higher: 31.1% (2007); Master's degree or higher: 11.5% (2007).
Housing: Homeownership rate: 87.1% (2007); Median home value: $229,338 (2007); Median rent: $513 per month (2000); Median age of housing: 29 years (2000).
Health: Birth rate: 121.8 per 10,000 population (2007); Death rate: 76.8 per 10,000 population (2007); Age-adjusted cancer mortality rate: 152.2 deaths per 100,000 population (2005); Air Quality Index: 91.2% good, 8.8% moderate, 0.0% unhealthy for sensitive individuals, 0.0% unhealthy (percent of days in 2007); Number of physicians: 23.1 per 10,000 population (2005); Hospital beds: 47.5 per 10,000 population (2004); Hospital admissions: 1,179.5 per 10,000 population (2004).
Elections: 2004 Presidential election results: 60.2% Bush, 39.4% Kerry, 0.0% Nader, 0.2% Badnarik
National and State Parks: Auburn State Wildlife Area; Punderson State Park
Additional Information Contacts
Geauga County Government . . . . (440) 285-2222
http://www.co.geauga.oh.us
Burton Chamber of Commerce . . . . (440) 834-1853
http://www.burtonchamberofcommerce.org
Chardon Area Chamber of Commerce . . . . (440) 285-9050
http://www.chardonchamber.com
Chesterland Chamber of Commerce . . . . (440) 729-7297
http://www.chesterlandchamber.com
Geauga County Tourism Council . . . . (440) 632-1538
http://www.tourgeauga.com
Middlefield Chamber of Commerce . . . . (440) 632-5705
http://www.middlefielddcc.com
Village of Chardon . . . . (440) 286-2600
http://www.chardon.cc
Village of Middlefield . . . . (440) 632-5248
http://www.middlefieldohio.com
Village of South Russell . . . . (440) 338-6700
http://www.southrussell.com

Geauga County Communities

AQUILLA (village). Aka Lake Aquilla. Covers a land area of 0.140 square miles and a water area of 0 square miles. Located at 41.54° N. Lat.; 81.17° W. Long. Elevation is 1,266 feet.
Population: 360 (1990); 372 (2000); 363 (2007); 359 (2012 projected); Race: 97.2% White, 0.6% Black, 1.9% Asian, 0.0% Hispanic of any race (2007); Density: 2,594.1 persons per square mile (2007); Average household size: 2.59 (2007); Median age: 37.7 (2007); Males per 100 females: 88.1 (2007); Marriage status: 29.2% never married, 51.5% now married, 5.3% widowed, 14.0% divorced (2000); Foreign born: 1.4% (2000); Ancestry (includes multiple ancestries): 19.1% German, 15.5% English, 12.8% Irish, 9.8% Italian, 7.6% United States or American (2000).
Economy: Employment by occupation: 13.8% management, 12.3% professional, 16.7% services, 17.2% sales, 0.0% farming, 12.8% construction, 27.1% production (2000).
Income: Per capita income: $22,321 (2007); Median household income: $55,385 (2007); Average household income: $57,875 (2007); Percent of households with income of $100,000 or more: 7.9% (2007); Poverty rate: 1.6% (2000).
Education: Percent of population age 25 and over with: High school diploma (including GED) or higher: 78.8% (2007); Bachelor's degree or higher: 13.9% (2007); Master's degree or higher: 2.4% (2007).
Housing: Homeownership rate: 82.1% (2007); Median home value: $120,479 (2007); Median rent: $533 per month (2000); Median age of housing: 52 years (2000).
Transportation: Commute to work: 93.1% car, 1.0% public transportation, 0.0% walk, 4.4% work from home (2000); Travel time to work: 30.9% less than 15 minutes, 25.8% 15 to 30 minutes, 27.8% 30 to 45 minutes, 10.3% 45 to 60 minutes, 5.2% 60 minutes or more (2000)

BAINBRIDGE (CDP). Covers a land area of 3.371 square miles and a water area of 0.066 square miles. Located at 41.39° N. Lat.; 81.33° W. Long. Elevation is 1,165 feet.
Population: 3,602 (1990); 3,417 (2000); 3,423 (2007); 3,459 (2012 projected); Race: 96.4% White, 1.2% Black, 0.9% Asian, 0.6% Hispanic of any race (2007); Density: 1,015.3 persons per square mile (2007); Average household size: 2.63 (2007); Median age: 44.1 (2007); Males per 100 females: 93.2 (2007); Marriage status: 16.7% never married, 71.2% now married, 5.4% widowed, 6.7% divorced (2000); Foreign born: 3.4% (2000); Ancestry (includes multiple ancestries): 23.8% German, 19.0% Irish, 14.8% English, 12.7% Italian, 7.5% Polish (2000).
Economy: Employment by occupation: 28.3% management, 29.9% professional, 9.1% services, 24.6% sales, 0.0% farming, 2.9% construction, 5.3% production (2000).
Income: Per capita income: $44,239 (2007); Median household income: $96,196 (2007); Average household income: $115,725 (2007); Percent of households with income of $100,000 or more: 47.3% (2007); Poverty rate: 2.1% (2000).
Education: Percent of population age 25 and over with: High school diploma (including GED) or higher: 94.5% (2007); Bachelor's degree or higher: 62.6% (2007); Master's degree or higher: 22.1% (2007).

School District(s)
Paint Valley Local (PK-12)
2005-06 Enrollment: 1,141 . . . . (740) 634-2826
Housing: Homeownership rate: 92.9% (2007); Median home value: $262,500 (2007); Median rent: $1,208 per month (2000); Median age of housing: 31 years (2000).
Transportation: Commute to work: 88.5% car, 1.2% public transportation, 0.0% walk, 9.8% work from home (2000); Travel time to work: 27.5% less than 15 minutes, 33.8% 15 to 30 minutes, 26.8% 30 to 45 minutes, 8.4% 45 to 60 minutes, 3.5% 60 minutes or more (2000)

BURTON (village). Covers a land area of 1.109 square miles and a water area of 0 square miles. Located at 41.47° N. Lat.; 81.14° W. Long. Elevation is 1,316 feet.
Population: 1,349 (1990); 1,450 (2000); 1,529 (2007); 1,581 (2012 projected); Race: 96.6% White, 1.2% Black, 0.4% Asian, 1.4% Hispanic of any race (2007); Density: 1,379.3 persons per square mile (2007); Average household size: 2.42 (2007); Median age: 40.7 (2007); Males per 100 females: 92.1 (2007); Marriage status: 23.4% never married, 53.6% now married, 11.6% widowed, 11.4% divorced (2000); Foreign born: 1.3% (2000); Ancestry (includes multiple ancestries): 28.4% German, 18.4% English, 15.9% Irish, 8.9% Other groups, 8.8% Italian (2000).
Economy: Employment by occupation: 12.1% management, 18.5% professional, 17.4% services, 23.2% sales, 0.0% farming, 12.1% construction, 16.8% production (2000).
Income: Per capita income: $24,287 (2007); Median household income: $49,758 (2007); Average household income: $57,060 (2007); Percent of households with income of $100,000 or more: 11.4% (2007); Poverty rate: 7.2% (2000).
Education: Percent of population age 25 and over with: High school diploma (including GED) or higher: 86.2% (2007); Bachelor's degree or higher: 23.4% (2007); Master's degree or higher: 8.7% (2007).

School District(s)
Berkshire Local (PK-12)
2005-06 Enrollment: 1,299 . . . . (440) 834-4123

Two-year College(s)
Kent State University-Geauga Campus (Public)
Fall 2007 Enrollment: 1,265. . . . . (440) 834-4187
2007-08 Tuition: In-state $4,770; Out-of-state $12,202

Housing: Homeownership rate: 51.8% (2007); Median home value: $173,713 (2007); Median rent: $471 per month (2000); Median age of housing: 41 years (2000).
Transportation: Commute to work: 90.9% car, 0.0% public transportation, 4.0% walk, 4.4% work from home (2000); Travel time to work: 39.9% less than 15 minutes, 30.4% 15 to 30 minutes, 16.3% 30 to 45 minutes, 9.8% 45 to 60 minutes, 3.5% 60 minutes or more (2000)
Additional Information Contacts
Burton Chamber of Commerce . . . . (440) 834-1853
http://www.burtonchamberofcommerce.org

CHARDON (village). County seat. Covers a land area of 4.603 square miles and a water area of 0.007 square miles. Located at 41.57° N. Lat.; 81.20° W. Long. Elevation is 1,299 feet.
History: Chardon was named for Peter Chardon Brooks, first owner of the site. The town developed as the maple syrup and sugar center of Ohio, from its location on the crest of a hill, surrounded by maple groves.
Population: 4,600 (1990); 5,156 (2000); 5,280 (2007); 5,363 (2012 projected); Race: 97.3% White, 0.7% Black, 0.4% Asian, 0.5% Hispanic of any race (2007); Density: 1,147.0 persons per square mile (2007); Average household size: 2.34 (2007); Median age: 39.8 (2007); Males per 100 females: 86.8 (2007); Marriage status: 20.2% never married, 56.5% now married, 11.5% widowed, 11.9% divorced (2000); Foreign born: 1.5% (2000); Ancestry (includes multiple ancestries): 25.8% German, 21.1% Irish, 16.8% English, 9.9% Italian, 8.7% Polish (2000).
Economy: Employment by occupation: 11.5% management, 23.1% professional, 12.2% services, 32.1% sales, 0.0% farming, 7.2% construction, 13.9% production (2000).
Income: Per capita income: $25,816 (2007); Median household income: $51,700 (2007); Average household income: $59,838 (2007); Percent of households with income of $100,000 or more: 14.6% (2007); Poverty rate: 3.8% (2000).
Education: Percent of population age 25 and over with: High school diploma (including GED) or higher: 89.1% (2007); Bachelor's degree or higher: 27.1% (2007); Master's degree or higher: 8.8% (2007).

School District(s)

Chardon Local (PK-12)
2005-06 Enrollment: 3,334 . . . . (440) 285-4052
Housing: Homeownership rate: 59.5% (2007); Median home value: $196,954 (2007); Median rent: $528 per month (2000); Median age of housing: 30 years (2000).
Hospitals: Heather Hill Hospital & Health Partnership (118 beds)
Safety: Violent crime rate: 5.7 per 10,000 population; Property crime rate: 219.0 per 10,000 population (2007).
Transportation: Commute to work: 95.0% car, 0.3% public transportation, 1.3% walk, 3.4% work from home (2000); Travel time to work: 39.9% less than 15 minutes, 26.2% 15 to 30 minutes, 20.5% 30 to 45 minutes, 8.9% 45 to 60 minutes, 4.5% 60 minutes or more (2000)
Additional Information Contacts
Chardon Area Chamber of Commerce . . . . (440) 285-9050
http://www.chardonchamber.com
Village of Chardon . . . . (440) 286-2600
http://www.chardon.cc

CHESTERLAND (CDP). Covers a land area of 4.398 square miles and a water area of 0.005 square miles. Located at 41.52° N. Lat.; 81.33° W. Long. Elevation is 1,214 feet.
Population: 2,750 (1990); 2,646 (2000); 2,658 (2007); 2,663 (2012 projected); Race: 98.6% White, 0.5% Black, 0.6% Asian, 1.1% Hispanic of any race (2007); Density: 604.4 persons per square mile (2007); Average household size: 2.54 (2007); Median age: 46.6 (2007); Males per 100 females: 97.6 (2007); Marriage status: 21.1% never married, 62.7% now married, 6.2% widowed, 10.0% divorced (2000); Foreign born: 7.7% (2000); Ancestry (includes multiple ancestries): 23.7% German, 21.2% Italian, 13.3% English, 12.5% Irish, 6.8% Hungarian (2000).
Economy: Employment by occupation: 10.0% management, 21.4% professional, 14.2% services, 27.5% sales, 0.0% farming, 12.3% construction, 14.5% production (2000).
Income: Per capita income: $32,869 (2007); Median household income: $66,733 (2007); Average household income: $81,515 (2007); Percent of households with income of $100,000 or more: 25.1% (2007); Poverty rate: 3.2% (2000).
Education: Percent of population age 25 and over with: High school diploma (including GED) or higher: 85.3% (2007); Bachelor's degree or higher: 23.5% (2007); Master's degree or higher: 8.1% (2007).

School District(s)

West Geauga Local (PK-12)
2005-06 Enrollment: 2,490 . . . . (440) 729-5900
Housing: Homeownership rate: 90.0% (2007); Median home value: $192,177 (2007); Median rent: $519 per month (2000); Median age of housing: 37 years (2000).
Transportation: Commute to work: 95.5% car, 0.0% public transportation, 0.0% walk, 3.8% work from home (2000); Travel time to work: 22.0% less than 15 minutes, 34.8% 15 to 30 minutes, 27.1% 30 to 45 minutes, 10.8% 45 to 60 minutes, 5.2% 60 minutes or more (2000)
Additional Information Contacts
Chesterland Chamber of Commerce . . . . (440) 729-7297
http://www.chesterlandchamber.com

HUNTSBURG (unincorporated postal area, zip code 44046). Covers a land area of 17.711 square miles and a water area of 0.597 square miles. Located at 41.54° N. Lat.; 81.08° W. Long. Elevation is 1,280 feet.
Population: 2,023 (2000); Race: 97.9% White, 1.9% Black, 0.0% Asian, 0.1% Hispanic of any race (2000); Density: 114.2 persons per square mile (2000); Age: 31.1% under 18, 11.7% over 64 (2000); Marriage status: 17.9% never married, 65.6% now married, 8.7% widowed, 7.7% divorced (2000); Foreign born: 0.6% (2000); Ancestry (includes multiple ancestries): 26.5% German, 19.0% Irish, 14.0% English, 7.4% Italian, 7.1% Polish (2000).
Economy: Employment by occupation: 6.4% management, 15.0% professional, 9.1% services, 30.2% sales, 1.9% farming, 19.8% construction, 17.6% production (2000).
Income: Per capita income: $22,630 (2000); Median household income: $58,810 (2000); Poverty rate: 3.9% (2000).
Education: Percent of population age 25 and over with: High school diploma (including GED) or higher: 84.9% (2000); Bachelor's degree or higher: 14.9% (2000).

School District(s)

Cardinal Local (KG-12)
2005-06 Enrollment: 1,467 . . . . (440) 632-0261
Housing: Homeownership rate: 88.4% (2000); Median home value: $157,300 (2000); Median rent: $475 per month (2000); Median age of housing: 28 years (2000).
Transportation: Commute to work: 93.1% car, 0.0% public transportation, 1.4% walk, 4.4% work from home (2000); Travel time to work: 21.0% less than 15 minutes, 31.3% 15 to 30 minutes, 23.0% 30 to 45 minutes, 15.2% 45 to 60 minutes, 9.4% 60 minutes or more (2000)

MIDDLEFIELD (village). Covers a land area of 3.005 square miles and a water area of 0 square miles. Located at 41.46° N. Lat.; 81.07° W. Long. Elevation is 1,125 feet.
Population: 2,257 (1990); 2,233 (2000); 2,480 (2007); 2,638 (2012 projected); Race: 97.6% White, 0.8% Black, 0.6% Asian, 0.9% Hispanic of any race (2007); Density: 825.3 persons per square mile (2007); Average household size: 2.27 (2007); Median age: 39.0 (2007); Males per 100 females: 90.0 (2007); Marriage status: 23.1% never married, 51.4% now married, 13.6% widowed, 11.9% divorced (2000); Foreign born: 1.1% (2000); Ancestry (includes multiple ancestries): 27.7% German, 15.7% Irish, 13.5% English, 8.2% Italian, 7.8% United States or American (2000).
Economy: Employment by occupation: 11.2% management, 13.0% professional, 14.9% services, 28.0% sales, 0.2% farming, 7.8% construction, 25.0% production (2000).
Income: Per capita income: $24,608 (2007); Median household income: $45,367 (2007); Average household income: $54,751 (2007); Percent of households with income of $100,000 or more: 10.2% (2007); Poverty rate: 9.0% (2000).
Education: Percent of population age 25 and over with: High school diploma (including GED) or higher: 77.5% (2007); Bachelor's degree or higher: 13.8% (2007); Master's degree or higher: 2.6% (2007).

School District(s)

Cardinal Local (KG-12)
2005-06 Enrollment: 1,467 . . . . (440) 632-0261
Housing: Homeownership rate: 49.7% (2007); Median home value: $149,885 (2007); Median rent: $471 per month (2000); Median age of housing: 29 years (2000).
Safety: Violent crime rate: 4.1 per 10,000 population; Property crime rate: 192.9 per 10,000 population (2007).
Transportation: Commute to work: 93.4% car, 0.0% public transportation, 4.2% walk, 1.6% work from home (2000); Travel time to work: 47.2% less

than 15 minutes, 22.1% 15 to 30 minutes, 13.3% 30 to 45 minutes, 12.9% 45 to 60 minutes, 4.4% 60 minutes or more (2000)
Airports: Geauga County (general aviation)
Additional Information Contacts
Geauga County Tourism Council. . . . . (440) 632-1538
http://www.tourgeauga.com
Middlefield Chamber of Commerce . . . . (440) 632-5705
http://www.middlefieldcc.com
Village of Middlefield . . . . (440) 632-5248
http://www.middlefieldohio.com

MONTVILLE (unincorporated postal area, zip code 44064). Covers a land area of 20.168 square miles and a water area of 0.026 square miles. Located at 41.61° N. Lat.; 81.05° W. Long. Elevation is 1,200 feet.
Population: 1,659 (2000); Race: 96.6% White, 0.3% Black, 0.8% Asian, 0.0% Hispanic of any race (2000); Density: 82.3 persons per square mile (2000); Age: 25.6% under 18, 14.9% over 64 (2000); Marriage status: 15.8% never married, 71.1% now married, 9.0% widowed, 4.1% divorced (2000); Foreign born: 1.7% (2000); Ancestry (includes multiple ancestries): 24.4% German, 14.1% Polish, 13.9% English, 12.0% Irish, 7.3% Hungarian (2000).
Economy: Employment by occupation: 14.7% management, 14.4% professional, 12.5% services, 25.5% sales, 2.3% farming, 14.1% construction, 16.5% production (2000).
Income: Per capita income: $22,160 (2000); Median household income: $52,134 (2000); Poverty rate: 1.7% (2000).
Education: Percent of population age 25 and over with: High school diploma (including GED) or higher: 83.6% (2000); Bachelor's degree or higher: 14.0% (2000).
Housing: Homeownership rate: 92.1% (2000); Median home value: $131,100 (2000); Median rent: $347 per month (2000); Median age of housing: 32 years (2000).
Transportation: Commute to work: 93.8% car, 1.0% public transportation, 0.0% walk, 4.5% work from home (2000); Travel time to work: 16.8% less than 15 minutes, 35.2% 15 to 30 minutes, 24.0% 30 to 45 minutes, 11.5% 45 to 60 minutes, 12.4% 60 minutes or more (2000)

NEWBURY (unincorporated postal area, zip code 44065). Aka Newbury Center. Covers a land area of 19.431 square miles and a water area of 0.173 square miles. Located at 41.47° N. Lat.; 81.24° W. Long.
Population: 4,135 (2000); Race: 97.0% White, 0.2% Black, 1.7% Asian, 0.0% Hispanic of any race (2000); Density: 212.8 persons per square mile (2000); Age: 27.0% under 18, 10.1% over 64 (2000); Marriage status: 24.4% never married, 61.4% now married, 5.3% widowed, 8.9% divorced (2000); Foreign born: 3.2% (2000); Ancestry (includes multiple ancestries): 26.5% German, 17.9% Irish, 14.8% English, 14.4% Italian, 6.5% Polish (2000).
Economy: Employment by occupation: 13.4% management, 18.3% professional, 13.3% services, 27.3% sales, 1.6% farming, 10.3% construction, 15.8% production (2000).
Income: Per capita income: $24,822 (2000); Median household income: $58,583 (2000); Poverty rate: 5.6% (2000).
Education: Percent of population age 25 and over with: High school diploma (including GED) or higher: 87.9% (2000); Bachelor's degree or higher: 23.2% (2000).

School District(s)

Newbury Local (PK-12)
2005-06 Enrollment: 784 . . . . (440) 564-5501
Housing: Homeownership rate: 83.9% (2000); Median home value: $160,900 (2000); Median rent: $538 per month (2000); Median age of housing: 38 years (2000).
Transportation: Commute to work: 96.3% car, 0.2% public transportation, 1.0% walk, 2.6% work from home (2000); Travel time to work: 28.3% less than 15 minutes, 25.1% 15 to 30 minutes, 27.3% 30 to 45 minutes, 17.2% 45 to 60 minutes, 2.0% 60 minutes or more (2000)

SOUTH RUSSELL (village). Covers a land area of 3.854 square miles and a water area of 0.030 square miles. Located at 41.43° N. Lat.; 81.34° W. Long. Elevation is 1,122 feet.
Population: 3,402 (1990); 4,022 (2000); 3,983 (2007); 3,955 (2012 projected); Race: 97.7% White, 0.4% Black, 1.4% Asian, 1.1% Hispanic of any race (2007); Density: 1,033.4 persons per square mile (2007); Average household size: 2.91 (2007); Median age: 42.7 (2007); Males per 100 females: 96.3 (2007); Marriage status: 15.9% never married, 74.3% now married, 4.9% widowed, 4.9% divorced (2000); Foreign born: 4.5% (2000); Ancestry (includes multiple ancestries): 30.2% German, 23.5% English, 22.8% Irish, 6.4% Polish, 5.8% Italian (2000).
Economy: Single-family building permits issued: 3 (2007); Multi-family building permits issued: 0 (2007); Employment by occupation: 31.6% management, 30.0% professional, 6.6% services, 25.0% sales, 0.3% farming, 4.0% construction, 2.5% production (2000).
Income: Per capita income: $47,007 (2007); Median household income: $105,310 (2007); Average household income: $136,962 (2007); Percent of households with income of $100,000 or more: 52.4% (2007); Poverty rate: 0.6% (2000).
Education: Percent of population age 25 and over with: High school diploma (including GED) or higher: 97.3% (2007); Bachelor's degree or higher: 65.5% (2007); Master's degree or higher: 27.5% (2007).
Housing: Homeownership rate: 97.7% (2007); Median home value: $336,232 (2007); Median rent: $907 per month (2000); Median age of housing: 26 years (2000).
Safety: Violent crime rate: 0.0 per 10,000 population; Property crime rate: 30.1 per 10,000 population (2007).
Transportation: Commute to work: 91.0% car, 2.0% public transportation, 0.6% walk, 6.4% work from home (2000); Travel time to work: 28.6% less than 15 minutes, 27.1% 15 to 30 minutes, 28.1% 30 to 45 minutes, 12.3% 45 to 60 minutes, 3.9% 60 minutes or more (2000)
Additional Information Contacts
Village of South Russell. . . . . (440) 338-6700
http://www.southrussell.com

THOMPSON (unincorporated postal area, zip code 44086). Covers a land area of 26.245 square miles and a water area of 0.083 square miles. Located at 41.67° N. Lat.; 81.05° W. Long. Elevation is 1,273 feet.
Population: 2,310 (2000); Race: 97.5% White, 1.1% Black, 0.0% Asian, 0.5% Hispanic of any race (2000); Density: 88.0 persons per square mile (2000); Age: 25.7% under 18, 7.1% over 64 (2000); Marriage status: 26.4% never married, 61.2% now married, 2.5% widowed, 9.8% divorced (2000); Foreign born: 0.4% (2000); Ancestry (includes multiple ancestries): 36.4% German, 24.4% English, 14.3% Irish, 7.5% Italian, 6.7% Other groups (2000).
Economy: Employment by occupation: 9.4% management, 16.4% professional, 14.7% services, 24.2% sales, 0.4% farming, 15.8% construction, 19.1% production (2000).
Income: Per capita income: $21,324 (2000); Median household income: $51,076 (2000); Poverty rate: 3.3% (2000).
Education: Percent of population age 25 and over with: High school diploma (including GED) or higher: 88.3% (2000); Bachelor's degree or higher: 14.2% (2000).

School District(s)

Ledgemont Local (PK-12)
2005-06 Enrollment: 663 . . . . (440) 298-3341
Housing: Homeownership rate: 90.2% (2000); Median home value: $138,800 (2000); Median rent: $425 per month (2000); Median age of housing: 27 years (2000).
Transportation: Commute to work: 91.0% car, 0.6% public transportation, 3.6% walk, 3.8% work from home (2000); Travel time to work: 11.2% less than 15 minutes, 30.9% 15 to 30 minutes, 34.9% 30 to 45 minutes, 14.2% 45 to 60 minutes, 8.7% 60 minutes or more (2000)

Greene County

Located in southwest central Ohio; crossed by the Little Miami and Mad Rivers. Covers a land area of 414.88 square miles, a water area of 1.34 square miles, and is located in the Eastern Time Zone. The county was founded in 1803. County seat is Xenia.

Greene County is part of the Dayton, OH Metropolitan Statistical Area. The entire metro area includes: Greene County, OH; Miami County, OH; Montgomery County, OH; Preble County, OH

Weather Station: Xenia 6 SSE Elevation: 967 feet

	Jan	Feb	Mar	Apr	May	Jun	Jul	Aug	Sep	Oct	Nov	Dec
High	36	41	52	63	73	80	84	82	76	65	52	41
Low	19	22	32	40	51	59	63	60	53	42	34	25
Precip	2.5	2.2	3.2	3.9	4.4	3.9	4.1	3.7	2.7	2.8	3.2	3.0
Snow	8.8	5.6	3.5	0.4	tr	0.0	0.0	0.0	0.0	0.2	0.9	3.3

High and Low temperatures in degrees Fahrenheit; Precipitation and Snow in inches

Population: 136,731 (1990); 147,886 (2000); 152,863 (2007); 155,573 (2012 projected); Race: 88.3% White, 6.3% Black, 2.5% Asian, 1.7%

Hispanic of any race (2007); Density: 368.5 persons per square mile (2007); Average household size: 2.60 (2007); Median age: 36.5 (2007); Males per 100 females: 96.1 (2007).
Religion: Five largest groups: 9.0% Catholic Church, 3.8% Southern Baptist Convention, 2.5% The United Methodist Church, 2.4% Christian Churches and Churches of Christ, 2.3% Independent, Non-Charismatic Churches (2000).
Economy: Unemployment rate: 6.5% (6/2008); Total civilian labor force: 78,967 (6/2008); Leading industries: 21.5% retail trade; 15.7% professional, scientific & technical services; 13.7% accommodation & food services (2005); Farms: 819 totaling 168,568 acres (2002); Companies that employ 500 or more persons: 3 (2006); Companies that employ 100 to 499 persons: 89 (2006); Companies that employ less than 100 persons: 2,995 (2006); Black-owned businesses: 181 (2002); Hispanic-owned businesses: n/a (2002); Asian-owned businesses: 186 (2002); Women-owned businesses: 3,371 (2002); Retail sales per capita: $14,128 (2008). Single-family building permits issued: 517 (2007); Multi-family building permits issued: 48 (2007).
Income: Per capita income: $28,030 (2007); Median household income: $57,404 (2007); Average household income: $71,420 (2007); Percent of households with income of $100,000 or more: 21.5% (2007); Poverty rate: 9.4% (2005); Bankruptcy rate: 3.50% (2007).
Taxes: Total county taxes per capita: $347 (2006); County property taxes per capita: $185 (2006).
Education: Percent of population age 25 and over with: High school diploma (including GED) or higher: 88.1% (2007); Bachelor's degree or higher: 31.7% (2007); Master's degree or higher: 14.2% (2007).
Housing: Homeownership rate: 70.0% (2007); Median home value: $146,429 (2007); Median rent: $492 per month (2000); Median age of housing: 31 years (2000).
Health: Birth rate: 118.5 per 10,000 population (2007); Death rate: 80.6 per 10,000 population (2007); Age-adjusted cancer mortality rate: 180.7 deaths per 100,000 population (2005); Air Quality Index: 66.2% good, 31.2% moderate, 2.7% unhealthy for sensitive individuals, 0.0% unhealthy (percent of days in 2007); Number of physicians: 25.2 per 10,000 population (2005); Hospital beds: 12.0 per 10,000 population (2004); Hospital admissions: 507.1 per 10,000 population (2004).
Elections: 2004 Presidential election results: 61.0% Bush, 38.5% Kerry, 0.0% Nader, 0.3% Badnarik
National and State Parks: Beaver Creek State Wildlife Area; Dayton Aviation Heritage National Historical Park; Glen Thompson State Reserve; Huffman Prairie National Historic Landmark; John Bryan State Park; Little Miami State Forest Preserve; The Narrows State Scenic River Reserve; Williamson Mound State Memorial

Additional Information Contacts

Greene County Government . . . . (937) 562-5006
http://www.co.greene.oh.us
Beavercreek Chamber of Commerce . . . . (937) 426-2202
http://www.beavercreekchamber.org
Bellbrook-Sugarcreek Area Chamber of Commerce . . . . . . (937) 848-4930
http://www.bellbrooksugarcreekchamber.com
City of Beavercreek . . . . (937) 427-5510
http://www.ci.beavercreek.oh.us
City of Bellbrook. . . . . (937) 848-4666
http://www.cityofbellbrook.org
City of Fairborn . . . . (937) 754-3016
http://www.ci.fairborn.oh.us
City of Xenia. . . . . (937) 376-7232
http://www.ci.xenia.oh.us
Fairborn Area Chamber of Commerce. . . . . (937) 878-3191
http://www.fairborn.com
Greene County Convention & Visitors Bureau. . . . . (937) 429-9100
http://www.greenecountyohio.org
Village of Yellow Springs . . . . (937) 767-7202
http://www.yso.com
Xenia Area Chamber of Commerce. . . . . (937) 372-3591
http://www.xacc.com
Yellow Springs Chamber of Commerce. . . . . (937) 767-2686
http://www.yellowspringsohio.org

Greene County Communities

BEAVERCREEK (city). Covers a land area of 26.392 square miles and a water area of 0 square miles. Located at 39.72° N. Lat.; 84.06° W. Long. Elevation is 873 feet.
Population: 33,946 (1990); 37,984 (2000); 39,794 (2007); 40,817 (2012 projected); Race: 91.6% White, 1.7% Black, 4.6% Asian, 1.6% Hispanic of any race (2007); Density: 1,507.8 persons per square mile (2007); Average household size: 2.59 (2007); Median age: 42.8 (2007); Males per 100 females: 98.6 (2007); Marriage status: 19.1% never married, 69.3% now married, 4.8% widowed, 6.8% divorced (2000); Foreign born: 4.7% (2000); Ancestry (includes multiple ancestries): 30.2% German, 14.4% Irish, 14.3% English, 10.3% United States or American, 8.8% Other groups (2000).
Economy: Unemployment rate: 5.6% (6/2008); Total civilian labor force: 21,001 (6/2008); Employment by occupation: 18.9% management, 32.3% professional, 8.9% services, 25.4% sales, 0.2% farming, 5.4% construction, 9.0% production (2000).
Income: Per capita income: $36,713 (2007); Median household income: $80,790 (2007); Average household income: $94,104 (2007); Percent of households with income of $100,000 or more: 35.2% (2007); Poverty rate: 2.4% (2000).
Education: Percent of population age 25 and over with: High school diploma (including GED) or higher: 92.7% (2007); Bachelor's degree or higher: 43.9% (2007); Master's degree or higher: 21.3% (2007).

School District(s)

Beavercreek City (PK-12)
2005-06 Enrollment: 7,626 . . . . (937) 426-1522
Housing: Homeownership rate: 83.5% (2007); Median home value: $169,628 (2007); Median rent: $705 per month (2000); Median age of housing: 27 years (2000).
Safety: Violent crime rate: 7.6 per 10,000 population; Property crime rate: 340.3 per 10,000 population (2007).
Transportation: Commute to work: 95.9% car, 0.1% public transportation, 0.6% walk, 3.2% work from home (2000); Travel time to work: 32.1% less than 15 minutes, 54.2% 15 to 30 minutes, 9.5% 30 to 45 minutes, 1.7% 45 to 60 minutes, 2.5% 60 minutes or more (2000)

Additional Information Contacts

Beavercreek Chamber of Commerce . . . . (937) 426-2202
http://www.beavercreekchamber.org
City of Beavercreek . . . . (937) 427-5510
http://www.ci.beavercreek.oh.us
Greene County Convention & Visitors Bureau. . . . . (937) 429-9100
http://www.greenecountyohio.org

BELLBROOK (city). Covers a land area of 3.123 square miles and a water area of 0 square miles. Located at 39.63° N. Lat.; 84.08° W. Long. Elevation is 778 feet.
Population: 6,520 (1990); 7,009 (2000); 6,839 (2007); 6,686 (2012 projected); Race: 96.3% White, 1.1% Black, 1.3% Asian, 1.9% Hispanic of any race (2007); Density: 2,190.0 persons per square mile (2007); Average household size: 2.61 (2007); Median age: 39.0 (2007); Males per 100 females: 97.8 (2007); Marriage status: 20.8% never married, 68.0% now married, 4.3% widowed, 6.9% divorced (2000); Foreign born: 3.9% (2000); Ancestry (includes multiple ancestries): 31.9% German, 15.3% English, 12.4% Irish, 10.7% United States or American, 6.8% Other groups (2000).
Economy: Employment by occupation: 17.2% management, 28.1% professional, 9.2% services, 29.2% sales, 0.4% farming, 5.3% construction, 10.6% production (2000).
Income: Per capita income: $30,659 (2007); Median household income: $72,354 (2007); Average household income: $79,999 (2007); Percent of households with income of $100,000 or more: 27.7% (2007); Poverty rate: 2.3% (2000).
Education: Percent of population age 25 and over with: High school diploma (including GED) or higher: 93.7% (2007); Bachelor's degree or higher: 40.1% (2007); Master's degree or higher: 16.3% (2007).

School District(s)

Sugarcreek Local (PK-12)
2005-06 Enrollment: 2,836 . . . . (937) 848-6251
Housing: Homeownership rate: 82.4% (2007); Median home value: $155,127 (2007); Median rent: $663 per month (2000); Median age of housing: 32 years (2000).
Safety: Violent crime rate: 1.5 per 10,000 population; Property crime rate: 172.7 per 10,000 population (2007).
Transportation: Commute to work: 95.5% car, 0.2% public transportation, 0.6% walk, 3.2% work from home (2000); Travel time to work: 22.0% less than 15 minutes, 55.3% 15 to 30 minutes, 15.5% 30 to 45 minutes, 2.8% 45 to 60 minutes, 4.6% 60 minutes or more (2000)

Additional Information Contacts

Bellbrook-Sugarcreek Area Chamber of Commerce . . . . . . (937) 848-4930
http://www.bellbrooksugarcreekchamber.com

City of Bellbrook . . . . (937) 848-4666
http://www.cityofbellbrook.org

BOWERSVILLE (village). Covers a land area of 0.138 square miles and a water area of 0 square miles. Located at 39.58° N. Lat.; 83.72° W. Long. Elevation is 1,089 feet.
Population: 225 (1990); 290 (2000); 325 (2007); 345 (2012 projected); Race: 98.2% White, 0.0% Black, 0.3% Asian, 0.6% Hispanic of any race (2007); Density: 2,354.9 persons per square mile (2007); Average household size: 2.52 (2007); Median age: 40.5 (2007); Males per 100 females: 108.3 (2007); Marriage status: 20.6% never married, 58.3% now married, 6.1% widowed, 14.9% divorced (2000); Foreign born: 0.0% (2000); Ancestry (includes multiple ancestries): 16.7% Other groups, 14.4% United States or American, 11.9% Irish, 10.6% German, 5.1% English (2000).
Economy: Employment by occupation: 6.1% management, 15.2% professional, 15.2% services, 26.5% sales, 3.0% farming, 6.1% construction, 28.0% production (2000).
Income: Per capita income: $19,431 (2007); Median household income: $45,833 (2007); Average household income: $48,953 (2007); Percent of households with income of $100,000 or more: 7.0% (2007); Poverty rate: 2.2% (2000).
Education: Percent of population age 25 and over with: High school diploma (including GED) or higher: 66.7% (2007); Bachelor's degree or higher: 6.1% (2007); Master's degree or higher: 0.0% (2007).
Housing: Homeownership rate: 81.4% (2007); Median home value: $80,417 (2007); Median rent: $341 per month (2000); Median age of housing: 60+ years (2000).
Transportation: Commute to work: 95.9% car, 0.0% public transportation, 4.1% walk, 0.0% work from home (2000); Travel time to work: 31.7% less than 15 minutes, 29.3% 15 to 30 minutes, 15.4% 30 to 45 minutes, 22.0% 45 to 60 minutes, 1.6% 60 minutes or more (2000)

CEDARVILLE (village). Covers a land area of 1.065 square miles and a water area of 0.012 square miles. Located at 39.74° N. Lat.; 83.80° W. Long. Elevation is 1,050 feet.
History: Cedarville was settled in 1805 and developed around Cedarville College, chartered in 1887 and opened in 1894 under the Reformed Presbyterian Church.
Population: 3,216 (1990); 3,828 (2000); 4,761 (2007); 5,243 (2012 projected); Race: 94.8% White, 1.4% Black, 1.2% Asian, 1.3% Hispanic of any race (2007); Density: 4,470.7 persons per square mile (2007); Average household size: 5.61 (2007); Median age: 20.9 (2007); Males per 100 females: 87.4 (2007); Marriage status: 62.6% never married, 33.2% now married, 2.3% widowed, 1.9% divorced (2000); Foreign born: 0.9% (2000); Ancestry (includes multiple ancestries): 30.2% German, 17.7% English, 10.1% Other groups, 10.0% Irish, 5.6% United States or American (2000).
Economy: Employment by occupation: 5.2% management, 22.5% professional, 32.6% services, 28.9% sales, 0.4% farming, 3.9% construction, 6.5% production (2000).
Income: Per capita income: $11,582 (2007); Median household income: $46,327 (2007); Average household income: $52,659 (2007); Percent of households with income of $100,000 or more: 10.4% (2007); Poverty rate: 13.8% (2000).
Education: Percent of population age 25 and over with: High school diploma (including GED) or higher: 89.7% (2007); Bachelor's degree or higher: 39.0% (2007); Master's degree or higher: 15.5% (2007).

School District(s)

Cedar Cliff Local (PK-12)
2005-06 Enrollment: 669 . . . . (937) 766-6000

Four-year College(s)

Cedarville University (Private, Not-for-profit, Baptist)
Fall 2007 Enrollment: 3,055 . . . . (937) 766-2211
2007-08 Tuition: In-state $19,680; Out-of-state $19,680
Housing: Homeownership rate: 54.7% (2007); Median home value: $123,473 (2007); Median rent: $365 per month (2000); Median age of housing: 38 years (2000).
Transportation: Commute to work: 56.2% car, 0.2% public transportation, 38.6% walk, 3.9% work from home (2000); Travel time to work: 60.7% less than 15 minutes, 21.8% 15 to 30 minutes, 12.5% 30 to 45 minutes, 2.0% 45 to 60 minutes, 2.9% 60 minutes or more (2000)

CLIFTON (village). Covers a land area of 0.177 square miles and a water area of 0.001 square miles. Located at 39.79° N. Lat.; 83.82° W. Long. Elevation is 1,004 feet.
History: Clifton was settled on the Little Miami River where water-power was plentiful. Isaac Kaufman Funk, who formed a partnership with college classmate Adam Willis Wagnalls, was born in Clifton in 1839. Funk was the editor of "A Standard Dictionary of the English Language."
Population: 165 (1990); 179 (2000); 203 (2007); 218 (2012 projected); Race: 86.2% White, 2.0% Black, 0.0% Asian, 0.0% Hispanic of any race (2007); Density: 1,147.5 persons per square mile (2007); Average household size: 2.54 (2007); Median age: 44.4 (2007); Males per 100 females: 105.1 (2007); Marriage status: 27.1% never married, 53.5% now married, 9.7% widowed, 9.7% divorced (2000); Foreign born: 0.0% (2000); Ancestry (includes multiple ancestries): 21.5% English, 18.3% United States or American, 14.5% German, 8.1% Other groups, 5.9% Scottish (2000).
Economy: Employment by occupation: 6.3% management, 32.3% professional, 28.1% services, 12.5% sales, 0.0% farming, 8.3% construction, 12.5% production (2000).
Income: Per capita income: $24,988 (2007); Median household income: $47,143 (2007); Average household income: $63,406 (2007); Percent of households with income of $100,000 or more: 18.8% (2007); Poverty rate: 5.4% (2000).
Education: Percent of population age 25 and over with: High school diploma (including GED) or higher: 83.6% (2007); Bachelor's degree or higher: 18.6% (2007); Master's degree or higher: 7.1% (2007).
Housing: Homeownership rate: 72.5% (2007); Median home value: $98,571 (2007); Median rent: $481 per month (2000); Median age of housing: 60+ years (2000).
Transportation: Commute to work: 96.8% car, 0.0% public transportation, 0.0% walk, 0.0% work from home (2000); Travel time to work: 22.6% less than 15 minutes, 34.4% 15 to 30 minutes, 20.4% 30 to 45 minutes, 4.3% 45 to 60 minutes, 18.3% 60 minutes or more (2000)

FAIRBORN (city). Aka Fairfield. Covers a land area of 13.064 square miles and a water area of 0 square miles. Located at 39.80° N. Lat.; 84.02° W. Long. Elevation is 837 feet.
History: Air Force Museum nearby. Settled 1799, incorporated 1950 with the merging of Osborn and Fairborn.
Population: 31,928 (1990); 32,052 (2000); 32,141 (2007); 32,089 (2012 projected); Race: 84.9% White, 7.3% Black, 4.1% Asian, 2.3% Hispanic of any race (2007); Density: 2,460.2 persons per square mile (2007); Average household size: 2.27 (2007); Median age: 33.4 (2007); Males per 100 females: 96.7 (2007); Marriage status: 33.1% never married, 48.8% now married, 5.7% widowed, 12.4% divorced (2000); Foreign born: 4.6% (2000); Ancestry (includes multiple ancestries): 21.1% German, 17.6% Other groups, 12.1% Irish, 10.4% United States or American, 10.2% English (2000).
Economy: Unemployment rate: 7.2% (6/2008); Total civilian labor force: 16,523 (6/2008); Single-family building permits issued: 78 (2007); Multi-family building permits issued: 0 (2007); Employment by occupation: 10.7% management, 20.1% professional, 18.9% services, 27.4% sales, 0.1% farming, 9.0% construction, 13.8% production (2000).
Income: Per capita income: $22,488 (2007); Median household income: $41,419 (2007); Average household income: $50,524 (2007); Percent of households with income of $100,000 or more: 9.9% (2007); Poverty rate: 14.1% (2000).
Education: Percent of population age 25 and over with: High school diploma (including GED) or higher: 84.3% (2007); Bachelor's degree or higher: 22.8% (2007); Master's degree or higher: 9.2% (2007).

School District(s)

Fairborn City (PK-12)
2005-06 Enrollment: 4,748 . . . . (937) 878-3961
Fairborn Digital Academy (02-12)
2005-06 Enrollment: 100 . . . . (937) 878-3961
Housing: Homeownership rate: 51.1% (2007); Median home value: $108,463 (2007); Median rent: $487 per month (2000); Median age of housing: 34 years (2000).
Safety: Violent crime rate: 35.0 per 10,000 population; Property crime rate: 363.0 per 10,000 population (2007).
Transportation: Commute to work: 94.5% car, 0.3% public transportation, 3.4% walk, 1.1% work from home (2000); Travel time to work: 40.3% less than 15 minutes, 42.5% 15 to 30 minutes, 12.3% 30 to 45 minutes, 1.9% 45 to 60 minutes, 2.9% 60 minutes or more (2000)
Additional Information Contacts
City of Fairborn . . . . (937) 754-3016
http://www.ci.fairborn.oh.us

Fairborn Area Chamber of Commerce. . . . . (937) 878-3191
http://www.fairborn.com

JAMESTOWN (village). Covers a land area of 1.214 square miles and a water area of <.001 square miles. Located at 39.65° N. Lat.; 83.73° W. Long. Elevation is 1,060 feet.

History: Jamestown was settled near the old route of Chiuxso's Trail, a wagon road through the forest connecting Ripley on the Ohio River with the Mad River Valley. The town was rebuilt after a cyclone destroyed the buildings in 1844.

Population: 1,947 (1990); 1,917 (2000); 1,955 (2007); 1,975 (2012 projected); Race: 95.7% White, 2.8% Black, 0.5% Asian, 0.7% Hispanic of any race (2007); Density: 1,610.6 persons per square mile (2007); Average household size: 2.48 (2007); Median age: 34.0 (2007); Males per 100 females: 94.1 (2007); Marriage status: 21.6% never married, 55.1% now married, 8.0% widowed, 15.4% divorced (2000); Foreign born: 0.5% (2000); Ancestry (includes multiple ancestries): 19.2% United States or American, 17.4% German, 13.3% Irish, 11.1% Other groups, 8.2% English (2000).

Economy: Employment by occupation: 5.6% management, 12.9% professional, 17.4% services, 21.6% sales, 0.6% farming, 11.5% construction, 30.3% production (2000).

Income: Per capita income: $21,191 (2007); Median household income: $48,073 (2007); Average household income: $52,506 (2007); Percent of households with income of $100,000 or more: 8.9% (2007); Poverty rate: 11.2% (2000).

Education: Percent of population age 25 and over with: High school diploma (including GED) or higher: 81.4% (2007); Bachelor's degree or higher: 9.5% (2007); Master's degree or higher: 3.1% (2007).

School District(s)

Greeneview Local (PK-12)
2005-06 Enrollment: 1,568 . . . . (937) 675-2728

Housing: Homeownership rate: 66.5% (2007); Median home value: $103,351 (2007); Median rent: $414 per month (2000); Median age of housing: 47 years (2000).

Transportation: Commute to work: 93.4% car, 0.9% public transportation, 2.6% walk, 2.5% work from home (2000); Travel time to work: 23.6% less than 15 minutes, 31.5% 15 to 30 minutes, 24.5% 30 to 45 minutes, 12.6% 45 to 60 minutes, 7.9% 60 minutes or more (2000)

SHAWNEE HILLS (CDP). Covers a land area of 2.661 square miles and a water area of 0.239 square miles. Located at 39.65° N. Lat.; 83.77° W. Long. Elevation is 1,047 feet.

Population: 2,199 (1990); 2,355 (2000); 2,457 (2007); 2,517 (2012 projected); Race: 96.3% White, 1.3% Black, 0.5% Asian, 1.1% Hispanic of any race (2007); Density: 923.3 persons per square mile (2007); Average household size: 2.76 (2007); Median age: 37.3 (2007); Males per 100 females: 100.7 (2007); Marriage status: 18.4% never married, 68.7% now married, 2.4% widowed, 10.5% divorced (2000); Foreign born: 1.9% (2000); Ancestry (includes multiple ancestries): 20.4% German, 16.3% Other groups, 15.5% English, 11.6% Irish, 7.2% United States or American (2000).

Economy: Employment by occupation: 13.1% management, 15.5% professional, 12.0% services, 31.2% sales, 0.3% farming, 8.2% construction, 19.7% production (2000).

Income: Per capita income: $26,682 (2007); Median household income: $65,879 (2007); Average household income: $73,660 (2007); Percent of households with income of $100,000 or more: 19.1% (2007); Poverty rate: 3.2% (2000).

Education: Percent of population age 25 and over with: High school diploma (including GED) or higher: 88.6% (2007); Bachelor's degree or higher: 15.6% (2007); Master's degree or higher: 3.4% (2007).

Housing: Homeownership rate: 95.1% (2007); Median home value: $130,429 (2007); Median rent: $457 per month (2000); Median age of housing: 25 years (2000).

Transportation: Commute to work: 97.7% car, 0.6% public transportation, 0.0% walk, 0.9% work from home (2000); Travel time to work: 12.8% less than 15 minutes, 42.5% 15 to 30 minutes, 33.1% 30 to 45 minutes, 6.8% 45 to 60 minutes, 4.7% 60 minutes or more (2000)

SPRING VALLEY (village). Covers a land area of 0.278 square miles and a water area of 0 square miles. Located at 39.60° N. Lat.; 84.00° W. Long. Elevation is 761 feet.

History: Spring Valley was named for the nearby springs, whose water was bottled and shipped from the town. Spring Valley developed as a farming community, with tobacco grown here as early as 1825.

Population: 507 (1990); 510 (2000); 499 (2007); 494 (2012 projected); Race: 94.4% White, 2.6% Black, 0.4% Asian, 0.0% Hispanic of any race (2007); Density: 1,793.3 persons per square mile (2007); Average household size: 2.51 (2007); Median age: 40.6 (2007); Males per 100 females: 104.5 (2007); Marriage status: 25.0% never married, 53.5% now married, 6.7% widowed, 14.8% divorced (2000); Foreign born: 0.4% (2000); Ancestry (includes multiple ancestries): 30.5% German, 15.9% Irish, 13.7% United States or American, 12.7% English, 6.8% Other groups (2000).

Economy: Employment by occupation: 11.0% management, 20.3% professional, 14.1% services, 26.2% sales, 1.4% farming, 13.1% construction, 13.8% production (2000).

Income: Per capita income: $24,704 (2007); Median household income: $49,722 (2007); Average household income: $61,947 (2007); Percent of households with income of $100,000 or more: 11.1% (2007); Poverty rate: 2.8% (2000).

Education: Percent of population age 25 and over with: High school diploma (including GED) or higher: 91.7% (2007); Bachelor's degree or higher: 16.6% (2007); Master's degree or higher: 6.3% (2007).

Housing: Homeownership rate: 83.9% (2007); Median home value: $108,750 (2007); Median rent: $375 per month (2000); Median age of housing: 60+ years (2000).

Transportation: Commute to work: 93.8% car, 0.0% public transportation, 1.4% walk, 2.8% work from home (2000); Travel time to work: 15.7% less than 15 minutes, 46.4% 15 to 30 minutes, 28.2% 30 to 45 minutes, 3.2% 45 to 60 minutes, 6.4% 60 minutes or more (2000)

WILBERFORCE (CDP). Covers a land area of 3.092 square miles and a water area of 0.052 square miles. Located at 39.71° N. Lat.; 83.88° W. Long. Elevation is 1,007 feet.

History: Wilberforce was named for William Wilberforce, an English reformer. The town grew around Wilberforce University, opened in 1856 by the Methodist Episcopal Church and purchased in 1863 by the African M.E. Church.

Population: 2,639 (1990); 1,579 (2000); 1,707 (2007); 1,842 (2012 projected); Race: 20.3% White, 73.1% Black, 0.1% Asian, 1.9% Hispanic of any race (2007); Density: 552.1 persons per square mile (2007); Average household size: 9.70 (2007); Median age: 20.9 (2007); Males per 100 females: 96.9 (2007); Marriage status: 72.0% never married, 23.1% now married, 3.0% widowed, 2.0% divorced (2000); Foreign born: 5.1% (2000); Ancestry (includes multiple ancestries): 76.6% Other groups, 4.0% African, 2.3% German, 2.0% United States or American, 1.5% Nigerian (2000).

Economy: Employment by occupation: 7.2% management, 32.5% professional, 18.6% services, 36.9% sales, 2.8% farming, 0.0% construction, 2.1% production (2000).

Income: Per capita income: $10,227 (2007); Median household income: $38,235 (2007); Average household income: $57,813 (2007); Percent of households with income of $100,000 or more: 18.2% (2007); Poverty rate: 6.5% (2000).

Education: Percent of population age 25 and over with: High school diploma (including GED) or higher: 84.6% (2007); Bachelor's degree or higher: 55.4% (2007); Master's degree or higher: 20.6% (2007).

Four-year College(s)

Central State University (Public, Historically black)
Fall 2007 Enrollment: 2,022. . . . . (937) 376-6011
2007-08 Tuition: In-state $5,294; Out-of-state $11,462

Payne Theological Seminary (Private, Not-for-profit, African Methodist Episcopal)
Fall 2007 Enrollment: 120 . . . . (937) 376-2946

Wilberforce University (Private, Not-for-profit, Historically black, African Methodist Episcopal)
Fall 2007 Enrollment: 834 . . . . (937) 376-2911
2007-08 Tuition: In-state $11,560; Out-of-state $11,560

Housing: Homeownership rate: 84.1% (2007); Median home value: $170,588 (2007); Median rent: $725 per month (2000); Median age of housing: 33 years (2000).

Transportation: Commute to work: 62.1% car, 0.0% public transportation, 28.6% walk, 7.8% work from home (2000); Travel time to work: 65.4% less than 15 minutes, 19.4% 15 to 30 minutes, 13.2% 30 to 45 minutes, 2.0% 45 to 60 minutes, 0.0% 60 minutes or more (2000)

XENIA (city). County seat. Covers a land area of 12.147 square miles and a water area of 0 square miles. Located at 39.68° N. Lat.; 83.93° W. Long. Elevation is 932 feet.
History: Xenia developed around an agricultural area. An early industry was the production of rope and twine.
Population: 25,481 (1990); 24,164 (2000); 23,555 (2007); 23,169 (2012 projected); Race: 83.5% White, 12.7% Black, 0.3% Asian, 1.7% Hispanic of any race (2007); Density: 1,939.2 persons per square mile (2007); Average household size: 2.49 (2007); Median age: 35.4 (2007); Males per 100 females: 92.5 (2007); Marriage status: 23.5% never married, 56.8% now married, 7.0% widowed, 12.7% divorced (2000); Foreign born: 1.9% (2000); Ancestry (includes multiple ancestries): 20.1% Other groups, 16.8% German, 14.3% United States or American, 10.4% Irish, 8.8% English (2000).
Economy: Unemployment rate: 7.8% (6/2008); Total civilian labor force: 11,490 (6/2008); Employment by occupation: 9.0% management, 16.3% professional, 17.9% services, 26.0% sales, 0.1% farming, 10.3% construction, 20.5% production (2000).
Income: Per capita income: $20,423 (2007); Median household income: $43,113 (2007); Average household income: $49,221 (2007); Percent of households with income of $100,000 or more: 7.6% (2007); Poverty rate: 11.6% (2000).
Taxes: Total city taxes per capita: $480 (2006); City property taxes per capita: $74 (2006).
Education: Percent of population age 25 and over with: High school diploma (including GED) or higher: 81.5% (2007); Bachelor's degree or higher: 15.1% (2007); Master's degree or higher: 5.5% (2007).

School District(s)

Greene County Jt Voc Sd (07-12)
2005-06 Enrollment: n/a . . . . (937) 372-6941
Summit Academy-Xenia (01-09)
2005-06 Enrollment: 39 . . . . (937) 372-5210
Xenia Community City (PK-12)
2005-06 Enrollment: 5,109 . . . . (937) 376-2961

Vocational/Technical School(s)

Greene County Career Center (Public)
Fall 2007 Enrollment: 1,089. . . . . (937) 372-6941
2007-08 Tuition: $3,350
Housing: Homeownership rate: 66.8% (2007); Median home value: $97,780 (2007); Median rent: $398 per month (2000); Median age of housing: 35 years (2000).
Hospitals: Greene Memorial Hospital (231 beds)
Safety: Violent crime rate: 18.4 per 10,000 population; Property crime rate: 484.3 per 10,000 population (2007).
Newspapers: Fairborn Daily Herald (Local news; Circulation 4,350); Greene County Shopper (Community news; Circulation 16,900); Xenia Daily Gazette (Local news; Circulation 9,758)
Transportation: Commute to work: 95.3% car, 0.5% public transportation, 2.2% walk, 1.5% work from home (2000); Travel time to work: 37.0% less than 15 minutes, 32.9% 15 to 30 minutes, 22.1% 30 to 45 minutes, 3.8% 45 to 60 minutes, 4.2% 60 minutes or more (2000)
Airports: Greene County-Lewis A Jackson Regional (general aviation)
Additional Information Contacts
City of Xenia. . . . . (937) 376-7232
http://www.ci.xenia.oh.us
Xenia Area Chamber of Commerce. . . . . (937) 372-3591
http://www.xacc.com

YELLOW SPRINGS (village). Covers a land area of 1.898 square miles and a water area of 0 square miles. Located at 39.80° N. Lat.; 83.89° W. Long. Elevation is 968 feet.
History: Yellow Springs was founded in 1804 and named for the yellowed water of the nearby iron springs. Antioch College was founded here in 1853 with Horace Mann as its first president.
Population: 4,008 (1990); 3,761 (2000); 3,713 (2007); 3,691 (2012 projected); Race: 79.2% White, 11.3% Black, 1.6% Asian, 2.9% Hispanic of any race (2007); Density: 1,956.0 persons per square mile (2007); Average household size: 2.31 (2007); Median age: 45.6 (2007); Males per 100 females: 79.8 (2007); Marriage status: 24.7% never married, 54.1% now married, 6.7% widowed, 14.6% divorced (2000); Foreign born: 3.9% (2000); Ancestry (includes multiple ancestries): 23.2% Other groups, 21.7% German, 13.7% English, 11.8% Irish, 4.2% Scottish (2000).
Economy: Employment by occupation: 16.1% management, 44.2% professional, 12.5% services, 14.6% sales, 0.6% farming, 3.8% construction, 8.3% production (2000).
Income: Per capita income: $32,760 (2007); Median household income: $59,248 (2007); Average household income: $73,995 (2007); Percent of households with income of $100,000 or more: 24.1% (2007); Poverty rate: 7.0% (2000).
Education: Percent of population age 25 and over with: High school diploma (including GED) or higher: 95.4% (2007); Bachelor's degree or higher: 58.5% (2007); Master's degree or higher: 31.7% (2007).

School District(s)

Yellow Springs Exempted Village (PK-12)
2005-06 Enrollment: 672 . . . . (937) 767-7381

Four-year College(s)

Antioch College (Private, Not-for-profit)
Fall 2007 Enrollment: 229 . . . . (937) 769-1000
2007-08 Tuition: In-state $28,573; Out-of-state $28,573
Antioch University McGregor (Private, Not-for-profit)
Fall 2007 Enrollment: 681 . . . . (937) 769-1800
Antioch University PhD Program in Leadership and Change (Private, Not-for-profit)
Fall 2007 Enrollment: 125 . . . . (937) 769-1360
Housing: Homeownership rate: 62.5% (2007); Median home value: $189,478 (2007); Median rent: $459 per month (2000); Median age of housing: 43 years (2000).
Newspapers: Yellow Springs News (Community news; Circulation 1,850)
Transportation: Commute to work: 79.2% car, 0.3% public transportation, 12.5% walk, 5.6% work from home (2000); Travel time to work: 36.6% less than 15 minutes, 36.8% 15 to 30 minutes, 16.8% 30 to 45 minutes, 1.1% 45 to 60 minutes, 8.7% 60 minutes or more (2000)
Additional Information Contacts
Village of Yellow Springs . . . . (937) 767-7202
http://www.yso.com
Yellow Springs Chamber of Commerce. . . . . (937) 767-2686
http://www.yellowspringsohio.org

Guernsey County

Located in eastern Ohio; drained by Wills Creek; includes Salt Fork Lake. Covers a land area of 521.90 square miles, a water area of 6.39 square miles, and is located in the Eastern Time Zone. The county was founded in 1810. County seat is Cambridge.

Guernsey County is part of the Cambridge, OH Micropolitan Statistical Area. The entire metro area includes: Guernsey County, OH

Weather Station: Cambridge — Elevation: 797 feet

	Jan	Feb	Mar	Apr	May	Jun	Jul	Aug	Sep	Oct	Nov	Dec
High	37	42	53	65	74	82	85	84	77	66	53	42
Low	20	22	31	39	49	58	62	61	54	42	34	26
Precip	2.7	2.3	3.0	3.4	4.0	4.1	4.3	3.9	3.0	2.6	3.3	2.8
Snow	7.4	4.1	2.9	0.6	tr	0.0	0.0	0.0	0.0	tr	0.8	2.6

High and Low temperatures in degrees Fahrenheit; Precipitation and Snow in inches

Population: 39,024 (1990); 40,792 (2000); 41,106 (2007); 41,093 (2012 projected); Race: 96.2% White, 1.6% Black, 0.2% Asian, 0.9% Hispanic of any race (2007); Density: 78.8 persons per square mile (2007); Average household size: 2.51 (2007); Median age: 39.0 (2007); Males per 100 females: 95.3 (2007).
Religion: Five largest groups: 10.0% The United Methodist Church, 4.5% Catholic Church, 3.1% Presbyterian Church (U.S.A.), 2.1% Churches of Christ, 2.0% American Baptist Churches in the USA (2000).
Economy: Unemployment rate: 7.3% (6/2008); Total civilian labor force: 20,381 (6/2008); Leading industries: 24.2% manufacturing; 19.3% health care and social assistance; 14.6% retail trade (2005); Farms: 910 totaling 137,443 acres (2002); Companies that employ 500 or more persons: 2 (2006); Companies that employ 100 to 499 persons: 18 (2006); Companies that employ less than 100 persons: 907 (2006); Black-owned businesses: n/a (2002); Hispanic-owned businesses: n/a (2002); Asian-owned businesses: n/a (2002); Women-owned businesses: 982 (2002); Retail sales per capita: $12,604 (2008). Single-family building permits issued: 57 (2007); Multi-family building permits issued: 0 (2007).
Income: Per capita income: $18,073 (2007); Median household income: $35,233 (2007); Average household income: $44,993 (2007); Percent of households with income of $100,000 or more: 6.3% (2007); Poverty rate: 17.2% (2005); Bankruptcy rate: 3.56% (2007).

Education: Percent of population age 25 and over with: High school diploma (including GED) or higher: 78.6% (2007); Bachelor's degree or higher: 10.1% (2007); Master's degree or higher: 4.0% (2007).
Housing: Homeownership rate: 73.7% (2007); Median home value: $85,513 (2007); Median rent: $303 per month (2000); Median age of housing: 35 years (2000).
Health: Birth rate: 125.5 per 10,000 population (2007); Death rate: 109.4 per 10,000 population (2007); Age-adjusted cancer mortality rate: 205.1 deaths per 100,000 population (2005); Number of physicians: 15.7 per 10,000 population (2005); Hospital beds: 89.1 per 10,000 population (2004); Hospital admissions: 1,590.9 per 10,000 population (2004).
Elections: 2004 Presidential election results: 55.8% Bush, 43.5% Kerry, 0.0% Nader, 0.3% Badnarik
National and State Parks: Salt Fork State Park and Wildlife Area
Additional Information Contacts
Guernsey County Government . . . . (740) 432-9200
http://www.guernseycounty.org
Cambridge Area Chamber of Commerce . . . . (740) 439-6688
http://www.cambridgeohiochamber.com
Cambridge/Guernsey County Visitors & Convention Bureau. . . . . (740) 432-2022
http://www.visitguernseycounty.com
City of Cambridge . . . . (740) 439-1050
http://www.cambridgeoh.org

Guernsey County Communities

BYESVILLE (village). Covers a land area of 0.974 square miles and a water area of 0 square miles. Located at 39.96° N. Lat.; 81.54° W. Long. Elevation is 817 feet.
History: Byesville was named for Jonathan Bye, who built a flour mill here in the early 1800's. Later, the town's economy depended on coal mining.
Population: 2,547 (1990); 2,574 (2000); 2,376 (2007); 2,305 (2012 projected); Race: 98.0% White, 0.3% Black, 0.3% Asian, 0.8% Hispanic of any race (2007); Density: 2,439.4 persons per square mile (2007); Average household size: 2.37 (2007); Median age: 36.3 (2007); Males per 100 females: 87.7 (2007); Marriage status: 22.0% never married, 57.6% now married, 7.8% widowed, 12.6% divorced (2000); Foreign born: 0.7% (2000); Ancestry (includes multiple ancestries): 18.3% German, 16.4% Irish, 10.6% English, 10.2% United States or American, 5.9% Other groups (2000).
Economy: Employment by occupation: 4.8% management, 10.4% professional, 16.4% services, 27.5% sales, 0.0% farming, 10.5% construction, 30.5% production (2000).
Income: Per capita income: $15,476 (2007); Median household income: $32,337 (2007); Average household income: $36,624 (2007); Percent of households with income of $100,000 or more: 3.1% (2007); Poverty rate: 15.2% (2000).
Education: Percent of population age 25 and over with: High school diploma (including GED) or higher: 82.6% (2007); Bachelor's degree or higher: 4.6% (2007); Master's degree or higher: 1.9% (2007).

School District(s)

Rolling Hills Local (PK-12)
2005-06 Enrollment: 2,151 . . . . (740) 432-5370
Housing: Homeownership rate: 64.0% (2007); Median home value: $71,265 (2007); Median rent: $294 per month (2000); Median age of housing: 48 years (2000).
Newspapers: Byesville Village Reporter (Community news)
Transportation: Commute to work: 95.2% car, 0.4% public transportation, 2.8% walk, 0.0% work from home (2000); Travel time to work: 52.2% less than 15 minutes, 31.1% 15 to 30 minutes, 9.4% 30 to 45 minutes, 1.6% 45 to 60 minutes, 5.7% 60 minutes or more (2000)

CAMBRIDGE (city). County seat. Covers a land area of 5.606 square miles and a water area of 0.004 square miles. Located at 40.02° N. Lat.; 81.58° W. Long. Elevation is 830 feet.
History: Cambridge was laid out in 1806 by Jacob Gomber and Zacheus Beatty, and named for Cambridge, Maryland, the former home of many of the first settlers. Oil and gas discovered in the area in the 1880's led to industrial development, including a glass factory founded in 1901.
Population: 11,871 (1990); 11,520 (2000); 11,440 (2007); 11,397 (2012 projected); Race: 92.7% White, 4.0% Black, 0.3% Asian, 1.4% Hispanic of any race (2007); Density: 2,040.8 persons per square mile (2007); Average household size: 2.33 (2007); Median age: 37.1 (2007); Males per 100 females: 87.8 (2007); Marriage status: 26.6% never married, 48.5% now married, 10.3% widowed, 14.5% divorced (2000); Foreign born: 1.8% (2000); Ancestry (includes multiple ancestries): 17.0% German, 14.4% Irish, 12.0% English, 10.8% Other groups, 9.1% United States or American (2000).
Economy: Employment by occupation: 8.7% management, 12.7% professional, 22.7% services, 20.6% sales, 0.3% farming, 9.6% construction, 25.5% production (2000).
Income: Per capita income: $16,453 (2007); Median household income: $28,045 (2007); Average household income: $37,833 (2007); Percent of households with income of $100,000 or more: 4.8% (2007); Poverty rate: 21.2% (2000).
Education: Percent of population age 25 and over with: High school diploma (including GED) or higher: 75.2% (2007); Bachelor's degree or higher: 12.4% (2007); Master's degree or higher: 4.7% (2007).

School District(s)

Cambridge City (PK-12)
2005-06 Enrollment: 2,686 . . . . (740) 439-5021
East Muskingum Local (PK-12)
2005-06 Enrollment: 2,170 . . . . (740) 826-7655

Vocational/Technical School(s)

Valley Beauty School (Private, For-profit)
Fall 2007 Enrollment: 5 . . . . (740) 373-3617
2007-08 Tuition: $9,000
Housing: Homeownership rate: 53.5% (2007); Median home value: $70,871 (2007); Median rent: $301 per month (2000); Median age of housing: 53 years (2000).
Hospitals: Appalachian Behavioral Healthcare (132 beds); Southeastern Ohio Regional Medical Center (209 beds)
Safety: Violent crime rate: 48.1 per 10,000 population; Property crime rate: 753.2 per 10,000 population (2007).
Newspapers: The Daily Jeffersonian (Local news; Circulation 14,500); Guernsey Noble Advertiser (Community news; Circulation 12,898); New Concord Leader (Community news; Circulation 1,250)
Transportation: Commute to work: 90.3% car, 1.5% public transportation, 5.2% walk, 1.9% work from home (2000); Travel time to work: 60.0% less than 15 minutes, 22.1% 15 to 30 minutes, 8.8% 30 to 45 minutes, 2.9% 45 to 60 minutes, 6.1% 60 minutes or more (2000)
Additional Information Contacts
Cambridge Area Chamber of Commerce . . . . (740) 439-6688
http://www.cambridgeohiochamber.com
Cambridge/Guernsey County Visitors & Convention Bureau. . . . . (740) 432-2022
http://www.visitguernseycounty.com
City of Cambridge . . . . (740) 439-1050
http://www.cambridgeoh.org

CUMBERLAND (village). Covers a land area of 0.483 square miles and a water area of 0 square miles. Located at 39.85° N. Lat.; 81.65° W. Long. Elevation is 843 feet.
Population: 318 (1990); 402 (2000); 406 (2007); 376 (2012 projected); Race: 99.0% White, 0.5% Black, 0.0% Asian, 0.0% Hispanic of any race (2007); Density: 840.2 persons per square mile (2007); Average household size: 2.74 (2007); Median age: 35.2 (2007); Males per 100 females: 106.1 (2007); Marriage status: 20.7% never married, 60.3% now married, 4.5% widowed, 14.5% divorced (2000); Foreign born: 0.5% (2000); Ancestry (includes multiple ancestries): 13.5% German, 12.3% United States or American, 11.0% Irish, 8.3% English, 7.8% Other groups (2000).
Economy: Employment by occupation: 9.6% management, 8.2% professional, 13.0% services, 20.5% sales, 2.7% farming, 13.7% construction, 32.2% production (2000).
Income: Per capita income: $13,214 (2007); Median household income: $35,000 (2007); Average household income: $36,250 (2007); Percent of households with income of $100,000 or more: 2.7% (2007); Poverty rate: 20.1% (2000).
Education: Percent of population age 25 and over with: High school diploma (including GED) or higher: 71.1% (2007); Bachelor's degree or higher: 2.8% (2007); Master's degree or higher: 0.0% (2007).
Housing: Homeownership rate: 79.7% (2007); Median home value: $49,500 (2007); Median rent: $275 per month (2000); Median age of housing: 60+ years (2000).
Transportation: Commute to work: 95.7% car, 0.0% public transportation, 0.0% walk, 4.3% work from home (2000); Travel time to work: 18.2% less than 15 minutes, 46.2% 15 to 30 minutes, 21.2% 30 to 45 minutes, 3.0% 45 to 60 minutes, 11.4% 60 minutes or more (2000)

FAIRVIEW (village). Covers a land area of 0.425 square miles and a water area of 0 square miles. Located at 40.05° N. Lat.; 81.23° W. Long. Elevation is 1,227 feet.
History: Fairview was once the leading U.S. producer of pennyroyal, an herb used in early medicines.
Population: 79 (1990); 81 (2000); 81 (2007); 77 (2012 projected); Race: 100.0% White, 0.0% Black, 0.0% Asian, 0.0% Hispanic of any race (2007); Density: 190.8 persons per square mile (2007); Average household size: 3.24 (2007); Median age: 44.4 (2007); Males per 100 females: 102.5 (2007); Marriage status: 15.9% never married, 74.6% now married, 3.2% widowed, 6.3% divorced (2000); Foreign born: 0.0% (2000); Ancestry (includes multiple ancestries): 26.1% Irish, 22.7% German, 14.8% Other groups, 11.4% United States or American, 10.2% English (2000).
Economy: Employment by occupation: 0.0% management, 0.0% professional, 21.4% services, 7.1% sales, 0.0% farming, 25.0% construction, 46.4% production (2000).
Income: Per capita income: $14,167 (2007); Median household income: $43,125 (2007); Average household income: $45,900 (2007); Percent of households with income of $100,000 or more: 0.0% (2007); Poverty rate: 9.1% (2000).
Education: Percent of population age 25 and over with: High school diploma (including GED) or higher: 72.7% (2007); Bachelor's degree or higher: 0.0% (2007); Master's degree or higher: 0.0% (2007).
Housing: Homeownership rate: 96.0% (2007); Median home value: $50,000 (2007); Median rent: $n/a per month (2000); Median age of housing: 60+ years (2000).
Transportation: Commute to work: 75.0% car, 17.9% public transportation, 0.0% walk, 0.0% work from home (2000); Travel time to work: 17.9% less than 15 minutes, 35.7% 15 to 30 minutes, 14.3% 30 to 45 minutes, 10.7% 45 to 60 minutes, 21.4% 60 minutes or more (2000)

KIMBOLTON (village). Covers a land area of 0.239 square miles and a water area of 0 square miles. Located at 40.15° N. Lat.; 81.57° W. Long. Elevation is 801 feet.
Population: 134 (1990); 190 (2000); 195 (2007); 193 (2012 projected); Race: 90.3% White, 3.6% Black, 0.0% Asian, 0.0% Hispanic of any race (2007); Density: 815.1 persons per square mile (2007); Average household size: 3.20 (2007); Median age: 46.0 (2007); Males per 100 females: 105.3 (2007); Marriage status: 30.6% never married, 48.6% now married, 12.5% widowed, 8.3% divorced (2000); Foreign born: 1.1% (2000); Ancestry (includes multiple ancestries): 14.5% United States or American, 10.2% English, 8.1% French (except Basque), 7.0% Irish, 5.4% European (2000).
Economy: Employment by occupation: 8.1% management, 11.3% professional, 14.5% services, 25.8% sales, 0.0% farming, 17.7% construction, 22.6% production (2000).
Income: Per capita income: $17,204 (2007); Median household income: $27,500 (2007); Average household income: $48,934 (2007); Percent of households with income of $100,000 or more: 4.9% (2007); Poverty rate: 30.5% (2000).
Education: Percent of population age 25 and over with: High school diploma (including GED) or higher: 66.9% (2007); Bachelor's degree or higher: 12.7% (2007); Master's degree or higher: 11.3% (2007).
Housing: Homeownership rate: 86.9% (2007); Median home value: $43,500 (2007); Median rent: $458 per month (2000); Median age of housing: 35 years (2000).
Transportation: Commute to work: 90.3% car, 0.0% public transportation, 6.5% walk, 3.2% work from home (2000); Travel time to work: 31.7% less than 15 minutes, 43.3% 15 to 30 minutes, 13.3% 30 to 45 minutes, 3.3% 45 to 60 minutes, 8.3% 60 minutes or more (2000)

LORE CITY (village). Covers a land area of 0.334 square miles and a water area of 0 square miles. Located at 39.98° N. Lat.; 81.45° W. Long. Elevation is 820 feet.
History: Lore City grew around the coal mines. Morgan's Confederate raiders burned buildings here on their flight across Ohio.
Population: 384 (1990); 305 (2000); 295 (2007); 289 (2012 projected); Race: 94.2% White, 0.0% Black, 0.0% Asian, 0.3% Hispanic of any race (2007); Density: 884.2 persons per square mile (2007); Average household size: 2.36 (2007); Median age: 40.7 (2007); Males per 100 females: 90.3 (2007); Marriage status: 22.8% never married, 65.3% now married, 7.8% widowed, 4.1% divorced (2000); Foreign born: 0.0% (2000); Ancestry (includes multiple ancestries): 15.6% German, 13.5% Irish, 12.8% United States or American, 12.8% English, 10.4% Dutch (2000).
Economy: Employment by occupation: 5.0% management, 17.1% professional, 23.6% services, 22.9% sales, 0.0% farming, 12.9% construction, 18.6% production (2000).
Income: Per capita income: $19,661 (2007); Median household income: $36,250 (2007); Average household income: $46,400 (2007); Percent of households with income of $100,000 or more: 3.2% (2007); Poverty rate: 14.2% (2000).
Education: Percent of population age 25 and over with: High school diploma (including GED) or higher: 78.9% (2007); Bachelor's degree or higher: 9.8% (2007); Master's degree or higher: 2.5% (2007).

School District(s)

East Guernsey Local (PK-12)
2005-06 Enrollment: 1,283 . . . . (740) 489-5190

Housing: Homeownership rate: 84.0% (2007); Median home value: $59,167 (2007); Median rent: $368 per month (2000); Median age of housing: 60+ years (2000).
Transportation: Commute to work: 90.4% car, 0.0% public transportation, 3.0% walk, 6.7% work from home (2000); Travel time to work: 18.3% less than 15 minutes, 54.8% 15 to 30 minutes, 7.1% 30 to 45 minutes, 10.3% 45 to 60 minutes, 9.5% 60 minutes or more (2000)

OLD WASHINGTON (village). Aka Washington. Covers a land area of 0.657 square miles and a water area of 0 square miles. Located at 40.03° N. Lat.; 81.44° W. Long. Elevation is 1,014 feet.
History: Old Washington was a stagecoach stop on the National Road, with several inns providing rooms and meals for travelers.
Population: 281 (1990); 265 (2000); 253 (2007); 244 (2012 projected); Race: 96.4% White, 2.4% Black, 1.2% Asian, 0.4% Hispanic of any race (2007); Density: 384.9 persons per square mile (2007); Average household size: 2.32 (2007); Median age: 46.1 (2007); Males per 100 females: 80.7 (2007); Marriage status: 19.1% never married, 58.2% now married, 8.8% widowed, 13.9% divorced (2000); Foreign born: 0.0% (2000); Ancestry (includes multiple ancestries): 18.1% Irish, 17.8% German, 11.5% United States or American, 9.1% English, 8.0% Other groups (2000).
Economy: Employment by occupation: 3.4% management, 10.9% professional, 15.1% services, 25.2% sales, 0.0% farming, 16.0% construction, 29.4% production (2000).
Income: Per capita income: $22,342 (2007); Median household income: $30,833 (2007); Average household income: $51,858 (2007); Percent of households with income of $100,000 or more: 6.4% (2007); Poverty rate: 13.9% (2000).
Education: Percent of population age 25 and over with: High school diploma (including GED) or higher: 83.8% (2007); Bachelor's degree or higher: 5.6% (2007); Master's degree or higher: 2.8% (2007).

School District(s)

East Guernsey Local (PK-12)
2005-06 Enrollment: 1,283 . . . . (740) 489-5190

Housing: Homeownership rate: 78.9% (2007); Median home value: $85,455 (2007); Median rent: $331 per month (2000); Median age of housing: 53 years (2000).
Transportation: Commute to work: 91.1% car, 0.0% public transportation, 8.0% walk, 0.9% work from home (2000); Travel time to work: 25.2% less than 15 minutes, 39.6% 15 to 30 minutes, 17.1% 30 to 45 minutes, 0.9% 45 to 60 minutes, 17.1% 60 minutes or more (2000)

PLEASANT CITY (village). Covers a land area of 0.186 square miles and a water area of 0 square miles. Located at 39.90° N. Lat.; 81.54° W. Long. Elevation is 823 feet.
History: Pleasant City, first called Point Pleasant, developed around the coal mines in the 1890's.
Population: 419 (1990); 439 (2000); 321 (2007); 324 (2012 projected); Race: 98.1% White, 0.6% Black, 0.0% Asian, 0.0% Hispanic of any race (2007); Density: 1,729.5 persons per square mile (2007); Average household size: 2.45 (2007); Median age: 38.5 (2007); Males per 100 females: 81.4 (2007); Marriage status: 22.0% never married, 59.1% now married, 8.7% widowed, 10.2% divorced (2000); Foreign born: 1.8% (2000); Ancestry (includes multiple ancestries): 19.5% German, 14.7% Irish, 12.7% United States or American, 11.3% Other groups, 7.7% English (2000).
Economy: Employment by occupation: 14.2% management, 9.7% professional, 21.6% services, 15.9% sales, 0.0% farming, 14.8% construction, 23.9% production (2000).
Income: Per capita income: $15,927 (2007); Median household income: $34,583 (2007); Average household income: $39,027 (2007); Percent of

households with income of $100,000 or more: 2.3% (2007); Poverty rate: 17.2% (2000).
Education: Percent of population age 25 and over with: High school diploma (including GED) or higher: 77.8% (2007); Bachelor's degree or higher: 8.3% (2007); Master's degree or higher: 3.2% (2007).
Housing: Homeownership rate: 77.9% (2007); Median home value: $51,111 (2007); Median rent: $278 per month (2000); Median age of housing: 60+ years (2000).
Transportation: Commute to work: 95.4% car, 1.7% public transportation, 2.9% walk, 0.0% work from home (2000); Travel time to work: 28.9% less than 15 minutes, 53.2% 15 to 30 minutes, 7.5% 30 to 45 minutes, 2.3% 45 to 60 minutes, 8.1% 60 minutes or more (2000)

QUAKER CITY (village). Covers a land area of 0.529 square miles and a water area of 0 square miles. Located at 39.97° N. Lat.; 81.29° W. Long. Elevation is 853 feet.
Population: 560 (1990); 563 (2000); 449 (2007); 452 (2012 projected); Race: 98.9% White, 0.2% Black, 0.0% Asian, 0.7% Hispanic of any race (2007); Density: 848.2 persons per square mile (2007); Average household size: 2.60 (2007); Median age: 35.2 (2007); Males per 100 females: 96.1 (2007); Marriage status: 19.2% never married, 61.4% now married, 9.3% widowed, 10.1% divorced (2000); Foreign born: 0.3% (2000); Ancestry (includes multiple ancestries): 22.7% United States or American, 15.0% Irish, 9.9% German, 9.0% English, 3.9% Scotch-Irish (2000).
Economy: Employment by occupation: 6.1% management, 7.0% professional, 16.5% services, 23.9% sales, 0.0% farming, 13.5% construction, 33.0% production (2000).
Income: Per capita income: $12,622 (2007); Median household income: $28,026 (2007); Average household income: $32,760 (2007); Percent of households with income of $100,000 or more: 1.2% (2007); Poverty rate: 16.0% (2000).
Education: Percent of population age 25 and over with: High school diploma (including GED) or higher: 79.8% (2007); Bachelor's degree or higher: 8.6% (2007); Master's degree or higher: 3.4% (2007).

School District(s)

East Guernsey Local (PK-12)
2005-06 Enrollment: 1,283 . . . . (740) 489-5190
Housing: Homeownership rate: 69.9% (2007); Median home value: $51,786 (2007); Median rent: $256 per month (2000); Median age of housing: 60+ years (2000).
Transportation: Commute to work: 92.4% car, 0.0% public transportation, 4.9% walk, 2.7% work from home (2000); Travel time to work: 18.3% less than 15 minutes, 22.9% 15 to 30 minutes, 39.4% 30 to 45 minutes, 11.9% 45 to 60 minutes, 7.3% 60 minutes or more (2000)

SALESVILLE (village). Covers a land area of 0.098 square miles and a water area of 0 square miles. Located at 39.97° N. Lat.; 81.33° W. Long. Elevation is 866 feet.
History: Salesville was established near Leatherwood Creek, and was the setting for William Dean Howells' novel "The Leatherwood God."
Population: 84 (1990); 154 (2000); 147 (2007); 142 (2012 projected); Race: 98.6% White, 0.0% Black, 0.0% Asian, 0.0% Hispanic of any race (2007); Density: 1,496.3 persons per square mile (2007); Average household size: 2.88 (2007); Median age: 38.7 (2007); Males per 100 females: 88.5 (2007); Marriage status: 14.7% never married, 63.8% now married, 8.6% widowed, 12.9% divorced (2000); Foreign born: 0.0% (2000); Ancestry (includes multiple ancestries): 33.6% German, 17.4% Irish, 14.8% United States or American, 6.0% Scottish, 4.7% French (except Basque) (2000).
Economy: Employment by occupation: 4.4% management, 0.0% professional, 4.4% services, 32.4% sales, 0.0% farming, 29.4% construction, 29.4% production (2000).
Income: Per capita income: $14,507 (2007); Median household income: $42,500 (2007); Average household income: $41,814 (2007); Percent of households with income of $100,000 or more: 0.0% (2007); Poverty rate: 12.3% (2000).
Education: Percent of population age 25 and over with: High school diploma (including GED) or higher: 86.6% (2007); Bachelor's degree or higher: 5.2% (2007); Master's degree or higher: 0.0% (2007).
Housing: Homeownership rate: 96.1% (2007); Median home value: $51,250 (2007); Median rent: $225 per month (2000); Median age of housing: 58 years (2000).
Transportation: Commute to work: 97.1% car, 0.0% public transportation, 2.9% walk, 0.0% work from home (2000); Travel time to work: 13.2% less than 15 minutes, 58.8% 15 to 30 minutes, 17.6% 30 to 45 minutes, 0.0% 45 to 60 minutes, 10.3% 60 minutes or more (2000)

SENECAVILLE (village). Covers a land area of 0.486 square miles and a water area of 0 square miles. Located at 39.93° N. Lat.; 81.46° W. Long. Elevation is 892 feet.
Population: 434 (1990); 453 (2000); 443 (2007); 434 (2012 projected); Race: 100.0% White, 0.0% Black, 0.0% Asian, 0.0% Hispanic of any race (2007); Density: 910.7 persons per square mile (2007); Average household size: 2.53 (2007); Median age: 37.6 (2007); Males per 100 females: 86.9 (2007); Marriage status: 22.3% never married, 55.6% now married, 7.4% widowed, 14.6% divorced (2000); Foreign born: 0.4% (2000); Ancestry (includes multiple ancestries): 17.4% English, 16.2% German, 13.4% Irish, 11.9% United States or American, 5.7% Slovak (2000).
Economy: Employment by occupation: 2.6% management, 17.2% professional, 23.4% services, 18.8% sales, 0.5% farming, 14.1% construction, 23.4% production (2000).
Income: Per capita income: $15,948 (2007); Median household income: $32,115 (2007); Average household income: $40,371 (2007); Percent of households with income of $100,000 or more: 8.0% (2007); Poverty rate: 17.2% (2000).
Education: Percent of population age 25 and over with: High school diploma (including GED) or higher: 83.2% (2007); Bachelor's degree or higher: 6.2% (2007); Master's degree or higher: 1.0% (2007).

School District(s)

Mid-East Career and Technology Centers (PK-12)
2005-06 Enrollment: n/a . . . . (740) 454-0105
Rolling Hills Local (PK-12)
2005-06 Enrollment: 2,151 . . . . (740) 432-5370
Housing: Homeownership rate: 77.1% (2007); Median home value: $63,000 (2007); Median rent: $311 per month (2000); Median age of housing: 60+ years (2000).
Transportation: Commute to work: 95.2% car, 0.0% public transportation, 3.8% walk, 0.0% work from home (2000); Travel time to work: 14.5% less than 15 minutes, 57.0% 15 to 30 minutes, 10.2% 30 to 45 minutes, 6.5% 45 to 60 minutes, 11.8% 60 minutes or more (2000)

Hamilton County

Located in southwestern Ohio; bounded on the west by Indiana, and on the south by the Ohio River and the Kentucky border; drained by Great Miami, Little Miami, and Whitewater Rivers. Covers a land area of 407.36 square miles, a water area of 5.42 square miles, and is located in the Eastern Time Zone. The county was founded in 1790. County seat is Cincinnati.

Hamilton County is part of the Cincinnati-Middletown, OH-KY-IN Metropolitan Statistical Area. The entire metro area includes: Dearborn County, IN; Franklin County, IN; Ohio County, IN; Boone County, KY; Bracken County, KY; Campbell County, KY; Gallatin County, KY; Grant County, KY; Kenton County, KY; Pendleton County, KY; Brown County, OH; Butler County, OH; Clermont County, OH; Hamilton County, OH; Warren County, OH

Weather Station: Cincinnati Fernbank — Elevation: 498 feet

	Jan	Feb	Mar	Apr	May	Jun	Jul	Aug	Sep	Oct	Nov	Dec
High	38	44	54	65	75	82	87	85	79	67	55	44
Low	20	23	31	40	50	60	64	63	55	43	35	26
Precip	3.5	2.9	4.4	4.4	5.5	4.6	4.5	4.1	2.9	3.3	3.7	3.6
Snow	6.7	na	2.6	0.1	tr	0.0	0.0	0.0	0.0	tr	0.4	2.2

High and Low temperatures in degrees Fahrenheit; Precipitation and Snow in inches

Weather Station: Cincinnati Lunken Airport — Elevation: 488 feet

	Jan	Feb	Mar	Apr	May	Jun	Jul	Aug	Sep	Oct	Nov	Dec
High	38	43	54	65	75	83	87	85	79	67	55	44
Low	22	25	34	43	53	62	67	65	57	45	36	28
Precip	2.7	2.4	3.9	3.7	4.6	4.0	3.8	4.1	3.1	3.0	3.4	3.2
Snow	4.6	3.7	2.6	0.2	tr	tr	tr	0.0	0.0	0.1	0.4	1.6

High and Low temperatures in degrees Fahrenheit; Precipitation and Snow in inches

Population: 866,228 (1990); 845,303 (2000); 795,920 (2007); 758,800 (2012 projected); Race: 70.8% White, 25.0% Black, 1.7% Asian, 1.5% Hispanic of any race (2007); Density: 1,953.8 persons per square mile (2007); Average household size: 2.38 (2007); Median age: 37.7 (2007); Males per 100 females: 92.2 (2007).

Religion: Five largest groups: 26.8% Catholic Church, 3.6% The United Methodist Church, 2.7% Jewish Estimate, 2.3% Presbyterian Church (U.S.A.), 1.8% Southern Baptist Convention (2000).
Economy: Unemployment rate: 5.9% (6/2008); Total civilian labor force: 438,200 (6/2008); Leading industries: 16.8% health care and social assistance; 11.8% manufacturing; 10.9% retail trade (2005); Farms: 399 totaling 29,520 acres (2002); Companies that employ 500 or more persons: 83 (2006); Companies that employ 100 to 499 persons: 726 (2006); Companies that employ less than 100 persons: 22,530 (2006); Black-owned businesses: 6,000 (2002); Hispanic-owned businesses: 684 (2002); Asian-owned businesses: 1,337 (2002); Women-owned businesses: 18,645 (2002); Retail sales per capita: $17,228 (2008). Single-family building permits issued: 693 (2007); Multi-family building permits issued: 583 (2007).
Income: Per capita income: $28,829 (2007); Median household income: $47,988 (2007); Average household income: $68,064 (2007); Percent of households with income of $100,000 or more: 18.3% (2007); Poverty rate: 14.0% (2005); Bankruptcy rate: 3.87% (2007).
Education: Percent of population age 25 and over with: High school diploma (including GED) or higher: 82.9% (2007); Bachelor's degree or higher: 29.2% (2007); Master's degree or higher: 10.7% (2007).
Housing: Homeownership rate: 60.7% (2007); Median home value: $133,751 (2007); Median rent: $424 per month (2000); Median age of housing: 42 years (2000).
Health: Birth rate: 131.1 per 10,000 population (2007); Death rate: 94.8 per 10,000 population (2007); Age-adjusted cancer mortality rate: 191.5 deaths per 100,000 population (2005); Air Quality Index: 52.9% good, 36.4% moderate, 10.1% unhealthy for sensitive individuals, 0.5% unhealthy (percent of days in 2007); Number of physicians: 48.3 per 10,000 population (2005); Hospital beds: 43.4 per 10,000 population (2004); Hospital admissions: 2,010.5 per 10,000 population (2004).
Elections: 2004 Presidential election results: 52.5% Bush, 47.1% Kerry, 0.0% Nader, 0.2% Badnarik
National and State Parks: Harrison State Park; Kroger Hills State Reserve; LIttle Miami State Scenic River; Little Miami Scenic State Park; William Howard Taft National Historic Site
Additional Information Contacts
Hamilton County Government . . . . (513) 946-4400
http://www.hamilton-co.org
Anderson Area Chamber of Commerce. . . . . (513) 474-4802
http://www.andersonareachamber.org
Cincinnati USA Convention & Visitors Bureau. . . . . (513) 621-2142
http://www.cincyusa.com
Cincinnati USA Regional Chamber . . . . (513) 579-3100
http://www.cincinnatichamber.com
City of Blue Ash . . . . (513) 745-8500
http://www.blueash.com
City of Cheviot . . . . (513) 661-2700
http://www.cheviot.org
City of Cincinnati . . . . (513) 591-6000
http://www.cincinnati-oh.gov
City of Forest Park . . . . (513) 595-5200
http://www.forestpark.org
City of Harrison . . . . (513) 367-3730
http://www.harrisonoh.org
City of Loveland . . . . (513) 683-0150
http://www.lovelandoh.com
City of Madeira. . . . . (513) 561-7228
http://www.madeiracity.com
City of Montgomery . . . . (513) 891-2424
http://www.ci.montgomery.oh.us
City of Mount Healthy. . . . . (513) 931-8840
http://www.mthealthy.org
City of North College Hill . . . . (513) 521-7413
http://www.northcollegehill.org
City of Norwood . . . . (513) 458-4501
http://www.norwood-ohio.com
City of Reading . . . . (513) 733-3725
http://www.readingohio.org
City of Sharonville . . . . (513) 563-1144
http://www.sharonville.org
City of Springdale. . . . . (513) 346-5700
http://www.springdale.org
City of Wyoming. . . . . (513) 821-7600
http://www.wyoming.oh.us
Grandview-Marble Cliff Area Chamber of Commerce . . . . . (614) 486-0196
http://www.grandviewchamber.org
Loveland Area Chamber of Commerce . . . . (513) 683-1544
http://www.lovelandchamber.org
Northern Cincinnati Convention & Visitors Bureau . . . . (513) 771-5353
http://www.cincynorth.com
Norwood Chamber of Commerce . . . . (513) 956-7935
http://www.norwoodchamber.org
Over-the-Rhine Chamber of Commerce . . . . (513) 241-2690
http://www.otrchamber.com
Reading Chamber of Commerce . . . . (513) 786-7274
http://www.readingohiochamber.org
Sharonville Chamber of Commerce. . . . . (513) 554-1722
http://www.sharonvillechamber.com
Village of Cleves . . . . (513) 941-5127
http://www.cleves.org
Village of Fairfax . . . . (513) 527-6503
http://www.fairfaxohio.org
Village of Glendale. . . . . (513) 771-7200
http://www.glendaleohio.org
Village of Golf Manor . . . . (513) 531-7418
http://www.golfmanor.org
Village of Greenhills. . . . . (513) 825-2100
http://www.greenhillsohio.org
Village of Lockland. . . . . (513) 761-1124
http://www.lockland.com

Hamilton County Communities

ADDYSTON (village). Covers a land area of 0.867 square miles and a water area of 0.041 square miles. Located at 39.13° N. Lat.; 84.71° W. Long. Elevation is 472 feet.
History: Addyston became a town in 1871 when Matthew Addy of Cincinnati established a pipe foundry.
Population: 1,198 (1990); 1,010 (2000); 787 (2007); 751 (2012 projected); Race: 88.7% White, 6.6% Black, 0.5% Asian, 2.3% Hispanic of any race (2007); Density: 907.9 persons per square mile (2007); Average household size: 2.70 (2007); Median age: 32.9 (2007); Males per 100 females: 96.8 (2007); Marriage status: 30.3% never married, 49.1% now married, 7.1% widowed, 13.5% divorced (2000); Foreign born: 1.2% (2000); Ancestry (includes multiple ancestries): 26.5% Other groups, 25.2% German, 15.6% Irish, 14.2% United States or American, 8.1% English (2000).
Economy: Single-family building permits issued: 0 (2007); Multi-family building permits issued: 0 (2007); Employment by occupation: 11.2% management, 8.5% professional, 25.6% services, 18.4% sales, 0.0% farming, 22.1% construction, 14.1% production (2000).
Income: Per capita income: $18,412 (2007); Median household income: $43,068 (2007); Average household income: $49,794 (2007); Percent of households with income of $100,000 or more: 9.3% (2007); Poverty rate: 11.6% (2000).
Education: Percent of population age 25 and over with: High school diploma (including GED) or higher: 61.0% (2007); Bachelor's degree or higher: 2.4% (2007); Master's degree or higher: 0.6% (2007).

School District(s)

Three Rivers Local (PK-12)
2005-06 Enrollment: 1,993 . . . . (513) 941-6400
Housing: Homeownership rate: 55.7% (2007); Median home value: $70,000 (2007); Median rent: $423 per month (2000); Median age of housing: 60+ years (2000).
Transportation: Commute to work: 93.8% car, 3.0% public transportation, 2.2% walk, 0.5% work from home (2000); Travel time to work: 26.4% less than 15 minutes, 27.4% 15 to 30 minutes, 28.3% 30 to 45 minutes, 11.1% 45 to 60 minutes, 6.8% 60 minutes or more (2000)

AMBERLEY (village). Covers a land area of 3.476 square miles and a water area of 0 square miles. Located at 39.19° N. Lat.; 84.42° W. Long. Elevation is 797 feet.
Population: 3,108 (1990); 3,425 (2000); 3,319 (2007); 3,180 (2012 projected); Race: 84.1% White, 11.8% Black, 2.5% Asian, 0.6% Hispanic of any race (2007); Density: 954.9 persons per square mile (2007); Average household size: 2.56 (2007); Median age: 50.5 (2007); Males per 100 females: 96.0 (2007); Marriage status: 12.1% never married, 76.3% now married, 6.7% widowed, 4.8% divorced (2000); Foreign born: 6.7% (2000); Ancestry (includes multiple ancestries): 21.9% German, 16.6% Other groups, 9.8% Irish, 9.5% United States or American, 9.2% Polish (2000).

Economy: Employment by occupation: 26.9% management, 33.7% professional, 5.8% services, 27.3% sales, 0.0% farming, 2.3% construction, 3.9% production (2000).
Income: Per capita income: $52,306 (2007); Median household income: $93,750 (2007); Average household income: $134,058 (2007); Percent of households with income of $100,000 or more: 46.7% (2007); Poverty rate: 3.5% (2000).
Education: Percent of population age 25 and over with: High school diploma (including GED) or higher: 94.6% (2007); Bachelor's degree or higher: 63.1% (2007); Master's degree or higher: 31.5% (2007).
Housing: Homeownership rate: 97.9% (2007); Median home value: $252,108 (2007); Median rent: $1,500 per month (2000); Median age of housing: 42 years (2000).
Safety: Violent crime rate: 3.1 per 10,000 population; Property crime rate: 156.1 per 10,000 population (2007).
Transportation: Commute to work: 95.4% car, 1.9% public transportation, 0.0% walk, 2.6% work from home (2000); Travel time to work: 24.8% less than 15 minutes, 56.1% 15 to 30 minutes, 15.2% 30 to 45 minutes, 2.0% 45 to 60 minutes, 2.1% 60 minutes or more (2000)

ARLINGTON HEIGHTS (village). Covers a land area of 0.257 square miles and a water area of 0 square miles. Located at 39.21° N. Lat.; 84.45° W. Long. Elevation is 554 feet.
Population: 1,084 (1990); 899 (2000); 798 (2007); 728 (2012 projected); Race: 91.7% White, 2.8% Black, 0.0% Asian, 0.8% Hispanic of any race (2007); Density: 3,101.5 persons per square mile (2007); Average household size: 2.27 (2007); Median age: 36.7 (2007); Males per 100 females: 98.5 (2007); Marriage status: 27.4% never married, 46.1% now married, 8.0% widowed, 18.4% divorced (2000); Foreign born: 0.7% (2000); Ancestry (includes multiple ancestries): 26.7% German, 18.0% United States or American, 12.6% Irish, 10.7% Other groups, 7.0% English (2000).
Economy: Single-family building permits issued: 0 (2007); Multi-family building permits issued: 0 (2007); Employment by occupation: 8.1% management, 6.8% professional, 19.1% services, 26.3% sales, 0.0% farming, 15.9% construction, 23.8% production (2000).
Income: Per capita income: $20,977 (2007); Median household income: $35,132 (2007); Average household income: $47,692 (2007); Percent of households with income of $100,000 or more: 7.1% (2007); Poverty rate: 13.0% (2000).
Education: Percent of population age 25 and over with: High school diploma (including GED) or higher: 68.1% (2007); Bachelor's degree or higher: 4.6% (2007); Master's degree or higher: 0.8% (2007).
Housing: Homeownership rate: 56.4% (2007); Median home value: $87,222 (2007); Median rent: $388 per month (2000); Median age of housing: 60+ years (2000).
Transportation: Commute to work: 96.0% car, 0.9% public transportation, 1.3% walk, 0.9% work from home (2000); Travel time to work: 24.2% less than 15 minutes, 52.1% 15 to 30 minutes, 16.7% 30 to 45 minutes, 4.1% 45 to 60 minutes, 2.8% 60 minutes or more (2000)

BLUE ASH (city). Covers a land area of 7.655 square miles and a water area of 0.014 square miles. Located at 39.24° N. Lat.; 84.37° W. Long. Elevation is 846 feet.
Population: 11,905 (1990); 12,513 (2000); 11,514 (2007); 10,788 (2012 projected); Race: 85.2% White, 5.5% Black, 7.5% Asian, 1.3% Hispanic of any race (2007); Density: 1,504.1 persons per square mile (2007); Average household size: 2.46 (2007); Median age: 42.2 (2007); Males per 100 females: 93.5 (2007); Marriage status: 24.0% never married, 60.4% now married, 6.3% widowed, 9.2% divorced (2000); Foreign born: 10.0% (2000); Ancestry (includes multiple ancestries): 29.8% German, 16.4% Other groups, 13.4% Irish, 11.5% English, 6.7% United States or American (2000).
Economy: Single-family building permits issued: 15 (2007); Multi-family building permits issued: 0 (2007); Employment by occupation: 18.2% management, 34.9% professional, 8.9% services, 25.2% sales, 0.2% farming, 4.3% construction, 8.2% production (2000).
Income: Per capita income: $42,590 (2007); Median household income: $72,941 (2007); Average household income: $104,251 (2007); Percent of households with income of $100,000 or more: 34.0% (2007); Poverty rate: 4.7% (2000).
Taxes: Total city taxes per capita: $2,184 (2006); City property taxes per capita: $193 (2006).
Education: Percent of population age 25 and over with: High school diploma (including GED) or higher: 90.7% (2007); Bachelor's degree or higher: 49.4% (2007); Master's degree or higher: 23.7% (2007).

Four-year College(s)

University of Cincinnati-Raymond Walters College (Public)
Fall 2007 Enrollment: 4,257. . . . . (513) 745-5600
2007-08 Tuition: In-state $5,232; Out-of-state $13,566

Housing: Homeownership rate: 73.8% (2007); Median home value: $179,205 (2007); Median rent: $724 per month (2000); Median age of housing: 25 years (2000).
Safety: Violent crime rate: 7.0 per 10,000 population; Property crime rate: 220.0 per 10,000 population (2007).
Transportation: Commute to work: 92.9% car, 1.5% public transportation, 1.4% walk, 3.4% work from home (2000); Travel time to work: 30.3% less than 15 minutes, 49.1% 15 to 30 minutes, 16.6% 30 to 45 minutes, 2.6% 45 to 60 minutes, 1.4% 60 minutes or more (2000)

Additional Information Contacts

City of Blue Ash . . . . (513) 745-8500
http://www.blueash.com

BRIDGETOWN NORTH (CDP). Covers a land area of 3.365 square miles and a water area of 0 square miles. Located at 39.15° N. Lat.; 84.63° W. Long.
Population: 11,760 (1990); 12,569 (2000); 12,224 (2007); 11,901 (2012 projected); Race: 97.8% White, 0.5% Black, 0.7% Asian, 0.7% Hispanic of any race (2007); Density: 3,632.6 persons per square mile (2007); Average household size: 2.40 (2007); Median age: 40.9 (2007); Males per 100 females: 89.8 (2007); Marriage status: 22.2% never married, 58.7% now married, 11.2% widowed, 8.0% divorced (2000); Foreign born: 1.7% (2000); Ancestry (includes multiple ancestries): 57.0% German, 18.0% Irish, 9.4% English, 7.4% Italian, 5.7% United States or American (2000).
Economy: Employment by occupation: 11.9% management, 18.7% professional, 14.3% services, 34.1% sales, 0.0% farming, 10.1% construction, 11.0% production (2000).
Income: Per capita income: $27,023 (2007); Median household income: $52,608 (2007); Average household income: $64,900 (2007); Percent of households with income of $100,000 or more: 15.2% (2007); Poverty rate: 3.3% (2000).
Education: Percent of population age 25 and over with: High school diploma (including GED) or higher: 86.3% (2007); Bachelor's degree or higher: 19.0% (2007); Master's degree or higher: 5.0% (2007).
Housing: Homeownership rate: 86.8% (2007); Median home value: $123,515 (2007); Median rent: $467 per month (2000); Median age of housing: 42 years (2000).
Transportation: Commute to work: 95.0% car, 1.8% public transportation, 1.0% walk, 1.7% work from home (2000); Travel time to work: 24.9% less than 15 minutes, 38.1% 15 to 30 minutes, 27.2% 30 to 45 minutes, 6.8% 45 to 60 minutes, 3.0% 60 minutes or more (2000)

CAMP DENNISON (unincorporated postal area, zip code 45111). Covers a land area of 1.636 square miles and a water area of 0 square miles. Located at 39.19° N. Lat.; 84.29° W. Long. Elevation is 577 feet.
Population: 430 (2000); Race: 71.6% White, 26.4% Black, 0.0% Asian, 13.1% Hispanic of any race (2000); Density: 262.9 persons per square mile (2000); Age: 13.1% under 18, 17.3% over 64 (2000); Marriage status: 29.2% never married, 40.3% now married, 13.3% widowed, 17.2% divorced (2000); Foreign born: 3.8% (2000); Ancestry (includes multiple ancestries): 39.4% Other groups, 26.6% Irish, 20.1% German, 17.1% English, 7.5% United States or American (2000).
Economy: Employment by occupation: 15.4% management, 9.4% professional, 7.7% services, 43.2% sales, 0.0% farming, 16.2% construction, 8.1% production (2000).
Income: Per capita income: $29,257 (2000); Median household income: $63,250 (2000); Poverty rate: 0.0% (2000).
Education: Percent of population age 25 and over with: High school diploma (including GED) or higher: 79.6% (2000); Bachelor's degree or higher: 32.2% (2000).
Housing: Homeownership rate: 81.3% (2000); Median home value: $89,000 (2000); Median rent: $529 per month (2000); Median age of housing: 51 years (2000).
Transportation: Commute to work: 93.2% car, 3.4% public transportation, 0.0% walk, 3.4% work from home (2000); Travel time to work: 20.4% less than 15 minutes, 55.3% 15 to 30 minutes, 18.1% 30 to 45 minutes, 0.0% 45 to 60 minutes, 6.2% 60 minutes or more (2000)

CHERRY GROVE (CDP). Covers a land area of 1.128 square miles and a water area of 0 square miles. Located at 39.08° N. Lat.; 84.31° W. Long. Elevation is 873 feet.
Population: 4,972 (1990); 4,555 (2000); 4,193 (2007); 3,912 (2012 projected); Race: 95.5% White, 1.4% Black, 1.7% Asian, 1.1% Hispanic of any race (2007); Density: 3,717.2 persons per square mile (2007); Average household size: 2.90 (2007); Median age: 38.9 (2007); Males per 100 females: 93.5 (2007); Marriage status: 17.3% never married, 71.2% now married, 4.0% widowed, 7.5% divorced (2000); Foreign born: 2.4% (2000); Ancestry (includes multiple ancestries): 41.8% German, 22.8% Irish, 12.7% English, 10.9% Italian, 6.2% Other groups (2000).
Economy: Employment by occupation: 15.3% management, 27.1% professional, 10.9% services, 32.2% sales, 0.0% farming, 4.3% construction, 10.2% production (2000).
Income: Per capita income: $28,142 (2007); Median household income: $75,599 (2007); Average household income: $81,716 (2007); Percent of households with income of $100,000 or more: 27.4% (2007); Poverty rate: 0.5% (2000).
Education: Percent of population age 25 and over with: High school diploma (including GED) or higher: 94.4% (2007); Bachelor's degree or higher: 33.2% (2007); Master's degree or higher: 9.9% (2007).
Housing: Homeownership rate: 95.7% (2007); Median home value: $157,135 (2007); Median rent: $813 per month (2000); Median age of housing: 31 years (2000).
Transportation: Commute to work: 90.3% car, 3.1% public transportation, 2.3% walk, 3.6% work from home (2000); Travel time to work: 22.6% less than 15 minutes, 35.0% 15 to 30 minutes, 32.1% 30 to 45 minutes, 7.2% 45 to 60 minutes, 3.1% 60 minutes or more (2000)

CHEVIOT (city). Covers a land area of 1.163 square miles and a water area of <.001 square miles. Located at 39.15° N. Lat.; 84.61° W. Long. Elevation is 909 feet.
History: Settled early 1800s; incorporated 1904.
Population: 9,629 (1990); 9,015 (2000); 8,042 (2007); 7,359 (2012 projected); Race: 96.5% White, 0.7% Black, 0.6% Asian, 1.5% Hispanic of any race (2007); Density: 6,916.6 persons per square mile (2007); Average household size: 2.15 (2007); Median age: 37.9 (2007); Males per 100 females: 90.6 (2007); Marriage status: 24.8% never married, 52.2% now married, 10.7% widowed, 12.3% divorced (2000); Foreign born: 1.6% (2000); Ancestry (includes multiple ancestries): 44.7% German, 15.4% Irish, 9.3% United States or American, 7.7% English, 5.2% Italian (2000).
Economy: Single-family building permits issued: 1 (2007); Multi-family building permits issued: 0 (2007); Employment by occupation: 10.7% management, 16.7% professional, 15.7% services, 31.4% sales, 0.0% farming, 14.4% construction, 11.1% production (2000).
Income: Per capita income: $23,250 (2007); Median household income: $39,897 (2007); Average household income: $49,353 (2007); Percent of households with income of $100,000 or more: 7.1% (2007); Poverty rate: 7.6% (2000).
Education: Percent of population age 25 and over with: High school diploma (including GED) or higher: 77.2% (2007); Bachelor's degree or higher: 16.4% (2007); Master's degree or higher: 3.8% (2007).
Housing: Homeownership rate: 61.6% (2007); Median home value: $107,502 (2007); Median rent: $387 per month (2000); Median age of housing: 55 years (2000).
Transportation: Commute to work: 91.9% car, 4.0% public transportation, 2.5% walk, 1.2% work from home (2000); Travel time to work: 22.0% less than 15 minutes, 46.1% 15 to 30 minutes, 26.4% 30 to 45 minutes, 4.2% 45 to 60 minutes, 1.4% 60 minutes or more (2000)
Additional Information Contacts
City of Cheviot . . . . (513) 661-2700
http://www.cheviot.org

CINCINNATI (city). County seat. Covers a land area of 77.968 square miles and a water area of 1.599 square miles. Located at 39.13° N. Lat.; 84.50° W. Long. Elevation is 627 feet.
History: Cincinnati was settled at an Ohio River crossroads in 1788 when developers platted a village that they named Losantiville. In 1790 the name was changed to Cincinnati by General Arthur St. Clair, Governor of the Northwest Territory, in honor of the Revolutionary Officers' Society. The Ohio River was the avenue down which settlers came to find space to establish farms, and Cincinnati became the center of commerce. Immigrants from Germany and Ireland joined other Europeans who came straight to Cincinnati. Steamboat travel on the Ohio River and the opening of the Miami & Erie Canal spurred trading. When Charles Dickens visited Cincinnati in 1842, he described it as "a place that commends itself... favorably and pleasantly to a stranger." The Civil War tore Cincinnati apart. Its sympathies were with the North, but its trade was with the South, and there was great rejoicing when the war ended.
Population: 363,974 (1990); 331,285 (2000); 302,545 (2007); 282,712 (2012 projected); Race: 49.1% White, 46.0% Black, 1.7% Asian, 1.8% Hispanic of any race (2007); Density: 3,880.4 persons per square mile (2007); Average household size: 2.18 (2007); Median age: 34.8 (2007); Males per 100 females: 91.1 (2007); Marriage status: 42.4% never married, 37.9% now married, 7.6% widowed, 12.1% divorced (2000); Foreign born: 3.8% (2000); Ancestry (includes multiple ancestries): 40.7% Other groups, 19.9% German, 10.4% Irish, 5.4% English, 4.8% United States or American (2000).
Economy: Unemployment rate: 6.4% (6/2008); Total civilian labor force: 168,910 (6/2008); Single-family building permits issued: 102 (2007); Multi-family building permits issued: 356 (2007); Employment by occupation: 12.6% management, 23.2% professional, 17.9% services, 26.3% sales, 0.1% farming, 6.4% construction, 13.5% production (2000).
Income: Per capita income: $23,691 (2007); Median household income: $33,981 (2007); Average household income: $50,597 (2007); Percent of households with income of $100,000 or more: 10.8% (2007); Poverty rate: 21.9% (2000).
Taxes: Total city taxes per capita: $1,221 (2006); City property taxes per capita: $204 (2006).
Education: Percent of population age 25 and over with: High school diploma (including GED) or higher: 77.0% (2007); Bachelor's degree or higher: 27.0% (2007); Master's degree or higher: 10.4% (2007).

School District(s)

A.B. Miree Fundamental Academy (KG-08)
2005-06 Enrollment: 467 . . . . (513) 351-8034
Alliance Academy of Cincinnati (KG-07)
2005-06 Enrollment: 493 . . . . (513) 751-5555
Cincinnati City (PK-12)
2005-06 Enrollment: 36,872 . . . . (513) 363-0000
Cincinnati College Preparatory Academy (KG-08)
2005-06 Enrollment: 531 . . . . (513) 684-0777
Cincinnati Leadership Academy
2005-06 Enrollment: n/a . . . . (513) 651-9624
Cincinnati Preparatory and Fitness Academy (KG-05)
2005-06 Enrollment: 33 . . . . (513) 587-6280
Cincinnati Speech & Reading Intervention Center (01-10)
2005-06 Enrollment: 224 . . . . (513) 651-9624
Deer Park Community City (PK-12)
2005-06 Enrollment: 1,422 . . . . (513) 891-0222
Dohn Community (09-12)
2005-06 Enrollment: 53 . . . . (513) 281-6100
East End Comm Heritage School (KG-12)
2005-06 Enrollment: 189 . . . . (937) 222-7355
Finneytown Local (PK-12)
2005-06 Enrollment: 1,733 . . . . (513) 728-3700
Forest Hills Local (PK-12)
2005-06 Enrollment: 7,634 . . . . (513) 231-3600
Great Oaks Inst of Technology (PK-12)
2005-06 Enrollment: n/a . . . . (513) 771-8840
Harmony Community School (06-12)
2005-06 Enrollment: 762 . . . . (513) 921-5260
Horizon Science Academy-Cincinnati (05-08)
2005-06 Enrollment: 179 . . . . (513) 242-0099
Indian Hill Exempted Village (PK-12)
2005-06 Enrollment: 2,251 . . . . (513) 272-4500
International College Preparatory Academy (KG-08)
2005-06 Enrollment: 509 . . . . (513) 241-1141
King Academy Community School (KG-08)
2005-06 Enrollment: 144 . . . . (513) 421-7519
Lakota Local (PK-12)
2005-06 Enrollment: 17,455 . . . . (513) 874-5505
Life Skills Center of Hamilton County (09-12)
2005-06 Enrollment: 221 . . . . (513) 821-6695
Life Skills Ctr of Cincinnati (09-12)
2005-06 Enrollment: 308 . . . . (513) 475-0222
Lighthouse Community Sch Inc (06-12)
2005-06 Enrollment: 61 . . . . (513) 561-7888
Lockland Local (PK-12)
2005-06 Enrollment: 694 . . . . (513) 563-5000

Madeira City (PK-12)
2005-06 Enrollment: 1,552 . . . . (513) 985-6070
Mariemont City (PK-12)
2005-06 Enrollment: 1,658 . . . . (513) 272-7500
Maud Booth Academy (KG-06)
2005-06 Enrollment: 126 . . . . (513) 241-1121
Mount Healthy City (PK-12)
2005-06 Enrollment: 3,729 . . . . (513) 729-0077
Mount Healthy Preparatory and Fitness Academy (KG-05)
2005-06 Enrollment: 35. . . . .
New Richmond Exempted Village (PK-12)
2005-06 Enrollment: 2,502 . . . . (513) 553-2616
North College Hill City (PK-12)
2005-06 Enrollment: 1,587 . . . . (513) 728-4770
Northwest Local (PK-12)
2005-06 Enrollment: 10,600 . . . . (513) 923-1000
Oak Hills Local (PK-12)
2005-06 Enrollment: 8,204 . . . . (513) 574-3200
Oak Tree Montessori (KG-05)
2005-06 Enrollment: 39 . . . . (513) 241-0448
Ohio Connections Academy Inc (KG-09)
2005-06 Enrollment: 810 . . . . (513) 533-3230
Orion Academy (KG-06)
2005-06 Enrollment: 471 . . . . (513) 251-6000
P.A.C.E. High School (09-12)
2005-06 Enrollment: 423 . . . . (513) 751-7223
Phoenix Community Learning Ctr (KG-08)
2005-06 Enrollment: 348 . . . . (513) 351-5801
Princeton City (PK-12)
2005-06 Enrollment: 5,713 . . . . (513) 771-8560
Riverside Academy (KG-08)
2005-06 Enrollment: 535 . . . . (513) 921-7777
St Bernard-Elmwood Place City (PK-12)
2005-06 Enrollment: 1,120 . . . . (513) 482-7121
Summit Academy Cincinnati (KG-06)
2005-06 Enrollment: 36 . . . . (513) 321-0561
Summit Academy Middle School - Cincinnati (05-09)
2005-06 Enrollment: 41 . . . . (513) 321-0561
Summit Academy Secondary School - Cincinnati
2005-06 Enrollment: n/a . . . .
Sycamore Community City (PK-12)
2005-06 Enrollment: 5,686 . . . . (513) 686-1700
T.C.P. World Academy (KG-06)
2005-06 Enrollment: 333 . . . . (513) 531-9500
Three Rivers Local (PK-12)
2005-06 Enrollment: 1,993 . . . . (513) 941-6400
V L T Academy (KG-08)
2005-06 Enrollment: 79 . . . . (513) 421-1464
Veritas Academy (01-09)
2005-06 Enrollment: 28 . . . . (513) 651-9624
W.E.B. Dubois (01-11)
2005-06 Enrollment: 230 . . . . (513) 702-3057
West Clermont Local (PK-12)
2005-06 Enrollment: 9,272 . . . . (513) 943-5000
Winton Woods City (PK-12)
2005-06 Enrollment: 4,059 . . . . (513) 619-2300

Four-year College(s)

Art Academy of Cincinnati (Private, Not-for-profit)
Fall 2007 Enrollment: 144 . . . . (513) 562-6262
2007-08 Tuition: In-state $20,340; Out-of-state $20,340
Athenaeum of Ohio (Private, Not-for-profit, Roman Catholic)
Fall 2007 Enrollment: 238 . . . . (513) 231-2223
2007-08 Tuition: In-state $17,100; Out-of-state $17,100
Cincinnati Christian University (Private, Not-for-profit, Christian Churches and Churches of Christ)
Fall 2007 Enrollment: 1,051. . . . . (513) 244-8100
2007-08 Tuition: In-state $11,520; Out-of-state $11,520
Cincinnati College of Mortuary Science (Private, Not-for-profit)
Fall 2007 Enrollment: 99 . . . . (513) 761-2020
2007-08 Tuition: In-state $14,510; Out-of-state $14,510
College of Mount St. Joseph (Private, Not-for-profit, Roman Catholic)
Fall 2007 Enrollment: 2,282. . . . . (513) 244-4200
2007-08 Tuition: In-state $21,200; Out-of-state $21,200
Gods Bible School and College (Private, Not-for-profit, Other Protestant)
Fall 2007 Enrollment: 285 . . . . (513) 721-7944
2007-08 Tuition: In-state $4,980; Out-of-state $4,980
Hebrew Union College-Jewish Institute of Religion (Private, Not-for-profit, Jewish)
Fall 2007 Enrollment: 232 . . . . (513) 221-1875
Temple Baptist College (Private, Not-for-profit, Baptist)
Fall 2007 Enrollment: 60 . . . . (513) 851-3800
2007-08 Tuition: In-state $8,670; Out-of-state $8,670
Union Institute & University (Private, Not-for-profit)
Fall 2007 Enrollment: 1,719. . . . . (800) 486-3116
2007-08 Tuition: In-state $9,844; Out-of-state $9,844
University of Cincinnati-Main Campus (Public)
Fall 2007 Enrollment: 29,319. . . . . (513) 556-6000
2007-08 Tuition: In-state $9,399; Out-of-state $23,932
Xavier University (Private, Not-for-profit, Roman Catholic)
Fall 2007 Enrollment: 6,646. . . . . (513) 745-3000
2007-08 Tuition: In-state $25,270; Out-of-state $25,270

Two-year College(s)

Academy of Court Reporting-Cincinnati (Private, For-profit)
Fall 2007 Enrollment: 247 . . . . (513) 723-0551
2007-08 Tuition: In-state $8,685; Out-of-state $8,685
Antonelli College (Private, For-profit)
Fall 2007 Enrollment: 377 . . . . (513) 241-4338
2007-08 Tuition: In-state $15,127; Out-of-state $15,127
Bohecker College-Cincinnati (Private, For-profit)
Fall 2007 Enrollment: 147 . . . . (513) 771-2795
2007-08 Tuition: In-state $12,457; Out-of-state $12,457
Brown Mackie College-Cincinnati (Private, For-profit)
Fall 2007 Enrollment: 1,339. . . . . (513) 771-2424
2007-08 Tuition: In-state $8,028; Out-of-state $8,028
Cincinnati State Technical and Community College (Public)
Fall 2007 Enrollment: 8,507. . . . . (513) 569-1500
2007-08 Tuition: In-state $4,755; Out-of-state $9,166
Good Samaritan College of Nursing & Health Science (Private, Not-for-profit, Roman Catholic)
Fall 2007 Enrollment: 304 . . . . (513) 872-2631
2007-08 Tuition: In-state $14,992; Out-of-state $14,992
Great Oaks Institute of Technology and Career Development (Public)
Fall 2007 Enrollment: 471 . . . . (513) 771-8925
International Academy of Hair Design (Private, For-profit)
Fall 2007 Enrollment: 111 . . . . (513) 741-4777
Moler Hollywood Beauty Academy (Private, For-profit)
Fall 2007 Enrollment: 93 . . . . (513) 621-5262
Moore University of Hair Design (Private, For-profit)
Fall 2007 Enrollment: 15 . . . . (513) 531-3100
Southwestern College (Private, For-profit)
Fall 2007 Enrollment: 821 . . . . (513) 874-0432
2007-08 Tuition: In-state $12,500; Out-of-state $12,500
Southwestern College (Private, For-profit)
Fall 2007 Enrollment: 342 . . . . (513) 421-3212
2007-08 Tuition: In-state $13,400; Out-of-state $13,400
The Art Institute of Cincinnati (Private, For-profit)
Fall 2007 Enrollment: 65 . . . . (513) 751-1206
2007-08 Tuition: In-state $17,886; Out-of-state $17,886
The Art Institute of Ohio-Cincinnati (Private, For-profit)
Fall 2007 Enrollment: 569 . . . . (513) 833-2400
2007-08 Tuition: In-state $15,759; Out-of-state $15,759
The Christ College of Nursing and Health Sciences (Private, Not-for-profit)
Fall 2007 Enrollment: 338 . . . . (513) 585-2498
2007-08 Tuition: In-state $10,625; Out-of-state $10,625
Western Hills School of Beauty and Hair Design (Private, For-profit)
Fall 2007 Enrollment: 308 . . . . (513) 574-3818

Vocational/Technical School(s)

Eastern Hills Academy of Hair Design (Private, For-profit)
Fall 2007 Enrollment: 101 . . . . (513) 231-8621
2007-08 Tuition: $11,495
Institute of Medical-Dental Technology (Private, For-profit)
Fall 2007 Enrollment: 150 . . . . (513) 851-8500
2007-08 Tuition: $7,080
Ohio Center for Broadcasting (Private, For-profit)
Fall 2007 Enrollment: 59 . . . . (513) 271-6060
2007-08 Tuition: In-state $12,221; Out-of-state $12,221

Regency Beauty Institute (Private, For-profit)
Fall 2007 Enrollment: 10 . . . . (513) 753-1888
2007-08 Tuition: $14,200

Housing: Homeownership rate: 39.3% (2007); Median home value: $115,304 (2007); Median rent: $392 per month (2000); Median age of housing: 52 years (2000).

Hospitals: Bethesda Hospital (412 beds); Bethesda North Hospital (314 beds); Christ Hospital; Cincinnati Children's Hospital Medical Center (450 beds); Deaconess Hospital (273 beds); Department of Veterans Affairs Medical Center (378 beds); Drake Center (356 beds); Franciscan Hospital-Western Hills (290 beds); Good Samaritan Hospital (700 beds); Health Alliance of Greater Cincinnati (550 beds); Jewish Hospital of Cincinnati (175 beds); Mercy Franciscan Hospital - Mt. Airy (269 beds); Mercy Hospital Anderson (186 beds); Shriners Hospitals for Children (30 beds); Summit Behavior Health Center (274 beds); University Hospital Health Alliance (650 beds)

Safety: Violent crime rate: 107.9 per 10,000 population; Property crime rate: 617.7 per 10,000 population (2007).

Newspapers: American Israelite (National news; Circulation 7,000); Catholic Telegraph (Regional news; Circulation 60,000); Christian Standard (Local news; Circulation 59,000); CiN Weekly (Regional news; Circulation 60,000); Cincinnati Citybeat (Local news; Circulation 50,000); Cincinnati Court Index (Local news; Circulation 2,000); Cincinnati Enquirer (Local news; Circulation 202,973); Cincinnati Herald (Community news; Circulation 10,000); The Community Press (Local news); Delhi Press (Community news; Circulation 17,727); Express Cincinnati (Community news; Circulation 8,000); Hilltop Press (Community news; Circulation 17,565); La Jornada Latina (Circulation 12,000); Northwest Press (Community news; Circulation 17,160); Price Hill Press (Community news; Circulation 9,500); The Spanish Journal (Regional news; Circulation 15,000); Tri-County Press (Community news; Circulation 8,130); Weekend - Cincinnati Enquirer (Local news); Western Hills Press (Community news; Circulation 20,770)

Transportation: Commute to work: 80.9% car, 10.1% public transportation, 5.5% walk, 2.6% work from home (2000); Travel time to work: 26.0% less than 15 minutes, 46.5% 15 to 30 minutes, 18.3% 30 to 45 minutes, 4.7% 45 to 60 minutes, 4.6% 60 minutes or more (2000); Amtrak: Service available.

Airports: Cincinnati Municipal Airport Lunken Field (general aviation); Cincinnati-Blue Ash (general aviation)

Additional Information Contacts

Anderson Area Chamber of Commerce. . . . . (513) 474-4802
http://www.andersonareachamber.org
Cincinnati USA Convention & Visitors Bureau. . . . . (513) 621-2142
http://www.cincyusa.com
Cincinnati USA Regional Chamber . . . . (513) 579-3100
http://www.cincinnatichamber.com
City of Cincinnati . . . . (513) 591-6000
http://www.cincinnati-oh.gov
Northern Cincinnati Convention & Visitors Bureau . . . . (513) 771-5353
http://www.cincynorth.com
Over-the-Rhine Chamber of Commerce . . . . (513) 241-2690
http://www.otrchamber.com

CLEVES (village). Covers a land area of 1.590 square miles and a water area of 0.002 square miles. Located at 39.16° N. Lat.; 84.75° W. Long. Elevation is 495 feet.

History: Cleves was platted in 1818 and named for John Cleves Symmes, a pioneer who had founded North Bend.

Population: 2,122 (1990); 2,790 (2000); 2,763 (2007); 2,573 (2012 projected); Race: 97.7% White, 0.7% Black, 0.2% Asian, 0.3% Hispanic of any race (2007); Density: 1,737.7 persons per square mile (2007); Average household size: 2.85 (2007); Median age: 34.8 (2007); Males per 100 females: 101.1 (2007); Marriage status: 21.6% never married, 63.9% now married, 5.9% widowed, 8.6% divorced (2000); Foreign born: 0.8% (2000); Ancestry (includes multiple ancestries): 30.1% German, 16.0% English, 15.4% Irish, 12.3% United States or American, 6.7% Other groups (2000).

Economy: Single-family building permits issued: 8 (2007); Multi-family building permits issued: 0 (2007); Employment by occupation: 8.9% management, 12.7% professional, 19.3% services, 26.9% sales, 0.0% farming, 18.4% construction, 13.8% production (2000).

Income: Per capita income: $22,468 (2007); Median household income: $58,133 (2007); Average household income: $64,132 (2007); Percent of households with income of $100,000 or more: 15.7% (2007); Poverty rate: 7.6% (2000).

Education: Percent of population age 25 and over with: High school diploma (including GED) or higher: 79.1% (2007); Bachelor's degree or higher: 13.6% (2007); Master's degree or higher: 4.5% (2007).

School District(s)

Three Rivers Local (PK-12)
2005-06 Enrollment: 1,993 . . . . (513) 941-6400

Housing: Homeownership rate: 78.1% (2007); Median home value: $122,904 (2007); Median rent: $387 per month (2000); Median age of housing: 42 years (2000).

Safety: Violent crime rate: 4.0 per 10,000 population; Property crime rate: 299.9 per 10,000 population (2007).

Transportation: Commute to work: 95.8% car, 1.1% public transportation, 1.1% walk, 1.5% work from home (2000); Travel time to work: 22.2% less than 15 minutes, 33.5% 15 to 30 minutes, 30.0% 30 to 45 minutes, 10.4% 45 to 60 minutes, 4.0% 60 minutes or more (2000)

Additional Information Contacts

Village of Cleves . . . . (513) 941-5127
http://www.cleves.org

COVEDALE (CDP). Covers a land area of 2.796 square miles and a water area of 0 square miles. Located at 39.12° N. Lat.; 84.62° W. Long. Elevation is 886 feet.

Population: 6,674 (1990); 6,360 (2000); 6,261 (2007); 6,084 (2012 projected); Race: 98.4% White, 0.5% Black, 0.2% Asian, 0.8% Hispanic of any race (2007); Density: 2,238.9 persons per square mile (2007); Average household size: 2.54 (2007); Median age: 42.3 (2007); Males per 100 females: 94.0 (2007); Marriage status: 21.9% never married, 64.5% now married, 8.4% widowed, 5.2% divorced (2000); Foreign born: 2.0% (2000); Ancestry (includes multiple ancestries): 54.1% German, 23.3% Irish, 9.4% English, 8.4% United States or American, 6.2% Italian (2000).

Economy: Employment by occupation: 19.8% management, 23.1% professional, 9.9% services, 29.8% sales, 0.0% farming, 8.1% construction, 9.3% production (2000).

Income: Per capita income: $34,145 (2007); Median household income: $65,715 (2007); Average household income: $86,596 (2007); Percent of households with income of $100,000 or more: 26.9% (2007); Poverty rate: 1.9% (2000).

Education: Percent of population age 25 and over with: High school diploma (including GED) or higher: 91.4% (2007); Bachelor's degree or higher: 31.7% (2007); Master's degree or higher: 11.1% (2007).

Housing: Homeownership rate: 92.7% (2007); Median home value: $149,238 (2007); Median rent: $570 per month (2000); Median age of housing: 43 years (2000).

Transportation: Commute to work: 94.8% car, 2.3% public transportation, 0.3% walk, 2.3% work from home (2000); Travel time to work: 23.8% less than 15 minutes, 34.7% 15 to 30 minutes, 32.8% 30 to 45 minutes, 5.8% 45 to 60 minutes, 2.9% 60 minutes or more (2000)

DEER PARK (city). Covers a land area of 0.857 square miles and a water area of 0 square miles. Located at 39.20° N. Lat.; 84.39° W. Long. Elevation is 869 feet.

Population: 6,181 (1990); 5,982 (2000); 5,518 (2007); 5,188 (2012 projected); Race: 95.4% White, 2.4% Black, 0.7% Asian, 1.0% Hispanic of any race (2007); Density: 6,437.7 persons per square mile (2007); Average household size: 2.21 (2007); Median age: 41.1 (2007); Males per 100 females: 87.9 (2007); Marriage status: 24.2% never married, 51.8% now married, 10.9% widowed, 13.2% divorced (2000); Foreign born: 2.2% (2000); Ancestry (includes multiple ancestries): 38.2% German, 16.2% Irish, 10.6% United States or American, 9.3% English, 7.5% Other groups (2000).

Economy: Single-family building permits issued: 0 (2007); Multi-family building permits issued: 0 (2007); Employment by occupation: 11.1% management, 18.0% professional, 16.2% services, 31.4% sales, 0.0% farming, 10.0% construction, 13.4% production (2000).

Income: Per capita income: $25,916 (2007); Median household income: $46,572 (2007); Average household income: $56,848 (2007); Percent of households with income of $100,000 or more: 11.5% (2007); Poverty rate: 5.3% (2000).

Taxes: Total city taxes per capita: $355 (2006); City property taxes per capita: $52 (2006).

Education: Percent of population age 25 and over with: High school diploma (including GED) or higher: 79.9% (2007); Bachelor's degree or higher: 16.6% (2007); Master's degree or higher: 3.2% (2007).

Housing: Homeownership rate: 72.4% (2007); Median home value: $117,686 (2007); Median rent: $441 per month (2000); Median age of housing: 54 years (2000).
Safety: Violent crime rate: 16.6 per 10,000 population; Property crime rate: 206.2 per 10,000 population (2007).
Transportation: Commute to work: 94.6% car, 0.7% public transportation, 1.8% walk, 2.7% work from home (2000); Travel time to work: 31.3% less than 15 minutes, 50.9% 15 to 30 minutes, 13.3% 30 to 45 minutes, 3.7% 45 to 60 minutes, 0.7% 60 minutes or more (2000)

DENT (CDP). Covers a land area of 6.006 square miles and a water area of 0 square miles. Located at 39.19° N. Lat.; 84.66° W. Long. Elevation is 843 feet.
Population: 6,416 (1990); 7,612 (2000); 8,879 (2007); 9,643 (2012 projected); Race: 97.6% White, 1.0% Black, 0.2% Asian, 0.6% Hispanic of any race (2007); Density: 1,478.4 persons per square mile (2007); Average household size: 2.33 (2007); Median age: 41.9 (2007); Males per 100 females: 94.0 (2007); Marriage status: 23.9% never married, 59.3% now married, 6.5% widowed, 10.3% divorced (2000); Foreign born: 0.9% (2000); Ancestry (includes multiple ancestries): 53.9% German, 16.7% Irish, 10.8% English, 7.7% Italian, 5.3% United States or American (2000).
Economy: Employment by occupation: 15.0% management, 22.5% professional, 12.0% services, 30.4% sales, 0.0% farming, 9.2% construction, 10.9% production (2000).
Income: Per capita income: $29,760 (2007); Median household income: $57,699 (2007); Average household income: $69,409 (2007); Percent of households with income of $100,000 or more: 19.7% (2007); Poverty rate: 3.7% (2000).
Education: Percent of population age 25 and over with: High school diploma (including GED) or higher: 89.8% (2007); Bachelor's degree or higher: 24.5% (2007); Master's degree or higher: 8.6% (2007).
Housing: Homeownership rate: 72.9% (2007); Median home value: $146,980 (2007); Median rent: $553 per month (2000); Median age of housing: 19 years (2000).
Transportation: Commute to work: 95.3% car, 1.0% public transportation, 1.1% walk, 2.0% work from home (2000); Travel time to work: 22.2% less than 15 minutes, 47.1% 15 to 30 minutes, 25.0% 30 to 45 minutes, 3.2% 45 to 60 minutes, 2.4% 60 minutes or more (2000)

DILLONVALE (CDP). Covers a land area of 0.902 square miles and a water area of 0 square miles. Located at 39.21° N. Lat.; 84.40° W. Long. Elevation is 784 feet.
Population: 4,209 (1990); 3,716 (2000); 3,260 (2007); 2,973 (2012 projected); Race: 95.1% White, 2.2% Black, 0.4% Asian, 1.3% Hispanic of any race (2007); Density: 3,612.9 persons per square mile (2007); Average household size: 2.24 (2007); Median age: 44.3 (2007); Males per 100 females: 88.3 (2007); Marriage status: 23.5% never married, 55.2% now married, 10.4% widowed, 11.0% divorced (2000); Foreign born: 3.0% (2000); Ancestry (includes multiple ancestries): 41.7% German, 18.0% Irish, 11.8% English, 9.7% United States or American, 7.6% Other groups (2000).
Economy: Employment by occupation: 16.3% management, 17.7% professional, 12.7% services, 30.7% sales, 0.0% farming, 9.5% construction, 13.1% production (2000).
Income: Per capita income: $26,194 (2007); Median household income: $50,345 (2007); Average household income: $58,568 (2007); Percent of households with income of $100,000 or more: 11.5% (2007); Poverty rate: 3.8% (2000).
Education: Percent of population age 25 and over with: High school diploma (including GED) or higher: 86.1% (2007); Bachelor's degree or higher: 20.4% (2007); Master's degree or higher: 5.5% (2007).

School District(s)

Martins Ferry City (PK-12)
2005-06 Enrollment: 1,565 . . . . (740) 633-1732
Housing: Homeownership rate: 87.1% (2007); Median home value: $129,030 (2007); Median rent: $519 per month (2000); Median age of housing: 45 years (2000).
Transportation: Commute to work: 94.8% car, 1.2% public transportation, 0.7% walk, 3.3% work from home (2000); Travel time to work: 29.5% less than 15 minutes, 50.5% 15 to 30 minutes, 17.5% 30 to 45 minutes, 1.3% 45 to 60 minutes, 1.2% 60 minutes or more (2000)

DRY RUN (CDP). Covers a land area of 4.754 square miles and a water area of 0 square miles. Located at 39.10° N. Lat.; 84.33° W. Long. Elevation is 873 feet.
Population: 5,389 (1990); 6,553 (2000); 7,058 (2007); 7,313 (2012 projected); Race: 95.9% White, 0.9% Black, 2.0% Asian, 1.1% Hispanic of any race (2007); Density: 1,484.5 persons per square mile (2007); Average household size: 3.09 (2007); Median age: 40.0 (2007); Males per 100 females: 100.8 (2007); Marriage status: 18.3% never married, 75.2% now married, 2.6% widowed, 4.0% divorced (2000); Foreign born: 3.6% (2000); Ancestry (includes multiple ancestries): 42.8% German, 25.4% Irish, 15.1% English, 7.2% Italian, 5.9% United States or American (2000).
Economy: Employment by occupation: 28.1% management, 30.9% professional, 8.2% services, 23.3% sales, 0.1% farming, 3.7% construction, 5.8% production (2000).
Income: Per capita income: $50,800 (2007); Median household income: $120,492 (2007); Average household income: $157,120 (2007); Percent of households with income of $100,000 or more: 61.0% (2007); Poverty rate: 2.0% (2000).
Education: Percent of population age 25 and over with: High school diploma (including GED) or higher: 97.2% (2007); Bachelor's degree or higher: 63.2% (2007); Master's degree or higher: 22.2% (2007).
Housing: Homeownership rate: 97.2% (2007); Median home value: $239,228 (2007); Median rent: $738 per month (2000); Median age of housing: 22 years (2000).
Transportation: Commute to work: 92.6% car, 1.2% public transportation, 0.2% walk, 5.9% work from home (2000); Travel time to work: 23.5% less than 15 minutes, 40.8% 15 to 30 minutes, 27.9% 30 to 45 minutes, 3.7% 45 to 60 minutes, 4.1% 60 minutes or more (2000)

ELMWOOD PLACE (village). Covers a land area of 0.331 square miles and a water area of 0 square miles. Located at 39.18° N. Lat.; 84.48° W. Long. Elevation is 518 feet.
History: Settled 1875, incorporated 1890.
Population: 2,937 (1990); 2,681 (2000); 2,367 (2007); 2,148 (2012 projected); Race: 89.9% White, 6.6% Black, 0.3% Asian, 2.6% Hispanic of any race (2007); Density: 7,157.0 persons per square mile (2007); Average household size: 2.47 (2007); Median age: 34.8 (2007); Males per 100 females: 104.6 (2007); Marriage status: 29.9% never married, 45.5% now married, 8.0% widowed, 16.6% divorced (2000); Foreign born: 1.0% (2000); Ancestry (includes multiple ancestries): 21.2% United States or American, 14.2% Other groups, 12.1% German, 7.4% Irish, 5.9% English (2000).
Economy: Single-family building permits issued: 0 (2007); Multi-family building permits issued: 0 (2007); Employment by occupation: 4.0% management, 6.0% professional, 17.0% services, 27.1% sales, 0.0% farming, 10.7% construction, 35.3% production (2000).
Income: Per capita income: $14,774 (2007); Median household income: $31,506 (2007); Average household income: $36,465 (2007); Percent of households with income of $100,000 or more: 1.9% (2007); Poverty rate: 19.0% (2000).
Education: Percent of population age 25 and over with: High school diploma (including GED) or higher: 54.0% (2007); Bachelor's degree or higher: 4.0% (2007); Master's degree or higher: 0.9% (2007).
Housing: Homeownership rate: 46.4% (2007); Median home value: $75,608 (2007); Median rent: $330 per month (2000); Median age of housing: 60+ years (2000).
Safety: Violent crime rate: 38.4 per 10,000 population; Property crime rate: 209.1 per 10,000 population (2007).
Transportation: Commute to work: 85.5% car, 3.9% public transportation, 7.2% walk, 1.8% work from home (2000); Travel time to work: 35.6% less than 15 minutes, 42.2% 15 to 30 minutes, 15.5% 30 to 45 minutes, 2.1% 45 to 60 minutes, 4.6% 60 minutes or more (2000)

EVENDALE (village). Covers a land area of 4.771 square miles and a water area of 0 square miles. Located at 39.24° N. Lat.; 84.43° W. Long. Elevation is 594 feet.
Population: 3,175 (1990); 3,090 (2000); 2,805 (2007); 2,591 (2012 projected); Race: 84.9% White, 8.8% Black, 5.0% Asian, 0.5% Hispanic of any race (2007); Density: 587.9 persons per square mile (2007); Average household size: 2.82 (2007); Median age: 45.8 (2007); Males per 100 females: 101.7 (2007); Marriage status: 18.9% never married, 72.7% now married, 2.3% widowed, 6.1% divorced (2000); Foreign born: 4.7% (2000); Ancestry (includes multiple ancestries): 34.8% German, 16.1% Irish, 13.7% English, 13.0% Other groups, 7.4% United States or American (2000).
Economy: Single-family building permits issued: 1 (2007); Multi-family building permits issued: 0 (2007); Employment by occupation: 22.8% management, 31.6% professional, 6.3% services, 29.1% sales, 0.0% farming, 4.4% construction, 5.9% production (2000).

Income: Per capita income: $51,292 (2007); Median household income: $108,485 (2007); Average household income: $144,889 (2007); Percent of households with income of $100,000 or more: 54.7% (2007); Poverty rate: 0.3% (2000).
Education: Percent of population age 25 and over with: High school diploma (including GED) or higher: 93.1% (2007); Bachelor's degree or higher: 55.8% (2007); Master's degree or higher: 25.3% (2007).
Housing: Homeownership rate: 95.6% (2007); Median home value: $246,818 (2007); Median rent: $531 per month (2000); Median age of housing: 21 years (2000).
Transportation: Commute to work: 93.6% car, 0.5% public transportation, 0.6% walk, 5.3% work from home (2000); Travel time to work: 31.1% less than 15 minutes, 47.9% 15 to 30 minutes, 15.7% 30 to 45 minutes, 3.2% 45 to 60 minutes, 2.1% 60 minutes or more (2000)

FAIRFAX (village). Covers a land area of 0.756 square miles and a water area of 0 square miles. Located at 39.14° N. Lat.; 84.39° W. Long. Elevation is 564 feet.
Population: 1,990 (1990); 1,938 (2000); 1,734 (2007); 1,586 (2012 projected); Race: 95.6% White, 1.5% Black, 1.2% Asian, 0.2% Hispanic of any race (2007); Density: 2,294.1 persons per square mile (2007); Average household size: 2.48 (2007); Median age: 38.7 (2007); Males per 100 females: 90.1 (2007); Marriage status: 27.1% never married, 52.9% now married, 8.1% widowed, 11.9% divorced (2000); Foreign born: 0.2% (2000); Ancestry (includes multiple ancestries): 39.8% German, 16.0% Irish, 10.3% English, 6.9% United States or American, 6.7% Other groups (2000).
Economy: Single-family building permits issued: 0 (2007); Multi-family building permits issued: 0 (2007); Employment by occupation: 12.2% management, 19.6% professional, 20.8% services, 26.2% sales, 0.0% farming, 8.0% construction, 13.2% production (2000).
Income: Per capita income: $23,049 (2007); Median household income: $49,018 (2007); Average household income: $57,260 (2007); Percent of households with income of $100,000 or more: 9.9% (2007); Poverty rate: 5.1% (2000).
Education: Percent of population age 25 and over with: High school diploma (including GED) or higher: 74.0% (2007); Bachelor's degree or higher: 15.7% (2007); Master's degree or higher: 4.2% (2007).
Housing: Homeownership rate: 80.8% (2007); Median home value: $116,122 (2007); Median rent: $535 per month (2000); Median age of housing: 55 years (2000).
Transportation: Commute to work: 88.6% car, 5.3% public transportation, 3.6% walk, 2.5% work from home (2000); Travel time to work: 32.5% less than 15 minutes, 42.0% 15 to 30 minutes, 16.3% 30 to 45 minutes, 5.6% 45 to 60 minutes, 3.6% 60 minutes or more (2000)
Additional Information Contacts
Village of Fairfax . . . . (513) 527-6503
http://www.fairfaxohio.org

FINNEYTOWN (CDP). Covers a land area of 3.988 square miles and a water area of 0 square miles. Located at 39.21° N. Lat.; 84.52° W. Long. Elevation is 889 feet.
Population: 13,094 (1990); 13,492 (2000); 12,433 (2007); 11,565 (2012 projected); Race: 67.2% White, 29.3% Black, 0.9% Asian, 0.9% Hispanic of any race (2007); Density: 3,117.3 persons per square mile (2007); Average household size: 2.52 (2007); Median age: 40.7 (2007); Males per 100 females: 88.6 (2007); Marriage status: 23.3% never married, 59.8% now married, 7.1% widowed, 9.8% divorced (2000); Foreign born: 2.8% (2000); Ancestry (includes multiple ancestries): 33.0% German, 28.1% Other groups, 13.2% Irish, 10.1% English, 5.5% United States or American (2000).
Economy: Employment by occupation: 15.5% management, 26.4% professional, 12.5% services, 28.5% sales, 0.0% farming, 5.8% construction, 11.3% production (2000).
Income: Per capita income: $29,228 (2007); Median household income: $59,300 (2007); Average household income: $73,368 (2007); Percent of households with income of $100,000 or more: 19.5% (2007); Poverty rate: 5.9% (2000).
Education: Percent of population age 25 and over with: High school diploma (including GED) or higher: 88.4% (2007); Bachelor's degree or higher: 36.3% (2007); Master's degree or higher: 12.5% (2007).
Housing: Homeownership rate: 80.1% (2007); Median home value: $129,142 (2007); Median rent: $567 per month (2000); Median age of housing: 41 years (2000).
Transportation: Commute to work: 92.5% car, 1.9% public transportation, 1.7% walk, 3.6% work from home (2000); Travel time to work: 21.3% less than 15 minutes, 50.5% 15 to 30 minutes, 23.0% 30 to 45 minutes, 3.6% 45 to 60 minutes, 1.6% 60 minutes or more (2000)

FOREST PARK (city). Covers a land area of 6.509 square miles and a water area of 0 square miles. Located at 39.28° N. Lat.; 84.52° W. Long. Elevation is 837 feet.
Population: 18,625 (1990); 19,463 (2000); 17,705 (2007); 16,356 (2012 projected); Race: 27.9% White, 63.8% Black, 4.3% Asian, 1.9% Hispanic of any race (2007); Density: 2,720.3 persons per square mile (2007); Average household size: 2.51 (2007); Median age: 36.8 (2007); Males per 100 females: 92.3 (2007); Marriage status: 29.3% never married, 53.8% now married, 5.5% widowed, 11.4% divorced (2000); Foreign born: 5.7% (2000); Ancestry (includes multiple ancestries): 54.5% Other groups, 14.6% German, 6.6% Irish, 5.8% English, 3.7% United States or American (2000).
Economy: Single-family building permits issued: 3 (2007); Multi-family building permits issued: 0 (2007); Employment by occupation: 12.5% management, 21.8% professional, 14.3% services, 30.6% sales, 0.0% farming, 4.2% construction, 16.6% production (2000).
Income: Per capita income: $25,555 (2007); Median household income: $55,235 (2007); Average household income: $63,967 (2007); Percent of households with income of $100,000 or more: 14.4% (2007); Poverty rate: 6.0% (2000).
Taxes: Total city taxes per capita: $618 (2006); City property taxes per capita: $253 (2006).
Education: Percent of population age 25 and over with: High school diploma (including GED) or higher: 88.5% (2007); Bachelor's degree or higher: 26.5% (2007); Master's degree or higher: 7.4% (2007).
Housing: Homeownership rate: 62.2% (2007); Median home value: $119,252 (2007); Median rent: $613 per month (2000); Median age of housing: 29 years (2000).
Safety: Violent crime rate: 31.5 per 10,000 population; Property crime rate: 374.9 per 10,000 population (2007).
Transportation: Commute to work: 92.9% car, 2.7% public transportation, 1.2% walk, 2.2% work from home (2000); Travel time to work: 23.1% less than 15 minutes, 42.9% 15 to 30 minutes, 23.5% 30 to 45 minutes, 6.2% 45 to 60 minutes, 4.3% 60 minutes or more (2000)
Additional Information Contacts
City of Forest Park . . . . (513) 595-5200
http://www.forestpark.org

FORESTVILLE (CDP). Covers a land area of 3.682 square miles and a water area of 0 square miles. Located at 39.07° N. Lat.; 84.33° W. Long. Elevation is 820 feet.
Population: 9,185 (1990); 10,978 (2000); 10,283 (2007); 9,746 (2012 projected); Race: 94.7% White, 1.1% Black, 2.6% Asian, 1.5% Hispanic of any race (2007); Density: 2,792.9 persons per square mile (2007); Average household size: 2.43 (2007); Median age: 41.3 (2007); Males per 100 females: 88.1 (2007); Marriage status: 20.4% never married, 62.0% now married, 10.3% widowed, 7.3% divorced (2000); Foreign born: 4.4% (2000); Ancestry (includes multiple ancestries): 38.7% German, 22.2% Irish, 13.7% English, 6.9% Other groups, 5.9% United States or American (2000).
Economy: Employment by occupation: 25.9% management, 23.5% professional, 11.5% services, 26.4% sales, 0.0% farming, 4.5% construction, 8.3% production (2000).
Income: Per capita income: $34,622 (2007); Median household income: $67,628 (2007); Average household income: $84,244 (2007); Percent of households with income of $100,000 or more: 30.2% (2007); Poverty rate: 3.6% (2000).
Education: Percent of population age 25 and over with: High school diploma (including GED) or higher: 92.0% (2007); Bachelor's degree or higher: 45.1% (2007); Master's degree or higher: 17.1% (2007).
Housing: Homeownership rate: 73.4% (2007); Median home value: $179,310 (2007); Median rent: $710 per month (2000); Median age of housing: 20 years (2000).
Transportation: Commute to work: 93.0% car, 1.9% public transportation, 0.7% walk, 3.5% work from home (2000); Travel time to work: 23.5% less than 15 minutes, 39.4% 15 to 30 minutes, 29.4% 30 to 45 minutes, 4.4% 45 to 60 minutes, 3.2% 60 minutes or more (2000)

FRUIT HILL (CDP). Covers a land area of 1.251 square miles and a water area of 0 square miles. Located at 39.07° N. Lat.; 84.36° W. Long. Elevation is 725 feet.
Population: 4,168 (1990); 3,945 (2000); 3,545 (2007); 3,219 (2012 projected); Race: 97.2% White, 1.1% Black, 0.9% Asian, 0.7% Hispanic of any race (2007); Density: 2,833.4 persons per square mile (2007); Average household size: 2.68 (2007); Median age: 41.4 (2007); Males per 100 females: 92.5 (2007); Marriage status: 18.6% never married, 71.5% now married, 4.8% widowed, 5.0% divorced (2000); Foreign born: 2.2% (2000); Ancestry (includes multiple ancestries): 51.3% German, 17.9% Irish, 16.5% English, 5.7% Other groups, 5.2% Italian (2000).
Economy: Employment by occupation: 17.5% management, 25.9% professional, 13.0% services, 33.7% sales, 0.0% farming, 5.8% construction, 4.1% production (2000).
Income: Per capita income: $35,702 (2007); Median household income: $72,579 (2007); Average household income: $95,216 (2007); Percent of households with income of $100,000 or more: 30.7% (2007); Poverty rate: 2.5% (2000).
Education: Percent of population age 25 and over with: High school diploma (including GED) or higher: 90.5% (2007); Bachelor's degree or higher: 39.7% (2007); Master's degree or higher: 15.9% (2007).
Housing: Homeownership rate: 91.2% (2007); Median home value: $144,731 (2007); Median rent: $631 per month (2000); Median age of housing: 37 years (2000).
Transportation: Commute to work: 90.3% car, 2.1% public transportation, 0.0% walk, 6.0% work from home (2000); Travel time to work: 22.2% less than 15 minutes, 40.6% 15 to 30 minutes, 24.8% 30 to 45 minutes, 5.5% 45 to 60 minutes, 7.0% 60 minutes or more (2000)

GLENDALE (village). Covers a land area of 1.666 square miles and a water area of 0 square miles. Located at 39.27° N. Lat.; 84.46° W. Long. Elevation is 630 feet.
History: Incorporated 1855.
Population: 2,445 (1990); 2,188 (2000); 2,116 (2007); 2,054 (2012 projected); Race: 82.5% White, 13.8% Black, 0.7% Asian, 1.8% Hispanic of any race (2007); Density: 1,269.7 persons per square mile (2007); Average household size: 2.25 (2007); Median age: 48.3 (2007); Males per 100 females: 94.7 (2007); Marriage status: 20.0% never married, 59.6% now married, 8.5% widowed, 11.9% divorced (2000); Foreign born: 0.8% (2000); Ancestry (includes multiple ancestries): 25.7% German, 19.4% Other groups, 13.6% Irish, 12.9% English, 5.6% Italian (2000).
Economy: Single-family building permits issued: 5 (2007); Multi-family building permits issued: 0 (2007); Employment by occupation: 21.3% management, 31.8% professional, 8.6% services, 25.5% sales, 0.0% farming, 5.4% construction, 7.5% production (2000).
Income: Per capita income: $58,029 (2007); Median household income: $95,978 (2007); Average household income: $130,498 (2007); Percent of households with income of $100,000 or more: 48.0% (2007); Poverty rate: 2.1% (2000).
Education: Percent of population age 25 and over with: High school diploma (including GED) or higher: 90.7% (2007); Bachelor's degree or higher: 56.1% (2007); Master's degree or higher: 16.8% (2007).
Housing: Homeownership rate: 84.9% (2007); Median home value: $248,098 (2007); Median rent: $597 per month (2000); Median age of housing: 53 years (2000).
Safety: Violent crime rate: 14.4 per 10,000 population; Property crime rate: 167.5 per 10,000 population (2007).
Transportation: Commute to work: 90.4% car, 0.6% public transportation, 3.7% walk, 4.6% work from home (2000); Travel time to work: 36.9% less than 15 minutes, 37.0% 15 to 30 minutes, 19.3% 30 to 45 minutes, 3.1% 45 to 60 minutes, 3.7% 60 minutes or more (2000)
Additional Information Contacts
Village of Glendale. . . . . (513) 771-7200
http://www.glendaleohio.org

GOLF MANOR (village). Covers a land area of 0.580 square miles and a water area of 0 square miles. Located at 39.18° N. Lat.; 84.44° W. Long. Elevation is 659 feet.
History: Incorporated 1947.
Population: 4,154 (1990); 3,999 (2000); 3,599 (2007); 3,308 (2012 projected); Race: 25.1% White, 71.5% Black, 0.8% Asian, 0.7% Hispanic of any race (2007); Density: 6,206.5 persons per square mile (2007); Average household size: 2.24 (2007); Median age: 40.6 (2007); Males per 100 females: 83.3 (2007); Marriage status: 32.7% never married, 46.5% now married, 7.5% widowed, 13.3% divorced (2000); Foreign born: 6.0% (2000); Ancestry (includes multiple ancestries): 58.3% Other groups, 11.2% German, 6.2% Irish, 3.7% English, 3.0% Italian (2000).
Economy: Single-family building permits issued: 0 (2007); Multi-family building permits issued: 0 (2007); Employment by occupation: 9.6% management, 22.8% professional, 18.7% services, 27.5% sales, 0.0% farming, 5.4% construction, 16.0% production (2000).
Income: Per capita income: $21,939 (2007); Median household income: $42,215 (2007); Average household income: $49,227 (2007); Percent of households with income of $100,000 or more: 6.7% (2007); Poverty rate: 10.7% (2000).
Education: Percent of population age 25 and over with: High school diploma (including GED) or higher: 81.7% (2007); Bachelor's degree or higher: 20.6% (2007); Master's degree or higher: 8.0% (2007).
Housing: Homeownership rate: 55.5% (2007); Median home value: $94,693 (2007); Median rent: $435 per month (2000); Median age of housing: 47 years (2000).
Transportation: Commute to work: 85.2% car, 8.4% public transportation, 1.9% walk, 3.1% work from home (2000); Travel time to work: 23.2% less than 15 minutes, 51.9% 15 to 30 minutes, 18.1% 30 to 45 minutes, 3.5% 45 to 60 minutes, 3.3% 60 minutes or more (2000)
Additional Information Contacts
Village of Golf Manor . . . . (513) 531-7418
http://www.golfmanor.org

GRANDVIEW (CDP). Covers a land area of 4.357 square miles and a water area of 0.342 square miles. Located at 39.19° N. Lat.; 84.72° W. Long. Elevation is 646 feet.
Population: 1,301 (1990); 1,391 (2000); 1,545 (2007); 1,617 (2012 projected); Race: 97.9% White, 0.1% Black, 0.3% Asian, 0.4% Hispanic of any race (2007); Density: 354.6 persons per square mile (2007); Average household size: 2.72 (2007); Median age: 37.1 (2007); Males per 100 females: 107.4 (2007); Marriage status: 22.2% never married, 60.6% now married, 10.1% widowed, 7.1% divorced (2000); Foreign born: 0.4% (2000); Ancestry (includes multiple ancestries): 49.4% German, 15.2% United States or American, 11.9% Irish, 11.5% English, 7.5% Italian (2000).
Economy: Employment by occupation: 3.3% management, 19.3% professional, 6.7% services, 38.1% sales, 0.0% farming, 15.2% construction, 17.4% production (2000).
Income: Per capita income: $23,743 (2007); Median household income: $41,726 (2007); Average household income: $64,468 (2007); Percent of households with income of $100,000 or more: 19.9% (2007); Poverty rate: 14.9% (2000).
Education: Percent of population age 25 and over with: High school diploma (including GED) or higher: 74.2% (2007); Bachelor's degree or higher: 16.4% (2007); Master's degree or higher: 6.1% (2007).
Housing: Homeownership rate: 84.4% (2007); Median home value: $121,918 (2007); Median rent: $420 per month (2000); Median age of housing: 27 years (2000).
Transportation: Commute to work: 100.0% car, 0.0% public transportation, 0.0% walk, 0.0% work from home (2000); Travel time to work: 17.2% less than 15 minutes, 43.2% 15 to 30 minutes, 30.1% 30 to 45 minutes, 6.0% 45 to 60 minutes, 3.6% 60 minutes or more (2000)
Additional Information Contacts
Grandview-Marble Cliff Area Chamber of Commerce . . . . . (614) 486-0196
http://www.grandviewchamber.org

GREENHILLS (village). Covers a land area of 1.232 square miles and a water area of 0 square miles. Located at 39.26° N. Lat.; 84.51° W. Long. Elevation is 804 feet.
History: Greenhills was completed in 1937 as a Resettlement Administration project to provide housing.
Population: 4,393 (1990); 4,103 (2000); 3,637 (2007); 3,317 (2012 projected); Race: 92.8% White, 3.9% Black, 0.2% Asian, 1.5% Hispanic of any race (2007); Density: 2,951.2 persons per square mile (2007); Average household size: 2.43 (2007); Median age: 38.2 (2007); Males per 100 females: 89.9 (2007); Marriage status: 24.2% never married, 56.1% now married, 6.3% widowed, 13.4% divorced (2000); Foreign born: 2.3% (2000); Ancestry (includes multiple ancestries): 40.7% German, 22.8% Irish, 9.6% Other groups, 9.1% English, 5.3% United States or American (2000).
Economy: Single-family building permits issued: 1 (2007); Multi-family building permits issued: 0 (2007); Employment by occupation: 15.2%

management, 24.8% professional, 13.6% services, 28.5% sales, 1.0% farming, 7.5% construction, 9.4% production (2000).
Income: Per capita income: $27,285 (2007); Median household income: $50,652 (2007); Average household income: $65,399 (2007); Percent of households with income of $100,000 or more: 16.9% (2007); Poverty rate: 3.8% (2000).
Education: Percent of population age 25 and over with: High school diploma (including GED) or higher: 91.6% (2007); Bachelor's degree or higher: 31.1% (2007); Master's degree or higher: 10.2% (2007).
Housing: Homeownership rate: 69.1% (2007); Median home value: $119,452 (2007); Median rent: $503 per month (2000); Median age of housing: 48 years (2000).
Transportation: Commute to work: 92.1% car, 2.5% public transportation, 1.2% walk, 4.0% work from home (2000); Travel time to work: 28.0% less than 15 minutes, 42.7% 15 to 30 minutes, 20.1% 30 to 45 minutes, 7.3% 45 to 60 minutes, 1.9% 60 minutes or more (2000)
Additional Information Contacts
Village of Greenhills . . . . (513) 825-2100
http://www.greenhillsohio.org

GROESBECK (CDP). Covers a land area of 2.938 square miles and a water area of 0 square miles. Located at 39.22° N. Lat.; 84.59° W. Long. Elevation is 866 feet.
Population: 6,684 (1990); 7,202 (2000); 6,537 (2007); 6,060 (2012 projected); Race: 89.5% White, 7.7% Black, 0.5% Asian, 0.7% Hispanic of any race (2007); Density: 2,224.7 persons per square mile (2007); Average household size: 2.55 (2007); Median age: 37.7 (2007); Males per 100 females: 96.2 (2007); Marriage status: 24.6% never married, 59.3% now married, 8.6% widowed, 7.5% divorced (2000); Foreign born: 0.8% (2000); Ancestry (includes multiple ancestries): 46.6% German, 14.7% Irish, 10.5% Other groups, 8.9% United States or American, 7.5% English (2000).
Economy: Employment by occupation: 13.6% management, 17.7% professional, 11.3% services, 34.4% sales, 0.2% farming, 10.2% construction, 12.6% production (2000).
Income: Per capita income: $25,799 (2007); Median household income: $57,805 (2007); Average household income: $65,690 (2007); Percent of households with income of $100,000 or more: 16.8% (2007); Poverty rate: 5.6% (2000).
Education: Percent of population age 25 and over with: High school diploma (including GED) or higher: 85.5% (2007); Bachelor's degree or higher: 19.8% (2007); Master's degree or higher: 6.7% (2007).
Housing: Homeownership rate: 83.6% (2007); Median home value: $121,340 (2007); Median rent: $522 per month (2000); Median age of housing: 32 years (2000).
Transportation: Commute to work: 95.1% car, 2.5% public transportation, 0.3% walk, 1.8% work from home (2000); Travel time to work: 21.7% less than 15 minutes, 51.9% 15 to 30 minutes, 20.4% 30 to 45 minutes, 3.5% 45 to 60 minutes, 2.5% 60 minutes or more (2000)

HARRISON (city). Covers a land area of 3.698 square miles and a water area of 0.028 square miles. Located at 39.25° N. Lat.; 84.80° W. Long. Elevation is 522 feet.
History: Harrison was settled before 1800, and the town was laid out in 1813 on the Ohio-Indiana border. It was named for William Henry Harrison.
Population: 7,904 (1990); 7,487 (2000); 7,953 (2007); 8,219 (2012 projected); Race: 97.7% White, 0.2% Black, 0.4% Asian, 0.8% Hispanic of any race (2007); Density: 2,150.5 persons per square mile (2007); Average household size: 2.69 (2007); Median age: 34.6 (2007); Males per 100 females: 95.0 (2007); Marriage status: 24.0% never married, 60.0% now married, 6.9% widowed, 9.0% divorced (2000); Foreign born: 0.6% (2000); Ancestry (includes multiple ancestries): 37.6% German, 15.2% Irish, 11.1% United States or American, 11.0% English, 9.4% Other groups (2000).
Economy: Single-family building permits issued: 34 (2007); Multi-family building permits issued: 98 (2007); Employment by occupation: 7.8% management, 17.7% professional, 17.2% services, 31.7% sales, 0.0% farming, 11.2% construction, 14.3% production (2000).
Income: Per capita income: $21,566 (2007); Median household income: $53,487 (2007); Average household income: $57,912 (2007); Percent of households with income of $100,000 or more: 10.8% (2007); Poverty rate: 6.8% (2000).
Education: Percent of population age 25 and over with: High school diploma (including GED) or higher: 79.6% (2007); Bachelor's degree or higher: 12.8% (2007); Master's degree or higher: 3.7% (2007).

School District(s)
Southwest Local (PK-12)
2005-06 Enrollment: 3,865 . . . . (513) 367-4139
Housing: Homeownership rate: 73.1% (2007); Median home value: $127,036 (2007); Median rent: $428 per month (2000); Median age of housing: 30 years (2000).
Safety: Violent crime rate: 8.3 per 10,000 population; Property crime rate: 419.4 per 10,000 population (2007).
Newspapers: Harrison Press (Local news; Circulation 5,382)
Transportation: Commute to work: 96.6% car, 0.7% public transportation, 1.4% walk, 0.7% work from home (2000); Travel time to work: 29.8% less than 15 minutes, 23.7% 15 to 30 minutes, 34.1% 30 to 45 minutes, 9.5% 45 to 60 minutes, 2.9% 60 minutes or more (2000)
Additional Information Contacts
City of Harrison . . . . (513) 367-3730
http://www.harrisonoh.org

KENWOOD (CDP). Covers a land area of 2.333 square miles and a water area of 0 square miles. Located at 39.20° N. Lat.; 84.37° W. Long. Elevation is 801 feet.
Population: 7,437 (1990); 7,423 (2000); 6,715 (2007); 6,260 (2012 projected); Race: 87.3% White, 6.0% Black, 5.5% Asian, 2.5% Hispanic of any race (2007); Density: 2,878.8 persons per square mile (2007); Average household size: 2.19 (2007); Median age: 47.5 (2007); Males per 100 females: 80.6 (2007); Marriage status: 18.2% never married, 59.1% now married, 14.9% widowed, 7.8% divorced (2000); Foreign born: 9.0% (2000); Ancestry (includes multiple ancestries): 32.0% German, 15.0% Irish, 14.8% English, 13.3% Other groups, 7.0% United States or American (2000).
Economy: Employment by occupation: 20.5% management, 35.6% professional, 10.6% services, 25.3% sales, 0.0% farming, 2.4% construction, 5.5% production (2000).
Income: Per capita income: $38,677 (2007); Median household income: $59,896 (2007); Average household income: $83,327 (2007); Percent of households with income of $100,000 or more: 27.3% (2007); Poverty rate: 3.3% (2000).
Education: Percent of population age 25 and over with: High school diploma (including GED) or higher: 91.5% (2007); Bachelor's degree or higher: 49.9% (2007); Master's degree or higher: 19.8% (2007).
Housing: Homeownership rate: 63.2% (2007); Median home value: $215,569 (2007); Median rent: $882 per month (2000); Median age of housing: 34 years (2000).
Transportation: Commute to work: 89.1% car, 1.5% public transportation, 1.5% walk, 6.7% work from home (2000); Travel time to work: 24.3% less than 15 minutes, 51.6% 15 to 30 minutes, 20.2% 30 to 45 minutes, 2.0% 45 to 60 minutes, 2.0% 60 minutes or more (2000)

LINCOLN HEIGHTS (village). Covers a land area of 0.739 square miles and a water area of 0 square miles. Located at 39.24° N. Lat.; 84.45° W. Long. Elevation is 594 feet.
History: Incorporated 1946.
Population: 4,805 (1990); 4,113 (2000); 3,725 (2007); 3,439 (2012 projected); Race: 1.2% White, 97.4% Black, 0.0% Asian, 1.4% Hispanic of any race (2007); Density: 5,041.0 persons per square mile (2007); Average household size: 2.50 (2007); Median age: 31.0 (2007); Males per 100 females: 77.0 (2007); Marriage status: 39.3% never married, 38.0% now married, 9.6% widowed, 13.1% divorced (2000); Foreign born: 0.7% (2000); Ancestry (includes multiple ancestries): 83.8% Other groups, 1.4% African, 1.2% Irish, 0.8% German, 0.6% United States or American (2000).
Economy: Single-family building permits issued: 0 (2007); Multi-family building permits issued: 0 (2007); Employment by occupation: 5.5% management, 9.7% professional, 29.1% services, 25.7% sales, 0.0% farming, 2.4% construction, 27.6% production (2000).
Income: Per capita income: $13,865 (2007); Median household income: $21,392 (2007); Average household income: $34,663 (2007); Percent of households with income of $100,000 or more: 4.2% (2007); Poverty rate: 29.9% (2000).
Education: Percent of population age 25 and over with: High school diploma (including GED) or higher: 67.1% (2007); Bachelor's degree or higher: 5.8% (2007); Master's degree or higher: 1.6% (2007).
Housing: Homeownership rate: 35.2% (2007); Median home value: $75,116 (2007); Median rent: $281 per month (2000); Median age of housing: 44 years (2000).
Transportation: Commute to work: 87.4% car, 5.6% public transportation, 5.4% walk, 1.6% work from home (2000); Travel time to work: 29.7% less

than 15 minutes, 44.5% 15 to 30 minutes, 16.3% 30 to 45 minutes, 5.3% 45 to 60 minutes, 4.2% 60 minutes or more (2000)

LOCKLAND (village). Covers a land area of 1.223 square miles and a water area of 0 square miles. Located at 39.22° N. Lat.; 84.45° W. Long. Elevation is 581 feet.

History: Plotted 1828, incorporated 1865.

Population: 4,357 (1990); 3,707 (2000); 3,307 (2007); 3,022 (2012 projected); Race: 67.9% White, 27.9% Black, 0.5% Asian, 2.4% Hispanic of any race (2007); Density: 2,703.8 persons per square mile (2007); Average household size: 2.23 (2007); Median age: 38.5 (2007); Males per 100 females: 102.0 (2007); Marriage status: 33.0% never married, 43.1% now married, 8.9% widowed, 15.0% divorced (2000); Foreign born: 4.9% (2000); Ancestry (includes multiple ancestries): 27.1% Other groups, 21.6% German, 9.7% Irish, 8.1% English, 6.9% United States or American (2000).

Economy: Single-family building permits issued: 3 (2007); Multi-family building permits issued: 0 (2007); Employment by occupation: 7.3% management, 10.4% professional, 20.4% services, 26.2% sales, 0.0% farming, 8.6% construction, 27.1% production (2000).

Income: Per capita income: $18,087 (2007); Median household income: $32,289 (2007); Average household income: $40,387 (2007); Percent of households with income of $100,000 or more: 5.2% (2007); Poverty rate: 17.1% (2000).

Education: Percent of population age 25 and over with: High school diploma (including GED) or higher: 71.3% (2007); Bachelor's degree or higher: 8.5% (2007); Master's degree or higher: 2.7% (2007).

School District(s)

Lockland Local (PK-12)
2005-06 Enrollment: 694 . . . . (513) 563-5000

Housing: Homeownership rate: 49.6% (2007); Median home value: $87,589 (2007); Median rent: $361 per month (2000); Median age of housing: 57 years (2000).

Transportation: Commute to work: 90.4% car, 5.8% public transportation, 1.7% walk, 1.7% work from home (2000); Travel time to work: 26.4% less than 15 minutes, 46.7% 15 to 30 minutes, 22.1% 30 to 45 minutes, 3.5% 45 to 60 minutes, 1.3% 60 minutes or more (2000)

Additional Information Contacts

Village of Lockland. . . . . (513) 761-1124
http://www.lockland.com

LOVELAND (city). Covers a land area of 4.646 square miles and a water area of 0.055 square miles. Located at 39.26° N. Lat.; 84.27° W. Long. Elevation is 594 feet.

Population: 10,756 (1990); 11,677 (2000); 11,323 (2007); 11,242 (2012 projected); Race: 95.5% White, 1.3% Black, 1.1% Asian, 1.7% Hispanic of any race (2007); Density: 2,437.3 persons per square mile (2007); Average household size: 2.53 (2007); Median age: 37.9 (2007); Males per 100 females: 91.8 (2007); Marriage status: 22.8% never married, 61.8% now married, 6.1% widowed, 9.3% divorced (2000); Foreign born: 2.9% (2000); Ancestry (includes multiple ancestries): 31.5% German, 17.5% Irish, 12.4% English, 9.4% Other groups, 8.5% United States or American (2000).

Economy: Single-family building permits issued: 25 (2007); Multi-family building permits issued: 0 (2007); Employment by occupation: 18.3% management, 20.2% professional, 12.9% services, 30.7% sales, 0.1% farming, 6.9% construction, 10.9% production (2000).

Income: Per capita income: $33,105 (2007); Median household income: $64,663 (2007); Average household income: $83,398 (2007); Percent of households with income of $100,000 or more: 25.7% (2007); Poverty rate: 5.7% (2000).

Education: Percent of population age 25 and over with: High school diploma (including GED) or higher: 89.7% (2007); Bachelor's degree or higher: 35.1% (2007); Master's degree or higher: 12.2% (2007).

School District(s)

Loveland City (PK-12)
2005-06 Enrollment: 4,599 . . . . (513) 683-5600
Milford Exempted Village (PK-12)
2005-06 Enrollment: 6,673 . . . . (513) 831-1314
Sycamore Community City (PK-12)
2005-06 Enrollment: 5,686 . . . . (513) 686-1700

Housing: Homeownership rate: 74.5% (2007); Median home value: $157,806 (2007); Median rent: $530 per month (2000); Median age of housing: 25 years (2000).

Newspapers: Bethel Journal (Community news; Circulation 2,035); Community Journal Clermont (Community news; Circulation 24,035); Community Journal North Clermont (Community news; Circulation 14,656); Community Press - Mason and Deerfield (Community news; Circulation 11,350); Eastern Hills Journal (Community news; Circulation 12,818); Forest Hills Journal (Community news; Circulation 14,110); Indian Hill Journal (Community news; Circulation 28,000); Loveland Herald (Community news; Circulation 6,274); Milford-Miami Advertiser (Community news; Circulation 7,370); Northeast Suburban Life (Community news; Circulation 8,011); Suburban Life (Community news; Circulation 8,370)

Transportation: Commute to work: 95.3% car, 0.7% public transportation, 0.4% walk, 3.2% work from home (2000); Travel time to work: 25.6% less than 15 minutes, 43.0% 15 to 30 minutes, 22.2% 30 to 45 minutes, 6.1% 45 to 60 minutes, 3.1% 60 minutes or more (2000)

Additional Information Contacts

City of Loveland . . . . (513) 683-0150
http://www.lovelandoh.com
Loveland Area Chamber of Commerce . . . . (513) 683-1544
http://www.lovelandchamber.org

MACK NORTH (CDP). Aka Mack. Covers a land area of 3.076 square miles and a water area of 0 square miles. Located at 39.16° N. Lat.; 84.66° W. Long.

Population: 2,816 (1990); 3,529 (2000); 3,669 (2007); 3,728 (2012 projected); Race: 97.3% White, 1.3% Black, 0.1% Asian, 1.0% Hispanic of any race (2007); Density: 1,192.7 persons per square mile (2007); Average household size: 3.09 (2007); Median age: 39.4 (2007); Males per 100 females: 101.5 (2007); Marriage status: 21.0% never married, 69.0% now married, 5.0% widowed, 4.9% divorced (2000); Foreign born: 1.4% (2000); Ancestry (includes multiple ancestries): 51.0% German, 18.6% Irish, 8.4% English, 7.5% Italian, 4.0% United States or American (2000).

Economy: Employment by occupation: 16.4% management, 18.9% professional, 9.7% services, 30.9% sales, 0.0% farming, 12.0% construction, 12.1% production (2000).

Income: Per capita income: $37,629 (2007); Median household income: $93,221 (2007); Average household income: $116,310 (2007); Percent of households with income of $100,000 or more: 45.4% (2007); Poverty rate: 4.0% (2000).

Education: Percent of population age 25 and over with: High school diploma (including GED) or higher: 88.8% (2007); Bachelor's degree or higher: 29.6% (2007); Master's degree or higher: 10.6% (2007).

Housing: Homeownership rate: 96.5% (2007); Median home value: $197,234 (2007); Median rent: $566 per month (2000); Median age of housing: 27 years (2000).

Transportation: Commute to work: 94.7% car, 2.1% public transportation, 1.0% walk, 2.3% work from home (2000); Travel time to work: 21.0% less than 15 minutes, 39.4% 15 to 30 minutes, 30.3% 30 to 45 minutes, 7.6% 45 to 60 minutes, 1.7% 60 minutes or more (2000)

MACK SOUTH (CDP). Covers a land area of 3.696 square miles and a water area of 0 square miles. Located at 39.14° N. Lat.; 84.67° W. Long.

Population: 5,767 (1990); 5,837 (2000); 5,959 (2007); 6,010 (2012 projected); Race: 98.8% White, 0.1% Black, 0.5% Asian, 0.3% Hispanic of any race (2007); Density: 1,612.3 persons per square mile (2007); Average household size: 2.95 (2007); Median age: 43.1 (2007); Males per 100 females: 97.4 (2007); Marriage status: 23.3% never married, 70.7% now married, 3.8% widowed, 2.2% divorced (2000); Foreign born: 1.2% (2000); Ancestry (includes multiple ancestries): 63.8% German, 19.3% Irish, 9.1% Italian, 7.4% English, 7.3% United States or American (2000).

Economy: Employment by occupation: 20.5% management, 25.8% professional, 12.2% services, 30.1% sales, 0.0% farming, 6.4% construction, 5.1% production (2000).

Income: Per capita income: $41,427 (2007); Median household income: $97,928 (2007); Average household income: $122,149 (2007); Percent of households with income of $100,000 or more: 48.5% (2007); Poverty rate: 0.4% (2000).

Education: Percent of population age 25 and over with: High school diploma (including GED) or higher: 95.1% (2007); Bachelor's degree or higher: 38.5% (2007); Master's degree or higher: 11.3% (2007).

Housing: Homeownership rate: 98.1% (2007); Median home value: $211,013 (2007); Median rent: $435 per month (2000); Median age of housing: 29 years (2000).

Transportation: Commute to work: 94.0% car, 2.1% public transportation, 0.4% walk, 3.2% work from home (2000); Travel time to work: 19.7% less than 15 minutes, 36.2% 15 to 30 minutes, 33.1% 30 to 45 minutes, 6.3% 45 to 60 minutes, 4.7% 60 minutes or more (2000)

MADEIRA (city). Covers a land area of 3.366 square miles and a water area of 0 square miles. Located at 39.18° N. Lat.; 84.36° W. Long. Elevation is 758 feet.
Population: 9,143 (1990); 8,923 (2000); 8,195 (2007); 7,656 (2012 projected); Race: 95.1% White, 1.5% Black, 1.9% Asian, 1.0% Hispanic of any race (2007); Density: 2,434.7 persons per square mile (2007); Average household size: 2.59 (2007); Median age: 44.0 (2007); Males per 100 females: 89.7 (2007); Marriage status: 18.2% never married, 66.2% now married, 8.4% widowed, 7.2% divorced (2000); Foreign born: 2.8% (2000); Ancestry (includes multiple ancestries): 43.0% German, 20.5% Irish, 14.3% English, 6.2% United States or American, 4.9% Italian (2000).
Economy: Single-family building permits issued: 15 (2007); Multi-family building permits issued: 0 (2007); Employment by occupation: 18.0% management, 33.3% professional, 9.9% services, 27.2% sales, 0.0% farming, 4.3% construction, 7.4% production (2000).
Income: Per capita income: $37,514 (2007); Median household income: $70,500 (2007); Average household income: $95,204 (2007); Percent of households with income of $100,000 or more: 32.3% (2007); Poverty rate: 1.3% (2000).
Education: Percent of population age 25 and over with: High school diploma (including GED) or higher: 92.0% (2007); Bachelor's degree or higher: 44.6% (2007); Master's degree or higher: 16.9% (2007).
Housing: Homeownership rate: 91.6% (2007); Median home value: $194,567 (2007); Median rent: $456 per month (2000); Median age of housing: 45 years (2000).
Safety: Violent crime rate: 2.5 per 10,000 population; Property crime rate: 83.2 per 10,000 population (2007).
Transportation: Commute to work: 92.5% car, 1.3% public transportation, 1.0% walk, 5.1% work from home (2000); Travel time to work: 27.9% less than 15 minutes, 54.8% 15 to 30 minutes, 14.0% 30 to 45 minutes, 1.2% 45 to 60 minutes, 2.2% 60 minutes or more (2000)
Additional Information Contacts
City of Madeira. . . . . (513) 561-7228
http://www.madeiracity.com

MARIEMONT (village). Covers a land area of 0.854 square miles and a water area of 0.009 square miles. Located at 39.14° N. Lat.; 84.37° W. Long. Elevation is 587 feet.
History: Mariemont was laid out in 1922 along the Little Miami River on land owned by Marie Emery of Cincinnati. A large stone tower on a knoll above the town housed the Bells of Mariemont, 23 bells weighing from 100 pounds to two tons.
Population: 3,169 (1990); 3,408 (2000); 3,061 (2007); 2,815 (2012 projected); Race: 95.7% White, 1.6% Black, 1.0% Asian, 1.5% Hispanic of any race (2007); Density: 3,585.3 persons per square mile (2007); Average household size: 2.35 (2007); Median age: 40.1 (2007); Males per 100 females: 80.2 (2007); Marriage status: 18.1% never married, 61.9% now married, 10.9% widowed, 9.1% divorced (2000); Foreign born: 3.9% (2000); Ancestry (includes multiple ancestries): 37.9% German, 20.2% English, 18.6% Irish, 6.3% Scottish, 4.9% Italian (2000).
Economy: Single-family building permits issued: 0 (2007); Multi-family building permits issued: 0 (2007); Employment by occupation: 20.9% management, 41.0% professional, 10.8% services, 23.7% sales, 0.0% farming, 1.4% construction, 2.2% production (2000).
Income: Per capita income: $37,714 (2007); Median household income: $68,646 (2007); Average household income: $87,676 (2007); Percent of households with income of $100,000 or more: 31.1% (2007); Poverty rate: 5.0% (2000).
Education: Percent of population age 25 and over with: High school diploma (including GED) or higher: 93.3% (2007); Bachelor's degree or higher: 63.2% (2007); Master's degree or higher: 27.8% (2007).
Housing: Homeownership rate: 62.0% (2007); Median home value: $254,911 (2007); Median rent: $644 per month (2000); Median age of housing: 55 years (2000).
Safety: Violent crime rate: 3.3 per 10,000 population; Property crime rate: 239.1 per 10,000 population (2007).
Transportation: Commute to work: 90.6% car, 3.1% public transportation, 1.8% walk, 4.5% work from home (2000); Travel time to work: 22.4% less than 15 minutes, 58.7% 15 to 30 minutes, 17.7% 30 to 45 minutes, 0.8% 45 to 60 minutes, 0.3% 60 minutes or more (2000)

MONFORT HEIGHTS EAST (CDP). Covers a land area of 1.439 square miles and a water area of 0 square miles. Located at 39.18° N. Lat.; 84.58° W. Long.
Population: 3,645 (1990); 3,880 (2000); 3,958 (2007); 3,999 (2012 projected); Race: 89.0% White, 7.7% Black, 1.6% Asian, 0.8% Hispanic of any race (2007); Density: 2,750.4 persons per square mile (2007); Average household size: 2.45 (2007); Median age: 35.7 (2007); Males per 100 females: 95.8 (2007); Marriage status: 24.1% never married, 63.1% now married, 6.3% widowed, 6.6% divorced (2000); Foreign born: 1.7% (2000); Ancestry (includes multiple ancestries): 49.8% German, 13.9% Irish, 9.5% Other groups, 7.7% English, 6.8% Italian (2000).
Economy: Employment by occupation: 14.3% management, 25.3% professional, 10.9% services, 31.4% sales, 0.0% farming, 7.9% construction, 10.2% production (2000).
Income: Per capita income: $26,802 (2007); Median household income: $56,522 (2007); Average household income: $65,511 (2007); Percent of households with income of $100,000 or more: 15.2% (2007); Poverty rate: 7.5% (2000).
Education: Percent of population age 25 and over with: High school diploma (including GED) or higher: 92.2% (2007); Bachelor's degree or higher: 30.5% (2007); Master's degree or higher: 6.7% (2007).
Housing: Homeownership rate: 75.2% (2007); Median home value: $131,944 (2007); Median rent: $531 per month (2000); Median age of housing: 35 years (2000).
Transportation: Commute to work: 89.8% car, 2.6% public transportation, 2.6% walk, 4.7% work from home (2000); Travel time to work: 18.6% less than 15 minutes, 48.9% 15 to 30 minutes, 26.2% 30 to 45 minutes, 3.7% 45 to 60 minutes, 2.6% 60 minutes or more (2000)

MONFORT HEIGHTS SOUTH (CDP). Aka Monfort Heights. Covers a land area of 3.108 square miles and a water area of <.001 square miles. Located at 39.17° N. Lat.; 84.60° W. Long.
Population: 4,399 (1990); 4,466 (2000); 4,782 (2007); 4,952 (2012 projected); Race: 97.5% White, 0.7% Black, 0.6% Asian, 0.6% Hispanic of any race (2007); Density: 1,538.7 persons per square mile (2007); Average household size: 2.59 (2007); Median age: 42.3 (2007); Males per 100 females: 99.2 (2007); Marriage status: 21.8% never married, 63.8% now married, 8.3% widowed, 6.1% divorced (2000); Foreign born: 1.9% (2000); Ancestry (includes multiple ancestries): 52.4% German, 17.3% Irish, 11.5% English, 11.4% United States or American, 6.6% Italian (2000).
Economy: Employment by occupation: 16.7% management, 20.9% professional, 13.3% services, 31.0% sales, 0.0% farming, 7.0% construction, 11.2% production (2000).
Income: Per capita income: $36,692 (2007); Median household income: $70,853 (2007); Average household income: $95,132 (2007); Percent of households with income of $100,000 or more: 29.0% (2007); Poverty rate: 5.6% (2000).
Education: Percent of population age 25 and over with: High school diploma (including GED) or higher: 89.2% (2007); Bachelor's degree or higher: 25.7% (2007); Master's degree or higher: 7.3% (2007).
Housing: Homeownership rate: 94.1% (2007); Median home value: $143,302 (2007); Median rent: $513 per month (2000); Median age of housing: 38 years (2000).
Transportation: Commute to work: 95.1% car, 2.5% public transportation, 0.0% walk, 2.2% work from home (2000); Travel time to work: 22.1% less than 15 minutes, 49.4% 15 to 30 minutes, 23.8% 30 to 45 minutes, 2.5% 45 to 60 minutes, 2.3% 60 minutes or more (2000)

MONTGOMERY (city). Covers a land area of 5.325 square miles and a water area of 0 square miles. Located at 39.24° N. Lat.; 84.34° W. Long. Elevation is 801 feet.
Population: 9,896 (1990); 10,163 (2000); 9,806 (2007); 9,534 (2012 projected); Race: 93.8% White, 1.9% Black, 2.8% Asian, 1.0% Hispanic of any race (2007); Density: 1,841.6 persons per square mile (2007); Average household size: 2.74 (2007); Median age: 45.4 (2007); Males per 100 females: 93.4 (2007); Marriage status: 16.1% never married, 72.9% now married, 7.0% widowed, 4.0% divorced (2000); Foreign born: 7.0% (2000); Ancestry (includes multiple ancestries): 34.2% German, 16.7% Irish, 14.9% English, 7.4% Other groups, 5.9% United States or American (2000).
Economy: Single-family building permits issued: 44 (2007); Multi-family building permits issued: 0 (2007); Employment by occupation: 30.1% management, 33.4% professional, 6.6% services, 23.5% sales, 0.2% farming, 2.2% construction, 4.0% production (2000).
Income: Per capita income: $51,150 (2007); Median household income: $100,528 (2007); Average household income: $139,742 (2007); Percent of households with income of $100,000 or more: 50.3% (2007); Poverty rate: 2.8% (2000).

Taxes: Total city taxes per capita: $1,100 (2006); City property taxes per capita: $391 (2006).
Education: Percent of population age 25 and over with: High school diploma (including GED) or higher: 95.7% (2007); Bachelor's degree or higher: 62.9% (2007); Master's degree or higher: 26.0% (2007).
Housing: Homeownership rate: 91.1% (2007); Median home value: $263,455 (2007); Median rent: $841 per month (2000); Median age of housing: 27 years (2000).
Safety: Violent crime rate: 1.0 per 10,000 population; Property crime rate: 202.7 per 10,000 population (2007).
Transportation: Commute to work: 90.7% car, 0.9% public transportation, 1.6% walk, 6.4% work from home (2000); Travel time to work: 29.0% less than 15 minutes, 44.3% 15 to 30 minutes, 19.4% 30 to 45 minutes, 2.6% 45 to 60 minutes, 4.6% 60 minutes or more (2000)
Additional Information Contacts
City of Montgomery . . . . (513) 891-2424
http://www.ci.montgomery.oh.us

MOUNT HEALTHY (city). Covers a land area of 1.423 square miles and a water area of 0 square miles. Located at 39.23° N. Lat.; 84.54° W. Long. Elevation is 837 feet.
History: Mount Healthy was founded in 1817 by John Laboyteaux and Samuel Hill. It was first called Mount Pleasant, but the name was later changed to reflect the village's escape from the cholera epidemic of the 1850's.
Population: 7,580 (1990); 7,149 (2000); 7,325 (2007); 7,405 (2012 projected); Race: 68.1% White, 28.4% Black, 0.5% Asian, 1.4% Hispanic of any race (2007); Density: 5,145.8 persons per square mile (2007); Average household size: 2.15 (2007); Median age: 39.1 (2007); Males per 100 females: 79.5 (2007); Marriage status: 28.7% never married, 46.8% now married, 12.7% widowed, 11.8% divorced (2000); Foreign born: 2.3% (2000); Ancestry (includes multiple ancestries): 32.0% German, 28.8% Other groups, 10.0% Irish, 8.0% English, 7.4% United States or American (2000).
Economy: Single-family building permits issued: 3 (2007); Multi-family building permits issued: 0 (2007); Employment by occupation: 11.1% management, 19.3% professional, 15.6% services, 30.3% sales, 0.0% farming, 6.2% construction, 17.5% production (2000).
Income: Per capita income: $22,388 (2007); Median household income: $38,681 (2007); Average household income: $46,656 (2007); Percent of households with income of $100,000 or more: 6.2% (2007); Poverty rate: 8.9% (2000).
Education: Percent of population age 25 and over with: High school diploma (including GED) or higher: 77.3% (2007); Bachelor's degree or higher: 16.2% (2007); Master's degree or higher: 5.0% (2007).

School District(s)
Hamilton Cnty Math & Science (KG-04)
2005-06 Enrollment: 285 . . . . (513) 728-8620
Housing: Homeownership rate: 47.8% (2007); Median home value: $103,997 (2007); Median rent: $466 per month (2000); Median age of housing: 43 years (2000).
Transportation: Commute to work: 92.1% car, 2.5% public transportation, 2.0% walk, 2.6% work from home (2000); Travel time to work: 23.0% less than 15 minutes, 44.6% 15 to 30 minutes, 23.7% 30 to 45 minutes, 6.4% 45 to 60 minutes, 2.2% 60 minutes or more (2000)
Additional Information Contacts
City of Mount Healthy. . . . . (513) 931-8840
http://www.mthealthy.org

MOUNT HEALTHY HEIGHTS (CDP). Covers a land area of 0.768 square miles and a water area of 0 square miles. Located at 39.27° N. Lat.; 84.57° W. Long. Elevation is 846 feet.
Population: 3,863 (1990); 3,450 (2000); 3,075 (2007); 2,837 (2012 projected); Race: 65.0% White, 30.6% Black, 1.6% Asian, 1.3% Hispanic of any race (2007); Density: 4,001.7 persons per square mile (2007); Average household size: 2.62 (2007); Median age: 33.7 (2007); Males per 100 females: 96.0 (2007); Marriage status: 30.3% never married, 56.8% now married, 3.4% widowed, 9.6% divorced (2000); Foreign born: 2.2% (2000); Ancestry (includes multiple ancestries): 36.5% German, 26.5% Other groups, 10.0% Irish, 4.5% United States or American, 4.0% English (2000).
Economy: Employment by occupation: 9.5% management, 17.1% professional, 11.6% services, 30.4% sales, 0.0% farming, 10.7% construction, 20.7% production (2000).
Income: Per capita income: $23,727 (2007); Median household income: $52,965 (2007); Average household income: $62,147 (2007); Percent of households with income of $100,000 or more: 11.6% (2007); Poverty rate: 4.2% (2000).
Education: Percent of population age 25 and over with: High school diploma (including GED) or higher: 84.5% (2007); Bachelor's degree or higher: 16.6% (2007); Master's degree or higher: 4.2% (2007).
Housing: Homeownership rate: 66.9% (2007); Median home value: $104,550 (2007); Median rent: $608 per month (2000); Median age of housing: 30 years (2000).
Transportation: Commute to work: 96.6% car, 1.9% public transportation, 0.0% walk, 1.5% work from home (2000); Travel time to work: 17.7% less than 15 minutes, 44.5% 15 to 30 minutes, 26.3% 30 to 45 minutes, 6.5% 45 to 60 minutes, 5.0% 60 minutes or more (2000)

NEWTOWN (village). Covers a land area of 2.322 square miles and a water area of 0 square miles. Located at 39.12° N. Lat.; 84.35° W. Long. Elevation is 499 feet.
History: Laid out 1801.
Population: 1,589 (1990); 2,420 (2000); 3,012 (2007); 3,364 (2012 projected); Race: 95.1% White, 2.9% Black, 0.9% Asian, 1.9% Hispanic of any race (2007); Density: 1,297.4 persons per square mile (2007); Average household size: 2.54 (2007); Median age: 38.9 (2007); Males per 100 females: 95.2 (2007); Marriage status: 26.3% never married, 60.4% now married, 5.0% widowed, 8.2% divorced (2000); Foreign born: 2.0% (2000); Ancestry (includes multiple ancestries): 37.5% German, 16.3% Irish, 10.1% English, 8.4% United States or American, 6.5% Other groups (2000).
Economy: Single-family building permits issued: 3 (2007); Multi-family building permits issued: 0 (2007); Employment by occupation: 20.3% management, 15.4% professional, 14.0% services, 24.8% sales, 0.0% farming, 12.3% construction, 13.1% production (2000).
Income: Per capita income: $38,544 (2007); Median household income: $60,554 (2007); Average household income: $97,970 (2007); Percent of households with income of $100,000 or more: 26.9% (2007); Poverty rate: 7.1% (2000).
Education: Percent of population age 25 and over with: High school diploma (including GED) or higher: 84.1% (2007); Bachelor's degree or higher: 33.1% (2007); Master's degree or higher: 12.3% (2007).
Housing: Homeownership rate: 70.3% (2007); Median home value: $129,576 (2007); Median rent: $689 per month (2000); Median age of housing: 36 years (2000).
Safety: Violent crime rate: 2.5 per 10,000 population; Property crime rate: 174.0 per 10,000 population (2007).
Transportation: Commute to work: 92.9% car, 0.4% public transportation, 5.2% walk, 0.7% work from home (2000); Travel time to work: 22.0% less than 15 minutes, 48.6% 15 to 30 minutes, 22.4% 30 to 45 minutes, 4.7% 45 to 60 minutes, 2.3% 60 minutes or more (2000)

NORTH BEND (village). Covers a land area of 1.076 square miles and a water area of 0.092 square miles. Located at 39.15° N. Lat.; 84.74° W. Long. Elevation is 574 feet.
History: North Bend was founded in 1789 by John Cleves Symmes. William Henry Harrison lived here until he became the 9th President of the U.S. in 1841. This was the birthplace of his grandson, William Henry Harrison (1833-1901), the 23rd U.S. President.
Population: 541 (1990); 603 (2000); 512 (2007); 475 (2012 projected); Race: 99.8% White, 0.2% Black, 0.0% Asian, 0.0% Hispanic of any race (2007); Density: 475.8 persons per square mile (2007); Average household size: 2.33 (2007); Median age: 46.6 (2007); Males per 100 females: 93.9 (2007); Marriage status: 21.7% never married, 59.4% now married, 6.2% widowed, 12.6% divorced (2000); Foreign born: 0.3% (2000); Ancestry (includes multiple ancestries): 41.1% German, 22.6% Irish, 11.0% English, 8.0% United States or American, 6.8% Italian (2000).
Economy: Employment by occupation: 20.2% management, 17.3% professional, 15.8% services, 27.9% sales, 0.0% farming, 7.0% construction, 11.8% production (2000).
Income: Per capita income: $41,802 (2007); Median household income: $70,200 (2007); Average household income: $97,284 (2007); Percent of households with income of $100,000 or more: 32.3% (2007); Poverty rate: 6.5% (2000).
Education: Percent of population age 25 and over with: High school diploma (including GED) or higher: 86.1% (2007); Bachelor's degree or higher: 26.5% (2007); Master's degree or higher: 7.2% (2007).

School District(s)
Southwest Local (PK-12)
2005-06 Enrollment: 3,865 . . . . (513) 367-4139

Three Rivers Local (PK-12)
2005-06 Enrollment: 1,993 . . . . (513) 941-6400
Housing: Homeownership rate: 68.2% (2007); Median home value: $183,333 (2007); Median rent: $400 per month (2000); Median age of housing: 43 years (2000).
Transportation: Commute to work: 89.2% car, 1.1% public transportation, 4.5% walk, 3.3% work from home (2000); Travel time to work: 26.5% less than 15 minutes, 36.9% 15 to 30 minutes, 28.8% 30 to 45 minutes, 6.5% 45 to 60 minutes, 1.2% 60 minutes or more (2000)

NORTH COLLEGE HILL (city). Covers a land area of 1.836 square miles and a water area of 0.001 square miles. Located at 39.21° N. Lat.; 84.55° W. Long. Elevation is 823 feet.
History: Named for its location north of Cincinnati. Revolutionary War cemetery is in the city. Incorporated as a city 1940.
Population: 11,002 (1990); 10,082 (2000); 9,097 (2007); 8,442 (2012 projected); Race: 67.2% White, 30.3% Black, 0.2% Asian, 0.7% Hispanic of any race (2007); Density: 4,954.6 persons per square mile (2007); Average household size: 2.34 (2007); Median age: 38.5 (2007); Males per 100 females: 86.7 (2007); Marriage status: 30.3% never married, 49.7% now married, 9.7% widowed, 10.3% divorced (2000); Foreign born: 1.7% (2000); Ancestry (includes multiple ancestries): 34.9% German, 21.3% Other groups, 13.5% United States or American, 10.7% Irish, 7.2% English (2000).
Economy: Single-family building permits issued: 2 (2007); Multi-family building permits issued: 0 (2007); Employment by occupation: 9.3% management, 14.4% professional, 17.7% services, 33.2% sales, 0.3% farming, 10.3% construction, 14.8% production (2000).
Income: Per capita income: $21,687 (2007); Median household income: $42,545 (2007); Average household income: $49,972 (2007); Percent of households with income of $100,000 or more: 7.1% (2007); Poverty rate: 8.7% (2000).
Education: Percent of population age 25 and over with: High school diploma (including GED) or higher: 81.6% (2007); Bachelor's degree or higher: 13.7% (2007); Master's degree or higher: 4.5% (2007).
Housing: Homeownership rate: 68.7% (2007); Median home value: $101,367 (2007); Median rent: $476 per month (2000); Median age of housing: 48 years (2000).
Transportation: Commute to work: 89.0% car, 6.0% public transportation, 2.5% walk, 2.5% work from home (2000); Travel time to work: 21.5% less than 15 minutes, 47.3% 15 to 30 minutes, 23.5% 30 to 45 minutes, 4.2% 45 to 60 minutes, 3.5% 60 minutes or more (2000)
Additional Information Contacts
City of North College Hill . . . . (513) 521-7413
http://www.northcollegehill.org

NORTHBROOK (CDP). Covers a land area of 1.939 square miles and a water area of 0 square miles. Located at 39.24° N. Lat.; 84.57° W. Long. Elevation is 830 feet.
Population: 11,471 (1990); 11,076 (2000); 9,891 (2007); 9,049 (2012 projected); Race: 77.3% White, 18.2% Black, 1.1% Asian, 2.1% Hispanic of any race (2007); Density: 5,101.8 persons per square mile (2007); Average household size: 2.57 (2007); Median age: 36.6 (2007); Males per 100 females: 90.8 (2007); Marriage status: 25.0% never married, 54.3% now married, 7.5% widowed, 13.2% divorced (2000); Foreign born: 0.9% (2000); Ancestry (includes multiple ancestries): 31.8% German, 18.1% Other groups, 12.8% Irish, 8.9% English, 8.8% United States or American (2000).
Economy: Employment by occupation: 9.2% management, 11.4% professional, 18.2% services, 34.5% sales, 0.0% farming, 10.3% construction, 16.4% production (2000).
Income: Per capita income: $22,583 (2007); Median household income: $50,483 (2007); Average household income: $58,034 (2007); Percent of households with income of $100,000 or more: 10.2% (2007); Poverty rate: 7.0% (2000).
Education: Percent of population age 25 and over with: High school diploma (including GED) or higher: 75.5% (2007); Bachelor's degree or higher: 11.1% (2007); Master's degree or higher: 3.0% (2007).
Housing: Homeownership rate: 79.3% (2007); Median home value: $94,822 (2007); Median rent: $593 per month (2000); Median age of housing: 33 years (2000).
Transportation: Commute to work: 95.1% car, 1.6% public transportation, 1.2% walk, 1.3% work from home (2000); Travel time to work: 22.4% less than 15 minutes, 44.5% 15 to 30 minutes, 26.4% 30 to 45 minutes, 4.4% 45 to 60 minutes, 2.3% 60 minutes or more (2000)

NORTHGATE (CDP). Covers a land area of 2.522 square miles and a water area of 0.021 square miles. Located at 39.25° N. Lat.; 84.58° W. Long. Elevation is 883 feet.
Population: 7,864 (1990); 8,016 (2000); 7,409 (2007); 6,967 (2012 projected); Race: 83.1% White, 12.6% Black, 1.5% Asian, 1.9% Hispanic of any race (2007); Density: 2,937.9 persons per square mile (2007); Average household size: 2.82 (2007); Median age: 38.4 (2007); Males per 100 females: 98.4 (2007); Marriage status: 26.4% never married, 60.0% now married, 6.5% widowed, 7.1% divorced (2000); Foreign born: 0.6% (2000); Ancestry (includes multiple ancestries): 40.6% German, 17.2% Other groups, 15.6% Irish, 8.4% United States or American, 6.4% English (2000).
Economy: Employment by occupation: 9.7% management, 12.4% professional, 16.8% services, 35.6% sales, 0.3% farming, 8.8% construction, 16.5% production (2000).
Income: Per capita income: $25,289 (2007); Median household income: $61,424 (2007); Average household income: $70,985 (2007); Percent of households with income of $100,000 or more: 18.3% (2007); Poverty rate: 3.7% (2000).
Education: Percent of population age 25 and over with: High school diploma (including GED) or higher: 81.8% (2007); Bachelor's degree or higher: 14.3% (2007); Master's degree or higher: 4.0% (2007).
Housing: Homeownership rate: 86.5% (2007); Median home value: $119,185 (2007); Median rent: $616 per month (2000); Median age of housing: 32 years (2000).
Transportation: Commute to work: 93.8% car, 1.1% public transportation, 1.6% walk, 2.2% work from home (2000); Travel time to work: 25.1% less than 15 minutes, 47.8% 15 to 30 minutes, 18.4% 30 to 45 minutes, 3.9% 45 to 60 minutes, 4.8% 60 minutes or more (2000)

NORWOOD (city). Covers a land area of 3.116 square miles and a water area of 0 square miles. Located at 39.16° N. Lat.; 84.45° W. Long. Elevation is 656 feet.
History: Named for the shortened form of north woods. Norwood began in the early 1800's, and until 1888 was called Sharpsburg, for early settler John Sharp. The U.S. Playing Card Company was established here, and maintained a Playing Card Museum.
Population: 23,635 (1990); 21,675 (2000); 19,481 (2007); 17,911 (2012 projected); Race: 92.4% White, 3.2% Black, 0.8% Asian, 2.7% Hispanic of any race (2007); Density: 6,252.4 persons per square mile (2007); Average household size: 2.27 (2007); Median age: 37.2 (2007); Males per 100 females: 96.2 (2007); Marriage status: 34.0% never married, 44.5% now married, 8.1% widowed, 13.5% divorced (2000); Foreign born: 2.3% (2000); Ancestry (includes multiple ancestries): 28.2% German, 19.0% Irish, 11.7% Other groups, 10.5% United States or American, 9.8% English (2000).
Economy: Unemployment rate: 6.4% (6/2008); Total civilian labor force: 10,765 (6/2008); Single-family building permits issued: 0 (2007); Multi-family building permits issued: 0 (2007); Employment by occupation: 9.2% management, 14.6% professional, 17.3% services, 28.4% sales, 0.0% farming, 10.2% construction, 20.3% production (2000).
Income: Per capita income: $21,414 (2007); Median household income: $38,134 (2007); Average household income: $48,394 (2007); Percent of households with income of $100,000 or more: 8.7% (2007); Poverty rate: 12.9% (2000).
Education: Percent of population age 25 and over with: High school diploma (including GED) or higher: 70.8% (2007); Bachelor's degree or higher: 14.1% (2007); Master's degree or higher: 3.6% (2007).

School District(s)

Norwood City (PK-12)
2005-06 Enrollment: 2,578 . . . . (513) 924-2500

Two-year College(s)

ITT Technical Institute-Norwood (Private, For-profit)
Fall 2007 Enrollment: 775 . . . . (513) 531-8300
2007-08 Tuition: In-state $15,600; Out-of-state $15,600
Housing: Homeownership rate: 51.5% (2007); Median home value: $112,378 (2007); Median rent: $387 per month (2000); Median age of housing: 60+ years (2000).
Transportation: Commute to work: 90.0% car, 3.5% public transportation, 4.0% walk, 1.6% work from home (2000); Travel time to work: 38.4% less than 15 minutes, 42.9% 15 to 30 minutes, 12.8% 30 to 45 minutes, 2.9% 45 to 60 minutes, 3.0% 60 minutes or more (2000)
Additional Information Contacts
City of Norwood . . . . (513) 458-4501
http://www.norwood-ohio.com

Norwood Chamber of Commerce . . . . (513) 956-7935
http://www.norwoodchamber.org

PLEASANT RUN (CDP). Covers a land area of 2.072 square miles and a water area of 0 square miles. Located at 39.29° N. Lat.; 84.56° W. Long. Elevation is 748 feet.
Population: 4,964 (1990); 5,267 (2000); 5,059 (2007); 4,891 (2012 projected); Race: 86.1% White, 9.4% Black, 2.3% Asian, 1.4% Hispanic of any race (2007); Density: 2,441.2 persons per square mile (2007); Average household size: 2.88 (2007); Median age: 36.6 (2007); Males per 100 females: 97.9 (2007); Marriage status: 21.8% never married, 64.6% now married, 6.8% widowed, 6.8% divorced (2000); Foreign born: 2.2% (2000); Ancestry (includes multiple ancestries): 33.9% German, 14.0% Other groups, 14.0% Irish, 10.7% United States or American, 10.6% English (2000).
Economy: Employment by occupation: 10.8% management, 17.0% professional, 12.7% services, 32.9% sales, 0.0% farming, 11.0% construction, 15.6% production (2000).
Income: Per capita income: $25,020 (2007); Median household income: $65,530 (2007); Average household income: $71,924 (2007); Percent of households with income of $100,000 or more: 18.1% (2007); Poverty rate: 3.0% (2000).
Education: Percent of population age 25 and over with: High school diploma (including GED) or higher: 88.0% (2007); Bachelor's degree or higher: 17.5% (2007); Master's degree or higher: 4.4% (2007).
Housing: Homeownership rate: 95.5% (2007); Median home value: $119,951 (2007); Median rent: $698 per month (2000); Median age of housing: 29 years (2000).
Transportation: Commute to work: 97.4% car, 0.2% public transportation, 0.2% walk, 1.8% work from home (2000); Travel time to work: 16.6% less than 15 minutes, 50.0% 15 to 30 minutes, 24.9% 30 to 45 minutes, 4.4% 45 to 60 minutes, 4.1% 60 minutes or more (2000)

PLEASANT RUN FARM (CDP). Covers a land area of 1.049 square miles and a water area of 0 square miles. Located at 39.29° N. Lat.; 84.55° W. Long. Elevation is 764 feet.
Population: 4,529 (1990); 4,731 (2000); 4,400 (2007); 4,284 (2012 projected); Race: 65.1% White, 31.4% Black, 1.4% Asian, 0.8% Hispanic of any race (2007); Density: 4,195.8 persons per square mile (2007); Average household size: 2.80 (2007); Median age: 34.0 (2007); Males per 100 females: 91.8 (2007); Marriage status: 25.2% never married, 62.6% now married, 3.2% widowed, 9.0% divorced (2000); Foreign born: 2.0% (2000); Ancestry (includes multiple ancestries): 34.1% German, 21.0% Other groups, 12.5% Irish, 8.6% United States or American, 7.5% English (2000).
Economy: Employment by occupation: 15.8% management, 25.5% professional, 7.2% services, 29.8% sales, 0.0% farming, 6.4% construction, 15.3% production (2000).
Income: Per capita income: $26,550 (2007); Median household income: $70,805 (2007); Average household income: $74,219 (2007); Percent of households with income of $100,000 or more: 22.3% (2007); Poverty rate: 4.8% (2000).
Education: Percent of population age 25 and over with: High school diploma (including GED) or higher: 92.0% (2007); Bachelor's degree or higher: 30.2% (2007); Master's degree or higher: 11.4% (2007).
Housing: Homeownership rate: 83.0% (2007); Median home value: $143,884 (2007); Median rent: $533 per month (2000); Median age of housing: 25 years (2000).
Transportation: Commute to work: 93.6% car, 2.3% public transportation, 0.4% walk, 3.5% work from home (2000); Travel time to work: 19.7% less than 15 minutes, 45.3% 15 to 30 minutes, 24.9% 30 to 45 minutes, 5.2% 45 to 60 minutes, 5.0% 60 minutes or more (2000)

READING (city). Covers a land area of 2.920 square miles and a water area of 0 square miles. Located at 39.22° N. Lat.; 84.43° W. Long. Elevation is 561 feet.
History: Reading was platted in 1798 by Adam Vorhees, and named Vorheestown. The name was changed to honor Redingbo, William Penn's son-in-law.
Population: 12,038 (1990); 11,292 (2000); 10,064 (2007); 9,165 (2012 projected); Race: 91.5% White, 4.5% Black, 1.4% Asian, 1.1% Hispanic of any race (2007); Density: 3,447.0 persons per square mile (2007); Average household size: 2.24 (2007); Median age: 40.4 (2007); Males per 100 females: 95.4 (2007); Marriage status: 27.2% never married, 51.2% now married, 7.5% widowed, 14.0% divorced (2000); Foreign born: 2.7% (2000); Ancestry (includes multiple ancestries): 39.6% German, 17.8% Irish, 9.1% English, 8.6% Other groups, 8.5% United States or American (2000).
Economy: Single-family building permits issued: 1 (2007); Multi-family building permits issued: 0 (2007); Employment by occupation: 10.4% management, 14.7% professional, 15.6% services, 31.8% sales, 0.1% farming, 10.4% construction, 17.0% production (2000).
Income: Per capita income: $26,091 (2007); Median household income: $44,414 (2007); Average household income: $58,210 (2007); Percent of households with income of $100,000 or more: 12.9% (2007); Poverty rate: 7.3% (2000).
Taxes: Total city taxes per capita: $492 (2006); City property taxes per capita: $37 (2006).
Education: Percent of population age 25 and over with: High school diploma (including GED) or higher: 78.9% (2007); Bachelor's degree or higher: 16.2% (2007); Master's degree or higher: 5.9% (2007).

School District(s)

Reading Community City (PK-12)
2005-06 Enrollment: 1,407 . . . . (513) 554-1800
Housing: Homeownership rate: 58.6% (2007); Median home value: $116,434 (2007); Median rent: $410 per month (2000); Median age of housing: 44 years (2000).
Safety: Violent crime rate: 29.2 per 10,000 population; Property crime rate: 392.5 per 10,000 population (2007).
Transportation: Commute to work: 95.4% car, 0.6% public transportation, 1.4% walk, 1.7% work from home (2000); Travel time to work: 30.5% less than 15 minutes, 51.9% 15 to 30 minutes, 11.9% 30 to 45 minutes, 2.8% 45 to 60 minutes, 2.9% 60 minutes or more (2000)
Additional Information Contacts
City of Reading . . . . (513) 733-3725
http://www.readingohio.org
Reading Chamber of Commerce . . . . (513) 786-7274
http://www.readingohiochamber.org

SAINT BERNARD (city). Covers a land area of 1.541 square miles and a water area of 0 square miles. Located at 39.16° N. Lat.; 84.49° W. Long. Elevation is 558 feet.
Population: 5,344 (1990); 4,924 (2000); 4,423 (2007); 4,062 (2012 projected); Race: 89.2% White, 8.2% Black, 0.7% Asian, 0.9% Hispanic of any race (2007); Density: 2,870.9 persons per square mile (2007); Average household size: 2.33 (2007); Median age: 38.6 (2007); Males per 100 females: 92.1 (2007); Marriage status: 28.7% never married, 50.3% now married, 10.4% widowed, 10.6% divorced (2000); Foreign born: 2.5% (2000); Ancestry (includes multiple ancestries): 41.1% German, 17.1% Irish, 10.7% Other groups, 10.5% United States or American, 9.9% English (2000).
Economy: Single-family building permits issued: 0 (2007); Multi-family building permits issued: 0 (2007); Employment by occupation: 10.4% management, 15.7% professional, 15.5% services, 28.4% sales, 0.3% farming, 11.4% construction, 18.3% production (2000).
Income: Per capita income: $21,401 (2007); Median household income: $42,645 (2007); Average household income: $49,726 (2007); Percent of households with income of $100,000 or more: 7.9% (2007); Poverty rate: 8.7% (2000).
Education: Percent of population age 25 and over with: High school diploma (including GED) or higher: 81.0% (2007); Bachelor's degree or higher: 13.4% (2007); Master's degree or higher: 4.5% (2007).

School District(s)

St Bernard-Elmwood Place City (PK-12)
2005-06 Enrollment: 1,120 . . . . (513) 482-7121
Housing: Homeownership rate: 64.1% (2007); Median home value: $110,927 (2007); Median rent: $391 per month (2000); Median age of housing: 60+ years (2000).
Safety: Violent crime rate: 32.1 per 10,000 population; Property crime rate: 387.3 per 10,000 population (2007).
Transportation: Commute to work: 89.2% car, 3.9% public transportation, 5.1% walk, 1.4% work from home (2000); Travel time to work: 35.7% less than 15 minutes, 48.0% 15 to 30 minutes, 9.8% 30 to 45 minutes, 3.8% 45 to 60 minutes, 2.8% 60 minutes or more (2000)

SHARONVILLE (city). Covers a land area of 9.806 square miles and a water area of 0.055 square miles. Located at 39.28° N. Lat.; 84.39° W. Long. Elevation is 584 feet.
History: Named for Sharon, Pennsylvania, which was named for the region in Palestine mentioned in the Bible. Sharonville was surveyed in

1796 by Simon Hegerman, and became a transportation center when the New York Central Lines built their freight yards and shops here.
Population: 13,092 (1990); 13,804 (2000); 12,910 (2007); 12,248 (2012 projected); Race: 85.1% White, 6.8% Black, 4.6% Asian, 3.6% Hispanic of any race (2007); Density: 1,316.5 persons per square mile (2007); Average household size: 2.15 (2007); Median age: 41.7 (2007); Males per 100 females: 93.3 (2007); Marriage status: 24.4% never married, 54.5% now married, 8.6% widowed, 12.6% divorced (2000); Foreign born: 6.4% (2000); Ancestry (includes multiple ancestries): 37.5% German, 14.8% Other groups, 12.7% Irish, 10.7% English, 8.9% United States or American (2000).
Economy: Single-family building permits issued: 0 (2007); Multi-family building permits issued: 0 (2007); Employment by occupation: 16.1% management, 24.8% professional, 13.7% services, 26.8% sales, 0.2% farming, 5.9% construction, 12.6% production (2000).
Income: Per capita income: $33,266 (2007); Median household income: $52,997 (2007); Average household income: $70,622 (2007); Percent of households with income of $100,000 or more: 19.9% (2007); Poverty rate: 4.0% (2000).
Education: Percent of population age 25 and over with: High school diploma (including GED) or higher: 87.8% (2007); Bachelor's degree or higher: 34.4% (2007); Master's degree or higher: 11.4% (2007).
Housing: Homeownership rate: 63.8% (2007); Median home value: $139,229 (2007); Median rent: $610 per month (2000); Median age of housing: 28 years (2000).
Transportation: Commute to work: 95.2% car, 0.6% public transportation, 1.6% walk, 2.1% work from home (2000); Travel time to work: 36.5% less than 15 minutes, 41.1% 15 to 30 minutes, 16.4% 30 to 45 minutes, 4.0% 45 to 60 minutes, 2.1% 60 minutes or more (2000)
Additional Information Contacts
City of Sharonville . . . . (513) 563-1144
http://www.sharonville.org
Sharonville Chamber of Commerce. . . . . (513) 554-1722
http://www.sharonvillechamber.com

SHERWOOD (CDP). Covers a land area of 1.109 square miles and a water area of 0 square miles. Located at 39.08° N. Lat.; 84.36° W. Long.
Population: 3,709 (1990); 3,907 (2000); 3,574 (2007); 3,409 (2012 projected); Race: 95.5% White, 0.8% Black, 2.0% Asian, 1.7% Hispanic of any race (2007); Density: 3,222.4 persons per square mile (2007); Average household size: 2.83 (2007); Median age: 37.2 (2007); Males per 100 females: 95.0 (2007); Marriage status: 18.1% never married, 74.9% now married, 3.5% widowed, 3.5% divorced (2000); Foreign born: 2.5% (2000); Ancestry (includes multiple ancestries): 44.6% German, 21.3% Irish, 15.3% English, 9.9% United States or American, 4.3% Italian (2000).
Economy: Employment by occupation: 19.7% management, 29.2% professional, 8.0% services, 28.6% sales, 0.0% farming, 5.8% construction, 8.6% production (2000).
Income: Per capita income: $37,224 (2007); Median household income: $88,736 (2007); Average household income: $105,253 (2007); Percent of households with income of $100,000 or more: 40.3% (2007); Poverty rate: 1.5% (2000).
Education: Percent of population age 25 and over with: High school diploma (including GED) or higher: 96.7% (2007); Bachelor's degree or higher: 53.6% (2007); Master's degree or higher: 17.8% (2007).

School District(s)

Central Local (PK-12)
2005-06 Enrollment: 1,220 . . . . (419) 658-2808
Housing: Homeownership rate: 95.5% (2007); Median home value: $165,711 (2007); Median rent: $844 per month (2000); Median age of housing: 32 years (2000).
Transportation: Commute to work: 90.7% car, 3.8% public transportation, 0.5% walk, 4.4% work from home (2000); Travel time to work: 24.6% less than 15 minutes, 36.7% 15 to 30 minutes, 30.2% 30 to 45 minutes, 6.1% 45 to 60 minutes, 2.4% 60 minutes or more (2000)

SILVERTON (city). Covers a land area of 1.114 square miles and a water area of 0 square miles. Located at 39.19° N. Lat.; 84.40° W. Long. Elevation is 850 feet.
History: Silverton developed as a residential community on the outskirts of Cincinnati.
Population: 5,859 (1990); 5,178 (2000); 4,615 (2007); 4,228 (2012 projected); Race: 42.5% White, 52.5% Black, 0.8% Asian, 1.7% Hispanic of any race (2007); Density: 4,142.5 persons per square mile (2007); Average household size: 1.98 (2007); Median age: 42.2 (2007); Males per 100 females: 81.8 (2007); Marriage status: 29.6% never married, 45.4% now married, 10.3% widowed, 14.6% divorced (2000); Foreign born: 0.2% (2000); Ancestry (includes multiple ancestries): 46.6% Other groups, 19.4% German, 9.9% Irish, 4.2% English, 3.6% United States or American (2000).
Economy: Single-family building permits issued: 0 (2007); Multi-family building permits issued: 0 (2007); Employment by occupation: 13.6% management, 16.8% professional, 17.4% services, 30.7% sales, 0.4% farming, 8.9% construction, 12.2% production (2000).
Income: Per capita income: $22,976 (2007); Median household income: $40,084 (2007); Average household income: $44,851 (2007); Percent of households with income of $100,000 or more: 5.8% (2007); Poverty rate: 9.5% (2000).
Education: Percent of population age 25 and over with: High school diploma (including GED) or higher: 78.8% (2007); Bachelor's degree or higher: 19.2% (2007); Master's degree or higher: 6.2% (2007).
Housing: Homeownership rate: 55.1% (2007); Median home value: $114,157 (2007); Median rent: $408 per month (2000); Median age of housing: 50 years (2000).
Safety: Violent crime rate: 24.1 per 10,000 population; Property crime rate: 289.7 per 10,000 population (2007).
Transportation: Commute to work: 90.0% car, 6.8% public transportation, 0.7% walk, 1.9% work from home (2000); Travel time to work: 22.5% less than 15 minutes, 48.1% 15 to 30 minutes, 19.5% 30 to 45 minutes, 3.7% 45 to 60 minutes, 6.2% 60 minutes or more (2000)

SPRINGDALE (city). Covers a land area of 4.957 square miles and a water area of 0.012 square miles. Located at 39.29° N. Lat.; 84.48° W. Long. Elevation is 738 feet.
History: Springdale was the site in 1801-1802 of a meeting of the religious sect called the New Lights, who evidenced pronounced physical manifestations of jerking, rolling, whirling, falling, and barking.
Population: 10,601 (1990); 10,563 (2000); 9,618 (2007); 8,900 (2012 projected); Race: 59.6% White, 33.2% Black, 2.7% Asian, 5.6% Hispanic of any race (2007); Density: 1,940.4 persons per square mile (2007); Average household size: 2.32 (2007); Median age: 41.0 (2007); Males per 100 females: 84.4 (2007); Marriage status: 23.8% never married, 56.1% now married, 8.3% widowed, 11.7% divorced (2000); Foreign born: 5.7% (2000); Ancestry (includes multiple ancestries): 30.5% Other groups, 21.2% German, 9.4% Irish, 8.3% English, 7.9% United States or American (2000).
Economy: Single-family building permits issued: 0 (2007); Multi-family building permits issued: 30 (2007); Employment by occupation: 16.6% management, 22.1% professional, 12.5% services, 26.6% sales, 0.6% farming, 5.8% construction, 15.7% production (2000).
Income: Per capita income: $27,341 (2007); Median household income: $48,854 (2007); Average household income: $62,972 (2007); Percent of households with income of $100,000 or more: 15.8% (2007); Poverty rate: 8.9% (2000).
Education: Percent of population age 25 and over with: High school diploma (including GED) or higher: 85.5% (2007); Bachelor's degree or higher: 27.8% (2007); Master's degree or higher: 9.1% (2007).

Vocational/Technical School(s)

Regency Beauty Institute (Private, For-profit)
Fall 2007 Enrollment: 27 . . . . (513) 771-4900
2007-08 Tuition: $14,200
Housing: Homeownership rate: 60.1% (2007); Median home value: $126,691 (2007); Median rent: $608 per month (2000); Median age of housing: 29 years (2000).
Safety: Violent crime rate: 30.5 per 10,000 population; Property crime rate: 840.3 per 10,000 population (2007).
Transportation: Commute to work: 94.7% car, 1.9% public transportation, 1.5% walk, 1.8% work from home (2000); Travel time to work: 30.7% less than 15 minutes, 36.2% 15 to 30 minutes, 22.8% 30 to 45 minutes, 6.6% 45 to 60 minutes, 3.7% 60 minutes or more (2000)
Additional Information Contacts
City of Springdale. . . . . (513) 346-5700
http://www.springdale.org

TERRACE PARK (village). Covers a land area of 1.203 square miles and a water area of 0.063 square miles. Located at 39.16° N. Lat.; 84.30° W. Long. Elevation is 561 feet.
History: Terrace Park developed as a suburban community near Cincinnati.

Population: 2,133 (1990); 2,273 (2000); 2,090 (2007); 1,951 (2012 projected); Race: 98.4% White, 0.2% Black, 0.8% Asian, 1.2% Hispanic of any race (2007); Density: 1,737.6 persons per square mile (2007); Average household size: 3.02 (2007); Median age: 39.7 (2007); Males per 100 females: 99.2 (2007); Marriage status: 16.2% never married, 75.7% now married, 3.8% widowed, 4.3% divorced (2000); Foreign born: 2.6% (2000); Ancestry (includes multiple ancestries): 40.3% German, 20.6% English, 13.9% Irish, 4.1% Scotch-Irish, 4.0% United States or American (2000).
Economy: Single-family building permits issued: 7 (2007); Multi-family building permits issued: 0 (2007); Employment by occupation: 27.7% management, 32.2% professional, 6.6% services, 27.9% sales, 0.3% farming, 1.8% construction, 3.6% production (2000).
Income: Per capita income: $49,953 (2007); Median household income: $116,000 (2007); Average household income: $150,871 (2007); Percent of households with income of $100,000 or more: 59.2% (2007); Poverty rate: 2.0% (2000).
Education: Percent of population age 25 and over with: High school diploma (including GED) or higher: 98.5% (2007); Bachelor's degree or higher: 71.0% (2007); Master's degree or higher: 26.2% (2007).

School District(s)

Mariemont City (PK-12)
2005-06 Enrollment: 1,658 . . . . (513) 272-7500
Housing: Homeownership rate: 94.9% (2007); Median home value: $387,698 (2007); Median rent: $1,028 per month (2000); Median age of housing: 49 years (2000).
Transportation: Commute to work: 88.3% car, 2.8% public transportation, 0.4% walk, 8.5% work from home (2000); Travel time to work: 23.0% less than 15 minutes, 43.8% 15 to 30 minutes, 25.9% 30 to 45 minutes, 4.8% 45 to 60 minutes, 2.4% 60 minutes or more (2000)

THE VILLAGE OF INDIAN HILL (city). Covers a land area of 18.534 square miles and a water area of 0.056 square miles. Located at 39.19° N. Lat.; 84.34° W. Long. Elevation is 561 feet.
Population: 5,382 (1990); 5,907 (2000); 5,610 (2007); 5,415 (2012 projected); Race: 94.2% White, 0.5% Black, 3.8% Asian, 0.7% Hispanic of any race (2007); Density: 302.7 persons per square mile (2007); Average household size: 2.81 (2007); Median age: 46.9 (2007); Males per 100 females: 95.6 (2007); Marriage status: 18.2% never married, 76.1% now married, 3.4% widowed, 2.3% divorced (2000); Foreign born: 7.9% (2000); Ancestry (includes multiple ancestries): 37.8% German, 23.3% English, 17.5% Irish, 7.9% Other groups, 5.8% Italian (2000).
Economy: Employment by occupation: 39.2% management, 29.1% professional, 3.1% services, 23.3% sales, 0.0% farming, 1.2% construction, 4.2% production (2000).
Income: Per capita income: $88,742 (2007); Median household income: $180,482 (2007); Average household income: $249,172 (2007); Percent of households with income of $100,000 or more: 73.6% (2007); Poverty rate: 2.4% (2000).
Education: Percent of population age 25 and over with: High school diploma (including GED) or higher: 97.7% (2007); Bachelor's degree or higher: 77.0% (2007); Master's degree or higher: 34.7% (2007).
Housing: Homeownership rate: 96.1% (2007); Median home value: $879,751 (2007); Median rent: $532 per month (2000); Median age of housing: 40 years (2000).
Safety: Violent crime rate: 1.8 per 10,000 population; Property crime rate: 99.8 per 10,000 population (2007).
Transportation: Commute to work: 89.5% car, 0.0% public transportation, 1.0% walk, 7.8% work from home (2000); Travel time to work: 21.3% less than 15 minutes, 58.5% 15 to 30 minutes, 17.8% 30 to 45 minutes, 0.0% 45 to 60 minutes, 2.4% 60 minutes or more (2000)

TURPIN HILLS (CDP). Covers a land area of 2.973 square miles and a water area of <.001 square miles. Located at 39.10° N. Lat.; 84.37° W. Long. Elevation is 650 feet.
Population: 4,908 (1990); 4,960 (2000); 5,369 (2007); 5,559 (2012 projected); Race: 95.8% White, 0.7% Black, 2.0% Asian, 1.6% Hispanic of any race (2007); Density: 1,806.1 persons per square mile (2007); Average household size: 2.77 (2007); Median age: 41.6 (2007); Males per 100 females: 95.5 (2007); Marriage status: 17.8% never married, 75.1% now married, 3.6% widowed, 3.5% divorced (2000); Foreign born: 4.0% (2000); Ancestry (includes multiple ancestries): 35.8% German, 18.5% Irish, 12.8% English, 12.2% Italian, 6.9% United States or American (2000).
Economy: Employment by occupation: 28.2% management, 30.0% professional, 11.7% services, 22.3% sales, 0.0% farming, 2.4% construction, 5.4% production (2000).
Income: Per capita income: $47,733 (2007); Median household income: $98,583 (2007); Average household income: $132,375 (2007); Percent of households with income of $100,000 or more: 49.1% (2007); Poverty rate: 1.0% (2000).
Education: Percent of population age 25 and over with: High school diploma (including GED) or higher: 95.3% (2007); Bachelor's degree or higher: 63.1% (2007); Master's degree or higher: 23.1% (2007).
Housing: Homeownership rate: 87.7% (2007); Median home value: $242,618 (2007); Median rent: $578 per month (2000); Median age of housing: 26 years (2000).
Transportation: Commute to work: 93.2% car, 0.8% public transportation, 0.2% walk, 5.8% work from home (2000); Travel time to work: 23.3% less than 15 minutes, 52.7% 15 to 30 minutes, 17.9% 30 to 45 minutes, 2.8% 45 to 60 minutes, 3.3% 60 minutes or more (2000)

WHITE OAK (CDP). Covers a land area of 4.094 square miles and a water area of 0 square miles. Located at 39.21° N. Lat.; 84.59° W. Long. Elevation is 915 feet.
Population: 12,430 (1990); 13,277 (2000); 12,591 (2007); 12,030 (2012 projected); Race: 92.1% White, 4.9% Black, 1.0% Asian, 1.6% Hispanic of any race (2007); Density: 3,075.1 persons per square mile (2007); Average household size: 2.45 (2007); Median age: 38.6 (2007); Males per 100 females: 94.9 (2007); Marriage status: 23.6% never married, 58.5% now married, 7.7% widowed, 10.2% divorced (2000); Foreign born: 1.5% (2000); Ancestry (includes multiple ancestries): 48.1% German, 16.5% Irish, 8.8% United States or American, 7.6% Other groups, 7.1% English (2000).
Economy: Employment by occupation: 15.5% management, 17.6% professional, 14.9% services, 29.1% sales, 0.0% farming, 9.2% construction, 13.8% production (2000).
Income: Per capita income: $28,713 (2007); Median household income: $53,226 (2007); Average household income: $70,401 (2007); Percent of households with income of $100,000 or more: 20.9% (2007); Poverty rate: 5.1% (2000).
Education: Percent of population age 25 and over with: High school diploma (including GED) or higher: 84.3% (2007); Bachelor's degree or higher: 22.8% (2007); Master's degree or higher: 6.1% (2007).
Housing: Homeownership rate: 71.6% (2007); Median home value: $133,674 (2007); Median rent: $485 per month (2000); Median age of housing: 35 years (2000).
Transportation: Commute to work: 94.2% car, 2.1% public transportation, 1.0% walk, 2.1% work from home (2000); Travel time to work: 20.9% less than 15 minutes, 50.8% 15 to 30 minutes, 22.5% 30 to 45 minutes, 3.1% 45 to 60 minutes, 2.6% 60 minutes or more (2000)

WHITE OAK EAST (CDP). Covers a land area of 0.799 square miles and a water area of 0 square miles. Located at 39.20° N. Lat.; 84.59° W. Long.
Population: 3,544 (1990); 3,508 (2000); 3,390 (2007); 3,311 (2012 projected); Race: 96.2% White, 2.0% Black, 0.8% Asian, 0.7% Hispanic of any race (2007); Density: 4,245.3 persons per square mile (2007); Average household size: 2.37 (2007); Median age: 39.5 (2007); Males per 100 females: 91.6 (2007); Marriage status: 23.1% never married, 60.0% now married, 8.6% widowed, 8.3% divorced (2000); Foreign born: 1.6% (2000); Ancestry (includes multiple ancestries): 51.9% German, 23.8% Irish, 11.7% United States or American, 8.9% Other groups, 6.9% Italian (2000).
Economy: Employment by occupation: 15.4% management, 23.3% professional, 10.8% services, 30.6% sales, 0.0% farming, 7.7% construction, 12.2% production (2000).
Income: Per capita income: $31,239 (2007); Median household income: $64,961 (2007); Average household income: $74,108 (2007); Percent of households with income of $100,000 or more: 20.7% (2007); Poverty rate: 2.5% (2000).
Education: Percent of population age 25 and over with: High school diploma (including GED) or higher: 90.4% (2007); Bachelor's degree or higher: 31.3% (2007); Master's degree or higher: 10.1% (2007).
Housing: Homeownership rate: 79.4% (2007); Median home value: $134,606 (2007); Median rent: $387 per month (2000); Median age of housing: 38 years (2000).
Transportation: Commute to work: 96.4% car, 0.4% public transportation, 0.4% walk, 2.8% work from home (2000); Travel time to work: 15.9% less than 15 minutes, 55.6% 15 to 30 minutes, 19.8% 30 to 45 minutes, 5.8% 45 to 60 minutes, 2.9% 60 minutes or more (2000)

WHITE OAK WEST (CDP). Covers a land area of 1.342 square miles and a water area of 0 square miles. Located at 39.20° N. Lat.; 84.61° W. Long.

Population: 2,879 (1990); 2,932 (2000); 3,183 (2007); 3,329 (2012 projected); Race: 97.0% White, 1.7% Black, 0.5% Asian, 0.3% Hispanic of any race (2007); Density: 2,372.0 persons per square mile (2007); Average household size: 2.54 (2007); Median age: 43.3 (2007); Males per 100 females: 95.8 (2007); Marriage status: 23.3% never married, 65.7% now married, 5.5% widowed, 5.5% divorced (2000); Foreign born: 0.9% (2000); Ancestry (includes multiple ancestries): 54.9% German, 18.7% Irish, 10.5% English, 8.1% United States or American, 5.4% Other groups (2000).
Economy: Employment by occupation: 17.4% management, 23.2% professional, 13.0% services, 33.7% sales, 0.4% farming, 4.9% construction, 7.3% production (2000).
Income: Per capita income: $40,963 (2007); Median household income: $66,906 (2007); Average household income: $103,975 (2007); Percent of households with income of $100,000 or more: 32.1% (2007); Poverty rate: 3.0% (2000).
Education: Percent of population age 25 and over with: High school diploma (including GED) or higher: 94.1% (2007); Bachelor's degree or higher: 35.2% (2007); Master's degree or higher: 11.4% (2007).
Housing: Homeownership rate: 84.6% (2007); Median home value: $179,581 (2007); Median rent: $466 per month (2000); Median age of housing: 32 years (2000).
Transportation: Commute to work: 92.1% car, 1.3% public transportation, 2.2% walk, 4.4% work from home (2000); Travel time to work: 25.5% less than 15 minutes, 46.5% 15 to 30 minutes, 23.2% 30 to 45 minutes, 4.5% 45 to 60 minutes, 0.4% 60 minutes or more (2000)

WOODLAWN (village). Covers a land area of 2.585 square miles and a water area of 0 square miles. Located at 39.25° N. Lat.; 84.47° W. Long. Elevation is 584 feet.

Population: 2,674 (1990); 2,816 (2000); 2,567 (2007); 2,387 (2012 projected); Race: 28.9% White, 65.3% Black, 3.2% Asian, 1.8% Hispanic of any race (2007); Density: 992.9 persons per square mile (2007); Average household size: 2.18 (2007); Median age: 39.1 (2007); Males per 100 females: 94.8 (2007); Marriage status: 35.8% never married, 43.1% now married, 8.7% widowed, 12.3% divorced (2000); Foreign born: 4.9% (2000); Ancestry (includes multiple ancestries): 65.3% Other groups, 8.1% German, 4.4% Irish, 3.6% English, 1.4% Italian (2000).
Economy: Single-family building permits issued: 0 (2007); Multi-family building permits issued: 0 (2007); Employment by occupation: 14.2% management, 28.1% professional, 15.5% services, 23.4% sales, 0.0% farming, 5.8% construction, 12.9% production (2000).
Income: Per capita income: $28,485 (2007); Median household income: $48,962 (2007); Average household income: $62,104 (2007); Percent of households with income of $100,000 or more: 13.5% (2007); Poverty rate: 10.4% (2000).
Education: Percent of population age 25 and over with: High school diploma (including GED) or higher: 89.5% (2007); Bachelor's degree or higher: 28.3% (2007); Master's degree or higher: 10.6% (2007).
Housing: Homeownership rate: 54.5% (2007); Median home value: $99,468 (2007); Median rent: $650 per month (2000); Median age of housing: 34 years (2000).
Safety: Violent crime rate: 36.1 per 10,000 population; Property crime rate: 525.7 per 10,000 population (2007).
Transportation: Commute to work: 93.6% car, 3.2% public transportation, 0.8% walk, 2.2% work from home (2000); Travel time to work: 28.1% less than 15 minutes, 44.5% 15 to 30 minutes, 18.5% 30 to 45 minutes, 4.8% 45 to 60 minutes, 4.0% 60 minutes or more (2000)

WYOMING (city). Covers a land area of 2.883 square miles and a water area of 0 square miles. Located at 39.22° N. Lat.; 84.47° W. Long. Elevation is 574 feet.

History: Settled 1865, incorporated 1874.
Population: 8,318 (1990); 8,261 (2000); 7,464 (2007); 6,900 (2012 projected); Race: 87.8% White, 9.1% Black, 1.3% Asian, 1.6% Hispanic of any race (2007); Density: 2,589.4 persons per square mile (2007); Average household size: 2.74 (2007); Median age: 42.2 (2007); Males per 100 females: 90.4 (2007); Marriage status: 19.6% never married, 68.0% now married, 5.2% widowed, 7.2% divorced (2000); Foreign born: 3.7% (2000); Ancestry (includes multiple ancestries): 33.8% German, 16.4% Other groups, 14.0% Irish, 13.6% English, 6.2% Italian (2000).
Economy: Single-family building permits issued: 5 (2007); Multi-family building permits issued: 0 (2007); Employment by occupation: 26.9% management, 38.5% professional, 7.2% services, 21.9% sales, 0.0% farming, 2.1% construction, 3.5% production (2000).
Income: Per capita income: $47,468 (2007); Median household income: $102,409 (2007); Average household income: $129,974 (2007); Percent of households with income of $100,000 or more: 51.1% (2007); Poverty rate: 1.4% (2000).
Education: Percent of population age 25 and over with: High school diploma (including GED) or higher: 96.6% (2007); Bachelor's degree or higher: 67.9% (2007); Master's degree or higher: 32.5% (2007).

School District(s)

Wyoming City (PK-12)
2005-06 Enrollment: 1,995 . . . . (513) 772-2343

Housing: Homeownership rate: 86.6% (2007); Median home value: $298,340 (2007); Median rent: $508 per month (2000); Median age of housing: 49 years (2000).
Safety: Violent crime rate: 8.0 per 10,000 population; Property crime rate: 169.7 per 10,000 population (2007).
Transportation: Commute to work: 90.8% car, 0.7% public transportation, 1.1% walk, 7.1% work from home (2000); Travel time to work: 24.7% less than 15 minutes, 53.4% 15 to 30 minutes, 17.6% 30 to 45 minutes, 2.0% 45 to 60 minutes, 2.3% 60 minutes or more (2000)

Additional Information Contacts

City of Wyoming. . . . . (513) 821-7600
http://www.wyoming.oh.us

Hancock County

Located in northwestern Ohio; crossed by the Blanchard River. Covers a land area of 531.35 square miles, a water area of 2.24 square miles, and is located in the Eastern Time Zone. The county was founded in 1820. County seat is Findlay.

Hancock County is part of the Findlay, OH Micropolitan Statistical Area. The entire metro area includes: Hancock County, OH

Weather Station: Findlay Airport — Elevation: 797 feet

	Jan	Feb	Mar	Apr	May	Jun	Jul	Aug	Sep	Oct	Nov	Dec
High	31	35	46	59	70	79	83	81	74	62	48	37
Low	18	20	29	39	50	59	63	61	54	43	34	24
Precip	1.8	1.7	2.5	3.2	3.7	4.1	3.9	3.7	2.8	2.2	2.7	2.4
Snow	8.2	5.3	3.2	0.7	tr	tr	0.0	0.0	tr	0.1	1.2	5.5

High and Low temperatures in degrees Fahrenheit; Precipitation and Snow in inches

Weather Station: Findlay WPCC — Elevation: 767 feet

	Jan	Feb	Mar	Apr	May	Jun	Jul	Aug	Sep	Oct	Nov	Dec
High	31	35	46	59	71	80	84	81	75	62	48	36
Low	17	20	29	39	50	60	64	61	54	43	33	23
Precip	2.2	2.0	2.7	3.3	3.9	4.1	3.9	4.1	3.0	2.4	2.8	2.7
Snow	10.2	6.2	4.3	1.2	tr	0.0	0.0	0.0	0.0	0.2	1.4	6.0

High and Low temperatures in degrees Fahrenheit; Precipitation and Snow in inches

Population: 65,536 (1990); 71,295 (2000); 73,888 (2007); 75,250 (2012 projected); Race: 94.2% White, 1.4% Black, 1.6% Asian, 3.3% Hispanic of any race (2007); Density: 139.1 persons per square mile (2007); Average household size: 2.51 (2007); Median age: 37.4 (2007); Males per 100 females: 95.3 (2007).
Religion: Five largest groups: 12.3% The United Methodist Church, 12.0% Catholic Church, 6.4% Evangelical Lutheran Church in America, 3.1% Presbyterian Church (U.S.A.), 1.8% Christian Churches and Churches of Christ (2000).
Economy: Unemployment rate: 5.7% (6/2008); Total civilian labor force: 42,196 (6/2008); Leading industries: 28.3% manufacturing; 12.0% retail trade; 11.5% health care and social assistance (2005); Farms: 976 totaling 262,095 acres (2002); Companies that employ 500 or more persons: 10 (2006); Companies that employ 100 to 499 persons: 58 (2006); Companies that employ less than 100 persons: 1,757 (2006); Black-owned businesses: n/a (2002); Hispanic-owned businesses: n/a (2002); Asian-owned businesses: n/a (2002); Women-owned businesses: 1,522 (2002); Retail sales per capita: $19,359 (2008). Single-family building permits issued: 638 (2007); Multi-family building permits issued: 19 (2007).
Income: Per capita income: $24,786 (2007); Median household income: $49,630 (2007); Average household income: $61,272 (2007); Percent of households with income of $100,000 or more: 13.9% (2007); Poverty rate: 9.6% (2005); Bankruptcy rate: 3.42% (2007).

Taxes: Total county taxes per capita: $213 (2006); County property taxes per capita: $101 (2006).
Education: Percent of population age 25 and over with: High school diploma (including GED) or higher: 88.5% (2007); Bachelor's degree or higher: 21.7% (2007); Master's degree or higher: 7.5% (2007).
Housing: Homeownership rate: 73.8% (2007); Median home value: $123,156 (2007); Median rent: $413 per month (2000); Median age of housing: 37 years (2000).
Health: Birth rate: 131.1 per 10,000 population (2007); Death rate: 84.2 per 10,000 population (2007); Age-adjusted cancer mortality rate: 203.8 deaths per 100,000 population (2005); Number of physicians: 18.1 per 10,000 population (2005); Hospital beds: 14.2 per 10,000 population (2004); Hospital admissions: 1,095.2 per 10,000 population (2004).
Elections: 2004 Presidential election results: 70.5% Bush, 29.1% Kerry, 0.0% Nader, 0.2% Badnarik
National and State Parks: Van Buren Lake State Park
Additional Information Contacts
Hancock County Government . . . . (419) 424-7044
http://www.co.hancock.oh.us
City of Findlay . . . . (419) 424-7137
http://www.ci.findlay.oh.us
Greater Findlay Inc.-A Partnership for Growth. . . . . (419) 422-3313
http://www.findlayhancockchamber.com
Hancock County Convention & Visitors Bureau. . . . . (419) 422-3315
http://www.visitfindlay.com

Hancock County Communities

ARCADIA (village). Covers a land area of 0.260 square miles and a water area of 0 square miles. Located at 41.11° N. Lat.; 83.51° W. Long. Elevation is 807 feet.
Population: 544 (1990); 537 (2000); 477 (2007); 457 (2012 projected); Race: 98.5% White, 0.0% Black, 0.0% Asian, 2.3% Hispanic of any race (2007); Density: 1,836.4 persons per square mile (2007); Average household size: 2.61 (2007); Median age: 32.2 (2007); Males per 100 females: 98.8 (2007); Marriage status: 23.6% never married, 61.7% now married, 3.9% widowed, 10.9% divorced (2000); Foreign born: 0.8% (2000); Ancestry (includes multiple ancestries): 50.3% German, 13.1% Other groups, 10.9% Irish, 9.2% English, 6.8% United States or American (2000).
Economy: Single-family building permits issued: 0 (2007); Multi-family building permits issued: 0 (2007); Employment by occupation: 4.6% management, 9.2% professional, 17.3% services, 21.2% sales, 0.0% farming, 14.5% construction, 33.2% production (2000).
Income: Per capita income: $22,416 (2007); Median household income: $49,750 (2007); Average household income: $58,429 (2007); Percent of households with income of $100,000 or more: 13.1% (2007); Poverty rate: 8.2% (2000).
Education: Percent of population age 25 and over with: High school diploma (including GED) or higher: 92.4% (2007); Bachelor's degree or higher: 5.8% (2007); Master's degree or higher: 0.0% (2007).
School District(s)
Arcadia Local (PK-12)
2005-06 Enrollment: 661 . . . . (419) 894-6431
Housing: Homeownership rate: 84.7% (2007); Median home value: $80,577 (2007); Median rent: $336 per month (2000); Median age of housing: 54 years (2000).
Transportation: Commute to work: 94.3% car, 0.0% public transportation, 4.6% walk, 0.0% work from home (2000); Travel time to work: 39.4% less than 15 minutes, 50.7% 15 to 30 minutes, 7.1% 30 to 45 minutes, 1.4% 45 to 60 minutes, 1.4% 60 minutes or more (2000)

ARLINGTON (village). Covers a land area of 0.730 square miles and a water area of 0 square miles. Located at 40.89° N. Lat.; 83.65° W. Long. Elevation is 863 feet.
Population: 1,236 (1990); 1,351 (2000); 1,267 (2007); 1,272 (2012 projected); Race: 99.4% White, 0.1% Black, 0.0% Asian, 0.2% Hispanic of any race (2007); Density: 1,736.6 persons per square mile (2007); Average household size: 2.54 (2007); Median age: 39.5 (2007); Males per 100 females: 88.8 (2007); Marriage status: 22.5% never married, 57.2% now married, 13.9% widowed, 6.4% divorced (2000); Foreign born: 0.5% (2000); Ancestry (includes multiple ancestries): 45.5% German, 9.9% United States or American, 9.3% English, 9.0% Irish, 5.1% French (except Basque) (2000).
Economy: Single-family building permits issued: 1 (2007); Multi-family building permits issued: 0 (2007); Employment by occupation: 9.3% management, 15.5% professional, 16.0% services, 24.2% sales, 0.3% farming, 10.3% construction, 24.5% production (2000).
Income: Per capita income: $23,905 (2007); Median household income: $47,727 (2007); Average household income: $58,876 (2007); Percent of households with income of $100,000 or more: 12.9% (2007); Poverty rate: 5.4% (2000).
Education: Percent of population age 25 and over with: High school diploma (including GED) or higher: 91.7% (2007); Bachelor's degree or higher: 15.8% (2007); Master's degree or higher: 3.5% (2007).
School District(s)
Arlington Local (PK-12)
2005-06 Enrollment: 652 . . . . (419) 365-5121
Housing: Homeownership rate: 76.3% (2007); Median home value: $112,634 (2007); Median rent: $397 per month (2000); Median age of housing: 50 years (2000).
Transportation: Commute to work: 95.8% car, 0.0% public transportation, 2.2% walk, 1.6% work from home (2000); Travel time to work: 22.8% less than 15 minutes, 60.6% 15 to 30 minutes, 9.8% 30 to 45 minutes, 4.1% 45 to 60 minutes, 2.8% 60 minutes or more (2000)

BENTON RIDGE (village). Covers a land area of 0.464 square miles and a water area of 0 square miles. Located at 41.00° N. Lat.; 83.79° W. Long. Elevation is 791 feet.
Population: 351 (1990); 315 (2000); 283 (2007); 278 (2012 projected); Race: 98.9% White, 0.7% Black, 0.0% Asian, 0.7% Hispanic of any race (2007); Density: 609.6 persons per square mile (2007); Average household size: 2.62 (2007); Median age: 35.8 (2007); Males per 100 females: 99.3 (2007); Marriage status: 30.4% never married, 52.6% now married, 7.7% widowed, 9.3% divorced (2000); Foreign born: 0.0% (2000); Ancestry (includes multiple ancestries): 31.8% United States or American, 29.1% German, 9.9% English, 9.3% Irish, 6.6% Other groups (2000).
Economy: Employment by occupation: 5.9% management, 4.6% professional, 20.4% services, 15.8% sales, 0.0% farming, 20.4% construction, 32.9% production (2000).
Income: Per capita income: $23,834 (2007); Median household income: $57,000 (2007); Average household income: $62,454 (2007); Percent of households with income of $100,000 or more: 15.7% (2007); Poverty rate: 2.3% (2000).
Education: Percent of population age 25 and over with: High school diploma (including GED) or higher: 92.3% (2007); Bachelor's degree or higher: 7.2% (2007); Master's degree or higher: 0.6% (2007).
Housing: Homeownership rate: 88.9% (2007); Median home value: $109,848 (2007); Median rent: $285 per month (2000); Median age of housing: 60+ years (2000).
Transportation: Commute to work: 91.4% car, 0.0% public transportation, 4.6% walk, 3.9% work from home (2000); Travel time to work: 19.2% less than 15 minutes, 61.0% 15 to 30 minutes, 14.4% 30 to 45 minutes, 0.0% 45 to 60 minutes, 5.5% 60 minutes or more (2000)

FINDLAY (city). County seat. Covers a land area of 17.194 square miles and a water area of 0.110 square miles. Located at 41.04° N. Lat.; 83.64° W. Long. Elevation is 778 feet.
History: Findlay was laid out in 1821 by Joseph Vance and Elnathan Cory, and named for Fort Findlay, an outpost built under the direction of General Hull during the War of 1812. After the Civil War, the Findlay Natural Gas Company began to make commercial use of the gas and oil beneath the city. It was in the Findlay "Jeffersonian" in 1860 that Petroleum V. Nasby (pen name of David Ross Locke, the editor) wrote satirical letters attacking the institution of slavery.
Population: 36,546 (1990); 38,967 (2000); 38,768 (2007); 38,713 (2012 projected); Race: 92.4% White, 1.8% Black, 2.4% Asian, 4.3% Hispanic of any race (2007); Density: 2,254.7 persons per square mile (2007); Average household size: 2.40 (2007); Median age: 36.6 (2007); Males per 100 females: 92.4 (2007); Marriage status: 25.5% never married, 56.5% now married, 7.1% widowed, 10.9% divorced (2000); Foreign born: 2.7% (2000); Ancestry (includes multiple ancestries): 35.5% German, 10.7% Irish, 10.6% English, 9.5% United States or American, 9.5% Other groups (2000).
Economy: Unemployment rate: 5.9% (6/2008); Total civilian labor force: 22,184 (6/2008); Single-family building permits issued: 66 (2007); Multi-family building permits issued: 5 (2007); Employment by occupation: 12.5% management, 17.6% professional, 15.0% services, 22.7% sales, 0.2% farming, 8.0% construction, 24.0% production (2000).

Income: Per capita income: $24,765 (2007); Median household income: $44,944 (2007); Average household income: $58,227 (2007); Percent of households with income of $100,000 or more: 12.9% (2007); Poverty rate: 9.1% (2000).
Education: Percent of population age 25 and over with: High school diploma (including GED) or higher: 87.5% (2007); Bachelor's degree or higher: 23.9% (2007); Master's degree or higher: 8.0% (2007).

School District(s)

Findlay City (PK-12)
2005-06 Enrollment: 6,281 . . . . (419) 425-8212
Findlay Digital Academy (09-12)
2005-06 Enrollment: 44 . . . . (419) 425-3598
Hancock
2005-06 Enrollment: n/a . . . . (419) 422-7525
Liberty-Benton Local (PK-12)
2005-06 Enrollment: 1,255 . . . . (419) 422-8526

Four-year College(s)

The University of Findlay (Private, Not-for-profit, Church of God)
Fall 2007 Enrollment: 5,388. . . . . (419) 422-8313
2007-08 Tuition: In-state $23,890; Out-of-state $23,890
Winebrenner Theological Seminary (Private, Not-for-profit, Other Protestant)
Fall 2007 Enrollment: 112 . . . . (419) 434-4200

Two-year College(s)

Brown Mackie College-Findlay (Private, For-profit)
Fall 2007 Enrollment: 723 . . . . (419) 423-2211
2007-08 Tuition: In-state $12,650; Out-of-state $12,650

Housing: Homeownership rate: 65.0% (2007); Median home value: $119,549 (2007); Median rent: $416 per month (2000); Median age of housing: 39 years (2000).
Hospitals: Blanchard Valley Regional Health Center (150 beds)
Safety: Violent crime rate: 15.5 per 10,000 population; Property crime rate: 336.8 per 10,000 population (2007).
Newspapers: Courier (Community news; Circulation 23,000)
Transportation: Commute to work: 91.5% car, 1.1% public transportation, 3.7% walk, 2.6% work from home (2000); Travel time to work: 60.6% less than 15 minutes, 26.8% 15 to 30 minutes, 6.7% 30 to 45 minutes, 2.9% 45 to 60 minutes, 3.0% 60 minutes or more (2000)
Airports: Findlay (general aviation)

Additional Information Contacts

City of Findlay . . . . (419) 424-7137
http://www.ci.findlay.oh.us
Greater Findlay Inc.-A Partnership for Growth. . . . . (419) 422-3313
http://www.findlayhancockchamber.com
Hancock County Convention & Visitors Bureau. . . . . (419) 422-3315
http://www.visitfindlay.com

JENERA (village). Covers a land area of 0.376 square miles and a water area of 0 square miles. Located at 40.90° N. Lat.; 83.72° W. Long. Elevation is 853 feet.
Population: 285 (1990); 235 (2000); 234 (2007); 232 (2012 projected); Race: 96.6% White, 1.7% Black, 0.0% Asian, 0.4% Hispanic of any race (2007); Density: 622.8 persons per square mile (2007); Average household size: 2.39 (2007); Median age: 37.0 (2007); Males per 100 females: 105.3 (2007); Marriage status: 19.4% never married, 57.5% now married, 15.6% widowed, 7.5% divorced (2000); Foreign born: 0.0% (2000); Ancestry (includes multiple ancestries): 70.0% German, 9.3% English, 4.4% Swiss, 4.4% Other groups, 3.5% Irish (2000).
Economy: Employment by occupation: 13.6% management, 9.7% professional, 12.6% services, 26.2% sales, 0.0% farming, 12.6% construction, 25.2% production (2000).
Income: Per capita income: $22,596 (2007); Median household income: $46,875 (2007); Average household income: $53,954 (2007); Percent of households with income of $100,000 or more: 9.2% (2007); Poverty rate: 3.1% (2000).
Education: Percent of population age 25 and over with: High school diploma (including GED) or higher: 89.0% (2007); Bachelor's degree or higher: 11.0% (2007); Master's degree or higher: 3.2% (2007).
Housing: Homeownership rate: 85.7% (2007); Median home value: $85,714 (2007); Median rent: $438 per month (2000); Median age of housing: 60+ years (2000).
Transportation: Commute to work: 90.3% car, 0.0% public transportation, 7.8% walk, 1.9% work from home (2000); Travel time to work: 20.8% less than 15 minutes, 51.5% 15 to 30 minutes, 23.8% 30 to 45 minutes, 0.0% 45 to 60 minutes, 4.0% 60 minutes or more (2000)

MCCOMB (village). Covers a land area of 0.913 square miles and a water area of 0.036 square miles. Located at 41.10° N. Lat.; 83.79° W. Long. Elevation is 771 feet.
Population: 1,555 (1990); 1,676 (2000); 1,460 (2007); 1,438 (2012 projected); Race: 95.8% White, 0.4% Black, 0.9% Asian, 4.5% Hispanic of any race (2007); Density: 1,598.8 persons per square mile (2007); Average household size: 2.78 (2007); Median age: 31.7 (2007); Males per 100 females: 97.6 (2007); Marriage status: 22.1% never married, 60.7% now married, 5.1% widowed, 12.1% divorced (2000); Foreign born: 1.0% (2000); Ancestry (includes multiple ancestries): 36.0% German, 11.1% English, 10.1% Other groups, 8.7% Irish, 6.4% United States or American (2000).
Economy: Single-family building permits issued: 0 (2007); Multi-family building permits issued: 0 (2007); Employment by occupation: 6.9% management, 11.7% professional, 13.4% services, 22.4% sales, 0.2% farming, 11.6% construction, 33.7% production (2000).
Income: Per capita income: $19,750 (2007); Median household income: $45,179 (2007); Average household income: $54,819 (2007); Percent of households with income of $100,000 or more: 9.5% (2007); Poverty rate: 8.6% (2000).
Education: Percent of population age 25 and over with: High school diploma (including GED) or higher: 88.7% (2007); Bachelor's degree or higher: 14.3% (2007); Master's degree or higher: 4.3% (2007).

School District(s)

Mccomb Local (PK-12)
2005-06 Enrollment: 832 . . . . (419) 293-3979

Housing: Homeownership rate: 77.2% (2007); Median home value: $105,114 (2007); Median rent: $439 per month (2000); Median age of housing: 45 years (2000).
Safety: Violent crime rate: 18.1 per 10,000 population; Property crime rate: 181.5 per 10,000 population (2007).
Transportation: Commute to work: 93.1% car, 0.0% public transportation, 2.5% walk, 3.6% work from home (2000); Travel time to work: 28.3% less than 15 minutes, 55.4% 15 to 30 minutes, 7.8% 30 to 45 minutes, 3.7% 45 to 60 minutes, 4.9% 60 minutes or more (2000)

MOUNT BLANCHARD (village). Covers a land area of 0.540 square miles and a water area of 0 square miles. Located at 40.90° N. Lat.; 83.55° W. Long. Elevation is 846 feet.
Population: 491 (1990); 484 (2000); 532 (2007); 555 (2012 projected); Race: 97.6% White, 0.4% Black, 0.0% Asian, 1.7% Hispanic of any race (2007); Density: 984.6 persons per square mile (2007); Average household size: 2.45 (2007); Median age: 35.0 (2007); Males per 100 females: 91.4 (2007); Marriage status: 18.2% never married, 66.4% now married, 6.2% widowed, 9.2% divorced (2000); Foreign born: 0.0% (2000); Ancestry (includes multiple ancestries): 34.5% German, 12.6% English, 8.8% Irish, 8.4% United States or American, 4.8% Other groups (2000).
Economy: Single-family building permits issued: 0 (2007); Multi-family building permits issued: 0 (2007); Employment by occupation: 11.8% management, 11.8% professional, 12.7% services, 22.6% sales, 0.0% farming, 9.0% construction, 32.1% production (2000).
Income: Per capita income: $23,026 (2007); Median household income: $49,125 (2007); Average household income: $56,452 (2007); Percent of households with income of $100,000 or more: 12.0% (2007); Poverty rate: 4.8% (2000).
Education: Percent of population age 25 and over with: High school diploma (including GED) or higher: 83.9% (2007); Bachelor's degree or higher: 11.3% (2007); Master's degree or higher: 4.2% (2007).

School District(s)

Riverdale Local (PK-12)
2005-06 Enrollment: 1,030 . . . . (419) 694-4994

Housing: Homeownership rate: 75.6% (2007); Median home value: $99,565 (2007); Median rent: $408 per month (2000); Median age of housing: 60+ years (2000).
Transportation: Commute to work: 90.0% car, 0.0% public transportation, 5.9% walk, 4.1% work from home (2000); Travel time to work: 18.4% less than 15 minutes, 56.1% 15 to 30 minutes, 21.2% 30 to 45 minutes, 1.9% 45 to 60 minutes, 2.4% 60 minutes or more (2000)

MOUNT CORY (village). Covers a land area of 0.384 square miles and a water area of 0 square miles. Located at 40.93° N. Lat.; 83.82° W. Long. Elevation is 814 feet.
Population: 245 (1990); 203 (2000); 215 (2007); 222 (2012 projected); Race: 96.3% White, 0.0% Black, 0.0% Asian, 0.9% Hispanic of any race

(2007); Density: 559.3 persons per square mile (2007); Average household size: 2.47 (2007); Median age: 41.4 (2007); Males per 100 females: 92.0 (2007); Marriage status: 27.2% never married, 60.4% now married, 5.9% widowed, 6.5% divorced (2000); Foreign born: 0.0% (2000); Ancestry (includes multiple ancestries): 38.9% German, 10.9% Irish, 9.8% Dutch, 5.7% Swiss, 5.2% English (2000).
Economy: Employment by occupation: 5.3% management, 8.4% professional, 17.9% services, 25.3% sales, 0.0% farming, 13.7% construction, 29.5% production (2000).
Income: Per capita income: $22,209 (2007); Median household income: $45,500 (2007); Average household income: $54,885 (2007); Percent of households with income of $100,000 or more: 8.0% (2007); Poverty rate: 1.0% (2000).
Education: Percent of population age 25 and over with: High school diploma (including GED) or higher: 87.7% (2007); Bachelor's degree or higher: 5.5% (2007); Master's degree or higher: 2.7% (2007).
Housing: Homeownership rate: 93.1% (2007); Median home value: $86,944 (2007); Median rent: $325 per month (2000); Median age of housing: 60+ years (2000).
Transportation: Commute to work: 91.4% car, 0.0% public transportation, 2.2% walk, 6.5% work from home (2000); Travel time to work: 25.3% less than 15 minutes, 52.9% 15 to 30 minutes, 18.4% 30 to 45 minutes, 0.0% 45 to 60 minutes, 3.4% 60 minutes or more (2000)

RAWSON (village). Covers a land area of 0.398 square miles and a water area of 0 square miles. Located at 40.95° N. Lat.; 83.78° W. Long. Elevation is 814 feet.
Population: 482 (1990); 465 (2000); 466 (2007); 462 (2012 projected); Race: 97.6% White, 0.0% Black, 0.0% Asian, 0.6% Hispanic of any race (2007); Density: 1,171.1 persons per square mile (2007); Average household size: 2.84 (2007); Median age: 35.8 (2007); Males per 100 females: 103.5 (2007); Marriage status: 24.8% never married, 64.0% now married, 1.8% widowed, 9.4% divorced (2000); Foreign born: 0.6% (2000); Ancestry (includes multiple ancestries): 26.6% German, 24.0% United States or American, 8.9% Irish, 7.1% English, 4.8% Other groups (2000).
Economy: Employment by occupation: 6.1% management, 8.3% professional, 10.1% services, 24.1% sales, 0.0% farming, 14.9% construction, 36.4% production (2000).
Income: Per capita income: $18,240 (2007); Median household income: $49,231 (2007); Average household income: $51,829 (2007); Percent of households with income of $100,000 or more: 3.7% (2007); Poverty rate: 5.9% (2000).
Education: Percent of population age 25 and over with: High school diploma (including GED) or higher: 80.8% (2007); Bachelor's degree or higher: 5.7% (2007); Master's degree or higher: 0.0% (2007).

School District(s)

Cory-Rawson Local (PK-12)
2005-06 Enrollment: 721 . . . . (419) 963-3415
Housing: Homeownership rate: 83.5% (2007); Median home value: $79,722 (2007); Median rent: $475 per month (2000); Median age of housing: 60+ years (2000).
Transportation: Commute to work: 93.9% car, 0.0% public transportation, 0.0% walk, 5.3% work from home (2000); Travel time to work: 18.5% less than 15 minutes, 58.8% 15 to 30 minutes, 13.9% 30 to 45 minutes, 2.8% 45 to 60 minutes, 6.0% 60 minutes or more (2000)

VAN BUREN (village). Covers a land area of 0.249 square miles and a water area of 0 square miles. Located at 41.13° N. Lat.; 83.64° W. Long. Elevation is 768 feet.
History: Van Buren was named for President Martin Van Buren. For a time, Van Buren was an oil center.
Population: 337 (1990); 313 (2000); 375 (2007); 397 (2012 projected); Race: 96.5% White, 0.3% Black, 0.0% Asian, 5.9% Hispanic of any race (2007); Density: 1,506.5 persons per square mile (2007); Average household size: 2.70 (2007); Median age: 38.9 (2007); Males per 100 females: 93.3 (2007); Marriage status: 14.2% never married, 69.8% now married, 6.5% widowed, 9.5% divorced (2000); Foreign born: 0.3% (2000); Ancestry (includes multiple ancestries): 45.6% German, 14.4% English, 8.4% French (except Basque), 8.4% Polish, 8.1% Dutch (2000).
Economy: Single-family building permits issued: 1 (2007); Multi-family building permits issued: 0 (2007); Employment by occupation: 10.4% management, 21.5% professional, 10.4% services, 16.0% sales, 0.0% farming, 6.7% construction, 35.0% production (2000).
Income: Per capita income: $22,513 (2007); Median household income: $56,458 (2007); Average household income: $60,737 (2007); Percent of households with income of $100,000 or more: 10.8% (2007); Poverty rate: 1.7% (2000).
Education: Percent of population age 25 and over with: High school diploma (including GED) or higher: 93.0% (2007); Bachelor's degree or higher: 15.2% (2007); Master's degree or higher: 6.1% (2007).

School District(s)

Van Buren Local (PK-12)
2005-06 Enrollment: 922 . . . . (419) 299-3578
Housing: Homeownership rate: 97.1% (2007); Median home value: $117,151 (2007); Median rent: $n/a per month (2000); Median age of housing: 60+ years (2000).
Transportation: Commute to work: 95.0% car, 0.0% public transportation, 1.3% walk, 3.8% work from home (2000); Travel time to work: 32.5% less than 15 minutes, 52.6% 15 to 30 minutes, 7.8% 30 to 45 minutes, 2.6% 45 to 60 minutes, 4.5% 60 minutes or more (2000)

VANLUE (village). Covers a land area of 0.280 square miles and a water area of 0.007 square miles. Located at 40.97° N. Lat.; 83.48° W. Long. Elevation is 823 feet.
Population: 373 (1990); 371 (2000); 372 (2007); 364 (2012 projected); Race: 95.4% White, 0.3% Black, 0.0% Asian, 1.6% Hispanic of any race (2007); Density: 1,329.4 persons per square mile (2007); Average household size: 2.57 (2007); Median age: 33.8 (2007); Males per 100 females: 95.8 (2007); Marriage status: 24.3% never married, 56.3% now married, 7.7% widowed, 11.6% divorced (2000); Foreign born: 0.0% (2000); Ancestry (includes multiple ancestries): 47.0% German, 11.4% Irish, 10.4% Other groups, 9.6% English, 5.7% French (except Basque) (2000).
Economy: Single-family building permits issued: 0 (2007); Multi-family building permits issued: 0 (2007); Employment by occupation: 7.0% management, 7.6% professional, 16.8% services, 24.3% sales, 1.1% farming, 7.0% construction, 36.2% production (2000).
Income: Per capita income: $17,177 (2007); Median household income: $37,292 (2007); Average household income: $44,069 (2007); Percent of households with income of $100,000 or more: 3.4% (2007); Poverty rate: 3.7% (2000).
Education: Percent of population age 25 and over with: High school diploma (including GED) or higher: 84.8% (2007); Bachelor's degree or higher: 6.3% (2007); Master's degree or higher: 2.1% (2007).

School District(s)

Vanlue Local (PK-12)
2005-06 Enrollment: 305 . . . . (419) 387-7724
Housing: Homeownership rate: 82.8% (2007); Median home value: $91,818 (2007); Median rent: $311 per month (2000); Median age of housing: 60+ years (2000).
Transportation: Commute to work: 89.5% car, 0.0% public transportation, 4.4% walk, 3.9% work from home (2000); Travel time to work: 20.7% less than 15 minutes, 65.5% 15 to 30 minutes, 6.9% 30 to 45 minutes, 2.3% 45 to 60 minutes, 4.6% 60 minutes or more (2000)

Hardin County

Located in west central Ohio; crossed by the Sciota, Blanchard, and Ottawa Rivers. Covers a land area of 470.29 square miles, a water area of 0.25 square miles, and is located in the Eastern Time Zone. The county was founded in 1820. County seat is Kenton.

Weather Station: Kenton Elevation: 994 feet

	Jan	Feb	Mar	Apr	May	Jun	Jul	Aug	Sep	Oct	Nov	Dec
High	32	37	47	60	72	81	85	83	76	64	50	38
Low	16	19	28	38	49	58	62	60	53	41	32	22
Precip	2.2	2.0	2.8	3.5	3.8	3.5	4.0	3.3	2.6	2.1	2.8	2.7
Snow	10.0	6.4	4.2	0.6	0.0	0.0	0.0	0.0	0.0	tr	1.2	5.4

High and Low temperatures in degrees Fahrenheit; Precipitation and Snow in inches

Population: 31,111 (1990); 31,945 (2000); 32,111 (2007); 32,160 (2012 projected); Race: 97.2% White, 0.9% Black, 0.5% Asian, 1.0% Hispanic of any race (2007); Density: 68.3 persons per square mile (2007); Average household size: 2.66 (2007); Median age: 33.6 (2007); Males per 100 females: 96.8 (2007).
Religion: Five largest groups: 12.5% The United Methodist Church, 5.6% Catholic Church, 4.4% Christian Churches and Churches of Christ, 4.1% United Church of Christ, 1.9% Christian Church (Disciples of Christ) (2000).
Economy: Unemployment rate: 7.3% (6/2008); Total civilian labor force: 15,874 (6/2008); Leading industries: 28.0% manufacturing; 13.8% retail trade; 10.4% health care and social assistance (2005); Farms: 842 totaling

246,393 acres (2002); Companies that employ 500 or more persons: 1 (2006); Companies that employ 100 to 499 persons: 10 (2006); Companies that employ less than 100 persons: 474 (2006); Black-owned businesses: n/a (2002); Hispanic-owned businesses: n/a (2002); Asian-owned businesses: n/a (2002); Women-owned businesses: 306 (2002); Retail sales per capita: $7,804 (2008). Single-family building permits issued: 34 (2007); Multi-family building permits issued: 2 (2007).
Income: Per capita income: $18,329 (2007); Median household income: $38,632 (2007); Average household income: $47,604 (2007); Percent of households with income of $100,000 or more: 7.2% (2007); Poverty rate: 15.4% (2005); Bankruptcy rate: 3.67% (2007).
Education: Percent of population age 25 and over with: High school diploma (including GED) or higher: 80.7% (2007); Bachelor's degree or higher: 12.0% (2007); Master's degree or higher: 4.7% (2007).
Housing: Homeownership rate: 72.9% (2007); Median home value: $96,217 (2007); Median rent: $311 per month (2000); Median age of housing: 44 years (2000).
Health: Birth rate: 125.8 per 10,000 population (2007); Death rate: 101.1 per 10,000 population (2007); Age-adjusted cancer mortality rate: 194.2 deaths per 100,000 population (2005); Number of physicians: 6.6 per 10,000 population (2005); Hospital beds: 7.8 per 10,000 population (2004); Hospital admissions: 461.7 per 10,000 population (2004).
Elections: 2004 Presidential election results: 63.0% Bush, 36.5% Kerry, 0.0% Nader, 0.2% Badnarik

Additional Information Contacts

Hardin County Government . . . . (419) 674-2205
http://www.co.hardin.oh.us
Ada Area Chamber of Commerce . . . . (419) 634-0936
http://www.adafirst.com

Hardin County Communities

ADA (village). Covers a land area of 1.871 square miles and a water area of 0 square miles. Located at 40.76° N. Lat.; 83.82° W. Long. Elevation is 958 feet.
History: Ada grew up around Ohio Northern University, founded in 1871 as the Northwestern Ohio Normal School by Henry Solomon Lehr.
Population: 5,437 (1990); 5,582 (2000); 6,058 (2007); 6,344 (2012 projected); Race: 95.0% White, 2.2% Black, 1.3% Asian, 0.6% Hispanic of any race (2007); Density: 3,237.1 persons per square mile (2007); Average household size: 3.24 (2007); Median age: 22.1 (2007); Males per 100 females: 97.2 (2007); Marriage status: 53.5% never married, 35.3% now married, 3.3% widowed, 7.9% divorced (2000); Foreign born: 2.8% (2000); Ancestry (includes multiple ancestries): 31.8% German, 11.9% United States or American, 10.1% English, 10.0% Irish, 9.4% Other groups (2000).
Economy: Single-family building permits issued: 3 (2007); Multi-family building permits issued: 2 (2007); Employment by occupation: 5.3% management, 32.1% professional, 17.6% services, 25.5% sales, 0.0% farming, 4.5% construction, 14.9% production (2000).
Income: Per capita income: $13,199 (2007); Median household income: $27,226 (2007); Average household income: $38,088 (2007); Percent of households with income of $100,000 or more: 4.9% (2007); Poverty rate: 21.9% (2000).
Education: Percent of population age 25 and over with: High school diploma (including GED) or higher: 86.5% (2007); Bachelor's degree or higher: 33.0% (2007); Master's degree or higher: 13.4% (2007).

School District(s)

Ada Exempted Village (PK-12)
2005-06 Enrollment: 865 . . . . (419) 634-6421

Four-year College(s)

Ohio Northern University (Private, Not-for-profit, United Methodist)
Fall 2007 Enrollment: 3,603. . . . . (419) 772-2000
2007-08 Tuition: In-state $29,685; Out-of-state $29,685

Housing: Homeownership rate: 49.3% (2007); Median home value: $85,878 (2007); Median rent: $339 per month (2000); Median age of housing: 38 years (2000).
Newspapers: Ada Herald (Community news; Circulation 2,700)
Transportation: Commute to work: 68.7% car, 0.5% public transportation, 27.2% walk, 2.3% work from home (2000); Travel time to work: 55.9% less than 15 minutes, 24.2% 15 to 30 minutes, 13.7% 30 to 45 minutes, 3.1% 45 to 60 minutes, 3.1% 60 minutes or more (2000)

Additional Information Contacts

Ada Area Chamber of Commerce . . . . (419) 634-0936
http://www.adafirst.com

ALGER (village). Covers a land area of 0.283 square miles and a water area of 0 square miles. Located at 40.70° N. Lat.; 83.84° W. Long. Elevation is 978 feet.
Population: 893 (1990); 888 (2000); 886 (2007); 867 (2012 projected); Race: 99.5% White, 0.0% Black, 0.0% Asian, 0.0% Hispanic of any race (2007); Density: 3,130.9 persons per square mile (2007); Average household size: 2.34 (2007); Median age: 34.4 (2007); Males per 100 females: 82.3 (2007); Marriage status: 18.9% never married, 57.6% now married, 9.5% widowed, 13.9% divorced (2000); Foreign born: 0.3% (2000); Ancestry (includes multiple ancestries): 25.9% United States or American, 12.3% German, 10.3% Irish, 5.2% Other groups, 4.4% English (2000).
Economy: Employment by occupation: 1.9% management, 7.4% professional, 14.8% services, 19.2% sales, 0.0% farming, 11.5% construction, 45.2% production (2000).
Income: Per capita income: $15,982 (2007); Median household income: $28,382 (2007); Average household income: $37,460 (2007); Percent of households with income of $100,000 or more: 2.9% (2007); Poverty rate: 18.8% (2000).
Education: Percent of population age 25 and over with: High school diploma (including GED) or higher: 68.7% (2007); Bachelor's degree or higher: 3.6% (2007); Master's degree or higher: 0.3% (2007).
Housing: Homeownership rate: 66.4% (2007); Median home value: $64,808 (2007); Median rent: $252 per month (2000); Median age of housing: 39 years (2000).
Transportation: Commute to work: 91.2% car, 1.1% public transportation, 3.4% walk, 2.0% work from home (2000); Travel time to work: 22.8% less than 15 minutes, 42.9% 15 to 30 minutes, 25.1% 30 to 45 minutes, 6.1% 45 to 60 minutes, 3.2% 60 minutes or more (2000)

DOLA (unincorporated postal area, zip code 45835). Covers a land area of 18.971 square miles and a water area of 0 square miles. Located at 40.76° N. Lat.; 83.70° W. Long. Elevation is 948 feet.
Population: 456 (2000); Race: 96.9% White, 0.0% Black, 1.8% Asian, 2.9% Hispanic of any race (2000); Density: 24.0 persons per square mile (2000); Age: 25.1% under 18, 14.2% over 64 (2000); Marriage status: 9.5% never married, 72.6% now married, 5.2% widowed, 12.7% divorced (2000); Foreign born: 0.0% (2000); Ancestry (includes multiple ancestries): 34.2% German, 11.6% Other groups, 10.4% English, 9.6% Irish, 7.1% Scottish (2000).
Economy: Employment by occupation: 23.9% management, 3.7% professional, 4.9% services, 17.8% sales, 0.0% farming, 4.3% construction, 45.4% production (2000).
Income: Per capita income: $21,228 (2000); Median household income: $46,023 (2000); Poverty rate: 20.4% (2000).
Education: Percent of population age 25 and over with: High school diploma (including GED) or higher: 84.0% (2000); Bachelor's degree or higher: 11.1% (2000).

School District(s)

Hardin Northern Local (PK-12)
2005-06 Enrollment: 478 . . . . (419) 759-2331

Housing: Homeownership rate: 82.4% (2000); Median home value: $81,100 (2000); Median rent: $323 per month (2000); Median age of housing: 43 years (2000).
Transportation: Commute to work: 89.0% car, 0.0% public transportation, 3.1% walk, 8.0% work from home (2000); Travel time to work: 18.7% less than 15 minutes, 40.0% 15 to 30 minutes, 30.0% 30 to 45 minutes, 0.0% 45 to 60 minutes, 11.3% 60 minutes or more (2000)

DUNKIRK (village). Covers a land area of 0.666 square miles and a water area of 0.059 square miles. Located at 40.78° N. Lat.; 83.64° W. Long. Elevation is 945 feet.
Population: 885 (1990); 952 (2000); 939 (2007); 936 (2012 projected); Race: 98.9% White, 0.0% Black, 0.1% Asian, 0.1% Hispanic of any race (2007); Density: 1,409.1 persons per square mile (2007); Average household size: 2.62 (2007); Median age: 34.4 (2007); Males per 100 females: 102.4 (2007); Marriage status: 22.1% never married, 63.7% now married, 5.0% widowed, 9.2% divorced (2000); Foreign born: 0.7% (2000); Ancestry (includes multiple ancestries): 21.1% German, 14.9% United States or American, 12.6% English, 5.1% Irish, 4.0% Other groups (2000).
Economy: Employment by occupation: 7.8% management, 8.9% professional, 20.2% services, 15.3% sales, 0.4% farming, 8.6% construction, 38.8% production (2000).

Income: Per capita income: $20,859 (2007); Median household income: $47,632 (2007); Average household income: $54,616 (2007); Percent of households with income of $100,000 or more: 8.7% (2007); Poverty rate: 9.3% (2000).
Education: Percent of population age 25 and over with: High school diploma (including GED) or higher: 78.7% (2007); Bachelor's degree or higher: 8.5% (2007); Master's degree or higher: 2.0% (2007).
Housing: Homeownership rate: 81.8% (2007); Median home value: $78,833 (2007); Median rent: $273 per month (2000); Median age of housing: 56 years (2000).
Transportation: Commute to work: 95.9% car, 0.7% public transportation, 1.6% walk, 1.8% work from home (2000); Travel time to work: 21.4% less than 15 minutes, 41.5% 15 to 30 minutes, 25.8% 30 to 45 minutes, 7.1% 45 to 60 minutes, 4.1% 60 minutes or more (2000)

FOREST (village). Covers a land area of 1.187 square miles and a water area of 0 square miles. Located at 40.80° N. Lat.; 83.51° W. Long. Elevation is 932 feet.
Population: 1,594 (1990); 1,488 (2000); 1,399 (2007); 1,369 (2012 projected); Race: 98.4% White, 0.5% Black, 0.0% Asian, 0.8% Hispanic of any race (2007); Density: 1,178.4 persons per square mile (2007); Average household size: 2.47 (2007); Median age: 32.7 (2007); Males per 100 females: 95.7 (2007); Marriage status: 21.6% never married, 58.0% now married, 6.9% widowed, 13.5% divorced (2000); Foreign born: 0.0% (2000); Ancestry (includes multiple ancestries): 26.5% German, 14.9% United States or American, 9.5% Irish, 7.0% English, 5.8% Other groups (2000).
Economy: Single-family building permits issued: 2 (2007); Multi-family building permits issued: 0 (2007); Employment by occupation: 5.5% management, 9.1% professional, 13.3% services, 20.9% sales, 0.4% farming, 6.1% construction, 44.7% production (2000).
Income: Per capita income: $17,829 (2007); Median household income: $38,611 (2007); Average household income: $43,990 (2007); Percent of households with income of $100,000 or more: 3.9% (2007); Poverty rate: 9.7% (2000).
Education: Percent of population age 25 and over with: High school diploma (including GED) or higher: 84.7% (2007); Bachelor's degree or higher: 6.5% (2007); Master's degree or higher: 1.9% (2007).
Housing: Homeownership rate: 79.7% (2007); Median home value: $84,737 (2007); Median rent: $290 per month (2000); Median age of housing: 47 years (2000).
Transportation: Commute to work: 93.3% car, 0.9% public transportation, 3.7% walk, 1.9% work from home (2000); Travel time to work: 24.9% less than 15 minutes, 36.0% 15 to 30 minutes, 25.1% 30 to 45 minutes, 6.4% 45 to 60 minutes, 7.6% 60 minutes or more (2000)

KENTON (city). County seat. Covers a land area of 4.480 square miles and a water area of 0.094 square miles. Located at 40.64° N. Lat.; 83.60° W. Long. Elevation is 991 feet.
History: Kenton was platted in 1833 on the Scioto River, and named for pioneer Simon Kenton. The town's economic base moved from agriculture to ornamental iron fences and then back to agriculture.
Population: 8,777 (1990); 8,336 (2000); 8,049 (2007); 7,842 (2012 projected); Race: 96.9% White, 1.0% Black, 0.5% Asian, 1.1% Hispanic of any race (2007); Density: 1,796.5 persons per square mile (2007); Average household size: 2.35 (2007); Median age: 36.8 (2007); Males per 100 females: 89.2 (2007); Marriage status: 21.0% never married, 53.9% now married, 9.9% widowed, 15.1% divorced (2000); Foreign born: 0.8% (2000); Ancestry (includes multiple ancestries): 22.0% German, 16.4% United States or American, 11.9% Irish, 11.3% English, 9.1% Other groups (2000).
Economy: Single-family building permits issued: 6 (2007); Multi-family building permits issued: 0 (2007); Employment by occupation: 5.0% management, 9.4% professional, 17.5% services, 18.7% sales, 1.0% farming, 7.9% construction, 40.5% production (2000).
Income: Per capita income: $17,524 (2007); Median household income: $31,774 (2007); Average household income: $39,764 (2007); Percent of households with income of $100,000 or more: 4.1% (2007); Poverty rate: 16.2% (2000).
Education: Percent of population age 25 and over with: High school diploma (including GED) or higher: 77.0% (2007); Bachelor's degree or higher: 6.3% (2007); Master's degree or higher: 2.7% (2007).

School District(s)

Kenton City (PK-12)
2005-06 Enrollment: 2,128 . . . . (419) 673-0775

Housing: Homeownership rate: 63.2% (2007); Median home value: $82,674 (2007); Median rent: $296 per month (2000); Median age of housing: 51 years (2000).
Hospitals: Hardin Memorial Hospital (103 beds)
Safety: Violent crime rate: 4.9 per 10,000 population; Property crime rate: 433.3 per 10,000 population (2007).
Newspapers: Kenton Times (Local news; Circulation 7,000)
Transportation: Commute to work: 93.8% car, 0.4% public transportation, 3.5% walk, 2.0% work from home (2000); Travel time to work: 50.9% less than 15 minutes, 13.5% 15 to 30 minutes, 22.2% 30 to 45 minutes, 9.3% 45 to 60 minutes, 4.1% 60 minutes or more (2000)

MCGUFFEY (village). Covers a land area of 0.366 square miles and a water area of 0 square miles. Located at 40.69° N. Lat.; 83.78° W. Long. Elevation is 971 feet.
History: McGuffey was settled in a marshy region, and took to the growing of onions. Those who tended the onion fields were sometimes called "marsh rats."
Population: 550 (1990); 522 (2000); 544 (2007); 543 (2012 projected); Race: 97.4% White, 0.0% Black, 0.4% Asian, 1.1% Hispanic of any race (2007); Density: 1,486.8 persons per square mile (2007); Average household size: 2.47 (2007); Median age: 34.8 (2007); Males per 100 females: 100.7 (2007); Marriage status: 27.4% never married, 43.0% now married, 11.0% widowed, 18.7% divorced (2000); Foreign born: 0.0% (2000); Ancestry (includes multiple ancestries): 28.4% United States or American, 12.6% German, 10.0% English, 8.8% Irish, 8.4% Other groups (2000).
Economy: Employment by occupation: 6.8% management, 5.0% professional, 23.0% services, 13.0% sales, 0.0% farming, 11.2% construction, 41.0% production (2000).
Income: Per capita income: $12,293 (2007); Median household income: $24,423 (2007); Average household income: $30,398 (2007); Percent of households with income of $100,000 or more: 0.9% (2007); Poverty rate: 19.7% (2000).
Education: Percent of population age 25 and over with: High school diploma (including GED) or higher: 60.5% (2007); Bachelor's degree or higher: 1.7% (2007); Master's degree or higher: 0.3% (2007).

School District(s)

Upper Scioto Valley Local (PK-12)
2005-06 Enrollment: 794 . . . . (419) 757-4451

Housing: Homeownership rate: 74.1% (2007); Median home value: $56,905 (2007); Median rent: $263 per month (2000); Median age of housing: 43 years (2000).
Transportation: Commute to work: 91.7% car, 1.3% public transportation, 7.0% walk, 0.0% work from home (2000); Travel time to work: 15.9% less than 15 minutes, 51.6% 15 to 30 minutes, 19.1% 30 to 45 minutes, 8.9% 45 to 60 minutes, 4.5% 60 minutes or more (2000)

MOUNT VICTORY (village). Covers a land area of 0.758 square miles and a water area of 0 square miles. Located at 40.53° N. Lat.; 83.52° W. Long. Elevation is 1,040 feet.
Population: 551 (1990); 600 (2000); 609 (2007); 613 (2012 projected); Race: 98.9% White, 0.0% Black, 0.0% Asian, 1.5% Hispanic of any race (2007); Density: 803.1 persons per square mile (2007); Average household size: 2.43 (2007); Median age: 35.3 (2007); Males per 100 females: 95.2 (2007); Marriage status: 23.1% never married, 54.9% now married, 9.4% widowed, 12.7% divorced (2000); Foreign born: 1.1% (2000); Ancestry (includes multiple ancestries): 23.6% United States or American, 21.1% German, 11.1% Other groups, 8.8% Irish, 7.7% English (2000).
Economy: Employment by occupation: 8.1% management, 8.4% professional, 11.7% services, 18.1% sales, 0.3% farming, 14.1% construction, 39.3% production (2000).
Income: Per capita income: $20,735 (2007); Median household income: $47,115 (2007); Average household income: $50,309 (2007); Percent of households with income of $100,000 or more: 8.0% (2007); Poverty rate: 6.9% (2000).
Education: Percent of population age 25 and over with: High school diploma (including GED) or higher: 82.2% (2007); Bachelor's degree or higher: 6.1% (2007); Master's degree or higher: 1.5% (2007).

School District(s)

Ridgemont Local (PK-12)
2005-06 Enrollment: 643 . . . . (937) 354-2441

Housing: Homeownership rate: 78.9% (2007); Median home value: $85,909 (2007); Median rent: $249 per month (2000); Median age of housing: 54 years (2000).

Transportation: Commute to work: 93.8% car, 1.0% public transportation, 2.1% walk, 2.4% work from home (2000); Travel time to work: 21.4% less than 15 minutes, 32.4% 15 to 30 minutes, 34.2% 30 to 45 minutes, 5.7% 45 to 60 minutes, 6.4% 60 minutes or more (2000)

PATTERSON (village). Covers a land area of 0.107 square miles and a water area of 0 square miles. Located at 40.78° N. Lat.; 83.52° W. Long. Elevation is 922 feet.
Population: 145 (1990); 138 (2000); 130 (2007); 127 (2012 projected); Race: 97.7% White, 0.0% Black, 0.0% Asian, 0.8% Hispanic of any race (2007); Density: 1,213.8 persons per square mile (2007); Average household size: 2.50 (2007); Median age: 46.0 (2007); Males per 100 females: 85.7 (2007); Marriage status: 15.8% never married, 65.8% now married, 13.2% widowed, 5.3% divorced (2000); Foreign born: 0.0% (2000); Ancestry (includes multiple ancestries): 20.4% German, 12.9% United States or American, 7.5% Irish, 6.8% Other groups, 4.1% Welsh (2000).
Economy: Employment by occupation: 0.0% management, 10.4% professional, 17.9% services, 7.5% sales, 0.0% farming, 3.0% construction, 61.2% production (2000).
Income: Per capita income: $23,577 (2007); Median household income: $42,500 (2007); Average household income: $58,942 (2007); Percent of households with income of $100,000 or more: 11.5% (2007); Poverty rate: 1.4% (2000).
Education: Percent of population age 25 and over with: High school diploma (including GED) or higher: 76.6% (2007); Bachelor's degree or higher: 4.3% (2007); Master's degree or higher: 0.0% (2007).
Housing: Homeownership rate: 90.4% (2007); Median home value: $64,167 (2007); Median rent: $344 per month (2000); Median age of housing: 60+ years (2000).
Transportation: Commute to work: 100.0% car, 0.0% public transportation, 0.0% walk, 0.0% work from home (2000); Travel time to work: 9.4% less than 15 minutes, 65.6% 15 to 30 minutes, 15.6% 30 to 45 minutes, 6.3% 45 to 60 minutes, 3.1% 60 minutes or more (2000)

RIDGEWAY (village). Covers a land area of 0.601 square miles and a water area of 0 square miles. Located at 40.51° N. Lat.; 83.57° W. Long. Elevation is 1,060 feet.
Population: 378 (1990); 354 (2000); 388 (2007); 401 (2012 projected); Race: 98.2% White, 1.3% Black, 0.0% Asian, 0.0% Hispanic of any race (2007); Density: 646.1 persons per square mile (2007); Average household size: 2.85 (2007); Median age: 34.6 (2007); Males per 100 females: 96.0 (2007); Marriage status: 23.8% never married, 64.7% now married, 6.7% widowed, 4.8% divorced (2000); Foreign born: 0.9% (2000); Ancestry (includes multiple ancestries): 27.3% German, 13.5% Irish, 7.8% United States or American, 7.2% English, 5.2% Dutch (2000).
Economy: Single-family building permits issued: 0 (2007); Multi-family building permits issued: 0 (2007); Employment by occupation: 8.7% management, 7.0% professional, 20.9% services, 9.3% sales, 1.2% farming, 12.2% construction, 40.7% production (2000).
Income: Per capita income: $22,043 (2007); Median household income: $51,053 (2007); Average household income: $62,886 (2007); Percent of households with income of $100,000 or more: 11.0% (2007); Poverty rate: 2.9% (2000).
Education: Percent of population age 25 and over with: High school diploma (including GED) or higher: 80.3% (2007); Bachelor's degree or higher: 4.8% (2007); Master's degree or higher: 0.8% (2007).

School District(s)

Ridgemont Local (PK-12)
2005-06 Enrollment: 643 . . . . (937) 354-2441

Housing: Homeownership rate: 90.4% (2007); Median home value: $65,000 (2007); Median rent: $258 per month (2000); Median age of housing: 60+ years (2000).
Transportation: Commute to work: 95.3% car, 0.0% public transportation, 2.4% walk, 1.2% work from home (2000); Travel time to work: 17.4% less than 15 minutes, 42.5% 15 to 30 minutes, 30.5% 30 to 45 minutes, 3.6% 45 to 60 minutes, 6.0% 60 minutes or more (2000)

Harrison County

Located in eastern Ohio; drained by Stillwater and Conotton Creeks; includes Tappan and Clendening Lakes. Covers a land area of 403.53 square miles, a water area of 7.26 square miles, and is located in the Eastern Time Zone. The county was founded in 1813. County seat is Cadiz.

Weather Station: Cadiz — Elevation: 1,259 feet

	Jan	Feb	Mar	Apr	May	Jun	Jul	Aug	Sep	Oct	Nov	Dec
High	35	39	50	62	71	79	83	82	76	64	51	40
Low	19	22	30	39	50	58	63	61	54	43	34	25
Precip	2.8	2.4	3.2	3.4	4.1	4.4	4.4	4.1	3.2	2.6	3.3	3.0
Snow	11.5	6.5	5.1	1.2	0.0	0.0	0.0	0.0	0.0	tr	1.7	6.3

High and Low temperatures in degrees Fahrenheit; Precipitation and Snow in inches

Population: 16,085 (1990); 15,856 (2000); 15,928 (2007); 15,915 (2012 projected); Race: 96.8% White, 2.1% Black, 0.1% Asian, 0.3% Hispanic of any race (2007); Density: 39.5 persons per square mile (2007); Average household size: 2.41 (2007); Median age: 42.4 (2007); Males per 100 females: 95.1 (2007).
Religion: Five largest groups: 15.9% The United Methodist Church, 6.2% Presbyterian Church (U.S.A.), 3.5% Catholic Church, 2.6% Christian Churches and Churches of Christ, 1.1% Church of the Nazarene (2000).
Economy: Unemployment rate: 7.5% (6/2008); Total civilian labor force: 7,372 (6/2008); Leading industries: 22.6% manufacturing; 20.2% health care and social assistance; 13.1% mining (2005); Farms: 450 totaling 138,423 acres (2002); Companies that employ 500 or more persons: 0 (2006); Companies that employ 100 to 499 persons: 7 (2006); Companies that employ less than 100 persons: 302 (2006); Black-owned businesses: n/a (2002); Hispanic-owned businesses: n/a (2002); Asian-owned businesses: n/a (2002); Women-owned businesses: 325 (2002); Retail sales per capita: $5,133 (2008). Single-family building permits issued: 2 (2007); Multi-family building permits issued: 0 (2007).
Income: Per capita income: $19,229 (2007); Median household income: $34,968 (2007); Average household income: $45,916 (2007); Percent of households with income of $100,000 or more: 6.8% (2007); Poverty rate: 15.0% (2005); Bankruptcy rate: 3.68% (2007).
Taxes: Total county taxes per capita: $189 (2006); County property taxes per capita: $102 (2006).
Education: Percent of population age 25 and over with: High school diploma (including GED) or higher: 79.7% (2007); Bachelor's degree or higher: 9.3% (2007); Master's degree or higher: 3.1% (2007).
Housing: Homeownership rate: 77.8% (2007); Median home value: $76,699 (2007); Median rent: $268 per month (2000); Median age of housing: 42 years (2000).
Health: Birth rate: 113.5 per 10,000 population (2007); Death rate: 129.0 per 10,000 population (2007); Age-adjusted cancer mortality rate: 216.3 deaths per 100,000 population (2005); Number of physicians: 7.7 per 10,000 population (2005); Hospital beds: 16.0 per 10,000 population (2004); Hospital admissions: 495.2 per 10,000 population (2004).
Elections: 2004 Presidential election results: 52.7% Bush, 46.6% Kerry, 0.0% Nader, 0.3% Badnarik
National and State Parks: Harrison County State Forest
Additional Information Contacts
Harrison County Government . . . . (740) 942-4623
http://www.harrisoncountyohio.org

Harrison County Communities

BOWERSTON (village). Covers a land area of 0.507 square miles and a water area of 0 square miles. Located at 40.42° N. Lat.; 81.18° W. Long. Elevation is 951 feet.
Population: 343 (1990); 414 (2000); 405 (2007); 390 (2012 projected); Race: 100.0% White, 0.0% Black, 0.0% Asian, 0.0% Hispanic of any race (2007); Density: 799.1 persons per square mile (2007); Average household size: 2.74 (2007); Median age: 41.4 (2007); Males per 100 females: 89.3 (2007); Marriage status: 12.9% never married, 68.2% now married, 9.1% widowed, 9.7% divorced (2000); Foreign born: 1.7% (2000); Ancestry (includes multiple ancestries): 24.4% German, 17.3% Irish, 7.6% English, 7.3% United States or American, 4.4% Italian (2000).
Economy: Employment by occupation: 4.5% management, 15.6% professional, 15.6% services, 25.1% sales, 0.0% farming, 8.9% construction, 30.2% production (2000).
Income: Per capita income: $18,141 (2007); Median household income: $42,143 (2007); Average household income: $46,672 (2007); Percent of households with income of $100,000 or more: 6.1% (2007); Poverty rate: 6.5% (2000).
Education: Percent of population age 25 and over with: High school diploma (including GED) or higher: 81.1% (2007); Bachelor's degree or higher: 11.5% (2007); Master's degree or higher: 3.5% (2007).

School District(s)

Conotton Valley Union Local (PK-12)
2005-06 Enrollment: 571 . . . . (740) 269-2000

Housing: Homeownership rate: 72.3% (2007); Median home value: $65,000 (2007); Median rent: $225 per month (2000); Median age of housing: 60+ years (2000).
Transportation: Commute to work: 94.9% car, 0.0% public transportation, 4.0% walk, 1.1% work from home (2000); Travel time to work: 34.5% less than 15 minutes, 23.0% 15 to 30 minutes, 27.6% 30 to 45 minutes, 8.6% 45 to 60 minutes, 6.3% 60 minutes or more (2000)

CADIZ (village). County seat. Covers a land area of 8.834 square miles and a water area of 0.099 square miles. Located at 40.27° N. Lat.; 80.99° W. Long. Elevation is 1,263 feet.
History: The town of Cadiz, settled at the junction of the Mingo and Moravian trails, was surveyed in 1803, and in 1830 became the seat of Harrison County.
Population: 3,468 (1990); 3,308 (2000); 3,392 (2007); 3,428 (2012 projected); Race: 88.9% White, 8.4% Black, 0.5% Asian, 0.3% Hispanic of any race (2007); Density: 384.0 persons per square mile (2007); Average household size: 2.32 (2007); Median age: 42.7 (2007); Males per 100 females: 85.1 (2007); Marriage status: 18.2% never married, 59.8% now married, 11.9% widowed, 10.1% divorced (2000); Foreign born: 1.0% (2000); Ancestry (includes multiple ancestries): 15.6% German, 12.4% United States or American, 12.0% English, 11.8% Other groups, 10.6% Irish (2000).
Economy: Employment by occupation: 5.6% management, 14.3% professional, 17.9% services, 25.7% sales, 1.1% farming, 13.4% construction, 21.9% production (2000).
Income: Per capita income: $20,553 (2007); Median household income: $33,911 (2007); Average household income: $47,063 (2007); Percent of households with income of $100,000 or more: 8.2% (2007); Poverty rate: 15.7% (2000).
Education: Percent of population age 25 and over with: High school diploma (including GED) or higher: 81.1% (2007); Bachelor's degree or higher: 10.6% (2007); Master's degree or higher: 4.5% (2007).

School District(s)

Belmont-Harrison (09-12)
2005-06 Enrollment: n/a . . . . (740) 695-9130
Harrison Hills City (PK-12)
2005-06 Enrollment: 2,045 . . . . (740) 942-7800

Housing: Homeownership rate: 66.1% (2007); Median home value: $81,940 (2007); Median rent: $280 per month (2000); Median age of housing: 46 years (2000).
Hospitals: Harrison Community Hospital (48 beds)
Safety: Violent crime rate: 23.7 per 10,000 population; Property crime rate: 242.7 per 10,000 population (2007).
Newspapers: Harrison News Herald (Local news; Circulation 6,000)
Transportation: Commute to work: 92.8% car, 0.0% public transportation, 3.8% walk, 3.5% work from home (2000); Travel time to work: 54.3% less than 15 minutes, 11.7% 15 to 30 minutes, 15.8% 30 to 45 minutes, 9.3% 45 to 60 minutes, 9.0% 60 minutes or more (2000)

DEERSVILLE (village). Covers a land area of 0.349 square miles and a water area of 0 square miles. Located at 40.30° N. Lat.; 81.18° W. Long. Elevation is 1,234 feet.
Population: 91 (1990); 82 (2000); 85 (2007); 84 (2012 projected); Race: 100.0% White, 0.0% Black, 0.0% Asian, 1.2% Hispanic of any race (2007); Density: 243.6 persons per square mile (2007); Average household size: 2.07 (2007); Median age: 50.8 (2007); Males per 100 females: 107.3 (2007); Marriage status: 24.1% never married, 57.8% now married, 10.8% widowed, 7.2% divorced (2000); Foreign born: 0.0% (2000); Ancestry (includes multiple ancestries): 23.3% United States or American, 18.9% Irish, 10.0% German, 8.9% English, 6.7% Scotch-Irish (2000).
Economy: Employment by occupation: 13.5% management, 18.9% professional, 13.5% services, 32.4% sales, 0.0% farming, 0.0% construction, 21.6% production (2000).
Income: Per capita income: $18,588 (2007); Median household income: $29,643 (2007); Average household income: $38,537 (2007); Percent of households with income of $100,000 or more: 9.8% (2007); Poverty rate: 14.4% (2000).
Education: Percent of population age 25 and over with: High school diploma (including GED) or higher: 80.3% (2007); Bachelor's degree or higher: 5.6% (2007); Master's degree or higher: 2.8% (2007).
Housing: Homeownership rate: 73.2% (2007); Median home value: $86,000 (2007); Median rent: $125 per month (2000); Median age of housing: 47 years (2000).
Transportation: Commute to work: 78.4% car, 0.0% public transportation, 16.2% walk, 5.4% work from home (2000); Travel time to work: 31.4% less than 15 minutes, 25.7% 15 to 30 minutes, 22.9% 30 to 45 minutes, 5.7% 45 to 60 minutes, 14.3% 60 minutes or more (2000)

FREEPORT (village). Covers a land area of 0.599 square miles and a water area of 0 square miles. Located at 40.21° N. Lat.; 81.26° W. Long. Elevation is 997 feet.
Population: 475 (1990); 398 (2000); 377 (2007); 373 (2012 projected); Race: 98.9% White, 0.0% Black, 0.5% Asian, 0.0% Hispanic of any race (2007); Density: 629.4 persons per square mile (2007); Average household size: 2.27 (2007); Median age: 42.0 (2007); Males per 100 females: 90.4 (2007); Marriage status: 22.2% never married, 48.6% now married, 17.3% widowed, 11.9% divorced (2000); Foreign born: 0.0% (2000); Ancestry (includes multiple ancestries): 16.7% German, 10.7% United States or American, 8.5% Irish, 7.5% English, 7.5% Other groups (2000).
Economy: Employment by occupation: 2.9% management, 24.7% professional, 18.2% services, 13.5% sales, 0.0% farming, 14.7% construction, 25.9% production (2000).
Income: Per capita income: $17,003 (2007); Median household income: $21,905 (2007); Average household income: $38,614 (2007); Percent of households with income of $100,000 or more: 4.8% (2007); Poverty rate: 19.4% (2000).
Education: Percent of population age 25 and over with: High school diploma (including GED) or higher: 73.9% (2007); Bachelor's degree or higher: 10.7% (2007); Master's degree or higher: 5.9% (2007).

School District(s)

Harrison Hills City (PK-12)
2005-06 Enrollment: 2,045 . . . . (740) 942-7800

Housing: Homeownership rate: 69.3% (2007); Median home value: $50,500 (2007); Median rent: $159 per month (2000); Median age of housing: 60+ years (2000).
Transportation: Commute to work: 72.4% car, 0.0% public transportation, 25.9% walk, 1.8% work from home (2000); Travel time to work: 39.5% less than 15 minutes, 21.0% 15 to 30 minutes, 23.4% 30 to 45 minutes, 10.8% 45 to 60 minutes, 5.4% 60 minutes or more (2000)

HARRISVILLE (village). Covers a land area of 0.151 square miles and a water area of 0 square miles. Located at 40.18° N. Lat.; 80.88° W. Long. Elevation is 1,250 feet.
Population: 308 (1990); 259 (2000); 234 (2007); 226 (2012 projected); Race: 99.6% White, 0.0% Black, 0.4% Asian, 0.0% Hispanic of any race (2007); Density: 1,547.9 persons per square mile (2007); Average household size: 2.34 (2007); Median age: 39.8 (2007); Males per 100 females: 105.3 (2007); Marriage status: 19.2% never married, 53.0% now married, 14.1% widowed, 13.6% divorced (2000); Foreign born: 0.0% (2000); Ancestry (includes multiple ancestries): 25.0% Irish, 18.9% Polish, 17.2% German, 13.9% Italian, 12.7% United States or American (2000).
Economy: Employment by occupation: 10.6% management, 10.6% professional, 13.8% services, 26.6% sales, 0.0% farming, 19.1% construction, 19.1% production (2000).
Income: Per capita income: $16,261 (2007); Median household income: $30,417 (2007); Average household income: $38,050 (2007); Percent of households with income of $100,000 or more: 2.0% (2007); Poverty rate: 5.7% (2000).
Education: Percent of population age 25 and over with: High school diploma (including GED) or higher: 73.9% (2007); Bachelor's degree or higher: 8.7% (2007); Master's degree or higher: 0.0% (2007).
Housing: Homeownership rate: 80.0% (2007); Median home value: $47,600 (2007); Median rent: $238 per month (2000); Median age of housing: 60 years (2000).
Transportation: Commute to work: 100.0% car, 0.0% public transportation, 0.0% walk, 0.0% work from home (2000); Travel time to work: 11.7% less than 15 minutes, 26.6% 15 to 30 minutes, 28.7% 30 to 45 minutes, 10.6% 45 to 60 minutes, 22.3% 60 minutes or more (2000)

HOPEDALE (village). Covers a land area of 0.716 square miles and a water area of 0 square miles. Located at 40.32° N. Lat.; 80.89° W. Long. Elevation is 1,158 feet.
History: Hopedale was the home of motion picture actor Clark Gable, who spent part of his boyhood here. The town developed around the coal mines.
Population: 920 (1990); 984 (2000); 958 (2007); 942 (2012 projected); Race: 99.3% White, 0.3% Black, 0.0% Asian, 0.4% Hispanic of any race (2007); Density: 1,338.4 persons per square mile (2007); Average

household size: 2.49 (2007); Median age: 45.5 (2007); Males per 100 females: 95.9 (2007); Marriage status: 16.0% never married, 63.9% now married, 11.0% widowed, 9.1% divorced (2000); Foreign born: 0.6% (2000); Ancestry (includes multiple ancestries): 18.6% German, 16.3% Italian, 12.6% English, 12.6% Irish, 12.0% United States or American (2000).
Economy: Employment by occupation: 7.7% management, 12.9% professional, 16.8% services, 24.8% sales, 0.0% farming, 14.3% construction, 23.4% production (2000).
Income: Per capita income: $19,725 (2007); Median household income: $37,589 (2007); Average household income: $47,286 (2007); Percent of households with income of $100,000 or more: 8.8% (2007); Poverty rate: 11.8% (2000).
Education: Percent of population age 25 and over with: High school diploma (including GED) or higher: 80.5% (2007); Bachelor's degree or higher: 7.9% (2007); Master's degree or higher: 2.6% (2007).

School District(s)

Harrison Hills City (PK-12)
2005-06 Enrollment: 2,045 . . . . (740) 942-7800
Housing: Homeownership rate: 77.7% (2007); Median home value: $75,682 (2007); Median rent: $288 per month (2000); Median age of housing: 45 years (2000).
Transportation: Commute to work: 96.3% car, 0.0% public transportation, 1.7% walk, 1.1% work from home (2000); Travel time to work: 26.7% less than 15 minutes, 39.7% 15 to 30 minutes, 16.1% 30 to 45 minutes, 6.6% 45 to 60 minutes, 10.9% 60 minutes or more (2000)

JEWETT (village). Covers a land area of 0.512 square miles and a water area of 0 square miles. Located at 40.36° N. Lat.; 81.00° W. Long. Elevation is 994 feet.
History: Laid out 1851, incorporated 1886.
Population: 778 (1990); 784 (2000); 759 (2007); 754 (2012 projected); Race: 98.9% White, 0.0% Black, 0.0% Asian, 0.3% Hispanic of any race (2007); Density: 1,483.3 persons per square mile (2007); Average household size: 2.54 (2007); Median age: 36.2 (2007); Males per 100 females: 97.7 (2007); Marriage status: 18.5% never married, 62.4% now married, 9.5% widowed, 9.7% divorced (2000); Foreign born: 0.4% (2000); Ancestry (includes multiple ancestries): 16.7% Irish, 15.3% German, 13.5% United States or American, 12.2% English, 10.2% Other groups (2000).
Economy: Single-family building permits issued: 1 (2007); Multi-family building permits issued: 0 (2007); Employment by occupation: 5.9% management, 9.5% professional, 22.7% services, 22.7% sales, 1.5% farming, 12.5% construction, 25.3% production (2000).
Income: Per capita income: $15,007 (2007); Median household income: $31,146 (2007); Average household income: $38,094 (2007); Percent of households with income of $100,000 or more: 4.3% (2007); Poverty rate: 21.7% (2000).
Education: Percent of population age 25 and over with: High school diploma (including GED) or higher: 77.0% (2007); Bachelor's degree or higher: 6.2% (2007); Master's degree or higher: 1.9% (2007).

School District(s)

Harrison Hills City (PK-12)
2005-06 Enrollment: 2,045 . . . . (740) 942-7800
Housing: Homeownership rate: 72.6% (2007); Median home value: $58,594 (2007); Median rent: $313 per month (2000); Median age of housing: 60+ years (2000).
Transportation: Commute to work: 91.2% car, 0.8% public transportation, 5.4% walk, 2.7% work from home (2000); Travel time to work: 21.7% less than 15 minutes, 36.4% 15 to 30 minutes, 11.9% 30 to 45 minutes, 18.2% 45 to 60 minutes, 11.9% 60 minutes or more (2000)

NEW ATHENS (village). Covers a land area of 0.283 square miles and a water area of 0 square miles. Located at 40.18° N. Lat.; 80.99° W. Long. Elevation is 1,184 feet.
Population: 370 (1990); 342 (2000); 310 (2007); 298 (2012 projected); Race: 98.7% White, 0.6% Black, 0.0% Asian, 0.0% Hispanic of any race (2007); Density: 1,096.9 persons per square mile (2007); Average household size: 2.44 (2007); Median age: 40.9 (2007); Males per 100 females: 86.7 (2007); Marriage status: 23.5% never married, 55.7% now married, 10.4% widowed, 10.4% divorced (2000); Foreign born: 0.0% (2000); Ancestry (includes multiple ancestries): 23.7% German, 19.6% Irish, 14.2% English, 4.7% Scotch-Irish, 3.6% Other groups (2000).
Economy: Employment by occupation: 3.4% management, 12.2% professional, 15.0% services, 28.6% sales, 0.0% farming, 14.3% construction, 26.5% production (2000).
Income: Per capita income: $14,274 (2007); Median household income: $30,179 (2007); Average household income: $34,843 (2007); Percent of households with income of $100,000 or more: 0.0% (2007); Poverty rate: 19.6% (2000).
Education: Percent of population age 25 and over with: High school diploma (including GED) or higher: 81.7% (2007); Bachelor's degree or higher: 5.0% (2007); Master's degree or higher: 2.3% (2007).
Housing: Homeownership rate: 82.7% (2007); Median home value: $61,154 (2007); Median rent: $255 per month (2000); Median age of housing: 60+ years (2000).
Transportation: Commute to work: 96.6% car, 0.0% public transportation, 0.0% walk, 0.0% work from home (2000); Travel time to work: 11.7% less than 15 minutes, 53.8% 15 to 30 minutes, 14.5% 30 to 45 minutes, 6.9% 45 to 60 minutes, 13.1% 60 minutes or more (2000)

PIEDMONT (unincorporated postal area, zip code 43983). Covers a land area of 18.890 square miles and a water area of 0.010 square miles. Located at 40.14° N. Lat.; 81.20° W. Long. Elevation is 890 feet.
Population: 433 (2000); Race: 100.0% White, 0.0% Black, 0.0% Asian, 0.0% Hispanic of any race (2000); Density: 22.9 persons per square mile (2000); Age: 7.5% under 18, 20.1% over 64 (2000); Marriage status: 11.9% never married, 61.3% now married, 13.2% widowed, 13.6% divorced (2000); Foreign born: 0.0% (2000); Ancestry (includes multiple ancestries): 29.1% German, 15.0% English, 13.0% United States or American, 13.0% Irish, 9.4% French (except Basque) (2000).
Economy: Employment by occupation: 19.2% management, 25.0% professional, 19.2% services, 10.6% sales, 0.0% farming, 12.5% construction, 13.5% production (2000).
Income: Per capita income: $21,099 (2000); Median household income: $29,643 (2000); Poverty rate: 8.3% (2000).
Education: Percent of population age 25 and over with: High school diploma (including GED) or higher: 79.5% (2000); Bachelor's degree or higher: 16.0% (2000).
Housing: Homeownership rate: 100.0% (2000); Median home value: $49,800 (2000); Median rent: $n/a per month (2000); Median age of housing: 30 years (2000).
Transportation: Commute to work: 86.5% car, 0.0% public transportation, 5.8% walk, 0.0% work from home (2000); Travel time to work: 5.8% less than 15 minutes, 38.5% 15 to 30 minutes, 10.6% 30 to 45 minutes, 28.8% 45 to 60 minutes, 16.3% 60 minutes or more (2000)

SCIO (village). Covers a land area of 0.552 square miles and a water area of 0 square miles. Located at 40.39° N. Lat.; 81.08° W. Long. Elevation is 991 feet.
Population: 854 (1990); 799 (2000); 728 (2007); 714 (2012 projected); Race: 99.7% White, 0.1% Black, 0.0% Asian, 0.8% Hispanic of any race (2007); Density: 1,318.3 persons per square mile (2007); Average household size: 2.17 (2007); Median age: 39.2 (2007); Males per 100 females: 84.8 (2007); Marriage status: 21.6% never married, 50.9% now married, 12.0% widowed, 15.6% divorced (2000); Foreign born: 0.0% (2000); Ancestry (includes multiple ancestries): 19.3% German, 15.0% Irish, 12.3% United States or American, 8.2% Other groups, 7.7% English (2000).
Economy: Single-family building permits issued: 1 (2007); Multi-family building permits issued: 0 (2007); Employment by occupation: 5.9% management, 11.8% professional, 16.7% services, 24.1% sales, 0.0% farming, 5.9% construction, 35.6% production (2000).
Income: Per capita income: $17,356 (2007); Median household income: $27,833 (2007); Average household income: $37,604 (2007); Percent of households with income of $100,000 or more: 3.3% (2007); Poverty rate: 13.9% (2000).
Education: Percent of population age 25 and over with: High school diploma (including GED) or higher: 79.8% (2007); Bachelor's degree or higher: 8.1% (2007); Master's degree or higher: 3.4% (2007).

School District(s)

Harrison Hills City (PK-12)
2005-06 Enrollment: 2,045 . . . . (740) 942-7800
Housing: Homeownership rate: 66.7% (2007); Median home value: $67,308 (2007); Median rent: $238 per month (2000); Median age of housing: 60+ years (2000).
Transportation: Commute to work: 92.6% car, 0.3% public transportation, 4.3% walk, 2.8% work from home (2000); Travel time to work: 29.0% less than 15 minutes, 24.8% 15 to 30 minutes, 18.2% 30 to 45 minutes, 9.2% 45 to 60 minutes, 18.8% 60 minutes or more (2000)

TIPPECANOE (unincorporated postal area, zip code 44699). Covers a land area of 51.622 square miles and a water area of 0.044 square miles. Located at 40.28° N. Lat.; 81.28° W. Long. Elevation is 875 feet.
Population: 987 (2000); Race: 100.0% White, 0.0% Black, 0.0% Asian, 0.8% Hispanic of any race (2000); Density: 19.1 persons per square mile (2000); Age: 23.7% under 18, 14.0% over 64 (2000); Marriage status: 16.8% never married, 69.2% now married, 6.1% widowed, 7.9% divorced (2000); Foreign born: 1.5% (2000); Ancestry (includes multiple ancestries): 23.1% German, 16.3% Irish, 6.8% Other groups, 6.4% English, 6.4% United States or American (2000).
Economy: Employment by occupation: 11.3% management, 13.1% professional, 15.6% services, 20.1% sales, 2.8% farming, 9.0% construction, 28.1% production (2000).
Income: Per capita income: $14,292 (2000); Median household income: $31,333 (2000); Poverty rate: 17.2% (2000).
Education: Percent of population age 25 and over with: High school diploma (including GED) or higher: 77.7% (2000); Bachelor's degree or higher: 8.2% (2000).
Housing: Homeownership rate: 77.0% (2000); Median home value: $45,500 (2000); Median rent: $283 per month (2000); Median age of housing: 34 years (2000).
Transportation: Commute to work: 91.0% car, 0.0% public transportation, 7.7% walk, 1.3% work from home (2000); Travel time to work: 10.9% less than 15 minutes, 29.8% 15 to 30 minutes, 36.0% 30 to 45 minutes, 9.3% 45 to 60 minutes, 14.0% 60 minutes or more (2000)

Henry County

Located in northwestern Ohio; crossed by the Maumee River. Covers a land area of 416.50 square miles, a water area of 3.47 square miles, and is located in the Eastern Time Zone. The county was founded in 1820. County seat is Napoleon.

Weather Station: Napoleon — Elevation: 679 feet

	Jan	Feb	Mar	Apr	May	Jun	Jul	Aug	Sep	Oct	Nov	Dec
High	31	35	47	60	72	81	85	83	76	64	50	37
Low	15	18	27	37	48	57	62	59	52	41	33	22
Precip	2.0	1.7	2.7	3.6	3.5	3.4	3.9	3.4	2.7	2.5	2.9	2.5
Snow	8.7	5.8	2.8	1.1	0.0	0.0	0.0	0.0	0.0	0.1	0.9	5.2

High and Low temperatures in degrees Fahrenheit; Precipitation and Snow in inches

Population: 29,108 (1990); 29,210 (2000); 29,522 (2007); 29,639 (2012 projected); Race: 94.8% White, 0.8% Black, 0.5% Asian, 6.0% Hispanic of any race (2007); Density: 70.9 persons per square mile (2007); Average household size: 2.61 (2007); Median age: 38.3 (2007); Males per 100 females: 98.6 (2007).
Religion: Five largest groups: 19.9% Lutheran Church—Missouri Synod, 14.7% Evangelical Lutheran Church in America, 12.7% Catholic Church, 11.8% The United Methodist Church, 2.7% United Church of Christ (2000).
Economy: Unemployment rate: 7.9% (6/2008); Total civilian labor force: 15,785 (6/2008); Leading industries: 36.0% manufacturing; 12.6% health care and social assistance; 10.6% retail trade (2005); Farms: 844 totaling 236,273 acres (2002); Companies that employ 500 or more persons: 2 (2006); Companies that employ 100 to 499 persons: 14 (2006); Companies that employ less than 100 persons: 609 (2006); Black-owned businesses: n/a (2002); Hispanic-owned businesses: n/a (2002); Asian-owned businesses: n/a (2002); Women-owned businesses: 724 (2002); Retail sales per capita: $9,469 (2008). Single-family building permits issued: 62 (2007); Multi-family building permits issued: 0 (2007).
Income: Per capita income: $21,786 (2007); Median household income: $48,382 (2007); Average household income: $56,583 (2007); Percent of households with income of $100,000 or more: 10.5% (2007); Poverty rate: 7.1% (2005); Bankruptcy rate: 2.83% (2007).
Education: Percent of population age 25 and over with: High school diploma (including GED) or higher: 83.5% (2007); Bachelor's degree or higher: 10.9% (2007); Master's degree or higher: 2.9% (2007).
Housing: Homeownership rate: 80.9% (2007); Median home value: $107,451 (2007); Median rent: $360 per month (2000); Median age of housing: 42 years (2000).
Health: Birth rate: 133.4 per 10,000 population (2007); Death rate: 100.6 per 10,000 population (2007); Age-adjusted cancer mortality rate: 165.0 deaths per 100,000 population (2005); Number of physicians: 6.2 per 10,000 population (2005); Hospital beds: 10.3 per 10,000 population (2004); Hospital admissions: 270.3 per 10,000 population (2004).
Elections: 2004 Presidential election results: 65.6% Bush, 33.8% Kerry, 0.0% Nader, 0.3% Badnarik
National and State Parks: Maumee State Forest; North Turkeyfoot State Park
Additional Information Contacts
Henry County Government . . . . (419) 592-4876
http://www.henrycountyohio.com
City of Napoleon . . . . (419) 592-4010
http://www.napoleonohio.com
Napoleon-Henry County Chamber of Commerce . . . . (419) 592-1786
http://www.ohiohenrycounty.com

Henry County Communities

DESHLER (village). Covers a land area of 2.264 square miles and a water area of 0.027 square miles. Located at 41.20° N. Lat.; 83.90° W. Long. Elevation is 712 feet.
Population: 1,876 (1990); 1,831 (2000); 1,867 (2007); 1,867 (2012 projected); Race: 93.1% White, 0.1% Black, 0.6% Asian, 7.7% Hispanic of any race (2007); Density: 824.7 persons per square mile (2007); Average household size: 2.55 (2007); Median age: 36.5 (2007); Males per 100 females: 100.1 (2007); Marriage status: 20.0% never married, 60.2% now married, 9.8% widowed, 10.1% divorced (2000); Foreign born: 2.2% (2000); Ancestry (includes multiple ancestries): 43.5% German, 11.1% Other groups, 8.5% Irish, 6.5% English, 6.3% United States or American (2000).
Economy: Employment by occupation: 6.9% management, 12.1% professional, 14.2% services, 17.5% sales, 0.2% farming, 13.0% construction, 36.0% production (2000).
Income: Per capita income: $18,705 (2007); Median household income: $39,669 (2007); Average household income: $47,595 (2007); Percent of households with income of $100,000 or more: 6.0% (2007); Poverty rate: 7.5% (2000).
Education: Percent of population age 25 and over with: High school diploma (including GED) or higher: 77.3% (2007); Bachelor's degree or higher: 8.7% (2007); Master's degree or higher: 3.2% (2007).
School District(s)
Patrick Henry Local (PK-12)
2005-06 Enrollment: 1,087 . . . . (419) 274-5451
Housing: Homeownership rate: 82.8% (2007); Median home value: $82,721 (2007); Median rent: $316 per month (2000); Median age of housing: 50 years (2000).
Newspapers: Deshler Flag (Community news; Circulation 1,500)
Transportation: Commute to work: 91.7% car, 0.4% public transportation, 5.4% walk, 1.1% work from home (2000); Travel time to work: 36.8% less than 15 minutes, 20.2% 15 to 30 minutes, 27.8% 30 to 45 minutes, 8.7% 45 to 60 minutes, 6.5% 60 minutes or more (2000)

FLORIDA (village). Covers a land area of 0.227 square miles and a water area of 0 square miles. Located at 41.32° N. Lat.; 84.20° W. Long. Elevation is 673 feet.
Population: 304 (1990); 246 (2000); 253 (2007); 254 (2012 projected); Race: 95.3% White, 0.0% Black, 0.4% Asian, 7.5% Hispanic of any race (2007); Density: 1,113.3 persons per square mile (2007); Average household size: 2.46 (2007); Median age: 40.4 (2007); Males per 100 females: 88.8 (2007); Marriage status: 19.0% never married, 62.0% now married, 5.5% widowed, 13.5% divorced (2000); Foreign born: 2.7% (2000); Ancestry (includes multiple ancestries): 49.0% German, 10.2% Other groups, 9.8% Irish, 8.6% United States or American, 5.1% English (2000).
Economy: Employment by occupation: 0.8% management, 12.3% professional, 9.8% services, 22.1% sales, 0.0% farming, 13.9% construction, 41.0% production (2000).
Income: Per capita income: $18,864 (2007); Median household income: $45,417 (2007); Average household income: $46,335 (2007); Percent of households with income of $100,000 or more: 1.0% (2007); Poverty rate: 9.0% (2000).
Education: Percent of population age 25 and over with: High school diploma (including GED) or higher: 71.7% (2007); Bachelor's degree or higher: 4.0% (2007); Master's degree or higher: 1.2% (2007).
Housing: Homeownership rate: 76.7% (2007); Median home value: $90,556 (2007); Median rent: $389 per month (2000); Median age of housing: 49 years (2000).
Transportation: Commute to work: 100.0% car, 0.0% public transportation, 0.0% walk, 0.0% work from home (2000); Travel time to

work: 16.4% less than 15 minutes, 62.3% 15 to 30 minutes, 15.6% 30 to 45 minutes, 3.3% 45 to 60 minutes, 2.5% 60 minutes or more (2000)

HAMLER (village). Covers a land area of 0.572 square miles and a water area of 0.003 square miles. Located at 41.22° N. Lat.; 84.03° W. Long. Elevation is 709 feet.
Population: 627 (1990); 650 (2000); 622 (2007); 622 (2012 projected); Race: 87.5% White, 1.0% Black, 0.0% Asian, 23.0% Hispanic of any race (2007); Density: 1,088.1 persons per square mile (2007); Average household size: 2.68 (2007); Median age: 33.8 (2007); Males per 100 females: 93.2 (2007); Marriage status: 21.9% never married, 62.9% now married, 5.9% widowed, 9.3% divorced (2000); Foreign born: 1.9% (2000); Ancestry (includes multiple ancestries): 44.5% German, 25.0% Other groups, 4.8% Irish, 3.8% United States or American, 3.6% Dutch (2000).
Economy: Single-family building permits issued: 0 (2007); Multi-family building permits issued: 0 (2007); Employment by occupation: 7.6% management, 14.8% professional, 14.1% services, 13.1% sales, 0.7% farming, 10.7% construction, 39.2% production (2000).
Income: Per capita income: $18,666 (2007); Median household income: $43,333 (2007); Average household income: $50,043 (2007); Percent of households with income of $100,000 or more: 5.2% (2007); Poverty rate: 6.3% (2000).
Education: Percent of population age 25 and over with: High school diploma (including GED) or higher: 77.4% (2007); Bachelor's degree or higher: 10.3% (2007); Master's degree or higher: 3.9% (2007).

School District(s)

Patrick Henry Local (PK-12)
2005-06 Enrollment: 1,087 . . . . (419) 274-5451
Housing: Homeownership rate: 80.6% (2007); Median home value: $81,667 (2007); Median rent: $360 per month (2000); Median age of housing: 48 years (2000).
Transportation: Commute to work: 95.1% car, 0.0% public transportation, 4.6% walk, 0.4% work from home (2000); Travel time to work: 24.5% less than 15 minutes, 42.9% 15 to 30 minutes, 16.3% 30 to 45 minutes, 11.7% 45 to 60 minutes, 4.6% 60 minutes or more (2000)

HOLGATE (village). Covers a land area of 0.980 square miles and a water area of 0 square miles. Located at 41.25° N. Lat.; 84.13° W. Long. Elevation is 712 feet.
Population: 1,290 (1990); 1,194 (2000); 1,095 (2007); 1,090 (2012 projected); Race: 93.8% White, 0.1% Black, 0.1% Asian, 17.7% Hispanic of any race (2007); Density: 1,117.7 persons per square mile (2007); Average household size: 2.64 (2007); Median age: 35.7 (2007); Males per 100 females: 95.2 (2007); Marriage status: 22.1% never married, 54.5% now married, 8.9% widowed, 14.5% divorced (2000); Foreign born: 3.5% (2000); Ancestry (includes multiple ancestries): 35.0% German, 24.1% Other groups, 8.2% United States or American, 6.5% Irish, 5.8% English (2000).
Economy: Single-family building permits issued: 2 (2007); Multi-family building permits issued: 0 (2007); Employment by occupation: 5.4% management, 11.7% professional, 15.4% services, 14.4% sales, 0.0% farming, 10.9% construction, 42.2% production (2000).
Income: Per capita income: $19,024 (2007); Median household income: $40,714 (2007); Average household income: $49,668 (2007); Percent of households with income of $100,000 or more: 8.0% (2007); Poverty rate: 10.5% (2000).
Education: Percent of population age 25 and over with: High school diploma (including GED) or higher: 75.0% (2007); Bachelor's degree or higher: 7.5% (2007); Master's degree or higher: 3.2% (2007).

School District(s)

Holgate Local (PK-12)
2005-06 Enrollment: 533 . . . . (419) 264-5141
Housing: Homeownership rate: 77.5% (2007); Median home value: $72,900 (2007); Median rent: $377 per month (2000); Median age of housing: 51 years (2000).
Transportation: Commute to work: 95.6% car, 0.4% public transportation, 2.2% walk, 1.4% work from home (2000); Travel time to work: 19.3% less than 15 minutes, 49.3% 15 to 30 minutes, 20.1% 30 to 45 minutes, 7.2% 45 to 60 minutes, 4.0% 60 minutes or more (2000)

LIBERTY CENTER (village). Covers a land area of 1.045 square miles and a water area of 0 square miles. Located at 41.44° N. Lat.; 84.00° W. Long. Elevation is 679 feet.
Population: 1,084 (1990); 1,109 (2000); 1,082 (2007); 1,073 (2012 projected); Race: 98.4% White, 0.0% Black, 0.2% Asian, 1.6% Hispanic of any race (2007); Density: 1,035.1 persons per square mile (2007); Average household size: 2.55 (2007); Median age: 35.9 (2007); Males per 100 females: 95.7 (2007); Marriage status: 21.4% never married, 61.4% now married, 6.3% widowed, 10.8% divorced (2000); Foreign born: 0.3% (2000); Ancestry (includes multiple ancestries): 43.2% German, 15.2% Irish, 9.1% United States or American, 8.4% Other groups, 7.3% French (except Basque) (2000).
Economy: Single-family building permits issued: 1 (2007); Multi-family building permits issued: 0 (2007); Employment by occupation: 6.0% management, 12.1% professional, 12.5% services, 15.3% sales, 0.6% farming, 11.5% construction, 42.1% production (2000).
Income: Per capita income: $20,619 (2007); Median household income: $47,941 (2007); Average household income: $52,618 (2007); Percent of households with income of $100,000 or more: 6.1% (2007); Poverty rate: 6.7% (2000).
Education: Percent of population age 25 and over with: High school diploma (including GED) or higher: 87.4% (2007); Bachelor's degree or higher: 10.8% (2007); Master's degree or higher: 2.5% (2007).

School District(s)

Liberty Center Local (PK-12)
2005-06 Enrollment: 1,170 . . . . (419) 533-5011
Housing: Homeownership rate: 80.9% (2007); Median home value: $99,688 (2007); Median rent: $360 per month (2000); Median age of housing: 50 years (2000).
Newspapers: Liberty Press (Community news; Circulation 1,300)
Transportation: Commute to work: 97.0% car, 0.0% public transportation, 1.4% walk, 1.2% work from home (2000); Travel time to work: 25.7% less than 15 minutes, 42.2% 15 to 30 minutes, 20.8% 30 to 45 minutes, 5.8% 45 to 60 minutes, 5.6% 60 minutes or more (2000)

MALINTA (village). Covers a land area of 0.771 square miles and a water area of 0 square miles. Located at 41.32° N. Lat.; 84.03° W. Long. Elevation is 686 feet.
Population: 295 (1990); 285 (2000); 285 (2007); 282 (2012 projected); Race: 98.2% White, 0.0% Black, 0.0% Asian, 6.0% Hispanic of any race (2007); Density: 369.8 persons per square mile (2007); Average household size: 2.46 (2007); Median age: 38.8 (2007); Males per 100 females: 103.6 (2007); Marriage status: 24.3% never married, 55.3% now married, 8.0% widowed, 12.4% divorced (2000); Foreign born: 0.0% (2000); Ancestry (includes multiple ancestries): 46.5% German, 11.1% Other groups, 9.4% Irish, 8.4% Dutch, 6.1% Belgian (2000).
Economy: Single-family building permits issued: 0 (2007); Multi-family building permits issued: 0 (2007); Employment by occupation: 9.2% management, 8.4% professional, 7.6% services, 16.8% sales, 0.0% farming, 14.5% construction, 43.5% production (2000).
Income: Per capita income: $20,763 (2007); Median household income: $46,250 (2007); Average household income: $51,013 (2007); Percent of households with income of $100,000 or more: 5.2% (2007); Poverty rate: 2.7% (2000).
Education: Percent of population age 25 and over with: High school diploma (including GED) or higher: 80.9% (2007); Bachelor's degree or higher: 6.4% (2007); Master's degree or higher: 1.1% (2007).

School District(s)

Patrick Henry Local (PK-12)
2005-06 Enrollment: 1,087 . . . . (419) 274-5451
Housing: Homeownership rate: 84.5% (2007); Median home value: $84,375 (2007); Median rent: $311 per month (2000); Median age of housing: 60+ years (2000).
Transportation: Commute to work: 96.9% car, 0.0% public transportation, 2.3% walk, 0.0% work from home (2000); Travel time to work: 26.0% less than 15 minutes, 51.1% 15 to 30 minutes, 13.7% 30 to 45 minutes, 6.1% 45 to 60 minutes, 3.1% 60 minutes or more (2000)

MCCLURE (village). Covers a land area of 0.494 square miles and a water area of 0 square miles. Located at 41.37° N. Lat.; 83.94° W. Long. Elevation is 676 feet.
Population: 828 (1990); 761 (2000); 747 (2007); 743 (2012 projected); Race: 97.2% White, 0.0% Black, 0.1% Asian, 5.4% Hispanic of any race (2007); Density: 1,511.1 persons per square mile (2007); Average household size: 2.60 (2007); Median age: 37.2 (2007); Males per 100 females: 103.0 (2007); Marriage status: 20.8% never married, 66.3% now married, 5.6% widowed, 7.3% divorced (2000); Foreign born: 0.5% (2000); Ancestry (includes multiple ancestries): 35.0% German, 10.6% Other groups, 8.9% Irish, 8.5% English, 7.2% United States or American (2000).

Economy: Single-family building permits issued: 2 (2007); Multi-family building permits issued: 0 (2007); Employment by occupation: 7.1% management, 8.8% professional, 14.8% services, 19.2% sales, 0.8% farming, 13.7% construction, 35.6% production (2000).
Income: Per capita income: $21,345 (2007); Median household income: $50,341 (2007); Average household income: $55,557 (2007); Percent of households with income of $100,000 or more: 8.7% (2007); Poverty rate: 7.9% (2000).
Education: Percent of population age 25 and over with: High school diploma (including GED) or higher: 85.2% (2007); Bachelor's degree or higher: 6.0% (2007); Master's degree or higher: 1.2% (2007).
Housing: Homeownership rate: 85.0% (2007); Median home value: $81,250 (2007); Median rent: $313 per month (2000); Median age of housing: 48 years (2000).
Transportation: Commute to work: 96.4% car, 0.0% public transportation, 0.8% walk, 2.8% work from home (2000); Travel time to work: 14.0% less than 15 minutes, 48.9% 15 to 30 minutes, 24.6% 30 to 45 minutes, 8.3% 45 to 60 minutes, 4.3% 60 minutes or more (2000)

NAPOLEON (city). County seat. Covers a land area of 5.586 square miles and a water area of 0.382 square miles. Located at 41.39° N. Lat.; 84.12° W. Long. Elevation is 679 feet.
History: Napoleon was named by a group of Frenchmen who settled here in the midst of a predominantly German population. Napoleon developed as the seat of Henry County, and as the market center for a rural area.
Population: 9,127 (1990); 9,318 (2000); 9,187 (2007); 9,078 (2012 projected); Race: 92.2% White, 1.3% Black, 0.8% Asian, 7.6% Hispanic of any race (2007); Density: 1,644.6 persons per square mile (2007); Average household size: 2.39 (2007); Median age: 37.6 (2007); Males per 100 females: 91.6 (2007); Marriage status: 20.2% never married, 59.3% now married, 8.9% widowed, 11.6% divorced (2000); Foreign born: 1.5% (2000); Ancestry (includes multiple ancestries): 50.4% German, 12.8% Other groups, 8.7% Irish, 6.3% United States or American, 6.3% English (2000).
Economy: Single-family building permits issued: 11 (2007); Multi-family building permits issued: 0 (2007); Employment by occupation: 8.0% management, 14.3% professional, 14.0% services, 21.2% sales, 0.1% farming, 10.4% construction, 32.1% production (2000).
Income: Per capita income: $20,434 (2007); Median household income: $40,094 (2007); Average household income: $48,180 (2007); Percent of households with income of $100,000 or more: 7.1% (2007); Poverty rate: 10.1% (2000).
Education: Percent of population age 25 and over with: High school diploma (including GED) or higher: 82.9% (2007); Bachelor's degree or higher: 13.5% (2007); Master's degree or higher: 3.4% (2007).

School District(s)

Napoleon Area City (PK-12)
2005-06 Enrollment: 2,390 . . . . (419) 599-7015

Housing: Homeownership rate: 69.5% (2007); Median home value: $105,075 (2007); Median rent: $363 per month (2000); Median age of housing: 36 years (2000).
Safety: Violent crime rate: 15.4 per 10,000 population; Property crime rate: 446.5 per 10,000 population (2007).
Newspapers: Napoleon Northwest Signal (Local news; Circulation 4,300)
Transportation: Commute to work: 94.6% car, 0.5% public transportation, 1.7% walk, 2.4% work from home (2000); Travel time to work: 51.1% less than 15 minutes, 32.7% 15 to 30 minutes, 9.6% 30 to 45 minutes, 2.9% 45 to 60 minutes, 3.7% 60 minutes or more (2000)

Additional Information Contacts

City of Napoleon . . . . (419) 592-4010
http://www.napoleonohio.com
Napoleon-Henry County Chamber of Commerce . . . . (419) 592-1786
http://www.ohiohenrycounty.com

NEW BAVARIA (village). Covers a land area of 0.062 square miles and a water area of 0 square miles. Located at 41.20° N. Lat.; 84.16° W. Long. Elevation is 735 feet.
Population: 92 (1990); 78 (2000); 76 (2007); 73 (2012 projected); Race: 97.4% White, 0.0% Black, 2.6% Asian, 0.0% Hispanic of any race (2007); Density: 1,231.1 persons per square mile (2007); Average household size: 2.24 (2007); Median age: 40.0 (2007); Males per 100 females: 111.1 (2007); Marriage status: 25.4% never married, 71.2% now married, 0.0% widowed, 3.4% divorced (2000); Foreign born: 0.0% (2000); Ancestry (includes multiple ancestries): 40.8% German, 11.8% United States or American, 11.8% Swedish, 3.9% Italian, 2.6% Other groups (2000).
Economy: Employment by occupation: 8.1% management, 10.8% professional, 5.4% services, 8.1% sales, 8.1% farming, 16.2% construction, 43.2% production (2000).
Income: Per capita income: $23,289 (2007); Median household income: $42,000 (2007); Average household income: $52,059 (2007); Percent of households with income of $100,000 or more: 5.9% (2007); Poverty rate: 6.6% (2000).
Education: Percent of population age 25 and over with: High school diploma (including GED) or higher: 72.5% (2007); Bachelor's degree or higher: 3.9% (2007); Master's degree or higher: 3.9% (2007).
Housing: Homeownership rate: 85.3% (2007); Median home value: $68,750 (2007); Median rent: <$100 per month (2000); Median age of housing: 56 years (2000).
Transportation: Commute to work: 100.0% car, 0.0% public transportation, 0.0% walk, 0.0% work from home (2000); Travel time to work: 21.6% less than 15 minutes, 56.8% 15 to 30 minutes, 18.9% 30 to 45 minutes, 0.0% 45 to 60 minutes, 2.7% 60 minutes or more (2000)

Highland County

Located in southwestern Ohio; drained by the East Fork of Little Miami River, and by several creeks. Covers a land area of 553.28 square miles, a water area of 4.56 square miles, and is located in the Eastern Time Zone. The county was founded in 1805. County seat is Hillsboro.

Weather Station: Hillsboro Elevation: 1,099 feet

	Jan	Feb	Mar	Apr	May	Jun	Jul	Aug	Sep	Oct	Nov	Dec
High	36	40	51	63	72	79	83	82	76	65	52	41
Low	20	23	32	41	51	60	64	62	56	44	35	26
Precip	2.9	2.7	3.8	4.1	4.7	4.2	4.0	4.3	3.4	2.9	3.2	3.1
Snow	7.3	5.0	3.8	0.6	tr	0.0	0.0	0.0	0.0	0.2	0.8	2.8

High and Low temperatures in degrees Fahrenheit; Precipitation and Snow in inches

Population: 35,728 (1990); 40,875 (2000); 43,294 (2007); 44,776 (2012 projected); Race: 96.7% White, 1.5% Black, 0.5% Asian, 0.7% Hispanic of any race (2007); Density: 78.2 persons per square mile (2007); Average household size: 2.59 (2007); Median age: 36.7 (2007); Males per 100 females: 95.2 (2007).
Religion: Five largest groups: 8.4% Christian Churches and Churches of Christ, 7.8% The United Methodist Church, 2.8% American Baptist Churches in the USA, 2.7% Catholic Church, 1.6% Church of God (Cleveland, Tennessee) (2000).
Economy: Unemployment rate: 7.0% (6/2008); Total civilian labor force: 21,317 (6/2008); Leading industries: 30.1% manufacturing; 17.3% retail trade; 16.8% health care and social assistance (2005); Farms: 1,381 totaling 273,263 acres (2002); Companies that employ 500 or more persons: 1 (2006); Companies that employ 100 to 499 persons: 18 (2006); Companies that employ less than 100 persons: 730 (2006); Black-owned businesses: n/a (2002); Hispanic-owned businesses: n/a (2002); Asian-owned businesses: n/a (2002); Women-owned businesses: 950 (2002); Retail sales per capita: $12,433 (2008). Single-family building permits issued: 71 (2007); Multi-family building permits issued: 36 (2007).
Income: Per capita income: $19,879 (2007); Median household income: $41,545 (2007); Average household income: $51,219 (2007); Percent of households with income of $100,000 or more: 9.3% (2007); Poverty rate: 12.3% (2005); Bankruptcy rate: 4.22% (2007).
Education: Percent of population age 25 and over with: High school diploma (including GED) or higher: 76.2% (2007); Bachelor's degree or higher: 9.6% (2007); Master's degree or higher: 3.9% (2007).
Housing: Homeownership rate: 75.6% (2007); Median home value: $113,490 (2007); Median rent: $334 per month (2000); Median age of housing: 30 years (2000).
Health: Birth rate: 145.8 per 10,000 population (2007); Death rate: 100.3 per 10,000 population (2007); Age-adjusted cancer mortality rate: 189.6 deaths per 100,000 population (2005); Number of physicians: 8.5 per 10,000 population (2005); Hospital beds: 22.2 per 10,000 population (2004); Hospital admissions: 821.5 per 10,000 population (2004).
Elections: 2004 Presidential election results: 66.1% Bush, 33.5% Kerry, 0.0% Nader, 0.2% Badnarik
National and State Parks: Fallsville State Wildlife Area; Fort Hill State Memorial; Oldaker State Wildlife Area; Rocky Fork State Park

Additional Information Contacts

Highland County Government . . . . (937) 393-1911

Highland County Chamber of Commerce . . . . (937) 393-1111
http://www.highlandcountychamber.com

Highland County Communities

GREENFIELD (city). Covers a land area of 1.934 square miles and a water area of 0 square miles. Located at 39.35° N. Lat.; 83.38° W. Long. Elevation is 912 feet.
History: Platted 1798, incorporated 1841.
Population: 5,218 (1990); 4,906 (2000); 5,027 (2007); 5,081 (2012 projected); Race: 95.8% White, 2.2% Black, 0.1% Asian, 1.0% Hispanic of any race (2007); Density: 2,598.8 persons per square mile (2007); Average household size: 2.48 (2007); Median age: 36.1 (2007); Males per 100 females: 87.3 (2007); Marriage status: 22.0% never married, 56.2% now married, 9.4% widowed, 12.4% divorced (2000); Foreign born: 0.3% (2000); Ancestry (includes multiple ancestries): 23.0% United States or American, 16.3% German, 10.2% Irish, 9.9% Other groups, 6.1% English (2000).
Economy: Single-family building permits issued: 2 (2007); Multi-family building permits issued: 2 (2007); Employment by occupation: 5.3% management, 11.4% professional, 14.7% services, 20.8% sales, 0.3% farming, 11.3% construction, 36.2% production (2000).
Income: Per capita income: $16,910 (2007); Median household income: $35,183 (2007); Average household income: $41,161 (2007); Percent of households with income of $100,000 or more: 5.2% (2007); Poverty rate: 15.1% (2000).
Education: Percent of population age 25 and over with: High school diploma (including GED) or higher: 70.8% (2007); Bachelor's degree or higher: 8.2% (2007); Master's degree or higher: 2.4% (2007).

School District(s)

Greenfield Exempted Village (PK-12)
2005-06 Enrollment: 2,301 . . . . (937) 981-2152
Housing: Homeownership rate: 60.1% (2007); Median home value: $86,988 (2007); Median rent: $299 per month (2000); Median age of housing: 53 years (2000).
Hospitals: Greenfield Area Medical Center (46 beds)
Safety: Violent crime rate: 15.5 per 10,000 population; Property crime rate: 585.8 per 10,000 population (2007).
Transportation: Commute to work: 88.8% car, 0.6% public transportation, 5.6% walk, 4.7% work from home (2000); Travel time to work: 42.6% less than 15 minutes, 22.9% 15 to 30 minutes, 17.6% 30 to 45 minutes, 10.0% 45 to 60 minutes, 6.8% 60 minutes or more (2000)

HIGHLAND (village). Covers a land area of 0.165 square miles and a water area of 0 square miles. Located at 39.34° N. Lat.; 83.59° W. Long. Elevation is 1,063 feet.
Population: 234 (1990); 283 (2000); 267 (2007); 265 (2012 projected); Race: 96.6% White, 0.4% Black, 0.0% Asian, 0.7% Hispanic of any race (2007); Density: 1,616.6 persons per square mile (2007); Average household size: 2.59 (2007); Median age: 34.9 (2007); Males per 100 females: 105.4 (2007); Marriage status: 28.3% never married, 54.3% now married, 7.6% widowed, 9.9% divorced (2000); Foreign born: 1.0% (2000); Ancestry (includes multiple ancestries): 37.6% United States or American, 10.1% Other groups, 9.4% Irish, 9.1% English, 5.7% German (2000).
Economy: Employment by occupation: 6.9% management, 5.6% professional, 7.6% services, 20.1% sales, 0.0% farming, 18.1% construction, 41.7% production (2000).
Income: Per capita income: $21,236 (2007); Median household income: $56,071 (2007); Average household income: $55,049 (2007); Percent of households with income of $100,000 or more: 6.8% (2007); Poverty rate: 10.1% (2000).
Education: Percent of population age 25 and over with: High school diploma (including GED) or higher: 79.8% (2007); Bachelor's degree or higher: 5.5% (2007); Master's degree or higher: 3.8% (2007).
Housing: Homeownership rate: 78.6% (2007); Median home value: $86,500 (2007); Median rent: $314 per month (2000); Median age of housing: 56 years (2000).
Transportation: Commute to work: 99.3% car, 0.0% public transportation, 0.0% walk, 0.7% work from home (2000); Travel time to work: 23.7% less than 15 minutes, 51.8% 15 to 30 minutes, 11.5% 30 to 45 minutes, 4.3% 45 to 60 minutes, 8.6% 60 minutes or more (2000)

HILLSBORO (city). County seat. Covers a land area of 5.189 square miles and a water area of 0 square miles. Located at 39.20° N. Lat.; 83.61° W. Long. Elevation is 1,122 feet.
History: Hillsboro was platted in 1807, and developed around brickyards, tanneries, and grist and woolen mills. In 1873, The Women's Temperance Crusade was organized and managed to close all of the saloons in the town when the women marched into each in turn and held a prayer meeting.
Population: 6,441 (1990); 6,368 (2000); 6,639 (2007); 6,796 (2012 projected); Race: 90.2% White, 6.4% Black, 1.7% Asian, 1.1% Hispanic of any race (2007); Density: 1,279.3 persons per square mile (2007); Average household size: 2.33 (2007); Median age: 37.6 (2007); Males per 100 females: 84.6 (2007); Marriage status: 21.0% never married, 53.3% now married, 11.9% widowed, 13.8% divorced (2000); Foreign born: 1.9% (2000); Ancestry (includes multiple ancestries): 17.7% German, 17.5% United States or American, 16.8% Other groups, 11.1% English, 9.9% Irish (2000).
Economy: Single-family building permits issued: 14 (2007); Multi-family building permits issued: 11 (2007); Employment by occupation: 8.4% management, 17.2% professional, 14.0% services, 20.1% sales, 0.0% farming, 7.5% construction, 32.8% production (2000).
Income: Per capita income: $17,658 (2007); Median household income: $29,540 (2007); Average household income: $40,424 (2007); Percent of households with income of $100,000 or more: 6.2% (2007); Poverty rate: 18.1% (2000).
Education: Percent of population age 25 and over with: High school diploma (including GED) or higher: 73.5% (2007); Bachelor's degree or higher: 11.0% (2007); Master's degree or higher: 6.3% (2007).

School District(s)

Bright Local (PK-12)
2005-06 Enrollment: 846 . . . . (937) 442-3114
Great Oaks Inst of Technology (PK-12)
2005-06 Enrollment: n/a . . . . (513) 771-8840
Hillsboro City (PK-12)
2005-06 Enrollment: 2,795 . . . . (937) 393-3475

Two-year College(s)

Southern State Community College (Public)
Fall 2007 Enrollment: 2,436. . . . . (937) 393-3431
2007-08 Tuition: In-state $3,390; Out-of-state $6,528
Housing: Homeownership rate: 56.2% (2007); Median home value: $108,270 (2007); Median rent: $324 per month (2000); Median age of housing: 35 years (2000).
Hospitals: Highland District Hospital (65 beds)
Safety: Violent crime rate: 4.5 per 10,000 population; Property crime rate: 420.1 per 10,000 population (2007).
Newspapers: Highland County Shopper (Community news; Circulation 2,000); SkyWrighter (Local news); Times-Gazette (Local news; Circulation 7,000)
Transportation: Commute to work: 93.0% car, 0.2% public transportation, 2.5% walk, 3.7% work from home (2000); Travel time to work: 47.7% less than 15 minutes, 22.9% 15 to 30 minutes, 18.9% 30 to 45 minutes, 5.5% 45 to 60 minutes, 5.1% 60 minutes or more (2000)
Additional Information Contacts
Highland County Chamber of Commerce . . . . (937) 393-1111
http://www.highlandcountychamber.com

LEESBURG (village). Covers a land area of 0.803 square miles and a water area of 0 square miles. Located at 39.34° N. Lat.; 83.55° W. Long. Elevation is 1,014 feet.
History: Shortly after Leesburg was founded in 1802, Quakers from Pennsylvania settled here. Prior to 1900, Leesburg hosted the annual meeting of the Society of Friends, attended by members from all parts of the United States.
Population: 1,194 (1990); 1,253 (2000); 1,216 (2007); 1,199 (2012 projected); Race: 98.8% White, 0.4% Black, 0.1% Asian, 0.1% Hispanic of any race (2007); Density: 1,514.0 persons per square mile (2007); Average household size: 2.46 (2007); Median age: 33.1 (2007); Males per 100 females: 100.0 (2007); Marriage status: 24.8% never married, 57.7% now married, 5.6% widowed, 11.8% divorced (2000); Foreign born: 0.5% (2000); Ancestry (includes multiple ancestries): 28.2% United States or American, 11.1% German, 9.2% Irish, 5.5% English, 4.6% Other groups (2000).
Economy: Employment by occupation: 6.5% management, 9.7% professional, 13.1% services, 17.9% sales, 0.0% farming, 15.3% construction, 37.5% production (2000).
Income: Per capita income: $21,686 (2007); Median household income: $44,500 (2007); Average household income: $53,381 (2007); Percent of households with income of $100,000 or more: 10.5% (2007); Poverty rate: 6.3% (2000).

Education: Percent of population age 25 and over with: High school diploma (including GED) or higher: 83.8% (2007); Bachelor's degree or higher: 8.8% (2007); Master's degree or higher: 3.1% (2007).

School District(s)

Fairfield Local (PK-12)
2005-06 Enrollment: 915 . . . . (937) 780-2221

Housing: Homeownership rate: 65.4% (2007); Median home value: $99,872 (2007); Median rent: $350 per month (2000); Median age of housing: 36 years (2000).

Safety: Violent crime rate: 7.4 per 10,000 population; Property crime rate: 356.9 per 10,000 population (2007).

Transportation: Commute to work: 93.0% car, 1.6% public transportation, 3.5% walk, 1.9% work from home (2000); Travel time to work: 32.6% less than 15 minutes, 35.9% 15 to 30 minutes, 16.6% 30 to 45 minutes, 5.1% 45 to 60 minutes, 9.8% 60 minutes or more (2000)

LYNCHBURG (village). Covers a land area of 0.878 square miles and a water area of 0 square miles. Located at 39.24° N. Lat.; 83.79° W. Long. Elevation is 1,007 feet.

Population: 1,322 (1990); 1,350 (2000); 1,236 (2007); 1,239 (2012 projected); Race: 98.3% White, 0.4% Black, 0.3% Asian, 0.0% Hispanic of any race (2007); Density: 1,408.5 persons per square mile (2007); Average household size: 2.56 (2007); Median age: 33.8 (2007); Males per 100 females: 91.3 (2007); Marriage status: 21.3% never married, 59.3% now married, 8.2% widowed, 11.2% divorced (2000); Foreign born: 0.6% (2000); Ancestry (includes multiple ancestries): 27.9% United States or American, 18.0% German, 17.2% Irish, 11.2% English, 7.5% Other groups (2000).

Economy: Employment by occupation: 6.8% management, 11.1% professional, 11.1% services, 26.7% sales, 0.0% farming, 12.2% construction, 32.0% production (2000).

Income: Per capita income: $20,144 (2007); Median household income: $42,581 (2007); Average household income: $51,655 (2007); Percent of households with income of $100,000 or more: 8.3% (2007); Poverty rate: 9.1% (2000).

Taxes: Total city taxes per capita: $85 (2006); City property taxes per capita: $85 (2006).

Education: Percent of population age 25 and over with: High school diploma (including GED) or higher: 78.3% (2007); Bachelor's degree or higher: 9.4% (2007); Master's degree or higher: 3.9% (2007).

School District(s)

Lynchburg-Clay Local (PK-12)
2005-06 Enrollment: 1,395 . . . . (937) 364-2338

Housing: Homeownership rate: 69.3% (2007); Median home value: $110,955 (2007); Median rent: $371 per month (2000); Median age of housing: 45 years (2000).

Safety: Violent crime rate: 7.0 per 10,000 population; Property crime rate: 182.2 per 10,000 population (2007).

Transportation: Commute to work: 95.6% car, 0.0% public transportation, 1.6% walk, 2.3% work from home (2000); Travel time to work: 20.1% less than 15 minutes, 39.2% 15 to 30 minutes, 17.8% 30 to 45 minutes, 9.6% 45 to 60 minutes, 13.3% 60 minutes or more (2000)

MOWRYSTOWN (village). Covers a land area of 0.483 square miles and a water area of 0.007 square miles. Located at 39.03° N. Lat.; 83.75° W. Long. Elevation is 997 feet.

Population: 460 (1990); 373 (2000); 360 (2007); 357 (2012 projected); Race: 98.9% White, 0.0% Black, 0.0% Asian, 0.0% Hispanic of any race (2007); Density: 745.9 persons per square mile (2007); Average household size: 2.59 (2007); Median age: 33.6 (2007); Males per 100 females: 105.7 (2007); Marriage status: 25.8% never married, 56.7% now married, 7.6% widowed, 9.8% divorced (2000); Foreign born: 0.0% (2000); Ancestry (includes multiple ancestries): 34.6% United States or American, 22.2% Other groups, 11.0% Irish, 10.1% German, 9.5% English (2000).

Economy: Employment by occupation: 2.5% management, 3.1% professional, 9.4% services, 19.4% sales, 0.0% farming, 21.9% construction, 43.8% production (2000).

Income: Per capita income: $18,458 (2007); Median household income: $47,031 (2007); Average household income: $47,806 (2007); Percent of households with income of $100,000 or more: 4.3% (2007); Poverty rate: 10.1% (2000).

Education: Percent of population age 25 and over with: High school diploma (including GED) or higher: 63.2% (2007); Bachelor's degree or higher: 0.9% (2007); Master's degree or higher: 0.0% (2007).

School District(s)

Bright Local (PK-12)
2005-06 Enrollment: 846 . . . . (937) 442-3114

Housing: Homeownership rate: 79.9% (2007); Median home value: $83,571 (2007); Median rent: $338 per month (2000); Median age of housing: 60+ years (2000).

Transportation: Commute to work: 93.1% car, 0.0% public transportation, 2.5% walk, 1.3% work from home (2000); Travel time to work: 10.8% less than 15 minutes, 23.4% 15 to 30 minutes, 26.6% 30 to 45 minutes, 16.5% 45 to 60 minutes, 22.8% 60 minutes or more (2000)

SINKING SPRING (village). Covers a land area of 0.468 square miles and a water area of 0 square miles. Located at 39.07° N. Lat.; 83.38° W. Long. Elevation is 866 feet.

History: Nearby are Fort Hill and Serpent Mound, prehistoric earthworks.

Population: 189 (1990); 158 (2000); 139 (2007); 141 (2012 projected); Race: 97.1% White, 0.0% Black, 0.0% Asian, 0.0% Hispanic of any race (2007); Density: 297.0 persons per square mile (2007); Average household size: 2.73 (2007); Median age: 37.1 (2007); Males per 100 females: 93.1 (2007); Marriage status: 34.3% never married, 54.7% now married, 8.0% widowed, 2.9% divorced (2000); Foreign born: 0.0% (2000); Ancestry (includes multiple ancestries): 38.1% United States or American, 15.5% German, 15.5% Irish, 10.3% Other groups, 5.2% English (2000).

Economy: Employment by occupation: 1.5% management, 9.1% professional, 9.1% services, 25.8% sales, 1.5% farming, 12.1% construction, 40.9% production (2000).

Income: Per capita income: $17,752 (2007); Median household income: $45,500 (2007); Average household income: $48,382 (2007); Percent of households with income of $100,000 or more: 5.9% (2007); Poverty rate: 7.7% (2000).

Education: Percent of population age 25 and over with: High school diploma (including GED) or higher: 63.9% (2007); Bachelor's degree or higher: 4.1% (2007); Master's degree or higher: 0.0% (2007).

Housing: Homeownership rate: 76.5% (2007); Median home value: $97,500 (2007); Median rent: $188 per month (2000); Median age of housing: 48 years (2000).

Transportation: Commute to work: 89.1% car, 0.0% public transportation, 0.0% walk, 4.7% work from home (2000); Travel time to work: 3.3% less than 15 minutes, 24.6% 15 to 30 minutes, 27.9% 30 to 45 minutes, 9.8% 45 to 60 minutes, 34.4% 60 minutes or more (2000)

Hocking County

Located in south central Ohio; crossed by the Hocking River. Covers a land area of 422.75 square miles, a water area of 0.85 square miles, and is located in the Eastern Time Zone. The county was founded in 1818. County seat is Logan.

Population: 25,533 (1990); 28,241 (2000); 29,219 (2007); 29,797 (2012 projected); Race: 97.3% White, 1.1% Black, 0.2% Asian, 0.6% Hispanic of any race (2007); Density: 69.1 persons per square mile (2007); Average household size: 2.55 (2007); Median age: 39.0 (2007); Males per 100 females: 99.7 (2007).

Religion: Five largest groups: 8.6% The United Methodist Church, 3.4% Catholic Church, 2.8% Southern Baptist Convention, 2.1% Evangelical Lutheran Church in America, 1.4% Christian Churches and Churches of Christ (2000).

Economy: Unemployment rate: 7.2% (6/2008); Total civilian labor force: 14,301 (6/2008); Leading industries: 18.5% retail trade; 17.9% health care and social assistance; 17.4% manufacturing (2005); Farms: 434 totaling 49,866 acres (2002); Companies that employ 500 or more persons: 0 (2006); Companies that employ 100 to 499 persons: 8 (2006); Companies that employ less than 100 persons: 522 (2006); Black-owned businesses: n/a (2002); Hispanic-owned businesses: n/a (2002); Asian-owned businesses: n/a (2002); Women-owned businesses: 751 (2002); Retail sales per capita: $10,808 (2008). Single-family building permits issued: 8 (2007); Multi-family building permits issued: 0 (2007).

Income: Per capita income: $19,089 (2007); Median household income: $39,458 (2007); Average household income: $48,128 (2007); Percent of households with income of $100,000 or more: 7.4% (2007); Poverty rate: 15.5% (2005); Bankruptcy rate: 4.45% (2007).

Taxes: Total county taxes per capita: $259 (2006); County property taxes per capita: $165 (2006).

Education: Percent of population age 25 and over with: High school diploma (including GED) or higher: 77.7% (2007); Bachelor's degree or higher: 9.7% (2007); Master's degree or higher: 3.6% (2007).

Housing: Homeownership rate: 76.1% (2007); Median home value: $111,274 (2007); Median rent: $295 per month (2000); Median age of housing: 30 years (2000).
Health: Birth rate: 125.3 per 10,000 population (2007); Death rate: 101.2 per 10,000 population (2007); Age-adjusted cancer mortality rate: 284.3 deaths per 100,000 population (2005); Number of physicians: 8.7 per 10,000 population (2005); Hospital beds: 32.0 per 10,000 population (2004); Hospital admissions: 615.2 per 10,000 population (2004).
Elections: 2004 Presidential election results: 52.5% Bush, 46.8% Kerry, 0.0% Nader, 0.3% Badnarik
National and State Parks: Hocking Hills State Park; Hocking State Forest; Lake Logan State Park; Sunday Creek State Wildlife Area; Wayne National Forest - Athens Ranger District
Additional Information Contacts
Hocking County Government. . . . . (740) 385-5195
http://www.co.hocking.oh.us
Logan-Hocking Chamber of Commerce . . . . (740) 385-6836
http://www.logan-hockingchamber.com

Hocking County Communities

LAURELVILLE (village). Covers a land area of 0.205 square miles and a water area of 0 square miles. Located at 39.47° N. Lat.; 82.73° W. Long. Elevation is 735 feet.
Population: 605 (1990); 533 (2000); 462 (2007); 460 (2012 projected); Race: 98.7% White, 0.0% Black, 0.0% Asian, 1.1% Hispanic of any race (2007); Density: 2,258.0 persons per square mile (2007); Average household size: 2.01 (2007); Median age: 41.5 (2007); Males per 100 females: 91.7 (2007); Marriage status: 21.7% never married, 47.7% now married, 12.6% widowed, 18.0% divorced (2000); Foreign born: 0.0% (2000); Ancestry (includes multiple ancestries): 19.4% German, 12.7% United States or American, 11.0% Irish, 7.2% Other groups, 5.7% English (2000).
Economy: Employment by occupation: 9.8% management, 10.7% professional, 27.7% services, 16.5% sales, 0.4% farming, 13.4% construction, 21.4% production (2000).
Income: Per capita income: $18,469 (2007); Median household income: $25,417 (2007); Average household income: $37,098 (2007); Percent of households with income of $100,000 or more: 3.5% (2007); Poverty rate: 13.5% (2000).
Education: Percent of population age 25 and over with: High school diploma (including GED) or higher: 64.7% (2007); Bachelor's degree or higher: 3.9% (2007); Master's degree or higher: 0.3% (2007).
School District(s)
Logan Elm Local (PK-12)
2005-06 Enrollment: 2,304 . . . . (740) 474-7501
Housing: Homeownership rate: 51.7% (2007); Median home value: $101,645 (2007); Median rent: $294 per month (2000); Median age of housing: 54 years (2000).
Transportation: Commute to work: 88.7% car, 0.9% public transportation, 9.0% walk, 0.9% work from home (2000); Travel time to work: 23.6% less than 15 minutes, 27.3% 15 to 30 minutes, 17.7% 30 to 45 minutes, 9.1% 45 to 60 minutes, 22.3% 60 minutes or more (2000)

LOGAN (city). County seat. Covers a land area of 3.082 square miles and a water area of 0 square miles. Located at 39.53° N. Lat.; 82.40° W. Long. Elevation is 741 feet.
History: Logan was founded in 1816 by Governor Thomas Worthington, who purchased a tract near the Hocking Falls and set up mills. Logan flourished with the opening of the Hocking Canal in 1840, and the completion of the Hocking Valley Railroad in 1869.
Population: 6,799 (1990); 6,704 (2000); 6,860 (2007); 6,995 (2012 projected); Race: 97.9% White, 0.5% Black, 0.2% Asian, 0.7% Hispanic of any race (2007); Density: 2,225.8 persons per square mile (2007); Average household size: 2.36 (2007); Median age: 38.7 (2007); Males per 100 females: 86.6 (2007); Marriage status: 20.9% never married, 54.6% now married, 11.7% widowed, 12.8% divorced (2000); Foreign born: 0.6% (2000); Ancestry (includes multiple ancestries): 24.4% German, 14.7% United States or American, 14.5% Irish, 10.7% English, 6.4% Other groups (2000).
Economy: Single-family building permits issued: 8 (2007); Multi-family building permits issued: 0 (2007); Employment by occupation: 8.4% management, 17.4% professional, 15.0% services, 24.5% sales, 0.2% farming, 12.3% construction, 22.2% production (2000).
Income: Per capita income: $17,661 (2007); Median household income: $32,542 (2007); Average household income: $40,924 (2007); Percent of households with income of $100,000 or more: 5.5% (2007); Poverty rate: 17.7% (2000).
Education: Percent of population age 25 and over with: High school diploma (including GED) or higher: 79.0% (2007); Bachelor's degree or higher: 10.1% (2007); Master's degree or higher: 4.3% (2007).
School District(s)
Logan-Hocking Local (PK-12)
2005-06 Enrollment: 4,157 . . . . (740) 385-8517
Housing: Homeownership rate: 61.3% (2007); Median home value: $104,697 (2007); Median rent: $297 per month (2000); Median age of housing: 48 years (2000).
Hospitals: Hocking Valley Community Hospital (93 beds)
Safety: Violent crime rate: 13.5 per 10,000 population; Property crime rate: 588.5 per 10,000 population (2007).
Newspapers: Logan Daily News (Local news; Circulation 4,224)
Transportation: Commute to work: 94.0% car, 0.5% public transportation, 3.9% walk, 1.4% work from home (2000); Travel time to work: 50.7% less than 15 minutes, 16.1% 15 to 30 minutes, 11.5% 30 to 45 minutes, 4.1% 45 to 60 minutes, 17.6% 60 minutes or more (2000)
Additional Information Contacts
Logan-Hocking Chamber of Commerce . . . . (740) 385-6836
http://www.logan-hockingchamber.com

MURRAY CITY (village). Covers a land area of 0.299 square miles and a water area of 0 square miles. Located at 39.51° N. Lat.; 82.16° W. Long. Elevation is 709 feet.
Population: 513 (1990); 452 (2000); 435 (2007); 432 (2012 projected); Race: 97.9% White, 0.0% Black, 0.0% Asian, 0.0% Hispanic of any race (2007); Density: 1,452.6 persons per square mile (2007); Average household size: 2.33 (2007); Median age: 35.3 (2007); Males per 100 females: 96.8 (2007); Marriage status: 25.1% never married, 56.8% now married, 8.5% widowed, 9.6% divorced (2000); Foreign born: 0.0% (2000); Ancestry (includes multiple ancestries): 14.6% German, 12.6% Irish, 12.4% English, 9.0% Other groups, 7.0% United States or American (2000).
Economy: Employment by occupation: 3.0% management, 8.4% professional, 22.2% services, 24.0% sales, 0.0% farming, 18.6% construction, 24.0% production (2000).
Income: Per capita income: $14,287 (2007); Median household income: $30,179 (2007); Average household income: $33,235 (2007); Percent of households with income of $100,000 or more: 1.1% (2007); Poverty rate: 19.8% (2000).
Education: Percent of population age 25 and over with: High school diploma (including GED) or higher: 69.1% (2007); Bachelor's degree or higher: 4.3% (2007); Master's degree or higher: 0.7% (2007).
Housing: Homeownership rate: 67.4% (2007); Median home value: $52,857 (2007); Median rent: $258 per month (2000); Median age of housing: 60+ years (2000).
Transportation: Commute to work: 96.4% car, 0.0% public transportation, 2.4% walk, 1.2% work from home (2000); Travel time to work: 13.3% less than 15 minutes, 27.3% 15 to 30 minutes, 21.8% 30 to 45 minutes, 11.5% 45 to 60 minutes, 26.1% 60 minutes or more (2000)

ROCKBRIDGE (unincorporated postal area, zip code 43149). Covers a land area of 56.031 square miles and a water area of 0.011 square miles. Located at 39.54° N. Lat.; 82.57° W. Long. Elevation is 760 feet.
Population: 2,596 (2000); Race: 99.3% White, 0.0% Black, 0.0% Asian, 0.3% Hispanic of any race (2000); Density: 46.3 persons per square mile (2000); Age: 24.7% under 18, 8.5% over 64 (2000); Marriage status: 21.0% never married, 63.6% now married, 4.3% widowed, 11.1% divorced (2000); Foreign born: 0.4% (2000); Ancestry (includes multiple ancestries): 22.2% German, 11.3% Irish, 9.6% United States or American, 9.5% English, 3.2% Other groups (2000).
Economy: Employment by occupation: 7.7% management, 10.5% professional, 14.9% services, 21.2% sales, 0.7% farming, 18.1% construction, 26.9% production (2000).
Income: Per capita income: $18,129 (2000); Median household income: $38,177 (2000); Poverty rate: 8.3% (2000).
Education: Percent of population age 25 and over with: High school diploma (including GED) or higher: 80.9% (2000); Bachelor's degree or higher: 14.4% (2000).
School District(s)
Logan-Hocking Local (PK-12)
2005-06 Enrollment: 4,157 . . . . (740) 385-8517

Housing: Homeownership rate: 81.2% (2000); Median home value: $89,800 (2000); Median rent: $348 per month (2000); Median age of housing: 22 years (2000).
Transportation: Commute to work: 96.4% car, 0.6% public transportation, 0.3% walk, 2.1% work from home (2000); Travel time to work: 9.8% less than 15 minutes, 36.0% 15 to 30 minutes, 22.0% 30 to 45 minutes, 11.4% 45 to 60 minutes, 20.9% 60 minutes or more (2000)

SOUTH BLOOMINGVILLE (unincorporated postal area, zip code 43152). Covers a land area of 55.684 square miles and a water area of 0 square miles. Located at 39.38° N. Lat.; 82.62° W. Long. Elevation is 696 feet.
Population: 1,098 (2000); Race: 99.4% White, 0.6% Black, 0.0% Asian, 0.0% Hispanic of any race (2000); Density: 19.7 persons per square mile (2000); Age: 24.6% under 18, 9.5% over 64 (2000); Marriage status: 21.1% never married, 65.6% now married, 4.5% widowed, 8.8% divorced (2000); Foreign born: 0.0% (2000); Ancestry (includes multiple ancestries): 30.3% United States or American, 16.0% German, 11.0% Irish, 6.1% Other groups, 5.8% English (2000).
Economy: Employment by occupation: 5.0% management, 8.2% professional, 23.5% services, 19.5% sales, 4.0% farming, 13.7% construction, 26.1% production (2000).
Income: Per capita income: $15,049 (2000); Median household income: $36,071 (2000); Poverty rate: 13.2% (2000).
Education: Percent of population age 25 and over with: High school diploma (including GED) or higher: 79.2% (2000); Bachelor's degree or higher: 10.4% (2000).

School District(s)

Logan-Hocking Local (PK-12)
2005-06 Enrollment: 4,157 . . . . (740) 385-8517
Housing: Homeownership rate: 78.6% (2000); Median home value: $102,700 (2000); Median rent: $214 per month (2000); Median age of housing: 26 years (2000).
Transportation: Commute to work: 96.0% car, 0.0% public transportation, 0.0% walk, 4.0% work from home (2000); Travel time to work: 10.2% less than 15 minutes, 10.8% 15 to 30 minutes, 29.4% 30 to 45 minutes, 16.0% 45 to 60 minutes, 33.5% 60 minutes or more (2000)

Holmes County

Located in central Ohio; crossed by Killbuck Creek and Walhonding River. Covers a land area of 422.99 square miles, a water area of 1.03 square miles, and is located in the Eastern Time Zone. The county was founded in 1824. County seat is Millersburg.
Population: 32,849 (1990); 38,943 (2000); 42,179 (2007); 44,191 (2012 projected); Race: 99.0% White, 0.4% Black, 0.0% Asian, 0.8% Hispanic of any race (2007); Density: 99.7 persons per square mile (2007); Average household size: 3.40 (2007); Median age: 29.2 (2007); Males per 100 females: 100.2 (2007).
Religion: Five largest groups: 15.9% Old Order Amish Church, 5.6% Christian Churches and Churches of Christ, 4.6% Mennonite Church USA, 3.9% The United Methodist Church, 3.1% Amish; Other Groups (2000).
Economy: Unemployment rate: 4.9% (6/2008); Total civilian labor force: 20,071 (6/2008); Leading industries: 36.7% manufacturing; 12.5% retail trade; 11.2% construction (2005); Farms: 1,809 totaling 206,603 acres (2002); Companies that employ 500 or more persons: 2 (2006); Companies that employ 100 to 499 persons: 27 (2006); Companies that employ less than 100 persons: 1,035 (2006); Black-owned businesses: n/a (2002); Hispanic-owned businesses: n/a (2002); Asian-owned businesses: n/a (2002); Women-owned businesses: 932 (2002); Retail sales per capita: $10,765 (2008). Single-family building permits issued: 8 (2007); Multi-family building permits issued: 0 (2007).
Income: Per capita income: $16,801 (2007); Median household income: $43,467 (2007); Average household income: $56,017 (2007); Percent of households with income of $100,000 or more: 10.0% (2007); Poverty rate: 11.5% (2005); Bankruptcy rate: 1.55% (2007).
Taxes: Total county taxes per capita: $267 (2006); County property taxes per capita: $146 (2006).
Education: Percent of population age 25 and over with: High school diploma (including GED) or higher: 50.2% (2007); Bachelor's degree or higher: 7.9% (2007); Master's degree or higher: 2.4% (2007).
Housing: Homeownership rate: 77.1% (2007); Median home value: $148,443 (2007); Median rent: $331 per month (2000); Median age of housing: 27 years (2000).
Health: Birth rate: 200.9 per 10,000 population (2007); Death rate: 69.1 per 10,000 population (2007); Age-adjusted cancer mortality rate: 190.7 deaths per 100,000 population (2005); Number of physicians: 7.8 per 10,000 population (2005); Hospital beds: 9.7 per 10,000 population (2004); Hospital admissions: 518.1 per 10,000 population (2004).
Elections: 2004 Presidential election results: 75.5% Bush, 24.0% Kerry, 0.0% Nader, 0.2% Badnarik

Additional Information Contacts

Holmes County Government . . . . (330) 674-0286
http://www.holmescounty.com/gov
Holmes County Chamber of Commerce . . . . (330) 674-3975
http://www.holmescountychamber.com
Village of Millersburg . . . . (330) 674-1886
http://www.millersburgohio.com

Holmes County Communities

BIG PRAIRIE (unincorporated postal area, zip code 44611). Covers a land area of 27.924 square miles and a water area of 0.010 square miles. Located at 40.63° N. Lat.; 82.08° W. Long. Elevation is 947 feet.
Population: 2,028 (2000); Race: 99.7% White, 0.0% Black, 0.0% Asian, 0.9% Hispanic of any race (2000); Density: 72.6 persons per square mile (2000); Age: 33.4% under 18, 6.5% over 64 (2000); Marriage status: 24.2% never married, 66.4% now married, 3.1% widowed, 6.2% divorced (2000); Foreign born: 0.1% (2000); Ancestry (includes multiple ancestries): 26.0% German, 18.9% United States or American, 9.1% Irish, 8.0% Other groups, 7.7% English (2000).
Economy: Employment by occupation: 7.0% management, 12.7% professional, 10.0% services, 17.9% sales, 1.9% farming, 8.0% construction, 42.4% production (2000).
Income: Per capita income: $13,305 (2000); Median household income: $35,814 (2000); Poverty rate: 10.3% (2000).
Education: Percent of population age 25 and over with: High school diploma (including GED) or higher: 77.9% (2000); Bachelor's degree or higher: 6.8% (2000).
Housing: Homeownership rate: 84.5% (2000); Median home value: $92,100 (2000); Median rent: $407 per month (2000); Median age of housing: 27 years (2000).
Transportation: Commute to work: 84.0% car, 0.0% public transportation, 3.4% walk, 11.6% work from home (2000); Travel time to work: 15.7% less than 15 minutes, 44.6% 15 to 30 minutes, 29.7% 30 to 45 minutes, 1.6% 45 to 60 minutes, 8.4% 60 minutes or more (2000)

GLENMONT (village). Covers a land area of 0.271 square miles and a water area of 0 square miles. Located at 40.51° N. Lat.; 82.09° W. Long. Elevation is 879 feet.
History: Glenmont grew up around the sandstone quarries that furnished the material for some of New York's brownstone houses.
Population: 246 (1990); 283 (2000); 296 (2007); 304 (2012 projected); Race: 100.0% White, 0.0% Black, 0.0% Asian, 1.0% Hispanic of any race (2007); Density: 1,091.9 persons per square mile (2007); Average household size: 2.41 (2007); Median age: 38.6 (2007); Males per 100 females: 102.7 (2007); Marriage status: 11.7% never married, 65.0% now married, 11.2% widowed, 12.1% divorced (2000); Foreign born: 0.7% (2000); Ancestry (includes multiple ancestries): 23.0% German, 21.3% Irish, 12.8% English, 12.1% United States or American, 7.1% Other groups (2000).
Economy: Employment by occupation: 3.6% management, 6.5% professional, 15.8% services, 15.8% sales, 0.0% farming, 19.4% construction, 38.8% production (2000).
Income: Per capita income: $19,603 (2007); Median household income: $43,500 (2007); Average household income: $47,175 (2007); Percent of households with income of $100,000 or more: 6.5% (2007); Poverty rate: 11.4% (2000).
Education: Percent of population age 25 and over with: High school diploma (including GED) or higher: 76.3% (2007); Bachelor's degree or higher: 7.6% (2007); Master's degree or higher: 2.5% (2007).
Housing: Homeownership rate: 74.0% (2007); Median home value: $71,923 (2007); Median rent: $300 per month (2000); Median age of housing: 49 years (2000).
Transportation: Commute to work: 94.9% car, 0.0% public transportation, 1.5% walk, 1.5% work from home (2000); Travel time to work: 23.7% less than 15 minutes, 25.9% 15 to 30 minutes, 34.1% 30 to 45 minutes, 11.1% 45 to 60 minutes, 5.2% 60 minutes or more (2000)

HOLMESVILLE (village). Covers a land area of 0.239 square miles and a water area of 0 square miles. Located at 40.62° N. Lat.; 81.92° W. Long. Elevation is 860 feet.
Population: 419 (1990); 386 (2000); 427 (2007); 455 (2012 projected); Race: 97.7% White, 0.0% Black, 0.0% Asian, 3.0% Hispanic of any race (2007); Density: 1,789.2 persons per square mile (2007); Average household size: 2.51 (2007); Median age: 36.5 (2007); Males per 100 females: 109.3 (2007); Marriage status: 29.7% never married, 53.4% now married, 4.8% widowed, 12.1% divorced (2000); Foreign born: 0.0% (2000); Ancestry (includes multiple ancestries): 20.6% German, 16.2% United States or American, 7.9% Other groups, 6.1% Irish, 4.4% English (2000).
Economy: Employment by occupation: 5.4% management, 5.9% professional, 12.3% services, 19.1% sales, 1.0% farming, 10.3% construction, 46.1% production (2000).
Income: Per capita income: $19,619 (2007); Median household income: $46,471 (2007); Average household income: $49,279 (2007); Percent of households with income of $100,000 or more: 2.9% (2007); Poverty rate: 6.4% (2000).
Education: Percent of population age 25 and over with: High school diploma (including GED) or higher: 71.8% (2007); Bachelor's degree or higher: 3.1% (2007); Master's degree or higher: 0.0% (2007).

School District(s)

Southeast Local (PK-12)
2005-06 Enrollment: 1,733 . . . . (330) 698-3001
Housing: Homeownership rate: 74.1% (2007); Median home value: $93,529 (2007); Median rent: $346 per month (2000); Median age of housing: 60+ years (2000).
Transportation: Commute to work: 96.4% car, 0.0% public transportation, 0.0% walk, 1.0% work from home (2000); Travel time to work: 44.3% less than 15 minutes, 30.9% 15 to 30 minutes, 13.4% 30 to 45 minutes, 7.2% 45 to 60 minutes, 4.1% 60 minutes or more (2000)

KILLBUCK (village). Covers a land area of 0.283 square miles and a water area of 0 square miles. Located at 40.49° N. Lat.; 81.98° W. Long. Elevation is 804 feet.
History: Killbuck was settled in 1811, and named for the creek on which it was established.
Population: 809 (1990); 839 (2000); 871 (2007); 891 (2012 projected); Race: 99.4% White, 0.0% Black, 0.0% Asian, 0.6% Hispanic of any race (2007); Density: 3,074.4 persons per square mile (2007); Average household size: 2.29 (2007); Median age: 37.4 (2007); Males per 100 females: 91.9 (2007); Marriage status: 22.1% never married, 55.2% now married, 7.1% widowed, 15.6% divorced (2000); Foreign born: 0.0% (2000); Ancestry (includes multiple ancestries): 23.3% German, 13.4% United States or American, 12.2% Irish, 8.3% English, 6.8% Other groups (2000).
Economy: Employment by occupation: 4.9% management, 9.6% professional, 10.8% services, 19.1% sales, 0.9% farming, 7.5% construction, 47.1% production (2000).
Income: Per capita income: $17,968 (2007); Median household income: $34,688 (2007); Average household income: $41,184 (2007); Percent of households with income of $100,000 or more: 4.2% (2007); Poverty rate: 12.2% (2000).
Education: Percent of population age 25 and over with: High school diploma (including GED) or higher: 75.5% (2007); Bachelor's degree or higher: 4.2% (2007); Master's degree or higher: 1.9% (2007).

School District(s)

West Holmes Local (KG-12)
2005-06 Enrollment: 2,806 . . . . (330) 674-3546
Housing: Homeownership rate: 64.2% (2007); Median home value: $91,212 (2007); Median rent: $319 per month (2000); Median age of housing: 52 years (2000).
Transportation: Commute to work: 93.7% car, 0.0% public transportation, 3.9% walk, 2.4% work from home (2000); Travel time to work: 39.5% less than 15 minutes, 36.7% 15 to 30 minutes, 15.4% 30 to 45 minutes, 5.7% 45 to 60 minutes, 2.7% 60 minutes or more (2000)

LAKEVILLE (unincorporated postal area, zip code 44638). Covers a land area of 29.839 square miles and a water area of 0.305 square miles. Located at 40.65° N. Lat.; 82.13° W. Long. Elevation is 988 feet.
Population: 1,533 (2000); Race: 97.2% White, 0.0% Black, 0.5% Asian, 2.6% Hispanic of any race (2000); Density: 51.4 persons per square mile (2000); Age: 31.2% under 18, 11.6% over 64 (2000); Marriage status: 23.7% never married, 60.6% now married, 6.1% widowed, 9.6% divorced (2000); Foreign born: 0.9% (2000); Ancestry (includes multiple ancestries): 28.4% German, 11.5% Irish, 10.0% United States or American, 7.9% Other groups, 5.1% English (2000).
Economy: Employment by occupation: 10.5% management, 10.3% professional, 14.7% services, 18.2% sales, 3.3% farming, 16.6% construction, 26.3% production (2000).
Income: Per capita income: $14,270 (2000); Median household income: $32,500 (2000); Poverty rate: 19.7% (2000).
Education: Percent of population age 25 and over with: High school diploma (including GED) or higher: 83.2% (2000); Bachelor's degree or higher: 14.8% (2000).

School District(s)

West Holmes Local (KG-12)
2005-06 Enrollment: 2,806 . . . . (330) 674-3546
Housing: Homeownership rate: 77.1% (2000); Median home value: $88,300 (2000); Median rent: $325 per month (2000); Median age of housing: 35 years (2000).
Transportation: Commute to work: 89.4% car, 2.4% public transportation, 0.0% walk, 7.2% work from home (2000); Travel time to work: 25.7% less than 15 minutes, 37.4% 15 to 30 minutes, 26.6% 30 to 45 minutes, 4.3% 45 to 60 minutes, 6.0% 60 minutes or more (2000)

MILLERSBURG (village). County seat. Covers a land area of 2.017 square miles and a water area of 0 square miles. Located at 40.55° N. Lat.; 81.91° W. Long. Elevation is 899 feet.
History: Settlement in Millersburg began in 1816, when many "Pennsylvania Dutch" came here. The town has been the seat of Holmes County since 1824.
Population: 3,307 (1990); 3,326 (2000); 3,511 (2007); 3,594 (2012 projected); Race: 97.0% White, 1.8% Black, 0.1% Asian, 2.0% Hispanic of any race (2007); Density: 1,740.7 persons per square mile (2007); Average household size: 2.73 (2007); Median age: 37.7 (2007); Males per 100 females: 96.4 (2007); Marriage status: 26.0% never married, 50.5% now married, 8.3% widowed, 15.2% divorced (2000); Foreign born: 3.4% (2000); Ancestry (includes multiple ancestries): 25.9% German, 15.1% United States or American, 10.0% Irish, 9.9% English, 8.5% Other groups (2000).
Economy: Single-family building permits issued: 8 (2007); Multi-family building permits issued: 0 (2007); Employment by occupation: 7.3% management, 13.1% professional, 16.6% services, 25.6% sales, 0.9% farming, 9.7% construction, 26.8% production (2000).
Income: Per capita income: $16,918 (2007); Median household income: $37,295 (2007); Average household income: $43,936 (2007); Percent of households with income of $100,000 or more: 4.9% (2007); Poverty rate: 12.2% (2000).
Education: Percent of population age 25 and over with: High school diploma (including GED) or higher: 75.3% (2007); Bachelor's degree or higher: 16.0% (2007); Master's degree or higher: 5.7% (2007).

School District(s)

East Holmes Local (KG-12)
2005-06 Enrollment: 1,906 . . . . (330) 893-2610
West Holmes Local (KG-12)
2005-06 Enrollment: 2,806 . . . . (330) 674-3546
Housing: Homeownership rate: 54.7% (2007); Median home value: $98,519 (2007); Median rent: $327 per month (2000); Median age of housing: 42 years (2000).
Hospitals: Joel Pomerene Memorial Hospital (55 beds)
Safety: Violent crime rate: 11.1 per 10,000 population; Property crime rate: 232.7 per 10,000 population (2007).
Newspapers: The Daily Record - Millersburg Bureau (Regional news; Circulation 25,000); Holmes County Hub (Community news; Circulation 4,550)
Transportation: Commute to work: 93.9% car, 0.0% public transportation, 4.2% walk, 1.7% work from home (2000); Travel time to work: 54.0% less than 15 minutes, 25.3% 15 to 30 minutes, 12.5% 30 to 45 minutes, 5.3% 45 to 60 minutes, 2.9% 60 minutes or more (2000)

Additional Information Contacts

Holmes County Chamber of Commerce . . . . (330) 674-3975
http://www.holmescountychamber.com
Village of Millersburg . . . . (330) 674-1886
http://www.millersburgohio.com

NASHVILLE (village). Covers a land area of 0.071 square miles and a water area of 0 square miles. Located at 40.59° N. Lat.; 82.11° W. Long. Elevation is 1,224 feet.
Population: 181 (1990); 172 (2000); 182 (2007); 185 (2012 projected); Race: 97.8% White, 0.0% Black, 0.0% Asian, 2.2% Hispanic of any race (2007); Density: 2,557.1 persons per square mile (2007); Average household size: 2.53 (2007); Median age: 36.3 (2007); Males per 100 females: 124.7 (2007); Marriage status: 20.3% never married, 66.2% now married, 6.8% widowed, 6.8% divorced (2000); Foreign born: 0.0% (2000); Ancestry (includes multiple ancestries): 33.5% German, 18.0% English, 16.8% Irish, 5.6% Other groups, 3.1% Dutch (2000).
Economy: Employment by occupation: 10.5% management, 9.3% professional, 19.8% services, 15.1% sales, 0.0% farming, 10.5% construction, 34.9% production (2000).
Income: Per capita income: $17,294 (2007); Median household income: $36,000 (2007); Average household income: $43,715 (2007); Percent of households with income of $100,000 or more: 4.2% (2007); Poverty rate: 11.2% (2000).
Education: Percent of population age 25 and over with: High school diploma (including GED) or higher: 79.7% (2007); Bachelor's degree or higher: 6.8% (2007); Master's degree or higher: 0.0% (2007).

School District(s)

West Holmes Local (KG-12)
2005-06 Enrollment: 2,806 . . . . (330) 674-3546
Housing: Homeownership rate: 83.3% (2007); Median home value: $67,500 (2007); Median rent: $356 per month (2000); Median age of housing: 60+ years (2000).
Transportation: Commute to work: 90.7% car, 0.0% public transportation, 9.3% walk, 0.0% work from home (2000); Travel time to work: 12.8% less than 15 minutes, 33.7% 15 to 30 minutes, 48.8% 30 to 45 minutes, 4.7% 45 to 60 minutes, 0.0% 60 minutes or more (2000)

Huron County

Located in northern Ohio; drained by the Huron and Vermilion Rivers. Covers a land area of 492.69 square miles, a water area of 1.83 square miles, and is located in the Eastern Time Zone. The county was founded in 1815. County seat is Norwalk.

Huron County is part of the Norwalk, OH Micropolitan Statistical Area. The entire metro area includes: Huron County, OH

Weather Station: Norwalk WWTP Elevation: 669 feet

	Jan	Feb	Mar	Apr	May	Jun	Jul	Aug	Sep	Oct	Nov	Dec
High	32	35	45	58	69	79	83	81	74	62	49	38
Low	16	19	27	37	48	57	62	60	52	41	33	23
Precip	2.2	1.8	2.7	3.3	3.5	4.2	3.7	3.8	3.2	2.4	3.0	2.8
Snow	8.6	6.2	4.8	0.8	tr	0.0	0.0	tr	0.0	tr	0.9	5.4

High and Low temperatures in degrees Fahrenheit; Precipitation and Snow in inches

Population: 56,101 (1990); 59,487 (2000); 60,648 (2007); 61,258 (2012 projected); Race: 95.2% White, 1.0% Black, 0.3% Asian, 4.8% Hispanic of any race (2007); Density: 123.1 persons per square mile (2007); Average household size: 2.62 (2007); Median age: 36.5 (2007); Males per 100 females: 96.4 (2007).
Religion: Five largest groups: 25.1% Catholic Church, 6.6% The United Methodist Church, 4.9% Evangelical Lutheran Church in America, 1.9% The Christian and Missionary Alliance, 1.4% United Church of Christ (2000).
Economy: Unemployment rate: 8.1% (6/2008); Total civilian labor force: 29,629 (6/2008); Leading industries: 37.4% manufacturing; 12.0% retail trade; 11.4% health care and social assistance (2005); Farms: 865 totaling 228,346 acres (2002); Companies that employ 500 or more persons: 5 (2006); Companies that employ 100 to 499 persons: 25 (2006); Companies that employ less than 100 persons: 1,228 (2006); Black-owned businesses: n/a (2002); Hispanic-owned businesses: n/a (2002); Asian-owned businesses: n/a (2002); Women-owned businesses: 1,141 (2002); Retail sales per capita: $10,497 (2008). Single-family building permits issued: 57 (2007); Multi-family building permits issued: 65 (2007).
Income: Per capita income: $20,681 (2007); Median household income: $45,214 (2007); Average household income: $53,822 (2007); Percent of households with income of $100,000 or more: 9.2% (2007); Poverty rate: 10.9% (2005); Bankruptcy rate: 4.06% (2007).
Taxes: Total county taxes per capita: $220 (2006); County property taxes per capita: $78 (2006).
Education: Percent of population age 25 and over with: High school diploma (including GED) or higher: 81.1% (2007); Bachelor's degree or higher: 10.9% (2007); Master's degree or higher: 3.3% (2007).
Housing: Homeownership rate: 72.5% (2007); Median home value: $120,762 (2007); Median rent: $370 per month (2000); Median age of housing: 40 years (2000).
Health: Birth rate: 144.8 per 10,000 population (2007); Death rate: 91.3 per 10,000 population (2007); Age-adjusted cancer mortality rate: 201.4 deaths per 100,000 population (2005); Number of physicians: 16.3 per 10,000 population (2005); Hospital beds: 35.6 per 10,000 population (2004); Hospital admissions: 1,268.6 per 10,000 population (2004).
Elections: 2004 Presidential election results: 58.0% Bush, 41.3% Kerry, 0.0% Nader, 0.3% Badnarik

Additional Information Contacts

Huron County Government . . . . (419) 668-3092
http://www.hccommissioners.com
City of Norwalk. . . . . (419) 663-6700
http://www.norwalkoh.com
City of Willard. . . . . (419) 933-2581
http://www.willardohio.com
Norwalk Area-Huron County Chamber of Commerce . . . . . (419) 668-4155
http://www.norwalkareachamber.com
Village of Monroeville. . . . . (419) 465-4443
http://www.monroevilleohio.com
Village of New London . . . . (419) 929-1809
http://www.newlondonohio.com
Willard Area Chamber of Commerce. . . . . (419) 935-1888
http://www.willardohio.com

Huron County Communities

COLLINS (unincorporated postal area, zip code 44826). Covers a land area of 30.599 square miles and a water area of 0 square miles. Located at 41.22° N. Lat.; 82.48° W. Long. Elevation is 885 feet.
Population: 1,733 (2000); Race: 99.0% White, 0.0% Black, 0.3% Asian, 0.8% Hispanic of any race (2000); Density: 56.6 persons per square mile (2000); Age: 25.5% under 18, 15.2% over 64 (2000); Marriage status: 22.5% never married, 62.7% now married, 7.7% widowed, 7.1% divorced (2000); Foreign born: 1.6% (2000); Ancestry (includes multiple ancestries): 32.7% German, 15.1% English, 11.5% Irish, 7.6% United States or American, 6.5% Other groups (2000).
Economy: Employment by occupation: 11.2% management, 12.6% professional, 8.5% services, 21.3% sales, 0.0% farming, 19.6% construction, 26.9% production (2000).
Income: Per capita income: $18,648 (2000); Median household income: $40,573 (2000); Poverty rate: 7.2% (2000).
Education: Percent of population age 25 and over with: High school diploma (including GED) or higher: 83.1% (2000); Bachelor's degree or higher: 6.3% (2000).

School District(s)

Western Reserve Local (PK-12)
2005-06 Enrollment: 1,401 . . . . (419) 660-8508
Housing: Homeownership rate: 91.4% (2000); Median home value: $112,500 (2000); Median rent: $350 per month (2000); Median age of housing: 40 years (2000).
Transportation: Commute to work: 98.6% car, 0.0% public transportation, 0.5% walk, 0.5% work from home (2000); Travel time to work: 30.9% less than 15 minutes, 30.1% 15 to 30 minutes, 23.2% 30 to 45 minutes, 12.5% 45 to 60 minutes, 3.3% 60 minutes or more (2000)

GREENWICH (village). Covers a land area of 1.357 square miles and a water area of 0.017 square miles. Located at 41.03° N. Lat.; 82.51° W. Long. Elevation is 1,030 feet.
History: Greenwich was incorporated in 1879 and named for the town in Connecticut.
Population: 1,442 (1990); 1,525 (2000); 1,529 (2007); 1,526 (2012 projected); Race: 97.9% White, 0.0% Black, 0.0% Asian, 1.1% Hispanic of any race (2007); Density: 1,126.9 persons per square mile (2007); Average household size: 2.57 (2007); Median age: 35.0 (2007); Males per 100 females: 90.9 (2007); Marriage status: 25.0% never married, 56.3% now married, 9.1% widowed, 9.7% divorced (2000); Foreign born: 0.3% (2000); Ancestry (includes multiple ancestries): 23.0% German, 14.5% English, 11.4% United States or American, 9.4% Other groups, 6.4% Irish (2000).
Economy: Single-family building permits issued: 2 (2007); Multi-family building permits issued: 0 (2007); Employment by occupation: 8.0%

management, 10.1% professional, 11.3% services, 20.1% sales, 1.4% farming, 9.4% construction, 39.7% production (2000).
Income: Per capita income: $16,485 (2007); Median household income: $35,125 (2007); Average household income: $42,433 (2007); Percent of households with income of $100,000 or more: 3.5% (2007); Poverty rate: 10.1% (2000).
Education: Percent of population age 25 and over with: High school diploma (including GED) or higher: 75.6% (2007); Bachelor's degree or higher: 5.4% (2007); Master's degree or higher: 1.4% (2007).

School District(s)

South Central Local (PK-12)
2005-06 Enrollment: 965 . . . . (419) 752-3815
Housing: Homeownership rate: 72.1% (2007); Median home value: $101,754 (2007); Median rent: $325 per month (2000); Median age of housing: 46 years (2000).
Transportation: Commute to work: 95.2% car, 0.7% public transportation, 1.6% walk, 2.4% work from home (2000); Travel time to work: 25.7% less than 15 minutes, 46.0% 15 to 30 minutes, 20.0% 30 to 45 minutes, 5.2% 45 to 60 minutes, 3.1% 60 minutes or more (2000)

MONROEVILLE (village). Covers a land area of 1.431 square miles and a water area of 0 square miles. Located at 41.24° N. Lat.; 82.69° W. Long. Elevation is 709 feet.
Population: 1,387 (1990); 1,433 (2000); 1,459 (2007); 1,472 (2012 projected); Race: 98.2% White, 0.1% Black, 0.0% Asian, 1.1% Hispanic of any race (2007); Density: 1,019.4 persons per square mile (2007); Average household size: 2.68 (2007); Median age: 34.2 (2007); Males per 100 females: 98.5 (2007); Marriage status: 27.2% never married, 55.9% now married, 6.4% widowed, 10.5% divorced (2000); Foreign born: 0.3% (2000); Ancestry (includes multiple ancestries): 43.7% German, 12.5% Irish, 10.8% United States or American, 8.6% English, 4.5% Other groups (2000).
Economy: Single-family building permits issued: 0 (2007); Multi-family building permits issued: 0 (2007); Employment by occupation: 7.0% management, 9.3% professional, 12.3% services, 19.2% sales, 0.0% farming, 11.7% construction, 40.5% production (2000).
Income: Per capita income: $20,126 (2007); Median household income: $48,100 (2007); Average household income: $53,115 (2007); Percent of households with income of $100,000 or more: 8.4% (2007); Poverty rate: 3.8% (2000).
Education: Percent of population age 25 and over with: High school diploma (including GED) or higher: 86.4% (2007); Bachelor's degree or higher: 9.0% (2007); Master's degree or higher: 2.4% (2007).

School District(s)

Monroeville Local (PK-12)
2005-06 Enrollment: 749 . . . . (419) 465-2610
Willard City (PK-12)
2005-06 Enrollment: 2,172 . . . . (419) 935-1541
Housing: Homeownership rate: 65.5% (2007); Median home value: $115,481 (2007); Median rent: $362 per month (2000); Median age of housing: 60+ years (2000).
Transportation: Commute to work: 95.0% car, 0.0% public transportation, 2.2% walk, 2.4% work from home (2000); Travel time to work: 47.8% less than 15 minutes, 36.3% 15 to 30 minutes, 10.1% 30 to 45 minutes, 2.7% 45 to 60 minutes, 3.1% 60 minutes or more (2000)
Additional Information Contacts
Village of Monroeville . . . . (419) 465-4443
http://www.monroevilleohio.com

NEW LONDON (village). Covers a land area of 2.103 square miles and a water area of 0.404 square miles. Located at 41.08° N. Lat.; 82.39° W. Long. Elevation is 981 feet.
History: New London was settled in 1816 and developed as a rural trading and shipping center. The C.E. Ward Company was established here to produce band uniforms, graduation caps and gowns, church vestments, and other regalia for a worldwide market.
Population: 2,765 (1990); 2,696 (2000); 2,641 (2007); 2,615 (2012 projected); Race: 96.1% White, 2.4% Black, 0.2% Asian, 0.9% Hispanic of any race (2007); Density: 1,255.7 persons per square mile (2007); Average household size: 2.56 (2007); Median age: 35.3 (2007); Males per 100 females: 94.9 (2007); Marriage status: 22.9% never married, 57.8% now married, 7.9% widowed, 11.5% divorced (2000); Foreign born: 0.1% (2000); Ancestry (includes multiple ancestries): 22.1% German, 12.0% Other groups, 12.0% Irish, 11.6% English, 11.2% United States or American (2000).
Economy: Single-family building permits issued: 2 (2007); Multi-family building permits issued: 0 (2007); Employment by occupation: 6.2% management, 17.4% professional, 14.3% services, 17.2% sales, 0.3% farming, 13.3% construction, 31.2% production (2000).
Income: Per capita income: $17,740 (2007); Median household income: $37,750 (2007); Average household income: $44,518 (2007); Percent of households with income of $100,000 or more: 5.8% (2007); Poverty rate: 10.7% (2000).
Education: Percent of population age 25 and over with: High school diploma (including GED) or higher: 76.4% (2007); Bachelor's degree or higher: 10.5% (2007); Master's degree or higher: 4.6% (2007).

School District(s)

New London Local (PK-12)
2005-06 Enrollment: 1,271 . . . . (419) 929-8433
Housing: Homeownership rate: 66.9% (2007); Median home value: $96,525 (2007); Median rent: $320 per month (2000); Median age of housing: 42 years (2000).
Safety: Violent crime rate: 7.7 per 10,000 population; Property crime rate: 123.5 per 10,000 population (2007).
Newspapers: New London Record (Community news; Circulation 3,000)
Transportation: Commute to work: 91.0% car, 0.3% public transportation, 6.0% walk, 0.7% work from home (2000); Travel time to work: 38.4% less than 15 minutes, 24.1% 15 to 30 minutes, 16.3% 30 to 45 minutes, 10.9% 45 to 60 minutes, 10.2% 60 minutes or more (2000)
Additional Information Contacts
Village of New London . . . . (419) 929-1809
http://www.newlondonohio.com

NORTH FAIRFIELD (village). Covers a land area of 0.466 square miles and a water area of 0 square miles. Located at 41.10° N. Lat.; 82.61° W. Long. Elevation is 928 feet.
Population: 504 (1990); 573 (2000); 590 (2007); 600 (2012 projected); Race: 94.9% White, 0.0% Black, 0.5% Asian, 9.8% Hispanic of any race (2007); Density: 1,265.7 persons per square mile (2007); Average household size: 3.14 (2007); Median age: 30.5 (2007); Males per 100 females: 111.5 (2007); Marriage status: 24.3% never married, 64.1% now married, 3.9% widowed, 7.6% divorced (2000); Foreign born: 0.7% (2000); Ancestry (includes multiple ancestries): 22.4% German, 14.0% Irish, 12.0% Other groups, 7.7% English, 6.3% United States or American (2000).
Economy: Single-family building permits issued: 0 (2007); Multi-family building permits issued: 0 (2007); Employment by occupation: 3.4% management, 2.3% professional, 14.5% services, 22.1% sales, 0.0% farming, 9.5% construction, 48.1% production (2000).
Income: Per capita income: $19,952 (2007); Median household income: $50,769 (2007); Average household income: $60,718 (2007); Percent of households with income of $100,000 or more: 8.5% (2007); Poverty rate: 9.9% (2000).
Education: Percent of population age 25 and over with: High school diploma (including GED) or higher: 72.3% (2007); Bachelor's degree or higher: 2.8% (2007); Master's degree or higher: 0.8% (2007).
Housing: Homeownership rate: 87.8% (2007); Median home value: $94,333 (2007); Median rent: $331 per month (2000); Median age of housing: 60+ years (2000).
Transportation: Commute to work: 96.1% car, 0.0% public transportation, 0.8% walk, 2.3% work from home (2000); Travel time to work: 4.3% less than 15 minutes, 64.8% 15 to 30 minutes, 19.4% 30 to 45 minutes, 9.1% 45 to 60 minutes, 2.4% 60 minutes or more (2000)

NORWALK (city). County seat. Covers a land area of 8.326 square miles and a water area of 0.248 square miles. Located at 41.24° N. Lat.; 82.61° W. Long. Elevation is 719 feet.
History: Norwalk was founded in 1816 by Platt Benedict, and named for the Connecticut town which had been the home of many of its first settlers.
Population: 14,920 (1990); 16,238 (2000); 16,221 (2007); 16,196 (2012 projected); Race: 93.3% White, 2.1% Black, 0.4% Asian, 5.2% Hispanic of any race (2007); Density: 1,948.2 persons per square mile (2007); Average household size: 2.50 (2007); Median age: 35.4 (2007); Males per 100 females: 92.9 (2007); Marriage status: 23.5% never married, 55.9% now married, 7.8% widowed, 12.8% divorced (2000); Foreign born: 2.4% (2000); Ancestry (includes multiple ancestries): 34.2% German, 11.2% English, 10.8% Irish, 10.4% Other groups, 9.2% United States or American (2000).
Economy: Single-family building permits issued: 15 (2007); Multi-family building permits issued: 65 (2007); Employment by occupation: 8.5%

management, 14.4% professional, 14.4% services, 24.0% sales, 0.6% farming, 7.2% construction, 30.9% production (2000).
Income: Per capita income: $20,781 (2007); Median household income: $41,563 (2007); Average household income: $51,278 (2007); Percent of households with income of $100,000 or more: 8.6% (2007); Poverty rate: 8.8% (2000).
Education: Percent of population age 25 and over with: High school diploma (including GED) or higher: 81.1% (2007); Bachelor's degree or higher: 14.9% (2007); Master's degree or higher: 4.5% (2007).

School District(s)

Norwalk City (PK-12)
2005-06 Enrollment: 3,085 . . . . (419) 668-2779
Housing: Homeownership rate: 62.2% (2007); Median home value: $118,141 (2007); Median rent: $391 per month (2000); Median age of housing: 40 years (2000).
Hospitals: Fisher-Titus Medical Center (112 beds)
Safety: Violent crime rate: 9.0 per 10,000 population; Property crime rate: 259.3 per 10,000 population (2007).
Newspapers: Morning Journal - Norwalk Bureau (Regional news); Norwalk Reflector (Regional news; Circulation 9,000)
Transportation: Commute to work: 92.8% car, 0.5% public transportation, 3.2% walk, 1.9% work from home (2000); Travel time to work: 59.2% less than 15 minutes, 23.7% 15 to 30 minutes, 9.5% 30 to 45 minutes, 3.9% 45 to 60 minutes, 3.6% 60 minutes or more (2000)
Airports: Norwalk-Huron County (general aviation)
Additional Information Contacts
City of Norwalk. . . . . (419) 663-6700
http://www.norwalkoh.com
Norwalk Area-Huron County Chamber of Commerce . . . . . (419) 668-4155
http://www.norwalkareachamber.com

WAKEMAN (village). Covers a land area of 0.795 square miles and a water area of 0.004 square miles. Located at 41.25° N. Lat.; 82.40° W. Long. Elevation is 830 feet.
History: Wakeman was the home of the C.S. Clark Seed Company, founded in 1878 and specializing in varieties of seed corn.
Population: 948 (1990); 951 (2000); 913 (2007); 914 (2012 projected); Race: 99.1% White, 0.0% Black, 0.0% Asian, 1.4% Hispanic of any race (2007); Density: 1,148.2 persons per square mile (2007); Average household size: 2.59 (2007); Median age: 38.5 (2007); Males per 100 females: 98.5 (2007); Marriage status: 19.5% never married, 60.6% now married, 6.6% widowed, 13.2% divorced (2000); Foreign born: 1.5% (2000); Ancestry (includes multiple ancestries): 30.8% German, 16.0% Irish, 13.7% English, 9.3% United States or American, 9.1% Other groups (2000).
Economy: Single-family building permits issued: 0 (2007); Multi-family building permits issued: 0 (2007); Employment by occupation: 6.6% management, 15.4% professional, 12.7% services, 17.4% sales, 1.0% farming, 14.1% construction, 32.8% production (2000).
Income: Per capita income: $21,468 (2007); Median household income: $51,585 (2007); Average household income: $55,524 (2007); Percent of households with income of $100,000 or more: 10.2% (2007); Poverty rate: 3.2% (2000).
Education: Percent of population age 25 and over with: High school diploma (including GED) or higher: 84.4% (2007); Bachelor's degree or higher: 10.0% (2007); Master's degree or higher: 4.1% (2007).
Housing: Homeownership rate: 78.2% (2007); Median home value: $123,707 (2007); Median rent: $431 per month (2000); Median age of housing: 51 years (2000).
Transportation: Commute to work: 93.3% car, 0.0% public transportation, 4.0% walk, 1.7% work from home (2000); Travel time to work: 18.2% less than 15 minutes, 38.1% 15 to 30 minutes, 26.1% 30 to 45 minutes, 9.4% 45 to 60 minutes, 8.1% 60 minutes or more (2000)

WILLARD (city). Covers a land area of 3.467 square miles and a water area of 0.026 square miles. Located at 41.05° N. Lat.; 82.72° W. Long. Elevation is 928 feet.
Population: 6,263 (1990); 6,806 (2000); 6,857 (2007); 6,814 (2012 projected); Race: 88.2% White, 1.6% Black, 0.4% Asian, 16.7% Hispanic of any race (2007); Density: 1,977.8 persons per square mile (2007); Average household size: 2.64 (2007); Median age: 33.4 (2007); Males per 100 females: 91.1 (2007); Marriage status: 24.3% never married, 53.7% now married, 8.6% widowed, 13.4% divorced (2000); Foreign born: 4.8% (2000); Ancestry (includes multiple ancestries): 21.8% German, 16.6% Other groups, 13.9% United States or American, 10.7% English, 7.2% Irish (2000).
Economy: Single-family building permits issued: 3 (2007); Multi-family building permits issued: 0 (2007); Employment by occupation: 4.7% management, 11.9% professional, 14.5% services, 20.2% sales, 1.8% farming, 5.9% construction, 40.9% production (2000).
Income: Per capita income: $15,327 (2007); Median household income: $31,514 (2007); Average household income: $40,171 (2007); Percent of households with income of $100,000 or more: 4.6% (2007); Poverty rate: 16.2% (2000).
Education: Percent of population age 25 and over with: High school diploma (including GED) or higher: 74.3% (2007); Bachelor's degree or higher: 7.6% (2007); Master's degree or higher: 2.4% (2007).

School District(s)

Willard City (PK-12)
2005-06 Enrollment: 2,172 . . . . (419) 935-1541
Housing: Homeownership rate: 56.1% (2007); Median home value: $90,111 (2007); Median rent: $357 per month (2000); Median age of housing: 45 years (2000).
Safety: Violent crime rate: 16.3 per 10,000 population; Property crime rate: 392.2 per 10,000 population (2007).
Newspapers: Willard Times Junction (Local news; Circulation 4,200)
Transportation: Commute to work: 92.9% car, 0.4% public transportation, 3.8% walk, 1.9% work from home (2000); Travel time to work: 62.3% less than 15 minutes, 18.8% 15 to 30 minutes, 12.1% 30 to 45 minutes, 4.9% 45 to 60 minutes, 1.8% 60 minutes or more (2000)
Additional Information Contacts
City of Willard. . . . . (419) 933-2581
http://www.willardohio.com
Willard Area Chamber of Commerce . . . . (419) 935-1888
http://www.willardohio.com

Jackson County

Located in southern Ohio; drained by the Little Scioto River. Covers a land area of 420.28 square miles, a water area of 1.22 square miles, and is located in the Eastern Time Zone. The county was founded in 1816. County seat is Jackson.

Weather Station: Jackson 3 NW Elevation: 797 feet

	Jan	Feb	Mar	Apr	May	Jun	Jul	Aug	Sep	Oct	Nov	Dec
High	38	43	53	65	74	81	85	83	77	66	54	43
Low	19	22	30	38	48	57	62	60	53	41	32	24
Precip	2.8	2.8	3.8	3.4	4.0	4.1	4.0	3.9	3.2	2.8	3.1	3.3
Snow	na	na	na	0.7	0.0	0.0	0.0	0.0	0.0	0.0	na	na

High and Low temperatures in degrees Fahrenheit; Precipitation and Snow in inches

Population: 30,230 (1990); 32,641 (2000); 33,820 (2007); 34,565 (2012 projected); Race: 97.4% White, 0.7% Black, 0.3% Asian, 1.3% Hispanic of any race (2007); Density: 80.5 persons per square mile (2007); Average household size: 2.54 (2007); Median age: 37.6 (2007); Males per 100 females: 93.7 (2007).
Religion: Five largest groups: 8.5% The United Methodist Church, 8.0% Church of God (Cleveland, Tennessee), 2.5% Church of the Nazarene, 2.0% The Wesleyan Church, 1.9% Presbyterian Church (U.S.A.) (2000).
Economy: Unemployment rate: 8.2% (6/2008); Total civilian labor force: 15,790 (6/2008); Leading industries: 38.4% manufacturing; 13.9% finance & insurance; 13.7% retail trade (2005); Farms: 458 totaling 73,800 acres (2002); Companies that employ 500 or more persons: 3 (2006); Companies that employ 100 to 499 persons: 8 (2006); Companies that employ less than 100 persons: 606 (2006); Black-owned businesses: n/a (2002); Hispanic-owned businesses: n/a (2002); Asian-owned businesses: n/a (2002); Women-owned businesses: 368 (2002); Retail sales per capita: $11,017 (2008). Single-family building permits issued: 84 (2007); Multi-family building permits issued: 0 (2007).
Income: Per capita income: $17,379 (2007); Median household income: $35,611 (2007); Average household income: $43,628 (2007); Percent of households with income of $100,000 or more: 6.5% (2007); Poverty rate: 16.5% (2005); Bankruptcy rate: 3.39% (2007).
Taxes: Total county taxes per capita: $175 (2006); County property taxes per capita: $79 (2006).
Education: Percent of population age 25 and over with: High school diploma (including GED) or higher: 73.2% (2007); Bachelor's degree or higher: 11.0% (2007); Master's degree or higher: 3.9% (2007).

Housing: Homeownership rate: 74.1% (2007); Median home value: $86,512 (2007); Median rent: $284 per month (2000); Median age of housing: 32 years (2000).
Health: Birth rate: 138.4 per 10,000 population (2007); Death rate: 113.5 per 10,000 population (2007); Age-adjusted cancer mortality rate: 238.6 deaths per 100,000 population (2005); Number of physicians: 8.7 per 10,000 population (2005); Hospital beds: 0.0 per 10,000 population (2004); Hospital admissions: 0.0 per 10,000 population (2004).
Elections: 2004 Presidential election results: 59.9% Bush, 39.8% Kerry, 0.0% Nader, 0.2% Badnarik
National and State Parks: Buckeye Furnace State Memorial; Jackson Lake State Reserve; Leo Petroglyph State Memorial; Richland Furnace State Forest
Additional Information Contacts
Jackson County Government. . . . . (740) 286-3301

Jackson Area Chamber of Commerce. . . . . (740) 286-2722
http://www.jacksonohio.org

Jackson County Communities

COALTON (village). Covers a land area of 0.549 square miles and a water area of 0 square miles. Located at 39.11° N. Lat.; 82.61° W. Long. Elevation is 692 feet.
History: During the 1880's, Coalton was a busy coal town.
Population: 553 (1990); 545 (2000); 618 (2007); 666 (2012 projected); Race: 96.1% White, 1.8% Black, 0.6% Asian, 2.4% Hispanic of any race (2007); Density: 1,124.8 persons per square mile (2007); Average household size: 2.55 (2007); Median age: 34.2 (2007); Males per 100 females: 94.3 (2007); Marriage status: 19.4% never married, 60.7% now married, 6.4% widowed, 13.5% divorced (2000); Foreign born: 0.5% (2000); Ancestry (includes multiple ancestries): 22.5% United States or American, 9.8% Other groups, 9.3% Irish, 8.0% German, 4.5% English (2000).
Economy: Single-family building permits issued: 0 (2007); Multi-family building permits issued: 0 (2007); Employment by occupation: 4.8% management, 10.8% professional, 18.3% services, 23.7% sales, 2.7% farming, 8.1% construction, 31.7% production (2000).
Income: Per capita income: $14,167 (2007); Median household income: $27,955 (2007); Average household income: $36,178 (2007); Percent of households with income of $100,000 or more: 4.5% (2007); Poverty rate: 27.5% (2000).
Education: Percent of population age 25 and over with: High school diploma (including GED) or higher: 66.7% (2007); Bachelor's degree or higher: 5.2% (2007); Master's degree or higher: 0.5% (2007).
Housing: Homeownership rate: 62.0% (2007); Median home value: $48,462 (2007); Median rent: $300 per month (2000); Median age of housing: 49 years (2000).
Transportation: Commute to work: 96.2% car, 0.0% public transportation, 1.6% walk, 2.2% work from home (2000); Travel time to work: 40.1% less than 15 minutes, 21.4% 15 to 30 minutes, 8.8% 30 to 45 minutes, 13.7% 45 to 60 minutes, 15.9% 60 minutes or more (2000)

JACKSON (city). County seat. Covers a land area of 7.511 square miles and a water area of 0.251 square miles. Located at 39.05° N. Lat.; 82.64° W. Long. Elevation is 692 feet.
History: Jackson was platted in 1817, and grew around the railroad that arrived in 1853. Many of Jackson's early settlers were Welsh who came to farm and later worked in the iron furnaces and coal mines.
Population: 6,351 (1990); 6,184 (2000); 6,294 (2007); 6,373 (2012 projected); Race: 97.6% White, 0.4% Black, 0.4% Asian, 1.9% Hispanic of any race (2007); Density: 838.0 persons per square mile (2007); Average household size: 2.28 (2007); Median age: 38.1 (2007); Males per 100 females: 86.7 (2007); Marriage status: 21.3% never married, 52.8% now married, 11.5% widowed, 14.4% divorced (2000); Foreign born: 2.2% (2000); Ancestry (includes multiple ancestries): 15.8% United States or American, 12.8% German, 8.4% Irish, 7.6% Other groups, 7.0% Welsh (2000).
Economy: Single-family building permits issued: 3 (2007); Multi-family building permits issued: 0 (2007); Employment by occupation: 9.9% management, 20.8% professional, 14.7% services, 25.6% sales, 0.4% farming, 8.1% construction, 20.4% production (2000).
Income: Per capita income: $17,170 (2007); Median household income: $30,498 (2007); Average household income: $39,035 (2007); Percent of households with income of $100,000 or more: 5.9% (2007); Poverty rate: 18.7% (2000).
Taxes: Total city taxes per capita: $250 (2006); City property taxes per capita: $115 (2006).
Education: Percent of population age 25 and over with: High school diploma (including GED) or higher: 72.4% (2007); Bachelor's degree or higher: 13.7% (2007); Master's degree or higher: 4.7% (2007).

School District(s)

Jackson City (PK-12)
2005-06 Enrollment: 2,787 . . . . (740) 286-6442

Two-year College(s)

Southeastern Business College (Private, For-profit)
Fall 2007 Enrollment: 14 . . . . (740) 286-1554
Housing: Homeownership rate: 62.4% (2007); Median home value: $98,860 (2007); Median rent: $307 per month (2000); Median age of housing: 46 years (2000).
Newspapers: Times-Journal (Community news; Circulation 9,200)
Transportation: Commute to work: 93.5% car, 0.0% public transportation, 3.9% walk, 1.6% work from home (2000); Travel time to work: 57.2% less than 15 minutes, 17.3% 15 to 30 minutes, 13.1% 30 to 45 minutes, 3.9% 45 to 60 minutes, 8.4% 60 minutes or more (2000)
Airports: James A Rhodes (general aviation)
Additional Information Contacts
Jackson Area Chamber of Commerce. . . . . (740) 286-2722
http://www.jacksonohio.org

OAK HILL (village). Covers a land area of 1.143 square miles and a water area of 0 square miles. Located at 38.89° N. Lat.; 82.57° W. Long. Elevation is 699 feet.
Population: 1,831 (1990); 1,685 (2000); 1,742 (2007); 1,782 (2012 projected); Race: 97.9% White, 0.4% Black, 0.3% Asian, 0.2% Hispanic of any race (2007); Density: 1,524.3 persons per square mile (2007); Average household size: 2.45 (2007); Median age: 36.3 (2007); Males per 100 females: 84.5 (2007); Marriage status: 22.2% never married, 54.0% now married, 11.3% widowed, 12.4% divorced (2000); Foreign born: 0.6% (2000); Ancestry (includes multiple ancestries): 19.4% United States or American, 15.4% German, 10.4% Welsh, 9.1% Irish, 7.5% Other groups (2000).
Economy: Single-family building permits issued: 0 (2007); Multi-family building permits issued: 0 (2007); Employment by occupation: 7.9% management, 17.7% professional, 19.1% services, 19.8% sales, 2.4% farming, 8.6% construction, 24.4% production (2000).
Income: Per capita income: $16,399 (2007); Median household income: $31,900 (2007); Average household income: $39,743 (2007); Percent of households with income of $100,000 or more: 4.9% (2007); Poverty rate: 20.6% (2000).
Education: Percent of population age 25 and over with: High school diploma (including GED) or higher: 74.3% (2007); Bachelor's degree or higher: 13.3% (2007); Master's degree or higher: 4.7% (2007).

School District(s)

Oak Hill Union Local (PK-12)
2005-06 Enrollment: 1,301 . . . . (740) 682-7595
Housing: Homeownership rate: 65.8% (2007); Median home value: $69,405 (2007); Median rent: $280 per month (2000); Median age of housing: 47 years (2000).
Transportation: Commute to work: 92.4% car, 1.1% public transportation, 4.5% walk, 1.4% work from home (2000); Travel time to work: 34.0% less than 15 minutes, 33.3% 15 to 30 minutes, 15.3% 30 to 45 minutes, 9.0% 45 to 60 minutes, 8.4% 60 minutes or more (2000)

WELLSTON (city). Covers a land area of 6.967 square miles and a water area of 0.083 square miles. Located at 39.12° N. Lat.; 82.53° W. Long. Elevation is 741 feet.
History: Wellston was named for Harvey Wells, who constructed a blast furnace in 1874 and platted a town around it.
Population: 6,062 (1990); 6,078 (2000); 5,970 (2007); 5,892 (2012 projected); Race: 97.4% White, 0.6% Black, 0.3% Asian, 1.1% Hispanic of any race (2007); Density: 856.9 persons per square mile (2007); Average household size: 2.53 (2007); Median age: 35.7 (2007); Males per 100 females: 89.9 (2007); Marriage status: 20.7% never married, 53.1% now married, 12.4% widowed, 13.8% divorced (2000); Foreign born: 0.8% (2000); Ancestry (includes multiple ancestries): 19.3% German, 14.7% United States or American, 12.1% Irish, 9.2% Other groups, 7.8% English (2000).

Economy: Single-family building permits issued: 13 (2007); Multi-family building permits issued: 0 (2007); Employment by occupation: 5.8% management, 14.2% professional, 16.8% services, 18.3% sales, 0.3% farming, 14.5% construction, 30.1% production (2000).
Income: Per capita income: $15,857 (2007); Median household income: $34,524 (2007); Average household income: $39,110 (2007); Percent of households with income of $100,000 or more: 4.0% (2007); Poverty rate: 18.8% (2000).
Education: Percent of population age 25 and over with: High school diploma (including GED) or higher: 72.4% (2007); Bachelor's degree or higher: 8.9% (2007); Master's degree or higher: 2.5% (2007).

School District(s)

Wellston City (PK-12)
2005-06 Enrollment: 1,786 . . . . (740) 384-2152
Housing: Homeownership rate: 66.6% (2007); Median home value: $68,758 (2007); Median rent: $259 per month (2000); Median age of housing: 43 years (2000).
Newspapers: Wellston Telegram (Local news; Circulation 6,200)
Transportation: Commute to work: 95.9% car, 0.0% public transportation, 1.0% walk, 3.1% work from home (2000); Travel time to work: 41.7% less than 15 minutes, 20.4% 15 to 30 minutes, 12.8% 30 to 45 minutes, 9.3% 45 to 60 minutes, 15.8% 60 minutes or more (2000)

Jefferson County

Located in eastern Ohio; bounded on the east by the Ohio River and the West Virginia border; drained by Yellow and Cross Creeks. Covers a land area of 409.61 square miles, a water area of 1.27 square miles, and is located in the Eastern Time Zone. The county was founded in 1797. County seat is Steubenville.

Jefferson County is part of the Weirton-Steubenville, WV-OH Metropolitan Statistical Area. The entire metro area includes: Jefferson County, OH; Brooke County, WV; Hancock County, WV

Weather Station: Steubenville Elevation: 990 feet

	Jan	Feb	Mar	Apr	May	Jun	Jul	Aug	Sep	Oct	Nov	Dec
High	36	40	51	62	72	80	83	82	76	64	52	42
Low	20	23	30	39	50	58	63	62	55	43	35	26
Precip	2.8	2.4	3.3	3.2	4.0	4.5	4.2	3.7	3.3	2.6	3.4	3.0
Snow	na	na	na	tr	0.0	0.0	0.0	0.0	0.0	0.2	0.3	na

High and Low temperatures in degrees Fahrenheit; Precipitation and Snow in inches

Population: 80,298 (1990); 73,894 (2000); 69,716 (2007); 66,592 (2012 projected); Race: 92.4% White, 5.7% Black, 0.5% Asian, 0.8% Hispanic of any race (2007); Density: 170.2 persons per square mile (2007); Average household size: 2.36 (2007); Median age: 43.5 (2007); Males per 100 females: 91.4 (2007).
Religion: Five largest groups: 19.9% Catholic Church, 9.2% The United Methodist Church, 3.3% Presbyterian Church (U.S.A.), 2.3% Christian Churches and Churches of Christ, 1.1% Serbian Orthodox Church in the USA (2000).
Economy: Unemployment rate: 7.4% (6/2008); Total civilian labor force: 32,093 (6/2008); Leading industries: 19.9% health care and social assistance; 17.4% retail trade; 14.6% manufacturing (2005); Farms: 461 totaling 67,231 acres (2002); Companies that employ 500 or more persons: 6 (2006); Companies that employ 100 to 499 persons: 22 (2006); Companies that employ less than 100 persons: 1,446 (2006); Black-owned businesses: n/a (2002); Hispanic-owned businesses: n/a (2002); Asian-owned businesses: n/a (2002); Women-owned businesses: 848 (2002); Retail sales per capita: $11,133 (2008). Single-family building permits issued: 18 (2007); Multi-family building permits issued: 106 (2007).
Income: Per capita income: $20,036 (2007); Median household income: $36,264 (2007); Average household income: $46,519 (2007); Percent of households with income of $100,000 or more: 7.7% (2007); Poverty rate: 16.3% (2005); Bankruptcy rate: 4.90% (2007).
Taxes: Total county taxes per capita: $289 (2006); County property taxes per capita: $147 (2006).
Education: Percent of population age 25 and over with: High school diploma (including GED) or higher: 81.8% (2007); Bachelor's degree or higher: 12.1% (2007); Master's degree or higher: 4.2% (2007).
Housing: Homeownership rate: 74.7% (2007); Median home value: $79,137 (2007); Median rent: $281 per month (2000); Median age of housing: 45 years (2000).
Health: Birth rate: 105.3 per 10,000 population (2007); Death rate: 144.0 per 10,000 population (2007); Age-adjusted cancer mortality rate: 240.4 deaths per 100,000 population (2005); Air Quality Index: 72.3% good, 24.4% moderate, 3.3% unhealthy for sensitive individuals, 0.0% unhealthy (percent of days in 2007); Number of physicians: 15.4 per 10,000 population (2005); Hospital beds: 47.7 per 10,000 population (2004); Hospital admissions: 1,769.4 per 10,000 population (2004).
Elections: 2004 Presidential election results: 47.2% Bush, 52.3% Kerry, 0.0% Nader, 0.2% Badnarik
National and State Parks: Fernwood State Forest; Jefferson Lake State Park
Additional Information Contacts
Jefferson County Government. . . . . (740) 283-8500
http://www.jeffersoncountyoh.com
City of Steubenville . . . . (740) 283-6000
http://www.ci.steubenville.oh.us
Jefferson County Chamber of Commerce . . . . (740) 282-6226
http://www.jeffersoncountychamber.com

Jefferson County Communities

ADENA (village). Covers a land area of 0.538 square miles and a water area of 0 square miles. Located at 40.21° N. Lat.; 80.87° W. Long. Elevation is 863 feet.
Population: 842 (1990); 815 (2000); 751 (2007); 716 (2012 projected); Race: 98.4% White, 1.1% Black, 0.1% Asian, 0.0% Hispanic of any race (2007); Density: 1,396.0 persons per square mile (2007); Average household size: 2.28 (2007); Median age: 45.0 (2007); Males per 100 females: 89.2 (2007); Marriage status: 18.5% never married, 62.8% now married, 10.4% widowed, 8.2% divorced (2000); Foreign born: 1.1% (2000); Ancestry (includes multiple ancestries): 30.1% Polish, 13.1% German, 10.5% Italian, 10.4% Irish, 9.6% United States or American (2000).
Economy: Single-family building permits issued: 0 (2007); Multi-family building permits issued: 0 (2007); Employment by occupation: 7.6% management, 13.5% professional, 15.9% services, 32.7% sales, 0.0% farming, 16.5% construction, 13.8% production (2000).
Income: Per capita income: $18,309 (2007); Median household income: $31,406 (2007); Average household income: $41,667 (2007); Percent of households with income of $100,000 or more: 7.3% (2007); Poverty rate: 20.6% (2000).
Education: Percent of population age 25 and over with: High school diploma (including GED) or higher: 80.1% (2007); Bachelor's degree or higher: 6.8% (2007); Master's degree or higher: 2.5% (2007).

School District(s)

Buckeye Local (PK-12)
2005-06 Enrollment: 2,443 . . . . (740) 769-7395
Housing: Homeownership rate: 82.4% (2007); Median home value: $50,256 (2007); Median rent: $217 per month (2000); Median age of housing: 60+ years (2000).
Transportation: Commute to work: 91.8% car, 0.0% public transportation, 5.4% walk, 1.6% work from home (2000); Travel time to work: 20.5% less than 15 minutes, 21.2% 15 to 30 minutes, 41.3% 30 to 45 minutes, 7.1% 45 to 60 minutes, 9.9% 60 minutes or more (2000)

AMSTERDAM (village). Covers a land area of 0.315 square miles and a water area of 0 square miles. Located at 40.47° N. Lat.; 80.92° W. Long. Elevation is 935 feet.
History: Settled 1830, incorporated 1904.
Population: 669 (1990); 568 (2000); 508 (2007); 479 (2012 projected); Race: 98.6% White, 0.0% Black, 0.0% Asian, 0.2% Hispanic of any race (2007); Density: 1,614.8 persons per square mile (2007); Average household size: 2.37 (2007); Median age: 35.7 (2007); Males per 100 females: 93.2 (2007); Marriage status: 19.3% never married, 63.1% now married, 8.9% widowed, 8.7% divorced (2000); Foreign born: 0.3% (2000); Ancestry (includes multiple ancestries): 22.8% German, 16.1% English, 15.9% Irish, 9.2% Polish, 7.0% Other groups (2000).
Economy: Employment by occupation: 1.6% management, 8.1% professional, 20.0% services, 16.8% sales, 1.1% farming, 18.4% construction, 34.1% production (2000).
Income: Per capita income: $15,915 (2007); Median household income: $32,000 (2007); Average household income: $37,780 (2007); Percent of households with income of $100,000 or more: 4.2% (2007); Poverty rate: 23.7% (2000).
Education: Percent of population age 25 and over with: High school diploma (including GED) or higher: 73.8% (2007); Bachelor's degree or higher: 4.1% (2007); Master's degree or higher: 0.9% (2007).

Housing: Homeownership rate: 69.2% (2007); Median home value: $51,818 (2007); Median rent: $258 per month (2000); Median age of housing: 60+ years (2000).
Transportation: Commute to work: 95.6% car, 0.0% public transportation, 1.1% walk, 3.3% work from home (2000); Travel time to work: 10.9% less than 15 minutes, 24.1% 15 to 30 minutes, 31.0% 30 to 45 minutes, 17.8% 45 to 60 minutes, 16.1% 60 minutes or more (2000)

BERGHOLZ (village). Covers a land area of 0.556 square miles and a water area of 0 square miles. Located at 40.52° N. Lat.; 80.88° W. Long. Elevation is 925 feet.
History: Settled 1885, incorporated 1906.
Population: 713 (1990); 769 (2000); 655 (2007); 634 (2012 projected); Race: 98.5% White, 0.6% Black, 0.0% Asian, 0.2% Hispanic of any race (2007); Density: 1,178.6 persons per square mile (2007); Average household size: 2.56 (2007); Median age: 38.8 (2007); Males per 100 females: 91.0 (2007); Marriage status: 27.4% never married, 56.9% now married, 7.9% widowed, 7.8% divorced (2000); Foreign born: 0.6% (2000); Ancestry (includes multiple ancestries): 14.3% Irish, 13.4% German, 10.3% United States or American, 7.8% English, 6.5% Italian (2000).
Economy: Employment by occupation: 5.8% management, 10.8% professional, 19.8% services, 28.5% sales, 2.9% farming, 11.9% construction, 20.3% production (2000).
Income: Per capita income: $20,646 (2007); Median household income: $40,769 (2007); Average household income: $52,754 (2007); Percent of households with income of $100,000 or more: 10.9% (2007); Poverty rate: 16.2% (2000).
Education: Percent of population age 25 and over with: High school diploma (including GED) or higher: 75.4% (2007); Bachelor's degree or higher: 10.8% (2007); Master's degree or higher: 5.0% (2007).

School District(s)

Edison Local (PK-12)
2005-06 Enrollment: 2,638 . . . . (330) 532-3199
Housing: Homeownership rate: 76.6% (2007); Median home value: $65,455 (2007); Median rent: $237 per month (2000); Median age of housing: 59 years (2000).
Transportation: Commute to work: 96.2% car, 0.0% public transportation, 2.3% walk, 0.6% work from home (2000); Travel time to work: 29.0% less than 15 minutes, 14.1% 15 to 30 minutes, 20.8% 30 to 45 minutes, 14.1% 45 to 60 minutes, 22.0% 60 minutes or more (2000)

BLOOMINGDALE (village). Covers a land area of 0.108 square miles and a water area of 0 square miles. Located at 40.34° N. Lat.; 80.81° W. Long. Elevation is 1,263 feet.
History: Laid out 1816. Also called Bloomfield.
Population: 227 (1990); 221 (2000); 217 (2007); 200 (2012 projected); Race: 98.2% White, 0.0% Black, 0.5% Asian, 0.0% Hispanic of any race (2007); Density: 2,017.7 persons per square mile (2007); Average household size: 2.61 (2007); Median age: 41.3 (2007); Males per 100 females: 88.7 (2007); Marriage status: 22.1% never married, 60.5% now married, 9.2% widowed, 8.2% divorced (2000); Foreign born: 0.0% (2000); Ancestry (includes multiple ancestries): 32.3% German, 23.7% Irish, 18.5% English, 9.5% United States or American, 7.3% Italian (2000).
Economy: Single-family building permits issued: 0 (2007); Multi-family building permits issued: 0 (2007); Employment by occupation: 2.6% management, 5.3% professional, 17.5% services, 22.8% sales, 0.0% farming, 18.4% construction, 33.3% production (2000).
Income: Per capita income: $23,214 (2007); Median household income: $60,313 (2007); Average household income: $60,693 (2007); Percent of households with income of $100,000 or more: 14.5% (2007); Poverty rate: 4.3% (2000).
Education: Percent of population age 25 and over with: High school diploma (including GED) or higher: 86.7% (2007); Bachelor's degree or higher: 13.3% (2007); Master's degree or higher: 4.0% (2007).

School District(s)

Indian Creek Local (PK-12)
2005-06 Enrollment: 2,375 . . . . (740) 264-3502
Jefferson County (09-12)
2005-06 Enrollment: n/a . . . . (740) 264-5545
Housing: Homeownership rate: 80.7% (2007); Median home value: $70,625 (2007); Median rent: $250 per month (2000); Median age of housing: 60+ years (2000).
Transportation: Commute to work: 91.5% car, 0.0% public transportation, 1.9% walk, 0.9% work from home (2000); Travel time to work: 24.8% less than 15 minutes, 51.4% 15 to 30 minutes, 8.6% 30 to 45 minutes, 6.7% 45 to 60 minutes, 8.6% 60 minutes or more (2000)

BRILLIANT (unincorporated postal area, zip code 43913). Covers a land area of 4.858 square miles and a water area of 0.012 square miles. Located at 40.32° N. Lat.; 80.76° W. Long. Elevation is 700 feet.
Population: 1,728 (2000); Race: 99.5% White, 0.0% Black, 0.0% Asian, 0.0% Hispanic of any race (2000); Density: 355.7 persons per square mile (2000); Age: 22.8% under 18, 16.4% over 64 (2000); Marriage status: 17.7% never married, 62.3% now married, 10.5% widowed, 9.4% divorced (2000); Foreign born: 0.0% (2000); Ancestry (includes multiple ancestries): 17.7% German, 13.3% Irish, 12.4% United States or American, 8.7% English, 6.9% Italian (2000).
Economy: Employment by occupation: 6.8% management, 15.8% professional, 21.3% services, 27.7% sales, 0.0% farming, 9.3% construction, 19.1% production (2000).
Income: Per capita income: $13,091 (2000); Median household income: $26,450 (2000); Poverty rate: 13.1% (2000).
Education: Percent of population age 25 and over with: High school diploma (including GED) or higher: 83.0% (2000); Bachelor's degree or higher: 7.7% (2000).

School District(s)

Buckeye Local (PK-12)
2005-06 Enrollment: 2,443 . . . . (740) 769-7395
Housing: Homeownership rate: 72.7% (2000); Median home value: $51,800 (2000); Median rent: $241 per month (2000); Median age of housing: 45 years (2000).
Transportation: Commute to work: 91.9% car, 0.5% public transportation, 4.3% walk, 3.0% work from home (2000); Travel time to work: 30.0% less than 15 minutes, 50.9% 15 to 30 minutes, 11.5% 30 to 45 minutes, 3.0% 45 to 60 minutes, 4.7% 60 minutes or more (2000)

DILLONVALE (village). Covers a land area of 0.413 square miles and a water area of 0.009 square miles. Located at 40.19° N. Lat.; 80.77° W. Long. Elevation is 735 feet.
History: Dillonvale grew in the center of a large coal-mining region.
Population: 857 (1990); 781 (2000); 723 (2007); 675 (2012 projected); Race: 98.1% White, 0.7% Black, 0.1% Asian, 0.0% Hispanic of any race (2007); Density: 1,749.2 persons per square mile (2007); Average household size: 2.23 (2007); Median age: 43.8 (2007); Males per 100 females: 90.8 (2007); Marriage status: 24.4% never married, 49.0% now married, 13.6% widowed, 12.9% divorced (2000); Foreign born: 0.0% (2000); Ancestry (includes multiple ancestries): 19.9% Polish, 16.1% Irish, 12.3% Italian, 12.1% German, 7.0% Czech (2000).
Economy: Single-family building permits issued: 0 (2007); Multi-family building permits issued: 0 (2007); Employment by occupation: 5.1% management, 10.2% professional, 19.5% services, 22.2% sales, 0.0% farming, 13.2% construction, 29.7% production (2000).
Income: Per capita income: $19,070 (2007); Median household income: $34,194 (2007); Average household income: $42,554 (2007); Percent of households with income of $100,000 or more: 6.2% (2007); Poverty rate: 11.9% (2000).
Education: Percent of population age 25 and over with: High school diploma (including GED) or higher: 80.3% (2007); Bachelor's degree or higher: 3.6% (2007); Master's degree or higher: 1.3% (2007).

School District(s)

Martins Ferry City (PK-12)
2005-06 Enrollment: 1,565 . . . . (740) 633-1732
Housing: Homeownership rate: 86.7% (2007); Median home value: $44,239 (2007); Median rent: $268 per month (2000); Median age of housing: 60+ years (2000).
Transportation: Commute to work: 94.6% car, 0.0% public transportation, 4.7% walk, 0.6% work from home (2000); Travel time to work: 20.1% less than 15 minutes, 25.2% 15 to 30 minutes, 37.3% 30 to 45 minutes, 4.8% 45 to 60 minutes, 12.7% 60 minutes or more (2000)

EMPIRE (village). Covers a land area of 0.329 square miles and a water area of 0 square miles. Located at 40.51° N. Lat.; 80.62° W. Long. Elevation is 682 feet.
Population: 364 (1990); 300 (2000); 249 (2007); 245 (2012 projected); Race: 97.2% White, 0.8% Black, 0.0% Asian, 2.0% Hispanic of any race (2007); Density: 757.9 persons per square mile (2007); Average household size: 2.33 (2007); Median age: 36.0 (2007); Males per 100 females: 93.0 (2007); Marriage status: 24.4% never married, 48.7% now married, 10.7% widowed, 16.2% divorced (2000); Foreign born: 0.0% (2000); Ancestry

(includes multiple ancestries): 24.3% Irish, 16.0% English, 15.3% German, 10.0% United States or American, 9.3% Other groups (2000).
Economy: Employment by occupation: 3.4% management, 7.6% professional, 18.6% services, 22.9% sales, 0.0% farming, 14.4% construction, 33.1% production (2000).
Income: Per capita income: $13,504 (2007); Median household income: $24,038 (2007); Average household income: $31,425 (2007); Percent of households with income of $100,000 or more: 3.7% (2007); Poverty rate: 16.3% (2000).
Education: Percent of population age 25 and over with: High school diploma (including GED) or higher: 82.4% (2007); Bachelor's degree or higher: 3.1% (2007); Master's degree or higher: 1.9% (2007).
Housing: Homeownership rate: 69.2% (2007); Median home value: $41,538 (2007); Median rent: $273 per month (2000); Median age of housing: 31 years (2000).
Transportation: Commute to work: 98.3% car, 0.0% public transportation, 1.7% walk, 0.0% work from home (2000); Travel time to work: 46.1% less than 15 minutes, 29.6% 15 to 30 minutes, 18.3% 30 to 45 minutes, 2.6% 45 to 60 minutes, 3.5% 60 minutes or more (2000)

HAMMONDSVILLE (unincorporated postal area, zip code 43930). Covers a land area of 27.112 square miles and a water area of 0.025 square miles. Located at 40.56° N. Lat.; 80.76° W. Long. Elevation is 687 feet.
Population: 743 (2000); Race: 100.0% White, 0.0% Black, 0.0% Asian, 0.0% Hispanic of any race (2000); Density: 27.4 persons per square mile (2000); Age: 27.4% under 18, 12.9% over 64 (2000); Marriage status: 21.3% never married, 63.0% now married, 6.9% widowed, 8.8% divorced (2000); Foreign born: 0.3% (2000); Ancestry (includes multiple ancestries): 17.4% German, 13.0% United States or American, 8.7% English, 8.6% Irish, 6.8% Polish (2000).
Economy: Employment by occupation: 6.1% management, 17.2% professional, 16.1% services, 17.7% sales, 1.1% farming, 11.6% construction, 30.2% production (2000).
Income: Per capita income: $15,401 (2000); Median household income: $38,500 (2000); Poverty rate: 8.8% (2000).
Education: Percent of population age 25 and over with: High school diploma (including GED) or higher: 82.4% (2000); Bachelor's degree or higher: 14.3% (2000).

School District(s)

Edison Local (PK-12)
2005-06 Enrollment: 2,638 . . . . (330) 532-3199
Housing: Homeownership rate: 90.6% (2000); Median home value: $88,800 (2000); Median rent: $n/a per month (2000); Median age of housing: 30 years (2000).
Transportation: Commute to work: 94.7% car, 0.0% public transportation, 0.0% walk, 5.3% work from home (2000); Travel time to work: 12.8% less than 15 minutes, 28.5% 15 to 30 minutes, 33.0% 30 to 45 minutes, 9.5% 45 to 60 minutes, 16.2% 60 minutes or more (2000)

IRONDALE (village). Covers a land area of 1.401 square miles and a water area of 0.024 square miles. Located at 40.57° N. Lat.; 80.72° W. Long. Elevation is 709 feet.
Population: 382 (1990); 418 (2000); 367 (2007); 354 (2012 projected); Race: 94.8% White, 3.8% Black, 0.5% Asian, 1.6% Hispanic of any race (2007); Density: 262.0 persons per square mile (2007); Average household size: 2.60 (2007); Median age: 35.6 (2007); Males per 100 females: 102.8 (2007); Marriage status: 22.1% never married, 57.7% now married, 13.5% widowed, 6.7% divorced (2000); Foreign born: 0.0% (2000); Ancestry (includes multiple ancestries): 28.5% German, 23.5% Irish, 12.7% English, 5.5% Other groups, 5.5% United States or American (2000).
Economy: Employment by occupation: 4.0% management, 12.0% professional, 17.0% services, 17.0% sales, 0.0% farming, 15.0% construction, 35.0% production (2000).
Income: Per capita income: $19,285 (2007); Median household income: $39,318 (2007); Average household income: $50,195 (2007); Percent of households with income of $100,000 or more: 12.8% (2007); Poverty rate: 20.5% (2000).
Education: Percent of population age 25 and over with: High school diploma (including GED) or higher: 72.7% (2007); Bachelor's degree or higher: 3.9% (2007); Master's degree or higher: 0.0% (2007).

School District(s)

Edison Local (PK-12)
2005-06 Enrollment: 2,638 . . . . (330) 532-3199
Housing: Homeownership rate: 84.4% (2007); Median home value: $38,036 (2007); Median rent: $278 per month (2000); Median age of housing: 60+ years (2000).
Transportation: Commute to work: 91.0% car, 0.0% public transportation, 5.0% walk, 4.0% work from home (2000); Travel time to work: 14.6% less than 15 minutes, 40.6% 15 to 30 minutes, 22.9% 30 to 45 minutes, 2.1% 45 to 60 minutes, 19.8% 60 minutes or more (2000)

MINGO JUNCTION (village). Covers a land area of 2.538 square miles and a water area of 0 square miles. Located at 40.32° N. Lat.; 80.61° W. Long. Elevation is 797 feet.
History: Mingo Junction developed near Steubenville as a steel town.
Population: 4,406 (1990); 3,631 (2000); 3,355 (2007); 3,149 (2012 projected); Race: 95.5% White, 2.9% Black, 0.0% Asian, 0.8% Hispanic of any race (2007); Density: 1,321.9 persons per square mile (2007); Average household size: 2.27 (2007); Median age: 44.9 (2007); Males per 100 females: 88.4 (2007); Marriage status: 20.7% never married, 57.8% now married, 10.1% widowed, 11.4% divorced (2000); Foreign born: 0.4% (2000); Ancestry (includes multiple ancestries): 22.6% Italian, 21.2% German, 16.3% Irish, 8.0% Slovak, 7.6% English (2000).
Economy: Single-family building permits issued: 1 (2007); Multi-family building permits issued: 0 (2007); Employment by occupation: 5.3% management, 15.8% professional, 19.1% services, 30.2% sales, 0.0% farming, 7.5% construction, 22.0% production (2000).
Income: Per capita income: $19,825 (2007); Median household income: $34,844 (2007); Average household income: $45,093 (2007); Percent of households with income of $100,000 or more: 6.5% (2007); Poverty rate: 12.8% (2000).
Education: Percent of population age 25 and over with: High school diploma (including GED) or higher: 84.8% (2007); Bachelor's degree or higher: 9.0% (2007); Master's degree or higher: 1.8% (2007).

School District(s)

Indian Creek Local (PK-12)
2005-06 Enrollment: 2,375 . . . . (740) 264-3502
Housing: Homeownership rate: 73.5% (2007); Median home value: $77,207 (2007); Median rent: $259 per month (2000); Median age of housing: 46 years (2000).
Safety: Violent crime rate: 65.2 per 10,000 population; Property crime rate: 195.7 per 10,000 population (2007).
Transportation: Commute to work: 93.2% car, 0.0% public transportation, 4.0% walk, 1.9% work from home (2000); Travel time to work: 43.8% less than 15 minutes, 41.3% 15 to 30 minutes, 6.4% 30 to 45 minutes, 4.2% 45 to 60 minutes, 4.4% 60 minutes or more (2000)

MOUNT PLEASANT (village). Covers a land area of 0.250 square miles and a water area of 0 square miles. Located at 40.17° N. Lat.; 80.80° W. Long. Elevation is 1,240 feet.
History: Mount Pleasant began in the early 1800's as a Quaker community. The town was an abolitionist stronghold, and a refuge for fugitive slaves from the south long before the Civil War. The first abolitionist newspaper, the "Philanthopist," was published here in 1817 by Charles Osborn.
Population: 498 (1990); 535 (2000); 510 (2007); 480 (2012 projected); Race: 97.8% White, 0.4% Black, 1.0% Asian, 0.0% Hispanic of any race (2007); Density: 2,036.7 persons per square mile (2007); Average household size: 2.58 (2007); Median age: 42.9 (2007); Males per 100 females: 96.2 (2007); Marriage status: 23.1% never married, 63.8% now married, 7.5% widowed, 5.7% divorced (2000); Foreign born: 0.4% (2000); Ancestry (includes multiple ancestries): 20.1% Polish, 19.4% German, 16.9% Italian, 14.4% Irish, 10.0% English (2000).
Economy: Single-family building permits issued: 0 (2007); Multi-family building permits issued: 0 (2007); Employment by occupation: 6.6% management, 10.9% professional, 13.1% services, 28.4% sales, 0.0% farming, 17.9% construction, 23.1% production (2000).
Income: Per capita income: $22,848 (2007); Median household income: $55,185 (2007); Average household income: $58,851 (2007); Percent of households with income of $100,000 or more: 11.1% (2007); Poverty rate: 9.3% (2000).
Education: Percent of population age 25 and over with: High school diploma (including GED) or higher: 83.1% (2007); Bachelor's degree or higher: 5.4% (2007); Master's degree or higher: 4.3% (2007).
Housing: Homeownership rate: 87.4% (2007); Median home value: $63,421 (2007); Median rent: $294 per month (2000); Median age of housing: 60+ years (2000).

Transportation: Commute to work: 93.9% car, 0.0% public transportation, 3.5% walk, 0.9% work from home (2000); Travel time to work: 13.2% less than 15 minutes, 47.1% 15 to 30 minutes, 26.9% 30 to 45 minutes, 7.0% 45 to 60 minutes, 5.7% 60 minutes or more (2000)

NEW ALEXANDRIA (village). Covers a land area of 0.361 square miles and a water area of 0 square miles. Located at 40.29° N. Lat.; 80.67° W. Long. Elevation is 1,224 feet.

Population: 257 (1990); 222 (2000); 210 (2007); 205 (2012 projected); Race: 97.1% White, 0.0% Black, 0.0% Asian, 0.0% Hispanic of any race (2007); Density: 581.4 persons per square mile (2007); Average household size: 2.41 (2007); Median age: 45.0 (2007); Males per 100 females: 82.6 (2007); Marriage status: 15.4% never married, 67.9% now married, 7.1% widowed, 9.6% divorced (2000); Foreign born: 0.0% (2000); Ancestry (includes multiple ancestries): 26.3% Irish, 17.0% German, 11.1% English, 9.4% Polish, 8.8% Other groups (2000).

Economy: Employment by occupation: 6.6% management, 13.1% professional, 32.8% services, 8.2% sales, 0.0% farming, 18.0% construction, 21.3% production (2000).

Income: Per capita income: $18,643 (2007); Median household income: $36,563 (2007); Average household income: $45,000 (2007); Percent of households with income of $100,000 or more: 11.5% (2007); Poverty rate: 15.8% (2000).

Education: Percent of population age 25 and over with: High school diploma (including GED) or higher: 71.4% (2007); Bachelor's degree or higher: 2.5% (2007); Master's degree or higher: 0.0% (2007).

Housing: Homeownership rate: 81.6% (2007); Median home value: $52,333 (2007); Median rent: $163 per month (2000); Median age of housing: 50 years (2000).

Transportation: Commute to work: 96.4% car, 0.0% public transportation, 0.0% walk, 0.0% work from home (2000); Travel time to work: 23.6% less than 15 minutes, 56.4% 15 to 30 minutes, 14.5% 30 to 45 minutes, 5.5% 45 to 60 minutes, 0.0% 60 minutes or more (2000)

RAYLAND (village). Covers a land area of 0.434 square miles and a water area of 0 square miles. Located at 40.18° N. Lat.; 80.69° W. Long. Elevation is 679 feet.

Population: 490 (1990); 434 (2000); 372 (2007); 351 (2012 projected); Race: 98.4% White, 1.1% Black, 0.0% Asian, 0.3% Hispanic of any race (2007); Density: 856.2 persons per square mile (2007); Average household size: 2.40 (2007); Median age: 44.6 (2007); Males per 100 females: 79.7 (2007); Marriage status: 21.4% never married, 62.5% now married, 9.3% widowed, 6.8% divorced (2000); Foreign born: 0.0% (2000); Ancestry (includes multiple ancestries): 22.2% Italian, 20.6% German, 16.4% Irish, 10.9% Hungarian, 10.6% Polish (2000).

Economy: Employment by occupation: 1.3% management, 9.4% professional, 20.1% services, 28.9% sales, 0.0% farming, 14.5% construction, 25.8% production (2000).

Income: Per capita income: $17,157 (2007); Median household income: $34,375 (2007); Average household income: $41,177 (2007); Percent of households with income of $100,000 or more: 5.2% (2007); Poverty rate: 23.3% (2000).

Education: Percent of population age 25 and over with: High school diploma (including GED) or higher: 84.7% (2007); Bachelor's degree or higher: 8.2% (2007); Master's degree or higher: 2.6% (2007).

School District(s)

Buckeye Local (PK-12)
2005-06 Enrollment: 2,443 . . . . (740) 769-7395

Housing: Homeownership rate: 81.3% (2007); Median home value: $65,455 (2007); Median rent: $236 per month (2000); Median age of housing: 60+ years (2000).

Transportation: Commute to work: 97.4% car, 0.0% public transportation, 1.3% walk, 0.0% work from home (2000); Travel time to work: 27.9% less than 15 minutes, 25.3% 15 to 30 minutes, 29.9% 30 to 45 minutes, 7.1% 45 to 60 minutes, 9.7% 60 minutes or more (2000)

RICHMOND (village). Covers a land area of 0.531 square miles and a water area of 0 square miles. Located at 40.43° N. Lat.; 80.77° W. Long. Elevation is 1,243 feet.

Population: 446 (1990); 471 (2000); 360 (2007); 358 (2012 projected); Race: 97.5% White, 0.0% Black, 1.9% Asian, 0.3% Hispanic of any race (2007); Density: 677.5 persons per square mile (2007); Average household size: 2.32 (2007); Median age: 43.3 (2007); Males per 100 females: 83.7 (2007); Marriage status: 17.6% never married, 59.3% now married, 11.0% widowed, 12.1% divorced (2000); Foreign born: 0.0% (2000); Ancestry (includes multiple ancestries): 24.4% Irish, 22.8% German, 11.5% English, 11.0% Italian, 6.5% French (except Basque) (2000).

Economy: Employment by occupation: 2.6% management, 9.8% professional, 18.7% services, 21.2% sales, 0.0% farming, 15.0% construction, 32.6% production (2000).

Income: Per capita income: $16,500 (2007); Median household income: $33,036 (2007); Average household income: $38,323 (2007); Percent of households with income of $100,000 or more: 3.2% (2007); Poverty rate: 11.0% (2000).

Education: Percent of population age 25 and over with: High school diploma (including GED) or higher: 81.3% (2007); Bachelor's degree or higher: 5.9% (2007); Master's degree or higher: 2.3% (2007).

School District(s)

Edison Local (PK-12)
2005-06 Enrollment: 2,638 . . . . (330) 532-3199

Housing: Homeownership rate: 82.6% (2007); Median home value: $74,286 (2007); Median rent: $291 per month (2000); Median age of housing: 47 years (2000).

Transportation: Commute to work: 96.9% car, 0.0% public transportation, 0.0% walk, 3.1% work from home (2000); Travel time to work: 18.7% less than 15 minutes, 55.6% 15 to 30 minutes, 17.6% 30 to 45 minutes, 2.7% 45 to 60 minutes, 5.3% 60 minutes or more (2000)

SMITHFIELD (village). Covers a land area of 0.959 square miles and a water area of 0 square miles. Located at 40.27° N. Lat.; 80.78° W. Long. Elevation is 1,247 feet.

Population: 957 (1990); 867 (2000); 789 (2007); 743 (2012 projected); Race: 90.0% White, 7.4% Black, 0.0% Asian, 0.1% Hispanic of any race (2007); Density: 823.1 persons per square mile (2007); Average household size: 2.37 (2007); Median age: 41.3 (2007); Males per 100 females: 91.0 (2007); Marriage status: 19.3% never married, 58.8% now married, 8.8% widowed, 13.1% divorced (2000); Foreign born: 0.8% (2000); Ancestry (includes multiple ancestries): 19.7% Irish, 18.7% Other groups, 15.3% German, 10.1% Italian, 8.5% United States or American (2000).

Economy: Single-family building permits issued: 0 (2007); Multi-family building permits issued: 0 (2007); Employment by occupation: 5.5% management, 15.4% professional, 16.5% services, 24.0% sales, 0.0% farming, 14.2% construction, 24.4% production (2000).

Income: Per capita income: $17,447 (2007); Median household income: $27,031 (2007); Average household income: $41,111 (2007); Percent of households with income of $100,000 or more: 7.5% (2007); Poverty rate: 28.8% (2000).

Education: Percent of population age 25 and over with: High school diploma (including GED) or higher: 72.3% (2007); Bachelor's degree or higher: 4.5% (2007); Master's degree or higher: 0.9% (2007).

Housing: Homeownership rate: 67.3% (2007); Median home value: $60,714 (2007); Median rent: $267 per month (2000); Median age of housing: 53 years (2000).

Transportation: Commute to work: 93.4% car, 0.0% public transportation, 6.6% walk, 0.0% work from home (2000); Travel time to work: 19.5% less than 15 minutes, 44.4% 15 to 30 minutes, 24.1% 30 to 45 minutes, 5.8% 45 to 60 minutes, 6.2% 60 minutes or more (2000)

STEUBENVILLE (city). County seat. Covers a land area of 10.322 square miles and a water area of 0.005 square miles. Located at 40.36° N. Lat.; 80.63° W. Long. Elevation is 1,047 feet.

History: Jacob Walker came to the Ohio River in 1765. He was followed in 1786 by government scouts who selected this site for a fort, called Fort Steuben for Baron Frederick William von Steuben, a Prussian drillmaster who aided the colonies in the Revolutionary War. A community called La Belle sprang up around the fort, and when the fort was destroyed in 1790, the settlement remained. Bezaleel Wells and James Ross laid out the town in 1797. It was named Steubenville, and became the seat of Jefferson County. Industries began in the early 1800's with a pottery, a drift coal mine, nail factory and foundry. As river traffic increased, Steubenville became an important port. The Frazier, Kilgore and Company rolling mill, using the labels of Wheeling Steel and Weirton Steel, was erected in 1856.

Population: 22,298 (1990); 19,015 (2000); 18,258 (2007); 17,656 (2012 projected); Race: 79.3% White, 17.4% Black, 1.0% Asian, 1.1% Hispanic of any race (2007); Density: 1,768.8 persons per square mile (2007); Average household size: 2.22 (2007); Median age: 44.4 (2007); Males per 100 females: 86.8 (2007); Marriage status: 26.6% never married, 51.4% now married, 11.3% widowed, 10.7% divorced (2000); Foreign born: 2.4% (2000); Ancestry (includes multiple ancestries): 18.9% Italian, 18.3% Other groups, 12.9% German, 12.7% Irish, 6.9% Polish (2000).

Economy: Single-family building permits issued: 5 (2007); Multi-family building permits issued: 0 (2007); Employment by occupation: 9.4% management, 21.5% professional, 19.9% services, 27.2% sales, 0.2% farming, 7.1% construction, 14.6% production (2000).
Income: Per capita income: $21,634 (2007); Median household income: $32,034 (2007); Average household income: $46,829 (2007); Percent of households with income of $100,000 or more: 9.9% (2007); Poverty rate: 20.4% (2000).
Education: Percent of population age 25 and over with: High school diploma (including GED) or higher: 79.6% (2007); Bachelor's degree or higher: 18.1% (2007); Master's degree or higher: 7.4% (2007).

School District(s)

Edison Local (PK-12)
2005-06 Enrollment: 2,638 . . . . (330) 532-3199
Steubenville City (PK-12)
2005-06 Enrollment: 2,352 . . . . (740) 283-3767

Four-year College(s)

Franciscan University of Steubenville (Private, Not-for-profit, Roman Catholic)
Fall 2007 Enrollment: 2,434. . . . . (740) 283-3771
2007-08 Tuition: In-state $18,180; Out-of-state $18,180

Two-year College(s)

Jefferson Community College (Public)
Fall 2007 Enrollment: 1,744. . . . . (740) 264-5591
2007-08 Tuition: In-state $2,880; Out-of-state $3,690
The Ohio Academy Paul Mitchell Partner School (Private, For-profit)
Fall 2007 Enrollment: 5 . . . . (740) 282-3312
Trinity Health System School of Nursing (Private, Not-for-profit, Roman Catholic)
Fall 2007 Enrollment: 147 . . . . (740) 283-7467
2007-08 Tuition: In-state $5,034; Out-of-state $5,412

Housing: Homeownership rate: 60.4% (2007); Median home value: $83,986 (2007); Median rent: $282 per month (2000); Median age of housing: 50 years (2000).
Hospitals: Trinity Medical Center - East (401 beds); Trinity Medical Center - West (231 beds)
Safety: Violent crime rate: 41.3 per 10,000 population; Property crime rate: 486.2 per 10,000 population (2007).
Newspapers: Brooke Scene (Community news; Circulation 12,000); The Herald-Star (Local news; Circulation 19,231); Steubenville Register (Regional news; Circulation 17,600)
Transportation: Commute to work: 93.2% car, 0.9% public transportation, 3.0% walk, 2.7% work from home (2000); Travel time to work: 55.9% less than 15 minutes, 27.4% 15 to 30 minutes, 8.4% 30 to 45 minutes, 4.1% 45 to 60 minutes, 4.3% 60 minutes or more (2000)

Additional Information Contacts

City of Steubenville . . . . (740) 283-6000
http://www.ci.steubenville.oh.us
Jefferson County Chamber of Commerce . . . . (740) 282-6226
http://www.jeffersoncountychamber.com

STRATTON (village). Covers a land area of 0.532 square miles and a water area of 0 square miles. Located at 40.52° N. Lat.; 80.62° W. Long. Elevation is 659 feet.
Population: 278 (1990); 277 (2000); 233 (2007); 228 (2012 projected); Race: 96.6% White, 0.0% Black, 3.4% Asian, 0.4% Hispanic of any race (2007); Density: 438.2 persons per square mile (2007); Average household size: 1.91 (2007); Median age: 46.4 (2007); Males per 100 females: 91.0 (2007); Marriage status: 23.0% never married, 40.9% now married, 22.1% widowed, 14.0% divorced (2000); Foreign born: 0.0% (2000); Ancestry (includes multiple ancestries): 19.8% German, 16.2% Irish, 15.8% English, 10.8% United States or American, 5.4% Slovak (2000).
Economy: Single-family building permits issued: 0 (2007); Multi-family building permits issued: 0 (2007); Employment by occupation: 10.8% management, 14.4% professional, 19.8% services, 27.9% sales, 0.0% farming, 6.3% construction, 20.7% production (2000).
Income: Per capita income: $20,944 (2007); Median household income: $29,444 (2007); Average household income: $40,000 (2007); Percent of households with income of $100,000 or more: 7.4% (2007); Poverty rate: 7.6% (2000).
Education: Percent of population age 25 and over with: High school diploma (including GED) or higher: 80.2% (2007); Bachelor's degree or higher: 2.9% (2007); Master's degree or higher: 0.0% (2007).
Housing: Homeownership rate: 80.3% (2007); Median home value: $31,667 (2007); Median rent: $230 per month (2000); Median age of housing: 50 years (2000).
Transportation: Commute to work: 85.6% car, 0.0% public transportation, 11.7% walk, 2.7% work from home (2000); Travel time to work: 36.1% less than 15 minutes, 53.7% 15 to 30 minutes, 1.9% 30 to 45 minutes, 8.3% 45 to 60 minutes, 0.0% 60 minutes or more (2000)

TILTONSVILLE (village). Aka Tiltonville. Covers a land area of 0.556 square miles and a water area of 0 square miles. Located at 40.17° N. Lat.; 80.69° W. Long. Elevation is 669 feet.
Population: 1,517 (1990); 1,329 (2000); 1,212 (2007); 1,126 (2012 projected); Race: 98.8% White, 0.0% Black, 0.0% Asian, 0.2% Hispanic of any race (2007); Density: 2,181.6 persons per square mile (2007); Average household size: 2.11 (2007); Median age: 46.6 (2007); Males per 100 females: 83.1 (2007); Marriage status: 19.5% never married, 54.9% now married, 14.2% widowed, 11.5% divorced (2000); Foreign born: 1.6% (2000); Ancestry (includes multiple ancestries): 21.0% Italian, 20.9% German, 16.6% Irish, 15.9% Polish, 9.6% Hungarian (2000).
Economy: Single-family building permits issued: 0 (2007); Multi-family building permits issued: 0 (2007); Employment by occupation: 10.5% management, 14.3% professional, 16.7% services, 32.4% sales, 0.0% farming, 10.5% construction, 15.7% production (2000).
Income: Per capita income: $19,594 (2007); Median household income: $34,324 (2007); Average household income: $41,372 (2007); Percent of households with income of $100,000 or more: 6.4% (2007); Poverty rate: 13.9% (2000).
Education: Percent of population age 25 and over with: High school diploma (including GED) or higher: 81.8% (2007); Bachelor's degree or higher: 9.2% (2007); Master's degree or higher: 1.8% (2007).

School District(s)

Buckeye Local (PK-12)
2005-06 Enrollment: 2,443 . . . . (740) 769-7395

Housing: Homeownership rate: 66.6% (2007); Median home value: $68,571 (2007); Median rent: $256 per month (2000); Median age of housing: 59 years (2000).
Transportation: Commute to work: 93.1% car, 0.0% public transportation, 4.8% walk, 1.7% work from home (2000); Travel time to work: 30.1% less than 15 minutes, 48.2% 15 to 30 minutes, 12.7% 30 to 45 minutes, 3.8% 45 to 60 minutes, 5.1% 60 minutes or more (2000)

TORONTO (city). Covers a land area of 1.883 square miles and a water area of 0.004 square miles. Located at 40.46° N. Lat.; 80.60° W. Long. Elevation is 702 feet.
History: Toronto was laid out in 1818 by John Depuy when it was called Newburg, and later Sloan's Station. In 1881 it was renamed Toronto for a prominent citizen who had come from Toronto, Canada.
Population: 6,127 (1990); 5,676 (2000); 5,282 (2007); 4,959 (2012 projected); Race: 97.7% White, 0.8% Black, 0.3% Asian, 0.6% Hispanic of any race (2007); Density: 2,805.3 persons per square mile (2007); Average household size: 2.24 (2007); Median age: 41.9 (2007); Males per 100 females: 86.1 (2007); Marriage status: 21.0% never married, 57.3% now married, 10.6% widowed, 11.1% divorced (2000); Foreign born: 0.6% (2000); Ancestry (includes multiple ancestries): 19.5% German, 19.2% Irish, 13.0% United States or American, 10.5% English, 9.1% Other groups (2000).
Economy: Single-family building permits issued: 3 (2007); Multi-family building permits issued: 0 (2007); Employment by occupation: 5.1% management, 11.4% professional, 17.4% services, 29.7% sales, 0.0% farming, 12.6% construction, 23.9% production (2000).
Income: Per capita income: $18,235 (2007); Median household income: $34,944 (2007); Average household income: $40,822 (2007); Percent of households with income of $100,000 or more: 3.9% (2007); Poverty rate: 13.4% (2000).
Education: Percent of population age 25 and over with: High school diploma (including GED) or higher: 84.2% (2007); Bachelor's degree or higher: 7.8% (2007); Master's degree or higher: 2.5% (2007).

School District(s)

Toronto City (PK-12)
2005-06 Enrollment: 956 . . . . (740) 537-2456

Housing: Homeownership rate: 70.3% (2007); Median home value: $78,279 (2007); Median rent: $257 per month (2000); Median age of housing: 53 years (2000).
Transportation: Commute to work: 92.3% car, 0.0% public transportation, 5.6% walk, 1.1% work from home (2000); Travel time to work: 41.6% less

than 15 minutes, 42.5% 15 to 30 minutes, 7.9% 30 to 45 minutes, 3.9% 45 to 60 minutes, 4.1% 60 minutes or more (2000)

WINTERSVILLE (village). Covers a land area of 3.523 square miles and a water area of 0.004 square miles. Located at 40.37° N. Lat.; 80.70° W. Long. Elevation is 1,263 feet.
History: Land office here for first land sales in Northwest Territory. Incorporated 1947.
Population: 4,368 (1990); 4,067 (2000); 4,057 (2007); 4,030 (2012 projected); Race: 93.5% White, 5.5% Black, 0.1% Asian, 0.8% Hispanic of any race (2007); Density: 1,151.6 persons per square mile (2007); Average household size: 2.27 (2007); Median age: 46.8 (2007); Males per 100 females: 94.3 (2007); Marriage status: 20.5% never married, 60.4% now married, 9.5% widowed, 9.6% divorced (2000); Foreign born: 1.4% (2000); Ancestry (includes multiple ancestries): 24.0% Italian, 19.4% Irish, 19.0% German, 10.6% English, 8.6% Other groups (2000).
Economy: Single-family building permits issued: 9 (2007); Multi-family building permits issued: 40 (2007); Employment by occupation: 5.9% management, 18.5% professional, 15.4% services, 29.0% sales, 0.0% farming, 11.6% construction, 19.7% production (2000).
Income: Per capita income: $22,874 (2007); Median household income: $39,636 (2007); Average household income: $51,059 (2007); Percent of households with income of $100,000 or more: 8.8% (2007); Poverty rate: 6.9% (2000).
Education: Percent of population age 25 and over with: High school diploma (including GED) or higher: 86.7% (2007); Bachelor's degree or higher: 16.5% (2007); Master's degree or higher: 5.2% (2007).

School District(s)

Indian Creek Local (PK-12)
2005-06 Enrollment: 2,375 . . . . (740) 264-3502
Housing: Homeownership rate: 71.8% (2007); Median home value: $97,400 (2007); Median rent: $377 per month (2000); Median age of housing: 39 years (2000).
Safety: Violent crime rate: 0.0 per 10,000 population; Property crime rate: 228.0 per 10,000 population (2007).
Transportation: Commute to work: 95.4% car, 0.4% public transportation, 0.5% walk, 3.0% work from home (2000); Travel time to work: 37.4% less than 15 minutes, 47.9% 15 to 30 minutes, 6.9% 30 to 45 minutes, 4.2% 45 to 60 minutes, 3.6% 60 minutes or more (2000)

YORKVILLE (village). Covers a land area of 0.611 square miles and a water area of 0 square miles. Located at 40.15° N. Lat.; 80.70° W. Long.
History: Yorkville grew around the Wheeling Steel Corporation's mill. It was named for York, Pennsylvania, the former home of many of the early settlers.
Population: 1,246 (1990); 1,230 (2000); 1,150 (2007); 1,092 (2012 projected); Race: 96.8% White, 1.6% Black, 0.0% Asian, 0.6% Hispanic of any race (2007); Density: 1,882.0 persons per square mile (2007); Average household size: 2.25 (2007); Median age: 43.6 (2007); Males per 100 females: 95.6 (2007); Marriage status: 22.2% never married, 51.5% now married, 12.0% widowed, 14.3% divorced (2000); Foreign born: 2.3% (2000); Ancestry (includes multiple ancestries): 25.4% Italian, 19.1% German, 16.4% Irish, 12.5% Polish, 7.8% Hungarian (2000).
Economy: Single-family building permits issued: 0 (2007); Multi-family building permits issued: 0 (2007); Employment by occupation: 7.1% management, 19.7% professional, 19.1% services, 24.1% sales, 0.0% farming, 6.6% construction, 23.4% production (2000).
Income: Per capita income: $19,841 (2007); Median household income: $36,218 (2007); Average household income: $44,247 (2007); Percent of households with income of $100,000 or more: 6.3% (2007); Poverty rate: 10.0% (2000).
Education: Percent of population age 25 and over with: High school diploma (including GED) or higher: 84.5% (2007); Bachelor's degree or higher: 14.0% (2007); Master's degree or higher: 4.1% (2007).

School District(s)

Buckeye Local (PK-12)
2005-06 Enrollment: 2,443 . . . . (740) 769-7395
Housing: Homeownership rate: 60.7% (2007); Median home value: $68,276 (2007); Median rent: $290 per month (2000); Median age of housing: 49 years (2000).
Transportation: Commute to work: 88.2% car, 1.4% public transportation, 8.1% walk, 1.6% work from home (2000); Travel time to work: 32.1% less than 15 minutes, 47.1% 15 to 30 minutes, 13.0% 30 to 45 minutes, 3.8% 45 to 60 minutes, 4.0% 60 minutes or more (2000)

Knox County

Located in central Ohio; drained by the Kokosing and Mohican Rivers and the North Fork of the Licking River. Covers a land area of 527.12 square miles, a water area of 2.41 square miles, and is located in the Eastern Time Zone. The county was founded in 1808. County seat is Mount Vernon.

Knox County is part of the Mount Vernon, OH Micropolitan Statistical Area. The entire metro area includes: Knox County, OH

Weather Station: Centerburg 2 SE Elevation: 1,204 feet

	Jan	Feb	Mar	Apr	May	Jun	Jul	Aug	Sep	Oct	Nov	Dec
High	32	36	47	60	70	79	82	81	74	62	49	37
Low	16	19	28	38	48	57	61	60	52	40	32	22
Precip	2.5	2.1	3.0	3.7	4.0	4.6	4.6	3.9	3.2	2.8	3.6	3.0
Snow	na	3.2	na	0.3	tr	0.0	0.0	0.0	0.0	tr	0.9	na

High and Low temperatures in degrees Fahrenheit; Precipitation and Snow in inches

Weather Station: Danville 2 W Elevation: 967 feet

	Jan	Feb	Mar	Apr	May	Jun	Jul	Aug	Sep	Oct	Nov	Dec
High	34	38	50	62	72	80	84	83	76	64	51	40
Low	16	18	27	35	45	54	58	57	49	38	30	22
Precip	2.6	2.4	3.1	3.7	4.2	4.7	4.3	3.8	3.3	2.7	3.4	3.1
Snow	12.4	8.4	4.6	1.3	tr	0.0	0.0	0.0	0.0	tr	1.8	7.0

High and Low temperatures in degrees Fahrenheit; Precipitation and Snow in inches

Weather Station: Fredericktown 4 S Elevation: 1,049 feet

	Jan	Feb	Mar	Apr	May	Jun	Jul	Aug	Sep	Oct	Nov	Dec
High	32	37	47	60	70	79	83	81	75	63	50	39
Low	13	16	26	35	45	55	58	56	49	38	30	22
Precip	2.6	2.1	3.0	3.6	4.3	4.4	4.2	3.7	3.3	2.6	3.3	2.9
Snow	7.8	5.3	3.1	0.7	tr	0.0	0.0	0.0	0.0	0.0	1.0	3.5

High and Low temperatures in degrees Fahrenheit; Precipitation and Snow in inches

Population: 47,473 (1990); 54,500 (2000); 59,402 (2007); 62,545 (2012 projected); Race: 97.3% White, 1.0% Black, 0.5% Asian, 0.8% Hispanic of any race (2007); Density: 112.7 persons per square mile (2007); Average household size: 2.71 (2007); Median age: 37.0 (2007); Males per 100 females: 95.2 (2007).
Religion: Five largest groups: 7.7% The United Methodist Church, 5.7% Catholic Church, 5.6% Christian Churches and Churches of Christ, 3.6% Church of the Nazarene, 2.0% American Baptist Churches in the USA (2000).
Economy: Unemployment rate: 6.5% (6/2008); Total civilian labor force: 31,202 (6/2008); Leading industries: 25.5% manufacturing; 13.4% educational services; 12.6% health care and social assistance (2005); Farms: 1,258 totaling 209,067 acres (2002); Companies that employ 500 or more persons: 7 (2006); Companies that employ 100 to 499 persons: 22 (2006); Companies that employ less than 100 persons: 1,090 (2006); Black-owned businesses: n/a (2002); Hispanic-owned businesses: n/a (2002); Asian-owned businesses: n/a (2002); Women-owned businesses: 1,050 (2002); Retail sales per capita: $9,437 (2008). Single-family building permits issued: 200 (2007); Multi-family building permits issued: 9 (2007).
Income: Per capita income: $21,116 (2007); Median household income: $45,845 (2007); Average household income: $56,266 (2007); Percent of households with income of $100,000 or more: 11.7% (2007); Poverty rate: 11.6% (2005); Bankruptcy rate: 3.14% (2007).
Education: Percent of population age 25 and over with: High school diploma (including GED) or higher: 81.9% (2007); Bachelor's degree or higher: 16.5% (2007); Master's degree or higher: 6.1% (2007).
Housing: Homeownership rate: 76.3% (2007); Median home value: $128,849 (2007); Median rent: $360 per month (2000); Median age of housing: 37 years (2000).
Health: Birth rate: 131.3 per 10,000 population (2007); Death rate: 101.3 per 10,000 population (2007); Age-adjusted cancer mortality rate: 190.4 deaths per 100,000 population (2005); Air Quality Index: 73.5% good, 24.2% moderate, 2.3% unhealthy for sensitive individuals, 0.0% unhealthy (percent of days in 2007); Number of physicians: 12.2 per 10,000 population (2005); Hospital beds: 14.1 per 10,000 population (2004); Hospital admissions: 673.7 per 10,000 population (2004).
Elections: 2004 Presidential election results: 63.1% Bush, 36.3% Kerry, 0.0% Nader, 0.3% Badnarik
National and State Parks: Knox Lake State Wildlife Area
Additional Information Contacts
Knox County Government . . . . (740) 393-6703
http://www.co.knox.oh.us

City of Mount Vernon . . . . (740) 393-9517
http://www.mountvernonohio.org
Knox County Convention & Visitors Bureau . . . . (740) 392-6102
http://www.visitknoxohio.org
Mount Vernon-Knox County Chamber of Commerce . . . . . (740) 393-1111
http://www.knoxchamber.com

Knox County Communities

BRINKHAVEN (unincorporated postal area, zip code 43006). Aka Brink Haven. Covers a land area of 20.423 square miles and a water area of 0 square miles. Located at 40.47° N. Lat.; 82.19° W. Long. Elevation is 920 feet.

Population: 597 (2000); Race: 99.2% White, 0.0% Black, 0.0% Asian, 0.3% Hispanic of any race (2000); Density: 29.2 persons per square mile (2000); Age: 27.8% under 18, 12.3% over 64 (2000); Marriage status: 19.0% never married, 66.4% now married, 4.5% widowed, 10.1% divorced (2000); Foreign born: 0.0% (2000); Ancestry (includes multiple ancestries): 18.0% German, 17.5% United States or American, 11.7% English, 6.6% Other groups, 5.2% Irish (2000).

Economy: Employment by occupation: 6.6% management, 5.1% professional, 20.6% services, 12.9% sales, 5.1% farming, 9.6% construction, 40.1% production (2000).

Income: Per capita income: $13,105 (2000); Median household income: $37,885 (2000); Poverty rate: 16.0% (2000).

Education: Percent of population age 25 and over with: High school diploma (including GED) or higher: 77.2% (2000); Bachelor's degree or higher: 6.4% (2000).

Housing: Homeownership rate: 85.3% (2000); Median home value: $64,600 (2000); Median rent: $208 per month (2000); Median age of housing: 47 years (2000).

Transportation: Commute to work: 95.1% car, 0.0% public transportation, 1.9% walk, 3.0% work from home (2000); Travel time to work: 19.8% less than 15 minutes, 23.3% 15 to 30 minutes, 28.0% 30 to 45 minutes, 10.5% 45 to 60 minutes, 18.3% 60 minutes or more (2000)

CENTERBURG (village). Covers a land area of 0.643 square miles and a water area of 0 square miles. Located at 40.30° N. Lat.; 82.69° W. Long. Elevation is 1,220 feet.

History: Centerburg was settled in 1806 and named for its position near the geographical center of the state.

Population: 1,311 (1990); 1,432 (2000); 1,557 (2007); 1,631 (2012 projected); Race: 98.0% White, 0.5% Black, 0.2% Asian, 0.1% Hispanic of any race (2007); Density: 2,423.1 persons per square mile (2007); Average household size: 2.82 (2007); Median age: 36.5 (2007); Males per 100 females: 100.1 (2007); Marriage status: 21.7% never married, 61.2% now married, 7.2% widowed, 9.9% divorced (2000); Foreign born: 0.2% (2000); Ancestry (includes multiple ancestries): 20.0% German, 17.0% English, 13.1% United States or American, 13.0% Irish, 8.8% Other groups (2000).

Economy: Single-family building permits issued: 7 (2007); Multi-family building permits issued: 0 (2007); Employment by occupation: 10.2% management, 14.9% professional, 16.6% services, 27.2% sales, 1.3% farming, 14.7% construction, 15.2% production (2000).

Income: Per capita income: $20,133 (2007); Median household income: $47,697 (2007); Average household income: $55,231 (2007); Percent of households with income of $100,000 or more: 9.0% (2007); Poverty rate: 5.6% (2000).

Education: Percent of population age 25 and over with: High school diploma (including GED) or higher: 77.7% (2007); Bachelor's degree or higher: 11.5% (2007); Master's degree or higher: 3.7% (2007).

School District(s)

Centerburg Local (PK-12)
2005-06 Enrollment: 1,194 . . . . (740) 625-6346

Housing: Homeownership rate: 62.0% (2007); Median home value: $131,094 (2007); Median rent: $409 per month (2000); Median age of housing: 56 years (2000).

Transportation: Commute to work: 92.8% car, 0.0% public transportation, 3.3% walk, 3.1% work from home (2000); Travel time to work: 17.5% less than 15 minutes, 21.6% 15 to 30 minutes, 30.0% 30 to 45 minutes, 23.3% 45 to 60 minutes, 7.6% 60 minutes or more (2000)

DANVILLE (village). Covers a land area of 0.537 square miles and a water area of 0 square miles. Located at 40.44° N. Lat.; 82.26° W. Long. Elevation is 994 feet.

Population: 1,034 (1990); 1,104 (2000); 1,088 (2007); 1,106 (2012 projected); Race: 97.9% White, 0.2% Black, 0.4% Asian, 0.5% Hispanic of any race (2007); Density: 2,025.3 persons per square mile (2007); Average household size: 2.48 (2007); Median age: 33.6 (2007); Males per 100 females: 99.3 (2007); Marriage status: 18.6% never married, 59.1% now married, 9.1% widowed, 13.2% divorced (2000); Foreign born: 0.5% (2000); Ancestry (includes multiple ancestries): 19.7% United States or American, 16.8% German, 10.6% Irish, 9.9% English, 5.1% Other groups (2000).

Economy: Single-family building permits issued: 0 (2007); Multi-family building permits issued: 0 (2007); Employment by occupation: 7.5% management, 12.8% professional, 15.3% services, 21.9% sales, 1.8% farming, 11.2% construction, 29.6% production (2000).

Income: Per capita income: $16,515 (2007); Median household income: $32,326 (2007); Average household income: $40,742 (2007); Percent of households with income of $100,000 or more: 5.7% (2007); Poverty rate: 15.2% (2000).

Education: Percent of population age 25 and over with: High school diploma (including GED) or higher: 76.8% (2007); Bachelor's degree or higher: 10.8% (2007); Master's degree or higher: 2.9% (2007).

School District(s)

Danville Local (PK-12)
2005-06 Enrollment: 675 . . . . (740) 599-6116

Housing: Homeownership rate: 62.1% (2007); Median home value: $100,316 (2007); Median rent: $319 per month (2000); Median age of housing: 46 years (2000).

Safety: Violent crime rate: 0.0 per 10,000 population; Property crime rate: 120.3 per 10,000 population (2007).

Transportation: Commute to work: 90.0% car, 0.2% public transportation, 7.0% walk, 2.1% work from home (2000); Travel time to work: 30.5% less than 15 minutes, 31.0% 15 to 30 minutes, 25.7% 30 to 45 minutes, 4.3% 45 to 60 minutes, 8.6% 60 minutes or more (2000)

FREDERICKTOWN (village). Covers a land area of 1.412 square miles and a water area of 0.035 square miles. Located at 40.48° N. Lat.; 82.54° W. Long. Elevation is 1,099 feet.

Population: 2,541 (1990); 2,428 (2000); 2,352 (2007); 2,353 (2012 projected); Race: 98.6% White, 0.3% Black, 0.0% Asian, 0.5% Hispanic of any race (2007); Density: 1,665.5 persons per square mile (2007); Average household size: 2.32 (2007); Median age: 36.4 (2007); Males per 100 females: 96.0 (2007); Marriage status: 16.6% never married, 59.1% now married, 9.7% widowed, 14.6% divorced (2000); Foreign born: 0.6% (2000); Ancestry (includes multiple ancestries): 22.8% German, 15.9% United States or American, 11.5% Irish, 10.8% English, 4.6% Other groups (2000).

Economy: Single-family building permits issued: 5 (2007); Multi-family building permits issued: 0 (2007); Employment by occupation: 9.5% management, 17.0% professional, 14.6% services, 26.1% sales, 0.0% farming, 7.8% construction, 25.1% production (2000).

Income: Per capita income: $21,509 (2007); Median household income: $41,992 (2007); Average household income: $49,941 (2007); Percent of households with income of $100,000 or more: 9.4% (2007); Poverty rate: 7.1% (2000).

Education: Percent of population age 25 and over with: High school diploma (including GED) or higher: 82.4% (2007); Bachelor's degree or higher: 16.4% (2007); Master's degree or higher: 5.3% (2007).

School District(s)

Fredericktown Local (PK-12)
2005-06 Enrollment: 1,211 . . . . (740) 694-2956

Housing: Homeownership rate: 71.0% (2007); Median home value: $108,920 (2007); Median rent: $374 per month (2000); Median age of housing: 45 years (2000).

Safety: Violent crime rate: 0.0 per 10,000 population; Property crime rate: 275.5 per 10,000 population (2007).

Newspapers: Knox County Citizen (Community news; Circulation 1,500)

Transportation: Commute to work: 93.9% car, 0.0% public transportation, 2.2% walk, 2.9% work from home (2000); Travel time to work: 28.7% less than 15 minutes, 44.8% 15 to 30 minutes, 14.4% 30 to 45 minutes, 2.5% 45 to 60 minutes, 9.6% 60 minutes or more (2000)

GAMBIER (village). Covers a land area of 0.936 square miles and a water area of 0 square miles. Located at 40.37° N. Lat.; 82.39° W. Long. Elevation is 1,079 feet.

History: Gambier was the site of the founding of Kenyon College, established in 1824 by Philander Chase, first Episcopal bishop of Ohio, as

a Theological Seminary. The college was located on land donated by Lord Gambier, for whom the town was named.
Population: 2,073 (1990); 1,871 (2000); 1,820 (2007); 1,817 (2012 projected); Race: 93.2% White, 4.0% Black, 0.9% Asian, 2.1% Hispanic of any race (2007); Density: 1,944.0 persons per square mile (2007); Average household size: 6.74 (2007); Median age: 20.9 (2007); Males per 100 females: 81.3 (2007); Marriage status: 79.0% never married, 15.6% now married, 1.9% widowed, 3.5% divorced (2000); Foreign born: 1.2% (2000); Ancestry (includes multiple ancestries): 10.4% German, 7.4% English, 5.6% Irish, 2.3% Other groups, 2.0% United States or American (2000).
Economy: Single-family building permits issued: 1 (2007); Multi-family building permits issued: 0 (2007); Employment by occupation: 9.5% management, 41.9% professional, 9.1% services, 33.2% sales, 0.3% farming, 2.7% construction, 3.2% production (2000).
Income: Per capita income: $11,789 (2007); Median household income: $63,750 (2007); Average household income: $66,519 (2007); Percent of households with income of $100,000 or more: 20.7% (2007); Poverty rate: 8.0% (2000).
Education: Percent of population age 25 and over with: High school diploma (including GED) or higher: 89.3% (2007); Bachelor's degree or higher: 55.9% (2007); Master's degree or higher: 36.2% (2007).

School District(s)

Mount Vernon City (PK-12)
2005-06 Enrollment: 4,200 . . . . (740) 397-7422

Four-year College(s)

Kenyon College (Private, Not-for-profit)
Fall 2007 Enrollment: 1,662. . . . . (740) 427-5000
2007-08 Tuition: In-state $38,140; Out-of-state $38,140
Housing: Homeownership rate: 57.0% (2007); Median home value: $152,500 (2007); Median rent: $429 per month (2000); Median age of housing: 41 years (2000).
Transportation: Commute to work: 48.7% car, 0.0% public transportation, 49.2% walk, 1.6% work from home (2000); Travel time to work: 80.9% less than 15 minutes, 13.2% 15 to 30 minutes, 1.0% 30 to 45 minutes, 1.0% 45 to 60 minutes, 3.9% 60 minutes or more (2000)

GANN (village). Aka Brinkhaven. Covers a land area of 0.191 square miles and a water area of 0 square miles. Located at 40.46° N. Lat.; 82.19° W. Long. Elevation is 902 feet.
Population: 179 (1990); 143 (2000); 146 (2007); 146 (2012 projected); Race: 100.0% White, 0.0% Black, 0.0% Asian, 1.4% Hispanic of any race (2007); Density: 765.3 persons per square mile (2007); Average household size: 2.81 (2007); Median age: 32.1 (2007); Males per 100 females: 92.1 (2007); Marriage status: 27.7% never married, 57.1% now married, 5.4% widowed, 9.8% divorced (2000); Foreign born: 0.0% (2000); Ancestry (includes multiple ancestries): 17.7% United States or American, 10.2% German, 8.2% Italian, 4.8% Canadian, 4.8% Irish (2000).
Economy: Employment by occupation: 0.0% management, 4.3% professional, 34.3% services, 7.1% sales, 12.9% farming, 0.0% construction, 41.4% production (2000).
Income: Per capita income: $14,127 (2007); Median household income: $41,250 (2007); Average household income: $39,663 (2007); Percent of households with income of $100,000 or more: 0.0% (2007); Poverty rate: 17.7% (2000).
Education: Percent of population age 25 and over with: High school diploma (including GED) or higher: 72.8% (2007); Bachelor's degree or higher: 3.3% (2007); Master's degree or higher: 0.0% (2007).
Housing: Homeownership rate: 76.9% (2007); Median home value: $55,000 (2007); Median rent: $125 per month (2000); Median age of housing: 60+ years (2000).
Transportation: Commute to work: 100.0% car, 0.0% public transportation, 0.0% walk, 0.0% work from home (2000); Travel time to work: 19.1% less than 15 minutes, 33.8% 15 to 30 minutes, 30.9% 30 to 45 minutes, 2.9% 45 to 60 minutes, 13.2% 60 minutes or more (2000)

HOWARD (unincorporated postal area, zip code 43028). Covers a land area of 51.489 square miles and a water area of 0.824 square miles. Located at 40.42° N. Lat.; 82.31° W. Long. Elevation is 930 feet.
Population: 5,564 (2000); Race: 98.7% White, 0.3% Black, 0.2% Asian, 0.0% Hispanic of any race (2000); Density: 108.1 persons per square mile (2000); Age: 22.8% under 18, 13.2% over 64 (2000); Marriage status: 15.4% never married, 70.8% now married, 4.8% widowed, 9.0% divorced (2000); Foreign born: 1.0% (2000); Ancestry (includes multiple ancestries): 27.9% German, 13.3% Irish, 12.4% United States or American, 11.1% English, 5.6% Other groups (2000).
Economy: Employment by occupation: 7.7% management, 20.0% professional, 11.6% services, 27.3% sales, 0.8% farming, 14.1% construction, 18.4% production (2000).
Income: Per capita income: $21,519 (2000); Median household income: $46,344 (2000); Poverty rate: 5.5% (2000).
Education: Percent of population age 25 and over with: High school diploma (including GED) or higher: 86.9% (2000); Bachelor's degree or higher: 18.3% (2000).

School District(s)

East Knox Local (PK-12)
2005-06 Enrollment: 1,235 . . . . (740) 599-7493
Housing: Homeownership rate: 91.7% (2000); Median home value: $104,200 (2000); Median rent: $422 per month (2000); Median age of housing: 14 years (2000).
Transportation: Commute to work: 94.3% car, 0.8% public transportation, 0.7% walk, 3.6% work from home (2000); Travel time to work: 16.0% less than 15 minutes, 48.7% 15 to 30 minutes, 10.8% 30 to 45 minutes, 4.8% 45 to 60 minutes, 19.8% 60 minutes or more (2000)

MARTINSBURG (village). Covers a land area of 0.180 square miles and a water area of 0 square miles. Located at 40.27° N. Lat.; 82.35° W. Long. Elevation is 1,175 feet.
Population: 213 (1990); 185 (2000); 197 (2007); 205 (2012 projected); Race: 100.0% White, 0.0% Black, 0.0% Asian, 0.0% Hispanic of any race (2007); Density: 1,092.8 persons per square mile (2007); Average household size: 2.46 (2007); Median age: 38.0 (2007); Males per 100 females: 91.3 (2007); Marriage status: 16.4% never married, 56.6% now married, 13.1% widowed, 13.9% divorced (2000); Foreign born: 0.0% (2000); Ancestry (includes multiple ancestries): 21.7% German, 14.0% English, 12.1% United States or American, 8.9% Other groups, 3.2% Dutch (2000).
Economy: Employment by occupation: 0.0% management, 12.7% professional, 9.5% services, 19.0% sales, 0.0% farming, 17.5% construction, 41.3% production (2000).
Income: Per capita income: $14,784 (2007); Median household income: $40,714 (2007); Average household income: $36,406 (2007); Percent of households with income of $100,000 or more: 1.3% (2007); Poverty rate: 14.0% (2000).
Education: Percent of population age 25 and over with: High school diploma (including GED) or higher: 66.9% (2007); Bachelor's degree or higher: 0.0% (2007); Master's degree or higher: 0.0% (2007).
Housing: Homeownership rate: 70.0% (2007); Median home value: $78,667 (2007); Median rent: $367 per month (2000); Median age of housing: 60+ years (2000).
Transportation: Commute to work: 100.0% car, 0.0% public transportation, 0.0% walk, 0.0% work from home (2000); Travel time to work: 4.8% less than 15 minutes, 33.9% 15 to 30 minutes, 30.6% 30 to 45 minutes, 4.8% 45 to 60 minutes, 25.8% 60 minutes or more (2000)

MOUNT VERNON (city). County seat. Covers a land area of 8.404 square miles and a water area of 0.040 square miles. Located at 40.39° N. Lat.; 82.48° W. Long. Elevation is 1,001 feet.
History: Mount Vernon was laid out in 1805 by Benjamin Butler, Thomas Patterson, and Joseph Walker, all of whom became prominent citizens here. The town developed as a rural commercial center, and later as a manufacturer of steam, diesel, and gas engines. John Chapman, known as Johnny Appleseed, owned lots in Mount Vernon. This was the birthplace of Daniel Decatur Emmett (1815-1904) who wrote the song "Dixie."
Population: 15,215 (1990); 14,375 (2000); 14,859 (2007); 15,140 (2012 projected); Race: 96.1% White, 1.5% Black, 0.8% Asian, 1.1% Hispanic of any race (2007); Density: 1,768.0 persons per square mile (2007); Average household size: 2.31 (2007); Median age: 37.4 (2007); Males per 100 females: 87.7 (2007); Marriage status: 23.3% never married, 52.7% now married, 9.4% widowed, 14.6% divorced (2000); Foreign born: 1.6% (2000); Ancestry (includes multiple ancestries): 19.7% German, 15.6% United States or American, 12.5% Irish, 10.3% English, 8.1% Other groups (2000).
Economy: Single-family building permits issued: 49 (2007); Multi-family building permits issued: 0 (2007); Employment by occupation: 9.3% management, 17.0% professional, 20.4% services, 23.1% sales, 0.9% farming, 7.8% construction, 21.5% production (2000).
Income: Per capita income: $19,050 (2007); Median household income: $33,596 (2007); Average household income: $43,391 (2007); Percent of households with income of $100,000 or more: 6.5% (2007); Poverty rate: 15.6% (2000).

Education: Percent of population age 25 and over with: High school diploma (including GED) or higher: 80.2% (2007); Bachelor's degree or higher: 18.2% (2007); Master's degree or higher: 7.3% (2007).

School District(s)

Knox County (PK-12)
2005-06 Enrollment: n/a . . . . (740) 397-5820
Mount Vernon City (PK-12)
2005-06 Enrollment: 4,200 . . . . (740) 397-7422

Four-year College(s)

Mount Vernon Nazarene University (Private, Not-for-profit, Church of the Nazarene)
Fall 2007 Enrollment: 2,675. . . . . (740) 392-6868
2007-08 Tuition: In-state $18,064; Out-of-state $18,064

Vocational/Technical School(s)

Knox County Career Center (Public)
Fall 2007 Enrollment: 110 . . . . (740) 393-2933
2007-08 Tuition: $10,630

Housing: Homeownership rate: 56.8% (2007); Median home value: $105,029 (2007); Median rent: $353 per month (2000); Median age of housing: 48 years (2000).
Hospitals: Knox Community Hospital (115 beds)
Newspapers: Mount Vernon News (Local news; Circulation 10,300)
Transportation: Commute to work: 91.2% car, 1.7% public transportation, 2.8% walk, 3.3% work from home (2000); Travel time to work: 58.5% less than 15 minutes, 18.2% 15 to 30 minutes, 7.0% 30 to 45 minutes, 7.2% 45 to 60 minutes, 9.2% 60 minutes or more (2000)
Airports: Knox County (general aviation)

Additional Information Contacts

City of Mount Vernon . . . . (740) 393-9517
http://www.mountvernonohio.org
Knox County Convention & Visitors Bureau . . . . (740) 392-6102
http://www.visitknoxohio.org
Mount Vernon-Knox County Chamber of Commerce . . . . . (740) 393-1111
http://www.knoxchamber.com

Lake County

Located in northeastern Ohio; bounded on the north by Lake Erie; drained by the Grand and Chagrin Rivers. Covers a land area of 228.21 square miles, a water area of 750.65 square miles, and is located in the Eastern Time Zone. The county was founded in 1840. County seat is Painesville.

Lake County is part of the Cleveland-Elyria-Mentor, OH Metropolitan Statistical Area. The entire metro area includes: Cuyahoga County, OH; Geauga County, OH; Lake County, OH; Lorain County, OH; Medina County, OH

Weather Station: Painesville 4 NW Elevation: 597 feet

	Jan	Feb	Mar	Apr	May	Jun	Jul	Aug	Sep	Oct	Nov	Dec
High	34	37	46	56	68	77	81	80	74	63	51	40
Low	20	21	29	39	50	59	64	63	57	46	37	27
Precip	2.3	1.8	2.8	3.2	3.0	3.8	3.1	3.7	4.1	3.3	3.5	2.9
Snow	10.2	7.3	5.2	1.2	tr	0.0	0.0	0.0	0.0	tr	2.1	8.8

High and Low temperatures in degrees Fahrenheit; Precipitation and Snow in inches

Population: 215,499 (1990); 227,511 (2000); 233,551 (2007); 236,710 (2012 projected); Race: 93.7% White, 2.7% Black, 1.2% Asian, 2.7% Hispanic of any race (2007); Density: 1,023.4 persons per square mile (2007); Average household size: 2.47 (2007); Median age: 41.0 (2007); Males per 100 females: 95.3 (2007).
Religion: Five largest groups: 35.7% Catholic Church, 4.0% The United Methodist Church, 1.6% Lutheran Church—Missouri Synod, 1.3% Southern Baptist Convention, 1.3% United Church of Christ (2000).
Economy: Unemployment rate: 6.9% (6/2008); Total civilian labor force: 133,770 (6/2008); Leading industries: 22.9% manufacturing; 16.5% retail trade; 12.0% health care and social assistance (2005); Farms: 333 totaling 19,785 acres (2002); Companies that employ 500 or more persons: 7 (2006); Companies that employ 100 to 499 persons: 142 (2006); Companies that employ less than 100 persons: 6,384 (2006); Black-owned businesses: n/a (2002); Hispanic-owned businesses: n/a (2002); Asian-owned businesses: 178 (2002); Women-owned businesses: 3,487 (2002); Retail sales per capita: $20,567 (2008). Single-family building permits issued: 514 (2007); Multi-family building permits issued: 131 (2007).
Income: Per capita income: $26,910 (2007); Median household income: $54,086 (2007); Average household income: $65,836 (2007); Percent of households with income of $100,000 or more: 16.5% (2007); Poverty rate: 7.8% (2005); Bankruptcy rate: 3.60% (2007).
Taxes: Total county taxes per capita: $328 (2006); County property taxes per capita: $209 (2006).
Education: Percent of population age 25 and over with: High school diploma (including GED) or higher: 86.4% (2007); Bachelor's degree or higher: 21.7% (2007); Master's degree or higher: 7.0% (2007).
Housing: Homeownership rate: 77.8% (2007); Median home value: $159,057 (2007); Median rent: $553 per month (2000); Median age of housing: 34 years (2000).
Health: Birth rate: 111.2 per 10,000 population (2007); Death rate: 93.9 per 10,000 population (2007); Age-adjusted cancer mortality rate: 201.8 deaths per 100,000 population (2005); Air Quality Index: 77.5% good, 20.5% moderate, 1.9% unhealthy for sensitive individuals, 0.0% unhealthy (percent of days in 2007); Number of physicians: 15.9 per 10,000 population (2005); Hospital beds: 19.5 per 10,000 population (2004); Hospital admissions: 825.7 per 10,000 population (2004).
Elections: 2004 Presidential election results: 51.1% Bush, 48.5% Kerry, 0.0% Nader, 0.3% Badnarik
National and State Parks: Chaplin State Forest; Headlands Beach State Park; James A Garfield National Historic Site; Mentor Marsh State Nature Preserve

Additional Information Contacts

Lake County Government . . . . (440) 350-2500
http://www.lakecountyohio.org
City of Eastlake . . . . (440) 951-1416
http://www.eastlakeohio.com
City of Kirtland . . . . (440) 256-3332
http://kirtlandohio.com
City of Mentor. . . . . (440) 255-1100
http://www.cityofmentor.com
City of Painesville. . . . . (440) 352-9301
http://www.painesville.com
City of Wickliffe . . . . (440) 943-7100
http://www.cityofwickliffe.com
City of Willoughby . . . . (440) 951-2800
http://www.willoughbyohio.com
City of Willowick. . . . . (440) 585-3700
http://www.cityofwillowick.com
Madison-Perry Area Chamber of Commerce. . . . . (440) 428-3760
http://www.mpacc.org
Mentor Area Chamber of Commerce. . . . . (440) 255-1616
http://www.mentorchamber.org
Painesville Area Chamber of Commerce. . . . . (440) 357-7572
http://www.painesvilleohchamber.org
Village of Madison . . . . (440) 428-7526
http://www.madisonvillage.org
Village of North Perry. . . . . (440) 259-4994
http://www.northperry.org
Wickliffe Chamber of Commerce . . . . (440) 943-1134
http://www.westernlakecountychamber.org
Willoughby Area Chamber of Commerce . . . . (440) 942-1632
http://www.willoughbyareachamber.com

Lake County Communities

EASTLAKE (city). Covers a land area of 6.397 square miles and a water area of 0.121 square miles. Located at 41.66° N. Lat.; 81.43° W. Long. Elevation is 620 feet.
Population: 21,161 (1990); 20,255 (2000); 19,633 (2007); 19,138 (2012 projected); Race: 96.5% White, 0.9% Black, 1.3% Asian, 1.1% Hispanic of any race (2007); Density: 3,069.3 persons per square mile (2007); Average household size: 2.42 (2007); Median age: 40.4 (2007); Males per 100 females: 96.0 (2007); Marriage status: 25.3% never married, 57.6% now married, 6.8% widowed, 10.4% divorced (2000); Foreign born: 5.0% (2000); Ancestry (includes multiple ancestries): 24.3% German, 20.3% Irish, 17.0% Italian, 9.8% English, 9.6% Polish (2000).
Economy: Single-family building permits issued: 6 (2007); Multi-family building permits issued: 0 (2007); Employment by occupation: 8.6% management, 15.2% professional, 14.4% services, 28.7% sales, 0.0% farming, 10.2% construction, 23.0% production (2000).
Income: Per capita income: $22,981 (2007); Median household income: $47,332 (2007); Average household income: $55,501 (2007); Percent of households with income of $100,000 or more: 10.2% (2007); Poverty rate: 5.0% (2000).

Taxes: Total city taxes per capita: $588 (2006); City property taxes per capita: $239 (2006).
Education: Percent of population age 25 and over with: High school diploma (including GED) or higher: 82.8% (2007); Bachelor's degree or higher: 12.6% (2007); Master's degree or higher: 3.4% (2007).

School District(s)

Willoughby-Eastlake City (PK-12)
2005-06 Enrollment: 8,826 . . . . (440) 946-5000
Housing: Homeownership rate: 77.4% (2007); Median home value: $137,043 (2007); Median rent: $538 per month (2000); Median age of housing: 35 years (2000).
Safety: Violent crime rate: 14.3 per 10,000 population; Property crime rate: 227.7 per 10,000 population (2007).
Transportation: Commute to work: 95.6% car, 1.0% public transportation, 1.2% walk, 1.6% work from home (2000); Travel time to work: 31.1% less than 15 minutes, 45.2% 15 to 30 minutes, 15.9% 30 to 45 minutes, 4.4% 45 to 60 minutes, 3.4% 60 minutes or more (2000)
Additional Information Contacts
City of Eastlake . . . . (440) 951-1416
http://www.eastlakeohio.com
Wickliffe Chamber of Commerce . . . . (440) 943-1134
http://www.westernlakecountychamber.org

FAIRPORT HARBOR (village). Aka Fairport. Covers a land area of 1.042 square miles and a water area of 0.078 square miles. Located at 41.75° N. Lat.; 81.27° W. Long. Elevation is 610 feet.
History: Fairport Harbor grew around fishing, salt-making, and the shipping of iron ore. Many of the early residents were Hungarians and Finns.
Population: 3,017 (1990); 3,180 (2000); 3,230 (2007); 3,262 (2012 projected); Race: 97.0% White, 0.9% Black, 0.2% Asian, 2.5% Hispanic of any race (2007); Density: 3,100.1 persons per square mile (2007); Average household size: 2.18 (2007); Median age: 38.8 (2007); Males per 100 females: 98.9 (2007); Marriage status: 28.5% never married, 48.5% now married, 8.3% widowed, 14.7% divorced (2000); Foreign born: 2.7% (2000); Ancestry (includes multiple ancestries): 18.8% German, 14.9% Irish, 14.1% Hungarian, 10.9% Finnish, 9.4% Italian (2000).
Economy: Employment by occupation: 8.5% management, 13.7% professional, 19.6% services, 26.1% sales, 0.0% farming, 11.8% construction, 20.2% production (2000).
Income: Per capita income: $23,763 (2007); Median household income: $41,078 (2007); Average household income: $51,841 (2007); Percent of households with income of $100,000 or more: 8.7% (2007); Poverty rate: 7.4% (2000).
Education: Percent of population age 25 and over with: High school diploma (including GED) or higher: 83.3% (2007); Bachelor's degree or higher: 15.0% (2007); Master's degree or higher: 4.4% (2007).

School District(s)

Fairport Harbor Exempted Village (PK-12)
2005-06 Enrollment: 582 . . . . (440) 354-5400
Housing: Homeownership rate: 61.0% (2007); Median home value: $118,729 (2007); Median rent: $444 per month (2000); Median age of housing: 60+ years (2000).
Safety: Violent crime rate: 55.8 per 10,000 population; Property crime rate: 474.4 per 10,000 population (2007).
Transportation: Commute to work: 92.9% car, 2.1% public transportation, 1.7% walk, 2.4% work from home (2000); Travel time to work: 34.6% less than 15 minutes, 42.4% 15 to 30 minutes, 14.3% 30 to 45 minutes, 5.6% 45 to 60 minutes, 3.0% 60 minutes or more (2000)

GRAND RIVER (village). Aka Richmond. Covers a land area of 0.550 square miles and a water area of 0.100 square miles. Located at 41.73° N. Lat.; 81.28° W. Long. Elevation is 610 feet.
History: Formerly Richmond.
Population: 295 (1990); 345 (2000); 322 (2007); 305 (2012 projected); Race: 99.7% White, 0.0% Black, 0.3% Asian, 0.9% Hispanic of any race (2007); Density: 585.3 persons per square mile (2007); Average household size: 2.85 (2007); Median age: 41.5 (2007); Males per 100 females: 103.8 (2007); Marriage status: 16.0% never married, 63.1% now married, 5.2% widowed, 15.7% divorced (2000); Foreign born: 2.1% (2000); Ancestry (includes multiple ancestries): 31.7% German, 16.9% Irish, 16.3% Italian, 12.4% English, 11.5% Polish (2000).
Economy: Employment by occupation: 6.0% management, 8.4% professional, 25.3% services, 16.9% sales, 0.0% farming, 13.9% construction, 29.5% production (2000).
Income: Per capita income: $19,953 (2007); Median household income: $53,929 (2007); Average household income: $56,858 (2007); Percent of households with income of $100,000 or more: 12.4% (2007); Poverty rate: 5.9% (2000).
Education: Percent of population age 25 and over with: High school diploma (including GED) or higher: 90.7% (2007); Bachelor's degree or higher: 4.0% (2007); Master's degree or higher: 2.2% (2007).
Housing: Homeownership rate: 78.8% (2007); Median home value: $147,794 (2007); Median rent: $565 per month (2000); Median age of housing: 49 years (2000).
Transportation: Commute to work: 100.0% car, 0.0% public transportation, 0.0% walk, 0.0% work from home (2000); Travel time to work: 40.1% less than 15 minutes, 27.4% 15 to 30 minutes, 15.3% 30 to 45 minutes, 14.6% 45 to 60 minutes, 2.5% 60 minutes or more (2000)

KIRTLAND (city). Covers a land area of 16.600 square miles and a water area of 0.111 square miles. Located at 41.60° N. Lat.; 81.34° W. Long. Elevation is 663 feet.
History: Kirtland was the location in 1831 where Joseph Smith led a group of his followers. The town flourished as a Mormon stronghold until 1838, when Smith moved on. The Kirtland Temple built by the group remained a dominant factor in the town.
Population: 5,881 (1990); 6,670 (2000); 7,409 (2007); 7,850 (2012 projected); Race: 97.8% White, 0.4% Black, 0.5% Asian, 0.9% Hispanic of any race (2007); Density: 446.3 persons per square mile (2007); Average household size: 2.66 (2007); Median age: 45.3 (2007); Males per 100 females: 97.6 (2007); Marriage status: 21.0% never married, 65.3% now married, 7.2% widowed, 6.5% divorced (2000); Foreign born: 6.4% (2000); Ancestry (includes multiple ancestries): 27.0% German, 18.9% Irish, 14.3% Italian, 12.0% English, 6.6% Slovene (2000).
Economy: Employment by occupation: 18.4% management, 24.0% professional, 10.8% services, 24.2% sales, 0.3% farming, 10.1% construction, 12.1% production (2000).
Income: Per capita income: $37,263 (2007); Median household income: $73,125 (2007); Average household income: $98,134 (2007); Percent of households with income of $100,000 or more: 33.3% (2007); Poverty rate: 2.3% (2000).
Education: Percent of population age 25 and over with: High school diploma (including GED) or higher: 87.9% (2007); Bachelor's degree or higher: 32.4% (2007); Master's degree or higher: 11.1% (2007).

School District(s)

Kirtland Local (PK-12)
2005-06 Enrollment: 1,129 . . . . (440) 256-3311

Two-year College(s)

Lakeland Community College (Public)
Fall 2007 Enrollment: 8,934 . . . . (440) 525-7000
2007-08 Tuition: In-state $3,333; Out-of-state $7,095
Housing: Homeownership rate: 86.5% (2007); Median home value: $246,063 (2007); Median rent: $560 per month (2000); Median age of housing: 33 years (2000).
Safety: Violent crime rate: 0.0 per 10,000 population; Property crime rate: 94.6 per 10,000 population (2007).
Transportation: Commute to work: 95.3% car, 0.2% public transportation, 1.1% walk, 3.3% work from home (2000); Travel time to work: 22.2% less than 15 minutes, 51.3% 15 to 30 minutes, 18.3% 30 to 45 minutes, 5.8% 45 to 60 minutes, 2.3% 60 minutes or more (2000)
Additional Information Contacts
City of Kirtland . . . . (440) 256-3332
http://kirtlandohio.com

KIRTLAND HILLS (village). Covers a land area of 5.585 square miles and a water area of 0.072 square miles. Located at 41.64° N. Lat.; 81.31° W. Long. Elevation is 801 feet.
History: The first Mormon temple was built here (1833-1836) by Joseph Smith and his followers. Settled 1808, incorporated 1926.
Population: 628 (1990); 597 (2000); 799 (2007); 921 (2012 projected); Race: 97.4% White, 0.6% Black, 0.1% Asian, 1.0% Hispanic of any race (2007); Density: 143.1 persons per square mile (2007); Average household size: 2.58 (2007); Median age: 47.4 (2007); Males per 100 females: 93.5 (2007); Marriage status: 19.8% never married, 69.0% now married, 5.6% widowed, 5.6% divorced (2000); Foreign born: 2.3% (2000); Ancestry (includes multiple ancestries): 21.5% German, 20.9% Irish, 17.2% Italian, 9.7% English, 8.2% Slovene (2000).

Economy: Employment by occupation: 32.5% management, 27.4% professional, 2.9% services, 23.6% sales, 0.0% farming, 8.3% construction, 5.4% production (2000).
Income: Per capita income: $81,230 (2007); Median household income: $119,565 (2007); Average household income: $209,363 (2007); Percent of households with income of $100,000 or more: 55.8% (2007); Poverty rate: 3.2% (2000).
Education: Percent of population age 25 and over with: High school diploma (including GED) or higher: 93.7% (2007); Bachelor's degree or higher: 47.6% (2007); Master's degree or higher: 20.0% (2007).
Housing: Homeownership rate: 90.0% (2007); Median home value: $517,857 (2007); Median rent: $525 per month (2000); Median age of housing: 28 years (2000).
Safety: Violent crime rate: 0.0 per 10,000 population; Property crime rate: 100.9 per 10,000 population (2007).
Transportation: Commute to work: 90.5% car, 0.7% public transportation, 0.7% walk, 8.2% work from home (2000); Travel time to work: 22.5% less than 15 minutes, 51.4% 15 to 30 minutes, 16.1% 30 to 45 minutes, 5.0% 45 to 60 minutes, 5.0% 60 minutes or more (2000)

LAKELINE (village). Covers a land area of 0.076 square miles and a water area of 0 square miles. Located at 41.65° N. Lat.; 81.45° W. Long. Elevation is 620 feet.
Population: 210 (1990); 165 (2000); 226 (2007); 263 (2012 projected); Race: 100.0% White, 0.0% Black, 0.0% Asian, 0.0% Hispanic of any race (2007); Density: 2,977.5 persons per square mile (2007); Average household size: 2.46 (2007); Median age: 44.0 (2007); Males per 100 females: 107.3 (2007); Marriage status: 23.6% never married, 52.8% now married, 10.2% widowed, 13.4% divorced (2000); Foreign born: 2.4% (2000); Ancestry (includes multiple ancestries): 28.3% Irish, 24.1% German, 19.9% Other groups, 8.4% Italian, 7.8% English (2000).
Economy: Employment by occupation: 7.0% management, 8.5% professional, 16.9% services, 32.4% sales, 0.0% farming, 4.2% construction, 31.0% production (2000).
Income: Per capita income: $21,803 (2007); Median household income: $51,429 (2007); Average household income: $53,560 (2007); Percent of households with income of $100,000 or more: 6.5% (2007); Poverty rate: 5.0% (2000).
Education: Percent of population age 25 and over with: High school diploma (including GED) or higher: 74.1% (2007); Bachelor's degree or higher: 8.6% (2007); Master's degree or higher: 3.1% (2007).
Housing: Homeownership rate: 91.3% (2007); Median home value: $150,000 (2007); Median rent: $469 per month (2000); Median age of housing: 53 years (2000).
Transportation: Commute to work: 97.2% car, 0.0% public transportation, 2.8% walk, 0.0% work from home (2000); Travel time to work: 21.1% less than 15 minutes, 62.0% 15 to 30 minutes, 9.9% 30 to 45 minutes, 1.4% 45 to 60 minutes, 5.6% 60 minutes or more (2000)
Additional Information Contacts
Wickliffe Chamber of Commerce . . . . (440) 943-1134
http://www.westernlakecountychamber.org

MADISON (village). Covers a land area of 4.578 square miles and a water area of 0 square miles. Located at 41.77° N. Lat.; 81.05° W. Long. Elevation is 728 feet.
History: Madison grew around its orchards, nurseries, and potato fields. It was known for Madison Willowcraft, the product of its basket-making industry.
Population: 2,480 (1990); 2,921 (2000); 3,105 (2007); 3,218 (2012 projected); Race: 97.8% White, 0.8% Black, 0.2% Asian, 1.5% Hispanic of any race (2007); Density: 678.3 persons per square mile (2007); Average household size: 2.54 (2007); Median age: 39.4 (2007); Males per 100 females: 99.7 (2007); Marriage status: 21.1% never married, 64.0% now married, 5.7% widowed, 9.2% divorced (2000); Foreign born: 1.3% (2000); Ancestry (includes multiple ancestries): 27.0% German, 20.3% Irish, 13.5% English, 10.7% United States or American, 9.0% Italian (2000).
Economy: Employment by occupation: 11.9% management, 22.1% professional, 11.7% services, 29.6% sales, 0.3% farming, 7.5% construction, 16.9% production (2000).
Income: Per capita income: $25,622 (2007); Median household income: $58,381 (2007); Average household income: $64,619 (2007); Percent of households with income of $100,000 or more: 13.6% (2007); Poverty rate: 3.4% (2000).
Education: Percent of population age 25 and over with: High school diploma (including GED) or higher: 88.3% (2007); Bachelor's degree or higher: 22.9% (2007); Master's degree or higher: 7.5% (2007).

School District(s)

Madison Local (PK-12)
2005-06 Enrollment: 3,744 . . . . (440) 428-2166
Housing: Homeownership rate: 76.2% (2007); Median home value: $158,745 (2007); Median rent: $476 per month (2000); Median age of housing: 28 years (2000).
Newspapers: Free Enterprise (Local news; Circulation 17,500); Lake County Gazette (Community news; Circulation 5,000); Tribune (Local news; Circulation 3,020)
Transportation: Commute to work: 96.2% car, 0.2% public transportation, 1.8% walk, 1.7% work from home (2000); Travel time to work: 24.2% less than 15 minutes, 31.4% 15 to 30 minutes, 29.3% 30 to 45 minutes, 9.9% 45 to 60 minutes, 5.2% 60 minutes or more (2000)
Additional Information Contacts
Madison-Perry Area Chamber of Commerce. . . . . (440) 428-3760
http://www.mpacc.org
Village of Madison . . . . (440) 428-7526
http://www.madisonvillage.org

MENTOR (city). Covers a land area of 26.769 square miles and a water area of 1.307 square miles. Located at 41.69° N. Lat.; 81.34° W. Long. Elevation is 692 feet.
History: Named, possibly, for Hiram Mentor, an early settler. Mentor was founded in 1799. James A. Garfield lived in Mentor prior to his time as president of the U.S.
Population: 47,358 (1990); 50,278 (2000); 51,770 (2007); 52,619 (2012 projected); Race: 96.2% White, 1.1% Black, 1.5% Asian, 1.0% Hispanic of any race (2007); Density: 1,934.0 persons per square mile (2007); Average household size: 2.59 (2007); Median age: 41.5 (2007); Males per 100 females: 94.7 (2007); Marriage status: 21.5% never married, 62.5% now married, 6.8% widowed, 9.2% divorced (2000); Foreign born: 3.8% (2000); Ancestry (includes multiple ancestries): 26.6% German, 19.5% Irish, 16.2% Italian, 12.8% English, 8.4% Polish (2000).
Economy: Unemployment rate: 6.2% (6/2008); Total civilian labor force: 30,722 (6/2008); Single-family building permits issued: 63 (2007); Multi-family building permits issued: 4 (2007); Employment by occupation: 15.3% management, 20.8% professional, 11.1% services, 28.7% sales, 0.2% farming, 7.0% construction, 16.9% production (2000).
Income: Per capita income: $28,662 (2007); Median household income: $63,593 (2007); Average household income: $73,546 (2007); Percent of households with income of $100,000 or more: 22.2% (2007); Poverty rate: 2.7% (2000).
Taxes: Total city taxes per capita: $679 (2006); City property taxes per capita: $107 (2006).
Education: Percent of population age 25 and over with: High school diploma (including GED) or higher: 89.3% (2007); Bachelor's degree or higher: 27.8% (2007); Master's degree or higher: 9.0% (2007).

School District(s)

Mentor Exempted Village (PK-12)
2005-06 Enrollment: 9,153 . . . . (440) 255-4444

Two-year College(s)

Brown Aveda Institute
Fall 2007 Enrollment: 116 . . . . (440) 255-9494

Vocational/Technical School(s)

Cleveland Institute of Dental-Medical Assistants (Private, For-profit)
Fall 2007 Enrollment: 163 . . . . (216) 241-2930
2007-08 Tuition: $8,295
Housing: Homeownership rate: 87.7% (2007); Median home value: $177,736 (2007); Median rent: $614 per month (2000); Median age of housing: 28 years (2000).
Safety: Violent crime rate: 8.5 per 10,000 population; Property crime rate: 233.3 per 10,000 population (2007).
Newspapers: The Plain Dealer - Lake County Bureau (Local news)
Transportation: Commute to work: 95.6% car, 0.9% public transportation, 1.0% walk, 2.2% work from home (2000); Travel time to work: 29.5% less than 15 minutes, 39.5% 15 to 30 minutes, 20.8% 30 to 45 minutes, 7.2% 45 to 60 minutes, 3.0% 60 minutes or more (2000)
Additional Information Contacts
City of Mentor. . . . . (440) 255-1100
http://www.cityofmentor.com
Mentor Area Chamber of Commerce. . . . . (440) 255-1616
http://www.mentorchamber.org

MENTOR-ON-THE-LAKE (city). Covers a land area of 1.633 square miles and a water area of 0.034 square miles. Located at 41.71° N. Lat.; 81.36° W. Long. Elevation is 620 feet.
Population: 8,271 (1990); 8,127 (2000); 8,319 (2007); 8,435 (2012 projected); Race: 96.1% White, 1.2% Black, 0.8% Asian, 1.8% Hispanic of any race (2007); Density: 5,093.8 persons per square mile (2007); Average household size: 2.37 (2007); Median age: 37.7 (2007); Males per 100 females: 96.1 (2007); Marriage status: 25.2% never married, 56.4% now married, 6.5% widowed, 11.9% divorced (2000); Foreign born: 1.1% (2000); Ancestry (includes multiple ancestries): 26.8% German, 21.2% Irish, 14.0% Italian, 10.3% English, 9.0% Polish (2000).
Economy: Employment by occupation: 12.2% management, 15.6% professional, 15.1% services, 30.2% sales, 0.0% farming, 8.9% construction, 18.0% production (2000).
Income: Per capita income: $23,507 (2007); Median household income: $48,475 (2007); Average household income: $55,714 (2007); Percent of households with income of $100,000 or more: 9.8% (2007); Poverty rate: 5.7% (2000).
Education: Percent of population age 25 and over with: High school diploma (including GED) or higher: 87.8% (2007); Bachelor's degree or higher: 14.6% (2007); Master's degree or higher: 5.2% (2007).

School District(s)

Mentor Exempted Village (PK-12)
2005-06 Enrollment: 9,153 . . . . (440) 255-4444

Housing: Homeownership rate: 68.4% (2007); Median home value: $146,448 (2007); Median rent: $609 per month (2000); Median age of housing: 30 years (2000).
Safety: Violent crime rate: 1.2 per 10,000 population; Property crime rate: 80.6 per 10,000 population (2007).
Transportation: Commute to work: 96.7% car, 0.7% public transportation, 0.7% walk, 1.6% work from home (2000); Travel time to work: 27.0% less than 15 minutes, 42.3% 15 to 30 minutes, 19.4% 30 to 45 minutes, 5.9% 45 to 60 minutes, 5.3% 60 minutes or more (2000)

NORTH MADISON (CDP). Covers a land area of 4.010 square miles and a water area of 0 square miles. Located at 41.83° N. Lat.; 81.05° W. Long. Elevation is 676 feet.
Population: 8,695 (1990); 8,451 (2000); 9,098 (2007); 9,482 (2012 projected); Race: 97.3% White, 0.2% Black, 0.5% Asian, 2.5% Hispanic of any race (2007); Density: 2,269.1 persons per square mile (2007); Average household size: 2.64 (2007); Median age: 36.1 (2007); Males per 100 females: 98.6 (2007); Marriage status: 21.1% never married, 61.3% now married, 5.3% widowed, 12.3% divorced (2000); Foreign born: 1.2% (2000); Ancestry (includes multiple ancestries): 22.5% German, 18.4% Irish, 10.9% Italian, 10.2% English, 10.1% United States or American (2000).
Economy: Employment by occupation: 7.7% management, 11.2% professional, 13.6% services, 26.3% sales, 0.5% farming, 14.0% construction, 26.6% production (2000).
Income: Per capita income: $21,523 (2007); Median household income: $49,701 (2007); Average household income: $56,726 (2007); Percent of households with income of $100,000 or more: 8.4% (2007); Poverty rate: 5.9% (2000).
Education: Percent of population age 25 and over with: High school diploma (including GED) or higher: 82.4% (2007); Bachelor's degree or higher: 9.5% (2007); Master's degree or higher: 3.7% (2007).
Housing: Homeownership rate: 82.0% (2007); Median home value: $122,145 (2007); Median rent: $496 per month (2000); Median age of housing: 35 years (2000).
Transportation: Commute to work: 97.2% car, 0.2% public transportation, 0.6% walk, 1.6% work from home (2000); Travel time to work: 16.9% less than 15 minutes, 30.7% 15 to 30 minutes, 33.1% 30 to 45 minutes, 10.9% 45 to 60 minutes, 8.4% 60 minutes or more (2000)

NORTH PERRY (village). Covers a land area of 3.890 square miles and a water area of 0 square miles. Located at 41.80° N. Lat.; 81.12° W. Long. Elevation is 682 feet.
Population: 830 (1990); 838 (2000); 951 (2007); 1,019 (2012 projected); Race: 98.7% White, 0.2% Black, 0.3% Asian, 0.5% Hispanic of any race (2007); Density: 244.5 persons per square mile (2007); Average household size: 2.68 (2007); Median age: 43.5 (2007); Males per 100 females: 97.7 (2007); Marriage status: 22.8% never married, 63.5% now married, 6.8% widowed, 6.8% divorced (2000); Foreign born: 1.3% (2000); Ancestry (includes multiple ancestries): 29.6% German, 23.3% Irish, 18.0% English, 8.0% Italian, 7.0% United States or American (2000).
Economy: Employment by occupation: 15.2% management, 13.7% professional, 14.9% services, 28.4% sales, 0.0% farming, 8.9% construction, 18.8% production (2000).
Income: Per capita income: $22,408 (2007); Median household income: $48,026 (2007); Average household income: $60,028 (2007); Percent of households with income of $100,000 or more: 13.8% (2007); Poverty rate: 6.0% (2000).
Education: Percent of population age 25 and over with: High school diploma (including GED) or higher: 85.6% (2007); Bachelor's degree or higher: 16.0% (2007); Master's degree or higher: 5.1% (2007).
Housing: Homeownership rate: 88.2% (2007); Median home value: $179,741 (2007); Median rent: $606 per month (2000); Median age of housing: 40 years (2000).
Transportation: Commute to work: 92.7% car, 0.7% public transportation, 1.7% walk, 4.9% work from home (2000); Travel time to work: 30.6% less than 15 minutes, 36.0% 15 to 30 minutes, 17.2% 30 to 45 minutes, 9.5% 45 to 60 minutes, 6.7% 60 minutes or more (2000)
Additional Information Contacts
Village of North Perry . . . . (440) 259-4994
http://www.northperry.org

PAINESVILLE (city). County seat. Covers a land area of 5.977 square miles and a water area of 0.710 square miles. Located at 41.72° N. Lat.; 81.25° W. Long. Elevation is 676 feet.
History: Named for Edward Paine, first settler, who had been a general in the American Revolution. Painesville was settled in the early 1800's by pioneers from Connecticut. Architect-builder Jonathan Goldsmith lived in Painesville from 1811 until his death in 1847, and the town had several examples of Goldsmith's work.
Population: 15,712 (1990); 17,503 (2000); 17,780 (2007); 17,915 (2012 projected); Race: 69.4% White, 15.9% Black, 0.5% Asian, 21.5% Hispanic of any race (2007); Density: 2,975.0 persons per square mile (2007); Average household size: 2.66 (2007); Median age: 33.0 (2007); Males per 100 females: 97.8 (2007); Marriage status: 29.7% never married, 50.5% now married, 7.3% widowed, 12.5% divorced (2000); Foreign born: 10.1% (2000); Ancestry (includes multiple ancestries): 26.7% Other groups, 18.7% German, 13.7% Irish, 10.5% English, 9.3% Italian (2000).
Economy: Single-family building permits issued: 95 (2007); Multi-family building permits issued: 100 (2007); Employment by occupation: 7.2% management, 13.0% professional, 17.8% services, 25.7% sales, 2.6% farming, 9.2% construction, 24.5% production (2000).
Income: Per capita income: $17,492 (2007); Median household income: $38,216 (2007); Average household income: $45,088 (2007); Percent of households with income of $100,000 or more: 6.0% (2007); Poverty rate: 16.0% (2000).
Taxes: Total city taxes per capita: $482 (2006); City property taxes per capita: $32 (2006).
Education: Percent of population age 25 and over with: High school diploma (including GED) or higher: 74.0% (2007); Bachelor's degree or higher: 12.5% (2007); Master's degree or higher: 4.3% (2007).

School District(s)

Auburn (09-12)
2005-06 Enrollment: n/a . . . . (440) 357-7542
Painesville Local (PK-12)
2005-06 Enrollment: 2,998 . . . . (440) 392-5060
Painesville Township Local (PK-12)
2005-06 Enrollment: 4,748 . . . . (440) 352-0668
Summit Academy Community School - Painesville (01-08)
2005-06 Enrollment: 35 . . . . (440) 358-0877

Four-year College(s)

Lake Erie College (Private, Not-for-profit)
Fall 2007 Enrollment: 941 . . . . (440) 375-7000
2007-08 Tuition: In-state $23,886; Out-of-state $23,886

Vocational/Technical School(s)

Auburn Career Center (Public)
Fall 2007 Enrollment: 399 . . . . (800) 544-9750
2007-08 Tuition: $10,000

Housing: Homeownership rate: 52.4% (2007); Median home value: $114,486 (2007); Median rent: $462 per month (2000); Median age of housing: 46 years (2000).
Hospitals: Lake Hospital System - East (359 beds)
Newspapers: Healthsense (Local news; Circulation 30,000)

Transportation: Commute to work: 92.9% car, 0.9% public transportation, 3.8% walk, 1.3% work from home (2000); Travel time to work: 32.4% less than 15 minutes, 41.6% 15 to 30 minutes, 17.4% 30 to 45 minutes, 5.4% 45 to 60 minutes, 3.2% 60 minutes or more (2000)

Additional Information Contacts

City of Painesville. . . . . (440) 352-9301
http://www.painesville.com

Painesville Area Chamber of Commerce. . . . . (440) 357-7572
http://www.painesvilleohchamber.org

PERRY (village). Covers a land area of 2.180 square miles and a water area of 0 square miles. Located at 41.75° N. Lat.; 81.13° W. Long. Elevation is 699 feet.

Population: 1,036 (1990); 1,195 (2000); 1,285 (2007); 1,338 (2012 projected); Race: 97.7% White, 0.2% Black, 1.2% Asian, 0.5% Hispanic of any race (2007); Density: 589.4 persons per square mile (2007); Average household size: 2.70 (2007); Median age: 40.8 (2007); Males per 100 females: 94.1 (2007); Marriage status: 21.2% never married, 62.6% now married, 5.0% widowed, 11.2% divorced (2000); Foreign born: 2.9% (2000); Ancestry (includes multiple ancestries): 31.2% German, 18.7% Irish, 15.6% Italian, 15.1% English, 6.2% Other groups (2000).

Economy: Employment by occupation: 9.4% management, 21.6% professional, 16.6% services, 24.4% sales, 0.3% farming, 12.1% construction, 15.5% production (2000).

Income: Per capita income: $26,352 (2007); Median household income: $62,500 (2007); Average household income: $71,140 (2007); Percent of households with income of $100,000 or more: 18.9% (2007); Poverty rate: 2.7% (2000).

Education: Percent of population age 25 and over with: High school diploma (including GED) or higher: 91.8% (2007); Bachelor's degree or higher: 22.4% (2007); Master's degree or higher: 7.5% (2007).

School District(s)

Perry Local (PK-12)
2005-06 Enrollment: 1,852 . . . . (440) 259-3881

Housing: Homeownership rate: 83.4% (2007); Median home value: $181,250 (2007); Median rent: $504 per month (2000); Median age of housing: 36 years (2000).

Transportation: Commute to work: 97.0% car, 0.3% public transportation, 1.2% walk, 1.5% work from home (2000); Travel time to work: 32.9% less than 15 minutes, 38.2% 15 to 30 minutes, 16.6% 30 to 45 minutes, 8.1% 45 to 60 minutes, 4.2% 60 minutes or more (2000)

TIMBERLAKE (village). Covers a land area of 0.214 square miles and a water area of 0 square miles. Located at 41.66° N. Lat.; 81.44° W. Long. Elevation is 620 feet.

Population: 833 (1990); 775 (2000); 740 (2007); 714 (2012 projected); Race: 98.6% White, 0.0% Black, 0.3% Asian, 2.2% Hispanic of any race (2007); Density: 3,450.9 persons per square mile (2007); Average household size: 2.42 (2007); Median age: 48.4 (2007); Males per 100 females: 100.5 (2007); Marriage status: 22.9% never married, 58.3% now married, 6.1% widowed, 12.7% divorced (2000); Foreign born: 3.4% (2000); Ancestry (includes multiple ancestries): 30.1% German, 18.9% Irish, 16.7% Italian, 13.4% English, 8.5% Slovene (2000).

Economy: Single-family building permits issued: 0 (2007); Multi-family building permits issued: 0 (2007); Employment by occupation: 12.9% management, 17.0% professional, 14.8% services, 33.7% sales, 0.0% farming, 8.0% construction, 13.6% production (2000).

Income: Per capita income: $25,973 (2007); Median household income: $55,000 (2007); Average household income: $62,810 (2007); Percent of households with income of $100,000 or more: 19.6% (2007); Poverty rate: 1.4% (2000).

Education: Percent of population age 25 and over with: High school diploma (including GED) or higher: 87.9% (2007); Bachelor's degree or higher: 22.5% (2007); Master's degree or higher: 7.8% (2007).

Housing: Homeownership rate: 95.1% (2007); Median home value: $193,409 (2007); Median rent: $771 per month (2000); Median age of housing: 44 years (2000).

Transportation: Commute to work: 92.9% car, 1.5% public transportation, 0.7% walk, 3.9% work from home (2000); Travel time to work: 30.9% less than 15 minutes, 37.1% 15 to 30 minutes, 23.0% 30 to 45 minutes, 6.1% 45 to 60 minutes, 2.8% 60 minutes or more (2000)

Additional Information Contacts

Wickliffe Chamber of Commerce . . . . (440) 943-1134
http://www.westernlakecountychamber.org

WAITE HILL (village). Covers a land area of 4.213 square miles and a water area of 0.059 square miles. Located at 41.61° N. Lat.; 81.38° W. Long. Elevation is 768 feet.

Population: 454 (1990); 446 (2000); 482 (2007); 503 (2012 projected); Race: 97.5% White, 0.0% Black, 1.2% Asian, 0.0% Hispanic of any race (2007); Density: 114.4 persons per square mile (2007); Average household size: 2.36 (2007); Median age: 54.8 (2007); Males per 100 females: 104.2 (2007); Marriage status: 11.6% never married, 78.7% now married, 4.3% widowed, 5.4% divorced (2000); Foreign born: 5.8% (2000); Ancestry (includes multiple ancestries): 19.7% English, 19.5% German, 11.3% Irish, 8.9% Italian, 6.7% Slovene (2000).

Economy: Employment by occupation: 35.3% management, 35.8% professional, 5.5% services, 15.6% sales, 0.0% farming, 0.9% construction, 6.9% production (2000).

Income: Per capita income: $69,481 (2007); Median household income: $98,913 (2007); Average household income: $164,167 (2007); Percent of households with income of $100,000 or more: 49.5% (2007); Poverty rate: 0.9% (2000).

Education: Percent of population age 25 and over with: High school diploma (including GED) or higher: 95.9% (2007); Bachelor's degree or higher: 57.0% (2007); Master's degree or higher: 26.4% (2007).

Housing: Homeownership rate: 85.8% (2007); Median home value: $515,625 (2007); Median rent: $833 per month (2000); Median age of housing: 56 years (2000).

Safety: Violent crime rate: 0.0 per 10,000 population; Property crime rate: 36.1 per 10,000 population (2007).

Transportation: Commute to work: 87.5% car, 0.9% public transportation, 2.8% walk, 7.9% work from home (2000); Travel time to work: 25.6% less than 15 minutes, 44.2% 15 to 30 minutes, 25.1% 30 to 45 minutes, 4.0% 45 to 60 minutes, 1.0% 60 minutes or more (2000)

WICKLIFFE (city). Covers a land area of 4.653 square miles and a water area of 0.003 square miles. Located at 41.60° N. Lat.; 81.47° W. Long. Elevation is 768 feet.

History: Named for Charles A. Wickliffe, a Kentucky lawyer. Borromeo College of Ohio and the Rabbinical College of Telshe are here. Incorporated 1916.

Population: 14,558 (1990); 13,484 (2000); 13,084 (2007); 12,774 (2012 projected); Race: 94.0% White, 3.7% Black, 1.0% Asian, 0.8% Hispanic of any race (2007); Density: 2,812.2 persons per square mile (2007); Average household size: 2.33 (2007); Median age: 44.7 (2007); Males per 100 females: 95.3 (2007); Marriage status: 23.5% never married, 57.2% now married, 10.1% widowed, 9.2% divorced (2000); Foreign born: 4.6% (2000); Ancestry (includes multiple ancestries): 21.2% German, 20.3% Italian, 18.0% Irish, 10.8% Polish, 9.9% Slovene (2000).

Economy: Single-family building permits issued: 14 (2007); Multi-family building permits issued: 0 (2007); Employment by occupation: 12.3% management, 17.8% professional, 15.8% services, 27.7% sales, 0.0% farming, 10.3% construction, 16.1% production (2000).

Income: Per capita income: $24,333 (2007); Median household income: $47,682 (2007); Average household income: $55,598 (2007); Percent of households with income of $100,000 or more: 10.2% (2007); Poverty rate: 6.5% (2000).

Education: Percent of population age 25 and over with: High school diploma (including GED) or higher: 85.5% (2007); Bachelor's degree or higher: 16.3% (2007); Master's degree or higher: 6.0% (2007).

School District(s)

Wickliffe City (PK-12)
2005-06 Enrollment: 1,519 . . . . (440) 943-6900

Four-year College(s)

Rabbinical College Telshe (Private, Not-for-profit, Jewish)
Fall 2007 Enrollment: 43 . . . . (440) 943-5300
2007-08 Tuition: In-state $7,500; Out-of-state $7,500

Housing: Homeownership rate: 84.4% (2007); Median home value: $141,554 (2007); Median rent: $489 per month (2000); Median age of housing: 44 years (2000).

Transportation: Commute to work: 93.8% car, 2.1% public transportation, 1.6% walk, 1.9% work from home (2000); Travel time to work: 36.7% less than 15 minutes, 42.5% 15 to 30 minutes, 15.4% 30 to 45 minutes, 3.5% 45 to 60 minutes, 1.9% 60 minutes or more (2000)

Additional Information Contacts

City of Wickliffe . . . . (440) 943-7100
http://www.cityofwickliffe.com

Wickliffe Chamber of Commerce . . . . (440) 943-1134
http://www.westernlakecountychamber.org

WILLOUGHBY (city). Covers a land area of 10.166 square miles and a water area of 0.064 square miles. Located at 41.65° N. Lat.; 81.40° W. Long. Elevation is 659 feet.

History: Willoughby was first called Chagrin, but was renamed for an instructor in the Willoughby Medical College, established in 1834. The college had a good reputation until 1843, when a local resident discovered her newly buried husband was missing from his grave. The medical school's method of acquiring cadavers for research soon brought about its own demise.

Population: 20,510 (1990); 22,621 (2000); 22,202 (2007); 21,881 (2012 projected); Race: 95.0% White, 1.8% Black, 1.5% Asian, 1.0% Hispanic of any race (2007); Density: 2,184.0 persons per square mile (2007); Average household size: 2.12 (2007); Median age: 41.5 (2007); Males per 100 females: 86.6 (2007); Marriage status: 26.0% never married, 49.9% now married, 9.8% widowed, 14.4% divorced (2000); Foreign born: 3.7% (2000); Ancestry (includes multiple ancestries): 26.4% German, 18.9% Irish, 15.6% Italian, 11.3% English, 6.5% Polish (2000).

Economy: Single-family building permits issued: 94 (2007); Multi-family building permits issued: 27 (2007); Employment by occupation: 15.0% management, 19.7% professional, 13.0% services, 28.1% sales, 0.1% farming, 7.9% construction, 16.1% production (2000).

Income: Per capita income: $27,608 (2007); Median household income: $47,342 (2007); Average household income: $58,017 (2007); Percent of households with income of $100,000 or more: 12.6% (2007); Poverty rate: 5.8% (2000).

Education: Percent of population age 25 and over with: High school diploma (including GED) or higher: 87.8% (2007); Bachelor's degree or higher: 24.0% (2007); Master's degree or higher: 6.4% (2007).

School District(s)

Lake
2005-06 Enrollment: n/a . . . . (440) 350-2563
Willoughby-Eastlake City (PK-12)
2005-06 Enrollment: 8,826 . . . . (440) 946-5000

Vocational/Technical School(s)

Willoughby-Eastlake School of Practical Nursing (Public)
Fall 2007 Enrollment: 70 . . . . (440) 946-7085
2007-08 Tuition: In-state $8,394; Out-of-state $8,394

Housing: Homeownership rate: 59.4% (2007); Median home value: $155,735 (2007); Median rent: $600 per month (2000); Median age of housing: 30 years (2000).

Hospitals: Lake Hospital System - West (359 beds); Laurelwood Hospital and Counseling Centers (160 beds)

Safety: Violent crime rate: 6.7 per 10,000 population; Property crime rate: 167.1 per 10,000 population (2007).

Newspapers: The Lake County Women's Journal (Local news; Circulation 56,000); News-Herald (Local news; Circulation 50,000)

Transportation: Commute to work: 95.4% car, 0.8% public transportation, 1.6% walk, 1.5% work from home (2000); Travel time to work: 29.5% less than 15 minutes, 42.2% 15 to 30 minutes, 21.2% 30 to 45 minutes, 4.2% 45 to 60 minutes, 2.8% 60 minutes or more (2000)

Airports: Willoughby Lost Nation Municipal (general aviation)

Additional Information Contacts

City of Willoughby . . . . (440) 951-2800
http://www.willoughbyohio.com
Willoughby Area Chamber of Commerce . . . . (440) 942-1632
http://www.willoughbyareachamber.com

WILLOUGHBY HILLS (city). Covers a land area of 10.765 square miles and a water area of 0.086 square miles. Located at 41.58° N. Lat.; 81.44° W. Long. Elevation is 804 feet.

Population: 8,427 (1990); 8,595 (2000); 8,406 (2007); 8,262 (2012 projected); Race: 82.2% White, 10.7% Black, 5.6% Asian, 0.9% Hispanic of any race (2007); Density: 780.9 persons per square mile (2007); Average household size: 2.17 (2007); Median age: 45.5 (2007); Males per 100 females: 92.4 (2007); Marriage status: 25.6% never married, 55.9% now married, 7.5% widowed, 11.0% divorced (2000); Foreign born: 11.3% (2000); Ancestry (includes multiple ancestries): 21.2% German, 16.3% Italian, 15.0% Irish, 12.2% Slovene, 10.9% Other groups (2000).

Economy: Single-family building permits issued: 12 (2007); Multi-family building permits issued: 0 (2007); Employment by occupation: 17.0% management, 24.5% professional, 13.2% services, 28.7% sales, 0.0% farming, 5.2% construction, 11.5% production (2000).

Income: Per capita income: $29,974 (2007); Median household income: $51,998 (2007); Average household income: $65,036 (2007); Percent of households with income of $100,000 or more: 16.4% (2007); Poverty rate: 3.4% (2000).

Education: Percent of population age 25 and over with: High school diploma (including GED) or higher: 87.5% (2007); Bachelor's degree or higher: 32.1% (2007); Master's degree or higher: 11.7% (2007).

Four-year College(s)

Bryant and Stratton College-Willoughby Hills (Private, For-profit)
Fall 2007 Enrollment: 599 . . . . (440) 944-6800
2007-08 Tuition: In-state $19,645; Out-of-state $19,645

Housing: Homeownership rate: 55.2% (2007); Median home value: $270,468 (2007); Median rent: $620 per month (2000); Median age of housing: 32 years (2000).

Safety: Violent crime rate: 11.9 per 10,000 population; Property crime rate: 155.4 per 10,000 population (2007).

Transportation: Commute to work: 95.3% car, 0.9% public transportation, 1.5% walk, 1.7% work from home (2000); Travel time to work: 24.7% less than 15 minutes, 43.4% 15 to 30 minutes, 22.6% 30 to 45 minutes, 6.0% 45 to 60 minutes, 3.3% 60 minutes or more (2000)

WILLOWICK (city). Covers a land area of 2.515 square miles and a water area of 0 square miles. Located at 41.63° N. Lat.; 81.46° W. Long. Elevation is 620 feet.

History: Named for the Willoughby and Wickliff families. Incorporated 1924.

Population: 15,269 (1990); 14,361 (2000); 13,862 (2007); 13,476 (2012 projected); Race: 97.1% White, 1.1% Black, 0.6% Asian, 1.2% Hispanic of any race (2007); Density: 5,510.8 persons per square mile (2007); Average household size: 2.28 (2007); Median age: 43.5 (2007); Males per 100 females: 92.8 (2007); Marriage status: 21.3% never married, 56.7% now married, 12.1% widowed, 9.9% divorced (2000); Foreign born: 4.6% (2000); Ancestry (includes multiple ancestries): 23.8% German, 19.3% Italian, 17.6% Irish, 11.9% Polish, 9.6% Slovene (2000).

Economy: Single-family building permits issued: 11 (2007); Multi-family building permits issued: 0 (2007); Employment by occupation: 12.0% management, 16.7% professional, 12.9% services, 32.4% sales, 0.0% farming, 8.2% construction, 17.8% production (2000).

Income: Per capita income: $24,762 (2007); Median household income: $47,971 (2007); Average household income: $56,340 (2007); Percent of households with income of $100,000 or more: 9.7% (2007); Poverty rate: 4.5% (2000).

Education: Percent of population age 25 and over with: High school diploma (including GED) or higher: 84.0% (2007); Bachelor's degree or higher: 14.3% (2007); Master's degree or higher: 3.9% (2007).

School District(s)

Willoughby-Eastlake City (PK-12)
2005-06 Enrollment: 8,826 . . . . (440) 946-5000

Housing: Homeownership rate: 82.9% (2007); Median home value: $136,305 (2007); Median rent: $596 per month (2000); Median age of housing: 44 years (2000).

Safety: Violent crime rate: 9.4 per 10,000 population; Property crime rate: 142.0 per 10,000 population (2007).

Transportation: Commute to work: 95.0% car, 1.7% public transportation, 1.0% walk, 1.8% work from home (2000); Travel time to work: 32.5% less than 15 minutes, 42.2% 15 to 30 minutes, 17.7% 30 to 45 minutes, 4.8% 45 to 60 minutes, 2.8% 60 minutes or more (2000)

Additional Information Contacts

City of Willowick . . . . (440) 585-3700
http://www.cityofwillowick.com
Wickliffe Chamber of Commerce . . . . (440) 943-1134
http://www.westernlakecountychamber.org

Lawrence County

Located in southern Ohio; bounded on the south by the Ohio River and the Kentucky and West Virginia borders. Covers a land area of 454.96 square miles, a water area of 2.32 square miles, and is located in the Eastern Time Zone. The county was founded in 1815. County seat is Ironton.

Lawrence County is part of the Huntington-Ashland, WV-KY-OH Metropolitan Statistical Area. The entire metro area includes: Boyd County, KY; Greenup County, KY; Lawrence County, OH; Cabell County, WV; Wayne County, WV

Population: 61,834 (1990); 62,319 (2000); 63,548 (2007); 64,363 (2012 projected); Race: 96.3% White, 2.1% Black, 0.4% Asian, 0.6% Hispanic of any race (2007); Density: 139.7 persons per square mile (2007); Average household size: 2.44 (2007); Median age: 38.9 (2007); Males per 100 females: 93.1 (2007).
Religion: Five largest groups: 4.7% The United Methodist Church, 3.3% Southern Baptist Convention, 3.1% Catholic Church, 2.9% Christian Churches and Churches of Christ, 2.3% Church of the Nazarene (2000).
Economy: Unemployment rate: 6.1% (6/2008); Total civilian labor force: 30,002 (6/2008); Leading industries: 23.8% retail trade; 23.0% health care and social assistance; 11.4% accommodation & food services (2005); Farms: 644 totaling 65,326 acres (2002); Companies that employ 500 or more persons: 0 (2006); Companies that employ 100 to 499 persons: 17 (2006); Companies that employ less than 100 persons: 854 (2006); Black-owned businesses: n/a (2002); Hispanic-owned businesses: n/a (2002); Asian-owned businesses: n/a (2002); Women-owned businesses: 880 (2002); Retail sales per capita: $9,467 (2008). Single-family building permits issued: 11 (2007); Multi-family building permits issued: 2 (2007).
Income: Per capita income: $18,011 (2007); Median household income: $34,191 (2007); Average household income: $43,704 (2007); Percent of households with income of $100,000 or more: 6.9% (2007); Poverty rate: 20.3% (2005); Bankruptcy rate: 1.95% (2007).
Education: Percent of population age 25 and over with: High school diploma (including GED) or higher: 75.7% (2007); Bachelor's degree or higher: 10.3% (2007); Master's degree or higher: 3.8% (2007).
Housing: Homeownership rate: 74.9% (2007); Median home value: $83,295 (2007); Median rent: $314 per month (2000); Median age of housing: 31 years (2000).
Health: Birth rate: 124.6 per 10,000 population (2007); Death rate: 117.6 per 10,000 population (2007); Age-adjusted cancer mortality rate: 230.8 deaths per 100,000 population (2005); Air Quality Index: 70.7% good, 26.8% moderate, 2.5% unhealthy for sensitive individuals, 0.0% unhealthy (percent of days in 2007); Number of physicians: 8.3 per 10,000 population (2005); Hospital beds: 0.0 per 10,000 population (2004); Hospital admissions: 0.0 per 10,000 population (2004).
Elections: 2004 Presidential election results: 55.8% Bush, 43.7% Kerry, 0.0% Nader, 0.3% Badnarik
National and State Parks: Dean State Forest; Wayne National Forest - Ironton Ranger District
Additional Information Contacts
Lawrence County Government . . . . (740) 533-4300
http://www.lawrencecountyohio.org
City of Ironton. . . . . (740) 532-3833
http://www.ironton-ohio.com
Greater Lawrence County Chamber of Commerce . . . . (740) 377-4550
http://www.lawrencecountyohio.org
Village of South Point. . . . . (740) 377-4838
http://www.villageofsouthpoint.com

Lawrence County Communities

ATHALIA (village). Covers a land area of 0.688 square miles and a water area of 0 square miles. Located at 38.51° N. Lat.; 82.30° W. Long. Elevation is 554 feet.
Population: 346 (1990); 328 (2000); 322 (2007); 324 (2012 projected); Race: 97.8% White, 0.0% Black, 1.6% Asian, 0.0% Hispanic of any race (2007); Density: 468.0 persons per square mile (2007); Average household size: 2.30 (2007); Median age: 37.0 (2007); Males per 100 females: 89.4 (2007); Marriage status: 25.4% never married, 57.4% now married, 6.6% widowed, 10.5% divorced (2000); Foreign born: 0.0% (2000); Ancestry (includes multiple ancestries): 14.1% English, 12.6% Other groups, 8.3% German, 7.7% United States or American, 6.4% Irish (2000).
Economy: Employment by occupation: 6.8% management, 14.4% professional, 18.6% services, 28.0% sales, 0.0% farming, 16.9% construction, 15.3% production (2000).
Income: Per capita income: $16,188 (2007); Median household income: $31,667 (2007); Average household income: $37,232 (2007); Percent of households with income of $100,000 or more: 3.6% (2007); Poverty rate: 12.9% (2000).
Education: Percent of population age 25 and over with: High school diploma (including GED) or higher: 76.2% (2007); Bachelor's degree or higher: 10.8% (2007); Master's degree or higher: 7.6% (2007).
Housing: Homeownership rate: 77.9% (2007); Median home value: $73,571 (2007); Median rent: $329 per month (2000); Median age of housing: 30 years (2000).
Transportation: Commute to work: 92.2% car, 1.7% public transportation, 0.0% walk, 0.9% work from home (2000); Travel time to work: 20.9% less than 15 minutes, 33.0% 15 to 30 minutes, 21.7% 30 to 45 minutes, 12.2% 45 to 60 minutes, 12.2% 60 minutes or more (2000)

BURLINGTON (CDP). Covers a land area of 1.425 square miles and a water area of 0 square miles. Located at 38.40° N. Lat.; 82.52° W. Long. Elevation is 558 feet.
History: Burlington was founded by Reverend Plymale, a Baptist minister in Virginia who had been a slave-holder. He purchased the land in Ohio and presented each of his former slaves with an equal portion of it. In 1817 Burlington became the first seat of Lawrence County.
Population: 3,003 (1990); 2,794 (2000); 2,856 (2007); 2,918 (2012 projected); Race: 89.7% White, 7.2% Black, 0.2% Asian, 1.8% Hispanic of any race (2007); Density: 2,004.6 persons per square mile (2007); Average household size: 2.39 (2007); Median age: 44.5 (2007); Males per 100 females: 85.6 (2007); Marriage status: 16.8% never married, 60.2% now married, 12.8% widowed, 10.2% divorced (2000); Foreign born: 0.4% (2000); Ancestry (includes multiple ancestries): 18.1% United States or American, 14.0% Other groups, 8.6% Irish, 7.5% English, 5.7% German (2000).
Economy: Employment by occupation: 9.6% management, 11.0% professional, 18.9% services, 32.3% sales, 0.9% farming, 13.4% construction, 13.8% production (2000).
Income: Per capita income: $18,411 (2007); Median household income: $27,942 (2007); Average household income: $41,876 (2007); Percent of households with income of $100,000 or more: 7.3% (2007); Poverty rate: 16.6% (2000).
Education: Percent of population age 25 and over with: High school diploma (including GED) or higher: 70.2% (2007); Bachelor's degree or higher: 8.8% (2007); Master's degree or higher: 4.2% (2007).
School District(s)
South Point Local (KG-12)
2005-06 Enrollment: 1,880 . . . . (740) 377-4315
Housing: Homeownership rate: 69.9% (2007); Median home value: $72,000 (2007); Median rent: $336 per month (2000); Median age of housing: 29 years (2000).
Transportation: Commute to work: 93.0% car, 1.0% public transportation, 2.0% walk, 2.9% work from home (2000); Travel time to work: 29.0% less than 15 minutes, 58.1% 15 to 30 minutes, 8.4% 30 to 45 minutes, 2.1% 45 to 60 minutes, 2.4% 60 minutes or more (2000)

CHESAPEAKE (village). Covers a land area of 0.553 square miles and a water area of 0.032 square miles. Located at 38.42° N. Lat.; 82.45° W. Long. Elevation is 554 feet.
History: Chesapeake developed as a residential community, with many of its citizens commuting to Huntington, across the Ohio River in West Virginia.
Population: 1,073 (1990); 842 (2000); 819 (2007); 822 (2012 projected); Race: 97.9% White, 0.2% Black, 0.4% Asian, 1.6% Hispanic of any race (2007); Density: 1,482.1 persons per square mile (2007); Average household size: 2.06 (2007); Median age: 41.0 (2007); Males per 100 females: 88.7 (2007); Marriage status: 21.0% never married, 54.7% now married, 12.4% widowed, 11.9% divorced (2000); Foreign born: 2.0% (2000); Ancestry (includes multiple ancestries): 29.2% United States or American, 9.2% German, 8.8% English, 7.7% Other groups, 6.7% Irish (2000).
Economy: Employment by occupation: 5.5% management, 21.8% professional, 23.9% services, 25.8% sales, 0.0% farming, 14.1% construction, 8.9% production (2000).
Income: Per capita income: $18,660 (2007); Median household income: $28,854 (2007); Average household income: $38,398 (2007); Percent of households with income of $100,000 or more: 4.5% (2007); Poverty rate: 15.5% (2000).
Education: Percent of population age 25 and over with: High school diploma (including GED) or higher: 72.9% (2007); Bachelor's degree or higher: 10.2% (2007); Master's degree or higher: 2.2% (2007).
School District(s)
Chesapeake Union Exempted Village (KG-12)
2005-06 Enrollment: 1,432 . . . . (740) 867-3135
Lawrence County (09-12)
2005-06 Enrollment: n/a . . . . (740) 867-6641
Two-year College(s)
O C Collins Career Center (Public)
Fall 2007 Enrollment: 492 . . . . (740) 867-6641

Housing: Homeownership rate: 61.8% (2007); Median home value: $82,143 (2007); Median rent: $331 per month (2000); Median age of housing: 43 years (2000).
Transportation: Commute to work: 92.8% car, 0.6% public transportation, 3.1% walk, 2.8% work from home (2000); Travel time to work: 52.8% less than 15 minutes, 28.2% 15 to 30 minutes, 14.6% 30 to 45 minutes, 1.9% 45 to 60 minutes, 2.6% 60 minutes or more (2000)

COAL GROVE (village). Covers a land area of 1.972 square miles and a water area of 0.166 square miles. Located at 38.50° N. Lat.; 82.64° W. Long. Elevation is 577 feet.
Population: 2,251 (1990); 2,027 (2000); 2,077 (2007); 2,112 (2012 projected); Race: 98.7% White, 0.1% Black, 0.0% Asian, 0.8% Hispanic of any race (2007); Density: 1,053.5 persons per square mile (2007); Average household size: 2.42 (2007); Median age: 39.3 (2007); Males per 100 females: 91.8 (2007); Marriage status: 19.7% never married, 59.5% now married, 8.5% widowed, 12.3% divorced (2000); Foreign born: 0.0% (2000); Ancestry (includes multiple ancestries): 22.9% United States or American, 11.1% German, 10.2% English, 10.0% Irish, 6.3% Other groups (2000).
Economy: Single-family building permits issued: 2 (2007); Multi-family building permits issued: 0 (2007); Employment by occupation: 5.2% management, 12.0% professional, 17.8% services, 32.4% sales, 0.1% farming, 11.4% construction, 21.1% production (2000).
Income: Per capita income: $17,759 (2007); Median household income: $30,437 (2007); Average household income: $42,360 (2007); Percent of households with income of $100,000 or more: 6.3% (2007); Poverty rate: 18.6% (2000).
Education: Percent of population age 25 and over with: High school diploma (including GED) or higher: 73.3% (2007); Bachelor's degree or higher: 6.9% (2007); Master's degree or higher: 2.4% (2007).

School District(s)

Dawson-Bryant Local (KG-12)
2005-06 Enrollment: 1,283 . . . . (740) 532-6451

Housing: Homeownership rate: 71.0% (2007); Median home value: $72,208 (2007); Median rent: $300 per month (2000); Median age of housing: 43 years (2000).
Transportation: Commute to work: 92.1% car, 1.7% public transportation, 1.7% walk, 3.4% work from home (2000); Travel time to work: 45.6% less than 15 minutes, 34.7% 15 to 30 minutes, 11.2% 30 to 45 minutes, 2.8% 45 to 60 minutes, 5.7% 60 minutes or more (2000)

HANGING ROCK (village). Covers a land area of 0.620 square miles and a water area of 0.064 square miles. Located at 38.55° N. Lat.; 82.72° W. Long. Elevation is 541 feet.
History: Hanging Rock was named for the sandstone cliff, 400 feet high, which has an overhang at the top. Hanging Rock was founded in 1820 and developed around an iron furnace.
Population: 306 (1990); 279 (2000); 257 (2007); 256 (2012 projected); Race: 99.6% White, 0.0% Black, 0.0% Asian, 0.0% Hispanic of any race (2007); Density: 414.3 persons per square mile (2007); Average household size: 2.47 (2007); Median age: 40.9 (2007); Males per 100 females: 99.2 (2007); Marriage status: 24.0% never married, 61.1% now married, 9.2% widowed, 5.7% divorced (2000); Foreign born: 0.0% (2000); Ancestry (includes multiple ancestries): 28.0% United States or American, 9.7% German, 9.0% Other groups, 8.7% French (except Basque), 8.7% English (2000).
Economy: Employment by occupation: 5.5% management, 14.7% professional, 20.2% services, 25.7% sales, 0.0% farming, 11.9% construction, 22.0% production (2000).
Income: Per capita income: $17,656 (2007); Median household income: $35,000 (2007); Average household income: $43,630 (2007); Percent of households with income of $100,000 or more: 7.7% (2007); Poverty rate: 17.0% (2000).
Education: Percent of population age 25 and over with: High school diploma (including GED) or higher: 74.7% (2007); Bachelor's degree or higher: 6.0% (2007); Master's degree or higher: 3.3% (2007).
Housing: Homeownership rate: 84.6% (2007); Median home value: $74,286 (2007); Median rent: $311 per month (2000); Median age of housing: 29 years (2000).
Transportation: Commute to work: 98.2% car, 0.0% public transportation, 1.8% walk, 0.0% work from home (2000); Travel time to work: 57.8% less than 15 minutes, 34.9% 15 to 30 minutes, 3.7% 30 to 45 minutes, 0.0% 45 to 60 minutes, 3.7% 60 minutes or more (2000)

IRONTON (city). County seat. Covers a land area of 4.135 square miles and a water area of 0.263 square miles. Located at 38.53° N. Lat.; 82.67° W. Long. Elevation is 551 feet.
History: Ironton was founded in 1848 by John Campbell, one of the first ironmasters of the region. The ore deposits in the Ironton district were discovered about 1826, and a charcoal furnace was set up to make pigiron. The iron industry supported Ironton for a century.
Population: 12,708 (1990); 11,211 (2000); 11,355 (2007); 11,431 (2012 projected); Race: 92.7% White, 5.6% Black, 0.5% Asian, 0.5% Hispanic of any race (2007); Density: 2,746.1 persons per square mile (2007); Average household size: 2.22 (2007); Median age: 42.6 (2007); Males per 100 females: 84.1 (2007); Marriage status: 20.6% never married, 51.3% now married, 13.0% widowed, 15.2% divorced (2000); Foreign born: 0.8% (2000); Ancestry (includes multiple ancestries): 18.1% United States or American, 13.8% German, 11.6% Irish, 9.6% English, 9.3% Other groups (2000).
Economy: Single-family building permits issued: 3 (2007); Multi-family building permits issued: 0 (2007); Employment by occupation: 7.6% management, 22.4% professional, 17.1% services, 27.8% sales, 0.4% farming, 6.8% construction, 17.9% production (2000).
Income: Per capita income: $17,955 (2007); Median household income: $26,559 (2007); Average household income: $39,331 (2007); Percent of households with income of $100,000 or more: 7.0% (2007); Poverty rate: 23.1% (2000).
Taxes: Total city taxes per capita: $187 (2006); City property taxes per capita: $56 (2006).
Education: Percent of population age 25 and over with: High school diploma (including GED) or higher: 75.4% (2007); Bachelor's degree or higher: 10.8% (2007); Master's degree or higher: 4.2% (2007).

School District(s)

Dawson-Bryant Local (KG-12)
2005-06 Enrollment: 1,283 . . . . (740) 532-6451
Ironton City (PK-12)
2005-06 Enrollment: 1,669 . . . . (740) 532-4133
Rock Hill Local (PK-12)
2005-06 Enrollment: 1,951 . . . . (740) 532-7030

Four-year College(s)

Ohio University-Southern Campus (Public)
Fall 2007 Enrollment: 1,699. . . . . (740) 533-4600
2007-08 Tuition: In-state $4,395; Out-of-state $5,715

Housing: Homeownership rate: 63.5% (2007); Median home value: $81,445 (2007); Median rent: $289 per month (2000); Median age of housing: 50 years (2000).
Newspapers: The Ironton Tribune (Local news)
Transportation: Commute to work: 92.6% car, 1.0% public transportation, 4.1% walk, 1.6% work from home (2000); Travel time to work: 51.4% less than 15 minutes, 31.4% 15 to 30 minutes, 9.6% 30 to 45 minutes, 2.4% 45 to 60 minutes, 5.2% 60 minutes or more (2000)

Additional Information Contacts

City of Ironton. . . . . (740) 532-3833
http://www.ironton-ohio.com

KITTS HILL (unincorporated postal area, zip code 45645). Covers a land area of 46.166 square miles and a water area of 0.013 square miles. Located at 38.55° N. Lat.; 82.53° W. Long. Elevation is 897 feet.
Population: 2,911 (2000); Race: 98.2% White, 0.2% Black, 0.5% Asian, 1.3% Hispanic of any race (2000); Density: 63.1 persons per square mile (2000); Age: 26.5% under 18, 9.9% over 64 (2000); Marriage status: 16.5% never married, 71.2% now married, 6.2% widowed, 6.1% divorced (2000); Foreign born: 0.5% (2000); Ancestry (includes multiple ancestries): 23.8% United States or American, 7.6% German, 6.4% Other groups, 6.0% English, 5.8% Irish (2000).
Economy: Employment by occupation: 7.7% management, 18.5% professional, 8.9% services, 27.2% sales, 0.0% farming, 20.1% construction, 17.6% production (2000).
Income: Per capita income: $13,753 (2000); Median household income: $33,021 (2000); Poverty rate: 18.6% (2000).
Education: Percent of population age 25 and over with: High school diploma (including GED) or higher: 84.9% (2000); Bachelor's degree or higher: 12.7% (2000).
Housing: Homeownership rate: 88.1% (2000); Median home value: $59,500 (2000); Median rent: $315 per month (2000); Median age of housing: 27 years (2000).

Transportation: Commute to work: 96.3% car, 0.6% public transportation, 0.6% walk, 1.9% work from home (2000); Travel time to work: 14.8% less than 15 minutes, 38.2% 15 to 30 minutes, 25.6% 30 to 45 minutes, 10.3% 45 to 60 minutes, 11.2% 60 minutes or more (2000)

PEDRO (unincorporated postal area, zip code 45659). Covers a land area of 101.909 square miles and a water area of 0.361 square miles. Located at 38.67° N. Lat.; 82.61° W. Long. Elevation is 615 feet.
Population: 3,154 (2000); Race: 98.9% White, 0.0% Black, 0.0% Asian, 0.5% Hispanic of any race (2000); Density: 30.9 persons per square mile (2000); Age: 30.1% under 18, 8.4% over 64 (2000); Marriage status: 18.7% never married, 62.6% now married, 7.4% widowed, 11.3% divorced (2000); Foreign born: 0.2% (2000); Ancestry (includes multiple ancestries): 20.5% United States or American, 13.0% Irish, 11.5% German, 5.0% Other groups, 3.3% English (2000).
Economy: Employment by occupation: 2.5% management, 10.2% professional, 21.7% services, 24.2% sales, 1.5% farming, 13.1% construction, 26.8% production (2000).
Income: Per capita income: $11,157 (2000); Median household income: $23,617 (2000); Poverty rate: 27.3% (2000).
Education: Percent of population age 25 and over with: High school diploma (including GED) or higher: 68.1% (2000); Bachelor's degree or higher: 4.8% (2000).
Housing: Homeownership rate: 76.9% (2000); Median home value: $62,200 (2000); Median rent: $266 per month (2000); Median age of housing: 24 years (2000).
Transportation: Commute to work: 96.7% car, 1.0% public transportation, 1.0% walk, 0.8% work from home (2000); Travel time to work: 7.6% less than 15 minutes, 22.8% 15 to 30 minutes, 38.1% 30 to 45 minutes, 19.3% 45 to 60 minutes, 12.2% 60 minutes or more (2000)

PROCTORVILLE (village). Covers a land area of 0.241 square miles and a water area of 0.026 square miles. Located at 38.43° N. Lat.; 82.38° W. Long. Elevation is 554 feet.
Population: 798 (1990); 620 (2000); 572 (2007); 575 (2012 projected); Race: 98.3% White, 0.7% Black, 0.0% Asian, 0.3% Hispanic of any race (2007); Density: 2,377.9 persons per square mile (2007); Average household size: 2.17 (2007); Median age: 39.0 (2007); Males per 100 females: 91.3 (2007); Marriage status: 22.3% never married, 49.0% now married, 12.6% widowed, 16.2% divorced (2000); Foreign born: 0.0% (2000); Ancestry (includes multiple ancestries): 16.6% German, 12.2% Irish, 10.4% English, 9.1% United States or American, 6.8% Other groups (2000).
Economy: Employment by occupation: 7.9% management, 14.9% professional, 19.4% services, 29.3% sales, 0.0% farming, 9.1% construction, 19.4% production (2000).
Income: Per capita income: $17,268 (2007); Median household income: $26,357 (2007); Average household income: $37,557 (2007); Percent of households with income of $100,000 or more: 4.2% (2007); Poverty rate: 18.6% (2000).
Education: Percent of population age 25 and over with: High school diploma (including GED) or higher: 73.2% (2007); Bachelor's degree or higher: 5.8% (2007); Master's degree or higher: 1.8% (2007).

School District(s)

Fairland Local (KG-12)
2005-06 Enrollment: 1,808 . . . . (740) 886-3100
Housing: Homeownership rate: 57.8% (2007); Median home value: $78,571 (2007); Median rent: $316 per month (2000); Median age of housing: 42 years (2000).
Transportation: Commute to work: 93.6% car, 0.0% public transportation, 3.4% walk, 0.0% work from home (2000); Travel time to work: 38.6% less than 15 minutes, 42.9% 15 to 30 minutes, 9.9% 30 to 45 minutes, 0.9% 45 to 60 minutes, 7.7% 60 minutes or more (2000)

SCOTTOWN (unincorporated postal area, zip code 45678). Covers a land area of 39.858 square miles and a water area of 0.468 square miles. Located at 38.61° N. Lat.; 82.38° W. Long. Elevation is 595 feet.
Population: 1,078 (2000); Race: 95.9% White, 0.0% Black, 3.5% Asian, 0.0% Hispanic of any race (2000); Density: 27.0 persons per square mile (2000); Age: 23.0% under 18, 12.6% over 64 (2000); Marriage status: 23.7% never married, 59.4% now married, 8.1% widowed, 8.8% divorced (2000); Foreign born: 1.4% (2000); Ancestry (includes multiple ancestries): 22.3% United States or American, 11.2% Other groups, 9.1% German, 5.5% English, 3.6% Irish (2000).
Economy: Employment by occupation: 7.9% management, 15.5% professional, 28.3% services, 15.2% sales, 0.0% farming, 0.0% construction, 33.1% production (2000).
Income: Per capita income: $14,233 (2000); Median household income: $32,250 (2000); Poverty rate: 16.8% (2000).
Education: Percent of population age 25 and over with: High school diploma (including GED) or higher: 58.9% (2000); Bachelor's degree or higher: 4.4% (2000).
Housing: Homeownership rate: 80.6% (2000); Median home value: $42,300 (2000); Median rent: $180 per month (2000); Median age of housing: 33 years (2000).
Transportation: Commute to work: 100.0% car, 0.0% public transportation, 0.0% walk, 0.0% work from home (2000); Travel time to work: 0.0% less than 15 minutes, 30.5% 15 to 30 minutes, 47.2% 30 to 45 minutes, 15.1% 45 to 60 minutes, 7.2% 60 minutes or more (2000)

SOUTH POINT (village). Covers a land area of 2.419 square miles and a water area of 0 square miles. Located at 38.41° N. Lat.; 82.58° W. Long. Elevation is 564 feet.
History: South Point was named for its location at the southern tip of Ohio. The residents of South Point enjoyed a view of three states: Kentucky, West Virginia, and Ohio.
Population: 3,902 (1990); 3,742 (2000); 3,924 (2007); 4,040 (2012 projected); Race: 95.2% White, 2.9% Black, 0.2% Asian, 0.4% Hispanic of any race (2007); Density: 1,622.3 persons per square mile (2007); Average household size: 2.44 (2007); Median age: 39.2 (2007); Males per 100 females: 91.3 (2007); Marriage status: 20.6% never married, 62.5% now married, 7.1% widowed, 9.8% divorced (2000); Foreign born: 0.3% (2000); Ancestry (includes multiple ancestries): 20.5% United States or American, 13.1% English, 12.9% Irish, 11.3% German, 7.9% Other groups (2000).
Economy: Single-family building permits issued: 6 (2007); Multi-family building permits issued: 2 (2007); Employment by occupation: 8.8% management, 20.1% professional, 17.9% services, 29.4% sales, 0.0% farming, 5.1% construction, 18.7% production (2000).
Income: Per capita income: $17,514 (2007); Median household income: $36,461 (2007); Average household income: $42,255 (2007); Percent of households with income of $100,000 or more: 5.7% (2007); Poverty rate: 11.3% (2000).
Education: Percent of population age 25 and over with: High school diploma (including GED) or higher: 81.8% (2007); Bachelor's degree or higher: 14.6% (2007); Master's degree or higher: 6.1% (2007).

School District(s)

South Point Local (KG-12)
2005-06 Enrollment: 1,880 . . . . (740) 377-4315

Four-year College(s)

Tri-State Bible College (Private, Not-for-profit, Undenominational)
Fall 2007 Enrollment: 41 . . . . (740) 377-2520
2007-08 Tuition: In-state $5,000; Out-of-state $5,000
Housing: Homeownership rate: 71.8% (2007); Median home value: $99,321 (2007); Median rent: $348 per month (2000); Median age of housing: 30 years (2000).
Transportation: Commute to work: 95.5% car, 0.5% public transportation, 1.0% walk, 1.1% work from home (2000); Travel time to work: 33.3% less than 15 minutes, 52.7% 15 to 30 minutes, 6.1% 30 to 45 minutes, 2.0% 45 to 60 minutes, 5.9% 60 minutes or more (2000)
Additional Information Contacts
Greater Lawrence County Chamber of Commerce . . . . (740) 377-4550
http://www.lawrencecountyohio.org
Village of South Point. . . . . (740) 377-4838
http://www.villageofsouthpoint.com

WATERLOO (unincorporated postal area, zip code 45688). Covers a land area of 36.160 square miles and a water area of 0.010 square miles. Located at 38.73° N. Lat.; 82.52° W. Long. Elevation is 620 feet.
Population: 440 (2000); Race: 94.0% White, 0.0% Black, 0.0% Asian, 0.0% Hispanic of any race (2000); Density: 12.2 persons per square mile (2000); Age: 32.6% under 18, 9.4% over 64 (2000); Marriage status: 29.9% never married, 42.5% now married, 6.4% widowed, 21.1% divorced (2000); Foreign born: 0.0% (2000); Ancestry (includes multiple ancestries): 28.6% United States or American, 15.0% German, 12.5% Other groups, 5.8% Irish, 4.3% Dutch (2000).
Economy: Employment by occupation: 7.2% management, 4.2% professional, 25.3% services, 19.3% sales, 6.0% farming, 9.0% construction, 28.9% production (2000).

Income: Per capita income: $8,787 (2000); Median household income: $20,804 (2000); Poverty rate: 39.1% (2000).
Education: Percent of population age 25 and over with: High school diploma (including GED) or higher: 49.2% (2000); Bachelor's degree or higher: 3.8% (2000).
Housing: Homeownership rate: 75.0% (2000); Median home value: $42,000 (2000); Median rent: $279 per month (2000); Median age of housing: 30 years (2000).
Transportation: Commute to work: 100.0% car, 0.0% public transportation, 0.0% walk, 0.0% work from home (2000); Travel time to work: 0.0% less than 15 minutes, 3.0% 15 to 30 minutes, 42.8% 30 to 45 minutes, 36.7% 45 to 60 minutes, 17.5% 60 minutes or more (2000)

WILLOW WOOD (unincorporated postal area, zip code 45696). Covers a land area of 34.810 square miles and a water area of 0.040 square miles. Located at 38.59° N. Lat.; 82.46° W. Long. Elevation is 580 feet.
Population: 1,366 (2000); Race: 97.7% White, 0.5% Black, 0.0% Asian, 0.4% Hispanic of any race (2000); Density: 39.2 persons per square mile (2000); Age: 31.6% under 18, 8.2% over 64 (2000); Marriage status: 19.7% never married, 60.8% now married, 9.1% widowed, 10.4% divorced (2000); Foreign born: 0.4% (2000); Ancestry (includes multiple ancestries): 30.6% United States or American, 12.7% English, 9.2% Other groups, 6.9% German, 6.4% Irish (2000).
Economy: Employment by occupation: 2.7% management, 13.3% professional, 23.6% services, 18.9% sales, 0.0% farming, 17.9% construction, 23.6% production (2000).
Income: Per capita income: $10,968 (2000); Median household income: $25,179 (2000); Poverty rate: 27.9% (2000).
Education: Percent of population age 25 and over with: High school diploma (including GED) or higher: 74.1% (2000); Bachelor's degree or higher: 7.2% (2000).

School District(s)

Symmes Valley Local (KG-12)
2005-06 Enrollment: 917 . . . . (740) 643-2451

Housing: Homeownership rate: 86.7% (2000); Median home value: $71,800 (2000); Median rent: $275 per month (2000); Median age of housing: 30 years (2000).
Transportation: Commute to work: 100.0% car, 0.0% public transportation, 0.0% walk, 0.0% work from home (2000); Travel time to work: 14.7% less than 15 minutes, 25.5% 15 to 30 minutes, 45.2% 30 to 45 minutes, 4.6% 45 to 60 minutes, 10.0% 60 minutes or more (2000)

Licking County

Located in central Ohio; drained by the Licking River and Raccoon Creek; includes part of Buckeye Lake. Covers a land area of 686.50 square miles, a water area of 1.88 square miles, and is located in the Eastern Time Zone. The county was founded in 1808. County seat is Newark.

Licking County is part of the Columbus, OH Metropolitan Statistical Area. The entire metro area includes: Delaware County, OH; Fairfield County, OH; Franklin County, OH; Licking County, OH; Madison County, OH; Morrow County, OH; Pickaway County, OH; Union County, OH

Weather Station: Newark Water Works Elevation: 833 feet

	Jan	Feb	Mar	Apr	May	Jun	Jul	Aug	Sep	Oct	Nov	Dec
High	35	40	51	63	73	81	85	83	77	65	52	41
Low	19	22	30	39	49	58	62	60	53	41	33	25
Precip	2.8	2.5	3.2	3.9	4.3	4.4	4.5	4.2	3.0	2.7	3.4	3.2
Snow	8.4	5.3	2.8	0.9	tr	0.0	0.0	0.0	0.0	tr	0.5	2.7

High and Low temperatures in degrees Fahrenheit; Precipitation and Snow in inches

Population: 128,300 (1990); 145,491 (2000); 157,581 (2007); 165,549 (2012 projected); Race: 94.7% White, 2.6% Black, 0.7% Asian, 0.9% Hispanic of any race (2007); Density: 229.5 persons per square mile (2007); Average household size: 2.59 (2007); Median age: 38.0 (2007); Males per 100 females: 95.7 (2007).
Religion: Five largest groups: 8.4% Catholic Church, 6.6% The United Methodist Church, 4.6% Southern Baptist Convention, 2.8% Christian Churches and Churches of Christ, 2.0% Presbyterian Church (U.S.A.) (2000).
Economy: Unemployment rate: 6.1% (6/2008); Total civilian labor force: 86,263 (6/2008); Leading industries: 17.3% manufacturing; 14.3% retail trade; 12.7% health care and social assistance (2005); Farms: 1,482 totaling 237,285 acres (2002); Companies that employ 500 or more persons: 8 (2006); Companies that employ 100 to 499 persons: 73 (2006); Companies that employ less than 100 persons: 2,903 (2006); Black-owned businesses: n/a (2002); Hispanic-owned businesses: n/a (2002); Asian-owned businesses: n/a (2002); Women-owned businesses: 3,551 (2002); Retail sales per capita: $11,793 (2008). Single-family building permits issued: 370 (2007); Multi-family building permits issued: 105 (2007).
Income: Per capita income: $24,756 (2007); Median household income: $52,158 (2007); Average household income: $63,682 (2007); Percent of households with income of $100,000 or more: 16.2% (2007); Poverty rate: 10.2% (2005); Bankruptcy rate: 4.15% (2007).
Taxes: Total county taxes per capita: $239 (2006); County property taxes per capita: $112 (2006).
Education: Percent of population age 25 and over with: High school diploma (including GED) or higher: 85.0% (2007); Bachelor's degree or higher: 19.0% (2007); Master's degree or higher: 5.9% (2007).
Housing: Homeownership rate: 74.9% (2007); Median home value: $141,207 (2007); Median rent: $405 per month (2000); Median age of housing: 31 years (2000).
Health: Birth rate: 138.4 per 10,000 population (2007); Death rate: 87.1 per 10,000 population (2007); Age-adjusted cancer mortality rate: 214.8 deaths per 100,000 population (2005); Air Quality Index: 69.8% good, 28.4% moderate, 1.9% unhealthy for sensitive individuals, 0.0% unhealthy (percent of days in 2007); Number of physicians: 11.5 per 10,000 population (2005); Hospital beds: 15.6 per 10,000 population (2004); Hospital admissions: 471.1 per 10,000 population (2004).
Elections: 2004 Presidential election results: 61.7% Bush, 37.8% Kerry, 0.0% Nader, 0.2% Badnarik
National and State Parks: Black Hand State Nature Preserve; Moundbuilders State Memorial; Octagon State Memorial

Additional Information Contacts

Licking County Government. . . . . (740) 349-6066
http://www.lcounty.com
City of Newark . . . . (740) 670-7500
http://www.ci.newark.oh.us
City of Pataskala . . . . (740) 964-2416
http://www.ci.pataskala.oh.us
Granville Chamber of Commerce . . . . (740) 587-4490
http://granvilleoh.com
Greater Buckeye Lake Chamber of Commerce. . . . . (740) 928-2048
http://www.buckeyelakecc.com
Greater Licking Co. Convention & Visitors Bureau . . . . (740) 345-8224
http://www.lccvb.com
Johnstown Area Chamber of Commerce. . . . . (740) 967-2334
http://www.johnstown.ws/villagegov.html
Licking County Chamber of Commerce. . . . . (740) 345-9757
http://www.lickingcountychamber.com
Pataskala Area Chamber of Commerce . . . . (740) 964-6100
http://www.pataskalachamber.com
Village of Granville. . . . . (740) 587-0707
http://www.granville.oh.us
Village of Hebron . . . . (740) 928-2261
http://www.hebronvillage.com
Village of Johnstown . . . . (740) 967-3177
http://www.villageofjohnstown.org

Licking County Communities

ALEXANDRIA (village). Covers a land area of 0.162 square miles and a water area of 0 square miles. Located at 40.09° N. Lat.; 82.61° W. Long. Elevation is 971 feet.
Population: 468 (1990); 85 (2000); 76 (2007); 73 (2012 projected); Race: 98.7% White, 0.0% Black, 0.0% Asian, 1.3% Hispanic of any race (2007); Density: 467.7 persons per square mile (2007); Average household size: 3.04 (2007); Median age: 35.0 (2007); Males per 100 females: 117.1 (2007); Marriage status: 0.0% never married, 66.7% now married, 33.3% widowed, 0.0% divorced (2000); Foreign born: 0.0% (2000); Ancestry (includes multiple ancestries): 82.4% German, 23.5% Scotch-Irish, 17.6% Other groups (2000).
Economy: Employment by occupation: 0.0% management, 0.0% professional, 100.0% services, 0.0% sales, 0.0% farming, 0.0% construction, 0.0% production (2000).
Income: Per capita income: $14,046 (2007); Median household income: $39,167 (2007); Average household income: $42,700 (2007); Percent of

households with income of $100,000 or more: 0.0% (2007); Poverty rate: 0.0% (2000).
Education: Percent of population age 25 and over with: High school diploma (including GED) or higher: 100.0% (2007); Bachelor's degree or higher: 42.2% (2007); Master's degree or higher: 0.0% (2007).

School District(s)

Northridge Local (PK-12)
2005-06 Enrollment: 1,489 . . . . (740) 967-6631
Housing: Homeownership rate: 96.0% (2007); Median home value: $197,500 (2007); Median rent: $n/a per month (2000); Median age of housing: 11 years (2000).
Transportation: Commute to work: 100.0% car, 0.0% public transportation, 0.0% walk, 0.0% work from home (2000); Travel time to work: 0.0% less than 15 minutes, 0.0% 15 to 30 minutes, 100.0% 30 to 45 minutes, 0.0% 45 to 60 minutes, 0.0% 60 minutes or more (2000)

BEECHWOOD TRAILS (CDP). Covers a land area of 3.453 square miles and a water area of 0 square miles. Located at 40.02° N. Lat.; 82.65° W. Long. Elevation is 1,207 feet.
Population: 1,367 (1990); 2,258 (2000); 2,691 (2007); 2,975 (2012 projected); Race: 96.7% White, 1.0% Black, 0.4% Asian, 0.6% Hispanic of any race (2007); Density: 779.2 persons per square mile (2007); Average household size: 2.95 (2007); Median age: 40.3 (2007); Males per 100 females: 100.8 (2007); Marriage status: 18.3% never married, 73.1% now married, 1.3% widowed, 7.4% divorced (2000); Foreign born: 0.9% (2000); Ancestry (includes multiple ancestries): 27.9% German, 13.1% Irish, 10.9% English, 10.3% United States or American, 9.6% Other groups (2000).
Economy: Employment by occupation: 19.2% management, 23.3% professional, 11.1% services, 31.0% sales, 0.5% farming, 9.3% construction, 5.5% production (2000).
Income: Per capita income: $30,753 (2007); Median household income: $87,933 (2007); Average household income: $90,842 (2007); Percent of households with income of $100,000 or more: 37.8% (2007); Poverty rate: 1.2% (2000).
Education: Percent of population age 25 and over with: High school diploma (including GED) or higher: 96.9% (2007); Bachelor's degree or higher: 32.6% (2007); Master's degree or higher: 7.0% (2007).
Housing: Homeownership rate: 97.8% (2007); Median home value: $189,143 (2007); Median rent: $675 per month (2000); Median age of housing: 16 years (2000).
Transportation: Commute to work: 93.7% car, 0.0% public transportation, 0.0% walk, 6.3% work from home (2000); Travel time to work: 11.4% less than 15 minutes, 35.6% 15 to 30 minutes, 34.3% 30 to 45 minutes, 15.3% 45 to 60 minutes, 3.5% 60 minutes or more (2000)

BUCKEYE LAKE (village). Covers a land area of 2.036 square miles and a water area of 0.011 square miles. Located at 39.93° N. Lat.; 82.48° W. Long. Elevation is 899 feet.
History: Beside lake created for Ohio Canal c.1827.
Population: 2,989 (1990); 3,049 (2000); 3,065 (2007); 3,094 (2012 projected); Race: 96.2% White, 1.0% Black, 0.1% Asian, 0.7% Hispanic of any race (2007); Density: 1,505.6 persons per square mile (2007); Average household size: 2.42 (2007); Median age: 35.9 (2007); Males per 100 females: 97.1 (2007); Marriage status: 21.0% never married, 52.1% now married, 8.0% widowed, 18.8% divorced (2000); Foreign born: 0.7% (2000); Ancestry (includes multiple ancestries): 23.7% German, 15.8% Irish, 10.4% Other groups, 10.1% United States or American, 8.4% English (2000).
Economy: Single-family building permits issued: 0 (2007); Multi-family building permits issued: 0 (2007); Employment by occupation: 8.6% management, 6.0% professional, 18.3% services, 23.7% sales, 0.0% farming, 13.6% construction, 29.9% production (2000).
Income: Per capita income: $19,644 (2007); Median household income: $36,580 (2007); Average household income: $47,597 (2007); Percent of households with income of $100,000 or more: 6.2% (2007); Poverty rate: 16.1% (2000).
Education: Percent of population age 25 and over with: High school diploma (including GED) or higher: 72.3% (2007); Bachelor's degree or higher: 4.4% (2007); Master's degree or higher: 1.8% (2007).
Housing: Homeownership rate: 68.4% (2007); Median home value: $55,833 (2007); Median rent: $357 per month (2000); Median age of housing: 31 years (2000).
Safety: Violent crime rate: 72.0 per 10,000 population; Property crime rate: 635.0 per 10,000 population (2007).
Newspapers: Buckeye Lake Beacon (Community news)
Transportation: Commute to work: 89.7% car, 0.4% public transportation, 4.8% walk, 3.0% work from home (2000); Travel time to work: 29.3% less than 15 minutes, 27.9% 15 to 30 minutes, 22.8% 30 to 45 minutes, 12.4% 45 to 60 minutes, 7.6% 60 minutes or more (2000)
Additional Information Contacts
Greater Buckeye Lake Chamber of Commerce. . . . . (740) 928-2048
http://www.buckeyelakecc.com

CROTON (unincorporated postal area, zip code 43013). Aka Hartford. Covers a land area of 19.844 square miles and a water area of 0 square miles. Located at 40.11° N. Lat.; 82.69° W. Long. Elevation is 1,168 feet.
Population: 979 (2000); Race: 99.4% White, 0.0% Black, 0.0% Asian, 1.4% Hispanic of any race (2000); Density: 49.3 persons per square mile (2000); Age: 28.6% under 18, 12.4% over 64 (2000); Marriage status: 17.4% never married, 66.2% now married, 8.1% widowed, 8.3% divorced (2000); Foreign born: 0.2% (2000); Ancestry (includes multiple ancestries): 23.4% German, 19.1% United States or American, 16.0% English, 11.1% Irish, 8.1% Other groups (2000).
Economy: Employment by occupation: 16.3% management, 13.8% professional, 15.1% services, 24.4% sales, 5.3% farming, 13.4% construction, 11.7% production (2000).
Income: Per capita income: $18,127 (2000); Median household income: $51,429 (2000); Poverty rate: 7.6% (2000).
Education: Percent of population age 25 and over with: High school diploma (including GED) or higher: 86.0% (2000); Bachelor's degree or higher: 16.8% (2000).

School District(s)

Northridge Local (PK-12)
2005-06 Enrollment: 1,489 . . . . (740) 967-6631
Housing: Homeownership rate: 78.2% (2000); Median home value: $99,400 (2000); Median rent: $409 per month (2000); Median age of housing: 47 years (2000).
Transportation: Commute to work: 91.6% car, 0.0% public transportation, 0.2% walk, 8.1% work from home (2000); Travel time to work: 23.3% less than 15 minutes, 19.6% 15 to 30 minutes, 32.4% 30 to 45 minutes, 19.1% 45 to 60 minutes, 5.6% 60 minutes or more (2000)

GRANVILLE (village). Covers a land area of 4.007 square miles and a water area of 0 square miles. Located at 40.06° N. Lat.; 82.51° W. Long. Elevation is 961 feet.
History: Granville was laid out in 1806 and named for the Massachusetts home of its early settlers. In 1831 the Granville Literary and Theological Institute was established, becoming Denison University in 1856.
Population: 4,196 (1990); 3,167 (2000); 3,669 (2007); 3,997 (2012 projected); Race: 96.3% White, 0.7% Black, 0.9% Asian, 1.3% Hispanic of any race (2007); Density: 915.7 persons per square mile (2007); Average household size: 2.47 (2007); Median age: 44.3 (2007); Males per 100 females: 95.8 (2007); Marriage status: 17.5% never married, 66.8% now married, 8.1% widowed, 7.6% divorced (2000); Foreign born: 3.4% (2000); Ancestry (includes multiple ancestries): 29.7% German, 24.7% English, 21.3% Irish, 7.9% Polish, 6.1% Italian (2000).
Economy: Employment by occupation: 31.6% management, 40.0% professional, 7.5% services, 17.7% sales, 0.0% farming, 1.2% construction, 2.0% production (2000).
Income: Per capita income: $43,624 (2007); Median household income: $84,800 (2007); Average household income: $107,638 (2007); Percent of households with income of $100,000 or more: 41.3% (2007); Poverty rate: 3.8% (2000).
Education: Percent of population age 25 and over with: High school diploma (including GED) or higher: 98.1% (2007); Bachelor's degree or higher: 68.2% (2007); Master's degree or higher: 32.1% (2007).

School District(s)

Granville Exempted Village (PK-12)
2005-06 Enrollment: 2,346 . . . . (740) 587-8101

Four-year College(s)

Denison University (Private, Not-for-profit)
Fall 2007 Enrollment: 2,242. . . . . (740) 587-0810
2007-08 Tuition: In-state $33,010; Out-of-state $33,010
Housing: Homeownership rate: 75.3% (2007); Median home value: $250,325 (2007); Median rent: $572 per month (2000); Median age of housing: 41 years (2000).
Safety: Violent crime rate: 5.7 per 10,000 population; Property crime rate: 124.4 per 10,000 population (2007).
Newspapers: Granville Sentinel (Community news; Circulation 2,000)

Transportation: Commute to work: 88.5% car, 1.4% public transportation, 4.0% walk, 6.1% work from home (2000); Travel time to work: 48.5% less than 15 minutes, 23.6% 15 to 30 minutes, 14.7% 30 to 45 minutes, 8.0% 45 to 60 minutes, 5.1% 60 minutes or more (2000)

Additional Information Contacts

Granville Chamber of Commerce . . . . (740) 587-4490
http://granvilleoh.com

Village of Granville . . . . (740) 587-0707
http://www.granville.oh.us

GRANVILLE SOUTH (CDP). Covers a land area of 6.110 square miles and a water area of 0.025 square miles. Located at 40.05° N. Lat.; 82.54° W. Long.

Population: 1,124 (1990); 1,194 (2000); 1,244 (2007); 1,268 (2012 projected); Race: 97.0% White, 0.0% Black, 1.1% Asian, 0.8% Hispanic of any race (2007); Density: 203.6 persons per square mile (2007); Average household size: 2.89 (2007); Median age: 46.4 (2007); Males per 100 females: 92.0 (2007); Marriage status: 16.7% never married, 76.2% now married, 2.9% widowed, 4.2% divorced (2000); Foreign born: 2.0% (2000); Ancestry (includes multiple ancestries): 41.3% German, 25.7% English, 11.6% Irish, 7.5% Italian, 6.7% Welsh (2000).

Economy: Employment by occupation: 14.5% management, 32.6% professional, 11.3% services, 27.5% sales, 0.0% farming, 3.9% construction, 10.2% production (2000).

Income: Per capita income: $28,808 (2007); Median household income: $79,348 (2007); Average household income: $83,343 (2007); Percent of households with income of $100,000 or more: 32.3% (2007); Poverty rate: 1.3% (2000).

Education: Percent of population age 25 and over with: High school diploma (including GED) or higher: 97.9% (2007); Bachelor's degree or higher: 46.5% (2007); Master's degree or higher: 14.6% (2007).

Housing: Homeownership rate: 93.0% (2007); Median home value: $218,932 (2007); Median rent: $433 per month (2000); Median age of housing: 27 years (2000).

Transportation: Commute to work: 91.0% car, 0.8% public transportation, 0.0% walk, 7.0% work from home (2000); Travel time to work: 43.2% less than 15 minutes, 21.3% 15 to 30 minutes, 23.4% 30 to 45 minutes, 4.0% 45 to 60 minutes, 8.1% 60 minutes or more (2000)

GRATIOT (village). Covers a land area of 0.119 square miles and a water area of 0 square miles. Located at 39.95° N. Lat.; 82.21° W. Long. Elevation is 988 feet.

Population: 195 (1990); 187 (2000); 209 (2007); 223 (2012 projected); Race: 97.1% White, 1.9% Black, 0.0% Asian, 0.0% Hispanic of any race (2007); Density: 1,749.7 persons per square mile (2007); Average household size: 2.40 (2007); Median age: 42.7 (2007); Males per 100 females: 115.5 (2007); Marriage status: 19.2% never married, 64.8% now married, 8.0% widowed, 8.0% divorced (2000); Foreign born: 0.0% (2000); Ancestry (includes multiple ancestries): 27.3% German, 16.3% Irish, 11.6% United States or American, 9.3% English, 5.8% Italian (2000).

Economy: Employment by occupation: 7.0% management, 11.6% professional, 15.1% services, 25.6% sales, 1.2% farming, 8.1% construction, 31.4% production (2000).

Income: Per capita income: $21,687 (2007); Median household income: $44,583 (2007); Average household income: $52,098 (2007); Percent of households with income of $100,000 or more: 8.0% (2007); Poverty rate: 9.3% (2000).

Education: Percent of population age 25 and over with: High school diploma (including GED) or higher: 86.0% (2007); Bachelor's degree or higher: 4.7% (2007); Master's degree or higher: 0.0% (2007).

Housing: Homeownership rate: 82.8% (2007); Median home value: $112,838 (2007); Median rent: $342 per month (2000); Median age of housing: 60+ years (2000).

Transportation: Commute to work: 91.8% car, 0.0% public transportation, 5.9% walk, 2.4% work from home (2000); Travel time to work: 15.7% less than 15 minutes, 47.0% 15 to 30 minutes, 28.9% 30 to 45 minutes, 4.8% 45 to 60 minutes, 3.6% 60 minutes or more (2000)

HANOVER (village). Covers a land area of 1.000 square miles and a water area of 0 square miles. Located at 40.07° N. Lat.; 82.27° W. Long. Elevation is 823 feet.

Population: 853 (1990); 885 (2000); 995 (2007); 1,067 (2012 projected); Race: 98.6% White, 0.4% Black, 0.0% Asian, 0.2% Hispanic of any race (2007); Density: 995.2 persons per square mile (2007); Average household size: 2.78 (2007); Median age: 39.5 (2007); Males per 100 females: 99.8 (2007); Marriage status: 21.1% never married, 67.1% now married, 5.0% widowed, 6.7% divorced (2000); Foreign born: 1.0% (2000); Ancestry (includes multiple ancestries): 20.5% German, 12.9% Irish, 12.1% English, 11.3% United States or American, 8.1% Other groups (2000).

Economy: Single-family building permits issued: 3 (2007); Multi-family building permits issued: 0 (2007); Employment by occupation: 9.1% management, 15.6% professional, 15.4% services, 21.3% sales, 0.2% farming, 13.7% construction, 24.7% production (2000).

Income: Per capita income: $23,590 (2007); Median household income: $60,000 (2007); Average household income: $65,566 (2007); Percent of households with income of $100,000 or more: 13.1% (2007); Poverty rate: 4.4% (2000).

Education: Percent of population age 25 and over with: High school diploma (including GED) or higher: 82.5% (2007); Bachelor's degree or higher: 4.4% (2007); Master's degree or higher: 0.9% (2007).

Housing: Homeownership rate: 88.8% (2007); Median home value: $132,051 (2007); Median rent: $428 per month (2000); Median age of housing: 29 years (2000).

Transportation: Commute to work: 94.3% car, 0.0% public transportation, 2.1% walk, 3.4% work from home (2000); Travel time to work: 14.6% less than 15 minutes, 59.3% 15 to 30 minutes, 12.0% 30 to 45 minutes, 7.2% 45 to 60 minutes, 7.0% 60 minutes or more (2000)

HARBOR HILLS (CDP). Covers a land area of 2.725 square miles and a water area of 0.721 square miles. Located at 39.93° N. Lat.; 82.43° W. Long. Elevation is 928 feet.

Population: 1,372 (1990); 1,303 (2000); 1,334 (2007); 1,349 (2012 projected); Race: 98.3% White, 0.2% Black, 0.1% Asian, 0.1% Hispanic of any race (2007); Density: 489.5 persons per square mile (2007); Average household size: 2.24 (2007); Median age: 50.3 (2007); Males per 100 females: 102.1 (2007); Marriage status: 13.5% never married, 70.0% now married, 7.5% widowed, 9.0% divorced (2000); Foreign born: 3.2% (2000); Ancestry (includes multiple ancestries): 28.2% German, 10.9% Irish, 10.4% United States or American, 9.1% English, 7.3% Italian (2000).

Economy: Employment by occupation: 14.8% management, 16.8% professional, 12.9% services, 32.2% sales, 0.0% farming, 9.8% construction, 13.5% production (2000).

Income: Per capita income: $32,314 (2007); Median household income: $57,391 (2007); Average household income: $72,328 (2007); Percent of households with income of $100,000 or more: 20.6% (2007); Poverty rate: 2.4% (2000).

Education: Percent of population age 25 and over with: High school diploma (including GED) or higher: 87.0% (2007); Bachelor's degree or higher: 14.2% (2007); Master's degree or higher: 3.5% (2007).

Housing: Homeownership rate: 89.9% (2007); Median home value: $178,814 (2007); Median rent: $425 per month (2000); Median age of housing: 41 years (2000).

Transportation: Commute to work: 93.9% car, 1.2% public transportation, 0.0% walk, 4.9% work from home (2000); Travel time to work: 22.3% less than 15 minutes, 28.1% 15 to 30 minutes, 21.5% 30 to 45 minutes, 19.7% 45 to 60 minutes, 8.4% 60 minutes or more (2000)

HARTFORD (village). Covers a land area of 0.536 square miles and a water area of 0 square miles. Located at 40.23° N. Lat.; 82.68° W. Long. Elevation is 1,168 feet.

Population: 418 (1990); 412 (2000); 460 (2007); 491 (2012 projected); Race: 97.2% White, 0.0% Black, 0.2% Asian, 1.1% Hispanic of any race (2007); Density: 858.7 persons per square mile (2007); Average household size: 2.72 (2007); Median age: 34.6 (2007); Males per 100 females: 124.4 (2007); Marriage status: 22.0% never married, 61.5% now married, 7.2% widowed, 9.3% divorced (2000); Foreign born: 0.5% (2000); Ancestry (includes multiple ancestries): 29.9% United States or American, 14.3% German, 9.5% Irish, 6.8% English, 4.0% Other groups (2000).

Economy: Single-family building permits issued: 0 (2007); Multi-family building permits issued: 0 (2007); Employment by occupation: 7.1% management, 9.6% professional, 21.2% services, 22.7% sales, 2.5% farming, 14.6% construction, 22.2% production (2000).

Income: Per capita income: $20,304 (2007); Median household income: $47,656 (2007); Average household income: $55,266 (2007); Percent of households with income of $100,000 or more: 8.3% (2007); Poverty rate: 6.0% (2000).

Education: Percent of population age 25 and over with: High school diploma (including GED) or higher: 89.5% (2007); Bachelor's degree or higher: 12.1% (2007); Master's degree or higher: 2.6% (2007).

School District(s)

Joseph Badger Local (PK-12)
2005-06 Enrollment: 1,028 . . . . (330) 876-1051

Housing: Homeownership rate: 74.6% (2007); Median home value: $109,483 (2007); Median rent: $407 per month (2000); Median age of housing: 60+ years (2000).

Transportation: Commute to work: 97.9% car, 0.0% public transportation, 0.5% walk, 1.5% work from home (2000); Travel time to work: 27.2% less than 15 minutes, 18.3% 15 to 30 minutes, 23.0% 30 to 45 minutes, 23.6% 45 to 60 minutes, 7.9% 60 minutes or more (2000)

HEATH (city). Aka Fourmile Lock. Covers a land area of 10.442 square miles and a water area of 0.007 square miles. Located at 40.03° N. Lat.; 82.43° W. Long. Elevation is 860 feet.

History: Former Newark Air Force Base nearby that specialized in guidance of navigation systems; closed base scheduled for privatization.

Population: 7,414 (1990); 8,527 (2000); 8,888 (2007); 9,166 (2012 projected); Race: 94.9% White, 2.4% Black, 0.8% Asian, 1.4% Hispanic of any race (2007); Density: 851.2 persons per square mile (2007); Average household size: 2.48 (2007); Median age: 38.7 (2007); Males per 100 females: 91.9 (2007); Marriage status: 20.5% never married, 58.1% now married, 7.5% widowed, 13.9% divorced (2000); Foreign born: 0.5% (2000); Ancestry (includes multiple ancestries): 25.8% German, 14.2% Irish, 13.0% United States or American, 10.6% English, 9.6% Other groups (2000).

Economy: Employment by occupation: 13.0% management, 13.4% professional, 17.1% services, 28.8% sales, 0.1% farming, 8.5% construction, 19.1% production (2000).

Income: Per capita income: $22,449 (2007); Median household income: $43,767 (2007); Average household income: $54,691 (2007); Percent of households with income of $100,000 or more: 9.1% (2007); Poverty rate: 8.5% (2000).

Education: Percent of population age 25 and over with: High school diploma (including GED) or higher: 82.5% (2007); Bachelor's degree or higher: 13.7% (2007); Master's degree or higher: 3.4% (2007).

School District(s)

Heath City (PK-12)
2005-06 Enrollment: 1,733 . . . . (740) 522-2816

Housing: Homeownership rate: 69.9% (2007); Median home value: $121,780 (2007); Median rent: $422 per month (2000); Median age of housing: 29 years (2000).

Safety: Violent crime rate: 17.9 per 10,000 population; Property crime rate: 616.6 per 10,000 population (2007).

Transportation: Commute to work: 95.6% car, 0.9% public transportation, 1.1% walk, 1.7% work from home (2000); Travel time to work: 44.4% less than 15 minutes, 31.1% 15 to 30 minutes, 9.1% 30 to 45 minutes, 8.9% 45 to 60 minutes, 6.5% 60 minutes or more (2000)

Additional Information Contacts

Greater Licking Co. Convention & Visitors Bureau . . . . (740) 345-8224
http://www.lccvb.com

HEBRON (village). Covers a land area of 2.683 square miles and a water area of 0 square miles. Located at 39.96° N. Lat.; 82.49° W. Long. Elevation is 889 feet.

History: Hebron developed as a commercial center on the Ohio & Erie Canal and the old National Road.

Population: 2,216 (1990); 2,034 (2000); 2,169 (2007); 2,268 (2012 projected); Race: 96.4% White, 0.3% Black, 0.7% Asian, 1.7% Hispanic of any race (2007); Density: 808.5 persons per square mile (2007); Average household size: 2.24 (2007); Median age: 37.2 (2007); Males per 100 females: 89.1 (2007); Marriage status: 23.6% never married, 51.2% now married, 9.9% widowed, 15.3% divorced (2000); Foreign born: 1.0% (2000); Ancestry (includes multiple ancestries): 25.0% German, 15.8% Irish, 11.6% United States or American, 10.2% English, 6.9% Other groups (2000).

Economy: Employment by occupation: 12.1% management, 7.7% professional, 18.2% services, 30.6% sales, 0.2% farming, 10.9% construction, 20.4% production (2000).

Income: Per capita income: $20,644 (2007); Median household income: $38,576 (2007); Average household income: $46,306 (2007); Percent of households with income of $100,000 or more: 5.6% (2007); Poverty rate: 9.5% (2000).

Education: Percent of population age 25 and over with: High school diploma (including GED) or higher: 82.7% (2007); Bachelor's degree or higher: 6.8% (2007); Master's degree or higher: 1.4% (2007).

School District(s)

Lakewood Digital Academy (KG-12)
2005-06 Enrollment: 26 . . . . (740) 928-5878

Lakewood Local (PK-12)
2005-06 Enrollment: 2,250 . . . . (740) 928-5878

Housing: Homeownership rate: 62.7% (2007); Median home value: $101,256 (2007); Median rent: $344 per month (2000); Median age of housing: 35 years (2000).

Safety: Violent crime rate: 4.6 per 10,000 population; Property crime rate: 415.7 per 10,000 population (2007).

Transportation: Commute to work: 95.1% car, 0.3% public transportation, 2.4% walk, 1.2% work from home (2000); Travel time to work: 33.8% less than 15 minutes, 25.7% 15 to 30 minutes, 21.8% 30 to 45 minutes, 10.8% 45 to 60 minutes, 7.9% 60 minutes or more (2000)

Additional Information Contacts

Village of Hebron . . . . (740) 928-2261
http://www.hebronvillage.com

JOHNSTOWN (village). Covers a land area of 2.094 square miles and a water area of 0 square miles. Located at 40.14° N. Lat.; 82.68° W. Long. Elevation is 1,152 feet.

History: Johnstown was the site of the discovery in 1926 of the skeleton of a mastodon. A farmer digging in his garden uncovered the bones of an animal that had been 8 feet tall and 15 feet long. The skeleton was purchased by the Cleveland Museum of Natural History.

Population: 3,272 (1990); 3,440 (2000); 3,907 (2007); 4,205 (2012 projected); Race: 98.3% White, 0.1% Black, 0.2% Asian, 0.5% Hispanic of any race (2007); Density: 1,866.0 persons per square mile (2007); Average household size: 2.42 (2007); Median age: 36.4 (2007); Males per 100 females: 92.9 (2007); Marriage status: 21.2% never married, 59.5% now married, 9.6% widowed, 9.7% divorced (2000); Foreign born: 1.4% (2000); Ancestry (includes multiple ancestries): 28.6% German, 16.0% United States or American, 14.3% Irish, 11.5% English, 4.8% Other groups (2000).

Economy: Single-family building permits issued: 11 (2007); Multi-family building permits issued: 0 (2007); Employment by occupation: 12.2% management, 17.6% professional, 11.8% services, 27.8% sales, 0.6% farming, 12.8% construction, 17.2% production (2000).

Income: Per capita income: $24,788 (2007); Median household income: $50,070 (2007); Average household income: $59,698 (2007); Percent of households with income of $100,000 or more: 13.7% (2007); Poverty rate: 7.6% (2000).

Education: Percent of population age 25 and over with: High school diploma (including GED) or higher: 80.1% (2007); Bachelor's degree or higher: 15.6% (2007); Master's degree or higher: 3.9% (2007).

School District(s)

Johnstown-Monroe Local (PK-12)
2005-06 Enrollment: 1,607 . . . . (740) 967-6846

Northridge Local (PK-12)
2005-06 Enrollment: 1,489 . . . . (740) 967-6631

Housing: Homeownership rate: 63.6% (2007); Median home value: $120,783 (2007); Median rent: $359 per month (2000); Median age of housing: 40 years (2000).

Safety: Violent crime rate: 7.4 per 10,000 population; Property crime rate: 91.7 per 10,000 population (2007).

Transportation: Commute to work: 93.7% car, 0.6% public transportation, 2.1% walk, 3.6% work from home (2000); Travel time to work: 29.5% less than 15 minutes, 29.5% 15 to 30 minutes, 26.9% 30 to 45 minutes, 9.2% 45 to 60 minutes, 4.9% 60 minutes or more (2000)

Additional Information Contacts

Johnstown Area Chamber of Commerce. . . . . (740) 967-2334
http://www.johnstown.ws/villagegov.html

Village of Johnstown . . . . (740) 967-3177
http://www.villageofjohnstown.org

KIRKERSVILLE (village). Covers a land area of 1.963 square miles and a water area of 0 square miles. Located at 39.95° N. Lat.; 82.59° W. Long. Elevation is 932 feet.

Population: 563 (1990); 520 (2000); 496 (2007); 496 (2012 projected); Race: 96.6% White, 2.0% Black, 0.2% Asian, 4.4% Hispanic of any race (2007); Density: 252.6 persons per square mile (2007); Average household size: 2.92 (2007); Median age: 39.1 (2007); Males per 100 females: 103.3 (2007); Marriage status: 23.8% never married, 59.6% now married, 4.6% widowed, 11.9% divorced (2000); Foreign born: 0.6% (2000); Ancestry

(includes multiple ancestries): 29.0% German, 19.8% Irish, 10.1% English, 9.0% Other groups, 7.7% United States or American (2000).
Economy: Employment by occupation: 14.2% management, 10.8% professional, 11.5% services, 21.5% sales, 0.0% farming, 24.2% construction, 17.7% production (2000).
Income: Per capita income: $21,716 (2007); Median household income: $56,667 (2007); Average household income: $62,191 (2007); Percent of households with income of $100,000 or more: 16.5% (2007); Poverty rate: 8.0% (2000).
Education: Percent of population age 25 and over with: High school diploma (including GED) or higher: 74.9% (2007); Bachelor's degree or higher: 13.5% (2007); Master's degree or higher: 3.0% (2007).

School District(s)

Southwest Licking Local (PK-12)
2005-06 Enrollment: 3,615 . . . . (740) 927-3941
Housing: Homeownership rate: 75.9% (2007); Median home value: $117,230 (2007); Median rent: $413 per month (2000); Median age of housing: 58 years (2000).
Transportation: Commute to work: 93.8% car, 0.4% public transportation, 2.3% walk, 0.8% work from home (2000); Travel time to work: 21.2% less than 15 minutes, 35.7% 15 to 30 minutes, 29.4% 30 to 45 minutes, 9.4% 45 to 60 minutes, 4.3% 60 minutes or more (2000)

NEWARK (city). County seat. Covers a land area of 19.554 square miles and a water area of 0.245 square miles. Located at 40.06° N. Lat.; 82.41° W. Long. Elevation is 833 feet.
History: In 1802, near the ancient mounds of a vanished people, General William Schenck platted a settlement and named it for his hometown in New Jersey. When Newark became the seat of Licking County in 1808, its citizens hammered together a one-room log cabin, with slab benches on a sawdust floor, as the courthouse. The canal came to Newark in 1832, and the population tripled, only to be cut again by a cholera epidemic in 1849. Natural gas discovered here in 1887 attracted iron and glass industries with its cheap fuel, and Newark again grew.
Population: 45,070 (1990); 46,279 (2000); 47,531 (2007); 48,387 (2012 projected); Race: 93.3% White, 3.5% Black, 0.7% Asian, 0.9% Hispanic of any race (2007); Density: 2,430.8 persons per square mile (2007); Average household size: 2.36 (2007); Median age: 36.7 (2007); Males per 100 females: 91.3 (2007); Marriage status: 23.4% never married, 53.8% now married, 8.2% widowed, 14.6% divorced (2000); Foreign born: 1.1% (2000); Ancestry (includes multiple ancestries): 23.1% German, 14.4% Irish, 13.6% United States or American, 10.8% English, 8.5% Other groups (2000).
Economy: Unemployment rate: 6.5% (6/2008); Total civilian labor force: 24,555 (6/2008); Single-family building permits issued: 356 (2007); Multi-family building permits issued: 105 (2007); Employment by occupation: 9.6% management, 14.1% professional, 18.0% services, 28.3% sales, 0.1% farming, 9.0% construction, 20.9% production (2000).
Income: Per capita income: $21,170 (2007); Median household income: $39,502 (2007); Average household income: $49,458 (2007); Percent of households with income of $100,000 or more: 8.9% (2007); Poverty rate: 13.0% (2000).
Taxes: Total city taxes per capita: $485 (2006); City property taxes per capita: $55 (2006).
Education: Percent of population age 25 and over with: High school diploma (including GED) or higher: 81.0% (2007); Bachelor's degree or higher: 15.1% (2007); Master's degree or higher: 4.7% (2007).

School District(s)

Career and Technology Educational Centers (09-12)
2005-06 Enrollment: n/a . . . . (740) 366-3351
Licking Valley Local (PK-12)
2005-06 Enrollment: 2,136 . . . . (740) 763-3525
Newark City (PK-12)
2005-06 Enrollment: 6,756 . . . . (740) 345-9891
Newark Digital Academy (02-12)
2005-06 Enrollment: 45 . . . . (740) 328-2022
North Fork Local (PK-12)
2005-06 Enrollment: 1,886 . . . . (740) 892-3666
Par Excellence Academy
2005-06 Enrollment: n/a . . . .

Four-year College(s)

Ohio State University-Newark Campus (Public)
Fall 2007 Enrollment: 2,505. . . . . (740) 366-9333
2007-08 Tuition: In-state $5,664; Out-of-state $18,273

Two-year College(s)

Central Ohio Technical College (Public)
Fall 2007 Enrollment: 3,100. . . . . (740) 366-1351
2007-08 Tuition: In-state $3,600; Out-of-state $6,300

Vocational/Technical School(s)

Career and Technology Education Centers of Licking County (Public)
Fall 2007 Enrollment: 430 . . . . (614) 364-2333
2007-08 Tuition: $8,449
Housing: Homeownership rate: 57.9% (2007); Median home value: $106,870 (2007); Median rent: $394 per month (2000); Median age of housing: 42 years (2000).
Hospitals: Licking Memorial Hospital (195 beds)
Safety: Violent crime rate: 26.0 per 10,000 population; Property crime rate: 530.9 per 10,000 population (2007).
Newspapers: Newark Advocate (Local news; Circulation 22,243)
Transportation: Commute to work: 94.9% car, 1.0% public transportation, 1.5% walk, 1.9% work from home (2000); Travel time to work: 44.5% less than 15 minutes, 30.8% 15 to 30 minutes, 10.3% 30 to 45 minutes, 8.7% 45 to 60 minutes, 5.6% 60 minutes or more (2000)
Airports: Newark-Heath (general aviation)
Additional Information Contacts
City of Newark . . . . (740) 670-7500
http://www.ci.newark.oh.us
Licking County Chamber of Commerce. . . . . (740) 345-9757
http://www.lickingcountychamber.com

PATASKALA (city). Covers a land area of 28.507 square miles and a water area of 0.022 square miles. Located at 39.99° N. Lat.; 82.69° W. Long. Elevation is 1,001 feet.
Population: 7,698 (1990); 10,249 (2000); 13,147 (2007); 14,979 (2012 projected); Race: 94.0% White, 3.1% Black, 0.6% Asian, 1.3% Hispanic of any race (2007); Density: 461.2 persons per square mile (2007); Average household size: 2.58 (2007); Median age: 36.2 (2007); Males per 100 females: 96.7 (2007); Marriage status: 19.9% never married, 62.9% now married, 5.1% widowed, 12.1% divorced (2000); Foreign born: 1.2% (2000); Ancestry (includes multiple ancestries): 26.4% German, 16.9% Irish, 12.2% English, 10.5% Other groups, 9.9% United States or American (2000).
Economy: Employment by occupation: 15.2% management, 17.2% professional, 10.7% services, 29.6% sales, 0.1% farming, 10.9% construction, 16.3% production (2000).
Income: Per capita income: $26,960 (2007); Median household income: $62,681 (2007); Average household income: $69,095 (2007); Percent of households with income of $100,000 or more: 18.9% (2007); Poverty rate: 5.4% (2000).
Education: Percent of population age 25 and over with: High school diploma (including GED) or higher: 86.5% (2007); Bachelor's degree or higher: 20.7% (2007); Master's degree or higher: 6.9% (2007).

School District(s)

Licking Heights Local (PK-12)
2005-06 Enrollment: 2,503 . . . . (740) 927-6926
Southwest Licking Local (PK-12)
2005-06 Enrollment: 3,615 . . . . (740) 927-3941
Housing: Homeownership rate: 75.9% (2007); Median home value: $162,357 (2007); Median rent: $459 per month (2000); Median age of housing: 21 years (2000).
Safety: Violent crime rate: 9.2 per 10,000 population; Property crime rate: 230.7 per 10,000 population (2007).
Newspapers: Pataskala Post (Community news; Circulation 11,200); Pataskala Standard (Local news); Standard (Community news; Circulation 5,200)
Transportation: Commute to work: 95.8% car, 0.6% public transportation, 0.8% walk, 2.4% work from home (2000); Travel time to work: 18.6% less than 15 minutes, 35.0% 15 to 30 minutes, 34.6% 30 to 45 minutes, 9.5% 45 to 60 minutes, 2.4% 60 minutes or more (2000)
Additional Information Contacts
City of Pataskala . . . . (740) 964-2416
http://www.ci.pataskala.oh.us
Pataskala Area Chamber of Commerce . . . . (740) 964-6100
http://www.pataskalachamber.com

SAINT LOUISVILLE (village). Covers a land area of 0.247 square miles and a water area of 0 square miles. Located at 40.17° N. Lat.; 82.41° W. Long. Elevation is 892 feet.

Population: 372 (1990); 346 (2000); 351 (2007); 348 (2012 projected); Race: 98.0% White, 0.0% Black, 0.0% Asian, 0.0% Hispanic of any race (2007); Density: 1,422.3 persons per square mile (2007); Average household size: 2.85 (2007); Median age: 34.9 (2007); Males per 100 females: 100.6 (2007); Marriage status: 26.2% never married, 50.4% now married, 10.5% widowed, 12.9% divorced (2000); Foreign born: 0.0% (2000); Ancestry (includes multiple ancestries): 38.0% German, 14.9% Other groups, 11.4% English, 10.2% Irish, 6.1% United States or American (2000).
Economy: Single-family building permits issued: 0 (2007); Multi-family building permits issued: 0 (2007); Employment by occupation: 2.7% management, 9.6% professional, 17.1% services, 31.5% sales, 0.0% farming, 15.8% construction, 23.3% production (2000).
Income: Per capita income: $17,301 (2007); Median household income: $47,955 (2007); Average household income: $49,370 (2007); Percent of households with income of $100,000 or more: 6.5% (2007); Poverty rate: 7.5% (2000).
Education: Percent of population age 25 and over with: High school diploma (including GED) or higher: 88.5% (2007); Bachelor's degree or higher: 6.0% (2007); Master's degree or higher: 1.4% (2007).
Housing: Homeownership rate: 86.2% (2007); Median home value: $107,065 (2007); Median rent: $404 per month (2000); Median age of housing: 60+ years (2000).
Transportation: Commute to work: 96.6% car, 0.0% public transportation, 0.0% walk, 2.1% work from home (2000); Travel time to work: 11.2% less than 15 minutes, 46.9% 15 to 30 minutes, 20.3% 30 to 45 minutes, 7.7% 45 to 60 minutes, 14.0% 60 minutes or more (2000)

UTICA (village). Covers a land area of 1.697 square miles and a water area of 0 square miles. Located at 40.23° N. Lat.; 82.44° W. Long. Elevation is 958 feet.
Population: 2,148 (1990); 2,130 (2000); 2,021 (2007); 2,048 (2012 projected); Race: 98.3% White, 0.1% Black, 0.1% Asian, 1.1% Hispanic of any race (2007); Density: 1,190.7 persons per square mile (2007); Average household size: 2.57 (2007); Median age: 38.2 (2007); Males per 100 females: 97.9 (2007); Marriage status: 19.4% never married, 55.8% now married, 10.2% widowed, 14.6% divorced (2000); Foreign born: 1.2% (2000); Ancestry (includes multiple ancestries): 21.8% German, 15.3% Irish, 11.6% United States or American, 11.1% English, 7.5% Other groups (2000).
Economy: Employment by occupation: 6.7% management, 12.9% professional, 14.1% services, 22.2% sales, 1.6% farming, 11.3% construction, 31.3% production (2000).
Income: Per capita income: $19,508 (2007); Median household income: $39,750 (2007); Average household income: $49,316 (2007); Percent of households with income of $100,000 or more: 7.4% (2007); Poverty rate: 6.2% (2000).
Education: Percent of population age 25 and over with: High school diploma (including GED) or higher: 79.6% (2007); Bachelor's degree or higher: 9.2% (2007); Master's degree or higher: 2.1% (2007).

School District(s)

North Fork Local (PK-12)
2005-06 Enrollment: 1,886 . . . . (740) 892-3666
Housing: Homeownership rate: 69.1% (2007); Median home value: $96,786 (2007); Median rent: $346 per month (2000); Median age of housing: 50 years (2000).
Newspapers: Utica Herald (Local news; Circulation 2,100)
Transportation: Commute to work: 94.4% car, 0.0% public transportation, 2.7% walk, 2.5% work from home (2000); Travel time to work: 21.5% less than 15 minutes, 35.7% 15 to 30 minutes, 20.9% 30 to 45 minutes, 12.7% 45 to 60 minutes, 9.2% 60 minutes or more (2000)

Logan County

Located in west central Ohio; drained by the Great Miami and Mad Rivers; includes Campbell Hill, the highest point in the state (1,550 ft). Covers a land area of 458.44 square miles, a water area of 8.34 square miles, and is located in the Eastern Time Zone. The county was founded in 1817. County seat is Bellefontaine.

Logan County is part of the Bellefontaine, OH Micropolitan Statistical Area. The entire metro area includes: Logan County, OH

Weather Station: Bellefontaine Elevation: 1,184 feet

	Jan	Feb	Mar	Apr	May	Jun	Jul	Aug	Sep	Oct	Nov	Dec
High	32	37	48	61	72	80	83	81	76	64	50	38
Low	17	20	29	39	50	59	63	61	54	43	33	23
Precip	2.3	2.0	2.8	3.6	4.0	4.0	3.9	3.4	2.7	2.4	3.1	3.0
Snow	6.9	4.1	1.7	0.4	tr	0.0	0.0	0.0	0.0	0.2	0.8	3.7

High and Low temperatures in degrees Fahrenheit; Precipitation and Snow in inches

Population: 42,310 (1990); 46,005 (2000); 46,711 (2007); 47,017 (2012 projected); Race: 95.9% White, 1.7% Black, 0.5% Asian, 0.8% Hispanic of any race (2007); Density: 101.9 persons per square mile (2007); Average household size: 2.52 (2007); Median age: 38.3 (2007); Males per 100 females: 96.4 (2007).
Religion: Five largest groups: 9.0% The United Methodist Church, 5.6% Catholic Church, 2.3% Christian Church (Disciples of Christ), 2.3% General Association of Regular Baptist Churches, 2.3% Presbyterian Church (U.S.A.) (2000).
Economy: Unemployment rate: 6.1% (6/2008); Total civilian labor force: 25,424 (6/2008); Leading industries: 32.8% manufacturing; 11.7% retail trade; 10.6% health care and social assistance (2005); Farms: 1,055 totaling 225,093 acres (2002); Companies that employ 500 or more persons: 6 (2006); Companies that employ 100 to 499 persons: 22 (2006); Companies that employ less than 100 persons: 917 (2006); Black-owned businesses: n/a (2002); Hispanic-owned businesses: n/a (2002); Asian-owned businesses: n/a (2002); Women-owned businesses: 999 (2002); Retail sales per capita: $10,459 (2008). Single-family building permits issued: 100 (2007); Multi-family building permits issued: 53 (2007).
Income: Per capita income: $22,849 (2007); Median household income: $47,922 (2007); Average household income: $57,098 (2007); Percent of households with income of $100,000 or more: 12.5% (2007); Poverty rate: 11.4% (2005); Bankruptcy rate: 4.82% (2007).
Education: Percent of population age 25 and over with: High school diploma (including GED) or higher: 83.7% (2007); Bachelor's degree or higher: 11.6% (2007); Master's degree or higher: 4.6% (2007).
Housing: Homeownership rate: 75.9% (2007); Median home value: $111,861 (2007); Median rent: $377 per month (2000); Median age of housing: 38 years (2000).
Health: Birth rate: 133.3 per 10,000 population (2007); Death rate: 97.5 per 10,000 population (2007); Age-adjusted cancer mortality rate: 248.8 deaths per 100,000 population (2005); Number of physicians: 11.9 per 10,000 population (2005); Hospital beds: 23.7 per 10,000 population (2004); Hospital admissions: 759.0 per 10,000 population (2004).
Elections: 2004 Presidential election results: 67.6% Bush, 31.9% Kerry, 0.0% Nader, 0.2% Badnarik
National and State Parks: Fox Island State Park; Indian Lake State Park; Indian Lake State Wildlife Area
Additional Information Contacts
Logan County Government . . . . (937) 599-7283
http://www.co.logan.oh.us
City of Bellefontaine . . . . (937) 592-4376
http://ci.bellefontaine.oh.us
Logan County Area Chamber of Commerce . . . . (937) 599-5121
http://www.logancountyohio.com
Village of Huntsville . . . . (937) 686-4329
http://huntsvilleohio.com

Logan County Communities

BELLE CENTER (village). Covers a land area of 0.689 square miles and a water area of 0.013 square miles. Located at 40.50° N. Lat.; 83.74° W. Long. Elevation is 1,043 feet.
History: Belle Center developed as a rural trading village. A large butter and cheese plant was established here.
Population: 816 (1990); 807 (2000); 789 (2007); 783 (2012 projected); Race: 100.0% White, 0.0% Black, 0.0% Asian, 0.5% Hispanic of any race (2007); Density: 1,144.9 persons per square mile (2007); Average household size: 2.42 (2007); Median age: 37.7 (2007); Males per 100 females: 93.9 (2007); Marriage status: 18.8% never married, 61.2% now married, 8.9% widowed, 11.1% divorced (2000); Foreign born: 0.6% (2000); Ancestry (includes multiple ancestries): 26.3% German, 17.4% United States or American, 11.5% English, 10.4% Irish, 7.6% Other groups (2000).
Economy: Single-family building permits issued: 0 (2007); Multi-family building permits issued: 0 (2007); Employment by occupation: 2.9% management, 14.4% professional, 12.5% services, 22.5% sales, 0.0% farming, 7.0% construction, 40.8% production (2000).

Income: Per capita income: $24,902 (2007); Median household income: $53,095 (2007); Average household income: $59,018 (2007); Percent of households with income of $100,000 or more: 13.5% (2007); Poverty rate: 8.5% (2000).
Education: Percent of population age 25 and over with: High school diploma (including GED) or higher: 83.9% (2007); Bachelor's degree or higher: 10.2% (2007); Master's degree or higher: 5.5% (2007).
Housing: Homeownership rate: 87.1% (2007); Median home value: $92,424 (2007); Median rent: $339 per month (2000); Median age of housing: 60+ years (2000).
Transportation: Commute to work: 97.0% car, 0.0% public transportation, 2.2% walk, 0.5% work from home (2000); Travel time to work: 13.3% less than 15 minutes, 60.3% 15 to 30 minutes, 18.8% 30 to 45 minutes, 4.3% 45 to 60 minutes, 3.5% 60 minutes or more (2000)

BELLEFONTAINE (city). County seat. Covers a land area of 8.764 square miles and a water area of 0 square miles. Located at 40.36° N. Lat.; 83.75° W. Long. Elevation is 1,243 feet.
History: Bellefontaine was settled in 1806, and became the seat of Logan County in 1820. The name means "beautiful fountain," referring to the natural springs at the site.
Population: 12,328 (1990); 13,069 (2000); 12,969 (2007); 12,832 (2012 projected); Race: 90.6% White, 4.9% Black, 1.1% Asian, 1.3% Hispanic of any race (2007); Density: 1,479.9 persons per square mile (2007); Average household size: 2.41 (2007); Median age: 34.2 (2007); Males per 100 females: 91.8 (2007); Marriage status: 24.0% never married, 52.6% now married, 8.3% widowed, 15.1% divorced (2000); Foreign born: 2.5% (2000); Ancestry (includes multiple ancestries): 22.4% German, 16.5% United States or American, 13.1% Other groups, 10.7% Irish, 8.3% English (2000).
Economy: Employment by occupation: 7.3% management, 12.4% professional, 16.5% services, 22.3% sales, 0.1% farming, 8.6% construction, 32.9% production (2000).
Income: Per capita income: $20,393 (2007); Median household income: $38,827 (2007); Average household income: $48,910 (2007); Percent of households with income of $100,000 or more: 8.7% (2007); Poverty rate: 14.6% (2000).
Education: Percent of population age 25 and over with: High school diploma (including GED) or higher: 84.6% (2007); Bachelor's degree or higher: 13.5% (2007); Master's degree or higher: 6.7% (2007).

School District(s)

Bellefontaine City (PK-12)
2005-06 Enrollment: 2,800 . . . . (937) 593-9060
Benjamin Logan Local (KG-12)
2005-06 Enrollment: 1,946 . . . . (937) 593-9211
Ohio Hi-Point Career Center (07-12)
2005-06 Enrollment: n/a . . . . (937) 599-3010

Vocational/Technical School(s)

Ohio Hi Point Joint Vocational School District (Public)
Fall 2007 Enrollment: 805 . . . . (937) 599-3010
2007-08 Tuition: In-state $10,269; Out-of-state $10,269
Housing: Homeownership rate: 58.0% (2007); Median home value: $102,040 (2007); Median rent: $381 per month (2000); Median age of housing: 44 years (2000).
Hospitals: Mary Rutan Hospital (105 beds)
Safety: Violent crime rate: 26.6 per 10,000 population; Property crime rate: 518.3 per 10,000 population (2007).
Newspapers: Bellefontaine Examiner (Local news; Circulation 10,000)
Transportation: Commute to work: 93.8% car, 0.1% public transportation, 3.2% walk, 2.0% work from home (2000); Travel time to work: 53.4% less than 15 minutes, 30.3% 15 to 30 minutes, 8.2% 30 to 45 minutes, 2.6% 45 to 60 minutes, 5.4% 60 minutes or more (2000)
Additional Information Contacts
City of Bellefontaine . . . . (937) 592-4376
http://ci.bellefontaine.oh.us
Logan County Area Chamber of Commerce . . . . (937) 599-5121
http://www.logancountyohio.com

DE GRAFF (village). Aka Degraff. Covers a land area of 0.857 square miles and a water area of 0 square miles. Located at 40.31° N. Lat.; 83.91° W. Long. Elevation is 1,001 feet.
History: Sometimes spelled Degraff.
Population: 1,331 (1990); 1,212 (2000); 1,088 (2007); 1,104 (2012 projected); Race: 99.7% White, 0.2% Black, 0.1% Asian, 0.3% Hispanic of any race (2007); Density: 1,269.7 persons per square mile (2007); Average household size: 2.46 (2007); Median age: 36.3 (2007); Males per 100 females: 99.3 (2007); Marriage status: 23.2% never married, 57.0% now married, 9.2% widowed, 10.6% divorced (2000); Foreign born: 0.7% (2000); Ancestry (includes multiple ancestries): 22.9% German, 19.8% United States or American, 8.0% English, 6.6% Irish, 2.6% Other groups (2000).
Economy: Single-family building permits issued: 0 (2007); Multi-family building permits issued: 0 (2007); Employment by occupation: 7.9% management, 9.6% professional, 12.1% services, 19.5% sales, 0.9% farming, 11.8% construction, 38.3% production (2000).
Income: Per capita income: $21,039 (2007); Median household income: $39,444 (2007); Average household income: $51,787 (2007); Percent of households with income of $100,000 or more: 12.0% (2007); Poverty rate: 8.2% (2000).
Education: Percent of population age 25 and over with: High school diploma (including GED) or higher: 83.7% (2007); Bachelor's degree or higher: 8.4% (2007); Master's degree or higher: 2.6% (2007).

School District(s)

Riverside Local (KG-12)
2005-06 Enrollment: 802 . . . . (937) 585-5981
Housing: Homeownership rate: 79.4% (2007); Median home value: $99,659 (2007); Median rent: $342 per month (2000); Median age of housing: 53 years (2000).
Transportation: Commute to work: 93.7% car, 0.0% public transportation, 3.8% walk, 2.3% work from home (2000); Travel time to work: 19.1% less than 15 minutes, 43.7% 15 to 30 minutes, 26.6% 30 to 45 minutes, 5.2% 45 to 60 minutes, 5.5% 60 minutes or more (2000)

EAST LIBERTY (unincorporated postal area, zip code 43319). Covers a land area of 20.961 square miles and a water area of 0.012 square miles. Located at 40.30° N. Lat.; 83.56° W. Long. Elevation is 1,130 feet.
Population: 967 (2000); Race: 96.5% White, 0.5% Black, 1.4% Asian, 0.5% Hispanic of any race (2000); Density: 46.1 persons per square mile (2000); Age: 28.5% under 18, 10.6% over 64 (2000); Marriage status: 19.4% never married, 62.6% now married, 3.6% widowed, 14.4% divorced (2000); Foreign born: 2.3% (2000); Ancestry (includes multiple ancestries): 26.7% German, 16.9% United States or American, 13.0% English, 11.7% Irish, 9.7% Other groups (2000).
Economy: Employment by occupation: 11.9% management, 5.7% professional, 9.6% services, 23.4% sales, 3.0% farming, 9.8% construction, 36.6% production (2000).
Income: Per capita income: $21,140 (2000); Median household income: $55,625 (2000); Poverty rate: 2.8% (2000).
Education: Percent of population age 25 and over with: High school diploma (including GED) or higher: 85.5% (2000); Bachelor's degree or higher: 4.3% (2000).
Housing: Homeownership rate: 86.1% (2000); Median home value: $89,700 (2000); Median rent: $455 per month (2000); Median age of housing: 60+ years (2000).
Transportation: Commute to work: 91.1% car, 0.0% public transportation, 4.0% walk, 4.9% work from home (2000); Travel time to work: 46.6% less than 15 minutes, 27.7% 15 to 30 minutes, 15.5% 30 to 45 minutes, 4.2% 45 to 60 minutes, 6.1% 60 minutes or more (2000)

HUNTSVILLE (village). Covers a land area of 0.337 square miles and a water area of 0 square miles. Located at 40.44° N. Lat.; 83.80° W. Long. Elevation is 1,079 feet.
Population: 343 (1990); 454 (2000); 442 (2007); 439 (2012 projected); Race: 96.6% White, 0.2% Black, 0.7% Asian, 0.7% Hispanic of any race (2007); Density: 1,311.2 persons per square mile (2007); Average household size: 2.53 (2007); Median age: 36.2 (2007); Males per 100 females: 93.0 (2007); Marriage status: 18.8% never married, 65.0% now married, 4.7% widowed, 11.6% divorced (2000); Foreign born: 0.0% (2000); Ancestry (includes multiple ancestries): 32.2% German, 17.9% Irish, 11.9% English, 9.9% United States or American, 6.8% Other groups (2000).
Economy: Single-family building permits issued: 3 (2007); Multi-family building permits issued: 0 (2007); Employment by occupation: 9.7% management, 6.5% professional, 24.1% services, 25.5% sales, 0.9% farming, 7.9% construction, 25.5% production (2000).
Income: Per capita income: $20,741 (2007); Median household income: $46,184 (2007); Average household income: $52,386 (2007); Percent of households with income of $100,000 or more: 8.6% (2007); Poverty rate: 8.4% (2000).

Education: Percent of population age 25 and over with: High school diploma (including GED) or higher: 85.7% (2007); Bachelor's degree or higher: 2.8% (2007); Master's degree or higher: 0.0% (2007).

School District(s)

Indian Lake Local (KG-12)
2005-06 Enrollment: 1,998 . . . . (937) 686-8601

Housing: Homeownership rate: 73.7% (2007); Median home value: $95,270 (2007); Median rent: $423 per month (2000); Median age of housing: 51 years (2000).

Transportation: Commute to work: 91.7% car, 0.0% public transportation, 1.9% walk, 5.1% work from home (2000); Travel time to work: 43.9% less than 15 minutes, 39.5% 15 to 30 minutes, 10.2% 30 to 45 minutes, 1.0% 45 to 60 minutes, 5.4% 60 minutes or more (2000)

Additional Information Contacts

Village of Huntsville . . . . (937) 686-4329
http://huntsvilleohio.com

LAKEVIEW (village). Covers a land area of 0.684 square miles and a water area of 0.005 square miles. Located at 40.48° N. Lat.; 83.92° W. Long. Elevation is 994 feet.

History: Lakeview developed as a resort on Indian Lake.

Population: 1,083 (1990); 1,074 (2000); 1,060 (2007); 1,052 (2012 projected); Race: 96.3% White, 0.1% Black, 0.7% Asian, 0.5% Hispanic of any race (2007); Density: 1,549.7 persons per square mile (2007); Average household size: 2.44 (2007); Median age: 36.7 (2007); Males per 100 females: 96.7 (2007); Marriage status: 19.3% never married, 56.5% now married, 8.6% widowed, 15.6% divorced (2000); Foreign born: 1.3% (2000); Ancestry (includes multiple ancestries): 22.7% German, 17.6% United States or American, 11.0% English, 9.6% Irish, 5.6% Other groups (2000).

Economy: Single-family building permits issued: 1 (2007); Multi-family building permits issued: 0 (2007); Employment by occupation: 7.4% management, 13.9% professional, 14.1% services, 17.2% sales, 0.0% farming, 12.1% construction, 35.2% production (2000).

Income: Per capita income: $18,535 (2007); Median household income: $39,048 (2007); Average household income: $45,271 (2007); Percent of households with income of $100,000 or more: 6.9% (2007); Poverty rate: 10.9% (2000).

Education: Percent of population age 25 and over with: High school diploma (including GED) or higher: 70.4% (2007); Bachelor's degree or higher: 4.0% (2007); Master's degree or higher: 0.9% (2007).

School District(s)

Indian Lake Local (KG-12)
2005-06 Enrollment: 1,998 . . . . (937) 686-8601

Housing: Homeownership rate: 74.0% (2007); Median home value: $69,483 (2007); Median rent: $354 per month (2000); Median age of housing: 42 years (2000).

Transportation: Commute to work: 96.8% car, 0.0% public transportation, 1.3% walk, 1.5% work from home (2000); Travel time to work: 26.7% less than 15 minutes, 38.0% 15 to 30 minutes, 17.5% 30 to 45 minutes, 7.9% 45 to 60 minutes, 9.8% 60 minutes or more (2000)

LEWISTOWN (unincorporated postal area, zip code 43333). Covers a land area of 29.227 square miles and a water area of 0.016 square miles. Located at 40.43° N. Lat.; 83.92° W. Long. Elevation is 1,022 feet.

Population: 693 (2000); Race: 100.0% White, 0.0% Black, 0.0% Asian, 0.0% Hispanic of any race (2000); Density: 23.7 persons per square mile (2000); Age: 23.0% under 18, 10.2% over 64 (2000); Marriage status: 21.6% never married, 58.3% now married, 8.9% widowed, 11.2% divorced (2000); Foreign born: 0.0% (2000); Ancestry (includes multiple ancestries): 33.1% German, 29.1% United States or American, 16.4% Irish, 8.5% English, 3.0% Other groups (2000).

Economy: Employment by occupation: 16.7% management, 20.1% professional, 22.0% services, 8.5% sales, 0.0% farming, 7.5% construction, 25.2% production (2000).

Income: Per capita income: $20,187 (2000); Median household income: $36,534 (2000); Poverty rate: 8.9% (2000).

Education: Percent of population age 25 and over with: High school diploma (including GED) or higher: 83.1% (2000); Bachelor's degree or higher: 7.3% (2000).

School District(s)

Indian Lake Local (KG-12)
2005-06 Enrollment: 1,998 . . . . (937) 686-8601

Housing: Homeownership rate: 78.4% (2000); Median home value: $87,800 (2000); Median rent: $407 per month (2000); Median age of housing: 60+ years (2000).

Transportation: Commute to work: 91.5% car, 0.0% public transportation, 0.0% walk, 8.5% work from home (2000); Travel time to work: 35.7% less than 15 minutes, 44.7% 15 to 30 minutes, 12.4% 30 to 45 minutes, 1.1% 45 to 60 minutes, 6.1% 60 minutes or more (2000)

QUINCY (village). Covers a land area of 1.132 square miles and a water area of 0 square miles. Located at 40.29° N. Lat.; 83.97° W. Long. Elevation is 1,053 feet.

Population: 697 (1990); 734 (2000); 708 (2007); 692 (2012 projected); Race: 98.2% White, 0.0% Black, 0.1% Asian, 1.0% Hispanic of any race (2007); Density: 625.3 persons per square mile (2007); Average household size: 2.81 (2007); Median age: 30.8 (2007); Males per 100 females: 101.7 (2007); Marriage status: 24.1% never married, 60.0% now married, 5.8% widowed, 10.0% divorced (2000); Foreign born: 0.0% (2000); Ancestry (includes multiple ancestries): 17.0% German, 12.6% English, 10.6% United States or American, 9.8% Irish, 5.9% Other groups (2000).

Economy: Single-family building permits issued: 1 (2007); Multi-family building permits issued: 0 (2007); Employment by occupation: 5.8% management, 6.4% professional, 18.0% services, 18.6% sales, 1.0% farming, 7.7% construction, 42.4% production (2000).

Income: Per capita income: $16,476 (2007); Median household income: $36,923 (2007); Average household income: $46,290 (2007); Percent of households with income of $100,000 or more: 7.5% (2007); Poverty rate: 14.9% (2000).

Education: Percent of population age 25 and over with: High school diploma (including GED) or higher: 79.7% (2007); Bachelor's degree or higher: 7.7% (2007); Master's degree or higher: 3.5% (2007).

Housing: Homeownership rate: 71.8% (2007); Median home value: $74,677 (2007); Median rent: $375 per month (2000); Median age of housing: 58 years (2000).

Transportation: Commute to work: 93.8% car, 0.0% public transportation, 4.9% walk, 1.3% work from home (2000); Travel time to work: 15.6% less than 15 minutes, 45.4% 15 to 30 minutes, 23.8% 30 to 45 minutes, 6.3% 45 to 60 minutes, 8.9% 60 minutes or more (2000)

RUSHSYLVANIA (village). Covers a land area of 0.758 square miles and a water area of 0 square miles. Located at 40.46° N. Lat.; 83.67° W. Long. Elevation is 1,237 feet.

Population: 573 (1990); 543 (2000); 485 (2007); 472 (2012 projected); Race: 97.5% White, 0.0% Black, 0.6% Asian, 0.8% Hispanic of any race (2007); Density: 640.1 persons per square mile (2007); Average household size: 2.65 (2007); Median age: 34.3 (2007); Males per 100 females: 104.6 (2007); Marriage status: 21.5% never married, 59.8% now married, 5.4% widowed, 13.3% divorced (2000); Foreign born: 0.2% (2000); Ancestry (includes multiple ancestries): 19.3% United States or American, 17.3% German, 10.1% Irish, 6.6% Other groups, 6.6% English (2000).

Economy: Single-family building permits issued: 1 (2007); Multi-family building permits issued: 0 (2007); Employment by occupation: 9.7% management, 8.9% professional, 17.4% services, 14.7% sales, 1.2% farming, 11.2% construction, 36.8% production (2000).

Income: Per capita income: $20,660 (2007); Median household income: $50,192 (2007); Average household income: $54,754 (2007); Percent of households with income of $100,000 or more: 8.7% (2007); Poverty rate: 10.9% (2000).

Education: Percent of population age 25 and over with: High school diploma (including GED) or higher: 80.9% (2007); Bachelor's degree or higher: 9.2% (2007); Master's degree or higher: 2.9% (2007).

Housing: Homeownership rate: 83.6% (2007); Median home value: $83,571 (2007); Median rent: $288 per month (2000); Median age of housing: 60+ years (2000).

Transportation: Commute to work: 93.8% car, 0.8% public transportation, 0.0% walk, 5.4% work from home (2000); Travel time to work: 16.8% less than 15 minutes, 57.4% 15 to 30 minutes, 12.7% 30 to 45 minutes, 4.5% 45 to 60 minutes, 8.6% 60 minutes or more (2000)

RUSSELLS POINT (village). Covers a land area of 0.934 square miles and a water area of 0.081 square miles. Located at 40.47° N. Lat.; 83.89° W. Long. Elevation is 1,004 feet.

History: Russells Point developed as a resort and vacation center on Indian Lake.

Population: 1,545 (1990); 1,619 (2000); 1,567 (2007); 1,550 (2012 projected); Race: 97.3% White, 0.2% Black, 1.0% Asian, 1.5% Hispanic of

any race (2007); Density: 1,677.5 persons per square mile (2007); Average household size: 2.19 (2007); Median age: 36.2 (2007); Males per 100 females: 88.3 (2007); Marriage status: 21.6% never married, 48.7% now married, 8.4% widowed, 21.2% divorced (2000); Foreign born: 0.6% (2000); Ancestry (includes multiple ancestries): 22.2% German, 18.5% United States or American, 10.3% Other groups, 9.8% Irish, 6.8% English (2000).
Economy: Single-family building permits issued: 0 (2007); Multi-family building permits issued: 0 (2007); Employment by occupation: 3.7% management, 12.7% professional, 16.0% services, 22.2% sales, 0.0% farming, 10.0% construction, 35.5% production (2000).
Income: Per capita income: $19,974 (2007); Median household income: $33,333 (2007); Average household income: $43,838 (2007); Percent of households with income of $100,000 or more: 6.7% (2007); Poverty rate: 20.2% (2000).
Education: Percent of population age 25 and over with: High school diploma (including GED) or higher: 72.8% (2007); Bachelor's degree or higher: 6.8% (2007); Master's degree or higher: 2.3% (2007).
Housing: Homeownership rate: 59.0% (2007); Median home value: $76,875 (2007); Median rent: $316 per month (2000); Median age of housing: 32 years (2000).
Transportation: Commute to work: 93.2% car, 0.8% public transportation, 2.9% walk, 2.9% work from home (2000); Travel time to work: 33.6% less than 15 minutes, 31.1% 15 to 30 minutes, 23.0% 30 to 45 minutes, 5.8% 45 to 60 minutes, 6.4% 60 minutes or more (2000)

VALLEY HI (village). Covers a land area of 0.659 square miles and a water area of 0 square miles. Located at 40.31° N. Lat.; 83.68° W. Long. Elevation is 1,270 feet.
Population: 217 (1990); 244 (2000); 237 (2007); 236 (2012 projected); Race: 97.9% White, 0.0% Black, 0.0% Asian, 0.8% Hispanic of any race (2007); Density: 359.8 persons per square mile (2007); Average household size: 2.49 (2007); Median age: 33.5 (2007); Males per 100 females: 106.1 (2007); Marriage status: 24.6% never married, 52.1% now married, 3.5% widowed, 19.9% divorced (2000); Foreign born: 0.0% (2000); Ancestry (includes multiple ancestries): 29.8% German, 13.4% Other groups, 13.2% Irish, 8.8% English, 5.3% French (except Basque) (2000).
Economy: Single-family building permits issued: 0 (2007); Multi-family building permits issued: 0 (2007); Employment by occupation: 11.1% management, 3.2% professional, 15.1% services, 31.0% sales, 0.0% farming, 9.1% construction, 30.6% production (2000).
Income: Per capita income: $20,876 (2007); Median household income: $50,250 (2007); Average household income: $52,079 (2007); Percent of households with income of $100,000 or more: 7.4% (2007); Poverty rate: 4.7% (2000).
Education: Percent of population age 25 and over with: High school diploma (including GED) or higher: 87.4% (2007); Bachelor's degree or higher: 6.6% (2007); Master's degree or higher: 0.0% (2007).
Housing: Homeownership rate: 76.8% (2007); Median home value: <$10,000 (2007); Median rent: $462 per month (2000); Median age of housing: 16 years (2000).
Transportation: Commute to work: 99.2% car, 0.0% public transportation, 0.0% walk, 0.8% work from home (2000); Travel time to work: 11.7% less than 15 minutes, 57.7% 15 to 30 minutes, 18.1% 30 to 45 minutes, 5.6% 45 to 60 minutes, 6.9% 60 minutes or more (2000)

WEST LIBERTY (village). Covers a land area of 1.107 square miles and a water area of 0 square miles. Located at 40.25° N. Lat.; 83.75° W. Long. Elevation is 1,089 feet.
History: West Liberty developed as a rural trading center around a milk plant, a flour mill, and grain elevators.
Population: 1,947 (1990); 1,813 (2000); 1,731 (2007); 1,720 (2012 projected); Race: 98.4% White, 0.1% Black, 0.3% Asian, 0.1% Hispanic of any race (2007); Density: 1,563.6 persons per square mile (2007); Average household size: 2.72 (2007); Median age: 45.7 (2007); Males per 100 females: 76.5 (2007); Marriage status: 20.1% never married, 53.4% now married, 17.4% widowed, 9.1% divorced (2000); Foreign born: 0.5% (2000); Ancestry (includes multiple ancestries): 27.1% German, 11.5% United States or American, 11.4% English, 8.2% Irish, 5.6% Other groups (2000).
Economy: Single-family building permits issued: 0 (2007); Multi-family building permits issued: 0 (2007); Employment by occupation: 7.8% management, 16.3% professional, 16.4% services, 28.9% sales, 0.0% farming, 9.0% construction, 21.6% production (2000).
Income: Per capita income: $23,941 (2007); Median household income: $47,202 (2007); Average household income: $56,868 (2007); Percent of households with income of $100,000 or more: 11.6% (2007); Poverty rate: 5.3% (2000).
Education: Percent of population age 25 and over with: High school diploma (including GED) or higher: 87.0% (2007); Bachelor's degree or higher: 18.3% (2007); Master's degree or higher: 5.1% (2007).

School District(s)

West Liberty-Salem Local (PK-12)
2005-06 Enrollment: 1,230 . . . . (937) 465-1075
Housing: Homeownership rate: 72.8% (2007); Median home value: $112,580 (2007); Median rent: $354 per month (2000); Median age of housing: 60+ years (2000).
Transportation: Commute to work: 90.7% car, 0.2% public transportation, 3.4% walk, 5.2% work from home (2000); Travel time to work: 44.4% less than 15 minutes, 38.7% 15 to 30 minutes, 9.3% 30 to 45 minutes, 2.7% 45 to 60 minutes, 5.1% 60 minutes or more (2000)

WEST MANSFIELD (village). Covers a land area of 0.825 square miles and a water area of 0.025 square miles. Located at 40.40° N. Lat.; 83.54° W. Long. Elevation is 1,089 feet.
Population: 843 (1990); 700 (2000); 609 (2007); 602 (2012 projected); Race: 97.5% White, 0.2% Black, 0.0% Asian, 0.3% Hispanic of any race (2007); Density: 738.5 persons per square mile (2007); Average household size: 2.49 (2007); Median age: 36.9 (2007); Males per 100 females: 82.3 (2007); Marriage status: 19.8% never married, 60.5% now married, 8.0% widowed, 11.6% divorced (2000); Foreign born: 0.3% (2000); Ancestry (includes multiple ancestries): 23.2% United States or American, 19.3% German, 11.9% English, 11.2% Irish, 7.4% Other groups (2000).
Economy: Single-family building permits issued: 2 (2007); Multi-family building permits issued: 6 (2007); Employment by occupation: 6.5% management, 7.3% professional, 15.6% services, 21.3% sales, 0.8% farming, 11.3% construction, 37.2% production (2000).
Income: Per capita income: $21,938 (2007); Median household income: $47,500 (2007); Average household income: $54,531 (2007); Percent of households with income of $100,000 or more: 11.4% (2007); Poverty rate: 3.4% (2000).
Education: Percent of population age 25 and over with: High school diploma (including GED) or higher: 85.9% (2007); Bachelor's degree or higher: 7.3% (2007); Master's degree or higher: 2.7% (2007).
Housing: Homeownership rate: 81.6% (2007); Median home value: $94,583 (2007); Median rent: $350 per month (2000); Median age of housing: 60+ years (2000).
Transportation: Commute to work: 92.4% car, 0.0% public transportation, 4.9% walk, 1.9% work from home (2000); Travel time to work: 23.6% less than 15 minutes, 49.2% 15 to 30 minutes, 19.4% 30 to 45 minutes, 5.8% 45 to 60 minutes, 1.9% 60 minutes or more (2000)

ZANESFIELD (village). Covers a land area of 0.118 square miles and a water area of 0 square miles. Located at 40.33° N. Lat.; 83.67° W. Long. Elevation is 1,175 feet.
History: Zanesfield was settled in 1819 on the site of a blockhouse built by the English during the French and Indian War. The land once belonged to Isaac Zane, who was adopted by the Wyandot tribe when he was nine years old, and married the daughter of Chief Tarhe. He was known as White Eagle.
Population: 183 (1990); 220 (2000); 216 (2007); 215 (2012 projected); Race: 99.5% White, 0.0% Black, 0.0% Asian, 0.0% Hispanic of any race (2007); Density: 1,833.7 persons per square mile (2007); Average household size: 2.25 (2007); Median age: 36.8 (2007); Males per 100 females: 91.2 (2007); Marriage status: 18.3% never married, 65.1% now married, 8.6% widowed, 8.0% divorced (2000); Foreign born: 1.4% (2000); Ancestry (includes multiple ancestries): 19.0% German, 18.5% English, 13.3% Irish, 12.3% Other groups, 9.5% United States or American (2000).
Economy: Single-family building permits issued: 0 (2007); Multi-family building permits issued: 0 (2007); Employment by occupation: 1.8% management, 17.9% professional, 11.6% services, 27.7% sales, 0.0% farming, 8.9% construction, 32.1% production (2000).
Income: Per capita income: $21,725 (2007); Median household income: $47,500 (2007); Average household income: $48,880 (2007); Percent of households with income of $100,000 or more: 3.1% (2007); Poverty rate: 0.9% (2000).
Education: Percent of population age 25 and over with: High school diploma (including GED) or higher: 94.0% (2007); Bachelor's degree or higher: 17.9% (2007); Master's degree or higher: 5.3% (2007).

Housing: Homeownership rate: 71.9% (2007); Median home value: $85,833 (2007); Median rent: $425 per month (2000); Median age of housing: 60+ years (2000).
Transportation: Commute to work: 90.6% car, 0.0% public transportation, 4.7% walk, 4.7% work from home (2000); Travel time to work: 37.6% less than 15 minutes, 36.6% 15 to 30 minutes, 10.9% 30 to 45 minutes, 4.0% 45 to 60 minutes, 10.9% 60 minutes or more (2000)

Lorain County

Located in northern Ohio; bounded on the north by Lake Erie; drained by the Black and Vermilion Rivers. Covers a land area of 492.50 square miles, a water area of 430.52 square miles, and is located in the Eastern Time Zone. The county was founded in 1822. County seat is Elyria.

Lorain County is part of the Cleveland-Elyria-Mentor, OH Metropolitan Statistical Area. The entire metro area includes: Cuyahoga County, OH; Geauga County, OH; Lake County, OH; Lorain County, OH; Medina County, OH

Weather Station: Elyria 3 E Elevation: 728 feet

	Jan	Feb	Mar	Apr	May	Jun	Jul	Aug	Sep	Oct	Nov	Dec
High	34	38	48	60	72	81	85	83	76	64	51	39
Low	19	21	29	38	49	58	63	61	55	44	35	25
Precip	2.4	2.2	2.7	3.2	3.4	4.0	3.7	3.8	3.5	2.7	3.2	3.1
Snow	12.0	10.2	7.2	1.7	tr	tr	0.0	0.0	0.0	0.1	3.2	9.2

High and Low temperatures in degrees Fahrenheit; Precipitation and Snow in inches

Weather Station: Oberlin Elevation: 813 feet

	Jan	Feb	Mar	Apr	May	Jun	Jul	Aug	Sep	Oct	Nov	Dec
High	33	37	47	60	71	80	84	82	75	63	50	38
Low	16	18	27	36	47	56	60	58	51	40	32	22
Precip	2.2	2.0	2.7	3.2	3.6	3.9	3.7	3.4	3.3	2.5	3.2	2.8
Snow	11.9	9.7	7.1	1.6	tr	0.0	0.0	0.0	0.0	tr	2.5	8.6

High and Low temperatures in degrees Fahrenheit; Precipitation and Snow in inches

Population: 271,126 (1990); 284,664 (2000); 299,951 (2007); 309,897 (2012 projected); Race: 84.9% White, 8.2% Black, 0.8% Asian, 7.4% Hispanic of any race (2007); Density: 609.0 persons per square mile (2007); Average household size: 2.62 (2007); Median age: 37.8 (2007); Males per 100 females: 96.3 (2007).
Religion: Five largest groups: 25.6% Catholic Church, 3.5% The United Methodist Church, 3.3% United Church of Christ, 2.8% Southern Baptist Convention, 1.5% Lutheran Church—Missouri Synod (2000).
Economy: Unemployment rate: 7.8% (6/2008); Total civilian labor force: 159,841 (6/2008); Leading industries: 20.8% manufacturing; 15.4% retail trade; 14.6% health care and social assistance (2005); Farms: 975 totaling 161,918 acres (2002); Companies that employ 500 or more persons: 10 (2006); Companies that employ 100 to 499 persons: 116 (2006); Companies that employ less than 100 persons: 5,909 (2006); Black-owned businesses: 439 (2002); Hispanic-owned businesses: 427 (2002); Asian-owned businesses: 218 (2002); Women-owned businesses: 6,198 (2002); Retail sales per capita: $13,431 (2008). Single-family building permits issued: 974 (2007); Multi-family building permits issued: 102 (2007).
Income: Per capita income: $24,884 (2007); Median household income: $51,608 (2007); Average household income: $64,257 (2007); Percent of households with income of $100,000 or more: 16.4% (2007); Poverty rate: 11.7% (2005); Bankruptcy rate: 4.61% (2007).
Taxes: Total county taxes per capita: $246 (2006); County property taxes per capita: $171 (2006).
Education: Percent of population age 25 and over with: High school diploma (including GED) or higher: 83.3% (2007); Bachelor's degree or higher: 17.2% (2007); Master's degree or higher: 5.9% (2007).
Housing: Homeownership rate: 74.9% (2007); Median home value: $142,999 (2007); Median rent: $435 per month (2000); Median age of housing: 37 years (2000).
Health: Birth rate: 127.1 per 10,000 population (2007); Death rate: 89.2 per 10,000 population (2007); Age-adjusted cancer mortality rate: 202.6 deaths per 100,000 population (2005); Air Quality Index: 73.7% good, 24.4% moderate, 1.5% unhealthy for sensitive individuals, 0.4% unhealthy (percent of days in 2007); Number of physicians: 16.3 per 10,000 population (2005); Hospital beds: 21.6 per 10,000 population (2004); Hospital admissions: 998.3 per 10,000 population (2004).
Elections: 2004 Presidential election results: 43.5% Bush, 56.1% Kerry, 0.0% Nader, 0.2% Badnarik

National and State Parks: Findley State Park
Additional Information Contacts
Lorain County Government . . . . (440) 329-5000
http://www.loraincounty.us
City of Amherst . . . . (440) 988-4380
http://www.amherstohio.org
City of Avon . . . . (440) 937-7800
http://www.cityofavon.com
City of Avon Lake. . . . . (440) 933-6141
http://www.avonlake.org
City of Elyria. . . . . (440) 326-1400
http://www.cityofelyria.org
City of Lorain . . . . (440) 204-2002
http://www.cityoflorain.org
City of North Ridgeville . . . . (440) 353-0819
http://www.ci.north-ridgeville.oh.us
Columbia Chamber of Commerce . . . . (440) 236-9053
http://www.columbiastation.com
Lorain County Chamber of Commerce . . . . (440) 328-2550
http://www.loraincountychamber.com
North Coast Regional Chamber of Commerce . . . . (440) 933-9311
http://www.avonlakeavoncc.com
North Ridgeville Chamber of Commerce. . . . . (440) 327-3737
http://www.nrchamber.com
Oberlin Area Chamber of Commerce . . . . (440) 774-6262
http://www.oberlinchamber.org
Vermilion Chamber of Commerce . . . . (440) 967-4477
Wellington Chamber of Commerce . . . . (440) 647-2222

Lorain County Communities

AMHERST (city). Covers a land area of 7.167 square miles and a water area of 0.006 square miles. Located at 41.40° N. Lat.; 82.22° W. Long. Elevation is 689 feet.
History: Named for Baron Jeffrey Amherst (1717-1797), British general in the French and Indian Wars. Amherst grew around an extensive sandstone quarry.
Population: 10,723 (1990); 11,797 (2000); 12,015 (2007); 12,146 (2012 projected); Race: 96.0% White, 0.6% Black, 1.0% Asian, 3.3% Hispanic of any race (2007); Density: 1,676.5 persons per square mile (2007); Average household size: 2.59 (2007); Median age: 42.2 (2007); Males per 100 females: 92.4 (2007); Marriage status: 17.8% never married, 67.2% now married, 7.3% widowed, 7.7% divorced (2000); Foreign born: 2.1% (2000); Ancestry (includes multiple ancestries): 30.2% German, 15.0% English, 14.7% Irish, 13.1% Polish, 9.3% Italian (2000).
Economy: Single-family building permits issued: 23 (2007); Multi-family building permits issued: 12 (2007); Employment by occupation: 12.8% management, 20.9% professional, 10.7% services, 27.2% sales, 0.1% farming, 9.2% construction, 19.1% production (2000).
Income: Per capita income: $28,852 (2007); Median household income: $61,387 (2007); Average household income: $74,225 (2007); Percent of households with income of $100,000 or more: 21.6% (2007); Poverty rate: 2.1% (2000).
Education: Percent of population age 25 and over with: High school diploma (including GED) or higher: 88.8% (2007); Bachelor's degree or higher: 22.2% (2007); Master's degree or higher: 7.9% (2007).

School District(s)

Amherst Exempted Village (PK-12)
2005-06 Enrollment: 4,295 . . . . (440) 988-4406
Housing: Homeownership rate: 85.2% (2007); Median home value: $168,401 (2007); Median rent: $485 per month (2000); Median age of housing: 35 years (2000).
Hospitals: Amherst Hospital (71 beds)
Safety: Violent crime rate: 11.0 per 10,000 population; Property crime rate: 194.1 per 10,000 population (2007).
Transportation: Commute to work: 95.9% car, 0.5% public transportation, 0.7% walk, 2.5% work from home (2000); Travel time to work: 35.4% less than 15 minutes, 37.9% 15 to 30 minutes, 17.4% 30 to 45 minutes, 5.0% 45 to 60 minutes, 4.3% 60 minutes or more (2000)
Additional Information Contacts
City of Amherst . . . . (440) 988-4380
http://www.amherstohio.org

AVON (city). Covers a land area of 20.872 square miles and a water area of 0.016 square miles. Located at 41.45° N. Lat.; 82.02° W. Long. Elevation is 666 feet.
History: Named for Avon, New York. Settled c.1814. Incorporated 1918.
Population: 7,337 (1990); 11,446 (2000); 17,003 (2007); 20,427 (2012 projected); Race: 95.9% White, 0.9% Black, 1.6% Asian, 1.5% Hispanic of any race (2007); Density: 814.6 persons per square mile (2007); Average household size: 2.69 (2007); Median age: 39.4 (2007); Males per 100 females: 95.1 (2007); Marriage status: 18.4% never married, 67.6% now married, 6.9% widowed, 7.1% divorced (2000); Foreign born: 3.7% (2000); Ancestry (includes multiple ancestries): 35.0% German, 18.2% Irish, 10.8% Italian, 10.4% English, 9.7% Polish (2000).
Economy: Single-family building permits issued: 180 (2007); Multi-family building permits issued: 0 (2007); Employment by occupation: 20.0% management, 24.5% professional, 8.9% services, 27.3% sales, 0.4% farming, 8.4% construction, 10.4% production (2000).
Income: Per capita income: $34,728 (2007); Median household income: $79,358 (2007); Average household income: $92,554 (2007); Percent of households with income of $100,000 or more: 35.8% (2007); Poverty rate: 1.9% (2000).
Education: Percent of population age 25 and over with: High school diploma (including GED) or higher: 90.7% (2007); Bachelor's degree or higher: 32.2% (2007); Master's degree or higher: 9.6% (2007).

School District(s)

Avon Local (PK-12)
2005-06 Enrollment: 2,987 . . . . (440) 937-4680
Housing: Homeownership rate: 87.9% (2007); Median home value: $220,829 (2007); Median rent: $650 per month (2000); Median age of housing: 18 years (2000).
Transportation: Commute to work: 93.6% car, 2.0% public transportation, 0.4% walk, 3.6% work from home (2000); Travel time to work: 22.9% less than 15 minutes, 45.1% 15 to 30 minutes, 20.4% 30 to 45 minutes, 8.7% 45 to 60 minutes, 3.0% 60 minutes or more (2000)
Additional Information Contacts
City of Avon . . . . (440) 937-7800
http://www.cityofavon.com
North Coast Regional Chamber of Commerce . . . . (440) 933-9311
http://www.avonlakeavoncc.com

AVON LAKE (city). Covers a land area of 11.132 square miles and a water area of 0 square miles. Located at 41.50° N. Lat.; 82.00° W. Long. Elevation is 607 feet.
History: Named for Avon New York, which was named for the river in England. Avon Lake developed as a vacation area, with beaches for water sports.
Population: 15,066 (1990); 18,145 (2000); 21,210 (2007); 23,157 (2012 projected); Race: 96.5% White, 0.5% Black, 1.2% Asian, 1.5% Hispanic of any race (2007); Density: 1,905.4 persons per square mile (2007); Average household size: 2.64 (2007); Median age: 40.3 (2007); Males per 100 females: 95.4 (2007); Marriage status: 18.2% never married, 68.7% now married, 5.3% widowed, 7.8% divorced (2000); Foreign born: 3.4% (2000); Ancestry (includes multiple ancestries): 36.2% German, 22.7% Irish, 13.9% English, 11.4% Italian, 7.3% Polish (2000).
Economy: Single-family building permits issued: 142 (2007); Multi-family building permits issued: 0 (2007); Employment by occupation: 20.6% management, 25.5% professional, 9.4% services, 27.1% sales, 0.2% farming, 7.1% construction, 10.2% production (2000).
Income: Per capita income: $37,319 (2007); Median household income: $74,586 (2007); Average household income: $98,391 (2007); Percent of households with income of $100,000 or more: 33.2% (2007); Poverty rate: 2.3% (2000).
Taxes: Total city taxes per capita: $690 (2006); City property taxes per capita: $244 (2006).
Education: Percent of population age 25 and over with: High school diploma (including GED) or higher: 94.8% (2007); Bachelor's degree or higher: 42.8% (2007); Master's degree or higher: 15.9% (2007).

School District(s)

Avon Lake City (PK-12)
2005-06 Enrollment: 3,489 . . . . (440) 933-6210
Housing: Homeownership rate: 86.5% (2007); Median home value: $209,663 (2007); Median rent: $572 per month (2000); Median age of housing: 29 years (2000).
Newspapers: Avon Lake Press (Local news; Circulation 8,700); The North Ridgeville Press and Light (Community news; Circulation 4,500); The Press (Local news; Circulation 8,700)
Transportation: Commute to work: 94.6% car, 1.0% public transportation, 0.3% walk, 3.3% work from home (2000); Travel time to work: 24.7% less than 15 minutes, 35.1% 15 to 30 minutes, 28.5% 30 to 45 minutes, 7.9% 45 to 60 minutes, 3.7% 60 minutes or more (2000)
Additional Information Contacts
City of Avon Lake. . . . . (440) 933-6141
http://www.avonlake.org
North Coast Regional Chamber of Commerce . . . . (440) 933-9311
http://www.avonlakeavoncc.com

COLUMBIA STATION (unincorporated postal area, zip code 44028). Covers a land area of 34.113 square miles and a water area of 0.344 square miles. Located at 41.31° N. Lat.; 81.93° W. Long. Elevation is 804 feet.
Population: 10,199 (2000); Race: 88.2% White, 9.6% Black, 0.2% Asian, 1.5% Hispanic of any race (2000); Density: 299.0 persons per square mile (2000); Age: 20.7% under 18, 8.8% over 64 (2000); Marriage status: 30.2% never married, 56.3% now married, 4.2% widowed, 9.3% divorced (2000); Foreign born: 2.6% (2000); Ancestry (includes multiple ancestries): 29.2% German, 16.2% Irish, 11.6% English, 9.4% Polish, 8.7% Other groups (2000).
Economy: Employment by occupation: 11.2% management, 15.1% professional, 13.9% services, 27.4% sales, 0.9% farming, 16.2% construction, 15.3% production (2000).
Income: Per capita income: $23,015 (2000); Median household income: $57,596 (2000); Poverty rate: 2.8% (2000).
Education: Percent of population age 25 and over with: High school diploma (including GED) or higher: 85.4% (2000); Bachelor's degree or higher: 14.4% (2000).

School District(s)

Columbia Local (PK-12)
2005-06 Enrollment: 1,162 . . . . (440) 236-5008
Housing: Homeownership rate: 90.2% (2000); Median home value: $148,100 (2000); Median rent: $541 per month (2000); Median age of housing: 36 years (2000).
Newspapers: Rural-Urban Record (Community news; Circulation 17,139)
Transportation: Commute to work: 95.1% car, 0.9% public transportation, 1.2% walk, 2.4% work from home (2000); Travel time to work: 20.1% less than 15 minutes, 42.0% 15 to 30 minutes, 22.5% 30 to 45 minutes, 9.6% 45 to 60 minutes, 5.7% 60 minutes or more (2000)
Additional Information Contacts
Columbia Chamber of Commerce . . . . (440) 236-9053
http://www.columbiastation.com

EATON ESTATES (CDP). Covers a land area of 0.880 square miles and a water area of 0 square miles. Located at 41.30° N. Lat.; 82.00° W. Long. Elevation is 801 feet.
Population: 1,586 (1990); 1,409 (2000); 1,373 (2007); 1,338 (2012 projected); Race: 97.1% White, 0.9% Black, 0.4% Asian, 2.4% Hispanic of any race (2007); Density: 1,560.7 persons per square mile (2007); Average household size: 2.98 (2007); Median age: 34.8 (2007); Males per 100 females: 96.7 (2007); Marriage status: 24.3% never married, 61.6% now married, 3.2% widowed, 10.9% divorced (2000); Foreign born: 0.5% (2000); Ancestry (includes multiple ancestries): 36.2% German, 28.9% Irish, 9.3% Other groups, 8.5% United States or American, 7.8% English (2000).
Economy: Employment by occupation: 3.6% management, 3.5% professional, 12.6% services, 26.9% sales, 0.0% farming, 9.8% construction, 43.7% production (2000).
Income: Per capita income: $19,148 (2007); Median household income: $55,556 (2007); Average household income: $57,152 (2007); Percent of households with income of $100,000 or more: 8.5% (2007); Poverty rate: 7.0% (2000).
Education: Percent of population age 25 and over with: High school diploma (including GED) or higher: 69.8% (2007); Bachelor's degree or higher: 3.2% (2007); Master's degree or higher: 0.0% (2007).
Housing: Homeownership rate: 90.4% (2007); Median home value: $112,146 (2007); Median rent: $492 per month (2000); Median age of housing: 44 years (2000).
Transportation: Commute to work: 96.3% car, 1.1% public transportation, 0.0% walk, 1.7% work from home (2000); Travel time to work: 12.9% less

than 15 minutes, 46.8% 15 to 30 minutes, 29.1% 30 to 45 minutes, 6.8% 45 to 60 minutes, 4.4% 60 minutes or more (2000)

ELYRIA (city). County seat. Covers a land area of 19.886 square miles and a water area of 0.026 square miles. Located at 41.37° N. Lat.; 82.10° W. Long. Elevation is 715 feet.

History: Named for Herman Ely (1775-1852), merchant and founder of the town. Settlement at Elyria began in 1817 when Heman Ely, a New Englander, acquired land around the falls of the Black River and built a dam, grist mill, sawmill, and house. Novelist Sherwood Anderson managed a paint factory in Elyria before he became a writer.

Population: 57,491 (1990); 55,953 (2000); 55,547 (2007); 55,434 (2012 projected); Race: 80.6% White, 13.7% Black, 0.8% Asian, 3.5% Hispanic of any race (2007); Density: 2,793.3 persons per square mile (2007); Average household size: 2.43 (2007); Median age: 36.0 (2007); Males per 100 females: 93.0 (2007); Marriage status: 26.6% never married, 52.9% now married, 7.0% widowed, 13.6% divorced (2000); Foreign born: 1.5% (2000); Ancestry (includes multiple ancestries): 23.8% German, 20.3% Other groups, 14.3% Irish, 10.9% English, 7.5% Polish (2000).

Economy: Unemployment rate: 7.8% (6/2008); Total civilian labor force: 29,800 (6/2008); Single-family building permits issued: 37 (2007); Multi-family building permits issued: 54 (2007); Employment by occupation: 8.3% management, 15.7% professional, 17.2% services, 24.9% sales, 0.3% farming, 9.4% construction, 24.3% production (2000).

Income: Per capita income: $21,769 (2007); Median household income: $42,359 (2007); Average household income: $52,262 (2007); Percent of households with income of $100,000 or more: 9.6% (2007); Poverty rate: 11.7% (2000).

Taxes: Total city taxes per capita: $485 (2006); City property taxes per capita: $67 (2006).

Education: Percent of population age 25 and over with: High school diploma (including GED) or higher: 82.1% (2007); Bachelor's degree or higher: 13.4% (2007); Master's degree or higher: 4.3% (2007).

School District(s)

Elyria City (PK-12)
2005-06 Enrollment: 7,760 . . . . (440) 284-8000
Elyria Community School (KG-07)
2005-06 Enrollment: 240 . . . . (440) 366-5225
Life Skills Center of Elyria (09-12)
2005-06 Enrollment: 278 . . . . (440) 324-1755

Two-year College(s)

Lorain County Community College (Public)
Fall 2007 Enrollment: 10,769 . . . . (440) 366-5222
2007-08 Tuition: In-state $2,890; Out-of-state $5,837

Housing: Homeownership rate: 64.7% (2007); Median home value: $114,661 (2007); Median rent: $430 per month (2000); Median age of housing: 38 years (2000).

Hospitals: EMH Regional Medical Center (348 beds)

Safety: Violent crime rate: 39.9 per 10,000 population; Property crime rate: 409.0 per 10,000 population (2007).

Newspapers: The Chronicle Telegram (Local news; Circulation 23,918); Plain Dealer - Lorain Bureau (Local news; Circulation 350,000)

Transportation: Commute to work: 94.1% car, 0.9% public transportation, 2.6% walk, 1.6% work from home (2000); Travel time to work: 38.3% less than 15 minutes, 37.3% 15 to 30 minutes, 16.1% 30 to 45 minutes, 5.1% 45 to 60 minutes, 3.1% 60 minutes or more (2000); Amtrak: Service available.

Additional Information Contacts

City of Elyria . . . . (440) 326-1400
http://www.cityofelyria.org
Lorain County Chamber of Commerce . . . . (440) 328-2550
http://www.loraincountychamber.com

GRAFTON (village). Covers a land area of 4.514 square miles and a water area of 0 square miles. Located at 41.27° N. Lat.; 82.05° W. Long. Elevation is 804 feet.

Population: 3,593 (1990); 2,302 (2000); 2,236 (2007); 2,223 (2012 projected); Race: 96.6% White, 1.2% Black, 0.4% Asian, 1.2% Hispanic of any race (2007); Density: 495.3 persons per square mile (2007); Average household size: 2.67 (2007); Median age: 36.3 (2007); Males per 100 females: 94.3 (2007); Marriage status: 23.1% never married, 60.8% now married, 6.3% widowed, 9.8% divorced (2000); Foreign born: 0.8% (2000); Ancestry (includes multiple ancestries): 29.4% German, 14.1% Irish, 13.6% Polish, 12.5% English, 10.2% Italian (2000).

Economy: Single-family building permits issued: 11 (2007); Multi-family building permits issued: 0 (2007); Employment by occupation: 9.4% management, 10.3% professional, 14.7% services, 26.3% sales, 0.0% farming, 10.1% construction, 29.2% production (2000).

Income: Per capita income: $24,034 (2007); Median household income: $58,989 (2007); Average household income: $64,273 (2007); Percent of households with income of $100,000 or more: 15.9% (2007); Poverty rate: 2.4% (2000).

Education: Percent of population age 25 and over with: High school diploma (including GED) or higher: 86.3% (2007); Bachelor's degree or higher: 9.5% (2007); Master's degree or higher: 2.9% (2007).

School District(s)

Midview Local (PK-12)
2005-06 Enrollment: 3,546 . . . . (440) 926-3737

Housing: Homeownership rate: 82.1% (2007); Median home value: $150,000 (2007); Median rent: $425 per month (2000); Median age of housing: 36 years (2000).

Transportation: Commute to work: 94.5% car, 0.0% public transportation, 2.7% walk, 1.7% work from home (2000); Travel time to work: 28.9% less than 15 minutes, 42.7% 15 to 30 minutes, 21.2% 30 to 45 minutes, 4.6% 45 to 60 minutes, 2.7% 60 minutes or more (2000)

KIPTON (village). Covers a land area of 0.462 square miles and a water area of 0 square miles. Located at 41.26° N. Lat.; 82.30° W. Long. Elevation is 850 feet.

Population: 283 (1990); 265 (2000); 277 (2007); 287 (2012 projected); Race: 98.6% White, 0.4% Black, 0.0% Asian, 0.7% Hispanic of any race (2007); Density: 599.2 persons per square mile (2007); Average household size: 2.43 (2007); Median age: 39.5 (2007); Males per 100 females: 108.3 (2007); Marriage status: 25.2% never married, 57.5% now married, 2.8% widowed, 14.5% divorced (2000); Foreign born: 0.0% (2000); Ancestry (includes multiple ancestries): 31.7% German, 21.8% English, 11.4% Irish, 11.1% Italian, 8.5% Other groups (2000).

Economy: Single-family building permits issued: 0 (2007); Multi-family building permits issued: 0 (2007); Employment by occupation: 2.9% management, 14.3% professional, 5.7% services, 20.0% sales, 9.3% farming, 26.4% construction, 21.4% production (2000).

Income: Per capita income: $25,469 (2007); Median household income: $53,529 (2007); Average household income: $61,886 (2007); Percent of households with income of $100,000 or more: 9.6% (2007); Poverty rate: 4.5% (2000).

Education: Percent of population age 25 and over with: High school diploma (including GED) or higher: 90.4% (2007); Bachelor's degree or higher: 12.7% (2007); Master's degree or higher: 4.6% (2007).

Housing: Homeownership rate: 82.5% (2007); Median home value: $113,281 (2007); Median rent: $400 per month (2000); Median age of housing: 60+ years (2000).

Transportation: Commute to work: 100.0% car, 0.0% public transportation, 0.0% walk, 0.0% work from home (2000); Travel time to work: 36.8% less than 15 minutes, 33.1% 15 to 30 minutes, 18.4% 30 to 45 minutes, 5.9% 45 to 60 minutes, 5.9% 60 minutes or more (2000)

LAGRANGE (village). Covers a land area of 1.759 square miles and a water area of 0 square miles. Located at 41.23° N. Lat.; 82.12° W. Long. Elevation is 820 feet.

Population: 1,220 (1990); 1,815 (2000); 1,957 (2007); 2,034 (2012 projected); Race: 96.2% White, 0.9% Black, 0.2% Asian, 1.8% Hispanic of any race (2007); Density: 1,112.6 persons per square mile (2007); Average household size: 2.84 (2007); Median age: 34.5 (2007); Males per 100 females: 94.1 (2007); Marriage status: 24.8% never married, 61.6% now married, 4.4% widowed, 9.2% divorced (2000); Foreign born: 0.8% (2000); Ancestry (includes multiple ancestries): 33.9% German, 19.2% Irish, 15.3% English, 7.3% Other groups, 6.7% Polish (2000).

Economy: Single-family building permits issued: 4 (2007); Multi-family building permits issued: 3 (2007); Employment by occupation: 10.2% management, 13.3% professional, 14.7% services, 26.2% sales, 0.5% farming, 15.1% construction, 20.1% production (2000).

Income: Per capita income: $26,202 (2007); Median household income: $61,603 (2007); Average household income: $74,423 (2007); Percent of households with income of $100,000 or more: 21.8% (2007); Poverty rate: 6.2% (2000).

Education: Percent of population age 25 and over with: High school diploma (including GED) or higher: 87.7% (2007); Bachelor's degree or higher: 11.8% (2007); Master's degree or higher: 3.2% (2007).

School District(s)

Keystone Local (PK-12)
2005-06 Enrollment: 1,859 . . . . (440) 355-5131

Housing: Homeownership rate: 75.8% (2007); Median home value: $172,525 (2007); Median rent: $503 per month (2000); Median age of housing: 26 years (2000).

Transportation: Commute to work: 93.3% car, 0.6% public transportation, 2.7% walk, 3.2% work from home (2000); Travel time to work: 25.9% less than 15 minutes, 41.4% 15 to 30 minutes, 22.9% 30 to 45 minutes, 5.7% 45 to 60 minutes, 4.1% 60 minutes or more (2000)

LORAIN (city). Covers a land area of 24.016 square miles and a water area of 0.231 square miles. Located at 41.44° N. Lat.; 82.16° W. Long. Elevation is 610 feet.

History: Named for the province of Lorraine in France. Lorain had its beginnings in 1807 when Nathan Perry and the Azariah Beebes established a trading post on the south shore of Lake Erie, at the mouth of the Black River. In 1810 others arrived, including John Reid, whose home became the post office, justice's office, and tavern. By 1819 shipbuilding began in Lorain. The town had first been known as Mouth of Black River, but in 1836 it was incorporated as Charleston. When the Cleveland, Lorain & Wheeling Railroad arrived in 1872, a new charter was granted under the name of Lorain. The first steel company came to Lorain in 1894, and was later acquired by the United States Steel Corporation, bringing immigrants from many countries to work here.

Population: 71,245 (1990); 68,652 (2000); 67,618 (2007); 67,017 (2012 projected); Race: 67.4% White, 16.3% Black, 0.4% Asian, 23.0% Hispanic of any race (2007); Density: 2,815.6 persons per square mile (2007); Average household size: 2.52 (2007); Median age: 35.2 (2007); Males per 100 females: 90.7 (2007); Marriage status: 28.3% never married, 50.5% now married, 8.4% widowed, 12.8% divorced (2000); Foreign born: 3.6% (2000); Ancestry (includes multiple ancestries): 36.9% Other groups, 16.0% German, 11.0% Irish, 7.8% Polish, 6.7% Italian (2000).

Economy: Unemployment rate: 9.3% (6/2008); Total civilian labor force: 33,613 (6/2008); Single-family building permits issued: 118 (2007); Multi-family building permits issued: 0 (2007); Employment by occupation: 7.4% management, 13.0% professional, 16.7% services, 25.7% sales, 0.6% farming, 9.6% construction, 27.0% production (2000).

Income: Per capita income: $18,911 (2007); Median household income: $37,829 (2007); Average household income: $47,261 (2007); Percent of households with income of $100,000 or more: 8.2% (2007); Poverty rate: 17.1% (2000).

Taxes: Total city taxes per capita: $359 (2006); City property taxes per capita: $63 (2006).

Education: Percent of population age 25 and over with: High school diploma (including GED) or higher: 74.5% (2007); Bachelor's degree or higher: 10.1% (2007); Master's degree or higher: 3.5% (2007).

School District(s)

Academy of Arts and Sciences (KG-05)
2005-06 Enrollment: 101 . . . . (440) 244-0156

Arts Academy The (KG-08)
2005-06 Enrollment: 254 . . . . (440) 960-0470

Clearview Local (PK-12)
2005-06 Enrollment: 1,525 . . . . (440) 233-5412

Lorain Academy for Gifted Students (KG-07)
2005-06 Enrollment: 66 . . . . (440) 244-0855

Lorain Alternative Academy (09-12)
2005-06 Enrollment: 21 . . . . (440) 282-4087

Lorain City (PK-12)
2005-06 Enrollment: 9,718 . . . . (440) 233-2271

Lorain Community School (KG-07)
2005-06 Enrollment: 241 . . . . (440) 204-2130

Lorain Elementary Digital (KG-06)
2005-06 Enrollment: 21 . . . . (440) 282-4087

Lorain High School Digital (09-12)
2005-06 Enrollment: 63 . . . . (440) 282-4087

Lorain Middle School Digital (07-08)
2005-06 Enrollment: 37 . . . . (440) 282-4087

Mansfield Preparatory Academy
2005-06 Enrollment: n/a . . . .

Summit Academy Middle School - Lorain (06-08)
2005-06 Enrollment: 45 . . . . (440) 245-2593

Summit Academy Secondary - Lorain (08-11)
2005-06 Enrollment: 30 . . . . (440) 245-2593

Summit Academy-Lorain (01-06)
2005-06 Enrollment: 63 . . . . (440) 277-4110

Two-year College(s)

Ohio Business College-Lorain (Private, For-profit)
Fall 2007 Enrollment: 231 . . . . (440) 277-0021
2007-08 Tuition: In-state $7,380; Out-of-state $7,380

Vocational/Technical School(s)

Northern Institute of Cosmetology (Private, For-profit)
Fall 2007 Enrollment: 26 . . . . (440) 244-4282
2007-08 Tuition: $5,695

Housing: Homeownership rate: 61.2% (2007); Median home value: $106,757 (2007); Median rent: $408 per month (2000); Median age of housing: 43 years (2000).

Hospitals: St. Joseph Community Center (328 beds)

Safety: Violent crime rate: 46.3 per 10,000 population; Property crime rate: 339.1 per 10,000 population (2007).

Newspapers: Morning Journal (Regional news; Circulation 14,600)

Transportation: Commute to work: 95.5% car, 0.7% public transportation, 1.7% walk, 1.3% work from home (2000); Travel time to work: 32.6% less than 15 minutes, 41.9% 15 to 30 minutes, 15.3% 30 to 45 minutes, 5.8% 45 to 60 minutes, 4.4% 60 minutes or more (2000)

Airports: Lorain County Regional (general aviation)

Additional Information Contacts

City of Lorain . . . . (440) 204-2002
http://www.cityoflorain.org

NORTH RIDGEVILLE (city). Covers a land area of 23.370 square miles and a water area of 0.141 square miles. Located at 41.39° N. Lat.; 82.00° W. Long. Elevation is 728 feet.

Population: 21,564 (1990); 22,338 (2000); 27,285 (2007); 30,383 (2012 projected); Race: 95.5% White, 0.9% Black, 1.3% Asian, 2.3% Hispanic of any race (2007); Density: 1,167.5 persons per square mile (2007); Average household size: 2.60 (2007); Median age: 40.6 (2007); Males per 100 females: 96.4 (2007); Marriage status: 21.7% never married, 63.8% now married, 6.4% widowed, 8.1% divorced (2000); Foreign born: 3.3% (2000); Ancestry (includes multiple ancestries): 32.9% German, 19.2% Irish, 12.6% English, 10.7% Polish, 9.0% Italian (2000).

Economy: Unemployment rate: 6.3% (6/2008); Total civilian labor force: 16,451 (6/2008); Single-family building permits issued: 273 (2007); Multi-family building permits issued: 16 (2007); Employment by occupation: 11.3% management, 16.2% professional, 12.8% services, 29.8% sales, 0.3% farming, 11.4% construction, 18.1% production (2000).

Income: Per capita income: $27,024 (2007); Median household income: $60,993 (2007); Average household income: $69,967 (2007); Percent of households with income of $100,000 or more: 19.1% (2007); Poverty rate: 3.2% (2000).

Education: Percent of population age 25 and over with: High school diploma (including GED) or higher: 85.9% (2007); Bachelor's degree or higher: 16.2% (2007); Master's degree or higher: 4.2% (2007).

School District(s)

North Ridgeville City (PK-12)
2005-06 Enrollment: 3,733 . . . . (440) 327-4444

Housing: Homeownership rate: 88.7% (2007); Median home value: $157,992 (2007); Median rent: $463 per month (2000); Median age of housing: 27 years (2000).

Safety: Violent crime rate: 4.3 per 10,000 population; Property crime rate: 106.6 per 10,000 population (2007).

Transportation: Commute to work: 96.1% car, 1.0% public transportation, 0.6% walk, 1.9% work from home (2000); Travel time to work: 18.8% less than 15 minutes, 44.4% 15 to 30 minutes, 24.8% 30 to 45 minutes, 7.2% 45 to 60 minutes, 4.8% 60 minutes or more (2000)

Additional Information Contacts

City of North Ridgeville . . . . (440) 353-0819
http://www.ci.north-ridgeville.oh.us

North Ridgeville Chamber of Commerce . . . . (440) 327-3737
http://www.nrchamber.com

OBERLIN (city). Covers a land area of 4.379 square miles and a water area of 0.026 square miles. Located at 41.28° N. Lat.; 82.21° W. Long. Elevation is 814 feet.

History: Oberlin College was founded in 1833 by John L. Shipherd, a Presbyterian minister from Elyria, and Philo P. Steward, a missionary. In 1837 four women applied for the regular college course. When they were accepted, Oberlin became the first coeducational college in the country.

Population: 8,327 (1990); 8,195 (2000); 8,375 (2007); 8,448 (2012 projected); Race: 73.6% White, 15.1% Black, 4.0% Asian, 3.6% Hispanic of any race (2007); Density: 1,912.6 persons per square mile (2007); Average

household size: 3.02 (2007); Median age: 26.8 (2007); Males per 100 females: 78.7 (2007); Marriage status: 50.0% never married, 35.2% now married, 7.9% widowed, 6.9% divorced (2000); Foreign born: 5.3% (2000); Ancestry (includes multiple ancestries): 27.7% Other groups, 17.0% German, 15.6% English, 10.4% Irish, 4.9% Italian (2000).
Economy: Single-family building permits issued: 4 (2007); Multi-family building permits issued: 0 (2007); Employment by occupation: 9.0% management, 34.8% professional, 21.5% services, 20.6% sales, 0.0% farming, 5.4% construction, 8.7% production (2000).
Income: Per capita income: $22,409 (2007); Median household income: $48,638 (2007); Average household income: $63,448 (2007); Percent of households with income of $100,000 or more: 18.0% (2007); Poverty rate: 19.4% (2000).
Taxes: Total city taxes per capita: $702 (2006); City property taxes per capita: $142 (2006).
Education: Percent of population age 25 and over with: High school diploma (including GED) or higher: 86.3% (2007); Bachelor's degree or higher: 41.4% (2007); Master's degree or higher: 24.4% (2007).

School District(s)

Firelands Local (PK-12)
2005-06 Enrollment: 2,141 . . . . (440) 965-5821
Lorain County (08-12)
2005-06 Enrollment: n/a . . . . (440) 774-1051
Oberlin City (PK-12)
2005-06 Enrollment: 1,096 . . . . (440) 774-1458

Four-year College(s)

Oberlin College (Private, Not-for-profit)
Fall 2007 Enrollment: 2,774. . . . . (440) 775-8411
2007-08 Tuition: In-state $36,282; Out-of-state $36,282

Vocational/Technical School(s)

Lorain County Joint Vocational School District (Public)
Fall 2007 Enrollment: 87 . . . . (440) 774-1051
2007-08 Tuition: $7,395

Housing: Homeownership rate: 50.3% (2007); Median home value: $145,177 (2007); Median rent: $444 per month (2000); Median age of housing: 41 years (2000).
Hospitals: Allen Medical Center (25 beds)
Safety: Violent crime rate: 17.0 per 10,000 population; Property crime rate: 185.5 per 10,000 population (2007).
Newspapers: Amherst News Times (Local news; Circulation 4,000); News-Tribune (Community news; Circulation 3,000)
Transportation: Commute to work: 52.9% car, 0.2% public transportation, 36.1% walk, 4.3% work from home (2000); Travel time to work: 65.9% less than 15 minutes, 20.9% 15 to 30 minutes, 7.4% 30 to 45 minutes, 3.1% 45 to 60 minutes, 2.7% 60 minutes or more (2000)

Additional Information Contacts

Oberlin Area Chamber of Commerce . . . . (440) 774-6262
http://www.oberlinchamber.org

ROCHESTER (village). Covers a land area of 1.102 square miles and a water area of 0 square miles. Located at 41.12° N. Lat.; 82.30° W. Long. Elevation is 928 feet.
Population: 206 (1990); 190 (2000); 219 (2007); 238 (2012 projected); Race: 100.0% White, 0.0% Black, 0.0% Asian, 0.0% Hispanic of any race (2007); Density: 198.8 persons per square mile (2007); Average household size: 2.70 (2007); Median age: 36.0 (2007); Males per 100 females: 119.0 (2007); Marriage status: 28.9% never married, 55.5% now married, 5.2% widowed, 10.4% divorced (2000); Foreign born: 1.0% (2000); Ancestry (includes multiple ancestries): 22.8% German, 19.3% United States or American, 15.8% Irish, 9.9% English, 5.0% French (except Basque) (2000).
Economy: Single-family building permits issued: 0 (2007); Multi-family building permits issued: 0 (2007); Employment by occupation: 4.2% management, 13.3% professional, 8.3% services, 10.0% sales, 5.0% farming, 16.7% construction, 42.5% production (2000).
Income: Per capita income: $19,395 (2007); Median household income: $46,500 (2007); Average household income: $52,438 (2007); Percent of households with income of $100,000 or more: 12.3% (2007); Poverty rate: 7.4% (2000).
Education: Percent of population age 25 and over with: High school diploma (including GED) or higher: 72.6% (2007); Bachelor's degree or higher: 6.2% (2007); Master's degree or higher: 1.4% (2007).
Housing: Homeownership rate: 81.5% (2007); Median home value: $112,500 (2007); Median rent: $425 per month (2000); Median age of housing: 60+ years (2000).
Transportation: Commute to work: 92.0% car, 0.0% public transportation, 5.4% walk, 2.7% work from home (2000); Travel time to work: 24.8% less than 15 minutes, 41.3% 15 to 30 minutes, 22.0% 30 to 45 minutes, 7.3% 45 to 60 minutes, 4.6% 60 minutes or more (2000)

SHEFFIELD (village). Aka Sheffield Village. Covers a land area of 10.817 square miles and a water area of 0.002 square miles. Located at 41.44° N. Lat.; 82.08° W. Long. Elevation is 633 feet.
History: Incorporated 1933.
Population: 1,943 (1990); 2,949 (2000); 3,431 (2007); 3,736 (2012 projected); Race: 89.1% White, 5.2% Black, 0.9% Asian, 6.5% Hispanic of any race (2007); Density: 317.2 persons per square mile (2007); Average household size: 2.63 (2007); Median age: 40.4 (2007); Males per 100 females: 94.5 (2007); Marriage status: 19.0% never married, 67.3% now married, 6.4% widowed, 7.3% divorced (2000); Foreign born: 4.3% (2000); Ancestry (includes multiple ancestries): 30.6% German, 14.3% Other groups, 13.9% Irish, 13.3% Polish, 10.1% English (2000).
Economy: Single-family building permits issued: 14 (2007); Multi-family building permits issued: 4 (2007); Employment by occupation: 19.7% management, 16.9% professional, 8.6% services, 22.0% sales, 0.9% farming, 11.2% construction, 20.6% production (2000).
Income: Per capita income: $29,984 (2007); Median household income: $68,625 (2007); Average household income: $78,831 (2007); Percent of households with income of $100,000 or more: 26.5% (2007); Poverty rate: 3.2% (2000).
Education: Percent of population age 25 and over with: High school diploma (including GED) or higher: 89.2% (2007); Bachelor's degree or higher: 22.7% (2007); Master's degree or higher: 5.5% (2007).

School District(s)

Sheffield-Sheffield Lake City (PK-12)
2005-06 Enrollment: 1,937 . . . . (440) 949-6181

Two-year College(s)

Ohio Institute of Health Careers-Sheffield Village (Private, For-profit)
Fall 2007 Enrollment: 182 . . . . (440) 934-3101
2007-08 Tuition: In-state $11,489; Out-of-state $11,489

Housing: Homeownership rate: 87.8% (2007); Median home value: $192,919 (2007); Median rent: $375 per month (2000); Median age of housing: 17 years (2000).
Transportation: Commute to work: 95.1% car, 0.0% public transportation, 0.9% walk, 3.7% work from home (2000); Travel time to work: 31.9% less than 15 minutes, 36.5% 15 to 30 minutes, 19.5% 30 to 45 minutes, 7.8% 45 to 60 minutes, 4.3% 60 minutes or more (2000)

Additional Information Contacts

North Coast Regional Chamber of Commerce . . . . (440) 933-9311
http://www.avonlakeavoncc.com

SHEFFIELD LAKE (city). Aka Sheffield Village. Covers a land area of 2.522 square miles and a water area of 0 square miles. Located at 41.48° N. Lat.; 82.10° W. Long. Elevation is 600 feet.
History: Incorporated 1920.
Population: 9,825 (1990); 9,371 (2000); 9,124 (2007); 8,969 (2012 projected); Race: 96.3% White, 1.1% Black, 0.3% Asian, 3.4% Hispanic of any race (2007); Density: 3,617.3 persons per square mile (2007); Average household size: 2.60 (2007); Median age: 37.4 (2007); Males per 100 females: 95.1 (2007); Marriage status: 25.8% never married, 60.6% now married, 4.8% widowed, 8.8% divorced (2000); Foreign born: 1.7% (2000); Ancestry (includes multiple ancestries): 30.2% German, 16.1% Irish, 10.4% Italian, 10.1% English, 9.4% Polish (2000).
Economy: Single-family building permits issued: 2 (2007); Multi-family building permits issued: 0 (2007); Employment by occupation: 9.7% management, 12.6% professional, 15.8% services, 27.3% sales, 0.3% farming, 12.2% construction, 22.1% production (2000).
Income: Per capita income: $23,193 (2007); Median household income: $52,707 (2007); Average household income: $60,186 (2007); Percent of households with income of $100,000 or more: 11.6% (2007); Poverty rate: 4.7% (2000).
Education: Percent of population age 25 and over with: High school diploma (including GED) or higher: 84.6% (2007); Bachelor's degree or higher: 13.2% (2007); Master's degree or higher: 3.3% (2007).

School District(s)

Sheffield-Sheffield Lake City (PK-12)
2005-06 Enrollment: 1,937 . . . . (440) 949-6181

Housing: Homeownership rate: 80.0% (2007); Median home value: $123,291 (2007); Median rent: $486 per month (2000); Median age of housing: 36 years (2000).

Safety: Violent crime rate: 7.7 per 10,000 population; Property crime rate: 217.7 per 10,000 population (2007).
Transportation: Commute to work: 95.7% car, 0.8% public transportation, 1.0% walk, 2.0% work from home (2000); Travel time to work: 22.0% less than 15 minutes, 40.1% 15 to 30 minutes, 24.7% 30 to 45 minutes, 9.9% 45 to 60 minutes, 3.4% 60 minutes or more (2000)
Additional Information Contacts
North Coast Regional Chamber of Commerce . . . . (440) 933-9311
http://www.avonlakeavoncc.com

SOUTH AMHERST (village). Covers a land area of 2.451 square miles and a water area of 0.008 square miles. Located at 41.35° N. Lat.; 82.24° W. Long. Elevation is 794 feet.
History: South Amherst was at one time called Podunk. The town developed as a quarrying center.
Population: 1,820 (1990); 1,863 (2000); 1,757 (2007); 1,685 (2012 projected); Race: 97.0% White, 0.5% Black, 0.2% Asian, 2.2% Hispanic of any race (2007); Density: 716.8 persons per square mile (2007); Average household size: 2.69 (2007); Median age: 40.7 (2007); Males per 100 females: 95.0 (2007); Marriage status: 21.7% never married, 65.5% now married, 5.9% widowed, 7.0% divorced (2000); Foreign born: 1.6% (2000); Ancestry (includes multiple ancestries): 27.4% German, 18.6% Irish, 15.1% English, 9.5% Other groups, 9.0% Polish (2000).
Economy: Single-family building permits issued: 1 (2007); Multi-family building permits issued: 0 (2007); Employment by occupation: 8.2% management, 16.8% professional, 16.1% services, 22.4% sales, 0.7% farming, 13.6% construction, 22.2% production (2000).
Income: Per capita income: $23,856 (2007); Median household income: $52,018 (2007); Average household income: $63,817 (2007); Percent of households with income of $100,000 or more: 15.9% (2007); Poverty rate: 4.2% (2000).
Education: Percent of population age 25 and over with: High school diploma (including GED) or higher: 83.1% (2007); Bachelor's degree or higher: 12.4% (2007); Master's degree or higher: 4.6% (2007).

School District(s)

Firelands Local (PK-12)
2005-06 Enrollment: 2,141 . . . . (440) 965-5821
Housing: Homeownership rate: 87.0% (2007); Median home value: $150,216 (2007); Median rent: $465 per month (2000); Median age of housing: 46 years (2000).
Transportation: Commute to work: 94.9% car, 1.5% public transportation, 0.7% walk, 2.6% work from home (2000); Travel time to work: 32.4% less than 15 minutes, 46.2% 15 to 30 minutes, 12.8% 30 to 45 minutes, 3.9% 45 to 60 minutes, 4.7% 60 minutes or more (2000)

VERMILION (city). Covers a land area of 10.791 square miles and a water area of 0.052 square miles. Located at 41.41° N. Lat.; 82.34° W. Long.
History: Vermilion was settled in 1808 along the Vermilion River, named for the red clay found along the river bottom. Vermilion developed as a fishing center and a tourist resort.
Population: 11,133 (1990); 10,927 (2000); 10,894 (2007); 10,898 (2012 projected); Race: 97.7% White, 0.2% Black, 0.3% Asian, 1.9% Hispanic of any race (2007); Density: 1,009.5 persons per square mile (2007); Average household size: 2.49 (2007); Median age: 40.6 (2007); Males per 100 females: 93.2 (2007); Marriage status: 20.2% never married, 64.0% now married, 7.3% widowed, 8.5% divorced (2000); Foreign born: 1.8% (2000); Ancestry (includes multiple ancestries): 34.0% German, 17.1% Irish, 13.8% English, 7.5% Other groups, 7.4% Italian (2000).
Economy: Single-family building permits issued: 16 (2007); Multi-family building permits issued: 0 (2007); Employment by occupation: 12.5% management, 15.6% professional, 12.8% services, 25.2% sales, 0.0% farming, 12.1% construction, 21.9% production (2000).
Income: Per capita income: $26,148 (2007); Median household income: $54,562 (2007); Average household income: $64,854 (2007); Percent of households with income of $100,000 or more: 13.9% (2007); Poverty rate: 5.4% (2000).
Education: Percent of population age 25 and over with: High school diploma (including GED) or higher: 86.4% (2007); Bachelor's degree or higher: 18.5% (2007); Master's degree or higher: 5.7% (2007).

School District(s)

Vermilion Local (PK-12)
2005-06 Enrollment: 2,466 . . . . (440) 967-5210
Housing: Homeownership rate: 75.4% (2007); Median home value: $133,433 (2007); Median rent: $501 per month (2000); Median age of housing: 36 years (2000).
Safety: Violent crime rate: 4.6 per 10,000 population; Property crime rate: 235.0 per 10,000 population (2007).
Newspapers: Vermilion Photo Journal (Local news; Circulation 4,000)
Transportation: Commute to work: 95.4% car, 0.4% public transportation, 1.6% walk, 2.6% work from home (2000); Travel time to work: 30.7% less than 15 minutes, 35.1% 15 to 30 minutes, 22.9% 30 to 45 minutes, 8.6% 45 to 60 minutes, 2.8% 60 minutes or more (2000)
Additional Information Contacts
Erie County Chamber of Commerce . . . . (419) 625-6421
http://www.eriecountyohiocofc.com
Vermilion Chamber of Commerce . . . . (440) 967-4477

WELLINGTON (village). Covers a land area of 2.936 square miles and a water area of 0.032 square miles. Located at 41.16° N. Lat.; 82.22° W. Long. Elevation is 850 feet.
History: Wellington developed in the dairy and grain area of Lorain County. It was an abolitionist center, and in 1858, when a Federal marshal stopped in Wellington with a runaway slave, the residents rescued the slave. Many of them were then arrested and charged with aiding a fugitive slave.
Population: 4,172 (1990); 4,511 (2000); 4,714 (2007); 4,875 (2012 projected); Race: 96.9% White, 1.2% Black, 0.1% Asian, 1.2% Hispanic of any race (2007); Density: 1,605.3 persons per square mile (2007); Average household size: 2.54 (2007); Median age: 36.1 (2007); Males per 100 females: 94.1 (2007); Marriage status: 25.4% never married, 52.1% now married, 10.8% widowed, 11.8% divorced (2000); Foreign born: 1.1% (2000); Ancestry (includes multiple ancestries): 24.1% German, 15.4% Irish, 14.4% English, 13.1% United States or American, 6.2% Other groups (2000).
Economy: Single-family building permits issued: 10 (2007); Multi-family building permits issued: 13 (2007); Employment by occupation: 6.0% management, 13.6% professional, 13.8% services, 24.2% sales, 1.0% farming, 12.1% construction, 29.4% production (2000).
Income: Per capita income: $21,428 (2007); Median household income: $46,302 (2007); Average household income: $53,730 (2007); Percent of households with income of $100,000 or more: 9.4% (2007); Poverty rate: 8.1% (2000).
Education: Percent of population age 25 and over with: High school diploma (including GED) or higher: 82.0% (2007); Bachelor's degree or higher: 11.7% (2007); Master's degree or higher: 2.7% (2007).

School District(s)

Keystone Local (PK-12)
2005-06 Enrollment: 1,859 . . . . (440) 355-5131
Wellington Exempted Village (PK-12)
2005-06 Enrollment: 1,643 . . . . (440) 647-4286
Housing: Homeownership rate: 66.0% (2007); Median home value: $132,083 (2007); Median rent: $399 per month (2000); Median age of housing: 46 years (2000).
Newspapers: Enterprise (Community news; Circulation 700)
Transportation: Commute to work: 94.6% car, 2.5% public transportation, 1.2% walk, 0.5% work from home (2000); Travel time to work: 41.0% less than 15 minutes, 21.6% 15 to 30 minutes, 23.9% 30 to 45 minutes, 8.4% 45 to 60 minutes, 5.1% 60 minutes or more (2000)
Additional Information Contacts
Wellington Chamber of Commerce . . . . (440) 647-2222

Lucas County

Located in northwestern Ohio; bounded on the north by Michigan, on the southeast by the Maumee River, and on the northeast by the west end of Lake Erie. Covers a land area of 340.46 square miles, a water area of 255.42 square miles, and is located in the Eastern Time Zone. The county was founded in 1835. County seat is Toledo.

Lucas County is part of the Toledo, OH Metropolitan Statistical Area. The entire metro area includes: Fulton County, OH; Lucas County, OH; Ottawa County, OH; Wood County, OH

Weather Station: Toledo Express Airport Elevation: 666 feet

	Jan	Feb	Mar	Apr	May	Jun	Jul	Aug	Sep	Oct	Nov	Dec
High	31	34	46	59	71	80	84	82	75	62	48	36
Low	16	18	27	37	48	57	61	59	52	41	32	22
Precip	1.9	1.9	2.7	3.3	3.1	3.8	2.9	3.2	2.9	2.3	2.8	2.6
Snow	10.9	8.2	5.7	1.4	tr	tr	tr	tr	tr	0.2	2.7	8.1

High and Low temperatures in degrees Fahrenheit; Precipitation and Snow in inches

Population: 462,361 (1990); 455,054 (2000); 445,674 (2007); 437,060 (2012 projected); Race: 75.8% White, 17.8% Black, 1.3% Asian, 5.2% Hispanic of any race (2007); Density: 1,309.0 persons per square mile (2007); Average household size: 2.45 (2007); Median age: 36.3 (2007); Males per 100 females: 93.9 (2007).
Religion: Five largest groups: 25.0% Catholic Church, 6.6% Evangelical Lutheran Church in America, 3.0% The United Methodist Church, 1.3% Jewish Estimate, 1.0% The Christian and Missionary Alliance (2000).
Economy: Unemployment rate: 7.8% (6/2008); Total civilian labor force: 226,221 (6/2008); Leading industries: 20.0% health care and social assistance; 12.6% retail trade; 12.1% manufacturing (2005); Farms: 405 totaling 77,823 acres (2002); Companies that employ 500 or more persons: 34 (2006); Companies that employ 100 to 499 persons: 300 (2006); Companies that employ less than 100 persons: 10,366 (2006); Black-owned businesses: 1,623 (2002); Hispanic-owned businesses: 473 (2002); Asian-owned businesses: 550 (2002); Women-owned businesses: 7,699 (2002); Retail sales per capita: $17,392 (2008). Single-family building permits issued: 511 (2007); Multi-family building permits issued: 565 (2007).
Income: Per capita income: $23,891 (2007); Median household income: $43,226 (2007); Average household income: $57,788 (2007); Percent of households with income of $100,000 or more: 13.7% (2007); Poverty rate: 17.5% (2005); Bankruptcy rate: 4.74% (2007).
Taxes: Total county taxes per capita: $420 (2006); County property taxes per capita: $238 (2006).
Education: Percent of population age 25 and over with: High school diploma (including GED) or higher: 83.4% (2007); Bachelor's degree or higher: 21.8% (2007); Master's degree or higher: 7.7% (2007).
Housing: Homeownership rate: 65.9% (2007); Median home value: $113,122 (2007); Median rent: $393 per month (2000); Median age of housing: 43 years (2000).
Health: Birth rate: 141.0 per 10,000 population (2007); Death rate: 96.7 per 10,000 population (2007); Age-adjusted cancer mortality rate: 222.5 deaths per 100,000 population (2005); Air Quality Index: 74.0% good, 23.8% moderate, 1.9% unhealthy for sensitive individuals, 0.3% unhealthy (percent of days in 2007); Number of physicians: 41.5 per 10,000 population (2005); Hospital beds: 55.3 per 10,000 population (2004); Hospital admissions: 2,106.6 per 10,000 population (2004).
Elections: 2004 Presidential election results: 39.5% Bush, 60.2% Kerry, 0.0% Nader, 0.1% Badnarik
National and State Parks: Cedar Point National Wildlife Refuge; Fallen Timbers State Memorial; Fort Miamis State Memorial; Mallard Club Marsh State Wildlife Area; Maumee Bay State Park; Missionary Island State Wildlife Area; West Sister Island National Wildlife Refuge

Additional Information Contacts

Lucas County Government . . . . (419) 213-4000
http://www.co.lucas.oh.us
City of Maumee . . . . (419) 897-7100
http://www.maumee.org
City of Oregon . . . . (419) 698-7045
http://www.ci.oregon.oh.us
City of Sylvania . . . . (419) 885-8925
http://www.cityofsylvania.com
City of Toledo. . . . . (419) 245-1001
http://www.ci.toledo.oh.us
Eastern Maumee Bay Chamber of Commerce . . . . (419) 693-5580
http://www.toledochamber.com
Greater Toledo Convention & Visitors Bureau. . . . . (800) 243-4667
http://www.dotoledo.org/gtcvb
Holland-Springfield Chamber of Commerce . . . . (419) 865-2110
http://www.hollandspringfieldcoc.org
Maumee Chamber of Commerce. (419) 893-5805
http://www.maumeechamber.com
Sylvania Area Chamber of Commerce . . . . (419) 882-2135
http://www.sylvaniachamber.org
Toldeo Regional Chamber of Commerce . . . . (419) 243-8191
http://www.toledochamber.com
Village of Ottawa Hills . . . . (419) 536-1111
http://www.ottawahills.org
Village of Waterville . . . . (419) 878-8100
http://www.waterville.org
Village of Whitehouse . . . . (419) 877-5383
http://www.whitehouseoh.com
Waterville Chamber of Commerce. . . . . (419) 878-5188
http://www.watervillechamber.com
Whitehouse Chamber of Commerce . . . . (419) 877-2747
http://www.whitehouseohchamber.com

Lucas County Communities

BERKEY (village). Covers a land area of 4.176 square miles and a water area of 0 square miles. Located at 41.71° N. Lat.; 83.83° W. Long. Elevation is 699 feet.
Population: 264 (1990); 265 (2000); 349 (2007); 397 (2012 projected); Race: 98.0% White, 0.0% Black, 0.6% Asian, 0.6% Hispanic of any race (2007); Density: 83.6 persons per square mile (2007); Average household size: 2.64 (2007); Median age: 38.4 (2007); Males per 100 females: 93.9 (2007); Marriage status: 17.6% never married, 69.5% now married, 11.0% widowed, 1.9% divorced (2000); Foreign born: 1.1% (2000); Ancestry (includes multiple ancestries): 44.8% German, 16.1% Irish, 13.0% English, 5.7% French (except Basque), 5.4% United States or American (2000).
Economy: Single-family building permits issued: 0 (2007); Multi-family building permits issued: 0 (2007); Employment by occupation: 12.4% management, 24.2% professional, 3.9% services, 30.7% sales, 0.0% farming, 10.5% construction, 18.3% production (2000).
Income: Per capita income: $33,073 (2007); Median household income: $71,250 (2007); Average household income: $87,443 (2007); Percent of households with income of $100,000 or more: 31.1% (2007); Poverty rate: 0.0% (2000).
Education: Percent of population age 25 and over with: High school diploma (including GED) or higher: 94.5% (2007); Bachelor's degree or higher: 25.0% (2007); Master's degree or higher: 7.7% (2007).
Housing: Homeownership rate: 90.9% (2007); Median home value: $175,000 (2007); Median rent: $363 per month (2000); Median age of housing: 56 years (2000).
Transportation: Commute to work: 98.6% car, 0.0% public transportation, 1.4% walk, 0.0% work from home (2000); Travel time to work: 12.5% less than 15 minutes, 36.8% 15 to 30 minutes, 34.0% 30 to 45 minutes, 6.9% 45 to 60 minutes, 9.7% 60 minutes or more (2000)

CURTICE (unincorporated postal area, zip code 43412). Covers a land area of 28.487 square miles and a water area of 0.105 square miles. Located at 41.63° N. Lat.; 83.30° W. Long. Elevation is 574 feet.
Population: 4,462 (2000); Race: 96.2% White, 0.5% Black, 0.3% Asian, 5.0% Hispanic of any race (2000); Density: 156.6 persons per square mile (2000); Age: 24.6% under 18, 11.5% over 64 (2000); Marriage status: 24.1% never married, 62.1% now married, 4.6% widowed, 9.2% divorced (2000); Foreign born: 1.3% (2000); Ancestry (includes multiple ancestries): 41.6% German, 11.9% Irish, 9.1% Other groups, 9.1% French (except Basque), 7.1% Polish (2000).
Economy: Employment by occupation: 9.3% management, 12.8% professional, 11.8% services, 23.3% sales, 1.7% farming, 14.3% construction, 26.8% production (2000).
Income: Per capita income: $20,778 (2000); Median household income: $53,393 (2000); Poverty rate: 7.5% (2000).
Education: Percent of population age 25 and over with: High school diploma (including GED) or higher: 85.2% (2000); Bachelor's degree or higher: 11.8% (2000).

School District(s)

Genoa Area Local (PK-12)
2005-06 Enrollment: 1,589 . . . . (419) 855-7741
Oregon City (PK-12)
2005-06 Enrollment: 3,929 . . . . (419) 693-0661

Housing: Homeownership rate: 89.0% (2000); Median home value: $117,500 (2000); Median rent: $356 per month (2000); Median age of housing: 41 years (2000).
Transportation: Commute to work: 95.7% car, 0.4% public transportation, 0.2% walk, 3.0% work from home (2000); Travel time to work: 17.6% less than 15 minutes, 50.7% 15 to 30 minutes, 17.7% 30 to 45 minutes, 7.3% 45 to 60 minutes, 6.6% 60 minutes or more (2000)

HARBOR VIEW (village). Covers a land area of 0.029 square miles and a water area of 0 square miles. Located at 41.69° N. Lat.; 83.44° W. Long. Elevation is 581 feet.

Population: 122 (1990); 99 (2000); 84 (2007); 86 (2012 projected); Race: 91.7% White, 0.0% Black, 0.0% Asian, 8.3% Hispanic of any race (2007); Density: 2,883.6 persons per square mile (2007); Average household size: 2.71 (2007); Median age: 40.5 (2007); Males per 100 females: 115.4 (2007); Marriage status: 23.2% never married, 52.4% now married, 6.1% widowed, 18.3% divorced (2000); Foreign born: 0.0% (2000); Ancestry (includes multiple ancestries): 24.1% German, 22.2% Other groups, 19.4% Irish, 18.5% United States or American, 6.5% Swedish (2000).

Economy: Employment by occupation: 0.0% management, 8.7% professional, 32.6% services, 28.3% sales, 0.0% farming, 21.7% construction, 8.7% production (2000).

Income: Per capita income: $17,708 (2007); Median household income: $40,833 (2007); Average household income: $47,984 (2007); Percent of households with income of $100,000 or more: 0.0% (2007); Poverty rate: 16.7% (2000).

Education: Percent of population age 25 and over with: High school diploma (including GED) or higher: 69.2% (2007); Bachelor's degree or higher: 0.0% (2007); Master's degree or higher: 0.0% (2007).

Housing: Homeownership rate: 93.5% (2007); Median home value: $54,167 (2007); Median rent: $425 per month (2000); Median age of housing: 60+ years (2000).

Transportation: Commute to work: 91.1% car, 0.0% public transportation, 8.9% walk, 0.0% work from home (2000); Travel time to work: 22.2% less than 15 minutes, 26.7% 15 to 30 minutes, 15.6% 30 to 45 minutes, 0.0% 45 to 60 minutes, 35.6% 60 minutes or more (2000)

HOLLAND (village). Covers a land area of 0.867 square miles and a water area of 0 square miles. Located at 41.61° N. Lat.; 83.71° W. Long. Elevation is 640 feet.

Population: 1,238 (1990); 1,306 (2000); 1,506 (2007); 1,620 (2012 projected); Race: 92.6% White, 2.6% Black, 2.9% Asian, 2.7% Hispanic of any race (2007); Density: 1,737.9 persons per square mile (2007); Average household size: 2.46 (2007); Median age: 42.8 (2007); Males per 100 females: 85.5 (2007); Marriage status: 18.5% never married, 46.9% now married, 21.7% widowed, 12.9% divorced (2000); Foreign born: 2.0% (2000); Ancestry (includes multiple ancestries): 27.7% German, 9.6% English, 9.3% Other groups, 9.1% United States or American, 9.1% Polish (2000).

Economy: Employment by occupation: 8.6% management, 11.7% professional, 15.7% services, 29.0% sales, 0.0% farming, 12.4% construction, 22.8% production (2000).

Income: Per capita income: $19,237 (2007); Median household income: $36,480 (2007); Average household income: $44,405 (2007); Percent of households with income of $100,000 or more: 7.0% (2007); Poverty rate: 7.9% (2000).

Education: Percent of population age 25 and over with: High school diploma (including GED) or higher: 74.9% (2007); Bachelor's degree or higher: 13.7% (2007); Master's degree or higher: 4.1% (2007).

School District(s)

Springfield Local (PK-12)
2005-06 Enrollment: 3,898 . . . . (419) 867-5600

Housing: Homeownership rate: 54.0% (2007); Median home value: $110,500 (2007); Median rent: $448 per month (2000); Median age of housing: 41 years (2000).

Safety: Violent crime rate: 31.4 per 10,000 population; Property crime rate: 1,310.8 per 10,000 population (2007).

Transportation: Commute to work: 95.1% car, 0.0% public transportation, 2.1% walk, 1.5% work from home (2000); Travel time to work: 35.3% less than 15 minutes, 40.8% 15 to 30 minutes, 13.5% 30 to 45 minutes, 3.8% 45 to 60 minutes, 6.6% 60 minutes or more (2000)

Additional Information Contacts

Holland-Springfield Chamber of Commerce . . . . (419) 865-2110
http://www.hollandspringfieldcoc.org

MAUMEE (city). Covers a land area of 9.935 square miles and a water area of 0.604 square miles. Located at 41.57° N. Lat.; 83.65° W. Long. Elevation is 633 feet.

History: A French-Canadian trading post was here from 1680 to 1693. In 1764 the British built Fort Miami. When a store opened in 1817, the town began to grow around it. Earlier names of Waynesville and South Toledo gave way to the name of Maumee, a corruption of the Indian name Miami.

Population: 15,569 (1990); 15,237 (2000); 14,141 (2007); 13,370 (2012 projected); Race: 95.7% White, 1.4% Black, 0.8% Asian, 2.1% Hispanic of any race (2007); Density: 1,423.3 persons per square mile (2007); Average household size: 2.34 (2007); Median age: 40.1 (2007); Males per 100 females: 94.0 (2007); Marriage status: 24.4% never married, 58.2% now married, 7.4% widowed, 10.0% divorced (2000); Foreign born: 2.2% (2000); Ancestry (includes multiple ancestries): 41.6% German, 15.5% Irish, 12.2% Polish, 10.0% English, 7.0% Other groups (2000).

Economy: Single-family building permits issued: 3 (2007); Multi-family building permits issued: 0 (2007); Employment by occupation: 13.4% management, 24.7% professional, 13.3% services, 28.4% sales, 0.1% farming, 7.9% construction, 12.2% production (2000).

Income: Per capita income: $27,202 (2007); Median household income: $52,672 (2007); Average household income: $63,560 (2007); Percent of households with income of $100,000 or more: 14.7% (2007); Poverty rate: 4.3% (2000).

Education: Percent of population age 25 and over with: High school diploma (including GED) or higher: 92.9% (2007); Bachelor's degree or higher: 29.2% (2007); Master's degree or higher: 8.6% (2007).

School District(s)

M.O.D.E.L. Community School (KG-12)
2005-06 Enrollment: 70 . . . . (419) 897-4400
Maumee City (PK-12)
2005-06 Enrollment: 2,895 . . . . (419) 893-3200
Ohio Virtual Academy (KG-09)
2005-06 Enrollment: 2,890 . . . . (419) 482-0948
Wildwood Environmental Academy (KG-08)
2005-06 Enrollment: 181 . . . . (419) 868-9885

Two-year College(s)

ITT Technical Institute-Maumee (Private, For-profit)
Fall 2007 Enrollment: 278 . . . . (419) 861-6500
2007-08 Tuition: In-state $15,600; Out-of-state $15,600
Stautzenberger College (Private, For-profit)
Fall 2007 Enrollment: 745 . . . . (419) 866-0261
2007-08 Tuition: In-state $7,290; Out-of-state $7,290

Housing: Homeownership rate: 72.3% (2007); Median home value: $140,654 (2007); Median rent: $461 per month (2000); Median age of housing: 40 years (2000).

Hospitals: St. Luke's Hospital (314 beds)

Transportation: Commute to work: 96.5% car, 0.5% public transportation, 1.0% walk, 2.0% work from home (2000); Travel time to work: 37.8% less than 15 minutes, 46.4% 15 to 30 minutes, 10.0% 30 to 45 minutes, 2.5% 45 to 60 minutes, 3.3% 60 minutes or more (2000)

Additional Information Contacts

City of Maumee . . . . (419) 897-7100
http://www.maumee.org
Maumee Chamber of Commerce. . . . . (419) 893-5805
http://www.maumeechamber.com

MONCLOVA (unincorporated postal area, zip code 43542). Covers a land area of 13.563 square miles and a water area of 0 square miles. Located at 41.57° N. Lat.; 83.76° W. Long. Elevation is 640 feet.

Population: 2,389 (2000); Race: 96.7% White, 0.0% Black, 0.2% Asian, 4.6% Hispanic of any race (2000); Density: 176.1 persons per square mile (2000); Age: 27.5% under 18, 10.5% over 64 (2000); Marriage status: 21.3% never married, 62.4% now married, 6.3% widowed, 10.0% divorced (2000); Foreign born: 0.3% (2000); Ancestry (includes multiple ancestries): 39.0% German, 15.5% English, 10.4% Other groups, 10.1% Irish, 8.5% Polish (2000).

Economy: Employment by occupation: 13.7% management, 20.9% professional, 13.9% services, 20.9% sales, 2.2% farming, 9.6% construction, 18.8% production (2000).

Income: Per capita income: $24,271 (2000); Median household income: $62,159 (2000); Poverty rate: 3.3% (2000).

Education: Percent of population age 25 and over with: High school diploma (including GED) or higher: 89.4% (2000); Bachelor's degree or higher: 20.2% (2000).

School District(s)

Anthony Wayne Local (PK-12)
2005-06 Enrollment: 4,249 . . . . (419) 877-5377

Housing: Homeownership rate: 89.6% (2000); Median home value: $136,100 (2000); Median rent: $530 per month (2000); Median age of housing: 35 years (2000).

Transportation: Commute to work: 93.3% car, 0.0% public transportation, 2.6% walk, 4.1% work from home (2000); Travel time to work: 34.2% less

than 15 minutes, 37.5% 15 to 30 minutes, 17.1% 30 to 45 minutes, 6.0% 45 to 60 minutes, 5.3% 60 minutes or more (2000)

OREGON (city). Covers a land area of 29.379 square miles and a water area of 8.712 square miles. Located at 41.64° N. Lat.; 83.46° W. Long. Elevation is 600 feet.
History: Incorporated 1958.
Population: 18,371 (1990); 19,355 (2000); 19,095 (2007); 18,808 (2012 projected); Race: 94.1% White, 1.0% Black, 0.8% Asian, 5.6% Hispanic of any race (2007); Density: 650.0 persons per square mile (2007); Average household size: 2.48 (2007); Median age: 41.0 (2007); Males per 100 females: 93.1 (2007); Marriage status: 22.9% never married, 59.7% now married, 7.7% widowed, 9.7% divorced (2000); Foreign born: 2.3% (2000); Ancestry (includes multiple ancestries): 33.8% German, 10.9% Irish, 9.9% Other groups, 8.9% Polish, 7.8% English (2000).
Economy: Single-family building permits issued: 52 (2007); Multi-family building permits issued: 2 (2007); Employment by occupation: 11.2% management, 17.5% professional, 13.3% services, 25.2% sales, 0.3% farming, 11.0% construction, 21.4% production (2000).
Income: Per capita income: $25,814 (2007); Median household income: $52,519 (2007); Average household income: $63,263 (2007); Percent of households with income of $100,000 or more: 17.1% (2007); Poverty rate: 4.8% (2000).
Education: Percent of population age 25 and over with: High school diploma (including GED) or higher: 85.0% (2007); Bachelor's degree or higher: 15.9% (2007); Master's degree or higher: 5.6% (2007).

School District(s)

Lucas
2005-06 Enrollment: n/a . . . . (419) 245-4150
Oregon City (PK-12)
2005-06 Enrollment: 3,929 . . . . (419) 693-0661

Two-year College(s)

Toledo Academy of Beauty Culture-East (Private, For-profit)
Fall 2007 Enrollment: 63 . . . . (419) 693-7257

Vocational/Technical School(s)

Oregon Career Center (Public)
Fall 2007 Enrollment: 305 . . . . (419) 697-3450
2007-08 Tuition: $3,174

Housing: Homeownership rate: 74.1% (2007); Median home value: $147,922 (2007); Median rent: $404 per month (2000); Median age of housing: 34 years (2000).
Hospitals: Bay Park Community Hospital (70 beds); St. Charles Hospital (386 beds)
Safety: Violent crime rate: 10.5 per 10,000 population; Property crime rate: 462.4 per 10,000 population (2007).
Transportation: Commute to work: 96.3% car, 0.0% public transportation, 1.5% walk, 1.6% work from home (2000); Travel time to work: 35.3% less than 15 minutes, 44.4% 15 to 30 minutes, 13.5% 30 to 45 minutes, 2.9% 45 to 60 minutes, 3.9% 60 minutes or more (2000)

Additional Information Contacts

City of Oregon . . . . (419) 698-7045
http://www.ci.oregon.oh.us
Eastern Maumee Bay Chamber of Commerce . . . . . . (419) 693-5580
http://www.toledochamber.com

OTTAWA HILLS (village). Covers a land area of 1.864 square miles and a water area of 0.009 square miles. Located at 41.67° N. Lat.; 83.64° W. Long. Elevation is 604 feet.
History: Settled 1916, incorporated 1924.
Population: 4,543 (1990); 4,564 (2000); 4,601 (2007); 4,619 (2012 projected); Race: 93.3% White, 1.2% Black, 2.7% Asian, 1.5% Hispanic of any race (2007); Density: 2,468.4 persons per square mile (2007); Average household size: 2.65 (2007); Median age: 44.9 (2007); Males per 100 females: 95.3 (2007); Marriage status: 18.4% never married, 69.1% now married, 6.1% widowed, 6.4% divorced (2000); Foreign born: 7.9% (2000); Ancestry (includes multiple ancestries): 28.1% German, 16.6% English, 15.0% Irish, 9.6% Other groups, 8.9% Polish (2000).
Economy: Employment by occupation: 26.4% management, 41.7% professional, 5.7% services, 19.4% sales, 0.0% farming, 4.0% construction, 2.8% production (2000).
Income: Per capita income: $59,187 (2007); Median household income: $103,047 (2007); Average household income: $157,138 (2007); Percent of households with income of $100,000 or more: 51.4% (2007); Poverty rate: 2.1% (2000).
Education: Percent of population age 25 and over with: High school diploma (including GED) or higher: 97.7% (2007); Bachelor's degree or higher: 69.0% (2007); Master's degree or higher: 40.0% (2007).
Housing: Homeownership rate: 87.9% (2007); Median home value: $303,417 (2007); Median rent: $730 per month (2000); Median age of housing: 46 years (2000).
Transportation: Commute to work: 95.6% car, 0.0% public transportation, 0.6% walk, 3.3% work from home (2000); Travel time to work: 42.0% less than 15 minutes, 49.2% 15 to 30 minutes, 3.6% 30 to 45 minutes, 1.5% 45 to 60 minutes, 3.6% 60 minutes or more (2000)

Additional Information Contacts

Village of Ottawa Hills . . . . (419) 536-1111
http://www.ottawahills.org

SYLVANIA (city). Covers a land area of 5.792 square miles and a water area of 0.045 square miles. Located at 41.71° N. Lat.; 83.70° W. Long. Elevation is 663 feet.
History: Incorporated 1867.
Population: 17,488 (1990); 18,670 (2000); 18,878 (2007); 18,999 (2012 projected); Race: 94.4% White, 1.1% Black, 2.4% Asian, 2.1% Hispanic of any race (2007); Density: 3,259.1 persons per square mile (2007); Average household size: 2.55 (2007); Median age: 39.6 (2007); Males per 100 females: 91.7 (2007); Marriage status: 20.9% never married, 63.1% now married, 7.8% widowed, 8.2% divorced (2000); Foreign born: 4.7% (2000); Ancestry (includes multiple ancestries): 32.8% German, 15.6% Irish, 11.4% English, 10.7% Polish, 6.7% Other groups (2000).
Economy: Employment by occupation: 15.7% management, 30.8% professional, 10.9% services, 26.9% sales, 0.2% farming, 5.6% construction, 9.8% production (2000).
Income: Per capita income: $32,107 (2007); Median household income: $65,265 (2007); Average household income: $81,661 (2007); Percent of households with income of $100,000 or more: 28.3% (2007); Poverty rate: 4.2% (2000).
Education: Percent of population age 25 and over with: High school diploma (including GED) or higher: 94.1% (2007); Bachelor's degree or higher: 43.5% (2007); Master's degree or higher: 15.4% (2007).

School District(s)

Sylvania City (PK-12)
2005-06 Enrollment: 7,713 . . . . (419) 824-8501

Four-year College(s)

Lourdes College (Private, Not-for-profit, Roman Catholic)
Fall 2007 Enrollment: 2,021. . . . . (419) 885-3211
2007-08 Tuition: In-state $11,232; Out-of-state $11,232

Housing: Homeownership rate: 75.4% (2007); Median home value: $184,762 (2007); Median rent: $445 per month (2000); Median age of housing: 28 years (2000).
Newspapers: Sylvania Herald (Community news; Circulation 24,000); Toledo Jewish News (Local news; Circulation 7,000); West Toledo Herald (Community news; Circulation 20,000)
Transportation: Commute to work: 94.3% car, 0.6% public transportation, 1.4% walk, 3.4% work from home (2000); Travel time to work: 30.6% less than 15 minutes, 49.6% 15 to 30 minutes, 11.8% 30 to 45 minutes, 2.5% 45 to 60 minutes, 5.5% 60 minutes or more (2000)

Additional Information Contacts

City of Sylvania . . . . (419) 885-8925
http://www.cityofsylvania.com
Sylvania Area Chamber of Commerce . . . . (419) 882-2135
http://www.sylvaniachamber.org

TOLEDO (city). County seat. Covers a land area of 80.622 square miles and a water area of 3.453 square miles. Located at 41.66° N. Lat.; 83.57° W. Long. Elevation is 614 feet.
History: Toledo was established along the Maumee River on the westernmost tip of Lake Erie. A stockade called Fort Industry was built here around 1800, but was short-lived. In 1833 two small settlements voted to consolidate, and the residents chose the name of Toledo for the new town. The early years were difficult for the town, with cholera, a drought, business failures, and the Toledo War of 1835, a protracted boundary dispute between Ohio and Michigan which ended with Michigan being given the Upper Peninsula in exchange for Ohio keeping the disputed territory. In the 1840's things improved, with Toledo the logical choice as terminus of the Wabash & Erie Canal, followed by the Miami & Erie Canal. When the 1850's came, Toledo was a station on the Underground Railroad for escaping slaves. Among the industries that developed after the Civil

War was the Libby Glass Company, which revolutionized the glass industry, and the Owens Bottle Machine Company.

Population: 332,921 (1990); 313,619 (2000); 297,162 (2007); 284,791 (2012 projected); Race: 67.4% White, 25.4% Black, 1.1% Asian, 6.3% Hispanic of any race (2007); Density: 3,685.9 persons per square mile (2007); Average household size: 2.38 (2007); Median age: 34.7 (2007); Males per 100 females: 93.5 (2007); Marriage status: 33.0% never married, 45.9% now married, 7.8% widowed, 13.3% divorced (2000); Foreign born: 3.0% (2000); Ancestry (includes multiple ancestries): 29.0% Other groups, 23.4% German, 10.8% Irish, 10.1% Polish, 6.0% English (2000).

Economy: Unemployment rate: 8.5% (6/2008); Total civilian labor force: 146,326 (6/2008); Single-family building permits issued: 82 (2007); Multi-family building permits issued: 185 (2007); Employment by occupation: 9.0% management, 16.7% professional, 17.9% services, 26.7% sales, 0.1% farming, 8.3% construction, 21.3% production (2000).

Income: Per capita income: $19,811 (2007); Median household income: $36,695 (2007); Average household income: $46,545 (2007); Percent of households with income of $100,000 or more: 8.1% (2007); Poverty rate: 17.9% (2000).

Taxes: Total city taxes per capita: $616 (2006); City property taxes per capita: $58 (2006).

Education: Percent of population age 25 and over with: High school diploma (including GED) or higher: 80.1% (2007); Bachelor's degree or higher: 17.2% (2007); Master's degree or higher: 5.6% (2007).

School District(s)

Academy of Business & Tech (KG-08)
2005-06 Enrollment: 337 . . . . (419) 242-7532
Alliance Academy of Toledo (KG-12)
2005-06 Enrollment: 361 . . . . (419) 418-5160
Alternative Education Academy (KG-12)
2005-06 Enrollment: 2,556 . . . . (330) 253-8680
Aurora Academy (KG-09)
2005-06 Enrollment: 195 . . . . (419) 693-6841
Bennett Venture Academy (KG-05)
2005-06 Enrollment: 417 . . . . (419) 269-2247
Brigadoon Academy Community School (07-12)
2005-06 Enrollment: 145 . . . . (419) 720-4523
Eagle Academy (KG-06)
2005-06 Enrollment: 112 . . . . (419) 691-4876
Englewood Peace Academy (KG-09)
2005-06 Enrollment: 229 . . . . (419) 243-7260
George A. Phillips Academy (KG-08)
2005-06 Enrollment: 270 . . . . (419) 534-4272
Glass City Academy (11-12)
2005-06 Enrollment: 218 . . . . (419) 720-6311
Horizon Science Academy Toledo (06-10)
2005-06 Enrollment: 287 . . . . (419) 244-5710
Horizon Science Academy-Springfield (05-08)
2005-06 Enrollment: 151 . . . . (419) 535-0524
Imani Learning Academy (KG-08)
2005-06 Enrollment: 172 . . . .
Lake Erie Academy (KG-08)
2005-06 Enrollment: 303 . . . . (419) 475-3876
Life Skills Center of Toledo (09-12)
2005-06 Enrollment: 265 . . . . (419) 241-5504
Lucas
2005-06 Enrollment: n/a . . . . (419) 245-4150
Meadows Choice Community (01-09)
2005-06 Enrollment: 104 . . . . (419) 385-5730
Ottawa Hills Local (PK-12)
2005-06 Enrollment: 996 . . . . (419) 536-6371
Paul Laurence Dunbar Academy (KG-06)
2005-06 Enrollment: 201 . . . . (419) 244-4202
Performing Arts School of Toledo (07-12)
2005-06 Enrollment: 123 . . . . (419) 243-4752
Phoenix Academy Community School (09-12)
2005-06 Enrollment: 594 . . . . (419) 720-4500
Polly Fox Academy Community School (07-12)
2005-06 Enrollment: 114 . . . . (419) 720-4500
Springfield Local (PK-12)
2005-06 Enrollment: 3,898 . . . . (419) 867-5600
Summit Academy Secondary School - Toledo (05-11)
2005-06 Enrollment: 73 . . . . (419) 476-7859
Summit Academy Toledo (KG-07)
2005-06 Enrollment: 117 . . . . (419) 476-7859
Sylvania City (PK-12)
2005-06 Enrollment: 7,713 . . . . (419) 824-8501
The Autism Academy of Learning (01-12)
2005-06 Enrollment: 51 . . . . (419) 865-7487
Toledo Academy of Learning (KG-10)
2005-06 Enrollment: 413 . . . . (419) 255-0253
Toledo Accelerated Academy (06-12)
2005-06 Enrollment: 150 . . . . (419) 539-7173
Toledo City (PK-12)
2005-06 Enrollment: 30,423 . . . . (419) 729-8200
Toledo School for the Arts (06-12)
2005-06 Enrollment: 389 . . . . (419) 246-8732
Victory Academy of Toledo (KG-08)
2005-06 Enrollment: 98 . . . . (419) 534-2304
Washington Local (PK-12)
2005-06 Enrollment: 6,926 . . . . (419) 473-8220
Winterfield Venture Academy (KG-06)
2005-06 Enrollment: 531 . . . . (419) 531-3285

Four-year College(s)

Mercy College of Northwest Ohio (Private, Not-for-profit, Roman Catholic)
Fall 2007 Enrollment: 804 . . . . (419) 251-1313
2007-08 Tuition: In-state $8,720; Out-of-state $8,720
The University of Toledo-Health Science Campus (Public)
Fall 2007 Enrollment: 1,358. . . . . (419) 383-4457
University of Toledo-Main Campus (Public)
Fall 2007 Enrollment: 19,767. . . . . (419) 530-4636
2007-08 Tuition: In-state $7,982; Out-of-state $16,794

Two-year College(s)

Davis College (Private, For-profit)
Fall 2007 Enrollment: 484 . . . . (419) 473-2700
2007-08 Tuition: In-state $8,700; Out-of-state $8,700
Professional Skills Institute (Private, For-profit)
Fall 2007 Enrollment: 292 . . . . (419) 531-9610
2007-08 Tuition: In-state $12,353; Out-of-state $12,353
Toledo Academy of Beauty Culture-South (Private, For-profit)
Fall 2007 Enrollment: 115 . . . . (419) 381-7218
Toledo School of Practical Nursing (Public)
Fall 2007 Enrollment: 309 . . . . (419) 671-8700
2007-08 Tuition: In-state $9,050; Out-of-state $9,450

Vocational/Technical School(s)

Toledo Academy of Beauty Culture-North (Private, For-profit)
Fall 2007 Enrollment: 65 . . . . (419) 478-5325
2007-08 Tuition: $11,050

Housing: Homeownership rate: 59.7% (2007); Median home value: $92,821 (2007); Median rent: $380 per month (2000); Median age of housing: 48 years (2000).

Hospitals: Medical College of Ohio Hospitals (319 beds); Northcoast Behavioral Healthcare Systems - Toledo Campus (96 beds); Saint Anne Mercy Hospital (88 beds); Saint Vincent Mercy Medical Center (588 beds); Toledo Hospital (774 beds)

Safety: Violent crime rate: 122.8 per 10,000 population; Property crime rate: 668.9 per 10,000 population (2007).

Newspapers: Ann Arbor Family (Local news; Circulation 25,000); The Blade (Local news; Circulation 145,929); Catholic Chronicle (Regional news; Circulation 19,651); El Tiempo (Local news; Circulation 10,000); La Prensa (Local news; Circulation 20,000); Point & Shoreland Journal (Community news; Circulation 8,700); Toledo City Paper (Local news; Circulation 30,000); The Toledo Journal (Local news; Circulation 22,500); Toledo Legal News (Local news; Circulation 500)

Transportation: Commute to work: 92.9% car, 2.5% public transportation, 2.3% walk, 1.5% work from home (2000); Travel time to work: 35.1% less than 15 minutes, 47.2% 15 to 30 minutes, 10.7% 30 to 45 minutes, 2.8% 45 to 60 minutes, 4.1% 60 minutes or more (2000); Amtrak: Service available.

Airports: Toledo Express (primary service)

Additional Information Contacts

City of Toledo. . . . . (419) 245-1001
http://www.ci.toledo.oh.us
Greater Toledo Convention & Visitors Bureau. . . . . (800) 243-4667
http://www.dotoledo.org/gtcvb
Toldeo Regional Chamber of Commerce . . . . (419) 243-8191
http://www.toledochamber.com

WATERVILLE (village). Covers a land area of 3.502 square miles and a water area of 0.115 square miles. Located at 41.50° N. Lat.; 83.72° W. Long. Elevation is 614 feet.

History: Waterville was platted in 1818 by John Pray. It grew as the center of a garden nursery region.

Population: 4,585 (1990); 4,828 (2000); 4,879 (2007); 4,912 (2012 projected); Race: 97.5% White, 0.1% Black, 0.2% Asian, 1.7% Hispanic of any race (2007); Density: 1,393.3 persons per square mile (2007); Average household size: 2.74 (2007); Median age: 40.8 (2007); Males per 100 females: 93.3 (2007); Marriage status: 20.5% never married, 67.8% now married, 5.4% widowed, 6.3% divorced (2000); Foreign born: 1.7% (2000); Ancestry (includes multiple ancestries): 34.6% German, 18.2% English, 14.6% Polish, 12.3% Irish, 5.5% Italian (2000).

Economy: Employment by occupation: 16.1% management, 30.2% professional, 11.2% services, 26.4% sales, 0.6% farming, 7.1% construction, 8.4% production (2000).

Income: Per capita income: $28,180 (2007); Median household income: $69,312 (2007); Average household income: $75,823 (2007); Percent of households with income of $100,000 or more: 26.1% (2007); Poverty rate: 1.8% (2000).

Education: Percent of population age 25 and over with: High school diploma (including GED) or higher: 94.6% (2007); Bachelor's degree or higher: 36.3% (2007); Master's degree or higher: 13.8% (2007).

School District(s)

Anthony Wayne Local (PK-12)
2005-06 Enrollment: 4,249 . . . . (419) 877-5377
Lucas
2005-06 Enrollment: n/a . . . . (419) 245-4150

Housing: Homeownership rate: 85.2% (2007); Median home value: $182,870 (2007); Median rent: $463 per month (2000); Median age of housing: 28 years (2000).

Transportation: Commute to work: 96.5% car, 0.3% public transportation, 1.1% walk, 2.1% work from home (2000); Travel time to work: 26.9% less than 15 minutes, 51.2% 15 to 30 minutes, 18.6% 30 to 45 minutes, 2.0% 45 to 60 minutes, 1.3% 60 minutes or more (2000)

Additional Information Contacts

Village of Waterville . . . . (419) 878-8100
http://www.waterville.org
Waterville Chamber of Commerce. (419) 878-5188
http://www.watervillechamber.com

WHITEHOUSE (village). Covers a land area of 3.454 square miles and a water area of 0 square miles. Located at 41.52° N. Lat.; 83.80° W. Long. Elevation is 653 feet.

Population: 2,646 (1990); 2,733 (2000); 3,236 (2007); 3,532 (2012 projected); Race: 98.5% White, 0.1% Black, 0.2% Asian, 1.1% Hispanic of any race (2007); Density: 936.8 persons per square mile (2007); Average household size: 2.58 (2007); Median age: 40.9 (2007); Males per 100 females: 94.6 (2007); Marriage status: 24.4% never married, 58.6% now married, 8.2% widowed, 8.8% divorced (2000); Foreign born: 1.8% (2000); Ancestry (includes multiple ancestries): 41.0% German, 15.3% Irish, 13.0% English, 9.4% French (except Basque), 6.9% Polish (2000).

Economy: Single-family building permits issued: 25 (2007); Multi-family building permits issued: 0 (2007); Employment by occupation: 14.5% management, 21.7% professional, 15.7% services, 19.5% sales, 0.4% farming, 9.1% construction, 19.0% production (2000).

Income: Per capita income: $29,349 (2007); Median household income: $62,990 (2007); Average household income: $75,353 (2007); Percent of households with income of $100,000 or more: 26.9% (2007); Poverty rate: 2.6% (2000).

Education: Percent of population age 25 and over with: High school diploma (including GED) or higher: 91.5% (2007); Bachelor's degree or higher: 24.8% (2007); Master's degree or higher: 9.2% (2007).

School District(s)

Anthony Wayne Local (PK-12)
2005-06 Enrollment: 4,249 . . . . (419) 877-5377

Housing: Homeownership rate: 77.5% (2007); Median home value: $163,704 (2007); Median rent: $410 per month (2000); Median age of housing: 27 years (2000).

Transportation: Commute to work: 97.9% car, 0.2% public transportation, 0.3% walk, 1.1% work from home (2000); Travel time to work: 30.3% less than 15 minutes, 43.1% 15 to 30 minutes, 21.5% 30 to 45 minutes, 2.9% 45 to 60 minutes, 2.3% 60 minutes or more (2000)

Additional Information Contacts

Village of Whitehouse . . . . (419) 877-5383
http://www.whitehouseoh.com
Whitehouse Chamber of Commerce . . . . (419) 877-2747
http://www.whitehouseohchamber.com

Madison County

Located in central Ohio; drained by Deer, Paint, and Darby Creeks. Covers a land area of 465.44 square miles, a water area of 0.74 square miles, and is located in the Eastern Time Zone. The county was founded in 1810. County seat is London.

Madison County is part of the Columbus, OH Metropolitan Statistical Area. The entire metro area includes: Delaware County, OH; Fairfield County, OH; Franklin County, OH; Licking County, OH; Madison County, OH; Morrow County, OH; Pickaway County, OH; Union County, OH

Weather Station: London Elevation: 1,017 feet

	Jan	Feb	Mar	Apr	May	Jun	Jul	Aug	Sep	Oct	Nov	Dec
High	34	39	50	63	73	81	85	83	77	65	51	40
Low	18	21	29	38	49	58	62	60	52	41	33	24
Precip	2.4	2.2	2.8	3.6	4.1	4.3	4.0	3.3	2.8	2.6	3.3	3.0
Snow	6.9	na	na	0.4	0.0	0.0	0.0	0.0	0.0	0.2	0.5	na

High and Low temperatures in degrees Fahrenheit; Precipitation and Snow in inches

Population: 37,076 (1990); 40,213 (2000); 41,690 (2007); 42,653 (2012 projected); Race: 91.0% White, 6.7% Black, 0.8% Asian, 0.9% Hispanic of any race (2007); Density: 89.6 persons per square mile (2007); Average household size: 2.88 (2007); Median age: 37.4 (2007); Males per 100 females: 118.7 (2007).

Religion: Five largest groups: 10.2% The United Methodist Church, 5.9% Catholic Church, 2.2% Presbyterian Church (U.S.A.), 2.0% Southern Baptist Convention, 1.9% Church of the Nazarene (2000).

Economy: Unemployment rate: 6.1% (6/2008); Total civilian labor force: 20,839 (6/2008); Leading industries: 25.9% manufacturing; 18.9% retail trade; 9.7% health care and social assistance (2005); Farms: 730 totaling 245,886 acres (2002); Companies that employ 500 or more persons: 1 (2006); Companies that employ 100 to 499 persons: 16 (2006); Companies that employ less than 100 persons: 774 (2006); Black-owned businesses: n/a (2002); Hispanic-owned businesses: n/a (2002); Asian-owned businesses: n/a (2002); Women-owned businesses: 799 (2002); Retail sales per capita: $14,914 (2008). Single-family building permits issued: 81 (2007); Multi-family building permits issued: 0 (2007).

Income: Per capita income: $23,001 (2007); Median household income: $52,904 (2007); Average household income: $63,382 (2007); Percent of households with income of $100,000 or more: 15.6% (2007); Poverty rate: 9.7% (2005); Bankruptcy rate: 4.31% (2007).

Taxes: Total county taxes per capita: $247 (2006); County property taxes per capita: $125 (2006).

Education: Percent of population age 25 and over with: High school diploma (including GED) or higher: 79.1% (2007); Bachelor's degree or higher: 13.3% (2007); Master's degree or higher: 3.8% (2007).

Housing: Homeownership rate: 72.0% (2007); Median home value: $125,057 (2007); Median rent: $389 per month (2000); Median age of housing: 31 years (2000).

Health: Birth rate: 118.8 per 10,000 population (2007); Death rate: 82.4 per 10,000 population (2007); Age-adjusted cancer mortality rate: 176.0 deaths per 100,000 population (2005); Air Quality Index: 63.6% good, 29.4% moderate, 7.0% unhealthy for sensitive individuals, 0.0% unhealthy (percent of days in 2007); Number of physicians: 10.0 per 10,000 population (2005); Hospital beds: 16.4 per 10,000 population (2004); Hospital admissions: 399.3 per 10,000 population (2004).

Elections: 2004 Presidential election results: 63.9% Bush, 35.7% Kerry, 0.0% Nader, 0.2% Badnarik

National and State Parks: Madison Lake State Park; Madison Lake State Reserve

Additional Information Contacts

Madison County Government . . . . (740) 852-2972
http://www.co.madison.oh.us
City of London . . . . (740) 852-3243
http://ci.london.oh.us
Madison County Chamber of Commerce. . . . . (740) 852-2250
http://www.madisoncountychamber.org
Village of West Jefferson . . . . (614) 879-7674
http://www.villageofwestjefferson.com

Madison County Communities

CHOCTAW LAKE (CDP). Aka Chocktou Lake. Covers a land area of 0.803 square miles and a water area of 0.402 square miles. Located at 39.96° N. Lat.; 83.48° W. Long. Elevation is 1,040 feet.
Population: 1,234 (1990); 1,562 (2000); 1,728 (2007); 1,844 (2012 projected); Race: 94.9% White, 0.1% Black, 3.6% Asian, 0.6% Hispanic of any race (2007); Density: 2,152.8 persons per square mile (2007); Average household size: 2.63 (2007); Median age: 42.5 (2007); Males per 100 females: 102.8 (2007); Marriage status: 18.7% never married, 69.9% now married, 4.7% widowed, 6.7% divorced (2000); Foreign born: 1.8% (2000); Ancestry (includes multiple ancestries): 31.9% German, 21.6% English, 11.8% Irish, 6.3% Other groups, 3.6% Scotch-Irish (2000).
Economy: Employment by occupation: 16.1% management, 26.2% professional, 10.6% services, 27.0% sales, 1.0% farming, 6.3% construction, 12.8% production (2000).
Income: Per capita income: $37,886 (2007); Median household income: $92,480 (2007); Average household income: $99,646 (2007); Percent of households with income of $100,000 or more: 44.1% (2007); Poverty rate: 6.9% (2000).
Education: Percent of population age 25 and over with: High school diploma (including GED) or higher: 94.2% (2007); Bachelor's degree or higher: 37.3% (2007); Master's degree or higher: 12.0% (2007).
Housing: Homeownership rate: 95.7% (2007); Median home value: $222,240 (2007); Median rent: $900 per month (2000); Median age of housing: 21 years (2000).
Transportation: Commute to work: 93.4% car, 0.0% public transportation, 0.0% walk, 5.2% work from home (2000); Travel time to work: 20.1% less than 15 minutes, 17.5% 15 to 30 minutes, 41.6% 30 to 45 minutes, 16.8% 45 to 60 minutes, 4.1% 60 minutes or more (2000)

LONDON (city). County seat. Covers a land area of 8.508 square miles and a water area of 0 square miles. Located at 39.88° N. Lat.; 83.44° W. Long. Elevation is 1,053 feet.
History: London was established on a site that had formerly been a swamp, known for malaria and ague. When the swamp was drained, the land was good for farming and livestock raising. The town was incorporated in 1831 and soon became a stockyard and trading center.
Population: 8,883 (1990); 8,771 (2000); 9,478 (2007); 9,917 (2012 projected); Race: 92.7% White, 4.2% Black, 0.8% Asian, 0.7% Hispanic of any race (2007); Density: 1,114.1 persons per square mile (2007); Average household size: 2.39 (2007); Median age: 37.3 (2007); Males per 100 females: 89.5 (2007); Marriage status: 19.2% never married, 58.2% now married, 9.7% widowed, 12.9% divorced (2000); Foreign born: 1.7% (2000); Ancestry (includes multiple ancestries): 20.7% German, 20.6% United States or American, 12.2% Other groups, 12.1% Irish, 9.3% English (2000).
Economy: Single-family building permits issued: 14 (2007); Multi-family building permits issued: 0 (2007); Employment by occupation: 12.2% management, 17.2% professional, 18.2% services, 23.6% sales, 0.0% farming, 8.6% construction, 20.2% production (2000).
Income: Per capita income: $22,391 (2007); Median household income: $42,233 (2007); Average household income: $52,290 (2007); Percent of households with income of $100,000 or more: 10.4% (2007); Poverty rate: 11.7% (2000).
Education: Percent of population age 25 and over with: High school diploma (including GED) or higher: 76.8% (2007); Bachelor's degree or higher: 15.1% (2007); Master's degree or higher: 5.0% (2007).

School District(s)

Jonathan Alder Local (PK-12)
2005-06 Enrollment: 1,991 . . . . (614) 873-5621
London City (PK-12)
2005-06 Enrollment: 2,090 . . . . (740) 852-5700
London Digital Academy (KG-12)
2005-06 Enrollment: 108 . . . . (740) 852-5700
Madison-Plains Local (KG-12)
2005-06 Enrollment: 1,503 . . . . (740) 852-0290

Housing: Homeownership rate: 56.3% (2007); Median home value: $112,538 (2007); Median rent: $375 per month (2000); Median age of housing: 37 years (2000).
Hospitals: Madison County Hospital (102 beds)
Safety: Violent crime rate: 10.4 per 10,000 population; Property crime rate: 346.8 per 10,000 population (2007).
Newspapers: Madison Press (Local news; Circulation 6,400); Mechanicsburg Telegram (Local news; Circulation 900); Plain City Advocate (Community news; Circulation 1,900); The Telegram (Community news; Circulation 1,800); Tribune (Local news; Circulation 6,924); Weekly Review (Local news; Circulation 12,000)
Transportation: Commute to work: 91.7% car, 0.8% public transportation, 3.0% walk, 2.8% work from home (2000); Travel time to work: 48.2% less than 15 minutes, 17.3% 15 to 30 minutes, 18.9% 30 to 45 minutes, 11.6% 45 to 60 minutes, 4.0% 60 minutes or more (2000)

Additional Information Contacts

City of London . . . . (740) 852-3243
http://ci.london.oh.us
Madison County Chamber of Commerce. . . . . (740) 852-2250
http://www.madisoncountychamber.org

MIDWAY (village). Aka Sedalia. Covers a land area of 0.278 square miles and a water area of 0 square miles. Located at 39.73° N. Lat.; 83.47° W. Long. Elevation is 1,063 feet.
History: Also called Sedalia.
Population: 289 (1990); 274 (2000); 265 (2007); 262 (2012 projected); Race: 99.2% White, 0.0% Black, 0.0% Asian, 1.1% Hispanic of any race (2007); Density: 952.5 persons per square mile (2007); Average household size: 2.43 (2007); Median age: 40.6 (2007); Males per 100 females: 93.4 (2007); Marriage status: 17.6% never married, 63.0% now married, 9.3% widowed, 10.2% divorced (2000); Foreign born: 0.7% (2000); Ancestry (includes multiple ancestries): 25.8% United States or American, 17.0% German, 10.0% English, 8.9% Irish, 5.5% Scotch-Irish (2000).
Economy: Employment by occupation: 9.8% management, 7.6% professional, 21.2% services, 25.8% sales, 0.8% farming, 11.4% construction, 23.5% production (2000).
Income: Per capita income: $21,726 (2007); Median household income: $45,750 (2007); Average household income: $52,821 (2007); Percent of households with income of $100,000 or more: 11.0% (2007); Poverty rate: 3.0% (2000).
Taxes: Total city taxes per capita: $19 (2006); City property taxes per capita: $19 (2006).
Education: Percent of population age 25 and over with: High school diploma (including GED) or higher: 70.2% (2007); Bachelor's degree or higher: 3.4% (2007); Master's degree or higher: 1.7% (2007).

School District(s)

Madison-Plains Local (KG-12)
2005-06 Enrollment: 1,503 . . . . (740) 852-0290

Housing: Homeownership rate: 85.3% (2007); Median home value: $103,241 (2007); Median rent: $338 per month (2000); Median age of housing: 60+ years (2000).
Transportation: Commute to work: 96.2% car, 0.0% public transportation, 2.3% walk, 1.5% work from home (2000); Travel time to work: 21.5% less than 15 minutes, 37.7% 15 to 30 minutes, 16.9% 30 to 45 minutes, 20.8% 45 to 60 minutes, 3.1% 60 minutes or more (2000)

MOUNT STERLING (village). Covers a land area of 0.983 square miles and a water area of 0 square miles. Located at 39.72° N. Lat.; 83.26° W. Long. Elevation is 902 feet.
History: Mount Sterling was founded in 1828 by John J. Smith, who named the town after his former home in Kentucky. An early industry was the Ohio Willow Wood Company, manufacturers of artificial limbs, polo balls and mallets.
Population: 1,647 (1990); 1,865 (2000); 1,750 (2007); 1,706 (2012 projected); Race: 96.9% White, 0.2% Black, 0.2% Asian, 3.0% Hispanic of any race (2007); Density: 1,780.9 persons per square mile (2007); Average household size: 2.36 (2007); Median age: 34.3 (2007); Males per 100 females: 90.4 (2007); Marriage status: 23.4% never married, 53.6% now married, 9.5% widowed, 13.6% divorced (2000); Foreign born: 0.9% (2000); Ancestry (includes multiple ancestries): 22.9% German, 19.3% United States or American, 15.9% Irish, 11.2% Other groups, 9.6% English (2000).
Economy: Single-family building permits issued: 1 (2007); Multi-family building permits issued: 0 (2007); Employment by occupation: 8.1% management, 11.0% professional, 13.4% services, 31.1% sales, 0.2% farming, 12.5% construction, 23.7% production (2000).
Income: Per capita income: $20,200 (2007); Median household income: $40,217 (2007); Average household income: $47,770 (2007); Percent of households with income of $100,000 or more: 6.5% (2007); Poverty rate: 9.4% (2000).
Education: Percent of population age 25 and over with: High school diploma (including GED) or higher: 78.2% (2007); Bachelor's degree or higher: 8.8% (2007); Master's degree or higher: 2.0% (2007).

School District(s)

Madison-Plains Local (KG-12)
2005-06 Enrollment: 1,503 . . . . (740) 852-0290
Miami Trace Local (PK-12)
2005-06 Enrollment: 2,770 . . . . (740) 335-3010

Housing: Homeownership rate: 53.1% (2007); Median home value: $109,758 (2007); Median rent: $356 per month (2000); Median age of housing: 45 years (2000).

Transportation: Commute to work: 90.4% car, 0.0% public transportation, 6.1% walk, 2.8% work from home (2000); Travel time to work: 32.1% less than 15 minutes, 22.9% 15 to 30 minutes, 27.0% 30 to 45 minutes, 11.4% 45 to 60 minutes, 6.6% 60 minutes or more (2000)

PLAIN CITY (village). Covers a land area of 1.812 square miles and a water area of 0 square miles. Located at 40.10° N. Lat.; 83.26° W. Long. Elevation is 935 feet.

History: Plain City was laid out in 1818 by Isaac Bigelow. It was first called Westminster, then Pleasant Valley, and finally named Plain City in 1851 because of its location on Big Darby Plain.

Population: 2,360 (1990); 2,832 (2000); 3,169 (2007); 3,416 (2012 projected); Race: 97.0% White, 0.4% Black, 0.6% Asian, 1.5% Hispanic of any race (2007); Density: 1,749.2 persons per square mile (2007); Average household size: 2.46 (2007); Median age: 35.9 (2007); Males per 100 females: 96.6 (2007); Marriage status: 23.5% never married, 53.7% now married, 9.5% widowed, 13.3% divorced (2000); Foreign born: 2.4% (2000); Ancestry (includes multiple ancestries): 23.4% German, 21.6% United States or American, 12.2% Irish, 9.9% English, 7.9% Other groups (2000).

Economy: Single-family building permits issued: 0 (2007); Multi-family building permits issued: 0 (2007); Employment by occupation: 8.4% management, 11.2% professional, 19.9% services, 30.4% sales, 0.0% farming, 11.4% construction, 18.7% production (2000).

Income: Per capita income: $26,911 (2007); Median household income: $55,216 (2007); Average household income: $66,263 (2007); Percent of households with income of $100,000 or more: 15.8% (2007); Poverty rate: 6.1% (2000).

Education: Percent of population age 25 and over with: High school diploma (including GED) or higher: 78.7% (2007); Bachelor's degree or higher: 14.2% (2007); Master's degree or higher: 3.2% (2007).

School District(s)

Jonathan Alder Local (PK-12)
2005-06 Enrollment: 1,991 . . . . (614) 873-5621
Tolles Career & Technical Center (09-12)
2005-06 Enrollment: n/a . . . . (614) 873-4666

Housing: Homeownership rate: 56.6% (2007); Median home value: $153,362 (2007); Median rent: $407 per month (2000); Median age of housing: 34 years (2000).

Safety: Violent crime rate: 2.7 per 10,000 population; Property crime rate: 73.9 per 10,000 population (2007).

Transportation: Commute to work: 95.6% car, 0.0% public transportation, 2.8% walk, 1.2% work from home (2000); Travel time to work: 30.7% less than 15 minutes, 40.1% 15 to 30 minutes, 21.4% 30 to 45 minutes, 5.3% 45 to 60 minutes, 2.5% 60 minutes or more (2000)

SOUTH SOLON (village). Covers a land area of 0.199 square miles and a water area of 0 square miles. Located at 39.73° N. Lat.; 83.61° W. Long. Elevation is 1,115 feet.

Population: 393 (1990); 405 (2000); 439 (2007); 455 (2012 projected); Race: 98.4% White, 0.0% Black, 0.7% Asian, 1.1% Hispanic of any race (2007); Density: 2,204.0 persons per square mile (2007); Average household size: 2.81 (2007); Median age: 32.9 (2007); Males per 100 females: 107.1 (2007); Marriage status: 23.2% never married, 58.4% now married, 7.5% widowed, 10.8% divorced (2000); Foreign born: 0.7% (2000); Ancestry (includes multiple ancestries): 28.0% United States or American, 14.6% German, 4.1% Other groups, 3.9% English, 3.9% French (except Basque) (2000).

Economy: Employment by occupation: 3.1% management, 12.2% professional, 16.3% services, 24.5% sales, 1.0% farming, 12.8% construction, 30.1% production (2000).

Income: Per capita income: $20,456 (2007); Median household income: $43,333 (2007); Average household income: $57,564 (2007); Percent of households with income of $100,000 or more: 9.6% (2007); Poverty rate: 10.0% (2000).

Education: Percent of population age 25 and over with: High school diploma (including GED) or higher: 75.6% (2007); Bachelor's degree or higher: 7.4% (2007); Master's degree or higher: 1.8% (2007).

Housing: Homeownership rate: 71.2% (2007); Median home value: $75,625 (2007); Median rent: $388 per month (2000); Median age of housing: 60+ years (2000).

Safety: Violent crime rate: 0.0 per 10,000 population; Property crime rate: 25.8 per 10,000 population (2007).

Transportation: Commute to work: 97.8% car, 0.0% public transportation, 1.1% walk, 1.1% work from home (2000); Travel time to work: 11.9% less than 15 minutes, 30.1% 15 to 30 minutes, 29.5% 30 to 45 minutes, 17.0% 45 to 60 minutes, 11.4% 60 minutes or more (2000)

WEST JEFFERSON (village). Aka Jefferson. Covers a land area of 3.316 square miles and a water area of 0.015 square miles. Located at 39.94° N. Lat.; 83.27° W. Long. Elevation is 909 feet.

Population: 4,623 (1990); 4,331 (2000); 4,109 (2007); 4,016 (2012 projected); Race: 99.0% White, 0.0% Black, 0.3% Asian, 0.8% Hispanic of any race (2007); Density: 1,239.0 persons per square mile (2007); Average household size: 2.60 (2007); Median age: 37.4 (2007); Males per 100 females: 97.4 (2007); Marriage status: 19.4% never married, 58.7% now married, 10.3% widowed, 11.6% divorced (2000); Foreign born: 0.4% (2000); Ancestry (includes multiple ancestries): 21.2% German, 18.5% United States or American, 10.9% English, 10.6% Irish, 6.0% Other groups (2000).

Economy: Single-family building permits issued: 13 (2007); Multi-family building permits issued: 0 (2007); Employment by occupation: 9.1% management, 9.6% professional, 14.5% services, 28.9% sales, 0.2% farming, 12.8% construction, 24.9% production (2000).

Income: Per capita income: $23,775 (2007); Median household income: $48,086 (2007); Average household income: $60,383 (2007); Percent of households with income of $100,000 or more: 12.2% (2007); Poverty rate: 5.9% (2000).

Education: Percent of population age 25 and over with: High school diploma (including GED) or higher: 75.7% (2007); Bachelor's degree or higher: 8.7% (2007); Master's degree or higher: 2.9% (2007).

School District(s)

Jefferson Local (PK-12)
2005-06 Enrollment: 1,304 . . . . (614) 879-7654

Housing: Homeownership rate: 72.3% (2007); Median home value: $110,009 (2007); Median rent: $434 per month (2000); Median age of housing: 38 years (2000).

Safety: Violent crime rate: 9.4 per 10,000 population; Property crime rate: 364.4 per 10,000 population (2007).

Transportation: Commute to work: 96.2% car, 0.5% public transportation, 1.0% walk, 1.6% work from home (2000); Travel time to work: 24.8% less than 15 minutes, 40.8% 15 to 30 minutes, 23.8% 30 to 45 minutes, 7.3% 45 to 60 minutes, 3.3% 60 minutes or more (2000)

Additional Information Contacts

Village of West Jefferson . . . . (614) 879-7674
http://www.villageofwestjefferson.com

Mahoning County

Located in eastern Ohio; bounded on the east by Pennsylvania; crossed by the Mahoning and Little Beaver Rivers. Covers a land area of 415.25 square miles, a water area of 8.14 square miles, and is located in the Eastern Time Zone. The county was founded in 1846. County seat is Youngstown.

Mahoning County is part of the Youngstown-Warren-Boardman, OH-PA Metropolitan Statistical Area. The entire metro area includes: Mahoning County, OH; Trumbull County, OH; Mercer County, PA

Weather Station: Canfield 1 S Elevation: 1,138 feet

	Jan	Feb	Mar	Apr	May	Jun	Jul	Aug	Sep	Oct	Nov	Dec
High	34	37	49	60	71	79	83	82	74	63	50	39
Low	16	17	26	34	45	54	58	56	49	38	31	22
Precip	2.0	1.8	2.9	3.0	3.9	4.2	4.4	3.6	3.8	2.8	3.1	2.7
Snow	na	na	3.3	0.7	0.0	0.0	0.0	0.0	0.0	0.3	1.1	na

High and Low temperatures in degrees Fahrenheit; Precipitation and Snow in inches

Population: 264,806 (1990); 257,555 (2000); 254,132 (2007); 251,505 (2012 projected); Race: 80.7% White, 15.6% Black, 0.7% Asian, 3.3% Hispanic of any race (2007); Density: 612.0 persons per square mile

(2007); Average household size: 2.52 (2007); Median age: 40.6 (2007); Males per 100 females: 93.1 (2007).
Religion: Five largest groups: 39.0% Catholic Church, 3.5% The United Methodist Church, 3.2% Evangelical Lutheran Church in America, 2.9% Assemblies of God, 2.7% Presbyterian Church (U.S.A.) (2000).
Economy: Unemployment rate: 7.1% (6/2008); Total civilian labor force: 120,361 (6/2008); Leading industries: 19.8% health care and social assistance; 15.6% retail trade; 10.7% manufacturing (2005); Farms: 652 totaling 76,543 acres (2002); Companies that employ 500 or more persons: 4 (2006); Companies that employ 100 to 499 persons: 137 (2006); Companies that employ less than 100 persons: 6,134 (2006); Black-owned businesses: 379 (2002); Hispanic-owned businesses: n/a (2002); Asian-owned businesses: 252 (2002); Women-owned businesses: 4,231 (2002); Retail sales per capita: $16,363 (2008). Single-family building permits issued: 277 (2007); Multi-family building permits issued: 32 (2007).
Income: Per capita income: $21,645 (2007); Median household income: $40,287 (2007); Average household income: $52,975 (2007); Percent of households with income of $100,000 or more: 11.1% (2007); Poverty rate: 14.3% (2005); Bankruptcy rate: 5.42% (2007).
Taxes: Total county taxes per capita: $231 (2006); County property taxes per capita: $136 (2006).
Education: Percent of population age 25 and over with: High school diploma (including GED) or higher: 82.2% (2007); Bachelor's degree or higher: 17.3% (2007); Master's degree or higher: 5.6% (2007).
Housing: Homeownership rate: 73.0% (2007); Median home value: $94,625 (2007); Median rent: $372 per month (2000); Median age of housing: 43 years (2000).
Health: Birth rate: 116.0 per 10,000 population (2007); Death rate: 123.5 per 10,000 population (2007); Age-adjusted cancer mortality rate: 199.1 deaths per 100,000 population (2005); Air Quality Index: 76.2% good, 21.4% moderate, 2.2% unhealthy for sensitive individuals, 0.3% unhealthy (percent of days in 2007); Number of physicians: 36.1 per 10,000 population (2005); Hospital beds: 36.3 per 10,000 population (2004); Hospital admissions: 1,669.4 per 10,000 population (2004).
Elections: 2004 Presidential election results: 36.7% Bush, 62.6% Kerry, 0.0% Nader, 0.4% Badnarik

Additional Information Contacts

Mahoning County Government . . . . (330) 740-2130

City of Campbell. . . . . (330) 755-1451
http://cityofcampbellohio.org
City of Canfield. . . . . (330) 533-1101
http://www.ci.canfield.oh.us
City of Struthers . . . . (330) 755-2181
http://www.cityofstruthers.com
City of Youngstown . . . . (330) 742-8701
http://www.cityofyoungstownoh.org
Village of Sebring. . . . . (330) 938-9340
http://www.sebringohio.net
Youngstown/Warren Regional Chamber of Commerce. . . . (330) 744-2131
http://www.regionalchamber.com

Mahoning County Communities

AUSTINTOWN (CDP). Covers a land area of 11.673 square miles and a water area of 0 square miles. Located at 41.09° N. Lat.; 80.73° W. Long. Elevation is 1,129 feet.
Population: 32,371 (1990); 31,627 (2000); 29,358 (2007); 28,123 (2012 projected); Race: 92.6% White, 4.6% Black, 0.9% Asian, 1.9% Hispanic of any race (2007); Density: 2,515.0 persons per square mile (2007); Average household size: 2.32 (2007); Median age: 41.7 (2007); Males per 100 females: 90.6 (2007); Marriage status: 24.8% never married, 55.5% now married, 8.5% widowed, 11.2% divorced (2000); Foreign born: 2.3% (2000); Ancestry (includes multiple ancestries): 26.1% German, 19.3% Italian, 17.8% Irish, 9.3% Other groups, 9.2% English (2000).
Economy: Employment by occupation: 8.1% management, 16.8% professional, 15.3% services, 29.4% sales, 0.0% farming, 8.1% construction, 22.2% production (2000).
Income: Per capita income: $22,224 (2007); Median household income: $43,078 (2007); Average household income: $50,524 (2007); Percent of households with income of $100,000 or more: 8.6% (2007); Poverty rate: 8.8% (2000).
Education: Percent of population age 25 and over with: High school diploma (including GED) or higher: 85.3% (2007); Bachelor's degree or higher: 15.9% (2007); Master's degree or higher: 4.3% (2007).
Housing: Homeownership rate: 66.2% (2007); Median home value: $99,374 (2007); Median rent: $422 per month (2000); Median age of housing: 34 years (2000).
Safety: Violent crime rate: 5.3 per 10,000 population; Property crime rate: 469.2 per 10,000 population (2007).
Transportation: Commute to work: 97.8% car, 0.4% public transportation, 0.7% walk, 0.7% work from home (2000); Travel time to work: 30.9% less than 15 minutes, 51.6% 15 to 30 minutes, 9.6% 30 to 45 minutes, 3.2% 45 to 60 minutes, 4.8% 60 minutes or more (2000)

BELOIT (village). Covers a land area of 0.768 square miles and a water area of 0 square miles. Located at 40.92° N. Lat.; 80.99° W. Long. Elevation is 1,129 feet.
Population: 1,037 (1990); 1,024 (2000); 929 (2007); 948 (2012 projected); Race: 98.4% White, 0.3% Black, 0.2% Asian, 0.0% Hispanic of any race (2007); Density: 1,209.3 persons per square mile (2007); Average household size: 2.33 (2007); Median age: 40.8 (2007); Males per 100 females: 85.4 (2007); Marriage status: 19.5% never married, 58.0% now married, 10.4% widowed, 12.1% divorced (2000); Foreign born: 0.0% (2000); Ancestry (includes multiple ancestries): 26.0% German, 16.3% English, 14.7% United States or American, 11.2% Irish, 6.0% Other groups (2000).
Economy: Employment by occupation: 4.7% management, 16.7% professional, 18.2% services, 20.3% sales, 0.0% farming, 6.2% construction, 33.8% production (2000).
Income: Per capita income: $21,391 (2007); Median household income: $38,519 (2007); Average household income: $49,931 (2007); Percent of households with income of $100,000 or more: 8.3% (2007); Poverty rate: 10.6% (2000).
Education: Percent of population age 25 and over with: High school diploma (including GED) or higher: 79.0% (2007); Bachelor's degree or higher: 9.3% (2007); Master's degree or higher: 2.8% (2007).

School District(s)

West Branch Local (PK-12)
2005-06 Enrollment: 2,485 . . . . (330) 938-9324
Housing: Homeownership rate: 73.6% (2007); Median home value: $76,591 (2007); Median rent: $281 per month (2000); Median age of housing: 47 years (2000).
Transportation: Commute to work: 94.2% car, 0.0% public transportation, 3.3% walk, 0.9% work from home (2000); Travel time to work: 35.5% less than 15 minutes, 41.5% 15 to 30 minutes, 12.3% 30 to 45 minutes, 7.4% 45 to 60 minutes, 3.3% 60 minutes or more (2000)

BERLIN CENTER (unincorporated postal area, zip code 44401). Covers a land area of 33.918 square miles and a water area of 0.059 square miles. Located at 41.03° N. Lat.; 80.95° W. Long. Elevation is 1,075 feet.
Population: 3,175 (2000); Race: 98.5% White, 0.0% Black, 0.2% Asian, 0.6% Hispanic of any race (2000); Density: 93.6 persons per square mile (2000); Age: 23.3% under 18, 10.7% over 64 (2000); Marriage status: 21.8% never married, 67.5% now married, 3.2% widowed, 7.6% divorced (2000); Foreign born: 2.8% (2000); Ancestry (includes multiple ancestries): 28.6% German, 15.0% Irish, 12.1% English, 11.8% Italian, 8.6% United States or American (2000).
Economy: Employment by occupation: 7.6% management, 15.4% professional, 11.9% services, 25.2% sales, 0.0% farming, 14.6% construction, 25.4% production (2000).
Income: Per capita income: $21,577 (2000); Median household income: $50,868 (2000); Poverty rate: 4.8% (2000).
Education: Percent of population age 25 and over with: High school diploma (including GED) or higher: 84.5% (2000); Bachelor's degree or higher: 14.7% (2000).

School District(s)

Western Reserve Local (PK-12)
2005-06 Enrollment: 794 . . . . (330) 547-4100
Housing: Homeownership rate: 89.1% (2000); Median home value: $119,700 (2000); Median rent: $343 per month (2000); Median age of housing: 30 years (2000).
Transportation: Commute to work: 95.7% car, 0.0% public transportation, 0.8% walk, 2.8% work from home (2000); Travel time to work: 19.3% less than 15 minutes, 41.6% 15 to 30 minutes, 25.9% 30 to 45 minutes, 6.1% 45 to 60 minutes, 7.1% 60 minutes or more (2000)

BOARDMAN (CDP). Covers a land area of 15.933 square miles and a water area of 0.101 square miles. Located at 41.03° N. Lat.; 80.66° W. Long. Elevation is 1,112 feet.
Population: 38,727 (1990); 37,215 (2000); 34,394 (2007); 32,880 (2012 projected); Race: 94.8% White, 2.4% Black, 1.2% Asian, 2.0% Hispanic of any race (2007); Density: 2,158.7 persons per square mile (2007); Average household size: 2.31 (2007); Median age: 44.0 (2007); Males per 100 females: 88.0 (2007); Marriage status: 23.7% never married, 55.6% now married, 10.7% widowed, 10.0% divorced (2000); Foreign born: 3.0% (2000); Ancestry (includes multiple ancestries): 26.5% Italian, 20.8% German, 17.7% Irish, 9.6% English, 9.5% Slovak (2000).
Economy: Employment by occupation: 14.0% management, 20.0% professional, 14.5% services, 30.5% sales, 0.0% farming, 7.0% construction, 14.0% production (2000).
Income: Per capita income: $25,832 (2007); Median household income: $46,349 (2007); Average household income: $58,516 (2007); Percent of households with income of $100,000 or more: 12.6% (2007); Poverty rate: 5.2% (2000).
Education: Percent of population age 25 and over with: High school diploma (including GED) or higher: 88.9% (2007); Bachelor's degree or higher: 24.4% (2007); Master's degree or higher: 7.7% (2007).

Two-year College(s)

Raphaels School of Beauty Culture (Private, For-profit)
Fall 2007 Enrollment: 36 . . . . (330) 782-3395

Housing: Homeownership rate: 71.1% (2007); Median home value: $113,512 (2007); Median rent: $423 per month (2000); Median age of housing: 36 years (2000).
Newspapers: Boardman News (Community news; Circulation 10,000)
Transportation: Commute to work: 96.9% car, 0.3% public transportation, 0.6% walk, 2.1% work from home (2000); Travel time to work: 37.3% less than 15 minutes, 41.6% 15 to 30 minutes, 13.9% 30 to 45 minutes, 2.4% 45 to 60 minutes, 4.8% 60 minutes or more (2000)

CAMPBELL (city). Covers a land area of 3.729 square miles and a water area of 0 square miles. Located at 41.07° N. Lat.; 80.59° W. Long. Elevation is 1,030 feet.
History: Until 1926, called East Youngstown.
Population: 10,038 (1990); 9,460 (2000); 8,507 (2007); 7,964 (2012 projected); Race: 78.6% White, 14.9% Black, 0.3% Asian, 12.1% Hispanic of any race (2007); Density: 2,281.2 persons per square mile (2007); Average household size: 2.49 (2007); Median age: 39.5 (2007); Males per 100 females: 87.5 (2007); Marriage status: 28.8% never married, 51.4% now married, 11.4% widowed, 8.4% divorced (2000); Foreign born: 6.2% (2000); Ancestry (includes multiple ancestries): 26.6% Other groups, 18.8% Italian, 12.8% Slovak, 10.4% Greek, 9.9% Irish (2000).
Economy: Single-family building permits issued: 2 (2007); Multi-family building permits issued: 0 (2007); Employment by occupation: 5.6% management, 11.7% professional, 18.7% services, 27.3% sales, 0.2% farming, 10.6% construction, 25.9% production (2000).
Income: Per capita income: $18,560 (2007); Median household income: $34,183 (2007); Average household income: $46,154 (2007); Percent of households with income of $100,000 or more: 6.5% (2007); Poverty rate: 18.3% (2000).
Education: Percent of population age 25 and over with: High school diploma (including GED) or higher: 75.2% (2007); Bachelor's degree or higher: 9.8% (2007); Master's degree or higher: 3.8% (2007).

School District(s)

Campbell City (PK-12)
2005-06 Enrollment: 1,497 . . . . (330) 799-8777

Housing: Homeownership rate: 75.4% (2007); Median home value: $73,053 (2007); Median rent: $330 per month (2000); Median age of housing: 46 years (2000).
Safety: Violent crime rate: 55.6 per 10,000 population; Property crime rate: 391.7 per 10,000 population (2007).
Transportation: Commute to work: 97.0% car, 0.2% public transportation, 0.8% walk, 1.7% work from home (2000); Travel time to work: 33.8% less than 15 minutes, 45.9% 15 to 30 minutes, 13.7% 30 to 45 minutes, 2.7% 45 to 60 minutes, 3.9% 60 minutes or more (2000)

Additional Information Contacts

City of Campbell. . . . . (330) 755-1451
http://cityofcampbellohio.org

CANFIELD (city). Covers a land area of 4.643 square miles and a water area of 0 square miles. Located at 41.03° N. Lat.; 80.76° W. Long. Elevation is 1,145 feet.
History: Canfield was surveyed in 1798. After a brief oil boom, the town turned to lumber, clay, coal, and farm products for its revenue source.
Population: 5,577 (1990); 7,374 (2000); 6,834 (2007); 6,519 (2012 projected); Race: 96.4% White, 0.4% Black, 2.2% Asian, 0.7% Hispanic of any race (2007); Density: 1,471.8 persons per square mile (2007); Average household size: 2.46 (2007); Median age: 43.6 (2007); Males per 100 females: 91.4 (2007); Marriage status: 19.1% never married, 66.9% now married, 8.3% widowed, 5.8% divorced (2000); Foreign born: 2.8% (2000); Ancestry (includes multiple ancestries): 27.0% German, 23.1% Italian, 17.3% Irish, 12.5% English, 9.9% Slovak (2000).
Economy: Employment by occupation: 20.3% management, 25.7% professional, 12.2% services, 28.2% sales, 0.0% farming, 4.6% construction, 9.1% production (2000).
Income: Per capita income: $36,944 (2007); Median household income: $70,401 (2007); Average household income: $90,983 (2007); Percent of households with income of $100,000 or more: 31.9% (2007); Poverty rate: 3.2% (2000).
Education: Percent of population age 25 and over with: High school diploma (including GED) or higher: 93.9% (2007); Bachelor's degree or higher: 40.6% (2007); Master's degree or higher: 16.4% (2007).

School District(s)

Canfield Local (PK-12)
2005-06 Enrollment: 3,110 . . . . (330) 533-3303
Mahoning Co Career & Tech Ctr (09-12)
2005-06 Enrollment: n/a . . . . (330) 729-4000

Vocational/Technical School(s)

Mahoning County Career and Technical Center (Public)
Fall 2007 Enrollment: 80 . . . . (330) 729-4100
2007-08 Tuition: In-state $4,000; Out-of-state $4,000

Housing: Homeownership rate: 83.7% (2007); Median home value: $162,958 (2007); Median rent: $445 per month (2000); Median age of housing: 31 years (2000).
Safety: Violent crime rate: 0.0 per 10,000 population; Property crime rate: 139.7 per 10,000 population (2007).
Transportation: Commute to work: 94.2% car, 0.2% public transportation, 0.7% walk, 4.2% work from home (2000); Travel time to work: 29.1% less than 15 minutes, 47.7% 15 to 30 minutes, 14.7% 30 to 45 minutes, 4.4% 45 to 60 minutes, 4.1% 60 minutes or more (2000)

Additional Information Contacts

City of Canfield. . . . . (330) 533-1101
http://www.ci.canfield.oh.us

CRAIG BEACH (village). Covers a land area of 0.929 square miles and a water area of 0.758 square miles. Located at 41.11° N. Lat.; 80.98° W. Long. Elevation is 958 feet.
Population: 1,402 (1990); 1,254 (2000); 1,315 (2007); 1,330 (2012 projected); Race: 97.6% White, 0.2% Black, 0.7% Asian, 0.7% Hispanic of any race (2007); Density: 1,416.0 persons per square mile (2007); Average household size: 2.54 (2007); Median age: 39.6 (2007); Males per 100 females: 92.0 (2007); Marriage status: 26.9% never married, 51.5% now married, 7.9% widowed, 13.7% divorced (2000); Foreign born: 1.1% (2000); Ancestry (includes multiple ancestries): 24.4% German, 19.1% Irish, 9.7% English, 9.1% Italian, 7.1% United States or American (2000).
Economy: Employment by occupation: 7.3% management, 10.3% professional, 16.8% services, 22.4% sales, 0.3% farming, 14.1% construction, 28.8% production (2000).
Income: Per capita income: $21,811 (2007); Median household income: $46,574 (2007); Average household income: $55,256 (2007); Percent of households with income of $100,000 or more: 12.2% (2007); Poverty rate: 13.0% (2000).
Education: Percent of population age 25 and over with: High school diploma (including GED) or higher: 80.8% (2007); Bachelor's degree or higher: 8.3% (2007); Master's degree or higher: 2.1% (2007).
Housing: Homeownership rate: 76.0% (2007); Median home value: $94,512 (2007); Median rent: $400 per month (2000); Median age of housing: 41 years (2000).
Transportation: Commute to work: 96.1% car, 0.0% public transportation, 1.1% walk, 1.2% work from home (2000); Travel time to work: 15.3% less than 15 minutes, 32.7% 15 to 30 minutes, 30.1% 30 to 45 minutes, 14.1% 45 to 60 minutes, 7.8% 60 minutes or more (2000)

LAKE MILTON (unincorporated postal area, zip code 44429). Covers a land area of 7.097 square miles and a water area of 0 square miles. Located at 41.10° N. Lat.; 80.98° W. Long. Elevation is 990 feet.
History: Incorporated 1930, disincorporated 1947.
Population: 2,884 (2000); Race: 98.1% White, 0.3% Black, 0.2% Asian, 1.2% Hispanic of any race (2000); Density: 406.4 persons per square mile (2000); Age: 23.9% under 18, 10.2% over 64 (2000); Marriage status: 25.5% never married, 57.0% now married, 6.7% widowed, 10.7% divorced (2000); Foreign born: 1.5% (2000); Ancestry (includes multiple ancestries): 23.3% German, 15.1% Irish, 12.4% United States or American, 11.2% English, 10.7% Italian (2000).
Economy: Employment by occupation: 6.8% management, 14.6% professional, 13.6% services, 26.2% sales, 0.1% farming, 12.8% construction, 25.9% production (2000).
Income: Per capita income: $17,000 (2000); Median household income: $39,816 (2000); Poverty rate: 12.2% (2000).
Education: Percent of population age 25 and over with: High school diploma (including GED) or higher: 82.5% (2000); Bachelor's degree or higher: 10.0% (2000).

Vocational/Technical School(s)

TDDS Technical Institute
Fall 2007 Enrollment: 491 . . . . (330) 538-2216
2007-08 Tuition: $5,645

Housing: Homeownership rate: 81.5% (2000); Median home value: $86,900 (2000); Median rent: $406 per month (2000); Median age of housing: 40 years (2000).
Transportation: Commute to work: 92.6% car, 0.2% public transportation, 3.8% walk, 2.7% work from home (2000); Travel time to work: 21.6% less than 15 minutes, 30.3% 15 to 30 minutes, 24.5% 30 to 45 minutes, 12.7% 45 to 60 minutes, 10.9% 60 minutes or more (2000)

LOWELLVILLE (village). Covers a land area of 1.437 square miles and a water area of 0 square miles. Located at 41.04° N. Lat.; 80.54° W. Long. Elevation is 820 feet.
History: Lowellville was settled in 1800 and incorporated in 1836. First a coal town, after 1845 the economy depended more on iron and steel.
Population: 1,349 (1990); 1,281 (2000); 1,151 (2007); 1,076 (2012 projected); Race: 99.0% White, 0.0% Black, 0.1% Asian, 2.1% Hispanic of any race (2007); Density: 801.0 persons per square mile (2007); Average household size: 2.39 (2007); Median age: 39.5 (2007); Males per 100 females: 91.8 (2007); Marriage status: 21.7% never married, 56.3% now married, 12.0% widowed, 10.0% divorced (2000); Foreign born: 2.1% (2000); Ancestry (includes multiple ancestries): 48.0% Italian, 18.6% German, 17.9% Irish, 7.8% Slovak, 5.4% English (2000).
Economy: Single-family building permits issued: 5 (2007); Multi-family building permits issued: 0 (2007); Employment by occupation: 10.6% management, 11.0% professional, 17.7% services, 24.8% sales, 0.0% farming, 10.6% construction, 25.2% production (2000).
Income: Per capita income: $17,022 (2007); Median household income: $33,672 (2007); Average household income: $40,733 (2007); Percent of households with income of $100,000 or more: 4.0% (2007); Poverty rate: 9.4% (2000).
Education: Percent of population age 25 and over with: High school diploma (including GED) or higher: 79.0% (2007); Bachelor's degree or higher: 8.1% (2007); Master's degree or higher: 3.0% (2007).

School District(s)

Lowellville Local (PK-12)
2005-06 Enrollment: 684 . . . . (330) 536-6318

Housing: Homeownership rate: 77.1% (2007); Median home value: $77,439 (2007); Median rent: $285 per month (2000); Median age of housing: 60+ years (2000).
Transportation: Commute to work: 92.2% car, 0.0% public transportation, 5.0% walk, 1.0% work from home (2000); Travel time to work: 33.9% less than 15 minutes, 40.0% 15 to 30 minutes, 17.9% 30 to 45 minutes, 2.8% 45 to 60 minutes, 5.3% 60 minutes or more (2000)

MAPLE RIDGE (CDP). Covers a land area of 2.011 square miles and a water area of 0 square miles. Located at 40.91° N. Lat.; 81.04° W. Long. Elevation is 1,102 feet.
Population: 1,018 (1990); 910 (2000); 964 (2007); 993 (2012 projected); Race: 98.9% White, 0.6% Black, 0.3% Asian, 0.3% Hispanic of any race (2007); Density: 479.4 persons per square mile (2007); Average household size: 2.48 (2007); Median age: 41.3 (2007); Males per 100 females: 91.7 (2007); Marriage status: 18.6% never married, 58.6% now married, 7.5% widowed, 15.3% divorced (2000); Foreign born: 0.0% (2000); Ancestry (includes multiple ancestries): 29.0% German, 19.6% Irish, 12.0% Italian, 10.1% United States or American, 9.6% English (2000).
Economy: Employment by occupation: 1.4% management, 7.2% professional, 22.8% services, 15.6% sales, 0.0% farming, 11.1% construction, 41.9% production (2000).
Income: Per capita income: $18,817 (2007); Median household income: $35,565 (2007); Average household income: $46,632 (2007); Percent of households with income of $100,000 or more: 5.7% (2007); Poverty rate: 5.8% (2000).
Education: Percent of population age 25 and over with: High school diploma (including GED) or higher: 73.4% (2007); Bachelor's degree or higher: 1.8% (2007); Master's degree or higher: 1.8% (2007).
Housing: Homeownership rate: 90.0% (2007); Median home value: $64,250 (2007); Median rent: $n/a per month (2000); Median age of housing: 48 years (2000).
Transportation: Commute to work: 100.0% car, 0.0% public transportation, 0.0% walk, 0.0% work from home (2000); Travel time to work: 53.2% less than 15 minutes, 33.4% 15 to 30 minutes, 7.8% 30 to 45 minutes, 2.9% 45 to 60 minutes, 2.6% 60 minutes or more (2000)

NEW MIDDLETOWN (village). Covers a land area of 0.871 square miles and a water area of 0 square miles. Located at 40.96° N. Lat.; 80.55° W. Long. Elevation is 1,253 feet.
Population: 1,966 (1990); 1,682 (2000); 1,648 (2007); 1,648 (2012 projected); Race: 99.3% White, 0.1% Black, 0.0% Asian, 0.8% Hispanic of any race (2007); Density: 1,892.9 persons per square mile (2007); Average household size: 2.36 (2007); Median age: 42.4 (2007); Males per 100 females: 84.3 (2007); Marriage status: 20.7% never married, 63.2% now married, 9.1% widowed, 7.0% divorced (2000); Foreign born: 1.1% (2000); Ancestry (includes multiple ancestries): 30.5% German, 16.6% Italian, 15.8% Irish, 11.7% English, 8.0% Slovak (2000).
Economy: Employment by occupation: 7.7% management, 15.1% professional, 17.9% services, 28.8% sales, 0.0% farming, 12.1% construction, 18.4% production (2000).
Income: Per capita income: $23,007 (2007); Median household income: $39,643 (2007); Average household income: $54,319 (2007); Percent of households with income of $100,000 or more: 11.0% (2007); Poverty rate: 7.7% (2000).
Education: Percent of population age 25 and over with: High school diploma (including GED) or higher: 85.8% (2007); Bachelor's degree or higher: 11.4% (2007); Master's degree or higher: 3.8% (2007).

School District(s)

Springfield Local (PK-12)
2005-06 Enrollment: 1,246 . . . . (330) 542-2929

Housing: Homeownership rate: 75.6% (2007); Median home value: $111,951 (2007); Median rent: $358 per month (2000); Median age of housing: 35 years (2000).
Transportation: Commute to work: 98.0% car, 0.0% public transportation, 0.6% walk, 1.1% work from home (2000); Travel time to work: 26.6% less than 15 minutes, 42.8% 15 to 30 minutes, 17.1% 30 to 45 minutes, 6.9% 45 to 60 minutes, 6.6% 60 minutes or more (2000)

NEW SPRINGFIELD (unincorporated postal area, zip code 44443). Covers a land area of 14.009 square miles and a water area of 0 square miles. Located at 40.91° N. Lat.; 80.60° W. Long. Elevation is 1,211 feet.
Population: 2,055 (2000); Race: 98.3% White, 1.3% Black, 0.0% Asian, 1.4% Hispanic of any race (2000); Density: 146.7 persons per square mile (2000); Age: 22.4% under 18, 17.4% over 64 (2000); Marriage status: 24.7% never married, 61.9% now married, 6.5% widowed, 6.9% divorced (2000); Foreign born: 0.0% (2000); Ancestry (includes multiple ancestries): 38.6% German, 12.3% English, 10.9% Irish, 9.6% Italian, 7.7% Slovak (2000).
Economy: Employment by occupation: 10.7% management, 16.9% professional, 11.0% services, 29.9% sales, 2.3% farming, 11.1% construction, 18.0% production (2000).
Income: Per capita income: $20,158 (2000); Median household income: $35,375 (2000); Poverty rate: 5.9% (2000).
Education: Percent of population age 25 and over with: High school diploma (including GED) or higher: 88.2% (2000); Bachelor's degree or higher: 14.7% (2000).
Housing: Homeownership rate: 82.9% (2000); Median home value: $106,100 (2000); Median rent: $345 per month (2000); Median age of housing: 35 years (2000).

Transportation: Commute to work: 86.7% car, 0.0% public transportation, 7.1% walk, 4.4% work from home (2000); Travel time to work: 30.9% less than 15 minutes, 41.4% 15 to 30 minutes, 17.6% 30 to 45 minutes, 6.1% 45 to 60 minutes, 4.0% 60 minutes or more (2000)

NORTH BENTON (unincorporated postal area, zip code 44449). Covers a land area of 11.222 square miles and a water area of 0.081 square miles. Located at 40.99° N. Lat.; 81.02° W. Long. Elevation is 1,080 feet.
Population: 1,305 (2000); Race: 100.0% White, 0.0% Black, 0.0% Asian, 0.6% Hispanic of any race (2000); Density: 116.3 persons per square mile (2000); Age: 25.2% under 18, 10.8% over 64 (2000); Marriage status: 19.2% never married, 62.7% now married, 4.1% widowed, 14.0% divorced (2000); Foreign born: 0.0% (2000); Ancestry (includes multiple ancestries): 19.6% United States or American, 19.4% German, 16.7% Irish, 7.4% English, 5.6% Other groups (2000).
Economy: Employment by occupation: 11.7% management, 14.7% professional, 10.8% services, 17.0% sales, 0.0% farming, 13.7% construction, 32.2% production (2000).
Income: Per capita income: $18,716 (2000); Median household income: $42,355 (2000); Poverty rate: 12.0% (2000).
Education: Percent of population age 25 and over with: High school diploma (including GED) or higher: 74.8% (2000); Bachelor's degree or higher: 11.1% (2000).
Housing: Homeownership rate: 84.5% (2000); Median home value: $115,100 (2000); Median rent: $289 per month (2000); Median age of housing: 35 years (2000).
Transportation: Commute to work: 97.6% car, 0.0% public transportation, 0.0% walk, 2.4% work from home (2000); Travel time to work: 11.4% less than 15 minutes, 36.4% 15 to 30 minutes, 33.0% 30 to 45 minutes, 16.0% 45 to 60 minutes, 3.2% 60 minutes or more (2000)

NORTH JACKSON (unincorporated postal area, zip code 44451). Covers a land area of 36.720 square miles and a water area of 0.152 square miles. Located at 41.09° N. Lat.; 80.86° W. Long. Elevation is 1,030 feet.
Population: 3,101 (2000); Race: 99.2% White, 0.3% Black, 0.2% Asian, 1.0% Hispanic of any race (2000); Density: 84.4 persons per square mile (2000); Age: 24.2% under 18, 10.1% over 64 (2000); Marriage status: 23.1% never married, 62.6% now married, 5.7% widowed, 8.6% divorced (2000); Foreign born: 1.8% (2000); Ancestry (includes multiple ancestries): 28.2% German, 20.3% Irish, 13.2% Italian, 9.2% United States or American, 9.0% English (2000).
Economy: Employment by occupation: 8.0% management, 15.1% professional, 9.7% services, 27.7% sales, 0.3% farming, 11.5% construction, 27.7% production (2000).
Income: Per capita income: $19,489 (2000); Median household income: $46,541 (2000); Poverty rate: 4.5% (2000).
Education: Percent of population age 25 and over with: High school diploma (including GED) or higher: 87.1% (2000); Bachelor's degree or higher: 15.9% (2000).

School District(s)

Jackson-Milton Local (PK-12)
2005-06 Enrollment: 916 . . . . (330) 538-3232
Housing: Homeownership rate: 83.2% (2000); Median home value: $120,300 (2000); Median rent: $357 per month (2000); Median age of housing: 37 years (2000).
Transportation: Commute to work: 93.3% car, 0.0% public transportation, 4.5% walk, 2.2% work from home (2000); Travel time to work: 29.5% less than 15 minutes, 39.2% 15 to 30 minutes, 20.9% 30 to 45 minutes, 4.7% 45 to 60 minutes, 5.7% 60 minutes or more (2000)

NORTH LIMA (unincorporated postal area, zip code 44452). Covers a land area of 14.674 square miles and a water area of 0 square miles. Located at 40.95° N. Lat.; 80.65° W. Long. Elevation is 1,103 feet.
Population: 2,724 (2000); Race: 97.9% White, 1.8% Black, 0.0% Asian, 2.6% Hispanic of any race (2000); Density: 185.6 persons per square mile (2000); Age: 26.1% under 18, 16.9% over 64 (2000); Marriage status: 24.4% never married, 60.3% now married, 6.5% widowed, 8.8% divorced (2000); Foreign born: 1.1% (2000); Ancestry (includes multiple ancestries): 30.2% German, 19.0% Irish, 17.9% Italian, 8.2% United States or American, 7.4% Polish (2000).
Economy: Employment by occupation: 9.2% management, 13.1% professional, 22.4% services, 23.8% sales, 1.1% farming, 12.9% construction, 17.4% production (2000).
Income: Per capita income: $16,355 (2000); Median household income: $43,232 (2000); Poverty rate: 4.3% (2000).
Education: Percent of population age 25 and over with: High school diploma (including GED) or higher: 80.9% (2000); Bachelor's degree or higher: 19.3% (2000).

School District(s)

South Range Local (PK-12)
2005-06 Enrollment: 1,346 . . . . (330) 549-5226

Two-year College(s)

Tri-State College
Fall 2007 Enrollment: 44 . . . . (330) 629-9998
2007-08 Tuition: In-state $6,740; Out-of-state $6,740
Housing: Homeownership rate: 85.5% (2000); Median home value: $104,600 (2000); Median rent: $331 per month (2000); Median age of housing: 40 years (2000).
Transportation: Commute to work: 95.7% car, 0.0% public transportation, 1.8% walk, 2.5% work from home (2000); Travel time to work: 41.1% less than 15 minutes, 39.0% 15 to 30 minutes, 13.8% 30 to 45 minutes, 2.8% 45 to 60 minutes, 3.3% 60 minutes or more (2000)

PETERSBURG (unincorporated postal area, zip code 44454). Covers a land area of 7.133 square miles and a water area of 0 square miles. Located at 40.91° N. Lat.; 80.53° W. Long. Elevation is 1,129 feet.
Population: 1,277 (2000); Race: 100.0% White, 0.0% Black, 0.0% Asian, 0.0% Hispanic of any race (2000); Density: 179.0 persons per square mile (2000); Age: 29.8% under 18, 4.6% over 64 (2000); Marriage status: 22.6% never married, 66.6% now married, 3.5% widowed, 7.3% divorced (2000); Foreign born: 1.0% (2000); Ancestry (includes multiple ancestries): 28.3% German, 22.7% English, 15.5% Irish, 12.5% Italian, 6.7% Welsh (2000).
Economy: Employment by occupation: 5.5% management, 18.7% professional, 12.6% services, 22.0% sales, 0.0% farming, 14.0% construction, 27.1% production (2000).
Income: Per capita income: $18,497 (2000); Median household income: $43,967 (2000); Poverty rate: 4.6% (2000).
Education: Percent of population age 25 and over with: High school diploma (including GED) or higher: 86.5% (2000); Bachelor's degree or higher: 16.1% (2000).
Housing: Homeownership rate: 86.2% (2000); Median home value: $87,800 (2000); Median rent: $250 per month (2000); Median age of housing: 32 years (2000).
Transportation: Commute to work: 93.0% car, 0.0% public transportation, 2.1% walk, 4.9% work from home (2000); Travel time to work: 19.9% less than 15 minutes, 37.2% 15 to 30 minutes, 33.3% 30 to 45 minutes, 2.2% 45 to 60 minutes, 7.3% 60 minutes or more (2000)

POLAND (village). Covers a land area of 1.244 square miles and a water area of 0 square miles. Located at 41.02° N. Lat.; 80.61° W. Long. Elevation is 1,043 feet.
History: Poland was settled in 1799 by Jonathan Fowler, and originally named for him. Fowler operated the Stone Tavern, a stop on the Pittsburgh to Cleveland stage route. The town became a residential suburb of Youngstown.
Population: 2,992 (1990); 2,866 (2000); 2,710 (2007); 2,602 (2012 projected); Race: 99.2% White, 0.2% Black, 0.1% Asian, 1.2% Hispanic of any race (2007); Density: 2,177.8 persons per square mile (2007); Average household size: 2.62 (2007); Median age: 44.9 (2007); Males per 100 females: 90.4 (2007); Marriage status: 18.9% never married, 61.8% now married, 10.8% widowed, 8.6% divorced (2000); Foreign born: 2.9% (2000); Ancestry (includes multiple ancestries): 26.8% Italian, 25.0% German, 21.7% Irish, 13.7% English, 13.0% Slovak (2000).
Economy: Employment by occupation: 13.7% management, 24.7% professional, 7.5% services, 34.5% sales, 0.0% farming, 11.0% construction, 8.6% production (2000).
Income: Per capita income: $27,964 (2007); Median household income: $54,265 (2007); Average household income: $70,970 (2007); Percent of households with income of $100,000 or more: 16.6% (2007); Poverty rate: 6.1% (2000).
Education: Percent of population age 25 and over with: High school diploma (including GED) or higher: 89.9% (2007); Bachelor's degree or higher: 32.6% (2007); Master's degree or higher: 11.4% (2007).

School District(s)

Poland Local (PK-12)
2005-06 Enrollment: 2,448 . . . . (330) 757-7000

Housing: Homeownership rate: 88.6% (2007); Median home value: $132,714 (2007); Median rent: $479 per month (2000); Median age of housing: 47 years (2000).
Safety: Violent crime rate: 3.7 per 10,000 population; Property crime rate: 80.8 per 10,000 population (2007).
Transportation: Commute to work: 96.7% car, 0.0% public transportation, 0.4% walk, 2.3% work from home (2000); Travel time to work: 40.9% less than 15 minutes, 38.1% 15 to 30 minutes, 12.6% 30 to 45 minutes, 2.2% 45 to 60 minutes, 6.1% 60 minutes or more (2000)

SEBRING (village). Covers a land area of 2.051 square miles and a water area of 0 square miles. Located at 40.92° N. Lat.; 81.02° W. Long. Elevation is 1,099 feet.
Population: 4,848 (1990); 4,912 (2000); 4,643 (2007); 4,436 (2012 projected); Race: 98.1% White, 0.5% Black, 0.3% Asian, 0.9% Hispanic of any race (2007); Density: 2,263.9 persons per square mile (2007); Average household size: 2.38 (2007); Median age: 45.4 (2007); Males per 100 females: 79.6 (2007); Marriage status: 17.0% never married, 54.6% now married, 16.5% widowed, 11.9% divorced (2000); Foreign born: 0.7% (2000); Ancestry (includes multiple ancestries): 21.8% German, 14.3% Irish, 13.0% English, 10.7% United States or American, 7.3% Italian (2000).
Economy: Single-family building permits issued: 2 (2007); Multi-family building permits issued: 0 (2007); Employment by occupation: 8.6% management, 9.4% professional, 14.0% services, 24.7% sales, 0.5% farming, 7.5% construction, 35.3% production (2000).
Income: Per capita income: $19,841 (2007); Median household income: $37,262 (2007); Average household income: $44,823 (2007); Percent of households with income of $100,000 or more: 6.1% (2007); Poverty rate: 10.9% (2000).
Education: Percent of population age 25 and over with: High school diploma (including GED) or higher: 81.9% (2007); Bachelor's degree or higher: 13.5% (2007); Master's degree or higher: 3.7% (2007).

School District(s)

Sebring Local (PK-12)
 2005-06 Enrollment: 743 . . . . (330) 938-6165
Housing: Homeownership rate: 55.1% (2007); Median home value: $91,705 (2007); Median rent: $434 per month (2000); Median age of housing: 48 years (2000).
Safety: Violent crime rate: 2.2 per 10,000 population; Property crime rate: 74.1 per 10,000 population (2007).
Transportation: Commute to work: 95.7% car, 0.0% public transportation, 2.4% walk, 0.6% work from home (2000); Travel time to work: 48.4% less than 15 minutes, 25.6% 15 to 30 minutes, 15.1% 30 to 45 minutes, 7.0% 45 to 60 minutes, 3.9% 60 minutes or more (2000)
Additional Information Contacts
Village of Sebring . . . . (330) 938-9340
 http://www.sebringohio.net

STRUTHERS (city). Covers a land area of 3.732 square miles and a water area of 0.013 square miles. Located at 41.05° N. Lat.; 80.59° W. Long. Elevation is 1,007 feet.
History: Principal steel industry has declined. Founded 1800, incorporated 1922.
Population: 12,284 (1990); 11,756 (2000); 10,883 (2007); 10,385 (2012 projected); Race: 97.3% White, 1.0% Black, 0.3% Asian, 1.9% Hispanic of any race (2007); Density: 2,916.3 persons per square mile (2007); Average household size: 2.44 (2007); Median age: 40.9 (2007); Males per 100 females: 89.1 (2007); Marriage status: 25.3% never married, 54.8% now married, 10.7% widowed, 9.1% divorced (2000); Foreign born: 1.7% (2000); Ancestry (includes multiple ancestries): 28.3% Italian, 20.0% German, 16.1% Slovak, 15.8% Irish, 6.4% Polish (2000).
Economy: Employment by occupation: 4.5% management, 14.6% professional, 16.5% services, 29.0% sales, 0.1% farming, 10.4% construction, 24.9% production (2000).
Income: Per capita income: $18,740 (2007); Median household income: $35,881 (2007); Average household income: $45,344 (2007); Percent of households with income of $100,000 or more: 6.2% (2007); Poverty rate: 12.0% (2000).
Education: Percent of population age 25 and over with: High school diploma (including GED) or higher: 80.4% (2007); Bachelor's degree or higher: 10.3% (2007); Master's degree or higher: 2.6% (2007).

School District(s)

Struthers City (PK-12)
 2005-06 Enrollment: 2,077 . . . . (330) 750-1061

Two-year College(s)

The Youngstown College of Massotherapy (Private, For-profit)
 Fall 2007 Enrollment: n/a . . . . (330) 755-1406
Housing: Homeownership rate: 77.6% (2007); Median home value: $75,464 (2007); Median rent: $336 per month (2000); Median age of housing: 50 years (2000).
Safety: Violent crime rate: 19.1 per 10,000 population; Property crime rate: 368.6 per 10,000 population (2007).
Newspapers: Journal (Local news; Circulation 4,100)
Transportation: Commute to work: 96.5% car, 0.4% public transportation, 1.9% walk, 0.7% work from home (2000); Travel time to work: 35.7% less than 15 minutes, 44.6% 15 to 30 minutes, 13.4% 30 to 45 minutes, 2.3% 45 to 60 minutes, 4.0% 60 minutes or more (2000)
Additional Information Contacts
City of Struthers . . . . (330) 755-2181
 http://www.cityofstruthers.com

YOUNGSTOWN (city). County seat. Covers a land area of 33.896 square miles and a water area of 0.350 square miles. Located at 41.09° N. Lat.; 80.64° W. Long. Elevation is 850 feet.
History: Youngstown, established along the Mahoning River, was shaped by the steel industry. In 1797 John Young of New York led a party of settlers to this site. By 1802 James and Daniel Heaton had set up a crude smelter on Yellow Creek, utilizing native bog ores and limestones. The first coal mine in the Mahoning Valley opened in 1826, and Mahoning coal was soon used in the reduction of iron ore. In 1892 the Union Iron & Steel Company built a plant in Youngstown, and the banks of the river were soon lined with Bessemer converters, open-hearth furnaces, strip and rolling mills, pipe plants, and manufactories of steel accessories and products.
Population: 95,732 (1990); 82,026 (2000); 86,296 (2007); 87,538 (2012 projected); Race: 52.4% White, 41.2% Black, 0.6% Asian, 5.9% Hispanic of any race (2007); Density: 2,545.9 persons per square mile (2007); Average household size: 2.65 (2007); Median age: 36.2 (2007); Males per 100 females: 97.6 (2007); Marriage status: 34.0% never married, 42.2% now married, 11.0% widowed, 12.8% divorced (2000); Foreign born: 2.0% (2000); Ancestry (includes multiple ancestries): 42.7% Other groups, 11.2% Italian, 10.3% German, 9.4% Irish, 5.3% Slovak (2000).
Economy: Unemployment rate: 8.5% (6/2008); Total civilian labor force: 32,141 (6/2008); Single-family building permits issued: 9 (2007); Multi-family building permits issued: 0 (2007); Employment by occupation: 5.7% management, 13.1% professional, 24.1% services, 25.5% sales, 0.2% farming, 7.2% construction, 24.2% production (2000).
Income: Per capita income: $14,669 (2007); Median household income: $27,438 (2007); Average household income: $35,908 (2007); Percent of households with income of $100,000 or more: 4.2% (2007); Poverty rate: 24.8% (2000).
Taxes: Total city taxes per capita: $561 (2006); City property taxes per capita: $25 (2006).
Education: Percent of population age 25 and over with: High school diploma (including GED) or higher: 73.1% (2007); Bachelor's degree or higher: 9.9% (2007); Master's degree or higher: 2.9% (2007).

School District(s)

Austintown Local (PK-12)
 2005-06 Enrollment: 5,102 . . . . (330) 797-3900
Boardman Local (PK-12)
 2005-06 Enrollment: 4,849 . . . . (330) 726-3404
Eagle Heights Academy (KG-08)
 2005-06 Enrollment: 965 . . . . (330) 742-9090
Legacy Acad for Leaders & Arts (KG-08)
 2005-06 Enrollment: 251 . . . . (330) 747-1620
Liberty Local (PK-12)
 2005-06 Enrollment: 1,812 . . . . (330) 759-0807
Life Skills Ctr of Youngstown (09-12)
 2005-06 Enrollment: 264 . . . . (330) 743-6698
Mahoning Educational Service Center
 2005-06 Enrollment: n/a . . . . (330) 965-7828
Mahoning Unlimited Classroom (05-12)
 2005-06 Enrollment: 177 . . . . (330) 965-7828
Mollie Kessler (01-08)
 2005-06 Enrollment: 62 . . . . (330) 746-3095
Summit Academy Community School - Youngstown (05-09)
 2005-06 Enrollment: 55 . . . . (330) 747-0950
Summit Academy Secondary - Youngstown (09-12)
 2005-06 Enrollment: 37 . . . . (330) 747-0950
Summit Academy-Youngstown (KG-09)
 2005-06 Enrollment: 204 . . . . (330) 259-0421

Youngstown Academy of Excellence (KG-05)
2005-06 Enrollment: 104 . . . . (330) 746-3970
Youngstown City (PK-12)
2005-06 Enrollment: 8,819 . . . . (330) 744-6900
Youngstown Community School (KG-06)
2005-06 Enrollment: 339 . . . . (330) 746-2240

Four-year College(s)

Youngstown State University (Public)
Fall 2007 Enrollment: 13,595. . . . . (877) 468-6978
2007-08 Tuition: In-state $6,721; Out-of-state $9,414

Two-year College(s)

Casal Aveda Institute (Private, For-profit)
Fall 2007 Enrollment: 137 . . . . (330) 792-6504
ITT Technical Institute-Youngstown (Private, For-profit)
Fall 2007 Enrollment: 656 . . . . (330) 270-1600
2007-08 Tuition: In-state $15,600; Out-of-state $15,600

Vocational/Technical School(s)

Choffin Career and Technical Center (Public)
Fall 2007 Enrollment: 160 . . . . (330) 744-8710
2007-08 Tuition: In-state $5,000; Out-of-state $5,000

Housing: Homeownership rate: 64.7% (2007); Median home value: $47,805 (2007); Median rent: $296 per month (2000); Median age of housing: 53 years (2000).
Hospitals: Forum Health - Western Reserve Care System (830 beds); St. Elizabeth Health Center (350 beds)
Safety: Violent crime rate: 99.6 per 10,000 population; Property crime rate: 503.1 per 10,000 population (2007).
Newspapers: Buckeye Review (Local news; Circulation 3,000); Catholic Exponent (Regional news; Circulation 41,300); Jewish Journal (Local news; Circulation 5,000); The Vindicator (Local news; Circulation 87,213)
Transportation: Commute to work: 91.8% car, 2.7% public transportation, 2.6% walk, 1.7% work from home (2000); Travel time to work: 38.4% less than 15 minutes, 43.4% 15 to 30 minutes, 11.0% 30 to 45 minutes, 2.2% 45 to 60 minutes, 5.0% 60 minutes or more (2000)
Airports: Youngstown Elser Metro (general aviation); Youngstown-Warren Regional (primary service)

Additional Information Contacts

City of Youngstown . . . . (330) 742-8701
http://www.cityofyoungstownoh.org
Youngstown/Warren Regional Chamber of Commerce. . . . (330) 744-2131
http://www.regionalchamber.com

Marion County

Located in central Ohio; crossed by the Scioto River; drained by the Olentangy and Little Scioto Rivers. Covers a land area of 403.84 square miles, a water area of 0.30 square miles, and is located in the Eastern Time Zone. The county was founded in 1820. County seat is Marion.

Marion County is part of the Marion, OH Micropolitan Statistical Area. The entire metro area includes: Marion County, OH

Weather Station: Marion 2 N Elevation: 964 feet

	Jan	Feb	Mar	Apr	May	Jun	Jul	Aug	Sep	Oct	Nov	Dec
High	32	37	47	60	71	80	84	82	76	63	50	38
Low	16	19	28	37	48	58	62	59	52	41	32	23
Precip	2.4	1.7	2.3	3.7	4.2	4.2	4.4	3.7	3.0	2.7	3.0	2.8
Snow	9.7	5.3	3.2	0.6	0.0	0.0	0.0	0.0	0.0	tr	0.8	4.4

High and Low temperatures in degrees Fahrenheit; Precipitation and Snow in inches

Population: 64,274 (1990); 66,217 (2000); 65,791 (2007); 65,219 (2012 projected); Race: 91.7% White, 6.1% Black, 0.6% Asian, 1.4% Hispanic of any race (2007); Density: 162.9 persons per square mile (2007); Average household size: 2.66 (2007); Median age: 38.6 (2007); Males per 100 females: 109.4 (2007).
Religion: Five largest groups: 8.6% The United Methodist Church, 5.7% Evangelical Lutheran Church in America, 4.3% Catholic Church, 2.8% Church of the Nazarene, 2.7% American Baptist Churches in the USA (2000).
Economy: Unemployment rate: 6.9% (6/2008); Total civilian labor force: 33,115 (6/2008); Leading industries: 30.7% manufacturing; 18.7% health care and social assistance; 12.6% retail trade (2005); Farms: 520 totaling 205,605 acres (2002); Companies that employ 500 or more persons: 4 (2006); Companies that employ 100 to 499 persons: 35 (2006); Companies that employ less than 100 persons: 1,252 (2006); Black-owned businesses: n/a (2002); Hispanic-owned businesses: n/a (2002); Asian-owned businesses: n/a (2002); Women-owned businesses: 1,114 (2002); Retail sales per capita: $13,153 (2008). Single-family building permits issued: 95 (2007); Multi-family building permits issued: 210 (2007).
Income: Per capita income: $20,952 (2007); Median household income: $44,167 (2007); Average household income: $53,547 (2007); Percent of households with income of $100,000 or more: 9.8% (2007); Poverty rate: 14.7% (2005); Bankruptcy rate: 4.11% (2007).
Taxes: Total county taxes per capita: $210 (2006); County property taxes per capita: $108 (2006).
Education: Percent of population age 25 and over with: High school diploma (including GED) or higher: 80.7% (2007); Bachelor's degree or higher: 11.4% (2007); Master's degree or higher: 3.9% (2007).
Housing: Homeownership rate: 73.6% (2007); Median home value: $95,042 (2007); Median rent: $379 per month (2000); Median age of housing: 43 years (2000).
Health: Birth rate: 118.2 per 10,000 population (2007); Death rate: 97.5 per 10,000 population (2007); Age-adjusted cancer mortality rate: 222.3 deaths per 100,000 population (2005); Number of physicians: 16.6 per 10,000 population (2005); Hospital beds: 19.9 per 10,000 population (2004); Hospital admissions: 1,565.2 per 10,000 population (2004).
Elections: 2004 Presidential election results: 58.7% Bush, 40.8% Kerry, 0.0% Nader, 0.3% Badnarik

Additional Information Contacts

Marion County Government. . . . . (740) 223-4001
http://www.co.marion.oh.us
City of Marion. . . . . (740) 387-3591
http://www.marionohio.us
Marion Area Chamber of Commerce . . . . (740) 382-2181
http://www.marionareachamber.org

Marion County Communities

CALEDONIA (village). Covers a land area of 0.225 square miles and a water area of 0 square miles. Located at 40.63° N. Lat.; 82.96° W. Long. Elevation is 994 feet.
History: Caledonia was the boyhood home of Warren G. Harding, 29th President of the United States.
Population: 644 (1990); 578 (2000); 596 (2007); 602 (2012 projected); Race: 99.3% White, 0.3% Black, 0.0% Asian, 0.5% Hispanic of any race (2007); Density: 2,648.0 persons per square mile (2007); Average household size: 2.45 (2007); Median age: 38.6 (2007); Males per 100 females: 100.7 (2007); Marriage status: 14.7% never married, 68.2% now married, 8.1% widowed, 9.0% divorced (2000); Foreign born: 0.0% (2000); Ancestry (includes multiple ancestries): 23.9% German, 18.1% United States or American, 6.3% English, 3.9% Irish, 2.7% Other groups (2000).
Economy: Single-family building permits issued: 0 (2007); Multi-family building permits issued: 0 (2007); Employment by occupation: 7.1% management, 8.9% professional, 20.8% services, 27.5% sales, 2.2% farming, 6.3% construction, 27.1% production (2000).
Income: Per capita income: $21,938 (2007); Median household income: $47,656 (2007); Average household income: $53,807 (2007); Percent of households with income of $100,000 or more: 12.8% (2007); Poverty rate: 4.9% (2000).
Taxes: Total city taxes per capita: $108 (2006); City property taxes per capita: $104 (2006).
Education: Percent of population age 25 and over with: High school diploma (including GED) or higher: 85.1% (2007); Bachelor's degree or higher: 4.7% (2007); Master's degree or higher: 2.2% (2007).

School District(s)

River Valley Digital Academy (KG-11)
2005-06 Enrollment: 46 . . . . (740) 725-5401
River Valley Local (PK-12)
2005-06 Enrollment: 1,882 . . . . (740) 725-5400

Housing: Homeownership rate: 82.7% (2007); Median home value: $91,667 (2007); Median rent: $375 per month (2000); Median age of housing: 51 years (2000).
Transportation: Commute to work: 94.3% car, 0.0% public transportation, 3.0% walk, 2.6% work from home (2000); Travel time to work: 27.1% less than 15 minutes, 58.1% 15 to 30 minutes, 9.7% 30 to 45 minutes, 0.8% 45 to 60 minutes, 4.3% 60 minutes or more (2000)

GREEN CAMP (village). Covers a land area of 0.339 square miles and a water area of 0 square miles. Located at 40.53° N. Lat.; 83.20° W. Long. Elevation is 912 feet.

Population: 393 (1990); 342 (2000); 314 (2007); 301 (2012 projected); Race: 99.7% White, 0.0% Black, 0.0% Asian, 0.0% Hispanic of any race (2007); Density: 925.3 persons per square mile (2007); Average household size: 2.51 (2007); Median age: 37.9 (2007); Males per 100 females: 113.6 (2007); Marriage status: 21.4% never married, 63.0% now married, 7.5% widowed, 8.2% divorced (2000); Foreign born: 0.6% (2000); Ancestry (includes multiple ancestries): 32.7% United States or American, 26.8% German, 9.4% Irish, 8.8% English, 1.5% Welsh (2000).
Economy: Single-family building permits issued: 0 (2007); Multi-family building permits issued: 0 (2007); Employment by occupation: 5.9% management, 6.4% professional, 15.5% services, 16.0% sales, 1.1% farming, 10.2% construction, 44.9% production (2000).
Income: Per capita income: $20,884 (2007); Median household income: $48,929 (2007); Average household income: $52,460 (2007); Percent of households with income of $100,000 or more: 8.0% (2007); Poverty rate: 9.1% (2000).
Education: Percent of population age 25 and over with: High school diploma (including GED) or higher: 84.7% (2007); Bachelor's degree or higher: 5.6% (2007); Master's degree or higher: 3.3% (2007).

School District(s)

Elgin Local (PK-12)
2005-06 Enrollment: 1,658 . . . . (740) 382-1101

Housing: Homeownership rate: 79.2% (2007); Median home value: $85,417 (2007); Median rent: $378 per month (2000); Median age of housing: 60+ years (2000).
Transportation: Commute to work: 90.0% car, 1.1% public transportation, 3.3% walk, 4.4% work from home (2000); Travel time to work: 30.8% less than 15 minutes, 47.1% 15 to 30 minutes, 9.9% 30 to 45 minutes, 8.7% 45 to 60 minutes, 3.5% 60 minutes or more (2000)

LA RUE (village). Covers a land area of 0.482 square miles and a water area of 0 square miles. Located at 40.57° N. Lat.; 83.38° W. Long. Elevation is 925 feet.
History: La Rue was the home of the Oorang Dog Kennels, which used Olympic athlete Jim Thorpe and other Indian athletes to play exhibition football games advertising their highly trained dogs.
Population: 818 (1990); 775 (2000); 710 (2007); 682 (2012 projected); Race: 99.3% White, 0.0% Black, 0.0% Asian, 0.1% Hispanic of any race (2007); Density: 1,473.6 persons per square mile (2007); Average household size: 2.47 (2007); Median age: 37.8 (2007); Males per 100 females: 96.7 (2007); Marriage status: 21.0% never married, 60.4% now married, 7.4% widowed, 11.2% divorced (2000); Foreign born: 0.3% (2000); Ancestry (includes multiple ancestries): 20.2% German, 13.4% United States or American, 10.4% English, 9.1% Irish, 6.4% Other groups (2000).
Economy: Single-family building permits issued: 0 (2007); Multi-family building permits issued: 0 (2007); Employment by occupation: 3.9% management, 11.8% professional, 14.9% services, 18.5% sales, 1.7% farming, 6.5% construction, 42.7% production (2000).
Income: Per capita income: $18,601 (2007); Median household income: $37,750 (2007); Average household income: $45,767 (2007); Percent of households with income of $100,000 or more: 6.3% (2007); Poverty rate: 7.8% (2000).
Education: Percent of population age 25 and over with: High school diploma (including GED) or higher: 81.7% (2007); Bachelor's degree or higher: 4.0% (2007); Master's degree or higher: 1.1% (2007).

School District(s)

Elgin Local (PK-12)
2005-06 Enrollment: 1,658 . . . . (740) 382-1101

Housing: Homeownership rate: 70.4% (2007); Median home value: $67,586 (2007); Median rent: $255 per month (2000); Median age of housing: 54 years (2000).
Transportation: Commute to work: 91.9% car, 0.0% public transportation, 4.5% walk, 3.7% work from home (2000); Travel time to work: 16.3% less than 15 minutes, 27.7% 15 to 30 minutes, 38.2% 30 to 45 minutes, 11.7% 45 to 60 minutes, 6.1% 60 minutes or more (2000)

MARION (city). County seat. Covers a land area of 11.346 square miles and a water area of 0.044 square miles. Located at 40.58° N. Lat.; 83.12° W. Long. Elevation is 981 feet.
History: The site of Marion was selected as the seat of Marion County in 1824 because of the abundance of well water, discovered when some thirsty travelers stuck a wooden spade in the ground and named the spot Jacob's Well. The Marion Steam Shovel Company was organized in 1884, sending the name of Marion all over the world on its digging equipment.
Population: 36,526 (1990); 35,318 (2000); 33,939 (2007); 32,812 (2012 projected); Race: 90.8% White, 6.6% Black, 0.6% Asian, 1.7% Hispanic of any race (2007); Density: 2,991.3 persons per square mile (2007); Average household size: 2.58 (2007); Median age: 36.6 (2007); Males per 100 females: 106.0 (2007); Marriage status: 26.0% never married, 50.4% now married, 8.1% widowed, 15.5% divorced (2000); Foreign born: 1.5% (2000); Ancestry (includes multiple ancestries): 18.6% United States or American, 17.5% German, 13.1% Other groups, 9.5% Irish, 7.7% English (2000).
Economy: Unemployment rate: 7.2% (6/2008); Total civilian labor force: 17,674 (6/2008); Single-family building permits issued: 15 (2007); Multi-family building permits issued: 18 (2007); Employment by occupation: 7.3% management, 11.9% professional, 17.6% services, 25.9% sales, 0.4% farming, 8.0% construction, 28.9% production (2000).
Income: Per capita income: $18,410 (2007); Median household income: $37,729 (2007); Average household income: $45,990 (2007); Percent of households with income of $100,000 or more: 6.6% (2007); Poverty rate: 13.8% (2000).
Taxes: Total city taxes per capita: $399 (2006); City property taxes per capita: $43 (2006).
Education: Percent of population age 25 and over with: High school diploma (including GED) or higher: 76.1% (2007); Bachelor's degree or higher: 9.2% (2007); Master's degree or higher: 3.0% (2007).

School District(s)

Buckeye Academy
2005-06 Enrollment: n/a . . . .
Department of Youth Services (06-12)
2005-06 Enrollment: 1,478 . . . . (614) 728-2489
Elgin Digital Academy (05-12)
2005-06 Enrollment: 27 . . . . (740) 392-1101
Elgin Local (PK-12)
2005-06 Enrollment: 1,658 . . . . (740) 382-1101
Marion City (PK-12)
2005-06 Enrollment: 5,250 . . . . (740) 387-3300
Marion City Digital Academy (05-12)
2005-06 Enrollment: 111 . . . . (740) 223-4417
Pleasant Community Digital (KG-12)
2005-06 Enrollment: 88 . . . . (740) 389-4476
Pleasant Local (PK-12)
2005-06 Enrollment: 1,370 . . . . (740) 389-4476
River Valley Local (PK-12)
2005-06 Enrollment: 1,882 . . . . (740) 725-5400
Treca Digital Academy (KG-12)
2005-06 Enrollment: 1,028 . . . . (740) 389-4798
Tri-Rivers (PK-12)
2005-06 Enrollment: n/a . . . . (740) 389-4681

Four-year College(s)

Ohio State University-Marion Campus (Public)
Fall 2007 Enrollment: 1,633. . . . . (740) 389-6786
2007-08 Tuition: In-state $5,664; Out-of-state $18,273

Two-year College(s)

Marion Technical College (Public)
Fall 2007 Enrollment: 2,125. . . . . (740) 389-4636
2007-08 Tuition: In-state $3,660; Out-of-state $5,568

Vocational/Technical School(s)

Tri-Rivers Career Center (Public)
Fall 2007 Enrollment: 222 . . . . (740) 389-4681
2007-08 Tuition: $7,300

Housing: Homeownership rate: 63.7% (2007); Median home value: $81,792 (2007); Median rent: $371 per month (2000); Median age of housing: 52 years (2000).
Safety: Violent crime rate: 27.0 per 10,000 population; Property crime rate: 483.9 per 10,000 population (2007).
Newspapers: Marion Star (Local news; Circulation 14,000)
Transportation: Commute to work: 94.7% car, 0.9% public transportation, 1.8% walk, 1.2% work from home (2000); Travel time to work: 53.3% less than 15 minutes, 25.5% 15 to 30 minutes, 9.3% 30 to 45 minutes, 5.7% 45 to 60 minutes, 6.2% 60 minutes or more (2000)
Airports: Marion Municipal (general aviation)

Additional Information Contacts

City of Marion. . . . . (740) 387-3591
http://www.marionohio.us
Marion Area Chamber of Commerce. . . . . (740) 382-2181
http://www.marionareachamber.org

MORRAL (village). Covers a land area of 2.714 square miles and a water area of 0 square miles. Located at 40.68° N. Lat.; 83.21° W. Long. Elevation is 909 feet.
Population: 373 (1990); 388 (2000); 375 (2007); 368 (2012 projected); Race: 99.5% White, 0.0% Black, 0.0% Asian, 0.0% Hispanic of any race (2007); Density: 138.2 persons per square mile (2007); Average household size: 2.55 (2007); Median age: 41.6 (2007); Males per 100 females: 110.7 (2007); Marriage status: 20.8% never married, 64.5% now married, 3.9% widowed, 10.8% divorced (2000); Foreign born: 0.7% (2000); Ancestry (includes multiple ancestries): 15.1% German, 8.9% Irish, 7.9% English, 7.7% United States or American, 6.7% Other groups (2000).
Economy: Single-family building permits issued: 1 (2007); Multi-family building permits issued: 0 (2007); Employment by occupation: 4.5% management, 12.6% professional, 17.6% services, 29.6% sales, 0.0% farming, 8.0% construction, 27.6% production (2000).
Income: Per capita income: $17,233 (2007); Median household income: $43,056 (2007); Average household income: $43,963 (2007); Percent of households with income of $100,000 or more: 0.7% (2007); Poverty rate: 6.5% (2000).
Education: Percent of population age 25 and over with: High school diploma (including GED) or higher: 75.4% (2007); Bachelor's degree or higher: 3.2% (2007); Master's degree or higher: 2.4% (2007).

School District(s)

Ridgedale Community School (06-12)
2005-06 Enrollment: 38 . . . . (740) 382-6065
Ridgedale Local (PK-12)
2005-06 Enrollment: 936 . . . . (740) 382-6065
Housing: Homeownership rate: 88.4% (2007); Median home value: $70,000 (2007); Median rent: $365 per month (2000); Median age of housing: 60+ years (2000).
Transportation: Commute to work: 95.9% car, 0.0% public transportation, 1.5% walk, 2.5% work from home (2000); Travel time to work: 22.9% less than 15 minutes, 55.7% 15 to 30 minutes, 8.9% 30 to 45 minutes, 4.2% 45 to 60 minutes, 8.3% 60 minutes or more (2000)

NEW BLOOMINGTON (village). Aka Agosta. Covers a land area of 0.439 square miles and a water area of 0 square miles. Located at 40.58° N. Lat.; 83.31° W. Long. Elevation is 942 feet.
Population: 429 (1990); 548 (2000); 508 (2007); 486 (2012 projected); Race: 97.0% White, 0.0% Black, 0.0% Asian, 3.0% Hispanic of any race (2007); Density: 1,155.9 persons per square mile (2007); Average household size: 2.82 (2007); Median age: 33.3 (2007); Males per 100 females: 96.1 (2007); Marriage status: 22.9% never married, 60.8% now married, 2.8% widowed, 13.4% divorced (2000); Foreign born: 2.0% (2000); Ancestry (includes multiple ancestries): 27.0% United States or American, 16.0% Other groups, 15.3% German, 6.5% Irish, 5.4% English (2000).
Economy: Employment by occupation: 3.2% management, 3.2% professional, 14.1% services, 18.9% sales, 2.4% farming, 14.1% construction, 44.2% production (2000).
Income: Per capita income: $15,650 (2007); Median household income: $37,857 (2007); Average household income: $44,167 (2007); Percent of households with income of $100,000 or more: 2.2% (2007); Poverty rate: 11.7% (2000).
Education: Percent of population age 25 and over with: High school diploma (including GED) or higher: 71.0% (2007); Bachelor's degree or higher: 3.3% (2007); Master's degree or higher: 1.0% (2007).
Housing: Homeownership rate: 92.2% (2007); Median home value: $37,500 (2007); Median rent: $300 per month (2000); Median age of housing: 29 years (2000).
Transportation: Commute to work: 97.5% car, 0.8% public transportation, 0.8% walk, 0.0% work from home (2000); Travel time to work: 13.1% less than 15 minutes, 47.3% 15 to 30 minutes, 18.1% 30 to 45 minutes, 18.1% 45 to 60 minutes, 3.4% 60 minutes or more (2000)

PROSPECT (village). Covers a land area of 0.725 square miles and a water area of 0 square miles. Located at 40.45° N. Lat.; 83.18° W. Long. Elevation is 909 feet.
History: Settled 1832, incorporated as village 1876.
Population: 1,237 (1990); 1,191 (2000); 1,149 (2007); 1,123 (2012 projected); Race: 99.5% White, 0.0% Black, 0.0% Asian, 0.0% Hispanic of any race (2007); Density: 1,585.0 persons per square mile (2007); Average household size: 2.48 (2007); Median age: 37.5 (2007); Males per 100 females: 98.1 (2007); Marriage status: 22.4% never married, 61.1% now married, 5.8% widowed, 10.7% divorced (2000); Foreign born: 0.3% (2000); Ancestry (includes multiple ancestries): 26.5% German, 13.6% United States or American, 12.4% Irish, 9.9% English, 4.2% Dutch (2000).
Economy: Single-family building permits issued: 0 (2007); Multi-family building permits issued: 0 (2007); Employment by occupation: 7.5% management, 19.2% professional, 13.1% services, 17.8% sales, 0.6% farming, 8.7% construction, 33.0% production (2000).
Income: Per capita income: $23,814 (2007); Median household income: $52,966 (2007); Average household income: $59,098 (2007); Percent of households with income of $100,000 or more: 12.7% (2007); Poverty rate: 2.6% (2000).
Education: Percent of population age 25 and over with: High school diploma (including GED) or higher: 91.0% (2007); Bachelor's degree or higher: 15.4% (2007); Master's degree or higher: 6.0% (2007).

School District(s)

Elgin Local (PK-12)
2005-06 Enrollment: 1,658 . . . . (740) 382-1101
Housing: Homeownership rate: 76.0% (2007); Median home value: $103,226 (2007); Median rent: $402 per month (2000); Median age of housing: 60+ years (2000).
Transportation: Commute to work: 95.1% car, 0.0% public transportation, 3.9% walk, 1.0% work from home (2000); Travel time to work: 16.1% less than 15 minutes, 45.3% 15 to 30 minutes, 23.0% 30 to 45 minutes, 8.0% 45 to 60 minutes, 7.6% 60 minutes or more (2000)

WALDO (village). Covers a land area of 0.650 square miles and a water area of 0 square miles. Located at 40.45° N. Lat.; 83.07° W. Long. Elevation is 942 feet.
Population: 340 (1990); 332 (2000); 306 (2007); 304 (2012 projected); Race: 99.3% White, 0.0% Black, 0.7% Asian, 0.0% Hispanic of any race (2007); Density: 470.5 persons per square mile (2007); Average household size: 2.25 (2007); Median age: 42.0 (2007); Males per 100 females: 83.2 (2007); Marriage status: 23.2% never married, 58.3% now married, 11.4% widowed, 7.0% divorced (2000); Foreign born: 0.9% (2000); Ancestry (includes multiple ancestries): 33.7% German, 22.2% Irish, 15.7% United States or American, 5.9% Scottish, 5.0% English (2000).
Economy: Single-family building permits issued: 0 (2007); Multi-family building permits issued: 0 (2007); Employment by occupation: 6.0% management, 14.7% professional, 17.4% services, 28.3% sales, 0.0% farming, 15.2% construction, 18.5% production (2000).
Income: Per capita income: $18,742 (2007); Median household income: $35,294 (2007); Average household income: $42,169 (2007); Percent of households with income of $100,000 or more: 4.4% (2007); Poverty rate: 10.4% (2000).
Education: Percent of population age 25 and over with: High school diploma (including GED) or higher: 94.9% (2007); Bachelor's degree or higher: 12.6% (2007); Master's degree or higher: 3.7% (2007).
Housing: Homeownership rate: 80.1% (2007); Median home value: $97,917 (2007); Median rent: $425 per month (2000); Median age of housing: 60+ years (2000).
Transportation: Commute to work: 97.2% car, 0.0% public transportation, 2.8% walk, 0.0% work from home (2000); Travel time to work: 32.0% less than 15 minutes, 45.9% 15 to 30 minutes, 13.3% 30 to 45 minutes, 6.6% 45 to 60 minutes, 2.2% 60 minutes or more (2000)

Medina County

Located in northern Ohio; drained by the Rocky and Black Rivers; includes Chippewa Lake. Covers a land area of 421.55 square miles, a water area of 1.57 square miles, and is located in the Eastern Time Zone. The county was founded in 1812. County seat is Medina.

Medina County is part of the Cleveland-Elyria-Mentor, OH Metropolitan Statistical Area. The entire metro area includes: Cuyahoga County, OH; Geauga County, OH; Lake County, OH; Lorain County, OH; Medina County, OH

Weather Station: Chippewa Lake Elevation: 1,177 feet

	Jan	Feb	Mar	Apr	May	Jun	Jul	Aug	Sep	Oct	Nov	Dec
High	33	37	47	60	71	79	83	81	75	63	50	38
Low	17	18	27	36	47	56	60	58	52	41	32	23
Precip	2.3	2.1	3.0	3.4	3.6	3.8	3.9	3.6	3.7	2.5	3.4	3.0
Snow	10.7	8.6	6.7	2.1	tr	0.0	0.0	0.0	0.0	0.2	3.3	8.2

High and Low temperatures in degrees Fahrenheit; Precipitation and Snow in inches

Population: 122,354 (1990); 151,095 (2000); 171,010 (2007); 183,939 (2012 projected); Race: 96.4% White, 1.1% Black, 1.0% Asian, 1.1% Hispanic of any race (2007); Density: 405.7 persons per square mile (2007); Average household size: 2.72 (2007); Median age: 38.2 (2007); Males per 100 females: 97.3 (2007).
Religion: Five largest groups: 18.0% Catholic Church, 5.4% The United Methodist Church, 3.4% Evangelical Lutheran Church in America, 1.6% United Church of Christ, 1.6% Lutheran Church—Missouri Synod (2000).
Economy: Unemployment rate: 6.8% (6/2008); Total civilian labor force: 95,914 (6/2008); Leading industries: 18.5% manufacturing; 16.3% retail trade; 12.1% health care and social assistance (2005); Farms: 1,188 totaling 122,682 acres (2002); Companies that employ 500 or more persons: 5 (2006); Companies that employ 100 to 499 persons: 81 (2006); Companies that employ less than 100 persons: 4,015 (2006); Black-owned businesses: n/a (2002); Hispanic-owned businesses: 132 (2002); Asian-owned businesses: 246 (2002); Women-owned businesses: 3,466 (2002); Retail sales per capita: $14,450 (2008). Single-family building permits issued: 938 (2007); Multi-family building permits issued: 144 (2007).
Income: Per capita income: $28,442 (2007); Median household income: $64,844 (2007); Average household income: $76,965 (2007); Percent of households with income of $100,000 or more: 23.4% (2007); Poverty rate: 5.4% (2005); Bankruptcy rate: 3.62% (2007).
Taxes: Total county taxes per capita: $205 (2006); County property taxes per capita: $137 (2006).
Education: Percent of population age 25 and over with: High school diploma (including GED) or higher: 88.8% (2007); Bachelor's degree or higher: 24.8% (2007); Master's degree or higher: 7.0% (2007).
Housing: Homeownership rate: 82.1% (2007); Median home value: $182,942 (2007); Median rent: $521 per month (2000); Median age of housing: 25 years (2000).
Health: Birth rate: 129.9 per 10,000 population (2007); Death rate: 68.8 per 10,000 population (2007); Age-adjusted cancer mortality rate: 185.6 deaths per 100,000 population (2005); Air Quality Index: 83.4% good, 16.6% moderate, 0.0% unhealthy for sensitive individuals, 0.0% unhealthy (percent of days in 2007); Number of physicians: 15.6 per 10,000 population (2005); Hospital beds: 13.4 per 10,000 population (2004); Hospital admissions: 537.0 per 10,000 population (2004).
Elections: 2004 Presidential election results: 56.8% Bush, 42.7% Kerry, 0.0% Nader, 0.3% Badnarik
National and State Parks: Spencer Lake State Wildlife Area
Additional Information Contacts
Medina County Government . . . . (330) 722-9208
http://www.co.medina.oh.us
Brunswick Area Chamber of Commerce . . . . (330) 225-8411
http://www.brunswickareachamber.org
City of Brunswick . . . . (330) 225-9144
http://www.brunswick.oh.us
City of Medina . . . . (330) 725-8861
http://www.medinaoh.org
City of Wadsworth . . . . (330) 335-1521
http://www.wadsworthcity.com
Greater Medina Chamber of Commerce . . . . (330) 723-8773
http://www.medinaohchamber.com
Lodi Area Chamber of Commerce . . . . (330) 948-8047
http://www.lodiohiochamber.com
Medina County Convention & Visitors Bureau . . . . (330) 722-5502
http://www.visitmedinacounty.com
Valley City Chamber of Commerce . . . . (330) 483-1111
http://www.valleycity.org
Village of Seville . . . . (330) 769-4146
http://www.villageofseville.com
Wadsworth Chamber of Commerce . . . . (330) 336-6150
http://www.wadsworthchamber.com

Medina County Communities

BRUNSWICK (city). Covers a land area of 12.541 square miles and a water area of 0.042 square miles. Located at 41.24° N. Lat.; 81.82° W. Long. Elevation is 1,171 feet.
History: Named for its pleasing sound to early residents. Small farm community for many years; population burgeoned with the housing boom after World War II. Settled 1815 as part of the Conn. Western Reserve. Incorporated 1960.
Population: 28,743 (1990); 33,388 (2000); 35,519 (2007); 36,975 (2012 projected); Race: 95.9% White, 1.2% Black, 1.3% Asian, 1.7% Hispanic of any race (2007); Density: 2,832.3 persons per square mile (2007); Average household size: 2.74 (2007); Median age: 36.3 (2007); Males per 100 females: 96.5 (2007); Marriage status: 22.7% never married, 63.6% now married, 5.1% widowed, 8.7% divorced (2000); Foreign born: 4.3% (2000); Ancestry (includes multiple ancestries): 29.0% German, 18.7% Irish, 12.6% Polish, 11.7% Italian, 8.3% English (2000).
Economy: Unemployment rate: 6.8% (6/2008); Total civilian labor force: 20,260 (6/2008); Single-family building permits issued: 39 (2007); Multi-family building permits issued: 0 (2007); Employment by occupation: 13.0% management, 18.0% professional, 12.6% services, 28.1% sales, 0.1% farming, 11.1% construction, 17.0% production (2000).
Income: Per capita income: $25,610 (2007); Median household income: $63,235 (2007); Average household income: $69,730 (2007); Percent of households with income of $100,000 or more: 18.4% (2007); Poverty rate: 4.6% (2000).
Education: Percent of population age 25 and over with: High school diploma (including GED) or higher: 87.3% (2007); Bachelor's degree or higher: 19.4% (2007); Master's degree or higher: 4.2% (2007).

School District(s)

Brunswick City (PK-12)
2005-06 Enrollment: 7,467 . . . . (330) 225-7731

Two-year College(s)

Raphaels School of Beauty Culture (Private, For-profit)
Fall 2007 Enrollment: 46 . . . . (330) 225-0195
Housing: Homeownership rate: 80.4% (2007); Median home value: $165,534 (2007); Median rent: $536 per month (2000); Median age of housing: 25 years (2000).
Transportation: Commute to work: 95.3% car, 1.0% public transportation, 0.5% walk, 2.4% work from home (2000); Travel time to work: 21.4% less than 15 minutes, 32.7% 15 to 30 minutes, 30.1% 30 to 45 minutes, 11.0% 45 to 60 minutes, 4.8% 60 minutes or more (2000)
Additional Information Contacts
Brunswick Area Chamber of Commerce . . . . (330) 225-8411
http://www.brunswickareachamber.org
City of Brunswick . . . . (330) 225-9144
http://www.brunswick.oh.us

CHIPPEWA LAKE (village). Aka Chippewa-on-the-Lake. Covers a land area of 0.271 square miles and a water area of 0.001 square miles. Located at 41.07° N. Lat.; 81.90° W. Long. Elevation is 1,020 feet.
Population: 938 (1990); 823 (2000); 853 (2007); 869 (2012 projected); Race: 98.6% White, 0.2% Black, 0.2% Asian, 0.9% Hispanic of any race (2007); Density: 3,145.9 persons per square mile (2007); Average household size: 2.42 (2007); Median age: 38.7 (2007); Males per 100 females: 108.0 (2007); Marriage status: 29.7% never married, 50.9% now married, 6.6% widowed, 12.8% divorced (2000); Foreign born: 1.3% (2000); Ancestry (includes multiple ancestries): 33.7% German, 16.3% Irish, 15.6% English, 7.9% Other groups, 7.2% Italian (2000).
Economy: Employment by occupation: 8.8% management, 7.9% professional, 20.4% services, 27.7% sales, 0.0% farming, 17.8% construction, 17.4% production (2000).
Income: Per capita income: $23,625 (2007); Median household income: $49,091 (2007); Average household income: $57,251 (2007); Percent of households with income of $100,000 or more: 11.4% (2007); Poverty rate: 9.2% (2000).
Education: Percent of population age 25 and over with: High school diploma (including GED) or higher: 83.1% (2007); Bachelor's degree or higher: 14.2% (2007); Master's degree or higher: 4.4% (2007).
Housing: Homeownership rate: 82.7% (2007); Median home value: $122,375 (2007); Median rent: $433 per month (2000); Median age of housing: 43 years (2000).
Transportation: Commute to work: 94.3% car, 1.8% public transportation, 0.0% walk, 3.4% work from home (2000); Travel time to work: 29.5% less than 15 minutes, 32.1% 15 to 30 minutes, 25.5% 30 to 45 minutes, 7.5% 45 to 60 minutes, 5.4% 60 minutes or more (2000)

GLORIA GLENS PARK (village). Covers a land area of 0.114 square miles and a water area of 0 square miles. Located at 41.05° N. Lat.; 81.90° W. Long. Elevation is 1,010 feet.
Population: 484 (1990); 538 (2000); 605 (2007); 646 (2012 projected); Race: 99.2% White, 0.0% Black, 0.0% Asian, 0.3% Hispanic of any race (2007); Density: 5,319.9 persons per square mile (2007); Average household size: 2.63 (2007); Median age: 35.9 (2007); Males per 100

females: 106.5 (2007); Marriage status: 22.7% never married, 56.6% now married, 6.5% widowed, 14.2% divorced (2000); Foreign born: 0.4% (2000); Ancestry (includes multiple ancestries): 30.2% German, 19.8% Irish, 12.1% English, 11.2% Polish, 5.7% Italian (2000).
Economy: Employment by occupation: 8.1% management, 13.0% professional, 18.5% services, 26.3% sales, 0.0% farming, 13.0% construction, 21.1% production (2000).
Income: Per capita income: $22,442 (2007); Median household income: $54,000 (2007); Average household income: $59,033 (2007); Percent of households with income of $100,000 or more: 10.0% (2007); Poverty rate: 1.3% (2000).
Education: Percent of population age 25 and over with: High school diploma (including GED) or higher: 87.5% (2007); Bachelor's degree or higher: 14.0% (2007); Master's degree or higher: 1.3% (2007).
Housing: Homeownership rate: 76.1% (2007); Median home value: $116,607 (2007); Median rent: $536 per month (2000); Median age of housing: 48 years (2000).
Transportation: Commute to work: 97.4% car, 0.3% public transportation, 0.3% walk, 1.6% work from home (2000); Travel time to work: 24.7% less than 15 minutes, 36.8% 15 to 30 minutes, 24.4% 30 to 45 minutes, 6.4% 45 to 60 minutes, 7.7% 60 minutes or more (2000)

HINCKLEY (unincorporated postal area, zip code 44233). Covers a land area of 26.816 square miles and a water area of 0.136 square miles. Located at 41.23° N. Lat.; 81.73° W. Long. Elevation is 1,100 feet.
Population: 6,777 (2000); Race: 99.8% White, 0.0% Black, 0.2% Asian, 1.0% Hispanic of any race (2000); Density: 252.7 persons per square mile (2000); Age: 25.3% under 18, 10.5% over 64 (2000); Marriage status: 19.7% never married, 70.7% now married, 4.6% widowed, 5.1% divorced (2000); Foreign born: 6.1% (2000); Ancestry (includes multiple ancestries): 28.6% German, 15.9% Polish, 15.1% Irish, 12.3% English, 12.0% Italian (2000).
Economy: Employment by occupation: 16.0% management, 20.0% professional, 12.4% services, 24.6% sales, 0.0% farming, 13.8% construction, 13.1% production (2000).
Income: Per capita income: $29,186 (2000); Median household income: $70,548 (2000); Poverty rate: 2.7% (2000).
Education: Percent of population age 25 and over with: High school diploma (including GED) or higher: 89.5% (2000); Bachelor's degree or higher: 26.2% (2000).

School District(s)

Highland Local (PK-12)
2005-06 Enrollment: 3,069 . . . . (330) 239-1901
Housing: Homeownership rate: 95.1% (2000); Median home value: $208,800 (2000); Median rent: $547 per month (2000); Median age of housing: 28 years (2000).
Transportation: Commute to work: 94.3% car, 0.4% public transportation, 1.1% walk, 3.7% work from home (2000); Travel time to work: 14.6% less than 15 minutes, 38.1% 15 to 30 minutes, 32.8% 30 to 45 minutes, 10.3% 45 to 60 minutes, 4.3% 60 minutes or more (2000)

HOMERVILLE (unincorporated postal area, zip code 44235). Covers a land area of 26.255 square miles and a water area of 0.030 square miles. Located at 41.02° N. Lat.; 82.11° W. Long. Elevation is 1,083 feet.
Population: 1,873 (2000); Race: 96.9% White, 1.8% Black, 0.0% Asian, 0.0% Hispanic of any race (2000); Density: 71.3 persons per square mile (2000); Age: 34.0% under 18, 6.0% over 64 (2000); Marriage status: 25.2% never married, 67.7% now married, 4.9% widowed, 2.3% divorced (2000); Foreign born: 1.2% (2000); Ancestry (includes multiple ancestries): 29.5% German, 22.5% United States or American, 15.7% English, 10.3% Polish, 9.9% Irish (2000).
Economy: Employment by occupation: 14.7% management, 16.2% professional, 8.0% services, 17.7% sales, 1.7% farming, 17.0% construction, 24.7% production (2000).
Income: Per capita income: $15,437 (2000); Median household income: $47,760 (2000); Poverty rate: 21.3% (2000).
Education: Percent of population age 25 and over with: High school diploma (including GED) or higher: 72.8% (2000); Bachelor's degree or higher: 14.5% (2000).
Housing: Homeownership rate: 88.0% (2000); Median home value: $119,700 (2000); Median rent: $417 per month (2000); Median age of housing: 26 years (2000).
Transportation: Commute to work: 82.9% car, 2.5% public transportation, 2.6% walk, 9.1% work from home (2000); Travel time to work: 18.3% less than 15 minutes, 16.2% 15 to 30 minutes, 31.2% 30 to 45 minutes, 10.4% 45 to 60 minutes, 23.9% 60 minutes or more (2000)

LITCHFIELD (unincorporated postal area, zip code 44253). Covers a land area of 25.487 square miles and a water area of 0.018 square miles. Located at 41.16° N. Lat.; 82.03° W. Long. Elevation is 1,010 feet.
Population: 3,312 (2000); Race: 96.5% White, 0.2% Black, 0.5% Asian, 0.5% Hispanic of any race (2000); Density: 130.0 persons per square mile (2000); Age: 30.2% under 18, 8.2% over 64 (2000); Marriage status: 21.0% never married, 67.0% now married, 4.1% widowed, 7.8% divorced (2000); Foreign born: 1.2% (2000); Ancestry (includes multiple ancestries): 37.5% German, 13.9% Irish, 11.6% English, 10.8% United States or American, 10.1% Polish (2000).
Economy: Employment by occupation: 11.4% management, 12.4% professional, 13.9% services, 25.0% sales, 0.4% farming, 15.9% construction, 21.0% production (2000).
Income: Per capita income: $20,288 (2000); Median household income: $56,563 (2000); Poverty rate: 5.6% (2000).
Education: Percent of population age 25 and over with: High school diploma (including GED) or higher: 87.0% (2000); Bachelor's degree or higher: 13.3% (2000).

School District(s)

Buckeye Local (PK-12)
2005-06 Enrollment: 2,384 . . . . (330) 722-8257
Housing: Homeownership rate: 92.9% (2000); Median home value: $150,800 (2000); Median rent: $658 per month (2000); Median age of housing: 24 years (2000).
Transportation: Commute to work: 95.3% car, 0.6% public transportation, 0.4% walk, 2.1% work from home (2000); Travel time to work: 14.8% less than 15 minutes, 42.9% 15 to 30 minutes, 18.3% 30 to 45 minutes, 12.3% 45 to 60 minutes, 11.6% 60 minutes or more (2000)

LODI (village). Covers a land area of 2.119 square miles and a water area of 0.008 square miles. Located at 41.03° N. Lat.; 82.01° W. Long. Elevation is 928 feet.
History: Lodi was founded in 1824 by Judge Joseph Harris, who built his house on an ancient Indian mound. The town developed as a distribution center for dairy products and fertilizers.
Population: 3,050 (1990); 3,061 (2000); 3,334 (2007); 3,518 (2012 projected); Race: 98.1% White, 0.0% Black, 0.2% Asian, 0.6% Hispanic of any race (2007); Density: 1,573.3 persons per square mile (2007); Average household size: 2.35 (2007); Median age: 37.1 (2007); Males per 100 females: 91.8 (2007); Marriage status: 21.6% never married, 52.8% now married, 8.1% widowed, 17.5% divorced (2000); Foreign born: 1.4% (2000); Ancestry (includes multiple ancestries): 29.4% German, 15.5% Irish, 10.4% English, 9.3% United States or American, 7.9% Other groups (2000).
Economy: Employment by occupation: 9.9% management, 4.3% professional, 18.5% services, 30.6% sales, 0.0% farming, 8.9% construction, 27.7% production (2000).
Income: Per capita income: $19,371 (2007); Median household income: $36,425 (2007); Average household income: $44,872 (2007); Percent of households with income of $100,000 or more: 5.7% (2007); Poverty rate: 10.1% (2000).
Education: Percent of population age 25 and over with: High school diploma (including GED) or higher: 78.2% (2007); Bachelor's degree or higher: 6.3% (2007); Master's degree or higher: 0.5% (2007).

School District(s)

Cloverleaf Local (PK-12)
2005-06 Enrollment: 3,390 . . . . (330) 948-2500
Housing: Homeownership rate: 65.6% (2007); Median home value: $109,511 (2007); Median rent: $419 per month (2000); Median age of housing: 36 years (2000).
Hospitals: Lodi Community Hospital (25 beds)
Transportation: Commute to work: 94.3% car, 0.6% public transportation, 2.7% walk, 2.2% work from home (2000); Travel time to work: 31.2% less than 15 minutes, 37.8% 15 to 30 minutes, 13.2% 30 to 45 minutes, 11.4% 45 to 60 minutes, 6.4% 60 minutes or more (2000)

Additional Information Contacts

Lodi Area Chamber of Commerce . . . . (330) 948-8047
http://www.lodiohiochamber.com

MEDINA (city). County seat. Covers a land area of 11.127 square miles and a water area of 0.194 square miles. Located at 41.13° N. Lat.; 81.86° W. Long. Elevation is 1,089 feet.

History: Named for the city of Hejaz, Saudi Arabia, to which Mohammed made his flight from Mecca in 622. Medina was platted in 1818 by a Captain Badger, who built a log cabin on the site. The town, first called Mecca, became known for its bee culture and honey products, calling itself the "sweetest town on earth."
Population: 19,807 (1990); 25,139 (2000); 26,900 (2007); 28,256 (2012 projected); Race: 93.3% White, 3.4% Black, 1.2% Asian, 1.2% Hispanic of any race (2007); Density: 2,417.6 persons per square mile (2007); Average household size: 2.64 (2007); Median age: 34.6 (2007); Males per 100 females: 93.3 (2007); Marriage status: 20.3% never married, 64.5% now married, 6.6% widowed, 8.7% divorced (2000); Foreign born: 2.7% (2000); Ancestry (includes multiple ancestries): 32.7% German, 16.7% Irish, 11.9% English, 9.6% Italian, 8.8% Polish (2000).
Economy: Unemployment rate: 6.6% (6/2008); Total civilian labor force: 14,344 (6/2008); Single-family building permits issued: 3 (2007); Multi-family building permits issued: 0 (2007); Employment by occupation: 15.0% management, 21.2% professional, 12.1% services, 29.8% sales, 0.1% farming, 7.4% construction, 14.3% production (2000).
Income: Per capita income: $26,219 (2007); Median household income: $58,201 (2007); Average household income: $67,953 (2007); Percent of households with income of $100,000 or more: 20.7% (2007); Poverty rate: 5.7% (2000).
Education: Percent of population age 25 and over with: High school diploma (including GED) or higher: 90.9% (2007); Bachelor's degree or higher: 33.2% (2007); Master's degree or higher: 8.4% (2007).

School District(s)

Buckeye Local (PK-12)
2005-06 Enrollment: 2,384 . . . . (330) 722-8257
Highland Local (PK-12)
2005-06 Enrollment: 3,069 . . . . (330) 239-1901
Medina City (PK-12)
2005-06 Enrollment: 7,488 . . . . (330) 636-3000
Medina County (PK-12)
2005-06 Enrollment: n/a . . . . (330) 725-8461

Vocational/Technical School(s)

Hamrick School (Private, For-profit)
Fall 2007 Enrollment: 140 . . . . (330) 239-2229
2007-08 Tuition: $5,877
Medina County Career Center (Public)
Fall 2007 Enrollment: 55 . . . . (330) 725-8461
2007-08 Tuition: $4,243

Housing: Homeownership rate: 68.0% (2007); Median home value: $170,125 (2007); Median rent: $525 per month (2000); Median age of housing: 23 years (2000).
Hospitals: Medina General Hospital (118 beds)
Newspapers: Brunswick Sun Times (Community news; Circulation 6,076); The Gazette (Local news; Circulation 16,500); The Medina County Women's Journal (Local news; Circulation 16,000); The Montrose Sun (Local news); Sun Banner Pride (Community news; Circulation 3,319); Sun Newspapers - Medina Bureau (Local news); West Akron Sun (Local news)
Transportation: Commute to work: 93.8% car, 0.7% public transportation, 1.6% walk, 2.9% work from home (2000); Travel time to work: 35.2% less than 15 minutes, 25.5% 15 to 30 minutes, 21.6% 30 to 45 minutes, 11.6% 45 to 60 minutes, 6.0% 60 minutes or more (2000)

Additional Information Contacts

City of Medina . . . . (330) 725-8861
http://www.medinaoh.org
Greater Medina Chamber of Commerce . . . . (330) 723-8773
http://www.medinaohchamber.com
Medina County Convention & Visitors Bureau. . . . . (330) 722-5502
http://www.visitmedinacounty.com

SEVILLE (village). Covers a land area of 2.017 square miles and a water area of 0 square miles. Located at 41.01° N. Lat.; 81.86° W. Long. Elevation is 978 feet.
Population: 1,812 (1990); 2,160 (2000); 2,436 (2007); 2,612 (2012 projected); Race: 99.0% White, 0.2% Black, 0.2% Asian, 0.8% Hispanic of any race (2007); Density: 1,207.8 persons per square mile (2007); Average household size: 2.61 (2007); Median age: 39.2 (2007); Males per 100 females: 89.7 (2007); Marriage status: 17.1% never married, 65.2% now married, 8.3% widowed, 9.4% divorced (2000); Foreign born: 0.9% (2000); Ancestry (includes multiple ancestries): 29.9% German, 14.8% Irish, 13.1% English, 5.1% Italian, 4.7% Other groups (2000).
Economy: Employment by occupation: 11.8% management, 13.2% professional, 14.0% services, 30.3% sales, 0.4% farming, 10.2% construction, 20.1% production (2000).
Income: Per capita income: $26,177 (2007); Median household income: $57,045 (2007); Average household income: $67,596 (2007); Percent of households with income of $100,000 or more: 16.6% (2007); Poverty rate: 3.7% (2000).
Education: Percent of population age 25 and over with: High school diploma (including GED) or higher: 89.2% (2007); Bachelor's degree or higher: 17.3% (2007); Master's degree or higher: 5.4% (2007).

School District(s)

Cloverleaf Local (PK-12)
2005-06 Enrollment: 3,390 . . . . (330) 948-2500

Housing: Homeownership rate: 82.3% (2007); Median home value: $140,064 (2007); Median rent: $479 per month (2000); Median age of housing: 26 years (2000).
Safety: Violent crime rate: 8.1 per 10,000 population; Property crime rate: 223.2 per 10,000 population (2007).
Transportation: Commute to work: 95.1% car, 0.0% public transportation, 2.3% walk, 2.3% work from home (2000); Travel time to work: 22.0% less than 15 minutes, 44.1% 15 to 30 minutes, 17.8% 30 to 45 minutes, 9.3% 45 to 60 minutes, 6.8% 60 minutes or more (2000)

Additional Information Contacts

Village of Seville. . . . . (330) 769-4146
http://www.villageofseville.com

SPENCER (village). Covers a land area of 0.988 square miles and a water area of 0.008 square miles. Located at 41.10° N. Lat.; 82.12° W. Long. Elevation is 912 feet.
Population: 726 (1990); 747 (2000); 939 (2007); 1,062 (2012 projected); Race: 98.4% White, 0.0% Black, 0.2% Asian, 1.2% Hispanic of any race (2007); Density: 950.1 persons per square mile (2007); Average household size: 2.54 (2007); Median age: 35.6 (2007); Males per 100 females: 96.9 (2007); Marriage status: 19.0% never married, 60.6% now married, 9.7% widowed, 10.7% divorced (2000); Foreign born: 1.5% (2000); Ancestry (includes multiple ancestries): 28.1% German, 24.8% United States or American, 12.4% Irish, 11.3% English, 6.1% Polish (2000).
Economy: Employment by occupation: 7.0% management, 11.0% professional, 13.0% services, 25.6% sales, 3.4% farming, 17.5% construction, 22.5% production (2000).
Income: Per capita income: $20,809 (2007); Median household income: $43,300 (2007); Average household income: $52,954 (2007); Percent of households with income of $100,000 or more: 8.9% (2007); Poverty rate: 3.9% (2000).
Education: Percent of population age 25 and over with: High school diploma (including GED) or higher: 85.3% (2007); Bachelor's degree or higher: 7.7% (2007); Master's degree or higher: 2.4% (2007).

School District(s)

Cloverleaf Local (PK-12)
2005-06 Enrollment: 3,390 . . . . (330) 948-2500

Housing: Homeownership rate: 69.6% (2007); Median home value: $117,952 (2007); Median rent: $470 per month (2000); Median age of housing: 60+ years (2000).
Safety: Violent crime rate: 0.0 per 10,000 population; Property crime rate: 84.8 per 10,000 population (2007).
Transportation: Commute to work: 94.2% car, 0.0% public transportation, 1.7% walk, 2.0% work from home (2000); Travel time to work: 15.6% less than 15 minutes, 36.9% 15 to 30 minutes, 26.8% 30 to 45 minutes, 8.8% 45 to 60 minutes, 11.8% 60 minutes or more (2000)

VALLEY CITY (unincorporated postal area, zip code 44280). Covers a land area of 24.786 square miles and a water area of 0.010 square miles. Located at 41.23° N. Lat.; 81.92° W. Long. Elevation is 815 feet.
Population: 4,150 (2000); Race: 98.1% White, 0.0% Black, 0.0% Asian, 1.5% Hispanic of any race (2000); Density: 167.4 persons per square mile (2000); Age: 22.9% under 18, 14.1% over 64 (2000); Marriage status: 18.6% never married, 67.7% now married, 6.6% widowed, 7.2% divorced (2000); Foreign born: 2.5% (2000); Ancestry (includes multiple ancestries): 38.0% German, 15.1% Irish, 12.5% English, 10.4% Polish, 7.7% Italian (2000).
Economy: Employment by occupation: 12.3% management, 19.4% professional, 17.0% services, 23.7% sales, 0.0% farming, 15.2% construction, 12.4% production (2000).
Income: Per capita income: $25,583 (2000); Median household income: $59,972 (2000); Poverty rate: 3.5% (2000).

Education: Percent of population age 25 and over with: High school diploma (including GED) or higher: 86.1% (2000); Bachelor's degree or higher: 20.3% (2000).
Housing: Homeownership rate: 92.6% (2000); Median home value: $166,100 (2000); Median rent: $637 per month (2000); Median age of housing: 26 years (2000).
Transportation: Commute to work: 91.6% car, 0.8% public transportation, 0.4% walk, 7.2% work from home (2000); Travel time to work: 20.8% less than 15 minutes, 33.2% 15 to 30 minutes, 26.6% 30 to 45 minutes, 12.4% 45 to 60 minutes, 7.0% 60 minutes or more (2000)
Additional Information Contacts
Valley City Chamber of Commerce . . . . (330) 483-1111
http://www.valleycity.org

WADSWORTH (city). Covers a land area of 9.501 square miles and a water area of 0 square miles. Located at 41.02° N. Lat.; 81.73° W. Long. Elevation is 1,168 feet.
History: Named for Colonel E. Wadsworth. Wadsworth developed as an industrial town, manufacturing matches, valves, locomotive appliances, and lubricators.
Population: 16,147 (1990); 18,437 (2000); 19,804 (2007); 20,751 (2012 projected); Race: 97.1% White, 0.4% Black, 1.0% Asian, 0.9% Hispanic of any race (2007); Density: 2,084.4 persons per square mile (2007); Average household size: 2.48 (2007); Median age: 38.6 (2007); Males per 100 females: 93.4 (2007); Marriage status: 17.9% never married, 65.0% now married, 8.3% widowed, 8.8% divorced (2000); Foreign born: 2.5% (2000); Ancestry (includes multiple ancestries): 34.5% German, 15.8% Irish, 11.7% English, 8.7% Italian, 7.5% United States or American (2000).
Economy: Single-family building permits issued: 50 (2007); Multi-family building permits issued: 144 (2007); Employment by occupation: 15.3% management, 19.7% professional, 14.2% services, 25.7% sales, 0.1% farming, 9.3% construction, 15.6% production (2000).
Income: Per capita income: $27,280 (2007); Median household income: $56,630 (2007); Average household income: $67,312 (2007); Percent of households with income of $100,000 or more: 18.3% (2007); Poverty rate: 5.4% (2000).
Taxes: Total city taxes per capita: $471 (2006); City property taxes per capita: $111 (2006).
Education: Percent of population age 25 and over with: High school diploma (including GED) or higher: 88.4% (2007); Bachelor's degree or higher: 27.2% (2007); Master's degree or higher: 7.1% (2007).

School District(s)

Wadsworth City (PK-12)
2005-06 Enrollment: 4,742 . . . . (330) 336-3571
Housing: Homeownership rate: 74.5% (2007); Median home value: $161,104 (2007); Median rent: $470 per month (2000); Median age of housing: 35 years (2000).
Hospitals: Wadsworth-Rittman Hospital (113 beds)
Safety: Violent crime rate: 7.4 per 10,000 population; Property crime rate: 204.0 per 10,000 population (2007).
Transportation: Commute to work: 94.3% car, 0.2% public transportation, 1.3% walk, 3.5% work from home (2000); Travel time to work: 34.6% less than 15 minutes, 44.0% 15 to 30 minutes, 12.6% 30 to 45 minutes, 5.0% 45 to 60 minutes, 3.9% 60 minutes or more (2000)
Additional Information Contacts
City of Wadsworth . . . . (330) 335-1521
http://www.wadsworthcity.com
Wadsworth Chamber of Commerce. . . . . (330) 336-6150
http://www.wadsworthchamber.com

WESTFIELD CENTER (village). Aka Leroy. Covers a land area of 2.113 square miles and a water area of 0 square miles. Located at 41.03° N. Lat.; 81.93° W. Long. Elevation is 1,099 feet.
Population: 915 (1990); 1,054 (2000); 1,090 (2007); 1,107 (2012 projected); Race: 98.6% White, 0.0% Black, 0.6% Asian, 0.6% Hispanic of any race (2007); Density: 515.9 persons per square mile (2007); Average household size: 2.56 (2007); Median age: 43.7 (2007); Males per 100 females: 99.3 (2007); Marriage status: 16.7% never married, 74.3% now married, 3.9% widowed, 5.2% divorced (2000); Foreign born: 1.3% (2000); Ancestry (includes multiple ancestries): 35.9% German, 21.8% English, 17.1% Irish, 7.8% Polish, 7.4% Italian (2000).
Economy: Employment by occupation: 22.2% management, 25.2% professional, 8.6% services, 33.6% sales, 0.0% farming, 4.7% construction, 5.7% production (2000).
Income: Per capita income: $39,901 (2007); Median household income: $78,716 (2007); Average household income: $102,095 (2007); Percent of households with income of $100,000 or more: 35.2% (2007); Poverty rate: 3.0% (2000).
Education: Percent of population age 25 and over with: High school diploma (including GED) or higher: 98.2% (2007); Bachelor's degree or higher: 47.1% (2007); Master's degree or higher: 12.8% (2007).

School District(s)

Cloverleaf Local (PK-12)
2005-06 Enrollment: 3,390 . . . . (330) 948-2500
Housing: Homeownership rate: 90.8% (2007); Median home value: $220,644 (2007); Median rent: $563 per month (2000); Median age of housing: 27 years (2000).
Transportation: Commute to work: 90.4% car, 0.7% public transportation, 4.0% walk, 4.3% work from home (2000); Travel time to work: 40.3% less than 15 minutes, 26.1% 15 to 30 minutes, 20.6% 30 to 45 minutes, 7.6% 45 to 60 minutes, 5.5% 60 minutes or more (2000)

Meigs County

Located in southeastern Ohio; bounded on the southeast by the Ohio River and the West Virginia border; drained by the Shade River and Leading Creek. Covers a land area of 429.42 square miles, a water area of 2.95 square miles, and is located in the Eastern Time Zone. The county was founded in 1819. County seat is Pomeroy.
Population: 22,987 (1990); 23,072 (2000); 23,280 (2007); 23,348 (2012 projected); Race: 97.7% White, 1.0% Black, 0.2% Asian, 0.5% Hispanic of any race (2007); Density: 54.2 persons per square mile (2007); Average household size: 2.43 (2007); Median age: 40.4 (2007); Males per 100 females: 96.1 (2007).
Religion: Five largest groups: 6.7% The United Methodist Church, 5.4% Christian Churches and Churches of Christ, 3.5% Church of the Nazarene, 1.7% Southern Baptist Convention, 1.5% Churches of Christ (2000).
Economy: Unemployment rate: 10.0% (6/2008); Total civilian labor force: 9,160 (6/2008); Leading industries: 24.1% retail trade; 20.4% health care and social assistance; 17.0% accommodation & food services (2005); Farms: 552 totaling 90,362 acres (2002); Companies that employ 500 or more persons: 0 (2006); Companies that employ 100 to 499 persons: 2 (2006); Companies that employ less than 100 persons: 330 (2006); Black-owned businesses: n/a (2002); Hispanic-owned businesses: n/a (2002); Asian-owned businesses: n/a (2002); Women-owned businesses: n/a (2002); Retail sales per capita: $6,683 (2008). Single-family building permits issued: 10 (2007); Multi-family building permits issued: 0 (2007).
Income: Per capita income: $15,970 (2007); Median household income: $30,058 (2007); Average household income: $38,617 (2007); Percent of households with income of $100,000 or more: 4.4% (2007); Poverty rate: 19.9% (2005); Bankruptcy rate: 2.01% (2007).
Education: Percent of population age 25 and over with: High school diploma (including GED) or higher: 73.1% (2007); Bachelor's degree or higher: 7.3% (2007); Master's degree or higher: 2.5% (2007).
Housing: Homeownership rate: 79.5% (2007); Median home value: $70,662 (2007); Median rent: $263 per month (2000); Median age of housing: 30 years (2000).
Health: Birth rate: 123.6 per 10,000 population (2007); Death rate: 110.5 per 10,000 population (2007); Age-adjusted cancer mortality rate: 245.8 deaths per 100,000 population (2005); Air Quality Index: 100.0% good, 0.0% moderate, 0.0% unhealthy for sensitive individuals, 0.0% unhealthy (percent of days in 2007); Number of physicians: 2.6 per 10,000 population (2005); Hospital beds: 0.0 per 10,000 population (2004); Hospital admissions: 0.0 per 10,000 population (2004).
Elections: 2004 Presidential election results: 58.2% Bush, 41.2% Kerry, 0.0% Nader, 0.3% Badnarik
National and State Parks: Buffington Island State Memorial; Forked Run State Park
Additional Information Contacts
Meigs County Government . . . . (740) 992-2895
http://www.meigscountyohio.com
Meigs County Chamber of Commerce. . . . . (740) 992-5005
http://www.meigscountychamber.com

Meigs County Communities

LANGSVILLE (unincorporated postal area, zip code 45741). Covers a land area of 46.721 square miles and a water area of 0.010 square miles. Located at 39.07° N. Lat.; 82.24° W. Long. Elevation is 590 feet.

Population: 918 (2000); Race: 95.5% White, 0.0% Black, 0.0% Asian, 0.0% Hispanic of any race (2000); Density: 19.6 persons per square mile (2000); Age: 25.5% under 18, 9.1% over 64 (2000); Marriage status: 24.7% never married, 63.6% now married, 4.0% widowed, 7.7% divorced (2000); Foreign born: 0.0% (2000); Ancestry (includes multiple ancestries): 29.2% United States or American, 13.1% German, 10.6% Other groups, 7.3% Irish, 6.4% English (2000).
Economy: Employment by occupation: 6.8% management, 17.5% professional, 14.5% services, 19.1% sales, 0.0% farming, 13.5% construction, 28.6% production (2000).
Income: Per capita income: $11,230 (2000); Median household income: $27,188 (2000); Poverty rate: 31.8% (2000).
Education: Percent of population age 25 and over with: High school diploma (including GED) or higher: 64.7% (2000); Bachelor's degree or higher: 4.5% (2000).
Housing: Homeownership rate: 80.3% (2000); Median home value: $53,600 (2000); Median rent: $225 per month (2000); Median age of housing: 29 years (2000).
Transportation: Commute to work: 93.1% car, 0.0% public transportation, 1.6% walk, 1.6% work from home (2000); Travel time to work: 13.4% less than 15 minutes, 38.2% 15 to 30 minutes, 32.2% 30 to 45 minutes, 7.6% 45 to 60 minutes, 8.6% 60 minutes or more (2000)

LONG BOTTOM (unincorporated postal area, zip code 45743). Covers a land area of 40.144 square miles and a water area of 0 square miles. Located at 39.07° N. Lat.; 81.84° W. Long. Elevation is 599 feet.
History: Long Bottom developed around a ferry that crossed the Ohio River to West Virginia.
Population: 1,593 (2000); Race: 97.5% White, 0.0% Black, 0.0% Asian, 1.8% Hispanic of any race (2000); Density: 39.7 persons per square mile (2000); Age: 21.9% under 18, 14.8% over 64 (2000); Marriage status: 19.0% never married, 62.8% now married, 6.7% widowed, 11.6% divorced (2000); Foreign born: 0.0% (2000); Ancestry (includes multiple ancestries): 29.4% United States or American, 15.6% German, 11.6% Irish, 8.2% English, 4.9% Other groups (2000).
Economy: Employment by occupation: 4.3% management, 9.4% professional, 22.8% services, 18.8% sales, 1.8% farming, 18.8% construction, 24.2% production (2000).
Income: Per capita income: $13,508 (2000); Median household income: $28,291 (2000); Poverty rate: 18.1% (2000).
Education: Percent of population age 25 and over with: High school diploma (including GED) or higher: 73.0% (2000); Bachelor's degree or higher: 6.3% (2000).
Housing: Homeownership rate: 83.7% (2000); Median home value: $58,300 (2000); Median rent: $239 per month (2000); Median age of housing: 26 years (2000).
Transportation: Commute to work: 94.0% car, 0.6% public transportation, 2.9% walk, 2.4% work from home (2000); Travel time to work: 11.8% less than 15 minutes, 34.8% 15 to 30 minutes, 21.0% 30 to 45 minutes, 18.1% 45 to 60 minutes, 14.3% 60 minutes or more (2000)

MIDDLEPORT (village). Covers a land area of 1.809 square miles and a water area of 0.093 square miles. Located at 38.99° N. Lat.; 82.05° W. Long. Elevation is 568 feet.
History: Middleport was an active river town along the Ohio River during the last half of the 1800's. The disastrous flooding of the river in 1937 destroyed Middleport's waterfront.
Population: 2,847 (1990); 2,525 (2000); 2,586 (2007); 2,599 (2012 projected); Race: 95.2% White, 3.3% Black, 0.2% Asian, 0.3% Hispanic of any race (2007); Density: 1,429.8 persons per square mile (2007); Average household size: 2.23 (2007); Median age: 41.3 (2007); Males per 100 females: 84.2 (2007); Marriage status: 20.4% never married, 54.1% now married, 12.0% widowed, 13.5% divorced (2000); Foreign born: 0.0% (2000); Ancestry (includes multiple ancestries): 23.7% United States or American, 17.4% German, 10.0% Irish, 8.4% English, 8.0% Other groups (2000).
Economy: Single-family building permits issued: 0 (2007); Multi-family building permits issued: 0 (2007); Employment by occupation: 2.8% management, 16.5% professional, 23.6% services, 20.0% sales, 1.6% farming, 12.5% construction, 23.0% production (2000).
Income: Per capita income: $15,194 (2007); Median household income: $25,160 (2007); Average household income: $33,171 (2007); Percent of households with income of $100,000 or more: 3.6% (2007); Poverty rate: 24.1% (2000).
Taxes: Total city taxes per capita: $138 (2006); City property taxes per capita: $56 (2006).
Education: Percent of population age 25 and over with: High school diploma (including GED) or higher: 68.2% (2007); Bachelor's degree or higher: 6.9% (2007); Master's degree or higher: 2.9% (2007).

School District(s)

Meigs Local (PK-12)
2005-06 Enrollment: 1,990 . . . . (740) 992-2153
Housing: Homeownership rate: 65.1% (2007); Median home value: $54,750 (2007); Median rent: $257 per month (2000); Median age of housing: 54 years (2000).
Transportation: Commute to work: 95.8% car, 0.6% public transportation, 2.5% walk, 0.0% work from home (2000); Travel time to work: 39.4% less than 15 minutes, 26.8% 15 to 30 minutes, 19.6% 30 to 45 minutes, 6.7% 45 to 60 minutes, 7.5% 60 minutes or more (2000)

POMEROY (village). County seat. Covers a land area of 3.236 square miles and a water area of 0.047 square miles. Located at 39.02° N. Lat.; 82.03° W. Long. Elevation is 571 feet.
History: Pomeroy began in 1804 when Samuel Pomeroy, a Boston merchant, purchased land here. Coal mining began in Pomeroy in the early 1800's, making the town the primary shipper of coal in Ohio prior to 1850. Salt making was also a leading early industry.
Population: 2,259 (1990); 1,966 (2000); 1,938 (2007); 1,896 (2012 projected); Race: 95.5% White, 2.3% Black, 0.1% Asian, 0.3% Hispanic of any race (2007); Density: 598.9 persons per square mile (2007); Average household size: 2.29 (2007); Median age: 36.3 (2007); Males per 100 females: 81.6 (2007); Marriage status: 24.1% never married, 48.8% now married, 13.2% widowed, 13.9% divorced (2000); Foreign born: 0.2% (2000); Ancestry (includes multiple ancestries): 23.2% German, 21.8% United States or American, 13.2% Irish, 9.3% Other groups, 4.4% English (2000).
Economy: Single-family building permits issued: 1 (2007); Multi-family building permits issued: 0 (2007); Employment by occupation: 4.9% management, 20.2% professional, 21.2% services, 20.2% sales, 6.0% farming, 12.3% construction, 15.2% production (2000).
Income: Per capita income: $12,468 (2007); Median household income: $21,716 (2007); Average household income: $28,401 (2007); Percent of households with income of $100,000 or more: 2.0% (2007); Poverty rate: 39.2% (2000).
Education: Percent of population age 25 and over with: High school diploma (including GED) or higher: 67.7% (2007); Bachelor's degree or higher: 9.3% (2007); Master's degree or higher: 4.5% (2007).

School District(s)

Meigs Local (PK-12)
2005-06 Enrollment: 1,990 . . . . (740) 992-2153
Housing: Homeownership rate: 61.8% (2007); Median home value: $48,291 (2007); Median rent: $246 per month (2000); Median age of housing: 57 years (2000).
Newspapers: Daily Sentinel (Pomeroy, OH) (Local news; Circulation 17,000)
Transportation: Commute to work: 91.6% car, 0.0% public transportation, 1.7% walk, 3.0% work from home (2000); Travel time to work: 45.5% less than 15 minutes, 27.5% 15 to 30 minutes, 10.6% 30 to 45 minutes, 9.6% 45 to 60 minutes, 6.8% 60 minutes or more (2000)
Additional Information Contacts
Meigs County Chamber of Commerce. . . . . (740) 992-5005
http://www.meigscountychamber.com

PORTLAND (unincorporated postal area, zip code 45770). Covers a land area of 18.387 square miles and a water area of 0 square miles. Located at 38.98° N. Lat.; 81.80° W. Long. Elevation is 610 feet.
Population: 542 (2000); Race: 100.0% White, 0.0% Black, 0.0% Asian, 0.0% Hispanic of any race (2000); Density: 29.5 persons per square mile (2000); Age: 13.6% under 18, 19.6% over 64 (2000); Marriage status: 22.7% never married, 53.1% now married, 12.1% widowed, 12.1% divorced (2000); Foreign born: 1.4% (2000); Ancestry (includes multiple ancestries): 14.4% German, 13.6% English, 10.3% Irish, 9.1% United States or American, 7.5% French (except Basque) (2000).
Economy: Employment by occupation: 15.2% management, 6.8% professional, 16.2% services, 10.5% sales, 10.5% farming, 18.8% construction, 22.0% production (2000).
Income: Per capita income: $12,589 (2000); Median household income: $29,896 (2000); Poverty rate: 9.9% (2000).

Education: Percent of population age 25 and over with: High school diploma (including GED) or higher: 57.5% (2000); Bachelor's degree or higher: 4.7% (2000).
Housing: Homeownership rate: 76.8% (2000); Median home value: $34,600 (2000); Median rent: $263 per month (2000); Median age of housing: 33 years (2000).
Transportation: Commute to work: 78.0% car, 0.0% public transportation, 0.0% walk, 14.7% work from home (2000); Travel time to work: 23.3% less than 15 minutes, 43.6% 15 to 30 minutes, 20.9% 30 to 45 minutes, 0.0% 45 to 60 minutes, 12.3% 60 minutes or more (2000)

RACINE (village). Covers a land area of 0.416 square miles and a water area of 0 square miles. Located at 38.96° N. Lat.; 81.91° W. Long. Elevation is 577 feet.
Population: 775 (1990); 746 (2000); 700 (2007); 684 (2012 projected); Race: 99.3% White, 0.3% Black, 0.3% Asian, 0.3% Hispanic of any race (2007); Density: 1,682.4 persons per square mile (2007); Average household size: 2.41 (2007); Median age: 38.7 (2007); Males per 100 females: 91.8 (2007); Marriage status: 25.4% never married, 58.4% now married, 6.5% widowed, 9.7% divorced (2000); Foreign born: 0.1% (2000); Ancestry (includes multiple ancestries): 31.8% United States or American, 17.6% German, 16.9% English, 6.7% Other groups, 5.2% Irish (2000).
Economy: Employment by occupation: 8.0% management, 12.2% professional, 20.7% services, 24.1% sales, 2.1% farming, 19.4% construction, 13.5% production (2000).
Income: Per capita income: $14,879 (2007); Median household income: $25,278 (2007); Average household income: $35,914 (2007); Percent of households with income of $100,000 or more: 3.8% (2007); Poverty rate: 26.4% (2000).
Education: Percent of population age 25 and over with: High school diploma (including GED) or higher: 77.4% (2007); Bachelor's degree or higher: 5.7% (2007); Master's degree or higher: 2.1% (2007).

School District(s)

Southern Local (PK-12)
2005-06 Enrollment: 748 . . . . (740) 949-2669
Housing: Homeownership rate: 71.7% (2007); Median home value: $73,333 (2007); Median rent: $289 per month (2000); Median age of housing: 45 years (2000).
Transportation: Commute to work: 97.0% car, 0.0% public transportation, 1.3% walk, 0.4% work from home (2000); Travel time to work: 25.8% less than 15 minutes, 37.8% 15 to 30 minutes, 16.7% 30 to 45 minutes, 10.7% 45 to 60 minutes, 9.0% 60 minutes or more (2000)

REEDSVILLE (unincorporated postal area, zip code 45772). Covers a land area of 41.108 square miles and a water area of 0.226 square miles. Located at 39.14° N. Lat.; 81.83° W. Long. Elevation is 640 feet.
Population: 2,083 (2000); Race: 97.3% White, 0.0% Black, 1.4% Asian, 1.1% Hispanic of any race (2000); Density: 50.7 persons per square mile (2000); Age: 25.5% under 18, 14.4% over 64 (2000); Marriage status: 16.8% never married, 69.2% now married, 7.1% widowed, 6.9% divorced (2000); Foreign born: 1.4% (2000); Ancestry (includes multiple ancestries): 20.3% United States or American, 12.6% German, 9.6% Irish, 8.5% English, 8.3% Other groups (2000).
Economy: Employment by occupation: 8.8% management, 8.3% professional, 16.5% services, 21.5% sales, 2.3% farming, 17.8% construction, 24.8% production (2000).
Income: Per capita income: $15,537 (2000); Median household income: $30,543 (2000); Poverty rate: 8.1% (2000).
Education: Percent of population age 25 and over with: High school diploma (including GED) or higher: 72.4% (2000); Bachelor's degree or higher: 6.4% (2000).

School District(s)

Eastern Local (PK-12)
2005-06 Enrollment: 828 . . . . (740) 667-6079
Housing: Homeownership rate: 87.9% (2000); Median home value: $60,900 (2000); Median rent: $180 per month (2000); Median age of housing: 29 years (2000).
Transportation: Commute to work: 96.3% car, 0.0% public transportation, 0.0% walk, 3.7% work from home (2000); Travel time to work: 20.9% less than 15 minutes, 18.5% 15 to 30 minutes, 35.4% 30 to 45 minutes, 13.1% 45 to 60 minutes, 12.1% 60 minutes or more (2000)

RUTLAND (village). Covers a land area of 0.821 square miles and a water area of 0 square miles. Located at 39.04° N. Lat.; 82.12° W. Long. Elevation is 574 feet.
Population: 469 (1990); 401 (2000); 403 (2007); 396 (2012 projected); Race: 99.3% White, 0.0% Black, 0.0% Asian, 0.0% Hispanic of any race (2007); Density: 490.7 persons per square mile (2007); Average household size: 2.40 (2007); Median age: 38.6 (2007); Males per 100 females: 92.8 (2007); Marriage status: 22.6% never married, 55.4% now married, 13.9% widowed, 8.0% divorced (2000); Foreign born: 0.0% (2000); Ancestry (includes multiple ancestries): 32.4% United States or American, 14.6% German, 6.3% English, 6.0% Irish, 4.3% Other groups (2000).
Economy: Employment by occupation: 5.8% management, 14.9% professional, 13.0% services, 26.0% sales, 0.0% farming, 21.4% construction, 18.8% production (2000).
Income: Per capita income: $15,397 (2007); Median household income: $30,500 (2007); Average household income: $36,935 (2007); Percent of households with income of $100,000 or more: 4.8% (2007); Poverty rate: 11.9% (2000).
Education: Percent of population age 25 and over with: High school diploma (including GED) or higher: 76.1% (2007); Bachelor's degree or higher: 6.6% (2007); Master's degree or higher: 4.0% (2007).

School District(s)

Meigs Local (PK-12)
2005-06 Enrollment: 1,990 . . . . (740) 992-2153
Housing: Homeownership rate: 80.4% (2007); Median home value: $55,000 (2007); Median rent: $279 per month (2000); Median age of housing: 39 years (2000).
Transportation: Commute to work: 93.4% car, 0.0% public transportation, 1.3% walk, 3.3% work from home (2000); Travel time to work: 28.6% less than 15 minutes, 36.7% 15 to 30 minutes, 23.8% 30 to 45 minutes, 4.1% 45 to 60 minutes, 6.8% 60 minutes or more (2000)

SYRACUSE (village). Covers a land area of 0.923 square miles and a water area of 0.033 square miles. Located at 39.00° N. Lat.; 81.97° W. Long. Elevation is 587 feet.
Population: 866 (1990); 879 (2000); 814 (2007); 802 (2012 projected); Race: 97.4% White, 1.5% Black, 0.0% Asian, 0.1% Hispanic of any race (2007); Density: 882.3 persons per square mile (2007); Average household size: 2.24 (2007); Median age: 42.4 (2007); Males per 100 females: 93.3 (2007); Marriage status: 17.5% never married, 62.7% now married, 9.6% widowed, 10.3% divorced (2000); Foreign born: 0.0% (2000); Ancestry (includes multiple ancestries): 30.7% United States or American, 17.0% German, 8.4% Irish, 7.3% English, 3.7% Other groups (2000).
Economy: Employment by occupation: 10.4% management, 21.2% professional, 11.6% services, 27.2% sales, 1.0% farming, 13.0% construction, 15.7% production (2000).
Income: Per capita income: $19,364 (2007); Median household income: $32,045 (2007); Average household income: $43,304 (2007); Percent of households with income of $100,000 or more: 6.0% (2007); Poverty rate: 15.5% (2000).
Education: Percent of population age 25 and over with: High school diploma (including GED) or higher: 81.5% (2007); Bachelor's degree or higher: 14.0% (2007); Master's degree or higher: 4.2% (2007).
Housing: Homeownership rate: 76.9% (2007); Median home value: $76,364 (2007); Median rent: $262 per month (2000); Median age of housing: 31 years (2000).
Transportation: Commute to work: 94.6% car, 0.0% public transportation, 1.5% walk, 3.4% work from home (2000); Travel time to work: 28.0% less than 15 minutes, 38.0% 15 to 30 minutes, 21.7% 30 to 45 minutes, 7.1% 45 to 60 minutes, 5.3% 60 minutes or more (2000)

Mercer County

Located in western Ohio; bounded on the west by Indiana; drained by the Wabash and St. Marys Rivers; includes part of Grand Lake. Covers a land area of 463.27 square miles, a water area of 10.03 square miles, and is located in the Eastern Time Zone. The county was founded in 1820. County seat is Celina.

Mercer County is part of the Celina, OH Micropolitan Statistical Area. The entire metro area includes: Mercer County, OH

Weather Station: Celina 3 NE   Elevation: 859 feet

	Jan	Feb	Mar	Apr	May	Jun	Jul	Aug	Sep	Oct	Nov	Dec
High	32	37	49	62	73	81	85	82	77	65	50	38
Low	18	21	30	40	51	60	64	61	55	44	34	24
Precip	2.1	2.1	2.8	3.5	3.6	3.8	4.5	3.5	2.7	2.3	3.0	2.6
Snow	11.4	7.7	4.7	1.1	0.0	0.0	0.0	0.0	0.0	0.3	1.6	6.3

High and Low temperatures in degrees Fahrenheit; Precipitation and Snow in inches

Population: 39,443 (1990); 40,924 (2000); 41,344 (2007); 41,547 (2012 projected); Race: 98.1% White, 0.2% Black, 0.6% Asian, 1.4% Hispanic of any race (2007); Density: 89.2 persons per square mile (2007); Average household size: 2.70 (2007); Median age: 37.6 (2007); Males per 100 females: 101.2 (2007).
Religion: Five largest groups: 61.2% Catholic Church, 8.6% The United Methodist Church, 5.5% Evangelical Lutheran Church in America, 2.5% Churches of God, General Conference, 1.1% The Missionary Church (2000).
Economy: Unemployment rate: 4.9% (6/2008); Total civilian labor force: 25,108 (6/2008); Leading industries: 25.6% manufacturing; 14.0% retail trade; 11.9% health care and social assistance (2005); Farms: 1,268 totaling 268,569 acres (2002); Companies that employ 500 or more persons: 1 (2006); Companies that employ 100 to 499 persons: 18 (2006); Companies that employ less than 100 persons: 968 (2006); Black-owned businesses: n/a (2002); Hispanic-owned businesses: n/a (2002); Asian-owned businesses: n/a (2002); Women-owned businesses: n/a (2002); Retail sales per capita: $12,214 (2008). Single-family building permits issued: 72 (2007); Multi-family building permits issued: 54 (2007).
Income: Per capita income: $22,308 (2007); Median household income: $50,322 (2007); Average household income: $59,552 (2007); Percent of households with income of $100,000 or more: 12.2% (2007); Poverty rate: 7.2% (2005); Bankruptcy rate: 2.30% (2007).
Taxes: Total county taxes per capita: $216 (2006); County property taxes per capita: $114 (2006).
Education: Percent of population age 25 and over with: High school diploma (including GED) or higher: 84.0% (2007); Bachelor's degree or higher: 12.6% (2007); Master's degree or higher: 5.1% (2007).
Housing: Homeownership rate: 80.2% (2007); Median home value: $116,257 (2007); Median rent: $346 per month (2000); Median age of housing: 36 years (2000).
Health: Birth rate: 146.0 per 10,000 population (2007); Death rate: 95.9 per 10,000 population (2007); Age-adjusted cancer mortality rate: 184.2 deaths per 100,000 population (2005); Number of physicians: 9.8 per 10,000 population (2005); Hospital beds: 14.7 per 10,000 population (2004); Hospital admissions: 488.0 per 10,000 population (2004).
Elections: 2004 Presidential election results: 74.9% Bush, 24.5% Kerry, 0.0% Nader, 0.4% Badnarik
National and State Parks: Grand Lake State Park; Harbor Point State Park
Additional Information Contacts
Mercer County Government. . . . . (419) 586-3178
http://www.mercercountyohio.org
Celina-Mercer County Chamber of Commerce . . . . (419) 586-2219
http://www.celinamercer.com
City of Celina . . . . (419) 586-6464
http://www.ci.celina.oh.us

Mercer County Communities

BURKETTSVILLE (village). Aka Gilberts. Covers a land area of 0.166 square miles and a water area of 0 square miles. Located at 40.35° N. Lat.; 84.64° W. Long. Elevation is 974 feet.
Population: 287 (1990); 254 (2000); 273 (2007); 282 (2012 projected); Race: 98.9% White, 0.0% Black, 0.0% Asian, 0.0% Hispanic of any race (2007); Density: 1,646.1 persons per square mile (2007); Average household size: 2.60 (2007); Median age: 35.3 (2007); Males per 100 females: 108.4 (2007); Marriage status: 36.8% never married, 57.8% now married, 4.5% widowed, 0.9% divorced (2000); Foreign born: 0.0% (2000); Ancestry (includes multiple ancestries): 74.4% German, 3.9% French (except Basque), 3.5% United States or American, 1.6% European, 0.8% Other groups (2000).
Economy: Employment by occupation: 4.1% management, 6.9% professional, 10.3% services, 14.5% sales, 8.3% farming, 15.2% construction, 40.7% production (2000).
Income: Per capita income: $23,223 (2007); Median household income: $53,500 (2007); Average household income: $60,381 (2007); Percent of households with income of $100,000 or more: 11.4% (2007); Poverty rate: 0.8% (2000).
Education: Percent of population age 25 and over with: High school diploma (including GED) or higher: 74.2% (2007); Bachelor's degree or higher: 7.7% (2007); Master's degree or higher: 1.5% (2007).
Housing: Homeownership rate: 86.7% (2007); Median home value: $97,857 (2007); Median rent: $325 per month (2000); Median age of housing: 47 years (2000).
Transportation: Commute to work: 86.4% car, 0.0% public transportation, 7.9% walk, 4.3% work from home (2000); Travel time to work: 35.1% less than 15 minutes, 44.8% 15 to 30 minutes, 14.9% 30 to 45 minutes, 0.0% 45 to 60 minutes, 5.2% 60 minutes or more (2000)

CELINA (city). County seat. Covers a land area of 4.390 square miles and a water area of 0.045 square miles. Located at 40.55° N. Lat.; 84.57° W. Long. Elevation is 876 feet.
History: Celina was settled in 1834 in a densely forested area. Lumber mills soon attracted woodworkers and cabinet makers, and furniture manufacture became the leading industry.
Population: 9,851 (1990); 10,303 (2000); 10,196 (2007); 10,130 (2012 projected); Race: 96.2% White, 0.4% Black, 1.4% Asian, 2.4% Hispanic of any race (2007); Density: 2,322.5 persons per square mile (2007); Average household size: 2.39 (2007); Median age: 37.9 (2007); Males per 100 females: 93.6 (2007); Marriage status: 21.1% never married, 57.8% now married, 8.7% widowed, 12.4% divorced (2000); Foreign born: 1.0% (2000); Ancestry (includes multiple ancestries): 48.8% German, 8.5% United States or American, 7.2% Irish, 6.6% Other groups, 6.5% English (2000).
Economy: Single-family building permits issued: 17 (2007); Multi-family building permits issued: 0 (2007); Employment by occupation: 8.5% management, 18.0% professional, 18.3% services, 20.5% sales, 0.3% farming, 7.4% construction, 27.0% production (2000).
Income: Per capita income: $20,982 (2007); Median household income: $40,555 (2007); Average household income: $49,353 (2007); Percent of households with income of $100,000 or more: 7.9% (2007); Poverty rate: 11.7% (2000).
Taxes: Total city taxes per capita: $299 (2006); City property taxes per capita: $36 (2006).
Education: Percent of population age 25 and over with: High school diploma (including GED) or higher: 84.8% (2007); Bachelor's degree or higher: 16.2% (2007); Master's degree or higher: 7.3% (2007).

School District(s)

Celina City (PK-12)
2005-06 Enrollment: 2,943 . . . . (419) 586-8300
Mercer
2005-06 Enrollment: n/a . . . . (419) 586-6628

Two-year College(s)

Wright State University-Lake Campus (Public)
Fall 2007 Enrollment: 845 . . . . (419) 586-0300
2007-08 Tuition: In-state $4,893; Out-of-state $11,619
Housing: Homeownership rate: 66.3% (2007); Median home value: $104,124 (2007); Median rent: $355 per month (2000); Median age of housing: 35 years (2000).
Safety: Violent crime rate: 20.2 per 10,000 population; Property crime rate: 317.2 per 10,000 population (2007).
Newspapers: The Daily Standard (Local news; Circulation 10,200)
Transportation: Commute to work: 96.3% car, 0.1% public transportation, 1.7% walk, 1.5% work from home (2000); Travel time to work: 52.0% less than 15 minutes, 25.7% 15 to 30 minutes, 12.0% 30 to 45 minutes, 5.1% 45 to 60 minutes, 5.2% 60 minutes or more (2000)
Airports: Lakefield (general aviation)
Additional Information Contacts
Celina-Mercer County Chamber of Commerce . . . . (419) 586-2219
http://www.celinamercer.com
City of Celina . . . . (419) 586-6464
http://www.ci.celina.oh.us

CHICKASAW (village). Covers a land area of 0.229 square miles and a water area of 0 square miles. Located at 40.43° N. Lat.; 84.49° W. Long. Elevation is 942 feet.
Population: 431 (1990); 364 (2000); 338 (2007); 339 (2012 projected); Race: 100.0% White, 0.0% Black, 0.0% Asian, 3.3% Hispanic of any race (2007); Density: 1,478.6 persons per square mile (2007); Average household size: 2.60 (2007); Median age: 38.3 (2007); Males per 100 females: 112.6 (2007); Marriage status: 24.7% never married, 64.2% now married, 8.2% widowed, 2.9% divorced (2000); Foreign born: 0.0% (2000); Ancestry (includes multiple ancestries): 70.8% German, 6.1% United States or American, 4.5% French (except Basque), 3.3% English, 2.5% Swedish (2000).
Economy: Single-family building permits issued: 1 (2007); Multi-family building permits issued: 0 (2007); Employment by occupation: 12.4% management, 13.0% professional, 9.9% services, 19.9% sales, 3.1% farming, 11.2% construction, 30.4% production (2000).

Income: Per capita income: $26,701 (2007); Median household income: $57,143 (2007); Average household income: $69,423 (2007); Percent of households with income of $100,000 or more: 13.1% (2007); Poverty rate: 5.0% (2000).
Education: Percent of population age 25 and over with: High school diploma (including GED) or higher: 87.0% (2007); Bachelor's degree or higher: 14.0% (2007); Master's degree or higher: 8.4% (2007).
Housing: Homeownership rate: 78.5% (2007); Median home value: $129,167 (2007); Median rent: $388 per month (2000); Median age of housing: 30 years (2000).
Transportation: Commute to work: 86.6% car, 0.0% public transportation, 7.6% walk, 5.7% work from home (2000); Travel time to work: 48.0% less than 15 minutes, 39.2% 15 to 30 minutes, 7.4% 30 to 45 minutes, 1.4% 45 to 60 minutes, 4.1% 60 minutes or more (2000)

COLDWATER (village). Covers a land area of 1.976 square miles and a water area of 0 square miles. Located at 40.48° N. Lat.; 84.62° W. Long. Elevation is 912 feet.
Population: 4,390 (1990); 4,482 (2000); 4,576 (2007); 4,635 (2012 projected); Race: 98.7% White, 0.2% Black, 0.2% Asian, 1.6% Hispanic of any race (2007); Density: 2,315.6 persons per square mile (2007); Average household size: 2.67 (2007); Median age: 37.3 (2007); Males per 100 females: 97.1 (2007); Marriage status: 20.1% never married, 64.9% now married, 9.2% widowed, 5.8% divorced (2000); Foreign born: 0.6% (2000); Ancestry (includes multiple ancestries): 73.5% German, 5.7% Irish, 4.2% United States or American, 3.6% Other groups, 2.9% French (except Basque) (2000).
Economy: Single-family building permits issued: 6 (2007); Multi-family building permits issued: 0 (2007); Employment by occupation: 5.6% management, 13.8% professional, 15.7% services, 29.3% sales, 0.3% farming, 6.9% construction, 28.4% production (2000).
Income: Per capita income: $22,885 (2007); Median household income: $50,438 (2007); Average household income: $60,402 (2007); Percent of households with income of $100,000 or more: 11.5% (2007); Poverty rate: 5.4% (2000).
Education: Percent of population age 25 and over with: High school diploma (including GED) or higher: 85.2% (2007); Bachelor's degree or higher: 11.0% (2007); Master's degree or higher: 2.8% (2007).

School District(s)

Coldwater Exempted Village (PK-12)
2005-06 Enrollment: 1,547 . . . . (419) 678-2611
Housing: Homeownership rate: 79.9% (2007); Median home value: $106,659 (2007); Median rent: $342 per month (2000); Median age of housing: 35 years (2000).
Hospitals: Mercer County Joint Township Community Hospital (76 beds)
Safety: Violent crime rate: 6.7 per 10,000 population; Property crime rate: 141.4 per 10,000 population (2007).
Newspapers: Mercer County Chronicle (Community news; Circulation 2,400)
Transportation: Commute to work: 94.5% car, 0.0% public transportation, 3.0% walk, 2.2% work from home (2000); Travel time to work: 52.8% less than 15 minutes, 29.7% 15 to 30 minutes, 11.5% 30 to 45 minutes, 3.3% 45 to 60 minutes, 2.7% 60 minutes or more (2000)

FORT RECOVERY (village). Covers a land area of 0.961 square miles and a water area of 0.015 square miles. Located at 40.41° N. Lat.; 84.77° W. Long. Elevation is 942 feet.
History: The original Fort Recovery was built by General Anthony Wayne in 1793.
Population: 1,392 (1990); 1,273 (2000); 1,212 (2007); 1,211 (2012 projected); Race: 98.3% White, 0.2% Black, 0.3% Asian, 1.6% Hispanic of any race (2007); Density: 1,261.4 persons per square mile (2007); Average household size: 2.42 (2007); Median age: 38.1 (2007); Males per 100 females: 98.7 (2007); Marriage status: 24.9% never married, 60.8% now married, 9.0% widowed, 5.3% divorced (2000); Foreign born: 0.7% (2000); Ancestry (includes multiple ancestries): 60.7% German, 7.7% Irish, 7.2% United States or American, 6.2% Other groups, 5.6% English (2000).
Economy: Single-family building permits issued: 3 (2007); Multi-family building permits issued: 0 (2007); Employment by occupation: 8.7% management, 10.4% professional, 12.4% services, 22.6% sales, 2.3% farming, 11.9% construction, 31.6% production (2000).
Income: Per capita income: $23,646 (2007); Median household income: $48,306 (2007); Average household income: $56,677 (2007); Percent of households with income of $100,000 or more: 8.8% (2007); Poverty rate: 3.9% (2000).
Education: Percent of population age 25 and over with: High school diploma (including GED) or higher: 82.7% (2007); Bachelor's degree or higher: 9.5% (2007); Master's degree or higher: 4.0% (2007).

School District(s)

Fort Recovery Local (PK-12)
2005-06 Enrollment: 1,086 . . . . (419) 375-4139
Housing: Homeownership rate: 79.0% (2007); Median home value: $99,730 (2007); Median rent: $313 per month (2000); Median age of housing: 51 years (2000).
Safety: Violent crime rate: 7.4 per 10,000 population; Property crime rate: 74.1 per 10,000 population (2007).
Transportation: Commute to work: 89.7% car, 0.6% public transportation, 5.4% walk, 2.8% work from home (2000); Travel time to work: 49.2% less than 15 minutes, 29.9% 15 to 30 minutes, 13.3% 30 to 45 minutes, 4.5% 45 to 60 minutes, 3.0% 60 minutes or more (2000)

MARIA STEIN (unincorporated postal area, zip code 45860). Covers a land area of 34.838 square miles and a water area of 0.012 square miles. Located at 40.40° N. Lat.; 84.51° W. Long. Elevation is 973 feet.
Population: 2,269 (2000); Race: 100.0% White, 0.0% Black, 0.0% Asian, 0.1% Hispanic of any race (2000); Density: 65.1 persons per square mile (2000); Age: 38.0% under 18, 12.4% over 64 (2000); Marriage status: 22.6% never married, 70.6% now married, 3.8% widowed, 3.0% divorced (2000); Foreign born: 0.0% (2000); Ancestry (includes multiple ancestries): 75.9% German, 9.2% United States or American, 6.1% French (except Basque), 1.7% Dutch, 1.7% Irish (2000).
Economy: Employment by occupation: 15.5% management, 16.6% professional, 7.8% services, 21.2% sales, 4.8% farming, 8.9% construction, 25.2% production (2000).
Income: Per capita income: $17,110 (2000); Median household income: $52,361 (2000); Poverty rate: 2.0% (2000).
Education: Percent of population age 25 and over with: High school diploma (including GED) or higher: 83.6% (2000); Bachelor's degree or higher: 10.5% (2000).

School District(s)

Marion Local (PK-12)
2005-06 Enrollment: 980 . . . . (419) 925-4294
Housing: Homeownership rate: 86.2% (2000); Median home value: $133,500 (2000); Median rent: $334 per month (2000); Median age of housing: 38 years (2000).
Transportation: Commute to work: 89.7% car, 0.0% public transportation, 3.0% walk, 7.4% work from home (2000); Travel time to work: 51.1% less than 15 minutes, 41.6% 15 to 30 minutes, 4.4% 30 to 45 minutes, 1.0% 45 to 60 minutes, 1.9% 60 minutes or more (2000)

MENDON (village). Covers a land area of 0.379 square miles and a water area of 0 square miles. Located at 40.67° N. Lat.; 84.51° W. Long. Elevation is 820 feet.
Population: 772 (1990); 697 (2000); 641 (2007); 643 (2012 projected); Race: 99.2% White, 0.0% Black, 0.0% Asian, 1.1% Hispanic of any race (2007); Density: 1,689.7 persons per square mile (2007); Average household size: 2.60 (2007); Median age: 34.8 (2007); Males per 100 females: 102.8 (2007); Marriage status: 23.9% never married, 58.5% now married, 5.5% widowed, 12.1% divorced (2000); Foreign born: 0.1% (2000); Ancestry (includes multiple ancestries): 39.0% German, 8.1% United States or American, 6.6% Irish, 5.5% Other groups, 3.8% English (2000).
Economy: Employment by occupation: 4.4% management, 7.3% professional, 18.8% services, 18.8% sales, 0.8% farming, 10.2% construction, 39.8% production (2000).
Income: Per capita income: $19,033 (2007); Median household income: $39,750 (2007); Average household income: $49,393 (2007); Percent of households with income of $100,000 or more: 8.1% (2007); Poverty rate: 5.3% (2000).
Education: Percent of population age 25 and over with: High school diploma (including GED) or higher: 82.3% (2007); Bachelor's degree or higher: 3.6% (2007); Master's degree or higher: 0.7% (2007).

School District(s)

Parkway Local (PK-12)
2005-06 Enrollment: 1,230 . . . . (419) 363-3045
Housing: Homeownership rate: 78.1% (2007); Median home value: $65,938 (2007); Median rent: $320 per month (2000); Median age of housing: 50 years (2000).
Transportation: Commute to work: 97.6% car, 0.8% public transportation, 1.6% walk, 0.0% work from home (2000); Travel time to work: 22.9% less

than 15 minutes, 51.3% 15 to 30 minutes, 16.5% 30 to 45 minutes, 5.1% 45 to 60 minutes, 4.3% 60 minutes or more (2000)

MONTEZUMA (village). Covers a land area of 0.115 square miles and a water area of <.001 square miles. Located at 40.48° N. Lat.; 84.54° W. Long. Elevation is 883 feet.
Population: 199 (1990); 191 (2000); 209 (2007); 220 (2012 projected); Race: 97.6% White, 0.0% Black, 0.0% Asian, 2.4% Hispanic of any race (2007); Density: 1,817.2 persons per square mile (2007); Average household size: 2.61 (2007); Median age: 38.4 (2007); Males per 100 females: 88.3 (2007); Marriage status: 31.3% never married, 53.7% now married, 4.5% widowed, 10.4% divorced (2000); Foreign born: 0.0% (2000); Ancestry (includes multiple ancestries): 55.1% German, 19.3% Irish, 13.1% English, 10.8% United States or American, 6.8% Other groups (2000).
Economy: Single-family building permits issued: 0 (2007); Multi-family building permits issued: 0 (2007); Employment by occupation: 7.4% management, 3.2% professional, 9.6% services, 25.5% sales, 3.2% farming, 11.7% construction, 39.4% production (2000).
Income: Per capita income: $22,010 (2007); Median household income: $50,000 (2007); Average household income: $57,500 (2007); Percent of households with income of $100,000 or more: 6.3% (2007); Poverty rate: 10.3% (2000).
Education: Percent of population age 25 and over with: High school diploma (including GED) or higher: 83.7% (2007); Bachelor's degree or higher: 6.7% (2007); Master's degree or higher: 3.0% (2007).
Housing: Homeownership rate: 91.3% (2007); Median home value: $83,750 (2007); Median rent: $415 per month (2000); Median age of housing: 50 years (2000).
Transportation: Commute to work: 92.6% car, 0.0% public transportation, 2.1% walk, 1.1% work from home (2000); Travel time to work: 36.6% less than 15 minutes, 45.2% 15 to 30 minutes, 12.9% 30 to 45 minutes, 5.4% 45 to 60 minutes, 0.0% 60 minutes or more (2000)

ROCKFORD (village). Covers a land area of 0.644 square miles and a water area of 0 square miles. Located at 40.69° N. Lat.; 84.64° W. Long. Elevation is 814 feet.
History: Rockford was settled after the Treaty of 1818 on the site of a trading post operated by Anthony Shane. The town was first called Shane's Crossing.
Population: 1,163 (1990); 1,126 (2000); 1,177 (2007); 1,192 (2012 projected); Race: 98.9% White, 0.6% Black, 0.0% Asian, 2.1% Hispanic of any race (2007); Density: 1,827.1 persons per square mile (2007); Average household size: 2.42 (2007); Median age: 38.1 (2007); Males per 100 females: 91.1 (2007); Marriage status: 26.1% never married, 56.5% now married, 7.6% widowed, 9.8% divorced (2000); Foreign born: 0.2% (2000); Ancestry (includes multiple ancestries): 51.5% German, 11.9% Irish, 8.6% Other groups, 7.6% English, 4.4% United States or American (2000).
Economy: Single-family building permits issued: 3 (2007); Multi-family building permits issued: 0 (2007); Employment by occupation: 6.8% management, 11.0% professional, 14.2% services, 22.2% sales, 0.5% farming, 4.3% construction, 40.9% production (2000).
Income: Per capita income: $23,156 (2007); Median household income: $44,634 (2007); Average household income: $51,245 (2007); Percent of households with income of $100,000 or more: 6.6% (2007); Poverty rate: 6.7% (2000).
Education: Percent of population age 25 and over with: High school diploma (including GED) or higher: 79.2% (2007); Bachelor's degree or higher: 9.9% (2007); Master's degree or higher: 3.8% (2007).

School District(s)

Parkway Local (PK-12)
2005-06 Enrollment: 1,230 . . . . (419) 363-3045
Housing: Homeownership rate: 76.5% (2007); Median home value: $80,926 (2007); Median rent: $289 per month (2000); Median age of housing: 51 years (2000).
Transportation: Commute to work: 92.3% car, 0.0% public transportation, 5.7% walk, 0.9% work from home (2000); Travel time to work: 30.8% less than 15 minutes, 43.7% 15 to 30 minutes, 17.6% 30 to 45 minutes, 4.3% 45 to 60 minutes, 3.6% 60 minutes or more (2000)

SAINT HENRY (village). Covers a land area of 1.439 square miles and a water area of 0 square miles. Located at 40.41° N. Lat.; 84.63° W. Long. Elevation is 971 feet.
Population: 2,121 (1990); 2,271 (2000); 2,331 (2007); 2,340 (2012 projected); Race: 98.7% White, 0.0% Black, 0.0% Asian, 1.9% Hispanic of any race (2007); Density: 1,619.9 persons per square mile (2007); Average household size: 3.04 (2007); Median age: 31.5 (2007); Males per 100 females: 105.0 (2007); Marriage status: 22.8% never married, 70.5% now married, 3.7% widowed, 2.9% divorced (2000); Foreign born: 1.1% (2000); Ancestry (includes multiple ancestries): 73.1% German, 6.0% United States or American, 4.3% Other groups, 3.6% Irish, 2.7% French (except Basque) (2000).
Economy: Single-family building permits issued: 11 (2007); Multi-family building permits issued: 0 (2007); Employment by occupation: 10.4% management, 16.7% professional, 13.4% services, 19.5% sales, 0.6% farming, 8.5% construction, 30.9% production (2000).
Income: Per capita income: $22,762 (2007); Median household income: $60,549 (2007); Average household income: $68,833 (2007); Percent of households with income of $100,000 or more: 16.0% (2007); Poverty rate: 3.6% (2000).
Education: Percent of population age 25 and over with: High school diploma (including GED) or higher: 84.7% (2007); Bachelor's degree or higher: 13.5% (2007); Master's degree or higher: 5.3% (2007).

School District(s)

St Henry Consolidated Local (PK-12)
2005-06 Enrollment: 1,145 . . . . (419) 678-4834
Housing: Homeownership rate: 82.5% (2007); Median home value: $127,399 (2007); Median rent: $368 per month (2000); Median age of housing: 30 years (2000).
Safety: Violent crime rate: 0.0 per 10,000 population; Property crime rate: 63.0 per 10,000 population (2007).
Transportation: Commute to work: 94.3% car, 0.0% public transportation, 4.0% walk, 0.7% work from home (2000); Travel time to work: 48.1% less than 15 minutes, 35.0% 15 to 30 minutes, 11.9% 30 to 45 minutes, 2.6% 45 to 60 minutes, 2.4% 60 minutes or more (2000)

Miami County

Located in western Ohio; crossed by the Great Miami and Stillwater Rivers. Covers a land area of 407.04 square miles, a water area of 2.18 square miles, and is located in the Eastern Time Zone. The county was founded in 1807. County seat is Troy.

Miami County is part of the Dayton, OH Metropolitan Statistical Area. The entire metro area includes: Greene County, OH; Miami County, OH; Montgomery County, OH; Preble County, OH

Population: 93,204 (1990); 98,868 (2000); 102,592 (2007); 105,002 (2012 projected); Race: 95.0% White, 2.0% Black, 1.1% Asian, 1.2% Hispanic of any race (2007); Density: 252.0 persons per square mile (2007); Average household size: 2.51 (2007); Median age: 39.3 (2007); Males per 100 females: 96.6 (2007).
Religion: Five largest groups: 12.9% Catholic Church, 6.6% The United Methodist Church, 4.2% United Church of Christ, 3.2% Church of the Brethren, 3.0% Evangelical Lutheran Church in America (2000).
Economy: Unemployment rate: 6.0% (6/2008); Total civilian labor force: 55,692 (6/2008); Leading industries: 28.9% manufacturing; 13.5% retail trade; 11.5% health care and social assistance (2005); Farms: 1,071 totaling 184,028 acres (2002); Companies that employ 500 or more persons: 6 (2006); Companies that employ 100 to 499 persons: 56 (2006); Companies that employ less than 100 persons: 2,225 (2006); Black-owned businesses: n/a (2002); Hispanic-owned businesses: n/a (2002); Asian-owned businesses: n/a (2002); Women-owned businesses: 2,679 (2002); Retail sales per capita: $13,659 (2008). Single-family building permits issued: 168 (2007); Multi-family building permits issued: 0 (2007).
Income: Per capita income: $25,029 (2007); Median household income: $49,799 (2007); Average household income: $62,279 (2007); Percent of households with income of $100,000 or more: 14.4% (2007); Poverty rate: 8.2% (2005); Bankruptcy rate: 4.16% (2007).
Taxes: Total county taxes per capita: $221 (2006); County property taxes per capita: $114 (2006).
Education: Percent of population age 25 and over with: High school diploma (including GED) or higher: 82.9% (2007); Bachelor's degree or higher: 16.5% (2007); Master's degree or higher: 5.5% (2007).
Housing: Homeownership rate: 72.7% (2007); Median home value: $134,981 (2007); Median rent: $423 per month (2000); Median age of housing: 39 years (2000).
Health: Birth rate: 127.9 per 10,000 population (2007); Death rate: 91.8 per 10,000 population (2007); Age-adjusted cancer mortality rate: 194.2 deaths per 100,000 population (2005); Air Quality Index: 79.1% good, 19.5% moderate, 1.4% unhealthy for sensitive individuals, 0.0% unhealthy

(percent of days in 2007); Number of physicians: 14.0 per 10,000 population (2005); Hospital beds: 16.4 per 10,000 population (2004); Hospital admissions: 965.7 per 10,000 population (2004).
Elections: 2004 Presidential election results: 65.7% Bush, 34.0% Kerry, 0.0% Nader, 0.2% Badnarik

Additional Information Contacts

Miami County Government . . . . (937) 332-7000
http://www.co.miami.oh.us
City of Piqua. . . . . (937) 778-2051
http://www.piquaoh.org
City of Tipp City . . . . (937) 667-8425
http://www.tippcityohio.gov
City of Troy. . . . . (937) 339-1221
http://www.troyohio.gov
Piqua Area Chamber of Commerce. . . . . (937) 773-2765
http://www.piquaareachamber.com
Tipp City Area Chamber of Commerce . . . . (937) 667-8300
http://www.tippcitychamber.org
Troy Area Chamber of Commerce. (937) 339-8769
http://www.troyohiochamber.com

Miami County Communities

BRADFORD (village). Covers a land area of 0.772 square miles and a water area of 0 square miles. Located at 40.12° N. Lat.; 84.43° W. Long. Elevation is 988 feet.
Population: 2,039 (1990); 1,859 (2000); 1,960 (2007); 2,004 (2012 projected); Race: 98.3% White, 0.0% Black, 0.2% Asian, 0.4% Hispanic of any race (2007); Density: 2,538.1 persons per square mile (2007); Average household size: 2.61 (2007); Median age: 35.0 (2007); Males per 100 females: 97.4 (2007); Marriage status: 20.7% never married, 60.1% now married, 8.0% widowed, 11.3% divorced (2000); Foreign born: 0.3% (2000); Ancestry (includes multiple ancestries): 29.1% German, 14.5% United States or American, 9.6% Irish, 5.4% English, 4.7% Other groups (2000).
Economy: Employment by occupation: 4.1% management, 7.3% professional, 15.9% services, 21.9% sales, 0.0% farming, 9.0% construction, 41.9% production (2000).
Income: Per capita income: $18,334 (2007); Median household income: $45,000 (2007); Average household income: $47,913 (2007); Percent of households with income of $100,000 or more: 3.2% (2007); Poverty rate: 6.7% (2000).
Education: Percent of population age 25 and over with: High school diploma (including GED) or higher: 76.7% (2007); Bachelor's degree or higher: 3.7% (2007); Master's degree or higher: 0.6% (2007).

School District(s)

Bradford Exempted Village (PK-12)
2005-06 Enrollment: 681 . . . . (937) 448-2770
Housing: Homeownership rate: 76.5% (2007); Median home value: $89,701 (2007); Median rent: $351 per month (2000); Median age of housing: 60+ years (2000).
Transportation: Commute to work: 94.6% car, 0.6% public transportation, 2.4% walk, 1.5% work from home (2000); Travel time to work: 21.6% less than 15 minutes, 48.6% 15 to 30 minutes, 18.0% 30 to 45 minutes, 6.2% 45 to 60 minutes, 5.5% 60 minutes or more (2000)

CASSTOWN (village). Covers a land area of 0.107 square miles and a water area of 0 square miles. Located at 40.05° N. Lat.; 84.12° W. Long. Elevation is 935 feet.
Population: 271 (1990); 322 (2000); 365 (2007); 393 (2012 projected); Race: 100.0% White, 0.0% Black, 0.0% Asian, 0.0% Hispanic of any race (2007); Density: 3,419.9 persons per square mile (2007); Average household size: 2.48 (2007); Median age: 41.7 (2007); Males per 100 females: 94.1 (2007); Marriage status: 22.0% never married, 61.8% now married, 7.9% widowed, 8.3% divorced (2000); Foreign born: 0.6% (2000); Ancestry (includes multiple ancestries): 32.3% German, 30.0% United States or American, 10.6% Irish, 7.1% English, 6.5% French (except Basque) (2000).
Economy: Employment by occupation: 6.3% management, 6.8% professional, 11.4% services, 25.0% sales, 1.7% farming, 14.8% construction, 34.1% production (2000).
Income: Per capita income: $20,411 (2007); Median household income: $48,125 (2007); Average household income: $50,680 (2007); Percent of households with income of $100,000 or more: 7.5% (2007); Poverty rate: 4.3% (2000).
Education: Percent of population age 25 and over with: High school diploma (including GED) or higher: 86.2% (2007); Bachelor's degree or higher: 5.9% (2007); Master's degree or higher: 0.4% (2007).

School District(s)

Miami East Local (PK-12)
2005-06 Enrollment: 1,325 . . . . (937) 335-7505
Housing: Homeownership rate: 78.9% (2007); Median home value: $97,727 (2007); Median rent: $393 per month (2000); Median age of housing: 60+ years (2000).
Transportation: Commute to work: 92.5% car, 0.0% public transportation, 1.2% walk, 4.0% work from home (2000); Travel time to work: 24.7% less than 15 minutes, 40.4% 15 to 30 minutes, 24.1% 30 to 45 minutes, 2.4% 45 to 60 minutes, 8.4% 60 minutes or more (2000)

CONOVER (unincorporated postal area, zip code 45317). Covers a land area of 21.354 square miles and a water area of 0 square miles. Located at 40.17° N. Lat.; 84.02° W. Long. Elevation is 1,138 feet.
Population: 1,078 (2000); Race: 99.0% White, 0.0% Black, 0.0% Asian, 0.0% Hispanic of any race (2000); Density: 50.5 persons per square mile (2000); Age: 20.5% under 18, 18.1% over 64 (2000); Marriage status: 18.8% never married, 61.3% now married, 7.4% widowed, 12.4% divorced (2000); Foreign born: 0.7% (2000); Ancestry (includes multiple ancestries): 28.7% German, 13.4% English, 10.0% Irish, 8.3% United States or American, 4.8% Norwegian (2000).
Economy: Employment by occupation: 8.2% management, 11.1% professional, 15.8% services, 18.4% sales, 0.0% farming, 11.7% construction, 34.8% production (2000).
Income: Per capita income: $20,023 (2000); Median household income: $41,156 (2000); Poverty rate: 3.0% (2000).
Education: Percent of population age 25 and over with: High school diploma (including GED) or higher: 83.3% (2000); Bachelor's degree or higher: 8.1% (2000).
Housing: Homeownership rate: 82.7% (2000); Median home value: $100,300 (2000); Median rent: $333 per month (2000); Median age of housing: 50 years (2000).
Transportation: Commute to work: 95.6% car, 0.0% public transportation, 2.0% walk, 2.4% work from home (2000); Travel time to work: 32.3% less than 15 minutes, 43.3% 15 to 30 minutes, 16.4% 30 to 45 minutes, 4.2% 45 to 60 minutes, 3.8% 60 minutes or more (2000)

COVINGTON (village). Covers a land area of 1.152 square miles and a water area of 0.028 square miles. Located at 40.11° N. Lat.; 84.35° W. Long. Elevation is 932 feet.
History: Covington was settled in 1807 on the site of an outpost built by General Anthony Wayne.
Population: 2,690 (1990); 2,559 (2000); 2,618 (2007); 2,662 (2012 projected); Race: 98.1% White, 0.2% Black, 0.1% Asian, 1.3% Hispanic of any race (2007); Density: 2,272.1 persons per square mile (2007); Average household size: 2.47 (2007); Median age: 39.6 (2007); Males per 100 females: 92.8 (2007); Marriage status: 19.5% never married, 62.7% now married, 8.2% widowed, 9.5% divorced (2000); Foreign born: 1.0% (2000); Ancestry (includes multiple ancestries): 34.6% German, 13.7% United States or American, 11.0% Irish, 8.2% English, 3.6% Dutch (2000).
Economy: Employment by occupation: 12.8% management, 11.8% professional, 16.2% services, 25.8% sales, 0.0% farming, 8.2% construction, 25.2% production (2000).
Income: Per capita income: $23,615 (2007); Median household income: $48,311 (2007); Average household income: $57,868 (2007); Percent of households with income of $100,000 or more: 10.1% (2007); Poverty rate: 2.6% (2000).
Education: Percent of population age 25 and over with: High school diploma (including GED) or higher: 81.6% (2007); Bachelor's degree or higher: 9.9% (2007); Master's degree or higher: 3.2% (2007).

School District(s)

Covington Exempted Village (PK-12)
2005-06 Enrollment: 878 . . . . (937) 473-9816
Housing: Homeownership rate: 76.0% (2007); Median home value: $113,419 (2007); Median rent: $383 per month (2000); Median age of housing: 56 years (2000).
Safety: Violent crime rate: 0.0 per 10,000 population; Property crime rate: 190.5 per 10,000 population (2007).
Newspapers: Stillwater Valley Advertiser (Community news; Circulation 10,661)
Transportation: Commute to work: 94.4% car, 0.4% public transportation, 4.0% walk, 1.0% work from home (2000); Travel time to work: 36.0% less

than 15 minutes, 42.6% 15 to 30 minutes, 12.8% 30 to 45 minutes, 5.4% 45 to 60 minutes, 3.1% 60 minutes or more (2000)

FLETCHER (village). Covers a land area of 0.309 square miles and a water area of 0 square miles. Located at 40.14° N. Lat.; 84.11° W. Long. Elevation is 1,043 feet.

Population: 545 (1990); 510 (2000); 521 (2007); 526 (2012 projected); Race: 97.3% White, 1.2% Black, 0.0% Asian, 1.0% Hispanic of any race (2007); Density: 1,687.5 persons per square mile (2007); Average household size: 2.64 (2007); Median age: 33.1 (2007); Males per 100 females: 102.7 (2007); Marriage status: 20.9% never married, 64.8% now married, 6.9% widowed, 7.4% divorced (2000); Foreign born: 1.9% (2000); Ancestry (includes multiple ancestries): 16.7% German, 13.2% United States or American, 9.4% Irish, 5.6% Other groups, 4.2% English (2000).
Economy: Employment by occupation: 6.4% management, 10.7% professional, 14.6% services, 25.3% sales, 1.7% farming, 12.4% construction, 28.8% production (2000).
Income: Per capita income: $22,438 (2007); Median household income: $49,167 (2007); Average household income: $59,340 (2007); Percent of households with income of $100,000 or more: 10.2% (2007); Poverty rate: 9.4% (2000).
Education: Percent of population age 25 and over with: High school diploma (including GED) or higher: 79.8% (2007); Bachelor's degree or higher: 2.5% (2007); Master's degree or higher: 0.0% (2007).

School District(s)

Miami East Local (PK-12)
2005-06 Enrollment: 1,325 . . . . (937) 335-7505

Housing: Homeownership rate: 83.8% (2007); Median home value: $94,310 (2007); Median rent: $427 per month (2000); Median age of housing: 60+ years (2000).
Transportation: Commute to work: 94.2% car, 0.0% public transportation, 2.2% walk, 2.7% work from home (2000); Travel time to work: 28.6% less than 15 minutes, 56.4% 15 to 30 minutes, 8.6% 30 to 45 minutes, 3.6% 45 to 60 minutes, 2.7% 60 minutes or more (2000)

LAURA (village). Covers a land area of 0.284 square miles and a water area of 0 square miles. Located at 39.99° N. Lat.; 84.40° W. Long. Elevation is 991 feet.

Population: 531 (1990); 487 (2000); 467 (2007); 463 (2012 projected); Race: 96.8% White, 0.0% Black, 0.2% Asian, 4.5% Hispanic of any race (2007); Density: 1,644.1 persons per square mile (2007); Average household size: 2.70 (2007); Median age: 37.0 (2007); Males per 100 females: 107.6 (2007); Marriage status: 20.5% never married, 62.9% now married, 2.1% widowed, 14.5% divorced (2000); Foreign born: 1.8% (2000); Ancestry (includes multiple ancestries): 25.4% German, 13.9% Irish, 12.9% United States or American, 12.1% Other groups, 3.8% English (2000).
Economy: Single-family building permits issued: 0 (2007); Multi-family building permits issued: 0 (2007); Employment by occupation: 3.9% management, 10.2% professional, 9.5% services, 25.4% sales, 4.6% farming, 16.6% construction, 29.7% production (2000).
Income: Per capita income: $22,088 (2007); Median household income: $51,136 (2007); Average household income: $59,624 (2007); Percent of households with income of $100,000 or more: 12.7% (2007); Poverty rate: 2.8% (2000).
Education: Percent of population age 25 and over with: High school diploma (including GED) or higher: 86.0% (2007); Bachelor's degree or higher: 6.5% (2007); Master's degree or higher: 2.0% (2007).
Housing: Homeownership rate: 83.2% (2007); Median home value: $99,583 (2007); Median rent: $375 per month (2000); Median age of housing: 60+ years (2000).
Transportation: Commute to work: 94.6% car, 0.7% public transportation, 2.9% walk, 1.1% work from home (2000); Travel time to work: 15.3% less than 15 minutes, 39.6% 15 to 30 minutes, 30.5% 30 to 45 minutes, 7.6% 45 to 60 minutes, 6.9% 60 minutes or more (2000)

LUDLOW FALLS (village). Covers a land area of 0.184 square miles and a water area of 0 square miles. Located at 39.99° N. Lat.; 84.34° W. Long. Elevation is 902 feet.

Population: 300 (1990); 210 (2000); 208 (2007); 205 (2012 projected); Race: 97.6% White, 0.0% Black, 0.0% Asian, 0.5% Hispanic of any race (2007); Density: 1,133.5 persons per square mile (2007); Average household size: 2.51 (2007); Median age: 35.0 (2007); Males per 100 females: 112.2 (2007); Marriage status: 26.3% never married, 51.5% now married, 5.3% widowed, 17.0% divorced (2000); Foreign born: 0.5% (2000); Ancestry (includes multiple ancestries): 38.6% United States or American, 33.2% German, 14.9% Irish, 7.9% English, 4.0% Swiss (2000).
Economy: Single-family building permits issued: 0 (2007); Multi-family building permits issued: 0 (2007); Employment by occupation: 9.2% management, 15.0% professional, 18.3% services, 11.7% sales, 0.0% farming, 18.3% construction, 27.5% production (2000).
Income: Per capita income: $19,063 (2007); Median household income: $45,938 (2007); Average household income: $47,771 (2007); Percent of households with income of $100,000 or more: 4.8% (2007); Poverty rate: 6.9% (2000).
Education: Percent of population age 25 and over with: High school diploma (including GED) or higher: 86.9% (2007); Bachelor's degree or higher: 5.8% (2007); Master's degree or higher: 0.0% (2007).
Housing: Homeownership rate: 72.3% (2007); Median home value: $101,471 (2007); Median rent: $350 per month (2000); Median age of housing: 60+ years (2000).
Transportation: Commute to work: 94.9% car, 0.0% public transportation, 2.5% walk, 2.5% work from home (2000); Travel time to work: 32.2% less than 15 minutes, 27.0% 15 to 30 minutes, 34.8% 30 to 45 minutes, 2.6% 45 to 60 minutes, 3.5% 60 minutes or more (2000)

PIQUA (city). Covers a land area of 10.694 square miles and a water area of 0.241 square miles. Located at 40.14° N. Lat.; 84.24° W. Long. Elevation is 873 feet.

History: Piqua was settled in 1797 and called Washington until 1816, when the legislature renamed it for a tribe of the Shawnee, who previously had villages near the site. The earlier fur trading was replaced by a flatboat business, as cargoes of lumber and farm products were sent to New Orleans. In 1815 Piqua became a producer of linseed oil. The Miami & Erie Canal and the railroads stimulated Piqua's growth in the later 1800's.
Population: 21,160 (1990); 20,738 (2000); 20,792 (2007); 20,786 (2012 projected); Race: 93.7% White, 3.4% Black, 0.5% Asian, 1.2% Hispanic of any race (2007); Density: 1,944.3 persons per square mile (2007); Average household size: 2.44 (2007); Median age: 36.6 (2007); Males per 100 females: 92.6 (2007); Marriage status: 22.6% never married, 55.1% now married, 8.7% widowed, 13.6% divorced (2000); Foreign born: 1.4% (2000); Ancestry (includes multiple ancestries): 28.1% German, 14.6% United States or American, 10.7% Irish, 10.4% Other groups, 8.2% English (2000).
Economy: Employment by occupation: 9.2% management, 10.0% professional, 15.1% services, 26.4% sales, 0.3% farming, 8.3% construction, 30.6% production (2000).
Income: Per capita income: $21,247 (2007); Median household income: $39,673 (2007); Average household income: $50,931 (2007); Percent of households with income of $100,000 or more: 8.2% (2007); Poverty rate: 12.2% (2000).
Taxes: Total city taxes per capita: $540 (2006); City property taxes per capita: $64 (2006).
Education: Percent of population age 25 and over with: High school diploma (including GED) or higher: 75.2% (2007); Bachelor's degree or higher: 10.4% (2007); Master's degree or higher: 3.4% (2007).

School District(s)

Piqua City (PK-12)
2005-06 Enrollment: 3,845 . . . . (937) 773-4321
Upper Valley (07-12)
2005-06 Enrollment: n/a . . . . (937) 778-1980

Four-year College(s)

Edison State Community College (Public)
Fall 2007 Enrollment: 3,025. . . . . (937) 778-8600
2007-08 Tuition: In-state $3,450; Out-of-state $6,420

Vocational/Technical School(s)

Upper Valley Joint Vocational School (Public)
Fall 2007 Enrollment: 633 . . . . (937) 778-1980
2007-08 Tuition: In-state $6,792; Out-of-state $6,792

Housing: Homeownership rate: 63.5% (2007); Median home value: $102,765 (2007); Median rent: $415 per month (2000); Median age of housing: 49 years (2000).
Safety: Violent crime rate: 16.3 per 10,000 population; Property crime rate: 533.2 per 10,000 population (2007).
Newspapers: Piqua Daily Call (Local news; Circulation 8,475)
Transportation: Commute to work: 93.1% car, 1.3% public transportation, 2.5% walk, 2.2% work from home (2000); Travel time to work: 49.9% less than 15 minutes, 33.5% 15 to 30 minutes, 10.2% 30 to 45 minutes, 3.6% 45 to 60 minutes, 2.7% 60 minutes or more (2000)
Additional Information Contacts

City of Piqua. . . . . (937) 778-2051
http://www.piquaoh.org
Piqua Area Chamber of Commerce. . . . . (937) 773-2765
http://www.piquaareachamber.com

PLEASANT HILL (village). Covers a land area of 0.474 square miles and a water area of 0 square miles. Located at 40.05° N. Lat.; 84.34° W. Long. Elevation is 932 feet.

Population: 1,124 (1990); 1,134 (2000); 1,214 (2007); 1,266 (2012 projected); Race: 99.2% White, 0.0% Black, 0.4% Asian, 0.2% Hispanic of any race (2007); Density: 2,561.8 persons per square mile (2007); Average household size: 2.62 (2007); Median age: 36.1 (2007); Males per 100 females: 92.4 (2007); Marriage status: 20.4% never married, 67.5% now married, 6.0% widowed, 6.1% divorced (2000); Foreign born: 0.5% (2000); Ancestry (includes multiple ancestries): 33.9% German, 15.6% United States or American, 11.4% English, 7.6% Irish, 5.4% Dutch (2000).

Economy: Employment by occupation: 10.8% management, 15.7% professional, 15.0% services, 23.0% sales, 0.0% farming, 9.1% construction, 26.3% production (2000).

Income: Per capita income: $24,821 (2007); Median household income: $57,593 (2007); Average household income: $64,941 (2007); Percent of households with income of $100,000 or more: 13.1% (2007); Poverty rate: 2.6% (2000).

Education: Percent of population age 25 and over with: High school diploma (including GED) or higher: 88.0% (2007); Bachelor's degree or higher: 13.0% (2007); Master's degree or higher: 5.0% (2007).

School District(s)

Newton Local (PK-12)
2005-06 Enrollment: 533 . . . . (937) 676-3271

Housing: Homeownership rate: 81.3% (2007); Median home value: $127,574 (2007); Median rent: $376 per month (2000); Median age of housing: 57 years (2000).

Transportation: Commute to work: 94.8% car, 0.0% public transportation, 2.6% walk, 2.2% work from home (2000); Travel time to work: 33.8% less than 15 minutes, 44.2% 15 to 30 minutes, 14.8% 30 to 45 minutes, 3.6% 45 to 60 minutes, 3.6% 60 minutes or more (2000)

POTSDAM (village). Covers a land area of 0.459 square miles and a water area of 0 square miles. Located at 39.96° N. Lat.; 84.41° W. Long. Elevation is 1,010 feet.

Population: 250 (1990); 203 (2000); 193 (2007); 191 (2012 projected); Race: 99.5% White, 0.0% Black, 0.0% Asian, 1.6% Hispanic of any race (2007); Density: 420.4 persons per square mile (2007); Average household size: 2.97 (2007); Median age: 37.5 (2007); Males per 100 females: 94.9 (2007); Marriage status: 25.2% never married, 64.4% now married, 2.2% widowed, 8.1% divorced (2000); Foreign born: 0.0% (2000); Ancestry (includes multiple ancestries): 34.4% United States or American, 18.0% German, 10.6% Irish, 8.5% Other groups, 2.6% Dutch (2000).

Economy: Employment by occupation: 3.8% management, 12.5% professional, 12.5% services, 32.5% sales, 0.0% farming, 16.3% construction, 22.5% production (2000).

Income: Per capita income: $20,829 (2007); Median household income: $48,125 (2007); Average household income: $61,846 (2007); Percent of households with income of $100,000 or more: 12.3% (2007); Poverty rate: 6.9% (2000).

Education: Percent of population age 25 and over with: High school diploma (including GED) or higher: 76.9% (2007); Bachelor's degree or higher: 5.1% (2007); Master's degree or higher: 4.3% (2007).

Housing: Homeownership rate: 87.7% (2007); Median home value: $109,375 (2007); Median rent: $506 per month (2000); Median age of housing: 60+ years (2000).

Transportation: Commute to work: 90.0% car, 0.0% public transportation, 0.0% walk, 10.0% work from home (2000); Travel time to work: 44.4% less than 15 minutes, 31.9% 15 to 30 minutes, 22.2% 30 to 45 minutes, 0.0% 45 to 60 minutes, 1.4% 60 minutes or more (2000)

TIPP CITY (city). Aka Tippecanoe City. Covers a land area of 6.178 square miles and a water area of 0.041 square miles. Located at 39.96° N. Lat.; 84.18° W. Long. Elevation is 827 feet.

History: Formerly called Tippecanoe City.

Population: 6,857 (1990); 9,221 (2000); 9,484 (2007); 9,658 (2012 projected); Race: 96.5% White, 0.3% Black, 1.4% Asian, 2.0% Hispanic of any race (2007); Density: 1,535.2 persons per square mile (2007); Average household size: 2.48 (2007); Median age: 36.9 (2007); Males per 100 females: 94.8 (2007); Marriage status: 19.3% never married, 59.1% now married, 8.5% widowed, 13.1% divorced (2000); Foreign born: 1.4% (2000); Ancestry (includes multiple ancestries): 35.8% German, 13.7% Irish, 12.2% English, 10.8% United States or American, 7.5% Other groups (2000).

Economy: Employment by occupation: 14.3% management, 20.2% professional, 11.2% services, 28.1% sales, 0.2% farming, 6.2% construction, 19.8% production (2000).

Income: Per capita income: $28,040 (2007); Median household income: $55,063 (2007); Average household income: $69,081 (2007); Percent of households with income of $100,000 or more: 20.1% (2007); Poverty rate: 5.2% (2000).

Education: Percent of population age 25 and over with: High school diploma (including GED) or higher: 89.7% (2007); Bachelor's degree or higher: 23.4% (2007); Master's degree or higher: 7.0% (2007).

School District(s)

Bethel Local (PK-12)
2005-06 Enrollment: 978 . . . . (937) 845-9414
Tipp Exempted Village (PK-12)
2005-06 Enrollment: 2,706 . . . . (937) 667-8444

Housing: Homeownership rate: 66.4% (2007); Median home value: $153,756 (2007); Median rent: $436 per month (2000); Median age of housing: 27 years (2000).

Safety: Violent crime rate: 13.9 per 10,000 population; Property crime rate: 256.0 per 10,000 population (2007).

Newspapers: Tipp City Herald (Local news; Circulation 7,200); West Milton Record (Community news; Circulation 3,000)

Transportation: Commute to work: 96.2% car, 0.1% public transportation, 1.6% walk, 1.4% work from home (2000); Travel time to work: 38.8% less than 15 minutes, 35.2% 15 to 30 minutes, 20.4% 30 to 45 minutes, 2.1% 45 to 60 minutes, 3.5% 60 minutes or more (2000)

Additional Information Contacts

City of Tipp City . . . . (937) 667-8425
http://www.tippcityohio.gov
Tipp City Area Chamber of Commerce . . . . (937) 667-8300
http://www.tippcitychamber.org

TROY (city). County seat. Covers a land area of 9.701 square miles and a water area of 0.067 square miles. Located at 40.04° N. Lat.; 84.20° W. Long. Elevation is 827 feet.

History: Troy was settled in 1798 by Michael Garver, who built a cabin here and encouraged other settlers to follow him. The coming of the canal in 1837 and the railroad in 1850 brought industrial growth to Troy.

Population: 19,956 (1990); 21,999 (2000); 22,189 (2007); 22,402 (2012 projected); Race: 89.7% White, 5.0% Black, 2.8% Asian, 1.3% Hispanic of any race (2007); Density: 2,287.4 persons per square mile (2007); Average household size: 2.40 (2007); Median age: 36.9 (2007); Males per 100 females: 95.5 (2007); Marriage status: 21.0% never married, 57.6% now married, 7.2% widowed, 14.1% divorced (2000); Foreign born: 2.1% (2000); Ancestry (includes multiple ancestries): 25.3% German, 14.6% United States or American, 11.7% Other groups, 11.4% Irish, 8.0% English (2000).

Economy: Employment by occupation: 12.7% management, 18.5% professional, 13.5% services, 24.7% sales, 0.5% farming, 5.1% construction, 25.1% production (2000).

Income: Per capita income: $22,658 (2007); Median household income: $43,124 (2007); Average household income: $53,316 (2007); Percent of households with income of $100,000 or more: 9.7% (2007); Poverty rate: 8.2% (2000).

Taxes: Total city taxes per capita: $662 (2006); City property taxes per capita: $86 (2006).

Education: Percent of population age 25 and over with: High school diploma (including GED) or higher: 81.4% (2007); Bachelor's degree or higher: 17.2% (2007); Master's degree or higher: 5.8% (2007).

School District(s)

Troy City (PK-12)
2005-06 Enrollment: 4,627 . . . . (937) 332-6700

Two-year College(s)

Miami-Jacobs Career College-Troy (Private, For-profit)
Fall 2007 Enrollment: 343 . . . . (937) 332-8580
2007-08 Tuition: In-state $10,440; Out-of-state $10,440

Vocational/Technical School(s)

Hobart Institute of Welding Technology (Private, Not-for-profit)
Fall 2007 Enrollment: 181 . . . . (937) 332-5000
2007-08 Tuition: $13,795

Housing: Homeownership rate: 59.9% (2007); Median home value: $119,009 (2007); Median rent: $435 per month (2000); Median age of housing: 37 years (2000).
Hospitals: Upper Valley Medical Center (128 beds)
Newspapers: Troy Advocate (Community news; Circulation 6,000); Troy Daily News (Local news; Circulation 15,113)
Transportation: Commute to work: 95.9% car, 0.6% public transportation, 1.6% walk, 0.8% work from home (2000); Travel time to work: 49.5% less than 15 minutes, 33.8% 15 to 30 minutes, 11.3% 30 to 45 minutes, 2.9% 45 to 60 minutes, 2.4% 60 minutes or more (2000)
Additional Information Contacts
City of Troy. . . . . (937) 339-1221
http://www.troyohio.gov
Troy Area Chamber of Commerce. (937) 339-8769
http://www.troyohiochamber.com

WEST MILTON (village). Aka Milton. Covers a land area of 2.414 square miles and a water area of 0.056 square miles. Located at 39.95° N. Lat.; 84.32° W. Long. Elevation is 906 feet.
History: Settled 1807, incorporated 1835.
Population: 4,499 (1990); 4,645 (2000); 4,732 (2007); 4,798 (2012 projected); Race: 98.4% White, 0.4% Black, 0.3% Asian, 1.2% Hispanic of any race (2007); Density: 1,959.9 persons per square mile (2007); Average household size: 2.43 (2007); Median age: 37.1 (2007); Males per 100 females: 93.9 (2007); Marriage status: 18.8% never married, 59.7% now married, 6.4% widowed, 15.1% divorced (2000); Foreign born: 0.2% (2000); Ancestry (includes multiple ancestries): 27.5% German, 16.7% United States or American, 9.7% Other groups, 9.7% Irish, 7.5% English (2000).
Economy: Employment by occupation: 8.7% management, 17.0% professional, 15.7% services, 25.1% sales, 1.4% farming, 9.0% construction, 23.2% production (2000).
Income: Per capita income: $22,195 (2007); Median household income: $45,732 (2007); Average household income: $53,971 (2007); Percent of households with income of $100,000 or more: 10.4% (2007); Poverty rate: 6.7% (2000).
Education: Percent of population age 25 and over with: High school diploma (including GED) or higher: 85.0% (2007); Bachelor's degree or higher: 14.2% (2007); Master's degree or higher: 4.8% (2007).

School District(s)

Milton-Union Exempted Village (PK-12)
2005-06 Enrollment: 1,731 . . . . (937) 884-7910
Housing: Homeownership rate: 65.9% (2007); Median home value: $117,840 (2007); Median rent: $402 per month (2000); Median age of housing: 39 years (2000).
Transportation: Commute to work: 96.4% car, 0.3% public transportation, 2.1% walk, 1.1% work from home (2000); Travel time to work: 19.1% less than 15 minutes, 44.6% 15 to 30 minutes, 27.1% 30 to 45 minutes, 4.7% 45 to 60 minutes, 4.4% 60 minutes or more (2000)

Monroe County

Located in eastern Ohio; bounded on the southeast by the Ohio River and the West Virginia border; drained by Little Muskingum River and Sunfish Creek. Covers a land area of 455.54 square miles, a water area of 1.92 square miles, and is located in the Eastern Time Zone. The county was founded in 1813. County seat is Woodsfield.

Weather Station: Hannibal Lock & Dam — Elevation: 620 feet

	Jan	Feb	Mar	Apr	May	Jun	Jul	Aug	Sep	Oct	Nov	Dec
High	37	42	51	63	73	81	84	83	76	65	54	42
Low	20	22	29	38	48	57	62	61	54	42	33	25
Precip	3.1	2.6	3.6	3.3	4.1	3.6	4.6	3.4	3.0	2.6	3.3	3.1
Snow	na	na	na	tr	0.0	0.0	0.0	0.0	0.0	0.0	tr	na

High and Low temperatures in degrees Fahrenheit; Precipitation and Snow in inches

Population: 15,497 (1990); 15,180 (2000); 14,515 (2007); 13,961 (2012 projected); Race: 98.9% White, 0.3% Black, 0.1% Asian, 0.5% Hispanic of any race (2007); Density: 31.9 persons per square mile (2007); Average household size: 2.45 (2007); Median age: 43.4 (2007); Males per 100 females: 98.3 (2007).
Religion: Five largest groups: 15.2% Churches of Christ, 10.5% The United Methodist Church, 6.1% Catholic Church, 6.0% United Church of Christ, 5.9% Southern Baptist Convention (2000).
Economy: Unemployment rate: 8.7% (6/2008); Total civilian labor force: 5,568 (6/2008); Leading industries: 13.9% retail trade; 8.9% transportation & warehousing; 5.2% other services (except public administration) (2005); Farms: 654 totaling 107,198 acres (2002); Companies that employ 500 or more persons: 0 (2006); Companies that employ 100 to 499 persons: 4 (2006); Companies that employ less than 100 persons: 277 (2006); Black-owned businesses: n/a (2002); Hispanic-owned businesses: n/a (2002); Asian-owned businesses: n/a (2002); Women-owned businesses: 239 (2002); Retail sales per capita: $4,611 (2008). Single-family building permits issued: 0 (2007); Multi-family building permits issued: 0 (2007).
Income: Per capita income: $18,089 (2007); Median household income: $36,141 (2007); Average household income: $44,032 (2007); Percent of households with income of $100,000 or more: 4.8% (2007); Poverty rate: 18.3% (2005); Bankruptcy rate: 2.10% (2007).
Education: Percent of population age 25 and over with: High school diploma (including GED) or higher: 78.6% (2007); Bachelor's degree or higher: 8.4% (2007); Master's degree or higher: 2.5% (2007).
Housing: Homeownership rate: 80.9% (2007); Median home value: $76,526 (2007); Median rent: $255 per month (2000); Median age of housing: 37 years (2000).
Health: Birth rate: 103.8 per 10,000 population (2007); Death rate: 132.6 per 10,000 population (2007); Age-adjusted cancer mortality rate: 228.9 deaths per 100,000 population (2005); Number of physicians: 4.1 per 10,000 population (2005); Hospital beds: 0.0 per 10,000 population (2004); Hospital admissions: 0.0 per 10,000 population (2004).
Elections: 2004 Presidential election results: 44.3% Bush, 54.9% Kerry, 0.0% Nader, 0.4% Badnarik
National and State Parks: Monroe Lake State Wildlife Area; Sunfish Creek State Forest; Wayne National Forest - Athens Ranger District
Additional Information Contacts
Monroe County Government . . . . (740) 472-1341

Monroe County Chamber of Commerce . . . . (740) 472-5499
http://www.monroechamber.com

Monroe County Communities

ANTIOCH (village). Covers a land area of 0.104 square miles and a water area of 0 square miles. Located at 39.66° N. Lat.; 81.06° W. Long. Elevation is 1,070 feet.
Population: 68 (1990); 89 (2000); 88 (2007); 84 (2012 projected); Race: 100.0% White, 0.0% Black, 0.0% Asian, 5.7% Hispanic of any race (2007); Density: 849.6 persons per square mile (2007); Average household size: 2.59 (2007); Median age: 42.1 (2007); Males per 100 females: 69.2 (2007); Marriage status: 12.9% never married, 67.1% now married, 18.6% widowed, 1.4% divorced (2000); Foreign born: 2.4% (2000); Ancestry (includes multiple ancestries): 54.2% German, 13.3% Irish, 12.0% English, 6.0% Dutch, 4.8% United States or American (2000).
Economy: Employment by occupation: 7.1% management, 35.7% professional, 7.1% services, 17.9% sales, 0.0% farming, 21.4% construction, 10.7% production (2000).
Income: Per capita income: $15,483 (2007); Median household income: $31,250 (2007); Average household income: $40,074 (2007); Percent of households with income of $100,000 or more: 2.9% (2007); Poverty rate: 10.8% (2000).
Education: Percent of population age 25 and over with: High school diploma (including GED) or higher: 75.8% (2007); Bachelor's degree or higher: 6.5% (2007); Master's degree or higher: 3.2% (2007).
Housing: Homeownership rate: 85.3% (2007); Median home value: $50,833 (2007); Median rent: $288 per month (2000); Median age of housing: 60+ years (2000).
Transportation: Commute to work: 100.0% car, 0.0% public transportation, 0.0% walk, 0.0% work from home (2000); Travel time to work: 14.3% less than 15 minutes, 71.4% 15 to 30 minutes, 7.1% 30 to 45 minutes, 0.0% 45 to 60 minutes, 7.1% 60 minutes or more (2000)

BEALLSVILLE (village). Covers a land area of 0.369 square miles and a water area of 0 square miles. Located at 39.84° N. Lat.; 81.03° W. Long. Elevation is 1,257 feet.
Population: 464 (1990); 423 (2000); 388 (2007); 374 (2012 projected); Race: 98.7% White, 0.0% Black, 0.0% Asian, 0.3% Hispanic of any race (2007); Density: 1,050.8 persons per square mile (2007); Average household size: 2.38 (2007); Median age: 35.9 (2007); Males per 100 females: 87.4 (2007); Marriage status: 24.2% never married, 53.8% now married, 7.3% widowed, 14.7% divorced (2000); Foreign born: 1.0% (2000); Ancestry (includes multiple ancestries): 25.6% German, 14.8%

Irish, 10.5% Other groups, 9.8% United States or American, 5.5% English (2000).
Economy: Employment by occupation: 1.3% management, 12.5% professional, 16.3% services, 14.4% sales, 2.5% farming, 19.4% construction, 33.8% production (2000).
Income: Per capita income: $17,371 (2007); Median household income: $29,808 (2007); Average household income: $41,350 (2007); Percent of households with income of $100,000 or more: 2.5% (2007); Poverty rate: 18.1% (2000).
Education: Percent of population age 25 and over with: High school diploma (including GED) or higher: 79.4% (2007); Bachelor's degree or higher: 3.4% (2007); Master's degree or higher: 1.1% (2007).

School District(s)

Switzerland of Ohio Local (PK-12)
2005-06 Enrollment: 2,692 . . . . (740) 472-5801
Housing: Homeownership rate: 66.9% (2007); Median home value: $54,231 (2007); Median rent: $150 per month (2000); Median age of housing: 54 years (2000).
Transportation: Commute to work: 88.0% car, 1.3% public transportation, 7.0% walk, 2.5% work from home (2000); Travel time to work: 22.1% less than 15 minutes, 23.4% 15 to 30 minutes, 31.8% 30 to 45 minutes, 12.3% 45 to 60 minutes, 10.4% 60 minutes or more (2000)

CLARINGTON (village). Covers a land area of 1.117 square miles and a water area of 0.141 square miles. Located at 39.77° N. Lat.; 80.86° W. Long. Elevation is 633 feet.
History: Clarington was originally settled by Swiss immigrants, who engaged in clock-making. Many of the later residents were of Slavic and Italian descent.
Population: 406 (1990); 444 (2000); 460 (2007); 439 (2012 projected); Race: 99.1% White, 0.9% Black, 0.0% Asian, 0.9% Hispanic of any race (2007); Density: 411.7 persons per square mile (2007); Average household size: 2.35 (2007); Median age: 43.5 (2007); Males per 100 females: 93.3 (2007); Marriage status: 21.8% never married, 52.5% now married, 7.5% widowed, 18.2% divorced (2000); Foreign born: 0.0% (2000); Ancestry (includes multiple ancestries): 28.4% German, 14.9% Irish, 14.9% United States or American, 10.1% English, 6.7% French (except Basque) (2000).
Economy: Employment by occupation: 6.6% management, 14.2% professional, 30.1% services, 17.5% sales, 0.0% farming, 8.7% construction, 23.0% production (2000).
Income: Per capita income: $16,484 (2007); Median household income: $31,176 (2007); Average household income: $38,686 (2007); Percent of households with income of $100,000 or more: 5.1% (2007); Poverty rate: 25.2% (2000).
Education: Percent of population age 25 and over with: High school diploma (including GED) or higher: 78.7% (2007); Bachelor's degree or higher: 6.4% (2007); Master's degree or higher: 1.2% (2007).
Housing: Homeownership rate: 79.1% (2007); Median home value: $61,923 (2007); Median rent: $230 per month (2000); Median age of housing: 51 years (2000).
Transportation: Commute to work: 93.6% car, 1.2% public transportation, 1.2% walk, 2.3% work from home (2000); Travel time to work: 15.0% less than 15 minutes, 36.5% 15 to 30 minutes, 19.8% 30 to 45 minutes, 16.8% 45 to 60 minutes, 12.0% 60 minutes or more (2000)

GRAYSVILLE (village). Covers a land area of 0.996 square miles and a water area of 0 square miles. Located at 39.66° N. Lat.; 81.17° W. Long. Elevation is 1,102 feet.
Population: 89 (1990); 113 (2000); 113 (2007); 106 (2012 projected); Race: 100.0% White, 0.0% Black, 0.0% Asian, 2.7% Hispanic of any race (2007); Density: 113.4 persons per square mile (2007); Average household size: 2.69 (2007); Median age: 36.6 (2007); Males per 100 females: 109.3 (2007); Marriage status: 7.7% never married, 76.9% now married, 2.6% widowed, 12.8% divorced (2000); Foreign born: 0.0% (2000); Ancestry (includes multiple ancestries): 11.2% Irish, 8.0% United States or American, 8.0% Other groups, 7.2% German, 5.6% English (2000).
Economy: Employment by occupation: 0.0% management, 0.0% professional, 22.9% services, 25.7% sales, 0.0% farming, 22.9% construction, 28.6% production (2000).
Income: Per capita income: $16,770 (2007); Median household income: $34,000 (2007); Average household income: $45,119 (2007); Percent of households with income of $100,000 or more: 4.8% (2007); Poverty rate: 28.8% (2000).
Education: Percent of population age 25 and over with: High school diploma (including GED) or higher: 70.6% (2007); Bachelor's degree or higher: 2.9% (2007); Master's degree or higher: 2.9% (2007).

School District(s)

Switzerland of Ohio Local (PK-12)
2005-06 Enrollment: 2,692 . . . . (740) 472-5801
Housing: Homeownership rate: 81.0% (2007); Median home value: $48,333 (2007); Median rent: $263 per month (2000); Median age of housing: 60+ years (2000).
Transportation: Commute to work: 94.1% car, 0.0% public transportation, 0.0% walk, 5.9% work from home (2000); Travel time to work: 6.3% less than 15 minutes, 37.5% 15 to 30 minutes, 0.0% 30 to 45 minutes, 34.4% 45 to 60 minutes, 21.9% 60 minutes or more (2000)

JERUSALEM (village). Covers a land area of 0.251 square miles and a water area of 0 square miles. Located at 39.85° N. Lat.; 81.09° W. Long. Elevation is 1,263 feet.
Population: 144 (1990); 152 (2000); 167 (2007); 169 (2012 projected); Race: 100.0% White, 0.0% Black, 0.0% Asian, 0.0% Hispanic of any race (2007); Density: 665.3 persons per square mile (2007); Average household size: 2.17 (2007); Median age: 48.2 (2007); Males per 100 females: 101.2 (2007); Marriage status: 19.5% never married, 50.0% now married, 11.0% widowed, 19.5% divorced (2000); Foreign born: 0.0% (2000); Ancestry (includes multiple ancestries): 26.6% German, 17.7% United States or American, 14.1% Irish, 8.3% English, 2.1% Welsh (2000).
Economy: Employment by occupation: 5.3% management, 5.3% professional, 14.7% services, 37.3% sales, 0.0% farming, 14.7% construction, 22.7% production (2000).
Income: Per capita income: $17,814 (2007); Median household income: $33,056 (2007); Average household income: $38,636 (2007); Percent of households with income of $100,000 or more: 6.5% (2007); Poverty rate: 13.5% (2000).
Education: Percent of population age 25 and over with: High school diploma (including GED) or higher: 86.1% (2007); Bachelor's degree or higher: 5.1% (2007); Master's degree or higher: 1.5% (2007).
Housing: Homeownership rate: 80.5% (2007); Median home value: $49,375 (2007); Median rent: $255 per month (2000); Median age of housing: 59 years (2000).
Transportation: Commute to work: 92.8% car, 4.3% public transportation, 2.9% walk, 0.0% work from home (2000); Travel time to work: 21.7% less than 15 minutes, 21.7% 15 to 30 minutes, 14.5% 30 to 45 minutes, 2.9% 45 to 60 minutes, 39.1% 60 minutes or more (2000)

LEWISVILLE (village). Covers a land area of 0.373 square miles and a water area of 0 square miles. Located at 39.76° N. Lat.; 81.21° W. Long. Elevation is 1,201 feet.
Population: 261 (1990); 233 (2000); 212 (2007); 203 (2012 projected); Race: 100.0% White, 0.0% Black, 0.0% Asian, 0.0% Hispanic of any race (2007); Density: 569.0 persons per square mile (2007); Average household size: 2.38 (2007); Median age: 43.2 (2007); Males per 100 females: 84.3 (2007); Marriage status: 19.9% never married, 59.7% now married, 13.4% widowed, 7.0% divorced (2000); Foreign born: 0.0% (2000); Ancestry (includes multiple ancestries): 42.3% German, 12.3% Irish, 5.7% United States or American, 4.4% English, 4.0% Other groups (2000).
Economy: Employment by occupation: 0.0% management, 10.7% professional, 18.7% services, 22.7% sales, 0.0% farming, 17.3% construction, 30.7% production (2000).
Income: Per capita income: $12,936 (2007); Median household income: $28,750 (2007); Average household income: $29,944 (2007); Percent of households with income of $100,000 or more: 0.0% (2007); Poverty rate: 10.1% (2000).
Education: Percent of population age 25 and over with: High school diploma (including GED) or higher: 73.4% (2007); Bachelor's degree or higher: 5.8% (2007); Master's degree or higher: 1.3% (2007).
Housing: Homeownership rate: 88.8% (2007); Median home value: $72,083 (2007); Median rent: $250 per month (2000); Median age of housing: 60+ years (2000).
Transportation: Commute to work: 97.3% car, 2.7% public transportation, 0.0% walk, 0.0% work from home (2000); Travel time to work: 25.3% less than 15 minutes, 30.7% 15 to 30 minutes, 16.0% 30 to 45 minutes, 12.0% 45 to 60 minutes, 16.0% 60 minutes or more (2000)

MILTONSBURG (village). Covers a land area of 0.077 square miles and a water area of 0 square miles. Located at 39.83° N. Lat.; 81.16° W. Long. Elevation is 1,296 feet.

Population: 56 (1990); 29 (2000); 31 (2007); 31 (2012 projected); Race: 100.0% White, 0.0% Black, 0.0% Asian, 0.0% Hispanic of any race (2007); Density: 402.2 persons per square mile (2007); Average household size: 2.58 (2007); Median age: 40.4 (2007); Males per 100 females: 158.3 (2007); Marriage status: 18.8% never married, 81.3% now married, 0.0% widowed, 0.0% divorced (2000); Foreign born: 0.0% (2000); Ancestry (includes multiple ancestries): 70.0% English, 35.0% French (except Basque), 15.0% Irish, 10.0% Russian, 10.0% Other groups (2000).
Economy: Employment by occupation: 0.0% management, 28.6% professional, 0.0% services, 0.0% sales, 0.0% farming, 0.0% construction, 71.4% production (2000).
Income: Per capita income: $21,613 (2007); Median household income: $55,000 (2007); Average household income: $55,833 (2007); Percent of households with income of $100,000 or more: 0.0% (2007); Poverty rate: 0.0% (2000).
Education: Percent of population age 25 and over with: High school diploma (including GED) or higher: 100.0% (2007); Bachelor's degree or higher: 4.8% (2007); Master's degree or higher: 4.8% (2007).
Housing: Homeownership rate: 100.0% (2007); Median home value: $130,000 (2007); Median rent: $n/a per month (2000); Median age of housing: 23 years (2000).
Transportation: Commute to work: 100.0% car, 0.0% public transportation, 0.0% walk, 0.0% work from home (2000); Travel time to work: 0.0% less than 15 minutes, 28.6% 15 to 30 minutes, 42.9% 30 to 45 minutes, 28.6% 45 to 60 minutes, 0.0% 60 minutes or more (2000)

SARDIS (unincorporated postal area, zip code 43946). Covers a land area of 56.186 square miles and a water area of 0.023 square miles. Located at 39.64° N. Lat.; 80.96° W. Long. Elevation is 668 feet.
Population: 2,057 (2000); Race: 97.4% White, 0.0% Black, 0.3% Asian, 0.0% Hispanic of any race (2000); Density: 36.6 persons per square mile (2000); Age: 18.1% under 18, 14.4% over 64 (2000); Marriage status: 22.6% never married, 65.8% now married, 5.5% widowed, 6.0% divorced (2000); Foreign born: 0.6% (2000); Ancestry (includes multiple ancestries): 24.1% German, 11.5% United States or American, 11.3% Irish, 11.1% English, 7.9% Other groups (2000).
Economy: Employment by occupation: 5.3% management, 9.8% professional, 10.2% services, 27.4% sales, 0.9% farming, 17.9% construction, 28.5% production (2000).
Income: Per capita income: $20,635 (2000); Median household income: $35,804 (2000); Poverty rate: 9.6% (2000).
Education: Percent of population age 25 and over with: High school diploma (including GED) or higher: 86.4% (2000); Bachelor's degree or higher: 8.2% (2000).

School District(s)

Switzerland of Ohio Local (PK-12)
2005-06 Enrollment: 2,692 . . . . (740) 472-5801
Housing: Homeownership rate: 82.7% (2000); Median home value: $80,200 (2000); Median rent: $311 per month (2000); Median age of housing: 33 years (2000).
Transportation: Commute to work: 96.5% car, 0.8% public transportation, 1.2% walk, 1.5% work from home (2000); Travel time to work: 34.9% less than 15 minutes, 36.3% 15 to 30 minutes, 12.3% 30 to 45 minutes, 5.5% 45 to 60 minutes, 11.0% 60 minutes or more (2000)

STAFFORD (village). Covers a land area of 0.338 square miles and a water area of 0 square miles. Located at 39.71° N. Lat.; 81.27° W. Long. Elevation is 1,079 feet.
Population: 97 (1990); 86 (2000); 78 (2007); 77 (2012 projected); Race: 98.7% White, 0.0% Black, 0.0% Asian, 0.0% Hispanic of any race (2007); Density: 230.6 persons per square mile (2007); Average household size: 2.23 (2007); Median age: 49.3 (2007); Males per 100 females: 116.7 (2007); Marriage status: 28.1% never married, 51.6% now married, 4.7% widowed, 15.6% divorced (2000); Foreign born: 0.0% (2000); Ancestry (includes multiple ancestries): 55.7% German, 18.6% Dutch, 15.7% Irish, 7.1% United States or American, 5.7% Italian (2000).
Economy: Employment by occupation: 5.0% management, 0.0% professional, 15.0% services, 50.0% sales, 0.0% farming, 10.0% construction, 20.0% production (2000).
Income: Per capita income: $16,731 (2007); Median household income: $29,722 (2007); Average household income: $37,286 (2007); Percent of households with income of $100,000 or more: 0.0% (2007); Poverty rate: 11.4% (2000).
Education: Percent of population age 25 and over with: High school diploma (including GED) or higher: 57.6% (2007); Bachelor's degree or higher: 6.8% (2007); Master's degree or higher: 0.0% (2007).
Housing: Homeownership rate: 68.6% (2007); Median home value: $63,333 (2007); Median rent: $250 per month (2000); Median age of housing: 60+ years (2000).
Transportation: Commute to work: 100.0% car, 0.0% public transportation, 0.0% walk, 0.0% work from home (2000); Travel time to work: 10.0% less than 15 minutes, 20.0% 15 to 30 minutes, 15.0% 30 to 45 minutes, 55.0% 45 to 60 minutes, 0.0% 60 minutes or more (2000)

WILSON (village). Covers a land area of 0.418 square miles and a water area of 0.064 square miles. Located at 39.86° N. Lat.; 81.07° W. Long. Elevation is 1,250 feet.
Population: 136 (1990); 118 (2000); 123 (2007); 125 (2012 projected); Race: 99.2% White, 0.0% Black, 0.0% Asian, 0.0% Hispanic of any race (2007); Density: 294.6 persons per square mile (2007); Average household size: 2.24 (2007); Median age: 51.0 (2007); Males per 100 females: 101.6 (2007); Marriage status: 9.6% never married, 73.4% now married, 5.3% widowed, 11.7% divorced (2000); Foreign born: 0.0% (2000); Ancestry (includes multiple ancestries): 19.8% German, 12.1% United States or American, 10.3% English, 9.5% Irish, 5.2% Italian (2000).
Economy: Employment by occupation: 4.5% management, 22.4% professional, 7.5% services, 19.4% sales, 0.0% farming, 13.4% construction, 32.8% production (2000).
Income: Per capita income: $27,785 (2007); Median household income: $38,214 (2007); Average household income: $62,136 (2007); Percent of households with income of $100,000 or more: 9.1% (2007); Poverty rate: 4.3% (2000).
Education: Percent of population age 25 and over with: High school diploma (including GED) or higher: 94.6% (2007); Bachelor's degree or higher: 19.6% (2007); Master's degree or higher: 12.0% (2007).
Housing: Homeownership rate: 98.2% (2007); Median home value: $68,889 (2007); Median rent: $n/a per month (2000); Median age of housing: 40 years (2000).
Transportation: Commute to work: 95.5% car, 0.0% public transportation, 0.0% walk, 1.5% work from home (2000); Travel time to work: 21.2% less than 15 minutes, 13.6% 15 to 30 minutes, 43.9% 30 to 45 minutes, 7.6% 45 to 60 minutes, 13.6% 60 minutes or more (2000)

WOODSFIELD (village). County seat. Covers a land area of 2.043 square miles and a water area of 0 square miles. Located at 39.76° N. Lat.; 81.11° W. Long. Elevation is 1,204 feet.
History: Settled 1815, incorporated 1834.
Population: 2,960 (1990); 2,598 (2000); 2,434 (2007); 2,296 (2012 projected); Race: 98.9% White, 0.1% Black, 0.2% Asian, 0.5% Hispanic of any race (2007); Density: 1,191.1 persons per square mile (2007); Average household size: 2.24 (2007); Median age: 45.2 (2007); Males per 100 females: 83.6 (2007); Marriage status: 21.0% never married, 59.8% now married, 10.4% widowed, 8.8% divorced (2000); Foreign born: 0.1% (2000); Ancestry (includes multiple ancestries): 27.9% German, 10.6% Irish, 10.4% English, 7.9% United States or American, 6.5% Other groups (2000).
Economy: Single-family building permits issued: 0 (2007); Multi-family building permits issued: 0 (2007); Employment by occupation: 10.5% management, 14.2% professional, 19.4% services, 25.0% sales, 0.6% farming, 10.1% construction, 20.3% production (2000).
Income: Per capita income: $16,259 (2007); Median household income: $27,701 (2007); Average household income: $35,946 (2007); Percent of households with income of $100,000 or more: 2.9% (2007); Poverty rate: 17.3% (2000).
Education: Percent of population age 25 and over with: High school diploma (including GED) or higher: 76.5% (2007); Bachelor's degree or higher: 12.4% (2007); Master's degree or higher: 3.8% (2007).

School District(s)

Switzerland of Ohio Local (PK-12)
2005-06 Enrollment: 2,692 . . . . (740) 472-5801
Housing: Homeownership rate: 65.4% (2007); Median home value: $70,220 (2007); Median rent: $238 per month (2000); Median age of housing: 47 years (2000).
Newspapers: Monroe County Beacon (Community news; Circulation 5,300)
Transportation: Commute to work: 89.1% car, 1.2% public transportation, 5.3% walk, 4.3% work from home (2000); Travel time to work: 53.5% less

than 15 minutes, 9.5% 15 to 30 minutes, 18.3% 30 to 45 minutes, 9.4% 45 to 60 minutes, 9.5% 60 minutes or more (2000)

Additional Information Contacts

Monroe County Chamber of Commerce . . . . (740) 472-5499
http://www.monroechamber.com

Montgomery County

Located in western Ohio; crossed by the Great Miami, Stillwater, and Mad Rivers. Covers a land area of 461.68 square miles, a water area of 2.67 square miles, and is located in the Eastern Time Zone. The county was founded in 1803. County seat is Dayton.

Montgomery County is part of the Dayton, OH Metropolitan Statistical Area. The entire metro area includes: Greene County, OH; Miami County, OH; Montgomery County, OH; Preble County, OH

Weather Station: Dayton Int'l Airport Elevation: 997 feet

	Jan	Feb	Mar	Apr	May	Jun	Jul	Aug	Sep	Oct	Nov	Dec
High	34	39	50	62	72	81	85	83	76	64	51	40
Low	19	22	31	41	51	60	65	62	55	44	34	25
Precip	2.5	2.3	3.3	4.1	4.2	4.2	3.7	3.4	2.6	2.7	3.3	3.1
Snow	9.7	6.6	4.7	0.8	tr	0.0	tr	0.0	0.0	0.4	1.5	4.4

High and Low temperatures in degrees Fahrenheit; Precipitation and Snow in inches

Weather Station: Dayton MCD Elevation: 744 feet

	Jan	Feb	Mar	Apr	May	Jun	Jul	Aug	Sep	Oct	Nov	Dec
High	35	40	50	63	74	83	87	85	79	66	52	41
Low	20	23	32	42	53	63	67	65	57	45	36	27
Precip	2.6	2.3	3.1	4.1	4.4	4.1	3.9	3.3	2.6	2.7	3.3	2.9
Snow	6.3	3.6	2.4	0.2	0.0	0.0	0.0	0.0	0.0	tr	0.4	2.8

High and Low temperatures in degrees Fahrenheit; Precipitation and Snow in inches

Population: 573,809 (1990); 559,062 (2000); 544,570 (2007); 532,897 (2012 projected); Race: 75.1% White, 20.7% Black, 1.5% Asian, 1.6% Hispanic of any race (2007); Density: 1,179.6 persons per square mile (2007); Average household size: 2.39 (2007); Median age: 38.3 (2007); Males per 100 females: 93.2 (2007).

Religion: Five largest groups: 16.0% Catholic Church, 4.9% Southern Baptist Convention, 4.5% The United Methodist Church, 2.3% Evangelical Lutheran Church in America, 1.9% American Baptist Churches in the USA (2000).

Economy: Unemployment rate: 7.3% (6/2008); Total civilian labor force: 274,650 (6/2008); Leading industries: 17.8% health care and social assistance; 14.8% manufacturing; 11.7% retail trade (2005); Farms: 832 totaling 101,912 acres (2002); Companies that employ 500 or more persons: 39 (2006); Companies that employ 100 to 499 persons: 337 (2006); Companies that employ less than 100 persons: 12,307 (2006); Black-owned businesses: 2,489 (2002); Hispanic-owned businesses: 239 (2002); Asian-owned businesses: 597 (2002); Women-owned businesses: 11,002 (2002); Retail sales per capita: $15,197 (2008). Single-family building permits issued: 753 (2007); Multi-family building permits issued: 28 (2007).

Income: Per capita income: $25,054 (2007); Median household income: $45,044 (2007); Average household income: $59,165 (2007); Percent of households with income of $100,000 or more: 14.1% (2007); Poverty rate: 14.7% (2005); Bankruptcy rate: 4.72% (2007).

Taxes: Total county taxes per capita: $353 (2006); County property taxes per capita: $210 (2006).

Education: Percent of population age 25 and over with: High school diploma (including GED) or higher: 83.8% (2007); Bachelor's degree or higher: 23.2% (2007); Master's degree or higher: 8.6% (2007).

Housing: Homeownership rate: 65.1% (2007); Median home value: $114,787 (2007); Median rent: $427 per month (2000); Median age of housing: 38 years (2000).

Health: Birth rate: 130.5 per 10,000 population (2007); Death rate: 102.2 per 10,000 population (2007); Age-adjusted cancer mortality rate: 191.6 deaths per 100,000 population (2005); Air Quality Index: 77.3% good, 21.1% moderate, 1.6% unhealthy for sensitive individuals, 0.0% unhealthy (percent of days in 2007); Number of physicians: 36.3 per 10,000 population (2005); Hospital beds: 50.3 per 10,000 population (2004); Hospital admissions: 1,865.0 per 10,000 population (2004).

Elections: 2004 Presidential election results: 49.0% Bush, 50.6% Kerry, 0.0% Nader, 0.2% Badnarik

National and State Parks: Miamisburg Mound State Memorial; Sycamore State Park

Additional Information Contacts

Montgomery County Government . . . . (937) 225-4690
http://www.co.montgomery.oh.us
Brookville Chamber of Commerce . . . . (937) 833-2375
http://www.brookvilleohio.com/inner/chamber%20_of_commerce.h
City of Centerville . . . . (937) 433-7151
http://www.ci.centerville.oh.us
City of Clayton . . . . (937) 836-3500
http://www.clayton.oh.us
City of Dayton . . . . (937) 333-3333
http://www.cityofdayton.org
City of Englewood . . . . (937) 836-5106
http://www.ci.englewood.oh.us
City of Huber Heights . . . . (937) 233-1423
http://www.ci.huber-heights.oh.us
City of Kettering . . . . (937) 296-2400
http://www.ketteringoh.org
City of Miamisburg . . . . (937) 866-3303
http://www.ci.miamisburg.oh.us
City of Moraine . . . . (937) 535-1000
http://www.ci.moraine.oh.us
City of Riverside . . . . (937) 233-1801
http://www.riverside.oh.us
City of Trotwood . . . . (937) 837-7771
http://www.trotwood.org
City of Union . . . . (937) 836-8624
http://www.ci.union.oh.us
City of Vandalia . . . . (937) 898-5891
http://www.ci.vandalia.oh.us
City of West Carrollton City . . . . (937) 859-5183
http://www.westcarrollton.org
Dayton Area Chamber of Commerce . . . . (937) 226-1444
http://www.daytonchamber.org
Dayton/Montgomery Co. Convention & Visitors Bureau . . . (937) 226-8211
http://www.daytoncvb.com
Huber Heights Chamber of Commerce . . . . (937) 233-5700
http://www.huberheightschamber.com
Kettering-Moraine-Oakwood Chamber of Commerce . . . . . (937) 299-3852
http://www.kmo-coc.org
Northmont Area Chamber of Commerce . . . . (937) 836-2550
http://northmont-area-coc.org
South Metro Regional Chamber of Commerce . . . . (937) 433-2032
http://www.smrcoc.org
Trotwood Chamber of Commerce . . . . (937) 837-1484
http://trotwoodchamber.org
Vandalia-Butler Chamber of Commerce . . . . (937) 898-5351
http://www.vandaliabutlerchamber.org
Village of Brookville . . . . (937) 833-2135
http://www.brookvilleohio.com
Village of Germantown . . . . (937) 855-7255
http://www.ci.germantown.oh.us
Village of New Lebanon . . . . (937) 687-1341
http://www.newlebanonoh.com

Montgomery County Communities

BROOKVILLE (city). Covers a land area of 3.368 square miles and a water area of 0 square miles. Located at 39.83° N. Lat.; 84.41° W. Long. Elevation is 1,030 feet.

Population: 5,087 (1990); 5,289 (2000); 5,549 (2007); 5,703 (2012 projected); Race: 98.4% White, 0.1% Black, 0.8% Asian, 0.5% Hispanic of any race (2007); Density: 1,647.8 persons per square mile (2007); Average household size: 2.33 (2007); Median age: 42.0 (2007); Males per 100 females: 88.3 (2007); Marriage status: 21.0% never married, 58.4% now married, 8.8% widowed, 11.8% divorced (2000); Foreign born: 0.5% (2000); Ancestry (includes multiple ancestries): 31.0% German, 13.3% United States or American, 10.2% Irish, 6.3% English, 4.8% Other groups (2000).

Economy: Single-family building permits issued: 26 (2007); Multi-family building permits issued: 10 (2007); Employment by occupation: 8.3% management, 17.9% professional, 14.4% services, 26.5% sales, 0.0% farming, 11.2% construction, 21.7% production (2000).

Income: Per capita income: $24,357 (2007); Median household income: $45,553 (2007); Average household income: $55,976 (2007); Percent of

households with income of $100,000 or more: 11.4% (2007); Poverty rate: 5.3% (2000).
Education: Percent of population age 25 and over with: High school diploma (including GED) or higher: 83.6% (2007); Bachelor's degree or higher: 18.6% (2007); Master's degree or higher: 7.7% (2007).

School District(s)

Brookville Local (PK-12)
2005-06 Enrollment: 1,605 . . . . (937) 833-2181
Housing: Homeownership rate: 67.0% (2007); Median home value: $119,444 (2007); Median rent: $445 per month (2000); Median age of housing: 38 years (2000).
Safety: Violent crime rate: 1.9 per 10,000 population; Property crime rate: 124.4 per 10,000 population (2007).
Newspapers: Brookville Star (Community news; Circulation 6,300)
Transportation: Commute to work: 93.5% car, 0.3% public transportation, 3.1% walk, 1.6% work from home (2000); Travel time to work: 34.9% less than 15 minutes, 28.7% 15 to 30 minutes, 26.9% 30 to 45 minutes, 4.7% 45 to 60 minutes, 4.7% 60 minutes or more (2000)
Additional Information Contacts
Brookville Chamber of Commerce . . . . (937) 833-2375
http://www.brookvilleohio.com/inner/chamber%20_of_commerce.h
Village of Brookville . . . . (937) 833-2135
http://www.brookvilleohio.com

CENTERVILLE (city). Covers a land area of 10.200 square miles and a water area of 0.019 square miles. Located at 39.63° N. Lat.; 84.14° W. Long. Elevation is 1,020 feet.
History: Incorporated 1879.
Population: 21,563 (1990); 23,024 (2000); 22,871 (2007); 22,815 (2012 projected); Race: 90.8% White, 3.7% Black, 3.6% Asian, 1.4% Hispanic of any race (2007); Density: 2,242.2 persons per square mile (2007); Average household size: 2.26 (2007); Median age: 44.2 (2007); Males per 100 females: 87.8 (2007); Marriage status: 20.2% never married, 61.7% now married, 7.9% widowed, 10.1% divorced (2000); Foreign born: 4.2% (2000); Ancestry (includes multiple ancestries): 34.1% German, 17.7% Irish, 14.9% English, 9.8% Other groups, 6.2% United States or American (2000).
Economy: Single-family building permits issued: 58 (2007); Multi-family building permits issued: 0 (2007); Employment by occupation: 18.8% management, 32.8% professional, 9.7% services, 28.3% sales, 0.0% farming, 3.9% construction, 6.6% production (2000).
Income: Per capita income: $35,532 (2007); Median household income: $63,032 (2007); Average household income: $78,932 (2007); Percent of households with income of $100,000 or more: 26.3% (2007); Poverty rate: 4.1% (2000).
Education: Percent of population age 25 and over with: High school diploma (including GED) or higher: 95.5% (2007); Bachelor's degree or higher: 45.8% (2007); Master's degree or higher: 17.9% (2007).

School District(s)

Centerville City (PK-12)
2005-06 Enrollment: 8,196 . . . . (937) 433-8841

Two-year College(s)

RETS Tech Center (Private, For-profit)
Fall 2007 Enrollment: 744 . . . . (937) 433-3410
2007-08 Tuition: In-state $8,641; Out-of-state $8,641

Vocational/Technical School(s)

David Curtis School of Floral Design (Private, For-profit)
Fall 2007 Enrollment: n/a. . . . . (937) 433-0566
Housing: Homeownership rate: 74.6% (2007); Median home value: $163,878 (2007); Median rent: $556 per month (2000); Median age of housing: 24 years (2000).
Safety: Violent crime rate: 4.8 per 10,000 population; Property crime rate: 243.8 per 10,000 population (2007).
Newspapers: Pursuit (Local news)
Transportation: Commute to work: 95.5% car, 1.0% public transportation, 0.5% walk, 2.8% work from home (2000); Travel time to work: 29.7% less than 15 minutes, 49.3% 15 to 30 minutes, 13.5% 30 to 45 minutes, 3.7% 45 to 60 minutes, 3.8% 60 minutes or more (2000)
Additional Information Contacts
City of Centerville. . . . . (937) 433-7151
http://www.ci.centerville.oh.us

CLAYTON (city). Covers a land area of 18.444 square miles and a water area of 0.113 square miles. Located at 39.85° N. Lat.; 84.31° W. Long. Elevation is 1,001 feet.
Population: 13,159 (1990); 13,347 (2000); 13,153 (2007); 12,989 (2012 projected); Race: 83.6% White, 12.9% Black, 1.6% Asian, 1.1% Hispanic of any race (2007); Density: 713.1 persons per square mile (2007); Average household size: 2.62 (2007); Median age: 41.4 (2007); Males per 100 females: 97.7 (2007); Marriage status: 20.8% never married, 66.0% now married, 4.6% widowed, 8.6% divorced (2000); Foreign born: 2.1% (2000); Ancestry (includes multiple ancestries): 32.2% German, 14.7% Other groups, 14.2% Irish, 9.7% English, 8.7% United States or American (2000).
Economy: Employment by occupation: 18.4% management, 24.7% professional, 11.3% services, 28.1% sales, 0.0% farming, 7.3% construction, 10.2% production (2000).
Income: Per capita income: $31,222 (2007); Median household income: $66,719 (2007); Average household income: $81,717 (2007); Percent of households with income of $100,000 or more: 25.2% (2007); Poverty rate: 4.4% (2000).
Taxes: Total city taxes per capita: $332 (2006); City property taxes per capita: $160 (2006).
Education: Percent of population age 25 and over with: High school diploma (including GED) or higher: 91.5% (2007); Bachelor's degree or higher: 32.5% (2007); Master's degree or higher: 12.7% (2007).

School District(s)

Miami Valley Career Tech (07-12)
2005-06 Enrollment: n/a . . . . (937) 837-7781
Northmont City (KG-12)
2005-06 Enrollment: 5,972 . . . . (937) 832-5000

Vocational/Technical School(s)

Miami Valley Career Technology Center (Public)
Fall 2007 Enrollment: 326 . . . . (800) 716-7161
2007-08 Tuition: $8,625
Housing: Homeownership rate: 85.2% (2007); Median home value: $153,331 (2007); Median rent: $472 per month (2000); Median age of housing: 29 years (2000).
Transportation: Commute to work: 95.3% car, 0.7% public transportation, 1.1% walk, 2.5% work from home (2000); Travel time to work: 26.1% less than 15 minutes, 44.6% 15 to 30 minutes, 22.2% 30 to 45 minutes, 3.3% 45 to 60 minutes, 3.9% 60 minutes or more (2000)
Additional Information Contacts
City of Clayton . . . . (937) 836-3500
http://www.clayton.oh.us

DAYTON (city). County seat. Covers a land area of 55.777 square miles and a water area of 0.851 square miles. Located at 39.76° N. Lat.; 84.19° W. Long. Elevation is 738 feet.
History: Settlers began coming in 1795 to the site where the Great Miami River was joined by the Stillwater and Mad Rivers and Wolf Creek. When Ohio became a state in 1803, Dayton became the Montgomery County seat, and two years later the town was incorporated. The opening of the canal system in the 1830's increased Dayton's river traffic, augmented by the railroad traffic that began in 1851. Industries such as the railroad car works and the National Cash Register Company were founded between 1850 and 1890, and by the early 1900's locally-made Stoddard-Dayton, Speedwell, and Big Four automobiles were wheeling around Dayton. Wilbur and Orville Wright used the Dayton Public Library to learn about aerodynamics, and soon established an experimental airplane factory here. Charles F. Kettering came to Dayton to work at the cash register plant, invented a quick-starting electric motor, and started the Dayton Engineering Laboratories Company (Delco). Dayton suffered recurring floods until a system of levees and dams to restrain the rivers was completed in 1921.
Population: 182,920 (1990); 166,179 (2000); 156,800 (2007); 149,884 (2012 projected); Race: 52.1% White, 43.8% Black, 0.7% Asian, 2.1% Hispanic of any race (2007); Density: 2,811.2 persons per square mile (2007); Average household size: 2.42 (2007); Median age: 34.4 (2007); Males per 100 females: 95.0 (2007); Marriage status: 38.7% never married, 39.2% now married, 7.8% widowed, 14.3% divorced (2000); Foreign born: 2.0% (2000); Ancestry (includes multiple ancestries): 40.1% Other groups, 14.4% German, 8.3% Irish, 7.7% United States or American, 4.9% English (2000).
Economy: Unemployment rate: 8.4% (6/2008); Total civilian labor force: 71,217 (6/2008); Single-family building permits issued: 134 (2007); Multi-family building permits issued: 0 (2007); Employment by occupation: 8.6% management, 17.1% professional, 21.1% services, 25.3% sales, 0.1% farming, 7.8% construction, 20.0% production (2000).
Income: Per capita income: $17,581 (2007); Median household income: $31,187 (2007); Average household income: $41,353 (2007); Percent of

households with income of $100,000 or more: 6.6% (2007); Poverty rate: 23.0% (2000).

Taxes: Total city taxes per capita: $877 (2006); City property taxes per capita: $143 (2006).

Education: Percent of population age 25 and over with: High school diploma (including GED) or higher: 75.6% (2007); Bachelor's degree or higher: 14.9% (2007); Master's degree or higher: 5.1% (2007).

School District(s)

Arise Sports Management Academy (09-12)
2005-06 Enrollment: 154 . . . . (937) 853-0560
Centerville City (PK-12)
2005-06 Enrollment: 8,196 . . . . (937) 433-8841
City Day Community School (KG-07)
2005-06 Enrollment: 180 . . . . (937) 223-8130
Colin Powell Leadership Acad (KG-09)
2005-06 Enrollment: 196 . . . . (937) 263-3937
Dayton Academy The (KG-08)
2005-06 Enrollment: 846 . . . . (937) 262-4080
Dayton City (PK-12)
2005-06 Enrollment: 17,054 . . . . (937) 542-3000
Dayton View Academy (KG-08)
2005-06 Enrollment: 778 . . . . (937) 567-9426
East End Community School (KG-05)
2005-06 Enrollment: 165 . . . . (937) 222-7355
Emerson Academy of Dayton (KG-06)
2005-06 Enrollment: 367 . . . . (937) 223-2889
General Chappie James Leadership Academy (09-12)
2005-06 Enrollment: 75 . . . . (937) 835-3580
Horizon Science Academy-Dayton (05-08)
2005-06 Enrollment: 99 . . . . (937) 277-1177
Jefferson Township Local (KG-12)
2005-06 Enrollment: 702 . . . . (937) 835-5682
Kettering City (PK-12)
2005-06 Enrollment: 7,605 . . . . (937) 499-1400
Life Skills Center of Dayton (09-12)
2005-06 Enrollment: 281 . . . . (937) 274-2841
Mad River Local (KG-12)
2005-06 Enrollment: 3,724 . . . . (937) 259-6606
Main Street Automotive Magnet School (08-12)
2005-06 Enrollment: 78 . . . . (937) 222-2725
Miami Valley Career Tech (07-12)
2005-06 Enrollment: n/a . . . . (937) 837-7781
Miamisburg City (PK-12)
2005-06 Enrollment: 5,548 . . . . (937) 866-3381
Moraine Community School (KG-12)
2005-06 Enrollment: 200 . . . . (937) 294-4522
Mound Street Health Careers Acadmy (09-12)
2005-06 Enrollment: 112 . . . . (937) 223-3041
Mound Street It Careers Academy (09-12)
2005-06 Enrollment: 110 . . . . (937) 223-3041
Mound Street Military Careers Academy (09-12)
2005-06 Enrollment: 97 . . . . (937) 223-3041
New City School (02-11)
2005-06 Enrollment: 59 . . . . (937) 277-7155
North Dayton School of Science & Discovery (KG-08)
2005-06 Enrollment: 676 . . . . (937) 278-6671
Northmont City (KG-12)
2005-06 Enrollment: 5,972 . . . . (937) 832-5000
Northridge Local (PK-12)
2005-06 Enrollment: 1,858 . . . . (937) 278-5885
Nu Bethel Center of Excellence (KG-06)
2005-06 Enrollment: 28 . . . . (937) 222-0338
Oakwood City (PK-12)
2005-06 Enrollment: 2,109 . . . . (937) 297-5332
Omega School of Excellence (05-08)
2005-06 Enrollment: 137 . . . . (937) 278-2372
Pathway School of Discovery (KG-07)
2005-06 Enrollment: 638 . . . . (937) 235-5498
Pete Entrepreneurship Training Academy (09-12)
2005-06 Enrollment: 130 . . . . (937) 853-0560
Rhea Academy Inc (02-09)
2005-06 Enrollment: 37 . . . . (937) 461-7432
Richard Allen Academy (01-08)
2005-06 Enrollment: 202 . . . . (937) 586-9815
Richard Allen Academy II (KG-08)
2005-06 Enrollment: 501 . . . . (937) 586-9756
Richard Allen Preparatory (01-08)
2005-06 Enrollment: 177 . . . . (937) 567-9124
Summit Academy Dayton (01-07)
2005-06 Enrollment: 57 . . . . (937) 223-3154
Summit Academy Secondary School - Dayton (07-10)
2005-06 Enrollment: 27 . . . . (937) 223-3154
Tech Con Institute (09-12)
2005-06 Enrollment: 47 . . . . (937) 854-4000
The Isus Institute of Construction Technology (11-12)
2005-06 Enrollment: 126 . . . . (937) 223-2323
The Isus Institute of Health Care (11-12)
2005-06 Enrollment: 36 . . . . (937) 223-2323
The Isus Institute of Manufacturing (11-12)
2005-06 Enrollment: 59 . . . . (937) 223-2323
The New Choices Community (07-09)
2005-06 Enrollment: 176 . . . . (937) 224-8201
Trotwood-Madison City (KG-12)
2005-06 Enrollment: 3,307 . . . . (937) 854-3050
Vandalia-Butler City (PK-12)
2005-06 Enrollment: 3,438 . . . . (937) 415-6400
West Carrollton City (PK-12)
2005-06 Enrollment: 3,821 . . . . (937) 859-5121
Wow Community School (KG-06)
2005-06 Enrollment: 357 . . . . (937) 542-3600
Wright-Dunbar Technology Academy (09-12)
2005-06 Enrollment: 69 . . . . (937) 835-0020

Four-year College(s)

Air Force Institute of Technology-Graduate School of Eng & Mgmt (Public)
Fall 2007 Enrollment: 834 . . . . (937) 255-3636
United Theological Seminary (Private, Not-for-profit, United Methodist)
Fall 2007 Enrollment: 248 . . . . (937) 529-2201
University of Dayton (Private, Not-for-profit, Roman Catholic)
Fall 2007 Enrollment: 10,395. . . . . (937) 229-1000
2007-08 Tuition: In-state $25,950; Out-of-state $25,950
Wright State University-Main Campus (Public)
Fall 2007 Enrollment: 16,151. . . . . (937) 775-3333
2007-08 Tuition: In-state $7,018; Out-of-state $13,744

Two-year College(s)

Carousel Beauty College (Private, For-profit)
Fall 2007 Enrollment: 39 . . . . (937) 223-3572
Creative Images Institute of Cosmetology (Private, For-profit)
Fall 2007 Enrollment: 157 . . . . (937) 454-1200
Creative Images Institute of Cosmetology (Private, For-profit)
Fall 2007 Enrollment: 113 . . . . (937) 433-1944
Dayton Barber College (Private, For-profit)
Fall 2007 Enrollment: 49 . . . . (937) 222-9101
ITT Technical Institute-Dayton (Private, For-profit)
Fall 2007 Enrollment: 452 . . . . (937) 264-7700
2007-08 Tuition: In-state $15,600; Out-of-state $15,600
International College of Broadcasting (Private, For-profit)
Fall 2007 Enrollment: 84 . . . . (937) 258-8251
2007-08 Tuition: In-state $8,520; Out-of-state $8,520
Miami-Jacobs Career College (Private, For-profit)
Fall 2007 Enrollment: 811 . . . . (937) 461-5174
2007-08 Tuition: In-state $10,440; Out-of-state $10,440
Ohio Institute of Photography and Technology (Private, For-profit)
Fall 2007 Enrollment: 569 . . . . (937) 294-6155
2007-08 Tuition: In-state $19,178; Out-of-state $19,178
Sinclair Community College (Public)
Fall 2007 Enrollment: 18,691. . . . . (937) 512-3000
2007-08 Tuition: In-state $2,646; Out-of-state $5,220
Southwestern College (Private, For-profit)
Fall 2007 Enrollment: 600 . . . . (937) 224-0061
2007-08 Tuition: In-state $9,625; Out-of-state $9,625

Vocational/Technical School(s)

Dayton School of Medical Massage (Private, For-profit)
Fall 2007 Enrollment: 706 . . . . (937) 294-6994
2007-08 Tuition: In-state $14,800; Out-of-state $14,800

Housing: Homeownership rate: 53.3% (2007); Median home value: $79,344 (2007); Median rent: $359 per month (2000); Median age of housing: 51 years (2000).

Hospitals: 74th Medical Group, Wright-Patterson Airforce Base (101 beds); Children's Medical Center (155 beds); Dayton Heart Hospital (47

beds); Dayton Veterans Affairs Medical Center (539 beds); Good Samaritan Hospital and Health Center (560 beds); Grandview Hospital and Medical Center (452 beds); Kindred Hospital Dayton (67 beds); Miami Valley Hospital (848 beds); Twin Valley Behavioral Healthcare-Dayton Campus
Safety: Violent crime rate: 102.7 per 10,000 population; Property crime rate: 672.9 per 10,000 population (2007).
Newspapers: Citizens Newspaper; Daily Court Reporter (Local news; Circulation 750); Dayton City Paper (Local news; Circulation 30,000); Dayton Daily News (Local news; Circulation 168,645); Down Towner (Local news; Circulation 24,500); Huber Heights Courier (Community news; Circulation 11,500); Oakwood Register (Community news; Circulation 6,900)
Transportation: Commute to work: 85.2% car, 7.0% public transportation, 5.3% walk, 1.6% work from home (2000); Travel time to work: 33.5% less than 15 minutes, 46.9% 15 to 30 minutes, 11.3% 30 to 45 minutes, 3.6% 45 to 60 minutes, 4.7% 60 minutes or more (2000)
Airports: Dayton-Wright Brothers (general aviation); James M Cox Dayton International (primary service/small hub); Wright-Patterson AFB (general aviation)
Additional Information Contacts
City of Dayton .... (937) 333-3333
http://www.cityofdayton.org
Dayton Area Chamber of Commerce.................. (937) 226-1444
http://www.daytonchamber.org
Dayton/Montgomery Co. Convention & Visitors Bureau ... (937) 226-8211
http://www.daytoncvb.com
South Metro Regional Chamber of Commerce .... (937) 433-2032
http://www.smrcoc.org

DREXEL (CDP). Covers a land area of 2.180 square miles and a water area of 0 square miles. Located at 39.74° N. Lat.; 84.29° W. Long. Elevation is 951 feet.
Population: 2,449 (1990); 2,057 (2000); 2,008 (2007); 1,967 (2012 projected); Race: 60.8% White, 35.4% Black, 0.2% Asian, 1.0% Hispanic of any race (2007); Density: 921.0 persons per square mile (2007); Average household size: 2.59 (2007); Median age: 32.0 (2007); Males per 100 females: 92.9 (2007); Marriage status: 37.6% never married, 38.8% now married, 12.2% widowed, 11.3% divorced (2000); Foreign born: 0.2% (2000); Ancestry (includes multiple ancestries): 38.2% Other groups, 14.5% United States or American, 13.1% Irish, 4.4% German, 2.4% Dutch (2000).
Economy: Employment by occupation: 2.2% management, 9.5% professional, 33.2% services, 16.6% sales, 0.0% farming, 12.6% construction, 25.9% production (2000).
Income: Per capita income: $11,545 (2007); Median household income: $23,353 (2007); Average household income: $29,352 (2007); Percent of households with income of $100,000 or more: 3.0% (2007); Poverty rate: 31.5% (2000).
Education: Percent of population age 25 and over with: High school diploma (including GED) or higher: 48.0% (2007); Bachelor's degree or higher: 5.5% (2007); Master's degree or higher: 1.2% (2007).
Housing: Homeownership rate: 61.0% (2007); Median home value: $59,224 (2007); Median rent: $297 per month (2000); Median age of housing: 50 years (2000).
Transportation: Commute to work: 87.0% car, 6.0% public transportation, 4.2% walk, 2.1% work from home (2000); Travel time to work: 21.4% less than 15 minutes, 48.7% 15 to 30 minutes, 17.9% 30 to 45 minutes, 6.9% 45 to 60 minutes, 5.0% 60 minutes or more (2000)

ENGLEWOOD (city). Covers a land area of 6.560 square miles and a water area of 0.045 square miles. Located at 39.86° N. Lat.; 84.30° W. Long. Elevation is 915 feet.
History: Englewood was established as a Mennonite community by descendants of a group that had been invited to Pennsylvania by William Penn.
Population: 11,620 (1990); 12,235 (2000); 12,897 (2007); 13,264 (2012 projected); Race: 90.4% White, 6.0% Black, 1.6% Asian, 1.1% Hispanic of any race (2007); Density: 1,966.0 persons per square mile (2007); Average household size: 2.35 (2007); Median age: 40.9 (2007); Males per 100 females: 90.4 (2007); Marriage status: 19.9% never married, 61.2% now married, 9.1% widowed, 9.8% divorced (2000); Foreign born: 2.5% (2000); Ancestry (includes multiple ancestries): 31.8% German, 11.4% Irish, 11.1% United States or American, 11.1% English, 10.8% Other groups (2000).
Economy: Single-family building permits issued: 36 (2007); Multi-family building permits issued: 6 (2007); Employment by occupation: 13.4% management, 22.6% professional, 13.6% services, 26.8% sales, 0.1% farming, 7.9% construction, 15.6% production (2000).
Income: Per capita income: $27,026 (2007); Median household income: $53,004 (2007); Average household income: $62,801 (2007); Percent of households with income of $100,000 or more: 16.9% (2007); Poverty rate: 5.1% (2000).
Education: Percent of population age 25 and over with: High school diploma (including GED) or higher: 88.1% (2007); Bachelor's degree or higher: 23.3% (2007); Master's degree or higher: 7.2% (2007).
School District(s)
Northmont City (KG-12)
2005-06 Enrollment: 5,972 .... (937) 832-5000
Housing: Homeownership rate: 72.9% (2007); Median home value: $134,576 (2007); Median rent: $459 per month (2000); Median age of housing: 27 years (2000).
Safety: Violent crime rate: 14.0 per 10,000 population; Property crime rate: 341.0 per 10,000 population (2007).
Newspapers: Englewood Independent (Community news; Circulation 6,500)
Transportation: Commute to work: 94.6% car, 0.4% public transportation, 2.1% walk, 2.0% work from home (2000); Travel time to work: 28.2% less than 15 minutes, 41.5% 15 to 30 minutes, 24.3% 30 to 45 minutes, 2.5% 45 to 60 minutes, 3.6% 60 minutes or more (2000)
Additional Information Contacts
City of Englewood .... (937) 836-5106
http://www.ci.englewood.oh.us
Northmont Area Chamber of Commerce............... (937) 836-2550
http://northmont-area-coc.org

FARMERSVILLE (village). Covers a land area of 0.705 square miles and a water area of 0 square miles. Located at 39.68° N. Lat.; 84.42° W. Long. Elevation is 879 feet.
Population: 934 (1990); 980 (2000); 1,017 (2007); 1,040 (2012 projected); Race: 98.9% White, 0.2% Black, 0.2% Asian, 0.5% Hispanic of any race (2007); Density: 1,442.1 persons per square mile (2007); Average household size: 2.69 (2007); Median age: 34.9 (2007); Males per 100 females: 96.0 (2007); Marriage status: 19.3% never married, 64.4% now married, 6.5% widowed, 9.8% divorced (2000); Foreign born: 0.2% (2000); Ancestry (includes multiple ancestries): 30.3% German, 24.7% United States or American, 6.8% Other groups, 6.8% Irish, 5.1% English (2000).
Economy: Employment by occupation: 6.3% management, 11.6% professional, 18.9% services, 27.1% sales, 0.2% farming, 12.0% construction, 23.9% production (2000).
Income: Per capita income: $20,501 (2007); Median household income: $50,000 (2007); Average household income: $55,159 (2007); Percent of households with income of $100,000 or more: 11.6% (2007); Poverty rate: 3.5% (2000).
Education: Percent of population age 25 and over with: High school diploma (including GED) or higher: 84.2% (2007); Bachelor's degree or higher: 8.0% (2007); Master's degree or higher: 2.7% (2007).
School District(s)
Valley View Local (PK-12)
2005-06 Enrollment: 2,079 .... (937) 855-6581
Housing: Homeownership rate: 79.6% (2007); Median home value: $109,056 (2007); Median rent: $400 per month (2000); Median age of housing: 47 years (2000).
Transportation: Commute to work: 93.4% car, 0.0% public transportation, 3.2% walk, 3.4% work from home (2000); Travel time to work: 23.7% less than 15 minutes, 39.6% 15 to 30 minutes, 29.2% 30 to 45 minutes, 4.6% 45 to 60 minutes, 2.9% 60 minutes or more (2000)

FORT MCKINLEY (CDP). Covers a land area of 1.332 square miles and a water area of 0 square miles. Located at 39.79° N. Lat.; 84.24° W. Long. Elevation is 919 feet.
Population: 4,238 (1990); 3,989 (2000); 3,774 (2007); 3,644 (2012 projected); Race: 32.7% White, 63.5% Black, 0.3% Asian, 0.6% Hispanic of any race (2007); Density: 2,833.0 persons per square mile (2007); Average household size: 2.44 (2007); Median age: 38.3 (2007); Males per 100 females: 85.8 (2007); Marriage status: 34.3% never married, 42.7% now married, 9.2% widowed, 13.8% divorced (2000); Foreign born: 3.8% (2000); Ancestry (includes multiple ancestries): 52.0% Other groups, 11.0% German, 5.4% United States or American, 5.0% Irish, 2.9% English (2000).

Economy: Employment by occupation: 8.9% management, 10.7% professional, 18.8% services, 23.8% sales, 0.0% farming, 10.8% construction, 27.0% production (2000).
Income: Per capita income: $17,282 (2007); Median household income: $34,320 (2007); Average household income: $41,787 (2007); Percent of households with income of $100,000 or more: 5.4% (2007); Poverty rate: 15.4% (2000).
Education: Percent of population age 25 and over with: High school diploma (including GED) or higher: 74.9% (2007); Bachelor's degree or higher: 9.6% (2007); Master's degree or higher: 2.6% (2007).
Housing: Homeownership rate: 78.0% (2007); Median home value: $68,773 (2007); Median rent: $398 per month (2000); Median age of housing: 42 years (2000).
Transportation: Commute to work: 94.6% car, 3.0% public transportation, 1.0% walk, 1.5% work from home (2000); Travel time to work: 19.6% less than 15 minutes, 57.9% 15 to 30 minutes, 16.2% 30 to 45 minutes, 2.1% 45 to 60 minutes, 4.2% 60 minutes or more (2000)

GERMANTOWN (village). Covers a land area of 3.588 square miles and a water area of 0 square miles. Located at 39.62° N. Lat.; 84.36° W. Long. Elevation is 722 feet.
History: Laid out 1814.
Population: 4,916 (1990); 4,884 (2000); 5,176 (2007); 5,355 (2012 projected); Race: 98.4% White, 0.3% Black, 0.4% Asian, 1.1% Hispanic of any race (2007); Density: 1,442.6 persons per square mile (2007); Average household size: 2.50 (2007); Median age: 38.8 (2007); Males per 100 females: 97.7 (2007); Marriage status: 18.4% never married, 63.1% now married, 6.2% widowed, 12.3% divorced (2000); Foreign born: 0.6% (2000); Ancestry (includes multiple ancestries): 25.3% German, 12.7% Irish, 11.2% Other groups, 8.5% United States or American, 7.9% English (2000).
Economy: Employment by occupation: 13.1% management, 16.0% professional, 12.4% services, 24.6% sales, 0.0% farming, 10.9% construction, 23.0% production (2000).
Income: Per capita income: $28,030 (2007); Median household income: $54,735 (2007); Average household income: $69,889 (2007); Percent of households with income of $100,000 or more: 18.7% (2007); Poverty rate: 5.8% (2000).
Education: Percent of population age 25 and over with: High school diploma (including GED) or higher: 86.0% (2007); Bachelor's degree or higher: 18.7% (2007); Master's degree or higher: 6.6% (2007).

School District(s)

Valley View Local (PK-12)
2005-06 Enrollment: 2,079 . . . . (937) 855-6581

Housing: Homeownership rate: 74.4% (2007); Median home value: $122,793 (2007); Median rent: $424 per month (2000); Median age of housing: 40 years (2000).
Safety: Violent crime rate: 9.8 per 10,000 population; Property crime rate: 156.1 per 10,000 population (2007).
Newspapers: Booster (Community news; Circulation 6,500); Press (Community news; Circulation 2,500)
Transportation: Commute to work: 94.1% car, 1.0% public transportation, 2.9% walk, 1.2% work from home (2000); Travel time to work: 19.7% less than 15 minutes, 39.8% 15 to 30 minutes, 27.9% 30 to 45 minutes, 6.5% 45 to 60 minutes, 6.1% 60 minutes or more (2000)

Additional Information Contacts

Village of Germantown. . . . . (937) 855-7255
http://www.ci.germantown.oh.us

HUBER HEIGHTS (city). Covers a land area of 21.027 square miles and a water area of 0.095 square miles. Located at 39.85° N. Lat.; 84.12° W. Long. Elevation is 932 feet.
Population: 38,478 (1990); 38,212 (2000); 37,774 (2007); 37,334 (2012 projected); Race: 82.9% White, 10.9% Black, 2.4% Asian, 1.9% Hispanic of any race (2007); Density: 1,796.4 persons per square mile (2007); Average household size: 2.58 (2007); Median age: 36.5 (2007); Males per 100 females: 95.1 (2007); Marriage status: 22.6% never married, 61.3% now married, 5.0% widowed, 11.1% divorced (2000); Foreign born: 3.2% (2000); Ancestry (includes multiple ancestries): 24.9% German, 18.0% Other groups, 11.5% Irish, 10.3% English, 9.7% United States or American (2000).
Economy: Unemployment rate: 6.6% (6/2008); Total civilian labor force: 20,066 (6/2008); Employment by occupation: 12.3% management, 17.8% professional, 13.9% services, 27.5% sales, 0.1% farming, 8.5% construction, 19.9% production (2000).
Income: Per capita income: $24,296 (2007); Median household income: $53,628 (2007); Average household income: $62,555 (2007); Percent of households with income of $100,000 or more: 13.5% (2007); Poverty rate: 5.9% (2000).
Taxes: Total city taxes per capita: $421 (2006); City property taxes per capita: $87 (2006).
Education: Percent of population age 25 and over with: High school diploma (including GED) or higher: 88.3% (2007); Bachelor's degree or higher: 19.2% (2007); Master's degree or higher: 6.8% (2007).

School District(s)

Huber Heights City (PK-12)
2005-06 Enrollment: 6,756 . . . . (937) 237-6300

Two-year College(s)

Carousel of Miami Valley Beauty College (Private, For-profit)
Fall 2007 Enrollment: 71 . . . . (937) 223-3572

Housing: Homeownership rate: 72.4% (2007); Median home value: $111,407 (2007); Median rent: $515 per month (2000); Median age of housing: 29 years (2000).
Safety: Violent crime rate: 17.0 per 10,000 population; Property crime rate: 314.2 per 10,000 population (2007).
Transportation: Commute to work: 96.2% car, 0.9% public transportation, 0.7% walk, 1.7% work from home (2000); Travel time to work: 25.3% less than 15 minutes, 51.7% 15 to 30 minutes, 16.4% 30 to 45 minutes, 3.1% 45 to 60 minutes, 3.5% 60 minutes or more (2000)

Additional Information Contacts

City of Huber Heights. . . . . (937) 233-1423
http://www.ci.huber-heights.oh.us
Huber Heights Chamber of Commerce . . . . (937) 233-5700
http://www.huberheightschamber.com

KETTERING (city). Covers a land area of 18.685 square miles and a water area of 0 square miles. Located at 39.69° N. Lat.; 84.15° W. Long. Elevation is 1,007 feet.
History: Settled c.1812, incorporated 1952.
Population: 60,570 (1990); 57,502 (2000); 54,597 (2007); 52,442 (2012 projected); Race: 94.3% White, 2.1% Black, 1.5% Asian, 1.4% Hispanic of any race (2007); Density: 2,922.0 persons per square mile (2007); Average household size: 2.19 (2007); Median age: 41.2 (2007); Males per 100 females: 91.4 (2007); Marriage status: 23.7% never married, 56.9% now married, 8.1% widowed, 11.3% divorced (2000); Foreign born: 2.7% (2000); Ancestry (includes multiple ancestries): 33.8% German, 15.5% Irish, 12.7% English, 8.6% United States or American, 8.6% Other groups (2000).
Economy: Unemployment rate: 6.0% (6/2008); Total civilian labor force: 29,529 (6/2008); Single-family building permits issued: 42 (2007); Multi-family building permits issued: 6 (2007); Employment by occupation: 15.3% management, 24.2% professional, 12.0% services, 28.8% sales, 0.2% farming, 6.5% construction, 13.0% production (2000).
Income: Per capita income: $30,380 (2007); Median household income: $50,127 (2007); Average household income: $66,391 (2007); Percent of households with income of $100,000 or more: 15.3% (2007); Poverty rate: 4.6% (2000).
Taxes: Total city taxes per capita: $701 (2006); City property taxes per capita: $161 (2006).
Education: Percent of population age 25 and over with: High school diploma (including GED) or higher: 91.0% (2007); Bachelor's degree or higher: 31.1% (2007); Master's degree or higher: 11.3% (2007).

School District(s)

Kettering City (PK-12)
2005-06 Enrollment: 7,605 . . . . (937) 499-1400
Montgomery
2005-06 Enrollment: n/a . . . . (937) 225-4598

Four-year College(s)

Kettering College of Medical Arts (Private, Not-for-profit, Seventh Day Adventists)
Fall 2007 Enrollment: 808 . . . . (937) 395-8601
2007-08 Tuition: In-state $7,548; Out-of-state $7,548

Two-year College(s)

Carousel Beauty College (Private, For-profit)
Fall 2007 Enrollment: 76 . . . . (937) 223-3572
School of Advertising Art Inc (Private, For-profit)
Fall 2007 Enrollment: 150 . . . . (937) 294-0592
2007-08 Tuition: In-state $18,390; Out-of-state $18,390

Housing: Homeownership rate: 66.8% (2007); Median home value: $129,754 (2007); Median rent: $494 per month (2000); Median age of housing: 41 years (2000).
Hospitals: Kettering Medical Center (669 beds)
Safety: Violent crime rate: 14.4 per 10,000 population; Property crime rate: 295.3 per 10,000 population (2007).
Newspapers: Centerville-Bellbrook Times (Community news; Circulation 21,175); Kettering-Oakwood Times (Community news; Circulation 30,000)
Transportation: Commute to work: 93.9% car, 1.1% public transportation, 1.4% walk, 2.9% work from home (2000); Travel time to work: 33.6% less than 15 minutes, 50.2% 15 to 30 minutes, 10.5% 30 to 45 minutes, 2.7% 45 to 60 minutes, 3.0% 60 minutes or more (2000)
Additional Information Contacts
City of Kettering . . . . (937) 296-2400
http://www.ketteringoh.org
Kettering-Moraine-Oakwood Chamber of Commerce . . . . . (937) 299-3852
http://www.kmo-coc.org

MIAMISBURG (city). Covers a land area of 11.190 square miles and a water area of 0.189 square miles. Located at 39.63° N. Lat.; 84.27° W. Long. Elevation is 699 feet.
History: Miamisburg was laid out in 1818 on the site of a blockhouse called Hole's Station, which had been built by Zachariah Hole about 1800. The Hoover and Gamble Company, manufacturer of reapers, was founded here in 1840. Tobacco warehouses were situated in Miamisburg in the late 1800's.
Population: 18,641 (1990); 19,489 (2000); 19,537 (2007); 19,517 (2012 projected); Race: 95.1% White, 1.9% Black, 0.7% Asian, 1.1% Hispanic of any race (2007); Density: 1,745.9 persons per square mile (2007); Average household size: 2.58 (2007); Median age: 39.4 (2007); Males per 100 females: 92.5 (2007); Marriage status: 19.9% never married, 64.0% now married, 5.7% widowed, 10.4% divorced (2000); Foreign born: 1.7% (2000); Ancestry (includes multiple ancestries): 26.5% German, 12.9% United States or American, 12.4% Irish, 11.0% English, 8.0% Other groups (2000).
Economy: Single-family building permits issued: 39 (2007); Multi-family building permits issued: 0 (2007); Employment by occupation: 11.9% management, 19.3% professional, 13.4% services, 30.2% sales, 0.0% farming, 8.5% construction, 16.7% production (2000).
Income: Per capita income: $27,260 (2007); Median household income: $57,998 (2007); Average household income: $69,490 (2007); Percent of households with income of $100,000 or more: 20.2% (2007); Poverty rate: 6.1% (2000).
Education: Percent of population age 25 and over with: High school diploma (including GED) or higher: 83.5% (2007); Bachelor's degree or higher: 19.3% (2007); Master's degree or higher: 5.5% (2007).

School District(s)

Miamisburg City (PK-12)
2005-06 Enrollment: 5,548 . . . . (937) 866-3381
Miamisburg Secondary Digital Academy (09-12)
2005-06 Enrollment: 49 . . . . (937) 866-3381
Housing: Homeownership rate: 72.6% (2007); Median home value: $141,497 (2007); Median rent: $419 per month (2000); Median age of housing: 33 years (2000).
Safety: Violent crime rate: 13.6 per 10,000 population; Property crime rate: 369.4 per 10,000 population (2007).
Newspapers: Miamisburg News (Local news; Circulation 6,500)
Transportation: Commute to work: 94.8% car, 1.0% public transportation, 1.8% walk, 2.1% work from home (2000); Travel time to work: 36.1% less than 15 minutes, 47.0% 15 to 30 minutes, 10.5% 30 to 45 minutes, 3.2% 45 to 60 minutes, 3.2% 60 minutes or more (2000)
Additional Information Contacts
City of Miamisburg . . . . (937) 866-3303
http://www.ci.miamisburg.oh.us

MORAINE (city). Covers a land area of 9.071 square miles and a water area of 0.273 square miles. Located at 39.69° N. Lat.; 84.22° W. Long. Elevation is 738 feet.
Population: 6,722 (1990); 6,897 (2000); 6,525 (2007); 6,292 (2012 projected); Race: 87.6% White, 7.2% Black, 2.5% Asian, 1.9% Hispanic of any race (2007); Density: 719.3 persons per square mile (2007); Average household size: 2.36 (2007); Median age: 35.0 (2007); Males per 100 females: 99.8 (2007); Marriage status: 24.8% never married, 54.2% now married, 5.2% widowed, 15.8% divorced (2000); Foreign born: 4.3% (2000); Ancestry (includes multiple ancestries): 17.3% Other groups, 17.2% German, 15.3% United States or American, 14.7% Irish, 13.3% English (2000).
Economy: Single-family building permits issued: 9 (2007); Multi-family building permits issued: 0 (2007); Employment by occupation: 10.8% management, 10.9% professional, 15.6% services, 26.3% sales, 0.1% farming, 14.1% construction, 22.1% production (2000).
Income: Per capita income: $19,291 (2007); Median household income: $38,057 (2007); Average household income: $45,202 (2007); Percent of households with income of $100,000 or more: 6.4% (2007); Poverty rate: 9.6% (2000).
Education: Percent of population age 25 and over with: High school diploma (including GED) or higher: 75.0% (2007); Bachelor's degree or higher: 8.8% (2007); Master's degree or higher: 2.7% (2007).
Housing: Homeownership rate: 61.2% (2007); Median home value: $88,005 (2007); Median rent: $455 per month (2000); Median age of housing: 32 years (2000).
Transportation: Commute to work: 93.0% car, 1.7% public transportation, 0.8% walk, 3.2% work from home (2000); Travel time to work: 42.6% less than 15 minutes, 40.2% 15 to 30 minutes, 10.2% 30 to 45 minutes, 2.5% 45 to 60 minutes, 4.5% 60 minutes or more (2000)
Additional Information Contacts
City of Moraine . . . . (937) 535-1000
http://www.ci.moraine.oh.us
Kettering-Moraine-Oakwood Chamber of Commerce . . . . . (937) 299-3852
http://www.kmo-coc.org

NEW LEBANON (village). Covers a land area of 1.999 square miles and a water area of 0 square miles. Located at 39.74° N. Lat.; 84.39° W. Long. Elevation is 906 feet.
History: New Lebanon was established as a community of Dunkards. A murder and the burning of the town in 1876 were attributed to a conflict between warring gangs.
Population: 4,501 (1990); 4,231 (2000); 4,322 (2007); 4,370 (2012 projected); Race: 98.2% White, 0.4% Black, 0.1% Asian, 1.1% Hispanic of any race (2007); Density: 2,162.5 persons per square mile (2007); Average household size: 2.62 (2007); Median age: 36.8 (2007); Males per 100 females: 91.2 (2007); Marriage status: 20.4% never married, 58.0% now married, 8.4% widowed, 13.2% divorced (2000); Foreign born: 0.7% (2000); Ancestry (includes multiple ancestries): 24.9% German, 22.7% United States or American, 9.7% English, 9.2% Other groups, 8.5% Irish (2000).
Economy: Employment by occupation: 9.4% management, 10.8% professional, 12.9% services, 20.6% sales, 0.0% farming, 17.7% construction, 28.5% production (2000).
Income: Per capita income: $20,945 (2007); Median household income: $46,064 (2007); Average household income: $53,843 (2007); Percent of households with income of $100,000 or more: 7.4% (2007); Poverty rate: 5.4% (2000).
Education: Percent of population age 25 and over with: High school diploma (including GED) or higher: 78.8% (2007); Bachelor's degree or higher: 4.5% (2007); Master's degree or higher: 1.5% (2007).

School District(s)

New Lebanon Local (KG-12)
2005-06 Enrollment: 1,247 . . . . (937) 687-1301
Housing: Homeownership rate: 74.8% (2007); Median home value: $105,342 (2007); Median rent: $370 per month (2000); Median age of housing: 35 years (2000).
Safety: Violent crime rate: 14.5 per 10,000 population; Property crime rate: 163.9 per 10,000 population (2007).
Transportation: Commute to work: 99.1% car, 0.0% public transportation, 0.5% walk, 0.4% work from home (2000); Travel time to work: 16.3% less than 15 minutes, 41.8% 15 to 30 minutes, 33.4% 30 to 45 minutes, 2.6% 45 to 60 minutes, 5.9% 60 minutes or more (2000)
Additional Information Contacts
Village of New Lebanon . . . . (937) 687-1341
http://www.newlebanonoh.com

NORTHRIDGE (CDP). Covers a land area of 2.273 square miles and a water area of 0 square miles. Located at 39.80° N. Lat.; 84.19° W. Long. Elevation is 801 feet.
Population: 9,432 (1990); 8,487 (2000); 8,051 (2007); 7,826 (2012 projected); Race: 83.5% White, 14.1% Black, 0.1% Asian, 1.0% Hispanic of any race (2007); Density: 3,542.0 persons per square mile (2007); Average household size: 2.43 (2007); Median age: 34.4 (2007); Males per 100 females: 89.7 (2007); Marriage status: 31.4% never married, 46.0% now

married, 6.9% widowed, 15.7% divorced (2000); Foreign born: 0.7% (2000); Ancestry (includes multiple ancestries): 18.8% Other groups, 14.8% United States or American, 12.7% German, 8.8% Irish, 6.5% English (2000).
Economy: Employment by occupation: 3.2% management, 7.1% professional, 14.3% services, 30.3% sales, 0.2% farming, 12.5% construction, 32.3% production (2000).
Income: Per capita income: $15,427 (2007); Median household income: $29,887 (2007); Average household income: $37,456 (2007); Percent of households with income of $100,000 or more: 3.4% (2007); Poverty rate: 21.9% (2000).
Education: Percent of population age 25 and over with: High school diploma (including GED) or higher: 64.6% (2007); Bachelor's degree or higher: 3.5% (2007); Master's degree or higher: 1.3% (2007).
Housing: Homeownership rate: 61.0% (2007); Median home value: $76,916 (2007); Median rent: $345 per month (2000); Median age of housing: 44 years (2000).
Transportation: Commute to work: 94.2% car, 3.7% public transportation, 1.0% walk, 0.3% work from home (2000); Travel time to work: 38.6% less than 15 minutes, 44.6% 15 to 30 minutes, 9.8% 30 to 45 minutes, 2.9% 45 to 60 minutes, 4.2% 60 minutes or more (2000)

OAKWOOD (city). Covers a land area of 2.189 square miles and a water area of 0 square miles. Located at 39.71° N. Lat.; 84.17° W. Long. Elevation is 988 feet.
History: Incorporated as village in 1907; became city after 1930.
Population: 8,957 (1990); 9,215 (2000); 8,640 (2007); 8,209 (2012 projected); Race: 96.8% White, 0.6% Black, 1.1% Asian, 1.7% Hispanic of any race (2007); Density: 3,946.4 persons per square mile (2007); Average household size: 2.56 (2007); Median age: 40.9 (2007); Males per 100 females: 90.2 (2007); Marriage status: 18.6% never married, 66.3% now married, 4.7% widowed, 10.4% divorced (2000); Foreign born: 2.5% (2000); Ancestry (includes multiple ancestries): 34.0% German, 19.3% English, 18.3% Irish, 5.9% United States or American, 5.3% Italian (2000).
Economy: Employment by occupation: 26.5% management, 38.5% professional, 6.6% services, 19.6% sales, 0.0% farming, 3.0% construction, 5.7% production (2000).
Income: Per capita income: $46,919 (2007); Median household income: $86,719 (2007); Average household income: $119,642 (2007); Percent of households with income of $100,000 or more: 41.7% (2007); Poverty rate: 3.3% (2000).
Education: Percent of population age 25 and over with: High school diploma (including GED) or higher: 95.5% (2007); Bachelor's degree or higher: 63.0% (2007); Master's degree or higher: 30.6% (2007).
Housing: Homeownership rate: 83.7% (2007); Median home value: $225,052 (2007); Median rent: $502 per month (2000); Median age of housing: 59 years (2000).
Transportation: Commute to work: 92.4% car, 0.9% public transportation, 3.0% walk, 3.5% work from home (2000); Travel time to work: 43.8% less than 15 minutes, 42.1% 15 to 30 minutes, 7.8% 30 to 45 minutes, 1.5% 45 to 60 minutes, 4.9% 60 minutes or more (2000)
Additional Information Contacts
Kettering-Moraine-Oakwood Chamber of Commerce . . . . . (937) 299-3852
http://www.kmo-coc.org

PHILLIPSBURG (village). Covers a land area of 0.266 square miles and a water area of 0 square miles. Located at 39.90° N. Lat.; 84.40° W. Long. Elevation is 1,037 feet.
Population: 687 (1990); 628 (2000); 637 (2007); 644 (2012 projected); Race: 97.8% White, 1.4% Black, 0.0% Asian, 1.4% Hispanic of any race (2007); Density: 2,399.1 persons per square mile (2007); Average household size: 2.45 (2007); Median age: 37.4 (2007); Males per 100 females: 96.0 (2007); Marriage status: 23.7% never married, 60.8% now married, 5.8% widowed, 9.6% divorced (2000); Foreign born: 0.5% (2000); Ancestry (includes multiple ancestries): 40.4% German, 11.8% Irish, 8.0% United States or American, 5.1% English, 3.4% Other groups (2000).
Economy: Employment by occupation: 8.6% management, 8.6% professional, 16.6% services, 20.2% sales, 0.0% farming, 14.2% construction, 31.8% production (2000).
Income: Per capita income: $24,741 (2007); Median household income: $51,111 (2007); Average household income: $60,615 (2007); Percent of households with income of $100,000 or more: 10.0% (2007); Poverty rate: 6.1% (2000).
Education: Percent of population age 25 and over with: High school diploma (including GED) or higher: 84.9% (2007); Bachelor's degree or higher: 6.4% (2007); Master's degree or higher: 1.4% (2007).
School District(s)
Northmont City (KG-12)
2005-06 Enrollment: 5,972 . . . . (937) 832-5000
Housing: Homeownership rate: 80.4% (2007); Median home value: $114,352 (2007); Median rent: $432 per month (2000); Median age of housing: 60+ years (2000).
Transportation: Commute to work: 93.9% car, 1.0% public transportation, 3.7% walk, 1.4% work from home (2000); Travel time to work: 24.7% less than 15 minutes, 44.9% 15 to 30 minutes, 19.9% 30 to 45 minutes, 5.5% 45 to 60 minutes, 5.1% 60 minutes or more (2000)

RIVERSIDE (city). Covers a land area of 7.857 square miles and a water area of 0.041 square miles. Located at 39.77° N. Lat.; 84.12° W. Long. Elevation is 781 feet.
Population: 25,374 (1990); 23,545 (2000); 22,910 (2007); 22,406 (2012 projected); Race: 90.0% White, 4.9% Black, 2.0% Asian, 2.0% Hispanic of any race (2007); Density: 2,915.7 persons per square mile (2007); Average household size: 2.36 (2007); Median age: 39.0 (2007); Males per 100 females: 94.9 (2007); Marriage status: 24.2% never married, 55.1% now married, 7.4% widowed, 13.3% divorced (2000); Foreign born: 2.9% (2000); Ancestry (includes multiple ancestries): 22.3% German, 15.8% Other groups, 14.4% United States or American, 13.4% Irish, 9.1% English (2000).
Economy: Unemployment rate: 7.7% (6/2008); Total civilian labor force: 11,110 (6/2008); Employment by occupation: 9.1% management, 15.2% professional, 15.8% services, 27.5% sales, 0.2% farming, 10.5% construction, 21.6% production (2000).
Income: Per capita income: $21,010 (2007); Median household income: $40,604 (2007); Average household income: $49,576 (2007); Percent of households with income of $100,000 or more: 8.2% (2007); Poverty rate: 10.1% (2000).
Education: Percent of population age 25 and over with: High school diploma (including GED) or higher: 78.8% (2007); Bachelor's degree or higher: 15.3% (2007); Master's degree or higher: 5.3% (2007).
Housing: Homeownership rate: 65.7% (2007); Median home value: $98,898 (2007); Median rent: $417 per month (2000); Median age of housing: 41 years (2000).
Safety: Violent crime rate: 29.1 per 10,000 population; Property crime rate: 436.9 per 10,000 population (2007).
Transportation: Commute to work: 95.7% car, 1.2% public transportation, 0.9% walk, 1.2% work from home (2000); Travel time to work: 33.9% less than 15 minutes, 50.7% 15 to 30 minutes, 8.0% 30 to 45 minutes, 2.9% 45 to 60 minutes, 4.6% 60 minutes or more (2000)
Additional Information Contacts
City of Riverside. . . . . (937) 233-1801
http://www.riverside.oh.us

SHILOH (CDP). Covers a land area of 3.838 square miles and a water area of 0.052 square miles. Located at 39.80° N. Lat.; 84.22° W. Long. Elevation is 814 feet.
Population: 11,673 (1990); 11,272 (2000); 10,934 (2007); 10,580 (2012 projected); Race: 51.6% White, 44.6% Black, 0.5% Asian, 1.3% Hispanic of any race (2007); Density: 2,848.8 persons per square mile (2007); Average household size: 1.94 (2007); Median age: 45.6 (2007); Males per 100 females: 84.4 (2007); Marriage status: 26.9% never married, 47.2% now married, 10.5% widowed, 15.3% divorced (2000); Foreign born: 4.0% (2000); Ancestry (includes multiple ancestries): 36.1% Other groups, 18.6% German, 7.3% Irish, 6.9% English, 6.4% United States or American (2000).
Economy: Employment by occupation: 11.1% management, 25.1% professional, 12.2% services, 29.6% sales, 0.0% farming, 5.8% construction, 16.3% production (2000).
Income: Per capita income: $24,728 (2007); Median household income: $36,844 (2007); Average household income: $47,215 (2007); Percent of households with income of $100,000 or more: 9.1% (2007); Poverty rate: 10.0% (2000).
Education: Percent of population age 25 and over with: High school diploma (including GED) or higher: 84.5% (2007); Bachelor's degree or higher: 26.7% (2007); Master's degree or higher: 11.4% (2007).
School District(s)
Plymouth-Shiloh Local (PK-12)
2005-06 Enrollment: 999 . . . . (419) 687-4733

Housing: Homeownership rate: 53.9% (2007); Median home value: $106,956 (2007); Median rent: $419 per month (2000); Median age of housing: 38 years (2000).
Transportation: Commute to work: 93.8% car, 2.2% public transportation, 1.2% walk, 2.1% work from home (2000); Travel time to work: 27.1% less than 15 minutes, 47.8% 15 to 30 minutes, 16.1% 30 to 45 minutes, 4.4% 45 to 60 minutes, 4.6% 60 minutes or more (2000)

TROTWOOD (city). Covers a land area of 30.530 square miles and a water area of 0.014 square miles. Located at 39.79° N. Lat.; 84.29° W. Long. Elevation is 840 feet.
Population: 29,395 (1990); 27,420 (2000); 26,355 (2007); 25,574 (2012 projected); Race: 32.1% White, 64.5% Black, 0.2% Asian, 1.0% Hispanic of any race (2007); Density: 863.3 persons per square mile (2007); Average household size: 2.40 (2007); Median age: 40.0 (2007); Males per 100 females: 84.1 (2007); Marriage status: 27.9% never married, 49.4% now married, 8.9% widowed, 13.7% divorced (2000); Foreign born: 1.2% (2000); Ancestry (includes multiple ancestries): 53.5% Other groups, 8.2% German, 7.6% United States or American, 4.6% Irish, 3.4% English (2000).
Economy: Unemployment rate: 8.8% (6/2008); Total civilian labor force: 12,172 (6/2008); Single-family building permits issued: 3 (2007); Multi-family building permits issued: 0 (2007); Employment by occupation: 9.2% management, 15.5% professional, 15.8% services, 27.2% sales, 0.0% farming, 7.3% construction, 25.1% production (2000).
Income: Per capita income: $20,150 (2007); Median household income: $37,758 (2007); Average household income: $47,529 (2007); Percent of households with income of $100,000 or more: 8.8% (2007); Poverty rate: 15.3% (2000).
Education: Percent of population age 25 and over with: High school diploma (including GED) or higher: 78.2% (2007); Bachelor's degree or higher: 15.2% (2007); Master's degree or higher: 6.6% (2007).

School District(s)

Academy of Dayton (KG-08)
2005-06 Enrollment: 138 . . . . (937) 567-1072
Trotwood Fitness & Prep Acad (KG-08)
2005-06 Enrollment: 251 . . . . (937) 854-4100
Trotwood-Madison City (KG-12)
2005-06 Enrollment: 3,307 . . . . (937) 854-3050

Housing: Homeownership rate: 62.1% (2007); Median home value: $95,564 (2007); Median rent: $449 per month (2000); Median age of housing: 35 years (2000).
Transportation: Commute to work: 93.4% car, 3.5% public transportation, 1.0% walk, 1.5% work from home (2000); Travel time to work: 20.4% less than 15 minutes, 48.7% 15 to 30 minutes, 20.7% 30 to 45 minutes, 5.2% 45 to 60 minutes, 5.0% 60 minutes or more (2000)

Additional Information Contacts

City of Trotwood . . . . (937) 837-7771
http://www.trotwood.org
Trotwood Chamber of Commerce . . . . (937) 837-1484
http://trotwoodchamber.org

UNION (city). Covers a land area of 4.281 square miles and a water area of 0.001 square miles. Located at 39.90° N. Lat.; 84.31° W. Long. Elevation is 922 feet.
Population: 5,736 (1990); 5,574 (2000); 5,805 (2007); 5,953 (2012 projected); Race: 96.3% White, 1.2% Black, 0.2% Asian, 1.5% Hispanic of any race (2007); Density: 1,355.9 persons per square mile (2007); Average household size: 2.61 (2007); Median age: 36.2 (2007); Males per 100 females: 93.3 (2007); Marriage status: 16.1% never married, 65.9% now married, 4.9% widowed, 13.1% divorced (2000); Foreign born: 0.5% (2000); Ancestry (includes multiple ancestries): 34.9% German, 16.5% Irish, 14.9% United States or American, 12.0% English, 10.5% Other groups (2000).
Economy: Single-family building permits issued: 16 (2007); Multi-family building permits issued: 0 (2007); Employment by occupation: 10.4% management, 17.2% professional, 13.6% services, 28.8% sales, 0.2% farming, 9.0% construction, 20.9% production (2000).
Income: Per capita income: $24,866 (2007); Median household income: $57,317 (2007); Average household income: $64,874 (2007); Percent of households with income of $100,000 or more: 12.8% (2007); Poverty rate: 3.7% (2000).
Education: Percent of population age 25 and over with: High school diploma (including GED) or higher: 85.4% (2007); Bachelor's degree or higher: 13.6% (2007); Master's degree or higher: 3.1% (2007).

School District(s)

Northmont City (KG-12)
2005-06 Enrollment: 5,972 . . . . (937) 832-5000

Housing: Homeownership rate: 86.1% (2007); Median home value: $110,576 (2007); Median rent: $509 per month (2000); Median age of housing: 27 years (2000).
Safety: Violent crime rate: 6.3 per 10,000 population; Property crime rate: 108.7 per 10,000 population (2007).
Transportation: Commute to work: 94.5% car, 0.8% public transportation, 2.6% walk, 2.1% work from home (2000); Travel time to work: 21.1% less than 15 minutes, 44.8% 15 to 30 minutes, 27.2% 30 to 45 minutes, 4.5% 45 to 60 minutes, 2.4% 60 minutes or more (2000)

Additional Information Contacts

City of Union . . . . (937) 836-8624
http://www.ci.union.oh.us

VANDALIA (city). Covers a land area of 11.810 square miles and a water area of 0.072 square miles. Located at 39.88° N. Lat.; 84.19° W. Long. Elevation is 994 feet.
History: Vandalia was settled in 1838 and named for Vandalia, Illinois. Vandalia was known as the site of the largest shotgun tournament in the world, held by the Amateur Trapshooters' Association.
Population: 14,297 (1990); 14,603 (2000); 14,306 (2007); 14,042 (2012 projected); Race: 94.9% White, 1.8% Black, 1.6% Asian, 1.2% Hispanic of any race (2007); Density: 1,211.4 persons per square mile (2007); Average household size: 2.30 (2007); Median age: 40.5 (2007); Males per 100 females: 94.3 (2007); Marriage status: 21.1% never married, 60.1% now married, 6.2% widowed, 12.6% divorced (2000); Foreign born: 2.2% (2000); Ancestry (includes multiple ancestries): 30.3% German, 12.8% Irish, 10.8% English, 9.8% United States or American, 7.4% Other groups (2000).
Economy: Single-family building permits issued: 44 (2007); Multi-family building permits issued: 0 (2007); Employment by occupation: 14.6% management, 20.1% professional, 12.1% services, 26.7% sales, 0.1% farming, 9.2% construction, 17.2% production (2000).
Income: Per capita income: $27,494 (2007); Median household income: $49,116 (2007); Average household income: $62,729 (2007); Percent of households with income of $100,000 or more: 15.5% (2007); Poverty rate: 5.2% (2000).
Education: Percent of population age 25 and over with: High school diploma (including GED) or higher: 87.3% (2007); Bachelor's degree or higher: 22.2% (2007); Master's degree or higher: 8.3% (2007).

School District(s)

Vandalia-Butler City (PK-12)
2005-06 Enrollment: 3,438 . . . . (937) 415-6400

Housing: Homeownership rate: 65.3% (2007); Median home value: $138,522 (2007); Median rent: $428 per month (2000); Median age of housing: 30 years (2000).
Safety: Violent crime rate: 14.1 per 10,000 population; Property crime rate: 301.3 per 10,000 population (2007).
Newspapers: Vandalia Drummer News (Local news; Circulation 5,300)
Transportation: Commute to work: 95.1% car, 0.5% public transportation, 1.2% walk, 2.7% work from home (2000); Travel time to work: 38.5% less than 15 minutes, 41.5% 15 to 30 minutes, 14.6% 30 to 45 minutes, 2.2% 45 to 60 minutes, 3.3% 60 minutes or more (2000)

Additional Information Contacts

City of Vandalia . . . . (937) 898-5891
http://www.ci.vandalia.oh.us
Vandalia-Butler Chamber of Commerce . . . . (937) 898-5351
http://www.vandaliabutlerchamber.org

WEST CARROLLTON CITY (city). Aka West Carrollton. Covers a land area of 6.308 square miles and a water area of 0.197 square miles. Located at 39.66° N. Lat.; 84.24° W. Long. Elevation is 702 feet.
Population: 14,403 (1990); 13,818 (2000); 13,010 (2007); 12,419 (2012 projected); Race: 91.0% White, 5.3% Black, 1.2% Asian, 2.1% Hispanic of any race (2007); Density: 2,062.6 persons per square mile (2007); Average household size: 2.19 (2007); Median age: 37.2 (2007); Males per 100 females: 93.2 (2007); Marriage status: 24.8% never married, 54.6% now married, 6.0% widowed, 14.6% divorced (2000); Foreign born: 2.5% (2000); Ancestry (includes multiple ancestries): 22.8% German, 14.9% Other groups, 14.3% United States or American, 10.7% English, 10.5% Irish (2000).
Economy: Single-family building permits issued: 3 (2007); Multi-family building permits issued: 0 (2007); Employment by occupation: 12.7%

management, 19.3% professional, 13.2% services, 26.1% sales, 0.2% farming, 7.3% construction, 21.2% production (2000).
Income: Per capita income: $23,438 (2007); Median household income: $44,466 (2007); Average household income: $51,151 (2007); Percent of households with income of $100,000 or more: 8.4% (2007); Poverty rate: 7.4% (2000).
Education: Percent of population age 25 and over with: High school diploma (including GED) or higher: 86.5% (2007); Bachelor's degree or higher: 17.1% (2007); Master's degree or higher: 5.0% (2007).

School District(s)

West Carrollton City (PK-12)
2005-06 Enrollment: 3,821 . . . . (937) 859-5121
Housing: Homeownership rate: 59.1% (2007); Median home value: $108,999 (2007); Median rent: $490 per month (2000); Median age of housing: 29 years (2000).
Safety: Violent crime rate: 32.6 per 10,000 population; Property crime rate: 361.3 per 10,000 population (2007).
Transportation: Commute to work: 96.0% car, 1.7% public transportation, 1.2% walk, 1.1% work from home (2000); Travel time to work: 38.2% less than 15 minutes, 42.8% 15 to 30 minutes, 12.9% 30 to 45 minutes, 2.5% 45 to 60 minutes, 3.6% 60 minutes or more (2000)
Additional Information Contacts
City of West Carrollton City . . . . (937) 859-5183
http://www.westcarrollton.org

WOODBOURNE-HYDE PARK (CDP). Covers a land area of 4.582 square miles and a water area of 0 square miles. Located at 39.66° N. Lat.; 84.17° W. Long.
Population: 7,867 (1990); 7,910 (2000); 7,392 (2007); 7,040 (2012 projected); Race: 95.6% White, 1.3% Black, 1.8% Asian, 1.1% Hispanic of any race (2007); Density: 1,613.2 persons per square mile (2007); Average household size: 2.63 (2007); Median age: 50.8 (2007); Males per 100 females: 90.9 (2007); Marriage status: 13.8% never married, 74.3% now married, 7.1% widowed, 4.9% divorced (2000); Foreign born: 4.6% (2000); Ancestry (includes multiple ancestries): 34.0% German, 16.1% Irish, 15.1% English, 5.9% Other groups, 5.6% United States or American (2000).
Economy: Employment by occupation: 23.6% management, 37.1% professional, 5.7% services, 25.1% sales, 0.7% farming, 2.5% construction, 5.3% production (2000).
Income: Per capita income: $45,999 (2007); Median household income: $90,763 (2007); Average household income: $118,404 (2007); Percent of households with income of $100,000 or more: 43.8% (2007); Poverty rate: 2.1% (2000).
Education: Percent of population age 25 and over with: High school diploma (including GED) or higher: 95.6% (2007); Bachelor's degree or higher: 53.6% (2007); Master's degree or higher: 25.1% (2007).
Housing: Homeownership rate: 96.8% (2007); Median home value: $192,075 (2007); Median rent: $1,040 per month (2000); Median age of housing: 37 years (2000).
Transportation: Commute to work: 93.4% car, 0.5% public transportation, 0.3% walk, 5.2% work from home (2000); Travel time to work: 32.2% less than 15 minutes, 50.0% 15 to 30 minutes, 12.3% 30 to 45 minutes, 3.1% 45 to 60 minutes, 2.4% 60 minutes or more (2000)

WRIGHT-PATTERSON AFB (CDP). Covers a land area of 11.693 square miles and a water area of 0.087 square miles. Located at 39.79° N. Lat.; 84.08° W. Long.
Population: 8,447 (1990); 6,656 (2000); 6,399 (2007); 6,235 (2012 projected); Race: 75.8% White, 15.2% Black, 1.8% Asian, 5.1% Hispanic of any race (2007); Density: 547.2 persons per square mile (2007); Average household size: 3.74 (2007); Median age: 23.3 (2007); Males per 100 females: 105.8 (2007); Marriage status: 16.3% never married, 80.6% now married, 0.4% widowed, 2.7% divorced (2000); Foreign born: 2.8% (2000); Ancestry (includes multiple ancestries): 29.0% Other groups, 20.2% German, 11.6% Irish, 10.3% English, 8.1% United States or American (2000).
Economy: Employment by occupation: 9.3% management, 24.1% professional, 23.5% services, 34.1% sales, 0.0% farming, 4.4% construction, 4.6% production (2000).
Income: Per capita income: $14,933 (2007); Median household income: $45,694 (2007); Average household income: $53,020 (2007); Percent of households with income of $100,000 or more: 6.2% (2007); Poverty rate: 1.8% (2000).
Education: Percent of population age 25 and over with: High school diploma (including GED) or higher: 97.2% (2007); Bachelor's degree or higher: 33.4% (2007); Master's degree or higher: 16.4% (2007).
Housing: Homeownership rate: 4.2% (2007); Median home value: $41,818 (2007); Median rent: $620 per month (2000); Median age of housing: 39 years (2000).
Transportation: Commute to work: 94.1% car, 0.9% public transportation, 1.5% walk, 2.9% work from home (2000); Travel time to work: 60.0% less than 15 minutes, 33.4% 15 to 30 minutes, 4.8% 30 to 45 minutes, 0.8% 45 to 60 minutes, 1.0% 60 minutes or more (2000)

Morgan County

Located in east central Ohio; crossed by the Muskingum River, and Meigs and Wolf Creeks. Covers a land area of 417.66 square miles, a water area of 4.20 square miles, and is located in the Eastern Time Zone. The county was founded in 1817. County seat is McConnelsville.

Weather Station: McConnelsville Lock 7 Elevation: 757 feet

	Jan	Feb	Mar	Apr	May	Jun	Jul	Aug	Sep	Oct	Nov	Dec
High	38	42	53	65	74	81	85	84	78	66	54	43
Low	18	19	28	37	47	56	61	60	52	39	32	24
Precip	3.0	2.5	3.5	3.6	4.4	4.1	4.9	4.4	3.2	2.8	3.4	3.2
Snow	7.9	5.7	3.4	0.9	0.0	0.0	0.0	0.0	0.0	0.0	0.7	2.6

High and Low temperatures in degrees Fahrenheit; Precipitation and Snow in inches

Population: 14,194 (1990); 14,897 (2000); 14,994 (2007); 15,025 (2012 projected); Race: 94.0% White, 3.3% Black, 0.1% Asian, 0.4% Hispanic of any race (2007); Density: 35.9 persons per square mile (2007); Average household size: 2.44 (2007); Median age: 40.3 (2007); Males per 100 females: 97.1 (2007).
Religion: Five largest groups: 12.5% The United Methodist Church, 7.4% Christian Churches and Churches of Christ, 2.8% Churches of Christ, 1.2% Southern Baptist Convention, 1.2% Catholic Church (2000).
Economy: Unemployment rate: 9.9% (6/2008); Total civilian labor force: 5,766 (6/2008); Leading industries: 23.4% manufacturing; 19.8% retail trade; 17.5% health care and social assistance (2005); Farms: 508 totaling 100,198 acres (2002); Companies that employ 500 or more persons: 0 (2006); Companies that employ 100 to 499 persons: 2 (2006); Companies that employ less than 100 persons: 173 (2006); Black-owned businesses: n/a (2002); Hispanic-owned businesses: n/a (2002); Asian-owned businesses: n/a (2002); Women-owned businesses: n/a (2002); Retail sales per capita: $4,780 (2008). Single-family building permits issued: 20 (2007); Multi-family building permits issued: 0 (2007).
Income: Per capita income: $16,312 (2007); Median household income: $32,342 (2007); Average household income: $39,418 (2007); Percent of households with income of $100,000 or more: 4.0% (2007); Poverty rate: 18.0% (2005); Bankruptcy rate: 2.46% (2007).
Taxes: Total county taxes per capita: $194 (2006); County property taxes per capita: $117 (2006).
Education: Percent of population age 25 and over with: High school diploma (including GED) or higher: 80.5% (2007); Bachelor's degree or higher: 9.2% (2007); Master's degree or higher: 4.0% (2007).
Housing: Homeownership rate: 78.7% (2007); Median home value: $85,787 (2007); Median rent: $266 per month (2000); Median age of housing: 35 years (2000).
Health: Birth rate: 121.1 per 10,000 population (2007); Death rate: 115.7 per 10,000 population (2007); Age-adjusted cancer mortality rate: 199.2 deaths per 100,000 population (2005); Air Quality Index: 99.2% good, 0.8% moderate, 0.0% unhealthy for sensitive individuals, 0.0% unhealthy (percent of days in 2007); Number of physicians: 1.4 per 10,000 population (2005); Hospital beds: 0.0 per 10,000 population (2004); Hospital admissions: 0.0 per 10,000 population (2004).
Elections: 2004 Presidential election results: 56.1% Bush, 42.9% Kerry, 0.0% Nader, 0.5% Badnarik
National and State Parks: Burr Oak State Park; Muskingum River Parkway State Park
Additional Information Contacts
Morgan County Government . . . . (740) 962-3183
http://www.morgancounty.org
Morgan County Chamber of Commerce . . . . (740) 962-3200
http://www.morgancounty.org/Chamber/default.aspx

Morgan County Communities

CHESTERHILL (village). Covers a land area of 0.544 square miles and a water area of 0 square miles. Located at 39.48° N. Lat.; 81.86° W. Long. Elevation is 974 feet.
Population: 309 (1990); 305 (2000); 274 (2007); 259 (2012 projected); Race: 82.8% White, 12.4% Black, 0.0% Asian, 0.4% Hispanic of any race (2007); Density: 503.8 persons per square mile (2007); Average household size: 2.23 (2007); Median age: 38.0 (2007); Males per 100 females: 95.7 (2007); Marriage status: 21.0% never married, 54.8% now married, 12.1% widowed, 12.1% divorced (2000); Foreign born: 0.0% (2000); Ancestry (includes multiple ancestries): 18.9% United States or American, 14.0% German, 13.7% English, 11.0% Irish, 7.6% Other groups (2000).
Economy: Employment by occupation: 10.8% management, 13.4% professional, 12.7% services, 20.4% sales, 0.0% farming, 11.5% construction, 31.2% production (2000).
Income: Per capita income: $17,080 (2007); Median household income: $28,125 (2007); Average household income: $38,049 (2007); Percent of households with income of $100,000 or more: 3.3% (2007); Poverty rate: 19.8% (2000).
Education: Percent of population age 25 and over with: High school diploma (including GED) or higher: 83.9% (2007); Bachelor's degree or higher: 6.3% (2007); Master's degree or higher: 2.1% (2007).
Housing: Homeownership rate: 79.7% (2007); Median home value: $56,429 (2007); Median rent: $267 per month (2000); Median age of housing: 60+ years (2000).
Transportation: Commute to work: 93.0% car, 0.0% public transportation, 3.8% walk, 3.2% work from home (2000); Travel time to work: 19.7% less than 15 minutes, 23.0% 15 to 30 minutes, 29.6% 30 to 45 minutes, 10.5% 45 to 60 minutes, 17.1% 60 minutes or more (2000)

MALTA (village). Covers a land area of 0.311 square miles and a water area of 0.032 square miles. Located at 39.65° N. Lat.; 81.86° W. Long. Elevation is 676 feet.
History: Malta was founded in 1816 by Simeon Pool and John Bell, who owned the land. The town was named for the island of Malta in the Mediterranean where Pool had visited.
Population: 802 (1990); 696 (2000); 551 (2007); 533 (2012 projected); Race: 90.2% White, 6.4% Black, 0.4% Asian, 0.0% Hispanic of any race (2007); Density: 1,774.2 persons per square mile (2007); Average household size: 2.39 (2007); Median age: 41.6 (2007); Males per 100 females: 85.5 (2007); Marriage status: 32.5% never married, 44.6% now married, 7.7% widowed, 15.2% divorced (2000); Foreign born: 0.1% (2000); Ancestry (includes multiple ancestries): 21.8% United States or American, 15.2% German, 12.7% Irish, 9.9% English, 9.0% Other groups (2000).
Economy: Single-family building permits issued: 2 (2007); Multi-family building permits issued: 0 (2007); Employment by occupation: 6.2% management, 8.2% professional, 29.6% services, 16.2% sales, 0.7% farming, 9.6% construction, 29.6% production (2000).
Income: Per capita income: $12,592 (2007); Median household income: $26,250 (2007); Average household income: $29,275 (2007); Percent of households with income of $100,000 or more: 0.0% (2007); Poverty rate: 25.3% (2000).
Education: Percent of population age 25 and over with: High school diploma (including GED) or higher: 81.0% (2007); Bachelor's degree or higher: 5.4% (2007); Master's degree or higher: 2.9% (2007).

School District(s)

Morgan Local (PK-12)
2005-06 Enrollment: 2,246 . . . . (740) 962-2782
Housing: Homeownership rate: 68.8% (2007); Median home value: $61,087 (2007); Median rent: $307 per month (2000); Median age of housing: 60+ years (2000).
Transportation: Commute to work: 88.0% car, 0.0% public transportation, 6.2% walk, 5.2% work from home (2000); Travel time to work: 48.6% less than 15 minutes, 20.7% 15 to 30 minutes, 8.3% 30 to 45 minutes, 6.5% 45 to 60 minutes, 15.9% 60 minutes or more (2000)

MCCONNELSVILLE (village). County seat. Covers a land area of 1.757 square miles and a water area of 0.067 square miles. Located at 39.64° N. Lat.; 81.85° W. Long. Elevation is 692 feet.
History: McConnelsville was platted in 1817 by General Robert McConnell, and became a Muskingum River shipping port for salt bound for Pittsburgh by keelboat.
Population: 1,824 (1990); 1,676 (2000); 1,664 (2007); 1,537 (2012 projected); Race: 95.2% White, 1.9% Black, 0.0% Asian, 0.2% Hispanic of any race (2007); Density: 946.8 persons per square mile (2007); Average household size: 2.02 (2007); Median age: 42.0 (2007); Males per 100 females: 81.3 (2007); Marriage status: 21.1% never married, 51.4% now married, 14.2% widowed, 13.4% divorced (2000); Foreign born: 0.2% (2000); Ancestry (includes multiple ancestries): 16.8% German, 14.2% United States or American, 11.1% Irish, 9.6% English, 6.6% Other groups (2000).
Economy: Single-family building permits issued: 0 (2007); Multi-family building permits issued: 0 (2007); Employment by occupation: 7.9% management, 17.9% professional, 15.1% services, 27.4% sales, 1.0% farming, 14.0% construction, 16.6% production (2000).
Income: Per capita income: $20,313 (2007); Median household income: $28,750 (2007); Average household income: $40,970 (2007); Percent of households with income of $100,000 or more: 6.5% (2007); Poverty rate: 18.1% (2000).
Education: Percent of population age 25 and over with: High school diploma (including GED) or higher: 85.6% (2007); Bachelor's degree or higher: 14.0% (2007); Master's degree or higher: 6.5% (2007).

School District(s)

Morgan Local (PK-12)
2005-06 Enrollment: 2,246 . . . . (740) 962-2782
Housing: Homeownership rate: 57.3% (2007); Median home value: $84,804 (2007); Median rent: $273 per month (2000); Median age of housing: 58 years (2000).
Newspapers: Morgan County Herald (Community news; Circulation 4,936)
Transportation: Commute to work: 90.0% car, 0.0% public transportation, 4.8% walk, 3.2% work from home (2000); Travel time to work: 61.4% less than 15 minutes, 10.1% 15 to 30 minutes, 7.4% 30 to 45 minutes, 6.8% 45 to 60 minutes, 14.2% 60 minutes or more (2000)
Additional Information Contacts
Morgan County Chamber of Commerce . . . . (740) 962-3200
http://www.morgancounty.org/Chamber/default.aspx

STOCKPORT (village). Covers a land area of 0.334 square miles and a water area of 0 square miles. Located at 39.54° N. Lat.; 81.79° W. Long. Elevation is 692 feet.
Population: 450 (1990); 540 (2000); 451 (2007); 447 (2012 projected); Race: 94.0% White, 2.9% Black, 0.0% Asian, 0.9% Hispanic of any race (2007); Density: 1,348.7 persons per square mile (2007); Average household size: 2.26 (2007); Median age: 34.7 (2007); Males per 100 females: 82.6 (2007); Marriage status: 21.1% never married, 57.6% now married, 10.0% widowed, 11.3% divorced (2000); Foreign born: 0.2% (2000); Ancestry (includes multiple ancestries): 19.1% United States or American, 13.5% English, 10.7% German, 9.3% Irish, 5.4% Other groups (2000).
Economy: Employment by occupation: 6.3% management, 12.7% professional, 23.8% services, 19.0% sales, 2.1% farming, 8.5% construction, 27.5% production (2000).
Income: Per capita income: $12,777 (2007); Median household income: $22,222 (2007); Average household income: $28,813 (2007); Percent of households with income of $100,000 or more: 1.0% (2007); Poverty rate: 39.6% (2000).
Education: Percent of population age 25 and over with: High school diploma (including GED) or higher: 84.8% (2007); Bachelor's degree or higher: 9.0% (2007); Master's degree or higher: 0.0% (2007).

School District(s)

Morgan Local (PK-12)
2005-06 Enrollment: 2,246 . . . . (740) 962-2782
Housing: Homeownership rate: 65.5% (2007); Median home value: $66,389 (2007); Median rent: $254 per month (2000); Median age of housing: 55 years (2000).
Transportation: Commute to work: 93.6% car, 0.0% public transportation, 3.2% walk, 3.2% work from home (2000); Travel time to work: 20.4% less than 15 minutes, 36.5% 15 to 30 minutes, 2.8% 30 to 45 minutes, 9.9% 45 to 60 minutes, 30.4% 60 minutes or more (2000)

Morrow County

Located in central Ohio; drained by the Kokosing River and Whetstone and Big Walnut Creeks. Covers a land area of 406.22 square miles, a water area of 1.13 square miles, and is located in the Eastern Time Zone. The county was founded in 1848. County seat is Mount Gilead.

Morrow County is part of the Columbus, OH Metropolitan Statistical Area. The entire metro area includes: Delaware County, OH; Fairfield County, OH; Franklin County, OH; Licking County, OH; Madison County, OH; Morrow County, OH; Pickaway County, OH; Union County, OH

Population: 27,749 (1990); 31,628 (2000); 34,908 (2007); 36,939 (2012 projected); Race: 97.9% White, 0.6% Black, 0.3% Asian, 1.0% Hispanic of any race (2007); Density: 85.9 persons per square mile (2007); Average household size: 2.69 (2007); Median age: 37.6 (2007); Males per 100 females: 99.3 (2007).

Religion: Five largest groups: 10.2% The United Methodist Church, 2.5% Christian Churches and Churches of Christ, 2.0% The Christian and Missionary Alliance, 1.6% American Baptist Churches in the USA, 1.5% Church of the Nazarene (2000).

Economy: Unemployment rate: 6.3% (6/2008); Total civilian labor force: 18,609 (6/2008); Leading industries: 30.1% manufacturing; 19.1% health care and social assistance; 16.0% retail trade (2005); Farms: 863 totaling 179,051 acres (2002); Companies that employ 500 or more persons: 1 (2006); Companies that employ 100 to 499 persons: 6 (2006); Companies that employ less than 100 persons: 418 (2006); Black-owned businesses: n/a (2002); Hispanic-owned businesses: n/a (2002); Asian-owned businesses: n/a (2002); Women-owned businesses: n/a (2002); Retail sales per capita: $5,505 (2008). Single-family building permits issued: 136 (2007); Multi-family building permits issued: 0 (2007).

Income: Per capita income: $21,582 (2007); Median household income: $48,410 (2007); Average household income: $57,726 (2007); Percent of households with income of $100,000 or more: 10.7% (2007); Poverty rate: 9.9% (2005); Bankruptcy rate: 3.68% (2007).

Taxes: Total county taxes per capita: $189 (2006); County property taxes per capita: $106 (2006).

Education: Percent of population age 25 and over with: High school diploma (including GED) or higher: 78.5% (2007); Bachelor's degree or higher: 9.4% (2007); Master's degree or higher: 3.0% (2007).

Housing: Homeownership rate: 82.4% (2007); Median home value: $124,423 (2007); Median rent: $343 per month (2000); Median age of housing: 29 years (2000).

Health: Birth rate: 128.3 per 10,000 population (2007); Death rate: 80.5 per 10,000 population (2007); Age-adjusted cancer mortality rate: 208.6 deaths per 100,000 population (2005); Number of physicians: 3.2 per 10,000 population (2005); Hospital beds: 15.7 per 10,000 population (2004); Hospital admissions: 358.9 per 10,000 population (2004).

Elections: 2004 Presidential election results: 64.1% Bush, 35.4% Kerry, 0.0% Nader, 0.2% Badnarik

National and State Parks: Mount Gilead State Park

Additional Information Contacts

Morrow County Government . . . . (419) 947-4085
http://www.morrowcounty.info

Morrow County Chamber of Commerce . . . . (419) 946-2821
http://www.morrowcochamber.com

Village of Mount Gilead . . . . (419) 946-8111
http://www.mountgilead.net

Morrow County Communities

CARDINGTON (village). Covers a land area of 1.864 square miles and a water area of 0 square miles. Located at 40.49° N. Lat.; 82.89° W. Long. Elevation is 1,010 feet.

History: Cardington was founded in 1822 and named for an old carding mill here. After the Civil War, Cardington became a lumber town.

Population: 1,847 (1990); 1,849 (2000); 2,059 (2007); 2,190 (2012 projected); Race: 98.0% White, 0.5% Black, 0.1% Asian, 0.3% Hispanic of any race (2007); Density: 1,104.9 persons per square mile (2007); Average household size: 2.40 (2007); Median age: 34.3 (2007); Males per 100 females: 92.4 (2007); Marriage status: 22.6% never married, 54.7% now married, 8.8% widowed, 13.8% divorced (2000); Foreign born: 0.7% (2000); Ancestry (includes multiple ancestries): 19.1% United States or American, 19.1% German, 10.7% English, 8.2% Irish, 7.7% Other groups (2000).

Economy: Single-family building permits issued: 5 (2007); Multi-family building permits issued: 0 (2007); Employment by occupation: 6.6% management, 12.4% professional, 23.6% services, 19.1% sales, 0.5% farming, 10.3% construction, 27.6% production (2000).

Income: Per capita income: $18,585 (2007); Median household income: $36,336 (2007); Average household income: $44,549 (2007); Percent of households with income of $100,000 or more: 4.9% (2007); Poverty rate: 16.7% (2000).

Education: Percent of population age 25 and over with: High school diploma (including GED) or higher: 77.4% (2007); Bachelor's degree or higher: 9.3% (2007); Master's degree or higher: 2.0% (2007).

School District(s)

Cardington Lincoln Local Digital Academy (03-12)
2005-06 Enrollment: 34 . . . . (419) 864-3691

Cardington-Lincoln Local (PK-12)
2005-06 Enrollment: 1,264 . . . . (419) 864-3691

Housing: Homeownership rate: 61.1% (2007); Median home value: $100,260 (2007); Median rent: $326 per month (2000); Median age of housing: 42 years (2000).

Safety: Violent crime rate: 9.9 per 10,000 population; Property crime rate: 303.3 per 10,000 population (2007).

Newspapers: Independent (Local news; Circulation 1,500); Morrow County Independent (Community news; Circulation 1,100)

Transportation: Commute to work: 92.5% car, 0.4% public transportation, 3.7% walk, 3.1% work from home (2000); Travel time to work: 30.4% less than 15 minutes, 24.0% 15 to 30 minutes, 23.2% 30 to 45 minutes, 13.4% 45 to 60 minutes, 8.9% 60 minutes or more (2000)

CHESTERVILLE (village). Covers a land area of 0.095 square miles and a water area of 0 square miles. Located at 40.48° N. Lat.; 82.68° W. Long. Elevation is 1,145 feet.

Population: 286 (1990); 193 (2000); 203 (2007); 208 (2012 projected); Race: 98.0% White, 0.0% Black, 0.0% Asian, 2.0% Hispanic of any race (2007); Density: 2,142.1 persons per square mile (2007); Average household size: 3.27 (2007); Median age: 44.9 (2007); Males per 100 females: 81.3 (2007); Marriage status: 19.3% never married, 50.0% now married, 23.9% widowed, 6.8% divorced (2000); Foreign born: 0.0% (2000); Ancestry (includes multiple ancestries): 26.2% German, 15.2% United States or American, 13.8% English, 9.5% Other groups, 7.1% Dutch (2000).

Economy: Single-family building permits issued: 0 (2007); Multi-family building permits issued: 0 (2007); Employment by occupation: 5.5% management, 16.4% professional, 17.3% services, 33.6% sales, 2.7% farming, 14.5% construction, 10.0% production (2000).

Income: Per capita income: $15,591 (2007); Median household income: $49,167 (2007); Average household income: $48,427 (2007); Percent of households with income of $100,000 or more: 4.8% (2007); Poverty rate: 9.9% (2000).

Education: Percent of population age 25 and over with: High school diploma (including GED) or higher: 79.3% (2007); Bachelor's degree or higher: 10.0% (2007); Master's degree or higher: 5.7% (2007).

School District(s)

Highland Local (PK-12)
2005-06 Enrollment: 1,766 . . . . (419) 768-2206

Housing: Homeownership rate: 80.6% (2007); Median home value: $75,000 (2007); Median rent: $475 per month (2000); Median age of housing: 60+ years (2000).

Transportation: Commute to work: 86.9% car, 0.0% public transportation, 10.3% walk, 2.8% work from home (2000); Travel time to work: 28.8% less than 15 minutes, 26.9% 15 to 30 minutes, 24.0% 30 to 45 minutes, 7.7% 45 to 60 minutes, 12.5% 60 minutes or more (2000)

EDISON (village). Covers a land area of 0.288 square miles and a water area of 0 square miles. Located at 40.55° N. Lat.; 82.86° W. Long. Elevation is 1,063 feet.

Population: 488 (1990); 437 (2000); 437 (2007); 433 (2012 projected); Race: 97.9% White, 0.0% Black, 0.2% Asian, 1.1% Hispanic of any race (2007); Density: 1,516.2 persons per square mile (2007); Average household size: 2.57 (2007); Median age: 36.0 (2007); Males per 100 females: 104.2 (2007); Marriage status: 24.9% never married, 51.1% now married, 8.8% widowed, 15.1% divorced (2000); Foreign born: 0.0% (2000); Ancestry (includes multiple ancestries): 17.6% German, 13.2% United States or American, 13.0% Other groups, 8.8% English, 8.6% Irish (2000).

Economy: Single-family building permits issued: 1 (2007); Multi-family building permits issued: 0 (2007); Employment by occupation: 3.8% management, 5.3% professional, 17.2% services, 31.6% sales, 0.0% farming, 19.6% construction, 22.5% production (2000).

Income: Per capita income: $21,516 (2007); Median household income: $47,917 (2007); Average household income: $55,309 (2007); Percent of households with income of $100,000 or more: 11.2% (2007); Poverty rate: 13.4% (2000).

Education: Percent of population age 25 and over with: High school diploma (including GED) or higher: 83.6% (2007); Bachelor's degree or higher: 10.9% (2007); Master's degree or higher: 2.0% (2007).

School District(s)

Goal Digital Academy (KG-12)
2005-06 Enrollment: 67 . . . . (419) 946-1903
Tomorrow Center (04-12)
2005-06 Enrollment: 37 . . . . (419) 946-1903

Housing: Homeownership rate: 78.8% (2007); Median home value: $94,500 (2007); Median rent: $415 per month (2000); Median age of housing: 60+ years (2000).
Transportation: Commute to work: 99.0% car, 0.0% public transportation, 1.0% walk, 0.0% work from home (2000); Travel time to work: 27.6% less than 15 minutes, 20.7% 15 to 30 minutes, 17.7% 30 to 45 minutes, 22.7% 45 to 60 minutes, 11.3% 60 minutes or more (2000)

FULTON (village). Covers a land area of 0.150 square miles and a water area of 0 square miles. Located at 40.46° N. Lat.; 82.82° W. Long. Elevation is 1,109 feet.
Population: 325 (1990); 264 (2000); 294 (2007); 311 (2012 projected); Race: 99.3% White, 0.0% Black, 0.0% Asian, 1.4% Hispanic of any race (2007); Density: 1,955.8 persons per square mile (2007); Average household size: 2.70 (2007); Median age: 41.1 (2007); Males per 100 females: 101.4 (2007); Marriage status: 33.7% never married, 50.4% now married, 7.0% widowed, 8.9% divorced (2000); Foreign born: 0.0% (2000); Ancestry (includes multiple ancestries): 24.7% German, 17.8% Irish, 15.1% United States or American, 10.9% English, 7.6% Other groups (2000).
Economy: Employment by occupation: 5.7% management, 5.1% professional, 21.7% services, 12.1% sales, 0.0% farming, 15.3% construction, 40.1% production (2000).
Income: Per capita income: $19,352 (2007); Median household income: $41,071 (2007); Average household income: $49,128 (2007); Percent of households with income of $100,000 or more: 8.3% (2007); Poverty rate: 11.3% (2000).
Education: Percent of population age 25 and over with: High school diploma (including GED) or higher: 47.1% (2007); Bachelor's degree or higher: 2.2% (2007); Master's degree or higher: 0.9% (2007).
Housing: Homeownership rate: 68.8% (2007); Median home value: $81,154 (2007); Median rent: $325 per month (2000); Median age of housing: 58 years (2000).
Transportation: Commute to work: 73.7% car, 21.1% public transportation, 2.6% walk, 2.6% work from home (2000); Travel time to work: 16.2% less than 15 minutes, 34.5% 15 to 30 minutes, 26.4% 30 to 45 minutes, 16.9% 45 to 60 minutes, 6.1% 60 minutes or more (2000)

MARENGO (village). Covers a land area of 0.178 square miles and a water area of 0 square miles. Located at 40.40° N. Lat.; 82.81° W. Long. Elevation is 1,158 feet.
Population: 393 (1990); 297 (2000); 346 (2007); 378 (2012 projected); Race: 95.7% White, 0.0% Black, 0.6% Asian, 1.2% Hispanic of any race (2007); Density: 1,944.2 persons per square mile (2007); Average household size: 2.54 (2007); Median age: 32.4 (2007); Males per 100 females: 98.9 (2007); Marriage status: 21.6% never married, 54.4% now married, 9.1% widowed, 14.9% divorced (2000); Foreign born: 0.0% (2000); Ancestry (includes multiple ancestries): 14.7% Other groups, 12.5% United States or American, 12.5% German, 9.2% Irish, 7.0% English (2000).
Economy: Employment by occupation: 5.3% management, 13.0% professional, 13.6% services, 21.3% sales, 0.0% farming, 24.9% construction, 21.9% production (2000).
Income: Per capita income: $18,526 (2007); Median household income: $43,571 (2007); Average household income: $47,132 (2007); Percent of households with income of $100,000 or more: 5.1% (2007); Poverty rate: 9.2% (2000).
Education: Percent of population age 25 and over with: High school diploma (including GED) or higher: 79.5% (2007); Bachelor's degree or higher: 8.7% (2007); Master's degree or higher: 4.1% (2007).

School District(s)

Highland Local (PK-12)
2005-06 Enrollment: 1,766 . . . . (419) 768-2206

Housing: Homeownership rate: 68.4% (2007); Median home value: $97,000 (2007); Median rent: $465 per month (2000); Median age of housing: 60+ years (2000).
Transportation: Commute to work: 89.2% car, 0.0% public transportation, 6.0% walk, 3.0% work from home (2000); Travel time to work: 21.6% less than 15 minutes, 27.2% 15 to 30 minutes, 37.0% 30 to 45 minutes, 9.9% 45 to 60 minutes, 4.3% 60 minutes or more (2000)

MOUNT GILEAD (village). County seat. Covers a land area of 3.176 square miles and a water area of 0.011 square miles. Located at 40.55° N. Lat.; 82.83° W. Long. Elevation is 1,135 feet.
History: Mount Gilead was settled in 1817 by Lewis and Ralph Hardenbrook, whose farm was in a tulip-tree forest. Until 1824 the settlement was called Whetstone, and later Youngstown. In 1832 the Ohio legislature changed the name again to honor Mount Gilead, Virginia.
Population: 3,216 (1990); 3,290 (2000); 3,352 (2007); 3,387 (2012 projected); Race: 95.7% White, 2.9% Black, 0.5% Asian, 1.8% Hispanic of any race (2007); Density: 1,055.3 persons per square mile (2007); Average household size: 2.49 (2007); Median age: 37.4 (2007); Males per 100 females: 92.6 (2007); Marriage status: 16.5% never married, 62.1% now married, 13.1% widowed, 8.3% divorced (2000); Foreign born: 1.4% (2000); Ancestry (includes multiple ancestries): 21.7% German, 16.3% United States or American, 11.9% Irish, 9.2% English, 9.0% Other groups (2000).
Economy: Single-family building permits issued: 40 (2007); Multi-family building permits issued: 0 (2007); Employment by occupation: 11.3% management, 13.4% professional, 14.8% services, 21.7% sales, 0.0% farming, 13.1% construction, 25.6% production (2000).
Income: Per capita income: $22,552 (2007); Median household income: $37,704 (2007); Average household income: $54,156 (2007); Percent of households with income of $100,000 or more: 11.6% (2007); Poverty rate: 13.2% (2000).
Education: Percent of population age 25 and over with: High school diploma (including GED) or higher: 75.7% (2007); Bachelor's degree or higher: 9.8% (2007); Master's degree or higher: 4.3% (2007).

School District(s)

Mount Gilead Exempted Village (PK-12)
2005-06 Enrollment: 1,336 . . . . (419) 946-1646

Housing: Homeownership rate: 63.2% (2007); Median home value: $114,989 (2007); Median rent: $274 per month (2000); Median age of housing: 48 years (2000).
Hospitals: Morrow County Hospital (79 beds)
Safety: Violent crime rate: 14.2 per 10,000 population; Property crime rate: 325.6 per 10,000 population (2007).
Newspapers: Morrow County Sentinel (Community news; Circulation 4,500)
Transportation: Commute to work: 93.4% car, 0.8% public transportation, 4.2% walk, 1.5% work from home (2000); Travel time to work: 39.3% less than 15 minutes, 18.3% 15 to 30 minutes, 17.4% 30 to 45 minutes, 11.7% 45 to 60 minutes, 13.4% 60 minutes or more (2000)
Airports: Morrow County (general aviation)
Additional Information Contacts
Morrow County Chamber of Commerce . . . . (419) 946-2821
http://www.morrowcochamber.com
Village of Mount Gilead . . . . (419) 946-8111
http://www.mountgilead.net

SPARTA (village). Covers a land area of 0.088 square miles and a water area of 0 square miles. Located at 40.39° N. Lat.; 82.70° W. Long. Elevation is 1,358 feet.
Population: 201 (1990); 191 (2000); 205 (2007); 213 (2012 projected); Race: 94.1% White, 3.9% Black, 0.0% Asian, 1.0% Hispanic of any race (2007); Density: 2,317.8 persons per square mile (2007); Average household size: 2.66 (2007); Median age: 37.8 (2007); Males per 100 females: 103.0 (2007); Marriage status: 22.4% never married, 60.2% now married, 1.9% widowed, 15.5% divorced (2000); Foreign born: 2.8% (2000); Ancestry (includes multiple ancestries): 22.9% United States or American, 21.0% German, 15.4% Irish, 6.5% Other groups, 5.1% Welsh (2000).
Economy: Employment by occupation: 11.6% management, 11.6% professional, 23.3% services, 18.6% sales, 0.0% farming, 4.7% construction, 30.2% production (2000).
Income: Per capita income: $15,329 (2007); Median household income: $35,357 (2007); Average household income: $40,812 (2007); Percent of households with income of $100,000 or more: 3.9% (2007); Poverty rate: 16.4% (2000).
Education: Percent of population age 25 and over with: High school diploma (including GED) or higher: 76.4% (2007); Bachelor's degree or higher: 5.6% (2007); Master's degree or higher: 0.0% (2007).

School District(s)

Highland Local (PK-12)
2005-06 Enrollment: 1,766 . . . . (419) 768-2206

Housing: Homeownership rate: 64.9% (2007); Median home value: $92,500 (2007); Median rent: $282 per month (2000); Median age of housing: 60+ years (2000).

Transportation: Commute to work: 97.5% car, 0.0% public transportation, 0.0% walk, 2.5% work from home (2000); Travel time to work: 16.7% less than 15 minutes, 24.4% 15 to 30 minutes, 21.8% 30 to 45 minutes, 24.4% 45 to 60 minutes, 12.8% 60 minutes or more (2000)

Muskingum County

Located in central Ohio; crossed by the Muskingum and Licking Rivers, and Salt and Jonathan Creeks. Covers a land area of 664.63 square miles, a water area of 7.97 square miles, and is located in the Eastern Time Zone. The county was founded in 1804. County seat is Zanesville.

Muskingum County is part of the Zanesville, OH Micropolitan Statistical Area. The entire metro area includes: Muskingum County, OH

Weather Station: Philo 3 SW Elevation: 1,017 feet

	Jan	Feb	Mar	Apr	May	Jun	Jul	Aug	Sep	Oct	Nov	Dec
High	35	40	50	62	71	78	82	81	74	63	51	40
Low	20	22	30	40	49	57	61	60	53	42	34	25
Precip	2.1	2.1	2.7	3.1	4.1	4.2	4.2	3.8	2.8	2.5	3.0	2.5
Snow	9.4	5.3	4.3	1.1	tr	0.0	0.0	0.0	0.0	tr	1.1	3.6

High and Low temperatures in degrees Fahrenheit; Precipitation and Snow in inches

Weather Station: Zanesville Municipal Airport Elevation: 879 feet

	Jan	Feb	Mar	Apr	May	Jun	Jul	Aug	Sep	Oct	Nov	Dec
High	36	41	51	62	72	80	84	82	76	64	52	41
Low	20	23	31	40	50	59	63	61	54	42	34	25
Precip	2.5	2.3	3.1	3.5	4.1	4.4	4.2	4.0	2.9	2.6	3.1	2.8
Snow	8.6	4.3	3.5	1.4	tr	tr	tr	0.0	tr	tr	1.2	3.5

High and Low temperatures in degrees Fahrenheit; Precipitation and Snow in inches

Population: 82,068 (1990); 84,585 (2000); 85,796 (2007); 86,295 (2012 projected); Race: 93.5% White, 4.1% Black, 0.4% Asian, 0.6% Hispanic of any race (2007); Density: 129.1 persons per square mile (2007); Average household size: 2.56 (2007); Median age: 38.1 (2007); Males per 100 females: 92.5 (2007).

Religion: Five largest groups: 11.4% The United Methodist Church, 6.3% Catholic Church, 5.1% American Baptist Churches in the USA, 3.0% Presbyterian Church (U.S.A.), 2.1% Evangelical Lutheran Church in America (2000).

Economy: Unemployment rate: 8.1% (6/2008); Total civilian labor force: 38,858 (6/2008); Leading industries: 20.1% health care and social assistance; 18.4% manufacturing; 16.7% retail trade (2005); Farms: 1,222 totaling 193,175 acres (2002); Companies that employ 500 or more persons: 5 (2006); Companies that employ 100 to 499 persons: 38 (2006); Companies that employ less than 100 persons: 1,944 (2006); Black-owned businesses: n/a (2002); Hispanic-owned businesses: n/a (2002); Asian-owned businesses: n/a (2002); Women-owned businesses: 1,683 (2002); Retail sales per capita: $18,352 (2008). Single-family building permits issued: 55 (2007); Multi-family building permits issued: 62 (2007).

Income: Per capita income: $20,699 (2007); Median household income: $40,691 (2007); Average household income: $52,019 (2007); Percent of households with income of $100,000 or more: 8.9% (2007); Poverty rate: 15.2% (2005); Bankruptcy rate: 4.88% (2007).

Taxes: Total county taxes per capita: $318 (2006); County property taxes per capita: $139 (2006).

Education: Percent of population age 25 and over with: High school diploma (including GED) or higher: 80.9% (2007); Bachelor's degree or higher: 13.0% (2007); Master's degree or higher: 4.7% (2007).

Housing: Homeownership rate: 74.1% (2007); Median home value: $102,873 (2007); Median rent: $331 per month (2000); Median age of housing: 38 years (2000).

Health: Birth rate: 129.1 per 10,000 population (2007); Death rate: 102.1 per 10,000 population (2007); Age-adjusted cancer mortality rate: 218.9 deaths per 100,000 population (2005); Number of physicians: 19.0 per 10,000 population (2005); Hospital beds: 43.2 per 10,000 population (2004); Hospital admissions: 2,011.3 per 10,000 population (2004).

Elections: 2004 Presidential election results: 57.3% Bush, 42.3% Kerry, 0.0% Nader, 0.2% Badnarik

National and State Parks: Blue Rock State Forest; Blue Rock State Park; Dillon State Park; Dillon State Wildlife Area; Monroe Basin State Wildlife Area; Muskingum River Parkway State Park; Powelson State Wildlife Area

Additional Information Contacts

Muskingum County Government . . . . (740) 455-7100
http://www.muskingumcounty.org

City of Zanesville . . . . (740) 455-0603
http://www.coz.org

Zanesfield-Muskingum County Chamber of Commerce . . . (740) 455-8282
http://www.zmchamber.com

Muskingum County Communities

ADAMSVILLE (village). Covers a land area of 0.051 square miles and a water area of 0 square miles. Located at 40.07° N. Lat.; 81.88° W. Long. Elevation is 1,020 feet.

Population: 151 (1990); 127 (2000); 127 (2007); 124 (2012 projected); Race: 100.0% White, 0.0% Black, 0.0% Asian, 0.0% Hispanic of any race (2007); Density: 2,483.6 persons per square mile (2007); Average household size: 2.70 (2007); Median age: 29.8 (2007); Males per 100 females: 111.7 (2007); Marriage status: 45.5% never married, 51.2% now married, 0.8% widowed, 2.5% divorced (2000); Foreign born: 0.0% (2000); Ancestry (includes multiple ancestries): 26.2% United States or American, 7.6% German, 4.8% Dutch, 4.8% Irish, 2.1% English (2000).

Economy: Employment by occupation: 5.0% management, 2.5% professional, 8.8% services, 8.8% sales, 0.0% farming, 26.3% construction, 48.8% production (2000).

Income: Per capita income: $15,886 (2007); Median household income: $36,875 (2007); Average household income: $42,926 (2007); Percent of households with income of $100,000 or more: 6.4% (2007); Poverty rate: 4.8% (2000).

Education: Percent of population age 25 and over with: High school diploma (including GED) or higher: 69.3% (2007); Bachelor's degree or higher: 2.7% (2007); Master's degree or higher: 2.7% (2007).

School District(s)

Tri-Valley Local (PK-12)
2005-06 Enrollment: 3,241 . . . . (740) 754-1572

Housing: Homeownership rate: 74.5% (2007); Median home value: $33,929 (2007); Median rent: $271 per month (2000); Median age of housing: 47 years (2000).

Transportation: Commute to work: 100.0% car, 0.0% public transportation, 0.0% walk, 0.0% work from home (2000); Travel time to work: 8.8% less than 15 minutes, 47.5% 15 to 30 minutes, 42.5% 30 to 45 minutes, 0.0% 45 to 60 minutes, 1.3% 60 minutes or more (2000)

BLUE ROCK (unincorporated postal area, zip code 43720). Aka Gaysport. Covers a land area of 44.288 square miles and a water area of 0.054 square miles. Located at 39.80° N. Lat.; 81.88° W. Long. Elevation is 680 feet.

Population: 1,206 (2000); Race: 97.7% White, 0.6% Black, 1.1% Asian, 0.0% Hispanic of any race (2000); Density: 27.2 persons per square mile (2000); Age: 31.6% under 18, 9.7% over 64 (2000); Marriage status: 17.6% never married, 71.3% now married, 2.2% widowed, 8.9% divorced (2000); Foreign born: 1.4% (2000); Ancestry (includes multiple ancestries): 19.9% United States or American, 13.8% German, 12.0% Irish, 7.3% English, 3.1% Other groups (2000).

Economy: Employment by occupation: 6.6% management, 12.2% professional, 15.0% services, 16.3% sales, 0.0% farming, 16.5% construction, 33.5% production (2000).

Income: Per capita income: $13,848 (2000); Median household income: $35,200 (2000); Poverty rate: 2.5% (2000).

Education: Percent of population age 25 and over with: High school diploma (including GED) or higher: 83.3% (2000); Bachelor's degree or higher: 3.1% (2000).

Housing: Homeownership rate: 87.8% (2000); Median home value: $78,300 (2000); Median rent: $246 per month (2000); Median age of housing: 29 years (2000).

Transportation: Commute to work: 96.7% car, 0.0% public transportation, 3.3% walk, 0.0% work from home (2000); Travel time to work: 9.0% less than 15 minutes, 32.6% 15 to 30 minutes, 32.1% 30 to 45 minutes, 10.3% 45 to 60 minutes, 16.1% 60 minutes or more (2000)

CHANDLERSVILLE (unincorporated postal area, zip code 43727). Covers a land area of 72.662 square miles and a water area of 0.682

square miles. Located at 39.87° N. Lat.; 81.81° W. Long. Elevation is 730 feet.
Population: 1,300 (2000); Race: 99.7% White, 0.0% Black, 0.0% Asian, 0.0% Hispanic of any race (2000); Density: 17.9 persons per square mile (2000); Age: 24.5% under 18, 15.6% over 64 (2000); Marriage status: 19.0% never married, 65.2% now married, 3.3% widowed, 12.5% divorced (2000); Foreign born: 0.4% (2000); Ancestry (includes multiple ancestries): 23.3% German, 14.5% Irish, 10.9% United States or American, 10.2% English, 5.7% Other groups (2000).
Economy: Employment by occupation: 10.9% management, 17.2% professional, 12.0% services, 20.1% sales, 3.3% farming, 12.7% construction, 23.9% production (2000).
Income: Per capita income: $15,815 (2000); Median household income: $40,602 (2000); Poverty rate: 6.6% (2000).
Education: Percent of population age 25 and over with: High school diploma (including GED) or higher: 84.5% (2000); Bachelor's degree or higher: 9.6% (2000).
Housing: Homeownership rate: 91.0% (2000); Median home value: $82,100 (2000); Median rent: $269 per month (2000); Median age of housing: 34 years (2000).
Transportation: Commute to work: 94.4% car, 0.0% public transportation, 1.3% walk, 4.3% work from home (2000); Travel time to work: 20.1% less than 15 minutes, 42.0% 15 to 30 minutes, 16.7% 30 to 45 minutes, 10.6% 45 to 60 minutes, 10.6% 60 minutes or more (2000)

DRESDEN (village). Covers a land area of 1.167 square miles and a water area of 0.044 square miles. Located at 40.12° N. Lat.; 82.01° W. Long. Elevation is 741 feet.
Population: 1,588 (1990); 1,423 (2000); 1,314 (2007); 1,320 (2012 projected); Race: 99.2% White, 0.2% Black, 0.0% Asian, 0.6% Hispanic of any race (2007); Density: 1,126.0 persons per square mile (2007); Average household size: 2.31 (2007); Median age: 39.6 (2007); Males per 100 females: 83.8 (2007); Marriage status: 21.1% never married, 55.7% now married, 11.1% widowed, 12.1% divorced (2000); Foreign born: 0.1% (2000); Ancestry (includes multiple ancestries): 25.4% German, 16.2% United States or American, 12.7% Irish, 8.4% English, 4.0% Other groups (2000).
Economy: Single-family building permits issued: 0 (2007); Multi-family building permits issued: 0 (2007); Employment by occupation: 10.9% management, 11.5% professional, 16.7% services, 18.0% sales, 0.3% farming, 8.0% construction, 34.5% production (2000).
Income: Per capita income: $24,404 (2007); Median household income: $45,903 (2007); Average household income: $56,274 (2007); Percent of households with income of $100,000 or more: 10.0% (2007); Poverty rate: 5.8% (2000).
Education: Percent of population age 25 and over with: High school diploma (including GED) or higher: 84.2% (2007); Bachelor's degree or higher: 10.5% (2007); Master's degree or higher: 3.5% (2007).

School District(s)

Tri-Valley Local (PK-12)
2005-06 Enrollment: 3,241 . . . . (740) 754-1572
Housing: Homeownership rate: 68.9% (2007); Median home value: $102,953 (2007); Median rent: $333 per month (2000); Median age of housing: 39 years (2000).
Newspapers: Dresden Transcript (Community news; Circulation 3,000)
Transportation: Commute to work: 93.4% car, 0.4% public transportation, 3.1% walk, 3.0% work from home (2000); Travel time to work: 44.1% less than 15 minutes, 32.3% 15 to 30 minutes, 13.5% 30 to 45 minutes, 5.2% 45 to 60 minutes, 4.9% 60 minutes or more (2000)

DUNCAN FALLS (unincorporated postal area, zip code 43734). Covers a land area of 3.393 square miles and a water area of 0 square miles. Located at 39.87° N. Lat.; 81.90° W. Long. Elevation is 690 feet.
History: Duncan Falls may have been named for a trapper who lived in the valley during the 1790's, and for the falls on the Muskingum River, which disappeared when a dam was built.
Population: 1,055 (2000); Race: 97.8% White, 0.0% Black, 0.0% Asian, 0.0% Hispanic of any race (2000); Density: 311.0 persons per square mile (2000); Age: 22.8% under 18, 12.3% over 64 (2000); Marriage status: 24.2% never married, 57.9% now married, 9.0% widowed, 8.9% divorced (2000); Foreign born: 0.0% (2000); Ancestry (includes multiple ancestries): 25.9% German, 14.0% English, 9.2% United States or American, 8.1% Irish, 2.7% Scotch-Irish (2000).
Economy: Employment by occupation: 9.3% management, 30.6% professional, 5.6% services, 23.9% sales, 0.0% farming, 12.5% construction, 18.2% production (2000).
Income: Per capita income: $19,383 (2000); Median household income: $40,417 (2000); Poverty rate: 8.5% (2000).
Education: Percent of population age 25 and over with: High school diploma (including GED) or higher: 94.7% (2000); Bachelor's degree or higher: 20.8% (2000).

School District(s)

Franklin Local (PK-12)
2005-06 Enrollment: 2,435 . . . . (740) 674-5203
Franklin Local Digital Academy (06-12)
2005-06 Enrollment: 33 . . . . (740) 674-5203
Housing: Homeownership rate: 80.1% (2000); Median home value: $109,200 (2000); Median rent: $351 per month (2000); Median age of housing: 42 years (2000).
Transportation: Commute to work: 90.9% car, 0.0% public transportation, 1.0% walk, 3.3% work from home (2000); Travel time to work: 18.1% less than 15 minutes, 53.0% 15 to 30 minutes, 12.3% 30 to 45 minutes, 9.8% 45 to 60 minutes, 6.8% 60 minutes or more (2000)

FRAZEYSBURG (village). Covers a land area of 0.760 square miles and a water area of 0 square miles. Located at 40.11° N. Lat.; 82.11° W. Long. Elevation is 741 feet.
Population: 1,165 (1990); 1,201 (2000); 1,140 (2007); 1,128 (2012 projected); Race: 96.6% White, 1.5% Black, 0.4% Asian, 0.4% Hispanic of any race (2007); Density: 1,499.2 persons per square mile (2007); Average household size: 2.42 (2007); Median age: 34.0 (2007); Males per 100 females: 86.3 (2007); Marriage status: 24.6% never married, 52.1% now married, 8.8% widowed, 14.6% divorced (2000); Foreign born: 0.3% (2000); Ancestry (includes multiple ancestries): 25.2% German, 12.1% English, 11.7% United States or American, 9.7% Irish, 4.9% Other groups (2000).
Economy: Employment by occupation: 5.7% management, 10.7% professional, 14.8% services, 15.8% sales, 0.0% farming, 12.8% construction, 40.2% production (2000).
Income: Per capita income: $20,046 (2007); Median household income: $40,662 (2007); Average household income: $48,519 (2007); Percent of households with income of $100,000 or more: 6.6% (2007); Poverty rate: 6.6% (2000).
Education: Percent of population age 25 and over with: High school diploma (including GED) or higher: 78.5% (2007); Bachelor's degree or higher: 5.2% (2007); Master's degree or higher: 1.4% (2007).

School District(s)

Tri-Valley Local (PK-12)
2005-06 Enrollment: 3,241 . . . . (740) 754-1572
Housing: Homeownership rate: 66.5% (2007); Median home value: $85,179 (2007); Median rent: $353 per month (2000); Median age of housing: 32 years (2000).
Transportation: Commute to work: 95.8% car, 0.0% public transportation, 3.0% walk, 0.8% work from home (2000); Travel time to work: 45.4% less than 15 minutes, 26.6% 15 to 30 minutes, 17.1% 30 to 45 minutes, 3.4% 45 to 60 minutes, 7.5% 60 minutes or more (2000)

FULTONHAM (village). Aka Uniontown. Covers a land area of 0.156 square miles and a water area of 0 square miles. Located at 39.85° N. Lat.; 82.14° W. Long. Elevation is 981 feet.
History: Fultonham developed around the Columbia Cement Company plant, which used the local desposits of limestone.
Population: 178 (1990); 151 (2000); 155 (2007); 158 (2012 projected); Race: 97.4% White, 1.3% Black, 0.0% Asian, 0.0% Hispanic of any race (2007); Density: 990.5 persons per square mile (2007); Average household size: 2.58 (2007); Median age: 38.1 (2007); Males per 100 females: 106.7 (2007); Marriage status: 36.9% never married, 43.9% now married, 9.6% widowed, 9.6% divorced (2000); Foreign born: 0.0% (2000); Ancestry (includes multiple ancestries): 18.5% German, 11.6% Irish, 11.0% English, 11.0% Other groups, 6.4% United States or American (2000).
Economy: Employment by occupation: 4.6% management, 18.5% professional, 7.7% services, 16.9% sales, 1.5% farming, 13.8% construction, 36.9% production (2000).
Income: Per capita income: $12,758 (2007); Median household income: $30,714 (2007); Average household income: $32,958 (2007); Percent of households with income of $100,000 or more: 0.0% (2007); Poverty rate: 13.3% (2000).

Education: Percent of population age 25 and over with: High school diploma (including GED) or higher: 75.7% (2007); Bachelor's degree or higher: 8.7% (2007); Master's degree or higher: 2.9% (2007).
Housing: Homeownership rate: 75.0% (2007); Median home value: $64,375 (2007); Median rent: $314 per month (2000); Median age of housing: 55 years (2000).
Transportation: Commute to work: 100.0% car, 0.0% public transportation, 0.0% walk, 0.0% work from home (2000); Travel time to work: 16.9% less than 15 minutes, 52.3% 15 to 30 minutes, 16.9% 30 to 45 minutes, 13.8% 45 to 60 minutes, 0.0% 60 minutes or more (2000)

HOPEWELL (unincorporated postal area, zip code 43746). Aka Mount Sterling. Covers a land area of 21.564 square miles and a water area of 0.036 square miles. Located at 39.96° N. Lat.; 82.18° W. Long. Elevation is 1,100 feet.
Population: 1,345 (2000); Race: 97.5% White, 0.0% Black, 1.4% Asian, 0.0% Hispanic of any race (2000); Density: 62.4 persons per square mile (2000); Age: 23.0% under 18, 6.2% over 64 (2000); Marriage status: 22.4% never married, 58.0% now married, 4.2% widowed, 15.4% divorced (2000); Foreign born: 1.1% (2000); Ancestry (includes multiple ancestries): 17.8% United States or American, 16.1% German, 14.5% English, 11.1% Irish, 6.7% Other groups (2000).
Economy: Employment by occupation: 15.2% management, 8.1% professional, 20.0% services, 23.0% sales, 1.2% farming, 10.9% construction, 21.5% production (2000).
Income: Per capita income: $20,739 (2000); Median household income: $45,469 (2000); Poverty rate: 4.6% (2000).
Education: Percent of population age 25 and over with: High school diploma (including GED) or higher: 84.6% (2000); Bachelor's degree or higher: 11.3% (2000).

School District(s)

West Muskingum Local (PK-12)
2005-06 Enrollment: 1,884 . . . . (740) 455-4050
Housing: Homeownership rate: 82.0% (2000); Median home value: $116,700 (2000); Median rent: $344 per month (2000); Median age of housing: 24 years (2000).
Transportation: Commute to work: 92.5% car, 1.2% public transportation, 1.5% walk, 4.8% work from home (2000); Travel time to work: 19.1% less than 15 minutes, 41.3% 15 to 30 minutes, 21.5% 30 to 45 minutes, 9.2% 45 to 60 minutes, 8.9% 60 minutes or more (2000)

NASHPORT (unincorporated postal area, zip code 43830). Covers a land area of 51.098 square miles and a water area of 0.030 square miles. Located at 40.06° N. Lat.; 82.16° W. Long. Elevation is 820 feet.
Population: 5,485 (2000); Race: 97.6% White, 1.5% Black, 0.2% Asian, 1.1% Hispanic of any race (2000); Density: 107.3 persons per square mile (2000); Age: 29.8% under 18, 8.2% over 64 (2000); Marriage status: 17.5% never married, 69.3% now married, 4.5% widowed, 8.7% divorced (2000); Foreign born: 0.4% (2000); Ancestry (includes multiple ancestries): 20.8% German, 13.6% United States or American, 13.6% English, 10.3% Irish, 6.4% Other groups (2000).
Economy: Employment by occupation: 10.8% management, 21.2% professional, 14.5% services, 19.7% sales, 0.3% farming, 8.0% construction, 25.6% production (2000).
Income: Per capita income: $20,546 (2000); Median household income: $48,464 (2000); Poverty rate: 6.3% (2000).
Education: Percent of population age 25 and over with: High school diploma (including GED) or higher: 87.9% (2000); Bachelor's degree or higher: 19.3% (2000).

School District(s)

Licking Valley Local (PK-12)
2005-06 Enrollment: 2,136 . . . . (740) 763-3525
Tri-Valley Local (PK-12)
2005-06 Enrollment: 3,241 . . . . (740) 754-1572
Housing: Homeownership rate: 81.2% (2000); Median home value: $109,500 (2000); Median rent: $386 per month (2000); Median age of housing: 23 years (2000).
Transportation: Commute to work: 94.0% car, 0.0% public transportation, 2.5% walk, 2.7% work from home (2000); Travel time to work: 20.6% less than 15 minutes, 50.1% 15 to 30 minutes, 14.8% 30 to 45 minutes, 5.2% 45 to 60 minutes, 9.4% 60 minutes or more (2000)

NEW CONCORD (village). Covers a land area of 1.497 square miles and a water area of 0 square miles. Located at 39.99° N. Lat.; 81.73° W. Long. Elevation is 863 feet.
History: New Concord began in 1807 when the National Road was opened. Muskingum College was founded here in 1836.
Population: 2,320 (1990); 2,651 (2000); 2,647 (2007); 2,658 (2012 projected); Race: 95.1% White, 1.9% Black, 2.0% Asian, 1.3% Hispanic of any race (2007); Density: 1,768.3 persons per square mile (2007); Average household size: 3.89 (2007); Median age: 22.2 (2007); Males per 100 females: 85.1 (2007); Marriage status: 58.9% never married, 31.7% now married, 4.8% widowed, 4.6% divorced (2000); Foreign born: 2.9% (2000); Ancestry (includes multiple ancestries): 29.7% German, 17.7% Irish, 12.1% English, 9.0% Other groups, 5.9% Italian (2000).
Economy: Single-family building permits issued: 0 (2007); Multi-family building permits issued: 0 (2007); Employment by occupation: 7.9% management, 23.8% professional, 21.9% services, 31.4% sales, 1.1% farming, 3.7% construction, 10.2% production (2000).
Income: Per capita income: $20,632 (2007); Median household income: $31,447 (2007); Average household income: $48,952 (2007); Percent of households with income of $100,000 or more: 10.4% (2007); Poverty rate: 24.6% (2000).
Education: Percent of population age 25 and over with: High school diploma (including GED) or higher: 87.1% (2007); Bachelor's degree or higher: 34.5% (2007); Master's degree or higher: 19.6% (2007).

School District(s)

East Muskingum Digital Academy
2005-06 Enrollment: n/a . . . . (740) 826-7641
East Muskingum Local (PK-12)
2005-06 Enrollment: 2,170 . . . . (740) 826-7655

Four-year College(s)

Muskingum College (Private, Not-for-profit, Presbyterian Church (USA))
Fall 2007 Enrollment: 2,099. . . . . (740) 826-8114
2007-08 Tuition: In-state $17,970; Out-of-state $17,970
Housing: Homeownership rate: 56.0% (2007); Median home value: $108,104 (2007); Median rent: $307 per month (2000); Median age of housing: 43 years (2000).
Transportation: Commute to work: 60.2% car, 0.0% public transportation, 35.7% walk, 2.4% work from home (2000); Travel time to work: 61.0% less than 15 minutes, 24.3% 15 to 30 minutes, 7.2% 30 to 45 minutes, 3.3% 45 to 60 minutes, 4.2% 60 minutes or more (2000)

NORTH ZANESVILLE (CDP). Covers a land area of 3.592 square miles and a water area of 0.003 square miles. Located at 39.98° N. Lat.; 82.00° W. Long. Elevation is 899 feet.
Population: 2,964 (1990); 3,013 (2000); 3,145 (2007); 3,218 (2012 projected); Race: 94.2% White, 2.1% Black, 2.2% Asian, 0.6% Hispanic of any race (2007); Density: 875.6 persons per square mile (2007); Average household size: 2.42 (2007); Median age: 47.4 (2007); Males per 100 females: 88.5 (2007); Marriage status: 19.7% never married, 65.5% now married, 5.6% widowed, 9.1% divorced (2000); Foreign born: 1.8% (2000); Ancestry (includes multiple ancestries): 25.7% German, 21.8% English, 11.9% Irish, 10.5% United States or American, 8.5% Other groups (2000).
Economy: Employment by occupation: 14.9% management, 30.3% professional, 12.0% services, 22.6% sales, 0.7% farming, 7.3% construction, 12.2% production (2000).
Income: Per capita income: $29,723 (2007); Median household income: $56,115 (2007); Average household income: $71,734 (2007); Percent of households with income of $100,000 or more: 18.2% (2007); Poverty rate: 5.2% (2000).
Education: Percent of population age 25 and over with: High school diploma (including GED) or higher: 88.9% (2007); Bachelor's degree or higher: 27.5% (2007); Master's degree or higher: 10.4% (2007).
Housing: Homeownership rate: 88.8% (2007); Median home value: $146,968 (2007); Median rent: $398 per month (2000); Median age of housing: 36 years (2000).
Transportation: Commute to work: 94.3% car, 1.8% public transportation, 0.4% walk, 3.5% work from home (2000); Travel time to work: 50.9% less than 15 minutes, 26.3% 15 to 30 minutes, 11.1% 30 to 45 minutes, 5.4% 45 to 60 minutes, 6.3% 60 minutes or more (2000)

NORWICH (village). Covers a land area of 0.096 square miles and a water area of 0 square miles. Located at 39.98° N. Lat.; 81.79° W. Long. Elevation is 971 feet.
History: The village of Norwich was reported in the 1800's to be the home of a headless creature which roamed Stumpy Hollow at night, frightening the residents and leaving them speechless.
Population: 133 (1990); 113 (2000); 120 (2007); 125 (2012 projected); Race: 100.0% White, 0.0% Black, 0.0% Asian, 0.0% Hispanic of any race

(2007); Density: 1,247.8 persons per square mile (2007); Average household size: 2.79 (2007); Median age: 39.4 (2007); Males per 100 females: 81.8 (2007); Marriage status: 21.9% never married, 69.9% now married, 2.7% widowed, 5.5% divorced (2000); Foreign born: 0.0% (2000); Ancestry (includes multiple ancestries): 43.8% German, 30.5% Scotch-Irish, 11.4% Irish, 8.6% French (except Basque), 8.6% Other groups (2000).
Economy: Employment by occupation: 1.9% management, 15.4% professional, 21.2% services, 11.5% sales, 0.0% farming, 0.0% construction, 50.0% production (2000).
Income: Per capita income: $19,208 (2007); Median household income: $43,500 (2007); Average household income: $53,605 (2007); Percent of households with income of $100,000 or more: 14.0% (2007); Poverty rate: 36.2% (2000).
Education: Percent of population age 25 and over with: High school diploma (including GED) or higher: 69.8% (2007); Bachelor's degree or higher: 3.5% (2007); Master's degree or higher: 3.5% (2007).
Housing: Homeownership rate: 81.4% (2007); Median home value: $71,250 (2007); Median rent: $225 per month (2000); Median age of housing: 41 years (2000).
Transportation: Commute to work: 62.0% car, 0.0% public transportation, 20.0% walk, 4.0% work from home (2000); Travel time to work: 50.0% less than 15 minutes, 27.1% 15 to 30 minutes, 2.1% 30 to 45 minutes, 4.2% 45 to 60 minutes, 16.7% 60 minutes or more (2000)

PHILO (village). Aka Taylorsville. Covers a land area of 0.418 square miles and a water area of 0 square miles. Located at 39.86° N. Lat.; 81.90° W. Long. Elevation is 735 feet.
Population: 810 (1990); 769 (2000); 808 (2007); 809 (2012 projected); Race: 98.4% White, 0.4% Black, 0.1% Asian, 0.0% Hispanic of any race (2007); Density: 1,931.0 persons per square mile (2007); Average household size: 2.66 (2007); Median age: 34.2 (2007); Males per 100 females: 90.6 (2007); Marriage status: 19.1% never married, 58.1% now married, 12.0% widowed, 10.8% divorced (2000); Foreign born: 0.4% (2000); Ancestry (includes multiple ancestries): 25.8% United States or American, 13.6% German, 7.4% Irish, 5.0% Other groups, 4.3% English (2000).
Economy: Single-family building permits issued: 0 (2007); Multi-family building permits issued: 0 (2007); Employment by occupation: 8.6% management, 12.9% professional, 17.2% services, 19.5% sales, 0.0% farming, 13.5% construction, 28.4% production (2000).
Income: Per capita income: $18,871 (2007); Median household income: $37,241 (2007); Average household income: $50,156 (2007); Percent of households with income of $100,000 or more: 4.3% (2007); Poverty rate: 15.5% (2000).
Education: Percent of population age 25 and over with: High school diploma (including GED) or higher: 78.1% (2007); Bachelor's degree or higher: 4.3% (2007); Master's degree or higher: 1.4% (2007).

School District(s)

Franklin Local (PK-12)
2005-06 Enrollment: 2,435 . . . . (740) 674-5203
Housing: Homeownership rate: 82.6% (2007); Median home value: $74,714 (2007); Median rent: $335 per month (2000); Median age of housing: 54 years (2000).
Transportation: Commute to work: 97.9% car, 0.0% public transportation, 1.0% walk, 1.0% work from home (2000); Travel time to work: 18.5% less than 15 minutes, 40.4% 15 to 30 minutes, 20.6% 30 to 45 minutes, 5.6% 45 to 60 minutes, 15.0% 60 minutes or more (2000)

PLEASANT GROVE (CDP). Covers a land area of 3.193 square miles and a water area of 0.007 square miles. Located at 39.94° N. Lat.; 81.96° W. Long. Elevation is 922 feet.
Population: 2,001 (1990); 2,016 (2000); 2,032 (2007); 2,025 (2012 projected); Race: 96.2% White, 2.4% Black, 0.3% Asian, 0.5% Hispanic of any race (2007); Density: 636.4 persons per square mile (2007); Average household size: 2.71 (2007); Median age: 46.2 (2007); Males per 100 females: 87.6 (2007); Marriage status: 19.2% never married, 56.7% now married, 13.5% widowed, 10.6% divorced (2000); Foreign born: 5.1% (2000); Ancestry (includes multiple ancestries): 18.7% German, 14.4% United States or American, 10.0% English, 7.7% Irish, 6.4% Other groups (2000).
Economy: Employment by occupation: 5.8% management, 16.6% professional, 18.3% services, 28.5% sales, 0.9% farming, 9.1% construction, 20.9% production (2000).
Income: Per capita income: $19,972 (2007); Median household income: $38,991 (2007); Average household income: $50,597 (2007); Percent of households with income of $100,000 or more: 8.5% (2007); Poverty rate: 11.3% (2000).
Education: Percent of population age 25 and over with: High school diploma (including GED) or higher: 80.5% (2007); Bachelor's degree or higher: 11.9% (2007); Master's degree or higher: 3.3% (2007).
Housing: Homeownership rate: 79.2% (2007); Median home value: $102,549 (2007); Median rent: $333 per month (2000); Median age of housing: 30 years (2000).
Transportation: Commute to work: 91.9% car, 1.2% public transportation, 2.1% walk, 3.8% work from home (2000); Travel time to work: 47.0% less than 15 minutes, 34.9% 15 to 30 minutes, 9.8% 30 to 45 minutes, 4.8% 45 to 60 minutes, 3.5% 60 minutes or more (2000)

SOUTH ZANESVILLE (village). Covers a land area of 0.730 square miles and a water area of 0 square miles. Located at 39.90° N. Lat.; 82.02° W. Long. Elevation is 738 feet.
Population: 2,056 (1990); 1,936 (2000); 1,980 (2007); 2,003 (2012 projected); Race: 97.6% White, 1.1% Black, 0.1% Asian, 0.4% Hispanic of any race (2007); Density: 2,713.5 persons per square mile (2007); Average household size: 2.39 (2007); Median age: 37.4 (2007); Males per 100 females: 90.6 (2007); Marriage status: 24.8% never married, 51.5% now married, 6.0% widowed, 17.7% divorced (2000); Foreign born: 0.7% (2000); Ancestry (includes multiple ancestries): 18.1% United States or American, 12.5% German, 9.6% Other groups, 6.6% Irish, 4.5% English (2000).
Economy: Single-family building permits issued: 0 (2007); Multi-family building permits issued: 0 (2007); Employment by occupation: 5.7% management, 12.4% professional, 14.3% services, 25.1% sales, 0.3% farming, 10.7% construction, 31.4% production (2000).
Income: Per capita income: $17,366 (2007); Median household income: $36,360 (2007); Average household income: $41,478 (2007); Percent of households with income of $100,000 or more: 3.5% (2007); Poverty rate: 11.1% (2000).
Education: Percent of population age 25 and over with: High school diploma (including GED) or higher: 77.2% (2007); Bachelor's degree or higher: 6.0% (2007); Master's degree or higher: 1.8% (2007).
Housing: Homeownership rate: 78.6% (2007); Median home value: $57,241 (2007); Median rent: $329 per month (2000); Median age of housing: 35 years (2000).
Transportation: Commute to work: 94.0% car, 0.5% public transportation, 1.1% walk, 3.3% work from home (2000); Travel time to work: 29.5% less than 15 minutes, 33.3% 15 to 30 minutes, 15.6% 30 to 45 minutes, 9.7% 45 to 60 minutes, 11.9% 60 minutes or more (2000)

ZANESVILLE (city). County seat. Covers a land area of 11.238 square miles and a water area of 0.262 square miles. Located at 39.94° N. Lat.; 82.01° W. Long. Elevation is 676 feet.
History: Zanesville, situated at the confluence of the Licking and Muskingum Rivers, was established in the late 1790's. Clay suitable for pottery-making was discovered in the vicinity, and by 1808 dishes, stoneware, and bricks were bearing the Zanesville imprint. Local sands were used in the glass plant started in Zanesville in 1815, making goblets and water pitchers that became prized collectors items. Zanesville was named for Ebenezer Zane, who surveyed Zane's Trace, an overland route through Ohio, in 1797. A descendant of Zane was western writer Zane Grey, who was born in Zanesville in 1875.
Population: 27,058 (1990); 25,586 (2000); 24,501 (2007); 23,829 (2012 projected); Race: 84.4% White, 11.4% Black, 0.3% Asian, 1.0% Hispanic of any race (2007); Density: 2,180.3 persons per square mile (2007); Average household size: 2.39 (2007); Median age: 35.9 (2007); Males per 100 females: 86.8 (2007); Marriage status: 25.5% never married, 49.1% now married, 9.6% widowed, 15.8% divorced (2000); Foreign born: 0.9% (2000); Ancestry (includes multiple ancestries): 16.7% Other groups, 15.1% United States or American, 14.6% German, 10.4% Irish, 7.4% English (2000).
Economy: Unemployment rate: 8.5% (6/2008); Total civilian labor force: 10,382 (6/2008); Single-family building permits issued: 55 (2007); Multi-family building permits issued: 8 (2007); Employment by occupation: 5.4% management, 17.4% professional, 18.2% services, 25.4% sales, 0.4% farming, 7.5% construction, 25.7% production (2000).
Income: Per capita income: $16,966 (2007); Median household income: $30,041 (2007); Average household income: $39,943 (2007); Percent of

households with income of $100,000 or more: 4.9% (2007); Poverty rate: 22.4% (2000).
Education: Percent of population age 25 and over with: High school diploma (including GED) or higher: 74.2% (2007); Bachelor's degree or higher: 11.8% (2007); Master's degree or higher: 4.5% (2007).

School District(s)

East Muskingum Local (PK-12)
2005-06 Enrollment: 2,170 . . . . (740) 826-7655
Foxfire Center for Student Success (09-12)
2005-06 Enrollment: 102 . . . . (740) 453-4509
Maysville Local (PK-12)
2005-06 Enrollment: 2,281 . . . . (740) 453-0754
Mid-East Career and Technology Centers (PK-12)
2005-06 Enrollment: n/a . . . . (740) 454-0105
West Muskingum Local (PK-12)
2005-06 Enrollment: 1,884 . . . . (740) 455-4050
Zanesville City (PK-12)
2005-06 Enrollment: 4,185 . . . . (740) 454-9751

Four-year College(s)

Ohio University-Zanesville Campus (Public)
Fall 2007 Enrollment: 1,805. . . . . (740) 453-0762
2007-08 Tuition: In-state $4,581; Out-of-state $8,904

Two-year College(s)

Valley Beauty School (Private, For-profit)
Fall 2007 Enrollment: 35 . . . . (740) 452-6821
Zane State College (Public)
Fall 2007 Enrollment: 2,049. . . . . (740) 454-2501
2007-08 Tuition: In-state $3,849; Out-of-state $7,698

Vocational/Technical School(s)

Adult Center for Education (Public)
Fall 2007 Enrollment: 245 . . . . (740) 455-3111
2007-08 Tuition: $5,720

Housing: Homeownership rate: 54.6% (2007); Median home value: $74,663 (2007); Median rent: $318 per month (2000); Median age of housing: 55 years (2000).
Hospitals: Bethesda Hospital (352 beds); Genesis-Good Samaritan (368 beds)
Safety: Violent crime rate: 46.6 per 10,000 population; Property crime rate: 626.9 per 10,000 population (2007).
Newspapers: Times Recorder (Local news; Circulation 21,542); Zanesville Muskingum Advertiser (Community news; Circulation 38,000)
Transportation: Commute to work: 92.8% car, 1.3% public transportation, 2.9% walk, 2.0% work from home (2000); Travel time to work: 49.6% less than 15 minutes, 26.3% 15 to 30 minutes, 10.2% 30 to 45 minutes, 6.0% 45 to 60 minutes, 8.0% 60 minutes or more (2000)
Airports: Zanesville Municipal (general aviation)
Additional Information Contacts
City of Zanesville . . . . (740) 455-0603
http://www.coz.org
Zanesfield-Muskingum County Chamber of Commerce . . . (740) 455-8282
http://www.zmchamber.com

Noble County

Located in eastern Ohio; drained by Wills, Duck, and Seneca Creeks. Covers a land area of 399.00 square miles, a water area of 5.59 square miles, and is located in the Eastern Time Zone. The county was founded in 1851. County seat is Caldwell.
Population: 11,336 (1990); 14,058 (2000); 14,192 (2007); 14,245 (2012 projected); Race: 92.0% White, 7.2% Black, 0.2% Asian, 0.7% Hispanic of any race (2007); Density: 35.6 persons per square mile (2007); Average household size: 3.10 (2007); Median age: 36.7 (2007); Males per 100 females: 136.5 (2007).
Religion: Five largest groups: 11.3% Catholic Church, 8.4% The United Methodist Church, 4.8% Churches of Christ, 1.8% Southern Baptist Convention, 1.7% Christian Churches and Churches of Christ (2000).
Economy: Unemployment rate: 7.7% (6/2008); Total civilian labor force: 5,815 (6/2008); Leading industries: 28.7% manufacturing; 20.0% health care and social assistance; 17.7% retail trade (2005); Farms: 602 totaling 106,957 acres (2002); Companies that employ 500 or more persons: 0 (2006); Companies that employ 100 to 499 persons: 4 (2006); Companies that employ less than 100 persons: 192 (2006); Black-owned businesses: n/a (2002); Hispanic-owned businesses: n/a (2002); Asian-owned businesses: n/a (2002); Women-owned businesses: n/a (2002); Retail sales per capita: $5,009 (2008). Single-family building permits issued: 25 (2007); Multi-family building permits issued: 0 (2007).
Income: Per capita income: $16,273 (2007); Median household income: $38,277 (2007); Average household income: $45,681 (2007); Percent of households with income of $100,000 or more: 5.5% (2007); Poverty rate: 14.5% (2005); Bankruptcy rate: 1.77% (2007).
Education: Percent of population age 25 and over with: High school diploma (including GED) or higher: 78.7% (2007); Bachelor's degree or higher: 8.2% (2007); Master's degree or higher: 2.4% (2007).
Housing: Homeownership rate: 79.7% (2007); Median home value: $85,964 (2007); Median rent: $273 per month (2000); Median age of housing: 34 years (2000).
Health: Birth rate: 106.4 per 10,000 population (2007); Death rate: 89.4 per 10,000 population (2007); Age-adjusted cancer mortality rate: 204.5 deaths per 100,000 population (2005); Number of physicians: 2.9 per 10,000 population (2005); Hospital beds: 0.0 per 10,000 population (2004); Hospital admissions: 0.0 per 10,000 population (2004).
Elections: 2004 Presidential election results: 58.7% Bush, 40.6% Kerry, 0.0% Nader, 0.4% Badnarik
National and State Parks: Wolf Run State Park
Additional Information Contacts
Noble County Government . . . . (740) 732-2969

Noble County Communities

BATESVILLE (village). Covers a land area of 0.248 square miles and a water area of 0 square miles. Located at 39.91° N. Lat.; 81.28° W. Long. Elevation is 909 feet.
Population: 95 (1990); 100 (2000); 111 (2007); 113 (2012 projected); Race: 100.0% White, 0.0% Black, 0.0% Asian, 0.0% Hispanic of any race (2007); Density: 447.0 persons per square mile (2007); Average household size: 2.52 (2007); Median age: 36.3 (2007); Males per 100 females: 101.8 (2007); Marriage status: 7.5% never married, 66.3% now married, 18.8% widowed, 7.5% divorced (2000); Foreign born: 0.0% (2000); Ancestry (includes multiple ancestries): 13.4% Irish, 10.9% German, 5.0% Other groups, 5.0% Russian, 1.7% Italian (2000).
Economy: Employment by occupation: 0.0% management, 10.8% professional, 37.8% services, 10.8% sales, 0.0% farming, 13.5% construction, 27.0% production (2000).
Income: Per capita income: $21,284 (2007); Median household income: $32,000 (2007); Average household income: $53,693 (2007); Percent of households with income of $100,000 or more: 6.8% (2007); Poverty rate: 17.6% (2000).
Education: Percent of population age 25 and over with: High school diploma (including GED) or higher: 72.9% (2007); Bachelor's degree or higher: 5.7% (2007); Master's degree or higher: 0.0% (2007).
Housing: Homeownership rate: 88.6% (2007); Median home value: $57,500 (2007); Median rent: $338 per month (2000); Median age of housing: 60+ years (2000).
Transportation: Commute to work: 89.2% car, 0.0% public transportation, 5.4% walk, 5.4% work from home (2000); Travel time to work: 20.0% less than 15 minutes, 42.9% 15 to 30 minutes, 25.7% 30 to 45 minutes, 0.0% 45 to 60 minutes, 11.4% 60 minutes or more (2000)

BELLE VALLEY (village). Covers a land area of 0.416 square miles and a water area of 0 square miles. Located at 39.78° N. Lat.; 81.55° W. Long. Elevation is 745 feet.
History: Belle Valley developed around a large coal mine. In the early 1900's the mine attracted many Eastern European immigrants who found work here.
Population: 290 (1990); 263 (2000); 253 (2007); 245 (2012 projected); Race: 97.2% White, 0.4% Black, 0.0% Asian, 0.8% Hispanic of any race (2007); Density: 608.6 persons per square mile (2007); Average household size: 2.46 (2007); Median age: 41.9 (2007); Males per 100 females: 91.7 (2007); Marriage status: 29.1% never married, 48.4% now married, 8.5% widowed, 14.1% divorced (2000); Foreign born: 0.4% (2000); Ancestry (includes multiple ancestries): 10.9% German, 7.9% Slovak, 7.5% Irish, 7.5% United States or American, 6.7% English (2000).
Economy: Employment by occupation: 5.2% management, 14.7% professional, 15.5% services, 13.8% sales, 2.6% farming, 7.8% construction, 40.5% production (2000).
Income: Per capita income: $16,087 (2007); Median household income: $35,682 (2007); Average household income: $39,515 (2007); Percent of

households with income of $100,000 or more: 2.9% (2007); Poverty rate: 19.9% (2000).
Education: Percent of population age 25 and over with: High school diploma (including GED) or higher: 80.7% (2007); Bachelor's degree or higher: 1.7% (2007); Master's degree or higher: 1.1% (2007).
Housing: Homeownership rate: 77.7% (2007); Median home value: $52,727 (2007); Median rent: $278 per month (2000); Median age of housing: 60+ years (2000).
Transportation: Commute to work: 96.5% car, 0.0% public transportation, 0.0% walk, 0.0% work from home (2000); Travel time to work: 24.8% less than 15 minutes, 45.1% 15 to 30 minutes, 14.2% 30 to 45 minutes, 4.4% 45 to 60 minutes, 11.5% 60 minutes or more (2000)

CALDWELL (village). County seat. Covers a land area of 0.979 square miles and a water area of 0 square miles. Located at 39.74° N. Lat.; 81.51° W. Long. Elevation is 741 feet.
History: Caldwell was founded in 1857 as the seat of Noble County, and named for the owners of the town site. Coal mining was Caldwell's primary industry.
Population: 1,797 (1990); 1,956 (2000); 2,058 (2007); 2,077 (2012 projected); Race: 98.9% White, 0.1% Black, 0.7% Asian, 0.2% Hispanic of any race (2007); Density: 2,102.4 persons per square mile (2007); Average household size: 2.32 (2007); Median age: 44.6 (2007); Males per 100 females: 86.1 (2007); Marriage status: 23.5% never married, 47.7% now married, 17.9% widowed, 11.0% divorced (2000); Foreign born: 0.0% (2000); Ancestry (includes multiple ancestries): 20.1% German, 11.5% Irish, 10.5% United States or American, 9.4% English, 4.8% Other groups (2000).
Economy: Employment by occupation: 9.8% management, 14.7% professional, 18.9% services, 25.6% sales, 1.3% farming, 8.2% construction, 21.6% production (2000).
Income: Per capita income: $17,330 (2007); Median household income: $29,750 (2007); Average household income: $37,753 (2007); Percent of households with income of $100,000 or more: 3.4% (2007); Poverty rate: 14.5% (2000).
Education: Percent of population age 25 and over with: High school diploma (including GED) or higher: 78.8% (2007); Bachelor's degree or higher: 10.4% (2007); Master's degree or higher: 2.0% (2007).

School District(s)

Caldwell Exempted Village (PK-12)
2005-06 Enrollment: 983 . . . . (740) 732-5637
Housing: Homeownership rate: 61.5% (2007); Median home value: $82,250 (2007); Median rent: $304 per month (2000); Median age of housing: 57 years (2000).
Newspapers: Journal & Leader (Local news; Circulation 5,000)
Transportation: Commute to work: 90.6% car, 0.0% public transportation, 5.4% walk, 4.0% work from home (2000); Travel time to work: 67.7% less than 15 minutes, 11.9% 15 to 30 minutes, 9.1% 30 to 45 minutes, 5.1% 45 to 60 minutes, 6.2% 60 minutes or more (2000)

DEXTER CITY (village). Covers a land area of 0.175 square miles and a water area of 0 square miles. Located at 39.65° N. Lat.; 81.47° W. Long. Elevation is 712 feet.
Population: 161 (1990); 166 (2000); 148 (2007); 142 (2012 projected); Race: 100.0% White, 0.0% Black, 0.0% Asian, 0.0% Hispanic of any race (2007); Density: 845.6 persons per square mile (2007); Average household size: 2.55 (2007); Median age: 38.5 (2007); Males per 100 females: 102.7 (2007); Marriage status: 29.8% never married, 48.9% now married, 8.5% widowed, 12.8% divorced (2000); Foreign born: 0.0% (2000); Ancestry (includes multiple ancestries): 28.7% German, 20.5% English, 11.1% Irish, 7.0% Other groups, 5.8% United States or American (2000).
Economy: Employment by occupation: 0.0% management, 13.2% professional, 35.5% services, 9.2% sales, 0.0% farming, 10.5% construction, 31.6% production (2000).
Income: Per capita income: $14,679 (2007); Median household income: $32,500 (2007); Average household income: $37,457 (2007); Percent of households with income of $100,000 or more: 0.0% (2007); Poverty rate: 21.6% (2000).
Education: Percent of population age 25 and over with: High school diploma (including GED) or higher: 69.6% (2007); Bachelor's degree or higher: 7.8% (2007); Master's degree or higher: 0.0% (2007).
Housing: Homeownership rate: 74.1% (2007); Median home value: $50,556 (2007); Median rent: $175 per month (2000); Median age of housing: 60+ years (2000).
Transportation: Commute to work: 97.4% car, 0.0% public transportation, 0.0% walk, 2.6% work from home (2000); Travel time to work: 27.0% less than 15 minutes, 35.1% 15 to 30 minutes, 25.7% 30 to 45 minutes, 6.8% 45 to 60 minutes, 5.4% 60 minutes or more (2000)

SARAHSVILLE (village). Covers a land area of 0.168 square miles and a water area of 0 square miles. Located at 39.80° N. Lat.; 81.46° W. Long. Elevation is 968 feet.
Population: 162 (1990); 198 (2000); 224 (2007); 232 (2012 projected); Race: 98.7% White, 0.9% Black, 0.0% Asian, 5.8% Hispanic of any race (2007); Density: 1,332.0 persons per square mile (2007); Average household size: 3.11 (2007); Median age: 32.5 (2007); Males per 100 females: 111.3 (2007); Marriage status: 28.7% never married, 61.9% now married, 5.6% widowed, 3.8% divorced (2000); Foreign born: 0.0% (2000); Ancestry (includes multiple ancestries): 8.7% German, 8.7% Irish, 5.1% French (except Basque), 3.6% Dutch, 3.6% United States or American (2000).
Economy: Employment by occupation: 10.0% management, 16.3% professional, 25.0% services, 10.0% sales, 2.5% farming, 16.3% construction, 20.0% production (2000).
Income: Per capita income: $15,324 (2007); Median household income: $42,500 (2007); Average household income: $47,674 (2007); Percent of households with income of $100,000 or more: 9.7% (2007); Poverty rate: 14.4% (2000).
Education: Percent of population age 25 and over with: High school diploma (including GED) or higher: 77.7% (2007); Bachelor's degree or higher: 0.0% (2007); Master's degree or higher: 0.0% (2007).

School District(s)

Noble Local (PK-12)
2005-06 Enrollment: 1,200 . . . . (740) 732-2084
Housing: Homeownership rate: 87.5% (2007); Median home value: $65,625 (2007); Median rent: $263 per month (2000); Median age of housing: 57 years (2000).
Transportation: Commute to work: 88.8% car, 0.0% public transportation, 3.8% walk, 7.5% work from home (2000); Travel time to work: 18.9% less than 15 minutes, 39.2% 15 to 30 minutes, 31.1% 30 to 45 minutes, 8.1% 45 to 60 minutes, 2.7% 60 minutes or more (2000)

SUMMERFIELD (village). Covers a land area of 0.370 square miles and a water area of 0 square miles. Located at 39.79° N. Lat.; 81.33° W. Long. Elevation is 1,201 feet.
Population: 295 (1990); 296 (2000); 249 (2007); 247 (2012 projected); Race: 100.0% White, 0.0% Black, 0.0% Asian, 0.0% Hispanic of any race (2007); Density: 672.4 persons per square mile (2007); Average household size: 2.86 (2007); Median age: 30.4 (2007); Males per 100 females: 91.5 (2007); Marriage status: 22.2% never married, 61.5% now married, 10.3% widowed, 6.0% divorced (2000); Foreign born: 0.0% (2000); Ancestry (includes multiple ancestries): 32.2% German, 11.0% Irish, 9.5% English, 6.3% United States or American, 6.3% Other groups (2000).
Economy: Employment by occupation: 5.9% management, 11.9% professional, 27.7% services, 15.8% sales, 0.0% farming, 13.9% construction, 24.8% production (2000).
Income: Per capita income: $12,018 (2007); Median household income: $26,500 (2007); Average household income: $34,397 (2007); Percent of households with income of $100,000 or more: 1.1% (2007); Poverty rate: 16.7% (2000).
Education: Percent of population age 25 and over with: High school diploma (including GED) or higher: 73.8% (2007); Bachelor's degree or higher: 7.1% (2007); Master's degree or higher: 1.4% (2007).
Housing: Homeownership rate: 81.6% (2007); Median home value: $42,333 (2007); Median rent: $194 per month (2000); Median age of housing: 60 years (2000).
Transportation: Commute to work: 85.7% car, 1.0% public transportation, 3.1% walk, 10.2% work from home (2000); Travel time to work: 14.8% less than 15 minutes, 40.9% 15 to 30 minutes, 8.0% 30 to 45 minutes, 13.6% 45 to 60 minutes, 22.7% 60 minutes or more (2000)

Ottawa County

Located in northern Ohio; bounded on the northeast by Lake Erie; drained by Portage River; includes the Bass Islands. Covers a land area of 254.95 square miles, a water area of 330.17 square miles, and is located in the Eastern Time Zone. The county was founded in 1840. County seat is Port Clinton.

Ottawa County is part of the Toledo, OH Metropolitan Statistical Area. The entire metro area includes: Fulton County, OH; Lucas County, OH; Ottawa County, OH; Wood County, OH

Weather Station: Put-In-Bay Elevation: 577 feet

	Jan	Feb	Mar	Apr	May	Jun	Jul	Aug	Sep	Oct	Nov	Dec
High	31	34	43	55	67	77	82	81	74	61	48	37
Low	18	20	29	39	51	61	67	66	59	48	37	26
Precip	1.6	1.4	5.2	2.9	3.3	3.4	3.1	3.3	3.2	2.6	2.7	2.2
Snow	7.3	5.3	2.8	0.4	tr	0.0	0.0	0.0	0.0	tr	0.2	3.7

High and Low temperatures in degrees Fahrenheit; Precipitation and Snow in inches

Population: 40,029 (1990); 40,985 (2000); 41,814 (2007); 42,299 (2012 projected); Race: 96.3% White, 0.8% Black, 0.3% Asian, 3.9% Hispanic of any race (2007); Density: 164.0 persons per square mile (2007); Average household size: 2.42 (2007); Median age: 43.1 (2007); Males per 100 females: 98.1 (2007).
Religion: Five largest groups: 21.9% Catholic Church, 17.1% Evangelical Lutheran Church in America, 7.0% United Church of Christ, 6.1% The United Methodist Church, 1.0% Lutheran Church—Missouri Synod (2000).
Economy: Unemployment rate: 7.2% (6/2008); Total civilian labor force: 21,656 (6/2008); Leading industries: 21.5% manufacturing; 17.5% retail trade; 13.7% health care and social assistance (2005); Farms: 517 totaling 114,430 acres (2002); Companies that employ 500 or more persons: 2 (2006); Companies that employ 100 to 499 persons: 10 (2006); Companies that employ less than 100 persons: 1,094 (2006); Black-owned businesses: n/a (2002); Hispanic-owned businesses: n/a (2002); Asian-owned businesses: n/a (2002); Women-owned businesses: 648 (2002); Retail sales per capita: $14,379 (2008). Single-family building permits issued: 207 (2007); Multi-family building permits issued: 69 (2007).
Income: Per capita income: $25,629 (2007); Median household income: $50,608 (2007); Average household income: $61,378 (2007); Percent of households with income of $100,000 or more: 15.1% (2007); Poverty rate: 7.3% (2005); Bankruptcy rate: 3.72% (2007).
Taxes: Total county taxes per capita: $338 (2006); County property taxes per capita: $186 (2006).
Education: Percent of population age 25 and over with: High school diploma (including GED) or higher: 84.1% (2007); Bachelor's degree or higher: 15.8% (2007); Master's degree or higher: 5.3% (2007).
Housing: Homeownership rate: 80.8% (2007); Median home value: $136,906 (2007); Median rent: $386 per month (2000); Median age of housing: 35 years (2000).
Health: Birth rate: 104.9 per 10,000 population (2007); Death rate: 108.6 per 10,000 population (2007); Age-adjusted cancer mortality rate: 215.9 deaths per 100,000 population (2005); Number of physicians: 12.8 per 10,000 population (2005); Hospital beds: 6.1 per 10,000 population (2004); Hospital admissions: 301.9 per 10,000 population (2004).
Elections: 2004 Presidential election results: 51.9% Bush, 47.8% Kerry, 0.0% Nader, 0.2% Badnarik
National and State Parks: Catawba Island State Park; Crane Creek State Park; East Harbor State Park; Ottawa National Wildlife Refuge; South Bass Island State Park
Additional Information Contacts
Ottawa County Government . . . . (419) 734-6710
http://www.co.ottawa.oh.us
City of Port Clinton . . . . (419) 734-5522
http://www.ci.port-clinton.oh.us
Marblehead Peninsula Chamber of Commerce . . . . (419) 734-9777
http://www.marbleheadpeninsula.com
Oak Harbor Area Chamber of Commerce . . . . (419) 898-0479
http://www.oakharborohio.net
Port Clinton Area Chamber of Commerce . . . . (419) 734-5503
http://www.portclintonchamber.com
Put-In-Bay Chamber of Commerce . . . . (419) 285-2832
http://www.put-in-bay.com
Village of Genoa . . . . (419) 855-7791
http://www.genoaohio.org
Village of Oak Harbor . . . . (419) 898-5561
http://www.oakharbor.oh.us

Ottawa County Communities

CLAY CENTER (village). Covers a land area of 0.903 square miles and a water area of 0 square miles. Located at 41.56° N. Lat.; 83.36° W. Long. Elevation is 610 feet.
Population: 303 (1990); 294 (2000); 312 (2007); 324 (2012 projected); Race: 99.0% White, 0.0% Black, 0.0% Asian, 5.4% Hispanic of any race (2007); Density: 345.6 persons per square mile (2007); Average household size: 2.62 (2007); Median age: 36.4 (2007); Males per 100 females: 98.7 (2007); Marriage status: 19.4% never married, 69.4% now married, 3.6% widowed, 7.7% divorced (2000); Foreign born: 0.0% (2000); Ancestry (includes multiple ancestries): 55.7% German, 10.1% Polish, 7.4% French (except Basque), 6.4% Other groups, 6.4% Irish (2000).
Economy: Single-family building permits issued: 1 (2007); Multi-family building permits issued: 0 (2007); Employment by occupation: 7.3% management, 9.3% professional, 16.0% services, 20.0% sales, 0.0% farming, 16.7% construction, 30.7% production (2000).
Income: Per capita income: $27,668 (2007); Median household income: $61,563 (2007); Average household income: $72,542 (2007); Percent of households with income of $100,000 or more: 14.3% (2007); Poverty rate: 3.0% (2000).
Education: Percent of population age 25 and over with: High school diploma (including GED) or higher: 85.4% (2007); Bachelor's degree or higher: 8.3% (2007); Master's degree or higher: 4.4% (2007).
Housing: Homeownership rate: 83.2% (2007); Median home value: $95,909 (2007); Median rent: $317 per month (2000); Median age of housing: 60+ years (2000).
Transportation: Commute to work: 91.3% car, 0.0% public transportation, 8.0% walk, 0.0% work from home (2000); Travel time to work: 43.3% less than 15 minutes, 33.3% 15 to 30 minutes, 18.7% 30 to 45 minutes, 1.3% 45 to 60 minutes, 3.3% 60 minutes or more (2000)

ELMORE (village). Covers a land area of 0.831 square miles and a water area of 0 square miles. Located at 41.47° N. Lat.; 83.29° W. Long. Elevation is 604 feet.
Population: 1,411 (1990); 1,426 (2000); 1,544 (2007); 1,608 (2012 projected); Race: 97.3% White, 0.2% Black, 0.0% Asian, 5.3% Hispanic of any race (2007); Density: 1,858.6 persons per square mile (2007); Average household size: 2.36 (2007); Median age: 37.4 (2007); Males per 100 females: 89.9 (2007); Marriage status: 17.5% never married, 64.5% now married, 9.7% widowed, 8.2% divorced (2000); Foreign born: 0.6% (2000); Ancestry (includes multiple ancestries): 48.1% German, 9.4% English, 9.4% Irish, 6.6% Other groups, 6.2% Hungarian (2000).
Economy: Employment by occupation: 11.9% management, 14.6% professional, 11.0% services, 29.7% sales, 1.2% farming, 7.9% construction, 23.7% production (2000).
Income: Per capita income: $23,269 (2007); Median household income: $47,563 (2007); Average household income: $55,019 (2007); Percent of households with income of $100,000 or more: 12.4% (2007); Poverty rate: 5.5% (2000).
Education: Percent of population age 25 and over with: High school diploma (including GED) or higher: 86.3% (2007); Bachelor's degree or higher: 18.2% (2007); Master's degree or higher: 5.2% (2007).

School District(s)
Woodmore Local (PK-12)
2005-06 Enrollment: 1,194 . . . . (419) 849-2381
Housing: Homeownership rate: 73.2% (2007); Median home value: $118,683 (2007); Median rent: $267 per month (2000); Median age of housing: 60+ years (2000).
Transportation: Commute to work: 93.5% car, 0.5% public transportation, 3.0% walk, 1.7% work from home (2000); Travel time to work: 27.9% less than 15 minutes, 31.9% 15 to 30 minutes, 30.8% 30 to 45 minutes, 6.3% 45 to 60 minutes, 3.1% 60 minutes or more (2000)

GENOA (village). Covers a land area of 1.496 square miles and a water area of 0 square miles. Located at 41.52° N. Lat.; 83.36° W. Long. Elevation is 627 feet.
History: Settled 1835 as Stony Ridge Station.
Population: 2,381 (1990); 2,230 (2000); 2,289 (2007); 2,293 (2012 projected); Race: 95.6% White, 0.7% Black, 0.4% Asian, 6.2% Hispanic of any race (2007); Density: 1,529.7 persons per square mile (2007); Average household size: 2.54 (2007); Median age: 40.5 (2007); Males per 100 females: 93.3 (2007); Marriage status: 21.3% never married, 54.3% now married, 12.8% widowed, 11.6% divorced (2000); Foreign born: 0.8% (2000); Ancestry (includes multiple ancestries): 32.1% German, 11.5% Irish, 10.6% Other groups, 9.6% English, 6.3% United States or American (2000).
Economy: Employment by occupation: 11.4% management, 13.3% professional, 16.0% services, 24.7% sales, 0.0% farming, 13.3% construction, 21.2% production (2000).

Income: Per capita income: $23,070 (2007); Median household income: $48,571 (2007); Average household income: $56,622 (2007); Percent of households with income of $100,000 or more: 9.8% (2007); Poverty rate: 2.0% (2000).
Education: Percent of population age 25 and over with: High school diploma (including GED) or higher: 84.9% (2007); Bachelor's degree or higher: 10.7% (2007); Master's degree or higher: 2.2% (2007).

School District(s)

Genoa Area Local (PK-12)
2005-06 Enrollment: 1,589 . . . . (419) 855-7741
Housing: Homeownership rate: 76.6% (2007); Median home value: $113,238 (2007); Median rent: $408 per month (2000); Median age of housing: 53 years (2000).
Safety: Violent crime rate: 0.0 per 10,000 population; Property crime rate: 219.9 per 10,000 population (2007).
Transportation: Commute to work: 96.5% car, 0.0% public transportation, 2.7% walk, 0.0% work from home (2000); Travel time to work: 25.2% less than 15 minutes, 39.6% 15 to 30 minutes, 24.4% 30 to 45 minutes, 8.0% 45 to 60 minutes, 2.8% 60 minutes or more (2000)
Additional Information Contacts
Village of Genoa . . . . (419) 855-7791
http://www.genoaohio.org

GRAYTOWN (unincorporated postal area, zip code 43432). Covers a land area of 24.748 square miles and a water area of 0.017 square miles. Located at 41.55° N. Lat.; 83.25° W. Long. Elevation is 595 feet.
Population: 1,357 (2000); Race: 97.1% White, 0.0% Black, 0.0% Asian, 6.4% Hispanic of any race (2000); Density: 54.8 persons per square mile (2000); Age: 29.5% under 18, 11.5% over 64 (2000); Marriage status: 20.6% never married, 70.9% now married, 2.9% widowed, 5.6% divorced (2000); Foreign born: 0.9% (2000); Ancestry (includes multiple ancestries): 52.2% German, 10.8% Irish, 6.9% Other groups, 3.8% Hungarian, 3.7% English (2000).
Economy: Employment by occupation: 10.9% management, 18.9% professional, 10.5% services, 20.9% sales, 1.4% farming, 8.9% construction, 28.5% production (2000).
Income: Per capita income: $20,032 (2000); Median household income: $61,750 (2000); Poverty rate: 4.6% (2000).
Education: Percent of population age 25 and over with: High school diploma (including GED) or higher: 88.9% (2000); Bachelor's degree or higher: 13.8% (2000).

School District(s)

Benton Carroll Salem Local (PK-12)
2005-06 Enrollment: 1,984 . . . . (419) 898-6210
Housing: Homeownership rate: 93.1% (2000); Median home value: $120,700 (2000); Median rent: $917 per month (2000); Median age of housing: 49 years (2000).
Transportation: Commute to work: 92.9% car, 0.0% public transportation, 2.9% walk, 4.2% work from home (2000); Travel time to work: 24.9% less than 15 minutes, 38.3% 15 to 30 minutes, 26.8% 30 to 45 minutes, 4.8% 45 to 60 minutes, 5.2% 60 minutes or more (2000)

LACARNE (unincorporated postal area, zip code 43439). Aka La Carne. Covers a land area of 0.017 square miles and a water area of 0 square miles. Located at 41.51° N. Lat.; 83.04° W. Long. Elevation is 577 feet.
Population: 74 (2000); Race: 100.0% White, 0.0% Black, 0.0% Asian, 0.0% Hispanic of any race (2000); Density: 4,360.1 persons per square mile (2000); Age: 38.3% under 18, 13.3% over 64 (2000); Marriage status: 21.6% never married, 35.1% now married, 0.0% widowed, 43.2% divorced (2000); Foreign born: 11.7% (2000); Ancestry (includes multiple ancestries): 51.7% German, 23.3% United States or American, 11.7% Irish, 11.7% Lithuanian, 10.0% Dutch (2000).
Economy: Employment by occupation: 0.0% management, 0.0% professional, 0.0% services, 0.0% sales, 0.0% farming, 0.0% construction, 100.0% production (2000).
Income: Per capita income: $15,100 (2000); Median household income: $27,500 (2000); Poverty rate: 0.0% (2000).
Education: Percent of population age 25 and over with: High school diploma (including GED) or higher: 100.0% (2000); Bachelor's degree or higher: 0.0% (2000).
Housing: Homeownership rate: 100.0% (2000); Median home value: $79,300 (2000); Median rent: $n/a per month (2000); Median age of housing: 60+ years (2000).
Transportation: Commute to work: 100.0% car, 0.0% public transportation, 0.0% walk, 0.0% work from home (2000); Travel time to work: 53.8% less than 15 minutes, 0.0% 15 to 30 minutes, 46.2% 30 to 45 minutes, 0.0% 45 to 60 minutes, 0.0% 60 minutes or more (2000)

LAKESIDE MARBLEHEAD (unincorporated postal area, zip code 43440). Part of the Village of Marblehead. Covers a land area of 15.362 square miles and a water area of 0.846 square miles. Located at 41.53° N. Lat.; 82.75° W. Long.
Population: 4,319 (2000); Race: 97.2% White, 0.8% Black, 0.0% Asian, 2.0% Hispanic of any race (2000); Density: 281.1 persons per square mile (2000); Age: 17.6% under 18, 22.8% over 64 (2000); Marriage status: 17.4% never married, 61.2% now married, 9.4% widowed, 11.9% divorced (2000); Foreign born: 1.3% (2000); Ancestry (includes multiple ancestries): 31.7% German, 12.3% English, 10.8% Irish, 8.6% Slovak, 8.1% Polish (2000).
Economy: Employment by occupation: 11.8% management, 14.4% professional, 17.1% services, 25.1% sales, 0.0% farming, 12.2% construction, 19.5% production (2000).
Income: Per capita income: $28,563 (2000); Median household income: $42,007 (2000); Poverty rate: 3.7% (2000).
Education: Percent of population age 25 and over with: High school diploma (including GED) or higher: 86.1% (2000); Bachelor's degree or higher: 18.7% (2000).

School District(s)

Danbury Local (PK-12)
2005-06 Enrollment: 616 . . . . (419) 798-5185
Housing: Homeownership rate: 82.5% (2000); Median home value: $127,900 (2000); Median rent: $416 per month (2000); Median age of housing: 33 years (2000).
Transportation: Commute to work: 89.0% car, 0.6% public transportation, 4.2% walk, 4.9% work from home (2000); Travel time to work: 33.1% less than 15 minutes, 36.8% 15 to 30 minutes, 14.7% 30 to 45 minutes, 5.0% 45 to 60 minutes, 10.4% 60 minutes or more (2000)

MARBLEHEAD (village). Covers a land area of 2.834 square miles and a water area of 0.979 square miles. Located at 41.53° N. Lat.; 82.72° W. Long. Elevation is 627 feet.
History: The Benajah Wolcott family settled here in 1809 and found three orchards which the French had planted earlier. Quarrying began in 1834 when John Clemens, a relative of Mark Twain, established himself here. Marblehead may have been called Marble Headland by an early visitor, who thought the white limestone cliffs were marble.
Population: 858 (1990); 762 (2000); 679 (2007); 673 (2012 projected); Race: 96.9% White, 0.6% Black, 0.4% Asian, 2.1% Hispanic of any race (2007); Density: 239.6 persons per square mile (2007); Average household size: 2.22 (2007); Median age: 51.7 (2007); Males per 100 females: 98.5 (2007); Marriage status: 20.5% never married, 67.2% now married, 6.9% widowed, 5.4% divorced (2000); Foreign born: 0.8% (2000); Ancestry (includes multiple ancestries): 30.3% German, 27.1% Slovak, 12.6% Irish, 11.6% English, 6.5% Polish (2000).
Economy: Employment by occupation: 12.2% management, 15.8% professional, 17.0% services, 23.3% sales, 0.0% farming, 14.3% construction, 17.3% production (2000).
Income: Per capita income: $31,995 (2007); Median household income: $53,409 (2007); Average household income: $69,314 (2007); Percent of households with income of $100,000 or more: 19.6% (2007); Poverty rate: 4.7% (2000).
Education: Percent of population age 25 and over with: High school diploma (including GED) or higher: 92.5% (2007); Bachelor's degree or higher: 24.6% (2007); Master's degree or higher: 11.6% (2007).
Housing: Homeownership rate: 85.3% (2007); Median home value: $172,917 (2007); Median rent: $411 per month (2000); Median age of housing: 30 years (2000).
Newspapers: Peninsula News (Community news; Circulation 1,800)
Transportation: Commute to work: 81.5% car, 0.9% public transportation, 4.3% walk, 10.1% work from home (2000); Travel time to work: 40.8% less than 15 minutes, 27.3% 15 to 30 minutes, 17.7% 30 to 45 minutes, 2.3% 45 to 60 minutes, 11.9% 60 minutes or more (2000)
Additional Information Contacts
Marblehead Peninsula Chamber of Commerce . . . . (419) 734-9777
http://www.marbleheadpeninsula.com

MARTIN (unincorporated postal area, zip code 43445). Covers a land area of 19.025 square miles and a water area of 0.129 square miles. Located at 41.59° N. Lat.; 83.29° W. Long. Elevation is 600 feet.

Population: 1,170 (2000); Race: 86.2% White, 0.0% Black, 0.0% Asian, 12.1% Hispanic of any race (2000); Density: 61.5 persons per square mile (2000); Age: 33.9% under 18, 7.9% over 64 (2000); Marriage status: 29.1% never married, 64.8% now married, 2.5% widowed, 3.7% divorced (2000); Foreign born: 2.0% (2000); Ancestry (includes multiple ancestries): 57.7% German, 15.3% Other groups, 11.1% Irish, 5.4% Hungarian, 5.2% Italian (2000).

Economy: Employment by occupation: 6.0% management, 10.1% professional, 15.3% services, 25.2% sales, 1.0% farming, 14.5% construction, 27.9% production (2000).

Income: Per capita income: $18,604 (2000); Median household income: $56,719 (2000); Poverty rate: 5.8% (2000).

Education: Percent of population age 25 and over with: High school diploma (including GED) or higher: 82.0% (2000); Bachelor's degree or higher: 12.7% (2000).

Housing: Homeownership rate: 87.1% (2000); Median home value: $109,600 (2000); Median rent: $375 per month (2000); Median age of housing: 44 years (2000).

Transportation: Commute to work: 95.2% car, 2.2% public transportation, 0.0% walk, 2.7% work from home (2000); Travel time to work: 23.7% less than 15 minutes, 40.6% 15 to 30 minutes, 29.5% 30 to 45 minutes, 4.8% 45 to 60 minutes, 1.4% 60 minutes or more (2000)

OAK HARBOR (village). Covers a land area of 1.327 square miles and a water area of 0.140 square miles. Located at 41.51° N. Lat.; 83.14° W. Long. Elevation is 581 feet.

History: Sometimes spelled Oakharbor.

Population: 2,637 (1990); 2,841 (2000); 2,820 (2007); 2,809 (2012 projected); Race: 97.8% White, 0.1% Black, 0.5% Asian, 2.4% Hispanic of any race (2007); Density: 2,124.4 persons per square mile (2007); Average household size: 2.39 (2007); Median age: 38.9 (2007); Males per 100 females: 91.8 (2007); Marriage status: 23.8% never married, 57.7% now married, 7.5% widowed, 11.0% divorced (2000); Foreign born: 0.5% (2000); Ancestry (includes multiple ancestries): 51.6% German, 9.9% Irish, 8.2% English, 7.1% Other groups, 5.2% United States or American (2000).

Economy: Single-family building permits issued: 11 (2007); Multi-family building permits issued: 0 (2007); Employment by occupation: 9.7% management, 18.9% professional, 14.5% services, 21.0% sales, 0.0% farming, 8.1% construction, 27.9% production (2000).

Income: Per capita income: $26,872 (2007); Median household income: $51,066 (2007); Average household income: $64,112 (2007); Percent of households with income of $100,000 or more: 15.2% (2007); Poverty rate: 3.5% (2000).

Taxes: Total city taxes per capita: $274 (2006); City property taxes per capita: $63 (2006).

Education: Percent of population age 25 and over with: High school diploma (including GED) or higher: 88.8% (2007); Bachelor's degree or higher: 17.2% (2007); Master's degree or higher: 6.1% (2007).

School District(s)

Benton Carroll Salem Local (PK-12)
2005-06 Enrollment: 1,984 . . . . (419) 898-6210

Housing: Homeownership rate: 71.3% (2007); Median home value: $118,408 (2007); Median rent: $346 per month (2000); Median age of housing: 55 years (2000).

Newspapers: Ottawa County Exponent (Community news; Circulation 3,000)

Transportation: Commute to work: 95.4% car, 0.0% public transportation, 2.1% walk, 2.0% work from home (2000); Travel time to work: 38.7% less than 15 minutes, 36.3% 15 to 30 minutes, 16.2% 30 to 45 minutes, 5.7% 45 to 60 minutes, 3.1% 60 minutes or more (2000)

Additional Information Contacts

Oak Harbor Area Chamber of Commerce . . . . (419) 898-0479
http://www.oakharborohio.net
Village of Oak Harbor. . . . . (419) 898-5561
http://www.oakharbor.oh.us

PORT CLINTON (city). County seat. Covers a land area of 2.106 square miles and a water area of 0.201 square miles. Located at 41.51° N. Lat.; 82.94° W. Long. Elevation is 581 feet.

History: Port Clinton was platted in 1828 and settled by some Scotch immigrants, bound for Chicago, who were shipwrecked at this point and settled here. The town was named for DeWitt Clinton.

Population: 7,170 (1990); 6,391 (2000); 6,339 (2007); 6,294 (2012 projected); Race: 92.7% White, 2.5% Black, 0.4% Asian, 6.1% Hispanic of any race (2007); Density: 3,009.4 persons per square mile (2007); Average household size: 2.23 (2007); Median age: 40.5 (2007); Males per 100 females: 95.6 (2007); Marriage status: 25.8% never married, 51.7% now married, 8.6% widowed, 13.9% divorced (2000); Foreign born: 1.2% (2000); Ancestry (includes multiple ancestries): 37.4% German, 12.3% Irish, 11.7% Other groups, 10.9% English, 6.5% United States or American (2000).

Economy: Employment by occupation: 10.0% management, 15.7% professional, 17.4% services, 26.4% sales, 0.4% farming, 9.6% construction, 20.5% production (2000).

Income: Per capita income: $21,828 (2007); Median household income: $39,277 (2007); Average household income: $48,121 (2007); Percent of households with income of $100,000 or more: 9.4% (2007); Poverty rate: 9.7% (2000).

Education: Percent of population age 25 and over with: High school diploma (including GED) or higher: 80.1% (2007); Bachelor's degree or higher: 12.0% (2007); Master's degree or higher: 5.3% (2007).

School District(s)

Port Clinton City (PK-12)
2005-06 Enrollment: 1,870 . . . . (419) 732-2102

Housing: Homeownership rate: 67.3% (2007); Median home value: $112,605 (2007); Median rent: $389 per month (2000); Median age of housing: 44 years (2000).

Hospitals: Magruder Hospital (98 beds)

Safety: Violent crime rate: 24.0 per 10,000 population; Property crime rate: 392.3 per 10,000 population (2007).

Newspapers: Beacon (Community news; Circulation 17,000); The Fishwrapper (Regional news); News-Herald (Local news; Circulation 3,250)

Transportation: Commute to work: 90.7% car, 1.3% public transportation, 3.8% walk, 2.8% work from home (2000); Travel time to work: 54.4% less than 15 minutes, 26.2% 15 to 30 minutes, 9.2% 30 to 45 minutes, 4.4% 45 to 60 minutes, 5.9% 60 minutes or more (2000)

Airports: Carl R Keller Field (general aviation)

Additional Information Contacts

City of Port Clinton . . . . (419) 734-5522
http://www.ci.port-clinton.oh.us
Port Clinton Area Chamber of Commerce . . . . (419) 734-5503
http://www.portclintonchamber.com

PUT-IN-BAY (village). Covers a land area of 0.458 square miles and a water area of 0.178 square miles. Located at 41.65° N. Lat.; 82.81° W. Long. Elevation is 571 feet.

History: Perry's Victory and International Peace Memorial national monument (est. 1936) is near here. A granite column 352 feet high commemorates battle of Lake Erie (1813), in which Admiral Perry's U.S. fleet defeated the British, and symbolizes century of peace between U.S. and Canada.

Population: 144 (1990); 128 (2000); 126 (2007); 126 (2012 projected); Race: 100.0% White, 0.0% Black, 0.0% Asian, 0.0% Hispanic of any race (2007); Density: 274.8 persons per square mile (2007); Average household size: 1.85 (2007); Median age: 49.4 (2007); Males per 100 females: 117.2 (2007); Marriage status: 23.1% never married, 62.3% now married, 8.5% widowed, 6.2% divorced (2000); Foreign born: 0.0% (2000); Ancestry (includes multiple ancestries): 54.4% German, 18.8% Irish, 11.4% Italian, 8.1% English, 6.7% Hungarian (2000).

Economy: Employment by occupation: 20.7% management, 24.1% professional, 12.6% services, 27.6% sales, 2.3% farming, 3.4% construction, 9.2% production (2000).

Income: Per capita income: $58,075 (2007); Median household income: $73,636 (2007); Average household income: $107,610 (2007); Percent of households with income of $100,000 or more: 38.2% (2007); Poverty rate: 0.0% (2000).

Education: Percent of population age 25 and over with: High school diploma (including GED) or higher: 92.2% (2007); Bachelor's degree or higher: 45.6% (2007); Master's degree or higher: 18.4% (2007).

School District(s)

Put-In-Bay Local (KG-12)
2005-06 Enrollment: 69 . . . . (419) 285-3614

Housing: Homeownership rate: 72.1% (2007); Median home value: $363,889 (2007); Median rent: $425 per month (2000); Median age of housing: 60+ years (2000).
Transportation: Commute to work: 65.5% car, 3.4% public transportation, 14.9% walk, 13.8% work from home (2000); Travel time to work: 70.7% less than 15 minutes, 20.0% 15 to 30 minutes, 5.3% 30 to 45 minutes, 0.0% 45 to 60 minutes, 4.0% 60 minutes or more (2000)
Airports: Put-in-Bay (general aviation)
Additional Information Contacts
Put-In-Bay Chamber of Commerce . . . . (419) 285-2832
http://www.put-in-bay.com

ROCKY RIDGE (village). Covers a land area of 1.018 square miles and a water area of 0.015 square miles. Located at 41.53° N. Lat.; 83.21° W. Long. Elevation is 607 feet.
Population: 425 (1990); 389 (2000); 377 (2007); 375 (2012 projected); Race: 98.9% White, 0.0% Black, 0.0% Asian, 5.8% Hispanic of any race (2007); Density: 370.4 persons per square mile (2007); Average household size: 2.88 (2007); Median age: 35.1 (2007); Males per 100 females: 102.7 (2007); Marriage status: 30.7% never married, 51.6% now married, 6.4% widowed, 11.3% divorced (2000); Foreign born: 1.0% (2000); Ancestry (includes multiple ancestries): 47.9% German, 12.2% Irish, 8.5% Other groups, 5.4% French (except Basque), 4.4% Polish (2000).
Economy: Employment by occupation: 5.8% management, 9.1% professional, 16.2% services, 13.0% sales, 0.0% farming, 8.4% construction, 47.4% production (2000).
Income: Per capita income: $17,779 (2007); Median household income: $44,773 (2007); Average household income: $51,164 (2007); Percent of households with income of $100,000 or more: 7.6% (2007); Poverty rate: 13.8% (2000).
Education: Percent of population age 25 and over with: High school diploma (including GED) or higher: 73.6% (2007); Bachelor's degree or higher: 4.1% (2007); Master's degree or higher: 0.8% (2007).

School District(s)

Benton Carroll Salem Local (PK-12)
2005-06 Enrollment: 1,984 . . . . (419) 898-6210
Housing: Homeownership rate: 77.9% (2007); Median home value: $102,381 (2007); Median rent: $325 per month (2000); Median age of housing: 45 years (2000).
Transportation: Commute to work: 95.4% car, 0.0% public transportation, 0.0% walk, 4.6% work from home (2000); Travel time to work: 24.1% less than 15 minutes, 41.4% 15 to 30 minutes, 22.8% 30 to 45 minutes, 10.3% 45 to 60 minutes, 1.4% 60 minutes or more (2000)

Paulding County

Located in northwestern Ohio; bounded on the west by Indiana; drained by the Auglaize and Maumee Rivers. Covers a land area of 416.26 square miles, a water area of 2.64 square miles, and is located in the Eastern Time Zone. The county was founded in 1820. County seat is Paulding.

Weather Station: Paulding Elevation: 725 feet

	Jan	Feb	Mar	Apr	May	Jun	Jul	Aug	Sep	Oct	Nov	Dec
High	30	35	46	59	71	80	84	82	75	63	49	37
Low	14	17	26	36	47	57	61	58	50	39	30	21
Precip	1.9	1.7	2.7	3.4	3.8	3.4	3.4	3.0	3.0	2.5	3.0	2.6
Snow	5.5	5.3	3.2	0.4	0.0	0.0	0.0	0.0	0.0	tr	1.2	4.1

High and Low temperatures in degrees Fahrenheit; Precipitation and Snow in inches

Population: 20,488 (1990); 20,293 (2000); 19,399 (2007); 18,770 (2012 projected); Race: 95.7% White, 1.1% Black, 0.1% Asian, 3.5% Hispanic of any race (2007); Density: 46.6 persons per square mile (2007); Average household size: 2.52 (2007); Median age: 39.7 (2007); Males per 100 females: 97.5 (2007).
Religion: Five largest groups: 13.6% Catholic Church, 9.4% The United Methodist Church, 4.1% Church of the Nazarene, 3.9% Evangelical Lutheran Church in America, 2.5% Apostolic Christian Church of America, Inc. (2000).
Economy: Unemployment rate: 7.2% (6/2008); Total civilian labor force: 11,268 (6/2008); Leading industries: 40.5% manufacturing; 16.0% health care and social assistance; 11.0% retail trade (2005); Farms: 651 totaling 238,497 acres (2002); Companies that employ 500 or more persons: 0 (2006); Companies that employ 100 to 499 persons: 6 (2006); Companies that employ less than 100 persons: 309 (2006); Black-owned businesses: n/a (2002); Hispanic-owned businesses: n/a (2002); Asian-owned businesses: n/a (2002); Women-owned businesses: n/a (2002); Retail sales per capita: $8,473 (2008). Single-family building permits issued: 21 (2007); Multi-family building permits issued: 0 (2007).
Income: Per capita income: $21,271 (2007); Median household income: $45,067 (2007); Average household income: $53,309 (2007); Percent of households with income of $100,000 or more: 8.6% (2007); Poverty rate: 9.1% (2005); Bankruptcy rate: 4.22% (2007).
Education: Percent of population age 25 and over with: High school diploma (including GED) or higher: 81.5% (2007); Bachelor's degree or higher: 7.8% (2007); Master's degree or higher: 3.3% (2007).
Housing: Homeownership rate: 84.2% (2007); Median home value: $94,439 (2007); Median rent: $305 per month (2000); Median age of housing: 36 years (2000).
Health: Birth rate: 132.4 per 10,000 population (2007); Death rate: 87.1 per 10,000 population (2007); Age-adjusted cancer mortality rate: 209.2 deaths per 100,000 population (2005); Number of physicians: 4.1 per 10,000 population (2005); Hospital beds: 12.8 per 10,000 population (2004); Hospital admissions: 293.4 per 10,000 population (2004).
Elections: 2004 Presidential election results: 62.8% Bush, 36.5% Kerry, 0.0% Nader, 0.3% Badnarik
Additional Information Contacts
Paulding County Government . . . . (419) 399-8215
http://www.pauldingcountycourt.com
Paulding Chamber of Commerce. . . . . (419) 399-5215
http://www.pauldingchamber.com

Paulding County Communities

ANTWERP (village). Covers a land area of 1.160 square miles and a water area of 0 square miles. Located at 41.18° N. Lat.; 84.73° W. Long. Elevation is 728 feet.
Population: 1,870 (1990); 1,740 (2000); 1,588 (2007); 1,532 (2012 projected); Race: 98.0% White, 0.4% Black, 0.0% Asian, 2.4% Hispanic of any race (2007); Density: 1,369.1 persons per square mile (2007); Average household size: 2.27 (2007); Median age: 37.8 (2007); Males per 100 females: 91.3 (2007); Marriage status: 22.2% never married, 55.6% now married, 9.4% widowed, 12.8% divorced (2000); Foreign born: 0.1% (2000); Ancestry (includes multiple ancestries): 36.6% German, 11.2% United States or American, 9.8% Irish, 7.7% English, 5.2% Other groups (2000).
Economy: Single-family building permits issued: 5 (2007); Multi-family building permits issued: 0 (2007); Employment by occupation: 8.4% management, 14.6% professional, 12.9% services, 22.6% sales, 0.5% farming, 9.5% construction, 31.5% production (2000).
Income: Per capita income: $22,014 (2007); Median household income: $35,955 (2007); Average household income: $50,011 (2007); Percent of households with income of $100,000 or more: 7.6% (2007); Poverty rate: 8.9% (2000).
Education: Percent of population age 25 and over with: High school diploma (including GED) or higher: 84.5% (2007); Bachelor's degree or higher: 9.3% (2007); Master's degree or higher: 3.6% (2007).

School District(s)

Antwerp Local (PK-12)
2005-06 Enrollment: 713 . . . . (419) 258-5421
Housing: Homeownership rate: 70.4% (2007); Median home value: $87,500 (2007); Median rent: $334 per month (2000); Median age of housing: 41 years (2000).
Newspapers: Antwerp Bee Argus (Community news; Circulation 1,500)
Transportation: Commute to work: 93.6% car, 0.9% public transportation, 2.9% walk, 2.0% work from home (2000); Travel time to work: 40.7% less than 15 minutes, 24.7% 15 to 30 minutes, 24.8% 30 to 45 minutes, 3.8% 45 to 60 minutes, 6.0% 60 minutes or more (2000)

BROUGHTON (village). Covers a land area of 0.216 square miles and a water area of 0 square miles. Located at 41.08° N. Lat.; 84.53° W. Long. Elevation is 719 feet.
Population: 151 (1990); 166 (2000); 179 (2007); 175 (2012 projected); Race: 96.1% White, 0.0% Black, 0.0% Asian, 3.9% Hispanic of any race (2007); Density: 828.3 persons per square mile (2007); Average household size: 2.80 (2007); Median age: 36.8 (2007); Males per 100 females: 123.8 (2007); Marriage status: 23.6% never married, 60.0% now married, 7.1% widowed, 9.3% divorced (2000); Foreign born: 0.0% (2000); Ancestry (includes multiple ancestries): 22.2% German, 10.6% Irish, 9.2% English, 5.8% United States or American, 3.4% Other groups (2000).

Economy: Employment by occupation: 6.6% management, 2.2% professional, 5.5% services, 20.9% sales, 0.0% farming, 2.2% construction, 62.6% production (2000).
Income: Per capita income: $16,885 (2007); Median household income: $38,333 (2007); Average household income: $47,227 (2007); Percent of households with income of $100,000 or more: 6.3% (2007); Poverty rate: 5.8% (2000).
Education: Percent of population age 25 and over with: High school diploma (including GED) or higher: 70.1% (2007); Bachelor's degree or higher: 1.7% (2007); Master's degree or higher: 1.7% (2007).
Housing: Homeownership rate: 95.3% (2007); Median home value: $63,750 (2007); Median rent: $225 per month (2000); Median age of housing: 36 years (2000).
Transportation: Commute to work: 94.0% car, 0.0% public transportation, 6.0% walk, 0.0% work from home (2000); Travel time to work: 47.6% less than 15 minutes, 17.9% 15 to 30 minutes, 27.4% 30 to 45 minutes, 4.8% 45 to 60 minutes, 2.4% 60 minutes or more (2000)

CECIL (village). Covers a land area of 1.467 square miles and a water area of 0 square miles. Located at 41.21° N. Lat.; 84.60° W. Long. Elevation is 722 feet.
Population: 249 (1990); 216 (2000); 225 (2007); 217 (2012 projected); Race: 97.8% White, 0.0% Black, 0.0% Asian, 2.7% Hispanic of any race (2007); Density: 153.3 persons per square mile (2007); Average household size: 2.68 (2007); Median age: 41.9 (2007); Males per 100 females: 122.8 (2007); Marriage status: 24.4% never married, 41.9% now married, 10.0% widowed, 23.8% divorced (2000); Foreign born: 0.0% (2000); Ancestry (includes multiple ancestries): 32.5% German, 9.6% Other groups, 8.1% Irish, 4.3% United States or American, 3.8% Polish (2000).
Economy: Employment by occupation: 13.5% management, 5.6% professional, 19.1% services, 15.7% sales, 0.0% farming, 10.1% construction, 36.0% production (2000).
Income: Per capita income: $13,822 (2007); Median household income: $32,143 (2007); Average household income: $37,024 (2007); Percent of households with income of $100,000 or more: 4.8% (2007); Poverty rate: 23.4% (2000).
Education: Percent of population age 25 and over with: High school diploma (including GED) or higher: 76.0% (2007); Bachelor's degree or higher: 8.4% (2007); Master's degree or higher: 4.5% (2007).
Housing: Homeownership rate: 92.9% (2007); Median home value: $45,000 (2007); Median rent: $225 per month (2000); Median age of housing: 60+ years (2000).
Transportation: Commute to work: 93.3% car, 0.0% public transportation, 6.7% walk, 0.0% work from home (2000); Travel time to work: 28.1% less than 15 minutes, 38.2% 15 to 30 minutes, 25.8% 30 to 45 minutes, 6.7% 45 to 60 minutes, 1.1% 60 minutes or more (2000)

GROVER HILL (village). Covers a land area of 0.290 square miles and a water area of 0 square miles. Located at 41.01° N. Lat.; 84.47° W. Long. Elevation is 722 feet.
Population: 498 (1990); 412 (2000); 350 (2007); 342 (2012 projected); Race: 96.0% White, 0.6% Black, 0.0% Asian, 4.0% Hispanic of any race (2007); Density: 1,206.7 persons per square mile (2007); Average household size: 2.38 (2007); Median age: 38.9 (2007); Males per 100 females: 93.4 (2007); Marriage status: 25.2% never married, 56.2% now married, 11.2% widowed, 7.3% divorced (2000); Foreign born: 0.7% (2000); Ancestry (includes multiple ancestries): 22.1% German, 19.2% Irish, 8.4% Other groups, 7.9% English, 4.7% United States or American (2000).
Economy: Single-family building permits issued: 0 (2007); Multi-family building permits issued: 0 (2007); Employment by occupation: 8.6% management, 7.5% professional, 19.5% services, 12.1% sales, 2.3% farming, 8.0% construction, 42.0% production (2000).
Income: Per capita income: $20,179 (2007); Median household income: $40,682 (2007); Average household income: $48,044 (2007); Percent of households with income of $100,000 or more: 7.5% (2007); Poverty rate: 17.7% (2000).
Education: Percent of population age 25 and over with: High school diploma (including GED) or higher: 78.0% (2007); Bachelor's degree or higher: 1.7% (2007); Master's degree or higher: 0.0% (2007).

School District(s)

Wayne Trace Local (PK-12)
2005-06 Enrollment: 1,109 . . . . (419) 399-4113

Housing: Homeownership rate: 88.4% (2007); Median home value: $55,484 (2007); Median rent: $406 per month (2000); Median age of housing: 56 years (2000).
Transportation: Commute to work: 95.8% car, 0.0% public transportation, 3.0% walk, 1.2% work from home (2000); Travel time to work: 11.5% less than 15 minutes, 44.8% 15 to 30 minutes, 18.8% 30 to 45 minutes, 9.7% 45 to 60 minutes, 15.2% 60 minutes or more (2000)

HAVILAND (village). Covers a land area of 0.287 square miles and a water area of 0 square miles. Located at 41.01° N. Lat.; 84.58° W. Long. Elevation is 735 feet.
Population: 229 (1990); 180 (2000); 162 (2007); 157 (2012 projected); Race: 97.5% White, 0.0% Black, 0.0% Asian, 1.2% Hispanic of any race (2007); Density: 563.9 persons per square mile (2007); Average household size: 2.57 (2007); Median age: 37.2 (2007); Males per 100 females: 95.2 (2007); Marriage status: 28.2% never married, 53.2% now married, 5.6% widowed, 12.9% divorced (2000); Foreign born: 0.0% (2000); Ancestry (includes multiple ancestries): 21.5% German, 12.3% Other groups, 8.6% United States or American, 8.0% Irish, 5.5% Swiss (2000).
Economy: Employment by occupation: 4.9% management, 8.2% professional, 26.2% services, 3.3% sales, 0.0% farming, 9.8% construction, 47.5% production (2000).
Income: Per capita income: $17,932 (2007); Median household income: $37,250 (2007); Average household income: $46,111 (2007); Percent of households with income of $100,000 or more: 9.5% (2007); Poverty rate: 13.1% (2000).
Education: Percent of population age 25 and over with: High school diploma (including GED) or higher: 66.1% (2007); Bachelor's degree or higher: 3.6% (2007); Master's degree or higher: 0.0% (2007).

School District(s)

Wayne Trace Local (PK-12)
2005-06 Enrollment: 1,109 . . . . (419) 399-4113

Housing: Homeownership rate: 81.0% (2007); Median home value: $61,000 (2007); Median rent: $219 per month (2000); Median age of housing: 60 years (2000).
Transportation: Commute to work: 98.4% car, 0.0% public transportation, 0.0% walk, 1.6% work from home (2000); Travel time to work: 31.7% less than 15 minutes, 35.0% 15 to 30 minutes, 20.0% 30 to 45 minutes, 11.7% 45 to 60 minutes, 1.7% 60 minutes or more (2000)

LATTY (village). Covers a land area of 0.267 square miles and a water area of 0 square miles. Located at 41.08° N. Lat.; 84.58° W. Long. Elevation is 728 feet.
Population: 205 (1990); 200 (2000); 215 (2007); 214 (2012 projected); Race: 87.9% White, 6.5% Black, 0.5% Asian, 2.8% Hispanic of any race (2007); Density: 804.4 persons per square mile (2007); Average household size: 2.50 (2007); Median age: 37.5 (2007); Males per 100 females: 100.9 (2007); Marriage status: 23.3% never married, 66.3% now married, 3.1% widowed, 7.4% divorced (2000); Foreign born: 0.0% (2000); Ancestry (includes multiple ancestries): 36.7% German, 22.2% Other groups, 10.1% Swiss, 8.7% United States or American, 6.3% English (2000).
Economy: Employment by occupation: 20.8% management, 6.5% professional, 7.8% services, 11.7% sales, 0.0% farming, 18.2% construction, 35.1% production (2000).
Income: Per capita income: $22,430 (2007); Median household income: $43,750 (2007); Average household income: $56,076 (2007); Percent of households with income of $100,000 or more: 8.1% (2007); Poverty rate: 12.6% (2000).
Education: Percent of population age 25 and over with: High school diploma (including GED) or higher: 79.3% (2007); Bachelor's degree or higher: 3.0% (2007); Master's degree or higher: 1.5% (2007).
Housing: Homeownership rate: 86.0% (2007); Median home value: $76,667 (2007); Median rent: $338 per month (2000); Median age of housing: 51 years (2000).
Transportation: Commute to work: 94.8% car, 0.0% public transportation, 2.6% walk, 2.6% work from home (2000); Travel time to work: 42.7% less than 15 minutes, 21.3% 15 to 30 minutes, 24.0% 30 to 45 minutes, 12.0% 45 to 60 minutes, 0.0% 60 minutes or more (2000)

MELROSE (village). Covers a land area of 0.860 square miles and a water area of 0 square miles. Located at 41.09° N. Lat.; 84.41° W. Long. Elevation is 709 feet.
Population: 307 (1990); 322 (2000); 323 (2007); 310 (2012 projected); Race: 96.3% White, 0.0% Black, 0.0% Asian, 3.7% Hispanic of any race (2007); Density: 375.5 persons per square mile (2007); Average household

size: 2.78 (2007); Median age: 30.9 (2007); Males per 100 females: 95.8 (2007); Marriage status: 30.7% never married, 48.4% now married, 8.9% widowed, 12.0% divorced (2000); Foreign born: 0.0% (2000); Ancestry (includes multiple ancestries): 30.1% German, 12.8% Irish, 11.8% Other groups, 8.1% United States or American, 6.1% English (2000).
Economy: Employment by occupation: 9.2% management, 2.3% professional, 6.9% services, 20.8% sales, 0.0% farming, 10.0% construction, 50.8% production (2000).
Income: Per capita income: $16,122 (2007); Median household income: $40,000 (2007); Average household income: $44,892 (2007); Percent of households with income of $100,000 or more: 2.6% (2007); Poverty rate: 14.5% (2000).
Education: Percent of population age 25 and over with: High school diploma (including GED) or higher: 63.1% (2007); Bachelor's degree or higher: 0.0% (2007); Master's degree or higher: 0.0% (2007).
Housing: Homeownership rate: 75.0% (2007); Median home value: $64,167 (2007); Median rent: $267 per month (2000); Median age of housing: 36 years (2000).
Transportation: Commute to work: 97.7% car, 0.0% public transportation, 0.0% walk, 0.0% work from home (2000); Travel time to work: 12.3% less than 15 minutes, 39.2% 15 to 30 minutes, 33.1% 30 to 45 minutes, 10.0% 45 to 60 minutes, 5.4% 60 minutes or more (2000)

OAKWOOD (village). Covers a land area of 0.585 square miles and a water area of 0 square miles. Located at 41.09° N. Lat.; 84.37° W. Long. Elevation is 709 feet.
Population: 709 (1990); 607 (2000); 541 (2007); 519 (2012 projected); Race: 99.1% White, 0.0% Black, 0.2% Asian, 0.2% Hispanic of any race (2007); Density: 924.2 persons per square mile (2007); Average household size: 2.48 (2007); Median age: 38.5 (2007); Males per 100 females: 88.5 (2007); Marriage status: 17.9% never married, 62.3% now married, 9.8% widowed, 10.0% divorced (2000); Foreign born: 0.3% (2000); Ancestry (includes multiple ancestries): 21.0% United States or American, 20.2% German, 12.4% Other groups, 6.6% Irish, 5.8% English (2000).
Economy: Single-family building permits issued: 1 (2007); Multi-family building permits issued: 0 (2007); Employment by occupation: 6.5% management, 11.4% professional, 14.6% services, 15.4% sales, 1.6% farming, 9.8% construction, 40.7% production (2000).
Income: Per capita income: $17,893 (2007); Median household income: $38,750 (2007); Average household income: $44,404 (2007); Percent of households with income of $100,000 or more: 4.1% (2007); Poverty rate: 10.9% (2000).
Education: Percent of population age 25 and over with: High school diploma (including GED) or higher: 79.3% (2007); Bachelor's degree or higher: 4.8% (2007); Master's degree or higher: 2.6% (2007).

School District(s)

Paulding Exempted Village (PK-12)
2005-06 Enrollment: 1,728 . . . . (419) 399-4656
Housing: Homeownership rate: 78.4% (2007); Median home value: $69,444 (2007); Median rent: $278 per month (2000); Median age of housing: 45 years (2000).
Transportation: Commute to work: 93.4% car, 0.0% public transportation, 5.8% walk, 0.8% work from home (2000); Travel time to work: 33.5% less than 15 minutes, 40.2% 15 to 30 minutes, 12.6% 30 to 45 minutes, 7.5% 45 to 60 minutes, 6.3% 60 minutes or more (2000)

PAULDING (village). County seat. Covers a land area of 2.280 square miles and a water area of 0.098 square miles. Located at 41.14° N. Lat.; 84.58° W. Long. Elevation is 719 feet.
Population: 3,637 (1990); 3,595 (2000); 3,388 (2007); 3,246 (2012 projected); Race: 90.9% White, 2.5% Black, 0.3% Asian, 7.4% Hispanic of any race (2007); Density: 1,486.3 persons per square mile (2007); Average household size: 2.37 (2007); Median age: 39.4 (2007); Males per 100 females: 91.8 (2007); Marriage status: 23.8% never married, 57.9% now married, 8.3% widowed, 10.0% divorced (2000); Foreign born: 0.8% (2000); Ancestry (includes multiple ancestries): 34.3% German, 16.5% Other groups, 12.5% United States or American, 7.2% Irish, 5.0% English (2000).
Economy: Single-family building permits issued: 4 (2007); Multi-family building permits issued: 0 (2007); Employment by occupation: 7.3% management, 13.6% professional, 14.5% services, 22.6% sales, 0.5% farming, 8.9% construction, 32.6% production (2000).
Income: Per capita income: $19,839 (2007); Median household income: $39,089 (2007); Average household income: $46,448 (2007); Percent of households with income of $100,000 or more: 5.6% (2007); Poverty rate: 9.0% (2000).
Education: Percent of population age 25 and over with: High school diploma (including GED) or higher: 84.1% (2007); Bachelor's degree or higher: 9.4% (2007); Master's degree or higher: 5.1% (2007).

School District(s)

Paulding Exempted Village (PK-12)
2005-06 Enrollment: 1,728 . . . . (419) 399-4656
Housing: Homeownership rate: 74.4% (2007); Median home value: $86,826 (2007); Median rent: $293 per month (2000); Median age of housing: 41 years (2000).
Hospitals: Paulding County Hospital (25 beds)
Safety: Violent crime rate: 8.8 per 10,000 population; Property crime rate: 67.8 per 10,000 population (2007).
Newspapers: Paulding Progress (Community news; Circulation 4,300)
Transportation: Commute to work: 92.0% car, 1.5% public transportation, 4.2% walk, 1.5% work from home (2000); Travel time to work: 54.2% less than 15 minutes, 13.6% 15 to 30 minutes, 17.7% 30 to 45 minutes, 8.8% 45 to 60 minutes, 5.7% 60 minutes or more (2000)

Additional Information Contacts

Paulding Chamber of Commerce. . . . . (419) 399-5215
http://www.pauldingchamber.com

PAYNE (village). Covers a land area of 0.538 square miles and a water area of 0 square miles. Located at 41.07° N. Lat.; 84.72° W. Long. Elevation is 745 feet.
Population: 1,325 (1990); 1,166 (2000); 1,014 (2007); 997 (2012 projected); Race: 96.5% White, 0.8% Black, 0.1% Asian, 4.4% Hispanic of any race (2007); Density: 1,885.9 persons per square mile (2007); Average household size: 2.20 (2007); Median age: 39.2 (2007); Males per 100 females: 89.5 (2007); Marriage status: 22.9% never married, 54.7% now married, 11.3% widowed, 11.1% divorced (2000); Foreign born: 0.8% (2000); Ancestry (includes multiple ancestries): 39.8% German, 14.0% Irish, 9.8% United States or American, 6.8% English, 5.1% Other groups (2000).
Economy: Single-family building permits issued: 1 (2007); Multi-family building permits issued: 0 (2007); Employment by occupation: 7.3% management, 13.1% professional, 15.0% services, 20.8% sales, 1.2% farming, 5.4% construction, 37.2% production (2000).
Income: Per capita income: $20,375 (2007); Median household income: $39,024 (2007); Average household income: $44,886 (2007); Percent of households with income of $100,000 or more: 5.7% (2007); Poverty rate: 5.3% (2000).
Education: Percent of population age 25 and over with: High school diploma (including GED) or higher: 81.5% (2007); Bachelor's degree or higher: 10.5% (2007); Master's degree or higher: 3.6% (2007).

School District(s)

Wayne Trace Local (PK-12)
2005-06 Enrollment: 1,109 . . . . (419) 399-4113
Housing: Homeownership rate: 73.9% (2007); Median home value: $80,000 (2007); Median rent: $264 per month (2000); Median age of housing: 44 years (2000).
Transportation: Commute to work: 93.5% car, 0.4% public transportation, 3.8% walk, 1.1% work from home (2000); Travel time to work: 30.9% less than 15 minutes, 33.9% 15 to 30 minutes, 21.2% 30 to 45 minutes, 6.4% 45 to 60 minutes, 7.6% 60 minutes or more (2000)

Perry County

Located in central Ohio; drained by Rush, Sunday, Jonathan, and Moxahala Creeks; includes part of Buckeye Lake. Covers a land area of 409.78 square miles, a water area of 2.82 square miles, and is located in the Eastern Time Zone. The county was founded in 1817. County seat is New Lexington.

Weather Station: New Lexington 2 NW — Elevation: 889 feet

	Jan	Feb	Mar	Apr	May	Jun	Jul	Aug	Sep	Oct	Nov	Dec
High	37	41	52	64	74	81	85	83	77	66	53	42
Low	18	20	28	37	47	56	60	59	52	40	31	23
Precip	2.9	2.6	3.4	3.8	4.3	4.3	4.7	3.9	2.8	2.7	3.4	3.1
Snow	9.2	5.9	3.6	0.5	tr	0.0	0.0	0.0	0.0	tr	0.7	3.0

High and Low temperatures in degrees Fahrenheit; Precipitation and Snow in inches

Population: 31,557 (1990); 34,078 (2000); 35,547 (2007); 36,428 (2012 projected); Race: 98.5% White, 0.3% Black, 0.1% Asian, 0.5% Hispanic of any race (2007); Density: 86.7 persons per square mile (2007); Average

household size: 2.69 (2007); Median age: 36.9 (2007); Males per 100 females: 98.9 (2007).
Religion: Five largest groups: 8.8% The United Methodist Church, 8.8% Catholic Church, 4.2% Evangelical Lutheran Church in America, 1.2% Christian Church (Disciples of Christ), 1.0% United Church of Christ (2000).
Economy: Unemployment rate: 8.1% (6/2008); Total civilian labor force: 16,437 (6/2008); Leading industries: 23.2% manufacturing; 17.6% health care and social assistance; 14.9% retail trade (2005); Farms: 639 totaling 91,907 acres (2002); Companies that employ 500 or more persons: 0 (2006); Companies that employ 100 to 499 persons: 8 (2006); Companies that employ less than 100 persons: 486 (2006); Black-owned businesses: n/a (2002); Hispanic-owned businesses: n/a (2002); Asian-owned businesses: n/a (2002); Women-owned businesses: 595 (2002); Retail sales per capita: $4,510 (2008). Single-family building permits issued: 51 (2007); Multi-family building permits issued: 4 (2007).
Income: Per capita income: $18,406 (2007); Median household income: $40,321 (2007); Average household income: $49,198 (2007); Percent of households with income of $100,000 or more: 7.4% (2007); Poverty rate: 14.1% (2005); Bankruptcy rate: 3.93% (2007).
Taxes: Total county taxes per capita: $201 (2006); County property taxes per capita: $137 (2006).
Education: Percent of population age 25 and over with: High school diploma (including GED) or higher: 78.7% (2007); Bachelor's degree or higher: 7.0% (2007); Master's degree or higher: 2.5% (2007).
Housing: Homeownership rate: 80.1% (2007); Median home value: $98,323 (2007); Median rent: $300 per month (2000); Median age of housing: 36 years (2000).
Health: Birth rate: 134.6 per 10,000 population (2007); Death rate: 101.0 per 10,000 population (2007); Age-adjusted cancer mortality rate: 202.9 deaths per 100,000 population (2005); Number of physicians: 4.6 per 10,000 population (2005); Hospital beds: 0.0 per 10,000 population (2004); Hospital admissions: 0.0 per 10,000 population (2004).
Elections: 2004 Presidential election results: 51.7% Bush, 47.8% Kerry, 0.0% Nader, 0.2% Badnarik
National and State Parks: Avondale State Wildlife Area; Perry State Forest
Additional Information Contacts
Perry County Government . . . . (740) 342-2045
http://www.perrycountyohiocofc.com/Govnment.htm
City of New Lexington . . . . (740) 342-2177
http://www.newlexington.org
Perry County Chamber of Commerce . . . . (740) 342-3547
http://www.perrycountyohiocofc.com
Village of Crooksville . . . . (740) 982-2656
http://www.crooksville.com

Perry County Communities

CORNING (village). Covers a land area of 0.436 square miles and a water area of 0 square miles. Located at 39.60° N. Lat.; 82.08° W. Long. Elevation is 725 feet.
Population: 703 (1990); 593 (2000); 554 (2007); 554 (2012 projected); Race: 97.5% White, 0.4% Black, 0.0% Asian, 0.2% Hispanic of any race (2007); Density: 1,270.6 persons per square mile (2007); Average household size: 2.43 (2007); Median age: 37.9 (2007); Males per 100 females: 88.4 (2007); Marriage status: 26.3% never married, 53.9% now married, 12.3% widowed, 7.5% divorced (2000); Foreign born: 0.0% (2000); Ancestry (includes multiple ancestries): 17.6% German, 15.1% English, 13.8% United States or American, 13.3% Irish, 5.6% Other groups (2000).
Economy: Employment by occupation: 4.6% management, 14.9% professional, 12.8% services, 25.6% sales, 0.0% farming, 14.9% construction, 27.2% production (2000).
Income: Per capita income: $17,022 (2007); Median household income: $34,565 (2007); Average household income: $41,360 (2007); Percent of households with income of $100,000 or more: 3.9% (2007); Poverty rate: 15.3% (2000).
Education: Percent of population age 25 and over with: High school diploma (including GED) or higher: 80.0% (2007); Bachelor's degree or higher: 7.1% (2007); Master's degree or higher: 3.7% (2007).

School District(s)

Southern Local (PK-12)
2005-06 Enrollment: 961 . . . . (740) 394-2402
Housing: Homeownership rate: 78.5% (2007); Median home value: $56,458 (2007); Median rent: $300 per month (2000); Median age of housing: 60+ years (2000).
Transportation: Commute to work: 95.7% car, 0.0% public transportation, 1.1% walk, 3.2% work from home (2000); Travel time to work: 14.9% less than 15 minutes, 40.9% 15 to 30 minutes, 18.8% 30 to 45 minutes, 6.6% 45 to 60 minutes, 18.8% 60 minutes or more (2000)

CROOKSVILLE (village). Covers a land area of 1.526 square miles and a water area of 0 square miles. Located at 39.76° N. Lat.; 82.09° W. Long. Elevation is 784 feet.
Population: 2,643 (1990); 2,483 (2000); 2,385 (2007); 2,346 (2012 projected); Race: 98.4% White, 0.4% Black, 0.1% Asian, 0.5% Hispanic of any race (2007); Density: 1,563.3 persons per square mile (2007); Average household size: 2.57 (2007); Median age: 34.4 (2007); Males per 100 females: 93.1 (2007); Marriage status: 20.5% never married, 58.1% now married, 10.2% widowed, 11.1% divorced (2000); Foreign born: 0.6% (2000); Ancestry (includes multiple ancestries): 17.3% German, 12.9% United States or American, 10.1% English, 9.0% Irish, 7.0% Other groups (2000).
Economy: Single-family building permits issued: 0 (2007); Multi-family building permits issued: 0 (2007); Employment by occupation: 4.9% management, 13.4% professional, 12.2% services, 20.0% sales, 0.0% farming, 12.2% construction, 37.2% production (2000).
Income: Per capita income: $16,524 (2007); Median household income: $32,796 (2007); Average household income: $42,422 (2007); Percent of households with income of $100,000 or more: 5.5% (2007); Poverty rate: 13.6% (2000).
Education: Percent of population age 25 and over with: High school diploma (including GED) or higher: 77.5% (2007); Bachelor's degree or higher: 4.1% (2007); Master's degree or higher: 1.7% (2007).

School District(s)

Crooksville Exempted Village (PK-12)
2005-06 Enrollment: 1,270 . . . . (740) 982-7040
Housing: Homeownership rate: 70.0% (2007); Median home value: $66,923 (2007); Median rent: $269 per month (2000); Median age of housing: 55 years (2000).
Safety: Violent crime rate: 20.3 per 10,000 population; Property crime rate: 77.0 per 10,000 population (2007).
Transportation: Commute to work: 91.3% car, 0.0% public transportation, 3.4% walk, 3.0% work from home (2000); Travel time to work: 34.5% less than 15 minutes, 19.7% 15 to 30 minutes, 20.7% 30 to 45 minutes, 10.4% 45 to 60 minutes, 14.7% 60 minutes or more (2000)
Additional Information Contacts
Village of Crooksville . . . . (740) 982-2656
http://www.crooksville.com

GLENFORD (village). Covers a land area of 0.130 square miles and a water area of 0 square miles. Located at 39.88° N. Lat.; 82.32° W. Long. Elevation is 846 feet.
History: Glenford was established near a prehistoric fortification known as Glenford Fort. A stone wall 7-10 feet high and 6,600 feet long enclosed an area with a central mound.
Population: 208 (1990); 198 (2000); 207 (2007); 209 (2012 projected); Race: 95.7% White, 1.9% Black, 0.0% Asian, 1.9% Hispanic of any race (2007); Density: 1,588.0 persons per square mile (2007); Average household size: 2.84 (2007); Median age: 33.3 (2007); Males per 100 females: 102.9 (2007); Marriage status: 27.7% never married, 62.8% now married, 4.7% widowed, 4.7% divorced (2000); Foreign born: 0.0% (2000); Ancestry (includes multiple ancestries): 28.6% German, 21.2% English, 10.6% Irish, 6.9% Other groups, 4.8% Italian (2000).
Economy: Single-family building permits issued: 0 (2007); Multi-family building permits issued: 0 (2007); Employment by occupation: 11.3% management, 8.5% professional, 11.3% services, 22.6% sales, 4.7% farming, 16.0% construction, 25.5% production (2000).
Income: Per capita income: $17,886 (2007); Median household income: $40,833 (2007); Average household income: $50,719 (2007); Percent of households with income of $100,000 or more: 6.8% (2007); Poverty rate: 1.6% (2000).
Education: Percent of population age 25 and over with: High school diploma (including GED) or higher: 84.5% (2007); Bachelor's degree or higher: 4.7% (2007); Master's degree or higher: 3.1% (2007).

School District(s)

Northern Local (PK-12)
2005-06 Enrollment: 2,337 . . . . (740) 743-1303

Housing: Homeownership rate: 74.0% (2007); Median home value: $97,500 (2007); Median rent: $425 per month (2000); Median age of housing: 60+ years (2000).
Transportation: Commute to work: 83.0% car, 0.0% public transportation, 15.1% walk, 1.9% work from home (2000); Travel time to work: 17.3% less than 15 minutes, 26.9% 15 to 30 minutes, 18.3% 30 to 45 minutes, 22.1% 45 to 60 minutes, 15.4% 60 minutes or more (2000)

HEMLOCK (village). Covers a land area of 0.379 square miles and a water area of 0 square miles. Located at 39.59° N. Lat.; 82.15° W. Long. Elevation is 761 feet.
Population: 203 (1990); 142 (2000); 147 (2007); 143 (2012 projected); Race: 95.2% White, 0.0% Black, 2.7% Asian, 3.4% Hispanic of any race (2007); Density: 387.4 persons per square mile (2007); Average household size: 2.83 (2007); Median age: 32.5 (2007); Males per 100 females: 88.5 (2007); Marriage status: 22.5% never married, 67.5% now married, 10.0% widowed, 0.0% divorced (2000); Foreign born: 0.0% (2000); Ancestry (includes multiple ancestries): 21.4% German, 15.7% Irish, 11.4% English, 11.4% Other groups, 7.9% United States or American (2000).
Economy: Employment by occupation: 0.0% management, 0.0% professional, 35.5% services, 16.1% sales, 0.0% farming, 12.9% construction, 35.5% production (2000).
Income: Per capita income: $10,544 (2007); Median household income: $28,333 (2007); Average household income: $29,808 (2007); Percent of households with income of $100,000 or more: 0.0% (2007); Poverty rate: 24.3% (2000).
Education: Percent of population age 25 and over with: High school diploma (including GED) or higher: 61.2% (2007); Bachelor's degree or higher: 0.0% (2007); Master's degree or higher: 0.0% (2007).
Housing: Homeownership rate: 92.3% (2007); Median home value: $36,000 (2007); Median rent: $331 per month (2000); Median age of housing: 60+ years (2000).
Transportation: Commute to work: 100.0% car, 0.0% public transportation, 0.0% walk, 0.0% work from home (2000); Travel time to work: 12.9% less than 15 minutes, 12.9% 15 to 30 minutes, 25.8% 30 to 45 minutes, 25.8% 45 to 60 minutes, 22.6% 60 minutes or more (2000)

JUNCTION CITY (village). Covers a land area of 0.641 square miles and a water area of 0 square miles. Located at 39.72° N. Lat.; 82.29° W. Long. Elevation is 833 feet.
Population: 770 (1990); 818 (2000); 752 (2007); 738 (2012 projected); Race: 99.3% White, 0.0% Black, 0.0% Asian, 0.8% Hispanic of any race (2007); Density: 1,173.4 persons per square mile (2007); Average household size: 2.71 (2007); Median age: 32.8 (2007); Males per 100 females: 99.5 (2007); Marriage status: 22.1% never married, 55.6% now married, 6.3% widowed, 16.0% divorced (2000); Foreign born: 0.0% (2000); Ancestry (includes multiple ancestries): 27.3% German, 16.9% Irish, 12.8% United States or American, 12.5% Other groups, 5.8% English (2000).
Economy: Employment by occupation: 2.8% management, 11.4% professional, 15.9% services, 18.4% sales, 0.3% farming, 13.4% construction, 37.9% production (2000).
Income: Per capita income: $14,362 (2007); Median household income: $35,568 (2007); Average household income: $38,989 (2007); Percent of households with income of $100,000 or more: 2.5% (2007); Poverty rate: 22.8% (2000).
Education: Percent of population age 25 and over with: High school diploma (including GED) or higher: 78.1% (2007); Bachelor's degree or higher: 4.5% (2007); Master's degree or higher: 0.9% (2007).

School District(s)

New Lexington City (PK-12)
2005-06 Enrollment: 1,903 . . . . (740) 342-4133
Housing: Homeownership rate: 66.1% (2007); Median home value: $80,278 (2007); Median rent: $339 per month (2000); Median age of housing: 48 years (2000).
Transportation: Commute to work: 94.6% car, 0.0% public transportation, 4.8% walk, 0.6% work from home (2000); Travel time to work: 26.6% less than 15 minutes, 26.6% 15 to 30 minutes, 14.2% 30 to 45 minutes, 8.8% 45 to 60 minutes, 23.8% 60 minutes or more (2000)

MOUNT PERRY (unincorporated postal area, zip code 43760). Covers a land area of 35.786 square miles and a water area of 0.093 square miles. Located at 39.88° N. Lat.; 82.19° W. Long. Elevation is 840 feet.
Population: 1,748 (2000); Race: 97.1% White, 0.0% Black, 0.6% Asian, 0.0% Hispanic of any race (2000); Density: 48.8 persons per square mile (2000); Age: 25.3% under 18, 11.3% over 64 (2000); Marriage status: 17.5% never married, 73.3% now married, 2.8% widowed, 6.4% divorced (2000); Foreign born: 1.3% (2000); Ancestry (includes multiple ancestries): 18.9% United States or American, 13.2% German, 11.5% English, 8.2% Irish, 4.9% Other groups (2000).
Economy: Employment by occupation: 7.3% management, 12.8% professional, 15.4% services, 16.6% sales, 1.5% farming, 19.5% construction, 26.9% production (2000).
Income: Per capita income: $20,616 (2000); Median household income: $40,476 (2000); Poverty rate: 5.5% (2000).
Education: Percent of population age 25 and over with: High school diploma (including GED) or higher: 74.0% (2000); Bachelor's degree or higher: 5.0% (2000).
Housing: Homeownership rate: 87.6% (2000); Median home value: $85,200 (2000); Median rent: $243 per month (2000); Median age of housing: 19 years (2000).
Transportation: Commute to work: 93.3% car, 1.6% public transportation, 0.0% walk, 5.1% work from home (2000); Travel time to work: 7.6% less than 15 minutes, 31.7% 15 to 30 minutes, 29.9% 30 to 45 minutes, 16.4% 45 to 60 minutes, 14.4% 60 minutes or more (2000)

NEW LEXINGTON (city). County seat. Covers a land area of 2.325 square miles and a water area of 0 square miles. Located at 39.71° N. Lat.; 82.21° W. Long. Elevation is 945 feet.
History: New Lexington developed around the tile and pottery works, which used the excellent clays found in the vicinity.
Population: 5,268 (1990); 4,689 (2000); 4,552 (2007); 4,477 (2012 projected); Race: 98.7% White, 0.3% Black, 0.2% Asian, 0.4% Hispanic of any race (2007); Density: 1,958.2 persons per square mile (2007); Average household size: 2.51 (2007); Median age: 33.9 (2007); Males per 100 females: 92.3 (2007); Marriage status: 24.7% never married, 54.5% now married, 10.3% widowed, 10.6% divorced (2000); Foreign born: 1.1% (2000); Ancestry (includes multiple ancestries): 22.3% United States or American, 20.0% German, 12.3% Irish, 7.2% English, 7.1% Other groups (2000).
Economy: Single-family building permits issued: 1 (2007); Multi-family building permits issued: 0 (2007); Employment by occupation: 6.7% management, 12.6% professional, 17.1% services, 20.0% sales, 0.0% farming, 9.6% construction, 34.1% production (2000).
Income: Per capita income: $15,711 (2007); Median household income: $31,376 (2007); Average household income: $38,028 (2007); Percent of households with income of $100,000 or more: 3.5% (2007); Poverty rate: 17.6% (2000).
Education: Percent of population age 25 and over with: High school diploma (including GED) or higher: 77.3% (2007); Bachelor's degree or higher: 7.6% (2007); Master's degree or higher: 3.7% (2007).

School District(s)

New Lexington City (PK-12)
2005-06 Enrollment: 1,903 . . . . (740) 342-4133
Housing: Homeownership rate: 63.0% (2007); Median home value: $87,923 (2007); Median rent: $289 per month (2000); Median age of housing: 48 years (2000).
Safety: Violent crime rate: 32.5 per 10,000 population; Property crime rate: 455.2 per 10,000 population (2007).
Newspapers: Perry County Tribune (Community news; Circulation 4,200)
Transportation: Commute to work: 91.9% car, 1.3% public transportation, 3.7% walk, 2.0% work from home (2000); Travel time to work: 43.2% less than 15 minutes, 13.9% 15 to 30 minutes, 16.9% 30 to 45 minutes, 9.4% 45 to 60 minutes, 16.6% 60 minutes or more (2000)
Additional Information Contacts
City of New Lexington . . . . (740) 342-2177
http://www.newlexington.org
Perry County Chamber of Commerce . . . . (740) 342-3547
http://www.perrycountyohiocofc.com

NEW STRAITSVILLE (village). Covers a land area of 1.313 square miles and a water area of 0 square miles. Located at 39.58° N. Lat.; 82.23° W. Long. Elevation is 787 feet.
History: New Straitsville was laid out in 1870 by a mining company. An undergound coal fire began to burn here in 1884, when some desperate miners set fire to loaded coal cars and pushed them down five mine shafts.
Population: 865 (1990); 774 (2000); 730 (2007); 713 (2012 projected); Race: 97.1% White, 0.1% Black, 0.0% Asian, 3.2% Hispanic of any race

(2007); Density: 555.9 persons per square mile (2007); Average household size: 2.43 (2007); Median age: 37.1 (2007); Males per 100 females: 91.6 (2007); Marriage status: 23.3% never married, 52.9% now married, 10.7% widowed, 13.1% divorced (2000); Foreign born: 0.0% (2000); Ancestry (includes multiple ancestries): 16.8% German, 10.2% Irish, 10.0% English, 7.2% United States or American, 4.0% Other groups (2000).
Economy: Employment by occupation: 4.3% management, 5.6% professional, 11.3% services, 23.5% sales, 0.0% farming, 10.6% construction, 44.7% production (2000).
Income: Per capita income: $15,017 (2007); Median household income: $31,618 (2007); Average household income: $36,542 (2007); Percent of households with income of $100,000 or more: 3.0% (2007); Poverty rate: 16.6% (2000).
Education: Percent of population age 25 and over with: High school diploma (including GED) or higher: 72.6% (2007); Bachelor's degree or higher: 4.3% (2007); Master's degree or higher: 1.6% (2007).
Housing: Homeownership rate: 78.7% (2007); Median home value: $49,412 (2007); Median rent: $257 per month (2000); Median age of housing: 60+ years (2000).
Transportation: Commute to work: 97.4% car, 0.0% public transportation, 2.0% walk, 0.7% work from home (2000); Travel time to work: 9.7% less than 15 minutes, 39.0% 15 to 30 minutes, 11.3% 30 to 45 minutes, 16.3% 45 to 60 minutes, 23.7% 60 minutes or more (2000)

RENDVILLE (village). Covers a land area of 0.310 square miles and a water area of 0 square miles. Located at 39.61° N. Lat.; 82.08° W. Long. Elevation is 741 feet.
Population: 32 (1990); 46 (2000); 46 (2007); 46 (2012 projected); Race: 95.7% White, 4.3% Black, 0.0% Asian, 0.0% Hispanic of any race (2007); Density: 148.5 persons per square mile (2007); Average household size: 2.42 (2007); Median age: 35.0 (2007); Males per 100 females: 109.1 (2007); Marriage status: 31.9% never married, 27.7% now married, 25.5% widowed, 14.9% divorced (2000); Foreign born: 0.0% (2000); Ancestry (includes multiple ancestries): 30.2% United States or American, 18.9% Other groups, 7.5% Irish, 5.7% German (2000).
Economy: Employment by occupation: 0.0% management, 15.4% professional, 23.1% services, 19.2% sales, 0.0% farming, 0.0% construction, 42.3% production (2000).
Income: Per capita income: $31,957 (2007); Median household income: $77,500 (2007); Average household income: $77,368 (2007); Percent of households with income of $100,000 or more: 26.3% (2007); Poverty rate: 13.2% (2000).
Education: Percent of population age 25 and over with: High school diploma (including GED) or higher: 46.9% (2007); Bachelor's degree or higher: 0.0% (2007); Master's degree or higher: 0.0% (2007).
Housing: Homeownership rate: 78.9% (2007); Median home value: $27,500 (2007); Median rent: $325 per month (2000); Median age of housing: 59 years (2000).
Transportation: Commute to work: 100.0% car, 0.0% public transportation, 0.0% walk, 0.0% work from home (2000); Travel time to work: 11.5% less than 15 minutes, 3.8% 15 to 30 minutes, 23.1% 30 to 45 minutes, 38.5% 45 to 60 minutes, 23.1% 60 minutes or more (2000)

ROSEVILLE (village). Covers a land area of 0.696 square miles and a water area of 0 square miles. Located at 39.80° N. Lat.; 82.07° W. Long.
Population: 1,973 (1990); 1,936 (2000); 1,956 (2007); 1,947 (2012 projected); Race: 98.1% White, 0.5% Black, 0.0% Asian, 0.4% Hispanic of any race (2007); Density: 2,811.0 persons per square mile (2007); Average household size: 2.64 (2007); Median age: 32.2 (2007); Males per 100 females: 90.6 (2007); Marriage status: 25.9% never married, 54.0% now married, 6.8% widowed, 13.2% divorced (2000); Foreign born: 0.1% (2000); Ancestry (includes multiple ancestries): 15.1% United States or American, 12.5% German, 12.3% Irish, 8.7% Other groups, 7.9% English (2000).
Economy: Single-family building permits issued: 0 (2007); Multi-family building permits issued: 0 (2007); Employment by occupation: 4.1% management, 8.2% professional, 23.8% services, 18.8% sales, 0.3% farming, 12.7% construction, 32.2% production (2000).
Income: Per capita income: $13,972 (2007); Median household income: $29,216 (2007); Average household income: $36,833 (2007); Percent of households with income of $100,000 or more: 3.8% (2007); Poverty rate: 27.6% (2000).
Education: Percent of population age 25 and over with: High school diploma (including GED) or higher: 72.3% (2007); Bachelor's degree or higher: 3.9% (2007); Master's degree or higher: 0.8% (2007).

School District(s)

Franklin Local (PK-12)
2005-06 Enrollment: 2,435 . . . . (740) 674-5203
Housing: Homeownership rate: 65.2% (2007); Median home value: $65,938 (2007); Median rent: $259 per month (2000); Median age of housing: 51 years (2000).
Transportation: Commute to work: 94.0% car, 0.8% public transportation, 1.0% walk, 2.4% work from home (2000); Travel time to work: 26.7% less than 15 minutes, 30.8% 15 to 30 minutes, 15.9% 30 to 45 minutes, 13.5% 45 to 60 minutes, 13.1% 60 minutes or more (2000)

SHAWNEE (village). Covers a land area of 1.993 square miles and a water area of 0.005 square miles. Located at 39.60° N. Lat.; 82.21° W. Long. Elevation is 853 feet.
Population: 742 (1990); 608 (2000); 512 (2007); 516 (2012 projected); Race: 99.4% White, 0.0% Black, 0.6% Asian, 0.0% Hispanic of any race (2007); Density: 257.0 persons per square mile (2007); Average household size: 2.86 (2007); Median age: 34.7 (2007); Males per 100 females: 101.6 (2007); Marriage status: 33.1% never married, 47.0% now married, 6.4% widowed, 13.5% divorced (2000); Foreign born: 0.0% (2000); Ancestry (includes multiple ancestries): 16.0% German, 15.2% United States or American, 14.3% Irish, 12.7% English, 5.4% Other groups (2000).
Economy: Employment by occupation: 5.2% management, 12.4% professional, 12.0% services, 17.2% sales, 0.0% farming, 21.0% construction, 32.2% production (2000).
Income: Per capita income: $15,034 (2007); Median household income: $37,639 (2007); Average household income: $43,003 (2007); Percent of households with income of $100,000 or more: 3.4% (2007); Poverty rate: 15.6% (2000).
Education: Percent of population age 25 and over with: High school diploma (including GED) or higher: 83.5% (2007); Bachelor's degree or higher: 1.5% (2007); Master's degree or higher: 0.3% (2007).
Housing: Homeownership rate: 82.7% (2007); Median home value: $58,571 (2007); Median rent: $275 per month (2000); Median age of housing: 60+ years (2000).
Newspapers: Community Life News (Local news; Circulation 750)
Transportation: Commute to work: 96.4% car, 0.0% public transportation, 0.9% walk, 1.8% work from home (2000); Travel time to work: 24.4% less than 15 minutes, 32.3% 15 to 30 minutes, 10.6% 30 to 45 minutes, 13.4% 45 to 60 minutes, 19.4% 60 minutes or more (2000)

SOMERSET (village). Covers a land area of 1.166 square miles and a water area of 0 square miles. Located at 39.80° N. Lat.; 82.30° W. Long. Elevation is 1,083 feet.
History: Somerset was laid out in 1810 by John Fink and Jacob Miller, and served as the seat of Perry County from 1829 to 1857. Civil War general Philip Henry Sheridan spent his boyhood in Somerset.
Population: 1,450 (1990); 1,549 (2000); 1,496 (2007); 1,481 (2012 projected); Race: 99.0% White, 0.0% Black, 0.1% Asian, 0.4% Hispanic of any race (2007); Density: 1,282.8 persons per square mile (2007); Average household size: 2.48 (2007); Median age: 41.0 (2007); Males per 100 females: 82.4 (2007); Marriage status: 22.5% never married, 49.9% now married, 14.2% widowed, 13.4% divorced (2000); Foreign born: 0.3% (2000); Ancestry (includes multiple ancestries): 28.4% German, 19.9% United States or American, 17.5% Irish, 7.9% English, 6.1% Other groups (2000).
Economy: Single-family building permits issued: 1 (2007); Multi-family building permits issued: 0 (2007); Employment by occupation: 7.8% management, 18.2% professional, 12.3% services, 20.1% sales, 0.0% farming, 13.3% construction, 28.4% production (2000).
Income: Per capita income: $16,763 (2007); Median household income: $33,821 (2007); Average household income: $40,448 (2007); Percent of households with income of $100,000 or more: 6.0% (2007); Poverty rate: 12.8% (2000).
Education: Percent of population age 25 and over with: High school diploma (including GED) or higher: 81.9% (2007); Bachelor's degree or higher: 7.3% (2007); Master's degree or higher: 2.1% (2007).

School District(s)

Northern Local (PK-12)
2005-06 Enrollment: 2,337 . . . . (740) 743-1303
Housing: Homeownership rate: 64.2% (2007); Median home value: $109,833 (2007); Median rent: $245 per month (2000); Median age of housing: 47 years (2000).
Transportation: Commute to work: 92.1% car, 1.2% public transportation, 4.5% walk, 1.3% work from home (2000); Travel time to work: 30.0% less

than 15 minutes, 22.9% 15 to 30 minutes, 20.0% 30 to 45 minutes, 10.2% 45 to 60 minutes, 16.9% 60 minutes or more (2000)

THORNVILLE (village). Covers a land area of 0.433 square miles and a water area of 0 square miles. Located at 39.89° N. Lat.; 82.42° W. Long. Elevation is 1,030 feet.

Population: 829 (1990); 731 (2000); 689 (2007); 695 (2012 projected); Race: 99.1% White, 0.0% Black, 0.0% Asian, 0.0% Hispanic of any race (2007); Density: 1,589.8 persons per square mile (2007); Average household size: 2.56 (2007); Median age: 39.6 (2007); Males per 100 females: 95.7 (2007); Marriage status: 18.5% never married, 67.3% now married, 6.4% widowed, 7.7% divorced (2000); Foreign born: 0.3% (2000); Ancestry (includes multiple ancestries): 36.0% German, 9.9% Irish, 8.5% English, 6.5% Other groups, 5.6% Italian (2000).
Economy: Single-family building permits issued: 1 (2007); Multi-family building permits issued: 0 (2007); Employment by occupation: 8.6% management, 19.5% professional, 12.0% services, 29.1% sales, 0.5% farming, 11.2% construction, 19.0% production (2000).
Income: Per capita income: $24,307 (2007); Median household income: $54,697 (2007); Average household income: $62,258 (2007); Percent of households with income of $100,000 or more: 15.2% (2007); Poverty rate: 4.2% (2000).
Education: Percent of population age 25 and over with: High school diploma (including GED) or higher: 93.9% (2007); Bachelor's degree or higher: 15.4% (2007); Master's degree or higher: 4.0% (2007).

School District(s)

Northern Local (PK-12)
2005-06 Enrollment: 2,337 . . . . (740) 743-1303

Housing: Homeownership rate: 79.9% (2007); Median home value: $136,080 (2007); Median rent: $409 per month (2000); Median age of housing: 57 years (2000).
Transportation: Commute to work: 95.2% car, 0.0% public transportation, 3.0% walk, 1.9% work from home (2000); Travel time to work: 15.1% less than 15 minutes, 31.5% 15 to 30 minutes, 19.7% 30 to 45 minutes, 23.0% 45 to 60 minutes, 10.7% 60 minutes or more (2000)

Pickaway County

Located in south central Ohio; crossed by the Scioto River. Covers a land area of 501.91 square miles, a water area of 4.88 square miles, and is located in the Eastern Time Zone. The county was founded in 1810. County seat is Circleville.

Pickaway County is part of the Columbus, OH Metropolitan Statistical Area. The entire metro area includes: Delaware County, OH; Fairfield County, OH; Franklin County, OH; Licking County, OH; Madison County, OH; Morrow County, OH; Pickaway County, OH; Union County, OH

Weather Station: Circleville — Elevation: 672 feet

	Jan	Feb	Mar	Apr	May	Jun	Jul	Aug	Sep	Oct	Nov	Dec
High	37	41	52	64	74	82	86	84	78	67	53	42
Low	21	23	31	40	51	60	64	61	54	43	35	26
Precip	2.4	2.1	2.8	3.5	4.6	3.9	3.9	3.9	3.1	2.6	3.1	2.7
Snow	5.9	4.0	2.0	0.4	0.0	0.0	0.0	0.0	0.0	0.1	0.7	1.8

High and Low temperatures in degrees Fahrenheit; Precipitation and Snow in inches

Population: 48,244 (1990); 52,727 (2000); 53,615 (2007); 54,504 (2012 projected); Race: 93.6% White, 4.9% Black, 0.3% Asian, 0.9% Hispanic of any race (2007); Density: 106.8 persons per square mile (2007); Average household size: 2.83 (2007); Median age: 37.8 (2007); Males per 100 females: 107.3 (2007).
Religion: Five largest groups: 10.1% The United Methodist Church, 3.8% Catholic Church, 3.8% Evangelical Lutheran Church in America, 2.3% Southern Baptist Convention, 1.1% Church of the Nazarene (2000).
Economy: Unemployment rate: 6.7% (6/2008); Total civilian labor force: 25,277 (6/2008); Leading industries: 26.5% manufacturing; 19.5% health care and social assistance; 14.0% retail trade (2005); Farms: 791 totaling 275,029 acres (2002); Companies that employ 500 or more persons: 1 (2006); Companies that employ 100 to 499 persons: 23 (2006); Companies that employ less than 100 persons: 827 (2006); Black-owned businesses: n/a (2002); Hispanic-owned businesses: n/a (2002); Asian-owned businesses: n/a (2002); Women-owned businesses: n/a (2002); Retail sales per capita: $8,991 (2008). Single-family building permits issued: 66 (2007); Multi-family building permits issued: 0 (2007).
Income: Per capita income: $21,620 (2007); Median household income: $50,335 (2007); Average household income: $59,352 (2007); Percent of households with income of $100,000 or more: 14.2% (2007); Poverty rate: 11.3% (2005); Bankruptcy rate: 4.53% (2007).
Taxes: Total county taxes per capita: $187 (2006); County property taxes per capita: $83 (2006).
Education: Percent of population age 25 and over with: High school diploma (including GED) or higher: 77.8% (2007); Bachelor's degree or higher: 11.8% (2007); Master's degree or higher: 4.0% (2007).
Housing: Homeownership rate: 75.3% (2007); Median home value: $133,464 (2007); Median rent: $381 per month (2000); Median age of housing: 30 years (2000).
Health: Birth rate: 127.7 per 10,000 population (2007); Death rate: 88.3 per 10,000 population (2007); Age-adjusted cancer mortality rate: 220.3 deaths per 100,000 population (2005); Number of physicians: 8.2 per 10,000 population (2005); Hospital beds: 16.4 per 10,000 population (2004); Hospital admissions: 787.8 per 10,000 population (2004).
Elections: 2004 Presidential election results: 62.0% Bush, 37.5% Kerry, 0.0% Nader, 0.3% Badnarik
National and State Parks: A W Marion State Park; Logan Elm State Memorial

Additional Information Contacts

Pickaway County Government. . . . . (740) 474-6093
http://www.pickaway.org
City of Circleville . . . . (740) 477-2551
http://www.ci.circleville.oh.us
Pickaway Chamber of Commerce . . . . (740) 474-4923
http://www.pickaway.com

Pickaway County Communities

ASHVILLE (village). Covers a land area of 1.559 square miles and a water area of 0 square miles. Located at 39.71° N. Lat.; 82.95° W. Long. Elevation is 709 feet.

Population: 2,728 (1990); 3,174 (2000); 3,449 (2007); 3,574 (2012 projected); Race: 97.9% White, 0.2% Black, 0.0% Asian, 1.7% Hispanic of any race (2007); Density: 2,212.2 persons per square mile (2007); Average household size: 2.50 (2007); Median age: 33.5 (2007); Males per 100 females: 88.3 (2007); Marriage status: 19.6% never married, 62.7% now married, 6.5% widowed, 11.1% divorced (2000); Foreign born: 0.0% (2000); Ancestry (includes multiple ancestries): 21.0% German, 12.4% United States or American, 12.3% Irish, 9.7% English, 5.3% Other groups (2000).
Economy: Employment by occupation: 8.5% management, 12.6% professional, 19.2% services, 25.6% sales, 0.0% farming, 12.0% construction, 22.0% production (2000).
Income: Per capita income: $20,810 (2007); Median household income: $48,022 (2007); Average household income: $52,122 (2007); Percent of households with income of $100,000 or more: 9.5% (2007); Poverty rate: 9.5% (2000).
Education: Percent of population age 25 and over with: High school diploma (including GED) or higher: 81.1% (2007); Bachelor's degree or higher: 11.9% (2007); Master's degree or higher: 3.7% (2007).

School District(s)

Teays Valley Local (PK-12)
2005-06 Enrollment: 3,539 . . . . (740) 983-4111

Housing: Homeownership rate: 57.0% (2007); Median home value: $146,406 (2007); Median rent: $369 per month (2000); Median age of housing: 27 years (2000).
Transportation: Commute to work: 94.1% car, 0.0% public transportation, 2.4% walk, 3.2% work from home (2000); Travel time to work: 26.4% less than 15 minutes, 29.3% 15 to 30 minutes, 28.7% 30 to 45 minutes, 11.1% 45 to 60 minutes, 4.4% 60 minutes or more (2000)

CIRCLEVILLE (city). County seat. Covers a land area of 6.620 square miles and a water area of 0.117 square miles. Located at 39.60° N. Lat.; 82.93° W. Long. Elevation is 696 feet.
History: Named for local circular earthworks made by prehistoric mound builders. Circleville was settled in 1810 on the site of two ancient forts erected by the mound builders, one of them a round enclosure from which Circleville took its name.
Population: 12,743 (1990); 13,485 (2000); 13,518 (2007); 13,408 (2012 projected); Race: 95.1% White, 2.8% Black, 0.6% Asian, 1.2% Hispanic of any race (2007); Density: 2,042.1 persons per square mile (2007); Average household size: 2.44 (2007); Median age: 37.0 (2007); Males per 100 females: 88.7 (2007); Marriage status: 22.5% never married, 57.5% now married, 8.3% widowed, 11.7% divorced (2000); Foreign born: 0.9%

(2000); Ancestry (includes multiple ancestries): 19.1% German, 16.3% United States or American, 9.7% Irish, 8.9% English, 7.4% Other groups (2000).

Economy: Single-family building permits issued: 16 (2007); Multi-family building permits issued: 0 (2007); Employment by occupation: 11.2% management, 14.8% professional, 16.3% services, 24.4% sales, 0.4% farming, 11.7% construction, 21.2% production (2000).

Income: Per capita income: $20,537 (2007); Median household income: $39,009 (2007); Average household income: $49,418 (2007); Percent of households with income of $100,000 or more: 9.8% (2007); Poverty rate: 13.3% (2000).

Taxes: Total city taxes per capita: $401 (2006); City property taxes per capita: $58 (2006).

Education: Percent of population age 25 and over with: High school diploma (including GED) or higher: 77.1% (2007); Bachelor's degree or higher: 13.3% (2007); Master's degree or higher: 4.1% (2007).

School District(s)

Circleville City (PK-12)
2005-06 Enrollment: 2,430 . . . . (740) 474-4340

Department of Youth Services (06-12)
2005-06 Enrollment: 1,478 . . . . (614) 728-2489

Logan Elm Local (PK-12)
2005-06 Enrollment: 2,304 . . . . (740) 474-7501

Four-year College(s)

Ohio Christian University (Private, Not-for-profit, Other Protestant)
Fall 2007 Enrollment: 636 . . . . (740) 474-8896
2007-08 Tuition: In-state $13,040; Out-of-state $13,040

Housing: Homeownership rate: 60.4% (2007); Median home value: $113,728 (2007); Median rent: $393 per month (2000); Median age of housing: 39 years (2000).

Hospitals: Berger Hospital (91 beds)

Safety: Violent crime rate: 13.9 per 10,000 population; Property crime rate: 806.0 per 10,000 population (2007).

Newspapers: The Circleville Herald (Community news; Circulation 6,486); The Pickaway County Paper (Community news; Circulation 15,000)

Transportation: Commute to work: 95.1% car, 0.3% public transportation, 2.7% walk, 1.6% work from home (2000); Travel time to work: 45.7% less than 15 minutes, 18.4% 15 to 30 minutes, 18.6% 30 to 45 minutes, 11.8% 45 to 60 minutes, 5.6% 60 minutes or more (2000)

Additional Information Contacts

City of Circleville . . . . (740) 477-2551
http://www.ci.circleville.oh.us

Pickaway Chamber of Commerce . . . . (740) 474-4923
http://www.pickaway.com

COMMERCIAL POINT (village). Covers a land area of 1.089 square miles and a water area of 0 square miles. Located at 39.77° N. Lat.; 83.06° W. Long. Elevation is 781 feet.

Population: 762 (1990); 776 (2000); 941 (2007); 980 (2012 projected); Race: 98.3% White, 0.2% Black, 0.3% Asian, 0.7% Hispanic of any race (2007); Density: 864.0 persons per square mile (2007); Average household size: 2.76 (2007); Median age: 35.2 (2007); Males per 100 females: 87.5 (2007); Marriage status: 23.6% never married, 64.6% now married, 3.1% widowed, 8.7% divorced (2000); Foreign born: 0.3% (2000); Ancestry (includes multiple ancestries): 18.6% German, 16.1% United States or American, 11.5% Irish, 7.9% Other groups, 6.9% English (2000).

Economy: Employment by occupation: 17.2% management, 9.7% professional, 9.2% services, 29.5% sales, 0.0% farming, 15.3% construction, 19.1% production (2000).

Income: Per capita income: $24,875 (2007); Median household income: $63,068 (2007); Average household income: $68,644 (2007); Percent of households with income of $100,000 or more: 14.4% (2007); Poverty rate: 9.0% (2000).

Education: Percent of population age 25 and over with: High school diploma (including GED) or higher: 74.9% (2007); Bachelor's degree or higher: 11.9% (2007); Master's degree or higher: 2.8% (2007).

School District(s)

Teays Valley Local (PK-12)
2005-06 Enrollment: 3,539 . . . . (740) 983-4111

Housing: Homeownership rate: 85.3% (2007); Median home value: $147,917 (2007); Median rent: $348 per month (2000); Median age of housing: 19 years (2000).

Transportation: Commute to work: 96.7% car, 0.3% public transportation, 2.0% walk, 1.0% work from home (2000); Travel time to work: 13.9% less than 15 minutes, 38.7% 15 to 30 minutes, 37.5% 30 to 45 minutes, 4.6% 45 to 60 minutes, 5.3% 60 minutes or more (2000)

DARBYVILLE (village). Covers a land area of 0.467 square miles and a water area of 0.016 square miles. Located at 39.69° N. Lat.; 83.11° W. Long. Elevation is 745 feet.

Population: 272 (1990); 293 (2000); 344 (2007); 370 (2012 projected); Race: 100.0% White, 0.0% Black, 0.0% Asian, 4.7% Hispanic of any race (2007); Density: 736.6 persons per square mile (2007); Average household size: 3.07 (2007); Median age: 36.0 (2007); Males per 100 females: 92.2 (2007); Marriage status: 20.1% never married, 52.6% now married, 7.7% widowed, 19.6% divorced (2000); Foreign born: 0.0% (2000); Ancestry (includes multiple ancestries): 33.9% United States or American, 12.1% German, 10.7% Irish, 10.4% Other groups, 5.9% English (2000).

Economy: Employment by occupation: 4.9% management, 3.3% professional, 18.9% services, 32.8% sales, 0.0% farming, 11.5% construction, 28.7% production (2000).

Income: Per capita income: $15,472 (2007); Median household income: $45,417 (2007); Average household income: $47,522 (2007); Percent of households with income of $100,000 or more: 2.7% (2007); Poverty rate: 22.0% (2000).

Education: Percent of population age 25 and over with: High school diploma (including GED) or higher: 70.3% (2007); Bachelor's degree or higher: 0.9% (2007); Master's degree or higher: 0.0% (2007).

Housing: Homeownership rate: 67.9% (2007); Median home value: $65,000 (2007); Median rent: $292 per month (2000); Median age of housing: 37 years (2000).

Transportation: Commute to work: 94.1% car, 0.0% public transportation, 4.2% walk, 0.0% work from home (2000); Travel time to work: 12.7% less than 15 minutes, 33.1% 15 to 30 minutes, 36.4% 30 to 45 minutes, 13.6% 45 to 60 minutes, 4.2% 60 minutes or more (2000)

LOGAN ELM VILLAGE (CDP). Covers a land area of 0.512 square miles and a water area of 0 square miles. Located at 39.57° N. Lat.; 82.95° W. Long. Elevation is 702 feet.

Population: 1,287 (1990); 1,062 (2000); 1,024 (2007); 1,001 (2012 projected); Race: 96.7% White, 1.7% Black, 1.1% Asian, 0.9% Hispanic of any race (2007); Density: 1,999.0 persons per square mile (2007); Average household size: 2.40 (2007); Median age: 44.1 (2007); Males per 100 females: 77.5 (2007); Marriage status: 15.7% never married, 59.4% now married, 11.4% widowed, 13.5% divorced (2000); Foreign born: 0.6% (2000); Ancestry (includes multiple ancestries): 22.3% United States or American, 16.8% German, 7.5% English, 6.1% Irish, 5.9% Other groups (2000).

Economy: Employment by occupation: 11.6% management, 18.8% professional, 9.7% services, 28.8% sales, 0.0% farming, 13.5% construction, 17.6% production (2000).

Income: Per capita income: $20,263 (2007); Median household income: $42,708 (2007); Average household income: $46,925 (2007); Percent of households with income of $100,000 or more: 6.1% (2007); Poverty rate: 10.6% (2000).

Education: Percent of population age 25 and over with: High school diploma (including GED) or higher: 64.9% (2007); Bachelor's degree or higher: 3.5% (2007); Master's degree or higher: 0.0% (2007).

Housing: Homeownership rate: 80.0% (2007); Median home value: $112,637 (2007); Median rent: $290 per month (2000); Median age of housing: 26 years (2000).

Transportation: Commute to work: 94.0% car, 0.0% public transportation, 2.6% walk, 3.3% work from home (2000); Travel time to work: 46.6% less than 15 minutes, 20.2% 15 to 30 minutes, 18.2% 30 to 45 minutes, 5.7% 45 to 60 minutes, 9.4% 60 minutes or more (2000)

NEW HOLLAND (village). Covers a land area of 1.869 square miles and a water area of 0 square miles. Located at 39.55° N. Lat.; 83.25° W. Long. Elevation is 853 feet.

History: New Holland was founded in 1818, and grew as a center for poultry and hog raising.

Population: 844 (1990); 785 (2000); 750 (2007); 743 (2012 projected); Race: 97.9% White, 0.5% Black, 0.0% Asian, 0.4% Hispanic of any race (2007); Density: 401.3 persons per square mile (2007); Average household size: 2.49 (2007); Median age: 38.6 (2007); Males per 100 females: 89.4 (2007); Marriage status: 18.0% never married, 63.8% now married, 10.3% widowed, 7.9% divorced (2000); Foreign born: 0.0% (2000); Ancestry (includes multiple ancestries): 13.9% German, 12.3% Irish, 10.6% Other groups, 7.9% United States or American, 7.9% English (2000).

Economy: Single-family building permits issued: 0 (2007); Multi-family building permits issued: 0 (2007); Employment by occupation: 5.9% management, 12.4% professional, 16.6% services, 24.9% sales, 0.9% farming, 8.6% construction, 30.8% production (2000).
Income: Per capita income: $18,173 (2007); Median household income: $35,147 (2007); Average household income: $45,282 (2007); Percent of households with income of $100,000 or more: 7.3% (2007); Poverty rate: 7.9% (2000).
Education: Percent of population age 25 and over with: High school diploma (including GED) or higher: 74.8% (2007); Bachelor's degree or higher: 5.5% (2007); Master's degree or higher: 3.5% (2007).

School District(s)

Miami Trace Local (PK-12)
2005-06 Enrollment: 2,770 . . . . (740) 335-3010

Housing: Homeownership rate: 77.1% (2007); Median home value: $93,810 (2007); Median rent: $326 per month (2000); Median age of housing: 56 years (2000).
Transportation: Commute to work: 93.5% car, 0.0% public transportation, 4.6% walk, 0.6% work from home (2000); Travel time to work: 14.3% less than 15 minutes, 40.4% 15 to 30 minutes, 23.9% 30 to 45 minutes, 12.4% 45 to 60 minutes, 9.0% 60 minutes or more (2000)

ORIENT (village). Aka Morgan. Covers a land area of 0.124 square miles and a water area of 0 square miles. Located at 39.80° N. Lat.; 83.15° W. Long. Elevation is 840 feet.
Population: 273 (1990); 269 (2000); 257 (2007); 241 (2012 projected); Race: 99.6% White, 0.0% Black, 0.0% Asian, 0.0% Hispanic of any race (2007); Density: 2,071.6 persons per square mile (2007); Average household size: 2.76 (2007); Median age: 32.5 (2007); Males per 100 females: 105.6 (2007); Marriage status: 26.5% never married, 59.1% now married, 4.8% widowed, 9.6% divorced (2000); Foreign born: 0.0% (2000); Ancestry (includes multiple ancestries): 39.4% United States or American, 17.2% Irish, 16.5% German, 9.0% English, 3.9% Other groups (2000).
Economy: Employment by occupation: 8.1% management, 8.1% professional, 14.1% services, 28.9% sales, 0.0% farming, 14.1% construction, 26.8% production (2000).
Income: Per capita income: $18,920 (2007); Median household income: $41,500 (2007); Average household income: $52,285 (2007); Percent of households with income of $100,000 or more: 15.1% (2007); Poverty rate: 11.5% (2000).
Education: Percent of population age 25 and over with: High school diploma (including GED) or higher: 45.5% (2007); Bachelor's degree or higher: 5.8% (2007); Master's degree or higher: 1.3% (2007).
Housing: Homeownership rate: 77.4% (2007); Median home value: $76,923 (2007); Median rent: $295 per month (2000); Median age of housing: 60+ years (2000).
Transportation: Commute to work: 100.0% car, 0.0% public transportation, 0.0% walk, 0.0% work from home (2000); Travel time to work: 15.4% less than 15 minutes, 25.5% 15 to 30 minutes, 28.2% 30 to 45 minutes, 26.8% 45 to 60 minutes, 4.0% 60 minutes or more (2000)

SOUTH BLOOMFIELD (village). Covers a land area of 1.149 square miles and a water area of 0 square miles. Located at 39.71° N. Lat.; 82.98° W. Long. Elevation is 696 feet.
Population: 1,031 (1990); 1,179 (2000); 1,418 (2007); 1,550 (2012 projected); Race: 98.8% White, 0.0% Black, 0.1% Asian, 1.8% Hispanic of any race (2007); Density: 1,234.3 persons per square mile (2007); Average household size: 2.43 (2007); Median age: 35.7 (2007); Males per 100 females: 91.4 (2007); Marriage status: 19.9% never married, 58.0% now married, 6.9% widowed, 15.3% divorced (2000); Foreign born: 0.9% (2000); Ancestry (includes multiple ancestries): 18.3% German, 15.2% United States or American, 9.3% Irish, 6.1% English, 5.3% Other groups (2000).
Economy: Single-family building permits issued: 2 (2007); Multi-family building permits issued: 0 (2007); Employment by occupation: 8.2% management, 5.8% professional, 19.2% services, 24.0% sales, 0.2% farming, 13.8% construction, 28.9% production (2000).
Income: Per capita income: $20,349 (2007); Median household income: $43,300 (2007); Average household income: $49,409 (2007); Percent of households with income of $100,000 or more: 6.3% (2007); Poverty rate: 7.8% (2000).
Education: Percent of population age 25 and over with: High school diploma (including GED) or higher: 73.9% (2007); Bachelor's degree or higher: 3.9% (2007); Master's degree or higher: 0.5% (2007).
Housing: Homeownership rate: 80.1% (2007); Median home value: $78,571 (2007); Median rent: $423 per month (2000); Median age of housing: 24 years (2000).
Transportation: Commute to work: 96.0% car, 0.0% public transportation, 2.5% walk, 1.6% work from home (2000); Travel time to work: 18.6% less than 15 minutes, 35.7% 15 to 30 minutes, 32.3% 30 to 45 minutes, 8.6% 45 to 60 minutes, 4.8% 60 minutes or more (2000)

TARLTON (village). Covers a land area of 0.420 square miles and a water area of 0 square miles. Located at 39.55° N. Lat.; 82.77° W. Long. Elevation is 902 feet.
History: Tarlton Cross Mound nearby.
Population: 315 (1990); 298 (2000); 294 (2007); 288 (2012 projected); Race: 100.0% White, 0.0% Black, 0.0% Asian, 0.0% Hispanic of any race (2007); Density: 700.6 persons per square mile (2007); Average household size: 2.91 (2007); Median age: 38.5 (2007); Males per 100 females: 97.3 (2007); Marriage status: 26.8% never married, 55.0% now married, 8.2% widowed, 10.0% divorced (2000); Foreign born: 0.0% (2000); Ancestry (includes multiple ancestries): 14.7% German, 12.9% United States or American, 9.8% English, 6.6% Dutch, 5.6% Irish (2000).
Economy: Employment by occupation: 3.1% management, 10.7% professional, 10.7% services, 18.3% sales, 0.0% farming, 16.0% construction, 41.2% production (2000).
Income: Per capita income: $15,374 (2007); Median household income: $37,083 (2007); Average household income: $44,752 (2007); Percent of households with income of $100,000 or more: 5.9% (2007); Poverty rate: 6.0% (2000).
Education: Percent of population age 25 and over with: High school diploma (including GED) or higher: 70.6% (2007); Bachelor's degree or higher: 1.1% (2007); Master's degree or higher: 0.0% (2007).
Housing: Homeownership rate: 83.2% (2007); Median home value: $90,000 (2007); Median rent: $300 per month (2000); Median age of housing: 59 years (2000).
Transportation: Commute to work: 89.8% car, 1.6% public transportation, 8.6% walk, 0.0% work from home (2000); Travel time to work: 26.6% less than 15 minutes, 33.6% 15 to 30 minutes, 18.0% 30 to 45 minutes, 10.2% 45 to 60 minutes, 11.7% 60 minutes or more (2000)

WILLIAMSPORT (village). Covers a land area of 1.341 square miles and a water area of 0 square miles. Located at 39.58° N. Lat.; 83.11° W. Long. Elevation is 758 feet.
Population: 851 (1990); 1,002 (2000); 1,045 (2007); 1,051 (2012 projected); Race: 98.6% White, 0.7% Black, 0.0% Asian, 0.0% Hispanic of any race (2007); Density: 779.4 persons per square mile (2007); Average household size: 2.80 (2007); Median age: 33.5 (2007); Males per 100 females: 83.7 (2007); Marriage status: 24.6% never married, 52.8% now married, 7.9% widowed, 14.7% divorced (2000); Foreign born: 0.5% (2000); Ancestry (includes multiple ancestries): 24.0% German, 19.7% United States or American, 11.1% English, 9.5% Irish, 8.3% Other groups (2000).
Economy: Employment by occupation: 7.4% management, 9.1% professional, 17.9% services, 31.4% sales, 0.4% farming, 12.2% construction, 21.7% production (2000).
Income: Per capita income: $16,395 (2007); Median household income: $36,742 (2007); Average household income: $44,718 (2007); Percent of households with income of $100,000 or more: 6.4% (2007); Poverty rate: 22.7% (2000).
Education: Percent of population age 25 and over with: High school diploma (including GED) or higher: 72.4% (2007); Bachelor's degree or higher: 6.6% (2007); Master's degree or higher: 1.2% (2007).

School District(s)

Westfall Local (PK-12)
2005-06 Enrollment: 1,724 . . . . (740) 986-3671

Housing: Homeownership rate: 69.4% (2007); Median home value: $103,940 (2007); Median rent: $336 per month (2000); Median age of housing: 43 years (2000).
Transportation: Commute to work: 93.8% car, 0.9% public transportation, 4.1% walk, 0.9% work from home (2000); Travel time to work: 19.4% less than 15 minutes, 35.8% 15 to 30 minutes, 13.6% 30 to 45 minutes, 20.5% 45 to 60 minutes, 10.8% 60 minutes or more (2000)

Pike County

Located in southern Ohio; crossed by the Scioto River. Covers a land area of 441.49 square miles, a water area of 2.46 square miles, and is located in the Eastern Time Zone. The county was founded in 1815. County seat is Waverly City.

Weather Station: Waverly Elevation: 557 feet

	Jan	Feb	Mar	Apr	May	Jun	Jul	Aug	Sep	Oct	Nov	Dec
High	39	44	55	67	75	83	86	85	79	68	56	45
Low	19	22	30	38	49	58	63	60	53	40	32	24
Precip	2.7	2.3	3.6	3.6	4.2	3.9	4.0	4.4	2.6	2.6	3.1	3.0
Snow	4.7	na	3.0	0.1	0.0	0.0	0.0	0.0	0.0	tr	0.1	1.5

High and Low temperatures in degrees Fahrenheit; Precipitation and Snow in inches

Population: 24,249 (1990); 27,695 (2000); 28,161 (2007); 28,298 (2012 projected); Race: 96.7% White, 1.0% Black, 0.3% Asian, 0.8% Hispanic of any race (2007); Density: 63.8 persons per square mile (2007); Average household size: 2.61 (2007); Median age: 36.7 (2007); Males per 100 females: 94.6 (2007).
Religion: Five largest groups: 5.6% Southern Baptist Convention, 4.2% The United Methodist Church, 1.5% Christian Churches and Churches of Christ, 1.2% Christian Union, 1.1% Catholic Church (2000).
Economy: Unemployment rate: 9.3% (6/2008); Total civilian labor force: 10,899 (6/2008); Leading industries: 40.2% manufacturing; 18.6% health care and social assistance; 12.4% retail trade (2005); Farms: 505 totaling 83,602 acres (2002); Companies that employ 500 or more persons: 2 (2006); Companies that employ 100 to 499 persons: 8 (2006); Companies that employ less than 100 persons: 448 (2006); Black-owned businesses: n/a (2002); Hispanic-owned businesses: n/a (2002); Asian-owned businesses: n/a (2002); Women-owned businesses: 589 (2002); Retail sales per capita: $8,951 (2008). Single-family building permits issued: 59 (2007); Multi-family building permits issued: 0 (2007).
Income: Per capita income: $18,389 (2007); Median household income: $36,904 (2007); Average household income: $47,498 (2007); Percent of households with income of $100,000 or more: 8.6% (2007); Poverty rate: 21.4% (2005); Bankruptcy rate: 3.51% (2007).
Taxes: Total county taxes per capita: $227 (2006); County property taxes per capita: $226 (2006).
Education: Percent of population age 25 and over with: High school diploma (including GED) or higher: 69.9% (2007); Bachelor's degree or higher: 9.5% (2007); Master's degree or higher: 3.3% (2007).
Housing: Homeownership rate: 70.5% (2007); Median home value: $91,591 (2007); Median rent: $313 per month (2000); Median age of housing: 26 years (2000).
Health: Birth rate: 138.6 per 10,000 population (2007); Death rate: 117.1 per 10,000 population (2007); Age-adjusted cancer mortality rate: 189.9 deaths per 100,000 population (2005); Number of physicians: 9.4 per 10,000 population (2005); Hospital beds: 13.2 per 10,000 population (2004); Hospital admissions: 502.4 per 10,000 population (2004).
Elections: 2004 Presidential election results: 51.8% Bush, 47.6% Kerry, 0.0% Nader, 0.3% Badnarik
National and State Parks: Lake White State Park
Additional Information Contacts
Pike County Government. . . . . (740) 947-4817

City of Waverly City . . . . (740) 947-5454
http://www.cityofwaverly.net
Pike County Chamber of Commerce . . . . (740) 947-7715
http://www.pikechamber.org

Pike County Communities

BEAVER (village). Covers a land area of 0.391 square miles and a water area of 0 square miles. Located at 39.03° N. Lat.; 82.82° W. Long. Elevation is 686 feet.
Population: 336 (1990); 464 (2000); 468 (2007); 469 (2012 projected); Race: 97.2% White, 0.0% Black, 0.4% Asian, 0.2% Hispanic of any race (2007); Density: 1,198.2 persons per square mile (2007); Average household size: 2.33 (2007); Median age: 33.2 (2007); Males per 100 females: 82.8 (2007); Marriage status: 20.1% never married, 57.7% now married, 8.7% widowed, 13.5% divorced (2000); Foreign born: 1.0% (2000); Ancestry (includes multiple ancestries): 13.7% United States or American, 12.9% German, 7.3% Irish, 6.3% Other groups, 3.9% Dutch (2000).
Economy: Employment by occupation: 5.6% management, 9.9% professional, 18.0% services, 18.6% sales, 1.2% farming, 26.1% construction, 20.5% production (2000).
Income: Per capita income: $14,151 (2007); Median household income: $25,781 (2007); Average household income: $32,948 (2007); Percent of households with income of $100,000 or more: 2.0% (2007); Poverty rate: 28.6% (2000).
Education: Percent of population age 25 and over with: High school diploma (including GED) or higher: 66.4% (2007); Bachelor's degree or higher: 6.4% (2007); Master's degree or higher: 1.1% (2007).

School District(s)

Eastern Local (PK-12)
2005-06 Enrollment: 814 . . . . (740) 226-4851
Housing: Homeownership rate: 47.8% (2007); Median home value: $100,000 (2007); Median rent: $273 per month (2000); Median age of housing: 37 years (2000).
Transportation: Commute to work: 82.0% car, 5.0% public transportation, 8.7% walk, 0.0% work from home (2000); Travel time to work: 28.0% less than 15 minutes, 36.6% 15 to 30 minutes, 15.5% 30 to 45 minutes, 8.7% 45 to 60 minutes, 11.2% 60 minutes or more (2000)

LATHAM (unincorporated postal area, zip code 45646). Covers a land area of 12.529 square miles and a water area of 0.014 square miles. Located at 39.08° N. Lat.; 83.31° W. Long. Elevation is 689 feet.
Population: 295 (2000); Race: 100.0% White, 0.0% Black, 0.0% Asian, 0.0% Hispanic of any race (2000); Density: 23.5 persons per square mile (2000); Age: 18.4% under 18, 18.4% over 64 (2000); Marriage status: 18.6% never married, 60.6% now married, 10.4% widowed, 10.4% divorced (2000); Foreign born: 0.0% (2000); Ancestry (includes multiple ancestries): 40.0% United States or American, 4.1% Irish, 3.4% German, 2.2% Other groups, 1.9% English (2000).
Economy: Employment by occupation: 4.5% management, 3.8% professional, 14.4% services, 29.5% sales, 0.0% farming, 18.9% construction, 28.8% production (2000).
Income: Per capita income: $13,250 (2000); Median household income: $29,583 (2000); Poverty rate: 25.6% (2000).
Education: Percent of population age 25 and over with: High school diploma (including GED) or higher: 49.6% (2000); Bachelor's degree or higher: 0.0% (2000).

School District(s)

Western Local (PK-12)
2005-06 Enrollment: 901 . . . . (740) 493-3113
Housing: Homeownership rate: 87.0% (2000); Median home value: $38,800 (2000); Median rent: $315 per month (2000); Median age of housing: 33 years (2000).
Transportation: Commute to work: 94.4% car, 0.0% public transportation, 0.0% walk, 5.6% work from home (2000); Travel time to work: 37.8% less than 15 minutes, 18.5% 15 to 30 minutes, 22.7% 30 to 45 minutes, 15.1% 45 to 60 minutes, 5.9% 60 minutes or more (2000)

PIKETON (village). Covers a land area of 1.996 square miles and a water area of 0.040 square miles. Located at 39.06° N. Lat.; 83.00° W. Long. Elevation is 574 feet.
History: Piketon was settled in 1814, when it was called Jefferson. Piketon served as the seat of Pike County until 1861.
Population: 1,700 (1990); 1,907 (2000); 1,855 (2007); 1,870 (2012 projected); Race: 96.1% White, 1.2% Black, 0.5% Asian, 0.2% Hispanic of any race (2007); Density: 929.6 persons per square mile (2007); Average household size: 2.70 (2007); Median age: 39.7 (2007); Males per 100 females: 76.5 (2007); Marriage status: 18.8% never married, 58.8% now married, 7.6% widowed, 14.7% divorced (2000); Foreign born: 0.3% (2000); Ancestry (includes multiple ancestries): 18.7% United States or American, 10.5% German, 6.8% Irish, 6.1% English, 5.1% Other groups (2000).
Economy: Single-family building permits issued: 2 (2007); Multi-family building permits issued: 0 (2007); Employment by occupation: 8.3% management, 11.6% professional, 23.0% services, 20.2% sales, 1.5% farming, 8.6% construction, 26.9% production (2000).
Income: Per capita income: $14,400 (2007); Median household income: $24,871 (2007); Average household income: $37,431 (2007); Percent of households with income of $100,000 or more: 6.1% (2007); Poverty rate: 30.3% (2000).
Education: Percent of population age 25 and over with: High school diploma (including GED) or higher: 67.6% (2007); Bachelor's degree or higher: 8.1% (2007); Master's degree or higher: 3.1% (2007).

School District(s)

Pike County Area (08-12)
2005-06 Enrollment: n/a . . . . (740) 289-2721
Scioto Valley Local (PK-12)
2005-06 Enrollment: 1,704 . . . . (740) 289-4456

Western Local (PK-12)
2005-06 Enrollment: 901 . . . . (740) 493-3113

Vocational/Technical School(s)

Pike County Joint Vocational School District (Public)
Fall 2007 Enrollment: 97 . . . . (740) 289-2282
2007-08 Tuition: $6,006

Housing: Homeownership rate: 52.3% (2007); Median home value: $101,933 (2007); Median rent: $263 per month (2000); Median age of housing: 30 years (2000).
Transportation: Commute to work: 92.7% car, 0.0% public transportation, 4.5% walk, 1.7% work from home (2000); Travel time to work: 52.0% less than 15 minutes, 23.6% 15 to 30 minutes, 13.2% 30 to 45 minutes, 4.4% 45 to 60 minutes, 6.8% 60 minutes or more (2000)

WAVERLY CITY (city). Aka Waverly. County seat. Covers a land area of 3.919 square miles and a water area of 0 square miles. Located at 39.12° N. Lat.; 82.98° W. Long. Elevation is 604 feet.
History: Waverly City (also known as Waverly) was founded in 1829 by James Emmitt and called Uniontown. The name was changed to Waverly in 1830 at the suggestion of Captain Francis Cleveland, a canal engineer, who had been reading Walter Scott's Waverly novels. Waverly managed to take the county seat from Piketon in 1861.
Population: 4,296 (1990); 4,433 (2000); 4,232 (2007); 4,148 (2012 projected); Race: 95.7% White, 1.8% Black, 1.1% Asian, 0.6% Hispanic of any race (2007); Density: 1,080.0 persons per square mile (2007); Average household size: 2.14 (2007); Median age: 44.5 (2007); Males per 100 females: 80.9 (2007); Marriage status: 17.0% never married, 57.2% now married, 12.5% widowed, 13.4% divorced (2000); Foreign born: 1.4% (2000); Ancestry (includes multiple ancestries): 16.2% German, 15.8% English, 13.9% United States or American, 10.9% Irish, 7.6% Other groups (2000).
Economy: Single-family building permits issued: 18 (2007); Multi-family building permits issued: 0 (2007); Employment by occupation: 9.0% management, 24.4% professional, 11.2% services, 28.6% sales, 0.0% farming, 5.5% construction, 21.4% production (2000).
Income: Per capita income: $21,585 (2007); Median household income: $37,121 (2007); Average household income: $45,532 (2007); Percent of households with income of $100,000 or more: 6.9% (2007); Poverty rate: 12.2% (2000).
Education: Percent of population age 25 and over with: High school diploma (including GED) or higher: 81.1% (2007); Bachelor's degree or higher: 21.5% (2007); Master's degree or higher: 7.0% (2007).

School District(s)

Waverly City (PK-12)
2005-06 Enrollment: 2,209 . . . . (740) 947-4770

Housing: Homeownership rate: 49.6% (2007); Median home value: $102,736 (2007); Median rent: $381 per month (2000); Median age of housing: 42 years (2000).
Hospitals: Pike Community Hospital (63 beds)
Safety: Violent crime rate: 0.0 per 10,000 population; Property crime rate: 246.0 per 10,000 population (2007).
Newspapers: The Paper (Community news; Circulation 42,000); Waverly News/Watchman (Local news; Circulation 5,000)
Transportation: Commute to work: 93.0% car, 0.7% public transportation, 4.2% walk, 1.8% work from home (2000); Travel time to work: 54.3% less than 15 minutes, 26.3% 15 to 30 minutes, 10.4% 30 to 45 minutes, 3.6% 45 to 60 minutes, 5.5% 60 minutes or more (2000)

Additional Information Contacts

City of Waverly City . . . . (740) 947-5454
http://www.cityofwaverly.net
Pike County Chamber of Commerce . . . . (740) 947-7715
http://www.pikechamber.org

Portage County

Located in northeastern Ohio; crossed by the Cuyahoga River and tributaries of the Mahoning; includes many small lakes. Covers a land area of 492.39 square miles, a water area of 14.72 square miles, and is located in the Eastern Time Zone. The county was founded in 1807. County seat is Ravenna.

Portage County is part of the Akron, OH Metropolitan Statistical Area. The entire metro area includes: Portage County, OH; Summit County, OH

Weather Station: Hiram Elevation: 1,227 feet

	Jan	Feb	Mar	Apr	May	Jun	Jul	Aug	Sep	Oct	Nov	Dec
High	32	36	46	58	70	77	82	80	73	61	49	37
Low	16	19	27	37	48	56	61	60	53	42	33	23
Precip	2.7	2.3	3.4	3.6	3.8	4.1	3.9	3.8	4.2	3.2	3.7	3.5
Snow	16.1	12.4	10.2	1.5	tr	0.0	0.0	0.0	0.0	0.2	6.0	15.2

High and Low temperatures in degrees Fahrenheit; Precipitation and Snow in inches

Population: 142,585 (1990); 152,061 (2000); 156,446 (2007); 158,814 (2012 projected); Race: 93.2% White, 3.6% Black, 1.2% Asian, 0.8% Hispanic of any race (2007); Density: 317.7 persons per square mile (2007); Average household size: 2.63 (2007); Median age: 35.8 (2007); Males per 100 females: 94.9 (2007).
Religion: Five largest groups: 19.4% Catholic Church, 3.7% The United Methodist Church, 1.7% United Church of Christ, 1.6% Christian Church (Disciples of Christ), 1.0% Independent, Non-Charismatic Churches (2000).
Economy: Unemployment rate: 6.3% (6/2008); Total civilian labor force: 92,009 (6/2008); Leading industries: 27.5% manufacturing; 13.9% retail trade; 11.3% health care and social assistance (2005); Farms: 962 totaling 96,874 acres (2002); Companies that employ 500 or more persons: 4 (2006); Companies that employ 100 to 499 persons: 72 (2006); Companies that employ less than 100 persons: 3,128 (2006); Black-owned businesses: 215 (2002); Hispanic-owned businesses: n/a (2002); Asian-owned businesses: 116 (2002); Women-owned businesses: 3,247 (2002); Retail sales per capita: $11,803 (2008). Single-family building permits issued: 473 (2007); Multi-family building permits issued: 32 (2007).
Income: Per capita income: $24,450 (2007); Median household income: $51,005 (2007); Average household income: $63,252 (2007); Percent of households with income of $100,000 or more: 15.5% (2007); Poverty rate: 10.9% (2005); Bankruptcy rate: 4.54% (2007).
Taxes: Total county taxes per capita: $259 (2006); County property taxes per capita: $166 (2006).
Education: Percent of population age 25 and over with: High school diploma (including GED) or higher: 86.1% (2007); Bachelor's degree or higher: 21.5% (2007); Master's degree or higher: 7.2% (2007).
Housing: Homeownership rate: 71.5% (2007); Median home value: $145,620 (2007); Median rent: $469 per month (2000); Median age of housing: 30 years (2000).
Health: Birth rate: 107.7 per 10,000 population (2007); Death rate: 76.0 per 10,000 population (2007); Age-adjusted cancer mortality rate: 208.6 deaths per 100,000 population (2005); Air Quality Index: 76.7% good, 20.2% moderate, 3.1% unhealthy for sensitive individuals, 0.0% unhealthy (percent of days in 2007); Number of physicians: 11.9 per 10,000 population (2005); Hospital beds: 7.6 per 10,000 population (2004); Hospital admissions: 529.8 per 10,000 population (2004).
Elections: 2004 Presidential election results: 46.4% Bush, 53.1% Kerry, 0.0% Nader, 0.3% Badnarik
National and State Parks: Nelson-Kennedy Ledges State Park; Tinkers Creek State Park; West Branch State Park

Additional Information Contacts

Portage County Government . . . . (330) 297-3600
http://www.co.portage.oh.us
Aurora Chamber of Commerce . . . . (330) 562-3355
http://www.auroraohiochamber.com
Brimfield Area Chamber of Commerce . . . . (330) 554-2236
http://www.brimfieldchamber.com
City of Aurora . . . . (330) 562-6131
http://www.auroraoh.com
City of Kent . . . . (330) 678-8007
http://www.kentohio.org
City of Ravenna . . . . (330) 296-3864
http://www.ci.ravenna.oh.us
City of Streetsboro . . . . (330) 626-4942
http://cityofstreetsboro.com
Garrettsville Area Chamber of Commerce . . . . (330) 527-2411
http://www.garrettsvillehiramarea.com
Kent Area Chamber of Commerce . . . . (330) 673-9855
http://www.kentbiz.com
Ravenna Area Chamber of Commerce . . . . (330) 296-3886
http://www.ravennaareachamber.com
Rootstown Area Chamber of Commerce . . . . (330) 325-2207
http://www.rootstownchamber.org
Streetsboro Area Chamber of Commerce . . . . (330) 626-4769
http://www.streetsborochamber.org
Streetsboro Visitors and Convention Bureau . . . . (330) 422-1770
http://www.streetsborovcb.com

Village of Garrettsville . . . . (330) 527-4424
http://www.garrettsville.org

Portage County Communities

ATWATER (unincorporated postal area, zip code 44201). Covers a land area of 52.866 square miles and a water area of 0.112 square miles. Located at 41.02° N. Lat.; 81.20° W. Long. Elevation is 1,168 feet.
Population: 6,915 (2000); Race: 99.2% White, 0.2% Black, 0.1% Asian, 0.0% Hispanic of any race (2000); Density: 130.8 persons per square mile (2000); Age: 27.0% under 18, 11.3% over 64 (2000); Marriage status: 21.1% never married, 67.4% now married, 3.9% widowed, 7.5% divorced (2000); Foreign born: 0.5% (2000); Ancestry (includes multiple ancestries): 31.9% German, 12.6% Irish, 11.4% English, 9.6% United States or American, 5.8% Other groups (2000).
Economy: Employment by occupation: 8.0% management, 9.8% professional, 11.4% services, 30.3% sales, 0.7% farming, 14.8% construction, 25.2% production (2000).
Income: Per capita income: $19,060 (2000); Median household income: $47,665 (2000); Poverty rate: 5.2% (2000).
Education: Percent of population age 25 and over with: High school diploma (including GED) or higher: 86.9% (2000); Bachelor's degree or higher: 10.3% (2000).

School District(s)

Waterloo Local (PK-12)
2005-06 Enrollment: 1,385 . . . . (330) 947-2664
Housing: Homeownership rate: 88.1% (2000); Median home value: $123,500 (2000); Median rent: $503 per month (2000); Median age of housing: 30 years (2000).
Transportation: Commute to work: 95.6% car, 0.0% public transportation, 1.1% walk, 2.3% work from home (2000); Travel time to work: 14.2% less than 15 minutes, 40.1% 15 to 30 minutes, 25.2% 30 to 45 minutes, 12.2% 45 to 60 minutes, 8.3% 60 minutes or more (2000)

AURORA (city). Covers a land area of 23.221 square miles and a water area of 0.872 square miles. Located at 41.31° N. Lat.; 81.35° W. Long. Elevation is 1,132 feet.
Population: 9,192 (1990); 13,556 (2000); 14,415 (2007); 14,934 (2012 projected); Race: 94.1% White, 2.7% Black, 2.1% Asian, 0.6% Hispanic of any race (2007); Density: 620.8 persons per square mile (2007); Average household size: 2.61 (2007); Median age: 42.8 (2007); Males per 100 females: 92.9 (2007); Marriage status: 17.3% never married, 70.0% now married, 5.5% widowed, 7.2% divorced (2000); Foreign born: 2.8% (2000); Ancestry (includes multiple ancestries): 26.1% German, 16.4% Irish, 13.9% Italian, 13.6% English, 9.8% Polish (2000).
Economy: Single-family building permits issued: 25 (2007); Multi-family building permits issued: 0 (2007); Employment by occupation: 26.0% management, 21.4% professional, 9.0% services, 28.4% sales, 0.1% farming, 5.9% construction, 9.1% production (2000).
Income: Per capita income: $42,131 (2007); Median household income: $82,878 (2007); Average household income: $109,285 (2007); Percent of households with income of $100,000 or more: 39.1% (2007); Poverty rate: 3.6% (2000).
Taxes: Total city taxes per capita: $1,019 (2006); City property taxes per capita: $286 (2006).
Education: Percent of population age 25 and over with: High school diploma (including GED) or higher: 93.2% (2007); Bachelor's degree or higher: 41.3% (2007); Master's degree or higher: 12.3% (2007).

School District(s)

Aurora City (PK-12)
2005-06 Enrollment: 2,953 . . . . (330) 562-6106
Housing: Homeownership rate: 81.3% (2007); Median home value: $236,646 (2007); Median rent: $890 per month (2000); Median age of housing: 18 years (2000).
Safety: Violent crime rate: 9.0 per 10,000 population; Property crime rate: 112.3 per 10,000 population (2007).
Transportation: Commute to work: 93.5% car, 0.1% public transportation, 0.5% walk, 5.5% work from home (2000); Travel time to work: 22.7% less than 15 minutes, 31.6% 15 to 30 minutes, 30.5% 30 to 45 minutes, 10.8% 45 to 60 minutes, 4.5% 60 minutes or more (2000)

Additional Information Contacts

Aurora Chamber of Commerce . . . . (330) 562-3355
http://www.auroraohiochamber.com
City of Aurora . . . . (330) 562-6131
http://www.auroraoh.com

BRADY LAKE (village). Aka Bradys Lake. Covers a land area of 0.316 square miles and a water area of 0.105 square miles. Located at 41.16° N. Lat.; 81.31° W. Long. Elevation is 1,076 feet.
Population: 498 (1990); 513 (2000); 548 (2007); 555 (2012 projected); Race: 95.4% White, 2.0% Black, 0.0% Asian, 1.1% Hispanic of any race (2007); Density: 1,736.5 persons per square mile (2007); Average household size: 2.49 (2007); Median age: 39.8 (2007); Males per 100 females: 95.7 (2007); Marriage status: 23.1% never married, 59.8% now married, 6.7% widowed, 10.4% divorced (2000); Foreign born: 0.8% (2000); Ancestry (includes multiple ancestries): 29.3% German, 18.7% Irish, 14.3% English, 9.8% United States or American, 8.4% Italian (2000).
Economy: Employment by occupation: 8.6% management, 20.0% professional, 14.8% services, 25.2% sales, 0.0% farming, 10.0% construction, 21.4% production (2000).
Income: Per capita income: $22,892 (2007); Median household income: $43,000 (2007); Average household income: $57,023 (2007); Percent of households with income of $100,000 or more: 12.7% (2007); Poverty rate: 3.8% (2000).
Education: Percent of population age 25 and over with: High school diploma (including GED) or higher: 78.5% (2007); Bachelor's degree or higher: 17.0% (2007); Master's degree or higher: 6.5% (2007).
Housing: Homeownership rate: 74.1% (2007); Median home value: $122,917 (2007); Median rent: $493 per month (2000); Median age of housing: 50 years (2000).
Transportation: Commute to work: 96.9% car, 0.7% public transportation, 0.0% walk, 1.7% work from home (2000); Travel time to work: 38.3% less than 15 minutes, 33.7% 15 to 30 minutes, 14.5% 30 to 45 minutes, 8.5% 45 to 60 minutes, 5.0% 60 minutes or more (2000)

BRIMFIELD (CDP). Covers a land area of 3.975 square miles and a water area of 0.028 square miles. Located at 41.09° N. Lat.; 81.34° W. Long. Elevation is 1,106 feet.
Population: 3,223 (1990); 3,248 (2000); 3,215 (2007); 3,146 (2012 projected); Race: 96.2% White, 1.6% Black, 0.2% Asian, 0.6% Hispanic of any race (2007); Density: 808.8 persons per square mile (2007); Average household size: 2.77 (2007); Median age: 37.7 (2007); Males per 100 females: 96.0 (2007); Marriage status: 23.2% never married, 57.6% now married, 8.1% widowed, 11.2% divorced (2000); Foreign born: 1.1% (2000); Ancestry (includes multiple ancestries): 24.5% German, 19.6% Irish, 11.1% English, 8.9% Other groups, 8.2% Italian (2000).
Economy: Employment by occupation: 8.7% management, 13.5% professional, 23.3% services, 27.6% sales, 0.0% farming, 7.2% construction, 19.7% production (2000).
Income: Per capita income: $21,230 (2007); Median household income: $45,819 (2007); Average household income: $58,704 (2007); Percent of households with income of $100,000 or more: 10.8% (2007); Poverty rate: 9.1% (2000).
Education: Percent of population age 25 and over with: High school diploma (including GED) or higher: 83.4% (2007); Bachelor's degree or higher: 13.7% (2007); Master's degree or higher: 4.2% (2007).
Housing: Homeownership rate: 84.7% (2007); Median home value: $120,758 (2007); Median rent: $619 per month (2000); Median age of housing: 35 years (2000).
Transportation: Commute to work: 95.6% car, 2.0% public transportation, 0.0% walk, 0.3% work from home (2000); Travel time to work: 26.0% less than 15 minutes, 44.1% 15 to 30 minutes, 20.9% 30 to 45 minutes, 3.5% 45 to 60 minutes, 5.6% 60 minutes or more (2000)

DEERFIELD (unincorporated postal area, zip code 44411). Covers a land area of 20.081 square miles and a water area of 0.561 square miles. Located at 41.02° N. Lat.; 81.05° W. Long. Elevation is 1,076 feet.
Population: 2,705 (2000); Race: 99.7% White, 0.3% Black, 0.0% Asian, 0.0% Hispanic of any race (2000); Density: 134.7 persons per square mile (2000); Age: 28.3% under 18, 9.6% over 64 (2000); Marriage status: 17.6% never married, 66.5% now married, 3.5% widowed, 12.4% divorced (2000); Foreign born: 0.0% (2000); Ancestry (includes multiple ancestries): 16.7% Irish, 16.6% German, 13.5% United States or American, 9.5% English, 5.6% Other groups (2000).
Economy: Employment by occupation: 9.4% management, 8.1% professional, 11.1% services, 22.9% sales, 0.4% farming, 15.8% construction, 32.4% production (2000).
Income: Per capita income: $17,585 (2000); Median household income: $46,920 (2000); Poverty rate: 4.1% (2000).

Education: Percent of population age 25 and over with: High school diploma (including GED) or higher: 81.3% (2000); Bachelor's degree or higher: 9.0% (2000).

School District(s)

Southeast Local (PK-12)
2005-06 Enrollment: 2,181 . . . . (330) 654-5841

Housing: Homeownership rate: 87.2% (2000); Median home value: $111,600 (2000); Median rent: $324 per month (2000); Median age of housing: 28 years (2000).

Transportation: Commute to work: 92.8% car, 0.5% public transportation, 0.9% walk, 3.9% work from home (2000); Travel time to work: 11.3% less than 15 minutes, 28.9% 15 to 30 minutes, 33.4% 30 to 45 minutes, 13.5% 45 to 60 minutes, 12.9% 60 minutes or more (2000)

DIAMOND (unincorporated postal area, zip code 44412). Covers a land area of 24.964 square miles and a water area of 0 square miles. Located at 41.09° N. Lat.; 81.00° W. Long. Elevation is 990 feet.

Population: 2,702 (2000); Race: 99.3% White, 0.0% Black, 0.3% Asian, 0.1% Hispanic of any race (2000); Density: 108.2 persons per square mile (2000); Age: 25.5% under 18, 12.0% over 64 (2000); Marriage status: 20.3% never married, 63.4% now married, 5.7% widowed, 10.5% divorced (2000); Foreign born: 0.5% (2000); Ancestry (includes multiple ancestries): 34.1% German, 14.7% Irish, 8.2% United States or American, 7.7% Italian, 7.7% English (2000).

Economy: Employment by occupation: 10.4% management, 12.5% professional, 13.9% services, 20.8% sales, 0.0% farming, 13.4% construction, 29.1% production (2000).

Income: Per capita income: $19,020 (2000); Median household income: $50,045 (2000); Poverty rate: 6.3% (2000).

Education: Percent of population age 25 and over with: High school diploma (including GED) or higher: 85.5% (2000); Bachelor's degree or higher: 9.9% (2000).

School District(s)

Southeast Local (PK-12)
2005-06 Enrollment: 2,181 . . . . (330) 654-5841

Housing: Homeownership rate: 86.4% (2000); Median home value: $116,400 (2000); Median rent: $433 per month (2000); Median age of housing: 26 years (2000).

Transportation: Commute to work: 97.5% car, 0.5% public transportation, 0.0% walk, 2.0% work from home (2000); Travel time to work: 9.1% less than 15 minutes, 40.3% 15 to 30 minutes, 25.2% 30 to 45 minutes, 12.5% 45 to 60 minutes, 13.0% 60 minutes or more (2000)

GARRETTSVILLE (village). Aka Garrettsville-Hiram. Covers a land area of 2.531 square miles and a water area of 0 square miles. Located at 41.28° N. Lat.; 81.09° W. Long. Elevation is 994 feet.

Population: 2,193 (1990); 2,262 (2000); 2,319 (2007); 2,357 (2012 projected); Race: 98.3% White, 0.2% Black, 0.1% Asian, 0.6% Hispanic of any race (2007); Density: 916.3 persons per square mile (2007); Average household size: 2.37 (2007); Median age: 38.6 (2007); Males per 100 females: 93.3 (2007); Marriage status: 21.1% never married, 63.3% now married, 6.8% widowed, 8.9% divorced (2000); Foreign born: 1.8% (2000); Ancestry (includes multiple ancestries): 31.7% German, 17.2% English, 15.2% Irish, 6.8% United States or American, 6.4% Polish (2000).

Economy: Employment by occupation: 13.4% management, 17.4% professional, 16.4% services, 22.5% sales, 0.4% farming, 9.9% construction, 20.0% production (2000).

Income: Per capita income: $26,218 (2007); Median household income: $56,907 (2007); Average household income: $62,041 (2007); Percent of households with income of $100,000 or more: 14.0% (2007); Poverty rate: 4.4% (2000).

Education: Percent of population age 25 and over with: High school diploma (including GED) or higher: 92.5% (2007); Bachelor's degree or higher: 21.8% (2007); Master's degree or higher: 6.3% (2007).

School District(s)

James A Garfield Local (PK-12)
2005-06 Enrollment: 1,605 . . . . (330) 527-4336

Housing: Homeownership rate: 64.9% (2007); Median home value: $166,260 (2007); Median rent: $430 per month (2000); Median age of housing: 38 years (2000).

Transportation: Commute to work: 92.8% car, 0.0% public transportation, 4.7% walk, 1.4% work from home (2000); Travel time to work: 34.0% less than 15 minutes, 21.8% 15 to 30 minutes, 27.9% 30 to 45 minutes, 10.2% 45 to 60 minutes, 6.0% 60 minutes or more (2000)

Additional Information Contacts

Garrettsville Area Chamber of Commerce. . . . . (330) 527-2411
http://www.garrettsvillehiramarea.com
Village of Garrettsville . . . . (330) 527-4424
http://www.garrettsville.org

HIRAM (village). Covers a land area of 0.908 square miles and a water area of 0 square miles. Located at 41.31° N. Lat.; 81.14° W. Long. Elevation is 1,253 feet.

History: Hiram grew up around Hiram College, founded in 1850 by the Disciples of Christ as the Western Reserve Eclectic Institute. President James A. Garfield was valedictorian of his class when he graduated from the Institute in 1853.

Population: 1,330 (1990); 1,242 (2000); 1,303 (2007); 1,357 (2012 projected); Race: 88.2% White, 7.0% Black, 2.2% Asian, 2.1% Hispanic of any race (2007); Density: 1,434.3 persons per square mile (2007); Average household size: 5.45 (2007); Median age: 21.0 (2007); Males per 100 females: 89.4 (2007); Marriage status: 71.4% never married, 23.6% now married, 1.4% widowed, 3.5% divorced (2000); Foreign born: 3.9% (2000); Ancestry (includes multiple ancestries): 21.9% German, 17.9% Irish, 14.7% English, 13.1% Other groups, 11.3% Italian (2000).

Economy: Employment by occupation: 3.9% management, 19.3% professional, 36.2% services, 26.0% sales, 2.5% farming, 5.0% construction, 7.2% production (2000).

Income: Per capita income: $20,347 (2007); Median household income: $54,464 (2007); Average household income: $61,224 (2007); Percent of households with income of $100,000 or more: 14.6% (2007); Poverty rate: 4.3% (2000).

Education: Percent of population age 25 and over with: High school diploma (including GED) or higher: 94.2% (2007); Bachelor's degree or higher: 44.2% (2007); Master's degree or higher: 23.4% (2007).

School District(s)

Crestwood Local (PK-12)
2005-06 Enrollment: 2,546 . . . . (330) 274-8511

Four-year College(s)

Hiram College (Private, Not-for-profit)
Fall 2007 Enrollment: 1,271. . . . . (330) 569-3211
2007-08 Tuition: In-state $24,885; Out-of-state $24,885

Housing: Homeownership rate: 46.4% (2007); Median home value: $172,500 (2007); Median rent: $414 per month (2000); Median age of housing: 43 years (2000).

Transportation: Commute to work: 59.0% car, 0.0% public transportation, 37.0% walk, 3.3% work from home (2000); Travel time to work: 50.1% less than 15 minutes, 30.5% 15 to 30 minutes, 7.2% 30 to 45 minutes, 7.6% 45 to 60 minutes, 4.6% 60 minutes or more (2000)

KENT (city). Covers a land area of 8.687 square miles and a water area of 0.021 square miles. Located at 41.15° N. Lat.; 81.36° W. Long. Elevation is 1,066 feet.

History: Kent developed around Kent State University, founded in 1910 as a state normal school and accredited as a university in 1935.

Population: 28,879 (1990); 27,906 (2000); 28,170 (2007); 28,270 (2012 projected); Race: 83.3% White, 10.6% Black, 3.0% Asian, 1.5% Hispanic of any race (2007); Density: 3,242.7 persons per square mile (2007); Average household size: 2.85 (2007); Median age: 24.4 (2007); Males per 100 females: 84.1 (2007); Marriage status: 57.7% never married, 30.4% now married, 4.1% widowed, 7.8% divorced (2000); Foreign born: 4.4% (2000); Ancestry (includes multiple ancestries): 26.0% German, 15.2% Other groups, 15.0% Irish, 11.0% English, 10.8% Italian (2000).

Economy: Unemployment rate: 5.6% (6/2008); Total civilian labor force: 17,552 (6/2008); Single-family building permits issued: 49 (2007); Multi-family building permits issued: 4 (2007); Employment by occupation: 9.3% management, 22.9% professional, 20.9% services, 29.0% sales, 0.1% farming, 4.8% construction, 13.1% production (2000).

Income: Per capita income: $17,827 (2007); Median household income: $34,446 (2007); Average household income: $47,363 (2007); Percent of households with income of $100,000 or more: 11.0% (2007); Poverty rate: 25.2% (2000).

Education: Percent of population age 25 and over with: High school diploma (including GED) or higher: 91.7% (2007); Bachelor's degree or higher: 37.7% (2007); Master's degree or higher: 16.3% (2007).

School District(s)

Field Local (PK-12)
2005-06 Enrollment: 2,358 . . . . (330) 673-2659
Kent City (PK-12)
2005-06 Enrollment: 3,654 . . . . (330) 673-6515

Kent Digital Academy (03-12)
2005-06 Enrollment: 20 . . . . (330) 676-7610

Four-year College(s)

Kent State University-Kent Campus (Public)
Fall 2007 Enrollment: 22,819. . . . . (330) 672-3000
2007-08 Tuition: In-state $8,430; Out-of-state $15,862

Vocational/Technical School(s)

Northcoast Medical Training Academy (Private, For-profit)
Fall 2007 Enrollment: 231 . . . . (330) 678-6600
2007-08 Tuition: In-state $9,350; Out-of-state $9,350

Housing: Homeownership rate: 38.2% (2007); Median home value: $134,160 (2007); Median rent: $458 per month (2000); Median age of housing: 35 years (2000).
Safety: Violent crime rate: 27.6 per 10,000 population; Property crime rate: 249.6 per 10,000 population (2007).
Newspapers: Record-Courier - Kent Bureau (Local news)
Transportation: Commute to work: 81.6% car, 2.2% public transportation, 13.1% walk, 2.3% work from home (2000); Travel time to work: 42.7% less than 15 minutes, 33.7% 15 to 30 minutes, 11.7% 30 to 45 minutes, 6.6% 45 to 60 minutes, 5.3% 60 minutes or more (2000)

Additional Information Contacts

Brimfield Area Chamber of Commerce . . . . (330) 554-2236
http://www.brimfieldchamber.com
City of Kent . . . . (330) 678-8007
http://www.kentohio.org
Kent Area Chamber of Commerce. (330) 673-9855
http://www.kentbiz.com

MANTUA (village). Covers a land area of 1.407 square miles and a water area of 0 square miles. Located at 41.28° N. Lat.; 81.22° W. Long. Elevation is 1,148 feet.
Population: 1,178 (1990); 1,046 (2000); 984 (2007); 998 (2012 projected); Race: 98.4% White, 0.5% Black, 0.3% Asian, 0.6% Hispanic of any race (2007); Density: 699.3 persons per square mile (2007); Average household size: 2.30 (2007); Median age: 38.1 (2007); Males per 100 females: 89.2 (2007); Marriage status: 22.6% never married, 55.8% now married, 7.1% widowed, 14.4% divorced (2000); Foreign born: 1.6% (2000); Ancestry (includes multiple ancestries): 29.1% German, 23.1% Irish, 16.8% English, 8.3% Italian, 7.8% Hungarian (2000).
Economy: Employment by occupation: 10.6% management, 15.4% professional, 13.3% services, 29.8% sales, 0.0% farming, 12.2% construction, 18.8% production (2000).
Income: Per capita income: $26,944 (2007); Median household income: $57,019 (2007); Average household income: $62,090 (2007); Percent of households with income of $100,000 or more: 12.9% (2007); Poverty rate: 3.4% (2000).
Education: Percent of population age 25 and over with: High school diploma (including GED) or higher: 89.8% (2007); Bachelor's degree or higher: 18.6% (2007); Master's degree or higher: 5.5% (2007).

School District(s)

Crestwood Local (PK-12)
2005-06 Enrollment: 2,546 . . . . (330) 274-8511

Housing: Homeownership rate: 63.2% (2007); Median home value: $149,167 (2007); Median rent: $454 per month (2000); Median age of housing: 60+ years (2000).
Transportation: Commute to work: 92.1% car, 0.2% public transportation, 4.8% walk, 2.9% work from home (2000); Travel time to work: 30.7% less than 15 minutes, 35.2% 15 to 30 minutes, 23.8% 30 to 45 minutes, 7.8% 45 to 60 minutes, 2.5% 60 minutes or more (2000)

RAVENNA (city). County seat. Covers a land area of 5.352 square miles and a water area of 0.012 square miles. Located at 41.15° N. Lat.; 81.24° W. Long. Elevation is 1,132 feet.
History: Ravenna was settled in 1799 by Benjamin Tappan, Jr., a New Englander and later U.S. senator from Ohio. The town was named for the Italian city.
Population: 12,237 (1990); 11,771 (2000); 11,205 (2007); 10,880 (2012 projected); Race: 92.1% White, 4.7% Black, 0.6% Asian, 1.1% Hispanic of any race (2007); Density: 2,093.5 persons per square mile (2007); Average household size: 2.32 (2007); Median age: 38.0 (2007); Males per 100 females: 90.0 (2007); Marriage status: 24.3% never married, 50.9% now married, 9.0% widowed, 15.8% divorced (2000); Foreign born: 1.0% (2000); Ancestry (includes multiple ancestries): 28.1% German, 17.2% Irish, 10.9% Italian, 10.5% English, 9.7% Other groups (2000).
Economy: Single-family building permits issued: 7 (2007); Multi-family building permits issued: 0 (2007); Employment by occupation: 8.3% management, 15.8% professional, 15.9% services, 25.6% sales, 0.5% farming, 8.2% construction, 25.8% production (2000).
Income: Per capita income: $20,531 (2007); Median household income: $38,754 (2007); Average household income: $46,229 (2007); Percent of households with income of $100,000 or more: 6.8% (2007); Poverty rate: 10.3% (2000).
Taxes: Total city taxes per capita: $666 (2006); City property taxes per capita: $59 (2006).
Education: Percent of population age 25 and over with: High school diploma (including GED) or higher: 80.3% (2007); Bachelor's degree or higher: 14.6% (2007); Master's degree or higher: 3.8% (2007).

School District(s)

Maplewood Career Center (11-12)
2005-06 Enrollment: n/a . . . . (330) 296-2892
Ravenna City (PK-12)
2005-06 Enrollment: 3,241 . . . . (330) 296-9679
Southeast Local (PK-12)
2005-06 Enrollment: 2,181 . . . . (330) 654-5841

Two-year College(s)

Bohecker College (Private, For-profit)
Fall 2007 Enrollment: 482 . . . . (330) 297-7319
2007-08 Tuition: In-state $8,694; Out-of-state $8,694

Housing: Homeownership rate: 54.4% (2007); Median home value: $116,230 (2007); Median rent: $405 per month (2000); Median age of housing: 48 years (2000).
Hospitals: Robinson Memorial Hospital (285 beds)
Newspapers: Real Estate Weekend - Record-Courier; Record-Courier (Local news; Circulation 18,337)
Transportation: Commute to work: 93.8% car, 0.9% public transportation, 3.0% walk, 1.6% work from home (2000); Travel time to work: 36.2% less than 15 minutes, 32.3% 15 to 30 minutes, 19.5% 30 to 45 minutes, 7.9% 45 to 60 minutes, 4.2% 60 minutes or more (2000)
Airports: Portage County (general aviation)

Additional Information Contacts

City of Ravenna . . . . (330) 296-3864
http://www.ci.ravenna.oh.us
Ravenna Area Chamber of Commerce . . . . (330) 296-3886
http://www.ravennaareachamber.com

ROOTSTOWN (unincorporated postal area, zip code 44272). Covers a land area of 20.213 square miles and a water area of 0.049 square miles. Located at 41.09° N. Lat.; 81.19° W. Long. Elevation is 1,126 feet.
Population: 4,047 (2000); Race: 98.5% White, 0.0% Black, 0.2% Asian, 0.2% Hispanic of any race (2000); Density: 200.2 persons per square mile (2000); Age: 26.3% under 18, 13.3% over 64 (2000); Marriage status: 19.5% never married, 64.7% now married, 6.0% widowed, 9.8% divorced (2000); Foreign born: 1.4% (2000); Ancestry (includes multiple ancestries): 33.3% German, 17.2% Irish, 16.8% English, 11.9% United States or American, 7.2% Other groups (2000).
Economy: Employment by occupation: 11.6% management, 13.8% professional, 14.5% services, 26.6% sales, 0.4% farming, 10.2% construction, 22.8% production (2000).
Income: Per capita income: $20,199 (2000); Median household income: $48,373 (2000); Poverty rate: 3.3% (2000).
Education: Percent of population age 25 and over with: High school diploma (including GED) or higher: 88.7% (2000); Bachelor's degree or higher: 13.3% (2000).

School District(s)

Rootstown Local (PK-12)
2005-06 Enrollment: 1,327 . . . . (330) 325-9911

Four-year College(s)

Northeastern Ohio Universities Colleges of Medicine and Pharmacy (Public)
Fall 2007 Enrollment: 533 . . . . (330) 325-2511

Housing: Homeownership rate: 78.7% (2000); Median home value: $125,900 (2000); Median rent: $513 per month (2000); Median age of housing: 32 years (2000).
Transportation: Commute to work: 96.3% car, 0.0% public transportation, 0.6% walk, 3.1% work from home (2000); Travel time to work: 28.5% less than 15 minutes, 35.5% 15 to 30 minutes, 24.8% 30 to 45 minutes, 6.4% 45 to 60 minutes, 4.7% 60 minutes or more (2000)

Additional Information Contacts

Rootstown Area Chamber of Commerce . . . . (330) 325-2207
http://www.rootstownchamber.org

STREETSBORO (city). Covers a land area of 24.017 square miles and a water area of 0.362 square miles. Located at 41.24° N. Lat.; 81.34° W. Long. Elevation is 1,132 feet.
History: Streetsboro was settled in 1822 and named for Titus Street, original owner of the land.
Population: 9,932 (1990); 12,311 (2000); 14,573 (2007); 15,915 (2012 projected); Race: 93.0% White, 2.9% Black, 2.5% Asian, 1.0% Hispanic of any race (2007); Density: 606.8 persons per square mile (2007); Average household size: 2.43 (2007); Median age: 37.0 (2007); Males per 100 females: 96.6 (2007); Marriage status: 22.6% never married, 60.1% now married, 5.3% widowed, 12.0% divorced (2000); Foreign born: 2.3% (2000); Ancestry (includes multiple ancestries): 27.8% German, 15.9% Irish, 11.5% Italian, 9.6% Polish, 9.0% English (2000).
Economy: Single-family building permits issued: 106 (2007); Multi-family building permits issued: 28 (2007); Employment by occupation: 11.9% management, 17.2% professional, 11.5% services, 25.6% sales, 0.1% farming, 8.7% construction, 25.1% production (2000).
Income: Per capita income: $25,574 (2007); Median household income: $54,790 (2007); Average household income: $61,967 (2007); Percent of households with income of $100,000 or more: 13.2% (2007); Poverty rate: 5.3% (2000).
Education: Percent of population age 25 and over with: High school diploma (including GED) or higher: 86.9% (2007); Bachelor's degree or higher: 20.3% (2007); Master's degree or higher: 4.8% (2007).

School District(s)

Streetsboro City (PK-12)
2005-06 Enrollment: 2,101 . . . . (330) 626-4900
Housing: Homeownership rate: 69.3% (2007); Median home value: $145,230 (2007); Median rent: $580 per month (2000); Median age of housing: 20 years (2000).
Transportation: Commute to work: 97.5% car, 0.3% public transportation, 0.9% walk, 1.2% work from home (2000); Travel time to work: 27.2% less than 15 minutes, 38.7% 15 to 30 minutes, 21.6% 30 to 45 minutes, 8.7% 45 to 60 minutes, 3.8% 60 minutes or more (2000)

Additional Information Contacts

City of Streetsboro . . . . (330) 626-4942
http://cityofstreetsboro.com
Streetsboro Area Chamber of Commerce . . . . (330) 626-4769
http://www.streetsborochamber.org
Streetsboro Visitors and Convention Bureau . . . . (330) 422-1770
http://www.streetsborovcb.com

SUGAR BUSH KNOLLS (village). Covers a land area of 0.228 square miles and a water area of 0.014 square miles. Located at 41.20° N. Lat.; 81.34° W. Long. Elevation is 1,096 feet.
Population: 211 (1990); 227 (2000); 301 (2007); 347 (2012 projected); Race: 99.0% White, 0.0% Black, 0.3% Asian, 0.7% Hispanic of any race (2007); Density: 1,320.2 persons per square mile (2007); Average household size: 2.74 (2007); Median age: 47.4 (2007); Males per 100 females: 102.0 (2007); Marriage status: 26.1% never married, 65.9% now married, 3.4% widowed, 4.5% divorced (2000); Foreign born: 6.2% (2000); Ancestry (includes multiple ancestries): 22.3% Irish, 21.3% German, 17.1% Italian, 13.7% English, 4.7% Slovene (2000).
Economy: Employment by occupation: 20.8% management, 31.7% professional, 2.5% services, 32.5% sales, 0.0% farming, 3.3% construction, 9.2% production (2000).
Income: Per capita income: $64,402 (2007); Median household income: $145,000 (2007); Average household income: $176,227 (2007); Percent of households with income of $100,000 or more: 65.5% (2007); Poverty rate: 2.8% (2000).
Education: Percent of population age 25 and over with: High school diploma (including GED) or higher: 97.2% (2007); Bachelor's degree or higher: 64.2% (2007); Master's degree or higher: 35.8% (2007).
Housing: Homeownership rate: 99.1% (2007); Median home value: $289,844 (2007); Median rent: $425 per month (2000); Median age of housing: 24 years (2000).
Transportation: Commute to work: 94.1% car, 0.0% public transportation, 0.0% walk, 3.4% work from home (2000); Travel time to work: 23.7% less than 15 minutes, 48.2% 15 to 30 minutes, 14.0% 30 to 45 minutes, 8.8% 45 to 60 minutes, 5.3% 60 minutes or more (2000)

WINDHAM (village). Covers a land area of 2.124 square miles and a water area of 0 square miles. Located at 41.23° N. Lat.; 81.03° W. Long. Elevation is 971 feet.
Population: 2,943 (1990); 2,806 (2000); 2,698 (2007); 2,676 (2012 projected); Race: 91.1% White, 6.3% Black, 0.1% Asian, 0.4% Hispanic of any race (2007); Density: 1,270.5 persons per square mile (2007); Average household size: 2.84 (2007); Median age: 29.3 (2007); Males per 100 females: 89.9 (2007); Marriage status: 28.3% never married, 48.2% now married, 6.6% widowed, 16.9% divorced (2000); Foreign born: 0.3% (2000); Ancestry (includes multiple ancestries): 21.2% United States or American, 18.8% German, 14.9% Irish, 9.6% Other groups, 9.3% English (2000).
Economy: Employment by occupation: 3.5% management, 8.0% professional, 16.9% services, 19.4% sales, 0.7% farming, 10.3% construction, 41.3% production (2000).
Income: Per capita income: $13,876 (2007); Median household income: $34,664 (2007); Average household income: $39,449 (2007); Percent of households with income of $100,000 or more: 4.3% (2007); Poverty rate: 23.8% (2000).
Education: Percent of population age 25 and over with: High school diploma (including GED) or higher: 75.5% (2007); Bachelor's degree or higher: 3.2% (2007); Master's degree or higher: 0.8% (2007).

School District(s)

Windham Exempted Village (PK-12)
2005-06 Enrollment: 958 . . . . (330) 326-2711
Housing: Homeownership rate: 48.9% (2007); Median home value: $96,404 (2007); Median rent: $319 per month (2000); Median age of housing: 51 years (2000).
Safety: Violent crime rate: 25.8 per 10,000 population; Property crime rate: 416.8 per 10,000 population (2007).
Transportation: Commute to work: 95.7% car, 0.0% public transportation, 1.2% walk, 1.9% work from home (2000); Travel time to work: 19.9% less than 15 minutes, 26.6% 15 to 30 minutes, 32.1% 30 to 45 minutes, 12.4% 45 to 60 minutes, 9.0% 60 minutes or more (2000)

Preble County

Located in western Ohio; bounded on the west by Indiana; drained by the East Fork of the Whitewater River. Covers a land area of 424.80 square miles, a water area of 1.52 square miles, and is located in the Eastern Time Zone. The county was founded in 1808. County seat is Eaton.

Preble County is part of the Dayton, OH Metropolitan Statistical Area. The entire metro area includes: Greene County, OH; Miami County, OH; Montgomery County, OH; Preble County, OH

Weather Station: Eaton Elevation: 1,000 feet

	Jan	Feb	Mar	Apr	May	Jun	Jul	Aug	Sep	Oct	Nov	Dec
High	33	38	49	61	72	81	85	83	77	65	51	39
Low	15	18	28	37	48	57	61	59	52	39	31	22
Precip	2.5	2.2	3.3	4.1	4.6	3.8	3.7	3.4	2.6	2.7	3.4	3.0
Snow	na	na	na	0.5	0.0	0.0	0.0	0.0	0.0	0.0	tr	na

High and Low temperatures in degrees Fahrenheit; Precipitation and Snow in inches

Population: 40,113 (1990); 42,337 (2000); 42,547 (2007); 42,519 (2012 projected); Race: 98.1% White, 0.5% Black, 0.5% Asian, 0.7% Hispanic of any race (2007); Density: 100.2 persons per square mile (2007); Average household size: 2.58 (2007); Median age: 39.8 (2007); Males per 100 females: 98.1 (2007).
Religion: Five largest groups: 7.1% Southern Baptist Convention, 5.6% Catholic Church, 5.2% The United Methodist Church, 4.9% Evangelical Lutheran Church in America, 3.9% Church of the Brethren (2000).
Economy: Unemployment rate: 6.5% (6/2008); Total civilian labor force: 22,090 (6/2008); Leading industries: 34.0% manufacturing; 16.6% retail trade; 11.7% health care and social assistance (2005); Farms: 1,065 totaling 198,048 acres (2002); Companies that employ 500 or more persons: 1 (2006); Companies that employ 100 to 499 persons: 18 (2006); Companies that employ less than 100 persons: 711 (2006); Black-owned businesses: n/a (2002); Hispanic-owned businesses: n/a (2002); Asian-owned businesses: n/a (2002); Women-owned businesses: n/a (2002); Retail sales per capita: $7,847 (2008). Single-family building permits issued: 63 (2007); Multi-family building permits issued: 0 (2007).
Income: Per capita income: $21,283 (2007); Median household income: $47,091 (2007); Average household income: $54,537 (2007); Percent of

households with income of $100,000 or more: 9.6% (2007); Poverty rate: 8.7% (2005); Bankruptcy rate: 4.62% (2007).
Education: Percent of population age 25 and over with: High school diploma (including GED) or higher: 81.7% (2007); Bachelor's degree or higher: 10.1% (2007); Master's degree or higher: 3.5% (2007).
Housing: Homeownership rate: 79.2% (2007); Median home value: $119,240 (2007); Median rent: $368 per month (2000); Median age of housing: 37 years (2000).
Health: Birth rate: 129.6 per 10,000 population (2007); Death rate: 98.5 per 10,000 population (2007); Age-adjusted cancer mortality rate: 196.5 deaths per 100,000 population (2005); Air Quality Index: 72.2% good, 26.6% moderate, 1.1% unhealthy for sensitive individuals, 0.0% unhealthy (percent of days in 2007); Number of physicians: 4.8 per 10,000 population (2005); Hospital beds: 0.0 per 10,000 population (2004); Hospital admissions: 0.0 per 10,000 population (2004).
Elections: 2004 Presidential election results: 65.0% Bush, 34.4% Kerry, 0.0% Nader, 0.3% Badnarik
National and State Parks: Fort Saint Clair State Park; Hueston Woods State Park
Additional Information Contacts
Preble County Government . . . . (937) 456-8143
http://www.prebco.org
Eaton-Preble County Chamber of Commerce . . . . (937) 456-4949
http://preblecountyohio.com

Preble County Communities

CAMDEN (village). Covers a land area of 1.231 square miles and a water area of 0 square miles. Located at 39.63° N. Lat.; 84.64° W. Long. Elevation is 837 feet.
Population: 2,210 (1990); 2,302 (2000); 2,092 (2007); 2,052 (2012 projected); Race: 97.9% White, 0.9% Black, 0.3% Asian, 1.1% Hispanic of any race (2007); Density: 1,699.5 persons per square mile (2007); Average household size: 2.48 (2007); Median age: 34.2 (2007); Males per 100 females: 89.3 (2007); Marriage status: 17.0% never married, 56.9% now married, 9.8% widowed, 16.2% divorced (2000); Foreign born: 0.0% (2000); Ancestry (includes multiple ancestries): 28.5% United States or American, 13.9% German, 6.6% Irish, 6.3% English, 5.8% Other groups (2000).
Economy: Employment by occupation: 8.1% management, 9.8% professional, 18.7% services, 21.6% sales, 0.6% farming, 12.0% construction, 29.1% production (2000).
Income: Per capita income: $16,580 (2007); Median household income: $34,846 (2007); Average household income: $41,194 (2007); Percent of households with income of $100,000 or more: 3.4% (2007); Poverty rate: 9.1% (2000).
Education: Percent of population age 25 and over with: High school diploma (including GED) or higher: 70.1% (2007); Bachelor's degree or higher: 4.8% (2007); Master's degree or higher: 1.4% (2007).
School District(s)
Preble Shawnee Board of Education Offices Local (PK-12)
2005-06 Enrollment: 1,538 . . . . (937) 452-3323
Housing: Homeownership rate: 69.6% (2007); Median home value: $79,250 (2007); Median rent: $354 per month (2000); Median age of housing: 33 years (2000).
Safety: Violent crime rate: 4.4 per 10,000 population; Property crime rate: 66.7 per 10,000 population (2007).
Transportation: Commute to work: 94.5% car, 0.0% public transportation, 1.6% walk, 3.9% work from home (2000); Travel time to work: 20.0% less than 15 minutes, 39.5% 15 to 30 minutes, 20.3% 30 to 45 minutes, 12.7% 45 to 60 minutes, 7.5% 60 minutes or more (2000)

COLLEGE CORNER (village). Covers a land area of 0.266 square miles and a water area of 0 square miles. Located at 39.56° N. Lat.; 84.81° W. Long. Elevation is 981 feet.
Population: 472 (1990); 424 (2000); 448 (2007); 464 (2012 projected); Race: 98.9% White, 0.2% Black, 0.0% Asian, 0.0% Hispanic of any race (2007); Density: 1,682.6 persons per square mile (2007); Average household size: 2.02 (2007); Median age: 34.5 (2007); Males per 100 females: 100.9 (2007); Marriage status: 23.8% never married, 63.0% now married, 5.1% widowed, 8.0% divorced (2000); Foreign born: 0.0% (2000); Ancestry (includes multiple ancestries): 21.7% German, 13.5% United States or American, 13.2% English, 11.8% Irish, 7.1% Other groups (2000).
Economy: Employment by occupation: 7.0% management, 11.4% professional, 23.1% services, 35.4% sales, 0.0% farming, 11.8% construction, 11.4% production (2000).
Income: Per capita income: $21,574 (2007); Median household income: $38,421 (2007); Average household income: $43,536 (2007); Percent of households with income of $100,000 or more: 4.5% (2007); Poverty rate: 8.8% (2000).
Education: Percent of population age 25 and over with: High school diploma (including GED) or higher: 83.9% (2007); Bachelor's degree or higher: 13.2% (2007); Master's degree or higher: 3.9% (2007).
School District(s)
College Corner Local (KG-12)
2005-06 Enrollment: 145 . . . . (765) 732-3183
Housing: Homeownership rate: 54.5% (2007); Median home value: $94,318 (2007); Median rent: $413 per month (2000); Median age of housing: 60+ years (2000).
Transportation: Commute to work: 91.6% car, 0.0% public transportation, 1.4% walk, 5.6% work from home (2000); Travel time to work: 44.1% less than 15 minutes, 31.2% 15 to 30 minutes, 7.9% 30 to 45 minutes, 6.4% 45 to 60 minutes, 10.4% 60 minutes or more (2000)

EATON (city). County seat. Covers a land area of 5.671 square miles and a water area of 0.008 square miles. Located at 39.74° N. Lat.; 84.63° W. Long. Elevation is 1,040 feet.
History: Eaton was founded in 1806 and named for General William Eaton, who served in the Tripolitan War of 1805.
Population: 7,407 (1990); 8,133 (2000); 8,124 (2007); 8,106 (2012 projected); Race: 97.6% White, 0.5% Black, 0.9% Asian, 1.0% Hispanic of any race (2007); Density: 1,432.6 persons per square mile (2007); Average household size: 2.42 (2007); Median age: 39.6 (2007); Males per 100 females: 89.6 (2007); Marriage status: 21.4% never married, 55.0% now married, 9.2% widowed, 14.4% divorced (2000); Foreign born: 1.5% (2000); Ancestry (includes multiple ancestries): 26.0% German, 11.1% United States or American, 9.4% Irish, 8.7% English, 6.9% Other groups (2000).
Economy: Single-family building permits issued: 20 (2007); Multi-family building permits issued: 0 (2007); Employment by occupation: 11.1% management, 13.1% professional, 14.7% services, 20.7% sales, 0.5% farming, 10.1% construction, 29.8% production (2000).
Income: Per capita income: $19,219 (2007); Median household income: $40,716 (2007); Average household income: $45,477 (2007); Percent of households with income of $100,000 or more: 4.9% (2007); Poverty rate: 8.7% (2000).
Education: Percent of population age 25 and over with: High school diploma (including GED) or higher: 79.5% (2007); Bachelor's degree or higher: 10.5% (2007); Master's degree or higher: 3.8% (2007).
School District(s)
Eaton Community Schools City (PK-12)
2005-06 Enrollment: 2,299 . . . . (937) 456-1107
Housing: Homeownership rate: 67.1% (2007); Median home value: $102,125 (2007); Median rent: $367 per month (2000); Median age of housing: 37 years (2000).
Safety: Violent crime rate: 19.5 per 10,000 population; Property crime rate: 403.0 per 10,000 population (2007).
Newspapers: Register Herald (Community news; Circulation 6,800)
Transportation: Commute to work: 94.2% car, 1.1% public transportation, 2.5% walk, 2.2% work from home (2000); Travel time to work: 48.3% less than 15 minutes, 20.6% 15 to 30 minutes, 14.4% 30 to 45 minutes, 8.6% 45 to 60 minutes, 8.0% 60 minutes or more (2000)
Additional Information Contacts
Eaton-Preble County Chamber of Commerce . . . . (937) 456-4949
http://preblecountyohio.com

ELDORADO (village). Covers a land area of 0.229 square miles and a water area of 0 square miles. Located at 39.90° N. Lat.; 84.67° W. Long. Elevation is 1,135 feet.
Population: 549 (1990); 543 (2000); 533 (2007); 529 (2012 projected); Race: 99.6% White, 0.0% Black, 0.0% Asian, 0.2% Hispanic of any race (2007); Density: 2,332.0 persons per square mile (2007); Average household size: 2.49 (2007); Median age: 37.1 (2007); Males per 100 females: 93.8 (2007); Marriage status: 17.7% never married, 64.5% now married, 8.1% widowed, 9.6% divorced (2000); Foreign born: 0.0% (2000); Ancestry (includes multiple ancestries): 28.0% German, 14.1% United States or American, 11.2% Irish, 8.5% English, 6.0% Other groups (2000).

Economy: Employment by occupation: 8.3% management, 9.4% professional, 15.9% services, 24.6% sales, 1.4% farming, 3.3% construction, 37.0% production (2000).
Income: Per capita income: $20,699 (2007); Median household income: $47,273 (2007); Average household income: $51,554 (2007); Percent of households with income of $100,000 or more: 8.4% (2007); Poverty rate: 2.3% (2000).
Education: Percent of population age 25 and over with: High school diploma (including GED) or higher: 85.5% (2007); Bachelor's degree or higher: 7.5% (2007); Master's degree or higher: 2.6% (2007).
Housing: Homeownership rate: 81.8% (2007); Median home value: $91,964 (2007); Median rent: $375 per month (2000); Median age of housing: 47 years (2000).
Transportation: Commute to work: 98.9% car, 0.0% public transportation, 0.4% walk, 0.7% work from home (2000); Travel time to work: 21.5% less than 15 minutes, 42.6% 15 to 30 minutes, 23.0% 30 to 45 minutes, 10.0% 45 to 60 minutes, 3.0% 60 minutes or more (2000)

GRATIS (village). Covers a land area of 0.944 square miles and a water area of 0 square miles. Located at 39.64° N. Lat.; 84.52° W. Long. Elevation is 879 feet.
Population: 998 (1990); 934 (2000); 847 (2007); 830 (2012 projected); Race: 98.9% White, 0.2% Black, 0.0% Asian, 0.8% Hispanic of any race (2007); Density: 897.1 persons per square mile (2007); Average household size: 2.60 (2007); Median age: 36.1 (2007); Males per 100 females: 106.6 (2007); Marriage status: 21.5% never married, 65.8% now married, 5.2% widowed, 7.4% divorced (2000); Foreign born: 0.0% (2000); Ancestry (includes multiple ancestries): 20.0% German, 14.8% United States or American, 9.4% Irish, 6.1% English, 5.8% Other groups (2000).
Economy: Employment by occupation: 9.4% management, 8.5% professional, 16.3% services, 16.7% sales, 0.0% farming, 17.9% construction, 31.2% production (2000).
Income: Per capita income: $18,703 (2007); Median household income: $40,517 (2007); Average household income: $48,405 (2007); Percent of households with income of $100,000 or more: 7.7% (2007); Poverty rate: 11.0% (2000).
Education: Percent of population age 25 and over with: High school diploma (including GED) or higher: 77.4% (2007); Bachelor's degree or higher: 2.8% (2007); Master's degree or higher: 0.7% (2007).
Housing: Homeownership rate: 81.9% (2007); Median home value: $102,712 (2007); Median rent: $393 per month (2000); Median age of housing: 35 years (2000).
Transportation: Commute to work: 97.2% car, 0.0% public transportation, 0.5% walk, 1.9% work from home (2000); Travel time to work: 13.3% less than 15 minutes, 31.4% 15 to 30 minutes, 28.3% 30 to 45 minutes, 21.9% 45 to 60 minutes, 5.0% 60 minutes or more (2000)

LEWISBURG (village). Covers a land area of 1.078 square miles and a water area of 0 square miles. Located at 39.84° N. Lat.; 84.54° W. Long. Elevation is 997 feet.
History: Lewisburg developed as a rural trade center. Tobacco was once a leading crop here.
Population: 1,865 (1990); 1,798 (2000); 1,778 (2007); 1,760 (2012 projected); Race: 97.7% White, 0.2% Black, 1.2% Asian, 0.6% Hispanic of any race (2007); Density: 1,650.1 persons per square mile (2007); Average household size: 2.59 (2007); Median age: 35.4 (2007); Males per 100 females: 94.1 (2007); Marriage status: 22.0% never married, 61.0% now married, 7.6% widowed, 9.4% divorced (2000); Foreign born: 0.5% (2000); Ancestry (includes multiple ancestries): 30.1% German, 12.8% Irish, 10.3% United States or American, 7.7% English, 7.3% Other groups (2000).
Economy: Employment by occupation: 9.4% management, 12.2% professional, 15.9% services, 20.5% sales, 0.2% farming, 16.7% construction, 25.1% production (2000).
Income: Per capita income: $22,008 (2007); Median household income: $48,258 (2007); Average household income: $56,958 (2007); Percent of households with income of $100,000 or more: 10.8% (2007); Poverty rate: 6.5% (2000).
Education: Percent of population age 25 and over with: High school diploma (including GED) or higher: 84.5% (2007); Bachelor's degree or higher: 9.1% (2007); Master's degree or higher: 2.2% (2007).

School District(s)

Tri-County North Local (PK-12)
2005-06 Enrollment: 1,141 . . . . (937) 962-2671

Housing: Homeownership rate: 72.8% (2007); Median home value: $110,947 (2007); Median rent: $386 per month (2000); Median age of housing: 57 years (2000).
Transportation: Commute to work: 91.1% car, 0.0% public transportation, 6.0% walk, 1.9% work from home (2000); Travel time to work: 38.7% less than 15 minutes, 27.3% 15 to 30 minutes, 23.5% 30 to 45 minutes, 6.8% 45 to 60 minutes, 3.6% 60 minutes or more (2000)

NEW PARIS (village). Covers a land area of 0.714 square miles and a water area of 0.016 square miles. Located at 39.85° N. Lat.; 84.79° W. Long. Elevation is 1,037 feet.
Population: 1,801 (1990); 1,623 (2000); 1,586 (2007); 1,564 (2012 projected); Race: 99.1% White, 0.4% Black, 0.1% Asian, 0.1% Hispanic of any race (2007); Density: 2,220.3 persons per square mile (2007); Average household size: 2.29 (2007); Median age: 37.5 (2007); Males per 100 females: 93.4 (2007); Marriage status: 19.9% never married, 55.1% now married, 8.4% widowed, 16.6% divorced (2000); Foreign born: 0.5% (2000); Ancestry (includes multiple ancestries): 23.0% German, 15.5% United States or American, 10.3% English, 9.8% Irish, 7.5% Other groups (2000).
Economy: Employment by occupation: 9.6% management, 8.2% professional, 14.8% services, 24.7% sales, 0.0% farming, 12.0% construction, 30.7% production (2000).
Income: Per capita income: $16,617 (2007); Median household income: $33,962 (2007); Average household income: $38,030 (2007); Percent of households with income of $100,000 or more: 3.0% (2007); Poverty rate: 10.1% (2000).
Education: Percent of population age 25 and over with: High school diploma (including GED) or higher: 75.6% (2007); Bachelor's degree or higher: 3.4% (2007); Master's degree or higher: 1.1% (2007).

School District(s)

National Trail Local (PK-12)
2005-06 Enrollment: 1,151 . . . . (937) 437-3333

Housing: Homeownership rate: 67.8% (2007); Median home value: $66,462 (2007); Median rent: $324 per month (2000); Median age of housing: 44 years (2000).
Transportation: Commute to work: 95.4% car, 0.3% public transportation, 2.6% walk, 0.3% work from home (2000); Travel time to work: 36.1% less than 15 minutes, 46.2% 15 to 30 minutes, 9.9% 30 to 45 minutes, 2.5% 45 to 60 minutes, 5.2% 60 minutes or more (2000)

VERONA (village). Covers a land area of 0.170 square miles and a water area of 0 square miles. Located at 39.90° N. Lat.; 84.48° W. Long. Elevation is 1,024 feet.
Population: 472 (1990); 430 (2000); 400 (2007); 387 (2012 projected); Race: 100.0% White, 0.0% Black, 0.0% Asian, 2.3% Hispanic of any race (2007); Density: 2,352.7 persons per square mile (2007); Average household size: 2.65 (2007); Median age: 34.4 (2007); Males per 100 females: 101.0 (2007); Marriage status: 19.0% never married, 62.7% now married, 5.1% widowed, 13.2% divorced (2000); Foreign born: 0.2% (2000); Ancestry (includes multiple ancestries): 24.7% German, 23.3% United States or American, 12.2% English, 11.1% Irish, 5.3% Dutch (2000).
Economy: Employment by occupation: 3.1% management, 15.5% professional, 10.4% services, 16.6% sales, 0.0% farming, 21.8% construction, 32.6% production (2000).
Income: Per capita income: $19,213 (2007); Median household income: $40,417 (2007); Average household income: $50,894 (2007); Percent of households with income of $100,000 or more: 5.3% (2007); Poverty rate: 8.4% (2000).
Education: Percent of population age 25 and over with: High school diploma (including GED) or higher: 78.9% (2007); Bachelor's degree or higher: 4.1% (2007); Master's degree or higher: 1.2% (2007).
Housing: Homeownership rate: 80.1% (2007); Median home value: $87,941 (2007); Median rent: $323 per month (2000); Median age of housing: 60+ years (2000).
Transportation: Commute to work: 98.4% car, 0.0% public transportation, 0.0% walk, 0.5% work from home (2000); Travel time to work: 17.7% less than 15 minutes, 42.5% 15 to 30 minutes, 24.2% 30 to 45 minutes, 11.3% 45 to 60 minutes, 4.3% 60 minutes or more (2000)

WEST ALEXANDRIA (village). Covers a land area of 0.723 square miles and a water area of 0 square miles. Located at 39.74° N. Lat.; 84.53° W. Long. Elevation is 889 feet.
Population: 1,488 (1990); 1,395 (2000); 1,404 (2007); 1,389 (2012 projected); Race: 98.5% White, 0.9% Black, 0.0% Asian, 0.6% Hispanic of

any race (2007); Density: 1,941.4 persons per square mile (2007); Average household size: 2.36 (2007); Median age: 38.0 (2007); Males per 100 females: 99.4 (2007); Marriage status: 24.1% never married, 53.6% now married, 10.5% widowed, 11.8% divorced (2000); Foreign born: 0.4% (2000); Ancestry (includes multiple ancestries): 33.3% German, 15.1% United States or American, 9.4% Irish, 8.4% Other groups, 6.3% English (2000).
Economy: Employment by occupation: 6.3% management, 14.5% professional, 17.8% services, 26.9% sales, 1.1% farming, 8.8% construction, 24.6% production (2000).
Income: Per capita income: $20,062 (2007); Median household income: $41,339 (2007); Average household income: $47,420 (2007); Percent of households with income of $100,000 or more: 6.6% (2007); Poverty rate: 7.4% (2000).
Education: Percent of population age 25 and over with: High school diploma (including GED) or higher: 83.3% (2007); Bachelor's degree or higher: 13.1% (2007); Master's degree or higher: 6.2% (2007).

School District(s)

Twin Valley Community Local (PK-12)
2005-06 Enrollment: 1,078 . . . . (937) 839-4688
Housing: Homeownership rate: 64.1% (2007); Median home value: $105,665 (2007); Median rent: $404 per month (2000); Median age of housing: 56 years (2000).
Safety: Violent crime rate: 15.1 per 10,000 population; Property crime rate: 233.4 per 10,000 population (2007).
Newspapers: Advertiser (Local news); The New Lebanon Advertiser (Local news; Circulation 10,000); Twin Valley News (Community news; Circulation 1,000)
Transportation: Commute to work: 93.5% car, 0.4% public transportation, 4.4% walk, 1.7% work from home (2000); Travel time to work: 29.8% less than 15 minutes, 27.6% 15 to 30 minutes, 27.3% 30 to 45 minutes, 10.1% 45 to 60 minutes, 5.2% 60 minutes or more (2000)

WEST ELKTON (village). Covers a land area of 0.506 square miles and a water area of 0 square miles. Located at 39.58° N. Lat.; 84.55° W. Long. Elevation is 1,030 feet.
Population: 154 (1990); 194 (2000); 203 (2007); 199 (2012 projected); Race: 98.5% White, 0.0% Black, 0.0% Asian, 0.5% Hispanic of any race (2007); Density: 401.0 persons per square mile (2007); Average household size: 2.64 (2007); Median age: 37.3 (2007); Males per 100 females: 111.5 (2007); Marriage status: 19.5% never married, 57.5% now married, 6.3% widowed, 16.7% divorced (2000); Foreign born: 0.9% (2000); Ancestry (includes multiple ancestries): 23.6% United States or American, 11.2% German, 7.3% Other groups, 5.6% Irish, 5.6% English (2000).
Economy: Employment by occupation: 7.4% management, 11.6% professional, 20.0% services, 28.4% sales, 0.0% farming, 15.8% construction, 16.8% production (2000).
Income: Per capita income: $21,047 (2007); Median household income: $43,214 (2007); Average household income: $55,487 (2007); Percent of households with income of $100,000 or more: 14.3% (2007); Poverty rate: 8.2% (2000).
Education: Percent of population age 25 and over with: High school diploma (including GED) or higher: 78.0% (2007); Bachelor's degree or higher: 3.8% (2007); Master's degree or higher: 2.3% (2007).

School District(s)

Preble Shawnee Board of Education Offices Local (PK-12)
2005-06 Enrollment: 1,538 . . . . (937) 452-3323
Housing: Homeownership rate: 83.1% (2007); Median home value: $111,765 (2007); Median rent: $420 per month (2000); Median age of housing: 60+ years (2000).
Transportation: Commute to work: 94.6% car, 0.0% public transportation, 3.3% walk, 2.2% work from home (2000); Travel time to work: 21.1% less than 15 minutes, 34.4% 15 to 30 minutes, 22.2% 30 to 45 minutes, 10.0% 45 to 60 minutes, 12.2% 60 minutes or more (2000)

WEST MANCHESTER (village). Covers a land area of 0.234 square miles and a water area of 0 square miles. Located at 39.90° N. Lat.; 84.62° W. Long. Elevation is 1,093 feet.
Population: 490 (1990); 433 (2000); 432 (2007); 427 (2012 projected); Race: 99.1% White, 0.0% Black, 0.0% Asian, 1.6% Hispanic of any race (2007); Density: 1,847.4 persons per square mile (2007); Average household size: 2.51 (2007); Median age: 33.6 (2007); Males per 100 females: 99.1 (2007); Marriage status: 21.0% never married, 63.9% now married, 7.2% widowed, 7.8% divorced (2000); Foreign born: 0.0% (2000); Ancestry (includes multiple ancestries): 15.6% Other groups, 14.6% United States or American, 14.3% Irish, 12.8% German, 10.1% English (2000).
Economy: Employment by occupation: 7.3% management, 13.3% professional, 7.8% services, 22.9% sales, 0.0% farming, 13.8% construction, 34.9% production (2000).
Income: Per capita income: $19,670 (2007); Median household income: $35,455 (2007); Average household income: $49,404 (2007); Percent of households with income of $100,000 or more: 8.7% (2007); Poverty rate: 7.7% (2000).
Education: Percent of population age 25 and over with: High school diploma (including GED) or higher: 82.9% (2007); Bachelor's degree or higher: 8.9% (2007); Master's degree or higher: 3.6% (2007).
Housing: Homeownership rate: 76.2% (2007); Median home value: $86,042 (2007); Median rent: $447 per month (2000); Median age of housing: 60+ years (2000).
Transportation: Commute to work: 93.1% car, 0.0% public transportation, 1.8% walk, 1.8% work from home (2000); Travel time to work: 11.7% less than 15 minutes, 54.9% 15 to 30 minutes, 20.7% 30 to 45 minutes, 8.9% 45 to 60 minutes, 3.8% 60 minutes or more (2000)

Putnam County

Located in northwestern Ohio; crossed by the Auglize and Blanchard Rivers. Covers a land area of 483.87 square miles, a water area of 0.36 square miles, and is located in the Eastern Time Zone. The county was founded in 1820. County seat is Ottawa.

Weather Station: Pandora Elevation: 767 feet

	Jan	Feb	Mar	Apr	May	Jun	Jul	Aug	Sep	Oct	Nov	Dec
High	32	36	47	60	72	81	84	82	75	63	49	37
Low	17	20	28	38	49	59	62	60	53	42	33	23
Precip	2.0	1.9	2.7	3.3	3.7	4.0	3.9	3.4	3.0	2.3	2.9	2.7
Snow	9.5	7.1	4.2	1.2	tr	0.0	0.0	0.0	tr	0.1	2.0	6.6

High and Low temperatures in degrees Fahrenheit; Precipitation and Snow in inches

Population: 33,819 (1990); 34,726 (2000); 35,055 (2007); 35,221 (2012 projected); Race: 96.0% White, 0.3% Black, 0.2% Asian, 4.8% Hispanic of any race (2007); Density: 72.4 persons per square mile (2007); Average household size: 2.75 (2007); Median age: 37.3 (2007); Males per 100 females: 100.3 (2007).
Religion: Five largest groups: 62.7% Catholic Church, 7.8% The United Methodist Church, 3.7% Mennonite Church USA, 1.6% Church of the Brethren, 1.0% United Church of Christ (2000).
Economy: Unemployment rate: 6.2% (6/2008); Total civilian labor force: 18,417 (6/2008); Leading industries: 30.8% manufacturing; 13.8% retail trade; 11.2% health care and social assistance (2005); Farms: 1,348 totaling 331,517 acres (2002); Companies that employ 500 or more persons: 0 (2006); Companies that employ 100 to 499 persons: 14 (2006); Companies that employ less than 100 persons: 734 (2006); Black-owned businesses: n/a (2002); Hispanic-owned businesses: n/a (2002); Asian-owned businesses: n/a (2002); Women-owned businesses: 730 (2002); Retail sales per capita: $8,020 (2008). Single-family building permits issued: 78 (2007); Multi-family building permits issued: 0 (2007).
Income: Per capita income: $22,267 (2007); Median household income: $52,980 (2007); Average household income: $60,668 (2007); Percent of households with income of $100,000 or more: 13.0% (2007); Poverty rate: 6.0% (2005); Bankruptcy rate: 1.65% (2007).
Education: Percent of population age 25 and over with: High school diploma (including GED) or higher: 86.1% (2007); Bachelor's degree or higher: 12.9% (2007); Master's degree or higher: 3.9% (2007).
Housing: Homeownership rate: 84.3% (2007); Median home value: $115,611 (2007); Median rent: $340 per month (2000); Median age of housing: 36 years (2000).
Health: Birth rate: 148.1 per 10,000 population (2007); Death rate: 88.1 per 10,000 population (2007); Age-adjusted cancer mortality rate: 240.4 deaths per 100,000 population (2005); Number of physicians: 5.5 per 10,000 population (2005); Hospital beds: 0.0 per 10,000 population (2004); Hospital admissions: 0.0 per 10,000 population (2004).
Elections: 2004 Presidential election results: 76.2% Bush, 23.3% Kerry, 0.0% Nader, 0.2% Badnarik

Additional Information Contacts

Putnam County Government . . . . (419) 523-3656
http://www.putnamcountyohio.com/county.html
Leipsic Area Chamber of Commerce. . . . . (419) 943-2009
http://www.leipsic.com

Ottawa Chamber of Commerce . . . . (419) 523-3141
http://www.ottawaohiochamber.com
Village of Ottawa . . . . (419) 523-5020
http://ottawaohio.us
Village of Ottoville . . . . (419) 453-2426
http://www.villageofottoville.org

Putnam County Communities

BELMORE (village). Covers a land area of 0.426 square miles and a water area of 0 square miles. Located at 41.15° N. Lat.; 83.94° W. Long. Elevation is 735 feet.
Population: 161 (1990); 171 (2000); 172 (2007); 171 (2012 projected); Race: 84.3% White, 0.0% Black, 0.0% Asian, 18.0% Hispanic of any race (2007); Density: 403.7 persons per square mile (2007); Average household size: 3.31 (2007); Median age: 34.1 (2007); Males per 100 females: 84.9 (2007); Marriage status: 34.6% never married, 49.6% now married, 9.4% widowed, 6.3% divorced (2000); Foreign born: 0.0% (2000); Ancestry (includes multiple ancestries): 52.0% Other groups, 14.3% German, 12.6% Irish, 4.6% United States or American, 2.9% Pennsylvania German (2000).
Economy: Employment by occupation: 0.0% management, 2.1% professional, 14.9% services, 6.4% sales, 0.0% farming, 6.4% construction, 70.2% production (2000).
Income: Per capita income: $15,756 (2007); Median household income: $52,222 (2007); Average household income: $52,115 (2007); Percent of households with income of $100,000 or more: 7.7% (2007); Poverty rate: 34.3% (2000).
Education: Percent of population age 25 and over with: High school diploma (including GED) or higher: 68.3% (2007); Bachelor's degree or higher: 0.0% (2007); Master's degree or higher: 0.0% (2007).
Housing: Homeownership rate: 80.8% (2007); Median home value: $41,000 (2007); Median rent: $150 per month (2000); Median age of housing: 60+ years (2000).
Transportation: Commute to work: 95.3% car, 0.0% public transportation, 4.7% walk, 0.0% work from home (2000); Travel time to work: 27.9% less than 15 minutes, 41.9% 15 to 30 minutes, 30.2% 30 to 45 minutes, 0.0% 45 to 60 minutes, 0.0% 60 minutes or more (2000)

CLOVERDALE (village). Covers a land area of 0.600 square miles and a water area of 0 square miles. Located at 41.02° N. Lat.; 84.30° W. Long. Elevation is 719 feet.
Population: 270 (1990); 201 (2000); 202 (2007); 204 (2012 projected); Race: 99.0% White, 0.0% Black, 0.0% Asian, 1.0% Hispanic of any race (2007); Density: 336.6 persons per square mile (2007); Average household size: 2.93 (2007); Median age: 53.7 (2007); Males per 100 females: 96.1 (2007); Marriage status: 31.6% never married, 50.6% now married, 4.0% widowed, 13.8% divorced (2000); Foreign born: 1.9% (2000); Ancestry (includes multiple ancestries): 30.4% German, 10.1% English, 9.2% United States or American, 5.8% Other groups, 3.4% Dutch (2000).
Economy: Single-family building permits issued: 0 (2007); Multi-family building permits issued: 0 (2007); Employment by occupation: 0.0% management, 13.0% professional, 20.8% services, 22.1% sales, 0.0% farming, 0.0% construction, 44.2% production (2000).
Income: Per capita income: $21,232 (2007); Median household income: $40,938 (2007); Average household income: $45,833 (2007); Percent of households with income of $100,000 or more: 1.4% (2007); Poverty rate: 19.9% (2000).
Education: Percent of population age 25 and over with: High school diploma (including GED) or higher: 70.5% (2007); Bachelor's degree or higher: 11.5% (2007); Master's degree or higher: 3.2% (2007).
Housing: Homeownership rate: 91.3% (2007); Median home value: $75,909 (2007); Median rent: $n/a per month (2000); Median age of housing: 42 years (2000).
Transportation: Commute to work: 100.0% car, 0.0% public transportation, 0.0% walk, 0.0% work from home (2000); Travel time to work: 29.3% less than 15 minutes, 21.3% 15 to 30 minutes, 41.3% 30 to 45 minutes, 5.3% 45 to 60 minutes, 2.7% 60 minutes or more (2000)

COLUMBUS GROVE (village). Covers a land area of 1.026 square miles and a water area of 0 square miles. Located at 40.91° N. Lat.; 84.06° W. Long. Elevation is 774 feet.
Population: 2,394 (1990); 2,200 (2000); 2,142 (2007); 2,099 (2012 projected); Race: 97.1% White, 0.0% Black, 0.0% Asian, 4.2% Hispanic of any race (2007); Density: 2,088.3 persons per square mile (2007); Average household size: 2.42 (2007); Median age: 36.7 (2007); Males per 100 females: 93.0 (2007); Marriage status: 23.7% never married, 60.3% now married, 6.8% widowed, 9.2% divorced (2000); Foreign born: 0.5% (2000); Ancestry (includes multiple ancestries): 45.2% German, 12.9% United States or American, 8.1% Irish, 5.8% English, 5.5% Other groups (2000).
Economy: Single-family building permits issued: 1 (2007); Multi-family building permits issued: 0 (2007); Employment by occupation: 8.6% management, 12.3% professional, 17.5% services, 19.5% sales, 2.0% farming, 10.2% construction, 30.0% production (2000).
Income: Per capita income: $21,879 (2007); Median household income: $47,868 (2007); Average household income: $53,015 (2007); Percent of households with income of $100,000 or more: 8.4% (2007); Poverty rate: 5.3% (2000).
Education: Percent of population age 25 and over with: High school diploma (including GED) or higher: 90.3% (2007); Bachelor's degree or higher: 9.2% (2007); Master's degree or higher: 1.4% (2007).

School District(s)

Columbus Grove Local (PK-12)
2005-06 Enrollment: 915 . . . . (419) 659-2639
Housing: Homeownership rate: 77.8% (2007); Median home value: $96,711 (2007); Median rent: $320 per month (2000); Median age of housing: 47 years (2000).
Newspapers: Pandora Times (Community news; Circulation 365); Putnam Cty Vidette/Pandora Times (Community news; Circulation 365)
Transportation: Commute to work: 95.4% car, 0.0% public transportation, 2.7% walk, 1.3% work from home (2000); Travel time to work: 29.8% less than 15 minutes, 48.7% 15 to 30 minutes, 16.0% 30 to 45 minutes, 2.2% 45 to 60 minutes, 3.2% 60 minutes or more (2000)

CONTINENTAL (village). Covers a land area of 0.709 square miles and a water area of 0.009 square miles. Located at 41.09° N. Lat.; 84.26° W. Long. Elevation is 722 feet.
Population: 1,239 (1990); 1,188 (2000); 1,158 (2007); 1,158 (2012 projected); Race: 98.4% White, 0.1% Black, 0.0% Asian, 2.4% Hispanic of any race (2007); Density: 1,632.8 persons per square mile (2007); Average household size: 2.38 (2007); Median age: 37.5 (2007); Males per 100 females: 92.7 (2007); Marriage status: 23.3% never married, 57.8% now married, 7.4% widowed, 11.5% divorced (2000); Foreign born: 0.5% (2000); Ancestry (includes multiple ancestries): 29.6% German, 16.2% United States or American, 7.5% Irish, 6.2% English, 5.3% Other groups (2000).
Economy: Single-family building permits issued: 3 (2007); Multi-family building permits issued: 0 (2007); Employment by occupation: 3.7% management, 11.6% professional, 16.6% services, 16.8% sales, 0.7% farming, 11.6% construction, 38.8% production (2000).
Income: Per capita income: $17,530 (2007); Median household income: $36,813 (2007); Average household income: $41,684 (2007); Percent of households with income of $100,000 or more: 2.7% (2007); Poverty rate: 9.3% (2000).
Education: Percent of population age 25 and over with: High school diploma (including GED) or higher: 79.4% (2007); Bachelor's degree or higher: 6.3% (2007); Master's degree or higher: 3.0% (2007).

School District(s)

Continental Local (PK-12)
2005-06 Enrollment: 625 . . . . (419) 596-3671
Housing: Homeownership rate: 76.2% (2007); Median home value: $77,258 (2007); Median rent: $302 per month (2000); Median age of housing: 39 years (2000).
Newspapers: Continental News-Review (Regional news; Circulation 1,000)
Transportation: Commute to work: 96.8% car, 0.2% public transportation, 0.7% walk, 0.6% work from home (2000); Travel time to work: 31.6% less than 15 minutes, 45.8% 15 to 30 minutes, 13.0% 30 to 45 minutes, 5.3% 45 to 60 minutes, 4.3% 60 minutes or more (2000)

DUPONT (village). Covers a land area of 0.931 square miles and a water area of 0 square miles. Located at 41.05° N. Lat.; 84.30° W. Long. Elevation is 725 feet.
Population: 279 (1990); 268 (2000); 270 (2007); 269 (2012 projected); Race: 95.2% White, 4.1% Black, 0.0% Asian, 4.1% Hispanic of any race (2007); Density: 290.0 persons per square mile (2007); Average household size: 2.78 (2007); Median age: 33.9 (2007); Males per 100 females: 98.5 (2007); Marriage status: 27.6% never married, 57.5% now married, 5.0% widowed, 9.9% divorced (2000); Foreign born: 0.0% (2000); Ancestry (includes multiple ancestries): 25.9% German, 8.5% Irish, 7.3% United States or American, 5.4% English, 3.1% French (except Basque) (2000).

Economy: Employment by occupation: 7.7% management, 9.9% professional, 18.7% services, 6.6% sales, 2.2% farming, 8.8% construction, 46.2% production (2000).
Income: Per capita income: $16,148 (2007); Median household income: $39,063 (2007); Average household income: $44,948 (2007); Percent of households with income of $100,000 or more: 6.2% (2007); Poverty rate: 7.7% (2000).
Education: Percent of population age 25 and over with: High school diploma (including GED) or higher: 74.8% (2007); Bachelor's degree or higher: 5.5% (2007); Master's degree or higher: 1.8% (2007).
Housing: Homeownership rate: 82.5% (2007); Median home value: $64,000 (2007); Median rent: $265 per month (2000); Median age of housing: 39 years (2000).
Transportation: Commute to work: 98.9% car, 0.0% public transportation, 1.1% walk, 0.0% work from home (2000); Travel time to work: 29.7% less than 15 minutes, 46.2% 15 to 30 minutes, 19.8% 30 to 45 minutes, 4.4% 45 to 60 minutes, 0.0% 60 minutes or more (2000)

FORT JENNINGS (village). Covers a land area of 0.507 square miles and a water area of 0 square miles. Located at 40.90° N. Lat.; 84.29° W. Long. Elevation is 745 feet.
Population: 436 (1990); 432 (2000); 473 (2007); 483 (2012 projected); Race: 99.4% White, 0.6% Black, 0.0% Asian, 0.0% Hispanic of any race (2007); Density: 933.1 persons per square mile (2007); Average household size: 2.44 (2007); Median age: 39.8 (2007); Males per 100 females: 96.3 (2007); Marriage status: 18.2% never married, 66.6% now married, 8.9% widowed, 6.3% divorced (2000); Foreign born: 0.0% (2000); Ancestry (includes multiple ancestries): 75.2% German, 6.0% Irish, 5.0% United States or American, 3.2% French (except Basque), 1.3% Other groups (2000).
Economy: Single-family building permits issued: 0 (2007); Multi-family building permits issued: 0 (2007); Employment by occupation: 7.5% management, 20.5% professional, 10.5% services, 23.4% sales, 0.8% farming, 11.3% construction, 25.9% production (2000).
Income: Per capita income: $25,291 (2007); Median household income: $51,176 (2007); Average household income: $61,662 (2007); Percent of households with income of $100,000 or more: 12.4% (2007); Poverty rate: 1.5% (2000).
Education: Percent of population age 25 and over with: High school diploma (including GED) or higher: 91.0% (2007); Bachelor's degree or higher: 12.7% (2007); Master's degree or higher: 3.0% (2007).

School District(s)

Jennings Local (PK-12)
2005-06 Enrollment: 449 . . . . (419) 286-2238
Housing: Homeownership rate: 90.2% (2007); Median home value: $95,286 (2007); Median rent: $404 per month (2000); Median age of housing: 37 years (2000).
Transportation: Commute to work: 97.0% car, 0.0% public transportation, 2.1% walk, 0.8% work from home (2000); Travel time to work: 33.8% less than 15 minutes, 31.2% 15 to 30 minutes, 25.6% 30 to 45 minutes, 6.0% 45 to 60 minutes, 3.4% 60 minutes or more (2000)

GILBOA (village). Covers a land area of 0.149 square miles and a water area of 0 square miles. Located at 41.01° N. Lat.; 83.92° W. Long. Elevation is 748 feet.
Population: 208 (1990); 170 (2000); 170 (2007); 167 (2012 projected); Race: 98.8% White, 0.0% Black, 0.0% Asian, 0.6% Hispanic of any race (2007); Density: 1,139.3 persons per square mile (2007); Average household size: 2.30 (2007); Median age: 39.0 (2007); Males per 100 females: 107.3 (2007); Marriage status: 28.0% never married, 53.0% now married, 9.1% widowed, 9.8% divorced (2000); Foreign born: 0.0% (2000); Ancestry (includes multiple ancestries): 46.2% German, 11.0% United States or American, 8.1% Irish, 8.1% Swiss, 7.5% English (2000).
Economy: Employment by occupation: 2.4% management, 10.8% professional, 8.4% services, 20.5% sales, 0.0% farming, 8.4% construction, 49.4% production (2000).
Income: Per capita income: $17,941 (2007); Median household income: $35,625 (2007); Average household income: $41,216 (2007); Percent of households with income of $100,000 or more: 1.4% (2007); Poverty rate: 5.2% (2000).
Education: Percent of population age 25 and over with: High school diploma (including GED) or higher: 74.6% (2007); Bachelor's degree or higher: 7.9% (2007); Master's degree or higher: 2.6% (2007).

School District(s)

Pandora-Gilboa Local (PK-12)
2005-06 Enrollment: 609 . . . . (419) 384-3227
Housing: Homeownership rate: 77.0% (2007); Median home value: $65,833 (2007); Median rent: $363 per month (2000); Median age of housing: 60+ years (2000).
Transportation: Commute to work: 96.4% car, 0.0% public transportation, 0.0% walk, 0.0% work from home (2000); Travel time to work: 47.0% less than 15 minutes, 36.1% 15 to 30 minutes, 9.6% 30 to 45 minutes, 4.8% 45 to 60 minutes, 2.4% 60 minutes or more (2000)

GLANDORF (village). Covers a land area of 1.533 square miles and a water area of 0 square miles. Located at 41.03° N. Lat.; 84.07° W. Long. Elevation is 728 feet.
Population: 829 (1990); 919 (2000); 790 (2007); 796 (2012 projected); Race: 98.5% White, 0.0% Black, 0.0% Asian, 1.6% Hispanic of any race (2007); Density: 515.3 persons per square mile (2007); Average household size: 3.12 (2007); Median age: 41.7 (2007); Males per 100 females: 92.2 (2007); Marriage status: 18.8% never married, 70.5% now married, 7.4% widowed, 3.3% divorced (2000); Foreign born: 0.3% (2000); Ancestry (includes multiple ancestries): 77.5% German, 5.2% Irish, 4.6% United States or American, 3.4% English, 2.5% French (except Basque) (2000).
Economy: Single-family building permits issued: 2 (2007); Multi-family building permits issued: 0 (2007); Employment by occupation: 10.5% management, 14.9% professional, 13.3% services, 24.9% sales, 0.0% farming, 12.3% construction, 24.1% production (2000).
Income: Per capita income: $24,780 (2007); Median household income: $63,827 (2007); Average household income: $72,273 (2007); Percent of households with income of $100,000 or more: 18.6% (2007); Poverty rate: 0.4% (2000).
Education: Percent of population age 25 and over with: High school diploma (including GED) or higher: 83.0% (2007); Bachelor's degree or higher: 17.0% (2007); Master's degree or higher: 5.0% (2007).

School District(s)

Ottawa-Glandorf Local (PK-12)
2005-06 Enrollment: 1,685 . . . . (419) 523-5261
Housing: Homeownership rate: 92.5% (2007); Median home value: $127,273 (2007); Median rent: $320 per month (2000); Median age of housing: 41 years (2000).
Transportation: Commute to work: 96.0% car, 0.7% public transportation, 2.4% walk, 0.9% work from home (2000); Travel time to work: 51.5% less than 15 minutes, 15.2% 15 to 30 minutes, 25.5% 30 to 45 minutes, 4.3% 45 to 60 minutes, 3.6% 60 minutes or more (2000)

KALIDA (village). Covers a land area of 1.115 square miles and a water area of 0 square miles. Located at 40.98° N. Lat.; 84.19° W. Long. Elevation is 725 feet.
Population: 1,044 (1990); 1,031 (2000); 1,114 (2007); 1,139 (2012 projected); Race: 98.9% White, 0.0% Black, 0.0% Asian, 1.3% Hispanic of any race (2007); Density: 998.8 persons per square mile (2007); Average household size: 2.58 (2007); Median age: 36.7 (2007); Males per 100 females: 104.4 (2007); Marriage status: 22.9% never married, 64.3% now married, 8.7% widowed, 4.1% divorced (2000); Foreign born: 0.4% (2000); Ancestry (includes multiple ancestries): 72.7% German, 7.7% United States or American, 5.1% Irish, 3.2% Other groups, 2.6% English (2000).
Economy: Single-family building permits issued: 6 (2007); Multi-family building permits issued: 0 (2007); Employment by occupation: 12.6% management, 19.8% professional, 11.4% services, 25.3% sales, 0.0% farming, 10.3% construction, 20.6% production (2000).
Income: Per capita income: $26,497 (2007); Median household income: $59,884 (2007); Average household income: $68,486 (2007); Percent of households with income of $100,000 or more: 19.0% (2007); Poverty rate: 4.4% (2000).
Education: Percent of population age 25 and over with: High school diploma (including GED) or higher: 86.8% (2007); Bachelor's degree or higher: 18.6% (2007); Master's degree or higher: 6.0% (2007).

School District(s)

Kalida Local (PK-12)
2005-06 Enrollment: 715 . . . . (419) 532-3534
Housing: Homeownership rate: 79.6% (2007); Median home value: $121,217 (2007); Median rent: $433 per month (2000); Median age of housing: 31 years (2000).
Transportation: Commute to work: 95.5% car, 0.4% public transportation, 3.2% walk, 0.4% work from home (2000); Travel time to work: 41.4% less

than 15 minutes, 26.3% 15 to 30 minutes, 22.9% 30 to 45 minutes, 4.3% 45 to 60 minutes, 5.0% 60 minutes or more (2000)

LEIPSIC (village). Covers a land area of 3.225 square miles and a water area of 0 square miles. Located at 41.10° N. Lat.; 83.98° W. Long. Elevation is 764 feet.

Population: 2,296 (1990); 2,236 (2000); 2,222 (2007); 2,220 (2012 projected); Race: 79.1% White, 0.6% Black, 0.4% Asian, 23.9% Hispanic of any race (2007); Density: 689.1 persons per square mile (2007); Average household size: 2.65 (2007); Median age: 39.7 (2007); Males per 100 females: 92.0 (2007); Marriage status: 23.6% never married, 54.6% now married, 14.4% widowed, 7.4% divorced (2000); Foreign born: 1.9% (2000); Ancestry (includes multiple ancestries): 32.1% German, 25.2% Other groups, 13.8% United States or American, 4.6% English, 4.3% French (except Basque) (2000).

Economy: Single-family building permits issued: 5 (2007); Multi-family building permits issued: 0 (2007); Employment by occupation: 3.0% management, 9.2% professional, 22.3% services, 20.2% sales, 1.4% farming, 7.4% construction, 36.5% production (2000).

Income: Per capita income: $19,120 (2007); Median household income: $40,714 (2007); Average household income: $49,042 (2007); Percent of households with income of $100,000 or more: 6.8% (2007); Poverty rate: 14.7% (2000).

Education: Percent of population age 25 and over with: High school diploma (including GED) or higher: 80.3% (2007); Bachelor's degree or higher: 7.9% (2007); Master's degree or higher: 3.2% (2007).

School District(s)

Leipsic Local (PK-12)
2005-06 Enrollment: 701 . . . . (419) 943-2165

Housing: Homeownership rate: 74.2% (2007); Median home value: $90,333 (2007); Median rent: $377 per month (2000); Median age of housing: 53 years (2000).

Newspapers: Leipsic Messenger (Community news; Circulation 1,500)

Transportation: Commute to work: 92.5% car, 0.4% public transportation, 5.6% walk, 0.5% work from home (2000); Travel time to work: 41.5% less than 15 minutes, 31.2% 15 to 30 minutes, 17.7% 30 to 45 minutes, 7.3% 45 to 60 minutes, 2.3% 60 minutes or more (2000)

Additional Information Contacts

Leipsic Area Chamber of Commerce. . . . . (419) 943-2009
http://www.leipsic.com

MILLER CITY (village). Aka Millers City. Covers a land area of 0.118 square miles and a water area of 0 square miles. Located at 41.10° N. Lat.; 84.13° W. Long. Elevation is 725 feet.

Population: 186 (1990); 136 (2000); 149 (2007); 156 (2012 projected); Race: 95.3% White, 0.0% Black, 0.0% Asian, 9.4% Hispanic of any race (2007); Density: 1,262.5 persons per square mile (2007); Average household size: 2.57 (2007); Median age: 34.8 (2007); Males per 100 females: 91.0 (2007); Marriage status: 28.4% never married, 53.4% now married, 9.1% widowed, 9.1% divorced (2000); Foreign born: 0.0% (2000); Ancestry (includes multiple ancestries): 52.4% German, 19.0% French (except Basque), 8.6% United States or American, 4.8% Irish (2000).

Economy: Single-family building permits issued: 0 (2007); Multi-family building permits issued: 0 (2007); Employment by occupation: 0.0% management, 8.5% professional, 8.5% services, 23.4% sales, 0.0% farming, 6.4% construction, 53.2% production (2000).

Income: Per capita income: $25,317 (2007); Median household income: $50,000 (2007); Average household income: $63,793 (2007); Percent of households with income of $100,000 or more: 13.8% (2007); Poverty rate: 1.0% (2000).

Education: Percent of population age 25 and over with: High school diploma (including GED) or higher: 90.3% (2007); Bachelor's degree or higher: 20.4% (2007); Master's degree or higher: 8.6% (2007).

School District(s)

Miller Local (PK-12)
2005-06 Enrollment: 488 . . . . (419) 876-3172

Housing: Homeownership rate: 93.1% (2007); Median home value: $91,429 (2007); Median rent: $425 per month (2000); Median age of housing: 42 years (2000).

Transportation: Commute to work: 93.6% car, 0.0% public transportation, 6.4% walk, 0.0% work from home (2000); Travel time to work: 19.1% less than 15 minutes, 34.0% 15 to 30 minutes, 31.9% 30 to 45 minutes, 12.8% 45 to 60 minutes, 2.1% 60 minutes or more (2000)

OTTAWA (village). County seat. Covers a land area of 3.876 square miles and a water area of 0.028 square miles. Located at 41.02° N. Lat.; 84.04° W. Long. Elevation is 728 feet.

History: Ottawa was established in 1833, and named for the Ottawa Indians. The Ohio Sugar Company, a beet-sugar refinery, was built here.

Population: 4,521 (1990); 4,367 (2000); 4,336 (2007); 4,283 (2012 projected); Race: 93.8% White, 0.3% Black, 0.4% Asian, 7.8% Hispanic of any race (2007); Density: 1,118.6 persons per square mile (2007); Average household size: 2.41 (2007); Median age: 39.7 (2007); Males per 100 females: 97.7 (2007); Marriage status: 24.4% never married, 56.1% now married, 8.3% widowed, 11.2% divorced (2000); Foreign born: 1.3% (2000); Ancestry (includes multiple ancestries): 62.1% German, 10.7% Other groups, 6.8% Irish, 5.7% United States or American, 3.5% English (2000).

Economy: Single-family building permits issued: 7 (2007); Multi-family building permits issued: 0 (2007); Employment by occupation: 13.2% management, 17.1% professional, 11.4% services, 19.0% sales, 0.5% farming, 7.6% construction, 31.2% production (2000).

Income: Per capita income: $24,856 (2007); Median household income: $42,601 (2007); Average household income: $59,441 (2007); Percent of households with income of $100,000 or more: 13.6% (2007); Poverty rate: 5.3% (2000).

Education: Percent of population age 25 and over with: High school diploma (including GED) or higher: 85.3% (2007); Bachelor's degree or higher: 19.5% (2007); Master's degree or higher: 6.9% (2007).

School District(s)

Ottawa-Glandorf Local (PK-12)
2005-06 Enrollment: 1,685 . . . . (419) 523-5261

Putnam
2005-06 Enrollment: n/a . . . . (419) 523-5951

Housing: Homeownership rate: 72.1% (2007); Median home value: $106,025 (2007); Median rent: $331 per month (2000); Median age of housing: 36 years (2000).

Newspapers: Putnam County Sentinel (Community news; Circulation 8,000)

Transportation: Commute to work: 91.8% car, 1.0% public transportation, 4.2% walk, 1.7% work from home (2000); Travel time to work: 55.7% less than 15 minutes, 17.3% 15 to 30 minutes, 21.5% 30 to 45 minutes, 2.8% 45 to 60 minutes, 2.7% 60 minutes or more (2000)

Additional Information Contacts

Ottawa Chamber of Commerce . . . . (419) 523-3141
http://www.ottawaohiochamber.com

Village of Ottawa . . . . (419) 523-5020
http://ottawaohio.us

OTTOVILLE (village). Covers a land area of 0.697 square miles and a water area of 0 square miles. Located at 40.93° N. Lat.; 84.33° W. Long. Elevation is 738 feet.

Population: 934 (1990); 873 (2000); 740 (2007); 747 (2012 projected); Race: 98.9% White, 0.0% Black, 0.3% Asian, 0.8% Hispanic of any race (2007); Density: 1,061.4 persons per square mile (2007); Average household size: 2.42 (2007); Median age: 40.2 (2007); Males per 100 females: 93.2 (2007); Marriage status: 19.6% never married, 65.1% now married, 8.4% widowed, 6.9% divorced (2000); Foreign born: 0.0% (2000); Ancestry (includes multiple ancestries): 77.9% German, 4.5% Irish, 3.8% United States or American, 2.2% Polish, 1.7% Other groups (2000).

Economy: Single-family building permits issued: 4 (2007); Multi-family building permits issued: 0 (2007); Employment by occupation: 11.4% management, 14.3% professional, 13.8% services, 27.2% sales, 0.4% farming, 9.6% construction, 23.2% production (2000).

Income: Per capita income: $23,828 (2007); Median household income: $52,000 (2007); Average household income: $57,623 (2007); Percent of households with income of $100,000 or more: 11.4% (2007); Poverty rate: 2.1% (2000).

Education: Percent of population age 25 and over with: High school diploma (including GED) or higher: 91.5% (2007); Bachelor's degree or higher: 12.9% (2007); Master's degree or higher: 4.6% (2007).

School District(s)

Ottoville Local (PK-12)
2005-06 Enrollment: 586 . . . . (419) 453-3356

Housing: Homeownership rate: 82.0% (2007); Median home value: $111,750 (2007); Median rent: $350 per month (2000); Median age of housing: 42 years (2000).

Transportation: Commute to work: 94.7% car, 0.0% public transportation, 3.1% walk, 1.1% work from home (2000); Travel time to work: 44.8% less than 15 minutes, 25.8% 15 to 30 minutes, 23.1% 30 to 45 minutes, 4.7% 45 to 60 minutes, 1.6% 60 minutes or more (2000)
Additional Information Contacts
Village of Ottoville . . . . (419) 453-2426
http://www.villageofottoville.org

PANDORA (village). Covers a land area of 0.813 square miles and a water area of 0 square miles. Located at 40.94° N. Lat.; 83.96° W. Long. Elevation is 774 feet.
Population: 1,078 (1990); 1,188 (2000); 1,155 (2007); 1,139 (2012 projected); Race: 98.5% White, 0.5% Black, 0.0% Asian, 1.4% Hispanic of any race (2007); Density: 1,421.4 persons per square mile (2007); Average household size: 2.60 (2007); Median age: 39.3 (2007); Males per 100 females: 93.5 (2007); Marriage status: 15.1% never married, 71.2% now married, 7.2% widowed, 6.5% divorced (2000); Foreign born: 0.5% (2000); Ancestry (includes multiple ancestries): 37.3% German, 18.6% Swiss, 11.7% United States or American, 7.2% Irish, 7.0% English (2000).
Economy: Single-family building permits issued: 1 (2007); Multi-family building permits issued: 0 (2007); Employment by occupation: 12.2% management, 16.2% professional, 12.2% services, 22.1% sales, 0.4% farming, 7.4% construction, 29.7% production (2000).
Income: Per capita income: $20,695 (2007); Median household income: $47,778 (2007); Average household income: $52,123 (2007); Percent of households with income of $100,000 or more: 6.5% (2007); Poverty rate: 4.0% (2000).
Education: Percent of population age 25 and over with: High school diploma (including GED) or higher: 88.0% (2007); Bachelor's degree or higher: 26.7% (2007); Master's degree or higher: 7.2% (2007).

School District(s)

Pandora-Gilboa Local (PK-12)
2005-06 Enrollment: 609 . . . . (419) 384-3227
Housing: Homeownership rate: 83.1% (2007); Median home value: $107,572 (2007); Median rent: $342 per month (2000); Median age of housing: 47 years (2000).
Transportation: Commute to work: 92.3% car, 1.7% public transportation, 1.9% walk, 3.7% work from home (2000); Travel time to work: 35.6% less than 15 minutes, 39.5% 15 to 30 minutes, 19.8% 30 to 45 minutes, 2.9% 45 to 60 minutes, 2.1% 60 minutes or more (2000)

WEST LEIPSIC (village). Covers a land area of 0.239 square miles and a water area of 0 square miles. Located at 41.10° N. Lat.; 84.00° W. Long. Elevation is 771 feet.
Population: 234 (1990); 271 (2000); 283 (2007); 289 (2012 projected); Race: 72.4% White, 0.0% Black, 0.0% Asian, 35.3% Hispanic of any race (2007); Density: 1,186.0 persons per square mile (2007); Average household size: 2.70 (2007); Median age: 34.8 (2007); Males per 100 females: 124.6 (2007); Marriage status: 23.8% never married, 62.7% now married, 5.4% widowed, 8.1% divorced (2000); Foreign born: 1.9% (2000); Ancestry (includes multiple ancestries): 38.4% German, 35.3% Other groups, 6.2% United States or American, 5.0% French (except Basque), 5.0% Irish (2000).
Economy: Employment by occupation: 2.7% management, 11.6% professional, 9.8% services, 11.6% sales, 0.0% farming, 4.5% construction, 59.8% production (2000).
Income: Per capita income: $22,818 (2007); Median household income: $47,500 (2007); Average household income: $61,500 (2007); Percent of households with income of $100,000 or more: 8.6% (2007); Poverty rate: 8.5% (2000).
Education: Percent of population age 25 and over with: High school diploma (including GED) or higher: 70.3% (2007); Bachelor's degree or higher: 2.9% (2007); Master's degree or higher: 0.0% (2007).
Housing: Homeownership rate: 84.8% (2007); Median home value: $67,857 (2007); Median rent: $288 per month (2000); Median age of housing: 60+ years (2000).
Transportation: Commute to work: 89.7% car, 0.0% public transportation, 2.8% walk, 4.7% work from home (2000); Travel time to work: 41.2% less than 15 minutes, 41.2% 15 to 30 minutes, 3.9% 30 to 45 minutes, 9.8% 45 to 60 minutes, 3.9% 60 minutes or more (2000)

Richland County

Located in north central Ohio; drained by forks of the Mohican River. Covers a land area of 496.88 square miles, a water area of 3.45 square miles, and is located in the Eastern Time Zone. The county was founded in 1813. County seat is Mansfield.

Richland County is part of the Mansfield, OH Metropolitan Statistical Area. The entire metro area includes: Richland County, OH

Weather Station: Mansfield 5 W Elevation: 1,348 feet

	Jan	Feb	Mar	Apr	May	Jun	Jul	Aug	Sep	Oct	Nov	Dec
High	32	36	47	59	70	78	82	80	74	62	49	37
Low	15	18	27	36	47	56	60	58	52	41	32	22
Precip	2.1	1.7	2.7	3.5	4.1	4.2	3.9	3.6	3.3	2.5	2.9	2.6
Snow	na	na	na	0.3	tr	0.0	0.0	0.0	0.0	tr	1.0	na

High and Low temperatures in degrees Fahrenheit; Precipitation and Snow in inches

Weather Station: Mansfield Lahm Municipal Airport Elevation: 1,292 feet

	Jan	Feb	Mar	Apr	May	Jun	Jul	Aug	Sep	Oct	Nov	Dec
High	32	36	46	59	69	78	82	80	73	62	49	38
Low	18	20	28	38	49	58	62	61	54	43	34	24
Precip	2.6	2.1	3.3	4.2	4.4	4.4	4.3	4.5	3.5	2.7	3.8	3.2
Snow	12.9	9.8	6.9	2.0	tr	tr	0.0	0.0	tr	0.6	2.5	8.6

High and Low temperatures in degrees Fahrenheit; Precipitation and Snow in inches

Population: 126,137 (1990); 128,852 (2000); 127,793 (2007); 126,692 (2012 projected); Race: 87.9% White, 9.4% Black, 0.6% Asian, 1.1% Hispanic of any race (2007); Density: 257.2 persons per square mile (2007); Average household size: 2.54 (2007); Median age: 39.4 (2007); Males per 100 females: 101.7 (2007).
Religion: Five largest groups: 9.3% Catholic Church, 5.1% Evangelical Lutheran Church in America, 4.6% The United Methodist Church, 1.7% Assemblies of God, 1.6% Independent, Non-Charismatic Churches (2000).
Economy: Unemployment rate: 7.1% (6/2008); Total civilian labor force: 62,565 (6/2008); Leading industries: 24.5% manufacturing; 15.3% health care and social assistance; 15.2% retail trade (2005); Farms: 1,086 totaling 158,653 acres (2002); Companies that employ 500 or more persons: 7 (2006); Companies that employ 100 to 499 persons: 77 (2006); Companies that employ less than 100 persons: 2,875 (2006); Black-owned businesses: 292 (2002); Hispanic-owned businesses: n/a (2002); Asian-owned businesses: 194 (2002); Women-owned businesses: 2,304 (2002); Retail sales per capita: $15,482 (2008). Single-family building permits issued: 128 (2007); Multi-family building permits issued: 74 (2007).
Income: Per capita income: $21,923 (2007); Median household income: $42,985 (2007); Average household income: $54,191 (2007); Percent of households with income of $100,000 or more: 11.2% (2007); Poverty rate: 12.1% (2005); Bankruptcy rate: 4.43% (2007).
Taxes: Total county taxes per capita: $292 (2006); County property taxes per capita: $162 (2006).
Education: Percent of population age 25 and over with: High school diploma (including GED) or higher: 80.4% (2007); Bachelor's degree or higher: 12.8% (2007); Master's degree or higher: 4.0% (2007).
Housing: Homeownership rate: 72.0% (2007); Median home value: $110,802 (2007); Median rent: $353 per month (2000); Median age of housing: 41 years (2000).
Health: Birth rate: 125.7 per 10,000 population (2007); Death rate: 97.9 per 10,000 population (2007); Age-adjusted cancer mortality rate: 187.5 deaths per 100,000 population (2005); Number of physicians: 18.6 per 10,000 population (2005); Hospital beds: 28.6 per 10,000 population (2004); Hospital admissions: 1,428.9 per 10,000 population (2004).
Elections: 2004 Presidential election results: 59.6% Bush, 39.8% Kerry, 0.0% Nader, 0.2% Badnarik
National and State Parks: Malabar Farm State Park
Additional Information Contacts
Richland County Government . . . . (419) 774-5599
http://www.richlandcountyoh.us
City of Mansfield . . . . (419) 755-9626
http://www.ci.mansfield.oh.us
City of Ontario . . . . (419) 529-3818
http://www.ontarioohio.org
Mansfield-Richland Area Chamber of Commerce . . . . (419) 522-3211
http://www.mrachamber.com
Shelby Chamber of Commerce . . . . (419) 342-2426
http://www.shelbyoh.com
Village of Bellville . . . . (419) 886-2245
http://www.bellvilleohio.net/villageadmin.htm
Village of Lexington . . . . (419) 884-0765
http://www.lexingtonohio.us

Richland County Communities

BELLVILLE (village). Covers a land area of 2.879 square miles and a water area of 0 square miles. Located at 40.62° N. Lat.; 82.51° W. Long. Elevation is 1,138 feet.

History: Bellville grew as a farm community surrounded by apple and peach orchards. Twice, the town's hopes for fortune were dashed. In 1853 Dr. James C. Lee, a former California miner, found gold here, but the amount turned out to be very small. In the 1890's it was thought that a spring might be of therapeutic value and a sanitarium was built, but failed to become a popular health spa.

Population: 1,744 (1990); 1,773 (2000); 1,820 (2007); 1,838 (2012 projected); Race: 98.6% White, 0.3% Black, 0.2% Asian, 1.3% Hispanic of any race (2007); Density: 632.3 persons per square mile (2007); Average household size: 2.28 (2007); Median age: 39.4 (2007); Males per 100 females: 90.0 (2007); Marriage status: 18.5% never married, 59.2% now married, 9.2% widowed, 13.1% divorced (2000); Foreign born: 0.7% (2000); Ancestry (includes multiple ancestries): 31.9% German, 14.8% Irish, 12.0% United States or American, 11.0% English, 5.8% Other groups (2000).

Economy: Employment by occupation: 9.9% management, 15.6% professional, 18.2% services, 27.9% sales, 0.7% farming, 9.7% construction, 18.0% production (2000).

Income: Per capita income: $22,214 (2007); Median household income: $39,484 (2007); Average household income: $50,728 (2007); Percent of households with income of $100,000 or more: 9.7% (2007); Poverty rate: 9.3% (2000).

Education: Percent of population age 25 and over with: High school diploma (including GED) or higher: 85.3% (2007); Bachelor's degree or higher: 11.3% (2007); Master's degree or higher: 2.2% (2007).

School District(s)

Clear Fork Valley Local (KG-12)
2005-06 Enrollment: 1,844 . . . . (419) 886-3855

Housing: Homeownership rate: 69.0% (2007); Median home value: $118,370 (2007); Median rent: $317 per month (2000); Median age of housing: 49 years (2000).

Safety: Violent crime rate: 11.6 per 10,000 population; Property crime rate: 317.7 per 10,000 population (2007).

Newspapers: Bellville Star & Tri-Forks Press (Community news; Circulation 1,900)

Transportation: Commute to work: 92.2% car, 0.0% public transportation, 3.7% walk, 3.2% work from home (2000); Travel time to work: 33.0% less than 15 minutes, 44.5% 15 to 30 minutes, 13.4% 30 to 45 minutes, 3.8% 45 to 60 minutes, 5.2% 60 minutes or more (2000)

Additional Information Contacts

Village of Bellville . . . . (419) 886-2245
http://www.bellvilleohio.net/villageadmin.htm

BUTLER (village). Covers a land area of 1.075 square miles and a water area of 0 square miles. Located at 40.58° N. Lat.; 82.42° W. Long. Elevation is 1,070 feet.

Population: 982 (1990); 921 (2000); 986 (2007); 1,024 (2012 projected); Race: 99.6% White, 0.0% Black, 0.1% Asian, 0.9% Hispanic of any race (2007); Density: 917.0 persons per square mile (2007); Average household size: 2.53 (2007); Median age: 36.8 (2007); Males per 100 females: 100.4 (2007); Marriage status: 18.8% never married, 64.9% now married, 6.2% widowed, 10.1% divorced (2000); Foreign born: 0.5% (2000); Ancestry (includes multiple ancestries): 30.7% German, 12.7% Irish, 10.1% United States or American, 10.0% English, 4.7% Other groups (2000).

Economy: Employment by occupation: 10.2% management, 10.4% professional, 16.2% services, 22.6% sales, 0.0% farming, 12.6% construction, 28.1% production (2000).

Income: Per capita income: $22,295 (2007); Median household income: $46,897 (2007); Average household income: $56,365 (2007); Percent of households with income of $100,000 or more: 11.8% (2007); Poverty rate: 4.9% (2000).

Education: Percent of population age 25 and over with: High school diploma (including GED) or higher: 82.8% (2007); Bachelor's degree or higher: 11.8% (2007); Master's degree or higher: 3.1% (2007).

School District(s)

Clear Fork Valley Local (KG-12)
2005-06 Enrollment: 1,844 . . . . (419) 886-3855

Housing: Homeownership rate: 79.7% (2007); Median home value: $109,245 (2007); Median rent: $346 per month (2000); Median age of housing: 60+ years (2000).

Transportation: Commute to work: 96.1% car, 0.0% public transportation, 2.8% walk, 1.1% work from home (2000); Travel time to work: 29.2% less than 15 minutes, 29.4% 15 to 30 minutes, 29.4% 30 to 45 minutes, 6.1% 45 to 60 minutes, 5.9% 60 minutes or more (2000)

LEXINGTON (village). Covers a land area of 3.671 square miles and a water area of 0 square miles. Located at 40.68° N. Lat.; 82.58° W. Long. Elevation is 1,217 feet.

Population: 4,228 (1990); 4,165 (2000); 4,164 (2007); 4,198 (2012 projected); Race: 96.5% White, 1.6% Black, 0.9% Asian, 1.1% Hispanic of any race (2007); Density: 1,134.4 persons per square mile (2007); Average household size: 2.47 (2007); Median age: 38.8 (2007); Males per 100 females: 93.5 (2007); Marriage status: 18.3% never married, 64.1% now married, 6.7% widowed, 10.8% divorced (2000); Foreign born: 1.4% (2000); Ancestry (includes multiple ancestries): 29.6% German, 15.6% English, 11.7% Irish, 7.4% United States or American, 6.6% Other groups (2000).

Economy: Employment by occupation: 17.9% management, 19.7% professional, 13.2% services, 27.0% sales, 0.0% farming, 4.9% construction, 17.2% production (2000).

Income: Per capita income: $28,599 (2007); Median household income: $55,259 (2007); Average household income: $70,591 (2007); Percent of households with income of $100,000 or more: 20.6% (2007); Poverty rate: 2.5% (2000).

Education: Percent of population age 25 and over with: High school diploma (including GED) or higher: 91.5% (2007); Bachelor's degree or higher: 26.0% (2007); Master's degree or higher: 6.8% (2007).

School District(s)

Lexington Local (PK-12)
2005-06 Enrollment: 2,784 . . . . (419) 884-2132

Housing: Homeownership rate: 73.1% (2007); Median home value: $141,621 (2007); Median rent: $385 per month (2000); Median age of housing: 31 years (2000).

Safety: Violent crime rate: 2.4 per 10,000 population; Property crime rate: 214.8 per 10,000 population (2007).

Transportation: Commute to work: 93.3% car, 0.0% public transportation, 3.2% walk, 3.4% work from home (2000); Travel time to work: 33.6% less than 15 minutes, 43.7% 15 to 30 minutes, 10.2% 30 to 45 minutes, 3.8% 45 to 60 minutes, 8.6% 60 minutes or more (2000)

Additional Information Contacts

Village of Lexington . . . . (419) 884-0765
http://www.lexingtonohio.us

LUCAS (village). Covers a land area of 0.598 square miles and a water area of 0 square miles. Located at 40.70° N. Lat.; 82.42° W. Long. Elevation is 1,093 feet.

Population: 761 (1990); 620 (2000); 615 (2007); 613 (2012 projected); Race: 97.1% White, 1.0% Black, 0.0% Asian, 0.5% Hispanic of any race (2007); Density: 1,028.7 persons per square mile (2007); Average household size: 2.43 (2007); Median age: 37.7 (2007); Males per 100 females: 95.2 (2007); Marriage status: 13.2% never married, 65.6% now married, 10.4% widowed, 10.8% divorced (2000); Foreign born: 1.7% (2000); Ancestry (includes multiple ancestries): 26.7% German, 20.7% United States or American, 10.9% Irish, 9.3% Other groups, 6.0% English (2000).

Economy: Employment by occupation: 7.4% management, 18.5% professional, 14.8% services, 19.2% sales, 2.6% farming, 11.8% construction, 25.8% production (2000).

Income: Per capita income: $21,154 (2007); Median household income: $45,568 (2007); Average household income: $51,423 (2007); Percent of households with income of $100,000 or more: 9.5% (2007); Poverty rate: 6.2% (2000).

Education: Percent of population age 25 and over with: High school diploma (including GED) or higher: 80.8% (2007); Bachelor's degree or higher: 3.4% (2007); Master's degree or higher: 2.0% (2007).

School District(s)

Lucas Local (PK-12)
2005-06 Enrollment: 586 . . . . (419) 892-2338

Housing: Homeownership rate: 70.0% (2007); Median home value: $89,500 (2007); Median rent: $409 per month (2000); Median age of housing: 49 years (2000).

Transportation: Commute to work: 96.2% car, 1.1% public transportation, 0.0% walk, 2.7% work from home (2000); Travel time to work: 25.0% less than 15 minutes, 63.3% 15 to 30 minutes, 6.6% 30 to 45 minutes, 2.3% 45 to 60 minutes, 2.7% 60 minutes or more (2000)

MANSFIELD (city). County seat. Covers a land area of 29.905 square miles and a water area of 0 square miles. Located at 40.75° N. Lat.; 82.52° W. Long. Elevation is 1,243 feet.

History: Mansfield was named for Jared Mansfield, U.S. Surveyor General, who directed the townsite to be laid out in 1808. Mansfield grew as the surrounding lands were cleared of timber and put under cultivation. During the War of 1812, Mansfield was threatened by British allies, but John Chapman (better known as Johnny Appleseed) made the 30-mile trip to bring troops from Mount Vernon, and Mansfield was saved. Mansfield's growth was slow, spurred only by the arrival of the railroad in 1846, until after the Civil War. By 1900 it was the home of the Ohio Brass Company, the Empire Sheet and Tin Plate Company, Tappan Stove Company, and a plant of the Westinghouse Electric and Manufacturing Company.

Population: 50,489 (1990); 49,346 (2000); 47,851 (2007); 46,730 (2012 projected); Race: 76.7% White, 19.3% Black, 0.7% Asian, 1.4% Hispanic of any race (2007); Density: 1,600.1 persons per square mile (2007); Average household size: 2.38 (2007); Median age: 38.1 (2007); Males per 100 females: 99.9 (2007); Marriage status: 27.2% never married, 49.2% now married, 9.1% widowed, 14.5% divorced (2000); Foreign born: 2.2% (2000); Ancestry (includes multiple ancestries): 22.4% German, 21.7% Other groups, 10.0% Irish, 9.0% United States or American, 7.9% English (2000).

Economy: Unemployment rate: 7.4% (6/2008); Total civilian labor force: 23,185 (6/2008); Single-family building permits issued: 5 (2007); Multi-family building permits issued: 44 (2007); Employment by occupation: 7.9% management, 15.3% professional, 19.1% services, 23.7% sales, 0.0% farming, 8.2% construction, 25.8% production (2000).

Income: Per capita income: $19,843 (2007); Median household income: $33,636 (2007); Average household income: $45,263 (2007); Percent of households with income of $100,000 or more: 7.7% (2007); Poverty rate: 16.3% (2000).

Taxes: Total city taxes per capita: $563 (2006); City property taxes per capita: $66 (2006).

Education: Percent of population age 25 and over with: High school diploma (including GED) or higher: 78.2% (2007); Bachelor's degree or higher: 13.7% (2007); Master's degree or higher: 4.7% (2007).

School District(s)

Interactive Media & Construction Inc. (09-12)
2005-06 Enrollment: 80 . . . . (419) 525-6409
Madison Local (PK-12)
2005-06 Enrollment: 3,399 . . . . (419) 589-2600
Mansfield City (PK-12)
2005-06 Enrollment: 5,424 . . . . (419) 525-6400
Mansfield Community (KG-06)
2005-06 Enrollment: 112 . . . . (419) 522-4578
Mansfield Enhancement Academy (09-12)
2005-06 Enrollment: 106 . . . . (419) 525-6305
Ontario Local (PK-12)
2005-06 Enrollment: 1,820 . . . . (419) 747-4311

Four-year College(s)

MedCentral College of Nursing (Private, Not-for-profit)
Fall 2007 Enrollment: 416 . . . . (419) 520-2600
2007-08 Tuition: In-state $10,545; Out-of-state $10,545
Ohio State University-Mansfield Campus (Public)
Fall 2007 Enrollment: 1,553 . . . . (419) 755-4011
2007-08 Tuition: In-state $5,664; Out-of-state $18,273

Two-year College(s)

North Central State College (Public)
Fall 2007 Enrollment: 3,148 . . . . (419) 755-4800
2007-08 Tuition: In-state $2,907; Out-of-state $5,814

Vocational/Technical School(s)

Madison Local Schools-Madison Adult Education (Public)
Fall 2007 Enrollment: 87 . . . . (419) 589-6363
2007-08 Tuition: $8,625

Housing: Homeownership rate: 58.1% (2007); Median home value: $88,608 (2007); Median rent: $347 per month (2000); Median age of housing: 47 years (2000).

Hospitals: MedCentral Health System/Mansfield Hospital (461 beds)

Safety: Violent crime rate: 32.6 per 10,000 population; Property crime rate: 577.2 per 10,000 population (2007).

Newspapers: Mansfield News-Journal (Local news; Circulation 35,230); Tribune Courier (Local news; Circulation 2,565)

Transportation: Commute to work: 94.1% car, 1.3% public transportation, 2.4% walk, 1.6% work from home (2000); Travel time to work: 47.3% less than 15 minutes, 39.5% 15 to 30 minutes, 6.4% 30 to 45 minutes, 2.3% 45 to 60 minutes, 4.6% 60 minutes or more (2000)

Airports: Mansfield Lahm Regional (general aviation)

Additional Information Contacts

City of Mansfield . . . . (419) 755-9626
http://www.ci.mansfield.oh.us
Mansfield-Richland Area Chamber of Commerce . . . . (419) 522-3211
http://www.mrachamber.com

ONTARIO (city). Covers a land area of 10.918 square miles and a water area of 0 square miles. Located at 40.76° N. Lat.; 82.60° W. Long. Elevation is 1,358 feet.

Population: 4,148 (1990); 5,303 (2000); 5,471 (2007); 5,563 (2012 projected); Race: 90.4% White, 4.9% Black, 2.3% Asian, 1.0% Hispanic of any race (2007); Density: 501.1 persons per square mile (2007); Average household size: 2.37 (2007); Median age: 41.8 (2007); Males per 100 females: 95.5 (2007); Marriage status: 16.6% never married, 64.9% now married, 9.1% widowed, 9.4% divorced (2000); Foreign born: 4.8% (2000); Ancestry (includes multiple ancestries): 33.7% German, 12.2% English, 12.1% Irish, 7.8% Other groups, 6.4% United States or American (2000).

Economy: Employment by occupation: 12.0% management, 16.7% professional, 14.5% services, 32.6% sales, 0.4% farming, 7.6% construction, 16.2% production (2000).

Income: Per capita income: $26,372 (2007); Median household income: $52,451 (2007); Average household income: $62,568 (2007); Percent of households with income of $100,000 or more: 14.3% (2007); Poverty rate: 6.2% (2000).

Education: Percent of population age 25 and over with: High school diploma (including GED) or higher: 84.6% (2007); Bachelor's degree or higher: 18.5% (2007); Master's degree or higher: 7.0% (2007).

Housing: Homeownership rate: 72.1% (2007); Median home value: $136,765 (2007); Median rent: $423 per month (2000); Median age of housing: 29 years (2000).

Safety: Violent crime rate: 17.0 per 10,000 population; Property crime rate: 1,060.2 per 10,000 population (2007).

Transportation: Commute to work: 93.2% car, 1.3% public transportation, 0.0% walk, 5.6% work from home (2000); Travel time to work: 54.5% less than 15 minutes, 31.7% 15 to 30 minutes, 7.1% 30 to 45 minutes, 2.9% 45 to 60 minutes, 3.7% 60 minutes or more (2000)

Additional Information Contacts

City of Ontario . . . . (419) 529-3818
http://www.ontarioohio.org

PLYMOUTH (village). Covers a land area of 2.219 square miles and a water area of 0.024 square miles. Located at 40.99° N. Lat.; 82.66° W. Long. Elevation is 1,017 feet.

Population: 1,951 (1990); 1,852 (2000); 1,970 (2007); 2,029 (2012 projected); Race: 98.2% White, 0.1% Black, 0.0% Asian, 1.2% Hispanic of any race (2007); Density: 887.6 persons per square mile (2007); Average household size: 2.70 (2007); Median age: 33.6 (2007); Males per 100 females: 94.3 (2007); Marriage status: 20.7% never married, 62.5% now married, 5.9% widowed, 10.9% divorced (2000); Foreign born: 0.3% (2000); Ancestry (includes multiple ancestries): 26.7% United States or American, 19.2% German, 10.0% Irish, 8.4% English, 8.3% Other groups (2000).

Economy: Single-family building permits issued: 0 (2007); Multi-family building permits issued: 0 (2007); Employment by occupation: 8.0% management, 11.6% professional, 13.5% services, 19.3% sales, 0.5% farming, 6.0% construction, 41.2% production (2000).

Income: Per capita income: $17,684 (2007); Median household income: $41,864 (2007); Average household income: $47,723 (2007); Percent of households with income of $100,000 or more: 6.7% (2007); Poverty rate: 13.3% (2000).

Education: Percent of population age 25 and over with: High school diploma (including GED) or higher: 75.5% (2007); Bachelor's degree or higher: 6.7% (2007); Master's degree or higher: 2.2% (2007).

School District(s)

Plymouth-Shiloh Local (PK-12)
2005-06 Enrollment: 999 . . . . (419) 687-4733

Housing: Homeownership rate: 66.8% (2007); Median home value: $94,390 (2007); Median rent: $365 per month (2000); Median age of housing: 52 years (2000).

Transportation: Commute to work: 95.5% car, 0.0% public transportation, 1.8% walk, 1.5% work from home (2000); Travel time to work: 39.8% less

than 15 minutes, 35.7% 15 to 30 minutes, 18.8% 30 to 45 minutes, 3.1% 45 to 60 minutes, 2.6% 60 minutes or more (2000)

SHELBY (city). Covers a land area of 5.038 square miles and a water area of 0.068 square miles. Located at 40.88° N. Lat.; 82.66° W. Long. Elevation is 1,102 feet.

Population: 9,672 (1990); 9,821 (2000); 9,555 (2007); 9,313 (2012 projected); Race: 98.1% White, 0.2% Black, 0.4% Asian, 1.4% Hispanic of any race (2007); Density: 1,896.5 persons per square mile (2007); Average household size: 2.34 (2007); Median age: 38.4 (2007); Males per 100 females: 92.1 (2007); Marriage status: 22.0% never married, 57.7% now married, 8.9% widowed, 11.4% divorced (2000); Foreign born: 1.1% (2000); Ancestry (includes multiple ancestries): 33.7% German, 14.0% Irish, 10.1% English, 10.1% United States or American, 7.7% Other groups (2000).

Economy: Single-family building permits issued: 4 (2007); Multi-family building permits issued: 0 (2007); Employment by occupation: 8.4% management, 10.8% professional, 16.3% services, 26.2% sales, 0.0% farming, 7.4% construction, 31.0% production (2000).

Income: Per capita income: $21,190 (2007); Median household income: $41,535 (2007); Average household income: $49,134 (2007); Percent of households with income of $100,000 or more: 7.9% (2007); Poverty rate: 10.2% (2000).

Education: Percent of population age 25 and over with: High school diploma (including GED) or higher: 81.6% (2007); Bachelor's degree or higher: 9.2% (2007); Master's degree or higher: 2.6% (2007).

School District(s)

Pioneer Career & Technology (PK-12)
2005-06 Enrollment: n/a . . . . (419) 347-7926

Shelby City (PK-12)
2005-06 Enrollment: 2,251 . . . . (419) 342-3520

Vocational/Technical School(s)

Pioneer Career and Technology Center (Public)
Fall 2007 Enrollment: 38 . . . . (419) 347-7744
2007-08 Tuition: $3,750

Housing: Homeownership rate: 65.5% (2007); Median home value: $99,529 (2007); Median rent: $318 per month (2000); Median age of housing: 46 years (2000).

Hospitals: MedCentral Health System/Shelby Hospital (68 beds)

Safety: Violent crime rate: 13.8 per 10,000 population; Property crime rate: 618.6 per 10,000 population (2007).

Newspapers: Daily Globe (Regional news; Circulation 4,058)

Transportation: Commute to work: 94.0% car, 0.6% public transportation, 2.2% walk, 2.4% work from home (2000); Travel time to work: 45.0% less than 15 minutes, 38.3% 15 to 30 minutes, 9.9% 30 to 45 minutes, 1.8% 45 to 60 minutes, 5.0% 60 minutes or more (2000)

Additional Information Contacts

Shelby Chamber of Commerce . . . . (419) 342-2426
http://www.shelbyoh.com

SHILOH (village). Covers a land area of 0.912 square miles and a water area of 0 square miles. Located at 40.97° N. Lat.; 82.60° W. Long. Elevation is 1,079 feet.

Population: 778 (1990); 721 (2000); 691 (2007); 685 (2012 projected); Race: 98.7% White, 0.0% Black, 0.0% Asian, 0.7% Hispanic of any race (2007); Density: 758.0 persons per square mile (2007); Average household size: 2.92 (2007); Median age: 32.5 (2007); Males per 100 females: 94.6 (2007); Marriage status: 22.5% never married, 60.7% now married, 6.6% widowed, 10.1% divorced (2000); Foreign born: 0.0% (2000); Ancestry (includes multiple ancestries): 20.2% United States or American, 15.8% German, 13.7% English, 6.2% Irish, 6.2% Other groups (2000).

Economy: Employment by occupation: 6.1% management, 8.4% professional, 14.8% services, 19.4% sales, 0.4% farming, 1.1% construction, 49.8% production (2000).

Income: Per capita income: $13,817 (2007); Median household income: $34,643 (2007); Average household income: $40,285 (2007); Percent of households with income of $100,000 or more: 2.5% (2007); Poverty rate: 17.3% (2000).

Education: Percent of population age 25 and over with: High school diploma (including GED) or higher: 64.5% (2007); Bachelor's degree or higher: 5.7% (2007); Master's degree or higher: 0.5% (2007).

School District(s)

Plymouth-Shiloh Local (PK-12)
2005-06 Enrollment: 999 . . . . (419) 687-4733

Housing: Homeownership rate: 78.1% (2007); Median home value: $64,524 (2007); Median rent: $333 per month (2000); Median age of housing: 60+ years (2000).

Transportation: Commute to work: 90.5% car, 0.0% public transportation, 4.4% walk, 4.4% work from home (2000); Travel time to work: 15.4% less than 15 minutes, 52.3% 15 to 30 minutes, 25.7% 30 to 45 minutes, 3.7% 45 to 60 minutes, 2.9% 60 minutes or more (2000)

Ross County

Located in southern Ohio; crossed by the Scioto River and several creeks. Covers a land area of 688.41 square miles, a water area of 4.55 square miles, and is located in the Eastern Time Zone. The county was founded in 1798. County seat is Chillicothe.

Ross County is part of the Chillicothe, OH Micropolitan Statistical Area. The entire metro area includes: Ross County, OH

Weather Station: Chillicothe Mound City Elevation: 649 feet

	Jan	Feb	Mar	Apr	May	Jun	Jul	Aug	Sep	Oct	Nov	Dec
High	38	42	53	64	74	82	86	85	79	67	54	43
Low	19	22	30	39	49	58	63	61	53	41	33	25
Precip	2.5	2.3	3.4	3.5	4.4	3.5	3.9	3.6	2.8	2.6	2.9	2.6
Snow	7.1	4.6	3.1	0.4	tr	0.0	0.0	0.0	0.0	0.1	0.4	2.2

High and Low temperatures in degrees Fahrenheit; Precipitation and Snow in inches

Population: 69,330 (1990); 73,345 (2000); 75,675 (2007); 77,006 (2012 projected); Race: 91.6% White, 6.3% Black, 0.4% Asian, 0.9% Hispanic of any race (2007); Density: 109.9 persons per square mile (2007); Average household size: 2.63 (2007); Median age: 38.3 (2007); Males per 100 females: 109.3 (2007).

Religion: Five largest groups: 6.4% The United Methodist Church, 3.9% Catholic Church, 2.5% Southern Baptist Convention, 1.7% American Baptist Churches in the USA, 1.6% The Wesleyan Church (2000).

Economy: Unemployment rate: 7.6% (6/2008); Total civilian labor force: 35,005 (6/2008); Leading industries: 23.3% health care and social assistance; 19.0% manufacturing; 15.6% retail trade (2005); Farms: 952 totaling 246,690 acres (2002); Companies that employ 500 or more persons: 4 (2006); Companies that employ 100 to 499 persons: 24 (2006); Companies that employ less than 100 persons: 1,311 (2006); Black-owned businesses: n/a (2002); Hispanic-owned businesses: n/a (2002); Asian-owned businesses: n/a (2002); Women-owned businesses: 1,177 (2002); Retail sales per capita: $11,871 (2008). Single-family building permits issued: 31 (2007); Multi-family building permits issued: 0 (2007).

Income: Per capita income: $20,624 (2007); Median household income: $41,970 (2007); Average household income: $51,834 (2007); Percent of households with income of $100,000 or more: 9.8% (2007); Poverty rate: 14.5% (2005); Bankruptcy rate: 4.54% (2007).

Taxes: Total county taxes per capita: $361 (2006); County property taxes per capita: $133 (2006).

Education: Percent of population age 25 and over with: High school diploma (including GED) or higher: 76.3% (2007); Bachelor's degree or higher: 11.6% (2007); Master's degree or higher: 4.1% (2007).

Housing: Homeownership rate: 74.1% (2007); Median home value: $101,323 (2007); Median rent: $329 per month (2000); Median age of housing: 35 years (2000).

Health: Birth rate: 121.9 per 10,000 population (2007); Death rate: 103.1 per 10,000 population (2007); Age-adjusted cancer mortality rate: 237.5 deaths per 100,000 population (2005); Number of physicians: 17.1 per 10,000 population (2005); Hospital beds: 65.5 per 10,000 population (2004); Hospital admissions: 1,986.8 per 10,000 population (2004).

Elections: 2004 Presidential election results: 54.4% Bush, 44.1% Kerry, 0.0% Nader, 1.2% Badnarik

National and State Parks: Adena State Memorial; Great Seal State Park; Hopewell Culture National Historical Park; Hopewell Culture National Historical Park; Paint Creek State Park; Ross County Lake State Wildlife Area; Scioto River Canal Lands Access State Wildlife Area; Scioto Trail State Forest; Seip Mound State Memorial; Story Mound State Memorial; Tar Hollow State Forest

Additional Information Contacts

Ross County Government . . . . (740) 702-3085
http://www.co.ross.oh.us

Chillicothe Ross Chamber of Commerce. . . . . (740) 702-2722
http://www.chillicotheohio.com

City of Chillicothe . . . . (740) 774-1185
http://ci.chillicothe.oh.us

Ross County Communities

ADELPHI (village). Covers a land area of 0.276 square miles and a water area of 0 square miles. Located at 39.46° N. Lat.; 82.74° W. Long. Elevation is 840 feet.

Population: 398 (1990); 371 (2000); 338 (2007); 333 (2012 projected); Race: 95.3% White, 4.1% Black, 0.0% Asian, 0.6% Hispanic of any race (2007); Density: 1,223.8 persons per square mile (2007); Average household size: 2.32 (2007); Median age: 37.9 (2007); Males per 100 females: 102.4 (2007); Marriage status: 24.1% never married, 59.5% now married, 9.4% widowed, 7.0% divorced (2000); Foreign born: 0.0% (2000); Ancestry (includes multiple ancestries): 19.7% United States or American, 18.4% German, 10.3% Other groups, 8.7% Irish, 5.8% English (2000).

Economy: Employment by occupation: 2.9% management, 6.3% professional, 13.7% services, 21.1% sales, 0.0% farming, 15.4% construction, 40.6% production (2000).

Income: Per capita income: $18,883 (2007); Median household income: $39,444 (2007); Average household income: $43,716 (2007); Percent of households with income of $100,000 or more: 6.2% (2007); Poverty rate: 13.6% (2000).

Education: Percent of population age 25 and over with: High school diploma (including GED) or higher: 65.7% (2007); Bachelor's degree or higher: 0.4% (2007); Master's degree or higher: 0.4% (2007).

Housing: Homeownership rate: 80.8% (2007); Median home value: $87,273 (2007); Median rent: $305 per month (2000); Median age of housing: 50 years (2000).

Transportation: Commute to work: 91.2% car, 2.9% public transportation, 2.9% walk, 1.8% work from home (2000); Travel time to work: 19.0% less than 15 minutes, 38.1% 15 to 30 minutes, 14.9% 30 to 45 minutes, 8.9% 45 to 60 minutes, 19.0% 60 minutes or more (2000)

BAINBRIDGE (village). Covers a land area of 0.512 square miles and a water area of 0 square miles. Located at 39.22° N. Lat.; 83.27° W. Long. Elevation is 722 feet.

History: Bainbridge was founded in 1805 by Nathaniel Massie, a landowner and surveyor. In 1826 Dr. John Harris established a school for teaching dentistry here, where Chapin A. Harris was trained. Harris later founded the dental college at Baltimore and the "American Journal of Dental Science."

Population: 968 (1990); 1,012 (2000); 889 (2007); 892 (2012 projected); Race: 99.7% White, 0.0% Black, 0.2% Asian, 0.1% Hispanic of any race (2007); Density: 1,735.7 persons per square mile (2007); Average household size: 2.48 (2007); Median age: 36.8 (2007); Males per 100 females: 86.0 (2007); Marriage status: 24.0% never married, 53.7% now married, 12.8% widowed, 9.6% divorced (2000); Foreign born: 0.3% (2000); Ancestry (includes multiple ancestries): 17.6% United States or American, 13.7% German, 10.7% Other groups, 7.7% Irish, 6.2% English (2000).

Economy: Employment by occupation: 5.1% management, 10.6% professional, 22.6% services, 19.6% sales, 2.3% farming, 6.5% construction, 33.3% production (2000).

Income: Per capita income: $17,026 (2007); Median household income: $30,000 (2007); Average household income: $41,159 (2007); Percent of households with income of $100,000 or more: 7.3% (2007); Poverty rate: 19.9% (2000).

Education: Percent of population age 25 and over with: High school diploma (including GED) or higher: 68.6% (2007); Bachelor's degree or higher: 6.5% (2007); Master's degree or higher: 2.4% (2007).

School District(s)

Paint Valley Local (PK-12)
2005-06 Enrollment: 1,141 . . . . (740) 634-2826

Housing: Homeownership rate: 63.4% (2007); Median home value: $77,414 (2007); Median rent: $255 per month (2000); Median age of housing: 49 years (2000).

Transportation: Commute to work: 90.2% car, 0.0% public transportation, 8.8% walk, 1.0% work from home (2000); Travel time to work: 30.1% less than 15 minutes, 12.0% 15 to 30 minutes, 27.7% 30 to 45 minutes, 14.5% 45 to 60 minutes, 15.7% 60 minutes or more (2000)

CHILLICOTHE (city). County seat. Covers a land area of 9.544 square miles and a water area of 0.198 square miles. Located at 39.33° N. Lat.; 82.98° W. Long. Elevation is 630 feet.

History: In 1796 Nathaniel Massie established a community of settlers on the Scioto River at the mouth of Paint Creek. When Edward Tiffin and other young men came from Virginia in 1798, the town of Chillicothe was founded and became the capitol of the Northwest Territory. Ohio became a state in 1803, and Chillicothe continued as the capitol until 1810. Then industrial growth replaced the business of state, and the first paper mill was founded in 1812. By 1815 a flour mill was turning out 50 barrels daily, and by 1835, when the canal made agriculture profitable, cereal mills constructed along its banks shipped their products east and south. By 1890 the town had factories manufacturing a variety of items, including the Champion bed lounge, Mosher ratchet jack, Neely razor blade, Scioto grain elevator, and Crown baking powder and spices.

Population: 22,771 (1990); 21,796 (2000); 21,594 (2007); 21,348 (2012 projected); Race: 89.6% White, 7.1% Black, 0.6% Asian, 1.2% Hispanic of any race (2007); Density: 2,262.6 persons per square mile (2007); Average household size: 2.24 (2007); Median age: 41.3 (2007); Males per 100 females: 89.7 (2007); Marriage status: 23.2% never married, 51.3% now married, 11.2% widowed, 14.2% divorced (2000); Foreign born: 1.0% (2000); Ancestry (includes multiple ancestries): 22.0% German, 13.9% United States or American, 13.4% Other groups, 11.8% Irish, 10.5% English (2000).

Economy: Single-family building permits issued: 20 (2007); Multi-family building permits issued: 0 (2007); Employment by occupation: 9.3% management, 21.5% professional, 17.3% services, 24.7% sales, 0.1% farming, 6.1% construction, 21.1% production (2000).

Income: Per capita income: $22,129 (2007); Median household income: $37,491 (2007); Average household income: $48,934 (2007); Percent of households with income of $100,000 or more: 8.6% (2007); Poverty rate: 12.4% (2000).

Taxes: Total city taxes per capita: $585 (2006); City property taxes per capita: $66 (2006).

Education: Percent of population age 25 and over with: High school diploma (including GED) or higher: 77.6% (2007); Bachelor's degree or higher: 17.6% (2007); Master's degree or higher: 7.1% (2007).

School District(s)

Chillicothe City (PK-12)
2005-06 Enrollment: 3,145 . . . . (740) 775-4250
Huntington Local (PK-12)
2005-06 Enrollment: 1,400 . . . . (740) 663-5892
Pickaway-Ross County Jvsd (PK-12)
2005-06 Enrollment: n/a . . . . (740) 642-1200
Southeastern Local (PK-12)
2005-06 Enrollment: 1,324 . . . . (740) 774-2003
Union-Scioto Local (PK-12)
2005-06 Enrollment: 2,053 . . . . (740) 773-4102
Zane Trace Local (PK-12)
2005-06 Enrollment: 1,671 . . . . (740) 775-1355

Four-year College(s)

Ohio University-Chillicothe Campus (Public)
Fall 2007 Enrollment: 1,836. . . . . (740) 774-7200
2007-08 Tuition: In-state $4,581; Out-of-state $8,904

Two-year College(s)

Samuel Stephen College (Private, For-profit)
Fall 2007 Enrollment: 62 . . . . (740) 774-6300
2007-08 Tuition: In-state $9,380; Out-of-state $9,380

Vocational/Technical School(s)

Pickaway Ross Joint Vocational School District (Public)
Fall 2007 Enrollment: 288 . . . . (740) 642-1200
2007-08 Tuition: In-state $4,950; Out-of-state $4,950

Housing: Homeownership rate: 62.3% (2007); Median home value: $98,544 (2007); Median rent: $345 per month (2000); Median age of housing: 50 years (2000).

Hospitals: Adena Regional Medical Center (238 beds); Veterans Affairs Medical Center (297 beds)

Newspapers: Chillicothe Gazette (Local news; Circulation 14,709)

Transportation: Commute to work: 93.3% car, 0.7% public transportation, 3.0% walk, 1.7% work from home (2000); Travel time to work: 56.9% less than 15 minutes, 22.9% 15 to 30 minutes, 7.8% 30 to 45 minutes, 4.0% 45 to 60 minutes, 8.5% 60 minutes or more (2000)

Airports: Ross County (general aviation)

Additional Information Contacts

Chillicothe Ross Chamber of Commerce. . . . . (740) 702-2722
http://www.chillicotheohio.com
City of Chillicothe . . . . (740) 774-1185
http://ci.chillicothe.oh.us

CLARKSBURG (village). Covers a land area of 0.186 square miles and a water area of 0 square miles. Located at 39.50° N. Lat.; 83.15° W. Long. Elevation is 771 feet.
Population: 567 (1990); 516 (2000); 506 (2007); 503 (2012 projected); Race: 97.0% White, 2.0% Black, 0.0% Asian, 0.0% Hispanic of any race (2007); Density: 2,719.2 persons per square mile (2007); Average household size: 2.80 (2007); Median age: 33.5 (2007); Males per 100 females: 96.9 (2007); Marriage status: 25.9% never married, 50.9% now married, 10.7% widowed, 12.5% divorced (2000); Foreign born: 0.0% (2000); Ancestry (includes multiple ancestries): 23.9% German, 15.4% Irish, 14.2% United States or American, 11.7% English, 9.1% Other groups (2000).
Economy: Employment by occupation: 5.0% management, 13.9% professional, 13.3% services, 20.6% sales, 1.7% farming, 15.0% construction, 30.6% production (2000).
Income: Per capita income: $14,184 (2007); Median household income: $39,038 (2007); Average household income: $39,185 (2007); Percent of households with income of $100,000 or more: 2.8% (2007); Poverty rate: 18.8% (2000).
Education: Percent of population age 25 and over with: High school diploma (including GED) or higher: 73.9% (2007); Bachelor's degree or higher: 5.3% (2007); Master's degree or higher: 1.9% (2007).
Housing: Homeownership rate: 71.3% (2007); Median home value: $80,357 (2007); Median rent: $318 per month (2000); Median age of housing: 60+ years (2000).
Transportation: Commute to work: 93.3% car, 0.0% public transportation, 5.6% walk, 1.1% work from home (2000); Travel time to work: 10.2% less than 15 minutes, 34.5% 15 to 30 minutes, 37.9% 30 to 45 minutes, 7.9% 45 to 60 minutes, 9.6% 60 minutes or more (2000)

FRANKFORT (village). Covers a land area of 0.564 square miles and a water area of 0 square miles. Located at 39.40° N. Lat.; 83.18° W. Long. Elevation is 738 feet.
History: Frankfort was established on the site of a Shawnee village that was burned and plundered by Simon Kenton in 1787.
Population: 1,176 (1990); 1,011 (2000); 904 (2007); 897 (2012 projected); Race: 93.3% White, 3.2% Black, 0.3% Asian, 0.1% Hispanic of any race (2007); Density: 1,603.1 persons per square mile (2007); Average household size: 2.20 (2007); Median age: 39.7 (2007); Males per 100 females: 90.3 (2007); Marriage status: 21.6% never married, 52.2% now married, 14.6% widowed, 11.6% divorced (2000); Foreign born: 1.7% (2000); Ancestry (includes multiple ancestries): 24.8% German, 16.1% English, 11.7% United States or American, 10.7% Other groups, 9.3% Irish (2000).
Economy: Employment by occupation: 9.5% management, 20.4% professional, 20.4% services, 18.3% sales, 0.9% farming, 10.4% construction, 20.0% production (2000).
Income: Per capita income: $20,353 (2007); Median household income: $36,552 (2007); Average household income: $44,768 (2007); Percent of households with income of $100,000 or more: 8.3% (2007); Poverty rate: 16.7% (2000).
Taxes: Total city taxes per capita: $49 (2006); City property taxes per capita: $26 (2006).
Education: Percent of population age 25 and over with: High school diploma (including GED) or higher: 78.8% (2007); Bachelor's degree or higher: 12.1% (2007); Master's degree or higher: 4.3% (2007).

School District(s)

Adena Local (PK-12)
2005-06 Enrollment: 1,291 . . . . (740) 998-4633
Housing: Homeownership rate: 68.5% (2007); Median home value: $96,607 (2007); Median rent: $287 per month (2000); Median age of housing: 46 years (2000).
Transportation: Commute to work: 92.7% car, 0.7% public transportation, 5.4% walk, 0.2% work from home (2000); Travel time to work: 23.8% less than 15 minutes, 51.2% 15 to 30 minutes, 14.9% 30 to 45 minutes, 4.0% 45 to 60 minutes, 6.1% 60 minutes or more (2000)

KINGSTON (village). Covers a land area of 0.369 square miles and a water area of 0 square miles. Located at 39.47° N. Lat.; 82.91° W. Long. Elevation is 791 feet.
Population: 1,153 (1990); 1,032 (2000); 981 (2007); 995 (2012 projected); Race: 98.6% White, 0.5% Black, 0.1% Asian, 0.6% Hispanic of any race (2007); Density: 2,657.7 persons per square mile (2007); Average household size: 2.18 (2007); Median age: 44.4 (2007); Males per 100 females: 86.1 (2007); Marriage status: 12.5% never married, 61.3% now married, 10.0% widowed, 16.2% divorced (2000); Foreign born: 0.7% (2000); Ancestry (includes multiple ancestries): 24.3% German, 18.7% United States or American, 15.6% Irish, 9.3% English, 7.7% Other groups (2000).
Economy: Employment by occupation: 8.6% management, 20.0% professional, 11.8% services, 25.7% sales, 0.7% farming, 9.9% construction, 23.5% production (2000).
Income: Per capita income: $23,307 (2007); Median household income: $36,000 (2007); Average household income: $48,939 (2007); Percent of households with income of $100,000 or more: 7.8% (2007); Poverty rate: 10.1% (2000).
Education: Percent of population age 25 and over with: High school diploma (including GED) or higher: 75.7% (2007); Bachelor's degree or higher: 11.4% (2007); Master's degree or higher: 2.9% (2007).

School District(s)

Logan Elm Local (PK-12)
2005-06 Enrollment: 2,304 . . . . (740) 474-7501
Housing: Homeownership rate: 73.1% (2007); Median home value: $105,021 (2007); Median rent: $281 per month (2000); Median age of housing: 57 years (2000).
Transportation: Commute to work: 95.9% car, 0.0% public transportation, 3.5% walk, 0.7% work from home (2000); Travel time to work: 21.6% less than 15 minutes, 45.9% 15 to 30 minutes, 9.5% 30 to 45 minutes, 10.4% 45 to 60 minutes, 12.5% 60 minutes or more (2000)

LONDONDERRY (unincorporated postal area, zip code 45647). Covers a land area of 48.747 square miles and a water area of 0.007 square miles. Located at 39.28° N. Lat.; 82.76° W. Long. Elevation is 685 feet.
History: Londonderry was named by its early settlers for their home county in Ireland.
Population: 1,889 (2000); Race: 99.3% White, 0.0% Black, 0.0% Asian, 0.7% Hispanic of any race (2000); Density: 38.8 persons per square mile (2000); Age: 23.5% under 18, 17.2% over 64 (2000); Marriage status: 18.8% never married, 62.5% now married, 8.9% widowed, 9.8% divorced (2000); Foreign born: 0.0% (2000); Ancestry (includes multiple ancestries): 21.1% United States or American, 10.1% German, 9.2% English, 7.4% Other groups, 5.3% Irish (2000).
Economy: Employment by occupation: 5.6% management, 10.5% professional, 17.0% services, 14.9% sales, 0.0% farming, 15.1% construction, 36.9% production (2000).
Income: Per capita income: $17,250 (2000); Median household income: $40,758 (2000); Poverty rate: 6.6% (2000).
Education: Percent of population age 25 and over with: High school diploma (including GED) or higher: 72.1% (2000); Bachelor's degree or higher: 5.9% (2000).
Housing: Homeownership rate: 82.4% (2000); Median home value: $76,000 (2000); Median rent: $296 per month (2000); Median age of housing: 31 years (2000).
Transportation: Commute to work: 97.0% car, 1.8% public transportation, 0.5% walk, 0.8% work from home (2000); Travel time to work: 11.0% less than 15 minutes, 49.6% 15 to 30 minutes, 18.8% 30 to 45 minutes, 7.6% 45 to 60 minutes, 13.0% 60 minutes or more (2000)

NORTH FORK VILLAGE (CDP). Covers a land area of 1.528 square miles and a water area of 0 square miles. Located at 39.33° N. Lat.; 83.02° W. Long. Elevation is 659 feet.
Population: 1,443 (1990); 1,726 (2000); 2,015 (2007); 2,190 (2012 projected); Race: 94.0% White, 5.1% Black, 0.5% Asian, 1.0% Hispanic of any race (2007); Density: 1,318.8 persons per square mile (2007); Average household size: 2.30 (2007); Median age: 39.0 (2007); Males per 100 females: 84.4 (2007); Marriage status: 16.9% never married, 67.6% now married, 5.0% widowed, 10.5% divorced (2000); Foreign born: 1.5% (2000); Ancestry (includes multiple ancestries): 21.6% German, 11.0% Other groups, 10.4% Irish, 9.9% English, 8.7% United States or American (2000).
Economy: Employment by occupation: 18.9% management, 20.7% professional, 17.5% services, 20.6% sales, 0.0% farming, 8.8% construction, 13.5% production (2000).
Income: Per capita income: $22,762 (2007); Median household income: $41,930 (2007); Average household income: $51,989 (2007); Percent of households with income of $100,000 or more: 9.4% (2007); Poverty rate: 4.4% (2000).

Education: Percent of population age 25 and over with: High school diploma (including GED) or higher: 86.1% (2007); Bachelor's degree or higher: 26.9% (2007); Master's degree or higher: 7.6% (2007).
Housing: Homeownership rate: 55.7% (2007); Median home value: $137,121 (2007); Median rent: $391 per month (2000); Median age of housing: 26 years (2000).
Transportation: Commute to work: 93.2% car, 0.0% public transportation, 3.7% walk, 3.1% work from home (2000); Travel time to work: 43.4% less than 15 minutes, 35.0% 15 to 30 minutes, 7.6% 30 to 45 minutes, 3.3% 45 to 60 minutes, 10.7% 60 minutes or more (2000)

RICHMOND DALE (unincorporated postal area, zip code 45673). Aka Richmondale. Covers a land area of 0.518 square miles and a water area of 0 square miles. Located at 39.20° N. Lat.; 82.81° W. Long. Elevation is 594 feet.
Population: 405 (2000); Race: 100.0% White, 0.0% Black, 0.0% Asian, 0.0% Hispanic of any race (2000); Density: 781.1 persons per square mile (2000); Age: 13.3% under 18, 12.0% over 64 (2000); Marriage status: 23.7% never married, 57.5% now married, 11.8% widowed, 6.9% divorced (2000); Foreign born: 0.0% (2000); Ancestry (includes multiple ancestries): 22.1% German, 12.5% United States or American, 11.2% Other groups, 9.6% European, 6.1% English (2000).
Economy: Employment by occupation: 0.0% management, 8.3% professional, 6.4% services, 21.1% sales, 0.0% farming, 6.4% construction, 57.8% production (2000).
Income: Per capita income: $16,708 (2000); Median household income: $33,365 (2000); Poverty rate: 3.5% (2000).
Education: Percent of population age 25 and over with: High school diploma (including GED) or higher: 73.9% (2000); Bachelor's degree or higher: 10.7% (2000).

School District(s)

Southeastern Local (PK-12)
2005-06 Enrollment: 1,324 . . . . (740) 774-2003
Housing: Homeownership rate: 74.0% (2000); Median home value: $58,300 (2000); Median rent: $315 per month (2000); Median age of housing: 56 years (2000).
Transportation: Commute to work: 92.5% car, 0.0% public transportation, 7.5% walk, 0.0% work from home (2000); Travel time to work: 23.1% less than 15 minutes, 57.3% 15 to 30 minutes, 7.5% 30 to 45 minutes, 4.0% 45 to 60 minutes, 8.0% 60 minutes or more (2000)

SOUTH SALEM (village). Covers a land area of 0.207 square miles and a water area of 0 square miles. Located at 39.33° N. Lat.; 83.30° W. Long. Elevation is 919 feet.
Population: 227 (1990); 213 (2000); 242 (2007); 260 (2012 projected); Race: 95.9% White, 0.8% Black, 0.0% Asian, 1.7% Hispanic of any race (2007); Density: 1,167.7 persons per square mile (2007); Average household size: 2.69 (2007); Median age: 37.4 (2007); Males per 100 females: 114.2 (2007); Marriage status: 26.2% never married, 58.7% now married, 7.0% widowed, 8.1% divorced (2000); Foreign born: 0.0% (2000); Ancestry (includes multiple ancestries): 21.2% German, 18.0% United States or American, 13.5% Irish, 12.6% Other groups, 9.9% Dutch (2000).
Economy: Employment by occupation: 7.9% management, 21.3% professional, 18.0% services, 10.1% sales, 1.1% farming, 10.1% construction, 31.5% production (2000).
Income: Per capita income: $16,405 (2007); Median household income: $37,500 (2007); Average household income: $44,111 (2007); Percent of households with income of $100,000 or more: 6.7% (2007); Poverty rate: 14.0% (2000).
Education: Percent of population age 25 and over with: High school diploma (including GED) or higher: 83.0% (2007); Bachelor's degree or higher: 5.1% (2007); Master's degree or higher: 1.7% (2007).

School District(s)

Greenfield Exempted Village (PK-12)
2005-06 Enrollment: 2,301 . . . . (937) 981-2152
Housing: Homeownership rate: 85.6% (2007); Median home value: $78,214 (2007); Median rent: $263 per month (2000); Median age of housing: 60+ years (2000).
Transportation: Commute to work: 100.0% car, 0.0% public transportation, 0.0% walk, 0.0% work from home (2000); Travel time to work: 28.1% less than 15 minutes, 30.3% 15 to 30 minutes, 30.3% 30 to 45 minutes, 9.0% 45 to 60 minutes, 2.2% 60 minutes or more (2000)

Sandusky County

Located in northern Ohio; bounded on the northeast by Sandusky Bay of Lake Erie; crossed by the Sandusky and Portage Rivers. Covers a land area of 409.18 square miles, a water area of 8.59 square miles, and is located in the Eastern Time Zone. The county was founded in 1820. County seat is Fremont.

Sandusky County is part of the Fremont, OH Micropolitan Statistical Area. The entire metro area includes: Sandusky County, OH

Weather Station: Fremont Elevation: 597 feet

	Jan	Feb	Mar	Apr	May	Jun	Jul	Aug	Sep	Oct	Nov	Dec
High	31	35	45	58	70	79	84	81	75	62	49	37
Low	16	18	27	38	49	58	63	60	53	41	33	22
Precip	2.1	1.9	2.7	3.3	3.7	4.3	3.4	3.3	3.1	2.6	2.9	2.7
Snow	6.7	5.2	3.6	0.3	tr	0.0	0.0	0.0	0.0	tr	0.6	na

High and Low temperatures in degrees Fahrenheit; Precipitation and Snow in inches

Population: 61,963 (1990); 61,792 (2000); 61,611 (2007); 61,246 (2012 projected); Race: 91.4% White, 2.8% Black, 0.4% Asian, 7.7% Hispanic of any race (2007); Density: 150.6 persons per square mile (2007); Average household size: 2.54 (2007); Median age: 38.8 (2007); Males per 100 females: 96.7 (2007).
Religion: Five largest groups: 20.5% Catholic Church, 11.5% Evangelical Lutheran Church in America, 8.1% The United Methodist Church, 1.8% Independent, Charismatic Churches, 1.6% Southern Baptist Convention (2000).
Economy: Unemployment rate: 6.3% (6/2008); Total civilian labor force: 34,224 (6/2008); Leading industries: 38.0% manufacturing; 13.4% health care and social assistance; 10.9% retail trade (2005); Farms: 802 totaling 196,152 acres (2002); Companies that employ 500 or more persons: 4 (2006); Companies that employ 100 to 499 persons: 39 (2006); Companies that employ less than 100 persons: 1,411 (2006); Black-owned businesses: n/a (2002); Hispanic-owned businesses: n/a (2002); Asian-owned businesses: n/a (2002); Women-owned businesses: 1,465 (2002); Retail sales per capita: $12,102 (2008). Single-family building permits issued: 60 (2007); Multi-family building permits issued: 0 (2007).
Income: Per capita income: $22,844 (2007); Median household income: $46,232 (2007); Average household income: $57,264 (2007); Percent of households with income of $100,000 or more: 11.2% (2007); Poverty rate: 8.9% (2005); Bankruptcy rate: 3.57% (2007).
Education: Percent of population age 25 and over with: High school diploma (including GED) or higher: 82.3% (2007); Bachelor's degree or higher: 11.9% (2007); Master's degree or higher: 4.2% (2007).
Housing: Homeownership rate: 75.6% (2007); Median home value: $111,489 (2007); Median rent: $365 per month (2000); Median age of housing: 46 years (2000).
Health: Birth rate: 134.3 per 10,000 population (2007); Death rate: 101.5 per 10,000 population (2007); Age-adjusted cancer mortality rate: 227.8 deaths per 100,000 population (2005); Number of physicians: 10.1 per 10,000 population (2005); Hospital beds: 49.5 per 10,000 population (2004); Hospital admissions: 666.7 per 10,000 population (2004).
Elections: 2004 Presidential election results: 55.9% Bush, 43.7% Kerry, 0.0% Nader, 0.2% Badnarik
National and State Parks: Pfizer State Park; Sandusky Scenic River State Access Area; Spiegel Grove State Park
Additional Information Contacts
Sandusky County Government . . . . (419) 334-6100
http://www.sandusky-county.org
Bellevue Area Chamber of Commerce . . . . (419) 483-2182
http://www.bellevuechamberofcommerce.org
Chamber of Commerce of Sandusky County . . . . (419) 332-1591
http://www.scchamber.org
City of Bellevue . . . . (419) 484-8400
http://www.cityofbellevue.com
City of Clyde. . . . . (419) 547-6898
http://www.clydeohio.org
City of Fremont . . . . (419) 334-5900
http://www.fremontohio.org

Sandusky County Communities

BALLVILLE (CDP). Covers a land area of 2.742 square miles and a water area of 0.204 square miles. Located at 41.32° N. Lat.; 83.13° W. Long. Elevation is 620 feet.

Population: 3,059 (1990); 3,255 (2000); 3,303 (2007); 3,335 (2012 projected); Race: 93.0% White, 1.5% Black, 1.2% Asian, 4.8% Hispanic of any race (2007); Density: 1,204.5 persons per square mile (2007); Average household size: 2.37 (2007); Median age: 47.0 (2007); Males per 100 females: 91.6 (2007); Marriage status: 14.4% never married, 68.1% now married, 9.3% widowed, 8.2% divorced (2000); Foreign born: 2.0% (2000); Ancestry (includes multiple ancestries): 48.5% German, 12.7% Irish, 10.4% English, 8.3% Other groups, 5.9% United States or American (2000).
Economy: Employment by occupation: 15.6% management, 23.7% professional, 10.8% services, 20.5% sales, 1.6% farming, 9.0% construction, 18.7% production (2000).
Income: Per capita income: $34,228 (2007); Median household income: $55,176 (2007); Average household income: $81,136 (2007); Percent of households with income of $100,000 or more: 20.4% (2007); Poverty rate: 5.1% (2000).
Education: Percent of population age 25 and over with: High school diploma (including GED) or higher: 91.3% (2007); Bachelor's degree or higher: 24.2% (2007); Master's degree or higher: 10.3% (2007).
Housing: Homeownership rate: 88.9% (2007); Median home value: $153,660 (2007); Median rent: $428 per month (2000); Median age of housing: 35 years (2000).
Transportation: Commute to work: 96.2% car, 0.0% public transportation, 0.0% walk, 2.8% work from home (2000); Travel time to work: 51.1% less than 15 minutes, 29.2% 15 to 30 minutes, 10.8% 30 to 45 minutes, 4.0% 45 to 60 minutes, 4.9% 60 minutes or more (2000)

BELLEVUE (city). Covers a land area of 5.058 square miles and a water area of 0.093 square miles. Located at 41.27° N. Lat.; 82.84° W. Long.
History: Bellevue was established as a railroad town in 1839 and named by James Bell, a railroad employee.
Population: 8,391 (1990); 8,193 (2000); 7,937 (2007); 7,737 (2012 projected); Race: 97.1% White, 0.4% Black, 0.3% Asian, 3.0% Hispanic of any race (2007); Density: 1,569.2 persons per square mile (2007); Average household size: 2.40 (2007); Median age: 37.1 (2007); Males per 100 females: 93.8 (2007); Marriage status: 21.7% never married, 56.8% now married, 8.7% widowed, 12.8% divorced (2000); Foreign born: 1.3% (2000); Ancestry (includes multiple ancestries): 38.0% German, 12.5% Irish, 11.6% United States or American, 9.6% Italian, 9.5% English (2000).
Economy: Single-family building permits issued: 8 (2007); Multi-family building permits issued: 0 (2007); Employment by occupation: 10.0% management, 14.6% professional, 14.4% services, 18.5% sales, 0.2% farming, 10.9% construction, 31.3% production (2000).
Income: Per capita income: $22,423 (2007); Median household income: $45,011 (2007); Average household income: $53,800 (2007); Percent of households with income of $100,000 or more: 9.3% (2007); Poverty rate: 5.8% (2000).
Education: Percent of population age 25 and over with: High school diploma (including GED) or higher: 83.1% (2007); Bachelor's degree or higher: 9.3% (2007); Master's degree or higher: 2.3% (2007).

School District(s)

Bellevue City (PK-12)
2005-06 Enrollment: 2,360 . . . . (419) 484-5000
Seneca East Local (PK-12)
2005-06 Enrollment: 992 . . . . (419) 426-7041

Housing: Homeownership rate: 70.0% (2007); Median home value: $108,197 (2007); Median rent: $375 per month (2000); Median age of housing: 50 years (2000).
Hospitals: Bellevue Hospital (64 beds)
Newspapers: Bellevue Gazette (Local news; Circulation 3,000)
Transportation: Commute to work: 94.1% car, 1.2% public transportation, 3.1% walk, 1.0% work from home (2000); Travel time to work: 49.1% less than 15 minutes, 28.4% 15 to 30 minutes, 13.8% 30 to 45 minutes, 2.0% 45 to 60 minutes, 6.6% 60 minutes or more (2000)

Additional Information Contacts

Bellevue Area Chamber of Commerce . . . . (419) 483-2182
http://www.bellevuechamberofcommerce.org
City of Bellevue . . . . (419) 484-8400
http://www.cityofbellevue.com

BURGOON (village). Covers a land area of 0.090 square miles and a water area of 0 square miles. Located at 41.26° N. Lat.; 83.25° W. Long. Elevation is 705 feet.
Population: 224 (1990); 199 (2000); 204 (2007); 205 (2012 projected); Race: 93.6% White, 0.0% Black, 3.4% Asian, 4.4% Hispanic of any race (2007); Density: 2,266.2 persons per square mile (2007); Average household size: 2.83 (2007); Median age: 36.9 (2007); Males per 100 females: 110.3 (2007); Marriage status: 16.7% never married, 68.2% now married, 4.5% widowed, 10.6% divorced (2000); Foreign born: 1.1% (2000); Ancestry (includes multiple ancestries): 37.8% German, 14.1% United States or American, 13.5% English, 8.6% Dutch, 8.1% Irish (2000).
Economy: Employment by occupation: 10.5% management, 20.0% professional, 15.8% services, 17.9% sales, 0.0% farming, 2.1% construction, 33.7% production (2000).
Income: Per capita income: $26,900 (2007); Median household income: $70,000 (2007); Average household income: $76,215 (2007); Percent of households with income of $100,000 or more: 12.5% (2007); Poverty rate: 1.1% (2000).
Education: Percent of population age 25 and over with: High school diploma (including GED) or higher: 90.6% (2007); Bachelor's degree or higher: 10.2% (2007); Master's degree or higher: 4.7% (2007).

School District(s)

Lakota Local (PK-12)
2005-06 Enrollment: 1,099 . . . . (419) 457-2911

Housing: Homeownership rate: 90.3% (2007); Median home value: $94,333 (2007); Median rent: $375 per month (2000); Median age of housing: 60+ years (2000).
Transportation: Commute to work: 94.9% car, 0.0% public transportation, 5.1% walk, 0.0% work from home (2000); Travel time to work: 26.3% less than 15 minutes, 45.5% 15 to 30 minutes, 14.1% 30 to 45 minutes, 10.1% 45 to 60 minutes, 4.0% 60 minutes or more (2000)

CLYDE (city). Covers a land area of 4.389 square miles and a water area of 0.052 square miles. Located at 41.30° N. Lat.; 82.97° W. Long. Elevation is 696 feet.
History: The story of Clyde's beginnings tells of an officer during the War of 1812 who drove a stake into the ground here and said: "At this spot I shall build my future home, which shall be the nucleus of a thriving town." It was 1820 when the soldier returned, recovered his chosen land, and the city of Clyde came into being. Writer Sherwood Anderson spent his boyhood in Clyde, and portrayed the town in the novel "Winesburg, Ohio."
Population: 6,207 (1990); 6,064 (2000); 6,118 (2007); 6,146 (2012 projected); Race: 95.3% White, 0.1% Black, 0.4% Asian, 4.8% Hispanic of any race (2007); Density: 1,393.8 persons per square mile (2007); Average household size: 2.56 (2007); Median age: 37.1 (2007); Males per 100 females: 93.2 (2007); Marriage status: 26.4% never married, 53.3% now married, 8.0% widowed, 12.4% divorced (2000); Foreign born: 0.3% (2000); Ancestry (includes multiple ancestries): 41.1% German, 13.0% Irish, 10.8% Other groups, 10.2% United States or American, 9.7% English (2000).
Economy: Single-family building permits issued: 6 (2007); Multi-family building permits issued: 0 (2007); Employment by occupation: 6.0% management, 12.9% professional, 13.6% services, 14.5% sales, 0.0% farming, 7.8% construction, 45.3% production (2000).
Income: Per capita income: $20,598 (2007); Median household income: $44,508 (2007); Average household income: $51,744 (2007); Percent of households with income of $100,000 or more: 8.7% (2007); Poverty rate: 8.6% (2000).
Education: Percent of population age 25 and over with: High school diploma (including GED) or higher: 76.9% (2007); Bachelor's degree or higher: 10.6% (2007); Master's degree or higher: 3.6% (2007).

School District(s)

Bellevue City (PK-12)
2005-06 Enrollment: 2,360 . . . . (419) 484-5000
Clyde-Green Springs Exempted Village (PK-12)
2005-06 Enrollment: 2,415 . . . . (419) 547-0588

Housing: Homeownership rate: 73.8% (2007); Median home value: $101,526 (2007); Median rent: $393 per month (2000); Median age of housing: 47 years (2000).
Safety: Violent crime rate: 4.9 per 10,000 population; Property crime rate: 359.7 per 10,000 population (2007).
Newspapers: Clyde Enterprise (Community news; Circulation 2,100)
Transportation: Commute to work: 90.4% car, 2.7% public transportation, 6.1% walk, 0.6% work from home (2000); Travel time to work: 51.5% less than 15 minutes, 27.6% 15 to 30 minutes, 13.5% 30 to 45 minutes, 1.7% 45 to 60 minutes, 5.7% 60 minutes or more (2000)

Additional Information Contacts

City of Clyde. . . . . (419) 547-6898
http://www.clydeohio.org

FREMONT (city). County seat. Covers a land area of 7.511 square miles and a water area of 0.218 square miles. Located at 41.34° N. Lat.; 83.11° W. Long. Elevation is 627 feet.

History: Settlement began here after the War of 1812, when the two small towns of Croghansville and Lower Sandusky were established on the Sandusky River. In 1829 the two united, and in 1849 the name was changed to Fremont, for explorer John C. Fremont. Fremont grew as a sugar-beet and cannery center.

Population: 18,243 (1990); 17,375 (2000); 16,603 (2007); 15,992 (2012 projected); Race: 80.2% White, 8.9% Black, 0.3% Asian, 14.2% Hispanic of any race (2007); Density: 2,210.4 persons per square mile (2007); Average household size: 2.47 (2007); Median age: 34.8 (2007); Males per 100 females: 91.3 (2007); Marriage status: 29.0% never married, 49.2% now married, 9.1% widowed, 12.7% divorced (2000); Foreign born: 2.3% (2000); Ancestry (includes multiple ancestries): 33.9% German, 22.4% Other groups, 9.4% Irish, 6.2% English, 6.0% United States or American (2000).

Economy: Single-family building permits issued: 5 (2007); Multi-family building permits issued: 0 (2007); Employment by occupation: 6.5% management, 14.1% professional, 14.8% services, 19.3% sales, 0.3% farming, 8.3% construction, 36.8% production (2000).

Income: Per capita income: $18,039 (2007); Median household income: $37,453 (2007); Average household income: $43,538 (2007); Percent of households with income of $100,000 or more: 4.5% (2007); Poverty rate: 12.9% (2000).

Taxes: Total city taxes per capita: $549 (2006); City property taxes per capita: $64 (2006).

Education: Percent of population age 25 and over with: High school diploma (including GED) or higher: 77.3% (2007); Bachelor's degree or higher: 10.1% (2007); Master's degree or higher: 3.4% (2007).

School District(s)

Fremont City (PK-12)
2005-06 Enrollment: 4,502 . . . . (419) 332-6454

Vanguard-Sentinel (07-12)
2005-06 Enrollment: n/a . . . . (419) 332-2626

Two-year College(s)

Terra State Community College (Public)
Fall 2007 Enrollment: 2,495. . . . . (419) 334-8400
2007-08 Tuition: In-state $3,590; Out-of-state $5,636

Vocational/Technical School(s)

Vanguard Career Center (Public)
Fall 2007 Enrollment: 20 . . . . (419) 334-6901
2007-08 Tuition: $3,988

Housing: Homeownership rate: 58.4% (2007); Median home value: $87,714 (2007); Median rent: $359 per month (2000); Median age of housing: 58 years (2000).

Hospitals: Memorial Hospital (186 beds)

Safety: Violent crime rate: 29.0 per 10,000 population; Property crime rate: 639.0 per 10,000 population (2007).

Newspapers: Fremont News-Messenger (Local news; Circulation 12,605)

Transportation: Commute to work: 94.6% car, 1.0% public transportation, 2.2% walk, 1.1% work from home (2000); Travel time to work: 57.2% less than 15 minutes, 26.8% 15 to 30 minutes, 9.7% 30 to 45 minutes, 3.3% 45 to 60 minutes, 2.9% 60 minutes or more (2000)

Airports: Sandusky County Regional (general aviation)

Additional Information Contacts

Chamber of Commerce of Sandusky County . . . . (419) 332-1591
http://www.scchamber.org

City of Fremont . . . . (419) 334-5900
http://www.fremontohio.org

GIBSONBURG (village). Covers a land area of 2.494 square miles and a water area of 0.039 square miles. Located at 41.38° N. Lat.; 83.32° W. Long. Elevation is 686 feet.

History: Founded 1871.

Population: 2,616 (1990); 2,506 (2000); 2,499 (2007); 2,469 (2012 projected); Race: 92.7% White, 0.4% Black, 0.4% Asian, 9.6% Hispanic of any race (2007); Density: 1,001.9 persons per square mile (2007); Average household size: 2.56 (2007); Median age: 37.0 (2007); Males per 100 females: 96.5 (2007); Marriage status: 20.7% never married, 59.6% now married, 10.6% widowed, 9.2% divorced (2000); Foreign born: 1.0% (2000); Ancestry (includes multiple ancestries): 44.1% German, 12.4% Other groups, 8.5% Irish, 6.4% English, 5.9% United States or American (2000).

Economy: Single-family building permits issued: 1 (2007); Multi-family building permits issued: 0 (2007); Employment by occupation: 10.5% management, 13.8% professional, 10.6% services, 19.2% sales, 0.0% farming, 11.5% construction, 34.5% production (2000).

Income: Per capita income: $20,813 (2007); Median household income: $47,617 (2007); Average household income: $51,587 (2007); Percent of households with income of $100,000 or more: 8.9% (2007); Poverty rate: 6.5% (2000).

Education: Percent of population age 25 and over with: High school diploma (including GED) or higher: 83.3% (2007); Bachelor's degree or higher: 10.5% (2007); Master's degree or higher: 5.2% (2007).

School District(s)

Gibsonburg Exempted Village (PK-12)
2005-06 Enrollment: 1,283 . . . . (419) 637-2479

Housing: Homeownership rate: 74.4% (2007); Median home value: $104,096 (2007); Median rent: $341 per month (2000); Median age of housing: 60+ years (2000).

Safety: Violent crime rate: 4.0 per 10,000 population; Property crime rate: 359.2 per 10,000 population (2007).

Transportation: Commute to work: 94.4% car, 0.0% public transportation, 3.5% walk, 1.0% work from home (2000); Travel time to work: 30.2% less than 15 minutes, 35.0% 15 to 30 minutes, 25.8% 30 to 45 minutes, 6.0% 45 to 60 minutes, 3.0% 60 minutes or more (2000)

HELENA (village). Covers a land area of 0.297 square miles and a water area of 0 square miles. Located at 41.34° N. Lat.; 83.29° W. Long. Elevation is 696 feet.

Population: 267 (1990); 236 (2000); 237 (2007); 236 (2012 projected); Race: 96.2% White, 0.0% Black, 0.0% Asian, 7.6% Hispanic of any race (2007); Density: 797.6 persons per square mile (2007); Average household size: 2.32 (2007); Median age: 42.0 (2007); Males per 100 females: 107.9 (2007); Marriage status: 16.6% never married, 66.3% now married, 5.2% widowed, 11.9% divorced (2000); Foreign born: 0.0% (2000); Ancestry (includes multiple ancestries): 47.7% German, 15.3% Irish, 9.4% United States or American, 7.7% Other groups, 7.2% English (2000).

Economy: Employment by occupation: 2.7% management, 11.7% professional, 22.5% services, 16.2% sales, 0.0% farming, 12.6% construction, 34.2% production (2000).

Income: Per capita income: $19,684 (2007); Median household income: $45,313 (2007); Average household income: $45,735 (2007); Percent of households with income of $100,000 or more: 2.0% (2007); Poverty rate: 12.4% (2000).

Education: Percent of population age 25 and over with: High school diploma (including GED) or higher: 88.4% (2007); Bachelor's degree or higher: 4.9% (2007); Master's degree or higher: 4.3% (2007).

Housing: Homeownership rate: 82.4% (2007); Median home value: $85,385 (2007); Median rent: $354 per month (2000); Median age of housing: 60+ years (2000).

Transportation: Commute to work: 98.2% car, 0.0% public transportation, 0.9% walk, 0.9% work from home (2000); Travel time to work: 24.5% less than 15 minutes, 53.6% 15 to 30 minutes, 11.8% 30 to 45 minutes, 2.7% 45 to 60 minutes, 7.3% 60 minutes or more (2000)

LINDSEY (village). Covers a land area of 1.541 square miles and a water area of 0 square miles. Located at 41.42° N. Lat.; 83.22° W. Long. Elevation is 620 feet.

Population: 529 (1990); 504 (2000); 441 (2007); 449 (2012 projected); Race: 92.3% White, 0.5% Black, 0.0% Asian, 9.8% Hispanic of any race (2007); Density: 286.1 persons per square mile (2007); Average household size: 2.44 (2007); Median age: 38.7 (2007); Males per 100 females: 102.3 (2007); Marriage status: 18.4% never married, 67.5% now married, 5.6% widowed, 8.5% divorced (2000); Foreign born: 0.0% (2000); Ancestry (includes multiple ancestries): 45.5% German, 13.1% Irish, 10.7% United States or American, 10.3% English, 8.7% French (except Basque) (2000).

Economy: Single-family building permits issued: 1 (2007); Multi-family building permits issued: 0 (2007); Employment by occupation: 3.7% management, 18.0% professional, 9.2% services, 19.5% sales, 0.4% farming, 13.2% construction, 36.0% production (2000).

Income: Per capita income: $25,471 (2007); Median household income: $53,400 (2007); Average household income: $62,058 (2007); Percent of households with income of $100,000 or more: 12.7% (2007); Poverty rate: 5.7% (2000).

Education: Percent of population age 25 and over with: High school diploma (including GED) or higher: 88.3% (2007); Bachelor's degree or higher: 15.0% (2007); Master's degree or higher: 5.3% (2007).

School District(s)

Fremont City (PK-12)
2005-06 Enrollment: 4,502 . . . . (419) 332-6454

Housing: Homeownership rate: 84.0% (2007); Median home value: $118,333 (2007); Median rent: $415 per month (2000); Median age of housing: 60+ years (2000).

Transportation: Commute to work: 97.4% car, 0.0% public transportation, 1.1% walk, 1.5% work from home (2000); Travel time to work: 16.8% less than 15 minutes, 53.1% 15 to 30 minutes, 16.4% 30 to 45 minutes, 10.3% 45 to 60 minutes, 3.4% 60 minutes or more (2000)

STONY PRAIRIE (CDP). Covers a land area of 1.542 square miles and a water area of 0 square miles. Located at 41.35° N. Lat.; 83.14° W. Long. Elevation is 633 feet.

Population: 894 (1990); 836 (2000); 777 (2007); 747 (2012 projected); Race: 92.8% White, 0.6% Black, 0.1% Asian, 19.4% Hispanic of any race (2007); Density: 504.0 persons per square mile (2007); Average household size: 2.33 (2007); Median age: 41.5 (2007); Males per 100 females: 96.7 (2007); Marriage status: 18.0% never married, 63.1% now married, 10.7% widowed, 8.2% divorced (2000); Foreign born: 3.2% (2000); Ancestry (includes multiple ancestries): 36.4% German, 18.1% Other groups, 12.8% United States or American, 9.3% Polish, 7.9% English (2000).

Economy: Employment by occupation: 3.6% management, 8.7% professional, 12.5% services, 19.8% sales, 0.0% farming, 8.9% construction, 46.5% production (2000).

Income: Per capita income: $21,271 (2007); Median household income: $43,235 (2007); Average household income: $49,484 (2007); Percent of households with income of $100,000 or more: 5.1% (2007); Poverty rate: 6.6% (2000).

Education: Percent of population age 25 and over with: High school diploma (including GED) or higher: 66.5% (2007); Bachelor's degree or higher: 6.9% (2007); Master's degree or higher: 2.1% (2007).

Housing: Homeownership rate: 78.7% (2007); Median home value: $81,310 (2007); Median rent: $292 per month (2000); Median age of housing: 46 years (2000).

Transportation: Commute to work: 98.8% car, 0.0% public transportation, 1.2% walk, 0.0% work from home (2000); Travel time to work: 60.5% less than 15 minutes, 32.4% 15 to 30 minutes, 5.5% 30 to 45 minutes, 1.7% 45 to 60 minutes, 0.0% 60 minutes or more (2000)

VICKERY (unincorporated postal area, zip code 43464). Covers a land area of 29.217 square miles and a water area of 0.048 square miles. Located at 41.40° N. Lat.; 82.92° W. Long. Elevation is 604 feet.

Population: 1,544 (2000); Race: 94.5% White, 1.2% Black, 0.8% Asian, 2.6% Hispanic of any race (2000); Density: 52.8 persons per square mile (2000); Age: 27.1% under 18, 7.5% over 64 (2000); Marriage status: 22.1% never married, 58.8% now married, 7.3% widowed, 11.8% divorced (2000); Foreign born: 0.8% (2000); Ancestry (includes multiple ancestries): 41.8% German, 12.6% Irish, 11.2% United States or American, 10.7% English, 10.5% Other groups (2000).

Economy: Employment by occupation: 8.4% management, 5.6% professional, 12.6% services, 17.3% sales, 3.4% farming, 14.1% construction, 38.6% production (2000).

Income: Per capita income: $17,336 (2000); Median household income: $39,956 (2000); Poverty rate: 7.4% (2000).

Education: Percent of population age 25 and over with: High school diploma (including GED) or higher: 83.0% (2000); Bachelor's degree or higher: 4.7% (2000).

School District(s)

Margaretta Local (PK-12)
2005-06 Enrollment: 1,418 . . . . (419) 684-5322

Housing: Homeownership rate: 86.5% (2000); Median home value: $82,000 (2000); Median rent: $252 per month (2000); Median age of housing: 41 years (2000).

Transportation: Commute to work: 91.2% car, 0.0% public transportation, 0.0% walk, 7.8% work from home (2000); Travel time to work: 21.4% less than 15 minutes, 54.4% 15 to 30 minutes, 15.8% 30 to 45 minutes, 2.8% 45 to 60 minutes, 5.7% 60 minutes or more (2000)

WOODVILLE (village). Covers a land area of 1.247 square miles and a water area of 0 square miles. Located at 41.45° N. Lat.; 83.36° W. Long. Elevation is 636 feet.

History: Woodville developed in the center of an extensive limestone area. The lime produced here was noted for its whiteness, plasticity, and sand-carrying qualities.

Population: 1,996 (1990); 1,977 (2000); 2,022 (2007); 2,063 (2012 projected); Race: 97.1% White, 0.2% Black, 0.0% Asian, 3.2% Hispanic of any race (2007); Density: 1,621.8 persons per square mile (2007); Average household size: 2.44 (2007); Median age: 38.5 (2007); Males per 100 females: 91.8 (2007); Marriage status: 19.2% never married, 63.4% now married, 7.7% widowed, 9.8% divorced (2000); Foreign born: 0.6% (2000); Ancestry (includes multiple ancestries): 54.4% German, 11.7% Irish, 10.2% English, 7.4% United States or American, 7.3% Other groups (2000).

Economy: Single-family building permits issued: 1 (2007); Multi-family building permits issued: 0 (2007); Employment by occupation: 10.5% management, 19.6% professional, 15.2% services, 21.2% sales, 0.5% farming, 12.6% construction, 20.5% production (2000).

Income: Per capita income: $24,874 (2007); Median household income: $52,671 (2007); Average household income: $60,816 (2007); Percent of households with income of $100,000 or more: 14.1% (2007); Poverty rate: 3.9% (2000).

Education: Percent of population age 25 and over with: High school diploma (including GED) or higher: 89.2% (2007); Bachelor's degree or higher: 18.5% (2007); Master's degree or higher: 5.7% (2007).

School District(s)

Woodmore Local (PK-12)
2005-06 Enrollment: 1,194 . . . . (419) 849-2381

Housing: Homeownership rate: 77.3% (2007); Median home value: $130,235 (2007); Median rent: $341 per month (2000); Median age of housing: 50 years (2000).

Transportation: Commute to work: 92.6% car, 0.0% public transportation, 3.6% walk, 3.0% work from home (2000); Travel time to work: 31.0% less than 15 minutes, 34.6% 15 to 30 minutes, 27.8% 30 to 45 minutes, 4.3% 45 to 60 minutes, 2.3% 60 minutes or more (2000)

Scioto County

Located in southern Ohio; bounded on the south by the Ohio River and the Kentucky border; crossed by the Scioto and Little Scioto Rivers. Covers a land area of 612.27 square miles, a water area of 3.80 square miles, and is located in the Eastern Time Zone. The county was founded in 1803. County seat is Portsmouth.

Scioto County is part of the Portsmouth, OH Micropolitan Statistical Area. The entire metro area includes: Scioto County, OH

Weather Station: Portsmouth Sciotoville — Elevation: 538 feet

	Jan	Feb	Mar	Apr	May	Jun	Jul	Aug	Sep	Oct	Nov	Dec
High	40	44	55	66	75	83	87	85	79	68	56	45
Low	22	25	33	42	51	60	64	62	55	43	35	27
Precip	3.2	2.8	3.7	3.4	4.4	3.9	4.1	4.0	3.1	2.6	3.0	3.3
Snow	5.5	3.7	2.3	0.3	tr	0.0	0.0	0.0	0.0	tr	0.3	1.2

High and Low temperatures in degrees Fahrenheit; Precipitation and Snow in inches

Population: 80,327 (1990); 79,195 (2000); 76,000 (2007); 73,652 (2012 projected); Race: 94.9% White, 2.5% Black, 0.4% Asian, 0.8% Hispanic of any race (2007); Density: 124.1 persons per square mile (2007); Average household size: 2.49 (2007); Median age: 37.9 (2007); Males per 100 females: 94.8 (2007).

Religion: Five largest groups: 5.9% The United Methodist Church, 4.3% Catholic Church, 2.7% Christian Churches and Churches of Christ, 2.2% General Association of Regular Baptist Churches, 2.2% National Association of Free Will Baptists (2000).

Economy: Unemployment rate: 8.3% (6/2008); Total civilian labor force: 32,788 (6/2008); Leading industries: 31.7% health care and social assistance; 17.4% retail trade; 14.4% accommodation & food services (2005); Farms: 709 totaling 96,449 acres (2002); Companies that employ 500 or more persons: 1 (2006); Companies that employ 100 to 499 persons: 28 (2006); Companies that employ less than 100 persons: 1,388 (2006); Black-owned businesses: n/a (2002); Hispanic-owned businesses: n/a (2002); Asian-owned businesses: 107 (2002); Women-owned businesses: 1,381 (2002); Retail sales per capita: $9,439 (2008). Single-family building permits issued: 2 (2007); Multi-family building permits issued: 40 (2007).

Income: Per capita income: $18,038 (2007); Median household income: $32,528 (2007); Average household income: $44,074 (2007); Percent of households with income of $100,000 or more: 7.2% (2007); Poverty rate: 25.3% (2005); Bankruptcy rate: 3.45% (2007).

Taxes: Total county taxes per capita: $173 (2006); County property taxes per capita: $61 (2006).

Education: Percent of population age 25 and over with: High school diploma (including GED) or higher: 74.3% (2007); Bachelor's degree or higher: 10.2% (2007); Master's degree or higher: 3.8% (2007).
Housing: Homeownership rate: 70.3% (2007); Median home value: $78,358 (2007); Median rent: $295 per month (2000); Median age of housing: 41 years (2000).
Health: Birth rate: 129.7 per 10,000 population (2007); Death rate: 120.2 per 10,000 population (2007); Age-adjusted cancer mortality rate: 217.7 deaths per 100,000 population (2005); Air Quality Index: 86.0% good, 13.7% moderate, 0.3% unhealthy for sensitive individuals, 0.0% unhealthy (percent of days in 2007); Number of physicians: 18.4 per 10,000 population (2005); Hospital beds: 29.1 per 10,000 population (2004); Hospital admissions: 1,508.8 per 10,000 population (2004).
Elections: 2004 Presidential election results: 51.9% Bush, 47.8% Kerry, 0.0% Nader, 0.2% Badnarik
National and State Parks: Brush Creek State Forest; Shawnee State Forest; Shawnee State Park
Additional Information Contacts
Scioto County Government . . . . (740) 355-8313
http://www.sciotocountyohio.com
City of Portsmouth . . . . (740) 354-8807
http://www.ci.portsmouth.oh.us
Portsmouth Area Chamber of Commerce . . . . (740) 353-7647
http://www.portsmouth.org

Scioto County Communities

FRANKLIN FURNACE (CDP). Covers a land area of 2.384 square miles and a water area of 0.357 square miles. Located at 38.62° N. Lat.; 82.84° W. Long. Elevation is 574 feet.
Population: 1,212 (1990); 1,537 (2000); 1,445 (2007); 1,408 (2012 projected); Race: 86.8% White, 11.5% Black, 0.1% Asian, 0.6% Hispanic of any race (2007); Density: 606.2 persons per square mile (2007); Average household size: 2.86 (2007); Median age: 31.2 (2007); Males per 100 females: 124.7 (2007); Marriage status: 22.8% never married, 55.6% now married, 5.8% widowed, 15.9% divorced (2000); Foreign born: 1.6% (2000); Ancestry (includes multiple ancestries): 16.5% United States or American, 14.7% German, 12.5% Other groups, 7.8% Irish, 6.1% English (2000).
Economy: Employment by occupation: 6.2% management, 10.9% professional, 24.9% services, 18.0% sales, 0.0% farming, 9.0% construction, 31.0% production (2000).
Income: Per capita income: $15,469 (2007); Median household income: $30,598 (2007); Average household income: $40,995 (2007); Percent of households with income of $100,000 or more: 6.7% (2007); Poverty rate: 12.5% (2000).
Education: Percent of population age 25 and over with: High school diploma (including GED) or higher: 70.0% (2007); Bachelor's degree or higher: 10.7% (2007); Master's degree or higher: 2.7% (2007).

School District(s)

Department of Youth Services (06-12)
2005-06 Enrollment: 1,478 . . . . (614) 728-2489
Green Local (PK-12)
2005-06 Enrollment: 706 . . . . (740) 354-9221
Housing: Homeownership rate: 75.0% (2007); Median home value: $96,875 (2007); Median rent: $355 per month (2000); Median age of housing: 23 years (2000).
Transportation: Commute to work: 93.7% car, 0.0% public transportation, 4.9% walk, 1.4% work from home (2000); Travel time to work: 29.7% less than 15 minutes, 34.0% 15 to 30 minutes, 17.4% 30 to 45 minutes, 8.4% 45 to 60 minutes, 10.5% 60 minutes or more (2000)

LUCASVILLE (CDP). Covers a land area of 2.515 square miles and a water area of 0.036 square miles. Located at 38.88° N. Lat.; 82.99° W. Long. Elevation is 548 feet.
History: Lucasville was founded in 1819 by John Lucas on land received by his father, William Lucas, for Revolutionary War service. The founder's son, Robert Lucas, was governor of Ohio (1832-1836) and territorial governor of Iowa (1838-1841).
Population: 1,575 (1990); 1,588 (2000); 1,278 (2007); 1,151 (2012 projected); Race: 96.9% White, 0.2% Black, 0.5% Asian, 0.3% Hispanic of any race (2007); Density: 508.1 persons per square mile (2007); Average household size: 2.62 (2007); Median age: 37.6 (2007); Males per 100 females: 90.2 (2007); Marriage status: 22.4% never married, 61.2% now married, 7.5% widowed, 9.0% divorced (2000); Foreign born: 0.0% (2000); Ancestry (includes multiple ancestries): 35.8% United States or American, 13.2% German, 10.4% English, 9.2% Irish, 8.3% Other groups (2000).
Economy: Employment by occupation: 6.8% management, 18.5% professional, 25.3% services, 18.5% sales, 0.0% farming, 9.7% construction, 21.2% production (2000).
Income: Per capita income: $15,945 (2007); Median household income: $30,833 (2007); Average household income: $41,843 (2007); Percent of households with income of $100,000 or more: 5.7% (2007); Poverty rate: 8.5% (2000).
Education: Percent of population age 25 and over with: High school diploma (including GED) or higher: 63.3% (2007); Bachelor's degree or higher: 14.6% (2007); Master's degree or higher: 6.8% (2007).

School District(s)

Scioto County Joint Vocational School (08-12)
2005-06 Enrollment: n/a . . . . (740) 259-5522
Valley Local (PK-12)
2005-06 Enrollment: 1,176 . . . . (740) 259-3115

Vocational/Technical School(s)

Scioto County Joint Vocational School District (Public)
Fall 2007 Enrollment: 421 . . . . (740) 259-5522
2007-08 Tuition: $7,744
Housing: Homeownership rate: 73.1% (2007); Median home value: $92,500 (2007); Median rent: $293 per month (2000); Median age of housing: 35 years (2000).
Transportation: Commute to work: 97.6% car, 0.0% public transportation, 1.0% walk, 0.0% work from home (2000); Travel time to work: 29.8% less than 15 minutes, 37.6% 15 to 30 minutes, 21.2% 30 to 45 minutes, 3.9% 45 to 60 minutes, 7.5% 60 minutes or more (2000)

MCDERMOTT (unincorporated postal area, zip code 45652). Covers a land area of 42.649 square miles and a water area of 0.028 square miles. Located at 38.83° N. Lat.; 83.07° W. Long. Elevation is 580 feet.
Population: 3,566 (2000); Race: 97.6% White, 0.0% Black, 1.0% Asian, 0.2% Hispanic of any race (2000); Density: 83.6 persons per square mile (2000); Age: 26.3% under 18, 13.7% over 64 (2000); Marriage status: 19.7% never married, 61.8% now married, 6.6% widowed, 11.8% divorced (2000); Foreign born: 0.3% (2000); Ancestry (includes multiple ancestries): 20.1% United States or American, 10.6% English, 10.0% German, 9.2% Other groups, 7.0% Irish (2000).
Economy: Employment by occupation: 10.1% management, 15.4% professional, 19.3% services, 20.4% sales, 2.3% farming, 12.0% construction, 20.5% production (2000).
Income: Per capita income: $16,655 (2000); Median household income: $28,468 (2000); Poverty rate: 18.7% (2000).
Education: Percent of population age 25 and over with: High school diploma (including GED) or higher: 76.6% (2000); Bachelor's degree or higher: 6.2% (2000).

School District(s)

Northwest Local (PK-12)
2005-06 Enrollment: 1,769 . . . . (740) 259-5558
Housing: Homeownership rate: 82.0% (2000); Median home value: $63,500 (2000); Median rent: $253 per month (2000); Median age of housing: 28 years (2000).
Transportation: Commute to work: 94.6% car, 0.8% public transportation, 3.0% walk, 1.6% work from home (2000); Travel time to work: 18.4% less than 15 minutes, 40.5% 15 to 30 minutes, 24.9% 30 to 45 minutes, 1.4% 45 to 60 minutes, 14.7% 60 minutes or more (2000)

MINFORD (unincorporated postal area, zip code 45653). Covers a land area of 47.606 square miles and a water area of 0.010 square miles. Located at 38.87° N. Lat.; 82.84° W. Long. Elevation is 657 feet.
Population: 4,163 (2000); Race: 99.3% White, 0.0% Black, 0.0% Asian, 0.2% Hispanic of any race (2000); Density: 87.4 persons per square mile (2000); Age: 25.7% under 18, 13.4% over 64 (2000); Marriage status: 19.8% never married, 65.3% now married, 5.9% widowed, 9.0% divorced (2000); Foreign born: 0.0% (2000); Ancestry (includes multiple ancestries): 21.6% United States or American, 16.0% German, 9.5% English, 7.4% Irish, 5.3% Other groups (2000).
Economy: Employment by occupation: 7.1% management, 19.1% professional, 15.6% services, 21.9% sales, 0.6% farming, 13.8% construction, 21.9% production (2000).
Income: Per capita income: $16,354 (2000); Median household income: $37,281 (2000); Poverty rate: 14.6% (2000).

Education: Percent of population age 25 and over with: High school diploma (including GED) or higher: 77.8% (2000); Bachelor's degree or higher: 11.7% (2000).

School District(s)

Minford Local (PK-12)
2005-06 Enrollment: 1,619 . . . . (740) 820-3896

Housing: Homeownership rate: 85.0% (2000); Median home value: $75,700 (2000); Median rent: $287 per month (2000); Median age of housing: 29 years (2000).

Transportation: Commute to work: 96.1% car, 0.0% public transportation, 0.7% walk, 3.0% work from home (2000); Travel time to work: 19.2% less than 15 minutes, 38.4% 15 to 30 minutes, 29.5% 30 to 45 minutes, 5.0% 45 to 60 minutes, 7.8% 60 minutes or more (2000)

NEW BOSTON (village). Covers a land area of 1.107 square miles and a water area of 0.052 square miles. Located at 38.75° N. Lat.; 82.93° W. Long. Elevation is 512 feet.

History: New Boston was founded in 1891 and named for Boston, whose capitalists financed a sawmill here. New Boston later became a river steel town.

Population: 2,717 (1990); 2,340 (2000); 2,238 (2007); 2,171 (2012 projected); Race: 97.7% White, 0.0% Black, 0.1% Asian, 0.7% Hispanic of any race (2007); Density: 2,022.2 persons per square mile (2007); Average household size: 2.06 (2007); Median age: 38.1 (2007); Males per 100 females: 74.0 (2007); Marriage status: 23.0% never married, 43.2% now married, 15.6% widowed, 18.2% divorced (2000); Foreign born: 0.0% (2000); Ancestry (includes multiple ancestries): 20.3% United States or American, 13.2% Other groups, 10.8% German, 9.5% Irish, 6.7% English (2000).

Economy: Single-family building permits issued: 0 (2007); Multi-family building permits issued: 0 (2007); Employment by occupation: 5.1% management, 10.3% professional, 23.2% services, 36.2% sales, 0.0% farming, 5.4% construction, 19.8% production (2000).

Income: Per capita income: $14,008 (2007); Median household income: $18,558 (2007); Average household income: $28,351 (2007); Percent of households with income of $100,000 or more: 1.9% (2007); Poverty rate: 32.2% (2000).

Education: Percent of population age 25 and over with: High school diploma (including GED) or higher: 58.2% (2007); Bachelor's degree or higher: 5.3% (2007); Master's degree or higher: 1.2% (2007).

School District(s)

New Boston Local (PK-12)
2005-06 Enrollment: 432 . . . . (740) 456-4626

Two-year College(s)

Southeastern Business College (Private, For-profit)
Fall 2007 Enrollment: 32 . . . . (740) 456-4124
2007-08 Tuition: In-state $9,380; Out-of-state $9,380

Housing: Homeownership rate: 39.1% (2007); Median home value: $55,267 (2007); Median rent: $246 per month (2000); Median age of housing: 53 years (2000).

Safety: Violent crime rate: 37.0 per 10,000 population; Property crime rate: 1,490.1 per 10,000 population (2007).

Transportation: Commute to work: 90.1% car, 0.9% public transportation, 5.7% walk, 1.0% work from home (2000); Travel time to work: 51.7% less than 15 minutes, 27.5% 15 to 30 minutes, 5.0% 30 to 45 minutes, 7.3% 45 to 60 minutes, 8.6% 60 minutes or more (2000)

OTWAY (village). Covers a land area of 0.222 square miles and a water area of 0 square miles. Located at 38.86° N. Lat.; 83.18° W. Long. Elevation is 597 feet.

Population: 105 (1990); 86 (2000); 77 (2007); 76 (2012 projected); Race: 93.5% White, 0.0% Black, 0.0% Asian, 5.2% Hispanic of any race (2007); Density: 347.5 persons per square mile (2007); Average household size: 2.08 (2007); Median age: 45.4 (2007); Males per 100 females: 83.3 (2007); Marriage status: 20.3% never married, 53.6% now married, 14.5% widowed, 11.6% divorced (2000); Foreign born: 0.0% (2000); Ancestry (includes multiple ancestries): 27.1% United States or American, 14.1% German, 7.1% Dutch, 7.1% Scotch-Irish, 4.7% Irish (2000).

Economy: Employment by occupation: 4.0% management, 0.0% professional, 12.0% services, 36.0% sales, 0.0% farming, 24.0% construction, 24.0% production (2000).

Income: Per capita income: $19,773 (2007); Median household income: $37,500 (2007); Average household income: $41,149 (2007); Percent of households with income of $100,000 or more: 5.4% (2007); Poverty rate: 14.1% (2000).

Education: Percent of population age 25 and over with: High school diploma (including GED) or higher: 67.2% (2007); Bachelor's degree or higher: 3.4% (2007); Master's degree or higher: 0.0% (2007).

Housing: Homeownership rate: 81.1% (2007); Median home value: $60,000 (2007); Median rent: $283 per month (2000); Median age of housing: 60+ years (2000).

Transportation: Commute to work: 92.0% car, 8.0% public transportation, 0.0% walk, 0.0% work from home (2000); Travel time to work: 8.0% less than 15 minutes, 36.0% 15 to 30 minutes, 44.0% 30 to 45 minutes, 0.0% 45 to 60 minutes, 12.0% 60 minutes or more (2000)

PORTSMOUTH (city). County seat. Covers a land area of 10.770 square miles and a water area of 0.288 square miles. Located at 38.74° N. Lat.; 82.96° W. Long. Elevation is 531 feet.

History: Portsmouth was founded in 1803 by Major Henry Massie, a Virginia land speculator. By 1815 Portsmouth was an incorporated town. Industry moved from lumbering and fur trading, to canal-boat center, to iron works and brickyards. In 1927, a suspension bridge was built across the Ohio River to connect the town with South Portsmouth in Kentucky.

Population: 22,676 (1990); 20,909 (2000); 19,840 (2007); 19,001 (2012 projected); Race: 91.0% White, 5.1% Black, 1.0% Asian, 1.3% Hispanic of any race (2007); Density: 1,842.2 persons per square mile (2007); Average household size: 2.24 (2007); Median age: 38.7 (2007); Males per 100 females: 85.2 (2007); Marriage status: 24.4% never married, 48.8% now married, 11.5% widowed, 15.2% divorced (2000); Foreign born: 1.1% (2000); Ancestry (includes multiple ancestries): 16.7% German, 15.9% United States or American, 12.8% Other groups, 12.5% Irish, 10.0% English (2000).

Economy: Single-family building permits issued: 0 (2007); Multi-family building permits issued: 40 (2007); Employment by occupation: 8.8% management, 20.3% professional, 21.6% services, 24.3% sales, 0.7% farming, 8.9% construction, 15.3% production (2000).

Income: Per capita income: $17,324 (2007); Median household income: $26,008 (2007); Average household income: $38,196 (2007); Percent of households with income of $100,000 or more: 5.6% (2007); Poverty rate: 23.6% (2000).

Education: Percent of population age 25 and over with: High school diploma (including GED) or higher: 74.1% (2007); Bachelor's degree or higher: 12.5% (2007); Master's degree or higher: 5.3% (2007).

School District(s)

Clay Local (KG-12)
2005-06 Enrollment: 608 . . . . (740) 354-6645
Portsmouth City (PK-12)
2005-06 Enrollment: 1,974 . . . . (740) 354-4727
Sciotoville (06-12)
2005-06 Enrollment: 429 . . . . (740) 776-6777

Four-year College(s)

Shawnee State University (Public)
Fall 2007 Enrollment: 3,699 . . . . (740) 354-3205
2007-08 Tuition: In-state $5,832; Out-of-state $9,972

Two-year College(s)

Paramount Beauty Academy (Private, For-profit)
Fall 2007 Enrollment: 54 . . . . (740) 353-2436

Housing: Homeownership rate: 53.8% (2007); Median home value: $67,146 (2007); Median rent: $302 per month (2000); Median age of housing: 58 years (2000).

Hospitals: Southern Ohio Medical Center (488 beds)

Safety: Violent crime rate: 62.4 per 10,000 population; Property crime rate: 1,067.4 per 10,000 population (2007).

Newspapers: Portsmouth Daily Times (Local news; Circulation 14,627)

Transportation: Commute to work: 90.5% car, 1.4% public transportation, 5.5% walk, 1.6% work from home (2000); Travel time to work: 55.2% less than 15 minutes, 26.3% 15 to 30 minutes, 9.3% 30 to 45 minutes, 2.2% 45 to 60 minutes, 7.0% 60 minutes or more (2000)

Airports: Greater Portsmouth Regional (general aviation)

Additional Information Contacts

City of Portsmouth . . . . (740) 354-8807
http://www.ci.portsmouth.oh.us
Portsmouth Area Chamber of Commerce . . . . (740) 353-7647
http://www.portsmouth.org

RARDEN (village). Covers a land area of 0.204 square miles and a water area of 0 square miles. Located at 38.92° N. Lat.; 83.24° W. Long. Elevation is 620 feet.

Population: 184 (1990); 176 (2000); 166 (2007); 160 (2012 projected); Race: 93.4% White, 0.0% Black, 0.0% Asian, 0.0% Hispanic of any race (2007); Density: 811.9 persons per square mile (2007); Average household size: 2.52 (2007); Median age: 36.7 (2007); Males per 100 females: 97.6 (2007); Marriage status: 31.7% never married, 49.0% now married, 11.4% widowed, 7.9% divorced (2000); Foreign born: 0.0% (2000); Ancestry (includes multiple ancestries): 27.7% United States or American, 13.5% Other groups, 10.0% Irish, 9.6% German, 2.7% Italian (2000).
Economy: Employment by occupation: 7.0% management, 9.0% professional, 12.0% services, 18.0% sales, 2.0% farming, 20.0% construction, 32.0% production (2000).
Income: Per capita income: $19,955 (2007); Median household income: $46,429 (2007); Average household income: $50,189 (2007); Percent of households with income of $100,000 or more: 4.5% (2007); Poverty rate: 1.2% (2000).
Education: Percent of population age 25 and over with: High school diploma (including GED) or higher: 72.7% (2007); Bachelor's degree or higher: 3.6% (2007); Master's degree or higher: 3.6% (2007).
Housing: Homeownership rate: 63.6% (2007); Median home value: $75,000 (2007); Median rent: $264 per month (2000); Median age of housing: 49 years (2000).
Transportation: Commute to work: 89.0% car, 0.0% public transportation, 6.0% walk, 3.0% work from home (2000); Travel time to work: 25.8% less than 15 minutes, 18.6% 15 to 30 minutes, 18.6% 30 to 45 minutes, 7.2% 45 to 60 minutes, 29.9% 60 minutes or more (2000)

ROSEMOUNT (CDP). Covers a land area of 5.754 square miles and a water area of 0 square miles. Located at 38.78° N. Lat.; 82.97° W. Long. Elevation is 607 feet.
Population: 2,277 (1990); 2,043 (2000); 2,015 (2007); 1,969 (2012 projected); Race: 98.3% White, 0.2% Black, 0.1% Asian, 0.3% Hispanic of any race (2007); Density: 350.2 persons per square mile (2007); Average household size: 2.35 (2007); Median age: 42.8 (2007); Males per 100 females: 87.1 (2007); Marriage status: 16.5% never married, 68.9% now married, 8.0% widowed, 6.6% divorced (2000); Foreign born: 0.6% (2000); Ancestry (includes multiple ancestries): 19.0% German, 18.0% United States or American, 10.2% Irish, 10.2% English, 7.8% Other groups (2000).
Economy: Employment by occupation: 17.0% management, 12.4% professional, 19.7% services, 28.4% sales, 0.0% farming, 7.6% construction, 14.8% production (2000).
Income: Per capita income: $22,297 (2007); Median household income: $42,269 (2007); Average household income: $52,302 (2007); Percent of households with income of $100,000 or more: 8.7% (2007); Poverty rate: 8.3% (2000).
Education: Percent of population age 25 and over with: High school diploma (including GED) or higher: 92.0% (2007); Bachelor's degree or higher: 17.3% (2007); Master's degree or higher: 3.3% (2007).
Housing: Homeownership rate: 81.0% (2007); Median home value: $94,694 (2007); Median rent: $383 per month (2000); Median age of housing: 43 years (2000).
Transportation: Commute to work: 95.6% car, 1.0% public transportation, 0.0% walk, 3.4% work from home (2000); Travel time to work: 49.1% less than 15 minutes, 34.0% 15 to 30 minutes, 13.5% 30 to 45 minutes, 2.6% 45 to 60 minutes, 0.9% 60 minutes or more (2000)

SCIOTODALE (CDP). Covers a land area of 1.968 square miles and a water area of <.001 square miles. Located at 38.75° N. Lat.; 82.86° W. Long. Elevation is 597 feet.
Population: 1,128 (1990); 982 (2000); 910 (2007); 917 (2012 projected); Race: 97.6% White, 0.1% Black, 0.2% Asian, 0.4% Hispanic of any race (2007); Density: 462.4 persons per square mile (2007); Average household size: 2.55 (2007); Median age: 41.1 (2007); Males per 100 females: 95.3 (2007); Marriage status: 19.6% never married, 57.4% now married, 5.5% widowed, 17.6% divorced (2000); Foreign born: 0.0% (2000); Ancestry (includes multiple ancestries): 14.9% Irish, 14.1% United States or American, 13.2% German, 10.0% English, 7.5% Other groups (2000).
Economy: Employment by occupation: 7.8% management, 12.4% professional, 19.7% services, 18.7% sales, 0.0% farming, 17.4% construction, 24.1% production (2000).
Income: Per capita income: $22,835 (2007); Median household income: $43,833 (2007); Average household income: $58,207 (2007); Percent of households with income of $100,000 or more: 13.2% (2007); Poverty rate: 24.2% (2000).
Education: Percent of population age 25 and over with: High school diploma (including GED) or higher: 82.4% (2007); Bachelor's degree or higher: 3.1% (2007); Master's degree or higher: 0.5% (2007).
Housing: Homeownership rate: 83.5% (2007); Median home value: $95,000 (2007); Median rent: $311 per month (2000); Median age of housing: 45 years (2000).
Transportation: Commute to work: 96.9% car, 0.0% public transportation, 0.0% walk, 1.8% work from home (2000); Travel time to work: 28.5% less than 15 minutes, 33.5% 15 to 30 minutes, 18.1% 30 to 45 minutes, 4.3% 45 to 60 minutes, 15.7% 60 minutes or more (2000)

SOUTH WEBSTER (village). Covers a land area of 1.306 square miles and a water area of 0.018 square miles. Located at 38.81° N. Lat.; 82.72° W. Long. Elevation is 715 feet.
Population: 806 (1990); 764 (2000); 673 (2007); 646 (2012 projected); Race: 97.6% White, 0.0% Black, 0.0% Asian, 1.0% Hispanic of any race (2007); Density: 515.1 persons per square mile (2007); Average household size: 2.38 (2007); Median age: 38.7 (2007); Males per 100 females: 86.9 (2007); Marriage status: 23.4% never married, 55.0% now married, 10.3% widowed, 11.3% divorced (2000); Foreign born: 0.3% (2000); Ancestry (includes multiple ancestries): 20.3% German, 13.5% United States or American, 7.9% Other groups, 6.4% Irish, 6.3% English (2000).
Economy: Employment by occupation: 4.3% management, 18.4% professional, 23.3% services, 23.1% sales, 1.7% farming, 12.7% construction, 16.4% production (2000).
Income: Per capita income: $19,502 (2007); Median household income: $35,833 (2007); Average household income: $46,378 (2007); Percent of households with income of $100,000 or more: 8.5% (2007); Poverty rate: 16.4% (2000).
Education: Percent of population age 25 and over with: High school diploma (including GED) or higher: 83.3% (2007); Bachelor's degree or higher: 12.8% (2007); Master's degree or higher: 6.6% (2007).

School District(s)

Bloom-Vernon Local (PK-12)
2005-06 Enrollment: 1,022 . . . . (740) 778-2281
Housing: Homeownership rate: 74.2% (2007); Median home value: $91,111 (2007); Median rent: $259 per month (2000); Median age of housing: 44 years (2000).
Transportation: Commute to work: 93.5% car, 1.2% public transportation, 2.1% walk, 1.2% work from home (2000); Travel time to work: 21.8% less than 15 minutes, 27.5% 15 to 30 minutes, 33.7% 30 to 45 minutes, 10.1% 45 to 60 minutes, 6.9% 60 minutes or more (2000)

STOUT (unincorporated postal area, zip code 45684). Covers a land area of 75.384 square miles and a water area of 0.046 square miles. Located at 38.78° N. Lat.; 83.10° W. Long.
Population: 1,827 (2000); Race: 99.1% White, 0.0% Black, 0.0% Asian, 0.1% Hispanic of any race (2000); Density: 24.2 persons per square mile (2000); Age: 23.5% under 18, 12.2% over 64 (2000); Marriage status: 16.6% never married, 63.3% now married, 7.4% widowed, 12.7% divorced (2000); Foreign born: 0.1% (2000); Ancestry (includes multiple ancestries): 24.3% United States or American, 12.3% German, 8.0% Other groups, 7.1% Irish, 7.1% English (2000).
Economy: Employment by occupation: 4.8% management, 16.4% professional, 15.0% services, 19.3% sales, 1.3% farming, 21.5% construction, 21.7% production (2000).
Income: Per capita income: $14,269 (2000); Median household income: $30,000 (2000); Poverty rate: 17.9% (2000).
Education: Percent of population age 25 and over with: High school diploma (including GED) or higher: 65.0% (2000); Bachelor's degree or higher: 9.0% (2000).
Housing: Homeownership rate: 81.4% (2000); Median home value: $64,300 (2000); Median rent: $244 per month (2000); Median age of housing: 26 years (2000).
Transportation: Commute to work: 91.8% car, 0.0% public transportation, 5.6% walk, 2.5% work from home (2000); Travel time to work: 15.5% less than 15 minutes, 32.6% 15 to 30 minutes, 23.3% 30 to 45 minutes, 13.0% 45 to 60 minutes, 15.5% 60 minutes or more (2000)

WEST PORTSMOUTH (CDP). Covers a land area of 4.747 square miles and a water area of 0 square miles. Located at 38.75° N. Lat.; 83.03° W. Long. Elevation is 617 feet.
Population: 3,551 (1990); 3,458 (2000); 3,092 (2007); 2,836 (2012 projected); Race: 96.8% White, 0.1% Black, 0.0% Asian, 0.1% Hispanic of any race (2007); Density: 651.4 persons per square mile (2007); Average

household size: 2.46 (2007); Median age: 37.4 (2007); Males per 100 females: 90.0 (2007); Marriage status: 20.1% never married, 59.6% now married, 7.8% widowed, 12.5% divorced (2000); Foreign born: 0.1% (2000); Ancestry (includes multiple ancestries): 17.0% United States or American, 13.4% Irish, 12.5% German, 9.8% Other groups, 5.6% English (2000).
Economy: Employment by occupation: 3.4% management, 12.1% professional, 28.8% services, 19.4% sales, 0.4% farming, 12.5% construction, 23.4% production (2000).
Income: Per capita income: $14,872 (2007); Median household income: $32,554 (2007); Average household income: $36,525 (2007); Percent of households with income of $100,000 or more: 3.4% (2007); Poverty rate: 22.1% (2000).
Education: Percent of population age 25 and over with: High school diploma (including GED) or higher: 70.1% (2007); Bachelor's degree or higher: 5.2% (2007); Master's degree or higher: 0.7% (2007).

School District(s)

Washington-Nile Local (PK-12)
2005-06 Enrollment: 1,689 . . . . (740) 858-1111
Housing: Homeownership rate: 75.9% (2007); Median home value: $48,750 (2007); Median rent: $310 per month (2000); Median age of housing: 45 years (2000).
Transportation: Commute to work: 95.3% car, 1.4% public transportation, 0.5% walk, 2.4% work from home (2000); Travel time to work: 41.7% less than 15 minutes, 32.5% 15 to 30 minutes, 13.5% 30 to 45 minutes, 4.4% 45 to 60 minutes, 7.8% 60 minutes or more (2000)

WHEELERSBURG (CDP). Covers a land area of 5.815 square miles and a water area of 0.080 square miles. Located at 38.73° N. Lat.; 82.84° W. Long. Elevation is 554 feet.
Population: 6,252 (1990); 6,471 (2000); 6,891 (2007); 7,099 (2012 projected); Race: 97.4% White, 0.4% Black, 0.2% Asian, 0.7% Hispanic of any race (2007); Density: 1,185.1 persons per square mile (2007); Average household size: 2.45 (2007); Median age: 40.6 (2007); Males per 100 females: 83.5 (2007); Marriage status: 18.5% never married, 61.6% now married, 9.2% widowed, 10.6% divorced (2000); Foreign born: 0.0% (2000); Ancestry (includes multiple ancestries): 21.2% German, 15.0% United States or American, 11.3% Irish, 7.8% English, 7.3% Other groups (2000).
Economy: Employment by occupation: 12.4% management, 23.5% professional, 22.8% services, 20.5% sales, 0.3% farming, 8.9% construction, 11.7% production (2000).
Income: Per capita income: $21,518 (2007); Median household income: $38,521 (2007); Average household income: $51,290 (2007); Percent of households with income of $100,000 or more: 9.2% (2007); Poverty rate: 14.2% (2000).
Education: Percent of population age 25 and over with: High school diploma (including GED) or higher: 79.1% (2007); Bachelor's degree or higher: 16.5% (2007); Master's degree or higher: 6.4% (2007).

School District(s)

Wheelersburg Local (PK-12)
2005-06 Enrollment: 1,536 . . . . (740) 574-8484
Housing: Homeownership rate: 68.3% (2007); Median home value: $108,333 (2007); Median rent: $322 per month (2000); Median age of housing: 30 years (2000).
Newspapers: Scioto Voice (Local news; Circulation 3,000)
Transportation: Commute to work: 97.2% car, 0.0% public transportation, 1.3% walk, 1.1% work from home (2000); Travel time to work: 32.3% less than 15 minutes, 42.7% 15 to 30 minutes, 12.9% 30 to 45 minutes, 6.7% 45 to 60 minutes, 5.5% 60 minutes or more (2000)

Seneca County

Located in northern Ohio; drained by the Sandusky River and its tributaries. Covers a land area of 550.59 square miles, a water area of 1.78 square miles, and is located in the Eastern Time Zone. The county was founded in 1820. County seat is Tiffin.

Seneca County is part of the Tiffin, OH Micropolitan Statistical Area. The entire metro area includes: Seneca County, OH

Weather Station: Tiffin Elevation: 738 feet

	Jan	Feb	Mar	Apr	May	Jun	Jul	Aug	Sep	Oct	Nov	Dec
High	32	36	48	60	72	80	84	82	76	63	49	38
Low	17	20	29	39	50	59	63	61	54	42	34	24
Precip	2.3	2.0	2.7	3.4	3.7	4.2	3.3	3.8	3.1	2.4	3.0	2.9
Snow	8.8	6.2	3.7	1.2	tr	0.0	0.0	0.0	0.0	tr	1.2	6.7

High and Low temperatures in degrees Fahrenheit; Precipitation and Snow in inches

Population: 59,733 (1990); 58,683 (2000); 57,175 (2007); 55,949 (2012 projected); Race: 94.5% White, 1.8% Black, 0.5% Asian, 3.8% Hispanic of any race (2007); Density: 103.8 persons per square mile (2007); Average household size: 2.57 (2007); Median age: 38.1 (2007); Males per 100 females: 98.5 (2007).
Religion: Five largest groups: 38.3% Catholic Church, 8.9% The United Methodist Church, 6.3% United Church of Christ, 4.5% Evangelical Lutheran Church in America, 1.0% Church of the Nazarene (2000).
Economy: Unemployment rate: 6.8% (6/2008); Total civilian labor force: 31,392 (6/2008); Leading industries: 28.1% manufacturing; 14.9% health care and social assistance; 11.8% retail trade (2005); Farms: 1,185 totaling 280,449 acres (2002); Companies that employ 500 or more persons: 3 (2006); Companies that employ 100 to 499 persons: 35 (2006); Companies that employ less than 100 persons: 1,254 (2006); Black-owned businesses: n/a (2002); Hispanic-owned businesses: n/a (2002); Asian-owned businesses: n/a (2002); Women-owned businesses: 779 (2002); Retail sales per capita: $10,619 (2008). Single-family building permits issued: 41 (2007); Multi-family building permits issued: 0 (2007).
Income: Per capita income: $20,253 (2007); Median household income: $43,395 (2007); Average household income: $51,338 (2007); Percent of households with income of $100,000 or more: 8.2% (2007); Poverty rate: 10.8% (2005); Bankruptcy rate: 3.19% (2007).
Taxes: Total county taxes per capita: $237 (2006); County property taxes per capita: $115 (2006).
Education: Percent of population age 25 and over with: High school diploma (including GED) or higher: 83.1% (2007); Bachelor's degree or higher: 12.5% (2007); Master's degree or higher: 4.3% (2007).
Housing: Homeownership rate: 75.7% (2007); Median home value: $105,117 (2007); Median rent: $339 per month (2000); Median age of housing: 49 years (2000).
Health: Birth rate: 132.3 per 10,000 population (2007); Death rate: 96.6 per 10,000 population (2007); Age-adjusted cancer mortality rate: 188.4 deaths per 100,000 population (2005); Number of physicians: 11.9 per 10,000 population (2005); Hospital beds: 18.4 per 10,000 population (2004); Hospital admissions: 634.6 per 10,000 population (2004).
Elections: 2004 Presidential election results: 58.9% Bush, 40.6% Kerry, 0.0% Nader, 0.3% Badnarik
National and State Parks: Sandusky Scenic River State Access Area; Springville Marsh State Natural Area
Additional Information Contacts
Seneca County Government . . . . (419) 447-4550

City of Fostoria. . . . . (419) 435-8282
http://www.ci.fostoria.oh.us
City of Tiffin . . . . (419) 448-5401
http://www.tiffinohio.com
Fostoria Area Chamber of Commerce. . . . . (419) 435-0486
http://www.fostoriaoh.org
Seneca County Convention and Visitors Bureau. . . . . (419) 447-5866
http://www.senecacounty.com/visitor
Tiffin Area Chamber of Commerce . . . . (419) 447-4141
http://www.tiffinchamber.com

Seneca County Communities

ALVADA (unincorporated postal area, zip code 44802). Aka Alveda. Covers a land area of 29.497 square miles and a water area of 0 square miles. Located at 41.05° N. Lat.; 83.41° W. Long. Elevation is 847 feet.
Population: 1,013 (2000); Race: 99.9% White, 0.0% Black, 0.0% Asian, 1.5% Hispanic of any race (2000); Density: 34.3 persons per square mile (2000); Age: 30.7% under 18, 12.0% over 64 (2000); Marriage status: 22.4% never married, 68.3% now married, 2.7% widowed, 6.5% divorced (2000); Foreign born: 0.2% (2000); Ancestry (includes multiple ancestries): 50.0% German, 12.1% English, 8.6% United States or American, 7.3% Irish, 4.9% French (except Basque) (2000).
Economy: Employment by occupation: 11.8% management, 9.6% professional, 10.0% services, 22.3% sales, 0.8% farming, 15.5% construction, 30.1% production (2000).

Income: Per capita income: $18,673 (2000); Median household income: $48,621 (2000); Poverty rate: 1.6% (2000).
Education: Percent of population age 25 and over with: High school diploma (including GED) or higher: 86.8% (2000); Bachelor's degree or higher: 8.8% (2000).
Housing: Homeownership rate: 87.5% (2000); Median home value: $108,100 (2000); Median rent: $331 per month (2000); Median age of housing: 44 years (2000).
Transportation: Commute to work: 90.3% car, 0.0% public transportation, 1.4% walk, 7.1% work from home (2000); Travel time to work: 27.0% less than 15 minutes, 58.4% 15 to 30 minutes, 10.0% 30 to 45 minutes, 0.9% 45 to 60 minutes, 3.7% 60 minutes or more (2000)

ATTICA (village). Covers a land area of 0.535 square miles and a water area of 0 square miles. Located at 41.06° N. Lat.; 82.88° W. Long. Elevation is 948 feet.
Population: 992 (1990); 955 (2000); 788 (2007); 777 (2012 projected); Race: 98.6% White, 0.0% Black, 0.0% Asian, 0.6% Hispanic of any race (2007); Density: 1,471.5 persons per square mile (2007); Average household size: 2.35 (2007); Median age: 39.0 (2007); Males per 100 females: 90.3 (2007); Marriage status: 21.0% never married, 61.9% now married, 5.7% widowed, 11.5% divorced (2000); Foreign born: 1.3% (2000); Ancestry (includes multiple ancestries): 44.9% German, 11.0% Irish, 9.0% United States or American, 8.5% English, 5.7% Other groups (2000).
Economy: Single-family building permits issued: 0 (2007); Multi-family building permits issued: 0 (2007); Employment by occupation: 7.6% management, 10.1% professional, 16.7% services, 16.5% sales, 0.4% farming, 9.3% construction, 39.3% production (2000).
Income: Per capita income: $21,504 (2007); Median household income: $44,783 (2007); Average household income: $50,432 (2007); Percent of households with income of $100,000 or more: 6.0% (2007); Poverty rate: 9.8% (2000).
Education: Percent of population age 25 and over with: High school diploma (including GED) or higher: 82.6% (2007); Bachelor's degree or higher: 11.2% (2007); Master's degree or higher: 5.6% (2007).

School District(s)

Seneca East Local (PK-12)
2005-06 Enrollment: 992 . . . . (419) 426-7041
Housing: Homeownership rate: 76.8% (2007); Median home value: $99,412 (2007); Median rent: $317 per month (2000); Median age of housing: 60 years (2000).
Newspapers: Attica Hub (Community news; Circulation 3,000); Bloomville Gazette (Community news; Circulation 400)
Transportation: Commute to work: 91.3% car, 0.0% public transportation, 5.7% walk, 3.0% work from home (2000); Travel time to work: 30.9% less than 15 minutes, 38.4% 15 to 30 minutes, 22.6% 30 to 45 minutes, 4.6% 45 to 60 minutes, 3.5% 60 minutes or more (2000)

BETTSVILLE (village). Covers a land area of 0.520 square miles and a water area of 0 square miles. Located at 41.24° N. Lat.; 83.23° W. Long. Elevation is 699 feet.
Population: 752 (1990); 784 (2000); 693 (2007); 690 (2012 projected); Race: 94.9% White, 0.1% Black, 0.4% Asian, 5.5% Hispanic of any race (2007); Density: 1,331.8 persons per square mile (2007); Average household size: 2.55 (2007); Median age: 35.4 (2007); Males per 100 females: 98.0 (2007); Marriage status: 23.0% never married, 61.0% now married, 4.3% widowed, 11.7% divorced (2000); Foreign born: 1.1% (2000); Ancestry (includes multiple ancestries): 44.7% German, 13.4% Other groups, 9.6% United States or American, 8.5% English, 8.3% Irish (2000).
Economy: Employment by occupation: 5.9% management, 8.1% professional, 13.8% services, 18.9% sales, 0.0% farming, 9.7% construction, 43.5% production (2000).
Income: Per capita income: $20,469 (2007); Median household income: $43,929 (2007); Average household income: $52,151 (2007); Percent of households with income of $100,000 or more: 4.8% (2007); Poverty rate: 7.4% (2000).
Education: Percent of population age 25 and over with: High school diploma (including GED) or higher: 81.2% (2007); Bachelor's degree or higher: 6.1% (2007); Master's degree or higher: 2.7% (2007).

School District(s)

Bettsville Local (PK-12)
2005-06 Enrollment: 228 . . . . (419) 986-5166
Housing: Homeownership rate: 80.5% (2007); Median home value: $85,536 (2007); Median rent: $288 per month (2000); Median age of housing: 58 years (2000).
Transportation: Commute to work: 91.1% car, 1.1% public transportation, 5.3% walk, 1.7% work from home (2000); Travel time to work: 18.9% less than 15 minutes, 59.0% 15 to 30 minutes, 11.3% 30 to 45 minutes, 6.5% 45 to 60 minutes, 4.2% 60 minutes or more (2000)

BLOOMVILLE (village). Covers a land area of 0.607 square miles and a water area of 0 square miles. Located at 41.05° N. Lat.; 83.01° W. Long. Elevation is 932 feet.
Population: 949 (1990); 1,045 (2000); 964 (2007); 922 (2012 projected); Race: 97.0% White, 0.5% Black, 0.0% Asian, 4.8% Hispanic of any race (2007); Density: 1,586.9 persons per square mile (2007); Average household size: 2.76 (2007); Median age: 33.4 (2007); Males per 100 females: 90.1 (2007); Marriage status: 21.1% never married, 62.6% now married, 5.5% widowed, 10.8% divorced (2000); Foreign born: 0.6% (2000); Ancestry (includes multiple ancestries): 39.9% German, 18.1% United States or American, 13.8% English, 11.7% Irish, 7.4% Other groups (2000).
Economy: Single-family building permits issued: 0 (2007); Multi-family building permits issued: 0 (2007); Employment by occupation: 5.0% management, 12.2% professional, 20.5% services, 17.9% sales, 0.0% farming, 12.4% construction, 32.0% production (2000).
Income: Per capita income: $16,440 (2007); Median household income: $41,196 (2007); Average household income: $44,950 (2007); Percent of households with income of $100,000 or more: 4.6% (2007); Poverty rate: 5.8% (2000).
Education: Percent of population age 25 and over with: High school diploma (including GED) or higher: 86.6% (2007); Bachelor's degree or higher: 13.6% (2007); Master's degree or higher: 4.6% (2007).

School District(s)

Buckeye Central Local (PK-12)
2005-06 Enrollment: 782 . . . . (419) 492-2864
Housing: Homeownership rate: 72.8% (2007); Median home value: $87,241 (2007); Median rent: $305 per month (2000); Median age of housing: 60+ years (2000).
Transportation: Commute to work: 93.4% car, 1.8% public transportation, 3.1% walk, 1.8% work from home (2000); Travel time to work: 20.9% less than 15 minutes, 47.5% 15 to 30 minutes, 19.1% 30 to 45 minutes, 5.2% 45 to 60 minutes, 7.2% 60 minutes or more (2000)

FOSTORIA (city). Covers a land area of 7.265 square miles and a water area of 0.218 square miles. Located at 41.15° N. Lat.; 83.41° W. Long. Elevation is 781 feet.
History: Fostoria grew from the union in 1854 of two rival settlements, Rome and Risdon, which had been established in 1832. The town was named for C.W. Foster, a local real estate developer whose son, Charles, served as governor of Ohio (1880-1884).
Population: 14,774 (1990); 13,931 (2000); 13,307 (2007); 12,777 (2012 projected); Race: 86.6% White, 5.8% Black, 0.6% Asian, 8.7% Hispanic of any race (2007); Density: 1,831.7 persons per square mile (2007); Average household size: 2.44 (2007); Median age: 37.0 (2007); Males per 100 females: 91.5 (2007); Marriage status: 26.4% never married, 49.6% now married, 10.2% widowed, 13.8% divorced (2000); Foreign born: 2.0% (2000); Ancestry (includes multiple ancestries): 33.2% German, 18.2% Other groups, 9.6% Irish, 7.6% English, 6.5% United States or American (2000).
Economy: Single-family building permits issued: 0 (2007); Multi-family building permits issued: 0 (2007); Employment by occupation: 6.9% management, 10.3% professional, 14.6% services, 18.9% sales, 0.2% farming, 8.0% construction, 41.2% production (2000).
Income: Per capita income: $17,431 (2007); Median household income: $34,291 (2007); Average household income: $41,938 (2007); Percent of households with income of $100,000 or more: 4.8% (2007); Poverty rate: 11.2% (2000).
Education: Percent of population age 25 and over with: High school diploma (including GED) or higher: 78.1% (2007); Bachelor's degree or higher: 8.8% (2007); Master's degree or higher: 2.6% (2007).

School District(s)

Fostoria City (PK-12)
2005-06 Enrollment: 2,176 . . . . (419) 435-8163
Lakota Local (PK-12)
2005-06 Enrollment: 1,099 . . . . (419) 457-2911

Housing: Homeownership rate: 70.7% (2007); Median home value: $71,994 (2007); Median rent: $325 per month (2000); Median age of housing: 53 years (2000).
Hospitals: Fostoria Community Hospital (66 beds)
Newspapers: The Fostoria Focus (Local news; Circulation 10,000); Fostoria Review-Times (Local news; Circulation 8,000)
Transportation: Commute to work: 92.1% car, 1.1% public transportation, 3.5% walk, 1.4% work from home (2000); Travel time to work: 46.0% less than 15 minutes, 28.5% 15 to 30 minutes, 16.2% 30 to 45 minutes, 4.5% 45 to 60 minutes, 4.8% 60 minutes or more (2000)
Airports: Fostoria Metropolitan (general aviation)
Additional Information Contacts
City of Fostoria . . . . (419) 435-8282
http://www.ci.fostoria.oh.us
Fostoria Area Chamber of Commerce . . . . (419) 435-0486
http://www.fostoriaoh.org

GREEN SPRINGS (village). Covers a land area of 1.072 square miles and a water area of 0.002 square miles. Located at 41.25° N. Lat.; 83.05° W. Long. Elevation is 709 feet.
History: Green Springs developed as a winter and summer resort and spa, attracting visitors for its waters.
Population: 1,446 (1990); 1,247 (2000); 1,201 (2007); 1,190 (2012 projected); Race: 94.1% White, 0.3% Black, 1.0% Asian, 5.0% Hispanic of any race (2007); Density: 1,120.2 persons per square mile (2007); Average household size: 2.75 (2007); Median age: 41.1 (2007); Males per 100 females: 91.9 (2007); Marriage status: 18.8% never married, 59.5% now married, 12.3% widowed, 9.4% divorced (2000); Foreign born: 0.5% (2000); Ancestry (includes multiple ancestries): 35.5% German, 12.3% Irish, 11.2% Other groups, 10.6% English, 9.1% United States or American (2000).
Economy: Employment by occupation: 5.6% management, 8.8% professional, 14.9% services, 22.8% sales, 0.0% farming, 13.0% construction, 35.0% production (2000).
Income: Per capita income: $17,605 (2007); Median household income: $38,173 (2007); Average household income: $46,013 (2007); Percent of households with income of $100,000 or more: 5.0% (2007); Poverty rate: 8.7% (2000).
Education: Percent of population age 25 and over with: High school diploma (including GED) or higher: 77.4% (2007); Bachelor's degree or higher: 6.4% (2007); Master's degree or higher: 1.7% (2007).
School District(s)
Clyde-Green Springs Exempted Village (PK-12)
2005-06 Enrollment: 2,415 . . . . (419) 547-0588
Housing: Homeownership rate: 68.2% (2007); Median home value: $90,769 (2007); Median rent: $322 per month (2000); Median age of housing: 60+ years (2000).
Hospitals: St. Francis Health Care Centre (186 beds)
Transportation: Commute to work: 92.3% car, 1.0% public transportation, 3.3% walk, 1.9% work from home (2000); Travel time to work: 34.4% less than 15 minutes, 45.7% 15 to 30 minutes, 10.6% 30 to 45 minutes, 2.4% 45 to 60 minutes, 6.8% 60 minutes or more (2000)

KANSAS (unincorporated postal area, zip code 44841). Covers a land area of 19.918 square miles and a water area of 0 square miles. Located at 41.25° N. Lat.; 83.29° W. Long. Elevation is 725 feet.
Population: 863 (2000); Race: 100.0% White, 0.0% Black, 0.0% Asian, 0.0% Hispanic of any race (2000); Density: 43.3 persons per square mile (2000); Age: 27.1% under 18, 7.5% over 64 (2000); Marriage status: 29.5% never married, 60.2% now married, 3.7% widowed, 6.6% divorced (2000); Foreign born: 1.9% (2000); Ancestry (includes multiple ancestries): 49.9% German, 16.3% United States or American, 10.1% Irish, 6.2% English, 2.7% French (except Basque) (2000).
Economy: Employment by occupation: 10.2% management, 12.9% professional, 8.9% services, 16.6% sales, 5.6% farming, 8.1% construction, 37.8% production (2000).
Income: Per capita income: $17,943 (2000); Median household income: $51,193 (2000); Poverty rate: 8.7% (2000).
Education: Percent of population age 25 and over with: High school diploma (including GED) or higher: 88.0% (2000); Bachelor's degree or higher: 5.6% (2000).
School District(s)
Lakota Local (PK-12)
2005-06 Enrollment: 1,099 . . . . (419) 457-2911
Housing: Homeownership rate: 90.3% (2000); Median home value: $82,900 (2000); Median rent: $385 per month (2000); Median age of housing: 49 years (2000).
Transportation: Commute to work: 95.8% car, 0.0% public transportation, 1.3% walk, 2.8% work from home (2000); Travel time to work: 23.4% less than 15 minutes, 48.9% 15 to 30 minutes, 12.4% 30 to 45 minutes, 7.6% 45 to 60 minutes, 7.6% 60 minutes or more (2000)

NEW RIEGEL (village). Covers a land area of 0.198 square miles and a water area of 0 square miles. Located at 41.05° N. Lat.; 83.31° W. Long. Elevation is 830 feet.
Population: 298 (1990); 226 (2000); 225 (2007); 221 (2012 projected); Race: 99.6% White, 0.0% Black, 0.0% Asian, 1.3% Hispanic of any race (2007); Density: 1,136.2 persons per square mile (2007); Average household size: 2.18 (2007); Median age: 43.1 (2007); Males per 100 females: 89.1 (2007); Marriage status: 24.6% never married, 56.3% now married, 7.1% widowed, 12.0% divorced (2000); Foreign born: 0.0% (2000); Ancestry (includes multiple ancestries): 75.0% German, 8.6% Other groups, 4.5% Italian, 4.1% Dutch, 2.7% United States or American (2000).
Economy: Employment by occupation: 0.9% management, 21.7% professional, 13.0% services, 20.0% sales, 0.0% farming, 12.2% construction, 32.2% production (2000).
Income: Per capita income: $20,584 (2007); Median household income: $35,938 (2007); Average household income: $44,660 (2007); Percent of households with income of $100,000 or more: 5.8% (2007); Poverty rate: 4.1% (2000).
Education: Percent of population age 25 and over with: High school diploma (including GED) or higher: 87.7% (2007); Bachelor's degree or higher: 8.0% (2007); Master's degree or higher: 1.9% (2007).
School District(s)
New Riegel Local (PK-12)
2005-06 Enrollment: 441 . . . . (419) 595-2265
Housing: Homeownership rate: 73.8% (2007); Median home value: $97,500 (2007); Median rent: $275 per month (2000); Median age of housing: 60+ years (2000).
Transportation: Commute to work: 77.5% car, 0.0% public transportation, 18.9% walk, 1.8% work from home (2000); Travel time to work: 33.9% less than 15 minutes, 45.0% 15 to 30 minutes, 13.8% 30 to 45 minutes, 5.5% 45 to 60 minutes, 1.8% 60 minutes or more (2000)

REPUBLIC (village). Covers a land area of 0.863 square miles and a water area of 0 square miles. Located at 41.12° N. Lat.; 83.01° W. Long. Elevation is 879 feet.
Population: 563 (1990); 614 (2000); 550 (2007); 552 (2012 projected); Race: 99.5% White, 0.0% Black, 0.0% Asian, 2.4% Hispanic of any race (2007); Density: 637.3 persons per square mile (2007); Average household size: 2.66 (2007); Median age: 33.5 (2007); Males per 100 females: 100.7 (2007); Marriage status: 22.6% never married, 62.8% now married, 8.3% widowed, 6.2% divorced (2000); Foreign born: 0.7% (2000); Ancestry (includes multiple ancestries): 43.8% German, 10.3% United States or American, 9.8% English, 9.3% Irish, 6.2% Other groups (2000).
Economy: Employment by occupation: 6.1% management, 9.6% professional, 17.9% services, 22.1% sales, 0.0% farming, 16.1% construction, 28.2% production (2000).
Income: Per capita income: $18,664 (2007); Median household income: $44,643 (2007); Average household income: $49,541 (2007); Percent of households with income of $100,000 or more: 7.2% (2007); Poverty rate: 7.6% (2000).
Education: Percent of population age 25 and over with: High school diploma (including GED) or higher: 83.6% (2007); Bachelor's degree or higher: 6.6% (2007); Master's degree or higher: 2.4% (2007).
School District(s)
Seneca East Local (PK-12)
2005-06 Enrollment: 992 . . . . (419) 426-7041
Housing: Homeownership rate: 77.8% (2007); Median home value: $75,250 (2007); Median rent: $331 per month (2000); Median age of housing: 60+ years (2000).
Transportation: Commute to work: 87.6% car, 2.5% public transportation, 6.2% walk, 1.8% work from home (2000); Travel time to work: 28.9% less than 15 minutes, 50.7% 15 to 30 minutes, 10.7% 30 to 45 minutes, 7.8% 45 to 60 minutes, 1.9% 60 minutes or more (2000)

TIFFIN (city). County seat. Covers a land area of 6.494 square miles and a water area of 0.142 square miles. Located at 41.11° N. Lat.; 83.17° W. Long. Elevation is 745 feet.
History: In 1817, Erastus Bowe built the Pan Yan Tavern on the north side of the Sandusky River, and a town called Oakley grew up around it. In 1820 Josiah Hedges established a settlement on the south side of the river opposite Oakley, calling it Tiffin after Edward Tiffin, the first governor of Ohio. The two villages were united as Tiffin in 1850.
Population: 19,009 (1990); 18,135 (2000); 17,132 (2007); 16,509 (2012 projected); Race: 95.6% White, 1.6% Black, 0.6% Asian, 2.7% Hispanic of any race (2007); Density: 2,637.9 persons per square mile (2007); Average household size: 2.41 (2007); Median age: 36.7 (2007); Males per 100 females: 96.5 (2007); Marriage status: 30.0% never married, 50.3% now married, 8.3% widowed, 11.4% divorced (2000); Foreign born: 1.3% (2000); Ancestry (includes multiple ancestries): 44.2% German, 11.0% Irish, 9.6% United States or American, 9.0% English, 8.4% Other groups (2000).
Economy: Single-family building permits issued: 7 (2007); Multi-family building permits issued: 0 (2007); Employment by occupation: 8.0% management, 16.0% professional, 17.0% services, 21.6% sales, 0.3% farming, 8.6% construction, 28.4% production (2000).
Income: Per capita income: $19,100 (2007); Median household income: $37,783 (2007); Average household income: $44,960 (2007); Percent of households with income of $100,000 or more: 5.0% (2007); Poverty rate: 11.1% (2000).
Education: Percent of population age 25 and over with: High school diploma (including GED) or higher: 83.8% (2007); Bachelor's degree or higher: 17.3% (2007); Master's degree or higher: 6.1% (2007).

School District(s)

Bridges Community Academy (KG-12)
2005-06 Enrollment: 119 .... (419) 455-9295
Tiffin City (PK-12)
2005-06 Enrollment: 3,002 .... (419) 447-2515
Tiffin City Digital Academy
2005-06 Enrollment: n/a ....
Vanguard-Sentinel (07-12)
2005-06 Enrollment: n/a .... (419) 332-2626

Four-year College(s)

Heidelberg College (Private, Not-for-profit, United Church of Christ)
Fall 2007 Enrollment: 1,584 .... (419) 448-2000
2007-08 Tuition: In-state $18,618; Out-of-state $18,618
Tiffin University (Private, Not-for-profit)
Fall 2007 Enrollment: 2,357 .... (800) 968-6446
2007-08 Tuition: In-state $16,800; Out-of-state $16,800

Two-year College(s)

Tiffin Academy of Hair Design (Private, For-profit)
Fall 2007 Enrollment: 64 .... (419) 447-3117
2007-08 Tuition: In-state $9,025; Out-of-state $9,025

Housing: Homeownership rate: 64.6% (2007); Median home value: $98,222 (2007); Median rent: $356 per month (2000); Median age of housing: 54 years (2000).
Hospitals: Mercy Hospital of Tiffin (105 beds)
Newspapers: Tiffin Advertiser-Tribune (Local news; Circulation 10,899)
Transportation: Commute to work: 88.8% car, 1.7% public transportation, 6.4% walk, 1.8% work from home (2000); Travel time to work: 60.2% less than 15 minutes, 18.9% 15 to 30 minutes, 12.6% 30 to 45 minutes, 3.8% 45 to 60 minutes, 4.5% 60 minutes or more (2000)
Airports: Seneca County (general aviation)
Additional Information Contacts
City of Tiffin .... (419) 448-5401
http://www.tiffinohio.com
Seneca County Convention and Visitors Bureau .... (419) 447-5866
http://www.senecacounty.com/visitor
Tiffin Area Chamber of Commerce .... (419) 447-4141
http://www.tiffinchamber.com

Shelby County

Located in western Ohio; crossed by the Great Miami River; includes Lake Loramie. Covers a land area of 409.27 square miles, a water area of 1.76 square miles, and is located in the Eastern Time Zone. The county was founded in 1819. County seat is Sidney.

Shelby County is part of the Sidney, OH Micropolitan Statistical Area. The entire metro area includes: Shelby County, OH

Population: 44,915 (1990); 47,910 (2000); 48,953 (2007); 49,500 (2012 projected); Race: 95.4% White, 1.7% Black, 1.1% Asian, 1.2% Hispanic of any race (2007); Density: 119.6 persons per square mile (2007); Average household size: 2.65 (2007); Median age: 36.5 (2007); Males per 100 females: 99.2 (2007).
Religion: Five largest groups: 28.1% Catholic Church, 7.6% Evangelical Lutheran Church in America, 6.4% The United Methodist Church, 3.0% Southern Baptist Convention, 2.5% United Church of Christ (2000).
Economy: Unemployment rate: 5.4% (6/2008); Total civilian labor force: 28,549 (6/2008); Leading industries: 51.8% manufacturing; 8.0% retail trade; 7.1% health care and social assistance (2005); Farms: 1,022 totaling 207,329 acres (2002); Companies that employ 500 or more persons: 6 (2006); Companies that employ 100 to 499 persons: 42 (2006); Companies that employ less than 100 persons: 998 (2006); Black-owned businesses: n/a (2002); Hispanic-owned businesses: n/a (2002); Asian-owned businesses: n/a (2002); Women-owned businesses: 689 (2002); Retail sales per capita: $12,871 (2008). Single-family building permits issued: 159 (2007); Multi-family building permits issued: 69 (2007).
Income: Per capita income: $23,737 (2007); Median household income: $51,293 (2007); Average household income: $61,674 (2007); Percent of households with income of $100,000 or more: 13.9% (2007); Poverty rate: 9.2% (2005); Bankruptcy rate: 3.56% (2007).
Taxes: Total county taxes per capita: $330 (2006); County property taxes per capita: $157 (2006).
Education: Percent of population age 25 and over with: High school diploma (including GED) or higher: 81.7% (2007); Bachelor's degree or higher: 12.8% (2007); Master's degree or higher: 4.0% (2007).
Housing: Homeownership rate: 74.7% (2007); Median home value: $123,900 (2007); Median rent: $380 per month (2000); Median age of housing: 34 years (2000).
Health: Birth rate: 150.5 per 10,000 population (2007); Death rate: 83.3 per 10,000 population (2007); Age-adjusted cancer mortality rate: 170.8 deaths per 100,000 population (2005); Number of physicians: 10.5 per 10,000 population (2005); Hospital beds: 18.6 per 10,000 population (2004); Hospital admissions: 812.6 per 10,000 population (2004).
Elections: 2004 Presidential election results: 70.9% Bush, 28.6% Kerry, 0.0% Nader, 0.2% Badnarik
National and State Parks: Lake Loramie State Park
Additional Information Contacts
Shelby County Government .... (937) 498-7226
http://www.co.shelby.oh.us
City of Sidney .... (937) 498-2335
http://www.sidneyoh.com
Sidney-Shelby County Chamber of Commerce .... (937) 492-9122
http://www.sidneyshelbychamber.com

Shelby County Communities

ANNA (village). Covers a land area of 0.837 square miles and a water area of 0 square miles. Located at 40.39° N. Lat.; 84.17° W. Long. Elevation is 1,033 feet.
Population: 1,211 (1990); 1,319 (2000); 1,465 (2007); 1,540 (2012 projected); Race: 96.2% White, 0.3% Black, 1.5% Asian, 0.7% Hispanic of any race (2007); Density: 1,751.2 persons per square mile (2007); Average household size: 2.71 (2007); Median age: 33.2 (2007); Males per 100 females: 101.8 (2007); Marriage status: 22.2% never married, 63.5% now married, 4.1% widowed, 10.3% divorced (2000); Foreign born: 1.8% (2000); Ancestry (includes multiple ancestries): 48.7% German, 10.8% Irish, 8.8% United States or American, 7.9% Other groups, 6.1% English (2000).
Economy: Single-family building permits issued: 5 (2007); Multi-family building permits issued: 0 (2007); Employment by occupation: 7.7% management, 14.0% professional, 13.3% services, 18.3% sales, 0.3% farming, 11.9% construction, 34.4% production (2000).
Income: Per capita income: $23,355 (2007); Median household income: $56,250 (2007); Average household income: $63,361 (2007); Percent of households with income of $100,000 or more: 13.3% (2007); Poverty rate: 3.6% (2000).
Education: Percent of population age 25 and over with: High school diploma (including GED) or higher: 87.1% (2007); Bachelor's degree or higher: 11.0% (2007); Master's degree or higher: 3.4% (2007).

School District(s)

Anna Local (KG-12)
2005-06 Enrollment: 1,225 . . . . (937) 394-2011

Housing: Homeownership rate: 77.8% (2007); Median home value: $111,047 (2007); Median rent: $438 per month (2000); Median age of housing: 31 years (2000).

Transportation: Commute to work: 95.4% car, 0.0% public transportation, 2.4% walk, 1.8% work from home (2000); Travel time to work: 44.4% less than 15 minutes, 43.9% 15 to 30 minutes, 5.7% 30 to 45 minutes, 3.0% 45 to 60 minutes, 3.0% 60 minutes or more (2000)

BOTKINS (village). Covers a land area of 0.919 square miles and a water area of 0 square miles. Located at 40.45° N. Lat.; 84.18° W. Long. Elevation is 1,001 feet.

Population: 1,390 (1990); 1,205 (2000); 1,288 (2007); 1,353 (2012 projected); Race: 99.1% White, 0.2% Black, 0.0% Asian, 0.9% Hispanic of any race (2007); Density: 1,401.3 persons per square mile (2007); Average household size: 2.55 (2007); Median age: 36.3 (2007); Males per 100 females: 105.1 (2007); Marriage status: 24.8% never married, 60.9% now married, 5.6% widowed, 8.7% divorced (2000); Foreign born: 0.7% (2000); Ancestry (includes multiple ancestries): 60.1% German, 9.7% United States or American, 9.0% Irish, 4.7% English, 2.4% Dutch (2000).

Economy: Single-family building permits issued: 1 (2007); Multi-family building permits issued: 0 (2007); Employment by occupation: 9.9% management, 14.6% professional, 12.8% services, 24.2% sales, 1.7% farming, 10.8% construction, 26.1% production (2000).

Income: Per capita income: $23,406 (2007); Median household income: $49,615 (2007); Average household income: $59,580 (2007); Percent of households with income of $100,000 or more: 13.6% (2007); Poverty rate: 3.6% (2000).

Education: Percent of population age 25 and over with: High school diploma (including GED) or higher: 89.9% (2007); Bachelor's degree or higher: 13.2% (2007); Master's degree or higher: 5.6% (2007).

School District(s)

Botkins Local (KG-12)
2005-06 Enrollment: 552 . . . . (937) 693-3756

Housing: Homeownership rate: 78.1% (2007); Median home value: $107,480 (2007); Median rent: $310 per month (2000); Median age of housing: 40 years (2000).

Transportation: Commute to work: 94.5% car, 0.0% public transportation, 4.8% walk, 0.3% work from home (2000); Travel time to work: 43.9% less than 15 minutes, 43.7% 15 to 30 minutes, 8.5% 30 to 45 minutes, 1.5% 45 to 60 minutes, 2.3% 60 minutes or more (2000)

FORT LORAMIE (village). Aka Loramie. Covers a land area of 0.727 square miles and a water area of 0 square miles. Located at 40.34° N. Lat.; 84.37° W. Long. Elevation is 948 feet.

History: Fort Loramie built here (1794) by Anthony Wayne.

Population: 1,191 (1990); 1,344 (2000); 1,260 (2007); 1,249 (2012 projected); Race: 99.6% White, 0.0% Black, 0.0% Asian, 0.2% Hispanic of any race (2007); Density: 1,733.2 persons per square mile (2007); Average household size: 2.72 (2007); Median age: 33.6 (2007); Males per 100 females: 96.0 (2007); Marriage status: 27.1% never married, 64.9% now married, 5.3% widowed, 2.8% divorced (2000); Foreign born: 0.2% (2000); Ancestry (includes multiple ancestries): 71.1% German, 10.2% French (except Basque), 8.5% Irish, 6.5% United States or American, 1.5% Other groups (2000).

Economy: Single-family building permits issued: 6 (2007); Multi-family building permits issued: 0 (2007); Employment by occupation: 9.8% management, 19.0% professional, 10.7% services, 24.9% sales, 0.0% farming, 8.4% construction, 27.2% production (2000).

Income: Per capita income: $26,296 (2007); Median household income: $66,500 (2007); Average household income: $71,406 (2007); Percent of households with income of $100,000 or more: 22.0% (2007); Poverty rate: 1.4% (2000).

Education: Percent of population age 25 and over with: High school diploma (including GED) or higher: 86.8% (2007); Bachelor's degree or higher: 15.6% (2007); Master's degree or higher: 4.4% (2007).

School District(s)

Fort Loramie Local (KG-12)
2005-06 Enrollment: 834 . . . . (937) 295-3931

Housing: Homeownership rate: 80.4% (2007); Median home value: $162,028 (2007); Median rent: $369 per month (2000); Median age of housing: 35 years (2000).

Transportation: Commute to work: 95.8% car, 0.0% public transportation, 2.6% walk, 1.3% work from home (2000); Travel time to work: 44.5% less than 15 minutes, 39.6% 15 to 30 minutes, 8.7% 30 to 45 minutes, 3.0% 45 to 60 minutes, 4.1% 60 minutes or more (2000)

HOUSTON (unincorporated postal area, zip code 45333). Covers a land area of 27.168 square miles and a water area of 0.017 square miles. Located at 40.26° N. Lat.; 84.33° W. Long. Elevation is 952 feet.

Population: 1,490 (2000); Race: 97.2% White, 0.0% Black, 2.8% Asian, 0.0% Hispanic of any race (2000); Density: 54.8 persons per square mile (2000); Age: 27.5% under 18, 8.9% over 64 (2000); Marriage status: 23.3% never married, 63.7% now married, 6.3% widowed, 6.7% divorced (2000); Foreign born: 2.8% (2000); Ancestry (includes multiple ancestries): 30.4% German, 13.5% United States or American, 12.1% Irish, 8.9% French (except Basque), 6.6% Other groups (2000).

Economy: Employment by occupation: 6.7% management, 10.8% professional, 13.4% services, 24.7% sales, 0.2% farming, 11.7% construction, 32.4% production (2000).

Income: Per capita income: $18,607 (2000); Median household income: $46,395 (2000); Poverty rate: 2.9% (2000).

Education: Percent of population age 25 and over with: High school diploma (including GED) or higher: 81.5% (2000); Bachelor's degree or higher: 8.9% (2000).

School District(s)

Hardin-Houston Local (KG-12)
2005-06 Enrollment: 938 . . . . (937) 295-3010

Housing: Homeownership rate: 90.3% (2000); Median home value: $98,300 (2000); Median rent: $338 per month (2000); Median age of housing: 27 years (2000).

Transportation: Commute to work: 97.5% car, 0.0% public transportation, 0.1% walk, 2.1% work from home (2000); Travel time to work: 19.7% less than 15 minutes, 60.2% 15 to 30 minutes, 15.7% 30 to 45 minutes, 2.8% 45 to 60 minutes, 1.6% 60 minutes or more (2000)

JACKSON CENTER (village). Covers a land area of 1.257 square miles and a water area of 0 square miles. Located at 40.44° N. Lat.; 84.03° W. Long. Elevation is 1,027 feet.

Population: 1,497 (1990); 1,369 (2000); 1,312 (2007); 1,292 (2012 projected); Race: 98.7% White, 0.8% Black, 0.0% Asian, 0.6% Hispanic of any race (2007); Density: 1,043.6 persons per square mile (2007); Average household size: 2.44 (2007); Median age: 33.7 (2007); Males per 100 females: 94.7 (2007); Marriage status: 16.6% never married, 64.7% now married, 8.2% widowed, 10.4% divorced (2000); Foreign born: 0.8% (2000); Ancestry (includes multiple ancestries): 33.3% German, 18.8% United States or American, 12.8% Irish, 7.5% Other groups, 6.5% English (2000).

Economy: Single-family building permits issued: 4 (2007); Multi-family building permits issued: 0 (2007); Employment by occupation: 10.9% management, 13.3% professional, 10.9% services, 20.0% sales, 0.3% farming, 6.7% construction, 38.0% production (2000).

Income: Per capita income: $21,759 (2007); Median household income: $48,704 (2007); Average household income: $53,062 (2007); Percent of households with income of $100,000 or more: 10.0% (2007); Poverty rate: 7.6% (2000).

Education: Percent of population age 25 and over with: High school diploma (including GED) or higher: 85.6% (2007); Bachelor's degree or higher: 12.1% (2007); Master's degree or higher: 5.2% (2007).

School District(s)

Jackson Center Local (PK-12)
2005-06 Enrollment: 548 . . . . (937) 596-6053

Housing: Homeownership rate: 74.3% (2007); Median home value: $103,947 (2007); Median rent: $343 per month (2000); Median age of housing: 31 years (2000).

Transportation: Commute to work: 94.6% car, 0.0% public transportation, 3.5% walk, 1.6% work from home (2000); Travel time to work: 43.8% less than 15 minutes, 33.2% 15 to 30 minutes, 15.4% 30 to 45 minutes, 4.6% 45 to 60 minutes, 3.0% 60 minutes or more (2000)

KETTLERSVILLE (village). Covers a land area of 1.020 square miles and a water area of 0.002 square miles. Located at 40.44° N. Lat.; 84.26° W. Long. Elevation is 974 feet.

History: Also spelled Kettlerville.

Population: 194 (1990); 175 (2000); 173 (2007); 171 (2012 projected); Race: 97.7% White, 0.6% Black, 0.0% Asian, 2.3% Hispanic of any race (2007); Density: 169.6 persons per square mile (2007); Average household

size: 2.84 (2007); Median age: 29.4 (2007); Males per 100 females: 101.2 (2007); Marriage status: 26.6% never married, 61.2% now married, 5.0% widowed, 7.2% divorced (2000); Foreign born: 0.0% (2000); Ancestry (includes multiple ancestries): 66.1% German, 10.0% Irish, 6.7% English, 4.4% Dutch, 3.3% Other groups (2000).
Economy: Single-family building permits issued: 0 (2007); Multi-family building permits issued: 0 (2007); Employment by occupation: 5.1% management, 12.2% professional, 18.4% services, 13.3% sales, 2.0% farming, 7.1% construction, 41.8% production (2000).
Income: Per capita income: $24,668 (2007); Median household income: $62,045 (2007); Average household income: $69,959 (2007); Percent of households with income of $100,000 or more: 23.0% (2007); Poverty rate: 1.2% (2000).
Education: Percent of population age 25 and over with: High school diploma (including GED) or higher: 85.7% (2007); Bachelor's degree or higher: 8.2% (2007); Master's degree or higher: 2.0% (2007).
Housing: Homeownership rate: 88.5% (2007); Median home value: $113,636 (2007); Median rent: $325 per month (2000); Median age of housing: 52 years (2000).
Transportation: Commute to work: 85.7% car, 0.0% public transportation, 8.2% walk, 6.1% work from home (2000); Travel time to work: 37.0% less than 15 minutes, 40.2% 15 to 30 minutes, 5.4% 30 to 45 minutes, 3.3% 45 to 60 minutes, 14.1% 60 minutes or more (2000)

LOCKINGTON (village). Covers a land area of 0.083 square miles and a water area of 0 square miles. Located at 40.20° N. Lat.; 84.23° W. Long. Elevation is 948 feet.
Population: 214 (1990); 208 (2000); 211 (2007); 213 (2012 projected); Race: 95.7% White, 3.3% Black, 0.0% Asian, 2.4% Hispanic of any race (2007); Density: 2,529.9 persons per square mile (2007); Average household size: 2.74 (2007); Median age: 35.6 (2007); Males per 100 females: 104.9 (2007); Marriage status: 19.4% never married, 67.5% now married, 5.6% widowed, 7.5% divorced (2000); Foreign born: 3.8% (2000); Ancestry (includes multiple ancestries): 36.3% German, 11.3% Irish, 8.0% English, 5.2% Other groups, 5.2% United States or American (2000).
Economy: Single-family building permits issued: 0 (2007); Multi-family building permits issued: 0 (2007); Employment by occupation: 9.8% management, 6.9% professional, 8.8% services, 10.8% sales, 2.0% farming, 18.6% construction, 43.1% production (2000).
Income: Per capita income: $20,711 (2007); Median household income: $44,643 (2007); Average household income: $56,753 (2007); Percent of households with income of $100,000 or more: 10.4% (2007); Poverty rate: 7.5% (2000).
Education: Percent of population age 25 and over with: High school diploma (including GED) or higher: 79.8% (2007); Bachelor's degree or higher: 5.4% (2007); Master's degree or higher: 0.0% (2007).
Housing: Homeownership rate: 76.6% (2007); Median home value: $88,750 (2007); Median rent: $263 per month (2000); Median age of housing: 59 years (2000).
Transportation: Commute to work: 93.9% car, 0.0% public transportation, 4.0% walk, 2.0% work from home (2000); Travel time to work: 33.0% less than 15 minutes, 41.2% 15 to 30 minutes, 14.4% 30 to 45 minutes, 7.2% 45 to 60 minutes, 4.1% 60 minutes or more (2000)

MAPLEWOOD (unincorporated postal area, zip code 45340). Covers a land area of 22.895 square miles and a water area of 0 square miles. Located at 40.37° N. Lat.; 84.05° W. Long. Elevation is 1,035 feet.
Population: 739 (2000); Race: 99.0% White, 0.0% Black, 0.3% Asian, 0.0% Hispanic of any race (2000); Density: 32.3 persons per square mile (2000); Age: 24.0% under 18, 8.1% over 64 (2000); Marriage status: 15.1% never married, 77.5% now married, 3.6% widowed, 3.8% divorced (2000); Foreign born: 0.3% (2000); Ancestry (includes multiple ancestries): 46.4% German, 12.7% United States or American, 9.5% English, 8.8% French (except Basque), 7.9% Irish (2000).
Economy: Employment by occupation: 14.4% management, 15.6% professional, 11.7% services, 12.7% sales, 2.7% farming, 11.0% construction, 31.8% production (2000).
Income: Per capita income: $19,271 (2000); Median household income: $51,917 (2000); Poverty rate: 3.8% (2000).
Education: Percent of population age 25 and over with: High school diploma (including GED) or higher: 86.3% (2000); Bachelor's degree or higher: 9.1% (2000).
Housing: Homeownership rate: 95.1% (2000); Median home value: $104,000 (2000); Median rent: $288 per month (2000); Median age of housing: 32 years (2000).
Transportation: Commute to work: 94.7% car, 0.0% public transportation, 0.0% walk, 5.3% work from home (2000); Travel time to work: 14.5% less than 15 minutes, 56.8% 15 to 30 minutes, 17.7% 30 to 45 minutes, 9.7% 45 to 60 minutes, 1.3% 60 minutes or more (2000)

PORT JEFFERSON (village). Covers a land area of 0.154 square miles and a water area of 0 square miles. Located at 40.33° N. Lat.; 84.09° W. Long. Elevation is 971 feet.
Population: 381 (1990); 321 (2000); 324 (2007); 325 (2012 projected); Race: 99.7% White, 0.0% Black, 0.3% Asian, 0.0% Hispanic of any race (2007); Density: 2,104.3 persons per square mile (2007); Average household size: 2.59 (2007); Median age: 38.0 (2007); Males per 100 females: 103.8 (2007); Marriage status: 19.9% never married, 62.9% now married, 7.2% widowed, 10.0% divorced (2000); Foreign born: 0.0% (2000); Ancestry (includes multiple ancestries): 28.5% German, 18.6% United States or American, 13.1% Irish, 6.5% English, 3.4% Other groups (2000).
Economy: Single-family building permits issued: 1 (2007); Multi-family building permits issued: 0 (2007); Employment by occupation: 2.5% management, 6.3% professional, 7.6% services, 10.8% sales, 0.0% farming, 18.4% construction, 54.4% production (2000).
Income: Per capita income: $21,049 (2007); Median household income: $45,625 (2007); Average household income: $54,560 (2007); Percent of households with income of $100,000 or more: 9.6% (2007); Poverty rate: 8.3% (2000).
Education: Percent of population age 25 and over with: High school diploma (including GED) or higher: 66.1% (2007); Bachelor's degree or higher: 1.3% (2007); Master's degree or higher: 1.3% (2007).
Housing: Homeownership rate: 79.2% (2007); Median home value: $83,182 (2007); Median rent: $350 per month (2000); Median age of housing: 49 years (2000).
Transportation: Commute to work: 100.0% car, 0.0% public transportation, 0.0% walk, 0.0% work from home (2000); Travel time to work: 9.7% less than 15 minutes, 76.6% 15 to 30 minutes, 10.4% 30 to 45 minutes, 3.2% 45 to 60 minutes, 0.0% 60 minutes or more (2000)

RUSSIA (village). Covers a land area of 0.645 square miles and a water area of 0 square miles. Located at 40.23° N. Lat.; 84.41° W. Long. Elevation is 968 feet.
Population: 491 (1990); 551 (2000); 604 (2007); 640 (2012 projected); Race: 99.3% White, 0.0% Black, 0.2% Asian, 2.2% Hispanic of any race (2007); Density: 936.1 persons per square mile (2007); Average household size: 2.73 (2007); Median age: 30.7 (2007); Males per 100 females: 104.7 (2007); Marriage status: 17.6% never married, 72.6% now married, 5.6% widowed, 4.2% divorced (2000); Foreign born: 0.2% (2000); Ancestry (includes multiple ancestries): 45.2% German, 35.6% French (except Basque), 13.9% United States or American, 8.1% Irish, 4.4% Other groups (2000).
Economy: Single-family building permits issued: 3 (2007); Multi-family building permits issued: 0 (2007); Employment by occupation: 9.8% management, 22.6% professional, 8.3% services, 16.5% sales, 0.8% farming, 8.3% construction, 33.8% production (2000).
Income: Per capita income: $29,123 (2007); Median household income: $61,630 (2007); Average household income: $79,593 (2007); Percent of households with income of $100,000 or more: 24.0% (2007); Poverty rate: 0.0% (2000).
Education: Percent of population age 25 and over with: High school diploma (including GED) or higher: 82.6% (2007); Bachelor's degree or higher: 19.7% (2007); Master's degree or higher: 2.6% (2007).

School District(s)

Russia Local (KG-12)
2005-06 Enrollment: 476 . . . . (937) 295-3454
Housing: Homeownership rate: 73.3% (2007); Median home value: $126,786 (2007); Median rent: $481 per month (2000); Median age of housing: 34 years (2000).
Transportation: Commute to work: 95.8% car, 0.0% public transportation, 3.4% walk, 0.8% work from home (2000); Travel time to work: 43.8% less than 15 minutes, 33.1% 15 to 30 minutes, 16.5% 30 to 45 minutes, 4.6% 45 to 60 minutes, 1.9% 60 minutes or more (2000)

SIDNEY (city). County seat. Covers a land area of 10.426 square miles and a water area of 0.068 square miles. Located at 40.29° N. Lat.; 84.16° W. Long. Elevation is 951 feet.
History: Sidney was platted in 1820 and named for Sir Philip Sidney, the English poet. The town developed around sawmills and woodworking mills.

In 1879, Benjamin Slusser built a factory to produce the sheet-steel road scraper that he had invented.
Population: 19,245 (1990); 20,211 (2000); 20,096 (2007); 19,947 (2012 projected); Race: 91.3% White, 3.5% Black, 2.2% Asian, 2.0% Hispanic of any race (2007); Density: 1,927.4 persons per square mile (2007); Average household size: 2.47 (2007); Median age: 35.7 (2007); Males per 100 females: 96.3 (2007); Marriage status: 22.1% never married, 57.8% now married, 8.0% widowed, 12.0% divorced (2000); Foreign born: 2.3% (2000); Ancestry (includes multiple ancestries): 31.4% German, 15.6% United States or American, 11.2% Other groups, 10.9% Irish, 9.1% English (2000).
Economy: Single-family building permits issued: 28 (2007); Multi-family building permits issued: 16 (2007); Employment by occupation: 10.9% management, 13.8% professional, 14.5% services, 19.2% sales, 0.3% farming, 8.1% construction, 33.3% production (2000).
Income: Per capita income: $21,995 (2007); Median household income: $43,033 (2007); Average household income: $53,733 (2007); Percent of households with income of $100,000 or more: 10.0% (2007); Poverty rate: 11.5% (2000).
Education: Percent of population age 25 and over with: High school diploma (including GED) or higher: 78.4% (2007); Bachelor's degree or higher: 13.8% (2007); Master's degree or higher: 4.3% (2007).

School District(s)

Fairlawn Local (KG-12)
2005-06 Enrollment: 549 . . . . (937) 492-1974
Hardin-Houston Local (KG-12)
2005-06 Enrollment: 938 . . . . (937) 295-3010
Sidney City (PK-12)
2005-06 Enrollment: 3,922 . . . . (937) 497-2200

Housing: Homeownership rate: 62.4% (2007); Median home value: $108,838 (2007); Median rent: $378 per month (2000); Median age of housing: 38 years (2000).
Hospitals: Wilson Memorial Hospital (112 beds)
Newspapers: Sidney Daily News (Local news; Circulation 14,700)
Transportation: Commute to work: 94.7% car, 0.4% public transportation, 2.0% walk, 2.3% work from home (2000); Travel time to work: 65.5% less than 15 minutes, 21.6% 15 to 30 minutes, 8.2% 30 to 45 minutes, 3.0% 45 to 60 minutes, 1.7% 60 minutes or more (2000)

Additional Information Contacts

City of Sidney. . . . . (937) 498-2335
http://www.sidneyoh.com
Sidney-Shelby County Chamber of Commerce . . . . (937) 492-9122
http://www.sidneyshelbychamber.com

Stark County

Located in east central Ohio; crossed by the Tuscarawas River. Covers a land area of 576.14 square miles, a water area of 4.77 square miles, and is located in the Eastern Time Zone. The county was founded in 1808. County seat is Canton.

Stark County is part of the Canton-Massillon, OH Metropolitan Statistical Area. The entire metro area includes: Carroll County, OH; Stark County, OH

Population: 367,585 (1990); 378,098 (2000); 381,111 (2007); 381,734 (2012 projected); Race: 89.6% White, 7.4% Black, 0.7% Asian, 1.0% Hispanic of any race (2007); Density: 661.5 persons per square mile (2007); Average household size: 2.51 (2007); Median age: 40.2 (2007); Males per 100 females: 93.2 (2007).
Religion: Five largest groups: 20.5% Catholic Church, 6.1% The United Methodist Church, 4.3% Independent, Non-Charismatic Churches, 3.2% Evangelical Lutheran Church in America, 2.7% Christian Churches and Churches of Christ (2000).
Economy: Unemployment rate: 6.7% (6/2008); Total civilian labor force: 193,653 (6/2008); Leading industries: 17.7% manufacturing; 17.2% health care and social assistance; 14.3% retail trade (2005); Farms: 1,337 totaling 145,163 acres (2002); Companies that employ 500 or more persons: 22 (2006); Companies that employ 100 to 499 persons: 206 (2006); Companies that employ less than 100 persons: 9,031 (2006); Black-owned businesses: 607 (2002); Hispanic-owned businesses: n/a (2002); Asian-owned businesses: 507 (2002); Women-owned businesses: 7,563 (2002); Retail sales per capita: $15,836 (2008). Single-family building permits issued: 614 (2007); Multi-family building permits issued: 110 (2007).
Income: Per capita income: $23,586 (2007); Median household income: $44,998 (2007); Average household income: $58,350 (2007); Percent of households with income of $100,000 or more: 12.7% (2007); Poverty rate: 12.0% (2005); Bankruptcy rate: 5.49% (2007).
Taxes: Total county taxes per capita: $186 (2006); County property taxes per capita: $145 (2006).
Education: Percent of population age 25 and over with: High school diploma (including GED) or higher: 83.6% (2007); Bachelor's degree or higher: 18.3% (2007); Master's degree or higher: 6.2% (2007).
Housing: Homeownership rate: 72.8% (2007); Median home value: $122,726 (2007); Median rent: $398 per month (2000); Median age of housing: 40 years (2000).
Health: Birth rate: 120.5 per 10,000 population (2007); Death rate: 103.8 per 10,000 population (2007); Age-adjusted cancer mortality rate: 184.8 deaths per 100,000 population (2005); Air Quality Index: 66.2% good, 25.6% moderate, 7.6% unhealthy for sensitive individuals, 0.6% unhealthy (percent of days in 2007); Number of physicians: 26.2 per 10,000 population (2005); Hospital beds: 42.9 per 10,000 population (2004); Hospital admissions: 1,523.4 per 10,000 population (2004).
Elections: 2004 Presidential election results: 48.9% Bush, 50.6% Kerry, 0.0% Nader, 0.3% Badnarik
National and State Parks: Quail Hollow State Park

Additional Information Contacts

Stark County Government . . . . (330) 451-7371
http://www.co.stark.oh.us
Alliance Area Chamber of Commerce . . . . (330) 823-6260
http://www.allianceohiochamber.org
Canton Regional Chamber of Commerce . . . . (330) 456-7253
http://www.cantonchamber.org
Canton-Stark County Convention & Visitors Bureau . . . . . . (330) 454-1439
http://www.visitcantonohio.com
City of Alliance . . . . (330) 821-3110
http://www.cityofalliance.com
City of Canton . . . . (330) 489-3283
http://www.ci.canton.oh.us
City of Louisville. . . . . (330) 875-3321
http://www.louisvilleohio.com
City of Massillon. . . . . (330) 830-1700
http://www.massillonohio.com
City of North Canton . . . . (330) 499-5081
http://www.northcantonohio.com
Green Chamber of Commerce. . . . . (330) 896-3023
http://www.greencoc.org
Lake Chamber of Commerce. . . . . (330) 877-5500
http://www.lakechamber.com
Louisville Area Chamber of Commerce . . . . (330) 875-7371
http://www.louisvilleohchamber.com
Massillon Area Chamber of Commerce . . . . (330) 833-3146
http://www.massillonohchamber.com
Minerva Area Chamber of Commerce . . . . (330) 868-7979
http://www.minervachamber.com
North Canton Area Chamber of Commerce. . . . . (330) 499-5100
http://www.northcantonchamber.org
Village of Navarre . . . . (330) 879-5508
http://www.navarreohio.net

Stark County Communities

ALLIANCE (city). Covers a land area of 8.612 square miles and a water area of 0.002 square miles. Located at 40.91° N. Lat.; 81.10° W. Long. Elevation is 1,158 feet.
History: Between 1805 and 1835, four small towns were established along the Mahoning River. In 1854 the four communities were united under the name of Alliance. Alliance was incorporated in 1889, and became known for its production of cranes and heavy mill machinery.
Population: 23,552 (1990); 23,253 (2000); 22,549 (2007); 22,025 (2012 projected); Race: 85.5% White, 10.8% Black, 1.0% Asian, 1.4% Hispanic of any race (2007); Density: 2,618.4 persons per square mile (2007); Average household size: 2.59 (2007); Median age: 35.2 (2007); Males per 100 females: 89.3 (2007); Marriage status: 31.4% never married, 48.1% now married, 8.4% widowed, 12.0% divorced (2000); Foreign born: 1.6% (2000); Ancestry (includes multiple ancestries): 22.5% German, 14.9% Other groups, 11.8% Irish, 9.9% Italian, 9.5% English (2000).
Economy: Single-family building permits issued: 14 (2007); Multi-family building permits issued: 0 (2007); Employment by occupation: 7.2%

management, 13.6% professional, 17.7% services, 25.5% sales, 0.6% farming, 7.4% construction, 27.9% production (2000).
Income: Per capita income: $16,959 (2007); Median household income: $34,031 (2007); Average household income: $42,642 (2007); Percent of households with income of $100,000 or more: 6.0% (2007); Poverty rate: 18.0% (2000).
Taxes: Total city taxes per capita: $430 (2006); City property taxes per capita: $59 (2006).
Education: Percent of population age 25 and over with: High school diploma (including GED) or higher: 79.8% (2007); Bachelor's degree or higher: 13.7% (2007); Master's degree or higher: 5.3% (2007).

School District(s)

Alliance City (PK-12)
2005-06 Enrollment: 3,175 . . . . (330) 821-2100
Marlington Local (PK-12)
2005-06 Enrollment: 2,645 . . . . (330) 823-7458
West Branch Local (PK-12)
2005-06 Enrollment: 2,485 . . . . (330) 938-9324

Four-year College(s)

Mount Union College (Private, Not-for-profit, United Methodist)
Fall 2007 Enrollment: 2,138. . . . . (800) 992-6682
2007-08 Tuition: In-state $22,050; Out-of-state $22,050

Two-year College(s)

Raphaels School of Beauty Culture (Private, For-profit)
Fall 2007 Enrollment: 52 . . . . (330) 823-3884

Vocational/Technical School(s)

Community Services Division-Alliance City (Public)
Fall 2007 Enrollment: 148 . . . . (330) 821-2102
2007-08 Tuition: In-state $4,335; Out-of-state $4,335

Housing: Homeownership rate: 60.7% (2007); Median home value: $85,762 (2007); Median rent: $337 per month (2000); Median age of housing: 53 years (2000).
Hospitals: Alliance Community Hospital (184 beds)
Safety: Violent crime rate: 47.1 per 10,000 population; Property crime rate: 486.7 per 10,000 population (2007).
Newspapers: The Review (Local news; Circulation 13,000); Sebring Times (Local news; Circulation 500)
Transportation: Commute to work: 90.2% car, 1.0% public transportation, 6.5% walk, 1.6% work from home (2000); Travel time to work: 56.0% less than 15 minutes, 23.0% 15 to 30 minutes, 11.4% 30 to 45 minutes, 4.3% 45 to 60 minutes, 5.3% 60 minutes or more (2000); Amtrak: Service available.

Additional Information Contacts

Alliance Area Chamber of Commerce . . . . (330) 823-6260
http://www.allianceohiochamber.org
City of Alliance . . . . (330) 821-3110
http://www.cityofalliance.com

BEACH CITY (village). Covers a land area of 0.463 square miles and a water area of 0 square miles. Located at 40.65° N. Lat.; 81.58° W. Long. Elevation is 1,001 feet.
History: Flood control dam completed in 1937 nearby.
Population: 1,051 (1990); 1,137 (2000); 1,117 (2007); 1,116 (2012 projected); Race: 98.5% White, 0.2% Black, 0.3% Asian, 1.6% Hispanic of any race (2007); Density: 2,411.6 persons per square mile (2007); Average household size: 2.44 (2007); Median age: 40.1 (2007); Males per 100 females: 94.9 (2007); Marriage status: 17.1% never married, 60.7% now married, 13.4% widowed, 8.8% divorced (2000); Foreign born: 0.2% (2000); Ancestry (includes multiple ancestries): 28.2% German, 20.1% United States or American, 10.9% Irish, 9.4% English, 6.2% Other groups (2000).
Economy: Single-family building permits issued: 0 (2007); Multi-family building permits issued: 0 (2007); Employment by occupation: 7.2% management, 12.1% professional, 18.6% services, 14.8% sales, 0.4% farming, 9.5% construction, 37.3% production (2000).
Income: Per capita income: $18,521 (2007); Median household income: $41,638 (2007); Average household income: $45,268 (2007); Percent of households with income of $100,000 or more: 2.8% (2007); Poverty rate: 8.1% (2000).
Education: Percent of population age 25 and over with: High school diploma (including GED) or higher: 79.5% (2007); Bachelor's degree or higher: 5.2% (2007); Master's degree or higher: 1.2% (2007).

School District(s)

Fairless Local (PK-12)
2005-06 Enrollment: 1,908 . . . . (330) 767-3577

Housing: Homeownership rate: 75.7% (2007); Median home value: $79,773 (2007); Median rent: $313 per month (2000); Median age of housing: 56 years (2000).
Transportation: Commute to work: 95.8% car, 0.0% public transportation, 2.6% walk, 1.3% work from home (2000); Travel time to work: 26.7% less than 15 minutes, 40.0% 15 to 30 minutes, 25.8% 30 to 45 minutes, 3.6% 45 to 60 minutes, 4.0% 60 minutes or more (2000)

BREWSTER (village). Covers a land area of 2.027 square miles and a water area of 0.008 square miles. Located at 40.71° N. Lat.; 81.59° W. Long. Elevation is 994 feet.
Population: 2,307 (1990); 2,324 (2000); 2,544 (2007); 2,669 (2012 projected); Race: 98.7% White, 0.0% Black, 0.2% Asian, 0.5% Hispanic of any race (2007); Density: 1,255.0 persons per square mile (2007); Average household size: 2.66 (2007); Median age: 39.6 (2007); Males per 100 females: 95.8 (2007); Marriage status: 18.2% never married, 60.5% now married, 11.7% widowed, 9.6% divorced (2000); Foreign born: 0.8% (2000); Ancestry (includes multiple ancestries): 38.5% German, 13.2% Irish, 10.9% United States or American, 8.6% Italian, 8.0% English (2000).
Economy: Employment by occupation: 8.9% management, 9.0% professional, 14.4% services, 23.3% sales, 0.2% farming, 7.8% construction, 36.5% production (2000).
Income: Per capita income: $20,419 (2007); Median household income: $43,119 (2007); Average household income: $52,406 (2007); Percent of households with income of $100,000 or more: 6.5% (2007); Poverty rate: 5.9% (2000).
Education: Percent of population age 25 and over with: High school diploma (including GED) or higher: 84.2% (2007); Bachelor's degree or higher: 6.5% (2007); Master's degree or higher: 1.7% (2007).

School District(s)

Fairless Local (PK-12)
2005-06 Enrollment: 1,908 . . . . (330) 767-3577

Housing: Homeownership rate: 78.8% (2007); Median home value: $102,033 (2007); Median rent: $382 per month (2000); Median age of housing: 44 years (2000).
Transportation: Commute to work: 95.2% car, 0.0% public transportation, 4.1% walk, 0.3% work from home (2000); Travel time to work: 40.0% less than 15 minutes, 39.1% 15 to 30 minutes, 14.8% 30 to 45 minutes, 5.0% 45 to 60 minutes, 1.2% 60 minutes or more (2000)

CANAL FULTON (village). Covers a land area of 2.421 square miles and a water area of 0.034 square miles. Located at 40.89° N. Lat.; 81.59° W. Long. Elevation is 951 feet.
History: Canal Fulton was first called Milan, but the name was changed during the construction of the Ohio & Erie Canal to honor Robert Fulton, inventor of the steamboat.
Population: 4,539 (1990); 5,061 (2000); 5,054 (2007); 5,061 (2012 projected); Race: 96.7% White, 1.0% Black, 0.5% Asian, 0.7% Hispanic of any race (2007); Density: 2,087.9 persons per square mile (2007); Average household size: 2.71 (2007); Median age: 36.6 (2007); Males per 100 females: 89.7 (2007); Marriage status: 22.1% never married, 64.4% now married, 4.7% widowed, 8.8% divorced (2000); Foreign born: 1.7% (2000); Ancestry (includes multiple ancestries): 34.2% German, 14.5% Irish, 14.0% English, 8.2% Italian, 6.8% United States or American (2000).
Economy: Employment by occupation: 11.9% management, 19.0% professional, 10.1% services, 32.8% sales, 0.0% farming, 9.3% construction, 16.8% production (2000).
Income: Per capita income: $23,649 (2007); Median household income: $52,388 (2007); Average household income: $62,390 (2007); Percent of households with income of $100,000 or more: 13.0% (2007); Poverty rate: 4.4% (2000).
Education: Percent of population age 25 and over with: High school diploma (including GED) or higher: 89.2% (2007); Bachelor's degree or higher: 17.3% (2007); Master's degree or higher: 3.5% (2007).

School District(s)

Northwest Local (PK-12)
2005-06 Enrollment: 2,459 . . . . (330) 854-2291

Housing: Homeownership rate: 65.0% (2007); Median home value: $141,579 (2007); Median rent: $467 per month (2000); Median age of housing: 25 years (2000).
Safety: Violent crime rate: 15.7 per 10,000 population; Property crime rate: 244.8 per 10,000 population (2007).
Transportation: Commute to work: 92.7% car, 2.4% public transportation, 1.5% walk, 3.1% work from home (2000); Travel time to work: 23.8% less

than 15 minutes, 41.5% 15 to 30 minutes, 23.6% 30 to 45 minutes, 4.1% 45 to 60 minutes, 7.1% 60 minutes or more (2000)

CANTON (city). County seat. Covers a land area of 20.546 square miles and a water area of 0.014 square miles. Located at 40.80° N. Lat.; 81.37° W. Long. Elevation is 1,060 feet.

History: Pioneer settlers from New England built homes along Nimishillen Creek in 1805. The town was platted in 1806 by Bezaleel Wells, the "Father of Canton," and incorporated in 1822. Canton's first major industry began in 1827 when Joshua Gibbs developed an improved metal plow. This was the start of Canton's future as a processor of steel, manufacturing reapers, roller bearings, and other products. German and Swiss artisans came to Canton to work in the Dueber-Hampden Watch Company. President William McKinley was a resident of Canton, and conducted his campaign for the presidency from his home here. After his assassination in Buffalo in 1901, his remains were brought back to Canton for burial.

Population: 84,082 (1990); 80,806 (2000); 78,373 (2007); 76,289 (2012 projected); Race: 72.0% White, 22.7% Black, 0.4% Asian, 1.3% Hispanic of any race (2007); Density: 3,814.6 persons per square mile (2007); Average household size: 2.46 (2007); Median age: 36.2 (2007); Males per 100 females: 88.8 (2007); Marriage status: 31.0% never married, 45.8% now married, 8.9% widowed, 14.2% divorced (2000); Foreign born: 1.7% (2000); Ancestry (includes multiple ancestries): 25.0% Other groups, 21.5% German, 11.4% Irish, 8.6% Italian, 6.9% English (2000).

Economy: Unemployment rate: 8.2% (6/2008); Total civilian labor force: 36,402 (6/2008); Single-family building permits issued: 54 (2007); Multi-family building permits issued: 0 (2007); Employment by occupation: 8.4% management, 13.1% professional, 20.0% services, 26.3% sales, 0.1% farming, 7.9% construction, 24.1% production (2000).

Income: Per capita income: $17,416 (2007); Median household income: $31,767 (2007); Average household income: $41,511 (2007); Percent of households with income of $100,000 or more: 6.1% (2007); Poverty rate: 19.2% (2000).

Taxes: Total city taxes per capita: $589 (2006); City property taxes per capita: $42 (2006).

Education: Percent of population age 25 and over with: High school diploma (including GED) or higher: 75.3% (2007); Bachelor's degree or higher: 12.2% (2007); Master's degree or higher: 4.1% (2007).

School District(s)

Aspire Academy The (07-08)
2005-06 Enrollment: 47 . . . . (330) 484-8010
Canton Arts Academy (03-06)
2005-06 Enrollment: 81 . . . . (330) 454-2254
Canton City (PK-12)
2005-06 Enrollment: 11,144 . . . . (330) 438-2500
Canton City Sch Digital Acdmy (03-12)
2005-06 Enrollment: 105 . . . . (330) 454-2418
Canton Local (PK-12)
2005-06 Enrollment: 2,298 . . . . (330) 484-8010
Canton Local Digital Academy (05-12)
2005-06 Enrollment: 37 . . . . (330) 484-8010
Golden Eagle Digital Academy (01-11)
2005-06 Enrollment: 21 . . . . (330) 492-3500
Hope Academy Canton Campus (KG-08)
2005-06 Enrollment: 432 . . . . (330) 454-3128
Jackson Local (PK-12)
2005-06 Enrollment: 5,786 . . . . (330) 830-8000
Life Skills Center Canton (09-12)
2005-06 Enrollment: 235 . . . .
Little Eagle Kindergarten Pgm (KG-KG)
2005-06 Enrollment: 25 . . . . (330) 492-3500
Perry Local (PK-12)
2005-06 Enrollment: 4,806 . . . . (330) 477-8121
Plain Local (PK-12)
2005-06 Enrollment: 6,052 . . . . (330) 492-3500
Plain Local Admy of Tech Inc (06-08)
2005-06 Enrollment: 27 . . . . (330) 492-3500
Project Rebuild Community School (09-12)
2005-06 Enrollment: 50 . . . . (330) 452-8414
Summit Academy Secondary - Canton (08-10)
2005-06 Enrollment: 30 . . . . (330) 453-8547
Summit Academy-Canton (01-08)
2005-06 Enrollment: 62 . . . . (330) 453-8547
The Canton Academy (09-12)
2005-06 Enrollment: 42 . . . . (330) 454-2208

Four-year College(s)

Malone College (Private, Not-for-profit, Friends)
Fall 2007 Enrollment: 2,371 . . . . (330) 471-8100
2007-08 Tuition: In-state $18,870; Out-of-state $18,870

Two-year College(s)

Aultman College of Nursing and Health Sciences (Private, Not-for-profit)
Fall 2007 Enrollment: 219 . . . . (330) 363-6347
2007-08 Tuition: In-state $13,000; Out-of-state $13,000
Brown Mackie College-North Canton (Private, For-profit)
Fall 2007 Enrollment: 1,081 . . . . (330) 494-1214
2007-08 Tuition: In-state $8,028; Out-of-state $8,028
Kent State University-Stark Campus (Public)
Fall 2007 Enrollment: 3,849 . . . . (330) 499-9600
2007-08 Tuition: In-state $4,770; Out-of-state $12,202

Vocational/Technical School(s)

National Beauty College (Private, For-profit)
Fall 2007 Enrollment: 77 . . . . (330) 499-5596
2007-08 Tuition: $7,825
Practical Nurse Program Canton City Schools (Public)
Fall 2007 Enrollment: 106 . . . . (330) 453-3271
2007-08 Tuition: $6,600

Housing: Homeownership rate: 59.9% (2007); Median home value: $80,056 (2007); Median rent: $352 per month (2000); Median age of housing: 55 years (2000).

Hospitals: Aultman Hospital (682 beds); Mercy Medical Center (476 beds)

Safety: Violent crime rate: 96.8 per 10,000 population; Property crime rate: 782.9 per 10,000 population (2007).

Newspapers: The Repository (Local news; Circulation 82,300)

Transportation: Commute to work: 91.8% car, 2.7% public transportation, 3.2% walk, 1.4% work from home (2000); Travel time to work: 43.8% less than 15 minutes, 39.3% 15 to 30 minutes, 9.8% 30 to 45 minutes, 3.2% 45 to 60 minutes, 3.9% 60 minutes or more (2000)

Additional Information Contacts

Canton Regional Chamber of Commerce . . . . (330) 456-7253
http://www.cantonchamber.org
Canton-Stark County Convention & Visitors Bureau . . . . . . (330) 454-1439
http://www.visitcantonohio.com
City of Canton . . . . (330) 489-3283
http://www.ci.canton.oh.us

EAST CANTON (village). Covers a land area of 1.326 square miles and a water area of 0 square miles. Located at 40.78° N. Lat.; 81.28° W. Long. Elevation is 1,165 feet.

History: East Canton was founded in 1805 as Osnaburg. The name was changed in 1821. The town developed as a residential suburb for Canton, and as a center for glazed brick making.

Population: 1,742 (1990); 1,629 (2000); 1,643 (2007); 1,651 (2012 projected); Race: 94.0% White, 4.3% Black, 0.1% Asian, 1.3% Hispanic of any race (2007); Density: 1,239.3 persons per square mile (2007); Average household size: 2.41 (2007); Median age: 40.3 (2007); Males per 100 females: 98.2 (2007); Marriage status: 27.0% never married, 54.3% now married, 6.5% widowed, 12.2% divorced (2000); Foreign born: 1.2% (2000); Ancestry (includes multiple ancestries): 32.8% German, 12.2% Irish, 10.5% United States or American, 9.5% English, 8.4% Other groups (2000).

Economy: Employment by occupation: 5.8% management, 13.7% professional, 16.6% services, 23.9% sales, 0.7% farming, 9.5% construction, 29.8% production (2000).

Income: Per capita income: $21,599 (2007); Median household income: $46,038 (2007); Average household income: $51,958 (2007); Percent of households with income of $100,000 or more: 6.9% (2007); Poverty rate: 8.1% (2000).

Education: Percent of population age 25 and over with: High school diploma (including GED) or higher: 83.7% (2007); Bachelor's degree or higher: 9.4% (2007); Master's degree or higher: 2.6% (2007).

School District(s)

East Canton Digital Academy (09-12)
2005-06 Enrollment: 26 . . . . (330) 488-0316
Osnaburg Local (PK-12)
2005-06 Enrollment: 923 . . . . (330) 488-1609

Housing: Homeownership rate: 68.2% (2007); Median home value: $111,236 (2007); Median rent: $431 per month (2000); Median age of housing: 43 years (2000).

Transportation: Commute to work: 93.5% car, 1.6% public transportation, 3.3% walk, 0.4% work from home (2000); Travel time to work: 29.6% less

than 15 minutes, 51.7% 15 to 30 minutes, 12.0% 30 to 45 minutes, 3.2% 45 to 60 minutes, 3.5% 60 minutes or more (2000)

EAST SPARTA (village). Covers a land area of 0.599 square miles and a water area of 0 square miles. Located at 40.67° N. Lat.; 81.35° W. Long. Elevation is 968 feet.
Population: 771 (1990); 806 (2000); 859 (2007); 892 (2012 projected); Race: 98.1% White, 0.2% Black, 0.0% Asian, 0.0% Hispanic of any race (2007); Density: 1,433.0 persons per square mile (2007); Average household size: 2.51 (2007); Median age: 40.9 (2007); Males per 100 females: 96.1 (2007); Marriage status: 18.8% never married, 64.4% now married, 6.7% widowed, 10.0% divorced (2000); Foreign born: 0.2% (2000); Ancestry (includes multiple ancestries): 30.3% German, 21.3% Irish, 8.6% United States or American, 8.4% English, 5.3% Other groups (2000).
Economy: Single-family building permits issued: 0 (2007); Multi-family building permits issued: 0 (2007); Employment by occupation: 6.2% management, 8.7% professional, 15.2% services, 26.7% sales, 0.0% farming, 13.5% construction, 29.7% production (2000).
Income: Per capita income: $20,908 (2007); Median household income: $45,000 (2007); Average household income: $52,515 (2007); Percent of households with income of $100,000 or more: 7.0% (2007); Poverty rate: 5.3% (2000).
Education: Percent of population age 25 and over with: High school diploma (including GED) or higher: 85.8% (2007); Bachelor's degree or higher: 4.4% (2007); Master's degree or higher: 0.5% (2007).

School District(s)

Sandy Valley Local (PK-12)
2005-06 Enrollment: 1,532 . . . . (330) 866-3339
Housing: Homeownership rate: 83.9% (2007); Median home value: $97,614 (2007); Median rent: $365 per month (2000); Median age of housing: 56 years (2000).
Transportation: Commute to work: 98.7% car, 0.0% public transportation, 0.8% walk, 0.5% work from home (2000); Travel time to work: 21.3% less than 15 minutes, 49.1% 15 to 30 minutes, 21.3% 30 to 45 minutes, 4.1% 45 to 60 minutes, 4.3% 60 minutes or more (2000)

GREENTOWN (CDP). Covers a land area of 2.744 square miles and a water area of 0 square miles. Located at 40.92° N. Lat.; 81.40° W. Long. Elevation is 1,201 feet.
Population: 1,856 (1990); 3,154 (2000); 3,199 (2007); 3,281 (2012 projected); Race: 96.2% White, 1.2% Black, 0.9% Asian, 1.2% Hispanic of any race (2007); Density: 1,165.7 persons per square mile (2007); Average household size: 2.99 (2007); Median age: 36.9 (2007); Males per 100 females: 99.3 (2007); Marriage status: 23.2% never married, 66.3% now married, 3.9% widowed, 6.6% divorced (2000); Foreign born: 1.3% (2000); Ancestry (includes multiple ancestries): 30.8% German, 17.2% Italian, 15.1% Irish, 11.2% English, 7.0% Other groups (2000).
Economy: Employment by occupation: 21.5% management, 20.8% professional, 12.1% services, 23.7% sales, 0.0% farming, 7.3% construction, 14.6% production (2000).
Income: Per capita income: $33,110 (2007); Median household income: $83,395 (2007); Average household income: $99,083 (2007); Percent of households with income of $100,000 or more: 37.3% (2007); Poverty rate: 0.9% (2000).
Education: Percent of population age 25 and over with: High school diploma (including GED) or higher: 94.6% (2007); Bachelor's degree or higher: 34.3% (2007); Master's degree or higher: 12.6% (2007).
Housing: Homeownership rate: 86.5% (2007); Median home value: $194,107 (2007); Median rent: $539 per month (2000); Median age of housing: 18 years (2000).
Transportation: Commute to work: 94.4% car, 1.1% public transportation, 0.0% walk, 3.1% work from home (2000); Travel time to work: 31.9% less than 15 minutes, 49.2% 15 to 30 minutes, 8.5% 30 to 45 minutes, 4.2% 45 to 60 minutes, 6.2% 60 minutes or more (2000)

HARTVILLE (village). Covers a land area of 1.833 square miles and a water area of 0 square miles. Located at 40.96° N. Lat.; 81.34° W. Long. Elevation is 1,168 feet.
Population: 2,327 (1990); 2,174 (2000); 1,979 (2007); 1,892 (2012 projected); Race: 98.1% White, 0.3% Black, 0.4% Asian, 0.8% Hispanic of any race (2007); Density: 1,079.8 persons per square mile (2007); Average household size: 2.46 (2007); Median age: 35.8 (2007); Males per 100 females: 98.1 (2007); Marriage status: 26.1% never married, 58.5% now married, 5.5% widowed, 9.9% divorced (2000); Foreign born: 1.4% (2000); Ancestry (includes multiple ancestries): 35.8% German, 16.2% Irish, 10.2% English, 7.2% Italian, 6.7% United States or American (2000).
Economy: Single-family building permits issued: 5 (2007); Multi-family building permits issued: 4 (2007); Employment by occupation: 13.1% management, 17.1% professional, 16.4% services, 28.0% sales, 0.7% farming, 11.2% construction, 13.5% production (2000).
Income: Per capita income: $22,654 (2007); Median household income: $45,057 (2007); Average household income: $55,102 (2007); Percent of households with income of $100,000 or more: 12.2% (2007); Poverty rate: 9.2% (2000).
Education: Percent of population age 25 and over with: High school diploma (including GED) or higher: 83.6% (2007); Bachelor's degree or higher: 22.8% (2007); Master's degree or higher: 5.4% (2007).

School District(s)

Lake Local (PK-12)
2005-06 Enrollment: 3,538 . . . . (330) 877-9383
Housing: Homeownership rate: 51.7% (2007); Median home value: $153,723 (2007); Median rent: $453 per month (2000); Median age of housing: 32 years (2000).
Safety: Violent crime rate: 3.9 per 10,000 population; Property crime rate: 105.3 per 10,000 population (2007).
Newspapers: Hartville News (Local news; Circulation 2,900)
Transportation: Commute to work: 93.7% car, 0.2% public transportation, 2.0% walk, 3.6% work from home (2000); Travel time to work: 33.0% less than 15 minutes, 35.5% 15 to 30 minutes, 22.7% 30 to 45 minutes, 3.0% 45 to 60 minutes, 5.8% 60 minutes or more (2000)
Additional Information Contacts
Lake Chamber of Commerce. . . . . (330) 877-5500
http://www.lakechamber.com

HILLS AND DALES (village). Covers a land area of 0.321 square miles and a water area of 0 square miles. Located at 40.82° N. Lat.; 81.44° W. Long. Elevation is 1,119 feet.
Population: 297 (1990); 260 (2000); 283 (2007); 297 (2012 projected); Race: 96.1% White, 0.7% Black, 2.8% Asian, 1.1% Hispanic of any race (2007); Density: 881.5 persons per square mile (2007); Average household size: 2.42 (2007); Median age: 53.8 (2007); Males per 100 females: 92.5 (2007); Marriage status: 17.2% never married, 73.1% now married, 6.3% widowed, 3.4% divorced (2000); Foreign born: 4.5% (2000); Ancestry (includes multiple ancestries): 32.9% German, 19.2% English, 14.7% Irish, 7.9% Other groups, 6.8% French (except Basque) (2000).
Economy: Employment by occupation: 45.7% management, 27.1% professional, 0.0% services, 24.8% sales, 0.0% farming, 1.6% construction, 0.8% production (2000).
Income: Per capita income: $72,774 (2007); Median household income: $113,816 (2007); Average household income: $176,026 (2007); Percent of households with income of $100,000 or more: 59.0% (2007); Poverty rate: 3.4% (2000).
Education: Percent of population age 25 and over with: High school diploma (including GED) or higher: 99.1% (2007); Bachelor's degree or higher: 69.1% (2007); Master's degree or higher: 35.5% (2007).
Housing: Homeownership rate: 98.3% (2007); Median home value: $447,917 (2007); Median rent: $n/a per month (2000); Median age of housing: 46 years (2000).
Transportation: Commute to work: 89.1% car, 0.0% public transportation, 0.0% walk, 9.3% work from home (2000); Travel time to work: 44.4% less than 15 minutes, 37.6% 15 to 30 minutes, 12.8% 30 to 45 minutes, 0.0% 45 to 60 minutes, 5.1% 60 minutes or more (2000)

LIMAVILLE (village). Covers a land area of 0.273 square miles and a water area of 0 square miles. Located at 40.98° N. Lat.; 81.14° W. Long. Elevation is 1,060 feet.
Population: 152 (1990); 193 (2000); 201 (2007); 207 (2012 projected); Race: 96.0% White, 0.0% Black, 0.0% Asian, 5.0% Hispanic of any race (2007); Density: 736.8 persons per square mile (2007); Average household size: 2.68 (2007); Median age: 39.4 (2007); Males per 100 females: 111.6 (2007); Marriage status: 24.3% never married, 60.1% now married, 2.3% widowed, 13.3% divorced (2000); Foreign born: 1.5% (2000); Ancestry (includes multiple ancestries): 18.9% Irish, 12.9% German, 10.4% English, 9.5% United States or American, 8.0% Other groups (2000).
Economy: Single-family building permits issued: 0 (2007); Multi-family building permits issued: 0 (2007); Employment by occupation: 5.8% management, 10.5% professional, 23.3% services, 16.3% sales, 0.0% farming, 16.3% construction, 27.9% production (2000).

Income: Per capita income: $18,035 (2007); Median household income: $43,250 (2007); Average household income: $48,333 (2007); Percent of households with income of $100,000 or more: 4.0% (2007); Poverty rate: 8.5% (2000).
Education: Percent of population age 25 and over with: High school diploma (including GED) or higher: 81.6% (2007); Bachelor's degree or higher: 5.0% (2007); Master's degree or higher: 2.8% (2007).
Housing: Homeownership rate: 88.0% (2007); Median home value: $100,000 (2007); Median rent: $365 per month (2000); Median age of housing: 60+ years (2000).
Transportation: Commute to work: 96.3% car, 0.0% public transportation, 0.0% walk, 3.7% work from home (2000); Travel time to work: 29.1% less than 15 minutes, 54.4% 15 to 30 minutes, 6.3% 30 to 45 minutes, 6.3% 45 to 60 minutes, 3.8% 60 minutes or more (2000)

LOUISVILLE (city). Covers a land area of 5.157 square miles and a water area of 0 square miles. Located at 40.83° N. Lat.; 81.25° W. Long. Elevation is 1,142 feet.
Population: 8,350 (1990); 8,904 (2000); 9,470 (2007); 9,804 (2012 projected); Race: 98.1% White, 0.5% Black, 0.3% Asian, 0.9% Hispanic of any race (2007); Density: 1,836.4 persons per square mile (2007); Average household size: 2.54 (2007); Median age: 37.4 (2007); Males per 100 females: 90.1 (2007); Marriage status: 21.4% never married, 60.8% now married, 8.0% widowed, 9.7% divorced (2000); Foreign born: 0.9% (2000); Ancestry (includes multiple ancestries): 32.5% German, 14.9% Irish, 9.8% Italian, 8.7% English, 7.9% French (except Basque) (2000).
Economy: Single-family building permits issued: 19 (2007); Multi-family building permits issued: 2 (2007); Employment by occupation: 11.1% management, 17.1% professional, 13.6% services, 26.6% sales, 0.0% farming, 6.8% construction, 24.8% production (2000).
Income: Per capita income: $23,358 (2007); Median household income: $46,398 (2007); Average household income: $58,948 (2007); Percent of households with income of $100,000 or more: 10.0% (2007); Poverty rate: 4.0% (2000).
Taxes: Total city taxes per capita: $378 (2006); City property taxes per capita: $39 (2006).
Education: Percent of population age 25 and over with: High school diploma (including GED) or higher: 88.7% (2007); Bachelor's degree or higher: 15.8% (2007); Master's degree or higher: 4.6% (2007).

School District(s)

Louisville City (PK-12)
2005-06 Enrollment: 3,335 . . . . (330) 875-9687
Marlington Local (PK-12)
2005-06 Enrollment: 2,645 . . . . (330) 823-7458

Housing: Homeownership rate: 64.5% (2007); Median home value: $135,645 (2007); Median rent: $416 per month (2000); Median age of housing: 31 years (2000).
Newspapers: Louisville Herald (Community news; Circulation 3,100)
Transportation: Commute to work: 93.4% car, 1.5% public transportation, 2.3% walk, 1.9% work from home (2000); Travel time to work: 27.3% less than 15 minutes, 45.5% 15 to 30 minutes, 17.7% 30 to 45 minutes, 5.0% 45 to 60 minutes, 4.5% 60 minutes or more (2000)

Additional Information Contacts

City of Louisville . . . . (330) 875-3321
http://www.louisvilleohio.com
Louisville Area Chamber of Commerce . . . . (330) 875-7371
http://www.louisvilleohchamber.com

MAGNOLIA (village). Covers a land area of 0.890 square miles and a water area of 0 square miles. Located at 40.65° N. Lat.; 81.29° W. Long. Elevation is 958 feet.
Population: 937 (1990); 931 (2000); 875 (2007); 871 (2012 projected); Race: 98.9% White, 0.7% Black, 0.0% Asian, 2.4% Hispanic of any race (2007); Density: 983.6 persons per square mile (2007); Average household size: 2.46 (2007); Median age: 41.4 (2007); Males per 100 females: 102.1 (2007); Marriage status: 22.2% never married, 62.6% now married, 6.4% widowed, 8.9% divorced (2000); Foreign born: 0.5% (2000); Ancestry (includes multiple ancestries): 35.1% German, 17.6% Irish, 16.8% Italian, 8.9% English, 4.8% Other groups (2000).
Economy: Employment by occupation: 10.1% management, 17.2% professional, 15.0% services, 20.6% sales, 0.0% farming, 14.4% construction, 22.7% production (2000).
Income: Per capita income: $22,360 (2007); Median household income: $44,052 (2007); Average household income: $55,113 (2007); Percent of households with income of $100,000 or more: 11.0% (2007); Poverty rate: 4.3% (2000).
Education: Percent of population age 25 and over with: High school diploma (including GED) or higher: 88.5% (2007); Bachelor's degree or higher: 14.1% (2007); Master's degree or higher: 4.2% (2007).

School District(s)

Cardinal Digital Academy Inc (07-12)
2005-06 Enrollment: 27 . . . . (330) 866-9371
Sandy Valley Local (PK-12)
2005-06 Enrollment: 1,532 . . . . (330) 866-3339

Housing: Homeownership rate: 78.0% (2007); Median home value: $113,426 (2007); Median rent: $327 per month (2000); Median age of housing: 57 years (2000).
Transportation: Commute to work: 95.4% car, 1.1% public transportation, 0.7% walk, 1.8% work from home (2000); Travel time to work: 27.5% less than 15 minutes, 45.3% 15 to 30 minutes, 20.7% 30 to 45 minutes, 2.7% 45 to 60 minutes, 3.8% 60 minutes or more (2000)

MASSILLON (city). Covers a land area of 16.749 square miles and a water area of 0.144 square miles. Located at 40.79° N. Lat.; 81.52° W. Long. Elevation is 948 feet.
History: Massillon came into existence in 1826 when the Ohio & Erie Canal was planned. The town was laid out on both sides of the Tuscarawas River by James Duncan and Ferdinand Hurxthal, and named for Jean Baptiste Massillon, a French divine and Mrs. Duncan's favorite writer. Two years later the canal was completed, and Massillon became a marketing and industrial town.
Population: 31,955 (1990); 31,325 (2000); 31,895 (2007); 32,132 (2012 projected); Race: 88.0% White, 9.1% Black, 0.3% Asian, 1.1% Hispanic of any race (2007); Density: 1,904.3 persons per square mile (2007); Average household size: 2.43 (2007); Median age: 39.2 (2007); Males per 100 females: 93.4 (2007); Marriage status: 23.0% never married, 56.2% now married, 8.2% widowed, 12.7% divorced (2000); Foreign born: 1.3% (2000); Ancestry (includes multiple ancestries): 33.6% German, 13.5% Irish, 12.8% Other groups, 8.3% English, 7.1% Italian (2000).
Economy: Unemployment rate: 6.7% (6/2008); Total civilian labor force: 16,050 (6/2008); Single-family building permits issued: 84 (2007); Multi-family building permits issued: 40 (2007); Employment by occupation: 8.3% management, 13.9% professional, 16.5% services, 26.1% sales, 0.2% farming, 7.9% construction, 27.1% production (2000).
Income: Per capita income: $20,402 (2007); Median household income: $37,941 (2007); Average household income: $48,896 (2007); Percent of households with income of $100,000 or more: 8.3% (2007); Poverty rate: 10.7% (2000).
Taxes: Total city taxes per capita: $483 (2006); City property taxes per capita: $65 (2006).
Education: Percent of population age 25 and over with: High school diploma (including GED) or higher: 80.7% (2007); Bachelor's degree or higher: 12.4% (2007); Master's degree or higher: 3.7% (2007).

School District(s)

Department of Youth Services (06-12)
2005-06 Enrollment: 1,478 . . . . (614) 728-2489
Jackson Local (PK-12)
2005-06 Enrollment: 5,786 . . . . (330) 830-8000
Massillon City (PK-12)
2005-06 Enrollment: 4,576 . . . . (330) 830-3900
Massillon Digital Academy Inc (KG-12)
2005-06 Enrollment: 39 . . . . (330) 830-3900
Perry Local (PK-12)
2005-06 Enrollment: 4,806 . . . . (330) 477-8121
Perry Panther Digital Academy (KG-12)
2005-06 Enrollment: 19 . . . . (330) 477-8121
Stark County Area (09-12)
2005-06 Enrollment: n/a . . . . (330) 832-1591
Tuslaw Local (PK-12)
2005-06 Enrollment: 1,495 . . . . (330) 837-7813

Housing: Homeownership rate: 69.4% (2007); Median home value: $99,514 (2007); Median rent: $356 per month (2000); Median age of housing: 50 years (2000).
Hospitals: Affinity Medical Center - Doctors Campus (130 beds); Hearthland Behavioral Healthcare (130 beds); Massillon Community Hospital (268 beds)
Newspapers: The Independent (Local news; Circulation 13,000)
Transportation: Commute to work: 94.3% car, 1.4% public transportation, 2.0% walk, 1.3% work from home (2000); Travel time to work: 39.1% less

than 15 minutes, 40.2% 15 to 30 minutes, 12.8% 30 to 45 minutes, 3.9% 45 to 60 minutes, 4.0% 60 minutes or more (2000)

Additional Information Contacts

City of Massillon . . . . (330) 830-1700
http://www.massillonohio.com

Massillon Area Chamber of Commerce . . . . (330) 833-3146
http://www.massillonohchamber.com

MEYERS LAKE (village). Aka Myers Lake. Covers a land area of 0.222 square miles and a water area of 0.211 square miles. Located at 40.81° N. Lat.; 81.41° W. Long. Elevation is 1,109 feet.

History: Former site of amusement park at streetcar line terminus.

Population: 493 (1990); 565 (2000); 555 (2007); 533 (2012 projected); Race: 95.0% White, 3.4% Black, 0.2% Asian, 1.3% Hispanic of any race (2007); Density: 2,503.3 persons per square mile (2007); Average household size: 1.80 (2007); Median age: 56.2 (2007); Males per 100 females: 78.5 (2007); Marriage status: 19.6% never married, 57.9% now married, 6.8% widowed, 15.7% divorced (2000); Foreign born: 3.2% (2000); Ancestry (includes multiple ancestries): 35.3% German, 17.0% English, 13.1% Irish, 7.8% Italian, 7.6% Other groups (2000).

Economy: Employment by occupation: 18.8% management, 25.6% professional, 11.8% services, 27.2% sales, 0.0% farming, 7.3% construction, 9.3% production (2000).

Income: Per capita income: $42,980 (2007); Median household income: $52,857 (2007); Average household income: $76,981 (2007); Percent of households with income of $100,000 or more: 21.1% (2007); Poverty rate: 6.6% (2000).

Education: Percent of population age 25 and over with: High school diploma (including GED) or higher: 91.4% (2007); Bachelor's degree or higher: 36.2% (2007); Master's degree or higher: 13.2% (2007).

Housing: Homeownership rate: 78.2% (2007); Median home value: $158,203 (2007); Median rent: $656 per month (2000); Median age of housing: 17 years (2000).

Transportation: Commute to work: 93.6% car, 0.6% public transportation, 1.0% walk, 4.8% work from home (2000); Travel time to work: 50.7% less than 15 minutes, 34.8% 15 to 30 minutes, 12.2% 30 to 45 minutes, 2.4% 45 to 60 minutes, 0.0% 60 minutes or more (2000)

MINERVA (village). Covers a land area of 2.138 square miles and a water area of 0 square miles. Located at 40.72° N. Lat.; 81.10° W. Long. Elevation is 1,056 feet.

History: Minerva was established as a town in 1835, when the Sandy & Beaver Canal was under construction. The town was named for the niece of John Whitacre, the founder.

Population: 4,318 (1990); 3,934 (2000); 3,922 (2007); 3,924 (2012 projected); Race: 99.0% White, 0.0% Black, 0.2% Asian, 0.7% Hispanic of any race (2007); Density: 1,834.6 persons per square mile (2007); Average household size: 2.40 (2007); Median age: 40.9 (2007); Males per 100 females: 90.5 (2007); Marriage status: 22.1% never married, 57.0% now married, 10.5% widowed, 10.4% divorced (2000); Foreign born: 0.9% (2000); Ancestry (includes multiple ancestries): 34.6% German, 17.5% Irish, 14.5% English, 7.0% Italian, 5.4% United States or American (2000).

Economy: Employment by occupation: 6.1% management, 12.5% professional, 16.5% services, 24.2% sales, 0.0% farming, 7.0% construction, 33.8% production (2000).

Income: Per capita income: $18,803 (2007); Median household income: $36,599 (2007); Average household income: $43,735 (2007); Percent of households with income of $100,000 or more: 5.1% (2007); Poverty rate: 9.8% (2000).

Education: Percent of population age 25 and over with: High school diploma (including GED) or higher: 87.1% (2007); Bachelor's degree or higher: 9.4% (2007); Master's degree or higher: 2.3% (2007).

School District(s)

Minerva Local (PK-12)
2005-06 Enrollment: 2,176 . . . . (330) 868-4332

Housing: Homeownership rate: 67.9% (2007); Median home value: $92,750 (2007); Median rent: $353 per month (2000); Median age of housing: 49 years (2000).

Safety: Violent crime rate: 25.2 per 10,000 population; Property crime rate: 443.7 per 10,000 population (2007).

Newspapers: The News Leader (Community news; Circulation 4,400); Press-News (Community news; Circulation 2,500)

Transportation: Commute to work: 93.6% car, 0.0% public transportation, 5.1% walk, 0.6% work from home (2000); Travel time to work: 56.3% less than 15 minutes, 16.7% 15 to 30 minutes, 19.3% 30 to 45 minutes, 4.9% 45 to 60 minutes, 2.8% 60 minutes or more (2000)

Additional Information Contacts

Minerva Area Chamber of Commerce . . . . (330) 868-7979
http://www.minervachamber.com

NAVARRE (village). Covers a land area of 1.503 square miles and a water area of 0.004 square miles. Located at 40.72° N. Lat.; 81.52° W. Long. Elevation is 958 feet.

History: Navarre was founded by James Duncan and named by his wife for a prince of Navarre. A lock of the Ohio & Erie Canal was located in Navarre, which became a shipping center for farm produce.

Population: 1,778 (1990); 1,440 (2000); 1,398 (2007); 1,391 (2012 projected); Race: 98.6% White, 0.4% Black, 0.0% Asian, 0.1% Hispanic of any race (2007); Density: 929.9 persons per square mile (2007); Average household size: 2.32 (2007); Median age: 47.8 (2007); Males per 100 females: 84.9 (2007); Marriage status: 18.3% never married, 53.2% now married, 14.6% widowed, 13.9% divorced (2000); Foreign born: 0.7% (2000); Ancestry (includes multiple ancestries): 37.4% German, 13.0% Irish, 9.9% English, 8.0% Italian, 4.4% United States or American (2000).

Economy: Single-family building permits issued: 1 (2007); Multi-family building permits issued: 0 (2007); Employment by occupation: 10.2% management, 14.2% professional, 16.8% services, 26.3% sales, 0.0% farming, 8.5% construction, 24.0% production (2000).

Income: Per capita income: $21,070 (2007); Median household income: $37,927 (2007); Average household income: $45,635 (2007); Percent of households with income of $100,000 or more: 6.8% (2007); Poverty rate: 5.7% (2000).

Education: Percent of population age 25 and over with: High school diploma (including GED) or higher: 78.4% (2007); Bachelor's degree or higher: 11.1% (2007); Master's degree or higher: 5.6% (2007).

School District(s)

Fairless Digital Academy (03-12)
2005-06 Enrollment: 29 . . . . (330) 767-3577

Fairless Local (PK-12)
2005-06 Enrollment: 1,908 . . . . (330) 767-3577

Perry Local (PK-12)
2005-06 Enrollment: 4,806 . . . . (330) 477-8121

Housing: Homeownership rate: 66.6% (2007); Median home value: $105,746 (2007); Median rent: $316 per month (2000); Median age of housing: 60+ years (2000).

Safety: Violent crime rate: 0.0 per 10,000 population; Property crime rate: 161.5 per 10,000 population (2007).

Transportation: Commute to work: 91.2% car, 0.0% public transportation, 6.0% walk, 2.4% work from home (2000); Travel time to work: 40.5% less than 15 minutes, 42.0% 15 to 30 minutes, 11.8% 30 to 45 minutes, 1.8% 45 to 60 minutes, 3.9% 60 minutes or more (2000)

Additional Information Contacts

Village of Navarre . . . . (330) 879-5508
http://www.navarreohio.net

NORTH CANTON (city). Covers a land area of 6.069 square miles and a water area of 0 square miles. Located at 40.87° N. Lat.; 81.40° W. Long. Elevation is 1,161 feet.

History: Settled c.1815, incorporated as a city 1961.

Population: 15,556 (1990); 16,369 (2000); 16,153 (2007); 15,979 (2012 projected); Race: 96.3% White, 1.4% Black, 1.1% Asian, 0.9% Hispanic of any race (2007); Density: 2,661.5 persons per square mile (2007); Average household size: 2.26 (2007); Median age: 43.8 (2007); Males per 100 females: 89.2 (2007); Marriage status: 20.8% never married, 58.3% now married, 10.4% widowed, 10.5% divorced (2000); Foreign born: 2.7% (2000); Ancestry (includes multiple ancestries): 34.1% German, 13.8% Irish, 13.0% English, 10.4% Italian, 5.3% Other groups (2000).

Economy: Single-family building permits issued: 30 (2007); Multi-family building permits issued: 0 (2007); Employment by occupation: 15.8% management, 26.9% professional, 10.2% services, 29.4% sales, 0.0% farming, 5.4% construction, 12.1% production (2000).

Income: Per capita income: $27,100 (2007); Median household income: $46,047 (2007); Average household income: $59,894 (2007); Percent of households with income of $100,000 or more: 13.7% (2007); Poverty rate: 5.7% (2000).

Education: Percent of population age 25 and over with: High school diploma (including GED) or higher: 91.4% (2007); Bachelor's degree or higher: 33.7% (2007); Master's degree or higher: 13.7% (2007).

School District(s)

Canton City (PK-12)
2005-06 Enrollment: 11,144 . . . . (330) 438-2500
North Canton City (PK-12)
2005-06 Enrollment: 4,892 . . . . (330) 497-5600

Four-year College(s)

Walsh University (Private, Not-for-profit, Roman Catholic)
Fall 2007 Enrollment: 2,522. . . . . (330) 499-7090
2007-08 Tuition: In-state $18,960; Out-of-state $18,960

Two-year College(s)

Stark State College of Technology (Public)
Fall 2007 Enrollment: 8,238. . . . . (330) 494-6170
2007-08 Tuition: In-state $3,302; Out-of-state $4,862

Housing: Homeownership rate: 68.2% (2007); Median home value: $140,416 (2007); Median rent: $506 per month (2000); Median age of housing: 34 years (2000).

Safety: Violent crime rate: 8.9 per 10,000 population; Property crime rate: 154.5 per 10,000 population (2007).

Transportation: Commute to work: 93.8% car, 0.1% public transportation, 2.7% walk, 2.8% work from home (2000); Travel time to work: 42.7% less than 15 minutes, 37.5% 15 to 30 minutes, 14.6% 30 to 45 minutes, 2.4% 45 to 60 minutes, 2.8% 60 minutes or more (2000)

Additional Information Contacts

City of North Canton . . . . (330) 499-5081
http://www.northcantonohio.com
North Canton Area Chamber of Commerce. . . . . (330) 499-5100
http://www.northcantonchamber.org

NORTH LAWRENCE

NORTH LAWRENCE (unincorporated postal area, zip code 44666). Covers a land area of 22.425 square miles and a water area of 0.105 square miles. Located at 40.84° N. Lat.; 81.62° W. Long. Elevation is 1,037 feet.

Population: 2,764 (2000); Race: 97.7% White, 1.3% Black, 1.0% Asian, 0.5% Hispanic of any race (2000); Density: 123.3 persons per square mile (2000); Age: 25.9% under 18, 10.9% over 64 (2000); Marriage status: 24.6% never married, 60.4% now married, 3.8% widowed, 11.1% divorced (2000); Foreign born: 0.9% (2000); Ancestry (includes multiple ancestries): 42.3% German, 14.3% Irish, 9.6% English, 8.6% Other groups, 5.9% United States or American (2000).

Economy: Employment by occupation: 8.6% management, 15.6% professional, 13.4% services, 23.9% sales, 1.0% farming, 10.1% construction, 27.3% production (2000).

Income: Per capita income: $22,225 (2000); Median household income: $48,214 (2000); Poverty rate: 5.8% (2000).

Education: Percent of population age 25 and over with: High school diploma (including GED) or higher: 86.0% (2000); Bachelor's degree or higher: 10.7% (2000).

Housing: Homeownership rate: 89.4% (2000); Median home value: $111,600 (2000); Median rent: $385 per month (2000); Median age of housing: 46 years (2000).

Transportation: Commute to work: 94.1% car, 0.5% public transportation, 0.7% walk, 3.6% work from home (2000); Travel time to work: 25.1% less than 15 minutes, 51.2% 15 to 30 minutes, 13.7% 30 to 45 minutes, 9.0% 45 to 60 minutes, 0.9% 60 minutes or more (2000)

PARIS

PARIS (unincorporated postal area, zip code 44669). Covers a land area of 18.160 square miles and a water area of 0.035 square miles. Located at 40.79° N. Lat.; 81.16° W. Long. Elevation is 1,260 feet.

Population: 1,564 (2000); Race: 97.9% White, 0.0% Black, 0.0% Asian, 0.0% Hispanic of any race (2000); Density: 86.1 persons per square mile (2000); Age: 34.3% under 18, 10.2% over 64 (2000); Marriage status: 21.6% never married, 66.8% now married, 2.8% widowed, 8.8% divorced (2000); Foreign born: 0.3% (2000); Ancestry (includes multiple ancestries): 33.5% German, 12.5% United States or American, 9.5% Irish, 8.6% English, 7.4% Italian (2000).

Economy: Employment by occupation: 13.9% management, 16.0% professional, 9.6% services, 19.1% sales, 2.8% farming, 13.6% construction, 24.9% production (2000).

Income: Per capita income: $16,669 (2000); Median household income: $47,292 (2000); Poverty rate: 9.6% (2000).

Education: Percent of population age 25 and over with: High school diploma (including GED) or higher: 84.5% (2000); Bachelor's degree or higher: 18.5% (2000).

Housing: Homeownership rate: 90.1% (2000); Median home value: $109,200 (2000); Median rent: $416 per month (2000); Median age of housing: 38 years (2000).

Transportation: Commute to work: 89.1% car, 0.0% public transportation, 1.1% walk, 9.7% work from home (2000); Travel time to work: 20.6% less than 15 minutes, 49.0% 15 to 30 minutes, 20.3% 30 to 45 minutes, 5.9% 45 to 60 minutes, 4.1% 60 minutes or more (2000)

PERRY HEIGHTS

PERRY HEIGHTS (CDP). Aka Genoa. Covers a land area of 2.917 square miles and a water area of 0.041 square miles. Located at 40.79° N. Lat.; 81.46° W. Long. Elevation is 1,099 feet.

Population: 9,418 (1990); 8,900 (2000); 8,653 (2007); 8,431 (2012 projected); Race: 94.1% White, 3.4% Black, 0.2% Asian, 1.7% Hispanic of any race (2007); Density: 2,966.2 persons per square mile (2007); Average household size: 2.46 (2007); Median age: 41.1 (2007); Males per 100 females: 92.2 (2007); Marriage status: 23.7% never married, 54.8% now married, 9.8% widowed, 11.8% divorced (2000); Foreign born: 1.7% (2000); Ancestry (includes multiple ancestries): 34.6% German, 14.9% Irish, 8.2% English, 7.9% Other groups, 7.6% Italian (2000).

Economy: Employment by occupation: 8.3% management, 15.4% professional, 13.8% services, 29.2% sales, 0.2% farming, 9.5% construction, 23.6% production (2000).

Income: Per capita income: $24,305 (2007); Median household income: $46,724 (2007); Average household income: $57,250 (2007); Percent of households with income of $100,000 or more: 11.0% (2007); Poverty rate: 6.9% (2000).

Education: Percent of population age 25 and over with: High school diploma (including GED) or higher: 85.8% (2007); Bachelor's degree or higher: 12.3% (2007); Master's degree or higher: 3.8% (2007).

Housing: Homeownership rate: 74.0% (2007); Median home value: $110,155 (2007); Median rent: $434 per month (2000); Median age of housing: 37 years (2000).

Transportation: Commute to work: 96.9% car, 0.8% public transportation, 0.4% walk, 1.5% work from home (2000); Travel time to work: 30.2% less than 15 minutes, 47.0% 15 to 30 minutes, 9.8% 30 to 45 minutes, 6.5% 45 to 60 minutes, 6.5% 60 minutes or more (2000)

UNIONTOWN

UNIONTOWN (CDP). Covers a land area of 2.496 square miles and a water area of 0.025 square miles. Located at 40.97° N. Lat.; 81.40° W. Long. Elevation is 1,119 feet.

Population: 3,074 (1990); 2,802 (2000); 2,707 (2007); 2,675 (2012 projected); Race: 97.7% White, 0.4% Black, 0.7% Asian, 0.6% Hispanic of any race (2007); Density: 1,084.5 persons per square mile (2007); Average household size: 2.41 (2007); Median age: 45.9 (2007); Males per 100 females: 90.6 (2007); Marriage status: 22.2% never married, 63.9% now married, 5.2% widowed, 8.7% divorced (2000); Foreign born: 2.5% (2000); Ancestry (includes multiple ancestries): 29.6% German, 21.1% English, 14.9% Irish, 9.5% Italian, 8.4% Other groups (2000).

Economy: Employment by occupation: 13.6% management, 23.2% professional, 9.4% services, 28.6% sales, 0.0% farming, 12.8% construction, 12.3% production (2000).

Income: Per capita income: $27,861 (2007); Median household income: $54,359 (2007); Average household income: $67,100 (2007); Percent of households with income of $100,000 or more: 18.4% (2007); Poverty rate: 2.7% (2000).

Education: Percent of population age 25 and over with: High school diploma (including GED) or higher: 88.8% (2007); Bachelor's degree or higher: 20.3% (2007); Master's degree or higher: 5.2% (2007).

School District(s)

Green Local (PK-12)
2005-06 Enrollment: 4,222 . . . . (330) 896-7500
Green Local (PK-12)
2005-06 Enrollment: 1,374 . . . . (330) 669-3921
Lake Local (PK-12)
2005-06 Enrollment: 3,538 . . . . (330) 877-9383

Housing: Homeownership rate: 85.4% (2007); Median home value: $159,898 (2007); Median rent: $484 per month (2000); Median age of housing: 31 years (2000).

Transportation: Commute to work: 97.1% car, 1.2% public transportation, 0.0% walk, 1.7% work from home (2000); Travel time to work: 24.5% less than 15 minutes, 42.7% 15 to 30 minutes, 22.6% 30 to 45 minutes, 2.7% 45 to 60 minutes, 7.4% 60 minutes or more (2000)

Additional Information Contacts

Green Chamber of Commerce. . . . . (330) 896-3023
http://www.greencoc.org

WAYNESBURG (village). Covers a land area of 0.516 square miles and a water area of 0 square miles. Located at 40.66° N. Lat.; 81.25° W. Long. Elevation is 997 feet.

Population: 1,068 (1990); 1,003 (2000); 900 (2007); 880 (2012 projected); Race: 95.3% White, 3.2% Black, 0.3% Asian, 0.7% Hispanic of any race (2007); Density: 1,744.8 persons per square mile (2007); Average household size: 2.51 (2007); Median age: 38.1 (2007); Males per 100 females: 97.4 (2007); Marriage status: 25.0% never married, 55.0% now married, 9.6% widowed, 10.4% divorced (2000); Foreign born: 2.4% (2000); Ancestry (includes multiple ancestries): 33.0% German, 23.3% Italian, 13.9% Irish, 10.3% Other groups, 8.0% United States or American (2000).

Economy: Employment by occupation: 6.0% management, 10.8% professional, 21.6% services, 22.8% sales, 0.7% farming, 13.7% construction, 24.5% production (2000).

Income: Per capita income: $19,533 (2007); Median household income: $39,722 (2007); Average household income: $48,969 (2007); Percent of households with income of $100,000 or more: 8.1% (2007); Poverty rate: 16.4% (2000).

Education: Percent of population age 25 and over with: High school diploma (including GED) or higher: 81.0% (2007); Bachelor's degree or higher: 5.4% (2007); Master's degree or higher: 3.5% (2007).

School District(s)

Sandy Valley Local (PK-12)
2005-06 Enrollment: 1,532 . . . . (330) 866-3339

Housing: Homeownership rate: 68.8% (2007); Median home value: $97,206 (2007); Median rent: $368 per month (2000); Median age of housing: 60+ years (2000).

Safety: Violent crime rate: 0.0 per 10,000 population; Property crime rate: 164.3 per 10,000 population (2007).

Transportation: Commute to work: 93.2% car, 0.7% public transportation, 3.4% walk, 2.7% work from home (2000); Travel time to work: 24.5% less than 15 minutes, 41.0% 15 to 30 minutes, 27.5% 30 to 45 minutes, 4.0% 45 to 60 minutes, 3.0% 60 minutes or more (2000)

WILMOT (village). Covers a land area of 0.164 square miles and a water area of 0 square miles. Located at 40.65° N. Lat.; 81.63° W. Long. Elevation is 1,014 feet.

History: Wilmot was platted in 1836, and developed as a trading center in the midst of the Amish country.

Population: 261 (1990); 335 (2000); 333 (2007); 331 (2012 projected); Race: 98.5% White, 0.0% Black, 0.6% Asian, 0.0% Hispanic of any race (2007); Density: 2,026.3 persons per square mile (2007); Average household size: 2.62 (2007); Median age: 33.2 (2007); Males per 100 females: 97.0 (2007); Marriage status: 22.7% never married, 61.1% now married, 5.3% widowed, 10.9% divorced (2000); Foreign born: 1.1% (2000); Ancestry (includes multiple ancestries): 23.4% German, 20.5% Other groups, 16.0% Irish, 14.2% Swiss, 8.8% English (2000).

Economy: Employment by occupation: 8.6% management, 17.1% professional, 9.2% services, 28.9% sales, 0.0% farming, 7.2% construction, 28.9% production (2000).

Income: Per capita income: $20,668 (2007); Median household income: $44,265 (2007); Average household income: $54,193 (2007); Percent of households with income of $100,000 or more: 4.7% (2007); Poverty rate: 6.6% (2000).

Education: Percent of population age 25 and over with: High school diploma (including GED) or higher: 77.7% (2007); Bachelor's degree or higher: 7.9% (2007); Master's degree or higher: 1.0% (2007).

Housing: Homeownership rate: 70.9% (2007); Median home value: $88,000 (2007); Median rent: $385 per month (2000); Median age of housing: 60+ years (2000).

Transportation: Commute to work: 87.4% car, 0.0% public transportation, 1.3% walk, 11.3% work from home (2000); Travel time to work: 19.4% less than 15 minutes, 58.2% 15 to 30 minutes, 14.9% 30 to 45 minutes, 4.5% 45 to 60 minutes, 3.0% 60 minutes or more (2000)

Summit County

Located in northeastern Ohio; drained by the Cuyahoga and Tuscarawas Rivers; includes Portage Lakes. Covers a land area of 412.72 square miles, a water area of 7.34 square miles, and is located in the Eastern Time Zone. The county was founded in 1840. County seat is Akron.

Summit County is part of the Akron, OH Metropolitan Statistical Area. The entire metro area includes: Portage County, OH; Summit County, OH

Weather Station: Akron-Canton Regional Airport Elevation: 1,207 feet

	Jan	Feb	Mar	Apr	May	Jun	Jul	Aug	Sep	Oct	Nov	Dec
High	33	37	47	59	70	78	82	81	73	62	49	38
Low	18	20	28	38	49	58	62	61	53	43	34	25
Precip	2.5	2.3	3.1	3.3	3.9	3.6	3.9	3.5	3.4	2.6	3.1	3.0
Snow	12.9	9.5	9.0	2.6	tr	tr	0.0	0.0	tr	0.6	3.2	9.1

High and Low temperatures in degrees Fahrenheit; Precipitation and Snow in inches

Population: 514,990 (1990); 542,899 (2000); 547,001 (2007); 547,448 (2012 projected); Race: 82.0% White, 14.0% Black, 1.8% Asian, 1.1% Hispanic of any race (2007); Density: 1,325.3 persons per square mile (2007); Average household size: 2.46 (2007); Median age: 39.1 (2007); Males per 100 females: 93.3 (2007).

Religion: Five largest groups: 22.4% Catholic Church, 4.0% Independent, Non-Charismatic Churches, 3.9% The United Methodist Church, 2.1% United Church of Christ, 1.3% Evangelical Lutheran Church in America (2000).

Economy: Unemployment rate: 6.2% (6/2008); Total civilian labor force: 299,282 (6/2008); Leading industries: 15.5% health care and social assistance; 14.3% manufacturing; 12.6% retail trade (2005); Farms: 377 totaling 21,117 acres (2002); Companies that employ 500 or more persons: 36 (2006); Companies that employ 100 to 499 persons: 406 (2006); Companies that employ less than 100 persons: 13,899 (2006); Black-owned businesses: 1,648 (2002); Hispanic-owned businesses: 378 (2002); Asian-owned businesses: 906 (2002); Women-owned businesses: 11,827 (2002); Retail sales per capita: $17,197 (2008). Single-family building permits issued: 906 (2007); Multi-family building permits issued: 183 (2007).

Income: Per capita income: $26,665 (2007); Median household income: $48,468 (2007); Average household income: $64,355 (2007); Percent of households with income of $100,000 or more: 16.3% (2007); Poverty rate: 11.6% (2005); Bankruptcy rate: 5.06% (2007).

Taxes: Total county taxes per capita: $335 (2006); County property taxes per capita: $231 (2006).

Education: Percent of population age 25 and over with: High school diploma (including GED) or higher: 85.9% (2007); Bachelor's degree or higher: 25.6% (2007); Master's degree or higher: 8.6% (2007).

Housing: Homeownership rate: 70.7% (2007); Median home value: $132,827 (2007); Median rent: $456 per month (2000); Median age of housing: 41 years (2000).

Health: Birth rate: 121.8 per 10,000 population (2007); Death rate: 99.5 per 10,000 population (2007); Age-adjusted cancer mortality rate: 199.4 deaths per 100,000 population (2005); Air Quality Index: 73.2% good, 20.8% moderate, 5.8% unhealthy for sensitive individuals, 0.3% unhealthy (percent of days in 2007); Number of physicians: 35.2 per 10,000 population (2005); Hospital beds: 38.2 per 10,000 population (2004); Hospital admissions: 1,549.0 per 10,000 population (2004).

Elections: 2004 Presidential election results: 42.9% Bush, 56.7% Kerry, 0.0% Nader, 0.2% Badnarik

National and State Parks: Cuyahoga Valley National Park; Portage Lakes State Park

Additional Information Contacts

Summit County Government . . . . (330) 643-2510
http://www.co.summit.oh.us

Akron-Summit Convention & Visitors Bureau . . . . (330) 374-7560
http://www.visitakron-summit.org

Barberton-South Summit Chamber of Commerce . . . . (330) 745-3141
http://www.southsummitchamber.org

City of Akron . . . . (330) 375-2345
http://www.ci.akron.oh.us

City of Barberton . . . . (330) 848-6719
http://www.cityofbarberton.com

City of Cuyahoga Falls . . . . (330) 971-8000
http://cfo.cityofcf.com/website/web2/view.do

City of Fairlawn . . . . (330) 668-9500
http://www.cityoffairlawn.com

City of Green . . . . (330) 896-5510
http://www.cityofgreen.org

City of Hudson . . . . (330) 650-1799
http://www.hudson.oh.us

City of Macedonia . . . . (330) 468-8300
http://www.macedonia.oh.us

City of Munroe Falls . . . . (330) 688-7491
http://www.munroefalls.com
City of Norton . . . . (330) 825-7815
http://www.cityofnorton.org
City of Stow . . . . (330) 689-2700
http://www.stow.oh.us
City of Tallmadge . . . . (330) 633-0857
http://www.tallmadge-ohio.org
City of Twinsburg . . . . (330) 425-7161
http://www.mytwinsburg.com
Cuyahoga Falls Chamber of Commerce . . . . (330) 929-6756
http://www.cuyahogafallschamberofcommerce.com
Fairlawn Area Chamber of Commerce . . . . (330) 849-0402
http://www.fairlawnareachamber.org
Greater Akron Chamber. . . . . (330) 376-5550
http://www.greaterakronchamber.org
Hudson Area Chamber of Commerce . . . . (330) 650-0621
http://www.hudsoncoc.org
Nordonia Hills Chamber of Commerce . . . . (330) 467-8956
http://www.nhcoc.org
Stow-Munroe Falls Chamber of Commerce. . . . . (330) 688-1579
http://www.smfcc.com
Tallmadge Chamber of Commerce . . . . (330) 633-5417
http://www.tallmadge-chamber.com
The British-American Chamber of Commerce . . . . (216) 621-0222
http://www.baccgl.org
Twinsburg Chamber of Commerce . . . . (330) 963-6249
http://www.twinsburgchamber.com
Village of Reminderville . . . . (330) 562-1234
http://www.reminderville.com
Village of Richfield . . . . (330) 659-9201
http://www.richfieldvillageohio.org

Summit County Communities

AKRON (city). County seat. Covers a land area of 62.069 square miles and a water area of 0.339 square miles. Located at 41.07° N. Lat.; 81.51° W. Long. Elevation is 955 feet.

History: The first settler in the Akron area was Captain Joseph Hart, who established Middlebury, now East Akron, in 1807. The city of Akron was laid out in 1825 by General Simon Perkins, commissioner of the Ohio Canal Fund, who saw a great future for a town on the summit of the course of the Ohio & Erie Canal. When the canal opened to traffic in 1827, the town grew rapidly. In 1840 trade was improved further with the opening of the Ohio & Pennsylvania Canal. In 1859, former resident John Brown was executed here for his raid at Harper's Ferry. Dr. Benjamin Franklin Goodrich came to Akron in 1870 and founded a plant for manufacturing fire hose and other articles from rubber. Around 1900 Akron was the national center for the manufacture of farm machinery, and the American Cereal Company (Quaker Oats) emerged as a leading cereal producer. But it was the rubber industry that by 1915 made Akron a boom town.

Population: 223,165 (1990); 217,074 (2000); 209,368 (2007); 203,372 (2012 projected); Race: 63.8% White, 31.1% Black, 1.8% Asian, 1.5% Hispanic of any race (2007); Density: 3,373.1 persons per square mile (2007); Average household size: 2.38 (2007); Median age: 36.1 (2007); Males per 100 females: 92.3 (2007); Marriage status: 33.0% never married, 45.2% now married, 8.0% widowed, 13.8% divorced (2000); Foreign born: 3.2% (2000); Ancestry (includes multiple ancestries): 29.9% Other groups, 18.1% German, 11.5% Irish, 7.2% English, 6.8% Italian (2000).

Economy: Unemployment rate: 6.8% (6/2008); Total civilian labor force: 109,025 (6/2008); Single-family building permits issued: 140 (2007); Multi-family building permits issued: 169 (2007); Employment by occupation: 9.0% management, 17.0% professional, 18.3% services, 28.3% sales, 0.1% farming, 7.7% construction, 19.6% production (2000).

Income: Per capita income: $19,918 (2007); Median household income: $35,993 (2007); Average household income: $46,437 (2007); Percent of households with income of $100,000 or more: 7.4% (2007); Poverty rate: 17.5% (2000).

Taxes: Total city taxes per capita: $776 (2006); City property taxes per capita: $144 (2006).

Education: Percent of population age 25 and over with: High school diploma (including GED) or higher: 80.2% (2007); Bachelor's degree or higher: 18.4% (2007); Master's degree or higher: 6.3% (2007).

School District(s)

Akron City (PK-12)
2005-06 Enrollment: 27,420 . . . . (330) 761-1661
Akron Digital Academy (KG-12)
2005-06 Enrollment: 590 . . . . (330) 237-2200
Coventry Local (PK-12)
2005-06 Enrollment: 2,411 . . . . (330) 644-8489
Edge Academy The (KG-08)
2005-06 Enrollment: 267 . . . . (330) 535-5023
Hope Academy Brown St Campus (KG-08)
2005-06 Enrollment: 262 . . . . (330) 785-0180
Hope Academy University (KG-08)
2005-06 Enrollment: 343 . . . . (330) 535-7728
Ida B Wells Community Academy (KG-08)
2005-06 Enrollment: 145 . . . . (330) 867-1085
Life Skills Center of Akron (09-12)
2005-06 Enrollment: 287 . . . . (330) 376-8700
Life Skills Center of North Akron (09-12)
2005-06 Enrollment: 121 . . . . (330) 633-5990
Life Skills Center of Summit County (09-12)
2005-06 Enrollment: 188 . . . . (330) 745-3678
Lighthouse Comm & Prof Dev (KG-08)
2005-06 Enrollment: 221 . . . . (330) 836-6370
Manchester Local (PK-12)
2005-06 Enrollment: 1,557 . . . . (330) 882-6926
Revere Local (PK-12)
2005-06 Enrollment: 2,868 . . . . (330) 666-4155
Springfield Local (PK-12)
2005-06 Enrollment: 2,934 . . . . (330) 798-1111
Summit Academy Secondary - Akron (09-12)
2005-06 Enrollment: 49 . . . . (330) 434-2343
Summit Academy of Alt Learners (01-06)
2005-06 Enrollment: 58 . . . . (330) 253-7441
Summit Academy of Creative Arts (06-09)
2005-06 Enrollment: 69 . . . . (330) 434-2343

Four-year College(s)

University of Akron Main Campus (Public)
Fall 2007 Enrollment: 23,007. . . . . (330) 972-7111
2007-08 Tuition: In-state $8,382; Out-of-state $17,631

Two-year College(s)

Academy of Court Reporting-Akron (Private, For-profit)
Fall 2007 Enrollment: 183 . . . . (330) 867-4030
2007-08 Tuition: In-state $9,555; Out-of-state $9,555
Akron Institute-A Division of Herzing Ohio Inc (Private, For-profit)
Fall 2007 Enrollment: 543 . . . . (330) 724-1600
2007-08 Tuition: In-state $12,460; Out-of-state $12,460
Brown Mackie College-Akron (Private, For-profit)
Fall 2007 Enrollment: 870 . . . . (330) 869-3600
2007-08 Tuition: In-state $7,164; Out-of-state $7,164
National Institute of Massotherapy (Private, For-profit)
Fall 2007 Enrollment: 132 . . . . (330) 867-1996
Ohio College of Massotherapy Inc (Private, Not-for-profit)
Fall 2007 Enrollment: 189 . . . . (330) 665-1084
2007-08 Tuition: In-state $8,475; Out-of-state $8,475

Vocational/Technical School(s)

Akron Adult Vocational Services (Public)
Fall 2007 Enrollment: 486 . . . . (330) 761-1385
2007-08 Tuition: $6,370
Akron School of Practical Nursing (Public)
Fall 2007 Enrollment: 129 . . . . (330) 761-3255
2007-08 Tuition: $8,250

Housing: Homeownership rate: 59.6% (2007); Median home value: $93,823 (2007); Median rent: $413 per month (2000); Median age of housing: 50 years (2000).

Hospitals: Akron Children's Hospital (267 beds); Akron City Hospital (505 beds); Akron General Health and Wellness Center; Akron General Medical Center (537 beds); Edwin Shaw Hospital for Rehabilitation (188 beds); St. Thomas Hospital (306 beds)

Safety: Violent crime rate: 75.1 per 10,000 population; Property crime rate: 502.8 per 10,000 population (2007).

Newspapers: The Akron Beacon Journal (Local news; Circulation 146,477); Akron Legal News (Local news; Circulation 1,000); Green Leader (Community news); Suburbanite (Local news; Circulation 31,600); Tomorrow's Technician; West Side Leader (Local news; Circulation 41,000)

Transportation: Commute to work: 91.7% car, 3.3% public transportation, 2.3% walk, 2.0% work from home (2000); Travel time to work: 34.3% less than 15 minutes, 43.0% 15 to 30 minutes, 13.2% 30 to 45 minutes, 4.7% 45 to 60 minutes, 4.9% 60 minutes or more (2000)
Airports: Akron Fulton International (general aviation); Akron-Canton Regional (primary service/small hub)
Additional Information Contacts
Akron-Summit Convention & Visitors Bureau . . . . (330) 374-7560
http://www.visitakron-summit.org
City of Akron . . . . (330) 375-2345
http://www.ci.akron.oh.us
Greater Akron Chamber. . . . . (330) 376-5550
http://www.greaterakronchamber.org

BARBERTON (city). Covers a land area of 9.014 square miles and a water area of 0.219 square miles. Located at 41.01° N. Lat.; 81.60° W. Long. Elevation is 974 feet.
History: Barberton was laid out in 1891 by Ohio Columbus Barber, the owner of the Diamond Match Company. Barber dominated the town until his death in 1920, spending millions of dollars on the Anna Dean Experimental Farm, known as Barber's Folly, where cows and horses lived in luxury.
Population: 27,931 (1990); 27,899 (2000); 26,911 (2007); 26,137 (2012 projected); Race: 91.6% White, 5.7% Black, 0.4% Asian, 0.9% Hispanic of any race (2007); Density: 2,985.6 persons per square mile (2007); Average household size: 2.38 (2007); Median age: 38.4 (2007); Males per 100 females: 88.5 (2007); Marriage status: 25.3% never married, 52.2% now married, 9.5% widowed, 13.0% divorced (2000); Foreign born: 1.9% (2000); Ancestry (includes multiple ancestries): 23.9% German, 13.1% Irish, 11.4% Other groups, 10.1% United States or American, 7.1% English (2000).
Economy: Unemployment rate: 7.3% (6/2008); Total civilian labor force: 13,848 (6/2008); Single-family building permits issued: 14 (2007); Multi-family building permits issued: 0 (2007); Employment by occupation: 8.0% management, 12.1% professional, 17.5% services, 27.4% sales, 0.2% farming, 10.7% construction, 24.1% production (2000).
Income: Per capita income: $20,269 (2007); Median household income: $36,877 (2007); Average household income: $47,606 (2007); Percent of households with income of $100,000 or more: 7.4% (2007); Poverty rate: 13.3% (2000).
Taxes: Total city taxes per capita: $426 (2006); City property taxes per capita: $50 (2006).
Education: Percent of population age 25 and over with: High school diploma (including GED) or higher: 79.2% (2007); Bachelor's degree or higher: 10.7% (2007); Master's degree or higher: 3.4% (2007).
School District(s)
Barberton City (PK-12)
2005-06 Enrollment: 4,355 . . . . (330) 753-1025
Housing: Homeownership rate: 65.4% (2007); Median home value: $96,029 (2007); Median rent: $380 per month (2000); Median age of housing: 49 years (2000).
Hospitals: Barberton Citizens Hospital (311 beds)
Safety: Violent crime rate: 21.2 per 10,000 population; Property crime rate: 436.5 per 10,000 population (2007).
Newspapers: Barberton Herald (Community news; Circulation 35,000)
Transportation: Commute to work: 94.4% car, 1.1% public transportation, 2.8% walk, 1.3% work from home (2000); Travel time to work: 38.8% less than 15 minutes, 39.1% 15 to 30 minutes, 13.7% 30 to 45 minutes, 4.6% 45 to 60 minutes, 3.9% 60 minutes or more (2000)
Additional Information Contacts
Barberton-South Summit Chamber of Commerce . . . . (330) 745-3141
http://www.southsummitchamber.org
City of Barberton . . . . (330) 848-6719
http://www.cityofbarberton.com

BOSTON HEIGHTS (village). Covers a land area of 6.897 square miles and a water area of 0.007 square miles. Located at 41.25° N. Lat.; 81.50° W. Long. Elevation is 1,070 feet.
Population: 733 (1990); 1,186 (2000); 1,529 (2007); 1,734 (2012 projected); Race: 95.8% White, 0.7% Black, 2.2% Asian, 1.2% Hispanic of any race (2007); Density: 221.7 persons per square mile (2007); Average household size: 2.91 (2007); Median age: 38.1 (2007); Males per 100 females: 102.2 (2007); Marriage status: 17.7% never married, 74.9% now married, 2.7% widowed, 4.7% divorced (2000); Foreign born: 3.0% (2000); Ancestry (includes multiple ancestries): 25.5% German, 18.8% Irish, 15.4% Polish, 13.7% Italian, 10.9% English (2000).
Economy: Single-family building permits issued: 5 (2007); Multi-family building permits issued: 0 (2007); Employment by occupation: 26.7% management, 22.0% professional, 12.2% services, 24.7% sales, 0.0% farming, 7.3% construction, 7.0% production (2000).
Income: Per capita income: $41,176 (2007); Median household income: $91,776 (2007); Average household income: $119,691 (2007); Percent of households with income of $100,000 or more: 45.2% (2007); Poverty rate: 1.6% (2000).
Education: Percent of population age 25 and over with: High school diploma (including GED) or higher: 93.7% (2007); Bachelor's degree or higher: 40.7% (2007); Master's degree or higher: 11.1% (2007).
Housing: Homeownership rate: 90.5% (2007); Median home value: $327,957 (2007); Median rent: $638 per month (2000); Median age of housing: 16 years (2000).
Transportation: Commute to work: 90.9% car, 0.0% public transportation, 0.4% walk, 7.7% work from home (2000); Travel time to work: 23.1% less than 15 minutes, 37.6% 15 to 30 minutes, 30.0% 30 to 45 minutes, 8.0% 45 to 60 minutes, 1.3% 60 minutes or more (2000)

CLINTON (village). Covers a land area of 3.554 square miles and a water area of 0.090 square miles. Located at 40.92° N. Lat.; 81.63° W. Long. Elevation is 948 feet.
Population: 1,175 (1990); 1,337 (2000); 1,432 (2007); 1,452 (2012 projected); Race: 97.1% White, 0.5% Black, 0.6% Asian, 0.6% Hispanic of any race (2007); Density: 402.9 persons per square mile (2007); Average household size: 2.63 (2007); Median age: 39.8 (2007); Males per 100 females: 102.5 (2007); Marriage status: 19.3% never married, 61.9% now married, 5.9% widowed, 12.8% divorced (2000); Foreign born: 1.5% (2000); Ancestry (includes multiple ancestries): 30.2% German, 15.7% Irish, 8.9% English, 7.7% Other groups, 6.3% Italian (2000).
Economy: Employment by occupation: 10.1% management, 15.7% professional, 16.0% services, 20.1% sales, 0.0% farming, 15.0% construction, 22.9% production (2000).
Income: Per capita income: $26,031 (2007); Median household income: $58,667 (2007); Average household income: $68,474 (2007); Percent of households with income of $100,000 or more: 16.2% (2007); Poverty rate: 4.9% (2000).
Education: Percent of population age 25 and over with: High school diploma (including GED) or higher: 87.3% (2007); Bachelor's degree or higher: 17.7% (2007); Master's degree or higher: 5.4% (2007).
School District(s)
Norton City (PK-12)
2005-06 Enrollment: 2,425 . . . . (330) 825-0863
Housing: Homeownership rate: 89.3% (2007); Median home value: $121,635 (2007); Median rent: $408 per month (2000); Median age of housing: 53 years (2000).
Transportation: Commute to work: 96.9% car, 0.0% public transportation, 1.0% walk, 1.8% work from home (2000); Travel time to work: 16.2% less than 15 minutes, 44.0% 15 to 30 minutes, 27.6% 30 to 45 minutes, 7.3% 45 to 60 minutes, 4.9% 60 minutes or more (2000)
Additional Information Contacts
Barberton-South Summit Chamber of Commerce . . . . (330) 745-3141
http://www.southsummitchamber.org

CUYAHOGA FALLS (city). Covers a land area of 25.544 square miles and a water area of 0.094 square miles. Located at 41.14° N. Lat.; 81.49° W. Long. Elevation is 1,050 feet.
History: The city greatly expanded its area by annexing Northampton township in the 1980s. Incorporated 1836.
Population: 48,814 (1990); 49,374 (2000); 50,608 (2007); 51,237 (2012 projected); Race: 94.6% White, 2.4% Black, 1.4% Asian, 0.8% Hispanic of any race (2007); Density: 1,981.2 persons per square mile (2007); Average household size: 2.24 (2007); Median age: 39.1 (2007); Males per 100 females: 91.0 (2007); Marriage status: 24.5% never married, 56.1% now married, 8.3% widowed, 11.2% divorced (2000); Foreign born: 3.1% (2000); Ancestry (includes multiple ancestries): 31.0% German, 17.4% Irish, 13.0% English, 12.4% Italian, 6.7% Other groups (2000).
Economy: Unemployment rate: 5.7% (6/2008); Total civilian labor force: 29,268 (6/2008); Single-family building permits issued: 92 (2007); Multi-family building permits issued: 0 (2007); Employment by occupation: 13.3% management, 21.2% professional, 13.5% services, 30.6% sales, 0.0% farming, 7.5% construction, 13.9% production (2000).

Income: Per capita income: $25,398 (2007); Median household income: $47,003 (2007); Average household income: $56,409 (2007); Percent of households with income of $100,000 or more: 11.3% (2007); Poverty rate: 6.1% (2000).
Taxes: Total city taxes per capita: $576 (2006); City property taxes per capita: $200 (2006).
Education: Percent of population age 25 and over with: High school diploma (including GED) or higher: 90.9% (2007); Bachelor's degree or higher: 25.7% (2007); Master's degree or higher: 7.7% (2007).

School District(s)

Cuyahoga Falls City (PK-12)
2005-06 Enrollment: 5,273 . . . . (330) 926-3800
Woodridge Local (PK-12)
2005-06 Enrollment: 1,819 . . . . (330) 928-9074

Two-year College(s)

National Institute of Technology (Private, For-profit)
Fall 2007 Enrollment: 486 . . . . (330) 923-9959
2007-08 Tuition: In-state $11,481; Out-of-state $11,481
Housing: Homeownership rate: 65.3% (2007); Median home value: $126,973 (2007); Median rent: $527 per month (2000); Median age of housing: 43 years (2000).
Hospitals: Cuyahoga Falls General Hospital (257 beds)
Safety: Violent crime rate: 15.0 per 10,000 population; Property crime rate: 306.5 per 10,000 population (2007).
Transportation: Commute to work: 95.1% car, 1.0% public transportation, 1.4% walk, 2.2% work from home (2000); Travel time to work: 32.7% less than 15 minutes, 41.5% 15 to 30 minutes, 14.8% 30 to 45 minutes, 5.8% 45 to 60 minutes, 5.1% 60 minutes or more (2000)

Additional Information Contacts

City of Cuyahoga Falls. . . . . (330) 971-8000
http://cfo.cityofcf.com/website/web2/view.do
Cuyahoga Falls Chamber of Commerce . . . . (330) 929-6756
http://www.cuyahogafallschamberofcommerce.com

FAIRLAWN (city). Covers a land area of 4.429 square miles and a water area of 0.011 square miles. Located at 41.13° N. Lat.; 81.61° W. Long. Elevation is 1,010 feet.
Population: 5,938 (1990); 7,307 (2000); 7,112 (2007); 6,948 (2012 projected); Race: 85.4% White, 7.8% Black, 4.4% Asian, 1.5% Hispanic of any race (2007); Density: 1,605.6 persons per square mile (2007); Average household size: 2.43 (2007); Median age: 46.1 (2007); Males per 100 females: 84.3 (2007); Marriage status: 20.1% never married, 58.1% now married, 11.9% widowed, 9.9% divorced (2000); Foreign born: 7.1% (2000); Ancestry (includes multiple ancestries): 22.6% German, 12.9% Irish, 11.7% Other groups, 10.2% Italian, 10.0% English (2000).
Economy: Single-family building permits issued: 0 (2007); Multi-family building permits issued: 0 (2007); Employment by occupation: 21.1% management, 34.5% professional, 6.8% services, 28.3% sales, 0.1% farming, 2.5% construction, 6.7% production (2000).
Income: Per capita income: $41,158 (2007); Median household income: $72,786 (2007); Average household income: $99,098 (2007); Percent of households with income of $100,000 or more: 33.1% (2007); Poverty rate: 1.5% (2000).
Education: Percent of population age 25 and over with: High school diploma (including GED) or higher: 92.5% (2007); Bachelor's degree or higher: 46.7% (2007); Master's degree or higher: 18.6% (2007).

School District(s)

Copley-Fairlawn City (PK-12)
2005-06 Enrollment: 3,352 . . . . (330) 664-4800

Vocational/Technical School(s)

Gerbers Akron Beauty School (Private, For-profit)
Fall 2007 Enrollment: 125 . . . . (330) 867-6200
2007-08 Tuition: $6,728
Housing: Homeownership rate: 67.0% (2007); Median home value: $188,766 (2007); Median rent: $666 per month (2000); Median age of housing: 31 years (2000).
Safety: Violent crime rate: 21.0 per 10,000 population; Property crime rate: 525.4 per 10,000 population (2007).
Transportation: Commute to work: 94.7% car, 0.6% public transportation, 0.8% walk, 3.1% work from home (2000); Travel time to work: 31.7% less than 15 minutes, 42.0% 15 to 30 minutes, 16.6% 30 to 45 minutes, 6.1% 45 to 60 minutes, 3.6% 60 minutes or more (2000)

Additional Information Contacts

City of Fairlawn . . . . (330) 668-9500
http://www.cityoffairlawn.com
Fairlawn Area Chamber of Commerce . . . . (330) 849-0402
http://www.fairlawnareachamber.org

GREEN (city). Covers a land area of 32.060 square miles and a water area of 1.471 square miles. Located at 40.95° N. Lat.; 81.48° W. Long. Elevation is 1,138 feet.
Population: 19,179 (1990); 22,817 (2000); 23,521 (2007); 23,939 (2012 projected); Race: 96.8% White, 1.0% Black, 1.0% Asian, 0.6% Hispanic of any race (2007); Density: 733.7 persons per square mile (2007); Average household size: 2.57 (2007); Median age: 41.2 (2007); Males per 100 females: 97.0 (2007); Marriage status: 20.8% never married, 63.0% now married, 6.5% widowed, 9.7% divorced (2000); Foreign born: 1.9% (2000); Ancestry (includes multiple ancestries): 28.3% German, 16.4% Irish, 10.9% English, 9.1% United States or American, 7.8% Italian (2000).
Economy: Employment by occupation: 14.7% management, 20.5% professional, 12.6% services, 27.4% sales, 0.2% farming, 9.2% construction, 15.4% production (2000).
Income: Per capita income: $30,902 (2007); Median household income: $63,492 (2007); Average household income: $79,065 (2007); Percent of households with income of $100,000 or more: 24.6% (2007); Poverty rate: 5.0% (2000).
Education: Percent of population age 25 and over with: High school diploma (including GED) or higher: 89.0% (2007); Bachelor's degree or higher: 26.4% (2007); Master's degree or higher: 7.6% (2007).

School District(s)

Green Local (PK-12)
2005-06 Enrollment: 4,222 . . . . (330) 896-7500
Portage Lakes (09-12)
2005-06 Enrollment: n/a . . . . (330) 896-8200

Two-year College(s)

Portage Lakes Career Center (Public)
Fall 2007 Enrollment: 53 . . . . (330) 896-8200

Vocational/Technical School(s)

W Howard Nicol School of Practical Nursing (Public)
Fall 2007 Enrollment: 35 . . . . (330) 896-8105
2007-08 Tuition: $8,505
Housing: Homeownership rate: 80.3% (2007); Median home value: $170,777 (2007); Median rent: $544 per month (2000); Median age of housing: 26 years (2000).
Transportation: Commute to work: 96.4% car, 0.5% public transportation, 0.5% walk, 2.1% work from home (2000); Travel time to work: 23.0% less than 15 minutes, 49.4% 15 to 30 minutes, 17.9% 30 to 45 minutes, 5.5% 45 to 60 minutes, 4.3% 60 minutes or more (2000)

Additional Information Contacts

City of Green . . . . (330) 896-5510
http://www.cityofgreen.org

HUDSON (city). Aka Hudson Village. Covers a land area of 25.588 square miles and a water area of 0.266 square miles. Located at 41.24° N. Lat.; 81.43° W. Long. Elevation is 1,066 feet.
Population: 17,128 (1990); 22,439 (2000); 23,175 (2007); 23,546 (2012 projected); Race: 93.4% White, 1.6% Black, 3.7% Asian, 1.1% Hispanic of any race (2007); Density: 905.7 persons per square mile (2007); Average household size: 3.03 (2007); Median age: 40.8 (2007); Males per 100 females: 97.4 (2007); Marriage status: 17.7% never married, 73.6% now married, 4.6% widowed, 4.1% divorced (2000); Foreign born: 5.2% (2000); Ancestry (includes multiple ancestries): 30.1% German, 19.8% Irish, 17.4% English, 10.6% Italian, 7.3% Polish (2000).
Economy: Employment by occupation: 29.8% management, 28.9% professional, 7.2% services, 27.1% sales, 0.1% farming, 2.5% construction, 4.4% production (2000).
Income: Per capita income: $48,510 (2007); Median household income: $110,967 (2007); Average household income: $146,434 (2007); Percent of households with income of $100,000 or more: 55.7% (2007); Poverty rate: 1.7% (2000).
Taxes: Total city taxes per capita: $753 (2006); City property taxes per capita: $189 (2006).
Education: Percent of population age 25 and over with: High school diploma (including GED) or higher: 97.3% (2007); Bachelor's degree or higher: 66.5% (2007); Master's degree or higher: 26.0% (2007).

School District(s)

Cleveland Municipal City (PK-12)
2005-06 Enrollment: 58,788 . . . . (216) 574-8193
Hudson City (PK-12)
2005-06 Enrollment: 5,355 . . . . (330) 653-1200

Housing: Homeownership rate: 90.3% (2007); Median home value: $277,042 (2007); Median rent: $1,131 per month (2000); Median age of housing: 20 years (2000).
Transportation: Commute to work: 91.8% car, 0.4% public transportation, 1.1% walk, 5.9% work from home (2000); Travel time to work: 27.8% less than 15 minutes, 31.0% 15 to 30 minutes, 22.8% 30 to 45 minutes, 13.3% 45 to 60 minutes, 5.2% 60 minutes or more (2000)
Additional Information Contacts
City of Hudson . . . . (330) 650-1799
http://www.hudson.oh.us
Hudson Area Chamber of Commerce . . . . (330) 650-0621
http://www.hudsoncoc.org
The British-American Chamber of Commerce . . . . (216) 621-0222
http://www.baccgl.org

LAKEMORE (village). Covers a land area of 1.462 square miles and a water area of 0.191 square miles. Located at 41.02° N. Lat.; 81.43° W. Long. Elevation is 1,086 feet.
History: Incorporated 1920.
Population: 2,684 (1990); 2,561 (2000); 2,608 (2007); 2,673 (2012 projected); Race: 97.4% White, 0.4% Black, 0.0% Asian, 0.6% Hispanic of any race (2007); Density: 1,783.9 persons per square mile (2007); Average household size: 2.58 (2007); Median age: 37.9 (2007); Males per 100 females: 98.9 (2007); Marriage status: 26.0% never married, 52.1% now married, 7.5% widowed, 14.3% divorced (2000); Foreign born: 0.6% (2000); Ancestry (includes multiple ancestries): 27.7% German, 20.7% Irish, 15.9% English, 12.8% Other groups, 6.6% United States or American (2000).
Economy: Single-family building permits issued: 22 (2007); Multi-family building permits issued: 0 (2007); Employment by occupation: 6.5% management, 9.0% professional, 18.8% services, 23.1% sales, 0.4% farming, 16.6% construction, 25.6% production (2000).
Income: Per capita income: $17,681 (2007); Median household income: $37,692 (2007); Average household income: $44,418 (2007); Percent of households with income of $100,000 or more: 5.0% (2007); Poverty rate: 10.1% (2000).
Education: Percent of population age 25 and over with: High school diploma (including GED) or higher: 72.2% (2007); Bachelor's degree or higher: 8.1% (2007); Master's degree or higher: 2.1% (2007).
School District(s)
Springfield Local (PK-12)
2005-06 Enrollment: 2,934 . . . . (330) 798-1111
Housing: Homeownership rate: 78.5% (2007); Median home value: $98,955 (2007); Median rent: $455 per month (2000); Median age of housing: 47 years (2000).
Safety: Violent crime rate: 10.8 per 10,000 population; Property crime rate: 478.8 per 10,000 population (2007).
Transportation: Commute to work: 93.5% car, 2.3% public transportation, 2.3% walk, 1.2% work from home (2000); Travel time to work: 30.2% less than 15 minutes, 43.0% 15 to 30 minutes, 17.3% 30 to 45 minutes, 5.3% 45 to 60 minutes, 4.2% 60 minutes or more (2000)

MACEDONIA (city). Covers a land area of 9.676 square miles and a water area of 0.038 square miles. Located at 41.31° N. Lat.; 81.50° W. Long. Elevation is 988 feet.
Population: 7,589 (1990); 9,224 (2000); 10,580 (2007); 11,390 (2012 projected); Race: 89.7% White, 6.5% Black, 2.4% Asian, 1.1% Hispanic of any race (2007); Density: 1,093.5 persons per square mile (2007); Average household size: 2.74 (2007); Median age: 40.6 (2007); Males per 100 females: 97.8 (2007); Marriage status: 19.7% never married, 69.0% now married, 3.4% widowed, 7.9% divorced (2000); Foreign born: 4.8% (2000); Ancestry (includes multiple ancestries): 21.7% German, 19.8% Italian, 15.0% Irish, 13.7% Polish, 12.1% English (2000).
Economy: Single-family building permits issued: 39 (2007); Multi-family building permits issued: 0 (2007); Employment by occupation: 19.2% management, 19.0% professional, 11.1% services, 31.9% sales, 0.1% farming, 6.8% construction, 11.9% production (2000).
Income: Per capita income: $32,797 (2007); Median household income: $80,613 (2007); Average household income: $89,998 (2007); Percent of households with income of $100,000 or more: 34.8% (2007); Poverty rate: 1.5% (2000).
Taxes: Total city taxes per capita: $889 (2006); City property taxes per capita: $195 (2006).
Education: Percent of population age 25 and over with: High school diploma (including GED) or higher: 93.2% (2007); Bachelor's degree or higher: 31.1% (2007); Master's degree or higher: 7.5% (2007).
School District(s)
Nordonia Hills City (PK-12)
2005-06 Enrollment: 3,967 . . . . (330) 467-0580
Housing: Homeownership rate: 95.6% (2007); Median home value: $196,908 (2007); Median rent: $653 per month (2000); Median age of housing: 26 years (2000).
Transportation: Commute to work: 96.5% car, 0.8% public transportation, 0.3% walk, 2.4% work from home (2000); Travel time to work: 30.0% less than 15 minutes, 38.0% 15 to 30 minutes, 22.6% 30 to 45 minutes, 5.4% 45 to 60 minutes, 4.0% 60 minutes or more (2000)
Additional Information Contacts
City of Macedonia . . . . (330) 468-8300
http://www.macedonia.oh.us
Nordonia Hills Chamber of Commerce . . . . (330) 467-8956
http://www.nhcoc.org

MOGADORE (village). Covers a land area of 2.092 square miles and a water area of 0.017 square miles. Located at 41.05° N. Lat.; 81.39° W. Long. Elevation is 1,148 feet.
Population: 4,066 (1990); 3,893 (2000); 3,923 (2007); 3,953 (2012 projected); Race: 98.3% White, 0.2% Black, 0.1% Asian, 0.2% Hispanic of any race (2007); Density: 1,875.1 persons per square mile (2007); Average household size: 2.56 (2007); Median age: 41.1 (2007); Males per 100 females: 96.5 (2007); Marriage status: 19.5% never married, 67.2% now married, 6.1% widowed, 7.2% divorced (2000); Foreign born: 0.6% (2000); Ancestry (includes multiple ancestries): 31.3% German, 13.4% Irish, 13.0% United States or American, 12.1% English, 6.9% Italian (2000).
Economy: Single-family building permits issued: 4 (2007); Multi-family building permits issued: 0 (2007); Employment by occupation: 10.6% management, 17.2% professional, 16.0% services, 27.6% sales, 0.0% farming, 7.9% construction, 20.7% production (2000).
Income: Per capita income: $24,317 (2007); Median household income: $55,383 (2007); Average household income: $61,389 (2007); Percent of households with income of $100,000 or more: 12.4% (2007); Poverty rate: 3.6% (2000).
Education: Percent of population age 25 and over with: High school diploma (including GED) or higher: 91.0% (2007); Bachelor's degree or higher: 17.8% (2007); Master's degree or higher: 4.8% (2007).
School District(s)
Field Local (PK-12)
2005-06 Enrollment: 2,358 . . . . (330) 673-2659
Mogadore Local (PK-12)
2005-06 Enrollment: 909 . . . . (330) 628-9946
Two-year College(s)
Carnegie Institute of Integrative Medicine and Massotherapy (Private, Not-for-profit)
Fall 2007 Enrollment: 207 . . . . (330) 630-1132
Housing: Homeownership rate: 85.0% (2007); Median home value: $128,872 (2007); Median rent: $459 per month (2000); Median age of housing: 43 years (2000).
Safety: Violent crime rate: 2.5 per 10,000 population; Property crime rate: 212.6 per 10,000 population (2007).
Transportation: Commute to work: 97.4% car, 0.0% public transportation, 0.9% walk, 1.4% work from home (2000); Travel time to work: 30.1% less than 15 minutes, 46.5% 15 to 30 minutes, 14.3% 30 to 45 minutes, 6.5% 45 to 60 minutes, 2.5% 60 minutes or more (2000)

MONTROSE-GHENT (CDP). Covers a land area of 9.422 square miles and a water area of 0.091 square miles. Located at 41.15° N. Lat.; 81.63° W. Long.
Population: 4,855 (1990); 5,261 (2000); 5,627 (2007); 5,852 (2012 projected); Race: 95.9% White, 1.0% Black, 2.1% Asian, 0.6% Hispanic of any race (2007); Density: 597.2 persons per square mile (2007); Average household size: 2.69 (2007); Median age: 47.7 (2007); Males per 100 females: 99.1 (2007); Marriage status: 16.8% never married, 70.1% now married, 5.6% widowed, 7.5% divorced (2000); Foreign born: 6.2% (2000); Ancestry (includes multiple ancestries): 33.5% German, 14.2% English, 13.1% Irish, 7.6% Italian, 5.3% Polish (2000).
Economy: Employment by occupation: 23.4% management, 36.3% professional, 9.3% services, 22.2% sales, 0.0% farming, 3.1% construction, 5.7% production (2000).

Income: Per capita income: $57,651 (2007); Median household income: $107,931 (2007); Average household income: $154,586 (2007); Percent of households with income of $100,000 or more: 53.0% (2007); Poverty rate: 0.7% (2000).
Education: Percent of population age 25 and over with: High school diploma (including GED) or higher: 96.2% (2007); Bachelor's degree or higher: 60.8% (2007); Master's degree or higher: 27.6% (2007).
Housing: Homeownership rate: 96.1% (2007); Median home value: $339,295 (2007); Median rent: $911 per month (2000); Median age of housing: 30 years (2000).
Transportation: Commute to work: 92.2% car, 0.3% public transportation, 0.4% walk, 6.9% work from home (2000); Travel time to work: 27.4% less than 15 minutes, 52.5% 15 to 30 minutes, 14.0% 30 to 45 minutes, 4.2% 45 to 60 minutes, 1.8% 60 minutes or more (2000)

MUNROE FALLS (city). Covers a land area of 2.739 square miles and a water area of 0.091 square miles. Located at 41.13° N. Lat.; 81.43° W. Long. Elevation is 1,030 feet.
Population: 5,359 (1990); 5,314 (2000); 5,295 (2007); 5,280 (2012 projected); Race: 96.7% White, 1.2% Black, 1.0% Asian, 1.0% Hispanic of any race (2007); Density: 1,932.9 persons per square mile (2007); Average household size: 2.66 (2007); Median age: 43.8 (2007); Males per 100 females: 93.4 (2007); Marriage status: 20.2% never married, 68.7% now married, 4.1% widowed, 7.0% divorced (2000); Foreign born: 2.3% (2000); Ancestry (includes multiple ancestries): 26.5% German, 15.0% Irish, 12.9% English, 12.8% Italian, 5.5% United States or American (2000).
Economy: Single-family building permits issued: 1 (2007); Multi-family building permits issued: 0 (2007); Employment by occupation: 20.4% management, 27.1% professional, 9.4% services, 25.4% sales, 0.0% farming, 5.9% construction, 11.8% production (2000).
Income: Per capita income: $31,871 (2007); Median household income: $68,253 (2007); Average household income: $82,757 (2007); Percent of households with income of $100,000 or more: 26.9% (2007); Poverty rate: 1.5% (2000).
Taxes: Total city taxes per capita: $406 (2006); City property taxes per capita: $150 (2006).
Education: Percent of population age 25 and over with: High school diploma (including GED) or higher: 89.5% (2007); Bachelor's degree or higher: 33.9% (2007); Master's degree or higher: 13.6% (2007).

School District(s)

Stow-Munroe Falls City (PK-12)
2005-06 Enrollment: 5,951 . . . . (330) 689-5445

Housing: Homeownership rate: 85.8% (2007); Median home value: $165,488 (2007); Median rent: $467 per month (2000); Median age of housing: 30 years (2000).
Safety: Violent crime rate: 0.0 per 10,000 population; Property crime rate: 64.7 per 10,000 population (2007).
Transportation: Commute to work: 97.3% car, 1.0% public transportation, 0.0% walk, 1.7% work from home (2000); Travel time to work: 28.7% less than 15 minutes, 47.2% 15 to 30 minutes, 13.9% 30 to 45 minutes, 4.8% 45 to 60 minutes, 5.5% 60 minutes or more (2000)

Additional Information Contacts

City of Munroe Falls . . . . (330) 688-7491
http://www.munroefalls.com

NEW FRANKLIN (city). Covers a land area of 2.224 square miles and a water area of 0.071 square miles. Located at 40.95° N. Lat.; 81.53° W. Long. Elevation is 1,093 feet.
History: In 1997 the village of New Franklin was incorporated from a section of Franklin Township to thwart annexation attempts from neighboring cities. New Franklin expanded significantly in November 2003 when the residents of Franklin Township and New Franklin voted to merge the two entities. The merger took effect January 1, 2005. The village officially became a city on March 6, 2006.
Population: 2,317 (1990); 2,191 (2000); 2,249 (2007); 2,274 (2012 projected); Race: 98.2% White, 0.6% Black, 0.3% Asian, 0.1% Hispanic of any race (2007); Density: 1,011.3 persons per square mile (2007); Average household size: 2.47 (2007); Median age: 43.5 (2007); Males per 100 females: 97.1 (2007); Marriage status: 18.5% never married, 68.1% now married, 7.6% widowed, 5.8% divorced (2000); Foreign born: 2.7% (2000); Ancestry (includes multiple ancestries): 35.2% German, 15.8% English, 13.0% Irish, 9.5% United States or American, 6.4% Other groups (2000).
Economy: Employment by occupation: 10.1% management, 17.4% professional, 15.5% services, 24.9% sales, 0.0% farming, 11.4% construction, 20.8% production (2000).
Income: Per capita income: $26,000 (2007); Median household income: $56,648 (2007); Average household income: $64,329 (2007); Percent of households with income of $100,000 or more: 15.6% (2007); Poverty rate: 4.8% (2000).
Education: Percent of population age 25 and over with: High school diploma (including GED) or higher: 89.5% (2007); Bachelor's degree or higher: 16.2% (2007); Master's degree or higher: 5.0% (2007).
Housing: Homeownership rate: 86.1% (2007); Median home value: $154,808 (2007); Median rent: $446 per month (2000); Median age of housing: 39 years (2000).
Safety: Violent crime rate: 4.6 per 10,000 population; Property crime rate: 77.6 per 10,000 population (2007).
Transportation: Commute to work: 96.5% car, 1.0% public transportation, 0.5% walk, 1.9% work from home (2000); Travel time to work: 16.3% less than 15 minutes, 49.3% 15 to 30 minutes, 20.8% 30 to 45 minutes, 8.0% 45 to 60 minutes, 5.7% 60 minutes or more (2000)

NORTHFIELD (village). Covers a land area of 1.073 square miles and a water area of 0 square miles. Located at 41.34° N. Lat.; 81.53° W. Long. Elevation is 1,050 feet.
Population: 3,437 (1990); 3,827 (2000); 3,691 (2007); 3,582 (2012 projected); Race: 90.2% White, 4.3% Black, 3.3% Asian, 0.7% Hispanic of any race (2007); Density: 3,441.3 persons per square mile (2007); Average household size: 2.38 (2007); Median age: 38.2 (2007); Males per 100 females: 98.5 (2007); Marriage status: 27.2% never married, 55.4% now married, 5.0% widowed, 12.3% divorced (2000); Foreign born: 3.1% (2000); Ancestry (includes multiple ancestries): 26.5% German, 17.8% Irish, 17.7% Italian, 15.0% Polish, 8.1% Other groups (2000).
Economy: Single-family building permits issued: 2 (2007); Multi-family building permits issued: 0 (2007); Employment by occupation: 8.8% management, 15.5% professional, 18.0% services, 28.3% sales, 0.4% farming, 8.5% construction, 20.5% production (2000).
Income: Per capita income: $20,476 (2007); Median household income: $42,338 (2007); Average household income: $48,352 (2007); Percent of households with income of $100,000 or more: 5.9% (2007); Poverty rate: 4.3% (2000).
Education: Percent of population age 25 and over with: High school diploma (including GED) or higher: 82.8% (2007); Bachelor's degree or higher: 13.2% (2007); Master's degree or higher: 2.8% (2007).

School District(s)

Nordonia Hills City (PK-12)
2005-06 Enrollment: 3,967 . . . . (330) 467-0580

Housing: Homeownership rate: 66.5% (2007); Median home value: $137,296 (2007); Median rent: $487 per month (2000); Median age of housing: 34 years (2000).
Hospitals: Northcoast Behavioral Healthcare Systems (272 beds)
Transportation: Commute to work: 91.4% car, 1.0% public transportation, 3.2% walk, 2.3% work from home (2000); Travel time to work: 30.2% less than 15 minutes, 41.1% 15 to 30 minutes, 21.1% 30 to 45 minutes, 4.3% 45 to 60 minutes, 3.2% 60 minutes or more (2000)

NORTON (city). Covers a land area of 20.117 square miles and a water area of 0.330 square miles. Located at 41.02° N. Lat.; 81.64° W. Long. Elevation is 1,066 feet.
Population: 11,487 (1990); 11,523 (2000); 11,535 (2007); 11,503 (2012 projected); Race: 96.8% White, 1.6% Black, 0.3% Asian, 0.4% Hispanic of any race (2007); Density: 573.4 persons per square mile (2007); Average household size: 2.59 (2007); Median age: 42.5 (2007); Males per 100 females: 96.6 (2007); Marriage status: 20.7% never married, 64.4% now married, 6.0% widowed, 8.9% divorced (2000); Foreign born: 1.9% (2000); Ancestry (includes multiple ancestries): 28.8% German, 13.7% English, 13.6% Irish, 8.6% United States or American, 7.3% Italian (2000).
Economy: Single-family building permits issued: 37 (2007); Multi-family building permits issued: 0 (2007); Employment by occupation: 10.3% management, 17.4% professional, 14.1% services, 28.2% sales, 0.6% farming, 11.6% construction, 18.0% production (2000).
Income: Per capita income: $24,669 (2007); Median household income: $54,990 (2007); Average household income: $63,573 (2007); Percent of households with income of $100,000 or more: 15.0% (2007); Poverty rate: 5.9% (2000).
Education: Percent of population age 25 and over with: High school diploma (including GED) or higher: 85.6% (2007); Bachelor's degree or higher: 17.4% (2007); Master's degree or higher: 4.8% (2007).

School District(s)

Norton City (PK-12)
2005-06 Enrollment: 2,425 . . . . (330) 825-0863

Vocational/Technical School(s)

Akron Machining Institute Inc (Private, Not-for-profit)
Fall 2007 Enrollment: n/a . . . . (330) 745-1111

Housing: Homeownership rate: 88.8% (2007); Median home value: $135,801 (2007); Median rent: $515 per month (2000); Median age of housing: 41 years (2000).

Transportation: Commute to work: 96.1% car, 0.1% public transportation, 0.7% walk, 2.9% work from home (2000); Travel time to work: 29.1% less than 15 minutes, 47.5% 15 to 30 minutes, 17.1% 30 to 45 minutes, 4.0% 45 to 60 minutes, 2.2% 60 minutes or more (2000)

Additional Information Contacts

Barberton-South Summit Chamber of Commerce . . . . (330) 745-3141
http://www.southsummitchamber.org

City of Norton . . . . (330) 825-7815
http://www.cityofnorton.org

PENINSULA (village). Covers a land area of 4.674 square miles and a water area of 0.010 square miles. Located at 41.24° N. Lat.; 81.55° W. Long. Elevation is 755 feet.

Population: 562 (1990); 602 (2000); 643 (2007); 663 (2012 projected); Race: 97.4% White, 0.6% Black, 0.5% Asian, 0.2% Hispanic of any race (2007); Density: 137.6 persons per square mile (2007); Average household size: 2.43 (2007); Median age: 47.3 (2007); Males per 100 females: 96.0 (2007); Marriage status: 20.4% never married, 59.4% now married, 6.7% widowed, 13.5% divorced (2000); Foreign born: 2.3% (2000); Ancestry (includes multiple ancestries): 37.3% German, 17.6% Irish, 11.0% English, 9.5% Polish, 7.7% Other groups (2000).

Economy: Employment by occupation: 18.3% management, 22.4% professional, 9.8% services, 27.5% sales, 0.0% farming, 11.2% construction, 10.8% production (2000).

Income: Per capita income: $37,825 (2007); Median household income: $77,851 (2007); Average household income: $89,311 (2007); Percent of households with income of $100,000 or more: 30.9% (2007); Poverty rate: 1.2% (2000).

Education: Percent of population age 25 and over with: High school diploma (including GED) or higher: 88.2% (2007); Bachelor's degree or higher: 38.9% (2007); Master's degree or higher: 17.6% (2007).

School District(s)

Woodridge Local (PK-12)
2005-06 Enrollment: 1,819 . . . . (330) 928-9074

Housing: Homeownership rate: 78.9% (2007); Median home value: $245,833 (2007); Median rent: $606 per month (2000); Median age of housing: 58 years (2000).

Transportation: Commute to work: 89.7% car, 0.0% public transportation, 1.1% walk, 9.2% work from home (2000); Travel time to work: 22.7% less than 15 minutes, 43.8% 15 to 30 minutes, 22.7% 30 to 45 minutes, 9.0% 45 to 60 minutes, 2.0% 60 minutes or more (2000)

PIGEON CREEK (CDP). Covers a land area of 0.893 square miles and a water area of 0 square miles. Located at 41.11° N. Lat.; 81.67° W. Long. Elevation is 1,040 feet.

Population: 1,008 (1990); 945 (2000); 1,123 (2007); 1,227 (2012 projected); Race: 95.4% White, 2.4% Black, 1.4% Asian, 0.1% Hispanic of any race (2007); Density: 1,257.9 persons per square mile (2007); Average household size: 2.87 (2007); Median age: 45.7 (2007); Males per 100 females: 95.6 (2007); Marriage status: 21.5% never married, 74.0% now married, 0.9% widowed, 3.6% divorced (2000); Foreign born: 5.6% (2000); Ancestry (includes multiple ancestries): 41.7% German, 10.7% English, 10.0% Other groups, 8.3% Italian, 7.8% Irish (2000).

Economy: Employment by occupation: 23.1% management, 34.0% professional, 8.6% services, 25.2% sales, 0.0% farming, 5.3% construction, 3.7% production (2000).

Income: Per capita income: $45,419 (2007); Median household income: $86,526 (2007); Average household income: $130,448 (2007); Percent of households with income of $100,000 or more: 39.4% (2007); Poverty rate: 0.0% (2000).

Education: Percent of population age 25 and over with: High school diploma (including GED) or higher: 98.7% (2007); Bachelor's degree or higher: 56.1% (2007); Master's degree or higher: 23.8% (2007).

Housing: Homeownership rate: 98.7% (2007); Median home value: $226,692 (2007); Median rent: $n/a per month (2000); Median age of housing: 27 years (2000).

Transportation: Commute to work: 95.8% car, 0.0% public transportation, 0.0% walk, 4.2% work from home (2000); Travel time to work: 26.5% less than 15 minutes, 32.8% 15 to 30 minutes, 22.5% 30 to 45 minutes, 14.7% 45 to 60 minutes, 3.4% 60 minutes or more (2000)

PORTAGE LAKES (CDP). Covers a land area of 6.571 square miles and a water area of 1.586 square miles. Located at 40.99° N. Lat.; 81.53° W. Long. Elevation is 1,053 feet.

Population: 10,288 (1990); 9,870 (2000); 9,668 (2007); 9,548 (2012 projected); Race: 97.3% White, 0.7% Black, 0.4% Asian, 0.7% Hispanic of any race (2007); Density: 1,471.2 persons per square mile (2007); Average household size: 2.31 (2007); Median age: 43.5 (2007); Males per 100 females: 98.9 (2007); Marriage status: 21.4% never married, 56.9% now married, 7.7% widowed, 14.0% divorced (2000); Foreign born: 1.5% (2000); Ancestry (includes multiple ancestries): 27.5% German, 15.5% Irish, 12.4% English, 9.9% United States or American, 5.5% Italian (2000).

Economy: Employment by occupation: 12.7% management, 20.2% professional, 13.4% services, 25.4% sales, 0.0% farming, 11.5% construction, 16.8% production (2000).

Income: Per capita income: $26,435 (2007); Median household income: $50,212 (2007); Average household income: $60,384 (2007); Percent of households with income of $100,000 or more: 12.7% (2007); Poverty rate: 5.0% (2000).

Education: Percent of population age 25 and over with: High school diploma (including GED) or higher: 86.8% (2007); Bachelor's degree or higher: 20.2% (2007); Master's degree or higher: 6.4% (2007).

Housing: Homeownership rate: 77.9% (2007); Median home value: $126,912 (2007); Median rent: $495 per month (2000); Median age of housing: 44 years (2000).

Transportation: Commute to work: 94.9% car, 0.1% public transportation, 1.3% walk, 3.2% work from home (2000); Travel time to work: 27.2% less than 15 minutes, 49.6% 15 to 30 minutes, 15.4% 30 to 45 minutes, 3.6% 45 to 60 minutes, 4.2% 60 minutes or more (2000)

REMINDERVILLE (village). Covers a land area of 1.992 square miles and a water area of 0.023 square miles. Located at 41.33° N. Lat.; 81.40° W. Long. Elevation is 1,010 feet.

Population: 2,163 (1990); 2,347 (2000); 2,260 (2007); 2,236 (2012 projected); Race: 94.7% White, 2.7% Black, 0.7% Asian, 1.2% Hispanic of any race (2007); Density: 1,134.5 persons per square mile (2007); Average household size: 2.51 (2007); Median age: 38.0 (2007); Males per 100 females: 99.8 (2007); Marriage status: 21.2% never married, 62.2% now married, 3.9% widowed, 12.7% divorced (2000); Foreign born: 5.0% (2000); Ancestry (includes multiple ancestries): 20.9% German, 16.0% Irish, 14.8% Italian, 11.7% Polish, 11.6% English (2000).

Economy: Single-family building permits issued: 78 (2007); Multi-family building permits issued: 9 (2007); Employment by occupation: 17.2% management, 21.8% professional, 12.1% services, 28.5% sales, 0.0% farming, 7.2% construction, 13.2% production (2000).

Income: Per capita income: $28,525 (2007); Median household income: $63,345 (2007); Average household income: $71,631 (2007); Percent of households with income of $100,000 or more: 19.2% (2007); Poverty rate: 4.4% (2000).

Education: Percent of population age 25 and over with: High school diploma (including GED) or higher: 95.5% (2007); Bachelor's degree or higher: 30.0% (2007); Master's degree or higher: 7.3% (2007).

Housing: Homeownership rate: 92.4% (2007); Median home value: $162,993 (2007); Median rent: $726 per month (2000); Median age of housing: 23 years (2000).

Safety: Violent crime rate: 3.9 per 10,000 population; Property crime rate: 55.0 per 10,000 population (2007).

Transportation: Commute to work: 95.8% car, 0.0% public transportation, 0.6% walk, 3.3% work from home (2000); Travel time to work: 15.7% less than 15 minutes, 40.9% 15 to 30 minutes, 29.0% 30 to 45 minutes, 10.9% 45 to 60 minutes, 3.5% 60 minutes or more (2000)

Additional Information Contacts

Village of Reminderville . . . . (330) 562-1234
http://www.reminderville.com

RICHFIELD (village). Covers a land area of 8.489 square miles and a water area of 0.003 square miles. Located at 41.23° N. Lat.; 81.63° W. Long. Elevation is 1,152 feet.

History: Richfield was the home of John Brown (1800-1859) during the 1840's, when he was a sheep raiser and wool broker. Brown became a symbol of the Northern sympathies in the Civil War after his raid on the

arsenal at Harpers Ferry in 1859, for which he was convicted of treason and hung.
Population: 3,256 (1990); 3,286 (2000); 3,716 (2007); 3,972 (2012 projected); Race: 96.3% White, 0.7% Black, 2.0% Asian, 0.2% Hispanic of any race (2007); Density: 437.7 persons per square mile (2007); Average household size: 2.62 (2007); Median age: 45.6 (2007); Males per 100 females: 96.9 (2007); Marriage status: 17.3% never married, 64.6% now married, 9.5% widowed, 8.7% divorced (2000); Foreign born: 5.7% (2000); Ancestry (includes multiple ancestries): 32.3% German, 14.3% Polish, 13.7% Irish, 13.1% English, 9.5% Italian (2000).
Economy: Employment by occupation: 18.5% management, 21.4% professional, 12.9% services, 25.2% sales, 0.5% farming, 9.5% construction, 12.0% production (2000).
Income: Per capita income: $37,956 (2007); Median household income: $77,122 (2007); Average household income: $97,108 (2007); Percent of households with income of $100,000 or more: 32.5% (2007); Poverty rate: 3.5% (2000).
Education: Percent of population age 25 and over with: High school diploma (including GED) or higher: 92.5% (2007); Bachelor's degree or higher: 24.8% (2007); Master's degree or higher: 8.5% (2007).

School District(s)

Revere Local (PK-12)
2005-06 Enrollment: 2,868 . . . . (330) 666-4155
Housing: Homeownership rate: 89.4% (2007); Median home value: $210,698 (2007); Median rent: $648 per month (2000); Median age of housing: 39 years (2000).
Transportation: Commute to work: 93.4% car, 0.9% public transportation, 1.4% walk, 4.0% work from home (2000); Travel time to work: 22.0% less than 15 minutes, 33.0% 15 to 30 minutes, 32.2% 30 to 45 minutes, 10.8% 45 to 60 minutes, 2.1% 60 minutes or more (2000)
Additional Information Contacts
Village of Richfield . . . . (330) 659-9201
http://www.richfieldvillageohio.org

SILVER LAKE (village). Covers a land area of 1.418 square miles and a water area of 0.181 square miles. Located at 41.15° N. Lat.; 81.46° W. Long. Elevation is 1,053 feet.
Population: 3,052 (1990); 3,019 (2000); 3,156 (2007); 3,238 (2012 projected); Race: 98.1% White, 0.2% Black, 0.5% Asian, 1.0% Hispanic of any race (2007); Density: 2,225.8 persons per square mile (2007); Average household size: 2.41 (2007); Median age: 49.9 (2007); Males per 100 females: 90.2 (2007); Marriage status: 13.7% never married, 73.4% now married, 7.9% widowed, 5.0% divorced (2000); Foreign born: 2.5% (2000); Ancestry (includes multiple ancestries): 32.3% German, 18.8% English, 15.0% Irish, 12.8% Italian, 6.4% Other groups (2000).
Economy: Employment by occupation: 22.5% management, 32.9% professional, 6.7% services, 30.7% sales, 0.0% farming, 3.7% construction, 3.4% production (2000).
Income: Per capita income: $41,334 (2007); Median household income: $80,178 (2007); Average household income: $99,202 (2007); Percent of households with income of $100,000 or more: 35.5% (2007); Poverty rate: 2.8% (2000).
Education: Percent of population age 25 and over with: High school diploma (including GED) or higher: 95.0% (2007); Bachelor's degree or higher: 49.8% (2007); Master's degree or higher: 19.3% (2007).

School District(s)

Cuyahoga Falls City (PK-12)
2005-06 Enrollment: 5,273 . . . . (330) 926-3800
Housing: Homeownership rate: 95.9% (2007); Median home value: $215,877 (2007); Median rent: $739 per month (2000); Median age of housing: 44 years (2000).
Transportation: Commute to work: 93.4% car, 0.8% public transportation, 1.3% walk, 4.6% work from home (2000); Travel time to work: 36.6% less than 15 minutes, 34.2% 15 to 30 minutes, 15.7% 30 to 45 minutes, 7.3% 45 to 60 minutes, 6.2% 60 minutes or more (2000)

STOW (city). Covers a land area of 17.112 square miles and a water area of 0.230 square miles. Located at 41.17° N. Lat.; 81.43° W. Long. Elevation is 1,093 feet.
History: Settled 1802, incorporated as a city 1960.
Population: 27,702 (1990); 32,139 (2000); 34,687 (2007); 36,200 (2012 projected); Race: 94.1% White, 1.9% Black, 2.3% Asian, 1.2% Hispanic of any race (2007); Density: 2,027.0 persons per square mile (2007); Average household size: 2.57 (2007); Median age: 38.8 (2007); Males per 100 females: 94.0 (2007); Marriage status: 21.8% never married, 63.5% now married, 5.5% widowed, 9.3% divorced (2000); Foreign born: 3.7% (2000); Ancestry (includes multiple ancestries): 29.7% German, 17.7% Irish, 14.3% English, 12.0% Italian, 7.5% Other groups (2000).
Economy: Unemployment rate: 5.4% (6/2008); Total civilian labor force: 20,260 (6/2008); Single-family building permits issued: 40 (2007); Multi-family building permits issued: 3 (2007); Employment by occupation: 15.8% management, 26.5% professional, 11.9% services, 27.2% sales, 0.0% farming, 6.1% construction, 12.5% production (2000).
Income: Per capita income: $29,949 (2007); Median household income: $65,252 (2007); Average household income: $76,185 (2007); Percent of households with income of $100,000 or more: 23.2% (2007); Poverty rate: 4.0% (2000).
Taxes: Total city taxes per capita: $557 (2006); City property taxes per capita: $188 (2006).
Education: Percent of population age 25 and over with: High school diploma (including GED) or higher: 93.2% (2007); Bachelor's degree or higher: 36.8% (2007); Master's degree or higher: 12.6% (2007).

School District(s)

Stow-Munroe Falls City (PK-12)
2005-06 Enrollment: 5,951 . . . . (330) 689-5445
Housing: Homeownership rate: 71.4% (2007); Median home value: $170,220 (2007); Median rent: $603 per month (2000); Median age of housing: 25 years (2000).
Safety: Violent crime rate: 6.9 per 10,000 population; Property crime rate: 238.3 per 10,000 population (2007).
Newspapers: Aurora Advocate (Community news; Circulation 6,900); Cuyahoga Falls News/Press (Local news; Circulation 25,500); Gateway News (Community news; Circulation 11,000); Hudson Hub-Times (Local news; Circulation 9,100); News Leader (Community news; Circulation 10,000); Record Publishing Company (Local news); Record-Courier - Stow Bureau (Regional news); Stow Sentry (Community news; Circulation 14,280); Tallmadge Express (Community news; Circulation 6,700); Twinsburg Bulletin (Community news; Circulation 8,000)
Transportation: Commute to work: 95.6% car, 0.4% public transportation, 0.6% walk, 2.9% work from home (2000); Travel time to work: 27.1% less than 15 minutes, 42.0% 15 to 30 minutes, 19.1% 30 to 45 minutes, 7.5% 45 to 60 minutes, 4.3% 60 minutes or more (2000)
Additional Information Contacts
City of Stow . . . . (330) 689-2700
http://www.stow.oh.us
Stow-Munroe Falls Chamber of Commerce. . . . . (330) 688-1579
http://www.smfcc.com

TALLMADGE (city). Covers a land area of 13.962 square miles and a water area of 0.023 square miles. Located at 41.09° N. Lat.; 81.42° W. Long. Elevation is 1,115 feet.
History: Settled 1807, incorporated 1950. Its historic architecture includes a 19th-century Congregational church near the city's center.
Population: 15,094 (1990); 16,390 (2000); 17,619 (2007); 18,357 (2012 projected); Race: 94.8% White, 2.6% Black, 1.0% Asian, 0.7% Hispanic of any race (2007); Density: 1,261.9 persons per square mile (2007); Average household size: 2.56 (2007); Median age: 43.8 (2007); Males per 100 females: 92.7 (2007); Marriage status: 21.0% never married, 63.7% now married, 7.4% widowed, 8.0% divorced (2000); Foreign born: 3.5% (2000); Ancestry (includes multiple ancestries): 29.0% German, 16.4% Irish, 13.1% English, 12.0% Italian, 8.0% United States or American (2000).
Economy: Single-family building permits issued: 55 (2007); Multi-family building permits issued: 0 (2007); Employment by occupation: 11.6% management, 22.6% professional, 12.2% services, 29.7% sales, 0.1% farming, 10.6% construction, 13.2% production (2000).
Income: Per capita income: $30,582 (2007); Median household income: $55,007 (2007); Average household income: $63,189 (2007); Percent of households with income of $100,000 or more: 16.0% (2007); Poverty rate: 4.7% (2000).
Taxes: Total city taxes per capita: $558 (2006); City property taxes per capita: $108 (2006).
Education: Percent of population age 25 and over with: High school diploma (including GED) or higher: 86.7% (2007); Bachelor's degree or higher: 24.3% (2007); Master's degree or higher: 8.0% (2007).

School District(s)

Tallmadge City (PK-12)
2005-06 Enrollment: 2,707 . . . . (330) 633-3291
Housing: Homeownership rate: 80.1% (2007); Median home value: $168,948 (2007); Median rent: $514 per month (2000); Median age of housing: 33 years (2000).

Safety: Violent crime rate: 13.1 per 10,000 population; Property crime rate: 227.9 per 10,000 population (2007).
Transportation: Commute to work: 96.0% car, 0.6% public transportation, 0.5% walk, 2.4% work from home (2000); Travel time to work: 32.9% less than 15 minutes, 46.4% 15 to 30 minutes, 12.6% 30 to 45 minutes, 3.0% 45 to 60 minutes, 5.0% 60 minutes or more (2000)
Additional Information Contacts
City of Tallmadge . . . . (330) 633-0857
http://www.tallmadge-ohio.org
Tallmadge Chamber of Commerce . . . . (330) 633-5417
http://www.tallmadge-chamber.com

TWINSBURG (city). Covers a land area of 12.443 square miles and a water area of 0.032 square miles. Located at 41.32° N. Lat.; 81.45° W. Long. Elevation is 1,001 feet.
History: Twinsburg was named for Moses and Aaron Wilcox, twins who built adjacent houses here in 1818.
Population: 9,759 (1990); 17,006 (2000); 18,103 (2007); 18,703 (2012 projected); Race: 83.6% White, 10.4% Black, 4.3% Asian, 1.4% Hispanic of any race (2007); Density: 1,454.9 persons per square mile (2007); Average household size: 2.51 (2007); Median age: 38.6 (2007); Males per 100 females: 92.5 (2007); Marriage status: 18.8% never married, 67.2% now married, 6.8% widowed, 7.2% divorced (2000); Foreign born: 4.1% (2000); Ancestry (includes multiple ancestries): 23.1% German, 15.0% Other groups, 15.0% Italian, 14.1% Irish, 11.4% Polish (2000).
Economy: Single-family building permits issued: 19 (2007); Multi-family building permits issued: 0 (2007); Employment by occupation: 21.1% management, 23.0% professional, 10.4% services, 28.9% sales, 0.0% farming, 6.0% construction, 10.6% production (2000).
Income: Per capita income: $33,426 (2007); Median household income: $71,863 (2007); Average household income: $83,298 (2007); Percent of households with income of $100,000 or more: 30.1% (2007); Poverty rate: 2.1% (2000).
Taxes: Total city taxes per capita: $1,216 (2006); City property taxes per capita: $71 (2006).
Education: Percent of population age 25 and over with: High school diploma (including GED) or higher: 92.4% (2007); Bachelor's degree or higher: 38.7% (2007); Master's degree or higher: 12.4% (2007).

School District(s)

Twinsburg City (PK-12)
2005-06 Enrollment: 4,103 . . . . (330) 486-2000
Housing: Homeownership rate: 77.0% (2007); Median home value: $210,403 (2007); Median rent: $687 per month (2000); Median age of housing: 12 years (2000).
Safety: Violent crime rate: 5.1 per 10,000 population; Property crime rate: 80.4 per 10,000 population (2007).
Transportation: Commute to work: 96.0% car, 0.4% public transportation, 0.4% walk, 2.7% work from home (2000); Travel time to work: 22.8% less than 15 minutes, 36.9% 15 to 30 minutes, 27.7% 30 to 45 minutes, 9.2% 45 to 60 minutes, 3.5% 60 minutes or more (2000)
Additional Information Contacts
City of Twinsburg . . . . (330) 425-7161
http://www.mytwinsburg.com
Twinsburg Chamber of Commerce . . . . (330) 963-6249
http://www.twinsburgchamber.com

Trumbull County

Located in northeastern Ohio; bounded on the east by Pennsylvania; drained by the Mahoning and Grand Rivers. Covers a land area of 616.48 square miles, a water area of 18.24 square miles, and is located in the Eastern Time Zone. The county was founded in 1800. County seat is Warren.

Trumbull County is part of the Youngstown-Warren-Boardman, OH-PA Metropolitan Statistical Area. The entire metro area includes: Mahoning County, OH; Trumbull County, OH; Mercer County, PA

Weather Station: Mineral Ridge Water Works Elevation: 889 feet

	Jan	Feb	Mar	Apr	May	Jun	Jul	Aug	Sep	Oct	Nov	Dec
High	35	40	50	62	74	82	86	84	77	65	52	41
Low	18	20	28	37	47	56	61	59	53	42	34	25
Precip	2.2	1.8	2.7	3.1	3.4	4.3	4.2	3.3	4.0	2.6	3.0	2.7
Snow	9.8	6.9	7.1	1.1	tr	0.0	0.0	0.0	0.0	tr	1.8	7.8

High and Low temperatures in degrees Fahrenheit; Precipitation and Snow in inches

Weather Station: Warren 3 S Elevation: 898 feet

	Jan	Feb	Mar	Apr	May	Jun	Jul	Aug	Sep	Oct	Nov	Dec
High	34	38	48	60	71	79	83	81	74	63	50	39
Low	16	18	26	34	44	54	58	57	50	39	31	23
Precip	2.2	1.7	3.0	3.3	3.6	4.0	4.2	3.3	3.9	2.7	3.1	2.8
Snow	11.1	8.2	5.5	0.5	tr	0.0	0.0	0.0	0.0	tr	1.3	7.3

High and Low temperatures in degrees Fahrenheit; Precipitation and Snow in inches

Weather Station: Youngstown Municipal Airport Elevation: 1,177 feet

	Jan	Feb	Mar	Apr	May	Jun	Jul	Aug	Sep	Oct	Nov	Dec
High	32	35	46	58	69	78	82	80	73	61	48	37
Low	17	19	27	37	47	55	60	58	51	41	33	24
Precip	2.3	2.0	3.1	3.3	3.4	3.9	4.1	3.4	3.9	2.5	3.2	3.0
Snow	14.1	10.5	10.7	2.2	tr	tr	tr	0.0	tr	0.6	4.5	12.1

High and Low temperatures in degrees Fahrenheit; Precipitation and Snow in inches

Population: 227,842 (1990); 225,116 (2000); 217,600 (2007); 211,549 (2012 projected); Race: 89.8% White, 8.2% Black, 0.4% Asian, 0.9% Hispanic of any race (2007); Density: 353.0 persons per square mile (2007); Average household size: 2.46 (2007); Median age: 41.3 (2007); Males per 100 females: 94.4 (2007).
Religion: Five largest groups: 23.1% Catholic Church, 5.1% The United Methodist Church, 2.5% Christian Church (Disciples of Christ), 1.9% Evangelical Lutheran Church in America, 1.3% Presbyterian Church (U.S.A.) (2000).
Economy: Unemployment rate: 7.8% (6/2008); Total civilian labor force: 107,447 (6/2008); Leading industries: 27.4% manufacturing; 14.3% health care and social assistance; 14.3% retail trade (2005); Farms: 1,016 totaling 125,962 acres (2002); Companies that employ 500 or more persons: 7 (2006); Companies that employ 100 to 499 persons: 96 (2006); Companies that employ less than 100 persons: 4,498 (2006); Black-owned businesses: 303 (2002); Hispanic-owned businesses: n/a (2002); Asian-owned businesses: 208 (2002); Women-owned businesses: 4,176 (2002); Retail sales per capita: $12,434 (2008). Single-family building permits issued: 152 (2007); Multi-family building permits issued: 168 (2007).
Income: Per capita income: $22,143 (2007); Median household income: $42,887 (2007); Average household income: $54,019 (2007); Percent of households with income of $100,000 or more: 11.1% (2007); Poverty rate: 11.5% (2005); Bankruptcy rate: 4.19% (2007).
Taxes: Total county taxes per capita: $208 (2006); County property taxes per capita: $129 (2006).
Education: Percent of population age 25 and over with: High school diploma (including GED) or higher: 82.5% (2007); Bachelor's degree or higher: 14.6% (2007); Master's degree or higher: 4.5% (2007).
Housing: Homeownership rate: 74.7% (2007); Median home value: $99,760 (2007); Median rent: $381 per month (2000); Median age of housing: 40 years (2000).
Health: Birth rate: 113.7 per 10,000 population (2007); Death rate: 113.8 per 10,000 population (2007); Age-adjusted cancer mortality rate: 207.3 deaths per 100,000 population (2005); Air Quality Index: 65.3% good, 27.5% moderate, 7.3% unhealthy for sensitive individuals, 0.0% unhealthy (percent of days in 2007); Number of physicians: 15.7 per 10,000 population (2005); Hospital beds: 22.7 per 10,000 population (2004); Hospital admissions: 1,010.2 per 10,000 population (2004).
Elections: 2004 Presidential election results: 37.9% Bush, 61.7% Kerry, 0.0% Nader, 0.2% Badnarik
National and State Parks: Grand River State Wildlife Area; Mosquito Creek State Park; Mosquito Creek State Wildlife Area
Additional Information Contacts
Trumbull County Government . . . . (330) 675-2451
http://www.co.trumbull.oh.us
City of Cortland . . . . (330) 637-4003
http://www.cityofcortland.org
City of Girard . . . . (330) 545-3879
http://www.cityofgirard.com
City of Hubbard . . . . (330) 534-3090
http://www.cityofhubbard.com
City of Niles . . . . (330) 544-9000
http://www.thecityofniles.com
City of Warren . . . . (330) 841-2601
http://www.warren.org
Youngstown/Warren Regional Chamber of Commerce . . . . (330) 392-6140
http://www.regionalchamber.com

Trumbull County Communities

BOLINDALE (CDP). Covers a land area of 0.959 square miles and a water area of 0 square miles. Located at 41.20° N. Lat.; 80.77° W. Long. Elevation is 951 feet.
Population: 2,827 (1990); 2,489 (2000); 2,166 (2007); 1,922 (2012 projected); Race: 92.9% White, 5.2% Black, 0.3% Asian, 1.6% Hispanic of any race (2007); Density: 2,258.4 persons per square mile (2007); Average household size: 2.43 (2007); Median age: 41.5 (2007); Males per 100 females: 92.7 (2007); Marriage status: 23.4% never married, 52.4% now married, 9.5% widowed, 14.7% divorced (2000); Foreign born: 2.7% (2000); Ancestry (includes multiple ancestries): 20.0% German, 18.4% Irish, 12.7% Italian, 7.9% Other groups, 7.8% United States or American (2000).
Economy: Employment by occupation: 7.5% management, 10.3% professional, 17.7% services, 17.5% sales, 1.0% farming, 10.3% construction, 35.7% production (2000).
Income: Per capita income: $19,625 (2007); Median household income: $40,274 (2007); Average household income: $47,761 (2007); Percent of households with income of $100,000 or more: 6.9% (2007); Poverty rate: 10.0% (2000).
Education: Percent of population age 25 and over with: High school diploma (including GED) or higher: 78.7% (2007); Bachelor's degree or higher: 8.5% (2007); Master's degree or higher: 2.0% (2007).
Housing: Homeownership rate: 79.3% (2007); Median home value: $84,851 (2007); Median rent: $347 per month (2000); Median age of housing: 40 years (2000).
Transportation: Commute to work: 97.1% car, 1.1% public transportation, 1.8% walk, 0.0% work from home (2000); Travel time to work: 37.1% less than 15 minutes, 47.1% 15 to 30 minutes, 6.1% 30 to 45 minutes, 5.1% 45 to 60 minutes, 4.7% 60 minutes or more (2000)

BRISTOLVILLE (unincorporated postal area, zip code 44402). Covers a land area of 33.696 square miles and a water area of 0 square miles. Located at 41.38° N. Lat.; 80.87° W. Long. Elevation is 899 feet.
Population: 3,325 (2000); Race: 98.4% White, 0.9% Black, 0.2% Asian, 0.0% Hispanic of any race (2000); Density: 98.7 persons per square mile (2000); Age: 25.0% under 18, 11.5% over 64 (2000); Marriage status: 18.8% never married, 66.7% now married, 5.1% widowed, 9.4% divorced (2000); Foreign born: 0.5% (2000); Ancestry (includes multiple ancestries): 23.1% German, 14.3% English, 13.3% Irish, 10.9% United States or American, 9.2% Italian (2000).
Economy: Employment by occupation: 5.1% management, 9.3% professional, 14.5% services, 21.5% sales, 1.1% farming, 10.6% construction, 37.9% production (2000).
Income: Per capita income: $18,059 (2000); Median household income: $48,316 (2000); Poverty rate: 4.6% (2000).
Education: Percent of population age 25 and over with: High school diploma (including GED) or higher: 81.1% (2000); Bachelor's degree or higher: 8.0% (2000).

School District(s)

Bristol Local (PK-12)
2005-06 Enrollment: 777 . . . . (330) 889-3882
Housing: Homeownership rate: 84.3% (2000); Median home value: $99,100 (2000); Median rent: $389 per month (2000); Median age of housing: 35 years (2000).
Transportation: Commute to work: 93.6% car, 0.2% public transportation, 2.1% walk, 2.6% work from home (2000); Travel time to work: 15.9% less than 15 minutes, 55.8% 15 to 30 minutes, 18.1% 30 to 45 minutes, 5.6% 45 to 60 minutes, 4.6% 60 minutes or more (2000)

BROOKFIELD (unincorporated postal area, zip code 44403). Covers a land area of 12.936 square miles and a water area of 0 square miles. Located at 41.23° N. Lat.; 80.57° W. Long. Elevation is 1,160 feet.
Population: 4,161 (2000); Race: 97.2% White, 1.8% Black, 0.9% Asian, 0.2% Hispanic of any race (2000); Density: 321.7 persons per square mile (2000); Age: 20.8% under 18, 22.8% over 64 (2000); Marriage status: 17.5% never married, 64.2% now married, 9.9% widowed, 8.5% divorced (2000); Foreign born: 2.2% (2000); Ancestry (includes multiple ancestries): 20.5% German, 14.8% Italian, 13.2% Irish, 10.8% English, 10.0% Polish (2000).
Economy: Employment by occupation: 11.0% management, 19.8% professional, 12.2% services, 24.6% sales, 0.3% farming, 14.4% construction, 17.8% production (2000).
Income: Per capita income: $20,059 (2000); Median household income: $38,131 (2000); Poverty rate: 10.0% (2000).
Education: Percent of population age 25 and over with: High school diploma (including GED) or higher: 83.8% (2000); Bachelor's degree or higher: 15.7% (2000).

School District(s)

Brookfield Local (PK-12)
2005-06 Enrollment: 1,402 . . . . (330) 448-4930
Housing: Homeownership rate: 86.1% (2000); Median home value: $111,400 (2000); Median rent: $389 per month (2000); Median age of housing: 28 years (2000).
Transportation: Commute to work: 96.8% car, 0.5% public transportation, 0.6% walk, 1.7% work from home (2000); Travel time to work: 29.3% less than 15 minutes, 53.0% 15 to 30 minutes, 9.2% 30 to 45 minutes, 4.1% 45 to 60 minutes, 4.3% 60 minutes or more (2000)

BROOKFIELD CENTER (CDP). Covers a land area of 2.858 square miles and a water area of 0 square miles. Located at 41.24° N. Lat.; 80.56° W. Long. Elevation is 1,070 feet.
Population: 1,396 (1990); 1,288 (2000); 1,302 (2007); 1,292 (2012 projected); Race: 98.6% White, 0.8% Black, 0.0% Asian, 1.3% Hispanic of any race (2007); Density: 455.6 persons per square mile (2007); Average household size: 2.30 (2007); Median age: 50.6 (2007); Males per 100 females: 97.0 (2007); Marriage status: 22.9% never married, 58.4% now married, 13.5% widowed, 5.2% divorced (2000); Foreign born: 3.0% (2000); Ancestry (includes multiple ancestries): 19.0% Italian, 16.3% Polish, 15.5% German, 13.1% Irish, 8.6% Slovak (2000).
Economy: Employment by occupation: 19.0% management, 21.6% professional, 11.0% services, 22.7% sales, 1.0% farming, 8.2% construction, 16.5% production (2000).
Income: Per capita income: $25,325 (2007); Median household income: $52,203 (2007); Average household income: $57,655 (2007); Percent of households with income of $100,000 or more: 15.5% (2007); Poverty rate: 6.2% (2000).
Education: Percent of population age 25 and over with: High school diploma (including GED) or higher: 80.4% (2007); Bachelor's degree or higher: 20.5% (2007); Master's degree or higher: 5.3% (2007).
Housing: Homeownership rate: 85.3% (2007); Median home value: $141,591 (2007); Median rent: $451 per month (2000); Median age of housing: 39 years (2000).
Transportation: Commute to work: 95.1% car, 1.6% public transportation, 2.0% walk, 0.0% work from home (2000); Travel time to work: 36.9% less than 15 minutes, 43.9% 15 to 30 minutes, 8.0% 30 to 45 minutes, 4.7% 45 to 60 minutes, 6.5% 60 minutes or more (2000)

BURGHILL (unincorporated postal area, zip code 44404). Covers a land area of 18.814 square miles and a water area of 0 square miles. Located at 41.34° N. Lat.; 80.53° W. Long. Elevation is 1,033 feet.
Population: 1,703 (2000); Race: 98.9% White, 0.0% Black, 0.1% Asian, 0.6% Hispanic of any race (2000); Density: 90.5 persons per square mile (2000); Age: 26.9% under 18, 11.2% over 64 (2000); Marriage status: 16.7% never married, 67.8% now married, 7.3% widowed, 8.2% divorced (2000); Foreign born: 0.1% (2000); Ancestry (includes multiple ancestries): 26.9% German, 15.6% Irish, 10.0% Italian, 9.8% United States or American, 8.6% English (2000).
Economy: Employment by occupation: 8.0% management, 11.1% professional, 13.4% services, 20.6% sales, 0.0% farming, 7.5% construction, 39.5% production (2000).
Income: Per capita income: $18,829 (2000); Median household income: $50,278 (2000); Poverty rate: 7.0% (2000).
Education: Percent of population age 25 and over with: High school diploma (including GED) or higher: 85.2% (2000); Bachelor's degree or higher: 8.3% (2000).
Housing: Homeownership rate: 87.1% (2000); Median home value: $87,700 (2000); Median rent: $336 per month (2000); Median age of housing: 43 years (2000).
Transportation: Commute to work: 90.8% car, 0.0% public transportation, 4.2% walk, 3.4% work from home (2000); Travel time to work: 21.9% less than 15 minutes, 40.3% 15 to 30 minutes, 21.2% 30 to 45 minutes, 10.4% 45 to 60 minutes, 6.2% 60 minutes or more (2000)

CHAMPION HEIGHTS (CDP). Aka Champion. Covers a land area of 3.401 square miles and a water area of 0 square miles. Located at 41.29° N. Lat.; 80.85° W. Long.

Population: 4,425 (1990); 4,727 (2000); 4,514 (2007); 4,335 (2012 projected); Race: 98.5% White, 0.5% Black, 0.0% Asian, 0.6% Hispanic of any race (2007); Density: 1,327.3 persons per square mile (2007); Average household size: 2.47 (2007); Median age: 42.3 (2007); Males per 100 females: 90.1 (2007); Marriage status: 18.4% never married, 62.6% now married, 10.8% widowed, 8.3% divorced (2000); Foreign born: 0.7% (2000); Ancestry (includes multiple ancestries): 27.5% German, 16.1% Irish, 15.8% English, 11.2% Italian, 8.9% United States or American (2000).
Economy: Employment by occupation: 10.3% management, 17.2% professional, 12.8% services, 28.0% sales, 0.3% farming, 8.3% construction, 23.2% production (2000).
Income: Per capita income: $22,786 (2007); Median household income: $45,573 (2007); Average household income: $55,665 (2007); Percent of households with income of $100,000 or more: 11.8% (2007); Poverty rate: 5.3% (2000).
Education: Percent of population age 25 and over with: High school diploma (including GED) or higher: 87.3% (2007); Bachelor's degree or higher: 13.4% (2007); Master's degree or higher: 3.4% (2007).
Housing: Homeownership rate: 83.5% (2007); Median home value: $108,526 (2007); Median rent: $415 per month (2000); Median age of housing: 42 years (2000).
Transportation: Commute to work: 96.2% car, 0.0% public transportation, 1.2% walk, 2.2% work from home (2000); Travel time to work: 35.2% less than 15 minutes, 42.6% 15 to 30 minutes, 13.1% 30 to 45 minutes, 5.0% 45 to 60 minutes, 4.1% 60 minutes or more (2000)

CHURCHILL (CDP). Covers a land area of 2.494 square miles and a water area of 0 square miles. Located at 41.17° N. Lat.; 80.67° W. Long. Elevation is 1,066 feet.
Population: 2,683 (1990); 2,601 (2000); 2,569 (2007); 2,630 (2012 projected); Race: 87.3% White, 10.2% Black, 0.3% Asian, 1.4% Hispanic of any race (2007); Density: 1,030.3 persons per square mile (2007); Average household size: 2.39 (2007); Median age: 44.4 (2007); Males per 100 females: 97.5 (2007); Marriage status: 22.8% never married, 51.8% now married, 9.8% widowed, 15.5% divorced (2000); Foreign born: 3.3% (2000); Ancestry (includes multiple ancestries): 21.5% German, 19.8% Irish, 19.0% Italian, 15.5% Other groups, 10.8% English (2000).
Economy: Employment by occupation: 11.8% management, 13.5% professional, 19.2% services, 25.1% sales, 0.0% farming, 8.7% construction, 21.7% production (2000).
Income: Per capita income: $23,590 (2007); Median household income: $40,913 (2007); Average household income: $56,479 (2007); Percent of households with income of $100,000 or more: 12.7% (2007); Poverty rate: 11.2% (2000).
Education: Percent of population age 25 and over with: High school diploma (including GED) or higher: 86.0% (2007); Bachelor's degree or higher: 15.6% (2007); Master's degree or higher: 3.9% (2007).
Housing: Homeownership rate: 78.7% (2007); Median home value: $93,409 (2007); Median rent: $347 per month (2000); Median age of housing: 35 years (2000).
Transportation: Commute to work: 95.4% car, 0.0% public transportation, 3.8% walk, 0.0% work from home (2000); Travel time to work: 37.2% less than 15 minutes, 55.9% 15 to 30 minutes, 4.4% 30 to 45 minutes, 2.0% 45 to 60 minutes, 0.6% 60 minutes or more (2000)

CORTLAND (city). Covers a land area of 4.479 square miles and a water area of 0 square miles. Located at 41.33° N. Lat.; 80.72° W. Long. Elevation is 1,024 feet.
Population: 5,841 (1990); 6,830 (2000); 6,628 (2007); 6,448 (2012 projected); Race: 97.4% White, 1.1% Black, 0.2% Asian, 0.9% Hispanic of any race (2007); Density: 1,479.7 persons per square mile (2007); Average household size: 2.42 (2007); Median age: 42.3 (2007); Males per 100 females: 91.0 (2007); Marriage status: 21.3% never married, 61.6% now married, 7.7% widowed, 9.3% divorced (2000); Foreign born: 1.2% (2000); Ancestry (includes multiple ancestries): 20.3% German, 18.3% English, 17.8% Irish, 14.4% Italian, 7.4% Slovak (2000).
Economy: Employment by occupation: 12.9% management, 22.3% professional, 14.1% services, 25.3% sales, 0.0% farming, 5.9% construction, 19.4% production (2000).
Income: Per capita income: $26,986 (2007); Median household income: $55,356 (2007); Average household income: $64,947 (2007); Percent of households with income of $100,000 or more: 19.4% (2007); Poverty rate: 5.3% (2000).
Taxes: Total city taxes per capita: $384 (2006); City property taxes per capita: $363 (2006).
Education: Percent of population age 25 and over with: High school diploma (including GED) or higher: 91.7% (2007); Bachelor's degree or higher: 29.7% (2007); Master's degree or higher: 9.7% (2007).

School District(s)

Lakeview Local (PK-12)
2005-06 Enrollment: 2,215 . . . . (330) 637-8741
Maplewood Local (PK-12)
2005-06 Enrollment: 1,101 . . . . (330) 637-7506
Mathews Local (PK-12)
2005-06 Enrollment: 933 . . . . (330) 394-1800

Housing: Homeownership rate: 73.9% (2007); Median home value: $148,677 (2007); Median rent: $427 per month (2000); Median age of housing: 23 years (2000).
Safety: Violent crime rate: 15.4 per 10,000 population; Property crime rate: 173.6 per 10,000 population (2007).
Transportation: Commute to work: 94.8% car, 0.1% public transportation, 1.0% walk, 3.3% work from home (2000); Travel time to work: 23.2% less than 15 minutes, 55.5% 15 to 30 minutes, 13.6% 30 to 45 minutes, 3.8% 45 to 60 minutes, 3.8% 60 minutes or more (2000)

Additional Information Contacts

City of Cortland . . . . (330) 637-4003
http://www.cityofcortland.org

FARMDALE (unincorporated postal area, zip code 44417). Covers a land area of 31.877 square miles and a water area of 0 square miles. Located at 41.42° N. Lat.; 80.65° W. Long. Elevation is 936 feet.
Population: 1,768 (2000); Race: 99.1% White, 0.9% Black, 0.0% Asian, 0.3% Hispanic of any race (2000); Density: 55.5 persons per square mile (2000); Age: 26.4% under 18, 11.6% over 64 (2000); Marriage status: 22.0% never married, 68.1% now married, 3.4% widowed, 6.5% divorced (2000); Foreign born: 0.7% (2000); Ancestry (includes multiple ancestries): 19.1% United States or American, 17.7% German, 16.1% English, 8.1% Italian, 7.5% Irish (2000).
Economy: Employment by occupation: 5.8% management, 11.9% professional, 17.4% services, 19.8% sales, 0.0% farming, 14.7% construction, 30.4% production (2000).
Income: Per capita income: $20,808 (2000); Median household income: $50,335 (2000); Poverty rate: 6.4% (2000).
Education: Percent of population age 25 and over with: High school diploma (including GED) or higher: 82.2% (2000); Bachelor's degree or higher: 7.4% (2000).

School District(s)

Joseph Badger Local (PK-12)
2005-06 Enrollment: 1,028 . . . . (330) 876-1051

Housing: Homeownership rate: 88.5% (2000); Median home value: $104,000 (2000); Median rent: $445 per month (2000); Median age of housing: 34 years (2000).
Transportation: Commute to work: 98.7% car, 0.0% public transportation, 0.0% walk, 0.7% work from home (2000); Travel time to work: 15.3% less than 15 minutes, 34.5% 15 to 30 minutes, 32.7% 30 to 45 minutes, 10.7% 45 to 60 minutes, 6.8% 60 minutes or more (2000)

FOWLER (unincorporated postal area, zip code 44418). Covers a land area of 17.112 square miles and a water area of 0 square miles. Located at 41.30° N. Lat.; 80.60° W. Long. Elevation is 1,140 feet.
Population: 1,237 (2000); Race: 97.0% White, 1.4% Black, 1.1% Asian, 0.9% Hispanic of any race (2000); Density: 72.3 persons per square mile (2000); Age: 23.4% under 18, 13.1% over 64 (2000); Marriage status: 19.6% never married, 63.8% now married, 6.1% widowed, 10.4% divorced (2000); Foreign born: 1.7% (2000); Ancestry (includes multiple ancestries): 21.6% German, 11.8% English, 10.4% Irish, 8.5% Italian, 7.9% Polish (2000).
Economy: Employment by occupation: 12.3% management, 19.0% professional, 12.3% services, 28.5% sales, 0.0% farming, 7.8% construction, 20.1% production (2000).
Income: Per capita income: $19,340 (2000); Median household income: $46,818 (2000); Poverty rate: 4.1% (2000).
Education: Percent of population age 25 and over with: High school diploma (including GED) or higher: 89.6% (2000); Bachelor's degree or higher: 17.5% (2000).

School District(s)

Mathews Local (PK-12)
2005-06 Enrollment: 933 . . . . (330) 394-1800

Housing: Homeownership rate: 85.2% (2000); Median home value: $105,600 (2000); Median rent: $396 per month (2000); Median age of housing: 34 years (2000).
Transportation: Commute to work: 93.9% car, 0.0% public transportation, 1.0% walk, 5.2% work from home (2000); Travel time to work: 17.3% less than 15 minutes, 54.6% 15 to 30 minutes, 18.7% 30 to 45 minutes, 4.1% 45 to 60 minutes, 5.3% 60 minutes or more (2000)

GIRARD (city). Covers a land area of 6.113 square miles and a water area of 0.485 square miles. Located at 41.15° N. Lat.; 80.69° W. Long. Elevation is 906 feet.
History: Girard was settled about 1800, but growth was slow until the Ohio & Erie Canal was completed. The town was probably named for Stephen Girard, philanthropist and founder of Girard College in Philadelphia, Pennsylvania.
Population: 11,550 (1990); 10,902 (2000); 10,325 (2007); 9,902 (2012 projected); Race: 95.2% White, 2.5% Black, 0.4% Asian, 0.8% Hispanic of any race (2007); Density: 1,689.1 persons per square mile (2007); Average household size: 2.29 (2007); Median age: 41.6 (2007); Males per 100 females: 89.8 (2007); Marriage status: 23.6% never married, 54.2% now married, 9.2% widowed, 13.0% divorced (2000); Foreign born: 2.0% (2000); Ancestry (includes multiple ancestries): 29.5% Italian, 21.8% German, 20.4% Irish, 8.6% English, 6.1% Other groups (2000).
Economy: Single-family building permits issued: 4 (2007); Multi-family building permits issued: 0 (2007); Employment by occupation: 7.1% management, 17.6% professional, 16.1% services, 24.8% sales, 0.0% farming, 9.6% construction, 24.8% production (2000).
Income: Per capita income: $20,282 (2007); Median household income: $36,537 (2007); Average household income: $46,423 (2007); Percent of households with income of $100,000 or more: 8.2% (2007); Poverty rate: 12.5% (2000).
Education: Percent of population age 25 and over with: High school diploma (including GED) or higher: 79.9% (2007); Bachelor's degree or higher: 16.4% (2007); Master's degree or higher: 5.1% (2007).

School District(s)

Girard City (PK-12)
2005-06 Enrollment: 1,760 . . . . (330) 545-2596

Housing: Homeownership rate: 67.7% (2007); Median home value: $87,403 (2007); Median rent: $373 per month (2000); Median age of housing: 46 years (2000).
Safety: Violent crime rate: 54.3 per 10,000 population; Property crime rate: 333.8 per 10,000 population (2007).
Transportation: Commute to work: 95.2% car, 0.2% public transportation, 1.4% walk, 1.9% work from home (2000); Travel time to work: 38.4% less than 15 minutes, 46.8% 15 to 30 minutes, 10.7% 30 to 45 minutes, 1.5% 45 to 60 minutes, 2.6% 60 minutes or more (2000)

Additional Information Contacts

City of Girard . . . . (330) 545-3879
http://www.cityofgirard.com

HILLTOP (CDP). Covers a land area of 0.568 square miles and a water area of 0 square miles. Located at 41.16° N. Lat.; 80.73° W. Long. Elevation is 978 feet.
Population: 576 (1990); 534 (2000); 540 (2007); 527 (2012 projected); Race: 96.9% White, 0.4% Black, 0.0% Asian, 1.5% Hispanic of any race (2007); Density: 951.0 persons per square mile (2007); Average household size: 2.60 (2007); Median age: 39.2 (2007); Males per 100 females: 97.8 (2007); Marriage status: 20.8% never married, 65.9% now married, 9.8% widowed, 3.5% divorced (2000); Foreign born: 0.0% (2000); Ancestry (includes multiple ancestries): 22.0% German, 18.8% Polish, 11.8% Slovak, 11.1% United States or American, 8.5% English (2000).
Economy: Employment by occupation: 3.6% management, 6.8% professional, 22.3% services, 21.4% sales, 0.0% farming, 17.3% construction, 28.6% production (2000).
Income: Per capita income: $19,588 (2007); Median household income: $49,667 (2007); Average household income: $50,853 (2007); Percent of households with income of $100,000 or more: 6.3% (2007); Poverty rate: 4.9% (2000).
Education: Percent of population age 25 and over with: High school diploma (including GED) or higher: 70.7% (2007); Bachelor's degree or higher: 2.1% (2007); Master's degree or higher: 0.0% (2007).
Housing: Homeownership rate: 88.0% (2007); Median home value: $67,885 (2007); Median rent: $325 per month (2000); Median age of housing: 55 years (2000).
Transportation: Commute to work: 100.0% car, 0.0% public transportation, 0.0% walk, 0.0% work from home (2000); Travel time to work: 35.9% less than 15 minutes, 22.7% 15 to 30 minutes, 10.9% 30 to 45 minutes, 13.6% 45 to 60 minutes, 16.8% 60 minutes or more (2000)

HOWLAND CENTER (CDP). Covers a land area of 4.036 square miles and a water area of 0 square miles. Located at 41.24° N. Lat.; 80.74° W. Long. Elevation is 892 feet.
Population: 6,805 (1990); 6,481 (2000); 6,452 (2007); 6,513 (2012 projected); Race: 95.4% White, 1.7% Black, 1.4% Asian, 0.9% Hispanic of any race (2007); Density: 1,598.7 persons per square mile (2007); Average household size: 2.55 (2007); Median age: 44.4 (2007); Males per 100 females: 96.3 (2007); Marriage status: 20.0% never married, 64.6% now married, 6.7% widowed, 8.6% divorced (2000); Foreign born: 2.7% (2000); Ancestry (includes multiple ancestries): 22.3% German, 18.4% Italian, 14.7% Irish, 14.4% English, 7.2% Slovak (2000).
Economy: Employment by occupation: 13.5% management, 24.0% professional, 12.6% services, 23.9% sales, 0.0% farming, 8.2% construction, 17.8% production (2000).
Income: Per capita income: $25,655 (2007); Median household income: $56,575 (2007); Average household income: $64,826 (2007); Percent of households with income of $100,000 or more: 13.1% (2007); Poverty rate: 2.0% (2000).
Education: Percent of population age 25 and over with: High school diploma (including GED) or higher: 92.0% (2007); Bachelor's degree or higher: 26.2% (2007); Master's degree or higher: 10.0% (2007).
Housing: Homeownership rate: 88.0% (2007); Median home value: $125,105 (2007); Median rent: $509 per month (2000); Median age of housing: 30 years (2000).
Transportation: Commute to work: 96.7% car, 0.4% public transportation, 1.1% walk, 1.7% work from home (2000); Travel time to work: 40.3% less than 15 minutes, 44.4% 15 to 30 minutes, 8.7% 30 to 45 minutes, 2.3% 45 to 60 minutes, 4.3% 60 minutes or more (2000)

HUBBARD (city). Covers a land area of 3.448 square miles and a water area of 0.007 square miles. Located at 41.15° N. Lat.; 80.56° W. Long. Elevation is 984 feet.
History: Hubbard was named for Nehemiah Hubbard, who purchased the land on which the town was founded in 1801. Until 1880, coal mining was the principal industry.
Population: 8,444 (1990); 8,284 (2000); 7,935 (2007); 7,644 (2012 projected); Race: 97.8% White, 1.0% Black, 0.2% Asian, 0.4% Hispanic of any race (2007); Density: 2,301.1 persons per square mile (2007); Average household size: 2.32 (2007); Median age: 42.6 (2007); Males per 100 females: 90.6 (2007); Marriage status: 22.9% never married, 59.1% now married, 9.8% widowed, 8.2% divorced (2000); Foreign born: 2.4% (2000); Ancestry (includes multiple ancestries): 24.4% German, 23.4% Italian, 18.3% Irish, 12.4% Slovak, 8.4% English (2000).
Economy: Employment by occupation: 8.3% management, 21.3% professional, 12.6% services, 32.1% sales, 0.2% farming, 8.8% construction, 16.7% production (2000).
Income: Per capita income: $20,972 (2007); Median household income: $37,621 (2007); Average household income: $48,626 (2007); Percent of households with income of $100,000 or more: 8.2% (2007); Poverty rate: 8.6% (2000).
Taxes: Total city taxes per capita: $243 (2006); City property taxes per capita: $46 (2006).
Education: Percent of population age 25 and over with: High school diploma (including GED) or higher: 85.9% (2007); Bachelor's degree or higher: 18.1% (2007); Master's degree or higher: 4.7% (2007).

School District(s)

Hubbard Exempted Village (PK-12)
2005-06 Enrollment: 2,306 . . . . (330) 534-1921

Housing: Homeownership rate: 72.2% (2007); Median home value: $97,249 (2007); Median rent: $376 per month (2000); Median age of housing: 42 years (2000).
Transportation: Commute to work: 96.4% car, 0.1% public transportation, 1.0% walk, 2.1% work from home (2000); Travel time to work: 31.0% less than 15 minutes, 46.4% 15 to 30 minutes, 15.3% 30 to 45 minutes, 2.8% 45 to 60 minutes, 4.5% 60 minutes or more (2000)

Additional Information Contacts

City of Hubbard . . . . (330) 534-3090
http://www.cityofhubbard.com

KINSMAN (unincorporated postal area, zip code 44428). Covers a land area of 52.479 square miles and a water area of 0.035 square miles. Located at 41.44° N. Lat.; 80.58° W. Long. Elevation is 932 feet.
History: Kinsman was settled in 1799 by John Kinsman. Clarence Darrow (1857-1938), noted criminal lawyer, was born in Kinsman, and described the village in his novel "Farmington" (1904).
Population: 3,487 (2000); Race: 100.0% White, 0.0% Black, 0.0% Asian, 0.0% Hispanic of any race (2000); Density: 66.4 persons per square mile (2000); Age: 23.1% under 18, 15.3% over 64 (2000); Marriage status: 21.6% never married, 61.7% now married, 7.2% widowed, 9.5% divorced (2000); Foreign born: 0.6% (2000); Ancestry (includes multiple ancestries): 23.5% German, 19.8% United States or American, 14.4% English, 14.0% Irish, 5.1% Italian (2000).
Economy: Employment by occupation: 10.4% management, 13.6% professional, 11.4% services, 19.1% sales, 0.6% farming, 7.0% construction, 37.9% production (2000).
Income: Per capita income: $15,885 (2000); Median household income: $37,089 (2000); Poverty rate: 7.9% (2000).
Education: Percent of population age 25 and over with: High school diploma (including GED) or higher: 82.5% (2000); Bachelor's degree or higher: 13.3% (2000).

School District(s)

Joseph Badger Local (PK-12)
2005-06 Enrollment: 1,028 . . . . (330) 876-1051
Housing: Homeownership rate: 84.4% (2000); Median home value: $90,300 (2000); Median rent: $320 per month (2000); Median age of housing: 40 years (2000).
Transportation: Commute to work: 90.1% car, 0.3% public transportation, 2.1% walk, 6.1% work from home (2000); Travel time to work: 26.0% less than 15 minutes, 24.5% 15 to 30 minutes, 32.7% 30 to 45 minutes, 10.2% 45 to 60 minutes, 6.5% 60 minutes or more (2000)

LEAVITTSBURG (CDP). Covers a land area of 1.668 square miles and a water area of 0.060 square miles. Located at 41.24° N. Lat.; 80.87° W. Long. Elevation is 909 feet.
Population: 2,112 (1990); 2,200 (2000); 2,133 (2007); 2,032 (2012 projected); Race: 98.9% White, 0.3% Black, 0.0% Asian, 1.2% Hispanic of any race (2007); Density: 1,279.0 persons per square mile (2007); Average household size: 2.62 (2007); Median age: 40.0 (2007); Males per 100 females: 95.5 (2007); Marriage status: 25.6% never married, 57.0% now married, 4.8% widowed, 12.7% divorced (2000); Foreign born: 1.1% (2000); Ancestry (includes multiple ancestries): 23.6% German, 18.8% United States or American, 18.0% Irish, 8.4% English, 7.6% Italian (2000).
Economy: Employment by occupation: 5.3% management, 9.2% professional, 18.9% services, 21.8% sales, 0.0% farming, 12.9% construction, 31.9% production (2000).
Income: Per capita income: $19,155 (2007); Median household income: $42,250 (2007); Average household income: $50,255 (2007); Percent of households with income of $100,000 or more: 8.6% (2007); Poverty rate: 8.9% (2000).
Education: Percent of population age 25 and over with: High school diploma (including GED) or higher: 73.7% (2007); Bachelor's degree or higher: 5.4% (2007); Master's degree or higher: 2.2% (2007).

School District(s)

Labrae Local (PK-12)
2005-06 Enrollment: 1,629 . . . . (330) 898-0800
Housing: Homeownership rate: 84.0% (2007); Median home value: $64,250 (2007); Median rent: $352 per month (2000); Median age of housing: 50 years (2000).
Transportation: Commute to work: 97.7% car, 0.0% public transportation, 0.0% walk, 1.3% work from home (2000); Travel time to work: 29.7% less than 15 minutes, 40.7% 15 to 30 minutes, 19.1% 30 to 45 minutes, 3.1% 45 to 60 minutes, 7.5% 60 minutes or more (2000)

LORDSTOWN (village). Covers a land area of 23.133 square miles and a water area of 0.001 square miles. Located at 41.17° N. Lat.; 80.86° W. Long. Elevation is 951 feet.
Population: 3,404 (1990); 3,633 (2000); 3,630 (2007); 3,623 (2012 projected); Race: 96.0% White, 2.6% Black, 0.4% Asian, 0.4% Hispanic of any race (2007); Density: 156.9 persons per square mile (2007); Average household size: 2.49 (2007); Median age: 42.3 (2007); Males per 100 females: 97.7 (2007); Marriage status: 19.2% never married, 64.0% now married, 6.4% widowed, 10.4% divorced (2000); Foreign born: 1.0% (2000); Ancestry (includes multiple ancestries): 21.7% German, 16.1% English, 13.0% Irish, 9.3% United States or American, 7.6% Other groups (2000).
Economy: Employment by occupation: 9.2% management, 11.5% professional, 14.0% services, 30.2% sales, 0.7% farming, 9.5% construction, 24.9% production (2000).
Income: Per capita income: $27,506 (2007); Median household income: $57,614 (2007); Average household income: $68,530 (2007); Percent of households with income of $100,000 or more: 15.6% (2007); Poverty rate: 4.4% (2000).
Education: Percent of population age 25 and over with: High school diploma (including GED) or higher: 87.7% (2007); Bachelor's degree or higher: 14.3% (2007); Master's degree or higher: 4.1% (2007).
Housing: Homeownership rate: 85.9% (2007); Median home value: $125,690 (2007); Median rent: $410 per month (2000); Median age of housing: 26 years (2000).
Safety: Violent crime rate: 0.0 per 10,000 population; Property crime rate: 199.4 per 10,000 population (2007).
Transportation: Commute to work: 93.1% car, 0.0% public transportation, 2.2% walk, 4.0% work from home (2000); Travel time to work: 40.7% less than 15 minutes, 37.7% 15 to 30 minutes, 16.4% 30 to 45 minutes, 3.8% 45 to 60 minutes, 1.4% 60 minutes or more (2000)

MAPLEWOOD PARK (CDP). Covers a land area of 0.750 square miles and a water area of 0 square miles. Located at 41.13° N. Lat.; 80.58° W. Long. Elevation is 1,089 feet.
Population: 390 (1990); 321 (2000); 289 (2007); 284 (2012 projected); Race: 47.8% White, 50.5% Black, 0.0% Asian, 0.0% Hispanic of any race (2007); Density: 385.3 persons per square mile (2007); Average household size: 2.54 (2007); Median age: 45.1 (2007); Males per 100 females: 100.7 (2007); Marriage status: 21.9% never married, 69.7% now married, 8.3% widowed, 0.0% divorced (2000); Foreign born: 0.0% (2000); Ancestry (includes multiple ancestries): 80.1% Other groups, 2.6% Slovak, 2.6% English, 2.6% Italian, 2.6% United States or American (2000).
Economy: Employment by occupation: 6.0% management, 20.7% professional, 12.1% services, 25.0% sales, 0.0% farming, 28.4% construction, 7.8% production (2000).
Income: Per capita income: $12,310 (2007); Median household income: $27,500 (2007); Average household income: $31,206 (2007); Percent of households with income of $100,000 or more: 1.8% (2007); Poverty rate: 19.1% (2000).
Education: Percent of population age 25 and over with: High school diploma (including GED) or higher: 71.6% (2007); Bachelor's degree or higher: 20.7% (2007); Master's degree or higher: 2.9% (2007).
Housing: Homeownership rate: 82.5% (2007); Median home value: $59,286 (2007); Median rent: $375 per month (2000); Median age of housing: 46 years (2000).
Transportation: Commute to work: 100.0% car, 0.0% public transportation, 0.0% walk, 0.0% work from home (2000); Travel time to work: 49.5% less than 15 minutes, 42.1% 15 to 30 minutes, 0.0% 30 to 45 minutes, 0.0% 45 to 60 minutes, 8.4% 60 minutes or more (2000)

MASURY (CDP). Covers a land area of 3.617 square miles and a water area of 0.034 square miles. Located at 41.20° N. Lat.; 80.53° W. Long. Elevation is 919 feet.
Population: 2,621 (1990); 2,618 (2000); 2,559 (2007); 2,451 (2012 projected); Race: 93.5% White, 3.9% Black, 0.2% Asian, 1.2% Hispanic of any race (2007); Density: 707.5 persons per square mile (2007); Average household size: 2.44 (2007); Median age: 42.4 (2007); Males per 100 females: 84.9 (2007); Marriage status: 21.4% never married, 60.0% now married, 7.6% widowed, 11.1% divorced (2000); Foreign born: 2.2% (2000); Ancestry (includes multiple ancestries): 26.0% German, 18.0% Italian, 16.4% Irish, 10.7% English, 6.9% Slovak (2000).
Economy: Employment by occupation: 8.3% management, 14.3% professional, 17.7% services, 25.1% sales, 0.7% farming, 10.2% construction, 23.7% production (2000).
Income: Per capita income: $21,769 (2007); Median household income: $41,400 (2007); Average household income: $51,676 (2007); Percent of households with income of $100,000 or more: 10.3% (2007); Poverty rate: 12.9% (2000).
Education: Percent of population age 25 and over with: High school diploma (including GED) or higher: 79.8% (2007); Bachelor's degree or higher: 13.5% (2007); Master's degree or higher: 5.0% (2007).

School District(s)

Brookfield Local (PK-12)
2005-06 Enrollment: 1,402 . . . . (330) 448-4930

Housing: Homeownership rate: 71.1% (2007); Median home value: $77,500 (2007); Median rent: $372 per month (2000); Median age of housing: 49 years (2000).
Transportation: Commute to work: 95.5% car, 0.0% public transportation, 0.9% walk, 2.5% work from home (2000); Travel time to work: 38.7% less than 15 minutes, 38.2% 15 to 30 minutes, 13.6% 30 to 45 minutes, 2.7% 45 to 60 minutes, 6.7% 60 minutes or more (2000)

MCDONALD (village). Covers a land area of 1.680 square miles and a water area of 0 square miles. Located at 41.16° N. Lat.; 80.72° W. Long. Elevation is 965 feet.
Population: 3,526 (1990); 3,481 (2000); 3,317 (2007); 3,184 (2012 projected); Race: 97.6% White, 1.1% Black, 0.1% Asian, 1.3% Hispanic of any race (2007); Density: 1,974.8 persons per square mile (2007); Average household size: 2.58 (2007); Median age: 40.6 (2007); Males per 100 females: 91.6 (2007); Marriage status: 22.0% never married, 62.2% now married, 9.4% widowed, 6.4% divorced (2000); Foreign born: 0.5% (2000); Ancestry (includes multiple ancestries): 24.0% German, 20.4% Irish, 17.2% Italian, 9.6% Slovak, 9.2% English (2000).
Economy: Single-family building permits issued: 1 (2007); Multi-family building permits issued: 0 (2007); Employment by occupation: 9.5% management, 18.4% professional, 13.1% services, 25.7% sales, 0.0% farming, 6.4% construction, 26.9% production (2000).
Income: Per capita income: $20,832 (2007); Median household income: $45,672 (2007); Average household income: $53,733 (2007); Percent of households with income of $100,000 or more: 10.2% (2007); Poverty rate: 4.0% (2000).
Education: Percent of population age 25 and over with: High school diploma (including GED) or higher: 88.1% (2007); Bachelor's degree or higher: 20.6% (2007); Master's degree or higher: 4.6% (2007).

School District(s)

Mcdonald Local (PK-12)
2005-06 Enrollment: 903 . . . . (330) 530-8051
Housing: Homeownership rate: 87.0% (2007); Median home value: $107,061 (2007); Median rent: $430 per month (2000); Median age of housing: 41 years (2000).
Transportation: Commute to work: 96.9% car, 0.0% public transportation, 1.7% walk, 1.4% work from home (2000); Travel time to work: 32.1% less than 15 minutes, 54.0% 15 to 30 minutes, 8.3% 30 to 45 minutes, 2.2% 45 to 60 minutes, 3.5% 60 minutes or more (2000)

MINERAL RIDGE (CDP). Covers a land area of 3.295 square miles and a water area of 0.013 square miles. Located at 41.14° N. Lat.; 80.76° W. Long. Elevation is 1,004 feet.
Population: 3,928 (1990); 3,900 (2000); 3,896 (2007); 3,825 (2012 projected); Race: 96.8% White, 1.4% Black, 0.1% Asian, 1.7% Hispanic of any race (2007); Density: 1,182.3 persons per square mile (2007); Average household size: 2.81 (2007); Median age: 42.2 (2007); Males per 100 females: 91.0 (2007); Marriage status: 25.3% never married, 61.4% now married, 6.1% widowed, 7.2% divorced (2000); Foreign born: 1.0% (2000); Ancestry (includes multiple ancestries): 28.4% German, 21.4% Irish, 15.3% Italian, 12.3% English, 6.4% Other groups (2000).
Economy: Employment by occupation: 6.9% management, 20.1% professional, 13.7% services, 21.9% sales, 0.0% farming, 13.4% construction, 24.1% production (2000).
Income: Per capita income: $22,827 (2007); Median household income: $53,758 (2007); Average household income: $62,045 (2007); Percent of households with income of $100,000 or more: 15.5% (2007); Poverty rate: 9.2% (2000).
Education: Percent of population age 25 and over with: High school diploma (including GED) or higher: 89.2% (2007); Bachelor's degree or higher: 16.9% (2007); Master's degree or higher: 6.8% (2007).

School District(s)

Weathersfield Local (PK-12)
2005-06 Enrollment: 1,012 . . . . (330) 652-0287
Housing: Homeownership rate: 76.6% (2007); Median home value: $114,193 (2007); Median rent: $370 per month (2000); Median age of housing: 28 years (2000).
Transportation: Commute to work: 98.0% car, 0.0% public transportation, 1.6% walk, 0.5% work from home (2000); Travel time to work: 35.0% less than 15 minutes, 49.5% 15 to 30 minutes, 12.5% 30 to 45 minutes, 1.4% 45 to 60 minutes, 1.6% 60 minutes or more (2000)

NEWTON FALLS (village). Covers a land area of 2.281 square miles and a water area of 0.075 square miles. Located at 41.18° N. Lat.; 80.97° W. Long. Elevation is 932 feet.
Population: 5,088 (1990); 5,002 (2000); 4,813 (2007); 4,652 (2012 projected); Race: 97.9% White, 0.4% Black, 0.1% Asian, 0.7% Hispanic of any race (2007); Density: 2,110.2 persons per square mile (2007); Average household size: 2.23 (2007); Median age: 39.1 (2007); Males per 100 females: 90.0 (2007); Marriage status: 21.8% never married, 53.4% now married, 9.7% widowed, 15.0% divorced (2000); Foreign born: 0.7% (2000); Ancestry (includes multiple ancestries): 23.7% German, 15.3% Irish, 11.4% English, 10.4% Other groups, 7.4% Italian (2000).
Economy: Employment by occupation: 6.8% management, 15.1% professional, 11.4% services, 24.3% sales, 0.3% farming, 11.1% construction, 31.0% production (2000).
Income: Per capita income: $19,397 (2007); Median household income: $37,649 (2007); Average household income: $43,265 (2007); Percent of households with income of $100,000 or more: 5.6% (2007); Poverty rate: 10.5% (2000).
Education: Percent of population age 25 and over with: High school diploma (including GED) or higher: 80.0% (2007); Bachelor's degree or higher: 12.7% (2007); Master's degree or higher: 2.8% (2007).

School District(s)

Newton Falls Exempted Village (PK-12)
2005-06 Enrollment: 1,499 . . . . (330) 872-5445
Housing: Homeownership rate: 54.9% (2007); Median home value: $98,791 (2007); Median rent: $383 per month (2000); Median age of housing: 44 years (2000).
Transportation: Commute to work: 97.1% car, 0.0% public transportation, 2.2% walk, 0.7% work from home (2000); Travel time to work: 27.7% less than 15 minutes, 37.3% 15 to 30 minutes, 20.8% 30 to 45 minutes, 6.6% 45 to 60 minutes, 7.6% 60 minutes or more (2000)

NILES (city). Covers a land area of 8.552 square miles and a water area of 0.018 square miles. Located at 41.18° N. Lat.; 80.75° W. Long. Elevation is 879 feet.
History: Niles was settled in 1806 by James Heaton, who built a gristmill and blast furnace in the area. It was known as Heaton's Furnace until 1834, when the name was changed to Nilestown for a Baltimore newspaper editor whom Heaton admired. The post office later shortened the name. William McKinley, the 25th president of the United States, was born in Niles in 1843.
Population: 21,353 (1990); 20,932 (2000); 19,730 (2007); 18,812 (2012 projected); Race: 95.7% White, 2.4% Black, 0.3% Asian, 0.9% Hispanic of any race (2007); Density: 2,306.9 persons per square mile (2007); Average household size: 2.29 (2007); Median age: 41.9 (2007); Males per 100 females: 89.9 (2007); Marriage status: 22.7% never married, 55.7% now married, 9.1% widowed, 12.6% divorced (2000); Foreign born: 1.9% (2000); Ancestry (includes multiple ancestries): 23.9% Italian, 21.4% German, 17.5% Irish, 10.6% English, 7.4% Other groups (2000).
Economy: Single-family building permits issued: 5 (2007); Multi-family building permits issued: 0 (2007); Employment by occupation: 7.7% management, 13.9% professional, 17.9% services, 26.7% sales, 0.1% farming, 7.8% construction, 25.9% production (2000).
Income: Per capita income: $22,877 (2007); Median household income: $40,000 (2007); Average household income: $51,678 (2007); Percent of households with income of $100,000 or more: 8.7% (2007); Poverty rate: 9.6% (2000).
Education: Percent of population age 25 and over with: High school diploma (including GED) or higher: 82.9% (2007); Bachelor's degree or higher: 11.7% (2007); Master's degree or higher: 2.8% (2007).

School District(s)

Niles City (PK-12)
2005-06 Enrollment: 2,875 . . . . (330) 652-2509

Two-year College(s)

ETI Technical College (Private, For-profit)
Fall 2007 Enrollment: 174 . . . . (330) 652-9919
2007-08 Tuition: In-state $7,050; Out-of-state $7,050
Raphaels School of Beauty Culture (Private, For-profit)
Fall 2007 Enrollment: 63 . . . . (330) 652-1559
Housing: Homeownership rate: 63.6% (2007); Median home value: $95,139 (2007); Median rent: $419 per month (2000); Median age of housing: 41 years (2000).
Safety: Violent crime rate: 40.2 per 10,000 population; Property crime rate: 620.6 per 10,000 population (2007).

Newspapers: Niles Times (Local news; Circulation 7,700)
Transportation: Commute to work: 96.3% car, 0.4% public transportation, 1.4% walk, 1.2% work from home (2000); Travel time to work: 40.4% less than 15 minutes, 46.0% 15 to 30 minutes, 7.8% 30 to 45 minutes, 2.2% 45 to 60 minutes, 3.6% 60 minutes or more (2000)
Additional Information Contacts
City of Niles . . . . (330) 544-9000
http://www.thecityofniles.com

NORTH BLOOMFIELD (unincorporated postal area, zip code 44450). Covers a land area of 48.401 square miles and a water area of 0.579 square miles. Located at 41.44° N. Lat.; 80.81° W. Long. Elevation is 900 feet.
Population: 2,115 (2000); Race: 96.5% White, 2.3% Black, 0.0% Asian, 0.7% Hispanic of any race (2000); Density: 43.7 persons per square mile (2000); Age: 31.8% under 18, 11.1% over 64 (2000); Marriage status: 25.1% never married, 57.5% now married, 8.2% widowed, 9.1% divorced (2000); Foreign born: 1.1% (2000); Ancestry (includes multiple ancestries): 23.6% German, 16.2% English, 11.1% United States or American, 10.0% Irish, 6.9% Other groups (2000).
Economy: Employment by occupation: 9.3% management, 10.2% professional, 10.4% services, 18.3% sales, 1.3% farming, 14.0% construction, 36.3% production (2000).
Income: Per capita income: $15,353 (2000); Median household income: $40,549 (2000); Poverty rate: 9.5% (2000).
Education: Percent of population age 25 and over with: High school diploma (including GED) or higher: 77.6% (2000); Bachelor's degree or higher: 8.4% (2000).

School District(s)

Bloomfield-Mespo Local (PK-12)
2005-06 Enrollment: 352 . . . . (440) 685-4752
Maplewood Local (PK-12)
2005-06 Enrollment: 1,101 . . . . (330) 637-7506
Housing: Homeownership rate: 78.4% (2000); Median home value: $87,300 (2000); Median rent: $345 per month (2000); Median age of housing: 39 years (2000).
Transportation: Commute to work: 90.8% car, 1.4% public transportation, 2.3% walk, 5.0% work from home (2000); Travel time to work: 17.9% less than 15 minutes, 39.9% 15 to 30 minutes, 26.4% 30 to 45 minutes, 9.6% 45 to 60 minutes, 6.2% 60 minutes or more (2000)

ORANGEVILLE (village). Covers a land area of 0.793 square miles and a water area of 0.322 square miles. Located at 41.34° N. Lat.; 80.52° W. Long. Elevation is 919 feet.
Population: 253 (1990); 189 (2000); 182 (2007); 178 (2012 projected); Race: 96.7% White, 0.0% Black, 0.0% Asian, 0.0% Hispanic of any race (2007); Density: 229.6 persons per square mile (2007); Average household size: 2.43 (2007); Median age: 41.2 (2007); Males per 100 females: 102.2 (2007); Marriage status: 18.1% never married, 69.8% now married, 4.0% widowed, 8.1% divorced (2000); Foreign born: 0.0% (2000); Ancestry (includes multiple ancestries): 42.4% German, 15.2% English, 13.6% United States or American, 13.1% Dutch, 9.4% Irish (2000).
Economy: Employment by occupation: 6.1% management, 9.1% professional, 12.1% services, 33.3% sales, 0.0% farming, 14.1% construction, 25.3% production (2000).
Income: Per capita income: $21,731 (2007); Median household income: $49,250 (2007); Average household income: $52,733 (2007); Percent of households with income of $100,000 or more: 0.0% (2007); Poverty rate: 0.0% (2000).
Education: Percent of population age 25 and over with: High school diploma (including GED) or higher: 89.1% (2007); Bachelor's degree or higher: 10.9% (2007); Master's degree or higher: 3.1% (2007).
Housing: Homeownership rate: 78.7% (2007); Median home value: $100,833 (2007); Median rent: $279 per month (2000); Median age of housing: 60+ years (2000).
Transportation: Commute to work: 93.9% car, 0.0% public transportation, 6.1% walk, 0.0% work from home (2000); Travel time to work: 18.2% less than 15 minutes, 40.4% 15 to 30 minutes, 34.3% 30 to 45 minutes, 6.1% 45 to 60 minutes, 1.0% 60 minutes or more (2000)

SOUTH CANAL (CDP). Covers a land area of 1.620 square miles and a water area of 0.038 square miles. Located at 41.17° N. Lat.; 80.98° W. Long. Elevation is 938 feet.
Population: 1,319 (1990); 1,346 (2000); 1,322 (2007); 1,297 (2012 projected); Race: 98.3% White, 0.3% Black, 0.1% Asian, 0.7% Hispanic of any race (2007); Density: 816.1 persons per square mile (2007); Average household size: 2.73 (2007); Median age: 46.9 (2007); Males per 100 females: 91.3 (2007); Marriage status: 19.8% never married, 61.1% now married, 9.0% widowed, 10.1% divorced (2000); Foreign born: 1.3% (2000); Ancestry (includes multiple ancestries): 16.6% German, 13.4% Slovak, 9.6% Italian, 9.4% English, 7.1% Irish (2000).
Economy: Employment by occupation: 3.0% management, 10.4% professional, 13.4% services, 37.4% sales, 0.0% farming, 15.2% construction, 20.6% production (2000).
Income: Per capita income: $23,428 (2007); Median household income: $54,118 (2007); Average household income: $62,288 (2007); Percent of households with income of $100,000 or more: 17.1% (2007); Poverty rate: 3.9% (2000).
Education: Percent of population age 25 and over with: High school diploma (including GED) or higher: 82.5% (2007); Bachelor's degree or higher: 7.5% (2007); Master's degree or higher: 2.6% (2007).
Housing: Homeownership rate: 90.9% (2007); Median home value: $118,443 (2007); Median rent: $465 per month (2000); Median age of housing: 36 years (2000).
Transportation: Commute to work: 98.4% car, 0.0% public transportation, 0.7% walk, 0.0% work from home (2000); Travel time to work: 25.9% less than 15 minutes, 43.5% 15 to 30 minutes, 17.6% 30 to 45 minutes, 7.2% 45 to 60 minutes, 5.9% 60 minutes or more (2000)

SOUTHINGTON (unincorporated postal area, zip code 44470). Covers a land area of 24.247 square miles and a water area of 0.030 square miles. Located at 41.29° N. Lat.; 80.95° W. Long. Elevation is 891 feet.
Population: 3,554 (2000); Race: 98.4% White, 1.1% Black, 0.0% Asian, 0.5% Hispanic of any race (2000); Density: 146.6 persons per square mile (2000); Age: 21.9% under 18, 13.6% over 64 (2000); Marriage status: 20.1% never married, 64.8% now married, 6.8% widowed, 8.3% divorced (2000); Foreign born: 0.7% (2000); Ancestry (includes multiple ancestries): 27.6% German, 18.0% English, 13.4% Irish, 8.7% United States or American, 5.2% Italian (2000).
Economy: Employment by occupation: 7.2% management, 12.1% professional, 11.7% services, 18.4% sales, 0.6% farming, 12.0% construction, 37.9% production (2000).
Income: Per capita income: $20,031 (2000); Median household income: $49,044 (2000); Poverty rate: 6.4% (2000).
Education: Percent of population age 25 and over with: High school diploma (including GED) or higher: 84.8% (2000); Bachelor's degree or higher: 10.0% (2000).

School District(s)

Southington Local (KG-12)
2005-06 Enrollment: 672 . . . . (330) 898-7480
Housing: Homeownership rate: 92.0% (2000); Median home value: $102,500 (2000); Median rent: $416 per month (2000); Median age of housing: 35 years (2000).
Transportation: Commute to work: 97.1% car, 0.0% public transportation, 1.0% walk, 1.5% work from home (2000); Travel time to work: 13.7% less than 15 minutes, 51.2% 15 to 30 minutes, 17.6% 30 to 45 minutes, 8.3% 45 to 60 minutes, 9.1% 60 minutes or more (2000)

VIENNA (unincorporated postal area, zip code 44473). Aka Vienna Center. Covers a land area of 25.220 square miles and a water area of 0.019 square miles. Located at 41.26° N. Lat.; 80.70° W. Long. Elevation is 1,050 feet.
Population: 4,215 (2000); Race: 97.4% White, 0.7% Black, 0.3% Asian, 0.2% Hispanic of any race (2000); Density: 167.1 persons per square mile (2000); Age: 22.7% under 18, 16.0% over 64 (2000); Marriage status: 19.4% never married, 64.0% now married, 7.7% widowed, 8.9% divorced (2000); Foreign born: 0.2% (2000); Ancestry (includes multiple ancestries): 23.0% German, 15.5% Irish, 12.3% English, 9.9% Italian, 5.8% United States or American (2000).
Economy: Employment by occupation: 9.4% management, 15.3% professional, 14.2% services, 23.8% sales, 1.0% farming, 12.2% construction, 24.0% production (2000).
Income: Per capita income: $19,652 (2000); Median household income: $45,556 (2000); Poverty rate: 4.4% (2000).
Education: Percent of population age 25 and over with: High school diploma (including GED) or higher: 88.4% (2000); Bachelor's degree or higher: 14.4% (2000).

School District(s)

Mathews Local (PK-12)
2005-06 Enrollment: 933 . . . . (330) 394-1800

Housing: Homeownership rate: 87.9% (2000); Median home value: $97,900 (2000); Median rent: $369 per month (2000); Median age of housing: 31 years (2000).

Transportation: Commute to work: 94.1% car, 0.6% public transportation, 1.7% walk, 3.1% work from home (2000); Travel time to work: 30.9% less than 15 minutes, 49.3% 15 to 30 minutes, 11.5% 30 to 45 minutes, 3.1% 45 to 60 minutes, 5.1% 60 minutes or more (2000)

VIENNA CENTER (CDP). Covers a land area of 4.236 square miles and a water area of 0 square miles. Located at 41.23° N. Lat.; 80.66° W. Long. Elevation is 1,148 feet.

Population: 1,066 (1990); 994 (2000); 971 (2007); 957 (2012 projected); Race: 98.2% White, 1.0% Black, 0.3% Asian, 0.6% Hispanic of any race (2007); Density: 229.2 persons per square mile (2007); Average household size: 2.58 (2007); Median age: 43.2 (2007); Males per 100 females: 105.3 (2007); Marriage status: 24.1% never married, 66.4% now married, 6.3% widowed, 3.2% divorced (2000); Foreign born: 0.0% (2000); Ancestry (includes multiple ancestries): 16.4% Irish, 16.3% German, 14.8% English, 9.1% Italian, 8.8% Other groups (2000).

Economy: Employment by occupation: 7.5% management, 21.6% professional, 12.9% services, 25.3% sales, 0.0% farming, 7.9% construction, 24.8% production (2000).

Income: Per capita income: $25,217 (2007); Median household income: $55,469 (2007); Average household income: $64,702 (2007); Percent of households with income of $100,000 or more: 19.4% (2007); Poverty rate: 3.1% (2000).

Education: Percent of population age 25 and over with: High school diploma (including GED) or higher: 88.3% (2007); Bachelor's degree or higher: 15.7% (2007); Master's degree or higher: 6.3% (2007).

Housing: Homeownership rate: 83.6% (2007); Median home value: $112,007 (2007); Median rent: $430 per month (2000); Median age of housing: 41 years (2000).

Transportation: Commute to work: 93.9% car, 0.0% public transportation, 4.3% walk, 1.8% work from home (2000); Travel time to work: 34.3% less than 15 minutes, 51.7% 15 to 30 minutes, 5.2% 30 to 45 minutes, 3.7% 45 to 60 minutes, 5.2% 60 minutes or more (2000)

WARREN (city). County seat. Covers a land area of 16.085 square miles and a water area of 0.027 square miles. Located at 41.23° N. Lat.; 80.81° W. Long. Elevation is 892 feet.

History: Warren was settled in 1798 when Ephraim Quinby and Richard Storr of the Connecticut Land Company came from Pennsylvania. In 1800 the settlement was made the seat of the newly formed Trumbull County. Warren, named for a surveyor, grew slowly, and was incorporated as a village in 1834. The opening of the canal brought a shipping industry, and manufacturing developed. In 1899 J. Ward Packard made the first Packard automobiles in Warren, as well as founding the forerunner of the Peerless Electric Company and other lamp manufacturing companies.

Population: 51,151 (1990); 46,832 (2000); 43,494 (2007); 41,195 (2012 projected); Race: 70.3% White, 26.6% Black, 0.4% Asian, 1.3% Hispanic of any race (2007); Density: 2,704.1 persons per square mile (2007); Average household size: 2.37 (2007); Median age: 38.1 (2007); Males per 100 females: 87.4 (2007); Marriage status: 26.7% never married, 49.5% now married, 9.0% widowed, 14.8% divorced (2000); Foreign born: 1.9% (2000); Ancestry (includes multiple ancestries): 25.3% Other groups, 15.2% German, 11.6% Irish, 10.3% Italian, 7.5% English (2000).

Economy: Unemployment rate: 9.1% (6/2008); Total civilian labor force: 19,920 (6/2008); Single-family building permits issued: 8 (2007); Multi-family building permits issued: 0 (2007); Employment by occupation: 7.8% management, 13.4% professional, 19.0% services, 23.3% sales, 0.2% farming, 8.3% construction, 28.1% production (2000).

Income: Per capita income: $17,990 (2007); Median household income: $32,642 (2007); Average household income: $41,914 (2007); Percent of households with income of $100,000 or more: 5.9% (2007); Poverty rate: 19.4% (2000).

Taxes: Total city taxes per capita: $500 (2006); City property taxes per capita: $33 (2006).

Education: Percent of population age 25 and over with: High school diploma (including GED) or higher: 77.5% (2007); Bachelor's degree or higher: 11.1% (2007); Master's degree or higher: 3.4% (2007).

School District(s)

Academy of Arts and Humanities (03-05)
2005-06 Enrollment: 28 . . . . (330) 399-6882
Arts and Science Academy (KG-02)
2005-06 Enrollment: 72 . . . . (330) 399-6882
Champion Local (PK-12)
2005-06 Enrollment: 1,719 . . . . (330) 847-2330
Howland Local (PK-12)
2005-06 Enrollment: 3,227 . . . . (330) 856-8200
Lakeview Local (PK-12)
2005-06 Enrollment: 2,215 . . . . (330) 637-8741
Life Skills of Trumbull County (09-12)
2005-06 Enrollment: 269 . . . . (330) 392-0231
Lordstown Local (PK-12)
2005-06 Enrollment: 562 . . . . (330) 824-2534
Summit Academy Middle School - Warren (06-09)
2005-06 Enrollment: 39 . . . . (330) 369-4233
Summit Academy Warren (01-06)
2005-06 Enrollment: 81 . . . . (330) 369-4233
Trumbull Career & Tech Ctr (09-12)
2005-06 Enrollment: n/a . . . . (330) 847-0503
Warren City (PK-12)
2005-06 Enrollment: 6,347 . . . . (330) 841-2321

Two-year College(s)

Kent State University-Trumbull Campus (Public)
Fall 2007 Enrollment: 2,120. . . . . (330) 847-0571
2007-08 Tuition: In-state $4,770; Out-of-state $12,202
Trumbull Business College (Private, For-profit)
Fall 2007 Enrollment: 296 . . . . (330) 369-3200
2007-08 Tuition: In-state $11,322; Out-of-state $11,322

Vocational/Technical School(s)

TCTC Adult Training Center (Public)
Fall 2007 Enrollment: 157 . . . . (330) 847-0503
2007-08 Tuition: $7,440

Housing: Homeownership rate: 58.9% (2007); Median home value: $72,973 (2007); Median rent: $355 per month (2000); Median age of housing: 47 years (2000).

Hospitals: Hillside Rehabilitation Hospital (93 beds); Trumbull Memorial Hospital (350 beds)

Safety: Violent crime rate: 113.2 per 10,000 population; Property crime rate: 555.5 per 10,000 population (2007).

Newspapers: Tribune Chronicle (Local news; Circulation 45,000); Vindicator -Warren Bureau (Local news; Circulation 5,500)

Transportation: Commute to work: 94.7% car, 0.2% public transportation, 1.8% walk, 1.7% work from home (2000); Travel time to work: 49.7% less than 15 minutes, 32.4% 15 to 30 minutes, 8.4% 30 to 45 minutes, 5.3% 45 to 60 minutes, 4.1% 60 minutes or more (2000)

Airports: Youngstown-Warren Regional (primary service)

Additional Information Contacts

City of Warren . . . . (330) 841-2601
http://www.warren.org
Youngstown/Warren Regional Chamber of Commerce. . . . (330) 392-6140
http://www.regionalchamber.com

WEST FARMINGTON (village). Covers a land area of 0.878 square miles and a water area of 0 square miles. Located at 41.39° N. Lat.; 80.97° W. Long. Elevation is 866 feet.

Population: 542 (1990); 519 (2000); 539 (2007); 543 (2012 projected); Race: 98.9% White, 0.7% Black, 0.0% Asian, 0.0% Hispanic of any race (2007); Density: 614.1 persons per square mile (2007); Average household size: 2.78 (2007); Median age: 34.1 (2007); Males per 100 females: 95.3 (2007); Marriage status: 19.9% never married, 58.8% now married, 9.7% widowed, 11.6% divorced (2000); Foreign born: 0.4% (2000); Ancestry (includes multiple ancestries): 30.4% German, 13.3% English, 13.1% Irish, 9.9% United States or American, 8.7% Dutch (2000).

Economy: Employment by occupation: 8.4% management, 14.9% professional, 7.4% services, 18.6% sales, 0.9% farming, 16.3% construction, 33.5% production (2000).

Income: Per capita income: $18,827 (2007); Median household income: $46,944 (2007); Average household income: $52,307 (2007); Percent of households with income of $100,000 or more: 7.2% (2007); Poverty rate: 8.9% (2000).

Education: Percent of population age 25 and over with: High school diploma (including GED) or higher: 78.8% (2007); Bachelor's degree or higher: 9.5% (2007); Master's degree or higher: 2.8% (2007).

School District(s)

Bristol Local (PK-12)
2005-06 Enrollment: 777 . . . . (330) 889-3882

Housing: Homeownership rate: 77.3% (2007); Median home value: $94,000 (2007); Median rent: $390 per month (2000); Median age of housing: 60+ years (2000).

Transportation: Commute to work: 93.4% car, 0.5% public transportation, 4.3% walk, 1.9% work from home (2000); Travel time to work: 13.5% less than 15 minutes, 47.3% 15 to 30 minutes, 23.7% 30 to 45 minutes, 9.7% 45 to 60 minutes, 5.8% 60 minutes or more (2000)

WEST HILL (CDP). Covers a land area of 1.634 square miles and a water area of 0 square miles. Located at 41.23° N. Lat.; 80.52° W. Long. Elevation is 1,043 feet.

Population: 2,954 (1990); 2,523 (2000); 2,323 (2007); 2,252 (2012 projected); Race: 89.8% White, 8.0% Black, 0.4% Asian, 0.9% Hispanic of any race (2007); Density: 1,421.3 persons per square mile (2007); Average household size: 2.37 (2007); Median age: 41.7 (2007); Males per 100 females: 92.6 (2007); Marriage status: 23.1% never married, 56.8% now married, 8.2% widowed, 11.9% divorced (2000); Foreign born: 3.6% (2000); Ancestry (includes multiple ancestries): 23.0% German, 17.9% Other groups, 14.1% Irish, 13.0% English, 11.5% Italian (2000).

Economy: Employment by occupation: 2.9% management, 7.9% professional, 22.5% services, 22.0% sales, 0.0% farming, 13.3% construction, 31.4% production (2000).

Income: Per capita income: $19,339 (2007); Median household income: $31,588 (2007); Average household income: $44,664 (2007); Percent of households with income of $100,000 or more: 5.1% (2007); Poverty rate: 13.3% (2000).

Education: Percent of population age 25 and over with: High school diploma (including GED) or higher: 78.1% (2007); Bachelor's degree or higher: 6.8% (2007); Master's degree or higher: 1.6% (2007).

Housing: Homeownership rate: 63.4% (2007); Median home value: $60,085 (2007); Median rent: $306 per month (2000); Median age of housing: 52 years (2000).

Transportation: Commute to work: 95.7% car, 0.0% public transportation, 0.0% walk, 0.9% work from home (2000); Travel time to work: 42.7% less than 15 minutes, 39.7% 15 to 30 minutes, 13.7% 30 to 45 minutes, 2.3% 45 to 60 minutes, 1.5% 60 minutes or more (2000)

YANKEE LAKE (village). Covers a land area of 0.549 square miles and a water area of 0 square miles. Located at 41.26° N. Lat.; 80.56° W. Long. Elevation is 1,007 feet.

Population: 88 (1990); 99 (2000); 103 (2007); 101 (2012 projected); Race: 100.0% White, 0.0% Black, 0.0% Asian, 0.0% Hispanic of any race (2007); Density: 187.7 persons per square mile (2007); Average household size: 2.34 (2007); Median age: 48.1 (2007); Males per 100 females: 123.9 (2007); Marriage status: 21.1% never married, 64.5% now married, 2.6% widowed, 11.8% divorced (2000); Foreign born: 0.0% (2000); Ancestry (includes multiple ancestries): 28.1% German, 19.1% English, 16.9% Slovak, 14.6% Croatian, 11.2% Italian (2000).

Economy: Employment by occupation: 10.2% management, 22.4% professional, 4.1% services, 14.3% sales, 0.0% farming, 30.6% construction, 18.4% production (2000).

Income: Per capita income: $24,660 (2007); Median household income: $52,500 (2007); Average household income: $57,727 (2007); Percent of households with income of $100,000 or more: 4.5% (2007); Poverty rate: 6.7% (2000).

Education: Percent of population age 25 and over with: High school diploma (including GED) or higher: 96.1% (2007); Bachelor's degree or higher: 13.2% (2007); Master's degree or higher: 3.9% (2007).

Housing: Homeownership rate: 88.6% (2007); Median home value: $114,881 (2007); Median rent: $288 per month (2000); Median age of housing: 36 years (2000).

Transportation: Commute to work: 100.0% car, 0.0% public transportation, 0.0% walk, 0.0% work from home (2000); Travel time to work: 10.2% less than 15 minutes, 51.0% 15 to 30 minutes, 30.6% 30 to 45 minutes, 4.1% 45 to 60 minutes, 4.1% 60 minutes or more (2000)

Tuscarawas County

Located in eastern Ohio; crossed by the Tuscarawas River. Covers a land area of 567.58 square miles, a water area of 3.91 square miles, and is located in the Eastern Time Zone. The county was founded in 1808. County seat is New Philadelphia.

Tuscarawas County is part of the New Philadelphia-Dover, OH Micropolitan Statistical Area. The entire metro area includes: Tuscarawas County, OH

Weather Station: New Philadelphia — Elevation: 892 feet

	Jan	Feb	Mar	Apr	May	Jun	Jul	Aug	Sep	Oct	Nov	Dec
High	35	39	49	61	72	80	84	83	76	64	51	40
Low	18	19	27	36	46	56	60	59	52	40	32	24
Precip	2.7	2.4	3.2	3.5	4.1	4.4	4.1	4.2	3.2	2.6	3.3	3.0
Snow	9.9	6.6	5.1	1.5	tr	0.0	0.0	0.0	0.0	tr	1.4	5.2

High and Low temperatures in degrees Fahrenheit; Precipitation and Snow in inches

Population: 84,090 (1990); 90,914 (2000); 92,086 (2007); 92,466 (2012 projected); Race: 97.4% White, 0.8% Black, 0.3% Asian, 1.1% Hispanic of any race (2007); Density: 162.2 persons per square mile (2007); Average household size: 2.51 (2007); Median age: 39.5 (2007); Males per 100 females: 96.1 (2007).

Religion: Five largest groups: 9.5% The United Methodist Church, 9.3% Catholic Church, 6.7% Evangelical Lutheran Church in America, 5.8% United Church of Christ, 3.4% Old Order Amish Church (2000).

Economy: Unemployment rate: 6.2% (6/2008); Total civilian labor force: 47,730 (6/2008); Leading industries: 27.5% manufacturing; 14.5% health care and social assistance; 14.5% retail trade (2005); Farms: 1,076 totaling 159,665 acres (2002); Companies that employ 500 or more persons: 3 (2006); Companies that employ 100 to 499 persons: 51 (2006); Companies that employ less than 100 persons: 2,329 (2006); Black-owned businesses: n/a (2002); Hispanic-owned businesses: n/a (2002); Asian-owned businesses: n/a (2002); Women-owned businesses: 1,707 (2002); Retail sales per capita: $12,872 (2008). Single-family building permits issued: 94 (2007); Multi-family building permits issued: 14 (2007).

Income: Per capita income: $20,270 (2007); Median household income: $40,866 (2007); Average household income: $50,638 (2007); Percent of households with income of $100,000 or more: 8.4% (2007); Poverty rate: 9.6% (2005); Bankruptcy rate: 4.16% (2007).

Taxes: Total county taxes per capita: $206 (2006); County property taxes per capita: $106 (2006).

Education: Percent of population age 25 and over with: High school diploma (including GED) or higher: 80.3% (2007); Bachelor's degree or higher: 12.3% (2007); Master's degree or higher: 4.1% (2007).

Housing: Homeownership rate: 75.3% (2007); Median home value: $110,151 (2007); Median rent: $354 per month (2000); Median age of housing: 41 years (2000).

Health: Birth rate: 131.1 per 10,000 population (2007); Death rate: 104.4 per 10,000 population (2007); Age-adjusted cancer mortality rate: 208.4 deaths per 100,000 population (2005); Air Quality Index: 99.7% good, 0.3% moderate, 0.0% unhealthy for sensitive individuals, 0.0% unhealthy (percent of days in 2007); Number of physicians: 12.3 per 10,000 population (2005); Hospital beds: 17.1 per 10,000 population (2004); Hospital admissions: 777.6 per 10,000 population (2004).

Elections: 2004 Presidential election results: 55.5% Bush, 43.9% Kerry, 0.0% Nader, 0.3% Badnarik

National and State Parks: Fort Laurens State Memorial

Additional Information Contacts

Tuscarawas County Government . . . . (330) 364-8811
http://www.co.tuscarawas.oh.us
City of Dover . . . . (330) 343-6726
http://www.doverohio.com
City of New Philadelphia . . . . (330) 364-4491
http://www.newphilaoh.com
Tuscarawas County Chamber of Commerce. . . . . (330) 343-4474
http://www.tuschamber.com
Twin City Chamber of Commerce . . . . (740) 922-5623
http://www.twincitychamber.org

Tuscarawas County Communities

BALTIC (village). Covers a land area of 0.834 square miles and a water area of 0 square miles. Located at 40.44° N. Lat.; 81.70° W. Long. Elevation is 1,066 feet.

Population: 755 (1990); 743 (2000); 750 (2007); 740 (2012 projected); Race: 98.4% White, 0.3% Black, 0.4% Asian, 0.1% Hispanic of any race (2007); Density: 899.4 persons per square mile (2007); Average household size: 2.68 (2007); Median age: 41.4 (2007); Males per 100 females: 103.3 (2007); Marriage status: 20.3% never married, 55.0% now married, 12.6% widowed, 12.0% divorced (2000); Foreign born: 0.0% (2000); Ancestry (includes multiple ancestries): 44.4% German, 11.7% Swiss, 7.1% Irish, 5.6% United States or American, 5.2% English (2000).

Economy: Single-family building permits issued: 0 (2007); Multi-family building permits issued: 0 (2007); Employment by occupation: 9.8% management, 8.0% professional, 13.2% services, 16.9% sales, 1.5% farming, 14.7% construction, 35.9% production (2000).
Income: Per capita income: $18,349 (2007); Median household income: $38,077 (2007); Average household income: $43,741 (2007); Percent of households with income of $100,000 or more: 3.2% (2007); Poverty rate: 5.7% (2000).
Education: Percent of population age 25 and over with: High school diploma (including GED) or higher: 69.1% (2007); Bachelor's degree or higher: 5.5% (2007); Master's degree or higher: 2.1% (2007).

School District(s)

Garaway Local (PK-12)
2005-06 Enrollment: 1,271 . . . . (330) 852-2421
Housing: Homeownership rate: 74.3% (2007); Median home value: $103,571 (2007); Median rent: $351 per month (2000); Median age of housing: 55 years (2000).
Transportation: Commute to work: 94.4% car, 0.0% public transportation, 2.2% walk, 1.9% work from home (2000); Travel time to work: 43.2% less than 15 minutes, 27.0% 15 to 30 minutes, 21.6% 30 to 45 minutes, 6.7% 45 to 60 minutes, 1.6% 60 minutes or more (2000)

BARNHILL (village). Covers a land area of 0.370 square miles and a water area of 0 square miles. Located at 40.44° N. Lat.; 81.36° W. Long. Elevation is 876 feet.
Population: 313 (1990); 364 (2000); 396 (2007); 416 (2012 projected); Race: 98.2% White, 0.5% Black, 0.0% Asian, 0.5% Hispanic of any race (2007); Density: 1,071.4 persons per square mile (2007); Average household size: 2.66 (2007); Median age: 33.8 (2007); Males per 100 females: 91.3 (2007); Marriage status: 24.2% never married, 56.3% now married, 8.7% widowed, 10.8% divorced (2000); Foreign born: 0.0% (2000); Ancestry (includes multiple ancestries): 19.2% German, 13.1% United States or American, 11.1% Other groups, 6.4% English, 6.4% Irish (2000).
Economy: Employment by occupation: 5.3% management, 7.3% professional, 18.7% services, 10.7% sales, 0.0% farming, 7.3% construction, 50.7% production (2000).
Income: Per capita income: $13,902 (2007); Median household income: $30,938 (2007); Average household income: $36,946 (2007); Percent of households with income of $100,000 or more: 2.7% (2007); Poverty rate: 19.5% (2000).
Education: Percent of population age 25 and over with: High school diploma (including GED) or higher: 71.0% (2007); Bachelor's degree or higher: 4.7% (2007); Master's degree or higher: 1.2% (2007).
Housing: Homeownership rate: 86.6% (2007); Median home value: $55,000 (2007); Median rent: $360 per month (2000); Median age of housing: 28 years (2000).
Transportation: Commute to work: 97.3% car, 0.0% public transportation, 0.0% walk, 0.0% work from home (2000); Travel time to work: 37.2% less than 15 minutes, 36.5% 15 to 30 minutes, 16.2% 30 to 45 minutes, 6.1% 45 to 60 minutes, 4.1% 60 minutes or more (2000)

BOLIVAR (village). Covers a land area of 0.505 square miles and a water area of 0.006 square miles. Located at 40.65° N. Lat.; 81.45° W. Long. Elevation is 925 feet.
History: Bolivar was an important grain market during the boom days of the Ohio & Erie and the Sandy & Beaver Canals. Near Bolivar was the site of the cabin built in 1761 by Christian Frederick Post, a Moravian missionary.
Population: 953 (1990); 894 (2000); 760 (2007); 762 (2012 projected); Race: 98.2% White, 0.0% Black, 0.9% Asian, 0.3% Hispanic of any race (2007); Density: 1,504.5 persons per square mile (2007); Average household size: 2.32 (2007); Median age: 41.4 (2007); Males per 100 females: 94.9 (2007); Marriage status: 16.8% never married, 66.3% now married, 10.4% widowed, 6.5% divorced (2000); Foreign born: 0.3% (2000); Ancestry (includes multiple ancestries): 40.4% German, 12.3% Irish, 12.2% English, 5.8% United States or American, 5.4% Other groups (2000).
Economy: Single-family building permits issued: 0 (2007); Multi-family building permits issued: 0 (2007); Employment by occupation: 15.9% management, 10.8% professional, 15.6% services, 20.3% sales, 0.0% farming, 12.5% construction, 24.9% production (2000).
Income: Per capita income: $21,513 (2007); Median household income: $43,587 (2007); Average household income: $50,000 (2007); Percent of households with income of $100,000 or more: 7.3% (2007); Poverty rate: 3.9% (2000).
Education: Percent of population age 25 and over with: High school diploma (including GED) or higher: 82.1% (2007); Bachelor's degree or higher: 14.0% (2007); Master's degree or higher: 3.7% (2007).

School District(s)

Tuscarawas Valley Local (PK-12)
2005-06 Enrollment: 1,704 . . . . (330) 859-2213
Housing: Homeownership rate: 84.4% (2007); Median home value: $113,690 (2007); Median rent: $373 per month (2000); Median age of housing: 49 years (2000).
Transportation: Commute to work: 92.4% car, 0.5% public transportation, 3.2% walk, 3.4% work from home (2000); Travel time to work: 32.4% less than 15 minutes, 47.7% 15 to 30 minutes, 12.2% 30 to 45 minutes, 3.8% 45 to 60 minutes, 3.8% 60 minutes or more (2000)

DENNISON (village). Covers a land area of 1.376 square miles and a water area of 0 square miles. Located at 40.39° N. Lat.; 81.33° W. Long. Elevation is 866 feet.
History: The site of Dennison was selected in 1864 by the Pittsburgh, Columbus & St. Louis Railroad for its division shops. The town was named for William Dennison, a Civil War governor of Ohio.
Population: 3,282 (1990); 2,992 (2000); 2,854 (2007); 2,789 (2012 projected); Race: 95.5% White, 1.9% Black, 0.1% Asian, 1.4% Hispanic of any race (2007); Density: 2,074.2 persons per square mile (2007); Average household size: 2.60 (2007); Median age: 34.8 (2007); Males per 100 females: 96.6 (2007); Marriage status: 24.1% never married, 56.8% now married, 8.7% widowed, 10.4% divorced (2000); Foreign born: 0.5% (2000); Ancestry (includes multiple ancestries): 22.8% German, 18.4% Irish, 10.0% Italian, 9.1% English, 8.6% United States or American (2000).
Economy: Single-family building permits issued: 0 (2007); Multi-family building permits issued: 0 (2007); Employment by occupation: 4.4% management, 11.0% professional, 19.1% services, 21.6% sales, 0.3% farming, 6.4% construction, 37.2% production (2000).
Income: Per capita income: $16,470 (2007); Median household income: $33,775 (2007); Average household income: $42,584 (2007); Percent of households with income of $100,000 or more: 5.6% (2007); Poverty rate: 17.2% (2000).
Education: Percent of population age 25 and over with: High school diploma (including GED) or higher: 75.3% (2007); Bachelor's degree or higher: 5.9% (2007); Master's degree or higher: 3.2% (2007).

School District(s)

Claymont City (PK-12)
2005-06 Enrollment: 2,267 . . . . (740) 922-5478
Housing: Homeownership rate: 67.3% (2007); Median home value: $74,889 (2007); Median rent: $340 per month (2000); Median age of housing: 60+ years (2000).
Hospitals: Twin City Hospital (25 beds)
Safety: Violent crime rate: 0.0 per 10,000 population; Property crime rate: 41.4 per 10,000 population (2007).
Transportation: Commute to work: 93.7% car, 0.0% public transportation, 2.8% walk, 2.1% work from home (2000); Travel time to work: 39.7% less than 15 minutes, 36.6% 15 to 30 minutes, 13.3% 30 to 45 minutes, 6.1% 45 to 60 minutes, 4.2% 60 minutes or more (2000)

DOVER (city). Covers a land area of 5.264 square miles and a water area of 0.069 square miles. Located at 40.52° N. Lat.; 81.47° W. Long. Elevation is 879 feet.
History: Dover was laid out in 1807 on land owned by Jesse Slingluff and Christian Deardorff, and settled by German immigrants from Pennsylvania. For a time it was known as Canal Dover, and was the collector's port for the Ohio & Erie Canal in Tuscarawas County.
Population: 11,544 (1990); 12,210 (2000); 12,293 (2007); 12,318 (2012 projected); Race: 96.6% White, 1.4% Black, 0.5% Asian, 0.9% Hispanic of any race (2007); Density: 2,335.4 persons per square mile (2007); Average household size: 2.41 (2007); Median age: 42.0 (2007); Males per 100 females: 88.3 (2007); Marriage status: 20.8% never married, 58.0% now married, 10.0% widowed, 11.2% divorced (2000); Foreign born: 0.7% (2000); Ancestry (includes multiple ancestries): 33.4% German, 12.3% Irish, 11.7% English, 11.2% Italian, 6.1% Other groups (2000).
Economy: Single-family building permits issued: 14 (2007); Multi-family building permits issued: 6 (2007); Employment by occupation: 10.8% management, 18.0% professional, 17.8% services, 25.2% sales, 0.1% farming, 6.4% construction, 21.6% production (2000).

Income: Per capita income: $21,479 (2007); Median household income: $41,574 (2007); Average household income: $51,361 (2007); Percent of households with income of $100,000 or more: 8.9% (2007); Poverty rate: 9.2% (2000).
Education: Percent of population age 25 and over with: High school diploma (including GED) or higher: 84.4% (2007); Bachelor's degree or higher: 17.8% (2007); Master's degree or higher: 6.1% (2007).

School District(s)

Dover City (PK-12)
2005-06 Enrollment: 2,619 . . . . (330) 364-1906
Housing: Homeownership rate: 72.2% (2007); Median home value: $118,903 (2007); Median rent: $383 per month (2000); Median age of housing: 47 years (2000).
Hospitals: Union Hospital (105 beds)
Safety: Violent crime rate: 12.0 per 10,000 population; Property crime rate: 116.5 per 10,000 population (2007).
Transportation: Commute to work: 95.7% car, 0.1% public transportation, 1.6% walk, 1.8% work from home (2000); Travel time to work: 52.3% less than 15 minutes, 29.3% 15 to 30 minutes, 12.1% 30 to 45 minutes, 2.9% 45 to 60 minutes, 3.3% 60 minutes or more (2000)
Additional Information Contacts
City of Dover . . . . (330) 343-6726
http://www.doverohio.com

DUNDEE (unincorporated postal area, zip code 44624). Covers a land area of 51.959 square miles and a water area of 0.025 square miles. Located at 40.60° N. Lat.; 81.65° W. Long. Elevation is 1,032 feet.
Population: 4,522 (2000); Race: 98.9% White, 0.0% Black, 0.0% Asian, 0.0% Hispanic of any race (2000); Density: 87.0 persons per square mile (2000); Age: 36.9% under 18, 6.2% over 64 (2000); Marriage status: 25.4% never married, 66.5% now married, 4.8% widowed, 3.3% divorced (2000); Foreign born: 0.0% (2000); Ancestry (includes multiple ancestries): 27.2% German, 13.8% United States or American, 6.6% Swiss, 5.2% Pennsylvania German, 3.4% Irish (2000).
Economy: Employment by occupation: 11.4% management, 4.8% professional, 13.1% services, 15.7% sales, 3.2% farming, 18.0% construction, 33.7% production (2000).
Income: Per capita income: $13,508 (2000); Median household income: $39,936 (2000); Poverty rate: 13.6% (2000).
Education: Percent of population age 25 and over with: High school diploma (including GED) or higher: 39.0% (2000); Bachelor's degree or higher: 2.1% (2000).

School District(s)

Garaway Local (PK-12)
2005-06 Enrollment: 1,271 . . . . (330) 852-2421
Housing: Homeownership rate: 84.5% (2000); Median home value: $112,800 (2000); Median rent: $379 per month (2000); Median age of housing: 25 years (2000).
Transportation: Commute to work: 71.5% car, 1.6% public transportation, 5.6% walk, 17.6% work from home (2000); Travel time to work: 33.4% less than 15 minutes, 41.3% 15 to 30 minutes, 15.7% 30 to 45 minutes, 5.1% 45 to 60 minutes, 4.6% 60 minutes or more (2000)

GNADENHUTTEN (village). Covers a land area of 0.999 square miles and a water area of <.001 square miles. Located at 40.36° N. Lat.; 81.43° W. Long. Elevation is 837 feet.
History: The name of Gnadenhutten is of German origin, meaning "tents of grace." A community was established here in 1772 by Joshua, a Mohican elder of a group of Indians from the Moravian mission founded by David Zeisberger at Schoenbrunn. The group was massacred by militiamen from Pennsylvania in 1782.
Population: 1,250 (1990); 1,280 (2000); 1,242 (2007); 1,238 (2012 projected); Race: 99.4% White, 0.1% Black, 0.0% Asian, 0.2% Hispanic of any race (2007); Density: 1,243.7 persons per square mile (2007); Average household size: 2.45 (2007); Median age: 39.4 (2007); Males per 100 females: 90.8 (2007); Marriage status: 18.0% never married, 65.1% now married, 8.2% widowed, 8.7% divorced (2000); Foreign born: 0.2% (2000); Ancestry (includes multiple ancestries): 29.3% German, 14.8% Irish, 11.5% United States or American, 10.0% English, 4.8% Italian (2000).
Economy: Single-family building permits issued: 0 (2007); Multi-family building permits issued: 0 (2007); Employment by occupation: 6.8% management, 12.0% professional, 19.8% services, 27.4% sales, 0.5% farming, 8.3% construction, 25.2% production (2000).
Income: Per capita income: $19,960 (2007); Median household income: $38,063 (2007); Average household income: $48,634 (2007); Percent of households with income of $100,000 or more: 6.1% (2007); Poverty rate: 8.8% (2000).
Education: Percent of population age 25 and over with: High school diploma (including GED) or higher: 85.6% (2007); Bachelor's degree or higher: 8.1% (2007); Master's degree or higher: 2.9% (2007).

School District(s)

Indian Valley Local (PK-12)
2005-06 Enrollment: 1,868 . . . . (740) 254-4334
Housing: Homeownership rate: 85.6% (2007); Median home value: $97,246 (2007); Median rent: $377 per month (2000); Median age of housing: 49 years (2000).
Transportation: Commute to work: 93.6% car, 0.7% public transportation, 3.5% walk, 2.2% work from home (2000); Travel time to work: 30.9% less than 15 minutes, 42.8% 15 to 30 minutes, 15.2% 30 to 45 minutes, 4.6% 45 to 60 minutes, 6.5% 60 minutes or more (2000)

MIDVALE (village). Covers a land area of 0.610 square miles and a water area of 0 square miles. Located at 40.43° N. Lat.; 81.37° W. Long. Elevation is 860 feet.
Population: 573 (1990); 547 (2000); 582 (2007); 603 (2012 projected); Race: 98.3% White, 0.0% Black, 0.0% Asian, 0.7% Hispanic of any race (2007); Density: 954.9 persons per square mile (2007); Average household size: 2.52 (2007); Median age: 38.7 (2007); Males per 100 females: 104.2 (2007); Marriage status: 21.4% never married, 59.5% now married, 9.2% widowed, 9.9% divorced (2000); Foreign born: 0.8% (2000); Ancestry (includes multiple ancestries): 23.0% German, 11.5% Italian, 10.0% Irish, 9.0% English, 8.8% Other groups (2000).
Economy: Single-family building permits issued: 0 (2007); Multi-family building permits issued: 0 (2007); Employment by occupation: 7.4% management, 5.8% professional, 21.8% services, 25.5% sales, 1.6% farming, 10.7% construction, 27.2% production (2000).
Income: Per capita income: $16,237 (2007); Median household income: $30,921 (2007); Average household income: $40,909 (2007); Percent of households with income of $100,000 or more: 5.6% (2007); Poverty rate: 12.2% (2000).
Education: Percent of population age 25 and over with: High school diploma (including GED) or higher: 69.6% (2007); Bachelor's degree or higher: 2.3% (2007); Master's degree or higher: 1.0% (2007).

School District(s)

Indian Valley Local (PK-12)
2005-06 Enrollment: 1,868 . . . . (740) 254-4334
Housing: Homeownership rate: 76.6% (2007); Median home value: $80,250 (2007); Median rent: $369 per month (2000); Median age of housing: 60+ years (2000).
Transportation: Commute to work: 96.7% car, 0.0% public transportation, 0.8% walk, 1.6% work from home (2000); Travel time to work: 34.7% less than 15 minutes, 47.7% 15 to 30 minutes, 9.2% 30 to 45 minutes, 0.0% 45 to 60 minutes, 8.4% 60 minutes or more (2000)

MINERAL CITY (village). Aka Zoarville. Covers a land area of 0.811 square miles and a water area of 0 square miles. Located at 40.60° N. Lat.; 81.36° W. Long. Elevation is 945 feet.
Population: 755 (1990); 841 (2000); 769 (2007); 754 (2012 projected); Race: 97.3% White, 0.0% Black, 0.0% Asian, 2.6% Hispanic of any race (2007); Density: 947.9 persons per square mile (2007); Average household size: 2.70 (2007); Median age: 35.9 (2007); Males per 100 females: 100.8 (2007); Marriage status: 20.6% never married, 59.6% now married, 6.6% widowed, 13.3% divorced (2000); Foreign born: 1.1% (2000); Ancestry (includes multiple ancestries): 26.8% German, 14.0% United States or American, 12.1% Irish, 7.6% Italian, 4.7% English (2000).
Economy: Single-family building permits issued: 0 (2007); Multi-family building permits issued: 0 (2007); Employment by occupation: 2.9% management, 8.0% professional, 15.3% services, 21.7% sales, 0.8% farming, 12.6% construction, 38.6% production (2000).
Income: Per capita income: $15,673 (2007); Median household income: $39,141 (2007); Average household income: $42,289 (2007); Percent of households with income of $100,000 or more: 2.1% (2007); Poverty rate: 8.9% (2000).
Education: Percent of population age 25 and over with: High school diploma (including GED) or higher: 77.0% (2007); Bachelor's degree or higher: 4.5% (2007); Master's degree or higher: 0.8% (2007).

School District(s)

Tuscarawas Valley Local (PK-12)
2005-06 Enrollment: 1,704 . . . . (330) 859-2213

Housing: Homeownership rate: 73.0% (2007); Median home value: $77,500 (2007); Median rent: $295 per month (2000); Median age of housing: 60+ years (2000).
Transportation: Commute to work: 96.9% car, 0.0% public transportation, 1.7% walk, 1.4% work from home (2000); Travel time to work: 15.7% less than 15 minutes, 43.4% 15 to 30 minutes, 26.3% 30 to 45 minutes, 3.4% 45 to 60 minutes, 11.1% 60 minutes or more (2000)

NEW PHILADELPHIA (city). County seat. Covers a land area of 7.795 square miles and a water area of 0.140 square miles. Located at 40.48° N. Lat.; 81.44° W. Long. Elevation is 906 feet.
History: New Philadelphia was founded in 1804 by John Knisely, and settled by many Swiss-German immigrants from Pennsylvania.
Population: 16,617 (1990); 17,056 (2000); 17,070 (2007); 17,021 (2012 projected); Race: 96.1% White, 1.3% Black, 0.5% Asian, 2.1% Hispanic of any race (2007); Density: 2,189.8 persons per square mile (2007); Average household size: 2.30 (2007); Median age: 39.3 (2007); Males per 100 females: 92.4 (2007); Marriage status: 22.2% never married, 54.9% now married, 9.8% widowed, 13.1% divorced (2000); Foreign born: 1.9% (2000); Ancestry (includes multiple ancestries): 29.8% German, 14.3% Irish, 10.7% English, 7.9% United States or American, 7.8% Italian (2000).
Economy: Single-family building permits issued: 14 (2007); Multi-family building permits issued: 6 (2007); Employment by occupation: 9.7% management, 15.1% professional, 15.8% services, 25.8% sales, 0.4% farming, 8.0% construction, 25.1% production (2000).
Income: Per capita income: $21,547 (2007); Median household income: $37,528 (2007); Average household income: $49,261 (2007); Percent of households with income of $100,000 or more: 7.9% (2007); Poverty rate: 10.2% (2000).
Education: Percent of population age 25 and over with: High school diploma (including GED) or higher: 83.3% (2007); Bachelor's degree or higher: 14.9% (2007); Master's degree or higher: 4.7% (2007).

School District(s)

Buckeye (07-12)
2005-06 Enrollment: n/a .... (330) 339-2288
New Philadelphia City (PK-12)
2005-06 Enrollment: 3,104 .... (330) 364-0600
Quaker Digital Academy (KG-12)
2005-06 Enrollment: 121 .... (330) 364-0600

Two-year College(s)

Kent State University-Tuscarawas Campus (Public)
Fall 2007 Enrollment: 2,039........................ (330) 339-3391
2007-08 Tuition: In-state $4,770; Out-of-state $12,202

Vocational/Technical School(s)

Buckeye Joint Vocational School (Public)
Fall 2007 Enrollment: 118 .... (330) 308-5720
2007-08 Tuition: $6,800

Housing: Homeownership rate: 66.4% (2007); Median home value: $104,628 (2007); Median rent: $350 per month (2000); Median age of housing: 44 years (2000).
Safety: Violent crime rate: 9.7 per 10,000 population; Property crime rate: 87.6 per 10,000 population (2007).
Newspapers: The Times-Reporter (Local news; Circulation 23,693)
Transportation: Commute to work: 94.3% car, 0.1% public transportation, 1.2% walk, 2.0% work from home (2000); Travel time to work: 54.5% less than 15 minutes, 23.6% 15 to 30 minutes, 14.1% 30 to 45 minutes, 3.7% 45 to 60 minutes, 4.1% 60 minutes or more (2000)
Airports: Harry Clever Field (general aviation)
Additional Information Contacts
City of New Philadelphia .... (330) 364-4491
http://www.newphilaoh.com
Tuscarawas County Chamber of Commerce............ (330) 343-4474
http://www.tuschamber.com

NEWCOMERSTOWN (village). Covers a land area of 2.475 square miles and a water area of 0.061 square miles. Located at 40.27° N. Lat.; 81.60° W. Long. Elevation is 810 feet.
History: First called Neighbor Town when it was settled in 1815 by the Neighbor brothers from New Jersey, the town became Newcomerstown in remembrance of Chief Eagle Feather who was called "the newcomer."
Population: 4,012 (1990); 4,008 (2000); 3,722 (2007); 3,589 (2012 projected); Race: 95.6% White, 2.6% Black, 0.1% Asian, 1.2% Hispanic of any race (2007); Density: 1,504.1 persons per square mile (2007); Average household size: 2.38 (2007); Median age: 39.2 (2007); Males per 100 females: 88.9 (2007); Marriage status: 19.6% never married, 55.7% now married, 12.7% widowed, 11.9% divorced (2000); Foreign born: 0.5% (2000); Ancestry (includes multiple ancestries): 19.8% German, 12.8% Irish, 10.8% Other groups, 10.6% English, 7.7% United States or American (2000).
Economy: Single-family building permits issued: 2 (2007); Multi-family building permits issued: 0 (2007); Employment by occupation: 5.8% management, 11.7% professional, 17.0% services, 20.0% sales, 1.4% farming, 9.7% construction, 34.4% production (2000).
Income: Per capita income: $18,642 (2007); Median household income: $34,167 (2007); Average household income: $43,350 (2007); Percent of households with income of $100,000 or more: 5.1% (2007); Poverty rate: 16.0% (2000).
Education: Percent of population age 25 and over with: High school diploma (including GED) or higher: 69.4% (2007); Bachelor's degree or higher: 5.9% (2007); Master's degree or higher: 2.2% (2007).

School District(s)

Newcomerstown Exempted Village (PK-12)
2005-06 Enrollment: 1,233 .... (740) 498-8373

Housing: Homeownership rate: 67.1% (2007); Median home value: $69,826 (2007); Median rent: $280 per month (2000); Median age of housing: 56 years (2000).
Safety: Violent crime rate: 7.7 per 10,000 population; Property crime rate: 283.5 per 10,000 population (2007).
Newspapers: Newcomerstown News (Community news; Circulation 3,500)
Transportation: Commute to work: 93.4% car, 0.0% public transportation, 4.1% walk, 1.1% work from home (2000); Travel time to work: 47.9% less than 15 minutes, 18.5% 15 to 30 minutes, 20.5% 30 to 45 minutes, 6.0% 45 to 60 minutes, 7.0% 60 minutes or more (2000)

PARRAL (village). Covers a land area of 0.181 square miles and a water area of 0 square miles. Located at 40.56° N. Lat.; 81.49° W. Long. Elevation is 912 feet.
Population: 255 (1990); 241 (2000); 270 (2007); 287 (2012 projected); Race: 98.9% White, 0.0% Black, 0.0% Asian, 0.0% Hispanic of any race (2007); Density: 1,492.4 persons per square mile (2007); Average household size: 2.25 (2007); Median age: 43.1 (2007); Males per 100 females: 114.3 (2007); Marriage status: 14.0% never married, 67.4% now married, 4.7% widowed, 14.0% divorced (2000); Foreign born: 0.0% (2000); Ancestry (includes multiple ancestries): 32.2% German, 12.0% Italian, 12.0% Irish, 11.6% United States or American, 10.7% Swiss (2000).
Economy: Single-family building permits issued: 0 (2007); Multi-family building permits issued: 0 (2007); Employment by occupation: 4.0% management, 12.8% professional, 13.6% services, 24.0% sales, 3.2% farming, 20.8% construction, 21.6% production (2000).
Income: Per capita income: $19,213 (2007); Median household income: $40,625 (2007); Average household income: $43,229 (2007); Percent of households with income of $100,000 or more: 2.5% (2007); Poverty rate: 7.0% (2000).
Education: Percent of population age 25 and over with: High school diploma (including GED) or higher: 90.4% (2007); Bachelor's degree or higher: 9.1% (2007); Master's degree or higher: 3.2% (2007).
Housing: Homeownership rate: 81.7% (2007); Median home value: $106,818 (2007); Median rent: $455 per month (2000); Median age of housing: 47 years (2000).
Transportation: Commute to work: 98.4% car, 0.0% public transportation, 0.0% walk, 0.0% work from home (2000); Travel time to work: 36.8% less than 15 minutes, 36.8% 15 to 30 minutes, 22.4% 30 to 45 minutes, 1.6% 45 to 60 minutes, 2.4% 60 minutes or more (2000)

PORT WASHINGTON (village). Covers a land area of 0.506 square miles and a water area of 0 square miles. Located at 40.32° N. Lat.; 81.52° W. Long. Elevation is 820 feet.
History: Port Washington was once a shipping center on the Ohio & Erie Canal. Nearby was the settlement of Salem, established in 1780 for members of the Lichtenau community.
Population: 513 (1990); 552 (2000); 539 (2007); 533 (2012 projected); Race: 97.0% White, 0.0% Black, 0.0% Asian, 2.2% Hispanic of any race (2007); Density: 1,065.5 persons per square mile (2007); Average household size: 2.71 (2007); Median age: 39.2 (2007); Males per 100 females: 98.9 (2007); Marriage status: 19.0% never married, 66.4% now married, 4.2% widowed, 10.4% divorced (2000); Foreign born: 0.4% (2000); Ancestry (includes multiple ancestries): 29.8% German, 10.2% United States or American, 9.5% Irish, 7.5% Other groups, 5.5% English (2000).

Economy: Single-family building permits issued: 2 (2007); Multi-family building permits issued: 0 (2007); Employment by occupation: 2.9% management, 13.2% professional, 11.8% services, 23.9% sales, 1.1% farming, 11.0% construction, 36.0% production (2000).
Income: Per capita income: $16,206 (2007); Median household income: $42,813 (2007); Average household income: $43,894 (2007); Percent of households with income of $100,000 or more: 1.5% (2007); Poverty rate: 6.1% (2000).
Education: Percent of population age 25 and over with: High school diploma (including GED) or higher: 77.5% (2007); Bachelor's degree or higher: 6.0% (2007); Master's degree or higher: 1.4% (2007).

School District(s)

Indian Valley Local (PK-12)
2005-06 Enrollment: 1,868 .... (740) 254-4334

Housing: Homeownership rate: 80.4% (2007); Median home value: $80,000 (2007); Median rent: $332 per month (2000); Median age of housing: 60+ years (2000).
Transportation: Commute to work: 92.5% car, 1.1% public transportation, 1.5% walk, 1.5% work from home (2000); Travel time to work: 31.4% less than 15 minutes, 29.5% 15 to 30 minutes, 27.3% 30 to 45 minutes, 3.4% 45 to 60 minutes, 8.3% 60 minutes or more (2000)

ROSWELL (village). Covers a land area of 0.272 square miles and a water area of 0 square miles. Located at 40.47° N. Lat.; 81.35° W. Long. Elevation is 945 feet.
Population: 257 (1990); 276 (2000); 307 (2007); 326 (2012 projected); Race: 98.7% White, 0.0% Black, 0.0% Asian, 0.0% Hispanic of any race (2007); Density: 1,128.0 persons per square mile (2007); Average household size: 2.95 (2007); Median age: 34.1 (2007); Males per 100 females: 98.1 (2007); Marriage status: 26.5% never married, 62.1% now married, 2.4% widowed, 9.0% divorced (2000); Foreign born: 0.0% (2000); Ancestry (includes multiple ancestries): 23.7% German, 17.3% Italian, 14.8% English, 12.7% Irish, 11.7% United States or American (2000).
Economy: Employment by occupation: 6.7% management, 5.7% professional, 17.1% services, 17.1% sales, 0.0% farming, 8.6% construction, 44.8% production (2000).
Income: Per capita income: $13,208 (2007); Median household income: $31,429 (2007); Average household income: $38,990 (2007); Percent of households with income of $100,000 or more: 4.8% (2007); Poverty rate: 21.6% (2000).
Education: Percent of population age 25 and over with: High school diploma (including GED) or higher: 57.5% (2007); Bachelor's degree or higher: 2.7% (2007); Master's degree or higher: 1.1% (2007).
Housing: Homeownership rate: 80.8% (2007); Median home value: $61,429 (2007); Median rent: $329 per month (2000); Median age of housing: 59 years (2000).
Transportation: Commute to work: 95.2% car, 0.0% public transportation, 2.9% walk, 1.9% work from home (2000); Travel time to work: 10.7% less than 15 minutes, 64.1% 15 to 30 minutes, 8.7% 30 to 45 minutes, 16.5% 45 to 60 minutes, 0.0% 60 minutes or more (2000)

STONE CREEK (village). Covers a land area of 0.431 square miles and a water area of <.001 square miles. Located at 40.39° N. Lat.; 81.55° W. Long. Elevation is 942 feet.
History: Stone Creek was laid out in 1854 by Phillip Leonard, and first called Phillipsburg. Settlers had come here as early as 1837 from Pennsylvania. The town grew around the iron ore mined in the area, and the clay used in brick plants. Early Swiss settlers also started a Swiss cheese industry.
Population: 181 (1990); 184 (2000); 180 (2007); 171 (2012 projected); Race: 100.0% White, 0.0% Black, 0.0% Asian, 0.0% Hispanic of any race (2007); Density: 417.6 persons per square mile (2007); Average household size: 2.73 (2007); Median age: 34.2 (2007); Males per 100 females: 102.2 (2007); Marriage status: 16.4% never married, 59.0% now married, 15.6% widowed, 9.0% divorced (2000); Foreign born: 0.0% (2000); Ancestry (includes multiple ancestries): 40.6% German, 15.0% United States or American, 10.0% English, 9.4% Irish, 4.4% Other groups (2000).
Economy: Single-family building permits issued: 0 (2007); Multi-family building permits issued: 0 (2007); Employment by occupation: 6.0% management, 7.5% professional, 19.4% services, 28.4% sales, 0.0% farming, 20.9% construction, 17.9% production (2000).
Income: Per capita income: $17,417 (2007); Median household income: $34,167 (2007); Average household income: $47,500 (2007); Percent of households with income of $100,000 or more: 9.1% (2007); Poverty rate: 8.8% (2000).
Education: Percent of population age 25 and over with: High school diploma (including GED) or higher: 78.1% (2007); Bachelor's degree or higher: 11.4% (2007); Master's degree or higher: 0.0% (2007).
Housing: Homeownership rate: 78.8% (2007); Median home value: $81,111 (2007); Median rent: $342 per month (2000); Median age of housing: 60+ years (2000).
Transportation: Commute to work: 97.0% car, 0.0% public transportation, 0.0% walk, 0.0% work from home (2000); Travel time to work: 14.9% less than 15 minutes, 53.7% 15 to 30 minutes, 9.0% 30 to 45 minutes, 17.9% 45 to 60 minutes, 4.5% 60 minutes or more (2000)

STRASBURG (village). Covers a land area of 1.193 square miles and a water area of 0 square miles. Located at 40.59° N. Lat.; 81.52° W. Long. Elevation is 912 feet.
History: Strasburg was notable as the location of the Garver Brothers Store, founded in 1866 by Phillip A. Garver. When his sons, Rudolph and Albert, took over the store in the 1880's, they made it the focal point of the community by keeping a card index record of every man, woman, and child living within 18 miles of Strasburg, and anticipating their needs.
Population: 2,032 (1990); 2,310 (2000); 2,371 (2007); 2,405 (2012 projected); Race: 97.1% White, 0.1% Black, 0.2% Asian, 3.2% Hispanic of any race (2007); Density: 1,987.9 persons per square mile (2007); Average household size: 2.40 (2007); Median age: 37.9 (2007); Males per 100 females: 95.1 (2007); Marriage status: 20.6% never married, 62.2% now married, 6.1% widowed, 11.1% divorced (2000); Foreign born: 1.3% (2000); Ancestry (includes multiple ancestries): 38.7% German, 11.9% Irish, 10.3% English, 8.1% United States or American, 6.0% Italian (2000).
Economy: Single-family building permits issued: 2 (2007); Multi-family building permits issued: 2 (2007); Employment by occupation: 8.7% management, 14.7% professional, 16.8% services, 23.5% sales, 0.3% farming, 8.1% construction, 28.1% production (2000).
Income: Per capita income: $19,182 (2007); Median household income: $41,356 (2007); Average household income: $46,123 (2007); Percent of households with income of $100,000 or more: 5.9% (2007); Poverty rate: 8.2% (2000).
Education: Percent of population age 25 and over with: High school diploma (including GED) or higher: 83.5% (2007); Bachelor's degree or higher: 11.3% (2007); Master's degree or higher: 3.5% (2007).

School District(s)

Strasburg-Franklin Local (PK-12)
2005-06 Enrollment: 714 .... (330) 878-5571

Housing: Homeownership rate: 63.1% (2007); Median home value: $107,917 (2007); Median rent: $360 per month (2000); Median age of housing: 41 years (2000).
Safety: Violent crime rate: 14.8 per 10,000 population; Property crime rate: 388.3 per 10,000 population (2007).
Transportation: Commute to work: 95.0% car, 0.0% public transportation, 2.1% walk, 2.4% work from home (2000); Travel time to work: 31.5% less than 15 minutes, 41.5% 15 to 30 minutes, 19.0% 30 to 45 minutes, 3.9% 45 to 60 minutes, 4.1% 60 minutes or more (2000)

SUGARCREEK (village). Aka Sugar Creek Station. Covers a land area of 3.799 square miles and a water area of 0 square miles. Located at 40.50° N. Lat.; 81.64° W. Long. Elevation is 1,004 feet.
Population: 2,296 (1990); 2,174 (2000); 2,144 (2007); 2,140 (2012 projected); Race: 99.0% White, 0.2% Black, 0.5% Asian, 0.1% Hispanic of any race (2007); Density: 564.3 persons per square mile (2007); Average household size: 2.48 (2007); Median age: 37.6 (2007); Males per 100 females: 96.3 (2007); Marriage status: 19.9% never married, 68.2% now married, 8.9% widowed, 2.9% divorced (2000); Foreign born: 0.0% (2000); Ancestry (includes multiple ancestries): 40.4% German, 16.7% Swiss, 10.2% United States or American, 7.2% Irish, 6.4% English (2000).
Economy: Single-family building permits issued: 12 (2007); Multi-family building permits issued: 0 (2007); Employment by occupation: 9.7% management, 12.0% professional, 12.8% services, 32.5% sales, 0.5% farming, 9.0% construction, 23.5% production (2000).
Income: Per capita income: $19,030 (2007); Median household income: $42,112 (2007); Average household income: $47,168 (2007); Percent of households with income of $100,000 or more: 7.4% (2007); Poverty rate: 7.2% (2000).
Education: Percent of population age 25 and over with: High school diploma (including GED) or higher: 70.4% (2007); Bachelor's degree or higher: 12.9% (2007); Master's degree or higher: 5.0% (2007).

School District(s)

Garaway Local (PK-12)
2005-06 Enrollment: 1,271 . . . . (330) 852-2421

Housing: Homeownership rate: 72.0% (2007); Median home value: $117,886 (2007); Median rent: $346 per month (2000); Median age of housing: 39 years (2000).

Newspapers: Sugarcreek Budget (Local news; Circulation 20,000)

Transportation: Commute to work: 92.7% car, 0.0% public transportation, 4.2% walk, 2.0% work from home (2000); Travel time to work: 51.7% less than 15 minutes, 31.2% 15 to 30 minutes, 6.1% 30 to 45 minutes, 5.7% 45 to 60 minutes, 5.2% 60 minutes or more (2000)

Additional Information Contacts

Bellbrook-Sugarcreek Area Chamber of Commerce . . . . . . (937) 848-4930
http://www.bellbrooksugarcreekchamber.com

TUSCARAWAS (village). Covers a land area of 0.709 square miles and a water area of 0.020 square miles. Located at 40.39° N. Lat.; 81.40° W. Long. Elevation is 850 feet.

Population: 879 (1990); 934 (2000); 900 (2007); 895 (2012 projected); Race: 98.6% White, 0.0% Black, 0.3% Asian, 0.0% Hispanic of any race (2007); Density: 1,270.1 persons per square mile (2007); Average household size: 2.46 (2007); Median age: 42.0 (2007); Males per 100 females: 94.0 (2007); Marriage status: 19.5% never married, 61.1% now married, 9.0% widowed, 10.4% divorced (2000); Foreign born: 0.4% (2000); Ancestry (includes multiple ancestries): 32.0% German, 11.8% Irish, 11.7% English, 8.1% United States or American, 6.9% Italian (2000).

Economy: Single-family building permits issued: 3 (2007); Multi-family building permits issued: 0 (2007); Employment by occupation: 7.2% management, 9.6% professional, 19.2% services, 24.0% sales, 0.0% farming, 9.6% construction, 30.5% production (2000).

Income: Per capita income: $18,922 (2007); Median household income: $41,087 (2007); Average household income: $46,530 (2007); Percent of households with income of $100,000 or more: 4.1% (2007); Poverty rate: 7.4% (2000).

Education: Percent of population age 25 and over with: High school diploma (including GED) or higher: 81.2% (2007); Bachelor's degree or higher: 7.7% (2007); Master's degree or higher: 1.7% (2007).

School District(s)

Indian Valley Local (PK-12)
2005-06 Enrollment: 1,868 . . . . (740) 254-4334

Housing: Homeownership rate: 83.9% (2007); Median home value: $102,896 (2007); Median rent: $338 per month (2000); Median age of housing: 47 years (2000).

Transportation: Commute to work: 94.7% car, 0.4% public transportation, 1.3% walk, 2.9% work from home (2000); Travel time to work: 36.0% less than 15 minutes, 45.4% 15 to 30 minutes, 8.7% 30 to 45 minutes, 4.8% 45 to 60 minutes, 5.0% 60 minutes or more (2000)

UHRICHSVILLE (city). Covers a land area of 2.858 square miles and a water area of 0.007 square miles. Located at 40.39° N. Lat.; 81.34° W. Long. Elevation is 856 feet.

History: Uhrichsville was settled in 1804 by Michael Uhrich of Pennsylvania, who purchased land in the area and built a flour mill. The town was platted in 1833 and became a center for the manufacture of vitrified clay products.

Population: 5,616 (1990); 5,662 (2000); 5,518 (2007); 5,369 (2012 projected); Race: 97.4% White, 1.0% Black, 0.1% Asian, 1.1% Hispanic of any race (2007); Density: 1,930.5 persons per square mile (2007); Average household size: 2.48 (2007); Median age: 35.5 (2007); Males per 100 females: 93.4 (2007); Marriage status: 21.1% never married, 55.3% now married, 9.9% widowed, 13.7% divorced (2000); Foreign born: 1.0% (2000); Ancestry (includes multiple ancestries): 22.3% German, 13.6% Irish, 10.0% United States or American, 9.9% Other groups, 8.7% English (2000).

Economy: Single-family building permits issued: 6 (2007); Multi-family building permits issued: 0 (2007); Employment by occupation: 6.5% management, 8.9% professional, 18.5% services, 21.8% sales, 0.0% farming, 9.9% construction, 34.5% production (2000).

Income: Per capita income: $15,021 (2007); Median household income: $30,993 (2007); Average household income: $37,088 (2007); Percent of households with income of $100,000 or more: 3.6% (2007); Poverty rate: 14.6% (2000).

Education: Percent of population age 25 and over with: High school diploma (including GED) or higher: 76.4% (2007); Bachelor's degree or higher: 6.2% (2007); Master's degree or higher: 3.7% (2007).

School District(s)

Claymont City (PK-12)
2005-06 Enrollment: 2,267 . . . . (740) 922-5478

Housing: Homeownership rate: 65.5% (2007); Median home value: $76,100 (2007); Median rent: $319 per month (2000); Median age of housing: 59 years (2000).

Safety: Violent crime rate: 3.6 per 10,000 population; Property crime rate: 387.7 per 10,000 population (2007).

Transportation: Commute to work: 96.2% car, 0.2% public transportation, 3.3% walk, 0.3% work from home (2000); Travel time to work: 40.0% less than 15 minutes, 32.3% 15 to 30 minutes, 10.9% 30 to 45 minutes, 9.8% 45 to 60 minutes, 7.0% 60 minutes or more (2000)

Additional Information Contacts

Twin City Chamber of Commerce . . . . (740) 922-5623
http://www.twincitychamber.org

ZOAR (village). Covers a land area of 0.550 square miles and a water area of 0.091 square miles. Located at 40.61° N. Lat.; 81.42° W. Long. Elevation is 902 feet.

History: Named for the biblical city to which Lot fled after leaving Sodom, Zoar was settled in 1817 by a group of Separatists from southern Germany who came seeking religious freedom. They established a communal corporation, chartered in 1832 as the Separatist Society of Zoar, which prospered for 80 years.

Population: 177 (1990); 193 (2000); 190 (2007); 186 (2012 projected); Race: 97.4% White, 0.0% Black, 1.6% Asian, 1.1% Hispanic of any race (2007); Density: 345.3 persons per square mile (2007); Average household size: 2.38 (2007); Median age: 51.0 (2007); Males per 100 females: 90.0 (2007); Marriage status: 15.2% never married, 62.9% now married, 9.9% widowed, 11.9% divorced (2000); Foreign born: 1.0% (2000); Ancestry (includes multiple ancestries): 39.1% German, 16.2% Irish, 11.7% English, 6.6% United States or American, 6.6% Italian (2000).

Economy: Single-family building permits issued: 1 (2007); Multi-family building permits issued: 0 (2007); Employment by occupation: 15.1% management, 26.7% professional, 16.3% services, 15.1% sales, 0.0% farming, 3.5% construction, 23.3% production (2000).

Income: Per capita income: $28,066 (2007); Median household income: $53,636 (2007); Average household income: $66,656 (2007); Percent of households with income of $100,000 or more: 18.8% (2007); Poverty rate: 3.6% (2000).

Education: Percent of population age 25 and over with: High school diploma (including GED) or higher: 92.4% (2007); Bachelor's degree or higher: 24.8% (2007); Master's degree or higher: 9.0% (2007).

Housing: Homeownership rate: 87.5% (2007); Median home value: $187,500 (2007); Median rent: $400 per month (2000); Median age of housing: 44 years (2000).

Transportation: Commute to work: 96.4% car, 0.0% public transportation, 0.0% walk, 0.0% work from home (2000); Travel time to work: 27.4% less than 15 minutes, 52.4% 15 to 30 minutes, 16.7% 30 to 45 minutes, 1.2% 45 to 60 minutes, 2.4% 60 minutes or more (2000)

Union County

Located in central Ohio; drained by Darby Creek. Covers a land area of 436.65 square miles, a water area of 0.33 square miles, and is located in the Eastern Time Zone. The county was founded in 1820. County seat is Marysville.

Union County is part of the Columbus, OH Metropolitan Statistical Area. The entire metro area includes: Delaware County, OH; Fairfield County, OH; Franklin County, OH; Licking County, OH; Madison County, OH; Morrow County, OH; Pickaway County, OH; Union County, OH

Weather Station: Irwin Elevation: 1,007 feet

	Jan	Feb	Mar	Apr	May	Jun	Jul	Aug	Sep	Oct	Nov	Dec
High	35	40	52	64	74	82	86	84	78	67	52	40
Low	17	20	29	38	49	58	61	59	52	41	33	23
Precip	2.3	1.9	2.6	3.5	4.1	4.3	4.7	3.7	2.9	2.6	3.1	2.7
Snow	6.8	4.5	2.5	0.8	tr	0.0	0.0	0.0	0.0	tr	1.0	na

High and Low temperatures in degrees Fahrenheit; Precipitation and Snow in inches

Weather Station: Marysville Elevation: 997 feet

	Jan	Feb	Mar	Apr	May	Jun	Jul	Aug	Sep	Oct	Nov	Dec
High	34	38	49	61	72	80	84	82	76	63	50	39
Low	18	21	29	39	50	59	63	61	54	42	33	24
Precip	2.3	1.9	2.6	3.4	3.9	4.3	4.1	3.3	2.6	2.4	3.0	2.7
Snow	6.5	4.8	3.3	0.9	0.0	0.0	0.0	0.0	0.0	tr	1.1	3.6

High and Low temperatures in degrees Fahrenheit; Precipitation and Snow in inches

Population: 31,969 (1990); 40,909 (2000); 47,092 (2007); 51,232 (2012 projected); Race: 94.4% White, 3.1% Black, 1.0% Asian, 1.2% Hispanic of any race (2007); Density: 107.8 persons per square mile (2007); Average household size: 2.83 (2007); Median age: 35.9 (2007); Males per 100 females: 93.2 (2007).
Religion: Five largest groups: 8.8% The United Methodist Church, 4.8% Lutheran Church—Missouri Synod, 4.6% Evangelical Lutheran Church in America, 3.8% Catholic Church, 2.4% Presbyterian Church (U.S.A.) (2000).
Economy: Unemployment rate: 5.4% (6/2008); Total civilian labor force: 26,159 (6/2008); Leading industries: 34.9% manufacturing; 9.8% administration, support, waste management, remediation services; 9.6% professional, scientific & technical services (2005); Farms: 1,021 totaling 256,024 acres (2002); Companies that employ 500 or more persons: 6 (2006); Companies that employ 100 to 499 persons: 22 (2006); Companies that employ less than 100 persons: 918 (2006); Black-owned businesses: n/a (2002); Hispanic-owned businesses: n/a (2002); Asian-owned businesses: n/a (2002); Women-owned businesses: 798 (2002); Retail sales per capita: $11,250 (2008). Single-family building permits issued: 221 (2007); Multi-family building permits issued: 0 (2007).
Income: Per capita income: $24,630 (2007); Median household income: $60,980 (2007); Average household income: $68,595 (2007); Percent of households with income of $100,000 or more: 19.4% (2007); Poverty rate: 6.2% (2005); Bankruptcy rate: 3.64% (2007).
Taxes: Total county taxes per capita: $437 (2006); County property taxes per capita: $262 (2006).
Education: Percent of population age 25 and over with: High school diploma (including GED) or higher: 86.4% (2007); Bachelor's degree or higher: 16.6% (2007); Master's degree or higher: 4.2% (2007).
Housing: Homeownership rate: 78.2% (2007); Median home value: $159,605 (2007); Median rent: $455 per month (2000); Median age of housing: 27 years (2000).
Health: Birth rate: 159.6 per 10,000 population (2007); Death rate: 64.8 per 10,000 population (2007); Age-adjusted cancer mortality rate: 238.0 deaths per 100,000 population (2005); Number of physicians: 9.7 per 10,000 population (2005); Hospital beds: 18.1 per 10,000 population (2004); Hospital admissions: 652.2 per 10,000 population (2004).
Elections: 2004 Presidential election results: 70.1% Bush, 29.5% Kerry, 0.0% Nader, 0.3% Badnarik
Additional Information Contacts
Union County Government . . . . (937) 645-3012
http://www.co.union.oh.us
City of Marysville . . . . (937) 642-6015
http://www.marysvilleohio.org

Union County Communities

IRWIN (unincorporated postal area, zip code 43029). Covers a land area of 23.353 square miles and a water area of 0 square miles. Located at 40.10° N. Lat.; 83.44° W. Long. Elevation is 1,012 feet.
Population: 621 (2000); Race: 99.2% White, 0.0% Black, 0.0% Asian, 0.0% Hispanic of any race (2000); Density: 26.6 persons per square mile (2000); Age: 32.9% under 18, 3.4% over 64 (2000); Marriage status: 38.9% never married, 57.3% now married, 1.7% widowed, 2.1% divorced (2000); Foreign born: 0.0% (2000); Ancestry (includes multiple ancestries): 37.5% German, 9.5% United States or American, 9.3% Hungarian, 8.3% Swiss, 6.6% English (2000).
Economy: Employment by occupation: 21.2% management, 4.3% professional, 12.2% services, 36.5% sales, 0.0% farming, 7.8% construction, 18.0% production (2000).
Income: Per capita income: $14,205 (2000); Median household income: $44,583 (2000); Poverty rate: 0.0% (2000).
Education: Percent of population age 25 and over with: High school diploma (including GED) or higher: 82.6% (2000); Bachelor's degree or higher: 21.8% (2000).

Two-year College(s)
Rosedale Bible College
Fall 2007 Enrollment: 81 . . . . (740) 857-1311
2007-08 Tuition: In-state $6,355; Out-of-state $6,355
Housing: Homeownership rate: 65.3% (2000); Median home value: $133,000 (2000); Median rent: $321 per month (2000); Median age of housing: 44 years (2000).
Transportation: Commute to work: 85.4% car, 0.0% public transportation, 6.5% walk, 6.8% work from home (2000); Travel time to work: 22.4% less than 15 minutes, 45.4% 15 to 30 minutes, 12.1% 30 to 45 minutes, 18.5% 45 to 60 minutes, 1.6% 60 minutes or more (2000)

MAGNETIC SPRINGS (village). Covers a land area of 0.244 square miles and a water area of 0 square miles. Located at 40.35° N. Lat.; 83.26° W. Long. Elevation is 932 feet.
Population: 373 (1990); 323 (2000); 307 (2007); 307 (2012 projected); Race: 96.4% White, 0.0% Black, 1.0% Asian, 0.0% Hispanic of any race (2007); Density: 1,259.4 persons per square mile (2007); Average household size: 2.74 (2007); Median age: 32.6 (2007); Males per 100 females: 107.4 (2007); Marriage status: 30.1% never married, 51.0% now married, 6.4% widowed, 12.4% divorced (2000); Foreign born: 0.3% (2000); Ancestry (includes multiple ancestries): 13.8% English, 13.8% German, 11.5% United States or American, 8.2% Irish, 5.6% Italian (2000).
Economy: Employment by occupation: 7.2% management, 10.5% professional, 21.6% services, 7.8% sales, 1.3% farming, 13.7% construction, 37.9% production (2000).
Income: Per capita income: $19,251 (2007); Median household income: $47,500 (2007); Average household income: $52,768 (2007); Percent of households with income of $100,000 or more: 8.0% (2007); Poverty rate: 6.0% (2000).
Education: Percent of population age 25 and over with: High school diploma (including GED) or higher: 73.2% (2007); Bachelor's degree or higher: 5.2% (2007); Master's degree or higher: 0.0% (2007).
School District(s)
North Union Local (PK-12)
2005-06 Enrollment: 1,491 . . . . (740) 943-2509
Housing: Homeownership rate: 58.9% (2007); Median home value: $97,143 (2007); Median rent: $370 per month (2000); Median age of housing: 60+ years (2000).
Transportation: Commute to work: 96.0% car, 0.0% public transportation, 4.0% walk, 0.0% work from home (2000); Travel time to work: 16.8% less than 15 minutes, 53.0% 15 to 30 minutes, 13.4% 30 to 45 minutes, 13.4% 45 to 60 minutes, 3.4% 60 minutes or more (2000)

MARYSVILLE (city). County seat. Covers a land area of 15.526 square miles and a water area of 0.076 square miles. Located at 40.23° N. Lat.; 83.36° W. Long. Elevation is 991 feet.
History: Marysville was settled in 1816 by Jonathan Summers, and platted in 1820 by Samuel Culbertson, who named the town for his daughter. The log cabin that became a symbol of William Henry Harrison's presidential campaign of 1840 came from Marysville.
Population: 11,003 (1990); 15,942 (2000); 18,330 (2007); 19,942 (2012 projected); Race: 89.9% White, 6.7% Black, 1.8% Asian, 1.5% Hispanic of any race (2007); Density: 1,180.6 persons per square mile (2007); Average household size: 2.86 (2007); Median age: 33.3 (2007); Males per 100 females: 79.5 (2007); Marriage status: 24.0% never married, 56.4% now married, 6.1% widowed, 13.6% divorced (2000); Foreign born: 1.3% (2000); Ancestry (includes multiple ancestries): 28.2% German, 13.3% Irish, 12.8% Other groups, 10.3% English, 10.2% United States or American (2000).
Economy: Employment by occupation: 10.9% management, 17.0% professional, 12.4% services, 28.1% sales, 0.3% farming, 7.0% construction, 24.3% production (2000).
Income: Per capita income: $21,897 (2007); Median household income: $54,486 (2007); Average household income: $60,003 (2007); Percent of households with income of $100,000 or more: 13.8% (2007); Poverty rate: 5.7% (2000).
Education: Percent of population age 25 and over with: High school diploma (including GED) or higher: 84.1% (2007); Bachelor's degree or higher: 17.6% (2007); Master's degree or higher: 3.3% (2007).
School District(s)
Marysville Digital Academy (01-12)
2005-06 Enrollment: 64 . . . . (937) 642-0010
Marysville Exempted Village (PK-12)
2005-06 Enrollment: 5,023 . . . . (937) 644-8105

Housing: Homeownership rate: 65.2% (2007); Median home value: $151,169 (2007); Median rent: $471 per month (2000); Median age of housing: 20 years (2000).
Hospitals: Memorial Hospital (82 beds)
Safety: Violent crime rate: 2.2 per 10,000 population; Property crime rate: 190.7 per 10,000 population (2007).
Newspapers: Marysville Journal Tribune (Local news; Circulation 6,200)
Transportation: Commute to work: 95.2% car, 0.2% public transportation, 1.8% walk, 2.1% work from home (2000); Travel time to work: 41.0% less than 15 minutes, 33.7% 15 to 30 minutes, 16.4% 30 to 45 minutes, 5.3% 45 to 60 minutes, 3.7% 60 minutes or more (2000)
Airports: Union County (general aviation)
Additional Information Contacts
City of Marysville . . . . (937) 642-6015
http://www.marysvilleohio.org

MILFORD CENTER (village). Covers a land area of 0.354 square miles and a water area of 0 square miles. Located at 40.17° N. Lat.; 83.43° W. Long. Elevation is 994 feet.
Population: 651 (1990); 626 (2000); 660 (2007); 679 (2012 projected); Race: 98.6% White, 0.0% Black, 0.0% Asian, 0.8% Hispanic of any race (2007); Density: 1,867.0 persons per square mile (2007); Average household size: 2.64 (2007); Median age: 35.9 (2007); Males per 100 females: 103.1 (2007); Marriage status: 22.2% never married, 57.6% now married, 10.1% widowed, 10.1% divorced (2000); Foreign born: 0.0% (2000); Ancestry (includes multiple ancestries): 29.4% German, 19.2% United States or American, 11.9% English, 9.0% Irish, 8.5% Other groups (2000).
Economy: Employment by occupation: 7.3% management, 6.4% professional, 22.4% services, 23.6% sales, 0.0% farming, 10.5% construction, 29.7% production (2000).
Income: Per capita income: $20,833 (2007); Median household income: $47,308 (2007); Average household income: $55,000 (2007); Percent of households with income of $100,000 or more: 10.8% (2007); Poverty rate: 1.0% (2000).
Education: Percent of population age 25 and over with: High school diploma (including GED) or higher: 79.0% (2007); Bachelor's degree or higher: 4.7% (2007); Master's degree or higher: 2.0% (2007).

School District(s)

Fairbanks Local (PK-12)
2005-06 Enrollment: 990 . . . . (937) 349-3731
Housing: Homeownership rate: 82.8% (2007); Median home value: $94,773 (2007); Median rent: $486 per month (2000); Median age of housing: 60+ years (2000).
Transportation: Commute to work: 91.8% car, 0.7% public transportation, 2.9% walk, 2.6% work from home (2000); Travel time to work: 27.2% less than 15 minutes, 44.6% 15 to 30 minutes, 17.4% 30 to 45 minutes, 7.0% 45 to 60 minutes, 3.7% 60 minutes or more (2000)

RAYMOND (unincorporated postal area, zip code 43067). Aka Raymonds. Covers a land area of 30.775 square miles and a water area of 0.036 square miles. Located at 40.35° N. Lat.; 83.46° W. Long. Elevation is 1,030 feet.
Population: 1,537 (2000); Race: 100.0% White, 0.0% Black, 0.0% Asian, 0.0% Hispanic of any race (2000); Density: 49.9 persons per square mile (2000); Age: 31.6% under 18, 6.9% over 64 (2000); Marriage status: 16.1% never married, 69.8% now married, 2.7% widowed, 11.4% divorced (2000); Foreign born: 0.9% (2000); Ancestry (includes multiple ancestries): 20.8% United States or American, 16.7% German, 7.1% Irish, 6.5% Other groups, 4.4% Scottish (2000).
Economy: Employment by occupation: 4.8% management, 10.5% professional, 13.0% services, 25.9% sales, 1.5% farming, 11.6% construction, 32.6% production (2000).
Income: Per capita income: $18,194 (2000); Median household income: $52,138 (2000); Poverty rate: 5.4% (2000).
Education: Percent of population age 25 and over with: High school diploma (including GED) or higher: 87.6% (2000); Bachelor's degree or higher: 6.4% (2000).

School District(s)

Marysville Exempted Village (PK-12)
2005-06 Enrollment: 5,023 . . . . (937) 644-8105
Housing: Homeownership rate: 89.9% (2000); Median home value: $99,500 (2000); Median rent: $521 per month (2000); Median age of housing: 39 years (2000).
Transportation: Commute to work: 97.8% car, 0.0% public transportation, 1.3% walk, 0.9% work from home (2000); Travel time to work: 26.9% less than 15 minutes, 50.9% 15 to 30 minutes, 10.0% 30 to 45 minutes, 6.9% 45 to 60 minutes, 5.4% 60 minutes or more (2000)

RICHWOOD (village). Covers a land area of 1.201 square miles and a water area of 0.019 square miles. Located at 40.42° N. Lat.; 83.29° W. Long. Elevation is 951 feet.
Population: 2,232 (1990); 2,156 (2000); 2,309 (2007); 2,401 (2012 projected); Race: 97.9% White, 0.2% Black, 0.1% Asian, 0.5% Hispanic of any race (2007); Density: 1,922.6 persons per square mile (2007); Average household size: 2.56 (2007); Median age: 33.7 (2007); Males per 100 females: 92.1 (2007); Marriage status: 21.0% never married, 57.7% now married, 10.7% widowed, 10.6% divorced (2000); Foreign born: 0.5% (2000); Ancestry (includes multiple ancestries): 19.5% German, 15.6% United States or American, 12.5% Irish, 7.7% Other groups, 6.8% English (2000).
Economy: Employment by occupation: 7.2% management, 11.7% professional, 20.1% services, 21.4% sales, 0.6% farming, 10.2% construction, 29.0% production (2000).
Income: Per capita income: $20,069 (2007); Median household income: $46,364 (2007); Average household income: $51,375 (2007); Percent of households with income of $100,000 or more: 8.8% (2007); Poverty rate: 8.4% (2000).
Education: Percent of population age 25 and over with: High school diploma (including GED) or higher: 81.7% (2007); Bachelor's degree or higher: 6.9% (2007); Master's degree or higher: 2.1% (2007).

School District(s)

North Union Local (PK-12)
2005-06 Enrollment: 1,491 . . . . (740) 943-2509
Housing: Homeownership rate: 68.4% (2007); Median home value: $103,795 (2007); Median rent: $340 per month (2000); Median age of housing: 55 years (2000).
Newspapers: The Richwood Gazette (Community news; Circulation 2,400)
Transportation: Commute to work: 94.7% car, 0.2% public transportation, 3.7% walk, 1.4% work from home (2000); Travel time to work: 22.6% less than 15 minutes, 41.0% 15 to 30 minutes, 22.9% 30 to 45 minutes, 7.9% 45 to 60 minutes, 5.6% 60 minutes or more (2000)

UNIONVILLE CENTER (village). Aka Unionville. Covers a land area of 0.160 square miles and a water area of 0 square miles. Located at 40.13° N. Lat.; 83.34° W. Long. Elevation is 971 feet.
Population: 238 (1990); 299 (2000); 323 (2007); 337 (2012 projected); Race: 99.7% White, 0.0% Black, 0.0% Asian, 1.5% Hispanic of any race (2007); Density: 2,024.9 persons per square mile (2007); Average household size: 2.65 (2007); Median age: 39.1 (2007); Males per 100 females: 105.7 (2007); Marriage status: 13.0% never married, 72.5% now married, 6.7% widowed, 7.8% divorced (2000); Foreign born: 0.0% (2000); Ancestry (includes multiple ancestries): 25.3% German, 20.8% Irish, 13.0% Other groups, 6.3% Dutch, 5.9% United States or American (2000).
Economy: Employment by occupation: 7.2% management, 2.9% professional, 15.1% services, 30.9% sales, 0.0% farming, 15.1% construction, 28.8% production (2000).
Income: Per capita income: $20,232 (2007); Median household income: $51,053 (2007); Average household income: $53,566 (2007); Percent of households with income of $100,000 or more: 4.9% (2007); Poverty rate: 6.3% (2000).
Education: Percent of population age 25 and over with: High school diploma (including GED) or higher: 84.5% (2007); Bachelor's degree or higher: 2.8% (2007); Master's degree or higher: 0.9% (2007).
Housing: Homeownership rate: 84.4% (2007); Median home value: $104,276 (2007); Median rent: $317 per month (2000); Median age of housing: 60+ years (2000).
Transportation: Commute to work: 97.0% car, 0.0% public transportation, 1.5% walk, 0.0% work from home (2000); Travel time to work: 18.5% less than 15 minutes, 31.9% 15 to 30 minutes, 35.6% 30 to 45 minutes, 11.9% 45 to 60 minutes, 2.2% 60 minutes or more (2000)

Van Wert County

Located in western Ohio; bounded on the west by Indiana; drained by the Little Auglaize River. Covers a land area of 410.09 square miles, a water area of 0.40 square miles, and is located in the Eastern Time Zone. The county was founded in 1820. County seat is Van Wert.

Van Wert County is part of the Van Wert, OH Micropolitan Statistical Area. The entire metro area includes: Van Wert County, OH

Weather Station: Van Wert 1 S Elevation: 787 feet

	Jan	Feb	Mar	Apr	May	Jun	Jul	Aug	Sep	Oct	Nov	Dec
High	32	36	48	61	73	81	85	83	77	64	50	38
Low	17	19	28	38	50	59	63	61	53	42	33	23
Precip	2.0	1.8	2.7	3.6	3.8	4.2	3.9	3.3	2.9	2.6	3.1	2.7
Snow	9.3	6.8	2.8	1.2	0.0	0.0	0.0	0.0	0.0	0.2	1.8	7.7

High and Low temperatures in degrees Fahrenheit; Precipitation and Snow in inches

Population: 30,464 (1990); 29,659 (2000); 29,043 (2007); 28,537 (2012 projected); Race: 97.0% White, 1.0% Black, 0.2% Asian, 1.9% Hispanic of any race (2007); Density: 70.8 persons per square mile (2007); Average household size: 2.50 (2007); Median age: 39.6 (2007); Males per 100 females: 95.8 (2007).
Religion: Five largest groups: 13.9% The United Methodist Church, 9.0% Catholic Church, 4.8% Lutheran Church—Missouri Synod, 4.1% Evangelical Lutheran Church in America, 2.9% Presbyterian Church (U.S.A.) (2000).
Economy: Unemployment rate: 7.9% (6/2008); Total civilian labor force: 15,760 (6/2008); Leading industries: 36.9% manufacturing; 16.3% health care and social assistance; 13.7% retail trade (2005); Farms: 681 totaling 250,224 acres (2002); Companies that employ 500 or more persons: 4 (2006); Companies that employ 100 to 499 persons: 12 (2006); Companies that employ less than 100 persons: 581 (2006); Black-owned businesses: n/a (2002); Hispanic-owned businesses: n/a (2002); Asian-owned businesses: n/a (2002); Women-owned businesses: 411 (2002); Retail sales per capita: $11,547 (2008). Single-family building permits issued: 38 (2007); Multi-family building permits issued: 4 (2007).
Income: Per capita income: $21,505 (2007); Median household income: $44,504 (2007); Average household income: $53,201 (2007); Percent of households with income of $100,000 or more: 8.4% (2007); Poverty rate: 7.2% (2005); Bankruptcy rate: 3.95% (2007).
Education: Percent of population age 25 and over with: High school diploma (including GED) or higher: 86.8% (2007); Bachelor's degree or higher: 12.1% (2007); Master's degree or higher: 4.1% (2007).
Housing: Homeownership rate: 82.1% (2007); Median home value: $95,305 (2007); Median rent: $315 per month (2000); Median age of housing: 49 years (2000).
Health: Birth rate: 139.2 per 10,000 population (2007); Death rate: 111.8 per 10,000 population (2007); Age-adjusted cancer mortality rate: 208.2 deaths per 100,000 population (2005); Number of physicians: 9.3 per 10,000 population (2005); Hospital beds: 27.4 per 10,000 population (2004); Hospital admissions: 586.1 per 10,000 population (2004).
Elections: 2004 Presidential election results: 72.0% Bush, 27.6% Kerry, 0.0% Nader, 0.2% Badnarik

Additional Information Contacts

Van Wert County Government. . . . . (419) 238-6159
http://www.vanwertcounty.org

City of Van Wert. . . . . (419) 238-0308
http://vanwert.org

Van Wert County Communities

CONVOY (village). Covers a land area of 0.557 square miles and a water area of 0 square miles. Located at 40.91° N. Lat.; 84.70° W. Long. Elevation is 784 feet.
Population: 1,205 (1990); 1,110 (2000); 1,050 (2007); 1,038 (2012 projected); Race: 97.0% White, 0.3% Black, 0.0% Asian, 1.3% Hispanic of any race (2007); Density: 1,885.4 persons per square mile (2007); Average household size: 2.55 (2007); Median age: 35.8 (2007); Males per 100 females: 93.0 (2007); Marriage status: 21.8% never married, 55.6% now married, 8.2% widowed, 14.3% divorced (2000); Foreign born: 0.8% (2000); Ancestry (includes multiple ancestries): 43.0% German, 15.1% Irish, 10.9% United States or American, 8.7% English, 6.9% Other groups (2000).
Economy: Single-family building permits issued: 1 (2007); Multi-family building permits issued: 0 (2007); Employment by occupation: 7.4% management, 8.7% professional, 20.0% services, 17.3% sales, 0.0% farming, 10.8% construction, 35.7% production (2000).
Income: Per capita income: $21,109 (2007); Median household income: $44,919 (2007); Average household income: $53,783 (2007); Percent of households with income of $100,000 or more: 8.3% (2007); Poverty rate: 6.3% (2000).
Education: Percent of population age 25 and over with: High school diploma (including GED) or higher: 85.1% (2007); Bachelor's degree or higher: 5.8% (2007); Master's degree or higher: 2.6% (2007).

School District(s)

Crestview Local (PK-12)
2005-06 Enrollment: 1,036 . . . . (419) 749-9100

Housing: Homeownership rate: 85.9% (2007); Median home value: $75,658 (2007); Median rent: $354 per month (2000); Median age of housing: 60 years (2000).
Transportation: Commute to work: 94.8% car, 0.4% public transportation, 3.5% walk, 1.3% work from home (2000); Travel time to work: 31.0% less than 15 minutes, 39.8% 15 to 30 minutes, 16.4% 30 to 45 minutes, 11.3% 45 to 60 minutes, 1.6% 60 minutes or more (2000)

ELGIN (village). Covers a land area of 0.226 square miles and a water area of 0 square miles. Located at 40.74° N. Lat.; 84.47° W. Long. Elevation is 814 feet.
Population: 71 (1990); 50 (2000); 52 (2007); 51 (2012 projected); Race: 100.0% White, 0.0% Black, 0.0% Asian, 0.0% Hispanic of any race (2007); Density: 229.9 persons per square mile (2007); Average household size: 2.60 (2007); Median age: 38.6 (2007); Males per 100 females: 62.5 (2007); Marriage status: 15.6% never married, 62.5% now married, 9.4% widowed, 12.5% divorced (2000); Foreign born: 0.0% (2000); Ancestry (includes multiple ancestries): 24.0% German, 16.0% English, 12.0% Other groups, 4.0% Swiss, 4.0% Welsh (2000).
Economy: Employment by occupation: 5.3% management, 0.0% professional, 0.0% services, 42.1% sales, 0.0% farming, 15.8% construction, 36.8% production (2000).
Income: Per capita income: $17,885 (2007); Median household income: $47,500 (2007); Average household income: $46,500 (2007); Percent of households with income of $100,000 or more: 10.0% (2007); Poverty rate: 22.0% (2000).
Education: Percent of population age 25 and over with: High school diploma (including GED) or higher: 100.0% (2007); Bachelor's degree or higher: 0.0% (2007); Master's degree or higher: 0.0% (2007).
Housing: Homeownership rate: 95.0% (2007); Median home value: $68,750 (2007); Median rent: $n/a per month (2000); Median age of housing: 57 years (2000).
Transportation: Commute to work: 94.7% car, 0.0% public transportation, 5.3% walk, 0.0% work from home (2000); Travel time to work: 15.8% less than 15 minutes, 63.2% 15 to 30 minutes, 21.1% 30 to 45 minutes, 0.0% 45 to 60 minutes, 0.0% 60 minutes or more (2000)

MIDDLE POINT (village). Aka Middlepoint. Covers a land area of 0.556 square miles and a water area of 0 square miles. Located at 40.85° N. Lat.; 84.44° W. Long. Elevation is 781 feet.
Population: 641 (1990); 593 (2000); 540 (2007); 543 (2012 projected); Race: 97.4% White, 0.0% Black, 0.0% Asian, 2.6% Hispanic of any race (2007); Density: 970.9 persons per square mile (2007); Average household size: 2.48 (2007); Median age: 39.1 (2007); Males per 100 females: 94.9 (2007); Marriage status: 24.2% never married, 56.9% now married, 7.1% widowed, 11.7% divorced (2000); Foreign born: 0.3% (2000); Ancestry (includes multiple ancestries): 46.3% German, 15.4% United States or American, 8.0% Other groups, 7.9% English, 6.7% Irish (2000).
Economy: Single-family building permits issued: 0 (2007); Multi-family building permits issued: 0 (2007); Employment by occupation: 7.4% management, 9.1% professional, 18.9% services, 15.8% sales, 1.0% farming, 8.8% construction, 39.1% production (2000).
Income: Per capita income: $18,287 (2007); Median household income: $38,750 (2007); Average household income: $45,298 (2007); Percent of households with income of $100,000 or more: 4.6% (2007); Poverty rate: 4.9% (2000).
Education: Percent of population age 25 and over with: High school diploma (including GED) or higher: 87.0% (2007); Bachelor's degree or higher: 4.4% (2007); Master's degree or higher: 2.2% (2007).
Housing: Homeownership rate: 90.4% (2007); Median home value: $64,750 (2007); Median rent: $370 per month (2000); Median age of housing: 59 years (2000).
Transportation: Commute to work: 95.2% car, 0.0% public transportation, 2.4% walk, 2.4% work from home (2000); Travel time to work: 31.3% less than 15 minutes, 46.5% 15 to 30 minutes, 12.0% 30 to 45 minutes, 6.0% 45 to 60 minutes, 4.2% 60 minutes or more (2000)

OHIO CITY (village). Covers a land area of 0.460 square miles and a water area of 0 square miles. Located at 40.77° N. Lat.; 84.61° W. Long. Elevation is 820 feet.

Population: 899 (1990); 784 (2000); 717 (2007); 698 (2012 projected); Race: 97.4% White, 0.3% Black, 0.1% Asian, 1.5% Hispanic of any race (2007); Density: 1,560.2 persons per square mile (2007); Average household size: 2.42 (2007); Median age: 36.1 (2007); Males per 100 females: 96.4 (2007); Marriage status: 20.5% never married, 63.7% now married, 5.6% widowed, 10.2% divorced (2000); Foreign born: 0.5% (2000); Ancestry (includes multiple ancestries): 34.7% German, 11.5% United States or American, 8.0% Irish, 5.6% English, 5.4% Other groups (2000).

Economy: Single-family building permits issued: 1 (2007); Multi-family building permits issued: 0 (2007); Employment by occupation: 4.9% management, 7.9% professional, 13.3% services, 15.1% sales, 0.0% farming, 9.5% construction, 49.4% production (2000).

Income: Per capita income: $19,780 (2007); Median household income: $42,308 (2007); Average household income: $47,914 (2007); Percent of households with income of $100,000 or more: 4.1% (2007); Poverty rate: 3.6% (2000).

Education: Percent of population age 25 and over with: High school diploma (including GED) or higher: 83.7% (2007); Bachelor's degree or higher: 5.5% (2007); Master's degree or higher: 1.7% (2007).

School District(s)

Van Wert City (PK-12)
2005-06 Enrollment: 2,236 . . . . (419) 238-0648

Housing: Homeownership rate: 83.1% (2007); Median home value: $66,000 (2007); Median rent: $271 per month (2000); Median age of housing: 52 years (2000).

Transportation: Commute to work: 89.6% car, 0.5% public transportation, 7.3% walk, 2.6% work from home (2000); Travel time to work: 43.6% less than 15 minutes, 37.0% 15 to 30 minutes, 9.0% 30 to 45 minutes, 6.1% 45 to 60 minutes, 4.3% 60 minutes or more (2000)

SCOTT (village). Covers a land area of 0.807 square miles and a water area of 0 square miles. Located at 40.98° N. Lat.; 84.58° W. Long. Elevation is 735 feet.

Population: 339 (1990); 322 (2000); 336 (2007); 347 (2012 projected); Race: 94.3% White, 4.2% Black, 0.0% Asian, 3.0% Hispanic of any race (2007); Density: 416.5 persons per square mile (2007); Average household size: 2.60 (2007); Median age: 34.6 (2007); Males per 100 females: 98.8 (2007); Marriage status: 20.3% never married, 70.3% now married, 2.6% widowed, 6.9% divorced (2000); Foreign born: 0.0% (2000); Ancestry (includes multiple ancestries): 39.8% German, 12.7% Other groups, 12.0% Irish, 8.6% United States or American, 5.6% English (2000).

Economy: Single-family building permits issued: 0 (2007); Multi-family building permits issued: 0 (2007); Employment by occupation: 3.5% management, 7.5% professional, 15.0% services, 21.4% sales, 1.2% farming, 6.4% construction, 45.1% production (2000).

Income: Per capita income: $22,582 (2007); Median household income: $44,318 (2007); Average household income: $58,818 (2007); Percent of households with income of $100,000 or more: 14.7% (2007); Poverty rate: 13.3% (2000).

Education: Percent of population age 25 and over with: High school diploma (including GED) or higher: 78.3% (2007); Bachelor's degree or higher: 4.1% (2007); Master's degree or higher: 0.0% (2007).

Housing: Homeownership rate: 88.4% (2007); Median home value: $61,875 (2007); Median rent: $258 per month (2000); Median age of housing: 47 years (2000).

Transportation: Commute to work: 97.5% car, 0.0% public transportation, 0.0% walk, 0.0% work from home (2000); Travel time to work: 19.9% less than 15 minutes, 52.2% 15 to 30 minutes, 21.7% 30 to 45 minutes, 5.0% 45 to 60 minutes, 1.2% 60 minutes or more (2000)

VAN WERT (city). County seat. Covers a land area of 5.926 square miles and a water area of 0.182 square miles. Located at 40.86° N. Lat.; 84.58° W. Long. Elevation is 778 feet.

History: The site of Van Wert was chosen in 1835 by Captain James Watson Riley, who correctly foresaw that the location would make it a thoroughfare. The town developed into the peony center of Ohio, raising many flowers.

Population: 11,092 (1990); 10,690 (2000); 10,119 (2007); 9,710 (2012 projected); Race: 95.6% White, 1.8% Black, 0.4% Asian, 2.7% Hispanic of any race (2007); Density: 1,707.4 persons per square mile (2007); Average household size: 2.29 (2007); Median age: 39.4 (2007); Males per 100 females: 90.0 (2007); Marriage status: 22.0% never married, 56.6% now married, 9.1% widowed, 12.4% divorced (2000); Foreign born: 0.9% (2000); Ancestry (includes multiple ancestries): 33.5% German, 11.2% Irish, 10.6% United States or American, 8.5% Other groups, 7.5% English (2000).

Economy: Single-family building permits issued: 10 (2007); Multi-family building permits issued: 0 (2007); Employment by occupation: 10.2% management, 12.3% professional, 14.8% services, 22.1% sales, 0.0% farming, 7.9% construction, 32.7% production (2000).

Income: Per capita income: $19,599 (2007); Median household income: $36,426 (2007); Average household income: $44,220 (2007); Percent of households with income of $100,000 or more: 5.1% (2007); Poverty rate: 7.1% (2000).

Education: Percent of population age 25 and over with: High school diploma (including GED) or higher: 85.2% (2007); Bachelor's degree or higher: 14.1% (2007); Master's degree or higher: 4.8% (2007).

School District(s)

Lincolnview Local (PK-12)
2005-06 Enrollment: 877 . . . . (419) 968-2226
Van Wert City (PK-12)
2005-06 Enrollment: 2,236 . . . . (419) 238-0648
Vantage (10-12)
2005-06 Enrollment: n/a . . . . (419) 238-5411

Vocational/Technical School(s)

Vantage Career Center (Public)
Fall 2007 Enrollment: 68 . . . . (419) 238-5411
2007-08 Tuition: $375

Housing: Homeownership rate: 71.9% (2007); Median home value: $87,296 (2007); Median rent: $314 per month (2000); Median age of housing: 52 years (2000).

Hospitals: Van Wert County Hospital (100 beds)

Safety: Violent crime rate: 27.9 per 10,000 population; Property crime rate: 479.7 per 10,000 population (2007).

Newspapers: The Times Bulletin (Local news; Circulation 6,600); Weekly Advertiser (Local news; Circulation 16,500)

Transportation: Commute to work: 93.9% car, 0.1% public transportation, 3.0% walk, 2.0% work from home (2000); Travel time to work: 67.2% less than 15 minutes, 15.6% 15 to 30 minutes, 8.6% 30 to 45 minutes, 5.8% 45 to 60 minutes, 2.8% 60 minutes or more (2000)

Additional Information Contacts

City of Van Wert. . . . . (419) 238-0308
http://vanwert.org

VENEDOCIA (village). Covers a land area of 0.134 square miles and a water area of 0 square miles. Located at 40.78° N. Lat.; 84.45° W. Long. Elevation is 804 feet.

Population: 158 (1990); 160 (2000); 167 (2007); 162 (2012 projected); Race: 97.6% White, 0.0% Black, 0.0% Asian, 1.2% Hispanic of any race (2007); Density: 1,249.1 persons per square mile (2007); Average household size: 2.61 (2007); Median age: 43.4 (2007); Males per 100 females: 83.5 (2007); Marriage status: 19.4% never married, 56.5% now married, 11.3% widowed, 12.9% divorced (2000); Foreign born: 0.0% (2000); Ancestry (includes multiple ancestries): 42.9% German, 19.0% Welsh, 14.1% United States or American, 12.9% Other groups, 11.7% Irish (2000).

Economy: Single-family building permits issued: 0 (2007); Multi-family building permits issued: 0 (2007); Employment by occupation: 4.5% management, 7.6% professional, 13.6% services, 10.6% sales, 0.0% farming, 15.2% construction, 48.5% production (2000).

Income: Per capita income: $14,446 (2007); Median household income: $35,833 (2007); Average household income: $37,695 (2007); Percent of households with income of $100,000 or more: 1.6% (2007); Poverty rate: 13.0% (2000).

Education: Percent of population age 25 and over with: High school diploma (including GED) or higher: 68.6% (2007); Bachelor's degree or higher: 4.2% (2007); Master's degree or higher: 0.8% (2007).

Housing: Homeownership rate: 81.3% (2007); Median home value: $70,000 (2007); Median rent: $279 per month (2000); Median age of housing: 60+ years (2000).

Transportation: Commute to work: 90.9% car, 0.0% public transportation, 6.1% walk, 0.0% work from home (2000); Travel time to work: 25.8% less than 15 minutes, 47.0% 15 to 30 minutes, 22.7% 30 to 45 minutes, 3.0% 45 to 60 minutes, 1.5% 60 minutes or more (2000)

WILLSHIRE (village). Covers a land area of 0.379 square miles and a water area of 0 square miles. Located at 40.74° N. Lat.; 84.79° W. Long. Elevation is 797 feet.

Population: 541 (1990); 463 (2000); 408 (2007); 405 (2012 projected); Race: 99.0% White, 0.0% Black, 0.0% Asian, 1.0% Hispanic of any race (2007); Density: 1,076.1 persons per square mile (2007); Average household size: 2.34 (2007); Median age: 38.9 (2007); Males per 100 females: 106.1 (2007); Marriage status: 20.3% never married, 57.5% now married, 10.0% widowed, 12.2% divorced (2000); Foreign born: 1.1% (2000); Ancestry (includes multiple ancestries): 38.9% German, 7.9% Other groups, 7.5% English, 7.5% Dutch, 6.8% Irish (2000).

Economy: Single-family building permits issued: 0 (2007); Multi-family building permits issued: 0 (2007); Employment by occupation: 4.4% management, 3.9% professional, 15.3% services, 14.8% sales, 0.9% farming, 12.7% construction, 48.0% production (2000).

Income: Per capita income: $21,795 (2007); Median household income: $48,333 (2007); Average household income: $51,106 (2007); Percent of households with income of $100,000 or more: 6.3% (2007); Poverty rate: 5.9% (2000).

Education: Percent of population age 25 and over with: High school diploma (including GED) or higher: 78.9% (2007); Bachelor's degree or higher: 3.9% (2007); Master's degree or higher: 1.1% (2007).

School District(s)

Parkway Local (PK-12)
2005-06 Enrollment: 1,230 . . . . (419) 363-3045

Housing: Homeownership rate: 81.6% (2007); Median home value: $60,000 (2007); Median rent: $329 per month (2000); Median age of housing: 54 years (2000).

Newspapers: Photo Star (Community news; Circulation 11,600)

Transportation: Commute to work: 96.4% car, 0.0% public transportation, 0.0% walk, 2.7% work from home (2000); Travel time to work: 24.8% less than 15 minutes, 51.8% 15 to 30 minutes, 14.7% 30 to 45 minutes, 6.9% 45 to 60 minutes, 1.8% 60 minutes or more (2000)

WREN (village). Covers a land area of 0.310 square miles and a water area of 0 square miles. Located at 40.80° N. Lat.; 84.77° W. Long. Elevation is 810 feet.

Population: 190 (1990); 199 (2000); 193 (2007); 187 (2012 projected); Race: 98.4% White, 0.0% Black, 0.0% Asian, 2.1% Hispanic of any race (2007); Density: 622.9 persons per square mile (2007); Average household size: 2.33 (2007); Median age: 40.5 (2007); Males per 100 females: 83.8 (2007); Marriage status: 26.8% never married, 48.8% now married, 7.9% widowed, 16.5% divorced (2000); Foreign born: 0.0% (2000); Ancestry (includes multiple ancestries): 32.0% German, 14.9% United States or American, 9.8% Irish, 7.2% Other groups, 6.7% English (2000).

Economy: Single-family building permits issued: 0 (2007); Multi-family building permits issued: 4 (2007); Employment by occupation: 2.0% management, 11.9% professional, 10.9% services, 24.8% sales, 2.0% farming, 7.9% construction, 40.6% production (2000).

Income: Per capita income: $19,806 (2007); Median household income: $39,464 (2007); Average household income: $46,054 (2007); Percent of households with income of $100,000 or more: 3.6% (2007); Poverty rate: 6.7% (2000).

Education: Percent of population age 25 and over with: High school diploma (including GED) or higher: 91.6% (2007); Bachelor's degree or higher: 5.6% (2007); Master's degree or higher: 0.0% (2007).

Housing: Homeownership rate: 88.0% (2007); Median home value: $62,917 (2007); Median rent: $318 per month (2000); Median age of housing: 60+ years (2000).

Transportation: Commute to work: 100.0% car, 0.0% public transportation, 0.0% walk, 0.0% work from home (2000); Travel time to work: 7.1% less than 15 minutes, 60.2% 15 to 30 minutes, 15.3% 30 to 45 minutes, 9.2% 45 to 60 minutes, 8.2% 60 minutes or more (2000)

Vinton County

Located in southern Ohio; drained by Raccoon Creek. Covers a land area of 414.08 square miles, a water area of 0.88 square miles, and is located in the Eastern Time Zone. The county was founded in 1850. County seat is McArthur.

Population: 11,098 (1990); 12,806 (2000); 13,586 (2007); 14,069 (2012 projected); Race: 98.2% White, 0.4% Black, 0.1% Asian, 0.6% Hispanic of any race (2007); Density: 32.8 persons per square mile (2007); Average household size: 2.57 (2007); Median age: 36.9 (2007); Males per 100 females: 99.2 (2007).

Religion: Five largest groups: 4.0% The United Methodist Church, 3.3% Christian Church (Disciples of Christ), 2.1% Southern Baptist Convention, 1.8% National Association of Free Will Baptists, 1.5% Catholic Church (2000).

Economy: Unemployment rate: 8.7% (6/2008); Total civilian labor force: 5,824 (6/2008); Leading industries: 39.5% manufacturing; 18.9% health care and social assistance; 4.2% transportation & warehousing (2005); Farms: 237 totaling 43,651 acres (2002); Companies that employ 500 or more persons: 0 (2006); Companies that employ 100 to 499 persons: 2 (2006); Companies that employ less than 100 persons: 166 (2006); Black-owned businesses: n/a (2002); Hispanic-owned businesses: n/a (2002); Asian-owned businesses: n/a (2002); Women-owned businesses: n/a (2002); Retail sales per capita: $3,307 (2008). Single-family building permits issued: 0 (2007); Multi-family building permits issued: 0 (2007).

Income: Per capita income: $16,248 (2007); Median household income: $33,647 (2007); Average household income: $41,453 (2007); Percent of households with income of $100,000 or more: 5.3% (2007); Poverty rate: 20.6% (2005); Bankruptcy rate: 3.89% (2007).

Education: Percent of population age 25 and over with: High school diploma (including GED) or higher: 71.2% (2007); Bachelor's degree or higher: 6.1% (2007); Master's degree or higher: 2.2% (2007).

Housing: Homeownership rate: 77.6% (2007); Median home value: $80,745 (2007); Median rent: $272 per month (2000); Median age of housing: 26 years (2000).

Health: Birth rate: 132.4 per 10,000 population (2007); Death rate: 109.2 per 10,000 population (2007); Age-adjusted cancer mortality rate: 185.6 deaths per 100,000 population (2005); Number of physicians: 0.0 per 10,000 population (2005); Hospital beds: 0.0 per 10,000 population (2004); Hospital admissions: 0.0 per 10,000 population (2004).

Elections: 2004 Presidential election results: 54.8% Bush, 44.7% Kerry, 0.0% Nader, 0.3% Badnarik

National and State Parks: Lake Alma State Reserve; Lake Hope State Park; Wayne National Forest; Zaleski State Forest

Additional Information Contacts

Vinton County Government . . . . (740) 596-4571
http://www.vintoncounty.com

Vinton County Convention and Visitors Bureau. . . . . (740) 596-5033
http://www.vintoncountytravel.com

Vinton County Communities

CREOLA (unincorporated postal area, zip code 45622). Covers a land area of 21.246 square miles and a water area of 0 square miles. Located at 39.36° N. Lat.; 82.49° W. Long. Elevation is 760 feet.

Population: 435 (2000); Race: 100.0% White, 0.0% Black, 0.0% Asian, 0.0% Hispanic of any race (2000); Density: 20.5 persons per square mile (2000); Age: 25.2% under 18, 11.1% over 64 (2000); Marriage status: 20.3% never married, 52.2% now married, 6.2% widowed, 21.4% divorced (2000); Foreign born: 0.0% (2000); Ancestry (includes multiple ancestries): 20.5% English, 17.0% United States or American, 14.1% Dutch, 10.9% Irish, 8.8% German (2000).

Economy: Employment by occupation: 4.7% management, 22.8% professional, 4.7% services, 6.3% sales, 6.3% farming, 24.4% construction, 30.7% production (2000).

Income: Per capita income: $17,312 (2000); Median household income: $33,977 (2000); Poverty rate: 18.5% (2000).

Education: Percent of population age 25 and over with: High school diploma (including GED) or higher: 67.2% (2000); Bachelor's degree or higher: 9.8% (2000).

Housing: Homeownership rate: 84.9% (2000); Median home value: $97,500 (2000); Median rent: $247 per month (2000); Median age of housing: 24 years (2000).

Transportation: Commute to work: 100.0% car, 0.0% public transportation, 0.0% walk, 0.0% work from home (2000); Travel time to work: 32.3% less than 15 minutes, 15.7% 15 to 30 minutes, 22.8% 30 to 45 minutes, 5.5% 45 to 60 minutes, 23.6% 60 minutes or more (2000)

HAMDEN (village). Covers a land area of 0.570 square miles and a water area of 0 square miles. Located at 39.16° N. Lat.; 82.52° W. Long. Elevation is 722 feet.

Population: 877 (1990); 871 (2000); 772 (2007); 774 (2012 projected); Race: 96.8% White, 0.0% Black, 0.0% Asian, 1.3% Hispanic of any race (2007); Density: 1,354.3 persons per square mile (2007); Average

household size: 2.48 (2007); Median age: 38.1 (2007); Males per 100 females: 95.4 (2007); Marriage status: 20.1% never married, 60.5% now married, 8.9% widowed, 10.5% divorced (2000); Foreign born: 0.0% (2000); Ancestry (includes multiple ancestries): 34.3% United States or American, 11.3% German, 8.7% Other groups, 7.5% Irish, 4.4% English (2000).
Economy: Employment by occupation: 8.7% management, 13.8% professional, 12.8% services, 14.1% sales, 2.2% farming, 14.7% construction, 33.7% production (2000).
Income: Per capita income: $15,829 (2007); Median household income: $30,093 (2007); Average household income: $39,293 (2007); Percent of households with income of $100,000 or more: 3.9% (2007); Poverty rate: 18.9% (2000).
Education: Percent of population age 25 and over with: High school diploma (including GED) or higher: 73.5% (2007); Bachelor's degree or higher: 6.6% (2007); Master's degree or higher: 3.8% (2007).

School District(s)

Vinton County Local (PK-12)
2005-06 Enrollment: 2,637 . . . . (740) 596-5218
Housing: Homeownership rate: 76.2% (2007); Median home value: $63,500 (2007); Median rent: $316 per month (2000); Median age of housing: 45 years (2000).
Transportation: Commute to work: 90.9% car, 0.0% public transportation, 5.0% walk, 4.0% work from home (2000); Travel time to work: 33.6% less than 15 minutes, 31.1% 15 to 30 minutes, 10.5% 30 to 45 minutes, 9.8% 45 to 60 minutes, 15.0% 60 minutes or more (2000)

MCARTHUR (village). County seat. Covers a land area of 1.333 square miles and a water area of 0 square miles. Located at 39.24° N. Lat.; 82.48° W. Long. Elevation is 764 feet.
History: McArthur was platted in 1815 and named McArthurstown for Duncan McArthur, later governor of Ohio. It was sited at the junction of two wilderness roads. Local clays were used in brickmaking, the town's early industry.
Population: 1,541 (1990); 1,888 (2000); 2,124 (2007); 2,215 (2012 projected); Race: 98.6% White, 0.1% Black, 0.0% Asian, 0.6% Hispanic of any race (2007); Density: 1,593.2 persons per square mile (2007); Average household size: 2.39 (2007); Median age: 33.0 (2007); Males per 100 females: 85.8 (2007); Marriage status: 24.0% never married, 52.2% now married, 10.6% widowed, 13.2% divorced (2000); Foreign born: 0.3% (2000); Ancestry (includes multiple ancestries): 26.0% United States or American, 13.0% Other groups, 10.8% Irish, 10.7% German, 9.4% English (2000).
Economy: Employment by occupation: 10.9% management, 13.9% professional, 14.0% services, 21.0% sales, 1.4% farming, 15.3% construction, 23.4% production (2000).
Income: Per capita income: $15,950 (2007); Median household income: $28,192 (2007); Average household income: $37,987 (2007); Percent of households with income of $100,000 or more: 5.8% (2007); Poverty rate: 27.8% (2000).
Education: Percent of population age 25 and over with: High school diploma (including GED) or higher: 79.9% (2007); Bachelor's degree or higher: 10.6% (2007); Master's degree or higher: 3.7% (2007).

School District(s)

Vinton County Local (PK-12)
2005-06 Enrollment: 2,637 . . . . (740) 596-5218
Housing: Homeownership rate: 60.7% (2007); Median home value: $80,667 (2007); Median rent: $275 per month (2000); Median age of housing: 39 years (2000).
Safety: Violent crime rate: 4.8 per 10,000 population; Property crime rate: 250.7 per 10,000 population (2007).
Transportation: Commute to work: 91.2% car, 0.1% public transportation, 5.0% walk, 3.3% work from home (2000); Travel time to work: 44.9% less than 15 minutes, 13.5% 15 to 30 minutes, 20.5% 30 to 45 minutes, 8.9% 45 to 60 minutes, 12.2% 60 minutes or more (2000)

Additional Information Contacts

Vinton County Convention and Visitors Bureau. . . . . (740) 596-5033
http://www.vintoncountytravel.com

NEW PLYMOUTH (unincorporated postal area, zip code 45654). Covers a land area of 53.669 square miles and a water area of 0.009 square miles. Located at 39.37° N. Lat.; 82.39° W. Long. Elevation is 764 feet.
Population: 1,026 (2000); Race: 95.3% White, 0.0% Black, 0.0% Asian, 0.0% Hispanic of any race (2000); Density: 19.1 persons per square mile (2000); Age: 26.2% under 18, 12.2% over 64 (2000); Marriage status: 20.2% never married, 56.2% now married, 9.0% widowed, 14.6% divorced (2000); Foreign born: 0.0% (2000); Ancestry (includes multiple ancestries): 13.9% United States or American, 12.2% German, 8.1% Other groups, 6.1% Irish, 5.7% English (2000).
Economy: Employment by occupation: 11.1% management, 9.9% professional, 11.8% services, 21.9% sales, 0.0% farming, 15.4% construction, 30.0% production (2000).
Income: Per capita income: $13,501 (2000); Median household income: $33,080 (2000); Poverty rate: 16.4% (2000).
Education: Percent of population age 25 and over with: High school diploma (including GED) or higher: 75.5% (2000); Bachelor's degree or higher: 3.7% (2000).
Housing: Homeownership rate: 85.9% (2000); Median home value: $70,800 (2000); Median rent: $325 per month (2000); Median age of housing: 28 years (2000).
Transportation: Commute to work: 94.5% car, 0.0% public transportation, 1.8% walk, 1.5% work from home (2000); Travel time to work: 14.8% less than 15 minutes, 37.2% 15 to 30 minutes, 26.0% 30 to 45 minutes, 1.8% 45 to 60 minutes, 20.2% 60 minutes or more (2000)

RAY (unincorporated postal area, zip code 45672). Covers a land area of 62.631 square miles and a water area of 0.022 square miles. Located at 39.20° N. Lat.; 82.69° W. Long. Elevation is 615 feet.
Population: 1,782 (2000); Race: 97.3% White, 2.3% Black, 0.0% Asian, 0.0% Hispanic of any race (2000); Density: 28.5 persons per square mile (2000); Age: 29.0% under 18, 10.8% over 64 (2000); Marriage status: 17.4% never married, 67.7% now married, 4.2% widowed, 10.6% divorced (2000); Foreign born: 0.0% (2000); Ancestry (includes multiple ancestries): 33.8% United States or American, 10.7% Irish, 9.9% English, 8.9% German, 6.8% Other groups (2000).
Economy: Employment by occupation: 8.1% management, 9.5% professional, 13.5% services, 17.5% sales, 1.7% farming, 14.7% construction, 34.9% production (2000).
Income: Per capita income: $15,479 (2000); Median household income: $30,553 (2000); Poverty rate: 17.3% (2000).
Education: Percent of population age 25 and over with: High school diploma (including GED) or higher: 74.2% (2000); Bachelor's degree or higher: 6.9% (2000).
Housing: Homeownership rate: 85.0% (2000); Median home value: $64,300 (2000); Median rent: $318 per month (2000); Median age of housing: 25 years (2000).
Transportation: Commute to work: 95.0% car, 0.0% public transportation, 2.5% walk, 1.4% work from home (2000); Travel time to work: 10.7% less than 15 minutes, 25.7% 15 to 30 minutes, 35.8% 30 to 45 minutes, 1.3% 45 to 60 minutes, 26.6% 60 minutes or more (2000)

WILKESVILLE (village). Covers a land area of 0.294 square miles and a water area of 0 square miles. Located at 39.07° N. Lat.; 82.32° W. Long. Elevation is 702 feet.
Population: 151 (1990); 151 (2000); 144 (2007); 145 (2012 projected); Race: 95.8% White, 0.0% Black, 0.0% Asian, 0.0% Hispanic of any race (2007); Density: 489.8 persons per square mile (2007); Average household size: 2.12 (2007); Median age: 47.0 (2007); Males per 100 females: 97.3 (2007); Marriage status: 13.9% never married, 61.6% now married, 13.9% widowed, 10.6% divorced (2000); Foreign born: 1.2% (2000); Ancestry (includes multiple ancestries): 30.3% United States or American, 23.6% German, 20.0% Irish, 4.8% English, 3.6% Dutch (2000).
Economy: Employment by occupation: 7.1% management, 2.4% professional, 12.9% services, 23.5% sales, 4.7% farming, 18.8% construction, 30.6% production (2000).
Income: Per capita income: $19,809 (2007); Median household income: $28,000 (2007); Average household income: $41,949 (2007); Percent of households with income of $100,000 or more: 7.4% (2007); Poverty rate: 18.8% (2000).
Education: Percent of population age 25 and over with: High school diploma (including GED) or higher: 67.6% (2007); Bachelor's degree or higher: 7.4% (2007); Master's degree or higher: 2.8% (2007).

School District(s)

Vinton County Local (PK-12)
2005-06 Enrollment: 2,637 . . . . (740) 596-5218
Housing: Homeownership rate: 92.6% (2007); Median home value: $72,500 (2007); Median rent: $125 per month (2000); Median age of housing: 39 years (2000).

Transportation: Commute to work: 94.1% car, 0.0% public transportation, 0.0% walk, 3.5% work from home (2000); Travel time to work: 19.5% less than 15 minutes, 25.6% 15 to 30 minutes, 39.0% 30 to 45 minutes, 1.2% 45 to 60 minutes, 14.6% 60 minutes or more (2000)

ZALESKI (village). Covers a land area of 0.477 square miles and a water area of 0 square miles. Located at 39.28° N. Lat.; 82.39° W. Long. Elevation is 755 feet.
History: Zaleski was settled in a forested area, the site of the Zaleski Resettlement Project that sought to rehabilitate timberlands.
Population: 294 (1990); 375 (2000); 411 (2007); 429 (2012 projected); Race: 98.3% White, 0.7% Black, 0.0% Asian, 0.0% Hispanic of any race (2007); Density: 861.8 persons per square mile (2007); Average household size: 2.48 (2007); Median age: 37.8 (2007); Males per 100 females: 95.7 (2007); Marriage status: 21.3% never married, 61.1% now married, 8.4% widowed, 9.1% divorced (2000); Foreign born: 0.0% (2000); Ancestry (includes multiple ancestries): 26.9% United States or American, 5.7% German, 5.4% Other groups, 3.6% Irish, 3.6% English (2000).
Economy: Employment by occupation: 3.1% management, 16.9% professional, 18.1% services, 17.5% sales, 0.6% farming, 28.7% construction, 15.0% production (2000).
Income: Per capita income: $15,298 (2007); Median household income: $33,125 (2007); Average household income: $37,877 (2007); Percent of households with income of $100,000 or more: 1.8% (2007); Poverty rate: 16.7% (2000).
Education: Percent of population age 25 and over with: High school diploma (including GED) or higher: 77.9% (2007); Bachelor's degree or higher: 3.8% (2007); Master's degree or higher: 2.8% (2007).
Housing: Homeownership rate: 81.3% (2007); Median home value: $48,056 (2007); Median rent: $290 per month (2000); Median age of housing: 40 years (2000).
Transportation: Commute to work: 92.5% car, 0.0% public transportation, 6.3% walk, 1.3% work from home (2000); Travel time to work: 25.9% less than 15 minutes, 28.5% 15 to 30 minutes, 29.7% 30 to 45 minutes, 6.3% 45 to 60 minutes, 9.5% 60 minutes or more (2000)

Warren County

Located in southwestern Ohio; crossed by the Little Miami River. Covers a land area of 399.63 square miles, a water area of 7.51 square miles, and is located in the Eastern Time Zone. The county was founded in 1803. County seat is Lebanon.

Warren County is part of the Cincinnati-Middletown, OH-KY-IN Metropolitan Statistical Area. The entire metro area includes: Dearborn County, IN; Franklin County, IN; Ohio County, IN; Boone County, KY; Bracken County, KY; Campbell County, KY; Gallatin County, KY; Grant County, KY; Kenton County, KY; Pendleton County, KY; Brown County, OH; Butler County, OH; Clermont County, OH; Hamilton County, OH; Warren County, OH

Weather Station: Franklin Elevation: 669 feet

	Jan	Feb	Mar	Apr	May	Jun	Jul	Aug	Sep	Oct	Nov	Dec
High	36	40	51	63	73	82	85	84	78	66	53	42
Low	18	21	30	39	49	59	63	60	52	40	33	24
Precip	2.5	2.3	3.2	3.9	4.4	3.7	4.2	3.3	2.7	3.0	3.3	3.0
Snow	na	2.4	1.6	tr	0.0	0.0	0.0	0.0	0.0	0.0	0.5	1.4

High and Low temperatures in degrees Fahrenheit; Precipitation and Snow in inches

Population: 113,967 (1990); 158,383 (2000); 206,750 (2007); 239,001 (2012 projected); Race: 91.9% White, 3.3% Black, 3.0% Asian, 1.6% Hispanic of any race (2007); Density: 517.4 persons per square mile (2007); Average household size: 2.76 (2007); Median age: 35.7 (2007); Males per 100 females: 100.2 (2007).
Religion: Five largest groups: 11.2% Catholic Church, 6.0% Southern Baptist Convention, 3.2% The United Methodist Church, 2.5% Christian Churches and Churches of Christ, 1.6% Presbyterian Church (U.S.A.) (2000).
Economy: Unemployment rate: 5.6% (6/2008); Total civilian labor force: 109,747 (6/2008); Leading industries: 18.3% manufacturing; 11.2% retail trade; 11.0% accommodation & food services (2005); Farms: 1,036 totaling 126,168 acres (2002); Companies that employ 500 or more persons: 12 (2006); Companies that employ 100 to 499 persons: 120 (2006); Companies that employ less than 100 persons: 3,513 (2006); Black-owned businesses: n/a (2002); Hispanic-owned businesses: 104 (2002); Asian-owned businesses: 174 (2002); Women-owned businesses: 4,235 (2002); Retail sales per capita: $10,325 (2008). Single-family building permits issued: 1,081 (2007); Multi-family building permits issued: 67 (2007).
Income: Per capita income: $30,725 (2007); Median household income: $68,332 (2007); Average household income: $84,114 (2007); Percent of households with income of $100,000 or more: 28.1% (2007); Poverty rate: 5.0% (2005); Bankruptcy rate: 3.34% (2007).
Taxes: Total county taxes per capita: $308 (2006); County property taxes per capita: $168 (2006).
Education: Percent of population age 25 and over with: High school diploma (including GED) or higher: 86.8% (2007); Bachelor's degree or higher: 29.5% (2007); Master's degree or higher: 9.5% (2007).
Housing: Homeownership rate: 80.1% (2007); Median home value: $178,369 (2007); Median rent: $504 per month (2000); Median age of housing: 20 years (2000).
Health: Birth rate: 150.2 per 10,000 population (2007); Death rate: 63.4 per 10,000 population (2007); Age-adjusted cancer mortality rate: 195.2 deaths per 100,000 population (2005); Air Quality Index: 57.5% good, 30.1% moderate, 12.0% unhealthy for sensitive individuals, 0.4% unhealthy (percent of days in 2007); Number of physicians: 22.0 per 10,000 population (2005); Hospital beds: 0.0 per 10,000 population (2004); Hospital admissions: 0.0 per 10,000 population (2004).
Elections: 2004 Presidential election results: 72.1% Bush, 27.6% Kerry, 0.0% Nader, 0.2% Badnarik
National and State Parks: Caesar Creek Gorge State Natural Area; Fort Ancient State Memorial
Additional Information Contacts
Warren County Government . . . . (513) 695-1250
http://www.co.warren.oh.us
City of Franklin . . . . (937) 746-9921
http://www.franklinohio.org
City of Lebanon . . . . (513) 932-3060
http://www.ci.lebanon.oh.us
City of Mason . . . . (513) 229-8500
http://www.imaginemason.org
City of Springboro . . . . (937) 748-4343
http://www.ci.springboro.oh.us
Franklin Area Chamber of Commerce . . . . (937) 746-8457
http://www.chamber45005.org
Lebanon Area Chamber of Commerce . . . . (513) 932-1100
http://www.lebanonchamber.org
Morrow Area Chamber of Commerce . . . . (513) 899-4466
http://www.morrow-today.org
Northeast Cincinnati Chamber of Commerce . . . . (513) 336-0125
http://www.necchamber.org
Springboro Chamber of Commerce . . . . (937) 748-0074
http://www.springboroohio.org
Village of Carlisle . . . . (937) 746-0555
http://www.carlisleoh.org
Waynesville Area Chamber of Commerce . . . . (513) 897-8855
http://www.waynesvilleohio.com

Warren County Communities

BUTLERVILLE (village). Covers a land area of 0.148 square miles and a water area of 0 square miles. Located at 39.30° N. Lat.; 84.08° W. Long. Elevation is 863 feet.
Population: 188 (1990); 231 (2000); 293 (2007); 335 (2012 projected); Race: 98.3% White, 0.0% Black, 0.0% Asian, 0.0% Hispanic of any race (2007); Density: 1,983.1 persons per square mile (2007); Average household size: 2.82 (2007); Median age: 33.5 (2007); Males per 100 females: 107.8 (2007); Marriage status: 25.7% never married, 70.3% now married, 1.1% widowed, 2.9% divorced (2000); Foreign born: 0.0% (2000); Ancestry (includes multiple ancestries): 20.9% United States or American, 20.5% German, 18.4% English, 7.7% Irish, 4.3% Italian (2000).
Economy: Single-family building permits issued: 0 (2007); Multi-family building permits issued: 0 (2007); Employment by occupation: 5.7% management, 3.3% professional, 14.6% services, 27.6% sales, 2.4% farming, 18.7% construction, 27.6% production (2000).
Income: Per capita income: $22,662 (2007); Median household income: $58,421 (2007); Average household income: $63,846 (2007); Percent of households with income of $100,000 or more: 11.5% (2007); Poverty rate: 0.9% (2000).

Education: Percent of population age 25 and over with: High school diploma (including GED) or higher: 85.3% (2007); Bachelor's degree or higher: 5.2% (2007); Master's degree or higher: 0.0% (2007).
Housing: Homeownership rate: 86.5% (2007); Median home value: $105,357 (2007); Median rent: $488 per month (2000); Median age of housing: 43 years (2000).
Transportation: Commute to work: 100.0% car, 0.0% public transportation, 0.0% walk, 0.0% work from home (2000); Travel time to work: 5.9% less than 15 minutes, 26.3% 15 to 30 minutes, 41.5% 30 to 45 minutes, 16.1% 45 to 60 minutes, 10.2% 60 minutes or more (2000)

CARLISLE (city). Covers a land area of 3.403 square miles and a water area of 0.161 square miles. Located at 39.58° N. Lat.; 84.31° W. Long. Elevation is 699 feet.
Population: 5,032 (1990); 5,121 (2000); 5,462 (2007); 5,718 (2012 projected); Race: 97.5% White, 0.2% Black, 0.7% Asian, 0.8% Hispanic of any race (2007); Density: 1,604.9 persons per square mile (2007); Average household size: 2.70 (2007); Median age: 36.1 (2007); Males per 100 females: 99.9 (2007); Marriage status: 16.8% never married, 69.4% now married, 5.0% widowed, 8.9% divorced (2000); Foreign born: 1.1% (2000); Ancestry (includes multiple ancestries): 18.9% United States or American, 17.7% German, 12.9% English, 10.7% Other groups, 10.4% Irish (2000).
Economy: Single-family building permits issued: 13 (2007); Multi-family building permits issued: 0 (2007); Employment by occupation: 6.0% management, 14.1% professional, 16.2% services, 23.6% sales, 0.0% farming, 11.2% construction, 28.8% production (2000).
Income: Per capita income: $21,506 (2007); Median household income: $50,815 (2007); Average household income: $57,315 (2007); Percent of households with income of $100,000 or more: 14.0% (2007); Poverty rate: 8.4% (2000).
Education: Percent of population age 25 and over with: High school diploma (including GED) or higher: 75.5% (2007); Bachelor's degree or higher: 7.0% (2007); Master's degree or higher: 2.0% (2007).

School District(s)

Carlisle Local (PK-12)
2005-06 Enrollment: 1,836 . . . . (937) 746-0710

Housing: Homeownership rate: 76.5% (2007); Median home value: $136,795 (2007); Median rent: $359 per month (2000); Median age of housing: 33 years (2000).
Transportation: Commute to work: 96.1% car, 0.0% public transportation, 1.2% walk, 1.8% work from home (2000); Travel time to work: 24.1% less than 15 minutes, 42.3% 15 to 30 minutes, 20.6% 30 to 45 minutes, 5.7% 45 to 60 minutes, 7.3% 60 minutes or more (2000)

Additional Information Contacts

Village of Carlisle . . . . (937) 746-0555
http://www.carlisleoh.org

CORWIN (village). Covers a land area of 0.299 square miles and a water area of 0 square miles. Located at 39.52° N. Lat.; 84.07° W. Long. Elevation is 738 feet.
Population: 263 (1990); 256 (2000); 347 (2007); 408 (2012 projected); Race: 99.4% White, 0.0% Black, 0.6% Asian, 0.0% Hispanic of any race (2007); Density: 1,159.7 persons per square mile (2007); Average household size: 2.48 (2007); Median age: 37.3 (2007); Males per 100 females: 96.0 (2007); Marriage status: 30.6% never married, 60.4% now married, 6.3% widowed, 2.7% divorced (2000); Foreign born: 0.0% (2000); Ancestry (includes multiple ancestries): 19.3% Irish, 15.8% German, 14.3% United States or American, 9.7% English, 5.4% Other groups (2000).
Economy: Employment by occupation: 7.0% management, 10.1% professional, 28.7% services, 13.2% sales, 1.6% farming, 17.1% construction, 22.5% production (2000).
Income: Per capita income: $27,810 (2007); Median household income: $61,800 (2007); Average household income: $68,929 (2007); Percent of households with income of $100,000 or more: 16.4% (2007); Poverty rate: 11.2% (2000).
Education: Percent of population age 25 and over with: High school diploma (including GED) or higher: 59.1% (2007); Bachelor's degree or higher: 6.9% (2007); Master's degree or higher: 0.0% (2007).
Housing: Homeownership rate: 75.7% (2007); Median home value: $123,077 (2007); Median rent: $458 per month (2000); Median age of housing: 50 years (2000).
Transportation: Commute to work: 87.4% car, 0.0% public transportation, 6.3% walk, 1.6% work from home (2000); Travel time to work: 34.4% less than 15 minutes, 36.8% 15 to 30 minutes, 23.2% 30 to 45 minutes, 1.6% 45 to 60 minutes, 4.0% 60 minutes or more (2000)

FIVE POINTS (CDP). Covers a land area of 2.886 square miles and a water area of 0.011 square miles. Located at 39.56° N. Lat.; 84.21° W. Long. Elevation is 991 feet.
Population: 1,503 (1990); 2,191 (2000); 3,625 (2007); 4,542 (2012 projected); Race: 97.6% White, 0.5% Black, 1.1% Asian, 1.8% Hispanic of any race (2007); Density: 1,256.0 persons per square mile (2007); Average household size: 2.94 (2007); Median age: 40.9 (2007); Males per 100 females: 105.4 (2007); Marriage status: 17.4% never married, 78.6% now married, 2.1% widowed, 1.9% divorced (2000); Foreign born: 1.8% (2000); Ancestry (includes multiple ancestries): 33.9% German, 16.9% Irish, 15.1% English, 10.6% Italian, 8.1% United States or American (2000).
Economy: Employment by occupation: 24.1% management, 31.2% professional, 6.0% services, 28.8% sales, 0.0% farming, 3.1% construction, 6.8% production (2000).
Income: Per capita income: $46,391 (2007); Median household income: $121,042 (2007); Average household income: $136,389 (2007); Percent of households with income of $100,000 or more: 62.3% (2007); Poverty rate: 0.3% (2000).
Education: Percent of population age 25 and over with: High school diploma (including GED) or higher: 94.9% (2007); Bachelor's degree or higher: 51.6% (2007); Master's degree or higher: 22.9% (2007).
Housing: Homeownership rate: 98.4% (2007); Median home value: $277,422 (2007); Median rent: $1,179 per month (2000); Median age of housing: 14 years (2000).
Transportation: Commute to work: 96.1% car, 0.6% public transportation, 1.0% walk, 2.3% work from home (2000); Travel time to work: 27.6% less than 15 minutes, 41.2% 15 to 30 minutes, 19.7% 30 to 45 minutes, 5.5% 45 to 60 minutes, 6.1% 60 minutes or more (2000)

FRANKLIN (city). Covers a land area of 9.110 square miles and a water area of 0.214 square miles. Located at 39.56° N. Lat.; 84.30° W. Long. Elevation is 679 feet.
History: Named for Benjamin Franklin, American statesman and inventor. Franklin was founded in 1796 by William Schenck, an officer in Harrison's Army in the War of 1812. The town was a port on the Great Miami River after the Miami & Erie Canal was built. Later, paper mills were established here.
Population: 11,274 (1990); 11,396 (2000); 12,731 (2007); 13,734 (2012 projected); Race: 96.6% White, 0.8% Black, 0.9% Asian, 1.2% Hispanic of any race (2007); Density: 1,397.5 persons per square mile (2007); Average household size: 2.42 (2007); Median age: 34.2 (2007); Males per 100 females: 90.3 (2007); Marriage status: 21.2% never married, 59.5% now married, 7.1% widowed, 12.2% divorced (2000); Foreign born: 1.1% (2000); Ancestry (includes multiple ancestries): 21.5% United States or American, 15.0% German, 10.4% Irish, 10.2% Other groups, 9.0% English (2000).
Economy: Single-family building permits issued: 12 (2007); Multi-family building permits issued: 0 (2007); Employment by occupation: 7.6% management, 13.2% professional, 15.5% services, 25.7% sales, 0.2% farming, 11.1% construction, 26.8% production (2000).
Income: Per capita income: $21,297 (2007); Median household income: $42,705 (2007); Average household income: $51,223 (2007); Percent of households with income of $100,000 or more: 10.1% (2007); Poverty rate: 10.1% (2000).
Education: Percent of population age 25 and over with: High school diploma (including GED) or higher: 74.3% (2007); Bachelor's degree or higher: 9.1% (2007); Master's degree or higher: 2.5% (2007).

School District(s)

Franklin City (PK-12)
2005-06 Enrollment: 2,838 . . . . (937) 746-1699

Two-year College(s)

Southwestern College (Private, For-profit)
Fall 2007 Enrollment: 280 . . . . (937) 746-6633
2007-08 Tuition: In-state $9,400; Out-of-state $9,400

Housing: Homeownership rate: 60.7% (2007); Median home value: $114,903 (2007); Median rent: $406 per month (2000); Median age of housing: 35 years (2000).
Newspapers: Chronicle (Local news; Circulation 2,205)
Transportation: Commute to work: 97.2% car, 0.2% public transportation, 1.2% walk, 1.2% work from home (2000); Travel time to work: 33.0% less than 15 minutes, 45.7% 15 to 30 minutes, 14.9% 30 to 45 minutes, 2.9% 45 to 60 minutes, 3.6% 60 minutes or more (2000)

Additional Information Contacts

City of Franklin . . . . (937) 746-9921
http://www.franklinohio.org
Franklin Area Chamber of Commerce . . . . (937) 746-8457
http://www.chamber45005.org

HARVEYSBURG (village). Covers a land area of 0.657 square miles and a water area of 0 square miles. Located at 39.50° N. Lat.; 84.00° W. Long. Elevation is 928 feet.
Population: 471 (1990); 563 (2000); 693 (2007); 776 (2012 projected); Race: 96.4% White, 1.6% Black, 0.0% Asian, 3.3% Hispanic of any race (2007); Density: 1,055.0 persons per square mile (2007); Average household size: 2.88 (2007); Median age: 31.7 (2007); Males per 100 females: 94.1 (2007); Marriage status: 23.0% never married, 57.7% now married, 7.8% widowed, 11.5% divorced (2000); Foreign born: 0.3% (2000); Ancestry (includes multiple ancestries): 20.3% German, 17.1% English, 16.1% United States or American, 9.6% Other groups, 8.4% Irish (2000).
Economy: Single-family building permits issued: 0 (2007); Multi-family building permits issued: 0 (2007); Employment by occupation: 12.5% management, 7.5% professional, 15.4% services, 27.5% sales, 1.1% farming, 17.1% construction, 18.9% production (2000).
Income: Per capita income: $21,562 (2007); Median household income: $52,778 (2007); Average household income: $62,002 (2007); Percent of households with income of $100,000 or more: 12.9% (2007); Poverty rate: 8.6% (2000).
Education: Percent of population age 25 and over with: High school diploma (including GED) or higher: 81.4% (2007); Bachelor's degree or higher: 13.8% (2007); Master's degree or higher: 2.6% (2007).
Housing: Homeownership rate: 75.1% (2007); Median home value: $116,741 (2007); Median rent: $497 per month (2000); Median age of housing: 42 years (2000).
Transportation: Commute to work: 93.8% car, 1.1% public transportation, 0.7% walk, 3.6% work from home (2000); Travel time to work: 22.3% less than 15 minutes, 25.3% 15 to 30 minutes, 35.1% 30 to 45 minutes, 14.0% 45 to 60 minutes, 3.4% 60 minutes or more (2000)

HUNTER (CDP). Covers a land area of 1.606 square miles and a water area of 0 square miles. Located at 39.49° N. Lat.; 84.29° W. Long. Elevation is 886 feet.
Population: 1,950 (1990); 1,737 (2000); 1,818 (2007); 1,871 (2012 projected); Race: 98.5% White, 0.2% Black, 0.1% Asian, 0.5% Hispanic of any race (2007); Density: 1,132.2 persons per square mile (2007); Average household size: 2.47 (2007); Median age: 42.0 (2007); Males per 100 females: 100.2 (2007); Marriage status: 19.4% never married, 62.5% now married, 5.8% widowed, 12.2% divorced (2000); Foreign born: 1.7% (2000); Ancestry (includes multiple ancestries): 19.9% United States or American, 15.5% German, 14.9% Other groups, 14.4% English, 11.6% Irish (2000).
Economy: Employment by occupation: 11.0% management, 17.8% professional, 16.5% services, 18.6% sales, 0.0% farming, 16.5% construction, 19.7% production (2000).
Income: Per capita income: $25,617 (2007); Median household income: $49,470 (2007); Average household income: $63,192 (2007); Percent of households with income of $100,000 or more: 11.9% (2007); Poverty rate: 1.0% (2000).
Education: Percent of population age 25 and over with: High school diploma (including GED) or higher: 85.9% (2007); Bachelor's degree or higher: 13.7% (2007); Master's degree or higher: 2.8% (2007).
Housing: Homeownership rate: 92.0% (2007); Median home value: $137,805 (2007); Median rent: $454 per month (2000); Median age of housing: 36 years (2000).
Transportation: Commute to work: 99.2% car, 0.0% public transportation, 0.0% walk, 0.0% work from home (2000); Travel time to work: 34.0% less than 15 minutes, 50.1% 15 to 30 minutes, 9.9% 30 to 45 minutes, 4.5% 45 to 60 minutes, 1.5% 60 minutes or more (2000)

KINGS MILLS (unincorporated postal area, zip code 45034). Covers a land area of 0.671 square miles and a water area of 0 square miles. Located at 39.35° N. Lat.; 84.24° W. Long. Elevation is 761 feet.
Population: 794 (2000); Race: 98.6% White, 0.0% Black, 0.0% Asian, 0.0% Hispanic of any race (2000); Density: 1,183.3 persons per square mile (2000); Age: 24.9% under 18, 4.5% over 64 (2000); Marriage status: 26.6% never married, 61.5% now married, 3.2% widowed, 8.7% divorced (2000); Foreign born: 0.0% (2000); Ancestry (includes multiple ancestries): 36.9% German, 19.7% Irish, 13.1% Other groups, 12.8% English, 8.0% United States or American (2000).
Economy: Employment by occupation: 11.9% management, 28.3% professional, 17.1% services, 17.7% sales, 0.0% farming, 11.9% construction, 13.2% production (2000).
Income: Per capita income: $26,323 (2000); Median household income: $59,038 (2000); Poverty rate: 0.9% (2000).
Education: Percent of population age 25 and over with: High school diploma (including GED) or higher: 93.7% (2000); Bachelor's degree or higher: 25.4% (2000).

School District(s)

Kings Local (PK-12)
2005-06 Enrollment: 3,839 . . . . (513) 398-8050
Housing: Homeownership rate: 84.2% (2000); Median home value: $178,700 (2000); Median rent: $343 per month (2000); Median age of housing: 5 years (2000).
Transportation: Commute to work: 92.5% car, 0.0% public transportation, 1.3% walk, 6.2% work from home (2000); Travel time to work: 24.6% less than 15 minutes, 47.2% 15 to 30 minutes, 28.2% 30 to 45 minutes, 0.0% 45 to 60 minutes, 0.0% 60 minutes or more (2000)

LANDEN (CDP). Covers a land area of 4.677 square miles and a water area of 0.083 square miles. Located at 39.30° N. Lat.; 84.28° W. Long. Elevation is 814 feet.
Population: 9,204 (1990); 12,766 (2000); 13,796 (2007); 14,591 (2012 projected); Race: 89.8% White, 1.5% Black, 5.8% Asian, 3.7% Hispanic of any race (2007); Density: 2,950.0 persons per square mile (2007); Average household size: 2.55 (2007); Median age: 34.9 (2007); Males per 100 females: 98.0 (2007); Marriage status: 22.0% never married, 65.3% now married, 3.0% widowed, 9.7% divorced (2000); Foreign born: 4.5% (2000); Ancestry (includes multiple ancestries): 36.4% German, 18.5% Irish, 12.4% English, 9.7% Other groups, 6.7% Italian (2000).
Economy: Employment by occupation: 24.8% management, 28.2% professional, 7.2% services, 28.0% sales, 0.0% farming, 5.3% construction, 6.6% production (2000).
Income: Per capita income: $34,369 (2007); Median household income: $71,104 (2007); Average household income: $87,676 (2007); Percent of households with income of $100,000 or more: 27.1% (2007); Poverty rate: 2.5% (2000).
Education: Percent of population age 25 and over with: High school diploma (including GED) or higher: 96.0% (2007); Bachelor's degree or higher: 50.6% (2007); Master's degree or higher: 15.1% (2007).
Housing: Homeownership rate: 67.8% (2007); Median home value: $174,856 (2007); Median rent: $742 per month (2000); Median age of housing: 13 years (2000).
Transportation: Commute to work: 92.7% car, 2.2% public transportation, 0.5% walk, 4.2% work from home (2000); Travel time to work: 25.1% less than 15 minutes, 38.7% 15 to 30 minutes, 23.8% 30 to 45 minutes, 7.0% 45 to 60 minutes, 5.4% 60 minutes or more (2000)

LEBANON (city). County seat. Covers a land area of 11.774 square miles and a water area of 0.005 square miles. Located at 39.42° N. Lat.; 84.21° W. Long. Elevation is 768 feet.
History: Named for the Semitic translation of "to be white". Lebanon was founded in 1803 and grew as the commercial center for the region between the two Miami Rivers. This was the home of Thomas Corwin (1794-1865) who was governor of Ohio, a U.S. senator, Secretary of the Treasury, and Minister to Mexico under Abraham Lincoln.
Population: 11,282 (1990); 16,962 (2000); 20,553 (2007); 22,872 (2012 projected); Race: 87.1% White, 8.7% Black, 1.3% Asian, 1.9% Hispanic of any race (2007); Density: 1,745.6 persons per square mile (2007); Average household size: 2.79 (2007); Median age: 32.5 (2007); Males per 100 females: 107.9 (2007); Marriage status: 19.8% never married, 59.3% now married, 5.7% widowed, 15.2% divorced (2000); Foreign born: 1.8% (2000); Ancestry (includes multiple ancestries): 20.5% German, 15.5% United States or American, 11.5% Irish, 9.0% English, 7.6% Other groups (2000).
Economy: Single-family building permits issued: 73 (2007); Multi-family building permits issued: 0 (2007); Employment by occupation: 13.5% management, 20.1% professional, 12.1% services, 27.8% sales, 0.1% farming, 8.9% construction, 17.6% production (2000).
Income: Per capita income: $24,578 (2007); Median household income: $54,867 (2007); Average household income: $66,371 (2007); Percent of households with income of $100,000 or more: 18.9% (2007); Poverty rate: 6.4% (2000).

Taxes: Total city taxes per capita: $465 (2006); City property taxes per capita: $150 (2006).
Education: Percent of population age 25 and over with: High school diploma (including GED) or higher: 86.2% (2007); Bachelor's degree or higher: 25.6% (2007); Master's degree or higher: 6.3% (2007).

School District(s)

Lebanon City (PK-12)
2005-06 Enrollment: 5,197 . . . . (513) 934-5770
Warren County (PK-12)
2005-06 Enrollment: n/a . . . . (513) 932-5677
Warren County Educational Service Center
2005-06 Enrollment: n/a . . . . (513) 695-2900
Warren County Virtual Community School (06-12)
2005-06 Enrollment: 128 . . . . (513) 695-2567

Vocational/Technical School(s)

Warren County Career Center (Public)
Fall 2007 Enrollment: 65 . . . . (513) 932-8145
2007-08 Tuition: $4,500
Housing: Homeownership rate: 60.5% (2007); Median home value: $160,254 (2007); Median rent: $495 per month (2000); Median age of housing: 22 years (2000).
Safety: Violent crime rate: 17.3 per 10,000 population; Property crime rate: 188.2 per 10,000 population (2007).
Newspapers: Dayton Daily News - Warren County Bureau (Local news); Today's Express (Community news; Circulation 9,800); Western Star (Community news; Circulation 16,300)
Transportation: Commute to work: 94.9% car, 0.7% public transportation, 1.3% walk, 2.5% work from home (2000); Travel time to work: 31.9% less than 15 minutes, 32.5% 15 to 30 minutes, 25.3% 30 to 45 minutes, 8.2% 45 to 60 minutes, 2.2% 60 minutes or more (2000)
Airports: Lebanon-Warren County (general aviation)
Additional Information Contacts
City of Lebanon . . . . (513) 932-3060
http://www.ci.lebanon.oh.us
Lebanon Area Chamber of Commerce . . . . (513) 932-1100
http://www.lebanonchamber.org

LOVELAND PARK (CDP). Covers a land area of 1.473 square miles and a water area of 0.068 square miles. Located at 39.29° N. Lat.; 84.26° W. Long. Elevation is 728 feet.
Population: 1,406 (1990); 1,799 (2000); 1,785 (2007); 1,768 (2012 projected); Race: 95.1% White, 1.0% Black, 2.6% Asian, 1.2% Hispanic of any race (2007); Density: 1,211.6 persons per square mile (2007); Average household size: 2.75 (2007); Median age: 38.6 (2007); Males per 100 females: 97.9 (2007); Marriage status: 21.0% never married, 63.0% now married, 3.6% widowed, 12.4% divorced (2000); Foreign born: 1.3% (2000); Ancestry (includes multiple ancestries): 29.1% German, 23.8% Irish, 14.6% United States or American, 9.4% English, 8.6% Other groups (2000).
Economy: Employment by occupation: 19.7% management, 14.3% professional, 16.3% services, 18.3% sales, 0.0% farming, 15.9% construction, 15.4% production (2000).
Income: Per capita income: $29,350 (2007); Median household income: $51,000 (2007); Average household income: $80,724 (2007); Percent of households with income of $100,000 or more: 21.1% (2007); Poverty rate: 1.8% (2000).
Education: Percent of population age 25 and over with: High school diploma (including GED) or higher: 80.8% (2007); Bachelor's degree or higher: 19.6% (2007); Master's degree or higher: 6.4% (2007).
Housing: Homeownership rate: 87.2% (2007); Median home value: $144,388 (2007); Median rent: $489 per month (2000); Median age of housing: 38 years (2000).
Transportation: Commute to work: 91.6% car, 1.0% public transportation, 1.0% walk, 6.3% work from home (2000); Travel time to work: 27.9% less than 15 minutes, 35.0% 15 to 30 minutes, 23.3% 30 to 45 minutes, 6.7% 45 to 60 minutes, 7.1% 60 minutes or more (2000)

MAINEVILLE (village). Covers a land area of 0.243 square miles and a water area of 0 square miles. Located at 39.31° N. Lat.; 84.22° W. Long. Elevation is 810 feet.
Population: 366 (1990); 885 (2000); 1,852 (2007); 2,472 (2012 projected); Race: 97.6% White, 0.3% Black, 0.2% Asian, 1.4% Hispanic of any race (2007); Density: 7,611.2 persons per square mile (2007); Average household size: 2.38 (2007); Median age: 38.3 (2007); Males per 100 females: 88.6 (2007); Marriage status: 20.8% never married, 58.6% now married, 7.7% widowed, 12.9% divorced (2000); Foreign born: 1.6% (2000); Ancestry (includes multiple ancestries): 30.3% German, 18.4% English, 18.2% Irish, 14.8% United States or American, 7.0% Other groups (2000).
Economy: Employment by occupation: 16.1% management, 20.0% professional, 11.2% services, 28.3% sales, 0.2% farming, 8.8% construction, 15.3% production (2000).
Income: Per capita income: $33,522 (2007); Median household income: $71,451 (2007); Average household income: $79,695 (2007); Percent of households with income of $100,000 or more: 25.5% (2007); Poverty rate: 3.2% (2000).
Education: Percent of population age 25 and over with: High school diploma (including GED) or higher: 85.6% (2007); Bachelor's degree or higher: 19.8% (2007); Master's degree or higher: 6.7% (2007).

School District(s)

Kings Local (PK-12)
2005-06 Enrollment: 3,839 . . . . (513) 398-8050
Little Miami Local (PK-12)
2005-06 Enrollment: 3,624 . . . . (513) 899-2264
Housing: Homeownership rate: 76.9% (2007); Median home value: $168,790 (2007); Median rent: $354 per month (2000); Median age of housing: 12 years (2000).
Transportation: Commute to work: 94.3% car, 0.6% public transportation, 0.0% walk, 4.3% work from home (2000); Travel time to work: 28.5% less than 15 minutes, 33.5% 15 to 30 minutes, 25.1% 30 to 45 minutes, 8.8% 45 to 60 minutes, 4.1% 60 minutes or more (2000)

MASON (city). Covers a land area of 17.613 square miles and a water area of 0.037 square miles. Located at 39.35° N. Lat.; 84.31° W. Long. Elevation is 810 feet.
Population: 12,046 (1990); 22,016 (2000); 30,484 (2007); 36,082 (2012 projected); Race: 90.5% White, 2.2% Black, 5.5% Asian, 1.4% Hispanic of any race (2007); Density: 1,730.8 persons per square mile (2007); Average household size: 2.81 (2007); Median age: 35.0 (2007); Males per 100 females: 95.2 (2007); Marriage status: 18.1% never married, 69.2% now married, 4.5% widowed, 8.1% divorced (2000); Foreign born: 4.0% (2000); Ancestry (includes multiple ancestries): 33.5% German, 18.3% Irish, 14.0% English, 9.3% Other groups, 8.2% United States or American (2000).
Economy: Unemployment rate: 4.7% (6/2008); Total civilian labor force: 16,260 (6/2008); Single-family building permits issued: 77 (2007); Multi-family building permits issued: 0 (2007); Employment by occupation: 20.8% management, 23.2% professional, 9.5% services, 29.7% sales, 0.1% farming, 5.0% construction, 11.7% production (2000).
Income: Per capita income: $36,701 (2007); Median household income: $81,913 (2007); Average household income: $103,096 (2007); Percent of households with income of $100,000 or more: 38.4% (2007); Poverty rate: 2.8% (2000).
Education: Percent of population age 25 and over with: High school diploma (including GED) or higher: 93.9% (2007); Bachelor's degree or higher: 41.4% (2007); Master's degree or higher: 12.8% (2007).

School District(s)

Mason City (PK-12)
2005-06 Enrollment: 9,778 . . . . (513) 398-0474
Housing: Homeownership rate: 86.1% (2007); Median home value: $196,220 (2007); Median rent: $527 per month (2000); Median age of housing: 12 years (2000).
Safety: Violent crime rate: 4.6 per 10,000 population; Property crime rate: 188.0 per 10,000 population (2007).
Newspapers: The Pulse-Journal (Community news; Circulation 34,000)
Transportation: Commute to work: 93.9% car, 1.0% public transportation, 0.3% walk, 4.5% work from home (2000); Travel time to work: 25.6% less than 15 minutes, 42.9% 15 to 30 minutes, 23.6% 30 to 45 minutes, 5.6% 45 to 60 minutes, 2.2% 60 minutes or more (2000)
Additional Information Contacts
City of Mason . . . . (513) 229-8500
http://www.imaginemason.org
Northeast Cincinnati Chamber of Commerce . . . . (513) 336-0125
http://www.necchamber.org

MORROW (village). Covers a land area of 1.691 square miles and a water area of 0.031 square miles. Located at 39.35° N. Lat.; 84.13° W. Long. Elevation is 640 feet.
History: Morrow was settled in 1844 and named for Jeremiah Morrow, Governor of Ohio from 1822 to 1826.

Population: 1,206 (1990); 1,286 (2000); 1,551 (2007); 1,724 (2012 projected); Race: 97.7% White, 0.6% Black, 0.2% Asian, 3.7% Hispanic of any race (2007); Density: 917.4 persons per square mile (2007); Average household size: 2.66 (2007); Median age: 38.6 (2007); Males per 100 females: 91.0 (2007); Marriage status: 17.2% never married, 59.3% now married, 8.4% widowed, 15.1% divorced (2000); Foreign born: 0.4% (2000); Ancestry (includes multiple ancestries): 20.0% German, 9.7% Irish, 9.5% United States or American, 9.0% English, 7.8% Other groups (2000).
Economy: Employment by occupation: 8.6% management, 10.9% professional, 16.0% services, 22.8% sales, 0.4% farming, 17.7% construction, 23.5% production (2000).
Income: Per capita income: $18,706 (2007); Median household income: $37,407 (2007); Average household income: $49,145 (2007); Percent of households with income of $100,000 or more: 10.7% (2007); Poverty rate: 15.5% (2000).
Education: Percent of population age 25 and over with: High school diploma (including GED) or higher: 70.3% (2007); Bachelor's degree or higher: 10.5% (2007); Master's degree or higher: 5.2% (2007).

School District(s)

Little Miami Local (PK-12)
2005-06 Enrollment: 3,624 . . . . (513) 899-2264

Housing: Homeownership rate: 57.2% (2007); Median home value: $117,700 (2007); Median rent: $394 per month (2000); Median age of housing: 49 years (2000).
Transportation: Commute to work: 91.0% car, 0.0% public transportation, 4.6% walk, 3.5% work from home (2000); Travel time to work: 24.0% less than 15 minutes, 37.0% 15 to 30 minutes, 23.2% 30 to 45 minutes, 9.7% 45 to 60 minutes, 6.1% 60 minutes or more (2000)

Additional Information Contacts

Morrow Area Chamber of Commerce . . . . (513) 899-4466
http://www.morrow-today.org

OREGONIA (unincorporated postal area, zip code 45054). Covers a land area of 31.745 square miles and a water area of 0.006 square miles. Located at 39.44° N. Lat.; 84.06° W. Long. Elevation is 690 feet.
Population: 1,689 (2000); Race: 99.7% White, 0.0% Black, 0.0% Asian, 0.4% Hispanic of any race (2000); Density: 53.2 persons per square mile (2000); Age: 27.3% under 18, 8.1% over 64 (2000); Marriage status: 15.5% never married, 66.0% now married, 4.0% widowed, 14.5% divorced (2000); Foreign born: 0.7% (2000); Ancestry (includes multiple ancestries): 23.5% German, 18.3% United States or American, 12.2% English, 11.5% Irish, 3.9% Dutch (2000).
Economy: Employment by occupation: 18.4% management, 18.8% professional, 15.9% services, 21.6% sales, 0.0% farming, 13.1% construction, 12.3% production (2000).
Income: Per capita income: $25,329 (2000); Median household income: $56,136 (2000); Poverty rate: 4.8% (2000).
Education: Percent of population age 25 and over with: High school diploma (including GED) or higher: 85.2% (2000); Bachelor's degree or higher: 23.6% (2000).
Housing: Homeownership rate: 87.5% (2000); Median home value: $141,700 (2000); Median rent: $421 per month (2000); Median age of housing: 25 years (2000).
Transportation: Commute to work: 95.7% car, 0.0% public transportation, 0.7% walk, 3.6% work from home (2000); Travel time to work: 12.7% less than 15 minutes, 35.5% 15 to 30 minutes, 35.4% 30 to 45 minutes, 10.5% 45 to 60 minutes, 5.9% 60 minutes or more (2000)

PLEASANT PLAIN (village). Covers a land area of 0.108 square miles and a water area of 0 square miles. Located at 39.28° N. Lat.; 84.10° W. Long. Elevation is 886 feet.
Population: 138 (1990); 156 (2000); 171 (2007); 180 (2012 projected); Race: 97.7% White, 0.0% Black, 2.3% Asian, 0.0% Hispanic of any race (2007); Density: 1,580.6 persons per square mile (2007); Average household size: 2.76 (2007); Median age: 36.8 (2007); Males per 100 females: 106.0 (2007); Marriage status: 18.9% never married, 60.4% now married, 5.7% widowed, 15.1% divorced (2000); Foreign born: 7.3% (2000); Ancestry (includes multiple ancestries): 35.1% German, 11.3% Other groups, 9.9% Italian, 8.6% Irish, 5.3% English (2000).
Economy: Employment by occupation: 17.4% management, 11.6% professional, 7.2% services, 33.3% sales, 0.0% farming, 21.7% construction, 8.7% production (2000).
Income: Per capita income: $20,629 (2007); Median household income: $55,000 (2007); Average household income: $56,895 (2007); Percent of households with income of $100,000 or more: 3.2% (2007); Poverty rate: 7.3% (2000).
Education: Percent of population age 25 and over with: High school diploma (including GED) or higher: 90.4% (2007); Bachelor's degree or higher: 19.3% (2007); Master's degree or higher: 1.8% (2007).
Housing: Homeownership rate: 82.3% (2007); Median home value: $95,667 (2007); Median rent: $575 per month (2000); Median age of housing: 60+ years (2000).
Transportation: Commute to work: 100.0% car, 0.0% public transportation, 0.0% walk, 0.0% work from home (2000); Travel time to work: 13.4% less than 15 minutes, 40.3% 15 to 30 minutes, 25.4% 30 to 45 minutes, 20.9% 45 to 60 minutes, 0.0% 60 minutes or more (2000)

SOUTH LEBANON (village). Covers a land area of 1.668 square miles and a water area of 0.030 square miles. Located at 39.37° N. Lat.; 84.21° W. Long. Elevation is 623 feet.
Population: 2,786 (1990); 2,538 (2000); 3,063 (2007); 3,414 (2012 projected); Race: 97.9% White, 0.0% Black, 0.4% Asian, 1.9% Hispanic of any race (2007); Density: 1,835.8 persons per square mile (2007); Average household size: 2.44 (2007); Median age: 33.6 (2007); Males per 100 females: 97.9 (2007); Marriage status: 20.1% never married, 61.7% now married, 7.9% widowed, 10.3% divorced (2000); Foreign born: 0.4% (2000); Ancestry (includes multiple ancestries): 31.5% United States or American, 10.0% Irish, 9.6% German, 9.1% Other groups, 5.7% English (2000).
Economy: Single-family building permits issued: 26 (2007); Multi-family building permits issued: 6 (2007); Employment by occupation: 3.4% management, 4.7% professional, 22.7% services, 16.4% sales, 0.0% farming, 19.1% construction, 33.7% production (2000).
Income: Per capita income: $18,597 (2007); Median household income: $41,019 (2007); Average household income: $45,461 (2007); Percent of households with income of $100,000 or more: 3.3% (2007); Poverty rate: 12.7% (2000).
Education: Percent of population age 25 and over with: High school diploma (including GED) or higher: 52.1% (2007); Bachelor's degree or higher: 2.2% (2007); Master's degree or higher: 1.0% (2007).
Housing: Homeownership rate: 68.6% (2007); Median home value: $86,406 (2007); Median rent: $396 per month (2000); Median age of housing: 38 years (2000).
Transportation: Commute to work: 96.4% car, 0.4% public transportation, 1.7% walk, 0.5% work from home (2000); Travel time to work: 31.6% less than 15 minutes, 41.7% 15 to 30 minutes, 18.1% 30 to 45 minutes, 3.6% 45 to 60 minutes, 5.0% 60 minutes or more (2000)

SPRINGBORO (city). Covers a land area of 8.810 square miles and a water area of 0 square miles. Located at 39.56° N. Lat.; 84.22° W. Long. Elevation is 774 feet.
Population: 7,772 (1990); 12,380 (2000); 17,032 (2007); 20,113 (2012 projected); Race: 92.9% White, 1.2% Black, 4.2% Asian, 1.5% Hispanic of any race (2007); Density: 1,933.2 persons per square mile (2007); Average household size: 2.89 (2007); Median age: 34.7 (2007); Males per 100 females: 95.1 (2007); Marriage status: 14.2% never married, 76.7% now married, 2.5% widowed, 6.6% divorced (2000); Foreign born: 2.1% (2000); Ancestry (includes multiple ancestries): 31.1% German, 17.4% Irish, 15.3% English, 11.0% United States or American, 8.9% Other groups (2000).
Economy: Single-family building permits issued: 69 (2007); Multi-family building permits issued: 0 (2007); Employment by occupation: 21.7% management, 26.2% professional, 8.6% services, 26.7% sales, 0.0% farming, 4.8% construction, 12.1% production (2000).
Income: Per capita income: $35,816 (2007); Median household income: $84,671 (2007); Average household income: $103,446 (2007); Percent of households with income of $100,000 or more: 40.3% (2007); Poverty rate: 3.0% (2000).
Taxes: Total city taxes per capita: $624 (2006); City property taxes per capita: $46 (2006).
Education: Percent of population age 25 and over with: High school diploma (including GED) or higher: 94.1% (2007); Bachelor's degree or higher: 43.8% (2007); Master's degree or higher: 16.1% (2007).

School District(s)

Springboro Community City (PK-12)
2005-06 Enrollment: 4,784 . . . . (937) 748-3960

Two-year College(s)

Miami-Jacobs Career College-Springboro Branch (Private, For-profit)
Fall 2007 Enrollment: 387 . . . . (937) 746-1830
2007-08 Tuition: In-state $10,440; Out-of-state $10,440

Housing: Homeownership rate: 87.9% (2007); Median home value: $214,443 (2007); Median rent: $476 per month (2000); Median age of housing: 11 years (2000).
Newspapers: Springboro Sun (Community news; Circulation 14,000)
Transportation: Commute to work: 94.4% car, 0.2% public transportation, 0.7% walk, 3.9% work from home (2000); Travel time to work: 26.9% less than 15 minutes, 44.2% 15 to 30 minutes, 20.0% 30 to 45 minutes, 4.9% 45 to 60 minutes, 4.0% 60 minutes or more (2000)
Additional Information Contacts
City of Springboro .... (937) 748-4343
http://www.ci.springboro.oh.us
Springboro Chamber of Commerce.................... (937) 748-0074
http://www.springboroohio.org

WAYNESVILLE (village). Covers a land area of 2.274 square miles and a water area of 0.066 square miles. Located at 39.53° N. Lat.; 84.08° W. Long. Elevation is 751 feet.
History: Waynesville was laid out in 1796 by Samuel Highway and Dr. Evan Banes, and was named for General Anthony Wayne. Many of the early residents were Quakers from Carolina and Pennsylvania.
Population: 1,954 (1990); 2,558 (2000); 3,049 (2007); 3,374 (2012 projected); Race: 97.9% White, 0.0% Black, 0.1% Asian, 1.3% Hispanic of any race (2007); Density: 1,340.7 persons per square mile (2007); Average household size: 2.45 (2007); Median age: 36.8 (2007); Males per 100 females: 90.2 (2007); Marriage status: 20.1% never married, 61.0% now married, 9.2% widowed, 9.8% divorced (2000); Foreign born: 0.3% (2000); Ancestry (includes multiple ancestries): 23.0% German, 15.8% United States or American, 14.1% English, 13.2% Irish, 5.9% Other groups (2000).
Economy: Employment by occupation: 15.2% management, 23.5% professional, 13.5% services, 22.3% sales, 0.5% farming, 9.1% construction, 15.9% production (2000).
Income: Per capita income: $26,994 (2007); Median household income: $54,722 (2007); Average household income: $65,215 (2007); Percent of households with income of $100,000 or more: 15.9% (2007); Poverty rate: 3.9% (2000).
Education: Percent of population age 25 and over with: High school diploma (including GED) or higher: 82.5% (2007); Bachelor's degree or higher: 22.8% (2007); Master's degree or higher: 8.4% (2007).

School District(s)

Wayne Local (PK-12)
2005-06 Enrollment: 1,480 .... (513) 897-6971
Housing: Homeownership rate: 68.5% (2007); Median home value: $157,027 (2007); Median rent: $429 per month (2000); Median age of housing: 25 years (2000).
Transportation: Commute to work: 94.7% car, 0.0% public transportation, 1.6% walk, 3.2% work from home (2000); Travel time to work: 22.0% less than 15 minutes, 36.3% 15 to 30 minutes, 30.8% 30 to 45 minutes, 7.1% 45 to 60 minutes, 3.7% 60 minutes or more (2000)
Additional Information Contacts
Waynesville Area Chamber of Commerce.............. (513) 897-8855
http://www.waynesvilleohio.com

Washington County

Located in southeastern Ohio; bounded on the southeast by the Ohio River and the West Virginia border; crossed by the Muskingum and Little Muskingum Rivers. Covers a land area of 635.15 square miles, a water area of 5.00 square miles, and is located in the Eastern Time Zone. The county was founded in 1788. County seat is Marietta.

Washington County is part of the Parkersburg-Marietta-Vienna, WV-OH Metropolitan Statistical Area. The entire metro area includes: Washington County, OH; Pleasants County, WV; Wirt County, WV; Wood County, WV

Weather Station: Marietta WWTP Elevation: 577 feet

	Jan	Feb	Mar	Apr	May	Jun	Jul	Aug	Sep	Oct	Nov	Dec
High	40	44	54	65	75	82	86	85	78	67	55	45
Low	22	24	32	41	50	59	64	62	55	43	35	27
Precip	3.1	2.8	3.7	3.1	4.0	4.4	4.2	4.2	3.3	2.9	3.2	3.4
Snow	7.2	na	3.4	0.5	0.0	0.0	0.0	0.0	0.0	tr	0.6	2.6

High and Low temperatures in degrees Fahrenheit; Precipitation and Snow in inches

Population: 62,254 (1990); 63,251 (2000); 61,915 (2007); 60,767 (2012 projected); Race: 97.3% White, 1.0% Black, 0.4% Asian, 0.7% Hispanic of any race (2007); Density: 97.5 persons per square mile (2007); Average household size: 2.47 (2007); Median age: 41.3 (2007); Males per 100 females: 95.1 (2007).
Religion: Five largest groups: 8.2% The United Methodist Church, 8.1% Catholic Church, 5.9% American Baptist Churches in the USA, 3.6% Churches of Christ, 2.0% Christian Churches and Churches of Christ (2000).
Economy: Unemployment rate: 5.6% (6/2008); Total civilian labor force: 33,082 (6/2008); Leading industries: 18.1% manufacturing; 17.6% health care and social assistance; 14.1% retail trade (2005); Farms: 952 totaling 141,455 acres (2002); Companies that employ 500 or more persons: 3 (2006); Companies that employ 100 to 499 persons: 32 (2006); Companies that employ less than 100 persons: 1,525 (2006); Black-owned businesses: n/a (2002); Hispanic-owned businesses: n/a (2002); Asian-owned businesses: n/a (2002); Women-owned businesses: 1,544 (2002); Retail sales per capita: $13,138 (2008). Single-family building permits issued: 24 (2007); Multi-family building permits issued: 0 (2007).
Income: Per capita income: $21,231 (2007); Median household income: $39,283 (2007); Average household income: $51,356 (2007); Percent of households with income of $100,000 or more: 9.6% (2007); Poverty rate: 13.3% (2005); Bankruptcy rate: 1.98% (2007).
Taxes: Total county taxes per capita: $312 (2006); County property taxes per capita: $150 (2006).
Education: Percent of population age 25 and over with: High school diploma (including GED) or higher: 84.4% (2007); Bachelor's degree or higher: 15.0% (2007); Master's degree or higher: 5.7% (2007).
Housing: Homeownership rate: 76.5% (2007); Median home value: $95,455 (2007); Median rent: $319 per month (2000); Median age of housing: 33 years (2000).
Health: Birth rate: 112.1 per 10,000 population (2007); Death rate: 115.3 per 10,000 population (2007); Age-adjusted cancer mortality rate: 216.5 deaths per 100,000 population (2005); Air Quality Index: 68.1% good, 24.9% moderate, 7.0% unhealthy for sensitive individuals, 0.0% unhealthy (percent of days in 2007); Number of physicians: 18.4 per 10,000 population (2005); Hospital beds: 35.5 per 10,000 population (2004); Hospital admissions: 1,340.0 per 10,000 population (2004).
Elections: 2004 Presidential election results: 58.0% Bush, 41.5% Kerry, 0.0% Nader, 0.3% Badnarik
National and State Parks: Howes State Park; Marietta State Forest Nursery
Additional Information Contacts
Washington County Government..................... (740) 373-6623
http://www.washingtongov.org
Belpre Area Chamber of Commerce .... (740) 423-8934
http://www.belprechamber.com
Beverly-Waterford Area Chamber of Commerce......... (740) 525-2044
http://www.bwchamber.net
City of Marietta.................................. (740) 373-1387
http://www.mariettaoh.net
Marietta Area Chamber of Commerce................. (740) 373-5176
http://www.mariettachamber.com

Washington County Communities

BELPRE (city). Covers a land area of 3.524 square miles and a water area of 0.027 square miles. Located at 39.28° N. Lat.; 81.58° W. Long. Elevation is 614 feet.
History: Belpre was established in 1789 by Captain Jonathan Stone who led a group of Revolutionary War veterans here from Marietta.
Population: 6,866 (1990); 6,660 (2000); 6,437 (2007); 6,252 (2012 projected); Race: 95.9% White, 2.3% Black, 0.4% Asian, 0.7% Hispanic of any race (2007); Density: 1,826.4 persons per square mile (2007); Average household size: 2.13 (2007); Median age: 42.9 (2007); Males per 100 females: 85.5 (2007); Marriage status: 20.3% never married, 55.4% now married, 9.9% widowed, 14.4% divorced (2000); Foreign born: 0.6% (2000); Ancestry (includes multiple ancestries): 18.3% German, 17.4% United States or American, 11.7% Irish, 10.1% English, 9.6% Other groups (2000).
Economy: Single-family building permits issued: 19 (2007); Multi-family building permits issued: 0 (2007); Employment by occupation: 10.6% management, 16.5% professional, 15.4% services, 32.4% sales, 0.0% farming, 8.1% construction, 17.1% production (2000).
Income: Per capita income: $20,738 (2007); Median household income: $34,000 (2007); Average household income: $44,018 (2007); Percent of households with income of $100,000 or more: 8.2% (2007); Poverty rate: 15.2% (2000).

Education: Percent of population age 25 and over with: High school diploma (including GED) or higher: 82.6% (2007); Bachelor's degree or higher: 13.5% (2007); Master's degree or higher: 4.1% (2007).

School District(s)

Belpre City (PK-12)
2005-06 Enrollment: 1,258 . . . . (740) 423-9511
Washington
2005-06 Enrollment: n/a . . . . (740) 373-6669

Housing: Homeownership rate: 66.0% (2007); Median home value: $94,135 (2007); Median rent: $334 per month (2000); Median age of housing: 34 years (2000).
Safety: Violent crime rate: 7.7 per 10,000 population; Property crime rate: 211.7 per 10,000 population (2007).
Transportation: Commute to work: 94.0% car, 0.4% public transportation, 2.4% walk, 1.9% work from home (2000); Travel time to work: 48.2% less than 15 minutes, 39.8% 15 to 30 minutes, 6.5% 30 to 45 minutes, 1.8% 45 to 60 minutes, 3.8% 60 minutes or more (2000)

Additional Information Contacts

Belpre Area Chamber of Commerce . . . . (740) 423-8934
http://www.belprechamber.com

BEVERLY (village). Covers a land area of 0.729 square miles and a water area of 0.055 square miles. Located at 39.54° N. Lat.; 81.63° W. Long. Elevation is 659 feet.
History: Beverly was settled in 1789 by a group of adventurers from Marietta. Fort Frye was erected, but it was abandoned in 1794 and a new community was established on the Muskingum River at the mouth of Olive Green Creek.
Population: 1,511 (1990); 1,282 (2000); 1,235 (2007); 1,215 (2012 projected); Race: 99.4% White, 0.4% Black, 0.1% Asian, 0.2% Hispanic of any race (2007); Density: 1,693.1 persons per square mile (2007); Average household size: 2.25 (2007); Median age: 45.4 (2007); Males per 100 females: 87.7 (2007); Marriage status: 19.1% never married, 63.0% now married, 9.3% widowed, 8.5% divorced (2000); Foreign born: 0.4% (2000); Ancestry (includes multiple ancestries): 28.4% German, 13.0% Irish, 9.6% English, 9.6% United States or American, 4.1% Italian (2000).
Economy: Single-family building permits issued: 1 (2007); Multi-family building permits issued: 0 (2007); Employment by occupation: 8.5% management, 14.9% professional, 18.2% services, 27.5% sales, 0.8% farming, 11.0% construction, 19.2% production (2000).
Income: Per capita income: $23,796 (2007); Median household income: $39,103 (2007); Average household income: $50,917 (2007); Percent of households with income of $100,000 or more: 9.1% (2007); Poverty rate: 9.8% (2000).
Education: Percent of population age 25 and over with: High school diploma (including GED) or higher: 84.8% (2007); Bachelor's degree or higher: 17.8% (2007); Master's degree or higher: 5.7% (2007).

School District(s)

Fort Frye Local (PK-12)
2005-06 Enrollment: 1,229 . . . . (740) 984-2497

Housing: Homeownership rate: 71.4% (2007); Median home value: $84,730 (2007); Median rent: $317 per month (2000); Median age of housing: 35 years (2000).
Safety: Violent crime rate: 0.0 per 10,000 population; Property crime rate: 435.1 per 10,000 population (2007).
Transportation: Commute to work: 92.8% car, 0.0% public transportation, 4.5% walk, 2.1% work from home (2000); Travel time to work: 40.8% less than 15 minutes, 16.6% 15 to 30 minutes, 32.6% 30 to 45 minutes, 4.0% 45 to 60 minutes, 6.1% 60 minutes or more (2000)

Additional Information Contacts

Beverly-Waterford Area Chamber of Commerce . . . . (740) 525-2044
http://www.bwchamber.net

CUTLER (unincorporated postal area, zip code 45724). Covers a land area of 52.092 square miles and a water area of 0.010 square miles. Located at 39.36° N. Lat.; 81.78° W. Long. Elevation is 780 feet.
Population: 1,547 (2000); Race: 91.2% White, 5.1% Black, 0.0% Asian, 0.0% Hispanic of any race (2000); Density: 29.7 persons per square mile (2000); Age: 25.1% under 18, 15.3% over 64 (2000); Marriage status: 17.1% never married, 66.4% now married, 7.4% widowed, 9.0% divorced (2000); Foreign born: 0.6% (2000); Ancestry (includes multiple ancestries): 13.7% German, 13.0% English, 12.5% United States or American, 8.5% Other groups, 7.8% Irish (2000).
Economy: Employment by occupation: 5.2% management, 18.3% professional, 17.9% services, 16.3% sales, 0.0% farming, 9.9% construction, 32.3% production (2000).
Income: Per capita income: $15,518 (2000); Median household income: $35,357 (2000); Poverty rate: 5.9% (2000).
Education: Percent of population age 25 and over with: High school diploma (including GED) or higher: 77.8% (2000); Bachelor's degree or higher: 9.7% (2000).

School District(s)

Warren Local (PK-12)
2005-06 Enrollment: 2,716 . . . . (740) 678-2366

Housing: Homeownership rate: 90.6% (2000); Median home value: $82,000 (2000); Median rent: $293 per month (2000); Median age of housing: 25 years (2000).
Transportation: Commute to work: 91.8% car, 0.0% public transportation, 2.3% walk, 3.4% work from home (2000); Travel time to work: 8.5% less than 15 minutes, 15.1% 15 to 30 minutes, 44.7% 30 to 45 minutes, 24.1% 45 to 60 minutes, 7.7% 60 minutes or more (2000)

DEVOLA (CDP). Covers a land area of 5.132 square miles and a water area of 0.223 square miles. Located at 39.47° N. Lat.; 81.47° W. Long. Elevation is 682 feet.
History: Also spelled De Vola.
Population: 2,736 (1990); 2,771 (2000); 2,701 (2007); 2,686 (2012 projected); Race: 97.7% White, 0.1% Black, 1.9% Asian, 0.1% Hispanic of any race (2007); Density: 526.3 persons per square mile (2007); Average household size: 2.53 (2007); Median age: 47.2 (2007); Males per 100 females: 93.9 (2007); Marriage status: 16.2% never married, 66.5% now married, 10.9% widowed, 6.4% divorced (2000); Foreign born: 0.0% (2000); Ancestry (includes multiple ancestries): 33.2% German, 13.5% English, 11.6% Irish, 8.3% United States or American, 5.0% Scottish (2000).
Economy: Employment by occupation: 15.4% management, 28.6% professional, 10.7% services, 24.3% sales, 1.5% farming, 10.3% construction, 9.2% production (2000).
Income: Per capita income: $24,400 (2007); Median household income: $48,085 (2007); Average household income: $61,184 (2007); Percent of households with income of $100,000 or more: 14.4% (2007); Poverty rate: 4.5% (2000).
Education: Percent of population age 25 and over with: High school diploma (including GED) or higher: 93.2% (2007); Bachelor's degree or higher: 29.0% (2007); Master's degree or higher: 11.5% (2007).
Housing: Homeownership rate: 90.4% (2007); Median home value: $125,370 (2007); Median rent: $468 per month (2000); Median age of housing: 35 years (2000).
Transportation: Commute to work: 96.9% car, 0.0% public transportation, 1.4% walk, 1.7% work from home (2000); Travel time to work: 38.2% less than 15 minutes, 42.2% 15 to 30 minutes, 10.9% 30 to 45 minutes, 2.4% 45 to 60 minutes, 6.3% 60 minutes or more (2000)

FLEMING (unincorporated postal area, zip code 45729). Covers a land area of 27.516 square miles and a water area of 0.049 square miles. Located at 39.42° N. Lat.; 81.59° W. Long. Elevation is 797 feet.
Population: 1,410 (2000); Race: 97.4% White, 0.6% Black, 0.0% Asian, 0.0% Hispanic of any race (2000); Density: 51.2 persons per square mile (2000); Age: 22.6% under 18, 12.6% over 64 (2000); Marriage status: 12.4% never married, 74.6% now married, 8.0% widowed, 5.0% divorced (2000); Foreign born: 0.0% (2000); Ancestry (includes multiple ancestries): 25.9% German, 18.5% United States or American, 16.8% Irish, 10.2% English, 4.6% Other groups (2000).
Economy: Employment by occupation: 5.6% management, 16.1% professional, 9.0% services, 33.1% sales, 0.0% farming, 12.5% construction, 23.6% production (2000).
Income: Per capita income: $19,008 (2000); Median household income: $40,667 (2000); Poverty rate: 8.3% (2000).
Education: Percent of population age 25 and over with: High school diploma (including GED) or higher: 85.8% (2000); Bachelor's degree or higher: 14.4% (2000).
Housing: Homeownership rate: 92.6% (2000); Median home value: $85,000 (2000); Median rent: $331 per month (2000); Median age of housing: 25 years (2000).
Transportation: Commute to work: 94.4% car, 0.0% public transportation, 2.4% walk, 2.6% work from home (2000); Travel time to work: 11.9% less than 15 minutes, 52.0% 15 to 30 minutes, 26.2% 30 to 45 minutes, 7.5% 45 to 60 minutes, 2.4% 60 minutes or more (2000)

LITTLE HOCKING (unincorporated postal area, zip code 45742). Covers a land area of 26.393 square miles and a water area of 0 square miles. Located at 39.27° N. Lat.; 81.70° W. Long. Elevation is 660 feet.
History: George Washington camped near the site of Little Hocking, on the river of the same name, while making a tour of the Ohio Valley in 1770. At that time the river was called the Little Hockhocking.
Population: 3,217 (2000); Race: 97.8% White, 0.3% Black, 0.0% Asian, 1.0% Hispanic of any race (2000); Density: 121.9 persons per square mile (2000); Age: 27.6% under 18, 11.0% over 64 (2000); Marriage status: 18.6% never married, 68.0% now married, 4.5% widowed, 8.9% divorced (2000); Foreign born: 0.8% (2000); Ancestry (includes multiple ancestries): 21.3% German, 19.4% United States or American, 10.3% English, 10.3% Irish, 5.7% Other groups (2000).
Economy: Employment by occupation: 5.9% management, 21.1% professional, 11.8% services, 30.1% sales, 0.0% farming, 9.1% construction, 22.0% production (2000).
Income: Per capita income: $16,633 (2000); Median household income: $39,583 (2000); Poverty rate: 5.5% (2000).
Education: Percent of population age 25 and over with: High school diploma (including GED) or higher: 83.4% (2000); Bachelor's degree or higher: 15.9% (2000).

School District(s)

Warren Local (PK-12)
2005-06 Enrollment: 2,716 . . . . (740) 678-2366

Housing: Homeownership rate: 87.1% (2000); Median home value: $73,100 (2000); Median rent: $308 per month (2000); Median age of housing: 26 years (2000).
Transportation: Commute to work: 90.6% car, 0.0% public transportation, 1.1% walk, 5.6% work from home (2000); Travel time to work: 18.9% less than 15 minutes, 50.6% 15 to 30 minutes, 21.4% 30 to 45 minutes, 1.4% 45 to 60 minutes, 7.8% 60 minutes or more (2000)

LOWELL (village). Covers a land area of 0.254 square miles and a water area of 0 square miles. Located at 39.52° N. Lat.; 81.50° W. Long. Elevation is 617 feet.
History: Lowell was founded in 1822 and grew around woolen mills. It was named for the textile town in Massachusetts.
Population: 614 (1990); 628 (2000); 623 (2007); 608 (2012 projected); Race: 99.5% White, 0.0% Black, 0.0% Asian, 0.6% Hispanic of any race (2007); Density: 2,456.6 persons per square mile (2007); Average household size: 2.38 (2007); Median age: 39.8 (2007); Males per 100 females: 101.0 (2007); Marriage status: 19.2% never married, 54.5% now married, 14.6% widowed, 11.6% divorced (2000); Foreign born: 0.7% (2000); Ancestry (includes multiple ancestries): 33.4% German, 19.2% United States or American, 12.7% Irish, 9.3% English, 6.3% Other groups (2000).
Economy: Single-family building permits issued: 0 (2007); Multi-family building permits issued: 0 (2007); Employment by occupation: 3.1% management, 10.0% professional, 21.2% services, 21.9% sales, 0.8% farming, 13.5% construction, 29.6% production (2000).
Income: Per capita income: $18,018 (2007); Median household income: $36,176 (2007); Average household income: $42,844 (2007); Percent of households with income of $100,000 or more: 4.6% (2007); Poverty rate: 14.5% (2000).
Education: Percent of population age 25 and over with: High school diploma (including GED) or higher: 84.6% (2007); Bachelor's degree or higher: 6.5% (2007); Master's degree or higher: 2.7% (2007).

School District(s)

Fort Frye Local (PK-12)
2005-06 Enrollment: 1,229 . . . . (740) 984-2497

Housing: Homeownership rate: 78.2% (2007); Median home value: $57,759 (2007); Median rent: $329 per month (2000); Median age of housing: 60+ years (2000).
Transportation: Commute to work: 93.3% car, 0.0% public transportation, 2.4% walk, 2.4% work from home (2000); Travel time to work: 14.6% less than 15 minutes, 63.6% 15 to 30 minutes, 15.4% 30 to 45 minutes, 3.2% 45 to 60 minutes, 3.2% 60 minutes or more (2000)

LOWER SALEM (village). Covers a land area of 0.079 square miles and a water area of 0 square miles. Located at 39.56° N. Lat.; 81.39° W. Long. Elevation is 650 feet.
History: Lower Salem was platted in 1850 by James Stanley.
Population: 103 (1990); 109 (2000); 105 (2007); 102 (2012 projected); Race: 92.4% White, 2.9% Black, 0.0% Asian, 0.0% Hispanic of any race (2007); Density: 1,322.8 persons per square mile (2007); Average household size: 3.09 (2007); Median age: 33.4 (2007); Males per 100 females: 66.7 (2007); Marriage status: 11.4% never married, 64.8% now married, 5.7% widowed, 18.2% divorced (2000); Foreign born: 0.0% (2000); Ancestry (includes multiple ancestries): 55.4% German, 21.6% Irish, 17.3% United States or American, 14.4% Swiss, 7.9% Dutch (2000).
Economy: Single-family building permits issued: 0 (2007); Multi-family building permits issued: 0 (2007); Employment by occupation: 15.7% management, 7.8% professional, 15.7% services, 27.5% sales, 0.0% farming, 11.8% construction, 21.6% production (2000).
Income: Per capita income: $16,071 (2007); Median household income: $45,000 (2007); Average household income: $49,632 (2007); Percent of households with income of $100,000 or more: 17.6% (2007); Poverty rate: 5.0% (2000).
Education: Percent of population age 25 and over with: High school diploma (including GED) or higher: 92.2% (2007); Bachelor's degree or higher: 7.8% (2007); Master's degree or higher: 3.1% (2007).

School District(s)

Fort Frye Local (PK-12)
2005-06 Enrollment: 1,229 . . . . (740) 984-2497

Housing: Homeownership rate: 82.4% (2007); Median home value: $54,000 (2007); Median rent: $225 per month (2000); Median age of housing: 60+ years (2000).
Transportation: Commute to work: 80.4% car, 3.9% public transportation, 5.9% walk, 9.8% work from home (2000); Travel time to work: 6.5% less than 15 minutes, 52.2% 15 to 30 minutes, 23.9% 30 to 45 minutes, 4.3% 45 to 60 minutes, 13.0% 60 minutes or more (2000)

MACKSBURG (village). Covers a land area of 0.233 square miles and a water area of 0 square miles. Located at 39.63° N. Lat.; 81.45° W. Long. Elevation is 702 feet.
Population: 218 (1990); 202 (2000); 197 (2007); 194 (2012 projected); Race: 99.5% White, 0.0% Black, 0.0% Asian, 2.0% Hispanic of any race (2007); Density: 845.0 persons per square mile (2007); Average household size: 2.46 (2007); Median age: 38.4 (2007); Males per 100 females: 121.3 (2007); Marriage status: 16.1% never married, 51.7% now married, 14.7% widowed, 17.5% divorced (2000); Foreign born: 0.0% (2000); Ancestry (includes multiple ancestries): 49.5% United States or American, 8.4% Irish, 8.4% German, 4.2% English, 3.2% Dutch (2000).
Economy: Employment by occupation: 0.0% management, 14.1% professional, 33.8% services, 8.5% sales, 8.5% farming, 12.7% construction, 22.5% production (2000).
Income: Per capita income: $11,751 (2007); Median household income: $26,250 (2007); Average household income: $28,938 (2007); Percent of households with income of $100,000 or more: 5.0% (2007); Poverty rate: 45.3% (2000).
Education: Percent of population age 25 and over with: High school diploma (including GED) or higher: 46.6% (2007); Bachelor's degree or higher: 1.5% (2007); Master's degree or higher: 1.5% (2007).
Housing: Homeownership rate: 77.5% (2007); Median home value: $36,250 (2007); Median rent: $225 per month (2000); Median age of housing: 58 years (2000).
Transportation: Commute to work: 93.7% car, 0.0% public transportation, 4.8% walk, 1.6% work from home (2000); Travel time to work: 30.6% less than 15 minutes, 22.6% 15 to 30 minutes, 30.6% 30 to 45 minutes, 9.7% 45 to 60 minutes, 6.5% 60 minutes or more (2000)

MARIETTA (city). County seat. Covers a land area of 8.309 square miles and a water area of 0.264 square miles. Located at 39.42° N. Lat.; 81.45° W. Long. Elevation is 614 feet.
History: Marietta was settled at the confluence of the Muskingum and Ohio Rivers in 1788 by the Ohio Company of Associates, a group of New Englanders looking for land to the west. At first they called the settlement Muskingum, but soon the name was officially declared to be Marietta, a tribute to Queen Marie Antoinette of France for her help in the American Revolution.
Population: 15,187 (1990); 14,515 (2000); 14,032 (2007); 13,638 (2012 projected); Race: 95.9% White, 1.4% Black, 0.8% Asian, 1.1% Hispanic of any race (2007); Density: 1,688.9 persons per square mile (2007); Average household size: 2.44 (2007); Median age: 40.1 (2007); Males per 100 females: 88.3 (2007); Marriage status: 26.2% never married, 49.3% now married, 10.6% widowed, 13.9% divorced (2000); Foreign born: 1.2% (2000); Ancestry (includes multiple ancestries): 26.7% German, 14.0% English, 14.0% Irish, 9.8% United States or American, 6.9% Other groups (2000).

Economy: Single-family building permits issued: 3 (2007); Multi-family building permits issued: 0 (2007); Employment by occupation: 12.1% management, 22.4% professional, 18.1% services, 26.1% sales, 0.1% farming, 6.5% construction, 14.8% production (2000).
Income: Per capita income: $21,006 (2007); Median household income: $33,088 (2007); Average household income: $47,544 (2007); Percent of households with income of $100,000 or more: 9.2% (2007); Poverty rate: 16.9% (2000).
Taxes: Total city taxes per capita: $593 (2006); City property taxes per capita: $48 (2006).
Education: Percent of population age 25 and over with: High school diploma (including GED) or higher: 83.7% (2007); Bachelor's degree or higher: 23.0% (2007); Master's degree or higher: 10.4% (2007).

School District(s)

Frontier Local (PK-12)
2005-06 Enrollment: 942 . . . . (740) 865-3473
Marietta City (PK-12)
2005-06 Enrollment: 3,038 . . . . (740) 374-6500
Warren Local (PK-12)
2005-06 Enrollment: 2,716 . . . . (740) 678-2366
Washington County (09-12)
2005-06 Enrollment: n/a . . . . (740) 373-2766

Four-year College(s)

Marietta College (Private, Not-for-profit)
Fall 2007 Enrollment: 1,605. . . . . (740) 376-4643
2007-08 Tuition: In-state $24,842; Out-of-state $24,842

Two-year College(s)

Washington State Community College (Public)
Fall 2007 Enrollment: 1,243. . . . . (740) 374-8716
2007-08 Tuition: In-state $3,336; Out-of-state $6,546

Vocational/Technical School(s)

Washington County Career Center-Adult Technical Training (Public)
Fall 2007 Enrollment: 273 . . . . (740) 373-6283
2007-08 Tuition: $7,000

Housing: Homeownership rate: 59.1% (2007); Median home value: $92,475 (2007); Median rent: $328 per month (2000); Median age of housing: 52 years (2000).
Hospitals: Marietta Memorial Hospital (204 beds); Selby General Hospital (80 beds)
Safety: Violent crime rate: 17.7 per 10,000 population; Property crime rate: 379.4 per 10,000 population (2007).
Newspapers: Marietta AM (Local news; Circulation 13,400); Marietta Times (Local news; Circulation 11,000)
Transportation: Commute to work: 89.1% car, 0.4% public transportation, 7.7% walk, 2.1% work from home (2000); Travel time to work: 57.3% less than 15 minutes, 28.3% 15 to 30 minutes, 7.8% 30 to 45 minutes, 1.9% 45 to 60 minutes, 4.7% 60 minutes or more (2000)

Additional Information Contacts

City of Marietta. . . . . (740) 373-1387
http://www.mariettaoh.net
Marietta Area Chamber of Commerce . . . . (740) 373-5176
http://www.mariettachamber.com

MATAMORAS (village). Aka New Matamoras. Covers a land area of 0.360 square miles and a water area of 0.025 square miles. Located at 39.52° N. Lat.; 81.06° W. Long. Elevation is 646 feet.
History: Matamoras, known as New Matamoras, was the center of a gas and oil boom during the latter decades of the 19th century.
Population: 1,007 (1990); 957 (2000); 788 (2007); 780 (2012 projected); Race: 99.1% White, 0.5% Black, 0.1% Asian, 0.3% Hispanic of any race (2007); Density: 2,187.3 persons per square mile (2007); Average household size: 2.26 (2007); Median age: 37.6 (2007); Males per 100 females: 82.8 (2007); Marriage status: 26.8% never married, 56.0% now married, 6.5% widowed, 10.6% divorced (2000); Foreign born: 0.2% (2000); Ancestry (includes multiple ancestries): 18.9% United States or American, 15.3% German, 14.3% Irish, 9.2% Other groups, 6.3% English (2000).
Economy: Single-family building permits issued: 1 (2007); Multi-family building permits issued: 0 (2007); Employment by occupation: 3.4% management, 9.1% professional, 27.2% services, 23.8% sales, 2.3% farming, 10.4% construction, 23.8% production (2000).
Income: Per capita income: $17,478 (2007); Median household income: $28,977 (2007); Average household income: $39,463 (2007); Percent of households with income of $100,000 or more: 8.3% (2007); Poverty rate: 29.3% (2000).
Education: Percent of population age 25 and over with: High school diploma (including GED) or higher: 74.8% (2007); Bachelor's degree or higher: 6.9% (2007); Master's degree or higher: 1.3% (2007).
Housing: Homeownership rate: 54.4% (2007); Median home value: $61,250 (2007); Median rent: $144 per month (2000); Median age of housing: 46 years (2000).
Transportation: Commute to work: 90.8% car, 0.0% public transportation, 6.5% walk, 1.1% work from home (2000); Travel time to work: 24.4% less than 15 minutes, 24.9% 15 to 30 minutes, 20.3% 30 to 45 minutes, 22.5% 45 to 60 minutes, 7.9% 60 minutes or more (2000)

NEW MATAMORAS (unincorporated postal area, zip code 45767). Aka Matamoras. Covers a land area of 102.833 square miles and a water area of 0.345 square miles. Located at 39.52° N. Lat.; 81.06° W. Long. Elevation is 627 feet.
Population: 2,840 (2000); Race: 97.4% White, 0.4% Black, 0.0% Asian, 0.1% Hispanic of any race (2000); Density: 27.6 persons per square mile (2000); Age: 22.5% under 18, 15.2% over 64 (2000); Marriage status: 18.0% never married, 65.3% now married, 8.4% widowed, 8.3% divorced (2000); Foreign born: 0.1% (2000); Ancestry (includes multiple ancestries): 19.0% German, 18.4% United States or American, 14.1% Irish, 9.7% English, 6.7% Other groups (2000).
Economy: Employment by occupation: 2.9% management, 8.8% professional, 25.9% services, 21.3% sales, 0.9% farming, 10.9% construction, 29.2% production (2000).
Income: Per capita income: $15,070 (2000); Median household income: $27,042 (2000); Poverty rate: 20.2% (2000).
Education: Percent of population age 25 and over with: High school diploma (including GED) or higher: 77.2% (2000); Bachelor's degree or higher: 6.0% (2000).

School District(s)

Frontier Local (PK-12)
2005-06 Enrollment: 942 . . . . (740) 865-3473

Housing: Homeownership rate: 75.6% (2000); Median home value: $59,600 (2000); Median rent: $169 per month (2000); Median age of housing: 41 years (2000).
Transportation: Commute to work: 95.5% car, 0.0% public transportation, 2.5% walk, 0.6% work from home (2000); Travel time to work: 20.1% less than 15 minutes, 21.6% 15 to 30 minutes, 31.7% 30 to 45 minutes, 18.7% 45 to 60 minutes, 7.9% 60 minutes or more (2000)

NEWPORT (unincorporated postal area, zip code 45768). Covers a land area of 31.197 square miles and a water area of 0.080 square miles. Located at 39.39° N. Lat.; 81.25° W. Long. Elevation is 651 feet.
Population: 1,926 (2000); Race: 100.0% White, 0.0% Black, 0.0% Asian, 0.0% Hispanic of any race (2000); Density: 61.7 persons per square mile (2000); Age: 25.1% under 18, 12.4% over 64 (2000); Marriage status: 19.6% never married, 69.3% now married, 2.8% widowed, 8.4% divorced (2000); Foreign born: 0.6% (2000); Ancestry (includes multiple ancestries): 26.7% United States or American, 14.9% German, 9.0% Irish, 7.4% English, 6.5% Other groups (2000).
Economy: Employment by occupation: 10.3% management, 9.1% professional, 23.5% services, 26.9% sales, 0.3% farming, 9.3% construction, 20.6% production (2000).
Income: Per capita income: $17,073 (2000); Median household income: $39,329 (2000); Poverty rate: 9.1% (2000).
Education: Percent of population age 25 and over with: High school diploma (including GED) or higher: 85.0% (2000); Bachelor's degree or higher: 6.5% (2000).

School District(s)

Frontier Local (PK-12)
2005-06 Enrollment: 942 . . . . (740) 865-3473

Housing: Homeownership rate: 79.7% (2000); Median home value: $75,400 (2000); Median rent: $253 per month (2000); Median age of housing: 28 years (2000).
Transportation: Commute to work: 92.7% car, 1.0% public transportation, 3.1% walk, 3.3% work from home (2000); Travel time to work: 19.2% less than 15 minutes, 40.9% 15 to 30 minutes, 25.7% 30 to 45 minutes, 12.4% 45 to 60 minutes, 1.8% 60 minutes or more (2000)

RENO (unincorporated postal area, zip code 45773). Covers a land area of 11.677 square miles and a water area of 0 square miles. Located at 39.47° N. Lat.; 81.28° W. Long. Elevation is 653 feet.
Population: 278 (2000); Race: 100.0% White, 0.0% Black, 0.0% Asian, 0.0% Hispanic of any race (2000); Density: 23.8 persons per square mile

(2000); Age: 24.0% under 18, 7.8% over 64 (2000); Marriage status: 9.9% never married, 80.1% now married, 1.2% widowed, 8.8% divorced (2000); Foreign born: 8.3% (2000); Ancestry (includes multiple ancestries): 24.0% German, 16.6% United States or American, 11.1% Irish, 8.3% Canadian, 8.3% Italian (2000).
Economy: Employment by occupation: 3.6% management, 21.4% professional, 11.9% services, 36.9% sales, 0.0% farming, 6.0% construction, 20.2% production (2000).
Income: Per capita income: $10,268 (2000); Median household income: $31,250 (2000); Poverty rate: 20.7% (2000).
Education: Percent of population age 25 and over with: High school diploma (including GED) or higher: 70.7% (2000); Bachelor's degree or higher: 0.0% (2000).

School District(s)

Marietta City (PK-12)
2005-06 Enrollment: 3,038 .... (740) 374-6500
Housing: Homeownership rate: 100.0% (2000); Median home value: $32,500 (2000); Median rent: $n/a per month (2000); Median age of housing: 32 years (2000).
Transportation: Commute to work: 100.0% car, 0.0% public transportation, 0.0% walk, 0.0% work from home (2000); Travel time to work: 0.0% less than 15 minutes, 56.0% 15 to 30 minutes, 29.8% 30 to 45 minutes, 0.0% 45 to 60 minutes, 14.3% 60 minutes or more (2000)

VINCENT (unincorporated postal area, zip code 45784). Covers a land area of 38.733 square miles and a water area of 0.212 square miles. Located at 39.38° N. Lat.; 81.68° W. Long. Elevation is 770 feet.
Population: 2,833 (2000); Race: 97.9% White, 0.0% Black, 0.0% Asian, 0.0% Hispanic of any race (2000); Density: 73.1 persons per square mile (2000); Age: 26.8% under 18, 10.8% over 64 (2000); Marriage status: 19.1% never married, 67.3% now married, 3.8% widowed, 9.8% divorced (2000); Foreign born: 0.3% (2000); Ancestry (includes multiple ancestries): 20.2% United States or American, 18.6% German, 11.2% English, 8.6% Irish, 5.1% Other groups (2000).
Economy: Employment by occupation: 13.3% management, 15.3% professional, 12.2% services, 27.1% sales, 1.3% farming, 10.2% construction, 20.7% production (2000).
Income: Per capita income: $18,320 (2000); Median household income: $41,964 (2000); Poverty rate: 8.3% (2000).
Education: Percent of population age 25 and over with: High school diploma (including GED) or higher: 90.7% (2000); Bachelor's degree or higher: 13.6% (2000).

School District(s)

Warren Local (PK-12)
2005-06 Enrollment: 2,716 .... (740) 678-2366
Housing: Homeownership rate: 89.3% (2000); Median home value: $96,900 (2000); Median rent: $298 per month (2000); Median age of housing: 24 years (2000).
Transportation: Commute to work: 93.4% car, 0.0% public transportation, 4.4% walk, 2.2% work from home (2000); Travel time to work: 16.3% less than 15 minutes, 41.1% 15 to 30 minutes, 31.4% 30 to 45 minutes, 6.0% 45 to 60 minutes, 5.2% 60 minutes or more (2000)

WATERFORD (unincorporated postal area, zip code 45786). Covers a land area of 56.396 square miles and a water area of 0.466 square miles. Located at 39.52° N. Lat.; 81.66° W. Long. Elevation is 675 feet.
Population: 2,989 (2000); Race: 97.4% White, 0.4% Black, 0.8% Asian, 0.0% Hispanic of any race (2000); Density: 53.0 persons per square mile (2000); Age: 28.1% under 18, 12.5% over 64 (2000); Marriage status: 16.5% never married, 67.1% now married, 5.1% widowed, 11.2% divorced (2000); Foreign born: 0.2% (2000); Ancestry (includes multiple ancestries): 32.5% German, 11.3% United States or American, 9.6% English, 9.6% Irish, 5.1% Other groups (2000).
Economy: Employment by occupation: 9.5% management, 12.1% professional, 16.2% services, 17.5% sales, 2.7% farming, 15.9% construction, 26.0% production (2000).
Income: Per capita income: $15,471 (2000); Median household income: $36,860 (2000); Poverty rate: 10.3% (2000).
Education: Percent of population age 25 and over with: High school diploma (including GED) or higher: 87.2% (2000); Bachelor's degree or higher: 7.5% (2000).

School District(s)

Wolf Creek Local (PK-12)
2005-06 Enrollment: 693 .... (740) 984-2373
Housing: Homeownership rate: 87.6% (2000); Median home value: $77,300 (2000); Median rent: $276 per month (2000); Median age of housing: 26 years (2000).
Transportation: Commute to work: 92.7% car, 0.0% public transportation, 2.7% walk, 3.4% work from home (2000); Travel time to work: 31.7% less than 15 minutes, 19.7% 15 to 30 minutes, 30.7% 30 to 45 minutes, 11.8% 45 to 60 minutes, 6.1% 60 minutes or more (2000)

WHIPPLE (unincorporated postal area, zip code 45788). Covers a land area of 33.202 square miles and a water area of 0.005 square miles. Located at 39.51° N. Lat.; 81.37° W. Long. Elevation is 646 feet.
Population: 1,001 (2000); Race: 98.4% White, 0.0% Black, 0.0% Asian, 0.8% Hispanic of any race (2000); Density: 30.1 persons per square mile (2000); Age: 22.8% under 18, 11.3% over 64 (2000); Marriage status: 21.9% never married, 65.8% now married, 6.1% widowed, 6.2% divorced (2000); Foreign born: 0.8% (2000); Ancestry (includes multiple ancestries): 26.1% German, 11.7% Irish, 11.6% United States or American, 8.5% Other groups, 2.4% English (2000).
Economy: Employment by occupation: 8.3% management, 6.5% professional, 13.9% services, 25.0% sales, 3.4% farming, 14.6% construction, 28.3% production (2000).
Income: Per capita income: $16,281 (2000); Median household income: $36,071 (2000); Poverty rate: 9.3% (2000).
Education: Percent of population age 25 and over with: High school diploma (including GED) or higher: 85.9% (2000); Bachelor's degree or higher: 3.4% (2000).
Housing: Homeownership rate: 85.1% (2000); Median home value: $61,600 (2000); Median rent: $168 per month (2000); Median age of housing: 30 years (2000).
Transportation: Commute to work: 83.9% car, 0.0% public transportation, 0.0% walk, 7.4% work from home (2000); Travel time to work: 16.0% less than 15 minutes, 49.0% 15 to 30 minutes, 29.1% 30 to 45 minutes, 4.9% 45 to 60 minutes, 1.0% 60 minutes or more (2000)

WINGETT RUN (unincorporated postal area, zip code 45789). Covers a land area of 16.651 square miles and a water area of 0 square miles. Located at 39.55° N. Lat.; 81.25° W. Long. Elevation is 660 feet.
Population: 308 (2000); Race: 100.0% White, 0.0% Black, 0.0% Asian, 0.0% Hispanic of any race (2000); Density: 18.5 persons per square mile (2000); Age: 29.3% under 18, 9.1% over 64 (2000); Marriage status: 28.4% never married, 41.9% now married, 2.3% widowed, 27.5% divorced (2000); Foreign born: 0.0% (2000); Ancestry (includes multiple ancestries): 45.1% United States or American, 19.5% Other groups, 13.1% English, 9.4% Scotch-Irish, 5.7% German (2000).
Economy: Employment by occupation: 0.0% management, 6.3% professional, 33.1% services, 15.0% sales, 0.0% farming, 22.0% construction, 23.6% production (2000).
Income: Per capita income: $10,017 (2000); Median household income: $27,050 (2000); Poverty rate: 23.0% (2000).
Education: Percent of population age 25 and over with: High school diploma (including GED) or higher: 72.7% (2000); Bachelor's degree or higher: 5.0% (2000).
Housing: Homeownership rate: 74.5% (2000); Median home value: $14,400 (2000); Median rent: $225 per month (2000); Median age of housing: 34 years (2000).
Transportation: Commute to work: 100.0% car, 0.0% public transportation, 0.0% walk, 0.0% work from home (2000); Travel time to work: 7.1% less than 15 minutes, 0.0% 15 to 30 minutes, 56.7% 30 to 45 minutes, 29.9% 45 to 60 minutes, 6.3% 60 minutes or more (2000)

Wayne County

Located in north central Ohio; crossed by the Lake Fork of the Mohican River. Covers a land area of 555.36 square miles, a water area of 0.96 square miles, and is located in the Eastern Time Zone. The county was founded in 1786. County seat is Wooster.

Wayne County is part of the Wooster, OH Micropolitan Statistical Area. The entire metro area includes: Wayne County, OH

Weather Station: Wooster Exp. Station Elevation: 1,017 feet

	Jan	Feb	Mar	Apr	May	Jun	Jul	Aug	Sep	Oct	Nov	Dec
High	32	36	47	59	69	78	82	80	73	61	49	38
Low	18	20	28	37	48	57	61	59	52	41	33	24
Precip	2.2	1.9	2.8	3.4	3.9	4.0	4.0	3.9	3.4	2.6	3.1	2.7
Snow	10.0	7.2	5.1	1.2	tr	0.0	0.0	tr	0.0	tr	1.9	6.3

High and Low temperatures in degrees Fahrenheit; Precipitation and Snow in inches

Population: 101,461 (1990); 111,564 (2000); 114,243 (2007); 115,675 (2012 projected); Race: 96.3% White, 1.5% Black, 0.8% Asian, 1.1% Hispanic of any race (2007); Density: 205.7 persons per square mile (2007); Average household size: 2.69 (2007); Median age: 37.0 (2007); Males per 100 females: 97.9 (2007).
Religion: Five largest groups: 7.8% Catholic Church, 7.0% The United Methodist Church, 4.4% Presbyterian Church (U.S.A.), 4.2% Evangelical Lutheran Church in America, 4.1% Old Order Amish Church (2000).
Economy: Unemployment rate: 5.6% (6/2008); Total civilian labor force: 60,338 (6/2008); Leading industries: 31.2% manufacturing; 13.3% retail trade; 12.7% health care and social assistance (2005); Farms: 1,894 totaling 267,169 acres (2002); Companies that employ 500 or more persons: 6 (2006); Companies that employ 100 to 499 persons: 63 (2006); Companies that employ less than 100 persons: 2,552 (2006); Black-owned businesses: n/a (2002); Hispanic-owned businesses: n/a (2002); Asian-owned businesses: n/a (2002); Women-owned businesses: 2,275 (2002); Retail sales per capita: $10,525 (2008). Single-family building permits issued: 239 (2007); Multi-family building permits issued: 104 (2007).
Income: Per capita income: $21,424 (2007); Median household income: $46,810 (2007); Average household income: $57,149 (2007); Percent of households with income of $100,000 or more: 11.4% (2007); Poverty rate: 10.5% (2005); Bankruptcy rate: 3.59% (2007).
Taxes: Total county taxes per capita: $232 (2006); County property taxes per capita: $143 (2006).
Education: Percent of population age 25 and over with: High school diploma (including GED) or higher: 79.9% (2007); Bachelor's degree or higher: 17.4% (2007); Master's degree or higher: 5.6% (2007).
Housing: Homeownership rate: 73.9% (2007); Median home value: $131,498 (2007); Median rent: $403 per month (2000); Median age of housing: 33 years (2000).
Health: Birth rate: 145.0 per 10,000 population (2007); Death rate: 86.3 per 10,000 population (2007); Age-adjusted cancer mortality rate: 194.4 deaths per 100,000 population (2005); Number of physicians: 14.0 per 10,000 population (2005); Hospital beds: 14.6 per 10,000 population (2004); Hospital admissions: 573.5 per 10,000 population (2004).
Elections: 2004 Presidential election results: 61.5% Bush, 38.2% Kerry, 0.0% Nader, 0.2% Badnarik
National and State Parks: Killbuck Marsh State Wildlife Area
Additional Information Contacts
Wayne County Government. . . . . (330) 287-5400
http://www.wayneohio.org
Apple Creek Area Chamber of Commerce . . . . (330) 698-2631
City of Orrville . . . . (330) 684-5000
http://www.orrville.com
City of Rittman . . . . (330) 925-2045
http://www.rittman.com
City of Wooster . . . . (330) 263-5200
http://www.woosteroh.com
Dalton Area Chamber of Commerce . . . . (330) 828-2281
http://www.daltonohchamber.com
Wayne County Convention & Visitors Bureau . . . . (330) 264-1800
http://www.waynecountycvb.org
Wooster Chamber of Commerce . . . . (330) 262-5735
http://www.woosterchamber.com

Wayne County Communities

APPLE CREEK (village). Covers a land area of 0.606 square miles and a water area of 0 square miles. Located at 40.75° N. Lat.; 81.83° W. Long. Elevation is 1,043 feet.
Population: 863 (1990); 999 (2000); 940 (2007); 928 (2012 projected); Race: 97.7% White, 0.0% Black, 0.6% Asian, 0.9% Hispanic of any race (2007); Density: 1,550.9 persons per square mile (2007); Average household size: 2.43 (2007); Median age: 36.2 (2007); Males per 100 females: 90.7 (2007); Marriage status: 21.0% never married, 65.3% now married, 4.8% widowed, 8.9% divorced (2000); Foreign born: 1.6% (2000); Ancestry (includes multiple ancestries): 32.8% German, 11.6% Irish, 9.3% Other groups, 7.2% United States or American, 6.9% English (2000).
Economy: Employment by occupation: 9.9% management, 17.4% professional, 12.8% services, 25.2% sales, 0.7% farming, 9.7% construction, 24.3% production (2000).
Income: Per capita income: $21,418 (2007); Median household income: $46,188 (2007); Average household income: $52,022 (2007); Percent of households with income of $100,000 or more: 7.0% (2007); Poverty rate: 5.5% (2000).
Education: Percent of population age 25 and over with: High school diploma (including GED) or higher: 81.0% (2007); Bachelor's degree or higher: 14.1% (2007); Master's degree or higher: 2.2% (2007).
School District(s)
Southeast Local (PK-12)
2005-06 Enrollment: 1,733 . . . . (330) 698-3001
Housing: Homeownership rate: 72.9% (2007); Median home value: $110,417 (2007); Median rent: $394 per month (2000); Median age of housing: 43 years (2000).
Transportation: Commute to work: 89.8% car, 0.0% public transportation, 3.4% walk, 6.7% work from home (2000); Travel time to work: 32.7% less than 15 minutes, 53.7% 15 to 30 minutes, 5.0% 30 to 45 minutes, 3.4% 45 to 60 minutes, 5.2% 60 minutes or more (2000)
Additional Information Contacts
Apple Creek Area Chamber of Commerce . . . . (330) 698-2631

BURBANK (village). Covers a land area of 0.331 square miles and a water area of 0 square miles. Located at 40.98° N. Lat.; 81.99° W. Long. Elevation is 955 feet.
Population: 289 (1990); 279 (2000); 298 (2007); 308 (2012 projected); Race: 97.7% White, 0.0% Black, 1.7% Asian, 1.7% Hispanic of any race (2007); Density: 899.6 persons per square mile (2007); Average household size: 2.64 (2007); Median age: 37.3 (2007); Males per 100 females: 108.4 (2007); Marriage status: 25.9% never married, 55.2% now married, 6.0% widowed, 12.9% divorced (2000); Foreign born: 1.4% (2000); Ancestry (includes multiple ancestries): 30.5% German, 17.0% United States or American, 16.7% Other groups, 5.7% English, 3.9% Welsh (2000).
Economy: Employment by occupation: 4.1% management, 6.9% professional, 14.5% services, 25.5% sales, 0.0% farming, 17.2% construction, 31.7% production (2000).
Income: Per capita income: $20,973 (2007); Median household income: $45,833 (2007); Average household income: $55,310 (2007); Percent of households with income of $100,000 or more: 6.2% (2007); Poverty rate: 7.2% (2000).
Education: Percent of population age 25 and over with: High school diploma (including GED) or higher: 82.1% (2007); Bachelor's degree or higher: 2.0% (2007); Master's degree or higher: 0.0% (2007).
School District(s)
North Central Local (PK-12)
2005-06 Enrollment: 1,473 . . . . (330) 435-6382
Housing: Homeownership rate: 80.5% (2007); Median home value: $102,232 (2007); Median rent: $367 per month (2000); Median age of housing: 60+ years (2000).
Transportation: Commute to work: 96.4% car, 0.0% public transportation, 1.4% walk, 0.0% work from home (2000); Travel time to work: 23.0% less than 15 minutes, 46.8% 15 to 30 minutes, 15.8% 30 to 45 minutes, 2.9% 45 to 60 minutes, 11.5% 60 minutes or more (2000)

CONGRESS (village). Covers a land area of 0.166 square miles and a water area of 0 square miles. Located at 40.92° N. Lat.; 82.05° W. Long. Elevation is 1,161 feet.
History: Congress was established in 1827.
Population: 162 (1990); 192 (2000); 197 (2007); 194 (2012 projected); Race: 97.0% White, 0.0% Black, 0.0% Asian, 0.0% Hispanic of any race (2007); Density: 1,184.3 persons per square mile (2007); Average household size: 2.90 (2007); Median age: 39.0 (2007); Males per 100 females: 105.2 (2007); Marriage status: 23.0% never married, 64.5% now married, 4.6% widowed, 7.9% divorced (2000); Foreign born: 0.0% (2000); Ancestry (includes multiple ancestries): 29.9% German, 18.3% Irish, 16.2% Other groups, 10.7% English, 3.6% Italian (2000).
Economy: Employment by occupation: 7.2% management, 7.2% professional, 15.5% services, 23.7% sales, 7.2% farming, 14.4% construction, 24.7% production (2000).
Income: Per capita income: $19,480 (2007); Median household income: $50,000 (2007); Average household income: $56,434 (2007); Percent of households with income of $100,000 or more: 5.9% (2007); Poverty rate: 4.1% (2000).
Education: Percent of population age 25 and over with: High school diploma (including GED) or higher: 60.3% (2007); Bachelor's degree or higher: 5.9% (2007); Master's degree or higher: 0.0% (2007).
Housing: Homeownership rate: 88.2% (2007); Median home value: $104,412 (2007); Median rent: $483 per month (2000); Median age of housing: 60+ years (2000).

Transportation: Commute to work: 96.9% car, 0.0% public transportation, 0.0% walk, 3.1% work from home (2000); Travel time to work: 12.8% less than 15 minutes, 54.3% 15 to 30 minutes, 23.4% 30 to 45 minutes, 2.1% 45 to 60 minutes, 7.4% 60 minutes or more (2000)

CRESTON (village). Covers a land area of 2.207 square miles and a water area of 0 square miles. Located at 40.98° N. Lat.; 81.89° W. Long. Elevation is 991 feet.

Population: 1,931 (1990); 2,161 (2000); 2,099 (2007); 2,084 (2012 projected); Race: 98.6% White, 0.3% Black, 0.0% Asian, 0.1% Hispanic of any race (2007); Density: 951.0 persons per square mile (2007); Average household size: 2.56 (2007); Median age: 38.4 (2007); Males per 100 females: 100.9 (2007); Marriage status: 17.7% never married, 64.8% now married, 8.1% widowed, 9.4% divorced (2000); Foreign born: 0.4% (2000); Ancestry (includes multiple ancestries): 28.4% German, 11.4% Irish, 11.3% English, 7.9% United States or American, 4.6% Other groups (2000).

Economy: Employment by occupation: 6.7% management, 13.5% professional, 16.3% services, 26.7% sales, 0.3% farming, 9.9% construction, 26.6% production (2000).

Income: Per capita income: $19,265 (2007); Median household income: $45,431 (2007); Average household income: $49,314 (2007); Percent of households with income of $100,000 or more: 6.3% (2007); Poverty rate: 4.9% (2000).

Education: Percent of population age 25 and over with: High school diploma (including GED) or higher: 72.6% (2007); Bachelor's degree or higher: 7.9% (2007); Master's degree or higher: 1.7% (2007).

School District(s)

North Central Local (PK-12)
2005-06 Enrollment: 1,473 . . . . (330) 435-6382

Housing: Homeownership rate: 79.6% (2007); Median home value: $116,802 (2007); Median rent: $381 per month (2000); Median age of housing: 34 years (2000).

Safety: Violent crime rate: 4.7 per 10,000 population; Property crime rate: 272.0 per 10,000 population (2007).

Transportation: Commute to work: 95.5% car, 0.8% public transportation, 1.5% walk, 1.4% work from home (2000); Travel time to work: 31.5% less than 15 minutes, 40.6% 15 to 30 minutes, 16.7% 30 to 45 minutes, 8.8% 45 to 60 minutes, 2.4% 60 minutes or more (2000)

DALTON (village). Covers a land area of 1.222 square miles and a water area of 0 square miles. Located at 40.79° N. Lat.; 81.69° W. Long. Elevation is 1,102 feet.

Population: 1,381 (1990); 1,605 (2000); 1,558 (2007); 1,547 (2012 projected); Race: 98.3% White, 0.1% Black, 0.3% Asian, 1.4% Hispanic of any race (2007); Density: 1,275.4 persons per square mile (2007); Average household size: 2.56 (2007); Median age: 36.5 (2007); Males per 100 females: 95.5 (2007); Marriage status: 22.6% never married, 62.2% now married, 5.2% widowed, 10.0% divorced (2000); Foreign born: 0.3% (2000); Ancestry (includes multiple ancestries): 39.9% German, 15.3% Irish, 11.4% Swiss, 7.3% English, 6.1% United States or American (2000).

Economy: Employment by occupation: 10.0% management, 16.7% professional, 15.2% services, 21.1% sales, 0.7% farming, 8.6% construction, 27.7% production (2000).

Income: Per capita income: $25,342 (2007); Median household income: $54,138 (2007); Average household income: $64,938 (2007); Percent of households with income of $100,000 or more: 12.7% (2007); Poverty rate: 4.5% (2000).

Education: Percent of population age 25 and over with: High school diploma (including GED) or higher: 87.5% (2007); Bachelor's degree or higher: 17.2% (2007); Master's degree or higher: 4.8% (2007).

School District(s)

Dalton Local (PK-12)
2005-06 Enrollment: 997 . . . . (330) 828-2267

Housing: Homeownership rate: 78.3% (2007); Median home value: $122,024 (2007); Median rent: $407 per month (2000); Median age of housing: 34 years (2000).

Newspapers: Dalton Gazette & Kidron News (Community news; Circulation 1,450)

Transportation: Commute to work: 93.9% car, 0.2% public transportation, 3.7% walk, 1.5% work from home (2000); Travel time to work: 44.5% less than 15 minutes, 40.5% 15 to 30 minutes, 10.0% 30 to 45 minutes, 3.4% 45 to 60 minutes, 1.7% 60 minutes or more (2000)

Additional Information Contacts

Dalton Area Chamber of Commerce . . . . (330) 828-2281
http://www.daltonohchamber.com

DOYLESTOWN (village). Covers a land area of 1.760 square miles and a water area of 0 square miles. Located at 40.97° N. Lat.; 81.69° W. Long. Elevation is 1,250 feet.

Population: 2,876 (1990); 2,799 (2000); 2,846 (2007); 2,875 (2012 projected); Race: 98.8% White, 0.1% Black, 0.1% Asian, 0.8% Hispanic of any race (2007); Density: 1,617.0 persons per square mile (2007); Average household size: 2.43 (2007); Median age: 41.5 (2007); Males per 100 females: 89.7 (2007); Marriage status: 21.5% never married, 62.2% now married, 6.8% widowed, 9.5% divorced (2000); Foreign born: 0.1% (2000); Ancestry (includes multiple ancestries): 33.0% German, 15.3% Irish, 13.0% English, 6.7% Italian, 6.5% United States or American (2000).

Economy: Single-family building permits issued: 5 (2007); Multi-family building permits issued: 0 (2007); Employment by occupation: 14.6% management, 21.9% professional, 12.5% services, 26.0% sales, 0.8% farming, 10.1% construction, 14.0% production (2000).

Income: Per capita income: $25,917 (2007); Median household income: $53,962 (2007); Average household income: $62,526 (2007); Percent of households with income of $100,000 or more: 15.9% (2007); Poverty rate: 5.2% (2000).

Education: Percent of population age 25 and over with: High school diploma (including GED) or higher: 88.4% (2007); Bachelor's degree or higher: 21.8% (2007); Master's degree or higher: 7.1% (2007).

School District(s)

Chippewa Local (PK-12)
2005-06 Enrollment: 1,526 . . . . (330) 658-6368

Housing: Homeownership rate: 69.5% (2007); Median home value: $150,670 (2007); Median rent: $482 per month (2000); Median age of housing: 35 years (2000).

Transportation: Commute to work: 96.9% car, 0.4% public transportation, 1.9% walk, 0.8% work from home (2000); Travel time to work: 24.8% less than 15 minutes, 50.4% 15 to 30 minutes, 17.7% 30 to 45 minutes, 4.1% 45 to 60 minutes, 2.9% 60 minutes or more (2000)

Additional Information Contacts

Barberton-South Summit Chamber of Commerce . . . . (330) 745-3141
http://www.southsummitchamber.org

FREDERICKSBURG (village). Covers a land area of 0.330 square miles and a water area of 0 square miles. Located at 40.67° N. Lat.; 81.87° W. Long. Elevation is 971 feet.

Population: 464 (1990); 487 (2000); 484 (2007); 482 (2012 projected); Race: 98.1% White, 0.0% Black, 0.0% Asian, 0.2% Hispanic of any race (2007); Density: 1,465.5 persons per square mile (2007); Average household size: 2.59 (2007); Median age: 36.3 (2007); Males per 100 females: 100.0 (2007); Marriage status: 28.1% never married, 57.8% now married, 8.1% widowed, 6.1% divorced (2000); Foreign born: 0.2% (2000); Ancestry (includes multiple ancestries): 24.8% German, 11.2% Irish, 9.6% Other groups, 7.7% English, 6.9% French (except Basque) (2000).

Economy: Employment by occupation: 4.5% management, 14.8% professional, 23.0% services, 19.8% sales, 0.0% farming, 10.3% construction, 27.6% production (2000).

Income: Per capita income: $15,760 (2007); Median household income: $36,912 (2007); Average household income: $40,642 (2007); Percent of households with income of $100,000 or more: 1.1% (2007); Poverty rate: 7.9% (2000).

Education: Percent of population age 25 and over with: High school diploma (including GED) or higher: 75.2% (2007); Bachelor's degree or higher: 10.6% (2007); Master's degree or higher: 1.9% (2007).

School District(s)

Southeast Local (PK-12)
2005-06 Enrollment: 1,733 . . . . (330) 698-3001

Housing: Homeownership rate: 72.7% (2007); Median home value: $92,500 (2007); Median rent: $356 per month (2000); Median age of housing: 60+ years (2000).

Transportation: Commute to work: 87.8% car, 3.0% public transportation, 5.5% walk, 3.8% work from home (2000); Travel time to work: 29.4% less than 15 minutes, 61.8% 15 to 30 minutes, 3.1% 30 to 45 minutes, 2.2% 45 to 60 minutes, 3.5% 60 minutes or more (2000)

MARSHALLVILLE (village). Covers a land area of 0.561 square miles and a water area of 0 square miles. Located at 40.90° N. Lat.; 81.73° W. Long. Elevation is 1,119 feet.

Population: 807 (1990); 826 (2000); 739 (2007); 721 (2012 projected); Race: 97.4% White, 0.3% Black, 0.0% Asian, 2.0% Hispanic of any race (2007); Density: 1,316.5 persons per square mile (2007); Average

household size: 2.66 (2007); Median age: 37.5 (2007); Males per 100 females: 100.8 (2007); Marriage status: 18.8% never married, 66.7% now married, 4.6% widowed, 9.8% divorced (2000); Foreign born: 1.6% (2000); Ancestry (includes multiple ancestries): 28.6% German, 16.4% Irish, 11.6% United States or American, 9.8% Other groups, 7.2% Swiss (2000).
Economy: Employment by occupation: 6.5% management, 8.5% professional, 16.7% services, 24.9% sales, 0.5% farming, 15.0% construction, 28.0% production (2000).
Income: Per capita income: $19,252 (2007); Median household income: $49,583 (2007); Average household income: $51,178 (2007); Percent of households with income of $100,000 or more: 3.2% (2007); Poverty rate: 5.9% (2000).
Education: Percent of population age 25 and over with: High school diploma (including GED) or higher: 83.3% (2007); Bachelor's degree or higher: 6.3% (2007); Master's degree or higher: 1.3% (2007).

School District(s)

Green Local (PK-12)
2005-06 Enrollment: 1,374 . . . . (330) 669-3921
Housing: Homeownership rate: 73.7% (2007); Median home value: $112,500 (2007); Median rent: $360 per month (2000); Median age of housing: 41 years (2000).
Transportation: Commute to work: 95.6% car, 0.5% public transportation, 2.2% walk, 1.2% work from home (2000); Travel time to work: 26.0% less than 15 minutes, 45.0% 15 to 30 minutes, 18.6% 30 to 45 minutes, 5.9% 45 to 60 minutes, 4.5% 60 minutes or more (2000)

MOUNT EATON (village). Covers a land area of 0.164 square miles and a water area of 0 square miles. Located at 40.69° N. Lat.; 81.70° W. Long. Elevation is 1,250 feet.
Population: 232 (1990); 246 (2000); 261 (2007); 271 (2012 projected); Race: 98.9% White, 0.4% Black, 0.0% Asian, 0.0% Hispanic of any race (2007); Density: 1,594.1 persons per square mile (2007); Average household size: 2.72 (2007); Median age: 33.6 (2007); Males per 100 females: 97.7 (2007); Marriage status: 27.7% never married, 60.9% now married, 2.7% widowed, 8.7% divorced (2000); Foreign born: 0.0% (2000); Ancestry (includes multiple ancestries): 33.2% German, 10.8% United States or American, 10.0% Swiss, 8.7% Other groups, 8.3% Irish (2000).
Economy: Employment by occupation: 8.1% management, 6.5% professional, 20.2% services, 18.5% sales, 0.0% farming, 9.7% construction, 37.1% production (2000).
Income: Per capita income: $20,613 (2007); Median household income: $50,000 (2007); Average household income: $56,042 (2007); Percent of households with income of $100,000 or more: 9.4% (2007); Poverty rate: 0.4% (2000).
Education: Percent of population age 25 and over with: High school diploma (including GED) or higher: 67.9% (2007); Bachelor's degree or higher: 8.5% (2007); Master's degree or higher: 4.8% (2007).

School District(s)

Southeast Local (PK-12)
2005-06 Enrollment: 1,733 . . . . (330) 698-3001
Housing: Homeownership rate: 74.0% (2007); Median home value: $95,000 (2007); Median rent: $373 per month (2000); Median age of housing: 60+ years (2000).
Transportation: Commute to work: 84.7% car, 0.0% public transportation, 6.5% walk, 7.3% work from home (2000); Travel time to work: 50.4% less than 15 minutes, 31.3% 15 to 30 minutes, 10.4% 30 to 45 minutes, 3.5% 45 to 60 minutes, 4.3% 60 minutes or more (2000)

ORRVILLE (city). Covers a land area of 5.342 square miles and a water area of 0.008 square miles. Located at 40.84° N. Lat.; 81.77° W. Long. Elevation is 1,060 feet.
History: Settled c.1850, incorporated 1864.
Population: 8,058 (1990); 8,551 (2000); 8,451 (2007); 8,348 (2012 projected); Race: 90.6% White, 5.7% Black, 1.3% Asian, 1.9% Hispanic of any race (2007); Density: 1,582.1 persons per square mile (2007); Average household size: 2.53 (2007); Median age: 37.1 (2007); Males per 100 females: 95.2 (2007); Marriage status: 21.1% never married, 61.8% now married, 5.6% widowed, 11.5% divorced (2000); Foreign born: 2.7% (2000); Ancestry (includes multiple ancestries): 30.2% German, 12.9% Other groups, 12.7% Irish, 9.3% English, 8.2% United States or American (2000).
Economy: Employment by occupation: 10.5% management, 13.4% professional, 16.5% services, 23.1% sales, 0.8% farming, 7.1% construction, 28.6% production (2000).
Income: Per capita income: $19,996 (2007); Median household income: $40,536 (2007); Average household income: $49,843 (2007); Percent of households with income of $100,000 or more: 9.0% (2007); Poverty rate: 7.7% (2000).
Education: Percent of population age 25 and over with: High school diploma (including GED) or higher: 83.9% (2007); Bachelor's degree or higher: 16.9% (2007); Master's degree or higher: 5.2% (2007).

School District(s)

Orrville City (PK-12)
2005-06 Enrollment: 1,828 . . . . (330) 682-4651

Two-year College(s)

University of Akron Wayne College (Public)
Fall 2007 Enrollment: 1,615. . . . . (800) 221-8308
2007-08 Tuition: In-state $5,331; Out-of-state $12,854
Housing: Homeownership rate: 62.2% (2007); Median home value: $124,245 (2007); Median rent: $411 per month (2000); Median age of housing: 41 years (2000).
Hospitals: Dunlap Memorial Hospital (51 beds)
Safety: Violent crime rate: 20.1 per 10,000 population; Property crime rate: 243.8 per 10,000 population (2007).
Transportation: Commute to work: 91.7% car, 0.0% public transportation, 3.4% walk, 2.5% work from home (2000); Travel time to work: 51.2% less than 15 minutes, 32.1% 15 to 30 minutes, 12.0% 30 to 45 minutes, 2.6% 45 to 60 minutes, 2.2% 60 minutes or more (2000)
Additional Information Contacts
City of Orrville . . . . (330) 684-5000
http://www.orrville.com

RITTMAN (city). Covers a land area of 6.031 square miles and a water area of 0.208 square miles. Located at 40.97° N. Lat.; 81.78° W. Long. Elevation is 981 feet.
Population: 6,155 (1990); 6,314 (2000); 6,282 (2007); 6,233 (2012 projected); Race: 97.9% White, 0.1% Black, 0.5% Asian, 1.2% Hispanic of any race (2007); Density: 1,041.6 persons per square mile (2007); Average household size: 2.54 (2007); Median age: 37.9 (2007); Males per 100 females: 96.6 (2007); Marriage status: 22.7% never married, 58.2% now married, 8.4% widowed, 10.8% divorced (2000); Foreign born: 2.5% (2000); Ancestry (includes multiple ancestries): 26.6% German, 14.6% Irish, 10.9% United States or American, 9.0% English, 7.1% Other groups (2000).
Economy: Employment by occupation: 7.6% management, 13.1% professional, 16.1% services, 21.5% sales, 1.1% farming, 11.4% construction, 29.2% production (2000).
Income: Per capita income: $18,109 (2007); Median household income: $38,201 (2007); Average household income: $45,735 (2007); Percent of households with income of $100,000 or more: 5.9% (2007); Poverty rate: 8.3% (2000).
Education: Percent of population age 25 and over with: High school diploma (including GED) or higher: 76.3% (2007); Bachelor's degree or higher: 9.5% (2007); Master's degree or higher: 2.6% (2007).

School District(s)

Rittman Digital Academy (07-12)
2005-06 Enrollment: 26 . . . . (330) 927-7401
Rittman Exempted Village (PK-12)
2005-06 Enrollment: 1,174 . . . . (330) 927-7400
Housing: Homeownership rate: 68.1% (2007); Median home value: $112,640 (2007); Median rent: $377 per month (2000); Median age of housing: 43 years (2000).
Safety: Violent crime rate: 7.9 per 10,000 population; Property crime rate: 241.6 per 10,000 population (2007).
Transportation: Commute to work: 96.2% car, 0.0% public transportation, 1.9% walk, 1.7% work from home (2000); Travel time to work: 40.8% less than 15 minutes, 30.7% 15 to 30 minutes, 19.3% 30 to 45 minutes, 5.4% 45 to 60 minutes, 3.7% 60 minutes or more (2000)
Additional Information Contacts
City of Rittman . . . . (330) 925-2045
http://www.rittman.com

SHREVE (village). Covers a land area of 0.846 square miles and a water area of 0 square miles. Located at 40.68° N. Lat.; 82.02° W. Long. Elevation is 902 feet.
Population: 1,584 (1990); 1,582 (2000); 1,487 (2007); 1,468 (2012 projected); Race: 98.2% White, 0.6% Black, 0.1% Asian, 0.8% Hispanic of any race (2007); Density: 1,758.0 persons per square mile (2007); Average household size: 2.35 (2007); Median age: 35.0 (2007); Males per 100

females: 92.9 (2007); Marriage status: 16.7% never married, 59.0% now married, 7.4% widowed, 16.9% divorced (2000); Foreign born: 0.4% (2000); Ancestry (includes multiple ancestries): 25.3% German, 17.8% United States or American, 11.8% Irish, 10.4% English, 8.5% Other groups (2000).
Economy: Single-family building permits issued: 0 (2007); Multi-family building permits issued: 0 (2007); Employment by occupation: 5.4% management, 12.0% professional, 14.0% services, 22.2% sales, 0.8% farming, 10.3% construction, 35.3% production (2000).
Income: Per capita income: $18,159 (2007); Median household income: $36,905 (2007); Average household income: $42,725 (2007); Percent of households with income of $100,000 or more: 5.5% (2007); Poverty rate: 10.4% (2000).
Education: Percent of population age 25 and over with: High school diploma (including GED) or higher: 80.5% (2007); Bachelor's degree or higher: 8.1% (2007); Master's degree or higher: 3.5% (2007).

School District(s)

Triway Local (PK-12)
2005-06 Enrollment: 2,166 . . . . (330) 264-9491
Housing: Homeownership rate: 67.2% (2007); Median home value: $93,154 (2007); Median rent: $282 per month (2000); Median age of housing: 44 years (2000).
Transportation: Commute to work: 90.7% car, 0.1% public transportation, 5.8% walk, 3.0% work from home (2000); Travel time to work: 37.2% less than 15 minutes, 43.8% 15 to 30 minutes, 12.1% 30 to 45 minutes, 2.6% 45 to 60 minutes, 4.2% 60 minutes or more (2000)

SMITHVILLE (village). Covers a land area of 1.235 square miles and a water area of 0 square miles. Located at 40.86° N. Lat.; 81.85° W. Long. Elevation is 1,063 feet.
Population: 1,387 (1990); 1,333 (2000); 1,236 (2007); 1,203 (2012 projected); Race: 98.4% White, 0.2% Black, 0.7% Asian, 0.7% Hispanic of any race (2007); Density: 1,000.9 persons per square mile (2007); Average household size: 2.36 (2007); Median age: 39.4 (2007); Males per 100 females: 91.3 (2007); Marriage status: 21.3% never married, 61.7% now married, 6.8% widowed, 10.2% divorced (2000); Foreign born: 1.0% (2000); Ancestry (includes multiple ancestries): 34.2% German, 11.1% English, 9.0% Irish, 8.7% Swiss, 6.6% United States or American (2000).
Economy: Employment by occupation: 8.9% management, 18.8% professional, 15.9% services, 23.4% sales, 0.7% farming, 8.4% construction, 23.8% production (2000).
Income: Per capita income: $21,143 (2007); Median household income: $44,583 (2007); Average household income: $49,871 (2007); Percent of households with income of $100,000 or more: 6.1% (2007); Poverty rate: 5.9% (2000).
Education: Percent of population age 25 and over with: High school diploma (including GED) or higher: 91.4% (2007); Bachelor's degree or higher: 18.7% (2007); Master's degree or higher: 7.2% (2007).

School District(s)

Green Local (PK-12)
2005-06 Enrollment: 1,374 . . . . (330) 669-3921
Wayne County Jvsd (07-12)
2005-06 Enrollment: n/a . . . . (330) 669-2134
Wooster City (PK-12)
2005-06 Enrollment: 3,952 . . . . (330) 264-0869

Vocational/Technical School(s)

Wayne County Schools Career Center (Public)
Fall 2007 Enrollment: 548 . . . . (330) 669-7070
2007-08 Tuition: $8,389
Housing: Homeownership rate: 63.4% (2007); Median home value: $135,843 (2007); Median rent: $431 per month (2000); Median age of housing: 38 years (2000).
Safety: Violent crime rate: 7.7 per 10,000 population; Property crime rate: 222.1 per 10,000 population (2007).
Transportation: Commute to work: 92.0% car, 0.3% public transportation, 2.5% walk, 4.3% work from home (2000); Travel time to work: 43.0% less than 15 minutes, 40.4% 15 to 30 minutes, 7.5% 30 to 45 minutes, 5.0% 45 to 60 minutes, 4.2% 60 minutes or more (2000)

STERLING (unincorporated postal area, zip code 44276). Covers a land area of 19.953 square miles and a water area of 0 square miles. Located at 40.95° N. Lat.; 81.82° W. Long. Elevation is 973 feet.
Population: 1,881 (2000); Race: 98.9% White, 0.0% Black, 0.0% Asian, 2.3% Hispanic of any race (2000); Density: 94.3 persons per square mile (2000); Age: 29.2% under 18, 9.2% over 64 (2000); Marriage status: 20.8% never married, 71.3% now married, 3.2% widowed, 4.6% divorced (2000); Foreign born: 0.5% (2000); Ancestry (includes multiple ancestries): 29.6% German, 15.7% Irish, 14.2% Swiss, 9.6% English, 6.3% United States or American (2000).
Economy: Employment by occupation: 10.8% management, 14.4% professional, 13.0% services, 22.5% sales, 3.7% farming, 14.0% construction, 21.7% production (2000).
Income: Per capita income: $17,370 (2000); Median household income: $51,215 (2000); Poverty rate: 2.5% (2000).
Education: Percent of population age 25 and over with: High school diploma (including GED) or higher: 83.3% (2000); Bachelor's degree or higher: 10.8% (2000).

School District(s)

North Central Local (PK-12)
2005-06 Enrollment: 1,473 . . . . (330) 435-6382
Housing: Homeownership rate: 81.1% (2000); Median home value: $108,500 (2000); Median rent: $468 per month (2000); Median age of housing: 36 years (2000).
Transportation: Commute to work: 89.7% car, 0.0% public transportation, 0.5% walk, 9.4% work from home (2000); Travel time to work: 28.8% less than 15 minutes, 43.9% 15 to 30 minutes, 15.0% 30 to 45 minutes, 3.5% 45 to 60 minutes, 8.9% 60 minutes or more (2000)

WEST SALEM (village). Covers a land area of 1.033 square miles and a water area of 0 square miles. Located at 40.97° N. Lat.; 82.11° W. Long. Elevation is 1,112 feet.
History: West Salem was laid out in 1834 by the Rickel brothers, who came from Wooster.
Population: 1,555 (1990); 1,501 (2000); 1,478 (2007); 1,496 (2012 projected); Race: 96.8% White, 0.1% Black, 0.6% Asian, 1.5% Hispanic of any race (2007); Density: 1,430.8 persons per square mile (2007); Average household size: 2.54 (2007); Median age: 34.2 (2007); Males per 100 females: 101.4 (2007); Marriage status: 24.2% never married, 56.9% now married, 7.0% widowed, 11.9% divorced (2000); Foreign born: 0.0% (2000); Ancestry (includes multiple ancestries): 29.0% German, 11.9% Irish, 11.4% English, 10.0% United States or American, 8.5% Other groups (2000).
Economy: Employment by occupation: 2.9% management, 7.8% professional, 13.8% services, 23.7% sales, 0.0% farming, 13.5% construction, 38.4% production (2000).
Income: Per capita income: $18,449 (2007); Median household income: $43,500 (2007); Average household income: $46,851 (2007); Percent of households with income of $100,000 or more: 5.0% (2007); Poverty rate: 7.9% (2000).
Education: Percent of population age 25 and over with: High school diploma (including GED) or higher: 75.0% (2007); Bachelor's degree or higher: 5.0% (2007); Master's degree or higher: 1.1% (2007).

School District(s)

Northwestern Local (KG-12)
2005-06 Enrollment: 1,464 . . . . (419) 846-3151
Housing: Homeownership rate: 77.0% (2007); Median home value: $93,590 (2007); Median rent: $389 per month (2000); Median age of housing: 31 years (2000).
Transportation: Commute to work: 93.3% car, 0.1% public transportation, 4.5% walk, 1.8% work from home (2000); Travel time to work: 24.6% less than 15 minutes, 29.0% 15 to 30 minutes, 29.1% 30 to 45 minutes, 8.7% 45 to 60 minutes, 8.7% 60 minutes or more (2000)

WOOSTER (city). County seat. Covers a land area of 14.374 square miles and a water area of 0.017 square miles. Located at 40.80° N. Lat.; 81.93° W. Long. Elevation is 997 feet.
History: Wooster was settled in 1807 by the Larwill family. The town that grew after the War of 1812 was named for Revolutionary War general David Wooster. Wooster claims to have had America's first Christmas tree in 1847, when a young German immigrant, August Imgard, cut and decorated a small spruce tree.
Population: 23,108 (1990); 24,811 (2000); 25,416 (2007); 25,817 (2012 projected); Race: 92.3% White, 3.7% Black, 1.9% Asian, 1.5% Hispanic of any race (2007); Density: 1,768.2 persons per square mile (2007); Average household size: 2.41 (2007); Median age: 37.3 (2007); Males per 100 females: 92.4 (2007); Marriage status: 29.3% never married, 51.5% now married, 6.7% widowed, 12.5% divorced (2000); Foreign born: 3.3% (2000); Ancestry (includes multiple ancestries): 30.4% German, 13.6% Irish, 11.9% English, 9.5% Other groups, 8.1% United States or American (2000).

Economy: Unemployment rate: 5.7% (6/2008); Total civilian labor force: 14,004 (6/2008); Single-family building permits issued: 53 (2007); Multi-family building permits issued: 76 (2007); Employment by occupation: 11.4% management, 21.4% professional, 14.6% services, 25.5% sales, 0.4% farming, 5.6% construction, 21.2% production (2000).
Income: Per capita income: $23,881 (2007); Median household income: $40,724 (2007); Average household income: $56,293 (2007); Percent of households with income of $100,000 or more: 11.4% (2007); Poverty rate: 10.4% (2000).
Taxes: Total city taxes per capita: $481 (2006); City property taxes per capita: $88 (2006).
Education: Percent of population age 25 and over with: High school diploma (including GED) or higher: 84.7% (2007); Bachelor's degree or higher: 27.6% (2007); Master's degree or higher: 10.5% (2007).

School District(s)

Triway Local (PK-12)
2005-06 Enrollment: 2,166 . . . . (330) 264-9491
Wooster City (PK-12)
2005-06 Enrollment: 3,952 . . . . (330) 264-0869

Four-year College(s)

The College of Wooster (Private, Not-for-profit)
Fall 2007 Enrollment: 1,781. . . . . (330) 263-2000
2007-08 Tuition: In-state $31,870; Out-of-state $31,870

Two-year College(s)

Ohio State University Agricultural Technical Institute (Public)
Fall 2007 Enrollment: 748 . . . . (330) 264-3911
2007-08 Tuition: In-state $5,859; Out-of-state $18,468

Housing: Homeownership rate: 61.0% (2007); Median home value: $122,568 (2007); Median rent: $418 per month (2000); Median age of housing: 35 years (2000).
Hospitals: Wooster Community Hospital (130 beds)
Safety: Violent crime rate: 21.2 per 10,000 population; Property crime rate: 378.9 per 10,000 population (2007).
Newspapers: The Daily Record (Local news; Circulation 22,328)
Transportation: Commute to work: 86.9% car, 0.9% public transportation, 9.2% walk, 2.6% work from home (2000); Travel time to work: 64.7% less than 15 minutes, 21.1% 15 to 30 minutes, 6.7% 30 to 45 minutes, 4.0% 45 to 60 minutes, 3.5% 60 minutes or more (2000)
Airports: Wayne County (general aviation)

Additional Information Contacts

City of Wooster . . . . (330) 263-5200
http://www.woosteroh.com
Wayne County Convention & Visitors Bureau . . . . . . (330) 264-1800
http://www.waynecountycvb.org
Wooster Chamber of Commerce . . . . (330) 262-5735
http://www.woosterchamber.com

Williams County

Located in northwestern Ohio; bounded on the north by Michigan, and on the west by Indiana; crossed by the St. Joseph and Tiffin Rivers. Covers a land area of 421.74 square miles, a water area of 1.31 square miles, and is located in the Eastern Time Zone. The county was founded in 1820. County seat is Bryan.

Weather Station: Montpelier Elevation: 859 feet

	Jan	Feb	Mar	Apr	May	Jun	Jul	Aug	Sep	Oct	Nov	Dec
High	30	34	45	58	71	80	84	82	75	62	48	36
Low	13	16	25	35	46	55	60	57	49	38	30	20
Precip	1.9	1.9	2.9	3.6	3.5	3.5	3.5	3.6	3.2	2.6	3.1	2.5
Snow	9.9	8.5	4.5	0.8	0.0	0.0	0.0	0.0	0.0	0.2	1.9	8.1

High and Low temperatures in degrees Fahrenheit; Precipitation and Snow in inches

Population: 36,956 (1990); 39,188 (2000); 38,548 (2007); 37,968 (2012 projected); Race: 96.2% White, 0.9% Black, 0.5% Asian, 3.1% Hispanic of any race (2007); Density: 91.4 persons per square mile (2007); Average household size: 2.54 (2007); Median age: 39.2 (2007); Males per 100 females: 99.3 (2007).
Religion: Five largest groups: 11.6% Catholic Church, 10.5% The United Methodist Church, 6.6% Evangelical Lutheran Church in America, 3.8% Christian Churches and Churches of Christ, 2.9% Presbyterian Church (U.S.A.) (2000).
Economy: Unemployment rate: 7.0% (6/2008); Total civilian labor force: 19,741 (6/2008); Leading industries: 47.0% manufacturing; 10.7% health care and social assistance; 10.0% retail trade (2005); Farms: 1,099 totaling 213,265 acres (2002); Companies that employ 500 or more persons: 1 (2006); Companies that employ 100 to 499 persons: 31 (2006); Companies that employ less than 100 persons: 850 (2006); Black-owned businesses: n/a (2002); Hispanic-owned businesses: n/a (2002); Asian-owned businesses: n/a (2002); Women-owned businesses: 746 (2002); Retail sales per capita: $9,037 (2008). Single-family building permits issued: 51 (2007); Multi-family building permits issued: 41 (2007).
Income: Per capita income: $21,444 (2007); Median household income: $45,556 (2007); Average household income: $53,489 (2007); Percent of households with income of $100,000 or more: 8.4% (2007); Poverty rate: 9.2% (2005); Bankruptcy rate: 3.36% (2007).
Taxes: Total county taxes per capita: $236 (2006); County property taxes per capita: $101 (2006).
Education: Percent of population age 25 and over with: High school diploma (including GED) or higher: 82.9% (2007); Bachelor's degree or higher: 10.7% (2007); Master's degree or higher: 3.6% (2007).
Housing: Homeownership rate: 77.1% (2007); Median home value: $111,754 (2007); Median rent: $375 per month (2000); Median age of housing: 39 years (2000).
Health: Birth rate: 124.6 per 10,000 population (2007); Death rate: 87.8 per 10,000 population (2007); Age-adjusted cancer mortality rate: 198.3 deaths per 100,000 population (2005); Number of physicians: 11.2 per 10,000 population (2005); Hospital beds: 29.3 per 10,000 population (2004); Hospital admissions: 972.5 per 10,000 population (2004).
Elections: 2004 Presidential election results: 64.6% Bush, 34.8% Kerry, 0.0% Nader, 0.3% Badnarik

Additional Information Contacts

Williams County Government . . . . (419) 636-2059
http://www.co.williams.oh.us
Bryan Area Chamber of Commerce. . . . . (419) 636-2247
http://www.bryanchamber.org
Montpelier Area Chamber of Commerce . . . . (419) 485-4416
http://www.montpelierchamber.com

Williams County Communities

ALVORDTON (village). Covers a land area of 0.258 square miles and a water area of 0 square miles. Located at 41.66° N. Lat.; 84.43° W. Long. Elevation is 860 feet.
Population: 298 (1990); 305 (2000); 296 (2007); 286 (2012 projected); Race: 95.6% White, 1.0% Black, 0.0% Asian, 3.0% Hispanic of any race (2007); Density: 1,148.7 persons per square mile (2007); Average household size: 2.93 (2007); Median age: 39.8 (2007); Males per 100 females: 120.9 (2007); Marriage status: 25.8% never married, 46.5% now married, 4.2% widowed, 23.5% divorced (2000); Foreign born: 1.7% (2000); Ancestry (includes multiple ancestries): 25.9% German, 14.1% United States or American, 13.3% Other groups, 6.9% Irish, 3.7% French (except Basque) (2000).
Economy: Employment by occupation: 4.8% management, 1.8% professional, 11.4% services, 9.6% sales, 2.4% farming, 4.2% construction, 65.7% production (2000).
Income: Per capita income: $20,804 (2007); Median household income: $42,917 (2007); Average household income: $41,485 (2007); Percent of households with income of $100,000 or more: 2.0% (2007); Poverty rate: 11.5% (2000).
Education: Percent of population age 25 and over with: High school diploma (including GED) or higher: 77.4% (2007); Bachelor's degree or higher: 4.1% (2007); Master's degree or higher: 1.4% (2007).
Housing: Homeownership rate: 73.3% (2007); Median home value: $51,111 (2007); Median rent: $275 per month (2000); Median age of housing: 60+ years (2000).
Transportation: Commute to work: 95.8% car, 0.0% public transportation, 1.2% walk, 3.0% work from home (2000); Travel time to work: 26.7% less than 15 minutes, 57.8% 15 to 30 minutes, 6.2% 30 to 45 minutes, 6.2% 45 to 60 minutes, 3.1% 60 minutes or more (2000)

BLAKESLEE (village). Aka Blakesley. Covers a land area of 0.106 square miles and a water area of 0 square miles. Located at 41.52° N. Lat.; 84.73° W. Long. Elevation is 863 feet.
Population: 128 (1990); 130 (2000); 129 (2007); 125 (2012 projected); Race: 99.2% White, 0.0% Black, 0.0% Asian, 0.0% Hispanic of any race (2007); Density: 1,217.3 persons per square mile (2007); Average household size: 2.63 (2007); Median age: 31.0 (2007); Males per 100 females: 95.5 (2007); Marriage status: 8.8% never married, 75.0% now married, 6.3% widowed, 10.0% divorced (2000); Foreign born: 0.0% (2000); Ancestry (includes multiple ancestries): 38.0% German, 16.5%

United States or American, 8.3% Syrian, 8.3% Other groups, 7.4% Irish (2000).
Economy: Employment by occupation: 22.6% management, 0.0% professional, 15.1% services, 13.2% sales, 0.0% farming, 13.2% construction, 35.8% production (2000).
Income: Per capita income: $18,818 (2007); Median household income: $46,875 (2007); Average household income: $49,541 (2007); Percent of households with income of $100,000 or more: 6.1% (2007); Poverty rate: 1.7% (2000).
Education: Percent of population age 25 and over with: High school diploma (including GED) or higher: 87.0% (2007); Bachelor's degree or higher: 2.6% (2007); Master's degree or higher: 0.0% (2007).
Housing: Homeownership rate: 69.4% (2007); Median home value: $96,667 (2007); Median rent: $300 per month (2000); Median age of housing: 57 years (2000).
Transportation: Commute to work: 94.3% car, 0.0% public transportation, 1.9% walk, 3.8% work from home (2000); Travel time to work: 13.7% less than 15 minutes, 51.0% 15 to 30 minutes, 25.5% 30 to 45 minutes, 9.8% 45 to 60 minutes, 0.0% 60 minutes or more (2000)

BRYAN (city). County seat. Covers a land area of 4.574 square miles and a water area of 0 square miles. Located at 41.47° N. Lat.; 84.55° W. Long. Elevation is 768 feet.
History: Bryan's early growth was attributed to its artesian wells, their supposed medicinal value creating a temporary business for the town, which became a trading and industrial center and the seat of Williams County.
Population: 8,575 (1990); 8,333 (2000); 8,043 (2007); 7,833 (2012 projected); Race: 96.1% White, 0.4% Black, 0.7% Asian, 4.3% Hispanic of any race (2007); Density: 1,758.3 persons per square mile (2007); Average household size: 2.31 (2007); Median age: 39.6 (2007); Males per 100 females: 91.5 (2007); Marriage status: 20.2% never married, 56.1% now married, 9.4% widowed, 14.3% divorced (2000); Foreign born: 1.5% (2000); Ancestry (includes multiple ancestries): 34.9% German, 11.7% United States or American, 11.2% Irish, 11.0% Other groups, 9.7% English (2000).
Economy: Single-family building permits issued: 17 (2007); Multi-family building permits issued: 41 (2007); Employment by occupation: 9.5% management, 14.4% professional, 12.3% services, 19.4% sales, 0.2% farming, 7.1% construction, 37.0% production (2000).
Income: Per capita income: $21,625 (2007); Median household income: $40,585 (2007); Average household income: $49,348 (2007); Percent of households with income of $100,000 or more: 7.8% (2007); Poverty rate: 6.0% (2000).
Education: Percent of population age 25 and over with: High school diploma (including GED) or higher: 82.8% (2007); Bachelor's degree or higher: 14.7% (2007); Master's degree or higher: 3.6% (2007).

School District(s)

Bryan City (PK-12)
2005-06 Enrollment: 2,282 . . . . (419) 636-6973
Housing: Homeownership rate: 63.3% (2007); Median home value: $116,875 (2007); Median rent: $399 per month (2000); Median age of housing: 41 years (2000).
Hospitals: Community Hospitals and Wellness Centers (131 beds)
Safety: Violent crime rate: 7.2 per 10,000 population; Property crime rate: 231.8 per 10,000 population (2007).
Newspapers: Bryan Times (Local news; Circulation 10,938)
Transportation: Commute to work: 91.8% car, 0.6% public transportation, 3.9% walk, 3.0% work from home (2000); Travel time to work: 56.3% less than 15 minutes, 29.3% 15 to 30 minutes, 9.5% 30 to 45 minutes, 2.5% 45 to 60 minutes, 2.4% 60 minutes or more (2000); Amtrak: Service available.
Airports: Williams County (general aviation)
Additional Information Contacts
Bryan Area Chamber of Commerce. . . . . (419) 636-2247
http://www.bryanchamber.org

EDGERTON (village). Covers a land area of 1.861 square miles and a water area of 0 square miles. Located at 41.44° N. Lat.; 84.74° W. Long. Elevation is 840 feet.
Population: 2,167 (1990); 2,117 (2000); 1,967 (2007); 1,908 (2012 projected); Race: 97.0% White, 0.2% Black, 0.1% Asian, 2.6% Hispanic of any race (2007); Density: 1,057.1 persons per square mile (2007); Average household size: 2.54 (2007); Median age: 38.2 (2007); Males per 100 females: 92.3 (2007); Marriage status: 20.2% never married, 56.6% now married, 11.0% widowed, 12.3% divorced (2000); Foreign born: 0.4% (2000); Ancestry (includes multiple ancestries): 43.2% German, 12.8% United States or American, 8.5% Other groups, 7.4% Irish, 6.8% English (2000).
Economy: Single-family building permits issued: 1 (2007); Multi-family building permits issued: 0 (2007); Employment by occupation: 6.9% management, 13.1% professional, 10.0% services, 21.8% sales, 0.4% farming, 8.8% construction, 39.1% production (2000).
Income: Per capita income: $20,860 (2007); Median household income: $44,868 (2007); Average household income: $52,526 (2007); Percent of households with income of $100,000 or more: 8.3% (2007); Poverty rate: 8.9% (2000).
Education: Percent of population age 25 and over with: High school diploma (including GED) or higher: 80.9% (2007); Bachelor's degree or higher: 10.1% (2007); Master's degree or higher: 3.9% (2007).

School District(s)

Edgerton Local (PK-12)
2005-06 Enrollment: 703 . . . . (419) 298-2112
Housing: Homeownership rate: 76.7% (2007); Median home value: $98,833 (2007); Median rent: $381 per month (2000); Median age of housing: 43 years (2000).
Safety: Violent crime rate: 5.0 per 10,000 population; Property crime rate: 260.4 per 10,000 population (2007).
Newspapers: Earth (Community news; Circulation 1,475)
Transportation: Commute to work: 93.1% car, 0.2% public transportation, 3.5% walk, 1.9% work from home (2000); Travel time to work: 48.9% less than 15 minutes, 34.2% 15 to 30 minutes, 11.4% 30 to 45 minutes, 2.5% 45 to 60 minutes, 3.0% 60 minutes or more (2000)

EDON (village). Covers a land area of 1.040 square miles and a water area of 0 square miles. Located at 41.55° N. Lat.; 84.76° W. Long. Elevation is 899 feet.
Population: 911 (1990); 898 (2000); 842 (2007); 843 (2012 projected); Race: 98.9% White, 0.0% Black, 0.5% Asian, 0.4% Hispanic of any race (2007); Density: 809.3 persons per square mile (2007); Average household size: 2.43 (2007); Median age: 38.5 (2007); Males per 100 females: 90.5 (2007); Marriage status: 21.3% never married, 62.2% now married, 7.8% widowed, 8.7% divorced (2000); Foreign born: 0.2% (2000); Ancestry (includes multiple ancestries): 45.5% German, 14.1% United States or American, 10.7% Irish, 6.3% English, 5.1% French (except Basque) (2000).
Economy: Single-family building permits issued: 2 (2007); Multi-family building permits issued: 0 (2007); Employment by occupation: 9.4% management, 9.6% professional, 13.3% services, 19.3% sales, 0.5% farming, 4.1% construction, 43.8% production (2000).
Income: Per capita income: $23,073 (2007); Median household income: $49,143 (2007); Average household income: $56,149 (2007); Percent of households with income of $100,000 or more: 7.2% (2007); Poverty rate: 5.2% (2000).
Education: Percent of population age 25 and over with: High school diploma (including GED) or higher: 88.0% (2007); Bachelor's degree or higher: 9.6% (2007); Master's degree or higher: 3.0% (2007).

School District(s)

Edon-Northwest Local (PK-12)
2005-06 Enrollment: 704 . . . . (419) 272-3213
Housing: Homeownership rate: 79.8% (2007); Median home value: $88,286 (2007); Median rent: $335 per month (2000); Median age of housing: 59 years (2000).
Transportation: Commute to work: 94.7% car, 0.0% public transportation, 3.0% walk, 2.1% work from home (2000); Travel time to work: 44.7% less than 15 minutes, 34.4% 15 to 30 minutes, 13.8% 30 to 45 minutes, 2.1% 45 to 60 minutes, 5.0% 60 minutes or more (2000)

HOLIDAY CITY (village). Covers a land area of 1.328 square miles and a water area of 0.022 square miles. Located at 41.61° N. Lat.; 84.55° W. Long. Elevation is 899 feet.
Population: 45 (1990); 49 (2000); 47 (2007); 47 (2012 projected); Race: 93.6% White, 0.0% Black, 6.4% Asian, 0.0% Hispanic of any race (2007); Density: 35.4 persons per square mile (2007); Average household size: 2.94 (2007); Median age: 31.9 (2007); Males per 100 females: 88.0 (2007); Marriage status: 13.3% never married, 76.7% now married, 10.0% widowed, 0.0% divorced (2000); Foreign born: 0.0% (2000); Ancestry (includes multiple ancestries): 58.8% United States or American, 17.6% Other groups, 9.8% German, 3.9% Polish, 3.9% Lebanese (2000).

Economy: Employment by occupation: 15.8% management, 15.8% professional, 0.0% services, 10.5% sales, 0.0% farming, 10.5% construction, 47.4% production (2000).
Income: Per capita income: $12,021 (2007); Median household income: $32,500 (2007); Average household income: $35,313 (2007); Percent of households with income of $100,000 or more: 0.0% (2007); Poverty rate: 6.3% (2000).
Education: Percent of population age 25 and over with: High school diploma (including GED) or higher: 64.3% (2007); Bachelor's degree or higher: 17.9% (2007); Master's degree or higher: 0.0% (2007).
Housing: Homeownership rate: 75.0% (2007); Median home value: $80,000 (2007); Median rent: $408 per month (2000); Median age of housing: 29 years (2000).
Transportation: Commute to work: 100.0% car, 0.0% public transportation, 0.0% walk, 0.0% work from home (2000); Travel time to work: 12.5% less than 15 minutes, 87.5% 15 to 30 minutes, 0.0% 30 to 45 minutes, 0.0% 45 to 60 minutes, 0.0% 60 minutes or more (2000)

MONTPELIER (village). Covers a land area of 2.698 square miles and a water area of 0 square miles. Located at 41.58° N. Lat.; 84.60° W. Long. Elevation is 856 feet.
History: Settled 1855, incorporated 1875.
Population: 4,254 (1990); 4,320 (2000); 4,062 (2007); 3,864 (2012 projected); Race: 96.4% White, 0.4% Black, 1.6% Asian, 1.8% Hispanic of any race (2007); Density: 1,505.4 persons per square mile (2007); Average household size: 2.41 (2007); Median age: 35.8 (2007); Males per 100 females: 91.8 (2007); Marriage status: 21.3% never married, 57.7% now married, 7.8% widowed, 13.2% divorced (2000); Foreign born: 1.0% (2000); Ancestry (includes multiple ancestries): 30.2% German, 17.8% United States or American, 9.6% English, 9.1% Irish, 7.4% Other groups (2000).
Economy: Single-family building permits issued: 4 (2007); Multi-family building permits issued: 0 (2007); Employment by occupation: 4.0% management, 7.4% professional, 14.4% services, 18.8% sales, 0.0% farming, 6.4% construction, 48.9% production (2000).
Income: Per capita income: $17,228 (2007); Median household income: $35,161 (2007); Average household income: $41,307 (2007); Percent of households with income of $100,000 or more: 2.4% (2007); Poverty rate: 6.2% (2000).
Education: Percent of population age 25 and over with: High school diploma (including GED) or higher: 83.2% (2007); Bachelor's degree or higher: 6.5% (2007); Master's degree or higher: 3.0% (2007).

School District(s)

Montpelier Exempted Village (PK-12)
2005-06 Enrollment: 1,188 . . . . (419) 485-3676
Housing: Homeownership rate: 67.2% (2007); Median home value: $85,104 (2007); Median rent: $341 per month (2000); Median age of housing: 56 years (2000).
Safety: Violent crime rate: 24.5 per 10,000 population; Property crime rate: 573.2 per 10,000 population (2007).
Newspapers: Leader Enterprise (Local news; Circulation 1,700)
Transportation: Commute to work: 90.7% car, 0.6% public transportation, 5.5% walk, 2.6% work from home (2000); Travel time to work: 54.8% less than 15 minutes, 31.7% 15 to 30 minutes, 8.6% 30 to 45 minutes, 2.0% 45 to 60 minutes, 2.8% 60 minutes or more (2000)
Additional Information Contacts
Montpelier Area Chamber of Commerce . . . . (419) 485-4416
http://www.montpelierchamber.com

PIONEER (village). Covers a land area of 1.601 square miles and a water area of 0.063 square miles. Located at 41.68° N. Lat.; 84.55° W. Long. Elevation is 879 feet.
Population: 1,328 (1990); 1,460 (2000); 1,340 (2007); 1,307 (2012 projected); Race: 97.2% White, 0.4% Black, 0.2% Asian, 2.2% Hispanic of any race (2007); Density: 836.9 persons per square mile (2007); Average household size: 2.39 (2007); Median age: 38.0 (2007); Males per 100 females: 95.9 (2007); Marriage status: 21.0% never married, 60.1% now married, 5.5% widowed, 13.4% divorced (2000); Foreign born: 0.5% (2000); Ancestry (includes multiple ancestries): 32.4% German, 13.0% United States or American, 8.5% Other groups, 7.6% English, 7.5% Irish (2000).
Economy: Single-family building permits issued: 0 (2007); Multi-family building permits issued: 0 (2007); Employment by occupation: 8.5% management, 14.1% professional, 12.3% services, 17.2% sales, 0.1% farming, 9.9% construction, 37.9% production (2000).
Income: Per capita income: $22,845 (2007); Median household income: $46,346 (2007); Average household income: $54,665 (2007); Percent of households with income of $100,000 or more: 9.6% (2007); Poverty rate: 6.5% (2000).
Education: Percent of population age 25 and over with: High school diploma (including GED) or higher: 82.5% (2007); Bachelor's degree or higher: 10.7% (2007); Master's degree or higher: 3.5% (2007).

School District(s)

North Central Local (PK-12)
2005-06 Enrollment: 678 . . . . (419) 737-2392
Housing: Homeownership rate: 70.0% (2007); Median home value: $113,462 (2007); Median rent: $378 per month (2000); Median age of housing: 26 years (2000).
Transportation: Commute to work: 93.1% car, 0.3% public transportation, 4.3% walk, 1.6% work from home (2000); Travel time to work: 47.3% less than 15 minutes, 32.1% 15 to 30 minutes, 14.2% 30 to 45 minutes, 3.0% 45 to 60 minutes, 3.4% 60 minutes or more (2000)

STRYKER (village). Covers a land area of 0.810 square miles and a water area of 0 square miles. Located at 41.50° N. Lat.; 84.41° W. Long. Elevation is 712 feet.
Population: 1,468 (1990); 1,406 (2000); 1,274 (2007); 1,269 (2012 projected); Race: 96.3% White, 0.2% Black, 0.2% Asian, 8.7% Hispanic of any race (2007); Density: 1,573.2 persons per square mile (2007); Average household size: 2.52 (2007); Median age: 34.3 (2007); Males per 100 females: 92.4 (2007); Marriage status: 23.0% never married, 61.8% now married, 4.2% widowed, 11.1% divorced (2000); Foreign born: 1.3% (2000); Ancestry (includes multiple ancestries): 34.4% German, 13.9% Other groups, 9.0% English, 8.1% French (except Basque), 7.3% Irish (2000).
Economy: Single-family building permits issued: 0 (2007); Multi-family building permits issued: 0 (2007); Employment by occupation: 4.8% management, 9.1% professional, 11.4% services, 17.6% sales, 0.7% farming, 9.7% construction, 46.7% production (2000).
Income: Per capita income: $19,876 (2007); Median household income: $45,234 (2007); Average household income: $50,144 (2007); Percent of households with income of $100,000 or more: 6.3% (2007); Poverty rate: 5.4% (2000).
Education: Percent of population age 25 and over with: High school diploma (including GED) or higher: 82.0% (2007); Bachelor's degree or higher: 9.2% (2007); Master's degree or higher: 2.8% (2007).

School District(s)

Stryker Local (KG-12)
2005-06 Enrollment: 522 . . . . (419) 682-6961
Housing: Homeownership rate: 78.0% (2007); Median home value: $84,444 (2007); Median rent: $318 per month (2000); Median age of housing: 53 years (2000).
Transportation: Commute to work: 93.2% car, 0.0% public transportation, 2.9% walk, 1.5% work from home (2000); Travel time to work: 50.0% less than 15 minutes, 37.3% 15 to 30 minutes, 5.9% 30 to 45 minutes, 1.9% 45 to 60 minutes, 4.9% 60 minutes or more (2000)

WEST UNITY (village). Covers a land area of 1.033 square miles and a water area of 0 square miles. Located at 41.58° N. Lat.; 84.43° W. Long. Elevation is 787 feet.
Population: 1,731 (1990); 1,790 (2000); 1,727 (2007); 1,696 (2012 projected); Race: 97.4% White, 0.4% Black, 0.1% Asian, 3.2% Hispanic of any race (2007); Density: 1,671.9 persons per square mile (2007); Average household size: 2.39 (2007); Median age: 34.5 (2007); Males per 100 females: 96.5 (2007); Marriage status: 25.7% never married, 56.3% now married, 6.8% widowed, 11.2% divorced (2000); Foreign born: 0.6% (2000); Ancestry (includes multiple ancestries): 37.6% German, 9.8% English, 8.2% Other groups, 8.1% United States or American, 8.0% Irish (2000).
Economy: Single-family building permits issued: 0 (2007); Multi-family building permits issued: 0 (2007); Employment by occupation: 6.2% management, 10.1% professional, 11.6% services, 21.1% sales, 0.4% farming, 8.6% construction, 41.9% production (2000).
Income: Per capita income: $18,525 (2007); Median household income: $38,564 (2007); Average household income: $43,634 (2007); Percent of households with income of $100,000 or more: 3.6% (2007); Poverty rate: 8.0% (2000).
Education: Percent of population age 25 and over with: High school diploma (including GED) or higher: 81.6% (2007); Bachelor's degree or higher: 8.1% (2007); Master's degree or higher: 3.1% (2007).

School District(s)

Millcreek-West Unity Local (PK-12)
2005-06 Enrollment: 754 . . . . (419) 924-2365

Housing: Homeownership rate: 67.5% (2007); Median home value: $105,099 (2007); Median rent: $320 per month (2000); Median age of housing: 38 years (2000).

Newspapers: Advance-Reporter (Community news; Circulation 1,975); Edon Commercial (Community news; Circulation 1,500)

Transportation: Commute to work: 95.0% car, 0.0% public transportation, 2.3% walk, 2.2% work from home (2000); Travel time to work: 35.7% less than 15 minutes, 49.1% 15 to 30 minutes, 9.3% 30 to 45 minutes, 1.6% 45 to 60 minutes, 4.4% 60 minutes or more (2000)

Wood County

Located in northwestern Ohio; bounded on the northwest by the Maumee River; crossed by the Portage River. Covers a land area of 617.32 square miles, a water area of 3.22 square miles, and is located in the Eastern Time Zone. The county was founded in 1820. County seat is Bowling Green.

Wood County is part of the Toledo, OH Metropolitan Statistical Area. The entire metro area includes: Fulton County, OH; Lucas County, OH; Ottawa County, OH; Wood County, OH

Weather Station: Bowling Green WWTP Elevation: 672 feet

	Jan	Feb	Mar	Apr	May	Jun	Jul	Aug	Sep	Oct	Nov	Dec
High	31	35	47	60	72	81	85	82	76	63	49	37
Low	16	19	28	37	48	58	62	59	52	41	32	23
Precip	1.7	1.6	2.4	3.3	3.5	3.5	3.7	3.3	2.6	2.5	2.7	2.3
Snow	7.2	5.4	3.1	0.7	tr	0.0	0.0	0.0	0.0	tr	0.7	4.8

High and Low temperatures in degrees Fahrenheit; Precipitation and Snow in inches

Weather Station: Hoytville 2 NE Elevation: 698 feet

	Jan	Feb	Mar	Apr	May	Jun	Jul	Aug	Sep	Oct	Nov	Dec
High	31	35	46	59	71	80	84	81	75	63	49	37
Low	15	18	27	36	48	57	61	58	51	40	32	22
Precip	1.8	1.7	2.5	3.3	3.4	3.6	3.9	3.5	2.6	2.4	2.8	2.4
Snow	7.5	5.5	3.4	1.0	tr	0.0	0.0	0.0	0.0	tr	1.3	5.2

High and Low temperatures in degrees Fahrenheit; Precipitation and Snow in inches

Population: 113,269 (1990); 121,065 (2000); 124,791 (2007); 127,010 (2012 projected); Race: 94.0% White, 1.6% Black, 1.2% Asian, 3.9% Hispanic of any race (2007); Density: 202.1 persons per square mile (2007); Average household size: 2.59 (2007); Median age: 33.6 (2007); Males per 100 females: 94.2 (2007).

Religion: Five largest groups: 18.2% Catholic Church, 9.2% Evangelical Lutheran Church in America, 6.7% The United Methodist Church, 3.3% Muslim Estimate, 1.7% Assemblies of God (2000).

Economy: Unemployment rate: 6.6% (6/2008); Total civilian labor force: 68,967 (6/2008); Leading industries: 26.2% manufacturing; 12.7% retail trade; 10.6% accommodation & food services (2005); Farms: 1,066 totaling 305,834 acres (2002); Companies that employ 500 or more persons: 8 (2006); Companies that employ 100 to 499 persons: 88 (2006); Companies that employ less than 100 persons: 2,711 (2006); Black-owned businesses: n/a (2002); Hispanic-owned businesses: 169 (2002); Asian-owned businesses: n/a (2002); Women-owned businesses: 2,283 (2002); Retail sales per capita: $13,294 (2008). Single-family building permits issued: 439 (2007); Multi-family building permits issued: 82 (2007).

Income: Per capita income: $25,125 (2007); Median household income: $50,189 (2007); Average household income: $64,109 (2007); Percent of households with income of $100,000 or more: 16.3% (2007); Poverty rate: 11.5% (2005); Bankruptcy rate: 3.20% (2007).

Taxes: Total county taxes per capita: $333 (2006); County property taxes per capita: $196 (2006).

Education: Percent of population age 25 and over with: High school diploma (including GED) or higher: 88.6% (2007); Bachelor's degree or higher: 26.3% (2007); Master's degree or higher: 10.4% (2007).

Housing: Homeownership rate: 71.1% (2007); Median home value: $140,058 (2007); Median rent: $427 per month (2000); Median age of housing: 29 years (2000).

Health: Birth rate: 113.7 per 10,000 population (2007); Death rate: 74.5 per 10,000 population (2007); Age-adjusted cancer mortality rate: 201.1 deaths per 100,000 population (2005); Air Quality Index: 78.6% good, 19.1% moderate, 2.3% unhealthy for sensitive individuals, 0.0% unhealthy (percent of days in 2007); Number of physicians: 18.4 per 10,000 population (2005); Hospital beds: 7.8 per 10,000 population (2004); Hospital admissions: 260.9 per 10,000 population (2004).

Elections: 2004 Presidential election results: 53.0% Bush, 46.4% Kerry, 0.0% Nader, 0.3% Badnarik

National and State Parks: Fort Meigs State Memorial; Thurston State Park

Additional Information Contacts

Wood County Government . . . . (419) 354-9100
http://www.co.wood.oh.us
Bowling Green Chamber of Commerce . . . . (419) 353-7945
http://www.bgchamber.net
Bowling Green Convention & Visitors Bureau . . . . (419) 353-9445
http://www.visitbgohio.org
City of Bowling Green . . . . (419) 354-6204
http://www.bgohio.org
City of Northwood . . . . (419) 693-9320
http://www.ci.northwood.oh.us
City of Perrysburg . . . . (419) 872-8010
http://www.ci.perrysburg.oh.us
City of Rossford . . . . (419) 666-0210
http://www.rossfordohio.com
Perrysburg Area Chamber of Commerce . . . . (419) 874-9147
http://www.perrysburgchamber.com
Village of Grand Rapids . . . . (419) 832-5305
http://www.grandrapidsohio.com
Village of Pemberville . . . . (419) 287-3832
http://pembervillelibrary.org/pemberville

Wood County Communities

BAIRDSTOWN (village). Covers a land area of 0.267 square miles and a water area of 0 square miles. Located at 41.17° N. Lat.; 83.60° W. Long. Elevation is 735 feet.

Population: 133 (1990); 130 (2000); 154 (2007); 170 (2012 projected); Race: 95.5% White, 0.0% Black, 0.0% Asian, 0.6% Hispanic of any race (2007); Density: 576.6 persons per square mile (2007); Average household size: 2.57 (2007); Median age: 43.3 (2007); Males per 100 females: 102.6 (2007); Marriage status: 24.6% never married, 60.7% now married, 9.8% widowed, 4.9% divorced (2000); Foreign born: 2.3% (2000); Ancestry (includes multiple ancestries): 42.7% United States or American, 17.6% German, 9.9% Other groups, 3.1% Scottish, 3.1% Pennsylvania German (2000).

Economy: Single-family building permits issued: 0 (2007); Multi-family building permits issued: 0 (2007); Employment by occupation: 0.0% management, 0.0% professional, 18.3% services, 11.7% sales, 0.0% farming, 23.3% construction, 46.7% production (2000).

Income: Per capita income: $19,107 (2007); Median household income: $47,500 (2007); Average household income: $49,042 (2007); Percent of households with income of $100,000 or more: 5.0% (2007); Poverty rate: 7.6% (2000).

Education: Percent of population age 25 and over with: High school diploma (including GED) or higher: 77.5% (2007); Bachelor's degree or higher: 2.5% (2007); Master's degree or higher: 2.5% (2007).

Housing: Homeownership rate: 83.3% (2007); Median home value: $72,000 (2007); Median rent: $281 per month (2000); Median age of housing: 37 years (2000).

Transportation: Commute to work: 100.0% car, 0.0% public transportation, 0.0% walk, 0.0% work from home (2000); Travel time to work: 29.3% less than 15 minutes, 48.3% 15 to 30 minutes, 12.1% 30 to 45 minutes, 0.0% 45 to 60 minutes, 10.3% 60 minutes or more (2000)

BLOOMDALE (village). Covers a land area of 0.669 square miles and a water area of 0.004 square miles. Located at 41.17° N. Lat.; 83.55° W. Long. Elevation is 748 feet.

Population: 632 (1990); 724 (2000); 861 (2007); 949 (2012 projected); Race: 98.1% White, 0.0% Black, 0.2% Asian, 1.4% Hispanic of any race (2007); Density: 1,287.5 persons per square mile (2007); Average household size: 2.72 (2007); Median age: 32.9 (2007); Males per 100 females: 99.8 (2007); Marriage status: 20.7% never married, 63.7% now married, 8.5% widowed, 7.2% divorced (2000); Foreign born: 1.2% (2000); Ancestry (includes multiple ancestries): 38.4% German, 14.4% English, 11.5% Irish, 7.8% United States or American, 5.3% Other groups (2000).

Economy: Single-family building permits issued: 0 (2007); Multi-family building permits issued: 0 (2007); Employment by occupation: 11.2%

management, 5.5% professional, 12.4% services, 17.0% sales, 0.0% farming, 8.9% construction, 45.1% production (2000).
Income: Per capita income: $19,257 (2007); Median household income: $47,130 (2007); Average household income: $52,303 (2007); Percent of households with income of $100,000 or more: 7.3% (2007); Poverty rate: 3.7% (2000).
Education: Percent of population age 25 and over with: High school diploma (including GED) or higher: 88.6% (2007); Bachelor's degree or higher: 13.9% (2007); Master's degree or higher: 2.6% (2007).

School District(s)

Elmwood Local (PK-12)
2005-06 Enrollment: 1,312 . . . . (419) 655-2583
Housing: Homeownership rate: 87.7% (2007); Median home value: $101,316 (2007); Median rent: $354 per month (2000); Median age of housing: 60+ years (2000).
Transportation: Commute to work: 96.4% car, 0.0% public transportation, 1.2% walk, 2.4% work from home (2000); Travel time to work: 20.6% less than 15 minutes, 55.2% 15 to 30 minutes, 15.8% 30 to 45 minutes, 4.2% 45 to 60 minutes, 4.2% 60 minutes or more (2000)

BOWLING GREEN (city). County seat. Covers a land area of 10.153 square miles and a water area of 0.033 square miles. Located at 41.37° N. Lat.; 83.65° W. Long. Elevation is 696 feet.
History: Bowling Green was laid out in 1835 and named by Joseph Gordon for his home town in Kentucky. Oil was found here in 1886, bringing an industrial boom. In 1914 the H.J. Heinz Company established a tomato-products plant in Bowling Green, and the same year Bowling Green State University opened as a normal school.
Population: 29,038 (1990); 29,636 (2000); 30,286 (2007); 30,684 (2012 projected); Race: 90.7% White, 3.4% Black, 1.8% Asian, 4.2% Hispanic of any race (2007); Density: 2,983.0 persons per square mile (2007); Average household size: 2.78 (2007); Median age: 23.9 (2007); Males per 100 females: 87.3 (2007); Marriage status: 54.7% never married, 35.8% now married, 3.7% widowed, 5.8% divorced (2000); Foreign born: 3.6% (2000); Ancestry (includes multiple ancestries): 31.4% German, 11.7% Irish, 10.6% English, 10.2% Other groups, 5.1% United States or American (2000).
Economy: Unemployment rate: 5.7% (6/2008); Total civilian labor force: 16,640 (6/2008); Employment by occupation: 9.9% management, 26.1% professional, 21.2% services, 24.6% sales, 0.2% farming, 3.7% construction, 14.2% production (2000).
Income: Per capita income: $18,422 (2007); Median household income: $34,859 (2007); Average household income: $48,234 (2007); Percent of households with income of $100,000 or more: 10.0% (2007); Poverty rate: 25.3% (2000).
Taxes: Total city taxes per capita: $529 (2006); City property taxes per capita: $67 (2006).
Education: Percent of population age 25 and over with: High school diploma (including GED) or higher: 90.8% (2007); Bachelor's degree or higher: 43.6% (2007); Master's degree or higher: 21.8% (2007).

School District(s)

Bowling Green City (PK-12)
2005-06 Enrollment: 3,133 . . . . (419) 352-3576

Four-year College(s)

Bowling Green State University-Main Campus (Public)
Fall 2007 Enrollment: 18,619. . . . . (419) 372-2531
2007-08 Tuition: In-state $9,060; Out-of-state $16,368
Housing: Homeownership rate: 42.9% (2007); Median home value: $152,733 (2007); Median rent: $434 per month (2000); Median age of housing: 28 years (2000).
Hospitals: Wood County Hospital (162 beds)
Safety: Violent crime rate: 10.1 per 10,000 population; Property crime rate: 377.0 per 10,000 population (2007).
Newspapers: The Blade - Bowling Green Bureau (Local news); Real Estate - Sentinel-Tribune; Sentinel-Tribune (Local news; Circulation 13,000)
Transportation: Commute to work: 83.7% car, 0.6% public transportation, 11.9% walk, 1.7% work from home (2000); Travel time to work: 62.2% less than 15 minutes, 19.0% 15 to 30 minutes, 14.3% 30 to 45 minutes, 2.6% 45 to 60 minutes, 1.9% 60 minutes or more (2000)
Airports: Wood County (general aviation)
Additional Information Contacts
Bowling Green Chamber of Commerce. . . . . (419) 353-7945
http://www.bgchamber.net
Bowling Green Convention & Visitors Bureau . . . . (419) 353-9445
http://www.visitbgohio.org
City of Bowling Green . . . . (419) 354-6204
http://www.bgohio.org

BRADNER (village). Covers a land area of 0.611 square miles and a water area of 0 square miles. Located at 41.32° N. Lat.; 83.43° W. Long. Elevation is 696 feet.
Population: 1,076 (1990); 1,171 (2000); 1,228 (2007); 1,255 (2012 projected); Race: 98.9% White, 0.0% Black, 0.0% Asian, 3.4% Hispanic of any race (2007); Density: 2,008.7 persons per square mile (2007); Average household size: 2.53 (2007); Median age: 34.9 (2007); Males per 100 females: 99.7 (2007); Marriage status: 24.9% never married, 57.7% now married, 7.1% widowed, 10.3% divorced (2000); Foreign born: 0.3% (2000); Ancestry (includes multiple ancestries): 34.6% German, 16.9% United States or American, 9.9% Irish, 7.6% Other groups, 7.5% English (2000).
Economy: Employment by occupation: 5.0% management, 8.5% professional, 13.1% services, 20.4% sales, 1.1% farming, 13.6% construction, 38.3% production (2000).
Income: Per capita income: $18,432 (2007); Median household income: $39,191 (2007); Average household income: $46,670 (2007); Percent of households with income of $100,000 or more: 4.9% (2007); Poverty rate: 12.2% (2000).
Education: Percent of population age 25 and over with: High school diploma (including GED) or higher: 78.4% (2007); Bachelor's degree or higher: 4.8% (2007); Master's degree or higher: 1.4% (2007).

School District(s)

Lakota Local (PK-12)
2005-06 Enrollment: 1,099 . . . . (419) 457-2911
Housing: Homeownership rate: 72.4% (2007); Median home value: $96,184 (2007); Median rent: $371 per month (2000); Median age of housing: 60+ years (2000).
Transportation: Commute to work: 92.8% car, 0.4% public transportation, 3.4% walk, 2.3% work from home (2000); Travel time to work: 22.7% less than 15 minutes, 44.9% 15 to 30 minutes, 22.2% 30 to 45 minutes, 5.0% 45 to 60 minutes, 5.2% 60 minutes or more (2000)

CUSTAR (village). Covers a land area of 0.251 square miles and a water area of 0 square miles. Located at 41.28° N. Lat.; 83.84° W. Long. Elevation is 692 feet.
Population: 209 (1990); 208 (2000); 205 (2007); 199 (2012 projected); Race: 97.6% White, 0.0% Black, 0.0% Asian, 4.9% Hispanic of any race (2007); Density: 818.2 persons per square mile (2007); Average household size: 2.77 (2007); Median age: 36.0 (2007); Males per 100 females: 91.6 (2007); Marriage status: 26.4% never married, 57.1% now married, 6.7% widowed, 9.8% divorced (2000); Foreign born: 0.5% (2000); Ancestry (includes multiple ancestries): 32.2% German, 10.9% Other groups, 5.4% English, 5.4% Dutch, 5.4% Irish (2000).
Economy: Employment by occupation: 12.0% management, 12.0% professional, 18.0% services, 15.0% sales, 0.0% farming, 8.0% construction, 35.0% production (2000).
Income: Per capita income: $18,357 (2007); Median household income: $42,083 (2007); Average household income: $48,007 (2007); Percent of households with income of $100,000 or more: 8.1% (2007); Poverty rate: 12.9% (2000).
Education: Percent of population age 25 and over with: High school diploma (including GED) or higher: 89.7% (2007); Bachelor's degree or higher: 1.5% (2007); Master's degree or higher: 1.5% (2007).

School District(s)

Bowling Green City (PK-12)
2005-06 Enrollment: 3,133 . . . . (419) 352-3576
Housing: Homeownership rate: 89.2% (2007); Median home value: $97,500 (2007); Median rent: $275 per month (2000); Median age of housing: 60+ years (2000).
Transportation: Commute to work: 85.9% car, 0.0% public transportation, 9.1% walk, 5.1% work from home (2000); Travel time to work: 16.0% less than 15 minutes, 27.7% 15 to 30 minutes, 26.6% 30 to 45 minutes, 12.8% 45 to 60 minutes, 17.0% 60 minutes or more (2000)

CYGNET (village). Covers a land area of 0.337 square miles and a water area of 0.001 square miles. Located at 41.24° N. Lat.; 83.64° W. Long. Elevation is 705 feet.
Population: 560 (1990); 564 (2000); 583 (2007); 589 (2012 projected); Race: 96.6% White, 0.5% Black, 0.0% Asian, 2.7% Hispanic of any race (2007); Density: 1,728.4 persons per square mile (2007); Average household size: 2.57 (2007); Median age: 36.3 (2007); Males per 100

females: 101.0 (2007); Marriage status: 19.1% never married, 58.6% now married, 8.0% widowed, 14.3% divorced (2000); Foreign born: 0.2% (2000); Ancestry (includes multiple ancestries): 35.6% German, 10.8% United States or American, 10.6% Irish, 9.5% English, 4.0% Other groups (2000).

Economy: Employment by occupation: 9.5% management, 7.6% professional, 15.6% services, 22.5% sales, 1.1% farming, 13.4% construction, 30.2% production (2000).

Income: Per capita income: $18,040 (2007); Median household income: $42,625 (2007); Average household income: $46,333 (2007); Percent of households with income of $100,000 or more: 3.5% (2007); Poverty rate: 4.6% (2000).

Education: Percent of population age 25 and over with: High school diploma (including GED) or higher: 82.8% (2007); Bachelor's degree or higher: 6.4% (2007); Master's degree or higher: 2.8% (2007).

School District(s)

Elmwood Local (PK-12)
2005-06 Enrollment: 1,312 . . . . (419) 655-2583

Housing: Homeownership rate: 86.8% (2007); Median home value: $91,042 (2007); Median rent: $347 per month (2000); Median age of housing: 60+ years (2000).

Transportation: Commute to work: 93.9% car, 1.9% public transportation, 3.4% walk, 0.8% work from home (2000); Travel time to work: 15.0% less than 15 minutes, 64.2% 15 to 30 minutes, 13.5% 30 to 45 minutes, 1.9% 45 to 60 minutes, 5.4% 60 minutes or more (2000)

GRAND RAPIDS (village). Covers a land area of 0.503 square miles and a water area of 0.088 square miles. Located at 41.41° N. Lat.; 83.86° W. Long. Elevation is 659 feet.

History: Grand Rapids developed as a rural trading center. It was the location of locks on the Miami & Erie Canal.

Population: 1,042 (1990); 1,002 (2000); 1,075 (2007); 1,121 (2012 projected); Race: 96.5% White, 0.3% Black, 0.5% Asian, 4.0% Hispanic of any race (2007); Density: 2,135.8 persons per square mile (2007); Average household size: 2.39 (2007); Median age: 37.7 (2007); Males per 100 females: 92.3 (2007); Marriage status: 19.3% never married, 60.6% now married, 8.1% widowed, 12.0% divorced (2000); Foreign born: 2.2% (2000); Ancestry (includes multiple ancestries): 36.2% German, 14.0% English, 11.0% Irish, 9.9% United States or American, 9.7% Other groups (2000).

Economy: Employment by occupation: 10.7% management, 15.8% professional, 14.1% services, 20.4% sales, 0.8% farming, 13.9% construction, 24.4% production (2000).

Income: Per capita income: $25,827 (2007); Median household income: $50,508 (2007); Average household income: $60,400 (2007); Percent of households with income of $100,000 or more: 10.7% (2007); Poverty rate: 5.7% (2000).

Education: Percent of population age 25 and over with: High school diploma (including GED) or higher: 85.0% (2007); Bachelor's degree or higher: 15.6% (2007); Master's degree or higher: 3.9% (2007).

School District(s)

Otsego Local (PK-12)
2005-06 Enrollment: 1,783 . . . . (419) 823-4381

Housing: Homeownership rate: 80.4% (2007); Median home value: $109,375 (2007); Median rent: $382 per month (2000); Median age of housing: 39 years (2000).

Transportation: Commute to work: 91.9% car, 0.0% public transportation, 6.1% walk, 1.2% work from home (2000); Travel time to work: 22.1% less than 15 minutes, 34.8% 15 to 30 minutes, 26.8% 30 to 45 minutes, 11.1% 45 to 60 minutes, 5.1% 60 minutes or more (2000)

Additional Information Contacts

Village of Grand Rapids . . . . (419) 832-5305
http://www.grandrapidsohio.com

HASKINS (village). Covers a land area of 1.527 square miles and a water area of 0 square miles. Located at 41.46° N. Lat.; 83.70° W. Long. Elevation is 656 feet.

Population: 549 (1990); 638 (2000); 758 (2007); 832 (2012 projected); Race: 97.8% White, 0.0% Black, 0.8% Asian, 3.2% Hispanic of any race (2007); Density: 496.2 persons per square mile (2007); Average household size: 2.54 (2007); Median age: 35.1 (2007); Males per 100 females: 101.6 (2007); Marriage status: 25.1% never married, 61.0% now married, 7.0% widowed, 7.0% divorced (2000); Foreign born: 0.3% (2000); Ancestry (includes multiple ancestries): 40.9% German, 12.8% English, 10.3% Irish, 8.8% United States or American, 7.9% French (except Basque) (2000).

Economy: Employment by occupation: 13.3% management, 22.1% professional, 13.9% services, 15.9% sales, 0.0% farming, 13.6% construction, 21.2% production (2000).

Income: Per capita income: $24,205 (2007); Median household income: $55,000 (2007); Average household income: $61,569 (2007); Percent of households with income of $100,000 or more: 15.8% (2007); Poverty rate: 4.8% (2000).

Education: Percent of population age 25 and over with: High school diploma (including GED) or higher: 93.6% (2007); Bachelor's degree or higher: 20.3% (2007); Master's degree or higher: 5.2% (2007).

School District(s)

Otsego Local (PK-12)
2005-06 Enrollment: 1,783 . . . . (419) 823-4381

Housing: Homeownership rate: 82.6% (2007); Median home value: $122,500 (2007); Median rent: $391 per month (2000); Median age of housing: 60+ years (2000).

Transportation: Commute to work: 95.8% car, 0.0% public transportation, 2.7% walk, 1.2% work from home (2000); Travel time to work: 30.2% less than 15 minutes, 50.8% 15 to 30 minutes, 13.6% 30 to 45 minutes, 3.3% 45 to 60 minutes, 2.1% 60 minutes or more (2000)

HOYTVILLE (village). Covers a land area of 0.744 square miles and a water area of 0.012 square miles. Located at 41.19° N. Lat.; 83.78° W. Long. Elevation is 709 feet.

Population: 301 (1990); 296 (2000); 360 (2007); 399 (2012 projected); Race: 83.3% White, 0.0% Black, 1.9% Asian, 14.4% Hispanic of any race (2007); Density: 483.9 persons per square mile (2007); Average household size: 3.16 (2007); Median age: 28.9 (2007); Males per 100 females: 90.5 (2007); Marriage status: 27.5% never married, 49.4% now married, 8.6% widowed, 14.6% divorced (2000); Foreign born: 0.0% (2000); Ancestry (includes multiple ancestries): 46.7% German, 22.6% Other groups, 10.3% Irish, 9.1% United States or American, 8.5% English (2000).

Economy: Single-family building permits issued: 0 (2007); Multi-family building permits issued: 0 (2007); Employment by occupation: 4.3% management, 2.5% professional, 9.3% services, 13.0% sales, 6.2% farming, 9.9% construction, 54.9% production (2000).

Income: Per capita income: $15,493 (2007); Median household income: $47,273 (2007); Average household income: $48,925 (2007); Percent of households with income of $100,000 or more: 3.5% (2007); Poverty rate: 10.7% (2000).

Education: Percent of population age 25 and over with: High school diploma (including GED) or higher: 72.3% (2007); Bachelor's degree or higher: 1.0% (2007); Master's degree or higher: 1.0% (2007).

School District(s)

Mccomb Local (PK-12)
2005-06 Enrollment: 832 . . . . (419) 293-3979

Housing: Homeownership rate: 86.0% (2007); Median home value: $54,286 (2007); Median rent: $311 per month (2000); Median age of housing: 60+ years (2000).

Transportation: Commute to work: 94.9% car, 0.0% public transportation, 5.1% walk, 0.0% work from home (2000); Travel time to work: 21.0% less than 15 minutes, 38.2% 15 to 30 minutes, 29.9% 30 to 45 minutes, 9.6% 45 to 60 minutes, 1.3% 60 minutes or more (2000)

JERRY CITY (village). Covers a land area of 1.007 square miles and a water area of 0 square miles. Located at 41.25° N. Lat.; 83.60° W. Long. Elevation is 696 feet.

Population: 517 (1990); 453 (2000); 484 (2007); 501 (2012 projected); Race: 99.6% White, 0.0% Black, 0.0% Asian, 2.3% Hispanic of any race (2007); Density: 480.7 persons per square mile (2007); Average household size: 2.72 (2007); Median age: 33.9 (2007); Males per 100 females: 101.7 (2007); Marriage status: 23.8% never married, 57.5% now married, 5.1% widowed, 13.6% divorced (2000); Foreign born: 0.0% (2000); Ancestry (includes multiple ancestries): 28.1% German, 19.6% United States or American, 14.9% Other groups, 8.4% English, 3.7% Irish (2000).

Economy: Single-family building permits issued: 0 (2007); Multi-family building permits issued: 0 (2007); Employment by occupation: 9.9% management, 8.5% professional, 9.0% services, 15.7% sales, 1.8% farming, 16.6% construction, 38.6% production (2000).

Income: Per capita income: $19,194 (2007); Median household income: $45,000 (2007); Average household income: $52,191 (2007); Percent of households with income of $100,000 or more: 7.9% (2007); Poverty rate: 9.8% (2000).

Education: Percent of population age 25 and over with: High school diploma (including GED) or higher: 76.7% (2007); Bachelor's degree or higher: 2.7% (2007); Master's degree or higher: 0.0% (2007).
Housing: Homeownership rate: 87.6% (2007); Median home value: $86,786 (2007); Median rent: $403 per month (2000); Median age of housing: 47 years (2000).
Transportation: Commute to work: 98.6% car, 0.0% public transportation, 0.0% walk, 1.4% work from home (2000); Travel time to work: 12.9% less than 15 minutes, 53.1% 15 to 30 minutes, 26.8% 30 to 45 minutes, 4.3% 45 to 60 minutes, 2.9% 60 minutes or more (2000)

LUCKEY (village). Covers a land area of 0.677 square miles and a water area of 0.001 square miles. Located at 41.45° N. Lat.; 83.48° W. Long. Elevation is 666 feet.
Population: 848 (1990); 998 (2000); 931 (2007); 929 (2012 projected); Race: 95.5% White, 0.2% Black, 0.0% Asian, 4.8% Hispanic of any race (2007); Density: 1,376.0 persons per square mile (2007); Average household size: 2.69 (2007); Median age: 34.0 (2007); Males per 100 females: 93.6 (2007); Marriage status: 18.3% never married, 64.9% now married, 6.8% widowed, 10.0% divorced (2000); Foreign born: 1.9% (2000); Ancestry (includes multiple ancestries): 45.8% German, 11.6% Irish, 8.5% English, 8.4% United States or American, 5.7% Polish (2000).
Economy: Employment by occupation: 9.7% management, 15.9% professional, 15.9% services, 23.9% sales, 0.4% farming, 10.1% construction, 23.9% production (2000).
Income: Per capita income: $21,807 (2007); Median household income: $54,348 (2007); Average household income: $58,678 (2007); Percent of households with income of $100,000 or more: 11.0% (2007); Poverty rate: 5.4% (2000).
Education: Percent of population age 25 and over with: High school diploma (including GED) or higher: 89.1% (2007); Bachelor's degree or higher: 11.6% (2007); Master's degree or higher: 3.5% (2007).

School District(s)

Eastwood Local (PK-12)
2005-06 Enrollment: 1,926 . . . . (419) 833-6411
Housing: Homeownership rate: 85.0% (2007); Median home value: $133,333 (2007); Median rent: $393 per month (2000); Median age of housing: 56 years (2000).
Transportation: Commute to work: 94.7% car, 0.7% public transportation, 1.8% walk, 1.8% work from home (2000); Travel time to work: 20.8% less than 15 minutes, 48.8% 15 to 30 minutes, 22.1% 30 to 45 minutes, 4.7% 45 to 60 minutes, 3.6% 60 minutes or more (2000)

MILLBURY (village). Covers a land area of 0.983 square miles and a water area of 0 square miles. Located at 41.56° N. Lat.; 83.42° W. Long. Elevation is 614 feet.
Population: 1,111 (1990); 1,161 (2000); 1,208 (2007); 1,230 (2012 projected); Race: 99.0% White, 0.0% Black, 0.1% Asian, 0.6% Hispanic of any race (2007); Density: 1,228.9 persons per square mile (2007); Average household size: 2.64 (2007); Median age: 38.4 (2007); Males per 100 females: 95.5 (2007); Marriage status: 19.2% never married, 68.5% now married, 5.1% widowed, 7.3% divorced (2000); Foreign born: 1.8% (2000); Ancestry (includes multiple ancestries): 44.8% German, 11.8% English, 9.9% Irish, 8.9% United States or American, 7.5% French (except Basque) (2000).
Economy: Employment by occupation: 8.1% management, 15.3% professional, 13.3% services, 36.9% sales, 0.3% farming, 9.6% construction, 16.5% production (2000).
Income: Per capita income: $25,019 (2007); Median household income: $61,875 (2007); Average household income: $66,132 (2007); Percent of households with income of $100,000 or more: 18.4% (2007); Poverty rate: 2.6% (2000).
Education: Percent of population age 25 and over with: High school diploma (including GED) or higher: 88.6% (2007); Bachelor's degree or higher: 12.9% (2007); Master's degree or higher: 2.9% (2007).

School District(s)

Lake Local (PK-12)
2005-06 Enrollment: 1,733 . . . . (419) 836-2552
Housing: Homeownership rate: 82.3% (2007); Median home value: $155,224 (2007); Median rent: $494 per month (2000); Median age of housing: 32 years (2000).
Newspapers: Metro Press (Local news; Circulation 21,000); Press (Local news; Circulation 1,000)
Transportation: Commute to work: 98.1% car, 0.3% public transportation, 0.3% walk, 0.9% work from home (2000); Travel time to work: 26.2% less than 15 minutes, 51.9% 15 to 30 minutes, 17.7% 30 to 45 minutes, 1.6% 45 to 60 minutes, 2.6% 60 minutes or more (2000)

MILTON CENTER (village). Aka Milton. Covers a land area of 0.399 square miles and a water area of 0 square miles. Located at 41.30° N. Lat.; 83.82° W. Long. Elevation is 689 feet.
Population: 200 (1990); 195 (2000); 192 (2007); 189 (2012 projected); Race: 92.7% White, 0.0% Black, 0.0% Asian, 19.3% Hispanic of any race (2007); Density: 480.8 persons per square mile (2007); Average household size: 2.78 (2007); Median age: 35.5 (2007); Males per 100 females: 102.1 (2007); Marriage status: 25.3% never married, 51.9% now married, 7.8% widowed, 14.9% divorced (2000); Foreign born: 1.0% (2000); Ancestry (includes multiple ancestries): 27.6% German, 21.2% Other groups, 10.8% United States or American, 7.9% Irish, 6.9% Italian (2000).
Economy: Employment by occupation: 3.8% management, 9.0% professional, 14.1% services, 19.2% sales, 0.0% farming, 21.8% construction, 32.1% production (2000).
Income: Per capita income: $13,763 (2007); Median household income: $32,500 (2007); Average household income: $38,297 (2007); Percent of households with income of $100,000 or more: 4.3% (2007); Poverty rate: 9.7% (2000).
Education: Percent of population age 25 and over with: High school diploma (including GED) or higher: 67.2% (2007); Bachelor's degree or higher: 8.8% (2007); Master's degree or higher: 2.4% (2007).
Housing: Homeownership rate: 84.1% (2007); Median home value: $70,000 (2007); Median rent: $292 per month (2000); Median age of housing: 60+ years (2000).
Transportation: Commute to work: 100.0% car, 0.0% public transportation, 0.0% walk, 0.0% work from home (2000); Travel time to work: 24.4% less than 15 minutes, 37.2% 15 to 30 minutes, 14.1% 30 to 45 minutes, 17.9% 45 to 60 minutes, 6.4% 60 minutes or more (2000)

NORTH BALTIMORE (village). Covers a land area of 2.223 square miles and a water area of 0.028 square miles. Located at 41.18° N. Lat.; 83.67° W. Long. Elevation is 732 feet.
History: Settled 1834.
Population: 3,169 (1990); 3,361 (2000); 3,385 (2007); 3,407 (2012 projected); Race: 96.7% White, 0.0% Black, 0.3% Asian, 3.5% Hispanic of any race (2007); Density: 1,523.0 persons per square mile (2007); Average household size: 2.54 (2007); Median age: 34.8 (2007); Males per 100 females: 92.8 (2007); Marriage status: 21.7% never married, 57.1% now married, 9.0% widowed, 12.2% divorced (2000); Foreign born: 0.6% (2000); Ancestry (includes multiple ancestries): 31.3% German, 15.8% United States or American, 11.8% Irish, 11.2% Other groups, 7.4% English (2000).
Economy: Employment by occupation: 7.7% management, 7.9% professional, 14.2% services, 25.4% sales, 0.0% farming, 9.6% construction, 35.2% production (2000).
Income: Per capita income: $20,782 (2007); Median household income: $43,958 (2007); Average household income: $51,934 (2007); Percent of households with income of $100,000 or more: 8.9% (2007); Poverty rate: 8.8% (2000).
Education: Percent of population age 25 and over with: High school diploma (including GED) or higher: 81.2% (2007); Bachelor's degree or higher: 10.4% (2007); Master's degree or higher: 3.6% (2007).

School District(s)

North Baltimore Local (PK-12)
2005-06 Enrollment: 871 . . . . (419) 257-3531
Housing: Homeownership rate: 74.0% (2007); Median home value: $92,390 (2007); Median rent: $299 per month (2000); Median age of housing: 50 years (2000).
Newspapers: North Baltimore News (Community news; Circulation 1,200)
Transportation: Commute to work: 95.8% car, 0.0% public transportation, 2.3% walk, 1.9% work from home (2000); Travel time to work: 42.5% less than 15 minutes, 41.7% 15 to 30 minutes, 12.6% 30 to 45 minutes, 2.3% 45 to 60 minutes, 0.9% 60 minutes or more (2000)

NORTHWOOD (city). Covers a land area of 8.403 square miles and a water area of 0.013 square miles. Located at 41.61° N. Lat.; 83.49° W. Long. Elevation is 614 feet.
Population: 5,506 (1990); 5,471 (2000); 5,477 (2007); 5,485 (2012 projected); Race: 94.0% White, 0.8% Black, 1.1% Asian, 5.1% Hispanic of any race (2007); Density: 651.8 persons per square mile (2007); Average household size: 2.60 (2007); Median age: 37.1 (2007); Males per 100 females: 96.2 (2007); Marriage status: 26.5% never married, 56.5% now

married, 5.7% widowed, 11.2% divorced (2000); Foreign born: 2.6% (2000); Ancestry (includes multiple ancestries): 34.0% German, 11.5% Irish, 11.4% Other groups, 9.7% English, 8.7% United States or American (2000).
Economy: Employment by occupation: 14.6% management, 14.2% professional, 13.9% services, 26.9% sales, 0.0% farming, 7.9% construction, 22.5% production (2000).
Income: Per capita income: $25,126 (2007); Median household income: $58,421 (2007); Average household income: $64,992 (2007); Percent of households with income of $100,000 or more: 16.7% (2007); Poverty rate: 10.2% (2000).
Education: Percent of population age 25 and over with: High school diploma (including GED) or higher: 84.0% (2007); Bachelor's degree or higher: 12.6% (2007); Master's degree or higher: 2.3% (2007).

School District(s)

Northwood Local (PK-12)
2005-06 Enrollment: 997 . . . . (419) 691-3888
Housing: Homeownership rate: 87.3% (2007); Median home value: $126,310 (2007); Median rent: $355 per month (2000); Median age of housing: 29 years (2000).
Safety: Violent crime rate: 16.4 per 10,000 population; Property crime rate: 563.7 per 10,000 population (2007).
Transportation: Commute to work: 98.2% car, 0.0% public transportation, 1.1% walk, 0.4% work from home (2000); Travel time to work: 33.9% less than 15 minutes, 47.7% 15 to 30 minutes, 11.3% 30 to 45 minutes, 1.9% 45 to 60 minutes, 5.3% 60 minutes or more (2000)
Additional Information Contacts
City of Northwood . . . . (419) 693-9320
http://www.ci.northwood.oh.us

PEMBERVILLE (village). Covers a land area of 1.107 square miles and a water area of 0 square miles. Located at 41.41° N. Lat.; 83.45° W. Long. Elevation is 650 feet.
History: Settled 1834, incorporated 1876.
Population: 1,304 (1990); 1,365 (2000); 1,342 (2007); 1,360 (2012 projected); Race: 94.9% White, 0.0% Black, 0.0% Asian, 5.4% Hispanic of any race (2007); Density: 1,211.9 persons per square mile (2007); Average household size: 2.41 (2007); Median age: 39.1 (2007); Males per 100 females: 90.4 (2007); Marriage status: 22.7% never married, 62.8% now married, 6.4% widowed, 8.2% divorced (2000); Foreign born: 1.6% (2000); Ancestry (includes multiple ancestries): 51.9% German, 9.2% English, 7.6% Irish, 7.1% Other groups, 3.0% United States or American (2000).
Economy: Employment by occupation: 10.8% management, 20.7% professional, 12.9% services, 27.1% sales, 0.6% farming, 9.3% construction, 18.7% production (2000).
Income: Per capita income: $26,857 (2007); Median household income: $59,609 (2007); Average household income: $64,708 (2007); Percent of households with income of $100,000 or more: 14.2% (2007); Poverty rate: 3.4% (2000).
Education: Percent of population age 25 and over with: High school diploma (including GED) or higher: 89.4% (2007); Bachelor's degree or higher: 22.5% (2007); Master's degree or higher: 9.2% (2007).

School District(s)

Eastwood Local (PK-12)
2005-06 Enrollment: 1,926 . . . . (419) 833-6411
Housing: Homeownership rate: 76.8% (2007); Median home value: $134,341 (2007); Median rent: $411 per month (2000); Median age of housing: 60+ years (2000).
Transportation: Commute to work: 90.2% car, 0.3% public transportation, 5.4% walk, 3.1% work from home (2000); Travel time to work: 32.9% less than 15 minutes, 41.0% 15 to 30 minutes, 18.6% 30 to 45 minutes, 4.2% 45 to 60 minutes, 3.3% 60 minutes or more (2000)
Additional Information Contacts
Village of Pemberville . . . . (419) 287-3832
http://pembervillelibrary.org/pemberville

PERRYSBURG (city). Covers a land area of 8.922 square miles and a water area of 0.212 square miles. Located at 41.55° N. Lat.; 83.63° W. Long. Elevation is 630 feet.
History: Perrysburg was settled in 1816 and named for Oliver Hazard Perry. Its site on the Maumee River made it a shipping and shipbuilding center. From 1822 to 1866, Perrysburg served as the seat of Wood County.
Population: 14,412 (1990); 16,945 (2000); 16,851 (2007); 16,735 (2012 projected); Race: 93.9% White, 1.5% Black, 2.5% Asian, 2.3% Hispanic of any race (2007); Density: 1,888.6 persons per square mile (2007); Average household size: 2.54 (2007); Median age: 38.9 (2007); Males per 100 females: 94.4 (2007); Marriage status: 19.3% never married, 65.7% now married, 6.9% widowed, 8.2% divorced (2000); Foreign born: 3.8% (2000); Ancestry (includes multiple ancestries): 39.6% German, 14.1% English, 13.5% Irish, 8.0% Polish, 6.5% Other groups (2000).
Economy: Employment by occupation: 20.4% management, 31.3% professional, 9.1% services, 25.2% sales, 0.0% farming, 4.2% construction, 9.8% production (2000).
Income: Per capita income: $34,664 (2007); Median household income: $68,589 (2007); Average household income: $87,785 (2007); Percent of households with income of $100,000 or more: 29.7% (2007); Poverty rate: 2.8% (2000).
Education: Percent of population age 25 and over with: High school diploma (including GED) or higher: 94.8% (2007); Bachelor's degree or higher: 47.4% (2007); Master's degree or higher: 19.0% (2007).

School District(s)

Eastwood Local (PK-12)
2005-06 Enrollment: 1,926 . . . . (419) 833-6411
Maritime Academy of Toledo The
2005-06 Enrollment: n/a . . . . (419) 661-1477
Penta Career Center (07-12)
2005-06 Enrollment: n/a . . . . (419) 666-1120
Perrysburg Digital Academy (KG-12)
2005-06 Enrollment: 67 . . . . (419) 872-8820
Perrysburg Exempted Village (PK-12)
2005-06 Enrollment: 4,454 . . . . (419) 874-9131
Rossford Exempted Village (PK-12)
2005-06 Enrollment: 2,041 . . . . (419) 666-2010

Two-year College(s)

Owens Community College (Public)
Fall 2007 Enrollment: 19,853. . . . . (567) 661-7000
2007-08 Tuition: In-state $3,594; Out-of-state $6,174

Vocational/Technical School(s)

Healing Arts Institute (Private, For-profit)
Fall 2007 Enrollment: 44 . . . . (419) 874-4496
Penta County Joint Vocational School (Public)
Fall 2007 Enrollment: 195 . . . . (419) 661-6555
2007-08 Tuition: $4,705
Housing: Homeownership rate: 75.4% (2007); Median home value: $195,313 (2007); Median rent: $516 per month (2000); Median age of housing: 24 years (2000).
Newspapers: American Recycler (National news); Messenger Journal (Local news; Circulation 13,500)
Transportation: Commute to work: 94.8% car, 0.5% public transportation, 1.1% walk, 3.0% work from home (2000); Travel time to work: 32.7% less than 15 minutes, 52.6% 15 to 30 minutes, 9.1% 30 to 45 minutes, 2.0% 45 to 60 minutes, 3.6% 60 minutes or more (2000)
Additional Information Contacts
City of Perrysburg . . . . (419) 872-8010
http://www.ci.perrysburg.oh.us
Perrysburg Area Chamber of Commerce . . . . (419) 874-9147
http://www.perrysburgchamber.com

PORTAGE (village). Covers a land area of 1.497 square miles and a water area of 0 square miles. Located at 41.32° N. Lat.; 83.65° W. Long. Elevation is 686 feet.
History: Portage began as a trading post in 1824 and grew during the oil and gas boom of the 1880's and 1890's.
Population: 501 (1990); 428 (2000); 486 (2007); 524 (2012 projected); Race: 89.9% White, 1.9% Black, 0.0% Asian, 11.3% Hispanic of any race (2007); Density: 324.7 persons per square mile (2007); Average household size: 2.70 (2007); Median age: 40.4 (2007); Males per 100 females: 105.1 (2007); Marriage status: 29.6% never married, 53.8% now married, 7.4% widowed, 9.2% divorced (2000); Foreign born: 2.5% (2000); Ancestry (includes multiple ancestries): 36.0% German, 11.3% Other groups, 9.7% English, 9.7% Irish, 5.5% Scottish (2000).
Economy: Single-family building permits issued: 0 (2007); Multi-family building permits issued: 0 (2007); Employment by occupation: 8.7% management, 13.5% professional, 11.3% services, 21.7% sales, 0.0% farming, 7.4% construction, 37.4% production (2000).
Income: Per capita income: $19,331 (2007); Median household income: $42,955 (2007); Average household income: $51,042 (2007); Percent of households with income of $100,000 or more: 8.3% (2007); Poverty rate: 10.4% (2000).

Education: Percent of population age 25 and over with: High school diploma (including GED) or higher: 76.9% (2007); Bachelor's degree or higher: 15.4% (2007); Master's degree or higher: 5.0% (2007).

School District(s)

Elmwood Local (PK-12)
2005-06 Enrollment: 1,312 . . . . (419) 655-2583

Housing: Homeownership rate: 70.6% (2007); Median home value: $106,419 (2007); Median rent: $431 per month (2000); Median age of housing: 60+ years (2000).

Transportation: Commute to work: 85.2% car, 12.2% public transportation, 0.0% walk, 1.7% work from home (2000); Travel time to work: 41.6% less than 15 minutes, 34.5% 15 to 30 minutes, 16.4% 30 to 45 minutes, 3.5% 45 to 60 minutes, 4.0% 60 minutes or more (2000)

RISINGSUN (village). Aka Rising Sun. Covers a land area of 0.577 square miles and a water area of 0 square miles. Located at 41.26° N. Lat.; 83.42° W. Long. Elevation is 715 feet.

Population: 659 (1990); 620 (2000); 598 (2007); 598 (2012 projected); Race: 97.5% White, 0.0% Black, 0.0% Asian, 2.3% Hispanic of any race (2007); Density: 1,035.7 persons per square mile (2007); Average household size: 2.57 (2007); Median age: 34.9 (2007); Males per 100 females: 83.4 (2007); Marriage status: 28.4% never married, 57.6% now married, 5.6% widowed, 8.4% divorced (2000); Foreign born: 0.8% (2000); Ancestry (includes multiple ancestries): 33.9% German, 20.1% United States or American, 9.0% Other groups, 6.6% Irish, 5.8% English (2000).

Economy: Employment by occupation: 5.3% management, 6.7% professional, 16.0% services, 25.7% sales, 0.0% farming, 8.0% construction, 38.3% production (2000).

Income: Per capita income: $19,578 (2007); Median household income: $42,344 (2007); Average household income: $50,247 (2007); Percent of households with income of $100,000 or more: 9.4% (2007); Poverty rate: 7.2% (2000).

Education: Percent of population age 25 and over with: High school diploma (including GED) or higher: 83.3% (2007); Bachelor's degree or higher: 3.8% (2007); Master's degree or higher: 1.9% (2007).

School District(s)

Lakota Local (PK-12)
2005-06 Enrollment: 1,099 . . . . (419) 457-2911

Housing: Homeownership rate: 73.4% (2007); Median home value: $80,789 (2007); Median rent: $362 per month (2000); Median age of housing: 60+ years (2000).

Transportation: Commute to work: 96.6% car, 0.0% public transportation, 1.0% walk, 1.0% work from home (2000); Travel time to work: 22.9% less than 15 minutes, 41.7% 15 to 30 minutes, 28.5% 30 to 45 minutes, 3.1% 45 to 60 minutes, 3.8% 60 minutes or more (2000)

ROSSFORD (city). Covers a land area of 4.300 square miles and a water area of 0.285 square miles. Located at 41.59° N. Lat.; 83.56° W. Long. Elevation is 617 feet.

History: Rossford began in 1896 when Edward Ford established a glass company that later merged with the Libbey-Owens corporation.

Population: 5,996 (1990); 6,406 (2000); 6,172 (2007); 6,048 (2012 projected); Race: 96.1% White, 1.3% Black, 0.7% Asian, 1.8% Hispanic of any race (2007); Density: 1,435.3 persons per square mile (2007); Average household size: 2.37 (2007); Median age: 38.3 (2007); Males per 100 females: 92.9 (2007); Marriage status: 24.7% never married, 57.7% now married, 8.8% widowed, 8.9% divorced (2000); Foreign born: 3.4% (2000); Ancestry (includes multiple ancestries): 35.3% German, 19.6% Polish, 11.8% Irish, 8.6% English, 6.6% Slovak (2000).

Economy: Employment by occupation: 11.5% management, 20.3% professional, 15.7% services, 24.4% sales, 0.0% farming, 9.7% construction, 18.3% production (2000).

Income: Per capita income: $26,635 (2007); Median household income: $48,418 (2007); Average household income: $63,252 (2007); Percent of households with income of $100,000 or more: 13.9% (2007); Poverty rate: 3.7% (2000).

Education: Percent of population age 25 and over with: High school diploma (including GED) or higher: 89.1% (2007); Bachelor's degree or higher: 20.8% (2007); Master's degree or higher: 5.8% (2007).

School District(s)

Rossford Exempted Village (PK-12)
2005-06 Enrollment: 2,041 . . . . (419) 666-2010

Housing: Homeownership rate: 71.2% (2007); Median home value: $138,474 (2007); Median rent: $383 per month (2000); Median age of housing: 41 years (2000).

Safety: Violent crime rate: 9.5 per 10,000 population; Property crime rate: 258.3 per 10,000 population (2007).

Newspapers: Rossford Record (Local news; Circulation 1,714)

Transportation: Commute to work: 95.8% car, 0.7% public transportation, 1.6% walk, 1.5% work from home (2000); Travel time to work: 38.0% less than 15 minutes, 50.5% 15 to 30 minutes, 4.3% 30 to 45 minutes, 2.2% 45 to 60 minutes, 5.0% 60 minutes or more (2000)

Additional Information Contacts

City of Rossford . . . . (419) 666-0210
http://www.rossfordohio.com

RUDOLPH (unincorporated postal area, zip code 43462). Covers a land area of 24.956 square miles and a water area of 0.025 square miles. Located at 41.28° N. Lat.; 83.69° W. Long. Elevation is 690 feet.

Population: 1,247 (2000); Race: 94.8% White, 0.0% Black, 0.0% Asian, 9.7% Hispanic of any race (2000); Density: 50.0 persons per square mile (2000); Age: 25.6% under 18, 11.1% over 64 (2000); Marriage status: 26.8% never married, 51.5% now married, 6.7% widowed, 14.9% divorced (2000); Foreign born: 0.0% (2000); Ancestry (includes multiple ancestries): 29.0% German, 15.3% Other groups, 13.1% United States or American, 12.3% Irish, 6.8% French (except Basque) (2000).

Economy: Employment by occupation: 9.6% management, 8.3% professional, 17.9% services, 20.6% sales, 1.6% farming, 7.8% construction, 34.2% production (2000).

Income: Per capita income: $17,684 (2000); Median household income: $40,066 (2000); Poverty rate: 4.5% (2000).

Education: Percent of population age 25 and over with: High school diploma (including GED) or higher: 75.8% (2000); Bachelor's degree or higher: 9.6% (2000).

Housing: Homeownership rate: 82.9% (2000); Median home value: $87,100 (2000); Median rent: $387 per month (2000); Median age of housing: 31 years (2000).

Transportation: Commute to work: 99.1% car, 0.0% public transportation, 0.0% walk, 0.9% work from home (2000); Travel time to work: 16.3% less than 15 minutes, 62.2% 15 to 30 minutes, 5.9% 30 to 45 minutes, 10.6% 45 to 60 minutes, 4.9% 60 minutes or more (2000)

TONTOGANY (village). Covers a land area of 0.182 square miles and a water area of 0 square miles. Located at 41.42° N. Lat.; 83.74° W. Long. Elevation is 656 feet.

Population: 364 (1990); 364 (2000); 378 (2007); 385 (2012 projected); Race: 98.7% White, 0.0% Black, 0.0% Asian, 3.7% Hispanic of any race (2007); Density: 2,072.8 persons per square mile (2007); Average household size: 2.57 (2007); Median age: 34.5 (2007); Males per 100 females: 101.1 (2007); Marriage status: 20.7% never married, 63.2% now married, 8.1% widowed, 8.1% divorced (2000); Foreign born: 0.0% (2000); Ancestry (includes multiple ancestries): 49.5% German, 24.2% English, 10.2% Other groups, 7.5% Irish, 5.9% Polish (2000).

Economy: Employment by occupation: 11.4% management, 12.9% professional, 15.8% services, 33.7% sales, 0.0% farming, 8.9% construction, 17.3% production (2000).

Income: Per capita income: $19,960 (2007); Median household income: $45,417 (2007); Average household income: $51,327 (2007); Percent of households with income of $100,000 or more: 7.5% (2007); Poverty rate: 5.1% (2000).

Education: Percent of population age 25 and over with: High school diploma (including GED) or higher: 91.5% (2007); Bachelor's degree or higher: 15.0% (2007); Master's degree or higher: 6.0% (2007).

School District(s)

Otsego Local (PK-12)
2005-06 Enrollment: 1,783 . . . . (419) 823-4381

Housing: Homeownership rate: 78.9% (2007); Median home value: $118,382 (2007); Median rent: $435 per month (2000); Median age of housing: 60+ years (2000).

Transportation: Commute to work: 95.0% car, 0.0% public transportation, 2.5% walk, 2.5% work from home (2000); Travel time to work: 34.9% less than 15 minutes, 44.6% 15 to 30 minutes, 16.9% 30 to 45 minutes, 0.0% 45 to 60 minutes, 3.6% 60 minutes or more (2000)

WALBRIDGE (village). Covers a land area of 1.662 square miles and a water area of 0.015 square miles. Located at 41.58° N. Lat.; 83.49° W. Long. Elevation is 617 feet.

Population: 2,736 (1990); 2,546 (2000); 2,534 (2007); 2,526 (2012 projected); Race: 97.0% White, 0.8% Black, 0.3% Asian, 2.9% Hispanic of any race (2007); Density: 1,524.8 persons per square mile (2007); Average

household size: 2.27 (2007); Median age: 40.0 (2007); Males per 100 females: 91.4 (2007); Marriage status: 19.5% never married, 58.4% now married, 10.0% widowed, 12.0% divorced (2000); Foreign born: 1.3% (2000); Ancestry (includes multiple ancestries): 33.1% German, 16.9% United States or American, 12.9% Irish, 11.0% English, 9.3% Other groups (2000).
Economy: Employment by occupation: 9.3% management, 13.5% professional, 11.8% services, 27.6% sales, 0.0% farming, 12.3% construction, 25.5% production (2000).
Income: Per capita income: $23,769 (2007); Median household income: $45,439 (2007); Average household income: $53,822 (2007); Percent of households with income of $100,000 or more: 12.3% (2007); Poverty rate: 4.7% (2000).
Education: Percent of population age 25 and over with: High school diploma (including GED) or higher: 84.2% (2007); Bachelor's degree or higher: 7.0% (2007); Master's degree or higher: 3.1% (2007).

School District(s)

Lake Local (PK-12)
2005-06 Enrollment: 1,733 . . . . (419) 836-2552

Housing: Homeownership rate: 72.0% (2007); Median home value: $123,002 (2007); Median rent: $397 per month (2000); Median age of housing: 40 years (2000).
Safety: Violent crime rate: 0.0 per 10,000 population; Property crime rate: 217.7 per 10,000 population (2007).
Transportation: Commute to work: 98.1% car, 0.6% public transportation, 0.0% walk, 1.2% work from home (2000); Travel time to work: 25.9% less than 15 minutes, 49.3% 15 to 30 minutes, 16.0% 30 to 45 minutes, 3.6% 45 to 60 minutes, 5.2% 60 minutes or more (2000)
Airports: Metcalf Field (general aviation)

WAYNE (village). Covers a land area of 0.322 square miles and a water area of 0 square miles. Located at 41.30° N. Lat.; 83.47° W. Long. Elevation is 699 feet.
History: Wayne was known as strongly abolitionist in sentiment prior to the Civil War. In the winter of 1858, Wayne was a transfer point for several hundred rifles headed for John Brown's hide-out in Maryland.
Population: 803 (1990); 842 (2000); 887 (2007); 911 (2012 projected); Race: 94.1% White, 0.5% Black, 0.0% Asian, 4.3% Hispanic of any race (2007); Density: 2,753.4 persons per square mile (2007); Average household size: 2.58 (2007); Median age: 36.1 (2007); Males per 100 females: 101.1 (2007); Marriage status: 26.5% never married, 59.8% now married, 6.2% widowed, 7.4% divorced (2000); Foreign born: 1.4% (2000); Ancestry (includes multiple ancestries): 35.2% German, 13.4% Other groups, 9.3% English, 8.9% Irish, 7.8% United States or American (2000).
Economy: Single-family building permits issued: 1 (2007); Multi-family building permits issued: 0 (2007); Employment by occupation: 5.9% management, 12.3% professional, 14.6% services, 19.5% sales, 0.0% farming, 13.6% construction, 34.0% production (2000).
Income: Per capita income: $22,024 (2007); Median household income: $52,500 (2007); Average household income: $56,788 (2007); Percent of households with income of $100,000 or more: 10.5% (2007); Poverty rate: 7.6% (2000).
Education: Percent of population age 25 and over with: High school diploma (including GED) or higher: 85.0% (2007); Bachelor's degree or higher: 11.1% (2007); Master's degree or higher: 2.6% (2007).

School District(s)

Elmwood Local (PK-12)
2005-06 Enrollment: 1,312 . . . . (419) 655-2583

Housing: Homeownership rate: 79.1% (2007); Median home value: $94,839 (2007); Median rent: $410 per month (2000); Median age of housing: 60+ years (2000).
Transportation: Commute to work: 96.8% car, 0.0% public transportation, 1.3% walk, 1.9% work from home (2000); Travel time to work: 17.6% less than 15 minutes, 53.0% 15 to 30 minutes, 20.0% 30 to 45 minutes, 5.7% 45 to 60 minutes, 3.7% 60 minutes or more (2000)

WEST MILLGROVE (village). Covers a land area of 0.260 square miles and a water area of 0 square miles. Located at 41.24° N. Lat.; 83.49° W. Long. Elevation is 712 feet.
Population: 171 (1990); 78 (2000); 75 (2007); 75 (2012 projected); Race: 100.0% White, 0.0% Black, 0.0% Asian, 0.0% Hispanic of any race (2007); Density: 288.9 persons per square mile (2007); Average household size: 3.00 (2007); Median age: 32.1 (2007); Males per 100 females: 102.7 (2007); Marriage status: 31.1% never married, 55.4% now married, 5.4% widowed, 8.1% divorced (2000); Foreign born: 0.0% (2000); Ancestry (includes multiple ancestries): 38.8% Irish, 28.2% German, 21.4% English, 17.5% United States or American, 6.8% Other groups (2000).
Economy: Employment by occupation: 0.0% management, 8.6% professional, 2.9% services, 25.7% sales, 0.0% farming, 37.1% construction, 25.7% production (2000).
Income: Per capita income: $16,400 (2007); Median household income: $58,333 (2007); Average household income: $49,200 (2007); Percent of households with income of $100,000 or more: 0.0% (2007); Poverty rate: 10.1% (2000).
Education: Percent of population age 25 and over with: High school diploma (including GED) or higher: 87.0% (2007); Bachelor's degree or higher: 6.5% (2007); Master's degree or higher: 6.5% (2007).
Housing: Homeownership rate: 76.0% (2007); Median home value: $61,667 (2007); Median rent: $367 per month (2000); Median age of housing: 60+ years (2000).
Transportation: Commute to work: 100.0% car, 0.0% public transportation, 0.0% walk, 0.0% work from home (2000); Travel time to work: 11.4% less than 15 minutes, 34.3% 15 to 30 minutes, 22.9% 30 to 45 minutes, 31.4% 45 to 60 minutes, 0.0% 60 minutes or more (2000)

WESTON (village). Covers a land area of 1.124 square miles and a water area of 0.003 square miles. Located at 41.34° N. Lat.; 83.79° W. Long. Elevation is 679 feet.
Population: 1,754 (1990); 1,659 (2000); 1,776 (2007); 1,878 (2012 projected); Race: 93.4% White, 0.2% Black, 0.1% Asian, 9.5% Hispanic of any race (2007); Density: 1,580.3 persons per square mile (2007); Average household size: 2.50 (2007); Median age: 32.9 (2007); Males per 100 females: 95.2 (2007); Marriage status: 26.5% never married, 55.9% now married, 4.8% widowed, 12.8% divorced (2000); Foreign born: 0.6% (2000); Ancestry (includes multiple ancestries): 30.1% German, 18.1% Other groups, 17.9% United States or American, 6.8% English, 6.7% Irish (2000).
Economy: Employment by occupation: 7.3% management, 11.5% professional, 15.7% services, 16.9% sales, 0.0% farming, 11.5% construction, 37.2% production (2000).
Income: Per capita income: $20,410 (2007); Median household income: $42,606 (2007); Average household income: $50,981 (2007); Percent of households with income of $100,000 or more: 8.6% (2007); Poverty rate: 9.9% (2000).
Education: Percent of population age 25 and over with: High school diploma (including GED) or higher: 82.4% (2007); Bachelor's degree or higher: 6.7% (2007); Master's degree or higher: 2.2% (2007).

School District(s)

Otsego Local (PK-12)
2005-06 Enrollment: 1,783 . . . . (419) 823-4381

Housing: Homeownership rate: 75.8% (2007); Median home value: $78,676 (2007); Median rent: $337 per month (2000); Median age of housing: 39 years (2000).
Transportation: Commute to work: 96.6% car, 0.0% public transportation, 1.4% walk, 1.3% work from home (2000); Travel time to work: 16.1% less than 15 minutes, 52.2% 15 to 30 minutes, 17.4% 30 to 45 minutes, 9.8% 45 to 60 minutes, 4.4% 60 minutes or more (2000)

Wyandot County

Located in north central Ohio; drained by the Sandusky River. Covers a land area of 405.61 square miles, a water area of 2.01 square miles, and is located in the Eastern Time Zone. The county was founded in 1845. County seat is Upper Sandusky.

Weather Station: Upper Sandusky Elevation: 853 feet

	Jan	Feb	Mar	Apr	May	Jun	Jul	Aug	Sep	Oct	Nov	Dec
High	32	37	48	60	72	81	84	83	76	64	50	38
Low	17	20	29	38	49	58	62	60	53	42	33	24
Precip	2.1	1.8	2.6	3.5	4.0	3.7	4.2	3.2	3.0	2.2	3.1	2.6
Snow	8.3	5.8	3.6	1.2	tr	0.0	0.0	0.0	0.0	tr	1.4	6.3

High and Low temperatures in degrees Fahrenheit; Precipitation and Snow in inches

Population: 22,254 (1990); 22,908 (2000); 22,823 (2007); 22,714 (2012 projected); Race: 97.7% White, 0.3% Black, 0.4% Asian, 1.9% Hispanic of any race (2007); Density: 56.3 persons per square mile (2007); Average household size: 2.52 (2007); Median age: 39.6 (2007); Males per 100 females: 96.6 (2007).
Religion: Five largest groups: 20.5% Catholic Church, 12.5% The United Methodist Church, 11.5% Evangelical Lutheran Church in America, 4.8% United Church of Christ, 1.6% Church of the Nazarene (2000).

Economy: Unemployment rate: 6.8% (6/2008); Total civilian labor force: 12,174 (6/2008); Leading industries: 37.4% manufacturing; 11.8% accommodation & food services; 9.5% health care and social assistance (2005); Farms: 607 totaling 201,146 acres (2002); Companies that employ 500 or more persons: 1 (2006); Companies that employ 100 to 499 persons: 14 (2006); Companies that employ less than 100 persons: 535 (2006); Black-owned businesses: n/a (2002); Hispanic-owned businesses: n/a (2002); Asian-owned businesses: n/a (2002); Women-owned businesses: 565 (2002); Retail sales per capita: $6,839 (2008). Single-family building permits issued: 27 (2007); Multi-family building permits issued: 0 (2007).
Income: Per capita income: $21,375 (2007); Median household income: $46,021 (2007); Average household income: $53,408 (2007); Percent of households with income of $100,000 or more: 8.3% (2007); Poverty rate: 6.8% (2005); Bankruptcy rate: 3.92% (2007).
Education: Percent of population age 25 and over with: High school diploma (including GED) or higher: 82.3% (2007); Bachelor's degree or higher: 9.7% (2007); Master's degree or higher: 2.8% (2007).
Housing: Homeownership rate: 75.0% (2007); Median home value: $108,342 (2007); Median rent: $313 per month (2000); Median age of housing: 48 years (2000).
Health: Birth rate: 135.3 per 10,000 population (2007); Death rate: 103.2 per 10,000 population (2007); Age-adjusted cancer mortality rate: 199.9 deaths per 100,000 population (2005); Number of physicians: 7.1 per 10,000 population (2005); Hospital beds: 13.6 per 10,000 population (2004); Hospital admissions: 471.6 per 10,000 population (2004).
Elections: 2004 Presidential election results: 65.7% Bush, 33.6% Kerry, 0.0% Nader, 0.5% Badnarik

Additional Information Contacts

Wyandot County Government . . . . (419) 294-3836
http://www.co.wyandot.oh.us
Carey Area Chamber of Commerce . . . . (419) 396-7856
http://www.careychamber.com
Upper Sandusky Area Chamber of Commerce . . . . (419) 294-3349
http://www.uppersanduskychamber.com

Wyandot County Communities

CAREY (village). Covers a land area of 1.973 square miles and a water area of 0.007 square miles. Located at 40.95° N. Lat.; 83.38° W. Long. Elevation is 820 feet.
History: Carey was platted in 1843, and grew as a trading and shipping center for onions and celery. The Shrine of Our Lady of Consolation was established here in 1875 by Father Joseph P. Gloden.
Population: 3,756 (1990); 3,901 (2000); 3,868 (2007); 3,829 (2012 projected); Race: 96.6% White, 0.2% Black, 1.6% Asian, 1.5% Hispanic of any race (2007); Density: 1,960.8 persons per square mile (2007); Average household size: 2.46 (2007); Median age: 36.0 (2007); Males per 100 females: 95.4 (2007); Marriage status: 27.6% never married, 53.4% now married, 9.2% widowed, 9.9% divorced (2000); Foreign born: 1.4% (2000); Ancestry (includes multiple ancestries): 32.3% German, 10.7% United States or American, 10.6% Other groups, 10.0% Irish, 4.6% Italian (2000).
Economy: Single-family building permits issued: 2 (2007); Multi-family building permits issued: 0 (2007); Employment by occupation: 6.1% management, 12.1% professional, 14.0% services, 18.1% sales, 0.8% farming, 14.2% construction, 34.8% production (2000).
Income: Per capita income: $18,557 (2007); Median household income: $38,008 (2007); Average household income: $45,407 (2007); Percent of households with income of $100,000 or more: 5.3% (2007); Poverty rate: 8.6% (2000).
Education: Percent of population age 25 and over with: High school diploma (including GED) or higher: 75.4% (2007); Bachelor's degree or higher: 9.2% (2007); Master's degree or higher: 1.6% (2007).

School District(s)

Carey Exempted Village (PK-12)
2005-06 Enrollment: 889 . . . . (419) 396-7922

Housing: Homeownership rate: 69.8% (2007); Median home value: $100,039 (2007); Median rent: $297 per month (2000); Median age of housing: 49 years (2000).
Newspapers: Carey Progressor Times (Community news; Circulation 4,000); Mohawk Leader (Local news; Circulation 800)
Transportation: Commute to work: 93.3% car, 0.6% public transportation, 2.1% walk, 1.6% work from home (2000); Travel time to work: 40.3% less than 15 minutes, 43.3% 15 to 30 minutes, 7.6% 30 to 45 minutes, 2.8% 45 to 60 minutes, 6.0% 60 minutes or more (2000)

Additional Information Contacts

Carey Area Chamber of Commerce . . . . (419) 396-7856
http://www.careychamber.com

HARPSTER (village). Covers a land area of 1.947 square miles and a water area of 0 square miles. Located at 40.73° N. Lat.; 83.25° W. Long. Elevation is 906 feet.
Population: 233 (1990); 203 (2000); 203 (2007); 200 (2012 projected); Race: 97.0% White, 3.0% Black, 0.0% Asian, 0.0% Hispanic of any race (2007); Density: 104.3 persons per square mile (2007); Average household size: 2.31 (2007); Median age: 47.0 (2007); Males per 100 females: 97.1 (2007); Marriage status: 14.1% never married, 64.7% now married, 7.1% widowed, 14.1% divorced (2000); Foreign born: 0.0% (2000); Ancestry (includes multiple ancestries): 24.6% German, 18.8% United States or American, 12.9% English, 6.3% Other groups, 4.9% Irish (2000).
Economy: Employment by occupation: 15.6% management, 4.6% professional, 14.7% services, 28.4% sales, 0.0% farming, 9.2% construction, 27.5% production (2000).
Income: Per capita income: $22,057 (2007); Median household income: $43,571 (2007); Average household income: $50,881 (2007); Percent of households with income of $100,000 or more: 8.0% (2007); Poverty rate: 2.2% (2000).
Education: Percent of population age 25 and over with: High school diploma (including GED) or higher: 79.5% (2007); Bachelor's degree or higher: 2.7% (2007); Master's degree or higher: 0.0% (2007).
Housing: Homeownership rate: 87.5% (2007); Median home value: $68,500 (2007); Median rent: $455 per month (2000); Median age of housing: 60+ years (2000).
Transportation: Commute to work: 93.6% car, 0.0% public transportation, 0.0% walk, 2.8% work from home (2000); Travel time to work: 41.5% less than 15 minutes, 51.9% 15 to 30 minutes, 4.7% 30 to 45 minutes, 1.9% 45 to 60 minutes, 0.0% 60 minutes or more (2000)

KIRBY (village). Covers a land area of 0.107 square miles and a water area of 0 square miles. Located at 40.81° N. Lat.; 83.41° W. Long. Elevation is 876 feet.
Population: 155 (1990); 132 (2000); 141 (2007); 145 (2012 projected); Race: 100.0% White, 0.0% Black, 0.0% Asian, 0.0% Hispanic of any race (2007); Density: 1,316.4 persons per square mile (2007); Average household size: 2.47 (2007); Median age: 36.6 (2007); Males per 100 females: 98.6 (2007); Marriage status: 18.7% never married, 52.7% now married, 8.8% widowed, 19.8% divorced (2000); Foreign born: 0.0% (2000); Ancestry (includes multiple ancestries): 70.3% German, 6.3% United States or American, 3.6% Irish, 2.7% English, 1.8% French (except Basque) (2000).
Economy: Employment by occupation: 3.4% management, 8.6% professional, 6.9% services, 24.1% sales, 0.0% farming, 10.3% construction, 46.6% production (2000).
Income: Per capita income: $24,149 (2007); Median household income: $42,500 (2007); Average household income: $59,737 (2007); Percent of households with income of $100,000 or more: 7.0% (2007); Poverty rate: 9.0% (2000).
Education: Percent of population age 25 and over with: High school diploma (including GED) or higher: 86.5% (2007); Bachelor's degree or higher: 11.5% (2007); Master's degree or higher: 0.0% (2007).
Housing: Homeownership rate: 73.7% (2007); Median home value: $75,000 (2007); Median rent: $363 per month (2000); Median age of housing: 60+ years (2000).
Transportation: Commute to work: 94.0% car, 0.0% public transportation, 6.0% walk, 0.0% work from home (2000); Travel time to work: 18.0% less than 15 minutes, 50.0% 15 to 30 minutes, 32.0% 30 to 45 minutes, 0.0% 45 to 60 minutes, 0.0% 60 minutes or more (2000)

MARSEILLES (village). Covers a land area of 0.096 square miles and a water area of 0 square miles. Located at 40.70° N. Lat.; 83.39° W. Long. Elevation is 876 feet.
Population: 130 (1990); 124 (2000); 132 (2007); 135 (2012 projected); Race: 97.0% White, 3.0% Black, 0.0% Asian, 0.0% Hispanic of any race (2007); Density: 1,378.4 persons per square mile (2007); Average household size: 2.54 (2007); Median age: 39.2 (2007); Males per 100 females: 91.3 (2007); Marriage status: 20.0% never married, 51.4% now married, 7.6% widowed, 21.0% divorced (2000); Foreign born: 0.0% (2000); Ancestry (includes multiple ancestries): 30.9% Other groups, 14.0% United States or American, 14.0% German, 7.4% Pennsylvania German, 6.6% Irish (2000).

Economy: Employment by occupation: 6.0% management, 13.4% professional, 19.4% services, 11.9% sales, 0.0% farming, 6.0% construction, 43.3% production (2000).
Income: Per capita income: $21,420 (2007); Median household income: $54,286 (2007); Average household income: $54,375 (2007); Percent of households with income of $100,000 or more: 5.8% (2007); Poverty rate: 5.9% (2000).
Education: Percent of population age 25 and over with: High school diploma (including GED) or higher: 71.3% (2007); Bachelor's degree or higher: 7.4% (2007); Master's degree or higher: 3.2% (2007).
Housing: Homeownership rate: 82.7% (2007); Median home value: $65,000 (2007); Median rent: $295 per month (2000); Median age of housing: 53 years (2000).
Transportation: Commute to work: 93.8% car, 0.0% public transportation, 6.3% walk, 0.0% work from home (2000); Travel time to work: 20.3% less than 15 minutes, 43.8% 15 to 30 minutes, 28.1% 30 to 45 minutes, 4.7% 45 to 60 minutes, 3.1% 60 minutes or more (2000)

MCCUTCHENVILLE (unincorporated postal area, zip code 44844). Covers a land area of 16.280 square miles and a water area of 0.015 square miles. Located at 40.99° N. Lat.; 83.26° W. Long. Elevation is 794 feet.
Population: 759 (2000); Race: 98.5% White, 0.0% Black, 0.0% Asian, 0.0% Hispanic of any race (2000); Density: 46.6 persons per square mile (2000); Age: 28.7% under 18, 10.5% over 64 (2000); Marriage status: 27.1% never married, 62.2% now married, 5.6% widowed, 5.1% divorced (2000); Foreign born: 0.0% (2000); Ancestry (includes multiple ancestries): 50.2% German, 11.5% English, 8.4% United States or American, 4.3% Irish, 3.2% Other groups (2000).
Economy: Employment by occupation: 7.1% management, 13.1% professional, 17.2% services, 19.5% sales, 0.0% farming, 9.9% construction, 33.1% production (2000).
Income: Per capita income: $15,501 (2000); Median household income: $48,750 (2000); Poverty rate: 6.4% (2000).
Education: Percent of population age 25 and over with: High school diploma (including GED) or higher: 79.4% (2000); Bachelor's degree or higher: 7.2% (2000).

School District(s)

Mohawk Local (PK-12)
2005-06 Enrollment: 1,055 . . . . (419) 927-2414
Housing: Homeownership rate: 89.6% (2000); Median home value: $74,600 (2000); Median rent: $325 per month (2000); Median age of housing: 46 years (2000).
Transportation: Commute to work: 89.3% car, 1.9% public transportation, 1.4% walk, 7.3% work from home (2000); Travel time to work: 22.3% less than 15 minutes, 63.2% 15 to 30 minutes, 9.0% 30 to 45 minutes, 2.3% 45 to 60 minutes, 3.3% 60 minutes or more (2000)

NEVADA (village). Covers a land area of 1.032 square miles and a water area of 0.001 square miles. Located at 40.81° N. Lat.; 83.13° W. Long. Elevation is 928 feet.
Population: 849 (1990); 814 (2000); 784 (2007); 782 (2012 projected); Race: 96.9% White, 1.1% Black, 0.1% Asian, 1.4% Hispanic of any race (2007); Density: 759.7 persons per square mile (2007); Average household size: 2.52 (2007); Median age: 37.8 (2007); Males per 100 females: 102.1 (2007); Marriage status: 22.8% never married, 58.6% now married, 7.8% widowed, 10.8% divorced (2000); Foreign born: 1.5% (2000); Ancestry (includes multiple ancestries): 31.6% German, 17.8% United States or American, 11.2% Irish, 8.3% English, 6.2% Other groups (2000).
Economy: Single-family building permits issued: 1 (2007); Multi-family building permits issued: 0 (2007); Employment by occupation: 5.5% management, 11.8% professional, 11.8% services, 17.3% sales, 0.8% farming, 8.3% construction, 44.6% production (2000).
Income: Per capita income: $18,651 (2007); Median household income: $43,241 (2007); Average household income: $47,018 (2007); Percent of households with income of $100,000 or more: 2.6% (2007); Poverty rate: 4.9% (2000).
Education: Percent of population age 25 and over with: High school diploma (including GED) or higher: 73.1% (2007); Bachelor's degree or higher: 4.0% (2007); Master's degree or higher: 2.3% (2007).
Housing: Homeownership rate: 75.6% (2007); Median home value: $84,167 (2007); Median rent: $345 per month (2000); Median age of housing: 60+ years (2000).
Transportation: Commute to work: 93.6% car, 1.0% public transportation, 2.6% walk, 1.0% work from home (2000); Travel time to work: 23.5% less than 15 minutes, 51.8% 15 to 30 minutes, 11.9% 30 to 45 minutes, 6.4% 45 to 60 minutes, 6.4% 60 minutes or more (2000)

SYCAMORE (village). Covers a land area of 0.588 square miles and a water area of 0 square miles. Located at 40.95° N. Lat.; 83.17° W. Long. Elevation is 850 feet.
Population: 919 (1990); 914 (2000); 810 (2007); 807 (2012 projected); Race: 99.4% White, 0.0% Black, 0.0% Asian, 0.4% Hispanic of any race (2007); Density: 1,377.6 persons per square mile (2007); Average household size: 2.28 (2007); Median age: 39.5 (2007); Males per 100 females: 84.9 (2007); Marriage status: 20.1% never married, 58.1% now married, 12.2% widowed, 9.6% divorced (2000); Foreign born: 0.4% (2000); Ancestry (includes multiple ancestries): 39.9% German, 13.6% Irish, 12.6% Other groups, 12.5% United States or American, 8.4% English (2000).
Economy: Single-family building permits issued: 1 (2007); Multi-family building permits issued: 0 (2007); Employment by occupation: 5.0% management, 9.7% professional, 15.6% services, 22.5% sales, 0.0% farming, 10.4% construction, 36.9% production (2000).
Income: Per capita income: $22,349 (2007); Median household income: $43,804 (2007); Average household income: $50,993 (2007); Percent of households with income of $100,000 or more: 5.9% (2007); Poverty rate: 4.9% (2000).
Education: Percent of population age 25 and over with: High school diploma (including GED) or higher: 82.5% (2007); Bachelor's degree or higher: 9.3% (2007); Master's degree or higher: 4.0% (2007).

School District(s)

Mohawk Local (PK-12)
2005-06 Enrollment: 1,055 . . . . (419) 927-2414
Housing: Homeownership rate: 76.1% (2007); Median home value: $83,548 (2007); Median rent: $329 per month (2000); Median age of housing: 60+ years (2000).
Transportation: Commute to work: 92.1% car, 0.0% public transportation, 7.5% walk, 0.4% work from home (2000); Travel time to work: 29.0% less than 15 minutes, 51.4% 15 to 30 minutes, 10.9% 30 to 45 minutes, 4.2% 45 to 60 minutes, 4.4% 60 minutes or more (2000)

UPPER SANDUSKY (city). County seat. Covers a land area of 5.242 square miles and a water area of 0.053 square miles. Located at 40.83° N. Lat.; 83.27° W. Long. Elevation is 846 feet.
History: Upper Sandusky was laid out in 1843 on land that had belonged to the Wyandot tribe. The town of Upper Sandusky was preceded by Fort Ferree, built during the War of 1812 by General William Henry Harrison.
Population: 6,197 (1990); 6,533 (2000); 6,410 (2007); 6,316 (2012 projected); Race: 96.5% White, 0.5% Black, 0.5% Asian, 3.7% Hispanic of any race (2007); Density: 1,222.8 persons per square mile (2007); Average household size: 2.33 (2007); Median age: 41.0 (2007); Males per 100 females: 88.7 (2007); Marriage status: 20.1% never married, 57.7% now married, 10.9% widowed, 11.2% divorced (2000); Foreign born: 1.0% (2000); Ancestry (includes multiple ancestries): 38.6% German, 14.6% United States or American, 9.0% Other groups, 8.8% English, 7.9% Irish (2000).
Economy: Single-family building permits issued: 6 (2007); Multi-family building permits issued: 0 (2007); Employment by occupation: 9.9% management, 12.7% professional, 17.5% services, 19.9% sales, 0.3% farming, 7.8% construction, 31.9% production (2000).
Income: Per capita income: $21,447 (2007); Median household income: $41,758 (2007); Average household income: $49,372 (2007); Percent of households with income of $100,000 or more: 6.5% (2007); Poverty rate: 4.7% (2000).
Education: Percent of population age 25 and over with: High school diploma (including GED) or higher: 82.5% (2007); Bachelor's degree or higher: 12.5% (2007); Master's degree or higher: 3.8% (2007).

School District(s)

Upper Sandusky Exempted Village (PK-12)
2005-06 Enrollment: 1,792 . . . . (419) 294-2307
Housing: Homeownership rate: 61.2% (2007); Median home value: $106,614 (2007); Median rent: $309 per month (2000); Median age of housing: 42 years (2000).
Hospitals: Wyandot Memorial Hospital (45 beds)
Newspapers: The Daily Chief-Union (Local news; Circulation 5,000)
Transportation: Commute to work: 94.4% car, 0.2% public transportation, 2.5% walk, 2.1% work from home (2000); Travel time to work: 59.9% less than 15 minutes, 21.4% 15 to 30 minutes, 10.0% 30 to 45 minutes, 1.8% 45 to 60 minutes, 7.0% 60 minutes or more (2000)

Additional Information Contacts
Upper Sandusky Area Chamber of Commerce . . . . (419) 294-3349
http://www.uppersanduskychamber.com

WHARTON (village). Covers a land area of 1.257 square miles and a water area of 0 square miles. Located at 40.86° N. Lat.; 83.46° W. Long. Elevation is 883 feet.
Population: 378 (1990); 409 (2000); 388 (2007); 388 (2012 projected); Race: 99.5% White, 0.0% Black, 0.3% Asian, 0.3% Hispanic of any race (2007); Density: 308.6 persons per square mile (2007); Average household size: 2.73 (2007); Median age: 35.2 (2007); Males per 100 females: 101.0 (2007); Marriage status: 19.4% never married, 65.0% now married, 2.5% widowed, 13.1% divorced (2000); Foreign born: 0.3% (2000); Ancestry (includes multiple ancestries): 33.3% German, 12.5% United States or American, 12.0% Other groups, 10.9% English, 6.9% Irish (2000).
Economy: Employment by occupation: 6.0% management, 8.8% professional, 8.2% services, 12.1% sales, 1.1% farming, 14.8% construction, 48.9% production (2000).
Income: Per capita income: $18,840 (2007); Median household income: $45,625 (2007); Average household income: $51,479 (2007); Percent of households with income of $100,000 or more: 8.5% (2007); Poverty rate: 2.6% (2000).
Education: Percent of population age 25 and over with: High school diploma (including GED) or higher: 87.9% (2007); Bachelor's degree or higher: 1.7% (2007); Master's degree or higher: 1.7% (2007).
Housing: Homeownership rate: 78.9% (2007); Median home value: $81,538 (2007); Median rent: $295 per month (2000); Median age of housing: 60+ years (2000).
Transportation: Commute to work: 96.6% car, 0.0% public transportation, 1.1% walk, 0.6% work from home (2000); Travel time to work: 23.3% less than 15 minutes, 55.1% 15 to 30 minutes, 15.3% 30 to 45 minutes, 4.0% 45 to 60 minutes, 2.3% 60 minutes or more (2000);

A

Aberdeen village *Brown County*, 25
Ada village *Hardin County*, 141
Adams County, 1 - 2
Adamsville village *Muskingum County*, 232
Addyston village *Hamilton County*, 121
Adelphi village *Ross County*, 266
Adena village *Jefferson County*, 158
Akron city *Summit County*, 289
Albany village *Athens County*, 14
Alexandria village *Licking County*, 175
Alger village *Hardin County*, 141
Alledonia postal area *Belmont County*, 21
Allen County, 3 - 5
Alliance city *Stark County*, 281
Alvada postal area *Seneca County*, 275
Alvordton village *Williams County*, 330
Amanda village *Fairfield County*, 90
Amberley village *Hamilton County*, 121
Amelia village *Clermont County*, 41
Amesville village *Athens County*, 14
Amherst city *Lorain County*, 184
Amlin postal area *Franklin County*, 96
Amsterdam village *Jefferson County*, 158
Andover village *Ashtabula County*, 10
Anna village *Shelby County*, 278
Ansonia village *Darke County*, 77
Antioch village *Monroe County*, 217
Antwerp village *Paulding County*, 241
Apple Creek village *Wayne County*, 326
Aquilla village *Geauga County*, 111
Arcadia village *Hancock County*, 138
Arcanum village *Darke County*, 77
Archbold village *Fulton County*, 106
Arlington Heights village *Hamilton County*, 122
Arlington village *Hancock County*, 138
Ashland County, 6 - 8
Ashland city *Ashland County*, 7
Ashley village *Delaware County*, 84
Ashtabula County, 9 - 13
Ashtabula city *Ashtabula County*, 10
Ashville village *Pickaway County*, 247
Athalia village *Lawrence County*, 172
Athens County, 14 - 17
Athens city *Athens County*, 15
Attica village *Seneca County*, 276
Atwater postal area *Portage County*, 252
Auglaize County, 18 - 20
Aurora city *Portage County*, 252
Austinburg postal area *Ashtabula County*, 10
Austintown CDP *Mahoning County*, 197
Avon Lake city *Lorain County*, 185
Avon city *Lorain County*, 185

B

Bailey Lakes village *Ashland County*, 7
Bainbridge CDP *Geauga County*, 111
Bainbridge village *Ross County*, 266
Bairdstown village *Wood County*, 333
Ballville CDP *Sandusky County*, 268
Baltic village *Tuscarawas County*, 304
Baltimore village *Fairfield County*, 90
Barberton city *Summit County*, 290
Barnesville village *Belmont County*, 21
Barnhill village *Tuscarawas County*, 305
Batavia village *Clermont County*, 42
Batesville village *Noble County*, 236
Bay View village *Erie County*, 86
Bay Village city *Cuyahoga County*, 59
Beach City village *Stark County*, 282
Beachwood city *Cuyahoga County*, 60
Beallsville village *Monroe County*, 217
Beaver village *Pike County*, 250
Beavercreek city *Greene County*, 114
Beaverdam village *Allen County*, 3
Beckett Ridge CDP *Butler County*, 28
Bedford Heights city *Cuyahoga County*, 60
Bedford city *Cuyahoga County*, 60
Beechwood Trails CDP *Licking County*, 176
Bellaire village *Belmont County*, 22
Bellbrook city *Greene County*, 114
Belle Center village *Logan County*, 180
Belle Valley village *Noble County*, 236
Bellefontaine city *Logan County*, 181
Bellevue city *Sandusky County*, 269
Bellville village *Richland County*, 263
Belmont County, 21 - 24
Belmont village *Belmont County*, 22
Belmore village *Putnam County*, 259
Beloit village *Mahoning County*, 197
Belpre city *Washington County*, 321
Bentleyville village *Cuyahoga County*, 61
Benton Ridge village *Hancock County*, 138
Berea city *Cuyahoga County*, 61
Bergholz village *Jefferson County*, 159
Berkey village *Lucas County*, 190
Berlin Center postal area *Mahoning County*, 197
Berlin Heights village *Erie County*, 87
Bethel village *Clermont County*, 42
Bethesda village *Belmont County*, 22
Bettsville village *Seneca County*, 276
Beverly village *Washington County*, 322
Bexley city *Franklin County*, 96
Bidwell postal area *Gallia County*, 108
Big Prairie postal area *Holmes County*, 152
Blacklick Estates CDP *Franklin County*, 96
Blacklick postal area *Franklin County*, 96
Blakeslee village *Williams County*, 330
Blanchester village *Clinton County*, 46
Bloomdale village *Wood County*, 333
Bloomingburg village *Fayette County*, 94
Bloomingdale village *Jefferson County*, 159
Bloomville village *Seneca County*, 276
Blue Ash city *Hamilton County*, 122
Blue Creek postal area *Adams County*, 1
Blue Rock postal area *Muskingum County*, 232
Bluffton village *Allen County*, 3
Boardman CDP *Mahoning County*, 198
Bolindale CDP *Trumbull County*, 297
Bolivar village *Tuscarawas County*, 305
Boston Heights village *Summit County*, 290
Botkins village *Shelby County*, 279
Bowerston village *Harrison County*, 143
Bowersville village *Greene County*, 115
Bowling Green city *Wood County*, 334
Bradford village *Miami County*, 214
Bradner village *Wood County*, 334
Brady Lake village *Portage County*, 252
Bratenahl village *Cuyahoga County*, 61
Brecksville city *Cuyahoga County*, 61
Bremen village *Fairfield County*, 90
Brewster village *Stark County*, 282
Brice village *Franklin County*, 97
Bridgeport village *Belmont County*, 22
Bridgetown North CDP *Hamilton County*, 122
Brilliant postal area *Jefferson County*, 159
Brimfield CDP *Portage County*, 252
Brinkhaven postal area *Knox County*, 164
Bristolville postal area *Trumbull County*, 297
Broadview Heights city *Cuyahoga County*, 62
Brook Park city *Cuyahoga County*, 62
Brookfield Center CDP *Trumbull County*, 297
Brookfield postal area *Trumbull County*, 297
Brooklyn Heights village *Cuyahoga County*, 63
Brooklyn city *Cuyahoga County*, 62
Brookside village *Belmont County*, 22
Brookville city *Montgomery County*, 220
Broughton village *Paulding County*, 241
Brown County, 25 - 27
Brunswick city *Medina County*, 205
Bryan city *Williams County*, 331
Buchtel village *Athens County*, 15
Buckeye Lake village *Licking County*, 176
Buckland village *Auglaize County*, 18
Bucyrus city *Crawford County*, 56
Burbank village *Wayne County*, 326
Burghill postal area *Trumbull County*, 297
Burgoon village *Sandusky County*, 269
Burkettsville village *Mercer County*, 211
Burlington CDP *Lawrence County*, 172
Burton village *Geauga County*, 111
Butler County, 28 - 32
Butler village *Richland County*, 263
Butlerville village *Warren County*, 316
Byesville village *Guernsey County*, 118

C

Cable postal area *Champaign County*, 35
Cadiz village *Harrison County*, 144
Cairo village *Allen County*, 4
Calcutta CDP *Columbiana County*, 49
Caldwell village *Noble County*, 237
Caledonia village *Marion County*, 202
Cambridge city *Guernsey County*, 118
Camden village *Preble County*, 256
Camp Dennison postal area *Hamilton County*, 122
Campbell city *Mahoning County*, 198
Canal Fulton village *Stark County*, 282
Canal Winchester village *Franklin County*, 97
Canfield city *Mahoning County*, 198
Canton city *Stark County*, 283
Cardington village *Morrow County*, 230
Carey village *Wyandot County*, 340
Carlisle city *Warren County*, 317
Carroll County, 33
Carroll village *Fairfield County*, 90
Carrollton village *Carroll County*, 33
Casstown village *Miami County*, 214
Castalia village *Erie County*, 87
Castine village *Darke County*, 78
Catawba village *Clark County*, 37
Cecil village *Paulding County*, 242
Cedarville village *Greene County*, 115
Celina city *Mercer County*, 211
Centerburg village *Knox County*, 164
Centerville city *Montgomery County*, 221
Centerville village *Gallia County*, 108
Chagrin Falls village *Cuyahoga County*, 63

CDP = Census Designated Place

Champaign County, 34 - 36
Champion Heights CDP *Trumbull County*, 297
Chandlersville postal area *Muskingum County*, 232
Chardon village *Geauga County*, 112
Chatfield village *Crawford County*, 57
Chauncey village *Athens County*, 15
Cherry Fork village *Adams County*, 1
Cherry Grove CDP *Hamilton County*, 123
Chesapeake village *Lawrence County*, 172
Cheshire village *Gallia County*, 109
Chesterhill village *Morgan County*, 229
Chesterland CDP *Geauga County*, 112
Chesterville village *Morrow County*, 230
Cheviot city *Hamilton County*, 123
Chickasaw village *Mercer County*, 211
Chillicothe city *Ross County*, 266
Chilo village *Clermont County*, 42
Chippewa Lake village *Medina County*, 205
Choctaw Lake CDP *Madison County*, 195
Christiansburg village *Champaign County*, 35
Churchill CDP *Trumbull County*, 298
Cincinnati city *Hamilton County*, 123
Circleville city *Pickaway County*, 247
Clarington village *Monroe County*, 218
Clark County, 37 - 40
Clarksburg village *Ross County*, 267
Clarksville village *Clinton County*, 46
Clay Center village *Ottawa County*, 238
Clayton city *Montgomery County*, 221
Clermont County, 41 - 45
Cleveland Heights city *Cuyahoga County*, 65
Cleveland city *Cuyahoga County*, 63
Cleves village *Hamilton County*, 125
Clifton village *Greene County*, 115
Clinton County, 46 - 47
Clinton village *Summit County*, 290
Cloverdale village *Putnam County*, 259
Clyde city *Sandusky County*, 269
Coal Grove village *Lawrence County*, 173
Coalton village *Jackson County*, 157
Coldwater village *Mercer County*, 212
College Corner village *Preble County*, 256
Collins postal area *Huron County*, 154
Columbia Station postal area *Lorain County*, 185
Columbiana County, 48 - 52
Columbiana city *Columbiana County*, 49
Columbus Grove village *Putnam County*, 259
Columbus city *Franklin County*, 97
Commercial Point village *Pickaway County*, 248
Conesville village *Coshocton County*, 54
Congress village *Wayne County*, 326
Conneaut city *Ashtabula County*, 11
Conover postal area *Miami County*, 214
Continental village *Putnam County*, 259
Convoy village *Van Wert County*, 312
Coolville village *Athens County*, 15
Corning village *Perry County*, 244
Cortland city *Trumbull County*, 298
Corwin village *Warren County*, 317
Coshocton County, 53 - 55
Coshocton city *Coshocton County*, 54
Covedale CDP *Hamilton County*, 125
Covington village *Miami County*, 214
Craig Beach village *Mahoning County*, 198
Crawford County, 56 - 57
Creola postal area *Vinton County*, 314
Crestline city *Crawford County*, 57
Creston village *Wayne County*, 327
Cridersville village *Auglaize County*, 18
Crooksville village *Perry County*, 244
Croton postal area *Licking County*, 176
Crown City village *Gallia County*, 109
Crystal Lakes CDP *Clark County*, 37
Cumberland village *Guernsey County*, 118
Curtice postal area *Lucas County*, 190
Custar village *Wood County*, 334
Cutler postal area *Washington County*, 322
Cuyahoga County, 58 - 76
Cuyahoga Falls city *Summit County*, 290
Cuyahoga Heights village *Cuyahoga County*, 65
Cygnet village *Wood County*, 334

D

Dalton village *Wayne County*, 327
Danville village *Knox County*, 164
Darbyville village *Pickaway County*, 248
Darke County, 77 - 80
Day Heights CDP *Clermont County*, 42
Dayton city *Montgomery County*, 221
De Graff village *Logan County*, 181
Deer Park city *Hamilton County*, 125
Deerfield postal area *Portage County*, 252
Deersville village *Harrison County*, 144
Defiance County, 81 - 82
Defiance city *Defiance County*, 82
Delaware County, 83 - 85
Delaware city *Delaware County*, 84
Dellroy village *Carroll County*, 33
Delphos city *Allen County*, 4
Delta village *Fulton County*, 106
Dennison village *Tuscarawas County*, 305
Dent CDP *Hamilton County*, 126
Deshler village *Henry County*, 146
Devola CDP *Washington County*, 322
Dexter City village *Noble County*, 237
Diamond postal area *Portage County*, 253
Dillonvale CDP *Hamilton County*, 126
Dillonvale village *Jefferson County*, 159
Dola postal area *Hardin County*, 141
Donnelsville village *Clark County*, 37
Dorset postal area *Ashtabula County*, 11
Dover city *Tuscarawas County*, 305
Doylestown village *Wayne County*, 327
Dresden village *Muskingum County*, 233
Drexel CDP *Montgomery County*, 223
Dry Run CDP *Hamilton County*, 126
Dublin city *Franklin County*, 99
Duncan Falls postal area *Muskingum County*, 233
Dundee postal area *Tuscarawas County*, 306
Dunkirk village *Hardin County*, 141
Dupont village *Putnam County*, 259

E

East Canton village *Stark County*, 283
East Cleveland city *Cuyahoga County*, 65
East Liberty postal area *Logan County*, 181
East Liverpool city *Columbiana County*, 49
East Palestine city *Columbiana County*, 50
East Rochester postal area *Columbiana County*, 50
East Sparta village *Stark County*, 284
Eastlake city *Lake County*, 166
Eaton Estates CDP *Lorain County*, 185
Eaton city *Preble County*, 256
Edgerton village *Williams County*, 331
Edgewood CDP *Ashtabula County*, 11
Edison village *Morrow County*, 230
Edon village *Williams County*, 331
Eldorado village *Preble County*, 256
Elgin village *Van Wert County*, 312
Elida village *Allen County*, 4
Elmore village *Ottawa County*, 238
Elmwood Place village *Hamilton County*, 126
Elyria city *Lorain County*, 186
Empire village *Jefferson County*, 159
Englewood city *Montgomery County*, 223
Enon village *Clark County*, 38
Erie County, 86 - 88
Euclid city *Cuyahoga County*, 66
Evendale village *Hamilton County*, 126

F

Fairborn city *Greene County*, 115
Fairfax village *Hamilton County*, 127
Fairfield Beach CDP *Fairfield County*, 90
Fairfield County, 89 - 92
Fairfield city *Butler County*, 28
Fairlawn city *Summit County*, 291
Fairport Harbor village *Lake County*, 167
Fairview Lanes CDP *Erie County*, 87
Fairview Park city *Cuyahoga County*, 66
Fairview village *Guernsey County*, 119
Farmdale postal area *Trumbull County*, 298
Farmersville village *Montgomery County*, 223
Fayette County, 93 - 94
Fayette village *Fulton County*, 107
Fayetteville village *Brown County*, 26
Felicity village *Clermont County*, 43
Findlay city *Hancock County*, 138
Finneytown CDP *Hamilton County*, 127
Five Points CDP *Warren County*, 317
Fleming postal area *Washington County*, 322
Fletcher village *Miami County*, 215
Florida village *Henry County*, 146
Flushing village *Belmont County*, 23
Forest Park city *Hamilton County*, 127
Forest village *Hardin County*, 142
Forestville CDP *Hamilton County*, 127
Fort Jennings village *Putnam County*, 260
Fort Loramie village *Shelby County*, 279
Fort McKinley CDP *Montgomery County*, 223
Fort Recovery village *Mercer County*, 212
Fort Shawnee village *Allen County*, 4
Fostoria city *Seneca County*, 276
Fowler postal area *Trumbull County*, 298
Frankfort village *Ross County*, 267
Franklin County, 95 - 104
Franklin Furnace CDP *Scioto County*, 272
Franklin city *Warren County*, 317
Frazeysburg village *Muskingum County*, 233
Fredericksburg village *Wayne County*, 327
Fredericktown village *Knox County*, 164
Freeport village *Harrison County*, 144
Fremont city *Sandusky County*, 270
Fresno postal area *Coshocton County*, 55
Fruit Hill CDP *Hamilton County*, 128
Fulton County, 105 - 107

CDP = Census Designated Place

Fulton village *Morrow County*, 231
Fultonham village *Muskingum County*, 233

G

Gahanna city *Franklin County*, 99
Galena village *Delaware County*, 84
Galion city *Crawford County*, 57
Gallia County, 108 - 109
Gallipolis city *Gallia County*, 109
Galloway postal area *Franklin County*, 100
Gambier village *Knox County*, 164
Gann village *Knox County*, 165
Garfield Heights city *Cuyahoga County*, 66
Garrettsville village *Portage County*, 253
Gates Mills village *Cuyahoga County*, 67
Geauga County, 110 - 112
Geneva city *Ashtabula County*, 11
Geneva-on-the-Lake village *Ashtabula County*, 11
Genoa village *Ottawa County*, 238
Georgetown village *Brown County*, 26
Germantown village *Montgomery County*, 224
Gettysburg village *Darke County*, 78
Gibsonburg village *Sandusky County*, 270
Gilboa village *Putnam County*, 260
Girard city *Trumbull County*, 299
Glandorf village *Putnam County*, 260
Glendale village *Hamilton County*, 128
Glenford village *Perry County*, 244
Glenmont village *Holmes County*, 152
Glenmoor CDP *Columbiana County*, 50
Glenwillow village *Cuyahoga County*, 67
Gloria Glens Park village *Medina County*, 205
Glouster village *Athens County*, 16
Gnadenhutten village *Tuscarawas County*, 306
Golf Manor village *Hamilton County*, 128
Gomer postal area *Allen County*, 5
Gordon village *Darke County*, 78
Goshen postal area *Clermont County*, 43
Grafton village *Lorain County*, 186
Grand Rapids village *Wood County*, 335
Grand River village *Lake County*, 167
Grandview Heights city *Franklin County*, 100
Grandview CDP *Hamilton County*, 128
Granville South CDP *Licking County*, 177
Granville village *Licking County*, 176
Gratiot village *Licking County*, 177
Gratis village *Preble County*, 257
Graysville village *Monroe County*, 218
Graytown postal area *Ottawa County*, 239
Green Camp village *Marion County*, 202
Green Meadows CDP *Clark County*, 38
Green Springs village *Seneca County*, 277
Green city *Summit County*, 291
Greene County, 113 - 116
Greenfield city *Highland County*, 149
Greenhills village *Hamilton County*, 128
Greentown CDP *Stark County*, 284
Greenville city *Darke County*, 78
Greenwich village *Huron County*, 154
Groesbeck CDP *Hamilton County*, 129
Grove City city *Franklin County*, 100
Groveport village *Franklin County*, 100
Grover Hill village *Paulding County*, 242
Guernsey County, 117 - 119
Guysville postal area *Athens County*, 16

H

Hamden village *Vinton County*, 314
Hamersville village *Brown County*, 26
Hamilton County, 120 - 136
Hamilton city *Butler County*, 29
Hamler village *Henry County*, 147
Hammondsville postal area *Jefferson County*, 160
Hancock County, 137 - 139
Hanging Rock village *Lawrence County*, 173
Hanover village *Licking County*, 177
Hanoverton village *Columbiana County*, 50
Harbor Hills CDP *Licking County*, 177
Harbor View village *Lucas County*, 191
Hardin County, 140 - 142
Harpster village *Wyandot County*, 340
Harrisburg village *Franklin County*, 101
Harrison County, 143 - 145
Harrison city *Hamilton County*, 129
Harrisville village *Harrison County*, 144
Harrod village *Allen County*, 5
Hartford village *Licking County*, 177
Hartville village *Stark County*, 284
Harveysburg village *Warren County*, 318
Haskins village *Wood County*, 335
Haviland village *Paulding County*, 242
Hayesville village *Ashland County*, 7
Heath city *Licking County*, 178
Hebron village *Licking County*, 178
Helena village *Sandusky County*, 270
Hemlock village *Perry County*, 245
Henry County, 146 - 147
Hicksville village *Defiance County*, 82
Higginsport village *Brown County*, 26
Highland County, 148 - 149
Highland Heights city *Cuyahoga County*, 67
Highland Hills village *Cuyahoga County*, 67
Highland village *Highland County*, 149
Hilliard city *Franklin County*, 101
Hills and Dales village *Stark County*, 284
Hillsboro city *Highland County*, 149
Hilltop CDP *Trumbull County*, 299
Hinckley postal area *Medina County*, 206
Hiram village *Portage County*, 253
Hocking County, 150 - 151
Holgate village *Henry County*, 147
Holiday City village *Williams County*, 331
Holiday Valley CDP *Clark County*, 38
Holland village *Lucas County*, 191
Hollansburg village *Darke County*, 79
Holloway village *Belmont County*, 23
Holmes County, 152 - 153
Holmesville village *Holmes County*, 153
Homerville postal area *Medina County*, 206
Homeworth postal area *Columbiana County*, 50
Hopedale village *Harrison County*, 144
Hopewell postal area *Muskingum County*, 234
Houston postal area *Shelby County*, 279
Howard postal area *Knox County*, 165
Howland Center CDP *Trumbull County*, 299
Hoytville village *Wood County*, 335
Hubbard city *Trumbull County*, 299
Huber Heights city *Montgomery County*, 224
Huber Ridge CDP *Franklin County*, 101
Hudson city *Summit County*, 291
Hunter CDP *Warren County*, 318
Hunting Valley village *Cuyahoga County*, 68
Huntsburg postal area *Geauga County*, 112
Huntsville village *Logan County*, 181
Huron County, 154 - 155
Huron city *Erie County*, 87

I

Independence city *Cuyahoga County*, 68
Irondale village *Jefferson County*, 160
Ironton city *Lawrence County*, 173
Irwin postal area *Union County*, 310
Ithaca village *Darke County*, 79

J

Jackson Center village *Shelby County*, 279
Jackson County, 156 - 157
Jackson city *Jackson County*, 157
Jacksonburg village *Butler County*, 29
Jacksonville village *Athens County*, 16
Jacobsburg postal area *Belmont County*, 23
Jamestown village *Greene County*, 116
Jefferson County, 158 - 162
Jefferson village *Ashtabula County*, 12
Jeffersonville village *Fayette County*, 94
Jenera village *Hancock County*, 139
Jeromesville village *Ashland County*, 7
Jerry City village *Wood County*, 335
Jerusalem village *Monroe County*, 218
Jewett village *Harrison County*, 145
Johnstown village *Licking County*, 178
Junction City village *Perry County*, 245

K

Kalida village *Putnam County*, 260
Kansas postal area *Seneca County*, 277
Kelleys Island village *Erie County*, 88
Kensington postal area *Columbiana County*, 51
Kent city *Portage County*, 253
Kenton city *Hardin County*, 142
Kenwood CDP *Hamilton County*, 129
Kettering city *Montgomery County*, 224
Kettlersville village *Shelby County*, 279
Killbuck village *Holmes County*, 153
Kimbolton village *Guernsey County*, 119
Kings Mills postal area *Warren County*, 318
Kingston village *Ross County*, 267
Kingsville postal area *Ashtabula County*, 12
Kinsman postal area *Trumbull County*, 300
Kipton village *Lorain County*, 186
Kirby village *Wyandot County*, 340
Kirkersville village *Licking County*, 178
Kirtland Hills village *Lake County*, 167
Kirtland city *Lake County*, 167
Kitts Hill postal area *Lawrence County*, 173
Knox County, 163 - 165

L

La Croft CDP *Columbiana County*, 51
La Rue village *Marion County*, 203
Lacarne postal area *Ottawa County*, 239
Lafayette village *Allen County*, 5
Lagrange village *Lorain County*, 186
Lake County, 166 - 170
Lake Darby CDP *Franklin County*, 101
Lake Milton postal area *Mahoning County*, 199
Lakeline village *Lake County*, 168

CDP = Census Designated Place

Lakemore village *Summit County*, 292
Lakeside Marblehead postal area *Ottawa County*, 239
Lakeview village *Logan County*, 182
Lakeville postal area *Holmes County*, 153
Lakewood city *Cuyahoga County*, 68
Lancaster city *Fairfield County*, 91
Landen CDP *Warren County*, 318
Langsville postal area *Meigs County*, 208
Latham postal area *Pike County*, 250
Latty village *Paulding County*, 242
Laura village *Miami County*, 215
Laurelville village *Hocking County*, 151
Lawrence County, 171 - 174
Lawrenceville village *Clark County*, 38
Leavittsburg CDP *Trumbull County*, 300
Lebanon city *Warren County*, 318
Leesburg village *Highland County*, 149
Leesville village *Carroll County*, 33
Leetonia village *Columbiana County*, 51
Leipsic village *Putnam County*, 261
Lewis Center postal area *Delaware County*, 85
Lewisburg village *Preble County*, 257
Lewistown postal area *Logan County*, 182
Lewisville village *Monroe County*, 218
Lexington village *Richland County*, 263
Liberty Center village *Henry County*, 147
Licking County, 175 - 179
Lima city *Allen County*, 5
Limaville village *Stark County*, 284
Lincoln Heights village *Hamilton County*, 129
Lincoln Village CDP *Franklin County*, 102
Lindsey village *Sandusky County*, 270
Linndale village *Cuyahoga County*, 68
Lisbon village *Columbiana County*, 51
Litchfield postal area *Medina County*, 206
Lithopolis village *Fairfield County*, 91
Little Hocking postal area *Washington County*, 323
Lockbourne village *Franklin County*, 102
Lockington village *Shelby County*, 280
Lockland village *Hamilton County*, 130
Lodi village *Medina County*, 206
Logan County, 180 - 183
Logan Elm Village CDP *Pickaway County*, 248
Logan city *Hocking County*, 151
London city *Madison County*, 195
Londonderry postal area *Ross County*, 267
Long Bottom postal area *Meigs County*, 209
Lorain County, 184 - 188
Lorain city *Lorain County*, 187
Lordstown village *Trumbull County*, 300
Lore City village *Guernsey County*, 119
Loudonville village *Ashland County*, 8
Louisville city *Stark County*, 285
Loveland Park CDP *Warren County*, 319
Loveland city *Hamilton County*, 130
Lowell village *Washington County*, 323
Lowellville village *Mahoning County*, 199
Lower Salem village *Washington County*, 323
Lucas County, 189 - 193
Lucas village *Richland County*, 263
Lucasville CDP *Scioto County*, 272
Luckey village *Wood County*, 336
Ludlow Falls village *Miami County*, 215
Lynchburg village *Highland County*, 150
Lyndhurst city *Cuyahoga County*, 69
Lyons village *Fulton County*, 107

M

Macedonia city *Summit County*, 292
Mack North CDP *Hamilton County*, 130
Mack South CDP *Hamilton County*, 130
Macksburg village *Washington County*, 323
Madeira city *Hamilton County*, 131
Madison County, 194 - 195
Madison village *Lake County*, 168
Magnetic Springs village *Union County*, 310
Magnolia village *Stark County*, 285
Mahoning County, 196 - 201
Maineville village *Warren County*, 319
Malinta village *Henry County*, 147
Malta village *Morgan County*, 229
Malvern village *Carroll County*, 34
Manchester village *Adams County*, 1
Mansfield city *Richland County*, 264
Mantua village *Portage County*, 254
Maple Heights city *Cuyahoga County*, 69
Maple Ridge CDP *Mahoning County*, 199
Maplewood Park CDP *Trumbull County*, 300
Maplewood postal area *Shelby County*, 280
Marble Cliff village *Franklin County*, 102
Marblehead village *Ottawa County*, 239
Marengo village *Morrow County*, 231
Maria Stein postal area *Mercer County*, 212
Mariemont village *Hamilton County*, 131
Marietta city *Washington County*, 323
Marion County, 202 - 203
Marion city *Marion County*, 203
Mark Center postal area *Defiance County*, 82
Marseilles village *Wyandot County*, 340
Marshallville village *Wayne County*, 327
Martin postal area *Ottawa County*, 240
Martins Ferry city *Belmont County*, 23
Martinsburg village *Knox County*, 165
Martinsville village *Clinton County*, 47
Marysville city *Union County*, 310
Mason city *Warren County*, 319
Massillon city *Stark County*, 285
Masury CDP *Trumbull County*, 300
Matamoras village *Washington County*, 324
Maumee city *Lucas County*, 191
Mayfield Heights city *Cuyahoga County*, 70
Mayfield village *Cuyahoga County*, 69
McArthur village *Vinton County*, 315
McClure village *Henry County*, 147
McComb village *Hancock County*, 139
McConnelsville village *Morgan County*, 229
McCutchenville postal area *Wyandot County*, 341
McDermott postal area *Scioto County*, 272
McDonald village *Trumbull County*, 301
McGuffey village *Hardin County*, 142
Mechanicsburg village *Champaign County*, 35
Mechanicstown postal area *Carroll County*, 34
Medina County, 204 - 207
Medina city *Medina County*, 206
Medway postal area *Clark County*, 38
Meigs County, 208 - 209
Melrose village *Paulding County*, 242
Mendon village *Mercer County*, 212
Mentor city *Lake County*, 168
Mentor-on-the-Lake city *Lake County*, 169
Mercer County, 210 - 212
Metamora village *Fulton County*, 107
Meyers Lake village *Stark County*, 286
Miami County, 213 - 216
Miamisburg city *Montgomery County*, 225
Middle Point village *Van Wert County*, 312
Middleburg Heights city *Cuyahoga County*, 70
Middlefield village *Geauga County*, 112
Middleport village *Meigs County*, 209
Middletown city *Butler County*, 29
Midland village *Clinton County*, 47
Midvale village *Tuscarawas County*, 306
Midway village *Madison County*, 195
Mifflin village *Ashland County*, 8
Milan village *Erie County*, 88
Milford Center village *Union County*, 311
Milford city *Clermont County*, 43
Millbury village *Wood County*, 336
Milledgeville village *Fayette County*, 94
Miller City village *Putnam County*, 261
Millersburg village *Holmes County*, 153
Millersport village *Fairfield County*, 91
Millfield postal area *Athens County*, 16
Millville village *Butler County*, 30
Milton Center village *Wood County*, 336
Miltonsburg village *Monroe County*, 218
Mineral City village *Tuscarawas County*, 306
Mineral Ridge CDP *Trumbull County*, 301
Minerva Park village *Franklin County*, 102
Minerva village *Stark County*, 286
Minford postal area *Scioto County*, 272
Mingo Junction village *Jefferson County*, 160
Minster village *Auglaize County*, 19
Mogadore village *Summit County*, 292
Monclova postal area *Lucas County*, 191
Monfort Heights East CDP *Hamilton County*, 131
Monfort Heights South CDP *Hamilton County*, 131
Monroe County, 217 - 219
Monroe city *Butler County*, 30
Monroeville village *Huron County*, 155
Montezuma village *Mercer County*, 213
Montgomery County, 220 - 227
Montgomery city *Hamilton County*, 131
Montpelier village *Williams County*, 332
Montrose-Ghent CDP *Summit County*, 292
Montville postal area *Geauga County*, 113
Moraine city *Montgomery County*, 225
Moreland Hills village *Cuyahoga County*, 70
Morgan County, 228
Morral village *Marion County*, 204
Morristown village *Belmont County*, 24
Morrow County, 229 - 231
Morrow village *Warren County*, 319
Moscow village *Clermont County*, 43
Mount Blanchard village *Hancock County*, 139
Mount Carmel CDP *Clermont County*, 44
Mount Cory village *Hancock County*, 139
Mount Eaton village *Wayne County*, 328
Mount Gilead village *Morrow County*, 231
Mount Healthy Heights CDP *Hamilton County*, 132
Mount Healthy city *Hamilton County*, 132
Mount Orab village *Brown County*, 26

CDP = Census Designated Place

Mount Perry postal area *Perry County*, 245
Mount Pleasant village *Jefferson County*, 160
Mount Repose CDP *Clermont County*, 44
Mount Sterling village *Madison County*, 195
Mount Vernon city *Knox County*, 165
Mount Victory village *Hardin County*, 142
Mowrystown village *Highland County*, 150
Mulberry CDP *Clermont County*, 44
Munroe Falls city *Summit County*, 293
Murray City village *Hocking County*, 151
Muskingum County, 232 - 235
Mutual village *Champaign County*, 35

N

Napoleon city *Henry County*, 148
Nashport postal area *Muskingum County*, 234
Nashville village *Holmes County*, 154
Navarre village *Stark County*, 286
Neffs CDP *Belmont County*, 24
Negley postal area *Columbiana County*, 52
Nellie village *Coshocton County*, 55
Nelsonville city *Athens County*, 16
Nevada village *Wyandot County*, 341
Neville village *Clermont County*, 44
New Albany village *Franklin County*, 102
New Alexandria village *Jefferson County*, 161
New Athens village *Harrison County*, 145
New Bavaria village *Henry County*, 148
New Bloomington village *Marion County*, 204
New Boston village *Scioto County*, 273
New Bremen village *Auglaize County*, 19
New Carlisle city *Clark County*, 39
New Concord village *Muskingum County*, 234
New Franklin city *Summit County*, 293
New Holland village *Pickaway County*, 248
New Knoxville village *Auglaize County*, 19
New Lebanon village *Montgomery County*, 225
New Lexington city *Perry County*, 245
New London village *Huron County*, 155
New Madison village *Darke County*, 79
New Marshfield postal area *Athens County*, 17
New Matamoras postal area *Washington County*, 324
New Miami village *Butler County*, 30
New Middletown village *Mahoning County*, 199
New Paris village *Preble County*, 257
New Philadelphia city *Tuscarawas County*, 307
New Plymouth postal area *Vinton County*, 315
New Richmond village *Clermont County*, 44
New Riegel village *Seneca County*, 277
New Rome village *Franklin County*, 103
New Springfield postal area *Mahoning County*, 199
New Straitsville village *Perry County*, 245
New Vienna village *Clinton County*, 47
New Washington village *Crawford County*, 57
New Waterford village *Columbiana County*, 52
New Weston village *Darke County*, 79
Newark city *Licking County*, 179
Newburgh Heights village *Cuyahoga County*, 70
Newbury postal area *Geauga County*, 113
Newcomerstown village *Tuscarawas County*, 307
Newport postal area *Washington County*, 324
Newton Falls village *Trumbull County*, 301
Newtonsville village *Clermont County*, 45
Newtown village *Hamilton County*, 132
Ney village *Defiance County*, 83
Niles city *Trumbull County*, 301
Noble County, 236
North Baltimore village *Wood County*, 336
North Bend village *Hamilton County*, 132
North Benton postal area *Mahoning County*, 200
North Bloomfield postal area *Trumbull County*, 302
North Canton city *Stark County*, 286
North College Hill city *Hamilton County*, 133
North Fairfield village *Huron County*, 155
North Fork Village CDP *Ross County*, 267
North Hampton village *Clark County*, 39
North Jackson postal area *Mahoning County*, 200
North Kingsville village *Ashtabula County*, 12
North Lawrence postal area *Stark County*, 287
North Lewisburg village *Champaign County*, 36
North Lima postal area *Mahoning County*, 200
North Madison CDP *Lake County*, 169
North Olmsted city *Cuyahoga County*, 71
North Perry village *Lake County*, 169
North Randall village *Cuyahoga County*, 71
North Ridgeville city *Lorain County*, 187
North Robinson village *Crawford County*, 58
North Royalton city *Cuyahoga County*, 71
North Star village *Darke County*, 79
North Zanesville CDP *Muskingum County*, 234
Northbrook CDP *Hamilton County*, 133
Northfield village *Summit County*, 293
Northgate CDP *Hamilton County*, 133
Northridge CDP *Clark County*, 39
Northridge CDP *Montgomery County*, 225
Northwood city *Wood County*, 336
Norton city *Summit County*, 293
Norwalk city *Huron County*, 155
Norwich village *Muskingum County*, 234
Norwood city *Hamilton County*, 133
Nova postal area *Ashland County*, 8

O

Oak Harbor village *Ottawa County*, 240
Oak Hill village *Jackson County*, 157
Oakwood city *Montgomery County*, 226
Oakwood village *Cuyahoga County*, 71
Oakwood village *Paulding County*, 243
Oberlin city *Lorain County*, 187
Obetz village *Franklin County*, 103
Octa village *Fayette County*, 94
Ohio City village *Van Wert County*, 313
Okeana postal area *Butler County*, 31
Old Washington village *Guernsey County*, 119
Olde West Chester CDP *Butler County*, 31
Olmsted Falls city *Cuyahoga County*, 72
Ontario city *Richland County*, 264
Orange village *Cuyahoga County*, 72
Orangeville village *Trumbull County*, 302
Oregon city *Lucas County*, 192
Oregonia postal area *Warren County*, 320
Orient village *Pickaway County*, 249
Orrville city *Wayne County*, 328
Orwell village *Ashtabula County*, 12
Osgood village *Darke County*, 80
Ostrander village *Delaware County*, 85
Ottawa County, 237 - 240
Ottawa Hills village *Lucas County*, 192
Ottawa village *Putnam County*, 261
Ottoville village *Putnam County*, 261
Otway village *Scioto County*, 273
Owensville village *Clermont County*, 45
Oxford city *Butler County*, 31

P

Painesville city *Lake County*, 169
Palestine village *Darke County*, 80
Pandora village *Putnam County*, 262
Paris postal area *Stark County*, 287
Park Layne CDP *Clark County*, 39
Parma Heights city *Cuyahoga County*, 73
Parma city *Cuyahoga County*, 72
Parral village *Tuscarawas County*, 307
Pataskala city *Licking County*, 179
Patriot postal area *Gallia County*, 109
Patterson village *Hardin County*, 143
Paulding County, 241 - 242
Paulding village *Paulding County*, 243
Payne village *Paulding County*, 243
Pedro postal area *Lawrence County*, 174
Peebles village *Adams County*, 2
Pemberville village *Wood County*, 337
Peninsula village *Summit County*, 294
Pepper Pike city *Cuyahoga County*, 73
Perry County, 243 - 246
Perry Heights CDP *Stark County*, 287
Perry village *Lake County*, 170
Perrysburg city *Wood County*, 337
Perrysville village *Ashland County*, 8
Petersburg postal area *Mahoning County*, 200
Phillipsburg village *Montgomery County*, 226
Philo village *Muskingum County*, 235
Pickaway County, 247 - 248
Pickerington city *Fairfield County*, 92
Piedmont postal area *Harrison County*, 145
Pierpont postal area *Ashtabula County*, 13
Pigeon Creek CDP *Summit County*, 294
Pike County, 249 - 250
Piketon village *Pike County*, 250
Pioneer village *Williams County*, 332
Piqua city *Miami County*, 215
Pitsburg village *Darke County*, 80
Plain City village *Madison County*, 196
Plainfield village *Coshocton County*, 55
Pleasant City village *Guernsey County*, 119
Pleasant Grove CDP *Muskingum County*, 235
Pleasant Hill village *Miami County*, 216
Pleasant Plain village *Warren County*, 320
Pleasant Run Farm CDP *Hamilton County*, 134
Pleasant Run CDP *Hamilton County*, 134
Pleasantville village *Fairfield County*, 92
Plymouth village *Richland County*, 264
Poland village *Mahoning County*, 200
Polk village *Ashland County*, 9

Pomeroy village *Meigs County*, 209
Port Clinton city *Ottawa County*, 240
Port Jefferson village *Shelby County*, 280
Port Washington village *Tuscarawas County*, 307
Port William village *Clinton County*, 47
Portage County, 251 - 254
Portage Lakes CDP *Summit County*, 294
Portage village *Wood County*, 337
Portland postal area *Meigs County*, 209
Portsmouth city *Scioto County*, 273
Potsdam village *Miami County*, 216
Powell city *Delaware County*, 85
Powhatan Point village *Belmont County*, 24
Preble County, 255 - 257
Proctorville village *Lawrence County*, 174
Prospect village *Marion County*, 204
Put-in-Bay village *Ottawa County*, 240
Putnam County, 258 - 261

Q

Quaker City village *Guernsey County*, 120
Quincy village *Logan County*, 182

R

Racine village *Meigs County*, 210
Radnor postal area *Delaware County*, 85
Rarden village *Scioto County*, 273
Ravenna city *Portage County*, 254
Rawson village *Hancock County*, 140
Ray postal area *Vinton County*, 315
Rayland village *Jefferson County*, 161
Raymond postal area *Union County*, 311
Reading city *Hamilton County*, 134
Reedsville postal area *Meigs County*, 210
Reminderville village *Summit County*, 294
Rendville village *Perry County*, 246
Reno postal area *Washington County*, 324
Republic village *Seneca County*, 277
Reynoldsburg city *Franklin County*, 103
Richfield village *Summit County*, 294
Richland County, 262 - 264
Richmond Dale postal area *Ross County*, 268
Richmond Heights city *Cuyahoga County*, 73
Richmond village *Jefferson County*, 161
Richwood village *Union County*, 311
Ridgeway village *Hardin County*, 143
Rio Grande village *Gallia County*, 110
Ripley village *Brown County*, 27
Risingsun village *Wood County*, 338
Rittman city *Wayne County*, 328
Riverlea village *Franklin County*, 103
Riverside city *Montgomery County*, 226
Roaming Shores village *Ashtabula County*, 13
Rochester village *Lorain County*, 188
Rock Creek village *Ashtabula County*, 13
Rockbridge postal area *Hocking County*, 151
Rockford village *Mercer County*, 213
Rocky Ridge village *Ottawa County*, 241
Rocky River city *Cuyahoga County*, 73
Rogers village *Columbiana County*, 52
Rome postal area *Ashtabula County*, 13
Rome village *Adams County*, 2
Rootstown postal area *Portage County*, 254
Rosemount CDP *Scioto County*, 274
Roseville village *Perry County*, 246
Ross County, 265 - 267
Ross CDP *Butler County*, 31
Rossburg village *Darke County*, 80
Rossford city *Wood County*, 338
Roswell village *Tuscarawas County*, 308
Rudolph postal area *Wood County*, 338
Rushsylvania village *Logan County*, 182
Rushville village *Fairfield County*, 92
Russells Point village *Logan County*, 182
Russellville village *Brown County*, 27
Russia village *Shelby County*, 280
Rutland village *Meigs County*, 210

S

Sabina village *Clinton County*, 48
Saint Bernard city *Hamilton County*, 134
Saint Clairsville city *Belmont County*, 24
Saint Henry village *Mercer County*, 213
Saint Louisville village *Licking County*, 179
Saint Martin village *Brown County*, 27
Saint Marys city *Auglaize County*, 20
Saint Paris village *Champaign County*, 36
Salem city *Columbiana County*, 52
Salesville village *Guernsey County*, 120
Salineville village *Columbiana County*, 53
Sandusky County, 268 - 270
Sandusky South CDP *Erie County*, 89
Sandusky city *Erie County*, 88
Sarahsville village *Noble County*, 237
Sardinia village *Brown County*, 27
Sardis postal area *Monroe County*, 219
Savannah village *Ashland County*, 9
Scio village *Harrison County*, 145
Scioto County, 271 - 274
Sciotodale CDP *Scioto County*, 274
Scott village *Van Wert County*, 313
Scottown postal area *Lawrence County*, 174
Seaman village *Adams County*, 2
Sebring village *Mahoning County*, 201
Seneca County, 275 - 277
Senecaville village *Guernsey County*, 120
Seven Hills city *Cuyahoga County*, 74
Seven Mile village *Butler County*, 32
Seville village *Medina County*, 207
Shade postal area *Athens County*, 17
Shadyside village *Belmont County*, 25
Shaker Heights city *Cuyahoga County*, 74
Sharonville city *Hamilton County*, 134
Shawnee Hills CDP *Greene County*, 116
Shawnee Hills village *Delaware County*, 86
Shawnee village *Perry County*, 246
Sheffield Lake city *Lorain County*, 188
Sheffield village *Lorain County*, 188
Shelby County, 278 - 280
Shelby city *Richland County*, 265
Sherrodsville village *Carroll County*, 34
Sherwood CDP *Hamilton County*, 135
Sherwood village *Defiance County*, 83
Shiloh CDP *Montgomery County*, 226
Shiloh village *Richland County*, 265
Shreve village *Wayne County*, 328
Sidney city *Shelby County*, 280
Silver Lake village *Summit County*, 295
Silverton city *Hamilton County*, 135
Sinking Spring village *Highland County*, 150
Smithfield village *Jefferson County*, 161
Smithville village *Wayne County*, 329
Solon city *Cuyahoga County*, 74
Somerset village *Perry County*, 246
Somerville village *Butler County*, 32
South Amherst village *Lorain County*, 189
South Bloomfield village *Pickaway County*, 249
South Bloomingville postal area *Hocking County*, 152
South Canal CDP *Trumbull County*, 302
South Charleston village *Clark County*, 39
South Euclid city *Cuyahoga County*, 74
South Lebanon village *Warren County*, 320
South Middletown CDP *Butler County*, 32
South Point village *Lawrence County*, 174
South Russell village *Geauga County*, 113
South Salem village *Ross County*, 268
South Solon village *Madison County*, 196
South Vienna village *Clark County*, 40
South Webster village *Scioto County*, 274
South Zanesville village *Muskingum County*, 235
Southington postal area *Trumbull County*, 302
Sparta village *Morrow County*, 231
Spencer village *Medina County*, 207
Spencerville village *Allen County*, 6
Spring Valley village *Greene County*, 116
Springboro city *Warren County*, 320
Springdale city *Hamilton County*, 135
Springfield city *Clark County*, 40
Stafford village *Monroe County*, 219
Stark County, 281 - 287
Sterling postal area *Wayne County*, 329
Steubenville city *Jefferson County*, 161
Stewart postal area *Athens County*, 17
Stockport village *Morgan County*, 229
Stone Creek village *Tuscarawas County*, 308
Stony Prairie CDP *Sandusky County*, 271
Stout postal area *Scioto County*, 274
Stoutsville village *Fairfield County*, 92
Stow city *Summit County*, 295
Strasburg village *Tuscarawas County*, 308
Stratton village *Jefferson County*, 162
Streetsboro city *Portage County*, 255
Strongsville city *Cuyahoga County*, 75
Struthers city *Mahoning County*, 201
Stryker village *Williams County*, 332
Sugar Bush Knolls village *Portage County*, 255
Sugar Grove village *Fairfield County*, 93
Sugarcreek village *Tuscarawas County*, 308
Sullivan postal area *Ashland County*, 9
Summerfield village *Noble County*, 237
Summerside CDP *Clermont County*, 45
Summit County, 288 - 295
Summitville village *Columbiana County*, 53
Sunbury village *Delaware County*, 86
Swanton village *Fulton County*, 107
Sycamore village *Wyandot County*, 341
Sylvania city *Lucas County*, 192
Syracuse village *Meigs County*, 210

T

Tallmadge city *Summit County*, 295
Tarlton village *Pickaway County*, 249
Terrace Park village *Hamilton County*, 135
The Plains CDP *Athens County*, 17
The Village of Indian Hill city *Hamilton County*, 136

CDP = Census Designated Place

Thompson postal area *Geauga County*, 113
Thornville village *Perry County*, 247
Thurman postal area *Gallia County*, 110
Thurston village *Fairfield County*, 93
Tiffin city *Seneca County*, 278
Tiltonsville village *Jefferson County*, 162
Timberlake village *Lake County*, 170
Tipp City city *Miami County*, 216
Tippecanoe postal area *Harrison County*, 146
Tiro village *Crawford County*, 58
Toledo city *Lucas County*, 192
Tontogany village *Wood County*, 338
Toronto city *Jefferson County*, 162
Tremont City village *Clark County*, 41
Trenton city *Butler County*, 32
Trimble village *Athens County*, 18
Trotwood city *Montgomery County*, 227
Troy city *Miami County*, 216
Trumbull County, 296 - 303
Turpin Hills CDP *Hamilton County*, 136
Tuscarawas County, 304 - 308
Tuscarawas village *Tuscarawas County*, 309
Twinsburg city *Summit County*, 296

U

Uhrichsville city *Tuscarawas County*, 309
Union City village *Darke County*, 80
Union County, 309 - 310
Union city *Montgomery County*, 227
Uniontown CDP *Stark County*, 287
Unionville Center village *Union County*, 311
Uniopolis village *Auglaize County*, 20
University Heights city *Cuyahoga County*, 75
Upper Arlington city *Franklin County*, 104
Upper Sandusky city *Wyandot County*, 341
Urbana city *Champaign County*, 36
Urbancrest village *Franklin County*, 104
Utica village *Licking County*, 180

V

Valley City postal area *Medina County*, 207
Valley Hi village *Logan County*, 183
Valley View village *Cuyahoga County*, 75
Valleyview village *Franklin County*, 104
Van Buren village *Hancock County*, 140
Van Wert County, 311 - 313
Van Wert city *Van Wert County*, 313
Vandalia city *Montgomery County*, 227
Vanlue village *Hancock County*, 140
Venedocia village *Van Wert County*, 313
Vermilion city *Lorain County*, 189
Verona village *Preble County*, 257
Versailles village *Darke County*, 81
Vickery postal area *Sandusky County*, 271
Vienna Center CDP *Trumbull County*, 303
Vienna postal area *Trumbull County*, 302
Vincent postal area *Washington County*, 325
Vinton County, 314 - 315
Vinton village *Gallia County*, 110

W

Wadsworth city *Medina County*, 208
Waite Hill village *Lake County*, 170
Wakeman village *Huron County*, 156
Walbridge village *Wood County*, 338
Waldo village *Marion County*, 204
Walhonding postal area *Coshocton County*, 55
Walton Hills village *Cuyahoga County*, 76
Wapakoneta city *Auglaize County*, 20
Warren County, 316 - 320
Warren city *Trumbull County*, 303
Warrensville Heights city *Cuyahoga County*, 76
Warsaw village *Coshocton County*, 55
Washington County, 321 - 324
Washington Court House city *Fayette County*, 94
Washingtonville village *Columbiana County*, 53
Waterford postal area *Washington County*, 325
Waterloo postal area *Lawrence County*, 174
Waterville village *Lucas County*, 194
Wauseon city *Fulton County*, 108
Waverly City city *Pike County*, 251
Wayne County, 325 - 329
Wayne Lakes village *Darke County*, 81
Wayne village *Wood County*, 339
Waynesburg village *Stark County*, 288
Waynesfield village *Auglaize County*, 20
Waynesville village *Warren County*, 321
Wellington village *Lorain County*, 189
Wellston city *Jackson County*, 157
Wellsville village *Columbiana County*, 53
West Alexandria village *Preble County*, 257
West Carrollton City city *Montgomery County*, 227
West Elkton village *Preble County*, 258
West Farmington village *Trumbull County*, 303
West Hill CDP *Trumbull County*, 304
West Jefferson village *Madison County*, 196
West Lafayette village *Coshocton County*, 56
West Leipsic village *Putnam County*, 262
West Liberty village *Logan County*, 183
West Manchester village *Preble County*, 258
West Mansfield village *Logan County*, 183
West Millgrove village *Wood County*, 339
West Milton village *Miami County*, 217
West Portsmouth CDP *Scioto County*, 274
West Rushville village *Fairfield County*, 93
West Salem village *Wayne County*, 329
West Union village *Adams County*, 2
West Unity village *Williams County*, 332
Westerville city *Franklin County*, 104
Westfield Center village *Medina County*, 208
Westlake city *Cuyahoga County*, 76
Weston village *Wood County*, 339
Wetherington CDP *Butler County*, 32
Wharton village *Wyandot County*, 342
Wheelersburg CDP *Scioto County*, 275
Whipple postal area *Washington County*, 325
White Oak East CDP *Hamilton County*, 136
White Oak West CDP *Hamilton County*, 137
White Oak CDP *Hamilton County*, 136
Whitehall city *Franklin County*, 105
Whitehouse village *Lucas County*, 194
Wickliffe city *Lake County*, 170
Wilberforce CDP *Greene County*, 116
Wilkesville village *Vinton County*, 315
Willard city *Huron County*, 156
Williams County, 330 - 332
Williamsburg village *Clermont County*, 45
Williamsfield postal area *Ashtabula County*, 13
Williamsport village *Pickaway County*, 249
Willoughby Hills city *Lake County*, 171
Willoughby city *Lake County*, 171
Willow Wood postal area *Lawrence County*, 175
Willowick city *Lake County*, 171
Willshire village *Van Wert County*, 314
Wilmington city *Clinton County*, 48
Wilmot village *Stark County*, 288
Wilson village *Monroe County*, 219
Winchester village *Adams County*, 2
Windham village *Portage County*, 255
Windsor postal area *Ashtabula County*, 14
Wingett Run postal area *Washington County*, 325
Wintersville village *Jefferson County*, 163
Withamsville CDP *Clermont County*, 46
Wood County, 333 - 338
Woodbourne-Hyde Park CDP *Montgomery County*, 228
Woodlawn village *Hamilton County*, 137
Woodmere village *Cuyahoga County*, 76
Woodsfield village *Monroe County*, 219
Woodstock village *Champaign County*, 36
Woodville village *Sandusky County*, 271
Wooster city *Wayne County*, 329
Worthington city *Franklin County*, 105
Wren village *Van Wert County*, 314
Wright-Patterson AFB CDP *Montgomery County*, 228
Wyandot County, 339 - 343
Wyoming city *Hamilton County*, 137

X

Xenia city *Greene County*, 117

Y

Yankee Lake village *Trumbull County*, 304
Yellow Springs village *Greene County*, 117
Yorkshire village *Darke County*, 81
Yorkville village *Jefferson County*, 163
Youngstown city *Mahoning County*, 201

Z

Zaleski village *Vinton County*, 316
Zanesfield village *Logan County*, 183
Zanesville city *Muskingum County*, 235
Zoar village *Tuscarawas County*, 309

Comparative Statistics

Population

Place	1990	2000	2007 Estimate	2012 Projection
Akron city *Summit Co.*	223,165	217,074	209,368	203,372
Alliance city *Stark Co.*	23,552	23,253	22,549	22,025
Ashland city *Ashland Co.*	20,355	21,249	21,694	22,043
Ashtabula city *Ashtabula Co.*	21,626	20,962	20,185	19,587
Athens city *Athens Co.*	21,362	21,342	20,316	19,535
Austintown CDP *Mahoning Co.*	32,371	31,627	29,358	28,123
Avon Lake city *Lorain Co.*	15,066	18,145	21,210	23,157
Barberton city *Summit Co.*	27,931	27,899	26,911	26,137
Beavercreek city *Greene Co.*	33,946	37,984	39,794	40,817
Berea city *Cuyahoga Co.*	19,045	18,970	18,129	17,472
Boardman CDP *Mahoning Co.*	38,727	37,215	34,394	32,880
Bowling Green city *Wood Co.*	29,038	29,636	30,286	30,684
Broadview Heights city *Cuyahoga Co.*	12,219	15,967	18,000	19,182
Brook Park city *Cuyahoga Co.*	22,961	21,218	19,733	18,613
Brunswick city *Medina Co.*	28,743	33,388	35,519	36,975
Canton city *Stark Co.*	84,082	80,806	78,373	76,289
Centerville city *Montgomery Co.*	21,563	23,024	22,871	22,815
Chillicothe city *Ross Co.*	22,771	21,796	21,594	21,348
Cincinnati city *Hamilton Co.*	363,974	331,285	302,545	282,712
Cleveland city *Cuyahoga Co.*	505,333	478,403	445,680	421,286
Cleveland Heights city *Cuyahoga Co.*	54,052	49,958	46,489	43,955
Columbus city *Franklin Co.*	648,656	711,470	732,084	742,773
Cuyahoga Falls city *Summit Co.*	48,814	49,374	50,608	51,237
Dayton city *Montgomery Co.*	182,920	166,179	156,800	149,884
Delaware city *Delaware Co.*	21,106	25,243	33,067	38,511
Dublin city *Franklin Co.*	17,231	31,392	35,862	38,751
East Cleveland city *Cuyahoga Co.*	33,096	27,217	25,329	23,928
Eastlake city *Lake Co.*	21,161	20,255	19,633	19,138
Elyria city *Lorain Co.*	57,491	55,953	55,547	55,434
Euclid city *Cuyahoga Co.*	54,875	52,717	48,676	45,739
Fairborn city *Greene Co.*	31,928	32,052	32,141	32,089
Fairfield city *Butler Co.*	40,084	42,097	42,217	42,398
Findlay city *Hancock Co.*	36,546	38,967	38,768	38,713
Forest Park city *Hamilton Co.*	18,625	19,463	17,705	16,356
Gahanna city *Franklin Co.*	24,610	32,636	32,473	32,255
Garfield Heights city *Cuyahoga Co.*	31,739	30,734	28,535	26,898
Green city *Summit Co.*	19,179	22,817	23,521	23,939
Grove City city *Franklin Co.*	21,241	27,075	29,709	31,262
Hamilton city *Butler Co.*	61,618	60,690	62,285	63,448
Hilliard city *Franklin Co.*	12,516	24,230	27,143	28,913
Huber Heights city *Montgomery Co.*	38,478	38,212	37,774	37,334
Hudson city *Summit Co.*	17,128	22,439	23,175	23,546
Kent city *Portage Co.*	28,879	27,906	28,170	28,270
Kettering city *Montgomery Co.*	60,570	57,502	54,597	52,442
Lakewood city *Cuyahoga Co.*	59,718	56,646	52,313	49,165
Lancaster city *Fairfield Co.*	35,664	35,335	36,375	37,307
Lebanon city *Warren Co.*	11,282	16,962	20,553	22,872
Lima city *Allen Co.*	45,620	40,081	36,337	33,869
Lorain city *Lorain Co.*	71,245	68,652	67,618	67,017
Mansfield city *Richland Co.*	50,489	49,346	47,851	46,730

Place	1990	2000	2007 Estimate	2012 Projection
Maple Heights city *Cuyahoga Co.*	27,089	26,156	24,312	22,890
Marion city *Marion Co.*	36,526	35,318	33,939	32,812
Marysville city *Union Co.*	11,003	15,942	18,330	19,942
Mason city *Warren Co.*	12,046	22,016	30,484	36,082
Massillon city *Stark Co.*	31,955	31,325	31,895	32,132
Mayfield Heights city *Cuyahoga Co.*	19,847	19,386	18,131	17,155
Medina city *Medina Co.*	19,807	25,139	26,900	28,256
Mentor city *Lake Co.*	47,358	50,278	51,770	52,619
Miamisburg city *Montgomery Co.*	18,641	19,489	19,537	19,517
Middletown city *Butler Co.*	52,003	51,605	51,325	51,275
Newark city *Licking Co.*	45,070	46,279	47,531	48,387
Niles city *Trumbull Co.*	21,353	20,932	19,730	18,812
North Olmsted city *Cuyahoga Co.*	34,240	34,113	32,152	30,671
North Ridgeville city *Lorain Co.*	21,564	22,338	27,285	30,383
North Royalton city *Cuyahoga Co.*	23,197	28,648	29,673	30,190
Norwood city *Hamilton Co.*	23,635	21,675	19,481	17,911
Oregon city *Lucas Co.*	18,371	19,355	19,095	18,808
Oxford city *Butler Co.*	21,307	21,943	22,194	22,485
Painesville city *Lake Co.*	15,712	17,503	17,780	17,915
Parma city *Cuyahoga Co.*	87,876	85,655	80,088	75,855
Parma Heights city *Cuyahoga Co.*	21,448	21,659	20,328	19,319
Piqua city *Miami Co.*	21,160	20,738	20,792	20,786
Portsmouth city *Scioto Co.*	22,676	20,909	19,840	19,001
Reynoldsburg city *Franklin Co.*	26,344	32,069	33,240	33,960
Riverside city *Montgomery Co.*	25,374	23,545	22,910	22,406
Rocky River city *Cuyahoga Co.*	20,410	20,735	19,379	18,339
Sandusky city *Erie Co.*	29,764	27,844	26,395	25,297
Shaker Heights city *Cuyahoga Co.*	30,831	29,405	27,239	25,617
Sidney city *Shelby Co.*	19,245	20,211	20,096	19,947
Solon city *Cuyahoga Co.*	18,548	21,802	22,421	22,679
South Euclid city *Cuyahoga Co.*	23,866	23,537	21,824	20,546
Springfield city *Clark Co.*	71,064	65,358	61,594	58,974
Steubenville city *Jefferson Co.*	22,298	19,015	18,258	17,656
Stow city *Summit Co.*	27,702	32,139	34,687	36,200
Strongsville city *Cuyahoga Co.*	35,308	43,858	43,708	43,303
Sylvania city *Lucas Co.*	17,488	18,670	18,878	18,999
Toledo city *Lucas Co.*	332,921	313,619	297,162	284,791
Trotwood city *Montgomery Co.*	29,395	27,420	26,355	25,574
Troy city *Miami Co.*	19,956	21,999	22,189	22,402
Twinsburg city *Summit Co.*	9,759	17,006	18,103	18,703
Upper Arlington city *Franklin Co.*	34,171	33,686	30,952	29,049
Wadsworth city *Medina Co.*	16,147	18,437	19,804	20,751
Warren city *Trumbull Co.*	51,151	46,832	43,494	41,195
Westerville city *Franklin Co.*	30,722	35,318	34,490	34,123
Westlake city *Cuyahoga Co.*	27,018	31,719	31,153	30,624
Willoughby city *Lake Co.*	20,510	22,621	22,202	21,881
Wooster city *Wayne Co.*	23,108	24,811	25,416	25,817
Xenia city *Greene Co.*	25,481	24,164	23,555	23,169
Youngstown city *Mahoning Co.*	95,732	82,026	86,296	87,538
Zanesville city *Muskingum Co.*	27,058	25,586	24,501	23,829

Physical Characteristics

Place	Density (persons per square mile)	Land Area (square miles)	Water Area (square miles)	Elevation (feet)
Akron city *Summit Co.*	3,373.1	62.07	0.34	955
Alliance city *Stark Co.*	2,618.4	8.61	0.00	1,158
Ashland city *Ashland Co.*	2,094.5	10.36	0.04	1,066
Ashtabula city *Ashtabula Co.*	2,673.0	7.55	0.17	673
Athens city *Athens Co.*	2,437.3	8.34	0.00	719
Austintown CDP *Mahoning Co.*	2,515.0	11.67	0.00	1,129
Avon Lake city *Lorain Co.*	1,905.4	11.13	0.00	607
Barberton city *Summit Co.*	2,985.6	9.01	0.22	974
Beavercreek city *Greene Co.*	1,507.8	26.39	0.00	873
Berea city *Cuyahoga Co.*	3,321.8	5.46	0.11	764
Boardman CDP *Mahoning Co.*	2,158.7	15.93	0.10	1,112
Bowling Green city *Wood Co.*	2,983.0	10.15	0.03	696
Broadview Heights city *Cuyahoga Co.*	1,378.4	13.06	0.00	1,198
Brook Park city *Cuyahoga Co.*	2,618.0	7.54	0.00	797
Brunswick city *Medina Co.*	2,832.3	12.54	0.04	1,171
Canton city *Stark Co.*	3,814.6	20.55	0.01	1,060
Centerville city *Montgomery Co.*	2,242.2	10.20	0.02	1,020
Chillicothe city *Ross Co.*	2,262.6	9.54	0.20	630
Cincinnati city *Hamilton Co.*	3,880.4	77.97	1.60	627
Cleveland city *Cuyahoga Co.*	5,744.8	77.58	4.84	653
Cleveland Heights city *Cuyahoga Co.*	5,732.4	8.11	0.02	935
Columbus city *Franklin Co.*	3,481.7	210.27	2.28	771
Cuyahoga Falls city *Summit Co.*	1,981.2	25.54	0.09	1,050
Dayton city *Montgomery Co.*	2,811.2	55.78	0.85	738
Delaware city *Delaware Co.*	2,204.5	15.00	0.10	869
Dublin city *Franklin Co.*	1,697.8	21.12	0.02	830
East Cleveland city *Cuyahoga Co.*	8,154.1	3.11	0.00	689
Eastlake city *Lake Co.*	3,069.3	6.40	0.12	620
Elyria city *Lorain Co.*	2,793.3	19.89	0.03	715
Euclid city *Cuyahoga Co.*	4,545.8	10.71	0.86	617
Fairborn city *Greene Co.*	2,460.2	13.06	0.00	837
Fairfield city *Butler Co.*	2,011.3	20.99	0.09	591
Findlay city *Hancock Co.*	2,254.7	17.19	0.11	778
Forest Park city *Hamilton Co.*	2,720.3	6.51	0.00	837
Gahanna city *Franklin Co.*	2,619.7	12.40	0.00	794
Garfield Heights city *Cuyahoga Co.*	3,948.7	7.23	0.08	955
Green city *Summit Co.*	733.7	32.06	1.47	1,138
Grove City city *Franklin Co.*	2,130.0	13.95	0.01	850
Hamilton city *Butler Co.*	2,882.0	21.61	0.47	594
Hilliard city *Franklin Co.*	2,436.3	11.14	0.00	935
Huber Heights city *Montgomery Co.*	1,796.4	21.03	0.09	932
Hudson city *Summit Co.*	905.7	25.59	0.27	1,066
Kent city *Portage Co.*	3,242.7	8.69	0.02	1,066
Kettering city *Montgomery Co.*	2,922.0	18.69	0.00	1,007
Lakewood city *Cuyahoga Co.*	9,427.7	5.55	1.15	705
Lancaster city *Fairfield Co.*	2,013.5	18.07	0.01	879
Lebanon city *Warren Co.*	1,745.6	11.77	0.00	768
Lima city *Allen Co.*	2,842.2	12.78	0.10	879
Lorain city *Lorain Co.*	2,815.6	24.02	0.23	610
Mansfield city *Richland Co.*	1,600.1	29.91	0.00	1,243

Place	Density (persons per square mile)	Land Area (square miles)	Water Area (square miles)	Elevation (feet)
Maple Heights city *Cuyahoga Co.*	4,683.8	5.19	0.00	899
Marion city *Marion Co.*	2,991.3	11.35	0.04	981
Marysville city *Union Co.*	1,180.6	15.53	0.08	991
Mason city *Warren Co.*	1,730.8	17.61	0.04	810
Massillon city *Stark Co.*	1,904.3	16.75	0.14	948
Mayfield Heights city *Cuyahoga Co.*	4,298.5	4.22	0.00	1,089
Medina city *Medina Co.*	2,417.6	11.13	0.19	1,089
Mentor city *Lake Co.*	1,934.0	26.77	1.31	692
Miamisburg city *Montgomery Co.*	1,745.9	11.19	0.19	699
Middletown city *Butler Co.*	2,000.4	25.66	0.14	656
Newark city *Licking Co.*	2,430.8	19.55	0.24	833
Niles city *Trumbull Co.*	2,306.9	8.55	0.02	879
North Olmsted city *Cuyahoga Co.*	2,764.3	11.63	0.00	761
North Ridgeville city *Lorain Co.*	1,167.5	23.37	0.14	728
North Royalton city *Cuyahoga Co.*	1,394.0	21.29	0.00	1,201
Norwood city *Hamilton Co.*	6,252.4	3.12	0.00	656
Oregon city *Lucas Co.*	650.0	29.38	8.71	600
Oxford city *Butler Co.*	3,777.1	5.88	0.00	928
Painesville city *Lake Co.*	2,975.0	5.98	0.71	676
Parma city *Cuyahoga Co.*	4,012.4	19.96	0.02	866
Parma Heights city *Cuyahoga Co.*	4,841.6	4.20	0.00	856
Piqua city *Miami Co.*	1,944.3	10.69	0.24	873
Portsmouth city *Scioto Co.*	1,842.2	10.77	0.29	531
Reynoldsburg city *Franklin Co.*	3,140.7	10.58	0.00	879
Riverside city *Montgomery Co.*	2,915.7	7.86	0.04	781
Rocky River city *Cuyahoga Co.*	4,075.6	4.75	0.87	689
Sandusky city *Erie Co.*	2,626.4	10.05	11.94	597
Shaker Heights city *Cuyahoga Co.*	4,339.9	6.28	0.04	1,050
Sidney city *Shelby Co.*	1,927.4	10.43	0.07	951
Solon city *Cuyahoga Co.*	1,091.0	20.55	0.04	1,040
South Euclid city *Cuyahoga Co.*	4,653.9	4.69	0.00	958
Springfield city *Clark Co.*	2,740.8	22.47	0.04	978
Steubenville city *Jefferson Co.*	1,768.8	10.32	0.00	1,047
Stow city *Summit Co.*	2,027.0	17.11	0.23	1,093
Strongsville city *Cuyahoga Co.*	1,773.5	24.64	0.01	932
Sylvania city *Lucas Co.*	3,259.1	5.79	0.04	663
Toledo city *Lucas Co.*	3,685.9	80.62	3.45	614
Trotwood city *Montgomery Co.*	863.3	30.53	0.01	840
Troy city *Miami Co.*	2,287.4	9.70	0.07	827
Twinsburg city *Summit Co.*	1,454.9	12.44	0.03	1,001
Upper Arlington city *Franklin Co.*	3,170.2	9.76	0.02	810
Wadsworth city *Medina Co.*	2,084.4	9.50	0.00	1,168
Warren city *Trumbull Co.*	2,704.1	16.08	0.03	892
Westerville city *Franklin Co.*	2,784.3	12.39	0.00	869
Westlake city *Cuyahoga Co.*	1,959.6	15.90	0.00	709
Willoughby city *Lake Co.*	2,184.0	10.17	0.06	659
Wooster city *Wayne Co.*	1,768.2	14.37	0.02	997
Xenia city *Greene Co.*	1,939.2	12.15	0.00	932
Youngstown city *Mahoning Co.*	2,545.9	33.90	0.35	850
Zanesville city *Muskingum Co.*	2,180.3	11.24	0.26	676

NOTE: Population Density figures as of 2007; Land Area and Water Area figures as of 2000.

Population by Race/Hispanic Origin

Place	White Alone[1] (%)	Black Alone[1] (%)	Asian Alone[1] (%)	Hispanic[2] (%)
Akron city *Summit Co.*	63.8	31.1	1.8	1.5
Alliance city *Stark Co.*	85.5	10.8	1.0	1.4
Ashland city *Ashland Co.*	96.0	1.2	1.4	1.0
Ashtabula city *Ashtabula Co.*	82.6	10.9	0.4	6.9
Athens city *Athens Co.*	88.6	3.5	5.2	1.5
Austintown CDP *Mahoning Co.*	92.6	4.6	0.9	1.9
Avon Lake city *Lorain Co.*	96.5	0.5	1.2	1.5
Barberton city *Summit Co.*	91.6	5.7	0.4	0.9
Beavercreek city *Greene Co.*	91.6	1.7	4.6	1.6
Berea city *Cuyahoga Co.*	90.6	5.4	1.0	1.7
Boardman CDP *Mahoning Co.*	94.8	2.4	1.2	2.0
Bowling Green city *Wood Co.*	90.7	3.4	1.8	4.2
Broadview Heights city *Cuyahoga Co.*	94.0	0.8	3.7	1.0
Brook Park city *Cuyahoga Co.*	93.2	2.4	1.6	2.1
Brunswick city *Medina Co.*	95.9	1.2	1.3	1.7
Canton city *Stark Co.*	72.0	22.7	0.4	1.3
Centerville city *Montgomery Co.*	90.8	3.7	3.6	1.4
Chillicothe city *Ross Co.*	89.6	7.1	0.6	1.2
Cincinnati city *Hamilton Co.*	49.1	46.0	1.7	1.8
Cleveland city *Cuyahoga Co.*	38.0	53.0	1.7	8.4
Cleveland Heights city *Cuyahoga Co.*	48.0	45.4	2.9	1.7
Columbus city *Franklin Co.*	63.6	26.8	4.0	3.8
Cuyahoga Falls city *Summit Co.*	94.6	2.4	1.4	0.8
Dayton city *Montgomery Co.*	52.1	43.8	0.7	2.1
Delaware city *Delaware Co.*	89.6	4.6	2.0	2.0
Dublin city *Franklin Co.*	86.3	2.5	9.4	1.6
East Cleveland city *Cuyahoga Co.*	4.3	93.2	0.2	0.8
Eastlake city *Lake Co.*	96.5	0.9	1.3	1.1
Elyria city *Lorain Co.*	80.6	13.7	0.8	3.5
Euclid city *Cuyahoga Co.*	57.5	38.8	1.0	1.3
Fairborn city *Greene Co.*	84.9	7.3	4.1	2.3
Fairfield city *Butler Co.*	85.4	9.2	2.9	2.4
Findlay city *Hancock Co.*	92.4	1.8	2.4	4.3
Forest Park city *Hamilton Co.*	27.9	63.8	4.3	1.9
Gahanna city *Franklin Co.*	83.1	9.9	4.1	1.9
Garfield Heights city *Cuyahoga Co.*	78.4	18.4	1.2	1.4
Green city *Summit Co.*	96.8	1.0	1.0	0.6
Grove City city *Franklin Co.*	94.8	2.2	0.8	1.8
Hamilton city *Butler Co.*	86.6	8.5	0.6	4.2
Hilliard city *Franklin Co.*	89.8	2.2	4.8	2.8
Huber Heights city *Montgomery Co.*	82.9	10.9	2.4	1.9
Hudson city *Summit Co.*	93.4	1.6	3.7	1.1
Kent city *Portage Co.*	83.3	10.6	3.0	1.5
Kettering city *Montgomery Co.*	94.3	2.1	1.5	1.4
Lakewood city *Cuyahoga Co.*	91.0	2.7	1.7	2.5
Lancaster city *Fairfield Co.*	95.9	1.3	0.6	1.3
Lebanon city *Warren Co.*	87.1	8.7	1.3	1.9
Lima city *Allen Co.*	68.8	25.9	0.8	2.4
Lorain city *Lorain Co.*	67.4	16.3	0.4	23.0
Mansfield city *Richland Co.*	76.7	19.3	0.7	1.4

Place	White Alone[1] (%)	Black Alone[1] (%)	Asian Alone[1] (%)	Hispanic[2] (%)
Maple Heights city *Cuyahoga Co.*	41.7	53.4	2.2	1.4
Marion city *Marion Co.*	90.8	6.6	0.6	1.7
Marysville city *Union Co.*	89.9	6.7	1.8	1.5
Mason city *Warren Co.*	90.5	2.2	5.5	1.4
Massillon city *Stark Co.*	88.0	9.1	0.3	1.1
Mayfield Heights city *Cuyahoga Co.*	89.8	3.7	5.1	1.2
Medina city *Medina Co.*	93.3	3.4	1.2	1.2
Mentor city *Lake Co.*	96.2	1.1	1.5	1.0
Miamisburg city *Montgomery Co.*	95.1	1.9	0.7	1.1
Middletown city *Butler Co.*	83.8	13.0	0.5	1.4
Newark city *Licking Co.*	93.3	3.5	0.7	0.9
Niles city *Trumbull Co.*	95.7	2.4	0.3	0.9
North Olmsted city *Cuyahoga Co.*	92.4	1.3	3.4	1.9
North Ridgeville city *Lorain Co.*	95.5	0.9	1.3	2.3
North Royalton city *Cuyahoga Co.*	95.4	0.9	2.3	1.1
Norwood city *Hamilton Co.*	92.4	3.2	0.8	2.7
Oregon city *Lucas Co.*	94.1	1.0	0.8	5.6
Oxford city *Butler Co.*	89.0	5.6	2.7	2.3
Painesville city *Lake Co.*	69.4	15.9	0.5	21.5
Parma city *Cuyahoga Co.*	94.6	1.3	1.9	1.8
Parma Heights city *Cuyahoga Co.*	92.8	1.7	3.2	2.0
Piqua city *Miami Co.*	93.7	3.4	0.5	1.2
Portsmouth city *Scioto Co.*	91.0	5.1	1.0	1.3
Reynoldsburg city *Franklin Co.*	79.5	14.8	1.9	2.8
Riverside city *Montgomery Co.*	90.0	4.9	2.0	2.0
Rocky River city *Cuyahoga Co.*	96.2	0.5	1.4	1.4
Sandusky city *Erie Co.*	73.9	20.8	0.4	3.7
Shaker Heights city *Cuyahoga Co.*	55.6	37.0	3.9	1.1
Sidney city *Shelby Co.*	91.3	3.5	2.2	2.0
Solon city *Cuyahoga Co.*	84.2	8.0	6.3	0.9
South Euclid city *Cuyahoga Co.*	68.6	27.6	1.6	1.1
Springfield city *Clark Co.*	76.9	18.7	0.9	1.6
Steubenville city *Jefferson Co.*	79.3	17.4	1.0	1.1
Stow city *Summit Co.*	94.1	1.9	2.3	1.2
Strongsville city *Cuyahoga Co.*	92.9	1.6	3.8	1.4
Sylvania city *Lucas Co.*	94.4	1.1	2.4	2.1
Toledo city *Lucas Co.*	67.4	25.4	1.1	6.3
Trotwood city *Montgomery Co.*	32.1	64.5	0.2	1.0
Troy city *Miami Co.*	89.7	5.0	2.8	1.3
Twinsburg city *Summit Co.*	83.6	10.4	4.3	1.4
Upper Arlington city *Franklin Co.*	93.6	0.8	4.0	1.4
Wadsworth city *Medina Co.*	97.1	0.4	1.0	0.9
Warren city *Trumbull Co.*	70.3	26.6	0.4	1.3
Westerville city *Franklin Co.*	90.9	4.4	2.3	1.6
Westlake city *Cuyahoga Co.*	91.4	1.2	4.9	1.4
Willoughby city *Lake Co.*	95.0	1.8	1.5	1.0
Wooster city *Wayne Co.*	92.3	3.7	1.9	1.5
Xenia city *Greene Co.*	83.5	12.7	0.3	1.7
Youngstown city *Mahoning Co.*	52.4	41.2	0.6	5.9
Zanesville city *Muskingum Co.*	84.4	11.4	0.3	1.0

NOTE: Data as of 2007; (1) Figures are not in combination with any other race; (2) Persons of Hispanic Origin may be of any race

Avg. Household Size, Median Age, Male/Female Ratio & Foreign Born

Place	Average Household Size (persons)	Median Age (years)	Male/Female Ratio (males per 100 females)	Foreign Born (%)
Akron city *Summit Co.*	2.38	36.1	92.3	3.2
Alliance city *Stark Co.*	2.59	35.2	89.3	1.6
Ashland city *Ashland Co.*	2.55	35.3	87.3	1.5
Ashtabula city *Ashtabula Co.*	2.44	36.2	89.9	2.7
Athens city *Athens Co.*	3.26	21.8	87.4	6.3
Austintown CDP *Mahoning Co.*	2.32	41.7	90.6	2.3
Avon Lake city *Lorain Co.*	2.64	40.3	95.4	3.4
Barberton city *Summit Co.*	2.38	38.4	88.5	1.9
Beavercreek city *Greene Co.*	2.59	42.8	98.6	4.7
Berea city *Cuyahoga Co.*	2.61	38.1	90.6	3.2
Boardman CDP *Mahoning Co.*	2.31	44.0	88.0	3.0
Bowling Green city *Wood Co.*	2.78	23.9	87.3	3.6
Broadview Heights city *Cuyahoga Co.*	2.45	41.5	92.6	8.9
Brook Park city *Cuyahoga Co.*	2.51	43.1	94.9	4.3
Brunswick city *Medina Co.*	2.74	36.3	96.5	4.3
Canton city *Stark Co.*	2.46	36.2	88.8	1.7
Centerville city *Montgomery Co.*	2.26	44.2	87.8	4.2
Chillicothe city *Ross Co.*	2.24	41.3	89.7	1.0
Cincinnati city *Hamilton Co.*	2.18	34.8	91.1	3.8
Cleveland city *Cuyahoga Co.*	2.47	35.0	91.0	4.5
Cleveland Heights city *Cuyahoga Co.*	2.33	38.1	87.7	8.3
Columbus city *Franklin Co.*	2.33	32.9	96.3	6.7
Cuyahoga Falls city *Summit Co.*	2.24	39.1	91.0	3.1
Dayton city *Montgomery Co.*	2.42	34.4	95.0	2.0
Delaware city *Delaware Co.*	2.59	31.6	93.5	1.6
Dublin city *Franklin Co.*	2.75	35.8	98.6	9.1
East Cleveland city *Cuyahoga Co.*	2.37	35.6	80.3	2.9
Eastlake city *Lake Co.*	2.42	40.4	96.0	5.0
Elyria city *Lorain Co.*	2.43	36.0	93.0	1.5
Euclid city *Cuyahoga Co.*	2.13	41.6	85.0	5.3
Fairborn city *Greene Co.*	2.27	33.4	96.7	4.6
Fairfield city *Butler Co.*	2.43	36.7	95.4	3.6
Findlay city *Hancock Co.*	2.40	36.6	92.4	2.7
Forest Park city *Hamilton Co.*	2.51	36.8	92.3	5.7
Gahanna city *Franklin Co.*	2.68	38.3	95.2	4.9
Garfield Heights city *Cuyahoga Co.*	2.41	40.6	88.5	4.4
Green city *Summit Co.*	2.57	41.2	97.0	1.9
Grove City city *Franklin Co.*	2.63	36.4	96.0	1.2
Hamilton city *Butler Co.*	2.45	35.7	94.0	2.2
Hilliard city *Franklin Co.*	2.84	34.9	97.4	4.2
Huber Heights city *Montgomery Co.*	2.58	36.5	95.1	3.2
Hudson city *Summit Co.*	3.03	40.8	97.4	5.2
Kent city *Portage Co.*	2.85	24.4	84.1	4.4
Kettering city *Montgomery Co.*	2.19	41.2	91.4	2.7
Lakewood city *Cuyahoga Co.*	2.08	37.8	92.9	8.7
Lancaster city *Fairfield Co.*	2.31	35.9	90.2	0.9
Lebanon city *Warren Co.*	2.79	32.5	107.9	1.8
Lima city *Allen Co.*	2.50	33.5	97.8	1.1
Lorain city *Lorain Co.*	2.52	35.2	90.7	3.6
Mansfield city *Richland Co.*	2.38	38.1	99.9	2.2

Place	Average Household Size (persons)	Median Age (years)	Male/Female Ratio (males per 100 females)	Foreign Born (%)
Maple Heights city *Cuyahoga Co.*	2.45	40.0	88.6	2.9
Marion city *Marion Co.*	2.58	36.6	106.0	1.5
Marysville city *Union Co.*	2.86	33.3	79.5	1.3
Mason city *Warren Co.*	2.81	35.0	95.2	4.0
Massillon city *Stark Co.*	2.43	39.2	93.4	1.3
Mayfield Heights city *Cuyahoga Co.*	1.93	46.1	83.3	18.1
Medina city *Medina Co.*	2.64	34.6	93.3	2.7
Mentor city *Lake Co.*	2.59	41.5	94.7	3.8
Miamisburg city *Montgomery Co.*	2.58	39.4	92.5	1.7
Middletown city *Butler Co.*	2.34	36.9	92.6	1.0
Newark city *Licking Co.*	2.36	36.7	91.3	1.1
Niles city *Trumbull Co.*	2.29	41.9	89.9	1.9
North Olmsted city *Cuyahoga Co.*	2.44	42.5	93.0	7.8
North Ridgeville city *Lorain Co.*	2.60	40.6	96.4	3.3
North Royalton city *Cuyahoga Co.*	2.49	41.4	94.7	6.8
Norwood city *Hamilton Co.*	2.27	37.2	96.2	2.3
Oregon city *Lucas Co.*	2.48	41.0	93.1	2.3
Oxford city *Butler Co.*	3.58	21.6	90.8	3.7
Painesville city *Lake Co.*	2.66	33.0	97.8	10.1
Parma city *Cuyahoga Co.*	2.38	41.8	91.6	9.1
Parma Heights city *Cuyahoga Co.*	2.17	44.4	87.2	10.2
Piqua city *Miami Co.*	2.44	36.6	92.6	1.4
Portsmouth city *Scioto Co.*	2.24	38.7	85.2	1.1
Reynoldsburg city *Franklin Co.*	2.46	37.2	92.5	3.6
Riverside city *Montgomery Co.*	2.36	39.0	94.9	2.9
Rocky River city *Cuyahoga Co.*	2.08	46.4	83.0	7.0
Sandusky city *Erie Co.*	2.28	37.8	89.4	1.7
Shaker Heights city *Cuyahoga Co.*	2.37	41.8	84.4	7.2
Sidney city *Shelby Co.*	2.47	35.7	96.3	2.3
Solon city *Cuyahoga Co.*	2.87	41.7	95.7	8.6
South Euclid city *Cuyahoga Co.*	2.42	40.5	86.1	9.4
Springfield city *Clark Co.*	2.43	36.0	90.4	1.2
Steubenville city *Jefferson Co.*	2.22	44.4	86.8	2.4
Stow city *Summit Co.*	2.57	38.8	94.0	3.7
Strongsville city *Cuyahoga Co.*	2.65	41.7	94.7	6.5
Sylvania city *Lucas Co.*	2.55	39.6	91.7	4.7
Toledo city *Lucas Co.*	2.38	34.7	93.5	3.0
Trotwood city *Montgomery Co.*	2.40	40.0	84.1	1.2
Troy city *Miami Co.*	2.40	36.9	95.5	2.1
Twinsburg city *Summit Co.*	2.51	38.6	92.5	4.1
Upper Arlington city *Franklin Co.*	2.39	44.4	90.5	6.3
Wadsworth city *Medina Co.*	2.48	38.6	93.4	2.5
Warren city *Trumbull Co.*	2.37	38.1	87.4	1.9
Westerville city *Franklin Co.*	2.74	38.7	91.4	3.2
Westlake city *Cuyahoga Co.*	2.41	44.9	89.5	8.4
Willoughby city *Lake Co.*	2.12	41.5	86.6	3.7
Wooster city *Wayne Co.*	2.41	37.3	92.4	3.3
Xenia city *Greene Co.*	2.49	35.4	92.5	1.9
Youngstown city *Mahoning Co.*	2.65	36.2	97.6	2.0
Zanesville city *Muskingum Co.*	2.39	35.9	86.8	0.9

NOTE: Average Household Size, Median Age, and Male/Female Ratio figures as of 2007. Foreign Born figures as of 2000.

Five Largest Ancestry Groups

Place	Group 1	Group 2	Group 3	Group 4	Group 5
Akron city *Summit Co.*	Other (29.9%)	German (18.1%)	Irish (11.5%)	English (7.2%)	Italian (6.8%)
Alliance city *Stark Co.*	German (22.5%)	Other (14.9%)	Irish (11.8%)	Italian (9.9%)	English (9.5%)
Ashland city *Ashland Co.*	German (31.5%)	Irish (11.7%)	American (11.3%)	English (10.8%)	Other (7.0%)
Ashtabula city *Ashtabula Co.*	Other (18.7%)	German (16.9%)	Italian (15.0%)	Irish (11.5%)	English (9.2%)
Athens city *Athens Co.*	German (28.3%)	Irish (17.1%)	Other (12.6%)	English (10.6%)	Italian (8.3%)
Austintown CDP *Mahoning Co.*	German (26.1%)	Italian (19.3%)	Irish (17.8%)	Other (9.3%)	English (9.2%)
Avon Lake city *Lorain Co.*	German (36.2%)	Irish (22.7%)	English (13.9%)	Italian (11.4%)	Polish (7.3%)
Barberton city *Summit Co.*	German (23.9%)	Irish (13.1%)	Other (11.4%)	American (10.1%)	English (7.1%)
Beavercreek city *Greene Co.*	German (30.2%)	Irish (14.4%)	English (14.3%)	American (10.3%)	Other (8.8%)
Berea city *Cuyahoga Co.*	German (27.8%)	Irish (17.8%)	English (13.5%)	Polish (10.7%)	Italian (9.8%)
Boardman CDP *Mahoning Co.*	Italian (26.5%)	German (20.8%)	Irish (17.7%)	English (9.6%)	Slovak (9.5%)
Bowling Green city *Wood Co.*	German (31.4%)	Irish (11.7%)	English (10.6%)	Other (10.2%)	American (5.1%)
Broadview Heights city *Cuyahoga Co.*	German (23.6%)	Italian (16.8%)	Polish (16.1%)	Irish (13.4%)	Slovak (7.4%)
Brook Park city *Cuyahoga Co.*	German (26.5%)	Irish (18.5%)	Polish (14.1%)	Italian (13.2%)	English (7.2%)
Brunswick city *Medina Co.*	German (29.0%)	Irish (18.7%)	Polish (12.6%)	Italian (11.7%)	English (8.3%)
Canton city *Stark Co.*	Other (25.0%)	German (21.5%)	Irish (11.4%)	Italian (8.6%)	English (6.9%)
Centerville city *Montgomery Co.*	German (34.1%)	Irish (17.7%)	English (14.9%)	Other (9.8%)	American (6.2%)
Chillicothe city *Ross Co.*	German (22.0%)	American (13.9%)	Other (13.4%)	Irish (11.8%)	English (10.5%)
Cincinnati city *Hamilton Co.*	Other (40.7%)	German (19.9%)	Irish (10.4%)	English (5.4%)	American (4.8%)
Cleveland city *Cuyahoga Co.*	Other (50.9%)	German (9.2%)	Irish (8.1%)	Polish (4.8%)	Italian (4.6%)
Cleveland Heights city *Cuyahoga Co.*	Other (44.5%)	German (12.1%)	Irish (10.3%)	English (7.5%)	Italian (5.8%)
Columbus city *Franklin Co.*	Other (30.0%)	German (19.4%)	Irish (11.7%)	English (7.9%)	American (7.2%)
Cuyahoga Falls city *Summit Co.*	German (31.0%)	Irish (17.4%)	English (13.0%)	Italian (12.4%)	Other (6.7%)
Dayton city *Montgomery Co.*	Other (40.1%)	German (14.4%)	Irish (8.3%)	American (7.7%)	English (4.9%)
Delaware city *Delaware Co.*	German (25.7%)	Irish (11.8%)	English (11.4%)	Other (10.1%)	American (9.0%)
Dublin city *Franklin Co.*	German (31.3%)	Irish (17.0%)	Other (12.9%)	English (12.3%)	Italian (9.4%)
East Cleveland city *Cuyahoga Co.*	Other (80.1%)	African (1.1%)	American (1.1%)	German (0.7%)	Italian (0.6%)
Eastlake city *Lake Co.*	German (24.3%)	Irish (20.3%)	Italian (17.0%)	English (9.8%)	Polish (9.6%)
Elyria city *Lorain Co.*	German (23.8%)	Other (20.3%)	Irish (14.3%)	English (10.9%)	Polish (7.5%)
Euclid city *Cuyahoga Co.*	Other (29.9%)	German (15.2%)	Irish (12.6%)	Italian (9.6%)	Slovene (8.8%)
Fairborn city *Greene Co.*	German (21.1%)	Other (17.6%)	Irish (12.1%)	American (10.4%)	English (10.2%)
Fairfield city *Butler Co.*	German (31.7%)	Irish (14.4%)	Other (12.9%)	English (11.2%)	American (9.0%)
Findlay city *Hancock Co.*	German (35.5%)	Irish (10.7%)	English (10.6%)	American (9.5%)	Other (9.5%)
Forest Park city *Hamilton Co.*	Other (54.5%)	German (14.6%)	Irish (6.6%)	English (5.8%)	American (3.7%)
Gahanna city *Franklin Co.*	German (26.3%)	Other (16.0%)	Irish (14.4%)	English (12.9%)	American (7.8%)
Garfield Heights city *Cuyahoga Co.*	Polish (26.1%)	Other (17.4%)	German (14.9%)	Italian (14.0%)	Irish (10.2%)
Green city *Summit Co.*	German (28.3%)	Irish (16.4%)	English (10.9%)	American (9.1%)	Italian (7.8%)
Grove City city *Franklin Co.*	German (29.6%)	Irish (16.8%)	American (12.0%)	English (11.3%)	Other (7.4%)
Hamilton city *Butler Co.*	German (21.6%)	American (15.0%)	Other (14.7%)	Irish (11.8%)	English (8.6%)
Hilliard city *Franklin Co.*	German (30.1%)	Irish (17.2%)	English (12.7%)	Other (8.4%)	American (8.3%)
Huber Heights city *Montgomery Co.*	German (24.9%)	Other (18.0%)	Irish (11.5%)	English (10.3%)	American (9.7%)
Hudson city *Summit Co.*	German (30.1%)	Irish (19.8%)	English (17.4%)	Italian (10.6%)	Polish (7.3%)
Kent city *Portage Co.*	German (26.0%)	Other (15.2%)	Irish (15.0%)	English (11.0%)	Italian (10.8%)
Kettering city *Montgomery Co.*	German (33.8%)	Irish (15.5%)	English (12.7%)	American (8.6%)	Other (8.6%)
Lakewood city *Cuyahoga Co.*	German (25.2%)	Irish (23.6%)	English (9.8%)	Italian (8.9%)	Polish (7.8%)
Lancaster city *Fairfield Co.*	German (27.6%)	American (15.2%)	Irish (13.4%)	English (8.8%)	Other (8.2%)
Lebanon city *Warren Co.*	German (20.5%)	American (15.5%)	Irish (11.5%)	English (9.0%)	Other (7.6%)
Lima city *Allen Co.*	Other (27.6%)	German (20.9%)	Irish (11.0%)	American (9.6%)	English (5.2%)
Lorain city *Lorain Co.*	Other (36.9%)	German (16.0%)	Irish (11.0%)	Polish (7.8%)	Italian (6.7%)
Mansfield city *Richland Co.*	German (22.4%)	Other (21.7%)	Irish (10.0%)	American (9.0%)	English (7.9%)

Place	Group 1	Group 2	Group 3	Group 4	Group 5
Maple Heights city *Cuyahoga Co.*	Other (42.4%)	Italian (10.0%)	Polish (9.9%)	German (8.6%)	Irish (6.4%)
Marion city *Marion Co.*	American (18.6%)	German (17.5%)	Other (13.1%)	Irish (9.5%)	English (7.7%)
Marysville city *Union Co.*	German (28.2%)	Irish (13.3%)	Other (12.8%)	English (10.3%)	American (10.2%)
Mason city *Warren Co.*	German (33.5%)	Irish (18.3%)	English (14.0%)	Other (9.3%)	American (8.2%)
Massillon city *Stark Co.*	German (33.6%)	Irish (13.5%)	Other (12.8%)	English (8.3%)	Italian (7.1%)
Mayfield Heights city *Cuyahoga Co.*	Italian (26.1%)	German (15.4%)	Other (12.6%)	Irish (9.0%)	Russian (6.8%)
Medina city *Medina Co.*	German (32.7%)	Irish (16.7%)	English (11.9%)	Italian (9.6%)	Polish (8.8%)
Mentor city *Lake Co.*	German (26.6%)	Irish (19.5%)	Italian (16.2%)	English (12.8%)	Polish (8.4%)
Miamisburg city *Montgomery Co.*	German (26.5%)	American (12.9%)	Irish (12.4%)	English (11.0%)	Other (8.0%)
Middletown city *Butler Co.*	Other (17.2%)	German (16.9%)	American (15.4%)	Irish (11.5%)	English (10.0%)
Newark city *Licking Co.*	German (23.1%)	Irish (14.4%)	American (13.6%)	English (10.8%)	Other (8.5%)
Niles city *Trumbull Co.*	Italian (23.9%)	German (21.4%)	Irish (17.5%)	English (10.6%)	Other (7.4%)
North Olmsted city *Cuyahoga Co.*	German (29.9%)	Irish (22.8%)	Italian (10.7%)	Polish (9.9%)	English (9.6%)
North Ridgeville city *Lorain Co.*	German (32.9%)	Irish (19.2%)	English (12.6%)	Polish (10.7%)	Italian (9.0%)
North Royalton city *Cuyahoga Co.*	German (25.4%)	Polish (18.4%)	Irish (14.0%)	Italian (12.3%)	English (8.3%)
Norwood city *Hamilton Co.*	German (28.2%)	Irish (19.0%)	Other (11.7%)	American (10.5%)	English (9.8%)
Oregon city *Lucas Co.*	German (33.8%)	Irish (10.9%)	Other (9.9%)	Polish (8.9%)	English (7.8%)
Oxford city *Butler Co.*	German (31.6%)	Irish (15.9%)	Other (11.1%)	English (10.8%)	Italian (8.2%)
Painesville city *Lake Co.*	Other (26.7%)	German (18.7%)	Irish (13.7%)	English (10.5%)	Italian (9.3%)
Parma city *Cuyahoga Co.*	German (24.5%)	Polish (18.1%)	Irish (14.6%)	Italian (13.5%)	Slovak (9.3%)
Parma Heights city *Cuyahoga Co.*	German (25.0%)	Irish (16.3%)	Polish (13.1%)	Italian (12.0%)	Slovak (7.8%)
Piqua city *Miami Co.*	German (28.1%)	American (14.6%)	Irish (10.7%)	Other (10.4%)	English (8.2%)
Portsmouth city *Scioto Co.*	German (16.7%)	American (15.9%)	Other (12.8%)	Irish (12.5%)	English (10.0%)
Reynoldsburg city *Franklin Co.*	German (26.8%)	Other (17.1%)	Irish (14.5%)	English (10.7%)	American (8.6%)
Riverside city *Montgomery Co.*	German (22.3%)	Other (15.8%)	American (14.4%)	Irish (13.4%)	English (9.1%)
Rocky River city *Cuyahoga Co.*	German (28.1%)	Irish (26.9%)	English (12.4%)	Italian (9.4%)	Polish (6.6%)
Sandusky city *Erie Co.*	German (32.1%)	Other (24.7%)	Irish (12.4%)	English (7.8%)	Italian (7.4%)
Shaker Heights city *Cuyahoga Co.*	Other (36.6%)	German (13.2%)	Irish (9.4%)	English (9.2%)	Russian (5.1%)
Sidney city *Shelby Co.*	German (31.4%)	American (15.6%)	Other (11.2%)	Irish (10.9%)	English (9.1%)
Solon city *Cuyahoga Co.*	German (16.8%)	Italian (14.5%)	Other (13.8%)	Irish (11.6%)	Polish (10.0%)
South Euclid city *Cuyahoga Co.*	Other (25.6%)	Italian (15.4%)	German (13.9%)	Irish (13.7%)	Russian (6.1%)
Springfield city *Clark Co.*	Other (21.9%)	German (17.9%)	American (13.8%)	Irish (10.4%)	English (6.5%)
Steubenville city *Jefferson Co.*	Italian (18.9%)	Other (18.3%)	German (12.9%)	Irish (12.7%)	Polish (6.9%)
Stow city *Summit Co.*	German (29.7%)	Irish (17.7%)	English (14.3%)	Italian (12.0%)	Other (7.5%)
Strongsville city *Cuyahoga Co.*	German (29.1%)	Irish (18.0%)	Italian (13.4%)	Polish (12.6%)	English (10.7%)
Sylvania city *Lucas Co.*	German (32.8%)	Irish (15.6%)	English (11.4%)	Polish (10.7%)	Other (6.7%)
Toledo city *Lucas Co.*	Other (29.0%)	German (23.4%)	Irish (10.8%)	Polish (10.1%)	English (6.0%)
Trotwood city *Montgomery Co.*	Other (53.5%)	German (8.2%)	American (7.6%)	Irish (4.6%)	English (3.4%)
Troy city *Miami Co.*	German (25.3%)	American (14.6%)	Other (11.7%)	Irish (11.4%)	English (8.0%)
Twinsburg city *Summit Co.*	German (23.1%)	Other (15.0%)	Italian (15.0%)	Irish (14.1%)	Polish (11.4%)
Upper Arlington city *Franklin Co.*	German (30.6%)	English (19.2%)	Irish (15.1%)	Other (7.7%)	Italian (6.8%)
Wadsworth city *Medina Co.*	German (34.5%)	Irish (15.8%)	English (11.7%)	Italian (8.7%)	American (7.5%)
Warren city *Trumbull Co.*	Other (25.3%)	German (15.2%)	Irish (11.6%)	Italian (10.3%)	English (7.5%)
Westerville city *Franklin Co.*	German (29.6%)	Irish (15.4%)	English (14.3%)	American (9.1%)	Other (8.6%)
Westlake city *Cuyahoga Co.*	German (26.2%)	Irish (23.3%)	Italian (11.6%)	English (10.0%)	Other (8.2%)
Willoughby city *Lake Co.*	German (26.4%)	Irish (18.9%)	Italian (15.6%)	English (11.3%)	Polish (6.5%)
Wooster city *Wayne Co.*	German (30.4%)	Irish (13.6%)	English (11.9%)	Other (9.5%)	American (8.1%)
Xenia city *Greene Co.*	Other (20.1%)	German (16.8%)	American (14.3%)	Irish (10.4%)	English (8.8%)
Youngstown city *Mahoning Co.*	Other (42.7%)	Italian (11.2%)	German (10.3%)	Irish (9.4%)	Slovak (5.3%)
Zanesville city *Muskingum Co.*	Other (16.7%)	American (15.1%)	German (14.6%)	Irish (10.4%)	English (7.4%)

NOTE: Data as of 2000; "Other" includes Hispanic and race groups; "French" excludes Basque; Please refer to the Explanation of Data for more information.

Marriage Status

Place	Never Married (%)	Now Married (%)	Widowed (%)	Divorced (%)
Akron city *Summit Co.*	33.0	45.2	8.0	13.8
Alliance city *Stark Co.*	31.4	48.1	8.4	12.0
Ashland city *Ashland Co.*	26.6	54.8	8.1	10.5
Ashtabula city *Ashtabula Co.*	27.4	49.1	9.8	13.8
Athens city *Athens Co.*	70.0	24.6	2.3	3.1
Austintown CDP *Mahoning Co.*	24.8	55.5	8.5	11.2
Avon Lake city *Lorain Co.*	18.2	68.7	5.3	7.8
Barberton city *Summit Co.*	25.3	52.2	9.5	13.0
Beavercreek city *Greene Co.*	19.1	69.3	4.8	6.8
Berea city *Cuyahoga Co.*	33.1	48.7	7.3	10.9
Boardman CDP *Mahoning Co.*	23.7	55.6	10.7	10.0
Bowling Green city *Wood Co.*	54.7	35.8	3.7	5.8
Broadview Heights city *Cuyahoga Co.*	23.0	60.0	7.2	9.8
Brook Park city *Cuyahoga Co.*	23.8	58.2	8.4	9.5
Brunswick city *Medina Co.*	22.7	63.6	5.1	8.7
Canton city *Stark Co.*	31.0	45.8	8.9	14.2
Centerville city *Montgomery Co.*	20.2	61.7	7.9	10.1
Chillicothe city *Ross Co.*	23.2	51.3	11.2	14.2
Cincinnati city *Hamilton Co.*	42.4	37.9	7.6	12.1
Cleveland city *Cuyahoga Co.*	38.9	38.2	9.0	13.9
Cleveland Heights city *Cuyahoga Co.*	36.7	47.5	6.1	9.7
Columbus city *Franklin Co.*	38.3	44.0	5.4	12.4
Cuyahoga Falls city *Summit Co.*	24.5	56.1	8.3	11.2
Dayton city *Montgomery Co.*	38.7	39.2	7.8	14.3
Delaware city *Delaware Co.*	25.3	57.4	5.8	11.5
Dublin city *Franklin Co.*	18.9	72.2	2.9	6.0
East Cleveland city *Cuyahoga Co.*	42.3	32.0	10.5	15.3
Eastlake city *Lake Co.*	25.3	57.6	6.8	10.4
Elyria city *Lorain Co.*	26.6	52.9	7.0	13.6
Euclid city *Cuyahoga Co.*	30.3	45.8	10.4	13.5
Fairborn city *Greene Co.*	33.1	48.8	5.7	12.4
Fairfield city *Butler Co.*	25.3	59.1	5.0	10.6
Findlay city *Hancock Co.*	25.5	56.5	7.1	10.9
Forest Park city *Hamilton Co.*	29.3	53.8	5.5	11.4
Gahanna city *Franklin Co.*	21.6	63.5	4.8	10.2
Garfield Heights city *Cuyahoga Co.*	26.6	52.8	10.4	10.2
Green city *Summit Co.*	20.8	63.0	6.5	9.7
Grove City city *Franklin Co.*	20.7	62.7	5.9	10.7
Hamilton city *Butler Co.*	24.7	52.5	8.6	14.2
Hilliard city *Franklin Co.*	19.8	68.1	3.6	8.4
Huber Heights city *Montgomery Co.*	22.6	61.3	5.0	11.1
Hudson city *Summit Co.*	17.7	73.6	4.6	4.1
Kent city *Portage Co.*	57.7	30.4	4.1	7.8
Kettering city *Montgomery Co.*	23.7	56.9	8.1	11.3
Lakewood city *Cuyahoga Co.*	38.3	43.1	6.5	12.1
Lancaster city *Fairfield Co.*	22.2	55.9	8.3	13.6
Lebanon city *Warren Co.*	19.8	59.3	5.7	15.2
Lima city *Allen Co.*	33.6	43.0	8.5	14.9
Lorain city *Lorain Co.*	28.3	50.5	8.4	12.8
Mansfield city *Richland Co.*	27.2	49.2	9.1	14.5

Place	Never Married (%)	Now Married (%)	Widowed (%)	Divorced (%)
Maple Heights city *Cuyahoga Co.*	27.4	52.1	10.0	10.6
Marion city *Marion Co.*	26.0	50.4	8.1	15.5
Marysville city *Union Co.*	24.0	56.4	6.1	13.6
Mason city *Warren Co.*	18.1	69.2	4.5	8.1
Massillon city *Stark Co.*	23.0	56.2	8.2	12.7
Mayfield Heights city *Cuyahoga Co.*	24.4	50.7	14.0	10.9
Medina city *Medina Co.*	20.3	64.5	6.6	8.7
Mentor city *Lake Co.*	21.5	62.5	6.8	9.2
Miamisburg city *Montgomery Co.*	19.9	64.0	5.7	10.4
Middletown city *Butler Co.*	23.7	53.5	8.3	14.6
Newark city *Licking Co.*	23.4	53.8	8.2	14.6
Niles city *Trumbull Co.*	22.7	55.7	9.1	12.6
North Olmsted city *Cuyahoga Co.*	23.9	59.6	7.3	9.2
North Ridgeville city *Lorain Co.*	21.7	63.8	6.4	8.1
North Royalton city *Cuyahoga Co.*	24.8	59.8	6.9	8.5
Norwood city *Hamilton Co.*	34.0	44.5	8.1	13.5
Oregon city *Lucas Co.*	22.9	59.7	7.7	9.7
Oxford city *Butler Co.*	70.4	24.1	2.4	3.2
Painesville city *Lake Co.*	29.7	50.5	7.3	12.5
Parma city *Cuyahoga Co.*	24.7	57.0	9.7	8.7
Parma Heights city *Cuyahoga Co.*	23.6	53.1	12.3	10.9
Piqua city *Miami Co.*	22.6	55.1	8.7	13.6
Portsmouth city *Scioto Co.*	24.4	48.8	11.5	15.2
Reynoldsburg city *Franklin Co.*	23.5	58.4	5.4	12.8
Riverside city *Montgomery Co.*	24.2	55.1	7.4	13.3
Rocky River city *Cuyahoga Co.*	21.0	57.3	11.4	10.3
Sandusky city *Erie Co.*	29.0	48.9	9.1	13.0
Shaker Heights city *Cuyahoga Co.*	25.5	56.3	7.6	10.6
Sidney city *Shelby Co.*	22.1	57.8	8.0	12.0
Solon city *Cuyahoga Co.*	18.9	68.4	5.2	7.5
South Euclid city *Cuyahoga Co.*	26.1	55.2	8.0	10.8
Springfield city *Clark Co.*	29.0	47.6	9.7	13.6
Steubenville city *Jefferson Co.*	26.6	51.4	11.3	10.7
Stow city *Summit Co.*	21.8	63.5	5.5	9.3
Strongsville city *Cuyahoga Co.*	20.7	66.9	5.3	7.2
Sylvania city *Lucas Co.*	20.9	63.1	7.8	8.2
Toledo city *Lucas Co.*	33.0	45.9	7.8	13.3
Trotwood city *Montgomery Co.*	27.9	49.4	8.9	13.7
Troy city *Miami Co.*	21.0	57.6	7.2	14.1
Twinsburg city *Summit Co.*	18.8	67.2	6.8	7.2
Upper Arlington city *Franklin Co.*	20.2	63.8	7.7	8.3
Wadsworth city *Medina Co.*	17.9	65.0	8.3	8.8
Warren city *Trumbull Co.*	26.7	49.5	9.0	14.8
Westerville city *Franklin Co.*	24.6	63.2	4.7	7.5
Westlake city *Cuyahoga Co.*	21.4	61.0	9.1	8.5
Willoughby city *Lake Co.*	26.0	49.9	9.8	14.4
Wooster city *Wayne Co.*	29.3	51.5	6.7	12.5
Xenia city *Greene Co.*	23.5	56.8	7.0	12.7
Youngstown city *Mahoning Co.*	34.0	42.2	11.0	12.8
Zanesville city *Muskingum Co.*	25.5	49.1	9.6	15.8

NOTE: Data as of 2000

Employment and Building Permits Issued

Place	Unemployment Rate (%)	Total Civilian Labor Force	Single-Family Building Permits	Multi-Family Building Permits
Akron city *Summit Co.*	6.8	109,025	140	169
Alliance city *Stark Co.*	n/a	n/a	14	0
Ashland city *Ashland Co.*	n/a	n/a	16	12
Ashtabula city *Ashtabula Co.*	n/a	n/a	1	0
Athens city *Athens Co.*	n/a	n/a	69	0
Austintown CDP *Mahoning Co.*	n/a	n/a	n/a	n/a
Avon Lake city *Lorain Co.*	n/a	n/a	142	0
Barberton city *Summit Co.*	7.3	13,848	14	0
Beavercreek city *Greene Co.*	5.6	21,001	n/a	n/a
Berea city *Cuyahoga Co.*	n/a	n/a	80	0
Boardman CDP *Mahoning Co.*	n/a	n/a	n/a	n/a
Bowling Green city *Wood Co.*	5.7	16,640	n/a	n/a
Broadview Heights city *Cuyahoga Co.*	n/a	n/a	30	0
Brook Park city *Cuyahoga Co.*	7.8	10,690	8	0
Brunswick city *Medina Co.*	6.8	20,260	39	0
Canton city *Stark Co.*	8.2	36,402	54	0
Centerville city *Montgomery Co.*	n/a	n/a	58	0
Chillicothe city *Ross Co.*	n/a	n/a	20	0
Cincinnati city *Hamilton Co.*	6.4	168,910	102	356
Cleveland city *Cuyahoga Co.*	10.1	190,735	184	64
Cleveland Heights city *Cuyahoga Co.*	6.4	27,404	7	22
Columbus city *Franklin Co.*	5.7	427,028	1,008	1,698
Cuyahoga Falls city *Summit Co.*	5.7	29,268	92	0
Dayton city *Montgomery Co.*	8.4	71,217	134	0
Delaware city *Delaware Co.*	5.6	17,808	204	0
Dublin city *Franklin Co.*	4.4	20,058	131	54
East Cleveland city *Cuyahoga Co.*	10.0	9,885	5	0
Eastlake city *Lake Co.*	n/a	n/a	6	0
Elyria city *Lorain Co.*	7.8	29,800	37	54
Euclid city *Cuyahoga Co.*	8.2	25,695	12	0
Fairborn city *Greene Co.*	7.2	16,523	78	0
Fairfield city *Butler Co.*	5.3	25,459	21	0
Findlay city *Hancock Co.*	5.9	22,184	66	5
Forest Park city *Hamilton Co.*	n/a	n/a	3	0
Gahanna city *Franklin Co.*	5.0	19,347	32	10
Garfield Heights city *Cuyahoga Co.*	8.4	14,855	1	0
Green city *Summit Co.*	n/a	n/a	n/a	n/a
Grove City city *Franklin Co.*	5.4	18,198	256	20
Hamilton city *Butler Co.*	6.6	30,938	68	26
Hilliard city *Franklin Co.*	4.4	15,713	92	34
Huber Heights city *Montgomery Co.*	6.6	20,066	n/a	n/a
Hudson city *Summit Co.*	n/a	n/a	n/a	n/a
Kent city *Portage Co.*	5.6	17,552	49	4
Kettering city *Montgomery Co.*	6.0	29,529	42	6
Lakewood city *Cuyahoga Co.*	7.0	32,465	9	0
Lancaster city *Fairfield Co.*	6.4	19,272	26	26
Lebanon city *Warren Co.*	n/a	n/a	73	0
Lima city *Allen Co.*	9.2	17,446	7	7
Lorain city *Lorain Co.*	9.3	33,613	118	0
Mansfield city *Richland Co.*	7.4	23,185	5	44

Place	Unemployment Rate (%)	Total Civilian Labor Force	Single-Family Building Permits	Multi-Family Building Permits
Maple Heights city *Cuyahoga Co.*	9.3	12,896	8	0
Marion city *Marion Co.*	7.2	17,674	15	18
Marysville city *Union Co.*	n/a	n/a	n/a	n/a
Mason city *Warren Co.*	4.7	16,260	77	0
Massillon city *Stark Co.*	6.7	16,050	84	40
Mayfield Heights city *Cuyahoga Co.*	n/a	n/a	27	0
Medina city *Medina Co.*	6.6	14,344	3	0
Mentor city *Lake Co.*	6.2	30,722	63	4
Miamisburg city *Montgomery Co.*	n/a	n/a	39	0
Middletown city *Butler Co.*	7.6	26,680	33	0
Newark city *Licking Co.*	6.5	24,555	356	105
Niles city *Trumbull Co.*	n/a	n/a	5	0
North Olmsted city *Cuyahoga Co.*	6.9	18,565	9	0
North Ridgeville city *Lorain Co.*	6.3	16,451	273	16
North Royalton city *Cuyahoga Co.*	6.4	17,751	91	30
Norwood city *Hamilton Co.*	6.4	10,765	0	0
Oregon city *Lucas Co.*	n/a	n/a	52	2
Oxford city *Butler Co.*	n/a	n/a	24	14
Painesville city *Lake Co.*	n/a	n/a	95	100
Parma city *Cuyahoga Co.*	7.8	42,948	20	0
Parma Heights city *Cuyahoga Co.*	n/a	n/a	0	0
Piqua city *Miami Co.*	n/a	n/a	n/a	n/a
Portsmouth city *Scioto Co.*	n/a	n/a	0	40
Reynoldsburg city *Franklin Co.*	5.5	19,503	14	0
Riverside city *Montgomery Co.*	7.7	11,110	n/a	n/a
Rocky River city *Cuyahoga Co.*	n/a	n/a	2	0
Sandusky city *Erie Co.*	6.5	15,106	7	0
Shaker Heights city *Cuyahoga Co.*	6.1	14,952	2	0
Sidney city *Shelby Co.*	n/a	n/a	28	16
Solon city *Cuyahoga Co.*	n/a	n/a	23	2
South Euclid city *Cuyahoga Co.*	6.8	12,521	9	0
Springfield city *Clark Co.*	7.3	29,333	84	200
Steubenville city *Jefferson Co.*	n/a	n/a	5	0
Stow city *Summit Co.*	5.4	20,260	40	3
Strongsville city *Cuyahoga Co.*	6.3	25,149	77	0
Sylvania city *Lucas Co.*	n/a	n/a	n/a	n/a
Toledo city *Lucas Co.*	8.5	146,326	82	185
Trotwood city *Montgomery Co.*	8.8	12,172	3	0
Troy city *Miami Co.*	n/a	n/a	n/a	n/a
Twinsburg city *Summit Co.*	n/a	n/a	19	0
Upper Arlington city *Franklin Co.*	4.7	16,980	41	0
Wadsworth city *Medina Co.*	n/a	n/a	50	144
Warren city *Trumbull Co.*	9.1	19,920	8	0
Westerville city *Franklin Co.*	4.8	20,305	65	53
Westlake city *Cuyahoga Co.*	6.5	16,828	72	0
Willoughby city *Lake Co.*	n/a	n/a	94	27
Wooster city *Wayne Co.*	5.7	14,004	53	76
Xenia city *Greene Co.*	7.8	11,490	n/a	n/a
Youngstown city *Mahoning Co.*	8.5	32,141	9	0
Zanesville city *Muskingum Co.*	8.5	10,382	55	8

NOTE: Unemployment Rate and Civilian Labor Force as of April 2008; Building permit data covers 2007; n/a not available.

Employment by Occupation

Place	Sales	Prof.	Mgmt	Services	Production	Constr.
Akron city *Summit Co.*	28.3	17.0	9.0	18.3	19.6	7.7
Alliance city *Stark Co.*	25.5	13.6	7.2	17.7	27.9	7.4
Ashland city *Ashland Co.*	24.8	17.9	9.6	15.5	24.9	6.8
Ashtabula city *Ashtabula Co.*	23.7	13.1	6.6	19.4	28.5	8.4
Athens city *Athens Co.*	24.8	37.4	8.2	22.5	4.7	2.3
Austintown CDP *Mahoning Co.*	29.4	16.8	8.1	15.3	22.2	8.1
Avon Lake city *Lorain Co.*	27.1	25.5	20.6	9.4	10.2	7.1
Barberton city *Summit Co.*	27.4	12.1	8.0	17.5	24.1	10.7
Beavercreek city *Greene Co.*	25.4	32.3	18.9	8.9	9.0	5.4
Berea city *Cuyahoga Co.*	33.5	21.4	12.1	13.3	12.8	6.7
Boardman CDP *Mahoning Co.*	30.5	20.0	14.0	14.5	14.0	7.0
Bowling Green city *Wood Co.*	24.6	26.1	9.9	21.2	14.2	3.7
Broadview Heights city *Cuyahoga Co.*	28.3	25.6	19.6	9.6	11.1	5.7
Brook Park city *Cuyahoga Co.*	30.1	12.3	9.7	16.0	20.6	11.3
Brunswick city *Medina Co.*	28.1	18.0	13.0	12.6	17.0	11.1
Canton city *Stark Co.*	26.3	13.1	8.4	20.0	24.1	7.9
Centerville city *Montgomery Co.*	28.3	32.8	18.8	9.7	6.6	3.9
Chillicothe city *Ross Co.*	24.7	21.5	9.3	17.3	21.1	6.1
Cincinnati city *Hamilton Co.*	26.3	23.2	12.6	17.9	13.5	6.4
Cleveland city *Cuyahoga Co.*	26.7	14.3	8.2	20.9	22.3	7.5
Cleveland Heights city *Cuyahoga Co.*	22.6	38.2	15.3	12.0	8.6	3.3
Columbus city *Franklin Co.*	30.1	21.5	13.9	15.2	12.7	6.5
Cuyahoga Falls city *Summit Co.*	30.6	21.2	13.3	13.5	13.9	7.5
Dayton city *Montgomery Co.*	25.3	17.1	8.6	21.1	20.0	7.8
Delaware city *Delaware Co.*	28.0	22.3	15.1	13.1	14.7	6.5
Dublin city *Franklin Co.*	28.3	29.9	29.9	6.5	3.3	2.0
East Cleveland city *Cuyahoga Co.*	27.2	13.8	6.6	27.4	19.0	6.0
Eastlake city *Lake Co.*	28.7	15.2	8.6	14.4	23.0	10.2
Elyria city *Lorain Co.*	24.9	15.7	8.3	17.2	24.3	9.4
Euclid city *Cuyahoga Co.*	30.8	18.7	11.9	15.2	16.5	6.8
Fairborn city *Greene Co.*	27.4	20.1	10.7	18.9	13.8	9.0
Fairfield city *Butler Co.*	30.6	23.5	15.9	10.4	12.4	7.1
Findlay city *Hancock Co.*	22.7	17.6	12.5	15.0	24.0	8.0
Forest Park city *Hamilton Co.*	30.6	21.8	12.5	14.3	16.6	4.2
Gahanna city *Franklin Co.*	29.7	25.7	20.7	10.1	8.1	5.7
Garfield Heights city *Cuyahoga Co.*	34.6	14.2	9.7	15.1	18.3	8.0
Green city *Summit Co.*	27.4	20.5	14.7	12.6	15.4	9.2
Grove City city *Franklin Co.*	32.6	18.2	15.8	13.1	11.6	8.6
Hamilton city *Butler Co.*	28.0	13.7	8.8	16.7	21.8	10.8
Hilliard city *Franklin Co.*	27.9	27.3	19.4	10.9	8.4	6.1
Huber Heights city *Montgomery Co.*	27.5	17.8	12.3	13.9	19.9	8.5
Hudson city *Summit Co.*	27.1	28.9	29.8	7.2	4.4	2.5
Kent city *Portage Co.*	29.0	22.9	9.3	20.9	13.1	4.8
Kettering city *Montgomery Co.*	28.8	24.2	15.3	12.0	13.0	6.5
Lakewood city *Cuyahoga Co.*	28.0	25.1	15.9	13.8	10.4	6.7
Lancaster city *Fairfield Co.*	29.2	14.7	9.1	17.1	18.5	11.4
Lebanon city *Warren Co.*	27.8	20.1	13.5	12.1	17.6	8.9
Lima city *Allen Co.*	22.0	12.0	6.4	20.8	29.9	8.5
Lorain city *Lorain Co.*	25.7	13.0	7.4	16.7	27.0	9.6
Mansfield city *Richland Co.*	23.7	15.3	7.9	19.1	25.8	8.2

Place	Sales	Prof.	Mgmt	Services	Production	Constr.
Maple Heights city *Cuyahoga Co.*	30.6	15.5	9.7	14.8	21.9	7.2
Marion city *Marion Co.*	25.9	11.9	7.3	17.6	28.9	8.0
Marysville city *Union Co.*	28.1	17.0	10.9	12.4	24.3	7.0
Mason city *Warren Co.*	29.7	23.2	20.8	9.5	11.7	5.0
Massillon city *Stark Co.*	26.1	13.9	8.3	16.5	27.1	7.9
Mayfield Heights city *Cuyahoga Co.*	31.5	23.5	14.5	14.0	9.3	7.1
Medina city *Medina Co.*	29.8	21.2	15.0	12.1	14.3	7.4
Mentor city *Lake Co.*	28.7	20.8	15.3	11.1	16.9	7.0
Miamisburg city *Montgomery Co.*	30.2	19.3	11.9	13.4	16.7	8.5
Middletown city *Butler Co.*	25.5	16.0	8.3	16.3	24.2	9.6
Newark city *Licking Co.*	28.3	14.1	9.6	18.0	20.9	9.0
Niles city *Trumbull Co.*	26.7	13.9	7.7	17.9	25.9	7.8
North Olmsted city *Cuyahoga Co.*	30.6	21.6	16.1	12.4	11.8	7.3
North Ridgeville city *Lorain Co.*	29.8	16.2	11.3	12.8	18.1	11.4
North Royalton city *Cuyahoga Co.*	30.1	19.9	17.2	11.6	12.7	8.4
Norwood city *Hamilton Co.*	28.4	14.6	9.2	17.3	20.3	10.2
Oregon city *Lucas Co.*	25.2	17.5	11.2	13.3	21.4	11.0
Oxford city *Butler Co.*	24.1	31.3	8.3	25.6	7.0	3.7
Painesville city *Lake Co.*	25.7	13.0	7.2	17.8	24.5	9.2
Parma city *Cuyahoga Co.*	31.9	17.7	12.3	14.2	15.3	8.6
Parma Heights city *Cuyahoga Co.*	35.0	18.3	12.2	12.2	14.3	7.9
Piqua city *Miami Co.*	26.4	10.0	9.2	15.1	30.6	8.3
Portsmouth city *Scioto Co.*	24.3	20.3	8.8	21.6	15.3	8.9
Reynoldsburg city *Franklin Co.*	31.7	20.1	15.9	13.8	11.8	6.6
Riverside city *Montgomery Co.*	27.5	15.2	9.1	15.8	21.6	10.5
Rocky River city *Cuyahoga Co.*	32.2	27.3	21.7	9.6	5.4	3.8
Sandusky city *Erie Co.*	24.9	12.0	7.0	21.1	27.1	7.8
Shaker Heights city *Cuyahoga Co.*	21.7	42.1	21.2	7.7	5.5	1.7
Sidney city *Shelby Co.*	19.2	13.8	10.9	14.5	33.3	8.1
Solon city *Cuyahoga Co.*	28.5	30.4	22.8	7.9	6.4	3.9
South Euclid city *Cuyahoga Co.*	31.4	27.2	13.1	12.7	10.4	5.1
Springfield city *Clark Co.*	25.2	16.0	8.5	17.9	24.1	8.1
Steubenville city *Jefferson Co.*	27.2	21.5	9.4	19.9	14.6	7.1
Stow city *Summit Co.*	27.2	26.5	15.8	11.9	12.5	6.1
Strongsville city *Cuyahoga Co.*	30.8	22.4	19.9	10.1	10.4	6.3
Sylvania city *Lucas Co.*	26.9	30.8	15.7	10.9	9.8	5.6
Toledo city *Lucas Co.*	26.7	16.7	9.0	17.9	21.3	8.3
Trotwood city *Montgomery Co.*	27.2	15.5	9.2	15.8	25.1	7.3
Troy city *Miami Co.*	24.7	18.5	12.7	13.5	25.1	5.1
Twinsburg city *Summit Co.*	28.9	23.0	21.1	10.4	10.6	6.0
Upper Arlington city *Franklin Co.*	24.7	39.9	24.2	6.2	2.9	2.0
Wadsworth city *Medina Co.*	25.7	19.7	15.3	14.2	15.6	9.3
Warren city *Trumbull Co.*	23.3	13.4	7.8	19.0	28.1	8.3
Westerville city *Franklin Co.*	29.8	26.0	21.6	10.8	7.0	4.7
Westlake city *Cuyahoga Co.*	27.8	26.4	26.5	8.8	5.8	4.7
Willoughby city *Lake Co.*	28.1	19.7	15.0	13.0	16.1	7.9
Wooster city *Wayne Co.*	25.5	21.4	11.4	14.6	21.2	5.6
Xenia city *Greene Co.*	26.0	16.3	9.0	17.9	20.5	10.3
Youngstown city *Mahoning Co.*	25.5	13.1	5.7	24.1	24.2	7.2
Zanesville city *Muskingum Co.*	25.4	17.4	5.4	18.2	25.7	7.5

NOTE: Data as of 2000

Educational Attainment

Place	Percent of Population 25 Years and Over with: High School Diploma including Equivalency	Bachelor's Degree or Higher	Masters's Degree or Higher
Akron city *Summit Co.*	80.2	18.4	6.3
Alliance city *Stark Co.*	79.8	13.7	5.3
Ashland city *Ashland Co.*	83.6	19.7	6.9
Ashtabula city *Ashtabula Co.*	77.7	10.4	3.1
Athens city *Athens Co.*	93.2	61.5	36.0
Austintown CDP *Mahoning Co.*	85.3	15.9	4.3
Avon Lake city *Lorain Co.*	94.8	42.8	15.9
Barberton city *Summit Co.*	79.2	10.7	3.4
Beavercreek city *Greene Co.*	92.7	43.9	21.3
Berea city *Cuyahoga Co.*	89.0	29.0	9.7
Boardman CDP *Mahoning Co.*	88.9	24.4	7.7
Bowling Green city *Wood Co.*	90.8	43.6	21.8
Broadview Heights city *Cuyahoga Co.*	90.4	36.9	13.1
Brook Park city *Cuyahoga Co.*	80.7	9.8	2.5
Brunswick city *Medina Co.*	87.3	19.4	4.2
Canton city *Stark Co.*	75.3	12.2	4.1
Centerville city *Montgomery Co.*	95.5	45.8	17.9
Chillicothe city *Ross Co.*	77.6	17.6	7.1
Cincinnati city *Hamilton Co.*	77.0	27.0	10.4
Cleveland city *Cuyahoga Co.*	69.1	11.7	3.9
Cleveland Heights city *Cuyahoga Co.*	91.5	49.8	25.2
Columbus city *Franklin Co.*	84.7	30.1	9.4
Cuyahoga Falls city *Summit Co.*	90.9	25.7	7.7
Dayton city *Montgomery Co.*	75.6	14.9	5.1
Delaware city *Delaware Co.*	88.3	27.0	8.1
Dublin city *Franklin Co.*	97.2	63.6	22.2
East Cleveland city *Cuyahoga Co.*	69.2	8.8	3.7
Eastlake city *Lake Co.*	82.8	12.6	3.4
Elyria city *Lorain Co.*	82.1	13.4	4.3
Euclid city *Cuyahoga Co.*	82.0	19.7	5.9
Fairborn city *Greene Co.*	84.3	22.8	9.2
Fairfield city *Butler Co.*	89.2	27.7	8.3
Findlay city *Hancock Co.*	87.5	23.9	8.0
Forest Park city *Hamilton Co.*	88.5	26.5	7.4
Gahanna city *Franklin Co.*	93.7	41.3	14.1
Garfield Heights city *Cuyahoga Co.*	80.1	11.9	3.3
Green city *Summit Co.*	89.0	26.4	7.6
Grove City city *Franklin Co.*	89.3	23.3	5.7
Hamilton city *Butler Co.*	73.7	12.5	3.8
Hilliard city *Franklin Co.*	92.5	45.9	14.4
Huber Heights city *Montgomery Co.*	88.3	19.2	6.8
Hudson city *Summit Co.*	97.3	66.5	26.0
Kent city *Portage Co.*	91.7	37.7	16.3
Kettering city *Montgomery Co.*	91.0	31.1	11.3
Lakewood city *Cuyahoga Co.*	88.7	35.6	11.9
Lancaster city *Fairfield Co.*	83.5	13.6	4.4
Lebanon city *Warren Co.*	86.2	25.6	6.3
Lima city *Allen Co.*	76.0	9.9	3.2
Lorain city *Lorain Co.*	74.5	10.1	3.5
Mansfield city *Richland Co.*	78.2	13.7	4.7

Place	Percent of Population 25 Years and Over with: High School Diploma including Equivalency	Bachelor's Degree or Higher	Masters's Degree or Higher
Maple Heights city *Cuyahoga Co.*	82.2	12.9	3.0
Marion city *Marion Co.*	76.1	9.2	3.0
Marysville city *Union Co.*	84.1	17.6	3.3
Mason city *Warren Co.*	93.9	41.4	12.8
Massillon city *Stark Co.*	80.7	12.4	3.7
Mayfield Heights city *Cuyahoga Co.*	85.8	27.7	10.7
Medina city *Medina Co.*	90.9	33.2	8.4
Mentor city *Lake Co.*	89.3	27.8	9.0
Miamisburg city *Montgomery Co.*	83.5	19.3	5.5
Middletown city *Butler Co.*	77.4	13.4	5.0
Newark city *Licking Co.*	81.0	15.1	4.7
Niles city *Trumbull Co.*	82.9	11.7	2.8
North Olmsted city *Cuyahoga Co.*	90.3	27.3	9.3
North Ridgeville city *Lorain Co.*	85.9	16.2	4.2
North Royalton city *Cuyahoga Co.*	88.0	29.4	8.5
Norwood city *Hamilton Co.*	70.8	14.1	3.6
Oregon city *Lucas Co.*	85.0	15.9	5.6
Oxford city *Butler Co.*	90.1	54.4	29.5
Painesville city *Lake Co.*	74.0	12.5	4.3
Parma city *Cuyahoga Co.*	83.4	17.9	5.2
Parma Heights city *Cuyahoga Co.*	82.7	18.7	5.8
Piqua city *Miami Co.*	75.2	10.4	3.4
Portsmouth city *Scioto Co.*	74.1	12.5	5.3
Reynoldsburg city *Franklin Co.*	90.5	27.4	7.8
Riverside city *Montgomery Co.*	78.8	15.3	5.3
Rocky River city *Cuyahoga Co.*	93.3	46.6	17.9
Sandusky city *Erie Co.*	79.6	11.2	3.3
Shaker Heights city *Cuyahoga Co.*	94.6	61.6	35.5
Sidney city *Shelby Co.*	78.4	13.8	4.3
Solon city *Cuyahoga Co.*	94.6	50.7	22.1
South Euclid city *Cuyahoga Co.*	90.0	36.6	13.0
Springfield city *Clark Co.*	77.0	13.0	4.8
Steubenville city *Jefferson Co.*	79.6	18.1	7.4
Stow city *Summit Co.*	93.2	36.8	12.6
Strongsville city *Cuyahoga Co.*	93.1	37.5	13.1
Sylvania city *Lucas Co.*	94.1	43.5	15.4
Toledo city *Lucas Co.*	80.1	17.2	5.6
Trotwood city *Montgomery Co.*	78.2	15.2	6.6
Troy city *Miami Co.*	81.4	17.2	5.8
Twinsburg city *Summit Co.*	92.4	38.7	12.4
Upper Arlington city *Franklin Co.*	97.9	67.5	29.8
Wadsworth city *Medina Co.*	88.4	27.2	7.1
Warren city *Trumbull Co.*	77.5	11.1	3.4
Westerville city *Franklin Co.*	94.7	45.2	13.9
Westlake city *Cuyahoga Co.*	92.1	45.4	17.9
Willoughby city *Lake Co.*	87.8	24.0	6.4
Wooster city *Wayne Co.*	84.7	27.6	10.5
Xenia city *Greene Co.*	81.5	15.1	5.5
Youngstown city *Mahoning Co.*	73.1	9.9	2.9
Zanesville city *Muskingum Co.*	74.2	11.8	4.5

NOTE: Data as of 2007

Income and Poverty

Place	Average Household Income ($)	Median Household Income ($)	Per Capita Income ($)	Households w/$100,000+ Income (%)	Poverty Rate[1] (%)
Akron city *Summit Co.*	46,437	35,993	19,918	7.4	17.5
Alliance city *Stark Co.*	42,642	34,031	16,959	6.0	18.0
Ashland city *Ashland Co.*	47,057	37,675	19,082	7.8	10.5
Ashtabula city *Ashtabula Co.*	38,769	30,843	16,052	4.2	21.4
Athens city *Athens Co.*	37,188	18,885	12,769	8.5	51.9
Austintown CDP *Mahoning Co.*	50,524	43,078	22,224	8.6	8.8
Avon Lake city *Lorain Co.*	98,391	74,586	37,319	33.2	2.3
Barberton city *Summit Co.*	47,606	36,877	20,269	7.4	13.3
Beavercreek city *Greene Co.*	94,104	80,790	36,713	35.2	2.4
Berea city *Cuyahoga Co.*	61,591	50,169	24,192	15.4	5.5
Boardman CDP *Mahoning Co.*	58,516	46,349	25,832	12.6	5.2
Bowling Green city *Wood Co.*	48,234	34,859	18,422	10.0	25.3
Broadview Heights city *Cuyahoga Co.*	90,081	66,754	36,880	29.3	3.2
Brook Park city *Cuyahoga Co.*	59,007	51,160	23,618	11.7	4.6
Brunswick city *Medina Co.*	69,730	63,235	25,610	18.4	4.6
Canton city *Stark Co.*	41,511	31,767	17,416	6.1	19.2
Centerville city *Montgomery Co.*	78,932	63,032	35,532	26.3	4.1
Chillicothe city *Ross Co.*	48,934	37,491	22,129	8.6	12.4
Cincinnati city *Hamilton Co.*	50,597	33,981	23,691	10.8	21.9
Cleveland city *Cuyahoga Co.*	39,282	29,186	16,197	5.5	26.3
Cleveland Heights city *Cuyahoga Co.*	70,254	51,388	30,376	18.9	10.6
Columbus city *Franklin Co.*	55,908	44,253	24,196	12.1	14.8
Cuyahoga Falls city *Summit Co.*	56,409	47,003	25,398	11.3	6.1
Dayton city *Montgomery Co.*	41,353	31,187	17,581	6.6	23.0
Delaware city *Delaware Co.*	60,250	51,475	23,696	13.7	7.3
Dublin city *Franklin Co.*	130,187	102,571	47,352	51.4	2.7
East Cleveland city *Cuyahoga Co.*	32,341	22,344	13,834	3.7	32.0
Eastlake city *Lake Co.*	55,501	47,332	22,981	10.2	5.0
Elyria city *Lorain Co.*	52,262	42,359	21,769	9.6	11.7
Euclid city *Cuyahoga Co.*	46,056	37,741	21,784	6.7	9.7
Fairborn city *Greene Co.*	50,524	41,419	22,488	9.9	14.1
Fairfield city *Butler Co.*	66,476	55,571	27,458	16.3	4.2
Findlay city *Hancock Co.*	58,227	44,944	24,765	12.9	9.1
Forest Park city *Hamilton Co.*	63,967	55,235	25,555	14.4	6.0
Gahanna city *Franklin Co.*	95,138	77,820	35,537	35.2	3.7
Garfield Heights city *Cuyahoga Co.*	51,739	43,950	21,615	7.9	8.5
Green city *Summit Co.*	79,065	63,492	30,902	24.6	5.0
Grove City city *Franklin Co.*	73,664	64,320	28,192	22.8	4.6
Hamilton city *Butler Co.*	48,623	39,626	20,121	7.6	13.4
Hilliard city *Franklin Co.*	100,215	86,024	35,419	39.2	2.2
Huber Heights city *Montgomery Co.*	62,555	53,628	24,296	13.5	5.9
Hudson city *Summit Co.*	146,434	110,967	48,510	55.7	1.7
Kent city *Portage Co.*	47,363	34,446	17,827	11.0	25.2
Kettering city *Montgomery Co.*	66,391	50,127	30,380	15.3	4.6
Lakewood city *Cuyahoga Co.*	57,436	45,231	27,818	12.8	8.9
Lancaster city *Fairfield Co.*	47,805	37,438	20,764	7.0	10.6
Lebanon city *Warren Co.*	66,371	54,867	24,578	18.9	6.4
Lima city *Allen Co.*	38,786	29,993	15,844	4.7	22.7
Lorain city *Lorain Co.*	47,261	37,829	18,911	8.2	17.1
Mansfield city *Richland Co.*	45,263	33,636	19,843	7.7	16.3

Place	Average Household Income ($)	Median Household Income ($)	Per Capita Income ($)	Households w/$100,000+ Income (%)	Poverty Rate[1] (%)
Maple Heights city *Cuyahoga Co.*	49,870	43,544	20,436	6.8	5.9
Marion city *Marion Co.*	45,990	37,729	18,410	6.6	13.8
Marysville city *Union Co.*	60,003	54,486	21,897	13.8	5.7
Mason city *Warren Co.*	103,096	81,913	36,701	38.4	2.8
Massillon city *Stark Co.*	48,896	37,941	20,402	8.3	10.7
Mayfield Heights city *Cuyahoga Co.*	54,209	41,932	28,194	10.1	6.3
Medina city *Medina Co.*	67,953	58,201	26,219	20.7	5.7
Mentor city *Lake Co.*	73,546	63,593	28,662	22.2	2.7
Miamisburg city *Montgomery Co.*	69,490	57,998	27,260	20.2	6.1
Middletown city *Butler Co.*	51,206	40,002	22,008	9.7	12.6
Newark city *Licking Co.*	49,458	39,502	21,170	8.9	13.0
Niles city *Trumbull Co.*	51,678	40,000	22,877	8.7	9.6
North Olmsted city *Cuyahoga Co.*	68,884	58,903	28,362	19.5	4.1
North Ridgeville city *Lorain Co.*	69,967	60,993	27,024	19.1	3.2
North Royalton city *Cuyahoga Co.*	79,487	66,000	32,094	26.3	2.3
Norwood city *Hamilton Co.*	48,394	38,134	21,414	8.7	12.9
Oregon city *Lucas Co.*	63,263	52,519	25,814	17.1	4.8
Oxford city *Butler Co.*	48,785	28,855	14,876	13.7	43.7
Painesville city *Lake Co.*	45,088	38,216	17,492	6.0	16.0
Parma city *Cuyahoga Co.*	57,231	48,791	24,252	11.5	4.9
Parma Heights city *Cuyahoga Co.*	49,902	41,282	23,160	8.6	7.6
Piqua city *Miami Co.*	50,931	39,673	21,247	8.2	12.2
Portsmouth city *Scioto Co.*	38,196	26,008	17,324	5.6	23.6
Reynoldsburg city *Franklin Co.*	67,200	58,484	27,363	18.4	5.5
Riverside city *Montgomery Co.*	49,576	40,604	21,010	8.2	10.1
Rocky River city *Cuyahoga Co.*	81,903	57,585	39,534	24.1	2.3
Sandusky city *Erie Co.*	45,236	34,128	20,027	6.4	15.3
Shaker Heights city *Cuyahoga Co.*	107,193	70,809	45,463	34.1	6.9
Sidney city *Shelby Co.*	53,733	43,033	21,995	10.0	11.5
Solon city *Cuyahoga Co.*	121,448	92,856	42,375	45.7	2.5
South Euclid city *Cuyahoga Co.*	62,468	54,090	25,943	14.9	4.5
Springfield city *Clark Co.*	45,127	35,017	18,884	7.2	16.9
Steubenville city *Jefferson Co.*	46,829	32,034	21,634	9.9	20.4
Stow city *Summit Co.*	76,185	65,252	29,949	23.2	4.0
Strongsville city *Cuyahoga Co.*	94,972	78,837	35,920	35.4	2.2
Sylvania city *Lucas Co.*	81,661	65,265	32,107	28.3	4.2
Toledo city *Lucas Co.*	46,545	36,695	19,811	8.1	17.9
Trotwood city *Montgomery Co.*	47,529	37,758	20,150	8.8	15.3
Troy city *Miami Co.*	53,316	43,124	22,658	9.7	8.2
Twinsburg city *Summit Co.*	83,298	71,863	33,426	30.1	2.1
Upper Arlington city *Franklin Co.*	115,017	85,394	48,208	40.4	2.4
Wadsworth city *Medina Co.*	67,312	56,630	27,280	18.3	5.4
Warren city *Trumbull Co.*	41,914	32,642	17,990	5.9	19.4
Westerville city *Franklin Co.*	99,164	83,225	36,517	39.8	3.5
Westlake city *Cuyahoga Co.*	107,174	73,817	45,017	33.7	2.5
Willoughby city *Lake Co.*	58,017	47,342	27,608	12.6	5.8
Wooster city *Wayne Co.*	56,293	40,724	23,881	11.4	10.4
Xenia city *Greene Co.*	49,221	43,113	20,423	7.6	11.6
Youngstown city *Mahoning Co.*	35,908	27,438	14,669	4.2	24.8
Zanesville city *Muskingum Co.*	39,943	30,041	16,966	4.9	22.4

NOTE: Data as of 2007 except for Poverty Rate which is from 2000; (1) Percentage of population with income below the poverty level

Taxes

Place	Total City Taxes Per Capita ($)	City Property Taxes Per Capita ($)
Akron city *Summit Co.*	776	144
Alliance city *Stark Co.*	430	59
Ashland city *Ashland Co.*	n/a	n/a
Ashtabula city *Ashtabula Co.*	n/a	n/a
Athens city *Athens Co.*	473	33
Austintown CDP *Mahoning Co.*	n/a	n/a
Avon Lake city *Lorain Co.*	690	244
Barberton city *Summit Co.*	426	50
Beavercreek city *Greene Co.*	n/a	n/a
Berea city *Cuyahoga Co.*	906	324
Boardman CDP *Mahoning Co.*	n/a	n/a
Bowling Green city *Wood Co.*	529	67
Broadview Heights city *Cuyahoga Co.*	n/a	n/a
Brook Park city *Cuyahoga Co.*	1,272	132
Brunswick city *Medina Co.*	n/a	n/a
Canton city *Stark Co.*	589	42
Centerville city *Montgomery Co.*	n/a	n/a
Chillicothe city *Ross Co.*	585	66
Cincinnati city *Hamilton Co.*	1,221	204
Cleveland city *Cuyahoga Co.*	931	149
Cleveland Heights city *Cuyahoga Co.*	709	223
Columbus city *Franklin Co.*	764	55
Cuyahoga Falls city *Summit Co.*	576	200
Dayton city *Montgomery Co.*	877	143
Delaware city *Delaware Co.*	n/a	n/a
Dublin city *Franklin Co.*	1,925	198
East Cleveland city *Cuyahoga Co.*	n/a	n/a
Eastlake city *Lake Co.*	588	239
Elyria city *Lorain Co.*	485	67
Euclid city *Cuyahoga Co.*	578	126
Fairborn city *Greene Co.*	n/a	n/a
Fairfield city *Butler Co.*	642	125
Findlay city *Hancock Co.*	n/a	n/a
Forest Park city *Hamilton Co.*	618	253
Gahanna city *Franklin Co.*	n/a	n/a
Garfield Heights city *Cuyahoga Co.*	660	307
Green city *Summit Co.*	n/a	n/a
Grove City city *Franklin Co.*	n/a	n/a
Hamilton city *Butler Co.*	519	133
Hilliard city *Franklin Co.*	629	44
Huber Heights city *Montgomery Co.*	421	87
Hudson city *Summit Co.*	753	189
Kent city *Portage Co.*	n/a	n/a
Kettering city *Montgomery Co.*	701	161
Lakewood city *Cuyahoga Co.*	618	268
Lancaster city *Fairfield Co.*	459	63
Lebanon city *Warren Co.*	465	150
Lima city *Allen Co.*	485	34
Lorain city *Lorain Co.*	359	63
Mansfield city *Richland Co.*	563	66

Place	Total City Taxes Per Capita ($)	City Property Taxes Per Capita ($)
Maple Heights city *Cuyahoga Co.*	548	240
Marion city *Marion Co.*	399	43
Marysville city *Union Co.*	n/a	n/a
Mason city *Warren Co.*	n/a	n/a
Massillon city *Stark Co.*	483	65
Mayfield Heights city *Cuyahoga Co.*	n/a	n/a
Medina city *Medina Co.*	n/a	n/a
Mentor city *Lake Co.*	679	107
Miamisburg city *Montgomery Co.*	n/a	n/a
Middletown city *Butler Co.*	474	116
Newark city *Licking Co.*	485	55
Niles city *Trumbull Co.*	n/a	n/a
North Olmsted city *Cuyahoga Co.*	n/a	n/a
North Ridgeville city *Lorain Co.*	n/a	n/a
North Royalton city *Cuyahoga Co.*	471	149
Norwood city *Hamilton Co.*	n/a	n/a
Oregon city *Lucas Co.*	n/a	n/a
Oxford city *Butler Co.*	n/a	n/a
Painesville city *Lake Co.*	482	32
Parma city *Cuyahoga Co.*	540	88
Parma Heights city *Cuyahoga Co.*	n/a	n/a
Piqua city *Miami Co.*	540	64
Portsmouth city *Scioto Co.*	n/a	n/a
Reynoldsburg city *Franklin Co.*	n/a	n/a
Riverside city *Montgomery Co.*	n/a	n/a
Rocky River city *Cuyahoga Co.*	n/a	n/a
Sandusky city *Erie Co.*	575	85
Shaker Heights city *Cuyahoga Co.*	1,225	269
Sidney city *Shelby Co.*	n/a	n/a
Solon city *Cuyahoga Co.*	n/a	n/a
South Euclid city *Cuyahoga Co.*	522	232
Springfield city *Clark Co.*	531	48
Steubenville city *Jefferson Co.*	n/a	n/a
Stow city *Summit Co.*	557	188
Strongsville city *Cuyahoga Co.*	n/a	n/a
Sylvania city *Lucas Co.*	n/a	n/a
Toledo city *Lucas Co.*	616	58
Trotwood city *Montgomery Co.*	n/a	n/a
Troy city *Miami Co.*	662	86
Twinsburg city *Summit Co.*	1,216	71
Upper Arlington city *Franklin Co.*	786	249
Wadsworth city *Medina Co.*	471	111
Warren city *Trumbull Co.*	500	33
Westerville city *Franklin Co.*	902	299
Westlake city *Cuyahoga Co.*	1,026	398
Willoughby city *Lake Co.*	n/a	n/a
Wooster city *Wayne Co.*	481	88
Xenia city *Greene Co.*	480	74
Youngstown city *Mahoning Co.*	561	25
Zanesville city *Muskingum Co.*	n/a	n/a

NOTE: Data as of 2006.

Housing

Place	Homeownership Rate (%)	Median Home Value ($)	Median Age of Housing (years)	Median Rent ($/month)
Akron city *Summit Co.*	59.6	93,823	50	413
Alliance city *Stark Co.*	60.7	85,762	53	337
Ashland city *Ashland Co.*	64.6	113,586	45	370
Ashtabula city *Ashtabula Co.*	58.4	90,217	52	369
Athens city *Athens Co.*	30.0	148,064	37	423
Austintown CDP *Mahoning Co.*	66.2	99,374	34	422
Avon Lake city *Lorain Co.*	86.5	209,663	29	572
Barberton city *Summit Co.*	65.4	96,029	49	380
Beavercreek city *Greene Co.*	83.5	169,628	27	705
Berea city *Cuyahoga Co.*	71.1	145,441	42	508
Boardman CDP *Mahoning Co.*	71.1	113,512	36	423
Bowling Green city *Wood Co.*	42.9	152,733	28	434
Broadview Heights city *Cuyahoga Co.*	76.3	213,950	25	637
Brook Park city *Cuyahoga Co.*	83.7	137,180	38	565
Brunswick city *Medina Co.*	80.4	165,534	25	536
Canton city *Stark Co.*	59.9	80,056	55	352
Centerville city *Montgomery Co.*	74.6	163,878	24	556
Chillicothe city *Ross Co.*	62.3	98,544	50	345
Cincinnati city *Hamilton Co.*	39.3	115,304	52	392
Cleveland city *Cuyahoga Co.*	48.4	88,857	60	379
Cleveland Heights city *Cuyahoga Co.*	62.8	136,892	60+	580
Columbus city *Franklin Co.*	49.8	124,172	30	490
Cuyahoga Falls city *Summit Co.*	65.3	126,973	43	527
Dayton city *Montgomery Co.*	53.3	79,344	51	359
Delaware city *Delaware Co.*	61.5	156,833	25	474
Dublin city *Franklin Co.*	75.4	290,601	9	839
East Cleveland city *Cuyahoga Co.*	35.1	81,238	56	397
Eastlake city *Lake Co.*	77.4	137,043	35	538
Elyria city *Lorain Co.*	64.7	114,661	38	430
Euclid city *Cuyahoga Co.*	58.5	111,295	45	483
Fairborn city *Greene Co.*	51.1	108,463	34	487
Fairfield city *Butler Co.*	65.9	145,294	23	593
Findlay city *Hancock Co.*	65.0	119,549	39	416
Forest Park city *Hamilton Co.*	62.2	119,252	29	613
Gahanna city *Franklin Co.*	77.8	184,388	18	582
Garfield Heights city *Cuyahoga Co.*	79.6	109,693	47	483
Green city *Summit Co.*	80.3	170,777	26	544
Grove City city *Franklin Co.*	74.4	151,526	23	517
Hamilton city *Butler Co.*	60.9	104,201	47	402
Hilliard city *Franklin Co.*	73.9	201,545	9	653
Huber Heights city *Montgomery Co.*	72.4	111,407	29	515
Hudson city *Summit Co.*	90.3	277,042	20	1,131
Kent city *Portage Co.*	38.2	134,160	35	458
Kettering city *Montgomery Co.*	66.8	129,754	41	494
Lakewood city *Cuyahoga Co.*	45.4	144,689	60+	492
Lancaster city *Fairfield Co.*	59.8	114,542	43	414
Lebanon city *Warren Co.*	60.5	160,254	22	495
Lima city *Allen Co.*	57.4	66,014	51	344
Lorain city *Lorain Co.*	61.2	106,757	43	408
Mansfield city *Richland Co.*	58.1	88,608	47	347

Place	Homeownership Rate (%)	Median Home Value ($)	Median Age of Housing (years)	Median Rent ($/month)
Maple Heights city *Cuyahoga Co.*	83.6	102,954	45	462
Marion city *Marion Co.*	63.7	81,792	52	371
Marysville city *Union Co.*	65.2	151,169	20	471
Mason city *Warren Co.*	86.1	196,220	12	527
Massillon city *Stark Co.*	69.4	99,514	50	356
Mayfield Heights city *Cuyahoga Co.*	50.9	153,376	36	624
Medina city *Medina Co.*	68.0	170,125	23	525
Mentor city *Lake Co.*	87.7	177,736	28	614
Miamisburg city *Montgomery Co.*	72.6	141,497	33	419
Middletown city *Butler Co.*	59.8	110,892	41	414
Newark city *Licking Co.*	57.9	106,870	42	394
Niles city *Trumbull Co.*	63.6	95,139	41	419
North Olmsted city *Cuyahoga Co.*	79.1	168,664	34	577
North Ridgeville city *Lorain Co.*	88.7	157,992	27	463
North Royalton city *Cuyahoga Co.*	74.2	209,476	21	587
Norwood city *Hamilton Co.*	51.5	112,378	60+	387
Oregon city *Lucas Co.*	74.1	147,922	34	404
Oxford city *Butler Co.*	34.0	161,994	27	443
Painesville city *Lake Co.*	52.4	114,486	46	462
Parma city *Cuyahoga Co.*	77.3	136,924	42	534
Parma Heights city *Cuyahoga Co.*	59.1	137,001	40	526
Piqua city *Miami Co.*	63.5	102,765	49	415
Portsmouth city *Scioto Co.*	53.8	67,146	58	302
Reynoldsburg city *Franklin Co.*	65.9	149,405	22	559
Riverside city *Montgomery Co.*	65.7	98,898	41	417
Rocky River city *Cuyahoga Co.*	71.6	215,385	41	614
Sandusky city *Erie Co.*	56.8	89,679	50	387
Shaker Heights city *Cuyahoga Co.*	65.2	221,489	55	679
Sidney city *Shelby Co.*	62.4	108,838	38	378
Solon city *Cuyahoga Co.*	87.6	264,832	23	753
South Euclid city *Cuyahoga Co.*	84.1	128,727	47	614
Springfield city *Clark Co.*	57.9	85,681	50	364
Steubenville city *Jefferson Co.*	60.4	83,986	50	282
Stow city *Summit Co.*	71.4	170,220	25	603
Strongsville city *Cuyahoga Co.*	83.0	208,068	21	573
Sylvania city *Lucas Co.*	75.4	184,762	28	445
Toledo city *Lucas Co.*	59.7	92,821	48	380
Trotwood city *Montgomery Co.*	62.1	95,564	35	449
Troy city *Miami Co.*	59.9	119,009	37	435
Twinsburg city *Summit Co.*	77.0	210,403	12	687
Upper Arlington city *Franklin Co.*	81.1	265,031	42	661
Wadsworth city *Medina Co.*	74.5	161,104	35	470
Warren city *Trumbull Co.*	58.9	72,973	47	355
Westerville city *Franklin Co.*	79.3	194,111	22	530
Westlake city *Cuyahoga Co.*	75.5	226,399	20	781
Willoughby city *Lake Co.*	59.4	155,735	30	600
Wooster city *Wayne Co.*	61.0	122,568	35	418
Xenia city *Greene Co.*	66.8	97,780	35	398
Youngstown city *Mahoning Co.*	64.7	47,805	53	296
Zanesville city *Muskingum Co.*	54.6	74,663	55	318

NOTE: Homeownership Rate and Median Home Value as of 2007; Median Rent and Median Age of Housing as of 2000.

Commute to Work

Place	Automobile (%)	Public Transportation (%)	Walk (%)	Work from Home (%)
Akron city *Summit Co.*	91.7	3.3	2.3	2.0
Alliance city *Stark Co.*	90.2	1.0	6.5	1.6
Ashland city *Ashland Co.*	90.3	0.6	5.7	2.4
Ashtabula city *Ashtabula Co.*	92.6	2.1	2.9	1.6
Athens city *Athens Co.*	51.1	1.0	40.6	4.2
Austintown CDP *Mahoning Co.*	97.8	0.4	0.7	0.7
Avon Lake city *Lorain Co.*	94.6	1.0	0.3	3.3
Barberton city *Summit Co.*	94.4	1.1	2.8	1.3
Beavercreek city *Greene Co.*	95.9	0.1	0.6	3.2
Berea city *Cuyahoga Co.*	86.6	2.8	7.1	2.7
Boardman CDP *Mahoning Co.*	96.9	0.3	0.6	2.1
Bowling Green city *Wood Co.*	83.7	0.6	11.9	1.7
Broadview Heights city *Cuyahoga Co.*	92.9	1.9	0.6	3.5
Brook Park city *Cuyahoga Co.*	94.1	2.5	0.9	1.3
Brunswick city *Medina Co.*	95.3	1.0	0.5	2.4
Canton city *Stark Co.*	91.8	2.7	3.2	1.4
Centerville city *Montgomery Co.*	95.5	1.0	0.5	2.8
Chillicothe city *Ross Co.*	93.3	0.7	3.0	1.7
Cincinnati city *Hamilton Co.*	80.9	10.1	5.5	2.6
Cleveland city *Cuyahoga Co.*	81.3	12.0	4.0	1.6
Cleveland Heights city *Cuyahoga Co.*	85.7	5.8	3.6	3.8
Columbus city *Franklin Co.*	89.7	3.9	3.2	2.3
Cuyahoga Falls city *Summit Co.*	95.1	1.0	1.4	2.2
Dayton city *Montgomery Co.*	85.2	7.0	5.3	1.6
Delaware city *Delaware Co.*	91.2	0.4	4.1	3.3
Dublin city *Franklin Co.*	93.3	0.4	0.5	5.4
East Cleveland city *Cuyahoga Co.*	75.5	17.9	3.9	1.9
Eastlake city *Lake Co.*	95.6	1.0	1.2	1.6
Elyria city *Lorain Co.*	94.1	0.9	2.6	1.6
Euclid city *Cuyahoga Co.*	90.6	5.7	1.7	1.5
Fairborn city *Greene Co.*	94.5	0.3	3.4	1.1
Fairfield city *Butler Co.*	95.7	1.1	0.5	2.3
Findlay city *Hancock Co.*	91.5	1.1	3.7	2.6
Forest Park city *Hamilton Co.*	92.9	2.7	1.2	2.2
Gahanna city *Franklin Co.*	94.4	0.9	0.7	3.7
Garfield Heights city *Cuyahoga Co.*	92.5	3.2	2.0	1.6
Green city *Summit Co.*	96.4	0.5	0.5	2.1
Grove City city *Franklin Co.*	95.1	1.1	0.9	2.0
Hamilton city *Butler Co.*	94.2	1.0	2.5	1.5
Hilliard city *Franklin Co.*	93.8	0.7	0.7	4.4
Huber Heights city *Montgomery Co.*	96.2	0.9	0.7	1.7
Hudson city *Summit Co.*	91.8	0.4	1.1	5.9
Kent city *Portage Co.*	81.6	2.2	13.1	2.3
Kettering city *Montgomery Co.*	93.9	1.1	1.4	2.9
Lakewood city *Cuyahoga Co.*	85.1	7.8	3.6	2.6
Lancaster city *Fairfield Co.*	93.3	0.5	3.2	2.1
Lebanon city *Warren Co.*	94.9	0.7	1.3	2.5
Lima city *Allen Co.*	94.0	1.7	1.7	1.6
Lorain city *Lorain Co.*	95.5	0.7	1.7	1.3
Mansfield city *Richland Co.*	94.1	1.3	2.4	1.6

Place	Automobile (%)	Public Transportation (%)	Walk (%)	Work from Home (%)
Maple Heights city *Cuyahoga Co.*	92.8	4.1	1.5	1.0
Marion city *Marion Co.*	94.7	0.9	1.8	1.2
Marysville city *Union Co.*	95.2	0.2	1.8	2.1
Mason city *Warren Co.*	93.9	1.0	0.3	4.5
Massillon city *Stark Co.*	94.3	1.4	2.0	1.3
Mayfield Heights city *Cuyahoga Co.*	91.5	2.1	2.5	3.1
Medina city *Medina Co.*	93.8	0.7	1.6	2.9
Mentor city *Lake Co.*	95.6	0.9	1.0	2.2
Miamisburg city *Montgomery Co.*	94.8	1.0	1.8	2.1
Middletown city *Butler Co.*	94.7	1.1	1.8	1.7
Newark city *Licking Co.*	94.9	1.0	1.5	1.9
Niles city *Trumbull Co.*	96.3	0.4	1.4	1.2
North Olmsted city *Cuyahoga Co.*	92.4	2.7	1.5	2.9
North Ridgeville city *Lorain Co.*	96.1	1.0	0.6	1.9
North Royalton city *Cuyahoga Co.*	92.8	1.7	1.0	3.9
Norwood city *Hamilton Co.*	90.0	3.5	4.0	1.6
Oregon city *Lucas Co.*	96.3	0.0	1.5	1.6
Oxford city *Butler Co.*	63.5	2.0	27.7	3.9
Painesville city *Lake Co.*	92.9	0.9	3.8	1.3
Parma city *Cuyahoga Co.*	93.3	3.1	1.4	1.6
Parma Heights city *Cuyahoga Co.*	93.1	3.5	1.2	1.8
Piqua city *Miami Co.*	93.1	1.3	2.5	2.2
Portsmouth city *Scioto Co.*	90.5	1.4	5.5	1.6
Reynoldsburg city *Franklin Co.*	94.8	1.3	1.2	2.2
Riverside city *Montgomery Co.*	95.7	1.2	0.9	1.2
Rocky River city *Cuyahoga Co.*	88.7	3.5	2.8	4.4
Sandusky city *Erie Co.*	94.6	0.6	2.3	1.4
Shaker Heights city *Cuyahoga Co.*	85.6	8.1	1.4	4.1
Sidney city *Shelby Co.*	94.7	0.4	2.0	2.3
Solon city *Cuyahoga Co.*	94.7	0.5	0.7	3.9
South Euclid city *Cuyahoga Co.*	91.6	3.3	1.3	3.3
Springfield city *Clark Co.*	91.7	1.5	4.2	1.6
Steubenville city *Jefferson Co.*	93.2	0.9	3.0	2.7
Stow city *Summit Co.*	95.6	0.4	0.6	2.9
Strongsville city *Cuyahoga Co.*	93.2	2.2	0.7	3.4
Sylvania city *Lucas Co.*	94.3	0.6	1.4	3.4
Toledo city *Lucas Co.*	92.9	2.5	2.3	1.5
Trotwood city *Montgomery Co.*	93.4	3.5	1.0	1.5
Troy city *Miami Co.*	95.9	0.6	1.6	0.8
Twinsburg city *Summit Co.*	96.0	0.4	0.4	2.7
Upper Arlington city *Franklin Co.*	90.3	1.5	1.4	5.8
Wadsworth city *Medina Co.*	94.3	0.2	1.3	3.5
Warren city *Trumbull Co.*	94.7	0.2	1.8	1.7
Westerville city *Franklin Co.*	92.6	1.0	2.1	3.9
Westlake city *Cuyahoga Co.*	92.6	2.3	0.6	3.9
Willoughby city *Lake Co.*	95.4	0.8	1.6	1.5
Wooster city *Wayne Co.*	86.9	0.9	9.2	2.6
Xenia city *Greene Co.*	95.3	0.5	2.2	1.5
Youngstown city *Mahoning Co.*	91.8	2.7	2.6	1.7
Zanesville city *Muskingum Co.*	92.8	1.3	2.9	2.0

NOTE: Data as of 2000

Travel Time to Work

Place	Less than 15 Minutes (%)	15 to 30 Minutes (%)	30 to 45 Minutes (%)	45 to 60 Minutes (%)	60 Minutes or More (%)
Akron city *Summit Co.*	34.3	43.0	13.2	4.7	4.9
Alliance city *Stark Co.*	56.0	23.0	11.4	4.3	5.3
Ashland city *Ashland Co.*	64.9	17.9	10.1	2.7	4.4
Ashtabula city *Ashtabula Co.*	50.1	27.5	9.8	6.7	5.9
Athens city *Athens Co.*	74.2	20.0	3.3	0.6	1.8
Austintown CDP *Mahoning Co.*	30.9	51.6	9.6	3.2	4.8
Avon Lake city *Lorain Co.*	24.7	35.1	28.5	7.9	3.7
Barberton city *Summit Co.*	38.8	39.1	13.7	4.6	3.9
Beavercreek city *Greene Co.*	32.1	54.2	9.5	1.7	2.5
Berea city *Cuyahoga Co.*	33.0	36.4	21.3	6.0	3.3
Boardman CDP *Mahoning Co.*	37.3	41.6	13.9	2.4	4.8
Bowling Green city *Wood Co.*	62.2	19.0	14.3	2.6	1.9
Broadview Heights city *Cuyahoga Co.*	16.6	43.9	29.4	7.2	2.9
Brook Park city *Cuyahoga Co.*	30.8	43.0	18.6	4.5	3.1
Brunswick city *Medina Co.*	21.4	32.7	30.1	11.0	4.8
Canton city *Stark Co.*	43.8	39.3	9.8	3.2	3.9
Centerville city *Montgomery Co.*	29.7	49.3	13.5	3.7	3.8
Chillicothe city *Ross Co.*	56.9	22.9	7.8	4.0	8.5
Cincinnati city *Hamilton Co.*	26.0	46.5	18.3	4.7	4.6
Cleveland city *Cuyahoga Co.*	22.0	45.0	20.7	5.6	6.7
Cleveland Heights city *Cuyahoga Co.*	22.3	44.3	23.8	4.9	4.7
Columbus city *Franklin Co.*	26.1	49.1	17.7	3.6	3.4
Cuyahoga Falls city *Summit Co.*	32.7	41.5	14.8	5.8	5.1
Dayton city *Montgomery Co.*	33.5	46.9	11.3	3.6	4.7
Delaware city *Delaware Co.*	31.5	27.1	23.2	11.4	6.7
Dublin city *Franklin Co.*	28.2	37.4	26.3	4.4	3.7
East Cleveland city *Cuyahoga Co.*	17.8	37.6	26.8	8.1	9.7
Eastlake city *Lake Co.*	31.1	45.2	15.9	4.4	3.4
Elyria city *Lorain Co.*	38.3	37.3	16.1	5.1	3.1
Euclid city *Cuyahoga Co.*	25.1	43.3	22.7	4.2	4.8
Fairborn city *Greene Co.*	40.3	42.5	12.3	1.9	2.9
Fairfield city *Butler Co.*	27.1	43.9	20.5	6.1	2.4
Findlay city *Hancock Co.*	60.6	26.8	6.7	2.9	3.0
Forest Park city *Hamilton Co.*	23.1	42.9	23.5	6.2	4.3
Gahanna city *Franklin Co.*	26.6	51.4	15.9	2.4	3.7
Garfield Heights city *Cuyahoga Co.*	25.5	47.0	20.5	3.2	3.9
Green city *Summit Co.*	23.0	49.4	17.9	5.5	4.3
Grove City city *Franklin Co.*	26.3	44.3	22.8	3.9	2.7
Hamilton city *Butler Co.*	32.2	36.9	20.0	6.5	4.4
Hilliard city *Franklin Co.*	28.8	43.7	19.4	4.4	3.7
Huber Heights city *Montgomery Co.*	25.3	51.7	16.4	3.1	3.5
Hudson city *Summit Co.*	27.8	31.0	22.8	13.3	5.2
Kent city *Portage Co.*	42.7	33.7	11.7	6.6	5.3
Kettering city *Montgomery Co.*	33.6	50.2	10.5	2.7	3.0
Lakewood city *Cuyahoga Co.*	26.4	45.9	20.4	4.3	2.9
Lancaster city *Fairfield Co.*	40.3	23.6	14.7	12.8	8.6
Lebanon city *Warren Co.*	31.9	32.5	25.3	8.2	2.2
Lima city *Allen Co.*	50.7	34.3	8.1	3.3	3.5
Lorain city *Lorain Co.*	32.6	41.9	15.3	5.8	4.4
Mansfield city *Richland Co.*	47.3	39.5	6.4	2.3	4.6

Place	Less than 15 Minutes (%)	15 to 30 Minutes (%)	30 to 45 Minutes (%)	45 to 60 Minutes (%)	60 Minutes or More (%)
Maple Heights city *Cuyahoga Co.*	24.9	43.6	21.7	5.9	3.9
Marion city *Marion Co.*	53.3	25.5	9.3	5.7	6.2
Marysville city *Union Co.*	41.0	33.7	16.4	5.3	3.7
Mason city *Warren Co.*	25.6	42.9	23.6	5.6	2.2
Massillon city *Stark Co.*	39.1	40.2	12.8	3.9	4.0
Mayfield Heights city *Cuyahoga Co.*	32.4	40.3	20.3	4.3	2.7
Medina city *Medina Co.*	35.2	25.5	21.6	11.6	6.0
Mentor city *Lake Co.*	29.5	39.5	20.8	7.2	3.0
Miamisburg city *Montgomery Co.*	36.1	47.0	10.5	3.2	3.2
Middletown city *Butler Co.*	42.5	32.4	17.0	4.7	3.3
Newark city *Licking Co.*	44.5	30.8	10.3	8.7	5.6
Niles city *Trumbull Co.*	40.4	46.0	7.8	2.2	3.6
North Olmsted city *Cuyahoga Co.*	25.5	41.2	23.3	6.6	3.5
North Ridgeville city *Lorain Co.*	18.8	44.4	24.8	7.2	4.8
North Royalton city *Cuyahoga Co.*	18.3	37.6	28.6	10.4	5.1
Norwood city *Hamilton Co.*	38.4	42.9	12.8	2.9	3.0
Oregon city *Lucas Co.*	35.3	44.4	13.5	2.9	3.9
Oxford city *Butler Co.*	63.9	17.9	8.4	6.1	3.7
Painesville city *Lake Co.*	32.4	41.6	17.4	5.4	3.2
Parma city *Cuyahoga Co.*	22.8	43.1	23.9	6.5	3.7
Parma Heights city *Cuyahoga Co.*	25.7	41.2	22.2	7.1	3.8
Piqua city *Miami Co.*	49.9	33.5	10.2	3.6	2.7
Portsmouth city *Scioto Co.*	55.2	26.3	9.3	2.2	7.0
Reynoldsburg city *Franklin Co.*	25.1	44.4	23.3	4.4	2.9
Riverside city *Montgomery Co.*	33.9	50.7	8.0	2.9	4.6
Rocky River city *Cuyahoga Co.*	27.7	44.4	21.2	4.5	2.2
Sandusky city *Erie Co.*	59.1	28.5	6.7	1.8	4.0
Shaker Heights city *Cuyahoga Co.*	22.0	47.9	22.1	5.1	2.9
Sidney city *Shelby Co.*	65.5	21.6	8.2	3.0	1.7
Solon city *Cuyahoga Co.*	28.1	36.7	25.2	7.2	2.8
South Euclid city *Cuyahoga Co.*	24.2	43.9	22.4	6.0	3.6
Springfield city *Clark Co.*	45.8	33.3	11.3	5.4	4.2
Steubenville city *Jefferson Co.*	55.9	27.4	8.4	4.1	4.3
Stow city *Summit Co.*	27.1	42.0	19.1	7.5	4.3
Strongsville city *Cuyahoga Co.*	22.9	34.0	28.5	10.1	4.5
Sylvania city *Lucas Co.*	30.6	49.6	11.8	2.5	5.5
Toledo city *Lucas Co.*	35.1	47.2	10.7	2.8	4.1
Trotwood city *Montgomery Co.*	20.4	48.7	20.7	5.2	5.0
Troy city *Miami Co.*	49.5	33.8	11.3	2.9	2.4
Twinsburg city *Summit Co.*	22.8	36.9	27.7	9.2	3.5
Upper Arlington city *Franklin Co.*	30.7	55.4	10.1	1.4	2.4
Wadsworth city *Medina Co.*	34.6	44.0	12.6	5.0	3.9
Warren city *Trumbull Co.*	49.7	32.4	8.4	5.3	4.1
Westerville city *Franklin Co.*	29.6	42.3	22.1	3.1	2.8
Westlake city *Cuyahoga Co.*	23.4	38.8	27.4	7.2	3.2
Willoughby city *Lake Co.*	29.5	42.2	21.2	4.2	2.8
Wooster city *Wayne Co.*	64.7	21.1	6.7	4.0	3.5
Xenia city *Greene Co.*	37.0	32.9	22.1	3.8	4.2
Youngstown city *Mahoning Co.*	38.4	43.4	11.0	2.2	5.0
Zanesville city *Muskingum Co.*	49.6	26.3	10.2	6.0	8.0

NOTE: Data as of 2000

Crime

Place	Violent Crime Rate (crimes per 10,000 population)	Property Crime Rate (crimes per 10,000 population)
Akron city *Summit Co.*	75.1	502.8
Alliance city *Stark Co.*	47.1	486.7
Ashland city *Ashland Co.*	8.7	251.2
Ashtabula city *Ashtabula Co.*	n/a	n/a
Athens city *Athens Co.*	19.2	230.9
Austintown CDP *Mahoning Co.*	5.3	469.2
Avon Lake city *Lorain Co.*	n/a	n/a
Barberton city *Summit Co.*	21.2	436.5
Beavercreek city *Greene Co.*	7.6	340.3
Berea city *Cuyahoga Co.*	7.8	175.3
Boardman CDP *Mahoning Co.*	n/a	n/a
Bowling Green city *Wood Co.*	10.1	377.0
Broadview Heights city *Cuyahoga Co.*	4.5	40.5
Brook Park city *Cuyahoga Co.*	10.8	148.2
Brunswick city *Medina Co.*	n/a	n/a
Canton city *Stark Co.*	96.8	782.9
Centerville city *Montgomery Co.*	4.8	243.8
Chillicothe city *Ross Co.*	n/a	n/a
Cincinnati city *Hamilton Co.*	107.9	617.7
Cleveland city *Cuyahoga Co.*	146.5	614.2
Cleveland Heights city *Cuyahoga Co.*	6.0	116.9
Columbus city *Franklin Co.*	85.2	699.6
Cuyahoga Falls city *Summit Co.*	15.0	306.5
Dayton city *Montgomery Co.*	102.7	672.9
Delaware city *Delaware Co.*	28.6	295.1
Dublin city *Franklin Co.*	6.7	202.8
East Cleveland city *Cuyahoga Co.*	n/a	n/a
Eastlake city *Lake Co.*	14.3	227.7
Elyria city *Lorain Co.*	39.9	409.0
Euclid city *Cuyahoga Co.*	41.5	338.5
Fairborn city *Greene Co.*	35.0	363.0
Fairfield city *Butler Co.*	52.8	351.8
Findlay city *Hancock Co.*	15.5	336.8
Forest Park city *Hamilton Co.*	31.5	374.9
Gahanna city *Franklin Co.*	36.2	277.9
Garfield Heights city *Cuyahoga Co.*	49.6	317.8
Green city *Summit Co.*	n/a	n/a
Grove City city *Franklin Co.*	20.3	367.1
Hamilton city *Butler Co.*	80.4	664.8
Hilliard city *Franklin Co.*	12.1	305.3
Huber Heights city *Montgomery Co.*	17.0	314.2
Hudson city *Summit Co.*	n/a	n/a
Kent city *Portage Co.*	27.6	249.6
Kettering city *Montgomery Co.*	14.4	295.3
Lakewood city *Cuyahoga Co.*	17.4	256.9
Lancaster city *Fairfield Co.*	24.0	526.2
Lebanon city *Warren Co.*	17.3	188.2
Lima city *Allen Co.*	92.9	697.2
Lorain city *Lorain Co.*	46.3	339.1
Mansfield city *Richland Co.*	32.6	577.2

Place	Violent Crime Rate (crimes per 10,000 population)	Property Crime Rate (crimes per 10,000 population)
Maple Heights city *Cuyahoga Co.*	n/a	n/a
Marion city *Marion Co.*	27.0	483.9
Marysville city *Union Co.*	2.2	190.7
Mason city *Warren Co.*	4.6	188.0
Massillon city *Stark Co.*	n/a	n/a
Mayfield Heights city *Cuyahoga Co.*	5.0	175.6
Medina city *Medina Co.*	n/a	n/a
Mentor city *Lake Co.*	8.5	233.3
Miamisburg city *Montgomery Co.*	13.6	369.4
Middletown city *Butler Co.*	43.5	788.4
Newark city *Licking Co.*	26.0	530.9
Niles city *Trumbull Co.*	40.2	620.6
North Olmsted city *Cuyahoga Co.*	12.2	184.3
North Ridgeville city *Lorain Co.*	4.3	106.6
North Royalton city *Cuyahoga Co.*	n/a	n/a
Norwood city *Hamilton Co.*	n/a	n/a
Oregon city *Lucas Co.*	10.5	462.4
Oxford city *Butler Co.*	43.6	271.2
Painesville city *Lake Co.*	n/a	n/a
Parma city *Cuyahoga Co.*	22.7	215.1
Parma Heights city *Cuyahoga Co.*	8.5	217.8
Piqua city *Miami Co.*	16.3	533.2
Portsmouth city *Scioto Co.*	62.4	1,067.4
Reynoldsburg city *Franklin Co.*	30.7	376.1
Riverside city *Montgomery Co.*	29.1	436.9
Rocky River city *Cuyahoga Co.*	n/a	n/a
Sandusky city *Erie Co.*	86.6	612.1
Shaker Heights city *Cuyahoga Co.*	n/a	n/a
Sidney city *Shelby Co.*	n/a	n/a
Solon city *Cuyahoga Co.*	9.0	118.7
South Euclid city *Cuyahoga Co.*	19.5	269.0
Springfield city *Clark Co.*	73.8	866.1
Steubenville city *Jefferson Co.*	41.3	486.2
Stow city *Summit Co.*	6.9	238.3
Strongsville city *Cuyahoga Co.*	n/a	n/a
Sylvania city *Lucas Co.*	n/a	n/a
Toledo city *Lucas Co.*	122.8	668.9
Trotwood city *Montgomery Co.*	n/a	n/a
Troy city *Miami Co.*	n/a	n/a
Twinsburg city *Summit Co.*	5.1	80.4
Upper Arlington city *Franklin Co.*	2.9	120.6
Wadsworth city *Medina Co.*	7.4	204.0
Warren city *Trumbull Co.*	113.2	555.5
Westerville city *Franklin Co.*	9.7	263.0
Westlake city *Cuyahoga Co.*	n/a	n/a
Willoughby city *Lake Co.*	6.7	167.1
Wooster city *Wayne Co.*	21.2	378.9
Xenia city *Greene Co.*	18.4	484.3
Youngstown city *Mahoning Co.*	99.6	503.1
Zanesville city *Muskingum Co.*	46.6	626.9

NOTE: Data as of 2007.

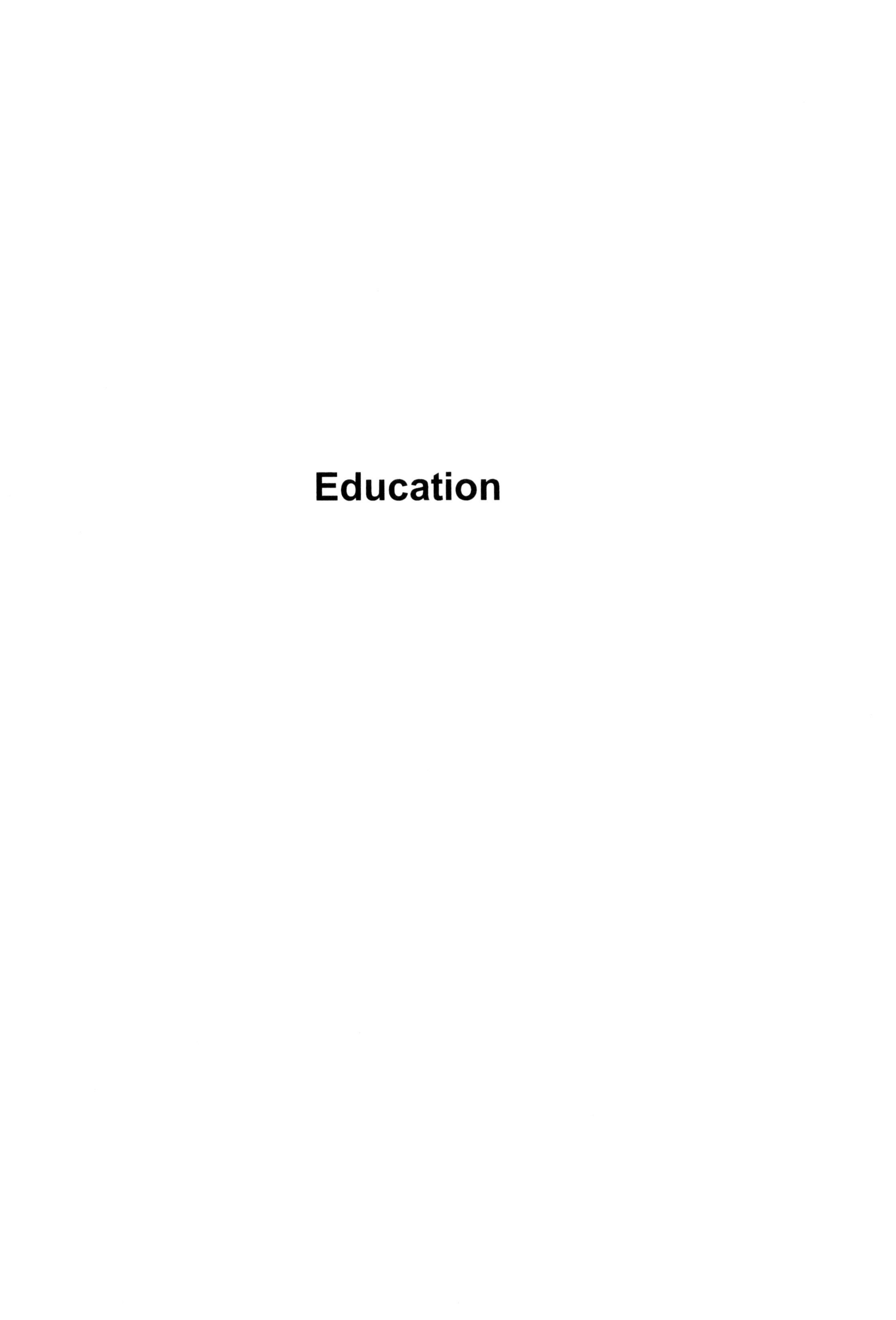

Education

Ohio Public School Educational Profile

Category	Value	Category	Value
Schools *(2005-2006)*	4,013	**Diploma Recipients** *(2004-2005)*	116,702
Instructional Level		White, Non-Hispanic	97,704
Primary	2,151	Black, Non-Hispanic	14,308
Middle	734	Asian/Pacific Islander	1,726
High	840	American Indian/Alaskan Native	128
Other Level	283	Hispanic	1,723
Curriculum		**High School Drop-out Rate** (%) *(2001-2002)*	3.1
Regular	3,910	White, Non-Hispanic	2.4
Special Education	13	Black, Non-Hispanic	7.2
Vocational	76	Asian/Pacific Islander	2.0
Alternative	9	American Indian/Alaskan Native	6.6
Type		Hispanic	6.6
Magnet	0	**Staff** *(2005-2006)*	
Charter	317	Teachers	117,976.1
Title I Eligible	2,755	Average Salary ($)	49,438
School-wide Title I	984	Librarians/Media Specialists	1,555.9
Students *(2005-2006)*	1,840,049	Guidance Counselors	3,839.6
Gender (%)		**Ratios** *(2005-2006)*	
Male	51.4	Student/Teacher Ratio	15.6 to 1
Female	48.6	Student/Librarian Ratio	1,182.6 to 1
Race/Ethnicity (%)		Student/Counselor Ratio	479.2 to 1
White, Non-Hispanic	76.9	**College Entrance Exam Scores** *(2006)*	
Black, Non-Hispanic	16.6	SAT Reasoning Test™	
Asian/Pacific Islander	1.4	Participation Rate (%)	28
American Indian/Alaskan Native	0.1	Mean SAT Critical Reading Score	535
Hispanic	2.4	Mean SAT Writing Score	521
Classification (%)		Mean SAT Math Score	544
Individual Education Program (IEP)	14.5	American College Testing Program (ACT)	
Migrant *(2004-2005)*	0.2	Participation Rate (%)	66
English Language Learner (ELL)	1.6	Average Composite Score	21.5
Eligible for Free Lunch Program	26.4	Average English Score	20.8
Eligible for Reduced-Price Lunch Program	6.2	Average Math Score	21.3
Current Spending *($ per student in FY 2005)*	8,765	Average Reading Score	21.9
Instruction	5,120	Average Science Score	21.5
Support Services	3,337		

Note: *For an explanation of data, please refer to the User's Guide in the front of the book*

Number of Schools

Rank	Number	District Name	City
1	147	Columbus City	Columbus
2	104	Cleveland Municipal City	Cleveland
3	79	Cincinnati City	Cincinnati
4	62	Akron City	Akron
5	58	Toledo City	Toledo
6	39	Dayton City	Dayton
7	36	South-Western City	Grove City
8	28	Canton City	Canton
9	26	Youngstown City	Youngstown
10	23	Westerville City	Westerville
11	22	Parma City	Parma
12	20	Hilliard City	Hilliard
13	19	Dublin City	Dublin
13	19	Elyria City	Elyria
13	19	Hamilton City	Hamilton
13	19	Lakota Local	Liberty Twp
17	18	Lorain City	Lorain
17	18	Springfield City	Springfield
17	18	Worthington City	Worthington
20	15	Findlay City	Findlay
20	15	Olentangy Local	Lewis Center
22	14	Cleveland Hgts-University Hgts	University Hgts
22	14	Mansfield City	Mansfield
22	14	Mentor Exempted Village	Mentor
22	14	Middletown City	Middletown
22	14	Newark City	Newark
22	14	Northwest Local	Cincinnati
28	13	Ashtabula Area City	Ashtabula
28	13	Berea City	Berea
28	13	Warren City	Warren
28	13	Willoughby-Eastlake City	Willoughby
32	12	Centerville City	Centerville
32	12	Kettering City	Kettering
32	12	Lakewood City	Lakewood
32	12	Strongsville City	Strongsville
32	12	Sylvania City	Sylvania
32	12	Washington Local	Toledo
32	12	West Clermont Local	Cincinnati
39	11	Brunswick City	Brunswick
39	11	Gahanna-Jefferson City	Gahanna
39	11	Lancaster City	Lancaster
39	11	Pickerington Local	Pickerington
39	11	Sandusky City	Sandusky
44	10	Cuyahoga Falls City	Cuyahoga Falls
44	10	East Holmes Local	Berlin
44	10	Euclid City	Euclid
44	10	Fairfield City	Fairfield
44	10	Groveport Madison Local	Groveport
44	10	Huber Heights City	Huber Heights
44	10	Lima City	Lima
44	10	Plain Local	Canton
44	10	Princeton City	Cincinnati
44	10	Reynoldsburg City	Reynoldsburg
44	10	Switzerland of Ohio Local	Woodsfield
44	10	Wooster City	Wooster
44	10	Xenia Community City	Xenia
57	9	Barberton City	Barberton
57	9	Delaware City	Delaware
57	9	Forest Hills Local	Cincinnati
57	9	Fremont City	Fremont
57	9	Logan-Hocking Local	Logan
57	9	Marion City	Marion
57	9	Marysville Exempted Village	Marysville
57	9	Medina City	Medina
57	9	Miami Trace Local	Washington CH
57	9	Miamisburg City	Miamisburg
57	9	Milford Exempted Village	Milford
57	9	Mount Healthy City	Cincinnati
57	9	North Olmsted City	North Olmsted
57	9	Northmont City	Englewood
57	9	Oak Hills Local	Cincinnati
57	9	Perry Local	Massillon
57	9	Piqua City	Piqua
57	9	Ravenna City	Ravenna
57	9	Shaker Heights City	Shaker Heights
57	9	Sidney City	Sidney
57	9	South Euclid-Lyndhurst City	Lyndhurst
57	9	Stow-Munroe Falls City	Stow
57	9	Troy City	Troy
57	9	Zanesville City	Zanesville
81	8	Ashland City	Ashland
81	8	Austintown Local	Youngstown
81	8	Beavercreek City	Beavercreek
81	8	Bowling Green City	Bowling Green
81	8	Carrollton Exempted Village	Carrollton
81	8	Gallia County Local	Gallipolis
81	8	Massillon City	Massillon
81	8	Mount Vernon City	Mount Vernon
81	8	Painesville Township Local	Painesville
81	8	Southwest Local	Harrison
81	8	Upper Arlington City	Upper Arlington
81	8	Wadsworth City	Wadsworth
93	7	Adams County/Ohio Valley Local	West Union
93	7	Athens City	The Plains
93	7	Avon Lake City	Avon Lake
93	7	Bedford City	Bedford
93	7	Bellevue City	Bellevue
93	7	Boardman Local	Youngstown
93	7	Buckeye Local	Dillonvale
93	7	Chillicothe City	Chillicothe
93	7	Defiance City	Defiance
93	7	East Cleveland City	East Cleveland
93	7	Edison Local	Hammondsville
93	7	Franklin City	Franklin
93	7	Geneva Area City	Geneva
93	7	Greenville City	Greenville
93	7	Kent City	Kent
93	7	Kenton City	Kenton
93	7	Mad River Local	Dayton
93	7	Madison Local	Mansfield
93	7	Mayfield City	Mayfield Hgts
93	7	New Philadel. City	New Philadel.
93	7	North Canton City	North Canton
93	7	N Ridgeville City	N Ridgeville
93	7	Northeastern Local	Springfield
93	7	Oregon City	Oregon
93	7	Painesville Local	Painesville
93	7	River View Local	Warsaw
93	7	Solon City	Solon
93	7	Springfield Local	Akron
93	7	Steubenville City	Steubenville
93	7	Sycamore Community City	Cincinnati
93	7	Tecumseh Local	New Carlisle
93	7	Tiffin City	Tiffin
93	7	Tri-Valley Local	Dresden
93	7	Trotwood-Madison City	Trotwood
93	7	Van Wert City	Van Wert
93	7	Vinton County Local	Mcarthur
93	7	Washington CH City	Washington CH
93	7	West Carrollton City	West Carrollton
93	7	West Holmes Local	Millersburg
93	7	Westlake City	Westlake
93	7	Winton Woods City	Cincinnati
134	6	Alliance City	Alliance
134	6	Amherst Exempted Village	Amherst
134	6	Anthony Wayne Local	Whitehouse
134	6	Avon Local	Avon
134	6	Bellefontaine City	Bellefontaine
134	6	Benton Carroll Salem Local	Oak Harbor
134	6	Brecksville-Broadview Heights City	Brecksville
134	6	Buckeye Local	Ashtabula
134	6	Celina City	Celina
134	6	Chardon Local	Chardon
134	6	Circleville City	Circleville
134	6	Claymont City	Dennison
134	6	Coventry Local	Akron
134	6	East Muskingum Local	New Concord
134	6	Eastwood Local	Pemberville
134	6	Harrison Hills City	Hopedale
134	6	Hillsboro City	Hillsboro
134	6	Howland Local	Warren
134	6	Hudson City	Hudson
134	6	Indian Creek Local	Wintersville
134	6	Ironton City	Ironton
134	6	Jackson Local	Massillon
134	6	Kings Local	Kings Mills
134	6	Lebanon City	Lebanon
134	6	Licking Valley Local	Newark
134	6	Little Miami Local	Morrow
134	6	Logan Elm Local	Circleville
134	6	Louisville City	Louisville
134	6	Loveland City	Loveland
134	6	Maple Heights City	Maple Heights
134	6	Marietta City	Marietta
134	6	Mason City	Mason
134	6	Maumee City	Maumee
134	6	Niles City	Niles
134	6	Nordonia Hills City	Northfield
134	6	North Royalton City	North Royalton
134	6	Norton City	Norton
134	6	Norwalk City	Norwalk
134	6	Norwood City	Norwood
134	6	Perrysburg Exempted Village	Perrysburg
134	6	Poland Local	Poland
134	6	Port Clinton City	Port Clinton
134	6	Portsmouth City	Portsmouth
134	6	Rossford Exempted Village	Rossford
134	6	Salem City	Salem
134	6	Sheffield-Sheffield Lake City	Sheffield Vllg
134	6	Southeast Local	Apple Creek
134	6	Southwest Licking Local	Etna
134	6	Springfield Local	Holland
134	6	Tallmadge City	Tallmadge
134	6	Urbana City	Urbana
134	6	Vandalia-Butler City	Vandalia
134	6	Warren Local	Vincent
134	6	Warrensville Hgts City	Warrensville Hgts
134	6	Whitehall City	Whitehall
134	6	Willard City	Willard
190	5	Beaver Local	Lisbon
190	5	Bexley City	Bexley
190	5	Big Walnut Local	Galena
190	5	Buckeye Valley Local	Delaware
190	5	Bucyrus City	Bucyrus
190	5	Cambridge City	Cambridge
190	5	Canal Wnchstr Local	Canal Wnchstr
190	5	Canton Local	Canton
190	5	Clark-Shawnee Local	Springfield
190	5	Cloverleaf Local	Lodi
190	5	Clyde-Green Springs Ex Vill	Clyde
190	5	Conneaut Area City	Conneaut
190	5	Copley-Fairlawn City	Copley
190	5	Coshocton City	Coshocton
190	5	Crestwood Local	Mantua
190	5	Dover City	Dover
190	5	East Liverpool City	East Liverpool
190	5	Edgewood City	Trenton
190	5	Fairfield Union Local	West Rushville
190	5	Fairless Local	Navarre
190	5	Fairview Park City	Fairview Park
190	5	Field Local	Mogadore
190	5	Fostoria City	Fostoria
190	5	Franklin Local	Duncan Falls
190	5	Galion City	Galion
190	5	Gallipolis City	Gallipolis
190	5	Garfield Hgts City	Garfield Hgts
190	5	Green Local	Green
190	5	Greenfield Exempted Village	Greenfield
190	5	Hamilton Local	Columbus
190	5	Highland Local	Medina
190	5	Highland Local	Sparta
190	5	Jackson City	Jackson
190	5	Jonathan Alder Local	Plain City
190	5	Kenston Local	Chagrin Falls
190	5	Lake Local	Millbury
190	5	Lake Local	Uniontown
190	5	Lakewood Local	Hebron
190	5	Lexington Local	Lexington
190	5	Madison Local	Madison
190	5	Madison-Plains Local	London
190	5	Mariemont City	Cincinnati
190	5	Marlington Local	Alliance
190	5	Martins Ferry City	Martins Ferry
190	5	Midview Local	Grafton
190	5	Morgan Local	Mcconnelsville
190	5	Napoleon Area City	Napoleon
190	5	New Richmond Exempted Village	New Richmond
190	5	Northern Local	Thornville
190	5	Northridge Local	Dayton
190	5	Northwest Local	Canal Fulton
190	5	Oakwood City	Dayton
190	5	Orrville City	Orrville
190	5	Otsego Local	Tontogany
190	5	Revere Local	Bath
190	5	Rolling Hills Local	Cambridge
190	5	Shelby City	Shelby
190	5	Southeast Local	Ravenna
190	5	Springboro Community City	Springboro
190	5	Streetsboro City	Streetsboro
190	5	Sugarcreek Local	Bellbrook
190	5	Teays Valley Local	Ashville
190	5	Three Rivers Local	Cleves
190	5	Tipp Exempted Village	Tipp City
190	5	Triway Local	Wooster
190	5	Tuscarawas Valley Local	Zoarville
190	5	Twinsburg City	Twinsburg
190	5	Upper Sandusky Exempted Village	Upper Sandusky
190	5	Wapakoneta City	Wapakoneta

190	5	West Branch Local	Beloit
190	5	West Muskingum Local	Zanesville
190	5	Wilmington City	Wilmington
190	5	Wyoming City	Wyoming
263	4	Amanda-Clearcreek Local	Amanda
263	4	Aurora City	Aurora
263	4	Bay Village City	Bay Village
263	4	Berlin-Milan Local	Milan
263	4	Bethel-Tate Local	Bethel
263	4	Blanchester Local	Blanchester
263	4	Bloom-Carroll Local	Carroll
263	4	Bryan City	Bryan
263	4	Buckeye Local	Medina
263	4	Canfield Local	Canfield
263	4	Carlisle Local	Carlisle
263	4	Chagrin Falls Exempted Village	Chagrin Falls
263	4	Clear Fork Valley Local	Bellville
263	4	Clermont Northeastern Local	Batavia
263	4	East Clinton Local	Lees Creek
263	4	Eastern Local	Sardinia
263	4	Eaton Community Schools City	Eaton
263	4	Elgin Local	Marion
263	4	Elida Local	Elida
263	4	Fairborn City	Fairborn
263	4	Fairland Local	Proctorville
263	4	Finneytown Local	Cincinnati
263	4	Genoa Area Local	Genoa
263	4	Girard City	Girard
263	4	Goshen Local	Goshen
263	4	Graham Local	Saint Paris
263	4	Granville Exempted Village	Granville
263	4	Greenon Local	Enon
263	4	Heath City	Heath
263	4	Indian Hill Exempted Village	Cincinnati
263	4	Indian Lake Local	Lewistown
263	4	James A Garfield Local	Garrettsville
263	4	Johnstown-Monroe Local	Johnstown
263	4	Keystone Local	Lagrange
263	4	Labrae Local	Leavittsburg
263	4	Lakeview Local	Cortland
263	4	London City	London
263	4	Meigs Local	Pomeroy
263	4	Minerva Local	Minerva
263	4	New Albany-Plain Local	New Albany
263	4	New Lexington City	New Lexington
263	4	North College Hill City	Cincinnati
263	4	North Fork Local	Utica
263	4	Olmsted Falls City	Olmsted Falls
263	4	Ontario Local	Mansfield
263	4	Orange City	Cleveland
263	4	Ottawa-Glandorf Local	Ottawa
263	4	Paulding Exempted Village	Paulding
263	4	Perkins Local	Sandusky
263	4	Pike-Delta-York Local	Delta
263	4	Preble Shawnee Board of Education	Camden
263	4	River Valley Local	Caledonia
263	4	Rock Hill Local	Ironton
263	4	Rocky River City	Rocky River
263	4	Ross Local	Hamilton
263	4	Saint Marys City	Saint Marys
263	4	Sandy Valley Local	Magnolia
263	4	Shawnee Local	Lima
263	4	South Point Local	South Point
263	4	Talawanda City	Oxford
263	4	Valley View Local	Germantown
263	4	Vermilion Local	Vermilion
263	4	Wauseon Exempted Village	Wauseon
263	4	Waverly City	Waverly
263	4	Wellston City	Wellston
263	4	West Geauga Local	Chesterland
263	4	Western Brown Local	Mount Orab
263	4	Woodridge Local	Peninsula
331	3	Alexander Local	Albany
331	3	Batavia Local	Batavia
331	3	Bath Local	Lima
331	3	Bellaire Local	Bellaire
331	3	Benjamin Logan Local	Bellefontaine
331	3	Black River Local	Sullivan
331	3	Brookville Local	Brookville
331	3	Champion Local	Warren
331	3	Chippewa Local	Doylestown
331	3	Clearview Local	Lorain
331	3	Clinton-Massie Local	Clarksville
331	3	Coldwater Exempted Village	Coldwater
331	3	Firelands Local	Oberlin
331	3	Greeneview Local	Jamestown
331	3	Hubbard Exempted Village	Hubbard
331	3	Huron City	Huron
331	3	Indian Valley Local	Gnadenhutten
331	3	Jefferson Area Local	Jefferson
331	3	Liberty Local	Youngstown
331	3	Licking Heights Local	Summit Station
331	3	Madeira City	Cincinnati
331	3	Madison Local	Middletown
331	3	Manchester Local	Akron
331	3	Maysville Local	Zanesville
331	3	Milton-Union Exempted Village	West Milton
331	3	Minford Local	Minford
331	3	Monroe Local	Monroe
331	3	Northwest Local	Mcdermott
331	3	Northwestern Local	Springfield
331	3	Perry Local	Perry
331	3	Saint Clairsville-Richland City	Saint Clairsville
331	3	Scioto Valley Local	Piketon
331	3	Struthers City	Struthers
331	3	Union-Scioto Local	Chillicothe
331	3	Washington-Nile Local	West Portsmouth
331	3	Wellington Exempted Village	Wellington
331	3	Westfall Local	Williamsport
331	3	Wheelersburg Local	Wheelersburg
331	3	Wickliffe City	Wickliffe
331	3	Zane Trace Local	Chillicothe
371	1	Alternative Education Academy	Toledo
371	1	Electronic Classroom of Tomorrow	Columbus
371	1	Ohio Virtual Academy	Maumee

Number of Teachers

Rank	Number	District Name	City
1	3,737	Cleveland Municipal City	Cleveland
2	3,405	Columbus City	Columbus
3	2,656	Akron City	Akron
4	2,356	Cincinnati City	Cincinnati
5	1,852	Toledo City	Toledo
6	1,305	South-Western City	Grove City
7	1,095	Dayton City	Dayton
8	921	Lakota Local	Liberty Twp
9	900	Hilliard City	Hilliard
10	827	Dublin City	Dublin
11	791	Parma City	Parma
12	752	Westerville City	Westerville
13	722	Canton City	Canton
14	660	Youngstown City	Youngstown
15	645	Olentangy Local	Lewis Center
16	637	Worthington City	Worthington
17	607	Northwest Local	Cincinnati
18	567	Hamilton City	Hamilton
19	563	Lorain City	Lorain
20	557	Mentor Exempted Village	Mentor
21	532	Mason City	Mason
22	516	Pickerington Local	Pickerington
23	513	Willoughby-Eastlake City	Willoughby
24	510	West Clermont Local	Cincinnati
25	508	Elyria City	Elyria
26	504	Fairfield City	Fairfield
27	497	Springfield City	Springfield
28	496	Kettering City	Kettering
29	487	Washington Local	Toledo
30	479	Cleveland Hgts-University Hgts	University Hgts
31	469	Huber Heights City	Huber Heights
32	464	Sylvania City	Sylvania
33	453	Berea City	Berea
34	447	Medina City	Medina
35	446	Middletown City	Middletown
36	444	Oak Hills Local	Cincinnati
37	443	Gahanna-Jefferson City	Gahanna
38	440	Mansfield City	Mansfield
39	439	Centerville City	Centerville
40	438	Newark City	Newark
41	432	Princeton City	Cincinnati
42	430	Warren City	Warren
43	429	Forest Hills Local	Cincinnati
44	428	Strongsville City	Strongsville
45	428	Shaker Heights City	Shaker Heights
46	425	Findlay City	Findlay
47	412	Lakewood City	Lakewood
48	402	Upper Arlington City	Upper Arlington
49	401	Euclid City	Euclid
50	398	Beavercreek City	Beavercreek
51	389	Brunswick City	Brunswick
52	388	Plain Local	Canton
53	376	Reynoldsburg City	Reynoldsburg
54	364	Solon City	Solon
55	364	Sycamore Community City	Cincinnati
56	359	Lima City	Lima
57	357	Milford Exempted Village	Milford
58	350	Groveport Madison Local	Groveport
59	347	Hudson City	Hudson
60	343	Northmont City	Englewood
61	339	Stow-Munroe Falls City	Stow
62	332	Lancaster City	Lancaster
63	326	Marion City	Marion
64	322	Miamisburg City	Miamisburg
65	318	Jackson Local	Massillon
66	318	Mayfield City	Mayfield Hgts
67	315	Austintown Local	Youngstown
68	314	Marysville Exempted Village	Marysville
69	312	Cuyahoga Falls City	Cuyahoga Falls
70	306	Boardman Local	Youngstown
71	297	South Euclid-Lyndhurst City	Lyndhurst
72	293	Adams County/Ohio Valley Local	West Union
73	293	North Olmsted City	North Olmsted
74	293	Kent City	Kent
75	290	Xenia Community City	Xenia
76	289	North Canton City	North Canton
77	288	Sandusky City	Sandusky
78	288	Ashtabula Area City	Ashtabula
79	287	Perrysburg Exempted Village	Perrysburg
80	284	Massillon City	Massillon
81	277	Delaware City	Delaware
82	276	Winton Woods City	Cincinnati
83	276	Mount Vernon City	Mount Vernon
84	266	Perry Local	Massillon
85	265	Barberton City	Barberton
86	264	Fairborn City	Fairborn
87	262	Oregon City	Oregon
88	262	Zanesville City	Zanesville
89	261	Brecksville-Broadview Heights City	Brecksville
90	258	North Royalton City	North Royalton
91	257	East Cleveland City	East Cleveland
92	255	Lebanon City	Lebanon
93	250	Fremont City	Fremont
94	250	Wadsworth City	Wadsworth
95	249	Painesville Township Local	Painesville
96	248	West Carrollton City	West Carrollton
97	248	Westlake City	Westlake
98	247	Wooster City	Wooster
99	245	Mount Healthy City	Cincinnati
100	242	Maple Heights City	Maple Heights
101	241	Bedford City	Bedford
102	241	Loveland City	Loveland
102	241	Troy City	Troy
104	240	Madison Local	Mansfield
105	238	Anthony Wayne Local	Whitehouse
106	237	Mad River Local	Dayton
107	235	Springfield Local	Holland
108	232	Springboro Community City	Springboro
109	231	Logan-Hocking Local	Logan
110	227	Vandalia-Butler City	Vandalia
111	227	Twinsburg City	Twinsburg
112	226	Green Local	Green
113	225	Nordonia Hills City	Northfield
114	223	Sidney City	Sidney
115	221	Amherst Exempted Village	Amherst
116	217	Ashland City	Ashland
117	216	Kings Local	Kings Mills
118	215	New Albany-Plain Local	New Albany
119	215	Avon Lake City	Avon Lake
120	215	Alliance City	Alliance
121	214	N Ridgeville City	N Ridgeville
122	212	Athens City	The Plains
123	211	Greenville City	Greenville
124	210	Kenston Local	Chagrin Falls
125	210	Southwest Licking Local	Etna
126	209	Teays Valley Local	Ashville
126	209	Tecumseh Local	New Carlisle
128	208	Bowling Green City	Bowling Green
129	207	Springfield Local	Akron
130	207	Edgewood City	Trenton
131	207	Copley-Fairlawn City	Copley
132	206	Switzerland of Ohio Local	Woodsfield
133	204	Southwest Local	Harrison
134	203	Olmsted Falls City	Olmsted Falls
135	201	Piqua City	Piqua
136	199	Electronic Classroom of Tomorrow	Columbus
137	198	Madison Local	Madison
138	198	Painesville Local	Painesville
139	197	Garfield Hgts City	Garfield Hgts
140	197	Lake Local	Uniontown
141	197	Ravenna City	Ravenna

142	196	Orange City	Cleveland
143	195	Northeastern Local	Springfield
144	195	Talawanda City	Oxford
145	194	Howland Local	Warren
146	194	Chardon Local	Chardon
147	194	New Philadel. City	New Philadel.
148	193	Little Miami Local	Morrow
149	191	Louisville City	Louisville
150	187	Whitehall City	Whitehall
151	186	Bellefontaine City	Bellefontaine
152	186	Celina City	Celina
153	184	Hillsboro City	Hillsboro
153	184	Lexington Local	Lexington
155	182	Cloverleaf Local	Lodi
156	181	Canfield Local	Canfield
157	180	Trotwood-Madison City	Trotwood
158	179	East Liverpool City	East Liverpool
159	179	Defiance City	Defiance
160	179	Wilmington City	Wilmington
161	178	Tri-Valley Local	Dresden
162	178	Chillicothe City	Chillicothe
162	178	Midview Local	Grafton
164	178	Western Brown Local	Mount Orab
165	177	Maumee City	Maumee
166	177	West Holmes Local	Millersburg
167	175	Tallmadge City	Tallmadge
168	175	Revere Local	Bath
169	173	Niles City	Niles
170	173	Aurora City	Aurora
170	173	Canal Wnchstr Local	Canal Wnchstr
172	173	Highland Local	Medina
173	171	Tiffin City	Tiffin
174	171	Vinton County Local	Mcarthur
175	170	Hamilton Local	Columbus
176	169	Warrensville Hgts City	Warrensville Hgts
177	168	Cambridge City	Cambridge
178	167	Norwalk City	Norwalk
179	167	Miami Trace Local	Washington CH
180	166	Marietta City	Marietta
181	166	Canton Local	Canton
182	166	Big Walnut Local	Galena
183	165	Norwood City	Norwood
184	164	Franklin City	Franklin
185	163	Buckeye Local	Dillonvale
186	163	Morgan Local	Mcconnelsville
187	162	Wapakoneta City	Wapakoneta
188	161	Bay Village City	Bay Village
189	160	Lakewood Local	Hebron
190	159	Indian Hill Exempted Village	Cincinnati
191	159	Northwest Local	Canal Fulton
192	159	Rocky River City	Rocky River
193	158	Dover City	Dover
194	158	New Richmond Exempted Village	New Richmond
195	156	Marlington Local	Alliance
196	156	Warren Local	Vincent
197	155	Gallia County Local	Gallipolis
198	154	Avon Local	Avon
199	154	Bexley City	Bexley
200	153	Indian Creek Local	Wintersville
201	153	Franklin Local	Duncan Falls
202	153	Gallipolis City	Gallipolis
203	152	Conneaut Area City	Conneaut
204	151	Edison Local	Hammondsville
205	150	Urbana City	Urbana
206	150	Geneva Area City	Geneva
207	150	Norton City	Norton
208	149	Licking Heights Local	Summit Station
209	149	Jackson City	Jackson
210	149	Vermilion Local	Vermilion
211	148	Ross Local	Hamilton
212	147	Bryan City	Bryan
212	147	Meigs Local	Pomeroy
214	147	Streetsboro City	Streetsboro
215	147	Tipp Exempted Village	Tipp City
216	146	West Geauga Local	Chesterland
217	146	Claymont City	Dennison
218	145	Crestwood Local	Mantua
219	145	Goshen Local	Goshen
220	144	Northern Local	Thornville
221	144	Bellevue City	Bellevue
222	144	Galion City	Galion
223	143	Carrollton Exempted Village	Carrollton
224	142	Saint Marys City	Saint Marys
225	141	Oakwood City	Dayton
226	141	Van Wert City	Van Wert
227	141	Buckeye Local	Ashtabula
228	140	Granville Exempted Village	Granville
229	140	West Branch Local	Beloit
230	139	Washington CH City	Washington CH
231	139	Coventry Local	Akron
232	139	Clark-Shawnee Local	Springfield
233	138	Steubenville City	Steubenville
233	138	Sugarcreek Local	Bellbrook
235	138	Salem City	Salem
236	138	Beaver Local	Lisbon
236	138	Harrison Hills City	Hopedale
238	138	Chagrin Falls Exempted Village	Chagrin Falls
239	137	River View Local	Warsaw
240	137	Elida Local	Elida
241	136	Shawnee Local	Lima
242	136	Rossford Exempted Village	Rossford
243	135	Hubbard Exempted Village	Hubbard
243	135	Portsmouth City	Portsmouth
245	134	Field Local	Mogadore
246	134	Kenton City	Kenton
247	133	Napoleon Area City	Napoleon
248	133	London City	London
249	133	Wyoming City	Wyoming
250	132	Buckeye Valley Local	Delaware
251	132	Rock Hill Local	Ironton
252	132	Blanchester Local	Blanchester
253	131	Circleville City	Circleville
254	131	East Holmes Local	Berlin
255	131	Triway Local	Wooster
256	130	Poland Local	Poland
257	130	Licking Valley Local	Newark
258	130	Minerva Local	Minerva
259	129	Fairview Park City	Fairview Park
260	129	Logan Elm Local	Circleville
261	128	Fostoria City	Fostoria
262	128	Perkins Local	Sandusky
262	128	Valley View Local	Germantown
262	128	Woodridge Local	Peninsula
265	128	Rolling Hills Local	Cambridge
266	127	Clyde-Green Springs Ex Vill	Clyde
267	126	Waverly City	Waverly
268	126	Maysville Local	Zanesville
269	126	Shelby City	Shelby
269	126	Willard City	Willard
271	126	New Lexington City	New Lexington
272	125	Graham Local	Saint Paris
272	125	Southeast Local	Ravenna
274	125	East Muskingum Local	New Concord
275	122	Greenfield Exempted Village	Greenfield
276	122	Lakeview Local	Cortland
277	122	Buckeye Local	Medina
278	122	Eaton Community Schools City	Eaton
279	122	Indian Lake Local	Lewistown
280	122	Port Clinton City	Port Clinton
281	121	Wauseon Exempted Village	Wauseon
282	121	Benjamin Logan Local	Bellefontaine
283	121	Coshocton City	Coshocton
284	121	Wellston City	Wellston
285	120	Fairless Local	Navarre
286	119	Mariemont City	Cincinnati
287	118	Perry Local	Perry
288	118	Indian Valley Local	Gnadenhutten
289	116	Paulding Exempted Village	Paulding
290	116	Struthers City	Struthers
291	115	Alexander Local	Albany
292	114	Bucyrus City	Bucyrus
292	114	Orrville City	Orrville
294	114	Benton Carroll Salem Local	Oak Harbor
295	113	Northridge Local	Dayton
296	113	Carlisle Local	Carlisle
297	112	Jefferson Area Local	Jefferson
298	112	Southeast Local	Apple Creek
299	112	Sheffield-Sheffield Lake City	Sheffield Vllg
300	111	Firelands Local	Oberlin
301	111	Greenon Local	Enon
302	110	South Point Local	South Point
303	110	West Muskingum Local	Zanesville
304	109	Fairfield Union Local	West Rushville
304	109	Three Rivers Local	Cleves
306	109	Clermont Northeastern Local	Batavia
307	109	North Fork Local	Utica
308	109	Elgin Local	Marion
308	109	Liberty Local	Youngstown
310	109	Ironton City	Ironton
310	109	Northwest Local	Mcdermott
312	108	River Valley Local	Caledonia
313	108	Sandy Valley Local	Magnolia
314	108	Clear Fork Valley Local	Bellville
315	108	Bellaire Local	Bellaire
316	108	Batavia Local	Batavia
316	108	Otsego Local	Tontogany
318	106	Champion Local	Warren
319	105	Highland Local	Sparta
320	105	Bethel-Tate Local	Bethel
321	104	Northwestern Local	Springfield
322	104	Finneytown Local	Cincinnati
323	103	Jonathan Alder Local	Plain City
324	103	Black River Local	Sullivan
325	102	Milton-Union Exempted Village	West Milton
326	102	Bath Local	Lima
327	101	Eastwood Local	Pemberville
327	101	Monroe Local	Monroe
329	101	Washington-Nile Local	West Portsmouth
330	100	Genoa Area Local	Genoa
331	100	Girard City	Girard
332	100	Pike-Delta-York Local	Delta
333	100	Union-Scioto Local	Chillicothe
334	100	Amanda-Clearcreek Local	Amanda
335	100	Tuscarawas Valley Local	Zoarville
336	100	Fairland Local	Proctorville
337	99	Wickliffe City	Wickliffe
338	98	Madeira City	Cincinnati
339	98	Preble Shawnee Board of Education	Camden
340	98	Upper Sandusky Exempted Village	Upper Sandusky
341	98	Madison Local	Middletown
342	97	Heath City	Heath
343	97	Westfall Local	Williamsport
344	97	Berlin-Milan Local	Milan
345	96	Clinton-Massie Local	Clarksville
346	94	Keystone Local	Lagrange
347	94	Scioto Valley Local	Piketon
348	94	Saint Clairsville-Richland City	Saint Clairsville
349	93	Clearview Local	Lorain
349	93	Ontario Local	Mansfield
351	92	Johnstown-Monroe Local	Johnstown
352	91	Minford Local	Minford
353	90	Ottawa-Glandorf Local	Ottawa
354	90	Madison-Plains Local	London
355	90	Eastern Local	Sardinia
356	90	Martins Ferry City	Martins Ferry
357	89	East Clinton Local	Lees Creek
358	89	Wellington Exempted Village	Wellington
359	89	James A Garfield Local	Garrettsville
360	89	Lake Local	Millbury
361	88	Labrae Local	Leavittsburg
362	88	Bloom-Carroll Local	Carroll
363	87	Coldwater Exempted Village	Coldwater
364	86	Zane Trace Local	Chillicothe
365	86	Wheelersburg Local	Wheelersburg
366	85	Brookville Local	Brookville
367	85	Huron City	Huron
368	83	Greeneview Local	Jamestown
368	83	North College Hill City	Cincinnati
370	81	Alternative Education Academy	Toledo
371	79	Manchester Local	Akron
372	76	Chippewa Local	Doylestown
373	62	Ohio Virtual Academy	Maumee

Number of Students

Rank	Number	District Name	City
1	58,961	Columbus City	Columbus
2	58,788	Cleveland Municipal City	Cleveland
3	36,872	Cincinnati City	Cincinnati
4	30,423	Toledo City	Toledo
5	27,420	Akron City	Akron
6	21,583	South-Western City	Grove City
7	17,455	Lakota Local	Liberty Twp
8	17,054	Dayton City	Dayton
9	14,851	Hilliard City	Hilliard
10	14,062	Westerville City	Westerville
11	12,988	Parma City	Parma
12	12,939	Dublin City	Dublin
13	11,144	Canton City	Canton
14	10,801	Olentangy Local	Lewis Center
15	10,600	Northwest Local	Cincinnati
16	9,857	Fairfield City	Fairfield
17	9,787	Pickerington Local	Pickerington
18	9,778	Mason City	Mason
19	9,718	Lorain City	Lorain
20	9,553	Worthington City	Worthington
21	9,272	West Clermont Local	Cincinnati
22	9,234	Hamilton City	Hamilton
23	9,153	Mentor Exempted Village	Mentor
24	8,826	Willoughby-Eastlake City	Willoughby

Rank	Number	District Name	City
25	8,819	Youngstown City	Youngstown
26	8,668	Springfield City	Springfield
27	8,204	Oak Hills Local	Cincinnati
28	8,196	Centerville City	Centerville
29	7,821	Berea City	Berea
30	7,760	Elyria City	Elyria
31	7,713	Sylvania City	Sylvania
32	7,634	Forest Hills Local	Cincinnati
33	7,626	Beavercreek City	Beavercreek
34	7,605	Kettering City	Kettering
35	7,488	Medina City	Medina
36	7,467	Brunswick City	Brunswick
37	7,400	Strongsville City	Strongsville
38	6,926	Washington Local	Toledo
39	6,925	Middletown City	Middletown
40	6,905	Gahanna-Jefferson City	Gahanna
41	6,781	Reynoldsburg City	Reynoldsburg
42	6,756	Huber Heights City	Huber Heights
42	6,756	Newark City	Newark
44	6,673	Milford Exempted Village	Milford
45	6,509	Euclid City	Euclid
46	6,376	Cleveland Hgts-University Hgts	University Hgts
47	6,361	Lakewood City	Lakewood
48	6,347	Warren City	Warren
49	6,281	Findlay City	Findlay
50	6,245	Electronic Classroom of Tomorrow	Columbus
51	6,172	Groveport Madison Local	Groveport
52	6,052	Plain Local	Canton
53	6,044	Lancaster City	Lancaster
54	5,972	Northmont City	Englewood
55	5,951	Stow-Munroe Falls City	Stow
56	5,786	Jackson Local	Massillon
57	5,713	Princeton City	Cincinnati
58	5,686	Sycamore Community City	Cincinnati
59	5,631	Shaker Heights City	Shaker Heights
60	5,629	Upper Arlington City	Upper Arlington
61	5,548	Miamisburg City	Miamisburg
62	5,424	Mansfield City	Mansfield
63	5,355	Hudson City	Hudson
64	5,345	Solon City	Solon
65	5,273	Cuyahoga Falls City	Cuyahoga Falls
66	5,250	Marion City	Marion
67	5,197	Lebanon City	Lebanon
68	5,109	Xenia Community City	Xenia
69	5,102	Austintown Local	Youngstown
70	5,071	Lima City	Lima
71	5,023	Marysville Exempted Village	Marysville
72	4,892	North Canton City	North Canton
73	4,849	Boardman Local	Youngstown
74	4,806	Perry Local	Massillon
75	4,784	Springboro Community City	Springboro
76	4,748	Fairborn City	Fairborn
76	4,748	Painesville Township Local	Painesville
78	4,742	Wadsworth City	Wadsworth
79	4,720	Brecksville-Broadview Heights City	Brecksville
80	4,683	Delaware City	Delaware
81	4,627	Troy City	Troy
82	4,613	North Olmsted City	North Olmsted
83	4,599	Loveland City	Loveland
84	4,588	North Royalton City	North Royalton
85	4,576	Massillon City	Massillon
86	4,528	South Euclid-Lyndhurst City	Lyndhurst
87	4,502	Fremont City	Fremont
88	4,454	Perrysburg Exempted Village	Perrysburg
89	4,434	Ashtabula Area City	Ashtabula
90	4,355	Barberton City	Barberton
90	4,355	East Cleveland City	East Cleveland
92	4,295	Amherst Exempted Village	Amherst
93	4,249	Anthony Wayne Local	Whitehouse
94	4,222	Green Local	Green
95	4,200	Mount Vernon City	Mount Vernon
96	4,190	Adams County/Ohio Valley Local	West Union
97	4,185	Zanesville City	Zanesville
98	4,157	Logan-Hocking Local	Logan
99	4,109	Sandusky City	Sandusky
100	4,103	Twinsburg City	Twinsburg
101	4,081	Garfield Hgts City	Garfield Hgts
102	4,067	Westlake City	Westlake
103	4,059	Winton Woods City	Cincinnati
104	3,967	Nordonia Hills City	Northfield
105	3,952	Wooster City	Wooster
106	3,949	Maple Heights City	Maple Heights
107	3,935	Mayfield City	Mayfield Hgts
108	3,929	Oregon City	Oregon
109	3,922	Sidney City	Sidney
110	3,898	Springfield Local	Holland
111	3,865	Southwest Local	Harrison
112	3,845	Piqua City	Piqua
113	3,839	Kings Local	Kings Mills
114	3,823	Northeastern Local	Springfield
115	3,821	West Carrollton City	West Carrollton
116	3,812	Bedford City	Bedford
117	3,789	Edgewood City	Trenton
118	3,744	Madison Local	Madison
119	3,733	N Ridgeville City	N Ridgeville
120	3,729	Mount Healthy City	Cincinnati
121	3,724	Mad River Local	Dayton
122	3,695	Ashland City	Ashland
123	3,654	Kent City	Kent
124	3,624	Little Miami Local	Morrow
125	3,615	Southwest Licking Local	Etna
126	3,560	Tecumseh Local	New Carlisle
127	3,546	Midview Local	Grafton
128	3,539	Teays Valley Local	Ashville
129	3,538	Lake Local	Uniontown
130	3,518	Olmsted Falls City	Olmsted Falls
131	3,489	Avon Lake City	Avon Lake
132	3,438	Vandalia-Butler City	Vandalia
133	3,429	New Albany-Plain Local	New Albany
134	3,399	Madison Local	Mansfield
135	3,390	Cloverleaf Local	Lodi
136	3,386	Western Brown Local	Mount Orab
137	3,352	Copley-Fairlawn City	Copley
138	3,335	Louisville City	Louisville
139	3,334	Chardon Local	Chardon
140	3,307	Trotwood-Madison City	Trotwood
141	3,296	Greenville City	Greenville
142	3,287	Wilmington City	Wilmington
143	3,241	Ravenna City	Ravenna
143	3,241	Tri-Valley Local	Dresden
145	3,227	Howland Local	Warren
146	3,218	Kenston Local	Chagrin Falls
147	3,175	Alliance City	Alliance
148	3,145	Chillicothe City	Chillicothe
149	3,133	Bowling Green City	Bowling Green
150	3,110	Canfield Local	Canfield
151	3,105	Wapakoneta City	Wapakoneta
152	3,104	New Philadel. City	New Philadel.
153	3,085	Norwalk City	Norwalk
154	3,076	Canal Wnchstr Local	Canal Wnchstr
155	3,069	Highland Local	Medina
156	3,038	Marietta City	Marietta
157	3,014	Talawanda City	Oxford
158	3,002	Tiffin City	Tiffin
159	2,998	Painesville Local	Painesville
160	2,987	Avon Local	Avon
161	2,964	Athens City	The Plains
162	2,953	Aurora City	Aurora
163	2,943	Celina City	Celina
164	2,934	Springfield Local	Akron
165	2,929	Geneva Area City	Geneva
166	2,918	Whitehall City	Whitehall
167	2,897	Ross Local	Hamilton
168	2,895	Maumee City	Maumee
169	2,890	Ohio Virtual Academy	Maumee
170	2,875	Niles City	Niles
171	2,868	Revere Local	Bath
172	2,855	Warrensville Hgts City	Warrensville Hgts
173	2,838	Franklin City	Franklin
174	2,837	Carrollton Exempted Village	Carrollton
175	2,836	Sugarcreek Local	Bellbrook
176	2,817	Hamilton Local	Columbus
177	2,806	West Holmes Local	Millersburg
178	2,800	Bellefontaine City	Bellefontaine
179	2,795	Hillsboro City	Hillsboro
180	2,787	Jackson City	Jackson
181	2,784	Lexington Local	Lexington
182	2,770	Miami Trace Local	Washington CH
183	2,732	Big Walnut Local	Galena
184	2,716	Warren Local	Vincent
185	2,707	Tallmadge City	Tallmadge
186	2,706	Tipp Exempted Village	Tipp City
187	2,692	Switzerland of Ohio Local	Woodsfield
188	2,687	East Liverpool City	East Liverpool
189	2,686	Cambridge City	Cambridge
190	2,674	Shawnee Local	Lima
191	2,645	Marlington Local	Alliance
192	2,641	Rocky River City	Rocky River
193	2,638	Edison Local	Hammondsville
194	2,637	Vinton County Local	Mcarthur
195	2,619	Dover City	Dover
196	2,578	Norwood City	Norwood
197	2,556	Alternative Education Academy	Toledo
198	2,548	Goshen Local	Goshen
199	2,546	Crestwood Local	Mantua
200	2,530	Defiance City	Defiance
201	2,515	Bay Village City	Bay Village
202	2,503	Clark-Shawnee Local	Springfield
202	2,503	Licking Heights Local	Summit Station
204	2,502	New Richmond Exempted Village	New Richmond
205	2,492	Gallia County Local	Gallipolis
206	2,490	West Geauga Local	Chesterland
207	2,485	West Branch Local	Beloit
208	2,466	Vermilion Local	Vermilion
209	2,459	Elida Local	Elida
209	2,459	Northwest Local	Canal Fulton
211	2,448	Poland Local	Poland
212	2,443	Buckeye Local	Dillonvale
213	2,438	Conneaut Area City	Conneaut
214	2,435	Franklin Local	Duncan Falls
215	2,432	River View Local	Warsaw
216	2,430	Circleville City	Circleville
217	2,425	Norton City	Norton
218	2,415	Clyde-Green Springs Ex Vill	Clyde
219	2,413	Saint Marys City	Saint Marys
220	2,411	Coventry Local	Akron
221	2,390	Napoleon Area City	Napoleon
222	2,387	Beaver Local	Lisbon
223	2,384	Buckeye Local	Medina
224	2,383	Gallipolis City	Gallipolis
225	2,375	Indian Creek Local	Wintersville
226	2,360	Bellevue City	Bellevue
227	2,358	Field Local	Mogadore
228	2,352	Steubenville City	Steubenville
229	2,346	Granville Exempted Village	Granville
230	2,337	Northern Local	Thornville
230	2,337	Salem City	Salem
232	2,333	Buckeye Local	Ashtabula
233	2,326	Washington CH City	Washington CH
234	2,319	Buckeye Valley Local	Delaware
235	2,317	Graham Local	Saint Paris
236	2,316	Urbana City	Urbana
237	2,306	Hubbard Exempted Village	Hubbard
238	2,304	Logan Elm Local	Circleville
239	2,301	Greenfield Exempted Village	Greenfield
240	2,299	Eaton Community Schools City	Eaton
241	2,298	Canton Local	Canton
242	2,282	Bryan City	Bryan
243	2,281	Maysville Local	Zanesville
244	2,275	Orange City	Cleveland
245	2,267	Claymont City	Dennison
246	2,251	Indian Hill Exempted Village	Cincinnati
246	2,251	Shelby City	Shelby
248	2,250	Lakewood Local	Hebron
249	2,246	Morgan Local	Mcconnelsville
250	2,236	Van Wert City	Van Wert
251	2,215	Lakeview Local	Cortland
252	2,209	Waverly City	Waverly
253	2,192	Perkins Local	Sandusky
254	2,181	Southeast Local	Ravenna
255	2,176	Fostoria City	Fostoria
255	2,176	Minerva Local	Minerva
257	2,175	Jefferson Area Local	Jefferson
258	2,172	Willard City	Willard
259	2,170	East Muskingum Local	New Concord
260	2,166	Triway Local	Wooster
261	2,161	Bexley City	Bexley
262	2,151	Rolling Hills Local	Cambridge
263	2,149	Galion City	Galion
264	2,141	Firelands Local	Oberlin
265	2,136	Licking Valley Local	Newark
266	2,128	Kenton City	Kenton
267	2,112	Wauseon Exempted Village	Wauseon
268	2,109	Oakwood City	Dayton
269	2,101	Streetsboro City	Streetsboro
270	2,090	London City	London
271	2,079	Valley View Local	Germantown
272	2,077	Struthers City	Struthers
273	2,062	Fairfield Union Local	West Rushville
274	2,053	Union-Scioto Local	Chillicothe
275	2,045	Harrison Hills City	Hopedale
276	2,041	Rossford Exempted Village	Rossford
277	2,031	Greenon Local	Enon
278	1,998	Indian Lake Local	Lewistown
279	1,995	Wyoming City	Wyoming
280	1,993	Three Rivers Local	Cleves
281	1,991	Jonathan Alder Local	Plain City
282	1,990	Meigs Local	Pomeroy
283	1,985	Bethel-Tate Local	Bethel
284	1,984	Bath Local	Lima
284	1,984	Benton Carroll Salem Local	Oak Harbor

286	1,982	Chagrin Falls Exempted Village	Chagrin Falls
287	1,974	Portsmouth City	Portsmouth
288	1,967	Coshocton City	Coshocton
289	1,959	Batavia Local	Batavia
290	1,951	Rock Hill Local	Ironton
291	1,947	Northwestern Local	Springfield
292	1,946	Benjamin Logan Local	Bellefontaine
293	1,937	Sheffield-Sheffield Lake City	Sheffield Vllg
294	1,926	Eastwood Local	Pemberville
295	1,922	Clermont Northeastern Local	Batavia
296	1,908	Fairless Local	Navarre
297	1,906	East Holmes Local	Berlin
298	1,903	New Lexington City	New Lexington
299	1,886	North Fork Local	Utica
300	1,884	West Muskingum Local	Zanesville
301	1,882	River Valley Local	Caledonia
302	1,880	South Point Local	South Point
303	1,877	Monroe Local	Monroe
304	1,870	Port Clinton City	Port Clinton
305	1,868	Indian Valley Local	Gnadenhutten
306	1,859	Keystone Local	Lagrange
307	1,858	Northridge Local	Dayton
308	1,852	Perry Local	Perry
309	1,847	Blanchester Local	Blanchester
310	1,844	Clear Fork Valley Local	Bellville
311	1,836	Carlisle Local	Carlisle
312	1,828	Orrville City	Orrville
313	1,823	Berlin-Milan Local	Milan
314	1,820	Ontario Local	Mansfield
315	1,819	Woodridge Local	Peninsula
316	1,815	Clinton-Massie Local	Clarksville
317	1,812	Liberty Local	Youngstown
318	1,810	Fairview Park City	Fairview Park
319	1,808	Fairland Local	Proctorville
320	1,792	Upper Sandusky Exempted Village	Upper Sandusky
321	1,786	Wellston City	Wellston
322	1,783	Otsego Local	Tontogany
323	1,779	Black River Local	Sullivan
324	1,769	Northwest Local	Mcdermott
325	1,766	Highland Local	Sparta
326	1,760	Girard City	Girard
327	1,748	Bucyrus City	Bucyrus
328	1,733	Finneytown Local	Cincinnati
328	1,733	Heath City	Heath
328	1,733	Lake Local	Millbury
328	1,733	Southeast Local	Apple Creek
332	1,731	Milton-Union Exempted Village	West Milton
333	1,728	Paulding Exempted Village	Paulding
334	1,724	Westfall Local	Williamsport
335	1,719	Champion Local	Warren
336	1,704	Scioto Valley Local	Piketon
336	1,704	Tuscarawas Valley Local	Zoarville
338	1,689	Washington-Nile Local	West Portsmouth
339	1,685	Ottawa-Glandorf Local	Ottawa
340	1,671	Zane Trace Local	Chillicothe
341	1,669	Ironton City	Ironton
342	1,658	Elgin Local	Marion
342	1,658	Mariemont City	Cincinnati
344	1,654	Alexander Local	Albany
345	1,643	Wellington Exempted Village	Wellington
346	1,629	Labrae Local	Leavittsburg
346	1,629	Saint Clairsville-Richland City	Saint Clairsville
348	1,619	Minford Local	Minford
349	1,607	Johnstown-Monroe Local	Johnstown
350	1,605	Brookville Local	Brookville
350	1,605	James A Garfield Local	Garrettsville
352	1,603	Amanda-Clearcreek Local	Amanda
353	1,589	Genoa Area Local	Genoa
354	1,587	North College Hill City	Cincinnati
355	1,578	Bloom-Carroll Local	Carroll
356	1,568	Greeneview Local	Jamestown
357	1,565	Martins Ferry City	Martins Ferry
358	1,564	Madison Local	Middletown
359	1,557	Manchester Local	Akron
360	1,552	East Clinton Local	Lees Creek
360	1,552	Madeira City	Cincinnati
362	1,547	Coldwater Exempted Village	Coldwater
363	1,543	Eastern Local	Sardinia
364	1,538	Preble Shawnee Board of Education	Camden
365	1,536	Wheelersburg Local	Wheelersburg
366	1,532	Sandy Valley Local	Magnolia
367	1,526	Chippewa Local	Doylestown
368	1,525	Clearview Local	Lorain
369	1,520	Pike-Delta-York Local	Delta
370	1,519	Wickliffe City	Wickliffe
371	1,518	Huron City	Huron
372	1,504	Bellaire Local	Bellaire
373	1,503	Madison-Plains Local	London

Male Students

Rank	Percent	District Name	City
1	55.3	Genoa Area Local	Genoa
2	54.6	Wickliffe City	Wickliffe
3	54.4	Portsmouth City	Portsmouth
4	54.2	Preble Shawnee Board of Education	Camden
5	54.1	Massillon City	Massillon
6	54.1	Piqua City	Piqua
7	54.0	Tallmadge City	Tallmadge
8	53.8	Lakewood Local	Hebron
9	53.8	Claymont City	Dennison
10	53.7	Saint Marys City	Saint Marys
11	53.5	Harrison Hills City	Hopedale
12	53.5	Chagrin Falls Exempted Village	Chagrin Falls
13	53.5	Northwest Local	Mcdermott
14	53.5	Black River Local	Sullivan
15	53.5	Morgan Local	Mcconnelsville
16	53.3	Madison Local	Mansfield
17	53.3	Maumee City	Maumee
18	53.3	Southeast Local	Ravenna
19	53.3	Fairfield Union Local	West Rushville
20	53.3	Green Local	Green
21	53.3	Licking Valley Local	Newark
22	53.2	Milton-Union Exempted Village	West Milton
23	53.2	Orange City	Cleveland
24	53.2	Amanda-Clearcreek Local	Amanda
25	53.2	Highland Local	Sparta
26	53.1	Finneytown Local	Cincinnati
27	53.1	North College Hill City	Cincinnati
28	53.1	Southwest Local	Harrison
29	53.1	Bloom-Carroll Local	Carroll
30	53.1	Ironton City	Ironton
31	53.1	Bellaire Local	Bellaire
32	53.1	Rossford Exempted Village	Rossford
33	53.0	Celina City	Celina
34	53.0	Three Rivers Local	Cleves
35	53.0	Shelby City	Shelby
36	53.0	Champion Local	Warren
37	52.9	Steubenville City	Steubenville
38	52.9	Perry Local	Massillon
39	52.9	Hudson City	Hudson
40	52.9	Madeira City	Cincinnati
41	52.9	Ross Local	Hamilton
42	52.9	Marysville Exempted Village	Marysville
43	52.9	Berlin-Milan Local	Milan
44	52.9	Fairland Local	Proctorville
45	52.9	Canton Local	Canton
46	52.9	Franklin Local	Duncan Falls
47	52.8	Greenfield Exempted Village	Greenfield
48	52.7	Warren Local	Vincent
49	52.6	Ravenna City	Ravenna
50	52.6	Berea City	Berea
51	52.6	Lake Local	Uniontown
52	52.6	Eaton Community Schools City	Eaton
53	52.6	Alliance City	Alliance
54	52.6	Minford Local	Minford
55	52.6	Rock Hill Local	Ironton
56	52.6	Southeast Local	Apple Creek
57	52.6	Kings Local	Kings Mills
58	52.6	Cambridge City	Cambridge
59	52.5	Indian Hill Exempted Village	Cincinnati
60	52.5	Defiance City	Defiance
61	52.5	Washington CH City	Washington CH
62	52.5	Franklin City	Franklin
63	52.5	West Geauga Local	Chesterland
64	52.5	Dublin City	Dublin
65	52.5	Conneaut Area City	Conneaut
66	52.5	Gallipolis City	Gallipolis
67	52.4	River View Local	Warsaw
68	52.4	Springfield Local	Holland
69	52.4	Lexington Local	Lexington
70	52.4	Logan-Hocking Local	Logan
71	52.4	Maple Heights City	Maple Heights
72	52.4	Trotwood-Madison City	Trotwood
73	52.4	Mount Healthy City	Cincinnati
74	52.4	Ashland City	Ashland
75	52.4	Garfield Hgts City	Garfield Hgts
76	52.4	Union-Scioto Local	Chillicothe
77	52.4	Princeton City	Cincinnati
78	52.4	Coldwater Exempted Village	Coldwater
79	52.4	Lancaster City	Lancaster
80	52.4	Euclid City	Euclid
81	52.3	Mayfield City	Mayfield Hgts
82	52.3	Streetsboro City	Streetsboro
83	52.3	Ashtabula Area City	Ashtabula
84	52.2	East Muskingum Local	New Concord
85	52.2	Orrville City	Orrville
86	52.2	Delaware City	Delaware
87	52.2	West Carrollton City	West Carrollton
88	52.2	Avon Lake City	Avon Lake
89	52.2	Brookville Local	Brookville
90	52.2	Mansfield City	Mansfield
91	52.2	Milford Exempted Village	Milford
92	52.2	Waverly City	Waverly
93	52.2	Tiffin City	Tiffin
94	52.2	Fairview Park City	Fairview Park
95	52.1	Tri-Valley Local	Dresden
96	52.1	Norwood City	Norwood
97	52.1	Northwest Local	Cincinnati
98	52.1	Kent City	Kent
99	52.1	Tuscarawas Valley Local	Zoarville
100	52.1	N Ridgeville City	N Ridgeville
101	52.1	Kenton City	Kenton
102	52.1	Wheelersburg Local	Wheelersburg
103	52.1	Springfield City	Springfield
104	52.1	Jonathan Alder Local	Plain City
105	52.1	Teays Valley Local	Ashville
106	52.1	Wooster City	Wooster
107	52.0	Norwalk City	Norwalk
108	52.0	Pickerington Local	Pickerington
109	52.0	Winton Woods City	Cincinnati
110	52.0	Hilliard City	Hilliard
111	52.0	Paulding Exempted Village	Paulding
112	52.0	Crestwood Local	Mantua
113	52.0	Wapakoneta City	Wapakoneta
114	52.0	Edgewood City	Trenton
115	52.0	Scioto Valley Local	Piketon
116	52.0	Urbana City	Urbana
117	52.0	Lima City	Lima
118	52.0	Nordonia Hills City	Northfield
119	52.0	Gahanna-Jefferson City	Gahanna
120	52.0	Miami Trace Local	Washington CH
121	52.0	Washington Local	Toledo
122	52.0	Field Local	Mogadore
123	52.0	Fairborn City	Fairborn
124	52.0	Martins Ferry City	Martins Ferry
125	51.9	Jefferson Area Local	Jefferson
126	51.9	Revere Local	Bath
127	51.9	Woodridge Local	Peninsula
128	51.9	Indian Valley Local	Gnadenhutten
129	51.9	Xenia Community City	Xenia
130	51.9	Mount Vernon City	Mount Vernon
131	51.9	Beavercreek City	Beavercreek
132	51.9	Greeneview Local	Jamestown
133	51.9	Struthers City	Struthers
134	51.8	Elida Local	Elida
135	51.8	Worthington City	Worthington
136	51.8	Toledo City	Toledo
137	51.8	Kenston Local	Chagrin Falls
138	51.8	Troy City	Troy
139	51.8	Bellevue City	Bellevue
140	51.8	Sandy Valley Local	Magnolia
141	51.8	Goshen Local	Goshen
142	51.8	New Richmond Exempted Village	New Richmond
143	51.8	Hamilton City	Hamilton
144	51.7	North Fork Local	Utica
145	51.7	Oregon City	Oregon
146	51.7	West Clermont Local	Cincinnati
147	51.7	North Olmsted City	North Olmsted
148	51.7	Huber Heights City	Huber Heights
149	51.7	Barberton City	Barberton
150	51.7	Perkins Local	Sandusky
151	51.7	Batavia Local	Batavia
152	51.7	Firelands Local	Oberlin
153	51.7	Dover City	Dover
154	51.7	Minerva Local	Minerva
155	51.7	Washington-Nile Local	West Portsmouth
156	51.7	West Branch Local	Beloit
157	51.6	Parma City	Parma
158	51.6	Bowling Green City	Bowling Green
159	51.6	Westerville City	Westerville
160	51.6	Stow-Munroe Falls City	Stow
161	51.6	Mad River Local	Dayton
162	51.6	Kettering City	Kettering
163	51.6	Wilmington City	Wilmington
164	51.6	Solon City	Solon
165	51.6	Hillsboro City	Hillsboro
166	51.6	Strongsville City	Strongsville
167	51.6	Austintown Local	Youngstown
168	51.6	Wadsworth City	Wadsworth

169	51.6	Bexley City	Bexley
170	51.6	Northmont City	Englewood
171	51.6	Tipp Exempted Village	Tipp City
172	51.6	Perrysburg Exempted Village	Perrysburg
173	51.6	Boardman Local	Youngstown
174	51.6	Beaver Local	Lisbon
175	51.6	Port Clinton City	Port Clinton
176	51.6	Saint Clairsville-Richland City	Saint Clairsville
177	51.6	Centerville City	Centerville
178	51.5	Lakota Local	Liberty Twp
179	51.5	Springboro Community City	Springboro
180	51.5	Clear Fork Valley Local	Bellville
181	51.5	Northern Local	Thornville
182	51.5	Bellefontaine City	Bellefontaine
183	51.5	Upper Arlington City	Upper Arlington
184	51.5	Ohio Virtual Academy	Maumee
185	51.5	Copley-Fairlawn City	Copley
186	51.5	Lakewood City	Lakewood
187	51.5	Buckeye Valley Local	Delaware
188	51.5	Cloverleaf Local	Lodi
189	51.4	Springfield Local	Akron
190	51.4	Fremont City	Fremont
191	51.4	Plain Local	Canton
192	51.4	Vandalia-Butler City	Vandalia
193	51.4	Jackson City	Jackson
193	51.4	Reynoldsburg City	Reynoldsburg
195	51.4	Willoughby-Eastlake City	Willoughby
196	51.4	Oak Hills Local	Cincinnati
197	51.4	Aurora City	Aurora
198	51.4	Benjamin Logan Local	Bellefontaine
199	51.4	Bedford City	Bedford
200	51.4	Elgin Local	Marion
200	51.4	Vinton County Local	Mcarthur
202	51.4	Sycamore Community City	Cincinnati
203	51.4	Groveport Madison Local	Groveport
204	51.4	Graham Local	Saint Paris
205	51.3	East Liverpool City	East Liverpool
206	51.3	Whitehall City	Whitehall
207	51.3	Van Wert City	Van Wert
208	51.3	Sandusky City	Sandusky
209	51.3	Sylvania City	Sylvania
210	51.3	Chippewa Local	Doylestown
211	51.3	Shaker Heights City	Shaker Heights
212	51.3	Canfield Local	Canfield
213	51.3	Miamisburg City	Miamisburg
214	51.3	Huron City	Huron
215	51.2	Clermont Northeastern Local	Batavia
216	51.2	Lorain City	Lorain
217	51.2	Northwest Local	Canal Fulton
218	51.2	Northeastern Local	Springfield
219	51.2	Vermilion Local	Vermilion
220	51.2	Eastwood Local	Pemberville
221	51.2	Madison Local	Madison
222	51.2	River Valley Local	Caledonia
223	51.2	Westfall Local	Williamsport
224	51.2	Midview Local	Grafton
225	51.2	Alexander Local	Albany
226	51.2	London City	London
227	51.1	Canal Wnchstr Local	Canal Wnchstr
228	51.1	Granville Exempted Village	Granville
229	51.1	Canton City	Canton
230	51.1	Bryan City	Bryan
231	51.1	Geneva Area City	Geneva
232	51.1	Buckeye Local	Dillonvale
233	51.1	Monroe Local	Monroe
234	51.1	Twinsburg City	Twinsburg
235	51.1	New Albany-Plain Local	New Albany
236	51.1	Dayton City	Dayton
237	51.1	Clark-Shawnee Local	Springfield
238	51.1	Wyoming City	Wyoming
239	51.1	Mariemont City	Cincinnati
240	51.1	Brunswick City	Brunswick
241	51.1	Loveland City	Loveland
242	51.1	Tecumseh Local	New Carlisle
243	51.1	Logan Elm Local	Circleville
244	51.1	Sidney City	Sidney
245	51.0	Upper Sandusky Exempted Village	Upper Sandusky
246	51.0	Otsego Local	Tontogany
247	51.0	Coshocton City	Coshocton
248	51.0	Bethel-Tate Local	Bethel
249	51.0	Middletown City	Middletown
250	51.0	West Holmes Local	Millersburg
251	51.0	Switzerland of Ohio Local	Woodsfield
252	51.0	Salem City	Salem
253	51.0	Howland Local	Warren
254	51.0	Chardon Local	Chardon
255	51.0	North Canton City	North Canton
256	50.9	Cleveland Municipal City	Cleveland
257	50.9	Akron City	Akron
258	50.9	Edison Local	Hammondsville
259	50.9	Southwest Licking Local	Etna
260	50.9	Olentangy Local	Lewis Center
261	50.9	Triway Local	Wooster
262	50.9	Marietta City	Marietta
263	50.9	Brecksville-Broadview Heights City	Brecksville
264	50.9	Clyde-Green Springs Ex Vill	Clyde
265	50.9	Greenon Local	Enon
266	50.9	Johnstown-Monroe Local	Johnstown
267	50.9	Fairless Local	Navarre
268	50.9	Marion City	Marion
269	50.9	Highland Local	Medina
270	50.9	Mason City	Mason
271	50.9	Talawanda City	Oxford
272	50.9	Liberty Local	Youngstown
273	50.8	Amherst Exempted Village	Amherst
274	50.8	Newark City	Newark
275	50.8	South-Western City	Grove City
276	50.8	Fairfield City	Fairfield
277	50.8	Sugarcreek Local	Bellbrook
278	50.8	Hamilton Local	Columbus
279	50.8	Carrollton Exempted Village	Carrollton
280	50.8	South Euclid-Lyndhurst City	Lyndhurst
281	50.8	Forest Hills Local	Cincinnati
282	50.8	Western Brown Local	Mount Orab
283	50.8	Big Walnut Local	Galena
284	50.7	Elyria City	Elyria
285	50.7	Olmsted Falls City	Olmsted Falls
286	50.7	Heath City	Heath
287	50.7	Wauseon Exempted Village	Wauseon
288	50.7	Painesville Township Local	Painesville
289	50.7	Mentor Exempted Village	Mentor
290	50.7	Niles City	Niles
291	50.7	Warrensville Hgts City	Warrensville Hgts
292	50.7	Cuyahoga Falls City	Cuyahoga Falls
293	50.7	Poland Local	Poland
294	50.7	Cleveland Hgts-University Hgts	University Hgts
295	50.6	Lebanon City	Lebanon
296	50.6	Eastern Local	Sardinia
297	50.6	Blanchester Local	Blanchester
298	50.6	Greenville City	Greenville
299	50.6	Wellston City	Wellston
300	50.6	Indian Creek Local	Wintersville
301	50.6	Indian Lake Local	Lewistown
302	50.6	Painesville City Local	Painesville
303	50.6	Clinton-Massie Local	Clarksville
304	50.6	Findlay City	Findlay
305	50.6	Madison-Plains Local	London
306	50.5	Lake Local	Millbury
307	50.5	Columbus City	Columbus
308	50.5	Bay Village City	Bay Village
309	50.5	Youngstown City	Youngstown
310	50.5	Perry Local	Perry
311	50.5	Circleville City	Circleville
312	50.5	Medina City	Medina
313	50.4	Anthony Wayne Local	Whitehouse
314	50.4	Chillicothe City	Chillicothe
315	50.4	Napoleon Area City	Napoleon
316	50.4	Maysville Local	Zanesville
317	50.4	New Lexington City	New Lexington
318	50.4	East Holmes Local	Berlin
319	50.4	Warren City	Warren
320	50.3	New Philadel. City	New Philadel.
321	50.3	Carlisle Local	Carlisle
322	50.3	Athens City	The Plains
323	50.3	Northwestern Local	Springfield
324	50.3	Willard City	Willard
325	50.3	Wellington Exempted Village	Wellington
326	50.3	Pike-Delta-York Local	Delta
327	50.3	Northridge Local	Dayton
328	50.3	North Royalton City	North Royalton
329	50.2	Meigs Local	Pomeroy
330	50.2	Westlake City	Westlake
331	50.2	Jackson Local	Massillon
332	50.2	Ontario Local	Mansfield
333	50.2	Keystone Local	Lagrange
334	50.2	James A Garfield Local	Garrettsville
335	50.2	Shawnee Local	Lima
336	50.2	Bucyrus City	Bucyrus
337	50.1	Fostoria City	Fostoria
338	50.1	Little Miami Local	Morrow
339	50.1	Buckeye Local	Medina
340	50.0	Zanesville City	Zanesville
341	50.0	West Muskingum Local	Zanesville
342	50.0	Madison Local	Middletown
343	50.0	Benton Carroll Salem Local	Oak Harbor
344	49.9	Cincinnati City	Cincinnati
345	49.9	South Point Local	South Point
346	49.9	Zane Trace Local	Chillicothe
347	49.9	Valley View Local	Germantown
348	49.8	Lakeview Local	Cortland
349	49.8	Licking Heights Local	Summit Station
350	49.8	Bath Local	Lima
351	49.8	Hubbard Exempted Village	Hubbard
352	49.7	Gallia County Local	Gallipolis
353	49.6	Rocky River City	Rocky River
354	49.6	Rolling Hills Local	Cambridge
355	49.6	Louisville City	Louisville
356	49.5	Oakwood City	Dayton
357	49.5	Coventry Local	Akron
358	49.3	Manchester Local	Akron
359	49.2	Sheffield-Sheffield Lake City	Sheffield Vllg
360	49.1	Labrae Local	Leavittsburg
361	49.1	East Clinton Local	Lees Creek
362	49.1	Girard City	Girard
363	49.0	Marlington Local	Alliance
364	49.0	Adams County/Ohio Valley Local	West Union
365	48.9	Avon Local	Avon
366	48.8	Norton City	Norton
367	48.8	Ottawa-Glandorf Local	Ottawa
368	48.5	East Cleveland City	East Cleveland
369	48.2	Buckeye Local	Ashtabula
370	47.8	Galion City	Galion
371	47.6	Clearview Local	Lorain
372	47.5	Alternative Education Academy	Toledo
373	43.5	Electronic Classroom of Tomorrow	Columbus

Female Students

Rank	Percent	District Name	City
1	56.4	Electronic Classroom of Tomorrow	Columbus
2	52.4	Alternative Education Academy	Toledo
3	52.3	Clearview Local	Lorain
4	52.1	Galion City	Galion
5	51.7	Buckeye Local	Ashtabula
6	51.4	East Cleveland City	East Cleveland
7	51.1	Ottawa-Glandorf Local	Ottawa
8	51.1	Norton City	Norton
9	51.0	Avon Local	Avon
10	50.9	Adams County/Ohio Valley Local	West Union
11	50.9	Marlington Local	Alliance
12	50.8	Girard City	Girard
13	50.8	East Clinton Local	Lees Creek
14	50.8	Labrae Local	Leavittsburg
15	50.7	Sheffield-Sheffield Lake City	Sheffield Vllg
16	50.6	Manchester Local	Akron
17	50.4	Coventry Local	Akron
18	50.4	Oakwood City	Dayton
19	50.3	Louisville City	Louisville
20	50.3	Rolling Hills Local	Cambridge
21	50.3	Rocky River City	Rocky River
22	50.2	Gallia County Local	Gallipolis
23	50.1	Hubbard Exempted Village	Hubbard
24	50.1	Bath Local	Lima
25	50.1	Licking Heights Local	Summit Station
26	50.1	Lakeview Local	Cortland
27	50.0	Valley View Local	Germantown
28	50.0	Zane Trace Local	Chillicothe
29	50.0	South Point Local	South Point
30	50.0	Cincinnati City	Cincinnati
31	50.0	Benton Carroll Salem Local	Oak Harbor
32	49.9	Madison Local	Middletown
33	49.9	West Muskingum Local	Zanesville
34	49.9	Zanesville City	Zanesville
35	49.8	Buckeye Local	Medina
36	49.8	Little Miami Local	Morrow
37	49.8	Fostoria City	Fostoria
38	49.7	Bucyrus City	Bucyrus
39	49.7	Shawnee Local	Lima
40	49.7	James A Garfield Local	Garrettsville
41	49.7	Keystone Local	Lagrange
42	49.7	Ontario Local	Mansfield
43	49.7	Jackson Local	Massillon
44	49.7	Westlake City	Westlake
45	49.7	Meigs Local	Pomeroy
46	49.6	North Royalton City	North Royalton
47	49.6	Northridge Local	Dayton
48	49.6	Pike-Delta-York Local	Delta
49	49.6	Wellington Exempted Village	Wellington
50	49.6	Willard City	Willard
51	49.6	Northwestern Local	Springfield

Rank	Score	District	City
52	49.6	Athens City	The Plains
53	49.6	Carlisle Local	Carlisle
54	49.6	New Philadel. City	New Philadel.
55	49.5	Warren City	Warren
56	49.5	East Holmes Local	Berlin
57	49.5	New Lexington City	New Lexington
58	49.5	Maysville Local	Zanesville
59	49.5	Napoleon Area City	Napoleon
60	49.5	Chillicothe City	Chillicothe
61	49.5	Anthony Wayne Local	Whitehouse
62	49.4	Medina City	Medina
63	49.4	Circleville City	Circleville
64	49.4	Perry Local	Perry
65	49.4	Youngstown City	Youngstown
66	49.4	Bay Village City	Bay Village
67	49.4	Columbus City	Columbus
68	49.4	Lake Local	Millbury
69	49.3	Madison-Plains Local	London
70	49.3	Findlay City	Findlay
71	49.3	Clinton-Massie Local	Clarksville
72	49.3	Painesville Local	Painesville
73	49.3	Indian Lake Local	Lewistown
74	49.3	Indian Creek Local	Wintersville
75	49.3	Wellston City	Wellston
76	49.3	Greenville City	Greenville
77	49.3	Blanchester Local	Blanchester
78	49.3	Eastern Local	Sardinia
79	49.3	Lebanon City	Lebanon
80	49.2	Cleveland Hgts-University Hgts	University Hgts
81	49.2	Poland Local	Poland
82	49.2	Cuyahoga Falls City	Cuyahoga Falls
83	49.2	Warrensville Hgts City	Warrensville Hgts
84	49.2	Niles City	Niles
85	49.2	Mentor Exempted Village	Mentor
86	49.2	Painesville Township Local	Painesville
87	49.2	Wauseon Exempted Village	Wauseon
88	49.2	Heath City	Heath
89	49.2	Olmsted Falls City	Olmsted Falls
90	49.2	Elyria City	Elyria
91	49.1	Big Walnut Local	Galena
92	49.1	Western Brown Local	Mount Orab
93	49.1	Forest Hills Local	Cincinnati
94	49.1	South Euclid-Lyndhurst City	Lyndhurst
95	49.1	Carrollton Exempted Village	Carrollton
96	49.1	Hamilton Local	Columbus
97	49.1	Sugarcreek Local	Bellbrook
98	49.1	Fairfield City	Fairfield
99	49.1	South-Western City	Grove City
100	49.1	Newark City	Newark
101	49.1	Amherst Exempted Village	Amherst
102	49.0	Liberty Local	Youngstown
103	49.0	Talawanda City	Oxford
104	49.0	Mason City	Mason
105	49.0	Highland Local	Medina
106	49.0	Marion City	Marion
107	49.0	Fairless Local	Navarre
108	49.0	Johnstown-Monroe Local	Johnstown
109	49.0	Greenon Local	Enon
110	49.0	Clyde-Green Springs Ex Vill	Clyde
111	49.0	Brecksville-Broadview Heights City	Brecksville
112	49.0	Marietta City	Marietta
113	49.0	Triway Local	Wooster
114	49.0	Olentangy Local	Lewis Center
115	49.0	Southwest Licking Local	Etna
116	49.0	Edison Local	Hammondsville
117	49.0	Akron City	Akron
118	49.0	Cleveland Municipal City	Cleveland
119	48.9	North Canton City	North Canton
120	48.9	Chardon Local	Chardon
121	48.9	Howland Local	Warren
122	48.9	Salem City	Salem
123	48.9	Switzerland of Ohio Local	Woodsfield
124	48.9	West Holmes Local	Millersburg
125	48.9	Middletown City	Middletown
126	48.9	Bethel-Tate Local	Bethel
127	48.9	Coshocton City	Coshocton
128	48.9	Otsego Local	Tontogany
129	48.9	Upper Sandusky Exempted Village	Upper Sandusky
130	48.8	Sidney City	Sidney
131	48.8	Logan Elm Local	Circleville
132	48.8	Tecumseh Local	New Carlisle
133	48.8	Loveland City	Loveland
134	48.8	Brunswick City	Brunswick
135	48.8	Mariemont City	Cincinnati
136	48.8	Wyoming City	Wyoming
137	48.8	Clark-Shawnee Local	Springfield
138	48.8	Dayton City	Dayton
139	48.8	New Albany-Plain Local	New Albany
140	48.8	Twinsburg City	Twinsburg
141	48.8	Monroe Local	Monroe
142	48.8	Buckeye Local	Dillonvale
143	48.8	Geneva Area City	Geneva
144	48.8	Bryan City	Bryan
145	48.8	Canton City	Canton
146	48.8	Granville Exempted Village	Granville
147	48.8	Canal Wnchstr Local	Canal Wnchstr
148	48.7	London City	London
149	48.7	Alexander Local	Albany
150	48.7	Midview Local	Grafton
151	48.7	Westfall Local	Williamsport
152	48.7	River Valley Local	Caledonia
153	48.7	Madison Local	Madison
154	48.7	Eastwood Local	Pemberville
155	48.7	Vermilion Local	Vermilion
156	48.7	Northeastern Local	Springfield
157	48.7	Northwest Local	Canal Fulton
158	48.7	Lorain City	Lorain
159	48.7	Clermont Northeastern Local	Batavia
160	48.6	Huron City	Huron
161	48.6	Miamisburg City	Miamisburg
162	48.6	Canfield Local	Canfield
163	48.6	Shaker Heights City	Shaker Heights
164	48.6	Chippewa Local	Doylestown
165	48.6	Sylvania City	Sylvania
166	48.6	Sandusky City	Sandusky
167	48.6	Van Wert City	Van Wert
168	48.6	Whitehall City	Whitehall
169	48.6	East Liverpool City	East Liverpool
170	48.5	Graham Local	Saint Paris
171	48.5	Groveport Madison Local	Groveport
172	48.5	Sycamore Community City	Cincinnati
173	48.5	Elgin Local	Marion
173	48.5	Vinton County Local	Mcarthur
175	48.5	Bedford City	Bedford
176	48.5	Benjamin Logan Local	Bellefontaine
177	48.5	Aurora City	Aurora
178	48.5	Oak Hills Local	Cincinnati
179	48.5	Willoughby-Eastlake City	Willoughby
180	48.5	Jackson City	Jackson
180	48.5	Reynoldsburg City	Reynoldsburg
182	48.5	Vandalia-Butler City	Vandalia
183	48.5	Plain Local	Canton
184	48.5	Fremont City	Fremont
185	48.5	Springfield Local	Akron
186	48.4	Cloverleaf Local	Lodi
187	48.4	Buckeye Valley Local	Delaware
188	48.4	Lakewood City	Lakewood
189	48.4	Copley-Fairlawn City	Copley
190	48.4	Ohio Virtual Academy	Maumee
191	48.4	Upper Arlington City	Upper Arlington
192	48.4	Bellefontaine City	Bellefontaine
193	48.4	Northern Local	Thornville
194	48.4	Clear Fork Valley Local	Bellville
195	48.4	Springboro Community City	Springboro
196	48.4	Lakota Local	Liberty Twp
197	48.3	Centerville City	Centerville
198	48.3	Saint Clairsville-Richland City	Saint Clairsville
199	48.3	Port Clinton City	Port Clinton
200	48.3	Beaver Local	Lisbon
201	48.3	Boardman Local	Youngstown
202	48.3	Perrysburg Exempted Village	Perrysburg
203	48.3	Tipp Exempted Village	Tipp City
204	48.3	Northmont City	Englewood
205	48.3	Bexley City	Bexley
206	48.3	Wadsworth City	Wadsworth
207	48.3	Austintown Local	Youngstown
208	48.3	Strongsville City	Strongsville
209	48.3	Hillsboro City	Hillsboro
210	48.3	Solon City	Solon
211	48.3	Wilmington City	Wilmington
212	48.3	Kettering City	Kettering
213	48.3	Mad River Local	Dayton
214	48.3	Stow-Munroe Falls City	Stow
215	48.3	Westerville City	Westerville
216	48.3	Bowling Green City	Bowling Green
217	48.3	Parma City	Parma
218	48.2	West Branch Local	Beloit
219	48.2	Washington-Nile Local	West Portsmouth
220	48.2	Minerva Local	Minerva
221	48.2	Dover City	Dover
222	48.2	Firelands Local	Oberlin
223	48.2	Batavia Local	Batavia
224	48.2	Perkins Local	Sandusky
225	48.2	Barberton City	Barberton
226	48.2	Huber Heights City	Huber Heights
227	48.2	North Olmsted City	North Olmsted
228	48.2	West Clermont Local	Cincinnati
229	48.2	Oregon City	Oregon
230	48.2	North Fork Local	Utica
231	48.1	Hamilton City	Hamilton
232	48.1	New Richmond Exempted Village	New Richmond
233	48.1	Goshen Local	Goshen
234	48.1	Sandy Valley Local	Magnolia
235	48.1	Bellevue City	Bellevue
236	48.1	Troy City	Troy
237	48.1	Kenston Local	Chagrin Falls
238	48.1	Toledo City	Toledo
239	48.1	Worthington City	Worthington
240	48.1	Elida Local	Elida
241	48.0	Struthers City	Struthers
242	48.0	Greeneview Local	Jamestown
243	48.0	Beavercreek City	Beavercreek
244	48.0	Mount Vernon City	Mount Vernon
245	48.0	Xenia Community City	Xenia
246	48.0	Indian Valley Local	Gnadenhutten
247	48.0	Woodridge Local	Peninsula
248	48.0	Revere Local	Bath
249	48.0	Jefferson Area Local	Jefferson
250	47.9	Martins Ferry City	Martins Ferry
251	47.9	Fairborn City	Fairborn
252	47.9	Field Local	Mogadore
253	47.9	Washington Local	Toledo
254	47.9	Miami Trace Local	Washington CH
255	47.9	Gahanna-Jefferson City	Gahanna
256	47.9	Nordonia Hills City	Northfield
257	47.9	Lima City	Lima
258	47.9	Urbana City	Urbana
259	47.9	Scioto Valley Local	Piketon
260	47.9	Edgewood City	Trenton
261	47.9	Wapakoneta City	Wapakoneta
262	47.9	Crestwood Local	Mantua
263	47.9	Paulding Exempted Village	Paulding
264	47.9	Hilliard City	Hilliard
265	47.9	Winton Woods City	Cincinnati
266	47.9	Pickerington Local	Pickerington
267	47.9	Norwalk City	Norwalk
268	47.8	Wooster City	Wooster
269	47.8	Teays Valley Local	Ashville
270	47.8	Jonathan Alder Local	Plain City
271	47.8	Springfield City	Springfield
272	47.8	Wheelersburg Local	Wheelersburg
273	47.8	Kenton City	Kenton
274	47.8	N Ridgeville City	N Ridgeville
275	47.8	Tuscarawas Valley Local	Zoarville
276	47.8	Kent City	Kent
277	47.8	Northwest Local	Cincinnati
278	47.8	Norwood City	Norwood
279	47.8	Tri-Valley Local	Dresden
280	47.7	Fairview Park City	Fairview Park
281	47.7	Tiffin City	Tiffin
282	47.7	Waverly City	Waverly
283	47.7	Milford Exempted Village	Milford
284	47.7	Mansfield City	Mansfield
285	47.7	Brookville Local	Brookville
286	47.7	Avon Lake City	Avon Lake
287	47.7	West Carrollton City	West Carrollton
288	47.7	Delaware City	Delaware
289	47.7	Orrville City	Orrville
290	47.7	East Muskingum Local	New Concord
291	47.6	Ashtabula Area City	Ashtabula
292	47.6	Streetsboro City	Streetsboro
293	47.6	Mayfield City	Mayfield Hgts
294	47.5	Euclid City	Euclid
295	47.5	Lancaster City	Lancaster
296	47.5	Coldwater Exempted Village	Coldwater
297	47.5	Princeton City	Cincinnati
298	47.5	Union-Scioto Local	Chillicothe
299	47.5	Garfield Hgts City	Garfield Hgts
300	47.5	Ashland City	Ashland
301	47.5	Mount Healthy City	Cincinnati
302	47.5	Trotwood-Madison City	Trotwood
303	47.5	Maple Heights City	Maple Heights
304	47.5	Logan-Hocking Local	Logan
305	47.5	Lexington Local	Lexington
306	47.5	Springfield Local	Holland
307	47.5	River View Local	Warsaw
308	47.5	Gallipolis City	Gallipolis
309	47.4	Conneaut Area City	Conneaut
310	47.4	Dublin City	Dublin
311	47.4	West Geauga Local	Chesterland
312	47.4	Franklin City	Franklin

313	47.4	Washington CH City	Washington CH
314	47.4	Defiance City	Defiance
315	47.4	Indian Hill Exempted Village	Cincinnati
316	47.3	Cambridge City	Cambridge
317	47.3	Kings Local	Kings Mills
318	47.3	Southeast Local	Apple Creek
319	47.3	Rock Hill Local	Ironton
320	47.3	Minford Local	Minford
321	47.3	Alliance City	Alliance
322	47.3	Eaton Community Schools City	Eaton
323	47.3	Lake Local	Uniontown
324	47.3	Berea City	Berea
325	47.3	Ravenna City	Ravenna
326	47.2	Warren Local	Vincent
327	47.1	Greenfield Exempted Village	Greenfield
328	47.0	Franklin Local	Duncan Falls
329	47.0	Canton Local	Canton
330	47.0	Fairland Local	Proctorville
331	47.0	Berlin-Milan Local	Milan
332	47.0	Marysville Exempted Village	Marysville
333	47.0	Ross Local	Hamilton
334	47.0	Madeira City	Cincinnati
335	47.0	Hudson City	Hudson
336	47.0	Perry Local	Massillon
337	47.0	Steubenville City	Steubenville
338	46.9	Champion Local	Warren
339	46.9	Shelby City	Shelby
340	46.9	Three Rivers Local	Cleves
341	46.9	Celina City	Celina
342	46.8	Rossford Exempted Village	Rossford
343	46.8	Bellaire Local	Bellaire
344	46.8	Ironton City	Ironton
345	46.8	Bloom-Carroll Local	Carroll
346	46.8	Southwest Local	Harrison
347	46.8	North College Hill City	Cincinnati
348	46.8	Finneytown Local	Cincinnati
349	46.7	Highland Local	Sparta
350	46.7	Amanda-Clearcreek Local	Amanda
351	46.7	Orange City	Cleveland
352	46.7	Milton-Union Exempted Village	West Milton
353	46.6	Licking Valley Local	Newark
354	46.6	Green Local	Green
355	46.6	Fairfield Union Local	West Rushville
356	46.6	Southeast Local	Ravenna
357	46.6	Maumee City	Maumee
358	46.6	Madison Local	Mansfield
359	46.4	Morgan Local	Mcconnelsville
360	46.4	Black River Local	Sullivan
361	46.4	Northwest Local	Mcdermott
362	46.4	Chagrin Falls Exempted Village	Chagrin Falls
363	46.4	Harrison Hills City	Hopedale
364	46.2	Saint Marys City	Saint Marys
365	46.1	Claymont City	Dennison
366	46.1	Lakewood Local	Hebron
367	45.9	Tallmadge City	Tallmadge
368	45.8	Piqua City	Piqua
369	45.8	Massillon City	Massillon
370	45.7	Preble Shawnee Board of Education	Camden
371	45.5	Portsmouth City	Portsmouth
372	45.3	Wickliffe City	Wickliffe
373	44.6	Genoa Area Local	Genoa

Individual Education Program Students

Rank	Percent	District Name	City
1	27.7	Harrison Hills City	Hopedale
2	24.1	Coshocton City	Coshocton
3	23.5	Zanesville City	Zanesville
4	23.0	Dayton City	Dayton
5	22.7	Alexander Local	Albany
6	22.5	Claymont City	Dennison
7	22.4	Gallipolis City	Gallipolis
8	22.1	Bellaire Local	Bellaire
9	22.0	Sandusky City	Sandusky
10	21.8	Lima City	Lima
11	21.4	Napoleon Area City	Napoleon
12	21.0	Celina City	Celina
12	21.0	Marion City	Marion
14	20.9	Cincinnati City	Cincinnati
14	20.9	South Point Local	South Point
16	20.8	East Liverpool City	East Liverpool
17	20.7	Mount Vernon City	Mount Vernon
18	20.3	Urbana City	Urbana
18	20.3	Warren City	Warren
20	20.0	Mansfield City	Mansfield
20	20.0	Paulding Exempted Village	Paulding
20	20.0	Youngstown City	Youngstown
23	19.9	Wellston City	Wellston
24	19.8	New Philadel. City	New Philadel.
25	19.7	Meigs Local	Pomeroy
25	19.7	Sidney City	Sidney
27	19.6	Ashtabula Area City	Ashtabula
27	19.6	Defiance City	Defiance
29	19.4	Bellevue City	Bellevue
30	19.2	Hamilton City	Hamilton
30	19.2	Saint Marys City	Saint Marys
32	19.1	Cleveland Municipal City	Cleveland
32	19.1	Tiffin City	Tiffin
34	19.0	Ravenna City	Ravenna
35	18.9	Bellefontaine City	Bellefontaine
35	18.9	Galion City	Galion
35	18.9	Middletown City	Middletown
38	18.8	Gallia County Local	Gallipolis
39	18.7	Findlay City	Findlay
40	18.6	Port Clinton City	Port Clinton
41	18.4	Ironton City	Ironton
42	18.3	Mayfield City	Mayfield Hgts
42	18.3	Winton Woods City	Cincinnati
44	18.2	Alliance City	Alliance
44	18.2	Buckeye Local	Dillonvale
44	18.2	Euclid City	Euclid
47	18.1	Fostoria City	Fostoria
48	18.0	Portsmouth City	Portsmouth
49	17.9	Springfield Local	Holland
50	17.8	Parma City	Parma
50	17.8	Switzerland of Ohio Local	Woodsfield
50	17.8	Van Wert City	Van Wert
53	17.7	Akron City	Akron
53	17.7	Bucyrus City	Bucyrus
53	17.7	Groveport Madison Local	Groveport
53	17.7	Springfield Local	Akron
53	17.7	Vinton County Local	Mcarthur
58	17.5	Greenville City	Greenville
58	17.5	River View Local	Warsaw
60	17.4	Athens City	The Plains
61	17.3	Edgewood City	Trenton
61	17.3	Goshen Local	Goshen
61	17.3	Massillon City	Massillon
64	17.2	Logan-Hocking Local	Logan
65	17.1	Toledo City	Toledo
66	17.0	South Euclid-Lyndhurst City	Lyndhurst
67	16.9	Cambridge City	Cambridge
67	16.9	Circleville City	Circleville
67	16.9	Graham Local	Saint Paris
67	16.9	Mount Healthy City	Cincinnati
71	16.8	Shelby City	Shelby
72	16.7	Indian Lake Local	Lewistown
72	16.7	Kettering City	Kettering
72	16.7	Marysville Exempted Village	Marysville
72	16.7	Piqua City	Piqua
76	16.6	Clermont Northeastern Local	Batavia
76	16.6	Electronic Classroom of Tomorrow	Columbus
76	16.6	Kenton City	Kenton
76	16.6	N Ridgeville City	N Ridgeville
76	16.6	Northwest Local	Mcdermott
76	16.6	Upper Sandusky Exempted Village	Upper Sandusky
82	16.3	Cleveland Hgts-University Hgts	University Hgts
82	16.3	Indian Creek Local	Wintersville
84	16.2	Canton City	Canton
84	16.2	Lakewood City	Lakewood
84	16.2	Pike-Delta-York Local	Delta
84	16.2	Waverly City	Waverly
88	16.1	Austintown Local	Youngstown
88	16.1	Fairless Local	Navarre
88	16.1	Fremont City	Fremont
88	16.1	Gahanna-Jefferson City	Gahanna
88	16.1	Northern Local	Thornville
88	16.1	Springfield City	Springfield
88	16.1	Warrensville Hgts City	Warrensville Hgts
88	16.1	Wickliffe City	Wickliffe
88	16.1	Xenia Community City	Xenia
97	16.0	Adams County/Ohio Valley Local	West Union
97	16.0	Dover City	Dover
97	16.0	Indian Valley Local	Gnadenhutten
97	16.0	Lorain City	Lorain
97	16.0	Southeast Local	Ravenna
97	16.0	Whitehall City	Whitehall
103	15.9	Rolling Hills Local	Cambridge
103	15.9	Sandy Valley Local	Magnolia
103	15.9	Shaker Heights City	Shaker Heights
103	15.9	Vandalia-Butler City	Vandalia
107	15.8	Jackson City	Jackson
107	15.8	London City	London
107	15.8	Maysville Local	Zanesville
107	15.8	Washington CH City	Washington CH
111	15.7	Ashland City	Ashland
111	15.7	Martins Ferry City	Martins Ferry
113	15.6	Alternative Education Academy	Toledo
113	15.6	Delaware City	Delaware
113	15.6	Southwest Licking Local	Etna
113	15.6	Three Rivers Local	Cleves
117	15.5	Barberton City	Barberton
117	15.5	Beaver Local	Lisbon
117	15.5	Clyde-Green Springs Ex Vill	Clyde
117	15.5	Elyria City	Elyria
117	15.5	Franklin City	Franklin
117	15.5	Minerva Local	Minerva
117	15.5	Wooster City	Wooster
124	15.4	Highland Local	Sparta
124	15.4	Marietta City	Marietta
124	15.4	Vermilion Local	Vermilion
124	15.4	Willard City	Willard
128	15.3	Blanchester Local	Blanchester
128	15.3	Clear Fork Valley Local	Bellville
128	15.3	Columbus City	Columbus
128	15.3	Perkins Local	Sandusky
128	15.3	Perry Local	Massillon
128	15.3	Streetsboro City	Streetsboro
134	15.2	Maumee City	Maumee
134	15.2	Princeton City	Cincinnati
136	15.1	Field Local	Mogadore
136	15.1	Geneva Area City	Geneva
136	15.1	Marlington Local	Alliance
139	15.0	Benjamin Logan Local	Bellefontaine
139	15.0	Madison Local	Mansfield
139	15.0	Norwalk City	Norwalk
142	14.9	Canton Local	Canton
142	14.9	Medina City	Medina
142	14.9	Newark City	Newark
142	14.9	Painesville Local	Painesville
142	14.9	Steubenville City	Steubenville
147	14.8	Fairborn City	Fairborn
147	14.8	Otsego Local	Tontogany
147	14.8	Rock Hill Local	Ironton
147	14.8	Willoughby-Eastlake City	Willoughby
151	14.7	Logan Elm Local	Circleville
152	14.6	Berea City	Berea
152	14.6	Big Walnut Local	Galena
152	14.6	Franklin Local	Duncan Falls
152	14.6	Salem City	Salem
152	14.6	Wapakoneta City	Wapakoneta
152	14.6	Washington Local	Toledo
158	14.5	Bedford City	Bedford
158	14.5	Crestwood Local	Mantua
158	14.5	West Muskingum Local	Zanesville
161	14.4	Bowling Green City	Bowling Green
161	14.4	Carrollton Exempted Village	Carrollton
161	14.4	Cuyahoga Falls City	Cuyahoga Falls
161	14.4	Garfield Hgts City	Garfield Hgts
161	14.4	Lakewood Local	Hebron
161	14.4	West Geauga Local	Chesterland
167	14.3	Amherst Exempted Village	Amherst
167	14.3	Heath City	Heath
167	14.3	North Fork Local	Utica
167	14.3	Northridge Local	Dayton
167	14.3	West Holmes Local	Millersburg
172	14.2	Bay Village City	Bay Village
172	14.2	Coldwater Exempted Village	Coldwater
172	14.2	Conneaut Area City	Conneaut
172	14.2	East Cleveland City	East Cleveland
172	14.2	Fairview Park City	Fairview Park
172	14.2	Mad River Local	Dayton
172	14.2	Rossford Exempted Village	Rossford
172	14.2	Southwest Local	Harrison
180	14.1	Brookville Local	Brookville
180	14.1	Elgin Local	Marion
180	14.1	Lancaster City	Lancaster
180	14.1	Licking Valley Local	Newark
180	14.1	South-Western City	Grove City
180	14.1	Southeast Local	Apple Creek
186	14.0	Benton Carroll Salem Local	Oak Harbor
186	14.0	Girard City	Girard
186	14.0	Woodridge Local	Peninsula
189	13.9	Bryan City	Bryan
189	13.9	Morgan Local	Mcconnelsville
189	13.9	North College Hill City	Cincinnati
189	13.9	Trotwood-Madison City	Trotwood
193	13.8	Huber Heights City	Huber Heights
193	13.8	James A Garfield Local	Garrettsville
193	13.8	Sheffield-Sheffield Lake City	Sheffield Vllg

196	13.7	Chagrin Falls Exempted Village	Chagrin Falls
196	13.7	Warren Local	Vincent
198	13.6	Amanda-Clearcreek Local	Amanda
198	13.6	East Clinton Local	Lees Creek
198	13.6	Lexington Local	Lexington
198	13.6	Oak Hills Local	Cincinnati
198	13.6	Reynoldsburg City	Reynoldsburg
198	13.6	Scioto Valley Local	Piketon
204	13.5	Beavercreek City	Beavercreek
204	13.5	East Muskingum Local	New Concord
204	13.5	Kings Local	Kings Mills
204	13.5	Mentor Exempted Village	Mentor
208	13.4	Finneytown Local	Cincinnati
208	13.4	Lakeview Local	Cortland
208	13.4	Niles City	Niles
211	13.3	Berlin-Milan Local	Milan
211	13.3	Licking Heights Local	Summit Station
211	13.3	River Valley Local	Caledonia
211	13.3	Teays Valley Local	Ashville
211	13.3	West Carrollton City	West Carrollton
211	13.3	Westlake City	Westlake
217	13.2	East Holmes Local	Berlin
217	13.2	Labrae Local	Leavittsburg
217	13.2	New Richmond Exempted Village	New Richmond
217	13.2	North Olmsted City	North Olmsted
221	13.1	Chillicothe City	Chillicothe
221	13.1	Northmont City	Englewood
221	13.1	Rocky River City	Rocky River
221	13.1	Tri-Valley Local	Dresden
221	13.1	Tuscarawas Valley Local	Zoarville
226	13.0	Edison Local	Hammondsville
226	13.0	Miami Trace Local	Washington CH
226	13.0	Miamisburg City	Miamisburg
226	13.0	Orrville City	Orrville
230	12.9	Huron City	Huron
230	12.9	Maple Heights City	Maple Heights
230	12.9	Northwest Local	Cincinnati
230	12.9	Sylvania City	Sylvania
230	12.9	Triway Local	Wooster
230	12.9	Zane Trace Local	Chillicothe
236	12.8	Hudson City	Hudson
236	12.8	Johnstown-Monroe Local	Johnstown
236	12.8	Madison-Plains Local	London
239	12.7	Bloom-Carroll Local	Carroll
239	12.7	New Lexington City	New Lexington
239	12.7	Springboro Community City	Springboro
239	12.7	Struthers City	Struthers
239	12.7	Troy City	Troy
244	12.6	Centerville City	Centerville
244	12.6	Milford Exempted Village	Milford
244	12.6	Northwest Local	Canal Fulton
244	12.6	Orange City	Cleveland
244	12.6	West Clermont Local	Cincinnati
249	12.5	Howland Local	Warren
249	12.5	Plain Local	Canton
249	12.5	Strongsville City	Strongsville
252	12.4	Canal Wnchstr Local	Canal Wnchstr
252	12.4	Cloverleaf Local	Lodi
252	12.4	Greeneview Local	Jamestown
252	12.4	Westfall Local	Williamsport
256	12.3	Chardon Local	Chardon
256	12.3	Ross Local	Hamilton
258	12.2	Buckeye Valley Local	Delaware
258	12.2	Green Local	Green
258	12.2	Norwood City	Norwood
258	12.2	Ottawa-Glandorf Local	Ottawa
262	12.0	Hamilton Local	Columbus
262	12.0	Madison Local	Middletown
262	12.0	Tallmadge City	Tallmadge
265	11.9	Jefferson Area Local	Jefferson
265	11.9	Jonathan Alder Local	Plain City
265	11.9	Union-Scioto Local	Chillicothe
268	11.8	Fairfield City	Fairfield
268	11.8	Fairland Local	Proctorville
268	11.8	Lake Local	Millbury
271	11.7	Granville Exempted Village	Granville
271	11.7	Hillsboro City	Hillsboro
271	11.7	Kent City	Kent
271	11.7	Preble Shawnee Board of Education	Camden
275	11.6	Clearview Local	Lorain
275	11.6	Greenfield Exempted Village	Greenfield
275	11.6	Milton-Union Exempted Village	West Milton
275	11.6	Wauseon Exempted Village	Wauseon
279	11.5	Champion Local	Warren
279	11.5	Hilliard City	Hilliard
279	11.5	Solon City	Solon
279	11.5	Tecumseh Local	New Carlisle
283	11.4	Black River Local	Sullivan
283	11.4	Eaton Community Schools City	Eaton
283	11.4	Firelands Local	Oberlin
283	11.4	Nordonia Hills City	Northfield
283	11.4	Oregon City	Oregon
288	11.3	Bath Local	Lima
288	11.3	Boardman Local	Youngstown
288	11.3	Westerville City	Westerville
288	11.3	Wilmington City	Wilmington
292	11.2	Lake Local	Uniontown
292	11.2	Talawanda City	Oxford
294	11.1	Avon Local	Avon
294	11.1	Clinton-Massie Local	Clarksville
294	11.1	Painesville Township Local	Painesville
294	11.1	Worthington City	Worthington
298	11.0	Copley-Fairlawn City	Copley
298	11.0	Keystone Local	Lagrange
298	11.0	Olmsted Falls City	Olmsted Falls
298	11.0	Poland Local	Poland
302	10.9	Bexley City	Bexley
302	10.9	Buckeye Local	Ashtabula
302	10.9	Carlisle Local	Carlisle
302	10.9	Stow-Munroe Falls City	Stow
306	10.8	Forest Hills Local	Cincinnati
306	10.8	Highland Local	Medina
306	10.8	Hubbard Exempted Village	Hubbard
306	10.8	Louisville City	Louisville
306	10.8	Saint Clairsville-Richland City	Saint Clairsville
306	10.8	Valley View Local	Germantown
312	10.7	Canfield Local	Canfield
312	10.7	Lebanon City	Lebanon
312	10.7	Little Miami Local	Morrow
312	10.7	Wellington Exempted Village	Wellington
316	10.6	Avon Lake City	Avon Lake
316	10.6	North Canton City	North Canton
318	10.5	Buckeye Local	Medina
318	10.5	Elida Local	Elida
318	10.5	Greenon Local	Enon
318	10.5	Madeira City	Cincinnati
318	10.5	Midview Local	Grafton
323	10.4	Brunswick City	Brunswick
323	10.4	Eastern Local	Sardinia
323	10.4	Kenston Local	Chagrin Falls
323	10.4	West Branch Local	Beloit
327	10.3	Sugarcreek Local	Bellbrook
327	10.3	Tipp Exempted Village	Tipp City
327	10.3	Twinsburg City	Twinsburg
330	10.2	Coventry Local	Akron
330	10.2	Minford Local	Minford
330	10.2	Sycamore Community City	Cincinnati
333	10.1	Madison Local	Madison
333	10.1	Monroe Local	Monroe
333	10.1	North Royalton City	North Royalton
333	10.1	Northwestern Local	Springfield
333	10.1	Olentangy Local	Lewis Center
333	10.1	Washington-Nile Local	West Portsmouth
339	10.0	Dublin City	Dublin
339	10.0	Manchester Local	Akron
341	9.9	Genoa Area Local	Genoa
341	9.9	Loveland City	Loveland
343	9.8	Batavia Local	Batavia
343	9.8	New Albany-Plain Local	New Albany
345	9.7	Mariemont City	Cincinnati
345	9.7	Mason City	Mason
345	9.7	Wyoming City	Wyoming
348	9.5	Pickerington Local	Pickerington
349	9.4	Clark-Shawnee Local	Springfield
349	9.4	Fairfield Union Local	West Rushville
349	9.4	Upper Arlington City	Upper Arlington
352	9.3	Aurora City	Aurora
352	9.3	Chippewa Local	Doylestown
352	9.3	Western Brown Local	Mount Orab
355	9.2	Indian Hill Exempted Village	Cincinnati
356	8.9	Brecksville-Broadview Heights City	Brecksville
356	8.9	Northeastern Local	Springfield
356	8.9	Revere Local	Bath
359	8.8	Perrysburg Exempted Village	Perrysburg
360	8.7	Eastwood Local	Pemberville
360	8.7	Lakota Local	Liberty Twp
360	8.7	Liberty Local	Youngstown
360	8.7	Oakwood City	Dayton
360	8.7	Perry Local	Perry
365	8.6	Shawnee Local	Lima
366	8.5	Norton City	Norton
367	8.1	Bethel-Tate Local	Bethel
368	8.0	Wheelersburg Local	Wheelersburg
369	7.8	Wadsworth City	Wadsworth
370	7.7	Jackson Local	Massillon
371	6.7	Anthony Wayne Local	Whitehouse
372	6.2	Ohio Virtual Academy	Maumee
373	5.6	Ontario Local	Mansfield

English Language Learner Students

Rank	Percent	District Name	City
1	56.5	East Holmes Local	Berlin
2	23.6	Painesville Local	Painesville
3	15.2	Southeast Local	Apple Creek
4	11.2	Whitehall City	Whitehall
5	9.1	Columbus City	Columbus
6	7.8	South-Western City	Grove City
7	7.7	Fremont City	Fremont
8	7.6	North Olmsted City	North Olmsted
9	7.1	Lakewood City	Lakewood
10	6.8	Dublin City	Dublin
11	6.6	Westerville City	Westerville
12	5.6	Hamilton City	Hamilton
12	5.6	Sycamore Community City	Cincinnati
14	5.3	Licking Heights Local	Summit Station
15	5.1	Ashtabula Area City	Ashtabula
16	4.7	Princeton City	Cincinnati
17	4.6	Cleveland Municipal City	Cleveland
18	4.3	Hilliard City	Hilliard
19	4.1	Norwood City	Norwood
20	4.0	Copley-Fairlawn City	Copley
20	4.0	Fairview Park City	Fairview Park
22	3.9	West Carrollton City	West Carrollton
23	3.8	Parma City	Parma
24	3.7	Mayfield City	Mayfield Hgts
25	3.3	Winton Woods City	Cincinnati
25	3.3	Worthington City	Worthington
27	3.1	Fostoria City	Fostoria
27	3.1	Huber Heights City	Huber Heights
29	3.0	Fairfield City	Fairfield
29	3.0	Tecumseh Local	New Carlisle
29	3.0	Wauseon Exempted Village	Wauseon
32	2.7	Lorain City	Lorain
33	2.5	Mason City	Mason
33	2.5	Solon City	Solon
33	2.5	Willard City	Willard
36	2.4	Middletown City	Middletown
37	2.3	Cincinnati City	Cincinnati
38	2.2	Centerville City	Centerville
38	2.2	Lake Local	Uniontown
38	2.2	Reynoldsburg City	Reynoldsburg
38	2.2	Shaker Heights City	Shaker Heights
42	2.1	Sidney City	Sidney
42	2.1	Willoughby-Eastlake City	Willoughby
42	2.1	Woodridge Local	Peninsula
45	2.0	Clearview Local	Lorain
45	2.0	Lakota Local	Liberty Twp
45	2.0	Nordonia Hills City	Northfield
48	1.9	Olentangy Local	Lewis Center
48	1.9	Strongsville City	Strongsville
50	1.8	Brecksville-Broadview Heights City	Brecksville
50	1.8	Canal Wnchstr Local	Canal Wnchstr
50	1.8	Groveport Madison Local	Groveport
50	1.8	Napoleon Area City	Napoleon
50	1.8	Troy City	Troy
55	1.7	Akron City	Akron
55	1.7	Delaware City	Delaware
55	1.7	North Royalton City	North Royalton
55	1.7	Pickerington Local	Pickerington
55	1.7	Rocky River City	Rocky River
60	1.6	Mentor Exempted Village	Mentor
60	1.6	Northmont City	Englewood
60	1.6	Youngstown City	Youngstown
63	1.5	Cuyahoga Falls City	Cuyahoga Falls
63	1.5	Madeira City	Cincinnati
63	1.5	Northwest Local	Cincinnati
63	1.5	Tipp Exempted Village	Tipp City
63	1.5	Upper Arlington City	Upper Arlington
63	1.5	Washington Local	Toledo
69	1.4	Boardman Local	Youngstown
69	1.4	Dayton City	Dayton
69	1.4	Kings Local	Kings Mills
69	1.4	Stow-Munroe Falls City	Stow
69	1.4	Sylvania City	Sylvania
74	1.3	Athens City	The Plains
74	1.3	Bellefontaine City	Bellefontaine
74	1.3	Kettering City	Kettering
74	1.3	Mount Healthy City	Cincinnati
74	1.3	Twinsburg City	Twinsburg

Rank	Value	District	City
79	1.2	Findlay City	Findlay
79	1.2	Indian Hill Exempted Village	Cincinnati
79	1.2	Jackson Local	Massillon
79	1.2	Marion City	Marion
79	1.2	Marlington Local	Alliance
79	1.2	Orange City	Cleveland
85	1.1	Beavercreek City	Beavercreek
85	1.1	Berea City	Berea
85	1.1	Bucyrus City	Bucyrus
85	1.1	Gahanna-Jefferson City	Gahanna
85	1.1	Green Local	Green
85	1.1	Lebanon City	Lebanon
85	1.1	London City	London
85	1.1	New Philadel. City	New Philadel.
85	1.1	Ohio Virtual Academy	Maumee
85	1.1	Pike-Delta-York Local	Delta
85	1.1	Sugarcreek Local	Bellbrook
85	1.1	Wyoming City	Wyoming
97	1.0	Cleveland Hgts-University Hgts	University Hgts
97	1.0	Fairborn City	Fairborn
97	1.0	Lake Local	Millbury
97	1.0	Norwalk City	Norwalk
101	0.9	Bowling Green City	Bowling Green
101	0.9	Granville Exempted Village	Granville
101	0.9	Miamisburg City	Miamisburg
101	0.9	Springfield Local	Holland
101	0.9	West Clermont Local	Cincinnati
106	0.8	Brunswick City	Brunswick
106	0.8	Elgin Local	Marion
106	0.8	Lima City	Lima
106	0.8	Monroe Local	Monroe
106	0.8	Oregon City	Oregon
106	0.8	Springfield City	Springfield
106	0.8	Streetsboro City	Streetsboro
106	0.8	Talawanda City	Oxford
106	0.8	Wilmington City	Wilmington
115	0.7	Bay Village City	Bay Village
115	0.7	Chagrin Falls Exempted Village	Chagrin Falls
115	0.7	Coventry Local	Akron
115	0.7	Defiance City	Defiance
115	0.7	Dover City	Dover
115	0.7	Eaton Community Schools City	Eaton
115	0.7	Field Local	Mogadore
115	0.7	Forest Hills Local	Cincinnati
115	0.7	Hudson City	Hudson
115	0.7	Kenston Local	Chagrin Falls
115	0.7	Loveland City	Loveland
115	0.7	New Albany-Plain Local	New Albany
115	0.7	Vandalia-Butler City	Vandalia
128	0.6	Alliance City	Alliance
128	0.6	Finneytown Local	Cincinnati
128	0.6	Garfield Hgts City	Garfield Hgts
128	0.6	Howland Local	Warren
128	0.6	Lexington Local	Lexington
128	0.6	Maple Heights City	Maple Heights
128	0.6	Perry Local	Massillon
128	0.6	Piqua City	Piqua
128	0.6	Tallmadge City	Tallmadge
128	0.6	Upper Sandusky Exempted Village	Upper Sandusky
138	0.5	Barberton City	Barberton
138	0.5	Batavia Local	Batavia
138	0.5	Franklin City	Franklin
138	0.5	Geneva Area City	Geneva
138	0.5	Kent City	Kent
138	0.5	Little Miami Local	Morrow
138	0.5	Saint Marys City	Saint Marys
138	0.5	Sandusky City	Sandusky
138	0.5	Springboro Community City	Springboro
138	0.5	West Holmes Local	Millersburg
138	0.5	Westlake City	Westlake
149	0.4	Avon Local	Avon
149	0.4	Bedford City	Bedford
149	0.4	Elida Local	Elida
149	0.4	Euclid City	Euclid
149	0.4	Greeneview Local	Jamestown
149	0.4	Mad River Local	Dayton
149	0.4	Madison-Plains Local	London
149	0.4	Miami Trace Local	Washington CH
149	0.4	Norton City	Norton
149	0.4	Painesville Township Local	Painesville
149	0.4	Perrysburg Exempted Village	Perrysburg
149	0.4	Portsmouth City	Portsmouth
149	0.4	Ravenna City	Ravenna
149	0.4	Saint Clairsville-Richland City	Saint Clairsville
149	0.4	Tiffin City	Tiffin
149	0.4	Wooster City	Wooster
165	0.3	Aurora City	Aurora
165	0.3	Avon Lake City	Avon Lake
165	0.3	Brookville Local	Brookville
165	0.3	Canton City	Canton
165	0.3	Girard City	Girard
165	0.3	Goshen Local	Goshen
165	0.3	Hillsboro City	Hillsboro
165	0.3	Jonathan Alder Local	Plain City
165	0.3	Midview Local	Grafton
165	0.3	Minerva Local	Minerva
165	0.3	Newark City	Newark
165	0.3	Oakwood City	Dayton
165	0.3	Olmsted Falls City	Olmsted Falls
165	0.3	Plain Local	Canton
165	0.3	South Euclid-Lyndhurst City	Lyndhurst
165	0.3	Wadsworth City	Wadsworth
165	0.3	Wapakoneta City	Wapakoneta
182	0.2	Anthony Wayne Local	Whitehouse
182	0.2	Ashland City	Ashland
182	0.2	Austintown Local	Youngstown
182	0.2	Bryan City	Bryan
182	0.2	Buckeye Local	Ashtabula
182	0.2	Canfield Local	Canfield
182	0.2	Clermont Northeastern Local	Batavia
182	0.2	East Cleveland City	East Cleveland
182	0.2	Elyria City	Elyria
182	0.2	Greenville City	Greenville
182	0.2	Hamilton Local	Columbus
182	0.2	Indian Lake Local	Lewistown
182	0.2	Kenton City	Kenton
182	0.2	Louisville City	Louisville
182	0.2	Madison Local	Madison
182	0.2	Marysville Exempted Village	Marysville
182	0.2	Medina City	Medina
182	0.2	N Ridgeville City	N Ridgeville
182	0.2	Ontario Local	Mansfield
182	0.2	Revere Local	Bath
182	0.2	Rolling Hills Local	Cambridge
182	0.2	Rossford Exempted Village	Rossford
182	0.2	Three Rivers Local	Cleves
182	0.2	Toledo City	Toledo
182	0.2	Triway Local	Wooster
182	0.2	Warren City	Warren
182	0.2	West Muskingum Local	Zanesville
182	0.2	Xenia Community City	Xenia
210	0.1	Amherst Exempted Village	Amherst
210	0.1	Bellaire Local	Bellaire
210	0.1	Benjamin Logan Local	Bellefontaine
210	0.1	Berlin-Milan Local	Milan
210	0.1	Bethel-Tate Local	Bethel
210	0.1	Big Walnut Local	Galena
210	0.1	Chardon Local	Chardon
210	0.1	Chippewa Local	Doylestown
210	0.1	Cloverleaf Local	Lodi
210	0.1	Coldwater Exempted Village	Coldwater
210	0.1	Eastwood Local	Pemberville
210	0.1	Edgewood City	Trenton
210	0.1	Galion City	Galion
210	0.1	Genoa Area Local	Genoa
210	0.1	Greenon Local	Enon
210	0.1	Highland Local	Medina
210	0.1	Hubbard Exempted Village	Hubbard
210	0.1	James A Garfield Local	Garrettsville
210	0.1	Jefferson Area Local	Jefferson
210	0.1	Massillon City	Massillon
210	0.1	Maumee City	Maumee
210	0.1	Maysville Local	Zanesville
210	0.1	Mount Vernon City	Mount Vernon
210	0.1	New Lexington City	New Lexington
210	0.1	North Canton City	North Canton
210	0.1	Northeastern Local	Springfield
210	0.1	Northern Local	Thornville
210	0.1	Northwestern Local	Springfield
210	0.1	Orrville City	Orrville
210	0.1	Ottawa-Glandorf Local	Ottawa
210	0.1	Port Clinton City	Port Clinton
210	0.1	Salem City	Salem
210	0.1	Sheffield-Sheffield Lake City	Sheffield Vllg
210	0.1	Southeast Local	Ravenna
210	0.1	Southwest Licking Local	Etna
210	0.1	Southwest Local	Harrison
210	0.1	Teays Valley Local	Ashville
210	0.1	Trotwood-Madison City	Trotwood
210	0.1	Urbana City	Urbana
210	0.1	Vermilion Local	Vermilion
210	0.1	Washington CH City	Washington CH
210	0.1	West Geauga Local	Chesterland
210	0.1	Westfall Local	Williamsport
210	0.1	Wickliffe City	Wickliffe
254	0.0	Beaver Local	Lisbon
254	0.0	Celina City	Celina
254	0.0	Chillicothe City	Chillicothe
254	0.0	Clyde-Green Springs Ex Vill	Clyde
254	0.0	Firelands Local	Oberlin
254	0.0	Lancaster City	Lancaster
254	0.0	Madison Local	Mansfield
254	0.0	Mansfield City	Mansfield
254	0.0	Marietta City	Marietta
254	0.0	Perkins Local	Sandusky
254	0.0	Shawnee Local	Lima
254	0.0	Valley View Local	Germantown
266	0.0	Adams County/Ohio Valley Local	West Union
266	0.0	Alexander Local	Albany
266	0.0	Alternative Education Academy	Toledo
266	0.0	Amanda-Clearcreek Local	Amanda
266	0.0	Bath Local	Lima
266	0.0	Bellevue City	Bellevue
266	0.0	Benton Carroll Salem Local	Oak Harbor
266	0.0	Bexley City	Bexley
266	0.0	Black River Local	Sullivan
266	0.0	Blanchester Local	Blanchester
266	0.0	Bloom-Carroll Local	Carroll
266	0.0	Buckeye Local	Dillonvale
266	0.0	Buckeye Local	Medina
266	0.0	Buckeye Valley Local	Delaware
266	0.0	Cambridge City	Cambridge
266	0.0	Canton Local	Canton
266	0.0	Carlisle Local	Carlisle
266	0.0	Carrollton Exempted Village	Carrollton
266	0.0	Champion Local	Warren
266	0.0	Circleville City	Circleville
266	0.0	Clark-Shawnee Local	Springfield
266	0.0	Claymont City	Dennison
266	0.0	Clear Fork Valley Local	Bellville
266	0.0	Clinton-Massie Local	Clarksville
266	0.0	Conneaut Area City	Conneaut
266	0.0	Coshocton City	Coshocton
266	0.0	Crestwood Local	Mantua
266	0.0	East Clinton Local	Lees Creek
266	0.0	East Liverpool City	East Liverpool
266	0.0	East Muskingum Local	New Concord
266	0.0	Eastern Local	Sardinia
266	0.0	Edison Local	Hammondsville
266	0.0	Electronic Classroom of Tomorrow	Columbus
266	0.0	Fairfield Union Local	West Rushville
266	0.0	Fairland Local	Proctorville
266	0.0	Fairless Local	Navarre
266	0.0	Franklin Local	Duncan Falls
266	0.0	Gallia County Local	Gallipolis
266	0.0	Gallipolis City	Gallipolis
266	0.0	Graham Local	Saint Paris
266	0.0	Greenfield Exempted Village	Greenfield
266	0.0	Harrison Hills City	Hopedale
266	0.0	Heath City	Heath
266	0.0	Highland Local	Sparta
266	0.0	Huron City	Huron
266	0.0	Indian Creek Local	Wintersville
266	0.0	Indian Valley Local	Gnadenhutten
266	0.0	Ironton City	Ironton
266	0.0	Jackson City	Jackson
266	0.0	Johnstown-Monroe Local	Johnstown
266	0.0	Keystone Local	Lagrange
266	0.0	Labrae Local	Leavittsburg
266	0.0	Lakeview Local	Cortland
266	0.0	Lakewood Local	Hebron
266	0.0	Liberty Local	Youngstown
266	0.0	Licking Valley Local	Newark
266	0.0	Logan Elm Local	Circleville
266	0.0	Logan-Hocking Local	Logan
266	0.0	Madison Local	Middletown
266	0.0	Manchester Local	Akron
266	0.0	Mariemont City	Cincinnati
266	0.0	Martins Ferry City	Martins Ferry
266	0.0	Meigs Local	Pomeroy
266	0.0	Milford Exempted Village	Milford
266	0.0	Milton-Union Exempted Village	West Milton
266	0.0	Minford Local	Minford
266	0.0	Morgan Local	Mcconnelsville
266	0.0	New Richmond Exempted Village	New Richmond
266	0.0	Niles City	Niles
266	0.0	North College Hill City	Cincinnati
266	0.0	North Fork Local	Utica
266	0.0	Northridge Local	Dayton
266	0.0	Northwest Local	Mcdermott
266	0.0	Northwest Local	Canal Fulton

266	0.0	Oak Hills Local	Cincinnati
266	0.0	Otsego Local	Tontogany
266	0.0	Paulding Exempted Village	Paulding
266	0.0	Perry Local	Perry
266	0.0	Poland Local	Poland
266	0.0	Preble Shawnee Board of Education	Camden
266	0.0	River Valley Local	Caledonia
266	0.0	River View Local	Warsaw
266	0.0	Rock Hill Local	Ironton
266	0.0	Ross Local	Hamilton
266	0.0	Sandy Valley Local	Magnolia
266	0.0	Scioto Valley Local	Piketon
266	0.0	Shelby City	Shelby
266	0.0	South Point Local	South Point
266	0.0	Springfield Local	Akron
266	0.0	Steubenville City	Steubenville
266	0.0	Struthers City	Struthers
266	0.0	Switzerland of Ohio Local	Woodsfield
266	0.0	Tri-Valley Local	Dresden
266	0.0	Tuscarawas Valley Local	Zoarville
266	0.0	Union-Scioto Local	Chillicothe
266	0.0	Van Wert City	Van Wert
266	0.0	Vinton County Local	Mcarthur
266	0.0	Warren Local	Vincent
266	0.0	Warrensville Hgts City	Warrensville Hgts
266	0.0	Washington-Nile Local	West Portsmouth
266	0.0	Waverly City	Waverly
266	0.0	Wellington Exempted Village	Wellington
266	0.0	Wellston City	Wellston
266	0.0	West Branch Local	Beloit
266	0.0	Western Brown Local	Mount Orab
266	0.0	Wheelersburg Local	Wheelersburg
266	0.0	Zane Trace Local	Chillicothe
266	0.0	Zanesville City	Zanesville

Migrant Students

Rank	Percent	District Name	City
1	56.4	Ohio Virtual Academy	Maumee
2	16.8	Painesville Local	Painesville
3	8.4	Willard City	Willard
4	2.4	Fremont City	Fremont
5	2.1	Ottawa-Glandorf Local	Ottawa
6	1.8	Marlington Local	Alliance
6	1.8	Napoleon Area City	Napoleon
8	1.7	Woodridge Local	Peninsula
9	1.0	Tecumseh Local	New Carlisle
10	0.8	Tipp Exempted Village	Tipp City
11	0.5	Fostoria City	Fostoria
11	0.5	Reynoldsburg City	Reynoldsburg
11	0.5	Urbana City	Urbana
14	0.4	Sylvania City	Sylvania
14	0.4	Wauseon Exempted Village	Wauseon
16	0.3	Alliance City	Alliance
16	0.3	Berlin-Milan Local	Milan
16	0.3	Clearview Local	Lorain
16	0.3	Genoa Area Local	Genoa
16	0.3	North Royalton City	North Royalton
16	0.3	Otsego Local	Tontogany
22	0.2	Columbus City	Columbus
22	0.2	Hamilton City	Hamilton
22	0.2	Highland Local	Medina
22	0.2	Pike-Delta-York Local	Delta
22	0.2	Vermilion Local	Vermilion
27	0.1	Black River Local	Sullivan
27	0.1	Chagrin Falls Exempted Village	Chagrin Falls
27	0.1	Champion Local	Warren
27	0.1	Chardon Local	Chardon
27	0.1	Cloverleaf Local	Lodi
27	0.1	Clyde-Green Springs Ex Vill	Clyde
27	0.1	Eastwood Local	Pemberville
27	0.1	Fairview Park City	Fairview Park
27	0.1	Kenston Local	Chagrin Falls
27	0.1	Lorain City	Lorain
27	0.1	Madison-Plains Local	London
27	0.1	Marion City	Marion
27	0.1	N Ridgeville City	N Ridgeville
27	0.1	Oregon City	Oregon
27	0.1	Painesville Township Local	Painesville
27	0.1	Sheffield-Sheffield Lake City	Sheffield Vllg
27	0.1	Springfield City	Springfield
27	0.1	Westlake City	Westlake
45	0.0	Amherst Exempted Village	Amherst
45	0.0	Ashtabula Area City	Ashtabula
45	0.0	Bay Village City	Bay Village
45	0.0	Bellevue City	Bellevue
45	0.0	Centerville City	Centerville
45	0.0	Elida Local	Elida
45	0.0	Elyria City	Elyria
45	0.0	Gahanna-Jefferson City	Gahanna
45	0.0	Greenville City	Greenville
45	0.0	Kettering City	Kettering
45	0.0	Lakota Local	Liberty Twp
45	0.0	Loveland City	Loveland
45	0.0	Mad River Local	Dayton
45	0.0	Maumee City	Maumee
45	0.0	Medina City	Medina
45	0.0	Middletown City	Middletown
45	0.0	North Olmsted City	North Olmsted
45	0.0	Olentangy Local	Lewis Center
45	0.0	Orange City	Cleveland
45	0.0	South-Western City	Grove City
45	0.0	Strongsville City	Strongsville
45	0.0	Zanesville City	Zanesville
67	0.0	Adams County/Ohio Valley Local	West Union
67	0.0	Akron City	Akron
67	0.0	Alexander Local	Albany
67	0.0	Alternative Education Academy	Toledo
67	0.0	Amanda-Clearcreek Local	Amanda
67	0.0	Anthony Wayne Local	Whitehouse
67	0.0	Ashland City	Ashland
67	0.0	Athens City	The Plains
67	0.0	Aurora City	Aurora
67	0.0	Austintown Local	Youngstown
67	0.0	Avon Lake City	Avon Lake
67	0.0	Avon Local	Avon
67	0.0	Barberton City	Barberton
67	0.0	Batavia Local	Batavia
67	0.0	Bath Local	Lima
67	0.0	Beaver Local	Lisbon
67	0.0	Beavercreek City	Beavercreek
67	0.0	Bedford City	Bedford
67	0.0	Bellaire Local	Bellaire
67	0.0	Bellefontaine City	Bellefontaine
67	0.0	Benjamin Logan Local	Bellefontaine
67	0.0	Benton Carroll Salem Local	Oak Harbor
67	0.0	Berea City	Berea
67	0.0	Bethel-Tate Local	Bethel
67	0.0	Bexley City	Bexley
67	0.0	Big Walnut Local	Galena
67	0.0	Blanchester Local	Blanchester
67	0.0	Bloom-Carroll Local	Carroll
67	0.0	Boardman Local	Youngstown
67	0.0	Bowling Green City	Bowling Green
67	0.0	Brecksville-Broadview Heights City	Brecksville
67	0.0	Brookville Local	Brookville
67	0.0	Brunswick City	Brunswick
67	0.0	Bryan City	Bryan
67	0.0	Buckeye Local	Ashtabula
67	0.0	Buckeye Local	Dillonvale
67	0.0	Buckeye Local	Medina
67	0.0	Buckeye Valley Local	Delaware
67	0.0	Bucyrus City	Bucyrus
67	0.0	Cambridge City	Cambridge
67	0.0	Canal Wnchstr Local	Canal Wnchstr
67	0.0	Canfield Local	Canfield
67	0.0	Canton City	Canton
67	0.0	Canton Local	Canton
67	0.0	Carlisle Local	Carlisle
67	0.0	Carrollton Exempted Village	Carrollton
67	0.0	Celina City	Celina
67	0.0	Chillicothe City	Chillicothe
67	0.0	Chippewa Local	Doylestown
67	0.0	Cincinnati City	Cincinnati
67	0.0	Circleville City	Circleville
67	0.0	Clark-Shawnee Local	Springfield
67	0.0	Claymont City	Dennison
67	0.0	Clear Fork Valley Local	Bellville
67	0.0	Clermont Northeastern Local	Batavia
67	0.0	Cleveland Hgts-University Hgts	University Hgts
67	0.0	Cleveland Municipal City	Cleveland
67	0.0	Clinton-Massie Local	Clarksville
67	0.0	Coldwater Exempted Village	Coldwater
67	0.0	Conneaut Area City	Conneaut
67	0.0	Copley-Fairlawn City	Copley
67	0.0	Coshocton City	Coshocton
67	0.0	Coventry Local	Akron
67	0.0	Crestwood Local	Mantua
67	0.0	Cuyahoga Falls City	Cuyahoga Falls
67	0.0	Dayton City	Dayton
67	0.0	Defiance City	Defiance
67	0.0	Delaware City	Delaware
67	0.0	Dover City	Dover
67	0.0	Dublin City	Dublin
67	0.0	East Cleveland City	East Cleveland
67	0.0	East Clinton Local	Lees Creek
67	0.0	East Holmes Local	Berlin
67	0.0	East Liverpool City	East Liverpool
67	0.0	East Muskingum Local	New Concord
67	0.0	Eastern Local	Sardinia
67	0.0	Eaton Community Schools City	Eaton
67	0.0	Edgewood City	Trenton
67	0.0	Edison Local	Hammondsville
67	0.0	Electronic Classroom of Tomorrow	Columbus
67	0.0	Elgin Local	Marion
67	0.0	Euclid City	Euclid
67	0.0	Fairborn City	Fairborn
67	0.0	Fairfield City	Fairfield
67	0.0	Fairfield Union Local	West Rushville
67	0.0	Fairland Local	Proctorville
67	0.0	Fairless Local	Navarre
67	0.0	Field Local	Mogadore
67	0.0	Findlay City	Findlay
67	0.0	Finneytown Local	Cincinnati
67	0.0	Firelands Local	Oberlin
67	0.0	Forest Hills Local	Cincinnati
67	0.0	Franklin City	Franklin
67	0.0	Franklin Local	Duncan Falls
67	0.0	Galion City	Galion
67	0.0	Gallia County Local	Gallipolis
67	0.0	Gallipolis City	Gallipolis
67	0.0	Garfield Hgts City	Garfield Hgts
67	0.0	Geneva Area City	Geneva
67	0.0	Girard City	Girard
67	0.0	Goshen Local	Goshen
67	0.0	Graham Local	Saint Paris
67	0.0	Granville Exempted Village	Granville
67	0.0	Green Local	Green
67	0.0	Greeneview Local	Jamestown
67	0.0	Greenfield Exempted Village	Greenfield
67	0.0	Greenon Local	Enon
67	0.0	Groveport Madison Local	Groveport
67	0.0	Hamilton Local	Columbus
67	0.0	Harrison Hills City	Hopedale
67	0.0	Heath City	Heath
67	0.0	Highland Local	Sparta
67	0.0	Hilliard City	Hilliard
67	0.0	Hillsboro City	Hillsboro
67	0.0	Howland Local	Warren
67	0.0	Hubbard Exempted Village	Hubbard
67	0.0	Huber Heights City	Huber Heights
67	0.0	Hudson City	Hudson
67	0.0	Huron City	Huron
67	0.0	Indian Creek Local	Wintersville
67	0.0	Indian Hill Exempted Village	Cincinnati
67	0.0	Indian Lake Local	Lewistown
67	0.0	Indian Valley Local	Gnadenhutten
67	0.0	Ironton City	Ironton
67	0.0	Jackson City	Jackson
67	0.0	Jackson Local	Massillon
67	0.0	James A Garfield Local	Garrettsville
67	0.0	Jefferson Area Local	Jefferson
67	0.0	Johnstown-Monroe Local	Johnstown
67	0.0	Jonathan Alder Local	Plain City
67	0.0	Kent City	Kent
67	0.0	Kenton City	Kenton
67	0.0	Keystone Local	Lagrange
67	0.0	Kings Local	Kings Mills
67	0.0	Labrae Local	Leavittsburg
67	0.0	Lake Local	Millbury
67	0.0	Lake Local	Uniontown
67	0.0	Lakeview Local	Cortland
67	0.0	Lakewood City	Lakewood
67	0.0	Lakewood Local	Hebron
67	0.0	Lancaster City	Lancaster
67	0.0	Lebanon City	Lebanon
67	0.0	Lexington Local	Lexington
67	0.0	Liberty Local	Youngstown
67	0.0	Licking Heights Local	Summit Station
67	0.0	Licking Valley Local	Newark
67	0.0	Lima City	Lima
67	0.0	Little Miami Local	Morrow
67	0.0	Logan Elm Local	Circleville
67	0.0	Logan-Hocking Local	Logan
67	0.0	London City	London
67	0.0	Louisville City	Louisville
67	0.0	Madeira City	Cincinnati
67	0.0	Madison Local	Mansfield
67	0.0	Madison Local	Madison
67	0.0	Madison Local	Middletown

67	0.0	Manchester Local	Akron
67	0.0	Mansfield City	Mansfield
67	0.0	Maple Heights City	Maple Heights
67	0.0	Mariemont City	Cincinnati
67	0.0	Marietta City	Marietta
67	0.0	Martins Ferry City	Martins Ferry
67	0.0	Marysville Exempted Village	Marysville
67	0.0	Mason City	Mason
67	0.0	Massillon City	Massillon
67	0.0	Mayfield City	Mayfield Hgts
67	0.0	Maysville Local	Zanesville
67	0.0	Meigs Local	Pomeroy
67	0.0	Mentor Exempted Village	Mentor
67	0.0	Miami Trace Local	Washington CH
67	0.0	Miamisburg City	Miamisburg
67	0.0	Midview Local	Grafton
67	0.0	Milford Exempted Village	Milford
67	0.0	Milton-Union Exempted Village	West Milton
67	0.0	Minerva Local	Minerva
67	0.0	Minford Local	Minford
67	0.0	Monroe Local	Monroe
67	0.0	Morgan Local	Mcconnelsville
67	0.0	Mount Healthy City	Cincinnati
67	0.0	Mount Vernon City	Mount Vernon
67	0.0	New Albany-Plain Local	New Albany
67	0.0	New Lexington City	New Lexington
67	0.0	New Philadel. City	New Philadel.
67	0.0	New Richmond Exempted Village	New Richmond
67	0.0	Newark City	Newark
67	0.0	Niles City	Niles
67	0.0	Nordonia Hills City	Northfield
67	0.0	North Canton City	North Canton
67	0.0	North College Hill City	Cincinnati
67	0.0	North Fork Local	Utica
67	0.0	Northeastern Local	Springfield
67	0.0	Northern Local	Thornville
67	0.0	Northmont City	Englewood
67	0.0	Northridge Local	Dayton
67	0.0	Northwest Local	Cincinnati
67	0.0	Northwest Local	Canal Fulton
67	0.0	Northwest Local	Mcdermott
67	0.0	Northwestern Local	Springfield
67	0.0	Norton City	Norton
67	0.0	Norwalk City	Norwalk
67	0.0	Norwood City	Norwood
67	0.0	Oak Hills Local	Cincinnati
67	0.0	Oakwood City	Dayton
67	0.0	Olmsted Falls City	Olmsted Falls
67	0.0	Ontario Local	Mansfield
67	0.0	Orrville City	Orrville
67	0.0	Parma City	Parma
67	0.0	Paulding Exempted Village	Paulding
67	0.0	Perkins Local	Sandusky
67	0.0	Perry Local	Massillon
67	0.0	Perry Local	Perry
67	0.0	Perrysburg Exempted Village	Perrysburg
67	0.0	Pickerington Local	Pickerington
67	0.0	Piqua City	Piqua
67	0.0	Plain Local	Canton
67	0.0	Poland Local	Poland
67	0.0	Port Clinton City	Port Clinton
67	0.0	Portsmouth City	Portsmouth
67	0.0	Preble Shawnee Board of Education	Camden
67	0.0	Princeton City	Cincinnati
67	0.0	Ravenna City	Ravenna
67	0.0	Revere Local	Bath
67	0.0	River Valley Local	Caledonia
67	0.0	River View Local	Warsaw
67	0.0	Rock Hill Local	Ironton
67	0.0	Rocky River City	Rocky River
67	0.0	Rolling Hills Local	Cambridge
67	0.0	Ross Local	Hamilton
67	0.0	Rossford Exempted Village	Rossford
67	0.0	Saint Clairsville-Richland City	Saint Clairsville
67	0.0	Saint Marys City	Saint Marys
67	0.0	Salem City	Salem
67	0.0	Sandusky City	Sandusky
67	0.0	Sandy Valley Local	Magnolia
67	0.0	Scioto Valley Local	Piketon
67	0.0	Shaker Heights City	Shaker Heights
67	0.0	Shawnee Local	Lima
67	0.0	Shelby City	Shelby
67	0.0	Sidney City	Sidney
67	0.0	Solon City	Solon
67	0.0	South Euclid-Lyndhurst City	Lyndhurst
67	0.0	South Point Local	South Point
67	0.0	Southeast Local	Ravenna
67	0.0	Southeast Local	Apple Creek
67	0.0	Southwest Licking Local	Etna
67	0.0	Southwest Local	Harrison
67	0.0	Springboro Community City	Springboro
67	0.0	Springfield Local	Akron
67	0.0	Springfield Local	Holland
67	0.0	Steubenville City	Steubenville
67	0.0	Stow-Munroe Falls City	Stow
67	0.0	Streetsboro City	Streetsboro
67	0.0	Struthers City	Struthers
67	0.0	Sugarcreek Local	Bellbrook
67	0.0	Switzerland of Ohio Local	Woodsfield
67	0.0	Sycamore Community City	Cincinnati
67	0.0	Talawanda City	Oxford
67	0.0	Tallmadge City	Tallmadge
67	0.0	Teays Valley Local	Ashville
67	0.0	Three Rivers Local	Cleves
67	0.0	Tiffin City	Tiffin
67	0.0	Toledo City	Toledo
67	0.0	Tri-Valley Local	Dresden
67	0.0	Triway Local	Wooster
67	0.0	Trotwood-Madison City	Trotwood
67	0.0	Troy City	Troy
67	0.0	Tuscarawas Valley Local	Zoarville
67	0.0	Twinsburg City	Twinsburg
67	0.0	Union-Scioto Local	Chillicothe
67	0.0	Upper Arlington City	Upper Arlington
67	0.0	Upper Sandusky Exempted Village	Upper Sandusky
67	0.0	Valley View Local	Germantown
67	0.0	Van Wert City	Van Wert
67	0.0	Vandalia-Butler City	Vandalia
67	0.0	Vinton County Local	Mcarthur
67	0.0	Wadsworth City	Wadsworth
67	0.0	Wapakoneta City	Wapakoneta
67	0.0	Warren City	Warren
67	0.0	Warren Local	Vincent
67	0.0	Warrensville Hgts City	Warrensville Hgts
67	0.0	Washington CH City	Washington CH
67	0.0	Washington Local	Toledo
67	0.0	Washington-Nile Local	West Portsmouth
67	0.0	Waverly City	Waverly
67	0.0	Wellington Exempted Village	Wellington
67	0.0	Wellston City	Wellston
67	0.0	West Branch Local	Beloit
67	0.0	West Carrollton City	West Carrollton
67	0.0	West Clermont Local	Cincinnati
67	0.0	West Geauga Local	Chesterland
67	0.0	West Holmes Local	Millersburg
67	0.0	West Muskingum Local	Zanesville
67	0.0	Western Brown Local	Mount Orab
67	0.0	Westerville City	Westerville
67	0.0	Westfall Local	Williamsport
67	0.0	Wheelersburg Local	Wheelersburg
67	0.0	Whitehall City	Whitehall
67	0.0	Wickliffe City	Wickliffe
67	0.0	Willoughby-Eastlake City	Willoughby
67	0.0	Wilmington City	Wilmington
67	0.0	Winton Woods City	Cincinnati
67	0.0	Wooster City	Wooster
67	0.0	Worthington City	Worthington
67	0.0	Wyoming City	Wyoming
67	0.0	Xenia Community City	Xenia
67	0.0	Youngstown City	Youngstown
67	0.0	Zane Trace Local	Chillicothe

Students Eligible for Free Lunch

Rank	Percent	District Name	City
1	75.9	Youngstown City	Youngstown
2	74.4	Cleveland Municipal City	Cleveland
3	70.2	Lima City	Lima
4	68.6	Dayton City	Dayton
5	67.9	Painesville Local	Painesville
6	67.3	Zanesville City	Zanesville
7	65.7	Lorain City	Lorain
8	63.9	East Liverpool City	East Liverpool
9	63.8	Portsmouth City	Portsmouth
10	59.9	Trotwood-Madison City	Trotwood
11	59.5	Canton City	Canton
12	59.2	East Cleveland City	East Cleveland
13	57.5	Mansfield City	Mansfield
14	57.2	Toledo City	Toledo
15	55.2	Akron City	Akron
16	54.9	Alliance City	Alliance
17	54.7	Cincinnati City	Cincinnati
17	54.7	Sandusky City	Sandusky
19	54.1	Springfield City	Springfield
20	53.7	Warrensville Hgts City	Warrensville Hgts
21	53.5	Steubenville City	Steubenville
22	52.6	Northridge Local	Dayton
23	50.5	Bellaire Local	Bellaire
23	50.5	Columbus City	Columbus
25	49.7	Rock Hill Local	Ironton
26	47.9	Northwest Local	Mcdermott
27	47.7	Marion City	Marion
28	47.5	Mount Healthy City	Cincinnati
29	46.7	Ironton City	Ironton
29	46.7	Whitehall City	Whitehall
31	45.8	Clearview Local	Lorain
32	45.6	Warren City	Warren
33	45.4	Vinton County Local	Mcarthur
34	45.1	Barberton City	Barberton
34	45.1	Coshocton City	Coshocton
36	45.0	Struthers City	Struthers
37	44.9	Maple Heights City	Maple Heights
37	44.9	North College Hill City	Cincinnati
39	44.6	Fostoria City	Fostoria
40	44.5	Washington-Nile Local	West Portsmouth
41	44.4	Euclid City	Euclid
41	44.4	Massillon City	Massillon
43	44.0	Meigs Local	Pomeroy
44	43.7	Cambridge City	Cambridge
45	43.3	South Point Local	South Point
46	43.1	Norwood City	Norwood
47	42.8	Gallia County Local	Gallipolis
48	42.3	Elyria City	Elyria
49	41.2	Adams County/Ohio Valley Local	West Union
50	40.9	Cleveland Hgts-University Hgts	University Hgts
50	40.9	Martins Ferry City	Martins Ferry
52	40.4	Ashtabula Area City	Ashtabula
53	40.2	Conneaut Area City	Conneaut
54	40.1	Scioto Valley Local	Piketon
55	39.9	Wellston City	Wellston
56	39.7	Claymont City	Dennison
57	38.6	Morgan Local	Mcconnelsville
58	38.3	Middletown City	Middletown
59	37.9	Chillicothe City	Chillicothe
59	37.9	New Lexington City	New Lexington
61	37.2	South-Western City	Grove City
62	36.6	Indian Creek Local	Wintersville
63	36.2	Edison Local	Hammondsville
63	36.2	Niles City	Niles
65	35.5	Gallipolis City	Gallipolis
66	35.4	Rolling Hills Local	Cambridge
67	35.2	Fremont City	Fremont
68	35.0	Logan-Hocking Local	Logan
69	34.4	Liberty Local	Youngstown
70	34.3	Franklin Local	Duncan Falls
71	34.1	Girard City	Girard
72	33.8	Buckeye Local	Dillonvale
72	33.8	Harrison Hills City	Hopedale
72	33.8	Waverly City	Waverly
75	33.4	Wilmington City	Wilmington
76	33.2	Xenia Community City	Xenia
77	33.1	Switzerland of Ohio Local	Woodsfield
78	33.0	Princeton City	Cincinnati
79	32.3	Geneva Area City	Geneva
80	32.2	Willard City	Willard
81	32.0	Kenton City	Kenton
82	31.9	Bedford City	Bedford
83	31.7	Jackson City	Jackson
83	31.7	Maysville Local	Zanesville
85	31.5	Mad River Local	Dayton
86	31.3	Wooster City	Wooster
87	30.8	Groveport Madison Local	Groveport
88	30.7	Newark City	Newark
89	30.5	Lancaster City	Lancaster
90	30.4	Bucyrus City	Bucyrus
91	30.2	Garfield Hgts City	Garfield Hgts
91	30.2	Piqua City	Piqua
93	29.6	Minford Local	Minford
93	29.6	Ravenna City	Ravenna
95	29.2	Lakewood City	Lakewood
96	29.0	Goshen Local	Goshen
97	28.9	New Richmond Exempted Village	New Richmond
98	28.8	Circleville City	Circleville
98	28.8	Springfield Local	Akron
100	28.7	Port Clinton City	Port Clinton
101	28.6	Norwalk City	Norwalk
102	28.5	Union-Scioto Local	Chillicothe
103	28.4	Winton Woods City	Cincinnati
104	28.1	Hamilton Local	Columbus
104	28.1	Hillsboro City	Hillsboro

Rank	Value	District	City
106	28.0	Beaver Local	Lisbon
107	27.9	Athens City	The Plains
107	27.9	Urbana City	Urbana
109	27.6	Labrae Local	Leavittsburg
109	27.6	Madison Local	Mansfield
111	27.3	Canton Local	Canton
111	27.3	Carrollton Exempted Village	Carrollton
111	27.3	Galion City	Galion
114	27.0	River View Local	Warsaw
115	26.9	Tecumseh Local	New Carlisle
116	26.8	Buckeye Local	Ashtabula
117	26.5	Bellefontaine City	Bellefontaine
117	26.5	Sidney City	Sidney
119	26.4	Hamilton City	Hamilton
120	26.2	Fairland Local	Proctorville
121	26.0	Lakewood Local	Hebron
122	25.6	Minerva Local	Minerva
123	25.2	Batavia Local	Batavia
124	25.0	Indian Valley Local	Gnadenhutten
124	25.0	Mount Vernon City	Mount Vernon
126	24.9	Blanchester Local	Blanchester
127	24.8	Hubbard Exempted Village	Hubbard
127	24.8	Western Brown Local	Mount Orab
129	24.7	Washington CH City	Washington CH
130	24.5	Elgin Local	Marion
130	24.5	Washington Local	Toledo
132	24.4	Sandy Valley Local	Magnolia
132	24.4	West Holmes Local	Millersburg
134	24.1	Salem City	Salem
135	23.8	Findlay City	Findlay
135	23.8	London City	London
137	23.7	Bethel-Tate Local	Bethel
138	23.5	Fairless Local	Navarre
138	23.5	Rossford Exempted Village	Rossford
140	23.4	Ashland City	Ashland
140	23.4	Greenfield Exempted Village	Greenfield
142	22.8	Woodridge Local	Peninsula
143	22.7	Eastern Local	Sardinia
143	22.7	Wheelersburg Local	Wheelersburg
145	22.6	Kent City	Kent
145	22.6	Milton-Union Exempted Village	West Milton
147	22.5	Fairborn City	Fairborn
147	22.5	Orrville City	Orrville
149	22.3	South Euclid-Lyndhurst City	Lyndhurst
150	22.1	Marietta City	Marietta
151	22.0	West Muskingum Local	Zanesville
152	21.9	Celina City	Celina
152	21.9	Highland Local	Sparta
152	21.9	Indian Lake Local	Lewistown
152	21.9	Jefferson Area Local	Jefferson
152	21.9	Northern Local	Thornville
152	21.9	Springfield Local	Holland
158	21.2	Shelby City	Shelby
159	21.0	North Fork Local	Utica
159	21.0	Preble Shawnee Board of Education	Camden
161	20.9	Miami Trace Local	Washington CH
162	20.7	Defiance City	Defiance
162	20.7	Saint Clairsville-Richland City	Saint Clairsville
164	20.5	Delaware City	Delaware
165	20.4	Tri-Valley Local	Dresden
165	20.4	Westfall Local	Williamsport
167	20.3	West Carrollton City	West Carrollton
168	20.2	Alexander Local	Albany
168	20.2	Plain Local	Canton
170	20.1	Austintown Local	Youngstown
170	20.1	Tiffin City	Tiffin
172	19.9	Sheffield-Sheffield Lake City	Sheffield Vllg
173	19.7	Amanda-Clearcreek Local	Amanda
174	19.6	Clear Fork Valley Local	Bellville
174	19.6	Paulding Exempted Village	Paulding
176	19.5	Elida Local	Elida
177	19.4	Perry Local	Massillon
178	19.3	Greenville City	Greenville
179	19.2	Bath Local	Lima
179	19.2	Madison Local	Madison
181	19.0	Clermont Northeastern Local	Batavia
181	19.0	Kettering City	Kettering
181	19.0	Oregon City	Oregon
184	18.9	Shaker Heights City	Shaker Heights
184	18.9	Vermilion Local	Vermilion
186	18.8	East Muskingum Local	New Concord
186	18.8	Logan Elm Local	Circleville
188	18.7	Napoleon Area City	Napoleon
188	18.7	Northwest Local	Cincinnati
190	18.6	Van Wert City	Van Wert
191	18.5	Warren Local	Vincent
192	18.4	West Branch Local	Beloit
193	18.3	Wapakoneta City	Wapakoneta
194	18.2	Clyde-Green Springs Ex Vill	Clyde
194	18.2	Southeast Local	Apple Creek
194	18.2	Three Rivers Local	Cleves
197	18.1	Finneytown Local	Cincinnati
197	18.1	Licking Heights Local	Summit Station
197	18.1	Wellington Exempted Village	Wellington
200	18.0	Berea City	Berea
200	18.0	Coventry Local	Akron
200	18.0	Reynoldsburg City	Reynoldsburg
200	18.0	Troy City	Troy
204	17.9	Miamisburg City	Miamisburg
205	17.8	New Philadel. City	New Philadel.
205	17.8	Pike-Delta-York Local	Delta
207	17.7	East Clinton Local	Lees Creek
208	17.6	Fairfield Union Local	West Rushville
208	17.6	Triway Local	Wooster
208	17.6	Upper Sandusky Exempted Village	Upper Sandusky
211	17.5	Southeast Local	Ravenna
212	17.4	Eaton Community Schools City	Eaton
212	17.4	Marlington Local	Alliance
214	17.3	Parma City	Parma
215	17.2	Franklin City	Franklin
216	17.0	Huber Heights City	Huber Heights
217	16.8	River Valley Local	Caledonia
218	16.7	Heath City	Heath
219	16.4	Bellevue City	Bellevue
220	15.9	Teays Valley Local	Ashville
221	15.8	Southwest Local	Harrison
221	15.8	Talawanda City	Oxford
223	15.5	Black River Local	Sullivan
223	15.5	Zane Trace Local	Chillicothe
225	15.4	Cuyahoga Falls City	Cuyahoga Falls
226	15.3	Benton Carroll Salem Local	Oak Harbor
226	15.3	North Olmsted City	North Olmsted
228	15.2	Boardman Local	Youngstown
228	15.2	Edgewood City	Trenton
228	15.2	Wauseon Exempted Village	Wauseon
231	15.1	Fairview Park City	Fairview Park
232	15.0	Lake Local	Millbury
232	15.0	Willoughby-Eastlake City	Willoughby
234	14.9	Field Local	Mogadore
234	14.9	Saint Marys City	Saint Marys
236	14.8	James A Garfield Local	Garrettsville
237	14.7	Canal Wnchstr Local	Canal Wnchstr
237	14.7	East Holmes Local	Berlin
237	14.7	Streetsboro City	Streetsboro
240	14.6	Bowling Green City	Bowling Green
241	14.3	Tuscarawas Valley Local	Zoarville
242	14.2	Lebanon City	Lebanon
243	14.1	Bryan City	Bryan
243	14.1	Licking Valley Local	Newark
243	14.1	Louisville City	Louisville
246	14.0	Graham Local	Saint Paris
247	13.9	Jonathan Alder Local	Plain City
247	13.9	Northwestern Local	Springfield
249	13.7	Midview Local	Grafton
250	13.5	West Clermont Local	Cincinnati
251	13.2	Madison Local	Middletown
252	12.8	Cloverleaf Local	Lodi
253	12.7	Chippewa Local	Doylestown
254	12.6	Madison-Plains Local	London
255	12.5	Dover City	Dover
256	12.3	Champion Local	Warren
256	12.3	Clark-Shawnee Local	Springfield
256	12.3	Shawnee Local	Lima
259	12.2	Howland Local	Warren
259	12.2	N Ridgeville City	N Ridgeville
261	12.0	Huron City	Huron
262	11.6	Genoa Area Local	Genoa
262	11.6	Monroe Local	Monroe
262	11.6	Norton City	Norton
265	11.2	Berlin-Milan Local	Milan
266	11.1	Crestwood Local	Mantua
266	11.1	Vandalia-Butler City	Vandalia
268	11.0	Marysville Exempted Village	Marysville
268	11.0	Southwest Licking Local	Etna
270	10.9	Carlisle Local	Carlisle
270	10.9	Greeneview Local	Jamestown
270	10.9	Lexington Local	Lexington
273	10.7	Firelands Local	Oberlin
273	10.7	Otsego Local	Tontogany
273	10.7	Painesville Township Local	Painesville
276	10.6	Buckeye Local	Medina
276	10.6	Maumee City	Maumee
276	10.6	Westerville City	Westerville
279	10.4	Brookville Local	Brookville
279	10.4	Hilliard City	Hilliard
281	10.3	Tipp Exempted Village	Tipp City
282	10.2	Ottawa-Glandorf Local	Ottawa
283	10.1	Big Walnut Local	Galena
283	10.1	Keystone Local	Lagrange
285	10.0	Northwest Local	Canal Fulton
286	9.9	Clinton-Massie Local	Clarksville
287	9.8	Eastwood Local	Pemberville
288	9.7	Buckeye Valley Local	Delaware
288	9.7	Greenon Local	Enon
288	9.7	Mentor Exempted Village	Mentor
291	9.5	Little Miami Local	Morrow
291	9.5	Milford Exempted Village	Milford
293	9.4	Fairfield City	Fairfield
293	9.4	Tallmadge City	Tallmadge
295	9.1	Benjamin Logan Local	Bellefontaine
295	9.1	Northmont City	Englewood
297	8.9	Green Local	Green
297	8.9	Twinsburg City	Twinsburg
297	8.9	Wadsworth City	Wadsworth
300	8.7	Avon Local	Avon
300	8.7	Lakeview Local	Cortland
302	8.6	Chardon Local	Chardon
303	8.4	Ontario Local	Mansfield
303	8.4	Perkins Local	Sandusky
305	8.3	Gahanna-Jefferson City	Gahanna
305	8.3	Johnstown-Monroe Local	Johnstown
307	8.2	Brunswick City	Brunswick
307	8.2	Worthington City	Worthington
309	7.9	Amherst Exempted Village	Amherst
310	7.7	Bloom-Carroll Local	Carroll
311	7.6	Mayfield City	Mayfield Hgts
311	7.6	Northeastern Local	Springfield
313	7.4	Perry Local	Perry
314	7.3	Copley-Fairlawn City	Copley
314	7.3	Pickerington Local	Pickerington
316	7.1	Kings Local	Kings Mills
317	6.9	Valley View Local	Germantown
318	6.7	Lake Local	Uniontown
319	6.6	Olmsted Falls City	Olmsted Falls
320	6.5	Loveland City	Loveland
321	6.4	Medina City	Medina
321	6.4	Ross Local	Hamilton
321	6.4	Sugarcreek Local	Bellbrook
324	6.3	Sycamore Community City	Cincinnati
325	6.2	Strongsville City	Strongsville
325	6.2	Sylvania City	Sylvania
327	6.1	Beavercreek City	Beavercreek
328	6.0	Jackson Local	Massillon
328	6.0	Manchester Local	Akron
330	5.8	Stow-Munroe Falls City	Stow
331	5.7	Coldwater Exempted Village	Coldwater
331	5.7	Nordonia Hills City	Northfield
333	5.5	North Canton City	North Canton
333	5.5	Westlake City	Westlake
335	5.3	Bexley City	Bexley
335	5.3	North Royalton City	North Royalton
337	5.1	Lakota Local	Liberty Twp
338	5.0	Dublin City	Dublin
338	5.0	Kenston Local	Chagrin Falls
340	4.6	Centerville City	Centerville
340	4.6	Highland Local	Medina
342	4.5	Anthony Wayne Local	Whitehouse
343	4.3	Mariemont City	Cincinnati
344	4.2	Avon Lake City	Avon Lake
344	4.2	Perrysburg Exempted Village	Perrysburg
344	4.2	Poland Local	Poland
347	4.1	Brecksville-Broadview Heights City	Brecksville
348	4.0	Olentangy Local	Lewis Center
349	3.8	Canfield Local	Canfield
350	3.6	Orange City	Cleveland
351	3.4	Aurora City	Aurora
351	3.4	Forest Hills Local	Cincinnati
351	3.4	Wyoming City	Wyoming
354	3.3	Bay Village City	Bay Village
355	3.2	West Geauga Local	Chesterland
356	3.0	Rocky River City	Rocky River
357	2.6	New Albany-Plain Local	New Albany
357	2.6	Solon City	Solon
359	2.4	Mason City	Mason
359	2.4	Springboro Community City	Springboro
361	2.2	Revere Local	Bath
362	1.8	Madeira City	Cincinnati
362	1.8	Oak Hills Local	Cincinnati
364	1.3	Hudson City	Hudson
365	1.2	Indian Hill Exempted Village	Cincinnati
366	0.9	Chagrin Falls Exempted Village	Chagrin Falls

366	0.9	Upper Arlington City	Upper Arlington
368	0.7	Oakwood City	Dayton
369	0.5	Granville Exempted Village	Granville
370	0.0	Alternative Education Academy	Toledo
370	0.0	Electronic Classroom of Tomorrow	Columbus
370	0.0	Ohio Virtual Academy	Maumee
370	0.0	Wickliffe City	Wickliffe

Students Eligible for Reduced-Price Lunch

Rank	Percent	District Name	City
1	16.8	Southeast Local	Apple Creek
2	14.8	Rock Hill Local	Ironton
3	14.7	New Lexington City	New Lexington
4	13.8	West Holmes Local	Millersburg
5	13.7	Mad River Local	Dayton
6	13.4	Labrae Local	Leavittsburg
7	13.0	Carrollton Exempted Village	Carrollton
8	12.4	Euclid City	Euclid
9	12.3	Barberton City	Barberton
9	12.3	Buckeye Local	Ashtabula
9	12.3	Switzerland of Ohio Local	Woodsfield
12	12.2	Alliance City	Alliance
13	12.1	Springfield Local	Akron
13	12.1	Struthers City	Struthers
15	12.0	Bucyrus City	Bucyrus
16	11.9	Fostoria City	Fostoria
17	11.7	Warrensville Hgts City	Warrensville Hgts
18	11.6	Adams County/Ohio Valley Local	West Union
18	11.6	Clearview Local	Lorain
20	11.5	Hubbard Exempted Village	Hubbard
21	11.2	Whitehall City	Whitehall
22	11.1	Garfield Hgts City	Garfield Hgts
22	11.1	Maple Heights City	Maple Heights
24	11.0	North College Hill City	Cincinnati
24	11.0	Ravenna City	Ravenna
24	11.0	Wellington Exempted Village	Wellington
27	10.9	Eastern Local	Sardinia
27	10.9	Sandusky City	Sandusky
29	10.8	Fairless Local	Navarre
29	10.8	Norwood City	Norwood
31	10.7	Mansfield City	Mansfield
31	10.7	Minerva Local	Minerva
31	10.7	Piqua City	Piqua
34	10.6	Canton Local	Canton
34	10.6	Massillon City	Massillon
36	10.5	Edison Local	Hammondsville
36	10.5	Sidney City	Sidney
38	10.4	Northridge Local	Dayton
39	10.3	Greenfield Exempted Village	Greenfield
40	10.2	Dayton City	Dayton
40	10.2	East Holmes Local	Berlin
40	10.2	Geneva Area City	Geneva
40	10.2	Madison Local	Mansfield
40	10.2	Wellston City	Wellston
45	10.0	Conneaut Area City	Conneaut
45	10.0	Jefferson Area Local	Jefferson
47	9.9	Lake Local	Millbury
47	9.9	Logan-Hocking Local	Logan
47	9.9	Southeast Local	Ravenna
47	9.9	Tiffin City	Tiffin
51	9.7	Cambridge City	Cambridge
51	9.7	Trotwood-Madison City	Trotwood
53	9.6	Akron City	Akron
53	9.6	Bellaire Local	Bellaire
55	9.5	Galion City	Galion
55	9.5	Martins Ferry City	Martins Ferry
55	9.5	Meigs Local	Pomeroy
58	9.4	Alexander Local	Albany
58	9.4	Ashtabula Area City	Ashtabula
58	9.4	Bedford City	Bedford
58	9.4	Canton City	Canton
58	9.4	Cuyahoga Falls City	Cuyahoga Falls
58	9.4	Harrison Hills City	Hopedale
64	9.3	Austintown Local	Youngstown
64	9.3	Beaver Local	Lisbon
64	9.3	Indian Valley Local	Gnadenhutten
67	9.2	Orrville City	Orrville
68	9.1	Ashland City	Ashland
68	9.1	Minford Local	Minford
68	9.1	South-Western City	Grove City
71	9.0	Northwest Local	Mcdermott
71	9.0	Norwalk City	Norwalk
71	9.0	Preble Shawnee Board of Education	Camden
71	9.0	Shelby City	Shelby
71	9.0	Westfall Local	Williamsport
76	8.9	Elgin Local	Marion
76	8.9	Hamilton Local	Columbus
76	8.9	Maysville Local	Zanesville
76	8.9	Parma City	Parma
76	8.9	Vinton County Local	Mcarthur
76	8.9	Wapakoneta City	Wapakoneta
76	8.9	Western Brown Local	Mount Orab
83	8.8	Bellevue City	Bellevue
83	8.8	Buckeye Local	Dillonvale
83	8.8	Jackson City	Jackson
83	8.8	North Fork Local	Utica
87	8.7	Tecumseh Local	New Carlisle
87	8.7	Urbana City	Urbana
87	8.7	Wooster City	Wooster
90	8.6	Fremont City	Fremont
90	8.6	Morgan Local	Mcconnelsville
90	8.6	Vermilion Local	Vermilion
93	8.5	Elida Local	Elida
93	8.5	Elyria City	Elyria
93	8.5	Gallia County Local	Gallipolis
93	8.5	Mount Healthy City	Cincinnati
93	8.5	Painesville Local	Painesville
93	8.5	Rossford Exempted Village	Rossford
99	8.4	Clear Fork Valley Local	Bellville
99	8.4	Coventry Local	Akron
101	8.3	Claymont City	Dennison
101	8.3	Clyde-Green Springs Ex Vill	Clyde
101	8.3	Scioto Valley Local	Piketon
104	8.2	Goshen Local	Goshen
104	8.2	Niles City	Niles
104	8.2	Oregon City	Oregon
104	8.2	Perry Local	Massillon
104	8.2	Triway Local	Wooster
109	8.1	Bath Local	Lima
109	8.1	James A Garfield Local	Garrettsville
109	8.1	Lorain City	Lorain
109	8.1	Napoleon Area City	Napoleon
113	8.0	Marion City	Marion
113	8.0	Warren City	Warren
115	7.9	Berea City	Berea
115	7.9	Cleveland Hgts-University Hgts	University Hgts
115	7.9	Lancaster City	Lancaster
115	7.9	Pike-Delta-York Local	Delta
115	7.9	Van Wert City	Van Wert
120	7.8	Liberty Local	Youngstown
120	7.8	Portsmouth City	Portsmouth
120	7.8	Princeton City	Cincinnati
120	7.8	Rolling Hills Local	Cambridge
120	7.8	Streetsboro City	Streetsboro
125	7.7	Benton Carroll Salem Local	Oak Harbor
125	7.7	Cleveland Municipal City	Cleveland
125	7.7	Newark City	Newark
125	7.7	Northwest Local	Cincinnati
125	7.7	Willoughby-Eastlake City	Willoughby
130	7.6	Amanda-Clearcreek Local	Amanda
130	7.6	Celina City	Celina
130	7.6	Lima City	Lima
130	7.6	Saint Marys City	Saint Marys
130	7.6	Sandy Valley Local	Magnolia
130	7.6	Wauseon Exempted Village	Wauseon
136	7.5	Louisville City	Louisville
136	7.5	Wilmington City	Wilmington
138	7.4	Cloverleaf Local	Lodi
138	7.4	Greenville City	Greenville
138	7.4	Groveport Madison Local	Groveport
138	7.4	Lakewood City	Lakewood
138	7.4	Madison-Plains Local	London
138	7.4	Paulding Exempted Village	Paulding
138	7.4	Port Clinton City	Port Clinton
145	7.3	East Muskingum Local	New Concord
145	7.3	Findlay City	Findlay
145	7.3	Miami Trace Local	Washington CH
145	7.3	Northern Local	Thornville
149	7.2	Bellefontaine City	Bellefontaine
149	7.2	Girard City	Girard
149	7.2	Huber Heights City	Huber Heights
152	7.0	Kenton City	Kenton
152	7.0	Lakewood Local	Hebron
152	7.0	Middletown City	Middletown
152	7.0	Sheffield-Sheffield Lake City	Sheffield Vllg
152	7.0	West Branch Local	Beloit
157	6.9	Franklin Local	Duncan Falls
158	6.8	Batavia Local	Batavia
158	6.8	Hillsboro City	Hillsboro
158	6.8	Kettering City	Kettering
158	6.8	Madison Local	Madison
158	6.8	Troy City	Troy
163	6.7	Bethel-Tate Local	Bethel
163	6.7	New Richmond Exempted Village	New Richmond
163	6.7	Washington Local	Toledo
163	6.7	West Muskingum Local	Zanesville
167	6.5	East Clinton Local	Lees Creek
167	6.5	Marlington Local	Alliance
169	6.4	Black River Local	Sullivan
169	6.4	Blanchester Local	Blanchester
169	6.4	Midview Local	Grafton
169	6.4	New Philadel. City	New Philadel.
169	6.4	Norton City	Norton
169	6.4	Waverly City	Waverly
175	6.3	Keystone Local	Lagrange
175	6.3	Saint Clairsville-Richland City	Saint Clairsville
175	6.3	Upper Sandusky Exempted Village	Upper Sandusky
178	6.2	East Cleveland City	East Cleveland
178	6.2	Milton-Union Exempted Village	West Milton
178	6.2	Northwest Local	Canal Fulton
178	6.2	Tri-Valley Local	Dresden
178	6.2	Tuscarawas Valley Local	Zoarville
178	6.2	Washington-Nile Local	West Portsmouth
178	6.2	Wheelersburg Local	Wheelersburg
178	6.2	Zanesville City	Zanesville
186	6.1	Bryan City	Bryan
186	6.1	Defiance City	Defiance
186	6.1	Finneytown Local	Cincinnati
186	6.1	Shawnee Local	Lima
186	6.1	Youngstown City	Youngstown
191	6.0	Cincinnati City	Cincinnati
191	6.0	Circleville City	Circleville
191	6.0	Fairborn City	Fairborn
191	6.0	North Olmsted City	North Olmsted
191	6.0	Northmont City	Englewood
191	6.0	Perry Local	Perry
191	6.0	Washington CH City	Washington CH
198	5.9	Graham Local	Saint Paris
198	5.9	Logan Elm Local	Circleville
198	5.9	Warren Local	Vincent
198	5.9	West Carrollton City	West Carrollton
202	5.8	Brookville Local	Brookville
202	5.8	Miamisburg City	Miamisburg
202	5.8	Plain Local	Canton
205	5.7	Chillicothe City	Chillicothe
205	5.7	Clark-Shawnee Local	Springfield
205	5.7	Clermont Northeastern Local	Batavia
205	5.7	Coldwater Exempted Village	Coldwater
205	5.7	Genoa Area Local	Genoa
205	5.7	Heath City	Heath
205	5.7	Indian Creek Local	Wintersville
205	5.7	Licking Valley Local	Newark
205	5.7	Marietta City	Marietta
214	5.6	Athens City	The Plains
214	5.6	Chippewa Local	Doylestown
214	5.6	Eastwood Local	Pemberville
214	5.6	Edgewood City	Trenton
214	5.6	South Euclid-Lyndhurst City	Lyndhurst
219	5.5	Berlin-Milan Local	Milan
219	5.5	Boardman Local	Youngstown
219	5.5	Columbus City	Columbus
219	5.5	Crestwood Local	Mantua
219	5.5	Highland Local	Sparta
219	5.5	River Valley Local	Caledonia
219	5.5	South Point Local	South Point
219	5.5	Willard City	Willard
219	5.5	Xenia Community City	Xenia
228	5.4	Carlisle Local	Carlisle
228	5.4	Coshocton City	Coshocton
228	5.4	Fairfield Union Local	West Rushville
228	5.4	Field Local	Mogadore
228	5.4	Teays Valley Local	Ashville
228	5.4	Winton Woods City	Cincinnati
234	5.3	Benjamin Logan Local	Bellefontaine
234	5.3	Champion Local	Warren
234	5.3	Southwest Licking Local	Etna
234	5.3	Southwest Local	Harrison
234	5.3	Springfield Local	Holland
234	5.3	Zane Trace Local	Chillicothe
240	5.2	Licking Heights Local	Summit Station
241	5.1	Amherst Exempted Village	Amherst
241	5.1	Dover City	Dover
241	5.1	Franklin City	Franklin
241	5.1	Hamilton City	Hamilton
241	5.1	Huron City	Huron
241	5.1	Kent City	Kent
241	5.1	Lakeview Local	Cortland
241	5.1	Maumee City	Maumee

249	5.0	Fairview Park City	Fairview Park
249	5.0	Ironton City	Ironton
249	5.0	Salem City	Salem
252	4.9	River View Local	Warsaw
252	4.9	Union-Scioto Local	Chillicothe
252	4.9	Vandalia-Butler City	Vandalia
255	4.8	Fairland Local	Proctorville
255	4.8	Howland Local	Warren
255	4.8	Lexington Local	Lexington
255	4.8	London City	London
259	4.7	Delaware City	Delaware
259	4.7	Manchester Local	Akron
259	4.7	Ontario Local	Mansfield
259	4.7	Steubenville City	Steubenville
259	4.7	West Clermont Local	Cincinnati
259	4.7	Woodridge Local	Peninsula
265	4.6	Bowling Green City	Bowling Green
265	4.6	Mentor Exempted Village	Mentor
267	4.5	Indian Lake Local	Lewistown
267	4.5	Mount Vernon City	Mount Vernon
267	4.5	Otsego Local	Tontogany
267	4.5	Perkins Local	Sandusky
267	4.5	Springfield City	Springfield
267	4.5	Toledo City	Toledo
273	4.4	Chardon Local	Chardon
273	4.4	Madison Local	Middletown
273	4.4	Marysville Exempted Village	Marysville
273	4.4	Northwestern Local	Springfield
273	4.4	Twinsburg City	Twinsburg
278	4.3	Brunswick City	Brunswick
278	4.3	Monroe Local	Monroe
280	4.2	Firelands Local	Oberlin
281	4.1	Lebanon City	Lebanon
281	4.1	North Canton City	North Canton
281	4.1	Talawanda City	Oxford
284	4.0	Eaton Community Schools City	Eaton
284	4.0	Gallipolis City	Gallipolis
284	4.0	Jonathan Alder Local	Plain City
284	4.0	Reynoldsburg City	Reynoldsburg
288	3.9	East Liverpool City	East Liverpool
288	3.9	Three Rivers Local	Cleves
290	3.8	Greeneview Local	Jamestown
291	3.7	Clinton-Massie Local	Clarksville
291	3.7	Fairfield City	Fairfield
291	3.7	Olmsted Falls City	Olmsted Falls
291	3.7	Ross Local	Hamilton
295	3.6	Painesville Township Local	Painesville
295	3.6	Wadsworth City	Wadsworth
297	3.5	Johnstown-Monroe Local	Johnstown
298	3.4	Buckeye Local	Medina
298	3.4	Canal Wnchstr Local	Canal Wnchstr
298	3.4	Lake Local	Uniontown
298	3.4	Milford Exempted Village	Milford
298	3.4	Westerville City	Westerville
303	3.3	Big Walnut Local	Galena
303	3.3	Ottawa-Glandorf Local	Ottawa
303	3.3	Poland Local	Poland
306	3.2	Beavercreek City	Beavercreek
306	3.2	Jackson Local	Massillon
306	3.2	Shaker Heights City	Shaker Heights
306	3.2	Stow-Munroe Falls City	Stow
306	3.2	Tallmadge City	Tallmadge
311	3.1	Hilliard City	Hilliard
311	3.1	Northeastern Local	Springfield
313	3.0	Gahanna-Jefferson City	Gahanna
313	3.0	Mayfield City	Mayfield Hgts
313	3.0	Medina City	Medina
313	3.0	Nordonia Hills City	Northfield
313	3.0	Pickerington Local	Pickerington
318	2.9	Kings Local	Kings Mills
318	2.9	North Royalton City	North Royalton
320	2.8	Greenon Local	Enon
321	2.7	Buckeye Valley Local	Delaware
321	2.7	N Ridgeville City	N Ridgeville
321	2.7	Valley View Local	Germantown
324	2.6	Avon Lake City	Avon Lake
324	2.6	Strongsville City	Strongsville
324	2.6	Worthington City	Worthington
327	2.5	Copley-Fairlawn City	Copley
327	2.5	Orange City	Cleveland
327	2.5	Sycamore Community City	Cincinnati
327	2.5	Tipp Exempted Village	Tipp City
331	2.4	Highland Local	Medina
332	2.3	Bay Village City	Bay Village
332	2.3	Green Local	Green
334	2.2	Perrysburg Exempted Village	Perrysburg
335	2.1	Kenston Local	Chagrin Falls
336	2.0	Loveland City	Loveland
336	2.0	Sylvania City	Sylvania
336	2.0	Westlake City	Westlake
339	1.9	Avon Local	Avon
339	1.9	Brecksville-Broadview Heights City	Brecksville
339	1.9	Olentangy Local	Lewis Center
342	1.7	Bexley City	Bexley
342	1.7	Bloom-Carroll Local	Carroll
342	1.7	Dublin City	Dublin
342	1.7	Sugarcreek Local	Bellbrook
346	1.6	Mariemont City	Cincinnati
346	1.6	West Geauga Local	Chesterland
348	1.5	Centerville City	Centerville
348	1.5	Forest Hills Local	Cincinnati
348	1.5	Lakota Local	Liberty Twp
348	1.5	Mason City	Mason
352	1.4	Canfield Local	Canfield
353	1.3	Aurora City	Aurora
353	1.3	New Albany-Plain Local	New Albany
353	1.3	Solon City	Solon
353	1.3	Springboro Community City	Springboro
357	1.2	Anthony Wayne Local	Whitehouse
357	1.2	Little Miami Local	Morrow
359	1.0	Wyoming City	Wyoming
360	0.9	Indian Hill Exempted Village	Cincinnati
361	0.8	Rocky River City	Rocky River
362	0.7	Madeira City	Cincinnati
362	0.7	Oak Hills Local	Cincinnati
364	0.6	Revere Local	Bath
364	0.6	Upper Arlington City	Upper Arlington
366	0.5	Chagrin Falls Exempted Village	Chagrin Falls
367	0.4	Granville Exempted Village	Granville
368	0.3	Hudson City	Hudson
368	0.3	Oakwood City	Dayton
370	0.0	Alternative Education Academy	Toledo
370	0.0	Electronic Classroom of Tomorrow	Columbus
370	0.0	Ohio Virtual Academy	Maumee
370	0.0	Wickliffe City	Wickliffe

Student/Teacher Ratio

Rank	Ratio	District Name	City
1	46.1	Ohio Virtual Academy	Maumee
2	31.4	Electronic Classroom of Tomorrow	Columbus
3	31.2	Alternative Education Academy	Toledo
4	20.7	Garfield Hgts City	Garfield Hgts
5	20.6	Springboro Community City	Springboro
6	20.4	Sugarcreek Local	Bellbrook
6	20.4	Union-Scioto Local	Chillicothe
8	20.3	Lebanon City	Lebanon
9	19.9	Chippewa Local	Doylestown
10	19.7	Carrollton Exempted Village	Carrollton
10	19.7	Midview Local	Grafton
12	19.6	Manchester Local	Akron
12	19.6	Shawnee Local	Lima
14	19.5	Fairfield City	Fairfield
14	19.5	Lake Local	Millbury
14	19.5	Northeastern Local	Springfield
14	19.5	Ross Local	Hamilton
18	19.4	Amherst Exempted Village	Amherst
18	19.4	Bath Local	Lima
18	19.4	Buckeye Local	Medina
18	19.4	Ontario Local	Mansfield
22	19.3	Jonathan Alder Local	Plain City
22	19.3	Keystone Local	Lagrange
22	19.3	Zane Trace Local	Chillicothe
25	19.2	Brunswick City	Brunswick
25	19.2	Geneva Area City	Geneva
25	19.2	Jefferson Area Local	Jefferson
28	19.1	Beavercreek City	Beavercreek
28	19.1	Loveland City	Loveland
28	19.1	Piqua City	Piqua
28	19.1	Wapakoneta City	Wapakoneta
32	19.0	Avon Local	Avon
32	19.0	Firelands Local	Oberlin
32	19.0	North College Hill City	Cincinnati
32	19.0	Pickerington Local	Pickerington
32	19.0	Troy City	Troy
32	19.0	Wadsworth City	Wadsworth
32	19.0	Western Brown Local	Mount Orab
39	18.9	Clinton-Massie Local	Clarksville
39	18.9	Clyde-Green Springs Ex Vill	Clyde
39	18.9	Eastwood Local	Pemberville
39	18.9	Lakota Local	Liberty Twp
39	18.9	Painesville Township Local	Painesville
39	18.9	Southwest Local	Harrison
45	18.8	Berlin-Milan Local	Milan
45	18.8	Bethel-Tate Local	Bethel
45	18.8	Brookville Local	Brookville
45	18.8	Eaton Community Schools City	Eaton
45	18.8	Fairfield Union Local	West Rushville
45	18.8	Greeneview Local	Jamestown
45	18.8	Madison Local	Madison
52	18.7	Greenfield Exempted Village	Greenfield
52	18.7	Jackson City	Jackson
52	18.7	Little Miami Local	Morrow
52	18.7	Milford Exempted Village	Milford
52	18.7	Poland Local	Poland
52	18.7	Westerville City	Westerville
58	18.6	Centerville City	Centerville
58	18.6	Cloverleaf Local	Lodi
58	18.6	Green Local	Green
58	18.6	Northwestern Local	Springfield
58	18.6	Ottawa-Glandorf Local	Ottawa
63	18.5	Norwalk City	Norwalk
64	18.4	Circleville City	Circleville
64	18.4	Graham Local	Saint Paris
64	18.4	Mason City	Mason
64	18.4	Monroe Local	Monroe
64	18.4	Oak Hills Local	Cincinnati
69	18.3	Edgewood City	Trenton
69	18.3	Greenon Local	Enon
69	18.3	Marietta City	Marietta
69	18.3	Tipp Exempted Village	Tipp City
69	18.3	Trotwood-Madison City	Trotwood
69	18.3	Wellington Exempted Village	Wellington
69	18.3	Wilmington City	Wilmington
76	18.2	Jackson Local	Massillon
76	18.2	Lancaster City	Lancaster
76	18.2	Three Rivers Local	Cleves
76	18.2	Upper Sandusky Exempted Village	Upper Sandusky
80	18.1	Batavia Local	Batavia
80	18.1	Fairland Local	Proctorville
80	18.1	Tri-Valley Local	Dresden
80	18.1	West Clermont Local	Cincinnati
84	18.0	Brecksville-Broadview Heights City	Brecksville
84	18.0	Clark-Shawnee Local	Springfield
84	18.0	Fremont City	Fremont
84	18.0	Lake Local	Uniontown
84	18.0	Maysville Local	Zanesville
84	18.0	Perry Local	Massillon
84	18.0	Reynoldsburg City	Reynoldsburg
84	18.0	Scioto Valley Local	Piketon
84	18.0	Twinsburg City	Twinsburg
93	17.9	Bloom-Carroll Local	Carroll
93	17.9	Elida Local	Elida
93	17.9	Fairborn City	Fairborn
93	17.9	James A Garfield Local	Garrettsville
93	17.9	Labrae Local	Leavittsburg
93	17.9	Logan-Hocking Local	Logan
93	17.9	Struthers City	Struthers
100	17.8	Anthony Wayne Local	Whitehouse
100	17.8	Forest Hills Local	Cincinnati
100	17.8	Huron City	Huron
100	17.8	Lakeview Local	Cortland
100	17.8	Logan Elm Local	Circleville
100	17.8	Minford Local	Minford
100	17.8	Napoleon Area City	Napoleon
100	17.8	North Royalton City	North Royalton
100	17.8	Shelby City	Shelby
100	17.8	Wheelersburg Local	Wheelersburg
110	17.7	Canal Wnchstr Local	Canal Wnchstr
110	17.7	Coldwater Exempted Village	Coldwater
110	17.7	Heath City	Heath
110	17.7	Highland Local	Medina
110	17.7	Kings Local	Kings Mills
110	17.7	River View Local	Warsaw
110	17.7	West Branch Local	Beloit
110	17.7	Westfall Local	Williamsport
118	17.6	Chillicothe City	Chillicothe
118	17.6	Groveport Madison Local	Groveport
118	17.6	Nordonia Hills City	Northfield
118	17.6	Xenia Community City	Xenia
122	17.5	Buckeye Valley Local	Delaware
122	17.5	Clermont Northeastern Local	Batavia
122	17.5	Crestwood Local	Mantua
122	17.5	Field Local	Mogadore
122	17.5	Girard City	Girard
122	17.5	Goshen Local	Goshen
122	17.5	Sidney City	Sidney
122	17.5	Stow-Munroe Falls City	Stow
122	17.5	Tiffin City	Tiffin
131	17.4	Benton Carroll Salem Local	Oak Harbor

131	17.4	Edison Local	Hammondsville
131	17.4	Johnstown-Monroe Local	Johnstown
131	17.4	Louisville City	Louisville
131	17.4	Martins Ferry City	Martins Ferry
131	17.4	N Ridgeville City	N Ridgeville
131	17.4	Northmont City	Englewood
131	17.4	Northwest Local	Cincinnati
131	17.4	Springfield City	Springfield
131	17.4	Warren Local	Vincent
131	17.4	Waverly City	Waverly
142	17.3	Black River Local	Sullivan
142	17.3	Columbus City	Columbus
142	17.3	Coventry Local	Akron
142	17.3	East Clinton Local	Lees Creek
142	17.3	East Muskingum Local	New Concord
142	17.3	Franklin City	Franklin
142	17.3	Lorain City	Lorain
142	17.3	Olmsted Falls City	Olmsted Falls
142	17.3	River Valley Local	Caledonia
142	17.3	Saint Clairsville-Richland City	Saint Clairsville
142	17.3	Sheffield-Sheffield Lake City	Sheffield Vllg
142	17.3	Southeast Local	Ravenna
142	17.3	Wauseon Exempted Village	Wauseon
155	17.2	Beaver Local	Lisbon
155	17.2	Berea City	Berea
155	17.2	Canfield Local	Canfield
155	17.2	Miamisburg City	Miamisburg
155	17.2	North Fork Local	Utica
155	17.2	Southwest Licking Local	Etna
155	17.2	Willard City	Willard
155	17.2	Willoughby-Eastlake City	Willoughby
163	17.1	Eastern Local	Sardinia
163	17.1	Strongsville City	Strongsville
163	17.1	West Muskingum Local	Zanesville
166	17.0	Ashland City	Ashland
166	17.0	Aurora City	Aurora
166	17.0	Chardon Local	Chardon
166	17.0	Clear Fork Valley Local	Bellville
166	17.0	Hubbard Exempted Village	Hubbard
166	17.0	Perkins Local	Sandusky
166	17.0	South Point Local	South Point
166	17.0	Tecumseh Local	New Carlisle
166	17.0	Tuscarawas Valley Local	Zoarville
166	17.0	West Geauga Local	Chesterland
176	16.9	Cuyahoga Falls City	Cuyahoga Falls
176	16.9	Delaware City	Delaware
176	16.9	East Cleveland City	East Cleveland
176	16.9	Fostoria City	Fostoria
176	16.9	Marlington Local	Alliance
176	16.9	North Canton City	North Canton
176	16.9	Saint Marys City	Saint Marys
176	16.9	Salem City	Salem
176	16.9	Steubenville City	Steubenville
176	16.9	Teays Valley Local	Ashville
176	16.9	Warrensville Hgts City	Warrensville Hgts
187	16.8	Medina City	Medina
187	16.8	Milton-Union Exempted Village	West Milton
187	16.8	Rolling Hills Local	Cambridge
190	16.7	Granville Exempted Village	Granville
190	16.7	Highland Local	Sparta
190	16.7	Licking Heights Local	Summit Station
190	16.7	Minerva Local	Minerva
190	16.7	Olentangy Local	Lewis Center
190	16.7	Washington-Nile Local	West Portsmouth
196	16.6	Finneytown Local	Cincinnati
196	16.6	Liberty Local	Youngstown
196	16.6	Madison-Plains Local	London
196	16.6	Miami Trace Local	Washington CH
196	16.6	Niles City	Niles
196	16.6	Rocky River City	Rocky River
196	16.6	Springfield Local	Holland
196	16.6	Sylvania City	Sylvania
196	16.6	Washington CH City	Washington CH
205	16.5	Buckeye Local	Ashtabula
205	16.5	Dover City	Dover
205	16.5	Hamilton Local	Columbus
205	16.5	Hilliard City	Hilliard
205	16.5	Howland Local	Warren
205	16.5	Otsego Local	Tontogany
205	16.5	Ravenna City	Ravenna
205	16.5	South-Western City	Grove City
205	16.5	Triway Local	Wooster
205	16.5	Vermilion Local	Vermilion
215	16.4	Barberton City	Barberton
215	16.4	Big Walnut Local	Galena
215	16.4	Indian Lake Local	Lewistown
215	16.4	Licking Valley Local	Newark
215	16.4	Mentor Exempted Village	Mentor
215	16.4	Northridge Local	Dayton
215	16.4	Parma City	Parma
215	16.4	Revere Local	Bath
215	16.4	Toledo City	Toledo
215	16.4	Westlake City	Westlake
225	16.3	Bellevue City	Bellevue
225	16.3	Hamilton City	Hamilton
225	16.3	Maple Heights City	Maple Heights
225	16.3	Maumee City	Maumee
229	16.2	Austintown Local	Youngstown
229	16.2	Avon Lake City	Avon Lake
229	16.2	Carlisle Local	Carlisle
229	16.2	Clearview Local	Lorain
229	16.2	Copley-Fairlawn City	Copley
229	16.2	Coshocton City	Coshocton
229	16.2	Euclid City	Euclid
229	16.2	Northwest Local	Mcdermott
229	16.2	Valley View Local	Germantown
238	16.1	Champion Local	Warren
238	16.1	Marion City	Marion
238	16.1	Massillon City	Massillon
238	16.1	Norton City	Norton
242	16.0	Amanda-Clearcreek Local	Amanda
242	16.0	Benjamin Logan Local	Bellefontaine
242	16.0	Cambridge City	Cambridge
242	16.0	Conneaut Area City	Conneaut
242	16.0	Gallia County Local	Gallipolis
242	16.0	Marysville Exempted Village	Marysville
242	16.0	New Philadel. City	New Philadel.
242	16.0	Northern Local	Thornville
242	16.0	Orrville City	Orrville
242	16.0	Wooster City	Wooster
242	16.0	Zanesville City	Zanesville
253	15.9	Franklin Local	Duncan Falls
253	15.9	Kenton City	Kenton
253	15.9	Madison Local	Middletown
253	15.9	New Albany-Plain Local	New Albany
257	15.8	Bedford City	Bedford
257	15.8	Boardman Local	Youngstown
257	15.8	Celina City	Celina
257	15.8	Fairless Local	Navarre
257	15.8	Genoa Area Local	Genoa
257	15.8	New Richmond Exempted Village	New Richmond
257	15.8	Van Wert City	Van Wert
257	15.8	West Holmes Local	Millersburg
265	15.7	Cleveland Municipal City	Cleveland
265	15.7	Indian Valley Local	Gnadenhutten
265	15.7	London City	London
265	15.7	Mad River Local	Dayton
265	15.7	Madeira City	Cincinnati
265	15.7	North Olmsted City	North Olmsted
271	15.6	Bay Village City	Bay Village
271	15.6	Dayton City	Dayton
271	15.6	Dublin City	Dublin
271	15.6	Gahanna-Jefferson City	Gahanna
271	15.6	Gallipolis City	Gallipolis
271	15.6	Norwood City	Norwood
271	15.6	Plain Local	Canton
271	15.6	Preble Shawnee Board of Education	Camden
271	15.6	Sycamore Community City	Cincinnati
271	15.6	Whitehall City	Whitehall
281	15.5	Claymont City	Dennison
281	15.5	Indian Creek Local	Wintersville
281	15.5	Middletown City	Middletown
281	15.5	Perry Local	Perry
281	15.5	Perrysburg Exempted Village	Perrysburg
281	15.5	Tallmadge City	Tallmadge
287	15.4	Ashtabula Area City	Ashtabula
287	15.4	Bryan City	Bryan
287	15.4	Canton City	Canton
287	15.4	Cincinnati City	Cincinnati
287	15.4	Hudson City	Hudson
287	15.4	Lakewood City	Lakewood
287	15.4	Newark City	Newark
287	15.4	Northwest Local	Canal Fulton
287	15.4	Southeast Local	Apple Creek
287	15.4	Talawanda City	Oxford
287	15.4	Vinton County Local	Mcarthur
287	15.4	West Carrollton City	West Carrollton
299	15.3	Bucyrus City	Bucyrus
299	15.3	Elyria City	Elyria
299	15.3	Greenville City	Greenville
299	15.3	Ironton City	Ironton
299	15.3	Port Clinton City	Port Clinton
299	15.3	Urbana City	Urbana
299	15.3	Wickliffe City	Wickliffe
306	15.2	Elgin Local	Marion
306	15.2	Hillsboro City	Hillsboro
306	15.2	Mount Healthy City	Cincinnati
306	15.2	Mount Vernon City	Mount Vernon
306	15.2	South Euclid-Lyndhurst City	Lyndhurst
311	15.1	Lexington Local	Lexington
311	15.1	New Lexington City	New Lexington
311	15.1	Pike-Delta-York Local	Delta
311	15.1	Vandalia-Butler City	Vandalia
315	15.0	Bellefontaine City	Bellefontaine
315	15.0	Bowling Green City	Bowling Green
315	15.0	Kenston Local	Chagrin Falls
315	15.0	Kettering City	Kettering
315	15.0	Rossford Exempted Village	Rossford
315	15.0	Worthington City	Worthington
315	15.0	Wyoming City	Wyoming
322	14.9	Buckeye Local	Dillonvale
322	14.9	East Liverpool City	East Liverpool
322	14.9	Galion City	Galion
322	14.9	Oakwood City	Dayton
322	14.9	Oregon City	Oregon
327	14.8	Alliance City	Alliance
327	14.8	Harrison Hills City	Hopedale
327	14.8	Paulding Exempted Village	Paulding
327	14.8	Rock Hill Local	Ironton
331	14.7	Findlay City	Findlay
331	14.7	Solon City	Solon
331	14.7	Warren City	Warren
331	14.7	Wellston City	Wellston
331	14.7	Winton Woods City	Cincinnati
336	14.6	Portsmouth City	Portsmouth
337	14.5	East Holmes Local	Berlin
337	14.5	Painesville Local	Painesville
339	14.4	Alexander Local	Albany
339	14.4	Huber Heights City	Huber Heights
341	14.3	Adams County/Ohio Valley Local	West Union
341	14.3	Chagrin Falls Exempted Village	Chagrin Falls
341	14.3	Streetsboro City	Streetsboro
344	14.2	Madison Local	Mansfield
344	14.2	Sandusky City	Sandusky
346	14.1	Defiance City	Defiance
346	14.1	Indian Hill Exempted Village	Cincinnati
346	14.1	Lima City	Lima
346	14.1	Sandy Valley Local	Magnolia
346	14.1	Springfield Local	Akron
346	14.1	Washington Local	Toledo
346	14.1	Woodridge Local	Peninsula
353	14.0	Bexley City	Bexley
353	14.0	Blanchester Local	Blanchester
353	14.0	Fairview Park City	Fairview Park
353	14.0	Lakewood Local	Hebron
357	13.9	Athens City	The Plains
357	13.9	Bellaire Local	Bellaire
357	13.9	Mariemont City	Cincinnati
357	13.9	Upper Arlington City	Upper Arlington
361	13.8	Canton Local	Canton
362	13.7	Morgan Local	Mcconnelsville
363	13.5	Meigs Local	Pomeroy
364	13.3	Cleveland Hgts-University Hgts	University Hgts
365	13.2	Princeton City	Cincinnati
365	13.2	Shaker Heights City	Shaker Heights
367	13.1	Switzerland of Ohio Local	Woodsfield
368	13.0	Youngstown City	Youngstown
369	12.5	Kent City	Kent
370	12.4	Mayfield City	Mayfield Hgts
371	12.3	Mansfield City	Mansfield
372	11.6	Orange City	Cleveland
373	10.3	Akron City	Akron

Student/Librarian Ratio

Rank	Ratio	District Name	City
1	12,515.0	Licking Heights Local	Summit Station
2	9,340.0	Indian Valley Local	Gnadenhutten
3	8,204.0	Oak Hills Local	Cincinnati
4	6,281.0	Findlay City	Findlay
5	5,972.0	Northmont City	Englewood
6	4,889.0	Mason City	Mason
7	4,748.0	Fairborn City	Fairborn
8	4,434.0	Ashtabula Area City	Ashtabula
9	4,316.4	South-Western City	Grove City
10	4,190.0	Adams County/Ohio Valley Local	West Union
11	4,050.0	Circleville City	Circleville
12	3,952.0	Wooster City	Wooster
13	3,744.0	Madison Local	Madison
14	3,624.0	Little Miami Local	Morrow

Rank	Value	District	City
15	3,462.5	Middletown City	Middletown
16	3,352.0	Copley-Fairlawn City	Copley
17	3,303.8	Amherst Exempted Village	Amherst
18	3,241.0	Ravenna City	Ravenna
19	3,176.7	East Holmes Local	Berlin
20	3,156.0	Kenston Local	Chagrin Falls
21	3,105.0	Wapakoneta City	Wapakoneta
22	3,104.0	New Philadel. City	New Philadel.
23	3,024.5	Plain Local	Canton
24	2,964.0	Athens City	The Plains
25	2,945.0	Avon Local	Avon
26	2,943.0	Celina City	Celina
27	2,934.0	Springfield Local	Akron
28	2,837.0	Carrollton Exempted Village	Carrollton
29	2,777.8	Canton City	Canton
30	2,774.0	Miamisburg City	Miamisburg
31	2,732.0	Big Walnut Local	Galena
32	2,716.9	Northwest Local	Cincinnati
33	2,715.0	Willard City	Willard
34	2,705.6	Franklin Local	Duncan Falls
35	2,687.0	East Liverpool City	East Liverpool
36	2,674.0	Shawnee Local	Lima
37	2,638.0	Edison Local	Hammondsville
38	2,637.0	Vinton County Local	Mcarthur
39	2,625.0	Marion City	Marion
40	2,619.0	Dover City	Dover
41	2,503.0	Clark-Shawnee Local	Springfield
42	2,502.0	New Richmond Exempted Village	New Richmond
43	2,486.3	Kettering City	Kettering
44	2,485.0	West Branch Local	Beloit
44	2,485.0	West Geauga Local	Chesterland
46	2,459.0	Elida Local	Elida
47	2,446.0	North Canton City	North Canton
48	2,443.0	Buckeye Local	Dillonvale
49	2,438.0	Conneaut Area City	Conneaut
50	2,432.0	River View Local	Warsaw
51	2,429.5	Lorain City	Lorain
52	2,414.0	Clyde-Green Springs Ex Vill	Clyde
53	2,411.0	Coventry Local	Akron
54	2,392.0	Springboro Community City	Springboro
55	2,383.0	Gallipolis City	Gallipolis
56	2,375.0	Indian Creek Local	Wintersville
57	2,371.0	Wadsworth City	Wadsworth
58	2,363.0	Painesville Township Local	Painesville
59	2,352.0	Steubenville City	Steubenville
60	2,341.5	Delaware City	Delaware
61	2,337.0	Salem City	Salem
62	2,326.0	Buckeye Local	Ashtabula
63	2,318.0	Buckeye Valley Local	Delaware
64	2,316.0	Urbana City	Urbana
65	2,304.0	Logan Elm Local	Circleville
66	2,301.0	Greenfield Exempted Village	Greenfield
67	2,299.0	Eaton Community Schools City	Eaton
68	2,298.0	Canton Local	Canton
69	2,293.0	Troy City	Troy
70	2,263.5	South Euclid-Lyndhurst City	Lyndhurst
71	2,260.3	Reynoldsburg City	Reynoldsburg
72	2,252.0	Huber Heights City	Huber Heights
73	2,236.0	Van Wert City	Van Wert
74	2,227.0	Perrysburg Exempted Village	Perrysburg
75	2,224.3	Milford Exempted Village	Milford
76	2,218.3	Austintown Local	Youngstown
77	2,209.0	Waverly City	Waverly
78	2,196.7	North Olmsted City	North Olmsted
79	2,192.0	Perkins Local	Sandusky
80	2,177.5	East Cleveland City	East Cleveland
81	2,176.0	Fostoria City	Fostoria
81	2,176.0	Minerva Local	Minerva
83	2,169.7	Euclid City	Euclid
84	2,167.0	Jefferson Area Local	Jefferson
85	2,151.0	Rolling Hills Local	Cambridge
86	2,149.0	Galion City	Galion
87	2,139.4	Medina City	Medina
88	2,128.0	Kenton City	Kenton
89	2,124.5	Anthony Wayne Local	Whitehouse
90	2,122.0	Firelands Local	Oberlin
91	2,112.0	Wauseon Exempted Village	Wauseon
92	2,077.0	Struthers City	Struthers
93	2,062.0	Fairfield Union Local	West Rushville
94	2,045.0	Harrison Hills City	Hopedale
95	2,031.0	Greenon Local	Enon
96	1,998.0	Indian Lake Local	Lewistown
97	1,991.0	Jonathan Alder Local	Plain City
98	1,984.0	Bath Local	Lima
99	1,983.5	Nordonia Hills City	Northfield
100	1,967.7	Washington Local	Toledo
101	1,959.0	Batavia Local	Batavia
102	1,947.0	Northwestern Local	Springfield
103	1,937.0	Sheffield-Sheffield Lake City	Sheffield Vllg
104	1,928.7	Jackson Local	Massillon
105	1,926.0	Eastwood Local	Pemberville
106	1,922.5	Piqua City	Piqua
107	1,922.0	Clermont Northeastern Local	Batavia
108	1,910.5	West Carrollton City	West Carrollton
109	1,908.0	Fairless Local	Navarre
110	1,906.0	Bedford City	Bedford
111	1,889.5	Logan-Hocking Local	Logan
112	1,882.0	River Valley Local	Caledonia
113	1,880.0	South Point Local	South Point
114	1,877.0	Monroe Local	Monroe
115	1,870.0	Port Clinton City	Port Clinton
116	1,866.8	Brunswick City	Brunswick
117	1,866.5	N Ridgeville City	N Ridgeville
118	1,858.5	Mad River Local	Dayton
119	1,858.0	Northridge Local	Dayton
120	1,847.0	Blanchester Local	Blanchester
120	1,847.0	Perry Local	Perry
122	1,846.8	Hamilton City	Hamilton
123	1,846.7	Miami Trace Local	Washington CH
124	1,844.0	Clear Fork Valley Local	Bellville
125	1,834.0	Keystone Local	Lagrange
126	1,823.0	Berlin-Milan Local	Milan
127	1,820.0	Ontario Local	Mansfield
128	1,815.0	Clinton-Massie Local	Clarksville
129	1,810.0	Liberty Local	Youngstown
130	1,807.5	Southwest Licking Local	Etna
131	1,792.0	Upper Sandusky Exempted Village	Upper Sandusky
132	1,786.0	Wellston City	Wellston
133	1,780.0	Tecumseh Local	New Carlisle
134	1,777.0	Black River Local	Sullivan
135	1,769.5	Teays Valley Local	Ashville
136	1,766.0	Highland Local	Sparta
137	1,765.2	Willoughby-Eastlake City	Willoughby
138	1,760.0	Girard City	Girard
139	1,757.0	Midview Local	Grafton
140	1,733.0	Finneytown Local	Cincinnati
140	1,733.0	Lake Local	Millbury
142	1,728.0	Paulding Exempted Village	Paulding
143	1,724.0	Westfall Local	Williamsport
144	1,704.0	Scioto Valley Local	Piketon
144	1,704.0	Tuscarawas Valley Local	Zoarville
146	1,699.5	Madison Local	Mansfield
147	1,694.8	Springfield Local	Holland
148	1,693.5	Cloverleaf Local	Lodi
149	1,690.3	Lima City	Lima
150	1,674.3	Marysville Exempted Village	Marysville
151	1,671.0	Zane Trace Local	Chillicothe
152	1,667.5	Louisville City	Louisville
153	1,658.0	Elgin Local	Marion
153	1,658.0	Mariemont City	Cincinnati
155	1,654.0	Alexander Local	Albany
156	1,653.5	Trotwood-Madison City	Trotwood
157	1,643.5	Wilmington City	Wilmington
158	1,633.5	Lancaster City	Lancaster
159	1,629.0	Saint Clairsville-Richland City	Saint Clairsville
160	1,623.5	Parma City	Parma
161	1,620.5	Tri-Valley Local	Dresden
162	1,616.5	Greenville City	Greenville
163	1,616.3	Boardman Local	Youngstown
164	1,607.0	Johnstown-Monroe Local	Johnstown
165	1,605.0	James A Garfield Local	Garrettsville
166	1,603.0	Amanda-Clearcreek Local	Amanda
167	1,602.0	Perry Local	Massillon
168	1,589.0	Genoa Area Local	Genoa
169	1,587.5	Alliance City	Alliance
170	1,587.0	North College Hill City	Cincinnati
171	1,585.9	Loveland City	Loveland
172	1,584.0	Labrae Local	Leavittsburg
173	1,581.5	Warren City	Warren
174	1,579.2	Union-Scioto Local	Chillicothe
175	1,572.5	Chillicothe City	Chillicothe
176	1,564.2	Berea City	Berea
177	1,555.0	Canfield Local	Canfield
178	1,552.0	East Clinton Local	Lees Creek
179	1,550.4	Dayton City	Dayton
180	1,546.0	Southwest Local	Harrison
181	1,543.0	Eastern Local	Sardinia
182	1,542.6	Sylvania City	Sylvania
183	1,538.0	Preble Shawnee Board of Education	Camden
184	1,536.2	West Clermont Local	Cincinnati
185	1,526.0	Chippewa Local	Doylestown
186	1,525.3	Massillon City	Massillon
187	1,525.2	Beavercreek City	Beavercreek
188	1,521.0	Clearview Local	Lorain
189	1,520.0	Pike-Delta-York Local	Delta
190	1,519.0	Marietta City	Marietta
191	1,517.1	Akron City	Akron
192	1,503.0	Madison-Plains Local	London
193	1,501.0	Tiffin City	Tiffin
194	1,500.7	Fremont City	Fremont
195	1,451.7	Barberton City	Barberton
196	1,451.5	Stow-Munroe Falls City	Stow
197	1,445.5	Geneva Area City	Geneva
198	1,444.7	Springfield City	Springfield
199	1,442.0	Painesville Local	Painesville
200	1,408.5	Hamilton Local	Columbus
201	1,407.3	Green Local	Green
202	1,399.5	Bellefontaine City	Bellefontaine
203	1,395.0	Zanesville City	Zanesville
204	1,393.5	Jackson City	Jackson
205	1,369.7	Sandusky City	Sandusky
206	1,358.0	Warren Local	Vincent
207	1,351.2	Newark City	Newark
208	1,343.0	Cambridge City	Cambridge
209	1,342.5	Tipp Exempted Village	Tipp City
210	1,326.5	Mentor Exempted Village	Mentor
211	1,322.5	Marlington Local	Alliance
212	1,320.5	Rocky River City	Rocky River
213	1,316.3	Maple Heights City	Maple Heights
214	1,311.7	Mayfield City	Mayfield Hgts
215	1,310.9	North Royalton City	North Royalton
216	1,309.7	Oregon City	Oregon
217	1,307.3	Sidney City	Sidney
218	1,289.3	Lakota Local	Liberty Twp
219	1,279.7	Kings Local	Kings Mills
220	1,277.3	Xenia Community City	Xenia
221	1,274.0	Goshen Local	Goshen
222	1,273.0	Crestwood Local	Mantua
223	1,267.6	Lebanon City	Lebanon
224	1,265.0	Defiance City	Defiance
225	1,257.5	Bay Village City	Bay Village
226	1,256.0	West Muskingum Local	Zanesville
227	1,246.0	Gallia County Local	Gallipolis
228	1,243.0	Mount Healthy City	Cincinnati
229	1,241.1	Field Local	Mogadore
230	1,232.5	Vermilion Local	Vermilion
231	1,231.7	Ashland City	Ashland
232	1,229.5	Northwest Local	Canal Fulton
233	1,226.7	Toledo City	Toledo
234	1,224.0	Youngstown City	Youngstown
235	1,220.0	West Holmes Local	Millersburg
236	1,206.5	Saint Marys City	Saint Marys
237	1,195.0	Napoleon Area City	Napoleon
238	1,180.0	Bellevue City	Bellevue
239	1,172.7	Olmsted Falls City	Olmsted Falls
240	1,163.0	Avon Lake City	Avon Lake
241	1,162.5	Washington CH City	Washington CH
242	1,152.9	Cincinnati City	Cincinnati
243	1,151.4	Pickerington Local	Pickerington
244	1,142.6	Princeton City	Cincinnati
245	1,141.0	Bryan City	Bryan
246	1,140.5	Maysville Local	Zanesville
247	1,133.6	Garfield Hgts City	Garfield Hgts
248	1,133.5	Claymont City	Dennison
249	1,123.0	Morgan Local	Mcconnelsville
250	1,121.9	Cuyahoga Falls City	Cuyahoga Falls
251	1,085.0	East Muskingum Local	New Concord
252	1,084.8	Mansfield City	Mansfield
253	1,083.0	Triway Local	Wooster
254	1,072.0	Columbus City	Columbus
255	1,069.3	Howland Local	Warren
256	1,051.4	Northern Local	Thornville
257	1,047.1	Strongsville City	Strongsville
258	1,045.0	London City	London
259	1,040.8	Winton Woods City	Cincinnati
260	1,039.5	Valley View Local	Germantown
261	1,028.3	Norwalk City	Norwalk
262	1,025.8	Twinsburg City	Twinsburg
263	1,025.3	Canal Wnchstr Local	Canal Wnchstr
264	1,023.0	Highland Local	Medina
265	1,020.5	Rossford Exempted Village	Rossford
266	997.5	Wyoming City	Wyoming
267	996.5	Three Rivers Local	Cleves
268	992.5	Bethel-Tate Local	Bethel
269	992.0	Benton Carroll Salem Local	Oak Harbor
270	991.0	Chagrin Falls Exempted Village	Chagrin Falls
271	984.3	Aurora City	Aurora
272	983.5	Coshocton City	Coshocton
273	975.5	Rock Hill Local	Ironton
274	973.0	Benjamin Logan Local	Bellefontaine
275	966.3	Carlisle Local	Carlisle

276	965.7	Ross Local	Hamilton
277	965.0	Maumee City	Maumee
278	958.3	Niles City	Niles
279	956.0	Revere Local	Bath
280	955.8	Northeastern Local	Springfield
281	954.3	Forest Hills Local	Cincinnati
282	946.0	Franklin City	Franklin
283	944.0	Brecksville-Broadview Heights City	Brecksville
284	943.0	North Fork Local	Utica
285	940.0	Portsmouth City	Portsmouth
286	937.5	Westerville City	Westerville
287	928.0	Lexington Local	Lexington
288	914.0	Orrville City	Orrville
289	908.7	Lakewood City	Lakewood
290	897.3	Switzerland of Ohio Local	Woodsfield
291	891.5	Otsego Local	Tontogany
292	890.8	Solon City	Solon
293	884.5	Lake Local	Uniontown
293	884.5	Northwest Local	Mcdermott
295	874.0	Bucyrus City	Bucyrus
296	866.5	Heath City	Heath
297	865.5	Milton-Union Exempted Village	West Milton
298	862.2	Elyria City	Elyria
299	840.0	Mount Vernon City	Mount Vernon
300	834.5	Ironton City	Ironton
301	828.5	Chardon Local	Chardon
302	823.7	Martins Ferry City	Martins Ferry
303	823.1	Beaver Local	Lisbon
304	821.8	Fairland Local	Proctorville
305	821.5	Wellington Exempted Village	Wellington
306	816.0	Poland Local	Poland
307	806.2	Western Brown Local	Mount Orab
308	789.0	Bloom-Carroll Local	Carroll
309	784.0	Greeneview Local	Jamestown
310	783.3	Bowling Green City	Bowling Green
311	782.0	Granville Exempted Village	Granville
311	782.0	Madison Local	Middletown
313	778.5	Manchester Local	Akron
314	775.9	Lakewood Local	Hebron
315	772.3	Graham Local	Saint Paris
316	771.5	Olentangy Local	Lewis Center
317	768.7	Hubbard Exempted Village	Hubbard
318	768.0	Wheelersburg Local	Wheelersburg
319	766.0	Sandy Valley Local	Magnolia
320	765.0	Hudson City	Hudson
321	759.0	Huron City	Huron
322	757.8	Edgewood City	Trenton
323	750.3	Indian Hill Exempted Village	Cincinnati
324	730.8	Kent City	Kent
325	730.1	Fairfield City	Fairfield
326	729.3	Lakeview Local	Cortland
327	714.0	Hilliard City	Hilliard
328	713.5	Warrensville Hgts City	Warrensville Hgts
329	703.0	Oakwood City	Dayton
330	701.0	Westlake City	Westlake
331	685.8	New Albany-Plain Local	New Albany
332	676.8	Tallmadge City	Tallmadge
333	647.0	Dublin City	Dublin
334	634.3	New Lexington City	New Lexington
335	630.5	Centerville City	Centerville
336	623.8	Fairview Park City	Fairview Park
337	621.2	Upper Arlington City	Upper Arlington
338	606.3	Woodridge Local	Peninsula
339	606.0	Cleveland Municipal City	Cleveland
340	602.8	Talawanda City	Oxford
341	583.6	Whitehall City	Whitehall
342	579.6	Cleveland Hgts-University Hgts	University Hgts
343	572.7	Champion Local	Warren
344	565.2	Worthington City	Worthington
345	563.1	Shaker Heights City	Shaker Heights
346	563.0	Washington-Nile Local	West Portsmouth
347	562.8	Shelby City	Shelby
348	539.8	Bexley City	Bexley
349	539.7	Minford Local	Minford
350	535.0	Brookville Local	Brookville
351	534.0	Licking Valley Local	Newark
352	531.2	Gahanna-Jefferson City	Gahanna
353	517.3	Madeira City	Cincinnati
354	514.3	Groveport Madison Local	Groveport
355	497.5	Meigs Local	Pomeroy
356	473.8	Sycamore Community City	Cincinnati
357	465.8	Hillsboro City	Hillsboro
358	379.2	Orange City	Cleveland
359	350.2	Streetsboro City	Streetsboro
360	n/a	Alternative Education Academy	Toledo
360	n/a	Bellaire Local	Bellaire
360	n/a	Buckeye Local	Medina
360	n/a	Coldwater Exempted Village	Coldwater
360	n/a	Electronic Classroom of Tomorrow	Columbus
360	n/a	Norton City	Norton
360	n/a	Norwood City	Norwood
360	n/a	Ohio Virtual Academy	Maumee
360	n/a	Ottawa-Glandorf Local	Ottawa
360	n/a	Southeast Local	Apple Creek
360	n/a	Southeast Local	Ravenna
360	n/a	Sugarcreek Local	Bellbrook
360	n/a	Vandalia-Butler City	Vandalia
360	n/a	Wickliffe City	Wickliffe

Student/Counselor Ratio

Rank	Ratio	District Name	City
1	2,080.5	Cincinnati City	Cincinnati
2	1,908.0	Fairless Local	Navarre
3	1,748.0	Bucyrus City	Bucyrus
4	1,550.4	Dayton City	Dayton
5	1,318.5	Vinton County Local	Mcarthur
6	1,216.0	River View Local	Warsaw
7	1,191.5	Gallipolis City	Gallipolis
8	1,159.0	Buckeye Valley Local	Delaware
9	1,108.6	New Philadel. City	New Philadel.
10	975.5	Rock Hill Local	Ironton
11	972.7	Whitehall City	Whitehall
12	953.0	East Holmes Local	Berlin
13	945.7	Carrollton Exempted Village	Carrollton
14	942.0	West Muskingum Local	Zanesville
15	940.0	South Point Local	South Point
16	936.0	Madison Local	Madison
17	934.0	Indian Valley Local	Gnadenhutten
18	929.0	Jackson City	Jackson
19	928.0	Lexington Local	Lexington
20	921.7	West Clermont Local	Cincinnati
21	911.5	Berlin-Milan Local	Milan
22	907.4	Teays Valley Local	Ashville
23	886.8	Ashtabula Area City	Ashtabula
24	879.3	Edison Local	Hammondsville
25	871.0	East Cleveland City	East Cleveland
26	859.2	Fairfield Union Local	West Rushville
27	839.7	Franklin Local	Duncan Falls
28	830.7	Gallia County Local	Gallipolis
29	814.5	Saint Clairsville-Richland City	Saint Clairsville
30	812.7	Conneaut Area City	Conneaut
31	810.3	Tri-Valley Local	Dresden
32	810.0	Circleville City	Circleville
33	809.8	Lorain City	Lorain
34	803.5	Johnstown-Monroe Local	Johnstown
35	794.5	Genoa Area Local	Genoa
36	782.3	Norton City	Norton
37	779.0	Salem City	Salem
38	777.5	Canfield Local	Canfield
39	776.0	East Clinton Local	Lees Creek
40	775.3	Buckeye Local	Ashtabula
41	773.5	Coldwater Exempted Village	Coldwater
42	769.4	Middletown City	Middletown
43	768.0	Logan Elm Local	Circleville
44	767.7	Newark City	Newark
45	767.0	Greenfield Exempted Village	Greenfield
46	763.5	Bethel-Tate Local	Bethel
47	763.0	Chippewa Local	Doylestown
48	755.5	Lancaster City	Lancaster
49	752.0	Bellaire Local	Bellaire
50	751.5	Madison-Plains Local	London
51	748.7	Morgan Local	Mcconnelsville
52	744.2	South-Western City	Grove City
53	736.3	Avon Local	Avon
54	734.5	Norwalk City	Norwalk
55	731.9	New Lexington City	New Lexington
56	728.0	Amherst Exempted Village	Amherst
57	723.3	East Muskingum Local	New Concord
58	722.8	Geneva Area City	Geneva
58	722.8	Northern Local	Thornville
60	722.3	Jefferson Area Local	Jefferson
61	720.6	Hubbard Exempted Village	Hubbard
62	720.0	Paulding Exempted Village	Paulding
63	718.8	Niles City	Niles
64	715.1	Licking Heights Local	Summit Station
65	713.4	Oak Hills Local	Cincinnati
66	701.4	Eastern Local	Sardinia
67	697.5	Zanesville City	Zanesville
68	696.9	Little Miami Local	Morrow
69	696.7	London City	London
70	693.0	Valley View Local	Germantown
71	691.4	Clearview Local	Lorain
72	687.6	Vandalia-Butler City	Vandalia
73	681.7	Harrison Hills City	Hopedale
74	678.9	Willoughby-Eastlake City	Willoughby
75	677.0	Greenon Local	Enon
76	675.1	Painesville Township Local	Painesville
77	673.0	Switzerland of Ohio Local	Woodsfield
78	670.8	Wilmington City	Wilmington
79	664.3	Three Rivers Local	Cleves
80	663.3	Mentor Exempted Village	Mentor
81	663.1	Beaver Local	Lisbon
82	661.4	Trotwood-Madison City	Trotwood
83	661.3	Bath Local	Lima
84	659.3	Tecumseh Local	New Carlisle
85	655.7	Coshocton City	Coshocton
86	649.4	Parma City	Parma
87	649.3	Brunswick City	Brunswick
88	648.2	Ravenna City	Ravenna
89	647.1	Elida Local	Elida
90	644.5	Norwood City	Norwood
91	641.6	Lebanon City	Lebanon
92	641.5	Southeast Local	Ravenna
93	640.0	Medina City	Medina
94	636.8	West Carrollton City	West Carrollton
95	636.5	Crestwood Local	Mantua
96	635.9	Clear Fork Valley Local	Bellville
97	634.2	Winton Woods City	Cincinnati
98	633.9	Lima City	Lima
99	629.8	Logan-Hocking Local	Logan
100	623.3	Northwest Local	Cincinnati
101	619.3	Northridge Local	Dayton
102	615.7	Blanchester Local	Blanchester
103	611.3	Keystone Local	Lagrange
104	610.8	Buckeye Local	Dillonvale
105	609.3	Orrville City	Orrville
106	608.4	Northwestern Local	Springfield
107	607.6	Marietta City	Marietta
108	606.7	Ontario Local	Mansfield
109	605.1	Loveland City	Loveland
110	602.8	Coventry Local	Akron
111	601.1	Stow-Munroe Falls City	Stow
112	600.1	Reynoldsburg City	Reynoldsburg
113	599.2	Cuyahoga Falls City	Cuyahoga Falls
114	598.0	Springboro Community City	Springboro
115	595.3	Wellston City	Wellston
116	594.3	Otsego Local	Tontogany
117	593.8	Indian Creek Local	Wintersville
118	592.8	Wadsworth City	Wadsworth
119	592.3	Black River Local	Sullivan
120	590.2	Highland Local	Medina
121	589.7	Northwest Local	Mcdermott
122	589.5	Field Local	Mogadore
123	588.7	Highland Local	Sparta
124	588.6	Celina City	Celina
125	588.0	Steubenville City	Steubenville
126	586.7	Girard City	Girard
127	585.7	Midview Local	Grafton
128	584.7	Fremont City	Fremont
129	583.3	Marion City	Marion
130	583.0	Garfield Hgts City	Garfield Hgts
131	577.7	Southeast Local	Apple Creek
132	576.8	Painesville Local	Painesville
133	575.2	Mason City	Mason
134	575.1	Warren City	Warren
135	574.7	Westfall Local	Williamsport
136	571.4	Chardon Local	Chardon
137	570.7	Lakota Local	Liberty Twp
138	570.3	Maysville Local	Zanesville
139	568.0	Scioto Valley Local	Piketon
139	568.0	Tuscarawas Valley Local	Zoarville
141	566.5	Eastwood Local	Pemberville
142	565.9	South Euclid-Lyndhurst City	Lyndhurst
143	564.1	Maple Heights City	Maple Heights
144	563.4	Hamilton Local	Columbus
145	563.1	Shaker Heights City	Shaker Heights
146	562.5	Lakewood Local	Hebron
147	561.1	Groveport Madison Local	Groveport
148	558.9	Northwest Local	Canal Fulton
149	557.3	Akron City	Akron
150	557.0	Zane Trace Local	Chillicothe
151	556.9	Springfield Local	Holland
152	553.4	James A Garfield Local	Garrettsville
153	552.3	Waverly City	Waverly
154	551.0	Galion City	Galion
155	547.7	Wellington Exempted Village	Wellington
156	546.4	Big Walnut Local	Galena
157	546.3	Cloverleaf Local	Lodi
158	544.0	Minerva Local	Minerva

159	542.4	Euclid City	Euclid
160	541.3	Edgewood City	Trenton
161	540.9	Milton-Union Exempted Village	West Milton
162	537.8	Rolling Hills Local	Cambridge
163	535.0	Brookville Local	Brookville
164	534.3	Amanda-Clearcreek Local	Amanda
165	533.5	Alexander Local	Albany
166	532.0	Kenton City	Kenton
167	531.0	Mad River Local	Dayton
168	528.0	Labrae Local	Leavittsburg
168	528.0	Wauseon Exempted Village	Wauseon
170	527.9	Ashland City	Ashland
171	527.1	Troy City	Troy
172	526.0	Bloom-Carroll Local	Carroll
173	524.7	Barberton City	Barberton
174	524.2	Chillicothe City	Chillicothe
175	523.8	Adams County/Ohio Valley Local	West Union
175	523.8	Dover City	Dover
177	520.4	Electronic Classroom of Tomorrow	Columbus
178	519.7	Huber Heights City	Huber Heights
179	515.1	Westerville City	Westerville
180	514.3	Olentangy Local	Lewis Center
181	514.2	Massillon City	Massillon
182	512.7	Canal Wnchstr Local	Canal Wnchstr
183	512.0	Wheelersburg Local	Wheelersburg
184	511.9	North College Hill City	Cincinnati
185	510.3	Rossford Exempted Village	Rossford
186	509.7	Sheffield-Sheffield Lake City	Sheffield Vllg
187	509.6	Goshen Local	Goshen
188	508.9	Lakewood City	Lakewood
189	508.4	Beavercreek City	Beavercreek
190	506.3	Wickliffe City	Wickliffe
191	506.0	Huron City	Huron
192	505.2	Firelands Local	Oberlin
193	503.0	Northeastern Local	Springfield
194	502.6	Green Local	Green
195	500.6	Clark-Shawnee Local	Springfield
196	499.5	Indian Lake Local	Lewistown
197	497.8	Jonathan Alder Local	Plain City
198	497.0	West Branch Local	Beloit
198	497.0	West Geauga Local	Chesterland
200	496.8	Gahanna-Jefferson City	Gahanna
201	495.5	Southwest Local	Harrison
202	495.3	Springfield City	Springfield
203	494.6	Fairborn City	Fairborn
203	494.6	Findlay City	Findlay
205	494.0	Athens City	The Plains
206	493.0	Vermilion Local	Vermilion
207	491.7	Bellevue City	Bellevue
208	489.9	New Albany-Plain Local	New Albany
209	489.8	Batavia Local	Batavia
210	488.7	Strongsville City	Strongsville
211	486.5	Benjamin Logan Local	Bellefontaine
212	486.0	Miami Trace Local	Washington CH
213	485.6	Madison Local	Mansfield
214	485.0	Washington Local	Toledo
215	483.2	Forest Hills Local	Cincinnati
216	482.8	Clyde-Green Springs Ex Vill	Clyde
217	482.4	Miamisburg City	Miamisburg
218	482.2	Jackson Local	Massillon
219	481.9	Olmsted Falls City	Olmsted Falls
220	481.4	Heath City	Heath
221	480.6	Hilliard City	Hilliard
221	480.6	Piqua City	Piqua
223	480.5	Clermont Northeastern Local	Batavia
224	476.6	Milford Exempted Village	Milford
225	476.4	Louisville City	Louisville
226	476.2	Buckeye Local	Medina
227	476.1	Princeton City	Cincinnati
228	475.7	Warrensville Hgts City	Warrensville Hgts
229	473.1	Saint Marys City	Saint Marys
230	473.0	Franklin City	Franklin
231	472.1	Copley-Fairlawn City	Copley
232	471.0	Centerville City	Centerville
233	470.5	River Valley Local	Caledonia
233	470.5	Wapakoneta City	Wapakoneta
235	469.3	Monroe Local	Monroe
236	469.1	Columbus City	Columbus
237	468.3	Delaware City	Delaware
238	468.2	Worthington City	Worthington
239	467.7	West Holmes Local	Millersburg
240	467.3	Ross Local	Hamilton
241	466.5	Bellefontaine City	Bellefontaine
241	466.5	Cleveland Municipal City	Cleveland
243	465.7	Hudson City	Hudson
244	465.0	Fairfield City	Fairfield
245	464.9	Sugarcreek Local	Bellbrook
245	464.9	Wooster City	Wooster
247	463.8	Western Brown Local	Mount Orab
248	463.4	Graham Local	Saint Paris
249	463.0	Canton City	Canton
250	461.9	Greenville City	Greenville
251	461.8	Perry Local	Perry
252	459.6	Canton Local	Canton
253	459.4	Northmont City	Englewood
254	458.3	Howland Local	Warren
255	456.6	Marysville Exempted Village	Marysville
256	455.9	Twinsburg City	Twinsburg
257	455.4	Toledo City	Toledo
258	455.2	N Ridgeville City	N Ridgeville
259	454.3	Aurora City	Aurora
260	453.4	Claymont City	Dennison
261	452.5	Liberty Local	Youngstown
262	450.9	Kenston Local	Chagrin Falls
263	449.0	North Fork Local	Utica
264	447.5	Tipp Exempted Village	Tipp City
265	447.2	Van Wert City	Van Wert
266	445.7	Shawnee Local	Lima
267	445.4	Perrysburg Exempted Village	Perrysburg
267	445.4	Urbana City	Urbana
269	443.9	Hamilton City	Hamilton
270	442.7	Clinton-Massie Local	Clarksville
271	442.1	Eaton Community Schools City	Eaton
272	441.9	Berea City	Berea
273	440.9	Southwest Licking Local	Etna
274	440.8	Boardman Local	Youngstown
275	438.7	Portsmouth City	Portsmouth
276	438.4	Perkins Local	Sandusky
277	437.6	Lakeview Local	Cortland
278	435.0	Pickerington Local	Pickerington
279	434.5	Revere Local	Bath
280	433.3	Lake Local	Millbury
281	429.9	Kent City	Kent
282	429.5	Champion Local	Warren
283	429.1	North Canton City	North Canton
284	425.8	Xenia Community City	Xenia
285	425.2	Austintown Local	Youngstown
286	422.7	Washington CH City	Washington CH
287	421.8	Oakwood City	Dayton
288	421.3	Ottawa-Glandorf Local	Ottawa
289	420.8	Manchester Local	Akron
290	420.5	Fairland Local	Proctorville
291	420.2	Streetsboro City	Streetsboro
292	420.0	Mount Vernon City	Mount Vernon
293	417.1	North Royalton City	North Royalton
294	417.0	New Richmond Exempted Village	New Richmond
295	415.1	Sandusky City	Sandusky
296	413.2	Cambridge City	Cambridge
297	410.7	Westlake City	Westlake
298	410.4	Brecksville-Broadview Heights City	Brecksville
299	409.9	Mayfield City	Mayfield Hgts
300	408.6	Anthony Wayne Local	Whitehouse
301	405.6	Bay Village City	Bay Village
302	398.0	Meigs Local	Pomeroy
303	396.8	Benton Carroll Salem Local	Oak Harbor
304	396.4	Chagrin Falls Exempted Village	Chagrin Falls
305	395.9	Mansfield City	Mansfield
306	394.8	Union-Scioto Local	Chillicothe
307	392.9	Oregon City	Oregon
308	392.2	Sidney City	Sidney
309	391.6	Bowling Green City	Bowling Green
310	391.2	Springfield Local	Akron
311	390.7	Perry Local	Massillon
312	388.9	Nordonia Hills City	Northfield
313	387.7	Avon Lake City	Avon Lake
314	384.5	Preble Shawnee Board of Education	Camden
315	383.9	East Liverpool City	East Liverpool
316	383.0	Sandy Valley Local	Magnolia
317	381.8	Solon City	Solon
318	378.5	Madeira City	Cincinnati
319	378.4	Granville Exempted Village	Granville
320	378.3	Dublin City	Dublin
321	377.3	Rocky River City	Rocky River
322	374.0	Port Clinton City	Port Clinton
323	369.2	Fairview Park City	Fairview Park
324	367.3	Sylvania City	Sylvania
325	363.8	Woodridge Local	Peninsula
326	362.7	Fostoria City	Fostoria
327	362.0	Willard City	Willard
328	361.9	Maumee City	Maumee
329	361.4	Defiance City	Defiance
330	353.9	Bexley City	Bexley
331	349.7	Poland Local	Poland
332	346.6	Finneytown Local	Cincinnati
333	346.5	Bedford City	Bedford
334	338.8	Upper Arlington City	Upper Arlington
335	337.8	Washington-Nile Local	West Portsmouth
336	334.3	North Olmsted City	North Olmsted
337	330.0	Kettering City	Kettering
338	326.0	Bryan City	Bryan
339	323.8	Minford Local	Minford
340	321.0	Ironton City	Ironton
341	314.1	Licking Valley Local	Newark
342	313.6	Greeneview Local	Jamestown
343	300.2	Tiffin City	Tiffin
344	298.8	Napoleon Area City	Napoleon
345	298.7	Upper Sandusky Exempted Village	Upper Sandusky
346	295.3	Kings Local	Kings Mills
347	290.9	Elgin Local	Marion
348	288.6	Indian Hill Exempted Village	Cincinnati
349	285.6	Youngstown City	Youngstown
350	281.4	Marlington Local	Alliance
350	281.4	Shelby City	Shelby
352	271.6	Warren Local	Vincent
353	270.8	Triway Local	Wooster
354	264.6	Alliance City	Alliance
355	260.8	Martins Ferry City	Martins Ferry
356	259.6	Struthers City	Struthers
357	256.3	Plain Local	Canton
358	254.1	Hillsboro City	Hillsboro
359	253.3	Pike-Delta-York Local	Delta
359	253.3	Talawanda City	Oxford
361	242.5	Elyria City	Elyria
362	232.4	Carlisle Local	Carlisle
363	225.6	Tallmadge City	Tallmadge
364	224.2	Wyoming City	Wyoming
365	219.4	Mount Healthy City	Cincinnati
366	208.1	Lake Local	Uniontown
367	207.3	Mariemont City	Cincinnati
368	206.8	Orange City	Cleveland
369	205.0	Cleveland Hgts-University Hgts	University Hgts
370	203.1	Sycamore Community City	Cincinnati
371	156.4	Madison Local	Middletown
372	150.4	Alternative Education Academy	Toledo
373	n/a	Ohio Virtual Academy	Maumee

Current Spending per Student in FY2003

Rank	Dollars	District Name	City
1	16,402	Orange City	Cleveland
2	14,330	Perry Local	Perry
3	13,964	Shaker Heights City	Shaker Heights
4	13,825	Youngstown City	Youngstown
5	13,696	Cleveland Hgts-University Hgts	University Hgts
6	12,838	Cincinnati City	Cincinnati
7	12,138	Sycamore Community City	Cincinnati
8	12,094	Mayfield City	Mayfield Hgts
9	12,042	Indian Hill Exempted Village	Cincinnati
10	11,761	Princeton City	Cincinnati
11	11,623	Dayton City	Dayton
12	11,420	Columbus City	Columbus
13	11,382	Toledo City	Toledo
14	11,351	Bedford City	Bedford
15	11,307	East Cleveland City	East Cleveland
16	11,121	Worthington City	Worthington
17	11,063	Upper Arlington City	Upper Arlington
18	11,039	Bexley City	Bexley
19	11,026	Trotwood-Madison City	Trotwood
20	10,949	Akron City	Akron
21	10,907	Mansfield City	Mansfield
22	10,785	Euclid City	Euclid
23	10,686	Solon City	Solon
24	10,672	Warrensville Hgts City	Warrensville Hgts
25	10,648	Fairview Park City	Fairview Park
26	10,638	South Euclid-Lyndhurst City	Lyndhurst
27	10,499	Kent City	Kent
28	10,443	Westlake City	Westlake
29	10,379	Chagrin Falls Exempted Village	Chagrin Falls
30	10,358	Lorain City	Lorain
31	10,339	Canton City	Canton
32	10,283	Northridge Local	Dayton
33	10,270	Rocky River City	Rocky River
34	10,115	Cleveland Municipal City	Cleveland
35	10,031	Painesville Local	Painesville
36	9,998	Norwood City	Norwood
37	9,967	Rossford Exempted Village	Rossford
38	9,948	Dublin City	Dublin
39	9,933	Portsmouth City	Portsmouth
40	9,875	Lakewood City	Lakewood
40	9,875	Maumee City	Maumee

Rank	Value	District	City
42	9,856	Madeira City	Cincinnati
43	9,806	Warren City	Warren
44	9,774	Hudson City	Hudson
45	9,740	Bay Village City	Bay Village
46	9,733	Mariemont City	Cincinnati
47	9,731	Elyria City	Elyria
48	9,707	Sandusky City	Sandusky
49	9,699	North Olmsted City	North Olmsted
50	9,658	Oregon City	Oregon
51	9,657	Berea City	Berea
52	9,653	Port Clinton City	Port Clinton
53	9,601	Mount Healthy City	Cincinnati
54	9,527	Kettering City	Kettering
55	9,523	Springfield City	Springfield
56	9,516	Woodridge Local	Peninsula
57	9,479	Avon Lake City	Avon Lake
58	9,473	Whitehall City	Whitehall
59	9,471	Monroe Local	Monroe
59	9,471	New Albany-Plain Local	New Albany
61	9,470	New Richmond Exempted Village	New Richmond
62	9,449	Kenston Local	Chagrin Falls
63	9,415	Revere Local	Bath
64	9,409	Celina City	Celina
65	9,403	Wyoming City	Wyoming
66	9,398	Finneytown Local	Cincinnati
67	9,395	Parma City	Parma
68	9,340	Winton Woods City	Cincinnati
69	9,324	Wooster City	Wooster
70	9,322	Wickliffe City	Wickliffe
71	9,316	Middletown City	Middletown
72	9,304	East Liverpool City	East Liverpool
73	9,286	Zanesville City	Zanesville
74	9,263	Lima City	Lima
75	9,239	Benton Carroll Salem Local	Oak Harbor
76	9,234	Rock Hill Local	Ironton
77	9,214	Washington Local	Toledo
78	9,181	Oakwood City	Dayton
79	9,171	Bellaire Local	Bellaire
80	9,152	Canton Local	Canton
81	9,143	Groveport Madison Local	Groveport
82	9,123	Strongsville City	Strongsville
83	9,096	Olmsted Falls City	Olmsted Falls
84	9,075	Springfield Local	Akron
85	9,020	Sylvania City	Sylvania
86	9,013	Bowling Green City	Bowling Green
87	9,007	Athens City	The Plains
88	8,991	Gahanna-Jefferson City	Gahanna
89	8,968	Aurora City	Aurora
90	8,953	Massillon City	Massillon
91	8,936	South-Western City	Grove City
92	8,924	Champion Local	Warren
93	8,905	Meigs Local	Pomeroy
94	8,899	Olentangy Local	Lewis Center
95	8,898	Streetsboro City	Streetsboro
96	8,895	Mad River Local	Dayton
97	8,888	Eastwood Local	Pemberville
98	8,852	Alliance City	Alliance
99	8,841	Findlay City	Findlay
100	8,824	Hilliard City	Hilliard
101	8,797	Morgan Local	Mcconnelsville
102	8,794	Maple Heights City	Maple Heights
103	8,785	Cambridge City	Cambridge
104	8,754	Barberton City	Barberton
105	8,751	Vermilion Local	Vermilion
106	8,725	Milford Exempted Village	Milford
107	8,719	Springfield Local	Holland
108	8,651	Willoughby-Eastlake City	Willoughby
109	8,649	Medina City	Medina
110	8,640	Xenia Community City	Xenia
111	8,636	Switzerland of Ohio Local	Woodsfield
112	8,635	Ravenna City	Ravenna
112	8,635	Three Rivers Local	Cleves
114	8,609	Madison Local	Mansfield
115	8,581	West Geauga Local	Chesterland
116	8,571	Centerville City	Centerville
117	8,558	Tallmadge City	Tallmadge
117	8,558	Vandalia-Butler City	Vandalia
119	8,555	Brecksville-Broadview Heights City	Brecksville
119	8,555	Southeast Local	Apple Creek
121	8,553	Mentor Exempted Village	Mentor
122	8,517	Marysville Exempted Village	Marysville
123	8,508	Conneaut Area City	Conneaut
124	8,501	Huber Heights City	Huber Heights
125	8,499	Coshocton City	Coshocton
126	8,494	North Royalton City	North Royalton
127	8,493	Talawanda City	Oxford
128	8,484	Granville Exempted Village	Granville
129	8,477	Cuyahoga Falls City	Cuyahoga Falls
130	8,468	Newark City	Newark
131	8,439	Paulding Exempted Village	Paulding
132	8,414	Gallia County Local	Gallipolis
133	8,399	Urbana City	Urbana
134	8,392	Howland Local	Warren
134	8,392	West Carrollton City	West Carrollton
136	8,378	Nordonia Hills City	Northfield
137	8,370	Twinsburg City	Twinsburg
138	8,368	Vinton County Local	Mcarthur
139	8,359	Clearview Local	Lorain
139	8,359	Hamilton City	Hamilton
141	8,346	East Holmes Local	Berlin
142	8,336	Shelby City	Shelby
143	8,332	Lancaster City	Lancaster
144	8,320	Crestwood Local	Mantua
145	8,293	Struthers City	Struthers
146	8,269	Mason City	Mason
147	8,263	Delaware City	Delaware
148	8,235	Canal Wnchstr Local	Canal Wnchstr
149	8,230	Copley-Fairlawn City	Copley
150	8,211	Ashtabula Area City	Ashtabula
151	8,206	Jackson Local	Massillon
152	8,198	Sheffield-Sheffield Lake City	Sheffield Vllg
153	8,185	Perrysburg Exempted Village	Perrysburg
154	8,174	Marlington Local	Alliance
155	8,164	Salem City	Salem
156	8,158	Westerville City	Westerville
157	8,155	Bellefontaine City	Bellefontaine
158	8,149	Forest Hills Local	Cincinnati
159	8,132	Chardon Local	Chardon
160	8,121	Buckeye Valley Local	Delaware
161	8,120	Adams County/Ohio Valley Local	West Union
162	8,116	Wellston City	Wellston
163	8,097	Alexander Local	Albany
164	8,085	Austintown Local	Youngstown
165	8,082	Perkins Local	Sandusky
166	8,080	Boardman Local	Youngstown
167	8,078	Circleville City	Circleville
168	8,055	Pickerington Local	Pickerington
169	8,051	Sidney City	Sidney
170	8,040	Pike-Delta-York Local	Delta
171	8,024	Sandy Valley Local	Magnolia
172	8,023	Gallipolis City	Gallipolis
173	7,974	Highland Local	Medina
174	7,967	Kings Local	Kings Mills
175	7,962	London City	London
176	7,957	Logan Elm Local	Circleville
177	7,951	Galion City	Galion
178	7,950	Logan-Hocking Local	Logan
179	7,923	Steubenville City	Steubenville
180	7,918	Stow-Munroe Falls City	Stow
181	7,907	Goshen Local	Goshen
182	7,905	North College Hill City	Cincinnati
183	7,880	Perry Local	Massillon
184	7,867	Miamisburg City	Miamisburg
185	7,862	Labrae Local	Leavittsburg
186	7,851	Huron City	Huron
187	7,843	Northwest Local	Cincinnati
188	7,836	Big Walnut Local	Galena
189	7,831	West Holmes Local	Millersburg
190	7,830	Amanda-Clearcreek Local	Amanda
191	7,819	Southwest Local	Harrison
192	7,805	Brookville Local	Brookville
193	7,786	Fairborn City	Fairborn
194	7,777	Loveland City	Loveland
195	7,773	Troy City	Troy
196	7,766	Defiance City	Defiance
197	7,763	Brunswick City	Brunswick
198	7,760	Hillsboro City	Hillsboro
199	7,755	Buckeye Local	Ashtabula
199	7,755	Carlisle Local	Carlisle
201	7,741	Greenville City	Greenville
202	7,739	Greenfield Exempted Village	Greenfield
203	7,732	Orrville City	Orrville
204	7,728	Benjamin Logan Local	Bellefontaine
204	7,728	Wellington Exempted Village	Wellington
206	7,725	Lakewood Local	Hebron
207	7,724	Berlin-Milan Local	Milan
208	7,720	Plain Local	Canton
208	7,720	Triway Local	Wooster
210	7,703	Coldwater Exempted Village	Coldwater
211	7,702	Kenton City	Kenton
212	7,694	Northwest Local	Mcdermott
213	7,691	Clyde-Green Springs Ex Vill	Clyde
214	7,688	Fremont City	Fremont
215	7,687	Harrison Hills City	Hopedale
216	7,671	Bryan City	Bryan
217	7,662	Painesville Township Local	Painesville
218	7,659	Ironton City	Ironton
219	7,658	Miami Trace Local	Washington CH
220	7,640	Milton-Union Exempted Village	West Milton
221	7,639	Fairless Local	Navarre
222	7,637	Sugarcreek Local	Bellbrook
223	7,634	Buckeye Local	Medina
224	7,621	Highland Local	Sparta
225	7,619	Elgin Local	Marion
226	7,615	West Clermont Local	Cincinnati
227	7,614	Minerva Local	Minerva
228	7,613	North Canton City	North Canton
229	7,609	Lakota Local	Liberty Twp
230	7,604	Madison Local	Middletown
231	7,603	Anthony Wayne Local	Whitehouse
232	7,585	River View Local	Warsaw
233	7,581	Bucyrus City	Bucyrus
234	7,572	Norton City	Norton
235	7,565	Warren Local	Vincent
236	7,562	Bellevue City	Bellevue
237	7,558	Valley View Local	Germantown
238	7,556	Ontario Local	Mansfield
239	7,554	Chillicothe City	Chillicothe
240	7,552	Tecumseh Local	New Carlisle
241	7,548	East Muskingum Local	New Concord
242	7,539	Madison-Plains Local	London
242	7,539	Scioto Valley Local	Piketon
244	7,534	N Ridgeville City	N Ridgeville
245	7,533	Indian Lake Local	Lewistown
245	7,533	Preble Shawnee Board of Education	Camden
247	7,532	Saint Clairsville-Richland City	Saint Clairsville
248	7,527	Garfield Hgts City	Garfield Hgts
249	7,525	East Clinton Local	Lees Creek
250	7,521	Napoleon Area City	Napoleon
251	7,515	Minford Local	Minford
252	7,512	Beavercreek City	Beavercreek
253	7,504	Hubbard Exempted Village	Hubbard
253	7,504	Van Wert City	Van Wert
255	7,499	Hamilton Local	Columbus
256	7,495	Eaton Community Schools City	Eaton
257	7,494	Jackson City	Jackson
258	7,492	Southeast Local	Ravenna
259	7,490	Northmont City	Englewood
260	7,477	Black River Local	Sullivan
261	7,471	Washington-Nile Local	West Portsmouth
262	7,467	Bloom-Carroll Local	Carroll
263	7,460	Otsego Local	Tontogany
264	7,456	Ashland City	Ashland
265	7,454	Southwest Licking Local	Etna
266	7,449	New Lexington City	New Lexington
267	7,444	Franklin City	Franklin
267	7,444	Green Local	Green
269	7,432	West Muskingum Local	Zanesville
270	7,422	Mount Vernon City	Mount Vernon
271	7,420	Licking Valley Local	Newark
272	7,417	Coventry Local	Akron
273	7,412	Little Miami Local	Morrow
274	7,406	Fostoria City	Fostoria
275	7,389	Reynoldsburg City	Reynoldsburg
276	7,387	River Valley Local	Caledonia
277	7,382	Wilmington City	Wilmington
278	7,379	Northwest Local	Canal Fulton
279	7,378	Lexington Local	Lexington
280	7,375	Manchester Local	Akron
281	7,374	Saint Marys City	Saint Marys
282	7,371	Edison Local	Hammondsville
283	7,370	Indian Valley Local	Gnadenhutten
284	7,365	Lebanon City	Lebanon
285	7,363	Washington CH City	Washington CH
286	7,357	Marion City	Marion
287	7,343	Poland Local	Poland
288	7,341	Westfall Local	Williamsport
289	7,338	Amherst Exempted Village	Amherst
290	7,332	Field Local	Mogadore
291	7,328	North Fork Local	Utica
292	7,327	Liberty Local	Youngstown
293	7,325	Fairfield Union Local	West Rushville
294	7,316	Dover City	Dover
295	7,310	Buckeye Local	Dillonvale
296	7,302	Canfield Local	Canfield
297	7,297	Heath City	Heath
298	7,294	Graham Local	Saint Paris
299	7,287	Teays Valley Local	Ashville
300	7,284	Claymont City	Dennison
301	7,276	Piqua City	Piqua
302	7,272	West Branch Local	Beloit

303	7,271	Willard City	Willard
304	7,269	Maysville Local	Zanesville
305	7,265	Martins Ferry City	Martins Ferry
306	7,264	Franklin Local	Duncan Falls
307	7,257	Eastern Local	Sardinia
308	7,249	Blanchester Local	Blanchester
309	7,225	Waverly City	Waverly
310	7,219	Batavia Local	Batavia
311	7,215	Rolling Hills Local	Cambridge
312	7,202	Keystone Local	Lagrange
312	7,202	Upper Sandusky Exempted Village	Upper Sandusky
314	7,198	Niles City	Niles
315	7,189	New Philadel. City	New Philadel.
316	7,181	Northern Local	Thornville
317	7,180	Fairfield City	Fairfield
318	7,179	Lake Local	Uniontown
319	7,176	Clark-Shawnee Local	Springfield
320	7,168	Clinton-Massie Local	Clarksville
321	7,152	Cloverleaf Local	Lodi
322	7,140	Tiffin City	Tiffin
323	7,138	Shawnee Local	Lima
324	7,131	Oak Hills Local	Cincinnati
325	7,111	Greeneview Local	Jamestown
326	7,110	Louisville City	Louisville
327	7,105	Firelands Local	Oberlin
328	7,103	Madison Local	Madison
329	7,079	Northwestern Local	Springfield
330	7,061	Tri-Valley Local	Dresden
331	7,052	Lakeview Local	Cortland
332	7,037	Geneva Area City	Geneva
333	7,032	Wadsworth City	Wadsworth
334	7,028	Edgewood City	Trenton
334	7,028	Tuscarawas Valley Local	Zoarville
336	7,012	Electronic Classroom of Tomorrow	Columbus
337	7,006	Wapakoneta City	Wapakoneta
338	6,992	Greenon Local	Enon
339	6,991	Bath Local	Lima
340	6,982	Licking Heights Local	Summit Station
341	6,959	Girard City	Girard
342	6,944	Marietta City	Marietta
343	6,943	Tipp Exempted Village	Tipp City
344	6,931	Elida Local	Elida
345	6,930	South Point Local	South Point
346	6,923	Springboro Community City	Springboro
347	6,919	James A Garfield Local	Garrettsville
348	6,894	Wheelersburg Local	Wheelersburg
349	6,892	Northeastern Local	Springfield
350	6,884	Jefferson Area Local	Jefferson
351	6,855	Avon Local	Avon
352	6,844	Genoa Area Local	Genoa
353	6,840	Beaver Local	Lisbon
353	6,840	Carrollton Exempted Village	Carrollton
355	6,822	Fairland Local	Proctorville
356	6,737	Ottawa-Glandorf Local	Ottawa
357	6,730	Midview Local	Grafton
358	6,714	Western Brown Local	Mount Orab
359	6,708	Wauseon Exempted Village	Wauseon
360	6,707	Chippewa Local	Doylestown
361	6,701	Johnstown-Monroe Local	Johnstown
362	6,657	Indian Creek Local	Wintersville
362	6,657	Lake Local	Millbury
364	6,624	Ross Local	Hamilton
365	6,611	Clear Fork Valley Local	Bellville
366	6,602	Alternative Education Academy	Toledo
367	6,521	Jonathan Alder Local	Plain City
368	6,506	Union-Scioto Local	Chillicothe
369	6,490	Zane Trace Local	Chillicothe
370	6,486	Norwalk City	Norwalk
371	6,345	Clermont Northeastern Local	Batavia
372	6,313	Bethel-Tate Local	Bethel
373	6,032	Ohio Virtual Academy	Maumee

Number of Diploma Recipients

Rank	Number	District Name	City
1	2,600	Columbus City	Columbus
2	2,443	Cleveland Municipal City	Cleveland
3	1,526	Akron City	Akron
4	1,478	Toledo City	Toledo
5	1,305	Cincinnati City	Cincinnati
6	1,003	South-Western City	Grove City
7	970	Westerville City	Westerville
8	963	Lakota Local	Liberty Twp
9	886	Parma City	Parma
10	858	Dayton City	Dayton
11	803	Worthington City	Worthington
12	785	Hilliard City	Hilliard
13	767	Dublin City	Dublin
14	730	Mentor Exempted Village	Mentor
15	656	Northwest Local	Cincinnati
16	637	Willoughby-Eastlake City	Willoughby
17	633	Oak Hills Local	Cincinnati
18	611	Berea City	Berea
19	608	Fairfield City	Fairfield
20	599	Sylvania City	Sylvania
21	590	Centerville City	Centerville
22	585	Forest Hills Local	Cincinnati
23	534	Kettering City	Kettering
24	524	Hamilton City	Hamilton
25	520	West Clermont Local	Cincinnati
26	518	Lakewood City	Lakewood
27	508	Strongsville City	Strongsville
28	501	Medina City	Medina
29	495	Beavercreek City	Beavercreek
29	495	Canton City	Canton
31	494	Pickerington Local	Pickerington
32	476	Lorain City	Lorain
33	475	Brunswick City	Brunswick
34	458	Reynoldsburg City	Reynoldsburg
35	448	Washington Local	Toledo
36	437	Huber Heights City	Huber Heights
37	426	Findlay City	Findlay
38	425	Sycamore Community City	Cincinnati
39	424	Gahanna-Jefferson City	Gahanna
40	422	Jackson Local	Massillon
41	421	Upper Arlington City	Upper Arlington
41	421	Youngstown City	Youngstown
43	420	Stow-Munroe Falls City	Stow
44	417	Milford Exempted Village	Milford
45	411	Springfield City	Springfield
46	403	Princeton City	Cincinnati
47	393	Northmont City	Englewood
48	390	Plain Local	Canton
48	390	Solon City	Solon
50	389	Newark City	Newark
51	381	Hudson City	Hudson
52	380	Boardman Local	Youngstown
53	368	North Olmsted City	North Olmsted
54	367	Mason City	Mason
55	363	Euclid City	Euclid
56	362	Elyria City	Elyria
56	362	Shaker Heights City	Shaker Heights
58	360	Cuyahoga Falls City	Cuyahoga Falls
58	360	Middletown City	Middletown
60	358	Lancaster City	Lancaster
61	352	Warren City	Warren
62	351	Austintown Local	Youngstown
63	349	Fairborn City	Fairborn
64	346	Cleveland Hgts-University Hgts	University Hgts
65	342	Perry Local	Massillon
65	342	South Euclid-Lyndhurst City	Lyndhurst
67	341	Mayfield City	Mayfield Hgts
68	340	Brecksville-Broadview Heights City	Brecksville
69	335	North Royalton City	North Royalton
70	330	Miamisburg City	Miamisburg
71	328	Perrysburg Exempted Village	Perrysburg
72	327	Wadsworth City	Wadsworth
73	325	Fremont City	Fremont
74	319	North Canton City	North Canton
75	315	Olentangy Local	Lewis Center
76	314	Groveport Madison Local	Groveport
76	314	Xenia Community City	Xenia
78	309	Nordonia Hills City	Northfield
79	308	Kent City	Kent
80	306	Adams County/Ohio Valley Local	West Union
80	306	Painesville Township Local	Painesville
82	294	Troy City	Troy
83	288	Ashland City	Ashland
84	285	Chillicothe City	Chillicothe
84	285	Loveland City	Loveland
86	284	Mount Vernon City	Mount Vernon
87	282	Celina City	Celina
88	281	Amherst Exempted Village	Amherst
88	281	Wooster City	Wooster
90	280	Marion City	Marion
91	279	Lebanon City	Lebanon
92	277	Southwest Local	Harrison
93	276	Westlake City	Westlake
94	273	Cloverleaf Local	Lodi
95	267	Greenville City	Greenville
96	264	Barberton City	Barberton
97	263	Garfield Hgts City	Garfield Hgts
98	261	Delaware City	Delaware
99	260	Talawanda City	Oxford
100	258	Mansfield City	Mansfield
101	257	Marysville Exempted Village	Marysville
102	256	Bowling Green City	Bowling Green
103	255	Massillon City	Massillon
104	254	Madison Local	Madison
104	254	West Carrollton City	West Carrollton
106	252	East Cleveland City	East Cleveland
107	248	Lake Local	Uniontown
108	247	Green Local	Green
108	247	Tiffin City	Tiffin
110	244	Lima City	Lima
110	244	Vandalia-Butler City	Vandalia
112	243	Avon Lake City	Avon Lake
113	242	Maumee City	Maumee
114	240	Ashtabula Area City	Ashtabula
114	240	Dover City	Dover
116	238	New Philadel. City	New Philadel.
117	236	Springfield Local	Holland
118	233	Anthony Wayne Local	Whitehouse
118	233	Sidney City	Sidney
118	233	Southwest Licking Local	Etna
121	232	Chardon Local	Chardon
122	231	Bedford City	Bedford
122	231	Sandusky City	Sandusky
122	231	Springboro Community City	Springboro
122	231	Wapakoneta City	Wapakoneta
122	231	Wilmington City	Wilmington
127	230	Howland Local	Warren
128	228	Piqua City	Piqua
129	227	Logan-Hocking Local	Logan
130	225	Canfield Local	Canfield
130	225	Oregon City	Oregon
130	225	Revere Local	Bath
133	224	Geneva Area City	Geneva
133	224	Madison Local	Mansfield
133	224	Tecumseh Local	New Carlisle
136	223	Kings Local	Kings Mills
137	219	Olmsted Falls City	Olmsted Falls
138	218	Winton Woods City	Cincinnati
139	216	Marietta City	Marietta
140	215	Lexington Local	Lexington
141	214	Kenston Local	Chagrin Falls
142	213	Alliance City	Alliance
143	211	Copley-Fairlawn City	Copley
144	210	Niles City	Niles
145	208	Midview Local	Grafton
146	207	Defiance City	Defiance
147	206	Twinsburg City	Twinsburg
148	203	Clark-Shawnee Local	Springfield
148	203	Jackson City	Jackson
150	202	Switzerland of Ohio Local	Woodsfield
151	199	Bellefontaine City	Bellefontaine
151	199	Carrollton Exempted Village	Carrollton
151	199	Hubbard Exempted Village	Hubbard
151	199	Louisville City	Louisville
155	198	Mount Healthy City	Cincinnati
155	198	N Ridgeville City	N Ridgeville
155	198	Northeastern Local	Springfield
155	198	Poland Local	Poland
159	196	Crestwood Local	Mantua
159	196	Highland Local	Medina
161	195	West Geauga Local	Chesterland
162	194	Napoleon Area City	Napoleon
162	194	Tri-Valley Local	Dresden
164	193	Orange City	Cleveland
164	193	Saint Marys City	Saint Marys
166	192	Trotwood-Madison City	Trotwood
166	192	Whitehall City	Whitehall
168	191	Big Walnut Local	Galena
168	191	Springfield Local	Akron
170	190	Franklin City	Franklin
170	190	Warren Local	Vincent
172	189	Maple Heights City	Maple Heights
173	187	Elida Local	Elida
173	187	West Branch Local	Beloit
175	185	East Liverpool City	East Liverpool
175	185	Tallmadge City	Tallmadge
177	184	River View Local	Warsaw
177	184	Sugarcreek Local	Bellbrook
179	183	Buckeye Local	Dillonvale
179	183	Norton City	Norton
179	183	Salem City	Salem
182	182	Buckeye Local	Medina
182	182	Edgewood City	Trenton
182	182	Hillsboro City	Hillsboro
182	182	Mad River Local	Dayton

186	181	Zanesville City	Zanesville
187	180	Bellevue City	Bellevue
188	178	Coventry Local	Akron
189	177	Bexley City	Bexley
189	177	East Muskingum Local	New Concord
189	177	Edison Local	Hammondsville
192	175	Field Local	Mogadore
192	175	Lakeview Local	Cortland
192	175	Tipp Exempted Village	Tipp City
195	174	Ravenna City	Ravenna
196	171	Clyde-Green Springs Ex Vill	Clyde
196	171	Marlington Local	Alliance
196	171	Shawnee Local	Lima
196	171	Shelby City	Shelby
196	171	Southeast Local	Ravenna
196	171	Steubenville City	Steubenville
196	171	Vermilion Local	Vermilion
203	170	Galion City	Galion
203	170	Miami Trace Local	Washington CH
205	169	Little Miami Local	Morrow
205	169	Port Clinton City	Port Clinton
205	169	Ross Local	Hamilton
208	168	Bay Village City	Bay Village
208	168	Teays Valley Local	Ashville
210	167	Fairview Park City	Fairview Park
210	167	Logan Elm Local	Circleville
212	165	Franklin Local	Duncan Falls
212	165	Gallia County Local	Gallipolis
214	164	Ottawa-Glandorf Local	Ottawa
215	162	Canton Local	Canton
215	162	Conneaut Area City	Conneaut
217	161	Beaver Local	Lisbon
218	160	Buckeye Local	Ashtabula
218	160	Maysville Local	Zanesville
218	160	Norwalk City	Norwalk
218	160	Warrensville Hgts City	Warrensville Hgts
222	157	Buckeye Valley Local	Delaware
222	157	Morgan Local	Mcconnelsville
224	155	Lakewood Local	Hebron
224	155	New Richmond Exempted Village	New Richmond
226	154	Cambridge City	Cambridge
227	153	Upper Sandusky Exempted Village	Upper Sandusky
227	153	Van Wert City	Van Wert
229	152	Bath Local	Lima
229	152	Benton Carroll Salem Local	Oak Harbor
229	152	Granville Exempted Village	Granville
232	151	Indian Hill Exempted Village	Cincinnati
232	151	Northern Local	Thornville
232	151	Northwest Local	Canal Fulton
235	150	Liberty Local	Youngstown
235	150	Perkins Local	Sandusky
235	150	West Holmes Local	Millersburg
238	149	Aurora City	Aurora
238	149	Bryan City	Bryan
238	149	Gallipolis City	Gallipolis
241	148	Champion Local	Warren
242	147	Kenton City	Kenton
242	147	Monroe Local	Monroe
244	146	Chagrin Falls Exempted Village	Chagrin Falls
244	146	Goshen Local	Goshen
244	146	Greenon Local	Enon
244	146	Triway Local	Wooster
248	145	Claymont City	Dennison
248	145	Minerva Local	Minerva
248	145	Rocky River City	Rocky River
248	145	Wauseon Exempted Village	Wauseon
252	144	Vinton County Local	Mcarthur
252	144	Washington CH City	Washington CH
252	144	Willard City	Willard
255	143	Western Brown Local	Mount Orab
255	143	Wyoming City	Wyoming
257	142	Circleville City	Circleville
257	142	Fairfield Union Local	West Rushville
257	142	West Muskingum Local	Zanesville
260	141	Finneytown Local	Cincinnati
261	140	Chippewa Local	Doylestown
261	140	Eastwood Local	Pemberville
261	140	Firelands Local	Oberlin
261	140	Oakwood City	Dayton
265	139	Clear Fork Valley Local	Bellville
265	139	Jefferson Area Local	Jefferson
265	139	River Valley Local	Caledonia
268	138	Bethel-Tate Local	Bethel
268	138	Harrison Hills City	Hopedale
268	138	Valley View Local	Germantown
271	137	Lake Local	Millbury
271	137	Norwood City	Norwood
271	137	Rossford Exempted Village	Rossford
274	136	Huron City	Huron
274	136	Three Rivers Local	Cleves
276	135	Canal Wnchstr Local	Canal Wnchstr
276	135	Eaton Community Schools City	Eaton
276	135	Northwestern Local	Springfield
279	134	London City	London
279	134	Paulding Exempted Village	Paulding
281	133	Hamilton Local	Columbus
281	133	Manchester Local	Akron
281	133	Union-Scioto Local	Chillicothe
284	132	Berlin-Milan Local	Milan
284	132	Graham Local	Saint Paris
284	132	Greenfield Exempted Village	Greenfield
284	132	Indian Creek Local	Wintersville
284	132	Perry Local	Perry
289	131	Benjamin Logan Local	Bellefontaine
290	130	Indian Lake Local	Lewistown
290	130	Sheffield-Sheffield Lake City	Sheffield Vllg
292	129	Martins Ferry City	Martins Ferry
293	128	Ironton City	Ironton
294	127	Genoa Area Local	Genoa
294	127	Madison-Plains Local	London
294	127	Orrville City	Orrville
297	125	Elgin Local	Marion
297	125	Meigs Local	Pomeroy
299	124	Coldwater Exempted Village	Coldwater
299	124	Rolling Hills Local	Cambridge
301	123	Struthers City	Struthers
302	122	Coshocton City	Coshocton
302	122	Indian Valley Local	Gnadenhutten
304	121	Clermont Northeastern Local	Batavia
305	120	Alexander Local	Albany
305	120	Saint Clairsville-Richland City	Saint Clairsville
307	119	Fairless Local	Navarre
307	119	Girard City	Girard
307	119	Ontario Local	Mansfield
307	119	Streetsboro City	Streetsboro
311	118	Bucyrus City	Bucyrus
311	118	Northwest Local	Mcdermott
311	118	Urbana City	Urbana
314	117	Avon Local	Avon
314	117	Clinton-Massie Local	Clarksville
314	117	North Fork Local	Utica
314	117	Otsego Local	Tontogany
314	117	Wickliffe City	Wickliffe
319	116	Milton-Union Exempted Village	West Milton
319	116	Pike-Delta-York Local	Delta
319	116	Preble Shawnee Board of Education	Camden
322	115	Bloom-Carroll Local	Carroll
322	115	Fairland Local	Proctorville
322	115	Fostoria City	Fostoria
322	115	Licking Valley Local	Newark
326	114	Waverly City	Waverly
327	113	Keystone Local	Lagrange
327	113	Mariemont City	Cincinnati
327	113	Minford Local	Minford
327	113	Sandy Valley Local	Magnolia
327	113	Washington-Nile Local	West Portsmouth
332	111	Carlisle Local	Carlisle
333	110	Bellaire Local	Bellaire
334	109	Jonathan Alder Local	Plain City
334	109	Madeira City	Cincinnati
334	109	Wellington Exempted Village	Wellington
337	108	New Albany-Plain Local	New Albany
337	108	Tuscarawas Valley Local	Zoarville
339	106	Highland Local	Sparta
339	106	Wheelersburg Local	Wheelersburg
341	105	South Point Local	South Point
342	104	Brookville Local	Brookville
342	104	Heath City	Heath
344	102	Greeneview Local	Jamestown
344	102	Johnstown-Monroe Local	Johnstown
344	102	Labrae Local	Leavittsburg
344	102	Portsmouth City	Portsmouth
348	101	James A Garfield Local	Garrettsville
349	100	New Lexington City	New Lexington
349	100	Rock Hill Local	Ironton
351	98	Black River Local	Sullivan
352	97	Clearview Local	Lorain
352	97	Westfall Local	Williamsport
354	96	Southeast Local	Apple Creek
354	96	Woodridge Local	Peninsula
356	95	Eastern Local	Sardinia
356	95	Madison Local	Middletown
356	95	Zane Trace Local	Chillicothe
359	93	Blanchester Local	Blanchester
359	93	East Clinton Local	Lees Creek
359	93	Northridge Local	Dayton
362	92	Batavia Local	Batavia
362	92	Licking Heights Local	Summit Station
362	92	North College Hill City	Cincinnati
365	89	Scioto Valley Local	Piketon
366	88	Painesville Local	Painesville
367	87	Amanda-Clearcreek Local	Amanda
367	87	Athens City	The Plains
369	78	Wellston City	Wellston
370	63	East Holmes Local	Berlin
371	31	Electronic Classroom of Tomorrow	Columbus
372	n/a	Alternative Education Academy	Toledo
373	n/a	Ohio Virtual Academy	Maumee

High School Drop-out Rate

Rank	Percent	District Name	City
1	16.0	Canton City	Canton
2	15.1	Cleveland Municipal City	Cleveland
3	12.2	Lima City	Lima
4	10.7	East Cleveland City	East Cleveland
5	9.0	Newark City	Newark
6	8.7	Columbus City	Columbus
6	8.7	Youngstown City	Youngstown
8	8.5	Zanesville City	Zanesville
9	8.4	Dayton City	Dayton
10	8.2	Cincinnati City	Cincinnati
11	8.1	Norwood City	Norwood
12	7.8	Bedford City	Bedford
13	7.6	Portsmouth City	Portsmouth
14	7.2	Mad River Local	Dayton
15	6.9	Trotwood-Madison City	Trotwood
16	6.8	Hamilton City	Hamilton
16	6.8	Lorain City	Lorain
16	6.8	Marion City	Marion
16	6.8	New Lexington City	New Lexington
20	6.7	Toledo City	Toledo
21	6.2	Logan-Hocking Local	Logan
21	6.2	Springfield City	Springfield
23	6.1	Ashtabula Area City	Ashtabula
23	6.1	Washington Local	Toledo
25	6.0	Elyria City	Elyria
26	5.9	Alliance City	Alliance
26	5.9	Maple Heights City	Maple Heights
26	5.9	Painesville Local	Painesville
26	5.9	South-Western City	Grove City
26	5.9	Whitehall City	Whitehall
31	5.8	Mansfield City	Mansfield
31	5.8	New Richmond Exempted Village	New Richmond
33	5.7	Northridge Local	Dayton
34	5.6	West Clermont Local	Cincinnati
35	5.5	Fairborn City	Fairborn
36	5.4	Madison Local	Mansfield
37	5.3	Fostoria City	Fostoria
37	5.3	Franklin City	Franklin
37	5.3	Huber Heights City	Huber Heights
37	5.3	Warren City	Warren
41	5.2	Middletown City	Middletown
41	5.2	Northwest Local	Cincinnati
41	5.2	Norwalk City	Norwalk
41	5.2	Scioto Valley Local	Piketon
41	5.2	Steubenville City	Steubenville
41	5.2	Western Brown Local	Mount Orab
47	5.1	Massillon City	Massillon
48	5.0	Akron City	Akron
48	5.0	Morgan Local	Mcconnelsville
48	5.0	Parma City	Parma
48	5.0	Southwest Local	Harrison
48	5.0	Vinton County Local	Mcarthur
53	4.9	Ravenna City	Ravenna
53	4.9	Tiffin City	Tiffin
53	4.9	Xenia Community City	Xenia
56	4.8	Barberton City	Barberton
56	4.8	Defiance City	Defiance
58	4.7	Ironton City	Ironton
59	4.6	Fremont City	Fremont
59	4.6	Tecumseh Local	New Carlisle
59	4.6	Tuscarawas Valley Local	Zoarville
62	4.5	Bucyrus City	Bucyrus
62	4.5	Eaton Community Schools City	Eaton
62	4.5	Goshen Local	Goshen
62	4.5	London City	London
66	4.4	Indian Lake Local	Lewistown
66	4.4	Lancaster City	Lancaster
66	4.4	Mount Healthy City	Cincinnati

Rank	Value	District	City
69	4.3	Gallipolis City	Gallipolis
69	4.3	Groveport Madison Local	Groveport
71	4.2	Bethel-Tate Local	Bethel
71	4.2	Clermont Northeastern Local	Batavia
71	4.2	Rolling Hills Local	Cambridge
74	4.1	North Fork Local	Utica
75	4.0	Circleville City	Circleville
75	4.0	Princeton City	Cincinnati
75	4.0	Talawanda City	Oxford
78	3.9	Alexander Local	Albany
78	3.9	Batavia Local	Batavia
78	3.9	Delaware City	Delaware
78	3.9	Greenfield Exempted Village	Greenfield
78	3.9	Greenon Local	Enon
78	3.9	Hamilton Local	Columbus
78	3.9	Teays Valley Local	Ashville
78	3.9	Three Rivers Local	Cleves
78	3.9	Waverly City	Waverly
87	3.8	Fairland Local	Proctorville
88	3.7	Cambridge City	Cambridge
88	3.7	Gallia County Local	Gallipolis
88	3.7	Sandusky City	Sandusky
91	3.6	Bellaire Local	Bellaire
91	3.6	Minerva Local	Minerva
91	3.6	Napoleon Area City	Napoleon
91	3.6	Washington-Nile Local	West Portsmouth
95	3.5	Cleveland Hgts-University Hgts	University Hgts
95	3.5	Harrison Hills City	Hopedale
95	3.5	Mariemont City	Cincinnati
95	3.5	Washington CH City	Washington CH
99	3.4	Edgewood City	Trenton
99	3.4	Lakewood City	Lakewood
99	3.4	Madison Local	Madison
99	3.4	Rock Hill Local	Ironton
99	3.4	Willard City	Willard
104	3.3	Chillicothe City	Chillicothe
104	3.3	East Clinton Local	Lees Creek
104	3.3	Galion City	Galion
104	3.3	James A Garfield Local	Garrettsville
104	3.3	Miami Trace Local	Washington CH
104	3.3	Piqua City	Piqua
110	3.2	Adams County/Ohio Valley Local	West Union
110	3.2	Niles City	Niles
110	3.2	Port Clinton City	Port Clinton
110	3.2	Ross Local	Hamilton
110	3.2	Shelby City	Shelby
110	3.2	Union-Scioto Local	Chillicothe
110	3.2	Winton Woods City	Cincinnati
117	3.1	Kenton City	Kenton
117	3.1	Troy City	Troy
119	3.0	Buckeye Local	Ashtabula
119	3.0	Franklin Local	Duncan Falls
119	3.0	Garfield Hgts City	Garfield Hgts
119	3.0	Oregon City	Oregon
119	3.0	Willoughby-Eastlake City	Willoughby
124	2.9	Ashland City	Ashland
124	2.9	Bellefontaine City	Bellefontaine
124	2.9	Madison Local	Middletown
124	2.9	North College Hill City	Cincinnati
124	2.9	Orrville City	Orrville
124	2.9	Sidney City	Sidney
124	2.9	Valley View Local	Germantown
124	2.9	Van Wert City	Van Wert
132	2.8	Midview Local	Grafton
132	2.8	Mount Vernon City	Mount Vernon
132	2.8	Springfield Local	Holland
132	2.8	Urbana City	Urbana
132	2.8	Wickliffe City	Wickliffe
137	2.7	Bryan City	Bryan
137	2.7	Gahanna-Jefferson City	Gahanna
137	2.7	Heath City	Heath
137	2.7	Licking Valley Local	Newark
137	2.7	Switzerland of Ohio Local	Woodsfield
142	2.6	Canal Wnchstr Local	Canal Wnchstr
142	2.6	Findlay City	Findlay
142	2.6	Plain Local	Canton
142	2.6	River View Local	Warsaw
142	2.6	Rossford Exempted Village	Rossford
147	2.5	Brookville Local	Brookville
147	2.5	Finneytown Local	Cincinnati
147	2.5	Jackson City	Jackson
147	2.5	Licking Heights Local	Summit Station
147	2.5	Milton-Union Exempted Village	West Milton
147	2.5	Northwest Local	Mcdermott
147	2.5	Struthers City	Struthers
147	2.5	Warren Local	Vincent
155	2.4	Conneaut Area City	Conneaut
155	2.4	Madison-Plains Local	London
155	2.4	Monroe Local	Monroe
155	2.4	Preble Shawnee Board of Education	Camden
155	2.4	Southwest Licking Local	Etna
155	2.4	Woodridge Local	Peninsula
161	2.3	Beavercreek City	Beavercreek
161	2.3	Big Walnut Local	Galena
161	2.3	Clinton-Massie Local	Clarksville
161	2.3	Milford Exempted Village	Milford
161	2.3	South Point Local	South Point
161	2.3	Southeast Local	Ravenna
161	2.3	Upper Sandusky Exempted Village	Upper Sandusky
168	2.2	Benjamin Logan Local	Bellefontaine
168	2.2	East Liverpool City	East Liverpool
168	2.2	Eastern Local	Sardinia
168	2.2	Greeneview Local	Jamestown
168	2.2	Jonathan Alder Local	Plain City
168	2.2	Kent City	Kent
168	2.2	Tri-Valley Local	Dresden
168	2.2	Westerville City	Westerville
176	2.1	Athens City	The Plains
176	2.1	Bloom-Carroll Local	Carroll
176	2.1	Clyde-Green Springs Ex Vill	Clyde
176	2.1	Elida Local	Elida
176	2.1	New Philadel. City	New Philadel.
176	2.1	Nordonia Hills City	Northfield
176	2.1	Otsego Local	Tontogany
176	2.1	Wellston City	Wellston
176	2.1	Zane Trace Local	Chillicothe
185	2.0	Anthony Wayne Local	Whitehouse
185	2.0	Cuyahoga Falls City	Cuyahoga Falls
185	2.0	Greenville City	Greenville
185	2.0	Salem City	Salem
185	2.0	Sandy Valley Local	Magnolia
185	2.0	Shawnee Local	Lima
185	2.0	Springfield Local	Akron
185	2.0	Triway Local	Wooster
185	2.0	Vermilion Local	Vermilion
185	2.0	West Holmes Local	Millersburg
195	1.9	Beaver Local	Lisbon
195	1.9	Blanchester Local	Blanchester
195	1.9	Carlisle Local	Carlisle
195	1.9	East Muskingum Local	New Concord
195	1.9	Geneva Area City	Geneva
195	1.9	Little Miami Local	Morrow
195	1.9	Painesville Township Local	Painesville
195	1.9	Pike-Delta-York Local	Delta
195	1.9	Saint Clairsville-Richland City	Saint Clairsville
195	1.9	Wadsworth City	Wadsworth
195	1.9	Wellington Exempted Village	Wellington
206	1.8	Bath Local	Lima
206	1.8	Bellevue City	Bellevue
206	1.8	Celina City	Celina
206	1.8	Clark-Shawnee Local	Springfield
206	1.8	Genoa Area Local	Genoa
206	1.8	Northwestern Local	Springfield
206	1.8	Sylvania City	Sylvania
206	1.8	Westfall Local	Williamsport
214	1.7	Avon Lake City	Avon Lake
214	1.7	Clear Fork Valley Local	Bellville
214	1.7	Field Local	Mogadore
214	1.7	Hilliard City	Hilliard
214	1.7	Lebanon City	Lebanon
214	1.7	Loveland City	Loveland
214	1.7	Northeastern Local	Springfield
214	1.7	Rocky River City	Rocky River
214	1.7	Southeast Local	Apple Creek
223	1.6	Berea City	Berea
223	1.6	Cloverleaf Local	Lodi
223	1.6	Fairless Local	Navarre
223	1.6	Highland Local	Medina
223	1.6	Jefferson Area Local	Jefferson
223	1.6	Marietta City	Marietta
223	1.6	Miamisburg City	Miamisburg
223	1.6	New Albany-Plain Local	New Albany
223	1.6	N Ridgeville City	N Ridgeville
223	1.6	Olmsted Falls City	Olmsted Falls
223	1.6	Reynoldsburg City	Reynoldsburg
223	1.6	Sheffield-Sheffield Lake City	Sheffield Vllg
223	1.6	Twinsburg City	Twinsburg
223	1.6	Wapakoneta City	Wapakoneta
223	1.6	Wauseon Exempted Village	Wauseon
238	1.5	Amanda-Clearcreek Local	Amanda
238	1.5	Buckeye Local	Medina
238	1.5	Forest Hills Local	Cincinnati
238	1.5	Girard City	Girard
238	1.5	Highland Local	Sparta
238	1.5	Mason City	Mason
238	1.5	West Carrollton City	West Carrollton
245	1.4	Coventry Local	Akron
245	1.4	Elgin Local	Marion
245	1.4	Firelands Local	Oberlin
245	1.4	Graham Local	Saint Paris
245	1.4	Hubbard Exempted Village	Hubbard
245	1.4	Labrae Local	Leavittsburg
245	1.4	Logan Elm Local	Circleville
245	1.4	Maumee City	Maumee
245	1.4	Maysville Local	Zanesville
254	1.3	Berlin-Milan Local	Milan
254	1.3	Crestwood Local	Mantua
254	1.3	Dover City	Dover
254	1.3	Fairview Park City	Fairview Park
254	1.3	Manchester Local	Akron
254	1.3	Northern Local	Thornville
254	1.3	River Valley Local	Caledonia
254	1.3	Strongsville City	Strongsville
254	1.3	Wilmington City	Wilmington
263	1.2	Bay Village City	Bay Village
263	1.2	Boardman Local	Youngstown
263	1.2	Buckeye Local	Dillonvale
263	1.2	Champion Local	Warren
263	1.2	Chardon Local	Chardon
263	1.2	Fairfield City	Fairfield
263	1.2	Hillsboro City	Hillsboro
263	1.2	Lake Local	Millbury
263	1.2	Minford Local	Minford
263	1.2	North Olmsted City	North Olmsted
263	1.2	Ontario Local	Mansfield
263	1.2	Ottawa-Glandorf Local	Ottawa
263	1.2	Paulding Exempted Village	Paulding
263	1.2	Westlake City	Westlake
277	1.1	Brunswick City	Brunswick
277	1.1	Carrollton Exempted Village	Carrollton
277	1.1	Clearview Local	Lorain
277	1.1	Edison Local	Hammondsville
277	1.1	Indian Creek Local	Wintersville
277	1.1	Keystone Local	Lagrange
277	1.1	Kings Local	Kings Mills
277	1.1	Louisville City	Louisville
277	1.1	Oakwood City	Dayton
277	1.1	Springboro Community City	Springboro
277	1.1	Stow-Munroe Falls City	Stow
288	1.0	Aurora City	Aurora
288	1.0	Bowling Green City	Bowling Green
288	1.0	Dublin City	Dublin
288	1.0	Mayfield City	Mayfield Hgts
288	1.0	Orange City	Cleveland
288	1.0	Perrysburg Exempted Village	Perrysburg
288	1.0	Sugarcreek Local	Bellbrook
295	0.9	Centerville City	Centerville
295	0.9	Coldwater Exempted Village	Coldwater
295	0.9	Lakota Local	Liberty Twp
295	0.9	Liberty Local	Youngstown
295	0.9	Meigs Local	Pomeroy
295	0.9	Mentor Exempted Village	Mentor
295	0.9	Pickerington Local	Pickerington
295	0.9	Streetsboro City	Streetsboro
295	0.9	Sycamore Community City	Cincinnati
295	0.9	Vandalia-Butler City	Vandalia
295	0.9	Wheelersburg Local	Wheelersburg
295	0.9	Worthington City	Worthington
307	0.8	Black River Local	Sullivan
307	0.8	Lake Local	Uniontown
307	0.8	Lakewood Local	Hebron
307	0.8	Lexington Local	Lexington
307	0.8	Revere Local	Bath
307	0.8	Wooster City	Wooster
313	0.7	Benton Carroll Salem Local	Oak Harbor
313	0.7	Brecksville-Broadview Heights City	Brecksville
313	0.7	Buckeye Valley Local	Delaware
313	0.7	Coshocton City	Coshocton
313	0.7	Fairfield Union Local	West Rushville
313	0.7	Hudson City	Hudson
313	0.7	Huron City	Huron
313	0.7	Marysville Exempted Village	Marysville
313	0.7	Northmont City	Englewood
313	0.7	Northwest Local	Canal Fulton
313	0.7	Perry Local	Perry
313	0.7	Solon City	Solon
313	0.7	Tallmadge City	Tallmadge
326	0.6	Copley-Fairlawn City	Copley
326	0.6	Indian Hill Exempted Village	Cincinnati
326	0.6	Jackson Local	Massillon
326	0.6	North Canton City	North Canton

Rank	Value	District	City
326	0.6	South Euclid-Lyndhurst City	Lyndhurst
331	0.5	Bexley City	Bexley
331	0.5	Chagrin Falls Exempted Village	Chagrin Falls
331	0.5	Claymont City	Dennison
331	0.5	Eastwood Local	Pemberville
331	0.5	Howland Local	Warren
331	0.5	Indian Valley Local	Gnadenhutten
331	0.5	Kettering City	Kettering
331	0.5	North Royalton City	North Royalton
331	0.5	Norton City	Norton
331	0.5	Oak Hills Local	Cincinnati
331	0.5	Perkins Local	Sandusky
342	0.4	Avon Local	Avon
342	0.4	Green Local	Green
342	0.4	Kenston Local	Chagrin Falls
342	0.4	Madeira City	Cincinnati
342	0.4	Martins Ferry City	Martins Ferry
342	0.4	Olentangy Local	Lewis Center
342	0.4	Perry Local	Massillon
342	0.4	Tipp Exempted Village	Tipp City
342	0.4	West Branch Local	Beloit
342	0.4	West Geauga Local	Chesterland
352	0.3	Austintown Local	Youngstown
352	0.3	Canfield Local	Canfield
352	0.3	Granville Exempted Village	Granville
352	0.3	Lakeview Local	Cortland
352	0.3	Marlington Local	Alliance
352	0.3	Medina City	Medina
352	0.3	Saint Marys City	Saint Marys
352	0.3	Upper Arlington City	Upper Arlington
360	0.2	Amherst Exempted Village	Amherst
360	0.2	Canton Local	Canton
360	0.2	Chippewa Local	Doylestown
360	0.2	Johnstown-Monroe Local	Johnstown
360	0.2	Poland Local	Poland
360	0.2	West Muskingum Local	Zanesville
366	0.1	Euclid City	Euclid
366	0.1	Warrensville Hgts City	Warrensville Hgts
368	0.0	East Holmes Local	Berlin
368	0.0	Electronic Classroom of Tomorrow	Columbus
368	0.0	Shaker Heights City	Shaker Heights
368	0.0	Wyoming City	Wyoming
372	n/a	Alternative Education Academy	Toledo
373	n/a	Ohio Virtual Academy	Maumee

The National Assessment of Educational Progress (NAEP) assesses mathematics in five content areas: number properties and operations; measurement; geometry; data analysis and probability; and algebra. The NAEP mathematics scale ranges from 0 to 500.

Overall Mathematics Results for Ohio

- In 2007, the average scale score for fourth-grade students in Ohio was 245. This was not significantly different from their average score in 2005 (242) and was higher than their average score in 1992 (219).[1]
- Ohio's average score (245) in 2007 was higher than that of the nation's public schools (239).
- Of the 52 states and other jurisdictions that participated in the 2007 fourth-grade assessment, students' average scale score in Ohio was higher than those in 31 jurisdictions, not significantly different from those in 16 jurisdictions, and lower than those in 4 jurisdictions.[2]
- The percentage of students in Ohio who performed at or above the NAEP *Proficient* level was 46 percent in 2007. This percentage was not significantly different from that in 2005 (43 percent) and was greater than that in 1992 (16 percent).
- The percentage of students in Ohio who performed at or above the NAEP *Basic* level was 87 percent in 2007. This percentage was greater than that in 2005 (84 percent) and was greater than that in 1992 (57 percent).

Percentages at NAEP Achievement Levels and Average Score

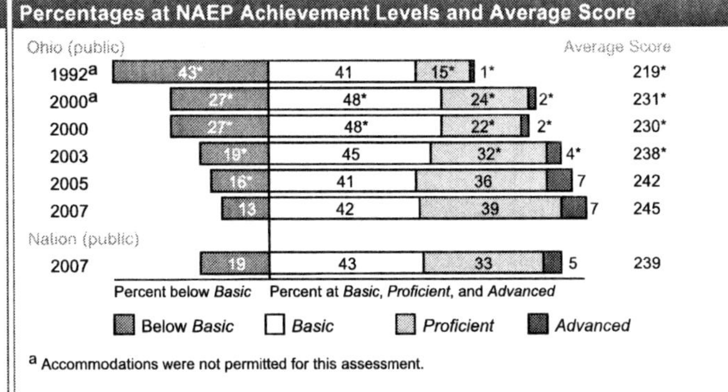

[a] Accommodations were not permitted for this assessment.

NOTE: The NAEP grade 4 mathematics achievement levels correspond to the following scale points: Below *Basic*, 213 or lower; *Basic*, 214–248; *Proficient*, 249–281; *Advanced*, 282 or above.

Performance of NAEP Reporting Groups in Ohio: 2007

Reporting groups	Percent of students	Average score	Percent below *Basic*	Percent of students at or above *Basic*	Percent of students at or above *Proficient*	Percent *Advanced*
Male	51	246	11	89	49	8
Female	49	243	14	86	43	5
White	75	250	7	93	53	8
Black	18	225	33	67	18	1
Hispanic	3	231	24	76	25	1
Asian/Pacific Islander	2	‡	‡	‡	‡	‡
American Indian/Alaska Native	#	‡	‡	‡	‡	‡
Eligible for National School Lunch Program	37	230	25	75	23	1
Not eligible for National School Lunch Program	63	253	5	95	59	9

Average Score Gaps Between Selected Groups

- In 2007, male students in Ohio had an average score that was higher than that of female students by 4 points. In 1992, there was no significant difference between the average score of male and female students.
- In 2007, Black students had an average score that was lower than that of White students by 25 points. In 1992, the average score for Black students was lower than that of White students by 28 points.
- In 2007, Hispanic students had an average score that was lower than that of White students by 18 points. Data are not reported for Hispanic students in 1992, because reporting standards were not met.
- In 2007, students who were eligible for free/reduced-price school lunch, a proxy for poverty, had an average score that was lower than that of students who were not eligible for free/reduced-price school lunch by 23 points. In 2000, the average score for students who were eligible for free/reduced-price school lunch was lower than the score of those not eligible by 22 points.
- In 2007, the score gap between students at the 75th percentile and students at the 25th percentile was 36 points. This performance gap was narrower than that of 1992 (42 points).

Mathematics Scores at Selected Percentiles

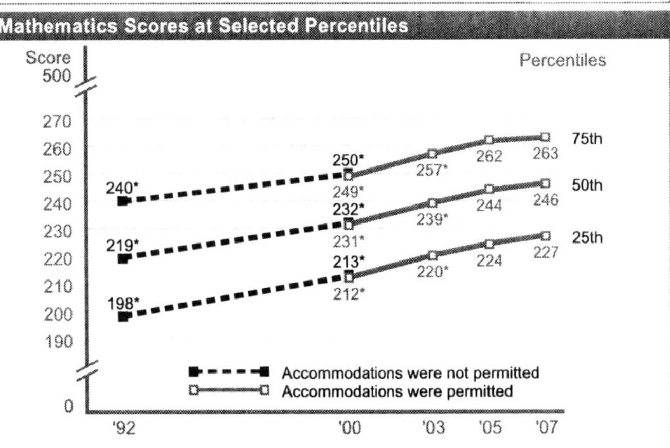

NOTE: Scores at selected percentiles on the NAEP mathematics scale indicate how well students at lower, middle, and higher levels performed.

\# Rounds to zero.
‡ Reporting standards not met.
* Significantly different from 2007.
↑ Significantly higher than 2005. ↓ Significantly lower than 2005.

[1] Comparisons (higher/lower/narrower/wider/not different) are based on statistical tests. The .05 level was used for testing statistical significance. Statistical comparisons are calculated on the basis of unrounded scale scores or percentages. Comparisons across jurisdictions and comparisons with the nation or within a jurisdiction across years may be affected by differences in exclusion rates for students with disabilities (SD) and English language learners (ELL). The exclusion rates for SD and ELL in Ohio were 4 percent and 1 percent in 2007, respectively.For more information on NAEP significance testing see http://nces.ed.gov/nationsreportcard/mathematics/interpret-results.asp#statistical.

[2] "Jurisdictions" refers to states and the District of Columbia and the Department of Defense Education Activity schools.

NOTE: Detail may not sum to totals because of rounding and because the "Information not available" category for the National School Lunch Program, which provides free and reduced-price lunches, and the "Unclassified" category for race/ethnicity are not displayed. Visit http://nces.ed.gov/nationsreportcard/states/ for additional results and detailed information.

SOURCE: U.S. Department of Education, Institute of Education Sciences, National Center for Education Statistics, National Assessment of Educational Progress (NAEP), various years, 1992–2007 Mathematics Assessments.

ies NATIONAL CENTER FOR EDUCATION STATISTICS Institute of Education Sciences
NCES 2007-497OH4

The Nation's Report Card Reading 2007 State Snapshot Report

Ohio
Grade 4
Public Schools

The National Assessment of Educational Progress (NAEP) assesses reading in two content areas in grade 4: reading for literary experience and to gain information. The NAEP reading scale ranges from 0 to 500.

Overall Reading Results for Ohio

- In 2007, the average scale score for fourth-grade students in Ohio was 226. This was not significantly different from their average score in 2005 (223) and was higher than their average score in 1992 (217).[1]
- Ohio's average score (226) in 2007 was higher than that of the nation's public schools (220).
- Of the 52 states and other jurisdictions that participated in the 2007 fourth-grade assessment, students' average scale score in Ohio was higher than those in 25 jurisdictions, not significantly different from those in 22 jurisdictions, and lower than those in 4 jurisdictions.[2]
- The percentage of students in Ohio who performed at or above the NAEP *Proficient* level was 36 percent in 2007. This percentage was not significantly different from that in 2005 (34 percent) and was greater than that in 1992 (27 percent).
- The percentage of students in Ohio who performed at or above the NAEP *Basic* level was 73 percent in 2007. This percentage was greater than that in 2005 (69 percent) and was greater than that in 1992 (63 percent).

Percentages at NAEP Achievement Levels and Average Score

	Below *Basic*	*Basic*	*Proficient*	*Advanced*	Average Score
Ohio (public)					
1992[a]	37*	36	22*	5*	217*
2002	32*	35	27	7	222
2003	31*	34	26	8	222*
2005	31*	34	27	8	223
2007	27	37	28	8	226
Nation (public)					
2007	34	34	24	7	220

Percent below *Basic* Percent at *Basic*, *Proficient*, and *Advanced*

[a] Accommodations were not permitted for this assessment.

NOTE: The NAEP grade 4 reading achievement levels correspond to the following scale points: Below *Basic*, 207 or lower; *Basic*, 208–237; *Proficient*, 238–267; *Advanced*, 268 or above.

Performance of NAEP Reporting Groups in Ohio: 2007

Reporting groups	Percent of students	Average score	Percent below *Basic*	Percent of students at or above *Basic*	Percent of students at or above *Proficient*	Percent *Advanced*
Male	51	223	29	71	33	6
Female	49	228	24	76	39	9
White	75	231	20	80	42	9
Black	17	204	54	46	14	1
Hispanic	2	214	45	55	21	2
Asian/Pacific Islander	1	‡	‡	‡	‡	‡
American Indian/Alaska Native	#	‡	‡	‡	‡	‡
Eligible for National School Lunch Program	36	211 ↑	42	58	19	2
Not eligible for National School Lunch Program	64	234	18	82	46	11

Average Score Gaps Between Selected Groups

- In 2007, male students in Ohio had an average score that was lower than that of female students by 6 points. In 1992, the average score for male students was lower than that of female students by 7 points.
- In 2007, Black students had an average score that was lower than that of White students by 27 points. In 1992, the average score for Black students was lower than that of White students by 23 points.
- In 2007, Hispanic students had an average score that was lower than that of White students by 17 points. Data are not reported for Hispanic students in 1992, because reporting standards were not met.
- In 2007, students who were eligible for free/reduced-price school lunch, a proxy for poverty, had an average score that was lower than that of students who were not eligible for free/reduced-price school lunch by 22 points. In 2002, the average score for students who were eligible for free/reduced-price school lunch was lower than the score of those not eligible by 24 points.
- In 2007, the score gap between students at the 75th percentile and students at the 25th percentile was 41 points. In 1992, the score gap between students at the 75th percentile and students at the 25th percentile was 43 points.

Reading Scores at Selected Percentiles

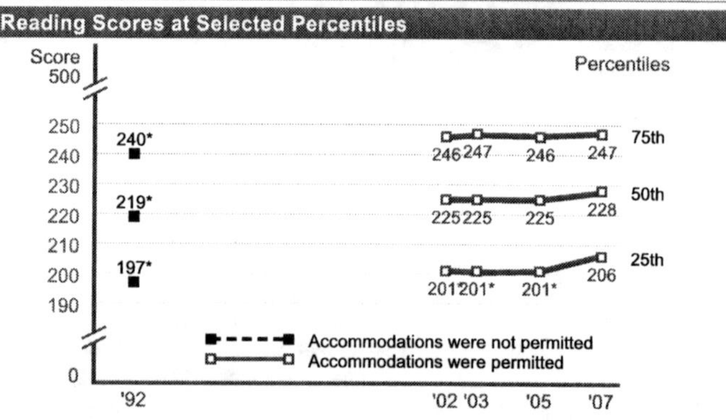

NOTE: Scores at selected percentiles on the NAEP reading scale indicate how well students at lower, middle, and higher levels performed.

\# Rounds to zero.
‡ Reporting standards not met.
* Significantly different from 2007.
↑ Significantly higher than 2005. ↓ Significantly lower than 2005.

[1] Comparisons (higher/lower/narrower/wider/not different) are based on statistical tests. The .05 level was used for testing statistical significance. Statistical comparisons are calculated on the basis of unrounded scale scores or percentages. Comparisons across jurisdictions and comparisons with the nation or within a jurisdiction across years may be affected by differences in exclusion rates for students with disabilities (SD) and English language learners (ELL). The exclusion rates for SD and ELL in Ohio were 7 percent and 1 percent in 2007, respectively.For more information on NAEP significance testing see http://nces.ed.gov/nationsreportcard/reading/interpret-results.asp#statistical.

[2] "Jurisdictions" refers to states and the District of Columbia and the Department of Defense Education Activity schools.

NOTE: Detail may not sum to totals because of rounding and because the "Information not available" category for the National School Lunch Program, which provides free and reduced-price lunches, and the "Unclassified" category for race/ethnicity are not displayed. Visit http://nces.ed.gov/nationsreportcard/states/ for additional results and detailed information.

SOURCE: U.S. Department of Education, Institute of Education Sciences, National Center for Education Statistics, National Assessment of Educational Progress (NAEP), various years, 1992–2007 Reading Assessments.

The writing assessment of the National Assessment of Educational Progress (NAEP) measures narrative, informative, and persuasive writing–three purposes identified in the NAEP framework. The NAEP writing scale ranges from 0 to 300.

Overall Writing Results for Ohio

- The average scale score for fourth-grade students in Ohio was 157.
- Ohio's average score (157) was higher[1] than that of the nation's public schools (153).
- Students' average scale scores in Ohio were higher than those in 26 jurisdictions[2], not significantly different from those in 17 jurisdictions, and lower than those in 4 jurisdictions.
- The percentage of students who performed at or above the NAEP *Proficient* level was 28 percent. The percentage of students who performed at or above the *Basic* level was 90 percent.

Student Percentage at Each Achievement Level

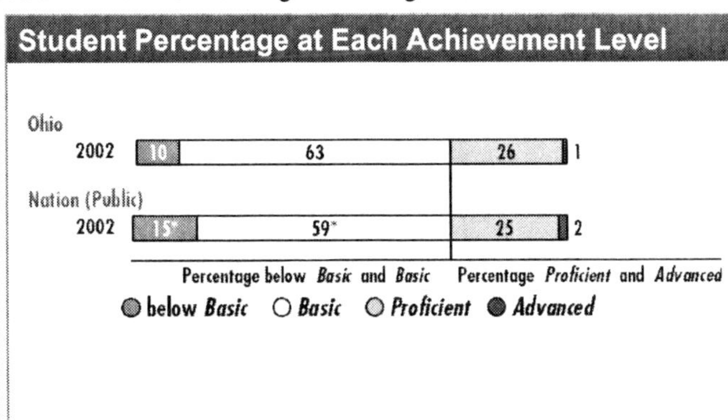

Performance of NAEP Reporting Groups in Ohio

Reporting groups	Percentage of students	Average Score	Below *Basic*	*Basic*	*Proficient*	*Advanced*
			Percentage of students at			
Male	50	150 ↑	13 ↓	67 ↑	19	1
Female	50	164	6 ↓	59	33	2
White	76	162	7 ↓	61 ↑	31	2
Black	20	140	20	68	11	#
Hispanic	2	---	---	---	---	---
Asian/Pacific Islander	1	---	---	---	---	---
American Indian/Alaska Native	#	---	---	---	---	---
Free/reduced-priced school lunch						
Eligible	32	143	18 ↓	69 ↑	14	#
Not eligible	61	164	5 ↓	60	33	2
Information not available	7	158	8	64	26	2

Average Score Gaps Between Selected Groups

- Female students in Ohio had an average score that was higher than that of male students (14 points). This performance gap was not significantly different from that of the Nation (18 points).
- White students had an average score that was higher than that of Black students (22 points). This performance gap was not significantly different from that of the Nation (20 points).
- The sample size was not sufficient to permit a reliable estimate for Hispanic students in Ohio.
- Students who were not eligible for free/reduced-price school lunch had an average score that was higher than that of students who were eligible (21 points). This performance gap was not significantly different from that of the Nation (22 points).

Writing Scale Scores at Selected Percentiles

Scale Score Distribution

	25th Percentile	50th Percentile	75th Percentile
Ohio	*135* ↑	*157* ↑	*179*
Nation (Public)	*128*	*153*	*178*

An examination of scores at different percentiles on the 0-300 NAEP writing scale at each grade indicates how well students at lower, middle, and higher levels of the distribution performed. For example, the data above shows that 75 percent of students in public schools nationally scored below *178,* while 75 percent of students in Ohio scored below *179.*

Percentage rounds to zero. --- Reporting standards not met; sample size insufficient to permit a reliable estimate.
* Significantly different from Ohio. ↑ Significantly higher than, ↓ lower than appropriate subgroup in the nation (public).
[1] Comparisons (higher/lower/not different) are based on statistical tests. The .05 level was used for testing statistical significance.
[2] "Jurisdictions" includes participating states and other jurisdictions (such as Guam or the District of Columbia).
NOTE: Detail may not sum to totals because of rounding. Score gaps are calculated based on differences between unrounded average scale scores.
Visit http://nces.ed.gov/nationsreportcard/states/ for additional results and detailed information.
SOURCE: U.S. Department of Education, Institute of Education Sciences, National Center for Education Statistics, National Assessment of Educational Progress (NAEP), 2002 Writing Assessment.

NCES National Center for Education Statistics | The Nation's Report Card State **Science 2005** | Ohio Grade 4 Public Schools

Snapshot Report

NCES 2006-467OH4

The National Assessment of Educational Progress (NAEP) assesses science in two major dimensions: Fields of Science (Earth, Physical, and Life) and Knowing and Doing Science (Conceptual Understanding, Scientific Investigation, and Practical Reasoning). The NAEP science scale ranges from 0 to 300. Scales are created separately for each grade.

Overall Science Results for Ohio

- In 2005, the average scale score for fourth-grade students in Ohio was 157. This was not significantly different from their average score in 2000 (155).[1]
- Ohio's average score (157) in 2005 was higher than that of the nation's public schools (149).
- Of the 44 states and one jurisdiction that participated in the 2005 fourth-grade assessment, students' average scale score in Ohio was higher than those in 25 jurisdictions, not significantly different from those in 12 jurisdictions, and lower than those in 7 jurisdictions.[2]
- The percentage of students in Ohio who performed at or above the NAEP *Proficient* level was 35 percent in 2005. This percentage was not significantly different from that in 2000 (31 percent).
- The percentage of students in Ohio who performed at or above the NAEP *Basic* level was 75 percent in 2005. This percentage was not significantly different from that in 2000 (73 percent).

Student Percentages at NAEP Achievement Levels

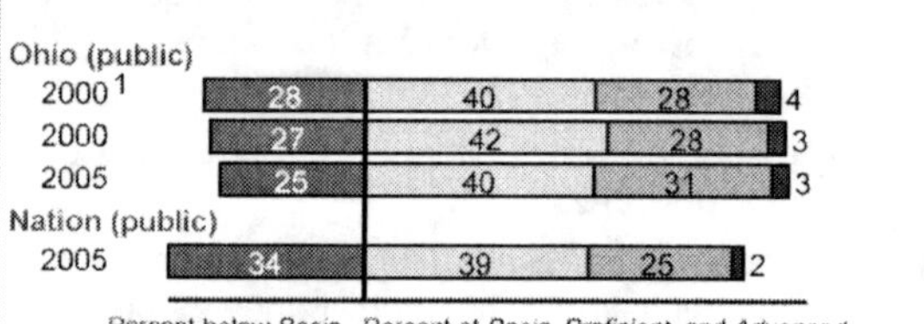

[1] Accommodations were not permitted for this assessment.

NOTE: The NAEP grade 4 science achievement levels correspond to the following scale points: Below *Basic*, 137 or lower; *Basic*, 138–169; *Proficient*, 170–204; *Advanced*, 205 or above.

Performance of NAEP Reporting Groups in Ohio: 2005

Reporting groups	Percent of students	Average score	Percent below *Basic*	Percent of students at or above *Basic*	Percent of students at or above *Proficient*	Percent *Advanced*
Male	53	159	23	77	39	4
Female	47	154	27	73	30	2
White	74	164	14	86	43	4
Black	20	130	61	39	7	#
Hispanic	2	146	39	61	22	1
Asian/Pacific Islander	1	‡	‡	‡	‡	‡
American Indian/Alaska Native	#	‡	‡	‡	‡	‡
Eligible for free/reduced-price school lunch	37	139	47	53	15	1
Not eligible for free/reduced-price school lunch	60	167	12	88	47	5

Average Score Gaps Between Selected Groups

- In 2005, male students in Ohio had an average score that was higher than that of female students by 5 points. In 2000, there was no significant difference between the average score of male and female students.
- In 2005, Black students had an average score that was lower than that of White students by 34 points. In 2000, the average score for Black students was lower than that of White students by 31 points.
- In 2005, Hispanic students had an average score that was lower than that of White students by 18 points. Data are not reported for Hispanic students in 2000, because reporting standards were not met. Therefore, the performance gap results are not reported.
- In 2005, students who were eligible for free/reduced-price school lunch, an indicator of poverty, had an average score that was lower than that of students who were not eligible for free/reduced-price school lunch by 28 points. In 2000, the average score for students who were eligible for free/reduced-price school lunch was lower than the score of those not eligible by 27 points.
- In 2005, the score gap between students at the 75th percentile and students at the 25th percentile was 39 points. In 2000, the score gap between students at the 75th percentile and students at the 25th percentile was 39 points.

Science Scale Scores at Selected Percentiles

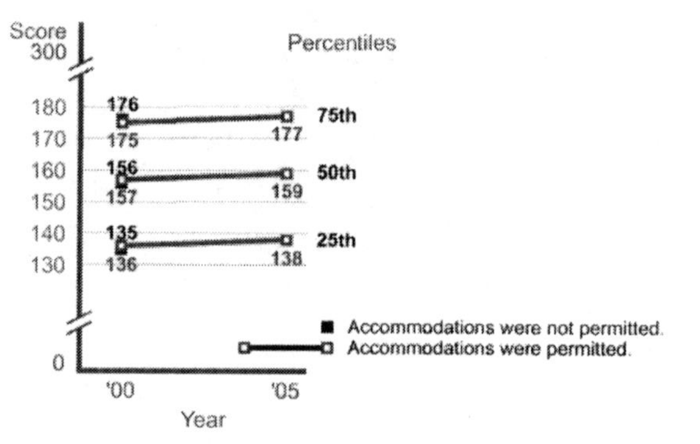

Scores at selected percentiles on the NAEP science scale indicate how well students at lower, middle, and higher levels performed.

The estimate rounds to zero.

‡ Reporting standards not met.

* Significantly different from 2005.

↑ Significantly higher than 2000. ↓ Significantly lower than 2000.

[1] Comparisons (higher/lower/not different) are based on statistical tests. The .05 level was used for testing statistical significance. Comparisons across jurisdictions and comparisons with the nation or within a jurisdiction across years may be affected by differences in exclusion rates for students with disabilities (SD) and English language learners (ELL). The exclusion rates for SD and ELL in Ohio were 3 percent and percentage rounds to zero in 2005, respectively. Statistical comparisons are calculated on the basis of unrounded scale scores or percentages.

[2] "Jurisdiction" refers to states and the Department of Defense Education Activity schools.

NOTE: Detail may not sum to totals because of rounding and because the "Information not available" category for free/reduced-price school lunch and the "Unclassifed" category for race/ethnicity are not displayed. Visit http://nces.ed.gov/nationsreportcard/states/ for additional results and detailed information.

SOURCE: U.S. Department of Education, Institute of Education Sciences, National Center for Education Statistics, National Assessment of Educational Progress (NAEP), 2000 and 2005 Science Assessments.

The National Assessment of Educational Progress (NAEP) assesses mathematics in five content areas: number properties and operations; measurement; geometry; data analysis and probability; and algebra. The NAEP mathematics scale ranges from 0 to 500.

Overall Mathematics Results for Ohio

- In 2007, the average scale score for eighth-grade students in Ohio was 285. This was not significantly different from their average score in 2005 (283) and was higher than their average score in 1990 (264).[1]
- Ohio's average score (285) in 2007 was higher than that of the nation's public schools (280).
- Of the 52 states and other jurisdictions that participated in the 2007 eighth-grade assessment, students' average scale score in Ohio was higher than those in 23 jurisdictions, not significantly different from those in 21 jurisdictions, and lower than those in 7 jurisdictions.[2]
- The percentage of students in Ohio who performed at or above the NAEP *Proficient* level was 35 percent in 2007. This percentage was not significantly different from that in 2005 (33 percent) and was greater than that in 1990 (15 percent).
- The percentage of students in Ohio who performed at or above the NAEP *Basic* level was 76 percent in 2007. This percentage was not significantly different from that in 2005 (74 percent) and was greater than that in 1990 (53 percent).

Percentages at NAEP Achievement Levels and Average Score

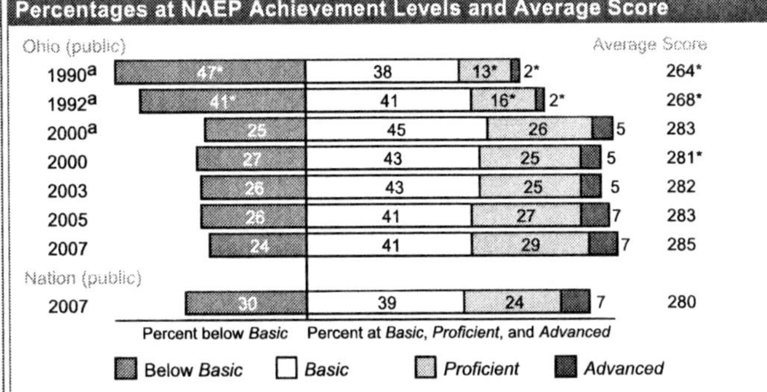

a Accommodations were not permitted for this assessment.

NOTE: The NAEP grade 8 mathematics achievement levels correspond to the following scale points: Below *Basic*, 261 or lower; *Basic*, 262–298; *Proficient*, 299–332; *Advanced*, 333 or above.

Performance of NAEP Reporting Groups in Ohio: 2007

Reporting groups	Percent of students	Average score	Percent below *Basic*	Percent of students at or above *Basic*	Percent of students at or above *Proficient*	Percent *Advanced*
Male	51	286	23	77	38	8
Female	49	283	24	76	33	5
White	76	291	17	83	42	8
Black	18	258	53	47	9	#
Hispanic	2	276	37	63	25	5
Asian/Pacific Islander	2	‡	‡	‡	‡	‡
American Indian/Alaska Native	#	‡	‡	‡	‡	‡
Eligible for National School Lunch Program	31	268	40	60	16	1
Not eligible for National School Lunch Program	67	293	16	84	44	9

Average Score Gaps Between Selected Groups

- In 2007, male students in Ohio had an average score that was not significantly different from that of female students. In 1990, the average score for male students was higher than that of female students by 5 points.
- In 2007, Black students had an average score that was lower than that of White students by 33 points. In 1990, the average score for Black students was lower than that of White students by 35 points.
- In 2007, Hispanic students had an average score that was lower than that of White students by 15 points. Data are not reported for Hispanic students in 1990, because reporting standards were not met.
- In 2007, students who were eligible for free/reduced-price school lunch, a proxy for poverty, had an average score that was lower than that of students who were not eligible for free/reduced-price school lunch by 25 points. In 2000, the average score for students who were eligible for free/reduced-price school lunch was lower than the score of those not eligible by 30 points.
- In 2007, the score gap between students at the 75th percentile and students at the 25th percentile was 44 points. In 1990, the score gap between students at the 75th percentile and students at the 25th percentile was 45 points.

Mathematics Scores at Selected Percentiles

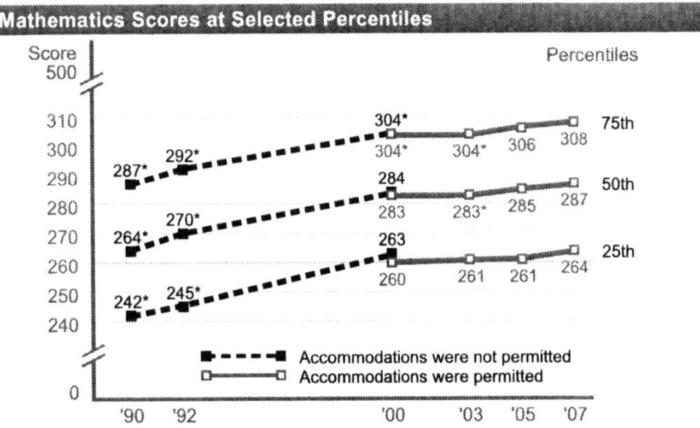

NOTE: Scores at selected percentiles on the NAEP mathematics scale indicate how well students at lower, middle, and higher levels performed.

\# Rounds to zero.
‡ Reporting standards not met.
* Significantly different from 2007.
↑ Significantly higher than 2005. ↓ Significantly lower than 2005.

[1] Comparisons (higher/lower/narrower/wider/not different) are based on statistical tests. The .05 level was used for testing statistical significance. Statistical comparisons are calculated on the basis of unrounded scale scores or percentages. Comparisons across jurisdictions and comparisons with the nation or within a jurisdiction across years may be affected by differences in exclusion rates for students with disabilities (SD) and English language learners (ELL). The exclusion rates for SD and ELL in Ohio were 7 percent and "percentage rounds to zero" in 2007, respectively.For more information on NAEP significance testing see http://nces.ed.gov/nationsreportcard/mathematics/interpret-results.asp#statistical.

[2] "Jurisdictions" refers to states and the District of Columbia and the Department of Defense Education Activity schools.

NOTE: Detail may not sum to totals because of rounding and because the "Information not available" category for the National School Lunch Program, which provides free and reduced-price lunches, and the "Unclassified" category for race/ethnicity are not displayed. Visit http://nces.ed.gov/nationsreportcard/states/ for additional results and detailed information.

SOURCE: U.S. Department of Education, Institute of Education Sciences, National Center for Education Statistics, National Assessment of Educational Progress (NAEP), various years, 1990–2007 Mathematics Assessments.

ies NATIONAL CENTER FOR EDUCATION STATISTICS Institute of Education Sciences
NCES 2007-497OH8

The Nation's Report Card **Reading 2007** State Snapshot Report

Ohio
Grade 8
Public Schools

The National Assessment of Educational Progress (NAEP) assesses reading in three content areas in grade 8: reading for literary experience, to gain information, and to perform a task. The NAEP reading scale ranges from 0 to 500.

Overall Reading Results for Ohio

- In 2007, the average scale score for eighth-grade students in Ohio was 268. This was not significantly different from their average score in 2005 (267) and was not significantly different from their average score in 2002 (268).[1]
- Ohio's average score (268) in 2007 was higher than that of the nation's public schools (261).
- Of the 52 states and other jurisdictions that participated in the 2007 eighth-grade assessment, students' average scale score in Ohio was higher than those in 29 jurisdictions, not significantly different from those in 19 jurisdictions, and lower than those in 3 jurisdictions.[2]
- The percentage of students in Ohio who performed at or above the NAEP *Proficient* level was 36 percent in 2007. This percentage was not significantly different from that in 2005 (36 percent) and was not significantly different from that in 2002 (35 percent).
- The percentage of students in Ohio who performed at or above the NAEP *Basic* level was 79 percent in 2007. This percentage was not significantly different from that in 2005 (78 percent) and was not significantly different from that in 2002 (82 percent).

Percentages at NAEP Achievement Levels and Average Score

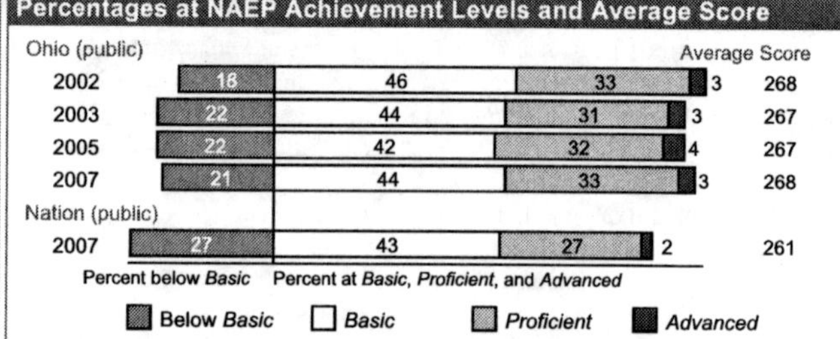

NOTE: The NAEP grade 8 reading achievement levels correspond to the following scale points: Below *Basic*, 242 or lower; *Basic*, 243–280; *Proficient*, 281–322; *Advanced*, 323 or above.

Performance of NAEP Reporting Groups in Ohio: 2007

Reporting groups	Percent of students	Average score	Percent below *Basic*	Percent of students at or above *Basic*	Percent of students at or above *Proficient*	Percent *Advanced*
Male	50	264	24	76	31	3
Female	50	272	17	83	40	4
White	76	274	15	85	42	4
Black	18	246	43	57	12	#
Hispanic	1	260	30	70	31	2
Asian/Pacific Islander	1	‡	‡	‡	‡	‡
American Indian/Alaska Native	#	‡	‡	‡	‡	‡
Eligible for National School Lunch Program	31	251	37	63	16	1
Not eligible for National School Lunch Program	67	275	13	87	45	4

Average Score Gaps Between Selected Groups

- In 2007, male students in Ohio had an average score that was lower than that of female students by 8 points. In 2002, the average score for male students was lower than that of female students by 6 points.
- In 2007, Black students had an average score that was lower than that of White students by 27 points. In 2002, the average score for Black students was lower than that of White students by 27 points.
- In 2007, Hispanic students had an average score that was not significantly different from that of White students (gap of 14 points). Data are not reported for Hispanic students in 2002, because reporting standards were not met.
- In 2007, students who were eligible for free/reduced-price school lunch, a proxy for poverty, had an average score that was lower than that of students who were not eligible for free/reduced-price school lunch by 24 points. In 2002, the average score for students who were eligible for free/reduced-price school lunch was lower than the score of those not eligible by 16 points.
- In 2007, the score gap between students at the 75th percentile and students at the 25th percentile was 42 points. In 2002, the score gap between students at the 75th percentile and students at the 25th percentile was 39 points.

Reading Scores at Selected Percentiles

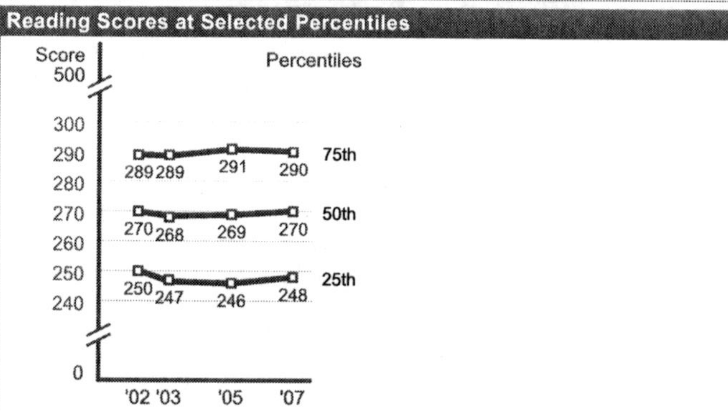

NOTE: Scores at selected percentiles on the NAEP reading scale indicate how well students at lower, middle, and higher levels performed.

\# Rounds to zero.
‡ Reporting standards not met.
* Significantly different from 2007.
↑ Significantly higher than 2005. ↓ Significantly lower than 2005.

[1] Comparisons (higher/lower/narrower/wider/not different) are based on statistical tests. The .05 level was used for testing statistical significance. Statistical comparisons are calculated on the basis of unrounded scale scores or percentages. Comparisons across jurisdictions and comparisons with the nation or within a jurisdiction across years may be affected by differences in exclusion rates for students with disabilities (SD) and English language learners (ELL). The exclusion rates for SD and ELL in Ohio were 9 percent and 1 percent in 2007, respectively.For more information on NAEP significance testing see http://nces.ed.gov/nationsreportcard/reading/interpret-results.asp#statistical.

[2] "Jurisdictions" refers to states and the District of Columbia and the Department of Defense Education Activity schools.

NOTE: Detail may not sum to totals because of rounding and because the "Information not available" category for the National School Lunch Program, which provides free and reduced-price lunches, and the "Unclassified" category for race/ethnicity are not displayed. Visit http://nces.ed.gov/nationsreportcard/states/ for additional results and detailed information.

SOURCE: U.S. Department of Education, Institute of Education Sciences, National Center for Education Statistics, National Assessment of Educational Progress (NAEP), various years, 2002–2007 Reading Assessments.

The National Assessment of Educational Progress (NAEP) assesses writing for three purposes identified in the NAEP framework: narrative, informative, and persuasive. The NAEP writing scale ranges from 0 to 300.

Overall Writing Results for Ohio

- In 2007, the average scale score for eighth-grade students in Ohio was 156. This was not significantly different from their average score in 2002 (160).[1]
- Ohio's average score (156) in 2007 was not significantly different from that of the nation's public schools (154).
- Of the 45 states and one other jurisdiction that participated in the 2007 eighth-grade assessment, students' average scale score in Ohio was higher than those in 15 jurisdictions, not significantly different from those in 22 jurisdictions, and lower than those in 8 jurisdictions.[2]
- The percentage of students in Ohio who performed at or above the NAEP *Proficient* level was 32 percent in 2007. This percentage was smaller than that in 2002 (38 percent).
- The percentage of students in Ohio who performed at or above the NAEP *Basic* level was 90 percent in 2007. This percentage was not significantly different from that in 2002 (89 percent).

Percentages at NAEP Achievement Levels and Average Score

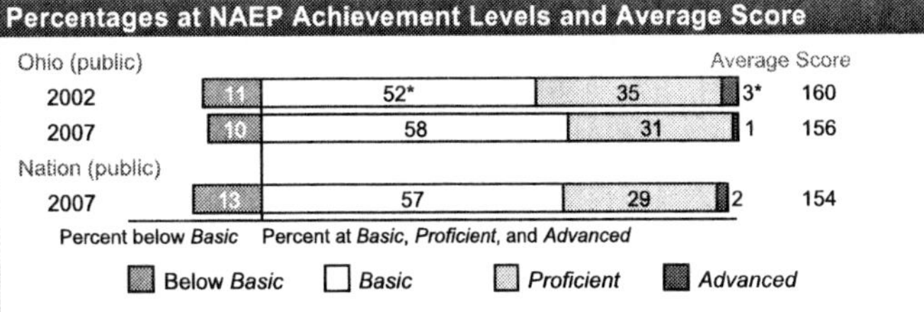

NOTE: The NAEP grade 8 writing achievement levels correspond to the following scale points: Below *Basic*, 113 or lower; *Basic*, 114–172; *Proficient*, 173–223; *Advanced*, 224 or above.

Performance of NAEP Reporting Groups in Ohio: 2007

Reporting groups	Percent of students	Average score	Percent below *Basic*	Percent of students at or above *Basic*	Percent of students at or above *Proficient*	Percent *Advanced*
Male	52	147	15	85	21	#
Female	48	166	5	95	43	2↓
White	76	160	8	92	36	1↓
Black	19	138	20	80	13	#
Hispanic	2	141	26	74	22	#
Asian/Pacific Islander	1	‡	‡	‡	‡	‡
American Indian/Alaska Native	#	‡	‡	‡	‡	‡
Eligible for National School Lunch Program	32	140	19	81	15	#
Not eligible for National School Lunch Program	66	163	6	94	39	1↓

Average Score Gaps Between Selected Groups

- In 2007, male students in Ohio had an average score that was lower than that of female students by 19 points. This performance gap was not significantly different from that of 2002 (20 points).
- In 2007, Black students had an average score that was lower than that of White students by 22 points. This performance gap was not significantly different from that of 2002 (33 points).
- In 2007, Hispanic students had an average score that was lower than that of White students by 20 points. Data are not reported for Hispanic students in 2002, because reporting standards were not met. Therefore, the performance gap results are not reported.
- In 2007, students who were eligible for free/reduced-price school lunch, an indicator of poverty, had an average score that was lower than that of students who were not eligible for free/reduced-price school lunch by 23 points. This performance gap was the same as that of 2002 (23 points).
- In 2007, the score gap between students at the 75th percentile and students at the 25th percentile was 44 points. This performance gap was not significantly different from that of 2002 (47 points).

Writing Scores at Selected Percentiles in Ohio

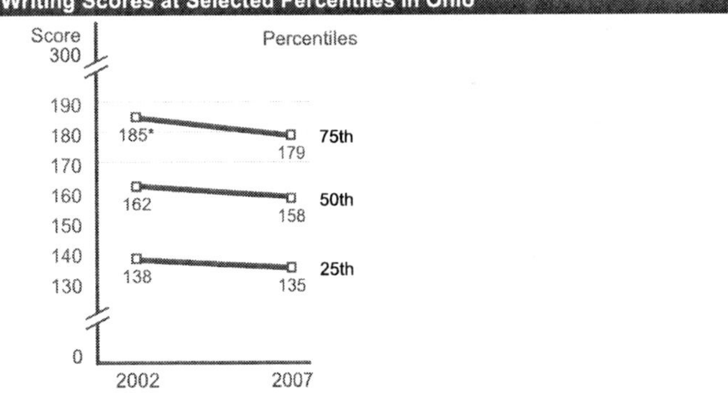

NOTE: Scores at selected percentiles on the NAEP writing scale indicate how well students at lower, middle, and higher levels performed.

\# Rounds to zero.
‡ Reporting standards not met.
* Significantly different from 2007.
↑ Significantly higher than 2002. ↓ Significantly lower than 2002.

[1] Comparisons (higher/lower/narrower/wider/not different) are based on statistical tests. The .05 level with appropriate adjustments for multiple comparisons was used for testing statistical significance. Statistical comparisons are calculated on the basis of unrounded scale scores or percentages. Comparisons across jurisdictions and comparisons with the nation or within a jurisdiction across years may be affected by differences in exclusion rates for students with disabilities (SD) and English language learners (ELL). The exclusion rates for SD and ELL in Ohio were 4 percent and "percentage rounds to zero" in 2007, respectively. For more information on NAEP significance testing, see http://nces.ed.gov/nationsreportcard/writing/interpret-results.asp#statistical.

[2] "Jurisdiction" refers to states, the District of Columbia, and the Department of Defense Education Activity schools.

NOTE: Detail may not sum to totals because of rounding and because the "Information not available" category for the National School Lunch Program, which provides free and reduced-price lunches, and the "Unclassified" category for race/ethnicity are not displayed. Visit http://nces.ed.gov/nationsreportcard/states/ for additional results and detailed information.

SOURCE: U.S. Department of Education, Institute of Education Sciences, National Center for Education Statistics, National Assessment of Educational Progress (NAEP), 2002 and 2007 Writing Assessments.

NCES National Center for Education Statistics

The Nation's Report Card
State **Science 2005**

Ohio
Grade 8
Public Schools

Snapshot Report

NCES 2006-467OH8

The National Assessment of Educational Progress (NAEP) assesses science in two major dimensions: Fields of Science (Earth, Physical, and Life) and Knowing and Doing Science (Conceptual Understanding, Scientific Investigation, and Practical Reasoning). The NAEP science scale ranges from 0 to 300. Scales are created separately for each grade.

Overall Science Results for Ohio

- In 2005, the average scale score for eighth-grade students in Ohio was 155. This was not significantly different from their average score in 2000 (159).[1]
- Ohio's average score (155) in 2005 was higher than that of the nation's public schools (147).
- Of the 44 states and one jurisdiction that participated in the 2005 eighth-grade assessment, students' average scale score in Ohio was higher than those in 23 jurisdictions, not significantly different from those in 13 jurisdictions, and lower than those in 8 jurisdictions.[2]
- The percentage of students in Ohio who performed at or above the NAEP *Proficient* level was 35 percent in 2005. This percentage was not significantly different from that in 2000 (39 percent).
- The percentage of students in Ohio who performed at or above the NAEP *Basic* level was 67 percent in 2005. This percentage was not significantly different from that in 2000 (72 percent).

Student Percentages at NAEP Achievement Levels

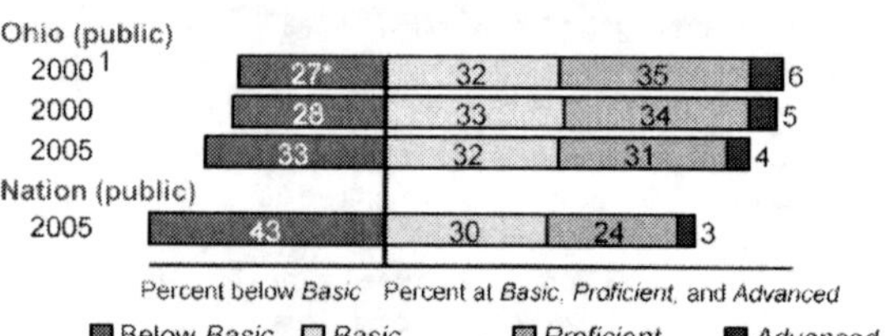

[1] Accommodations were not permitted for this assessment.

NOTE: The NAEP grade 8 science achievement levels correspond to the following scale points: Below *Basic*, 142 or lower; *Basic*, 143–169; *Proficient*, 170–207; *Advanced*, 208 or above.

Performance of NAEP Reporting Groups in Ohio: 2005

Reporting groups	Percent of students	Average score	Percent below *Basic*	Percent of students at or above *Basic*	Percent of students at or above *Proficient*	Percent *Advanced*
Male	48	157	31	69	38	5
Female	52	154	34	66	33	3
White	79↓	162	25	75	41	5
Black	16↑	124	71	29	7	#
Hispanic	1	142	48	52	24	#
Asian/Pacific Islander	1	‡	‡	‡	‡	‡
American Indian/Alaska Native	#	‡	‡	‡	‡	‡
Eligible for free/reduced-price school lunch	31↑	134	59	41	13	#
Not eligible for free/reduced-price school lunch	62↓	165	21	79	45	6

Average Score Gaps Between Selected Groups

- In 2005, male students in Ohio had an average score that was not significantly different from that of female students. In 2000, the average score for male students was higher than that of female students by 5 points.
- In 2005, Black students had an average score that was lower than that of White students by 38 points. In 2000, the average score for Black students was lower than that of White students by 36 points.
- In 2005, Hispanic students had an average score that was lower than that of White students by 20 points. Data are not reported for Hispanic students in 2000, because reporting standards were not met. Therefore, the performance gap results are not reported.
- In 2005, students who were eligible for free/reduced-price school lunch, an indicator of poverty, had an average score that was lower than that of students who were not eligible for free/reduced-price school lunch by 31 points. In 2000, the average score for students who were eligible for free/reduced-price school lunch was lower than the score of those not eligible by 22 points.
- In 2005, the score gap between students at the 75th percentile and students at the 25th percentile was 43 points. In 2000, the score gap between students at the 75th percentile and students at the 25th percentile was 42 points.

Science Scale Scores at Selected Percentiles

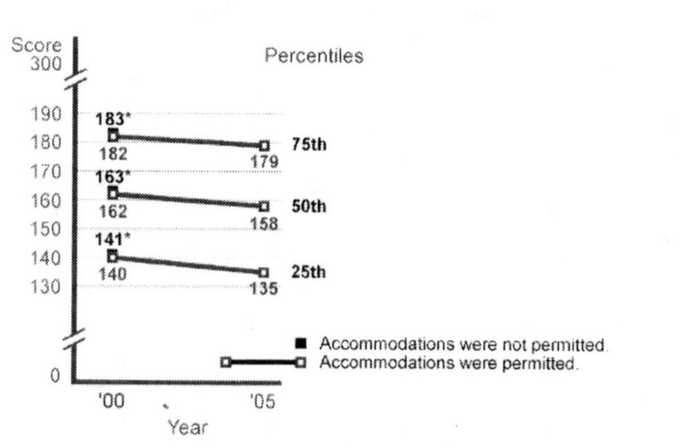

Scores at selected percentiles on the NAEP science scale indicate how well students at lower, middle, and higher levels performed.

\# The estimate rounds to zero.
‡ Reporting standards not met.
* Significantly different from 2005.
↑ Significantly higher than 2000. ↓ Significantly lower than 2000.

[1] Comparisons (higher/lower/not different) are based on statistical tests. The .05 level was used for testing statistical significance. Comparisons across jurisdictions and comparisons with the nation or within a jurisdiction across years may be affected by differences in exclusion rates for students with disabilities (SD) and English language learners (ELL). The exclusion rates for SD and ELL in Ohio were 4 percent and percentage rounds to zero in 2005, respectively. Statistical comparisons are calculated on the basis of unrounded scale scores or percentages.

[2] "Jurisdiction" refers to states and the Department of Defense Education Activity schools.

NOTE: Detail may not sum to totals because of rounding and because the "Information not available" category for free/reduced-price school lunch and the "Unclassifed" category for race/ethnicity are not displayed. Visit http://nces.ed.gov/nationsreportcard/states/ for additional results and detailed information.

SOURCE: U.S. Department of Education, Institute of Education Sciences, National Center for Education Statistics, National Assessment of Educational Progress (NAEP), 2000 and 2005 Science Assessments.

HIGHLIGHTS
OHIO ACHIEVEMENT TESTS PRELIMINARY RESULTS
MAY 2008 TEST ADMINISTRATION

INTRODUCTION

The Ohio Achievement Tests (OAT) were administered to students in grades 3-8 from April 21 through May 09, 2008.

The highlights were based on the preliminary results of the May 2008 test administration. Schools and districts have not verified those results. The final figures may be different due to appeals, late scoring and other changes. If a third-grade student took both the October 2007 test and May 2008 test in Reading, the higher score will be used for accountability purposes; however, the highlights reflect May 2008 results only.

TOTAL STUDENTS TESTED

Table 1 shows the total number of public and community school students tested during the May 2008 administration by subject.

Table 1 – Total number of public school students taking the OAT in May 2008

	Grade					
	Third	Fourth	Fifth	Sixth	Seventh	Eighth
Reading	124,102	129,651	128,084	129,421	133,907	135,718
Mathematics	129,418	129,683	127,959	129,269	133,556	135,630
Writing	-	129,552	-	-	133,669	-
Science	-	-	128,223	-	-	135,592
Soc. Studies	-	-	128,185	-	-	135,449

Note: Grade three students were also tested in Reading in October and some of them did not take the test again in May. Blank cells indicate that a grade cohort was not tested in that subject.

OVERALL PRELIMINARY RESULTS

Table 2 shows the percent of students who scored at proficient or above (accelerated or advanced) on each test in the May 2008 test administration.

Office of Assessment, Ohio Department of Education, July 2008

Table 2 – Percentage of students at or above the proficient standard in May 2008

	Grade					
	Third	Fourth	Fifth	Sixth	Seventh	Eighth
Reading	74 %	81 %	72 %	80 %	77 %	79 %
Mathematics	79 %	74 %	61 %	76 %	68 %	73 %
Writing	-	82 %	-	-	86 %	-
Science	-	-	66 %	-	-	62 %
Soc. Studies	-	-	64 %	-	-	53 %

Note: Grade three Reading Test data are for the May 2008 administration only; October 2007 administration data are not included. Blank cells indicate that a grade cohort was not tested in that subject.

TEST RESULTS BY RACE/ETHNICITY

Table 3 shows the percent of students who scored at proficient or above on each test disaggregated by ethnicity.

Table 3 – Ohio Achievement Tests, May 2008 Administration
Percentage of students at or above proficient level by race/ethnicity

		Grade					
		Third	Fourth	Fifth	Sixth	Seventh	Eighth
Reading	African-Amer.	52 %	58 %	44 %	58 %	53 %	58 %
	Asian	84 %	90 %	86 %	90 %	87 %	90 %
	Hispanic	59 %	68 %	58 %	68 %	60 %	65 %
	White	79 %	86 %	79 %	85 %	83 %	84 %
Mathematics	African-Amer.	52 %	48 %	31 %	48 %	37 %	44 %
	Asian	89 %	88 %	82 %	92 %	88 %	90 %
	Hispanic	63 %	59 %	43 %	61 %	51 %	57 %
	White	85 %	81%	68 %	83 %	75 %	79 %
Writing	African-Amer.	-	66 %	-	-	70 %	-
	Asian	-	92 %	-	-	93 %	-
	Hispanic	-	73 %	-	-	76 %	-
	White	-	85 %	-	-	89 %	-
Science	African-Amer.	-	-	32 %	-	-	27 %
	Asian	-	-	82 %	-	-	80 %
	Hispanic	-	-	46 %	-	-	41 %
	White	-	-	74 %	-	-	70 %
Soc. Studies	African-Amer.	-	-	30 %	-	-	22 %
	Asian	-	-	79 %	-	-	76 %
	Hispanic	-	-	44 %	-	-	33 %
	White	-	-	72 %	-	-	60 %

Note: Blank cells indicate that a grade cohort was not tested in a subject. Table includes data for both regular and accelerated testing.

TEST RESULTS BY GENDER

Table 4 shows the percent of students who scored at proficient or above on each test disaggregated by gender.

Table 4 – Ohio Achievement Tests, May 2008 Administration
Percentage of students at or above proficient level by gender

		Grade					
		Third	Fourth	Fifth	Sixth	Seventh	Eighth
Reading	Male	71 %	80 %	70 %	75 %	73 %	75 %
	Female	77 %	82 %	75 %	84 %	81 %	83 %
Mathematics	Male	79 %	74 %	61 %	76 %	68 %	72 %
	Female	78 %	74 %	61 %	76 %	68 %	73 %
Writing	Male	-	76 %	-	-	80 %	-
	Female	-	87 %	-	-	91 %	-
Science	Male	-	-	66 %	-	-	63 %
	Female	-	-	65 %	-	-	60 %
Soc. Studies	Male	-	-	65 %	-	-	54 %
	Female	-	-	63 %	-	-	51 %

Note: Blank cells indicate that a grade cohort was not tested in that subject. Table includes data for both regular and accelerated testing.

Many documents and materials for the Ohio Achievement Tests, such as manuals, interpretive guides, cut scores, can be found on the internet at http://www.ohiodocs.org/. You also can find additional information for the achievement tests at the ODE assessment Web site at http://www.ode.state.oh.us .

HIGHLIGHTS
OHIO GRADUATION TEST PRELIMINARY RESULTS
MARCH 2008 TEST ADMINISTRATION

The Ohio Graduation Tests (OGT) superseded the Ninth-Grade Proficiency Tests as a high school graduation requirement for the classes of 2007 and beyond. The tests were developed in compliance with the requirements of Ohio Senate Bill 1, Ohio House Bill 3, and the Federal *No Child Left Behind* Act.

The tests were administered during the two weeks beginning Monday, March 10, 2008, to tenth-graders in Ohio public schools, community schools and chartered non-public schools. Eleventh-graders, twelfth-graders, and members of earlier classes who had not achieved proficient scores on one or more tests also participated in the OGT.

The performance standards for the OGT were adopted by the Ohio Board of Education based on the recommendations of Ohio educators, parents and community members. The standards for the reading and mathematics tests were set after the March 2004 administration, and the standards for the remaining tests were set after the March 2005 administration. Consistent standards for later forms of the tests are maintained through a statistical process called equating. Students must demonstrate performance at the proficient level or above in all five subject areas to meet graduation requirements. Members of the classes of 2007 and beyond may also meet graduation requirements by achieving a proficient score on four of the five tests and meeting a series of alternative criteria. See Ohio Revised Code 3313.615, or Appendix O of the testing rules book, for additional information.

The highlights are based on the preliminary results of the March 2008 test administration. Schools and districts have not verified those results. The final figures may differ due to appeals, late scoring and other changes. Please visit the ODE Assessment Web site at www.ode.state.oh.us for additional information.

NUMBER OF STUDENTS TESTED

Table 1 shows the total number of tenth-grade students that took the OGT in March 2008 by subject and school classification. Community school students are included in the public totals.

Table 1 – Number of tenth-grade students tested

	Reading	Mathematics	Writing	Science	Social Studies	All five tests
Public	134,682	135,440	134,153	135,562	134,974	131,954
Non-Public	13,335	13,359	13,349	13,347	13,293	13,193
Total	148,017	148,799	147,502	148,909	148,267	145,147

Ohio Department of Education
June 2008

SCORE RANGES FOR PERFORMANCE LEVELS

Table 2 provides the raw and scaled scores associated with each of the five performance levels on each test for the March 2008 administration.

Table 2 – Score ranges for all subjects and all performance levels

Subject	Performance Level	Raw Score	Scaled Score
Reading	Advanced	38.5 – 48.0	448 – 552
	Accelerated	32.0 – 38.0	429 – 447
	Proficient	20.5 – 31.5	400 – 428
	Basic	14.5 – 20.0	383 – 399
	Limited	0.0 – 14.0	258 – 382
Mathematics	Advanced	35.5 – 46.0	444 – 560
	Accelerated	29.5 – 35.0	425 – 443
	Proficient	20.0 – 29.0	400 – 424
	Basic	14.5 – 19.5	384 – 399
	Limited	0.0 – 14.0	251 – 383
Writing	Advanced	40.5 – 48.0	476 – 630
	Accelerated	34.0 – 40.0	430 – 475
	Proficient	26.0 – 33.5	400 – 429
	Basic	19.0 – 25.5	378 – 399
	Limited	0.0 – 18.5	265 – 377
Science	Advanced	36.5 – 48.0	445 – 590
	Accelerated	31.0 – 36.0	425 – 444
	Proficient	22.5 – 30.5	400 – 424
	Basic	13.5 – 22.0	371 – 399
	Limited	0.0 – 13.0	216 – 370
Social Studies	Advanced	36.0 – 48.0	446 – 580
	Accelerated	31.0 – 35.5	429 – 445
	Proficient	21.5 – 30.5	400 – 428
	Basic	16.0 – 21.0	382 – 399
	Limited	0.0 – 15.5	225 – 381

Ohio Department of Education
June 2008

PRELIMINARY TEST RESULTS FOR PUBLIC SCHOOL STUDENTS

Table 3 presents a summary of tenth-grade student performance on the March 2008 OGT. Students with Individualized Education Plans (IEP) and/or Limited English Proficiency (LEP) are included in the figures. Nearly two thirds (65.0%) of public tenth graders who attempted all five tests achieved a result of proficient or above on all five tests. Community school students are included in the public school totals.

Table 3 – Results of the March 2008 OGT administration for public school students

Reading				
Performance Level		Number	Percent	
Proficient or above:	Advanced	24,078	17.9	85.1
	Accelerated	43,068	32.0	
	Proficient	47,427	35.2	
Below proficient:	Basic	11,282	8.4	14.9
	Limited	8,827	6.6	

Mathematics				
Performance Level		Number	Percent	
Proficient or above:	Advanced	45,873	33.9	79.0
	Accelerated	28,108	20.8	
	Proficient	32,969	24.3	
Below proficient:	Basic	14,034	10.4	21.0
	Limited	14,456	10.7	

Writing				
Performance Level		Number	Percent	
Proficient or above:	Advanced	3,105	2.3	84.9
	Accelerated	56,697	42.3	
	Proficient	54,043	40.3	
Below proficient:	Basic	14,632	10.9	15.1
	Limited	5,676	4.2	

Science				
Performance Level		Number	Percent	
Proficient or above:	Advanced	31,144	23.0	72.6
	Accelerated	29,023	21.4	
	Proficient	38,304	28.3	
Below proficient:	Basic	26,459	19.5	27.4
	Limited	10.632	7.8	

Ohio Department of Education
June 2008

Table 3 (public school students, continued)

Social Studies				
Performance Level		Number	Percent	
Proficient or above:	Advanced	39,071	28.9	78.4
	Accelerated	27,243	20.2	
	Proficient	39,484	29.3	
Below proficient:	Basic	14,813	11.0	21.6
	Limited	14,363	10.6	

Note: Percents may not add up to 100 percent due to rounding.

Table 4 summarizes results for each gender and ethnic group.

Table 4 – Results disaggregated by gender and ethnicity for public school students

Reading			
	Total Tested	Total Proficient	Percent Proficient
Grand Total	134,682	114,573	85.1
Male	67,959	55,778	82.1
Female	66,346	58,571	88.3
American Indian	200	156	78.0
Asian/Pacific Isl.	1,650	1,504	91.2
African American	20,062	13,530	67.4
Hispanic	2,749	2,031	73.9
White	106,031	94,245	88.9
Multi-Racial	3,008	2,492	82.8
Other	133	86	64.7

Mathematics			
	Total Tested	Total Proficient	Percent Proficient
Grand Total	135,440	106,950	79.0
Male	68,219	53,940	79.1
Female	66,835	52,830	79.0
American Indian	201	152	75.6
Asian/Pacific Isl.	1,666	1,530	91.8
African American	20,484	10,675	52.1
Hispanic	2,793	1,843	66.0
White	106,267	90,008	84.7
Multi-Racial	3,034	2,227	73.4
Other	134	70	52.2

Table 4 (public school students, continued)

Writing			
	Total Tested	Total Proficient	Percent Proficient
Grand Total	134,153	113,845	84.9
Male	67,728	53,788	79.4
Female	66,058	59,840	90.6
American Indian	198	160	80.8
Asian/Pacific Isl.	1,650	1,488	90.2
African American	19,809	13,650	68.9
Hispanic	2,730	2,000	73.3
White	105,821	93,475	88.3
Multi-Racial	2,987	2,459	82.3
Other	126	81	64.3

Science			
	Total Tested	Total Proficient	Percent Proficient
Grand Total	135,562	98,471	72.6
Male	68,231	50,781	74.4
Female	66,951	47,546	71.0
American Indian	199	133	66.8
Asian/Pacific Isl.	1,663	1,379	82.9
African American	20,527	8,368	40.8
Hispanic	2,792	1,554	55.7
White	106,363	84,578	79.5
Multi-Racial	3,043	2,039	67.0
Other	135	58	43.0

Social Studies			
	Total Tested	Total Proficient	Percent Proficient
Grand Total	134,974	105,798	78.4
Male	67,978	53,124	78.1
Female	66,629	52,511	78.8
American Indian	198	144	72.7
Asian/Pacific Isl.	1,661	1,476	88.9
African American	20,180	11,652	57.7
Hispanic	2,782	1,843	66.2
White	106,154	87,880	82.8
Multi-Racial	3,030	2,293	75.7
Other	133	74	55.6

Note: Grand totals include students for whom gender information was not available, so they are slightly higher than the sum of male and female students. Numbers and percentages of students achieving proficient scores include those who were accelerated or advanced.

Ohio Department of Education
June 2008

PRELIMINARY TEST RESULTS FOR CHARTERED NON-PUBLIC SCHOOL STUDENTS

Table 5 presents a summary of tenth-grade student performance on the March 2008 OGT. Students with Individualized Education Plans (IEP) and/or Limited English Proficiency (LEP) are included in the figures. Approximately 86.3% of non-public tenth graders who attempted all five tests achieved a result of proficient or above on all five tests.

Table 5 – Results of the March 2008 OGT administration for non-public students

Reading				
Performance Level		Number	Percent	
Proficient or above:	Advanced	4,744	35.6	97.7
	Accelerated	5,548	41.6	
	Proficient	2,740	20.5	
Below proficient:	Basic	207	1.6	2.3
	Limited	96	0.7	

Mathematics				
Performance Level		Number	Percent	
Proficient or above:	Advanced	6,681	50.0	93.2
	Accelerated	3,239	24.2	
	Proficient	2,526	18.9	
Below proficient:	Basic	608	4.6	6.8
	Limited	305	2.3	

Writing				
Performance Level		Number	Percent	
Proficient or above:	Advanced	708	5.3	97.6
	Accelerated	9,050	67.8	
	Proficient	3,268	24.5	
Below proficient:	Basic	250	1.9	2.4
	Limited	73	0.5	

Science				
Performance Level		Number	Percent	
Proficient or above:	Advanced	4,685	35.1	90.6
	Accelerated	3,953	29.6	
	Proficient	3,454	25.9	
Below proficient:	Basic	1,072	8.0	9.4
	Limited	183	1.4	

Ohio Department of Education
June 2008

Table 5 (non-public students, continued)

Social Studies				
Performance Level		Number	Percent	
Proficient or above:	Advanced	5,753	43.3	94.2
	Accelerated	3,465	26.1	
	Proficient	3,299	24.8	
Below proficient:	Basic	547	4.1	5.8
	Limited	229	1.7	

Note: Percents may not add up to 100 percent due to rounding.

Table 6 summarizes results for each gender and ethnic group.

Table 6 – Results disaggregated by gender and ethnicity for non-public students

Reading			
	Number Tested	Number Proficient	Percent Proficient
Grand Total	13,335	13,032	97.7
Male	6,692	6,490	97.0
Female	6,562	6,467	98.6
American Indian	37	37	100.0
Asian/Pacific Isl.	283	266	94.0
African American	1,144	1,042	91.1
Hispanic	244	237	97.1
White	10,764	10,613	98.6
Multi-Racial	336	323	96.1
Other	150	146	97.3

Mathematics			
	Total Tested	Total Proficient	Percent Proficient
Grand Total	13,359	12,446	93.2
Male	6,710	6,313	94.1
Female	6,568	6,061	92.3
American Indian	37	36	97.3
Asian/Pacific Isl.	284	278	97.9
African American	1,148	841	73.3
Hispanic	243	220	90.5
White	10,780	10,287	95.4
Multi-Racial	337	298	88.4
Other	150	137	91.3

Table 6 (non-public students, continued)

Writing			
	Total Tested	Total Proficient	Percent Proficient
Grand Total	13,349	13,026	97.6
Male	6,703	6,458	96.3
Female	6,563	6,490	98.9
American Indian	37	33	89.2
Asian/Pacific Isl.	284	267	94.0
African American	1,145	1,042	91.0
Hispanic	240	234	97.5
White	10,777	10,607	98.4
Multi-Racial	336	326	97.0
Other	150	146	97.3

Science			
	Total Tested	Total Proficient	Percent Proficient
Grand Total	13,347	12,092	90.6
Male	6,697	6,165	92.1
Female	6,566	5,851	89.1
American Indian	37	33	89.2
Asian/Pacific Isl.	282	253	89.7
African American	1,147	769	67.0
Hispanic	241	204	84.6
White	10,778	10,066	93.4
Multi-Racial	336	291	86.6
Other	147	134	91.2

Social Studies			
	Total Tested	Total Proficient	Percent Proficient
Grand Total	13,293	12,517	94.2
Male	6,676	6,306	94.5
Female	6,538	6,140	93.9
American Indian	37	37	100.0
Asian/Pacific Isl.	270	248	91.9
African American	1,142	932	81.6
Hispanic	243	226	93.0
White	10,740	10,281	95.7
Multi-Racial	336	300	89.3
Other	148	139	93.9

Note: Grand totals include students for whom gender information was not available, so they are slightly higher than the sum of male and female students. Numbers and percentages of students achieving proficient scores include those who were accelerated or advanced.

Ohio Department of Education
June 2008

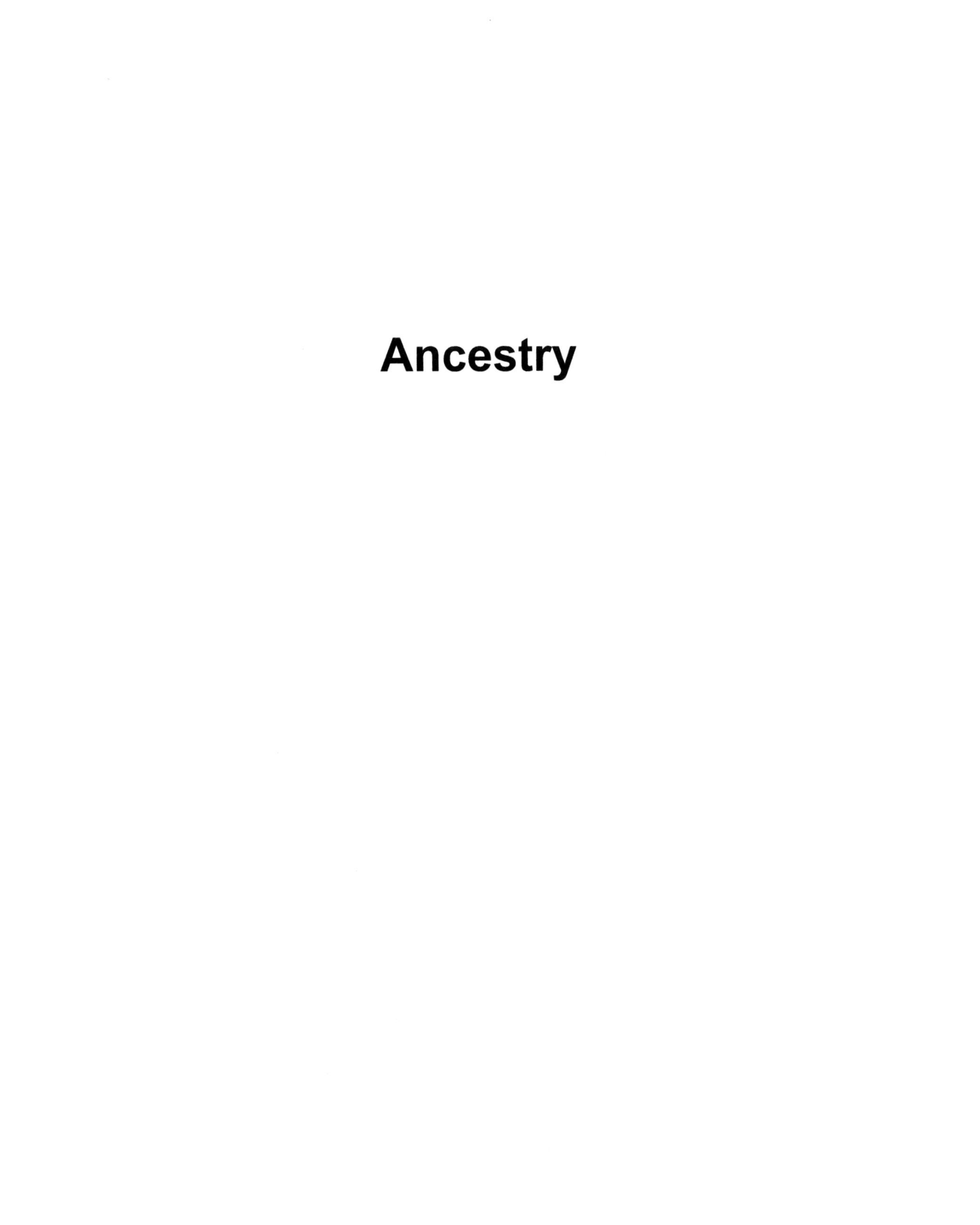

Ancestry

Acadian/Cajun

Top 10 Places Sorted by Number
Based on all places, regardless of population

Place	Number	%
Cincinnati (city) Hamilton County	60	0.02
Columbus (city) Franklin County	41	0.01
Loveland (city) Hamilton County	29	0.24
Mansfield (city) Richland County	27	0.05
Barberton (city) Summit County	23	0.08
Beavercreek (city) Greene County	22	0.06
Hamilton (city) Butler County	20	0.03
Norwood (city) Hamilton County	15	0.07
Toledo (city) Lucas County	12	0.00
Chardon (village) Geauga County	11	0.21

Top 10 Places Sorted by Percent
Based on all places, regardless of population

Place	Number	%
Pioneer (village) Williams County	5	0.34
Loveland (city) Hamilton County	29	0.24
Chardon (village) Geauga County	11	0.21
Luckey (village) Wood County	2	0.20
Waynesville (village) Warren County	3	0.11
Wapakoneta (city) Auglaize County	9	0.10
Cortland (city) Trumbull County	7	0.10
New Carlisle (city) Clark County	6	0.10
Sebring (village) Mahoning County	5	0.10
Barberton (city) Summit County	23	0.08

Top 10 Places Sorted by Percent
Based on places with populations of 10,000 or more

Place	Number	%
Loveland (city) Hamilton County	29	0.24
Barberton (city) Summit County	23	0.08
Norwood (city) Hamilton County	15	0.07
Beavercreek (city) Greene County	22	0.06
Steubenville (city) Jefferson County	11	0.06
Mansfield (city) Richland County	27	0.05
Vandalia (city) Montgomery County	8	0.05
Shiloh (cdp) Montgomery County	6	0.05
Lebanon (city) Warren County	7	0.04
Mount Vernon (city) Knox County	6	0.04

Afghan

Top 10 Places Sorted by Number
Based on all places, regardless of population

Place	Number	%
Columbus (city) Franklin County	98	0.01
Upper Arlington (city) Franklin County	26	0.08
Cleveland (city) Cuyahoga County	18	0.00
Canton (city) Stark County	12	0.01
Mansfield (city) Richland County	7	0.01
Lakewood (city) Cuyahoga County	6	0.01
Cincinnati (city) Hamilton County	5	0.00
Turpin Hills (cdp) Hamilton County	4	0.08

Top 10 Places Sorted by Percent
Based on all places, regardless of population

Place	Number	%
Upper Arlington (city) Franklin County	26	0.08
Turpin Hills (cdp) Hamilton County	4	0.08
Columbus (city) Franklin County	98	0.01
Canton (city) Stark County	12	0.01
Mansfield (city) Richland County	7	0.01
Lakewood (city) Cuyahoga County	6	0.01
Cleveland (city) Cuyahoga County	18	0.00
Cincinnati (city) Hamilton County	5	0.00

Top 10 Places Sorted by Percent
Based on places with populations of 10,000 or more

Place	Number	%
Upper Arlington (city) Franklin County	26	0.08
Columbus (city) Franklin County	98	0.01
Canton (city) Stark County	12	0.01
Mansfield (city) Richland County	7	0.01
Lakewood (city) Cuyahoga County	6	0.01
Cleveland (city) Cuyahoga County	18	0.00
Cincinnati (city) Hamilton County	5	0.00

African American/Black

Top 10 Places Sorted by Number
Based on all places, regardless of population

Place	Number	%
Cleveland (city) Cuyahoga County	249,192	52.09
Columbus (city) Franklin County	185,173	26.03
Cincinnati (city) Hamilton County	145,615	43.95
Toledo (city) Lucas County	77,765	24.80
Dayton (city) Montgomery County	73,552	44.26
Akron (city) Summit County	64,530	29.73
Youngstown (city) Mahoning County	37,301	45.47
East Cleveland (city) Cuyahoga County	25,752	94.62
Cleveland Heights (city) Cuyahoga County	21,649	43.33
Canton (city) Stark County	18,537	22.94

Top 10 Places Sorted by Percent
Based on all places, regardless of population

Place	Number	%
Lincoln Heights (village) Hamilton County	4,058	98.66
East Cleveland (city) Cuyahoga County	25,752	94.62
Warrensville Heights (city) Cuyahoga County	13,863	91.75
Wilberforce (cdp) Greene County	1,391	88.09
North Randall (village) Cuyahoga County	668	73.73
Woodlawn (village) Hamilton County	1,951	69.28
Bedford Heights (city) Cuyahoga County	7,855	69.05
Highland Hills (village) Cuyahoga County	1,090	67.37
Golf Manor (village) Hamilton County	2,578	64.47
Trotwood (city) Montgomery County	16,405	59.83

Top 10 Places Sorted by Percent
Based on places with populations of 10,000 or more

Place	Number	%
East Cleveland (city) Cuyahoga County	25,752	94.62
Warrensville Heights (city) Cuyahoga County	13,863	91.75
Bedford Heights (city) Cuyahoga County	7,855	69.05
Trotwood (city) Montgomery County	16,405	59.83
Forest Park (city) Hamilton County	11,269	57.90
Cleveland (city) Cuyahoga County	249,192	52.09
Youngstown (city) Mahoning County	37,301	45.47
Maple Heights (city) Cuyahoga County	11,879	45.42
Dayton (city) Montgomery County	73,552	44.26
Cincinnati (city) Hamilton County	145,615	43.95

African American/Black: Not Hispanic

Top 10 Places Sorted by Number
Based on all places, regardless of population

Place	Number	%
Cleveland (city) Cuyahoga County	245,890	51.40
Columbus (city) Franklin County	183,224	25.75
Cincinnati (city) Hamilton County	144,770	43.70
Toledo (city) Lucas County	76,563	24.41
Dayton (city) Montgomery County	73,073	43.97
Akron (city) Summit County	64,073	29.52
Youngstown (city) Mahoning County	36,561	44.57
East Cleveland (city) Cuyahoga County	25,596	94.04
Cleveland Heights (city) Cuyahoga County	21,460	42.96
Canton (city) Stark County	18,353	22.71

Top 10 Places Sorted by Percent
Based on all places, regardless of population

Place	Number	%
Lincoln Heights (village) Hamilton County	4,043	98.30
East Cleveland (city) Cuyahoga County	25,596	94.04
Warrensville Heights (city) Cuyahoga County	13,799	91.33
Wilberforce (cdp) Greene County	1,376	87.14
North Randall (village) Cuyahoga County	663	73.18
Woodlawn (village) Hamilton County	1,945	69.07
Bedford Heights (city) Cuyahoga County	7,793	68.51
Highland Hills (village) Cuyahoga County	1,085	67.06
Golf Manor (village) Hamilton County	2,567	64.19
Trotwood (city) Montgomery County	16,342	59.60

Top 10 Places Sorted by Percent
Based on places with populations of 10,000 or more

Place	Number	%
East Cleveland (city) Cuyahoga County	25,596	94.04
Warrensville Heights (city) Cuyahoga County	13,799	91.33
Bedford Heights (city) Cuyahoga County	7,793	68.51
Trotwood (city) Montgomery County	16,342	59.60
Forest Park (city) Hamilton County	11,216	57.63
Cleveland (city) Cuyahoga County	245,890	51.40
Maple Heights (city) Cuyahoga County	11,798	45.11
Youngstown (city) Mahoning County	36,561	44.57
Dayton (city) Montgomery County	73,073	43.97
Cincinnati (city) Hamilton County	144,770	43.70

African American/Black: Hispanic

Top 10 Places Sorted by Number
Based on all places, regardless of population

Place	Number	%
Cleveland (city) Cuyahoga County	3,302	0.69
Columbus (city) Franklin County	1,949	0.27
Toledo (city) Lucas County	1,202	0.38
Lorain (city) Lorain County	1,039	1.51
Cincinnati (city) Hamilton County	845	0.26
Youngstown (city) Mahoning County	740	0.90
Dayton (city) Montgomery County	479	0.29
Akron (city) Summit County	457	0.21
Cleveland Heights (city) Cuyahoga County	189	0.38
Elyria (city) Lorain County	185	0.33

Top 10 Places Sorted by Percent
Based on all places, regardless of population

Place	Number	%
Linndale (village) Cuyahoga County	4	3.42
Lorain (city) Lorain County	1,039	1.51
Van Buren (village) Hancock County	4	1.28
Jeromesville (village) Ashland County	6	1.26
Latty (village) Paulding County	2	1.00
Wilberforce (cdp) Greene County	15	0.95
Belmont (village) Belmont County	5	0.94
Bloomingburg (village) Fayette County	8	0.92
Youngstown (city) Mahoning County	740	0.90
Campbell (city) Mahoning County	74	0.78

Top 10 Places Sorted by Percent
Based on places with populations of 10,000 or more

Place	Number	%
Lorain (city) Lorain County	1,039	1.51
Youngstown (city) Mahoning County	740	0.90
Cleveland (city) Cuyahoga County	3,302	0.69
East Cleveland (city) Cuyahoga County	156	0.57
Painesville (city) Lake County	97	0.55
Bedford Heights (city) Cuyahoga County	62	0.55
Warrensville Heights (city) Cuyahoga County	64	0.42
Fremont (city) Sandusky County	72	0.41
Defiance (city) Defiance County	65	0.39
Toledo (city) Lucas County	1,202	0.38

Notes: (cdp) census designated place; Refer to the User's Guide in the front of the book for more detailed information.

African, sub-Saharan

Top 10 Places Sorted by Number

Based on all places, regardless of population

Place	Number	%
Columbus (city) Franklin County	15,914	2.24
Cincinnati (city) Hamilton County	7,196	2.18
Cleveland (city) Cuyahoga County	6,075	1.27
Akron (city) Summit County	3,687	1.70
Toledo (city) Lucas County	2,947	0.94
Dayton (city) Montgomery County	2,179	1.31
Youngstown (city) Mahoning County	1,031	1.26
Canton (city) Stark County	978	1.21
Trotwood (city) Montgomery County	638	2.32
Mansfield (city) Richland County	613	1.24

Top 10 Places Sorted by Percent

Based on all places, regardless of population

Place	Number	%
Wilberforce (cdp) Greene County	89	6.24
Lockland (village) Hamilton County	134	3.61
North Randall (village) Cuyahoga County	33	3.61
Forest Park (city) Hamilton County	539	2.78
Whitehall (city) Franklin County	514	2.67
Golf Manor (village) Hamilton County	95	2.38
Warrensville Heights (city) Cuyahoga County	363	2.36
Trotwood (city) Montgomery County	638	2.32
Columbus (city) Franklin County	15,914	2.24
North Robinson (village) Crawford County	5	2.23

Top 10 Places Sorted by Percent

Based on places with populations of 10,000 or more

Place	Number	%
Forest Park (city) Hamilton County	539	2.78
Whitehall (city) Franklin County	514	2.67
Warrensville Heights (city) Cuyahoga County	363	2.36
Trotwood (city) Montgomery County	638	2.32
Columbus (city) Franklin County	15,914	2.24
Cincinnati (city) Hamilton County	7,196	2.18
Akron (city) Summit County	3,687	1.70
Springdale (city) Hamilton County	178	1.68
Sandusky (city) Erie County	447	1.60
Shiloh (cdp) Montgomery County	178	1.58

African, Subsaharan: African

Top 10 Places Sorted by Number

Based on all places, regardless of population

Place	Number	%
Columbus (city) Franklin County	8,924	1.25
Cincinnati (city) Hamilton County	6,339	1.92
Cleveland (city) Cuyahoga County	5,696	1.19
Akron (city) Summit County	3,525	1.62
Toledo (city) Lucas County	2,668	0.85
Dayton (city) Montgomery County	1,766	1.06
Youngstown (city) Mahoning County	960	1.17
Canton (city) Stark County	914	1.13
Lima (city) Allen County	575	1.43
Mansfield (city) Richland County	543	1.10

Top 10 Places Sorted by Percent

Based on all places, regardless of population

Place	Number	%
Wilberforce (cdp) Greene County	57	4.00
North Randall (village) Cuyahoga County	27	2.95
Golf Manor (village) Hamilton County	95	2.38
North Robinson (village) Crawford County	5	2.23
Warrensville Heights (city) Cuyahoga County	329	2.13
Cincinnati (city) Hamilton County	6,339	1.92
Sugar Bush Knolls (village) Portage County	4	1.90
Athalia (village) Lawrence County	6	1.84
Bainbridge (cdp) Geauga County	63	1.81
Fort McKinley (cdp) Montgomery County	68	1.76

Top 10 Places Sorted by Percent

Based on places with populations of 10,000 or more

Place	Number	%
Warrensville Heights (city) Cuyahoga County	329	2.13
Cincinnati (city) Hamilton County	6,339	1.92
Trotwood (city) Montgomery County	478	1.74
Akron (city) Summit County	3,525	1.62
Sandusky (city) Erie County	447	1.60
Forest Park (city) Hamilton County	299	1.54
Springdale (city) Hamilton County	158	1.49
Lima (city) Allen County	575	1.43
Shiloh (cdp) Montgomery County	142	1.26
Columbus (city) Franklin County	8,924	1.25

African, Subsaharan: Cape Verdean

Top 10 Places Sorted by Number

Based on all places, regardless of population

Place	Number	%
Columbus (city) Franklin County	59	0.01
Cincinnati (city) Hamilton County	27	0.01
Cleveland (city) Cuyahoga County	25	0.01
Alliance (city) Stark County	22	0.09
Athens (city) Athens County	16	0.08
Canton (city) Stark County	15	0.02
Bowling Green (city) Wood County	12	0.04
Pleasant Run Farm (cdp) Hamilton County	11	0.24
Euclid (city) Cuyahoga County	11	0.02
Akron (city) Summit County	11	0.01

Top 10 Places Sorted by Percent

Based on all places, regardless of population

Place	Number	%
Pleasant Run Farm (cdp) Hamilton County	11	0.24
East Canton (village) Stark County	3	0.18
Alliance (city) Stark County	22	0.09
Athens (city) Athens County	16	0.08
Lincoln Village (cdp) Franklin County	7	0.07
Bedford (city) Cuyahoga County	8	0.06
Bowling Green (city) Wood County	12	0.04
Troy (city) Miami County	9	0.04
Struthers (city) Mahoning County	4	0.03
Canton (city) Stark County	15	0.02

Top 10 Places Sorted by Percent

Based on places with populations of 10,000 or more

Place	Number	%
Alliance (city) Stark County	22	0.09
Athens (city) Athens County	16	0.08
Bedford (city) Cuyahoga County	8	0.06
Bowling Green (city) Wood County	12	0.04
Troy (city) Miami County	9	0.04
Struthers (city) Mahoning County	4	0.03
Canton (city) Stark County	15	0.02
Euclid (city) Cuyahoga County	11	0.02
Cleveland Heights (city) Cuyahoga County	9	0.02
Columbus (city) Franklin County	59	0.01

African, Subsaharan: Ethiopian

Top 10 Places Sorted by Number

Based on all places, regardless of population

Place	Number	%
Columbus (city) Franklin County	1,241	0.17
Whitehall (city) Franklin County	162	0.84
Cincinnati (city) Hamilton County	143	0.04
Dayton (city) Montgomery County	65	0.04
Cleveland (city) Cuyahoga County	43	0.01
Mansfield (city) Richland County	35	0.07
University Heights (city) Cuyahoga County	33	0.23
Grandview Heights (city) Franklin County	20	0.30
Oberlin (city) Lorain County	19	0.23
Shaker Heights (city) Cuyahoga County	18	0.06

Top 10 Places Sorted by Percent

Based on all places, regardless of population

Place	Number	%
Whitehall (city) Franklin County	162	0.84
Yellow Springs (village) Greene County	12	0.33
Grandview Heights (city) Franklin County	20	0.30
Sardinia (village) Brown County	2	0.24
University Heights (city) Cuyahoga County	33	0.23
Oberlin (city) Lorain County	19	0.23
North Randall (village) Cuyahoga County	2	0.22
Columbus (city) Franklin County	1,241	0.17
Mount Healthy Heights (cdp) Hamilton County	5	0.14
Aurora (city) Portage County	16	0.1[illegible]

Top 10 Places Sorted by Percent

Based on places with populations of 10,000 or more

Place	Number	%
Whitehall (city) Franklin County	162	0.84
University Heights (city) Cuyahoga County	33	0.23
Columbus (city) Franklin County	1,241	0.17
Aurora (city) Portage County	16	0.12
Shiloh (cdp) Montgomery County	14	0.12
Mayfield Heights (city) Cuyahoga County	15	0.08
Mansfield (city) Richland County	35	0.07
Shaker Heights (city) Cuyahoga County	18	0.06
Cincinnati (city) Hamilton County	143	0.04
Dayton (city) Montgomery County	65	0.04

African, Subsaharan: Ghanian

Top 10 Places Sorted by Number

Based on all places, regardless of population

Place	Number	%
Columbus (city) Franklin County	731	0.10
Cincinnati (city) Hamilton County	54	0.02
Dayton (city) Montgomery County	43	0.03
Akron (city) Summit County	39	0.02
Fairfield (city) Butler County	28	0.07
Cleveland (city) Cuyahoga County	28	0.01
Fairlawn (city) Summit County	26	0.35
Cleveland Heights (city) Cuyahoga County	26	0.05
Wooster (city) Wayne County	25	0.10
Moreland Hills (village) Cuyahoga County	17	0.51

Top 10 Places Sorted by Percent

Based on all places, regardless of population

Place	Number	%
Berkey (village) Lucas County	3	1.15
Moreland Hills (village) Cuyahoga County	17	0.51
Fairlawn (city) Summit County	26	0.35
Columbus (city) Franklin County	731	0.10
Wooster (city) Wayne County	25	0.10
Wyoming (city) Hamilton County	8	0.10
Fairfield (city) Butler County	28	0.07
Blacklick Estates (cdp) Franklin County	7	0.07
Cleveland Heights (city) Cuyahoga County	26	0.05
Shaker Heights (city) Cuyahoga County	12	0.04

Top 10 Places Sorted by Percent

Based on places with populations of 10,000 or more

Place	Number	%
Columbus (city) Franklin County	731	0.10
Wooster (city) Wayne County	25	0.10
Fairfield (city) Butler County	28	0.07
Cleveland Heights (city) Cuyahoga County	26	0.05
Shaker Heights (city) Cuyahoga County	12	0.04
Bedford (city) Cuyahoga County	6	0.04
Dayton (city) Montgomery County	43	0.03
Mansfield (city) Richland County	15	0.03
North Olmsted (city) Cuyahoga County	11	0.03
Bowling Green (city) Wood County	8	0.03

Notes: (cdp) census designated place; Refer to the User's Guide in the front of the book for more detailed information.

African, Subsaharan: Kenyan

Top 10 Places Sorted by Number
Based on all places, regardless of population

Place	Number	%
Columbus (city) Franklin County	86	0.01
Cincinnati (city) Hamilton County	65	0.02
Reynoldsburg (city) Franklin County	45	0.14
Shaker Heights (city) Cuyahoga County	41	0.14
Pepper Pike (city) Cuyahoga County	31	0.51
Dayton (city) Montgomery County	23	0.01
Elyria (city) Lorain County	22	0.04
Toledo (city) Lucas County	19	0.01
Oberlin (city) Lorain County	18	0.22
Sylvania (city) Lucas County	15	0.08

Top 10 Places Sorted by Percent
Based on all places, regardless of population

Place	Number	%
Pepper Pike (city) Cuyahoga County	31	0.51
Oberlin (city) Lorain County	18	0.22
Jefferson (village) Ashtabula County	6	0.17
Reynoldsburg (city) Franklin County	45	0.14
Shaker Heights (city) Cuyahoga County	41	0.14
Ottawa Hills (village) Lucas County	5	0.11
Sylvania (city) Lucas County	15	0.08
Shiloh (cdp) Montgomery County	9	0.08
Elyria (city) Lorain County	22	0.04
Kent (city) Portage County	11	0.04

Top 10 Places Sorted by Percent
Based on places with populations of 10,000 or more

Place	Number	%
Reynoldsburg (city) Franklin County	45	0.14
Shaker Heights (city) Cuyahoga County	41	0.14
Sylvania (city) Lucas County	15	0.08
Shiloh (cdp) Montgomery County	9	0.08
Elyria (city) Lorain County	22	0.04
Kent (city) Portage County	11	0.04
Cincinnati (city) Hamilton County	65	0.02
Bowling Green (city) Wood County	6	0.02
Columbus (city) Franklin County	86	0.01
Dayton (city) Montgomery County	23	0.01

African, Subsaharan: Liberian

Top 10 Places Sorted by Number
Based on all places, regardless of population

Place	Number	%
Columbus (city) Franklin County	166	0.02
Toledo (city) Lucas County	64	0.02
Cleveland Heights (city) Cuyahoga County	52	0.10
Cleveland (city) Cuyahoga County	40	0.01
Kent (city) Portage County	37	0.13
Lakewood (city) Cuyahoga County	37	0.07
Trotwood (city) Montgomery County	27	0.10
Akron (city) Summit County	14	0.01
Warrensville Heights (city) Cuyahoga County	13	0.08
Euclid (city) Cuyahoga County	13	0.02

Top 10 Places Sorted by Percent
Based on all places, regardless of population

Place	Number	%
North Randall (village) Cuyahoga County	4	0.44
Ottawa Hills (village) Lucas County	11	0.24
Kent (city) Portage County	37	0.13
Harrison (city) Hamilton County	9	0.12
Cleveland Heights (city) Cuyahoga County	52	0.10
Trotwood (city) Montgomery County	27	0.10
Warrensville Heights (city) Cuyahoga County	13	0.08
Lakewood (city) Cuyahoga County	37	0.07
Green (city) Summit County	7	0.03
Columbus (city) Franklin County	166	0.02

Top 10 Places Sorted by Percent
Based on places with populations of 10,000 or more

Place	Number	%
Kent (city) Portage County	37	0.13
Cleveland Heights (city) Cuyahoga County	52	0.10
Trotwood (city) Montgomery County	27	0.10
Warrensville Heights (city) Cuyahoga County	13	0.08
Lakewood (city) Cuyahoga County	37	0.07
Green (city) Summit County	7	0.03
Columbus (city) Franklin County	166	0.02
Toledo (city) Lucas County	64	0.02
Euclid (city) Cuyahoga County	13	0.02
North Olmsted (city) Cuyahoga County	7	0.02

African, Subsaharan: Nigerian

Top 10 Places Sorted by Number
Based on all places, regardless of population

Place	Number	%
Columbus (city) Franklin County	813	0.11
Cincinnati (city) Hamilton County	232	0.07
Cleveland (city) Cuyahoga County	159	0.03
Dayton (city) Montgomery County	147	0.09
Toledo (city) Lucas County	135	0.04
Trotwood (city) Montgomery County	133	0.48
Forest Park (city) Hamilton County	132	0.68
University Heights (city) Cuyahoga County	93	0.66
Solon (city) Cuyahoga County	82	0.38
Youngstown (city) Mahoning County	71	0.09

Top 10 Places Sorted by Percent
Based on all places, regardless of population

Place	Number	%
Wilberforce (cdp) Greene County	22	1.54
Orange (village) Cuyahoga County	39	1.21
Ontario (village) Richland County	51	0.98
Albany (village) Athens County	7	0.85
Forest Park (city) Hamilton County	132	0.68
University Heights (city) Cuyahoga County	93	0.66
Forestville (cdp) Hamilton County	55	0.50
Trotwood (city) Montgomery County	133	0.48
Sebring (village) Mahoning County	20	0.41
The Plains (cdp) Athens County	12	0.41

Top 10 Places Sorted by Percent
Based on places with populations of 10,000 or more

Place	Number	%
Forest Park (city) Hamilton County	132	0.68
University Heights (city) Cuyahoga County	93	0.66
Forestville (cdp) Hamilton County	55	0.50
Trotwood (city) Montgomery County	133	0.48
Solon (city) Cuyahoga County	82	0.38
Sidney (city) Shelby County	63	0.31
Sharonville (city) Hamilton County	25	0.18
Sylvania (city) Lucas County	31	0.17
North College Hill (city) Hamilton County	13	0.13
Shiloh (cdp) Montgomery County	13	0.12

African, Subsaharan: Senegalese

Top 10 Places Sorted by Number
Based on all places, regardless of population

Place	Number	%
Columbus (city) Franklin County	95	0.01
Cincinnati (city) Hamilton County	26	0.01
Beachwood (city) Cuyahoga County	20	0.16
Fairborn (city) Greene County	20	0.06
Mansfield (city) Richland County	12	0.02
Wilberforce (cdp) Greene County	10	0.70
Lockland (village) Hamilton County	8	0.22
Upper Arlington (city) Franklin County	7	0.02
Cleveland (city) Cuyahoga County	5	0.00

Top 10 Places Sorted by Percent
Based on all places, regardless of population

Place	Number	%
Wilberforce (cdp) Greene County	10	0.70
Lockland (village) Hamilton County	8	0.22
Beachwood (city) Cuyahoga County	20	0.16
Fairborn (city) Greene County	20	0.06
Mansfield (city) Richland County	12	0.02
Upper Arlington (city) Franklin County	7	0.02
Columbus (city) Franklin County	95	0.01
Cincinnati (city) Hamilton County	26	0.01
Cleveland (city) Cuyahoga County	5	0.00

Top 10 Places Sorted by Percent
Based on places with populations of 10,000 or more

Place	Number	%
Beachwood (city) Cuyahoga County	20	0.16
Fairborn (city) Greene County	20	0.06
Mansfield (city) Richland County	12	0.02
Upper Arlington (city) Franklin County	7	0.02
Columbus (city) Franklin County	95	0.01
Cincinnati (city) Hamilton County	26	0.01
Cleveland (city) Cuyahoga County	5	0.00

African, Subsaharan: Sierra Leonean

Top 10 Places Sorted by Number
Based on all places, regardless of population

Place	Number	%
Columbus (city) Franklin County	88	0.01
Cincinnati (city) Hamilton County	32	0.01
Toledo (city) Lucas County	5	0.00
Willshire (village) Van Wert County	2	0.45

Top 10 Places Sorted by Percent
Based on all places, regardless of population

Place	Number	%
Willshire (village) Van Wert County	2	0.45
Columbus (city) Franklin County	88	0.01
Cincinnati (city) Hamilton County	32	0.01
Toledo (city) Lucas County	5	0.00

Top 10 Places Sorted by Percent
Based on places with populations of 10,000 or more

Place	Number	%
Columbus (city) Franklin County	88	0.01
Cincinnati (city) Hamilton County	32	0.01
Toledo (city) Lucas County	5	0.00

African, Subsaharan: Somalian

Top 10 Places Sorted by Number
Based on all places, regardless of population

Place	Number	%
Columbus (city) Franklin County	2,839	0.40
Blue Ash (city) Hamilton County	16	0.13
Toledo (city) Lucas County	12	0.00
Reynoldsburg (city) Franklin County	9	0.03
Bexley (city) Franklin County	7	0.05
Wooster (city) Wayne County	7	0.03
Urbancrest (village) Franklin County	4	0.48

Top 10 Places Sorted by Percent
Based on all places, regardless of population

Place	Number	%
Urbancrest (village) Franklin County	4	0.48
Columbus (city) Franklin County	2,839	0.40
Blue Ash (city) Hamilton County	16	0.13
Bexley (city) Franklin County	7	0.05
Reynoldsburg (city) Franklin County	9	0.03
Wooster (city) Wayne County	7	0.03
Toledo (city) Lucas County	12	0.00

Notes: (cdp) census designated place; Refer to the User's Guide in the front of the book for more detailed information.

Top 10 Places Sorted by Percent
Based on places with populations of 10,000 or more

Place	Number	%
Columbus (city) Franklin County	2,839	0.40
Blue Ash (city) Hamilton County	16	0.13
Bexley (city) Franklin County	7	0.05
Reynoldsburg (city) Franklin County	9	0.03
Wooster (city) Wayne County	7	0.03
Toledo (city) Lucas County	12	0.00

African, Subsaharan: South African

Top 10 Places Sorted by Number
Based on all places, regardless of population

Place	Number	%
Reynoldsburg (city) Franklin County	108	0.34
Beachwood (city) Cuyahoga County	55	0.45
Forest Park (city) Hamilton County	51	0.26
Columbus (city) Franklin County	50	0.01
Dublin (city) Franklin County	47	0.15
Loveland (city) Hamilton County	34	0.28
Landen (cdp) Warren County	31	0.25
Solon (city) Cuyahoga County	28	0.13
Richmond Heights (city) Cuyahoga County	27	0.25
Fostoria (city) Seneca County	27	0.19

Top 10 Places Sorted by Percent
Based on all places, regardless of population

Place	Number	%
Amelia (village) Clermont County	16	0.59
Peninsula (village) Summit County	3	0.58
Beachwood (city) Cuyahoga County	55	0.45
Moreland Hills (village) Cuyahoga County	13	0.39
Reynoldsburg (city) Franklin County	108	0.34
Loveland (city) Hamilton County	34	0.28
Turpin Hills (cdp) Hamilton County	14	0.28
Forest Park (city) Hamilton County	51	0.26
Landen (cdp) Warren County	31	0.25
Richmond Heights (city) Cuyahoga County	27	0.25

Top 10 Places Sorted by Percent
Based on places with populations of 10,000 or more

Place	Number	%
Beachwood (city) Cuyahoga County	55	0.45
Reynoldsburg (city) Franklin County	108	0.34
Loveland (city) Hamilton County	34	0.28
Forest Park (city) Hamilton County	51	0.26
Landen (cdp) Warren County	31	0.25
Richmond Heights (city) Cuyahoga County	27	0.25
Fostoria (city) Seneca County	27	0.19
Dublin (city) Franklin County	47	0.15
Solon (city) Cuyahoga County	28	0.13
Montgomery (city) Hamilton County	10	0.10

African, Subsaharan: Sudanese

Top 10 Places Sorted by Number
Based on all places, regardless of population

Place	Number	%
Whitehall (city) Franklin County	97	0.50
Brooklyn (city) Cuyahoga County	38	0.33
Cincinnati (city) Hamilton County	36	0.01
Cleveland Heights (city) Cuyahoga County	33	0.07
Xenia (city) Greene County	24	0.10
Columbus (city) Franklin County	22	0.00
Cleveland (city) Cuyahoga County	15	0.00
Euclid (city) Cuyahoga County	11	0.02
Wooster (city) Wayne County	8	0.03
Lima (city) Allen County	7	0.02

Top 10 Places Sorted by Percent
Based on all places, regardless of population

Place	Number	%
Whitehall (city) Franklin County	97	0.50
Woodmere (village) Cuyahoga County	3	0.36
Brooklyn (city) Cuyahoga County	38	0.33
Xenia (city) Greene County	24	0.10
Cleveland Heights (city) Cuyahoga County	33	0.07
Wooster (city) Wayne County	8	0.03
Euclid (city) Cuyahoga County	11	0.02
Lima (city) Allen County	7	0.02
Cincinnati (city) Hamilton County	36	0.01
Columbus (city) Franklin County	22	0.00

Top 10 Places Sorted by Percent
Based on places with populations of 10,000 or more

Place	Number	%
Whitehall (city) Franklin County	97	0.50
Brooklyn (city) Cuyahoga County	38	0.33
Xenia (city) Greene County	24	0.10
Cleveland Heights (city) Cuyahoga County	33	0.07
Wooster (city) Wayne County	8	0.03
Euclid (city) Cuyahoga County	11	0.02
Lima (city) Allen County	7	0.02
Cincinnati (city) Hamilton County	36	0.01
Columbus (city) Franklin County	22	0.00
Cleveland (city) Cuyahoga County	15	0.00

African, Subsaharan: Ugandan

Top 10 Places Sorted by Number
Based on all places, regardless of population

Place	Number	%
Cleveland Heights (city) Cuyahoga County	23	0.05
Groesbeck (cdp) Hamilton County	20	0.28
Hamilton (city) Butler County	19	0.03
Columbus (city) Franklin County	19	0.00
Cincinnati (city) Hamilton County	8	0.00
Lancaster (city) Fairfield County	7	0.02
Pepper Pike (city) Cuyahoga County	2	0.03

Top 10 Places Sorted by Percent
Based on all places, regardless of population

Place	Number	%
Groesbeck (cdp) Hamilton County	20	0.28
Cleveland Heights (city) Cuyahoga County	23	0.05
Hamilton (city) Butler County	19	0.03
Pepper Pike (city) Cuyahoga County	2	0.03
Lancaster (city) Fairfield County	7	0.02
Columbus (city) Franklin County	19	0.00
Cincinnati (city) Hamilton County	8	0.00

Top 10 Places Sorted by Percent
Based on places with populations of 10,000 or more

Place	Number	%
Cleveland Heights (city) Cuyahoga County	23	0.05
Hamilton (city) Butler County	19	0.03
Lancaster (city) Fairfield County	7	0.02
Columbus (city) Franklin County	19	0.00
Cincinnati (city) Hamilton County	8	0.00

African, Subsaharan: Zairian

Top 10 Places Sorted by Number
Based on all places, regardless of population

Place	Number	%

Top 10 Places Sorted by Percent
Based on all places, regardless of population

Place	Number	%

Top 10 Places Sorted by Percent
Based on places with populations of 10,000 or more

Place	Number	%

African, Subsaharan: Zimbabwean

Top 10 Places Sorted by Number
Based on all places, regardless of population

Place	Number	%
Columbus (city) Franklin County	82	0.01
Cincinnati (city) Hamilton County	19	0.01
Akron (city) Summit County	15	0.01
Cleveland Heights (city) Cuyahoga County	13	0.03
Kent (city) Portage County	8	0.03
Cleveland (city) Cuyahoga County	4	0.00
Waynesville (village) Warren County	2	0.08

Top 10 Places Sorted by Percent
Based on all places, regardless of population

Place	Number	%
Waynesville (village) Warren County	2	0.08
Cleveland Heights (city) Cuyahoga County	13	0.03
Kent (city) Portage County	8	0.03
Columbus (city) Franklin County	82	0.01
Cincinnati (city) Hamilton County	19	0.01
Akron (city) Summit County	15	0.01
Cleveland (city) Cuyahoga County	4	0.00

Top 10 Places Sorted by Percent
Based on places with populations of 10,000 or more

Place	Number	%
Cleveland Heights (city) Cuyahoga County	13	0.03
Kent (city) Portage County	8	0.03
Columbus (city) Franklin County	82	0.01
Cincinnati (city) Hamilton County	19	0.01
Akron (city) Summit County	15	0.01
Cleveland (city) Cuyahoga County	4	0.00

African, Subsaharan: Other

Top 10 Places Sorted by Number
Based on all places, regardless of population

Place	Number	%
Columbus (city) Franklin County	699	0.10
Cincinnati (city) Hamilton County	193	0.06
Dayton (city) Montgomery County	104	0.06
Lockland (village) Hamilton County	99	2.67
Sidney (city) Shelby County	54	0.27
Forest Park (city) Hamilton County	49	0.25
Whitehall (city) Franklin County	38	0.20
Cleveland (city) Cuyahoga County	29	0.01
Mount Carmel (cdp) Clermont County	19	0.44
Akron (city) Summit County	19	0.01

Top 10 Places Sorted by Percent
Based on all places, regardless of population

Place	Number	%
Lockland (village) Hamilton County	99	2.67
Vienna Center (cdp) Trumbull County	8	0.68
North Fork Village (cdp) Ross County	8	0.50
Mount Carmel (cdp) Clermont County	19	0.44
Mineral Ridge (cdp) Trumbull County	13	0.36

Notes: (cdp) census designated place; Refer to the User's Guide in the front of the book for more detailed information.

Place	Number	%
Sidney (city) Shelby County	54	0.27
Forest Park (city) Hamilton County	49	0.25
Moraine (city) Montgomery County	16	0.23
Oberlin (city) Lorain County	18	0.22
Whitehall (city) Franklin County	38	0.20

Top 10 Places Sorted by Percent
Based on places with populations of 10,000 or more

Place	Number	%
Sidney (city) Shelby County	54	0.27
Forest Park (city) Hamilton County	49	0.25
Whitehall (city) Franklin County	38	0.20
Springdale (city) Hamilton County	12	0.11
Columbus (city) Franklin County	699	0.10
Fremont (city) Sandusky County	17	0.10
Warrensville Heights (city) Cuyahoga County	12	0.08
Worthington (city) Franklin County	10	0.07
Cincinnati (city) Hamilton County	193	0.06
Dayton (city) Montgomery County	104	0.06

Alaska Native tribes, specified

Top 10 Places Sorted by Number
Based on all places, regardless of population

Place	Number	%
Columbus (city) Franklin County	44	0.01
Cleveland (city) Cuyahoga County	21	0.00
Cincinnati (city) Hamilton County	17	0.01
Akron (city) Summit County	14	0.01
Norwood (city) Hamilton County	13	0.06
Toledo (city) Lucas County	11	0.00
Parma (city) Cuyahoga County	10	0.01
Dayton (city) Montgomery County	8	0.00
Hamilton (city) Butler County	6	0.01
Ross (cdp) Butler County	5	0.25

Top 10 Places Sorted by Percent
Based on all places, regardless of population

Place	Number	%
West Manchester (village) Preble County	2	0.46
Cheshire (village) Gallia County	1	0.45
Eldorado (village) Preble County	2	0.37
Ross (cdp) Butler County	5	0.25
Brady Lake (village) Portage County	1	0.19
Lucas (village) Richland County	1	0.16
Bratenahl (village) Cuyahoga County	2	0.15
New Carlisle (city) Clark County	5	0.09
Fayette (village) Fulton County	1	0.07
Franklin Furnace (cdp) Scioto County	1	0.07

Top 10 Places Sorted by Percent
Based on places with populations of 10,000 or more

Place	Number	%
Norwood (city) Hamilton County	13	0.06
Bellefontaine (city) Logan County	4	0.03
Avon Lake (city) Lorain County	4	0.02
Bedford (city) Cuyahoga County	3	0.02
Columbus (city) Franklin County	44	0.01
Cincinnati (city) Hamilton County	17	0.01
Akron (city) Summit County	14	0.01
Parma (city) Cuyahoga County	10	0.01
Hamilton (city) Butler County	6	0.01
Fairborn (city) Greene County	4	0.01

Alaska Native: Alaska Athabascan

Top 10 Places Sorted by Number
Based on all places, regardless of population

Place	Number	%
Columbus (city) Franklin County	10	0.00
Cincinnati (city) Hamilton County	7	0.00
New Carlisle (city) Clark County	5	0.09
Cleveland (city) Cuyahoga County	5	0.00
Toledo (city) Lucas County	5	0.00
Trotwood (city) Montgomery County	3	0.01
Troy (city) Miami County	3	0.01
Northgate (cdp) Hamilton County	2	0.02
Dublin (city) Franklin County	2	0.01
Massillon (city) Stark County	2	0.01

Top 10 Places Sorted by Percent
Based on all places, regardless of population

Place	Number	%
Brady Lake (village) Portage County	1	0.19
Lucas (village) Richland County	1	0.16
New Carlisle (city) Clark County	5	0.09
Northgate (cdp) Hamilton County	2	0.02
Ada (village) Hardin County	1	0.02
Blanchester (village) Clinton County	1	0.02
Trotwood (city) Montgomery County	3	0.01
Troy (city) Miami County	3	0.01
Dublin (city) Franklin County	2	0.01
Massillon (city) Stark County	2	0.01

Top 10 Places Sorted by Percent
Based on places with populations of 10,000 or more

Place	Number	%
Trotwood (city) Montgomery County	3	0.01
Troy (city) Miami County	3	0.01
Dublin (city) Franklin County	2	0.01
Massillon (city) Stark County	2	0.01
Portsmouth (city) Scioto County	2	0.01
Aurora (city) Portage County	1	0.01
Coshocton (city) Coshocton County	1	0.01
Fostoria (city) Seneca County	1	0.01
Reading (city) Hamilton County	1	0.01
Columbus (city) Franklin County	10	0.00

Alaska Native: Aleut

Top 10 Places Sorted by Number
Based on all places, regardless of population

Place	Number	%
Norwood (city) Hamilton County	11	0.05
Akron (city) Summit County	8	0.00
Cincinnati (city) Hamilton County	6	0.00
Columbus (city) Franklin County	6	0.00
Bellefontaine (city) Logan County	4	0.03
Toledo (city) Lucas County	4	0.00
Fairborn (city) Greene County	3	0.01
Sidney (city) Shelby County	3	0.01
Dayton (city) Montgomery County	3	0.00
Cleveland (city) Cuyahoga County	2	0.00

Top 10 Places Sorted by Percent
Based on all places, regardless of population

Place	Number	%
Franklin Furnace (cdp) Scioto County	1	0.07
Norwood (city) Hamilton County	11	0.05
Lakemore (village) Summit County	1	0.04
Bellefontaine (city) Logan County	4	0.03
West Milton (village) Miami County	1	0.02
Wright-Patterson AFB (cdp) Montgomery County	1	0.02
Fairborn (city) Greene County	3	0.01
Sidney (city) Shelby County	3	0.01
Bedford (city) Cuyahoga County	1	0.01
Marietta (city) Washington County	1	0.01

Top 10 Places Sorted by Percent
Based on places with populations of 10,000 or more

Place	Number	%
Norwood (city) Hamilton County	11	0.05
Bellefontaine (city) Logan County	4	0.03
Fairborn (city) Greene County	3	0.01
Sidney (city) Shelby County	3	0.01
Bedford (city) Cuyahoga County	1	0.01
Marietta (city) Washington County	1	0.01
Miamisburg (city) Montgomery County	1	0.01
Akron (city) Summit County	8	0.00
Cincinnati (city) Hamilton County	6	0.00
Columbus (city) Franklin County	6	0.00

Alaska Native: Eskimo

Top 10 Places Sorted by Number
Based on all places, regardless of population

Place	Number	%
Columbus (city) Franklin County	16	0.00
Cleveland (city) Cuyahoga County	11	0.00
Ross (cdp) Butler County	5	0.25
Akron (city) Summit County	5	0.00
Delphos (city) Allen County	3	0.04
Dayton (city) Montgomery County	3	0.00
Youngstown (city) Mahoning County	3	0.00
Bratenahl (village) Cuyahoga County	2	0.15
Newton Falls (village) Trumbull County	2	0.04
Bedford (city) Cuyahoga County	2	0.01

Top 10 Places Sorted by Percent
Based on all places, regardless of population

Place	Number	%
Ross (cdp) Butler County	5	0.25
Bratenahl (village) Cuyahoga County	2	0.15
Glendale (village) Hamilton County	1	0.05
South Charleston (village) Clark County	1	0.05
Delphos (city) Allen County	3	0.04
Newton Falls (village) Trumbull County	2	0.04
North Kingsville (village) Ashtabula County	1	0.04
Obetz (village) Franklin County	1	0.03
Brookville (village) Montgomery County	1	0.02
West Milton (village) Miami County	1	0.02

Top 10 Places Sorted by Percent
Based on places with populations of 10,000 or more

Place	Number	%
Bedford (city) Cuyahoga County	2	0.01
North Olmsted (city) Cuyahoga County	2	0.01
Shaker Heights (city) Cuyahoga County	2	0.01
Berea (city) Cuyahoga County	1	0.01
Dover (city) Tuscarawas County	1	0.01
Maumee (city) Lucas County	1	0.01
Willowick (city) Lake County	1	0.01
Columbus (city) Franklin County	16	0.00
Cleveland (city) Cuyahoga County	11	0.00
Akron (city) Summit County	5	0.00

Alaska Native: Tlingit-Haida

Top 10 Places Sorted by Number
Based on all places, regardless of population

Place	Number	%
Columbus (city) Franklin County	11	0.00
Parma (city) Cuyahoga County	6	0.01
Avon Lake (city) Lorain County	4	0.02
Highland Heights (city) Cuyahoga County	3	0.04
Lakewood (city) Cuyahoga County	3	0.01
Cincinnati (city) Hamilton County	3	0.00
Cleveland (city) Cuyahoga County	3	0.00
North Ridgeville (city) Lorain County	2	0.01
Elyria (city) Lorain County	2	0.00
Hamilton (city) Butler County	2	0.00

Top 10 Places Sorted by Percent
Based on all places, regardless of population

Place	Number	%
Cheshire (village) Gallia County	1	0.45
Fayette (village) Fulton County	1	0.07
Highland Heights (city) Cuyahoga County	3	0.04
Amelia (village) Clermont County	1	0.04
Yellow Springs (village) Greene County	1	0.03

Notes: (cdp) census designated place; Refer to the User's Guide in the front of the book for more detailed information.

Place	Number	%
Avon Lake (city) Lorain County	4	0.02
Ada (village) Hardin County	1	0.02
Parma (city) Cuyahoga County	6	0.01
Lakewood (city) Cuyahoga County	3	0.01
North Ridgeville (city) Lorain County	2	0.01

Top 10 Places Sorted by Percent
Based on places with populations of 10,000 or more

Place	Number	%
Avon Lake (city) Lorain County	4	0.02
Parma (city) Cuyahoga County	6	0.01
Lakewood (city) Cuyahoga County	3	0.01
North Ridgeville (city) Lorain County	2	0.01
Columbus (city) Franklin County	11	0.00
Cincinnati (city) Hamilton County	3	0.00
Cleveland (city) Cuyahoga County	3	0.00
Elyria (city) Lorain County	2	0.00
Hamilton (city) Butler County	2	0.00
Middletown (city) Butler County	2	0.00

Alaska Native: All other tribes

Top 10 Places Sorted by Number
Based on all places, regardless of population

Place	Number	%
Hamilton (city) Butler County	3	0.00
Parma (city) Cuyahoga County	3	0.00
West Manchester (village) Preble County	2	0.46
Eldorado (village) Preble County	2	0.37
Brookville (village) Montgomery County	1	0.02
Columbus (city) Franklin County	1	0.00
Grove City (city) Franklin County	1	0.00
Norwood (city) Hamilton County	1	0.00
Springfield (city) Clark County	1	0.00

Top 10 Places Sorted by Percent
Based on all places, regardless of population

Place	Number	%
West Manchester (village) Preble County	2	0.46
Eldorado (village) Preble County	2	0.37
Brookville (village) Montgomery County	1	0.02
Hamilton (city) Butler County	3	0.00
Parma (city) Cuyahoga County	3	0.00
Columbus (city) Franklin County	1	0.00
Grove City (city) Franklin County	1	0.00
Norwood (city) Hamilton County	1	0.00
Springfield (city) Clark County	1	0.00

Top 10 Places Sorted by Percent
Based on places with populations of 10,000 or more

Place	Number	%
Hamilton (city) Butler County	3	0.00
Parma (city) Cuyahoga County	3	0.00
Columbus (city) Franklin County	1	0.00
Grove City (city) Franklin County	1	0.00
Norwood (city) Hamilton County	1	0.00
Springfield (city) Clark County	1	0.00

Alaska Native tribes, not specified

Top 10 Places Sorted by Number
Based on all places, regardless of population

Place	Number	%
Dayton (city) Montgomery County	4	0.00
Toledo (city) Lucas County	4	0.00
Masury (cdp) Trumbull County	3	0.11
Monfort Heights South (cdp) Hamilton County	3	0.07
Cambridge (city) Guernsey County	3	0.03
Akron (city) Summit County	3	0.00
Portsmouth (city) Scioto County	2	0.01
Lakewood (city) Cuyahoga County	2	0.00
Mount Gilead (village) Morrow County	1	0.03
Ontario (village) Richland County	1	0.02

Top 10 Places Sorted by Percent
Based on all places, regardless of population

Place	Number	%
Masury (cdp) Trumbull County	3	0.11
Monfort Heights South (cdp) Hamilton County	3	0.07
Cambridge (city) Guernsey County	3	0.03
Mount Gilead (village) Morrow County	1	0.03
Ontario (village) Richland County	1	0.02
Portsmouth (city) Scioto County	2	0.01
Broadview Heights (city) Cuyahoga County	1	0.01
Conneaut (city) Ashtabula County	1	0.01
Grandview Heights (city) Franklin County	1	0.01
Marietta (city) Washington County	1	0.01

Top 10 Places Sorted by Percent
Based on places with populations of 10,000 or more

Place	Number	%
Cambridge (city) Guernsey County	3	0.03
Portsmouth (city) Scioto County	2	0.01
Broadview Heights (city) Cuyahoga County	1	0.01
Conneaut (city) Ashtabula County	1	0.01
Marietta (city) Washington County	1	0.01
Vandalia (city) Montgomery County	1	0.01
Dayton (city) Montgomery County	4	0.00
Toledo (city) Lucas County	4	0.00
Akron (city) Summit County	3	0.00
Lakewood (city) Cuyahoga County	2	0.00

American Indian or Alaska Native, not specified

Top 10 Places Sorted by Number
Based on all places, regardless of population

Place	Number	%
Columbus (city) Franklin County	2,805	0.39
Cleveland (city) Cuyahoga County	1,858	0.39
Toledo (city) Lucas County	1,213	0.39
Cincinnati (city) Hamilton County	1,033	0.31
Akron (city) Summit County	792	0.36
Dayton (city) Montgomery County	677	0.41
Canton (city) Stark County	431	0.53
Youngstown (city) Mahoning County	361	0.44
Lorain (city) Lorain County	308	0.45
Springfield (city) Clark County	299	0.46

Top 10 Places Sorted by Percent
Based on all places, regardless of population

Place	Number	%
Clifton (village) Greene County	8	4.47
Rome (village) Adams County	5	4.27
Jacksonburg (village) Butler County	2	2.99
Rarden (village) Scioto County	5	2.84
Kimbolton (village) Guernsey County	5	2.63
Milton Center (village) Wood County	5	2.56
Port William (village) Clinton County	6	2.33
Catawba (village) Clark County	7	2.24
Jeromesville (village) Ashland County	8	1.67
North Fairfield (village) Huron County	9	1.57

Top 10 Places Sorted by Percent
Based on places with populations of 10,000 or more

Place	Number	%
Portsmouth (city) Scioto County	132	0.63
Zanesville (city) Muskingum County	149	0.58
Canton (city) Stark County	431	0.53
Whitehall (city) Franklin County	97	0.51
Chillicothe (city) Ross County	108	0.50
Warrensville Heights (city) Cuyahoga County	74	0.49
Cambridge (city) Guernsey County	57	0.49
Springfield (city) Clark County	299	0.46
East Cleveland (city) Cuyahoga County	125	0.46
Lorain (city) Lorain County	308	0.45

Albanian

Top 10 Places Sorted by Number
Based on all places, regardless of population

Place	Number	%
Lakewood (city) Cuyahoga County	593	1.05
Cleveland (city) Cuyahoga County	225	0.05
Akron (city) Summit County	160	0.07
Cincinnati (city) Hamilton County	155	0.05
Mansfield (city) Richland County	149	0.3[illegible]
Columbus (city) Franklin County	133	0.02
Massillon (city) Stark County	87	0.28
Niles (city) Trumbull County	74	0.35
Parma (city) Cuyahoga County	70	0.08
Mason (city) Warren County	58	0.26

Top 10 Places Sorted by Percent
Based on all places, regardless of population

Place	Number	%
Lakewood (city) Cuyahoga County	593	1.05
Enon (village) Clark County	26	0.98
Harbor Hills (cdp) Licking County	9	0.73
New Franklin (village) Summit County	13	0.62
Kelleys Island (village) Erie County	2	0.58
Ottawa Hills (village) Lucas County	22	0.48
Peninsula (village) Summit County	2	0.39
Tipp City (city) Miami County	35	0.38
Gloria Glens Park (village) Medina County	2	0.38
Midvale (village) Tuscarawas County	2	0.38

Top 10 Places Sorted by Percent
Based on places with populations of 10,000 or more

Place	Number	%
Lakewood (city) Cuyahoga County	593	1.05
Niles (city) Trumbull County	74	0.35
Avon (city) Lorain County	35	0.31
Reading (city) Hamilton County	35	0.31
Mansfield (city) Richland County	149	0.30
Massillon (city) Stark County	87	0.28
Mason (city) Warren County	58	0.26
Rocky River (city) Cuyahoga County	51	0.25
Berea (city) Cuyahoga County	32	0.17
Wickliffe (city) Lake County	16	0.12

Alsatian

Top 10 Places Sorted by Number
Based on all places, regardless of population

Place	Number	%
Cleveland (city) Cuyahoga County	41	0.01
Akron (city) Summit County	35	0.02
Cincinnati (city) Hamilton County	31	0.01
Toledo (city) Lucas County	28	0.01
Columbus (city) Franklin County	23	0.00
Hudson (city) Summit County	22	0.10
Wauseon (city) Fulton County	21	0.30
Centerville (city) Montgomery County	18	0.08
Worthington (city) Franklin County	16	0.11
Cuyahoga Falls (city) Summit County	14	0.03

Top 10 Places Sorted by Percent
Based on all places, regardless of population

Place	Number	%
Kirtland Hills (village) Lake County	5	0.83
Bay View (village) Erie County	3	0.43
Wauseon (city) Fulton County	21	0.30
Groveport (village) Franklin County	9	0.23
Silver Lake (village) Summit County	7	0.23
Clinton (village) Summit County	3	0.23
Fairfax (village) Hamilton County	4	0.21
Canal Fulton (village) Stark County	9	0.18
Beach City (village) Stark County	2	0.18
White Oak West (cdp) Hamilton County	5	0.17

Notes: (cdp) census designated place; Refer to the User's Guide in the front of the book for more detailed information.

Top 10 Places Sorted by Percent

Based on places with populations of 10,000 or more

Place	Number	%
Worthington (city) Franklin County	16	0.11
Hudson (city) Summit County	22	0.10
Washington (city) Fayette County	13	0.10
Montgomery (city) Hamilton County	10	0.10
Centerville (city) Montgomery County	18	0.08
Loveland (city) Hamilton County	10	0.08
Coshocton (city) Coshocton County	8	0.07
Fremont (city) Sandusky County	10	0.06
Seven Hills (city) Cuyahoga County	7	0.06
South Euclid (city) Cuyahoga County	11	0.05

American Indian tribes, specified

Top 10 Places Sorted by Number

Based on all places, regardless of population

Place	Number	%
Columbus (city) Franklin County	4,012	0.56
Cleveland (city) Cuyahoga County	2,235	0.47
Toledo (city) Lucas County	1,665	0.53
Cincinnati (city) Hamilton County	1,458	0.44
Akron (city) Summit County	1,187	0.55
Dayton (city) Montgomery County	869	0.52
Canton (city) Stark County	812	1.00
Lorain (city) Lorain County	504	0.73
Youngstown (city) Mahoning County	484	0.59
Springfield (city) Clark County	430	0.66

Top 10 Places Sorted by Percent

Based on all places, regardless of population

Place	Number	%
Wilkesville (village) Vinton County	7	4.64
Congress (village) Wayne County	8	4.17
Linndale (village) Cuyahoga County	4	3.42
Rarden (village) Scioto County	6	3.41
Bairdstown (village) Wood County	4	3.08
Latty (village) Paulding County	6	3.00
Nellie (village) Coshocton County	4	2.99
West Leipsic (village) Putnam County	8	2.95
Hamden (village) Vinton County	25	2.87
Amesville (village) Athens County	5	2.72

Top 10 Places Sorted by Percent

Based on places with populations of 10,000 or more

Place	Number	%
Portsmouth (city) Scioto County	225	1.08
Canton (city) Stark County	812	1.00
Celina (city) Mercer County	88	0.85
Chillicothe (city) Ross County	184	0.84
Fairborn (city) Greene County	241	0.75
Lorain (city) Lorain County	504	0.73
Elyria (city) Lorain County	408	0.73
Zanesville (city) Muskingum County	180	0.70
Xenia (city) Greene County	167	0.69
Norwood (city) Hamilton County	149	0.69

American Indian: Apache

Top 10 Places Sorted by Number

Based on all places, regardless of population

Place	Number	%
Columbus (city) Franklin County	121	0.02
Cleveland (city) Cuyahoga County	56	0.01
Toledo (city) Lucas County	53	0.02
Cincinnati (city) Hamilton County	36	0.01
Canton (city) Stark County	33	0.04
Akron (city) Summit County	20	0.01
Dayton (city) Montgomery County	18	0.01
Lorain (city) Lorain County	15	0.02
Springfield (city) Clark County	15	0.02
Parma (city) Cuyahoga County	14	0.02

Top 10 Places Sorted by Percent

Based on all places, regardless of population

Place	Number	%
Lyons (village) Fulton County	4	0.72
Thurston (village) Fairfield County	3	0.54
Belle Valley (village) Noble County	1	0.38
Jamestown (village) Greene County	7	0.37
Wayne (village) Wood County	3	0.36
Lore City (village) Guernsey County	1	0.33
Lucasville (cdp) Scioto County	5	0.31
Edison (village) Morrow County	1	0.23
Fayette (village) Fulton County	3	0.22
Pemberville (village) Wood County	3	0.22

Top 10 Places Sorted by Percent

Based on places with populations of 10,000 or more

Place	Number	%
Celina (city) Mercer County	7	0.07
Sandusky (city) Erie County	13	0.05
Urbana (city) Champaign County	6	0.05
Canton (city) Stark County	33	0.04
Zanesville (city) Muskingum County	11	0.04
Tiffin (city) Seneca County	7	0.04
Fostoria (city) Seneca County	5	0.04
Northbrook (cdp) Hamilton County	4	0.04
Shiloh (cdp) Montgomery County	4	0.04
Huber Heights (city) Montgomery County	10	0.03

American Indian: Blackfeet

Top 10 Places Sorted by Number

Based on all places, regardless of population

Place	Number	%
Columbus (city) Franklin County	407	0.06
Cleveland (city) Cuyahoga County	271	0.06
Toledo (city) Lucas County	175	0.06
Akron (city) Summit County	155	0.07
Cincinnati (city) Hamilton County	143	0.04
Dayton (city) Montgomery County	70	0.04
Elyria (city) Lorain County	58	0.10
Canton (city) Stark County	49	0.06
Lorain (city) Lorain County	48	0.07
Cleveland Heights (city) Cuyahoga County	40	0.08

Top 10 Places Sorted by Percent

Based on all places, regardless of population

Place	Number	%
Kimbolton (village) Guernsey County	3	1.58
Congress (village) Wayne County	3	1.56
Galena (village) Delaware County	4	1.31
Butlerville (village) Warren County	3	1.30
Marshallville (village) Wayne County	7	0.85
Beallsville (village) Monroe County	3	0.71
Hamden (village) Vinton County	6	0.69
Byesville (village) Guernsey County	14	0.54
Lyons (village) Fulton County	3	0.54
Mowrystown (village) Highland County	2	0.54

Top 10 Places Sorted by Percent

Based on places with populations of 10,000 or more

Place	Number	%
Bellefontaine (city) Logan County	18	0.14
Painesville (city) Lake County	21	0.12
Conneaut (city) Ashtabula County	14	0.11
Elyria (city) Lorain County	58	0.10
Ashtabula (city) Ashtabula County	20	0.10
Portsmouth (city) Scioto County	20	0.10
East Cleveland (city) Cuyahoga County	24	0.09
Sandusky (city) Erie County	24	0.09
Cleveland Heights (city) Cuyahoga County	40	0.08
Bucyrus (city) Crawford County	11	0.08

American Indian: Cherokee

Top 10 Places Sorted by Number

Based on all places, regardless of population

Place	Number	%
Columbus (city) Franklin County	2,100	0.30
Cleveland (city) Cuyahoga County	984	0.21
Toledo (city) Lucas County	763	0.24
Cincinnati (city) Hamilton County	756	0.23
Akron (city) Summit County	662	0.30
Dayton (city) Montgomery County	490	0.29
Canton (city) Stark County	389	0.48
Youngstown (city) Mahoning County	295	0.36
Lorain (city) Lorain County	262	0.38
Springfield (city) Clark County	249	0.38

Top 10 Places Sorted by Percent

Based on all places, regardless of population

Place	Number	%
Bairdstown (village) Wood County	4	3.08
Nellie (village) Coshocton County	4	2.99
Wilkesville (village) Vinton County	4	2.65
Congress (village) Wayne County	5	2.60
Alvordton (village) Williams County	7	2.30
Rarden (village) Scioto County	4	2.27
Rendville (village) Perry County	1	2.17
Beaver (village) Pike County	10	2.16
Hemlock (village) Perry County	3	2.11
Chesterville (village) Morrow County	4	2.07

Top 10 Places Sorted by Percent

Based on places with populations of 10,000 or more

Place	Number	%
Portsmouth (city) Scioto County	126	0.60
Canton (city) Stark County	389	0.48
Chillicothe (city) Ross County	102	0.47
Fairborn (city) Greene County	145	0.45
Celina (city) Mercer County	46	0.45
Norwood (city) Hamilton County	95	0.44
Mansfield (city) Richland County	206	0.42
Zanesville (city) Muskingum County	103	0.40
Lorain (city) Lorain County	262	0.38
Springfield (city) Clark County	249	0.38

American Indian: Cheyenne

Top 10 Places Sorted by Number

Based on all places, regardless of population

Place	Number	%
Columbus (city) Franklin County	32	0.00
Cleveland (city) Cuyahoga County	19	0.00
Akron (city) Summit County	11	0.01
Youngstown (city) Mahoning County	10	0.01
Toledo (city) Lucas County	10	0.00
Cincinnati (city) Hamilton County	9	0.00
Norwood (city) Hamilton County	6	0.03
Lorain (city) Lorain County	6	0.01
New Vienna (village) Clinton County	5	0.39
Brook Park (city) Cuyahoga County	5	0.02

Top 10 Places Sorted by Percent

Based on all places, regardless of population

Place	Number	%
Gettysburg (village) Darke County	4	0.72
New Vienna (village) Clinton County	5	0.39
Anna (village) Shelby County	3	0.23
Piketon (village) Pike County	3	0.16
Stony Prairie (cdp) Sandusky County	1	0.12
Lakemore (village) Summit County	2	0.08
Wellsville (village) Columbiana County	3	0.07
Martins Ferry (city) Belmont County	4	0.06
Granville (village) Licking County	2	0.06
New Middletown (village) Mahoning County	1	0.06

Notes: (cdp) census designated place; Refer to the User's Guide in the front of the book for more detailed information.

Top 10 Places Sorted by Percent
Based on places with populations of 10,000 or more

Place	Number	%
Springdale (city) Hamilton County	4	0.04
Norwood (city) Hamilton County	6	0.03
Norton (city) Summit County	4	0.03
Brook Park (city) Cuyahoga County	5	0.02
Portsmouth (city) Scioto County	4	0.02
Marietta (city) Washington County	3	0.02
Whitehall (city) Franklin County	3	0.02
Amherst (city) Lorain County	2	0.02
Bedford Heights (city) Cuyahoga County	2	0.02
Akron (city) Summit County	11	0.01

American Indian: Chickasaw

Top 10 Places Sorted by Number
Based on all places, regardless of population

Place	Number	%
Columbus (city) Franklin County	16	0.00
Cleveland (city) Cuyahoga County	11	0.00
Cincinnati (city) Hamilton County	10	0.00
Akron (city) Summit County	7	0.00
Galion (city) Crawford County	5	0.04
Hamilton (city) Butler County	5	0.01
Dillonvale (cdp) Hamilton County	4	0.11
Oxford (city) Butler County	4	0.02
Canton (city) Stark County	4	0.00
Amanda (village) Fairfield County	3	0.42

Top 10 Places Sorted by Percent
Based on all places, regardless of population

Place	Number	%
Latty (village) Paulding County	2	1.00
Donnelsville (village) Clark County	2	0.68
Amanda (village) Fairfield County	3	0.42
Midland (village) Clinton County	1	0.38
Clarksville (village) Clinton County	1	0.20
Manchester (village) Adams County	3	0.15
Dillonvale (cdp) Hamilton County	4	0.11
Fruit Hill (cdp) Hamilton County	3	0.08
North Baltimore (village) Wood County	2	0.06
Carey (village) Wyandot County	2	0.05

Top 10 Places Sorted by Percent
Based on places with populations of 10,000 or more

Place	Number	%
Galion (city) Crawford County	5	0.04
Brooklyn (city) Cuyahoga County	3	0.03
Oxford (city) Butler County	4	0.02
Hamilton (city) Butler County	5	0.01
Barberton (city) Summit County	3	0.01
Centerville (city) Montgomery County	3	0.01
East Cleveland (city) Cuyahoga County	3	0.01
Fairfield (city) Butler County	3	0.01
Garfield Heights (city) Cuyahoga County	3	0.01
Kent (city) Portage County	3	0.01

American Indian: Chippewa

Top 10 Places Sorted by Number
Based on all places, regardless of population

Place	Number	%
Toledo (city) Lucas County	105	0.03
Columbus (city) Franklin County	90	0.01
Cleveland (city) Cuyahoga County	77	0.02
Akron (city) Summit County	34	0.02
Cincinnati (city) Hamilton County	29	0.01
Canton (city) Stark County	19	0.02
Dayton (city) Montgomery County	18	0.01
Cuyahoga Falls (city) Summit County	14	0.03
Ashtabula (city) Ashtabula County	13	0.06
Hamilton (city) Butler County	12	0.02

Top 10 Places Sorted by Percent
Based on all places, regardless of population

Place	Number	%
Port William (village) Clinton County	3	1.16
Rushville (village) Fairfield County	2	0.75
Rushsylvania (village) Logan County	3	0.55
Orangeville (village) Trumbull County	1	0.53
Cecil (village) Paulding County	1	0.46
Kingston (village) Ross County	3	0.29
Shiloh (village) Richland County	2	0.28
Aquilla (village) Geauga County	1	0.27
Elmwood Place (village) Hamilton County	7	0.26
Shawnee Hills (cdp) Greene County	6	0.25

Top 10 Places Sorted by Percent
Based on places with populations of 10,000 or more

Place	Number	%
Ashtabula (city) Ashtabula County	13	0.06
Conneaut (city) Ashtabula County	8	0.06
Marietta (city) Washington County	8	0.06
Greenville (city) Darke County	7	0.05
North College Hill (city) Hamilton County	5	0.05
Parma Heights (city) Cuyahoga County	8	0.04
Wadsworth (city) Medina County	8	0.04
Defiance (city) Defiance County	7	0.04
Washington (city) Fayette County	6	0.04
Springdale (city) Hamilton County	4	0.04

American Indian: Choctaw

Top 10 Places Sorted by Number
Based on all places, regardless of population

Place	Number	%
Cleveland (city) Cuyahoga County	68	0.01
Columbus (city) Franklin County	65	0.01
Toledo (city) Lucas County	40	0.01
Dayton (city) Montgomery County	28	0.02
Cincinnati (city) Hamilton County	28	0.01
Akron (city) Summit County	24	0.01
Elyria (city) Lorain County	18	0.03
East Cleveland (city) Cuyahoga County	14	0.05
Parma (city) Cuyahoga County	14	0.02
Canton (city) Stark County	10	0.01

Top 10 Places Sorted by Percent
Based on all places, regardless of population

Place	Number	%
Woodstock (village) Champaign County	3	0.95
Hartford (village) Licking County	2	0.49
Valley Hi (village) Logan County	1	0.41
New Holland (village) Pickaway County	3	0.38
Berkey (village) Lucas County	1	0.38
Wilmot (village) Stark County	1	0.30
Clarksville (village) Clinton County	1	0.20
Lindsey (village) Sandusky County	1	0.20
Beechwood Trails (cdp) Licking County	4	0.18
Thurston (village) Fairfield County	1	0.18

Top 10 Places Sorted by Percent
Based on places with populations of 10,000 or more

Place	Number	%
East Cleveland (city) Cuyahoga County	14	0.05
Englewood (city) Montgomery County	5	0.04
Elyria (city) Lorain County	18	0.03
Athens (city) Athens County	6	0.03
Wadsworth (city) Medina County	5	0.03
Whitehall (city) Franklin County	5	0.03
Brecksville (city) Cuyahoga County	4	0.03
Landen (cdp) Warren County	4	0.03
Springboro (city) Warren County	4	0.03
Amherst (city) Lorain County	3	0.03

American Indian: Colville

Top 10 Places Sorted by Number
Based on all places, regardless of population

Place	Number	%
Springboro (city) Warren County	1	0.01
Centerville (city) Montgomery County	1	0.0
Cleveland (city) Cuyahoga County	1	0.0
Cuyahoga Falls (city) Summit County	1	0.0
Fairborn (city) Greene County	1	0.0
Stow (city) Summit County	1	0.0
Wooster (city) Wayne County	1	0.0

Top 10 Places Sorted by Percent
Based on all places, regardless of population

Place	Number	%
Springboro (city) Warren County	1	0.01
Centerville (city) Montgomery County	1	0.0
Cleveland (city) Cuyahoga County	1	0.0
Cuyahoga Falls (city) Summit County	1	0.0
Fairborn (city) Greene County	1	0.0
Stow (city) Summit County	1	0.0
Wooster (city) Wayne County	1	0.0

Top 10 Places Sorted by Percent
Based on places with populations of 10,000 or more

Place	Number	%
Springboro (city) Warren County	1	0.01
Centerville (city) Montgomery County	1	0.0
Cleveland (city) Cuyahoga County	1	0.0
Cuyahoga Falls (city) Summit County	1	0.0
Fairborn (city) Greene County	1	0.0
Stow (city) Summit County	1	0.0
Wooster (city) Wayne County	1	0.0

American Indian: Comanche

Top 10 Places Sorted by Number
Based on all places, regardless of population

Place	Number	%
Columbus (city) Franklin County	19	0.0
Cleveland (city) Cuyahoga County	10	0.0
Urbana (city) Champaign County	7	0.06
Findlay (city) Hancock County	6	0.02
Cincinnati (city) Hamilton County	6	0.0
Toledo (city) Lucas County	6	0.0
Celina (city) Mercer County	5	0.05
Akron (city) Summit County	5	0.0
Warsaw (village) Coshocton County	4	0.51
Heath (city) Licking County	4	0.05

Top 10 Places Sorted by Percent
Based on all places, regardless of population

Place	Number	%
Warsaw (village) Coshocton County	4	0.51
Fairfield Beach (cdp) Fairfield County	2	0.17
Dalton (village) Wayne County	2	0.12
Chesapeake (village) Lawrence County	1	0.12
Millersport (village) Fairfield County	1	0.10
Roaming Shores (village) Ashtabula County	1	0.08
White Oak West (cdp) Hamilton County	2	0.07
Urbana (city) Champaign County	7	0.06
New Lexington (city) Perry County	3	0.06
Oak Hill (village) Jackson County	1	0.06

Top 10 Places Sorted by Percent
Based on places with populations of 10,000 or more

Place	Number	%
Urbana (city) Champaign County	7	0.06
Celina (city) Mercer County	5	0.05
Circleville (city) Pickaway County	4	0.03
Findlay (city) Hancock County	6	0.02
Chillicothe (city) Ross County	4	0.02

Notes: (cdp) census designated place; Refer to the User's Guide in the front of the book for more detailed information.

Place	Number	%
Englewood (city) Montgomery County	3	0.02
Ravenna (city) Portage County	2	0.02
Fairborn (city) Greene County	3	0.01
Lakewood (city) Cuyahoga County	3	0.01
Massillon (city) Stark County	3	0.01

American Indian: Cree

Top 10 Places Sorted by Number

Based on all places, regardless of population

Place	Number	%
Columbus (city) Franklin County	14	0.00
Cleveland (city) Cuyahoga County	13	0.00
Akron (city) Summit County	9	0.00
Toledo (city) Lucas County	7	0.00
North Royalton (city) Cuyahoga County	6	0.02
Lakewood (city) Cuyahoga County	5	0.01
Dayton (city) Montgomery County	5	0.00
Bridgetown North (cdp) Hamilton County	4	0.03
Conneaut (city) Ashtabula County	4	0.03
Alliance (city) Stark County	4	0.02

Top 10 Places Sorted by Percent

Based on all places, regardless of population

Place	Number	%
Rawson (village) Hancock County	1	0.22
North Fairfield (village) Huron County	1	0.17
Clinton (village) Summit County	1	0.07
West Salem (village) Wayne County	1	0.07
Gallipolis (city) Gallia County	2	0.05
Huber Ridge (cdp) Franklin County	2	0.04
Enon (village) Clark County	1	0.04
Bridgetown North (cdp) Hamilton County	4	0.03
Conneaut (city) Ashtabula County	4	0.03
Portage Lakes (cdp) Summit County	3	0.03

Top 10 Places Sorted by Percent

Based on places with populations of 10,000 or more

Place	Number	%
Bridgetown North (cdp) Hamilton County	4	0.03
Conneaut (city) Ashtabula County	4	0.03
North Royalton (city) Cuyahoga County	6	0.02
Alliance (city) Stark County	4	0.02
Northbrook (cdp) Hamilton County	2	0.02
Lakewood (city) Cuyahoga County	5	0.01
Beavercreek (city) Greene County	4	0.01
Elyria (city) Lorain County	4	0.01
Lorain (city) Lorain County	4	0.01
Sandusky (city) Erie County	4	0.01

American Indian: Creek

Top 10 Places Sorted by Number

Based on all places, regardless of population

Place	Number	%
Columbus (city) Franklin County	29	0.00
Cincinnati (city) Hamilton County	25	0.01
Dayton (city) Montgomery County	22	0.01
Cleveland (city) Cuyahoga County	18	0.00
Cleveland Heights (city) Cuyahoga County	9	0.02
Centerville (city) Montgomery County	8	0.03
Fairborn (city) Greene County	7	0.02
Akron (city) Summit County	7	0.00
Toledo (city) Lucas County	7	0.00
Forest Park (city) Hamilton County	6	0.03

Top 10 Places Sorted by Percent

Based on all places, regardless of population

Place	Number	%
Clifton (village) Greene County	2	1.12
Jacksonville (village) Athens County	2	0.37
New Bremen (village) Auglaize County	5	0.17
Caldwell (village) Noble County	3	0.15
Mack North (cdp) Hamilton County	5	0.14
Centerburg (village) Knox County	2	0.14
North Perry (village) Lake County	1	0.12
Blanchester (village) Clinton County	4	0.09
Richwood (village) Union County	2	0.09
Gnadenhutten (village) Tuscarawas County	1	0.08

Top 10 Places Sorted by Percent

Based on places with populations of 10,000 or more

Place	Number	%
Clayton (city) Montgomery County	5	0.04
Centerville (city) Montgomery County	8	0.03
Forest Park (city) Hamilton County	6	0.03
Avon (city) Lorain County	4	0.03
Norton (city) Summit County	3	0.03
Cleveland Heights (city) Cuyahoga County	9	0.02
Fairborn (city) Greene County	7	0.02
Massillon (city) Stark County	6	0.02
Xenia (city) Greene County	6	0.02
Zanesville (city) Muskingum County	6	0.02

American Indian: Crow

Top 10 Places Sorted by Number

Based on all places, regardless of population

Place	Number	%
Toledo (city) Lucas County	17	0.01
Columbus (city) Franklin County	11	0.00
Cleveland Heights (city) Cuyahoga County	9	0.02
Akron (city) Summit County	8	0.00
Cleveland (city) Cuyahoga County	8	0.00
New Philadelphia (city) Tuscarawas County	7	0.04
Cincinnati (city) Hamilton County	7	0.00
North Ridgeville (city) Lorain County	5	0.02
Dayton (city) Montgomery County	5	0.00
Thurston (village) Fairfield County	4	0.72

Top 10 Places Sorted by Percent

Based on all places, regardless of population

Place	Number	%
Thurston (village) Fairfield County	4	0.72
Tuscarawas (village) Tuscarawas County	3	0.32
Sherrodsville (village) Carroll County	1	0.32
Wharton (village) Wyandot County	1	0.24
Wayne Lakes (village) Darke County	1	0.15
Pleasantville (village) Fairfield County	1	0.11
Syracuse (village) Meigs County	1	0.11
Greentown (cdp) Stark County	3	0.10
Caldwell (village) Noble County	2	0.10
Edgerton (village) Williams County	2	0.09

Top 10 Places Sorted by Percent

Based on places with populations of 10,000 or more

Place	Number	%
New Philadelphia (city) Tuscarawas County	7	0.04
Cleveland Heights (city) Cuyahoga County	9	0.02
North Ridgeville (city) Lorain County	5	0.02
Sidney (city) Shelby County	4	0.02
Steubenville (city) Jefferson County	4	0.02
Miamisburg (city) Montgomery County	3	0.02
Sylvania (city) Lucas County	3	0.02
Vandalia (city) Montgomery County	3	0.02
Whitehall (city) Franklin County	3	0.02
Springdale (city) Hamilton County	2	0.02

American Indian: Delaware

Top 10 Places Sorted by Number

Based on all places, regardless of population

Place	Number	%
Canton (city) Stark County	86	0.11
Columbus (city) Franklin County	32	0.00
Lorain (city) Lorain County	9	0.01
Cleveland (city) Cuyahoga County	9	0.00
Zanesville (city) Muskingum County	8	0.03
Akron (city) Summit County	8	0.00
Cincinnati (city) Hamilton County	8	0.00
Alliance (city) Stark County	7	0.03
Canal Winchester (village) Franklin County	6	0.13
Celina (city) Mercer County	6	0.06

Top 10 Places Sorted by Percent

Based on all places, regardless of population

Place	Number	%
Plainfield (village) Coshocton County	1	0.63
Bolivar (village) Tuscarawas County	3	0.34
Galena (village) Delaware County	1	0.33
East Canton (village) Stark County	5	0.31
Aquilla (village) Geauga County	1	0.27
Irondale (village) Jefferson County	1	0.24
Glenmoor (cdp) Columbiana County	3	0.14
Canal Winchester (village) Franklin County	6	0.13
Mineral City (village) Tuscarawas County	1	0.12
Canton (city) Stark County	86	0.11

Top 10 Places Sorted by Percent

Based on places with populations of 10,000 or more

Place	Number	%
Canton (city) Stark County	86	0.11
Celina (city) Mercer County	6	0.06
Dover (city) Tuscarawas County	5	0.04
Pataskala (city) Licking County	4	0.04
Zanesville (city) Muskingum County	8	0.03
Alliance (city) Stark County	7	0.03
New Philadelphia (city) Tuscarawas County	5	0.03
Kent (city) Portage County	6	0.02
Coshocton (city) Coshocton County	2	0.02
Galion (city) Crawford County	2	0.02

American Indian: Houma

Top 10 Places Sorted by Number

Based on all places, regardless of population

Place	Number	%
Lake Darby (cdp) Franklin County	4	0.11
Canton (city) Stark County	4	0.00
Struthers (city) Mahoning County	3	0.03
Columbus (city) Franklin County	3	0.00
Risingsun (village) Wood County	2	0.32
Mentor (city) Lake County	2	0.00
Berea (city) Cuyahoga County	1	0.01
Ravenna (city) Portage County	1	0.01
Akron (city) Summit County	1	0.00
Cuyahoga Falls (city) Summit County	1	0.00

Top 10 Places Sorted by Percent

Based on all places, regardless of population

Place	Number	%
Risingsun (village) Wood County	2	0.32
Lake Darby (cdp) Franklin County	4	0.11
Struthers (city) Mahoning County	3	0.03
Berea (city) Cuyahoga County	1	0.01
Ravenna (city) Portage County	1	0.01
Canton (city) Stark County	4	0.00
Columbus (city) Franklin County	3	0.00
Mentor (city) Lake County	2	0.00
Akron (city) Summit County	1	0.00
Cuyahoga Falls (city) Summit County	1	0.00

Top 10 Places Sorted by Percent

Based on places with populations of 10,000 or more

Place	Number	%
Struthers (city) Mahoning County	3	0.03
Berea (city) Cuyahoga County	1	0.01
Ravenna (city) Portage County	1	0.01
Canton (city) Stark County	4	0.00
Columbus (city) Franklin County	3	0.00

Notes: (cdp) census designated place; Refer to the User's Guide in the front of the book for more detailed information.

Place	Number	%
Mentor (city) Lake County	2	0.00
Akron (city) Summit County	1	0.00
Cuyahoga Falls (city) Summit County	1	0.00
Reynoldsburg (city) Franklin County	1	0.00
Toledo (city) Lucas County	1	0.00

American Indian: Iroquois

Top 10 Places Sorted by Number

Based on all places, regardless of population

Place	Number	%
Columbus (city) Franklin County	118	0.02
Cleveland (city) Cuyahoga County	91	0.02
Canton (city) Stark County	89	0.11
Toledo (city) Lucas County	41	0.01
Lorain (city) Lorain County	38	0.06
Akron (city) Summit County	38	0.02
Cincinnati (city) Hamilton County	28	0.01
Dayton (city) Montgomery County	21	0.01
Bowling Green (city) Wood County	19	0.06
Lakewood (city) Cuyahoga County	18	0.03

Top 10 Places Sorted by Percent

Based on all places, regardless of population

Place	Number	%
West Leipsic (village) Putnam County	5	1.85
Polk (village) Ashland County	2	0.56
Freeport (village) Harrison County	2	0.50
Cloverdale (village) Putnam County	1	0.50
Urbancrest (village) Franklin County	4	0.46
Galena (village) Delaware County	1	0.33
Hunter (cdp) Warren County	5	0.29
Vanlue (village) Hancock County	1	0.27
Morrow (village) Warren County	3	0.23
Pleasant City (village) Guernsey County	1	0.23

Top 10 Places Sorted by Percent

Based on places with populations of 10,000 or more

Place	Number	%
Canton (city) Stark County	89	0.11
Maumee (city) Lucas County	10	0.07
Lorain (city) Lorain County	38	0.06
Bowling Green (city) Wood County	19	0.06
University Heights (city) Cuyahoga County	9	0.06
Marietta (city) Washington County	8	0.06
Delaware (city) Delaware County	13	0.05
Willoughby (city) Lake County	11	0.05
Middleburg Heights (city) Cuyahoga County	8	0.05
Aurora (city) Portage County	7	0.05

American Indian: Kiowa

Top 10 Places Sorted by Number

Based on all places, regardless of population

Place	Number	%
Columbus (city) Franklin County	10	0.00
Cleveland (city) Cuyahoga County	7	0.00
Dennison (village) Tuscarawas County	6	0.20
North Ridgeville (city) Lorain County	6	0.03
Akron (city) Summit County	5	0.00
Wheelersburg (cdp) Scioto County	3	0.05
Coshocton (city) Coshocton County	3	0.03
Middleburg Heights (city) Cuyahoga County	3	0.02
Toledo (city) Lucas County	3	0.00
Piketon (village) Pike County	2	0.10

Top 10 Places Sorted by Percent

Based on all places, regardless of population

Place	Number	%
Dennison (village) Tuscarawas County	6	0.20
Piketon (village) Pike County	2	0.10
Wheelersburg (cdp) Scioto County	3	0.05
North Ridgeville (city) Lorain County	6	0.03
Coshocton (city) Coshocton County	3	0.03
Middleburg Heights (city) Cuyahoga County	3	0.02
Blue Ash (city) Hamilton County	2	0.02
Finneytown (cdp) Hamilton County	2	0.01
Lebanon (city) Warren County	2	0.01
Circleville (city) Pickaway County	1	0.01

Top 10 Places Sorted by Percent

Based on places with populations of 10,000 or more

Place	Number	%
North Ridgeville (city) Lorain County	6	0.03
Coshocton (city) Coshocton County	3	0.03
Middleburg Heights (city) Cuyahoga County	3	0.02
Blue Ash (city) Hamilton County	2	0.02
Finneytown (cdp) Hamilton County	2	0.01
Lebanon (city) Warren County	2	0.01
Circleville (city) Pickaway County	1	0.01
West Carrollton City (city) Montgomery County	1	0.01
Columbus (city) Franklin County	10	0.00
Cleveland (city) Cuyahoga County	7	0.00

American Indian: Latin American Indians

Top 10 Places Sorted by Number

Based on all places, regardless of population

Place	Number	%
Columbus (city) Franklin County	160	0.02
Cleveland (city) Cuyahoga County	155	0.03
Cincinnati (city) Hamilton County	136	0.04
Toledo (city) Lucas County	118	0.04
Lorain (city) Lorain County	46	0.07
Cleveland Heights (city) Cuyahoga County	17	0.03
Dover (city) Tuscarawas County	15	0.12
Youngstown (city) Mahoning County	15	0.02
Norwood (city) Hamilton County	14	0.06
Akron (city) Summit County	14	0.01

Top 10 Places Sorted by Percent

Based on all places, regardless of population

Place	Number	%
Summitville (village) Columbiana County	1	0.93
Latty (village) Paulding County	1	0.50
Aberdeen (village) Brown County	7	0.44
West Leipsic (village) Putnam County	1	0.37
Castalia (village) Erie County	3	0.32
Waynesville (village) Warren County	8	0.31
West Unity (village) Williams County	5	0.28
Strasburg (village) Tuscarawas County	6	0.26
Rockford (village) Mercer County	2	0.18
Cridersville (village) Auglaize County	3	0.17

Top 10 Places Sorted by Percent

Based on places with populations of 10,000 or more

Place	Number	%
Dover (city) Tuscarawas County	15	0.12
Lorain (city) Lorain County	46	0.07
Norwood (city) Hamilton County	14	0.06
Struthers (city) Mahoning County	7	0.06
Fremont (city) Sandusky County	9	0.05
Celina (city) Mercer County	5	0.05
Cincinnati (city) Hamilton County	136	0.04
Toledo (city) Lucas County	118	0.04
Brunswick (city) Medina County	13	0.04
Sandusky (city) Erie County	10	0.04

American Indian: Lumbee

Top 10 Places Sorted by Number

Based on all places, regardless of population

Place	Number	%
Columbus (city) Franklin County	45	0.01
Parma (city) Cuyahoga County	17	0.02
Toledo (city) Lucas County	12	0.00
Elyria (city) Lorain County	11	0.0
Fostoria (city) Seneca County	8	0.0
Cleveland (city) Cuyahoga County	7	0.0
Reynoldsburg (city) Franklin County	6	0.0
Hilltop (cdp) Trumbull County	5	0.9
Walbridge (village) Wood County	5	0.2
Pleasant Run (cdp) Hamilton County	5	0.0

Top 10 Places Sorted by Percent

Based on all places, regardless of population

Place	Number	%
Hilltop (cdp) Trumbull County	5	0.9
Walbridge (village) Wood County	5	0.2
West Salem (village) Wayne County	3	0.2
Sunbury (village) Delaware County	3	0.1
Gratis (village) Preble County	1	0.1
Pleasant Run (cdp) Hamilton County	5	0.0
Logan (city) Hocking County	5	0.07
Lodi (village) Medina County	2	0.07
Navarre (village) Stark County	1	0.07
Fostoria (city) Seneca County	8	0.06

Top 10 Places Sorted by Percent

Based on places with populations of 10,000 or more

Place	Number	%
Fostoria (city) Seneca County	8	0.06
Landen (cdp) Warren County	4	0.03
Parma (city) Cuyahoga County	17	0.02
Elyria (city) Lorain County	11	0.02
Reynoldsburg (city) Franklin County	6	0.02
Delaware (city) Delaware County	5	0.02
Alliance (city) Stark County	4	0.02
Tallmadge (city) Summit County	4	0.02
Columbus (city) Franklin County	45	0.01
Westlake (city) Cuyahoga County	4	0.01

American Indian: Menominee

Top 10 Places Sorted by Number

Based on all places, regardless of population

Place	Number	%
Columbus (city) Franklin County	9	0.00
Lima (city) Allen County	6	0.01
Toledo (city) Lucas County	6	0.00
Fostoria (city) Seneca County	3	0.02
Norwalk (city) Huron County	3	0.02
Cambridge (city) Guernsey County	2	0.02
Dublin (city) Franklin County	2	0.01
Norwood (city) Hamilton County	2	0.01
Cincinnati (city) Hamilton County	2	0.00
Dayton (city) Montgomery County	2	0.00

Top 10 Places Sorted by Percent

Based on all places, regardless of population

Place	Number	%
Sugarcreek (village) Tuscarawas County	1	0.05
Fostoria (city) Seneca County	3	0.02
Norwalk (city) Huron County	3	0.02
Cambridge (city) Guernsey County	2	0.02
Lima (city) Allen County	6	0.01
Dublin (city) Franklin County	2	0.01
Norwood (city) Hamilton County	2	0.01
Bedford Heights (city) Cuyahoga County	1	0.01
Bryan (city) Williams County	1	0.01
Columbus (city) Franklin County	9	0.00

Top 10 Places Sorted by Percent

Based on places with populations of 10,000 or more

Place	Number	%
Fostoria (city) Seneca County	3	0.02
Norwalk (city) Huron County	3	0.02
Cambridge (city) Guernsey County	2	0.02
Lima (city) Allen County	6	0.01
Dublin (city) Franklin County	2	0.01

Notes: (cdp) census designated place; Refer to the User's Guide in the front of the book for more detailed information.

Place	Number	%
Norwood (city) Hamilton County	2	0.01
Bedford Heights (city) Cuyahoga County	1	0.01
Columbus (city) Franklin County	9	0.00
Toledo (city) Lucas County	6	0.00
Cincinnati (city) Hamilton County	2	0.00

American Indian: Navajo

Top 10 Places Sorted by Number

Based on all places, regardless of population

Place	Number	%
Columbus (city) Franklin County	73	0.01
Cleveland (city) Cuyahoga County	38	0.01
Cincinnati (city) Hamilton County	26	0.01
Toledo (city) Lucas County	22	0.01
Akron (city) Summit County	18	0.01
Dayton (city) Montgomery County	11	0.01
Lancaster (city) Fairfield County	9	0.03
Canton (city) Stark County	9	0.01
Northbrook (cdp) Hamilton County	7	0.06
Berea (city) Cuyahoga County	7	0.04

Top 10 Places Sorted by Percent

Based on all places, regardless of population

Place	Number	%
South Salem (village) Ross County	1	0.47
Marengo (village) Morrow County	1	0.34
Smithville (village) Wayne County	3	0.23
South Amherst (village) Lorain County	4	0.21
Pioneer (village) Williams County	3	0.21
Somerset (village) Perry County	3	0.19
Roseville (village) Perry County	3	0.15
Malta (village) Morgan County	1	0.14
Woodmere (village) Cuyahoga County	1	0.12
Bellville (village) Richland County	2	0.11

Top 10 Places Sorted by Percent

Based on places with populations of 10,000 or more

Place	Number	%
Northbrook (cdp) Hamilton County	7	0.06
Pataskala (city) Licking County	6	0.06
Berea (city) Cuyahoga County	7	0.04
Franklin (city) Warren County	5	0.04
Reading (city) Hamilton County	4	0.04
Lancaster (city) Fairfield County	9	0.03
Conneaut (city) Ashtabula County	4	0.03
Middleburg Heights (city) Cuyahoga County	4	0.03
Ravenna (city) Portage County	3	0.03
Huber Heights (city) Montgomery County	7	0.02

American Indian: Osage

Top 10 Places Sorted by Number

Based on all places, regardless of population

Place	Number	%
Columbus (city) Franklin County	15	0.00
Toledo (city) Lucas County	6	0.00
Zanesville (city) Muskingum County	5	0.02
Cleves (village) Hamilton County	4	0.14
Edgerton (village) Williams County	3	0.14
Lincoln Village (cdp) Franklin County	3	0.03
Ashtabula (city) Ashtabula County	3	0.01
Chillicothe (city) Ross County	3	0.01
Middletown (city) Butler County	3	0.01
Uhrichsville (city) Tuscarawas County	2	0.04

Top 10 Places Sorted by Percent

Based on all places, regardless of population

Place	Number	%
Jeromesville (village) Ashland County	1	0.21
Cleves (village) Hamilton County	4	0.14
Edgerton (village) Williams County	3	0.14
Clinton (village) Summit County	1	0.07
Uhrichsville (city) Tuscarawas County	2	0.04
Waterville (village) Lucas County	2	0.04
Lincoln Village (cdp) Franklin County	3	0.03
The Plains (cdp) Athens County	1	0.03
Zanesville (city) Muskingum County	5	0.02
Geneva (city) Ashtabula County	1	0.02

Top 10 Places Sorted by Percent

Based on places with populations of 10,000 or more

Place	Number	%
Zanesville (city) Muskingum County	5	0.02
Ashtabula (city) Ashtabula County	3	0.01
Chillicothe (city) Ross County	3	0.01
Middletown (city) Butler County	3	0.01
Trotwood (city) Montgomery County	2	0.01
Lyndhurst (city) Cuyahoga County	1	0.01
Marietta (city) Washington County	1	0.01
Mount Vernon (city) Knox County	1	0.01
Vandalia (city) Montgomery County	1	0.01
Columbus (city) Franklin County	15	0.00

American Indian: Ottawa

Top 10 Places Sorted by Number

Based on all places, regardless of population

Place	Number	%
Toledo (city) Lucas County	20	0.01
Cleveland (city) Cuyahoga County	16	0.00
Columbus (city) Franklin County	9	0.00
Canton (city) Stark County	8	0.01
Sylvania (city) Lucas County	6	0.03
Sandusky (city) Erie County	5	0.02
Bellbrook (city) Greene County	4	0.06
Lorain (city) Lorain County	4	0.01
Fairport Harbor (village) Lake County	3	0.09
Oregon (city) Lucas County	3	0.02

Top 10 Places Sorted by Percent

Based on all places, regardless of population

Place	Number	%
Convoy (village) Van Wert County	2	0.18
Wayne Lakes (village) Darke County	1	0.15
Fairport Harbor (village) Lake County	3	0.09
Fairfield Beach (cdp) Fairfield County	1	0.09
Bellbrook (city) Greene County	4	0.06
Amelia (village) Clermont County	1	0.04
Burlington (cdp) Lawrence County	1	0.04
Sylvania (city) Lucas County	6	0.03
Port Clinton (city) Ottawa County	2	0.03
Silver Lake (village) Summit County	1	0.03

Top 10 Places Sorted by Percent

Based on places with populations of 10,000 or more

Place	Number	%
Sylvania (city) Lucas County	6	0.03
Sandusky (city) Erie County	5	0.02
Oregon (city) Lucas County	3	0.02
Urbana (city) Champaign County	2	0.02
Toledo (city) Lucas County	20	0.01
Canton (city) Stark County	8	0.01
Lorain (city) Lorain County	4	0.01
Cuyahoga Falls (city) Summit County	3	0.01
Portsmouth (city) Scioto County	3	0.01
Massillon (city) Stark County	2	0.01

American Indian: Paiute

Top 10 Places Sorted by Number

Based on all places, regardless of population

Place	Number	%
East Cleveland (city) Cuyahoga County	15	0.06
Columbus (city) Franklin County	5	0.00
Forest Park (city) Hamilton County	4	0.02
Johnstown (village) Licking County	3	0.09
Avon (city) Lorain County	3	0.03
Cincinnati (city) Hamilton County	3	0.00
Cleveland (city) Cuyahoga County	3	0.00
Newark (city) Licking County	2	0.00
Toledo (city) Lucas County	2	0.00
Canal Winchester (village) Franklin County	1	0.02

Top 10 Places Sorted by Percent

Based on all places, regardless of population

Place	Number	%
Johnstown (village) Licking County	3	0.09
East Cleveland (city) Cuyahoga County	15	0.06
Avon (city) Lorain County	3	0.03
Forest Park (city) Hamilton County	4	0.02
Canal Winchester (village) Franklin County	1	0.02
Uhrichsville (city) Tuscarawas County	1	0.02
Columbus (city) Franklin County	5	0.00
Cincinnati (city) Hamilton County	3	0.00
Cleveland (city) Cuyahoga County	3	0.00
Newark (city) Licking County	2	0.00

Top 10 Places Sorted by Percent

Based on places with populations of 10,000 or more

Place	Number	%
East Cleveland (city) Cuyahoga County	15	0.06
Avon (city) Lorain County	3	0.03
Forest Park (city) Hamilton County	4	0.02
Columbus (city) Franklin County	5	0.00
Cincinnati (city) Hamilton County	3	0.00
Cleveland (city) Cuyahoga County	3	0.00
Newark (city) Licking County	2	0.00
Toledo (city) Lucas County	2	0.00
Elyria (city) Lorain County	1	0.00
Massillon (city) Stark County	1	0.00

American Indian: Pima

Top 10 Places Sorted by Number

Based on all places, regardless of population

Place	Number	%
Cleveland (city) Cuyahoga County	8	0.00
Columbus (city) Franklin County	7	0.00
Dayton (city) Montgomery County	4	0.00
Streetsboro (city) Portage County	3	0.02
Bryan (city) Williams County	2	0.02
Cincinnati (city) Hamilton County	2	0.00
South Amherst (village) Lorain County	1	0.05
Monfort Heights East (cdp) Hamilton County	1	0.03
Kettering (city) Montgomery County	1	0.00
Newark (city) Licking County	1	0.00

Top 10 Places Sorted by Percent

Based on all places, regardless of population

Place	Number	%
South Amherst (village) Lorain County	1	0.05
Monfort Heights East (cdp) Hamilton County	1	0.03
Streetsboro (city) Portage County	3	0.02
Bryan (city) Williams County	2	0.02
Cleveland (city) Cuyahoga County	8	0.00
Columbus (city) Franklin County	7	0.00
Dayton (city) Montgomery County	4	0.00
Cincinnati (city) Hamilton County	2	0.00
Kettering (city) Montgomery County	1	0.00
Newark (city) Licking County	1	0.00

Top 10 Places Sorted by Percent

Based on places with populations of 10,000 or more

Place	Number	%
Streetsboro (city) Portage County	3	0.02
Cleveland (city) Cuyahoga County	8	0.00
Columbus (city) Franklin County	7	0.00
Dayton (city) Montgomery County	4	0.00
Cincinnati (city) Hamilton County	2	0.00

Notes: (cdp) census designated place; Refer to the User's Guide in the front of the book for more detailed information.

Kettering (city) Montgomery County	1	0.00
Newark (city) Licking County	1	0.00
Riverside (city) Montgomery County	1	0.00

American Indian: Potawatomi

Top 10 Places Sorted by Number

Based on all places, regardless of population

Place	Number	%
Toledo (city) Lucas County	18	0.01
Columbus (city) Franklin County	12	0.00
Springfield (city) Clark County	8	0.01
Massillon (city) Stark County	6	0.02
Cincinnati (city) Hamilton County	6	0.00
Yellow Springs (village) Greene County	5	0.13
Xenia (city) Greene County	5	0.02
Cleveland (city) Cuyahoga County	5	0.00
Groveport (village) Franklin County	4	0.10
Austintown (cdp) Mahoning County	4	0.01

Top 10 Places Sorted by Percent

Based on all places, regardless of population

Place	Number	%
Port Washington (village) Tuscarawas County	1	0.18
Stryker (village) Williams County	2	0.14
Yellow Springs (village) Greene County	5	0.13
Reminderville (village) Summit County	3	0.13
McClure (village) Henry County	1	0.13
Lakemore (village) Summit County	3	0.12
Millville (village) Butler County	1	0.12
Groveport (village) Franklin County	4	0.10
Montpelier (village) Williams County	3	0.07
Huron (city) Erie County	3	0.04

Top 10 Places Sorted by Percent

Based on places with populations of 10,000 or more

Place	Number	%
Massillon (city) Stark County	6	0.02
Xenia (city) Greene County	5	0.02
Toledo (city) Lucas County	18	0.01
Springfield (city) Clark County	8	0.01
Austintown (cdp) Mahoning County	4	0.01
Kent (city) Portage County	3	0.01
Solon (city) Cuyahoga County	3	0.01
Westlake (city) Cuyahoga County	3	0.01
Ashland (city) Ashland County	2	0.01
Beavercreek (city) Greene County	2	0.01

American Indian: Pueblo

Top 10 Places Sorted by Number

Based on all places, regardless of population

Place	Number	%
Columbus (city) Franklin County	23	0.00
Toledo (city) Lucas County	17	0.01
Cleveland (city) Cuyahoga County	16	0.00
Akron (city) Summit County	10	0.00
Lorain (city) Lorain County	7	0.01
Cincinnati (city) Hamilton County	6	0.00
Dayton (city) Montgomery County	6	0.00
University Heights (city) Cuyahoga County	5	0.04
Northbrook (cdp) Hamilton County	4	0.04
Niles (city) Trumbull County	4	0.02

Top 10 Places Sorted by Percent

Based on all places, regardless of population

Place	Number	%
Holmesville (village) Holmes County	1	0.26
Rock Creek (village) Ashtabula County	1	0.17
Wayne Lakes (village) Darke County	1	0.15
Eaton Estates (cdp) Lorain County	2	0.14
Amanda (village) Fairfield County	1	0.14
Urbancrest (village) Franklin County	1	0.12
Alger (village) Hardin County	1	0.11
North Randall (village) Cuyahoga County	1	0.11
Addyston (village) Hamilton County	1	0.10
McDonald (village) Trumbull County	3	0.09

Top 10 Places Sorted by Percent

Based on places with populations of 10,000 or more

Place	Number	%
University Heights (city) Cuyahoga County	5	0.04
Northbrook (cdp) Hamilton County	4	0.04
Niles (city) Trumbull County	4	0.02
Riverside (city) Montgomery County	4	0.02
Rocky River (city) Cuyahoga County	4	0.02
Steubenville (city) Jefferson County	4	0.02
Toledo (city) Lucas County	17	0.01
Lorain (city) Lorain County	7	0.01
Garfield Heights (city) Cuyahoga County	4	0.01
Elyria (city) Lorain County	3	0.01

American Indian: Puget Sound Salish

Top 10 Places Sorted by Number

Based on all places, regardless of population

Place	Number	%
Dayton (city) Montgomery County	5	0.00
Summerside (cdp) Clermont County	3	0.05
Canton (city) Stark County	3	0.00
Gates Mills (village) Cuyahoga County	2	0.08
Rossford (city) Wood County	2	0.03
Bowling Green (city) Wood County	2	0.01
Heath (city) Licking County	1	0.01
Oberlin (city) Lorain County	1	0.01
Wauseon (city) Fulton County	1	0.01
Columbus (city) Franklin County	1	0.00

Top 10 Places Sorted by Percent

Based on all places, regardless of population

Place	Number	%
Gates Mills (village) Cuyahoga County	2	0.08
Summerside (cdp) Clermont County	3	0.05
Rossford (city) Wood County	2	0.03
Bowling Green (city) Wood County	2	0.01
Heath (city) Licking County	1	0.01
Oberlin (city) Lorain County	1	0.01
Wauseon (city) Fulton County	1	0.01
Dayton (city) Montgomery County	5	0.00
Canton (city) Stark County	3	0.00
Columbus (city) Franklin County	1	0.00

Top 10 Places Sorted by Percent

Based on places with populations of 10,000 or more

Place	Number	%
Bowling Green (city) Wood County	2	0.01
Dayton (city) Montgomery County	5	0.00
Canton (city) Stark County	3	0.00
Columbus (city) Franklin County	1	0.00
Findlay (city) Hancock County	1	0.00

American Indian: Seminole

Top 10 Places Sorted by Number

Based on all places, regardless of population

Place	Number	%
Cleveland (city) Cuyahoga County	41	0.01
Columbus (city) Franklin County	35	0.00
Toledo (city) Lucas County	27	0.01
Cincinnati (city) Hamilton County	18	0.01
Dayton (city) Montgomery County	16	0.01
Youngstown (city) Mahoning County	14	0.02
Akron (city) Summit County	14	0.01
Cleveland Heights (city) Cuyahoga County	11	0.02
Canton (city) Stark County	11	0.01
Elyria (city) Lorain County	7	0.01

Top 10 Places Sorted by Percent

Based on all places, regardless of population

Place	Number	%
New Bremen (village) Auglaize County	5	0.
Bay View (village) Erie County	1	0.
Philo (village) Muskingum County	1	0.
Bethesda (village) Belmont County	1	0.
West Salem (village) Wayne County	1	0.
Choctaw Lake (cdp) Madison County	1	0.
Mineral Ridge (cdp) Trumbull County	2	0.
Harrison (city) Hamilton County	3	0.
Northridge (cdp) Montgomery County	3	0.
Huber Ridge (cdp) Franklin County	2	0.

Top 10 Places Sorted by Percent

Based on places with populations of 10,000 or more

Place	Number	%
Steubenville (city) Jefferson County	6	0.
Youngstown (city) Mahoning County	14	0.0
Cleveland Heights (city) Cuyahoga County	11	0.0
Lancaster (city) Fairfield County	6	0.0
Kent (city) Portage County	5	0.0
Shaker Heights (city) Cuyahoga County	5	0.0
Mason (city) Warren County	4	0.0
Portsmouth (city) Scioto County	4	0.0
Fostoria (city) Seneca County	3	0.0
Fremont (city) Sandusky County	3	0.0

American Indian: Shoshone

Top 10 Places Sorted by Number

Based on all places, regardless of population

Place	Number	%
Akron (city) Summit County	6	0.0
Forestville (cdp) Hamilton County	3	0.0
Columbus (city) Franklin County	3	0.0
Lorain (city) Lorain County	3	0.0
Minerva (village) Stark County	2	0.0
South Point (village) Lawrence County	2	0.0
Port Clinton (city) Ottawa County	2	0.0
Sheffield Lake (city) Lorain County	2	0.0
Bedford (city) Cuyahoga County	2	0.0
East Cleveland (city) Cuyahoga County	2	0.0

Top 10 Places Sorted by Percent

Based on all places, regardless of population

Place	Number	%
Seaman (village) Adams County	1	0.1
Neffs (cdp) Belmont County	1	0.0
Minerva (village) Stark County	2	0.0
South Point (village) Lawrence County	2	0.0
Drexel (cdp) Montgomery County	1	0.0
Devola (cdp) Washington County	1	0.0
Woodsfield (village) Monroe County	1	0.0
Forestville (cdp) Hamilton County	3	0.0
Port Clinton (city) Ottawa County	2	0.0
Delta (village) Fulton County	1	0.0

Top 10 Places Sorted by Percent

Based on places with populations of 10,000 or more

Place	Number	%
Forestville (cdp) Hamilton County	3	0.0
Bedford (city) Cuyahoga County	2	0.01
East Cleveland (city) Cuyahoga County	2	0.01
Findlay (city) Hancock County	2	0.01
Garfield Heights (city) Cuyahoga County	2	0.01
Avon (city) Lorain County	1	0.01
Avon Lake (city) Lorain County	1	0.01
Greenville (city) Darke County	1	0.01
North Canton (city) Stark County	1	0.01
Norwalk (city) Huron County	1	0.01

Notes: (cdp) census designated place; Refer to the User's Guide in the front of the book for more detailed information.

American Indian: Sioux

Top 10 Places Sorted by Number
Based on all places, regardless of population

Place	Number	%
Columbus (city) Franklin County	178	0.03
Cleveland (city) Cuyahoga County	140	0.03
Akron (city) Summit County	63	0.03
Toledo (city) Lucas County	60	0.02
Dayton (city) Montgomery County	50	0.03
Cincinnati (city) Hamilton County	47	0.01
Lakewood (city) Cuyahoga County	26	0.05
Canton (city) Stark County	26	0.03
Newark (city) Licking County	20	0.04
Elyria (city) Lorain County	18	0.03

Top 10 Places Sorted by Percent
Based on all places, regardless of population

Place	Number	%
Rarden (village) Scioto County	2	1.14
Norwich (village) Muskingum County	1	0.88
Lore City (village) Guernsey County	2	0.66
Tremont City (village) Clark County	2	0.57
Orangeville (village) Trumbull County	1	0.53
Waynesfield (village) Auglaize County	4	0.50
Andover (village) Ashtabula County	5	0.39
West Leipsic (village) Putnam County	1	0.37
New Bloomington (village) Marion County	2	0.36
Phillipsburg (village) Montgomery County	2	0.32

Top 10 Places Sorted by Percent
Based on places with populations of 10,000 or more

Place	Number	%
Marysville (city) Union County	14	0.09
Bellefontaine (city) Logan County	9	0.07
Blue Ash (city) Hamilton County	7	0.06
Lakewood (city) Cuyahoga County	26	0.05
Kent (city) Portage County	15	0.05
Portsmouth (city) Scioto County	10	0.05
Cambridge (city) Guernsey County	6	0.05
Salem (city) Columbiana County	6	0.05
Newark (city) Licking County	20	0.04
Reynoldsburg (city) Franklin County	12	0.04

American Indian: Tohono O'Odham

Top 10 Places Sorted by Number
Based on all places, regardless of population

Place	Number	%
Cleveland (city) Cuyahoga County	9	0.00
Columbus (city) Franklin County	7	0.00
Cincinnati (city) Hamilton County	4	0.00
Dayton (city) Montgomery County	3	0.00
Youngstown (city) Mahoning County	2	0.00
Westfield Center (village) Medina County	1	0.09
Clinton (village) Summit County	1	0.07
Holiday Valley (cdp) Clark County	1	0.06
Sabina (village) Clinton County	1	0.04
Bedford Heights (city) Cuyahoga County	1	0.01

Top 10 Places Sorted by Percent
Based on all places, regardless of population

Place	Number	%
Westfield Center (village) Medina County	1	0.09
Clinton (village) Summit County	1	0.07
Holiday Valley (cdp) Clark County	1	0.06
Sabina (village) Clinton County	1	0.04
Bedford Heights (city) Cuyahoga County	1	0.01
Norton (city) Summit County	1	0.01
Orrville (city) Wayne County	1	0.01
Willowick (city) Lake County	1	0.01
Wilmington (city) Clinton County	1	0.01
Cleveland (city) Cuyahoga County	9	0.00

Top 10 Places Sorted by Percent
Based on places with populations of 10,000 or more

Place	Number	%
Bedford Heights (city) Cuyahoga County	1	0.01
Norton (city) Summit County	1	0.01
Willowick (city) Lake County	1	0.01
Wilmington (city) Clinton County	1	0.01
Cleveland (city) Cuyahoga County	9	0.00
Columbus (city) Franklin County	7	0.00
Cincinnati (city) Hamilton County	4	0.00
Dayton (city) Montgomery County	3	0.00
Youngstown (city) Mahoning County	2	0.00
Elyria (city) Lorain County	1	0.00

American Indian: Ute

Top 10 Places Sorted by Number
Based on all places, regardless of population

Place	Number	%
Brook Park (city) Cuyahoga County	4	0.02
Lancaster (city) Fairfield County	4	0.01
Hamden (village) Vinton County	3	0.34
Streetsboro (city) Portage County	3	0.02
Hudson (city) Summit County	3	0.01
Canton (city) Stark County	3	0.00
Woodsfield (village) Monroe County	2	0.08
Cleveland (city) Cuyahoga County	2	0.00
The Plains (cdp) Athens County	1	0.03
Berea (city) Cuyahoga County	1	0.01

Top 10 Places Sorted by Percent
Based on all places, regardless of population

Place	Number	%
Hamden (village) Vinton County	3	0.34
Woodsfield (village) Monroe County	2	0.08
The Plains (cdp) Athens County	1	0.03
Brook Park (city) Cuyahoga County	4	0.02
Streetsboro (city) Portage County	3	0.02
Lancaster (city) Fairfield County	4	0.01
Hudson (city) Summit County	3	0.01
Berea (city) Cuyahoga County	1	0.01
Marietta (city) Washington County	1	0.01
Mount Vernon (city) Knox County	1	0.01

Top 10 Places Sorted by Percent
Based on places with populations of 10,000 or more

Place	Number	%
Brook Park (city) Cuyahoga County	4	0.02
Streetsboro (city) Portage County	3	0.02
Lancaster (city) Fairfield County	4	0.01
Hudson (city) Summit County	3	0.01
Berea (city) Cuyahoga County	1	0.01
Marietta (city) Washington County	1	0.01
Mount Vernon (city) Knox County	1	0.01
Norwalk (city) Huron County	1	0.01
Canton (city) Stark County	3	0.00
Cleveland (city) Cuyahoga County	2	0.00

American Indian: Yakama

Top 10 Places Sorted by Number
Based on all places, regardless of population

Place	Number	%
Wellsville (village) Columbiana County	2	0.05
Cleveland (city) Cuyahoga County	2	0.00
Oberlin (city) Lorain County	1	0.01
Canton (city) Stark County	1	0.00
Toledo (city) Lucas County	1	0.00
Westerville (city) Franklin County	1	0.00

Top 10 Places Sorted by Percent
Based on all places, regardless of population

Place	Number	%
Wellsville (village) Columbiana County	2	0.05
Oberlin (city) Lorain County	1	0.01
Cleveland (city) Cuyahoga County	2	0.00
Canton (city) Stark County	1	0.00
Toledo (city) Lucas County	1	0.00
Westerville (city) Franklin County	1	0.00

Top 10 Places Sorted by Percent
Based on places with populations of 10,000 or more

Place	Number	%
Cleveland (city) Cuyahoga County	2	0.00
Canton (city) Stark County	1	0.00
Toledo (city) Lucas County	1	0.00
Westerville (city) Franklin County	1	0.00

American Indian: Yaqui

Top 10 Places Sorted by Number
Based on all places, regardless of population

Place	Number	%
Columbus (city) Franklin County	9	0.00
Belpre (city) Washington County	3	0.05
Cheviot (city) Hamilton County	3	0.03
Springfield (city) Clark County	3	0.00
Addyston (village) Hamilton County	2	0.20
Bryan (city) Williams County	2	0.02
Dover (city) Tuscarawas County	2	0.02
Ashtabula (city) Ashtabula County	2	0.01
Akron (city) Summit County	2	0.00
Euclid (city) Cuyahoga County	2	0.00

Top 10 Places Sorted by Percent
Based on all places, regardless of population

Place	Number	%
Addyston (village) Hamilton County	2	0.20
Forest (village) Hardin County	1	0.07
Belpre (city) Washington County	3	0.05
Bolindale (cdp) Trumbull County	1	0.04
Grafton (village) Lorain County	1	0.04
Cheviot (city) Hamilton County	3	0.03
Bryan (city) Williams County	2	0.02
Dover (city) Tuscarawas County	2	0.02
Uhrichsville (city) Tuscarawas County	1	0.02
Ashtabula (city) Ashtabula County	2	0.01

Top 10 Places Sorted by Percent
Based on places with populations of 10,000 or more

Place	Number	%
Dover (city) Tuscarawas County	2	0.02
Ashtabula (city) Ashtabula County	2	0.01
Avon Lake (city) Lorain County	1	0.01
Fremont (city) Sandusky County	1	0.01
Mount Vernon (city) Knox County	1	0.01
Tiffin (city) Seneca County	1	0.01
Columbus (city) Franklin County	9	0.00
Springfield (city) Clark County	3	0.00
Akron (city) Summit County	2	0.00
Euclid (city) Cuyahoga County	2	0.00

American Indian: Yuman

Top 10 Places Sorted by Number
Based on all places, regardless of population

Place	Number	%
Seaman (village) Adams County	2	0.19
Bowling Green (city) Wood County	2	0.01
Cleveland (city) Cuyahoga County	2	0.00
Portage (village) Wood County	1	0.23
Forest Park (city) Hamilton County	1	0.01
Martins Ferry (city) Belmont County	1	0.01

Notes: (cdp) census designated place; Refer to the User's Guide in the front of the book for more detailed information.

Richmond Heights (city) Cuyahoga County	1	0.01
Worthington (city) Franklin County	1	0.01
Canton (city) Stark County	1	0.00
Eastlake (city) Lake County	1	0.00

Top 10 Places Sorted by Percent

Based on all places, regardless of population

Place	Number	%
Portage (village) Wood County	1	0.23
Seaman (village) Adams County	2	0.19
Bowling Green (city) Wood County	2	0.01
Forest Park (city) Hamilton County	1	0.01
Martins Ferry (city) Belmont County	1	0.01
Richmond Heights (city) Cuyahoga County	1	0.01
Worthington (city) Franklin County	1	0.01
Cleveland (city) Cuyahoga County	2	0.00
Canton (city) Stark County	1	0.00
Eastlake (city) Lake County	1	0.00

Top 10 Places Sorted by Percent

Based on places with populations of 10,000 or more

Place	Number	%
Bowling Green (city) Wood County	2	0.01
Forest Park (city) Hamilton County	1	0.01
Richmond Heights (city) Cuyahoga County	1	0.01
Worthington (city) Franklin County	1	0.01
Cleveland (city) Cuyahoga County	2	0.00
Canton (city) Stark County	1	0.00
Eastlake (city) Lake County	1	0.00
Kettering (city) Montgomery County	1	0.00
Mansfield (city) Richland County	1	0.00
Massillon (city) Stark County	1	0.00

American Indian: All other tribes

Top 10 Places Sorted by Number

Based on all places, regardless of population

Place	Number	%
Columbus (city) Franklin County	353	0.05
Cleveland (city) Cuyahoga County	143	0.03
Toledo (city) Lucas County	117	0.04
Cincinnati (city) Hamilton County	108	0.03
Dayton (city) Montgomery County	64	0.04
Springfield (city) Clark County	58	0.09
Akron (city) Summit County	57	0.03
Canton (city) Stark County	37	0.05
Youngstown (city) Mahoning County	36	0.04
Urbana (city) Champaign County	28	0.24

Top 10 Places Sorted by Percent

Based on all places, regardless of population

Place	Number	%
Linndale (village) Cuyahoga County	3	2.56
Wilkesville (village) Vinton County	3	1.99
Rome (village) Adams County	2	1.71
Amesville (village) Athens County	3	1.63
Alexandria (village) Licking County	1	1.18
Harbor View (village) Lucas County	1	1.01
Hollansburg (village) Darke County	2	0.93
Rio Grande (village) Gallia County	7	0.77
McGuffey (village) Hardin County	4	0.77
Corning (village) Perry County	4	0.67

Top 10 Places Sorted by Percent

Based on places with populations of 10,000 or more

Place	Number	%
Urbana (city) Champaign County	28	0.24
Portsmouth (city) Scioto County	28	0.13
Chillicothe (city) Ross County	27	0.12
Xenia (city) Greene County	24	0.10
West Carrollton City (city) Montgomery County	14	0.10
Springfield (city) Clark County	58	0.09
Shiloh (cdp) Montgomery County	10	0.09
Celina (city) Mercer County	9	0.09

Oxford (city) Butler County	18	0.08
Troy (city) Miami County	18	0.08

American Indian tribes, not specified

Top 10 Places Sorted by Number

Based on all places, regardless of population

Place	Number	%
Columbus (city) Franklin County	329	0.05
Cleveland (city) Cuyahoga County	238	0.05
Toledo (city) Lucas County	179	0.06
Cincinnati (city) Hamilton County	135	0.04
Dayton (city) Montgomery County	91	0.05
Akron (city) Summit County	85	0.04
Canton (city) Stark County	59	0.07
Lorain (city) Lorain County	44	0.06
Youngstown (city) Mahoning County	42	0.05
Mansfield (city) Richland County	39	0.08

Top 10 Places Sorted by Percent

Based on all places, regardless of population

Place	Number	%
Pitsburg (village) Darke County	5	1.28
Moscow (village) Clermont County	3	1.23
Fredericksburg (village) Wayne County	5	1.03
Vanlue (village) Hancock County	3	0.81
Beallsville (village) Monroe County	3	0.71
Sinking Spring (village) Highland County	1	0.63
New Athens (village) Harrison County	2	0.58
Belmore (village) Putnam County	1	0.58
Zaleski (village) Vinton County	2	0.53
Sparta (village) Morrow County	1	0.52

Top 10 Places Sorted by Percent

Based on places with populations of 10,000 or more

Place	Number	%
Ravenna (city) Portage County	13	0.11
Troy (city) Miami County	22	0.10
Defiance (city) Defiance County	17	0.10
Lebanon (city) Warren County	16	0.09
Brooklyn (city) Cuyahoga County	11	0.09
Mansfield (city) Richland County	39	0.08
Bowling Green (city) Wood County	23	0.08
Canton (city) Stark County	59	0.07
Huber Heights (city) Montgomery County	26	0.07
Barberton (city) Summit County	19	0.07

Arab

Top 10 Places Sorted by Number

Based on all places, regardless of population

Place	Number	%
Columbus (city) Franklin County	4,512	0.63
Toledo (city) Lucas County	3,668	1.17
Cleveland (city) Cuyahoga County	2,916	0.61
Lakewood (city) Cuyahoga County	2,371	4.19
Akron (city) Summit County	1,453	0.67
Parma (city) Cuyahoga County	1,381	1.61
North Olmsted (city) Cuyahoga County	1,050	3.08
Cincinnati (city) Hamilton County	981	0.30
Westlake (city) Cuyahoga County	926	2.91
Strongsville (city) Cuyahoga County	623	1.42

Top 10 Places Sorted by Percent

Based on all places, regardless of population

Place	Number	%
Blakeslee (village) Williams County	10	8.26
Masury (cdp) Trumbull County	161	5.85
Fairlawn (city) Summit County	356	4.86
Lakewood (city) Cuyahoga County	2,371	4.19
Holiday City (village) Williams County	2	3.92
Gates Mills (village) Cuyahoga County	95	3.88
Moreland Hills (village) Cuyahoga County	126	3.82
Clay Center (village) Ottawa County	11	3.72
Sugar Bush Knolls (village) Portage County	7	3.32
Ottawa Hills (village) Lucas County	150	3.30

Top 10 Places Sorted by Percent

Based on places with populations of 10,000 or more

Place	Number	%
Lakewood (city) Cuyahoga County	2,371	4.19
North Olmsted (city) Cuyahoga County	1,050	3.08
Westlake (city) Cuyahoga County	926	2.91
Brooklyn (city) Cuyahoga County	317	2.74
Rocky River (city) Cuyahoga County	444	2.14
Fairview Park (city) Cuyahoga County	333	1.90
Brecksville (city) Cuyahoga County	245	1.84
Parma Heights (city) Cuyahoga County	389	1.80
Montgomery (city) Hamilton County	165	1.64
Parma (city) Cuyahoga County	1,381	1.61

Arab: Arab/Arabic

Top 10 Places Sorted by Number

Based on all places, regardless of population

Place	Number	%
Columbus (city) Franklin County	921	0.13
Cleveland (city) Cuyahoga County	805	0.17
Lakewood (city) Cuyahoga County	721	1.27
Toledo (city) Lucas County	359	0.11
North Olmsted (city) Cuyahoga County	335	0.98
Akron (city) Summit County	248	0.11
Westlake (city) Cuyahoga County	237	0.74
Westerville (city) Franklin County	159	0.45
Dayton (city) Montgomery County	144	0.09
Parma (city) Cuyahoga County	120	0.14

Top 10 Places Sorted by Percent

Based on all places, regardless of population

Place	Number	%
Chauncey (village) Athens County	19	1.77
Lakewood (city) Cuyahoga County	721	1.27
Richfield (village) Summit County	36	1.09
North Olmsted (city) Cuyahoga County	335	0.98
Saint Louisville (village) Licking County	3	0.88
Moreland Hills (village) Cuyahoga County	27	0.82
Rossford (city) Wood County	48	0.76
Westlake (city) Cuyahoga County	237	0.74
Mount Carmel (cdp) Clermont County	32	0.74
Marshallville (village) Wayne County	6	0.72

Top 10 Places Sorted by Percent

Based on places with populations of 10,000 or more

Place	Number	%
Lakewood (city) Cuyahoga County	721	1.27
North Olmsted (city) Cuyahoga County	335	0.98
Westlake (city) Cuyahoga County	237	0.74
West Carrollton City (city) Montgomery County	92	0.66
Westerville (city) Franklin County	159	0.45
Middleburg Heights (city) Cuyahoga County	66	0.42
Kent (city) Portage County	108	0.39
Bellefontaine (city) Logan County	51	0.39
Fairview Park (city) Cuyahoga County	64	0.36
Northbrook (cdp) Hamilton County	38	0.34

Arab: Egyptian

Top 10 Places Sorted by Number

Based on all places, regardless of population

Place	Number	%
Columbus (city) Franklin County	491	0.07
Cleveland (city) Cuyahoga County	329	0.07
Lakewood (city) Cuyahoga County	118	0.21
Parma (city) Cuyahoga County	103	0.12
Upper Arlington (city) Franklin County	101	0.30
Parma Heights (city) Cuyahoga County	98	0.45

Notes: (cdp) census designated place; Refer to the User's Guide in the front of the book for more detailed information.

Place	Number	%
Toledo (city) Lucas County	95	0.03
Cincinnati (city) Hamilton County	82	0.02
Mayfield Heights (city) Cuyahoga County	71	0.37
Westlake (city) Cuyahoga County	70	0.22

Top 10 Places Sorted by Percent

Based on all places, regardless of population

Place	Number	%
South Russell (village) Geauga County	46	1.14
Ottawa Hills (village) Lucas County	48	1.06
Rio Grande (village) Gallia County	9	1.01
Pepper Pike (city) Cuyahoga County	60	0.99
Woodmere (village) Cuyahoga County	6	0.72
The Village of Indian Hill (city) Hamilton County	40	0.69
Orange (village) Cuyahoga County	19	0.59
Parma Heights (city) Cuyahoga County	98	0.45
Mayfield Heights (city) Cuyahoga County	71	0.37
Marshallville (village) Wayne County	3	0.36

Top 10 Places Sorted by Percent

Based on places with populations of 10,000 or more

Place	Number	%
Parma Heights (city) Cuyahoga County	98	0.45
Mayfield Heights (city) Cuyahoga County	71	0.37
Upper Arlington (city) Franklin County	101	0.30
Worthington (city) Franklin County	37	0.26
Richmond Heights (city) Cuyahoga County	27	0.25
Westlake (city) Cuyahoga County	70	0.22
Lakewood (city) Cuyahoga County	118	0.21
Brooklyn (city) Cuyahoga County	22	0.19
Lyndhurst (city) Cuyahoga County	28	0.18
Blue Ash (city) Hamilton County	22	0.17

Arab: Iraqi

Top 10 Places Sorted by Number

Based on all places, regardless of population

Place	Number	%
Toledo (city) Lucas County	121	0.04
Columbus (city) Franklin County	111	0.02
Mayfield Heights (city) Cuyahoga County	46	0.24
Olmsted Falls (city) Cuyahoga County	40	0.51
Parma Heights (city) Cuyahoga County	31	0.14
Cleveland (city) Cuyahoga County	27	0.01
Clayton (city) Montgomery County	20	0.15
Solon (city) Cuyahoga County	20	0.09
Beachwood (city) Cuyahoga County	18	0.15
Brecksville (city) Cuyahoga County	13	0.10

Top 10 Places Sorted by Percent

Based on all places, regardless of population

Place	Number	%
Olmsted Falls (city) Cuyahoga County	40	0.51
Oakwood (village) Cuyahoga County	9	0.25
Mayfield Heights (city) Cuyahoga County	46	0.24
Golf Manor (village) Hamilton County	8	0.20
Clayton (city) Montgomery County	20	0.15
Beachwood (city) Cuyahoga County	18	0.15
Logan (city) Hocking County	10	0.15
Parma Heights (city) Cuyahoga County	31	0.14
Monfort Heights South (cdp) Hamilton County	6	0.13
Brecksville (city) Cuyahoga County	13	0.10

Top 10 Places Sorted by Percent

Based on places with populations of 10,000 or more

Place	Number	%
Mayfield Heights (city) Cuyahoga County	46	0.24
Clayton (city) Montgomery County	20	0.15
Beachwood (city) Cuyahoga County	18	0.15
Parma Heights (city) Cuyahoga County	31	0.14
Brecksville (city) Cuyahoga County	13	0.10
Solon (city) Cuyahoga County	20	0.09
Toledo (city) Lucas County	121	0.04
Shiloh (cdp) Montgomery County	4	0.04

Place	Number	%
Brunswick (city) Medina County	9	0.03
Riverside (city) Montgomery County	7	0.03

Arab: Jordanian

Top 10 Places Sorted by Number

Based on all places, regardless of population

Place	Number	%
Toledo (city) Lucas County	174	0.06
Akron (city) Summit County	150	0.07
Columbus (city) Franklin County	146	0.02
Cleveland (city) Cuyahoga County	135	0.03
Lakewood (city) Cuyahoga County	106	0.19
Miamisburg (city) Montgomery County	91	0.46
Fairfield (city) Butler County	77	0.18
Huber Heights (city) Montgomery County	46	0.12
Avon (city) Lorain County	37	0.32
Kettering (city) Montgomery County	37	0.06

Top 10 Places Sorted by Percent

Based on all places, regardless of population

Place	Number	%
Greenhills (village) Hamilton County	28	0.69
Miamisburg (city) Montgomery County	91	0.46
Mulberry (cdp) Clermont County	12	0.38
Montgomery (city) Hamilton County	35	0.35
Avon (city) Lorain County	37	0.32
Magnolia (village) Stark County	3	0.30
Landen (cdp) Warren County	35	0.28
Brooklyn (city) Cuyahoga County	30	0.26
Bay Village (city) Cuyahoga County	33	0.21
Lakewood (city) Cuyahoga County	106	0.19

Top 10 Places Sorted by Percent

Based on places with populations of 10,000 or more

Place	Number	%
Miamisburg (city) Montgomery County	91	0.46
Montgomery (city) Hamilton County	35	0.35
Avon (city) Lorain County	37	0.32
Landen (cdp) Warren County	35	0.28
Brooklyn (city) Cuyahoga County	30	0.26
Bay Village (city) Cuyahoga County	33	0.21
Lakewood (city) Cuyahoga County	106	0.19
Fairfield (city) Butler County	77	0.18
Fairview Park (city) Cuyahoga County	28	0.16
Huber Heights (city) Montgomery County	46	0.12

Arab: Lebanese

Top 10 Places Sorted by Number

Based on all places, regardless of population

Place	Number	%
Toledo (city) Lucas County	2,048	0.65
Columbus (city) Franklin County	1,291	0.18
Cleveland (city) Cuyahoga County	1,004	0.21
Parma (city) Cuyahoga County	958	1.12
Akron (city) Summit County	834	0.38
Lakewood (city) Cuyahoga County	645	1.14
Cincinnati (city) Hamilton County	559	0.17
Strongsville (city) Cuyahoga County	478	1.09
Boardman (cdp) Mahoning County	441	1.18
Westlake (city) Cuyahoga County	304	0.95

Top 10 Places Sorted by Percent

Based on all places, regardless of population

Place	Number	%
Holiday City (village) Williams County	2	3.92
Fairlawn (city) Summit County	255	3.48
Montrose-Ghent (cdp) Summit County	105	2.10
Gates Mills (village) Cuyahoga County	48	1.96
Sherwood (cdp) Hamilton County	57	1.47
Higginsport (village) Brown County	5	1.44
Loveland Park (cdp) Warren County	25	1.40

Place	Number	%
Hills and Dales (village) Stark County	4	1.37
Brooklyn (city) Cuyahoga County	154	1.33
North Randall (village) Cuyahoga County	12	1.31

Top 10 Places Sorted by Percent

Based on places with populations of 10,000 or more

Place	Number	%
Brooklyn (city) Cuyahoga County	154	1.33
Brecksville (city) Cuyahoga County	161	1.21
Boardman (cdp) Mahoning County	441	1.18
Lakewood (city) Cuyahoga County	645	1.14
Parma (city) Cuyahoga County	958	1.12
Strongsville (city) Cuyahoga County	478	1.09
Parma Heights (city) Cuyahoga County	233	1.08
Sylvania (city) Lucas County	201	1.07
Westlake (city) Cuyahoga County	304	0.95
Broadview Heights (city) Cuyahoga County	148	0.93

Arab: Moroccan

Top 10 Places Sorted by Number

Based on all places, regardless of population

Place	Number	%
Cleveland (city) Cuyahoga County	133	0.03
Columbus (city) Franklin County	121	0.02
Youngstown (city) Mahoning County	92	0.11
Bexley (city) Franklin County	69	0.52
South Euclid (city) Cuyahoga County	35	0.15
Cincinnati (city) Hamilton County	30	0.01
Lakewood (city) Cuyahoga County	26	0.05
Fairfield (city) Butler County	22	0.05
Fairview Park (city) Cuyahoga County	20	0.11
Englewood (city) Montgomery County	19	0.16

Top 10 Places Sorted by Percent

Based on all places, regardless of population

Place	Number	%
Bexley (city) Franklin County	69	0.52
Brookside (village) Belmont County	2	0.31
Englewood (city) Montgomery County	19	0.16
South Euclid (city) Cuyahoga County	35	0.15
Gallipolis (city) Gallia County	5	0.12
Youngstown (city) Mahoning County	92	0.11
Fairview Park (city) Cuyahoga County	20	0.11
Highland Heights (city) Cuyahoga County	9	0.11
Riverside (city) Montgomery County	18	0.08
Wilmington (city) Clinton County	9	0.08

Top 10 Places Sorted by Percent

Based on places with populations of 10,000 or more

Place	Number	%
Bexley (city) Franklin County	69	0.52
Englewood (city) Montgomery County	19	0.16
South Euclid (city) Cuyahoga County	35	0.15
Youngstown (city) Mahoning County	92	0.11
Fairview Park (city) Cuyahoga County	20	0.11
Riverside (city) Montgomery County	18	0.08
Wilmington (city) Clinton County	9	0.08
Vermilion (city) Lorain County	8	0.07
West Carrollton City (city) Montgomery County	9	0.06
Lakewood (city) Cuyahoga County	26	0.05

Arab: Palestinian

Top 10 Places Sorted by Number

Based on all places, regardless of population

Place	Number	%
Columbus (city) Franklin County	510	0.07
Lakewood (city) Cuyahoga County	473	0.84
North Olmsted (city) Cuyahoga County	354	1.04
Toledo (city) Lucas County	322	0.10
Cleveland (city) Cuyahoga County	244	0.05
Rocky River (city) Cuyahoga County	106	0.51

Notes: (cdp) census designated place; Refer to the User's Guide in the front of the book for more detailed information.

Westlake (city) Cuyahoga County	98	0.31
Parma (city) Cuyahoga County	87	0.10
Akron (city) Summit County	82	0.04
Cincinnati (city) Hamilton County	67	0.02

Top 10 Places Sorted by Percent
Based on all places, regardless of population

Place	Number	%
North Olmsted (city) Cuyahoga County	354	1.04
Lakewood (city) Cuyahoga County	473	0.84
Ottawa Hills (village) Lucas County	31	0.68
Rocky River (city) Cuyahoga County	106	0.51
Campbell (city) Mahoning County	47	0.50
Lowellville (village) Mahoning County	6	0.47
Brooklyn (city) Cuyahoga County	49	0.42
Montgomery (city) Hamilton County	35	0.35
Westlake (city) Cuyahoga County	98	0.31
Landen (cdp) Warren County	30	0.24

Top 10 Places Sorted by Percent
Based on places with populations of 10,000 or more

Place	Number	%
North Olmsted (city) Cuyahoga County	354	1.04
Lakewood (city) Cuyahoga County	473	0.84
Rocky River (city) Cuyahoga County	106	0.51
Brooklyn (city) Cuyahoga County	49	0.42
Montgomery (city) Hamilton County	35	0.35
Westlake (city) Cuyahoga County	98	0.31
Landen (cdp) Warren County	30	0.24
Tallmadge (city) Summit County	35	0.21
Fairview Park (city) Cuyahoga County	36	0.20
Middleburg Heights (city) Cuyahoga County	26	0.17

Arab: Syrian

Top 10 Places Sorted by Number
Based on all places, regardless of population

Place	Number	%
Columbus (city) Franklin County	381	0.05
Toledo (city) Lucas County	304	0.10
Canton (city) Stark County	278	0.34
Lakewood (city) Cuyahoga County	213	0.38
Cleveland (city) Cuyahoga County	187	0.04
Westlake (city) Cuyahoga County	156	0.49
Akron (city) Summit County	123	0.06
Cincinnati (city) Hamilton County	100	0.03
Amherst (city) Lorain County	88	0.74
Parma (city) Cuyahoga County	74	0.09

Top 10 Places Sorted by Percent
Based on all places, regardless of population

Place	Number	%
Blakeslee (village) Williams County	10	8.26
Clay Center (village) Ottawa County	11	3.72
Sugar Bush Knolls (village) Portage County	6	2.84
Stony Prairie (cdp) Sandusky County	24	2.68
Moreland Hills (village) Cuyahoga County	67	2.03
Gates Mills (village) Cuyahoga County	47	1.92
Waldo (village) Marion County	6	1.78
Sherwood (cdp) Hamilton County	41	1.06
Ottawa Hills (village) Lucas County	43	0.95
Meyers Lake (village) Stark County	5	0.88

Top 10 Places Sorted by Percent
Based on places with populations of 10,000 or more

Place	Number	%
Amherst (city) Lorain County	88	0.74
Westlake (city) Cuyahoga County	156	0.49
Lakewood (city) Cuyahoga County	213	0.38
Brecksville (city) Cuyahoga County	50	0.38
Montgomery (city) Hamilton County	38	0.38
Canton (city) Stark County	278	0.34
Fairview Park (city) Cuyahoga County	60	0.34
Sylvania (city) Lucas County	62	0.33

Brook Park (city) Cuyahoga County	65	0.31
Springboro (city) Warren County	37	0.30

Arab: Other

Top 10 Places Sorted by Number
Based on all places, regardless of population

Place	Number	%
Columbus (city) Franklin County	540	0.08
Toledo (city) Lucas County	228	0.07
Masury (cdp) Trumbull County	157	5.70
Dayton (city) Montgomery County	118	0.07
Youngstown (city) Mahoning County	81	0.10
Athens (city) Athens County	69	0.33
Fairlawn (city) Summit County	63	0.86
Brooklyn (city) Cuyahoga County	62	0.54
Lakewood (city) Cuyahoga County	62	0.11
Westlake (city) Cuyahoga County	61	0.19

Top 10 Places Sorted by Percent
Based on all places, regardless of population

Place	Number	%
Masury (cdp) Trumbull County	157	5.70
Woodmere (village) Cuyahoga County	11	1.33
Fairlawn (city) Summit County	63	0.86
North Lewisburg (village) Champaign County	11	0.69
Brooklyn (city) Cuyahoga County	62	0.54
Athens (city) Athens County	69	0.33
Sheffield Lake (city) Lorain County	31	0.33
Jeffersonville (village) Fayette County	4	0.31
Yellow Springs (village) Greene County	11	0.30
Middleport (village) Meigs County	7	0.28

Top 10 Places Sorted by Percent
Based on places with populations of 10,000 or more

Place	Number	%
Brooklyn (city) Cuyahoga County	62	0.54
Athens (city) Athens County	69	0.33
Blue Ash (city) Hamilton County	25	0.20
Westlake (city) Cuyahoga County	61	0.19
Miamisburg (city) Montgomery County	28	0.14
Lakewood (city) Cuyahoga County	62	0.11
Fairview Park (city) Cuyahoga County	20	0.11
Washington (city) Fayette County	15	0.11
Youngstown (city) Mahoning County	81	0.10
North Canton (city) Stark County	17	0.10

Armenian

Top 10 Places Sorted by Number
Based on all places, regardless of population

Place	Number	%
Columbus (city) Franklin County	216	0.03
Toledo (city) Lucas County	102	0.03
Westlake (city) Cuyahoga County	94	0.30
Upper Arlington (city) Franklin County	90	0.27
Akron (city) Summit County	88	0.04
North Royalton (city) Cuyahoga County	87	0.30
Cincinnati (city) Hamilton County	83	0.03
Westerville (city) Franklin County	81	0.23
Dayton (city) Montgomery County	62	0.04
Cleveland Heights (city) Cuyahoga County	60	0.12

Top 10 Places Sorted by Percent
Based on all places, regardless of population

Place	Number	%
West Leipsic (village) Putnam County	9	3.49
Hamler (village) Henry County	8	1.27
Riverlea (village) Franklin County	6	1.20
Bainbridge (cdp) Geauga County	38	1.09
Moreland Hills (village) Cuyahoga County	24	0.73
Granville (village) Licking County	21	0.72
Sebring (village) Mahoning County	31	0.63

Cherry Grove (cdp) Hamilton County	25	0.5
Beloit (village) Mahoning County	5	0.4
Glendale (village) Hamilton County	10	0.4

Top 10 Places Sorted by Percent
Based on places with populations of 10,000 or more

Place	Number	%
Westlake (city) Cuyahoga County	94	0.3
North Royalton (city) Cuyahoga County	87	0.3
Middleburg Heights (city) Cuyahoga County	47	0.3
Upper Arlington (city) Franklin County	90	0.2
Avon Lake (city) Lorain County	46	0.2
Sharonville (city) Hamilton County	34	0.2
Brecksville (city) Cuyahoga County	33	0.2
Broadview Heights (city) Cuyahoga County	39	0.2
Westerville (city) Franklin County	81	0.2
Tallmadge (city) Summit County	34	0.2

Asian

Top 10 Places Sorted by Number
Based on all places, regardless of population

Place	Number	%
Columbus (city) Franklin County	28,624	4.0
Cleveland (city) Cuyahoga County	7,910	1.6
Cincinnati (city) Hamilton County	6,187	1.8
Toledo (city) Lucas County	4,293	1.3
Akron (city) Summit County	3,919	1.8
Dublin (city) Franklin County	2,527	8.0
Parma (city) Cuyahoga County	1,634	1.9
Strongsville (city) Cuyahoga County	1,594	3.6
Dayton (city) Montgomery County	1,561	0.9
Beavercreek (city) Greene County	1,549	4.0

Top 10 Places Sorted by Percent
Based on all places, regardless of population

Place	Number	%
Urbancrest (village) Franklin County	129	14.8
Dublin (city) Franklin County	2,527	8.0
Woodmere (village) Cuyahoga County	64	7.7
Blue Ash (city) Hamilton County	845	6.7
Beckett Ridge (cdp) Butler County	522	6.0
Evendale (village) Hamilton County	179	5.7
Lower Salem (village) Washington County	6	5.5
Solon (city) Cuyahoga County	1,168	5.3
Richmond Heights (city) Cuyahoga County	582	5.3
Highland Heights (city) Cuyahoga County	410	5.0

Top 10 Places Sorted by Percent
Based on places with populations of 10,000 or more

Place	Number	%
Dublin (city) Franklin County	2,527	8.0
Blue Ash (city) Hamilton County	845	6.7
Solon (city) Cuyahoga County	1,168	5.3
Richmond Heights (city) Cuyahoga County	582	5.3
Athens (city) Athens County	1,080	5.0
Westlake (city) Cuyahoga County	1,506	4.7
Mayfield Heights (city) Cuyahoga County	878	4.5
Sharonville (city) Hamilton County	579	4.1
Forest Park (city) Hamilton County	802	4.1
Beavercreek (city) Greene County	1,549	4.0

Asian: Bangladeshi

Top 10 Places Sorted by Number
Based on all places, regardless of population

Place	Number	%
Columbus (city) Franklin County	194	0.0
Dayton (city) Montgomery County	22	0.01
Cincinnati (city) Hamilton County	17	0.01
Akron (city) Summit County	16	0.01
Strongsville (city) Cuyahoga County	14	0.0
Toledo (city) Lucas County	14	0.0

Notes: (cdp) census designated place; Refer to the User's Guide in the front of the book for more detailed information.

Place	Number	%
Dublin (city) Franklin County	13	0.04
Brecksville (city) Cuyahoga County	10	0.07
Beavercreek (city) Greene County	10	0.03
Moraine (city) Montgomery County	9	0.13

Top 10 Places Sorted by Percent

Based on all places, regardless of population

Place	Number	%
Lucasville (cdp) Scioto County	4	0.25
Holland (village) Lucas County	3	0.23
Moraine (city) Montgomery County	9	0.13
Powell (village) Delaware County	8	0.13
Ada (village) Hardin County	5	0.09
Willoughby Hills (city) Lake County	7	0.08
Groveport (village) Franklin County	3	0.08
Brecksville (city) Cuyahoga County	10	0.07
Bedford Heights (city) Cuyahoga County	8	0.07
Twinsburg (city) Summit County	9	0.05

Top 10 Places Sorted by Percent

Based on places with populations of 10,000 or more

Place	Number	%
Brecksville (city) Cuyahoga County	10	0.07
Bedford Heights (city) Cuyahoga County	8	0.07
Twinsburg (city) Summit County	9	0.05
Dublin (city) Franklin County	13	0.04
Riverside (city) Montgomery County	9	0.04
Forest Park (city) Hamilton County	8	0.04
Columbus (city) Franklin County	194	0.03
Strongsville (city) Cuyahoga County	14	0.03
Beavercreek (city) Greene County	10	0.03
Parma Heights (city) Cuyahoga County	7	0.03

Asian: Cambodian

Top 10 Places Sorted by Number

Based on all places, regardless of population

Place	Number	%
Columbus (city) Franklin County	1,366	0.19
Cleveland (city) Cuyahoga County	391	0.08
Cincinnati (city) Hamilton County	229	0.07
Dayton (city) Montgomery County	81	0.05
Urbancrest (village) Franklin County	58	6.68
Fairfield (city) Butler County	42	0.10
Parma (city) Cuyahoga County	40	0.05
Forest Park (city) Hamilton County	39	0.20
Gahanna (city) Franklin County	38	0.12
Akron (city) Summit County	37	0.02

Top 10 Places Sorted by Percent

Based on all places, regardless of population

Place	Number	%
Urbancrest (village) Franklin County	58	6.68
Valleyview (village) Franklin County	11	1.83
Madeira (city) Hamilton County	36	0.40
Lockland (village) Hamilton County	13	0.35
Pleasant Run (cdp) Hamilton County	17	0.32
Fairfax (village) Hamilton County	6	0.31
Harrisburg (village) Franklin County	1	0.30
New Richmond (village) Clermont County	6	0.27
Northgate (cdp) Hamilton County	20	0.25
Kenwood (cdp) Hamilton County	18	0.24

Top 10 Places Sorted by Percent

Based on places with populations of 10,000 or more

Place	Number	%
Forest Park (city) Hamilton County	39	0.20
Columbus (city) Franklin County	1,366	0.19
Brooklyn (city) Cuyahoga County	20	0.17
Celina (city) Mercer County	13	0.13
Gahanna (city) Franklin County	38	0.12
Fairfield (city) Butler County	42	0.10
Norwood (city) Hamilton County	19	0.09
Cleveland (city) Cuyahoga County	391	0.08

Place	Number	%
Hilliard (city) Franklin County	19	0.08
Oxford (city) Butler County	17	0.08

Asian: Chinese, except Taiwanese

Top 10 Places Sorted by Number

Based on all places, regardless of population

Place	Number	%
Columbus (city) Franklin County	5,977	0.84
Cleveland (city) Cuyahoga County	2,231	0.47
Cincinnati (city) Hamilton County	1,521	0.46
Toledo (city) Lucas County	1,040	0.33
Akron (city) Summit County	656	0.30
Upper Arlington (city) Franklin County	502	1.49
Dublin (city) Franklin County	476	1.52
Cleveland Heights (city) Cuyahoga County	465	0.93
Shaker Heights (city) Cuyahoga County	371	1.26
Solon (city) Cuyahoga County	355	1.63

Top 10 Places Sorted by Percent

Based on all places, regardless of population

Place	Number	%
Highland Heights (city) Cuyahoga County	141	1.74
Solon (city) Cuyahoga County	355	1.63
Athens (city) Athens County	339	1.59
Dublin (city) Franklin County	476	1.52
Upper Arlington (city) Franklin County	502	1.49
Riverlea (village) Franklin County	7	1.40
Richmond Heights (city) Cuyahoga County	144	1.32
Oberlin (city) Lorain County	107	1.31
Shaker Heights (city) Cuyahoga County	371	1.26
Jeromesville (village) Ashland County	6	1.26

Top 10 Places Sorted by Percent

Based on places with populations of 10,000 or more

Place	Number	%
Solon (city) Cuyahoga County	355	1.63
Athens (city) Athens County	339	1.59
Dublin (city) Franklin County	476	1.52
Upper Arlington (city) Franklin County	502	1.49
Richmond Heights (city) Cuyahoga County	144	1.32
Shaker Heights (city) Cuyahoga County	371	1.26
Hudson (city) Summit County	263	1.17
Blue Ash (city) Hamilton County	141	1.13
Mayfield Heights (city) Cuyahoga County	210	1.08
Worthington (city) Franklin County	138	0.98

Asian: Filipino

Top 10 Places Sorted by Number

Based on all places, regardless of population

Place	Number	%
Columbus (city) Franklin County	1,851	0.26
Cleveland (city) Cuyahoga County	955	0.20
Cincinnati (city) Hamilton County	598	0.18
Toledo (city) Lucas County	529	0.17
Parma (city) Cuyahoga County	340	0.40
Akron (city) Summit County	252	0.12
Dayton (city) Montgomery County	242	0.15
Huber Heights (city) Montgomery County	218	0.57
Strongsville (city) Cuyahoga County	211	0.48
Elyria (city) Lorain County	197	0.35

Top 10 Places Sorted by Percent

Based on all places, regardless of population

Place	Number	%
Hemlock (village) Perry County	4	2.82
Wright-Patterson AFB (cdp) Montgomery County	116	1.74
New Rome (village) Franklin County	1	1.67
Devola (cdp) Washington County	42	1.52
Hills and Dales (village) Stark County	3	1.15
Aquilla (village) Geauga County	4	1.08
Tiro (village) Crawford County	3	1.07

Place	Number	%
Holland (village) Lucas County	12	0.92
Gettysburg (village) Darke County	5	0.90
Trimble (village) Athens County	4	0.86

Top 10 Places Sorted by Percent

Based on places with populations of 10,000 or more

Place	Number	%
Seven Hills (city) Cuyahoga County	81	0.67
North Royalton (city) Cuyahoga County	170	0.59
Forest Park (city) Hamilton County	112	0.58
Huber Heights (city) Montgomery County	218	0.57
Fairborn (city) Greene County	171	0.53
Northbrook (cdp) Hamilton County	58	0.52
Brecksville (city) Cuyahoga County	68	0.51
Strongsville (city) Cuyahoga County	211	0.48
Broadview Heights (city) Cuyahoga County	76	0.48
Bedford Heights (city) Cuyahoga County	52	0.46

Asian: Hmong

Top 10 Places Sorted by Number

Based on all places, regardless of population

Place	Number	%
Akron (city) Summit County	280	0.13
Columbus (city) Franklin County	13	0.00
Toledo (city) Lucas County	8	0.00
Medina (city) Medina County	6	0.02
Cuyahoga Falls (city) Summit County	5	0.01
Canton (city) Stark County	3	0.00
Cincinnati (city) Hamilton County	3	0.00
Shaker Heights (city) Cuyahoga County	2	0.01
Sharonville (city) Hamilton County	1	0.01
Euclid (city) Cuyahoga County	1	0.00

Top 10 Places Sorted by Percent

Based on all places, regardless of population

Place	Number	%
Akron (city) Summit County	280	0.13
Medina (city) Medina County	6	0.02
Cuyahoga Falls (city) Summit County	5	0.01
Shaker Heights (city) Cuyahoga County	2	0.01
Sharonville (city) Hamilton County	1	0.01
Columbus (city) Franklin County	13	0.00
Toledo (city) Lucas County	8	0.00
Canton (city) Stark County	3	0.00
Cincinnati (city) Hamilton County	3	0.00
Euclid (city) Cuyahoga County	1	0.00

Top 10 Places Sorted by Percent

Based on places with populations of 10,000 or more

Place	Number	%
Akron (city) Summit County	280	0.13
Medina (city) Medina County	6	0.02
Cuyahoga Falls (city) Summit County	5	0.01
Shaker Heights (city) Cuyahoga County	2	0.01
Sharonville (city) Hamilton County	1	0.01
Columbus (city) Franklin County	13	0.00
Toledo (city) Lucas County	8	0.00
Canton (city) Stark County	3	0.00
Cincinnati (city) Hamilton County	3	0.00
Euclid (city) Cuyahoga County	1	0.00

Asian: Indian

Top 10 Places Sorted by Number

Based on all places, regardless of population

Place	Number	%
Columbus (city) Franklin County	7,025	0.99
Cincinnati (city) Hamilton County	1,633	0.49
Cleveland (city) Cuyahoga County	1,445	0.30
Toledo (city) Lucas County	908	0.29
Akron (city) Summit County	756	0.35
Strongsville (city) Cuyahoga County	738	1.68

Notes: (cdp) census designated place; Refer to the User's Guide in the front of the book for more detailed information.

Place	Number	%
Dublin (city) Franklin County	678	2.16
Westlake (city) Cuyahoga County	611	1.93
Parma (city) Cuyahoga County	603	0.70
Solon (city) Cuyahoga County	510	2.34

Top 10 Places Sorted by Percent
Based on all places, regardless of population

Place	Number	%
Lower Salem (village) Washington County	6	5.50
Holiday City (village) Williams County	2	4.08
Urbancrest (village) Franklin County	29	3.34
Blue Ash (city) Hamilton County	379	3.03
Evendale (village) Hamilton County	90	2.91
Woodmere (village) Cuyahoga County	20	2.42
Solon (city) Cuyahoga County	510	2.34
Beckett Ridge (cdp) Butler County	203	2.34
The Village of Indian Hill (city) Hamilton County	136	2.30
Pepper Pike (city) Cuyahoga County	136	2.25

Top 10 Places Sorted by Percent
Based on places with populations of 10,000 or more

Place	Number	%
Blue Ash (city) Hamilton County	379	3.03
Solon (city) Cuyahoga County	510	2.34
Richmond Heights (city) Cuyahoga County	240	2.19
Dublin (city) Franklin County	678	2.16
Sharonville (city) Hamilton County	290	2.10
Westlake (city) Cuyahoga County	611	1.93
Forest Park (city) Hamilton County	364	1.87
Mayfield Heights (city) Cuyahoga County	346	1.78
Strongsville (city) Cuyahoga County	738	1.68
Twinsburg (city) Summit County	265	1.56

Asian: Indonesian

Top 10 Places Sorted by Number
Based on all places, regardless of population

Place	Number	%
Columbus (city) Franklin County	490	0.07
Cleveland (city) Cuyahoga County	67	0.01
Lakewood (city) Cuyahoga County	46	0.08
Toledo (city) Lucas County	39	0.01
Cincinnati (city) Hamilton County	38	0.01
Athens (city) Athens County	22	0.10
Kettering (city) Montgomery County	18	0.03
Cleveland Heights (city) Cuyahoga County	16	0.03
Dayton (city) Montgomery County	15	0.01
Upper Arlington (city) Franklin County	13	0.04

Top 10 Places Sorted by Percent
Based on all places, regardless of population

Place	Number	%
Gates Mills (village) Cuyahoga County	4	0.16
Hiram (village) Portage County	2	0.16
Athens (city) Athens County	22	0.10
Lakewood (city) Cuyahoga County	46	0.08
Columbus (city) Franklin County	490	0.07
Fairview Park (city) Cuyahoga County	12	0.07
Pepper Pike (city) Cuyahoga County	4	0.07
Oberlin (city) Lorain County	5	0.06
White Oak East (cdp) Hamilton County	2	0.06
Hilliard (city) Franklin County	12	0.05

Top 10 Places Sorted by Percent
Based on places with populations of 10,000 or more

Place	Number	%
Athens (city) Athens County	22	0.10
Lakewood (city) Cuyahoga County	46	0.08
Columbus (city) Franklin County	490	0.07
Fairview Park (city) Cuyahoga County	12	0.07
Hilliard (city) Franklin County	12	0.05
Upper Arlington (city) Franklin County	13	0.04
Twinsburg (city) Summit County	6	0.04
Kettering (city) Montgomery County	18	0.03
Cleveland Heights (city) Cuyahoga County	16	0.03
Stow (city) Summit County	10	0.03

Asian: Japanese

Top 10 Places Sorted by Number
Based on all places, regardless of population

Place	Number	%
Columbus (city) Franklin County	2,458	0.35
Dublin (city) Franklin County	855	2.72
Cleveland (city) Cuyahoga County	343	0.07
Cincinnati (city) Hamilton County	336	0.10
Toledo (city) Lucas County	291	0.09
Findlay (city) Hancock County	285	0.73
Sidney (city) Shelby County	239	1.18
Hilliard (city) Franklin County	174	0.72
Troy (city) Miami County	172	0.78
Huber Heights (city) Montgomery County	169	0.44

Top 10 Places Sorted by Percent
Based on all places, regardless of population

Place	Number	%
Dublin (city) Franklin County	855	2.72
Choctaw Lake (cdp) Madison County	19	1.22
Sidney (city) Shelby County	239	1.18
Yellow Springs (village) Greene County	37	0.98
Gambier (village) Knox County	17	0.91
Mayfield (village) Cuyahoga County	29	0.84
Cuyahoga Heights (village) Cuyahoga County	5	0.83
Troy (city) Miami County	172	0.78
Montgomery (city) Hamilton County	77	0.76
Fairlawn (city) Summit County	55	0.75

Top 10 Places Sorted by Percent
Based on places with populations of 10,000 or more

Place	Number	%
Dublin (city) Franklin County	855	2.72
Sidney (city) Shelby County	239	1.18
Troy (city) Miami County	172	0.78
Montgomery (city) Hamilton County	77	0.76
Blue Ash (city) Hamilton County	92	0.74
Findlay (city) Hancock County	285	0.73
Hilliard (city) Franklin County	174	0.72
Mayfield Heights (city) Cuyahoga County	136	0.70
Athens (city) Athens County	146	0.68
Landen (cdp) Warren County	78	0.61

Asian: Korean

Top 10 Places Sorted by Number
Based on all places, regardless of population

Place	Number	%
Columbus (city) Franklin County	2,930	0.41
Cincinnati (city) Hamilton County	464	0.14
Cleveland (city) Cuyahoga County	380	0.08
Toledo (city) Lucas County	370	0.12
Akron (city) Summit County	366	0.17
Beavercreek (city) Greene County	284	0.75
Fairborn (city) Greene County	206	0.64
Westlake (city) Cuyahoga County	193	0.61
Dublin (city) Franklin County	191	0.61
Dayton (city) Montgomery County	161	0.10

Top 10 Places Sorted by Percent
Based on all places, regardless of population

Place	Number	%
Woodmere (village) Cuyahoga County	22	2.66
North Hampton (village) Clark County	8	2.16
Burgoon (village) Sandusky County	3	1.51
Chauncey (village) Athens County	15	1.41
Hoytville (village) Wood County	4	1.35
Pepper Pike (city) Cuyahoga County	65	1.08
Highland (village) Highland County	3	1.06
Zoar (village) Tuscarawas County	2	1.04
Blue Ash (city) Hamilton County	118	0.94
Belmont (village) Belmont County	5	0.94

Top 10 Places Sorted by Percent
Based on places with populations of 10,000 or more

Place	Number	%
Blue Ash (city) Hamilton County	118	0.94
Beavercreek (city) Greene County	284	0.75
Broadview Heights (city) Cuyahoga County	108	0.68
Fairborn (city) Greene County	206	0.64
Westlake (city) Cuyahoga County	193	0.61
Dublin (city) Franklin County	191	0.61
Beachwood (city) Cuyahoga County	69	0.57
Montgomery (city) Hamilton County	55	0.54
Athens (city) Athens County	106	0.50
Worthington (city) Franklin County	70	0.50

Asian: Laotian

Top 10 Places Sorted by Number
Based on all places, regardless of population

Place	Number	%
Columbus (city) Franklin County	1,290	0.18
Akron (city) Summit County	516	0.24
Toledo (city) Lucas County	146	0.05
Whitehall (city) Franklin County	75	0.39
Cleveland (city) Cuyahoga County	70	0.01
Orrville (city) Wayne County	67	0.78
Findlay (city) Hancock County	67	0.17
Carey (village) Wyandot County	59	1.51
Euclid (city) Cuyahoga County	50	0.09
Montpelier (village) Williams County	48	1.11

Top 10 Places Sorted by Percent
Based on all places, regardless of population

Place	Number	%
Carey (village) Wyandot County	59	1.51
Montpelier (village) Williams County	48	1.11
Orrville (city) Wayne County	67	0.78
Buckland (village) Auglaize County	2	0.78
Deshler (village) Henry County	13	0.71
Groveport (village) Franklin County	19	0.49
Whitehall (city) Franklin County	75	0.39
Sugarcreek (village) Tuscarawas County	8	0.37
Wauseon (city) Fulton County	21	0.30
Smithville (village) Wayne County	4	0.30

Top 10 Places Sorted by Percent
Based on places with populations of 10,000 or more

Place	Number	%
Whitehall (city) Franklin County	75	0.39
Akron (city) Summit County	516	0.24
Columbus (city) Franklin County	1,290	0.18
Findlay (city) Hancock County	67	0.17
Fostoria (city) Seneca County	18	0.13
Euclid (city) Cuyahoga County	50	0.09
Richmond Heights (city) Cuyahoga County	10	0.09
Oregon (city) Lucas County	15	0.08
Bexley (city) Franklin County	10	0.08
Wadsworth (city) Medina County	11	0.06

Asian: Malaysian

Top 10 Places Sorted by Number
Based on all places, regardless of population

Place	Number	%
Columbus (city) Franklin County	66	0.01
Toledo (city) Lucas County	43	0.01
Athens (city) Athens County	25	0.12
Cleveland (city) Cuyahoga County	18	0.00
Findlay (city) Hancock County	9	0.02
Akron (city) Summit County	8	0.00

Notes: (cdp) census designated place; Refer to the User's Guide in the front of the book for more detailed information.

Lakewood (city) Cuyahoga County	7	0.01
Monfort Heights East (cdp) Hamilton County	6	0.15
Maumee (city) Lucas County	6	0.04
Dublin (city) Franklin County	6	0.02

Top 10 Places Sorted by Percent

Based on all places, regardless of population

Place	Number	%
Woodmere (village) Cuyahoga County	2	0.24
Monfort Heights East (cdp) Hamilton County	6	0.15
Greentown (cdp) Stark County	4	0.13
Athens (city) Athens County	25	0.12
Gates Mills (village) Cuyahoga County	2	0.08
Boston Heights (village) Summit County	1	0.08
The Plains (cdp) Athens County	2	0.07
Ripley (village) Brown County	1	0.06
New Albany (village) Franklin County	2	0.05
South Russell (village) Geauga County	2	0.05

Top 10 Places Sorted by Percent

Based on places with populations of 10,000 or more

Place	Number	%
Athens (city) Athens County	25	0.12
Maumee (city) Lucas County	6	0.04
Reading (city) Hamilton County	3	0.03
Findlay (city) Hancock County	9	0.02
Dublin (city) Franklin County	6	0.02
Fairborn (city) Greene County	6	0.02
Riverside (city) Montgomery County	4	0.02
Clayton (city) Montgomery County	3	0.02
Fremont (city) Sandusky County	3	0.02
Urbana (city) Champaign County	2	0.02

Asian: Pakistani

Top 10 Places Sorted by Number

Based on all places, regardless of population

Place	Number	%
Columbus (city) Franklin County	434	0.06
Cincinnati (city) Hamilton County	85	0.03
Cleveland (city) Cuyahoga County	70	0.01
Toledo (city) Lucas County	68	0.02
Akron (city) Summit County	59	0.03
Westlake (city) Cuyahoga County	50	0.16
Lakewood (city) Cuyahoga County	48	0.08
Strongsville (city) Cuyahoga County	46	0.10
Forest Park (city) Hamilton County	42	0.22
Austintown (cdp) Mahoning County	31	0.10

Top 10 Places Sorted by Percent

Based on all places, regardless of population

Place	Number	%
Mount Cory (village) Hancock County	3	1.48
Orange (village) Cuyahoga County	13	0.40
Oak Hill (village) Jackson County	4	0.24
Woodmere (village) Cuyahoga County	2	0.24
Forest Park (city) Hamilton County	42	0.22
Richmond Heights (city) Cuyahoga County	20	0.18
Dry Run (cdp) Hamilton County	12	0.18
Westlake (city) Cuyahoga County	50	0.16
Amberley (village) Hamilton County	5	0.15
Marble Cliff (village) Franklin County	1	0.15

Top 10 Places Sorted by Percent

Based on places with populations of 10,000 or more

Place	Number	%
Forest Park (city) Hamilton County	42	0.22
Richmond Heights (city) Cuyahoga County	20	0.18
Westlake (city) Cuyahoga County	50	0.16
Middleburg Heights (city) Cuyahoga County	20	0.13
Brecksville (city) Cuyahoga County	17	0.13
Strongsville (city) Cuyahoga County	46	0.10
Austintown (cdp) Mahoning County	31	0.10
Mason (city) Warren County	19	0.09

Forestville (cdp) Hamilton County	10	0.09
Lakewood (city) Cuyahoga County	48	0.08

Asian: Sri Lankan

Top 10 Places Sorted by Number

Based on all places, regardless of population

Place	Number	%
Columbus (city) Franklin County	116	0.02
Cincinnati (city) Hamilton County	65	0.02
Hilliard (city) Franklin County	15	0.06
Fairborn (city) Greene County	14	0.04
Upper Arlington (city) Franklin County	12	0.04
Shaker Heights (city) Cuyahoga County	11	0.04
Akron (city) Summit County	11	0.01
Toledo (city) Lucas County	10	0.00
Solon (city) Cuyahoga County	9	0.04
Bowling Green (city) Wood County	9	0.03

Top 10 Places Sorted by Percent

Based on all places, regardless of population

Place	Number	%
Fairfax (village) Hamilton County	7	0.36
Gates Mills (village) Cuyahoga County	6	0.24
Mount Repose (cdp) Clermont County	5	0.12
Hilliard (city) Franklin County	15	0.06
Blue Ash (city) Hamilton County	7	0.06
Deer Park (city) Hamilton County	3	0.05
Glendale (village) Hamilton County	1	0.05
Fairborn (city) Greene County	14	0.04
Upper Arlington (city) Franklin County	12	0.04
Shaker Heights (city) Cuyahoga County	11	0.04

Top 10 Places Sorted by Percent

Based on places with populations of 10,000 or more

Place	Number	%
Hilliard (city) Franklin County	15	0.06
Blue Ash (city) Hamilton County	7	0.06
Fairborn (city) Greene County	14	0.04
Upper Arlington (city) Franklin County	12	0.04
Shaker Heights (city) Cuyahoga County	11	0.04
Solon (city) Cuyahoga County	9	0.04
Aurora (city) Portage County	6	0.04
Bowling Green (city) Wood County	9	0.03
Kent (city) Portage County	9	0.03
Athens (city) Athens County	7	0.03

Asian: Taiwanese

Top 10 Places Sorted by Number

Based on all places, regardless of population

Place	Number	%
Columbus (city) Franklin County	435	0.06
Upper Arlington (city) Franklin County	103	0.31
Cincinnati (city) Hamilton County	87	0.03
Dublin (city) Franklin County	80	0.25
Cleveland (city) Cuyahoga County	56	0.01
Athens (city) Athens County	47	0.22
Beavercreek (city) Greene County	46	0.12
Solon (city) Cuyahoga County	39	0.18
Westlake (city) Cuyahoga County	37	0.12
Hilliard (city) Franklin County	32	0.13

Top 10 Places Sorted by Percent

Based on all places, regardless of population

Place	Number	%
Evendale (village) Hamilton County	16	0.52
Shawnee Hills (village) Delaware County	2	0.48
Pigeon Creek (cdp) Summit County	4	0.42
Five Points (cdp) Warren County	7	0.32
Upper Arlington (city) Franklin County	103	0.31
Highland Heights (city) Cuyahoga County	25	0.31
Dublin (city) Franklin County	80	0.25

Athens (city) Athens County	47	0.22
Cherry Grove (cdp) Hamilton County	10	0.22
The Village of Indian Hill (city) Hamilton County	12	0.20

Top 10 Places Sorted by Percent

Based on places with populations of 10,000 or more

Place	Number	%
Upper Arlington (city) Franklin County	103	0.31
Dublin (city) Franklin County	80	0.25
Athens (city) Athens County	47	0.22
Solon (city) Cuyahoga County	39	0.18
Springdale (city) Hamilton County	19	0.18
Montgomery (city) Hamilton County	16	0.16
Sharonville (city) Hamilton County	21	0.15
Hilliard (city) Franklin County	32	0.13
Centerville (city) Montgomery County	29	0.13
Beavercreek (city) Greene County	46	0.12

Asian: Thai

Top 10 Places Sorted by Number

Based on all places, regardless of population

Place	Number	%
Columbus (city) Franklin County	472	0.07
Cleveland (city) Cuyahoga County	121	0.03
Cincinnati (city) Hamilton County	88	0.03
Akron (city) Summit County	79	0.04
Toledo (city) Lucas County	76	0.02
Dayton (city) Montgomery County	48	0.03
Fairborn (city) Greene County	41	0.13
Huber Heights (city) Montgomery County	40	0.10
Cleveland Heights (city) Cuyahoga County	37	0.07
Lakewood (city) Cuyahoga County	30	0.05

Top 10 Places Sorted by Percent

Based on all places, regardless of population

Place	Number	%
Riverlea (village) Franklin County	3	0.60
Kirtland Hills (village) Lake County	3	0.50
Richmond (village) Jefferson County	2	0.42
Hills and Dales (village) Stark County	1	0.38
Pigeon Creek (cdp) Summit County	3	0.32
Enon (village) Clark County	8	0.30
Wilmot (village) Stark County	1	0.30
Wright-Patterson AFB (cdp) Montgomery County	17	0.26
Green Springs (village) Seneca County	3	0.24
Rawson (village) Hancock County	1	0.22

Top 10 Places Sorted by Percent

Based on places with populations of 10,000 or more

Place	Number	%
Fairborn (city) Greene County	41	0.13
Athens (city) Athens County	28	0.13
Huber Heights (city) Montgomery County	40	0.10
Riverside (city) Montgomery County	22	0.09
Columbus (city) Franklin County	472	0.07
Cleveland Heights (city) Cuyahoga County	37	0.07
Gahanna (city) Franklin County	23	0.07
Whitehall (city) Franklin County	13	0.07
Ashland (city) Ashland County	12	0.06
Berea (city) Cuyahoga County	11	0.06

Asian: Vietnamese

Top 10 Places Sorted by Number

Based on all places, regardless of population

Place	Number	%
Columbus (city) Franklin County	2,089	0.29
Cleveland (city) Cuyahoga County	1,186	0.25
Cincinnati (city) Hamilton County	620	0.19
Akron (city) Summit County	434	0.20
Toledo (city) Lucas County	298	0.10
Huber Heights (city) Montgomery County	245	0.64

Notes: (cdp) census designated place; Refer to the User's Guide in the front of the book for more detailed information.

Dayton (city) Montgomery County	179	0.11
Fairborn (city) Greene County	145	0.45
Fairfield (city) Butler County	120	0.29
Kettering (city) Montgomery County	120	0.21

Top 10 Places Sorted by Percent
Based on all places, regardless of population

Place	Number	%
Moraine (city) Montgomery County	64	0.93
Olde West Chester (cdp) Butler County	2	0.86
Beckett Ridge (cdp) Butler County	66	0.76
Springdale (city) Hamilton County	74	0.70
Urbancrest (village) Franklin County	6	0.69
Huber Heights (city) Montgomery County	245	0.64
Magnetic Springs (village) Union County	2	0.62
Pleasant Run Farm (cdp) Hamilton County	28	0.59
Brooklyn (city) Cuyahoga County	67	0.58
Northgate (cdp) Hamilton County	46	0.57

Top 10 Places Sorted by Percent
Based on places with populations of 10,000 or more

Place	Number	%
Springdale (city) Hamilton County	74	0.70
Huber Heights (city) Montgomery County	245	0.64
Brooklyn (city) Cuyahoga County	67	0.58
Forest Park (city) Hamilton County	93	0.48
Fairborn (city) Greene County	145	0.45
Sharonville (city) Hamilton County	47	0.34
Columbus (city) Franklin County	2,089	0.29
Fairfield (city) Butler County	120	0.29
Riverside (city) Montgomery County	68	0.29
Parma Heights (city) Cuyahoga County	59	0.27

Asian: Other Asian, specified

Top 10 Places Sorted by Number
Based on all places, regardless of population

Place	Number	%
Columbus (city) Franklin County	103	0.01
Cincinnati (city) Hamilton County	44	0.01
Cleveland (city) Cuyahoga County	44	0.01
Akron (city) Summit County	39	0.02
Toledo (city) Lucas County	22	0.01
Hamilton (city) Butler County	15	0.02
Cleveland Heights (city) Cuyahoga County	14	0.03
Dayton (city) Montgomery County	13	0.01
Frankfort (village) Ross County	12	1.19
Franklin (city) Warren County	11	0.10

Top 10 Places Sorted by Percent
Based on all places, regardless of population

Place	Number	%
Frankfort (village) Ross County	12	1.19
Seven Mile (village) Butler County	5	0.74
Corning (village) Perry County	2	0.34
Rio Grande (village) Gallia County	3	0.33
Woodmere (village) Cuyahoga County	2	0.24
Crown City (village) Gallia County	1	0.24
Lucasville (cdp) Scioto County	3	0.19
Hiram (village) Portage County	2	0.16
Roseville (village) Perry County	3	0.15
Fort Loramie (village) Shelby County	2	0.15

Top 10 Places Sorted by Percent
Based on places with populations of 10,000 or more

Place	Number	%
Franklin (city) Warren County	11	0.10
Springboro (city) Warren County	11	0.09
University Heights (city) Cuyahoga County	10	0.07
Landen (cdp) Warren County	8	0.06
Oxford (city) Butler County	10	0.05
Richmond Heights (city) Cuyahoga County	5	0.05
Athens (city) Athens County	8	0.04
Blue Ash (city) Hamilton County	5	0.04
Finneytown (cdp) Hamilton County	5	0.04
Cleveland Heights (city) Cuyahoga County	14	0.03

Asian: Other Asian, not specified

Top 10 Places Sorted by Number
Based on all places, regardless of population

Place	Number	%
Columbus (city) Franklin County	1,315	0.18
Cleveland (city) Cuyahoga County	518	0.11
Toledo (city) Lucas County	399	0.13
Cincinnati (city) Hamilton County	341	0.10
Akron (city) Summit County	239	0.11
Dayton (city) Montgomery County	129	0.08
Parma (city) Cuyahoga County	107	0.12
North Olmsted (city) Cuyahoga County	91	0.27
Lakewood (city) Cuyahoga County	85	0.15
Westlake (city) Cuyahoga County	75	0.24

Top 10 Places Sorted by Percent
Based on all places, regardless of population

Place	Number	%
Urbancrest (village) Franklin County	34	3.92
Chauncey (village) Athens County	11	1.03
Put-in-Bay (village) Ottawa County	1	0.78
Old Washington (village) Guernsey County	2	0.75
Potsdam (village) Miami County	1	0.49
Powhatan Point (village) Belmont County	8	0.46
North Randall (village) Cuyahoga County	4	0.44
Pigeon Creek (cdp) Summit County	3	0.32
Fairlawn (city) Summit County	23	0.31
McComb (village) Hancock County	5	0.30

Top 10 Places Sorted by Percent
Based on places with populations of 10,000 or more

Place	Number	%
North Olmsted (city) Cuyahoga County	91	0.27
Westlake (city) Cuyahoga County	75	0.24
Miamisburg (city) Montgomery County	46	0.24
Athens (city) Athens County	46	0.22
Fairview Park (city) Cuyahoga County	35	0.20
Forestville (cdp) Hamilton County	22	0.20
Columbus (city) Franklin County	1,315	0.18
Bowling Green (city) Wood County	53	0.18
Centerville (city) Montgomery County	42	0.18
Fairborn (city) Greene County	54	0.17

Assyrian/Chaldean/Syriac

Top 10 Places Sorted by Number
Based on all places, regardless of population

Place	Number	%
Rocky River (city) Cuyahoga County	39	0.19
Defiance (city) Defiance County	20	0.12
Toledo (city) Lucas County	15	0.00
Middlefield (village) Geauga County	7	0.32
Aurora (city) Portage County	7	0.05
Dayton (city) Montgomery County	7	0.00
Cedarville (village) Greene County	6	0.16
Oregon (city) Lucas County	6	0.03
Gahanna (city) Franklin County	6	0.02
Kettering (city) Montgomery County	6	0.01

Top 10 Places Sorted by Percent
Based on all places, regardless of population

Place	Number	%
Middlefield (village) Geauga County	7	0.32
Rocky River (city) Cuyahoga County	39	0.19
Cedarville (village) Greene County	6	0.16
Defiance (city) Defiance County	20	0.12
Aurora (city) Portage County	7	0.05
Oregon (city) Lucas County	6	0.03
Gahanna (city) Franklin County	6	0.02
Parma Heights (city) Cuyahoga County	5	0.02
Kettering (city) Montgomery County	6	0.01
Lakewood (city) Cuyahoga County	6	0.01

Top 10 Places Sorted by Percent
Based on places with populations of 10,000 or more

Place	Number	%
Rocky River (city) Cuyahoga County	39	0.19
Defiance (city) Defiance County	20	0.12
Aurora (city) Portage County	7	0.05
Oregon (city) Lucas County	6	0.03
Gahanna (city) Franklin County	6	0.02
Parma Heights (city) Cuyahoga County	5	0.02
Kettering (city) Montgomery County	6	0.01
Lakewood (city) Cuyahoga County	6	0.01
Huber Heights (city) Montgomery County	5	0.01
Toledo (city) Lucas County	15	0.00

Australian

Top 10 Places Sorted by Number
Based on all places, regardless of population

Place	Number	%
Columbus (city) Franklin County	262	0.04
Toledo (city) Lucas County	107	0.03
Cincinnati (city) Hamilton County	65	0.02
Shaker Heights (city) Cuyahoga County	54	0.18
Solon (city) Cuyahoga County	51	0.23
Beachwood (city) Cuyahoga County	50	0.41
Mount Vernon (city) Knox County	50	0.34
Akron (city) Summit County	50	0.02
Elyria (city) Lorain County	46	0.08
Cleveland (city) Cuyahoga County	40	0.01

Top 10 Places Sorted by Percent
Based on all places, regardless of population

Place	Number	%
Carrollton (village) Carroll County	19	0.61
Germantown (village) Montgomery County	29	0.60
Lake Darby (cdp) Franklin County	20	0.55
New Riegel (village) Seneca County	1	0.45
Beachwood (city) Cuyahoga County	50	0.41
Timberlake (village) Lake County	3	0.39
Peninsula (village) Summit County	2	0.39
Wright-Patterson AFB (cdp) Montgomery County	25	0.38
Fort Shawnee (village) Allen County	14	0.35
Mount Vernon (city) Knox County	50	0.34

Top 10 Places Sorted by Percent
Based on places with populations of 10,000 or more

Place	Number	%
Beachwood (city) Cuyahoga County	50	0.41
Mount Vernon (city) Knox County	50	0.34
Loveland (city) Hamilton County	29	0.24
Solon (city) Cuyahoga County	51	0.23
Worthington (city) Franklin County	30	0.21
Shaker Heights (city) Cuyahoga County	54	0.18
Bexley (city) Franklin County	20	0.15
Hudson (city) Summit County	26	0.12
Dublin (city) Franklin County	35	0.11
Montgomery (city) Hamilton County	10	0.10

Austrian

Top 10 Places Sorted by Number
Based on all places, regardless of population

Place	Number	%
Columbus (city) Franklin County	1,483	0.21
Cincinnati (city) Hamilton County	804	0.24
Cleveland (city) Cuyahoga County	749	0.16
Akron (city) Summit County	602	0.28
Parma (city) Cuyahoga County	473	0.55
Toledo (city) Lucas County	396	0.13

Notes: (cdp) census designated place; Refer to the User's Guide in the front of the book for more detailed information.

Place	Number	%
Lakewood (city) Cuyahoga County	385	0.68
Strongsville (city) Cuyahoga County	312	0.71
Euclid (city) Cuyahoga County	310	0.59
Westlake (city) Cuyahoga County	269	0.84

Top 10 Places Sorted by Percent
Based on all places, regardless of population

Place	Number	%
Tuscarawas (village) Tuscarawas County	36	3.75
Peninsula (village) Summit County	14	2.70
Pepper Pike (city) Cuyahoga County	117	1.94
Orange (village) Cuyahoga County	58	1.79
Newton Falls (village) Trumbull County	90	1.78
Turpin Hills (cdp) Hamilton County	84	1.68
Aquilla (village) Geauga County	6	1.63
Beachwood (city) Cuyahoga County	198	1.62
New Concord (village) Muskingum County	42	1.56
North Perry (village) Lake County	13	1.55

Top 10 Places Sorted by Percent
Based on places with populations of 10,000 or more

Place	Number	%
Beachwood (city) Cuyahoga County	198	1.62
Mayfield Heights (city) Cuyahoga County	203	1.05
Lyndhurst (city) Cuyahoga County	159	1.04
Brecksville (city) Cuyahoga County	120	0.90
Avon (city) Lorain County	103	0.90
Rocky River (city) Cuyahoga County	176	0.85
New Philadelphia (city) Tuscarawas County	143	0.85
Westlake (city) Cuyahoga County	269	0.84
University Heights (city) Cuyahoga County	114	0.81
South Euclid (city) Cuyahoga County	187	0.79

Basque

Top 10 Places Sorted by Number
Based on all places, regardless of population

Place	Number	%
Columbus (city) Franklin County	37	0.01
Cleveland Heights (city) Cuyahoga County	19	0.04
Cleveland (city) Cuyahoga County	16	0.00
Reading (city) Hamilton County	15	0.13
Centerville (city) Montgomery County	13	0.06
Bowling Green (city) Wood County	12	0.04
Willoughby Hills (city) Lake County	11	0.13
Toledo (city) Lucas County	10	0.00
Westlake (city) Cuyahoga County	9	0.03
Hilliard (city) Franklin County	8	0.03

Top 10 Places Sorted by Percent
Based on all places, regardless of population

Place	Number	%
New Albany (village) Franklin County	6	0.16
Reading (city) Hamilton County	15	0.13
Willoughby Hills (city) Lake County	11	0.13
Centerville (city) Montgomery County	13	0.06
Chagrin Falls (village) Cuyahoga County	2	0.05
Cleveland Heights (city) Cuyahoga County	19	0.04
Bowling Green (city) Wood County	12	0.04
Bedford (city) Cuyahoga County	5	0.04
Westlake (city) Cuyahoga County	9	0.03
Hilliard (city) Franklin County	8	0.03

Top 10 Places Sorted by Percent
Based on places with populations of 10,000 or more

Place	Number	%
Reading (city) Hamilton County	15	0.13
Centerville (city) Montgomery County	13	0.06
Cleveland Heights (city) Cuyahoga County	19	0.04
Bowling Green (city) Wood County	12	0.04
Bedford (city) Cuyahoga County	5	0.04
Westlake (city) Cuyahoga County	9	0.03
Hilliard (city) Franklin County	8	0.03
Fairview Park (city) Cuyahoga County	5	0.03

Place	Number	%
Shaker Heights (city) Cuyahoga County	6	0.02
Rocky River (city) Cuyahoga County	5	0.02

Belgian

Top 10 Places Sorted by Number
Based on all places, regardless of population

Place	Number	%
Columbus (city) Franklin County	510	0.07
Toledo (city) Lucas County	458	0.15
Cincinnati (city) Hamilton County	167	0.05
Akron (city) Summit County	117	0.05
Cleveland (city) Cuyahoga County	98	0.02
Cleveland Heights (city) Cuyahoga County	95	0.19
Gahanna (city) Franklin County	92	0.28
Springfield (city) Clark County	91	0.14
Findlay (city) Hancock County	83	0.21
Sylvania (city) Lucas County	82	0.44

Top 10 Places Sorted by Percent
Based on all places, regardless of population

Place	Number	%
Malinta (village) Henry County	18	6.06
Vanlue (village) Hancock County	7	1.82
New Riegel (village) Seneca County	3	1.36
Lyons (village) Fulton County	7	1.27
Tiltonsville (village) Jefferson County	16	1.23
Granville (village) Licking County	35	1.20
Magnolia (village) Stark County	11	1.12
Cairo (village) Allen County	5	1.01
Montpelier (village) Williams County	41	0.95
Montrose-Ghent (cdp) Summit County	47	0.94

Top 10 Places Sorted by Percent
Based on places with populations of 10,000 or more

Place	Number	%
Maumee (city) Lucas County	72	0.47
Montgomery (city) Hamilton County	46	0.46
Mount Vernon (city) Knox County	65	0.45
Sylvania (city) Lucas County	82	0.44
Marietta (city) Washington County	51	0.35
Perrysburg (city) Wood County	55	0.32
Loveland (city) Hamilton County	38	0.32
Gahanna (city) Franklin County	92	0.28
Centerville (city) Montgomery County	63	0.27
Springboro (city) Warren County	33	0.27

Brazilian

Top 10 Places Sorted by Number
Based on all places, regardless of population

Place	Number	%
Columbus (city) Franklin County	272	0.04
Canton (city) Stark County	79	0.10
Cleveland (city) Cuyahoga County	69	0.01
Granville South (cdp) Licking County	64	5.26
Cincinnati (city) Hamilton County	54	0.02
Dayton (city) Montgomery County	42	0.03
Westlake (city) Cuyahoga County	35	0.11
Bowling Green (city) Wood County	32	0.11
North Canton (city) Stark County	31	0.19
Fairlawn (city) Summit County	30	0.41

Top 10 Places Sorted by Percent
Based on all places, regardless of population

Place	Number	%
Granville South (cdp) Licking County	64	5.26
Ridgeway (village) Hardin County	12	3.45
Fairlawn (city) Summit County	30	0.41
Cedarville (village) Greene County	14	0.37
Beckett Ridge (cdp) Butler County	30	0.35
Mulberry (cdp) Clermont County	11	0.35
North Canton (city) Stark County	31	0.19
Gloria Glens Park (village) Medina County	1	0.19
Loveland (city) Hamilton County	21	0.18
Amelia (village) Clermont County	5	0.18

Top 10 Places Sorted by Percent
Based on places with populations of 10,000 or more

Place	Number	%
North Canton (city) Stark County	31	0.19
Loveland (city) Hamilton County	21	0.18
Celina (city) Mercer County	16	0.15
Marietta (city) Washington County	21	0.14
Mayfield Heights (city) Cuyahoga County	26	0.13
Marysville (city) Union County	21	0.13
Westlake (city) Cuyahoga County	35	0.11
Bowling Green (city) Wood County	32	0.11
Canton (city) Stark County	79	0.10
North Ridgeville (city) Lorain County	20	0.09

British

Top 10 Places Sorted by Number
Based on all places, regardless of population

Place	Number	%
Columbus (city) Franklin County	3,186	0.45
Cincinnati (city) Hamilton County	1,188	0.36
Toledo (city) Lucas County	689	0.22
Akron (city) Summit County	663	0.31
Cleveland (city) Cuyahoga County	492	0.10
Dayton (city) Montgomery County	483	0.29
Upper Arlington (city) Franklin County	346	1.03
Cuyahoga Falls (city) Summit County	307	0.62
Hudson (city) Summit County	285	1.27
Canton (city) Stark County	280	0.35

Top 10 Places Sorted by Percent
Based on all places, regardless of population

Place	Number	%
Old Washington (village) Guernsey County	10	3.48
Chilo (village) Clermont County	3	3.30
Terrace Park (village) Hamilton County	66	2.90
Germantown (village) Montgomery County	126	2.63
Riverlea (village) Franklin County	12	2.40
Lindsey (village) Sandusky County	12	2.38
Beverly (village) Washington County	26	2.07
Hunting Valley (village) Cuyahoga County	15	2.04
Lucas (village) Richland County	12	2.00
College Corner (village) Preble County	8	1.89

Top 10 Places Sorted by Percent
Based on places with populations of 10,000 or more

Place	Number	%
Hudson (city) Summit County	285	1.27
Montgomery (city) Hamilton County	121	1.20
Worthington (city) Franklin County	157	1.10
Bay Village (city) Cuyahoga County	176	1.09
Rocky River (city) Cuyahoga County	220	1.06
Sharonville (city) Hamilton County	144	1.05
Upper Arlington (city) Franklin County	346	1.03
Oxford (city) Butler County	223	1.01
Vandalia (city) Montgomery County	143	0.98
Kent (city) Portage County	239	0.85

Bulgarian

Top 10 Places Sorted by Number
Based on all places, regardless of population

Place	Number	%
Columbus (city) Franklin County	217	0.03
Toledo (city) Lucas County	167	0.05
Cincinnati (city) Hamilton County	106	0.03
Cleveland (city) Cuyahoga County	79	0.02
Akron (city) Summit County	67	0.03
Oregon (city) Lucas County	63	0.33

Notes: (cdp) census designated place; Refer to the User's Guide in the front of the book for more detailed information.

Place	Number	%
Massillon (city) Stark County	56	0.18
Youngstown (city) Mahoning County	54	0.07
Rocky River (city) Cuyahoga County	51	0.25
Lebanon (city) Warren County	45	0.27

Top 10 Places Sorted by Percent
Based on all places, regardless of population

Place	Number	%
Burbank (village) Wayne County	7	2.48
Linndale (village) Cuyahoga County	3	2.48
Lyons (village) Fulton County	5	0.90
Sherwood (cdp) Hamilton County	34	0.88
New London (village) Huron County	17	0.63
Fruit Hill (cdp) Hamilton County	24	0.62
Waterville (village) Lucas County	27	0.57
Uniontown (cdp) Stark County	16	0.56
Willard (city) Huron County	35	0.51
Ada (village) Hardin County	28	0.51

Top 10 Places Sorted by Percent
Based on places with populations of 10,000 or more

Place	Number	%
Oregon (city) Lucas County	63	0.33
Lebanon (city) Warren County	45	0.27
Rocky River (city) Cuyahoga County	51	0.25
Fairview Park (city) Cuyahoga County	43	0.24
Mount Vernon (city) Knox County	34	0.23
Sylvania (city) Lucas County	42	0.22
Massillon (city) Stark County	56	0.18
Avon (city) Lorain County	19	0.17
Blue Ash (city) Hamilton County	19	0.15
Defiance (city) Defiance County	23	0.14

Canadian

Top 10 Places Sorted by Number
Based on all places, regardless of population

Place	Number	%
Columbus (city) Franklin County	1,034	0.15
Toledo (city) Lucas County	682	0.22
Cincinnati (city) Hamilton County	398	0.12
Cleveland (city) Cuyahoga County	359	0.08
Akron (city) Summit County	218	0.10
Dublin (city) Franklin County	214	0.68
Cleveland Heights (city) Cuyahoga County	198	0.40
Westerville (city) Franklin County	170	0.48
Upper Arlington (city) Franklin County	156	0.46
Mentor (city) Lake County	154	0.31

Top 10 Places Sorted by Percent
Based on all places, regardless of population

Place	Number	%
Gann (village) Knox County	7	4.76
Broughton (village) Paulding County	6	2.90
Hartford (village) Licking County	11	2.76
Huntsville (village) Logan County	10	2.21
Sciotodale (cdp) Scioto County	19	1.82
Gates Mills (village) Cuyahoga County	40	1.63
Reminderville (village) Summit County	34	1.45
Shawnee Hills (cdp) Greene County	34	1.44
Bentleyville (village) Cuyahoga County	13	1.37
The Village of Indian Hill (city) Hamilton County	75	1.29

Top 10 Places Sorted by Percent
Based on places with populations of 10,000 or more

Place	Number	%
Brecksville (city) Cuyahoga County	96	0.72
Dublin (city) Franklin County	214	0.68
Troy (city) Miami County	138	0.62
Rocky River (city) Cuyahoga County	118	0.57
Bay Village (city) Cuyahoga County	91	0.57
Twinsburg (city) Summit County	87	0.52
Hudson (city) Summit County	114	0.51
Defiance (city) Defiance County	80	0.49

Place	Number	%
Westerville (city) Franklin County	170	0.48
Upper Arlington (city) Franklin County	156	0.46

Carpatho Rusyn

Top 10 Places Sorted by Number
Based on all places, regardless of population

Place	Number	%
Akron (city) Summit County	51	0.02
Cleveland (city) Cuyahoga County	48	0.01
Columbus (city) Franklin County	41	0.01
North Royalton (city) Cuyahoga County	34	0.12
Parma (city) Cuyahoga County	34	0.04
Brooklyn (city) Cuyahoga County	30	0.26
Amherst (city) Lorain County	30	0.25
Perrysburg (city) Wood County	21	0.12
Parma Heights (city) Cuyahoga County	21	0.10
Warren (city) Trumbull County	21	0.04

Top 10 Places Sorted by Percent
Based on all places, regardless of population

Place	Number	%
Belle Valley (village) Noble County	1	0.37
Brooklyn (city) Cuyahoga County	30	0.26
Washingtonville (village) Columbiana County	2	0.26
Amherst (city) Lorain County	30	0.25
Shawnee Hills (village) Delaware County	1	0.24
Macedonia (city) Summit County	19	0.21
Newburgh Heights (village) Cuyahoga County	5	0.21
Campbell (city) Mahoning County	15	0.16
Bedford (city) Cuyahoga County	18	0.13
Geneva-on-the-Lake (village) Ashtabula County	2	0.13

Top 10 Places Sorted by Percent
Based on places with populations of 10,000 or more

Place	Number	%
Brooklyn (city) Cuyahoga County	30	0.26
Amherst (city) Lorain County	30	0.25
Bedford (city) Cuyahoga County	18	0.13
North Royalton (city) Cuyahoga County	34	0.12
Perrysburg (city) Wood County	21	0.12
Parma Heights (city) Cuyahoga County	21	0.10
Willoughby (city) Lake County	15	0.07
Solon (city) Cuyahoga County	14	0.06
Bay Village (city) Cuyahoga County	9	0.06
Vermilion (city) Lorain County	7	0.06

Celtic

Top 10 Places Sorted by Number
Based on all places, regardless of population

Place	Number	%
Columbus (city) Franklin County	222	0.03
Cincinnati (city) Hamilton County	67	0.02
Toledo (city) Lucas County	46	0.01
Sherwood (cdp) Hamilton County	45	1.16
Cleveland Heights (city) Cuyahoga County	44	0.09
Pickerington (city) Fairfield County	42	0.43
Akron (city) Summit County	38	0.02
Alliance (city) Stark County	32	0.14
Newark (city) Licking County	29	0.06
Steubenville (city) Jefferson County	26	0.14

Top 10 Places Sorted by Percent
Based on all places, regardless of population

Place	Number	%
Bowersville (village) Greene County	8	2.56
Belle Valley (village) Noble County	5	1.87
Sherwood (cdp) Hamilton County	45	1.16
Proctorville (village) Lawrence County	6	0.98
Casstown (village) Miami County	3	0.97
Harbor Hills (cdp) Licking County	11	0.89
Quincy (village) Logan County	5	0.71

Place	Number	%
Addyston (village) Hamilton County	6	0.6
Stoutsville (village) Fairfield County	3	0.5
Navarre (village) Stark County	8	0.5

Top 10 Places Sorted by Percent
Based on places with populations of 10,000 or more

Place	Number	%
Van Wert (city) Van Wert County	22	0.2
Aurora (city) Portage County	25	0.1
Alliance (city) Stark County	32	0.1
Steubenville (city) Jefferson County	26	0.1
Bay Village (city) Cuyahoga County	17	0.1
Forestville (cdp) Hamilton County	12	0.1
Cleveland Heights (city) Cuyahoga County	44	0.0
Centerville (city) Montgomery County	20	0.0
Montgomery (city) Hamilton County	9	0.0
Fairborn (city) Greene County	26	0.0

Croatian

Top 10 Places Sorted by Number
Based on all places, regardless of population

Place	Number	%
Cleveland (city) Cuyahoga County	2,219	0.4
Euclid (city) Cuyahoga County	1,705	3.2
Mentor (city) Lake County	1,173	2.3
Columbus (city) Franklin County	1,117	0.1
Youngstown (city) Mahoning County	1,013	1.2
Eastlake (city) Lake County	901	4.47
Boardman (cdp) Mahoning County	864	2.3
Akron (city) Summit County	856	0.3
Parma (city) Cuyahoga County	851	0.9
Lorain (city) Lorain County	830	1.21

Top 10 Places Sorted by Percent
Based on all places, regardless of population

Place	Number	%
Yankee Lake (village) Trumbull County	13	14.61
Aquilla (village) Geauga County	22	5.9
Eastlake (city) Lake County	901	4.47
Willoughby Hills (city) Lake County	383	4.4
Struthers (city) Mahoning County	506	4.3
Masury (cdp) Trumbull County	117	4.2
Hubbard (city) Trumbull County	326	3.9
Willowick (city) Lake County	555	3.8
Poland (village) Mahoning County	110	3.84
McDonald (village) Trumbull County	126	3.64

Top 10 Places Sorted by Percent
Based on places with populations of 10,000 or more

Place	Number	%
Eastlake (city) Lake County	901	4.47
Struthers (city) Mahoning County	506	4.30
Willowick (city) Lake County	555	3.85
Euclid (city) Cuyahoga County	1,705	3.23
Seven Hills (city) Cuyahoga County	329	2.72
Mentor (city) Lake County	1,173	2.33
Boardman (cdp) Mahoning County	864	2.32
Richmond Heights (city) Cuyahoga County	252	2.30
Wickliffe (city) Lake County	260	1.93
Amherst (city) Lorain County	226	1.90

Cypriot

Top 10 Places Sorted by Number
Based on all places, regardless of population

Place	Number	%
Akron (city) Summit County	51	0.02
Columbus (city) Franklin County	27	0.00
Toledo (city) Lucas County	24	0.01
Brecksville (city) Cuyahoga County	20	0.15
Boardman (cdp) Mahoning County	18	0.05
Bowling Green (city) Wood County	12	0.04

Notes: (cdp) census designated place; Refer to the User's Guide in the front of the book for more detailed information.

Place	Number	%
Elyria (city) Lorain County	9	0.02
Cuyahoga Falls (city) Summit County	8	0.02
Lakewood (city) Cuyahoga County	7	0.01

Top 10 Places Sorted by Percent
Based on all places, regardless of population

Place	Number	%
Brecksville (city) Cuyahoga County	20	0.15
Boardman (cdp) Mahoning County	18	0.05
Bowling Green (city) Wood County	12	0.04
Akron (city) Summit County	51	0.02
Elyria (city) Lorain County	9	0.02
Cuyahoga Falls (city) Summit County	8	0.02
Toledo (city) Lucas County	24	0.01
Lakewood (city) Cuyahoga County	7	0.01
Columbus (city) Franklin County	27	0.00

Top 10 Places Sorted by Percent
Based on places with populations of 10,000 or more

Place	Number	%
Brecksville (city) Cuyahoga County	20	0.15
Boardman (cdp) Mahoning County	18	0.05
Bowling Green (city) Wood County	12	0.04
Akron (city) Summit County	51	0.02
Elyria (city) Lorain County	9	0.02
Cuyahoga Falls (city) Summit County	8	0.02
Toledo (city) Lucas County	24	0.01
Lakewood (city) Cuyahoga County	7	0.01
Columbus (city) Franklin County	27	0.00

Czech

Top 10 Places Sorted by Number
Based on all places, regardless of population

Place	Number	%
Cleveland (city) Cuyahoga County	3,580	0.75
Parma (city) Cuyahoga County	2,554	2.98
Columbus (city) Franklin County	2,232	0.31
Garfield Heights (city) Cuyahoga County	1,445	4.72
Strongsville (city) Cuyahoga County	1,180	2.69
Lakewood (city) Cuyahoga County	1,014	1.79
Mentor (city) Lake County	990	1.97
Maple Heights (city) Cuyahoga County	964	3.69
North Royalton (city) Cuyahoga County	949	3.31
Solon (city) Cuyahoga County	757	3.47

Top 10 Places Sorted by Percent
Based on all places, regardless of population

Place	Number	%
Valley View (village) Cuyahoga County	157	7.22
Dillonvale (village) Jefferson County	54	6.97
Glenwillow (village) Cuyahoga County	31	6.97
Newburgh Heights (village) Cuyahoga County	155	6.49
Brooklyn Heights (village) Cuyahoga County	94	5.96
Seven Hills (city) Cuyahoga County	704	5.83
Independence (city) Cuyahoga County	347	4.82
Pigeon Creek (cdp) Summit County	43	4.81
Walton Hills (village) Cuyahoga County	114	4.77
Garfield Heights (city) Cuyahoga County	1,445	4.72

Top 10 Places Sorted by Percent
Based on places with populations of 10,000 or more

Place	Number	%
Seven Hills (city) Cuyahoga County	704	5.83
Garfield Heights (city) Cuyahoga County	1,445	4.72
Brecksville (city) Cuyahoga County	568	4.26
Broadview Heights (city) Cuyahoga County	610	3.82
Maple Heights (city) Cuyahoga County	964	3.69
Solon (city) Cuyahoga County	757	3.47
North Royalton (city) Cuyahoga County	949	3.31
Middleburg Heights (city) Cuyahoga County	484	3.11
Aurora (city) Portage County	412	3.04
Brooklyn (city) Cuyahoga County	350	3.02

Czechoslovakian

Top 10 Places Sorted by Number
Based on all places, regardless of population

Place	Number	%
Columbus (city) Franklin County	1,125	0.16
Cleveland (city) Cuyahoga County	1,096	0.23
Parma (city) Cuyahoga County	766	0.89
Toledo (city) Lucas County	569	0.18
Akron (city) Summit County	563	0.26
Lakewood (city) Cuyahoga County	446	0.79
Strongsville (city) Cuyahoga County	334	0.76
Westlake (city) Cuyahoga County	281	0.88
Cincinnati (city) Hamilton County	232	0.07
Mentor (city) Lake County	218	0.43

Top 10 Places Sorted by Percent
Based on all places, regardless of population

Place	Number	%
Morristown (village) Belmont County	16	5.25
Metamora (village) Fulton County	23	4.07
South Canal (cdp) Trumbull County	50	3.71
Rochester (village) Lorain County	5	2.48
Donnelsville (village) Clark County	6	2.47
Antioch (village) Monroe County	2	2.41
West Rushville (village) Fairfield County	3	2.33
Brooklyn Heights (village) Cuyahoga County	31	1.97
Fairport Harbor (village) Lake County	58	1.82
Riverlea (village) Franklin County	9	1.80

Top 10 Places Sorted by Percent
Based on places with populations of 10,000 or more

Place	Number	%
Brecksville (city) Cuyahoga County	184	1.38
Brooklyn (city) Cuyahoga County	140	1.21
Seven Hills (city) Cuyahoga County	127	1.05
Broadview Heights (city) Cuyahoga County	153	0.96
Bedford (city) Cuyahoga County	130	0.91
Parma (city) Cuyahoga County	766	0.89
Vermilion (city) Lorain County	97	0.89
Westlake (city) Cuyahoga County	281	0.88
Avon (city) Lorain County	96	0.84
Lakewood (city) Cuyahoga County	446	0.79

Danish

Top 10 Places Sorted by Number
Based on all places, regardless of population

Place	Number	%
Columbus (city) Franklin County	938	0.13
Toledo (city) Lucas County	467	0.15
Cincinnati (city) Hamilton County	374	0.11
Cleveland (city) Cuyahoga County	333	0.07
Mentor (city) Lake County	215	0.43
Akron (city) Summit County	209	0.10
Sandusky (city) Erie County	186	0.66
Strongsville (city) Cuyahoga County	184	0.42
Cuyahoga Falls (city) Summit County	177	0.36
Westerville (city) Franklin County	170	0.48

Top 10 Places Sorted by Percent
Based on all places, regardless of population

Place	Number	%
Peninsula (village) Summit County	12	2.32
Fulton (village) Morrow County	7	2.30
Zoar (village) Tuscarawas County	4	2.03
Castalia (village) Erie County	17	1.73
Port William (village) Clinton County	4	1.65
Port Clinton (city) Ottawa County	101	1.59
Waite Hill (village) Lake County	7	1.55
Newtown (village) Hamilton County	31	1.26
Cedarville (village) Greene County	47	1.23
Marblehead (village) Ottawa County	9	1.19

Top 10 Places Sorted by Percent
Based on places with populations of 10,000 or more

Place	Number	%
Fairview Park (city) Cuyahoga County	159	0.90
Lebanon (city) Warren County	128	0.76
Sandusky (city) Erie County	186	0.66
Bay Village (city) Cuyahoga County	101	0.63
Hudson (city) Summit County	132	0.59
Avon (city) Lorain County	66	0.58
Oxford (city) Butler County	115	0.52
Perrysburg (city) Wood County	88	0.51
Landen (cdp) Warren County	65	0.51
Lyndhurst (city) Cuyahoga County	77	0.50

Dutch

Top 10 Places Sorted by Number
Based on all places, regardless of population

Place	Number	%
Columbus (city) Franklin County	9,831	1.38
Toledo (city) Lucas County	4,309	1.37
Akron (city) Summit County	3,053	1.41
Cincinnati (city) Hamilton County	3,032	0.92
Cleveland (city) Cuyahoga County	2,847	0.60
Dayton (city) Montgomery County	1,802	1.08
Canton (city) Stark County	1,445	1.78
Springfield (city) Clark County	1,414	2.16
Kettering (city) Montgomery County	1,366	2.37
Mansfield (city) Richland County	1,082	2.19

Top 10 Places Sorted by Percent
Based on all places, regardless of population

Place	Number	%
Octa (village) Fayette County	14	18.92
Stafford (village) Monroe County	13	18.57
Catawba (village) Clark County	29	15.03
Uniopolis (village) Auglaize County	32	13.56
Orangeville (village) Trumbull County	25	13.09
Lore City (village) Guernsey County	34	10.40
South Salem (village) Ross County	22	9.91
Mount Cory (village) Hancock County	19	9.84
Lawrenceville (village) Clark County	28	9.52
Amesville (village) Athens County	18	9.47

Top 10 Places Sorted by Percent
Based on places with populations of 10,000 or more

Place	Number	%
Bellefontaine (city) Logan County	483	3.70
Greenville (city) Darke County	444	3.36
Norwalk (city) Huron County	509	3.13
Vermilion (city) Lorain County	335	3.08
Cambridge (city) Guernsey County	355	3.07
Englewood (city) Montgomery County	374	3.06
Lancaster (city) Fairfield County	1,025	2.91
Tallmadge (city) Summit County	474	2.90
Salem (city) Columbiana County	350	2.90
Piqua (city) Miami County	586	2.81

Eastern European

Top 10 Places Sorted by Number
Based on all places, regardless of population

Place	Number	%
Columbus (city) Franklin County	428	0.06
Beachwood (city) Cuyahoga County	391	3.21
Shaker Heights (city) Cuyahoga County	372	1.26
Cleveland Heights (city) Cuyahoga County	323	0.65
Cincinnati (city) Hamilton County	262	0.08
Bexley (city) Franklin County	223	1.69
University Heights (city) Cuyahoga County	198	1.40
Solon (city) Cuyahoga County	198	0.91
Gahanna (city) Franklin County	140	0.43
South Euclid (city) Cuyahoga County	124	0.53

Notes: (cdp) census designated place; Refer to the User's Guide in the front of the book for more detailed information.

Top 10 Places Sorted by Percent

Based on all places, regardless of population

Place	Number	%
Hills and Dales (village) Stark County	16	5.48
Beachwood (city) Cuyahoga County	391	3.21
Orange (village) Cuyahoga County	92	2.84
Amberley (village) Hamilton County	79	2.32
Bexley (city) Franklin County	223	1.69
Gates Mills (village) Cuyahoga County	41	1.67
Moreland Hills (village) Cuyahoga County	54	1.64
University Heights (city) Cuyahoga County	198	1.40
Shaker Heights (city) Cuyahoga County	372	1.26
Pepper Pike (city) Cuyahoga County	70	1.16

Top 10 Places Sorted by Percent

Based on places with populations of 10,000 or more

Place	Number	%
Beachwood (city) Cuyahoga County	391	3.21
Bexley (city) Franklin County	223	1.69
University Heights (city) Cuyahoga County	198	1.40
Shaker Heights (city) Cuyahoga County	372	1.26
Solon (city) Cuyahoga County	198	0.91
Blue Ash (city) Hamilton County	92	0.72
Cleveland Heights (city) Cuyahoga County	323	0.65
South Euclid (city) Cuyahoga County	124	0.53
Montgomery (city) Hamilton County	47	0.47
Gahanna (city) Franklin County	140	0.43

English

Top 10 Places Sorted by Number

Based on all places, regardless of population

Place	Number	%
Columbus (city) Franklin County	55,990	7.87
Toledo (city) Lucas County	18,854	6.01
Cincinnati (city) Hamilton County	18,016	5.45
Akron (city) Summit County	15,720	7.24
Cleveland (city) Cuyahoga County	13,169	2.75
Dayton (city) Montgomery County	8,170	4.92
Kettering (city) Montgomery County	7,303	12.69
Upper Arlington (city) Franklin County	6,462	19.23
Mentor (city) Lake County	6,457	12.84
Cuyahoga Falls (city) Summit County	6,410	12.99

Top 10 Places Sorted by Percent

Based on all places, regardless of population

Place	Number	%
Miltonsburg (village) Monroe County	14	70.00
La Croft (cdp) Columbiana County	373	26.16
Granville South (cdp) Licking County	313	25.74
Ithaca (village) Darke County	30	25.21
Granville (village) Licking County	721	24.72
Neville (village) Clermont County	33	24.63
Nellie (village) Coshocton County	33	24.44
Tontogany (village) Wood County	90	24.19
Riverlea (village) Franklin County	118	23.55
South Russell (village) Geauga County	946	23.52

Top 10 Places Sorted by Percent

Based on places with populations of 10,000 or more

Place	Number	%
Upper Arlington (city) Franklin County	6,462	19.23
Worthington (city) Franklin County	2,728	19.05
Hudson (city) Summit County	3,899	17.42
Bay Village (city) Cuyahoga County	2,493	15.50
Springboro (city) Warren County	1,870	15.32
Amherst (city) Lorain County	1,784	15.02
Centerville (city) Montgomery County	3,462	14.93
Montgomery (city) Hamilton County	1,494	14.88
Beavercreek (city) Greene County	5,470	14.33
Westerville (city) Franklin County	5,075	14.33

Estonian

Top 10 Places Sorted by Number

Based on all places, regardless of population

Place	Number	%
Broadview Heights (city) Cuyahoga County	44	0.28
Lakewood (city) Cuyahoga County	39	0.07
Parma (city) Cuyahoga County	34	0.04
Wetherington (cdp) Butler County	33	3.24
Sherwood (cdp) Hamilton County	28	0.72
Columbus (city) Franklin County	27	0.00
Parma Heights (city) Cuyahoga County	19	0.09
Mentor (city) Lake County	18	0.04
Stow (city) Summit County	16	0.05
Cleveland Heights (city) Cuyahoga County	15	0.03

Top 10 Places Sorted by Percent

Based on all places, regardless of population

Place	Number	%
Wetherington (cdp) Butler County	33	3.24
Sherwood (cdp) Hamilton County	28	0.72
Wakeman (village) Huron County	7	0.72
Maineville (village) Warren County	4	0.44
Bentleyville (village) Cuyahoga County	4	0.42
Newtown (village) Hamilton County	10	0.41
Lordstown (village) Trumbull County	12	0.33
Attica (village) Seneca County	3	0.31
Broadview Heights (city) Cuyahoga County	44	0.28
Dry Run (cdp) Hamilton County	13	0.20

Top 10 Places Sorted by Percent

Based on places with populations of 10,000 or more

Place	Number	%
Broadview Heights (city) Cuyahoga County	44	0.28
Parma Heights (city) Cuyahoga County	19	0.09
Painesville (city) Lake County	14	0.08
Lakewood (city) Cuyahoga County	39	0.07
Oregon (city) Lucas County	14	0.07
Ashland (city) Ashland County	13	0.06
Bridgetown North (cdp) Hamilton County	7	0.06
Stow (city) Summit County	16	0.05
Athens (city) Athens County	11	0.05
Centerville (city) Montgomery County	11	0.05

European

Top 10 Places Sorted by Number

Based on all places, regardless of population

Place	Number	%
Columbus (city) Franklin County	5,217	0.73
Cincinnati (city) Hamilton County	2,175	0.66
Cleveland (city) Cuyahoga County	949	0.20
Akron (city) Summit County	933	0.43
Dayton (city) Montgomery County	894	0.54
Toledo (city) Lucas County	785	0.25
Fairborn (city) Greene County	709	2.22
Cleveland Heights (city) Cuyahoga County	670	1.34
Kettering (city) Montgomery County	627	1.09
Fairfield (city) Butler County	503	1.20

Top 10 Places Sorted by Percent

Based on all places, regardless of population

Place	Number	%
Ostrander (village) Delaware County	42	11.63
Marseilles (village) Wyandot County	9	6.62
Donnelsville (village) Clark County	15	6.17
Kimbolton (village) Guernsey County	10	5.38
Lowell (village) Washington County	28	4.67
Gilboa (village) Putnam County	8	4.62
Clifton (village) Greene County	8	4.30
Chesterville (village) Morrow County	8	3.81
Beechwood Trails (cdp) Licking County	84	3.62
Murray City (village) Hocking County	15	3.38

Top 10 Places Sorted by Percent

Based on places with populations of 10,000 or more

Place	Number	%
Fairborn (city) Greene County	709	2.2
Montgomery (city) Hamilton County	191	1.9
Bexley (city) Franklin County	236	1.7
Athens (city) Athens County	374	1.7
Worthington (city) Franklin County	239	1.6
University Heights (city) Cuyahoga County	236	1.6
Pataskala (city) Licking County	169	1.6
Blue Ash (city) Hamilton County	192	1.5
Delaware (city) Delaware County	376	1.4
Shiloh (cdp) Montgomery County	160	1.4

Finnish

Top 10 Places Sorted by Number

Based on all places, regardless of population

Place	Number	%
Ashtabula (city) Ashtabula County	878	4.2
Columbus (city) Franklin County	822	0.1
Conneaut (city) Ashtabula County	741	5.9
Mentor (city) Lake County	508	1.0
Cleveland (city) Cuyahoga County	475	0.1
Fairport Harbor (village) Lake County	348	10.9
Painesville (city) Lake County	289	1.6
Edgewood (cdp) Ashtabula County	259	5.4
Toledo (city) Lucas County	215	0.0
Lakewood (city) Cuyahoga County	214	0.3

Top 10 Places Sorted by Percent

Based on all places, regardless of population

Place	Number	%
Fairport Harbor (village) Lake County	348	10.94
Conneaut (city) Ashtabula County	741	5.92
Edgewood (cdp) Ashtabula County	259	5.41
Grand River (village) Lake County	17	5.03
North Kingsville (village) Ashtabula County	125	4.71
Ashtabula (city) Ashtabula County	878	4.21
Cheshire (village) Gallia County	8	3.42
New Riegel (village) Seneca County	6	2.73
Andover (village) Ashtabula County	35	2.64
Logan Elm Village (cdp) Pickaway County	26	2.58

Top 10 Places Sorted by Percent

Based on places with populations of 10,000 or more

Place	Number	%
Conneaut (city) Ashtabula County	741	5.92
Ashtabula (city) Ashtabula County	878	4.21
Painesville (city) Lake County	289	1.65
Mentor (city) Lake County	508	1.01
Avon (city) Lorain County	92	0.80
Bay Village (city) Cuyahoga County	104	0.65
Niles (city) Trumbull County	134	0.64
Amherst (city) Lorain County	59	0.50
Solon (city) Cuyahoga County	105	0.48
Girard (city) Trumbull County	51	0.46

French, except Basque

Top 10 Places Sorted by Number

Based on all places, regardless of population

Place	Number	%
Toledo (city) Lucas County	14,382	4.59
Columbus (city) Franklin County	13,588	1.91
Cincinnati (city) Hamilton County	5,602	1.69
Cleveland (city) Cuyahoga County	4,106	0.86
Akron (city) Summit County	3,799	1.75
Dayton (city) Montgomery County	2,446	1.47
Kettering (city) Montgomery County	2,086	3.63
Canton (city) Stark County	1,988	2.45
Cuyahoga Falls (city) Summit County	1,586	3.21
Lakewood (city) Cuyahoga County	1,574	2.78

Notes: (cdp) census designated place; Refer to the User's Guide in the front of the book for more detailed information.

Top 10 Places Sorted by Percent

Based on all places, regardless of population

Place	Number	%
Russia (village) Shelby County	202	35.56
Miltonsburg (village) Monroe County	7	35.00
North Star (village) Darke County	51	24.88
Versailles (village) Darke County	567	21.40
Miller City (village) Putnam County	20	19.05
Osgood (village) Darke County	49	18.22
Fayetteville (village) Brown County	51	13.21
Olde West Chester (cdp) Butler County	32	12.03
Metamora (village) Fulton County	59	10.44
Fort Loramie (village) Shelby County	140	10.21

Top 10 Places Sorted by Percent

Based on places with populations of 10,000 or more

Place	Number	%
Oregon (city) Lucas County	1,445	7.47
Maumee (city) Lucas County	814	5.35
Montgomery (city) Hamilton County	535	5.33
Perrysburg (city) Wood County	832	4.86
Toledo (city) Lucas County	14,382	4.59
Sylvania (city) Lucas County	805	4.30
Piqua (city) Miami County	880	4.23
Clayton (city) Montgomery County	528	3.95
Centerville (city) Montgomery County	900	3.88
Mason (city) Warren County	822	3.75

French Canadian

Top 10 Places Sorted by Number

Based on all places, regardless of population

Place	Number	%
Toledo (city) Lucas County	2,604	0.83
Columbus (city) Franklin County	2,010	0.28
Cleveland (city) Cuyahoga County	873	0.18
Cincinnati (city) Hamilton County	768	0.23
Dayton (city) Montgomery County	505	0.30
Akron (city) Summit County	469	0.22
Kettering (city) Montgomery County	365	0.63
Lakewood (city) Cuyahoga County	339	0.60
Parma (city) Cuyahoga County	277	0.32
Elyria (city) Lorain County	259	0.46

Top 10 Places Sorted by Percent

Based on all places, regardless of population

Place	Number	%
Ney (village) Defiance County	15	4.05
Clay Center (village) Ottawa County	12	4.05
Swanton (village) Fulton County	120	3.59
West Rushville (village) Fairfield County	4	3.10
Olde West Chester (cdp) Butler County	8	3.01
Custar (village) Wood County	6	2.97
Berkey (village) Lucas County	7	2.68
Benton Ridge (village) Hancock County	7	2.32
Alvordton (village) Williams County	8	2.31
Saint Martin (village) Brown County	2	2.27

Top 10 Places Sorted by Percent

Based on places with populations of 10,000 or more

Place	Number	%
Sylvania (city) Lucas County	249	1.33
Maumee (city) Lucas County	174	1.14
Vermilion (city) Lorain County	114	1.05
Perrysburg (city) Wood County	176	1.03
Northbrook (cdp) Hamilton County	106	0.94
Oregon (city) Lucas County	178	0.92
Toledo (city) Lucas County	2,604	0.83
Eastlake (city) Lake County	158	0.78
Englewood (city) Montgomery County	95	0.78
Marietta (city) Washington County	100	0.69

German

Top 10 Places Sorted by Number

Based on all places, regardless of population

Place	Number	%
Columbus (city) Franklin County	137,761	19.36
Toledo (city) Lucas County	73,482	23.43
Cincinnati (city) Hamilton County	65,659	19.86
Cleveland (city) Cuyahoga County	44,172	9.23
Akron (city) Summit County	39,203	18.06
Dayton (city) Montgomery County	23,990	14.44
Parma (city) Cuyahoga County	21,013	24.53
Kettering (city) Montgomery County	19,450	33.81
Canton (city) Stark County	17,447	21.51
Cuyahoga Falls (city) Summit County	15,305	31.01

Top 10 Places Sorted by Percent

Based on all places, regardless of population

Place	Number	%
Alexandria (village) Licking County	14	82.35
Ottoville (village) Putnam County	677	77.91
Glandorf (village) Putnam County	719	77.48
Minster (village) Auglaize County	2,131	75.43
Fort Jennings (village) Putnam County	349	75.22
New Riegel (village) Seneca County	165	75.00
Burkettsville (village) Mercer County	189	74.41
Osgood (village) Darke County	198	73.61
Coldwater (village) Mercer County	3,392	73.55
Saint Henry (village) Mercer County	1,683	73.14

Top 10 Places Sorted by Percent

Based on places with populations of 10,000 or more

Place	Number	%
Bridgetown North (cdp) Hamilton County	7,249	56.98
Celina (city) Mercer County	5,089	48.85
White Oak (cdp) Hamilton County	6,375	48.11
Tiffin (city) Seneca County	8,025	44.25
Maumee (city) Lucas County	6,330	41.57
Perrysburg (city) Wood County	6,774	39.59
Reading (city) Hamilton County	4,432	39.56
Forestville (cdp) Hamilton County	4,281	38.70
Sharonville (city) Hamilton County	5,145	37.55
Landen (cdp) Warren County	4,604	36.41

German Russian

Top 10 Places Sorted by Number

Based on all places, regardless of population

Place	Number	%
Columbus (city) Franklin County	23	0.00
Euclid (city) Cuyahoga County	20	0.04
Lorain (city) Lorain County	18	0.03
Canfield (city) Mahoning County	16	0.21
Middletown (city) Butler County	16	0.03
Akron (city) Summit County	16	0.01
Clyde (city) Sandusky County	15	0.25
Cleveland (city) Cuyahoga County	13	0.00
Springfield (city) Clark County	12	0.02
Huber Heights (city) Montgomery County	11	0.03

Top 10 Places Sorted by Percent

Based on all places, regardless of population

Place	Number	%
Clyde (city) Sandusky County	15	0.25
Canfield (city) Mahoning County	16	0.21
Windham (village) Portage County	4	0.14
Geneva-on-the-Lake (village) Ashtabula County	2	0.13
McConnelsville (village) Morgan County	2	0.12
Willowick (city) Lake County	7	0.05
Euclid (city) Cuyahoga County	20	0.04
Lorain (city) Lorain County	18	0.03
Middletown (city) Butler County	16	0.03
Huber Heights (city) Montgomery County	11	0.03

Top 10 Places Sorted by Percent

Based on places with populations of 10,000 or more

Place	Number	%
Willowick (city) Lake County	7	0.05
Euclid (city) Cuyahoga County	20	0.04
Lorain (city) Lorain County	18	0.03
Middletown (city) Butler County	16	0.03
Huber Heights (city) Montgomery County	11	0.03
Beavercreek (city) Greene County	10	0.03
Sandusky (city) Erie County	7	0.03
Springfield (city) Clark County	12	0.02
Warren (city) Trumbull County	11	0.02
Akron (city) Summit County	16	0.01

Greek

Top 10 Places Sorted by Number

Based on all places, regardless of population

Place	Number	%
Columbus (city) Franklin County	2,702	0.38
Toledo (city) Lucas County	1,554	0.50
Cleveland (city) Cuyahoga County	1,385	0.29
Akron (city) Summit County	1,267	0.58
Canton (city) Stark County	1,059	1.31
Cincinnati (city) Hamilton County	1,040	0.31
Warren (city) Trumbull County	1,033	2.20
Campbell (city) Mahoning County	981	10.37
Parma (city) Cuyahoga County	867	1.01
Lakewood (city) Cuyahoga County	703	1.24

Top 10 Places Sorted by Percent

Based on all places, regardless of population

Place	Number	%
Campbell (city) Mahoning County	981	10.37
Yorkville (village) Jefferson County	55	4.40
Vienna Center (cdp) Trumbull County	35	2.95
Gratiot (village) Licking County	5	2.91
Wetherington (cdp) Butler County	28	2.75
Seven Hills (city) Cuyahoga County	310	2.57
Fairlawn (city) Summit County	172	2.35
Brimfield (cdp) Portage County	70	2.24
Ostrander (village) Delaware County	8	2.22
Warren (city) Trumbull County	1,033	2.20

Top 10 Places Sorted by Percent

Based on places with populations of 10,000 or more

Place	Number	%
Seven Hills (city) Cuyahoga County	310	2.57
Warren (city) Trumbull County	1,033	2.20
Westlake (city) Cuyahoga County	647	2.03
Brooklyn (city) Cuyahoga County	208	1.80
Upper Arlington (city) Franklin County	588	1.75
North Canton (city) Stark County	260	1.59
Middleburg Heights (city) Cuyahoga County	236	1.52
Fairview Park (city) Cuyahoga County	266	1.51
North Royalton (city) Cuyahoga County	406	1.42
Boardman (cdp) Mahoning County	508	1.36

Guyanese

Top 10 Places Sorted by Number

Based on all places, regardless of population

Place	Number	%
Cleveland (city) Cuyahoga County	159	0.03
Toledo (city) Lucas County	77	0.02
Columbus (city) Franklin County	61	0.01
Parma (city) Cuyahoga County	35	0.04
Euclid (city) Cuyahoga County	26	0.05
Cincinnati (city) Hamilton County	21	0.01
Shiloh (cdp) Montgomery County	19	0.17
Westlake (city) Cuyahoga County	18	0.06
Cleveland Heights (city) Cuyahoga County	18	0.04
North Ridgeville (city) Lorain County	16	0.07

Notes: (cdp) census designated place; Refer to the User's Guide in the front of the book for more detailed information.

Top 10 Places Sorted by Percent
Based on all places, regardless of population

Place	Number	%
Highland Hills (village) Cuyahoga County	5	0.38
Shiloh (cdp) Montgomery County	19	0.17
Sheffield (village) Lorain County	5	0.17
Richmond Heights (city) Cuyahoga County	14	0.13
North Ridgeville (city) Lorain County	16	0.07
Athens (city) Athens County	14	0.07
Westlake (city) Cuyahoga County	18	0.06
Bedford Heights (city) Cuyahoga County	7	0.06
Euclid (city) Cuyahoga County	26	0.05
Miamisburg (city) Montgomery County	10	0.05

Top 10 Places Sorted by Percent
Based on places with populations of 10,000 or more

Place	Number	%
Shiloh (cdp) Montgomery County	19	0.17
Richmond Heights (city) Cuyahoga County	14	0.13
North Ridgeville (city) Lorain County	16	0.07
Athens (city) Athens County	14	0.07
Westlake (city) Cuyahoga County	18	0.06
Bedford Heights (city) Cuyahoga County	7	0.06
Euclid (city) Cuyahoga County	26	0.05
Miamisburg (city) Montgomery County	10	0.05
Warrensville Heights (city) Cuyahoga County	8	0.05
Parma (city) Cuyahoga County	35	0.04

Hawaii Native/Pacific Islander

Top 10 Places Sorted by Number
Based on all places, regardless of population

Place	Number	%
Columbus (city) Franklin County	974	0.14
Cleveland (city) Cuyahoga County	514	0.11
Cincinnati (city) Hamilton County	338	0.10
Toledo (city) Lucas County	197	0.06
Akron (city) Summit County	178	0.08
Dayton (city) Montgomery County	149	0.09
Canton (city) Stark County	71	0.09
Youngstown (city) Mahoning County	63	0.08
Lorain (city) Lorain County	61	0.09
Hamilton (city) Butler County	57	0.09

Top 10 Places Sorted by Percent
Based on all places, regardless of population

Place	Number	%
Belmont (village) Belmont County	20	3.76
Frankfort (village) Ross County	12	1.19
Glenford (village) Perry County	2	1.01
Lore City (village) Guernsey County	3	0.98
Summitville (village) Columbiana County	1	0.93
Valley Hi (village) Logan County	2	0.82
Mowrystown (village) Highland County	3	0.80
Buckland (village) Auglaize County	2	0.78
Roswell (village) Tuscarawas County	2	0.72
Patterson (village) Hardin County	1	0.72

Top 10 Places Sorted by Percent
Based on places with populations of 10,000 or more

Place	Number	%
Landen (cdp) Warren County	30	0.23
University Heights (city) Cuyahoga County	28	0.20
Marietta (city) Washington County	27	0.19
Girard (city) Trumbull County	21	0.19
Sidney (city) Shelby County	31	0.15
Sharonville (city) Hamilton County	21	0.15
Columbus (city) Franklin County	974	0.14
Fairborn (city) Greene County	45	0.14
Delaware (city) Delaware County	36	0.14
Middleburg Heights (city) Cuyahoga County	21	0.14

Hawaii Native/Pacific Islander: Melanesian

Top 10 Places Sorted by Number
Based on all places, regardless of population

Place	Number	%
Cincinnati (city) Hamilton County	11	0.00
Columbus (city) Franklin County	5	0.00
Lore City (village) Guernsey County	2	0.66
Geneva (city) Ashtabula County	2	0.03
Dublin (city) Franklin County	2	0.01
Akron (city) Summit County	2	0.00
Urbana (city) Champaign County	1	0.01
Willard (city) Huron County	1	0.01
Chillicothe (city) Ross County	1	0.00
Dayton (city) Montgomery County	1	0.00

Top 10 Places Sorted by Percent
Based on all places, regardless of population

Place	Number	%
Lore City (village) Guernsey County	2	0.66
Geneva (city) Ashtabula County	2	0.03
Dublin (city) Franklin County	2	0.01
Urbana (city) Champaign County	1	0.01
Willard (city) Huron County	1	0.01
Cincinnati (city) Hamilton County	11	0.00
Columbus (city) Franklin County	5	0.00
Akron (city) Summit County	2	0.00
Chillicothe (city) Ross County	1	0.00
Dayton (city) Montgomery County	1	0.00

Top 10 Places Sorted by Percent
Based on places with populations of 10,000 or more

Place	Number	%
Dublin (city) Franklin County	2	0.01
Urbana (city) Champaign County	1	0.01
Cincinnati (city) Hamilton County	11	0.00
Columbus (city) Franklin County	5	0.00
Akron (city) Summit County	2	0.00
Chillicothe (city) Ross County	1	0.00
Dayton (city) Montgomery County	1	0.00
Mansfield (city) Richland County	1	0.00
Norwood (city) Hamilton County	1	0.00

Hawaii Native/Pacific Islander: Fijian

Top 10 Places Sorted by Number
Based on all places, regardless of population

Place	Number	%
Columbus (city) Franklin County	5	0.00
Lore City (village) Guernsey County	2	0.66
Geneva (city) Ashtabula County	2	0.03
Akron (city) Summit County	2	0.00
Urbana (city) Champaign County	1	0.01
Willard (city) Huron County	1	0.01
Dayton (city) Montgomery County	1	0.00
Mansfield (city) Richland County	1	0.00

Top 10 Places Sorted by Percent
Based on all places, regardless of population

Place	Number	%
Lore City (village) Guernsey County	2	0.66
Geneva (city) Ashtabula County	2	0.03
Urbana (city) Champaign County	1	0.01
Willard (city) Huron County	1	0.01
Columbus (city) Franklin County	5	0.00
Akron (city) Summit County	2	0.00
Dayton (city) Montgomery County	1	0.00
Mansfield (city) Richland County	1	0.00

Top 10 Places Sorted by Percent
Based on places with populations of 10,000 or more

Place	Number	%
Urbana (city) Champaign County	1	0.01
Columbus (city) Franklin County	5	0.0
Akron (city) Summit County	2	0.0
Dayton (city) Montgomery County	1	0.0
Mansfield (city) Richland County	1	0.0

Hawaii Native/Pacific Islander: Other Melanesian

Top 10 Places Sorted by Number
Based on all places, regardless of population

Place	Number	%
Cincinnati (city) Hamilton County	11	0.0
Dublin (city) Franklin County	2	0.0
Chillicothe (city) Ross County	1	0.0
Norwood (city) Hamilton County	1	0.0

Top 10 Places Sorted by Percent
Based on all places, regardless of population

Place	Number	%
Dublin (city) Franklin County	2	0.0
Cincinnati (city) Hamilton County	11	0.0
Chillicothe (city) Ross County	1	0.0
Norwood (city) Hamilton County	1	0.0

Top 10 Places Sorted by Percent
Based on places with populations of 10,000 or more

Place	Number	%
Dublin (city) Franklin County	2	0.0
Cincinnati (city) Hamilton County	11	0.0
Chillicothe (city) Ross County	1	0.0
Norwood (city) Hamilton County	1	0.0

Hawaii Native/Pacific Islander: Micronesian

Top 10 Places Sorted by Number
Based on all places, regardless of population

Place	Number	%
Columbus (city) Franklin County	126	0.02
Cleveland (city) Cuyahoga County	83	0.02
Cincinnati (city) Hamilton County	62	0.02
Dayton (city) Montgomery County	29	0.02
Akron (city) Summit County	23	0.01
Sidney (city) Shelby County	21	0.10
Toledo (city) Lucas County	19	0.01
Mansfield (city) Richland County	18	0.04
Canton (city) Stark County	17	0.02
Oberlin (city) Lorain County	14	0.17

Top 10 Places Sorted by Percent
Based on all places, regardless of population

Place	Number	%
Glenford (village) Perry County	2	1.01
Valley Hi (village) Logan County	2	0.82
North Robinson (village) Crawford County	1	0.47
Donnelsville (village) Clark County	1	0.34
Strasburg (village) Tuscarawas County	7	0.30
Perrysville (village) Ashland County	2	0.25
Waynesfield (village) Auglaize County	2	0.25
Anna (village) Shelby County	3	0.23
Crooksville (village) Perry County	5	0.20
Oberlin (city) Lorain County	14	0.17

Top 10 Places Sorted by Percent
Based on places with populations of 10,000 or more

Place	Number	%
Sidney (city) Shelby County	21	0.10
Springdale (city) Hamilton County	8	0.08
East Liverpool (city) Columbiana County	9	0.07
Girard (city) Trumbull County	8	0.07
Centerville (city) Montgomery County	13	0.06
Landen (cdp) Warren County	8	0.06
Ashland (city) Ashland County	10	0.05

Notes: (cdp) census designated place; Refer to the User's Guide in the front of the book for more detailed information.

Place	Number	%
Avon Lake (city) Lorain County	9	0.05
Northbrook (cdp) Hamilton County	5	0.05
Mansfield (city) Richland County	18	0.04

Hawaii Native/Pacific Islander: Guamanian or Chamorro

Top 10 Places Sorted by Number

Based on all places, regardless of population

Place	Number	%
Columbus (city) Franklin County	116	0.02
Cleveland (city) Cuyahoga County	78	0.02
Cincinnati (city) Hamilton County	59	0.02
Dayton (city) Montgomery County	27	0.02
Akron (city) Summit County	22	0.01
Toledo (city) Lucas County	19	0.01
Sidney (city) Shelby County	18	0.09
Mansfield (city) Richland County	18	0.04
Canton (city) Stark County	17	0.02
Oberlin (city) Lorain County	14	0.17

Top 10 Places Sorted by Percent

Based on all places, regardless of population

Place	Number	%
Glenford (village) Perry County	2	1.01
North Robinson (village) Crawford County	1	0.47
Strasburg (village) Tuscarawas County	7	0.30
Perrysville (village) Ashland County	2	0.25
Waynesfield (village) Auglaize County	2	0.25
Anna (village) Shelby County	3	0.23
Oberlin (city) Lorain County	14	0.17
Burton (village) Geauga County	2	0.14
Silver Lake (village) Summit County	4	0.13
Albany (village) Athens County	1	0.12

Top 10 Places Sorted by Percent

Based on places with populations of 10,000 or more

Place	Number	%
Sidney (city) Shelby County	18	0.09
Springdale (city) Hamilton County	8	0.08
Girard (city) Trumbull County	8	0.07
Landen (cdp) Warren County	8	0.06
Centerville (city) Montgomery County	12	0.05
Ashland (city) Ashland County	10	0.05
East Liverpool (city) Columbiana County	7	0.05
Northbrook (cdp) Hamilton County	5	0.05
Mansfield (city) Richland County	18	0.04
Fairborn (city) Greene County	13	0.04

Hawaii Native/Pacific Islander: Other Micronesian

Top 10 Places Sorted by Number

Based on all places, regardless of population

Place	Number	%
Columbus (city) Franklin County	10	0.00
Crooksville (village) Perry County	5	0.20
Medina (city) Medina County	5	0.02
Cleveland (city) Cuyahoga County	5	0.00
Mulberry (cdp) Clermont County	4	0.13
Parma (city) Cuyahoga County	4	0.00
West Liberty (village) Logan County	3	0.17
Bellefontaine (city) Logan County	3	0.02
Mayfield Heights (city) Cuyahoga County	3	0.02
Huber Heights (city) Montgomery County	3	0.01

Top 10 Places Sorted by Percent

Based on all places, regardless of population

Place	Number	%
Valley Hi (village) Logan County	2	0.82
Donnelsville (village) Clark County	1	0.34
Crooksville (village) Perry County	5	0.20
West Liberty (village) Logan County	3	0.17
Quincy (village) Logan County	1	0.14
Mulberry (cdp) Clermont County	4	0.13
Edgerton (village) Williams County	2	0.09
Bremen (village) Fairfield County	1	0.08
Amberley (village) Hamilton County	1	0.03
Cedarville (village) Greene County	1	0.03

Top 10 Places Sorted by Percent

Based on places with populations of 10,000 or more

Place	Number	%
Medina (city) Medina County	5	0.02
Bellefontaine (city) Logan County	3	0.02
Mayfield Heights (city) Cuyahoga County	3	0.02
Celina (city) Mercer County	2	0.02
East Liverpool (city) Columbiana County	2	0.02
Huber Heights (city) Montgomery County	3	0.01
Sidney (city) Shelby County	3	0.01
Avon Lake (city) Lorain County	2	0.01
Forest Park (city) Hamilton County	2	0.01
Perrysburg (city) Wood County	2	0.01

Hawaii Native/Pacific Islander: Polynesian

Top 10 Places Sorted by Number

Based on all places, regardless of population

Place	Number	%
Columbus (city) Franklin County	381	0.05
Cleveland (city) Cuyahoga County	169	0.04
Cincinnati (city) Hamilton County	114	0.03
Toledo (city) Lucas County	110	0.04
Akron (city) Summit County	81	0.04
Dayton (city) Montgomery County	57	0.03
Canton (city) Stark County	40	0.05
Delaware (city) Delaware County	29	0.11
Hamilton (city) Butler County	28	0.05
Parma (city) Cuyahoga County	27	0.03

Top 10 Places Sorted by Percent

Based on all places, regardless of population

Place	Number	%
Belmont (village) Belmont County	10	1.88
Mowrystown (village) Highland County	3	0.80
Roswell (village) Tuscarawas County	2	0.72
Patterson (village) Hardin County	1	0.72
Empire (village) Jefferson County	2	0.67
Fort Recovery (village) Mercer County	7	0.55
Pitsburg (village) Darke County	2	0.51
Hartford (village) Licking County	2	0.49
South Salem (village) Ross County	1	0.47
Dellroy (village) Carroll County	1	0.34

Top 10 Places Sorted by Percent

Based on places with populations of 10,000 or more

Place	Number	%
Tallmadge (city) Summit County	22	0.13
Delaware (city) Delaware County	29	0.11
Middleburg Heights (city) Cuyahoga County	17	0.11
Landen (cdp) Warren County	14	0.11
Bexley (city) Franklin County	12	0.09
Circleville (city) Pickaway County	11	0.08
Forest Park (city) Hamilton County	13	0.07
Miamisburg (city) Montgomery County	13	0.07
Warrensville Heights (city) Cuyahoga County	10	0.07
Finneytown (cdp) Hamilton County	9	0.07

Hawaii Native/Pacific Islander: Native Hawaiian

Top 10 Places Sorted by Number

Based on all places, regardless of population

Place	Number	%
Columbus (city) Franklin County	187	0.03
Cleveland (city) Cuyahoga County	105	0.02
Cincinnati (city) Hamilton County	66	0.02
Akron (city) Summit County	52	0.02
Toledo (city) Lucas County	51	0.02
Canton (city) Stark County	30	0.04
Delaware (city) Delaware County	26	0.10
Dayton (city) Montgomery County	24	0.01
Tallmadge (city) Summit County	22	0.13
Beavercreek (city) Greene County	21	0.06

Top 10 Places Sorted by Percent

Based on all places, regardless of population

Place	Number	%
Belmont (village) Belmont County	5	0.94
Mowrystown (village) Highland County	3	0.80
Patterson (village) Hardin County	1	0.72
Fort Recovery (village) Mercer County	7	0.55
Hartford (village) Licking County	2	0.49
South Salem (village) Ross County	1	0.47
Roaming Shores (village) Ashtabula County	4	0.32
Wetherington (cdp) Butler County	3	0.30
Quincy (village) Logan County	2	0.27
Pitsburg (village) Darke County	1	0.26

Top 10 Places Sorted by Percent

Based on places with populations of 10,000 or more

Place	Number	%
Tallmadge (city) Summit County	22	0.13
Delaware (city) Delaware County	26	0.10
Circleville (city) Pickaway County	11	0.08
Landen (cdp) Warren County	9	0.07
Beavercreek (city) Greene County	21	0.06
Finneytown (cdp) Hamilton County	8	0.06
Huber Heights (city) Montgomery County	18	0.05
Lancaster (city) Fairfield County	16	0.05
Chillicothe (city) Ross County	10	0.05
Painesville (city) Lake County	9	0.05

Hawaii Native/Pacific Islander: Samoan

Top 10 Places Sorted by Number

Based on all places, regardless of population

Place	Number	%
Columbus (city) Franklin County	186	0.03
Cleveland (city) Cuyahoga County	61	0.01
Toledo (city) Lucas County	49	0.02
Cincinnati (city) Hamilton County	42	0.01
Dayton (city) Montgomery County	30	0.02
Akron (city) Summit County	21	0.01
Hamilton (city) Butler County	17	0.03
Elyria (city) Lorain County	12	0.02
Willoughby (city) Lake County	11	0.05
Springfield (city) Clark County	11	0.02

Top 10 Places Sorted by Percent

Based on all places, regardless of population

Place	Number	%
Belmont (village) Belmont County	5	0.94
Roswell (village) Tuscarawas County	2	0.72
Empire (village) Jefferson County	2	0.67
Dellroy (village) Carroll County	1	0.34
Pitsburg (village) Darke County	1	0.26
Beallsville (village) Monroe County	1	0.24
Delta (village) Fulton County	6	0.20
West Salem (village) Wayne County	3	0.20
Drexel (cdp) Montgomery County	4	0.19
Genoa (village) Ottawa County	4	0.18

Top 10 Places Sorted by Percent

Based on places with populations of 10,000 or more

Place	Number	%
Willoughby (city) Lake County	11	0.05
Bexley (city) Franklin County	7	0.05
Landen (cdp) Warren County	5	0.04
Shiloh (cdp) Montgomery County	4	0.04

Notes: (cdp) census designated place; Refer to the User's Guide in the front of the book for more detailed information.

Columbus (city) Franklin County	186	0.03
Hamilton (city) Butler County	17	0.03
Miamisburg (city) Montgomery County	6	0.03
Rocky River (city) Cuyahoga County	6	0.03
Whitehall (city) Franklin County	6	0.03
Forest Park (city) Hamilton County	5	0.03

Hawaii Native/Pacific Islander: Tongan

Top 10 Places Sorted by Number

Based on all places, regardless of population

Place	Number	%
Middleburg Heights (city) Cuyahoga County	7	0.05
Toledo (city) Lucas County	5	0.00
Newark (city) Licking County	4	0.01
Strongsville (city) Cuyahoga County	4	0.01
Sidney (city) Shelby County	2	0.01
Parma (city) Cuyahoga County	2	0.00
Milford (city) Clermont County	1	0.02
Berea (city) Cuyahoga County	1	0.01
Cleveland Heights (city) Cuyahoga County	1	0.00
Columbus (city) Franklin County	1	0.00

Top 10 Places Sorted by Percent

Based on all places, regardless of population

Place	Number	%
Middleburg Heights (city) Cuyahoga County	7	0.05
Milford (city) Clermont County	1	0.02
Newark (city) Licking County	4	0.01
Strongsville (city) Cuyahoga County	4	0.01
Sidney (city) Shelby County	2	0.01
Berea (city) Cuyahoga County	1	0.01
Toledo (city) Lucas County	5	0.00
Parma (city) Cuyahoga County	2	0.00
Cleveland Heights (city) Cuyahoga County	1	0.00
Columbus (city) Franklin County	1	0.00

Top 10 Places Sorted by Percent

Based on places with populations of 10,000 or more

Place	Number	%
Middleburg Heights (city) Cuyahoga County	7	0.05
Newark (city) Licking County	4	0.01
Strongsville (city) Cuyahoga County	4	0.01
Sidney (city) Shelby County	2	0.01
Berea (city) Cuyahoga County	1	0.01
Toledo (city) Lucas County	5	0.00
Parma (city) Cuyahoga County	2	0.00
Cleveland Heights (city) Cuyahoga County	1	0.00
Columbus (city) Franklin County	1	0.00
Dayton (city) Montgomery County	1	0.00

Hawaii Native/Pacific Islander: Other Polynesian

Top 10 Places Sorted by Number

Based on all places, regardless of population

Place	Number	%
Akron (city) Summit County	8	0.00
Xenia (city) Greene County	7	0.03
Columbus (city) Franklin County	7	0.00
Cincinnati (city) Hamilton County	6	0.00
Warrensville Heights (city) Cuyahoga County	5	0.03
Toledo (city) Lucas County	5	0.00
Middleburg Heights (city) Cuyahoga County	4	0.03
Ashland (city) Ashland County	4	0.02
Austintown (cdp) Mahoning County	3	0.01
Boardman (cdp) Mahoning County	3	0.01

Top 10 Places Sorted by Percent

Based on all places, regardless of population

Place	Number	%
Hartville (village) Stark County	1	0.05
Xenia (city) Greene County	7	0.03
Warrensville Heights (city) Cuyahoga County	5	0.03
Middleburg Heights (city) Cuyahoga County	4	0.03
West Portsmouth (cdp) Scioto County	1	0.03
Ashland (city) Ashland County	4	0.02
Wellington (village) Lorain County	1	0.02
West Milton (village) Miami County	1	0.02
Austintown (cdp) Mahoning County	3	0.01
Boardman (cdp) Mahoning County	3	0.01

Top 10 Places Sorted by Percent

Based on places with populations of 10,000 or more

Place	Number	%
Xenia (city) Greene County	7	0.03
Warrensville Heights (city) Cuyahoga County	5	0.03
Middleburg Heights (city) Cuyahoga County	4	0.03
Ashland (city) Ashland County	4	0.02
Austintown (cdp) Mahoning County	3	0.01
Boardman (cdp) Mahoning County	3	0.01
Fairborn (city) Greene County	3	0.01
Mansfield (city) Richland County	3	0.01
Whitehall (city) Franklin County	1	0.01
Wilmington (city) Clinton County	1	0.01

Hawaii Native/Pacific Islander: Other Pacific Islander, specified

Top 10 Places Sorted by Number

Based on all places, regardless of population

Place	Number	%
Cleveland (city) Cuyahoga County	34	0.01
Columbus (city) Franklin County	26	0.00
Akron (city) Summit County	18	0.01
Cincinnati (city) Hamilton County	18	0.01
Toledo (city) Lucas County	15	0.00
Hamilton (city) Butler County	12	0.02
Dayton (city) Montgomery County	11	0.01
Frankfort (village) Ross County	10	0.99
East Cleveland (city) Cuyahoga County	9	0.03
Springboro (city) Warren County	8	0.06

Top 10 Places Sorted by Percent

Based on all places, regardless of population

Place	Number	%
Frankfort (village) Ross County	10	0.99
Crown City (village) Gallia County	1	0.24
Lucasville (cdp) Scioto County	3	0.19
Fort Loramie (village) Shelby County	2	0.15
Doylestown (village) Wayne County	3	0.11
Monfort Heights East (cdp) Hamilton County	4	0.10
Roseville (village) Perry County	2	0.10
Springboro (city) Warren County	8	0.06
University Heights (city) Cuyahoga County	7	0.05
Middlefield (village) Geauga County	1	0.04

Top 10 Places Sorted by Percent

Based on places with populations of 10,000 or more

Place	Number	%
Springboro (city) Warren County	8	0.06
University Heights (city) Cuyahoga County	7	0.05
East Cleveland (city) Cuyahoga County	9	0.03
Bedford Heights (city) Cuyahoga County	3	0.03
Cambridge (city) Guernsey County	3	0.03
Hamilton (city) Butler County	12	0.02
Stow (city) Summit County	5	0.02
Worthington (city) Franklin County	3	0.02
Shiloh (cdp) Montgomery County	2	0.02
Cleveland (city) Cuyahoga County	34	0.01

Hawaii Native/Pacific Islander: Other Pacific Islander, not specified

Top 10 Places Sorted by Number

Based on all places, regardless of population

Place	Number	%
Columbus (city) Franklin County	436	0.06
Cleveland (city) Cuyahoga County	228	0.05
Cincinnati (city) Hamilton County	133	0.04
Akron (city) Summit County	54	0.02
Toledo (city) Lucas County	53	0.02
Dayton (city) Montgomery County	51	0.03
Lorain (city) Lorain County	38	0.06
Youngstown (city) Mahoning County	29	0.04
Parma (city) Cuyahoga County	21	0.02
Dublin (city) Franklin County	20	0.06

Top 10 Places Sorted by Percent

Based on all places, regardless of population

Place	Number	%
Belmont (village) Belmont County	10	1.88
Summitville (village) Columbiana County	1	0.93
Buckland (village) Auglaize County	2	0.78
Kirkersville (village) Licking County	3	0.58
Bloomingdale (village) Jefferson County	1	0.45
Philo (village) Muskingum County	3	0.39
South Webster (village) Scioto County	3	0.39
Corning (village) Perry County	2	0.34
Lore City (village) Guernsey County	1	0.33
Jeffersonville (village) Fayette County	3	0.23

Top 10 Places Sorted by Percent

Based on places with populations of 10,000 or more

Place	Number	%
University Heights (city) Cuyahoga County	18	0.13
Marietta (city) Washington County	16	0.11
Lebanon (city) Warren County	15	0.09
Girard (city) Trumbull County	10	0.09
Montgomery (city) Hamilton County	9	0.09
Broadview Heights (city) Cuyahoga County	11	0.07
Sharonville (city) Hamilton County	10	0.07
Richmond Heights (city) Cuyahoga County	8	0.07
Columbus (city) Franklin County	436	0.06
Lorain (city) Lorain County	38	0.06

Hispanic or Latino

Top 10 Places Sorted by Number

Based on all places, regardless of population

Place	Number	%
Cleveland (city) Cuyahoga County	34,728	7.26
Columbus (city) Franklin County	17,471	2.46
Toledo (city) Lucas County	17,141	5.47
Lorain (city) Lorain County	14,438	21.03
Youngstown (city) Mahoning County	4,282	5.22
Cincinnati (city) Hamilton County	4,230	1.28
Dayton (city) Montgomery County	2,626	1.58
Akron (city) Summit County	2,513	1.16
Painesville (city) Lake County	2,256	12.89
Fremont (city) Sandusky County	2,140	12.32

Top 10 Places Sorted by Percent

Based on all places, regardless of population

Place	Number	%
West Leipsic (village) Putnam County	88	32.47
Belmore (village) Putnam County	44	25.73
Leipsic (village) Putnam County	535	23.93
Lorain (city) Lorain County	14,438	21.03
Hamler (village) Henry County	134	20.62
Holgate (village) Henry County	222	18.59
Milton Center (village) Wood County	34	17.44
Stony Prairie (cdp) Sandusky County	138	16.51
Hoytville (village) Wood County	48	16.22
Painesville (city) Lake County	2,256	12.89

Notes: (cdp) census designated place; Refer to the User's Guide in the front of the book for more detailed information.

Top 10 Places Sorted by Percent

Based on places with populations of 10,000 or more

Place	Number	%
Lorain (city) Lorain County	14,438	21.03
Painesville (city) Lake County	2,256	12.89
Defiance (city) Defiance County	2,100	12.75
Fremont (city) Sandusky County	2,140	12.32
Fostoria (city) Seneca County	1,104	7.92
Cleveland (city) Cuyahoga County	34,728	7.26
Toledo (city) Lucas County	17,141	5.47
Ashtabula (city) Ashtabula County	1,115	5.32
Youngstown (city) Mahoning County	4,282	5.22
Oregon (city) Lucas County	922	4.76

Hispanic: Central American

Top 10 Places Sorted by Number

Based on all places, regardless of population

Place	Number	%
Cleveland (city) Cuyahoga County	1,166	0.24
Columbus (city) Franklin County	1,040	0.15
Cincinnati (city) Hamilton County	397	0.12
Toledo (city) Lucas County	151	0.05
Akron (city) Summit County	134	0.06
Dayton (city) Montgomery County	72	0.04
New Philadelphia (city) Tuscarawas County	67	0.39
Canton (city) Stark County	62	0.08
Cleveland Heights (city) Cuyahoga County	60	0.12
Youngstown (city) Mahoning County	58	0.07

Top 10 Places Sorted by Percent

Based on all places, regardless of population

Place	Number	%
Harveysburg (village) Warren County	11	1.95
Milton Center (village) Wood County	3	1.54
Strasburg (village) Tuscarawas County	29	1.26
Shawnee Hills (village) Delaware County	5	1.19
Holgate (village) Henry County	7	0.59
Millersburg (village) Holmes County	18	0.54
Willard (city) Huron County	34	0.50
Sugar Bush Knolls (village) Portage County	1	0.44
Holiday Valley (cdp) Clark County	7	0.41
Riverlea (village) Franklin County	2	0.40

Top 10 Places Sorted by Percent

Based on places with populations of 10,000 or more

Place	Number	%
New Philadelphia (city) Tuscarawas County	67	0.39
Springdale (city) Hamilton County	27	0.26
Cleveland (city) Cuyahoga County	1,166	0.24
Sharonville (city) Hamilton County	32	0.23
Whitehall (city) Franklin County	40	0.21
Dover (city) Tuscarawas County	22	0.18
Landen (cdp) Warren County	20	0.16
Columbus (city) Franklin County	1,040	0.15
Norwood (city) Hamilton County	31	0.14
Painesville (city) Lake County	22	0.13

Hispanic: Costa Rican

Top 10 Places Sorted by Number

Based on all places, regardless of population

Place	Number	%
Columbus (city) Franklin County	67	0.01
Cleveland (city) Cuyahoga County	39	0.01
Cincinnati (city) Hamilton County	38	0.01
Dayton (city) Montgomery County	17	0.01
Lebanon (city) Warren County	12	0.07
Sharonville (city) Hamilton County	11	0.08
Bellefontaine (city) Logan County	8	0.06
Austintown (cdp) Mahoning County	8	0.03
Kettering (city) Montgomery County	8	0.01
Shelby (city) Richland County	7	0.07

Top 10 Places Sorted by Percent

Based on all places, regardless of population

Place	Number	%
Anna (village) Shelby County	3	0.23
Fredericksburg (village) Wayne County	1	0.21
Plain City (village) Madison County	5	0.18
Risingsun (village) Wood County	1	0.16
South Russell (village) Geauga County	5	0.12
Cherry Grove (cdp) Hamilton County	4	0.09
Sharonville (city) Hamilton County	11	0.08
Kenwood (cdp) Hamilton County	6	0.08
Lebanon (city) Warren County	12	0.07
Shelby (city) Richland County	7	0.07

Top 10 Places Sorted by Percent

Based on places with populations of 10,000 or more

Place	Number	%
Sharonville (city) Hamilton County	11	0.08
Lebanon (city) Warren County	12	0.07
Bellefontaine (city) Logan County	8	0.06
Perrysburg (city) Wood County	7	0.04
Marysville (city) Union County	6	0.04
Austintown (cdp) Mahoning County	8	0.03
North Olmsted (city) Cuyahoga County	6	0.02
Oxford (city) Butler County	5	0.02
Athens (city) Athens County	4	0.02
Painesville (city) Lake County	4	0.02

Hispanic: Guatemalan

Top 10 Places Sorted by Number

Based on all places, regardless of population

Place	Number	%
Cleveland (city) Cuyahoga County	431	0.09
Cincinnati (city) Hamilton County	211	0.06
Columbus (city) Franklin County	115	0.02
New Philadelphia (city) Tuscarawas County	65	0.38
Strasburg (village) Tuscarawas County	26	1.13
Toledo (city) Lucas County	23	0.01
Lakewood (city) Cuyahoga County	21	0.04
Akron (city) Summit County	21	0.01
Dover (city) Tuscarawas County	19	0.16
Lorain (city) Lorain County	15	0.02

Top 10 Places Sorted by Percent

Based on all places, regardless of population

Place	Number	%
Strasburg (village) Tuscarawas County	26	1.13
Holgate (village) Henry County	7	0.59
New Philadelphia (city) Tuscarawas County	65	0.38
Minerva Park (village) Franklin County	3	0.23
Moraine (city) Montgomery County	12	0.17
Dover (city) Tuscarawas County	19	0.16
Utica (village) Licking County	3	0.14
Burton (village) Geauga County	2	0.14
Monroeville (village) Huron County	2	0.14
Dennison (village) Tuscarawas County	4	0.13

Top 10 Places Sorted by Percent

Based on places with populations of 10,000 or more

Place	Number	%
New Philadelphia (city) Tuscarawas County	65	0.38
Dover (city) Tuscarawas County	19	0.16
Springdale (city) Hamilton County	13	0.12
Cleveland (city) Cuyahoga County	431	0.09
Cincinnati (city) Hamilton County	211	0.06
Lakewood (city) Cuyahoga County	21	0.04
Hilliard (city) Franklin County	10	0.04
South Euclid (city) Cuyahoga County	10	0.04
Athens (city) Athens County	9	0.04
Amherst (city) Lorain County	5	0.04

Hispanic: Honduran

Top 10 Places Sorted by Number

Based on all places, regardless of population

Place	Number	%
Cleveland (city) Cuyahoga County	170	0.04
Columbus (city) Franklin County	108	0.02
Akron (city) Summit County	48	0.02
Cincinnati (city) Hamilton County	47	0.01
Canton (city) Stark County	34	0.04
Norwood (city) Hamilton County	17	0.08
Toledo (city) Lucas County	15	0.00
North Canton (city) Stark County	13	0.08
Mount Carmel (cdp) Clermont County	10	0.23
Parma (city) Cuyahoga County	10	0.01

Top 10 Places Sorted by Percent

Based on all places, regardless of population

Place	Number	%
Milton Center (village) Wood County	3	1.54
Shawnee Hills (village) Delaware County	5	1.19
Sugar Bush Knolls (village) Portage County	1	0.44
Riverlea (village) Franklin County	2	0.40
Fairport Harbor (village) Lake County	9	0.28
Mount Carmel (cdp) Clermont County	10	0.23
Holiday Valley (cdp) Clark County	4	0.23
Jeffersonville (village) Fayette County	3	0.23
Millersburg (village) Holmes County	7	0.21
Hartville (village) Stark County	4	0.18

Top 10 Places Sorted by Percent

Based on places with populations of 10,000 or more

Place	Number	%
Norwood (city) Hamilton County	17	0.08
North Canton (city) Stark County	13	0.08
Sharonville (city) Hamilton County	8	0.06
Cleveland (city) Cuyahoga County	170	0.04
Canton (city) Stark County	34	0.04
Painesville (city) Lake County	6	0.03
Whitehall (city) Franklin County	6	0.03
Berea (city) Cuyahoga County	5	0.03
Columbus (city) Franklin County	108	0.02
Akron (city) Summit County	48	0.02

Hispanic: Nicaraguan

Top 10 Places Sorted by Number

Based on all places, regardless of population

Place	Number	%
Cleveland (city) Cuyahoga County	91	0.02
Columbus (city) Franklin County	73	0.01
Toledo (city) Lucas County	69	0.02
Cincinnati (city) Hamilton County	23	0.01
Painesville (city) Lake County	11	0.06
Bowling Green (city) Wood County	10	0.03
Middletown (city) Butler County	9	0.02
Akron (city) Summit County	9	0.00
Mentor (city) Lake County	8	0.02
Springdale (city) Hamilton County	7	0.07

Top 10 Places Sorted by Percent

Based on all places, regardless of population

Place	Number	%
Harveysburg (village) Warren County	6	1.07
Gambier (village) Knox County	6	0.32
Lucasville (cdp) Scioto County	3	0.19
Fayette (village) Fulton County	2	0.15
Grandview Heights (city) Franklin County	6	0.09
Summerside (cdp) Clermont County	5	0.09
Springdale (city) Hamilton County	7	0.07
Northridge (cdp) Clark County	5	0.07
Willard (city) Huron County	5	0.07
Navarre (village) Stark County	1	0.07

Notes: (cdp) census designated place; Refer to the User's Guide in the front of the book for more detailed information.

Top 10 Places Sorted by Percent

Based on places with populations of 10,000 or more

Place	Number	%
Springdale (city) Hamilton County	7	0.07
Painesville (city) Lake County	11	0.06
University Heights (city) Cuyahoga County	5	0.04
Wilmington (city) Clinton County	5	0.04
Bowling Green (city) Wood County	10	0.03
Loveland (city) Hamilton County	4	0.03
Cleveland (city) Cuyahoga County	91	0.02
Toledo (city) Lucas County	69	0.02
Middletown (city) Butler County	9	0.02
Mentor (city) Lake County	8	0.02

Hispanic: Panamanian

Top 10 Places Sorted by Number

Based on all places, regardless of population

Place	Number	%
Columbus (city) Franklin County	173	0.02
Cleveland (city) Cuyahoga County	47	0.01
Cincinnati (city) Hamilton County	45	0.01
Toledo (city) Lucas County	33	0.01
Dayton (city) Montgomery County	27	0.02
Youngstown (city) Mahoning County	20	0.02
Huber Heights (city) Montgomery County	18	0.05
Akron (city) Summit County	18	0.01
Mansfield (city) Richland County	17	0.03
Lorain (city) Lorain County	13	0.02

Top 10 Places Sorted by Percent

Based on all places, regardless of population

Place	Number	%
North Randall (village) Cuyahoga County	2	0.22
Gloria Glens Park (village) Medina County	1	0.19
Sherwood (cdp) Hamilton County	7	0.18
Hartville (village) Stark County	4	0.18
Holiday Valley (cdp) Clark County	3	0.18
Russia (village) Shelby County	1	0.18
Botkins (village) Shelby County	2	0.17
Lithopolis (village) Fairfield County	1	0.17
Wright-Patterson AFB (cdp) Montgomery County	7	0.11
Lockland (village) Hamilton County	4	0.11

Top 10 Places Sorted by Percent

Based on places with populations of 10,000 or more

Place	Number	%
Huber Heights (city) Montgomery County	18	0.05
Pataskala (city) Licking County	5	0.05
Forest Park (city) Hamilton County	7	0.04
Marysville (city) Union County	6	0.04
Finneytown (cdp) Hamilton County	5	0.04
Shiloh (cdp) Montgomery County	5	0.04
Bedford Heights (city) Cuyahoga County	4	0.04
Richmond Heights (city) Cuyahoga County	4	0.04
Mansfield (city) Richland County	17	0.03
Fairborn (city) Greene County	11	0.03

Hispanic: Salvadoran

Top 10 Places Sorted by Number

Based on all places, regardless of population

Place	Number	%
Columbus (city) Franklin County	455	0.06
Cleveland (city) Cuyahoga County	324	0.07
Akron (city) Summit County	30	0.01
Whitehall (city) Franklin County	28	0.15
Willard (city) Huron County	27	0.40
Cincinnati (city) Hamilton County	27	0.01
Cleveland Heights (city) Cuyahoga County	24	0.05
Youngstown (city) Mahoning County	20	0.02
Middletown (city) Butler County	14	0.03
North Olmsted (city) Cuyahoga County	12	0.04

Top 10 Places Sorted by Percent

Based on all places, regardless of population

Place	Number	%
Harveysburg (village) Warren County	5	0.89
Willard (city) Huron County	27	0.40
Arlington Heights (village) Hamilton County	2	0.22
Millersburg (village) Holmes County	7	0.21
Whitehall (city) Franklin County	28	0.15
Northgate (cdp) Hamilton County	11	0.14
Lincoln Village (cdp) Franklin County	11	0.12
Five Points (cdp) Warren County	2	0.09
Sharonville (city) Hamilton County	11	0.08
Bolindale (cdp) Trumbull County	2	0.08

Top 10 Places Sorted by Percent

Based on places with populations of 10,000 or more

Place	Number	%
Whitehall (city) Franklin County	28	0.15
Sharonville (city) Hamilton County	11	0.08
Cleveland (city) Cuyahoga County	324	0.07
University Heights (city) Cuyahoga County	10	0.07
Bellefontaine (city) Logan County	9	0.07
Columbus (city) Franklin County	455	0.06
Cleveland Heights (city) Cuyahoga County	24	0.05
Brooklyn (city) Cuyahoga County	6	0.05
Springdale (city) Hamilton County	5	0.05
North Olmsted (city) Cuyahoga County	12	0.04

Hispanic: Other Central American

Top 10 Places Sorted by Number

Based on all places, regardless of population

Place	Number	%
Cleveland (city) Cuyahoga County	64	0.01
Columbus (city) Franklin County	49	0.01
Tiffin (city) Seneca County	6	0.03
Cincinnati (city) Hamilton County	6	0.00
Finneytown (cdp) Hamilton County	5	0.04
Landen (cdp) Warren County	5	0.04
Millersburg (village) Holmes County	4	0.12
Cambridge (city) Guernsey County	4	0.03
Warrensville Heights (city) Cuyahoga County	4	0.03
Berea (city) Cuyahoga County	4	0.02

Top 10 Places Sorted by Percent

Based on all places, regardless of population

Place	Number	%
Marshallville (village) Wayne County	2	0.24
Grandview (cdp) Hamilton County	3	0.22
Strasburg (village) Tuscarawas County	3	0.13
Millersburg (village) Holmes County	4	0.12
Hiram (village) Portage County	1	0.08
Finneytown (cdp) Hamilton County	5	0.04
Landen (cdp) Warren County	5	0.04
Wyoming (city) Hamilton County	3	0.04
Tiffin (city) Seneca County	6	0.03
Cambridge (city) Guernsey County	4	0.03

Top 10 Places Sorted by Percent

Based on places with populations of 10,000 or more

Place	Number	%
Finneytown (cdp) Hamilton County	5	0.04
Landen (cdp) Warren County	5	0.04
Tiffin (city) Seneca County	6	0.03
Cambridge (city) Guernsey County	4	0.03
Warrensville Heights (city) Cuyahoga County	4	0.03
Berea (city) Cuyahoga County	4	0.02
Fairview Park (city) Cuyahoga County	4	0.02
Whitehall (city) Franklin County	3	0.02
Cleveland (city) Cuyahoga County	64	0.01
Columbus (city) Franklin County	49	0.01

Hispanic: Cuban

Top 10 Places Sorted by Number

Based on all places, regardless of population

Place	Number	%
Columbus (city) Franklin County	627	0.09
Cleveland (city) Cuyahoga County	512	0.11
Cincinnati (city) Hamilton County	220	0.07
Toledo (city) Lucas County	181	0.06
Dayton (city) Montgomery County	117	0.07
Akron (city) Summit County	74	0.03
Youngstown (city) Mahoning County	68	0.08
Lorain (city) Lorain County	64	0.09
Kettering (city) Montgomery County	61	0.11
Hamilton (city) Butler County	56	0.09

Top 10 Places Sorted by Percent

Based on all places, regardless of population

Place	Number	%
Glenford (village) Perry County	2	1.01
Sarahsville (village) Noble County	2	1.01
Kalida (village) Putnam County	5	0.48
Chauncey (village) Athens County	5	0.47
Sugar Grove (village) Fairfield County	2	0.45
Wetherington (cdp) Butler County	4	0.40
West Leipsic (village) Putnam County	1	0.37
North Randall (village) Cuyahoga County	3	0.33
Empire (village) Jefferson County	1	0.33
West Mansfield (village) Logan County	2	0.29

Top 10 Places Sorted by Percent

Based on places with populations of 10,000 or more

Place	Number	%
Landen (cdp) Warren County	30	0.23
Oxford (city) Butler County	34	0.15
Blue Ash (city) Hamilton County	19	0.15
Washington (city) Fayette County	18	0.13
Montgomery (city) Hamilton County	13	0.13
Rocky River (city) Cuyahoga County	24	0.12
Clayton (city) Montgomery County	16	0.12
Cleveland (city) Cuyahoga County	512	0.11
Kettering (city) Montgomery County	61	0.11
Brecksville (city) Cuyahoga County	15	0.11

Hispanic: Dominican Republic

Top 10 Places Sorted by Number

Based on all places, regardless of population

Place	Number	%
Cleveland (city) Cuyahoga County	542	0.11
Columbus (city) Franklin County	298	0.04
Hamilton (city) Butler County	91	0.15
Lorain (city) Lorain County	69	0.10
Cincinnati (city) Hamilton County	51	0.02
Dayton (city) Montgomery County	29	0.02
Lincoln Village (cdp) Franklin County	26	0.27
Toledo (city) Lucas County	23	0.01
Whitehall (city) Franklin County	22	0.11
Lakewood (city) Cuyahoga County	20	0.04

Top 10 Places Sorted by Percent

Based on all places, regardless of population

Place	Number	%
Phillipsburg (village) Montgomery County	5	0.80
Van Buren (village) Hancock County	2	0.64
Lincoln Village (cdp) Franklin County	26	0.27
Washingtonville (village) Columbiana County	2	0.25
Willard (city) Huron County	15	0.22
Genoa (village) Ottawa County	5	0.22
Gambier (village) Knox County	3	0.16
Hamilton (city) Butler County	91	0.15
Lake Darby (cdp) Franklin County	5	0.13
Green Meadows (cdp) Clark County	3	0.13

Notes: (cdp) census designated place; Refer to the User's Guide in the front of the book for more detailed information.

Top 10 Places Sorted by Percent
Based on places with populations of 10,000 or more

Place	Number	%
Hamilton (city) Butler County	91	0.15
Cleveland (city) Cuyahoga County	542	0.11
Whitehall (city) Franklin County	22	0.11
Lorain (city) Lorain County	69	0.10
Reading (city) Hamilton County	9	0.08
West Carrollton City (city) Montgomery County	10	0.07
Sharonville (city) Hamilton County	8	0.06
Pataskala (city) Licking County	6	0.06
Reynoldsburg (city) Franklin County	17	0.05
Austintown (cdp) Mahoning County	15	0.05

Hispanic: Mexican

Top 10 Places Sorted by Number
Based on all places, regardless of population

Place	Number	%
Toledo (city) Lucas County	13,320	4.25
Columbus (city) Franklin County	8,686	1.22
Cleveland (city) Cuyahoga County	2,973	0.62
Lorain (city) Lorain County	2,437	3.55
Painesville (city) Lake County	1,869	10.68
Fremont (city) Sandusky County	1,584	9.12
Cincinnati (city) Hamilton County	1,542	0.47
Defiance (city) Defiance County	1,371	8.33
Dayton (city) Montgomery County	1,360	0.82
Findlay (city) Hancock County	1,215	3.12

Top 10 Places Sorted by Percent
Based on all places, regardless of population

Place	Number	%
West Leipsic (village) Putnam County	60	22.14
Leipsic (village) Putnam County	441	19.72
Belmore (village) Putnam County	32	18.71
Hamler (village) Henry County	108	16.62
Hoytville (village) Wood County	45	15.20
Holgate (village) Henry County	168	14.07
Stony Prairie (cdp) Sandusky County	116	13.88
Milton Center (village) Wood County	24	12.31
Painesville (city) Lake County	1,869	10.68
Willard (city) Huron County	636	9.34

Top 10 Places Sorted by Percent
Based on places with populations of 10,000 or more

Place	Number	%
Painesville (city) Lake County	1,869	10.68
Fremont (city) Sandusky County	1,584	9.12
Defiance (city) Defiance County	1,371	8.33
Fostoria (city) Seneca County	948	6.80
Toledo (city) Lucas County	13,320	4.25
Oregon (city) Lucas County	689	3.56
Lorain (city) Lorain County	2,437	3.55
Findlay (city) Hancock County	1,215	3.12
Norwalk (city) Huron County	469	2.89
Springdale (city) Hamilton County	255	2.41

Hispanic: Puerto Rican

Top 10 Places Sorted by Number
Based on all places, regardless of population

Place	Number	%
Cleveland (city) Cuyahoga County	25,385	5.31
Lorain (city) Lorain County	10,536	15.35
Youngstown (city) Mahoning County	3,222	3.93
Columbus (city) Franklin County	2,790	0.39
Campbell (city) Mahoning County	873	9.23
Elyria (city) Lorain County	853	1.52
Toledo (city) Lucas County	742	0.24
Ashtabula (city) Ashtabula County	727	3.47
Parma (city) Cuyahoga County	695	0.81
Akron (city) Summit County	654	0.30

Top 10 Places Sorted by Percent
Based on all places, regardless of population

Place	Number	%
Lorain (city) Lorain County	10,536	15.35
Campbell (city) Mahoning County	873	9.23
Linndale (village) Cuyahoga County	9	7.69
Cleveland (city) Cuyahoga County	25,385	5.31
New Rome (village) Franklin County	3	5.00
Geneva (city) Ashtabula County	269	4.08
Youngstown (city) Mahoning County	3,222	3.93
Sheffield (village) Lorain County	108	3.66
Ashtabula (city) Ashtabula County	727	3.47
Brooklyn (city) Cuyahoga County	300	2.59

Top 10 Places Sorted by Percent
Based on places with populations of 10,000 or more

Place	Number	%
Lorain (city) Lorain County	10,536	15.35
Cleveland (city) Cuyahoga County	25,385	5.31
Youngstown (city) Mahoning County	3,222	3.93
Ashtabula (city) Ashtabula County	727	3.47
Brooklyn (city) Cuyahoga County	300	2.59
Elyria (city) Lorain County	853	1.52
Amherst (city) Lorain County	169	1.43
Painesville (city) Lake County	245	1.40
Defiance (city) Defiance County	193	1.17
Boardman (cdp) Mahoning County	422	1.13

Hispanic: South American

Top 10 Places Sorted by Number
Based on all places, regardless of population

Place	Number	%
Columbus (city) Franklin County	944	0.13
Cleveland (city) Cuyahoga County	557	0.12
Cincinnati (city) Hamilton County	320	0.10
Toledo (city) Lucas County	159	0.05
Lakewood (city) Cuyahoga County	116	0.20
Akron (city) Summit County	115	0.05
Cleveland Heights (city) Cuyahoga County	89	0.18
Shaker Heights (city) Cuyahoga County	78	0.27
Parma (city) Cuyahoga County	77	0.09
Upper Arlington (city) Franklin County	69	0.20

Top 10 Places Sorted by Percent
Based on all places, regardless of population

Place	Number	%
Urbancrest (village) Franklin County	9	1.04
Meyers Lake (village) Stark County	5	0.88
Albany (village) Athens County	7	0.87
Burlington (cdp) Lawrence County	22	0.79
Bratenahl (village) Cuyahoga County	9	0.67
Timberlake (village) Lake County	5	0.65
Hilltop (cdp) Trumbull County	3	0.56
Hunting Valley (village) Cuyahoga County	4	0.54
Bentleyville (village) Cuyahoga County	5	0.53
Kenwood (cdp) Hamilton County	33	0.44

Top 10 Places Sorted by Percent
Based on places with populations of 10,000 or more

Place	Number	%
Oxford (city) Butler County	66	0.30
Worthington (city) Franklin County	42	0.30
University Heights (city) Cuyahoga County	41	0.29
Athens (city) Athens County	60	0.28
Shaker Heights (city) Cuyahoga County	78	0.27
Richmond Heights (city) Cuyahoga County	30	0.27
Brecksville (city) Cuyahoga County	33	0.25
Gahanna (city) Franklin County	67	0.21
Landen (cdp) Warren County	27	0.21
Lakewood (city) Cuyahoga County	116	0.20

Hispanic: Argentinean

Top 10 Places Sorted by Number
Based on all places, regardless of population

Place	Number	%
Columbus (city) Franklin County	72	0.01
Cincinnati (city) Hamilton County	49	0.01
Cleveland (city) Cuyahoga County	43	0.01
Gahanna (city) Franklin County	24	0.07
Akron (city) Summit County	20	0.01
Shaker Heights (city) Cuyahoga County	18	0.06
Oberlin (city) Lorain County	16	0.20
Cleveland Heights (city) Cuyahoga County	16	0.03
Lakewood (city) Cuyahoga County	16	0.03
Toledo (city) Lucas County	11	0.00

Top 10 Places Sorted by Percent
Based on all places, regardless of population

Place	Number	%
Hunting Valley (village) Cuyahoga County	4	0.54
Bentleyville (village) Cuyahoga County	4	0.42
Hiram (village) Portage County	5	0.40
Oberlin (city) Lorain County	16	0.20
Yellow Springs (village) Greene County	5	0.13
Ottawa Hills (village) Lucas County	5	0.11
Gahanna (city) Franklin County	24	0.07
Pepper Pike (city) Cuyahoga County	4	0.07
Chagrin Falls (village) Cuyahoga County	3	0.07
South Russell (village) Geauga County	3	0.07

Top 10 Places Sorted by Percent
Based on places with populations of 10,000 or more

Place	Number	%
Gahanna (city) Franklin County	24	0.07
Shaker Heights (city) Cuyahoga County	18	0.06
Defiance (city) Defiance County	10	0.06
Beachwood (city) Cuyahoga County	7	0.06
University Heights (city) Cuyahoga County	7	0.05
Brooklyn (city) Cuyahoga County	6	0.05
Richmond Heights (city) Cuyahoga County	6	0.05
Kent (city) Portage County	10	0.04
Avon Lake (city) Lorain County	7	0.04
Twinsburg (city) Summit County	7	0.04

Hispanic: Bolivian

Top 10 Places Sorted by Number
Based on all places, regardless of population

Place	Number	%
Columbus (city) Franklin County	34	0.00
Burlington (cdp) Lawrence County	21	0.75
Cincinnati (city) Hamilton County	12	0.00
Cleveland (city) Cuyahoga County	10	0.00
Urbancrest (village) Franklin County	9	1.04
Kettering (city) Montgomery County	9	0.02
Miamisburg (city) Montgomery County	8	0.04
Centerville (city) Montgomery County	8	0.03
Toledo (city) Lucas County	8	0.00
Wauseon (city) Fulton County	6	0.08

Top 10 Places Sorted by Percent
Based on all places, regardless of population

Place	Number	%
Urbancrest (village) Franklin County	9	1.04
Burlington (cdp) Lawrence County	21	0.75
Fletcher (village) Miami County	2	0.39
Payne (village) Paulding County	1	0.09
Wauseon (city) Fulton County	6	0.08
Pandora (village) Putnam County	1	0.08
Mount Carmel (cdp) Clermont County	3	0.07
Bratenahl (village) Cuyahoga County	1	0.07
Pickerington (city) Fairfield County	6	0.06
Granville (village) Licking County	2	0.06

Notes: (cdp) census designated place; Refer to the User's Guide in the front of the book for more detailed information.

Top 10 Places Sorted by Percent
Based on places with populations of 10,000 or more

Place	Number	%
Miamisburg (city) Montgomery County	8	0.04
Centerville (city) Montgomery County	8	0.03
Brooklyn (city) Cuyahoga County	3	0.03
Kettering (city) Montgomery County	9	0.02
Tallmadge (city) Summit County	4	0.02
Fairview Park (city) Cuyahoga County	3	0.02
Worthington (city) Franklin County	3	0.02
Dover (city) Tuscarawas County	2	0.02
Upper Arlington (city) Franklin County	5	0.01
Lima (city) Allen County	4	0.01

Hispanic: Chilean

Top 10 Places Sorted by Number
Based on all places, regardless of population

Place	Number	%
Cleveland (city) Cuyahoga County	61	0.01
Columbus (city) Franklin County	51	0.01
Cincinnati (city) Hamilton County	21	0.01
Toledo (city) Lucas County	17	0.01
Westerville (city) Franklin County	15	0.04
Lakewood (city) Cuyahoga County	11	0.02
Wyoming (city) Hamilton County	10	0.12
Shaker Heights (city) Cuyahoga County	10	0.03
Wooster (city) Wayne County	9	0.04
University Heights (city) Cuyahoga County	8	0.06

Top 10 Places Sorted by Percent
Based on all places, regardless of population

Place	Number	%
Timberlake (village) Lake County	5	0.65
Elida (village) Allen County	3	0.16
Wyoming (city) Hamilton County	10	0.12
Hunter (cdp) Warren County	2	0.12
Woodlawn (village) Hamilton County	3	0.11
The Village of Indian Hill (city) Hamilton County	6	0.10
New Boston (village) Scioto County	2	0.09
Kenwood (cdp) Hamilton County	6	0.08
Fairlawn (city) Summit County	5	0.07
University Heights (city) Cuyahoga County	8	0.06

Top 10 Places Sorted by Percent
Based on places with populations of 10,000 or more

Place	Number	%
University Heights (city) Cuyahoga County	8	0.06
Worthington (city) Franklin County	7	0.05
Celina (city) Mercer County	5	0.05
Westerville (city) Franklin County	15	0.04
Wooster (city) Wayne County	9	0.04
Sylvania (city) Lucas County	7	0.04
Shaker Heights (city) Cuyahoga County	10	0.03
Kent (city) Portage County	8	0.03
South Euclid (city) Cuyahoga County	8	0.03
Westlake (city) Cuyahoga County	8	0.03

Hispanic: Colombian

Top 10 Places Sorted by Number
Based on all places, regardless of population

Place	Number	%
Columbus (city) Franklin County	289	0.04
Cleveland (city) Cuyahoga County	162	0.03
Cincinnati (city) Hamilton County	96	0.03
Toledo (city) Lucas County	44	0.01
Lakewood (city) Cuyahoga County	32	0.06
Dayton (city) Montgomery County	27	0.02
Oxford (city) Butler County	26	0.12
North Olmsted (city) Cuyahoga County	24	0.07
Cleveland Heights (city) Cuyahoga County	24	0.05
Kettering (city) Montgomery County	24	0.04

Top 10 Places Sorted by Percent
Based on all places, regardless of population

Place	Number	%
Meyers Lake (village) Stark County	5	0.88
Hilltop (cdp) Trumbull County	3	0.56
Albany (village) Athens County	3	0.37
Galena (village) Delaware County	1	0.33
New Straitsville (village) Perry County	2	0.26
Dillonvale (cdp) Hamilton County	9	0.24
Weston (village) Wood County	4	0.24
Bratenahl (village) Cuyahoga County	3	0.22
Granville (village) Licking County	6	0.19
North Lewisburg (village) Champaign County	3	0.19

Top 10 Places Sorted by Percent
Based on places with populations of 10,000 or more

Place	Number	%
Oxford (city) Butler County	26	0.12
Perrysburg (city) Wood County	16	0.09
Richmond Heights (city) Cuyahoga County	10	0.09
University Heights (city) Cuyahoga County	12	0.08
Worthington (city) Franklin County	12	0.08
North Olmsted (city) Cuyahoga County	24	0.07
Fairview Park (city) Cuyahoga County	12	0.07
Twinsburg (city) Summit County	12	0.07
Brecksville (city) Cuyahoga County	10	0.07
Landen (cdp) Warren County	9	0.07

Hispanic: Ecuadorian

Top 10 Places Sorted by Number
Based on all places, regardless of population

Place	Number	%
Columbus (city) Franklin County	97	0.01
Cleveland (city) Cuyahoga County	58	0.01
Cincinnati (city) Hamilton County	30	0.01
Dayton (city) Montgomery County	22	0.01
Akron (city) Summit County	20	0.01
Moraine (city) Montgomery County	17	0.25
Lorain (city) Lorain County	17	0.02
Hamilton (city) Butler County	15	0.02
Oxford (city) Butler County	11	0.05
Toledo (city) Lucas County	11	0.00

Top 10 Places Sorted by Percent
Based on all places, regardless of population

Place	Number	%
Sherrodsville (village) Carroll County	1	0.32
Moraine (city) Montgomery County	17	0.25
Jeromesville (village) Ashland County	1	0.21
Burton (village) Geauga County	2	0.14
Lincoln Village (cdp) Franklin County	10	0.11
South Amherst (village) Lorain County	2	0.11
Chagrin Falls (village) Cuyahoga County	4	0.10
University Heights (city) Cuyahoga County	9	0.06
Finneytown (cdp) Hamilton County	8	0.06
Orrville (city) Wayne County	5	0.06

Top 10 Places Sorted by Percent
Based on places with populations of 10,000 or more

Place	Number	%
University Heights (city) Cuyahoga County	9	0.06
Finneytown (cdp) Hamilton County	8	0.06
Oxford (city) Butler County	11	0.05
Athens (city) Athens County	10	0.05
Worthington (city) Franklin County	7	0.05
Avon Lake (city) Lorain County	7	0.04
Washington (city) Fayette County	6	0.04
Franklin (city) Warren County	5	0.04
Greenville (city) Darke County	4	0.03
Reading (city) Hamilton County	3	0.03

Hispanic: Paraguayan

Top 10 Places Sorted by Number
Based on all places, regardless of population

Place	Number	%
Toledo (city) Lucas County	7	0.0
Columbus (city) Franklin County	5	0.0
Brimfield (cdp) Portage County	4	0.1
Mayfield Heights (city) Cuyahoga County	4	0.0
Rocky River (city) Cuyahoga County	4	0.0
Cincinnati (city) Hamilton County	4	0.0
Sylvania (city) Lucas County	3	0.0
University Heights (city) Cuyahoga County	3	0.0
Cuyahoga Falls (city) Summit County	3	0.0
Cleveland (city) Cuyahoga County	3	0.0

Top 10 Places Sorted by Percent
Based on all places, regardless of population

Place	Number	%
Brimfield (cdp) Portage County	4	0.1
Sunbury (village) Delaware County	1	0.0
Mariemont (village) Hamilton County	1	0.0
Mayfield (village) Cuyahoga County	1	0.0
Mulberry (cdp) Clermont County	1	0.0
White Oak West (cdp) Hamilton County	1	0.0
Mayfield Heights (city) Cuyahoga County	4	0.0
Rocky River (city) Cuyahoga County	4	0.0
Sylvania (city) Lucas County	3	0.0
University Heights (city) Cuyahoga County	3	0.0

Top 10 Places Sorted by Percent
Based on places with populations of 10,000 or more

Place	Number	%
Mayfield Heights (city) Cuyahoga County	4	0.02
Rocky River (city) Cuyahoga County	4	0.02
Sylvania (city) Lucas County	3	0.02
University Heights (city) Cuyahoga County	3	0.02
Cuyahoga Falls (city) Summit County	3	0.01
Fairview Park (city) Cuyahoga County	2	0.01
Miamisburg (city) Montgomery County	2	0.01
Perrysburg (city) Wood County	2	0.01
Avon Lake (city) Lorain County	1	0.01
Bexley (city) Franklin County	1	0.01

Hispanic: Peruvian

Top 10 Places Sorted by Number
Based on all places, regardless of population

Place	Number	%
Columbus (city) Franklin County	179	0.03
Cleveland (city) Cuyahoga County	142	0.03
Cincinnati (city) Hamilton County	57	0.02
Parma (city) Cuyahoga County	44	0.05
Lakewood (city) Cuyahoga County	21	0.04
Maple Heights (city) Cuyahoga County	19	0.07
Gahanna (city) Franklin County	19	0.06
Toledo (city) Lucas County	18	0.01
Upper Arlington (city) Franklin County	17	0.05
Lorain (city) Lorain County	17	0.02

Top 10 Places Sorted by Percent
Based on all places, regardless of population

Place	Number	%
South Webster (village) Scioto County	2	0.26
Nevada (village) Wyandot County	2	0.25
Rayland (village) Jefferson County	1	0.23
Bratenahl (village) Cuyahoga County	3	0.22
Gambier (village) Knox County	3	0.16
Mount Sterling (village) Madison County	3	0.16
Amelia (village) Clermont County	4	0.15
Mount Healthy (city) Hamilton County	10	0.14
Fairfax (village) Hamilton County	2	0.10
Landen (cdp) Warren County	11	0.09

Notes: (cdp) census designated place; Refer to the User's Guide in the front of the book for more detailed information.

Top 10 Places Sorted by Percent
Based on places with populations of 10,000 or more

Place	Number	%
Landen (cdp) Warren County	11	0.09
Maple Heights (city) Cuyahoga County	19	0.07
Gahanna (city) Franklin County	19	0.06
Montgomery (city) Hamilton County	6	0.06
Parma (city) Cuyahoga County	44	0.05
Upper Arlington (city) Franklin County	17	0.05
North Olmsted (city) Cuyahoga County	16	0.05
South Euclid (city) Cuyahoga County	12	0.05
Athens (city) Athens County	10	0.05
Mayfield Heights (city) Cuyahoga County	9	0.05

Hispanic: Uruguayan

Top 10 Places Sorted by Number
Based on all places, regardless of population

Place	Number	%
Richmond Heights (city) Cuyahoga County	7	0.06
Massillon (city) Stark County	5	0.02
Cleveland (city) Cuyahoga County	5	0.00
Huber Heights (city) Montgomery County	4	0.01
Cleveland Heights (city) Cuyahoga County	3	0.01
Oxford (city) Butler County	3	0.01
Shaker Heights (city) Cuyahoga County	3	0.01
Columbus (city) Franklin County	3	0.00
Kenwood (cdp) Hamilton County	2	0.03
Stow (city) Summit County	2	0.01

Top 10 Places Sorted by Percent
Based on all places, regardless of population

Place	Number	%
Richmond Heights (city) Cuyahoga County	7	0.06
Day Heights (cdp) Clermont County	1	0.04
Kenwood (cdp) Hamilton County	2	0.03
Mogadore (village) Summit County	1	0.03
Massillon (city) Stark County	5	0.02
Huber Heights (city) Montgomery County	4	0.01
Cleveland Heights (city) Cuyahoga County	3	0.01
Oxford (city) Butler County	3	0.01
Shaker Heights (city) Cuyahoga County	3	0.01
Stow (city) Summit County	2	0.01

Top 10 Places Sorted by Percent
Based on places with populations of 10,000 or more

Place	Number	%
Richmond Heights (city) Cuyahoga County	7	0.06
Massillon (city) Stark County	5	0.02
Huber Heights (city) Montgomery County	4	0.01
Cleveland Heights (city) Cuyahoga County	3	0.01
Oxford (city) Butler County	3	0.01
Shaker Heights (city) Cuyahoga County	3	0.01
Stow (city) Summit County	2	0.01
Avon (city) Lorain County	1	0.01
Landen (cdp) Warren County	1	0.01
Loveland (city) Hamilton County	1	0.01

Hispanic: Venezuelan

Top 10 Places Sorted by Number
Based on all places, regardless of population

Place	Number	%
Columbus (city) Franklin County	180	0.03
Cleveland (city) Cuyahoga County	47	0.01
Cincinnati (city) Hamilton County	36	0.01
Toledo (city) Lucas County	27	0.01
Lakewood (city) Cuyahoga County	24	0.04
Upper Arlington (city) Franklin County	22	0.07
Akron (city) Summit County	20	0.01
Shaker Heights (city) Cuyahoga County	17	0.06
Cleveland Heights (city) Cuyahoga County	17	0.03
Dublin (city) Franklin County	16	0.05

Top 10 Places Sorted by Percent
Based on all places, regardless of population

Place	Number	%
Laurelville (village) Hocking County	2	0.38
Albany (village) Athens County	3	0.37
Nelsonville (city) Athens County	13	0.25
Bolindale (cdp) Trumbull County	6	0.24
South Canal (cdp) Trumbull County	3	0.22
Kenwood (cdp) Hamilton County	14	0.19
Lakemore (village) Summit County	4	0.16
Woodmere (village) Cuyahoga County	1	0.12
Bentleyville (village) Cuyahoga County	1	0.11
Greentown (cdp) Stark County	3	0.10

Top 10 Places Sorted by Percent
Based on places with populations of 10,000 or more

Place	Number	%
Upper Arlington (city) Franklin County	22	0.07
Athens (city) Athens County	14	0.07
Blue Ash (city) Hamilton County	9	0.07
Shaker Heights (city) Cuyahoga County	17	0.06
Rocky River (city) Cuyahoga County	13	0.06
Dublin (city) Franklin County	16	0.05
Fairborn (city) Greene County	15	0.05
Hudson (city) Summit County	12	0.05
Lakewood (city) Cuyahoga County	24	0.04
Riverside (city) Montgomery County	10	0.04

Hispanic: Other South American

Top 10 Places Sorted by Number
Based on all places, regardless of population

Place	Number	%
Columbus (city) Franklin County	34	0.00
Cleveland (city) Cuyahoga County	26	0.01
Toledo (city) Lucas County	16	0.01
Cincinnati (city) Hamilton County	14	0.00
Brecksville (city) Cuyahoga County	10	0.07
Akron (city) Summit County	8	0.00
Willowick (city) Lake County	7	0.05
Gahanna (city) Franklin County	7	0.02
Middleburg Heights (city) Cuyahoga County	5	0.03
Bowling Green (city) Wood County	5	0.02

Top 10 Places Sorted by Percent
Based on all places, regardless of population

Place	Number	%
Wharton (village) Wyandot County	1	0.24
Albany (village) Athens County	1	0.12
Wetherington (cdp) Butler County	1	0.10
Brecksville (city) Cuyahoga County	10	0.07
Mount Carmel (cdp) Clermont County	3	0.07
Bratenahl (village) Cuyahoga County	1	0.07
Willowick (city) Lake County	7	0.05
Powell (village) Delaware County	3	0.05
Yellow Springs (village) Greene County	2	0.05
Seville (village) Medina County	1	0.05

Top 10 Places Sorted by Percent
Based on places with populations of 10,000 or more

Place	Number	%
Brecksville (city) Cuyahoga County	10	0.07
Willowick (city) Lake County	7	0.05
Middleburg Heights (city) Cuyahoga County	5	0.03
Gahanna (city) Franklin County	7	0.02
Bowling Green (city) Wood County	5	0.02
Hilliard (city) Franklin County	5	0.02
Brook Park (city) Cuyahoga County	4	0.02
South Euclid (city) Cuyahoga County	4	0.02
Forest Park (city) Hamilton County	3	0.02
Lyndhurst (city) Cuyahoga County	3	0.02

Hispanic: Other

Top 10 Places Sorted by Number
Based on all places, regardless of population

Place	Number	%
Cleveland (city) Cuyahoga County	3,593	0.75
Columbus (city) Franklin County	3,086	0.43
Toledo (city) Lucas County	2,565	0.82
Lorain (city) Lorain County	1,229	1.79
Cincinnati (city) Hamilton County	1,052	0.32
Akron (city) Summit County	577	0.27
Dayton (city) Montgomery County	525	0.32
Defiance (city) Defiance County	508	3.09
Youngstown (city) Mahoning County	441	0.54
Fremont (city) Sandusky County	406	2.34

Top 10 Places Sorted by Percent
Based on all places, regardless of population

Place	Number	%
West Leipsic (village) Putnam County	26	9.59
Belmore (village) Putnam County	12	7.02
Leipsic (village) Putnam County	90	4.03
Holgate (village) Henry County	47	3.94
Hamler (village) Henry County	25	3.85
Antioch (village) Monroe County	3	3.37
Archbold (village) Fulton County	142	3.31
Defiance (city) Defiance County	508	3.09
Milton Center (village) Wood County	6	3.08
West Rushville (village) Fairfield County	4	3.03

Top 10 Places Sorted by Percent
Based on places with populations of 10,000 or more

Place	Number	%
Defiance (city) Defiance County	508	3.09
Fremont (city) Sandusky County	406	2.34
Lorain (city) Lorain County	1,229	1.79
Fostoria (city) Seneca County	140	1.00
Oregon (city) Lucas County	163	0.84
Toledo (city) Lucas County	2,565	0.82
Washington (city) Fayette County	108	0.80
Cleveland (city) Cuyahoga County	3,593	0.75
Bowling Green (city) Wood County	211	0.71
Sandusky (city) Erie County	169	0.61

Hungarian

Top 10 Places Sorted by Number
Based on all places, regardless of population

Place	Number	%
Cleveland (city) Cuyahoga County	8,385	1.75
Toledo (city) Lucas County	6,188	1.97
Columbus (city) Franklin County	5,889	0.83
Parma (city) Cuyahoga County	4,514	5.27
Akron (city) Summit County	4,025	1.85
Lorain (city) Lorain County	3,078	4.48
Lakewood (city) Cuyahoga County	2,674	4.72
Elyria (city) Lorain County	2,342	4.19
Mentor (city) Lake County	2,253	4.48
Strongsville (city) Cuyahoga County	1,885	4.30

Top 10 Places Sorted by Percent
Based on all places, regardless of population

Place	Number	%
Fairport Harbor (village) Lake County	448	14.09
Grand River (village) Lake County	38	11.24
Rayland (village) Jefferson County	49	10.86
Tiltonsville (village) Jefferson County	124	9.55
Reminderville (village) Summit County	193	8.25
Yankee Lake (village) Trumbull County	7	7.87
Yorkville (village) Jefferson County	98	7.83
Mantua (village) Portage County	85	7.79
Pepper Pike (city) Cuyahoga County	458	7.58
Sheffield (village) Lorain County	221	7.49

Notes: (cdp) census designated place; Refer to the User's Guide in the front of the book for more detailed information.

Top 10 Places Sorted by Percent
Based on places with populations of 10,000 or more

Place	Number	%
Lyndhurst (city) Cuyahoga County	1,127	7.38
Oregon (city) Lucas County	1,412	7.29
Beachwood (city) Cuyahoga County	830	6.81
Avon (city) Lorain County	708	6.19
Solon (city) Cuyahoga County	1,325	6.08
Twinsburg (city) Summit County	1,012	5.99
Amherst (city) Lorain County	711	5.98
Bedford (city) Cuyahoga County	841	5.92
Streetsboro (city) Portage County	721	5.85
Middleburg Heights (city) Cuyahoga County	875	5.63

Icelander

Top 10 Places Sorted by Number
Based on all places, regardless of population

Place	Number	%
Cuyahoga Falls (city) Summit County	36	0.07
Columbus (city) Franklin County	36	0.01
Dublin (city) Franklin County	32	0.10
Vermilion (city) Lorain County	31	0.29
Mariemont (village) Hamilton County	30	0.86
Cleveland (city) Cuyahoga County	25	0.01
Toledo (city) Lucas County	25	0.01
Cincinnati (city) Hamilton County	22	0.01
Terrace Park (village) Hamilton County	19	0.84
Parma (city) Cuyahoga County	18	0.02

Top 10 Places Sorted by Percent
Based on all places, regardless of population

Place	Number	%
Mariemont (village) Hamilton County	30	0.86
Terrace Park (village) Hamilton County	19	0.84
Stoutsville (village) Fairfield County	3	0.56
Enon (village) Clark County	12	0.45
Waite Hill (village) Lake County	2	0.44
Roseville (village) Perry County	7	0.36
Beechwood Trails (cdp) Licking County	8	0.34
Vermilion (city) Lorain County	31	0.29
Fruit Hill (cdp) Hamilton County	8	0.21
Dry Run (cdp) Hamilton County	9	0.14

Top 10 Places Sorted by Percent
Based on places with populations of 10,000 or more

Place	Number	%
Vermilion (city) Lorain County	31	0.29
North College Hill (city) Hamilton County	11	0.11
Dublin (city) Franklin County	32	0.10
Landen (cdp) Warren County	11	0.09
Streetsboro (city) Portage County	10	0.08
Cuyahoga Falls (city) Summit County	36	0.07
Maple Heights (city) Cuyahoga County	17	0.06
Middleburg Heights (city) Cuyahoga County	9	0.06
Sandusky (city) Erie County	13	0.05
Sharonville (city) Hamilton County	7	0.05

Iranian

Top 10 Places Sorted by Number
Based on all places, regardless of population

Place	Number	%
Columbus (city) Franklin County	725	0.10
Cincinnati (city) Hamilton County	159	0.05
Akron (city) Summit County	121	0.06
Mayfield Heights (city) Cuyahoga County	117	0.60
Upper Arlington (city) Franklin County	105	0.31
Cleveland Heights (city) Cuyahoga County	87	0.17
Dublin (city) Franklin County	82	0.26
Strongsville (city) Cuyahoga County	64	0.15
Westlake (city) Cuyahoga County	56	0.18
Pepper Pike (city) Cuyahoga County	54	0.89

Top 10 Places Sorted by Percent
Based on all places, regardless of population

Place	Number	%
Hunting Valley (village) Cuyahoga County	20	2.71
Waite Hill (village) Lake County	7	1.55
Riverlea (village) Franklin County	5	1.00
Montrose-Ghent (cdp) Summit County	47	0.94
Moreland Hills (village) Cuyahoga County	30	0.91
Pepper Pike (city) Cuyahoga County	54	0.89
Seven Mile (village) Butler County	6	0.85
Wetherington (cdp) Butler County	8	0.78
South Russell (village) Geauga County	28	0.70
Mulberry (cdp) Clermont County	20	0.64

Top 10 Places Sorted by Percent
Based on places with populations of 10,000 or more

Place	Number	%
Mayfield Heights (city) Cuyahoga County	117	0.60
Bexley (city) Franklin County	51	0.39
Upper Arlington (city) Franklin County	105	0.31
Beachwood (city) Cuyahoga County	37	0.30
Marietta (city) Washington County	42	0.29
Cambridge (city) Guernsey County	31	0.27
Forestville (cdp) Hamilton County	30	0.27
Dublin (city) Franklin County	82	0.26
Springboro (city) Warren County	26	0.21
Westlake (city) Cuyahoga County	56	0.18

Irish

Top 10 Places Sorted by Number
Based on all places, regardless of population

Place	Number	%
Columbus (city) Franklin County	83,226	11.69
Cleveland (city) Cuyahoga County	38,986	8.15
Cincinnati (city) Hamilton County	34,226	10.35
Toledo (city) Lucas County	33,738	10.76
Akron (city) Summit County	24,889	11.46
Dayton (city) Montgomery County	13,825	8.32
Lakewood (city) Cuyahoga County	13,379	23.62
Parma (city) Cuyahoga County	12,466	14.55
Mentor (city) Lake County	9,804	19.50
Canton (city) Stark County	9,213	11.36

Top 10 Places Sorted by Percent
Based on all places, regardless of population

Place	Number	%
West Millgrove (village) Wood County	40	38.83
Neffs (cdp) Belmont County	356	31.09
Eaton Estates (cdp) Lorain County	385	28.95
Lakeline (village) Lake County	47	28.31
Brice (village) Franklin County	18	27.69
Rocky River (city) Cuyahoga County	5,580	26.91
Bay Village (city) Cuyahoga County	4,310	26.79
Fairview Park (city) Cuyahoga County	4,694	26.71
New Alexandria (village) Jefferson County	45	26.32
Fairview (village) Guernsey County	23	26.14

Top 10 Places Sorted by Percent
Based on places with populations of 10,000 or more

Place	Number	%
Rocky River (city) Cuyahoga County	5,580	26.91
Bay Village (city) Cuyahoga County	4,310	26.79
Fairview Park (city) Cuyahoga County	4,694	26.71
Lakewood (city) Cuyahoga County	13,379	23.62
Westlake (city) Cuyahoga County	7,433	23.33
North Olmsted (city) Cuyahoga County	7,761	22.75
Avon Lake (city) Lorain County	4,116	22.68
Forestville (cdp) Hamilton County	2,455	22.20
Girard (city) Trumbull County	2,273	20.39
Eastlake (city) Lake County	4,104	20.35

Israeli

Top 10 Places Sorted by Number
Based on all places, regardless of population

Place	Number	%
Columbus (city) Franklin County	226	0.03
Beachwood (city) Cuyahoga County	178	1.46
South Euclid (city) Cuyahoga County	119	0.51
Pepper Pike (city) Cuyahoga County	98	1.62
Cincinnati (city) Hamilton County	91	0.03
Toledo (city) Lucas County	69	0.02
Cleveland Heights (city) Cuyahoga County	49	0.10
Orange (village) Cuyahoga County	40	1.24
Woodbourne-Hyde Park (cdp) Montgomery County	35	0.43
Bexley (city) Franklin County	33	0.25

Top 10 Places Sorted by Percent
Based on all places, regardless of population

Place	Number	%
Pepper Pike (city) Cuyahoga County	98	1.62
Beachwood (city) Cuyahoga County	178	1.46
Orange (village) Cuyahoga County	40	1.24
Peninsula (village) Summit County	3	0.58
South Euclid (city) Cuyahoga County	119	0.51
Woodbourne-Hyde Park (cdp) Montgomery County	35	0.43
Eldorado (village) Preble County	2	0.39
Mayfield (village) Cuyahoga County	12	0.34
Bexley (city) Franklin County	33	0.25
Clayton (city) Montgomery County	32	0.24

Top 10 Places Sorted by Percent
Based on places with populations of 10,000 or more

Place	Number	%
Beachwood (city) Cuyahoga County	178	1.46
South Euclid (city) Cuyahoga County	119	0.51
Bexley (city) Franklin County	33	0.25
Clayton (city) Montgomery County	32	0.24
Montgomery (city) Hamilton County	24	0.24
University Heights (city) Cuyahoga County	33	0.23
Blue Ash (city) Hamilton County	23	0.18
Mayfield Heights (city) Cuyahoga County	23	0.12
Cleveland Heights (city) Cuyahoga County	49	0.10
Brecksville (city) Cuyahoga County	12	0.09

Italian

Top 10 Places Sorted by Number
Based on all places, regardless of population

Place	Number	%
Columbus (city) Franklin County	35,236	4.95
Cleveland (city) Cuyahoga County	22,053	4.61
Akron (city) Summit County	14,705	6.77
Parma (city) Cuyahoga County	11,603	13.55
Cincinnati (city) Hamilton County	10,877	3.29
Boardman (cdp) Mahoning County	9,888	26.53
Toledo (city) Lucas County	9,383	2.99
Youngstown (city) Mahoning County	9,210	11.23
Mentor (city) Lake County	8,167	16.24
Canton (city) Stark County	6,940	8.56

Top 10 Places Sorted by Percent
Based on all places, regardless of population

Place	Number	%
Lowellville (village) Mahoning County	615	48.01
Highland Heights (city) Cuyahoga County	2,528	31.28
Girard (city) Trumbull County	3,285	29.46
Struthers (city) Mahoning County	3,332	28.34
Poland (village) Mahoning County	767	26.76
Boardman (cdp) Mahoning County	9,888	26.53
Mayfield Heights (city) Cuyahoga County	5,061	26.11
Yorkville (village) Jefferson County	318	25.42
Mayfield (village) Cuyahoga County	873	25.09
Wintersville (village) Jefferson County	966	24.02

Notes: (cdp) census designated place; Refer to the User's Guide in the front of the book for more detailed information.

Top 10 Places Sorted by Percent

Based on places with populations of 10,000 or more

Place	Number	%
Girard (city) Trumbull County	3,285	29.46
Struthers (city) Mahoning County	3,332	28.34
Boardman (cdp) Mahoning County	9,888	26.53
Mayfield Heights (city) Cuyahoga County	5,061	26.11
Niles (city) Trumbull County	5,011	23.94
Lyndhurst (city) Cuyahoga County	3,646	23.86
Wickliffe (city) Lake County	2,741	20.33
Willowick (city) Lake County	2,780	19.30
Austintown (cdp) Mahoning County	6,098	19.27
Steubenville (city) Jefferson County	3,613	18.92

Latvian

Top 10 Places Sorted by Number

Based on all places, regardless of population

Place	Number	%
Columbus (city) Franklin County	290	0.04
Cleveland (city) Cuyahoga County	213	0.04
Lakewood (city) Cuyahoga County	141	0.25
Parma (city) Cuyahoga County	131	0.15
Cincinnati (city) Hamilton County	102	0.03
Brook Park (city) Cuyahoga County	65	0.31
Toledo (city) Lucas County	65	0.02
Strongsville (city) Cuyahoga County	60	0.14
Cuyahoga Falls (city) Summit County	53	0.11
Cleveland Heights (city) Cuyahoga County	52	0.10

Top 10 Places Sorted by Percent

Based on all places, regardless of population

Place	Number	%
Wetherington (cdp) Butler County	33	3.24
Mifflin (village) Ashland County	2	1.52
Bentleyville (village) Cuyahoga County	8	0.84
Hiram (village) Portage County	9	0.74
Evendale (village) Hamilton County	19	0.61
McDonald (village) Trumbull County	20	0.58
South Russell (village) Geauga County	21	0.52
Bratenahl (village) Cuyahoga County	7	0.52
Cuyahoga Heights (village) Cuyahoga County	3	0.50
Highland Heights (city) Cuyahoga County	38	0.47

Top 10 Places Sorted by Percent

Based on places with populations of 10,000 or more

Place	Number	%
Broadview Heights (city) Cuyahoga County	51	0.32
Brook Park (city) Cuyahoga County	65	0.31
Lakewood (city) Cuyahoga County	141	0.25
Beachwood (city) Cuyahoga County	31	0.25
Mayfield Heights (city) Cuyahoga County	38	0.20
Norton (city) Summit County	23	0.20
North Royalton (city) Cuyahoga County	50	0.17
Worthington (city) Franklin County	23	0.16
Parma (city) Cuyahoga County	131	0.15
Fairview Park (city) Cuyahoga County	26	0.15

Lithuanian

Top 10 Places Sorted by Number

Based on all places, regardless of population

Place	Number	%
Cleveland (city) Cuyahoga County	1,444	0.30
Columbus (city) Franklin County	1,028	0.14
Euclid (city) Cuyahoga County	811	1.54
Parma (city) Cuyahoga County	527	0.62
Cincinnati (city) Hamilton County	496	0.15
Mentor (city) Lake County	426	0.85
Akron (city) Summit County	423	0.19
Beachwood (city) Cuyahoga County	308	2.53
Lakewood (city) Cuyahoga County	299	0.53
Cleveland Heights (city) Cuyahoga County	296	0.59

Top 10 Places Sorted by Percent

Based on all places, regardless of population

Place	Number	%
Donnelsville (village) Clark County	10	4.12
Salesville (village) Guernsey County	6	4.03
Grand River (village) Lake County	13	3.85
Beachwood (city) Cuyahoga County	308	2.53
Moscow (village) Clermont County	6	2.30
South Canal (cdp) Trumbull County	30	2.23
Willowick (city) Lake County	270	1.87
Brady Lake (village) Portage County	9	1.79
Waite Hill (village) Lake County	8	1.77
Amberley (village) Hamilton County	60	1.76

Top 10 Places Sorted by Percent

Based on places with populations of 10,000 or more

Place	Number	%
Beachwood (city) Cuyahoga County	308	2.53
Willowick (city) Lake County	270	1.87
Richmond Heights (city) Cuyahoga County	173	1.58
Euclid (city) Cuyahoga County	811	1.54
Eastlake (city) Lake County	262	1.30
Bexley (city) Franklin County	172	1.30
Lyndhurst (city) Cuyahoga County	167	1.09
Wickliffe (city) Lake County	147	1.09
Willoughby (city) Lake County	228	1.01
Bucyrus (city) Crawford County	125	0.95

Luxemburger

Top 10 Places Sorted by Number

Based on all places, regardless of population

Place	Number	%
Cincinnati (city) Hamilton County	66	0.02
Toledo (city) Lucas County	40	0.01
Dover (city) Tuscarawas County	29	0.24
Landen (cdp) Warren County	23	0.18
Vermilion (city) Lorain County	21	0.19
Fostoria (city) Seneca County	21	0.15
Mason (city) Warren County	19	0.09
Centerville (city) Montgomery County	19	0.08
Perrysburg (city) Wood County	18	0.11
Delaware (city) Delaware County	15	0.06

Top 10 Places Sorted by Percent

Based on all places, regardless of population

Place	Number	%
Bentleyville (village) Cuyahoga County	8	0.84
Milan (village) Erie County	5	0.34
South Russell (village) Geauga County	13	0.32
Doylestown (village) Wayne County	8	0.29
Five Points (cdp) Warren County	6	0.26
Timberlake (village) Lake County	2	0.26
Dover (city) Tuscarawas County	29	0.24
Pleasantville (village) Fairfield County	2	0.23
Mariemont (village) Hamilton County	7	0.20
Vermilion (city) Lorain County	21	0.19

Top 10 Places Sorted by Percent

Based on places with populations of 10,000 or more

Place	Number	%
Dover (city) Tuscarawas County	29	0.24
Vermilion (city) Lorain County	21	0.19
Landen (cdp) Warren County	23	0.18
Fostoria (city) Seneca County	21	0.15
Perrysburg (city) Wood County	18	0.11
Mason (city) Warren County	19	0.09
Centerville (city) Montgomery County	19	0.08
Aurora (city) Portage County	9	0.07
Delaware (city) Delaware County	15	0.06
Reading (city) Hamilton County	7	0.06

Macedonian

Top 10 Places Sorted by Number

Based on all places, regardless of population

Place	Number	%
Columbus (city) Franklin County	471	0.07
Gahanna (city) Franklin County	284	0.87
Akron (city) Summit County	214	0.10
Lorain (city) Lorain County	105	0.15
Cleveland (city) Cuyahoga County	101	0.02
Massillon (city) Stark County	92	0.29
Lakewood (city) Cuyahoga County	92	0.16
Green (city) Summit County	79	0.35
Whitehall (city) Franklin County	75	0.39
Cincinnati (city) Hamilton County	70	0.02

Top 10 Places Sorted by Percent

Based on all places, regardless of population

Place	Number	%
Brookfield Center (cdp) Trumbull County	17	1.46
Bloomingdale (village) Jefferson County	3	1.29
Ontario (village) Richland County	66	1.26
Gahanna (city) Franklin County	284	0.87
Fairlawn (city) Summit County	63	0.86
Mount Eaton (village) Wayne County	2	0.83
Mogadore (village) Summit County	30	0.81
Obetz (village) Franklin County	27	0.71
Meyers Lake (village) Stark County	3	0.53
Lexington (village) Richland County	21	0.50

Top 10 Places Sorted by Percent

Based on places with populations of 10,000 or more

Place	Number	%
Gahanna (city) Franklin County	284	0.87
Amherst (city) Lorain County	52	0.44
Whitehall (city) Franklin County	75	0.39
Green (city) Summit County	79	0.35
Broadview Heights (city) Cuyahoga County	50	0.31
Massillon (city) Stark County	92	0.29
Parma Heights (city) Cuyahoga County	57	0.26
Barberton (city) Summit County	59	0.21
North Canton (city) Stark County	35	0.21
Forestville (cdp) Hamilton County	20	0.18

Maltese

Top 10 Places Sorted by Number

Based on all places, regardless of population

Place	Number	%
Columbus (city) Franklin County	29	0.00
Moraine (city) Montgomery County	23	0.33
Hudson (city) Summit County	23	0.10
Beavercreek (city) Greene County	22	0.06
Cincinnati (city) Hamilton County	20	0.01
Silver Lake (village) Summit County	17	0.56
Gahanna (city) Franklin County	16	0.05
Garfield Heights (city) Cuyahoga County	16	0.05
Norwalk (city) Huron County	12	0.07
Toledo (city) Lucas County	11	0.00

Top 10 Places Sorted by Percent

Based on all places, regardless of population

Place	Number	%
Silver Lake (village) Summit County	17	0.56
Orwell (village) Ashtabula County	7	0.46
Felicity (village) Clermont County	3	0.34
Moraine (city) Montgomery County	23	0.33
Canal Winchester (village) Franklin County	10	0.22
South Russell (village) Geauga County	8	0.20
Gates Mills (village) Cuyahoga County	5	0.20
Plymouth (village) Richland County	3	0.16
De Graff (village) Logan County	2	0.16
Hudson (city) Summit County	23	0.10

Notes: (cdp) census designated place; Refer to the User's Guide in the front of the book for more detailed information.

Top 10 Places Sorted by Percent
Based on places with populations of 10,000 or more

Place	Number	%
Hudson (city) Summit County	23	0.10
Norwalk (city) Huron County	12	0.07
Beavercreek (city) Greene County	22	0.06
Gahanna (city) Franklin County	16	0.05
Garfield Heights (city) Cuyahoga County	16	0.05
Urbana (city) Champaign County	6	0.05
Wadsworth (city) Medina County	8	0.04
Sylvania (city) Lucas County	7	0.04
Delaware (city) Delaware County	8	0.03
Eastlake (city) Lake County	6	0.03

New Zealander

Top 10 Places Sorted by Number
Based on all places, regardless of population

Place	Number	%
Toledo (city) Lucas County	27	0.01
Cuyahoga Falls (city) Summit County	14	0.03
Delaware (city) Delaware County	10	0.04
New Albany (village) Franklin County	9	0.25
Kent (city) Portage County	7	0.03
Fairborn (city) Greene County	7	0.02
Brunswick (city) Medina County	6	0.02
Cleveland (city) Cuyahoga County	6	0.00
Winchester (village) Adams County	2	0.20

Top 10 Places Sorted by Percent
Based on all places, regardless of population

Place	Number	%
New Albany (village) Franklin County	9	0.25
Winchester (village) Adams County	2	0.20
Delaware (city) Delaware County	10	0.04
Cuyahoga Falls (city) Summit County	14	0.03
Kent (city) Portage County	7	0.03
Fairborn (city) Greene County	7	0.02
Brunswick (city) Medina County	6	0.02
Toledo (city) Lucas County	27	0.01
Cleveland (city) Cuyahoga County	6	0.00

Top 10 Places Sorted by Percent
Based on places with populations of 10,000 or more

Place	Number	%
Delaware (city) Delaware County	10	0.04
Cuyahoga Falls (city) Summit County	14	0.03
Kent (city) Portage County	7	0.03
Fairborn (city) Greene County	7	0.02
Brunswick (city) Medina County	6	0.02
Toledo (city) Lucas County	27	0.01
Cleveland (city) Cuyahoga County	6	0.00

Northern European

Top 10 Places Sorted by Number
Based on all places, regardless of population

Place	Number	%
Columbus (city) Franklin County	293	0.04
Cincinnati (city) Hamilton County	167	0.05
Shaker Heights (city) Cuyahoga County	71	0.24
Toledo (city) Lucas County	71	0.02
Kettering (city) Montgomery County	66	0.11
Mentor (city) Lake County	55	0.11
Centerville (city) Montgomery County	46	0.20
Dublin (city) Franklin County	46	0.15
Cleveland Heights (city) Cuyahoga County	45	0.09
Aurora (city) Portage County	43	0.32

Top 10 Places Sorted by Percent
Based on all places, regardless of population

Place	Number	%
South Solon (village) Madison County	10	2.43
Harrisburg (village) Franklin County	5	1.45
Granville South (cdp) Licking County	14	1.15
Granville (village) Licking County	33	1.13
Yellow Springs (village) Greene County	32	0.87
Newcomerstown (village) Tuscarawas County	33	0.83
Mariemont (village) Hamilton County	29	0.83
Swanton (village) Fulton County	20	0.60
Kirkersville (village) Licking County	3	0.56
Minerva Park (village) Franklin County	7	0.55

Top 10 Places Sorted by Percent
Based on places with populations of 10,000 or more

Place	Number	%
Aurora (city) Portage County	43	0.32
Bexley (city) Franklin County	36	0.27
Shaker Heights (city) Cuyahoga County	71	0.24
Marysville (city) Union County	33	0.21
Centerville (city) Montgomery County	46	0.20
Maumee (city) Lucas County	29	0.19
Pataskala (city) Licking County	19	0.19
Springdale (city) Hamilton County	19	0.18
White Oak (cdp) Hamilton County	22	0.17
Dublin (city) Franklin County	46	0.15

Norwegian

Top 10 Places Sorted by Number
Based on all places, regardless of population

Place	Number	%
Columbus (city) Franklin County	3,027	0.43
Cincinnati (city) Hamilton County	983	0.30
Toledo (city) Lucas County	961	0.31
Akron (city) Summit County	783	0.36
Cleveland (city) Cuyahoga County	570	0.12
Dayton (city) Montgomery County	494	0.30
Beavercreek (city) Greene County	465	1.22
Cuyahoga Falls (city) Summit County	447	0.91
Lakewood (city) Cuyahoga County	366	0.65
Kettering (city) Montgomery County	366	0.64

Top 10 Places Sorted by Percent
Based on all places, regardless of population

Place	Number	%
Wetherington (cdp) Butler County	47	4.61
Van Buren (village) Hancock County	13	4.36
Bentleyville (village) Cuyahoga County	34	3.59
Lawrenceville (village) Clark County	10	3.40
Helena (village) Sandusky County	8	3.40
Cedarville (village) Greene County	119	3.11
Wright-Patterson AFB (cdp) Montgomery County	174	2.63
Ottawa Hills (village) Lucas County	114	2.51
Lakeline (village) Lake County	4	2.41
Corwin (village) Warren County	6	2.32

Top 10 Places Sorted by Percent
Based on places with populations of 10,000 or more

Place	Number	%
Montgomery (city) Hamilton County	160	1.59
Hudson (city) Summit County	339	1.51
Beavercreek (city) Greene County	465	1.22
Worthington (city) Franklin County	170	1.19
Avon Lake (city) Lorain County	212	1.17
Oxford (city) Butler County	242	1.10
Springdale (city) Hamilton County	115	1.09
Perrysburg (city) Wood County	178	1.04
Upper Arlington (city) Franklin County	342	1.02
Berea (city) Cuyahoga County	189	0.99

Pennsylvania German

Top 10 Places Sorted by Number
Based on all places, regardless of population

Place	Number	%
Columbus (city) Franklin County	487	0.0
Akron (city) Summit County	405	0.1
Canton (city) Stark County	224	0.2
Toledo (city) Lucas County	223	0.
Cleveland (city) Cuyahoga County	192	0.0
Warren (city) Trumbull County	181	0.3
Austintown (cdp) Mahoning County	179	0.5
Youngstown (city) Mahoning County	175	0.2
Wadsworth (city) Medina County	154	0.8
Cincinnati (city) Hamilton County	114	0.0

Top 10 Places Sorted by Percent
Based on all places, regardless of population

Place	Number	%
Marseilles (village) Wyandot County	10	7.3
Hoytville (village) Wood County	13	4.08
Glenford (village) Perry County	7	3.7
Bairdstown (village) Wood County	4	3.05
Mount Eaton (village) Wayne County	7	2.9
Vienna Center (cdp) Trumbull County	34	2.87
Belmore (village) Putnam County	5	2.86
Sugar Bush Knolls (village) Portage County	6	2.84
North Hampton (village) Clark County	5	2.67
Wharton (village) Wyandot County	9	2.29

Top 10 Places Sorted by Percent
Based on places with populations of 10,000 or more

Place	Number	%
Wadsworth (city) Medina County	154	0.83
Austintown (cdp) Mahoning County	179	0.57
Dover (city) Tuscarawas County	59	0.48
Ashland (city) Ashland County	100	0.47
Salem (city) Columbiana County	54	0.45
Galion (city) Crawford County	52	0.45
Wooster (city) Wayne County	100	0.40
Warren (city) Trumbull County	181	0.39
Alliance (city) Stark County	87	0.37
Ashtabula (city) Ashtabula County	78	0.37

Polish

Top 10 Places Sorted by Number
Based on all places, regardless of population

Place	Number	%
Toledo (city) Lucas County	31,802	10.14
Cleveland (city) Cuyahoga County	22,978	4.80
Parma (city) Cuyahoga County	15,503	18.10
Columbus (city) Franklin County	14,510	2.04
Garfield Heights (city) Cuyahoga County	7,983	26.07
Strongsville (city) Cuyahoga County	5,536	12.62
Lorain (city) Lorain County	5,386	7.85
North Royalton (city) Cuyahoga County	5,278	18.42
Akron (city) Summit County	5,200	2.40
Lakewood (city) Cuyahoga County	4,406	7.78

Top 10 Places Sorted by Percent
Based on all places, regardless of population

Place	Number	%
Cuyahoga Heights (village) Cuyahoga County	239	39.90
Independence (city) Cuyahoga County	2,323	32.28
Adena (village) Jefferson County	249	30.11
Newburgh Heights (village) Cuyahoga County	706	29.55
Garfield Heights (city) Cuyahoga County	7,983	26.07
Valley View (village) Cuyahoga County	536	24.64
Brooklyn Heights (village) Cuyahoga County	368	23.34
Seven Hills (city) Cuyahoga County	2,732	22.62
Mount Pleasant (village) Jefferson County	113	20.14
Dillonvale (village) Jefferson County	154	19.87

Notes: (cdp) census designated place; Refer to the User's Guide in the front of the book for more detailed information.

Top 10 Places Sorted by Percent
Based on places with populations of 10,000 or more

Place	Number	%
Garfield Heights (city) Cuyahoga County	7,983	26.07
Seven Hills (city) Cuyahoga County	2,732	22.62
North Royalton (city) Cuyahoga County	5,278	18.42
Brecksville (city) Cuyahoga County	2,436	18.27
Parma (city) Cuyahoga County	15,503	18.10
Broadview Heights (city) Cuyahoga County	2,565	16.06
Brook Park (city) Cuyahoga County	2,998	14.13
Brooklyn (city) Cuyahoga County	1,629	14.06
Amherst (city) Lorain County	1,557	13.10
Parma Heights (city) Cuyahoga County	2,827	13.05

Portuguese

Top 10 Places Sorted by Number
Based on all places, regardless of population

Place	Number	%
Columbus (city) Franklin County	549	0.08
Cincinnati (city) Hamilton County	158	0.05
Toledo (city) Lucas County	157	0.05
Ashtabula (city) Ashtabula County	133	0.64
Cleveland (city) Cuyahoga County	115	0.02
Canton (city) Stark County	113	0.14
Kettering (city) Montgomery County	84	0.15
Akron (city) Summit County	70	0.03
Beavercreek (city) Greene County	65	0.17
North Olmsted (city) Cuyahoga County	64	0.19

Top 10 Places Sorted by Percent
Based on all places, regardless of population

Place	Number	%
Kipton (village) Lorain County	14	5.17
Wilson (village) Monroe County	3	2.59
Burgoon (village) Sandusky County	4	2.16
North Perry (village) Lake County	16	1.91
Granville South (cdp) Licking County	18	1.48
Buchtel (village) Athens County	8	1.43
Rossburg (village) Darke County	3	1.43
Arcadia (village) Hancock County	7	1.31
Ludlow Falls (village) Miami County	2	0.99
Rushsylvania (village) Logan County	5	0.92

Top 10 Places Sorted by Percent
Based on places with populations of 10,000 or more

Place	Number	%
Ashtabula (city) Ashtabula County	133	0.64
Forestville (cdp) Hamilton County	34	0.31
Conneaut (city) Ashtabula County	34	0.27
Perrysburg (city) Wood County	41	0.24
Landen (cdp) Warren County	30	0.24
Worthington (city) Franklin County	33	0.23
Streetsboro (city) Portage County	28	0.23
Avon Lake (city) Lorain County	40	0.22
Norton (city) Summit County	24	0.21
Mason (city) Warren County	44	0.20

Romanian

Top 10 Places Sorted by Number
Based on all places, regardless of population

Place	Number	%
Cleveland (city) Cuyahoga County	1,461	0.31
Columbus (city) Franklin County	954	0.13
Akron (city) Summit County	623	0.29
Lakewood (city) Cuyahoga County	582	1.03
Canton (city) Stark County	517	0.64
Parma (city) Cuyahoga County	506	0.59
Warren (city) Trumbull County	487	1.04
North Olmsted (city) Cuyahoga County	453	1.33
Boardman (cdp) Mahoning County	414	1.11
Alliance (city) Stark County	406	1.75

Top 10 Places Sorted by Percent
Based on all places, regardless of population

Place	Number	%
Yankee Lake (village) Trumbull County	6	6.74
Brookfield Center (cdp) Trumbull County	43	3.69
Limaville (village) Stark County	5	2.49
Sheffield (village) Lorain County	61	2.07
Perry Heights (cdp) Stark County	175	1.95
Alliance (city) Stark County	406	1.75
Howland Center (cdp) Trumbull County	108	1.64
Middleburg Heights (city) Cuyahoga County	249	1.60
Bolindale (cdp) Trumbull County	38	1.55
West Leipsic (village) Putnam County	4	1.55

Top 10 Places Sorted by Percent
Based on places with populations of 10,000 or more

Place	Number	%
Alliance (city) Stark County	406	1.75
Middleburg Heights (city) Cuyahoga County	249	1.60
Parma Heights (city) Cuyahoga County	327	1.51
North Olmsted (city) Cuyahoga County	453	1.33
Beachwood (city) Cuyahoga County	154	1.26
Rocky River (city) Cuyahoga County	237	1.14
Boardman (cdp) Mahoning County	414	1.11
North Canton (city) Stark County	177	1.08
Niles (city) Trumbull County	220	1.05
Warren (city) Trumbull County	487	1.04

Russian

Top 10 Places Sorted by Number
Based on all places, regardless of population

Place	Number	%
Columbus (city) Franklin County	4,333	0.61
Cleveland (city) Cuyahoga County	2,429	0.51
Cincinnati (city) Hamilton County	1,948	0.59
Beachwood (city) Cuyahoga County	1,894	15.54
Shaker Heights (city) Cuyahoga County	1,509	5.13
Akron (city) Summit County	1,469	0.68
Solon (city) Cuyahoga County	1,464	6.71
South Euclid (city) Cuyahoga County	1,439	6.11
Cleveland Heights (city) Cuyahoga County	1,438	2.88
Mayfield Heights (city) Cuyahoga County	1,318	6.80

Top 10 Places Sorted by Percent
Based on all places, regardless of population

Place	Number	%
Beachwood (city) Cuyahoga County	1,894	15.54
Moreland Hills (village) Cuyahoga County	331	10.02
Miltonsburg (village) Monroe County	2	10.00
Orange (village) Cuyahoga County	319	9.86
Pepper Pike (city) Cuyahoga County	552	9.14
Amberley (village) Hamilton County	295	8.67
Bexley (city) Franklin County	967	7.33
Mayfield Heights (city) Cuyahoga County	1,318	6.80
Solon (city) Cuyahoga County	1,464	6.71
Hunting Valley (village) Cuyahoga County	48	6.51

Top 10 Places Sorted by Percent
Based on places with populations of 10,000 or more

Place	Number	%
Beachwood (city) Cuyahoga County	1,894	15.54
Bexley (city) Franklin County	967	7.33
Mayfield Heights (city) Cuyahoga County	1,318	6.80
Solon (city) Cuyahoga County	1,464	6.71
University Heights (city) Cuyahoga County	880	6.22
South Euclid (city) Cuyahoga County	1,439	6.11
Lyndhurst (city) Cuyahoga County	893	5.84
Shaker Heights (city) Cuyahoga County	1,509	5.13
Richmond Heights (city) Cuyahoga County	496	4.53
Blue Ash (city) Hamilton County	454	3.56

Scandinavian

Top 10 Places Sorted by Number
Based on all places, regardless of population

Place	Number	%
Columbus (city) Franklin County	596	0.08
Cincinnati (city) Hamilton County	168	0.05
Toledo (city) Lucas County	122	0.04
Beavercreek (city) Greene County	108	0.28
Fairborn (city) Greene County	79	0.25
Cleveland Heights (city) Cuyahoga County	76	0.15
Huber Heights (city) Montgomery County	74	0.19
Cleveland (city) Cuyahoga County	72	0.02
Hudson (city) Summit County	71	0.32
Upper Arlington (city) Franklin County	62	0.18

Top 10 Places Sorted by Percent
Based on all places, regardless of population

Place	Number	%
Waldo (village) Marion County	7	2.07
Wilson (village) Monroe County	2	1.72
Saint Louisville (village) Licking County	5	1.46
Cloverdale (village) Putnam County	2	0.97
Westfield Center (village) Medina County	10	0.94
Sparta (village) Morrow County	2	0.93
North Fork Village (cdp) Ross County	14	0.87
Ross (cdp) Butler County	15	0.82
Granville South (cdp) Licking County	10	0.82
Saint Bernard (city) Hamilton County	34	0.69

Top 10 Places Sorted by Percent
Based on places with populations of 10,000 or more

Place	Number	%
Amherst (city) Lorain County	46	0.39
Springboro (city) Warren County	43	0.35
Hudson (city) Summit County	71	0.32
Perrysburg (city) Wood County	53	0.31
Bay Village (city) Cuyahoga County	48	0.30
Beavercreek (city) Greene County	108	0.28
Lebanon (city) Warren County	47	0.28
Maumee (city) Lucas County	41	0.27
Fairborn (city) Greene County	79	0.25
Norwood (city) Hamilton County	52	0.24

Scotch-Irish

Top 10 Places Sorted by Number
Based on all places, regardless of population

Place	Number	%
Columbus (city) Franklin County	9,675	1.36
Akron (city) Summit County	2,991	1.38
Cincinnati (city) Hamilton County	2,970	0.90
Toledo (city) Lucas County	2,923	0.93
Cleveland (city) Cuyahoga County	2,319	0.48
Dayton (city) Montgomery County	1,659	1.00
Cuyahoga Falls (city) Summit County	1,446	2.93
Kettering (city) Montgomery County	1,267	2.20
Upper Arlington (city) Franklin County	1,153	3.43
Canton (city) Stark County	1,114	1.37

Top 10 Places Sorted by Percent
Based on all places, regardless of population

Place	Number	%
Norwich (village) Muskingum County	32	30.48
Alexandria (village) Licking County	4	23.53
Holiday Valley (cdp) Clark County	224	12.33
Centerville (village) Gallia County	12	8.39
Brice (village) Franklin County	5	7.69
Otway (village) Scioto County	6	7.06
Lithopolis (village) Fairfield County	39	7.01
Freeport (village) Harrison County	28	6.97
Riverlea (village) Franklin County	34	6.79
Summitville (village) Columbiana County	6	6.74

Notes: (cdp) census designated place; Refer to the User's Guide in the front of the book for more detailed information.

Top 10 Places Sorted by Percent
Based on places with populations of 10,000 or more

Place	Number	%
Avon Lake (city) Lorain County	638	3.52
Upper Arlington (city) Franklin County	1,153	3.43
Worthington (city) Franklin County	443	3.09
Aurora (city) Portage County	414	3.05
Cuyahoga Falls (city) Summit County	1,446	2.93
Steubenville (city) Jefferson County	491	2.57
Hudson (city) Summit County	554	2.48
Mason (city) Warren County	535	2.44
Centerville (city) Montgomery County	550	2.37
Westerville (city) Franklin County	835	2.36

Scottish

Top 10 Places Sorted by Number
Based on all places, regardless of population

Place	Number	%
Columbus (city) Franklin County	11,819	1.66
Cincinnati (city) Hamilton County	4,086	1.24
Toledo (city) Lucas County	3,419	1.09
Akron (city) Summit County	3,134	1.44
Cleveland (city) Cuyahoga County	2,475	0.52
Dayton (city) Montgomery County	1,965	1.18
Kettering (city) Montgomery County	1,563	2.72
Lakewood (city) Cuyahoga County	1,393	2.46
Westerville (city) Franklin County	1,368	3.86
Cuyahoga Falls (city) Summit County	1,357	2.75

Top 10 Places Sorted by Percent
Based on all places, regardless of population

Place	Number	%
Zanesfield (village) Logan County	20	9.48
Summitville (village) Columbiana County	7	7.87
Riverlea (village) Franklin County	34	6.79
Waite Hill (village) Lake County	29	6.43
Mariemont (village) Hamilton County	220	6.29
South Vienna (village) Clark County	31	6.26
West Mansfield (village) Logan County	43	6.11
Salesville (village) Guernsey County	9	6.04
Waldo (village) Marion County	20	5.92
Clifton (village) Greene County	11	5.91

Top 10 Places Sorted by Percent
Based on places with populations of 10,000 or more

Place	Number	%
Avon Lake (city) Lorain County	794	4.38
Upper Arlington (city) Franklin County	1,326	3.95
Bay Village (city) Cuyahoga County	633	3.93
Westerville (city) Franklin County	1,368	3.86
Worthington (city) Franklin County	511	3.57
Wadsworth (city) Medina County	658	3.55
Aurora (city) Portage County	481	3.55
Bexley (city) Franklin County	463	3.51
North Canton (city) Stark County	557	3.40
Perrysburg (city) Wood County	573	3.35

Serbian

Top 10 Places Sorted by Number
Based on all places, regardless of population

Place	Number	%
Akron (city) Summit County	1,135	0.52
Parma (city) Cuyahoga County	941	1.10
Cleveland (city) Cuyahoga County	721	0.15
Columbus (city) Franklin County	651	0.09
Barberton (city) Summit County	334	1.19
Lorain (city) Lorain County	324	0.47
Broadview Heights (city) Cuyahoga County	314	1.97
Lakewood (city) Cuyahoga County	296	0.52
Strongsville (city) Cuyahoga County	266	0.61
Brunswick (city) Medina County	255	0.76

Top 10 Places Sorted by Percent
Based on all places, regardless of population

Place	Number	%
Maple Ridge (cdp) Mahoning County	34	3.71
Mingo Junction (village) Jefferson County	97	2.65
Burbank (village) Wayne County	7	2.48
Yankee Lake (village) Trumbull County	2	2.25
Broadview Heights (city) Cuyahoga County	314	1.97
Shadyside (village) Belmont County	68	1.87
Bellaire (city) Belmont County	88	1.78
Bloomingdale (village) Jefferson County	4	1.72
McDonald (village) Trumbull County	58	1.68
Morristown (village) Belmont County	5	1.64

Top 10 Places Sorted by Percent
Based on places with populations of 10,000 or more

Place	Number	%
Broadview Heights (city) Cuyahoga County	314	1.97
Norton (city) Summit County	158	1.37
Barberton (city) Summit County	334	1.19
Seven Hills (city) Cuyahoga County	135	1.12
Parma (city) Cuyahoga County	941	1.10
Steubenville (city) Jefferson County	192	1.01
Brooklyn (city) Cuyahoga County	105	0.91
North Royalton (city) Cuyahoga County	229	0.80
Brunswick (city) Medina County	255	0.76
Massillon (city) Stark County	222	0.71

Slavic

Top 10 Places Sorted by Number
Based on all places, regardless of population

Place	Number	%
Columbus (city) Franklin County	374	0.05
Cleveland (city) Cuyahoga County	189	0.04
North Royalton (city) Cuyahoga County	126	0.44
Parma (city) Cuyahoga County	112	0.13
Cincinnati (city) Hamilton County	106	0.03
Akron (city) Summit County	100	0.05
Lakewood (city) Cuyahoga County	91	0.16
Toledo (city) Lucas County	87	0.03
Youngstown (city) Mahoning County	80	0.10
Steubenville (city) Jefferson County	69	0.36

Top 10 Places Sorted by Percent
Based on all places, regardless of population

Place	Number	%
Brookfield Center (cdp) Trumbull County	52	4.47
Deersville (village) Harrison County	2	2.22
Sugar Bush Knolls (village) Portage County	3	1.42
Amsterdam (village) Jefferson County	7	1.20
Saint Louisville (village) Licking County	4	1.17
Pleasant City (village) Guernsey County	5	1.13
Chesterland (cdp) Geauga County	27	0.98
Powhatan Point (village) Belmont County	16	0.92
Willshire (village) Van Wert County	4	0.90
Stony Prairie (cdp) Sandusky County	8	0.89

Top 10 Places Sorted by Percent
Based on places with populations of 10,000 or more

Place	Number	%
North Royalton (city) Cuyahoga County	126	0.44
Brooklyn (city) Cuyahoga County	46	0.40
Steubenville (city) Jefferson County	69	0.36
Painesville (city) Lake County	59	0.34
Loveland (city) Hamilton County	39	0.33
Parma Heights (city) Cuyahoga County	66	0.30
Avon Lake (city) Lorain County	55	0.30
Willowick (city) Lake County	37	0.26
Barberton (city) Summit County	66	0.24
Worthington (city) Franklin County	35	0.24

Slovak

Top 10 Places Sorted by Number
Based on all places, regardless of population

Place	Number	%
Cleveland (city) Cuyahoga County	8,402	1.76
Parma (city) Cuyahoga County	7,940	9.27
Youngstown (city) Mahoning County	4,345	5.30
Boardman (cdp) Mahoning County	3,552	9.53
Lakewood (city) Cuyahoga County	3,006	5.31
Lorain (city) Lorain County	2,618	3.81
Columbus (city) Franklin County	2,491	0.35
Akron (city) Summit County	2,479	1.14
Strongsville (city) Cuyahoga County	2,467	5.62
Austintown (cdp) Mahoning County	2,411	7.62

Top 10 Places Sorted by Percent
Based on all places, regardless of population

Place	Number	%
Marblehead (village) Ottawa County	206	27.14
Yankee Lake (village) Trumbull County	15	16.85
Struthers (city) Mahoning County	1,887	16.05
South Canal (cdp) Trumbull County	181	13.44
Poland (village) Mahoning County	372	12.98
Campbell (city) Mahoning County	1,207	12.76
Hubbard (city) Trumbull County	1,024	12.42
Hilltop (cdp) Trumbull County	67	11.80
Canfield (city) Mahoning County	741	9.89
McDonald (village) Trumbull County	333	9.62

Top 10 Places Sorted by Percent
Based on places with populations of 10,000 or more

Place	Number	%
Struthers (city) Mahoning County	1,887	16.05
Boardman (cdp) Mahoning County	3,552	9.53
Brooklyn (city) Cuyahoga County	1,090	9.41
Parma (city) Cuyahoga County	7,940	9.27
Seven Hills (city) Cuyahoga County	1,081	8.95
North Royalton (city) Cuyahoga County	2,276	7.94
Middleburg Heights (city) Cuyahoga County	1,226	7.89
Parma Heights (city) Cuyahoga County	1,690	7.80
Austintown (cdp) Mahoning County	2,411	7.62
Broadview Heights (city) Cuyahoga County	1,177	7.37

Slovene

Top 10 Places Sorted by Number
Based on all places, regardless of population

Place	Number	%
Euclid (city) Cuyahoga County	4,640	8.80
Cleveland (city) Cuyahoga County	3,828	0.80
Mentor (city) Lake County	3,652	7.26
Eastlake (city) Lake County	1,558	7.72
Parma (city) Cuyahoga County	1,477	1.72
Willowick (city) Lake County	1,387	9.63
Willoughby (city) Lake County	1,346	5.96
Wickliffe (city) Lake County	1,336	9.91
Willoughby Hills (city) Lake County	1,060	12.23
Strongsville (city) Cuyahoga County	979	2.23

Top 10 Places Sorted by Percent
Based on all places, regardless of population

Place	Number	%
Willoughby Hills (city) Lake County	1,060	12.23
Wickliffe (city) Lake County	1,336	9.91
Willowick (city) Lake County	1,387	9.63
Euclid (city) Cuyahoga County	4,640	8.80
Timberlake (village) Lake County	65	8.46
Kirtland Hills (village) Lake County	49	8.18
Eastlake (city) Lake County	1,558	7.72
Highland Heights (city) Cuyahoga County	591	7.31
Mentor (city) Lake County	3,652	7.26
Waite Hill (village) Lake County	30	6.65

Notes: (cdp) census designated place; Refer to the User's Guide in the front of the book for more detailed information.

Top 10 Places Sorted by Percent
Based on places with populations of 10,000 or more

Place	Number	%
Wickliffe (city) Lake County	1,336	9.91
Willowick (city) Lake County	1,387	9.63
Euclid (city) Cuyahoga County	4,640	8.80
Eastlake (city) Lake County	1,558	7.72
Mentor (city) Lake County	3,652	7.26
Willoughby (city) Lake County	1,346	5.96
Richmond Heights (city) Cuyahoga County	613	5.60
Lyndhurst (city) Cuyahoga County	583	3.82
Broadview Heights (city) Cuyahoga County	515	3.23
Mayfield Heights (city) Cuyahoga County	507	2.62

Soviet Union

Top 10 Places Sorted by Number
Based on all places, regardless of population

Place	Number	%
Beachwood (city) Cuyahoga County	9	0.07
Columbus (city) Franklin County	6	0.00

Top 10 Places Sorted by Percent
Based on all places, regardless of population

Place	Number	%
Beachwood (city) Cuyahoga County	9	0.07
Columbus (city) Franklin County	6	0.00

Top 10 Places Sorted by Percent
Based on places with populations of 10,000 or more

Place	Number	%
Beachwood (city) Cuyahoga County	9	0.07
Columbus (city) Franklin County	6	0.00

Swedish

Top 10 Places Sorted by Number
Based on all places, regardless of population

Place	Number	%
Columbus (city) Franklin County	4,254	0.60
Toledo (city) Lucas County	1,640	0.52
Akron (city) Summit County	1,629	0.75
Cleveland (city) Cuyahoga County	1,331	0.28
Cincinnati (city) Hamilton County	1,318	0.40
Dublin (city) Franklin County	720	2.29
Beavercreek (city) Greene County	604	1.58
Cuyahoga Falls (city) Summit County	597	1.21
Parma (city) Cuyahoga County	597	0.70
Boardman (cdp) Mahoning County	592	1.59

Top 10 Places Sorted by Percent
Based on all places, regardless of population

Place	Number	%
New Bavaria (village) Henry County	9	11.84
Harbor View (village) Lucas County	7	6.48
South Middletown (cdp) Butler County	9	5.17
Blakeslee (village) Williams County	6	4.96
Put-in-Bay (village) Ottawa County	6	4.03
Granville (village) Licking County	110	3.77
South Russell (village) Geauga County	141	3.51
Edgewood (cdp) Ashtabula County	156	3.26
Pigeon Creek (cdp) Summit County	28	3.13
Hartville (village) Stark County	69	3.10

Top 10 Places Sorted by Percent
Based on places with populations of 10,000 or more

Place	Number	%
Dublin (city) Franklin County	720	2.29
Ashtabula (city) Ashtabula County	478	2.29
Hudson (city) Summit County	485	2.17
Bexley (city) Franklin County	282	2.14
Conneaut (city) Ashtabula County	244	1.95
Struthers (city) Mahoning County	205	1.74
Bay Village (city) Cuyahoga County	278	1.73
Springboro (city) Warren County	199	1.63
Boardman (cdp) Mahoning County	592	1.59
Beavercreek (city) Greene County	604	1.58

Swiss

Top 10 Places Sorted by Number
Based on all places, regardless of population

Place	Number	%
Columbus (city) Franklin County	2,640	0.37
Toledo (city) Lucas County	1,245	0.40
Akron (city) Summit County	976	0.45
Cincinnati (city) Hamilton County	800	0.24
Canton (city) Stark County	775	0.96
Orrville (city) Wayne County	654	7.66
Dover (city) Tuscarawas County	625	5.10
Wooster (city) Wayne County	573	2.29
Cleveland (city) Cuyahoga County	541	0.11
Alliance (city) Stark County	537	2.31

Top 10 Places Sorted by Percent
Based on all places, regardless of population

Place	Number	%
Pandora (village) Putnam County	227	18.64
Sugarcreek (village) Tuscarawas County	366	16.70
Lower Salem (village) Washington County	20	14.39
Wilmot (village) Stark County	50	14.25
Baltic (village) Tuscarawas County	86	11.75
Dalton (village) Wayne County	179	11.44
Parral (village) Tuscarawas County	26	10.74
Bluffton (village) Allen County	385	10.39
Olde West Chester (cdp) Butler County	27	10.15
Latty (village) Paulding County	21	10.14

Top 10 Places Sorted by Percent
Based on places with populations of 10,000 or more

Place	Number	%
Dover (city) Tuscarawas County	625	5.10
New Philadelphia (city) Tuscarawas County	418	2.48
Wadsworth (city) Medina County	432	2.33
Alliance (city) Stark County	537	2.31
Wooster (city) Wayne County	573	2.29
North Canton (city) Stark County	291	1.78
Massillon (city) Stark County	495	1.58
Maumee (city) Lucas County	179	1.18
Findlay (city) Hancock County	431	1.10
Upper Arlington (city) Franklin County	365	1.09

Turkish

Top 10 Places Sorted by Number
Based on all places, regardless of population

Place	Number	%
Columbus (city) Franklin County	454	0.06
Cleveland (city) Cuyahoga County	151	0.03
Cincinnati (city) Hamilton County	119	0.04
Upper Arlington (city) Franklin County	97	0.29
Kent (city) Portage County	81	0.29
Dublin (city) Franklin County	79	0.25
Toledo (city) Lucas County	66	0.02
Montgomery (city) Hamilton County	59	0.59
Solon (city) Cuyahoga County	49	0.22
Akron (city) Summit County	48	0.02

Top 10 Places Sorted by Percent
Based on all places, regardless of population

Place	Number	%
Fairport Harbor (village) Lake County	20	0.63
Montgomery (city) Hamilton County	59	0.59
Amelia (village) Clermont County	16	0.59
Pepper Pike (city) Cuyahoga County	27	0.45
Enon (village) Clark County	11	0.42
Bainbridge (cdp) Geauga County	13	0.37
Forestville (cdp) Hamilton County	37	0.33
Ottawa Hills (village) Lucas County	15	0.33
Cleves (village) Hamilton County	9	0.32
New Vienna (village) Clinton County	4	0.31

Top 10 Places Sorted by Percent
Based on places with populations of 10,000 or more

Place	Number	%
Montgomery (city) Hamilton County	59	0.59
Forestville (cdp) Hamilton County	37	0.33
Upper Arlington (city) Franklin County	97	0.29
Kent (city) Portage County	81	0.29
Dublin (city) Franklin County	79	0.25
Springboro (city) Warren County	29	0.24
Solon (city) Cuyahoga County	49	0.22
Loveland (city) Hamilton County	23	0.19
South Euclid (city) Cuyahoga County	43	0.18
Sylvania (city) Lucas County	32	0.17

Ukrainian

Top 10 Places Sorted by Number
Based on all places, regardless of population

Place	Number	%
Parma (city) Cuyahoga County	3,692	4.31
Cleveland (city) Cuyahoga County	3,224	0.67
Columbus (city) Franklin County	1,955	0.27
Youngstown (city) Mahoning County	1,111	1.35
Strongsville (city) Cuyahoga County	1,019	2.32
Akron (city) Summit County	844	0.39
North Royalton (city) Cuyahoga County	836	2.92
Lakewood (city) Cuyahoga County	663	1.17
Austintown (cdp) Mahoning County	651	2.06
Parma Heights (city) Cuyahoga County	622	2.87

Top 10 Places Sorted by Percent
Based on all places, regardless of population

Place	Number	%
Parma (city) Cuyahoga County	3,692	4.31
Wetherington (cdp) Butler County	44	4.31
Glenwillow (village) Cuyahoga County	19	4.27
Seven Hills (city) Cuyahoga County	501	4.15
Chatfield (village) Crawford County	9	4.02
Brooklyn Heights (village) Cuyahoga County	55	3.49
Middleburg Heights (city) Cuyahoga County	473	3.04
Olde West Chester (cdp) Butler County	8	3.01
North Royalton (city) Cuyahoga County	836	2.92
Peninsula (village) Summit County	15	2.90

Top 10 Places Sorted by Percent
Based on places with populations of 10,000 or more

Place	Number	%
Parma (city) Cuyahoga County	3,692	4.31
Seven Hills (city) Cuyahoga County	501	4.15
Middleburg Heights (city) Cuyahoga County	473	3.04
North Royalton (city) Cuyahoga County	836	2.92
Parma Heights (city) Cuyahoga County	622	2.87
Broadview Heights (city) Cuyahoga County	393	2.46
Strongsville (city) Cuyahoga County	1,019	2.32
Mayfield Heights (city) Cuyahoga County	416	2.15
Girard (city) Trumbull County	233	2.09
Austintown (cdp) Mahoning County	651	2.06

United States or American

Top 10 Places Sorted by Number
Based on all places, regardless of population

Place	Number	%
Columbus (city) Franklin County	51,427	7.23
Cincinnati (city) Hamilton County	15,919	4.81
Akron (city) Summit County	13,911	6.41

Notes: (cdp) census designated place; Refer to the User's Guide in the front of the book for more detailed information.

Place	Number	%
Cleveland (city) Cuyahoga County	13,063	2.73
Dayton (city) Montgomery County	12,783	7.69
Toledo (city) Lucas County	12,242	3.90
Hamilton (city) Butler County	9,129	15.05
Springfield (city) Clark County	9,036	13.83
Middletown (city) Butler County	7,955	15.36
Marion (city) Marion County	6,571	18.62

Top 10 Places Sorted by Percent
Based on all places, regardless of population

Place	Number	%
Holiday City (village) Williams County	30	58.82
South Middletown (cdp) Butler County	91	52.30
Macksburg (village) Washington County	94	49.47
Bairdstown (village) Wood County	56	42.75
Orient (village) Pickaway County	110	39.43
Ludlow Falls (village) Miami County	78	38.61
Sinking Spring (village) Highland County	59	38.06
Cherry Fork (village) Adams County	56	37.84
Highland (village) Highland County	112	37.58
Lucasville (cdp) Scioto County	587	35.81

Top 10 Places Sorted by Percent
Based on places with populations of 10,000 or more

Place	Number	%
Franklin (city) Warren County	2,482	21.51
Marion (city) Marion County	6,571	18.62
Ironton (city) Lawrence County	2,042	18.09
Washington (city) Fayette County	2,420	18.00
Bellefontaine (city) Logan County	2,155	16.51
Galion (city) Crawford County	1,879	16.35
Circleville (city) Pickaway County	2,206	16.26
Urbana (city) Champaign County	1,889	16.26
Portsmouth (city) Scioto County	3,315	15.91
Mount Vernon (city) Knox County	2,275	15.62

Welsh

Top 10 Places Sorted by Number
Based on all places, regardless of population

Place	Number	%
Columbus (city) Franklin County	9,969	1.40
Akron (city) Summit County	2,390	1.10
Cincinnati (city) Hamilton County	1,745	0.53
Toledo (city) Lucas County	1,611	0.51
Cleveland (city) Cuyahoga County	1,309	0.27
Cuyahoga Falls (city) Summit County	1,064	2.16
Upper Arlington (city) Franklin County	1,060	3.15
Canton (city) Stark County	1,012	1.25
Austintown (cdp) Mahoning County	990	3.13
Youngstown (city) Mahoning County	983	1.20

Top 10 Places Sorted by Percent
Based on all places, regardless of population

Place	Number	%
Venedocia (village) Van Wert County	31	19.02
Oak Hill (village) Jackson County	177	10.41
Catawba (village) Clark County	15	7.77
Cairo (village) Allen County	35	7.09
Jackson (city) Jackson County	417	6.97
Yankee Lake (village) Trumbull County	6	6.74
Granville South (cdp) Licking County	81	6.66
La Croft (cdp) Columbiana County	84	5.89
Rogers (village) Columbiana County	15	5.86
Washingtonville (village) Columbiana County	45	5.84

Top 10 Places Sorted by Percent
Based on places with populations of 10,000 or more

Place	Number	%
Niles (city) Trumbull County	819	3.91
Dover (city) Tuscarawas County	395	3.22
Grove City (city) Franklin County	856	3.17
Upper Arlington (city) Franklin County	1,060	3.15
Austintown (cdp) Mahoning County	990	3.13
Worthington (city) Franklin County	448	3.13
Girard (city) Trumbull County	303	2.72
Westerville (city) Franklin County	956	2.70
Boardman (cdp) Mahoning County	950	2.55
North Canton (city) Stark County	406	2.48

West Indian, excluding Hispanic

Top 10 Places Sorted by Number
Based on all places, regardless of population

Place	Number	%
Columbus (city) Franklin County	1,726	0.24
Cleveland (city) Cuyahoga County	1,651	0.35
Cincinnati (city) Hamilton County	634	0.19
Toledo (city) Lucas County	562	0.18
Dayton (city) Montgomery County	392	0.24
Akron (city) Summit County	378	0.17
Cleveland Heights (city) Cuyahoga County	322	0.64
Warrensville Heights (city) Cuyahoga County	194	1.26
Euclid (city) Cuyahoga County	175	0.33
South Euclid (city) Cuyahoga County	156	0.66

Top 10 Places Sorted by Percent
Based on all places, regardless of population

Place	Number	%
Warrensville Heights (city) Cuyahoga County	194	1.26
Mount Healthy (city) Hamilton County	87	1.20
The Plains (cdp) Athens County	34	1.15
Nelsonville (city) Athens County	51	1.00
Woodmere (village) Cuyahoga County	8	0.96
Woodlawn (village) Hamilton County	26	0.91
Golf Manor (village) Hamilton County	34	0.85
Shiloh (cdp) Montgomery County	88	0.78
Wilberforce (cdp) Greene County	11	0.77
Gettysburg (village) Darke County	4	0.73

Top 10 Places Sorted by Percent
Based on places with populations of 10,000 or more

Place	Number	%
Warrensville Heights (city) Cuyahoga County	194	1.26
Shiloh (cdp) Montgomery County	88	0.78
South Euclid (city) Cuyahoga County	156	0.66
Cleveland Heights (city) Cuyahoga County	322	0.64
University Heights (city) Cuyahoga County	82	0.58
Springdale (city) Hamilton County	58	0.55
Forest Park (city) Hamilton County	104	0.54
East Cleveland (city) Cuyahoga County	145	0.53
Bedford Heights (city) Cuyahoga County	52	0.46
Bedford (city) Cuyahoga County	57	0.40

West Indian: Bahamian, excluding Hispanic

Top 10 Places Sorted by Number
Based on all places, regardless of population

Place	Number	%
Dayton (city) Montgomery County	49	0.03
Strongsville (city) Cuyahoga County	33	0.08
Columbus (city) Franklin County	25	0.00
Cleveland (city) Cuyahoga County	21	0.00
Youngstown (city) Mahoning County	14	0.02
Findlay (city) Hancock County	10	0.03
Mayfield Heights (city) Cuyahoga County	9	0.05
Steubenville (city) Jefferson County	8	0.04
Cleveland Heights (city) Cuyahoga County	7	0.01
Toledo (city) Lucas County	6	0.00

Top 10 Places Sorted by Percent
Based on all places, regardless of population

Place	Number	%
Woodlawn (village) Hamilton County	4	0.14
Strongsville (city) Cuyahoga County	33	0.08
Mount Healthy (city) Hamilton County	4	0.06
Mayfield Heights (city) Cuyahoga County	9	0.05
Steubenville (city) Jefferson County	8	0.04
Dayton (city) Montgomery County	49	0.0
Findlay (city) Hancock County	10	0.03
Maumee (city) Lucas County	5	0.03
Youngstown (city) Mahoning County	14	0.02
Cleveland Heights (city) Cuyahoga County	7	0.01

Top 10 Places Sorted by Percent
Based on places with populations of 10,000 or more

Place	Number	%
Strongsville (city) Cuyahoga County	33	0.08
Mayfield Heights (city) Cuyahoga County	9	0.05
Steubenville (city) Jefferson County	8	0.04
Dayton (city) Montgomery County	49	0.03
Findlay (city) Hancock County	10	0.03
Maumee (city) Lucas County	5	0.03
Youngstown (city) Mahoning County	14	0.02
Cleveland Heights (city) Cuyahoga County	7	0.01
Columbus (city) Franklin County	25	0.0
Cleveland (city) Cuyahoga County	21	0.0

West Indian: Barbadian, excluding Hispanic

Top 10 Places Sorted by Number
Based on all places, regardless of population

Place	Number	%
Columbus (city) Franklin County	32	0.00
Forest Park (city) Hamilton County	22	0.11
Euclid (city) Cuyahoga County	19	0.04
Youngstown (city) Mahoning County	14	0.02
Clayton (city) Montgomery County	12	0.09
Piqua (city) Miami County	12	0.06
Austintown (cdp) Mahoning County	11	0.03
Kettering (city) Montgomery County	11	0.02
East Cleveland (city) Cuyahoga County	9	0.03
Mount Healthy (city) Hamilton County	6	0.08

Top 10 Places Sorted by Percent
Based on all places, regardless of population

Place	Number	%
Forest Park (city) Hamilton County	22	0.11
Clayton (city) Montgomery County	12	0.09
Mount Healthy (city) Hamilton County	6	0.08
Piqua (city) Miami County	12	0.06
Euclid (city) Cuyahoga County	19	0.04
Austintown (cdp) Mahoning County	11	0.03
East Cleveland (city) Cuyahoga County	9	0.03
Warrensville Heights (city) Cuyahoga County	5	0.03
Youngstown (city) Mahoning County	14	0.02
Kettering (city) Montgomery County	11	0.02

Top 10 Places Sorted by Percent
Based on places with populations of 10,000 or more

Place	Number	%
Forest Park (city) Hamilton County	22	0.11
Clayton (city) Montgomery County	12	0.09
Piqua (city) Miami County	12	0.06
Euclid (city) Cuyahoga County	19	0.04
Austintown (cdp) Mahoning County	11	0.03
East Cleveland (city) Cuyahoga County	9	0.03
Warrensville Heights (city) Cuyahoga County	5	0.03
Youngstown (city) Mahoning County	14	0.02
Kettering (city) Montgomery County	11	0.02
Maple Heights (city) Cuyahoga County	6	0.02

West Indian: Belizean, excluding Hispanic

Top 10 Places Sorted by Number
Based on all places, regardless of population

Place	Number	%
Columbus (city) Franklin County	25	0.00

Notes: (cdp) census designated place; Refer to the User's Guide in the front of the book for more detailed information.

Place	Number	%
Dayton (city) Montgomery County	21	0.01
Cleveland (city) Cuyahoga County	16	0.00
Mount Healthy Heights (cdp) Hamilton County	9	0.26
Euclid (city) Cuyahoga County	7	0.01
Chillicothe (city) Ross County	6	0.03
Shaker Heights (city) Cuyahoga County	6	0.02
Parma (city) Cuyahoga County	6	0.01
Gambier (village) Knox County	5	0.26
Bedford Heights (city) Cuyahoga County	5	0.04

Top 10 Places Sorted by Percent

Based on all places, regardless of population

Place	Number	%
Mount Healthy Heights (cdp) Hamilton County	9	0.26
Gambier (village) Knox County	5	0.26
Bedford Heights (city) Cuyahoga County	5	0.04
Chillicothe (city) Ross County	6	0.03
Shaker Heights (city) Cuyahoga County	6	0.02
Dayton (city) Montgomery County	21	0.01
Euclid (city) Cuyahoga County	7	0.01
Parma (city) Cuyahoga County	6	0.01
Columbus (city) Franklin County	25	0.00
Cleveland (city) Cuyahoga County	16	0.00

Top 10 Places Sorted by Percent

Based on places with populations of 10,000 or more

Place	Number	%
Bedford Heights (city) Cuyahoga County	5	0.04
Chillicothe (city) Ross County	6	0.03
Shaker Heights (city) Cuyahoga County	6	0.02
Dayton (city) Montgomery County	21	0.01
Euclid (city) Cuyahoga County	7	0.01
Parma (city) Cuyahoga County	6	0.01
Columbus (city) Franklin County	25	0.00
Cleveland (city) Cuyahoga County	16	0.00

West Indian: Bermudan, excluding Hispanic

Top 10 Places Sorted by Number

Based on all places, regardless of population

Place	Number	%
Columbus (city) Franklin County	28	0.00
Dayton (city) Montgomery County	15	0.01
Toledo (city) Lucas County	15	0.00
Pepper Pike (city) Cuyahoga County	12	0.20
Mount Healthy (city) Hamilton County	12	0.17
Warrensville Heights (city) Cuyahoga County	11	0.07
Akron (city) Summit County	9	0.00
Xenia (city) Greene County	7	0.03
Lakewood (city) Cuyahoga County	6	0.01
Cincinnati (city) Hamilton County	4	0.00

Top 10 Places Sorted by Percent

Based on all places, regardless of population

Place	Number	%
Pepper Pike (city) Cuyahoga County	12	0.20
Mount Healthy (city) Hamilton County	12	0.17
Warrensville Heights (city) Cuyahoga County	11	0.07
Xenia (city) Greene County	7	0.03
Dayton (city) Montgomery County	15	0.01
Lakewood (city) Cuyahoga County	6	0.01
Columbus (city) Franklin County	28	0.00
Toledo (city) Lucas County	15	0.00
Akron (city) Summit County	9	0.00
Cincinnati (city) Hamilton County	4	0.00

Top 10 Places Sorted by Percent

Based on places with populations of 10,000 or more

Place	Number	%
Warrensville Heights (city) Cuyahoga County	11	0.07
Xenia (city) Greene County	7	0.03
Dayton (city) Montgomery County	15	0.01
Lakewood (city) Cuyahoga County	6	0.01
Columbus (city) Franklin County	28	0.00
Toledo (city) Lucas County	15	0.00
Akron (city) Summit County	9	0.00
Cincinnati (city) Hamilton County	4	0.00

West Indian: British West Indian, excluding Hispanic

Top 10 Places Sorted by Number

Based on all places, regardless of population

Place	Number	%
Columbus (city) Franklin County	44	0.01
Fairview Park (city) Cuyahoga County	27	0.15
Cincinnati (city) Hamilton County	16	0.00
University Heights (city) Cuyahoga County	15	0.11
Gahanna (city) Franklin County	14	0.04
Akron (city) Summit County	14	0.01
Fairfield (city) Butler County	12	0.03
Toledo (city) Lucas County	11	0.00
Athens (city) Athens County	8	0.04
Clayton (city) Montgomery County	7	0.05

Top 10 Places Sorted by Percent

Based on all places, regardless of population

Place	Number	%
Fairview Park (city) Cuyahoga County	27	0.15
University Heights (city) Cuyahoga County	15	0.11
Clayton (city) Montgomery County	7	0.05
Gahanna (city) Franklin County	14	0.04
Athens (city) Athens County	8	0.04
Fairfield (city) Butler County	12	0.03
Fremont (city) Sandusky County	5	0.03
Ravenna (city) Portage County	4	0.03
Huber Heights (city) Montgomery County	7	0.02
Westlake (city) Cuyahoga County	6	0.02

Top 10 Places Sorted by Percent

Based on places with populations of 10,000 or more

Place	Number	%
Fairview Park (city) Cuyahoga County	27	0.15
University Heights (city) Cuyahoga County	15	0.11
Clayton (city) Montgomery County	7	0.05
Gahanna (city) Franklin County	14	0.04
Athens (city) Athens County	8	0.04
Fairfield (city) Butler County	12	0.03
Fremont (city) Sandusky County	5	0.03
Ravenna (city) Portage County	4	0.03
Huber Heights (city) Montgomery County	7	0.02
Westlake (city) Cuyahoga County	6	0.02

West Indian: Dutch West Indian, excluding Hispanic

Top 10 Places Sorted by Number

Based on all places, regardless of population

Place	Number	%
Lorain (city) Lorain County	44	0.06
Akron (city) Summit County	36	0.02
Columbus (city) Franklin County	33	0.00
Austintown (cdp) Mahoning County	18	0.06
Dayton (city) Montgomery County	16	0.01
Medina (city) Medina County	13	0.05
Crooksville (village) Perry County	11	0.45
Norwood (city) Hamilton County	11	0.05
Whitehall (city) Franklin County	10	0.05
Greenfield (city) Highland County	9	0.18

Top 10 Places Sorted by Percent

Based on all places, regardless of population

Place	Number	%
Crooksville (village) Perry County	11	0.45
Meyers Lake (village) Stark County	2	0.35
Fulton (village) Morrow County	1	0.33
Centerburg (village) Knox County	4	0.28
New Straitsville (village) Perry County	2	0.26
Mechanicsburg (village) Champaign County	4	0.22
Greenfield (city) Highland County	9	0.18
McArthur (village) Vinton County	3	0.16
New Waterford (village) Columbiana County	2	0.15
McComb (village) Hancock County	2	0.12

Top 10 Places Sorted by Percent

Based on places with populations of 10,000 or more

Place	Number	%
Lorain (city) Lorain County	44	0.06
Austintown (cdp) Mahoning County	18	0.06
Ravenna (city) Portage County	7	0.06
Medina (city) Medina County	13	0.05
Norwood (city) Hamilton County	11	0.05
Whitehall (city) Franklin County	10	0.05
Mayfield Heights (city) Cuyahoga County	7	0.04
Centerville (city) Montgomery County	7	0.03
Green (city) Summit County	6	0.03
Steubenville (city) Jefferson County	6	0.03

West Indian: Haitian, excluding Hispanic

Top 10 Places Sorted by Number

Based on all places, regardless of population

Place	Number	%
Columbus (city) Franklin County	131	0.02
Cincinnati (city) Hamilton County	70	0.02
Dayton (city) Montgomery County	52	0.03
Akron (city) Summit County	45	0.02
Cleveland (city) Cuyahoga County	43	0.01
The Plains (cdp) Athens County	34	1.15
Springdale (city) Hamilton County	31	0.29
Sidney (city) Shelby County	28	0.14
Northgate (cdp) Hamilton County	26	0.33
Wilmington (city) Clinton County	24	0.20

Top 10 Places Sorted by Percent

Based on all places, regardless of population

Place	Number	%
The Plains (cdp) Athens County	34	1.15
Northgate (cdp) Hamilton County	26	0.33
Springdale (city) Hamilton County	31	0.29
Wilmington (city) Clinton County	24	0.20
Sidney (city) Shelby County	28	0.14
Woodlawn (village) Hamilton County	4	0.14
Utica (village) Licking County	3	0.14
Mentor-on-the-Lake (city) Lake County	8	0.10
Portsmouth (city) Scioto County	14	0.07
Chillicothe (city) Ross County	14	0.06

Top 10 Places Sorted by Percent

Based on places with populations of 10,000 or more

Place	Number	%
Springdale (city) Hamilton County	31	0.29
Wilmington (city) Clinton County	24	0.20
Sidney (city) Shelby County	28	0.14
Portsmouth (city) Scioto County	14	0.07
Chillicothe (city) Ross County	14	0.06
Westerville (city) Franklin County	16	0.05
Barberton (city) Summit County	14	0.05
Warrensville Heights (city) Cuyahoga County	8	0.05
Centerville (city) Montgomery County	10	0.04
Rocky River (city) Cuyahoga County	9	0.04

West Indian: Jamaican, excluding Hispanic

Top 10 Places Sorted by Number

Based on all places, regardless of population

Place	Number	%
Cleveland (city) Cuyahoga County	1,194	0.25

Notes: (cdp) census designated place; Refer to the User's Guide in the front of the book for more detailed information.

Place	Number	%
Columbus (city) Franklin County	1,058	0.15
Toledo (city) Lucas County	480	0.15
Cincinnati (city) Hamilton County	437	0.13
Akron (city) Summit County	235	0.11
Cleveland Heights (city) Cuyahoga County	209	0.42
Dayton (city) Montgomery County	170	0.10
Euclid (city) Cuyahoga County	140	0.27
South Euclid (city) Cuyahoga County	124	0.53
East Cleveland (city) Cuyahoga County	118	0.43

Top 10 Places Sorted by Percent

Based on all places, regardless of population

Place	Number	%
Nelsonville (city) Athens County	51	1.00
Woodmere (village) Cuyahoga County	8	0.96
Golf Manor (village) Hamilton County	34	0.85
Shiloh (cdp) Montgomery County	88	0.78
Wilberforce (cdp) Greene County	11	0.77
Warrensville Heights (city) Cuyahoga County	108	0.70
North Bend (village) Hamilton County	4	0.65
Woodlawn (village) Hamilton County	18	0.63
Mount Healthy (city) Hamilton County	39	0.54
South Euclid (city) Cuyahoga County	124	0.53

Top 10 Places Sorted by Percent

Based on places with populations of 10,000 or more

Place	Number	%
Shiloh (cdp) Montgomery County	88	0.78
Warrensville Heights (city) Cuyahoga County	108	0.70
South Euclid (city) Cuyahoga County	124	0.53
University Heights (city) Cuyahoga County	67	0.47
East Cleveland (city) Cuyahoga County	118	0.43
Cleveland Heights (city) Cuyahoga County	209	0.42
Bedford Heights (city) Cuyahoga County	42	0.37
Bedford (city) Cuyahoga County	49	0.34
Forest Park (city) Hamilton County	57	0.29
Euclid (city) Cuyahoga County	140	0.27

West Indian: Trinidadian and Tobagonian, excluding Hispanic

Top 10 Places Sorted by Number

Based on all places, regardless of population

Place	Number	%
Cleveland (city) Cuyahoga County	184	0.04
Columbus (city) Franklin County	106	0.01
Warrensville Heights (city) Cuyahoga County	51	0.33
Huber Heights (city) Montgomery County	44	0.11
Middleburg Heights (city) Cuyahoga County	33	0.21
South Euclid (city) Cuyahoga County	29	0.12
The Village of Indian Hill (city) Hamilton County	20	0.34
Vandalia (city) Montgomery County	19	0.13
Edgewood (cdp) Ashtabula County	17	0.36
Toledo (city) Lucas County	17	0.01

Top 10 Places Sorted by Percent

Based on all places, regardless of population

Place	Number	%
Edgewood (cdp) Ashtabula County	17	0.36
The Village of Indian Hill (city) Hamilton County	20	0.34
Warrensville Heights (city) Cuyahoga County	51	0.33
Newtown (village) Hamilton County	8	0.33
Middleburg Heights (city) Cuyahoga County	33	0.21
Vandalia (city) Montgomery County	19	0.13
Northwood (city) Wood County	7	0.13
South Euclid (city) Cuyahoga County	29	0.12
Huber Heights (city) Montgomery County	44	0.11
Mount Healthy (city) Hamilton County	8	0.11

Top 10 Places Sorted by Percent

Based on places with populations of 10,000 or more

Place	Number	%
Warrensville Heights (city) Cuyahoga County	51	0.33
Middleburg Heights (city) Cuyahoga County	33	0.21
Vandalia (city) Montgomery County	19	0.13
South Euclid (city) Cuyahoga County	29	0.12
Huber Heights (city) Montgomery County	44	0.11
Bedford (city) Cuyahoga County	8	0.06
White Oak (cdp) Hamilton County	7	0.05
Cleveland (city) Cuyahoga County	184	0.04
Shaker Heights (city) Cuyahoga County	12	0.04
Kent (city) Portage County	11	0.04

West Indian: U.S. Virgin Islander, excluding Hispanic

Top 10 Places Sorted by Number

Based on all places, regardless of population

Place	Number	%
Columbus (city) Franklin County	43	0.01
Cleveland (city) Cuyahoga County	30	0.01
Dayton (city) Montgomery County	15	0.01
Akron (city) Summit County	11	0.01
Fairlawn (city) Summit County	9	0.12
Chillicothe (city) Ross County	6	0.03
Murray City (village) Hocking County	2	0.45

Top 10 Places Sorted by Percent

Based on all places, regardless of population

Place	Number	%
Murray City (village) Hocking County	2	0.45
Fairlawn (city) Summit County	9	0.12
Chillicothe (city) Ross County	6	0.03
Columbus (city) Franklin County	43	0.01
Cleveland (city) Cuyahoga County	30	0.01
Dayton (city) Montgomery County	15	0.01
Akron (city) Summit County	11	0.01

Top 10 Places Sorted by Percent

Based on places with populations of 10,000 or more

Place	Number	%
Chillicothe (city) Ross County	6	0.03
Columbus (city) Franklin County	43	0.01
Cleveland (city) Cuyahoga County	30	0.01
Dayton (city) Montgomery County	15	0.01
Akron (city) Summit County	11	0.01

West Indian: West Indian, excluding Hispanic

Top 10 Places Sorted by Number

Based on all places, regardless of population

Place	Number	%
Columbus (city) Franklin County	201	0.03
Cleveland (city) Cuyahoga County	154	0.03
Cincinnati (city) Hamilton County	93	0.03
Cleveland Heights (city) Cuyahoga County	85	0.17
Dayton (city) Montgomery County	32	0.02
Huber Ridge (cdp) Franklin County	31	0.63
Reynoldsburg (city) Franklin County	30	0.09
Painesville (city) Lake County	22	0.13
Lorain (city) Lorain County	21	0.03
Gahanna (city) Franklin County	20	0.06

Top 10 Places Sorted by Percent

Based on all places, regardless of population

Place	Number	%
Gettysburg (village) Darke County	4	0.73
Huber Ridge (cdp) Franklin County	31	0.63
Cridersville (village) Auglaize County	7	0.39
Sandusky South (cdp) Erie County	17	0.26
Mount Healthy (city) Hamilton County	18	0.25
Oakwood (village) Cuyahoga County	9	0.25
Edgewood (cdp) Ashtabula County	9	0.19
Oberlin (city) Lorain County	15	0.18
Amelia (village) Clermont County	5	0.18
Terrace Park (village) Hamilton County	4	0.18

Top 10 Places Sorted by Percent

Based on places with populations of 10,000 or more

Place	Number	%
Cleveland Heights (city) Cuyahoga County	85	0.1
Painesville (city) Lake County	22	0.1
Reynoldsburg (city) Franklin County	30	0.0
Forest Park (city) Hamilton County	18	0.0
Bridgetown North (cdp) Hamilton County	12	0.0
North College Hill (city) Hamilton County	9	0.0
Berea (city) Cuyahoga County	15	0.0
East Cleveland (city) Cuyahoga County	18	0.0
Warrensville Heights (city) Cuyahoga County	11	0.0
Gahanna (city) Franklin County	20	0.0

West Indian: Other, excluding Hispanic

Top 10 Places Sorted by Number

Based on all places, regardless of population

Place	Number	%
Mansfield (city) Richland County	19	0.0
Ripley (village) Brown County	2	0.1

Top 10 Places Sorted by Percent

Based on all places, regardless of population

Place	Number	%
Ripley (village) Brown County	2	0.1
Mansfield (city) Richland County	19	0.0

Top 10 Places Sorted by Percent

Based on places with populations of 10,000 or more

Place	Number	%
Mansfield (city) Richland County	19	0.0

White

Top 10 Places Sorted by Number

Based on all places, regardless of population

Place	Number	%
Columbus (city) Franklin County	496,425	69.7
Toledo (city) Lucas County	227,094	72.4
Cleveland (city) Cuyahoga County	206,487	43.1
Cincinnati (city) Hamilton County	179,453	54.1
Akron (city) Summit County	149,577	68.9
Dayton (city) Montgomery County	91,049	54.7
Parma (city) Cuyahoga County	82,806	96.6
Canton (city) Stark County	62,328	77.1
Kettering (city) Montgomery County	55,389	96.3
Hamilton (city) Butler County	54,699	90.1

Top 10 Places Sorted by Percent

Based on all places, regardless of population

Place	Number	%
Fort Loramie (village) Shelby County	1,344	100.0
Bremen (village) Fairfield County	1,265	100.0
Junction City (village) Perry County	818	100.0
Lowell (village) Washington County	628	100.0
Milford Center (village) Union County	626	100.0
Midvale (village) Tuscarawas County	547	100.0
Fredericksburg (village) Wayne County	487	100.0
Jerry City (village) Wood County	453	100.00
Senecaville (village) Guernsey County	453	100.00
Sugar Grove (village) Fairfield County	448	100.00

Top 10 Places Sorted by Percent

Based on places with populations of 10,000 or more

Place	Number	%
Vermilion (city) Lorain County	10,831	99.12
Salem (city) Columbiana County	12,068	98.94
Bridgetown North (cdp) Hamilton County	12,426	98.86
Galion (city) Crawford County	11,206	98.81
Bay Village (city) Cuyahoga County	15,875	98.68
Wadsworth (city) Medina County	18,164	98.52

Notes: (cdp) census designated place; Refer to the User's Guide in the front of the book for more detailed information.

Place	Number	%
Willowick (city) Lake County	14,147	98.51
Lancaster (city) Fairfield County	34,748	98.34
Franklin (city) Warren County	11,204	98.32
Greenville (city) Darke County	13,064	98.27

White: Not Hispanic

Top 10 Places Sorted by Number

Based on all places, regardless of population

Place	Number	%
Columbus (city) Franklin County	487,638	68.54
Toledo (city) Lucas County	217,906	69.48
Cleveland (city) Cuyahoga County	191,741	40.08
Cincinnati (city) Hamilton County	177,483	53.57
Akron (city) Summit County	148,161	68.25
Dayton (city) Montgomery County	89,683	53.97
Parma (city) Cuyahoga County	81,853	95.56
Canton (city) Stark County	61,720	76.38
Kettering (city) Montgomery County	54,906	95.49
Hamilton (city) Butler County	53,999	88.98

Top 10 Places Sorted by Percent

Based on all places, regardless of population

Place	Number	%
Senecaville (village) Guernsey County	453	100.00
Bowerston (village) Harrison County	414	100.00
Green Camp (village) Marion County	342	100.00
Casstown (village) Miami County	322	100.00
Tarlton (village) Pickaway County	298	100.00
Summerfield (village) Noble County	296	100.00
Hanging Rock (village) Lawrence County	279	100.00
Osgood (village) Darke County	255	100.00
Parral (village) Tuscarawas County	241	100.00
Butlerville (village) Warren County	231	100.00

Top 10 Places Sorted by Percent

Based on places with populations of 10,000 or more

Place	Number	%
Bridgetown North (cdp) Hamilton County	12,390	98.58
Salem (city) Columbiana County	12,015	98.51
Galion (city) Crawford County	11,130	98.14
Wadsworth (city) Medina County	18,072	98.02
Franklin (city) Warren County	11,156	97.89
Bay Village (city) Cuyahoga County	15,740	97.84
Willowick (city) Lake County	14,050	97.83
Green (city) Summit County	22,305	97.76
Norton (city) Summit County	11,260	97.72
Lancaster (city) Fairfield County	34,522	97.70

White: Hispanic

Top 10 Places Sorted by Number

Based on all places, regardless of population

Place	Number	%
Cleveland (city) Cuyahoga County	14,746	3.08
Toledo (city) Lucas County	9,188	2.93
Columbus (city) Franklin County	8,787	1.24
Lorain (city) Lorain County	6,929	10.09
Cincinnati (city) Hamilton County	1,970	0.59
Youngstown (city) Mahoning County	1,908	2.33
Akron (city) Summit County	1,416	0.65
Dayton (city) Montgomery County	1,366	0.82
Fremont (city) Sandusky County	1,090	6.27
Painesville (city) Lake County	1,052	6.01

Top 10 Places Sorted by Percent

Based on all places, regardless of population

Place	Number	%
Holgate (village) Henry County	134	11.22
Stony Prairie (cdp) Sandusky County	92	11.00
Milton Center (village) Wood County	21	10.77
Lorain (city) Lorain County	6,929	10.09
Hamler (village) Henry County	65	10.00
West Leipsic (village) Putnam County	25	9.23
Leipsic (village) Putnam County	177	7.92
Campbell (city) Mahoning County	660	6.98
Fremont (city) Sandusky County	1,090	6.27
Willard (city) Huron County	424	6.23

Top 10 Places Sorted by Percent

Based on places with populations of 10,000 or more

Place	Number	%
Lorain (city) Lorain County	6,929	10.09
Fremont (city) Sandusky County	1,090	6.27
Painesville (city) Lake County	1,052	6.01
Defiance (city) Defiance County	956	5.81
Fostoria (city) Seneca County	592	4.25
Cleveland (city) Cuyahoga County	14,746	3.08
Oregon (city) Lucas County	575	2.97
Toledo (city) Lucas County	9,188	2.93
Ashtabula (city) Ashtabula County	549	2.62
Youngstown (city) Mahoning County	1,908	2.33

Yugoslavian

Top 10 Places Sorted by Number

Based on all places, regardless of population

Place	Number	%
Columbus (city) Franklin County	631	0.09
Akron (city) Summit County	626	0.29
Cleveland (city) Cuyahoga County	599	0.13
Parma (city) Cuyahoga County	383	0.45
Lakewood (city) Cuyahoga County	254	0.45
Euclid (city) Cuyahoga County	226	0.43
Cincinnati (city) Hamilton County	213	0.06
Parma Heights (city) Cuyahoga County	182	0.84
Green (city) Summit County	168	0.74
Mansfield (city) Richland County	164	0.33

Top 10 Places Sorted by Percent

Based on all places, regardless of population

Place	Number	%
New Rome (village) Franklin County	9	13.85
Fultonham (village) Muskingum County	3	1.73
Ontario (village) Richland County	51	0.98
Peninsula (village) Summit County	5	0.97
Harrisburg (village) Franklin County	3	0.87
Parma Heights (city) Cuyahoga County	182	0.84
Apple Creek (village) Wayne County	8	0.82
Doylestown (village) Wayne County	21	0.77
Lexington (village) Richland County	32	0.76
Green (city) Summit County	168	0.74

Top 10 Places Sorted by Percent

Based on places with populations of 10,000 or more

Place	Number	%
Parma Heights (city) Cuyahoga County	182	0.84
Green (city) Summit County	168	0.74
Mayfield Heights (city) Cuyahoga County	131	0.68
North Royalton (city) Cuyahoga County	155	0.54
Eastlake (city) Lake County	104	0.52
Seven Hills (city) Cuyahoga County	57	0.47
Avon (city) Lorain County	54	0.47
Parma (city) Cuyahoga County	383	0.45
Lakewood (city) Cuyahoga County	254	0.45
Brecksville (city) Cuyahoga County	60	0.45

Notes: (cdp) census designated place; Refer to the User's Guide in the front of the book for more detailed information.

Hispanic Population

Population

Total Population

Top 10 Places Sorted by Number

Place	Number
Columbus, OH (city) Franklin County	711,644
Cleveland, OH (city) Cuyahoga County	478,393
Cincinnati, OH (city) Hamilton County	330,662
Toledo, OH (city) Lucas County	313,587
Akron, OH (city) Summit County	217,088
Dayton, OH (city) Montgomery County	166,193
Parma, OH (city) Cuyahoga County	85,655
Youngstown, OH (city) Mahoning County	82,026
Canton, OH (city) Stark County	81,118
Lorain, OH (city) Lorain County	68,655

Hispanic

Top 10 Places Sorted by Number

Place	Number
Cleveland, OH (city) Cuyahoga County	34,554
Columbus, OH (city) Franklin County	17,368
Toledo, OH (city) Lucas County	17,241
Lorain, OH (city) Lorain County	14,189
Cincinnati, OH (city) Hamilton County	4,089
Youngstown, OH (city) Mahoning County	4,088
Akron, OH (city) Summit County	2,367
Painesville, OH (city) Lake County	2,312
Defiance, OH (city) Defiance County	2,126
Dayton, OH (city) Montgomery County	2,079

Hispanic

Top 10 Places Sorted by Percent of Total Population

Place	Percent
Lorain, OH (city) Lorain County	20.67
Painesville, OH (city) Lake County	13.22
Defiance, OH (city) Defiance County	13.04
Fremont, OH (city) Sandusky County	11.73
Fostoria, OH (city) Seneca County	7.97
Cleveland, OH (city) Cuyahoga County	7.22
Ashtabula, OH (city) Ashtabula County	5.98
Toledo, OH (city) Lucas County	5.50
Youngstown, OH (city) Mahoning County	4.98
Oregon, OH (city) Lucas County	4.49

Argentinian

Top 10 Places Sorted by Number

Place	Number
No places met population threshold.	

Argentinian

Top 10 Places Sorted by Percent of Hispanic Population

Place	Percent
No places met population threshold.	

Argentinian

Top 10 Places Sorted by Percent of Total Population

Place	Percent
No places met population threshold.	

Bolivian

Top 10 Places Sorted by Number

Place	Number
No places met population threshold.	

Bolivian

Top 10 Places Sorted by Percent of Hispanic Population

Place	Percent
No places met population threshold.	

Bolivian

Top 10 Places Sorted by Percent of Total Population

Place	Percent
No places met population threshold.	

Central American

Top 10 Places Sorted by Number

Place	Number
Cleveland, OH (city) Cuyahoga County	1,677
Columbus, OH (city) Franklin County	784
Cincinnati, OH (city) Hamilton County	503

Central American

Top 10 Places Sorted by Percent of Hispanic Population

Place	Percent
Cincinnati, OH (city) Hamilton County	12.30
Cleveland, OH (city) Cuyahoga County	4.85
Columbus, OH (city) Franklin County	4.51

Central American

Top 10 Places Sorted by Percent of Total Population

Place	Percent
Cleveland, OH (city) Cuyahoga County	0.35
Cincinnati, OH (city) Hamilton County	0.15
Columbus, OH (city) Franklin County	0.11

Chilean

Top 10 Places Sorted by Number

Place	Number
No places met population threshold.	

Chilean

Top 10 Places Sorted by Percent of Hispanic Population

Place	Percent
No places met population threshold.	

Chilean

Top 10 Places Sorted by Percent of Total Population

Place	Percent
No places met population threshold.	

Colombian

Top 10 Places Sorted by Number

Place	Number
No places met population threshold.	

Colombian

Top 10 Places Sorted by Percent of Hispanic Population

Place	Percent
No places met population threshold.	

Colombian

Top 10 Places Sorted by Percent of Total Population

Place	Percent
No places met population threshold.	

Costa Rican

Top 10 Places Sorted by Number

Place	Number
No places met population threshold.	

Costa Rican

Top 10 Places Sorted by Percent of Hispanic Population

Place	Percent
No places met population threshold.	

Costa Rican

Top 10 Places Sorted by Percent of Total Population

Place	Percent
No places met population threshold.	

Cuban

Top 10 Places Sorted by Number

Place	Number
Columbus, OH (city) Franklin County	700
Cleveland, OH (city) Cuyahoga County	436

Cuban

Top 10 Places Sorted by Percent of Hispanic Population

Place	Percent
Columbus, OH (city) Franklin County	4.03
Cleveland, OH (city) Cuyahoga County	1.26

Cuban

Top 10 Places Sorted by Percent of Total Population

Place	Percent
Columbus, OH (city) Franklin County	0.10
Cleveland, OH (city) Cuyahoga County	0.09

Dominican

Top 10 Places Sorted by Number

Place	Number
Cleveland, OH (city) Cuyahoga County	619

Dominican

Top 10 Places Sorted by Percent of Hispanic Population

Place	Percent
Cleveland, OH (city) Cuyahoga County	1.79

Dominican

Top 10 Places Sorted by Percent of Total Population

Place	Percent
Cleveland, OH (city) Cuyahoga County	0.13

Ecuadorian

Top 10 Places Sorted by Number

Place	Number
No places met population threshold.	

Ecuadorian

Top 10 Places Sorted by Percent of Hispanic Population

Place	Percent
No places met population threshold.	

Ecuadorian

Top 10 Places Sorted by Percent of Total Population

Place	Percent
No places met population threshold.	

Guatelmalan

Top 10 Places Sorted by Number

Place	Number
Cleveland, OH (city) Cuyahoga County	452

Guatelmalan

Top 10 Places Sorted by Percent of Hispanic Population

Place	Percent
Cleveland, OH (city) Cuyahoga County	1.31

Notes: Please refer to the User's Guide for an explanation of data; tables include places with populations > 9,999 and reflect only those areas that meet Summary File 4 population thresholds, therefore there may be less than 10 places listed

Guatelmalan
Top 10 Places Sorted by Percent of Total Population

Place	Percent
Cleveland, OH (city) Cuyahoga County	0.09

Honduran
Top 10 Places Sorted by Number

Place	Number

No places met population threshold.

Honduran
Top 10 Places Sorted by Percent of Hispanic Population

Place	Percent

No places met population threshold.

Honduran
Top 10 Places Sorted by Percent of Total Population

Place	Percent

No places met population threshold.

Mexican
Top 10 Places Sorted by Number

Place	Number
Toledo, OH (city) Lucas County	12,901
Columbus, OH (city) Franklin County	8,496
Cleveland, OH (city) Cuyahoga County	3,351
Lorain, OH (city) Lorain County	2,327
Painesville, OH (city) Lake County	1,863
Cincinnati, OH (city) Hamilton County	1,554
Fremont, OH (city) Sandusky County	1,376
Defiance, OH (city) Defiance County	1,307
Findlay, OH (city) Hancock County	1,137
Dayton, OH (city) Montgomery County	984

Mexican
Top 10 Places Sorted by Percent of Hispanic Population

Place	Percent
Fostoria, OH (city) Seneca County	83.32
Painesville, OH (city) Lake County	80.58
Norwalk, OH (city) Huron County	75.88
Toledo, OH (city) Lucas County	74.83
Findlay, OH (city) Hancock County	74.56
Oregon, OH (city) Lucas County	72.53
Sandusky, OH (city) Erie County	72.25
Bowling Green, OH (city) Wood County	69.95
Fremont, OH (city) Sandusky County	67.62
Hamilton, OH (city) Butler County	65.29

Mexican
Top 10 Places Sorted by Percent of Total Population

Place	Percent
Painesville, OH (city) Lake County	10.65
Defiance, OH (city) Defiance County	8.02
Fremont, OH (city) Sandusky County	7.93
Fostoria, OH (city) Seneca County	6.64
Toledo, OH (city) Lucas County	4.11
Lorain, OH (city) Lorain County	3.39
Oregon, OH (city) Lucas County	3.26
Norwalk, OH (city) Huron County	3.17
Findlay, OH (city) Hancock County	2.90
Bowling Green, OH (city) Wood County	2.28

Nicaraguan
Top 10 Places Sorted by Number

Place	Number

No places met population threshold.

Nicaraguan
Top 10 Places Sorted by Percent of Hispanic Population

Place	Percent

No places met population threshold.

Nicaraguan
Top 10 Places Sorted by Percent of Total Population

Place	Percent

No places met population threshold.

Panamanian
Top 10 Places Sorted by Number

Place	Number

No places met population threshold.

Panamanian
Top 10 Places Sorted by Percent of Hispanic Population

Place	Percent

No places met population threshold.

Panamanian
Top 10 Places Sorted by Percent of Total Population

Place	Percent

No places met population threshold.

Paraguayan
Top 10 Places Sorted by Number

Place	Number

No places met population threshold.

Paraguayan
Top 10 Places Sorted by Percent of Hispanic Population

Place	Percent

No places met population threshold.

Paraguayan
Top 10 Places Sorted by Percent of Total Population

Place	Percent

No places met population threshold.

Peruvian
Top 10 Places Sorted by Number

Place	Number

No places met population threshold.

Peruvian
Top 10 Places Sorted by Percent of Hispanic Population

Place	Percent

No places met population threshold.

Peruvian
Top 10 Places Sorted by Percent of Total Population

Place	Percent

No places met population threshold.

Puerto Rican
Top 10 Places Sorted by Number

Place	Number
Cleveland, OH (city) Cuyahoga County	24,293
Lorain, OH (city) Lorain County	10,050
Columbus, OH (city) Franklin County	3,069
Youngstown, OH (city) Mahoning County	2,976
Toledo, OH (city) Lucas County	1,043
Elyria, OH (city) Lorain County	689
Ashtabula, OH (city) Ashtabula County	637
Akron, OH (city) Summit County	614
Boardman, OH (cdp) Mahoning County	584
Cincinnati, OH (city) Hamilton County	56

Puerto Rican
Top 10 Places Sorted by Percent of Hispanic Population

Place	Percent
Youngstown, OH (city) Mahoning County	72.8
Lorain, OH (city) Lorain County	70.83
Cleveland, OH (city) Cuyahoga County	70.3
Boardman, OH (cdp) Mahoning County	66.59
Ashtabula, OH (city) Ashtabula County	51.04
Elyria, OH (city) Lorain County	49.36
Lakewood, OH (city) Cuyahoga County	44.7
Parma, OH (city) Cuyahoga County	43.53
Akron, OH (city) Summit County	25.94
Columbus, OH (city) Franklin County	17.67

Puerto Rican
Top 10 Places Sorted by Percent of Total Population

Place	Percent
Lorain, OH (city) Lorain County	14.64
Cleveland, OH (city) Cuyahoga County	5.08
Youngstown, OH (city) Mahoning County	3.63
Ashtabula, OH (city) Ashtabula County	3.05
Boardman, OH (cdp) Mahoning County	1.57
Elyria, OH (city) Lorain County	1.23
Lakewood, OH (city) Cuyahoga County	0.99
Parma, OH (city) Cuyahoga County	0.64
Columbus, OH (city) Franklin County	0.43
Toledo, OH (city) Lucas County	0.33

Salvadoran
Top 10 Places Sorted by Number

Place	Number
Cleveland, OH (city) Cuyahoga County	454
Columbus, OH (city) Franklin County	404

Salvadoran
Top 10 Places Sorted by Percent of Hispanic Population

Place	Percent
Columbus, OH (city) Franklin County	2.33
Cleveland, OH (city) Cuyahoga County	1.31

Salvadoran
Top 10 Places Sorted by Percent of Total Population

Place	Percent
Cleveland, OH (city) Cuyahoga County	0.09
Columbus, OH (city) Franklin County	0.06

South American
Top 10 Places Sorted by Number

Place	Number
Columbus, OH (city) Franklin County	1,020
Cleveland, OH (city) Cuyahoga County	553
Cincinnati, OH (city) Hamilton County	473

South American
Top 10 Places Sorted by Percent of Hispanic Population

Place	Percent
Cincinnati, OH (city) Hamilton County	11.57
Columbus, OH (city) Franklin County	5.87
Cleveland, OH (city) Cuyahoga County	1.60

South American
Top 10 Places Sorted by Percent of Total Population

Place	Percent
Cincinnati, OH (city) Hamilton County	0.14
Columbus, OH (city) Franklin County	0.14
Cleveland, OH (city) Cuyahoga County	0.12

Notes: Please refer to the User's Guide for an explanation of data; tables include places with populations > 9,999 and reflect only those areas that meet Summary File 4 population thresholds, therefore there may be less than 10 places listed

Spaniard
Top 10 Places Sorted by Number

Place	Number
No places met population threshold.	

Spaniard
Top 10 Places Sorted by Percent of Hispanic Population

Place	Percent
No places met population threshold.	

Spaniard
Top 10 Places Sorted by Percent of Total Population

Place	Percent
No places met population threshold.	

Uruguayan
Top 10 Places Sorted by Number

Place	Number
No places met population threshold.	

Uruguayan
Top 10 Places Sorted by Percent of Hispanic Population

Place	Percent
No places met population threshold.	

Uruguayan
Top 10 Places Sorted by Percent of Total Population

Place	Percent
No places met population threshold.	

Venezuelan
Top 10 Places Sorted by Number

Place	Number
No places met population threshold.	

Venezuelan
Top 10 Places Sorted by Percent of Hispanic Population

Place	Percent
No places met population threshold.	

Venezuelan
Top 10 Places Sorted by Percent of Total Population

Place	Percent
No places met population threshold.	

Other Hispanic
Top 10 Places Sorted by Number

Place	Number
Cleveland, OH (city) Cuyahoga County	3,529
Columbus, OH (city) Franklin County	2,953
Toledo, OH (city) Lucas County	2,688
Lorain, OH (city) Lorain County	1,399
Cincinnati, OH (city) Hamilton County	712
Fremont, OH (city) Sandusky County	554
Defiance, OH (city) Defiance County	526
Akron, OH (city) Summit County	493
Youngstown, OH (city) Mahoning County	470
Dayton, OH (city) Montgomery County	445

Other Hispanic
Top 10 Places Sorted by Percent of Hispanic Population

Place	Percent
Fremont, OH (city) Sandusky County	27.22
Defiance, OH (city) Defiance County	24.74
Dayton, OH (city) Montgomery County	21.40
Akron, OH (city) Summit County	20.83
Cincinnati, OH (city) Hamilton County	17.41
Columbus, OH (city) Franklin County	17.00
Toledo, OH (city) Lucas County	15.59
Youngstown, OH (city) Mahoning County	11.50
Cleveland, OH (city) Cuyahoga County	10.21
Lorain, OH (city) Lorain County	9.86

Other Hispanic
Top 10 Places Sorted by Percent of Total Population

Place	Percent
Defiance, OH (city) Defiance County	3.23
Fremont, OH (city) Sandusky County	3.19
Lorain, OH (city) Lorain County	2.04
Toledo, OH (city) Lucas County	0.86
Cleveland, OH (city) Cuyahoga County	0.74
Youngstown, OH (city) Mahoning County	0.57
Columbus, OH (city) Franklin County	0.41
Dayton, OH (city) Montgomery County	0.27
Akron, OH (city) Summit County	0.23
Cincinnati, OH (city) Hamilton County	0.22

Median Age

Total Population
Top 10 Places Sorted by Number

Place	Years
Upper Arlington, OH (city) Franklin County	42.5
Parma Heights, OH (city) Cuyahoga County	42.1
Brooklyn, OH (city) Cuyahoga County	42.0
Westlake, OH (city) Cuyahoga County	41.9
Boardman, OH (cdp) Mahoning County	41.8
Beavercreek, OH (city) Greene County	40.6
Austintown, OH (cdp) Mahoning County	40.1
North Olmsted, OH (city) Cuyahoga County	39.8
Brook Park, OH (city) Cuyahoga County	39.6
Oregon, OH (city) Lucas County	39.5

Hispanic
Top 10 Places Sorted by Number

Place	Years
Parma Heights, OH (city) Cuyahoga County	38.9
Boardman, OH (cdp) Mahoning County	33.0
Riverside, OH (city) Montgomery County	32.0
Austintown, OH (cdp) Mahoning County	31.5
Kettering, OH (city) Montgomery County	31.0
Perrysburg, OH (city) Wood County	30.8
Brooklyn, OH (city) Cuyahoga County	30.2
Cleveland Heights, OH (city) Cuyahoga County	29.8
Parma, OH (city) Cuyahoga County	29.2
Upper Arlington, OH (city) Franklin County	29.2

Argentinian
Top 10 Places Sorted by Number

Place	Years
No places met population threshold.	

Bolivian
Top 10 Places Sorted by Number

Place	Years
No places met population threshold.	

Central American
Top 10 Places Sorted by Number

Place	Years
Columbus, OH (city) Franklin County	26.7
Cleveland, OH (city) Cuyahoga County	26.4
Cincinnati, OH (city) Hamilton County	25.0

Chilean
Top 10 Places Sorted by Number

Place	Years
No places met population threshold.	

Colombian
Top 10 Places Sorted by Number

Place	Years
No places met population threshold.	

Costa Rican
Top 10 Places Sorted by Number

Place	Years
No places met population threshold.	

Cuban
Top 10 Places Sorted by Number

Place	Years
Cleveland, OH (city) Cuyahoga County	31.3
Columbus, OH (city) Franklin County	27.1

Dominican
Top 10 Places Sorted by Number

Place	Years
Cleveland, OH (city) Cuyahoga County	26.8

Ecuadorian
Top 10 Places Sorted by Number

Place	Years
No places met population threshold.	

Guatelmalan
Top 10 Places Sorted by Number

Place	Years
Cleveland, OH (city) Cuyahoga County	26.5

Honduran
Top 10 Places Sorted by Number

Place	Years
No places met population threshold.	

Mexican
Top 10 Places Sorted by Number

Place	Years
Youngstown, OH (city) Mahoning County	30.8
Lorain, OH (city) Lorain County	27.2
Cleveland, OH (city) Cuyahoga County	27.0
Oregon, OH (city) Lucas County	26.5
Sandusky, OH (city) Erie County	25.8
Lakewood, OH (city) Cuyahoga County	25.7
Defiance, OH (city) Defiance County	25.4
Lima, OH (city) Allen County	25.1
Dayton, OH (city) Montgomery County	24.9
Hamilton, OH (city) Butler County	24.6

Nicaraguan
Top 10 Places Sorted by Number

Place	Years
No places met population threshold.	

Panamanian
Top 10 Places Sorted by Number

Place	Years
No places met population threshold.	

Paraguayan
Top 10 Places Sorted by Number

Place	Years
No places met population threshold.	

Notes: Please refer to the User's Guide for an explanation of data; tables include places with populations > 9,999 and reflect only those areas that meet Summary File 4 population thresholds, therefore there may be less than 10 places listed

Peruvian

Top 10 Places Sorted by Number

Place	Years
No places met population threshold.	

Puerto Rican

Top 10 Places Sorted by Number

Place	Years
Boardman, OH (cdp) Mahoning County	31.9
Parma, OH (city) Cuyahoga County	27.5
Lorain, OH (city) Lorain County	24.8
Cincinnati, OH (city) Hamilton County	24.4
Lakewood, OH (city) Cuyahoga County	24.2
Youngstown, OH (city) Mahoning County	24.2
Cleveland, OH (city) Cuyahoga County	24.1
Columbus, OH (city) Franklin County	23.7
Akron, OH (city) Summit County	22.3
Ashtabula, OH (city) Ashtabula County	22.1

Salvadoran

Top 10 Places Sorted by Number

Place	Years
Columbus, OH (city) Franklin County	25.0
Cleveland, OH (city) Cuyahoga County	23.8

South American

Top 10 Places Sorted by Number

Place	Years
Cincinnati, OH (city) Hamilton County	30.8
Cleveland, OH (city) Cuyahoga County	30.7
Columbus, OH (city) Franklin County	30.2

Spaniard

Top 10 Places Sorted by Number

Place	Years
No places met population threshold.	

Uruguayan

Top 10 Places Sorted by Number

Place	Years
No places met population threshold.	

Venezuelan

Top 10 Places Sorted by Number

Place	Years
No places met population threshold.	

Other Hispanic

Top 10 Places Sorted by Number

Place	Years
Akron, OH (city) Summit County	33.5
Cincinnati, OH (city) Hamilton County	30.1
Dayton, OH (city) Montgomery County	28.8
Columbus, OH (city) Franklin County	25.2
Defiance, OH (city) Defiance County	22.8
Youngstown, OH (city) Mahoning County	21.8
Toledo, OH (city) Lucas County	21.3
Fremont, OH (city) Sandusky County	20.5
Cleveland, OH (city) Cuyahoga County	18.6
Lorain, OH (city) Lorain County	15.4

Average Household Size

Total Population

Top 10 Places Sorted by Number

Place	Number
Brunswick, OH (city) Medina County	2.79
Strongsville, OH (city) Cuyahoga County	2.69
Westerville, OH (city) Franklin County	2.67
Beavercreek, OH (city) Greene County	2.66
Huber Heights, OH (city) Montgomery County	2.64
Perrysburg, OH (city) Wood County	2.61
Brook Park, OH (city) Cuyahoga County	2.58
Lorain, OH (city) Lorain County	2.57
Painesville, OH (city) Lake County	2.55
Xenia, OH (city) Greene County	2.52

Hispanic

Top 10 Places Sorted by Number

Place	Number
Painesville, OH (city) Lake County	4.97
Norwalk, OH (city) Huron County	3.62
Xenia, OH (city) Greene County	3.58
Ashtabula, OH (city) Ashtabula County	3.55
Hamilton, OH (city) Butler County	3.48
Strongsville, OH (city) Cuyahoga County	3.47
Maple Heights, OH (city) Cuyahoga County	3.25
Riverside, OH (city) Montgomery County	3.14
Brook Park, OH (city) Cuyahoga County	3.12
Lorain, OH (city) Lorain County	3.12

Argentinian

Top 10 Places Sorted by Number

Place	Number
No places met population threshold.	

Bolivian

Top 10 Places Sorted by Number

Place	Number
No places met population threshold.	

Central American

Top 10 Places Sorted by Number

Place	Number
Cincinnati, OH (city) Hamilton County	3.81
Cleveland, OH (city) Cuyahoga County	3.79
Columbus, OH (city) Franklin County	2.87

Chilean

Top 10 Places Sorted by Number

Place	Number
No places met population threshold.	

Colombian

Top 10 Places Sorted by Number

Place	Number
No places met population threshold.	

Costa Rican

Top 10 Places Sorted by Number

Place	Number
No places met population threshold.	

Cuban

Top 10 Places Sorted by Number

Place	Number
Columbus, OH (city) Franklin County	3.25
Cleveland, OH (city) Cuyahoga County	2.04

Dominican

Top 10 Places Sorted by Number

Place	Number
Cleveland, OH (city) Cuyahoga County	2.99

Ecuadorian

Top 10 Places Sorted by Number

Place	Number
No places met population threshold.	

Guatelmalan

Top 10 Places Sorted by Number

Place	Number
Cleveland, OH (city) Cuyahoga County	3.7

Honduran

Top 10 Places Sorted by Number

Place	Number
No places met population threshold.	

Mexican

Top 10 Places Sorted by Number

Place	Number
Painesville, OH (city) Lake County	5.51
Ashtabula, OH (city) Ashtabula County	4.80
Hamilton, OH (city) Butler County	4.39
Dayton, OH (city) Montgomery County	3.87
Norwalk, OH (city) Huron County	3.70
Canton, OH (city) Stark County	3.22
Columbus, OH (city) Franklin County	3.18
Oregon, OH (city) Lucas County	3.17
Lorain, OH (city) Lorain County	3.14
Lakewood, OH (city) Cuyahoga County	3.02

Nicaraguan

Top 10 Places Sorted by Number

Place	Number
No places met population threshold.	

Panamanian

Top 10 Places Sorted by Number

Place	Number
No places met population threshold.	

Paraguayan

Top 10 Places Sorted by Number

Place	Number
No places met population threshold.	

Peruvian

Top 10 Places Sorted by Number

Place	Number
No places met population threshold.	

Puerto Rican

Top 10 Places Sorted by Number

Place	Number
Toledo, OH (city) Lucas County	3.79
Lorain, OH (city) Lorain County	3.11
Cleveland, OH (city) Cuyahoga County	3.10
Ashtabula, OH (city) Ashtabula County	3.08
Boardman, OH (cdp) Mahoning County	2.93
Youngstown, OH (city) Mahoning County	2.88
Akron, OH (city) Summit County	2.63
Columbus, OH (city) Franklin County	2.59
Lakewood, OH (city) Cuyahoga County	2.43
Parma, OH (city) Cuyahoga County	2.36

Salvadoran

Top 10 Places Sorted by Number

Place	Number
Cleveland, OH (city) Cuyahoga County	4.11
Columbus, OH (city) Franklin County	3.54

Notes: Please refer to the User's Guide for an explanation of data; tables include places with populations > 9,999 and reflect only those areas that meet Summary File 4 population thresholds, therefore there may be less than 10 places listed

South American

Top 10 Places Sorted by Number

Place	Number
Cleveland, OH (city) Cuyahoga County	3.05
Columbus, OH (city) Franklin County	2.41
Cincinnati, OH (city) Hamilton County	2.15

Spaniard

Top 10 Places Sorted by Number

Place	Number
No places met population threshold.	

Uruguayan

Top 10 Places Sorted by Number

Place	Number
No places met population threshold.	

Venezuelan

Top 10 Places Sorted by Number

Place	Number
No places met population threshold.	

Other Hispanic

Top 10 Places Sorted by Number

Place	Number
Youngstown, OH (city) Mahoning County	3.60
Cleveland, OH (city) Cuyahoga County	3.20
Fremont, OH (city) Sandusky County	3.17
Defiance, OH (city) Defiance County	3.12
Lorain, OH (city) Lorain County	3.05
Toledo, OH (city) Lucas County	3.00
Akron, OH (city) Summit County	2.71
Columbus, OH (city) Franklin County	2.55
Dayton, OH (city) Montgomery County	2.34
Cincinnati, OH (city) Hamilton County	1.65

Language Spoken at Home: English Only

Total Population 5 Years and Over Who Speak English-Only at Home

Top 10 Places Sorted by Number

Place	Number
Columbus, OH (city) Franklin County	593,275
Cleveland, OH (city) Cuyahoga County	387,438
Cincinnati, OH (city) Hamilton County	286,454
Toledo, OH (city) Lucas County	269,728
Akron, OH (city) Summit County	189,917
Dayton, OH (city) Montgomery County	147,790
Canton, OH (city) Stark County	71,291
Parma, OH (city) Cuyahoga County	69,839
Youngstown, OH (city) Mahoning County	69,647
Springfield, OH (city) Clark County	58,165

Total Population 5 Years and Over Who Speak English-Only at Home

Top 10 Places Sorted by Percent

Place	Percent
Middletown, OH (city) Butler County	96.74
Springfield, OH (city) Clark County	96.52
Tiffin, OH (city) Seneca County	96.46
Marion, OH (city) Marion County	96.22
Elyria, OH (city) Lorain County	96.15
Lima, OH (city) Allen County	96.12
Xenia, OH (city) Greene County	95.99
Sandusky, OH (city) Erie County	95.77
Dayton, OH (city) Montgomery County	95.64
Norwood, OH (city) Hamilton County	95.39

Hispanics 5 Years and Over Who Speak English-Only at Home

Top 10 Places Sorted by Number

Place	Number
Toledo, OH (city) Lucas County	8,574
Cleveland, OH (city) Cuyahoga County	7,066
Columbus, OH (city) Franklin County	5,079
Lorain, OH (city) Lorain County	4,246
Cincinnati, OH (city) Hamilton County	1,493
Youngstown, OH (city) Mahoning County	1,155
Akron, OH (city) Summit County	1,149
Dayton, OH (city) Montgomery County	754
Findlay, OH (city) Hancock County	750
Elyria, OH (city) Lorain County	725

Hispanics 5 Years and Over Who Speak English-Only at Home

Top 10 Places Sorted by Percent

Place	Percent
Oregon, OH (city) Lucas County	67.78
Warren, OH (city) Trumbull County	66.30
Elyria, OH (city) Lorain County	65.08
Springfield, OH (city) Clark County	64.37
Austintown, OH (cdp) Mahoning County	63.12
Fostoria, OH (city) Seneca County	59.96
Riverside, OH (city) Montgomery County	59.10
Tiffin, OH (city) Seneca County	58.92
Findlay, OH (city) Hancock County	57.96
Mansfield, OH (city) Richland County	57.80

Argentinians 5 Years and Over Who Speak English-Only at Home

Top 10 Places Sorted by Number

Place	Number
No places met population threshold.	

Argentinians 5 Years and Over Who Speak English-Only at Home

Top 10 Places Sorted by Percent

Place	Percent
No places met population threshold.	

Bolivians 5 Years and Over Who Speak English-Only at Home

Top 10 Places Sorted by Number

Place	Number
No places met population threshold.	

Bolivians 5 Years and Over Who Speak English-Only at Home

Top 10 Places Sorted by Percent

Place	Percent
No places met population threshold.	

Central Americans 5 Years and Over Who Speak English-Only at Home

Top 10 Places Sorted by Number

Place	Number
Cleveland, OH (city) Cuyahoga County	157
Columbus, OH (city) Franklin County	114
Cincinnati, OH (city) Hamilton County	30

Central Americans 5 Years and Over Who Speak English-Only at Home

Top 10 Places Sorted by Percent

Place	Percent
Columbus, OH (city) Franklin County	15.51
Cleveland, OH (city) Cuyahoga County	10.20
Cincinnati, OH (city) Hamilton County	6.22

Chileans 5 Years and Over Who Speak English-Only at Home

Top 10 Places Sorted by Number

Place	Number
No places met population threshold.	

Chileans 5 Years and Over Who Speak English-Only at Home

Top 10 Places Sorted by Percent

Place	Percent
No places met population threshold.	

Colombians 5 Years and Over Who Speak English-Only at Home

Top 10 Places Sorted by Number

Place	Number
No places met population threshold.	

Colombians 5 Years and Over Who Speak English-Only at Home

Top 10 Places Sorted by Percent

Place	Percent
No places met population threshold.	

Costa Ricans 5 Years and Over Who Speak English-Only at Home

Top 10 Places Sorted by Number

Place	Number
No places met population threshold.	

Costa Ricans 5 Years and Over Who Speak English-Only at Home

Top 10 Places Sorted by Percent

Place	Percent
No places met population threshold.	

Cubans 5 Years and Over Who Speak English-Only at Home

Top 10 Places Sorted by Number

Place	Number
Columbus, OH (city) Franklin County	274
Cleveland, OH (city) Cuyahoga County	102

Cubans 5 Years and Over Who Speak English-Only at Home

Top 10 Places Sorted by Percent

Place	Percent
Columbus, OH (city) Franklin County	42.35
Cleveland, OH (city) Cuyahoga County	26.36

Dominicans 5 Years and Over Who Speak English-Only at Home

Top 10 Places Sorted by Number

Place	Number
Cleveland, OH (city) Cuyahoga County	29

Dominicans 5 Years and Over Who Speak English-Only at Home

Top 10 Places Sorted by Percent

Place	Percent
Cleveland, OH (city) Cuyahoga County	5.00

Ecuadorians 5 Years and Over Who Speak English-Only at Home

Top 10 Places Sorted by Number

Place	Number
No places met population threshold.	

Notes: Please refer to the User's Guide for an explanation of data; tables include places with populations > 9,999 and reflect only those areas that meet Summary File 4 population thresholds, therefore there may be less than 10 places listed

Ecuadorians 5 Years and Over Who Speak English-Only at Home
Top 10 Places Sorted by Percent

Place	Percent

No places met population threshold.

Guatelmalans 5 Years and Over Who Speak English-Only at Home
Top 10 Places Sorted by Number

Place	Number
Cleveland, OH (city) Cuyahoga County	35

Guatelmalans 5 Years and Over Who Speak English-Only at Home
Top 10 Places Sorted by Percent

Place	Percent
Cleveland, OH (city) Cuyahoga County	8.41

Hondurans 5 Years and Over Who Speak English-Only at Home
Top 10 Places Sorted by Number

Place	Number

No places met population threshold.

Hondurans 5 Years and Over Who Speak English-Only at Home
Top 10 Places Sorted by Percent

Place	Percent

No places met population threshold.

Mexicans 5 Years and Over Who Speak English-Only at Home
Top 10 Places Sorted by Number

Place	Number
Toledo, OH (city) Lucas County	6,533
Columbus, OH (city) Franklin County	1,993
Cleveland, OH (city) Cuyahoga County	1,569
Lorain, OH (city) Lorain County	1,048
Cincinnati, OH (city) Hamilton County	676
Findlay, OH (city) Hancock County	600
Defiance, OH (city) Defiance County	493
Fremont, OH (city) Sandusky County	469
Fostoria, OH (city) Seneca County	465
Akron, OH (city) Summit County	448

Mexicans 5 Years and Over Who Speak English-Only at Home
Top 10 Places Sorted by Percent

Place	Percent
Elyria, OH (city) Lorain County	82.39
Oregon, OH (city) Lucas County	73.27
Findlay, OH (city) Hancock County	61.29
Fostoria, OH (city) Seneca County	58.94
Toledo, OH (city) Lucas County	58.13
Akron, OH (city) Summit County	55.72
Springfield, OH (city) Clark County	55.19
Cleveland, OH (city) Cuyahoga County	53.11
Lima, OH (city) Allen County	52.23
Cincinnati, OH (city) Hamilton County	51.64

Nicaraguans 5 Years and Over Who Speak English-Only at Home
Top 10 Places Sorted by Number

Place	Number

No places met population threshold.

Nicaraguans 5 Years and Over Who Speak English-Only at Home
Top 10 Places Sorted by Percent

Place	Percent

No places met population threshold.

Panamanians 5 Years and Over Who Speak English-Only at Home
Top 10 Places Sorted by Number

Place	Number

No places met population threshold.

Panamanians 5 Years and Over Who Speak English-Only at Home
Top 10 Places Sorted by Percent

Place	Percent

No places met population threshold.

Paraguayans 5 Years and Over Who Speak English-Only at Home
Top 10 Places Sorted by Number

Place	Number

No places met population threshold.

Paraguayans 5 Years and Over Who Speak English-Only at Home
Top 10 Places Sorted by Percent

Place	Percent

No places met population threshold.

Peruvians 5 Years and Over Who Speak English-Only at Home
Top 10 Places Sorted by Number

Place	Number

No places met population threshold.

Peruvians 5 Years and Over Who Speak English-Only at Home
Top 10 Places Sorted by Percent

Place	Percent

No places met population threshold.

Puerto Ricans 5 Years and Over Who Speak English-Only at Home
Top 10 Places Sorted by Number

Place	Number
Cleveland, OH (city) Cuyahoga County	4,055
Lorain, OH (city) Lorain County	2,498
Columbus, OH (city) Franklin County	1,171
Youngstown, OH (city) Mahoning County	661
Toledo, OH (city) Lucas County	429
Elyria, OH (city) Lorain County	328
Lakewood, OH (city) Cuyahoga County	296
Akron, OH (city) Summit County	257
Boardman, OH (cdp) Mahoning County	205
Cincinnati, OH (city) Hamilton County	171

Puerto Ricans 5 Years and Over Who Speak English-Only at Home
Top 10 Places Sorted by Percent

Place	Percent
Lakewood, OH (city) Cuyahoga County	64.21
Elyria, OH (city) Lorain County	57.64
Akron, OH (city) Summit County	48.95
Toledo, OH (city) Lucas County	45.54
Columbus, OH (city) Franklin County	42.17
Boardman, OH (cdp) Mahoning County	38.75
Cincinnati, OH (city) Hamilton County	35.19
Parma, OH (city) Cuyahoga County	31.72
Lorain, OH (city) Lorain County	27.8
Ashtabula, OH (city) Ashtabula County	25.7

Salvadorans 5 Years and Over Who Speak English-Only at Home
Top 10 Places Sorted by Number

Place	Number
Columbus, OH (city) Franklin County	3
Cleveland, OH (city) Cuyahoga County	1

Salvadorans 5 Years and Over Who Speak English-Only at Home
Top 10 Places Sorted by Percent

Place	Percent
Columbus, OH (city) Franklin County	9.0
Cleveland, OH (city) Cuyahoga County	2.4

South Americans 5 Years and Over Who Speak English-Only at Home
Top 10 Places Sorted by Number

Place	Number
Columbus, OH (city) Franklin County	21
Cincinnati, OH (city) Hamilton County	9
Cleveland, OH (city) Cuyahoga County	6

South Americans 5 Years and Over Who Speak English-Only at Home
Top 10 Places Sorted by Percent

Place	Percent
Cincinnati, OH (city) Hamilton County	23.0
Columbus, OH (city) Franklin County	22.4
Cleveland, OH (city) Cuyahoga County	12.2

Spaniards 5 Years and Over Who Speak English-Only at Home
Top 10 Places Sorted by Number

Place	Number

No places met population threshold.

Spaniards 5 Years and Over Who Speak English-Only at Home
Top 10 Places Sorted by Percent

Place	Percent

No places met population threshold.

Uruguayans 5 Years and Over Who Speak English-Only at Home
Top 10 Places Sorted by Number

Place	Number

No places met population threshold.

Uruguayans 5 Years and Over Who Speak English-Only at Home
Top 10 Places Sorted by Percent

Place	Percent

No places met population threshold.

Venezuelans 5 Years and Over Who Speak English-Only at Home
Top 10 Places Sorted by Number

Place	Number

No places met population threshold.

Venezuelans 5 Years and Over Who Speak English-Only at Home
Top 10 Places Sorted by Percent

Place	Percent

No places met population threshold.

Notes: Please refer to the User's Guide for an explanation of data; tables include places with populations > 9,999 and reflect only those areas that meet Summary File 4 population thresholds, therefore there may be less than 10 places listed

Other Hispanics 5 Years and Over Who Speak English-Only at Home

Top 10 Places Sorted by Number

Place	Number
Toledo, OH (city) Lucas County	1,489
Columbus, OH (city) Franklin County	1,293
Cleveland, OH (city) Cuyahoga County	1,043
Lorain, OH (city) Lorain County	645
Cincinnati, OH (city) Hamilton County	372
Akron, OH (city) Summit County	343
Youngstown, OH (city) Mahoning County	274
Dayton, OH (city) Montgomery County	257
Fremont, OH (city) Sandusky County	136
Defiance, OH (city) Defiance County	100

Other Hispanics 5 Years and Over Who Speak English-Only at Home

Top 10 Places Sorted by Percent

Place	Percent
Akron, OH (city) Summit County	79.77
Toledo, OH (city) Lucas County	63.07
Youngstown, OH (city) Mahoning County	61.99
Dayton, OH (city) Montgomery County	61.93
Lorain, OH (city) Lorain County	56.73
Cincinnati, OH (city) Hamilton County	55.19
Columbus, OH (city) Franklin County	50.10
Cleveland, OH (city) Cuyahoga County	37.20
Fremont, OH (city) Sandusky County	28.69
Defiance, OH (city) Defiance County	21.14

Language Spoken at Home: Spanish

Total Population 5 Years and Over Who Speak Spanish at Home

Top 10 Places Sorted by Number

Place	Number
Cleveland, OH (city) Cuyahoga County	28,564
Columbus, OH (city) Franklin County	19,275
Toledo, OH (city) Lucas County	9,992
Lorain, OH (city) Lorain County	9,113
Cincinnati, OH (city) Hamilton County	6,720
Youngstown, OH (city) Mahoning County	3,546
Akron, OH (city) Summit County	3,122
Dayton, OH (city) Montgomery County	3,062
Painesville, OH (city) Lake County	2,069
Hamilton, OH (city) Butler County	1,701

Total Population 5 Years and Over Who Speak Spanish at Home

Top 10 Places Sorted by Percent

Place	Percent
Lorain, OH (city) Lorain County	14.40
Painesville, OH (city) Lake County	13.05
Defiance, OH (city) Defiance County	9.01
Fremont, OH (city) Sandusky County	8.70
Cleveland, OH (city) Cuyahoga County	6.50
Ashtabula, OH (city) Ashtabula County	5.42
Youngstown, OH (city) Mahoning County	4.65
Bowling Green, OH (city) Wood County	4.24
Whitehall, OH (city) Franklin County	4.23
Fostoria, OH (city) Seneca County	3.62

Hispanics 5 Years and Over Who Speak Spanish at Home

Top 10 Places Sorted by Number

Place	Number
Cleveland, OH (city) Cuyahoga County	23,081
Columbus, OH (city) Franklin County	10,201
Lorain, OH (city) Lorain County	8,318
Toledo, OH (city) Lucas County	6,372
Youngstown, OH (city) Mahoning County	2,486
Cincinnati, OH (city) Hamilton County	2,050
Painesville, OH (city) Lake County	1,826
Defiance, OH (city) Defiance County	1,162
Fremont, OH (city) Sandusky County	1,130
Dayton, OH (city) Montgomery County	1,056

Hispanics 5 Years and Over Who Speak Spanish at Home

Top 10 Places Sorted by Percent

Place	Percent
Painesville, OH (city) Lake County	91.39
Hamilton, OH (city) Butler County	80.15
Whitehall, OH (city) Franklin County	79.80
Ashtabula, OH (city) Ashtabula County	77.65
Cleveland, OH (city) Cuyahoga County	76.11
Youngstown, OH (city) Mahoning County	68.28
Lorain, OH (city) Lorain County	66.14
Columbus, OH (city) Franklin County	65.88
Fremont, OH (city) Sandusky County	64.02
Defiance, OH (city) Defiance County	62.74

Argentinians 5 Years and Over Who Speak Spanish at Home

Top 10 Places Sorted by Number

Place	Number
No places met population threshold.	

Argentinians 5 Years and Over Who Speak Spanish at Home

Top 10 Places Sorted by Percent

Place	Percent
No places met population threshold.	

Bolivians 5 Years and Over Who Speak Spanish at Home

Top 10 Places Sorted by Number

Place	Number
No places met population threshold.	

Bolivians 5 Years and Over Who Speak Spanish at Home

Top 10 Places Sorted by Percent

Place	Percent
No places met population threshold.	

Central Americans 5 Years and Over Who Speak Spanish at Home

Top 10 Places Sorted by Number

Place	Number
Cleveland, OH (city) Cuyahoga County	1,362
Columbus, OH (city) Franklin County	621
Cincinnati, OH (city) Hamilton County	441

Central Americans 5 Years and Over Who Speak Spanish at Home

Top 10 Places Sorted by Percent

Place	Percent
Cincinnati, OH (city) Hamilton County	91.49
Cleveland, OH (city) Cuyahoga County	88.50
Columbus, OH (city) Franklin County	84.49

Chileans 5 Years and Over Who Speak Spanish at Home

Top 10 Places Sorted by Number

Place	Number
No places met population threshold.	

Chileans 5 Years and Over Who Speak Spanish at Home

Top 10 Places Sorted by Percent

Place	Percent
No places met population threshold.	

Colombians 5 Years and Over Who Speak Spanish at Home

Top 10 Places Sorted by Number

Place	Number
No places met population threshold.	

Colombians 5 Years and Over Who Speak Spanish at Home

Top 10 Places Sorted by Percent

Place	Percent
No places met population threshold.	

Costa Ricans 5 Years and Over Who Speak Spanish at Home

Top 10 Places Sorted by Number

Place	Number
No places met population threshold.	

Costa Ricans 5 Years and Over Who Speak Spanish at Home

Top 10 Places Sorted by Percent

Place	Percent
No places met population threshold.	

Cubans 5 Years and Over Who Speak Spanish at Home

Top 10 Places Sorted by Number

Place	Number
Columbus, OH (city) Franklin County	368
Cleveland, OH (city) Cuyahoga County	285

Cubans 5 Years and Over Who Speak Spanish at Home

Top 10 Places Sorted by Percent

Place	Percent
Cleveland, OH (city) Cuyahoga County	73.64
Columbus, OH (city) Franklin County	56.88

Dominicans 5 Years and Over Who Speak Spanish at Home

Top 10 Places Sorted by Number

Place	Number
Cleveland, OH (city) Cuyahoga County	551

Dominicans 5 Years and Over Who Speak Spanish at Home

Top 10 Places Sorted by Percent

Place	Percent
Cleveland, OH (city) Cuyahoga County	95.00

Ecuadorians 5 Years and Over Who Speak Spanish at Home

Top 10 Places Sorted by Number

Place	Number
No places met population threshold.	

Ecuadorians 5 Years and Over Who Speak Spanish at Home

Top 10 Places Sorted by Percent

Place	Percent
No places met population threshold.	

Notes: Please refer to the User's Guide for an explanation of data; tables include places with populations > 9,999 and reflect only those areas that meet Summary File 4 population thresholds, therefore there may be less than 10 places listed

Guatelmalans 5 Years and Over Who Speak Spanish at Home
Top 10 Places Sorted by Number

Place	Number
Cleveland, OH (city) Cuyahoga County	381

Guatelmalans 5 Years and Over Who Speak Spanish at Home
Top 10 Places Sorted by Percent

Place	Percent
Cleveland, OH (city) Cuyahoga County	91.59

Hondurans 5 Years and Over Who Speak Spanish at Home
Top 10 Places Sorted by Number

Place	Number
No places met population threshold.	

Hondurans 5 Years and Over Who Speak Spanish at Home
Top 10 Places Sorted by Percent

Place	Percent
No places met population threshold.	

Mexicans 5 Years and Over Who Speak Spanish at Home
Top 10 Places Sorted by Number

Place	Number
Columbus, OH (city) Franklin County	5,430
Toledo, OH (city) Lucas County	4,679
Painesville, OH (city) Lake County	1,533
Cleveland, OH (city) Cuyahoga County	1,368
Lorain, OH (city) Lorain County	1,007
Fremont, OH (city) Sandusky County	734
Hamilton, OH (city) Butler County	672
Defiance, OH (city) Defiance County	618
Cincinnati, OH (city) Hamilton County	594
Dayton, OH (city) Montgomery County	550

Mexicans 5 Years and Over Who Speak Spanish at Home
Top 10 Places Sorted by Percent

Place	Percent
Painesville, OH (city) Lake County	95.16
Ashtabula, OH (city) Ashtabula County	86.13
Hamilton, OH (city) Butler County	84.00
Columbus, OH (city) Franklin County	72.59
Dayton, OH (city) Montgomery County	68.32
Fremont, OH (city) Sandusky County	61.01
Defiance, OH (city) Defiance County	55.63
Youngstown, OH (city) Mahoning County	54.99
Bowling Green, OH (city) Wood County	52.57
Lakewood, OH (city) Cuyahoga County	50.55

Nicaraguans 5 Years and Over Who Speak Spanish at Home
Top 10 Places Sorted by Number

Place	Number
No places met population threshold.	

Nicaraguans 5 Years and Over Who Speak Spanish at Home
Top 10 Places Sorted by Percent

Place	Percent
No places met population threshold.	

Panamanians 5 Years and Over Who Speak Spanish at Home
Top 10 Places Sorted by Number

Place	Number
No places met population threshold.	

Panamanians 5 Years and Over Who Speak Spanish at Home
Top 10 Places Sorted by Percent

Place	Percent
No places met population threshold.	

Paraguayans 5 Years and Over Who Speak Spanish at Home
Top 10 Places Sorted by Number

Place	Number
No places met population threshold.	

Paraguayans 5 Years and Over Who Speak Spanish at Home
Top 10 Places Sorted by Percent

Place	Percent
No places met population threshold.	

Peruvians 5 Years and Over Who Speak Spanish at Home
Top 10 Places Sorted by Number

Place	Number
No places met population threshold.	

Peruvians 5 Years and Over Who Speak Spanish at Home
Top 10 Places Sorted by Percent

Place	Percent
No places met population threshold.	

Puerto Ricans 5 Years and Over Who Speak Spanish at Home
Top 10 Places Sorted by Number

Place	Number
Cleveland, OH (city) Cuyahoga County	17,373
Lorain, OH (city) Lorain County	6,479
Youngstown, OH (city) Mahoning County	1,994
Columbus, OH (city) Franklin County	1,579
Toledo, OH (city) Lucas County	450
Ashtabula, OH (city) Ashtabula County	407
Parma, OH (city) Cuyahoga County	325
Boardman, OH (cdp) Mahoning County	324
Cincinnati, OH (city) Hamilton County	308
Akron, OH (city) Summit County	250

Puerto Ricans 5 Years and Over Who Speak Spanish at Home
Top 10 Places Sorted by Percent

Place	Percent
Cleveland, OH (city) Cuyahoga County	80.85
Youngstown, OH (city) Mahoning County	75.10
Ashtabula, OH (city) Ashtabula County	74.27
Lorain, OH (city) Lorain County	72.13
Parma, OH (city) Cuyahoga County	68.28
Cincinnati, OH (city) Hamilton County	63.37
Boardman, OH (cdp) Mahoning County	61.25
Columbus, OH (city) Franklin County	56.86
Toledo, OH (city) Lucas County	47.77
Akron, OH (city) Summit County	47.62

Salvadorans 5 Years and Over Who Speak Spanish at Home
Top 10 Places Sorted by Number

Place	Number
Cleveland, OH (city) Cuyahoga County	392
Columbus, OH (city) Franklin County	323

Salvadorans 5 Years and Over Who Speak Spanish at Home
Top 10 Places Sorted by Percent

Place	Percent
Cleveland, OH (city) Cuyahoga County	96.08
Columbus, OH (city) Franklin County	90.99

South Americans 5 Years and Over Who Speak Spanish at Home
Top 10 Places Sorted by Number

Place	Number
Columbus, OH (city) Franklin County	734
Cleveland, OH (city) Cuyahoga County	437
Cincinnati, OH (city) Hamilton County	330

South Americans 5 Years and Over Who Speak Spanish at Home
Top 10 Places Sorted by Percent

Place	Percent
Cleveland, OH (city) Cuyahoga County	87.75
Cincinnati, OH (city) Hamilton County	76.92
Columbus, OH (city) Franklin County	76.62

Spaniards 5 Years and Over Who Speak Spanish at Home
Top 10 Places Sorted by Number

Place	Number
No places met population threshold.	

Spaniards 5 Years and Over Who Speak Spanish at Home
Top 10 Places Sorted by Percent

Place	Percent
No places met population threshold.	

Uruguayans 5 Years and Over Who Speak Spanish at Home
Top 10 Places Sorted by Number

Place	Number
No places met population threshold.	

Uruguayans 5 Years and Over Who Speak Spanish at Home
Top 10 Places Sorted by Percent

Place	Percent
No places met population threshold.	

Venezuelans 5 Years and Over Who Speak Spanish at Home
Top 10 Places Sorted by Number

Place	Number
No places met population threshold.	

Venezuelans 5 Years and Over Who Speak Spanish at Home
Top 10 Places Sorted by Percent

Place	Percent
No places met population threshold.	

Notes: Please refer to the User's Guide for an explanation of data; tables include places with populations > 9,999 and reflect only those areas that meet Summary File 4 population thresholds, therefore there may be less than 10 places listed

Other Hispanics 5 Years and Over Who Speak Spanish at Home

Top 10 Places Sorted by Number

Place	Number
Cleveland, OH (city) Cuyahoga County	1,679
Columbus, OH (city) Franklin County	1,182
Toledo, OH (city) Lucas County	847
Lorain, OH (city) Lorain County	492
Defiance, OH (city) Defiance County	373
Fremont, OH (city) Sandusky County	338
Cincinnati, OH (city) Hamilton County	280
Youngstown, OH (city) Mahoning County	168
Dayton, OH (city) Montgomery County	153
Akron, OH (city) Summit County	84

Other Hispanics 5 Years and Over Who Speak Spanish at Home

Top 10 Places Sorted by Percent

Place	Percent
Defiance, OH (city) Defiance County	78.86
Fremont, OH (city) Sandusky County	71.31
Cleveland, OH (city) Cuyahoga County	59.88
Columbus, OH (city) Franklin County	45.80
Lorain, OH (city) Lorain County	43.27
Cincinnati, OH (city) Hamilton County	41.54
Youngstown, OH (city) Mahoning County	38.01
Dayton, OH (city) Montgomery County	36.87
Toledo, OH (city) Lucas County	35.87
Akron, OH (city) Summit County	19.53

Foreign Born

Total Population

Top 10 Places Sorted by Number

Place	Number
Columbus, OH (city) Franklin County	47,713
Cleveland, OH (city) Cuyahoga County	21,372
Cincinnati, OH (city) Hamilton County	12,461
Toledo, OH (city) Lucas County	9,475
Parma, OH (city) Cuyahoga County	7,797
Akron, OH (city) Summit County	6,911
Lakewood, OH (city) Cuyahoga County	4,945
Cleveland Heights, OH (city) Cuyahoga County	4,130
Dayton, OH (city) Montgomery County	3,245
Strongsville, OH (city) Cuyahoga County	2,841

Total Population

Top 10 Places Sorted by Percent

Place	Percent
Parma Heights, OH (city) Cuyahoga County	10.17
Painesville, OH (city) Lake County	10.07
Parma, OH (city) Cuyahoga County	9.10
Brooklyn, OH (city) Cuyahoga County	8.97
Lakewood, OH (city) Cuyahoga County	8.73
Westlake, OH (city) Cuyahoga County	8.39
Cleveland Heights, OH (city) Cuyahoga County	8.26
North Olmsted, OH (city) Cuyahoga County	7.85
Columbus, OH (city) Franklin County	6.70
Strongsville, OH (city) Cuyahoga County	6.48

Hispanic

Top 10 Places Sorted by Number

Place	Number
Columbus, OH (city) Franklin County	6,389
Cleveland, OH (city) Cuyahoga County	3,456
Toledo, OH (city) Lucas County	1,775
Painesville, OH (city) Lake County	1,611
Cincinnati, OH (city) Hamilton County	1,544
Lorain, OH (city) Lorain County	921
Hamilton, OH (city) Butler County	814
Dayton, OH (city) Montgomery County	618
Akron, OH (city) Summit County	469
Ashtabula, OH (city) Ashtabula County	271

Hispanic

Top 10 Places Sorted by Percent

Place	Percent
Painesville, OH (city) Lake County	69.68
Hamilton, OH (city) Butler County	58.02
Upper Arlington, OH (city) Franklin County	43.09
Norwood, OH (city) Hamilton County	41.93
Cincinnati, OH (city) Hamilton County	37.76
Columbus, OH (city) Franklin County	36.79
Middletown, OH (city) Butler County	35.91
Fairfield, OH (city) Butler County	34.69
Whitehall, OH (city) Franklin County	33.19
Dayton, OH (city) Montgomery County	29.73

Argentinian

Top 10 Places Sorted by Number

Place	Number
No places met population threshold.	

Argentinian

Top 10 Places Sorted by Percent

Place	Percent
No places met population threshold.	

Bolivian

Top 10 Places Sorted by Number

Place	Number
No places met population threshold.	

Bolivian

Top 10 Places Sorted by Percent

Place	Percent
No places met population threshold.	

Central American

Top 10 Places Sorted by Number

Place	Number
Cleveland, OH (city) Cuyahoga County	1,257
Columbus, OH (city) Franklin County	564
Cincinnati, OH (city) Hamilton County	466

Central American

Top 10 Places Sorted by Percent

Place	Percent
Cincinnati, OH (city) Hamilton County	92.64
Cleveland, OH (city) Cuyahoga County	74.96
Columbus, OH (city) Franklin County	71.94

Chilean

Top 10 Places Sorted by Number

Place	Number
No places met population threshold.	

Chilean

Top 10 Places Sorted by Percent

Place	Percent
No places met population threshold.	

Colombian

Top 10 Places Sorted by Number

Place	Number
No places met population threshold.	

Colombian

Top 10 Places Sorted by Percent

Place	Percent
No places met population threshold.	

Costa Rican

Top 10 Places Sorted by Number

Place	Number
No places met population threshold.	

Costa Rican

Top 10 Places Sorted by Percent

Place	Percent
No places met population threshold.	

Cuban

Top 10 Places Sorted by Number

Place	Number
Columbus, OH (city) Franklin County	202
Cleveland, OH (city) Cuyahoga County	162

Cuban

Top 10 Places Sorted by Percent

Place	Percent
Cleveland, OH (city) Cuyahoga County	37.16
Columbus, OH (city) Franklin County	28.86

Dominican

Top 10 Places Sorted by Number

Place	Number
Cleveland, OH (city) Cuyahoga County	369

Dominican

Top 10 Places Sorted by Percent

Place	Percent
Cleveland, OH (city) Cuyahoga County	59.61

Ecuadorian

Top 10 Places Sorted by Number

Place	Number
No places met population threshold.	

Ecuadorian

Top 10 Places Sorted by Percent

Place	Percent
No places met population threshold.	

Guatelmalan

Top 10 Places Sorted by Number

Place	Number
Cleveland, OH (city) Cuyahoga County	345

Guatelmalan

Top 10 Places Sorted by Percent

Place	Percent
Cleveland, OH (city) Cuyahoga County	76.33

Honduran

Top 10 Places Sorted by Number

Place	Number
No places met population threshold.	

Honduran

Top 10 Places Sorted by Percent

Place	Percent
No places met population threshold.	

Notes: Please refer to the User's Guide for an explanation of data; tables include places with populations > 9,999 and reflect only those areas that meet Summary File 4 population thresholds, therefore there may be less than 10 places listed

Mexican
Top 10 Places Sorted by Number

Place	Number
Columbus, OH (city) Franklin County	4,100
Painesville, OH (city) Lake County	1,572
Toledo, OH (city) Lucas County	1,205
Hamilton, OH (city) Butler County	669
Cleveland, OH (city) Cuyahoga County	597
Cincinnati, OH (city) Hamilton County	486
Lorain, OH (city) Lorain County	476
Dayton, OH (city) Montgomery County	363
Akron, OH (city) Summit County	233
Ashtabula, OH (city) Ashtabula County	217

Mexican
Top 10 Places Sorted by Percent

Place	Percent
Painesville, OH (city) Lake County	84.38
Hamilton, OH (city) Butler County	73.03
Ashtabula, OH (city) Ashtabula County	51.91
Columbus, OH (city) Franklin County	48.26
Dayton, OH (city) Montgomery County	36.89
Cincinnati, OH (city) Hamilton County	31.27
Norwalk, OH (city) Huron County	30.62
Lakewood, OH (city) Cuyahoga County	26.54
Akron, OH (city) Summit County	26.06
Canton, OH (city) Stark County	24.53

Nicaraguan
Top 10 Places Sorted by Number

Place	Number
No places met population threshold.	

Nicaraguan
Top 10 Places Sorted by Percent

Place	Percent
No places met population threshold.	

Panamanian
Top 10 Places Sorted by Number

Place	Number
No places met population threshold.	

Panamanian
Top 10 Places Sorted by Percent

Place	Percent
No places met population threshold.	

Paraguayan
Top 10 Places Sorted by Number

Place	Number
No places met population threshold.	

Paraguayan
Top 10 Places Sorted by Percent

Place	Percent
No places met population threshold.	

Peruvian
Top 10 Places Sorted by Number

Place	Number
No places met population threshold.	

Peruvian
Top 10 Places Sorted by Percent

Place	Percent
No places met population threshold.	

Puerto Rican
Top 10 Places Sorted by Number

Place	Number
Cleveland, OH (city) Cuyahoga County	136
Columbus, OH (city) Franklin County	36
Toledo, OH (city) Lucas County	25
Lorain, OH (city) Lorain County	21
Cincinnati, OH (city) Hamilton County	16
Akron, OH (city) Summit County	8
Parma, OH (city) Cuyahoga County	8
Ashtabula, OH (city) Ashtabula County	0
Boardman, OH (cdp) Mahoning County	0
Elyria, OH (city) Lorain County	0

Puerto Rican
Top 10 Places Sorted by Percent

Place	Percent
Cincinnati, OH (city) Hamilton County	2.83
Toledo, OH (city) Lucas County	2.40
Parma, OH (city) Cuyahoga County	1.45
Akron, OH (city) Summit County	1.30
Columbus, OH (city) Franklin County	1.17
Cleveland, OH (city) Cuyahoga County	0.56
Lorain, OH (city) Lorain County	0.21
Ashtabula, OH (city) Ashtabula County	0.00
Boardman, OH (cdp) Mahoning County	0.00
Elyria, OH (city) Lorain County	0.00

Salvadoran
Top 10 Places Sorted by Number

Place	Number
Cleveland, OH (city) Cuyahoga County	361
Columbus, OH (city) Franklin County	318

Salvadoran
Top 10 Places Sorted by Percent

Place	Percent
Cleveland, OH (city) Cuyahoga County	79.52
Columbus, OH (city) Franklin County	78.71

South American
Top 10 Places Sorted by Number

Place	Number
Columbus, OH (city) Franklin County	674
Cleveland, OH (city) Cuyahoga County	371
Cincinnati, OH (city) Hamilton County	326

South American
Top 10 Places Sorted by Percent

Place	Percent
Cincinnati, OH (city) Hamilton County	68.92
Cleveland, OH (city) Cuyahoga County	67.09
Columbus, OH (city) Franklin County	66.08

Spaniard
Top 10 Places Sorted by Number

Place	Number
No places met population threshold.	

Spaniard
Top 10 Places Sorted by Percent

Place	Percent
No places met population threshold.	

Uruguayan
Top 10 Places Sorted by Number

Place	Number
No places met population threshold.	

Uruguayan
Top 10 Places Sorted by Percent

Place	Percent
No places met population threshold.	

Venezuelan
Top 10 Places Sorted by Number

Place	Number
No places met population threshold.	

Venezuelan
Top 10 Places Sorted by Percent

Place	Percent
No places met population threshold.	

Other Hispanic
Top 10 Places Sorted by Number

Place	Number
Columbus, OH (city) Franklin County	571
Cleveland, OH (city) Cuyahoga County	538
Toledo, OH (city) Lucas County	239
Cincinnati, OH (city) Hamilton County	186
Lorain, OH (city) Lorain County	122
Dayton, OH (city) Montgomery County	85
Defiance, OH (city) Defiance County	65
Youngstown, OH (city) Mahoning County	52
Fremont, OH (city) Sandusky County	31
Akron, OH (city) Summit County	26

Other Hispanic
Top 10 Places Sorted by Percent

Place	Percent
Cincinnati, OH (city) Hamilton County	26.12
Columbus, OH (city) Franklin County	19.34
Dayton, OH (city) Montgomery County	19.10
Cleveland, OH (city) Cuyahoga County	15.25
Defiance, OH (city) Defiance County	12.36
Youngstown, OH (city) Mahoning County	11.06
Toledo, OH (city) Lucas County	8.89
Lorain, OH (city) Lorain County	8.72
Fremont, OH (city) Sandusky County	5.60
Akron, OH (city) Summit County	5.27

Foreign-Born Naturalized Citizens

Total Population
Top 10 Places Sorted by Number

Place	Number
Columbus, OH (city) Franklin County	14,197
Cleveland, OH (city) Cuyahoga County	9,755
Parma, OH (city) Cuyahoga County	4,567
Toledo, OH (city) Lucas County	4,487
Cincinnati, OH (city) Hamilton County	4,139
Akron, OH (city) Summit County	3,181
Lakewood, OH (city) Cuyahoga County	2,603
Cleveland Heights, OH (city) Cuyahoga County	1,926
Westlake, OH (city) Cuyahoga County	1,905
Strongsville, OH (city) Cuyahoga County	1,760

Total Population
Top 10 Places Sorted by Percent

Place	Percent
Westlake, OH (city) Cuyahoga County	5.98
Parma Heights, OH (city) Cuyahoga County	5.38
Parma, OH (city) Cuyahoga County	5.33
Brooklyn, OH (city) Cuyahoga County	5.26
North Olmsted, OH (city) Cuyahoga County	4.95
Lakewood, OH (city) Cuyahoga County	4.60
Strongsville, OH (city) Cuyahoga County	4.01
Cleveland Heights, OH (city) Cuyahoga County	3.85
Upper Arlington, OH (city) Franklin County	3.30

Notes: Please refer to the User's Guide for an explanation of data; tables include places with populations > 9,999 and reflect only those areas that meet Summary File 4 population thresholds, therefore there may be less than 10 places listed

Place	Percent
Euclid, OH (city) Cuyahoga County	3.26

Hispanic
Top 10 Places Sorted by Number

Place	Number
Columbus, OH (city) Franklin County	1,504
Cleveland, OH (city) Cuyahoga County	1,425
Toledo, OH (city) Lucas County	644
Cincinnati, OH (city) Hamilton County	426
Lorain, OH (city) Lorain County	340
Akron, OH (city) Summit County	217
Painesville, OH (city) Lake County	185
Parma, OH (city) Cuyahoga County	153
Fremont, OH (city) Sandusky County	138
Dayton, OH (city) Montgomery County	127

Hispanic
Top 10 Places Sorted by Percent

Place	Percent
Upper Arlington, OH (city) Franklin County	25.00
Fairfield, OH (city) Butler County	24.03
Middletown, OH (city) Butler County	21.55
Cleveland Heights, OH (city) Cuyahoga County	17.11
Brunswick, OH (city) Medina County	16.99
Beavercreek, OH (city) Greene County	14.86
Kettering, OH (city) Montgomery County	13.68
Xenia, OH (city) Greene County	13.26
Parma, OH (city) Cuyahoga County	12.07
North Olmsted, OH (city) Cuyahoga County	11.29

Argentinian
Top 10 Places Sorted by Number

Place	Number
No places met population threshold.	

Argentinian
Top 10 Places Sorted by Percent

Place	Percent
No places met population threshold.	

Bolivian
Top 10 Places Sorted by Number

Place	Number
No places met population threshold.	

Bolivian
Top 10 Places Sorted by Percent

Place	Percent
No places met population threshold.	

Central American
Top 10 Places Sorted by Number

Place	Number
Cleveland, OH (city) Cuyahoga County	462
Columbus, OH (city) Franklin County	134
Cincinnati, OH (city) Hamilton County	79

Central American
Top 10 Places Sorted by Percent

Place	Percent
Cleveland, OH (city) Cuyahoga County	27.55
Columbus, OH (city) Franklin County	17.09
Cincinnati, OH (city) Hamilton County	15.71

Chilean
Top 10 Places Sorted by Number

Place	Number
No places met population threshold.	

Chilean
Top 10 Places Sorted by Percent

Place	Percent
No places met population threshold.	

Colombian
Top 10 Places Sorted by Number

Place	Number
No places met population threshold.	

Colombian
Top 10 Places Sorted by Percent

Place	Percent
No places met population threshold.	

Costa Rican
Top 10 Places Sorted by Number

Place	Number
No places met population threshold.	

Costa Rican
Top 10 Places Sorted by Percent

Place	Percent
No places met population threshold.	

Cuban
Top 10 Places Sorted by Number

Place	Number
Columbus, OH (city) Franklin County	120
Cleveland, OH (city) Cuyahoga County	90

Cuban
Top 10 Places Sorted by Percent

Place	Percent
Cleveland, OH (city) Cuyahoga County	20.64
Columbus, OH (city) Franklin County	17.14

Dominican
Top 10 Places Sorted by Number

Place	Number
Cleveland, OH (city) Cuyahoga County	129

Dominican
Top 10 Places Sorted by Percent

Place	Percent
Cleveland, OH (city) Cuyahoga County	20.84

Ecuadorian
Top 10 Places Sorted by Number

Place	Number
No places met population threshold.	

Ecuadorian
Top 10 Places Sorted by Percent

Place	Percent
No places met population threshold.	

Guatelmalan
Top 10 Places Sorted by Number

Place	Number
Cleveland, OH (city) Cuyahoga County	98

Guatelmalan
Top 10 Places Sorted by Percent

Place	Percent
Cleveland, OH (city) Cuyahoga County	21.68

Honduran
Top 10 Places Sorted by Number

Place	Number
No places met population threshold.	

Honduran
Top 10 Places Sorted by Percent

Place	Percent
No places met population threshold.	

Mexican
Top 10 Places Sorted by Number

Place	Number
Columbus, OH (city) Franklin County	694
Toledo, OH (city) Lucas County	418
Cleveland, OH (city) Cuyahoga County	267
Painesville, OH (city) Lake County	177
Lorain, OH (city) Lorain County	131
Fremont, OH (city) Sandusky County	111
Cincinnati, OH (city) Hamilton County	89
Akron, OH (city) Summit County	72
Youngstown, OH (city) Mahoning County	65
Dayton, OH (city) Montgomery County	56

Mexican
Top 10 Places Sorted by Percent

Place	Percent
Youngstown, OH (city) Mahoning County	12.70
Lakewood, OH (city) Cuyahoga County	11.42
Canton, OH (city) Stark County	10.14
Painesville, OH (city) Lake County	9.50
Columbus, OH (city) Franklin County	8.17
Fremont, OH (city) Sandusky County	8.07
Akron, OH (city) Summit County	8.05
Cleveland, OH (city) Cuyahoga County	7.97
Ashtabula, OH (city) Ashtabula County	7.18
Cincinnati, OH (city) Hamilton County	5.73

Nicaraguan
Top 10 Places Sorted by Number

Place	Number
No places met population threshold.	

Nicaraguan
Top 10 Places Sorted by Percent

Place	Percent
No places met population threshold.	

Panamanian
Top 10 Places Sorted by Number

Place	Number
No places met population threshold.	

Panamanian
Top 10 Places Sorted by Percent

Place	Percent
No places met population threshold.	

Paraguayan
Top 10 Places Sorted by Number

Place	Number
No places met population threshold.	

Notes: Please refer to the User's Guide for an explanation of data; tables include places with populations > 9,999 and reflect only those areas that meet Summary File 4 population thresholds, therefore there may be less than 10 places listed

Paraguayan
Top 10 Places Sorted by Percent

Place	Percent
No places met population threshold.	

Peruvian
Top 10 Places Sorted by Number

Place	Number
No places met population threshold.	

Peruvian
Top 10 Places Sorted by Percent

Place	Percent
No places met population threshold.	

Puerto Rican
Top 10 Places Sorted by Number

Place	Number
Cleveland, OH (city) Cuyahoga County	47
Columbus, OH (city) Franklin County	36
Toledo, OH (city) Lucas County	12
Cincinnati, OH (city) Hamilton County	8
Akron, OH (city) Summit County	0
Ashtabula, OH (city) Ashtabula County	0
Boardman, OH (cdp) Mahoning County	0
Elyria, OH (city) Lorain County	0
Lakewood, OH (city) Cuyahoga County	0
Lorain, OH (city) Lorain County	0

Puerto Rican
Top 10 Places Sorted by Percent

Place	Percent
Cincinnati, OH (city) Hamilton County	1.41
Columbus, OH (city) Franklin County	1.17
Toledo, OH (city) Lucas County	1.15
Cleveland, OH (city) Cuyahoga County	0.19
Akron, OH (city) Summit County	0.00
Ashtabula, OH (city) Ashtabula County	0.00
Boardman, OH (cdp) Mahoning County	0.00
Elyria, OH (city) Lorain County	0.00
Lakewood, OH (city) Cuyahoga County	0.00
Lorain, OH (city) Lorain County	0.00

Salvadoran
Top 10 Places Sorted by Number

Place	Number
Cleveland, OH (city) Cuyahoga County	180
Columbus, OH (city) Franklin County	22

Salvadoran
Top 10 Places Sorted by Percent

Place	Percent
Cleveland, OH (city) Cuyahoga County	39.65
Columbus, OH (city) Franklin County	5.45

South American
Top 10 Places Sorted by Number

Place	Number
Columbus, OH (city) Franklin County	272
Cleveland, OH (city) Cuyahoga County	204
Cincinnati, OH (city) Hamilton County	107

South American
Top 10 Places Sorted by Percent

Place	Percent
Cleveland, OH (city) Cuyahoga County	36.89
Columbus, OH (city) Franklin County	26.67
Cincinnati, OH (city) Hamilton County	22.62

Spaniard
Top 10 Places Sorted by Number

Place	Number
No places met population threshold.	

Spaniard
Top 10 Places Sorted by Percent

Place	Percent
No places met population threshold.	

Uruguayan
Top 10 Places Sorted by Number

Place	Number
No places met population threshold.	

Uruguayan
Top 10 Places Sorted by Percent

Place	Percent
No places met population threshold.	

Venezuelan
Top 10 Places Sorted by Number

Place	Number
No places met population threshold.	

Venezuelan
Top 10 Places Sorted by Percent

Place	Percent
No places met population threshold.	

Other Hispanic
Top 10 Places Sorted by Number

Place	Number
Cleveland, OH (city) Cuyahoga County	216
Columbus, OH (city) Franklin County	179
Toledo, OH (city) Lucas County	119
Cincinnati, OH (city) Hamilton County	97
Lorain, OH (city) Lorain County	40
Defiance, OH (city) Defiance County	34
Fremont, OH (city) Sandusky County	27
Youngstown, OH (city) Mahoning County	26
Akron, OH (city) Summit County	20
Dayton, OH (city) Montgomery County	5

Other Hispanic
Top 10 Places Sorted by Percent

Place	Percent
Cincinnati, OH (city) Hamilton County	13.62
Defiance, OH (city) Defiance County	6.46
Cleveland, OH (city) Cuyahoga County	6.12
Columbus, OH (city) Franklin County	6.06
Youngstown, OH (city) Mahoning County	5.53
Fremont, OH (city) Sandusky County	4.87
Toledo, OH (city) Lucas County	4.43
Akron, OH (city) Summit County	4.06
Lorain, OH (city) Lorain County	2.86
Dayton, OH (city) Montgomery County	1.12

Educational Attainment: H.S. Graduates

Total Populations 25 Years and Over Who are High School Graduates
Top 10 Places Sorted by Number

Place	Number
Columbus, OH (city) Franklin County	369,376
Cleveland, OH (city) Cuyahoga County	204,829
Cincinnati, OH (city) Hamilton County	159,012
Toledo, OH (city) Lucas County	157,014
Akron, OH (city) Summit County	111,556
Dayton, OH (city) Montgomery County	75,651
Parma, OH (city) Cuyahoga County	50,540
Canton, OH (city) Stark County	38,747
Youngstown, OH (city) Mahoning County	38,543
Kettering, OH (city) Montgomery County	36,547

Total Populations 25 Years and Over Who are High School Graduates
Top 10 Places Sorted by Percent

Place	Percent
Upper Arlington, OH (city) Franklin County	97.93
Perrysburg, OH (city) Wood County	94.74
Westerville, OH (city) Franklin County	94.55
Strongsville, OH (city) Cuyahoga County	92.99
Beavercreek, OH (city) Greene County	92.38
Westlake, OH (city) Cuyahoga County	92.14
Cleveland Heights, OH (city) Cuyahoga County	91.58
Bowling Green, OH (city) Wood County	91.20
Kettering, OH (city) Montgomery County	90.97
North Olmsted, OH (city) Cuyahoga County	90.41

Hispanics 25 Years and Over Who are High School Graduates
Top 10 Places Sorted by Number

Place	Number
Cleveland, OH (city) Cuyahoga County	9,165
Columbus, OH (city) Franklin County	5,818
Toledo, OH (city) Lucas County	4,920
Lorain, OH (city) Lorain County	4,066
Cincinnati, OH (city) Hamilton County	1,671
Youngstown, OH (city) Mahoning County	1,159
Akron, OH (city) Summit County	824
Dayton, OH (city) Montgomery County	739
Defiance, OH (city) Defiance County	714
Parma, OH (city) Cuyahoga County	675

Hispanics 25 Years and Over Who are High School Graduates
Top 10 Places Sorted by Percent

Place	Percent
Beavercreek, OH (city) Greene County	98.05
Upper Arlington, OH (city) Franklin County	97.12
Reynoldsburg, OH (city) Franklin County	96.83
Perrysburg, OH (city) Wood County	95.83
Westlake, OH (city) Cuyahoga County	94.39
Berea, OH (city) Cuyahoga County	93.81
Fairborn, OH (city) Greene County	92.45
Huber Heights, OH (city) Montgomery County	91.23
North Olmsted, OH (city) Cuyahoga County	89.51
Austintown, OH (cdp) Mahoning County	89.38

Argentinians 25 Years and Over Who are High School Graduates
Top 10 Places Sorted by Number

Place	Number
No places met population threshold.	

Argentinians 25 Years and Over Who are High School Graduates
Top 10 Places Sorted by Percent

Place	Percent
No places met population threshold.	

Bolivians 25 Years and Over Who are High School Graduates
Top 10 Places Sorted by Number

Place	Number
No places met population threshold.	

Notes: Please refer to the User's Guide for an explanation of data; tables include places with populations > 9,999 and reflect only those areas that meet Summary File 4 population thresholds, therefore there may be less than 10 places listed

Bolivians 25 Years and Over Who are High School Graduates
Top 10 Places Sorted by Percent

Place	Percent
No places met population threshold.	

Central Americans 25 Years and Over Who are High School Graduates
Top 10 Places Sorted by Number

Place	Number
Cleveland, OH (city) Cuyahoga County	404
Columbus, OH (city) Franklin County	284
Cincinnati, OH (city) Hamilton County	126

Central Americans 25 Years and Over Who are High School Graduates
Top 10 Places Sorted by Percent

Place	Percent
Columbus, OH (city) Franklin County	64.40
Cincinnati, OH (city) Hamilton County	49.61
Cleveland, OH (city) Cuyahoga County	46.38

Chileans 25 Years and Over Who are High School Graduates
Top 10 Places Sorted by Number

Place	Number
No places met population threshold.	

Chileans 25 Years and Over Who are High School Graduates
Top 10 Places Sorted by Percent

Place	Percent
No places met population threshold.	

Colombians 25 Years and Over Who are High School Graduates
Top 10 Places Sorted by Number

Place	Number
No places met population threshold.	

Colombians 25 Years and Over Who are High School Graduates
Top 10 Places Sorted by Percent

Place	Percent
No places met population threshold.	

Costa Ricans 25 Years and Over Who are High School Graduates
Top 10 Places Sorted by Number

Place	Number
No places met population threshold.	

Costa Ricans 25 Years and Over Who are High School Graduates
Top 10 Places Sorted by Percent

Place	Percent
No places met population threshold.	

Cubans 25 Years and Over Who are High School Graduates
Top 10 Places Sorted by Number

Place	Number
Columbus, OH (city) Franklin County	309
Cleveland, OH (city) Cuyahoga County	151

Cubans 25 Years and Over Who are High School Graduates
Top 10 Places Sorted by Percent

Place	Percent
Columbus, OH (city) Franklin County	82.40
Cleveland, OH (city) Cuyahoga County	59.92

Dominicans 25 Years and Over Who are High School Graduates
Top 10 Places Sorted by Number

Place	Number
Cleveland, OH (city) Cuyahoga County	185

Dominicans 25 Years and Over Who are High School Graduates
Top 10 Places Sorted by Percent

Place	Percent
Cleveland, OH (city) Cuyahoga County	55.39

Ecuadorians 25 Years and Over Who are High School Graduates
Top 10 Places Sorted by Number

Place	Number
No places met population threshold.	

Ecuadorians 25 Years and Over Who are High School Graduates
Top 10 Places Sorted by Percent

Place	Percent
No places met population threshold.	

Guatelmalans 25 Years and Over Who are High School Graduates
Top 10 Places Sorted by Number

Place	Number
Cleveland, OH (city) Cuyahoga County	110

Guatelmalans 25 Years and Over Who are High School Graduates
Top 10 Places Sorted by Percent

Place	Percent
Cleveland, OH (city) Cuyahoga County	44.53

Hondurans 25 Years and Over Who are High School Graduates
Top 10 Places Sorted by Number

Place	Number
No places met population threshold.	

Hondurans 25 Years and Over Who are High School Graduates
Top 10 Places Sorted by Percent

Place	Percent
No places met population threshold.	

Mexicans 25 Years and Over Who are High School Graduates
Top 10 Places Sorted by Number

Place	Number
Toledo, OH (city) Lucas County	3,692
Columbus, OH (city) Franklin County	2,345
Cleveland, OH (city) Cuyahoga County	1,055
Lorain, OH (city) Lorain County	804
Cincinnati, OH (city) Hamilton County	503
Defiance, OH (city) Defiance County	465
Fremont, OH (city) Sandusky County	342
Findlay, OH (city) Hancock County	317
Akron, OH (city) Summit County	313
Dayton, OH (city) Montgomery County	283

Mexicans 25 Years and Over Who are High School Graduates
Top 10 Places Sorted by Percent

Place	Percent
Lakewood, OH (city) Cuyahoga County	81.67
Oregon, OH (city) Lucas County	76.00
Elyria, OH (city) Lorain County	74.56
Akron, OH (city) Summit County	71.79
Sandusky, OH (city) Erie County	70.32
Defiance, OH (city) Defiance County	69.72
Cincinnati, OH (city) Hamilton County	68.62
Bowling Green, OH (city) Wood County	67.60
Norwalk, OH (city) Huron County	66.99
Findlay, OH (city) Hancock County	63.27

Nicaraguans 25 Years and Over Who are High School Graduates
Top 10 Places Sorted by Number

Place	Number
No places met population threshold.	

Nicaraguans 25 Years and Over Who are High School Graduates
Top 10 Places Sorted by Percent

Place	Percent
No places met population threshold.	

Panamanians 25 Years and Over Who are High School Graduates
Top 10 Places Sorted by Number

Place	Number
No places met population threshold.	

Panamanians 25 Years and Over Who are High School Graduates
Top 10 Places Sorted by Percent

Place	Percent
No places met population threshold.	

Paraguayans 25 Years and Over Who are High School Graduates
Top 10 Places Sorted by Number

Place	Number
No places met population threshold.	

Paraguayans 25 Years and Over Who are High School Graduates
Top 10 Places Sorted by Percent

Place	Percent
No places met population threshold.	

Peruvians 25 Years and Over Who are High School Graduates
Top 10 Places Sorted by Number

Place	Number
No places met population threshold.	

Peruvians 25 Years and Over Who are High School Graduates
Top 10 Places Sorted by Percent

Place	Percent
No places met population threshold.	

Notes: Please refer to the User's Guide for an explanation of data; tables include places with populations > 9,999 and reflect only those areas that meet Summary File 4 population thresholds, therefore there may be less than 10 places listed

Puerto Ricans 25 Years and Over Who are High School Graduates

Top 10 Places Sorted by Number

Place	Number
Cleveland, OH (city) Cuyahoga County	6,255
Lorain, OH (city) Lorain County	2,819
Columbus, OH (city) Franklin County	1,131
Youngstown, OH (city) Mahoning County	819
Toledo, OH (city) Lucas County	303
Parma, OH (city) Cuyahoga County	259
Boardman, OH (cdp) Mahoning County	257
Lakewood, OH (city) Cuyahoga County	249
Cincinnati, OH (city) Hamilton County	233
Elyria, OH (city) Lorain County	202

Puerto Ricans 25 Years and Over Who are High School Graduates

Top 10 Places Sorted by Percent

Place	Percent
Lakewood, OH (city) Cuyahoga County	91.54
Parma, OH (city) Cuyahoga County	85.76
Cincinnati, OH (city) Hamilton County	85.66
Boardman, OH (cdp) Mahoning County	79.57
Toledo, OH (city) Lucas County	79.11
Columbus, OH (city) Franklin County	78.54
Akron, OH (city) Summit County	73.13
Elyria, OH (city) Lorain County	68.24
Youngstown, OH (city) Mahoning County	56.52
Lorain, OH (city) Lorain County	56.40

Salvadorans 25 Years and Over Who are High School Graduates

Top 10 Places Sorted by Number

Place	Number
Columbus, OH (city) Franklin County	89
Cleveland, OH (city) Cuyahoga County	46

Salvadorans 25 Years and Over Who are High School Graduates

Top 10 Places Sorted by Percent

Place	Percent
Columbus, OH (city) Franklin County	44.06
Cleveland, OH (city) Cuyahoga County	22.33

South Americans 25 Years and Over Who are High School Graduates

Top 10 Places Sorted by Number

Place	Number
Columbus, OH (city) Franklin County	560
Cleveland, OH (city) Cuyahoga County	318
Cincinnati, OH (city) Hamilton County	315

South Americans 25 Years and Over Who are High School Graduates

Top 10 Places Sorted by Percent

Place	Percent
Cincinnati, OH (city) Hamilton County	98.44
Columbus, OH (city) Franklin County	88.89
Cleveland, OH (city) Cuyahoga County	84.80

Spaniards 25 Years and Over Who are High School Graduates

Top 10 Places Sorted by Number

Place	Number

No places met population threshold.

Spaniards 25 Years and Over Who are High School Graduates

Top 10 Places Sorted by Percent

Place	Percent

No places met population threshold.

Uruguayans 25 Years and Over Who are High School Graduates

Top 10 Places Sorted by Number

Place	Number

No places met population threshold.

Uruguayans 25 Years and Over Who are High School Graduates

Top 10 Places Sorted by Percent

Place	Percent

No places met population threshold.

Venezuelans 25 Years and Over Who are High School Graduates

Top 10 Places Sorted by Number

Place	Number

No places met population threshold.

Venezuelans 25 Years and Over Who are High School Graduates

Top 10 Places Sorted by Percent

Place	Percent

No places met population threshold.

Other Hispanics 25 Years and Over Who are High School Graduates

Top 10 Places Sorted by Number

Place	Number
Columbus, OH (city) Franklin County	1,022
Cleveland, OH (city) Cuyahoga County	763
Toledo, OH (city) Lucas County	753
Cincinnati, OH (city) Hamilton County	349
Lorain, OH (city) Lorain County	293
Akron, OH (city) Summit County	203
Dayton, OH (city) Montgomery County	203
Defiance, OH (city) Defiance County	185
Youngstown, OH (city) Mahoning County	125
Fremont, OH (city) Sandusky County	113

Other Hispanics 25 Years and Over Who are High School Graduates

Top 10 Places Sorted by Percent

Place	Percent
Dayton, OH (city) Montgomery County	79.30
Cincinnati, OH (city) Hamilton County	76.37
Defiance, OH (city) Defiance County	74.00
Akron, OH (city) Summit County	70.73
Columbus, OH (city) Franklin County	68.22
Toledo, OH (city) Lucas County	62.49
Lorain, OH (city) Lorain County	61.43
Youngstown, OH (city) Mahoning County	58.14
Cleveland, OH (city) Cuyahoga County	52.73
Fremont, OH (city) Sandusky County	47.68

Educational Attainment: College Graduates

Total Populations 25 Years and Over Who are Four-Year College Graduates

Top 10 Places Sorted by Number

Place	Number
Columbus, OH (city) Franklin County	128,058
Cincinnati, OH (city) Hamilton County	55,215
Cleveland, OH (city) Cuyahoga County	33,949
Toledo, OH (city) Lucas County	33,09
Akron, OH (city) Summit County	25,11
Cleveland Heights, OH (city) Cuyahoga County	16,76
Upper Arlington, OH (city) Franklin County	16,06
Dayton, OH (city) Montgomery County	14,47
Lakewood, OH (city) Cuyahoga County	14,19
Kettering, OH (city) Montgomery County	12,45

Total Populations 25 Years and Over Who are Four-Year College Graduates

Top 10 Places Sorted by Percent

Place	Percent
Upper Arlington, OH (city) Franklin County	67.4
Cleveland Heights, OH (city) Cuyahoga County	50.0
Perrysburg, OH (city) Wood County	46.9
Westlake, OH (city) Cuyahoga County	45.3
Westerville, OH (city) Franklin County	44.5
Bowling Green, OH (city) Wood County	44.1
Beavercreek, OH (city) Greene County	42.9
Strongsville, OH (city) Cuyahoga County	36.9
Lakewood, OH (city) Cuyahoga County	35.9
Kettering, OH (city) Montgomery County	31.0

Hispanics 25 Years and Over Who are Four-Year College Graduates

Top 10 Places Sorted by Number

Place	Number
Columbus, OH (city) Franklin County	1,656
Cleveland, OH (city) Cuyahoga County	1,327
Cincinnati, OH (city) Hamilton County	857
Toledo, OH (city) Lucas County	677
Lorain, OH (city) Lorain County	326
Lakewood, OH (city) Cuyahoga County	216
Akron, OH (city) Summit County	204
Dayton, OH (city) Montgomery County	178
Cleveland Heights, OH (city) Cuyahoga County	167
Boardman, OH (cdp) Mahoning County	151

Hispanics 25 Years and Over Who are Four-Year College Graduates

Top 10 Places Sorted by Percent

Place	Percent
Upper Arlington, OH (city) Franklin County	65.87
Beavercreek, OH (city) Greene County	59.02
Westlake, OH (city) Cuyahoga County	50.93
Cleveland Heights, OH (city) Cuyahoga County	42.93
Riverside, OH (city) Montgomery County	41.49
Westerville, OH (city) Franklin County	39.13
Cincinnati, OH (city) Hamilton County	38.97
Fairborn, OH (city) Greene County	36.33
Fairfield, OH (city) Butler County	33.61
Berea, OH (city) Cuyahoga County	31.86

Argentinians 25 Years and Over Who are Four-Year College Graduates

Top 10 Places Sorted by Number

Place	Number

No places met population threshold.

Argentinians 25 Years and Over Who are Four-Year College Graduates

Top 10 Places Sorted by Percent

Place	Percent

No places met population threshold.

Bolivians 25 Years and Over Who are Four-Year College Graduates

Top 10 Places Sorted by Number

Place	Number

No places met population threshold.

Notes: Please refer to the User's Guide for an explanation of data; tables include places with populations > 9,999 and reflect only those areas that meet Summary File 4 population thresholds, therefore there may be less than 10 places listed

Bolivians 25 Years and Over Who are Four-Year College Graduates
Top 10 Places Sorted by Percent

Place	Percent
No places met population threshold.	

Central Americans 25 Years and Over Who are Four-Year College Graduates
Top 10 Places Sorted by Number

Place	Number
Columbus, OH (city) Franklin County	111
Cleveland, OH (city) Cuyahoga County	105
Cincinnati, OH (city) Hamilton County	71

Central Americans 25 Years and Over Who are Four-Year College Graduates
Top 10 Places Sorted by Percent

Place	Percent
Cincinnati, OH (city) Hamilton County	27.95
Columbus, OH (city) Franklin County	25.17
Cleveland, OH (city) Cuyahoga County	12.06

Chileans 25 Years and Over Who are Four-Year College Graduates
Top 10 Places Sorted by Number

Place	Number
No places met population threshold.	

Chileans 25 Years and Over Who are Four-Year College Graduates
Top 10 Places Sorted by Percent

Place	Percent
No places met population threshold.	

Colombians 25 Years and Over Who are Four-Year College Graduates
Top 10 Places Sorted by Number

Place	Number
No places met population threshold.	

Colombians 25 Years and Over Who are Four-Year College Graduates
Top 10 Places Sorted by Percent

Place	Percent
No places met population threshold.	

Costa Ricans 25 Years and Over Who are Four-Year College Graduates
Top 10 Places Sorted by Number

Place	Number
No places met population threshold.	

Costa Ricans 25 Years and Over Who are Four-Year College Graduates
Top 10 Places Sorted by Percent

Place	Percent
No places met population threshold.	

Cubans 25 Years and Over Who are Four-Year College Graduates
Top 10 Places Sorted by Number

Place	Number
Columbus, OH (city) Franklin County	122
Cleveland, OH (city) Cuyahoga County	42

Cubans 25 Years and Over Who are Four-Year College Graduates
Top 10 Places Sorted by Percent

Place	Percent
Columbus, OH (city) Franklin County	32.53
Cleveland, OH (city) Cuyahoga County	16.67

Dominicans 25 Years and Over Who are Four-Year College Graduates
Top 10 Places Sorted by Number

Place	Number
Cleveland, OH (city) Cuyahoga County	24

Dominicans 25 Years and Over Who are Four-Year College Graduates
Top 10 Places Sorted by Percent

Place	Percent
Cleveland, OH (city) Cuyahoga County	7.19

Ecuadorians 25 Years and Over Who are Four-Year College Graduates
Top 10 Places Sorted by Number

Place	Number
No places met population threshold.	

Ecuadorians 25 Years and Over Who are Four-Year College Graduates
Top 10 Places Sorted by Percent

Place	Percent
No places met population threshold.	

Guatelmalans 25 Years and Over Who are Four-Year College Graduates
Top 10 Places Sorted by Number

Place	Number
Cleveland, OH (city) Cuyahoga County	7

Guatelmalans 25 Years and Over Who are Four-Year College Graduates
Top 10 Places Sorted by Percent

Place	Percent
Cleveland, OH (city) Cuyahoga County	2.83

Hondurans 25 Years and Over Who are Four-Year College Graduates
Top 10 Places Sorted by Number

Place	Number
No places met population threshold.	

Hondurans 25 Years and Over Who are Four-Year College Graduates
Top 10 Places Sorted by Percent

Place	Percent
No places met population threshold.	

Mexicans 25 Years and Over Who are Four-Year College Graduates
Top 10 Places Sorted by Number

Place	Number
Columbus, OH (city) Franklin County	508
Toledo, OH (city) Lucas County	426
Cincinnati, OH (city) Hamilton County	249
Cleveland, OH (city) Cuyahoga County	192
Akron, OH (city) Summit County	87
Lakewood, OH (city) Cuyahoga County	72
Findlay, OH (city) Hancock County	53
Lorain, OH (city) Lorain County	51
Defiance, OH (city) Defiance County	47
Dayton, OH (city) Montgomery County	33

Mexicans 25 Years and Over Who are Four-Year College Graduates
Top 10 Places Sorted by Percent

Place	Percent
Lakewood, OH (city) Cuyahoga County	40.00
Cincinnati, OH (city) Hamilton County	33.97
Akron, OH (city) Summit County	19.95
Columbus, OH (city) Franklin County	12.76
Cleveland, OH (city) Cuyahoga County	10.87
Findlay, OH (city) Hancock County	10.58
Norwalk, OH (city) Huron County	9.71
Toledo, OH (city) Lucas County	7.15
Defiance, OH (city) Defiance County	7.05
Dayton, OH (city) Montgomery County	6.73

Nicaraguans 25 Years and Over Who are Four-Year College Graduates
Top 10 Places Sorted by Number

Place	Number
No places met population threshold.	

Nicaraguans 25 Years and Over Who are Four-Year College Graduates
Top 10 Places Sorted by Percent

Place	Percent
No places met population threshold.	

Panamanians 25 Years and Over Who are Four-Year College Graduates
Top 10 Places Sorted by Number

Place	Number
No places met population threshold.	

Panamanians 25 Years and Over Who are Four-Year College Graduates
Top 10 Places Sorted by Percent

Place	Percent
No places met population threshold.	

Paraguayans 25 Years and Over Who are Four-Year College Graduates
Top 10 Places Sorted by Number

Place	Number
No places met population threshold.	

Paraguayans 25 Years and Over Who are Four-Year College Graduates
Top 10 Places Sorted by Percent

Place	Percent
No places met population threshold.	

Peruvians 25 Years and Over Who are Four-Year College Graduates
Top 10 Places Sorted by Number

Place	Number
No places met population threshold.	

Peruvians 25 Years and Over Who are Four-Year College Graduates
Top 10 Places Sorted by Percent

Place	Percent
No places met population threshold.	

Notes: Please refer to the User's Guide for an explanation of data; tables include places with populations > 9,999 and reflect only those areas that meet Summary File 4 population thresholds, therefore there may be less than 10 places listed

Puerto Ricans 25 Years and Over Who are Four-Year College Graduates
Top 10 Places Sorted by Number

Place	Number
Cleveland, OH (city) Cuyahoga County	699
Columbus, OH (city) Franklin County	349
Lorain, OH (city) Lorain County	198
Cincinnati, OH (city) Hamilton County	107
Boardman, OH (cdp) Mahoning County	82
Youngstown, OH (city) Mahoning County	71
Lakewood, OH (city) Cuyahoga County	62
Toledo, OH (city) Lucas County	51
Parma, OH (city) Cuyahoga County	32
Akron, OH (city) Summit County	29

Puerto Ricans 25 Years and Over Who are Four-Year College Graduates
Top 10 Places Sorted by Percent

Place	Percent
Cincinnati, OH (city) Hamilton County	39.34
Boardman, OH (cdp) Mahoning County	25.39
Columbus, OH (city) Franklin County	24.24
Lakewood, OH (city) Cuyahoga County	22.79
Toledo, OH (city) Lucas County	13.32
Akron, OH (city) Summit County	10.82
Parma, OH (city) Cuyahoga County	10.60
Elyria, OH (city) Lorain County	8.45
Cleveland, OH (city) Cuyahoga County	5.92
Youngstown, OH (city) Mahoning County	4.90

Salvadorans 25 Years and Over Who are Four-Year College Graduates
Top 10 Places Sorted by Number

Place	Number
Columbus, OH (city) Franklin County	18
Cleveland, OH (city) Cuyahoga County	5

Salvadorans 25 Years and Over Who are Four-Year College Graduates
Top 10 Places Sorted by Percent

Place	Percent
Columbus, OH (city) Franklin County	8.91
Cleveland, OH (city) Cuyahoga County	2.43

South Americans 25 Years and Over Who are Four-Year College Graduates
Top 10 Places Sorted by Number

Place	Number
Columbus, OH (city) Franklin County	296
Cincinnati, OH (city) Hamilton County	219
Cleveland, OH (city) Cuyahoga County	98

South Americans 25 Years and Over Who are Four-Year College Graduates
Top 10 Places Sorted by Percent

Place	Percent
Cincinnati, OH (city) Hamilton County	68.44
Columbus, OH (city) Franklin County	46.98
Cleveland, OH (city) Cuyahoga County	26.13

Spaniards 25 Years and Over Who are Four-Year College Graduates
Top 10 Places Sorted by Number

Place	Number

No places met population threshold.

Spaniards 25 Years and Over Who are Four-Year College Graduates
Top 10 Places Sorted by Percent

Place	Percent

No places met population threshold.

Uruguayans 25 Years and Over Who are Four-Year College Graduates
Top 10 Places Sorted by Number

Place	Number

No places met population threshold.

Uruguayans 25 Years and Over Who are Four-Year College Graduates
Top 10 Places Sorted by Percent

Place	Percent

No places met population threshold.

Venezuelans 25 Years and Over Who are Four-Year College Graduates
Top 10 Places Sorted by Number

Place	Number

No places met population threshold.

Venezuelans 25 Years and Over Who are Four-Year College Graduates
Top 10 Places Sorted by Percent

Place	Percent

No places met population threshold.

Other Hispanics 25 Years and Over Who are Four-Year College Graduates
Top 10 Places Sorted by Number

Place	Number
Columbus, OH (city) Franklin County	194
Cleveland, OH (city) Cuyahoga County	145
Cincinnati, OH (city) Hamilton County	118
Toledo, OH (city) Lucas County	104
Akron, OH (city) Summit County	44
Lorain, OH (city) Lorain County	37
Dayton, OH (city) Montgomery County	36
Youngstown, OH (city) Mahoning County	15
Defiance, OH (city) Defiance County	11
Fremont, OH (city) Sandusky County	9

Other Hispanics 25 Years and Over Who are Four-Year College Graduates
Top 10 Places Sorted by Percent

Place	Percent
Cincinnati, OH (city) Hamilton County	25.82
Akron, OH (city) Summit County	15.33
Dayton, OH (city) Montgomery County	14.06
Columbus, OH (city) Franklin County	12.95
Cleveland, OH (city) Cuyahoga County	10.02
Toledo, OH (city) Lucas County	8.63
Lorain, OH (city) Lorain County	7.76
Youngstown, OH (city) Mahoning County	6.98
Defiance, OH (city) Defiance County	4.40
Fremont, OH (city) Sandusky County	3.80

Median Household Income

Total Population
Top 10 Places Sorted by Number

Place	Dollars
Upper Arlington, OH (city) Franklin County	72,116
Westerville, OH (city) Franklin County	69,135
Beavercreek, OH (city) Greene County	68,801
Strongsville, OH (city) Cuyahoga County	68,660
Westlake, OH (city) Cuyahoga County	64,963
Perrysburg, OH (city) Wood County	62,237
Brunswick, OH (city) Medina County	56,28[illegible]
North Olmsted, OH (city) Cuyahoga County	52,542
Reynoldsburg, OH (city) Franklin County	51,10[illegible]
Fairfield, OH (city) Butler County	50,316

Hispanic
Top 10 Places Sorted by Number

Place	Dollars
Strongsville, OH (city) Cuyahoga County	77,700
Upper Arlington, OH (city) Franklin County	73,977
Beavercreek, OH (city) Greene County	70,208
Brunswick, OH (city) Medina County	65,208
Westerville, OH (city) Franklin County	56,125
Riverside, OH (city) Montgomery County	55,431
Perrysburg, OH (city) Wood County	52,865
Fairfield, OH (city) Butler County	50,156
Reynoldsburg, OH (city) Franklin County	49,444
Huber Heights, OH (city) Montgomery County	48,897

Argentinian
Top 10 Places Sorted by Number

Place	Dollars

No places met population threshold.

Bolivian
Top 10 Places Sorted by Number

Place	Dollars

No places met population threshold.

Central American
Top 10 Places Sorted by Number

Place	Dollars
Columbus, OH (city) Franklin County	32,384
Cleveland, OH (city) Cuyahoga County	29,817
Cincinnati, OH (city) Hamilton County	24,318

Chilean
Top 10 Places Sorted by Number

Place	Dollars

No places met population threshold.

Colombian
Top 10 Places Sorted by Number

Place	Dollars

No places met population threshold.

Costa Rican
Top 10 Places Sorted by Number

Place	Dollars

No places met population threshold.

Cuban
Top 10 Places Sorted by Number

Place	Dollars
Columbus, OH (city) Franklin County	46,146
Cleveland, OH (city) Cuyahoga County	38,167

Dominican
Top 10 Places Sorted by Number

Place	Dollars
Cleveland, OH (city) Cuyahoga County	23,750

Ecuadorian
Top 10 Places Sorted by Number

Place	Dollars

No places met population threshold.

Notes: Please refer to the User's Guide for an explanation of data; tables include places with populations > 9,999 and reflect only those areas that meet Summary File 4 population thresholds, therefore there may be less than 10 places listed

Guatelmalan

Top 10 Places Sorted by Number

Place	Dollars
Cleveland, OH (city) Cuyahoga County	25,938

Honduran

Top 10 Places Sorted by Number

Place	Dollars

No places met population threshold.

Mexican

Top 10 Places Sorted by Number

Place	Dollars
Lakewood, OH (city) Cuyahoga County	61,250
Oregon, OH (city) Lucas County	41,417
Defiance, OH (city) Defiance County	41,210
Akron, OH (city) Summit County	39,489
Ashtabula, OH (city) Ashtabula County	37,500
Hamilton, OH (city) Butler County	35,795
Painesville, OH (city) Lake County	34,524
Lorain, OH (city) Lorain County	33,401
Columbus, OH (city) Franklin County	33,333
Toledo, OH (city) Lucas County	32,064

Nicaraguan

Top 10 Places Sorted by Number

Place	Dollars

No places met population threshold.

Panamanian

Top 10 Places Sorted by Number

Place	Dollars

No places met population threshold.

Paraguayan

Top 10 Places Sorted by Number

Place	Dollars

No places met population threshold.

Peruvian

Top 10 Places Sorted by Number

Place	Dollars

No places met population threshold.

Puerto Rican

Top 10 Places Sorted by Number

Place	Dollars
Lakewood, OH (city) Cuyahoga County	50,000
Parma, OH (city) Cuyahoga County	41,490
Boardman, OH (cdp) Mahoning County	36,500
Columbus, OH (city) Franklin County	29,972
Toledo, OH (city) Lucas County	27,083
Cincinnati, OH (city) Hamilton County	26,953
Elyria, OH (city) Lorain County	26,953
Lorain, OH (city) Lorain County	26,681
Cleveland, OH (city) Cuyahoga County	24,315
Akron, OH (city) Summit County	21,382

Salvadoran

Top 10 Places Sorted by Number

Place	Dollars
Columbus, OH (city) Franklin County	36,447
Cleveland, OH (city) Cuyahoga County	28,958

South American

Top 10 Places Sorted by Number

Place	Dollars
Cleveland, OH (city) Cuyahoga County	37,625
Columbus, OH (city) Franklin County	37,383
Cincinnati, OH (city) Hamilton County	34,750

Spaniard

Top 10 Places Sorted by Number

Place	Dollars

No places met population threshold.

Uruguayan

Top 10 Places Sorted by Number

Place	Dollars

No places met population threshold.

Venezuelan

Top 10 Places Sorted by Number

Place	Dollars

No places met population threshold.

Other Hispanic

Top 10 Places Sorted by Number

Place	Dollars
Lorain, OH (city) Lorain County	45,938
Defiance, OH (city) Defiance County	43,438
Columbus, OH (city) Franklin County	29,485
Cleveland, OH (city) Cuyahoga County	25,804
Cincinnati, OH (city) Hamilton County	24,844
Akron, OH (city) Summit County	23,750
Toledo, OH (city) Lucas County	22,258
Fremont, OH (city) Sandusky County	21,023
Dayton, OH (city) Montgomery County	19,000
Youngstown, OH (city) Mahoning County	18,917

Per Capita Income

Total Population

Top 10 Places Sorted by Number

Place	Dollars
Upper Arlington, OH (city) Franklin County	42,025
Westlake, OH (city) Cuyahoga County	37,142
Beavercreek, OH (city) Greene County	30,298
Strongsville, OH (city) Cuyahoga County	29,722
Perrysburg, OH (city) Wood County	29,652
Westerville, OH (city) Franklin County	29,401
Kettering, OH (city) Montgomery County	27,009
Cleveland Heights, OH (city) Cuyahoga County	25,804
Fairfield, OH (city) Butler County	24,556
North Olmsted, OH (city) Cuyahoga County	24,329

Hispanic

Top 10 Places Sorted by Number

Place	Dollars
Beavercreek, OH (city) Greene County	25,348
Strongsville, OH (city) Cuyahoga County	25,068
Upper Arlington, OH (city) Franklin County	22,260
Perrysburg, OH (city) Wood County	22,129
Brooklyn, OH (city) Cuyahoga County	21,291
Tiffin, OH (city) Seneca County	20,467
Kettering, OH (city) Montgomery County	20,046
Westlake, OH (city) Cuyahoga County	19,786
Austintown, OH (cdp) Mahoning County	19,734
Parma, OH (city) Cuyahoga County	19,491

Argentinian

Top 10 Places Sorted by Number

Place	Dollars

No places met population threshold.

Bolivian

Top 10 Places Sorted by Number

Place	Dollars

No places met population threshold.

Central American

Top 10 Places Sorted by Number

Place	Dollars
Columbus, OH (city) Franklin County	13,998
Cincinnati, OH (city) Hamilton County	10,708
Cleveland, OH (city) Cuyahoga County	9,358

Chilean

Top 10 Places Sorted by Number

Place	Dollars

No places met population threshold.

Colombian

Top 10 Places Sorted by Number

Place	Dollars

No places met population threshold.

Costa Rican

Top 10 Places Sorted by Number

Place	Dollars

No places met population threshold.

Cuban

Top 10 Places Sorted by Number

Place	Dollars
Columbus, OH (city) Franklin County	14,827
Cleveland, OH (city) Cuyahoga County	13,147

Dominican

Top 10 Places Sorted by Number

Place	Dollars
Cleveland, OH (city) Cuyahoga County	12,898

Ecuadorian

Top 10 Places Sorted by Number

Place	Dollars

No places met population threshold.

Guatelmalan

Top 10 Places Sorted by Number

Place	Dollars
Cleveland, OH (city) Cuyahoga County	8,042

Honduran

Top 10 Places Sorted by Number

Place	Dollars

No places met population threshold.

Mexican

Top 10 Places Sorted by Number

Place	Dollars
Lakewood, OH (city) Cuyahoga County	17,623
Youngstown, OH (city) Mahoning County	16,488
Akron, OH (city) Summit County	15,485
Defiance, OH (city) Defiance County	15,084
Cincinnati, OH (city) Hamilton County	14,457
Oregon, OH (city) Lucas County	14,447
Lorain, OH (city) Lorain County	13,123
Columbus, OH (city) Franklin County	12,776
Cleveland, OH (city) Cuyahoga County	12,633
Sandusky, OH (city) Erie County	12,290

Nicaraguan

Top 10 Places Sorted by Number

Place	Dollars

No places met population threshold.

Notes: Please refer to the User's Guide for an explanation of data; tables include places with populations > 9,999 and reflect only those areas that meet Summary File 4 population thresholds, therefore there may be less than 10 places listed

Panamanian
Top 10 Places Sorted by Number

Place	Dollars
No places met population threshold.	

Paraguayan
Top 10 Places Sorted by Number

Place	Dollars
No places met population threshold.	

Peruvian
Top 10 Places Sorted by Number

Place	Dollars
No places met population threshold.	

Puerto Rican
Top 10 Places Sorted by Number

Place	Dollars
Cincinnati, OH (city) Hamilton County	16,874
Boardman, OH (cdp) Mahoning County	16,306
Parma, OH (city) Cuyahoga County	15,514
Lakewood, OH (city) Cuyahoga County	14,449
Columbus, OH (city) Franklin County	13,984
Lorain, OH (city) Lorain County	10,790
Akron, OH (city) Summit County	10,339
Elyria, OH (city) Lorain County	10,028
Cleveland, OH (city) Cuyahoga County	9,718
Ashtabula, OH (city) Ashtabula County	9,522

Salvadoran
Top 10 Places Sorted by Number

Place	Dollars
Columbus, OH (city) Franklin County	13,382
Cleveland, OH (city) Cuyahoga County	8,782

South American
Top 10 Places Sorted by Number

Place	Dollars
Cincinnati, OH (city) Hamilton County	25,630
Columbus, OH (city) Franklin County	18,062
Cleveland, OH (city) Cuyahoga County	16,626

Spaniard
Top 10 Places Sorted by Number

Place	Dollars
No places met population threshold.	

Uruguayan
Top 10 Places Sorted by Number

Place	Dollars
No places met population threshold.	

Venezuelan
Top 10 Places Sorted by Number

Place	Dollars
No places met population threshold.	

Other Hispanic
Top 10 Places Sorted by Number

Place	Dollars
Akron, OH (city) Summit County	18,483
Defiance, OH (city) Defiance County	18,007
Cincinnati, OH (city) Hamilton County	16,210
Columbus, OH (city) Franklin County	14,694
Toledo, OH (city) Lucas County	14,608
Dayton, OH (city) Montgomery County	11,299
Lorain, OH (city) Lorain County	10,254
Cleveland, OH (city) Cuyahoga County	8,702
Fremont, OH (city) Sandusky County	8,527
Youngstown, OH (city) Mahoning County	8,149

Poverty Status

Total Populations with Income Below Poverty Level
Top 10 Places Sorted by Number

Place	Number
Cleveland, OH (city) Cuyahoga County	122,479
Columbus, OH (city) Franklin County	102,723
Cincinnati, OH (city) Hamilton County	69,722
Toledo, OH (city) Lucas County	54,903
Akron, OH (city) Summit County	36,975
Dayton, OH (city) Montgomery County	35,756
Youngstown, OH (city) Mahoning County	19,127
Canton, OH (city) Stark County	14,957
Lorain, OH (city) Lorain County	11,582
Springfield, OH (city) Clark County	10,577

Total Populations with Income Below Poverty Level
Top 10 Places Sorted by Percent

Place	Percent
Cleveland, OH (city) Cuyahoga County	26.27
Bowling Green, OH (city) Wood County	25.27
Youngstown, OH (city) Mahoning County	24.78
Dayton, OH (city) Montgomery County	22.99
Lima, OH (city) Allen County	22.67
Cincinnati, OH (city) Hamilton County	21.91
Ashtabula, OH (city) Ashtabula County	21.35
Warren, OH (city) Trumbull County	19.38
Canton, OH (city) Stark County	19.16
Toledo, OH (city) Lucas County	17.89

Hispanics with Income Below Poverty Level
Top 10 Places Sorted by Number

Place	Number
Cleveland, OH (city) Cuyahoga County	11,110
Toledo, OH (city) Lucas County	4,355
Lorain, OH (city) Lorain County	3,180
Columbus, OH (city) Franklin County	3,166
Youngstown, OH (city) Mahoning County	1,273
Cincinnati, OH (city) Hamilton County	909
Painesville, OH (city) Lake County	662
Dayton, OH (city) Montgomery County	592
Akron, OH (city) Summit County	471
Fremont, OH (city) Sandusky County	440

Hispanics with Income Below Poverty Level
Top 10 Places Sorted by Percent

Place	Percent
Warren, OH (city) Trumbull County	43.82
Cleveland, OH (city) Cuyahoga County	32.57
Youngstown, OH (city) Mahoning County	32.22
Ashtabula, OH (city) Ashtabula County	32.21
Marion, OH (city) Marion County	31.53
Dayton, OH (city) Montgomery County	31.04
Hamilton, OH (city) Butler County	30.17
Painesville, OH (city) Lake County	29.50
Canton, OH (city) Stark County	26.89
Lima, OH (city) Allen County	26.82

Argentinians with Income Below Poverty Level
Top 10 Places Sorted by Number

Place	Number
No places met population threshold.	

Argentinians with Income Below Poverty Level
Top 10 Places Sorted by Percent

Place	Percent
No places met population threshold.	

Bolivians with Income Below Poverty Level
Top 10 Places Sorted by Number

Place	Numbe
No places met population threshold.	

Bolivians with Income Below Poverty Level
Top 10 Places Sorted by Percent

Place	Percen
No places met population threshold.	

Central Americans with Income Below Poverty Leve
Top 10 Places Sorted by Number

Place	Numbe
Cleveland, OH (city) Cuyahoga County	31
Columbus, OH (city) Franklin County	16
Cincinnati, OH (city) Hamilton County	11

Central Americans with Income Below Poverty Leve
Top 10 Places Sorted by Percent

Place	Percen
Cincinnati, OH (city) Hamilton County	23.0
Columbus, OH (city) Franklin County	21.2
Cleveland, OH (city) Cuyahoga County	19.2

Chileans with Income Below Poverty Level
Top 10 Places Sorted by Number

Place	Numbe
No places met population threshold.	

Chileans with Income Below Poverty Level
Top 10 Places Sorted by Percent

Place	Percen
No places met population threshold.	

Colombians with Income Below Poverty Level
Top 10 Places Sorted by Number

Place	Numbe
No places met population threshold.	

Colombians with Income Below Poverty Level
Top 10 Places Sorted by Percent

Place	Percen
No places met population threshold.	

Costa Ricans with Income Below Poverty Level
Top 10 Places Sorted by Number

Place	Number
No places met population threshold.	

Costa Ricans with Income Below Poverty Level
Top 10 Places Sorted by Percent

Place	Percent
No places met population threshold.	

Cubans with Income Below Poverty Level
Top 10 Places Sorted by Number

Place	Number
Cleveland, OH (city) Cuyahoga County	178
Columbus, OH (city) Franklin County	59

Cubans with Income Below Poverty Level
Top 10 Places Sorted by Percent

Place	Percent
Cleveland, OH (city) Cuyahoga County	42.38
Columbus, OH (city) Franklin County	8.51

Notes: Please refer to the User's Guide for an explanation of data; tables include places with populations > 9,999 and reflect only those areas that meet Summary File 4 population thresholds, therefore there may be less than 10 places listed

Dominicans with Income Below Poverty Level
Top 10 Places Sorted by Number

Place	Number
Cleveland, OH (city) Cuyahoga County	171

Dominicans with Income Below Poverty Level
Top 10 Places Sorted by Percent

Place	Percent
Cleveland, OH (city) Cuyahoga County	27.63

Ecuadorians with Income Below Poverty Level
Top 10 Places Sorted by Number

Place	Number
No places met population threshold.	

Ecuadorians with Income Below Poverty Level
Top 10 Places Sorted by Percent

Place	Percent
No places met population threshold.	

Guatelmalans with Income Below Poverty Level
Top 10 Places Sorted by Number

Place	Number
Cleveland, OH (city) Cuyahoga County	118

Guatelmalans with Income Below Poverty Level
Top 10 Places Sorted by Percent

Place	Percent
Cleveland, OH (city) Cuyahoga County	27.00

Hondurans with Income Below Poverty Level
Top 10 Places Sorted by Number

Place	Number
No places met population threshold.	

Hondurans with Income Below Poverty Level
Top 10 Places Sorted by Percent

Place	Percent
No places met population threshold.	

Mexicans with Income Below Poverty Level
Top 10 Places Sorted by Number

Place	Number
Toledo, OH (city) Lucas County	3,057
Columbus, OH (city) Franklin County	1,836
Cleveland, OH (city) Cuyahoga County	960
Painesville, OH (city) Lake County	591
Lorain, OH (city) Lorain County	419
Cincinnati, OH (city) Hamilton County	354
Dayton, OH (city) Montgomery County	349
Hamilton, OH (city) Butler County	247
Defiance, OH (city) Defiance County	218
Fostoria, OH (city) Seneca County	214

Mexicans with Income Below Poverty Level
Top 10 Places Sorted by Percent

Place	Percent
Youngstown, OH (city) Mahoning County	39.75
Dayton, OH (city) Montgomery County	36.89
Canton, OH (city) Stark County	36.23
Painesville, OH (city) Lake County	31.95
Cleveland, OH (city) Cuyahoga County	29.34
Hamilton, OH (city) Butler County	27.78
Springfield, OH (city) Clark County	26.59
Lima, OH (city) Allen County	25.77
Ashtabula, OH (city) Ashtabula County	25.12
Toledo, OH (city) Lucas County	24.00

Nicaraguans with Income Below Poverty Level
Top 10 Places Sorted by Number

Place	Number
No places met population threshold.	

Nicaraguans with Income Below Poverty Level
Top 10 Places Sorted by Percent

Place	Percent
No places met population threshold.	

Panamanians with Income Below Poverty Level
Top 10 Places Sorted by Number

Place	Number
No places met population threshold.	

Panamanians with Income Below Poverty Level
Top 10 Places Sorted by Percent

Place	Percent
No places met population threshold.	

Paraguayans with Income Below Poverty Level
Top 10 Places Sorted by Number

Place	Number
No places met population threshold.	

Paraguayans with Income Below Poverty Level
Top 10 Places Sorted by Percent

Place	Percent
No places met population threshold.	

Peruvians with Income Below Poverty Level
Top 10 Places Sorted by Number

Place	Number
No places met population threshold.	

Peruvians with Income Below Poverty Level
Top 10 Places Sorted by Percent

Place	Percent
No places met population threshold.	

Puerto Ricans with Income Below Poverty Level
Top 10 Places Sorted by Number

Place	Number
Cleveland, OH (city) Cuyahoga County	8,433
Lorain, OH (city) Lorain County	2,300
Youngstown, OH (city) Mahoning County	874
Columbus, OH (city) Franklin County	404
Toledo, OH (city) Lucas County	374
Ashtabula, OH (city) Ashtabula County	294
Akron, OH (city) Summit County	145
Elyria, OH (city) Lorain County	113
Lakewood, OH (city) Cuyahoga County	68
Cincinnati, OH (city) Hamilton County	53

Puerto Ricans with Income Below Poverty Level
Top 10 Places Sorted by Percent

Place	Percent
Ashtabula, OH (city) Ashtabula County	46.15
Toledo, OH (city) Lucas County	36.52
Cleveland, OH (city) Cuyahoga County	35.04
Youngstown, OH (city) Mahoning County	29.83
Akron, OH (city) Summit County	23.62
Lorain, OH (city) Lorain County	22.96
Elyria, OH (city) Lorain County	16.99
Columbus, OH (city) Franklin County	13.85
Lakewood, OH (city) Cuyahoga County	12.19
Cincinnati, OH (city) Hamilton County	9.48

Salvadorans with Income Below Poverty Level
Top 10 Places Sorted by Number

Place	Number
Columbus, OH (city) Franklin County	73
Cleveland, OH (city) Cuyahoga County	53

Salvadorans with Income Below Poverty Level
Top 10 Places Sorted by Percent

Place	Percent
Columbus, OH (city) Franklin County	18.07
Cleveland, OH (city) Cuyahoga County	11.86

South Americans with Income Below Poverty Level
Top 10 Places Sorted by Number

Place	Number
Columbus, OH (city) Franklin County	150
Cincinnati, OH (city) Hamilton County	118
Cleveland, OH (city) Cuyahoga County	56

South Americans with Income Below Poverty Level
Top 10 Places Sorted by Percent

Place	Percent
Cincinnati, OH (city) Hamilton County	24.95
Columbus, OH (city) Franklin County	14.88
Cleveland, OH (city) Cuyahoga County	10.41

Spaniards with Income Below Poverty Level
Top 10 Places Sorted by Number

Place	Number
No places met population threshold.	

Spaniards with Income Below Poverty Level
Top 10 Places Sorted by Percent

Place	Percent
No places met population threshold.	

Uruguayans with Income Below Poverty Level
Top 10 Places Sorted by Number

Place	Number
No places met population threshold.	

Uruguayans with Income Below Poverty Level
Top 10 Places Sorted by Percent

Place	Percent
No places met population threshold.	

Venezuelans with Income Below Poverty Level
Top 10 Places Sorted by Number

Place	Number
No places met population threshold.	

Venezuelans with Income Below Poverty Level
Top 10 Places Sorted by Percent

Place	Percent
No places met population threshold.	

Other Hispanics with Income Below Poverty Level
Top 10 Places Sorted by Number

Place	Number
Cleveland, OH (city) Cuyahoga County	982
Toledo, OH (city) Lucas County	713
Columbus, OH (city) Franklin County	448
Lorain, OH (city) Lorain County	379
Fremont, OH (city) Sandusky County	244
Cincinnati, OH (city) Hamilton County	217
Youngstown, OH (city) Mahoning County	166
Dayton, OH (city) Montgomery County	133
Akron, OH (city) Summit County	111

Notes: Please refer to the User's Guide for an explanation of data; tables include places with populations > 9,999 and reflect only those areas that meet Summary File 4 population thresholds, therefore there may be less than 10 places listed

Place	Number
Defiance, OH (city) Defiance County	24

Other Hispanics with Income Below Poverty Level
Top 10 Places Sorted by Percent

Place	Percent
Fremont, OH (city) Sandusky County	44.04
Youngstown, OH (city) Mahoning County	39.24
Cincinnati, OH (city) Hamilton County	32.10
Dayton, OH (city) Montgomery County	31.52
Cleveland, OH (city) Cuyahoga County	28.51
Lorain, OH (city) Lorain County	27.58
Toledo, OH (city) Lucas County	26.82
Akron, OH (city) Summit County	24.89
Columbus, OH (city) Franklin County	15.44
Defiance, OH (city) Defiance County	4.71

Homeownership

Total Populations Who Own Their Own Homes
Top 10 Places Sorted by Number

Place	Number
Columbus, OH (city) Franklin County	148,315
Cleveland, OH (city) Cuyahoga County	92,498
Toledo, OH (city) Lucas County	77,028
Cincinnati, OH (city) Hamilton County	57,655
Akron, OH (city) Summit County	53,441
Dayton, OH (city) Montgomery County	35,536
Parma, OH (city) Cuyahoga County	27,222
Youngstown, OH (city) Mahoning County	20,600
Canton, OH (city) Stark County	19,375
Kettering, OH (city) Montgomery County	17,082

Total Populations Who Own Their Own Homes
Top 10 Places Sorted by Percent

Place	Percent
Beavercreek, OH (city) Greene County	84.21
Maple Heights, OH (city) Cuyahoga County	83.82
Brook Park, OH (city) Cuyahoga County	83.61
Strongsville, OH (city) Cuyahoga County	82.73
Upper Arlington, OH (city) Franklin County	81.11
Brunswick, OH (city) Medina County	80.90
Garfield Heights, OH (city) Cuyahoga County	80.12
North Olmsted, OH (city) Cuyahoga County	79.71
Westerville, OH (city) Franklin County	79.01
Parma, OH (city) Cuyahoga County	77.50

Hispanics Who Own Their Own Homes
Top 10 Places Sorted by Number

Place	Number
Cleveland, OH (city) Cuyahoga County	4,272
Toledo, OH (city) Lucas County	2,422
Lorain, OH (city) Lorain County	2,129
Columbus, OH (city) Franklin County	1,419
Youngstown, OH (city) Mahoning County	737
Defiance, OH (city) Defiance County	372
Akron, OH (city) Summit County	354
Cincinnati, OH (city) Hamilton County	338
Fremont, OH (city) Sandusky County	280
Dayton, OH (city) Montgomery County	236

Hispanics Who Own Their Own Homes
Top 10 Places Sorted by Percent

Place	Percent
Beavercreek, OH (city) Greene County	84.76
Brook Park, OH (city) Cuyahoga County	84.62
Strongsville, OH (city) Cuyahoga County	76.58
Maple Heights, OH (city) Cuyahoga County	74.34
Perrysburg, OH (city) Wood County	73.79
Garfield Heights, OH (city) Cuyahoga County	73.33
Brunswick, OH (city) Medina County	67.86
Westlake, OH (city) Cuyahoga County	67.24
Fostoria, OH (city) Seneca County	63.04
Xenia, OH (city) Greene County	62.14

Argentinians Who Own Their Own Homes
Top 10 Places Sorted by Number

Place	Number

No places met population threshold.

Argentinians Who Own Their Own Homes
Top 10 Places Sorted by Percent

Place	Percent

No places met population threshold.

Bolivians Who Own Their Own Homes
Top 10 Places Sorted by Number

Place	Number

No places met population threshold.

Bolivians Who Own Their Own Homes
Top 10 Places Sorted by Percent

Place	Percent

No places met population threshold.

Central Americans Who Own Their Own Homes
Top 10 Places Sorted by Number

Place	Number
Cleveland, OH (city) Cuyahoga County	196
Columbus, OH (city) Franklin County	43
Cincinnati, OH (city) Hamilton County	6

Central Americans Who Own Their Own Homes
Top 10 Places Sorted by Percent

Place	Percent
Cleveland, OH (city) Cuyahoga County	44.75
Columbus, OH (city) Franklin County	17.62
Cincinnati, OH (city) Hamilton County	4.92

Chileans Who Own Their Own Homes
Top 10 Places Sorted by Number

Place	Number

No places met population threshold.

Chileans Who Own Their Own Homes
Top 10 Places Sorted by Percent

Place	Percent

No places met population threshold.

Colombians Who Own Their Own Homes
Top 10 Places Sorted by Number

Place	Number

No places met population threshold.

Colombians Who Own Their Own Homes
Top 10 Places Sorted by Percent

Place	Percent

No places met population threshold.

Costa Ricans Who Own Their Own Homes
Top 10 Places Sorted by Number

Place	Number

No places met population threshold.

Costa Ricans Who Own Their Own Homes
Top 10 Places Sorted by Percent

Place	Percent

No places met population threshold.

Cubans Who Own Their Own Homes
Top 10 Places Sorted by Number

Place	Number
Columbus, OH (city) Franklin County	12[illegible]
Cleveland, OH (city) Cuyahoga County	70

Cubans Who Own Their Own Homes
Top 10 Places Sorted by Percent

Place	Percent
Columbus, OH (city) Franklin County	57.40
Cleveland, OH (city) Cuyahoga County	41.92

Dominicans Who Own Their Own Homes
Top 10 Places Sorted by Number

Place	Number
Cleveland, OH (city) Cuyahoga County	85

Dominicans Who Own Their Own Homes
Top 10 Places Sorted by Percent

Place	Percent
Cleveland, OH (city) Cuyahoga County	34.69

Ecuadorians Who Own Their Own Homes
Top 10 Places Sorted by Number

Place	Number

No places met population threshold.

Ecuadorians Who Own Their Own Homes
Top 10 Places Sorted by Percent

Place	Percent

No places met population threshold.

Guatelmalans Who Own Their Own Homes
Top 10 Places Sorted by Number

Place	Number
Cleveland, OH (city) Cuyahoga County	39

Guatelmalans Who Own Their Own Homes
Top 10 Places Sorted by Percent

Place	Percent
Cleveland, OH (city) Cuyahoga County	33.05

Hondurans Who Own Their Own Homes
Top 10 Places Sorted by Number

Place	Number

No places met population threshold.

Hondurans Who Own Their Own Homes
Top 10 Places Sorted by Percent

Place	Percent

No places met population threshold.

Mexicans Who Own Their Own Homes
Top 10 Places Sorted by Number

Place	Number
Toledo, OH (city) Lucas County	1,849
Columbus, OH (city) Franklin County	516
Lorain, OH (city) Lorain County	481
Cleveland, OH (city) Cuyahoga County	426
Defiance, OH (city) Defiance County	254
Fremont, OH (city) Sandusky County	190
Fostoria, OH (city) Seneca County	168
Oregon, OH (city) Lucas County	134
Akron, OH (city) Summit County	123
Findlay, OH (city) Hancock County	100

Notes: Please refer to the User's Guide for an explanation of data; tables include places with populations > 9,999 and reflect only those areas that meet Summary File 4 population thresholds, therefore there may be less than 10 places listed

Mexicans Who Own Their Own Homes
Top 10 Places Sorted by Percent

Place	Percent
Lorain, OH (city) Lorain County	63.96
Fostoria, OH (city) Seneca County	61.31
Oregon, OH (city) Lucas County	60.91
Defiance, OH (city) Defiance County	55.82
Youngstown, OH (city) Mahoning County	55.19
Lakewood, OH (city) Cuyahoga County	52.94
Norwalk, OH (city) Huron County	52.04
Toledo, OH (city) Lucas County	51.45
Fremont, OH (city) Sandusky County	48.10
Sandusky, OH (city) Erie County	41.27

Nicaraguans Who Own Their Own Homes
Top 10 Places Sorted by Number

Place	Number
No places met population threshold.	

Nicaraguans Who Own Their Own Homes
Top 10 Places Sorted by Percent

Place	Percent
No places met population threshold.	

Panamanians Who Own Their Own Homes
Top 10 Places Sorted by Number

Place	Number
No places met population threshold.	

Panamanians Who Own Their Own Homes
Top 10 Places Sorted by Percent

Place	Percent
No places met population threshold.	

Paraguayans Who Own Their Own Homes
Top 10 Places Sorted by Number

Place	Number
No places met population threshold.	

Paraguayans Who Own Their Own Homes
Top 10 Places Sorted by Percent

Place	Percent
No places met population threshold.	

Peruvians Who Own Their Own Homes
Top 10 Places Sorted by Number

Place	Number
No places met population threshold.	

Peruvians Who Own Their Own Homes
Top 10 Places Sorted by Percent

Place	Percent
No places met population threshold.	

Puerto Ricans Who Own Their Own Homes
Top 10 Places Sorted by Number

Place	Number
Cleveland, OH (city) Cuyahoga County	2,987
Lorain, OH (city) Lorain County	1,483
Youngstown, OH (city) Mahoning County	590
Columbus, OH (city) Franklin County	284
Toledo, OH (city) Lucas County	122
Boardman, OH (cdp) Mahoning County	97
Parma, OH (city) Cuyahoga County	78
Akron, OH (city) Summit County	77
Cincinnati, OH (city) Hamilton County	63
Elyria, OH (city) Lorain County	50

Puerto Ricans Who Own Their Own Homes
Top 10 Places Sorted by Percent

Place	Percent
Youngstown, OH (city) Mahoning County	64.34
Boardman, OH (cdp) Mahoning County	59.88
Toledo, OH (city) Lucas County	48.61
Lorain, OH (city) Lorain County	46.93
Akron, OH (city) Summit County	42.31
Cleveland, OH (city) Cuyahoga County	40.39
Parma, OH (city) Cuyahoga County	38.05
Cincinnati, OH (city) Hamilton County	28.77
Columbus, OH (city) Franklin County	27.20
Elyria, OH (city) Lorain County	26.74

Salvadorans Who Own Their Own Homes
Top 10 Places Sorted by Number

Place	Number
Cleveland, OH (city) Cuyahoga County	80
Columbus, OH (city) Franklin County	19

Salvadorans Who Own Their Own Homes
Top 10 Places Sorted by Percent

Place	Percent
Cleveland, OH (city) Cuyahoga County	72.07
Columbus, OH (city) Franklin County	14.96

South Americans Who Own Their Own Homes
Top 10 Places Sorted by Number

Place	Number
Cleveland, OH (city) Cuyahoga County	118
Columbus, OH (city) Franklin County	115
Cincinnati, OH (city) Hamilton County	49

South Americans Who Own Their Own Homes
Top 10 Places Sorted by Percent

Place	Percent
Cleveland, OH (city) Cuyahoga County	45.56
Columbus, OH (city) Franklin County	32.49
Cincinnati, OH (city) Hamilton County	22.27

Spaniards Who Own Their Own Homes
Top 10 Places Sorted by Number

Place	Number
No places met population threshold.	

Spaniards Who Own Their Own Homes
Top 10 Places Sorted by Percent

Place	Percent
No places met population threshold.	

Uruguayans Who Own Their Own Homes
Top 10 Places Sorted by Number

Place	Number
No places met population threshold.	

Uruguayans Who Own Their Own Homes
Top 10 Places Sorted by Percent

Place	Percent
No places met population threshold.	

Venezuelans Who Own Their Own Homes
Top 10 Places Sorted by Number

Place	Number
No places met population threshold.	

Venezuelans Who Own Their Own Homes
Top 10 Places Sorted by Percent

Place	Percent
No places met population threshold.	

Other Hispanics Who Own Their Own Homes
Top 10 Places Sorted by Number

Place	Number
Cleveland, OH (city) Cuyahoga County	375
Toledo, OH (city) Lucas County	372
Columbus, OH (city) Franklin County	302
Akron, OH (city) Summit County	128
Lorain, OH (city) Lorain County	123
Cincinnati, OH (city) Hamilton County	96
Defiance, OH (city) Defiance County	79
Fremont, OH (city) Sandusky County	74
Dayton, OH (city) Montgomery County	57
Youngstown, OH (city) Mahoning County	53

Other Hispanics Who Own Their Own Homes
Top 10 Places Sorted by Percent

Place	Percent
Akron, OH (city) Summit County	60.09
Defiance, OH (city) Defiance County	57.66
Toledo, OH (city) Lucas County	50.47
Youngstown, OH (city) Mahoning County	48.62
Cleveland, OH (city) Cuyahoga County	45.79
Fremont, OH (city) Sandusky County	45.12
Lorain, OH (city) Lorain County	38.56
Columbus, OH (city) Franklin County	33.86
Cincinnati, OH (city) Hamilton County	30.09
Dayton, OH (city) Montgomery County	27.80

Median Gross Rent

All Specified Renter-Occupied Housing Units
Top 10 Places Sorted by Number

Place	Dollars/Month
Westlake, OH (city) Cuyahoga County	866
Beavercreek, OH (city) Greene County	821
Upper Arlington, OH (city) Franklin County	776
Fairfield, OH (city) Butler County	667
Brook Park, OH (city) Cuyahoga County	659
Reynoldsburg, OH (city) Franklin County	653
Huber Heights, OH (city) Montgomery County	651
Cleveland Heights, OH (city) Cuyahoga County	640
North Olmsted, OH (city) Cuyahoga County	634
Brunswick, OH (city) Medina County	630

Specified Housing Units Rented by Hispanics
Top 10 Places Sorted by Number

Place	Dollars/Month
Beavercreek, OH (city) Greene County	1,028
Westlake, OH (city) Cuyahoga County	775
Reynoldsburg, OH (city) Franklin County	699
Brunswick, OH (city) Medina County	681
Upper Arlington, OH (city) Franklin County	667
Fairfield, OH (city) Butler County	638
Parma, OH (city) Cuyahoga County	633
Huber Heights, OH (city) Montgomery County	619
North Olmsted, OH (city) Cuyahoga County	618
Parma Heights, OH (city) Cuyahoga County	600

Specified Housing Units Rented by Argentinians
Top 10 Places Sorted by Number

Place	Dollars/Month
No places met population threshold.	

Notes: Please refer to the User's Guide for an explanation of data; tables include places with populations > 9,999 and reflect only those areas that meet Summary File 4 population thresholds, therefore there may be less than 10 places listed

Specified Housing Units Rented by Bolivians
Top 10 Places Sorted by Number

Place	Dollars/Month

No places met population threshold.

Specified Housing Units Rented by Central Americans
Top 10 Places Sorted by Number

Place	Dollars/Month
Columbus, OH (city) Franklin County	599
Cleveland, OH (city) Cuyahoga County	486
Cincinnati, OH (city) Hamilton County	397

Specified Housing Units Rented by Chileans
Top 10 Places Sorted by Number

Place	Dollars/Month

No places met population threshold.

Specified Housing Units Rented by Colombians
Top 10 Places Sorted by Number

Place	Dollars/Month

No places met population threshold.

Specified Housing Units Rented by Costa Ricans
Top 10 Places Sorted by Number

Place	Dollars/Month

No places met population threshold.

Specified Housing Units Rented by Cubans
Top 10 Places Sorted by Number

Place	Dollars/Month
Columbus, OH (city) Franklin County	599
Cleveland, OH (city) Cuyahoga County	479

Specified Housing Units Rented by Dominicans
Top 10 Places Sorted by Number

Place	Dollars/Month
Cleveland, OH (city) Cuyahoga County	460

Specified Housing Units Rented by Ecuadorians
Top 10 Places Sorted by Number

Place	Dollars/Month

No places met population threshold.

Specified Housing Units Rented by Guatelmalans
Top 10 Places Sorted by Number

Place	Dollars/Month
Cleveland, OH (city) Cuyahoga County	498

Specified Housing Units Rented by Hondurans
Top 10 Places Sorted by Number

Place	Dollars/Month

No places met population threshold.

Specified Housing Units Rented by Mexicans
Top 10 Places Sorted by Number

Place	Dollars/Month
Painesville, OH (city) Lake County	599
Lakewood, OH (city) Cuyahoga County	590
Hamilton, OH (city) Butler County	572
Dayton, OH (city) Montgomery County	555
Columbus, OH (city) Franklin County	541
Bowling Green, OH (city) Wood County	538
Elyria, OH (city) Lorain County	538
Canton, OH (city) Stark County	531
Lorain, OH (city) Lorain County	531
Akron, OH (city) Summit County	508

Specified Housing Units Rented by Nicaraguans
Top 10 Places Sorted by Number

Place	Dollars/Month

No places met population threshold.

Specified Housing Units Rented by Panamanians
Top 10 Places Sorted by Number

Place	Dollars/Month

No places met population threshold.

Specified Housing Units Rented by Paraguayans
Top 10 Places Sorted by Number

Place	Dollars/Month

No places met population threshold.

Specified Housing Units Rented by Peruvians
Top 10 Places Sorted by Number

Place	Dollars/Month

No places met population threshold.

Specified Housing Units Rented by Puerto Ricans
Top 10 Places Sorted by Number

Place	Dollars/Month
Parma, OH (city) Cuyahoga County	620
Columbus, OH (city) Franklin County	571
Boardman, OH (cdp) Mahoning County	563
Lakewood, OH (city) Cuyahoga County	554
Cincinnati, OH (city) Hamilton County	544
Elyria, OH (city) Lorain County	490
Toledo, OH (city) Lucas County	482
Cleveland, OH (city) Cuyahoga County	467
Lorain, OH (city) Lorain County	452
Akron, OH (city) Summit County	448

Specified Housing Units Rented by Salvadorans
Top 10 Places Sorted by Number

Place	Dollars/Month
Columbus, OH (city) Franklin County	584
Cleveland, OH (city) Cuyahoga County	442

Specified Housing Units Rented by South Americans
Top 10 Places Sorted by Number

Place	Dollars/Month
Columbus, OH (city) Franklin County	623
Cleveland, OH (city) Cuyahoga County	578
Cincinnati, OH (city) Hamilton County	534

Specified Housing Units Rented by Spaniards
Top 10 Places Sorted by Number

Place	Dollars/Month

No places met population threshold.

Specified Housing Units Rented by Uruguayans
Top 10 Places Sorted by Number

Place	Dollars/Month

No places met population threshold.

Specified Housing Units Rented by Venezuelans
Top 10 Places Sorted by Number

Place	Dollars/Month

No places met population threshold.

Specified Housing Units Rented by Other Hispanics
Top 10 Places Sorted by Number

Place	Dollars/Month
Columbus, OH (city) Franklin County	580
Lorain, OH (city) Lorain County	525
Youngstown, OH (city) Mahoning County	524
Cincinnati, OH (city) Hamilton County	49
Akron, OH (city) Summit County	491
Defiance, OH (city) Defiance County	48
Cleveland, OH (city) Cuyahoga County	44
Toledo, OH (city) Lucas County	44
Fremont, OH (city) Sandusky County	42
Dayton, OH (city) Montgomery County	40

Median Home Value

All Specified Owner-Occupied Housing Units
Top 10 Places Sorted by Number

Place	Dollars
Upper Arlington, OH (city) Franklin County	214,70
Westlake, OH (city) Cuyahoga County	201,00
Strongsville, OH (city) Cuyahoga County	170,20
Westerville, OH (city) Franklin County	161,50
Perrysburg, OH (city) Wood County	158,70
Beavercreek, OH (city) Greene County	143,30
North Olmsted, OH (city) Cuyahoga County	142,30
Brunswick, OH (city) Medina County	136,00
Bowling Green, OH (city) Wood County	130,30
Fairfield, OH (city) Butler County	125,00

Specified Housing Units Owned and Occupied by Hispanics
Top 10 Places Sorted by Number

Place	Dollars
Upper Arlington, OH (city) Franklin County	186,50
Westerville, OH (city) Franklin County	180,00
Beavercreek, OH (city) Greene County	164,80
Westlake, OH (city) Cuyahoga County	161,90
Reynoldsburg, OH (city) Franklin County	160,20
Brunswick, OH (city) Medina County	158,00
Strongsville, OH (city) Cuyahoga County	148,80
North Olmsted, OH (city) Cuyahoga County	144,50
Huber Heights, OH (city) Montgomery County	140,00
Brooklyn, OH (city) Cuyahoga County	133,00

Specified Housing Units Owned and Occupied by Argentinians
Top 10 Places Sorted by Number

Place	Dollars

No places met population threshold.

Specified Housing Units Owned and Occupied by Bolivians
Top 10 Places Sorted by Number

Place	Dollars

No places met population threshold.

Specified Housing Units Owned and Occupied by Central Americans
Top 10 Places Sorted by Number

Place	Dollars
Columbus, OH (city) Franklin County	108,900
Cleveland, OH (city) Cuyahoga County	76,300
Cincinnati, OH (city) Hamilton County	55,000

Specified Housing Units Owned and Occupied by Chileans
Top 10 Places Sorted by Number

Place	Dollars

No places met population threshold.

Specified Housing Units Owned and Occupied by Colombians
Top 10 Places Sorted by Number

Place	Dollars

No places met population threshold.

Notes: Please refer to the User's Guide for an explanation of data; tables include places with populations > 9,999 and reflect only those areas that meet Summary File 4 population thresholds, therefore there may be less than 10 places listed

Specified Housing Units Owned and Occupied by Costa Ricans

Top 10 Places Sorted by Number

Place	Dollars
No places met population threshold.	

Specified Housing Units Owned and Occupied by Cubans

Top 10 Places Sorted by Number

Place	Dollars
Columbus, OH (city) Franklin County	112,500
Cleveland, OH (city) Cuyahoga County	81,900

Specified Housing Units Owned and Occupied by Dominicans

Top 10 Places Sorted by Number

Place	Dollars
Cleveland, OH (city) Cuyahoga County	62,900

Specified Housing Units Owned and Occupied by Ecuadorians

Top 10 Places Sorted by Number

Place	Dollars
No places met population threshold.	

Specified Housing Units Owned and Occupied by Guatelmalans

Top 10 Places Sorted by Number

Place	Dollars
Cleveland, OH (city) Cuyahoga County	79,500

Specified Housing Units Owned and Occupied by Hondurans

Top 10 Places Sorted by Number

Place	Dollars
No places met population threshold.	

Specified Housing Units Owned and Occupied by Mexicans

Top 10 Places Sorted by Number

Place	Dollars
Oregon, OH (city) Lucas County	115,800
Cincinnati, OH (city) Hamilton County	115,400
Lakewood, OH (city) Cuyahoga County	111,900
Bowling Green, OH (city) Wood County	104,400
Columbus, OH (city) Franklin County	101,800
Akron, OH (city) Summit County	99,300
Springfield, OH (city) Clark County	91,400
Elyria, OH (city) Lorain County	85,000
Lorain, OH (city) Lorain County	78,000
Norwalk, OH (city) Huron County	75,600

Specified Housing Units Owned and Occupied by Nicaraguans

Top 10 Places Sorted by Number

Place	Dollars
No places met population threshold.	

Specified Housing Units Owned and Occupied by Panamanians

Top 10 Places Sorted by Number

Place	Dollars
No places met population threshold.	

Specified Housing Units Owned and Occupied by Paraguayans

Top 10 Places Sorted by Number

Place	Dollars
No places met population threshold.	

Specified Housing Units Owned and Occupied by Peruvians

Top 10 Places Sorted by Number

Place	Dollars
No places met population threshold.	

Specified Housing Units Owned and Occupied by Puerto Ricans

Top 10 Places Sorted by Number

Place	Dollars
Columbus, OH (city) Franklin County	133,300
Parma, OH (city) Cuyahoga County	117,300
Lakewood, OH (city) Cuyahoga County	107,300
Cincinnati, OH (city) Hamilton County	106,000
Lorain, OH (city) Lorain County	79,900
Boardman, OH (cdp) Mahoning County	76,600
Toledo, OH (city) Lucas County	74,400
Cleveland, OH (city) Cuyahoga County	72,000
Akron, OH (city) Summit County	65,800
Elyria, OH (city) Lorain County	65,800

Specified Housing Units Owned and Occupied by Salvadorans

Top 10 Places Sorted by Number

Place	Dollars
Columbus, OH (city) Franklin County	112,500
Cleveland, OH (city) Cuyahoga County	68,600

Specified Housing Units Owned and Occupied by South Americans

Top 10 Places Sorted by Number

Place	Dollars
Cincinnati, OH (city) Hamilton County	344,400
Columbus, OH (city) Franklin County	133,900
Cleveland, OH (city) Cuyahoga County	104,700

Specified Housing Units Owned and Occupied by Spaniards

Top 10 Places Sorted by Number

Place	Dollars
No places met population threshold.	

Specified Housing Units Owned and Occupied by Uruguayans

Top 10 Places Sorted by Number

Place	Dollars
No places met population threshold.	

Specified Housing Units Owned and Occupied by Venezuelans

Top 10 Places Sorted by Number

Place	Dollars
No places met population threshold.	

Specified Housing Units Owned and Occupied by Other Hispanics

Top 10 Places Sorted by Number

Place	Dollars
Columbus, OH (city) Franklin County	100,800
Lorain, OH (city) Lorain County	96,700
Akron, OH (city) Summit County	89,200
Defiance, OH (city) Defiance County	82,300
Cincinnati, OH (city) Hamilton County	80,800
Cleveland, OH (city) Cuyahoga County	74,300
Dayton, OH (city) Montgomery County	63,200
Fremont, OH (city) Sandusky County	63,100
Toledo, OH (city) Lucas County	54,600
Youngstown, OH (city) Mahoning County	40,000

Notes: Please refer to the User's Guide for an explanation of data; tables include places with populations > 9,999 and reflect only those areas that meet Summary File 4 population thresholds, therefore there may be less than 10 places listed

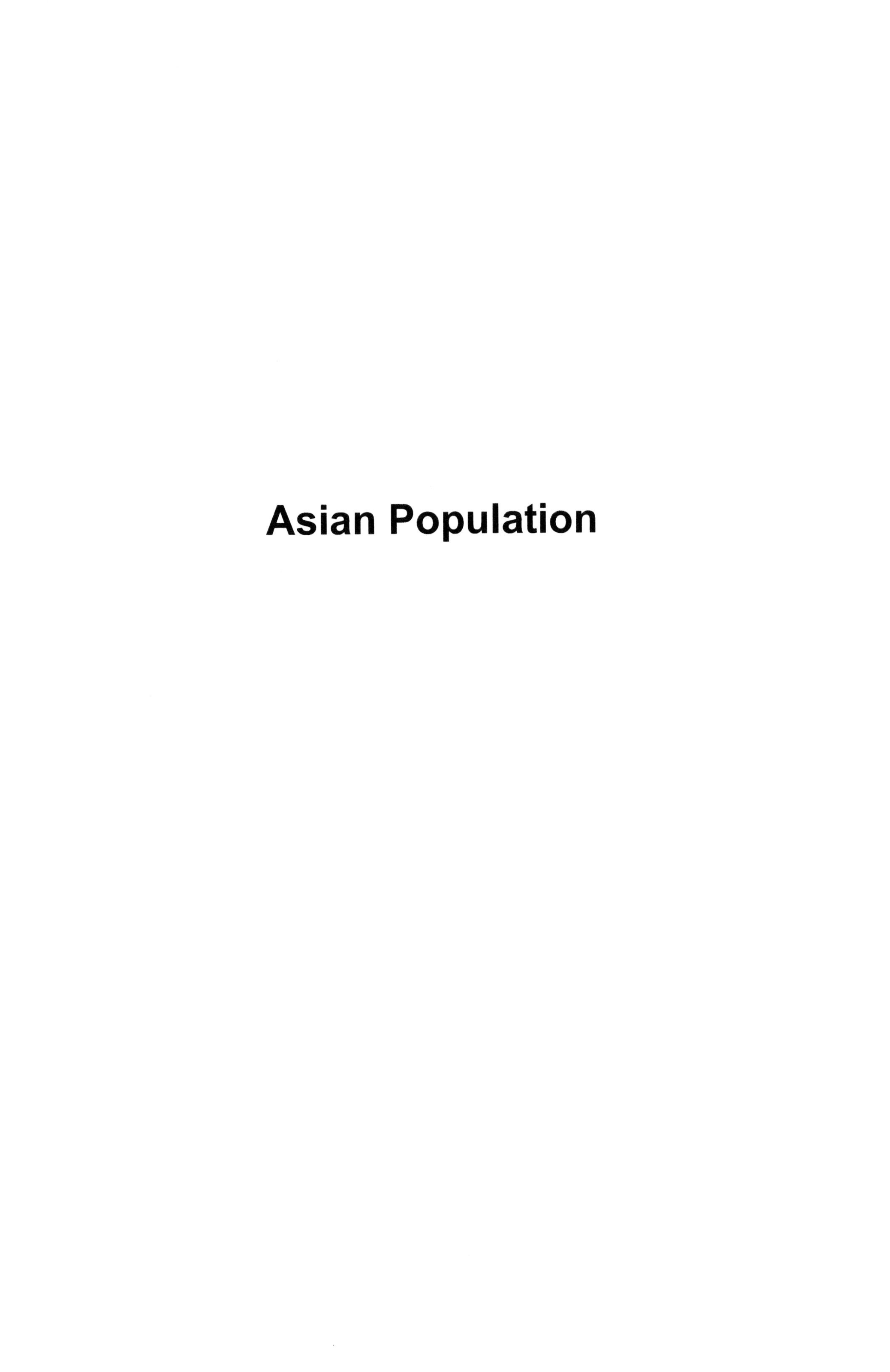

Asian Population

Population

Total Population
Top 10 Places Sorted by Number

Place	Number
Columbus, OH (city) Franklin County	711,644
Cleveland, OH (city) Cuyahoga County	478,393
Cincinnati, OH (city) Hamilton County	330,662
Toledo, OH (city) Lucas County	313,587
Akron, OH (city) Summit County	217,088
Dayton, OH (city) Montgomery County	166,193
Parma, OH (city) Cuyahoga County	85,655
Kettering, OH (city) Montgomery County	57,531
Lakewood, OH (city) Cuyahoga County	56,646
Mentor, OH (city) Lake County	50,278

Asian
Top 10 Places Sorted by Number

Place	Number
Columbus, OH (city) Franklin County	24,743
Cleveland, OH (city) Cuyahoga County	6,878
Cincinnati, OH (city) Hamilton County	4,962
Akron, OH (city) Summit County	3,148
Toledo, OH (city) Lucas County	2,994
Dublin, OH (city) Franklin County	2,497
Strongsville, OH (city) Cuyahoga County	1,470
Parma, OH (city) Cuyahoga County	1,410
Cleveland Heights, OH (city) Cuyahoga County	1,358
Westlake, OH (city) Cuyahoga County	1,354

Asian
Top 10 Places Sorted by Percent of Total Population

Place	Percent
Dublin, OH (city) Franklin County	7.93
Beckett Ridge, OH (cdp) Butler County	7.32
Blue Ash, OH (city) Hamilton County	7.04
Highland Heights, OH (city) Cuyahoga County	5.09
Kenwood, OH (cdp) Hamilton County	4.98
Solon, OH (city) Cuyahoga County	4.91
Richmond Heights, OH (city) Cuyahoga County	4.71
Westlake, OH (city) Cuyahoga County	4.25
Hilliard, OH (city) Franklin County	4.16
Athens, OH (city) Athens County	4.13

Native Hawaiian and Other Pacific Islander
Top 10 Places Sorted by Number

Place	Number
No places met population threshold.	

Native Hawaiian and Other Pacific Islander
Top 10 Places Sorted by Percent of Asian Population

Place	Percent
No places met population threshold.	

Native Hawaiian and Other Pacific Islander
Top 10 Places Sorted by Percent of Total Population

Place	Percent
No places met population threshold.	

Asian Indian
Top 10 Places Sorted by Number

Place	Number
Columbus, OH (city) Franklin County	6,413
Cincinnati, OH (city) Hamilton County	1,541
Cleveland, OH (city) Cuyahoga County	1,206
Toledo, OH (city) Lucas County	865
Strongsville, OH (city) Cuyahoga County	727
Dublin, OH (city) Franklin County	666
Parma, OH (city) Cuyahoga County	635
Akron, OH (city) Summit County	599
Cleveland Heights, OH (city) Cuyahoga County	553
Westlake, OH (city) Cuyahoga County	541

Asian Indian
Top 10 Places Sorted by Percent of Asian Population

Place	Percent
Sharonville, OH (city) Hamilton County	70.68
North Royalton, OH (city) Cuyahoga County	55.92
Strongsville, OH (city) Cuyahoga County	49.46
Mayfield Heights, OH (city) Cuyahoga County	48.62
North Olmsted, OH (city) Cuyahoga County	45.14
Blue Ash, OH (city) Hamilton County	45.10
Parma, OH (city) Cuyahoga County	45.04
Fairfield, OH (city) Butler County	44.41
Solon, OH (city) Cuyahoga County	43.93
Cleveland Heights, OH (city) Cuyahoga County	40.72

Asian Indian
Top 10 Places Sorted by Percent of Total Population

Place	Percent
Blue Ash, OH (city) Hamilton County	3.18
Sharonville, OH (city) Hamilton County	2.87
Solon, OH (city) Cuyahoga County	2.16
Dublin, OH (city) Franklin County	2.12
Mayfield Heights, OH (city) Cuyahoga County	2.00
Westlake, OH (city) Cuyahoga County	1.70
Strongsville, OH (city) Cuyahoga County	1.66
North Olmsted, OH (city) Cuyahoga County	1.25
Beavercreek, OH (city) Greene County	1.24
Cleveland Heights, OH (city) Cuyahoga County	1.11

Bangladeshi
Top 10 Places Sorted by Number

Place	Number
No places met population threshold.	

Bangladeshi
Top 10 Places Sorted by Percent of Asian Population

Place	Percent
No places met population threshold.	

Bangladeshi
Top 10 Places Sorted by Percent of Total Population

Place	Percent
No places met population threshold.	

Cambodian
Top 10 Places Sorted by Number

Place	Number
Columbus, OH (city) Franklin County	1,192

Cambodian
Top 10 Places Sorted by Percent of Asian Population

Place	Percent
Columbus, OH (city) Franklin County	4.82

Cambodian
Top 10 Places Sorted by Percent of Total Population

Place	Percent
Columbus, OH (city) Franklin County	0.17

Chinese (except Taiwanese)
Top 10 Places Sorted by Number

Place	Number
Columbus, OH (city) Franklin County	5,147
Cleveland, OH (city) Cuyahoga County	2,029
Cincinnati, OH (city) Hamilton County	1,322
Toledo, OH (city) Lucas County	774
Akron, OH (city) Summit County	535
Dublin, OH (city) Franklin County	510
Cleveland Heights, OH (city) Cuyahoga County	394
Hudson, OH (city) Summit County	359
Solon, OH (city) Cuyahoga County	346
Upper Arlington, OH (city) Franklin County	339

Chinese (except Taiwanese)
Top 10 Places Sorted by Percent of Asian Population

Place	Percent
Hudson, OH (city) Summit County	49.11
Upper Arlington, OH (city) Franklin County	33.43
Solon, OH (city) Cuyahoga County	32.34
Cleveland, OH (city) Cuyahoga County	29.50
Cleveland Heights, OH (city) Cuyahoga County	29.01
Cincinnati, OH (city) Hamilton County	26.64
Toledo, OH (city) Lucas County	25.85
Columbus, OH (city) Franklin County	20.80
Dublin, OH (city) Franklin County	20.42
Akron, OH (city) Summit County	16.99

Chinese (except Taiwanese)
Top 10 Places Sorted by Percent of Total Population

Place	Percent
Dublin, OH (city) Franklin County	1.62
Hudson, OH (city) Summit County	1.60
Solon, OH (city) Cuyahoga County	1.59
Upper Arlington, OH (city) Franklin County	1.01
Cleveland Heights, OH (city) Cuyahoga County	0.79
Columbus, OH (city) Franklin County	0.72
Cleveland, OH (city) Cuyahoga County	0.42
Cincinnati, OH (city) Hamilton County	0.40
Akron, OH (city) Summit County	0.25
Toledo, OH (city) Lucas County	0.25

Fijian
Top 10 Places Sorted by Number

Place	Number
No places met population threshold.	

Fijian
Top 10 Places Sorted by Percent of Asian Population

Place	Percent
No places met population threshold.	

Fijian
Top 10 Places Sorted by Percent of Total Population

Place	Percent
No places met population threshold.	

Filipino
Top 10 Places Sorted by Number

Place	Number
Columbus, OH (city) Franklin County	1,379
Cleveland, OH (city) Cuyahoga County	837
Cincinnati, OH (city) Hamilton County	480
Toledo, OH (city) Lucas County	372

Filipino
Top 10 Places Sorted by Percent of Asian Population

Place	Percent
Toledo, OH (city) Lucas County	12.42
Cleveland, OH (city) Cuyahoga County	12.17
Cincinnati, OH (city) Hamilton County	9.67
Columbus, OH (city) Franklin County	5.57

Filipino
Top 10 Places Sorted by Percent of Total Population

Place	Percent
Columbus, OH (city) Franklin County	0.19
Cleveland, OH (city) Cuyahoga County	0.17
Cincinnati, OH (city) Hamilton County	0.15
Toledo, OH (city) Lucas County	0.12

Guamanian or Chamorro
Top 10 Places Sorted by Number

Place	Number
No places met population threshold.	

Notes: Please refer to the User's Guide for an explanation of data; tables reflect only those areas that meet Summary File 4 population thresholds, therefore there may be less than 10 places listed

Guamanian or Chamorro
Top 10 Places Sorted by Percent of Asian Population

Place	Percent
No places met population threshold.	

Guamanian or Chamorro
Top 10 Places Sorted by Percent of Total Population

Place	Percent
No places met population threshold.	

Hawaiian, Native
Top 10 Places Sorted by Number

Place	Number
No places met population threshold.	

Hawaiian, Native
Top 10 Places Sorted by Percent of Asian Population

Place	Percent
No places met population threshold.	

Hawaiian, Native
Top 10 Places Sorted by Percent of Total Population

Place	Percent
No places met population threshold.	

Hmong
Top 10 Places Sorted by Number

Place	Number
No places met population threshold.	

Hmong
Top 10 Places Sorted by Percent of Asian Population

Place	Percent
No places met population threshold.	

Hmong
Top 10 Places Sorted by Percent of Total Population

Place	Percent
No places met population threshold.	

Indonesian
Top 10 Places Sorted by Number

Place	Number
Columbus, OH (city) Franklin County	514

Indonesian
Top 10 Places Sorted by Percent of Asian Population

Place	Percent
Columbus, OH (city) Franklin County	2.08

Indonesian
Top 10 Places Sorted by Percent of Total Population

Place	Percent
Columbus, OH (city) Franklin County	0.07

Japanese
Top 10 Places Sorted by Number

Place	Number
Columbus, OH (city) Franklin County	1,845
Dublin, OH (city) Franklin County	820

Japanese
Top 10 Places Sorted by Percent of Asian Population

Place	Percent
Dublin, OH (city) Franklin County	32.84
Columbus, OH (city) Franklin County	7.46

Japanese
Top 10 Places Sorted by Percent of Total Population

Place	Percent
Dublin, OH (city) Franklin County	2.60
Columbus, OH (city) Franklin County	0.26

Korean
Top 10 Places Sorted by Number

Place	Number
Columbus, OH (city) Franklin County	2,524

Korean
Top 10 Places Sorted by Percent of Asian Population

Place	Percent
Columbus, OH (city) Franklin County	10.20

Korean
Top 10 Places Sorted by Percent of Total Population

Place	Percent
Columbus, OH (city) Franklin County	0.35

Laotian
Top 10 Places Sorted by Number

Place	Number
Columbus, OH (city) Franklin County	979
Akron, OH (city) Summit County	572

Laotian
Top 10 Places Sorted by Percent of Asian Population

Place	Percent
Akron, OH (city) Summit County	18.17
Columbus, OH (city) Franklin County	3.96

Laotian
Top 10 Places Sorted by Percent of Total Population

Place	Percent
Akron, OH (city) Summit County	0.26
Columbus, OH (city) Franklin County	0.14

Malaysian
Top 10 Places Sorted by Number

Place	Number
No places met population threshold.	

Malaysian
Top 10 Places Sorted by Percent of Asian Population

Place	Percent
No places met population threshold.	

Malaysian
Top 10 Places Sorted by Percent of Total Population

Place	Percent
No places met population threshold.	

Pakistani
Top 10 Places Sorted by Number

Place	Number
No places met population threshold.	

Pakistani
Top 10 Places Sorted by Percent of Asian Population

Place	Percent
No places met population threshold.	

Pakistani
Top 10 Places Sorted by Percent of Total Population

Place	Percent
No places met population threshold.	

Samoan
Top 10 Places Sorted by Number

Place	Number
No places met population threshold.	

Samoan
Top 10 Places Sorted by Percent of Asian Population

Place	Percent
No places met population threshold.	

Samoan
Top 10 Places Sorted by Percent of Total Population

Place	Percent
No places met population threshold.	

Sri Lankan
Top 10 Places Sorted by Number

Place	Number
No places met population threshold.	

Sri Lankan
Top 10 Places Sorted by Percent of Asian Population

Place	Percent
No places met population threshold.	

Sri Lankan
Top 10 Places Sorted by Percent of Total Population

Place	Percent
No places met population threshold.	

Taiwanese
Top 10 Places Sorted by Number

Place	Number
Columbus, OH (city) Franklin County	463

Taiwanese
Top 10 Places Sorted by Percent of Asian Population

Place	Percent
Columbus, OH (city) Franklin County	1.87

Taiwanese
Top 10 Places Sorted by Percent of Total Population

Place	Percent
Columbus, OH (city) Franklin County	0.07

Thai
Top 10 Places Sorted by Number

Place	Number
Columbus, OH (city) Franklin County	389

Thai
Top 10 Places Sorted by Percent of Asian Population

Place	Percent
Columbus, OH (city) Franklin County	1.57

Thai
Top 10 Places Sorted by Percent of Total Population

Place	Percent
Columbus, OH (city) Franklin County	0.05

Notes: Please refer to the User's Guide for an explanation of data; tables reflect only those areas that meet Summary File 4 population thresholds, therefore there may be less than 10 places listed

Tongan
Top 10 Places Sorted by Number

Place	Number
No places met population threshold.	

Tongan
Top 10 Places Sorted by Percent of Asian Population

Place	Percent
No places met population threshold.	

Tongan
Top 10 Places Sorted by Percent of Total Population

Place	Percent
No places met population threshold.	

Vietnamese
Top 10 Places Sorted by Number

Place	Number
Columbus, OH (city) Franklin County	2,181
Cleveland, OH (city) Cuyahoga County	1,107
Akron, OH (city) Summit County	571

Vietnamese
Top 10 Places Sorted by Percent of Asian Population

Place	Percent
Akron, OH (city) Summit County	18.14
Cleveland, OH (city) Cuyahoga County	16.09
Columbus, OH (city) Franklin County	8.81

Vietnamese
Top 10 Places Sorted by Percent of Total Population

Place	Percent
Columbus, OH (city) Franklin County	0.31
Akron, OH (city) Summit County	0.26
Cleveland, OH (city) Cuyahoga County	0.23

Median Age

Total Population
Top 10 Places Sorted by Number

Place	Years
Beachwood, OH (city) Cuyahoga County	51.6
Kenwood, OH (cdp) Hamilton County	45.2
Worthington, OH (city) Franklin County	44.0
Mayfield Heights, OH (city) Cuyahoga County	43.9
Middleburg Heights, OH (city) Cuyahoga County	43.0
Upper Arlington, OH (city) Franklin County	42.5
Centerville, OH (city) Montgomery County	42.2
Highland Heights, OH (city) Cuyahoga County	42.2
Parma Heights, OH (city) Cuyahoga County	42.1
Westlake, OH (city) Cuyahoga County	41.9

Asian
Top 10 Places Sorted by Number

Place	Years
Westlake, OH (city) Cuyahoga County	43.2
Worthington, OH (city) Franklin County	40.6
Solon, OH (city) Cuyahoga County	39.7
Beavercreek, OH (city) Greene County	38.9
Highland Heights, OH (city) Cuyahoga County	38.6
Mentor, OH (city) Lake County	37.6
Westerville, OH (city) Franklin County	37.4
North Royalton, OH (city) Cuyahoga County	37.3
Hudson, OH (city) Summit County	37.0
Kenwood, OH (cdp) Hamilton County	36.7

Native Hawaiian and Other Pacific Islander
Top 10 Places Sorted by Number

Place	Years
No places met population threshold.	

Asian Indian
Top 10 Places Sorted by Number

Place	Years
Beavercreek, OH (city) Greene County	44.5
Westlake, OH (city) Cuyahoga County	41.2
Solon, OH (city) Cuyahoga County	41.0
North Royalton, OH (city) Cuyahoga County	32.5
North Olmsted, OH (city) Cuyahoga County	31.8
Strongsville, OH (city) Cuyahoga County	31.7
Fairfield, OH (city) Butler County	30.0
Parma, OH (city) Cuyahoga County	29.9
Mayfield Heights, OH (city) Cuyahoga County	29.8
Blue Ash, OH (city) Hamilton County	29.4

Bangladeshi
Top 10 Places Sorted by Number

Place	Years
No places met population threshold.	

Cambodian
Top 10 Places Sorted by Number

Place	Years
Columbus, OH (city) Franklin County	23.7

Chinese (except Taiwanese)
Top 10 Places Sorted by Number

Place	Years
Upper Arlington, OH (city) Franklin County	37.7
Solon, OH (city) Cuyahoga County	37.4
Hudson, OH (city) Summit County	35.8
Dublin, OH (city) Franklin County	35.1
Cleveland, OH (city) Cuyahoga County	32.1
Akron, OH (city) Summit County	31.7
Toledo, OH (city) Lucas County	31.5
Cincinnati, OH (city) Hamilton County	30.8
Columbus, OH (city) Franklin County	29.9
Cleveland Heights, OH (city) Cuyahoga County	28.2

Fijian
Top 10 Places Sorted by Number

Place	Years
No places met population threshold.	

Filipino
Top 10 Places Sorted by Number

Place	Years
Toledo, OH (city) Lucas County	37.1
Cleveland, OH (city) Cuyahoga County	35.5
Columbus, OH (city) Franklin County	33.6
Cincinnati, OH (city) Hamilton County	28.4

Guamanian or Chamorro
Top 10 Places Sorted by Number

Place	Years
No places met population threshold.	

Hawaiian, Native
Top 10 Places Sorted by Number

Place	Years
No places met population threshold.	

Hmong
Top 10 Places Sorted by Number

Place	Years
No places met population threshold.	

Indonesian
Top 10 Places Sorted by Number

Place	Years
Columbus, OH (city) Franklin County	21.9

Japanese
Top 10 Places Sorted by Number

Place	Years
Dublin, OH (city) Franklin County	33.4
Columbus, OH (city) Franklin County	30.3

Korean
Top 10 Places Sorted by Number

Place	Years
Columbus, OH (city) Franklin County	27.9

Laotian
Top 10 Places Sorted by Number

Place	Years
Columbus, OH (city) Franklin County	27.4
Akron, OH (city) Summit County	20.5

Malaysian
Top 10 Places Sorted by Number

Place	Years
No places met population threshold.	

Pakistani
Top 10 Places Sorted by Number

Place	Years
No places met population threshold.	

Samoan
Top 10 Places Sorted by Number

Place	Years
No places met population threshold.	

Sri Lankan
Top 10 Places Sorted by Number

Place	Years
No places met population threshold.	

Taiwanese
Top 10 Places Sorted by Number

Place	Years
Columbus, OH (city) Franklin County	26.9

Thai
Top 10 Places Sorted by Number

Place	Years
Columbus, OH (city) Franklin County	29.7

Tongan
Top 10 Places Sorted by Number

Place	Years
No places met population threshold.	

Vietnamese
Top 10 Places Sorted by Number

Place	Years
Cleveland, OH (city) Cuyahoga County	31.1
Columbus, OH (city) Franklin County	28.4
Akron, OH (city) Summit County	26.8

Average Household Size

Total Population
Top 10 Places Sorted by Number

Place	Number
Hudson, OH (city) Summit County	3.01
Highland Heights, OH (city) Cuyahoga County	2.90
Solon, OH (city) Cuyahoga County	2.88

Notes: Please refer to the User's Guide for an explanation of data; tables reflect only those areas that meet Summary File 4 population thresholds, therefore there may be less than 10 places listed

Beckett Ridge, OH (cdp) Butler County	2.80
Dublin, OH (city) Franklin County	2.80
Hilliard, OH (city) Franklin County	2.80
Brunswick, OH (city) Medina County	2.79
Mason, OH (city) Warren County	2.79
Gahanna, OH (city) Franklin County	2.70
Strongsville, OH (city) Cuyahoga County	2.69

Asian

Top 10 Places Sorted by Number

Place	Number
Beckett Ridge, OH (cdp) Butler County	4.27
Kenwood, OH (cdp) Hamilton County	4.26
North Royalton, OH (city) Cuyahoga County	3.76
Worthington, OH (city) Franklin County	3.68
Maple Heights, OH (city) Cuyahoga County	3.57
Hudson, OH (city) Summit County	3.54
Highland Heights, OH (city) Cuyahoga County	3.49
Twinsburg, OH (city) Summit County	3.47
Strongsville, OH (city) Cuyahoga County	3.46
Middleburg Heights, OH (city) Cuyahoga County	3.45

Native Hawaiian and Other Pacific Islander

Top 10 Places Sorted by Number

Place	Number
No places met population threshold.	

Asian Indian

Top 10 Places Sorted by Number

Place	Number
North Royalton, OH (city) Cuyahoga County	4.17
Strongsville, OH (city) Cuyahoga County	3.48
North Olmsted, OH (city) Cuyahoga County	3.21
Solon, OH (city) Cuyahoga County	3.21
Beavercreek, OH (city) Greene County	3.19
Dublin, OH (city) Franklin County	3.14
Blue Ash, OH (city) Hamilton County	3.12
Fairfield, OH (city) Butler County	2.73
Sharonville, OH (city) Hamilton County	2.73
Westlake, OH (city) Cuyahoga County	2.69

Bangladeshi

Top 10 Places Sorted by Number

Place	Number
No places met population threshold.	

Cambodian

Top 10 Places Sorted by Number

Place	Number
Columbus, OH (city) Franklin County	3.84

Chinese (except Taiwanese)

Top 10 Places Sorted by Number

Place	Number
Hudson, OH (city) Summit County	3.92
Dublin, OH (city) Franklin County	3.24
Solon, OH (city) Cuyahoga County	3.02
Upper Arlington, OH (city) Franklin County	2.59
Cleveland, OH (city) Cuyahoga County	2.47
Columbus, OH (city) Franklin County	2.30
Akron, OH (city) Summit County	2.28
Cincinnati, OH (city) Hamilton County	1.97
Toledo, OH (city) Lucas County	1.93
Cleveland Heights, OH (city) Cuyahoga County	1.81

Fijian

Top 10 Places Sorted by Number

Place	Number
No places met population threshold.	

Filipino

Top 10 Places Sorted by Number

Place	Number
Cleveland, OH (city) Cuyahoga County	2.87
Cincinnati, OH (city) Hamilton County	2.55
Toledo, OH (city) Lucas County	2.41
Columbus, OH (city) Franklin County	2.25

Guamanian or Chamorro

Top 10 Places Sorted by Number

Place	Number
No places met population threshold.	

Hawaiian, Native

Top 10 Places Sorted by Number

Place	Number
No places met population threshold.	

Hmong

Top 10 Places Sorted by Number

Place	Number
No places met population threshold.	

Indonesian

Top 10 Places Sorted by Number

Place	Number
Columbus, OH (city) Franklin County	2.04

Japanese

Top 10 Places Sorted by Number

Place	Number
Dublin, OH (city) Franklin County	3.20
Columbus, OH (city) Franklin County	2.17

Korean

Top 10 Places Sorted by Number

Place	Number
Columbus, OH (city) Franklin County	1.97

Laotian

Top 10 Places Sorted by Number

Place	Number
Akron, OH (city) Summit County	5.45
Columbus, OH (city) Franklin County	3.45

Malaysian

Top 10 Places Sorted by Number

Place	Number
No places met population threshold.	

Pakistani

Top 10 Places Sorted by Number

Place	Number
No places met population threshold.	

Samoan

Top 10 Places Sorted by Number

Place	Number
No places met population threshold.	

Sri Lankan

Top 10 Places Sorted by Number

Place	Number
No places met population threshold.	

Taiwanese

Top 10 Places Sorted by Number

Place	Number
Columbus, OH (city) Franklin County	2.1[illegible]

Thai

Top 10 Places Sorted by Number

Place	Number
Columbus, OH (city) Franklin County	2.9[illegible]

Tongan

Top 10 Places Sorted by Number

Place	Number
No places met population threshold.	

Vietnamese

Top 10 Places Sorted by Number

Place	Number
Akron, OH (city) Summit County	4.35
Cleveland, OH (city) Cuyahoga County	3.28
Columbus, OH (city) Franklin County	3.07

Language Spoken at Home: English Only

Total Population 5 Years and Over Who Speak English-Only at Home

Top 10 Places Sorted by Number

Place	Number
Columbus, OH (city) Franklin County	593,275
Cleveland, OH (city) Cuyahoga County	387,438
Cincinnati, OH (city) Hamilton County	286,454
Toledo, OH (city) Lucas County	269,728
Akron, OH (city) Summit County	189,917
Dayton, OH (city) Montgomery County	147,790
Parma, OH (city) Cuyahoga County	69,839
Kettering, OH (city) Montgomery County	51,686
Lakewood, OH (city) Cuyahoga County	46,390
Mentor, OH (city) Lake County	44,752

Total Population 5 Years and Over Who Speak English-Only at Home

Top 10 Places Sorted by Percent

Place	Percent
Dayton, OH (city) Montgomery County	95.64
Kettering, OH (city) Montgomery County	95.35
Westerville, OH (city) Franklin County	95.27
Cuyahoga Falls, OH (city) Summit County	95.23
Riverside, OH (city) Montgomery County	94.83
Sylvania, OH (city) Lucas County	94.71
Mentor, OH (city) Lake County	94.70
Findlay, OH (city) Hancock County	94.67
Reynoldsburg, OH (city) Franklin County	94.31
Mason, OH (city) Warren County	94.28

Asians 5 Years and Over Who Speak English-Only at Home

Top 10 Places Sorted by Number

Place	Number
Columbus, OH (city) Franklin County	3,508
Cincinnati, OH (city) Hamilton County	975
Cleveland, OH (city) Cuyahoga County	934
Toledo, OH (city) Lucas County	509
Akron, OH (city) Summit County	440
Cleveland Heights, OH (city) Cuyahoga County	344
Westlake, OH (city) Cuyahoga County	267
Dublin, OH (city) Franklin County	254
Kettering, OH (city) Montgomery County	240
Beavercreek, OH (city) Greene County	238

Notes: Please refer to the User's Guide for an explanation of data; tables reflect only those areas that meet Summary File 4 population thresholds, therefore there may be less than 10 places listed

Asians 5 Years and Over Who Speak English-Only at Home

Top 10 Places Sorted by Percent

Place	Percent
Reynoldsburg, OH (city) Franklin County	39.58
Sylvania, OH (city) Lucas County	37.30
Mentor, OH (city) Lake County	36.22
South Euclid, OH (city) Cuyahoga County	34.65
Highland Heights, OH (city) Cuyahoga County	33.50
Kettering, OH (city) Montgomery County	32.92
Oxford, OH (city) Butler County	29.19
Wooster, OH (city) Wayne County	28.72
Lakewood, OH (city) Cuyahoga County	28.57
Fairview Park, OH (city) Cuyahoga County	28.21

Native Hawaiian and Other Pacific Islanders 5 Years and Over Who Speak English-Only at Home

Top 10 Places Sorted by Number

Place	Number
No places met population threshold.	

Native Hawaiian and Other Pacific Islanders 5 Years and Over Who Speak English-Only at Home

Top 10 Places Sorted by Percent

Place	Percent
No places met population threshold.	

Asian Indians 5 Years and Over Who Speak English-Only at Home

Top 10 Places Sorted by Number

Place	Number
Columbus, OH (city) Franklin County	1,043
Cleveland, OH (city) Cuyahoga County	210
Toledo, OH (city) Lucas County	175
Cincinnati, OH (city) Hamilton County	174
Cleveland Heights, OH (city) Cuyahoga County	136
Westlake, OH (city) Cuyahoga County	134
Dublin, OH (city) Franklin County	117
Fairfield, OH (city) Butler County	107
Blue Ash, OH (city) Hamilton County	92
Beavercreek, OH (city) Greene County	87

Asian Indians 5 Years and Over Who Speak English-Only at Home

Top 10 Places Sorted by Percent

Place	Percent
Fairfield, OH (city) Butler County	25.85
Westlake, OH (city) Cuyahoga County	25.82
Cleveland Heights, OH (city) Cuyahoga County	25.76
Blue Ash, OH (city) Hamilton County	24.86
Toledo, OH (city) Lucas County	21.34
Dublin, OH (city) Franklin County	19.44
Beavercreek, OH (city) Greene County	19.29
Cleveland, OH (city) Cuyahoga County	18.55
Columbus, OH (city) Franklin County	17.64
Akron, OH (city) Summit County	13.87

Bangladeshis 5 Years and Over Who Speak English-Only at Home

Top 10 Places Sorted by Number

Place	Number
No places met population threshold.	

Bangladeshis 5 Years and Over Who Speak English-Only at Home

Top 10 Places Sorted by Percent

Place	Percent
No places met population threshold.	

Cambodians 5 Years and Over Who Speak English-Only at Home

Top 10 Places Sorted by Number

Place	Number
Columbus, OH (city) Franklin County	79

Cambodians 5 Years and Over Who Speak English-Only at Home

Top 10 Places Sorted by Percent

Place	Percent
Columbus, OH (city) Franklin County	7.41

Chinese (except Taiwanese) 5 Years and Over Who Speak English-Only at Home

Top 10 Places Sorted by Number

Place	Number
Columbus, OH (city) Franklin County	468
Cleveland, OH (city) Cuyahoga County	203
Cincinnati, OH (city) Hamilton County	186
Akron, OH (city) Summit County	86
Cleveland Heights, OH (city) Cuyahoga County	79
Toledo, OH (city) Lucas County	54
Solon, OH (city) Cuyahoga County	49
Hudson, OH (city) Summit County	30
Upper Arlington, OH (city) Franklin County	22
Dublin, OH (city) Franklin County	5

Chinese (except Taiwanese) 5 Years and Over Who Speak English-Only at Home

Top 10 Places Sorted by Percent

Place	Percent
Cleveland Heights, OH (city) Cuyahoga County	22.44
Akron, OH (city) Summit County	17.03
Cincinnati, OH (city) Hamilton County	15.53
Solon, OH (city) Cuyahoga County	15.51
Cleveland, OH (city) Cuyahoga County	11.10
Columbus, OH (city) Franklin County	9.66
Hudson, OH (city) Summit County	9.01
Toledo, OH (city) Lucas County	7.01
Upper Arlington, OH (city) Franklin County	6.98
Dublin, OH (city) Franklin County	1.14

Fijians 5 Years and Over Who Speak English-Only at Home

Top 10 Places Sorted by Number

Place	Number
No places met population threshold.	

Fijians 5 Years and Over Who Speak English-Only at Home

Top 10 Places Sorted by Percent

Place	Percent
No places met population threshold.	

Filipinos 5 Years and Over Who Speak English-Only at Home

Top 10 Places Sorted by Number

Place	Number
Columbus, OH (city) Franklin County	546
Cincinnati, OH (city) Hamilton County	214
Toledo, OH (city) Lucas County	143
Cleveland, OH (city) Cuyahoga County	134

Filipinos 5 Years and Over Who Speak English-Only at Home

Top 10 Places Sorted by Percent

Place	Percent
Cincinnati, OH (city) Hamilton County	47.03
Columbus, OH (city) Franklin County	41.52
Toledo, OH (city) Lucas County	40.74
Cleveland, OH (city) Cuyahoga County	17.59

Guamanians or Chamorros 5 Years and Over Who Speak English-Only at Home

Top 10 Places Sorted by Number

Place	Number
No places met population threshold.	

Guamanians or Chamorros 5 Years and Over Who Speak English-Only at Home

Top 10 Places Sorted by Percent

Place	Percent
No places met population threshold.	

Hawaiian Natives 5 Years and Over Who Speak English-Only at Home

Top 10 Places Sorted by Number

Place	Number
No places met population threshold.	

Hawaiian Natives 5 Years and Over Who Speak English-Only at Home

Top 10 Places Sorted by Percent

Place	Percent
No places met population threshold.	

Hmongs 5 Years and Over Who Speak English-Only at Home

Top 10 Places Sorted by Number

Place	Number
No places met population threshold.	

Hmongs 5 Years and Over Who Speak English-Only at Home

Top 10 Places Sorted by Percent

Place	Percent
No places met population threshold.	

Indonesians 5 Years and Over Who Speak English-Only at Home

Top 10 Places Sorted by Number

Place	Number
Columbus, OH (city) Franklin County	24

Indonesians 5 Years and Over Who Speak English-Only at Home

Top 10 Places Sorted by Percent

Place	Percent
Columbus, OH (city) Franklin County	4.79

Japanese 5 Years and Over Who Speak English-Only at Home

Top 10 Places Sorted by Number

Place	Number
Columbus, OH (city) Franklin County	340
Dublin, OH (city) Franklin County	31

Japanese 5 Years and Over Who Speak English-Only at Home

Top 10 Places Sorted by Percent

Place	Percent
Columbus, OH (city) Franklin County	20.04
Dublin, OH (city) Franklin County	4.30

Koreans 5 Years and Over Who Speak English-Only at Home

Top 10 Places Sorted by Number

Place	Number
Columbus, OH (city) Franklin County	519

Notes: Please refer to the User's Guide for an explanation of data; tables reflect only those areas that meet Summary File 4 population thresholds, therefore there may be less than 10 places listed

Koreans 5 Years and Over Who Speak English-Only at Home
Top 10 Places Sorted by Percent

Place	Percent
Columbus, OH (city) Franklin County	21.60

Laotians 5 Years and Over Who Speak English-Only at Home
Top 10 Places Sorted by Number

Place	Number
Akron, OH (city) Summit County	48
Columbus, OH (city) Franklin County	32

Laotians 5 Years and Over Who Speak English-Only at Home
Top 10 Places Sorted by Percent

Place	Percent
Akron, OH (city) Summit County	9.90
Columbus, OH (city) Franklin County	3.64

Malaysians 5 Years and Over Who Speak English-Only at Home
Top 10 Places Sorted by Number

Place	Number
No places met population threshold.	

Malaysians 5 Years and Over Who Speak English-Only at Home
Top 10 Places Sorted by Percent

Place	Percent
No places met population threshold.	

Pakistanis 5 Years and Over Who Speak English-Only at Home
Top 10 Places Sorted by Number

Place	Number
No places met population threshold.	

Pakistanis 5 Years and Over Who Speak English-Only at Home
Top 10 Places Sorted by Percent

Place	Percent
No places met population threshold.	

Samoans 5 Years and Over Who Speak English-Only at Home
Top 10 Places Sorted by Number

Place	Number
No places met population threshold.	

Samoans 5 Years and Over Who Speak English-Only at Home
Top 10 Places Sorted by Percent

Place	Percent
No places met population threshold.	

Sri Lankans 5 Years and Over Who Speak English-Only at Home
Top 10 Places Sorted by Number

Place	Number
No places met population threshold.	

Sri Lankans 5 Years and Over Who Speak English-Only at Home
Top 10 Places Sorted by Percent

Place	Percent
No places met population threshold.	

Taiwanese 5 Years and Over Who Speak English-Only at Home
Top 10 Places Sorted by Number

Place	Number
Columbus, OH (city) Franklin County	16

Taiwanese 5 Years and Over Who Speak English-Only at Home
Top 10 Places Sorted by Percent

Place	Percent
Columbus, OH (city) Franklin County	3.48

Thais 5 Years and Over Who Speak English-Only at Home
Top 10 Places Sorted by Number

Place	Number
Columbus, OH (city) Franklin County	38

Thais 5 Years and Over Who Speak English-Only at Home
Top 10 Places Sorted by Percent

Place	Percent
Columbus, OH (city) Franklin County	10.30

Tongans 5 Years and Over Who Speak English-Only at Home
Top 10 Places Sorted by Number

Place	Number
No places met population threshold.	

Tongans 5 Years and Over Who Speak English-Only at Home
Top 10 Places Sorted by Percent

Place	Percent
No places met population threshold.	

Vietnamese 5 Years and Over Who Speak English-Only at Home
Top 10 Places Sorted by Number

Place	Number
Columbus, OH (city) Franklin County	226
Cleveland, OH (city) Cuyahoga County	99
Akron, OH (city) Summit County	25

Vietnamese 5 Years and Over Who Speak English-Only at Home
Top 10 Places Sorted by Percent

Place	Percent
Columbus, OH (city) Franklin County	11.35
Cleveland, OH (city) Cuyahoga County	9.86
Akron, OH (city) Summit County	4.79

Foreign Born

Total Population
Top 10 Places Sorted by Number

Place	Number
Columbus, OH (city) Franklin County	47,713
Cleveland, OH (city) Cuyahoga County	21,372
Cincinnati, OH (city) Hamilton County	12,461
Toledo, OH (city) Lucas County	9,475
Parma, OH (city) Cuyahoga County	7,797
Akron, OH (city) Summit County	6,911
Lakewood, OH (city) Cuyahoga County	4,945
Cleveland Heights, OH (city) Cuyahoga County	4,130
Mayfield Heights, OH (city) Cuyahoga County	3,506
Dayton, OH (city) Montgomery County	3,245

Total Population
Top 10 Places Sorted by Percent

Place	Percent
Mayfield Heights, OH (city) Cuyahoga County	18.0
Richmond Heights, OH (city) Cuyahoga County	17.3
Beachwood, OH (city) Cuyahoga County	15.4
Highland Heights, OH (city) Cuyahoga County	11.1
Parma Heights, OH (city) Cuyahoga County	10.1
Blue Ash, OH (city) Hamilton County	9.9
South Euclid, OH (city) Cuyahoga County	9.4
Dublin, OH (city) Franklin County	9.1
Parma, OH (city) Cuyahoga County	9.1
Kenwood, OH (cdp) Hamilton County	9.0

Asian
Top 10 Places Sorted by Number

Place	Number
Columbus, OH (city) Franklin County	19,18
Cleveland, OH (city) Cuyahoga County	4,99
Cincinnati, OH (city) Hamilton County	3,80
Akron, OH (city) Summit County	2,43
Toledo, OH (city) Lucas County	2,37
Dublin, OH (city) Franklin County	1,91
Parma, OH (city) Cuyahoga County	1,11
Strongsville, OH (city) Cuyahoga County	1,05
Cleveland Heights, OH (city) Cuyahoga County	99
Westlake, OH (city) Cuyahoga County	99

Asian
Top 10 Places Sorted by Percent

Place	Percent
Fairborn, OH (city) Greene County	91.55
Findlay, OH (city) Hancock County	87.35
Sharonville, OH (city) Hamilton County	87.23
Bowling Green, OH (city) Wood County	86.39
Forest Park, OH (city) Hamilton County	84.33
Stow, OH (city) Summit County	82.60
Garfield Heights, OH (city) Cuyahoga County	82.25
Blue Ash, OH (city) Hamilton County	80.96
Maple Heights, OH (city) Cuyahoga County	80.91
Beachwood, OH (city) Cuyahoga County	80.90

Native Hawaiian and Other Pacific Islander
Top 10 Places Sorted by Number

Place	Number
No places met population threshold.	

Native Hawaiian and Other Pacific Islander
Top 10 Places Sorted by Percent

Place	Percent
No places met population threshold.	

Asian Indian
Top 10 Places Sorted by Number

Place	Number
Columbus, OH (city) Franklin County	5,131
Cincinnati, OH (city) Hamilton County	1,392
Cleveland, OH (city) Cuyahoga County	814
Toledo, OH (city) Lucas County	684
Parma, OH (city) Cuyahoga County	566
Strongsville, OH (city) Cuyahoga County	546
Dublin, OH (city) Franklin County	518
Akron, OH (city) Summit County	498
Cleveland Heights, OH (city) Cuyahoga County	430
Westlake, OH (city) Cuyahoga County	407

Asian Indian
Top 10 Places Sorted by Percent

Place	Percent
Sharonville, OH (city) Hamilton County	92.37
Cincinnati, OH (city) Hamilton County	90.33
Parma, OH (city) Cuyahoga County	89.13

Notes: Please refer to the User's Guide for an explanation of data; tables reflect only those areas that meet Summary File 4 population thresholds, therefore there may be less than 10 places listed

Place	Percent
Blue Ash, OH (city) Hamilton County	84.69
Akron, OH (city) Summit County	83.14
Mayfield Heights, OH (city) Cuyahoga County	82.22
Columbus, OH (city) Franklin County	80.01
Toledo, OH (city) Lucas County	79.08
Dublin, OH (city) Franklin County	77.78
Cleveland Heights, OH (city) Cuyahoga County	77.76

Bangladeshi
Top 10 Places Sorted by Number

Place	Number

No places met population threshold.

Bangladeshi
Top 10 Places Sorted by Percent

Place	Percent

No places met population threshold.

Cambodian
Top 10 Places Sorted by Number

Place	Number
Columbus, OH (city) Franklin County	783

Cambodian
Top 10 Places Sorted by Percent

Place	Percent
Columbus, OH (city) Franklin County	65.69

Chinese (except Taiwanese)
Top 10 Places Sorted by Number

Place	Number
Columbus, OH (city) Franklin County	4,168
Cleveland, OH (city) Cuyahoga County	1,516
Cincinnati, OH (city) Hamilton County	1,061
Toledo, OH (city) Lucas County	704
Akron, OH (city) Summit County	433
Dublin, OH (city) Franklin County	340
Upper Arlington, OH (city) Franklin County	270
Cleveland Heights, OH (city) Cuyahoga County	266
Solon, OH (city) Cuyahoga County	247
Hudson, OH (city) Summit County	227

Chinese (except Taiwanese)
Top 10 Places Sorted by Percent

Place	Percent
Toledo, OH (city) Lucas County	90.96
Columbus, OH (city) Franklin County	80.98
Akron, OH (city) Summit County	80.93
Cincinnati, OH (city) Hamilton County	80.26
Upper Arlington, OH (city) Franklin County	79.65
Cleveland, OH (city) Cuyahoga County	74.72
Solon, OH (city) Cuyahoga County	71.39
Cleveland Heights, OH (city) Cuyahoga County	67.51
Dublin, OH (city) Franklin County	66.67
Hudson, OH (city) Summit County	63.23

Fijian
Top 10 Places Sorted by Number

Place	Number

No places met population threshold.

Fijian
Top 10 Places Sorted by Percent

Place	Percent

No places met population threshold.

Filipino
Top 10 Places Sorted by Number

Place	Number
Columbus, OH (city) Franklin County	787
Cleveland, OH (city) Cuyahoga County	623
Toledo, OH (city) Lucas County	262
Cincinnati, OH (city) Hamilton County	233

Filipino
Top 10 Places Sorted by Percent

Place	Percent
Cleveland, OH (city) Cuyahoga County	74.43
Toledo, OH (city) Lucas County	70.43
Columbus, OH (city) Franklin County	57.07
Cincinnati, OH (city) Hamilton County	48.54

Guamanian or Chamorro
Top 10 Places Sorted by Number

Place	Number

No places met population threshold.

Guamanian or Chamorro
Top 10 Places Sorted by Percent

Place	Percent

No places met population threshold.

Hawaiian, Native
Top 10 Places Sorted by Number

Place	Number

No places met population threshold.

Hawaiian, Native
Top 10 Places Sorted by Percent

Place	Percent

No places met population threshold.

Hmong
Top 10 Places Sorted by Number

Place	Number

No places met population threshold.

Hmong
Top 10 Places Sorted by Percent

Place	Percent

No places met population threshold.

Indonesian
Top 10 Places Sorted by Number

Place	Number
Columbus, OH (city) Franklin County	501

Indonesian
Top 10 Places Sorted by Percent

Place	Percent
Columbus, OH (city) Franklin County	97.47

Japanese
Top 10 Places Sorted by Number

Place	Number
Columbus, OH (city) Franklin County	1,395
Dublin, OH (city) Franklin County	715

Japanese
Top 10 Places Sorted by Percent

Place	Percent
Dublin, OH (city) Franklin County	87.20
Columbus, OH (city) Franklin County	75.61

Korean
Top 10 Places Sorted by Number

Place	Number
Columbus, OH (city) Franklin County	2,019

Korean
Top 10 Places Sorted by Percent

Place	Percent
Columbus, OH (city) Franklin County	79.99

Laotian
Top 10 Places Sorted by Number

Place	Number
Columbus, OH (city) Franklin County	692
Akron, OH (city) Summit County	363

Laotian
Top 10 Places Sorted by Percent

Place	Percent
Columbus, OH (city) Franklin County	70.68
Akron, OH (city) Summit County	63.46

Malaysian
Top 10 Places Sorted by Number

Place	Number

No places met population threshold.

Malaysian
Top 10 Places Sorted by Percent

Place	Percent

No places met population threshold.

Pakistani
Top 10 Places Sorted by Number

Place	Number

No places met population threshold.

Pakistani
Top 10 Places Sorted by Percent

Place	Percent

No places met population threshold.

Samoan
Top 10 Places Sorted by Number

Place	Number

No places met population threshold.

Samoan
Top 10 Places Sorted by Percent

Place	Percent

No places met population threshold.

Sri Lankan
Top 10 Places Sorted by Number

Place	Number

No places met population threshold.

Sri Lankan
Top 10 Places Sorted by Percent

Place	Percent

No places met population threshold.

Taiwanese
Top 10 Places Sorted by Number

Place	Number
Columbus, OH (city) Franklin County	406

Taiwanese
Top 10 Places Sorted by Percent

Place	Percent
Columbus, OH (city) Franklin County	87.69

Notes: Please refer to the User's Guide for an explanation of data; tables reflect only those areas that meet Summary File 4 population thresholds, therefore there may be less than 10 places listed

Thai

Top 10 Places Sorted by Number

Place	Number
Columbus, OH (city) Franklin County	327

Thai

Top 10 Places Sorted by Percent

Place	Percent
Columbus, OH (city) Franklin County	84.06

Tongan

Top 10 Places Sorted by Number

Place	Number

No places met population threshold.

Tongan

Top 10 Places Sorted by Percent

Place	Percent

No places met population threshold.

Vietnamese

Top 10 Places Sorted by Number

Place	Number
Columbus, OH (city) Franklin County	1,740
Cleveland, OH (city) Cuyahoga County	758
Akron, OH (city) Summit County	468

Vietnamese

Top 10 Places Sorted by Percent

Place	Percent
Akron, OH (city) Summit County	81.96
Columbus, OH (city) Franklin County	79.78
Cleveland, OH (city) Cuyahoga County	68.47

Foreign-Born Naturalized Citizens

Total Population

Top 10 Places Sorted by Number

Place	Number
Columbus, OH (city) Franklin County	14,197
Cleveland, OH (city) Cuyahoga County	9,755
Parma, OH (city) Cuyahoga County	4,567
Toledo, OH (city) Lucas County	4,487
Cincinnati, OH (city) Hamilton County	4,139
Akron, OH (city) Summit County	3,181
Lakewood, OH (city) Cuyahoga County	2,603
Cleveland Heights, OH (city) Cuyahoga County	1,926
Westlake, OH (city) Cuyahoga County	1,905
Strongsville, OH (city) Cuyahoga County	1,760

Total Population

Top 10 Places Sorted by Percent

Place	Percent
Beachwood, OH (city) Cuyahoga County	10.35
Richmond Heights, OH (city) Cuyahoga County	9.59
Mayfield Heights, OH (city) Cuyahoga County	8.77
Highland Heights, OH (city) Cuyahoga County	7.76
Middleburg Heights, OH (city) Cuyahoga County	6.54
South Euclid, OH (city) Cuyahoga County	6.20
Westlake, OH (city) Cuyahoga County	5.98
Solon, OH (city) Cuyahoga County	5.44
Parma Heights, OH (city) Cuyahoga County	5.38
Parma, OH (city) Cuyahoga County	5.33

Asian

Top 10 Places Sorted by Number

Place	Number
Columbus, OH (city) Franklin County	5,679
Cleveland, OH (city) Cuyahoga County	1,852
Cincinnati, OH (city) Hamilton County	981
Toledo, OH (city) Lucas County	764
Akron, OH (city) Summit County	712
Westlake, OH (city) Cuyahoga County	665
Strongsville, OH (city) Cuyahoga County	645
Beavercreek, OH (city) Greene County	639
Dublin, OH (city) Franklin County	528
Parma, OH (city) Cuyahoga County	471

Asian

Top 10 Places Sorted by Percent

Place	Percent
Garfield Heights, OH (city) Cuyahoga County	52.48
Beavercreek, OH (city) Greene County	52.12
Brunswick, OH (city) Medina County	50.14
Westlake, OH (city) Cuyahoga County	49.11
Huber Heights, OH (city) Montgomery County	45.72
Maple Heights, OH (city) Cuyahoga County	45.34
Riverside, OH (city) Montgomery County	45.29
Strongsville, OH (city) Cuyahoga County	43.88
Beckett Ridge, OH (cdp) Butler County	43.53
Solon, OH (city) Cuyahoga County	43.46

Native Hawaiian and Other Pacific Islander

Top 10 Places Sorted by Number

Place	Number

No places met population threshold.

Native Hawaiian and Other Pacific Islander

Top 10 Places Sorted by Percent

Place	Percent

No places met population threshold.

Asian Indian

Top 10 Places Sorted by Number

Place	Number
Columbus, OH (city) Franklin County	1,102
Strongsville, OH (city) Cuyahoga County	322
Cincinnati, OH (city) Hamilton County	264
Westlake, OH (city) Cuyahoga County	258
Beavercreek, OH (city) Greene County	255
Solon, OH (city) Cuyahoga County	229
Parma, OH (city) Cuyahoga County	189
Cleveland, OH (city) Cuyahoga County	188
Cleveland Heights, OH (city) Cuyahoga County	176
North Olmsted, OH (city) Cuyahoga County	159

Asian Indian

Top 10 Places Sorted by Percent

Place	Percent
Beavercreek, OH (city) Greene County	53.80
Solon, OH (city) Cuyahoga County	48.72
Westlake, OH (city) Cuyahoga County	47.69
Strongsville, OH (city) Cuyahoga County	44.29
North Olmsted, OH (city) Cuyahoga County	37.24
Cleveland Heights, OH (city) Cuyahoga County	31.83
Parma, OH (city) Cuyahoga County	29.76
North Royalton, OH (city) Cuyahoga County	27.36
Fairfield, OH (city) Butler County	25.41
Dublin, OH (city) Franklin County	23.12

Bangladeshi

Top 10 Places Sorted by Number

Place	Number

No places met population threshold.

Bangladeshi

Top 10 Places Sorted by Percent

Place	Percent

No places met population threshold.

Cambodian

Top 10 Places Sorted by Number

Place	Number
Columbus, OH (city) Franklin County	32[illegible]

Cambodian

Top 10 Places Sorted by Percent

Place	Percent
Columbus, OH (city) Franklin County	27.0[illegible]

Chinese (except Taiwanese)

Top 10 Places Sorted by Number

Place	Number
Columbus, OH (city) Franklin County	1,15[illegible]
Cleveland, OH (city) Cuyahoga County	49[illegible]
Cincinnati, OH (city) Hamilton County	18[illegible]
Dublin, OH (city) Franklin County	17[illegible]
Toledo, OH (city) Lucas County	14[illegible]
Solon, OH (city) Cuyahoga County	13[illegible]
Upper Arlington, OH (city) Franklin County	10[illegible]
Hudson, OH (city) Summit County	10[illegible]
Cleveland Heights, OH (city) Cuyahoga County	10[illegible]
Akron, OH (city) Summit County	3[illegible]

Chinese (except Taiwanese)

Top 10 Places Sorted by Percent

Place	Percent
Solon, OH (city) Cuyahoga County	37.5[illegible]
Dublin, OH (city) Franklin County	33.5[illegible]
Upper Arlington, OH (city) Franklin County	30.6[illegible]
Hudson, OH (city) Summit County	28.4[illegible]
Cleveland Heights, OH (city) Cuyahoga County	25.3[illegible]
Cleveland, OH (city) Cuyahoga County	24.4[illegible]
Columbus, OH (city) Franklin County	22.4[illegible]
Toledo, OH (city) Lucas County	18.7[illegible]
Cincinnati, OH (city) Hamilton County	13.6[illegible]
Akron, OH (city) Summit County	7.2[illegible]

Fijian

Top 10 Places Sorted by Number

Place	Number

No places met population threshold.

Fijian

Top 10 Places Sorted by Percent

Place	Percent

No places met population threshold.

Filipino

Top 10 Places Sorted by Number

Place	Number
Columbus, OH (city) Franklin County	521
Cleveland, OH (city) Cuyahoga County	284
Toledo, OH (city) Lucas County	189
Cincinnati, OH (city) Hamilton County	123

Filipino

Top 10 Places Sorted by Percent

Place	Percent
Toledo, OH (city) Lucas County	50.81
Columbus, OH (city) Franklin County	37.78
Cleveland, OH (city) Cuyahoga County	33.93
Cincinnati, OH (city) Hamilton County	25.62

Guamanian or Chamorro

Top 10 Places Sorted by Number

Place	Number

No places met population threshold.

Notes: Please refer to the User's Guide for an explanation of data; tables reflect only those areas that meet Summary File 4 population thresholds, therefore there may be less than 10 places listed

Guamanian or Chamorro
Top 10 Places Sorted by Percent

Place	Percent
No places met population threshold.	

Hawaiian, Native
Top 10 Places Sorted by Number

Place	Number
No places met population threshold.	

Hawaiian, Native
Top 10 Places Sorted by Percent

Place	Percent
No places met population threshold.	

Hmong
Top 10 Places Sorted by Number

Place	Number
No places met population threshold.	

Hmong
Top 10 Places Sorted by Percent

Place	Percent
No places met population threshold.	

Indonesian
Top 10 Places Sorted by Number

Place	Number
Columbus, OH (city) Franklin County	0

Indonesian
Top 10 Places Sorted by Percent

Place	Percent
Columbus, OH (city) Franklin County	0.00

Japanese
Top 10 Places Sorted by Number

Place	Number
Columbus, OH (city) Franklin County	107
Dublin, OH (city) Franklin County	10

Japanese
Top 10 Places Sorted by Percent

Place	Percent
Columbus, OH (city) Franklin County	5.80
Dublin, OH (city) Franklin County	1.22

Korean
Top 10 Places Sorted by Number

Place	Number
Columbus, OH (city) Franklin County	634

Korean
Top 10 Places Sorted by Percent

Place	Percent
Columbus, OH (city) Franklin County	25.12

Laotian
Top 10 Places Sorted by Number

Place	Number
Columbus, OH (city) Franklin County	404
Akron, OH (city) Summit County	151

Laotian
Top 10 Places Sorted by Percent

Place	Percent
Columbus, OH (city) Franklin County	41.27
Akron, OH (city) Summit County	26.40

Malaysian
Top 10 Places Sorted by Number

Place	Number
No places met population threshold.	

Malaysian
Top 10 Places Sorted by Percent

Place	Percent
No places met population threshold.	

Pakistani
Top 10 Places Sorted by Number

Place	Number
No places met population threshold.	

Pakistani
Top 10 Places Sorted by Percent

Place	Percent
No places met population threshold.	

Samoan
Top 10 Places Sorted by Number

Place	Number
No places met population threshold.	

Samoan
Top 10 Places Sorted by Percent

Place	Percent
No places met population threshold.	

Sri Lankan
Top 10 Places Sorted by Number

Place	Number
No places met population threshold.	

Sri Lankan
Top 10 Places Sorted by Percent

Place	Percent
No places met population threshold.	

Taiwanese
Top 10 Places Sorted by Number

Place	Number
Columbus, OH (city) Franklin County	123

Taiwanese
Top 10 Places Sorted by Percent

Place	Percent
Columbus, OH (city) Franklin County	26.57

Thai
Top 10 Places Sorted by Number

Place	Number
Columbus, OH (city) Franklin County	65

Thai
Top 10 Places Sorted by Percent

Place	Percent
Columbus, OH (city) Franklin County	16.71

Tongan
Top 10 Places Sorted by Number

Place	Number
No places met population threshold.	

Tongan
Top 10 Places Sorted by Percent

Place	Percent
No places met population threshold.	

Vietnamese
Top 10 Places Sorted by Number

Place	Number
Columbus, OH (city) Franklin County	891
Cleveland, OH (city) Cuyahoga County	418
Akron, OH (city) Summit County	183

Vietnamese
Top 10 Places Sorted by Percent

Place	Percent
Columbus, OH (city) Franklin County	40.85
Cleveland, OH (city) Cuyahoga County	37.76
Akron, OH (city) Summit County	32.05

Educational Attainment: H.S. Graduates

Total Populations 25 Years and Over Who are High School Graduates
Top 10 Places Sorted by Number

Place	Number
Columbus, OH (city) Franklin County	369,376
Cleveland, OH (city) Cuyahoga County	204,829
Cincinnati, OH (city) Hamilton County	159,012
Toledo, OH (city) Lucas County	157,014
Akron, OH (city) Summit County	111,556
Dayton, OH (city) Montgomery County	75,651
Parma, OH (city) Cuyahoga County	50,540
Kettering, OH (city) Montgomery County	36,547
Lakewood, OH (city) Cuyahoga County	35,064
Cuyahoga Falls, OH (city) Summit County	31,140

Total Populations 25 Years and Over Who are High School Graduates
Top 10 Places Sorted by Percent

Place	Percent
Upper Arlington, OH (city) Franklin County	97.93
Dublin, OH (city) Franklin County	97.27
Hudson, OH (city) Summit County	97.25
Beckett Ridge, OH (cdp) Butler County	96.63
Worthington, OH (city) Franklin County	96.06
Centerville, OH (city) Montgomery County	95.54
Shaker Heights, OH (city) Cuyahoga County	94.63
Solon, OH (city) Cuyahoga County	94.60
Westerville, OH (city) Franklin County	94.55
Sylvania, OH (city) Lucas County	94.05

Asians 25 Years and Over Who are High School Graduates
Top 10 Places Sorted by Number

Place	Number
Columbus, OH (city) Franklin County	13,017
Cleveland, OH (city) Cuyahoga County	3,289
Cincinnati, OH (city) Hamilton County	3,042
Toledo, OH (city) Lucas County	1,816
Akron, OH (city) Summit County	1,509
Dublin, OH (city) Franklin County	1,464
Parma, OH (city) Cuyahoga County	945
Cleveland Heights, OH (city) Cuyahoga County	926
Strongsville, OH (city) Cuyahoga County	890
Westlake, OH (city) Cuyahoga County	866

Asians 25 Years and Over Who are High School Graduates
Top 10 Places Sorted by Percent

Place	Percent
Kent, OH (city) Portage County	100.00
Athens, OH (city) Athens County	98.17

Notes: Please refer to the User's Guide for an explanation of data; tables reflect only those areas that meet Summary File 4 population thresholds, therefore there may be less than 10 places listed

Findlay, OH (city) Hancock County	98.00
Beckett Ridge, OH (cdp) Butler County	97.86
Blue Ash, OH (city) Hamilton County	97.55
Kenwood, OH (cdp) Hamilton County	97.33
Centerville, OH (city) Montgomery County	97.17
South Euclid, OH (city) Cuyahoga County	96.89
Hudson, OH (city) Summit County	96.61
Mason, OH (city) Warren County	95.95

Native Hawaiian and Other Pacific Islanders 25 Years and Over Who are High School Graduates

Top 10 Places Sorted by Number

Place	Number

No places met population threshold.

Native Hawaiian and Other Pacific Islanders 25 Years and Over Who are High School Graduates

Top 10 Places Sorted by Percent

Place	Percent

No places met population threshold.

Asian Indians 25 Years and Over Who are High School Graduates

Top 10 Places Sorted by Number

Place	Number
Columbus, OH (city) Franklin County	3,693
Cincinnati, OH (city) Hamilton County	934
Cleveland, OH (city) Cuyahoga County	650
Toledo, OH (city) Lucas County	468
Strongsville, OH (city) Cuyahoga County	453
Dublin, OH (city) Franklin County	422
Parma, OH (city) Cuyahoga County	413
Westlake, OH (city) Cuyahoga County	386
Akron, OH (city) Summit County	340
Cleveland Heights, OH (city) Cuyahoga County	306

Asian Indians 25 Years and Over Who are High School Graduates

Top 10 Places Sorted by Percent

Place	Percent
Blue Ash, OH (city) Hamilton County	100.00
Dublin, OH (city) Franklin County	100.00
North Olmsted, OH (city) Cuyahoga County	98.46
Westlake, OH (city) Cuyahoga County	98.22
Sharonville, OH (city) Hamilton County	96.39
Mayfield Heights, OH (city) Cuyahoga County	94.81
Cleveland Heights, OH (city) Cuyahoga County	94.74
Strongsville, OH (city) Cuyahoga County	93.79
Toledo, OH (city) Lucas County	93.60
Cincinnati, OH (city) Hamilton County	93.49

Bangladeshis 25 Years and Over Who are High School Graduates

Top 10 Places Sorted by Number

Place	Number

No places met population threshold.

Bangladeshis 25 Years and Over Who are High School Graduates

Top 10 Places Sorted by Percent

Place	Percent

No places met population threshold.

Cambodians 25 Years and Over Who are High School Graduates

Top 10 Places Sorted by Number

Place	Number
Columbus, OH (city) Franklin County	266

Cambodians 25 Years and Over Who are High School Graduates

Top 10 Places Sorted by Percent

Place	Percent
Columbus, OH (city) Franklin County	46.67

Chinese (except Taiwanese) 25 Years and Over Who are High School Graduates

Top 10 Places Sorted by Number

Place	Number
Columbus, OH (city) Franklin County	3,087
Cincinnati, OH (city) Hamilton County	1,002
Cleveland, OH (city) Cuyahoga County	988
Toledo, OH (city) Lucas County	579
Akron, OH (city) Summit County	342
Cleveland Heights, OH (city) Cuyahoga County	269
Dublin, OH (city) Franklin County	268
Solon, OH (city) Cuyahoga County	220
Upper Arlington, OH (city) Franklin County	205
Hudson, OH (city) Summit County	195

Chinese (except Taiwanese) 25 Years and Over Who are High School Graduates

Top 10 Places Sorted by Percent

Place	Percent
Hudson, OH (city) Summit County	100.00
Solon, OH (city) Cuyahoga County	100.00
Cincinnati, OH (city) Hamilton County	97.85
Cleveland Heights, OH (city) Cuyahoga County	94.06
Dublin, OH (city) Franklin County	89.04
Upper Arlington, OH (city) Franklin County	88.36
Columbus, OH (city) Franklin County	86.45
Toledo, OH (city) Lucas County	85.40
Akron, OH (city) Summit County	81.04
Cleveland, OH (city) Cuyahoga County	68.52

Fijians 25 Years and Over Who are High School Graduates

Top 10 Places Sorted by Number

Place	Number

No places met population threshold.

Fijians 25 Years and Over Who are High School Graduates

Top 10 Places Sorted by Percent

Place	Percent

No places met population threshold.

Filipinos 25 Years and Over Who are High School Graduates

Top 10 Places Sorted by Number

Place	Number
Columbus, OH (city) Franklin County	883
Cleveland, OH (city) Cuyahoga County	527
Toledo, OH (city) Lucas County	288
Cincinnati, OH (city) Hamilton County	255

Filipinos 25 Years and Over Who are High School Graduates

Top 10 Places Sorted by Percent

Place	Percent
Toledo, OH (city) Lucas County	93.20
Cincinnati, OH (city) Hamilton County	93.07
Columbus, OH (city) Franklin County	90.47
Cleveland, OH (city) Cuyahoga County	82.99

Guamanians or Chamorros 25 Years and Over Who are High School Graduates

Top 10 Places Sorted by Number

Place	Number

No places met population threshold.

Guamanians or Chamorros 25 Years and Over Who are High School Graduates

Top 10 Places Sorted by Percent

Place	Percent

No places met population threshold.

Hawaiian Natives 25 Years and Over Who are High School Graduates

Top 10 Places Sorted by Number

Place	Number

No places met population threshold.

Hawaiian Natives 25 Years and Over Who are High School Graduates

Top 10 Places Sorted by Percent

Place	Percent

No places met population threshold.

Hmongs 25 Years and Over Who are High School Graduates

Top 10 Places Sorted by Number

Place	Number

No places met population threshold.

Hmongs 25 Years and Over Who are High School Graduates

Top 10 Places Sorted by Percent

Place	Percent

No places met population threshold.

Indonesians 25 Years and Over Who are High School Graduates

Top 10 Places Sorted by Number

Place	Number
Columbus, OH (city) Franklin County	90

Indonesians 25 Years and Over Who are High School Graduates

Top 10 Places Sorted by Percent

Place	Percent
Columbus, OH (city) Franklin County	100.00

Japanese 25 Years and Over Who are High School Graduates

Top 10 Places Sorted by Number

Place	Number
Columbus, OH (city) Franklin County	1,081
Dublin, OH (city) Franklin County	491

Japanese 25 Years and Over Who are High School Graduates

Top 10 Places Sorted by Percent

Place	Percent
Columbus, OH (city) Franklin County	96.95
Dublin, OH (city) Franklin County	96.27

Koreans 25 Years and Over Who are High School Graduates

Top 10 Places Sorted by Number

Place	Number
Columbus, OH (city) Franklin County	1,511

Koreans 25 Years and Over Who are High School Graduates

Top 10 Places Sorted by Percent

Place	Percent
Columbus, OH (city) Franklin County	91.69

Notes: Please refer to the User's Guide for an explanation of data; tables reflect only those areas that meet Summary File 4 population thresholds, therefore there may be less than 10 places listed

Laotians 25 Years and Over Who are High School Graduates
Top 10 Places Sorted by Number

Place	Number
Columbus, OH (city) Franklin County	320
Akron, OH (city) Summit County	132

Laotians 25 Years and Over Who are High School Graduates
Top 10 Places Sorted by Percent

Place	Percent
Akron, OH (city) Summit County	60.27
Columbus, OH (city) Franklin County	59.37

Malaysians 25 Years and Over Who are High School Graduates
Top 10 Places Sorted by Number

Place	Number

No places met population threshold.

Malaysians 25 Years and Over Who are High School Graduates
Top 10 Places Sorted by Percent

Place	Percent

No places met population threshold.

Pakistanis 25 Years and Over Who are High School Graduates
Top 10 Places Sorted by Number

Place	Number

No places met population threshold.

Pakistanis 25 Years and Over Who are High School Graduates
Top 10 Places Sorted by Percent

Place	Percent

No places met population threshold.

Samoans 25 Years and Over Who are High School Graduates
Top 10 Places Sorted by Number

Place	Number

No places met population threshold.

Samoans 25 Years and Over Who are High School Graduates
Top 10 Places Sorted by Percent

Place	Percent

No places met population threshold.

Sri Lankans 25 Years and Over Who are High School Graduates
Top 10 Places Sorted by Number

Place	Number

No places met population threshold.

Sri Lankans 25 Years and Over Who are High School Graduates
Top 10 Places Sorted by Percent

Place	Percent

No places met population threshold.

Taiwanese 25 Years and Over Who are High School Graduates
Top 10 Places Sorted by Number

Place	Number
Columbus, OH (city) Franklin County	295

Taiwanese 25 Years and Over Who are High School Graduates
Top 10 Places Sorted by Percent

Place	Percent
Columbus, OH (city) Franklin County	96.09

Thais 25 Years and Over Who are High School Graduates
Top 10 Places Sorted by Number

Place	Number
Columbus, OH (city) Franklin County	219

Thais 25 Years and Over Who are High School Graduates
Top 10 Places Sorted by Percent

Place	Percent
Columbus, OH (city) Franklin County	86.56

Tongans 25 Years and Over Who are High School Graduates
Top 10 Places Sorted by Number

Place	Number

No places met population threshold.

Tongans 25 Years and Over Who are High School Graduates
Top 10 Places Sorted by Percent

Place	Percent

No places met population threshold.

Vietnamese 25 Years and Over Who are High School Graduates
Top 10 Places Sorted by Number

Place	Number
Columbus, OH (city) Franklin County	870
Cleveland, OH (city) Cuyahoga County	381
Akron, OH (city) Summit County	222

Vietnamese 25 Years and Over Who are High School Graduates
Top 10 Places Sorted by Percent

Place	Percent
Akron, OH (city) Summit County	67.27
Columbus, OH (city) Franklin County	63.83
Cleveland, OH (city) Cuyahoga County	54.35

Educational Attainment: College Graduates

Total Populations 25 Years and Over Who are Four-Year College Graduates
Top 10 Places Sorted by Number

Place	Number
Columbus, OH (city) Franklin County	128,058
Cincinnati, OH (city) Hamilton County	55,215
Cleveland, OH (city) Cuyahoga County	33,949
Toledo, OH (city) Lucas County	33,091
Akron, OH (city) Summit County	25,110
Cleveland Heights, OH (city) Cuyahoga County	16,760
Upper Arlington, OH (city) Franklin County	16,063
Dayton, OH (city) Montgomery County	14,477
Lakewood, OH (city) Cuyahoga County	14,193
Dublin, OH (city) Franklin County	12,749

Total Populations 25 Years and Over Who are Four-Year College Graduates
Top 10 Places Sorted by Percent

Place	Percent
Upper Arlington, OH (city) Franklin County	67.46
Hudson, OH (city) Summit County	66.54
Dublin, OH (city) Franklin County	64.66
Athens, OH (city) Athens County	63.81
Shaker Heights, OH (city) Cuyahoga County	61.69
Worthington, OH (city) Franklin County	59.71
Beckett Ridge, OH (cdp) Butler County	54.49
Oxford, OH (city) Butler County	53.56
Beachwood, OH (city) Cuyahoga County	50.86
Kenwood, OH (cdp) Hamilton County	50.58

Asians 25 Years and Over Who are Four-Year College Graduates
Top 10 Places Sorted by Number

Place	Number
Columbus, OH (city) Franklin County	9,085
Cincinnati, OH (city) Hamilton County	2,357
Cleveland, OH (city) Cuyahoga County	1,907
Toledo, OH (city) Lucas County	1,183
Dublin, OH (city) Franklin County	1,027
Akron, OH (city) Summit County	950
Cleveland Heights, OH (city) Cuyahoga County	797
Westlake, OH (city) Cuyahoga County	731
Strongsville, OH (city) Cuyahoga County	703
Parma, OH (city) Cuyahoga County	662

Asians 25 Years and Over Who are Four-Year College Graduates
Top 10 Places Sorted by Percent

Place	Percent
Athens, OH (city) Athens County	86.50
Kent, OH (city) Portage County	84.21
Cleveland Heights, OH (city) Cuyahoga County	82.00
Kenwood, OH (cdp) Hamilton County	81.33
Centerville, OH (city) Montgomery County	81.09
Shaker Heights, OH (city) Cuyahoga County	80.58
Beachwood, OH (city) Cuyahoga County	79.58
Hudson, OH (city) Summit County	79.19
Richmond Heights, OH (city) Cuyahoga County	78.37
Beckett Ridge, OH (cdp) Butler County	77.21

Native Hawaiian and Other Pacific Islanders 25 Years and Over Who are Four-Year College Graduates
Top 10 Places Sorted by Number

Place	Number

No places met population threshold.

Native Hawaiian and Other Pacific Islanders 25 Years and Over Who are Four-Year College Graduates
Top 10 Places Sorted by Percent

Place	Percent

No places met population threshold.

Asian Indians 25 Years and Over Who are Four-Year College Graduates
Top 10 Places Sorted by Number

Place	Number
Columbus, OH (city) Franklin County	3,160
Cincinnati, OH (city) Hamilton County	838
Cleveland, OH (city) Cuyahoga County	504
Dublin, OH (city) Franklin County	380
Westlake, OH (city) Cuyahoga County	358
Strongsville, OH (city) Cuyahoga County	341
Toledo, OH (city) Lucas County	305
Parma, OH (city) Cuyahoga County	297
Akron, OH (city) Summit County	285
Solon, OH (city) Cuyahoga County	279

Asian Indians 25 Years and Over Who are Four-Year College Graduates
Top 10 Places Sorted by Percent

Place	Percent
Westlake, OH (city) Cuyahoga County	91.09
Dublin, OH (city) Franklin County	90.05
Sharonville, OH (city) Hamilton County	89.56

Notes: Please refer to the User's Guide for an explanation of data; tables reflect only those areas that meet Summary File 4 population thresholds, therefore there may be less than 10 places listed

Place	Percent
Blue Ash, OH (city) Hamilton County	86.64
Cleveland Heights, OH (city) Cuyahoga County	86.07
Solon, OH (city) Cuyahoga County	85.85
Cincinnati, OH (city) Hamilton County	83.88
Mayfield Heights, OH (city) Cuyahoga County	81.85
North Olmsted, OH (city) Cuyahoga County	79.23
Columbus, OH (city) Franklin County	78.12

Bangladeshis 25 Years and Over Who are Four-Year College Graduates

Top 10 Places Sorted by Number

Place	Number
No places met population threshold.	

Bangladeshis 25 Years and Over Who are Four-Year College Graduates

Top 10 Places Sorted by Percent

Place	Percent
No places met population threshold.	

Cambodians 25 Years and Over Who are Four-Year College Graduates

Top 10 Places Sorted by Number

Place	Number
Columbus, OH (city) Franklin County	54

Cambodians 25 Years and Over Who are Four-Year College Graduates

Top 10 Places Sorted by Percent

Place	Percent
Columbus, OH (city) Franklin County	9.47

Chinese (except Taiwanese) 25 Years and Over Who are Four-Year College Graduates

Top 10 Places Sorted by Number

Place	Number
Columbus, OH (city) Franklin County	2,428
Cincinnati, OH (city) Hamilton County	846
Cleveland, OH (city) Cuyahoga County	558
Toledo, OH (city) Lucas County	474
Akron, OH (city) Summit County	275
Dublin, OH (city) Franklin County	262
Cleveland Heights, OH (city) Cuyahoga County	215
Upper Arlington, OH (city) Franklin County	196
Hudson, OH (city) Summit County	185
Solon, OH (city) Cuyahoga County	165

Chinese (except Taiwanese) 25 Years and Over Who are Four-Year College Graduates

Top 10 Places Sorted by Percent

Place	Percent
Hudson, OH (city) Summit County	94.87
Dublin, OH (city) Franklin County	87.04
Upper Arlington, OH (city) Franklin County	84.48
Cincinnati, OH (city) Hamilton County	82.62
Cleveland Heights, OH (city) Cuyahoga County	75.17
Solon, OH (city) Cuyahoga County	75.00
Toledo, OH (city) Lucas County	69.91
Columbus, OH (city) Franklin County	67.99
Akron, OH (city) Summit County	65.17
Cleveland, OH (city) Cuyahoga County	38.70

Fijians 25 Years and Over Who are Four-Year College Graduates

Top 10 Places Sorted by Number

Place	Number
No places met population threshold.	

Fijians 25 Years and Over Who are Four-Year College Graduates

Top 10 Places Sorted by Percent

Place	Percent
No places met population threshold.	

Filipinos 25 Years and Over Who are Four-Year College Graduates

Top 10 Places Sorted by Number

Place	Number
Columbus, OH (city) Franklin County	518
Cleveland, OH (city) Cuyahoga County	342
Cincinnati, OH (city) Hamilton County	178
Toledo, OH (city) Lucas County	176

Filipinos 25 Years and Over Who are Four-Year College Graduates

Top 10 Places Sorted by Percent

Place	Percent
Cincinnati, OH (city) Hamilton County	64.96
Toledo, OH (city) Lucas County	56.96
Cleveland, OH (city) Cuyahoga County	53.86
Columbus, OH (city) Franklin County	53.07

Guamanians or Chamorros 25 Years and Over Who are Four-Year College Graduates

Top 10 Places Sorted by Number

Place	Number
No places met population threshold.	

Guamanians or Chamorros 25 Years and Over Who are Four-Year College Graduates

Top 10 Places Sorted by Percent

Place	Percent
No places met population threshold.	

Hawaiian Natives 25 Years and Over Who are Four-Year College Graduates

Top 10 Places Sorted by Number

Place	Number
No places met population threshold.	

Hawaiian Natives 25 Years and Over Who are Four-Year College Graduates

Top 10 Places Sorted by Percent

Place	Percent
No places met population threshold.	

Hmongs 25 Years and Over Who are Four-Year College Graduates

Top 10 Places Sorted by Number

Place	Number
No places met population threshold.	

Hmongs 25 Years and Over Who are Four-Year College Graduates

Top 10 Places Sorted by Percent

Place	Percent
No places met population threshold.	

Indonesians 25 Years and Over Who are Four-Year College Graduates

Top 10 Places Sorted by Number

Place	Number
Columbus, OH (city) Franklin County	59

Indonesians 25 Years and Over Who are Four-Year College Graduates

Top 10 Places Sorted by Percent

Place	Percent
Columbus, OH (city) Franklin County	65.5

Japanese 25 Years and Over Who are Four-Year College Graduates

Top 10 Places Sorted by Number

Place	Number
Columbus, OH (city) Franklin County	61
Dublin, OH (city) Franklin County	20

Japanese 25 Years and Over Who are Four-Year College Graduates

Top 10 Places Sorted by Percent

Place	Percent
Columbus, OH (city) Franklin County	54.9
Dublin, OH (city) Franklin County	39.6

Koreans 25 Years and Over Who are Four-Year College Graduates

Top 10 Places Sorted by Number

Place	Number
Columbus, OH (city) Franklin County	1,11

Koreans 25 Years and Over Who are Four-Year College Graduates

Top 10 Places Sorted by Percent

Place	Percent
Columbus, OH (city) Franklin County	67.9

Laotians 25 Years and Over Who are Four-Year College Graduates

Top 10 Places Sorted by Number

Place	Number
Columbus, OH (city) Franklin County	4
Akron, OH (city) Summit County	7

Laotians 25 Years and Over Who are Four-Year College Graduates

Top 10 Places Sorted by Percent

Place	Percent
Columbus, OH (city) Franklin County	7.98
Akron, OH (city) Summit County	3.20

Malaysians 25 Years and Over Who are Four-Year College Graduates

Top 10 Places Sorted by Number

Place	Number
No places met population threshold.	

Malaysians 25 Years and Over Who are Four-Year College Graduates

Top 10 Places Sorted by Percent

Place	Percent
No places met population threshold.	

Pakistanis 25 Years and Over Who are Four-Year College Graduates

Top 10 Places Sorted by Number

Place	Number
No places met population threshold.	

Notes: Please refer to the User's Guide for an explanation of data; tables reflect only those areas that meet Summary File 4 population thresholds, therefore there may be less than 10 places listed

Pakistanis 25 Years and Over Who are Four-Year College Graduates
Top 10 Places Sorted by Percent

Place	Percent
No places met population threshold.	

Samoans 25 Years and Over Who are Four-Year College Graduates
Top 10 Places Sorted by Number

Place	Number
No places met population threshold.	

Samoans 25 Years and Over Who are Four-Year College Graduates
Top 10 Places Sorted by Percent

Place	Percent
No places met population threshold.	

Sri Lankans 25 Years and Over Who are Four-Year College Graduates
Top 10 Places Sorted by Number

Place	Number
No places met population threshold.	

Sri Lankans 25 Years and Over Who are Four-Year College Graduates
Top 10 Places Sorted by Percent

Place	Percent
No places met population threshold.	

Taiwanese 25 Years and Over Who are Four-Year College Graduates
Top 10 Places Sorted by Number

Place	Number
Columbus, OH (city) Franklin County	241

Taiwanese 25 Years and Over Who are Four-Year College Graduates
Top 10 Places Sorted by Percent

Place	Percent
Columbus, OH (city) Franklin County	78.50

Thais 25 Years and Over Who are Four-Year College Graduates
Top 10 Places Sorted by Number

Place	Number
Columbus, OH (city) Franklin County	150

Thais 25 Years and Over Who are Four-Year College Graduates
Top 10 Places Sorted by Percent

Place	Percent
Columbus, OH (city) Franklin County	59.29

Tongans 25 Years and Over Who are Four-Year College Graduates
Top 10 Places Sorted by Number

Place	Number
No places met population threshold.	

Tongans 25 Years and Over Who are Four-Year College Graduates
Top 10 Places Sorted by Percent

Place	Percent
No places met population threshold.	

Vietnamese 25 Years and Over Who are Four-Year College Graduates
Top 10 Places Sorted by Number

Place	Number
Columbus, OH (city) Franklin County	283
Cleveland, OH (city) Cuyahoga County	99
Akron, OH (city) Summit County	75

Vietnamese 25 Years and Over Who are Four-Year College Graduates
Top 10 Places Sorted by Percent

Place	Percent
Akron, OH (city) Summit County	22.73
Columbus, OH (city) Franklin County	20.76
Cleveland, OH (city) Cuyahoga County	14.12

Median Household Income

Total Population
Top 10 Places Sorted by Number

Place	Dollars
Hudson, OH (city) Summit County	99,156
Dublin, OH (city) Franklin County	91,162
Beckett Ridge, OH (cdp) Butler County	80,090
Solon, OH (city) Cuyahoga County	78,903
Upper Arlington, OH (city) Franklin County	72,116
Highland Heights, OH (city) Cuyahoga County	69,750
Westerville, OH (city) Franklin County	69,135
Hilliard, OH (city) Franklin County	69,015
Beavercreek, OH (city) Greene County	68,801
Strongsville, OH (city) Cuyahoga County	68,660

Asian
Top 10 Places Sorted by Number

Place	Dollars
Gahanna, OH (city) Franklin County	110,928
Hudson, OH (city) Summit County	108,230
Westlake, OH (city) Cuyahoga County	105,940
Strongsville, OH (city) Cuyahoga County	102,156
Beckett Ridge, OH (cdp) Butler County	101,799
Solon, OH (city) Cuyahoga County	99,394
Highland Heights, OH (city) Cuyahoga County	90,401
Westerville, OH (city) Franklin County	88,669
Dublin, OH (city) Franklin County	86,889
Mason, OH (city) Warren County	84,308

Native Hawaiian and Other Pacific Islander
Top 10 Places Sorted by Number

Place	Dollars
No places met population threshold.	

Asian Indian
Top 10 Places Sorted by Number

Place	Dollars
Solon, OH (city) Cuyahoga County	134,386
Strongsville, OH (city) Cuyahoga County	107,297
Westlake, OH (city) Cuyahoga County	104,242
Dublin, OH (city) Franklin County	102,288
Beavercreek, OH (city) Greene County	91,015
North Olmsted, OH (city) Cuyahoga County	83,513
Blue Ash, OH (city) Hamilton County	75,506
Mayfield Heights, OH (city) Cuyahoga County	67,250
North Royalton, OH (city) Cuyahoga County	67,188
Fairfield, OH (city) Butler County	62,813

Bangladeshi
Top 10 Places Sorted by Number

Place	Dollars
No places met population threshold.	

Cambodian
Top 10 Places Sorted by Number

Place	Dollars
Columbus, OH (city) Franklin County	31,382

Chinese (except Taiwanese)
Top 10 Places Sorted by Number

Place	Dollars
Dublin, OH (city) Franklin County	118,591
Hudson, OH (city) Summit County	106,977
Solon, OH (city) Cuyahoga County	81,203
Upper Arlington, OH (city) Franklin County	77,418
Columbus, OH (city) Franklin County	34,942
Cleveland Heights, OH (city) Cuyahoga County	34,342
Cincinnati, OH (city) Hamilton County	34,013
Toledo, OH (city) Lucas County	27,031
Akron, OH (city) Summit County	26,528
Cleveland, OH (city) Cuyahoga County	23,313

Fijian
Top 10 Places Sorted by Number

Place	Dollars
No places met population threshold.	

Filipino
Top 10 Places Sorted by Number

Place	Dollars
Cincinnati, OH (city) Hamilton County	50,714
Toledo, OH (city) Lucas County	50,625
Columbus, OH (city) Franklin County	47,750
Cleveland, OH (city) Cuyahoga County	37,917

Guamanian or Chamorro
Top 10 Places Sorted by Number

Place	Dollars
No places met population threshold.	

Hawaiian, Native
Top 10 Places Sorted by Number

Place	Dollars
No places met population threshold.	

Hmong
Top 10 Places Sorted by Number

Place	Dollars
No places met population threshold.	

Indonesian
Top 10 Places Sorted by Number

Place	Dollars
Columbus, OH (city) Franklin County	3,208

Japanese
Top 10 Places Sorted by Number

Place	Dollars
Dublin, OH (city) Franklin County	80,830
Columbus, OH (city) Franklin County	48,243

Korean
Top 10 Places Sorted by Number

Place	Dollars
Columbus, OH (city) Franklin County	16,840

Laotian
Top 10 Places Sorted by Number

Place	Dollars
Akron, OH (city) Summit County	56,400
Columbus, OH (city) Franklin County	39,565

Notes: Please refer to the User's Guide for an explanation of data; tables reflect only those areas that meet Summary File 4 population thresholds, therefore there may be less than 10 places listed

Malaysian

Top 10 Places Sorted by Number

Place	Dollars
No places met population threshold.	

Pakistani

Top 10 Places Sorted by Number

Place	Dollars
No places met population threshold.	

Samoan

Top 10 Places Sorted by Number

Place	Dollars
No places met population threshold.	

Sri Lankan

Top 10 Places Sorted by Number

Place	Dollars
No places met population threshold.	

Taiwanese

Top 10 Places Sorted by Number

Place	Dollars
Columbus, OH (city) Franklin County	21,146

Thai

Top 10 Places Sorted by Number

Place	Dollars
Columbus, OH (city) Franklin County	16,125

Tongan

Top 10 Places Sorted by Number

Place	Dollars
No places met population threshold.	

Vietnamese

Top 10 Places Sorted by Number

Place	Dollars
Akron, OH (city) Summit County	41,080
Columbus, OH (city) Franklin County	36,611
Cleveland, OH (city) Cuyahoga County	33,295

Per Capita Income

Total Population

Top 10 Places Sorted by Number

Place	Dollars
Upper Arlington, OH (city) Franklin County	42,025
Shaker Heights, OH (city) Cuyahoga County	41,354
Dublin, OH (city) Franklin County	41,122
Hudson, OH (city) Summit County	40,915
Beachwood, OH (city) Cuyahoga County	40,509
Westlake, OH (city) Cuyahoga County	37,142
Solon, OH (city) Cuyahoga County	35,394
Worthington, OH (city) Franklin County	34,495
Beckett Ridge, OH (cdp) Butler County	33,835
Blue Ash, OH (city) Hamilton County	33,801

Asian

Top 10 Places Sorted by Number

Place	Dollars
Westlake, OH (city) Cuyahoga County	46,367
Solon, OH (city) Cuyahoga County	41,367
Gahanna, OH (city) Franklin County	38,218
Hudson, OH (city) Summit County	36,891
Upper Arlington, OH (city) Franklin County	35,630
Wooster, OH (city) Wayne County	34,538
Dublin, OH (city) Franklin County	33,203
Mason, OH (city) Warren County	32,153
Shaker Heights, OH (city) Cuyahoga County	31,910
Strongsville, OH (city) Cuyahoga County	31,692

Native Hawaiian and Other Pacific Islander

Top 10 Places Sorted by Number

Place	Dollars
No places met population threshold.	

Asian Indian

Top 10 Places Sorted by Number

Place	Dollars
Westlake, OH (city) Cuyahoga County	55,467
Solon, OH (city) Cuyahoga County	47,197
Beavercreek, OH (city) Greene County	39,369
Dublin, OH (city) Franklin County	38,436
Strongsville, OH (city) Cuyahoga County	35,842
Mayfield Heights, OH (city) Cuyahoga County	26,494
Fairfield, OH (city) Butler County	25,866
Blue Ash, OH (city) Hamilton County	25,038
Columbus, OH (city) Franklin County	24,873
Cincinnati, OH (city) Hamilton County	24,787

Bangladeshi

Top 10 Places Sorted by Number

Place	Dollars
No places met population threshold.	

Cambodian

Top 10 Places Sorted by Number

Place	Dollars
Columbus, OH (city) Franklin County	17,681

Chinese (except Taiwanese)

Top 10 Places Sorted by Number

Place	Dollars
Solon, OH (city) Cuyahoga County	37,218
Dublin, OH (city) Franklin County	35,393
Hudson, OH (city) Summit County	29,140
Cleveland Heights, OH (city) Cuyahoga County	26,672
Upper Arlington, OH (city) Franklin County	26,190
Columbus, OH (city) Franklin County	19,976
Cincinnati, OH (city) Hamilton County	17,631
Toledo, OH (city) Lucas County	16,701
Akron, OH (city) Summit County	13,508
Cleveland, OH (city) Cuyahoga County	12,750

Fijian

Top 10 Places Sorted by Number

Place	Dollars
No places met population threshold.	

Filipino

Top 10 Places Sorted by Number

Place	Dollars
Columbus, OH (city) Franklin County	29,897
Cincinnati, OH (city) Hamilton County	22,479
Toledo, OH (city) Lucas County	20,428
Cleveland, OH (city) Cuyahoga County	18,238

Guamanian or Chamorro

Top 10 Places Sorted by Number

Place	Dollars
No places met population threshold.	

Hawaiian, Native

Top 10 Places Sorted by Number

Place	Dollars
No places met population threshold.	

Hmong

Top 10 Places Sorted by Number

Place	Dollar
No places met population threshold.	

Indonesian

Top 10 Places Sorted by Number

Place	Dollar
Columbus, OH (city) Franklin County	9,66

Japanese

Top 10 Places Sorted by Number

Place	Dollar
Dublin, OH (city) Franklin County	31,85
Columbus, OH (city) Franklin County	21,84

Korean

Top 10 Places Sorted by Number

Place	Dollars
Columbus, OH (city) Franklin County	16,69

Laotian

Top 10 Places Sorted by Number

Place	Dollars
Columbus, OH (city) Franklin County	12,99
Akron, OH (city) Summit County	11,52

Malaysian

Top 10 Places Sorted by Number

Place	Dollars
No places met population threshold.	

Pakistani

Top 10 Places Sorted by Number

Place	Dollars
No places met population threshold.	

Samoan

Top 10 Places Sorted by Number

Place	Dollars
No places met population threshold.	

Sri Lankan

Top 10 Places Sorted by Number

Place	Dollars
No places met population threshold.	

Taiwanese

Top 10 Places Sorted by Number

Place	Dollars
Columbus, OH (city) Franklin County	26,570

Thai

Top 10 Places Sorted by Number

Place	Dollars
Columbus, OH (city) Franklin County	10,742

Tongan

Top 10 Places Sorted by Number

Place	Dollars
No places met population threshold.	

Vietnamese

Top 10 Places Sorted by Number

Place	Dollars
Akron, OH (city) Summit County	27,728
Cleveland, OH (city) Cuyahoga County	15,747

Notes: Please refer to the User's Guide for an explanation of data; tables reflect only those areas that meet Summary File 4 population thresholds, therefore there may be less than 10 places listed

Columbus, OH (city) Franklin County	15,203

Poverty Status

Total Populations with Income Below Poverty Level
Top 10 Places Sorted by Number

Place	Number
Cleveland, OH (city) Cuyahoga County	122,479
Columbus, OH (city) Franklin County	102,723
Cincinnati, OH (city) Hamilton County	69,722
Toledo, OH (city) Lucas County	54,903
Akron, OH (city) Summit County	36,975
Dayton, OH (city) Montgomery County	35,756
Athens, OH (city) Athens County	7,247
Oxford, OH (city) Butler County	6,296
Bowling Green, OH (city) Wood County	5,761
Kent, OH (city) Portage County	5,622

Total Populations with Income Below Poverty Level
Top 10 Places Sorted by Percent

Place	Percent
Athens, OH (city) Athens County	51.93
Oxford, OH (city) Butler County	43.66
Cleveland, OH (city) Cuyahoga County	26.27
Bowling Green, OH (city) Wood County	25.27
Kent, OH (city) Portage County	25.23
Dayton, OH (city) Montgomery County	22.99
Cincinnati, OH (city) Hamilton County	21.91
Toledo, OH (city) Lucas County	17.89
Akron, OH (city) Summit County	17.45
Columbus, OH (city) Franklin County	14.81

Asians with Income Below Poverty Level
Top 10 Places Sorted by Number

Place	Number
Columbus, OH (city) Franklin County	4,482
Cleveland, OH (city) Cuyahoga County	1,697
Cincinnati, OH (city) Hamilton County	993
Toledo, OH (city) Lucas County	743
Akron, OH (city) Summit County	631
Athens, OH (city) Athens County	410
Fairborn, OH (city) Greene County	374
Cleveland Heights, OH (city) Cuyahoga County	310
Kent, OH (city) Portage County	235
Oxford, OH (city) Butler County	197

Asians with Income Below Poverty Level
Top 10 Places Sorted by Percent

Place	Percent
Athens, OH (city) Athens County	54.23
Oxford, OH (city) Butler County	52.39
Kent, OH (city) Portage County	44.09
Fairborn, OH (city) Greene County	42.16
Cleveland, OH (city) Cuyahoga County	25.99
Parma Heights, OH (city) Cuyahoga County	25.87
Findlay, OH (city) Hancock County	25.13
Toledo, OH (city) Lucas County	25.09
Cleveland Heights, OH (city) Cuyahoga County	22.83
Beachwood, OH (city) Cuyahoga County	21.11

Native Hawaiian and Other Pacific Islanders with Income Below Poverty Level
Top 10 Places Sorted by Number

Place	Number
No places met population threshold.	

Native Hawaiian and Other Pacific Islanders with Income Below Poverty Level
Top 10 Places Sorted by Percent

Place	Percent
No places met population threshold.	

Asian Indians with Income Below Poverty Level
Top 10 Places Sorted by Number

Place	Number
Columbus, OH (city) Franklin County	948
Cleveland, OH (city) Cuyahoga County	463
Cincinnati, OH (city) Hamilton County	327
Toledo, OH (city) Lucas County	252
Akron, OH (city) Summit County	160
Cleveland Heights, OH (city) Cuyahoga County	134
Parma, OH (city) Cuyahoga County	45
Beavercreek, OH (city) Greene County	23
North Olmsted, OH (city) Cuyahoga County	23
Sharonville, OH (city) Hamilton County	8

Asian Indians with Income Below Poverty Level
Top 10 Places Sorted by Percent

Place	Percent
Cleveland, OH (city) Cuyahoga County	43.84
Toledo, OH (city) Lucas County	30.00
Akron, OH (city) Summit County	28.02
Cleveland Heights, OH (city) Cuyahoga County	24.23
Cincinnati, OH (city) Hamilton County	21.22
Columbus, OH (city) Franklin County	15.26
Parma, OH (city) Cuyahoga County	7.09
North Olmsted, OH (city) Cuyahoga County	5.46
Beavercreek, OH (city) Greene County	4.85
Sharonville, OH (city) Hamilton County	2.04

Bangladeshis with Income Below Poverty Level
Top 10 Places Sorted by Number

Place	Number
No places met population threshold.	

Bangladeshis with Income Below Poverty Level
Top 10 Places Sorted by Percent

Place	Percent
No places met population threshold.	

Cambodians with Income Below Poverty Level
Top 10 Places Sorted by Number

Place	Number
Columbus, OH (city) Franklin County	291

Cambodians with Income Below Poverty Level
Top 10 Places Sorted by Percent

Place	Percent
Columbus, OH (city) Franklin County	24.41

Chinese (except Taiwanese) with Income Below Poverty Level
Top 10 Places Sorted by Number

Place	Number
Columbus, OH (city) Franklin County	843
Cleveland, OH (city) Cuyahoga County	448
Cincinnati, OH (city) Hamilton County	236
Toledo, OH (city) Lucas County	218
Cleveland Heights, OH (city) Cuyahoga County	76
Akron, OH (city) Summit County	75
Upper Arlington, OH (city) Franklin County	61
Dublin, OH (city) Franklin County	25
Hudson, OH (city) Summit County	0
Solon, OH (city) Cuyahoga County	0

Chinese (except Taiwanese) with Income Below Poverty Level
Top 10 Places Sorted by Percent

Place	Percent
Toledo, OH (city) Lucas County	28.17
Cleveland, OH (city) Cuyahoga County	23.22
Cleveland Heights, OH (city) Cuyahoga County	19.29
Cincinnati, OH (city) Hamilton County	18.14
Upper Arlington, OH (city) Franklin County	17.99
Columbus, OH (city) Franklin County	16.88
Akron, OH (city) Summit County	14.18
Dublin, OH (city) Franklin County	4.90
Hudson, OH (city) Summit County	0.00
Solon, OH (city) Cuyahoga County	0.00

Fijians with Income Below Poverty Level
Top 10 Places Sorted by Number

Place	Number
No places met population threshold.	

Fijians with Income Below Poverty Level
Top 10 Places Sorted by Percent

Place	Percent
No places met population threshold.	

Filipinos with Income Below Poverty Level
Top 10 Places Sorted by Number

Place	Number
Columbus, OH (city) Franklin County	71
Cincinnati, OH (city) Hamilton County	54
Cleveland, OH (city) Cuyahoga County	46
Toledo, OH (city) Lucas County	24

Filipinos with Income Below Poverty Level
Top 10 Places Sorted by Percent

Place	Percent
Cincinnati, OH (city) Hamilton County	11.49
Toledo, OH (city) Lucas County	6.45
Cleveland, OH (city) Cuyahoga County	5.50
Columbus, OH (city) Franklin County	5.15

Guamanians or Chamorros with Income Below Poverty Level
Top 10 Places Sorted by Number

Place	Number
No places met population threshold.	

Guamanians or Chamorros with Income Below Poverty Level
Top 10 Places Sorted by Percent

Place	Percent
No places met population threshold.	

Hawaiian Natives with Income Below Poverty Level
Top 10 Places Sorted by Number

Place	Number
No places met population threshold.	

Hawaiian Natives with Income Below Poverty Level
Top 10 Places Sorted by Percent

Place	Percent
No places met population threshold.	

Hmongs with Income Below Poverty Level
Top 10 Places Sorted by Number

Place	Number
No places met population threshold.	

Hmongs with Income Below Poverty Level
Top 10 Places Sorted by Percent

Place	Percent
No places met population threshold.	

Indonesians with Income Below Poverty Level
Top 10 Places Sorted by Number

Place	Number
Columbus, OH (city) Franklin County	321

Notes: Please refer to the User's Guide for an explanation of data; tables reflect only those areas that meet Summary File 4 population thresholds, therefore there may be less than 10 places listed

Indonesians with Income Below Poverty Level
Top 10 Places Sorted by Percent

Place	Percent
Columbus, OH (city) Franklin County	63.31

Japanese with Income Below Poverty Level
Top 10 Places Sorted by Number

Place	Number
Columbus, OH (city) Franklin County	232
Dublin, OH (city) Franklin County	107

Japanese with Income Below Poverty Level
Top 10 Places Sorted by Percent

Place	Percent
Columbus, OH (city) Franklin County	13.35
Dublin, OH (city) Franklin County	13.05

Koreans with Income Below Poverty Level
Top 10 Places Sorted by Number

Place	Number
Columbus, OH (city) Franklin County	688

Koreans with Income Below Poverty Level
Top 10 Places Sorted by Percent

Place	Percent
Columbus, OH (city) Franklin County	28.64

Laotians with Income Below Poverty Level
Top 10 Places Sorted by Number

Place	Number
Columbus, OH (city) Franklin County	187
Akron, OH (city) Summit County	66

Laotians with Income Below Poverty Level
Top 10 Places Sorted by Percent

Place	Percent
Columbus, OH (city) Franklin County	19.10
Akron, OH (city) Summit County	11.81

Malaysians with Income Below Poverty Level
Top 10 Places Sorted by Number

Place	Number
No places met population threshold.	

Malaysians with Income Below Poverty Level
Top 10 Places Sorted by Percent

Place	Percent
No places met population threshold.	

Pakistanis with Income Below Poverty Level
Top 10 Places Sorted by Number

Place	Number
No places met population threshold.	

Pakistanis with Income Below Poverty Level
Top 10 Places Sorted by Percent

Place	Percent
No places met population threshold.	

Samoans with Income Below Poverty Level
Top 10 Places Sorted by Number

Place	Number
No places met population threshold.	

Samoans with Income Below Poverty Level
Top 10 Places Sorted by Percent

Place	Percent
No places met population threshold.	

Sri Lankans with Income Below Poverty Level
Top 10 Places Sorted by Number

Place	Number
No places met population threshold.	

Sri Lankans with Income Below Poverty Level
Top 10 Places Sorted by Percent

Place	Percent
No places met population threshold.	

Taiwanese with Income Below Poverty Level
Top 10 Places Sorted by Number

Place	Number
Columbus, OH (city) Franklin County	123

Taiwanese with Income Below Poverty Level
Top 10 Places Sorted by Percent

Place	Percent
Columbus, OH (city) Franklin County	30.90

Thais with Income Below Poverty Level
Top 10 Places Sorted by Number

Place	Number
Columbus, OH (city) Franklin County	128

Thais with Income Below Poverty Level
Top 10 Places Sorted by Percent

Place	Percent
Columbus, OH (city) Franklin County	33.60

Tongans with Income Below Poverty Level
Top 10 Places Sorted by Number

Place	Number
No places met population threshold.	

Tongans with Income Below Poverty Level
Top 10 Places Sorted by Percent

Place	Percent
No places met population threshold.	

Vietnamese with Income Below Poverty Level
Top 10 Places Sorted by Number

Place	Number
Cleveland, OH (city) Cuyahoga County	314
Columbus, OH (city) Franklin County	301
Akron, OH (city) Summit County	124

Vietnamese with Income Below Poverty Level
Top 10 Places Sorted by Percent

Place	Percent
Cleveland, OH (city) Cuyahoga County	28.36
Akron, OH (city) Summit County	21.72
Columbus, OH (city) Franklin County	14.03

Homeownership

Total Populations Who Own Their Own Homes
Top 10 Places Sorted by Number

Place	Number
Columbus, OH (city) Franklin County	148,315
Cleveland, OH (city) Cuyahoga County	92,498
Toledo, OH (city) Lucas County	77,028
Cincinnati, OH (city) Hamilton County	57,65
Akron, OH (city) Summit County	53,44
Dayton, OH (city) Montgomery County	35,53
Parma, OH (city) Cuyahoga County	27,22
Kettering, OH (city) Montgomery County	17,08
Mentor, OH (city) Lake County	16,43
Cuyahoga Falls, OH (city) Summit County	14,23

Total Populations Who Own Their Own Homes
Top 10 Places Sorted by Percent

Place	Percen
Highland Heights, OH (city) Cuyahoga County	97.3
Hudson, OH (city) Summit County	90.4
Solon, OH (city) Cuyahoga County	87.8
Mentor, OH (city) Lake County	87.4
Beckett Ridge, OH (cdp) Butler County	85.8
Worthington, OH (city) Franklin County	84.6
Beavercreek, OH (city) Greene County	84.2
Mason, OH (city) Warren County	84.1
South Euclid, OH (city) Cuyahoga County	83.9
Maple Heights, OH (city) Cuyahoga County	83.8

Asians Who Own Their Own Homes
Top 10 Places Sorted by Number

Place	Numbe
Columbus, OH (city) Franklin County	2,68
Cleveland, OH (city) Cuyahoga County	94
Akron, OH (city) Summit County	444
Dublin, OH (city) Franklin County	42
Cincinnati, OH (city) Hamilton County	37
Toledo, OH (city) Lucas County	370
Strongsville, OH (city) Cuyahoga County	319
Westlake, OH (city) Cuyahoga County	31
Beavercreek, OH (city) Greene County	280
Solon, OH (city) Cuyahoga County	250

Asians Who Own Their Own Homes
Top 10 Places Sorted by Percent

Place	Percen
Highland Heights, OH (city) Cuyahoga County	100.00
Mason, OH (city) Warren County	93.63
Beckett Ridge, OH (cdp) Butler County	89.82
Brunswick, OH (city) Medina County	85.19
Solon, OH (city) Cuyahoga County	84.46
Hudson, OH (city) Summit County	83.82
Twinsburg, OH (city) Summit County	78.99
Garfield Heights, OH (city) Cuyahoga County	75.81
Stow, OH (city) Summit County	74.63
Worthington, OH (city) Franklin County	74.02

Native Hawaiian and Other Pacific Islanders Who Own Their Own Homes
Top 10 Places Sorted by Number

Place	Number
No places met population threshold.	

Native Hawaiian and Other Pacific Islanders Who Own Their Own Homes
Top 10 Places Sorted by Percent

Place	Percent
No places met population threshold.	

Asian Indians Who Own Their Own Homes
Top 10 Places Sorted by Number

Place	Number
Columbus, OH (city) Franklin County	513
Strongsville, OH (city) Cuyahoga County	159
Dublin, OH (city) Franklin County	142
Westlake, OH (city) Cuyahoga County	128
Beavercreek, OH (city) Greene County	119
Solon, OH (city) Cuyahoga County	116
Cleveland, OH (city) Cuyahoga County	111
Cincinnati, OH (city) Hamilton County	108

Notes: Please refer to the User's Guide for an explanation of data; tables reflect only those areas that meet Summary File 4 population thresholds, therefore there may be less than 10 places listed

North Olmsted, OH (city) Cuyahoga County	79
Parma, OH (city) Cuyahoga County	78

Asian Indians Who Own Their Own Homes
Top 10 Places Sorted by Percent

Place	Percent
Solon, OH (city) Cuyahoga County	86.57
Beavercreek, OH (city) Greene County	74.84
Strongsville, OH (city) Cuyahoga County	70.67
North Royalton, OH (city) Cuyahoga County	67.35
North Olmsted, OH (city) Cuyahoga County	62.20
Dublin, OH (city) Franklin County	58.92
Westlake, OH (city) Cuyahoga County	58.72
Cleveland Heights, OH (city) Cuyahoga County	38.59
Blue Ash, OH (city) Hamilton County	36.62
Fairfield, OH (city) Butler County	35.06

Bangladeshis Who Own Their Own Homes
Top 10 Places Sorted by Number

Place	Number
No places met population threshold.	

Bangladeshis Who Own Their Own Homes
Top 10 Places Sorted by Percent

Place	Percent
No places met population threshold.	

Cambodians Who Own Their Own Homes
Top 10 Places Sorted by Number

Place	Number
Columbus, OH (city) Franklin County	125

Cambodians Who Own Their Own Homes
Top 10 Places Sorted by Percent

Place	Percent
Columbus, OH (city) Franklin County	42.96

Chinese (except Taiwanese) Who Own Their Own Homes
Top 10 Places Sorted by Number

Place	Number
Columbus, OH (city) Franklin County	670
Cleveland, OH (city) Cuyahoga County	281
Dublin, OH (city) Franklin County	115
Toledo, OH (city) Lucas County	96
Hudson, OH (city) Summit County	87
Solon, OH (city) Cuyahoga County	76
Akron, OH (city) Summit County	71
Cleveland Heights, OH (city) Cuyahoga County	68
Cincinnati, OH (city) Hamilton County	56
Upper Arlington, OH (city) Franklin County	54

Chinese (except Taiwanese) Who Own Their Own Homes
Top 10 Places Sorted by Percent

Place	Percent
Hudson, OH (city) Summit County	83.65
Solon, OH (city) Cuyahoga County	80.85
Dublin, OH (city) Franklin County	75.66
Upper Arlington, OH (city) Franklin County	47.79
Cleveland, OH (city) Cuyahoga County	37.22
Cleveland Heights, OH (city) Cuyahoga County	35.60
Akron, OH (city) Summit County	33.33
Columbus, OH (city) Franklin County	33.18
Toledo, OH (city) Lucas County	29.72
Cincinnati, OH (city) Hamilton County	9.57

Fijians Who Own Their Own Homes
Top 10 Places Sorted by Number

Place	Number
No places met population threshold.	

Fijians Who Own Their Own Homes
Top 10 Places Sorted by Percent

Place	Percent
No places met population threshold.	

Filipinos Who Own Their Own Homes
Top 10 Places Sorted by Number

Place	Number
Columbus, OH (city) Franklin County	218
Cleveland, OH (city) Cuyahoga County	135
Toledo, OH (city) Lucas County	98
Cincinnati, OH (city) Hamilton County	70

Filipinos Who Own Their Own Homes
Top 10 Places Sorted by Percent

Place	Percent
Toledo, OH (city) Lucas County	73.68
Columbus, OH (city) Franklin County	43.60
Cleveland, OH (city) Cuyahoga County	39.94
Cincinnati, OH (city) Hamilton County	37.43

Guamanians or Chamorros Who Own Their Own Homes
Top 10 Places Sorted by Number

Place	Number
No places met population threshold.	

Guamanians or Chamorros Who Own Their Own Homes
Top 10 Places Sorted by Percent

Place	Percent
No places met population threshold.	

Hawaiian Natives Who Own Their Own Homes
Top 10 Places Sorted by Number

Place	Number
No places met population threshold.	

Hawaiian Natives Who Own Their Own Homes
Top 10 Places Sorted by Percent

Place	Percent
No places met population threshold.	

Hmongs Who Own Their Own Homes
Top 10 Places Sorted by Number

Place	Number
No places met population threshold.	

Hmongs Who Own Their Own Homes
Top 10 Places Sorted by Percent

Place	Percent
No places met population threshold.	

Indonesians Who Own Their Own Homes
Top 10 Places Sorted by Number

Place	Number
Columbus, OH (city) Franklin County	0

Indonesians Who Own Their Own Homes
Top 10 Places Sorted by Percent

Place	Percent
Columbus, OH (city) Franklin County	0.00

Japanese Who Own Their Own Homes
Top 10 Places Sorted by Number

Place	Number
Columbus, OH (city) Franklin County	263
Dublin, OH (city) Franklin County	82

Japanese Who Own Their Own Homes
Top 10 Places Sorted by Percent

Place	Percent
Columbus, OH (city) Franklin County	35.44
Dublin, OH (city) Franklin County	29.93

Koreans Who Own Their Own Homes
Top 10 Places Sorted by Number

Place	Number
Columbus, OH (city) Franklin County	114

Koreans Who Own Their Own Homes
Top 10 Places Sorted by Percent

Place	Percent
Columbus, OH (city) Franklin County	10.09

Laotians Who Own Their Own Homes
Top 10 Places Sorted by Number

Place	Number
Columbus, OH (city) Franklin County	151
Akron, OH (city) Summit County	96

Laotians Who Own Their Own Homes
Top 10 Places Sorted by Percent

Place	Percent
Akron, OH (city) Summit County	86.49
Columbus, OH (city) Franklin County	50.50

Malaysians Who Own Their Own Homes
Top 10 Places Sorted by Number

Place	Number
No places met population threshold.	

Malaysians Who Own Their Own Homes
Top 10 Places Sorted by Percent

Place	Percent
No places met population threshold.	

Pakistanis Who Own Their Own Homes
Top 10 Places Sorted by Number

Place	Number
No places met population threshold.	

Pakistanis Who Own Their Own Homes
Top 10 Places Sorted by Percent

Place	Percent
No places met population threshold.	

Samoans Who Own Their Own Homes
Top 10 Places Sorted by Number

Place	Number
No places met population threshold.	

Samoans Who Own Their Own Homes
Top 10 Places Sorted by Percent

Place	Percent
No places met population threshold.	

Sri Lankans Who Own Their Own Homes
Top 10 Places Sorted by Number

Place	Number
No places met population threshold.	

Sri Lankans Who Own Their Own Homes
Top 10 Places Sorted by Percent

Place	Percent
No places met population threshold.	

Notes: Please refer to the User's Guide for an explanation of data; tables reflect only those areas that meet Summary File 4 population thresholds, therefore there may be less than 10 places listed

Taiwanese Who Own Their Own Homes
Top 10 Places Sorted by Number

Place	Number
Columbus, OH (city) Franklin County	50

Taiwanese Who Own Their Own Homes
Top 10 Places Sorted by Percent

Place	Percent
Columbus, OH (city) Franklin County	31.65

Thais Who Own Their Own Homes
Top 10 Places Sorted by Number

Place	Number
Columbus, OH (city) Franklin County	41

Thais Who Own Their Own Homes
Top 10 Places Sorted by Percent

Place	Percent
Columbus, OH (city) Franklin County	31.78

Tongans Who Own Their Own Homes
Top 10 Places Sorted by Number

Place	Number
No places met population threshold.	

Tongans Who Own Their Own Homes
Top 10 Places Sorted by Percent

Place	Percent
No places met population threshold.	

Vietnamese Who Own Their Own Homes
Top 10 Places Sorted by Number

Place	Number
Columbus, OH (city) Franklin County	359
Cleveland, OH (city) Cuyahoga County	211
Akron, OH (city) Summit County	96

Vietnamese Who Own Their Own Homes
Top 10 Places Sorted by Percent

Place	Percent
Akron, OH (city) Summit County	69.06
Cleveland, OH (city) Cuyahoga County	58.61
Columbus, OH (city) Franklin County	58.56

Median Gross Rent

All Specified Renter-Occupied Housing Units
Top 10 Places Sorted by Number

Place	Dollars/Month
Hudson, OH (city) Summit County	1,303
Beachwood, OH (city) Cuyahoga County	1,145
Beckett Ridge, OH (cdp) Butler County	1,019
Highland Heights, OH (city) Cuyahoga County	1,000
Kenwood, OH (cdp) Hamilton County	953
Dublin, OH (city) Franklin County	929
Westlake, OH (city) Cuyahoga County	866
Beavercreek, OH (city) Greene County	821
Blue Ash, OH (city) Hamilton County	816
Solon, OH (city) Cuyahoga County	814

Specified Housing Units Rented by Asians
Top 10 Places Sorted by Number

Place	Dollars/Month
Hudson, OH (city) Summit County	1,403
Beckett Ridge, OH (cdp) Butler County	1,264
Dublin, OH (city) Franklin County	1,036
Kenwood, OH (cdp) Hamilton County	1,000
Beavercreek, OH (city) Greene County	984
Beachwood, OH (city) Cuyahoga County	961
Westlake, OH (city) Cuyahoga County	943
Hilliard, OH (city) Franklin County	888
Twinsburg, OH (city) Summit County	789
North Royalton, OH (city) Cuyahoga County	783

Specified Housing Units Rented by Native Hawaiian and Other Pacific Islanders
Top 10 Places Sorted by Number

Place	Dollars/Month
No places met population threshold.	

Specified Housing Units Rented by Asian Indians
Top 10 Places Sorted by Number

Place	Dollars/Month
Westlake, OH (city) Cuyahoga County	998
Dublin, OH (city) Franklin County	910
Beavercreek, OH (city) Greene County	867
North Royalton, OH (city) Cuyahoga County	814
Solon, OH (city) Cuyahoga County	771
Blue Ash, OH (city) Hamilton County	757
North Olmsted, OH (city) Cuyahoga County	727
Strongsville, OH (city) Cuyahoga County	704
Fairfield, OH (city) Butler County	677
Cleveland Heights, OH (city) Cuyahoga County	651

Specified Housing Units Rented by Bangladeshis
Top 10 Places Sorted by Number

Place	Dollars/Month
No places met population threshold.	

Specified Housing Units Rented by Cambodians
Top 10 Places Sorted by Number

Place	Dollars/Month
Columbus, OH (city) Franklin County	445

Specified Housing Units Rented by Chinese (except Taiwanese)
Top 10 Places Sorted by Number

Place	Dollars/Month
Hudson, OH (city) Summit County	1,264
Dublin, OH (city) Franklin County	939
Upper Arlington, OH (city) Franklin County	710
Solon, OH (city) Cuyahoga County	675
Cleveland Heights, OH (city) Cuyahoga County	601
Columbus, OH (city) Franklin County	523
Cincinnati, OH (city) Hamilton County	469
Toledo, OH (city) Lucas County	449
Cleveland, OH (city) Cuyahoga County	448
Akron, OH (city) Summit County	428

Specified Housing Units Rented by Fijians
Top 10 Places Sorted by Number

Place	Dollars/Month
No places met population threshold.	

Specified Housing Units Rented by Filipinos
Top 10 Places Sorted by Number

Place	Dollars/Month
Columbus, OH (city) Franklin County	622
Toledo, OH (city) Lucas County	553
Cincinnati, OH (city) Hamilton County	522
Cleveland, OH (city) Cuyahoga County	446

Specified Housing Units Rented by Guamanians or Chamorros
Top 10 Places Sorted by Number

Place	Dollars/Month
No places met population threshold.	

Specified Housing Units Rented by Hawaiian Natives
Top 10 Places Sorted by Number

Place	Dollars/Month
No places met population threshold.	

Specified Housing Units Rented by Hmongs
Top 10 Places Sorted by Number

Place	Dollars/Month
No places met population threshold.	

Specified Housing Units Rented by Indonesians
Top 10 Places Sorted by Number

Place	Dollars/Month
Columbus, OH (city) Franklin County	71[illegible]

Specified Housing Units Rented by Japanese
Top 10 Places Sorted by Number

Place	Dollars/Month
Dublin, OH (city) Franklin County	1,438
Columbus, OH (city) Franklin County	693

Specified Housing Units Rented by Koreans
Top 10 Places Sorted by Number

Place	Dollars/Month
Columbus, OH (city) Franklin County	613

Specified Housing Units Rented by Laotians
Top 10 Places Sorted by Number

Place	Dollars/Month
Columbus, OH (city) Franklin County	553
Akron, OH (city) Summit County	247

Specified Housing Units Rented by Malaysians
Top 10 Places Sorted by Number

Place	Dollars/Month
No places met population threshold.	

Specified Housing Units Rented by Pakistanis
Top 10 Places Sorted by Number

Place	Dollars/Month
No places met population threshold.	

Specified Housing Units Rented by Samoans
Top 10 Places Sorted by Number

Place	Dollars/Month
No places met population threshold.	

Specified Housing Units Rented by Sri Lankans
Top 10 Places Sorted by Number

Place	Dollars/Month
No places met population threshold.	

Specified Housing Units Rented by Taiwanese
Top 10 Places Sorted by Number

Place	Dollars/Month
Columbus, OH (city) Franklin County	576

Specified Housing Units Rented by Thais
Top 10 Places Sorted by Number

Place	Dollars/Month
Columbus, OH (city) Franklin County	533

Specified Housing Units Rented by Tongans
Top 10 Places Sorted by Number

Place	Dollars/Month
No places met population threshold.	

Notes: Please refer to the User's Guide for an explanation of data; tables reflect only those areas that meet Summary File 4 population thresholds, therefore there may be less than 10 places listed

Specified Housing Units Rented by Vietnamese

Top 10 Places Sorted by Number

Place	Dollars/Month
Columbus, OH (city) Franklin County	534
Akron, OH (city) Summit County	453
Cleveland, OH (city) Cuyahoga County	400

Median Home Value

All Specified Owner-Occupied Housing Units

Top 10 Places Sorted by Number

Place	Dollars
Beachwood, OH (city) Cuyahoga County	244,700
Dublin, OH (city) Franklin County	243,200
Hudson, OH (city) Summit County	236,700
Highland Heights, OH (city) Cuyahoga County	217,500
Solon, OH (city) Cuyahoga County	217,000
Upper Arlington, OH (city) Franklin County	214,700
Shaker Heights, OH (city) Cuyahoga County	201,600
Westlake, OH (city) Cuyahoga County	201,000
Kenwood, OH (cdp) Hamilton County	184,800
Beckett Ridge, OH (cdp) Butler County	184,100

Specified Housing Units Owned and Occupied by Asians

Top 10 Places Sorted by Number

Place	Dollars
Solon, OH (city) Cuyahoga County	250,900
Westlake, OH (city) Cuyahoga County	248,200
Beachwood, OH (city) Cuyahoga County	246,400
Highland Heights, OH (city) Cuyahoga County	242,200
Gahanna, OH (city) Franklin County	232,500
Upper Arlington, OH (city) Franklin County	230,000
Dublin, OH (city) Franklin County	229,500
Hudson, OH (city) Summit County	228,400
Blue Ash, OH (city) Hamilton County	224,200
Strongsville, OH (city) Cuyahoga County	218,500

Specified Housing Units Owned and Occupied by Native Hawaiian and Other Pacific Islanders

Top 10 Places Sorted by Number

Place	Dollars

No places met population threshold.

Specified Housing Units Owned and Occupied by Asian Indians

Top 10 Places Sorted by Number

Place	Dollars
Westlake, OH (city) Cuyahoga County	297,700
Dublin, OH (city) Franklin County	256,400
Solon, OH (city) Cuyahoga County	240,200
Strongsville, OH (city) Cuyahoga County	215,400
North Royalton, OH (city) Cuyahoga County	210,500
Blue Ash, OH (city) Hamilton County	204,200
Beavercreek, OH (city) Greene County	198,300
Cincinnati, OH (city) Hamilton County	187,500
Sharonville, OH (city) Hamilton County	181,000
Fairfield, OH (city) Butler County	172,300

Specified Housing Units Owned and Occupied by Bangladeshis

Top 10 Places Sorted by Number

Place	Dollars

No places met population threshold.

Specified Housing Units Owned and Occupied by Cambodians

Top 10 Places Sorted by Number

Place	Dollars
Columbus, OH (city) Franklin County	88,000

Specified Housing Units Owned and Occupied by Chinese (except Taiwanese)

Top 10 Places Sorted by Number

Place	Dollars
Upper Arlington, OH (city) Franklin County	258,300
Dublin, OH (city) Franklin County	244,600
Solon, OH (city) Cuyahoga County	228,600
Hudson, OH (city) Summit County	215,000
Cincinnati, OH (city) Hamilton County	171,400
Columbus, OH (city) Franklin County	148,700
Cleveland Heights, OH (city) Cuyahoga County	101,800
Toledo, OH (city) Lucas County	98,800
Akron, OH (city) Summit County	85,500
Cleveland, OH (city) Cuyahoga County	82,500

Specified Housing Units Owned and Occupied by Fijians

Top 10 Places Sorted by Number

Place	Dollars

No places met population threshold.

Specified Housing Units Owned and Occupied by Filipinos

Top 10 Places Sorted by Number

Place	Dollars
Columbus, OH (city) Franklin County	141,100
Cincinnati, OH (city) Hamilton County	131,600
Cleveland, OH (city) Cuyahoga County	84,500
Toledo, OH (city) Lucas County	83,200

Specified Housing Units Owned and Occupied by Guamanians or Chamorros

Top 10 Places Sorted by Number

Place	Dollars

No places met population threshold.

Specified Housing Units Owned and Occupied by Hawaiian Natives

Top 10 Places Sorted by Number

Place	Dollars

No places met population threshold.

Specified Housing Units Owned and Occupied by Hmongs

Top 10 Places Sorted by Number

Place	Dollars

No places met population threshold.

Specified Housing Units Owned and Occupied by Indonesians

Top 10 Places Sorted by Number

Place	Dollars
Columbus, OH (city) Franklin County	0

Specified Housing Units Owned and Occupied by Japanese

Top 10 Places Sorted by Number

Place	Dollars
Dublin, OH (city) Franklin County	147,200
Columbus, OH (city) Franklin County	134,700

Specified Housing Units Owned and Occupied by Koreans

Top 10 Places Sorted by Number

Place	Dollars
Columbus, OH (city) Franklin County	122,700

Specified Housing Units Owned and Occupied by Laotians

Top 10 Places Sorted by Number

Place	Dollars
Columbus, OH (city) Franklin County	83,600
Akron, OH (city) Summit County	76,200

Specified Housing Units Owned and Occupied by Malaysians

Top 10 Places Sorted by Number

Place	Dollars

No places met population threshold.

Specified Housing Units Owned and Occupied by Pakistanis

Top 10 Places Sorted by Number

Place	Dollars

No places met population threshold.

Specified Housing Units Owned and Occupied by Samoans

Top 10 Places Sorted by Number

Place	Dollars

No places met population threshold.

Specified Housing Units Owned and Occupied by Sri Lankans

Top 10 Places Sorted by Number

Place	Dollars

No places met population threshold.

Specified Housing Units Owned and Occupied by Taiwanese

Top 10 Places Sorted by Number

Place	Dollars
Columbus, OH (city) Franklin County	245,000

Specified Housing Units Owned and Occupied by Thais

Top 10 Places Sorted by Number

Place	Dollars
Columbus, OH (city) Franklin County	119,100

Specified Housing Units Owned and Occupied by Tongans

Top 10 Places Sorted by Number

Place	Dollars

No places met population threshold.

Specified Housing Units Owned and Occupied by Vietnamese

Top 10 Places Sorted by Number

Place	Dollars
Columbus, OH (city) Franklin County	97,100
Cleveland, OH (city) Cuyahoga County	77,300
Akron, OH (city) Summit County	60,200

Notes: Please refer to the User's Guide for an explanation of data; tables reflect only those areas that meet Summary File 4 population thresholds, therefore there may be less than 10 places listed

OHIO

PHYSICAL FEATURES AND GENERAL CLIMATE. The climate of Ohio is remarkably varied. Less than one-half of its area is occupied by typical plains, while most of eastern and much of southern Ohio is hilly. Topography ranges in elevation from 430 feet above sea level at the junction of the Great Miami and Ohio Rivers up to 1,550 feet on a summit near Bellefontaine. In addition to this high point there are innumerable other hills which rise above 1,400 feet (mean sea level). These are located mainly along the dividing line between the Ohio River and Lake Erie drainage basins. Large areas in the State have elevations above 1,000 feet. An extensive area in northwestern Ohio is occupied by a flat lake plain — once the bottom of glacial Lake Maumee which was much larger than the present Lake Erie. The greater part of eastern Ohio is within the Allegheny Plateau, an unglaciated area consisting of picturesque hills, many of which rise above 1,300 feet and comprise many winding rivers and streams.

The Ohio River, which forms the southern and southeastern boundaries of Ohio, and its tributaries drain the greater portion of the State. A number of streams drain northward into Lake Erie. Although this area comprises nearly a third of the State, the divide between the two drainages is only 20 to 40 miles from the lake shore for a distance of more than 100 miles until it dips south of the arrowhead-shaped Maumee Basin. The largest streams in this region are the Maumee, Sandusky, and Cuyahoga Rivers. Principal tributaries flowing southward into the Ohio River include the Muskingum in the east, the Scioto in the central section, and the Great Miami in the west. A small portion in the west-central region drains westward into the Wabash River basin of Indiana.

Located west of the Appalachian Mountains, Ohio has a climate essentially continental in nature, characterized by moderate extremes of heat and cold, and wetness and dryness. Summers are moderately warm and humid, with occasional days when temperatures exceed 100°F.; winters are reasonably cold, with an average of about two days of subzero weather; and autumns are predominately cool, dry, and invigorating. Spring is the wettest season and vegetation is lush and profuse.

PRECIPITATION. Annual precipitation is slightly in excess of the national average and is well distributed, though with peaks in early spring and summer. In spite of the relatively small range in latitude and the compact shape of Ohio, rainfall varies considerably in amount and seasonal distribution. This is accounted for not only by the presence of Lake Erie on the north, but also by its topography and proximity to rain producing storm paths. Annual precipitation averages about 38 inches, being most generous in spring (about four inches in April) and least in the fall (about 2.5 inches in October). Greatest amounts are measured in the southwest where Wilmington has an average of 44.36 inches; the lake shore is driest, with Gilbralter Island having a normal of only 29.06 inches.

The southern half of the State is visited more frequently by productive rainstorms which, together with the general roughness of terrain, accounts for the larger total precipitation. The lifting of moist air masses over the hills tends to increase the yield of rainfall, especially in winter and spring. There is a marked tendency during the cold season for northeastern counties to receive snowfall amounts substantially in excess of those measured elsewhere. Northerly winds have a long fetch across Lake Huron and the widest part of Lake Erie, thus picking up moisture and heat from the lakes. This moisture is then forced to condense as the air is lifted abruptly over the divide a short distance from the lake. Average snowfall ranges from 60 inches in parts of Lake and adjoining counties down to 16 inches or less along the Ohio River.

TEMPERATURE. The normal annual temperature for the State ranges from 49.6°F. at Hiram in Portage County up to 56.9°F. at Portsmouth on the Ohio River. Variations over the State are due mainly to differences in latitude and topography, but the immediate lake shore area experiences a moderating effect due to its proximity to a large body of water. Widest temperature ranges are found generally among the eastern hills. In an average year, 90°F. heat may be expected about 20 times in summer with 100°F. or more once or twice. Readings of zero or lower are generally to be expected on two to four days each winter, and these are just as likely to occur in the south as the north. However, one winter out of six or eight will pass without experiencing zero readings anywhere in the State.

OTHER CLIMATIC ELEMENTS. The growing season, as defined by the period 32°F. or higher, ranges widely because of latitude and proximity to Lake Erie. The longest is about 200 days on the lake shore and the shortest is in the northeastern valleys within the Ohio River drainage. Dates of the average last freezing temperature in spring range from April 15 to May 18 and the mean first freeze date in fall varies from September 30 to November 6, the latter being on the western lake shore.

Damaging windstorms are mostly associated with heavy thunderstorms or line squalls. Three or four tornadoes may be expected to strike in Ohio each year. Most tornadoes, however, are of limited effect having paths that are short and narrow.

Most floods in Ohio are caused by unusual precipitation. The storms causing floods may bring rainfall of unusual intensity or of unusual duration and extent. Some floods may be caused by a series of ordinary storms which follow one another in rapid succession. Others may result from rain falling at relatively high temperatures on snow-covered areas. At times, though infrequent, flood conditions are caused or aggravated by ice gorges, especially in the tributary streams. Severe thunderstorms frequently cause local flash flooding. General flooding occurs most frequently during January to March and rarely occurs during August to October.

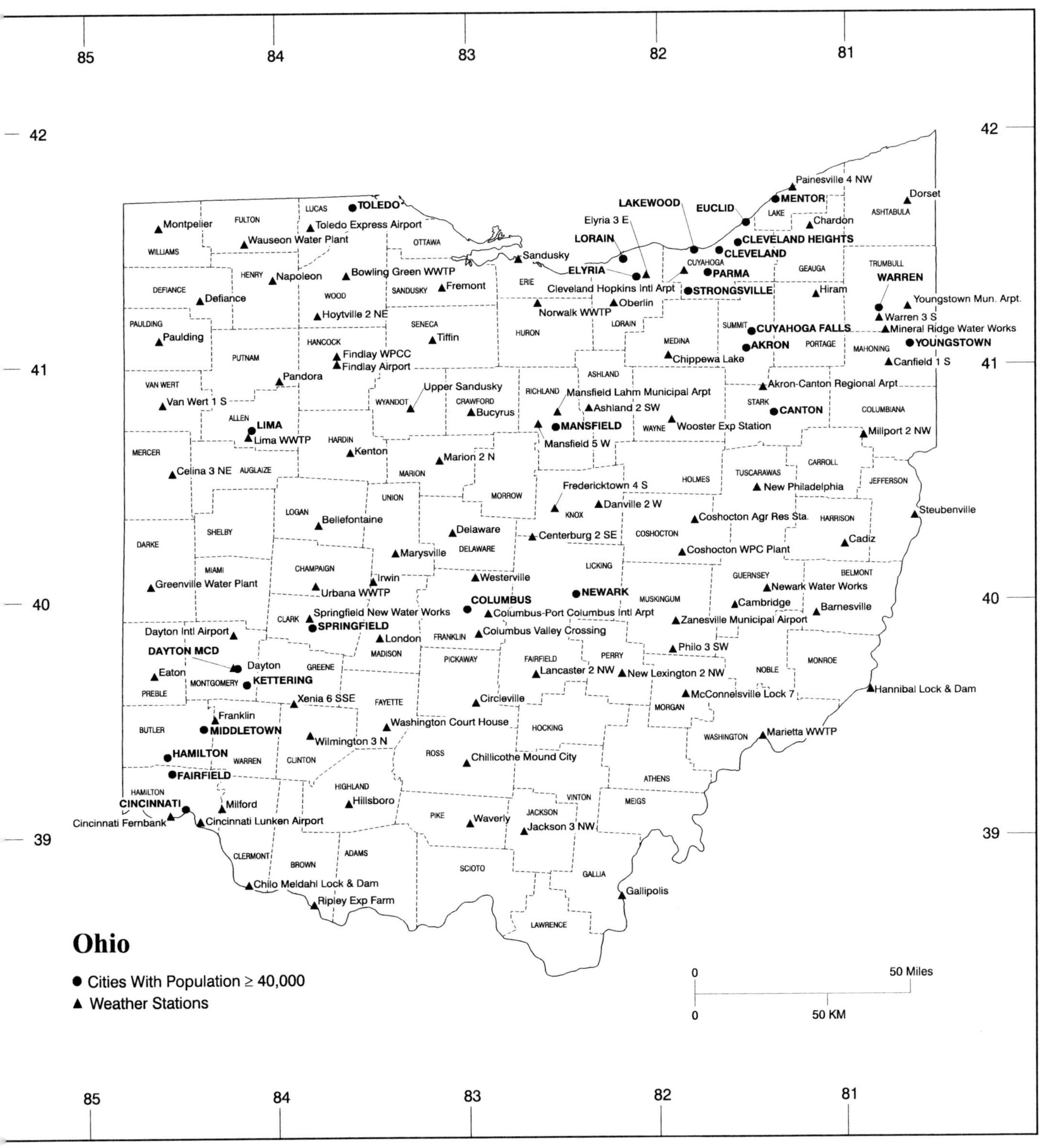
Ohio
Cities With Population ≥ 40,000
Weather Stations
TOLEDO
Toledo Express Airport
Wauseon Water Plant
Montpelier
Napoleon
Bowling Green WWTP
Fremont
Sandusky
Defiance
Hoytville 2 NE
Paulding
Tiffin
Findlay WPCC
Findlay Airport
Pandora
Upper Sandusky
Bucyrus
Van Wert 1 S
LIMA
Lima WWTP
Kenton
Celina 3 NE
Marion 2 N
Bellefontaine
Delaware
Marysville
Greenville Water Plant
Urbana WWTP
Irwin
Westerville
COLUMBUS
Columbus-Port Columbus Intl Arpt
Springfield New Water Works
SPRINGFIELD
London
Columbus Valley Crossing
Dayton Intl Airport
DAYTON MCD
Dayton
KETTERING
Eaton
Xenia 6 SSE
Franklin
MIDDLETOWN
HAMILTON
FAIRFIELD
Wilmington 3 N
Washington Court House
Circleville
Chillicothe Mound City
CINCINNATI
Milford
Cincinnati Fernbank
Cincinnati Lunken Airport
Hillsboro
Waverly
Jackson 3 NW
Chilo Meldahl Lock & Dam
Ripley Exp Farm
Gallipolis
LAKEWOOD
EUCLID
MENTOR
Painesville 4 NW
Dorset
Chardon
CLEVELAND HEIGHTS
CLEVELAND
Elyria 3 E
LORAIN
ELYRIA
PARMA
Cleveland Hopkins Intl Arpt
STRONGSVILLE
Oberlin
Norwalk WWTP
Hiram
WARREN
Youngstown Mun. Arpt.
Warren 3 S
Mineral Ridge Water Works
YOUNGSTOWN
Canfield 1 S
CUYAHOGA FALLS
AKRON
Chippewa Lake
Akron-Canton Regional Arpt
CANTON
Mansfield Lahm Municipal Arpt
Ashland 2 SW
MANSFIELD
Mansfield 5 W
Wooster Exp Station
Millport 2 NW
Fredericktown 4 S
Danville 2 W
New Philadelphia
Coshocton Agr Res Sta.
Steubenville
Centerburg 2 SE
Cadiz
Coshocton WPC Plant
NEWARK
Newark Water Works
Cambridge
Barnesville
Zanesville Municipal Airport
Philo 3 SW
Lancaster 2 NW
New Lexington 2 NW
McConnelsville Lock 7
Hannibal Lock & Dam
Marietta WWTP
LUCAS
FULTON
WILLIAMS
OTTAWA
HENRY
DEFIANCE
WOOD
SANDUSKY
ERIE
PAULDING
SENECA
HURON
LORAIN
HANCOCK
PUTNAM
VAN WERT
WYANDOT
CRAWFORD
RICHLAND
ASHLAND
ALLEN
HARDIN
MERCER
AUGLAIZE
MARION
UNION
MORROW
KNOX
LOGAN
SHELBY
DARKE
DELAWARE
MIAMI
CHAMPAIGN
LICKING
CLARK
FRANKLIN
MADISON
PICKAWAY
FAIRFIELD
PERRY
GREENE
MONTGOMERY
PREBLE
FAYETTE
BUTLER
WARREN
CLINTON
HOCKING
ROSS
HAMILTON
HIGHLAND
VINTON
MEIGS
ATHENS
PIKE
JACKSON
CLERMONT
BROWN
ADAMS
SCIOTO
GALLIA
LAWRENCE
CUYAHOGA
GEAUGA
LAKE
ASHTABULA
TRUMBULL
SUMMIT
MEDINA
PORTAGE
MAHONING
STARK
COLUMBIANA
WAYNE
HOLMES
TUSCARAWAS
CARROLL
JEFFERSON
HARRISON
COSHOCTON
GUERNSEY
BELMONT
MUSKINGUM
NOBLE
MONROE
MORGAN
WASHINGTON
85
84
83
82
81
42
41
40
39
0
50 Miles
50 KM

Ohio Weather Stations by County

County	Station Name
Allen	Lima WWTP
Ashland	Ashland 2 SW
Ashtabula	Dorset
Belmont	Barnesville
Boone	Cincinnati Covington Airport
Brown	Ripley Exp. Farm
Champaign	Urbana WWTP
Clark	Springfield New Water Works
Clermont	Chilo Meldahl Lock & Dam Milford
Clinton	Wilmington 3 N
Columbiana	Millport 2 NW
Coshocton	Coshocton Agr. Res. Station Coshocton WPC Plant
Crawford	Bucyrus
Cuyahoga	Cleveland Hopkins Int'l Airport
Darke	Greenville Water Plant
Defiance	Defiance
Delaware	Delaware
Erie	Sandusky
Fairfield	Lancaster 2 NW
Fayette	Washington Court House
Franklin	Columbus Valley Crossing Columbus-Port Columbus Int'l Westerville
Fulton	Wauseon Water Plant
Gallia	Gallipolis
Geauga	Chardon
Greene	Xenia 6 SSE
Guernsey	Cambridge
Hamilton	Cincinnati Fernbank Cincinnati Lunken Airport
Hancock	Findlay Airport Findlay WPCC
Hardin	Kenton

County	Station Name
Harrison	Cadiz
Henry	Napoleon
Highland	Hillsboro
Huron	Norwalk WWTP
Jackson	Jackson 3 NW
Jefferson	Steubenville
Knox	Centerburg 2 SE Danville 2 W Fredericktown 4 S
Lake	Painesville 4 NW
Licking	Newark Water Works
Logan	Bellefontaine
Lorain	Elyria 3 E Oberlin
Lucas	Toledo Express Airport
Madison	London
Mahoning	Canfield 1 S
Marion	Marion 2 N
Medina	Chippewa Lake
Mercer	Celina 3 NE
Monroe	Hannibal Lock & Dam
Montgomery	Dayton Int'l Airport Dayton MCD
Morgan	McConnelsville Lock 7
Muskingum	Philo 3 SW Zanesville Municipal Airport
Ottawa	Put-In-Bay
Paulding	Paulding
Perry	New Lexington 2 NW
Pickaway	Circleville
Pike	Waverly
Portage	Hiram
Preble	Eaton
Putnam	Pandora
Richland	Mansfield 5 W

County	Station Name
Richland (cont.)	Mansfield Lahm Municipal Airport
Ross	Chillicothe Mound City
Sandusky	Fremont
Scioto	Portsmouth Sciotoville
Seneca	Tiffin
Summit	Akron-Canton Regional Airport
Trumbull	Mineral Ridge Water Works Warren 3 S Youngstown Municipal Airport
Tuscarawas	New Philadelphia
Union	Irwin Marysville
Van Wert	Van Wert 1 S
Warren	Franklin
Washington	Marietta WWTP
Wayne	Wooster Exp. Station
Williams	Montpelier
Wood	Bowling Green WWTP Hoytville 2 NE
Wyandot	Upper Sandusky

Ohio Weather Stations by City

City	Station Name	Miles
Akron	Akron-Canton Regional Airport	12
Canton	Akron-Canton Regional Airport	8
Cincinnati	Cincinnati Covington Airport	11
	Cincinnati Fernbank	10
	Cincinnati Lunken Airport	5
	Milford	12
Cleveland	Cleveland Hopkins Int'l Airport	11
Cleveland Heights	Cleveland Hopkins Int'l Airport	17
Columbus	Columbus Valley Crossing	8
	Columbus-Port Columbus Int'l	6
	Westerville	9
Cuyahoga Falls	Akron-Canton Regional Airport	16
Dayton	Dayton MCD	1
	Dayton Int'l Airport	10
	Franklin	16
	Xenia 6 SSE	19
Elyria	Cleveland Hopkins Int'l Airport	13
	Elyria 3 E	3
	Oberlin	10
Euclid	Chardon	17
	Painesville 4 NW	16
Fairfield	Cincinnati Fernbank	17
	Cincinnati Lunken Airport	17
	Franklin	20
	Milford	17
Hamilton	Franklin	17
Kettering	Dayton MCD	5
	Dayton Int'l Airport	15
	Franklin	13
	Xenia 6 SSE	14
Lakewood	Cleveland Hopkins Int'l Airport	6
	Elyria 3 E	15
Lima	Lima WWTP	2
	Pandora	16
Lorain	Cleveland Hopkins Int'l Airport	17
	Elyria 3 E	8
	Oberlin	13
Mansfield	Ashland 2 SW	11
	Mansfield Lahm Municipal Airport	4
	Mansfield 5 W	5
Mentor	Chardon	11
	Painesville 4 NW	5
Middletown	Franklin	4
Parma	Cleveland Hopkins Int'l Airport	6
	Elyria 3 E	17

City	Station Name	Miles
Springfield	London	19
	Springfield New Water Works	3
	Urbana WWTP	12
Strongsville	Chippewa Lake	19
	Cleveland Hopkins Int'l Airport	6
	Elyria 3 E	12
Toledo	Monroe, MI	20
	Bowling Green WWTP	19
	Toledo Express Airport	13
Warren	Canfield 1 S	16
	Hiram	18
	Mineral Ridge Water Works	6
	Warren 3 S	3
	Youngstown Municipal Airport	8
Youngstown	Canfield 1 S	8
	Mineral Ridge Water Works	8
	Warren 3 S	11
	Youngstown Municipal Airport	11
	New Castle 1 N, PA	16

Note: Miles is the distance between the geographic center of the city and the weather station.

Ohio Weather Stations by Elevation

Feet	Station Name
1,348	Mansfield 5 W
1,292	Mansfield Lahm Muni Airport
1,263	Ashland 2 SW
1,259	Cadiz
1,240	Barnesville
1,227	Hiram
1,207	Akron-Canton Regional Airport
1,204	Centerburg 2 SE
1,184	Bellefontaine
1,177	Chippewa Lake
1,177	Youngstown Municipal Airport
1,148	Millport 2 NW
1,138	Canfield 1 S
1,138	Coshocton Agr. Res. Station
1,128	Chardon
1,099	Hillsboro
1,049	Fredericktown 4 S
1,026	Wilmington 3 N
1,023	Greenville Water Plant
1,017	London
1,017	Philo 3 SW
1,017	Wooster Exp. Station
1,007	Irwin
1,000	Eaton
997	Dayton Int'l Airport
997	Marysville
997	Urbana WWTP
994	Kenton
990	Steubenville
977	Dorset
967	Danville 2 W
967	Xenia 6 SSE
964	Marion 2 N
958	Washington Court House
954	Bucyrus
928	Springfield New Water Works
918	Delaware
898	Warren 3 S
892	New Philadelphia
889	Mineral Ridge Water Works
889	New Lexington 2 NW
879	Ripley Exp. Farm
879	Zanesville Municipal Airport
866	Cincinnati Covington Airport
859	Celina 3 NE
859	Lancaster 2 NW
859	Montpelier
853	Upper Sandusky
849	Lima WWTP
833	Newark Water Works
813	Oberlin
807	Columbus-Port Columbus Int'l
807	Westerville
797	Cambridge
797	Findlay Airport

Feet	Station Name
797	Jackson 3 NW
787	Van Wert 1 S
767	Cleveland Hopkins Int'l Airport
767	Findlay WPCC
767	Pandora
757	Coshocton WPC Plant
757	McConnelsville Lock 7
748	Wauseon Water Plant
744	Dayton MCD
738	Tiffin
734	Columbus Valley Crossing
728	Elyria 3 E
725	Paulding
698	Defiance
698	Hoytville 2 NE
679	Napoleon
672	Bowling Green WWTP
672	Circleville
669	Franklin
669	Norwalk WWTP
666	Toledo Express Airport
649	Chillicothe Mound City
620	Hannibal Lock & Dam
597	Fremont
597	Painesville 4 NW
583	Sandusky
577	Marietta WWTP
577	Put-In-Bay
567	Gallipolis
557	Waverly
538	Portsmouth Sciotoville
518	Milford
498	Chilo Meldahl Lock & Dam
498	Cincinnati Fernbank
488	Cincinnati Lunken Airport

Akron-Canton Regional Airport

The station at the Akron-Canton Airport is located about midway between Akron and Canton, a few miles south of the crest separating the Lake Erie and Muskingum River drainage areas. Precipitation at the station and southward drains through the Muskingum River into the Ohio, while northward of the crest the Cuyahoga and other streams flow into Lake Erie. The terrain is rolling with highest elevations near 1,300 feet above sea level and many small lakes provide water for local industry as well as recreational facilities for the densely populated region. The area is mainly industrial, agricultural operations having diminished rapidly in recent years.

Lake Erie has considerable influence on the area weather, tempering cold air masses during the late fall and winter, as well as contributing to the formation of brief, but heavy snow squalls until the lake freezes over.

The arrival of spring is late in this area, allowing growing of normally frost-susceptible fruits. Summers are moderately warm, but quite humid, while the months of September, October, and sometimes November are usually pleasant although with considerable morning fog. The average last occurrence of freezing temperatures in spring is the end of April, and the first occurrence in fall is late October. In past years, growing seasons for most vegetation has varied from 120 to 211 days. Temperatures and occurences of frost vary widely over the area because of the hilly terrain. Due to the influence of Lake Erie, snowfall is usually much heavier north of the station.

Akron-Canton Regional Airport *Summit County* Elevation: 1,207 ft. Latitude: 40° 55' N Longitude: 81° 26' W

	JAN	FEB	MAR	APR	MAY	JUN	JUL	AUG	SEP	OCT	NOV	DEC	YEAR
Mean Maximum Temp. (°F)	33.5	36.8	46.9	59.1	69.7	78.4	82.4	80.7	73.3	61.6	49.2	38.4	59.2
Mean Temp. (°F)	26.0	28.7	37.7	48.5	59.1	68.0	72.2	70.6	63.4	52.1	41.5	31.5	49.9
Mean Minimum Temp. (°F)	18.4	20.5	28.4	37.9	48.6	57.6	61.9	60.5	53.5	42.5	33.8	24.5	40.7
Extreme Maximum Temp. (°F)	65	70	81	88	93	100	101	97	93	81	75	76	101
Extreme Minimum Temp. (°F)	-25	-13	-3	14	27	32	43	41	35	22	2	-16	-25
Days Maximum Temp. ≥ 90°F	0	0	0	0	0	1	4	2	0	0	0	0	7
Days Maximum Temp. ≤ 32°F	14	11	4	0	0	0	0	0	0	0	2	9	40
Days Minimum Temp. ≤ 32°F	28	23	21	9	1	0	0	0	0	3	14	25	124
Days Minimum Temp. ≤ 0°F	3	2	0	0	0	0	0	0	0	0	0	1	6
Heating Degree Days (base 65°F)	1,204	1,020	841	494	216	46	7	14	116	398	697	1,031	6,084
Cooling Degree Days (base 65°F)	0	0	1	7	43	142	249	197	72	5	0	0	716
Mean Precipitation (in.)	2.50	2.30	3.13	3.34	3.94	3.63	3.90	3.52	3.40	2.61	3.08	2.96	38.31
Maximum Precipitation (in.)	8.7	5.2	8.8	6.5	9.6	8.4	11.4	8.2	9.0	8.4	9.4	6.7	65.7
Minimum Precipitation (in.)	0.7	0.3	1.0	0.9	1.0	0.4	0.7	0.5	0.2	0.4	0.6	0.3	23.8
Maximum 24-hr. Precipitation (in.)	2.8	2.0	3.2	2.0	2.6	2.8	3.3	3.7	3.7	2.6	1.9	1.6	3.7
Days With ≥ 0.1" Precipitation	7	6	8	8	8	7	7	7	6	6	7	7	84
Days With ≥ 1.0" Precipitation	0	0	0	1	1	1	1	1	1	0	0	1	7
Mean Snowfall (in.)	12.9	9.5	9.0	2.6	trace	trace	0.0	0.0	trace	0.6	3.2	9.1	46.9
Maximum Snowfall (in.)	38	20	21	21	3	0	0	0	0	7	22	29	72
Maximum 24-hr. Snowfall (in.)	9	10	8	20	3	0	0	0	0	4	7	16	20
Days With ≥ 1.0" Snow Depth	16	12	6	1	0	0	0	0	0	0	1	9	45
Thunderstorm Days	< 1	< 1	2	4	6	7	8	6	3	1	1	< 1	38
Foggy Days	13	12	13	13	14	15	17	19	17	15	13	14	175
Predominant Sky Cover	OVR	OVR	OVR	OVR	OVR	OVR	OVR	OVR	OVR	OVR	OVR	OVR	OVR
Mean Relative Humidity 7am (%)	80	80	79	77	77	80	84	87	88	84	80	81	82
Mean Relative Humidity 4pm (%)	69	65	59	53	52	54	54	55	56	56	64	70	59
Mean Dewpoint (°F)	19	20	27	36	47	56	61	60	53	42	32	24	40
Prevailing Wind Direction	SW	WSW	W	SW	SW	SW	SW	SW	S	S	S	WSW	SW
Prevailing Wind Speed (mph)	13	12	13	12	10	9	8	8	8	9	12	13	10
Maximum Wind Gust (mph)	76	58	64	60	56	63	68	62	52	51	58	61	76

Cincinnati Covington Airport

Greater Cincinnati Airport is located on a gently rolling plateau about 12 miles southwest of downtown Cincinnati and two miles south of the Ohio River at its nearest point. The river valley is rather narrow and steep-sided varying from one to three miles in width and the river bed is 500 feet below the level of the airport.

The climate is continental with a rather wide range of temperatures from winter to summer. A precipitation maximum occurs during winter and spring with a late summer and fall minimum. On the average, the maximum snowfall occurs during January, although the heaviest 24-hour amounts have been recorded during late November and February.

The heaviest precipitation, as well as the precipitation of the longest duration, is normally associated with low pressure disturbances moving in a general southwest to northeast direction through the Ohio valley and south of the Cincinnati area.

Summers are warm and rather humid. The temperature will reach 100 degrees or more in one year out of three. However, the temperature will reach 90 degrees or higher on about 19 days each year. Winters are moderately cold with frequent periods of extensive cloudiness.

The freeze free period lasts on the average 187 days from mid-April to the latter part of October.

Cincinnati Covington Airport *Boone County* Elevation: 866 ft. Latitude: 39° 03' N Longitude: 84° 40' W

	JAN	FEB	MAR	APR	MAY	JUN	JUL	AUG	SEP	OCT	NOV	DEC	YEAR
Mean Maximum Temp. (°F)	37.4	42.0	52.7	64.1	73.8	81.7	85.8	84.2	77.7	65.8	53.1	42.4	63.4
Mean Temp. (°F)	29.1	33.1	42.9	53.2	63.0	71.4	75.8	74.0	67.2	55.2	44.2	34.5	53.6
Mean Minimum Temp. (°F)	20.7	24.2	33.0	42.2	52.2	61.0	65.6	63.8	56.6	44.5	35.3	26.4	43.8
Extreme Maximum Temp. (°F)	70	74	84	89	92	102	103	101	95	87	81	75	103
Extreme Minimum Temp. (°F)	-25	-11	-11	15	30	39	48	43	31	19	1	-20	-25
Days Maximum Temp. ≥ 90°F	0	0	0	0	0	4	8	5	2	0	0	0	19
Days Maximum Temp. ≤ 32°F	11	7	1	0	0	0	0	0	0	0	1	6	26
Days Minimum Temp. ≤ 32°F	26	21	16	5	0	0	0	0	0	3	13	21	105
Days Minimum Temp. ≤ 0°F	3	1	0	0	0	0	0	0	0	0	0	1	5
Heating Degree Days (base 65°F)	1,108	894	681	363	132	17	1	2	64	315	618	941	5,136
Cooling Degree Days (base 65°F)	0	0	3	13	77	225	352	294	132	19	1	1	1,117
Mean Precipitation (in.)	2.81	2.61	3.95	4.06	4.48	4.46	3.75	3.79	2.79	3.00	3.46	3.29	42.45
Maximum Precipitation (in.)	9.4	6.7	12.2	7.2	9.5	7.4	8.4	7.7	8.6	8.6	7.5	7.9	57.6
Minimum Precipitation (in.)	0.6	0.3	1.1	1.0	1.1	0.9	1.2	0.3	0.2	0.3	0.4	0.5	28.0
Maximum 24-hr. Precipitation (in.)	4.0	2.8	5.2	2.1	3.0	3.3	3.9	3.5	3.2	4.3	3.3	2.5	5.2
Days With ≥ 0.1" Precipitation	6	6	9	8	8	7	7	7	5	6	7	7	83
Days With ≥ 1.0" Precipitation	0	1	1	1	1	1	1	1	1	1	1	1	11
Mean Snowfall (in.)	7.7	6.1	4.2	0.6	trace	trace	trace	0.0	0.0	0.4	1.3	3.3	23.6
Maximum Snowfall (in.)	32	20	13	4	trace	0	0	0	0	6	12	13	54
Maximum 24-hr. Snowfall (in.)	8	9	10	3	trace	0	0	0	0	6	9	8	10
Days With ≥ 1.0" Snow Depth	8	7	3	0	0	0	0	0	0	0	0	3	21
Thunderstorm Days	1	1	3	4	6	7	8	6	3	1	1	< 1	41
Foggy Days	13	12	12	9	12	13	16	19	16	14	12	14	162
Predominant Sky Cover	OVR	OVR	OVR	OVR	OVR	OVR	OVR	OVR	OVR	OVR	OVR	OVR	OVR
Mean Relative Humidity 7am (%)	80	79	77	76	80	82	85	88	87	83	79	80	81
Mean Relative Humidity 4pm (%)	65	60	55	50	52	53	54	53	52	51	59	65	56
Mean Dewpoint (°F)	22	24	31	40	51	60	64	63	56	44	34	26	43
Prevailing Wind Direction	SSW	SSW	SSW	SSW	SSW	SSW	SW	SSW	SSW	SSW	SSW	SSW	SSW
Prevailing Wind Speed (mph)	12	12	13	12	9	9	8	7	8	9	12	12	10
Maximum Wind Gust (mph)	71	55	64	71	59	67	83	62	54	59	56	61	83

Cleveland Hopkins Int'l Airport

Cleveland is on the south shore of Lake Erie in northeast Ohio. The metropolitan area has a lake frontage of 3l miles. The surrounding terrain is generally level except for an abrupt ridge on the eastern edge of the city which rises some 500 feet above the shore terrain. The Cuyahoga River, which flows through a rather deep but narrow north-south valley, bisects the city.

Local climate is continental in character but with strong modifying influences by Lake Erie. West to northerly winds blowing off Lake Erie tend to lower daily high temperatures in summer and raise temperatures in winter. Temperatures at Hopkins Airport which is 5 miles south of the lakeshore average from two to four degrees higher than the lakeshore in summer, while overnight low temperatures average from two to four degrees lower than the lakefront during all seasons.

In this area, summers are moderately warm and humid with occasional days when temperatures exceed 90 degrees. Winters are relatively cold and cloudy with an average of five days with sub-zero temperatures. Weather changes occur every few days from the passing of cold fronts.

The daily range in temperature is usually greatest in late summer and least in winter. Annual extremes in temperature normally occur soon after late June and December. Maximum temperatures below freezing occur most often in December, January, and February. Temperatures of 100 degrees or higher are rare. On the average, freezing temperatures in fall are first recorded in October while the last freezing temperature in spring normally occurs in April.

As is characteristic of continental climates, precipitation varies widely from year to year. However, it is normally abundant and well distributed throughout the year with spring being the wettest season. Showers and thunderstorms account for most of the rainfall during the growing season. Thunderstorms are most frequent from April through August. Snowfall may fluctuate widely. Mean annual snowfall increases from west to east in Cuyahoga County ranging from about 45 inches in the west to more than 90 inches in the extreme east.

Damaging winds of 50 mph or greater are usually associated with thunderstorms. Tornadoes, one of the most destructive of all atmospheric storms, occasionally occur in Cuyahoga County.

Cleveland Hopkins Int'l Airport *Cuyahoga Co.* Elevation: 767 ft. Latitude: 41° 24' N Longitude: 81° 51' W

	JAN	FEB	MAR	APR	MAY	JUN	JUL	AUG	SEP	OCT	NOV	DEC	YEAR
Mean Maximum Temp. (°F)	33.1	36.4	46.3	58.0	69.2	78.0	82.4	80.4	73.6	62.0	49.9	38.7	59.0
Mean Temp. (°F)	25.9	28.7	37.6	48.1	58.9	68.0	72.5	70.9	64.1	52.9	42.5	32.0	50.2
Mean Minimum Temp. (°F)	18.7	20.9	28.9	38.2	48.5	57.9	62.5	61.3	54.5	43.7	35.0	25.3	41.3
Extreme Maximum Temp. (°F)	67	71	82	88	91	104	100	99	95	84	77	77	104
Extreme Minimum Temp. (°F)	-20	-10	-5	11	27	31	45	38	34	19	3	-15	-20
Days Maximum Temp. ≥ 90°F	0	0	0	0	0	2	4	2	1	0	0	0	9
Days Maximum Temp. ≤ 32°F	15	12	4	0	0	0	0	0	0	0	1	9	41
Days Minimum Temp. ≤ 32°F	28	23	21	9	1	0	0	0	0	2	13	24	121
Days Minimum Temp. ≤ 0°F	3	2	0	0	0	0	0	0	0	0	0	1	6
Heating Degree Days (base 65°F)	1,205	1,019	844	508	227	51	6	12	106	376	670	1,016	6,040
Cooling Degree Days (base 65°F)	0	0	2	7	45	148	257	203	82	8	1	0	753
Mean Precipitation (in.)	2.43	2.27	2.96	3.34	3.42	3.87	3.57	3.56	3.77	2.75	3.42	3.12	38.48
Maximum Precipitation (in.)	7.0	4.7	6.1	6.6	9.1	9.1	9.1	9.0	7.3	9.5	8.8	8.6	53.8
Minimum Precipitation (in.)	0.4	0.5	0.8	1.2	1.0	0.6	1.2	0.5	0.7	0.6	0.8	0.7	18.8
Maximum 24-hr. Precipitation (in.)	2.5	2.0	2.8	2.1	3.4	3.0	2.7	3.5	2.3	3.4	2.2	2.4	3.5
Days With ≥ 0.1" Precipitation	7	6	8	8	8	7	6	7	7	7	8	8	87
Days With ≥ 1.0" Precipitation	0	0	0	0	1	1	1	1	1	0	1	0	6
Mean Snowfall (in.)	16.4	13.4	10.8	2.5	trace	trace	trace	0.0	trace	0.4	4.9	12.6	61.0
Maximum Snowfall (in.)	43	39	26	13	2	0	0	0	0	8	22	30	97
Maximum 24-hr. Snowfall (in.)	10	14	11	9	2	0	0	0	0	7	13	12	14
Days With ≥ 1.0" Snow Depth	17	14	7	1	0	0	0	0	0	0	3	10	52
Thunderstorm Days	< 1	< 1	2	3	5	6	6	5	3	2	1	< 1	33
Foggy Days	13	12	13	12	13	11	12	14	12	11	12	13	148
Predominant Sky Cover	OVR	OVR	OVR	OVR	OVR	OVR	OVR	OVR	OVR	OVR	OVR	OVR	OVR
Mean Relative Humidity 7am (%)	79	79	79	76	77	79	81	85	84	81	78	78	80
Mean Relative Humidity 4pm (%)	70	67	62	56	54	55	55	58	58	58	65	70	61
Mean Dewpoint (°F)	19	21	27	37	47	57	61	61	54	43	33	24	40
Prevailing Wind Direction	SW	SW	SW	S	N	SSW	SW	SW	S	SSW	SW	SW	SW
Prevailing Wind Speed (mph)	13	13	14	13	9	10	9	8	9	10	13	13	12
Maximum Wind Gust (mph)	82	64	63	78	55	77	67	51	58	54	59	71	82

Columbus-Port Columbus Int'l

Columbus is located in the center of the state and in the drainage area of the Ohio River. The airport is located at the eastern boundary of the city approximately seven miles from the center of the business district.

Four nearly parallel streams run through or adjacent to the city. The Scioto River is the principal stream and flows from the northwest into the center of the city and then flows straight south toward the Ohio River. The Olentangy River runs almost due south and empties into the Scioto just west of the business district. Alum Creek empties into the Big Walnut southeast of the city and the Big Walnut Creek empties into the Scioto a few miles downstream.

The narrow valleys associated with the streams flowing through the city supply the only variation in the micro-climate of the area. The city proper shows the typical metropolitan effect with shrubs and flowers blossoming earlier than in the immediate surroundings and in retarding light frost on clear quiet nights. Many small areas to the southeast and to the north and northeast show marked effects of air drainage as evidenced by the frequent formation of shallow ground fog at daybreak during the summer and fall months and the higher frequency of frost in the spring and fall.

The average occurrence of the last freezing temperature in the spring within the city proper is mid-April, and the first freeze in the fall is very late October, but in the immediate surroundings there is much variation. For example, at Valley Crossing located at the southeastern outskirts of the city, the average occurrence of the last 32 degree temperature in the spring is very early May, while the first 32 degree temperature in the fall is mid-October.

The records show a high frequency of calm or very low wind speeds during the late evening and early morning hours, from June through September. The rolling landscape is conducive to calm winds from the Weather Service location at the airport these are toward the northwest with the wind direction indicated as southeast, at speeds generally 4 mph or less.

Columbus is located in the area of changeable weather. Air masses from central and northwest Canada frequently invade this region. Air from the Gulf of Mexico often reaches central Ohio during the summer and to a much lesser extent in the fall and winter. There are also occasional weather changes brought about by cool outbreaks from the Hudson Bay region of Canada, especially during the spring months. At infrequent intervals the general circulation will bring showers or snow to Columbus from the Atlantic.

Columbus-Port Columbus Int'l *Franklin County* Elevation: 807 ft. Latitude: 39° 59' N Longitude: 82° 53' W

	JAN	FEB	MAR	APR	MAY	JUN	JUL	AUG	SEP	OCT	NOV	DEC	YEAR
Mean Maximum Temp. (°F)	35.2	39.4	50.6	62.4	72.7	81.0	84.7	83.1	76.5	64.5	51.6	40.6	61.9
Mean Temp. (°F)	27.6	31.2	41.0	51.4	61.8	70.4	74.5	72.9	66.0	54.0	43.2	33.4	52.3
Mean Minimum Temp. (°F)	19.9	22.8	31.4	40.3	50.8	59.7	64.2	62.6	55.4	43.5	34.7	26.1	42.6
Extreme Maximum Temp. (°F)	70	74	83	88	93	101	100	101	97	86	80	76	101
Extreme Minimum Temp. (°F)	-22	-13	-6	14	30	35	43	40	33	21	5	-17	-22
Days Maximum Temp. ≥ 90°F	0	0	0	0	1	3	6	4	1	0	0	0	15
Days Maximum Temp. ≤ 32°F	12	9	2	0	0	0	0	0	0	0	1	7	31
Days Minimum Temp. ≤ 32°F	27	22	18	6	0	0	0	0	0	3	13	23	112
Days Minimum Temp. ≤ 0°F	3	1	0	0	0	0	0	0	0	0	0	1	5
Heating Degree Days (base 65°F)	1,154	950	738	412	159	25	3	6	77	345	649	973	5,491
Cooling Degree Days (base 65°F)	0	0	2	9	66	201	319	267	114	12	1	0	991
Mean Precipitation (in.)	2.46	2.16	2.90	3.30	3.88	4.15	4.60	3.72	2.91	2.29	3.21	2.89	38.47
Maximum Precipitation (in.)	8.3	5.1	9.6	6.4	9.1	9.8	12.4	8.6	6.8	5.2	10.7	7.0	53.2
Minimum Precipitation (in.)	0.6	0.3	1.0	0.7	0.9	0.7	1.0	0.6	0.5	0.1	0.6	0.5	24.5
Maximum 24-hr. Precipitation (in.)	4.8	2.1	3.4	2.0	2.1	2.5	5.1	3.2	2.7	1.7	2.4	1.7	5.1
Days With ≥ 0.1" Precipitation	6	6	8	7	8	7	7	7	5	5	7	7	80
Days With ≥ 1.0" Precipitation	0	0	0	1	1	1	1	1	1	0	1	0	7
Mean Snowfall (in.)	10.5	6.1	4.3	1.2	trace	trace	trace	0.0	trace	0.2	1.6	4.5	28.4
Maximum Snowfall (in.)	34	16	14	13	1	0	0	0	trace	5	15	17	48
Maximum 24-hr. Snowfall (in.)	7	9	9	12	1	0	0	0	trace	4	8	8	12
Days With ≥ 1.0" Snow Depth	12	8	3	0	0	0	0	0	0	0	0	4	27
Thunderstorm Days	< 1	1	2	4	6	8	8	6	3	1	1	< 1	40
Foggy Days	13	11	12	10	13	14	16	19	15	14	12	14	163
Predominant Sky Cover	OVR	OVR	OVR	OVR	OVR	OVR	OVR	SCT	OVR	OVR	OVR	OVR	OVR
Mean Relative Humidity 7am (%)	78	78	76	76	79	81	84	87	87	83	80	80	81
Mean Relative Humidity 4pm (%)	67	62	55	51	52	53	54	53	53	52	61	67	57
Mean Dewpoint (°F)	20	22	29	38	49	59	63	62	55	43	34	25	42
Prevailing Wind Direction	S	S	WNW	S	S	S	S	S	S	S	S	S	S
Prevailing Wind Speed (mph)	9	9	12	9	8	8	7	7	8	8	9	9	9
Maximum Wind Gust (mph)	69	58	62	78	76	68	67	66	62	53	53	61	78

Dayton Int'l Airport

Dayton is located near the center of the Miami River Valley, which is a nearly flat plain, 50 to 200 feet below the general elevation of the adjacent rolling country. Three Miami River tributaries, the Mad River, the Stillwater River, and Wolf Creek converge, fanwise, from the north to join the master stream within the city limits of Dayton. Heavy rains in March 1913 caused the worst flood disaster in the history of the Miami Valley. During the flood more than 400 people lost their lives and property damage amounted to $100 million. After the 1913 flood, dams were built on the streams north of Dayton, forming retarding basins. No floods have occurred at Dayton since the construction of these dams.

The elevation of the city of Dayton is about 750 feet. Terrain north of the city slopes gradually upward to about 1,100 feet at Indian Lake. Ten miles southeast of Indian Lake, near Bellefontaine, is the highest point in the state, with an elevation of about 1,550 feet. South of the city, the terrain slopes gradually downward to about 450 feet where the Miami River empties into the Ohio River.

Precipitation, which is rather evenly distributed throughout the year, and moderate temperatures help to make the Miami Valley a rich agricultural region. High relative humidities during much of the year cause some discomfort to people with allergies. Temperatures of zero or below will be experienced in about four years out of five, while 100 degrees or higher will be recorded in about one year out of five. Extreme temperatures are usually of short duration. The downward slope of about 700 feet in the 163 miles of the Miami River may have some moderating influence on the winter temperatures in the Miami Valley.

Based on the 1951-1980 period, the average last occurrence in the spring of freezing temperatures is mid-April, and the average first occurrence in the autumn is late October.

Cold, polar air, flowing across the Great Lakes, causes much cloudiness during the winter, and is accompanied by frequent snow flurries. These add little to the total snowfall.

Dayton Int'l Airport *Montgomery County* Elevation: 997 ft. Latitude: 39° 54' N Longitude: 84° 13' W

	JAN	FEB	MAR	APR	MAY	JUN	JUL	AUG	SEP	OCT	NOV	DEC	YEAR
Mean Maximum Temp. (°F)	34.3	38.9	49.9	61.9	72.3	81.1	85.1	83.1	76.4	64.2	51.0	39.8	61.5
Mean Temp. (°F)	26.6	30.5	40.5	51.2	61.8	70.7	74.8	72.8	65.7	53.9	42.8	32.4	52.0
Mean Minimum Temp. (°F)	18.9	22.1	31.0	40.5	51.2	60.3	64.5	62.4	54.9	43.6	34.4	24.9	42.4
Extreme Maximum Temp. (°F)	66	73	82	88	92	102	102	102	96	86	79	72	102
Extreme Minimum Temp. (°F)	-25	-12	-7	15	28	40	44	41	32	23	5	-20	-25
Days Maximum Temp. ≥ 90°F	0	0	0	0	0	3	7	4	1	0	0	0	15
Days Maximum Temp. ≤ 32°F	13	9	3	0	0	0	0	0	0	0	1	8	34
Days Minimum Temp. ≤ 32°F	27	22	18	6	0	0	0	0	0	3	14	24	114
Days Minimum Temp. ≤ 0°F	3	2	0	0	0	0	0	0	0	0	0	1	6
Heating Degree Days (base 65°F)	1,184	967	755	417	161	22	2	6	85	349	662	1,006	5,616
Cooling Degree Days (base 65°F)	0	0	2	9	63	201	319	258	109	12	1	0	974
Mean Precipitation (in.)	2.53	2.26	3.29	4.07	4.16	4.21	3.73	3.44	2.59	2.70	3.28	3.06	39.32
Maximum Precipitation (in.)	9.9	5.8	7.6	6.8	9.0	10.9	8.5	8.0	5.7	6.3	8.1	10.0	59.8
Minimum Precipitation (in.)	0.3	0.2	1.1	0.6	1.5	0.3	0.5	0.3	0.3	0.2	0.5	0.4	24.2
Maximum 24-hr. Precipitation (in.)	4.2	2.6	2.9	3.1	3.2	3.8	3.2	3.4	2.6	3.5	2.8	2.8	4.2
Days With ≥ 0.1" Precipitation	6	5	8	8	8	7	7	6	5	6	7	7	80
Days With ≥ 1.0" Precipitation	0	0	0	1	1	1	1	1	1	0	1	1	8
Mean Snowfall (in.)	9.7	6.6	4.7	0.8	trace	0.0	trace	0.0	0.0	0.4	1.5	4.4	28.1
Maximum Snowfall (in.)	40	18	14	5	trace	0	0	0	0	6	13	16	53
Maximum 24-hr. Snowfall (in.)	12	7	11	5	trace	0	0	0	0	5	8	6	12
Days With ≥ 1.0" Snow Depth	12	9	3	0	0	0	0	0	0	0	1	5	30
Thunderstorm Days	< 1	1	2	4	6	7	8	6	3	2	1	< 1	40
Foggy Days	15	12	14	12	13	13	15	18	15	14	14	15	170
Predominant Sky Cover	OVR	OVR	OVR	OVR	OVR	OVR	OVR	OVR	OVR	OVR	OVR	OVR	OVR
Mean Relative Humidity 7am (%)	80	79	79	77	78	80	83	86	87	83	81	81	81
Mean Relative Humidity 4pm (%)	68	64	59	53	52	52	53	53	52	52	63	69	57
Mean Dewpoint (°F)	20	22	30	39	49	58	63	62	54	43	33	25	42
Prevailing Wind Direction	W	WNW	WNW	SSW	SSW	SSW	SW	SW	SSW	SSW	SSW	SSW	SSW
Prevailing Wind Speed (mph)	13	13	13	13	12	10	9	9	9	10	13	13	12
Maximum Wind Gust (mph)	69	52	67	63	60	60	71	61	48	46	54	62	71

Mansfield Lahm Municipal Airport

Mansfield is in the north central highlands at the geographical and climatological junction of central Ohio, northwest Ohio, and northeast Ohio. The station is on a plateau 3 miles north of the city of Mansfield and surrounded by rolling open farmland. The general elevation ranges from around 1,300 to 1,400 feet above sea level with the 1,000-foot contour east to west some 15 miles to the north. The climate is continental, with the modifying effects of Lake Erie most pronounced in winter. Lake Erie is just 38 miles due north.

The lake influence, plus the elevation, produce cloudy skies and considerable snow shower activity from late November into April with any wind flow from northwest through northeast. Because of this, any windshift with a cold frontal passage in winter does not bring the clearing skies, indeed, more snow is often measured from the flurry activity behind the front than from the pre-frontal conditions. A frozen Lake Erie will allow clearing skies, but an open lake dictates overcast and snow flurries. Usually the lake is open enough to set off the flurries and cloudy conditions. The major snow producer will be an intense storm moving out of the southwest with the Gulf of Mexico moisture available. Snow cover is almost constant from December through March due to almost daily snow flurries, but the depth of cover is rarely more than 8 inches. Daytime winter temperatures are not above the freezing mark too often.

Spring is a short period of rapid transition from hard winter to summer conditions. April usually brings abundant shower activity and the crops and vegetation get a quick start.

Summer is a pleasant season with low humidities and no extremely high temperatures. Rarely does the temperature climb above the 90 degree point. Thunderstorms average about once every three days during the season from June through September. Highest winds are associated with the heavier thunderstorms, and while hail does not occur often, it is of major concern to the applegrowers in the area. Flooding problems are confined to the flash-flood type on the small streams in the area.

The growing season is normally about 153 days. Autumn usually produces many clear warm days and cool invigorating nights. Ground fog is at a maximum incidence during the autumn. Little rainfall occurs to interfere with harvest time and county fair time.

Mansfield Lahm Municipal Airport *Richland Co.* Elevation: 1,292 ft. Latitude: 40° 49' N Longitude: 82° 31' W

	JAN	FEB	MAR	APR	MAY	JUN	JUL	AUG	SEP	OCT	NOV	DEC	YEAR
Mean Maximum Temp. (°F)	32.4	35.8	46.4	58.6	69.5	78.0	82.1	80.0	73.4	61.8	48.9	37.6	58.7
Mean Temp. (°F)	25.0	28.0	37.5	48.4	59.1	67.9	72.2	70.4	63.6	52.3	41.3	30.7	49.7
Mean Minimum Temp. (°F)	17.6	20.1	28.4	38.1	48.7	57.7	62.2	60.7	53.7	42.7	33.6	23.8	40.6
Extreme Maximum Temp. (°F)	65	68	82	86	90	101	100	97	92	84	76	73	101
Extreme Minimum Temp. (°F)	-22	-11	-6	8	26	37	43	42	33	20	2	-17	-22
Days Maximum Temp. ≥ 90°F	0	0	0	0	0	1	3	1	1	0	0	0	6
Days Maximum Temp. ≤ 32°F	16	12	4	0	0	0	0	0	0	0	2	10	44
Days Minimum Temp. ≤ 32°F	28	24	21	9	1	0	0	0	0	4	15	25	127
Days Minimum Temp. ≤ 0°F	4	2	0	0	0	0	0	0	0	0	0	1	7
Heating Degree Days (base 65°F)	1,234	1,038	848	499	219	50	7	17	115	396	706	1,056	6,185
Cooling Degree Days (base 65°F)	0	0	2	7	43	143	238	185	73	7	0	0	698
Mean Precipitation (in.)	2.57	2.11	3.33	4.20	4.42	4.42	4.30	4.45	3.51	2.70	3.80	3.24	43.05
Maximum Precipitation (in.)	11.5	5.4	7.0	7.0	8.8	10.0	13.2	8.6	7.8	6.4	12.8	11.2	67.2
Minimum Precipitation (in.)	0.4	0.3	1.2	0.8	1.1	0.6	0.9	0.6	0.7	0.4	0.7	0.7	21.8
Maximum 24-hr. Precipitation (in.)	2.7	2.8	2.4	2.3	2.6	3.7	3.4	3.8	2.3	3.3	3.1	2.6	3.8
Days With ≥ 0.1" Precipitation	6	5	8	9	9	7	7	7	6	6	7	7	84
Days With ≥ 1.0" Precipitation	0	0	1	1	1	1	1	1	1	0	1	1	9
Mean Snowfall (in.)	12.9	9.8	6.9	2.0	trace	trace	0.0	0.0	trace	0.6	2.5	8.6	43.3
Maximum Snowfall (in.)	42	18	17	13	1	0	0	0	0	10	12	23	59
Maximum 24-hr. Snowfall (in.)	10	9	8	12	1	0	0	0	0	8	5	12	12
Days With ≥ 1.0" Snow Depth	17	14	6	1	0	0	0	0	0	0	2	10	50
Thunderstorm Days	< 1	< 1	2	3	5	6	7	6	3	1	1	< 1	34
Foggy Days	13	12	14	13	14	13	14	17	15	13	13	15	166
Predominant Sky Cover	OVR	OVR	OVR	OVR	OVR	OVR	SCT	SCT	OVR	OVR	OVR	OVR	OVR
Mean Relative Humidity 7am (%)	82	81	81	78	78	81	83	87	87	83	82	83	82
Mean Relative Humidity 4pm (%)	72	69	64	56	55	56	56	57	58	56	67	74	62
Mean Dewpoint (°F)	20	21	28	37	47	58	62	61	54	42	33	24	40
Prevailing Wind Direction	WSW	WSW	WSW	WSW	SSW	SSW	SW	SSW	S	S	SW	WSW	WSW
Prevailing Wind Speed (mph)	15	14	15	14	13	12	10	10	9	10	14	14	13
Maximum Wind Gust (mph)	62	59	62	68	60	68	81	69	61	53	69	69	81

Toledo Express Airport

Toledo is located on the western end of Lake Erie at the mouth of the Maumee River. Except for a bank up from the river about 30 feet, the terrain is generally level with only a slight slope toward the river and Lake Erie. The city has quite a diversified industrial section and excellent harbor facilities, making it a large transportation center for rail, water, and motor freight. Generally rich agricultural land is found in the surrounding area, especially up the Maumee Valley toward the Indiana state line.

Rainfall is usually sufficient for general agriculture. The terrain is level and drainage rather poor, therefore, a little less than the normal precipitation during the growing season is better than excessive amounts. Snowfall is generally light in this area, distributed throughout the winter from November to March with frequent thaws.

The nearness of Lake Erie and the other Great Lakes has a moderating effect on the temperature, and extremes are seldom recorded. On average, only fifteen days a year experience temperatures of 90 degrees or higher, and only eight days when it drops to zero or lower. The growing season averages 160 days, but has ranged from over 220 to less than 125 days.

Humidity is rather high throughout the year in this area, and there is an excessive amount of cloudiness. In the winter months the sun shines during only about 30 percent of the daylight hours. December and January, the cloudiest months, sometimes have as little as 16 percent of the possible hours of sunshine.

Severe windstorms, causing more than minor damage, occur infrequently. There are on the average twenty-three days per year having a sustained wind velocity of 32 mph or more.

Flooding in the Toledo area is produced by several factors. Heavy rains of one inch or more will cause a sudden rise in creeks and drainage ditches to the point of overflow. The western shores of Lake Erie are subject to flooding when the lake level is high and prolonged periods of east to northeast winds prevail.

Toledo Express Airport *Lucas County* Elevation: 666 ft. Latitude: 41° 35' N Longitude: 83° 48' W

	JAN	FEB	MAR	APR	MAY	JUN	JUL	AUG	SEP	OCT	NOV	DEC	YEAR
Mean Maximum Temp. (°F)	30.9	34.5	45.8	58.9	70.9	79.9	84.0	81.7	74.6	62.3	48.4	36.4	59.0
Mean Temp. (°F)	23.5	26.5	36.6	48.0	59.3	68.4	72.8	70.6	63.2	51.4	40.2	29.3	49.1
Mean Minimum Temp. (°F)	16.0	18.4	27.3	37.1	47.6	56.9	61.5	59.4	51.8	40.5	31.9	22.2	39.2
Extreme Maximum Temp. (°F)	65	71	81	88	94	104	104	99	98	87	78	69	104
Extreme Minimum Temp. (°F)	-20	-14	-6	8	25	32	40	34	26	15	5	-19	-20
Days Maximum Temp. ≥ 90°F	0	0	0	0	1	3	6	3	1	0	0	0	14
Days Maximum Temp. ≤ 32°F	17	12	4	0	0	0	0	0	0	0	2	10	45
Days Minimum Temp. ≤ 32°F	29	25	22	10	1	0	0	0	0	6	17	26	136
Days Minimum Temp. ≤ 0°F	5	3	0	0	0	0	0	0	0	0	0	1	9
Heating Degree Days (base 65°F)	1,282	1,081	875	510	216	44	6	16	125	421	738	1,099	6,413
Cooling Degree Days (base 65°F)	0	0	1	6	47	161	270	206	77	6	0	0	774
Mean Precipitation (in.)	1.93	1.88	2.65	3.27	3.05	3.77	2.93	3.15	2.87	2.32	2.80	2.61	33.23
Maximum Precipitation (in.)	4.6	5.4	5.7	6.1	5.1	8.5	6.8	8.5	8.1	5.5	6.9	6.8	40.8
Minimum Precipitation (in.)	0.3	0.3	0.6	0.9	1.0	0.3	0.3	0.4	0.6	0.3	0.5	0.5	22.0
Maximum 24-hr. Precipitation (in.)	1.5	2.6	2.6	2.9	1.7	3.1	4.3	2.4	3.3	2.9	2.7	3.5	4.3
Days With ≥ 0.1" Precipitation	5	5	7	8	7	7	6	6	6	6	6	7	76
Days With ≥ 1.0" Precipitation	0	0	0	0	1	1	1	1	1	0	0	0	5
Mean Snowfall (in.)	10.9	8.2	5.7	1.4	trace	trace	trace	trace	trace	0.2	2.7	8.1	37.2
Maximum Snowfall (in.)	31	17	18	12	1	0	0	0	trace	2	18	24	72
Maximum 24-hr. Snowfall (in.)	10	8	9	7	1	0	0	0	trace	2	7	14	14
Days With ≥ 1.0" Snow Depth	17	14	5	1	0	0	0	0	0	0	1	10	48
Thunderstorm Days	< 1	1	2	4	5	7	7	6	4	1	1	< 1	38
Foggy Days	13	11	14	12	12	11	14	18	15	13	14	15	162
Predominant Sky Cover	OVR	OVR	OVR	OVR	OVR	OVR	SCT	SCT	OVR	OVR	OVR	OVR	OVR
Mean Relative Humidity 7am (%)	80	80	81	80	80	82	86	91	91	86	83	83	84
Mean Relative Humidity 4pm (%)	68	65	59	53	51	52	53	56	54	55	65	72	58
Mean Dewpoint (°F)	17	19	27	36	47	57	62	61	54	42	32	23	40
Prevailing Wind Direction	WSW	WSW	ENE	WSW	WSW	SW	SW	SW	SW	SW	WSW	WSW	WSW
Prevailing Wind Speed (mph)	13	13	12	13	12	9	8	8	9	10	13	13	12
Maximum Wind Gust (mph)	62	52	64	63	58	59	66	75	54	49	55	56	75

Youngstown Municipal Airport

The Youngstown Municipal Airport is located in northeastern Ohio approximately eight miles north of the city of Youngstown in Trumbull County. Airport elevation is 1,178 feet, about 200 feet higher than most communities in the Mahoning and Shenango River Valleys. There are numerous natural and man-made lakes in the region, including Lake Erie, 45 miles to the north. Drainage from the area flows southward through the Mahoning and Shenango Rivers which join to form the Beaver River at New Castle, Pennsylvania. The Beaver empties into the Ohio River at Rochester, Pennsylvania.

This entire area experiences frequent outbreaks of cold Canadian air masses which may be modified by passage over Lake Erie. This effect produces widespread cloudiness especially during the cool months of the year. The winter months are characterized by persistent cloudiness and intermittent snow flurries. The daily temperature range during most winter days is quite small. During most winters, the bulk of the snow falls as flurries of 2 inches or less per occurrence, although several snowstorms per year will produce amounts in the four to 10 inch range.

Destructive storms seldom occur, and tornadoes are not common. During recent years flood control projects have all but eliminated the threat of serious river flooding. Flash flooding of small streams and creeks rarely affects residential areas. Certain communities have well known areas of urban flooding during periods of prolonged heavy thunderstorms.

The climate of the Youngstown district has had an important role in the growth and development of this industrial area. Temperatures seldom reach extreme values especially during the summer months. However, high humidity during most days of the year tends to accentuate the temperature. Rainfall, reasonably well distributed throughout the year, provides a more than adequate supply of water for agriculture, industrial, and residential use.

Based on the 1951-1980 period, the average first occurrence of 32 degrees Fahrenheit in the fall is October 14 and the average last occurrence in the spring is May 6.

Youngstown Municipal Airport *Trumbull County* Elevation: 1,177 ft. Latitude: 41° 15' N Longitude: 80° 40' W

	JAN	FEB	MAR	APR	MAY	JUN	JUL	AUG	SEP	OCT	NOV	DEC	YEAR
Mean Maximum Temp. (°F)	31.9	35.5	45.7	58.3	69.4	77.6	81.9	80.1	72.5	60.9	48.3	37.3	58.3
Mean Temp. (°F)	24.7	27.5	36.5	47.7	58.1	66.4	70.7	69.1	62.0	51.1	40.9	30.7	48.8
Mean Minimum Temp. (°F)	17.5	19.5	27.3	37.0	46.7	55.2	59.5	58.1	51.4	41.4	33.5	24.0	39.3
Extreme Maximum Temp. (°F)	67	71	82	88	90	99	100	97	92	83	78	76	100
Extreme Minimum Temp. (°F)	-22	-14	-10	14	24	30	42	32	29	20	1	-12	-22
Days Maximum Temp. ≥ 90°F	0	0	0	0	0	1	3	2	0	0	0	0	6
Days Maximum Temp. ≤ 32°F	16	12	5	0	0	0	0	0	0	0	2	10	45
Days Minimum Temp. ≤ 32°F	28	24	22	11	1	0	0	0	0	5	15	25	131
Days Minimum Temp. ≤ 0°F	3	2	0	0	0	0	0	0	0	0	0	1	6
Heating Degree Days (base 65°F)	1,242	1,052	877	522	244	67	13	25	144	427	716	1,057	6,386
Cooling Degree Days (base 65°F)	0	0	2	7	35	118	208	163	59	6	1	0	599
Mean Precipitation (in.)	2.30	2.03	3.06	3.27	3.42	3.91	4.12	3.38	3.87	2.50	3.17	2.95	37.98
Maximum Precipitation (in.)	7.6	5.3	6.2	6.4	6.2	10.7	9.7	7.9	6.1	8.6	9.1	6.5	48.6
Minimum Precipitation (in.)	0.7	0.5	1.1	1.0	0.8	0.7	1.6	0.5	0.3	0.4	0.9	0.9	23.8
Maximum 24-hr. Precipitation (in.)	2.6	1.9	2.0	1.6	1.9	3.6	3.8	3.5	3.0	4.3	2.7	1.9	4.3
Days With ≥ 0.1" Precipitation	6	6	8	8	8	8	7	6	7	6	7	7	84
Days With ≥ 1.0" Precipitation	0	0	0	1	1	1	1	1	1	0	0	0	6
Mean Snowfall (in.)	14.1	10.5	10.7	2.2	trace	trace	trace	0.0	trace	0.6	4.5	12.1	54.7
Maximum Snowfall (in.)	36	23	31	12	5	0	0	0	trace	8	31	30	91
Maximum 24-hr. Snowfall (in.)	17	9	15	12	5	0	0	0	trace	5	17	12	17
Days With ≥ 1.0" Snow Depth	18	14	7	1	0	0	0	0	0	0	2	11	53
Thunderstorm Days	< 1	< 1	2	3	4	7	7	5	3	1	1	< 1	33
Foggy Days	13	12	14	13	15	16	17	20	17	15	13	14	179
Predominant Sky Cover	OVR	OVR	OVR	OVR	OVR	OVR	OVR	OVR	OVR	OVR	OVR	OVR	OVR
Mean Relative Humidity 7am (%)	81	80	80	77	79	82	85	88	89	85	81	82	82
Mean Relative Humidity 4pm (%)	70	66	60	54	52	54	55	55	57	57	66	72	60
Mean Dewpoint (°F)	18	19	26	36	46	56	60	60	53	42	32	23	39
Prevailing Wind Direction	WSW	WSW	W	SW	SW	SW	SW	SW	SW	SW	SW	WSW	SW
Prevailing Wind Speed (mph)	14	13	13	13	12	9	9	8	9	10	12	14	12
Maximum Wind Gust (mph)	67	54	78	75	70	58	66	58	62	51	53	62	78

Ashland 2 SW *Ashland County* Elevation: 1,263 ft. Latitude: 40° 50' N Longitude: 82° 21' W

	JAN	FEB	MAR	APR	MAY	JUN	JUL	AUG	SEP	OCT	NOV	DEC	YEAR
Mean Maximum Temp. (°F)	32.3	36.1	46.5	59.2	70.2	78.9	83.1	81.0	74.4	62.3	48.8	37.7	59.2
Mean Temp. (°F)	23.9	27.1	36.3	47.5	58.5	67.4	71.5	69.3	62.7	51.2	40.0	29.8	48.8
Mean Minimum Temp. (°F)	15.5	18.0	26.1	35.7	46.6	55.8	59.8	57.6	50.9	40.0	31.2	21.8	38.3
Extreme Maximum Temp. (°F)	65	69	80	87	90	100	99	96	94	85	76	74	100
Extreme Minimum Temp. (°F)	-23	-16	-15	6	25	31	39	37	29	20	0	-18	-23
Days Maximum Temp. ≥ 90°F	0	0	0	0	0	2	5	2	1	0	0	0	10
Days Maximum Temp. ≤ 32°F	16	11	4	0	0	0	0	0	0	0	2	10	43
Days Minimum Temp. ≤ 32°F	29	25	23	12	1	0	0	0	1	7	18	27	143
Days Minimum Temp. ≤ 0°F	5	3	1	0	0	0	0	0	0	0	0	1	10
Heating Degree Days (base 65°F)	1,268	1,064	883	525	235	57	12	23	133	427	744	1,086	6,457
Cooling Degree Days (base 65°F)	0	0	1	5	35	133	221	159	63	5	0	0	622
Mean Precipitation (in.)	2.36	2.10	2.80	3.55	4.05	3.96	4.22	4.09	3.40	2.57	3.17	2.66	38.93
Days With ≥ 0.1" Precipitation	6	5	7	8	9	8	7	6	6	6	7	7	82
Days With ≥ 1.0" Precipitation	0	0	0	1	1	1	1	1	1	0	1	0	7
Mean Snowfall (in.)	10.0	7.9	5.4	1.5	trace	0.0	0.0	0.0	0.0	trace	2.1	7.1	34.0
Days With ≥ 1.0" Snow Depth	16	13	5	1	0	0	0	0	0	0	2	9	46

Barnesville *Belmont County* Elevation: 1,240 ft. Latitude: 39° 59' N Longitude: 81° 09' W

	JAN	FEB	MAR	APR	MAY	JUN	JUL	AUG	SEP	OCT	NOV	DEC	YEAR
Mean Maximum Temp. (°F)	34.5	38.2	48.8	60.4	70.3	78.3	82.1	80.8	74.5	62.8	50.8	40.0	60.1
Mean Temp. (°F)	25.8	28.8	38.3	48.7	58.8	67.2	71.4	69.8	63.2	51.5	41.5	31.8	49.7
Mean Minimum Temp. (°F)	17.0	19.2	27.8	36.9	47.2	56.1	60.6	58.8	51.8	40.0	32.2	23.6	39.3
Extreme Maximum Temp. (°F)	71	72	82	87	90	96	100	96	94	83	77	75	100
Extreme Minimum Temp. (°F)	-23	-20	-5	13	22	31	42	38	28	16	0	-17	-23
Days Maximum Temp. ≥ 90°F	0	0	0	0	0	1	2	2	1	0	0	0	6
Days Maximum Temp. ≤ 32°F	14	10	3	0	0	0	0	0	0	0	1	8	36
Days Minimum Temp. ≤ 32°F	28	24	22	11	2	0	0	0	0	6	16	25	134
Days Minimum Temp. ≤ 0°F	4	2	0	0	0	0	0	0	0	0	0	1	7
Heating Degree Days (base 65°F)	1,208	1,015	821	491	221	51	9	18	118	417	698	1,022	6,089
Cooling Degree Days (base 65°F)	0	0	2	8	37	136	237	185	69	5	0	0	679
Mean Precipitation (in.)	3.01	2.69	3.53	3.85	4.35	4.88	4.73	3.90	3.54	2.97	3.69	3.20	44.34
Days With ≥ 0.1" Precipitation	7	6	8	9	9	8	8	7	6	6	8	8	90
Days With ≥ 1.0" Precipitation	0	0	1	1	1	1	1	1	1	1	1	0	9
Mean Snowfall (in.)	11.6	7.6	5.1	1.2	trace	0.0	0.0	trace	0.0	trace	1.7	5.7	32.9
Days With ≥ 1.0" Snow Depth	14	12	5	0	0	0	0	0	0	0	2	7	40

Bellefontaine *Logan County* Elevation: 1,184 ft. Latitude: 40° 21' N Longitude: 83° 46' W

	JAN	FEB	MAR	APR	MAY	JUN	JUL	AUG	SEP	OCT	NOV	DEC	YEAR
Mean Maximum Temp. (°F)	32.3	37.1	48.1	60.6	71.5	79.6	83.3	81.5	75.9	63.5	49.7	38.2	60.1
Mean Temp. (°F)	24.6	28.6	38.5	49.8	60.8	69.2	73.0	71.3	64.9	53.2	41.3	30.8	50.5
Mean Minimum Temp. (°F)	16.9	20.0	29.0	39.0	50.0	58.7	62.6	61.0	53.9	42.8	33.0	23.2	40.8
Extreme Maximum Temp. (°F)	64	71	82	87	90	101	99	101	95	85	77	71	101
Extreme Minimum Temp. (°F)	-27	-13	-12	9	25	37	45	39	30	17	5	-22	-27
Days Maximum Temp. ≥ 90°F	0	0	0	0	0	2	4	2	1	0	0	0	9
Days Maximum Temp. ≤ 32°F	15	11	3	0	0	0	0	0	0	0	2	9	40
Days Minimum Temp. ≤ 32°F	28	24	21	8	1	0	0	0	0	5	16	25	128
Days Minimum Temp. ≤ 0°F	4	2	0	0	0	0	0	0	0	0	0	1	7
Heating Degree Days (base 65°F)	1,245	1,022	814	457	180	35	4	11	94	370	704	1,054	5,990
Cooling Degree Days (base 65°F)	0	0	1	6	54	169	265	217	94	11	0	0	817
Mean Precipitation (in.)	2.25	1.98	2.75	3.56	3.95	3.97	3.92	3.42	2.67	2.44	3.06	2.95	36.92
Days With ≥ 0.1" Precipitation	6	5	7	8	8	7	7	6	5	6	7	7	79
Days With ≥ 1.0" Precipitation	0	0	0	1	1	1	1	1	1	0	0	1	7
Mean Snowfall (in.)	6.9	4.1	1.7	0.4	trace	0.0	0.0	0.0	0.0	0.2	0.8	3.7	17.8
Days With ≥ 1.0" Snow Depth	11	6	2	0	0	0	0	0	0	0	0	4	23

Bowling Green WWTP *Wood County* Elevation: 672 ft. Latitude: 41° 23' N Longitude: 83° 37' W

	JAN	FEB	MAR	APR	MAY	JUN	JUL	AUG	SEP	OCT	NOV	DEC	YEAR
Mean Maximum Temp. (°F)	31.3	35.4	46.5	59.6	71.7	81.1	84.6	82.2	76.0	63.5	49.2	37.2	59.8
Mean Temp. (°F)	23.8	27.4	37.0	48.4	60.0	69.6	73.3	70.8	64.1	52.4	40.7	29.9	49.8
Mean Minimum Temp. (°F)	16.2	19.3	27.5	37.2	48.3	58.2	61.9	59.4	52.2	41.3	32.2	22.6	39.7
Extreme Maximum Temp. (°F)	64	71	80	88	92	104	101	98	96	88	78	70	104
Extreme Minimum Temp. (°F)	-20	-13	-7	8	25	36	41	38	30	21	6	-19	-20
Days Maximum Temp. ≥ 90°F	0	0	0	0	1	4	6	3	1	0	0	0	15
Days Maximum Temp. ≤ 32°F	16	12	4	0	0	0	0	0	0	0	1	9	42
Days Minimum Temp. ≤ 32°F	29	25	23	10	1	0	0	0	0	5	17	26	136
Days Minimum Temp. ≤ 0°F	4	2	0	0	0	0	0	0	0	0	0	1	7
Heating Degree Days (base 65°F)	1,272	1,056	860	498	200	33	4	14	107	393	722	1,080	6,239
Cooling Degree Days (base 65°F)	0	0	1	7	49	177	269	197	80	9	0	0	789
Mean Precipitation (in.)	1.73	1.59	2.40	3.27	3.53	3.52	3.70	3.28	2.60	2.50	2.69	2.33	33.14
Days With ≥ 0.1" Precipitation	5	4	6	8	7	7	7	6	5	6	6	6	73
Days With ≥ 1.0" Precipitation	0	0	0	0	1	1	1	1	1	0	0	0	5
Mean Snowfall (in.)	7.2	5.4	3.1	0.7	trace	0.0	0.0	0.0	0.0	trace	0.7	4.8	21.9
Days With ≥ 1.0" Snow Depth	14	12	4	0	0	0	0	0	0	0	1	6	37

Bucyrus *Crawford County* Elevation: 954 ft. Latitude: 40° 49' N Longitude: 82° 58' W

	JAN	FEB	MAR	APR	MAY	JUN	JUL	AUG	SEP	OCT	NOV	DEC	YEAR
Mean Maximum Temp. (°F)	31.5	35.1	45.8	58.7	70.2	79.1	83.1	81.0	74.5	62.0	48.6	37.1	58.9
Mean Temp. (°F)	23.8	26.7	36.3	47.7	58.7	68.0	72.0	69.9	63.0	51.3	40.2	29.8	48.9
Mean Minimum Temp. (°F)	16.0	18.2	26.7	36.6	47.2	56.8	61.0	58.8	51.4	40.4	31.8	22.5	38.9
Extreme Maximum Temp. (°F)	64	69	81	88	91	102	100	99	93	85	76	72	102
Extreme Minimum Temp. (°F)	-26	-18	-11	10	26	37	43	39	27	18	3	-18	-26
Days Maximum Temp. ≥ 90°F	0	0	0	0	0	2	5	2	1	0	0	0	10
Days Maximum Temp. ≤ 32°F	16	12	4	0	0	0	0	0	0	0	2	10	44
Days Minimum Temp. ≤ 32°F	29	25	23	11	1	0	0	0	0	6	17	26	138
Days Minimum Temp. ≤ 0°F	4	3	0	0	0	0	0	0	0	0	0	1	8
Heating Degree Days (base 65°F)	1,271	1,077	885	520	230	49	9	20	128	425	736	1,085	6,435
Cooling Degree Days (base 65°F)	0	0	1	6	41	149	245	185	72	7	0	0	706
Mean Precipitation (in.)	2.24	1.90	2.67	3.52	3.95	4.40	4.48	3.83	3.16	2.37	3.10	2.76	38.38
Days With ≥ 0.1" Precipitation	6	5	7	8	8	7	7	6	6	6	7	7	80
Days With ≥ 1.0" Precipitation	0	0	0	1	1	1	1	1	1	0	1	0	7
Mean Snowfall (in.)	7.9	5.9	3.6	0.8	trace	0.0	0.0	0.0	0.0	trace	1.0	4.0	23.2
Days With ≥ 1.0" Snow Depth	15	10	4	0	0	0	0	0	0	0	1	6	36

Cadiz *Harrison County* Elevation: 1,259 ft. Latitude: 40° 16' N Longitude: 81° 00' W

	JAN	FEB	MAR	APR	MAY	JUN	JUL	AUG	SEP	OCT	NOV	DEC	YEAR
Mean Maximum Temp. (°F)	34.9	39.3	49.9	61.8	71.3	79.0	82.7	81.5	75.6	64.0	51.0	40.4	61.0
Mean Temp. (°F)	27.0	30.4	39.9	50.6	60.6	68.6	72.6	71.3	65.0	53.4	42.4	32.6	51.2
Mean Minimum Temp. (°F)	19.1	21.5	29.7	39.3	49.8	58.1	62.5	61.1	54.5	42.8	33.8	24.8	41.4
Extreme Maximum Temp. (°F)	69	72	81	89	89	97	101	96	94	84	79	75	101
Extreme Minimum Temp. (°F)	-24	-10	-6	14	23	33	42	40	33	21	1	-17	-24
Days Maximum Temp. ≥ 90°F	0	0	0	0	0	1	3	2	1	0	0	0	7
Days Maximum Temp. ≤ 32°F	13	9	3	0	0	0	0	0	0	0	1	8	34
Days Minimum Temp. ≤ 32°F	28	23	20	8	1	0	0	0	0	4	14	25	123
Days Minimum Temp. ≤ 0°F	3	2	0	0	0	0	0	0	0	0	0	1	6
Heating Degree Days (base 65°F)	1,171	970	775	439	180	36	5	9	87	361	670	997	5,700
Cooling Degree Days (base 65°F)	0	0	2	11	47	150	258	211	91	10	1	0	781
Mean Precipitation (in.)	2.79	2.38	3.18	3.39	4.09	4.37	4.43	4.13	3.23	2.59	3.28	3.00	40.86
Days With ≥ 0.1" Precipitation	7	6	8	9	9	8	8	7	6	6	7	7	88
Days With ≥ 1.0" Precipitation	0	0	0	0	1	1	1	1	1	0	0	0	5
Mean Snowfall (in.)	11.5	6.5	5.1	1.2	0.0	0.0	0.0	0.0	0.0	trace	1.7	6.3	32.3
Days With ≥ 1.0" Snow Depth	na	na	na	0	0	0	0	0	0	0	1	na	na

Cambridge *Guernsey County* Elevation: 797 ft. Latitude: 40° 01' N Longitude: 81° 35' W

	JAN	FEB	MAR	APR	MAY	JUN	JUL	AUG	SEP	OCT	NOV	DEC	YEAR
Mean Maximum Temp. (°F)	37.4	41.9	52.9	65.0	74.3	81.7	85.1	83.6	77.4	65.9	53.2	42.4	63.4
Mean Temp. (°F)	28.7	32.2	41.7	52.2	61.6	69.6	73.6	72.2	65.8	53.9	43.6	34.1	52.4
Mean Minimum Temp. (°F)	20.1	22.5	30.5	39.3	48.8	57.5	62.1	60.8	54.0	41.9	33.9	25.7	41.4
Extreme Maximum Temp. (°F)	71	73	83	90	92	99	102	99	96	85	79	77	102
Extreme Minimum Temp. (°F)	-32	-16	-3	14	25	30	42	37	32	19	0	-17	-32
Days Maximum Temp. ≥ 90°F	0	0	0	0	0	3	6	4	1	0	0	0	14
Days Maximum Temp. ≤ 32°F	10	7	1	0	0	0	0	0	0	0	0	6	24
Days Minimum Temp. ≤ 32°F	27	22	19	8	1	0	0	0	0	5	14	23	119
Days Minimum Temp. ≤ 0°F	3	2	0	0	0	0	0	0	0	0	0	1	6
Heating Degree Days (base 65°F)	1,118	920	717	389	154	26	3	7	77	347	638	952	5,348
Cooling Degree Days (base 65°F)	0	0	2	12	56	183	301	247	108	10	0	0	919
Mean Precipitation (in.)	2.67	2.25	2.99	3.39	3.96	4.07	4.32	3.87	2.97	2.61	3.25	2.84	39.19
Days With ≥ 0.1" Precipitation	7	6	8	7	8	8	8	7	6	6	7	7	85
Days With ≥ 1.0" Precipitation	0	0	0	1	1	1	1	1	1	0	1	0	7
Mean Snowfall (in.)	7.4	4.1	2.9	0.6	trace	0.0	0.0	0.0	0.0	trace	0.8	2.6	18.4
Days With ≥ 1.0" Snow Depth	11	7	2	0	0	0	0	0	0	0	0	4	24

Canfield 1 S *Mahoning County* Elevation: 1,138 ft. Latitude: 41° 01' N Longitude: 80° 46' W

	JAN	FEB	MAR	APR	MAY	JUN	JUL	AUG	SEP	OCT	NOV	DEC	YEAR
Mean Maximum Temp. (°F)	34.1	36.9	48.6	60.1	70.9	79.1	82.9	81.7	74.5	62.8	49.7	38.8	60.0
Mean Temp. (°F)	25.2	27.0	37.4	47.3	57.8	66.4	70.4	68.9	61.8	50.6	40.4	30.4	48.6
Mean Minimum Temp. (°F)	16.3	17.1	26.1	34.4	44.7	53.7	57.9	56.0	49.1	38.4	31.0	21.9	37.2
Extreme Maximum Temp. (°F)	65	70	84	94	89	96	101	98	92	84	75	74	101
Extreme Minimum Temp. (°F)	-24	-23	-15	12	20	29	38	27	26	15	-3	-16	-24
Days Maximum Temp. ≥ 90°F	0	0	0	0	0	1	4	2	0	0	0	0	7
Days Maximum Temp. ≤ 32°F	14	11	3	0	0	0	0	0	0	0	1	9	38
Days Minimum Temp. ≤ 32°F	28	25	23	14	4	0	0	0	1	9	18	27	149
Days Minimum Temp. ≤ 0°F	4	3	1	0	0	0	0	0	0	0	0	1	9
Heating Degree Days (base 65°F)	1,227	1,065	851	528	246	63	15	27	147	442	733	1,066	6,410
Cooling Degree Days (base 65°F)	0	0	1	4	28	112	200	153	51	3	0	0	552
Mean Precipitation (in.)	1.97	1.80	2.89	3.03	3.87	4.19	4.37	3.57	3.78	2.77	3.07	2.66	37.97
Days With ≥ 0.1" Precipitation	5	6	7	7	9	8	8	7	7	6	7	6	83
Days With ≥ 1.0" Precipitation	0	0	0	0	1	1	1	1	1	0	0	0	5
Mean Snowfall (in.)	na	na	3.3	0.7	0.0	0.0	0.0	0.0	0.0	0.3	1.1	na	na
Days With ≥ 1.0" Snow Depth	na	na	3	1	0	0	0	0	0	0	1	na	na

Celina 3 NE *Mercer County* Elevation: 859 ft. Latitude: 40° 34' N Longitude: 84° 32' W

	JAN	FEB	MAR	APR	MAY	JUN	JUL	AUG	SEP	OCT	NOV	DEC	YEAR
Mean Maximum Temp. (°F)	32.5	37.2	48.8	61.9	73.0	81.3	84.6	82.4	76.9	64.6	50.0	38.1	60.9
Mean Temp. (°F)	25.1	29.0	39.4	50.9	61.8	70.7	74.1	71.8	65.8	54.2	42.1	31.2	51.3
Mean Minimum Temp. (°F)	17.7	20.8	29.9	39.8	50.6	59.9	63.6	61.2	54.5	43.7	34.2	24.2	41.7
Extreme Maximum Temp. (°F)	62	69	82	86	94	103	101	101	96	88	76	70	103
Extreme Minimum Temp. (°F)	-23	-16	-9	9	28	40	43	39	30	20	6	-20	-23
Days Maximum Temp. ≥ 90°F	0	0	0	0	0	3	6	3	1	0	0	0	13
Days Maximum Temp. ≤ 32°F	15	10	3	0	0	0	0	0	0	0	1	9	38
Days Minimum Temp. ≤ 32°F	28	24	20	7	1	0	0	0	0	3	14	25	122
Days Minimum Temp. ≤ 0°F	4	2	0	0	0	0	0	0	0	0	0	1	7
Heating Degree Days (base 65°F)	1,230	1,009	788	426	159	25	3	10	83	342	680	1,042	5,797
Cooling Degree Days (base 65°F)	0	0	1	9	67	205	298	232	110	15	0	0	937
Mean Precipitation (in.)	2.13	2.06	2.79	3.52	3.63	3.80	4.51	3.53	2.66	2.33	2.97	2.63	36.56
Days With ≥ 0.1" Precipitation	6	5	7	8	8	7	7	6	6	6	6	7	79
Days With ≥ 1.0" Precipitation	0	0	0	1	1	1	1	1	1	0	0	0	6
Mean Snowfall (in.)	11.4	7.7	4.7	1.1	0.0	0.0	0.0	0.0	0.0	0.3	1.6	6.3	33.1
Days With ≥ 1.0" Snow Depth	14	9	3	0	0	0	0	0	0	0	1	6	33

Centerburg 2 SE *Knox County* Elevation: 1,204 ft. Latitude: 40° 18' N Longitude: 82° 39' W

	JAN	FEB	MAR	APR	MAY	JUN	JUL	AUG	SEP	OCT	NOV	DEC	YEAR
Mean Maximum Temp. (°F)	32.2	36.3	47.1	59.6	69.8	78.6	82.3	80.8	74.4	62.2	49.2	37.4	59.2
Mean Temp. (°F)	24.1	27.5	37.5	48.7	59.0	68.0	71.8	70.3	63.4	51.3	40.6	29.8	49.3
Mean Minimum Temp. (°F)	15.6	18.5	27.7	37.5	48.1	57.4	61.3	59.5	52.2	40.4	31.9	22.4	39.4
Extreme Maximum Temp. (°F)	66	72	82	86	89	99	99	97	94	87	78	70	99
Extreme Minimum Temp. (°F)	-29	-16	-6	11	25	32	43	38	31	20	0	-23	-29
Days Maximum Temp. ≥ 90°F	0	0	0	0	0	1	3	2	1	0	0	0	7
Days Maximum Temp. ≤ 32°F	15	11	4	0	0	0	0	0	0	0	2	10	42
Days Minimum Temp. ≤ 32°F	29	25	22	10	1	0	0	0	0	7	17	26	137
Days Minimum Temp. ≤ 0°F	4	3	0	0	0	0	0	0	0	0	0	1	8
Heating Degree Days (base 65°F)	1,262	1,053	848	491	219	44	8	17	118	424	727	1,086	6,297
Cooling Degree Days (base 65°F)	0	0	2	7	42	146	242	195	71	6	0	0	711
Mean Precipitation (in.)	2.45	2.13	2.98	3.66	4.03	4.59	4.56	3.85	3.21	2.80	3.61	3.02	40.89
Days With ≥ 0.1" Precipitation	6	6	7	8	8	8	8	6	5	6	7	7	82
Days With ≥ 1.0" Precipitation	0	0	0	1	1	1	1	1	1	1	1	1	9
Mean Snowfall (in.)	na	3.2	na	0.3	trace	0.0	0.0	0.0	0.0	trace	0.9	na	na
Days With ≥ 1.0" Snow Depth	9	6	3	1	0	0	0	0	0	0	1	5	25

Chardon *Geauga County* Elevation: 1,128 ft. Latitude: 41° 35' N Longitude: 81° 11' W

	JAN	FEB	MAR	APR	MAY	JUN	JUL	AUG	SEP	OCT	NOV	DEC	YEAR
Mean Maximum Temp. (°F)	31.4	34.5	43.9	56.1	67.7	76.3	80.1	78.7	71.9	60.4	48.0	37.0	57.2
Mean Temp. (°F)	22.8	24.8	33.9	44.9	55.9	64.7	69.0	67.5	60.7	49.8	39.8	29.5	46.9
Mean Minimum Temp. (°F)	14.1	15.1	23.8	33.7	44.1	53.1	57.8	56.2	49.3	39.2	31.6	21.9	36.7
Extreme Maximum Temp. (°F)	65	69	82	88	89	100	98	96	91	83	76	73	100
Extreme Minimum Temp. (°F)	-23	-26	-17	5	22	30	38	33	25	15	-2	-21	-26
Days Maximum Temp. ≥ 90°F	0	0	0	0	0	1	2	1	0	0	0	0	4
Days Maximum Temp. ≤ 32°F	17	13	6	1	0	0	0	0	0	0	2	10	49
Days Minimum Temp. ≤ 32°F	29	26	25	15	3	0	0	0	1	7	18	27	151
Days Minimum Temp. ≤ 0°F	5	4	1	0	0	0	0	0	0	0	0	1	11
Heating Degree Days (base 65°F)	1,303	1,130	959	600	296	94	30	40	173	466	748	1,095	6,934
Cooling Degree Days (base 65°F)	0	0	0	4	22	96	169	126	48	3	0	0	468
Mean Precipitation (in.)	3.22	2.70	3.44	3.77	4.08	4.42	4.00	4.58	4.49	3.88	4.29	4.14	47.01
Days With ≥ 0.1" Precipitation	10	8	9	9	9	8	8	7	9	9	10	11	107
Days With ≥ 1.0" Precipitation	0	0	0	1	1	1	1	1	1	1	1	0	8
Mean Snowfall (in.)	26.2	18.9	14.4	2.9	trace	0.0	0.0	0.0	0.0	0.9	10.1	23.6	97.0
Days With ≥ 1.0" Snow Depth	24	20	12	2	0	0	0	0	0	0	6	17	81

Chillicothe Mound City *Ross County* Elevation: 649 ft. Latitude: 39° 22' N Longitude: 83° 00' W

	JAN	FEB	MAR	APR	MAY	JUN	JUL	AUG	SEP	OCT	NOV	DEC	YEAR
Mean Maximum Temp. (°F)	37.6	41.9	52.7	64.0	74.0	82.0	86.2	85.1	78.6	66.5	53.9	42.7	63.8
Mean Temp. (°F)	28.4	31.8	41.5	51.7	61.7	70.2	74.5	72.9	65.8	53.8	43.6	33.7	52.5
Mean Minimum Temp. (°F)	19.1	21.6	30.2	39.3	49.4	58.4	62.8	60.8	52.9	40.7	33.2	24.5	41.1
Extreme Maximum Temp. (°F)	73	76	83	90	93	103	103	105	100	88	82	80	105
Extreme Minimum Temp. (°F)	-29	-14	-10	13	29	35	41	39	31	17	-2	-21	-29
Days Maximum Temp. ≥ 90°F	0	0	0	0	1	4	9	7	2	0	0	0	23
Days Maximum Temp. ≤ 32°F	10	7	2	0	0	0	0	0	0	0	0	6	25
Days Minimum Temp. ≤ 32°F	27	23	20	8	1	0	0	0	0	6	16	24	125
Days Minimum Temp. ≤ 0°F	3	2	0	0	0	0	0	0	0	0	0	1	6
Heating Degree Days (base 65°F)	1,128	932	723	405	159	27	2	7	83	354	637	965	5,422
Cooling Degree Days (base 65°F)	0	0	3	12	62	200	317	265	114	14	1	0	988
Mean Precipitation (in.)	2.49	2.34	3.38	3.52	4.37	3.45	3.91	3.59	2.80	2.55	2.93	2.63	37.96
Days With ≥ 0.1" Precipitation	6	5	7	8	8	7	7	6	5	5	6	6	76
Days With ≥ 1.0" Precipitation	0	1	1	1	1	1	1	1	1	1	0	1	10
Mean Snowfall (in.)	7.1	4.6	3.1	0.4	trace	0.0	0.0	0.0	0.0	0.1	0.4	2.2	17.9
Days With ≥ 1.0" Snow Depth	10	6	2	0	0	0	0	0	0	0	0	3	21

Chilo Meldahl Lock & Dam *Clermont County* Elevation: 498 ft. Latitude: 38° 48' N Longitude: 84° 10' W

	JAN	FEB	MAR	APR	MAY	JUN	JUL	AUG	SEP	OCT	NOV	DEC	YEAR
Mean Maximum Temp. (°F)	38.5	43.2	53.0	64.9	73.8	82.0	86.2	85.3	79.3	67.6	54.8	43.8	64.4
Mean Temp. (°F)	29.6	33.4	42.1	52.6	62.0	70.8	75.4	74.3	67.7	55.9	45.0	35.1	53.6
Mean Minimum Temp. (°F)	20.4	23.1	31.3	40.3	50.1	59.5	64.3	63.2	56.1	44.1	35.2	26.3	42.8
Extreme Maximum Temp. (°F)	71	73	82	89	91	98	101	107	98	90	82	73	107
Extreme Minimum Temp. (°F)	-22	-8	-4	20	29	39	47	44	33	21	5	-15	-22
Days Maximum Temp. ≥ 90°F	0	0	0	0	0	3	9	7	3	0	0	0	22
Days Maximum Temp. ≤ 32°F	9	6	1	0	0	0	0	0	0	0	0	5	21
Days Minimum Temp. ≤ 32°F	26	23	18	6	0	0	0	0	0	2	12	22	109
Days Minimum Temp. ≤ 0°F	2	1	0	0	0	0	0	0	0	0	0	1	4
Heating Degree Days (base 65°F)	1,091	888	704	373	145	20	1	2	54	289	595	921	5,083
Cooling Degree Days (base 65°F)	0	0	1	9	54	208	344	307	139	17	0	0	1,079
Mean Precipitation (in.)	3.04	2.97	4.17	3.81	4.48	4.29	3.79	3.94	3.11	2.88	3.28	3.29	43.05
Days With ≥ 0.1" Precipitation	7	5	8	8	7	7	6	6	5	5	6	6	76
Days With ≥ 1.0" Precipitation	1	1	1	1	1	1	1	1	1	1	1	1	12
Mean Snowfall (in.)	na	na	1.0	0.0	0.0	0.0	0.0	0.0	0.0	0.0	trace	1.5	na
Days With ≥ 1.0" Snow Depth	4	5	1	0	0	0	0	0	0	0	0	1	11

Chippewa Lake *Medina County* Elevation: 1,177 ft. Latitude: 41° 03' N Longitude: 81° 56' W

	JAN	FEB	MAR	APR	MAY	JUN	JUL	AUG	SEP	OCT	NOV	DEC	YEAR
Mean Maximum Temp. (°F)	32.7	36.7	47.0	59.7	70.7	79.1	83.0	81.3	74.5	62.8	49.6	38.0	59.6
Mean Temp. (°F)	24.6	27.6	36.9	47.9	58.7	67.4	71.5	69.9	63.0	51.9	41.0	30.5	49.2
Mean Minimum Temp. (°F)	16.7	18.3	26.7	36.0	46.5	55.7	59.9	58.3	51.5	40.9	32.3	22.9	38.8
Extreme Maximum Temp. (°F)	64	70	83	88	90	102	102	99	94	84	77	75	102
Extreme Minimum Temp. (°F)	-26	-17	-14	8	23	28	39	34	28	16	-2	-18	-26
Days Maximum Temp. ≥ 90°F	0	0	0	0	0	1	4	2	1	0	0	0	8
Days Maximum Temp. ≤ 32°F	15	11	4	0	0	0	0	0	0	0	2	9	41
Days Minimum Temp. ≤ 32°F	29	25	23	12	2	0	0	0	0	5	17	26	139
Days Minimum Temp. ≤ 0°F	4	3	0	0	0	0	0	0	0	0	0	1	8
Heating Degree Days (base 65°F)	1,244	1,051	864	511	226	52	10	18	123	406	715	1,064	6,284
Cooling Degree Days (base 65°F)	0	0	1	5	36	136	230	183	69	6	0	0	666
Mean Precipitation (in.)	2.28	2.11	2.98	3.37	3.64	3.81	3.88	3.58	3.67	2.51	3.39	3.00	38.22
Days With ≥ 0.1" Precipitation	7	6	8	9	8	8	7	7	6	7	8	8	89
Days With ≥ 1.0" Precipitation	0	0	0	0	1	1	1	1	1	0	1	0	6
Mean Snowfall (in.)	10.7	8.6	6.7	2.1	trace	0.0	0.0	0.0	0.0	0.2	3.3	8.2	39.8
Days With ≥ 1.0" Snow Depth	17	14	6	1	0	0	0	0	0	0	2	9	49

Cincinnati Fernbank *Hamilton County* Elevation: 498 ft. Latitude: 39° 07' N Longitude: 84° 42' W

	JAN	FEB	MAR	APR	MAY	JUN	JUL	AUG	SEP	OCT	NOV	DEC	YEAR
Mean Maximum Temp. (°F)	38.1	43.6	53.8	65.1	74.7	82.4	86.6	85.3	78.5	67.2	55.4	43.7	64.6
Mean Temp. (°F)	29.2	33.3	42.6	52.7	62.5	71.0	75.5	74.1	66.7	55.2	45.3	34.8	53.6
Mean Minimum Temp. (°F)	20.2	23.0	31.3	40.1	50.3	59.5	64.4	62.8	54.8	43.1	35.1	25.8	42.5
Extreme Maximum Temp. (°F)	70	77	84	90	93	106	107	105	96	87	88	78	107
Extreme Minimum Temp. (°F)	-25	-10	-10	17	29	41	46	42	33	18	1	-18	-25
Days Maximum Temp. ≥ 90°F	0	0	0	0	1	5	9	7	2	0	0	0	24
Days Maximum Temp. ≤ 32°F	10	6	1	0	0	0	0	0	0	0	0	5	22
Days Minimum Temp. ≤ 32°F	26	22	18	7	0	0	0	0	0	3	13	23	112
Days Minimum Temp. ≤ 0°F	3	1	0	0	0	0	0	0	0	0	0	1	5
Heating Degree Days (base 65°F)	1,104	888	691	377	142	20	1	3	69	315	586	930	5,126
Cooling Degree Days (base 65°F)	0	0	3	12	66	209	342	293	129	21	1	0	1,076
Mean Precipitation (in.)	3.46	2.91	4.35	4.42	5.51	4.62	4.52	4.08	2.88	3.30	3.74	3.64	47.43
Days With ≥ 0.1" Precipitation	7	6	9	10	9	8	7	7	5	6	8	7	89
Days With ≥ 1.0" Precipitation	1	1	1	1	2	1	2	1	1	1	1	1	14
Mean Snowfall (in.)	6.7	na	2.6	0.1	trace	0.0	0.0	0.0	0.0	trace	0.4	2.2	na
Days With ≥ 1.0" Snow Depth	7	6	2	0	0	0	0	0	0	0	0	3	18

Cincinnati Lunken Airport *Hamilton County* Elevation: 488 ft. Latitude: 39° 06' N Longitude: 84° 26' W

	JAN	FEB	MAR	APR	MAY	JUN	JUL	AUG	SEP	OCT	NOV	DEC	YEAR
Mean Maximum Temp. (°F)	38.5	43.5	54.2	65.4	74.7	82.8	86.8	85.2	78.6	67.1	54.6	43.9	64.6
Mean Temp. (°F)	30.4	34.4	44.2	54.3	63.8	72.4	76.8	75.1	68.1	56.0	45.4	35.8	54.7
Mean Minimum Temp. (°F)	22.2	25.4	34.2	43.1	52.9	62.0	66.7	64.9	57.4	44.9	36.1	27.7	44.8
Extreme Maximum Temp. (°F)	70	76	85	90	93	101	105	103	97	87	82	75	105
Extreme Minimum Temp. (°F)	-22	-9	-6	21	32	41	47	43	35	20	7	-14	-22
Days Maximum Temp. ≥ 90°F	0	0	0	0	1	5	11	7	3	0	0	0	27
Days Maximum Temp. ≤ 32°F	10	6	1	0	0	0	0	0	0	0	0	5	22
Days Minimum Temp. ≤ 32°F	25	21	14	3	0	0	0	0	0	2	12	21	98
Days Minimum Temp. ≤ 0°F	1	0	0	0	0	0	0	0	0	0	0	0	1
Heating Degree Days (base 65°F)	1,066	857	639	330	114	11	0	2	52	287	582	899	4,839
Cooling Degree Days (base 65°F)	0	0	2	14	82	243	387	327	142	17	1	0	1,215
Mean Precipitation (in.)	2.70	2.43	3.88	3.74	4.61	4.00	3.83	4.07	3.12	2.95	3.39	3.17	41.89
Days With ≥ 0.1" Precipitation	6	5	9	8	8	8	7	6	5	5	7	7	81
Days With ≥ 1.0" Precipitation	1	0	1	1	1	1	1	1	1	1	1	0	10
Mean Snowfall (in.)	4.6	3.7	2.6	0.2	trace	trace	trace	0.0	0.0	0.1	0.4	1.6	13.2
Days With ≥ 1.0" Snow Depth	7	6	2	0	0	0	0	0	0	0	0	2	17

Circleville *Pickaway County* Elevation: 672 ft. Latitude: 39° 37' N Longitude: 82° 57' W

	JAN	FEB	MAR	APR	MAY	JUN	JUL	AUG	SEP	OCT	NOV	DEC	YEAR
Mean Maximum Temp. (°F)	37.0	41.2	52.4	64.3	73.9	82.0	85.5	84.2	78.3	66.6	53.3	42.2	63.4
Mean Temp. (°F)	28.9	32.1	41.9	52.3	62.3	70.8	74.6	72.9	66.4	54.8	44.0	34.3	52.9
Mean Minimum Temp. (°F)	20.8	23.0	31.3	40.2	50.5	59.6	63.6	61.5	54.5	42.9	34.6	26.4	42.4
Extreme Maximum Temp. (°F)	70	75	83	90	91	100	100	101	97	87	81	79	101
Extreme Minimum Temp. (°F)	-22	-15	-5	17	30	35	42	40	31	19	5	-19	-22
Days Maximum Temp. ≥ 90°F	0	0	0	0	1	4	7	5	1	0	0	0	18
Days Maximum Temp. ≤ 32°F	11	7	2	0	0	0	0	0	0	0	1	6	27
Days Minimum Temp. ≤ 32°F	26	22	18	7	0	0	0	0	0	4	14	22	113
Days Minimum Temp. ≤ 0°F	2	2	0	0	0	0	0	0	0	0	0	1	5
Heating Degree Days (base 65°F)	1,111	921	713	388	148	21	2	6	71	325	625	944	5,275
Cooling Degree Days (base 65°F)	0	0	2	11	61	200	309	255	110	16	1	0	965
Mean Precipitation (in.)	2.35	2.14	2.77	3.48	4.62	3.88	3.87	3.85	3.11	2.64	3.07	2.67	38.45
Days With ≥ 0.1" Precipitation	6	5	7	8	8	7	7	6	5	6	7	6	78
Days With ≥ 1.0" Precipitation	0	0	0	1	1	1	1	1	1	0	1	0	7
Mean Snowfall (in.)	5.9	4.0	2.0	0.4	0.0	0.0	0.0	0.0	0.0	0.1	0.7	1.8	14.9
Days With ≥ 1.0" Snow Depth	9	6	2	0	0	0	0	0	0	0	0	4	21

Columbus Valley Crossing *Franklin County* Elevation: 734 ft. Latitude: 39° 54' N Longitude: 82° 56' W

	JAN	FEB	MAR	APR	MAY	JUN	JUL	AUG	SEP	OCT	NOV	DEC	YEAR
Mean Maximum Temp. (°F)	36.2	41.0	52.1	64.3	74.0	82.0	85.3	83.5	77.9	66.3	52.9	41.6	63.1
Mean Temp. (°F)	28.1	32.0	41.9	52.4	62.3	71.0	74.6	72.6	66.3	54.7	43.7	33.7	52.8
Mean Minimum Temp. (°F)	20.0	23.1	31.6	40.5	50.7	59.8	63.7	61.6	54.6	43.0	34.4	25.7	42.4
Extreme Maximum Temp. (°F)	70	74	83	90	93	100	100	100	95	87	79	76	100
Extreme Minimum Temp. (°F)	-28	-14	-2	17	30	37	45	38	28	19	2	-21	-28
Days Maximum Temp. ≥ 90°F	0	0	0	0	1	4	7	4	1	0	0	0	17
Days Maximum Temp. ≤ 32°F	11	7	2	0	0	0	0	0	0	0	1	6	27
Days Minimum Temp. ≤ 32°F	27	22	18	7	0	0	0	0	0	4	14	23	115
Days Minimum Temp. ≤ 0°F	3	1	0	0	0	0	0	0	0	0	0	1	5
Heating Degree Days (base 65°F)	1,138	924	712	381	141	18	1	5	72	326	635	965	5,318
Cooling Degree Days (base 65°F)	0	0	1	9	61	203	311	246	110	12	1	0	954
Mean Precipitation (in.)	2.51	2.03	3.00	3.72	4.34	4.08	4.39	4.26	2.88	2.52	3.34	2.89	39.96
Days With ≥ 0.1" Precipitation	6	5	7	7	8	7	7	7	5	6	7	6	78
Days With ≥ 1.0" Precipitation	0	0	0	1	1	1	1	1	1	0	1	0	7
Mean Snowfall (in.)	8.4	5.0	1.9	0.6	trace	0.0	0.0	0.0	0.0	trace	0.6	2.8	19.3
Days With ≥ 1.0" Snow Depth	9	na	1	0	0	0	0	0	0	0	0	3	na

Coshocton Agr. Res. Station *Coshocton County* Elevation: 1,138 ft. Latitude: 40° 22' N Longitude: 81° 48' W

	JAN	FEB	MAR	APR	MAY	JUN	JUL	AUG	SEP	OCT	NOV	DEC	YEAR
Mean Maximum Temp. (°F)	33.3	36.9	47.4	59.2	69.6	78.1	82.0	80.5	74.1	62.4	50.1	38.9	59.4
Mean Temp. (°F)	25.5	28.6	38.2	49.5	60.1	68.6	72.7	71.3	64.7	52.9	41.9	31.6	50.5
Mean Minimum Temp. (°F)	17.7	20.2	29.0	39.7	50.6	59.1	63.3	62.0	55.2	43.3	33.8	24.1	41.5
Extreme Maximum Temp. (°F)	68	71	82	85	91	98	101	97	94	83	78	74	101
Extreme Minimum Temp. (°F)	-26	-15	1	14	28	38	47	39	32	21	1	-17	-26
Days Maximum Temp. ≥ 90°F	0	0	0	0	0	1	3	2	1	0	0	0	7
Days Maximum Temp. ≤ 32°F	15	11	4	0	0	0	0	0	0	0	1	9	40
Days Minimum Temp. ≤ 32°F	28	24	21	7	0	0	0	0	0	3	15	25	123
Days Minimum Temp. ≤ 0°F	3	2	0	0	0	0	0	0	0	0	0	1	6
Heating Degree Days (base 65°F)	1,216	1,022	824	469	196	38	5	11	94	379	687	1,030	5,971
Cooling Degree Days (base 65°F)	0	0	2	9	48	163	270	225	92	10	1	0	820
Mean Precipitation (in.)	2.28	2.04	2.91	3.34	3.79	4.01	4.04	3.53	2.95	2.40	3.10	2.65	37.04
Days With ≥ 0.1" Precipitation	5	5	7	7	7	7	7	6	6	6	6	6	75
Days With ≥ 1.0" Precipitation	0	0	0	1	1	1	1	1	1	0	1	0	7
Mean Snowfall (in.)	na	na	na	trace	0.0	0.0	0.0	0.0	0.0	trace	0.2	na	na
Days With ≥ 1.0" Snow Depth	na	na	na	0	0	0	0	0	0	0	0	na	na

Coshocton WPC Plant *Coshocton County* Elevation: 757 ft. Latitude: 40° 14' N Longitude: 81° 52' W

	JAN	FEB	MAR	APR	MAY	JUN	JUL	AUG	SEP	OCT	NOV	DEC	YEAR
Mean Maximum Temp. (°F)	36.1	40.4	51.2	62.6	72.6	80.4	84.2	82.6	76.1	64.7	52.3	41.2	62.0
Mean Temp. (°F)	27.3	30.6	40.3	50.3	60.4	68.7	72.7	71.2	64.3	52.6	42.3	32.7	51.1
Mean Minimum Temp. (°F)	18.4	20.9	29.4	38.0	48.2	57.0	61.3	59.7	52.4	40.4	32.3	24.1	40.2
Extreme Maximum Temp. (°F)	69	72	84	89	92	101	101	99	96	86	80	77	101
Extreme Minimum Temp. (°F)	-24	-14	-6	12	20	31	41	39	29	19	1	-19	-24
Days Maximum Temp. ≥ 90°F	0	0	0	0	0	2	5	3	1	0	0	0	11
Days Maximum Temp. ≤ 32°F	12	8	2	0	0	0	0	0	0	0	1	6	29
Days Minimum Temp. ≤ 32°F	28	24	21	9	1	0	0	0	0	6	17	25	131
Days Minimum Temp. ≤ 0°F	3	2	0	0	0	0	0	0	0	0	0	1	6
Heating Degree Days (base 65°F)	1,163	964	759	440	182	34	5	11	98	384	673	996	5,709
Cooling Degree Days (base 65°F)	0	0	1	7	47	159	271	219	80	6	1	0	791
Mean Precipitation (in.)	2.54	2.36	3.16	3.79	4.11	4.03	4.45	4.15	3.21	2.69	3.47	3.00	40.96
Days With ≥ 0.1" Precipitation	7	6	8	8	8	8	8	7	6	6	8	7	87
Days With ≥ 1.0" Precipitation	0	0	0	1	1	1	1	1	1	0	1	0	7
Mean Snowfall (in.)	8.8	5.6	3.0	0.8	trace	0.0	0.0	0.0	0.0	trace	0.9	3.6	22.7
Days With ≥ 1.0" Snow Depth	13	8	3	0	0	0	0	0	0	0	1	5	30

Danville 2 W *Knox County* Elevation: 967 ft. Latitude: 40° 26' N Longitude: 82° 18' W

	JAN	FEB	MAR	APR	MAY	JUN	JUL	AUG	SEP	OCT	NOV	DEC	YEAR
Mean Maximum Temp. (°F)	34.0	38.5	49.6	61.6	72.0	80.3	84.3	82.7	76.2	64.2	51.0	39.6	61.2
Mean Temp. (°F)	25.0	28.4	38.1	48.2	58.4	67.3	71.4	69.7	62.8	50.9	40.7	30.9	49.3
Mean Minimum Temp. (°F)	16.0	18.3	26.7	34.7	44.8	54.2	58.5	56.7	49.3	37.5	30.3	22.1	37.4
Extreme Maximum Temp. (°F)	67	72	83	89	94	102	102	98	96	84	78	74	102
Extreme Minimum Temp. (°F)	-35	-22	-18	9	21	27	35	32	26	15	-2	-22	-35
Days Maximum Temp. ≥ 90°F	0	0	0	0	0	2	5	3	1	0	0	0	11
Days Maximum Temp. ≤ 32°F	14	9	3	0	0	0	0	0	0	0	1	8	35
Days Minimum Temp. ≤ 32°F	28	25	22	14	3	0	0	0	1	11	19	26	149
Days Minimum Temp. ≤ 0°F	5	3	0	0	0	0	0	0	0	0	0	2	10
Heating Degree Days (base 65°F)	1,234	1,026	827	502	230	51	10	21	130	434	724	1,051	6,240
Cooling Degree Days (base 65°F)	0	0	0	3	31	124	220	169	62	4	0	0	613
Mean Precipitation (in.)	2.62	2.38	3.12	3.67	4.22	4.68	4.32	3.75	3.33	2.65	3.37	3.10	41.21
Days With ≥ 0.1" Precipitation	6	6	8	8	9	8	7	6	6	6	7	7	84
Days With ≥ 1.0" Precipitation	0	0	0	1	1	1	1	1	1	0	1	1	8
Mean Snowfall (in.)	12.4	8.4	4.6	1.3	trace	0.0	0.0	0.0	0.0	trace	1.8	7.0	35.5
Days With ≥ 1.0" Snow Depth	16	11	4	1	0	0	0	0	0	0	2	8	42

Dayton MCD *Montgomery County* Elevation: 744 ft. Latitude: 39° 46' N Longitude: 84° 11' W

	JAN	FEB	MAR	APR	MAY	JUN	JUL	AUG	SEP	OCT	NOV	DEC	YEAR
Mean Maximum Temp. (°F)	34.9	39.8	50.5	63.0	74.1	83.1	87.3	85.4	78.8	65.8	52.2	41.0	63.0
Mean Temp. (°F)	27.7	31.5	41.3	52.6	63.7	72.9	77.1	75.0	68.1	55.6	44.2	33.9	53.6
Mean Minimum Temp. (°F)	20.4	23.2	32.0	42.3	53.2	62.6	66.9	64.6	57.3	45.3	36.1	26.7	44.2
Extreme Maximum Temp. (°F)	69	75	84	90	95	103	104	103	97	89	81	75	104
Extreme Minimum Temp. (°F)	-21	-6	2	18	33	42	51	45	35	24	8	-16	-21
Days Maximum Temp. ≥ 90°F	0	0	0	0	2	7	12	8	3	0	0	0	32
Days Maximum Temp. ≤ 32°F	13	8	2	0	0	0	0	0	0	0	1	7	31
Days Minimum Temp. ≤ 32°F	26	22	17	4	0	0	0	0	0	2	11	22	104
Days Minimum Temp. ≤ 0°F	2	1	0	0	0	0	0	0	0	0	0	1	4
Heating Degree Days (base 65°F)	1,152	939	732	382	129	15	1	2	57	306	619	958	5,292
Cooling Degree Days (base 65°F)	0	0	4	16	92	264	397	330	156	23	1	0	1,283
Mean Precipitation (in.)	2.57	2.32	3.07	4.07	4.38	4.11	3.90	3.28	2.57	2.68	3.25	2.93	39.13
Days With ≥ 0.1" Precipitation	6	6	7	8	8	7	7	6	5	5	6	6	77
Days With ≥ 1.0" Precipitation	0	0	0	1	1	1	1	1	1	1	1	1	9
Mean Snowfall (in.)	6.3	3.6	2.4	0.2	0.0	0.0	0.0	0.0	0.0	trace	0.4	2.8	15.7
Days With ≥ 1.0" Snow Depth	11	7	2	0	0	0	0	0	0	0	0	3	23

Defiance *Defiance County* Elevation: 698 ft. Latitude: 41° 17' N Longitude: 84° 23' W

	JAN	FEB	MAR	APR	MAY	JUN	JUL	AUG	SEP	OCT	NOV	DEC	YEAR
Mean Maximum Temp. (°F)	31.1	35.0	45.7	59.1	71.3	80.7	84.6	82.4	75.6	63.1	48.7	36.9	59.5
Mean Temp. (°F)	22.9	26.1	35.9	47.8	59.3	69.0	73.0	70.9	63.8	51.9	40.1	29.3	49.2
Mean Minimum Temp. (°F)	14.7	17.1	26.1	36.4	47.4	57.2	61.5	59.4	51.9	40.6	31.4	21.6	38.8
Extreme Maximum Temp. (°F)	64	71	80	89	92	104	104	99	95	88	77	70	104
Extreme Minimum Temp. (°F)	-22	-19	-6	4	26	38	45	43	29	18	6	-19	-22
Days Maximum Temp. ≥ 90°F	0	0	0	0	1	4	7	4	1	0	0	0	17
Days Maximum Temp. ≤ 32°F	16	12	4	0	0	0	0	0	0	0	1	10	43
Days Minimum Temp. ≤ 32°F	29	25	24	10	1	0	0	0	0	5	18	27	139
Days Minimum Temp. ≤ 0°F	5	4	0	0	0	0	0	0	0	0	0	2	11
Heating Degree Days (base 65°F)	1,298	1,094	895	519	215	41	6	13	114	409	741	1,099	6,444
Cooling Degree Days (base 65°F)	0	0	1	7	48	174	280	216	85	9	0	0	820
Mean Precipitation (in.)	1.90	1.79	2.68	3.45	3.59	3.72	4.03	3.13	3.16	2.62	3.00	2.57	35.64
Days With ≥ 0.1" Precipitation	5	5	7	8	8	7	7	6	6	6	6	6	77
Days With ≥ 1.0" Precipitation	0	0	0	1	1	1	1	1	1	0	1	0	7
Mean Snowfall (in.)	6.8	5.3	2.4	0.6	trace	0.0	0.0	0.0	0.0	trace	1.2	4.5	20.8
Days With ≥ 1.0" Snow Depth	16	12	4	0	0	0	0	0	0	0	1	8	41

Delaware *Delaware County* Elevation: 918 ft. Latitude: 40° 19' N Longitude: 83° 04' W

	JAN	FEB	MAR	APR	MAY	JUN	JUL	AUG	SEP	OCT	NOV	DEC	YEAR
Mean Maximum Temp. (°F)	33.3	37.2	47.9	60.5	71.3	80.0	83.9	82.4	76.2	63.9	49.9	38.9	60.5
Mean Temp. (°F)	24.7	27.8	37.7	48.9	59.5	68.6	72.6	70.7	63.8	51.9	40.6	30.8	49.8
Mean Minimum Temp. (°F)	16.2	18.5	27.5	37.1	47.6	57.1	61.2	59.0	51.4	39.9	31.3	22.6	39.1
Extreme Maximum Temp. (°F)	68	72	82	87	90	101	100	100	96	87	78	74	101
Extreme Minimum Temp. (°F)	-28	-16	-9	14	27	35	41	37	31	16	2	-27	-28
Days Maximum Temp. ≥ 90°F	0	0	0	0	0	3	6	3	1	0	0	0	13
Days Maximum Temp. ≤ 32°F	14	10	3	0	0	0	0	0	0	0	1	8	36
Days Minimum Temp. ≤ 32°F	28	24	22	10	1	0	0	0	0	7	18	25	135
Days Minimum Temp. ≤ 0°F	4	3	0	0	0	0	0	0	0	0	0	1	8
Heating Degree Days (base 65°F)	1,243	1,044	839	484	210	41	6	15	111	407	725	1,054	6,179
Cooling Degree Days (base 65°F)	0	0	1	6	46	161	266	206	81	9	0	0	776
Mean Precipitation (in.)	2.29	1.88	2.47	3.44	3.96	4.20	4.12	3.54	2.78	2.45	3.47	2.73	37.33
Days With ≥ 0.1" Precipitation	6	5	7	7	8	8	7	6	5	5	7	7	78
Days With ≥ 1.0" Precipitation	0	0	0	1	1	1	1	1	1	0	1	0	7
Mean Snowfall (in.)	8.1	4.3	2.9	0.9	0.0	0.0	0.0	0.0	0.0	trace	0.8	3.7	20.7
Days With ≥ 1.0" Snow Depth	13	9	3	0	0	0	0	0	0	0	1	5	31

Dorset *Ashtabula County* Elevation: 977 ft. Latitude: 41° 41' N Longitude: 80° 40' W

	JAN	FEB	MAR	APR	MAY	JUN	JUL	AUG	SEP	OCT	NOV	DEC	YEAR
Mean Maximum Temp. (°F)	31.4	34.7	44.3	56.6	68.3	76.9	81.2	79.7	73.1	61.3	48.4	37.0	57.8
Mean Temp. (°F)	23.1	25.3	34.5	45.5	56.3	65.1	69.4	67.9	61.4	50.4	40.3	29.6	47.4
Mean Minimum Temp. (°F)	14.6	15.8	24.7	34.3	44.2	53.2	57.4	56.0	49.6	39.5	32.1	22.2	37.0
Extreme Maximum Temp. (°F)	67	69	83	88	89	99	100	98	95	85	83	74	100
Extreme Minimum Temp. (°F)	-28	-28	-20	-4	22	30	37	30	26	17	2	-22	-28
Days Maximum Temp. ≥ 90°F	0	0	0	0	0	1	2	1	0	0	0	0	4
Days Maximum Temp. ≤ 32°F	17	12	6	1	0	0	0	0	0	0	2	10	48
Days Minimum Temp. ≤ 32°F	29	26	24	14	4	0	0	0	1	6	17	26	147
Days Minimum Temp. ≤ 0°F	5	4	1	0	0	0	0	0	0	0	0	1	11
Heating Degree Days (base 65°F)	1,294	1,116	938	583	290	88	28	36	162	448	736	1,090	6,809
Cooling Degree Days (base 65°F)	0	0	0	5	28	100	180	136	62	3	0	0	514
Mean Precipitation (in.)	2.60	2.26	3.16	3.55	3.69	4.53	4.20	4.06	4.31	3.79	3.88	3.27	43.30
Days With ≥ 0.1" Precipitation	7	7	9	9	9	8	7	7	8	9	10	9	99
Days With ≥ 1.0" Precipitation	0	0	0	0	1	1	1	1	1	1	0	0	6
Mean Snowfall (in.)	17.5	12.9	12.1	2.9	trace	0.0	0.0	0.0	0.0	0.6	8.7	18.4	73.1
Days With ≥ 1.0" Snow Depth	21	18	10	2	0	0	0	0	0	0	5	15	71

Eaton *Preble County* Elevation: 1,000 ft. Latitude: 39° 44' N Longitude: 84° 38' W

	JAN	FEB	MAR	APR	MAY	JUN	JUL	AUG	SEP	OCT	NOV	DEC	YEAR
Mean Maximum Temp. (°F)	33.4	38.4	49.3	61.4	72.3	80.8	84.7	83.3	77.2	64.7	50.9	39.2	61.3
Mean Temp. (°F)	24.4	28.3	38.5	48.9	60.2	68.9	72.8	71.2	64.4	52.1	41.0	30.8	50.1
Mean Minimum Temp. (°F)	15.4	18.2	27.6	36.8	48.0	56.9	60.8	59.0	51.5	39.3	31.1	22.1	38.9
Extreme Maximum Temp. (°F)	65	72	82	87	91	100	102	101	96	90	79	72	102
Extreme Minimum Temp. (°F)	-33	-20	-11	14	25	36	42	38	26	12	-3	-30	-33
Days Maximum Temp. ≥ 90°F	0	0	0	0	0	3	6	4	2	0	0	0	15
Days Maximum Temp. ≤ 32°F	14	10	3	0	0	0	0	0	0	0	1	8	36
Days Minimum Temp. ≤ 32°F	28	25	22	10	1	0	0	0	0	7	18	26	137
Days Minimum Temp. ≤ 0°F	5	3	0	0	0	0	0	0	0	0	0	2	10
Heating Degree Days (base 65°F)	1,251	1,029	816	481	189	36	6	9	103	401	714	1,054	6,089
Cooling Degree Days (base 65°F)	0	0	1	4	47	167	265	220	91	9	0	0	804
Mean Precipitation (in.)	2.46	2.24	3.25	4.11	4.64	3.81	3.65	3.38	2.57	2.72	3.41	3.02	39.26
Days With ≥ 0.1" Precipitation	6	6	7	8	8	7	6	6	5	5	7	6	77
Days With ≥ 1.0" Precipitation	0	0	1	1	1	1	1	1	1	1	1	1	10
Mean Snowfall (in.)	na	na	na	0.5	0.0	0.0	0.0	0.0	0.0	0.0	trace	na	na
Days With ≥ 1.0" Snow Depth	12	9	4	0	0	0	0	0	0	0	1	5	31

Elyria 3 E *Lorain County* Elevation: 728 ft. Latitude: 41° 23' N Longitude: 82° 03' W

	JAN	FEB	MAR	APR	MAY	JUN	JUL	AUG	SEP	OCT	NOV	DEC	YEAR
Mean Maximum Temp. (°F)	34.0	37.6	47.8	60.4	71.7	80.5	84.6	82.5	75.9	64.0	51.0	39.4	60.8
Mean Temp. (°F)	26.5	29.2	38.3	49.4	60.1	69.3	73.6	71.8	65.3	53.9	43.0	32.4	51.1
Mean Minimum Temp. (°F)	18.9	20.7	28.8	38.4	48.5	57.9	62.5	61.0	54.6	43.8	35.0	25.3	41.3
Extreme Maximum Temp. (°F)	66	72	84	89	93	104	102	100	95	86	78	76	104
Extreme Minimum Temp. (°F)	-22	-15	-10	11	27	33	44	40	32	18	7	-14	-22
Days Maximum Temp. ≥ 90°F	0	0	0	0	1	4	8	4	1	0	0	0	18
Days Maximum Temp. ≤ 32°F	14	10	3	0	0	0	0	0	0	0	1	7	35
Days Minimum Temp. ≤ 32°F	28	24	21	9	1	0	0	0	0	2	13	24	122
Days Minimum Temp. ≤ 0°F	3	2	0	0	0	0	0	0	0	0	0	1	6
Heating Degree Days (base 65°F)	1,187	1,005	822	470	196	35	4	9	85	346	653	1,003	5,815
Cooling Degree Days (base 65°F)	0	0	2	9	53	173	289	229	98	11	0	0	864
Mean Precipitation (in.)	2.37	2.17	2.74	3.19	3.42	3.98	3.65	3.76	3.54	2.69	3.18	3.07	37.76
Days With ≥ 0.1" Precipitation	7	6	7	8	8	7	7	7	7	7	8	8	87
Days With ≥ 1.0" Precipitation	0	0	0	0	0	1	1	1	1	0	0	0	4
Mean Snowfall (in.)	12.0	10.2	7.2	1.7	trace	trace	0.0	0.0	0.0	0.1	3.2	9.2	43.6
Days With ≥ 1.0" Snow Depth	16	13	5	0	0	0	0	0	0	0	1	9	44

Findlay Airport *Hancock County* Elevation: 797 ft. Latitude: 41° 01' N Longitude: 83° 40' W

	JAN	FEB	MAR	APR	MAY	JUN	JUL	AUG	SEP	OCT	NOV	DEC	YEAR
Mean Maximum Temp. (°F)	31.1	34.7	46.0	58.5	70.2	78.9	82.8	80.5	74.3	62.0	48.4	36.7	58.7
Mean Temp. (°F)	24.3	27.5	37.6	48.7	60.0	69.0	73.0	70.8	64.0	52.4	41.0	30.3	49.9
Mean Minimum Temp. (°F)	17.5	20.3	29.1	38.8	49.8	59.1	63.1	60.9	53.7	42.7	33.6	23.8	41.0
Extreme Maximum Temp. (°F)	66	72	80	86	94	104	102	99	94	86	79	70	104
Extreme Minimum Temp. (°F)	-20	-14	-12	10	28	39	44	40	30	21	7	-18	-20
Days Maximum Temp. ≥ 90°F	0	0	0	0	1	2	5	2	1	0	0	0	11
Days Maximum Temp. ≤ 32°F	16	12	4	0	0	0	0	0	0	0	2	11	45
Days Minimum Temp. ≤ 32°F	28	23	20	8	0	0	0	0	0	4	15	25	123
Days Minimum Temp. ≤ 0°F	4	2	0	0	0	0	0	0	0	0	0	1	7
Heating Degree Days (base 65°F)	1,252	1,051	844	490	200	36	4	13	108	392	712	1,068	6,170
Cooling Degree Days (base 65°F)	0	0	1	6	51	165	265	200	82	9	0	0	779
Mean Precipitation (in.)	1.80	1.65	2.52	3.24	3.74	4.07	3.88	3.66	2.83	2.17	2.73	2.39	34.68
Days With ≥ 0.1" Precipitation	5	4	7	8	7	7	6	6	6	5	6	6	73
Days With ≥ 1.0" Precipitation	0	0	0	0	1	1	1	1	1	0	0	0	5
Mean Snowfall (in.)	8.2	5.3	3.2	0.7	trace	trace	0.0	0.0	trace	0.1	1.2	5.5	24.2
Days With ≥ 1.0" Snow Depth	15	11	4	0	0	0	0	0	0	0	1	7	38

Findlay WPCC *Hancock County* Elevation: 767 ft. Latitude: 41° 03' N Longitude: 83° 40' W

	JAN	FEB	MAR	APR	MAY	JUN	JUL	AUG	SEP	OCT	NOV	DEC	YEAR
Mean Maximum Temp. (°F)	31.3	35.2	46.5	59.2	71.1	79.8	83.6	81.2	74.6	62.2	48.2	36.5	59.1
Mean Temp. (°F)	24.3	27.7	37.7	49.0	60.6	69.7	73.6	71.4	64.5	52.6	40.7	29.9	50.1
Mean Minimum Temp. (°F)	17.2	20.1	28.8	38.8	50.1	59.5	63.6	61.5	54.2	42.9	33.1	23.4	41.1
Extreme Maximum Temp. (°F)	66	71	81	86	93	104	101	99	96	88	78	70	104
Extreme Minimum Temp. (°F)	-20	-12	-11	8	26	40	47	42	31	19	6	-18	-20
Days Maximum Temp. ≥ 90°F	0	0	0	0	1	3	5	3	1	0	0	0	13
Days Maximum Temp. ≤ 32°F	16	12	4	0	0	0	0	0	0	0	2	11	45
Days Minimum Temp. ≤ 32°F	28	24	21	7	1	0	0	0	0	3	16	25	125
Days Minimum Temp. ≤ 0°F	4	2	0	0	0	0	0	0	0	0	0	1	7
Heating Degree Days (base 65°F)	1,256	1,047	841	480	186	32	3	11	100	387	724	1,080	6,147
Cooling Degree Days (base 65°F)	0	0	2	7	58	187	294	230	97	10	0	0	885
Mean Precipitation (in.)	2.15	1.98	2.72	3.28	3.92	4.13	3.91	4.05	2.95	2.35	2.78	2.73	36.95
Days With ≥ 0.1" Precipitation	6	5	7	8	8	8	6	6	6	6	7	6	79
Days With ≥ 1.0" Precipitation	0	0	0	1	1	1	1	1	1	0	0	0	6
Mean Snowfall (in.)	10.2	6.2	4.3	1.2	trace	0.0	0.0	0.0	0.0	0.2	1.4	6.0	29.5
Days With ≥ 1.0" Snow Depth	16	12	4	0	0	0	0	0	0	0	1	8	41

Franklin *Warren County* Elevation: 669 ft. Latitude: 39° 33' N Longitude: 84° 19' W

	JAN	FEB	MAR	APR	MAY	JUN	JUL	AUG	SEP	OCT	NOV	DEC	YEAR
Mean Maximum Temp. (°F)	36.0	40.5	51.1	62.8	73.2	81.6	85.5	84.2	78.0	65.6	52.8	41.7	62.7
Mean Temp. (°F)	27.2	30.8	40.5	51.1	61.3	70.1	74.1	72.3	65.3	53.0	42.9	33.1	51.8
Mean Minimum Temp. (°F)	18.4	21.0	29.9	39.3	49.3	58.6	62.7	60.4	52.5	40.2	32.9	24.4	40.8
Extreme Maximum Temp. (°F)	68	74	86	88	96	100	101	100	95	90	79	74	101
Extreme Minimum Temp. (°F)	-24	-12	-7	18	29	38	42	39	32	18	5	-21	-24
Days Maximum Temp. ≥ 90°F	0	0	0	0	0	4	7	5	2	0	0	0	18
Days Maximum Temp. ≤ 32°F	11	8	2	0	0	0	0	0	0	0	1	6	28
Days Minimum Temp. ≤ 32°F	27	23	20	8	1	0	0	0	0	7	16	24	126
Days Minimum Temp. ≤ 0°F	3	2	0	0	0	0	0	0	0	0	0	1	6
Heating Degree Days (base 65°F)	1,164	959	753	420	167	26	3	7	90	376	657	982	5,604
Cooling Degree Days (base 65°F)	0	0	2	7	55	188	298	245	99	9	0	0	903
Mean Precipitation (in.)	2.48	2.30	3.20	3.93	4.40	3.67	4.15	3.27	2.65	2.96	3.34	2.99	39.34
Days With ≥ 0.1" Precipitation	6	6	7	8	8	7	7	6	5	6	7	6	79
Days With ≥ 1.0" Precipitation	0	0	0	1	1	1	1	1	1	1	1	0	8
Mean Snowfall (in.)	na	2.4	1.6	trace	0.0	0.0	0.0	0.0	0.0	0.0	0.5	1.4	na
Days With ≥ 1.0" Snow Depth	8	7	2	0	0	0	0	0	0	0	0	2	19

Fredericktown 4 S *Knox County* Elevation: 1,049 ft. Latitude: 40° 25' N Longitude: 82° 32' W

	JAN	FEB	MAR	APR	MAY	JUN	JUL	AUG	SEP	OCT	NOV	DEC	YEAR
Mean Maximum Temp. (°F)	32.2	36.6	47.4	59.6	70.5	79.3	83.1	81.5	75.1	63.1	49.8	38.8	59.7
Mean Temp. (°F)	22.9	26.5	36.6	47.4	58.0	67.0	70.7	68.7	61.9	50.3	39.9	30.3	48.3
Mean Minimum Temp. (°F)	13.5	16.4	25.7	35.2	45.4	54.6	58.2	55.8	48.6	37.5	30.0	21.7	36.9
Extreme Maximum Temp. (°F)	66	70	82	88	91	100	98	98	94	87	78	75	100
Extreme Minimum Temp. (°F)	-30	-26	-21	12	21	34	38	32	26	15	0	-16	-30
Days Maximum Temp. ≥ 90°F	0	0	0	0	0	2	4	2	1	0	0	0	9
Days Maximum Temp. ≤ 32°F	15	11	4	0	0	0	0	0	0	0	1	8	39
Days Minimum Temp. ≤ 32°F	29	26	24	13	2	0	0	0	1	10	19	26	150
Days Minimum Temp. ≤ 0°F	6	4	1	0	0	0	0	0	0	0	0	2	13
Heating Degree Days (base 65°F)	1,300	1,081	876	526	246	56	14	29	147	452	745	1,070	6,542
Cooling Degree Days (base 65°F)	0	0	1	4	32	123	207	147	54	3	0	0	571
Mean Precipitation (in.)	2.58	2.14	2.97	3.56	4.26	4.37	4.15	3.73	3.29	2.61	3.30	2.94	39.90
Days With ≥ 0.1" Precipitation	6	5	7	8	8	8	7	6	6	6	7	7	81
Days With ≥ 1.0" Precipitation	0	0	0	1	1	1	1	1	1	1	1	1	9
Mean Snowfall (in.)	7.8	5.3	3.1	0.7	trace	0.0	0.0	0.0	0.0	0.0	1.0	3.5	21.4
Days With ≥ 1.0" Snow Depth	na	7	2	0	0	0	0	0	0	0	1	3	na

Fremont *Sandusky County* Elevation: 597 ft. Latitude: 41° 20' N Longitude: 83° 07' W

	JAN	FEB	MAR	APR	MAY	JUN	JUL	AUG	SEP	OCT	NOV	DEC	YEAR
Mean Maximum Temp. (°F)	31.3	34.5	44.9	58.1	70.3	79.1	83.5	81.2	74.7	62.2	49.2	36.8	58.8
Mean Temp. (°F)	23.7	26.4	36.2	48.0	59.6	68.8	73.1	70.6	63.7	51.5	41.0	29.6	49.3
Mean Minimum Temp. (°F)	16.0	18.3	27.5	37.9	48.8	58.4	62.5	60.0	52.6	40.7	32.8	22.3	39.8
Extreme Maximum Temp. (°F)	62	72	81	87	92	104	100	99	95	86	77	71	104
Extreme Minimum Temp. (°F)	-20	-11	-5	8	29	38	46	41	31	19	9	-17	-20
Days Maximum Temp. ≥ 90°F	0	0	0	0	1	3	6	2	1	0	0	0	13
Days Maximum Temp. ≤ 32°F	16	12	5	0	0	0	0	0	0	0	1	10	44
Days Minimum Temp. ≤ 32°F	29	25	23	8	0	0	0	0	0	5	15	26	131
Days Minimum Temp. ≤ 0°F	5	3	0	0	0	0	0	0	0	0	0	1	9
Heating Degree Days (base 65°F)	1,275	1,082	887	510	211	43	5	16	116	421	713	1,092	6,371
Cooling Degree Days (base 65°F)	0	0	2	7	53	165	275	201	82	9	0	0	794
Mean Precipitation (in.)	2.09	1.89	2.71	3.31	3.72	4.26	3.44	3.33	3.07	2.56	2.93	2.73	36.04
Days With ≥ 0.1" Precipitation	6	5	7	8	8	7	6	6	6	6	7	7	79
Days With ≥ 1.0" Precipitation	0	0	0	1	1	1	1	1	1	0	0	0	6
Mean Snowfall (in.)	6.7	5.2	3.6	0.3	trace	0.0	0.0	0.0	0.0	trace	0.6	na	na
Days With ≥ 1.0" Snow Depth	8	6	3	0	0	0	0	0	0	0	0	na	na

Gallipolis *Gallia County* Elevation: 567 ft. Latitude: 38° 49' N Longitude: 82° 11' W

	JAN	FEB	MAR	APR	MAY	JUN	JUL	AUG	SEP	OCT	NOV	DEC	YEAR
Mean Maximum Temp. (°F)	41.9	46.8	57.5	68.2	76.7	83.9	87.4	86.1	80.2	69.3	57.4	46.8	66.8
Mean Temp. (°F)	32.2	35.7	44.9	54.3	63.5	71.6	75.8	74.4	68.1	56.3	46.1	37.0	55.0
Mean Minimum Temp. (°F)	22.4	24.5	32.2	40.4	50.2	59.3	64.1	62.5	55.8	43.2	34.8	27.1	43.0
Extreme Maximum Temp. (°F)	76	77	86	91	96	102	105	105	98	87	82	80	105
Extreme Minimum Temp. (°F)	-28	-14	-8	16	26	34	44	40	31	17	6	-13	-28
Days Maximum Temp. ≥ 90°F	0	0	0	0	1	5	11	8	3	0	0	0	28
Days Maximum Temp. ≤ 32°F	7	4	1	0	0	0	0	0	0	0	0	3	15
Days Minimum Temp. ≤ 32°F	25	21	17	7	1	0	0	0	0	4	14	22	111
Days Minimum Temp. ≤ 0°F	2	1	0	0	0	0	0	0	0	0	0	0	3
Heating Degree Days (base 65°F)	1,012	821	621	329	119	14	1	3	49	281	562	861	4,673
Cooling Degree Days (base 65°F)	0	0	3	16	81	228	359	306	142	19	2	0	1,156
Mean Precipitation (in.)	2.90	2.90	3.60	3.29	3.98	3.88	4.32	3.66	2.98	2.79	3.09	3.27	40.66
Days With ≥ 0.1" Precipitation	7	7	8	8	8	8	7	7	6	6	7	7	86
Days With ≥ 1.0" Precipitation	0	0	0	0	1	1	1	1	1	1	1	1	8
Mean Snowfall (in.)	6.1	4.6	2.2	trace	0.0	0.0	0.0	0.0	0.0	trace	0.3	1.0	14.2
Days With ≥ 1.0" Snow Depth	7	6	1	0	0	0	0	0	0	0	0	1	15

Greenville Water Plant *Darke County* Elevation: 1,023 ft. Latitude: 40° 06' N Longitude: 84° 39' W

	JAN	FEB	MAR	APR	MAY	JUN	JUL	AUG	SEP	OCT	NOV	DEC	YEAR
Mean Maximum Temp. (°F)	32.2	36.7	47.7	60.4	71.5	80.2	84.1	82.4	76.6	64.1	50.0	38.3	60.3
Mean Temp. (°F)	23.6	27.2	37.6	49.0	59.8	68.9	72.7	70.3	63.5	51.6	40.6	29.9	49.6
Mean Minimum Temp. (°F)	15.0	17.7	27.5	37.6	48.1	57.6	61.1	58.2	50.4	39.0	31.1	21.5	38.7
Extreme Maximum Temp. (°F)	63	72	82	89	92	101	104	101	94	87	78	72	104
Extreme Minimum Temp. (°F)	-33	-23	-14	10	26	37	43	36	28	14	1	-21	-33
Days Maximum Temp. ≥ 90°F	0	0	0	0	0	3	5	3	2	0	0	0	13
Days Maximum Temp. ≤ 32°F	15	11	4	0	0	0	0	0	0	0	1	9	40
Days Minimum Temp. ≤ 32°F	29	25	23	9	1	0	0	0	0	8	18	26	139
Days Minimum Temp. ≤ 0°F	5	4	0	0	0	0	0	0	0	0	0	2	11
Heating Degree Days (base 65°F)	1,277	1,060	843	481	202	39	6	17	121	417	727	1,081	6,271
Cooling Degree Days (base 65°F)	0	0	1	6	48	168	260	193	80	8	0	0	764
Mean Precipitation (in.)	2.16	2.05	2.91	3.56	4.04	3.98	4.24	3.18	2.47	2.73	3.11	2.69	37.12
Days With ≥ 0.1" Precipitation	5	5	7	8	8	7	6	6	5	6	7	6	76
Days With ≥ 1.0" Precipitation	0	0	0	1	1	1	1	1	1	1	1	0	8
Mean Snowfall (in.)	8.3	5.6	3.0	0.5	trace	0.0	0.0	0.0	0.0	0.2	0.8	3.3	21.7
Days With ≥ 1.0" Snow Depth	na	na	2	0	0	0	0	0	0	0	na	na	na

Hannibal Lock & Dam *Monroe County* Elevation: 620 ft. Latitude: 39° 40' N Longitude: 80° 52' W

	JAN	FEB	MAR	APR	MAY	JUN	JUL	AUG	SEP	OCT	NOV	DEC	YEAR
Mean Maximum Temp. (°F)	37.1	41.5	51.4	63.0	72.6	80.6	84.1	82.7	76.4	65.0	53.6	42.2	62.5
Mean Temp. (°F)	28.4	31.6	40.3	50.3	60.3	68.6	73.3	72.1	65.4	53.5	43.6	33.6	51.8
Mean Minimum Temp. (°F)	19.6	21.7	29.0	37.6	47.8	56.6	62.4	61.4	54.4	41.9	33.4	25.1	40.9
Extreme Maximum Temp. (°F)	71	73	83	90	91	96	99	100	95	85	80	74	100
Extreme Minimum Temp. (°F)	-24	-11	-8	18	26	38	42	42	34	22	6	-14	-24
Days Maximum Temp. ≥ 90°F	0	0	0	0	0	2	6	4	1	0	0	0	13
Days Maximum Temp. ≤ 32°F	11	6	2	0	0	0	0	0	0	0	0	6	25
Days Minimum Temp. ≤ 32°F	27	23	21	9	1	0	0	0	0	3	15	24	123
Days Minimum Temp. ≤ 0°F	2	1	0	0	0	0	0	0	0	0	0	0	3
Heating Degree Days (base 65°F)	1,129	936	758	439	181	32	3	7	76	357	637	965	5,520
Cooling Degree Days (base 65°F)	0	0	0	5	37	147	272	235	91	8	0	0	795
Mean Precipitation (in.)	3.08	2.57	3.57	3.25	4.12	3.65	4.63	3.41	3.01	2.63	3.33	3.09	40.34
Days With ≥ 0.1" Precipitation	7	7	8	8	9	7	7	6	5	6	7	7	84
Days With ≥ 1.0" Precipitation	1	0	1	0	1	1	1	1	1	1	0	0	8
Mean Snowfall (in.)	na	na	na	trace	0.0	0.0	0.0	0.0	0.0	0.0	trace	na	na
Days With ≥ 1.0" Snow Depth	na	na	1	0	0	0	0	0	0	0	0	na	na

Hillsboro *Highland County* Elevation: 1,099 ft. Latitude: 39° 12' N Longitude: 83° 37' W

	JAN	FEB	MAR	APR	MAY	JUN	JUL	AUG	SEP	OCT	NOV	DEC	YEAR
Mean Maximum Temp. (°F)	35.6	40.5	51.1	62.7	71.7	79.3	83.3	81.9	76.3	64.9	52.3	41.3	61.7
Mean Temp. (°F)	27.8	31.6	41.4	52.0	61.6	69.7	73.9	72.1	65.9	54.6	43.6	33.5	52.3
Mean Minimum Temp. (°F)	19.9	22.8	31.5	41.4	51.4	60.0	64.3	62.3	55.5	44.1	34.9	25.7	42.8
Extreme Maximum Temp. (°F)	72	73	81	87	89	98	100	99	96	87	80	76	100
Extreme Minimum Temp. (°F)	-23	-9	-1	16	32	37	46	40	25	20	4	-21	-23
Days Maximum Temp. ≥ 90°F	0	0	0	0	0	1	4	2	1	0	0	0	8
Days Maximum Temp. ≤ 32°F	12	8	2	0	0	0	0	0	0	0	1	6	29
Days Minimum Temp. ≤ 32°F	27	22	18	5	0	0	0	0	0	3	14	23	112
Days Minimum Temp. ≤ 0°F	2	1	0	0	0	0	0	0	0	0	0	1	4
Heating Degree Days (base 65°F)	1,148	935	729	396	157	25	2	7	76	332	637	970	5,414
Cooling Degree Days (base 65°F)	0	0	2	14	54	176	289	238	105	16	1	0	895
Mean Precipitation (in.)	2.94	2.68	3.79	4.11	4.70	4.21	4.03	4.27	3.36	2.90	3.22	3.12	43.33
Days With ≥ 0.1" Precipitation	7	6	8	8	9	8	7	6	5	6	7	6	83
Days With ≥ 1.0" Precipitation	0	0	1	1	1	1	1	1	1	1	1	1	10
Mean Snowfall (in.)	7.3	5.0	3.8	0.6	trace	0.0	0.0	0.0	0.0	0.2	0.8	2.8	20.5
Days With ≥ 1.0" Snow Depth	9	8	3	0	0	0	0	0	0	0	0	4	24

Hiram *Portage County* Elevation: 1,227 ft. Latitude: 41° 18' N Longitude: 81° 09' W

	JAN	FEB	MAR	APR	MAY	JUN	JUL	AUG	SEP	OCT	NOV	DEC	YEAR
Mean Maximum Temp. (°F)	31.7	35.8	45.8	58.5	69.6	77.3	81.6	79.9	72.8	61.0	48.5	36.9	58.3
Mean Temp. (°F)	24.1	27.4	36.3	47.9	58.8	66.7	71.4	69.8	62.8	51.5	40.7	29.9	48.9
Mean Minimum Temp. (°F)	16.5	18.8	27.1	37.2	47.9	56.1	61.0	59.7	52.9	41.9	33.0	22.8	39.6
Extreme Maximum Temp. (°F)	65	69	81	87	90	100	99	95	91	81	75	73	100
Extreme Minimum Temp. (°F)	-25	-10	-6	12	25	34	44	38	32	21	1	-15	-25
Days Maximum Temp. ≥ 90°F	0	0	0	0	0	1	2	1	0	0	0	0	4
Days Maximum Temp. ≤ 32°F	16	12	4	0	0	0	0	0	0	0	1	10	43
Days Minimum Temp. ≤ 32°F	29	25	23	10	1	0	0	0	0	4	16	27	135
Days Minimum Temp. ≤ 0°F	3	2	0	0	0	0	0	0	0	0	0	1	6
Heating Degree Days (base 65°F)	1,261	1,056	883	514	225	61	9	18	123	418	722	1,082	6,372
Cooling Degree Days (base 65°F)	0	0	1	7	36	121	223	178	63	4	0	0	633
Mean Precipitation (in.)	2.67	2.30	3.38	3.55	3.75	4.08	3.89	3.79	4.15	3.23	3.65	3.47	41.91
Days With ≥ 0.1" Precipitation	8	7	9	9	8	8	7	7	8	8	9	9	97
Days With ≥ 1.0" Precipitation	0	0	0	0	0	1	1	1	1	1	0	0	5
Mean Snowfall (in.)	16.1	12.4	10.2	1.5	trace	0.0	0.0	0.0	0.0	0.2	6.0	15.2	61.6
Days With ≥ 1.0" Snow Depth	20	17	8	1	0	0	0	0	0	0	4	14	64

Hoytville 2 NE *Wood County* Elevation: 698 ft. Latitude: 41° 13' N Longitude: 83° 46' W

	JAN	FEB	MAR	APR	MAY	JUN	JUL	AUG	SEP	OCT	NOV	DEC	YEAR
Mean Maximum Temp. (°F)	31.1	34.8	46.0	59.1	71.2	80.1	83.8	81.4	75.5	63.1	48.8	36.8	59.3
Mean Temp. (°F)	23.1	26.3	36.3	47.7	59.4	68.8	72.5	69.9	63.3	51.5	40.3	29.3	49.0
Mean Minimum Temp. (°F)	15.0	17.7	26.6	36.3	47.5	57.4	61.1	58.3	51.0	39.8	31.7	21.7	38.7
Extreme Maximum Temp. (°F)	65	71	82	88	93	105	101	98	95	87	78	69	105
Extreme Minimum Temp. (°F)	-22	-15	-9	1	25	36	41	37	27	17	8	-19	-22
Days Maximum Temp. ≥ 90°F	0	0	0	0	1	4	5	3	1	0	0	0	14
Days Maximum Temp. ≤ 32°F	16	12	4	0	0	0	0	0	0	0	1	10	43
Days Minimum Temp. ≤ 32°F	29	25	23	11	1	0	0	0	0	7	18	27	141
Days Minimum Temp. ≤ 0°F	5	3	0	0	0	0	0	0	0	0	0	2	10
Heating Degree Days (base 65°F)	1,293	1,087	884	520	218	43	8	22	125	420	735	1,101	6,456
Cooling Degree Days (base 65°F)	0	0	1	7	48	162	255	183	76	8	0	0	740
Mean Precipitation (in.)	1.78	1.70	2.51	3.26	3.41	3.60	3.86	3.54	2.64	2.40	2.79	2.40	33.89
Days With ≥ 0.1" Precipitation	5	4	6	8	7	7	7	6	5	5	7	6	73
Days With ≥ 1.0" Precipitation	0	0	0	1	1	1	1	1	0	0	0	0	5
Mean Snowfall (in.)	7.5	5.5	3.4	1.0	trace	0.0	0.0	0.0	0.0	trace	1.3	5.2	23.9
Days With ≥ 1.0" Snow Depth	15	11	4	1	0	0	0	0	0	0	1	8	40

Irwin *Union County* Elevation: 1,007 ft. Latitude: 40° 07' N Longitude: 83° 29' W

	JAN	FEB	MAR	APR	MAY	JUN	JUL	AUG	SEP	OCT	NOV	DEC	YEAR
Mean Maximum Temp. (°F)	34.5	39.6	51.5	64.0	74.3	82.5	85.6	84.2	78.3	66.7	51.8	39.6	62.7
Mean Temp. (°F)	25.8	29.9	40.4	51.1	61.5	70.0	73.3	71.5	65.0	53.8	42.2	31.3	51.3
Mean Minimum Temp. (°F)	17.1	20.2	29.3	38.2	48.6	57.5	61.0	58.8	51.7	40.8	32.5	23.2	39.9
Extreme Maximum Temp. (°F)	66	72	82	88	93	101	101	101	95	88	79	72	101
Extreme Minimum Temp. (°F)	-28	-21	-17	11	27	34	41	35	28	15	2	-19	-28
Days Maximum Temp. ≥ 90°F	0	0	0	0	1	4	7	4	1	0	0	0	17
Days Maximum Temp. ≤ 32°F	13	9	2	0	0	0	0	0	0	0	1	7	32
Days Minimum Temp. ≤ 32°F	28	24	20	10	1	0	0	0	1	7	16	25	132
Days Minimum Temp. ≤ 0°F	5	3	0	0	0	0	0	0	0	0	0	1	9
Heating Degree Days (base 65°F)	1,208	984	759	419	163	24	4	11	90	352	678	1,037	5,729
Cooling Degree Days (base 65°F)	0	0	1	8	58	183	281	230	93	11	0	0	865
Mean Precipitation (in.)	2.25	1.93	2.62	3.52	4.14	4.28	4.67	3.67	2.92	2.57	3.13	2.68	38.38
Days With ≥ 0.1" Precipitation	5	4	6	7	8	7	7	6	5	5	6	6	72
Days With ≥ 1.0" Precipitation	0	0	0	1	1	1	1	1	1	0	1	1	8
Mean Snowfall (in.)	6.8	4.5	2.5	0.8	trace	0.0	0.0	0.0	0.0	trace	1.0	na	na
Days With ≥ 1.0" Snow Depth	10	7	2	0	0	0	0	0	0	0	1	na	na

Jackson 3 NW *Jackson County* Elevation: 797 ft. Latitude: 39° 05' N Longitude: 82° 42' W

	JAN	FEB	MAR	APR	MAY	JUN	JUL	AUG	SEP	OCT	NOV	DEC	YEAR
Mean Maximum Temp. (°F)	38.3	42.9	53.1	64.8	73.9	81.0	84.6	83.3	77.3	65.8	54.0	43.3	63.5
Mean Temp. (°F)	28.6	32.4	41.4	51.5	61.1	69.0	73.3	71.9	65.3	53.2	43.1	33.8	52.1
Mean Minimum Temp. (°F)	19.1	21.9	29.6	38.1	48.2	57.0	61.9	60.5	53.3	40.5	32.2	24.2	40.5
Extreme Maximum Temp. (°F)	74	76	85	91	91	100	101	102	96	86	81	79	102
Extreme Minimum Temp. (°F)	-28	-14	-15	16	26	31	40	36	30	17	-5	-20	-28
Days Maximum Temp. ≥ 90°F	0	0	0	0	0	2	6	4	1	0	0	0	13
Days Maximum Temp. ≤ 32°F	10	6	2	0	0	0	0	0	0	0	0	6	24
Days Minimum Temp. ≤ 32°F	27	23	19	9	2	0	0	0	0	7	16	24	127
Days Minimum Temp. ≤ 0°F	2	2	0	0	0	0	0	0	0	0	0	1	5
Heating Degree Days (base 65°F)	1,120	914	728	407	169	33	4	9	85	370	651	961	5,451
Cooling Degree Days (base 65°F)	0	0	3	10	57	171	288	240	103	12	1	0	885
Mean Precipitation (in.)	2.76	2.76	3.75	3.43	3.96	4.14	4.03	3.92	3.17	2.82	3.12	3.27	41.13
Days With ≥ 0.1" Precipitation	6	7	8	8	8	8	7	7	6	6	6	8	85
Days With ≥ 1.0" Precipitation	0	0	1	0	1	1	1	1	1	0	1	1	8
Mean Snowfall (in.)	na	na	na	0.7	0.0	0.0	0.0	0.0	0.0	0.0	na	na	na
Days With ≥ 1.0" Snow Depth	na	na	na	0	0	0	0	0	0	0	na	na	na

Kenton *Hardin County* Elevation: 994 ft. Latitude: 40° 39' N Longitude: 83° 36' W

	JAN	FEB	MAR	APR	MAY	JUN	JUL	AUG	SEP	OCT	NOV	DEC	YEAR
Mean Maximum Temp. (°F)	32.4	37.0	47.3	60.2	72.0	80.9	85.1	82.9	76.3	63.9	49.7	37.7	60.5
Mean Temp. (°F)	24.3	28.2	37.7	49.1	60.5	69.5	73.9	71.4	64.5	52.6	40.9	30.0	50.2
Mean Minimum Temp. (°F)	15.9	19.0	28.0	37.9	49.0	58.2	62.4	59.9	52.7	41.1	32.1	22.2	39.8
Extreme Maximum Temp. (°F)	64	71	82	89	93	104	103	103	96	87	78	71	104
Extreme Minimum Temp. (°F)	-22	-17	-5	10	26	36	42	39	27	16	3	-18	-22
Days Maximum Temp. ≥ 90°F	0	0	0	0	1	4	8	4	2	0	0	0	19
Days Maximum Temp. ≤ 32°F	15	10	4	0	0	0	0	0	0	0	2	9	40
Days Minimum Temp. ≤ 32°F	29	25	22	9	1	0	0	0	0	5	16	27	134
Days Minimum Temp. ≤ 0°F	4	3	0	0	0	0	0	0	0	0	0	1	8
Heating Degree Days (base 65°F)	1,256	1,032	841	478	189	37	4	14	103	389	715	1,080	6,138
Cooling Degree Days (base 65°F)	0	0	1	10	60	190	303	237	99	11	0	0	911
Mean Precipitation (in.)	2.23	2.02	2.75	3.48	3.84	3.53	4.01	3.30	2.61	2.14	2.84	2.72	35.47
Days With ≥ 0.1" Precipitation	6	6	7	8	7	7	7	6	5	5	7	7	78
Days With ≥ 1.0" Precipitation	0	0	0	1	1	1	1	1	1	0	0	0	6
Mean Snowfall (in.)	10.0	6.4	4.2	0.6	0.0	0.0	0.0	0.0	0.0	trace	1.2	5.4	27.8
Days With ≥ 1.0" Snow Depth	na	na	4	0	0	0	0	0	0	0	1	6	na

Lancaster 2 NW *Fairfield County* Elevation: 859 ft. Latitude: 39° 44' N Longitude: 82° 38' W

	JAN	FEB	MAR	APR	MAY	JUN	JUL	AUG	SEP	OCT	NOV	DEC	YEAR
Mean Maximum Temp. (°F)	34.5	38.7	49.6	61.6	71.8	80.4	84.2	82.9	76.9	65.1	51.8	40.5	61.5
Mean Temp. (°F)	25.8	29.1	38.9	49.5	59.7	68.9	72.8	71.4	64.6	52.8	42.1	32.0	50.6
Mean Minimum Temp. (°F)	17.0	19.4	28.2	37.4	47.6	57.3	61.6	59.8	52.4	40.4	32.4	23.4	39.7
Extreme Maximum Temp. (°F)	68	71	82	89	92	101	99	101	96	86	80	78	101
Extreme Minimum Temp. (°F)	-24	-15	-7	8	27	34	41	35	30	19	3	-20	-24
Days Maximum Temp. ≥ 90°F	0	0	0	0	0	2	6	4	1	0	0	0	13
Days Maximum Temp. ≤ 32°F	14	9	3	0	0	0	0	0	0	0	1	7	34
Days Minimum Temp. ≤ 32°F	28	23	22	10	1	0	0	0	0	7	16	24	131
Days Minimum Temp. ≤ 0°F	4	2	0	0	0	0	0	0	0	0	0	1	7
Heating Degree Days (base 65°F)	1,209	1,008	803	468	206	37	6	14	104	381	681	1,017	5,934
Cooling Degree Days (base 65°F)	0	0	2	11	48	170	273	233	99	11	1	0	848
Mean Precipitation (in.)	2.28	2.17	2.65	3.22	4.18	3.82	4.37	3.64	2.76	2.46	3.09	2.91	37.55
Days With ≥ 0.1" Precipitation	5	5	6	6	7	6	7	6	5	5	7	6	71
Days With ≥ 1.0" Precipitation	0	0	1	1	1	1	1	1	1	0	1	0	8
Mean Snowfall (in.)	na	na	na	0.7	0.0	0.0	0.0	0.0	0.0	trace	0.3	na	na
Days With ≥ 1.0" Snow Depth	na	na	na	0	0	0	0	0	0	0	na	na	na

Lima WWTP *Allen County* Elevation: 849 ft. Latitude: 40° 43' N Longitude: 84° 08' W

	JAN	FEB	MAR	APR	MAY	JUN	JUL	AUG	SEP	OCT	NOV	DEC	YEAR
Mean Maximum Temp. (°F)	33.1	37.6	48.3	60.9	72.5	80.9	84.7	82.5	76.6	64.3	50.4	38.7	60.9
Mean Temp. (°F)	25.6	29.4	39.1	50.3	61.6	70.5	74.4	72.4	66.0	54.1	42.5	31.7	51.5
Mean Minimum Temp. (°F)	18.0	21.1	29.9	39.7	50.7	60.0	64.1	62.2	55.3	43.9	34.4	24.5	42.0
Extreme Maximum Temp. (°F)	64	71	81	89	93	97	100	99	95	94	77	70	100
Extreme Minimum Temp. (°F)	-21	-15	-3	8	27	40	46	42	30	19	6	-17	-21
Days Maximum Temp. ≥ 90°F	0	0	0	0	1	3	6	3	1	0	0	0	14
Days Maximum Temp. ≤ 32°F	14	10	3	0	0	0	0	0	0	0	2	8	37
Days Minimum Temp. ≤ 32°F	28	23	20	7	1	0	0	0	0	3	14	24	120
Days Minimum Temp. ≤ 0°F	3	1	0	0	0	0	0	0	0	0	0	1	5
Heating Degree Days (base 65°F)	1,217	996	797	443	166	26	2	8	79	344	668	1,027	5,773
Cooling Degree Days (base 65°F)	0	0	2	10	66	201	310	251	113	15	0	0	968
Mean Precipitation (in.)	2.20	1.94	2.70	3.48	3.91	4.04	4.36	3.28	3.08	2.38	3.13	2.65	37.15
Days With ≥ 0.1" Precipitation	6	5	6	8	8	7	7	6	6	6	7	6	78
Days With ≥ 1.0" Precipitation	0	0	0	1	1	1	1	1	1	0	0	0	6
Mean Snowfall (in.)	na	na	na	0.1	0.0	0.0	0.0	0.0	0.0	trace	trace	na	na
Days With ≥ 1.0" Snow Depth	na	na	na	0	0	0	0	0	0	0	0	na	na

London *Madison County* Elevation: 1,017 ft. Latitude: 39° 53' N Longitude: 83° 27' W

	JAN	FEB	MAR	APR	MAY	JUN	JUL	AUG	SEP	OCT	NOV	DEC	YEAR
Mean Maximum Temp. (°F)	34.4	39.1	50.4	62.6	73.2	81.5	85.1	83.0	77.1	65.3	51.3	40.0	61.9
Mean Temp. (°F)	26.3	30.0	39.9	50.4	61.0	69.8	73.5	71.4	64.7	53.2	42.1	32.1	51.2
Mean Minimum Temp. (°F)	18.1	20.8	29.3	38.2	48.7	58.0	61.8	59.7	52.4	41.0	32.8	24.2	40.4
Extreme Maximum Temp. (°F)	67	71	82	88	92	102	100	101	95	88	79	74	102
Extreme Minimum Temp. (°F)	-24	-19	-14	12	26	35	42	38	30	16	0	-18	-24
Days Maximum Temp. ≥ 90°F	0	0	0	0	0	4	7	4	1	0	0	0	16
Days Maximum Temp. ≤ 32°F	13	9	2	0	0	0	0	0	0	0	1	7	32
Days Minimum Temp. ≤ 32°F	27	23	20	9	1	0	0	0	0	6	16	24	126
Days Minimum Temp. ≤ 0°F	4	2	0	0	0	0	0	0	0	0	0	1	7
Heating Degree Days (base 65°F)	1,194	982	774	440	174	30	4	12	99	370	681	1,014	5,774
Cooling Degree Days (base 65°F)	0	0	1	7	55	184	286	222	93	10	0	0	858
Mean Precipitation (in.)	2.38	2.16	2.80	3.59	4.07	4.30	3.99	3.34	2.82	2.58	3.28	2.96	38.27
Days With ≥ 0.1" Precipitation	5	5	7	8	8	7	7	6	5	5	7	7	77
Days With ≥ 1.0" Precipitation	0	0	0	1	1	1	1	1	1	0	1	0	7
Mean Snowfall (in.)	6.9	na	na	0.4	0.0	0.0	0.0	0.0	0.0	0.2	0.5	na	na
Days With ≥ 1.0" Snow Depth	na	na	2	0	0	0	0	0	0	0	0	na	na

Mansfield 5 W *Richland County* Elevation: 1,348 ft. Latitude: 40° 46' N Longitude: 82° 37' W

	JAN	FEB	MAR	APR	MAY	JUN	JUL	AUG	SEP	OCT	NOV	DEC	YEAR
Mean Maximum Temp. (°F)	31.9	35.9	46.6	59.2	69.9	78.2	81.9	80.2	73.5	61.8	48.7	37.5	58.8
Mean Temp. (°F)	23.7	27.1	36.7	47.8	58.5	66.9	70.8	69.2	62.7	51.3	40.2	29.7	48.7
Mean Minimum Temp. (°F)	15.4	18.3	26.7	36.3	47.0	55.5	59.7	58.2	51.7	40.7	31.6	21.9	38.6
Extreme Maximum Temp. (°F)	66	69	81	87	89	100	99	97	94	84	76	69	100
Extreme Minimum Temp. (°F)	-25	-22	-11	5	18	28	38	37	25	15	3	-19	-25
Days Maximum Temp. ≥ 90°F	0	0	0	0	0	1	3	1	0	0	0	0	5
Days Maximum Temp. ≤ 32°F	15	12	5	0	0	0	0	0	0	0	2	10	44
Days Minimum Temp. ≤ 32°F	29	25	23	12	2	0	0	0	1	6	17	26	141
Days Minimum Temp. ≤ 0°F	5	3	1	0	0	0	0	0	0	0	0	1	10
Heating Degree Days (base 65°F)	1,276	1,063	871	518	232	59	14	22	133	426	739	1,087	6,440
Cooling Degree Days (base 65°F)	0	0	1	6	36	127	212	164	66	7	0	0	619
Mean Precipitation (in.)	2.08	1.69	2.65	3.54	4.14	4.16	3.92	3.63	3.27	2.51	2.91	2.55	37.05
Days With ≥ 0.1" Precipitation	5	5	7	8	9	7	7	7	6	6	6	6	79
Days With ≥ 1.0" Precipitation	0	0	0	1	1	1	1	1	1	0	1	0	7
Mean Snowfall (in.)	na	na	na	0.3	trace	0.0	0.0	0.0	0.0	trace	1.0	na	na
Days With ≥ 1.0" Snow Depth	na	na	3	0	0	0	0	0	0	0	1	na	na

Marietta WWTP *Washington County* Elevation: 577 ft. Latitude: 39° 25' N Longitude: 81° 26' W

	JAN	FEB	MAR	APR	MAY	JUN	JUL	AUG	SEP	OCT	NOV	DEC	YEAR
Mean Maximum Temp. (°F)	39.5	43.8	54.2	65.5	74.7	82.2	85.8	84.5	78.2	66.9	54.9	44.7	64.6
Mean Temp. (°F)	30.8	33.9	43.1	53.1	62.6	70.8	74.9	73.5	66.9	55.1	44.8	36.0	53.8
Mean Minimum Temp. (°F)	22.1	24.0	31.9	40.6	50.5	59.4	64.0	62.5	55.5	43.2	34.8	27.2	43.0
Extreme Maximum Temp. (°F)	73	75	85	91	93	99	102	100	96	86	81	78	102
Extreme Minimum Temp. (°F)	-23	-10	0	19	29	37	44	38	33	20	10	-11	-23
Days Maximum Temp. ≥ 90°F	0	0	0	0	1	3	8	6	2	0	0	0	20
Days Maximum Temp. ≤ 32°F	9	5	1	0	0	0	0	0	0	0	0	4	19
Days Minimum Temp. ≤ 32°F	25	22	17	6	1	0	0	0	0	3	14	22	110
Days Minimum Temp. ≤ 0°F	1	1	0	0	0	0	0	0	0	0	0	0	2
Heating Degree Days (base 65°F)	1,053	872	674	362	134	19	1	4	61	313	599	892	4,984
Cooling Degree Days (base 65°F)	0	0	2	11	64	205	332	274	116	13	1	0	1,018
Mean Precipitation (in.)	3.12	2.75	3.69	3.10	4.04	4.40	4.22	4.16	3.31	2.87	3.17	3.37	42.20
Days With ≥ 0.1" Precipitation	8	7	8	8	9	8	7	7	6	6	7	8	89
Days With ≥ 1.0" Precipitation	0	0	1	0	1	1	1	1	1	1	0	0	7
Mean Snowfall (in.)	7.2	na	3.4	0.5	0.0	0.0	0.0	0.0	0.0	trace	0.6	2.6	na
Days With ≥ 1.0" Snow Depth	9	na	1	0	0	0	0	0	0	0	0	2	na

Marion 2 N *Marion County* Elevation: 964 ft. Latitude: 40° 37' N Longitude: 83° 08' W

	JAN	FEB	MAR	APR	MAY	JUN	JUL	AUG	SEP	OCT	NOV	DEC	YEAR
Mean Maximum Temp. (°F)	32.3	36.7	47.3	60.2	71.1	80.3	84.0	82.2	75.7	63.5	49.8	38.0	60.1
Mean Temp. (°F)	24.1	27.7	37.5	48.8	59.7	69.2	73.0	70.8	63.8	52.1	41.0	30.4	49.8
Mean Minimum Temp. (°F)	15.8	18.7	27.6	37.4	48.3	58.0	61.9	59.3	51.9	40.7	32.1	22.8	39.6
Extreme Maximum Temp. (°F)	67	72	81	87	91	103	100	99	97	90	79	73	103
Extreme Minimum Temp. (°F)	-23	-20	-5	8	25	36	43	35	24	17	4	-19	-23
Days Maximum Temp. ≥ 90°F	0	0	0	0	1	4	6	4	2	0	0	0	17
Days Maximum Temp. ≤ 32°F	15	11	4	0	0	0	0	0	0	0	1	9	40
Days Minimum Temp. ≤ 32°F	29	25	22	10	1	0	0	0	0	6	17	26	136
Days Minimum Temp. ≤ 0°F	4	3	0	0	0	0	0	0	0	0	0	1	8
Heating Degree Days (base 65°F)	1,262	1,047	848	488	210	39	6	18	116	401	714	1,064	6,213
Cooling Degree Days (base 65°F)	0	0	2	8	51	172	270	206	83	10	0	0	802
Mean Precipitation (in.)	2.35	1.72	2.31	3.69	4.17	4.24	4.38	3.69	3.03	2.73	3.01	2.84	38.16
Days With ≥ 0.1" Precipitation	5	5	6	9	8	7	7	6	6	6	7	7	79
Days With ≥ 1.0" Precipitation	0	0	0	1	1	1	1	1	1	1	1	0	8
Mean Snowfall (in.)	9.7	5.3	3.2	0.6	0.0	0.0	0.0	0.0	0.0	trace	0.8	4.4	24.0
Days With ≥ 1.0" Snow Depth	14	10	3	0	0	0	0	0	0	0	1	5	33

Marysville *Union County* Elevation: 997 ft. Latitude: 40° 14' N Longitude: 83° 22' W

	JAN	FEB	MAR	APR	MAY	JUN	JUL	AUG	SEP	OCT	NOV	DEC	YEAR
Mean Maximum Temp. (°F)	33.5	37.8	49.0	61.2	72.2	80.4	84.2	82.3	75.7	63.5	50.0	38.7	60.7
Mean Temp. (°F)	25.8	29.2	39.2	50.2	61.1	69.7	73.7	71.7	64.8	53.0	41.7	31.5	51.0
Mean Minimum Temp. (°F)	17.9	20.7	29.4	39.1	50.0	58.8	63.1	61.0	53.8	42.4	33.3	24.1	41.1
Extreme Maximum Temp. (°F)	66	72	82	88	92	101	100	99	96	86	78	72	101
Extreme Minimum Temp. (°F)	-23	-18	-11	12	29	36	44	41	31	18	4	-20	-23
Days Maximum Temp. ≥ 90°F	0	0	0	0	0	3	6	3	1	0	0	0	13
Days Maximum Temp. ≤ 32°F	14	10	3	0	0	0	0	0	0	0	1	8	36
Days Minimum Temp. ≤ 32°F	28	24	21	7	0	0	0	0	0	4	15	25	124
Days Minimum Temp. ≤ 0°F	4	2	0	0	0	0	0	0	0	0	0	1	7
Heating Degree Days (base 65°F)	1,210	1,004	794	445	173	29	3	9	95	374	694	1,033	5,863
Cooling Degree Days (base 65°F)	0	0	2	7	58	180	292	232	95	9	0	0	875
Mean Precipitation (in.)	2.26	1.93	2.59	3.38	3.88	4.32	4.05	3.27	2.64	2.44	2.95	2.66	36.37
Days With ≥ 0.1" Precipitation	6	5	7	7	8	7	7	7	5	6	7	6	78
Days With ≥ 1.0" Precipitation	0	0	0	1	1	1	1	1	1	0	1	0	7
Mean Snowfall (in.)	6.5	4.8	3.3	0.9	0.0	0.0	0.0	0.0	0.0	trace	1.1	3.6	20.2
Days With ≥ 1.0" Snow Depth	13	8	3	0	0	0	0	0	0	0	1	5	30

McConnelsville Lock 7 *Morgan County* Elevation: 757 ft. Latitude: 39° 39' N Longitude: 81° 51' W

	JAN	FEB	MAR	APR	MAY	JUN	JUL	AUG	SEP	OCT	NOV	DEC	YEAR
Mean Maximum Temp. (°F)	37.9	41.9	52.6	64.5	74.0	81.4	85.0	83.7	77.6	66.2	54.1	43.3	63.5
Mean Temp. (°F)	27.8	30.7	40.2	50.6	60.5	68.8	73.1	71.7	64.9	52.8	42.8	33.4	51.5
Mean Minimum Temp. (°F)	17.6	19.5	27.8	36.7	46.9	56.2	61.2	59.7	52.2	39.4	31.5	23.5	39.3
Extreme Maximum Temp. (°F)	74	75	84	91	94	99	102	99	97	87	81	77	102
Extreme Minimum Temp. (°F)	-32	-15	-11	15	26	32	40	39	31	18	1	-16	-32
Days Maximum Temp. ≥ 90°F	0	0	0	0	1	3	7	5	2	0	0	0	18
Days Maximum Temp. ≤ 32°F	11	6	1	0	0	0	0	0	0	0	0	5	23
Days Minimum Temp. ≤ 32°F	28	24	22	11	2	0	0	0	0	7	18	25	137
Days Minimum Temp. ≤ 0°F	3	3	0	0	0	0	0	0	0	0	0	1	7
Heating Degree Days (base 65°F)	1,145	962	761	433	180	32	4	9	91	377	659	973	5,626
Cooling Degree Days (base 65°F)	0	0	1	7	39	150	265	218	86	7	0	0	773
Mean Precipitation (in.)	3.03	2.49	3.48	3.64	4.37	4.14	4.85	4.35	3.22	2.79	3.38	3.22	42.96
Days With ≥ 0.1" Precipitation	8	7	8	8	9	7	8	7	6	6	7	8	89
Days With ≥ 1.0" Precipitation	0	0	1	1	1	1	1	1	1	1	1	0	9
Mean Snowfall (in.)	7.9	5.7	3.4	0.9	0.0	0.0	0.0	0.0	0.0	0.0	0.7	2.6	21.2
Days With ≥ 1.0" Snow Depth	na	5	2	0	0	0	0	0	0	0	0	2	na

Milford *Clermont County* Elevation: 518 ft. Latitude: 39° 11' N Longitude: 84° 17' W

	JAN	FEB	MAR	APR	MAY	JUN	JUL	AUG	SEP	OCT	NOV	DEC	YEAR
Mean Maximum Temp. (°F)	37.0	41.3	52.4	64.3	74.6	82.4	86.8	85.2	78.5	66.9	53.7	42.5	63.8
Mean Temp. (°F)	27.8	31.1	41.0	51.3	61.7	70.2	74.7	73.1	65.9	53.7	43.0	33.4	52.3
Mean Minimum Temp. (°F)	18.6	20.9	29.6	38.5	48.6	57.9	62.6	61.0	53.2	40.5	32.1	24.3	40.6
Extreme Maximum Temp. (°F)	72	76	84	89	93	97	104	101	98	88	81	75	104
Extreme Minimum Temp. (°F)	-25	-13	-10	18	27	36	40	41	26	12	-3	-22	-25
Days Maximum Temp. ≥ 90°F	0	0	0	0	1	4	10	8	2	0	0	0	25
Days Maximum Temp. ≤ 32°F	11	7	1	0	0	0	0	0	0	0	1	6	26
Days Minimum Temp. ≤ 32°F	27	23	20	9	1	0	0	0	0	6	16	24	126
Days Minimum Temp. ≤ 0°F	3	2	0	0	0	0	0	0	0	0	0	1	6
Heating Degree Days (base 65°F)	1,146	951	739	412	157	23	2	5	80	355	652	973	5,495
Cooling Degree Days (base 65°F)	0	0	2	8	65	202	335	279	112	13	0	0	1,016
Mean Precipitation (in.)	3.14	2.57	3.78	4.18	4.98	4.51	4.03	4.22	3.15	3.14	3.67	3.35	44.72
Days With ≥ 0.1" Precipitation	7	6	8	9	9	8	7	7	6	7	8	7	89
Days With ≥ 1.0" Precipitation	0	0	1	1	1	1	1	1	1	1	1	1	10
Mean Snowfall (in.)	5.8	4.9	2.1	0.4	trace	0.0	0.0	trace	0.0	0.1	0.4	2.2	15.9
Days With ≥ 1.0" Snow Depth	8	7	2	0	0	0	0	0	0	0	0	3	20

Millport 2 NW *Columbiana County* Elevation: 1,148 ft. Latitude: 40° 43' N Longitude: 80° 54' W

	JAN	FEB	MAR	APR	MAY	JUN	JUL	AUG	SEP	OCT	NOV	DEC	YEAR
Mean Maximum Temp. (°F)	34.7	39.1	49.5	61.5	71.3	79.6	83.3	82.0	75.1	63.4	50.7	39.8	60.8
Mean Temp. (°F)	25.6	28.9	38.3	48.5	58.4	66.8	70.8	69.2	62.5	51.1	40.9	31.3	49.4
Mean Minimum Temp. (°F)	16.5	18.7	26.9	35.5	45.4	54.0	58.3	56.5	49.8	38.7	31.1	22.7	37.8
Extreme Maximum Temp. (°F)	67	72	82	90	91	98	103	99	94	82	77	74	103
Extreme Minimum Temp. (°F)	-34	-21	-17	10	20	28	38	27	26	14	-5	-20	-34
Days Maximum Temp. ≥ 90°F	0	0	0	0	0	2	5	3	1	0	0	0	11
Days Maximum Temp. ≤ 32°F	13	8	3	0	0	0	0	0	0	0	1	8	33
Days Minimum Temp. ≤ 32°F	28	24	22	13	3	0	0	0	1	9	18	25	143
Days Minimum Temp. ≤ 0°F	5	3	1	0	0	0	0	0	0	0	0	1	10
Heating Degree Days (base 65°F)	1,214	1,012	823	492	229	54	11	22	131	428	716	1,038	6,170
Cooling Degree Days (base 65°F)	0	0	1	4	29	120	214	164	59	4	0	0	595
Mean Precipitation (in.)	2.47	2.31	3.11	3.24	4.09	3.83	4.15	3.12	3.27	2.53	3.25	3.12	38.49
Days With ≥ 0.1" Precipitation	7	7	8	8	9	8	8	6	7	6	8	8	90
Days With ≥ 1.0" Precipitation	0	0	0	0	1	1	1	1	1	0	0	0	5
Mean Snowfall (in.)	7.8	6.7	6.1	1.3	trace	0.0	0.0	0.0	0.0	trace	2.2	6.1	30.2
Days With ≥ 1.0" Snow Depth	na	na	na	0	0	0	0	0	0	0	1	na	na

Mineral Ridge Water Works *Trumbull County* Elevation: 889 ft. Latitude: 41° 09' N Longitude: 80° 47' W

	JAN	FEB	MAR	APR	MAY	JUN	JUL	AUG	SEP	OCT	NOV	DEC	YEAR
Mean Maximum Temp. (°F)	35.2	39.5	50.1	62.5	73.6	81.5	85.7	83.7	76.9	65.1	51.7	40.9	62.2
Mean Temp. (°F)	26.8	29.9	39.0	49.8	60.3	68.7	73.2	71.5	64.8	53.4	42.7	33.2	51.1
Mean Minimum Temp. (°F)	18.3	20.3	27.8	37.0	47.1	55.9	60.6	59.2	52.7	41.6	33.6	25.4	40.0
Extreme Maximum Temp. (°F)	67	73	82	90	92	98	102	100	94	91	79	74	102
Extreme Minimum Temp. (°F)	-24	-16	-6	13	24	29	41	34	26	14	4	-11	-24
Days Maximum Temp. ≥ 90°F	0	0	0	0	0	4	8	5	1	0	0	0	18
Days Maximum Temp. ≤ 32°F	12	8	2	0	0	0	0	0	0	0	1	7	30
Days Minimum Temp. ≤ 32°F	28	24	22	10	2	0	0	0	0	5	15	25	131
Days Minimum Temp. ≤ 0°F	3	2	0	0	0	0	0	0	0	0	0	0	5
Heating Degree Days (base 65°F)	1,178	984	801	457	188	38	5	12	93	361	664	980	5,761
Cooling Degree Days (base 65°F)	0	0	1	6	50	158	279	223	93	7	0	0	817
Mean Precipitation (in.)	2.16	1.82	2.67	3.11	3.41	4.32	4.19	3.34	3.97	2.55	2.99	2.68	37.21
Days With ≥ 0.1" Precipitation	6	6	7	7	8	8	7	6	7	6	7	7	82
Days With ≥ 1.0" Precipitation	0	0	0	0	0	1	1	1	1	0	0	0	4
Mean Snowfall (in.)	9.8	6.9	7.1	1.1	trace	0.0	0.0	0.0	0.0	trace	1.8	7.8	34.5
Days With ≥ 1.0" Snow Depth	16	13	4	0	0	0	0	0	0	0	1	7	41

Montpelier *Williams County* Elevation: 859 ft. Latitude: 41° 35' N Longitude: 84° 36' W

	JAN	FEB	MAR	APR	MAY	JUN	JUL	AUG	SEP	OCT	NOV	DEC	YEAR
Mean Maximum Temp. (°F)	30.3	34.4	45.0	58.3	70.7	80.2	84.1	81.9	74.9	62.1	48.0	36.1	58.8
Mean Temp. (°F)	21.8	25.1	35.1	46.8	58.3	67.8	71.9	69.7	62.2	50.1	39.0	28.3	48.0
Mean Minimum Temp. (°F)	13.3	15.7	25.1	35.2	45.8	55.5	59.7	57.4	49.5	38.1	29.9	20.4	37.1
Extreme Maximum Temp. (°F)	62	71	80	88	92	104	104	102	95	89	76	69	104
Extreme Minimum Temp. (°F)	-25	-22	-7	8	26	36	43	36	28	18	5	-19	-25
Days Maximum Temp. ≥ 90°F	0	0	0	0	1	4	6	3	1	0	0	0	15
Days Maximum Temp. ≤ 32°F	17	12	4	0	0	0	0	0	0	0	2	10	45
Days Minimum Temp. ≤ 32°F	30	27	25	12	2	0	0	0	1	9	20	28	154
Days Minimum Temp. ≤ 0°F	6	4	0	0	0	0	0	0	0	0	0	2	12
Heating Degree Days (base 65°F)	1,332	1,121	922	544	239	50	9	22	140	459	774	1,133	6,745
Cooling Degree Days (base 65°F)	0	0	1	5	39	152	248	187	64	4	0	0	700
Mean Precipitation (in.)	1.92	1.89	2.86	3.60	3.54	3.53	3.47	3.57	3.22	2.55	3.13	2.54	35.82
Days With ≥ 0.1" Precipitation	5	5	7	8	7	7	7	7	6	6	7	7	79
Days With ≥ 1.0" Precipitation	0	0	0	1	1	1	1	1	1	0	0	0	6
Mean Snowfall (in.)	9.9	8.5	4.5	0.8	0.0	0.0	0.0	0.0	0.0	0.2	1.9	8.1	33.9
Days With ≥ 1.0" Snow Depth	17	14	5	0	0	0	0	0	0	0	2	8	46

Napoleon *Henry County* Elevation: 679 ft. Latitude: 41° 22' N Longitude: 84° 00' W

	JAN	FEB	MAR	APR	MAY	JUN	JUL	AUG	SEP	OCT	NOV	DEC	YEAR
Mean Maximum Temp. (°F)	31.1	35.1	47.3	60.2	72.3	81.5	85.0	83.0	75.9	63.9	49.8	37.1	60.2
Mean Temp. (°F)	23.2	26.5	37.4	48.6	60.1	69.5	73.5	71.3	64.1	52.7	41.2	29.6	49.8
Mean Minimum Temp. (°F)	15.2	17.7	27.4	37.0	47.8	57.4	62.0	59.5	52.3	41.4	32.6	22.0	39.4
Extreme Maximum Temp. (°F)	62	69	80	88	93	105	104	99	95	88	77	70	105
Extreme Minimum Temp. (°F)	-24	-13	-7	5	28	39	40	38	27	22	6	-18	-24
Days Maximum Temp. ≥ 90°F	0	0	0	0	1	4	7	4	1	0	0	0	17
Days Maximum Temp. ≤ 32°F	16	11	3	0	0	0	0	0	0	0	1	9	40
Days Minimum Temp. ≤ 32°F	29	25	22	10	1	0	0	0	1	5	16	26	135
Days Minimum Temp. ≤ 0°F	4	3	0	0	0	0	0	0	0	0	0	2	9
Heating Degree Days (base 65°F)	1,290	1,083	850	493	200	33	4	14	110	383	708	1,091	6,259
Cooling Degree Days (base 65°F)	0	0	1	8	48	160	272	208	79	6	0	0	782
Mean Precipitation (in.)	1.96	1.65	2.68	3.62	3.52	3.40	3.94	3.42	2.72	2.52	2.91	2.47	34.81
Days With ≥ 0.1" Precipitation	5	5	6	8	7	7	7	6	6	6	6	7	76
Days With ≥ 1.0" Precipitation	0	0	0	1	1	1	1	1	0	0	0	0	5
Mean Snowfall (in.)	8.7	5.8	2.8	1.1	0.0	0.0	0.0	0.0	0.0	0.1	0.9	5.2	24.6
Days With ≥ 1.0" Snow Depth	15	12	3	0	0	0	0	0	0	0	1	7	38

New Lexington 2 NW *Perry County* Elevation: 889 ft. Latitude: 39° 44' N Longitude: 82° 13' W

	JAN	FEB	MAR	APR	MAY	JUN	JUL	AUG	SEP	OCT	NOV	DEC	YEAR
Mean Maximum Temp. (°F)	36.7	41.4	52.4	64.2	73.8	81.2	84.7	83.1	77.1	65.7	52.9	42.0	62.9
Mean Temp. (°F)	27.2	30.6	40.3	50.4	60.3	68.6	72.6	71.1	64.6	52.7	42.1	32.8	51.1
Mean Minimum Temp. (°F)	17.6	19.8	28.1	36.6	46.9	56.0	60.5	59.1	52.0	39.6	31.2	23.5	39.2
Extreme Maximum Temp. (°F)	72	74	84	91	92	100	101	100	95	85	80	77	101
Extreme Minimum Temp. (°F)	-35	-20	-11	14	27	32	40	37	30	17	-4	-24	-35
Days Maximum Temp. ≥ 90°F	0	0	0	0	1	3	6	4	1	0	0	0	15
Days Maximum Temp. ≤ 32°F	11	7	2	0	0	0	0	0	0	0	1	6	27
Days Minimum Temp. ≤ 32°F	28	24	21	12	2	0	0	0	0	8	17	25	137
Days Minimum Temp. ≤ 0°F	4	2	0	0	0	0	0	0	0	0	0	1	7
Heating Degree Days (base 65°F)	1,167	964	761	438	183	33	4	11	94	382	683	992	5,712
Cooling Degree Days (base 65°F)	0	0	1	6	39	144	251	203	81	6	0	0	731
Mean Precipitation (in.)	2.87	2.64	3.38	3.76	4.29	4.25	4.68	3.94	2.82	2.65	3.38	3.08	41.74
Days With ≥ 0.1" Precipitation	8	6	8	9	9	8	8	7	6	6	8	7	90
Days With ≥ 1.0" Precipitation	0	0	0	1	1	1	1	1	1	0	1	0	7
Mean Snowfall (in.)	9.2	5.9	3.6	0.5	trace	0.0	0.0	0.0	0.0	trace	0.7	3.0	22.9
Days With ≥ 1.0" Snow Depth	14	9	4	0	0	0	0	0	0	0	1	5	33

New Philadelphia *Tuscarawas County* Elevation: 892 ft. Latitude: 40° 30' N Longitude: 81° 28' W

	JAN	FEB	MAR	APR	MAY	JUN	JUL	AUG	SEP	OCT	NOV	DEC	YEAR
Mean Maximum Temp. (°F)	34.7	38.7	49.1	61.0	71.9	80.3	84.1	82.9	76.1	64.1	51.2	40.1	61.2
Mean Temp. (°F)	26.2	29.1	38.2	48.7	59.1	68.1	72.2	70.9	63.9	52.0	41.7	32.0	50.2
Mean Minimum Temp. (°F)	17.6	19.4	27.3	36.3	46.3	55.8	60.2	58.8	51.6	39.8	32.2	23.8	39.1
Extreme Maximum Temp. (°F)	69	73	84	90	91	99	102	99	96	87	79	76	102
Extreme Minimum Temp. (°F)	-22	-12	-5	13	25	30	42	36	30	18	4	-16	-22
Days Maximum Temp. ≥ 90°F	0	0	0	0	0	3	6	4	1	0	0	0	14
Days Maximum Temp. ≤ 32°F	13	9	3	0	0	0	0	0	0	0	1	7	33
Days Minimum Temp. ≤ 32°F	28	24	22	12	2	0	0	0	0	7	17	25	137
Days Minimum Temp. ≤ 0°F	3	3	0	0	0	0	0	0	0	0	0	1	7
Heating Degree Days (base 65°F)	1,197	1,008	824	491	218	46	8	16	112	402	692	1,017	6,031
Cooling Degree Days (base 65°F)	0	0	1	7	41	147	253	211	83	7	1	0	751
Mean Precipitation (in.)	2.74	2.40	3.22	3.54	4.08	4.43	4.10	4.21	3.22	2.62	3.28	3.04	40.88
Days With ≥ 0.1" Precipitation	6	6	8	8	8	8	7	7	6	6	7	7	84
Days With ≥ 1.0" Precipitation	0	0	0	1	1	1	1	1	1	0	1	0	7
Mean Snowfall (in.)	9.9	6.6	5.1	1.5	trace	0.0	0.0	0.0	0.0	trace	1.4	5.2	29.7
Days With ≥ 1.0" Snow Depth	15	11	5	0	0	0	0	0	0	0	1	6	38

Newark Water Works *Licking County* Elevation: 833 ft. Latitude: 40° 05' N Longitude: 81° 25' W

	JAN	FEB	MAR	APR	MAY	JUN	JUL	AUG	SEP	OCT	NOV	DEC	YEAR
Mean Maximum Temp. (°F)	35.4	39.9	51.0	63.1	73.3	81.3	84.9	83.0	76.5	64.6	51.8	40.6	62.1
Mean Temp. (°F)	27.3	30.8	40.6	51.1	61.0	69.5	73.4	71.7	64.9	53.0	42.5	32.7	51.5
Mean Minimum Temp. (°F)	19.1	21.6	30.2	39.0	48.7	57.7	61.9	60.3	53.2	41.4	33.1	24.8	40.9
Extreme Maximum Temp. (°F)	69	73	82	89	91	100	100	100	96	87	78	76	100
Extreme Minimum Temp. (°F)	-24	-14	-7	15	29	32	41	38	31	19	3	-17	-24
Days Maximum Temp. ≥ 90°F	0	0	0	0	0	3	6	4	1	0	0	0	14
Days Maximum Temp. ≤ 32°F	12	8	2	0	0	0	0	0	0	0	1	7	30
Days Minimum Temp. ≤ 32°F	27	23	19	9	1	0	0	0	0	5	15	24	123
Days Minimum Temp. ≤ 0°F	3	2	0	0	0	0	0	0	0	0	0	1	6
Heating Degree Days (base 65°F)	1,163	960	751	421	170	29	4	9	93	373	670	994	5,637
Cooling Degree Days (base 65°F)	0	0	1	7	49	170	280	224	90	8	1	0	830
Mean Precipitation (in.)	2.84	2.45	3.16	3.89	4.26	4.40	4.53	4.17	2.96	2.66	3.37	3.17	41.86
Days With ≥ 0.1" Precipitation	7	6	8	8	8	8	8	7	6	6	7	7	86
Days With ≥ 1.0" Precipitation	0	0	0	1	1	1	1	1	1	0	1	0	7
Mean Snowfall (in.)	8.4	5.3	2.8	0.9	trace	0.0	0.0	0.0	0.0	trace	0.5	2.7	20.6
Days With ≥ 1.0" Snow Depth	12	8	3	0	0	0	0	0	0	0	0	4	27

Norwalk WWTP *Huron County* Elevation: 669 ft. Latitude: 41° 16' N Longitude: 82° 37' W

	JAN	FEB	MAR	APR	MAY	JUN	JUL	AUG	SEP	OCT	NOV	DEC	YEAR
Mean Maximum Temp. (°F)	32.3	35.4	45.3	57.9	69.5	78.5	82.6	80.7	74.3	62.4	49.3	37.8	58.8
Mean Temp. (°F)	24.4	27.0	36.3	47.4	58.6	67.9	72.1	70.2	63.3	51.9	41.2	30.5	49.2
Mean Minimum Temp. (°F)	16.5	18.6	27.2	37.0	47.7	57.2	61.6	59.6	52.3	41.3	33.1	23.2	39.6
Extreme Maximum Temp. (°F)	65	70	81	87	91	103	98	98	94	85	77	73	103
Extreme Minimum Temp. (°F)	-21	-11	-7	7	26	33	41	41	30	17	6	-17	-21
Days Maximum Temp. ≥ 90°F	0	0	0	0	0	3	5	2	1	0	0	0	11
Days Maximum Temp. ≤ 32°F	16	12	4	0	0	0	0	0	0	0	1	9	42
Days Minimum Temp. ≤ 32°F	29	25	22	10	1	0	0	0	0	5	16	26	134
Days Minimum Temp. ≤ 0°F	4	3	0	0	0	0	0	0	0	0	0	1	8
Heating Degree Days (base 65°F)	1,253	1,065	885	529	237	56	12	20	124	408	708	1,062	6,359
Cooling Degree Days (base 65°F)	0	0	2	8	46	152	250	192	81	9	0	0	740
Mean Precipitation (in.)	2.16	1.79	2.72	3.32	3.50	4.22	3.72	3.81	3.24	2.41	2.98	2.75	36.62
Days With ≥ 0.1" Precipitation	6	5	7	8	8	7	7	6	7	6	7	7	81
Days With ≥ 1.0" Precipitation	0	0	0	0	1	1	1	1	1	0	0	0	5
Mean Snowfall (in.)	8.6	6.2	4.8	0.8	trace	0.0	0.0	trace	0.0	trace	0.9	5.4	26.7
Days With ≥ 1.0" Snow Depth	15	13	5	1	0	0	0	0	0	0	1	8	43

Oberlin *Lorain County* Elevation: 813 ft. Latitude: 41° 16' N Longitude: 82° 13' W

	JAN	FEB	MAR	APR	MAY	JUN	JUL	AUG	SEP	OCT	NOV	DEC	YEAR
Mean Maximum Temp. (°F)	33.0	36.8	46.9	59.6	71.2	79.9	83.9	82.0	75.3	63.3	50.0	38.3	60.0
Mean Temp. (°F)	24.6	27.6	36.9	48.0	59.0	67.9	72.2	70.1	63.2	51.8	41.0	30.3	49.4
Mean Minimum Temp. (°F)	16.1	18.4	26.7	36.4	46.8	56.0	60.5	58.2	51.0	40.3	32.1	22.3	38.7
Extreme Maximum Temp. (°F)	65	71	82	87	92	104	100	100	96	85	76	75	104
Extreme Minimum Temp. (°F)	-23	-18	-15	11	24	30	38	32	25	16	4	-18	-23
Days Maximum Temp. ≥ 90°F	0	0	0	0	0	3	6	3	1	0	0	0	13
Days Maximum Temp. ≤ 32°F	15	11	4	0	0	0	0	0	0	0	1	8	39
Days Minimum Temp. ≤ 32°F	29	25	23	11	2	0	0	0	0	5	17	26	138
Days Minimum Temp. ≤ 0°F	4	3	0	0	0	0	0	0	0	0	0	1	8
Heating Degree Days (base 65°F)	1,247	1,049	867	510	222	52	10	17	123	409	712	1,069	6,287
Cooling Degree Days (base 65°F)	0	0	2	6	44	146	246	184	71	6	0	0	705
Mean Precipitation (in.)	2.19	1.96	2.66	3.20	3.55	3.91	3.70	3.41	3.34	2.46	3.18	2.76	36.32
Days With ≥ 0.1" Precipitation	6	6	7	8	8	8	7	6	6	6	8	7	83
Days With ≥ 1.0" Precipitation	0	0	0	0	1	1	1	1	1	0	0	0	5
Mean Snowfall (in.)	11.9	9.7	7.1	1.6	trace	0.0	0.0	0.0	0.0	trace	2.5	8.6	41.4
Days With ≥ 1.0" Snow Depth	na	na	na	1	0	0	0	0	0	0	1	na	na

Painesville 4 NW *Lake County* Elevation: 597 ft. Latitude: 41° 45' N Longitude: 81° 18' W

	JAN	FEB	MAR	APR	MAY	JUN	JUL	AUG	SEP	OCT	NOV	DEC	YEAR
Mean Maximum Temp. (°F)	34.3	36.6	45.6	56.3	67.7	76.7	81.4	79.8	74.2	63.2	51.2	40.3	58.9
Mean Temp. (°F)	27.2	29.0	37.1	47.6	58.6	67.8	72.6	71.3	65.4	54.7	44.1	33.7	50.8
Mean Minimum Temp. (°F)	20.1	21.4	28.7	38.8	49.5	58.9	63.8	62.8	56.6	46.1	36.9	27.1	42.6
Extreme Maximum Temp. (°F)	67	74	82	91	92	98	96	93	91	86	78	75	98
Extreme Minimum Temp. (°F)	-19	-8	0	17	29	39	45	39	33	24	5	-11	-19
Days Maximum Temp. ≥ 90°F	0	0	0	0	0	1	2	1	0	0	0	0	4
Days Maximum Temp. ≤ 32°F	13	11	4	0	0	0	0	0	0	0	0	6	34
Days Minimum Temp. ≤ 32°F	27	24	21	7	0	0	0	0	0	1	9	22	111
Days Minimum Temp. ≤ 0°F	2	1	0	0	0	0	0	0	0	0	0	0	3
Heating Degree Days (base 65°F)	1,166	1,009	858	522	229	45	3	7	74	324	624	962	5,823
Cooling Degree Days (base 65°F)	0	0	1	5	38	135	257	213	94	11	0	0	754
Mean Precipitation (in.)	2.28	1.78	2.76	3.15	3.02	3.80	3.13	3.72	4.12	3.28	3.54	2.94	37.52
Days With ≥ 0.1" Precipitation	7	5	7	8	7	7	6	7	7	8	9	8	86
Days With ≥ 1.0" Precipitation	0	0	0	0	0	1	1	1	1	0	1	0	5
Mean Snowfall (in.)	10.2	7.3	5.2	1.2	trace	0.0	0.0	0.0	0.0	trace	2.1	8.8	34.8
Days With ≥ 1.0" Snow Depth	17	11	4	0	0	0	0	0	0	0	1	9	42

Pandora *Putnam County* Elevation: 767 ft. Latitude: 40° 57' N Longitude: 83° 58' W

	JAN	FEB	MAR	APR	MAY	JUN	JUL	AUG	SEP	OCT	NOV	DEC	YEAR
Mean Maximum Temp. (°F)	31.6	35.7	47.1	59.9	71.7	80.5	84.0	81.7	75.4	62.9	48.9	37.1	59.7
Mean Temp. (°F)	24.2	27.6	37.8	49.1	60.6	69.6	73.2	70.8	64.1	52.5	41.0	30.2	50.1
Mean Minimum Temp. (°F)	16.7	19.6	28.5	38.2	49.4	58.7	62.3	59.9	52.8	42.0	33.1	23.2	40.4
Extreme Maximum Temp. (°F)	65	71	82	89	94	103	101	100	96	87	78	71	103
Extreme Minimum Temp. (°F)	-21	-17	-13	6	25	37	44	40	28	19	8	-19	-21
Days Maximum Temp. ≥ 90°F	0	0	0	0	1	3	6	3	1	0	0	0	14
Days Maximum Temp. ≤ 32°F	16	12	4	0	0	0	0	0	0	0	2	10	44
Days Minimum Temp. ≤ 32°F	28	24	21	9	1	0	0	0	0	5	16	26	130
Days Minimum Temp. ≤ 0°F	5	3	0	0	0	0	0	0	0	0	0	1	9
Heating Degree Days (base 65°F)	1,260	1,048	838	481	190	32	4	14	107	390	714	1,073	6,151
Cooling Degree Days (base 65°F)	0	0	2	8	59	179	278	210	87	10	0	0	833
Mean Precipitation (in.)	2.04	1.86	2.74	3.32	3.65	3.97	3.86	3.35	3.01	2.31	2.86	2.66	35.63
Days With ≥ 0.1" Precipitation	6	5	7	8	7	7	7	6	6	5	7	6	77
Days With ≥ 1.0" Precipitation	0	0	0	0	1	1	1	1	1	0	0	0	5
Mean Snowfall (in.)	9.5	7.1	4.2	1.2	trace	0.0	0.0	0.0	trace	0.1	2.0	6.6	30.7
Days With ≥ 1.0" Snow Depth	16	12	5	1	0	0	0	0	0	0	1	8	43

Paulding *Paulding County* Elevation: 725 ft. Latitude: 41° 07' N Longitude: 84° 36' W

	JAN	FEB	MAR	APR	MAY	JUN	JUL	AUG	SEP	OCT	NOV	DEC	YEAR
Mean Maximum Temp. (°F)	30.4	34.5	45.8	58.9	70.9	80.3	84.2	81.9	75.4	62.5	48.7	36.6	59.2
Mean Temp. (°F)	22.0	25.6	36.0	47.6	59.1	68.7	72.4	69.8	62.9	50.7	39.6	28.7	48.6
Mean Minimum Temp. (°F)	13.7	16.6	26.2	36.2	47.2	57.1	60.5	57.7	50.2	38.8	30.4	20.8	37.9
Extreme Maximum Temp. (°F)	62	71	80	87	92	104	100	99	95	85	79	70	104
Extreme Minimum Temp. (°F)	-25	-20	-11	7	25	36	45	39	27	17	5	-20	-25
Days Maximum Temp. ≥ 90°F	0	0	0	0	0	3	6	3	1	0	0	0	13
Days Maximum Temp. ≤ 32°F	17	12	4	0	0	0	0	0	0	0	2	10	45
Days Minimum Temp. ≤ 32°F	30	26	24	10	1	0	0	0	1	7	19	27	145
Days Minimum Temp. ≤ 0°F	6	3	0	0	0	0	0	0	0	0	0	2	11
Heating Degree Days (base 65°F)	1,327	1,106	892	520	221	41	7	20	127	443	755	1,117	6,576
Cooling Degree Days (base 65°F)	0	0	0	4	45	159	251	179	74	5	0	0	717
Mean Precipitation (in.)	1.90	1.73	2.68	3.38	3.78	3.43	3.41	2.95	3.00	2.50	2.95	2.58	34.29
Days With ≥ 0.1" Precipitation	5	4	6	7	7	6	6	5	6	6	6	6	70
Days With ≥ 1.0" Precipitation	0	0	0	1	1	1	1	1	0	0	1	0	6
Mean Snowfall (in.)	5.5	5.3	3.2	0.4	0.0	0.0	0.0	0.0	0.0	trace	1.2	4.1	19.7
Days With ≥ 1.0" Snow Depth	na	na	na	0	0	0	0	0	0	0	1	na	na

Philo 3 SW *Muskingum County* Elevation: 1,017 ft. Latitude: 39° 50' N Longitude: 81° 55' W

	JAN	FEB	MAR	APR	MAY	JUN	JUL	AUG	SEP	OCT	NOV	DEC	YEAR
Mean Maximum Temp. (°F)	34.9	39.6	50.4	62.0	71.0	78.0	81.7	80.6	74.4	63.5	51.0	40.1	60.6
Mean Temp. (°F)	27.3	30.9	40.5	51.0	60.1	67.7	71.5	70.3	63.9	52.9	42.5	32.6	50.9
Mean Minimum Temp. (°F)	19.6	22.2	30.5	39.9	49.3	57.3	61.3	59.8	53.2	42.3	34.0	25.0	41.2
Extreme Maximum Temp. (°F)	67	73	83	89	89	98	102	99	97	85	80	76	102
Extreme Minimum Temp. (°F)	-27	-10	-2	12	25	33	43	39	28	19	2	-18	-27
Days Maximum Temp. ≥ 90°F	0	0	0	0	0	0	3	1	1	0	0	0	5
Days Maximum Temp. ≤ 32°F	13	9	3	0	0	0	0	0	0	0	2	8	35
Days Minimum Temp. ≤ 32°F	27	23	19	7	1	0	0	0	0	5	15	24	121
Days Minimum Temp. ≤ 0°F	2	1	0	0	0	0	0	0	0	0	0	1	4
Heating Degree Days (base 65°F)	1,164	958	759	428	192	42	9	16	109	377	669	998	5,721
Cooling Degree Days (base 65°F)	0	0	3	11	42	126	222	182	75	9	1	0	671
Mean Precipitation (in.)	2.09	2.07	2.70	3.11	4.08	4.18	4.19	3.77	2.83	2.50	2.97	2.54	37.03
Days With ≥ 0.1" Precipitation	6	5	7	7	8	8	7	6	6	6	7	6	79
Days With ≥ 1.0" Precipitation	0	0	0	1	1	1	1	1	1	0	0	0	6
Mean Snowfall (in.)	9.4	5.3	4.3	1.1	trace	0.0	0.0	0.0	0.0	trace	1.1	3.6	24.8
Days With ≥ 1.0" Snow Depth	13	9	3	0	0	0	0	0	0	0	1	5	31

Portsmouth Sciotoville *Scioto County* Elevation: 538 ft. Latitude: 38° 45' N Longitude: 82° 53' W

	JAN	FEB	MAR	APR	MAY	JUN	JUL	AUG	SEP	OCT	NOV	DEC	YEAR
Mean Maximum Temp. (°F)	39.7	44.4	55.1	66.4	75.5	82.8	86.7	85.4	79.3	67.9	55.9	45.2	65.3
Mean Temp. (°F)	30.9	34.6	44.2	54.1	63.5	71.5	75.5	73.8	67.2	55.4	45.4	36.2	54.4
Mean Minimum Temp. (°F)	22.1	24.8	33.4	42.0	51.5	60.0	64.2	62.2	55.0	42.9	34.8	27.1	43.3
Extreme Maximum Temp. (°F)	74	76	84	92	93	101	104	104	100	88	82	76	104
Extreme Minimum Temp. (°F)	-29	-8	0	12	28	38	40	35	31	22	7	-18	-29
Days Maximum Temp. ≥ 90°F	0	0	0	0	1	5	10	7	2	0	0	0	25
Days Maximum Temp. ≤ 32°F	8	5	1	0	0	0	0	0	0	0	0	4	18
Days Minimum Temp. ≤ 32°F	26	22	15	5	0	0	0	0	0	4	13	21	106
Days Minimum Temp. ≤ 0°F	1	1	0	0	0	0	0	0	0	0	0	1	3
Heating Degree Days (base 65°F)	1,049	851	640	337	120	17	1	5	63	306	584	887	4,860
Cooling Degree Days (base 65°F)	0	0	2	13	74	213	330	269	114	14	1	0	1,030
Mean Precipitation (in.)	3.16	2.82	3.65	3.44	4.37	3.86	4.06	4.00	3.05	2.63	3.02	3.33	41.39
Days With ≥ 0.1" Precipitation	7	7	8	8	9	7	8	6	5	6	7	7	85
Days With ≥ 1.0" Precipitation	1	1	1	1	1	1	1	1	1	0	1	1	11
Mean Snowfall (in.)	5.5	3.7	2.3	0.3	trace	0.0	0.0	0.0	0.0	trace	0.3	1.2	13.3
Days With ≥ 1.0" Snow Depth	7	6	2	0	0	0	0	0	0	0	0	1	16

Put-In-Bay *Ottawa County* Elevation: 577 ft. Latitude: 41° 39' N Longitude: 82° 48' W

	JAN	FEB	MAR	APR	MAY	JUN	JUL	AUG	SEP	OCT	NOV	DEC	YEAR
Mean Maximum Temp. (°F)	31.2	33.9	43.1	55.3	67.1	77.3	82.3	80.6	73.7	61.3	48.4	36.9	57.6
Mean Temp. (°F)	24.8	26.7	35.9	47.2	59.2	69.4	74.6	73.5	66.6	54.5	42.6	31.2	50.5
Mean Minimum Temp. (°F)	18.4	19.7	28.6	39.1	51.2	61.5	66.9	66.3	59.4	47.6	36.6	25.5	43.4
Extreme Maximum Temp. (°F)	60	63	78	87	91	99	100	95	97	84	79	68	100
Extreme Minimum Temp. (°F)	-18	-10	-2	13	33	41	51	50	37	30	11	-14	-18
Days Maximum Temp. ≥ 90°F	0	0	0	0	0	1	4	2	1	0	0	0	8
Days Maximum Temp. ≤ 32°F	16	13	4	0	0	0	0	0	0	0	1	8	42
Days Minimum Temp. ≤ 32°F	28	25	21	5	0	0	0	0	0	0	9	23	111
Days Minimum Temp. ≤ 0°F	2	1	0	0	0	0	0	0	0	0	0	1	4
Heating Degree Days (base 65°F)	1,239	1,075	896	532	211	27	1	3	61	329	667	1,040	6,081
Cooling Degree Days (base 65°F)	0	0	0	6	35	162	307	269	105	8	0	0	892
Mean Precipitation (in.)	1.58	1.44	5.21	2.91	3.33	3.41	3.06	3.31	3.16	2.55	2.68	2.15	34.79
Days With ≥ 0.1" Precipitation	5	4	5	7	7	6	6	6	6	6	6	5	69
Days With ≥ 1.0" Precipitation	0	0	0	0	1	1	1	1	1	0	0	0	5
Mean Snowfall (in.)	7.3	5.3	2.8	0.4	trace	0.0	0.0	0.0	0.0	trace	0.2	3.7	19.7
Days With ≥ 1.0" Snow Depth	17	12	5	0	0	0	0	0	0	0	0	7	41

Ripley Exp. Farm *Brown County* Elevation: 879 ft. Latitude: 38° 47' N Longitude: 83° 48' W

	JAN	FEB	MAR	APR	MAY	JUN	JUL	AUG	SEP	OCT	NOV	DEC	YEAR
Mean Maximum Temp. (°F)	38.0	42.8	53.1	64.3	73.4	81.5	85.2	84.0	78.1	66.3	53.6	43.4	63.6
Mean Temp. (°F)	29.1	32.9	42.3	52.7	62.2	70.5	74.4	72.8	66.2	54.3	43.9	34.4	53.0
Mean Minimum Temp. (°F)	20.2	22.9	31.5	41.0	50.9	59.6	63.5	61.6	54.3	42.2	34.1	25.4	42.3
Extreme Maximum Temp. (°F)	73	74	81	88	90	102	103	103	96	87	81	76	103
Extreme Minimum Temp. (°F)	-28	-11	-5	15	30	37	43	39	30	18	2	-22	-28
Days Maximum Temp. ≥ 90°F	0	0	0	0	0	3	7	5	2	0	0	0	17
Days Maximum Temp. ≤ 32°F	10	7	2	0	0	0	0	0	0	0	1	5	25
Days Minimum Temp. ≤ 32°F	27	22	18	6	0	0	0	0	0	5	14	23	115
Days Minimum Temp. ≤ 0°F	3	1	0	0	0	0	0	0	0	0	0	1	5
Heating Degree Days (base 65°F)	1,106	901	699	377	147	22	2	6	76	339	628	942	5,245
Cooling Degree Days (base 65°F)	0	0	2	11	66	200	314	262	111	14	1	0	981
Mean Precipitation (in.)	2.84	2.77	4.14	4.17	4.97	4.49	4.56	4.09	3.25	3.05	3.43	3.57	45.33
Days With ≥ 0.1" Precipitation	6	6	8	9	9	8	7	7	6	6	7	8	87
Days With ≥ 1.0" Precipitation	0	1	1	1	1	1	2	1	1	1	1	1	12
Mean Snowfall (in.)	7.5	5.6	4.1	0.5	trace	0.0	0.0	0.0	0.0	trace	0.9	2.9	21.5
Days With ≥ 1.0" Snow Depth	10	8	3	0	0	0	0	0	0	0	0	4	25

Sandusky *Erie County* Elevation: 583 ft. Latitude: 41° 27' N Longitude: 82° 43' W

	JAN	FEB	MAR	APR	MAY	JUN	JUL	AUG	SEP	OCT	NOV	DEC	YEAR
Mean Maximum Temp. (°F)	32.2	35.0	44.1	56.3	68.0	77.5	82.3	80.3	73.7	62.0	49.3	37.9	58.2
Mean Temp. (°F)	25.1	27.6	36.5	47.8	59.5	69.1	73.7	71.9	64.8	53.3	42.2	31.3	50.2
Mean Minimum Temp. (°F)	18.0	20.2	28.8	39.2	50.9	60.6	65.1	63.4	55.9	44.6	35.0	24.7	42.2
Extreme Maximum Temp. (°F)	65	71	81	88	93	103	99	98	94	86	77	73	103
Extreme Minimum Temp. (°F)	-20	-7	-7	16	32	43	41	45	36	24	9	-16	-20
Days Maximum Temp. ≥ 90°F	0	0	0	0	0	2	4	2	1	0	0	0	9
Days Maximum Temp. ≤ 32°F	16	12	5	0	0	0	0	0	0	0	1	9	43
Days Minimum Temp. ≤ 32°F	28	24	21	5	0	0	0	0	0	2	13	25	118
Days Minimum Temp. ≤ 0°F	3	2	0	0	0	0	0	0	0	0	0	1	6
Heating Degree Days (base 65°F)	1,230	1,049	878	518	212	36	3	7	92	365	678	1,039	6,107
Cooling Degree Days (base 65°F)	0	0	2	7	46	165	285	231	91	10	0	0	837
Mean Precipitation (in.)	1.86	1.71	2.48	3.06	3.29	4.10	3.38	3.58	3.13	2.32	2.75	2.53	34.19
Days With ≥ 0.1" Precipitation	5	4	6	7	7	7	6	6	6	6	6	6	72
Days With ≥ 1.0" Precipitation	0	0	0	0	1	1	1	1	1	0	0	0	5
Mean Snowfall (in.)	8.7	6.0	3.0	0.6	trace	0.0	0.0	0.0	0.0	trace	0.3	4.3	22.9
Days With ≥ 1.0" Snow Depth	14	8	3	0	0	0	0	0	0	0	0	6	31

Springfield New Water Works *Clark County* Elevation: 928 ft. Latitude: 39° 58' N Longitude: 83° 49' W

	JAN	FEB	MAR	APR	MAY	JUN	JUL	AUG	SEP	OCT	NOV	DEC	YEAR
Mean Maximum Temp. (°F)	33.7	37.9	48.6	60.5	71.4	80.0	83.8	82.4	76.3	63.9	50.7	39.6	60.7
Mean Temp. (°F)	25.2	28.5	38.5	49.2	59.9	69.2	72.8	70.9	64.0	52.0	41.5	31.5	50.3
Mean Minimum Temp. (°F)	16.5	19.1	28.4	37.8	48.4	58.2	61.8	59.3	51.7	40.1	32.2	23.3	39.7
Extreme Maximum Temp. (°F)	68	73	81	93	91	98	98	100	95	86	79	72	100
Extreme Minimum Temp. (°F)	-26	-18	-13	14	26	34	43	39	29	15	3	-26	-26
Days Maximum Temp. ≥ 90°F	0	0	0	0	0	2	5	3	1	0	0	0	11
Days Maximum Temp. ≤ 32°F	14	10	3	0	0	0	0	0	0	0	1	8	36
Days Minimum Temp. ≤ 32°F	28	24	21	10	1	0	0	0	0	7	17	25	133
Days Minimum Temp. ≤ 0°F	4	3	0	0	0	0	0	0	0	0	0	1	8
Heating Degree Days (base 65°F)	1,229	1,025	815	476	199	37	6	15	111	405	701	1,032	6,051
Cooling Degree Days (base 65°F)	0	0	2	6	49	176	270	213	86	9	0	0	811
Mean Precipitation (in.)	2.27	1.81	2.51	3.40	4.34	4.45	4.15	3.62	2.90	2.57	2.96	2.71	37.69
Days With ≥ 0.1" Precipitation	5	5	6	7	8	8	7	6	5	5	6	7	75
Days With ≥ 1.0" Precipitation	0	0	0	1	1	1	1	1	1	1	1	0	8
Mean Snowfall (in.)	na	na	na	trace	0.0	0.0	0.0	0.0	0.0	trace	0.1	na	na
Days With ≥ 1.0" Snow Depth	na	na	na	0	0	0	0	0	0	0	0	na	na

Steubenville *Jefferson County* Elevation: 990 ft. Latitude: 40° 23' N Longitude: 80° 38' W

	JAN	FEB	MAR	APR	MAY	JUN	JUL	AUG	SEP	OCT	NOV	DEC	YEAR
Mean Maximum Temp. (°F)	36.5	40.4	50.8	62.4	72.0	79.9	83.3	82.0	75.6	64.1	52.1	41.6	61.7
Mean Temp. (°F)	28.4	31.6	40.6	50.8	60.8	69.2	73.3	72.0	65.5	53.8	43.5	33.8	51.9
Mean Minimum Temp. (°F)	20.3	22.7	30.3	39.2	49.5	58.4	63.2	62.0	55.4	43.5	34.8	26.0	42.1
Extreme Maximum Temp. (°F)	72	74	83	89	90	98	102	96	95	84	80	77	102
Extreme Minimum Temp. (°F)	-22	-8	-1	16	27	34	45	42	34	22	5	-14	-22
Days Maximum Temp. ≥ 90°F	0	0	0	0	0	2	4	2	1	0	0	0	9
Days Maximum Temp. ≤ 32°F	12	8	2	0	0	0	0	0	0	0	1	7	30
Days Minimum Temp. ≤ 32°F	27	22	19	8	1	0	0	0	0	2	13	23	115
Days Minimum Temp. ≤ 0°F	2	1	0	0	0	0	0	0	0	0	0	0	3
Heating Degree Days (base 65°F)	1,128	937	753	427	172	30	3	7	78	348	640	961	5,484
Cooling Degree Days (base 65°F)	0	0	2	8	47	165	280	233	96	9	1	0	841
Mean Precipitation (in.)	2.80	2.43	3.31	3.20	3.98	4.45	4.20	3.72	3.25	2.61	3.42	3.00	40.37
Days With ≥ 0.1" Precipitation	7	6	8	8	9	8	8	7	6	6	8	7	88
Days With ≥ 1.0" Precipitation	0	0	0	0	1	1	1	1	1	0	1	0	6
Mean Snowfall (in.)	na	na	na	trace	0.0	0.0	0.0	0.0	0.0	0.2	0.3	na	na
Days With ≥ 1.0" Snow Depth	na	na	na	0	0	0	0	0	0	0	0	na	na

Tiffin *Seneca County* Elevation: 738 ft. Latitude: 41° 07' N Longitude: 83° 10' W

	JAN	FEB	MAR	APR	MAY	JUN	JUL	AUG	SEP	OCT	NOV	DEC	YEAR
Mean Maximum Temp. (°F)	32.1	36.1	47.6	60.2	71.9	80.3	84.4	82.2	76.0	63.3	49.5	37.8	60.1
Mean Temp. (°F)	24.8	28.2	38.4	49.5	60.7	69.5	73.7	71.4	64.8	52.7	41.6	30.8	50.5
Mean Minimum Temp. (°F)	17.5	20.2	29.2	38.7	49.5	58.6	63.0	60.6	53.6	42.0	33.6	23.8	40.9
Extreme Maximum Temp. (°F)	67	72	82	88	93	105	101	98	95	86	79	72	105
Extreme Minimum Temp. (°F)	-21	-15	-2	8	28	38	44	39	31	19	7	-18	-21
Days Maximum Temp. ≥ 90°F	0	0	0	0	1	3	6	3	1	0	0	0	14
Days Maximum Temp. ≤ 32°F	15	11	3	0	0	0	0	0	0	0	1	9	39
Days Minimum Temp. ≤ 32°F	28	24	20	8	0	0	0	0	0	4	15	25	124
Days Minimum Temp. ≤ 0°F	3	2	0	0	0	0	0	0	0	0	0	1	6
Heating Degree Days (base 65°F)	1,239	1,033	818	469	185	37	4	12	96	384	696	1,054	6,027
Cooling Degree Days (base 65°F)	0	0	2	9	59	178	290	220	93	9	0	0	860
Mean Precipitation (in.)	2.26	1.97	2.69	3.39	3.68	4.19	3.34	3.77	3.14	2.39	3.00	2.93	36.75
Days With ≥ 0.1" Precipitation	6	5	7	8	8	8	7	6	6	6	7	7	81
Days With ≥ 1.0" Precipitation	0	0	0	1	1	1	1	1	1	0	0	0	6
Mean Snowfall (in.)	8.8	6.2	3.7	1.2	trace	0.0	0.0	0.0	0.0	trace	1.2	6.7	27.8
Days With ≥ 1.0" Snow Depth	16	13	4	1	0	0	0	0	0	0	1	8	43

Upper Sandusky *Wyandot County* Elevation: 853 ft. Latitude: 40° 50' N Longitude: 83° 17' W

	JAN	FEB	MAR	APR	MAY	JUN	JUL	AUG	SEP	OCT	NOV	DEC	YEAR
Mean Maximum Temp. (°F)	32.4	36.6	47.6	60.4	71.7	80.6	84.4	82.7	76.4	63.9	49.8	38.1	60.4
Mean Temp. (°F)	24.8	28.2	38.2	49.3	60.3	69.5	73.4	71.5	64.7	52.8	41.4	30.8	50.4
Mean Minimum Temp. (°F)	17.2	19.8	28.7	38.1	48.9	58.3	62.2	60.1	53.0	41.8	32.9	23.5	40.4
Extreme Maximum Temp. (°F)	67	72	82	87	92	104	102	99	95	88	79	72	104
Extreme Minimum Temp. (°F)	-23	-16	-8	9	26	37	43	40	28	18	6	-20	-23
Days Maximum Temp. ≥ 90°F	0	0	0	0	1	3	6	4	1	0	0	0	15
Days Maximum Temp. ≤ 32°F	15	11	3	0	0	0	0	0	0	0	1	9	39
Days Minimum Temp. ≤ 32°F	28	24	20	9	1	0	0	0	0	5	16	25	128
Days Minimum Temp. ≤ 0°F	4	2	0	0	0	0	0	0	0	0	0	1	7
Heating Degree Days (base 65°F)	1,239	1,033	826	474	195	35	5	12	98	383	701	1,052	6,053
Cooling Degree Days (base 65°F)	0	0	2	7	52	174	275	219	90	11	0	0	830
Mean Precipitation (in.)	2.11	1.77	2.63	3.50	3.98	3.72	4.17	3.22	3.03	2.22	3.05	2.63	36.03
Days With ≥ 0.1" Precipitation	6	5	6	8	8	7	7	6	6	6	7	7	79
Days With ≥ 1.0" Precipitation	0	0	0	1	1	1	1	1	1	0	1	0	7
Mean Snowfall (in.)	8.3	5.8	3.6	1.2	trace	0.0	0.0	0.0	0.0	trace	1.4	6.3	26.6
Days With ≥ 1.0" Snow Depth	14	11	4	0	0	0	0	0	0	0	1	6	36

Urbana WWTP *Champaign County* Elevation: 997 ft. Latitude: 40° 06' N Longitude: 83° 47' W

	JAN	FEB	MAR	APR	MAY	JUN	JUL	AUG	SEP	OCT	NOV	DEC	YEAR
Mean Maximum Temp. (°F)	33.4	37.5	48.1	60.5	71.5	80.3	84.4	82.7	76.4	63.7	50.4	39.1	60.7
Mean Temp. (°F)	25.1	28.5	38.3	49.3	60.1	69.2	72.9	70.8	64.0	52.1	41.4	31.1	50.2
Mean Minimum Temp. (°F)	16.8	19.4	28.5	38.1	48.7	58.0	61.5	58.9	51.5	40.5	32.4	23.1	39.8
Extreme Maximum Temp. (°F)	66	68	80	87	93	99	100	101	96	87	76	72	101
Extreme Minimum Temp. (°F)	-26	-18	-8	14	28	36	42	39	28	18	1	-22	-26
Days Maximum Temp. ≥ 90°F	0	0	0	0	0	3	6	3	1	0	0	0	13
Days Maximum Temp. ≤ 32°F	14	10	3	0	0	0	0	0	0	0	1	8	36
Days Minimum Temp. ≤ 32°F	28	24	21	9	1	0	0	0	0	6	16	25	130
Days Minimum Temp. ≤ 0°F	4	3	0	0	0	0	0	0	0	0	0	1	8
Heating Degree Days (base 65°F)	1,230	1,025	820	470	194	35	5	14	108	400	700	1,043	6,044
Cooling Degree Days (base 65°F)	0	0	0	5	46	167	266	205	81	7	0	0	777
Mean Precipitation (in.)	2.33	2.09	2.85	3.52	4.37	4.46	4.97	3.61	2.87	2.78	3.05	2.90	39.80
Days With ≥ 0.1" Precipitation	6	5	7	8	8	8	7	6	5	6	7	6	79
Days With ≥ 1.0" Precipitation	1	0	0	1	1	1	2	1	1	1	1	1	11
Mean Snowfall (in.)	na	na	na	0.5	0.0	0.0	0.0	0.0	0.0	0.1	0.3	na	na
Days With ≥ 1.0" Snow Depth	na	na	na	0	0	0	0	0	0	0	0	na	na

Van Wert 1 S *Van Wert County* Elevation: 787 ft. Latitude: 40° 51' N Longitude: 84° 35' W

	JAN	FEB	MAR	APR	MAY	JUN	JUL	AUG	SEP	OCT	NOV	DEC	YEAR
Mean Maximum Temp. (°F)	32.2	36.3	47.6	60.7	72.6	81.5	85.2	82.9	76.6	64.1	49.6	37.6	60.6
Mean Temp. (°F)	24.4	27.8	38.0	49.6	61.1	70.4	74.1	71.8	64.9	52.9	41.2	30.3	50.5
Mean Minimum Temp. (°F)	16.6	19.1	28.3	38.4	49.6	59.2	63.0	60.6	53.1	41.6	32.8	23.0	40.5
Extreme Maximum Temp. (°F)	64	72	81	88	94	104	103	99	97	89	77	71	104
Extreme Minimum Temp. (°F)	-22	-14	-9	9	28	39	44	41	30	20	7	-18	-22
Days Maximum Temp. ≥ 90°F	0	0	0	0	1	4	7	4	2	0	0	0	18
Days Maximum Temp. ≤ 32°F	15	10	3	0	0	0	0	0	0	0	1	9	38
Days Minimum Temp. ≤ 32°F	29	25	21	8	1	0	0	0	0	4	16	26	130
Days Minimum Temp. ≤ 0°F	4	3	0	0	0	0	0	0	0	0	0	1	8
Heating Degree Days (base 65°F)	1,253	1,045	831	464	176	28	3	11	97	380	708	1,068	6,064
Cooling Degree Days (base 65°F)	0	0	1	8	62	198	301	232	97	11	0	0	910
Mean Precipitation (in.)	2.00	1.83	2.66	3.57	3.81	4.16	3.93	3.28	2.90	2.63	3.07	2.68	36.52
Days With ≥ 0.1" Precipitation	5	5	7	8	8	7	7	6	6	6	7	6	78
Days With ≥ 1.0" Precipitation	0	0	0	1	1	1	1	1	1	1	1	0	8
Mean Snowfall (in.)	9.3	6.8	2.8	1.2	0.0	0.0	0.0	0.0	0.0	0.2	1.8	7.7	29.8
Days With ≥ 1.0" Snow Depth	12	11	4	0	0	0	0	0	0	0	1	6	34

Warren 3 S *Trumbull County* Elevation: 898 ft. Latitude: 41° 12' N Longitude: 80° 49' W

	JAN	FEB	MAR	APR	MAY	JUN	JUL	AUG	SEP	OCT	NOV	DEC	YEAR
Mean Maximum Temp. (°F)	33.9	37.6	47.9	60.1	71.0	79.1	83.1	81.4	74.2	62.7	50.2	39.3	60.1
Mean Temp. (°F)	25.0	27.6	36.8	47.3	57.8	66.4	70.5	69.0	62.0	50.8	40.7	31.0	48.7
Mean Minimum Temp. (°F)	15.9	17.6	25.5	34.4	44.5	53.5	57.9	56.6	49.7	38.8	31.2	22.6	37.3
Extreme Maximum Temp. (°F)	67	73	82	90	91	99	101	99	93	83	78	76	101
Extreme Minimum Temp. (°F)	-26	-20	-11	10	20	28	38	30	27	16	-7	-17	-26
Days Maximum Temp. ≥ 90°F	0	0	0	0	0	2	4	2	1	0	0	0	9
Days Maximum Temp. ≤ 32°F	14	10	4	0	0	0	0	0	0	0	1	8	37
Days Minimum Temp. ≤ 32°F	29	25	24	14	4	0	0	0	1	9	18	26	150
Days Minimum Temp. ≤ 0°F	4	3	0	0	0	0	0	0	0	0	0	1	8
Heating Degree Days (base 65°F)	1,236	1,049	871	529	246	62	14	24	144	437	722	1,048	6,382
Cooling Degree Days (base 65°F)	0	0	1	5	30	114	208	162	58	3	0	0	581
Mean Precipitation (in.)	2.24	1.67	2.95	3.25	3.59	4.01	4.22	3.32	3.93	2.69	3.10	2.80	37.77
Days With ≥ 0.1" Precipitation	6	5	8	8	8	8	7	7	8	7	7	7	86
Days With ≥ 1.0" Precipitation	0	0	0	1	1	1	1	1	1	0	0	0	6
Mean Snowfall (in.)	11.1	8.2	5.5	0.5	trace	0.0	0.0	0.0	0.0	trace	1.3	7.3	33.9
Days With ≥ 1.0" Snow Depth	16	11	4	0	0	0	0	0	0	0	1	8	40

Washington Court House *Fayette County* Elevation: 958 ft. Latitude: 39° 31' N Longitude: 83° 25' W

	JAN	FEB	MAR	APR	MAY	JUN	JUL	AUG	SEP	OCT	NOV	DEC	YEAR
Mean Maximum Temp. (°F)	35.6	40.4	51.3	63.4	72.4	79.5	82.6	81.8	76.5	65.8	52.4	40.9	61.9
Mean Temp. (°F)	28.0	31.8	41.6	52.2	62.1	70.1	73.6	72.3	66.2	54.9	43.5	33.4	52.5
Mean Minimum Temp. (°F)	20.3	23.2	31.8	40.9	51.7	60.6	64.5	62.8	55.9	44.0	34.6	25.8	43.0
Extreme Maximum Temp. (°F)	69	73	83	89	91	93	97	97	95	86	80	77	97
Extreme Minimum Temp. (°F)	-27	-11	-4	16	30	39	47	42	33	19	1	-20	-27
Days Maximum Temp. ≥ 90°F	0	0	0	0	0	1	3	3	1	0	0	0	8
Days Maximum Temp. ≤ 32°F	12	8	2	0	0	0	0	0	0	0	1	7	30
Days Minimum Temp. ≤ 32°F	27	22	18	6	0	0	0	0	0	3	14	23	113
Days Minimum Temp. ≤ 0°F	2	1	0	0	0	0	0	0	0	0	0	1	4
Heating Degree Days (base 65°F)	1,140	930	722	388	148	22	2	6	71	319	640	974	5,362
Cooling Degree Days (base 65°F)	0	0	2	9	63	186	284	243	113	14	1	0	915
Mean Precipitation (in.)	2.43	2.35	3.32	3.60	4.70	3.79	3.95	3.85	2.64	2.65	3.01	2.81	39.10
Days With ≥ 0.1" Precipitation	6	6	8	8	8	7	7	6	5	6	6	7	80
Days With ≥ 1.0" Precipitation	0	0	1	0	1	1	1	1	1	1	1	0	8
Mean Snowfall (in.)	8.7	6.1	4.1	0.7	trace	0.0	0.0	0.0	0.0	0.2	1.0	3.5	24.3
Days With ≥ 1.0" Snow Depth	11	8	3	0	0	0	0	0	0	0	1	4	27

Wauseon Water Plant *Fulton County* Elevation: 748 ft. Latitude: 41° 31' N Longitude: 84° 09' W

	JAN	FEB	MAR	APR	MAY	JUN	JUL	AUG	SEP	OCT	NOV	DEC	YEAR
Mean Maximum Temp. (°F)	30.8	35.0	46.4	59.8	71.8	80.9	84.3	81.9	75.7	63.2	48.8	36.5	59.6
Mean Temp. (°F)	23.0	26.6	36.9	48.5	59.8	69.1	72.6	70.3	63.6	51.9	40.3	29.2	49.3
Mean Minimum Temp. (°F)	15.3	18.0	27.3	37.2	47.7	57.3	60.8	58.6	51.4	40.6	31.7	22.0	39.0
Extreme Maximum Temp. (°F)	62	69	79	88	93	103	101	98	95	88	76	68	103
Extreme Minimum Temp. (°F)	-24	-16	-7	2	26	37	40	37	28	17	5	-21	-24
Days Maximum Temp. ≥ 90°F	0	0	0	0	0	3	6	3	1	0	0	0	13
Days Maximum Temp. ≤ 32°F	16	11	3	0	0	0	0	0	0	0	2	10	42
Days Minimum Temp. ≤ 32°F	29	26	23	10	1	0	0	0	0	6	18	27	140
Days Minimum Temp. ≤ 0°F	5	3	0	0	0	0	0	0	0	0	0	1	9
Heating Degree Days (base 65°F)	1,295	1,080	867	493	203	34	5	15	112	404	736	1,102	6,346
Cooling Degree Days (base 65°F)	0	0	0	6	51	172	266	197	80	6	0	0	778
Mean Precipitation (in.)	1.85	1.61	2.53	3.37	3.39	3.69	3.44	3.65	3.09	2.60	2.95	2.42	34.59
Days With ≥ 0.1" Precipitation	5	4	6	8	7	7	6	7	6	6	7	6	75
Days With ≥ 1.0" Precipitation	0	0	0	0	1	1	1	1	1	0	0	0	5
Mean Snowfall (in.)	8.7	7.0	4.4	0.9	trace	0.0	0.0	0.0	0.0	trace	2.2	5.8	29.0
Days With ≥ 1.0" Snow Depth	14	12	4	0	0	0	0	0	0	0	2	7	39

Waverly *Pike County* Elevation: 557 ft. Latitude: 39° 07' N Longitude: 82° 59' W

	JAN	FEB	MAR	APR	MAY	JUN	JUL	AUG	SEP	OCT	NOV	DEC	YEAR
Mean Maximum Temp. (°F)	39.0	44.0	55.0	66.8	75.4	82.9	86.5	85.2	79.2	68.0	55.6	44.7	65.2
Mean Temp. (°F)	29.1	32.8	42.5	52.6	62.1	70.5	74.6	72.8	66.2	54.1	43.9	34.5	53.0
Mean Minimum Temp. (°F)	19.2	21.7	29.9	38.3	48.8	58.1	62.7	60.5	53.1	40.1	32.2	24.3	40.7
Extreme Maximum Temp. (°F)	75	77	88	92	96	101	102	102	99	87	81	79	102
Extreme Minimum Temp. (°F)	-31	-17	-12	15	27	31	41	38	28	17	7	-21	-31
Days Maximum Temp. ≥ 90°F	0	0	0	0	1	5	9	7	2	0	0	0	24
Days Maximum Temp. ≤ 32°F	8	5	1	0	0	0	0	0	0	0	0	4	18
Days Minimum Temp. ≤ 32°F	27	23	20	9	1	0	0	0	0	7	17	23	127
Days Minimum Temp. ≤ 0°F	2	1	0	0	0	0	0	0	0	0	0	1	4
Heating Degree Days (base 65°F)	1,106	902	696	376	146	21	2	6	74	343	627	939	5,238
Cooling Degree Days (base 65°F)	0	0	1	9	59	194	313	251	104	12	0	0	943
Mean Precipitation (in.)	2.69	2.27	3.62	3.56	4.18	3.86	3.99	4.40	2.63	2.56	3.08	3.02	39.86
Days With ≥ 0.1" Precipitation	5	5	8	8	8	7	7	6	5	5	7	7	78
Days With ≥ 1.0" Precipitation	0	0	1	1	1	1	1	1	1	1	0	1	9
Mean Snowfall (in.)	4.7	na	3.0	0.1	0.0	0.0	0.0	0.0	0.0	trace	0.1	1.5	na
Days With ≥ 1.0" Snow Depth	na	na	1	0	0	0	0	0	0	0	0	na	na

Westerville *Franklin County* Elevation: 807 ft. Latitude: 40° 08' N Longitude: 82° 57' W

	JAN	FEB	MAR	APR	MAY	JUN	JUL	AUG	SEP	OCT	NOV	DEC	YEAR
Mean Maximum Temp. (°F)	35.6	40.6	51.8	64.1	74.2	82.1	85.3	84.0	77.9	66.1	52.4	41.0	62.9
Mean Temp. (°F)	27.0	30.8	41.0	51.6	61.8	70.3	73.8	72.3	65.7	54.0	43.1	33.0	52.0
Mean Minimum Temp. (°F)	18.4	21.0	30.1	39.1	49.3	58.3	62.2	60.6	53.5	41.9	33.7	25.0	41.1
Extreme Maximum Temp. (°F)	68	73	82	88	92	100	101	101	97	86	79	76	101
Extreme Minimum Temp. (°F)	-27	-25	-8	14	27	33	41	36	29	17	3	-25	-27
Days Maximum Temp. ≥ 90°F	0	0	0	0	0	3	7	5	2	0	0	0	17
Days Maximum Temp. ≤ 32°F	12	8	2	0	0	0	0	0	0	0	1	7	30
Days Minimum Temp. ≤ 32°F	27	23	19	9	1	0	0	0	0	5	15	24	123
Days Minimum Temp. ≤ 0°F	4	3	0	0	0	0	0	0	0	0	0	1	8
Heating Degree Days (base 65°F)	1,171	959	739	404	155	24	3	8	82	346	652	985	5,528
Cooling Degree Days (base 65°F)	0	0	2	10	65	200	306	257	116	14	1	0	971
Mean Precipitation (in.)	2.52	2.23	2.79	3.61	4.03	4.64	4.04	3.51	2.90	2.62	3.36	2.91	39.16
Days With ≥ 0.1" Precipitation	6	5	7	8	8	8	7	6	5	6	7	7	80
Days With ≥ 1.0" Precipitation	0	0	0	1	1	1	1	1	1	0	1	0	7
Mean Snowfall (in.)	7.7	5.1	2.3	0.7	trace	0.0	0.0	0.0	0.0	trace	0.5	3.3	19.6
Days With ≥ 1.0" Snow Depth	12	7	2	0	0	0	0	0	0	0	0	4	25

Wilmington 3 N *Clinton County* Elevation: 1,026 ft. Latitude: 39° 29' N Longitude: 83° 49' W

	JAN	FEB	MAR	APR	MAY	JUN	JUL	AUG	SEP	OCT	NOV	DEC	YEAR
Mean Maximum Temp. (°F)	35.0	39.1	50.0	61.6	71.8	80.2	83.9	82.6	76.9	64.8	51.6	40.5	61.5
Mean Temp. (°F)	26.7	30.0	39.9	50.3	60.6	69.3	73.0	71.1	64.8	53.1	42.3	32.5	51.1
Mean Minimum Temp. (°F)	18.4	20.9	29.6	38.9	49.3	58.3	62.1	59.5	52.6	41.3	33.0	24.4	40.7
Extreme Maximum Temp. (°F)	69	72	82	87	90	99	99	99	95	86	78	73	99
Extreme Minimum Temp. (°F)	-25	-20	-10	12	27	37	40	37	30	12	2	-24	-25
Days Maximum Temp. ≥ 90°F	0	0	0	0	0	2	5	4	1	0	0	0	12
Days Maximum Temp. ≤ 32°F	13	9	3	0	0	0	0	0	0	0	1	7	33
Days Minimum Temp. ≤ 32°F	27	23	20	8	1	0	0	0	0	6	15	24	124
Days Minimum Temp. ≤ 0°F	3	3	0	0	0	0	0	0	0	0	0	1	7
Heating Degree Days (base 65°F)	1,181	981	774	444	181	32	4	14	98	373	675	1,002	5,759
Cooling Degree Days (base 65°F)	0	0	2	9	48	174	274	215	94	12	1	0	829
Mean Precipitation (in.)	2.57	2.38	3.40	4.06	4.81	4.25	4.35	3.33	2.81	2.89	3.36	2.91	41.12
Days With ≥ 0.1" Precipitation	6	6	8	9	9	8	8	6	5	6	7	6	84
Days With ≥ 1.0" Precipitation	1	0	1	1	1	1	1	1	1	1	1	0	10
Mean Snowfall (in.)	8.2	6.3	3.9	0.7	trace	0.0	0.0	0.0	0.0	0.2	1.4	3.0	23.7
Days With ≥ 1.0" Snow Depth	11	9	3	0	0	0	0	0	0	0	1	4	28

Wooster Exp. Station *Wayne County* Elevation: 1,017 ft. Latitude: 40° 47' N Longitude: 81° 55' W

	JAN	FEB	MAR	APR	MAY	JUN	JUL	AUG	SEP	OCT	NOV	DEC	YEAR
Mean Maximum Temp. (°F)	32.4	36.1	46.9	58.8	69.5	78.0	81.8	80.0	73.0	61.2	48.8	37.7	58.7
Mean Temp. (°F)	25.0	28.0	37.6	48.2	58.6	67.3	71.2	69.4	62.5	51.1	40.9	30.8	49.2
Mean Minimum Temp. (°F)	17.6	19.9	28.4	37.5	47.8	56.6	60.6	58.9	51.8	40.9	32.9	23.8	39.7
Extreme Maximum Temp. (°F)	64	70	80	86	90	100	101	95	92	83	75	74	101
Extreme Minimum Temp. (°F)	-24	-13	-6	14	25	31	41	36	30	17	5	-17	-24
Days Maximum Temp. ≥ 90°F	0	0	0	0	0	1	2	1	0	0	0	0	4
Days Maximum Temp. ≤ 32°F	16	11	4	0	0	0	0	0	0	0	2	10	43
Days Minimum Temp. ≤ 32°F	28	24	21	10	1	0	0	0	0	6	16	25	131
Days Minimum Temp. ≤ 0°F	4	2	0	0	0	0	0	0	0	0	0	1	7
Heating Degree Days (base 65°F)	1,233	1,038	842	503	226	53	10	21	134	429	717	1,055	6,261
Cooling Degree Days (base 65°F)	0	0	1	5	36	133	225	170	60	5	0	0	635
Mean Precipitation (in.)	2.22	1.94	2.76	3.44	3.92	4.02	4.00	3.91	3.43	2.61	3.07	2.65	37.97
Days With ≥ 0.1" Precipitation	6	5	7	8	8	8	7	7	6	6	7	6	81
Days With ≥ 1.0" Precipitation	0	0	0	1	1	1	1	1	1	0	0	0	6
Mean Snowfall (in.)	10.0	7.2	5.1	1.2	trace	0.0	0.0	trace	0.0	trace	1.9	6.3	31.7
Days With ≥ 1.0" Snow Depth	16	13	6	1	0	0	0	0	0	0	1	9	46

Xenia 6 SSE *Greene County* Elevation: 967 ft. Latitude: 39° 37' N Longitude: 83° 54' W

	JAN	FEB	MAR	APR	MAY	JUN	JUL	AUG	SEP	OCT	NOV	DEC	YEAR
Mean Maximum Temp. (°F)	35.8	40.7	52.0	63.4	73.0	80.4	83.7	82.1	76.3	65.1	52.3	41.2	62.2
Mean Temp. (°F)	27.6	31.6	41.9	51.9	61.8	69.8	73.2	71.2	64.9	53.8	43.1	33.1	52.0
Mean Minimum Temp. (°F)	19.3	22.5	31.8	40.4	50.6	59.2	62.7	60.2	53.5	42.4	33.8	24.9	41.8
Extreme Maximum Temp. (°F)	68	74	83	88	91	102	100	98	95	89	80	74	102
Extreme Minimum Temp. (°F)	-28	-20	-5	14	28	37	42	38	25	16	3	-24	-28
Days Maximum Temp. ≥ 90°F	0	0	0	0	0	2	4	2	1	0	0	0	9
Days Maximum Temp. ≤ 32°F	12	8	2	0	0	0	0	0	0	0	1	6	29
Days Minimum Temp. ≤ 32°F	26	22	18	7	1	0	0	0	0	5	15	24	118
Days Minimum Temp. ≤ 0°F	3	2	0	0	0	0	0	0	0	0	0	1	6
Heating Degree Days (base 65°F)	1,154	936	712	395	151	25	3	10	90	353	652	983	5,464
Cooling Degree Days (base 65°F)	0	0	2	10	61	185	279	216	96	12	1	0	862
Mean Precipitation (in.)	2.51	2.23	3.16	3.91	4.42	3.87	4.09	3.66	2.73	2.84	3.23	3.02	39.67
Days With ≥ 0.1" Precipitation	6	6	7	8	8	7	8	7	5	6	7	7	82
Days With ≥ 1.0" Precipitation	0	0	0	1	1	1	1	1	1	1	1	1	9
Mean Snowfall (in.)	8.8	5.6	3.5	0.4	trace	0.0	0.0	0.0	0.0	0.2	0.9	3.3	22.7
Days With ≥ 1.0" Snow Depth	na	na	1	0	0	0	0	0	0	0	0	na	na

Zanesville Municipal Airport *Muskingum County* Elevation: 879 ft. Latitude: 39° 57' N Longitude: 81° 54' W

	JAN	FEB	MAR	APR	MAY	JUN	JUL	AUG	SEP	OCT	NOV	DEC	YEAR
Mean Maximum Temp. (°F)	36.0	40.6	51.3	62.4	72.2	80.1	83.9	82.2	75.6	64.0	52.2	40.9	61.8
Mean Temp. (°F)	28.1	31.7	41.2	51.2	61.1	69.3	73.4	71.8	64.8	53.1	43.2	33.2	51.8
Mean Minimum Temp. (°F)	20.1	22.6	31.1	39.9	49.9	58.5	62.9	61.4	53.9	42.1	34.2	25.5	41.8
Extreme Maximum Temp. (°F)	70	72	83	88	90	101	103	98	96	84	79	76	103
Extreme Minimum Temp. (°F)	-25	-13	-2	16	26	37	42	37	30	18	2	-17	-25
Days Maximum Temp. ≥ 90°F	0	0	0	0	0	2	5	3	1	0	0	0	11
Days Maximum Temp. ≤ 32°F	12	8	2	0	0	0	0	0	0	0	1	7	30
Days Minimum Temp. ≤ 32°F	27	22	18	7	1	0	0	0	0	5	15	23	118
Days Minimum Temp. ≤ 0°F	2	2	0	0	0	0	0	0	0	0	0	1	5
Heating Degree Days (base 65°F)	1,137	934	733	418	170	30	3	9	93	371	648	979	5,525
Cooling Degree Days (base 65°F)	0	0	2	8	52	171	286	230	94	10	1	0	854
Mean Precipitation (in.)	2.53	2.31	3.09	3.54	4.11	4.39	4.19	3.96	2.94	2.56	3.10	2.75	39.47
Days With ≥ 0.1" Precipitation	7	6	8	8	8	7	7	7	6	6	7	7	84
Days With ≥ 1.0" Precipitation	0	0	0	1	1	1	1	1	1	0	0	0	6
Mean Snowfall (in.)	8.6	4.3	3.5	1.4	trace	trace	trace	0.0	trace	trace	1.2	3.5	22.5
Days With ≥ 1.0" Snow Depth	12	8	3	0	0	0	0	0	0	0	1	4	28

Note: See User's Guide for explanation of data.

Annual Extreme Maximum Temperature

Highest

Rank	Station Name	°F
1	Chilo Meldahl Lock & Dam	107
1	Cincinnati Fernbank	107
3	Chillicothe Mound City	105
3	Cincinnati Lunken Airport	105
3	Gallipolis	105
3	Hoytville 2 NE	105
3	Napoleon	105
3	Tiffin	105
9	Bowling Green WWTP	104
9	Cleveland Hopkins Int'l Airport	104
9	Dayton MCD	104
9	Defiance	104
9	Elyria 3 E	104
9	Findlay Airport	104
9	Findlay WPCC	104
9	Fremont	104
9	Greenville Water Plant	104
9	Kenton	104
9	Milford	104
9	Montpelier	104
9	Oberlin	104
9	Paulding	104
9	Portsmouth Sciotoville	104
9	Toledo Express Airport	104
9	Upper Sandusky	104

Lowest

Rank	Station Name	°F
1	Washington Court House	97
2	Painesville 4 NW	98
3	Centerburg 2 SE	99
3	Wilmington 3 N	99
5	Ashland 2 SW	100
5	Barnesville	100
5	Chardon	100
5	Columbus Valley Crossing	100
5	Dorset	100
5	Fredericktown 4 S	100
5	Hannibal Lock & Dam	100
5	Hillsboro	100
5	Hiram	100
5	Lima WWTP	100
5	Mansfield 5 W	100
5	Newark Water Works	100
5	Put-In-Bay	100
5	Springfield New Water Works	100
5	Youngstown Municipal Airport	100
20	Akron-Canton Regional Airport	101
20	Bellefontaine	101
20	Cadiz	101
20	Canfield 1 S	101
20	Circleville	101
20	Columbus-Port Columbus Int'l	101

Annual Mean Maximum Temperature

Highest

Rank	Station Name	°F
1	Gallipolis	66.8
2	Portsmouth Sciotoville	65.3
3	Waverly	65.2
4	Cincinnati Fernbank	64.6
4	Cincinnati Lunken Airport	64.6
4	Marietta WWTP	64.6
7	Chilo Meldahl Lock & Dam	64.4
8	Chillicothe Mound City	63.8
8	Milford	63.8
10	Ripley Exp. Farm	63.6
11	Jackson 3 NW	63.5
11	McConnelsville Lock 7	63.5
13	Cambridge	63.4
13	Circleville	63.4
15	Columbus Valley Crossing	63.1
16	Dayton MCD	63.0
17	New Lexington 2 NW	62.9
17	Westerville	62.9
19	Franklin	62.7
19	Irwin	62.7
21	Hannibal Lock & Dam	62.5
22	Mineral Ridge Water Works	62.2
22	Xenia 6 SSE	62.2
24	Newark Water Works	62.1
25	Coshocton WPC Plant	62.0

Lowest

Rank	Station Name	°F
1	Chardon	57.2
2	Put-In-Bay	57.6
3	Dorset	57.8
4	Sandusky	58.2
5	Hiram	58.3
5	Youngstown Municipal Airport	58.3
7	Findlay Airport	58.7
7	Mansfield Lahm Municipal Airport	58.7
7	Wooster Exp. Station	58.7
10	Fremont	58.8
10	Mansfield 5 W	58.8
10	Montpelier	58.8
10	Norwalk WWTP	58.8
14	Bucyrus	58.9
14	Painesville 4 NW	58.9
16	Cleveland Hopkins Int'l Airport	59.0
16	Toledo Express Airport	59.0
18	Findlay WPCC	59.1
19	Akron-Canton Regional Airport	59.2
19	Ashland 2 SW	59.2
19	Centerburg 2 SE	59.2
19	Paulding	59.2
23	Hoytville 2 NE	59.3
24	Coshocton Agr. Res. Station	59.4
25	Defiance	59.5

Annual Mean Temperature

Highest

Rank	Station Name	°F
1	Gallipolis	55.0
2	Cincinnati Lunken Airport	54.7
3	Portsmouth Sciotoville	54.4
4	Marietta WWTP	53.8
5	Chilo Meldahl Lock & Dam	53.6
5	Cincinnati Fernbank	53.6
5	Dayton MCD	53.6
8	Ripley Exp. Farm	53.0
8	Waverly	53.0
10	Circleville	52.9
11	Columbus Valley Crossing	52.8
12	Chillicothe Mound City	52.5
12	Washington Court House	52.5
14	Cambridge	52.4
15	Columbus-Port Columbus Int'l	52.3
15	Hillsboro	52.3
15	Milford	52.3
18	Jackson 3 NW	52.1
19	Dayton Int'l Airport	52.0
19	Westerville	52.0
19	Xenia 6 SSE	52.0
22	Steubenville	51.9
23	Franklin	51.8
23	Hannibal Lock & Dam	51.8
23	Zanesville Municipal Airport	51.8

Lowest

Rank	Station Name	°F
1	Chardon	46.9
2	Dorset	47.4
3	Montpelier	48.0
4	Fredericktown 4 S	48.3
5	Canfield 1 S	48.6
5	Paulding	48.6
7	Mansfield 5 W	48.7
7	Warren 3 S	48.7
9	Ashland 2 SW	48.8
9	Youngstown Municipal Airport	48.8
11	Bucyrus	48.9
11	Hiram	48.9
13	Hoytville 2 NE	49.0
14	Toledo Express Airport	49.1
15	Chippewa Lake	49.2
15	Defiance	49.2
15	Norwalk WWTP	49.2
15	Wooster Exp. Station	49.2
19	Centerburg 2 SE	49.3
19	Danville 2 W	49.3
19	Fremont	49.3
19	Wauseon Water Plant	49.3
23	Millport 2 NW	49.4
23	Oberlin	49.4
25	Greenville Water Plant	49.6

Annual Mean Minimum Temperature

Highest

Rank	Station Name	°F
1	Cincinnati Lunken Airport	44.8
2	Dayton MCD	44.2
3	Put-In-Bay	43.4
4	Portsmouth Sciotoville	43.3
5	Gallipolis	43.0
5	Marietta WWTP	43.0
5	Washington Court House	43.0
8	Chilo Meldahl Lock & Dam	42.8
8	Hillsboro	42.8
10	Columbus-Port Columbus Int'l	42.6
10	Painesville 4 NW	42.6
12	Cincinnati Fernbank	42.5
13	Circleville	42.4
13	Columbus Valley Crossing	42.4
13	Dayton Int'l Airport	42.4
16	Ripley Exp. Farm	42.3
17	Sandusky	42.2
18	Steubenville	42.1
19	Lima WWTP	42.0
20	Xenia 6 SSE	41.8
20	Zanesville Municipal Airport	41.8
22	Celina 3 NE	41.7
23	Coshocton Agr. Res. Station	41.5
24	Cadiz	41.4
24	Cambridge	41.4

Lowest

Rank	Station Name	°F
1	Chardon	36.7
2	Fredericktown 4 S	36.9
3	Dorset	37.0
4	Montpelier	37.1
5	Canfield 1 S	37.2
6	Warren 3 S	37.3
7	Danville 2 W	37.4
8	Millport 2 NW	37.8
9	Paulding	37.9
10	Ashland 2 SW	38.3
11	Mansfield 5 W	38.6
12	Greenville Water Plant	38.7
12	Hoytville 2 NE	38.7
12	Oberlin	38.7
15	Chippewa Lake	38.8
15	Defiance	38.8
17	Bucyrus	38.9
17	Eaton	38.9
19	Wauseon Water Plant	39.0
20	Delaware	39.1
20	New Philadelphia	39.1
22	New Lexington 2 NW	39.2
22	Toledo Express Airport	39.2
24	Barnesville	39.3
24	McConnelsville Lock 7	39.3

Annual Extreme Minimum Temperature

Highest

Rank	Station Name	°F
1	Put-In-Bay	-18
2	Painesville 4 NW	-19
3	Bowling Green WWTP	-20
3	Cleveland Hopkins Int'l Airport	-20
3	Findlay Airport	-20
3	Findlay WPCC	-20
3	Fremont	-20
3	Sandusky	-20
3	Toledo Express Airport	-20
10	Dayton MCD	-21
10	Lima WWTP	-21
10	Norwalk WWTP	-21
10	Pandora	-21
10	Tiffin	-21
15	Chilo Meldahl Lock & Dam	-22
15	Cincinnati Lunken Airport	-22
15	Circleville	-22
15	Columbus-Port Columbus Int'l	-22
15	Defiance	-22
15	Elyria 3 E	-22
15	Hoytville 2 NE	-22
15	Kenton	-22
15	Mansfield Lahm Municipal Airport	-22
15	New Philadelphia	-22
15	Steubenville	-22

Lowest

Rank	Station Name	°F
1	Danville 2 W	-35
1	New Lexington 2 NW	-35
3	Millport 2 NW	-34
4	Eaton	-33
4	Greenville Water Plant	-33
6	Cambridge	-32
6	McConnelsville Lock 7	-32
8	Waverly	-31
9	Fredericktown 4 S	-30
10	Centerburg 2 SE	-29
10	Chillicothe Mound City	-29
10	Portsmouth Sciotoville	-29
13	Columbus Valley Crossing	-28
13	Delaware	-28
13	Dorset	-28
13	Gallipolis	-28
13	Irwin	-28
13	Jackson 3 NW	-28
13	Ripley Exp. Farm	-28
13	Xenia 6 SSE	-28
21	Bellefontaine	-27
21	Philo 3 SW	-27
21	Washington Court House	-27
21	Westerville	-27
25	Bucyrus	-26

July Mean Maximum Temperature

Highest

Rank	Station Name	°F
1	Gallipolis	87.4
2	Dayton MCD	87.3
3	Cincinnati Lunken Airport	86.8
3	Milford	86.8
5	Portsmouth Sciotoville	86.7
6	Cincinnati Fernbank	86.6
7	Waverly	86.5
8	Chillicothe Mound City	86.2
8	Chilo Meldahl Lock & Dam	86.2
10	Marietta WWTP	85.8
11	Mineral Ridge Water Works	85.7
12	Irwin	85.6
13	Circleville	85.5
13	Franklin	85.5
15	Columbus Valley Crossing	85.3
15	Westerville	85.3
17	Ripley Exp. Farm	85.2
17	Van Wert 1 S	85.2
19	Cambridge	85.1
19	Dayton Int'l Airport	85.1
19	Kenton	85.1
19	London	85.1
23	McConnelsville Lock 7	85.0
23	Napoleon	85.0
25	Newark Water Works	84.9

Lowest

Rank	Station Name	°F
1	Chardon	80.1
2	Dorset	81.2
3	Painesville 4 NW	81.4
4	Hiram	81.6
5	Philo 3 SW	81.7
6	Wooster Exp. Station	81.8
7	Mansfield 5 W	81.9
7	Youngstown Municipal Airport	81.9
9	Coshocton Agr. Res. Station	82.0
10	Barnesville	82.1
10	Mansfield Lahm Municipal Airport	82.1
12	Centerburg 2 SE	82.3
12	Put-In-Bay	82.3
12	Sandusky	82.3
15	Akron-Canton Regional Airport	82.4
15	Cleveland Hopkins Int'l Airport	82.4
17	Norwalk WWTP	82.6
17	Washington Court House	82.6
19	Cadiz	82.7
20	Findlay Airport	82.8
21	Canfield 1 S	82.9
22	Chippewa Lake	83.0
23	Ashland 2 SW	83.1
23	Bucyrus	83.1
23	Fredericktown 4 S	83.1

January Mean Minimum Temperature

Highest

Rank	Station Name	°F
1	Gallipolis	22.4
2	Cincinnati Lunken Airport	22.2
3	Marietta WWTP	22.1
3	Portsmouth Sciotoville	22.1
5	Circleville	20.8
6	Chilo Meldahl Lock & Dam	20.4
6	Dayton MCD	20.4
8	Steubenville	20.3
8	Washington Court House	20.3
10	Cincinnati Fernbank	20.2
10	Ripley Exp. Farm	20.2
12	Cambridge	20.1
12	Painesville 4 NW	20.1
12	Zanesville Municipal Airport	20.1
15	Columbus Valley Crossing	20.0
16	Columbus-Port Columbus Int'l	19.9
16	Hillsboro	19.9
18	Hannibal Lock & Dam	19.6
18	Philo 3 SW	19.6
20	Xenia 6 SSE	19.3
21	Waverly	19.2
22	Cadiz	19.1
22	Chillicothe Mound City	19.1
22	Jackson 3 NW	19.1
22	Newark Water Works	19.1

Lowest

Rank	Station Name	°F
1	Montpelier	13.3
2	Fredericktown 4 S	13.5
3	Paulding	13.7
4	Chardon	14.1
5	Dorset	14.6
6	Defiance	14.7
7	Greenville Water Plant	15.0
7	Hoytville 2 NE	15.0
9	Napoleon	15.2
10	Wauseon Water Plant	15.3
11	Eaton	15.4
11	Mansfield 5 W	15.4
13	Ashland 2 SW	15.5
14	Centerburg 2 SE	15.6
15	Marion 2 N	15.8
16	Kenton	15.9
16	Warren 3 S	15.9
18	Bucyrus	16.0
18	Danville 2 W	16.0
18	Fremont	16.0
18	Toledo Express Airport	16.0
22	Oberlin	16.1
23	Bowling Green WWTP	16.2
23	Delaware	16.2
25	Canfield 1 S	16.3

Number of Annual Heating Degree Days

Highest

Rank	Station Name	Num.
1	Chardon	6,934
2	Dorset	6,809
3	Montpelier	6,745
4	Paulding	6,576
5	Fredericktown 4 S	6,542
6	Ashland 2 SW	6,457
7	Hoytville 2 NE	6,456
8	Defiance	6,444
9	Mansfield 5 W	6,440
10	Bucyrus	6,435
11	Toledo Express Airport	6,413
12	Canfield 1 S	6,410
13	Youngstown Municipal Airport	6,386
14	Warren 3 S	6,382
15	Hiram	6,372
16	Fremont	6,371
17	Norwalk WWTP	6,359
18	Wauseon Water Plant	6,346
19	Centerburg 2 SE	6,297
20	Oberlin	6,287
21	Chippewa Lake	6,284
22	Greenville Water Plant	6,271
23	Wooster Exp. Station	6,261
24	Napoleon	6,259
25	Danville 2 W	6,240

Lowest

Rank	Station Name	Num.
1	Gallipolis	4,673
2	Cincinnati Lunken Airport	4,839
3	Portsmouth Sciotoville	4,860
4	Marietta WWTP	4,984
5	Chilo Meldahl Lock & Dam	5,083
6	Cincinnati Fernbank	5,126
7	Waverly	5,238
8	Ripley Exp. Farm	5,245
9	Circleville	5,275
10	Dayton MCD	5,292
11	Columbus Valley Crossing	5,318
12	Cambridge	5,348
13	Washington Court House	5,362
14	Hillsboro	5,414
15	Chillicothe Mound City	5,422
16	Jackson 3 NW	5,451
17	Xenia 6 SSE	5,464
18	Steubenville	5,484
19	Columbus-Port Columbus Int'l	5,491
20	Milford	5,495
21	Hannibal Lock & Dam	5,520
22	Zanesville Municipal Airport	5,525
23	Westerville	5,528
24	Franklin	5,604
25	Dayton Int'l Airport	5,616

Number of Annual Cooling Degree Days

Highest			Lowest		
Rank	Station Name	Num.	Rank	Station Name	Num.
1	Dayton MCD	1,283	1	Chardon	468
2	Cincinnati Lunken Airport	1,215	2	Dorset	514
3	Gallipolis	1,156	3	Canfield 1 S	552
4	Chilo Meldahl Lock & Dam	1,079	4	Fredericktown 4 S	571
5	Cincinnati Fernbank	1,076	5	Warren 3 S	581
6	Portsmouth Sciotoville	1,030	6	Millport 2 NW	595
7	Marietta WWTP	1,018	7	Youngstown Municipal Airport	599
8	Milford	1,016	8	Danville 2 W	613
9	Columbus-Port Columbus Int'l	991	9	Mansfield 5 W	619
10	Chillicothe Mound City	988	10	Ashland 2 SW	622
11	Ripley Exp. Farm	981	11	Hiram	633
12	Dayton Int'l Airport	974	12	Wooster Exp. Station	635
13	Westerville	971	13	Chippewa Lake	666
14	Lima WWTP	968	14	Philo 3 SW	671
15	Circleville	965	15	Barnesville	679
16	Columbus Valley Crossing	954	16	Mansfield Lahm Municipal Airport	698
17	Waverly	943	17	Montpelier	700
18	Celina 3 NE	937	18	Oberlin	705
19	Cambridge	919	19	Bucyrus	706
20	Washington Court House	915	20	Centerburg 2 SE	711
21	Kenton	911	21	Akron-Canton Regional Airport	716
22	Van Wert 1 S	910	22	Paulding	717
23	Franklin	903	23	New Lexington 2 NW	731
24	Hillsboro	895	24	Hoytville 2 NE	740
25	Put-In-Bay	892	24	Norwalk WWTP	740

Annual Precipitation

Highest			Lowest		
Rank	Station Name	Inches	Rank	Station Name	Inches
1	Cincinnati Fernbank	47.43	1	Bowling Green WWTP	33.14
2	Chardon	47.01	2	Toledo Express Airport	33.23
3	Ripley Exp. Farm	45.33	3	Hoytville 2 NE	33.89
4	Milford	44.72	4	Sandusky	34.19
5	Barnesville	44.34	5	Paulding	34.29
6	Hillsboro	43.33	6	Wauseon Water Plant	34.59
7	Dorset	43.30	7	Findlay Airport	34.68
8	Chilo Meldahl Lock & Dam	43.05	8	Put-In-Bay	34.79
8	Mansfield Lahm Municipal Airport	43.05	9	Napoleon	34.81
10	McConnelsville Lock 7	42.96	10	Kenton	35.47
11	Marietta WWTP	42.20	11	Pandora	35.63
12	Hiram	41.91	12	Defiance	35.64
13	Cincinnati Lunken Airport	41.89	13	Montpelier	35.82
14	Newark Water Works	41.86	14	Upper Sandusky	36.03
15	New Lexington 2 NW	41.74	15	Fremont	36.04
16	Portsmouth Sciotoville	41.39	16	Oberlin	36.32
17	Danville 2 W	41.21	17	Marysville	36.37
18	Jackson 3 NW	41.13	18	Van Wert 1 S	36.52
19	Wilmington 3 N	41.12	19	Celina 3 NE	36.56
20	Coshocton WPC Plant	40.96	20	Norwalk WWTP	36.62
21	Centerburg 2 SE	40.89	21	Tiffin	36.75
22	New Philadelphia	40.88	22	Bellefontaine	36.92
23	Cadiz	40.86	23	Findlay WPCC	36.95
24	Gallipolis	40.66	24	Philo 3 SW	37.03
25	Steubenville	40.37	25	Coshocton Agr. Res. Station	37.04

Number of Days Annually With ≥ 0.1" Precipitation

Highest

Rank	Station Name	Days
1	Chardon	107
2	Dorset	99
3	Hiram	97
4	Barnesville	90
4	Millport 2 NW	90
4	New Lexington 2 NW	90
7	Chippewa Lake	89
7	Cincinnati Fernbank	89
7	Marietta WWTP	89
7	McConnelsville Lock 7	89
7	Milford	89
12	Cadiz	88
12	Steubenville	88
14	Cleveland Hopkins Int'l Airport	87
14	Coshocton WPC Plant	87
14	Elyria 3 E	87
14	Ripley Exp. Farm	87
18	Gallipolis	86
18	Newark Water Works	86
18	Painesville 4 NW	86
18	Warren 3 S	86
22	Cambridge	85
22	Jackson 3 NW	85
22	Portsmouth Sciotoville	85
25	Akron-Canton Regional Airport	84

Lowest

Rank	Station Name	Days
1	Put-In-Bay	69
2	Paulding	70
3	Lancaster 2 NW	71
4	Irwin	72
4	Sandusky	72
6	Bowling Green WWTP	73
6	Findlay Airport	73
6	Hoytville 2 NE	73
9	Coshocton Agr. Res. Station	75
9	Springfield New Water Works	75
9	Wauseon Water Plant	75
12	Chillicothe Mound City	76
12	Chilo Meldahl Lock & Dam	76
12	Greenville Water Plant	76
12	Napoleon	76
12	Toledo Express Airport	76
17	Dayton MCD	77
17	Defiance	77
17	Eaton	77
17	London	77
17	Pandora	77
22	Circleville	78
22	Columbus Valley Crossing	78
22	Delaware	78
22	Kenton	78

Number of Days Annually With ≥ 1.0" Precipitation

Highest

Rank	Station Name	Days
1	Cincinnati Fernbank	14
2	Chilo Meldahl Lock & Dam	12
2	Ripley Exp. Farm	12
4	Portsmouth Sciotoville	11
4	Urbana WWTP	11
6	Chillicothe Mound City	10
6	Cincinnati Lunken Airport	10
6	Eaton	10
6	Hillsboro	10
6	Milford	10
6	Wilmington 3 N	10
12	Barnesville	9
12	Centerburg 2 SE	9
12	Dayton MCD	9
12	Fredericktown 4 S	9
12	Mansfield Lahm Municipal Airport	9
12	McConnelsville Lock 7	9
12	Waverly	9
12	Xenia 6 SSE	9
20	Chardon	8
20	Danville 2 W	8
20	Dayton Int'l Airport	8
20	Franklin	8
20	Gallipolis	8
20	Greenville Water Plant	8

Lowest

Rank	Station Name	Days
1	Elyria 3 E	4
1	Mineral Ridge Water Works	4
3	Bowling Green WWTP	5
3	Cadiz	5
3	Canfield 1 S	5
3	Findlay Airport	5
3	Hiram	5
3	Hoytville 2 NE	5
3	Millport 2 NW	5
3	Napoleon	5
3	Norwalk WWTP	5
3	Oberlin	5
3	Painesville 4 NW	5
3	Pandora	5
3	Put-In-Bay	5
3	Sandusky	5
3	Toledo Express Airport	5
3	Wauseon Water Plant	5
19	Celina 3 NE	6
19	Chippewa Lake	6
19	Cleveland Hopkins Int'l Airport	6
19	Dorset	6
19	Findlay WPCC	6
19	Fremont	6
19	Kenton	6

Annual Snowfall

Highest

Rank	Station Name	Inches
1	Chardon	97.0
2	Dorset	73.1
3	Hiram	61.6
4	Cleveland Hopkins Int'l Airport	61.0
5	Youngstown Municipal Airport	54.7
6	Akron-Canton Regional Airport	46.9
7	Elyria 3 E	43.6
8	Mansfield Lahm Municipal Airport	43.3
9	Oberlin	41.4
10	Chippewa Lake	39.8
11	Toledo Express Airport	37.2
12	Danville 2 W	35.5
13	Painesville 4 NW	34.8
14	Mineral Ridge Water Works	34.5
15	Ashland 2 SW	34.0
16	Montpelier	33.9
16	Warren 3 S	33.9
18	Celina 3 NE	33.1
19	Barnesville	32.9
20	Cadiz	32.3
21	Wooster Exp. Station	31.7
22	Pandora	30.7
23	Millport 2 NW	30.2
24	Van Wert 1 S	29.8
25	New Philadelphia	29.7

Lowest

Rank	Station Name	Inches
1	Cincinnati Lunken Airport	13.2
2	Portsmouth Sciotoville	13.3
3	Gallipolis	14.2
4	Circleville	14.9
5	Dayton MCD	15.7
6	Milford	15.9
7	Bellefontaine	17.8
8	Chillicothe Mound City	17.9
9	Cambridge	18.4
10	Columbus Valley Crossing	19.3
11	Westerville	19.6
12	Paulding	19.7
12	Put-In-Bay	19.7
14	Marysville	20.2
15	Hillsboro	20.5
16	Newark Water Works	20.6
17	Delaware	20.7
18	Defiance	20.8
19	McConnelsville Lock 7	21.2
20	Fredericktown 4 S	21.4
21	Ripley Exp. Farm	21.5
22	Greenville Water Plant	21.7
23	Bowling Green WWTP	21.9
24	Zanesville Municipal Airport	22.5
25	Coshocton WPC Plant	22.7

Note: See User's Guide for explanation of data.

Deadliest Storm Events in Ohio: January 1950 - May 2008

Rank	Location or County	Date	Storm Event	Fatalities	Injuries	Property Damage ($mil.)	Crop Damage ($mil.)
1	Greene County	4/3/1974	Tornado (F5)	36	1,150	250.0	0.0
2	Lorain County	4/11/1965	Tornado (F4)	17	100	25.0	0.0
3	Lucas County	4/11/1965	Tornado (F4)	16	207	25.0	0.0
4	Northern Ohio	8/8/1995	Heat Wave	13	52	0.5	0.0
5	Statewide	7/20/1999	Excessive Heat	13	0	0.0	0.0
6	Allen County	4/11/1965	Tornado (F4)	11	100	2.5	0.0
7	Trumbull County	5/31/1985	Tornado (F5)	10	250	250.0	0.0
8	Scioto County	4/23/1968	Tornado (F5)	7	75	2.5	0.0
9	Cuyahoga County	6/8/1953	Tornado (F4)	6	300	0.0	0.0
10	Henry County	6/8/1953	Tornado (F4)	5	1	0.0	0.0
11	Huron County	5/10/1973	Tornado (F3)	5	100	2.5	0.0
12	Northern Ohio	8/3/1995	Heat Wave	5	11	0.0	0.0
13	Noble County	6/27/1998	Flash Flood	5	0	10.0	10.0
14	Cuyahoga County	8/20/1962	Tornado (F2)	4	20	2.5	0.0
15	Seneca County	4/11/1965	Tornado (F3)	4	30	0.3	0.0
16	Delaware County	4/11/1965	Tornado (F2)	4	35	2.5	0.0
17	Hamilton County	8/9/1969	Tornado (F3)	4	240	2.5	0.0
18	Morrow County	6/13/1981	Tornado (F3)	4	56	25.0	0.0
19	Statewide	2/11/1995	Extreme Cold	4	0	0.1	0.0
20	Northern Ohio	1/10/1997	Extreme Cold	4	0	0.2	0.0
21	Blue Ash	4/9/1999	Tornado (F4)	4	65	82.0	0.0
22	Wood County	6/8/1953	Tornado (F4)	3	8	0.0	0.0
23	Shelby County	4/11/1965	Tornado (F4)	3	50	2.5	0.0
24	Hamilton County	4/3/1974	Tornado (F5)	3	190	0.0	0.0
25	Lucas County	6/3/1990	Thunderstorm Wind	3	1	0.0	0.0
26	Cuyahoga County	9/6/1990	Thunderstorm Wind	3	3	0.0	0.0
27	Eastern Half of Scioto County	8/9/1995	Flash Flood	3	0	0.1	0.0
28	Northern Ohio	12/9/1995	Extreme Cold	3	0	0.2	0.0
29	Bay Village	7/24/1999	Thunderstorm Wind	3	0	0.0	0.0
30	Hamilton County	7/17/2001	Flash Flood	3	0	3.6	0.0
31	Summit County	7/21/2003	Flash Flood	3	0	100.0	0.0

Source: National Climatic Data Center, Storm Events Database

Most Destructive Storm Events in Ohio: January 1950 - May 2008

Rank	Location or County	Date	Storm Event	Fatalities	Injuries	Property Damage ($mil.)	Crop Damage ($mil.)
1	Knox, Stark, and Trumbull Counties	3/7/2008	Winter Storm	0	0	750.0	0.0
2	Lake County	7/28/2006	Flash Flood	1	0	320.0	0.0
3	Greene County	4/3/1974	Tornado (F5)	36	1,150	250.0	0.0
4	Portage County	5/31/1985	Tornado (F5)	0	0	250.0	0.0
5	Trumbull County	5/31/1985	Tornado (F5)	10	250	250.0	0.0
6	Trumbull County	5/31/1985	Tornado (F5)	0	0	250.0	0.0
7	Northern Ohio	1/5/2005	Ice Storm	0	0	124.9	0.0
8	Akron	6/8/2007	Hail (4.25 in.)	0	0	105.0	0.0
9	Summit County	7/21/2003	Flash Flood	3	0	100.0	0.0
10	Gahanna	10/4/2006	Hail (2.00 in.)	0	0	100.0	0.0
11	Pataskala	10/4/2006	Hail (1.75 in.)	0	1	100.0	0.0
12	Findlay	8/21/2007	Flash Flood	0	0	100.0	5.0
13	Blue Ash	4/9/1999	Tornado (F4)	4	65	82.0	0.0
14	Westerville	4/20/2003	Hail (1.75 in.)	0	0	80.0	0.0
15	Huber Heights	4/9/2001	Hail (1.75 in.)	0	0	70.0	0.0
16	Shelby	8/21/2007	Flash Flood	0	0	70.0	5.0
17	Powell	4/20/2003	Hail (1.50 in.)	0	0	65.0	0.0
18	Bucyrus	8/21/2007	Flash Flood	0	0	62.0	3.0
19	Northern Ohio	12/22/2004	Winter Storm	0	0	54.9	0.0
20	Stark County	7/27/2003	Flash Flood	0	0	52.0	0.0
21	Southern Ohio	2/8/1994	Ice Storm	1	1,568	50.0	5.0
22	New Albany	10/11/2006	Tornado (F2)	0	0	50.0	0.0
23	Crystal Springs	4/28/2002	Tornado (F2)	0	2	45.5	0.0
24	Lucas County	6/21/2006	Flash Flood	0	0	42.0	0.0

Source: National Climatic Data Center, Storm Events Database

Demographic and Reference Maps

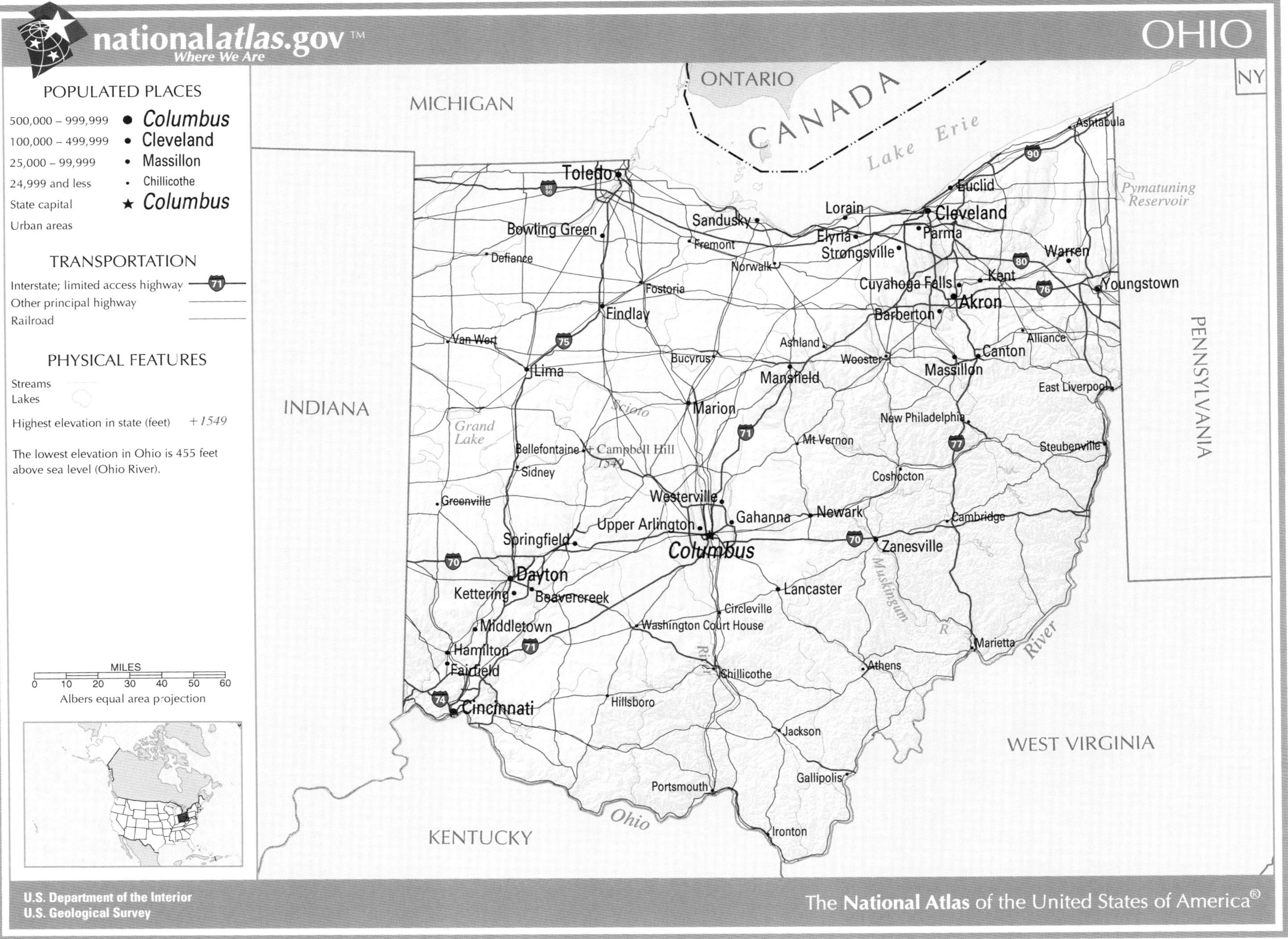
nationalatlas.gov™
Where We Are
OHIO
POPULATED PLACES
500,000 – 999,999 Columbus
100,000 – 499,999 Cleveland
25,000 – 99,999 Massillon
24,999 and less Chillicothe
State capital Columbus
Urban areas
TRANSPORTATION
Interstate; limited access highway
Other principal highway
Railroad
PHYSICAL FEATURES
Streams
Lakes
Highest elevation in state (feet) +1549
The lowest elevation in Ohio is 455 feet above sea level (Ohio River).
MILES
0 10 20 30 40 50 60
Albers equal area projection
U.S. Department of the Interior
U.S. Geological Survey
The National Atlas of the United States of America®
MICHIGAN
ONTARIO
CANADA
Lake Erie
NY
Pymatuning Reservoir
PENNSYLVANIA
INDIANA
WEST VIRGINIA
KENTUCKY
Grand Lake
Campbell Hill 1549
Scioto
Muskingum R
River
Ohio
Toledo
Bowling Green
Defiance
Van Wert
Lima
Findlay
Fostoria
Fremont
Sandusky
Norwalk
Lorain
Elyria
Strongsville
Cleveland
Euclid
Parma
Cuyahoga Falls
Akron
Barberton
Kent
Warren
Youngstown
Ashtabula
Alliance
Canton
Massillon
East Liverpool
Steubenville
New Philadelphia
Cambridge
Marietta
Zanesville
Coshocton
Wooster
Ashland
Mansfield
Mt Vernon
Newark
Bucyrus
Marion
Westerville
Gahanna
Columbus
Upper Arlington
Lancaster
Circleville
Athens
Washington Court House
Chillicothe
Jackson
Gallipolis
Ironton
Portsmouth
Hillsboro
Bellefontaine
Sidney
Greenville
Springfield
Dayton
Kettering
Beavercreek
Middletown
Hamilton
Fairfield
Cincinnati
90
80
76
77
70
71
75
74

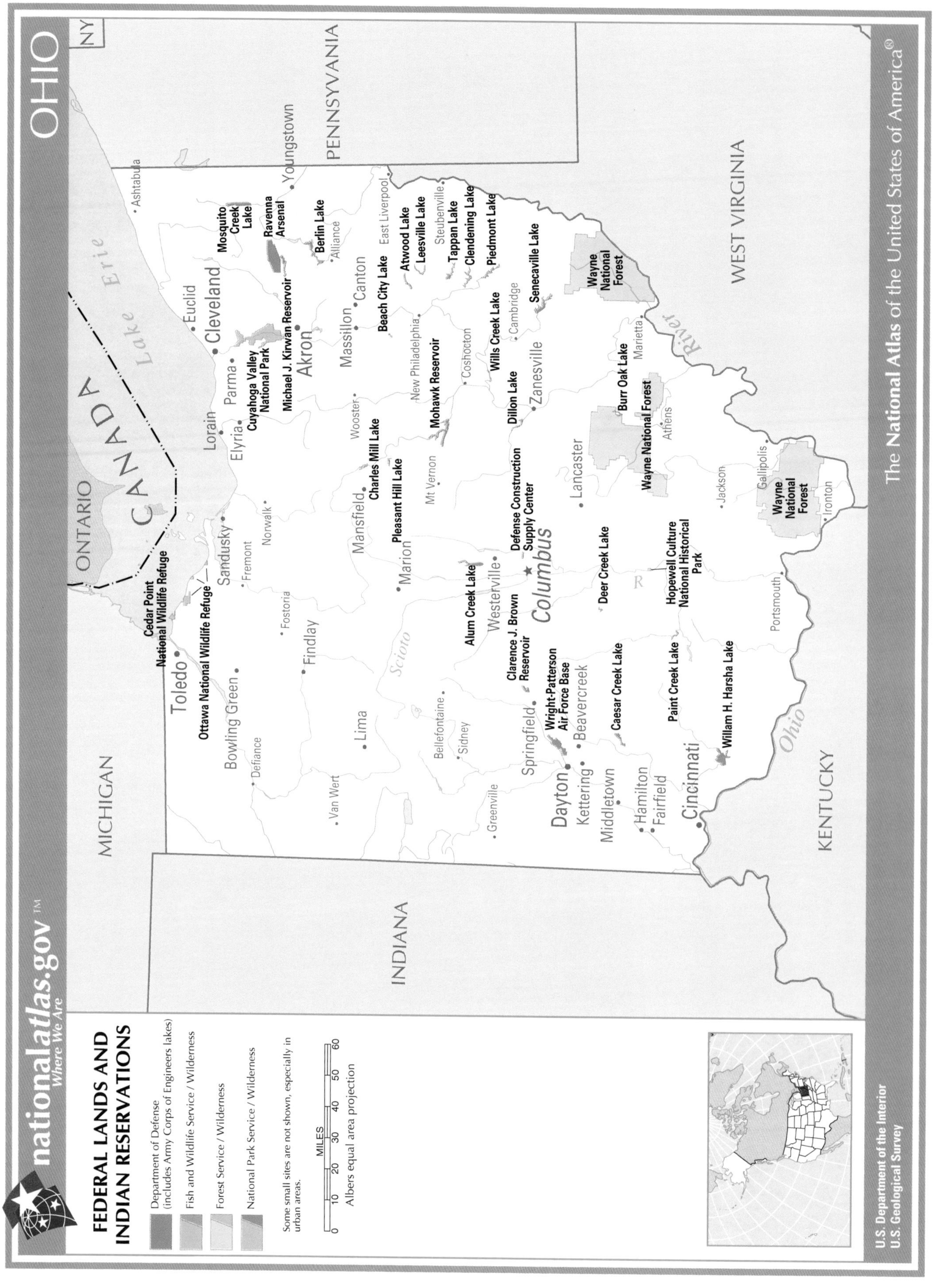
OHIO
nationalatlas.gov™
Where We Are
FEDERAL LANDS AND INDIAN RESERVATIONS
Department of Defense (includes Army Corps of Engineers lakes)
Fish and Wildlife Service / Wilderness
Forest Service / Wilderness
National Park Service / Wilderness
Some small sites are not shown, especially in urban areas.
MILES
0 10 20 30 40 50 60
Albers equal area projection
U.S. Department of the Interior
U.S. Geological Survey
The National Atlas of the United States of America®
NY
PENNSYVANIA
WEST VIRGINIA
KENTUCKY
INDIANA
MICHIGAN
ONTARIO
CANADA
Lake Erie
Ohio River
Scioto
Ashtabula
Youngstown
Mosquito Creek Lake
Ravenna Arsenal
Berlin Lake
Alliance
East Liverpool
Atwood Lake
Leesville Lake
Steubenville
Tappan Lake
Clendening Lake
Piedmont Lake
Senecaville Lake
Wayne National Forest
Euclid
Cleveland
Michael J. Kirwan Reservoir
Canton
Beach City Lake
New Philadelphia
Cambridge
Wills Creek Lake
Marietta
Akron
Massillon
Mohawk Reservoir
Coshocton
Zanesville
Dillon Lake
Burr Oak Lake
Wayne National Forest
Athens
Parma
Cuyahoga Valley National Park
Lorain
Elyria
Wooster
Charles Mill Lake
Pleasant Hill Lake
Mt Vernon
Lancaster
Defense Construction Supply Center
Columbus
Gallipolis
Jackson
Wayne National Forest
Ironton
Sandusky
Norwalk
Mansfield
Marion
Cedar Point National Wildlife Refuge
Fremont
Ottawa National Wildlife Refuge
Alum Creek Lake
Westerville
Deer Creek Lake
Hopewell Culture National Historical Park
Portsmouth
Toledo
Fostoria
Findlay
Clarence J. Brown Reservoir
Wright-Patterson Air Force Base
Beavercreek
Caesar Creek Lake
Paint Creek Lake
William H. Harsha Lake
Bowling Green
Defiance
Lima
Bellefontaine
Sidney
Springfield
Dayton
Kettering
Middletown
Hamilton
Fairfield
Cincinnati
Van Wert
Greenville

OHIO - Core Based Statistical Areas and Counties

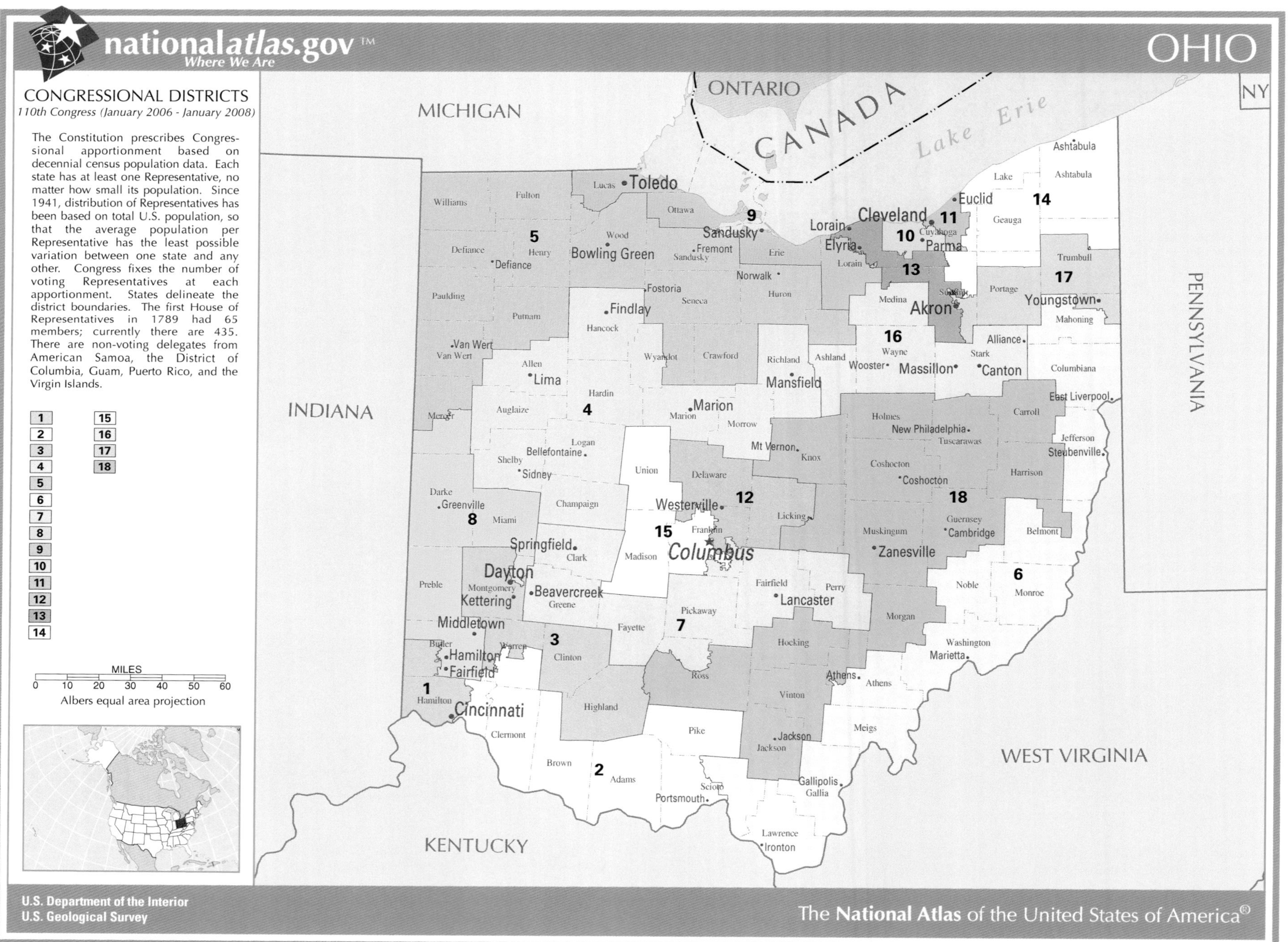
nationalatlas.gov™
Where We Are
OHIO
CONGRESSIONAL DISTRICTS
110th Congress (January 2006 - January 2008)
The Constitution prescribes Congressional apportionment based on decennial census population data. Each state has at least one Representative, no matter how small its population. Since 1941, distribution of Representatives has been based on total U.S. population, so that the average population per Representative has the least possible variation between one state and any other. Congress fixes the number of voting Representatives at each apportionment. States delineate the district boundaries. The first House of Representatives in 1789 had 65 members; currently there are 435. There are non-voting delegates from American Samoa, the District of Columbia, Guam, Puerto Rico, and the Virgin Islands.
1 2 3 4 5 6 7 8 9 10 11 12 13 14 15 16 17 18
MILES
0 10 20 30 40 50 60
Albers equal area projection
MICHIGAN
ONTARIO
CANADA
Lake Erie
PENNSYLVANIA
NY
INDIANA
WEST VIRGINIA
KENTUCKY
Toledo
Sandusky
Fremont
Bowling Green
Defiance
Van Wert
Fostoria
Findlay
Lima
Norwalk
Lorain
Elyria
Cleveland
Euclid
Parma
Akron
Youngstown
Alliance
Canton
Massillon
Wooster
Mansfield
Marion
Mt Vernon
Bellefontaine
Sidney
Greenville
Westerville
Columbus
Springfield
Dayton
Kettering
Beavercreek
Middletown
Hamilton
Fairfield
Cincinnati
Lancaster
Zanesville
Coshocton
Cambridge
New Philadelphia
East Liverpool
Steubenville
Marietta
Athens
Jackson
Gallipolis
Portsmouth
Ironton
Ashtabula
U.S. Department of the Interior
U.S. Geological Survey
The National Atlas of the United States of America®

Population (2007)

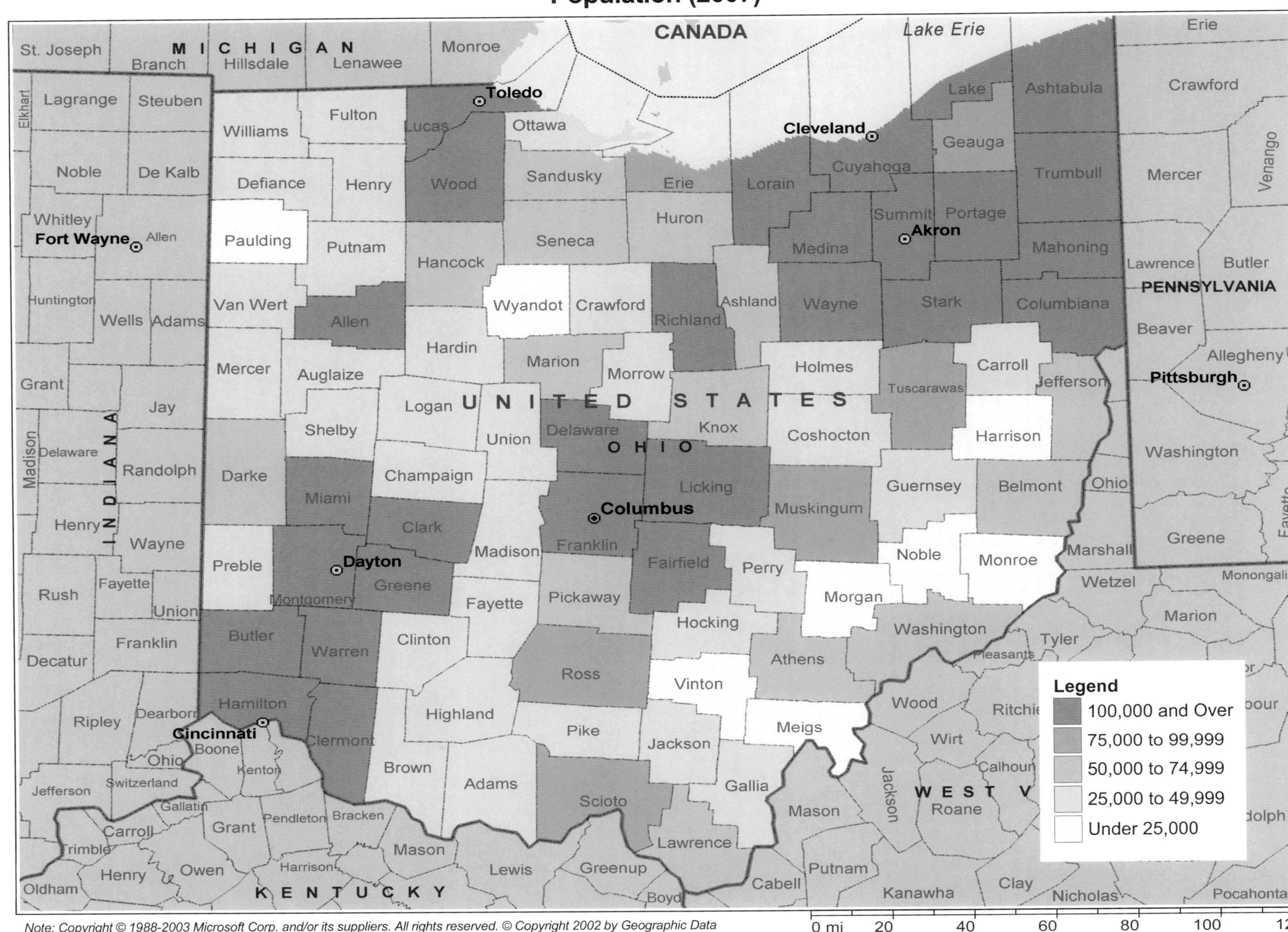

Percent White (2007)

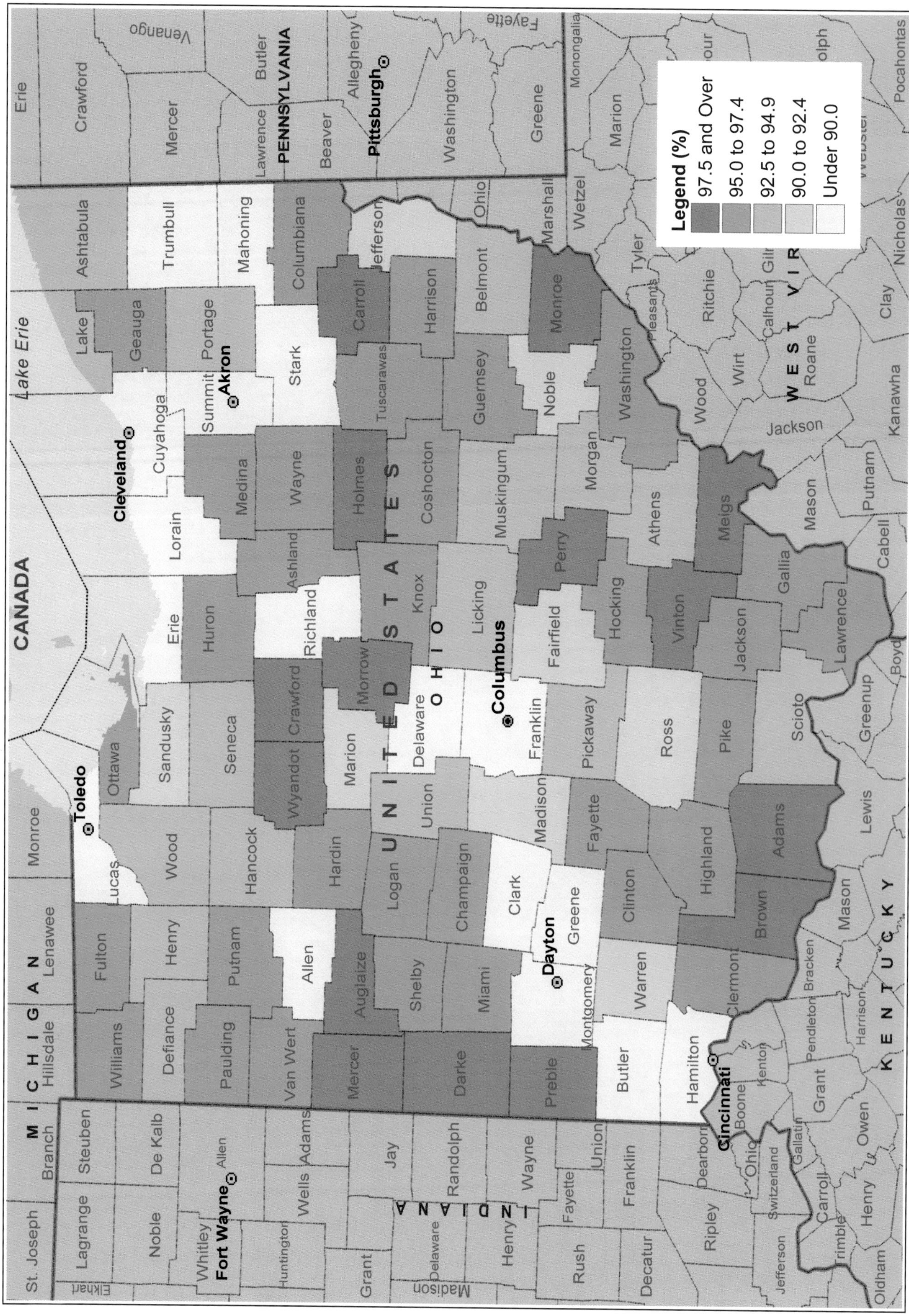

Legend (%)

- 97.5 and Over
- 95.0 to 97.4
- 92.5 to 94.9
- 90.0 to 92.4
- Under 90.0

0 mi 20 40 60 80 100 120

Percent Black (2007)

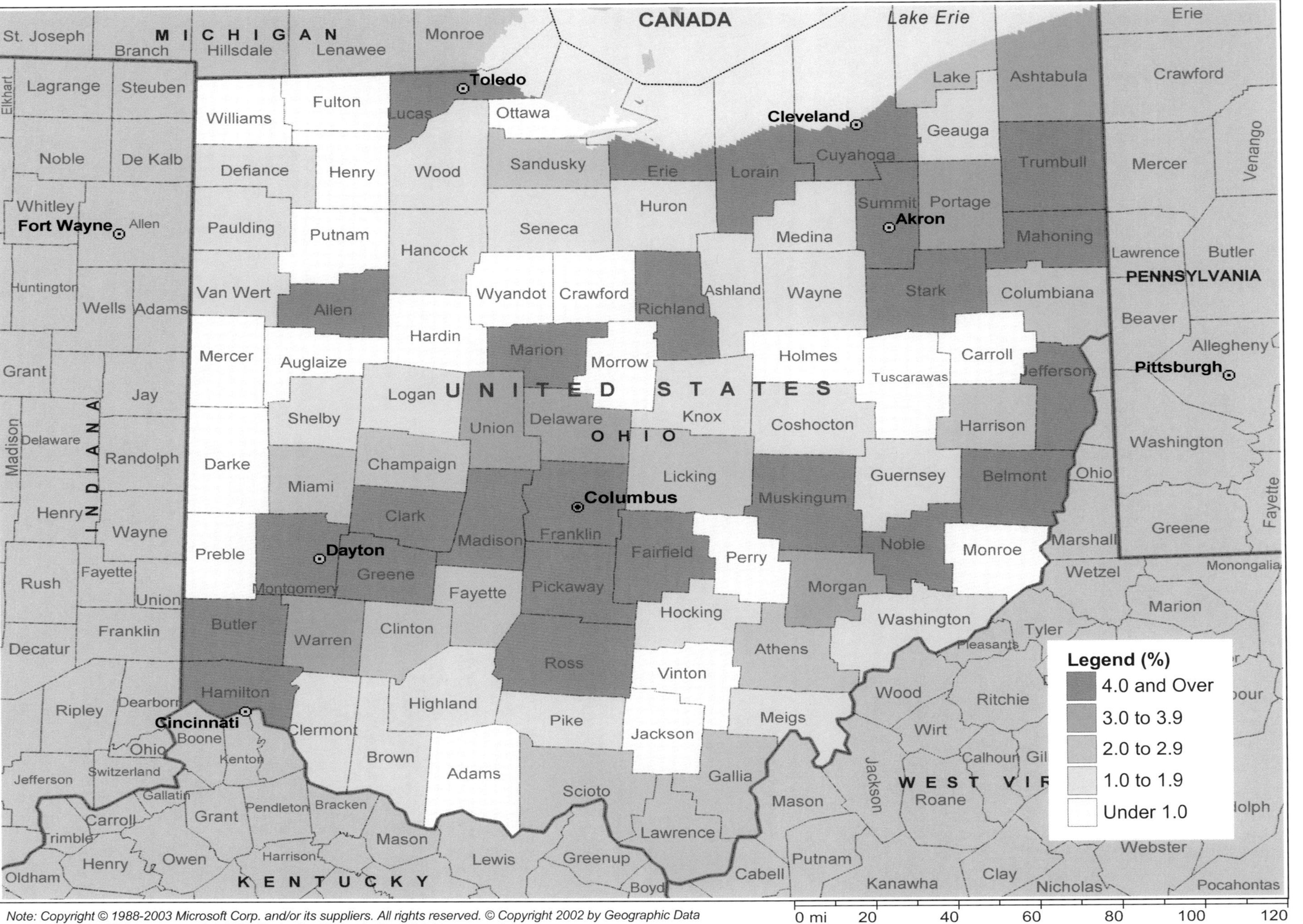

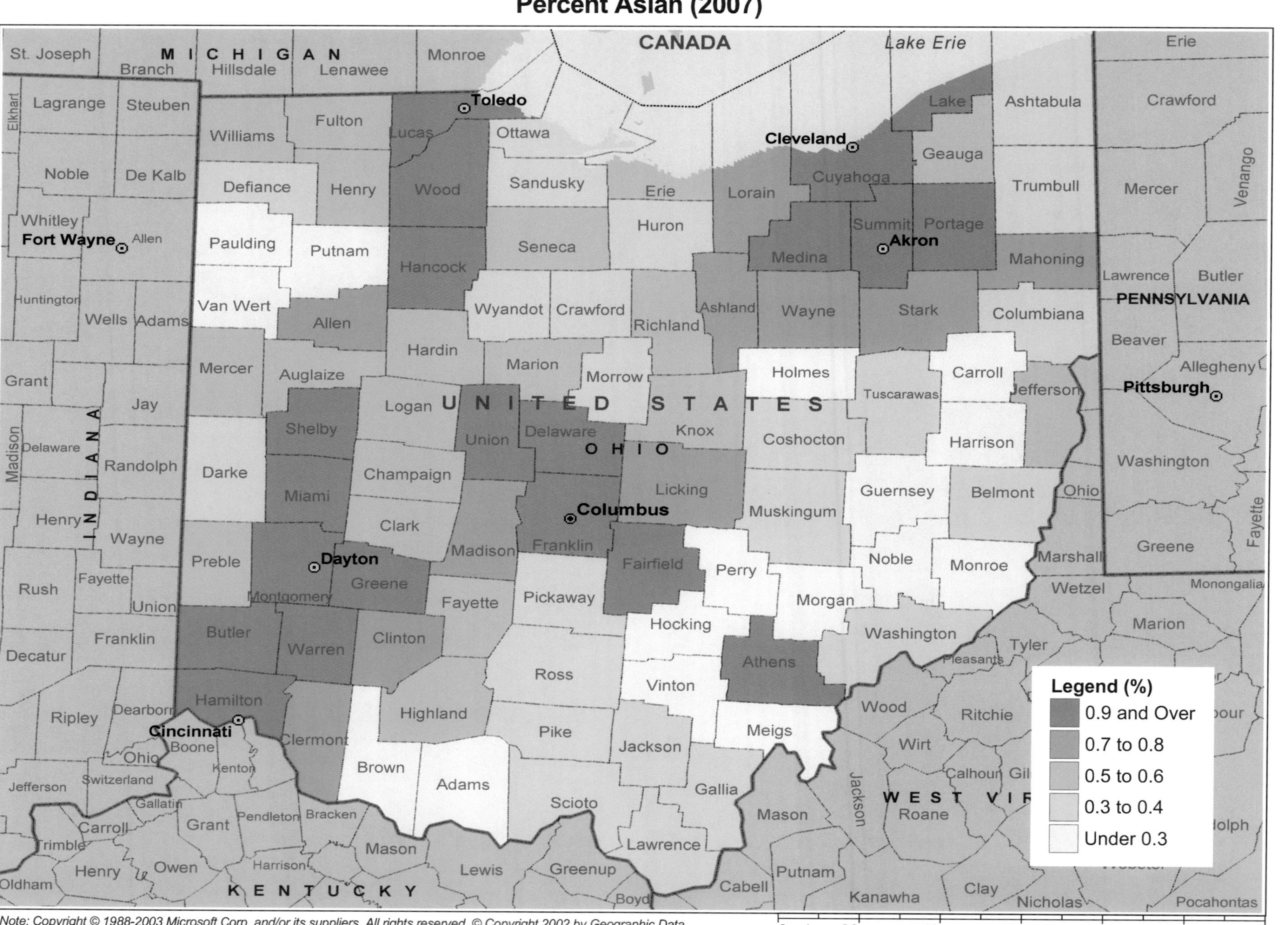
Percent Asian (2007)
Legend (%)
0.9 and Over
0.7 to 0.8
0.5 to 0.6
0.3 to 0.4
Under 0.3
0 mi 20 40 60 80 100 120
Note: Copyright © 1988-2003 Microsoft Corp. and/or its suppliers. All rights reserved. © Copyright 2002 by Geographic Data Technology, Inc. All rights reserved. © 2002 Navigation Technologies. All rights reserved.

Percent Hispanic (2007)

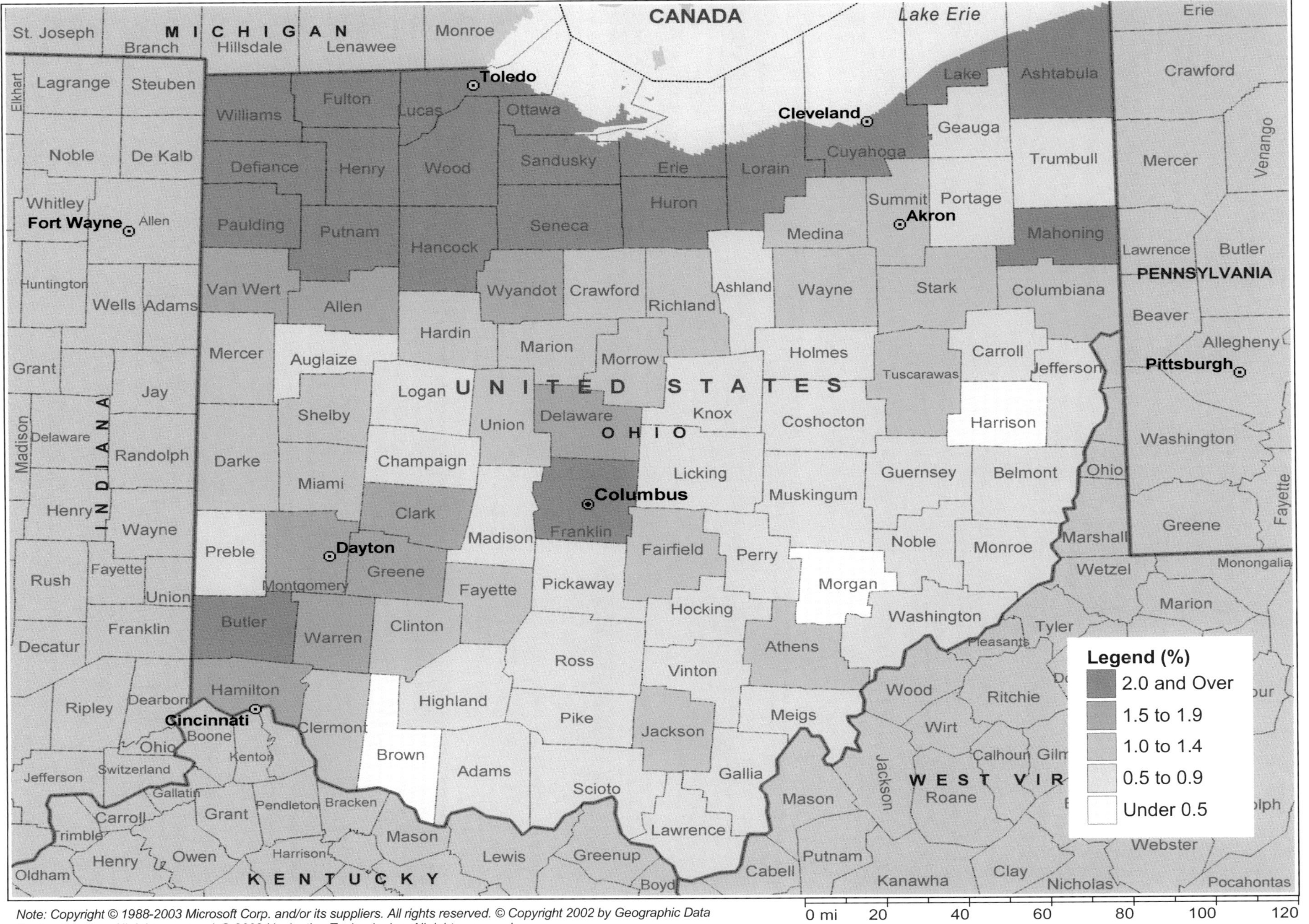

Note: Copyright © 1988-2003 Microsoft Corp. and/or its suppliers. All rights reserved. © Copyright 2002 by Geographic Data Technology, Inc. All rights reserved. © 2002 Navigation Technologies. All rights reserved.

Median Age (2007)

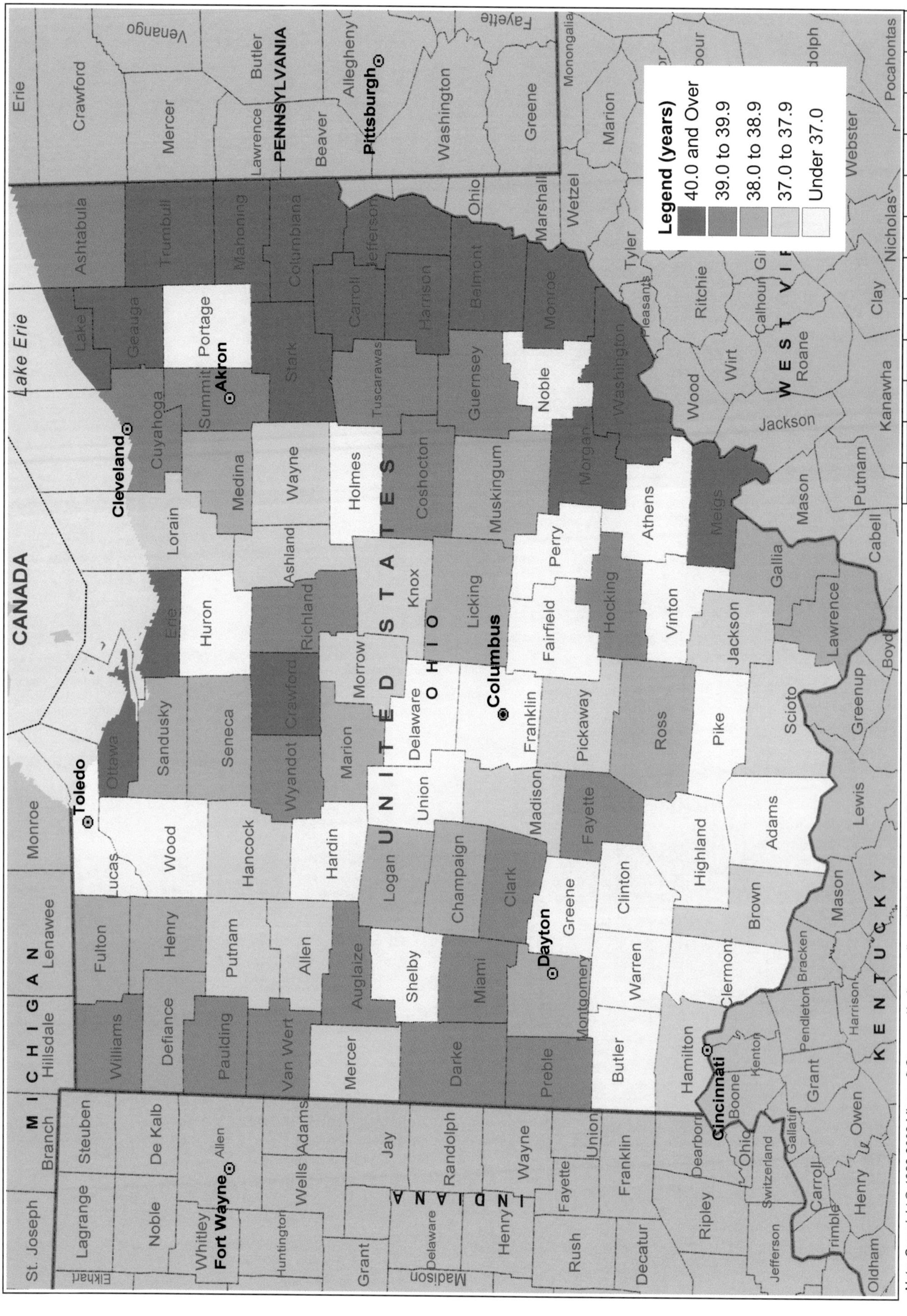

Legend (years)

- 40.0 and Over
- 39.0 to 39.9
- 38.0 to 38.9
- 37.0 to 37.9
- Under 37.0

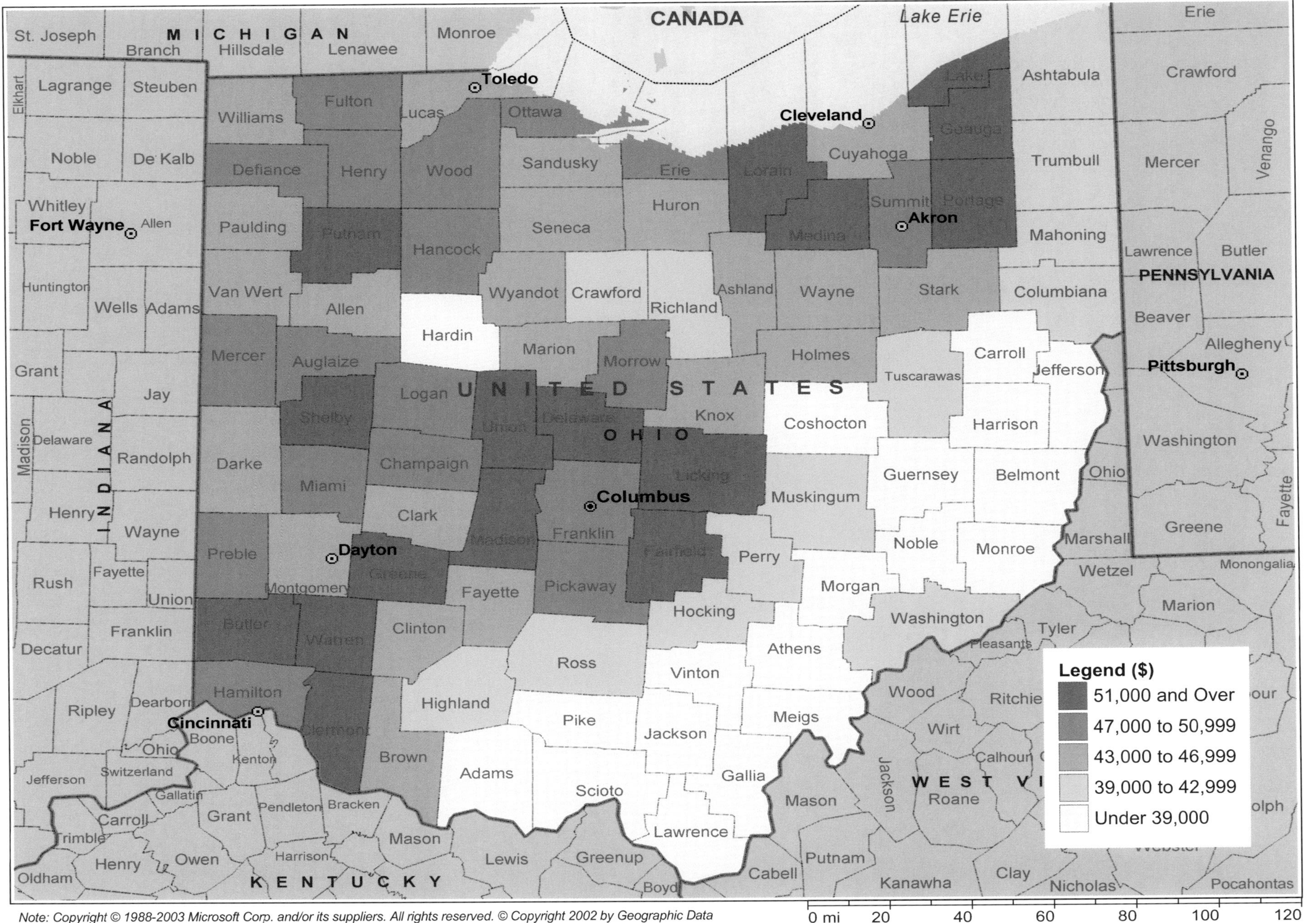
Median Household Income (2007)
Legend ($)
51,000 and Over
47,000 to 50,999
43,000 to 46,999
39,000 to 42,999
Under 39,000
0 mi 20 40 60 80 100 120

Median Home Value (2007)

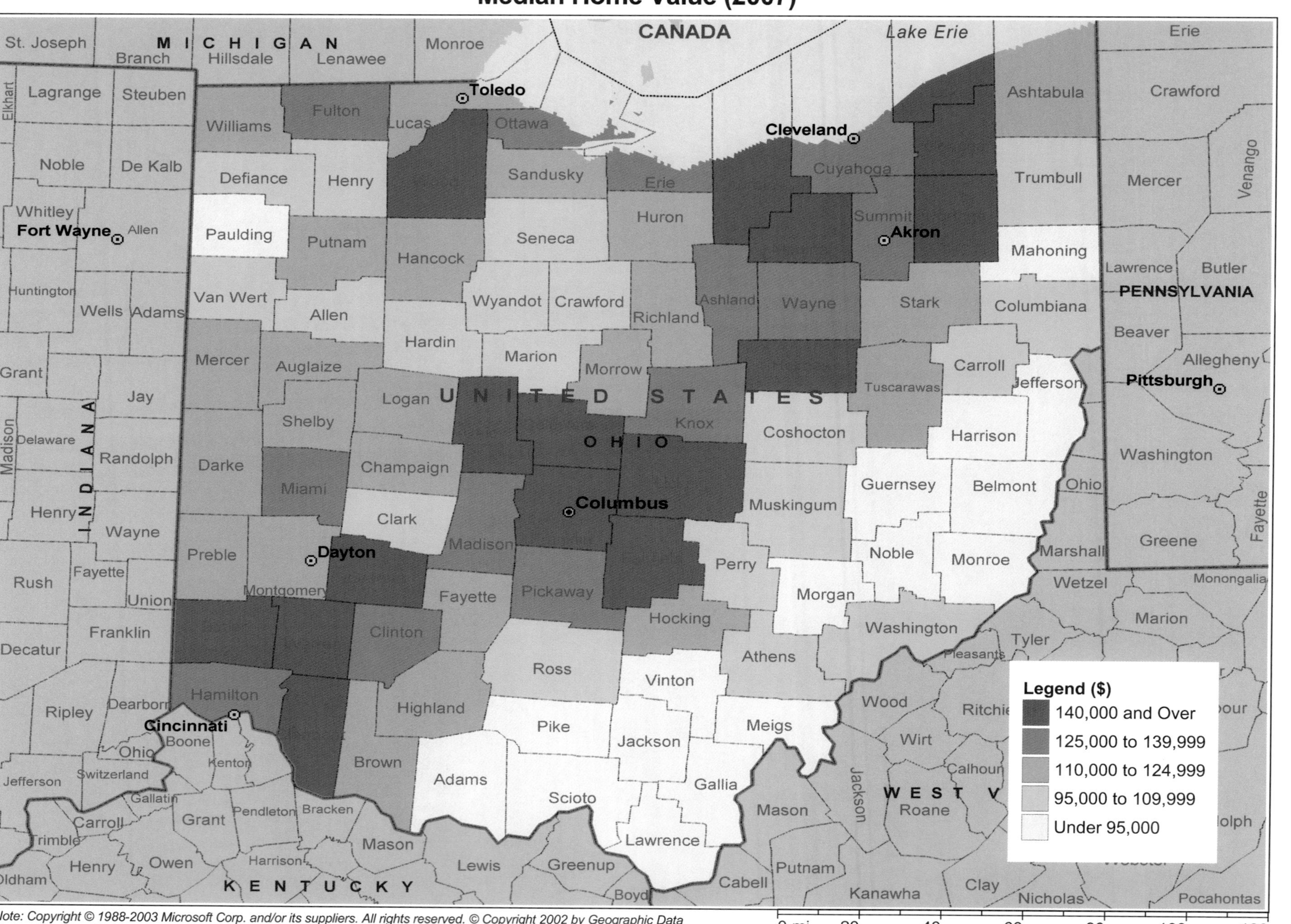

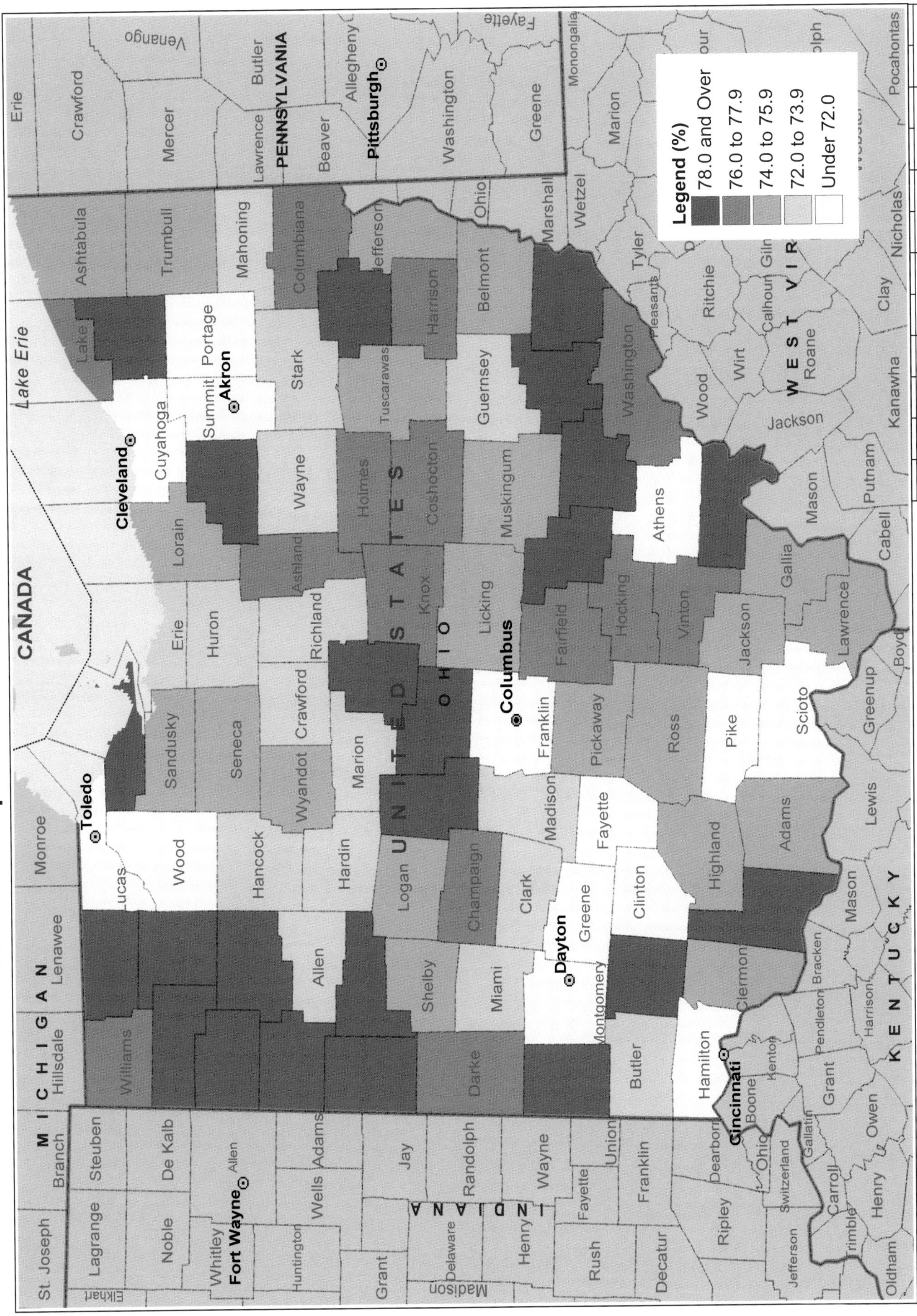

Legend (%)
- 78.0 and Over
- 76.0 to 77.9
- 74.0 to 75.9
- 72.0 to 73.9
- Under 72.0

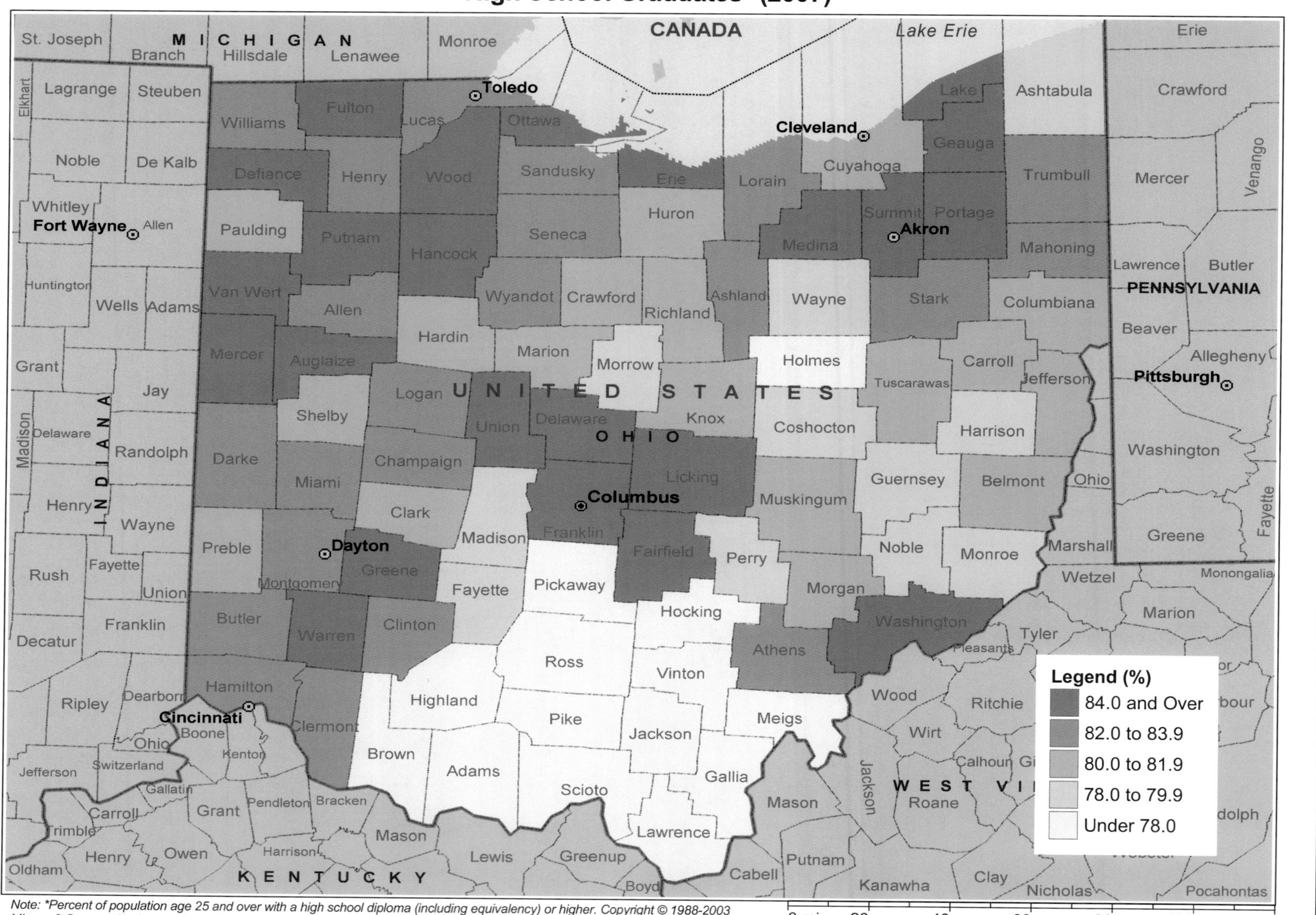
High School Graduates* (2007)
Legend (%)
84.0 and Over
82.0 to 83.9
80.0 to 81.9
78.0 to 79.9
Under 78.0
0 mi 20 40 60 80 100 120
Note: *Percent of population age 25 and over with a high school diploma (including equivalency) or higher. Copyright © 1988-2003 Microsoft Corp. and/or its suppliers. All rights reserved. © Copyright 2002 by Geographic Data Technology, Inc. All rights reserved. ©

College Graduates* (2007)

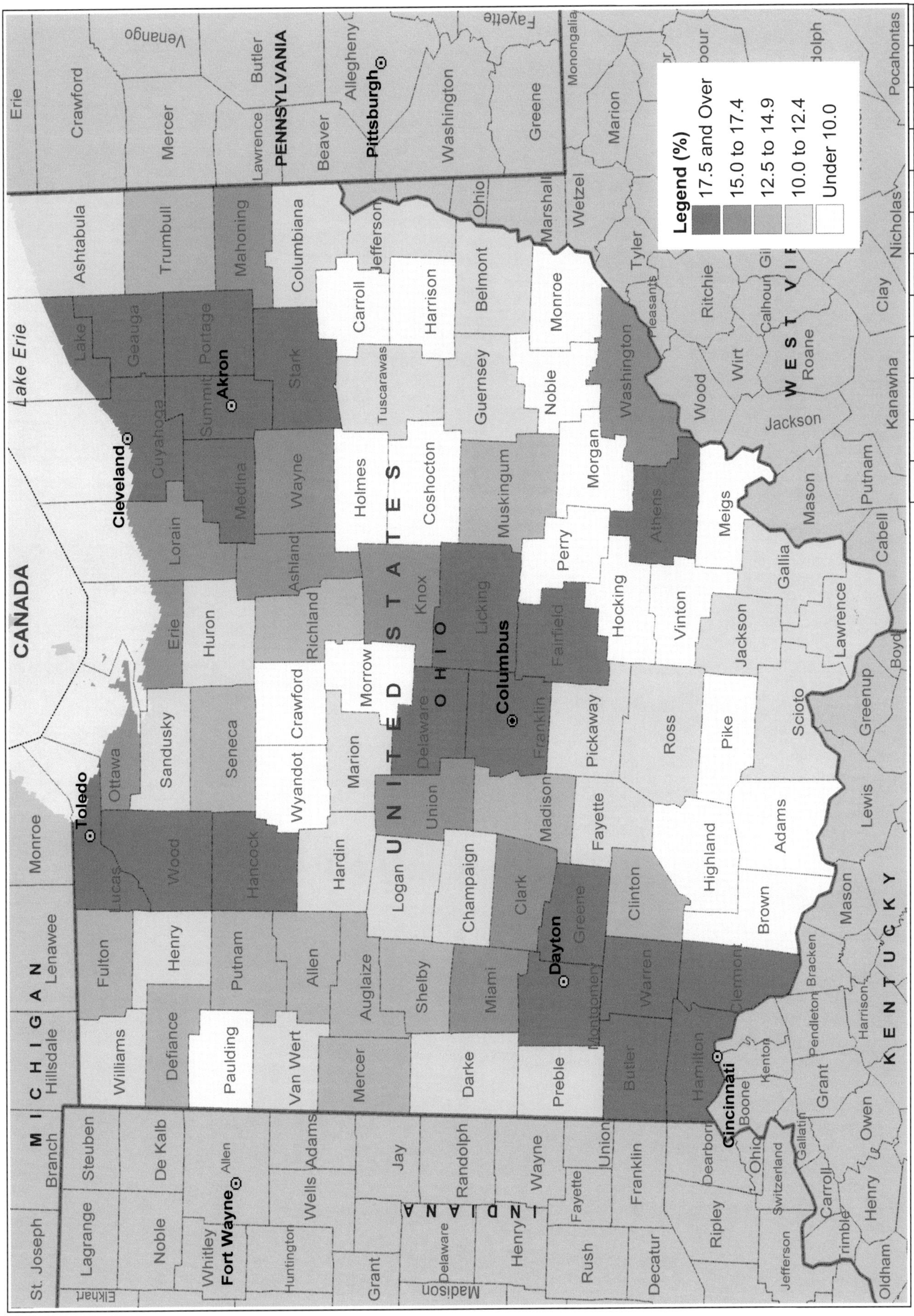

Note: *Percent of population age 25 and over with a Bachelor's Degree or higher.

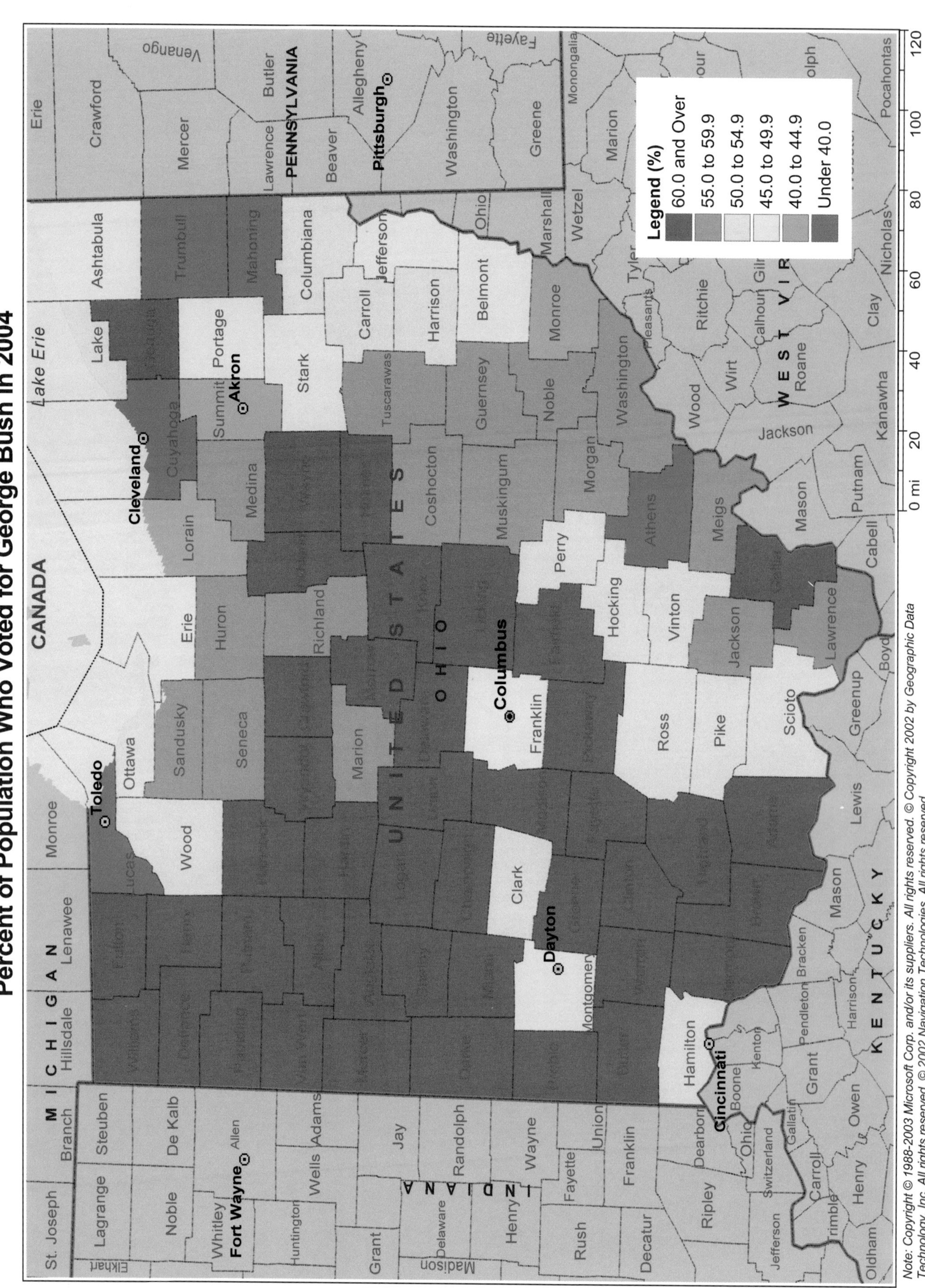
Percent of Population Who Voted for George Bush in 2004
Legend (%)
60.0 and Over
55.0 to 59.9
50.0 to 54.9
45.0 to 49.9
40.0 to 44.9
Under 40.0
0 mi 20 40 60 80 100 120
CANADA
Lake Erie
MICHIGAN
INDIANA
UNITED STATES
OHIO
PENNSYLVANIA
WEST VIRGINIA
KENTUCKY
Toledo
Cleveland
Akron
Columbus
Dayton
Cincinnati
Fort Wayne
Pittsburgh
Note: Copyright © 1988-2003 Microsoft Corp. and/or its suppliers. All rights reserved. © Copyright 2002 by Geographic Data Technology, Inc. All rights reserved. © 2002 Navigation Technologies. All rights reserved.

The Directory of Business Information Resources, 2009

With 100% verification, over 1,000 new listings and more than 12,000 updates, *The Directory of Business Information Resources* is the most up-to-date source for contacts in over 98 business areas – from advertising and agriculture to utilities and wholesalers. This carefully researched volume details: the Associations representing each industry; the Newsletters that keep members current; the Magazines and Journals - with their "Special Issues" - that are important to the trade, the Conventions that are "must attends," Databases, Directories and Industry Web Sites that provide access to must-have marketing resources. Includes contact names, phone & fax numbers, web sites and e-mail addresses. This one-volume resource is a gold mine of information and would be a welcome addition to any reference collection.

"This is a most useful and easy-to-use addition to any researcher's library." –The Information Professionals Institute

Softcover ISBN 978-1-59237-399-4, 2,500 pages, $195.00 | Online Database: http://gold.greyhouse.com Call (800) 562-2139 for quote

Hudson's Washington News Media Contacts Directory, 2009

With 100% verification of data, *Hudson's Washington News Media Contacts Directory* is the most accurate, most up-to-date source for media contacts in our nation's capital. With the largest concentration of news media in the world, having access to Washington's news media will get your message heard by these key media outlets. Published for over 40 years, Hudson's Washington News Media Contacts Directory brings you immediate access to: News Services & Newspapers, News Service Syndicates, DC Newspapers, Foreign Newspapers, Radio & TV, Magazines & Newsletters, and Freelance Writers & Photographers. The easy-to-read entries include contact names, phone & fax numbers, web sites and e-mail and more. For easy navigation, Hudson's Washington News Media Contacts Directory contains two indexes: Entry Index and Executive Index. This kind of comprehensive and up-to-date information would cost thousands of dollars to replicate or countless hours of searching to find. Don't miss this opportunity to have this important resource in your collection, and start saving time and money today. Hudson's Washington News Media Contacts Directory is the perfect research tool for Public Relations, Marketing, Networking and so much more. This resource is a gold mine of information and would be a welcome addition to any reference collection.

Softcover ISBN 978-1-59237-407-6, 800 pages, $289.00 | Online Database: http://gold.greyhouse.com Call (800) 562-2139 for quote

Nations of the World, 2009 A Political, Economic and Business Handbook

This completely revised edition covers all the nations of the world in an easy-to-use, single volume. Each nation is profiled in a single chapter that includes Key Facts, Political & Economic Issues, a Country Profile and Business Information. In this fast-changing world, it is extremely important to make sure that the most up-to-date information is included in your reference collection. This edition is just the answer. Each of the 200+ country chapters have been carefully reviewed by a political expert to make sure that the text reflects the most current information on Politics, Travel Advisories, Economics and more. You'll find such vital information as a Country Map, Population Characteristics, Inflation, Agricultural Production, Foreign Debt, Political History, Foreign Policy, Regional Insecurity, Economics, Trade & Tourism, Historical Profile, Political Systems, Ethnicity, Languages, Media, Climate, Hotels, Chambers of Commerce, Banking, Travel Information and more. Five Regional Chapters follow the main text and include a Regional Map, an Introductory Article, Key Indicators and Currencies for the Region. As an added bonus, an all-inclusive CD-ROM is available as a companion to the printed text. Noted for its sophisticated, up-to-date and reliable compilation of political, economic and business information, this brand new edition will be an important acquisition to any public, academic or special library reference collection.

"A useful addition to both general reference collections and business collections." –RUSQ

Softcover ISBN 978-1-59237-273-7, 1,700 pages, $175.00

The Directory of Venture Capital & Private Equity Firms, 2009

This edition has been extensively updated and broadly expanded to offer direct access to over 2,800 Domestic and International Venture Capital Firms, including address, phone & fax numbers, e-mail addresses and web sites for both primary and branch locations. Entries include details on the firm's Mission Statement, Industry Group Preferences, Geographic Preferences, Average and Minimum Investments and Investment Criteria. You'll also find details that are available nowhere else, including the Firm's Portfolio Companies and extensive information on each of the firm's Managing Partners, such as Education, Professional Background and Directorships held, along with the Partner's E-mail Address. *The Directory of Venture Capital & Private Equity Firms* offers five important indexes: Geographic Index, Executive Name Index, Portfolio Company Index, Industry Preference Index and College & University Index. With its comprehensive coverage and detailed, extensive information on each company, The Directory of Venture Capital & Private Equity Firms is an important addition to any finance collection.

"The sheer number of listings, the descriptive information and the outstanding indexing make this directory a better value than ...Pratt's Guide to Venture Capital Sources. Recommended for business collections in large public, academic and business libraries." –Choice

Softcover ISBN 978-1-59237-398-7, 1,300 pages, $565/$450 Lib | Online DB: http://gold.greyhouse.com Call (800) 562-2139 for quote

The Encyclopedia of Emerging Industries

*Published under an exclusive license from the Gale Group, Inc.

The fifth edition of the *Encyclopedia of Emerging Industries* details the inception, emergence, and current status of nearly 120 flourishing U.S. industries and industry segments. These focused essays unearth for users a wealth of relevant, current, factual data previously accessible only through a diverse variety of sources. This volume provides broad-based, highly-readable, industry information under such headings as Industry Snapshot, Organization & Structure, Background & Development, Industry Leaders, Current Conditions, America and the World, Pioneers, and Research & Technology. Essays in this new edition, arranged alphabetically for easy use, have been completely revised, with updated statistics and the most current information on industry trends and developments. In addition, there are new essays on some of the most interesting and influential new business fields, including Application Service Providers, Concierge Services, Entrepreneurial Training, Fuel Cells, Logistics Outsourcing Services, Pharmacogenomics, and Tissue Engineering. Two indexes, General and Industry, provide immediate access to this wealth of information. Plus, two conversion tables for SIC and NAICS codes, along with Suggested Further Readings, are provided to aid the user. *The Encyclopedia of Emerging Industries* pinpoints emerging industries while they are still in the spotlight. This important resource will be an important acquisition to any business reference collection.

"This well-designed source...should become another standard business source, nicely complementing Standard & Poor's Industry Surveys. It contains more information on each industry than Hoover's Handbook of Emerging Companies, is broader in scope than The Almanac of American Employers 1998-1999, but is less expansive than the Encyclopedia of Careers & Vocational Guidance. Highly recommended for all academic libraries and specialized business collections." –Library Journal

Hardcover ISBN 978-1-59237-242-3, 1,400 pages, $325.00

Encyclopedia of American Industries

*Published under an exclusive license from the Gale Group, Inc.

The Encyclopedia of American Industries is a major business reference tool that provides detailed, comprehensive information on a wide range of industries in every realm of American business. A two volume set, Volume I provides separate coverage of nearly 500 manufacturing industries, while Volume II presents nearly 600 essays covering the vast array of services and other non-manufacturing industries in the United States. Combined, these two volumes provide individual essays on every industry recognized by the U.S. Standard Industrial Classification (SIC) system. Both volumes are arranged numerically by SIC code, for easy use. Additionally, each entry includes the corresponding NAICS code(s). The *Encyclopedia's* business coverage includes information on historical events of consequence, as well as current trends and statistics. Essays include an Industry Snapshot, Organization & Structure, Background & Development, Current Conditions, Industry Leaders, Workforce, America and the World, Research & Technology along with Suggested Further Readings. Both SIC and NAICS code conversion tables and an all-encompassing Subject Index, with cross-references, complete the text. With its detailed, comprehensive information on a wide range of industries, this resource will be an important tool for both the industry newcomer and the seasoned professional.

"Encyclopedia of American Industries contains detailed, signed essays on virtually every industry in contemporary society. ... Highly recommended for all but the smallest libraries." -American Reference Books Annual

Two Volumes, Hardcover ISBN 978-1-59237-244-7, 3,000 pages, $650.00

Encyclopedia of Global Industries

*Published under an exclusive license from the Gale Group, Inc.

This fourth edition of the acclaimed *Encyclopedia of Global Industries* presents a thoroughly revised and expanded look at more than 125 business sectors of global significance. Detailed, insightful articles discuss the origins, development, trends, key statistics and current international character of the world's most lucrative, dynamic and widely researched industries – including hundreds of profiles of leading international corporations. Beginning researchers will gain from this book a solid understanding of how each industry operates and which countries and companies are significant participants, while experienced researchers will glean current and historical figures for comparison and analysis. The industries profiled in previous editions have been updated, and in some cases, expanded to reflect recent industry trends. Additionally, this edition provides both SIC and NAICS codes for all industries profiled. As in the original volumes, *The Encyclopedia of Global Industries* offers thorough studies of some of the biggest and most frequently researched industry sectors, including Aircraft, Biotechnology, Computers, Internet Services, Motor Vehicles, Pharmaceuticals, Semiconductors, Software and Telecommunications. An SIC and NAICS conversion table and an all-encompassing Subject Index, with cross-references, are provided to ensure easy access to this wealth of information. These and many others make the *Encyclopedia of Global Industries* the authoritative reference for studies of international industries.

"Provides detailed coverage of the history, development, and current status of 115 of "the world's most lucrative and high-profile industries." It far surpasses the Department of Commerce's U.S. Global Trade Outlook 1995-2000 (GPO, 1995) in scope and coverage. Recommended for comprehensive public and academic library business collections." -Booklist

Hardcover ISBN 978-1-59237-243-0, 1,400 pages, $495.00

The Directory of Mail Order Catalogs, 2009

Published since 1981, *The Directory of Mail Order Catalogs* is the premier source of information on the mail order catalog industry. It is the source that business professionals and librarians have come to rely on for the thousands of catalog companies in the US. Since the 2007 edition, *The Directory of Mail Order Catalogs* has been combined with its companion volume, *The Directory of Business to Business Catalogs*, to offer all 13,000 catalog companies in one easy-to-use volume. Section I: Consumer Catalogs, covers over 9,000 consumer catalog companies in 44 different product chapters from Animals to Toys & Games. Section II: Business to Business Catalogs, details 5,000 business catalogs, everything from computers to laboratory supplies, building construction and much more. Listings contain detailed contact information including mailing address, phone & fax numbers, web sites, e-mail addresses and key contacts along with important business details such as product descriptions, employee size, years in business, sales volume, catalog size, number of catalogs mailed and more. *The Directory of Mail Order Catalogs*, now with its expanded business to business catalogs, is the largest and most comprehensive resource covering this billion-dollar industry. It is the standard in its field. This important resource is a useful tool for entrepreneurs searching for catalogs to pick up their product, vendors looking to expand their customer base in the catalog industry, market researchers, small businesses investigating new supply vendors, along with the library patron who is exploring the available catalogs in their areas of interest.

"This is a godsend for those looking for information." –Reference Book Review

Softcover ISBN 978-1-59237-396-3, 1,700 pages, $350/$250 Lib | Online DB: http://gold.greyhouse.com Call (800) 562-2139 for quote

Sports Market Place Directory, 2008

For over 20 years, this comprehensive, up-to-date directory has offered direct access to the Who, What, When & Where of the Sports Industry. With over 20,000 updates and enhancements, the *Sports Market Place Directory* is the most detailed, comprehensive and current sports business reference source available. In 1,800 information-packed pages, *Sports Market Place Directory* profiles contact information and key executives for: Single Sport Organizations, Professional Leagues, Multi-Sport Organizations, Disabled Sports, High School & Youth Sports, Military Sports, Olympic Organizations, Media, Sponsors, Sponsorship & Marketing Event Agencies, Event & Meeting Calendars, Professional Services, College Sports, Manufacturers & Retailers, Facilities and much more. The Sports Market Place Directory provides organization's contact information with detailed descriptions including: Key Contacts, physical, mailing, email and web addresses plus phone and fax numbers. *Sports Market Place Directory* provides a one-stop resources for this billion-dollar industry. This will be an important resource for large public libraries, university libraries, university athletic programs, career services or job placement organizations, and is a must for anyone doing research on or marketing to the US and Canadian sports industry.

"Grey House is the new publisher and has produced an excellent edition...highly recommended for public libraries and academic libraries with sports management programs or strong interest in athletics." -Booklist

Softcover ISBN 978-1-59237-348-2, 1,800 pages, $225.00 | Online Database: http://gold.greyhouse.com Call (800) 562-2139 for quote

Food and Beverage Market Place, 2009

Food and Beverage Market Place is bigger and better than ever with thousands of new companies, thousands of updates to existing companies and two revised and enhanced product category indexes. This comprehensive directory profiles over 18,000 Food & Beverage Manufacturers, 12,000 Equipment & Supply Companies, 2,200 Transportation & Warehouse Companies, 2,000 Brokers & Wholesalers, 8,000 Importers & Exporters, 900 Industry Resources and hundreds of Mail Order Catalogs. Listings include detailed Contact Information, Sales Volumes, Key Contacts, Brand & Product Information, Packaging Details and much more. *Food and Beverage Market Place* is available as a three-volume printed set, a subscription-based Online Database via the Internet, on CD-ROM, as well as mailing lists and a licensable database.

"An essential purchase for those in the food industry but will also be useful in public libraries where needed. Much of the information will be difficult and time consuming to locate without this handy three-volume ready-reference source." –ARBA

3 Vol Set, Softcover ISBN 978-1-59237-361-1, 8,500 pages, $595 | Online DB: http://gold.greyhouse.com Call (800) 562-2139 for quote

The Grey House Performing Arts Directory, 2009

The Grey House Performing Arts Directory is the most comprehensive resource covering the Performing Arts. This important directory provides current information on over 8,500 Dance Companies, Instrumental Music Programs, Opera Companies, Choral Groups, Theater Companies, Performing Arts Series and Performing Arts Facilities. Plus, this edition now contains a brand new section on Artist Management Groups. In addition to mailing address, phone & fax numbers, e-mail addresses and web sites, dozens of other fields of available information include mission statement, key contacts, facilities, seating capacity, season, attendance and more. This directory also provides an important Information Resources section that covers hundreds of Performing Arts Associations, Magazines, Newsletters, Trade Shows, Directories, Databases and Industry Web Sites. Five indexes provide immediate access to this wealth of information: Entry Name, Executive Name, Performance Facilities, Geographic and Information Resources. *The Grey House Performing Arts Directory* pulls together thousands of Performing Arts Organizations, Facilities and Information Resources into an easy-to-use source – this kind of comprehensiveness and extensive detail is not available in any resource on the market place today.

"Immensely useful and user-friendly ... recommended for public, academic and certain special library reference collections." –Booklist

Softcover ISBN 978-1-59237-376-5, 1,500 pages, $185.00 | Online Database: http://gold.greyhouse.com Call (800) 562-2139 for quote

To preview any of our Directories Risk-Free for 30 days, call (800) 562-2139 or fax (518) 789-0556
www.greyhouse.com books@greyhouse.com

The Environmental Resource Handbook, 2008/09

The Environmental Resource Handbook is the most up-to-date and comprehensive source for Environmental Resources and Statistics. Section I: Resources provides detailed contact information for thousands of information sources, including Associations & Organizations, Awards & Honors, Conferences, Foundations & Grants, Environmental Health, Government Agencies, National Parks & Wildlife Refuges, Publications, Research Centers, Educational Programs, Green Product Catalogs, Consultants and much more. Section II: Statistics, provides statistics and rankings on hundreds of important topics, including Children's Environmental Index, Municipal Finances, Toxic Chemicals, Recycling, Climate, Air & Water Quality and more. This kind of up-to-date environmental data, all in one place, is not available anywhere else on the market place today. This vast compilation of resources and statistics is a must-have for all public and academic libraries as well as any organization with a primary focus on the environment.

"...the intrinsic value of the information make it worth consideration by libraries with environmental collections and environmentally concerned users." –Booklist

Softcover ISBN 978-1-59237-195-2, 1,000 pages, $155.00 | Online Database: http://gold.greyhouse.com Call (800) 562-2139 for quote

New York State Directory, 2008/09

The New York State Directory, published annually since 1983, is a comprehensive and easy-to-use guide to accessing public officials and private sector organizations and individuals who influence public policy in the state of New York. *The New York State Directory* includes important information on all New York state legislators and congressional representatives, including biographies and key committee assignments. It also includes staff rosters for all branches of New York state government and for federal agencies and departments that impact the state policy process. Following the state government section are 25 chapters covering policy areas from agriculture through veterans' affairs. Each chapter identifies the state, local and federal agencies and officials that formulate or implement policy. In addition, each chapter contains a roster of private sector experts and advocates who influence the policy process. The directory also offers appendices that include statewide party officials; chambers of commerce; lobbying organizations; public and private universities and colleges; television, radio and print media; and local government agencies and officials.

"This comprehensive directory covers not only New York State government offices and key personnel but pertinent U.S. government agencies and non-governmental entities. This directory is all encompassing... recommended." -Choice

New York State Directory - Softcover ISBN 978-1-59237-358-1, 800 pages, $145.00
Online Database: http://gold.greyhouse.com Call (800) 562-2139 for quote
New York State Directory with *Profiles of New York* – 2 Volumes, Softcover ISBN 978-1-59237-359-8, 1,600 pages, $225.00

The Grey House Homeland Security Directory, 2008

This updated edition features the latest contact information for government and private organizations involved with Homeland Security along with the latest product information and provides detailed profiles of nearly 1,000 Federal & State Organizations & Agencies and over 3,000 Officials and Key Executives involved with Homeland Security. These listings are incredibly detailed and include Mailing Address, Phone & Fax Numbers, Email Addresses & Web Sites, a complete Description of the Agency and a complete list of the Officials and Key Executives associated with the Agency. Next, *The Grey House Homeland Security Directory* provides the go-to source for Homeland Security Products & Services. This section features over 2,000 Companies that provide Consulting, Products or Services. With this Buyer's Guide at their fingertips, users can locate suppliers of everything from Training Materials to Access Controls, from Perimeter Security to BioTerrorism Countermeasures and everything in between – complete with contact information and product descriptions. A handy Product Locator Index is provided to quickly and easily locate suppliers of a particular product. This comprehensive, information-packed resource will be a welcome tool for any company or agency that is in need of Homeland Security information and will be a necessary acquisition for the reference collection of all public libraries and large school districts.

"Compiles this information in one place and is discerning in content. A useful purchase for public and academic libraries." –Booklist

Softcover ISBN 978-1-59237-196-6, 800 pages, $195.00 | Online Database: http://gold.greyhouse.com Call (800) 562-2139 for quote

The Grey House Safety & Security Directory, 2009

The Grey House Safety & Security Directory is the most comprehensive reference tool and buyer's guide for the safety and security industry. Arranged by safety topic, each chapter begins with OSHA regulations for the topic, followed by Training Articles written by top professionals in the field and Self-Inspection Checklists. Next, each topic contains Buyer's Guide sections that feature related products and services. Topics include Administration, Insurance, Loss Control & Consulting, Protective Equipment & Apparel, Noise & Vibration, Facilities Monitoring & Maintenance, Employee Health Maintenance & Ergonomics, Retail Food Services, Machine Guards, Process Guidelines & Tool Handling, Ordinary Materials Handling, Hazardous Materials Handling, Workplace Preparation & Maintenance, Electrical Lighting & Safety, Fire & Rescue and Security. Six important indexes make finding information and product manufacturers quick and easy: Geographical Index of Manufacturers and Distributors, Company Profile Index, Brand Name Index, Product Index, Index of Web Sites and Index of Advertisers. This comprehensive, up-to-date reference will provide every tool necessary to make sure a business is in compliance with OSHA regulations and locate the products and services needed to meet those regulations.

"Presents industrial safety information for engineers, plant managers, risk managers, and construction site supervisors..." –Choice

Softcover ISBN 978-1-59237-375-8, 1,500 pages, $165.00

The Grey House Transportation Security Directory & Handbook

This is the only reference of its kind that brings together current data on Transportation Security. With information on everything from Regulatory Authorities to Security Equipment, this top-flight database brings together the relevant information necessary for creating and maintaining a security plan for a wide range of transportation facilities. With this current, comprehensive directory at the ready you'll have immediate access to: Regulatory Authorities & Legislation; Information Resources; Sample Security Plans & Checklists; Contact Data for Major Airports, Seaports, Railroads, Trucking Companies and Oil Pipelines; Security Service Providers; Recommended Equipment & Product Information and more. Using the *Grey House Transportation Security Directory & Handbook*, managers will be able to quickly and easily assess their current security plans; develop contacts to create and maintain new security procedures; and source the products and services necessary to adequately maintain a secure environment. This valuable resource is a must for all Security Managers at Airports, Seaports, Railroads, Trucking Companies and Oil Pipelines.

"Highly recommended. Library collections that support all levels of readers, including professionals/practitioners; and schools/organizations offering education and training in transportation security." -Choice

Softcover ISBN 978-1-59237-075-7, 800 pages, $195.00

The Grey House Biometric Information Directory

This edition offers a complete, current overview of biometric companies and products – one of the fastest growing industries in today's economy. Detailed profiles of manufacturers of the latest biometric technology, including Finger, Voice, Face, Hand, Signature, Iris, Vein and Palm Identification systems. Data on the companies include key executives, company size and a detailed, indexed description of their product line. Information in the directory includes: Editorial on Advancements in Biometrics; Profiles of 700+ companies listed with contact information; Organizations, Trade & Educational Associations, Publications, Conferences, Trade Shows and Expositions Worldwide; Web Site Index; Biometric & Vendors Services Index by Types of Biometrics; and a Glossary of Biometric Terms. This resource will be an important source for anyone who is considering the use of a biometric product, investing in the development of biometric technology, support existing marketing and sales efforts and will be an important acquisition for the business reference collection for large public and business libraries.

"This book should prove useful to agencies or businesses seeking companies that deal with biometric technology. Summing Up: Recommended. Specialized collections serving researchers/faculty and professionals/practitioners." -Choice

Softcover ISBN 978-1-59237-121-1, 800 pages, $225.00

The Rauch Guide to the US Adhesives & Sealants, Cosmetics & Toiletries, Ink, Paint, Plastics, Pulp & Paper and Rubber Industries

The Rauch Guides save time and money by organizing widely scattered information and providing estimates for important business decisions, some of which are available nowhere else. Within each Guide, after a brief introduction, the ECONOMICS section provides data on industry shipments; long-term growth and forecasts; prices; company performance; employment, expenditures, and productivity; transportation and geographical patterns; packaging; foreign trade; and government regulations. Next, TECHNOLOGY & RAW MATERIALS provide market, technical, and raw material information for chemicals, equipment and related materials, including market size and leading suppliers, prices, end uses, and trends. PRODUCTS & MARKETS provide information for each major industry product, including market size and historical trends, leading suppliers, five-year forecasts, industry structure, and major end uses. Next, the COMPANY DIRECTORY profiles major industry companies, both public and private. Information includes complete contact information, web address, estimated total and domestic sales, product description, and recent mergers and acquisitions. *The Rauch Guides* will prove to be an invaluable source of market information, company data, trends and forecasts that anyone in these fast-paced industries.

"An invaluable and affordable publication. The comprehensive nature of the data and text offers considerable insights into the industry, market sizes, company activities, and applications of the products of the industry. The additions that have been made have certainly enhanced the value of the Guide." –Adhesives & Sealants Newsletter of the Rauch Guide to the US Adhesives & Sealants Industry

Paint Industry: Softcover ISBN 978-1-59237-127-3 $595 | Plastics Industry: Softcover ISBN 978-1-59237-128-0 $595 | Adhesives and Sealants Industry: Softcover ISBN 978-1-59237-129-7 $595 | Ink Industry: Softcover ISBN 978-1-59237-126-6 $595 | Rubber Industry: Softcover ISBN 978-1-59237-130-3 $595 | Pulp and Paper Industry: Softcover ISBN 978-1-59237-131-0 $595 | Cosmetic & Toiletries Industry: Softcover ISBN 978-1-59237-132-7 $895

Research Services Directory: Commercial & Corporate Research Centers

This ninth edition provides access to well over 8,000 independent Commercial Research Firms, Corporate Research Centers and Laboratories offering contract services for hands-on, basic or applied research. Research Services Directory covers the thousands of types of research companies, including Biotechnology & Pharmaceutical Developers, Consumer Product Research, Defense Contractors, Electronics & Software Engineers, Think Tanks, Forensic Investigators, Independent Commercial Laboratories, Information Brokers, Market & Survey Research Companies, Medical Diagnostic Facilities, Product Research & Development Firms and more. Each entry provides the company's name, mailing address, phone & fax numbers, key contacts, web site, e-mail address, as well as a company description and research and technical fields served. Four indexes provide immediate access to this wealth of information: Research Firms Index, Geographic Index, Personnel Name Index and Subject Index.

"An important source for organizations in need of information about laboratories, individuals and other facilities." –ARBA

Softcover ISBN 978-1-59237-003-0, 1,400 pages, $465.00

International Business and Trade Directories

Completely updated, the Third Edition of *International Business and Trade Directories* now contains more than 10,000 entries, over 2,000 more than the last edition, making this directory the most comprehensive resource of the worlds business and trade directories. Entries include content descriptions, price, publisher's name and address, web site and e-mail addresses, phone and fax numbers and editorial staff. Organized by industry group, and then by region, this resource puts over 10,000 industry-specific business and trade directories at the reader's fingertips. Three indexes are included for quick access to information: Geographic Index, Publisher Index and Title Index. Public, college and corporate libraries, as well as individuals and corporations seeking critical market information will want to add this directory to their marketing collection.

"Reasonably priced for a work of this type, this directory should appeal to larger academic, public and corporate libraries with an international focus." –Library Journal

Softcover ISBN 978-1-930956-63-6, 1,800 pages, $225.00

TheStreet.com Ratings Guide to Health Insurers

TheStreet.com Ratings Guide to Health Insurers is the first and only source to cover the financial stability of the nation's health care system, rating the financial safety of more than 6,000 health insurance providers, health maintenance organizations (HMOs) and all of the Blue Cross Blue Shield plans – updated quarterly to ensure the most accurate information. The Guide also provides a complete listing of all the major health insurers, including all Long-Term Care and Medigap insurers. Our *Guide to Health Insurers* includes comprehensive, timely coverage on the financial stability of HMOs and health insurers; the most accurate insurance company ratings available–the same quality ratings heralded by the U.S. General Accounting Office; separate listings for those companies offering Medigap and long-term care policies; the number of serious consumer complaints filed against most HMOs so you can see who is actually providing the best (or worst) service and more. The easy-to-use layout gives you a one-line summary analysis for each company that we track, followed by an in-depth, detailed analysis of all HMOs and the largest health insurers. The guide also includes a list of TheStreet.com Ratings Recommended Companies with information on how to contact them, and the reasoning behind any rating upgrades or downgrades.

"With 20 years behind its insurance-advocacy research [the rating guide] continues to offer a wealth of information that helps consumers weigh their healthcare options now and in the future." -Today's Librarian

Issues published quarterly, Softcover, 550 pages, $499.00 for four quarterly issues, $249.00 for a single issue

TheStreet.com Ratings Guide to Life & Annuity Insurers

TheStreet.com Safety Ratings are the most reliable source for evaluating an insurer's financial solvency risk. Consequently, policy-holders have come to rely on TheStreet.com's flagship publication, *TheStreet.com Ratings Guide to Life & Annuity Insurers*, to help them identify the safest companies to do business with. Each easy-to-use edition delivers TheStreet.com's independent ratings and analyses on more than 1,100 insurers, updated every quarter. Plus, your patrons will find a complete list of TheStreet.com Recommended Companies, including contact information, and the reasoning behind any rating upgrades or downgrades. This guide is perfect for those who are considering the purchase of a life insurance policy, placing money in an annuity, or advising clients about insurance and annuities. A life or health insurance policy or annuity is only as secure as the insurance company issuing it. Therefore, make sure your patrons have what they need to periodically monitor the financial condition of the companies with whom they have an investment. The TheStreet.com Ratings product line is designed to help them in their evaluations.

"Weiss has an excellent reputation and this title is held by hundreds of libraries. This guide is recommended for public and academic libraries." -ARBA

Issues published quarterly, Softcover, 360 pages, $499.00 for four quarterly issues, $249.00 for a single issue

TheStreet.com Ratings Guide to Property & Casualty Insurers

TheStreet.com Ratings Guide to Property and Casualty Insurers provides the most extensive coverage of insurers writing policies, helping consumers and businesses avoid financial headaches. Updated quarterly, this easy-to-use publication delivers the independent, unbiased TheStreet.com Safety Ratings and supporting analyses on more than 2,800 U.S. insurance companies, offering auto & homeowners insurance, business insurance, worker's compensation insurance, product liability insurance, medical malpractice and other professional liability insurance. Each edition includes a list of TheStreet.com Recommended Companies by type of insurance, including a contact number, plus helpful information about the coverage provided by the State Guarantee Associations.

"In contrast to the other major insurance rating agencies...Weiss does not have a financial relationship worth the companies it rates. A GAO study found that Weiss identified financial vulnerability earlier than the other rating agencies." -ARBA

Issues published quarterly, Softcover, 455 pages, $499.00 for four quarterly issues, $249.00 for a single issue

TheStreet.com Ratings Consumer Box Set

Deliver the critical information your patrons need to safeguard their personal finances with *TheStreet.com Ratings' Consumer Guide Box Set*. Each of the eight guides is packed with accurate, unbiased information and recommendations to help your patrons make sound financial decisions. TheStreet.com Ratings Consumer Guide Box Set provides your patrons with easy to understand guidance on important personal finance topics, including: *Consumer Guide to Variable Annuities, Consumer Guide to Medicare Supplement Insurance, Consumer Guide to Elder Care Choices, Consumer Guide to Automobile Insurance, Consumer Guide to Long-Term Care Insurance, Consumer Guide to Homeowners Insurance, Consumer Guide to Term Life Insurance, and Consumer Guide to Medicare Prescription Drug Coverage*. Each guide provides an easy-to-read overview of the topic, what to look out for when selecting a company or insurance plan to do business with, who are the recommended companies to work with and how to navigate through these often-times difficult decisions. Custom worksheets and step-by-step directions make these resources accessible to all types of users. Packaged in a handy custom display box, these helpful guides will prove to be a much-used addition to any reference collection.

Issues published twice per year, Softcover, 600 pages, $499.00 for two biennial issues

TheStreet.com Ratings Guide to Stock Mutual Funds

TheStreet.com Ratings Guide to Stock Mutual Funds offers ratings and analyses on more than 8,800 equity mutual funds – more than any other publication. The exclusive TheStreet.com Investment Ratings combine an objective evaluation of each fund's performance and risk to provide a single, user-friendly, composite rating, giving your patrons a better handle on a mutual fund's risk-adjusted performance. Each edition identifies the top-performing mutual funds based on risk category, type of fund, and overall risk-adjusted performance. TheStreet.com's unique investment rating system makes it easy to see exactly which stocks are on the rise and which ones should be avoided. For those investors looking to tailor their mutual fund selections based on age, income, and tolerance for risk, we've also assigned two component ratings to each fund: a performance rating and a risk rating. With these, you can identify those funds that are best suited to meet your - or your client's – individual needs and goals. Plus, we include a handy Risk Profile Quiz to help you assess your personal tolerance for risk. So whether you're an investing novice or professional, the *Guide to Stock Mutual Funds* gives you everything you need to find a mutual fund that is right for you.

"There is tremendous need for information such as that provided by this Weiss publication. This reasonably priced guide is recommended for public and academic libraries serving investors." -ARBA

Issues published quarterly, Softcover, 655 pages, $499 for four quarterly issues, $249 for a single issue

TheStreet.com Ratings Guide to Exchange-Traded Funds

TheStreet.com Ratings editors analyze hundreds of mutual funds each quarter, condensing all of the available data into a single composite opinion of each fund's risk-adjusted performance. The intuitive, consumer-friendly ratings allow investors to instantly identify those funds that have historically done well and those that have under-performed the market. Each quarterly edition identifies the top-performing exchange-traded funds based on risk category, type of fund, and overall risk-adjusted performance. The rating scale, A through F, gives you a better handle on an exchange-traded fund's risk-adjusted performance. Other features include Top & Bottom 200 Exchange-Traded Funds; Performance and Risk: 100 Best and Worst Exchange- Traded Funds; Investor Profile Quiz; Performance Benchmarks and Fund Type Descriptions. With the growing popularity of mutual fund investing, consumers need a reliable source to help them track and evaluate the performance of their mutual fund holdings. Plus, they need a way of identifying and monitoring other funds as potential new investments. Unfortunately, the hundreds of performance and risk measures available, multiplied by the vast number of mutual fund investments on the market today, can make this a daunting task for even the most sophisticated investor. This Guide will serve as a useful tool for both the first-time and seasoned investor.

Editions published quarterly, Softcover, 440 pages, $499.00 for four quarterly issues, $249.00 for a single issue

TheStreet.com Ratings Guide to Bond & Money Market Mutual Funds

TheStreet.com Ratings Guide to Bond & Money Market Mutual Funds has everything your patrons need to easily identify the top-performing fixed income funds on the market today. Each quarterly edition contains TheStreet.com's independent ratings and analyses on more than 4,600 fixed income funds – more than any other publication, including corporate bond funds, high-yield bond funds, municipal bond funds, mortgage security funds, money market funds, global bond funds and government bond funds. In addition, the fund's risk rating is combined with its three-year performance rating to get an overall picture of the fund's risk-adjusted performance. The resulting TheStreet.com Investment Rating gives a single, user-friendly, objective evaluation that makes it easy to compare one fund to another and select the right fund based on the level of risk tolerance. Most investors think of fixed income mutual funds as "safe" investments. That's not always the case, however, depending on the credit risk, interest rate risk, and prepayment risk of the securities owned by the fund. TheStreet.com Ratings assesses each of these risks and assigns each fund a risk rating to help investors quickly evaluate the fund's risk component. Plus, we include a handy Risk Profile Quiz to help you assess your personal tolerance for risk. So whether you're an investing novice or professional, the *Guide to Bond and Money Market Mutual Funds* gives you everything you need to find a mutual fund that is right for you.

"Comprehensive... It is easy to use and consumer-oriented, and can be recommended for larger public and academic libraries." -ARBA

Issues published quarterly, Softcover, 470 pages, $499.00 for four quarterly issues, $249.00 for a single issue

TheStreet.com Ratings Guide to Banks & Thrifts

Updated quarterly, for the most up-to-date information, *TheStreet.com Ratings Guide to Banks and Thrifts* offers accurate, intuitive safety ratings your patrons can trust; supporting ratios and analyses that show an institution's strong & weak points; identification of the TheStreet.com Recommended Companies with branches in your area; a complete list of institutions receiving upgrades/downgrades; and comprehensive coverage of every bank and thrift in the nation – more than 9,000. TheStreet.com Safety Ratings are then based on the analysts' review of publicly available information collected by the federal banking regulators. The easy-to-use layout gives you: the institution's TheStreet.com Safety Rating for the last 3 years; the five key indexes used to evaluate each institution; along with the primary ratios and statistics used in determining the company's rating. *TheStreet.com Ratings Guide to Banks & Thrifts* will be a must for individuals who are concerned about the safety of their CD or savings account; need to be sure that an existing line of credit will be there when they need it; or simply want to avoid the hassles of dealing with a failing or troubled institution.

"Large public and academic libraries most definitely need to acquire the work. Likewise, special libraries in large corporations will find this title indispensable." -ARBA

Issues published quarterly, Softcover, 370 pages, $499.00 for four quarterly issues, $249.00 for a single issue

TheStreet.com Ratings Guide to Common Stocks

TheStreet.com Ratings Guide to Common Stocks gives your patrons reliable insight into the risk-adjusted performance of common stocks listed on the NYSE, AMEX, and Nasdaq – over 5,800 stocks in all – more than any other publication. TheStreet.com's unique investment rating system makes it easy to see exactly which stocks are on the rise and which ones should be avoided. In addition, your patrons also get supporting analysis showing growth trends, profitability, debt levels, valuation levels, the top-rated stocks within each industry, and more. Plus, each stock is ranked with the easy-to-use buy-hold-sell equivalents commonly used by Wall Street. Whether they're selecting their own investments or checking up on a broker's recommendation, TheStreet.com Ratings can help them in their evaluations.

"Users... will find the information succinct and the explanations readable, easy to understand, and helpful to a novice." -Library Journal

Issues published quarterly, Softcover, 440 pages, $499.00 for four quarterly issues, $249.00 for a single issue

TheStreet.com Ratings Ultimate Guided Tour of Stock Investing

This important reference guide from TheStreet.com Ratings is just what librarians around the country have asked for: a step-by-step introduction to stock investing for the beginning to intermediate investor. This easy-to-navigate guide explores the basics of stock investing and includes the intuitive TheStreet.com Investment Rating on more than 5,800 stocks, complete with real-world investing information that can be put to use immediately with stocks that fit the concepts discussed in the guide; informative charts, graphs and worksheets; easy-to-understand explanations on topics like P/E, compound interest, marked indices, diversifications, brokers, and much more; along with financial safety ratings for every stock on the NYSE, American Stock Exchange and the Nasdaq. This consumer-friendly guide offers complete how-to information on stock investing that can be put to use right away; a friendly format complete with our "Wise Guide" who leads the reader on a safari to learn about the investing jungle; helpful charts, graphs and simple worksheets; the intuitive TheStreet.com Investment rating on over 6,000 stocks — every stock found on the NYSE, American Stock Exchange and the NASDAQ; and much more.

"Provides investors with an alternative to stock broker recommendations, which recently have been tarnished by conflicts of interest. In summary, the guide serves as a welcome addition for all public library collections." -ARBA

Issues published quarterly, Softcover, 370 pages, $499.00 for four quarterly issues, $249.00 for a single issue

TheStreet.com Ratings' Reports & Services

- Ratings Online — An on-line summary covering an individual company's TheStreet.com Financial Strength Rating or an investment's unique TheStreet.com Investment Rating with the factors contributing to that rating; available 24 hours a day by visiting www.thestreet.com/tscratings or calling (800) 289-9222.
- Unlimited Ratings Research — The ultimate research tool providing fast, easy online access to the very latest TheStreet.com Financial Strength Ratings and Investment Ratings. Price: $559 per industry.

Contact TheStreet.com for more information about Reports & Services at www.thestreet.com/tscratings or call (800) 289-9222

TheStreet.com Ratings' Custom Reports

TheStreet.com Ratings is pleased to offer two customized options for receiving ratings data. Each taps into TheStreet.com's vast data repositories and is designed to provide exactly the data you need. Choose from a variety of industries, companies, data variables, and delivery formats including print, Excel, SQL, Text or Access.

- Customized Reports - get right to the heart of your company's research and data needs with a report customized to your specifications.
- Complete Database Download – TheStreet.com will design and deliver the database; from there you can sort it, recalculate it, and format your results to suit your specific needs.

Contact TheStreet.com for more information about Custom Reports at www.thestreet.com/tscratings or call (800) 289-9222

The Value of a Dollar 1600-1859, The Colonial Era to The Civil War

Following the format of the widely acclaimed, *The Value of a Dollar, 1860-2004*, *The Value of a Dollar 1600-1859, The Colonial Era to The Civil War* records the actual prices of thousands of items that consumers purchased from the Colonial Era to the Civil War. Our editorial department had been flooded with requests from users of our *Value of a Dollar* for the same type of information, just from an earlier time period. This new volume is just the answer – with pricing data from 1600 to 1859. Arranged into five-year chapters, each 5-year chapter includes a Historical Snapshot, Consumer Expenditures, Investments, Selected Income, Income/Standard Jobs, Food Basket, Standard Prices and Miscellany. There is also a section on Trends. This informative section charts the change in price over time and provides added detail on the reasons prices changed within the time period, including industry developments, changes in consumer attitudes and important historical facts. This fascinating survey will serve a wide range of research needs and will be useful in all high school, public and academic library reference collections.

"The Value of a Dollar: Colonial Era to the Civil War, 1600-1865 will find a happy audience among students, researchers, and general browsers. It offers a fascinating and detailed look at early American history from the viewpoint of everyday people trying to make ends meet. This title and the earlier publication, The Value of a Dollar, 1860-2004, complement each other very well, and readers will appreciate finding them side-by-side on the shelf." -Booklist

Hardcover ISBN 978-1-59237-094-8, 600 pages, $145.00 | Ebook ISBN 978-1-59237-169-3 www.greyhouse.com/ebooks.htm

The Value of a Dollar 1860-2009, Fourth Edition

A guide to practical economy, *The Value of a Dollar* records the actual prices of thousands of items that consumers purchased from the Civil War to the present, along with facts about investment options and income opportunities. This brand new Third Edition boasts a brand new addition to each five-year chapter, a section on Trends. This informative section charts the change in price over time and provides added detail on the reasons prices changed within the time period, including industry developments, changes in consumer attitudes and important historical facts. Plus, a brand new chapter for 2005-2009 has been added. Each 5-year chapter includes a Historical Snapshot, Consumer Expenditures, Investments, Selected Income, Income/Standard Jobs, Food Basket, Standard Prices and Miscellany. This interesting and useful publication will be widely used in any reference collection.

"Business historians, reporters, writers and students will find this source... very helpful for historical research. Libraries will want to purchase it." –ARBA

Hardcover ISBN 978-1-59237-403-8, 600 pages, $145.00 | Ebook ISBN 978-1-59237-173-0 www.greyhouse.com/ebooks.htm

Working Americans 1880-1999
Volume I: The Working Class, Volume II: The Middle Class, Volume III: The Upper Class

Each of the volumes in the *Working Americans* series focuses on a particular class of Americans, The Working Class, The Middle Class and The Upper Class over the last 120 years. Chapters in each volume focus on one decade and profile three to five families. Family Profiles include real data on Income & Job Descriptions, Selected Prices of the Times, Annual Income, Annual Budgets, Family Finances, Life at Work, Life at Home, Life in the Community, Working Conditions, Cost of Living, Amusements and much more. Each chapter also contains an Economic Profile with Average Wages of other Professions, a selection of Typical Pricing, Key Events & Inventions, News Profiles, Articles from Local Media and Illustrations. The *Working Americans* series captures the lifestyles of each of the classes from the last twelve decades, covers a vast array of occupations and ethnic backgrounds and travels the entire nation. These interesting and useful compilations of portraits of the American Working, Middle and Upper Classes during the last 120 years will be an important addition to any high school, public or academic library reference collection.

"These interesting, unique compilations of economic and social facts, figures and graphs will support multiple research needs. They will engage and enlighten patrons in high school, public and academic library collections." –Booklist

Volume I: The Working Class Hardcover ISBN 978-1-891482-81-6, 558 pages, $145.00 | Volume II: The Middle Class Hardcover ISBN 978-1-891482-72-4, 591 pages, $145.00 | Volume III: The Upper Class Hardcover ISBN 978-1-930956-38-4, 567 pages, $145.00 | www.greyhouse.com/ebooks.htm

Working Americans 1880-1999 Volume IV: Their Children

This Fourth Volume in the highly successful *Working Americans* series focuses on American children, decade by decade from 1880 to 1999. This interesting and useful volume introduces the reader to three children in each decade, one from each of the Working, Middle and Upper classes. Like the first three volumes in the series, the individual profiles are created from interviews, diaries, statistical studies, biographies and news reports. Profiles cover a broad range of ethnic backgrounds, geographic area and lifestyles – everything from an orphan in Memphis in 1882, following the Yellow Fever epidemic of 1878 to an eleven-year-old nephew of a beer baron and owner of the New York Yankees in New York City in 1921. Chapters also contain important supplementary materials including News Features as well as information on everything from Schools to Parks, Infectious Diseases to Childhood Fears along with Entertainment, Family Life and much more to provide an informative overview of the lifestyles of children from each decade. This interesting account of what life was like for Children in the Working, Middle and Upper Classes will be a welcome addition to the reference collection of any high school, public or academic library.

Hardcover ISBN 978-1-930956-35-3, 600 pages, $145.00 | Ebook ISBN 978-1-59237-166-2 www.greyhouse.com/ebooks.htm

Working Americans 1880-2003 Volume V: Americans At War

Working Americans 1880-2003 Volume V: Americans At War is divided into 11 chapters, each covering a decade from 1880-2003 and examines the lives of Americans during the time of war, including declared conflicts, one-time military actions, protests, and preparations for war. Each decade includes several personal profiles, whether on the battlefield or on the homefront, that tell the stories of civilians, soldiers, and officers during the decade. The profiles examine: Life at Home; Life at Work; and Life in the Community. Each decade also includes an Economic Profile with statistical comparisons, a Historical Snapshot, News Profiles, local News Articles, and Illustrations that provide a solid historical background to the decade being examined. Profiles range widely not only geographically, but also emotionally, from that of a girl whose leg was torn off in a blast during WWI, to the boredom of being stationed in the Dakotas as the Indian Wars were drawing to a close. As in previous volumes of the *Working Americans* series, information is presented in narrative form, but hard facts and real-life situations back up each story. The basis of the profiles come from diaries, private print books, personal interviews, family histories, estate documents and magazine articles. For easy reference, *Working Americans 1880-2003 Volume V: Americans At War* includes an in-depth Subject Index. The Working Americans series has become an important reference for public libraries, academic libraries and high school libraries. This fifth volume will be a welcome addition to all of these types of reference collections.

Hardcover ISBN 978-1-59237-024-5, 600 pages, $145.00 | Ebook ISBN 978-1-59237-167-9 www.greyhouse.com/ebooks.htm

Working Americans 1880-2005 Volume VI: Women at Work

Unlike any other volume in the *Working Americans* series, this Sixth Volume, is the first to focus on a particular gender of Americans. *Volume VI: Women at Work*, traces what life was like for working women from the 1860's to the present time. Beginning with the life of a maid in 1890 and a store clerk in 1900 and ending with the life and times of the modern working women, this text captures the struggle, strengths and changing perception of the American woman at work. Each chapter focuses on one decade and profiles three to five women with real data on Income & Job Descriptions, Selected Prices of the Times, Annual Income, Annual Budgets, Family Finances, Life at Work, Life at Home, Life in the Community, Working Conditions, Cost of Living, Amusements and much more. For even broader access to the events, economics and attitude towards women throughout the past 130 years, each chapter is supplemented with News Profiles, Articles from Local Media, Illustrations, Economic Profiles, Typical Pricing, Key Events, Inventions and more. This important volume illustrates what life was like for working women over time and allows the reader to develop an understanding of the changing role of women at work. These interesting and useful compilations of portraits of women at work will be an important addition to any high school, public or academic library reference collection.

Hardcover ISBN 978-1-59237-063-4, 600 pages, $145.00 | Ebook ISBN 978-1-59237-168-6 www.greyhouse.com/ebooks.htm

Working Americans 1880-2005 Volume VII: Social Movements

Working Americans series, Volume VII: Social Movements explores how Americans sought and fought for change from the 1880s to the present time. Following the format of previous volumes in the Working Americans series, the text examines the lives of 34 individuals who have worked -- often behind the scenes --- to bring about change. Issues include topics as diverse as the Anti-smoking movement of 1901 to efforts by Native Americans to reassert their long lost rights. Along the way, the book will profile individuals brave enough to demand suffrage for Kansas women in 1912 or demand an end to lynching during a March on Washington in 1923. Each profile is enriched with real data on Income & Job Descriptions, Selected Prices of the Times, Annual Incomes & Budgets, Life at Work, Life at Home, Life in the Community, along with News Features, Key Events, and Illustrations. The depth of information contained in each profile allow the user to explore the private, financial and public lives of these subjects, deepening our understanding of how calls for change took place in our society. A must-purchase for the reference collections of high school libraries, public libraries and academic libraries.

Hardcover ISBN 978-1-59237-101-3, 600 pages, $145.00 | Ebook ISBN 978-1-59237-174-7 www.gale.com/gvrl/partners/grey.htm

Working Americans 1880-2005 Volume VIII: Immigrants

Working Americans 1880-2007 Volume VIII: Immigrants illustrates what life was like for families leaving their homeland and creating a new life in the United States. Each chapter covers one decade and introduces the reader to three immigrant families. Family profiles cover what life was like in their homeland, in their community in the United States, their home life, working conditions and so much more. As the reader moves through these pages, the families and individuals come to life, painting a picture of why they left their homeland, their experiences in setting roots in a new country, their struggles and triumphs, stretching from the 1800s to the present time. Profiles include a seven-year-old Swedish girl who meets her father for the first time at Ellis Island; a Chinese photographer's assistant; an Armenian who flees the genocide of his country to build Ford automobiles in Detroit; a 38-year-old German bachelor cigar maker who settles in Newark NJ, but contemplates tobacco farming in Virginia; a 19-year-old Irish domestic servant who is amazed at the easy life of American dogs; a 19-year-old Filipino who came to Hawaii against his parent's wishes to farm sugar cane; a French-Canadian who finds success as a boxer in Maine and many more. As in previous volumes, information is presented in narrative form, but hard facts and real-life situations back up each story. With the topic of immigration being so hotly debated in this country, this timely resource will prove to be a useful source for students, researchers, historians and library patrons to discover the issues facing immigrants in the United States. This title will be a useful addition to reference collections of public libraries, university libraries and high schools.

Hardcover ISBN 978-1-59237-197-6, 600 pages, $145.00 | Ebook ISBN 978-1-59237-232-4 www.greyhouse.com/ebooks.htm

Working Americans 1770-1896 Volume IX: From the Revolutionary War to the Civil War

Working Americans 1770-1869: From the Revolutionary War to the Civil War examines what life was like for the earliest of Americans. Like previous volumes in the successful Working Americans series, each chapter introduces the reader to three individuals or families. These profiles illustrate what life was like for that individual, at home, in the community and at work. The profiles are supplemented with information on current events, community issues, pricing of the times and news articles to give the reader a broader understanding of what was happening in that individual's world and how it shaped their life. Profiles extend through all walks of life, from farmers to merchants, the rich and poor, men, women and children. In these information-packed, fun-to-explore pages, the reader will be introduced to Ezra Stiles, a preacher and college president from 1776; Colonel Israel Angell, a continental officer from 1778; Thomas Vernon, a loyalist in 1776, Anna Green Winslow, a school girl in 1771; Sarah Pierce, a school teacher in 1792; Edward Hooker, an attorney in 1805; Jeremiah Greenman, a common soldier in 1775 and many others. Using these informationfilled profiles, the reader can develop an understanding of what life was like for all types of Americans in these interesting and changing times. This new edition will be an important acquisition for high school, public and academic libraries as well as history reference collections.

Hardcover ISBN 978-1-59237-371-0, 660 pages, $145.00

The Encyclopedia of Warrior Peoples & Fighting Groups

Many military groups throughout the world have excelled in their craft either by fortuitous circumstances, outstanding leadership, or intense training. This new second edition of *The Encyclopedia of Warrior Peoples and Fighting Groups* explores the origins and leadership of these outstanding combat forces, chronicles their conquests and accomplishments, examines the circumstances surrounding their decline or disbanding, and assesses their influence on the groups and methods of warfare that followed. Readers will encounter ferocious tribes, charismatic leaders, and daring militias, from ancient times to the present, including Amazons, Buffalo Soldiers, Green Berets, Iron Brigade, Kamikazes, Peoples of the Sea, Polish Winged Hussars, Teutonic Knights, and Texas Rangers. With over 100 alphabetical entries, numerous cross-references and illustrations, a comprehensive bibliography, and index, the *Encyclopedia of Warrior Peoples and Fighting Groups* is a valuable resource for readers seeking insight into the bold history of distinguished fighting forces.

"Especially useful for high school students, undergraduates, and general readers with an interest in military history." –Library Journal

Hardcover ISBN 978-1-59237-116-7, 660 pages, $135.00 | Ebook ISBN 978-1-59237-172-3 www.greyhouse.com/ebooks.htm

The Encyclopedia of Invasions & Conquests, From the Ancient Times to the Present

This second edition of the popular *Encyclopedia of Invasions & Conquests*, a comprehensive guide to over 150 invasions, conquests, battles and occupations from ancient times to the present, takes readers on a journey that includes the Roman conquest of Britain, the Portuguese colonization of Brazil, and the Iraqi invasion of Kuwait, to name a few. New articles will explore the late 20th and 21st centuries, with a specific focus on recent conflicts in Afghanistan, Kuwait, Iraq, Yugoslavia, Grenada and Chechnya. In addition to covering the military aspects of invasions and conquests, entries cover some of the political, economic, and cultural aspects, for example, the effects of a conquest on the invade country's political and monetary system and in its language and religion. The entries on leaders – among them Sargon, Alexander the Great, William the Conqueror, and Adolf Hitler – deal with the people who sought to gain control, expand power, or exert religious or political influence over others through military means. Revised and updated for this second edition, entries are arranged alphabetically within historical periods. Each chapter provides a map to help readers locate key areas and geographical features, and bibliographical references appear at the end of each entry. Other useful features include cross-references, a cumulative bibliography and a comprehensive subject index. This authoritative, well-organized, lucidly written volume will prove invaluable for a variety of readers, including high school students, military historians, members of the armed forces, history buffs and hobbyists.

"Engaging writing, sensible organization, nice illustrations, interesting and obscure facts, and useful maps make this book a pleasure to read." –ARBA

Hardcover ISBN 978-1-59237-114-3, 598 pages, $135.00 | Ebook ISBN 978-1-59237-171-6 www.gale.com/gvrl/partners/grey.htm

Encyclopedia of Prisoners of War & Internment

This authoritative second edition provides a valuable overview of the history of prisoners of war and interned civilians, from earliest times to the present. Written by an international team of experts in the field of POW studies, this fascinating and thought-provoking volume includes entries on a wide range of subjects including the Crusades, Plains Indian Warfare, concentration camps, the two world wars, and famous POWs throughout history, as well as atrocities, escapes, and much more. Written in a clear and easily understandable style, this informative reference details over 350 entries, 30% larger than the first edition, that survey the history of prisoners of war and interned civilians from the earliest times to the present, with emphasis on the 19th and 20th centuries. Medical conditions, international law, exchanges of prisoners, organizations working on behalf of POWs, and trials associated with the treatment of captives are just some of the themes explored. Entries are arranged alphabetically, plus illustrations and maps are provided for easy reference. The text also includes an introduction, bibliography, appendix of selected documents, and end-of-entry reading suggestions. This one-of-a-kind reference will be a helpful addition to the reference collections of all public libraries, high schools, and university libraries and will prove invaluable to historians and military enthusiasts.

"Thorough and detailed yet accessible to the lay reader. Of special interest to subject specialists and historians; recommended for public and academic libraries." - Library Journal

Hardcover ISBN 978-1-59237-120-4, 676 pages, $135.00 | Ebook ISBN 978-1-59237-170-9 www.greyhouse.com/ebooks.htm

The Encyclopedia of Rural America: the Land & People

History, sociology, anthropology, and public policy are combined to deliver the encyclopedia destined to become the standard reference work in American rural studies. From irrigation and marriage to games and mental health, this encyclopedia is the first to explore the contemporary landscape of rural America, placed in historical perspective. With over 300 articles prepared by leading experts from across the nation, this timely encyclopedia documents and explains the major themes, concepts, industries, concerns, and everyday life of the people and land who make up rural America. Entries range from the industrial sector and government policy to arts and humanities and social and family concerns. Articles explore every aspect of life in rural America. *Encyclopedia of Rural America*, with its broad range of coverage, will appeal to high school and college students as well as graduate students, faculty, scholars, and people whose work pertains to rural areas.

"This exemplary encyclopedia is guaranteed to educate our highly urban society about the uniqueness of rural America. Recommended for public and academic libraries." -Library Journal

Two Volumes, Hardcover, ISBN 978-1-59237-115-0, 800 pages, $250.00

The Religious Right, A Reference Handbook

Timely and unbiased, this third edition updates and expands its examination of the religious right and its influence on our government, citizens, society, and politics. From the fight to outlaw the teaching of Darwin's theory of evolution to the struggle to outlaw abortion, the religious right is continually exerting an influence on public policy. This text explores the influence of religion on legislation and society, while examining the alignment of the religious right with the political right. A historical survey of the movement highlights the shift to "hands-on" approach to politics and the struggle to present a unified front. The coverage offers a critical historical survey of the religious right movement, focusing on its increased involvement in the political arena, attempts to forge coalitions, and notable successes and failures. The text offers complete coverage of biographies of the men and women who have advanced the cause and an up to date chronology illuminate the movement's goals, including their accomplishments and failures. This edition offers an extensive update to all sections along with several brand new entries. Two new sections complement this third edition, a chapter on legal issues and court decisions and a chapter on demographic statistics and electoral patterns. To aid in further research, *The Religious Right*, offers an entire section of annotated listings of print and non-print resources, as well as of organizations affiliated with the religious right, and those opposing it. Comprehensive in its scope, this work offers easy-to-read, pertinent information for those seeking to understand the religious right and its evolving role in American society. A must for libraries of all sizes, university religion departments, activists, high schools and for those interested in the evolving role of the religious right.

" Recommended for all public and academic libraries." - Library Journal

Hardcover ISBN 978-1-59237-113-6, 600 pages, $135.00 | Ebook ISBN 978-1-59237-226-3 www.greyhouse.com/ebooks.htm

From Suffrage to the Senate, America's Political Women

From Suffrage to the Senate is a comprehensive and valuable compendium of biographies of leading women in U.S. politics, past and present, and an examination of the wide range of women's movements. Up to date through 2006, this dynamically illustrated reference work explores American women's path to political power and social equality from the struggle for the right to vote and the abolition of slavery to the first African American woman in the U.S. Senate and beyond. This new edition includes over 150 new entries and a brand new section on trends and demographics of women in politics. The in-depth coverage also traces the political heritage of the abolition, labor, suffrage, temperance, and reproductive rights movements. The alphabetically arranged entries include biographies of every woman from across the political spectrum who has served in the U.S. House and Senate, along with women in the Judiciary and the U.S. Cabinet and, new to this edition, biographies of activists and political consultants. Bibliographical references follow each entry. For easy reference, a handy chronology is provided detailing 150 years of women's history. This up-to-date reference will be a must-purchase for women's studies departments, high schools and public libraries and will be a handy resource for those researching the key players in women's politics, past and present.

"An engaging tool that would be useful in high school, public, and academic libraries looking for an overview of the political history of women in the US." –Booklist

Two Volumes, Hardcover ISBN 978-1-59237-117-4, 1,160 pages, $195.00 | Ebook ISBN 978-1-59237-227-0
www.gale.com/gvrl/partners/grey.htm

An African Biographical Dictionary

This landmark second edition is the only biographical dictionary to bring together, in one volume, cultural, social and political leaders – both historical and contemporary – of the sub-Saharan region. Over 800 biographical sketches of prominent Africans, as well as foreigners who have affected the continent's history, are featured, 150 more than the previous edition. The wide spectrum of leaders includes religious figures, writers, politicians, scientists, entertainers, sports personalities and more. Access to these fascinating individuals is provided in a user-friendly format. The biographies are arranged alphabetically, cross-referenced and indexed. Entries include the country or countries in which the person was significant and the commonly accepted dates of birth and death. Each biographical sketch is chronologically written; entries for cultural personalities add an evaluation of their work. This information is followed by a selection of references often found in university and public libraries, including autobiographies and principal biographical works. Appendixes list each individual by country and by field of accomplishment – rulers, musicians, explorers, missionaries, businessmen, physicists – nearly thirty categories in all. Another convenient appendix lists heads of state since independence by country. Up-to-date and representative of African societies as a whole, An African Biographical Dictionary provides a wealth of vital information for students of African culture and is an indispensable reference guide for anyone interested in African affairs.

"An unquestionable convenience to have these concise, informative biographies gathered into one source, indexed, and analyzed by appendixes listing entrants by nation and occupational field." –Wilson Library Bulletin

Hardcover ISBN 978-1-59237-112-9, 667 pages, $135.00 | Ebook ISBN 978-1-59237-229-4 www.greyhouse.com/ebooks.htm

American Environmental Leaders, From Colonial Times to the Present

A comprehensive and diverse award winning collection of biographies of the most important figures in American environmentalism. Few subjects arouse the passions the way the environment does. How will we feed an ever-increasing population and how can that food be made safe for consumption? Who decides how land is developed? How can environmental policies be made fair for everyone, including multiethnic groups, women, children, and the poor? *American Environmental Leaders* presents more than 350 biographies of men and women who have devoted their lives to studying, debating, and organizing these and other controversial issues over the last 200 years. In addition to the scientists who have analyzed how human actions affect nature, we are introduced to poets, landscape architects, presidents, painters, activists, even sanitation engineers, and others who have forever altered how we think about the environment. The easy to use A–Z format provides instant access to these fascinating individuals, and frequent cross references indicate others with whom individuals worked (and sometimes clashed). End of entry references provide users with a starting point for further research.

"Highly recommended for high school, academic, and public libraries needing environmental biographical information." –Library Journal/Starred Review

Two Volumes, Hardcover ISBN 978-1-59237-119-8, 900 pages $195.00 | Ebook ISBN 978-1-59237-230-0
www.greyhouse.com/ebooks.htm

World Cultural Leaders of the Twentieth & Twenty-First Centuries

World Cultural Leaders of the Twentieth & Twenty-First Centuries is a window into the arts, performances, movements, and music that shaped the world's cultural development since 1900. A remarkable around-the-world look at one-hundred-plus years of cultural development through the eyes of those that set the stage and stayed to play. This second edition offers over 120 new biographies along with a complete update of existing biographies. To further aid the reader, a handy fold-out timeline traces important events in all six cultural categories from 1900 through the present time. Plus, a new section of detailed material and resources for 100 selected individuals is also new to this edition, with further data on museums, homesteads, websites, artwork and more. This remarkable compilation will answer a wide range of questions. Who was the originator of the term "documentary"? Which poet married the daughter of the famed novelist Thomas Mann in order to help her escape Nazi Germany? Which British writer served as an agent in Russia against the Bolsheviks before the 1917 revolution? A handy two-volume set that makes it easy to look up 450 worldwide cultural icons: novelists, poets, playwrights, painters, sculptors, architects, dancers, choreographers, actors, directors, filmmakers, singers, composers, and musicians. *World Cultural Leaders of the Twentieth & Twenty-First Centuries* provides entries (many of them illustrated) covering the person's works, achievements, and professional career in a thorough essay and offers interesting facts and statistics. Entries are fully cross-referenced so that readers can learn how various individuals influenced others. An index of leaders by occupation, a useful glossary and a thorough general index complete the coverage. This remarkable resource will be an important acquisition for the reference collections of public libraries, university libraries and high schools.

"Fills a need for handy, concise information on a wide array of international cultural figures."-ARBA

Two Volumes, Hardcover ISBN 978-1-59237-118-1, 900 pages, $195.00 | Ebook ISBN 978-1-59237-231-7
www.greyhouse.com/ebooks.htm

Political Corruption in America: An Encyclopedia of Scandals, Power, and Greed

The complete scandal-filled history of American political corruption, focusing on the infamous people and cases, as well as society's electoral and judicial reactions. Since colonial times, there has been no shortage of politicians willing to take a bribe, skirt campaign finance laws, or act in their own interests. Corruption like the Whiskey Ring, Watergate, and Whitewater cases dominate American life, making political scandal a leading U.S. industry. From judges to senators, presidents to mayors, *Political Corruption in America* discusses the infamous people throughout history who have been accused of and implicated in crooked behavior. In this new second edition, more than 250 A–Z entries explore the people, crimes, investigations, and court cases behind 200 years of American political scandals. This unbiased volume also delves into the issues surrounding Koreagate, the Chinese campaign scandal, and other ethical lapses. Relevant statutes and terms, including the Independent Counsel Statute and impeachment as a tool of political punishment, are examined as well. Students, scholars, and other readers interested in American history, political science, and ethics will appreciate this survey of a wide range of corrupting influences. This title focuses on how politicians from all parties have fallen because of their greed and hubris, and how society has used electoral and judicial means against those who tested the accepted standards of political conduct. A full range of illustrations including political cartoons, photos of key figures such as Abe Fortas and Archibald Cox, graphs of presidential pardons, and tables showing the number of expulsions and censures in both the House and Senate round out the text. In addition, a comprehensive chronology of major political scandals in U.S. history from colonial times until the present. For further reading, an extensive bibliography lists sources including archival letters, newspapers, and private manuscript collections from the United States and Great Britain. With its comprehensive coverage of this interesting topic, *Political Corruption in America: An Encyclopedia of Scandals, Power, and Greed* will prove to be a useful addition to the reference collections of all public libraries, university libraries, history collections, political science collections and high schools.

"...this encyclopedia is a useful contribution to the field. Highly recommended." - CHOICE
"Political Corruption should be useful in most academic, high school, and public libraries." Booklist

Two Volumes, Hardcover ISBN 978-1-59237-297-3, 500 pages, $195.00 | Ebook ISBN 978-1-59237-308-6
www.greyhouse.com/ebooks.htm

Religion and Law: A Dictionary

This informative, easy-to-use reference work covers a wide range of legal issues that affect the roles of religion and law in American society. Extensive A–Z entries provide coverage of key court decisions, case studies, concepts, individuals, religious groups, organizations, and agencies shaping religion and law in today's society. This *Dictionary* focuses on topics involved with the constitutional theory and interpretation of religion and the law; terms providing a historical explanation of the ways in which America's ever increasing ethnic and religious diversity contributed to our current understanding of the mandates of the First and Fourteenth Amendments; terms and concepts describing the development of religion clause jurisprudence; an analytical examination of the distinct vocabulary used in this area of the law; the means by which American courts have attempted to balance religious liberty against other important individual and social interests in a wide variety of physical and regulatory environments, including the classroom, the workplace, the courtroom, religious group organization and structure, taxation, the clash of "secular" and "religious" values, and the relationship of the generalized idea of individual autonomy of the specific concept of religious liberty. Important legislation and legal cases affecting religion and society are thoroughly covered in this timely volume, including a detailed Table of Cases and Table of Statutes for more detailed research. A guide to further reading and an index are also included. This useful resource will be an important acquisition for the reference collections of all public libraries, university libraries, religion reference collections and high schools.

Two Volumes, Hardcover ISBN 978-1-59237-298-0, 500 pages, $195.00 | Ebook ISBN 978-1-59237-309-3
www.greyhouse.com/ebooks.htm

Human Rights in the United States: A Dictionary and Documents

This two volume set offers easy to grasp explanations of the basic concepts, laws, and case law in the field, with emphasis on human rights in the historical, political, and legal experience of the United States. Human rights is a term not fully understood by many Americans. Addressing this gap, the new second edition of *Human Rights in the United States: A Dictionary and Documents* offers a comprehensive introduction that places the history of human rights in the United States in an international context. It surveys the legal protection of human dignity in the United States, examines the sources of human rights norms, cites key legal cases, explains the role of international governmental and non-governmental organizations, and charts global, regional, and U.N. human rights measures. Over 240 dictionary entries of human rights terms are detailed—ranging from asylum and cultural relativism to hate crimes and torture. Each entry discusses the significance of the term, gives examples, and cites appropriate documents and court decisions. In addition, a Documents section is provided that contains 59 conventions, treaties, and protocols related to the most up to date international action on ethnic cleansing; freedom of expression and religion; violence against women; and much more. A bibliography, extensive glossary, and comprehensive index round out this indispensable volume. This comprehensive, timely volume is a must for large public libraries, university libraries and social science departments, along with high school libraries.

"...invaluable for anyone interested in human rights issues ... highly recommended for all reference collections."
- American Reference Books Annual

Two Volumes, Hardcover ISBN 978-1-59237-290-4, 750 pages, $225.00 | Ebook ISBN 978-1-59237-301-7
www.greyhouse.com/ebooks.htm

The Comparative Guide to American Elementary & Secondary Schools, 2008

The only guide of its kind, this award winning compilation offers a snapshot profile of every public school district in the United States serving 1,500 or more students – more than 5,900 districts are covered. Organized alphabetically by district within state, each chapter begins with a Statistical Overview of the state. Each district listing includes contact information (name, address, phone number and web site) plus Grades Served, the Numbers of Students and Teachers and the Number of Regular, Special Education, Alternative and Vocational Schools in the district along with statistics on Student/Classroom Teacher Ratios, Drop Out Rates, Ethnicity, the Numbers of Librarians and Guidance Counselors and District Expenditures per student. As an added bonus, *The Comparative Guide to American Elementary and Secondary Schools* provides important ranking tables, both by state and nationally, for each data element. For easy navigation through this wealth of information, this handbook contains a useful City Index that lists all districts that operate schools within a city. These important comparative statistics are necessary for anyone considering relocation or doing comparative research on their own district and would be a perfect acquisition for any public library or school district library.

"This straightforward guide is an easy way to find general information. Valuable for academic and large public library collections." –ARBA

Softcover ISBN 978-1-59237-223-2, 2,400 pages, $125.00 | Ebook ISBN 978-1-59237-238-6 www.greyhouse.com/ebooks.htm

The Complete Learning Disabilities Directory, 2009

The Complete Learning Disabilities Directory is the most comprehensive database of Programs, Services, Curriculum Materials, Professional Meetings & Resources, Camps, Newsletters and Support Groups for teachers, students and families concerned with learning disabilities. This information-packed directory includes information about Associations & Organizations, Schools, Colleges & Testing Materials, Government Agencies, Legal Resources and much more. For quick, easy access to information, this directory contains four indexes: Entry Name Index, Subject Index and Geographic Index. With every passing year, the field of learning disabilities attracts more attention and the network of caring, committed and knowledgeable professionals grows every day. This directory is an invaluable research tool for these parents, students and professionals.

"Due to its wealth and depth of coverage, parents, teachers and others... should find this an invaluable resource." -Booklist

Softcover ISBN 978-1-59237-368-0, 900 pages, $145.00 | Online Database $195.00 | Online Database & Directory Combo $280.00

Educators Resource Directory, 2007/08

Educators Resource Directory is a comprehensive resource that provides the educational professional with thousands of resources and statistical data for professional development. This directory saves hours of research time by providing immediate access to Associations & Organizations, Conferences & Trade Shows, Educational Research Centers, Employment Opportunities & Teaching Abroad, School Library Services, Scholarships, Financial Resources, Professional Consultants, Computer Software & Testing Resources and much more. Plus, this comprehensive directory also includes a section on Statistics and Rankings with over 100 tables, including statistics on Average Teacher Salaries, SAT/ACT scores, Revenues & Expenditures and more. These important statistics will allow the user to see how their school rates among others, make relocation decisions and so much more. For quick access to information, this directory contains four indexes: Entry & Publisher Index, Geographic Index, a Subject & Grade Index and Web Sites Index. *Educators Resource Directory* will be a well-used addition to the reference collection of any school district, education department or public library.

"Recommended for all collections that serve elementary and secondary school professionals." –Choice

Softcover ISBN 978-1-59237-179-2, 800 pages, $145.00 | Online Database $195.00 | Online Database & Directory Combo $280.00

Profiles of New York | Profiles of Florida | Profiles of Texas | Profiles of Illinois | Profiles of Michigan | Profiles of Ohio | Profiles of New Jersey | Profiles of Massachusetts | Profiles of Pennsylvania | Profiles of Wisconsin | Profiles of Connecticut & Rhode Island | Profiles of Indiana | Profiles of North Carolina & South Carolina | Profiles of Virginia | Profiles of California

The careful layout gives the user an easy-to-read snapshot of every single place and county in the state, from the biggest metropolis to the smallest unincorporated hamlet. The richness of each place or county profile is astounding in its depth, from history to weather, all packed in an easy-to-navigate, compact format. Each profile contains data on History, Geography, Climate, Population, Vital Statistics, Economy, Income, Taxes, Education, Housing, Health & Environment, Public Safety, Newspapers, Transportation, Presidential Election Results, Information Contacts and Chambers of Commerce. As an added bonus, there is a section on Selected Statistics, where data from the 100 largest towns and cities is arranged into easy-to-use charts. Each of 22 different data points has its own two-page spread with the cities listed in alpha order so researchers can easily compare and rank cities. A remarkable compilation that offers overviews and insights into each corner of the state, each volume goes beyond Census statistics, beyond metro area coverage, beyond the 100 best places to live. Drawn from official census information, other government statistics and original research, you will have at your fingertips data that's available nowhere else in one single source.

"The publisher claims that this is the 'most comprehensive portrait of the state of Florida ever published,' and this reviewer is inclined to believe it...Recommended. All levels." –Choice on Profiles of Florida

Each Profiles of... title ranges from 400-800 pages, priced at $149.00 each

America's Top-Rated Cities, 2008

America's Top-Rated Cities provides current, comprehensive statistical information and other essential data in one easy-to-use source on the 100 "top" cities that have been cited as the best for business and living in the U.S. This handbook allows readers to see, at a glance, a concise social, business, economic, demographic and environmental profile of each city, including brief evaluative comments. In addition to detailed data on Cost of Living, Finances, Real Estate, Education, Major Employers, Media, Crime and Climate, city reports now include Housing Vacancies, Tax Audits, Bankruptcy, Presidential Election Results and more. This outstanding source of information will be widely used in any reference collection.

"The only source of its kind that brings together all of this information into one easy-to-use source. It will be beneficial to many business and public libraries." –ARBA

Four Volumes, Softcover ISBN 978-1-59237-349-9, 2,500 pages, $195.00 | Ebook ISBN 978-1-59237-233-1
www.greyhouse.com/ebooks.htm

America's Top-Rated Smaller Cities, 2008/09

A perfect companion to *America's Top-Rated Cities, America's Top-Rated Smaller Cities* provides current, comprehensive business and living profiles of smaller cities (population 25,000-99,999) that have been cited as the best for business and living in the United States. Sixty cities make up this 2004 edition of America's Top-Rated Smaller Cities, all are top-ranked by Population Growth, Median Income, Unemployment Rate and Crime Rate. City reports reflect the most current data available on a wide-range of statistics, including Employment & Earnings, Household Income, Unemployment Rate, Population Characteristics, Taxes, Cost of Living, Education, Health Care, Public Safety, Recreation, Media, Air & Water Quality and much more. Plus, each city report contains a Background of the City, and an Overview of the State Finances. *America's Top-Rated Smaller Cities* offers a reliable, one-stop source for statistical data that, before now, could only be found scattered in hundreds of sources. This volume is designed for a wide range of readers: individuals considering relocating a residence or business; professionals considering expanding their business or changing careers; general and market researchers; real estate consultants; human resource personnel; urban planners and investors.

"Provides current, comprehensive statistical information in one easy-to-use source... Recommended for public and academic libraries and specialized collections." –Library Journal

Two Volumes, Softcover ISBN 978-1-59237-284-3, 1,100 pages, $195.00 | Ebook ISBN 978-1-59237-234-8
www.greyhouse.com/ebooks.htm

Profiles of America: Facts, Figures & Statistics for Every Populated Place in the United States

Profiles of America is the only source that pulls together, in one place, statistical, historical and descriptive information about every place in the United States in an easy-to-use format. This award winning reference set, now in its second edition, compiles statistics and data from over 20 different sources – the latest census information has been included along with more than nine brand new statistical topics. This Four-Volume Set details over 40,000 places, from the biggest metropolis to the smallest unincorporated hamlet, and provides statistical details and information on over 50 different topics including Geography, Climate, Population, Vital Statistics, Economy, Income, Taxes, Education, Housing, Health & Environment, Public Safety, Newspapers, Transportation, Presidential Election Results and Information Contacts or Chambers of Commerce. Profiles are arranged, for ease-of-use, by state and then by county. Each county begins with a County-Wide Overview and is followed by information for each Community in that particular county. The Community Profiles within the county are arranged alphabetically. *Profiles of America* is a virtual snapshot of America at your fingertips and a unique compilation of information that will be widely used in any reference collection.

A Library Journal Best Reference Book "An outstanding compilation." –Library Journal

Four Volumes, Softcover ISBN 978-1-891482-80-9, 10,000 pages, $595.00

The Comparative Guide to American Suburbs, 2007/08

The Comparative Guide to American Suburbs is a one-stop source for Statistics on the 2,000+ suburban communities surrounding the 50 largest metropolitan areas – their population characteristics, income levels, economy, school system and important data on how they compare to one another. Organized into 50 Metropolitan Area chapters, each chapter contains an overview of the Metropolitan Area, a detailed Map followed by a comprehensive Statistical Profile of each Suburban Community, including Contact Information, Physical Characteristics, Population Characteristics, Income, Economy, Unemployment Rate, Cost of Living, Education, Chambers of Commerce and more. Next, statistical data is sorted into Ranking Tables that rank the suburbs by twenty different criteria, including Population, Per Capita Income, Unemployment Rate, Crime Rate, Cost of Living and more. *The Comparative Guide to American Suburbs* is the best source for locating data on suburbs. Those looking to relocate, as well as those doing preliminary market research, will find this an invaluable timesaving resource.

"Public and academic libraries will find this compilation useful...The work draws together figures from many sources and will be especially helpful for job relocation decisions." – Booklist

Softcover ISBN 978-1-59237-180-8, 1,700 pages, $130.00 | Ebook ISBN 978-1-59237-235-5 www.greyhouse.com/ebooks.htm

The American Tally: Statistics & Comparative Rankings for U.S. Cities with Populations over 10,000

This important statistical handbook compiles, all in one place, comparative statistics on all U.S. cities and towns with a 10,000+ population. *The American Tally* provides statistical details on over 4,000 cities and towns and profiles how they compare with one another in Population Characteristics, Education, Language & Immigration, Income & Employment and Housing. Each section begins with an alphabetical listing of cities by state, allowing for quick access to both the statistics and relative rankings of any city. Next, the highest and lowest cities are listed in each statistic. These important, informative lists provide quick reference to which cities are at both extremes of the spectrum for each statistic. Unlike any other reference, *The American Tally* provides quick, easy access to comparative statistics – a must-have for any reference collection.

"A solid library reference." -Bookwatch

Softcover ISBN 978-1-930956-29-2, 500 pages, $125.00 | Ebook ISBN 978-1-59237-241-6 www.greyhouse.com/ebooks.htm

The Asian Databook: Statistics for all US Counties & Cities with Over 10,000 Population

This is the first-ever resource that compiles statistics and rankings on the US Asian population. *The Asian Databook* presents over 20 statistical data points for each city and county, arranged alphabetically by state, then alphabetically by place name. Data reported for each place includes Population, Languages Spoken at Home, Foreign-Born, Educational Attainment, Income Figures, Poverty Status, Homeownership, Home Values & Rent, and more. Next, in the Rankings Section, the top 75 places are listed for each data element. These easy-to-access ranking tables allow the user to quickly determine trends and population characteristics. This kind of comparative data can not be found elsewhere, in print or on the web, in a format that's as easy-to-use or more concise. A useful resource for those searching for demographics data, career search and relocation information and also for market research. With data ranging from Ancestry to Education, *The Asian Databook* presents a useful compilation of information that will be a much-needed resource in the reference collection of any public or academic library along with the marketing collection of any company whose primary focus in on the Asian population.

"This useful resource will help those searching for demographics data, and market research or relocation information... Accurate and clearly laid out, the publication is recommended for large public library and research collections." -Booklist

Softcover ISBN 978-1-59237-044-3, 1,000 pages, $150.00

The Hispanic Databook: Statistics for all US Counties & Cities with Over 10,000 Population

Previously published by Toucan Valley Publications, this second edition has been completely updated with figures from the latest census and has been broadly expanded to include dozens of new data elements and a brand new Rankings section. The Hispanic population in the United States has increased over 42% in the last 10 years and accounts for 12.5% of the total US population. For ease-of-use, *The Hispanic Databook* presents over 20 statistical data points for each city and county, arranged alphabetically by state, then alphabetically by place name. Data reported for each place includes Population, Languages Spoken at Home, Foreign-Born, Educational Attainment, Income Figures, Poverty Status, Homeownership, Home Values & Rent, and more. Next, in the Rankings Section, the top 75 places are listed for each data element. These easy-to-access ranking tables allow the user to quickly determine trends and population characteristics. This kind of comparative data can not be found elsewhere, in print or on the web, in a format that's as easy-to-use or more concise. A useful resource for those searching for demographics data, career search and relocation information and also for market research. With data ranging from Ancestry to Education, *The Hispanic Databook* presents a useful compilation of information that will be a much-needed resource in the reference collection of any public or academic library along with the marketing collection of any company whose primary focus in on the Hispanic population.

"This accurate, clearly presented volume of selected Hispanic demographics is recommended for large public libraries and research collections."-Library Journal

Softcover ISBN 978-1-59237-008-5, 1,000 pages, $150.00

Ancestry in America: A Comparative Guide to Over 200 Ethnic Backgrounds

This brand new reference work pulls together thousands of comparative statistics on the Ethnic Backgrounds of all populated places in the United States with populations over 10,000. Never before has this kind of information been reported in a single volume. Section One, Statistics by Place, is made up of a list of over 200 ancestry and race categories arranged alphabetically by each of the 5,000 different places with populations over 10,000. The population number of the ancestry group in that city or town is provided along with the percent that group represents of the total population. This informative city-by-city section allows the user to quickly and easily explore the ethnic makeup of all major population bases in the United States. Section Two, Comparative Rankings, contains three tables for each ethnicity and race. In the first table, the top 150 populated places are ranked by population number for that particular ancestry group, regardless of population. In the second table, the top 150 populated places are ranked by the percent of the total population for that ancestry group. In the third table, those top 150 populated places with 10,000 population are ranked by population number for each ancestry group. These easy-to-navigate tables allow users to see ancestry population patterns and make city-by-city comparisons as well. This brand new, information-packed resource will serve a wide-range or research requests for demographics, population characteristics, relocation information and much more. *Ancestry in America: A Comparative Guide to Over 200 Ethnic Backgrounds* will be an important acquisition to all reference collections.

"This compilation will serve a wide range of research requests for population characteristics … it offers much more detail than other sources." –Booklist

Softcover ISBN 978-1-59237-029-0, 1,500 pages, $225.00

Weather America, A Thirty-Year Summary of Statistical Weather Data and Rankings

This valuable resource provides extensive climatological data for over 4,000 National and Cooperative Weather Stations throughout the United States. Weather America begins with a new Major Storms section that details major storm events of the nation and a National Rankings section that details rankings for several data elements, such as Maximum Temperature and Precipitation. The main body of Weather America is organized into 50 state sections. Each section provides a Data Table on each Weather Station, organized alphabetically, that provides statistics on Maximum and Minimum Temperatures, Precipitation, Snowfall, Extreme Temperatures, Foggy Days, Humidity and more. State sections contain two brand new features in this edition – a City Index and a narrative Description of the climatic conditions of the state. Each section also includes a revised Map of the State that includes not only weather stations, but cities and towns.

"Best Reference Book of the Year." –Library Journal

Softcover ISBN 978-1-891482-29-8, 2,013 pages, $175.00 | Ebook ISBN 978-1-59237-237-9 www.greyhouse.com/ebooks.htm

Crime in America's Top-Rated Cities

This volume includes over 20 years of crime statistics in all major crime categories: violent crimes, property crimes and total crime. *Crime in America's Top-Rated Cities* is conveniently arranged by city and covers 76 top-rated cities. Crime in America's Top-Rated Cities offers details that compare the number of crimes and crime rates for the city, suburbs and metro area along with national crime trends for violent, property and total crimes. Also, this handbook contains important information and statistics on Anti-Crime Programs, Crime Risk, Hate Crimes, Illegal Drugs, Law Enforcement, Correctional Facilities, Death Penalty Laws and much more. A much-needed resource for people who are relocating, business professionals, general researchers, the press, law enforcement officials and students of criminal justice.

"Data is easy to access and will save hours of searching." –Global Enforcement Review

Softcover ISBN 978-1-891482-84-7, 832 pages, $155.00

The Complete Directory for People with Disabilities, 2009

A wealth of information, now in one comprehensive sourcebook. Completely updated, this edition contains more information than ever before, including thousands of new entries and enhancements to existing entries and thousands of additional web sites and e-mail addresses. This up-to-date directory is the most comprehensive resource available for people with disabilities, detailing Independent Living Centers, Rehabilitation Facilities, State & Federal Agencies, Associations, Support Groups, Periodicals & Books, Assistive Devices, Employment & Education Programs, Camps and Travel Groups. Each year, more libraries, schools, colleges, hospitals, rehabilitation centers and individuals add *The Complete Directory for People with Disabilities* to their collections, making sure that this information is readily available to the families, individuals and professionals who can benefit most from the amazing wealth of resources cataloged here.

"No other reference tool exists to meet the special needs of the disabled in one convenient resource for information." –Library Journal

Softcover ISBN 978-1-59237-367-3, 1,200 pages, $165.00 | Online Database: http://gold.greyhouse.com Call (800) 562-2139 for quote

The Complete Learning Disabilities Directory, 2009

The Complete Learning Disabilities Directory is the most comprehensive database of Programs, Services, Curriculum Materials, Professional Meetings & Resources, Camps, Newsletters and Support Groups for teachers, students and families concerned with learning disabilities. This information-packed directory includes information about Associations & Organizations, Schools, Colleges & Testing Materials, Government Agencies, Legal Resources and much more. For quick, easy access to information, this directory contains four indexes: Entry Name Index, Subject Index and Geographic Index. With every passing year, the field of learning disabilities attracts more attention and the network of caring, committed and knowledgeable professionals grows every day. This directory is an invaluable research tool for these parents, students and professionals.

"Due to its wealth and depth of coverage, parents, teachers and others... should find this an invaluable resource." -Booklist

Softcover ISBN 978-1-59237-368-0, 900 pages, $145.00 | Online Database: http://gold.greyhouse.com Call (800) 562-2139 for quote

The Complete Directory for People with Chronic Illness, 2007/08

Thousands of hours of research have gone into this completely updated edition – several new chapters have been added along with thousands of new entries and enhancements to existing entries. Plus, each chronic illness chapter has been reviewed by a medical expert in the field. This widely-hailed directory is structured around the 90 most prevalent chronic illnesses – from Asthma to Cancer to Wilson's Disease – and provides a comprehensive overview of the support services and information resources available for people diagnosed with a chronic illness. Each chronic illness has its own chapter and contains a brief description in layman's language, followed by important resources for National & Local Organizations, State Agencies, Newsletters, Books & Periodicals, Libraries & Research Centers, Support Groups & Hotlines, Web Sites and much more. This directory is an important resource for health care professionals, the collections of hospital and health care libraries, as well as an invaluable tool for people with a chronic illness and their support network.

"A must purchase for all hospital and health care libraries and is strongly recommended for all public library reference departments." –ARBA

Softcover ISBN 978-1-59237-183-9, 1,200 pages, $165.00 | Online Database: http://gold.greyhouse.com Call (800) 562-2139 for quote

The Complete Mental Health Directory, 2008/09

This is the most comprehensive resource covering the field of behavioral health, with critical information for both the layman and the mental health professional. For the layman, this directory offers understandable descriptions of 25 Mental Health Disorders as well as detailed information on Associations, Media, Support Groups and Mental Health Facilities. For the professional, The Complete Mental Health Directory offers critical and comprehensive information on Managed Care Organizations, Information Systems, Government Agencies and Provider Organizations. This comprehensive volume of needed information will be widely used in any reference collection.

"... the strength of this directory is that it consolidates widely dispersed information into a single volume." –Booklist

Softcover ISBN 978-1-59237-285-0, 800 pages, $165.00 | Online Database: http://gold.greyhouse.com Call (800) 562-2139 for quote

The Comparative Guide to American Hospitals, Second Edition

This new second edition compares all of the nation's hospitals by 24 measures of quality in the treatment of heart attack, heart failure, pneumonia, and, new to this edition, surgical procedures and pregnancy care. Plus, this second edition is now available in regional volumes, to make locating information about hospitals in your area quicker and easier than ever before. The Comparative Guide to American Hospitals provides a snapshot profile of each of the nations 4,200+ hospitals. These informative profiles illustrate how the hospital rates when providing 24 different treatments within four broad categories: Heart Attack Care, Heart Failure Care, Surgical Infection Prevention (NEW), and Pregnancy Care measures (NEW). Each profile includes the raw percentage for that hospital, the state average, the US average and data on the top hospital. For easy access to contact information, each profile includes the hospital's address, phone and fax numbers, email and web addresses, type and accreditation along with 5 top key administrations. These profiles will allow the user to quickly identify the quality of the hospital and have the necessary information at their fingertips to make contact with that hospital. Most importantly, *The Comparative Guide to American Hospitals* provides easy-to-use Regional State by State Statistical Summary Tables for each of the data elements to allow the user to quickly locate hospitals with the best level of service. Plus, a new 30-Day Mortality Chart, Glossary of Terms and Regional Hospital Profile Index make this a must-have source. This new, expanded edition will be a must for the reference collection at all public, medical and academic libraries.

"These data will help those with heart conditions and pneumonia make informed decisions about their healthcare and encourage hospitals to improve the quality of care they provide. Large medical, hospital, and public libraries are most likely to benefit from this weighty resource."-Library Journal

Four Volumes Softcover ISBN 978-1-59237-182-2, 3,500 pages, $325.00 | Regional Volumes $135.00 |
Ebook ISBN 978-1-59237-239-3 www.greyhouse.com/ebooks.htm

Older Americans Information Directory, 2008

Completely updated for 2008, this sixth edition has been completely revised and now contains 1,000 new listings, over 8,000 updates to existing listings and over 3,000 brand new e-mail addresses and web sites. You'll find important resources for Older Americans including National, Regional, State & Local Organizations, Government Agencies, Research Centers, Libraries & Information Centers, Legal Resources, Discount Travel Information, Continuing Education Programs, Disability Aids & Assistive Devices, Health, Print Media and Electronic Media. Three indexes: Entry Index, Subject Index and Geographic Index make it easy to find just the right source of information. This comprehensive guide to resources for Older Americans will be a welcome addition to any reference collection.

"Highly recommended for academic, public, health science and consumer libraries…" –Choice

1,200 pages; Softcover ISBN 978-1-59237-357-4, $165.00 | Online Database: http://gold.greyhouse.com Call (800) 562-2139 for quote

The Complete Directory for Pediatric Disorders, 2008

This important directory provides parents and caregivers with information about Pediatric Conditions, Disorders, Diseases and Disabilities, including Blood Disorders, Bone & Spinal Disorders, Brain Defects & Abnormalities, Chromosomal Disorders, Congenital Heart Defects, Movement Disorders, Neuromuscular Disorders and Pediatric Tumors & Cancers. This carefully written directory offers: understandable Descriptions of 15 major bodily systems; Descriptions of more than 200 Disorders and a Resources Section, detailing National Agencies & Associations, State Associations, Online Services, Libraries & Resource Centers, Research Centers, Support Groups & Hotlines, Camps, Books and Periodicals. This resource will provide immediate access to information crucial to families and caregivers when coping with children's illnesses.

"Recommended for public and consumer health libraries." –Library Journal

Softcover ISBN 978-1-59237-150-1, 1,200 pages, $165.00 | Online Database: http://gold.greyhouse.com Call (800) 562-2139 for quote

The Directory of Drug & Alcohol Residential Rehabilitation Facilities

This brand new directory is the first-ever resource to bring together, all in one place, data on the thousands of drug and alcohol residential rehabilitation facilities in the United States. The Directory of Drug & Alcohol Residential Rehabilitation Facilities covers over 1,000 facilities, with detailed contact information for each one, including mailing address, phone and fax numbers, email addresses and web sites, mission statement, type of treatment programs, cost, average length of stay, numbers of residents and counselors, accreditation, insurance plans accepted, type of environment, religious affiliation, education components and much more. It also contains a helpful chapter on General Resources that provides contact information for Associations, Print & Electronic Media, Support Groups and Conferences. Multiple indexes allow the user to pinpoint the facilities that meet very specific criteria. This time-saving tool is what so many counselors, parents and medical professionals have been asking for. *The Directory of Drug & Alcohol Residential Rehabilitation Facilities* will be a helpful tool in locating the right source for treatment for a wide range of individuals. This comprehensive directory will be an important acquisition for all reference collections: public and academic libraries, case managers, social workers, state agencies and many more.

"This is an excellent, much needed directory that fills an important gap…" –Booklist

Softcover ISBN 978-1-59237-031-3, 300 pages, $135.00

The Directory of Hospital Personnel, 2009

The Directory of Hospital Personnel is the best resource you can have at your fingertips when researching or marketing a product or service to the hospital market. A "Who's Who" of the hospital universe, this directory puts you in touch with over 150,000 key decision-makers. With 100% verification of data you can rest assured that you will reach the right person with just one call. Every hospital in the U.S. is profiled, listed alphabetically by city within state. Plus, three easy-to-use, cross-referenced indexes put the facts at your fingertips faster and more easily than any other directory: Hospital Name Index, Bed Size Index and Personnel Index. *The Directory of Hospital Personnel* is the only complete source for key hospital decision-makers by name. Whether you want to define or restructure sales territories... locate hospitals with the purchasing power to accept your proposals... keep track of important contacts or colleagues... or find information on which insurance plans are accepted, *The Directory of Hospital Personnel* gives you the information you need – easily, efficiently, effectively and accurately.

"Recommended for college, university and medical libraries." -ARBA

Softcover ISBN 978-1-59237-402-1, 2,500 pages, $325.00 | Online Database: http://gold.greyhouse.com Call (800) 562-2139 for quote

The HMO/PPO Directory, 2009

The HMO/PPO Directory is a comprehensive source that provides detailed information about Health Maintenance Organizations and Preferred Provider Organizations nationwide. This comprehensive directory details more information about more managed health care organizations than ever before. Over 1,100 HMOs, PPOs, Medicare Advantage Plans and affiliated companies are listed, arranged alphabetically by state. Detailed listings include Key Contact Information, Prescription Drug Benefits, Enrollment, Geographical Areas served, Affiliated Physicians & Hospitals, Federal Qualifications, Status, Year Founded, Managed Care Partners, Employer References, Fees & Payment Information and more. Plus, five years of historical information is included related to Revenues, Net Income, Medical Loss Ratios, Membership Enrollment and Number of Patient Complaints. Five easy-to-use, cross-referenced indexes will put this vast array of information at your fingertips immediately: HMO Index, PPO Index, Other Providers Index, Personnel Index and Enrollment Index. *The HMO/PPO Directory* provides the most comprehensive data on the most companies available on the market place today.

"Helpful to individuals requesting certain HMO/PPO issues such as co-payment costs, subscription costs and patient complaints. Individuals concerned (or those with questions) about their insurance may find this text to be of use to them." -ARBA

Softcover ISBN 978-1-59237-369-7, 600 pages, $325.00 | Online Database: http://gold.greyhouse.com Call (800) 562-2139 for quote

Medical Device Register, 2009

The only one-stop resource of every medical supplier licensed to sell products in the US. This award-winning directory offers immediate access to over 13,000 companies - and more than 65,000 products – in two information-packed volumes. This comprehensive resource saves hours of time and trouble when searching for medical equipment and supplies and the manufacturers who provide them. Volume I: The Product Directory, provides essential information for purchasing or specifying medical supplies for every medical device, supply, and diagnostic available in the US. Listings provide FDA codes & Federal Procurement Eligibility, Contact information for every manufacturer of the product along with Prices and Product Specifications. Volume 2 - Supplier Profiles, offers the most complete and important data about Suppliers, Manufacturers and Distributors. Company Profiles detail the number of employees, ownership, method of distribution, sales volume, net income, key executives detailed contact information medical products the company supplies, plus the medical specialties they cover. Four indexes provide immediate access to this wealth of information: Keyword Index, Trade Name Index, Supplier Geographical Index and OEM (Original Equipment Manufacturer) Index. *Medical Device Register* is the only one-stop source for locating suppliers and products; looking for new manufacturers or hard-to-find medical devices; comparing products and companies; know who's selling what and who to buy from cost effectively. This directory has become the standard in its field and will be a welcome addition to the reference collection of any medical library, large public library, university library along with the collections that serve the medical community.

"A wealth of information on medical devices, medical device companies... and key personnel in the industry is provide in this comprehensive reference work... A valuable reference work, one of the best hardcopy compilations available." -Doody Publishing

Two Volumes, Hardcover ISBN 978-1-59237-373-4, 3,000 pages, $325.00

The Directory of Health Care Group Purchasing Organizations, 2008

This comprehensive directory provides the important data you need to get in touch with over 800 Group Purchasing Organizations. By providing in-depth information on this growing market and its members, *The Directory of Health Care Group Purchasing Organizations* fills a major need for the most accurate and comprehensive information on over 800 GPOs – Mailing Address, Phone & Fax Numbers, E-mail Addresses, Key Contacts, Purchasing Agents, Group Descriptions, Membership Categorization, Standard Vendor Proposal Requirements, Membership Fees & Terms, Expanded Services, Total Member Beds & Outpatient Visits represented and more. Five Indexes provide a number of ways to locate the right GPO: Alphabetical Index, Expanded Services Index, Organization Type Index, Geographic Index and Member Institution Index. With its comprehensive and detailed information on each purchasing organization, *The Directory of Health Care Group Purchasing Organizations* is the go-to source for anyone looking to target this market.

"The information is clearly arranged and easy to access...recommended for those needing this very specialized information." –ARBA

1,000 pages; Softcover ISBN 978-1-59237-287-4, $325.00 | Online Database: http://gold.greyhouse.com Call (800) 562-2139 for quote

Canadian Almanac & Directory, 2009

The Canadian Almanac & Directory contains sixteen directories in one – giving you all the facts and figures you will ever need about Canada. No other single source provides users with the quality and depth of up-to-date information for all types of research. This national directory and guide gives you access to statistics, images and over 100,000 names and addresses for everything from Airlines to Zoos - updated every year. It's Ten Directories in One! Each section is a directory in itself, providing robust information on business and finance, communications, government, associations, arts and culture (museums, zoos, libraries, etc.), health, transportation, law, education, and more. Government information includes federal, provincial and territorial - and includes an easy-to-use quick index to find key information. A separate municipal government section includes every municipality in Canada, with full profiles of Canada's largest urban centers. A complete legal directory lists judges and judicial officials, court locations and law firms across the country. A wealth of general information, the *Canadian Almanac & Directory* also includes national statistics on population, employment, imports and exports, and more. National awards and honors are presented, along with forms of address, Commonwealth information and full color photos of Canadian symbols. Postal information, weights, measures, distances and other useful charts are also incorporated. Complete almanac information includes perpetual calendars, five-year holiday planners and astronomical information. Published continuously for 160 years, *The Canadian Almanac & Directory* is the best single reference source for business executives, managers and assistants; government and public affairs executives; lawyers; marketing, sales and advertising executives; researchers, editors and journalists.

Hardcover ISBN 978-1-59237-370-3, 1,600 pages, $325.00

Associations Canada, 2009

The Most Powerful Fact-Finder to Business, Trade, Professional and Consumer Organizations

Associations Canada covers Canadian organizations and international groups including industry, commercial and professional associations, registered charities, special interest and common interest organizations. This annually revised compendium provides detailed listings and abstracts for nearly 20,000 regional, national and international organizations. This popular volume provides the most comprehensive picture of Canada's non-profit sector. Detailed listings enable users to identify an organization's budget, founding date, scope of activity, licensing body, sources of funding, executive information, full address and complete contact information, just to name a few. Powerful indexes help researchers find information quickly and easily. The following indexes are included: subject, acronym, geographic, budget, executive name, conferences & conventions, mailing list, defunct and unreachable associations and registered charitable organizations. In addition to annual spending of over $1 billion on transportation and conventions alone, Canadian associations account for many millions more in pursuit of membership interests. *Associations Canada* provides complete access to this highly lucrative market. *Associations Canada* is a strong source of prospects for sales and marketing executives, tourism and convention officials, researchers, government officials - anyone who wants to locate non-profit interest groups and trade associations.

Hardcover ISBN 978-1-59237-401-4, 1,600 pages, $325.00

Financial Services Canada, 2008/09

Financial Services Canada is the only master file of current contacts and information that serves the needs of the entire financial services industry in Canada. With over 18,000 organizations and hard-to-find business information, Financial Services Canada is the most up-to-date source for names and contact numbers of industry professionals, senior executives, portfolio managers, financial advisors, agency bureaucrats and elected representatives. Financial Services Canada incorporates the latest changes in the industry to provide you with the most current details on each company, including: name, title, organization, telephone and fax numbers, e-mail and web addresses. *Financial Services Canada* also includes private company listings never before compiled, government agencies, association and consultant services - to ensure that you'll never miss a client or a contact. Current listings include: banks and branches, non-depository institutions, stock exchanges and brokers, investment management firms, insurance companies, major accounting and law firms, government agencies and financial associations. Powerful indexes assist researchers with locating the vital financial information they need. The following indexes are included: alphabetic, geographic, executive name, corporate web site/e-mail, government quick reference and subject. *Financial Services Canada* is a valuable resource for financial executives, bankers, financial planners, sales and marketing professionals, lawyers and chartered accountants, government officials, investment dealers, journalists, librarians and reference specialists.

Hardcover ISBN 978-1-59237-278-2, 900 pages, $315.00

Directory of Libraries in Canada, 2008/09

The Directory of Libraries in Canada brings together almost 7,000 listings including libraries and their branches, information resource centers, archives and library associations and learning centers. The directory offers complete and comprehensive information on Canadian libraries, resource centers, business information centers, professional associations, regional library systems, archives, library schools and library technical programs. *The Directory of Libraries in Canada* includes important features of each library and service, including library information; personnel details, including contact names and e-mail addresses; collection information; services available to users; acquisitions budgets; and computers and automated systems. Useful information on each library's electronic access is also included, such as Internet browser, connectivity and public Internet/CD-ROM/subscription database access. The directory also provides powerful indexes for subject, location, personal name and Web site/e-mail to assist researchers with locating the crucial information they need. *The Directory of Libraries in Canada* is a vital reference tool for publishers, advocacy groups, students, research institutions, computer hardware suppliers, and other diverse groups that provide products and services to this unique market.

Hardcover ISBN 978-1-59237-279-9, 850 pages, $315.00

Canadian Environmental Directory, 2009

The Canadian Environmental Directory is Canada's most complete and only national listing of environmental associations and organizations, government regulators and purchasing groups, product and service companies, special libraries, and more! The extensive Products and Services section provides detailed listings enabling users to identify the company name, address, phone, fax, e-mail, Web address, firm type, contact names (and titles), product and service information, affiliations, trade information, branch and affiliate data. The Government section gives you all the contact information you need at every government level – federal, provincial and municipal. We also include descriptions of current environmental initiatives, programs and agreements, names of environment-related acts administered by each ministry or department PLUS information and tips on who to contact and how to sell to governments in Canada. The Associations section provides complete contact information and a brief description of activities. Included are Canadian environmental organizations and international groups including industry, commercial and professional associations, registered charities, special interest and common interest organizations. All the Information you need about the Canadian environmental industry: directory of products and services, special libraries and resource, conferences, seminars and tradeshows, chronology of environmental events, law firms and major Canadian companies, *The Canadian Environmental Directory* is ideal for business, government, engineers and anyone conducting research on the environment.

Softcover ISBN 978-1-59237-374-1, 900 pages, $325.00

Canadian Parliamentary Guide, 2008

An indispensable guide to government in Canada, the annual *Canadian Parliamentary Guide* provides information on both federal and provincial governments, courts, and their elected and appointed members. The Guide is completely bilingual, with each record appearing both in English and then in French. The Guide contains biographical sketches of members of the Governor General's Household, the Privy Council, members of Canadian legislatures (federal, including both the House of Commons and the Senate, provincial and territorial), members of the federal superior courts (Supreme, Federal, Federal Appeal, Court Martial Appeal and Tax Courts) and the senior staff for these institutions. Biographies cover personal data, political career, private career and contact information. In addition, the Guide provides descriptions of each of the institutions, including brief historical information in text and chart format and significant facts (i.e. number of members and their salaries). The Guide covers the results of all federal general elections and by-elections from Confederations to the present and the results of the most recent provincial elections. A complete name index rounds out the text, making information easy to find. No other resources presents a more up-to-date, more complete picture of Canadian government and her political leaders. A must-have resource for all Canadian reference collections.

Hardcover ISBN 978-1-59237-310-9, 800 pages, $184.00